Official 1990 National Football League

NFL™

Record & Fact Book

P9-DBO-562

A National Football League Book.
Workman Publishing Co., New York.

National Football League, 1990

410 Park Avenue, New York, N.Y. 10022   (212) 758-1500

Commissioner: Paul Tagliabue
Executive Vice President and League Counsel: Jay Moyer
Vice President of Communications & Development:
    Joe Browne
Vice President of Broadcasting & Productions:
    Val Pinchbeck, Jr.
Executive Director for Special Events: Jim Steeg
Treasurer: Tom Sullivan

Pete Abitante: AFC Director of Information
Greg Aiello: Director of Communications
Phil Ayoub: Comptroller
Nancy Behar: Assistant Director of Broadcasting &
    Productions
Joel Bussert: Director of Player Personnel
John Buzzeo: Director of Administration
David Cornwell: Director of Equal Employment &
    Assistant Counsel
Roger Goodell: Director of Club Administration &
    International Development
Bill Granholm: Director of Special Projects
Jim Heffernan: Director of Public Relations
Charles R. Jackson: Assistant Director of Security
Dick Maxwell: Director of Broadcasting Services
Art McNally: Director of Officiating
Susan McCann Minogue: Assistant Director of Special
    Events
Jack Reader: Assistant Supervisor of Officials
Jan Van Duser: Director of Game Operations
Tony Veteri: Assistant Supervisor of Officials
Don Weiss: Director of Planning
Warren Welsh: Director of Security

Cover Photograph by Greg Trott.
Copyright © 1990 by the National Football League.
All rights reserved. The information in this publication
has been compiled for use by the news media to aid
in reporting of the games and teams of the National
Football League. No part of this book may be repro-
duced or transmitted in any form or by any means,
electronic or mechanical, including photocopying,
recording, or by any information storage and re-
trieval system, without permission in writing from the
National Football League.
Printed in the United States of America.

A National Football League Book.
Compiled by the NFL Public Relations Department
    and Seymour Siwoff, Elias Sports Bureau.
Edited by Leslie Hammond, NFL Public Relations and
    Chuck Garrity, Jr., NFLP Creative Services.
Statistics by Elias Sports Bureau.
Produced by NFL Properties, Inc., Creative Services
    Division.
Workman Publishing Co.
708 Broadway, New York, N.Y. 10003
Manufactured in the United States of America.
First printing, July 1990.
10 9 8 7 6 5 4 3 2 1

Index

1990 SCHEDULE AND NOTE CALENDAR

(All Times Local Except Tokyo, London, and Berlin which are ET)
Nationally televised games in parentheses.

Preseason/First Week

Saturday, August 4
Hall of Fame Game at Canton, Ohio (ABC) 1:00
  Chicago ___ vs. Cleveland ___
American Bowl '90 at Tokyo, Japan (ESPN) 10:00*
  Denver ___ vs. Seattle ___

Sunday, August 5
American Bowl '90 at London, England (NBC) 1:00*
  Los Angeles Raiders ___ vs. New Orleans ___

Thursday, August 9
Detroit ___ at Houston ___ 7:00
American Bowl '90 at Montreal, Canada
  New England ___ vs. Pittsburgh ___ 7:30

Saturday, August 11
American Bowl '90 at Berlin, Germany (NBC) 1:00*
  Los Angeles Rams ___ vs. Kansas City ___
Atlanta ___ vs. Washington ___ at Chapel Hill, N.C. 7:00
Cincinnati ___ at Tampa Bay ___ 7:00
Cleveland ___ at Green Bay ___ 6:00
Dallas ___ at San Diego ___ 7:00
Denver ___ at Indianapolis ___ 7:30
Los Angeles Raiders ___ at San Francisco ___ (CBS) 6:00
Miami ___ at Chicago ___ 6:00
New Orleans ___ at Minnesota ___ 7:00
New York Jets ___ at Philadelphia ___ 7:30
Seattle ___ at Phoenix ___ 7:30

Monday, August 13
New York Giants ___ at Buffalo ___ (ABC) 8:00

*(Tokyo game actual kickoff
11:00 a.m. August 5; London
game actual kickoff 6:00 p.m.
August 5; Berlin game actual
kickoff 7:00 p.m. August 11)

Preseason/Second Week

Friday, August 17
Buffalo ___ at Detroit ___ 7:30
Indianapolis ___ at Seattle ___ 7:30
Pittsburgh ___ at Washington ___ 8:00

Saturday, August 18
Chicago ___ at Phoenix ___ 7:30
Cincinnati ___ at Atlanta ___ 7:00
Dallas ___ at Los Angeles Raiders ___ 1:00
Miami ___ at Philadelphia ___ 7:30
New England ___ vs. Tampa Bay ___ at Jacksonville 8:00
New Orleans ___ vs. Green Bay ___ at Madison, Wis. 1:00
New York Giants ___ at Houston ___ (ESPN) 7:00
New York Jets ___ at Kansas City ___ 7:00
San Diego ___ at Los Angeles Rams ___ 7:00

Sunday, August 19
Minnesota ___ at Cleveland ___ (TNT) 8:00

Monday, August 20
San Francisco ___ at Denver ___ (ABC) 6:00

Preseason/Third Week

Friday, August 24
Cincinnati ___ at New England ___ 7:00
Kansas City ___ at Detroit ___ 7:30
Los Angeles Raiders ___ at Chicago ___ (NBC) 7:00
Tampa Bay ___ at Seattle ___ 6:00

Saturday, August 25
Atlanta ___ vs. Green Bay ___ at Milwaukee 6:00
Buffalo ___ at New Orleans ___ 7:00
Denver ___ at Miami ___ (TNT) 8:00
New York Jets ___ at New York Giants ___ 8:00
Phoenix ___ at Los Angeles Rams ___ 7:00
Pittsburgh ___ at Dallas ___ 8:00
San Francisco ___ at San Diego ___ 6:00
Washington ___ at Cleveland ___ 7:00

Sunday, August 26
Houston ___ at Minnesota ___ (CBS) 12:00

Monday, August 27
Philadelphia ___ at Indianapolis ___ (ABC) 7:00

4

Preseason/Fourth Week

Thursday, August 30	Buffalo ___ vs. Chicago ___ at Columbia, S.C.	(ESPN) 8:00
	New York Jets ___ at Tampa Bay ___	7:00
Friday, August 31	Atlanta ___ at New England ___	7:30
	Detroit ___ at Cincinnati ___	7:30
	Green Bay ___ at Kansas City ___	7:00
	Indianapolis ___ at New Orleans ___	7:00
	Los Angeles Rams ___ at Washington ___	(TNT) 8:00
	Minnesota ___ at Miami ___	8:00
	Phoenix ___ at Denver ___	7:00
	Seattle ___ at San Francisco ___	6:00
Saturday, September 1	Cleveland ___ at New York Giants ___	8:00
	Houston ___ at Dallas ___	8:00
	Philadelphia ___ at Pittsburgh ___	(CBS) 9:00
	San Diego ___ at Los Angeles Raiders ___	1:00

First Week

Sunday, September 9 **(NBC-TV National Weekend)**	Denver ___ at Los Angeles Raiders ___	(NBC) 1:00
	Houston ___ at Atlanta ___	4:00
	Indianapolis ___ at Buffalo ___	4:00
	Los Angeles Rams ___ at Green Bay ___	12:00
	Miami ___ at New England ___	4:00
	Minnesota ___ at Kansas City ___	12:00
	New York Jets ___ at Cincinnati ___	4:00
	Phoenix ___ at Washington ___	1:00
	Pittsburgh ___ at Cleveland ___	4:00
	San Diego ___ at Dallas ___	3:00
	Seattle ___ at Chicago ___	12:00
	Tampa Bay ___ at Detroit ___	1:00
Sunday Night	Philadelphia ___ at New York Giants ___	(TNT) 8:00
Monday, September 10	San Francisco ___ at New Orleans ___	(ABC) 8:00

Second Week

Sunday, September 16 **(CBS-TV National Weekend)**	Atlanta ___ at Detroit ___	1:00
	Buffalo ___ at Miami ___	1:00
	Chicago ___ at Green Bay ___	12:00
	Cincinnati ___ at San Diego ___	1:00
	Cleveland ___ at New York Jets ___	1:00
	Los Angeles Raiders ___ at Seattle ___	1:00
	Los Angeles Rams ___ at Tampa Bay ___	1:00
	New England ___ at Indianapolis ___	12:00
	New Orleans ___ at Minnesota ___	3:00
	New York Giants ___ at Dallas ___	3:00
	Phoenix ___ at Philadelphia ___	1:00
	Washington ___ at San Francisco ___	(CBS) 1:00
Sunday Night	Houston ___ at Pittsburgh ___	(TNT) 8:00
Monday, September 17	Kansas City ___ at Denver ___	(ABC) 7:00

Third Week

Sunday, September 23 **(CBS-TV National Weekend)**	Atlanta ___ at San Francisco ___	1:00
	Dallas ___ at Washington ___	1:00
	Indianapolis ___ at Houston ___	12:00
	Kansas City ___ at Green Bay ___	12:00
	Miami ___ at New York Giants ___	1:00
	Minnesota ___ at Chicago ___	12:00
	New England ___ at Cincinnati ___	1:00
	Philadelphia ___ at Los Angeles Rams ___	(CBS) 1:00
	Phoenix ___ at New Orleans ___	12:00
	Pittsburgh ___ at Los Angeles Raiders ___	1:00
	San Diego ___ at Cleveland ___	1:00
	Seattle ___ at Denver ___	2:00
Sunday Night	Detroit ___ at Tampa Bay ___	(TNT) 8:00
Monday, September 24	Buffalo ___ at New York Jets ___	(ABC) 9:00

5

Fourth Week

Open Date: Four NFC West Teams

Sunday, September 30
(NBC-TV National Weekend)

Chicago ____ at Los Angeles Raiders ____		1:00
Cleveland ____ at Kansas City ____	(NBC)	3:00
Dallas ____ at New York Giants ____		1:00
Denver ____ at Buffalo ____		1:00
Green Bay ____ at Detroit ____		1:00
Houston ____ at San Diego ____		1:00
Indianapolis ____ at Philadelphia ____		1:00
Miami ____ at Pittsburgh ____		1:00
New York Jets ____ at New England ____		4:00
Tampa Bay ____ at Minnesota ____		12:00

Sunday Night Washington ____ at Phoenix ____ (TNT) 5:00

Monday, October 1 Cincinnati ____ at Seattle ____ (ABC) 6:00

Fifth Week

Open Date: Four NFC East Teams

Sunday, October 7
(NBC-TV National Weekend)

Cincinnati ____ at Los Angeles Rams ____	(NBC)	1:00
Detroit ____ at Minnesota ____		12:00
Green Bay ____ at Chicago ____		3:00
Kansas City ____ at Indianapolis ____		12:00
New Orleans ____ at Atlanta ____		1:00
New York Jets ____ at Miami ____		1:00
San Diego ____ at Pittsburgh ____		1:00
San Francisco ____ at Houston ____		12:00
Seattle ____ at New England ____		1:00
Tampa Bay ____ at Dallas ____		12:00

Sunday Night Los Angeles Raiders ____ at Buffalo ____ (TNT) 7:30

Monday, October 8 Cleveland ____ at Denver ____ (ABC) 7:00

Sixth Week

Open Date: Four AFC East Teams

Sunday, October 14
(CBS-TV National Weekend)

Cleveland ____ at New Orleans ____		12:00
Dallas ____ at Phoenix ____		1:00
Detroit ____ at Kansas City ____		12:00
Green Bay ____ at Tampa Bay ____		1:00
Houston ____ at Cincinnati ____		1:00
New York Giants ____ at Washington ____	(CBS)	4:00
Pittsburgh ____ at Denver ____		2:00
San Diego ____ at New York Jets ____		1:00
San Francisco ____ at Atlanta ____		1:00
Seattle ____ at Los Angeles Raiders ____		1:00

Sunday Night Los Angeles Rams ____ at Chicago ____ (TNT) 6:30

Monday, October 15 Minnesota ____ at Philadelphia ____ (ABC) 9:00

Seventh Week

Open Date: Four NFC Central Teams

Thursday, October 18 New England ____ at Miami ____ (TNT) 8:00

Sunday, October 21
(NBC-TV National Weekend)

Atlanta ____ at Los Angeles Rams ____		1:00
Dallas ____ at Tampa Bay ____		1:00
Denver ____ at Indianapolis ____		12:00
Kansas City ____ at Seattle ____		1:00
Los Angeles Raiders ____ at San Diego ____		1:00
New Orleans ____ at Houston ____		12:00
New York Jets ____ at Buffalo ____		1:00
Philadelphia ____ at Washington ____		1:00
Phoenix ____ at New York Giants ____		4:00
Pittsburgh ____ at San Francisco ____	(NBC)	1:00

Monday, October 22 Cincinnati ____ at Cleveland ____ (ABC) 9:00

Eighth Week

Open Date: Four AFC West Teams

Sunday, October 28	Buffalo ___ at New England ___	1:00
(CBS-TV National Weekend)	Chicago ___ at Phoenix ___	2:00
	Cleveland ___ at San Francisco ___	1:00
	Detroit ___ at New Orleans ___	12:00
	Miami ___ at Indianapolis ___	1:00
	Minnesota ___ vs. Green Bay ___ at Milwaukee	12:00
	New York Jets ___ at Houston ___	12:00
	Philadelphia ___ at Dallas ___	12:00
	Tampa Bay ___ at San Diego ___	1:00
	Washington ___ at New York Giants ___	(CBS) 4:00
Sunday Night	Cincinnati ___ at Atlanta ___	(TNT) 8:00
Monday, October 29	Los Angeles Rams ___ at Pittsburgh ___	(ABC) 9:00

Ninth Week

Sunday, November 4	Atlanta ___ at Pittsburgh ___	1:00
(NBC-TV National Weekend)	Buffalo ___ at Cleveland ___	1:00
	Chicago ___ at Tampa Bay ___	4:00
	Dallas ___ at New York Jets ___	1:00
	Houston ___ at Los Angeles Rams ___	(NBC) 1:00
	Los Angeles Raiders ___ at Kansas City ___	12:00
	New England ___ at Philadelphia ___	1:00
	New Orleans ___ at Cincinnati ___	1:00
	Phoenix ___ at Miami ___	1:00
	San Diego ___ at Seattle ___	1:00
	San Francisco ___ at Green Bay ___	12:00
	Washington ___ at Detroit ___	1:00
Sunday Night	Denver ___ at Minnesota ___	(TNT) 7:00
Monday, November 5	New York Giants ___ at Indianapolis ___	(ABC) 9:00

Tenth Week

Open Date: Four AFC Central Teams

Sunday, November 11	Atlanta ___ at Chicago ___	12:00
(CBS-TV National Weekend)	Denver ___ at San Diego ___	1:00
	Green Bay ___ at Los Angeles Raiders ___	1:00
	Indianapolis ___ at New England ___	1:00
	Miami ___ at New York Jets ___	1:00
	Minnesota ___ at Detroit ___	1:00
	New York Giants ___ at Los Angeles Rams ___	(CBS) 1:00
	Phoenix ___ at Buffalo ___	1:00
	Seattle ___ at Kansas City ___	12:00
	Tampa Bay ___ at New Orleans ___	12:00
Sunday Night	San Francisco ___ at Dallas ___	(ESPN) 7:00
Monday, November 12	Washington ___ at Philadelphia ___	(ABC) 9:00

Eleventh Week

Sunday, November 18	Chicago ___ at Denver ___	(CBS) 2:00
(CBS-TV National Weekend)	Dallas ___ at Los Angeles Rams ___	1:00
	Detroit ___ at New York Giants ___	1:00
	Green Bay ___ at Phoenix ___	2:00
	Houston ___ at Cleveland ___	1:00
	Minnesota ___ at Seattle ___	1:00
	New England ___ at Buffalo ___	1:00
	New Orleans ___ at Washington ___	1:00
	New York Jets ___ at Indianapolis ___	4:00
	Philadelphia ___ at Atlanta ___	1:00
	San Diego ___ at Kansas City ___	12:00
	Tampa Bay ___ at San Francisco ___	1:00
Sunday Night	Pittsburgh ___ at Cincinnati ___	(ESPN) 8:00
Monday, November 19	Los Angeles Raiders ___ at Miami ___	(ABC) 9:00

Twelfth Week

Thursday, November 22	Denver ___ at Detroit ___	(NBC) 12:30
Thanksgiving Day	Washington ___ at Dallas ___	(CBS) 3:00
Sunday, November 25	Atlanta ___ at New Orleans ___	12:00
(NBC-TV National Weekend)	Chicago ___ at Minnesota ___	12:00
	Indianapolis ___ at Cincinnati ___	1:00
	Kansas City ___ at Los Angeles Raiders ___	(NBC) 1:00
	Los Angeles Rams ___ at San Francisco ___	1:00
	Miami ___ at Cleveland ___	1:00
	New England ___ at Phoenix ___	2:00
	New York Giants ___ at Philadelphia ___	1:00
	Pittsburgh ___ at New York Jets ___	4:00
	Tampa Bay ___ vs. Green Bay ___ at Milwaukee	12:00
Sunday Night	Seattle ___ at San Diego ___	(ESPN) 5:00
Monday, November 26	Buffalo ___ at Houston ___	(ABC) 8:00

Thirteenth Week

Sunday, December 2	Atlanta ___ at Tampa Bay ___	1:00
(NBC-TV National Weekend)	Cincinnati ___ at Pittsburgh ___	1:00
	Detroit ___ at Chicago ___	12:00
	Houston ___ at Seattle ___	1:00
	Indianapolis ___ at Phoenix ___	2:00
	Kansas City ___ at New England ___	1:00
	Los Angeles Raiders ___ at Denver ___	(NBC) 2:00
	Los Angeles Rams ___ at Cleveland ___	1:00
	Miami ___ at Washington ___	1:00
	New Orleans ___ at Dallas ___	3:00
	New York Jets ___ at San Diego ___	1:00
	Philadelphia ___ at Buffalo ___	1:00
Sunday Night	Green Bay ___ at Minnesota ___	(ESPN) 7:00
Monday, December 3	New York Giants ___ at San Francisco ___	(ABC) 6:00

Fourteenth Week
Open Date: Four 1989 Fifth-Place Teams

Sunday December 9	Buffalo ___ at Indianapolis ___	1:00
(CBS-TV National Weekend)	Chicago ___ at Washington ___	4:00
	Cleveland ___ at Houston ___	12:00
	Denver ___ at Kansas City ___	3:00
	Minnesota ___ at New York Giants ___	1:00
	New England ___ at Pittsburgh ___	1:00
	New Orleans ___ at Los Angeles Rams ___	(CBS) 1:00
	Phoenix ___ at Atlanta ___	1:00
	San Francisco ___ at Cincinnati ___	1:00
	Seattle ___ vs. Green Bay ___ at Milwaukee	12:00
Sunday Night	Philadelphia ___ at Miami ___	(ESPN) 8:00
Monday, December 10	Los Angeles Raiders ___ at Detroit ___	(ABC) 9:00

Fifteenth Week

Saturday, December 15	Buffalo ___ at New York Giants ___	(NBC) 12:30
	Washington ___ at New England ___	(CBS) 4:00
Sunday, December 16	Atlanta ___ at Cleveland ___	1:00
(NBC-TV National Weekend)	Cincinnati ___ at Los Angeles Raiders ___	(NBC) 1:00
	Green Bay ___ at Philadelphia ___	4:00
	Houston ___ at Kansas City ___	12:00
	Indianapolis ___ at New York Jets ___	1:00
	Minnesota ___ at Tampa Bay ___	1:00
	Phoenix ___ at Dallas ___	12:00
	Pittsburgh ___ at New Orleans ___	12:00
	San Diego ___ at Denver ___	2:00
	Seattle ___ at Miami ___	1:00
Sunday Night	Chicago ___ at Detroit ___	(ESPN) 8:00
Monday, December 17	San Francisco ___ at Los Angeles Rams ___	(ABC) 6:00

Sixteenth Week

Saturday, December 22	Detroit ____ at Green Bay ____	(CBS) 11:30
	Los Angeles Raiders ____ at Minnesota ____	(NBC) 3:00
	Washington ____ at Indianapolis ____	(ABC) 8:00
Sunday, December 23	Cincinnati ____ at Houston ____	12:00
(CBS-TV National Weekend)	Cleveland ____ at Pittsburgh ____	1:00
	Dallas ____ at Philadelphia ____	1:00
	Kansas City ____ at San Diego ____	1:00
	Los Angeles Rams ____ at Atlanta ____	1:00
	Miami ____ at Buffalo ____	1:00
	New England ____ at New York Jets ____	1:00
	New Orleans ____ at San Francisco ____	(CBS) 1:00
	New York Giants ____ at Phoenix ____	2:00
	Tampa Bay ____ at Chicago ____	12:00
Sunday Night	Denver ____ at Seattle ____	(ABC) 5:00

Seventeenth Week

Saturday, December 29	Kansas City ____ at Chicago ____	(NBC) 11:30
	Philadelphia ____ at Phoenix ____	(CBS) 2:00
Sunday, December 30	Buffalo ____ at Washington ____	1:00
(CBS-TV National Weekend)	Cleveland ____ at Cincinnati ____	1:00
	Dallas ____ at Atlanta ____	1:00
	Detroit ____ at Seattle ____	1:00
	Green Bay ____ at Denver ____	(CBS) 2:00
	Indianapolis ____ at Miami ____	1:00
	New York Giants ____ at New England ____	1:00
	New York Jets ____ at Tampa Bay ____	4:00
	San Diego ____ at Los Angeles Raiders ____	1:00
	San Francisco ____ at Minnesota ____	12:00
Sunday Night	Pittsburgh ____ at Houston ____	(ESPN) 7:00
Monday, December 31	Los Angeles Rams ____ at New Orleans ____	(ABC) 7:00

First-Round Playoff Games

Site Priorities
Three Wild Card teams (division non-champions with best three records) from each conference and the division champion with the third-best record in each conference will enter the first round of the playoffs. The division champion with the third-best record will play host to the Wild Card team with the third-best record. The Wild Card team with the best record will play host to the Wild Card team with the second-best record. There are no restrictions on intra-division games.

Saturday, January 5, 1991 American Football Conference

_____ at _____ (ABC)

National Football Conference

_____ at _____ (ABC)

Sunday, January 6, 1991 American Football Conference

_____ at _____ (NBC)

National Football Conference

_____ at _____ (CBS)

Second-Round Playoff Games

Site Priorities
In each conference, the two division champions with the highest won-lost-tied percentage during the regular season will play host to the First-Round winners. The division champion with the best record in each conference is assured of playing the Wild Card survivor with the poorest record. There are no restrictions on intra-division games.

Saturday, January 12, 1991 American Football Conference

_____ at _____ (NBC)

National Football Conference

_____ at _____ (CBS)

Sunday, January 13, 1991 American Football Conference

_____ at _____ (NBC)

National Football Conference

_____ at _____ (CBS)

Conference Championship Games, Super Bowl XXV, and AFC-NFC Pro Bowl

Site Priorities for Championship Games
The home teams will be the surviving playoff winners with the best won-lost-tied percentage during the regular season. A Wild Card team cannot play host unless two Wild Card teams are in the game, in which case the Wild Card team with the best record will play host.

Sunday, January 20, 1991 American Football Conference Championship Game

_____ at _____ (NBC)

National Football Conference Championship Game

_____ at _____ (CBS)

Sunday, January 27, 1991 Super Bowl XXV at Tampa Stadium, Tampa, Florida

_____ vs. _____ (ABC)

Sunday, February 3, 1991 AFC-NFC Pro Bowl at Honolulu, Hawaii

AFC _____ vs. NFC _____ (ESPN)

Postseason Games

Saturday, January 5	AFC and NFC First-Round Playoffs (ABC)
Sunday, January 6	AFC and NFC First-Round Playoffs (NBC and CBS)
Saturday, January 12	AFC and NFC Second-Round Playoffs (NBC and CBS)
Sunday, January 13	AFC and NFC Second-Round Playoffs (NBC and CBS)
Sunday, January 20	AFC and NFC Championship Games (NBC and CBS)
Sunday, January 27	Super Bowl XXV at Tampa Stadium, Tampa, Florida (ABC)
Sunday, February 3	AFC-NFC Pro Bowl at Honolulu, Hawaii (ESPN)

1990 Nationally Televised Games

(All games carried on CBS Radio Network.)

Regular Season

Sunday, September 9	Denver at Los Angeles Raiders (day, NBC)
	Philadelphia at New York Giants (night, TNT)
Monday, September 10	San Francisco at New Orleans (night, ABC)
Sunday, September 16	Washington at San Francisco (day, CBS)
	Houston at Pittsburgh (night, TNT)
Monday, September 17	Kansas City at Denver (night, ABC)
Sunday, September 23	Philadelphia at Los Angeles Rams (day, CBS)
	Detroit at Tampa Bay (night, TNT)
Monday, September 24	Buffalo at New York Jets (night, ABC)
Sunday, September 30	Cleveland at Kansas City (day, NBC)
	Washington at Phoenix (night, TNT)
Monday, October 1	Cincinnati at Seattle (night, ABC)
Sunday, October 7	Cincinnati at Los Angeles Rams (day, NBC)
	Los Angeles Raiders at Buffalo (night, TNT)
Monday, October 8	Cleveland at Denver (night, ABC)
Sunday, October 14	New York Giants at Washington (day, CBS)
	Los Angeles Rams at Chicago (night, TNT)
Monday, October 15	Minnesota at Philadelphia (night, ABC)
Thursday, October 18	New England at Miami (night, TNT)
Sunday, October 21	Pittsburgh at San Francisco (day, NBC)
Monday, October 22	Cincinnati at Cleveland (night, ABC)
Sunday, October 28	Washington at New York Giants (day, CBS)
	Cincinnati at Atlanta (night, TNT)
Monday, October 29	Los Angeles Rams at Pittsburgh (night, ABC)
Sunday, November 4	Houston at Los Angeles Rams (day, NBC)
	Denver at Minnesota (night, TNT)
Monday, November 5	New York Giants at Indianapolis (night, ABC)
Sunday, November 11	New York Giants at Los Angeles Rams (day, CBS)
	San Francisco at Dallas (night, ESPN)
Monday, November 12	Washington at Philadelphia (night, ABC)
Sunday, November 18	Chicago at Denver (day, NBC)
	Pittsburgh at Cincinnati (night, ESPN)
Monday, November 19	Los Angeles Raiders at Miami (night, ABC)
Thursday, November 22	Denver at Detroit (day, NBC)
	Washington at Dallas (day, CBS)
Sunday, November 25	Kansas City at Los Angeles Raiders (day, NBC)
	Seattle at San Diego (night, ESPN)
Monday, November 26	Buffalo at Houston (night, ABC)
Sunday, December 2	Los Angeles Raiders at Denver (day, NBC)
	Green Bay at Minnesota (night, ESPN)
Monday, December 3	New York Giants at San Francisco (night, ABC)
Sunday, December 9	New Orleans at Los Angeles Rams (day, CBS)
	Philadelphia at Miami (night, ESPN)
Monday, December 10	Los Angeles Raiders at Detroit (night, ABC)
Saturday, December 15	Buffalo at New York Giants (day, NBC)
	Washington at New England (day, CBS)
Sunday, December 16	Cincinnati at Los Angeles Raiders (day, NBC)
	Chicago at Detroit (night, ESPN)
Monday, December 17	San Francisco at Los Angeles Rams (night, ABC)
Saturday, December 22	Detroit at Green Bay (day, CBS)
	Los Angeles Raiders at Minnesota (day, NBC)
	Washington at Indianapolis (night, ABC)
Sunday, December 23	New Orleans at San Francisco (day, CBS)
	Denver at Seattle (night, ESPN)
Saturday, December 29	Kansas City at Chicago (day, NBC)
	Philadelphia at Phoenix (day, CBS)
Sunday, December 30	Green Bay at Denver (day, CBS)
	Pittsburgh at Houston (night, ESPN)
Monday, December 31	Los Angeles Rams at New Orleans (night, ABC)

1990 AFC-NFC Interconference Games

(All times local.)

September 9	Houston at Atlanta	4:00
	Minnesota at Kansas City	12:00
	San Diego at Dallas	3:00
	Seattle at Chicago	12:00
September 23	Kansas City at Green Bay	12:00
	Miami at New York Giants	1:00
September 30	Chicago at Los Angeles Raiders	1:00
	Indianapolis at Philadelphia	1:00
October 7	Cincinnati at Los Angeles Rams	1:00
	San Francisco at Houston	12:00
October 14	Cleveland at New Orleans	12:00
	Detroit at Kansas City	12:00
October 21	New Orleans at Houston	12:00
	Pittsburgh at San Francisco	1:00
October 28	Cleveland at San Francisco	1:00
	Tampa Bay at San Diego	1:00
	Cincinnati at Atlanta	8:00
October 29	Los Angeles Rams at Pittsburgh	9:00
November 4	Atlanta at Pittsburgh	1:00
	Dallas at New York Jets	1:00
	Houston at Los Angeles Rams	1:00
	New England at Philadelphia	1:00
	New Orleans at Cincinnati	1:00
	Phoenix at Miami	1:00
	Denver at Minnesota	7:00
November 5	New York Giants at Indianapolis	9:00
November 11	Green Bay at Los Angeles Raiders	1:00
	Phoenix at Buffalo	1:00
November 18	Chicago at Denver	2:00
	Minnesota at Seattle	1:00
November 22	Denver at Detroit	12:30
November 25	New England at Phoenix	2:00
December 2	Indianapolis at Phoenix	2:00
	Miami at Washington	1:00
	Los Angeles Rams at Cleveland	1:00
	Philadelphia at Buffalo	1:00
December 9	San Francisco at Cincinnati	1:00
	Seattle vs. Green Bay at Milwaukee	12:00
	Philadelphia at Miami	8:00
December 10	Los Angeles Raiders at Detroit	9:00
December 15	Buffalo at New York Giants	12:30
	Washington at New England	4:00
December 16	Atlanta at Cleveland	1:00
	Pittsburgh at New Orleans	12:00

December 22	Washington at Indianapolis	8:00
	Los Angeles Raiders at Minnesota	3:00
December 29	Kansas City at Chicago	11:30
December 30	Buffalo at Washington	1:00
	Detroit at Seattle	1:00
	Green Bay at Denver	2:00
	New York Giants at New England	1:00
	New York Jets at Tampa Bay	4:00

Thursday, Saturday, Sunday, and Monday Night Games at a Glance

(All games carried on CBS Radio Network.)

Sunday, September 9	Philadelphia at N.Y. Giants (TNT)	8:00
Monday, September 10	San Francisco at New Orleans (ABC)	8:00
Sunday, September 16	Houston at Pittsburgh (TNT)	8:00
Monday, September 17	Kansas City at Denver (ABC)	7:00
Sunday, September 23	Detroit at Tampa Bay (TNT)	8:00
Monday, September 24	Buffalo at New York Jets (ABC)	9:00
Sunday, September 30	Washington at Phoenix (TNT)	5:00
Monday, October 1	Cincinnati at Seattle (ABC)	6:00
Sunday, October 7	Los Angeles Raiders at Buffalo (TNT)	7:30
Monday, October 8	Cleveland at Denver (ABC)	7:00
Sunday, October 14	Los Angeles Rams at Chicago (TNT)	6:30
Monday, October 15	Minnesota at Philadelphia (ABC)	9:00
Thursday, October 18	New England at Miami (TNT)	8:00
Monday, October 22	Cincinnati at Cleveland (ABC)	9:00
Sunday, October 28	Cincinnati at Atlanta (TNT)	8:00
Monday, October 29	L.A. Rams at Pittsburgh (ABC)	9:00
Sunday, November 4	Denver at Minnesota (TNT)	7:00
Monday, November 5	N.Y. Giants at Indianapolis (ABC)	9:00
Sunday, November 11	San Francisco at Dallas (ESPN)	7:00
Monday, November 12	Washington at Philadelphia (ABC)	9:00
Sunday, November 18	Pittsburgh at Cincinnati (ESPN)	8:00
Monday, November 19	Los Angeles Raiders at Miami (ABC)	9:00
Sunday, November 25	Seattle at San Diego (ESPN)	5:00
Monday, November 26	Buffalo at Houston (ABC)	8:00
Sunday, December 2	Green Bay at Minnesota (ESPN)	7:00
Monday, December 3	N.Y. Giants at San Francisco (ABC)	6:00
Sunday, December 9	Philadelphia at Miami (ESPN)	8:00
Monday, December 10	Los Angeles Raiders at Detroit (ABC)	9:00
Saturday, December 15	Buffalo at New York Giants (NBC)	12:30
	Washington at New England (CBS)	4:00
Sunday, December 16	Chicago at Detroit (ESPN)	8:00
Monday, December 17	San Francisco at L.A. Rams (ABC)	6:00
Saturday, December 22	Detroit at Green Bay (CBS)	11:30
	L.A. Raiders at Minnesota (NBC)	3:00
	Washington at Indianapolis (ABC)	8:00
Sunday, December 23	Denver at Seattle (ESPN)	5:00
Saturday, December 29	Kansas City at Chicago (NBC)	11:30
	Philadelphia at Phoenix (CBS)	2:00
Sunday, December 30	Pittsburgh at Houston (ESPN)	7:00
Monday, December 31	L.A. Rams at New Orleans (ABC)	7:00

Important Dates

1990 Season

July 5	Claiming period of 24 hours begins in waiver system. All waiver requests for the year are no-recall and no-withdrawal.
Mid-July	Preseason training camps open.
August 4	Hall of Fame Game, Canton, Ohio: Cleveland vs. Chicago.
August 4	American Bowl '90, Tokyo, Japan: Denver vs. Seattle.
August 5	American Bowl '90, London, England: Los Angeles Raiders vs. New Orleans.
August 9	American Bowl '90, Montreal, Canada: New England vs. Pittsburgh.
August 9-13	First preseason weekend.
August 11	American Bowl '90, Berlin, Germany: Kansas City vs. Los Angeles Rams.
August 17-20	Second preseason weekend.
August 24-27	Third preseason weekend.
August 28	Roster cutdown to maximum of 60 players.
August 30-September 1	Fourth preseason weekend.
September 3	Roster cutdown to maximum of 47 players. Clubs may dress 45 players for each game. No later than 1:15 prior to kickoff of each game, clubs must establish an Inactive List of two players.
September 9-10	Regular season opens.
September 25	Priority on multiple waiver claims is now based on the current season's standings.
October 16	Trading of player contracts/rights ends at 4 P.M. New York Time.
October 16-17	NFL Fall Meeting, Chicago, Illinois.
December 1	Deadline for reinstatement of players in Reserve List categories of Retired, Did Not Report, and Veteran Free Agent Asked to Re-Sign.
December 17-18	Balloting for AFC-NFC Pro Bowl.
December 28	Deadline for waiver requests in 1990 for non-playoff teams.
January 5-6	AFC and NFC First-Round Playoff Games.
January 12-13	AFC and NFC Second-Round Playoff Games.
January 20	AFC and NFC Championship Games.
January 27	Super Bowl XXV, Tampa Stadium, Tampa, Florida.
January 28	Trading period begins.
February 1	Deadline for establishing Protected List of 37 players. All players who are not on Protected List will be eligible to sign as free agents with any other club through April 1.
February 3	AFC-NFC Pro Bowl at Aloha Stadium, Honolulu, Hawaii.

1991 Season

February 4	Waiver system begins for 1991.
February 6-10	Combine timing and testing of college players, Hoosier Dome, Indianapolis, Indiana.
March 17-22	NFL Annual Meeting, Kona, Hawaii.
April 1	Deadline for signing of offer sheets by veteran free agents and new clubs.
April 1	Expiration of free agency period for unprotected players.
April 21-22	56th Annual NFL Selection Meeting, New York, New York.
May 22-23	NFL Spring Meeting, Minneapolis, Minnesota.
July 27	Hall of Fame Game, Canton, Ohio: Miami vs. Detroit.
August 2-4	First preseason weekend.
September 1-2	Regular season opens.
December 23	Regular season closes.
December 28-29	AFC and NFC First-Round Playoff Games.
January 4-5	AFC and NFC Second-Round Playoff Games.
January 12	AFC and NFC Championship Games.
January 26	Super Bowl XXVI at Hubert H. Humphrey Metrodome, Minneapolis, Minnesota.
February 2	AFC-NFC Pro Bowl.

Future Pro Football Hall of Fame Games

1992	New York Jets (AFC) vs. Philadelphia Eagles (NFC)
1993	Los Angeles Raiders (AFC) vs. Green Bay Packers (NFC)
1994	Denver Broncos (AFC) vs. Dallas Cowboys (NFC)
1995	San Diego Chargers (AFC) vs. Atlanta Falcons (NFC)
1996	Indianapolis Colts (AFC) vs. New Orleans Saints (NFC)
1997	Seattle Seahawks (AFC) vs. Minnesota Vikings (NFC)
1998	Pittsburgh Steelers (AFC) vs. Tampa Bay Buccaneers (NFC)

Waivers

The waiver system is a procedure by which player contracts or NFL rights to players are made available by a club to other clubs in the League. During the procedure the 27 other clubs either file claims to obtain the players or waive the opportunity to do so—thus the term "waiver." Claiming clubs are assigned players on a priority based on the inverse of won-and-lost standing. The claiming period normally is 10 days during the offseason and 24 hours from early July through December. In some circumstances, another 24 hours is added on to allow the original club to rescind its action (known as a recall of a waiver request) and/or the claiming club to do the same (known as withdrawal of a claim). If a player passes through waivers unclaimed and is not recalled by the original club, he becomes a free agent. All waivers from July through December are no recall and no withdrawal. Under the Collective Bargaining Agreement, from February 1 through October 16, any veteran who has acquired four years of pension credit may, if about to be assigned to another club through the waiver system, reject such assignment and become a free agent.

Active List

The Active List is the principal status for players participating for a club. It consists of all players under contract, including option, who are eligible for preseason, regular season, and postseason games. In 1990, teams will be permitted to open training camp with no more than 80 players under contract and thereafter must meet a series of mandatory roster reductions prior to the season opener. Teams will be permitted to dress up to 45 players for each regular season and postseason game during the 1990 season; in addition, each club will have an Inactive List of two players. Maximum roster limits and dates for 1990 are:

August 28. . . . . active list of 60 players
September 3 . . . . active list of 45 players (plus two-player Inactive List)

In addition to the Active List limits described above, there also is an overall roster limit of 80 players that is applicable to players on a club's Active, Inactive, or Exempt Lists, and any players on Reserve as Injured, Physically Unable to Perform, Non-Football Illness/Injury, and Suspended.

Reserve List

The Reserve List is a status for players who, for reasons of injury, retirement, military service, or other circumstances, are not immediately available for participation with a club. Players on Reserve/Injured are not eligible to practice or return to the Active List until four regular-season games have been played.

Each club will have five free activations for players placed on Reserve/Injured after the final cutdown. Players also can be returned to the club's Active List if they clear Procedural Recall waivers. Any player placed on Reserve/Injured prior to or concurrent with the final cutdown on September 3 may not return to the club nor practice with the team that year. Clubs participating in postseason competition will be granted an additional activation for each postseason game, provided they have exhausted all previous activations.

Players in the category of Reserve/Retired, Reserve/Did Not Report, or Reserve/Veteran Free Agent Asked to Re-Sign may not be reinstated during the period from 30 days before the end of the regular season through the postseason.

Trades

Unrestricted trading between the AFC and NFC is allowed in 1990 through October 16, after which trading of player contracts/rights will end until January 28, 1991.

Annual Active Player Limits

NFL

Year(s)	Limit
1985-90	45
1983-84	49
1982	45†−49
1978−81	45
1975−77	43
1974	47
1964−73	40
1963	37
1961−62	36
1960	38
1959	36
1957−58	35
1951−56	33
1949−50	32
1948	35
1947	35*−34
1945−46	33
1943−44	28
1940−42	33
1938−39	30
1936−37	25
1935	24
1930−34	20
1926−29	18
1925	16

†45 for first two games
*35 for first three games

AFL

Year(s)	Limit
1966−69	40
1965	38
1964	34
1962−63	33
1960−61	35

Tie-Breaking Procedures

The following procedures will be used to break standings ties for postseason playoffs and to determine regular-season schedules.

To Break a Tie Within a Division

If, at the end of the regular season, two or more clubs in the same division finish with identical won-lost-tied percentages, the following steps will be taken until a champion is determined.

Two Clubs

1. Head-to-head (best won-lost-tied percentage in games between the clubs).
2. Best won-lost-tied percentage in games played within the division.
3. Best won-lost-tied percentage in games played within the conference.
4. Best won-lost-tied percentage in common games, if applicable.
5. Best net points in division games.
6. Best net points in all games.
7. Strength of schedule.
8. Best net touchdowns in all games.
9. Coin toss.

Three or More Clubs

(Note: If one team wins multiple-team tiebreaker to advance to playoff round, remaining teams revert to step 1 of applicable two-club format, i.e., either in division tiebreaker or Wild Card tiebreaker. If two teams in a multiple-team tie possess superior marks in a tiebreaking step, this pair of teams revert to top of applicable two-club format to break tie. One team advances to playoff round, while other returns to original group and step 1 of applicable tiebreaker).

1. Head-to-head (best won-lost-tied percentage in games among the clubs).
2. Best won-lost-tied percentage in games played within the division.
3. Best won-lost-tied percentage in games played within the conference.
4. Best won-lost-tied percentage in common games.
5. Best net points in division games.
6. Best net points in all games.
7. Strength of schedule.
8. Best net touchdowns in all games.
9. Coin toss.

To Break a Tie for the Wild Card Team

If it is necessary to break ties to determine the three Wild Card clubs from each conference, the following steps will be taken.

1. If the tied clubs are from the same division, apply division tiebreaker.
2. If the tied clubs are from different divisions, apply the following steps.

Two Clubs

1. Head-to-head, if applicable.
2. Best won-lost-tied percentage in games played within the conference.
3. Best won-lost-tied percentage in common games, minimum of four.
4. Best average net points in conference games.
5. Best net points in all games.
6. Strength of schedule.
7. Best net touchdowns in all games.
8. Coin toss.

Three or More Clubs

(Note: If one team wins multiple-team tiebreaker to advance to playoff round, remaining teams revert to step 1 of applicable two-club format, i.e., either in division tiebreaker or Wild Card tiebreaker. If two teams in a multiple-team tie possess superior marks in a tiebreaking step, this pair of teams revert to the top of the applicable two-club format to break tie. One team advances to playoff round, while other returns to original group and step 1 of applicable tiebreaker.)

1. Head-to-head sweep. (Applicable only if one club has defeated each of the others, or if one club has lost to each of the others.)
2. Best won-lost-tied percentage in games played within the conference.
3. Best won-lost-tied percentage in common games, minimum of four.
4. Best average net points in conference games.
5. Best net points in all games.
6. Strength of schedule.
7. Best net touchdowns in all games.
8. Coin toss.

Tie-Breaking Procedure for Selection Meeting

If two or more clubs are tied for selection order, the conventional strength of schedule tiebreaker will be applied, subject to the following exceptions for all playoff teams.

1. The Super Bowl winner will be last and the Super Bowl loser will be next-to-last.
2. Any non-Super Bowl playoff team involved in the tie moves down in drafting priority as follows:
    A. Participation by a club in the playoffs without a victory adds one-half victory to the club's regular-season won-lost-tied record.
    B. For each victory in the playoffs, one full victory will be added to the club's regular-season won-lost-tied record.
3. Clubs with the best won-lost-tied records after these steps are applied will drop to their appropriate spots at the bottom of the tied segment. In no case will the above process move a club lower than the segment in which it was initially tied.
4. Tied clubs will alternate priority throughout the 12 rounds of the draft. In case of a tie involving three or more teams, the club with priority in the first round will drop to the bottom of the tied segment in the second round and move its way back to the top of the segment in each succeeding round.

Instant Replay Approved for 1990

For the fifth consecutive season, NFL clubs have approved a limited system of Instant Replay on a one-year basis.

There is one significant change in the system from 1989. All replay reviews which involve contact to the field from the Replay Booth will be a maximum of two minutes in duration, timed from the moment when the Umpire signals timeout.

The Replay Official will be assigned to a regular officiating crew and will attend crew meetings the day before each game.

The following table outlines the number of reversals and plays closely reviewed by instant replay in each of the previous four seasons.

	Games	Reversals	Plays Closely Reviewed
1986	224	38	374
1987	210	57	490
1988	224	53	537
1989	224	65	492

In 1986, the system was approved by a 23-4-1 vote. In 1987, the vote was 21-7. In 1988, replay was cleared by a 23-5 margin. In 1989, the vote was 24-4. In 1990, the vote was 21-7.

The NFL has discussed Instant Replay in some degree or other since the early 1970s. The League experimented in 1976 and 1978 using two basic frameworks—an independent system using cameras, replay machines, and technicians separate from the network covering the games, and a "no-frills" approach using existing TV coverage.

In 1985, the NFL used the network feed of the nine nationally-televised preseason games to experiment with the basic system which later was adopted for 1986, 1987, and 1988. A total of 28 plays (17 confirmed calls, 4 inconclusive, 1 reversed, and 6 no replay shown) were closely examined in the 1985 experiment.

Q—What is the objective of this system?

A—The clubs feel that on certain plays the telecast viewed by the general public should be used to correct an indisputable error. The system will be used to reverse an on-field decision only when the Replay Official has **indisputable visual evidence** available to him that warrants the change.

Q—Who will be involved?

A—The Replay Official (a former NFL or collegiate official) will be positioned in a sideline Replay Booth, which will house two TV monitors and two high-speed VCRs plus radio communications to the on-field officials. The Replay Official makes the decision although a Communicator (normally a member of the League Office staff) and a Technician also will be there to lend logistical help.

Q—Why is the system referred to as "limited" Instant Replay?

A—This system will concentrate on plays of **possession** or **touching** (e.g. fumbles, receptions, interceptions, muffs) and most plays governed by the **sidelines, goal lines, end lines,** and **line of scrimmage** (e.g. receiver or runner in or out of bounds, forward or backward passes, breaking the plane of the goal line). It also will be used to determine whether there are more than 11 men on the field.

Q—Why aren't most fouls included in this system?

A—It is recognized that in most circumstances the on-field officials have the best vantage points involving fouls. It is for this reason that Instant Replay **will not review** a list of the following 26 fouls:

1. Clipping
2. Encroachment and offsides
3. Grasp of facemask
4. False start
5. Defensive pass interference
6. Offensive pass interference
7. Offensive holding and illegal use of hands
8. Illegal batting or punching ball
9. Illegal block on free kick or scrimmage kick
10. Illegal crackback
11. Illegal motion
12. Illegal use of forearm or elbow
13. Illegal use of hands by defense
14. Illegally kicking ball
15. Illegally snapping ball
16. Intentional grounding
17. Member of punting team downfield early
18. Illegal formation
19. Palpably unfair act
20. Piling on
21. Roughing the passer
22. Running into/roughing kicker
23. Striking, kicking, or kneeing
24. Unnecessary roughness
25. Unsportsmanlike conduct
26. Use of helmet as a weapon

Q—Is the television network carrying the game part of the review process?

A—No. Although the Replay Official will be viewing the live network feed, there is no communication to television personnel as to which plays to show or not to show. The Replay Official does not hear the TV commentators.

Q—What is the step-by-step procedure of a play review?

A—The Replay Official will view game action and a play will be replayed immediately on one of the two monitors, while the other one continues to record the live feed.

The Replay Official makes a determination if further study of the play is needed. If not, there is no contact with the field and play continues without interruption.

If the Replay Official believes an error may have been made the Umpire will be contacted via a headset.

The Replay Official will watch replay(s) on one or both monitors and complete his review within a reasonable period after the play is over.

The Replay Official will inform the Umpire of his decision, and the Referee will make the appropriate announcement on the wireless microphone.

Figuring the 1991 NFL Schedule

As soon as the final game of the 1990 NFL regular season (Los Angeles Rams at New Orleans on December 31) has been completed, it will be possible to determine the 1991 opponents of the 28 teams.

At the March, 1990, Owners' Meeting, the NFL announced it will play its 16-game schedule over 17 weeks in 1990 and 1991, and a 16-game schedule over 18 weeks in 1992 and 1993.

The 16-over-17 format provides each team one open weekend. The 16-over-18 format will provide each team two open weekends. Teams in groups of four by division, other than the NFL's four fifth-place finishers from the previous season, will be off on the same date. The four fifth-place teams also will be off on the same date. There will be 10 (out of 17) weeks in 1990 and 1991 when all 28 teams will be scheduled and four (out of 18) weeks in 1992 and 1993 when all 28 teams will play.

Each 1991 team schedule is based on a "common opponent" formula initiated for the 1978 season and most recently modified in 1987. Under the common opponent format, the first- through fourth-place teams in a division play at least 12 of their 16 games the following season against common opponents, and the fifth-place team in the division plays at least 10 common opponent games. It is not a position scheduling format in which the strong play the strong and the weak play the weak.

For years, the NFL had been seeking a more easily understood and balanced schedule that would provide both competitive equality and a variety of opponents. Under the old rotation scheduling system in effect from 1970-77, non-division opponents were determined by a pre-set formula. This often resulted in competitive imbalances.

With common opponents as the basis for scheduling, a more competitive and equitable method of determining division champions and postseason playoff representatives has developed. Teams battling for a division title are playing at least 75 percent of their games against common opponents.

In 1987, NFL owners passed two bylaw proposals designed to modify the common opponent scheduling format in the hopes of creating even more equity. The first concerns pairings with non-division opponents:

Prior Year's Finish in Division	Pairings in Non-Division Games Within Conference	Previous Pairings 1978-86
1	1-1-2-3	1-1-4-4
2	1-2-2-4	2-2-3-3
3	1-3-3-4	2-2-3-3
4	2-3-4-4	1-1-4-4

The second bylaw change further specified that: "site locations (for the non-division games listed above) will be assigned so that, where possible by formula, teams do not play a second consecutive regular-season home or road game with an opponent." The formula to determine 1991 site locations will be used on the final day of the 1990 season when the division finishes have been determined.

The NFL also has used the same philosophy in the determination of site locations for interconference games (AFC vs. NFC), avoiding a team playing two consecutive home or road games with an opponent, where possible by formula.

Under the common opponent format, schedules of any NFL team are figured according to one of the following three formulas. (The reference point for the figuring is the team's final division standing. Ties for a position in divisions are broken according to the tie-breaking procedures outlined on page 14. The chart on the following page is included for use as you go through each step.)

A. First- through fourth-place teams in a five-team division (AFC East, AFC West, NFC East, NFC Central).

1. Home-and-home round-robin within the division (8 games).
2. One game each with the first- through fourth-place teams in a division of the other conference (4 games). In 1991, the AFC East will play the NFC Central, the AFC Central will play the NFC East, and the AFC West will play the NFC West.

3. The first-place team plays the first-place teams in the other divisions within the conference plus a second- and third-place team within the conference. The second-place team plays the second-place teams in the other divisions within the conference plus a first- and fourth-place team within the conference. The third-place team plays the third-place teams in the other divisions within the conference plus a first- and fourth-place team within the conference. The fourth-place team plays the fourth-place teams in the other divisions within the conference plus a second- and third-place team within the conference (4 games).

This completes the 16-game schedule.

B. First- through fourth-place teams in a four-team division (AFC Central, NFC West).

1. Home-and-home round-robin within the division (6 games).
2. One game with each of the fifth-place teams in the conference (2 games).
3. The same procedure that is listed in step A2 (4 games).
4. The same procedure that is listed in step A3 (4 games).

This completes the 16-game schedule.

C. The fifth-place teams in a division (AFC East, AFC West, NFC East, NFC Central).

1. Home-and-home round-robin within the division (8 games).
2. One game with each team in the four-team division of the conference (4 games).
3. A home-and-home with the other fifth-place team in the conference (2 games).
4. One game each with the fifth-place teams in the other conference (2 games).

This completes the 16-game schedule.

The 1991 Opponent Breakdown chart on the following page does not include the round-robin games within the division. Those are automatically scheduled on a home-and-away basis.

1990 NFL Standings

AFC   NFC

EAST AE

1 _____
2 _____
3 _____
4 _____
5 _____

CENTRAL AC

1 _____
2 _____
3 _____
4 _____

WEST AW

1 _____
2 _____
3 _____
4 _____
5 _____

EAST NE

1 _____
2 _____
3 _____
4 _____
5 _____

WEST NW

1 _____
2 _____
3 _____
4 _____

CENTRAL NC

1 _____
2 _____
3 _____
4 _____
5 _____

A Team's 1991 Schedule

Team Name _____

_____
_____
_____
_____
_____
_____
_____
_____
_____
_____
_____
_____
_____
_____
_____
_____
_____

1991 Opponent Breakdown

(Certain game sites subject to change under NFL scheduling formulas.)

AE AFC East			AC AFC Central			AW AFC West			NE NFC East			NC NFC Central			NW NFC West		
	Home	Away		Home	Away		Home	Away		Home	Away		Home	Away		Home	Away
AE1	AC1	AW1	**AC1**	AW1	AE1	**AW1**	AE1	AC1	**NE1**	NW1	NC1	**NC1**	NE1	NW1	**NW1**	NC1	NE1
	AC3	AW2		AW3	AE2		AE3	AC2		NW3	NC2		NE3	NW2		NC3	NE2
	NC1	NC2		AE5	AW5		NW1	NW2		AC2	AC1		AE2	AE1		NE5	NC5
	NC3	NC4		NE1	NE2		NW3	NW4		AC4	AC3		AE4	AE3		AW2	AW1
				NE3	NE4											AW4	AW3
AE2	AC2	AW2	**AC2**	AW2	AE2	**AW2**	AE2	AC2	**NE2**	NW2	NC2	**NC2**	NE2	NW2	**NW2**	NC2	NE2
	AC1	AW4		AW1	AE4		AE1	AC4		NW1	NC4		NE1	NW4		NC1	NE4
	NC2	NC1		AW5	AE5		NW2	NW1		AC1	AC2		AE1	AE2		NC5	NE5
	NC4	NC3		NE2	NE1		NW4	NW3		AC3	AC4		AE3	AE4		AW1	AW2
				NE4	NE3											AW3	AW4
AE3	AC3	AW3	**AC3**	AW3	AE3	**AW3**	AE3	AC3	**NE3**	NW3	NC3	**NC3**	NE3	NW3	**NW3**	NC3	NE3
	AC4	AW1		AW4	AE1		AE4	AC1		NW4	NC1		NE4	NW1		NC4	NE1
	NC1	NC2		AE5	AW5		NW1	NW2		AC2	AC1		AE2	AE1		NE5	NC5
	NC3	NC4		NE1	NE2		NW3	NW4		AC4	AC3		AE4	AE3		AW2	AW1
				NE3	NE4											AW4	AW3
AE4	AC4	AW4	**AC4**	AW4	AE4	**AW4**	AE4	AC4	**NE4**	NW4	NC4	**NC4**	NE4	NW4	**NW4**	NC4	NE4
	AC2	AW3		AW2	AE3		AE2	AC3		NW2	NC3		NE2	NW3		NC2	NE3
	NC2	NC1		AW5	AE5		NW2	NW1		AC1	AC2		AE1	AE2		NC5	NE5
	NC4	NC3		NE2	NE1		NW4	NW3		AC3	AC4		AE3	AE4		AW1	AW2
				NE4	NE3											AW3	AW4
AE5	AC2	AC1				**AW5**	AC1	AC2	**NE5**	NW2	NW1	**NC5**	NW1	NW2			
	AC4	AC3					AC3	AC4		NW4	NW3		NW3	NW4			
	AW5	AW5					AE5	AE5		NC5	NC5		NE5	NE5			
	NC5	NE5					NE5	NC5		AE5	AW5		AW5	AE5			

AFC ACTIVE STATISTICAL LEADERS

LEADING ACTIVE PASSERS, AMERICAN FOOTBALL CONFERENCE

1,000 or more attempts

	Yrs.	Att.	Comp.	Pct. Comp.	Yards	Avg. Gain	TD	Pct. TD	Had Int.	Pct. Int.	Rate Pts.
Dan Marino, Mia.	7	3650	2174	59.6	27853	7.63	220	6.0	125	3.4	89.3
Boomer Esiason, Cin.	6	2285	1296	56.7	18350	8.03	126	5.5	76	3.3	87.3
Dave Krieg, Sea.	10	2843	1644	57.8	20858	7.34	169	5.9	116	4.1	83.7
Bernie Kosar, Clev.	5	1940	1134	58.5	13888	7.16	75	3.9	47	2.4	83.4
Ken O'Brien, N.Y.J.	6	2467	1471	59.6	17589	7.13	96	3.9	68	2.8	83.0
Jim Kelly, Buff.	4	1742	1032	59.2	12901	7.41	81	4.6	63	3.6	82.7
Tony Eason, N.Y.J.	7	1536	898	58.5	10987	7.15	61	4.0	50	3.3	80.3
Warren Moon, Hou.	6	2441	1339	54.9	18300	7.50	101	4.1	99	4.1	75.9
John Elway, Den.	7	3070	1665	54.2	21195	6.90	120	3.9	114	3.7	73.6
Ron Jaworski, K.C.	15	4117	2187	53.1	28190	6.85	179	4.3	164	4.0	72.8
Steve DeBerg, K.C.	12	3735	2118	56.7	25046	6.71	143	3.8	171	4.6	71.0
Jay Schroeder, Raiders	5	1467	721	49.1	10834	7.39	60	4.1	63	4.3	69.6
Steve Grogan, N.E.	15	3501	1829	52.2	26271	7.50	178	5.1	205	5.9	69.4
Marc Wilson, N.E.	9	1816	946	52.1	12766	7.03	80	4.4	91	5.0	68.6
Mike Pagel, Clev.	8	1305	665	51.0	8323	6.38	43	3.3	52	4.0	65.5
Jack Trudeau, Ind.	4	1042	536	51.4	6287	6.03	29	2.8	40	3.8	63.4

TOP 10 ACTIVE RUSHERS, AFC

2,000 or more yards

	Yrs.	Att.	Yards	TD
1. Eric Dickerson, Ind.	7	2450	11226	82
2. Marcus Allen, Raiders	8	1781	7275	63
3. Freeman McNeil, N.Y.J.	9	1605	7146	30
4. James Brooks, Cin.	9	1320	6343	42
5. Sammy Winder, Den.	8	1453	5307	37
6. Darrin Nelson, S.D.	8	979	4213	16
7. Johnny Hector, N.Y.J.	7	874	3491	39
8. James Jones, Sea.	7	960	3452	23
9. Mike Rozier, Hou.	5	900	3384	27
10. Kevin Mack, Clev.	5	757	3119	26

Other Leading Rushers

Larry Kinnebrew, Buff.	6	770	3115	43
Herman Heard, K.C.	6	651	2694	13
Christian Okoye, K.C.	3	632	2613	18
John L. Williams, Sea.	4	577	2414	6
Mosi Tatupu, N.E.	12	596	2359	18
Steve Grogan, N.E.	15	441	2181	35
Thurman Thomas, Buff.	2	505	2125	8
Bo Jackson, Raiders	3	390	2084	11
John Stephens, N.E.	2	541	2001	11

TOP 10 ACTIVE PASS RECEIVERS, AFC

200 or more receptions

	Yrs.	No.	Yards	TD
1. Ozzie Newsome, Clev.	12	639	7740	45
2. James Lofton, Buff.	12	607	11251	57
3. Mickey Shuler, N.Y.J.	12	438	4819	37
4. Mark Clayton, Mia.	7	405	6565	63
5. Marcus Allen, Raiders	8	388	3661	16
6. Drew Hill, Hou.	10	376	6696	48
7. Al Toon, N.Y.J.	5	355	4574	23
8. Mark Duper, Mia.	8	345	6212	42
9. Andre Reed, Buff.	5	317	4408	31
10. James Brooks, Cin.	9	315	3005	24

Other Leading Receivers

Stephone Paige, K.C.	7	303	5209	44
James Jones, Sea.	7	286	2326	10
Vance Johnson, Den.	5	268	3759	24
Darrin Nelson, S.D.	8	263	2388	5
Eddie Brown, Cin.	5	260	4601	30
Freeman McNeil, N.Y.J.	9	256	2521	12
Bruce Hardy, Mia.	12	256	2455	25
Louis Lipps, Pitt.	6	253	4665	34
Brian Brennan, Clev.	6	239	3255	16
Bill Brooks, Ind.	4	233	3639	18
Ernest Givins, Hou.	4	229	3765	17
Willie Gault, Raiders	7	228	4732	33
Rodney Holman, Cin.	8	221	3022	25
Jeff Chadwick, Sea.	7	214	3454	17
Eric Sievers, N.E.	9	206	2408	16
John L. Williams, Sea.	4	205	1947	12
Eric Dickerson, Ind.	7	202	1633	4

TOP 10 ACTIVE SCORERS, AFC

250 or more points

	Yrs.	TD	FG	PAT	TP
1. Pat Leahy, N.Y.J.	16	0	255	496	1261
2. Nick Lowery, K.C.	11	0	225	338	1013
3. Jim Breech, Cin.	11	0	184	418	970
4. Matt Bahr, Clev.	11	0	182	349	895
5. Gary Anderson, Pitt.	8	0	186	260	818
6. Norm Johnson, Sea.	8	0	136	300	708
7. Eric Dickerson, Ind.	7	86	0	0	516
8. Tony Zendejas, Hou.	5	0	110	177	507
9. Marcus Allen, Raiders	8	80	0	0	480
10. Scott Norwood, Buff.	5	0	95	165	450

Other Leading Scorers

James Brooks, Cin.	9	66	0	0	396*
Dean Biasucci, Ind.	5	0	86	133	391
Mark Clayton, Mia.	7	64	0	0	384
James Lofton, Buff.	12	58	0	0	348
Fuad Reveiz, S.D.	4	0	53	161	320
Drew Hill, Hou.	10	49	0	0	294
Ozzie Newsome, Clev.	12	47	0	0	282
Larry Kinnebrew, Buff.	6	46	0	0	276
Sammy Winder, Den.	8	46	0	0	276
Stephone Paige, K.C.	7	44	0	0	264
Mark Duper, Mia.	8	42	0	0	252
Johnny Hector, N.Y.J.	7	42	0	0	252
Freeman McNeil, N.Y.J.	9	42	0	0	252

*total includes safety scored

TOP 10 ACTIVE INTERCEPTORS, AFC

20 or more interceptions

	Yrs.	No.	Yards	TD
1. Deron Cherry, K.C.	9	43	617	1
2. Ray Clayborn, Clev.	13	36	555	1
3. Mike Harden, Raiders	10	35	644	4
4. Dwayne Woodruff, Pitt.	10	34	579	3
5. Vann McElroy, Raiders	8	31	296	1
6. Roland James, N.E.	10	29	383	0
7. Terry Kinard, Hou.	7	27	574	2
8. Albert Lewis, K.C.	7	26	232	0
9. Gill Byrd, S.D.	7	25	347	2
10. Fred Marion, N.E.	8	23	407	1
Felix Wright, Clev.	5	23	413	2

Other Leading Interceptors

Eugene Daniel, Ind.	6	22	201	1
Kevin Ross, K.C.	6	21	306	1
Lloyd Burruss, K.C.	9	20	412	4
David Fulcher, Cin.	4	20	175	1
Lionel Washington, Raiders	7	20	247	2

TOP 10 ACTIVE QUARTERBACK SACKERS, AFC

Official statistic since 1982

	No.
1. Jacob Green, Sea.	79
2. Andre Tippett, N.E.	72.5
3. Greg Townsend, Raiders	69.5
4. Al Baker, Clev.	62.5
5. Howie Long, Raiders	60
6. Lee Williams, S.D.	58
7. Bruce Smith, Buff.	57.5
8. Ezra Johnson, Hou.	53
9. Gary Jeter, N.E.	52
10. Bill Pickel, Raiders	51.5

Other Leading Sackers

Jeff Bryant, Sea.	49
Karl Mecklenburg, Den.	47
Keith Willis, Pitt.	47
Carl Hairston, Clev.	46.5

TOP 10 ACTIVE PUNT RETURNERS, AFC

40 or more punt returns

	Yrs.	No.	Yards	Avg.	TD
1. Clarence Verdin, Ind.	4	45	535	11.9	2
2. Louis Lipps, Pitt.	6	107	1212	11.3	3
3. Bobby J. Edmonds, Sea.	4	105	1178	11.2	1
4. JoJo Townsell, N.Y.J.	5	110	1206	11.0	2
5. Irving Fryar, N.E.	6	176	1912	10.9	3
James Brooks, Cin.	9	52	565	10.9	0
7. Mike Martin, Cin.	7	140	1381	9.9	1
8. Scott Schwedes, Mia.	3	66	643	9.7	1
9. Gerald McNeil, Hou.	4	161	1545	9.6	1
10. Roland James, N.E.	10	42	400	9.5	1

Other Leading Punt Returners

Pete Mandley, K.C.	6	162	1511	9.3	2
Mark Clayton, Mia.	7	52	485	9.3	1
Tim Brown, Raiders	2	53	487	9.2	1
Vance Johnson, Den.	5	46	423	9.2	0
Paul Skansi, Sea.	7	95	858	9.0	0
Mickey Sutton, Buff.	4	62	559	9.0	0
Lew Barnes, Buff.	3	93	830	8.9	0
Ricky Nattiel, Den.	3	44	373	8.5	0
Nesby Glasgow, Sea.	11	80	651	8.1	1
Rod Woodson, Pitt.	3	78	623	8.0	0
Brian Brennan, Clev.	6	44	352	8.0	1
Bill Brooks, Ind.	4	43	292	6.8	0
Robb Riddick, Buff.	6	46	289	6.3	0

TOP 10 ACTIVE KICKOFF RETURNERS, AFC

40 or more kickoff returns

	Yrs.	No.	Yards	Avg.	TD
1. Ray Clayborn, Clev.	13	57	1538	27.0	3
2. Tim Brown, Raiders	2	44	1161	26.4	1
3. Anthony Miller, S.D.	2	46	1181	25.7	0
4. Rod Woodson, Pitt.	3	86	2122	24.7	2
5. Sammy Martin, N.E.	2	55	1319	24.0	1
6. Darrin Nelson, S.D.	8	99	2315	23.4	1
7. Ron Brown, Raiders	6	157	3662	23.3	4
8. Nesby Glasgow, Sea.	11	84	1904	22.7	0
9. Mike Martin, Cin.	7	75	1643	21.9	0
10. Bobby J. Edmonds, Sea.	4	115	2499	21.7	0
Darryl Clack, Clev.	4	83	1802	21.7	0

Other Leading Kickoff Returners

Albert Bentley, Ind.	5	137	2964	21.6	0
Tim McGee, Cin.	4	58	1249	21.5	0
James Brooks, Cin.	9	118	2523	21.4	0
Paul Palmer, Cin.	3	72	1542	21.4	2
Ken Bell, Den.	4	104	2218	21.3	0
Steve Tasker, Buff.	5	42	896	21.3	0
Lorenzo Hampton, Den.	5	96	2025	21.1	0
Barry Redden, Clev.	8	66	1392	21.1	0
Dwight Stone, Pitt.	3	64	1351	21.1	1
Leonard Harris, Hou.	4	55	1159	21.1	0
Ronnie Harmon, S.D.	4	48	1009	21.0	0
JoJo Townsell, N.Y.J.	5	91	1890	20.8	1
Stanford Jennings, Cin.	6	107	2168	20.3	1
Gerald McNeil, Hou.	4	64	1301	20.3	1
Robb Riddick, Buff.	6	63	1276	20.3	0
Drew Hill, Hou.	10	172	3460	20.1	1
Clarence Verdin, Ind.	4	50	1000	20.0	0
Stefon Adams, Raiders	4	60	1191	19.9	0
Allen Pinkett, Hou.	4	50	978	19.6	0

TOP 10 ACTIVE PUNTERS, AFC

50 or more punts

	Yrs.	No.	Avg.	LG
1. Rohn Stark, Ind.	8	593	44.2	72
2. Reggie Roby, Mia.	7	394	43.4	77
3. Rick Donnelly, Sea.	4	296	42.6	71
4. Mike Horan, Den.	6	390	41.8	75
5. Greg Montgomery, Hou.	2	121	40.9	63
6. Jeff Gossett, Raiders	8	498	40.8	64
7. Lee Johnson, Cin.	5	313	40.7	66
8. John Kidd, S.D.	6	446	40.5	67
9. Bryan Wagner, Clev.	3	212	40.4	71
Kelly Goodburn, K.C.	3	202	40.4	59

Other Leading Punters

Ruben Rodriguez, Sea.	3	192	40.3	68
Joe Prokop, N.Y.J.	4	245	39.2	76
Jeff Feagles, N.E.	2	154	38.1	74

NFC ACTIVE STATISTICAL LEADERS

LEADING ACTIVE PASSERS, NATIONAL FOOTBALL CONFERENCE
1,000 or more attempts

	Yrs.	Att.	Comp.	Pct. Comp.	Yards	Avg. Gain	TD	Pct. TD	Had Int.	Pct. Int.	Rate Pts.
Joe Montana, S.F.	11	4059	2593	63.9	31054	7.65	216	5.3	107	2.6	94.0
Jim Everett, Rams	4	1484	847	57.1	11356	7.65	78	5.3	56	3.8	83.3
Bobby Hebert, N.O.	5	1385	804	58.1	9667	6.98	57	4.1	51	3.7	77.9
Don Majkowski, G.B.	3	1062	586	55.2	7312	6.89	41	3.9	34	3.2	76.3
Phil Simms, N.Y.G.	10	3658	1980	54.1	26235	7.17	156	4.3	137	3.7	75.7
Randall Cunningham, Phil.	5	1788	959	53.6	11933	6.67	77	4.3	58	3.2	75.4
Wade Wilson, Minn.	8	1397	775	55.5	10155	7.27	54	3.9	57	4.1	74.5
Gary Hogeboom, Phx.	10	1325	743	56.1	9436	7.12	49	3.7	60	4.5	71.9
Dave Wilson, N.O.	7	1039	551	53.0	6987	6.72	36	3.5	55	5.3	63.8
Vinny Testaverde, T.B.	3	1111	551	49.6	7454	6.71	38	3.4	63	5.7	59.1

TOP 10 ACTIVE RUSHERS, NFC
2,000 or more yards

	Yrs.	Att.	Yards	TD
1. Ottis Anderson, N.Y.G.	11	2274	9317	69
2. Gerald Riggs, Wash.	8	1788	7465	52
3. Curt Warner, Rams	7	1649	6705	55
4. Roger Craig, S.F.	7	1545	6625	49
5. James Wilder, Wash.	9	1575	5957	37
6. Joe Morris, N.Y.G.	7	1318	5296	48
7. Greg Bell, Rams	6	1157	4795	50
8. Stump Mitchell, Phx.	9	986	4649	32
9. Herschel Walker, Minn.	4	971	4057	31
10. Earnest Byner, Wash.	6	806	3293	30

Other Leading Rushers

Neal Anderson, Chi.	4	687	3113	26
Dalton Hilliard, N.O.	4	792	3018	30
Rueben Mayes, N.O.	3	699	2898	16
Randall Cunningham, Phil.	5	368	2495	18
Gary Anderson, T.B.	4	548	2250	11
Alfred Anderson, Minn.	6	541	2049	19

TOP 10 ACTIVE PASS RECEIVERS, NFC
200 or more receptions

	Yrs.	No.	Yards	TD
1. Art Monk, Wash.	10	662	9165	47
2. J.T. Smith, Phx.	12	526	6749	33
3. Roger Craig, S.F.	7	483	4241	16
4. Roy Green, Phx.	11	469	7699	62
5. James Wilder, Wash.	9	430	3492	9
6. Mike Quick, Phil.	8	354	6329	60
7. Jimmie Giles, Phil.	13	350	5084	41
8. Ottis Anderson, N.Y.G.	11	347	2882	5
9. Jerry Rice, S.F.	5	346	6364	66
10. Henry Ellard, Rams	7	345	5743	36

Other Leading Receivers

Gary Clark, Wash.	5	340	5378	35
Steve Jordan, Minn.	8	309	4074	20
Pete Holohan, Rams	9	281	3223	12
Eric Martin, N.O.	5	269	4148	31
John Spagnola, G.B.	10	263	2886	15
Earnest Byner, Wash.	6	258	2492	10
Anthony Carter, Minn.	5	256	4720	32
Mark Bavaro, N.Y.G.	5	233	3329	23
Herschel Walker, Minn.	4	229	2480	7
Lionel Manuel, N.Y.G.	6	221	3772	23
Don Warren, Wash.	11	220	2337	6
Hoby Brenner, N.O.	9	211	3125	18
Stump Mitchell, Phx.	9	209	1955	9
Ricky Sanders, Wash.	4	204	3202	21
Stacey Bailey, Atl.	8	202	3378	18

TOP 10 ACTIVE SCORERS, NFC
250 or more points

	Yrs.	TD	FG	PAT	TP
1. Eddie Murray, Det.	10	0	212	307	943
2. Rich Karlis, Minn.	8	0	168	271	775
3. Morten Andersen, N.O.	8	0	171	247	760
4. Mike Lansford, Rams	8	0	143	273	702
5. Raul Allegre, N.Y.G.	7	0	128	167	551
6. Paul McFadden, Atl.	6	0	120	160	520
7. Kevin Butler, Chi.	5	0	108	195	519
8. Ottis Anderson, N.Y.G.	11	74	0	0	444
9. Al Del Greco, Phx.	6	0	84	190	442
10. Jerry Rice, S.F.	5	70	0	0	420

Other Leading Scorers

Donald Igwebuike, T.B.	5	0	94	134	416
Roger Craig, S.F.	7	65	0	0	390
Roy Green, Phx.	11	65	0	0	390
Mike Quick, Phil.	8	60	0	0	360
Greg Bell, Rams	6	57	0	0	342
Gerald Riggs, Wash.	8	52	0	0	312
Joe Morris, N.Y.G.	7	50	0	0	300
Art Monk, Wash.	10	47	0	0	282
James Wilder, Wash.	9	46	0	0	276
Mike Cofer, S.F.	3	0	57	94	265
Stump Mitchell, Phx.	9	42	0	0	252

TOP 10 ACTIVE INTERCEPTORS, NFC
20 or more interceptions

	Yrs.	No.	Yards	TD
1. Dave Brown, G.B.	15	62	698	5
2. Ronnie Lott, S.F.	9	48	617	5
3. Everson Walls, N.Y.G.	9	44	391	0
4. Dave Waymer, S.F.	10	37	395	0
5. Mark Lee, G.B.	10	30	249	0
6. Hanford Dixon, S.F.	9	26	225	0
7. Joey Browner, Minn.	7	25	265	2
8. William Judson, Det.	8	24	368	2
Bobby Butler, Atl.	9	24	222	1
10. Carl Lee, Minn.	7	21	280	2
Jerry Holmes, G.B.	8	21	267	2
Scott Case, Atl.	6	21	191	0

Other Leading Interceptors

Darrell Green, Wash.	7	20	194	1

TOP 10 ACTIVE QUARTERBACK SACKERS, NFC
Official statistic since 1982

	No.
1. Lawrence Taylor, N.Y.G.	104
2. Richard Dent, Chi.	81
Reggie White, Phil.	81
4. Rickey Jackson, N.O.	72.5
5. Steve McMichael, Chi.	63
6. Jim Jeffcoat, Dall.	62.5
7. Leonard Marshall, N.Y.G.	60
8. Charles Mann, Wash.	59.5
9. Dan Hampton, Chi.	57
10. Doug Martin, Minn.	51
Keith Millard, Minn.	51

Other Leading Sackers

Michael Cofer, Det.	49.5
Tim Harris, G.B.	48
Kevin Greene, Rams	46.5

TOP 10 ACTIVE PUNT RETURNERS, NFC
40 or more punt returns

	Yrs.	No.	Yards	Avg.	TD
1. Dave Meggett, N.Y.G.	1	46	582	12.7	1
2. Mel Gray, Det.	4	60	733	12.2	1
3. John Taylor, S.F.	3	81	982	12.1	2
4. Vai Sikahema, Phx.	4	157	1846	11.8	3
5. Henry Ellard, Rams	7	131	1494	11.4	4
6. Darrell Green, Wash.	7	49	543	11.1	0
7. J.T. Smith, Phx.	12	264	2730	10.3	4
8. Leo Lewis, Minn.	9	138	1407	10.2	1
Derrick Shepard, Dall.	3	49	501	10.2	1
10. Walter Stanley, Wash.	5	123	1216	9.9	1

Other Leading Punt Returners

Don Griffin, S.F.	4	52	493	9.5	1
Dennis McKinnon, Dall.	6	127	1171	9.2	3
Stump Mitchell, Phx.	9	156	1377	8.8	1
Kelvin Martin, Dall.	3	70	608	8.7	0
Ron Pitts, G.B.	4	50	436	8.7	2
Willie Drewrey, T.B.	5	83	716	8.6	0
Bobby Futrell, T.B.	4	77	639	8.3	0
Eric Martin, N.O.	5	46	368	8.0	0
Evan Cooper, T.B.	6	101	763	7.6	0
Clifford Hicks, Rams	3	42	293	7.0	0

TOP 10 ACTIVE KICKOFF RETURNERS, NFC
40 or more kickoff returns

	Yrs.	No.	Yards	Avg.	TD
1. James Dixon, Dall.	1	47	1181	25.1	1
2. Mel Gray, Det.	4	117	2812	24.0	1
3. Dennis Gentry, Chi.	8	145	3408	23.5	3
4. Roy Green, Phx.	11	83	1917	23.1	1
5. Bobby Humphery, Rams	6	130	2974	22.9	2
6. Stump Mitchell, Phx.	9	177	4007	22.6	0
Sylvester Stamps, T.B.	6	92	2079	22.6	1
8. Vai Sikahema, Phx.	4	137	2957	21.6	0
9. Gene Lang, Atl.	6	62	1335	21.5	0
Willie Drewery, T.B.	5	61	1314	21.5	0

Other Leading Kickoff Returners

Brent Fullwood, G.B.	3	56	1174	21.0	0
Gary Anderson, T.B.	4	59	1217	20.6	1
Derrick Shepard, Dall.	3	44	878	20.0	0
Bobby Futrell, T.B.	4	42	820	19.5	0
Herman Fontenot, G.B.	5	47	909	19.3	0
Mark Lee, G.B.	10	45	859	19.1	0
Walter Stanley, Wash.	5	51	952	18.7	0
Evan Cooper, T.B.	6	43	790	18.4	0

TOP 10 ACTIVE PUNTERS, NFC
50 or more punts

	Yrs.	No.	Avg.	LG
1. Sean Landeta, N.Y.G.	5	301	43.3	71
2. Ralf Mojsiejenko, Wash.	5	354	42.9	74
3. Rich Camarillo, Phx.	9	584	42.5	76
4. Jim Arnold, Det.	7	545	42.4	69
5. Maury Buford, Chi.	7	432	41.6	71
6. Harry Newsome, Minn.	5	375	41.4	64
7. Bucky Scribner, Minn.	5	330	41.0	70
8. Mike Saxon, Dall.	5	394	40.8	63
9. Scott Fulhage, Atl.	3	180	40.6	65
10. Dale Hatcher, G.B.	5	369	40.4	67

Other Leading Punters

John Teltschik, Phil.	4	345	40.1	70
Hank Ilesic, Rams	1	76	40.1	64
Don Bracken, G.B.	5	304	40.0	65
Barry Helton, S.F.	2	133	39.8	56
Chris Mohr, T.B.	1	84	39.4	58

NFL Passer Rating System

The NFL rates its forward passers for statistical purposes against a pre-fixed performance standard based on statistical achievements of all qualified pro passers since 1960. The system now being used replaced one that rated passers in relation to their position in a total group based on various criteria. The current system, which was adopted in 1973, removes inequities that existed in the former method and, at the same time, provides a means of comparing passing performances from one season to the next.

It is important to remember that the system is used to rate **passers,** not **quarterbacks.** Statistics do not reflect leadership, play-calling, and other intangible factors that go into making a successful professional quarterback. Four categories are used as a basis for compiling a rating:
- —Percentage of touchdown passes per attempt
- —Percentage of completions per attempt
- —Percentage of interceptions per attempt
- —Average yards gained per attempt

The base, or **average** standard, is 1.000. The bottom is .000. To earn a 2.000 rating, a passer must perform at exceptional levels, i.e., 70 percent in completions, 10 percent in touchdowns, 1.5 percent in interceptions, and 11 yards average gain per pass attempt. The **maximum** a passer can receive in any category is 2.375.

For example, to gain a 2.375 in completion percentage, a passer would have to complete 77.5 percent of his passes. The NFL record is 70.55 by Ken Anderson (Cincinnati, 1982). To gain 2.375 in percentage of interceptions, a passer would have to go the entire season without an interception. The 2.375 figure in average yards is 12.50, compared with the NFL record of 11.17 by Tommy O'Connell (Cleveland, 1957). To earn a 2.375 in percentage of touchdowns, a passer would have to achieve an 11.9. The record is 13.9 by Sid Luckman (Chicago, 1943).

In order to make the rating more understandable, the point rating is then converted into a scale of 100. For instance, if a passer completes 11 of 23 passes for 114 yards, with one touchdown and no interceptions, the four components would be:

- —**Percentage of Completions**—11 of 23 is 47.8 percent. The point rating is 0.890.

- —**Percentage of Touchdown Passes**—1 touchdown in 23 attempts works out to 4.3 percent for a rating of 0.860.

- —**Percentage of Interceptions**—You can't do better than zero, so the passer receives a maximum rating of 2.375.

- —**Average Yards Gained Per Attempt**—23 attempts divided into 114 yards equals 4.96 yards per attempt for a corresponding rating of 0.490.

The sum of the four components is 4.615, which converts to a rating of 76.9. In order for a passer to achieve 100, his points would have to total 6.000. In rare cases, where statistical performance has been superior, it is possible for a passer to go over 100. However, such an instance is rare. The leading passers each year were checked from 1932 when the NFL began keeping official statistics, and only 10 passers in history have scored over 100 in the year they led the league in passing. The most recent passer to lead the league and score over 100 was San Francisco quarterback Joe Montana, who achieved an NFL-record 112.4 rating in 1989.

Active Coaches' Career Records

Start of 1990 Season

Coach	Team(s)	Regular Season					Postseason					Career			
		Yrs.	Won	Lost	Tied	Pct.	Won	Lost	Tied	Pct.		Won	Lost	Tied	Pct.
Don Shula	Baltimore Colts, Miami Dolphins	27	269	119	6	.690	16	13	0	.552		285	132	6	.681
Chuck Noll	Pittsburgh Steelers	21	177	132	1	.573	16	8	0	.667		193	140	1	.578
Chuck Knox	Los Angeles Rams, Buffalo Bills, Seattle Seahawks	17	155	98	1	.610	7	11	0	.389		162	109	1	.597
Joe Gibbs	Washington Redskins	9	91	45	0	.669	11	3	0	.786		102	48	0	.680
Dan Reeves	Denver Broncos	9	85	50	1	.629	6	5	0	.545		91	55	1	.622
Mike Ditka	Chicago Bears	8	79	41	0	.658	5	4	0	.556		84	45	0	.651
John Robinson	Los Angeles Rams	7	67	44	0	.604	4	6	0	.400		71	50	0	.587
Bill Parcells	New York Giants	7	64	46	1	.581	5	3	0	.625		69	49	1	.584
Marv Levy	Kansas City Chiefs, Buffalo Bills	9	61	66	0	.480	1	2	0	.333		62	68	0	.477
Marty Schottenheimer	Cleveland Browns, Kansas City Chiefs	6	52	34	1	.603	2	4	0	.333		54	38	1	.586
Sam Wyche	Cincinnati Benglas	6	49	46	0	.516	2	1	0	.667		51	47	0	.520
Ron Meyer	New England Patriots, Indianapolis Colts	7	47	36	0	.566	0	2	0	.000		47	38	0	.553
Jack Pardee	Chicago Bears, Washington Redskins, Houston Oilers	6	44	46	0	.489	0	1	0	.000		44	47	0	.485
Jerry Burns	Minnesota Vikings	4	38	25	0	.603	3	3	0	.500		41	28	0	.594
Jim Mora	New Orleans Saints	4	38	25	0	.603	0	1	0	.000		38	26	0	.594
Ray Perkins	New York Giants, Tampa Bay Buccaneers	7	37	67	0	.356	1	1	0	.500		38	68	0	.358
Jerry Glanville	Houston Oilers, Atlanta Falcons	5	33	32	0	.508	2	3	0	.400		35	35	0	.500
Buddy Ryan	Philadelphia Eagles	4	33	29	1	.532	0	2	0	.000		33	31	1	.515
Dan Henning	Atlanta Falcons, San Diego Chargers	5	28	51	1	.356	0	0	0	.000		28	51	1	.356
George Seifert	San Francisco 49ers	1	14	2	0	.875	3	0	0	1.000		17	2	0	.895
Lindy Infante	Green Bay Packers	2	14	18	0	.438	0	0	0	.000		14	18	0	.438
Bud Carson	Cleveland Browns	1	9	6	1	.594	1	1	0	.500		10	7	1	.556
Wayne Fontes	Detroit Lions	2	9	12	0	.429	0	0	0	.000		9	12	0	.429
Art Shell	Los Angeles Raiders	1	7	5	0	.583	0	0	0	.000		7	5	0	.583
Jimmy Johnson	Dallas Cowboys	1	1	15	0	.063	0	0	0	.000		1	15	0	.063
Joe Bugel	Phoenix Cardinals	0	0	0	0	.000	0	0	0	.000		0	0	0	.000
Bruce Coslet	New York Jets	0	0	0	0	.000	0	0	0	.000		0	0	0	.000
Rod Rust	New England Patriots	0	0	0	0	.000	0	0	0	.000		0	0	0	.000

Coaches With 100 Career Victories

Start of 1990 Season

Coach	Team(s)	Regular Season					Postseason					Career			
		Yrs.	Won	Lost	Tied	Pct.	Won	Lost	Tied	Pct.		Won	Lost	Tied	Pct.
George Halas	Chicago Bears	40	319	148	31	.672	6	3	0	.667		325	151	31	.672
Don Shula	Baltimore Colts, Miami Dolphins	27	269	119	6	.690	16	13	0	.552		285	132	6	.681
Tom Landry	Dallas Cowboys	29	250	162	6	.605	20	16	0	.556		270	178	6	.601
Earl (Curly) Lambeau	Green Bay Packers, Chicago Cardinals, Washington Redskins	33	226	132	22	.624	3	2	0	.600		229	134	22	.623
Chuck Noll	Pittsburgh Steelers	21	177	132	1	.573	16	8	0	.667		193	140	1	.578
Paul Brown	Cleveland Browns, Cincinnati Bengals	21	166	100	6	.621	4	8	0	.333		170	108	6	.609
Bud Grant	Minnesota Vikings	18	158	96	5	.620	10	12	0	.455		168	108	5	.607
Chuck Knox	Los Angeles Rams, Buffalo Bills, Seattle Seahawks	17	155	98	1	.610	7	11	0	.389		162	109	1	.597
Steve Owen	New York Giants	23	151	100	17	.595	2	8	0	.200		153	108	17	.581
Hank Stram	Dallas Texans-Kansas City Chiefs, New Orleans Saints	17	131	97	10	.571	5	3	0	.625		136	100	10	.573
Weeb Ewbank	Baltimore Colts, New York Jets	20	130	129	7	.502	4	1	0	.800		134	130	7	.507
Sid Gillman	Los Angeles Rams, Los Angeles-San Diego Chargers, Houston Oilers	18	122	99	7	.550	1	5	0	.167		123	104	7	.541
George Allen	Los Angeles Rams, Washington Redskins	12	116	47	5	.705	2	7	0	.222		118	54	5	.681
Don Coryell	St. Louis Cardinals, San Diego Chargers	14	111	83	1	.572	3	6	0	.333		114	89	1	.561
John Madden	Oakland Raiders	10	103	32	7	.750	9	7	0	.563		112	39	7	.731
Ray (Buddy) Parker	Chicago Cardinals, Detroit Lions, Pittsburgh Steelers	15	104	75	9	.577	3	1	0	.750		107	76	9	.581
Vince Lombardi	Green Bay Packers, Washington Redskins	10	96	34	6	.728	9	1	0	.900		105	35	6	.740
Joe Gibbs	Washington Redskins	9	91	45	0	.669	11	3	0	.786		102	48	0	.680
Bill Walsh	San Francisco 49ers	10	92	59	1	.609	10	4	0	.714		102	63	1	.617

55th Annual NFL Draft, April 22-23, 1990

Atlanta Falcons (Drafted 2nd)

1. Choice to Indianapolis
   Steve Broussard—20, RB, Washington State, from Washington
2. Darion Conner—27, LB, Jackson State
3. Oliver Barnett—55, DE, Kentucky
4. Choice to Indianapolis
5. Choice to Denver through Washington and New England
   Reggie Redding—121, TE, Cal State-Fullerton, from Indianapolis
6. Mike Pringle—139, RB, Cal State-Fullerton
7. Choice to New York Jets
8. Tory Epps—195, NT, Memphis State
9. Darrell Jordan—222, LB, Northern Arizona
10. Donnie Salum—250, LB, Arizona
11. Chris Ellison—278, DB, Houston
12. Shawn McCarthy—305, P, Purdue

Buffalo Bills (Drafted alternately 18-17-16-19)

1. James Williams—16, DB, Fresno State
2. Carwell Gardner—42, RB, Louisville
3. Glenn Parker—69, T, Arizona
4. Eddie Fuller—100, RB, Louisiana State
5. Choice to Kansas City
6. John Nies—154, P, Arizona
7. Brent Griffith—166, G, Minnesota-Duluth, from Dallas through New England
   Brent Collins—170, LB, Carson-Newman, from New England
   Fred De Riggi—181, NT, Syracuse
8. Marvcus Patton—208, LB, UCLA, from Kansas City
   Choice exercised in 1989 Supplemental Draft for Brett Young, DB, Oregon
9. Clarkston Hines—238, WR, Duke
10. Mike Lodish—265, DT, UCLA
11. Al Edwards—292, WR, Northwest Louisiana
12. Choice to New England

Chicago Bears (Drafted alternately 8-7)

1. Mark Carrier—6, DB, Southern California
2. Fred Washington—32, DT, Texas Christian
   Ron Cox—33, LB, Fresno State, from San Diego
3. Tim Ryan—61, DT, Southern California
   Peter Tom Willis—63, QB, Florida State, from Los Angeles Raiders
4. Tony Moss—88, WR, Louisiana State
5. Pat Chaffey—117, RB, Oregon State
6. John Mangum—144, DB, Alabama
7. Choice to L.A. Raiders
   Bill Anderson—176, C, Iowa, from Los Angeles Raiders
8. James Rouse—200, RB, Arkansas
9. Johnny Bailey—228, RB, Texas A&I
10. Terry Price—255, DT, Texas A&M
11. Brent White—284, DE, Michigan
    Roman Matusz—298, T, Pittsburgh, from Minnesota through L.A. Raiders
12. Anthony Cooney—310, DB, Arkansas

Cincinnati Bengals (Drafted alternately 14-13-12-11)

1. James Francis—12, LB, Baylor
2. Harold Green—38, RB, South Carolina
3. Bernard Clark—65, LB, Miami
4. Mike Brennan—91, T, Notre Dame
5. Lynn James—122, WR, Arizona State
6. Don Odegard—150, DB, Nevada-Las Vegas
7. Craig Ogletree—177, LB, Auburn
8. Doug Wellsandt—204, TE, Washington State
9. Mitchell Price—234, DB, Tulane
10. Eric Crigler—261, T, Murray State
11. Tim O'Connor—288, T, Virginia
12. Andre Riley—314, WR, Washington

Cleveland Browns (Drafted 20th)

1. Choice to Green Bay
2. Leroy Hoard—45, RB, Michigan
3. Anthony Pleasant—73, DE, Tennessee State
4. Harlon Barnett—101, DB, Michigan State
5. Rob Burnett—129, DE, Syracuse
6. Randy Hilliard—157, DB, Northwest Louisiana
7. Scott Galbraith—178, TE, Southern California, from Miami
   Choice to San Diego
8. Jock Jones—212, LB, Virginia Tech
9. Eugene Rowell—240, WR, Southern Mississippi
10. Michael Wallace—268, DB, Jackson State
11. Clemente Gordon—296, QB, Grambling
12. Kerry Simien—323, WR, Texas A&I

Dallas Cowboys (Drafted 1st)

1. Choice exercised in 1989 Supplemental Draft for Steve Walsh, QB, Miami
   Emmitt Smith—17, RB, Florida, from Pittsburgh
2. Alexander Wright—26, WR, Auburn
3. Choice to Minnesota
   Jimmie Jones—64, DT, Miami, from Seattle through New England
4. Choice to Denver
5. Choice to New England through Washington
6. Choice to San Diego
7. Choice to Buffalo through New England
8. Choice to Detroit
9. Kenneth Gant—221, DB, Albany State, Ga.
10. Choice to Minnesota
11. Dave Harper—277, LB, Humboldt State
12. Choice exercised in 1989 Supplemental Draft for Mike Lowman, RB, Coffeyville JC

Denver Broncos (Drafted 27th)

1. Choice exercised in 1989 Supplemental Draft for Bobby Humphrey, RB, Alabama
2. Alton Montgomery—52, DB, Houston
3. Choice to New England through Dallas
4. Jeroy Robinson—82, LB, Texas A&M, from Dallas
   Choice to Tampa Bay
5. Jeff Davidson—111, G, Ohio State, from Atlanta through Washington and New England
   Le-Lo Lang—136, DB, Washington
6. Ronnie Haliburton—164, TE, Louisiana State
7. Shannon Sharpe—192, WR, Savannah State
8. Brad Leggett—219, C, Southern California
9. Todd Ellis—247, QB, South Carolina
10. James Szymanski—259, DE, Michigan State, from Indianapolis through Dallas and Los Angeles Raiders
    Anthony Thompson—275, LB, East Carolina
11. Choice to L.A. Raiders
12. Choice to Phoenix

Detroit Lions (Drafted alternately 9-10)

1. Andre Ware—7, QB, Houston
2. Dan Owens—35, DE, Southern California
3. Marc Spindler—62, DE, Pittsburgh
4. Rob Hinckley—90, LB, Stanford
   Chris Oldham—105, DB, Oregon, from Los Angeles Rams
5. Jeff Campbell—118, WR, Colorado
6. Maurice Henry—147, LB, Kansas State
7. Tracy Hayworth—174, LB, Tennessee
8. Willie Green—194, WR, Mississippi, from Dallas
   Roman Fortin—203, G, San Diego State
9. Jack Linn—229, T, West Virginia
10. Bill Miller—258, WR, Illinois State
11. Reginald Warnsley—285, RB, Southern Mississippi
12. Robert Claiborne—313, WR, San Diego State

Green Bay Packers (Drafted alternately 21-23-22)

1. Tony Bennett—18, LB, Mississippi, from Cleveland
   Darrell Thompson—19, RB, Minnesota
2. LeRoy Butler—48, DB, Florida State
3. Bobby Houston—75, LB, North Carolina State
4. Jackie Harris—102, TE, Northeast Louisiana
5. Charles Wilson—132, WR, Memphis State
6. Bryce Paup—159, LB, Northern Iowa
7. Lester Archambeau—186, DE, Stanford
8. Roger Brown—215, DB, Virginia Tech
9. Kirk Baumgartner—242, QB, Wisconsin-Stevens Point
10. Jerome Martin—269, DB, Western Kentucky
11. Harry Jackson—299, RB, St. Cloud, Minn.
12. Kirk Maggio—325, P, UCLA

Houston Oilers (Drafted alternately 17-16-19-18)

1. Lamar Lathon—15, LB, Houston
2. Jeff Alm—41, DT, Notre Dame
3. Willis Peguese—72, DE, Miami
4. Eric Still—99, G, Tennessee
5. Richard Newbill—126, LB, Miami
6. Tony Jones—153, WR, Texas
7. Andy Murray—184, RB, Kentucky
8. Brett Tucker—211, DB, Northern Illinois
9. Pat Coleman—237, WR, Mississippi
10. Dee Thomas—264, DB, Nicholls State
11. Joey Banes—295, T, Houston
12. Reggie Slack—321, QB, Auburn

Indianapolis Colts (Drafted alternately 12-11-14-13)

1. Jeff George—1, QB, Illinois, from Atlanta
2. Anthony Johnson—36, RB, Notre Dame
3. Choice to San Diego
4. Stacey Simmons—83, WR, Florida, from Atlanta
   Bill Schultz—94, G, Southern California
   Alan Grant—103, DB, Stanford, from Washington
   Pat Cunningham—106, T, Texas A&M, from Philadelphia
5. Choice to Atlanta
6. Tony Walker—148, LB, Southeast Missouri
7. James Singletary—179, LB, East Carolina
8. Ken Clark—206, RB, Nebraska
   Harvey Wilson—213, DB, Southern University, from Washington
9. Darvell Huffman—232, WR, Boston University
10. Choice to Denver, through Dallas and Los Angeles Raiders
11. Carnel Smith—290, DE, Pittsburgh
12. Gene Benhart—311, QB, Western Illinois, from San Diego
    Dean Brown—316, G, Notre Dame

Kansas City Chiefs (Drafted 15th)

1. Percy Snow—13, LB, Michigan State
2. Tim Grunhard—40, C, Notre Dame
3. Choice to San Diego through Dallas
4. Fred Jones—96, WR, Grambling
5. Derrick Graham—124, T, Appalachian State
   Ken Hackemack—127, T, Texas, from Buffalo
6. Tom Sims—152, DT, Pittsburgh
7. Dave Szott—180, G, Penn State
8. Choice to Buffalo
9. Michael Owens—235, RB, Syracuse
10. Craig Hudson—263, TE, Wisconsin
11. Ernest Thompson—291, RB, Georgia Southern
12. Tony Jeffery—318, WR, San Jose State

Los Angeles Raiders (Drafted alternately 13-12-11-14)

1. Anthony Smith—11, DE, Arizona
2. Aaron Wallace—37, LB, Texas A&M
3. Choice to Chicago
4. Torin Dorn—95, DB, North Carolina
5. Stan Smagala—123, DB, Notre Dame
6. Marcus Wilson—149, RB, Virginia
7. Garry Lewis—173, DB, Alcorn State, from Chicago
   Choice to Chicago
8. Arthur Jimerson—197, LB, Norfolk State, from New England through Dallas
   Choice to New Orleans
9. Leon Perry—230, RB, Oklahoma, from Seattle through Dallas
   Choice to New Orleans
10. Choice to New Orleans
11. Choice to New Orleans
    Ron Lewis—303, WR, Jackson State, from Denver
    Myron Jones—304, RB, Fresno State, from San Francisco through Dallas
12. Major Harris—317, QB, West Virginia
    Demetrius Davis—331, TE, Nevada-Reno, from San Francisco

Los Angeles Rams (Drafted alternately 25-24)

1. Bern Brostek—23, C, Washington
2. Pat Terrell—49, DB, Notre Dame
3. Latin Berry—78, RB, Oregon
4. Choice to Detroit
5. Choice to New York Jets
6. Tim Stallworth—161, WR, Washington State
7. Kent Elmore—190, P, Tennessee
8. Ray Savage—198, LB, Virginia, from Tampa Bay
   Elbert Crawford—216, C, Arkansas
9. Tony Lomack—245, WR, Florida
10. Steve Bates—272, DE, James Madison
11. Bill Goldberg—301, DT, Georgia
12. David Lang—328, RB, Northern Arizona

Miami Dolphins (Drafted alternately 11-14-13-12)

1. Richmond Webb—9, T, Texas A&M
2. Keith Sims—39, G, Iowa State
3. Alfred Oglesby—66, DT, Houston
4. Scott Mitchell—93, QB, Utah
5. Choice to New England through Dallas
   Leroy Holt—137, RB, Southern California, from San Francisco through Los Angeles Raiders and Washington
6. Sean Vanhorse—151, DB, Howard
7. Choice to Cleveland
8. Thomas Woods—205, WR, Tennessee
9. Phil Ross—231, TE, Oregon State
10. Choice to Washington
11. Choice to San Francisco
12. Bobby Harden—315, DB, Miami

Minnesota Vikings (Drafted alternately 23-22-21)

1. Choice to Pittsburgh through Dallas
2. Choice to San Francisco through Dallas
3. Mike Jones—54, TE, Texas A&M, from Dallas
   Marion Hobby—74, DE, Tennessee
4. Alonzo Hampton—104, DB, Pittsburgh
5. Reggie Thornton—116, WR, Bowling Green, from San Diego through Dallas
   Cedric Smith—131, RB, Florida
6. Choice to New Orleans through Dallas and Los Angeles Raiders
7. John Levelis—188, LB, C.W. Post
8. Craig Schlichting—214, DE, Wyoming
9. Terry Allen—241, RB, Clemson
10. Pat Newman—249, WR, Utah State, from Dallas
    Donald Smith—271, DB, Liberty
11. Choice to Chicago through Los Angeles Raiders
12. Ron Goetz—324, LB, Minnesota

New England Patriots (Drafted alternately 5-4-6)

1. Choice to Seattle
   Chris Singleton—8, LB, Arizona, from Seattle
   Ray Agnew—10, DE, North Carolina State, from Indianapolis through Seattle
2. Choice to Seattle
3. Tommy Hodson—59, QB, Louisiana State
   Greg McMurtry—80, WR, Michigan, from Denver through Dallas
4. Choice to Washington
5. Junior Robinson—110, DB, East Carolina, from Dallas through Washington
   Jon Melander—113, T, Minnesota
   James Gray—120, RB, Texas Tech, from Miami through Dallas
6. Choice to San Diego through Dallas
7. Choice to Buffalo
8. Choice to L.A. Raiders through Dallas
9. Shawn Bouwens—226, G, Nebraska Wesleyan
10. Anthony Landry—253, RB, Stephen F. Austin
11. Sean Smith—280, DE, Georgia Tech
12. Ventson Donelson—309, DB, Michigan State
    Blaine Rose—322, G, Maryland, from Buffalo

New Orleans Saints (Drafted alternately 16-19-18-17)

1. Renaldo Turnbull—14, DE, West Virginia
2. Vince Buck—44, DB, Central State, Ohio
3. Joel Smeenge—71, DE, Western Michigan
4. DeMond Winston—98, LB, Vanderbilt
5. Charles Arbuckle—125, TE, UCLA
6. Mike Buck—156, QB, Maine
   James Williams—158, LB, Mississippi State, from Minnesota through Dallas and Los Angeles Raiders
7. Scott Hough—183, G, Maine
8. Gerry Gdowski—207, QB, Nebraska, from Los Angeles Raiders
   Derrick Carr—210, DE, Bowling Green
9. Broderick Graves—233, RB, Winston-Salem State, from Los Angeles Raiders
   Lonnie Brockman—236, LB, West Virginia
10. Gary Cooper—260, WR, Clemson, from Los Angeles Raiders
    Ernest Spears—267, DB, Southern California
11. Webbie Burnett—287, NT, Western Kentucky, from Los Angeles Raiders
    Choice to Philadelphia
12. Chris Port—320, G, Duke

New York Giants (Drafted 26th)

1. Rodney Hampton—24, RB, Georgia
2. Mike Fox—51, DT, West Virginia
3. Greg Mark—79, DE, Miami
4. David Whitmore—107, DB, Stephen F. Austin
5. Craig Kupp—135, QB, Pacific Lutheran
6. Choice to San Diego through Dallas
7. Aaron Emanuel—191, RB, Southern California
8. Barry Voorhees—218, T, Cal State-Northridge
9. Clint James—246, DE, Louisiana State
10. Otis Moore—274, DT, Clemson
11. Tim Downing—302, DE, Washington State
12. Matt Stover—329, K, Louisiana Tech

New York Jets (Drafted 3rd)

1. Blair Thomas—2, RB, Penn State
2. Reggie Rembert—28, WR, West Virginia
3. Tony Stargell—56, DB, Tennessee State
4. Troy Taylor—84, QB, California
5. Tony Savage—112, DT, Washington State
   Robert McWright—134, DB, Texas Christian, from Los Angeles Rams
6. Terance Mathis—140, WR, New Mexico
7. Dwayne White—167, G, Alcorn State, from Atlanta
   Basil Proctor—168, LB, West Virginia
8. Roger Duffy—196, C, Penn State
9. Dale Dawkins—223, WR, Miami
10. Brad Quast—251, LB, Iowa
11. Derrick Kelson—279, DB, Purdue
12. Darrell Davis—306, LB, Texas Christian

Philadelphia Eagles (Drafted alternately 24-25)

1. Ben Smith—22, DB, Georgia
2. Mike Bellamy—50, WR, Illinois
3. Fred Barnett—77, WR, Arkansas State
4. Choice to Indianapolis
5. Calvin Williams—133, WR, Purdue
6. Kevin Thompson—162, DB, Oklahoma
7. Terry Strouf—189, T, Wisconsin-LaCrosse
8. Curt Dykes—217, T, Oregon
9. Cecil Gray—244, DT, North Carolina
10. Orlando Adams—273, DT, Jacksonville State
11. John Hudson—294, C, Auburn, from New Orleans
    Tyrone Watson—300, WR, Tennessee State
12. Judd Garrett—327, RB, Princeton

Phoenix Cardinals (Drafted alternately 4-6-5)

1. Choice exercised in 1989 Supplemental Draft for Timm Rosenbach, QB, Washington State
2. Anthony Thompson—31, RB, Indiana
3. Ricky Proehl—58, WR, Wake Forest
4. Travis Davis—85, DT, Michigan State
5. Larry Centers—115, RB, Stephen F. Austin
6. Tyrone Shavers—142, WR, Lamar
7. Johnny Johnson—169, RB, San Jose State
8. Mickey Washington—199, DB, Texas A&M
9. David Bavaro—225, LB, Syracuse
10. Dave Elle—252, TE, South Dakota
11. Dempsey Norman—282, WR, St. Francis, Ill.
12. Donnie Riley—308, RB, Central Michigan
    Ken McMichel—330, DB, Oklahoma, from Denver

Pittsburgh Steelers (Drafted alternately 19-18-17-16)

1. Choice to Dallas
   Eric Green—21, TE, Liberty, from Minnesota through Dallas
2. Kenny Davidson—43, DE, Louisiana State
3. Neil O'Donnell—70, QB, Maryland
   Craig Veasey—81, DT, Houston, from San Francisco through Dallas
4. Chris Calloway—97, WR, Michigan
5. Barry Foster—128, RB, Arkansas
6. Ronald Heard—155, WR, Bowling Green
7. Dan Grayson—182, LB, Washington State
8. Karl Dunbar—209, DT, Louisiana State
9. Gary Jones—239, DB, Texas A&M
10. Eddie Miles—266, LB, Minnesota
11. Justin Strzelczyk—293, T, Maine
12. Richard Bell—319, RB, Nebraska

San Diego Chargers (Drafted alternately 7-8)

1. Junior Seau—5, LB, Southern California
2. Choice to Chicago
3. Jeff Mills—57, LB, Nebraska, from Tampa Bay
   Leo Goeas—60, G, Hawaii
   Walter Wilson—67, WR, East Carolina, from Indianapolis
4. Choice to San Francisco through Los Angeles Raiders
5. Choice to Minnesota through Dallas
6. John Friesz—138, QB, Idaho, from Dallas
   Frank Cornish—143, C, UCLA, from New England through Dallas
   David Pool—145, DB, Carson-Newman
   Derrick Walker—163, TE, Michigan, from New York Giants through Dallas
7. Jeff Novak—172, G, S.W. Texas State
7. Joe Staysniak—185, T, Ohio State, from Cleveland
   Nate Lewis—187, WR, Oregon Tech, from Washington
   Keith Collins—193, DB, Appalachian State, from San Francisco
8. J.J. Flannigan—201, RB, Colorado
9. Chris Goetz—227, G, Pittsburgh
10. Kenny Berry—256, DB, Miami
11. Tommie Stowers—283, TE, Missouri
12. Choice to Indianapolis
    Elliott Searcy—326, WR, Southern U., from Washington

San Francisco 49ers (Drafted 28th)

1. Dexter Carter—25, RB, Florida State
2. Dennis Brown—47, DT, Washington, from Minnesota through Dallas
   Eric Davis—53, DB, Jacksonville State
3. Ronald Lewis—68, WR, Florida State, from Kansas City through Dallas
   Choice to Pittsburgh through Dallas
4. Dean Caliguire—92, C, Pittsburgh, from San Diego through L.A. Raiders
   Choice to Washington through Los Angeles Raiders
5. Choice to Miami through L.A. Raiders and Washington
6. Frank Pollack—165, T, Northern Arizona
7. Choice to San Diego
8. Dwight Pickens—220, WR, Fresno State
9. Odell Haggins—248, DT, Florida State
10. Martin Harrison—276, DE, Washington
11. Anthony Shelton—289, DB, Tennessee State, from Miami
    Choice to L.A. Raiders through Dallas
12. Choice to L.A. Raiders

Seattle Seahawks (Drafted alternately 10-9)

1. Cortez Kennedy—3, DT, Miami, from New England
   Choice to New England
2. Terry Wooden—29, LB, Syracuse, from New England
   Robert Blackmon—34, DB, Baylor
3. Choice to Dallas through New England
4. Chris Warren—89, RB, Ferrum, Va.
5. Eric Hayes—119, DT, Florida State
6. Ned Bolcar—146, LB, Notre Dame
7. Bob Kula—175, T, Michigan State
8. Bill Hitchcock—202, T, Purdue
9. Choice to L.A. Raiders through Dallas
10. Robert Morris—257, DE, Valdosta State
11. Daryl Reed—286, DB, Oregon
12. John Gromos—312, QB, Vanderbilt

Tampa Bay Buccaneers (Drafted alternately 6-5-4)

1. Keith McCants—4, LB, Alabama
2. Reggie Cobb—30, RB, Tennessee
3. Choice to San Diego
4. Jesse Anderson—87, TE, Mississippi State
   Tony Mayberry—108, C, Wake Forest, from Denver
5. Ian Beckles—114, G, Indiana
6. Derrick Douglas—141, RB, Louisiana Tech
7. Donnie Gardner—171, DE, Kentucky
8. Choice to L.A. Rams
9. Terry Cook—224, DE, Fresno State
10. Mike Busch—254, TE, Iowa State
11. Terry Anthony—281, WR, Florida State
12. Todd Hammel—307, QB, Stephen F. Austin

Washington Redskins (Drafted alternately 22-21-23)

1. Choice to Atlanta
2. Andre Collins—46, LB, Penn State
3. Mohammed Elewonibi—76, G, Brigham Young
4. Cary Conklin—86, QB, Washington, from New England
   Choice to Indianapolis
   Rico Labbe—109, DB, Boston College, from San Francisco through L.A. Raiders
5. Brian Mitchell—130, RB, Southwestern Louisiana
6. Kent Wells—160, DT, Nebraska
7. Choice to San Diego
8. Choice to Indianapolis
9. Tim Moxley—243, G, Ohio State
10. D'Juan Francisco—262, DB, Notre Dame, from Miami
    Thomas Rayam—270, DT, Alabama
11. Jon Leverenz—297, LB, Minnesota
12. Choice to San Diego

23

Look for in 1990

Things that could happen in 1990

• **Eric Dickerson,** Indianapolis, starts the season with 11,226 yards rushing in seven NFL seasons, an average of 1,604 yards per season. He currently stands seventh on the all-time rushing list, but he's only 1,513 yards behind the number-two rusher on that list, Tony Dorsett.

• Dickerson could become the first player in NFL history to gain 1,000 yards rushing for eight consecutive seasons. He set the record of seven straight 1,000-yard rushing seasons in 1989.

• **Ottis Anderson,** New York Giants, starts 1990 in ninth place on the all-time list with 9,317 yards rushing. He needs 91 yards to pass Earl Campbell into eighth place, and needs 683 yards to become the eighth 10,000-yard rusher in NFL history.

• **Roger Craig,** San Francisco, has carried 1,545 times for 6,625 yards and 49 touchdowns. He needs 38 carries, 720 yards, and two touchdowns to break the 49ers' team records of 1,582 carries (held by Ken Willard), and 7,344 yards and 50 touchdowns (both held by Joe Perry).

• **James Brooks,** Cincinnati, has 4,872 yards rushing in six years with the team. He needs 550 yards to break the club record of 5,421 held by Pete Johnson.

• **Dalton Hilliard,** New Orleans, has scored 37 touchdowns in four seasons. He needs one more to break the team record he shares with Danny Abramowicz.

• **Dan Marino,** Miami, and **Joe Montana,** San Francisco, each have passed for 3,000 or more yards in six seasons, tying the NFL record set by Dan Fouts. Either Marino or Montana could become the first to have seven 3,000-yard seasons.

• Marino has had 16 games in his seven-year career in which he has thrown at least four touchdown passes. He is one short of the NFL record held by Johnny Unitas, who played for 18 seasons.

• Marino has thrown 220 touchdown passes, the eighth-highest total in NFL history. He needs 30 more to become only the fifth player with 250-or-more scoring passes; the others: Fran Tarkenton (342), Johnny Unitas (290), Sonny Jurgensen (255), and Dan Fouts (254).

• Montana starts 1990 with 2,593 completions, tied with Jim Hart for fifth on the all-time list. He needs 238 to move into third place past Hart, Ken Anderson (2,654), and John Unitas (2,830).

• Montana has gained 31,054 yards on 4,059 passes. He needs 495 yards and 433 passes to break the 49ers' club records of 31,548 and 4,491, both held by John Brodie.

• **Phil Simms,** New York Giants, who has thrown 156 touchdown passes, needs 18 to break Charlie Conerly's team record of 173.

• **Warren Moon,** Houston, has completed 1,339 passes for 18,300 yards in six years in the NFL. He needs 88 completions and 850 yards to break the Oilers' team records held by Dan Pastorini (1,426 completions) and George Blanda (19,149 yards).

• **Art Monk,** Washington, needs 38 receptions to become the third player in NFL history to amass 700 career receptions. Steve Largent had 819 catches, and Charlie Joiner had 750.

• **Roy Green,** Phoenix, has 469 career receptions for 7,699 yards. He needs 12 catches and 220 yards to break the franchise records in those categories (480 and 7,918), both held by Jackie Smith.

• **Henry Ellard,** Los Angeles Rams, starts 1990 with 345 receptions for 5,743 yards. He needs 56 receptions and 547 yards to break the Rams' team records of 400 receptions (held by Tom Fears) and 6,289 yards (held by Elroy (Crazylegs) Hirsch).

• **Mark Clayton,** Miami, has 64 career touchdowns and needs 12 to break the team record of 75 touchdowns held by Nat Moore.

• **Eric Martin,** New Orleans, has caught 269 passes in five seasons. He needs 41 receptions to break the Saints' team record of 309 established by Danny Abramowicz.

• **Dave Brown,** Green Bay, has 62 career interceptions, tied with Dick LeBeau for fifth place in NFL history. He needs three interceptions to tie Ken Riley for fourth place, and needs six to tie Dick (Night Train) Lane for third.

• **Gill Byrd,** San Diego, has 25 interceptions in seven seasons. He needs five to break the Chargers' team record of 29 held by Dick Harris.

• **Steve McMichael,** Chicago, has scored three safeties in his career, one shy of the NFL record of four shared by Ted Hendricks and Doug English.

• **Ron Brown,** L.A. Raiders, has scored four touchdowns on kickoff returns in his career. That total is two short of the NFL record of six, shared by Ollie Matson, Gale Sayers, and Travis Williams.

• **J. T. Smith,** Phoenix, has a career total of 264 punt returns. He is 18 shy of the NFL record set by Billy (White Shoes) Johnson.

• **Nick Lowery,** Kansas City, has scored at least 100 points in seven seasons, tying the total of Jan Stenerud. No NFL player has scored 100 points in eight seasons.

• **Jim Breech,** Cincinnati, has scored at least one point in 149 consecutive games. He needs three more games to break the NFL record of 151, established by Fred Cox.

• **Kevin Butler,** Chicago, has 108 field goals in five seasons. He needs 21 more to break the Bears' club record of 128 held by Bob Thomas.

• **Mike Webster,** Kansas City, has played in 236 NFL games, a total exceeded by only 10 players in NFL history. He needs three games to tie Charlie Joiner for tenth place on that list and is 14 games shy of the 250 mark, a plateau reached by only four players: George Blanda (340), Jim Marshall (282), Jan Stenerud (263), and Earl Morrall (255).

• **Don Shula,** Miami head coach, needs two victories to reach 200 victories since joining the team in 1970. Only three other coaches have had that many wins with one team: George Halas (319 with Chicago), Tom Landry (250 with Dallas), and Curly Lambeau (209 with Green Bay). Including his seven seasons as coach of Baltimore, Shula has a total of 269 wins, 50 shy of Halas's NFL record.

THE AFC

American Football Conference
Eastern Division

Team Colors: Royal Blue, Scarlet Red, and White

One Bills Drive
Orchard Park, New York 14127
Telephone: (716) 648-1800

Club Officials

President: Ralph C. Wilson, Jr.
Executive Vice President: David N. Olsen
General Manager and Vice President-
   Administration: Bill Polian
Vice President-Head Coach: Marv Levy
Treasurer: Jeffrey C. Littmann
Assistant General Manager/Director of
   Pro Personnel: Bob Ferguson
Assistant General Manager/Business Operations:
   Bill Munson
Director of Administration: Ed Stillwell
Business Manager: Jim Overdorf
Director of College Scouting: John Butler
Director of Marketing/Sales: Jerry Foran
Director of Public/Community Relations:
   Denny Lynch
Director of Stadium Operations: Steve Champlin
Box Office Comptroller: June Foran
Manager of Media Relations: Scott Berchtold
Equipment Manager: Dave Hojnowski
Strength and Conditioning Coordinator:
   Rusty Jones
Trainers: Ed Abramoski, Bud Carpenter
Video Director: Henry Kunttu

Stadium: Rich Stadium • **Capacity:** 80,290
   One Bills Drive
   Orchard Park, New York 14127

Playing Surface: AstroTurf

Training Camp: Fredonia State University
   Fredonia, New York 14063

1990 Schedule

Preseason
Aug. 13	**New York Giants**	8:00
Aug. 17	at Detroit	7:30
Aug. 25	at New Orleans	7:00
Aug. 30	vs. Chicago at Columbia, S.C.	8:00

Regular Season
Sept. 9	**Indianapolis**	4:00
Sept. 16	at Miami	1:00
Sept. 24	at New York Jets (Monday)	9:00
Sept. 30	**Denver**	1:00
Oct. 7	**Los Angeles Raiders**	7:30
Oct. 14	**Open Date**	
Oct. 21	**New York Jets**	1:00
Oct. 28	at New England	1:00
Nov. 4	at Cleveland	1:00
Nov. 11	**Phoenix**	1:00
Nov. 18	**New England**	1:00
Nov. 26	at Houston (Monday)	8:00
Dec. 2	**Philadelphia**	1:00
Dec. 9	at Indianapolis	1:00
Dec. 15	at N.Y. Giants (Saturday)	12:30
Dec. 23	**Miami**	1:00
Dec. 30	at Washington	1:00

Bills Coaching History

(189-250-8)

1960-61	Buster Ramsey	11-16-1
1962-65	Lou Saban	38-18-3
1966-68	Joe Collier*	13-17-1
1968	Harvey Johnson	1-10-1
1969-70	John Rauch	7-20-1
1971	Harvey Johnson	1-13-0
1972-76	Lou Saban**	32-29-1
1976-77	Jim Ringo	3-20-0
1978-82	Chuck Knox	38-38-0
1983-84	Kay Stephenson***	10-26-0
1985-86	Hank Bullough****	4-17-0
1986-89	Marv Levy	31-26-0

   *Released after two games in 1968
   **Resigned after five games in 1976
   ***Released after four games in 1985
   ****Released after nine games in 1986

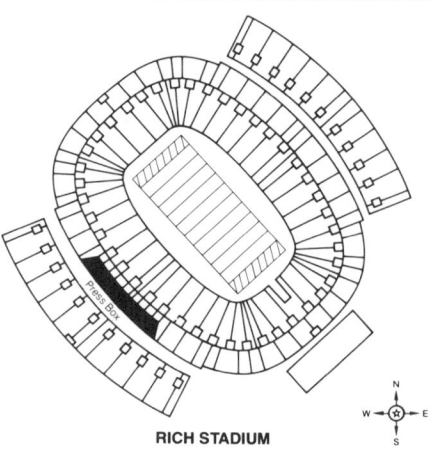

RICH STADIUM

Record Holders
Individual Records—Career

Category	Name	Performance
Rushing (Yds.)	O.J. Simpson, 1969-1977	10,183
Passing (Yds.)	Joe Ferguson, 1973-1984	27,590
Passing (TDs)	Joe Ferguson, 1973-1984	181
Receiving (No.)	Andre Reed, 1985-89	317
Receiving (Yds.)	Elbert Dubenion, 1960-67	5,304
Interceptions	George (Butch) Byrd, 1964-1970	40
Punting (Avg.)	Paul Maguire, 1964-1970	42.1
Punt Return (Avg.)	Keith Moody, 1976-79	10.5
Kickoff Return (Avg.)	Wallace Francis, 1973-74	27.2
Field Goals	Scott Norwood, 1985-89	97
Touchdowns (Tot.)	O.J. Simpson, 1969-1977	70
Points	Scott Norwood, 1985-89	465

Individual Records—Single Season

Category	Name	Performance
Rushing (Yds.)	O.J. Simpson, 1973	2,003
Passing (Yds.)	Joe Ferguson, 1981	3,652
Passing (TDs)	Joe Ferguson, 1983	26
Receiving (No.)	Andre Reed, 1989	88
Receiving (Yds.)	Andre Reed, 1989	1,312
Interceptions	Billy Atkins, 1961	10
	Tom Janik, 1967	10
Punting (Avg.)	Billy Atkins, 1961	44.5
Punt Return (Avg.)	Keith Moody, 1977	13.1
Kickoff Return (Avg.)	Ed Rutkowski, 1963	30.2
Field Goals	Scott Norwood, 1988	32
Touchdowns (Tot.)	O.J. Simpson, 1975	23
Points	O.J. Simpson, 1975	138

Individual Records—Single Game

Category	Name	Performance
Rushing (Yds.)	O.J. Simpson, 11-25-76	273
Passing (Yds.)	Joe Ferguson, 10-9-83	419
Passing (TDs)	Joe Ferguson, 9-23-79	5
	Joe Ferguson, 10-9-83	5
	Jim Kelly, 9-24-89	5
Receiving (No.)	Greg Bell, 9-8-85	13
	Andre Reed, 9-18-89	13
Receiving (Yds.)	Jerry Butler, 9-23-79	255
Interceptions	Many times	3
	Last time by Jeff Nixon, 9-7-80	
Field Goals	Pete Gogolak, 12-5-65	5
	Scott Norwood, 9-25-88	5
Touchdowns (Tot.)	Cookie Gilchrist, 12-8-63	5
Points	Cookie Gilchrist, 12-8-63	30

1989 Team Record

Preseason (1-4)

Date	Result		Opponents
8/5	L	6-31	vs. Washington at Canton, Ohio
8/13	L	20-24	at Cincinnati
8/19	W	10- 7	New Orleans
8/26	L	24-27	vs. Green Bay at Madison, Wis.
9/1	L	17-38	vs. Atlanta at Jacksonville, Fla.
		77-127	

Regular Season (9-7)

Date	Result		Opponents	Att.
9/10	W	27-24	at Miami	54,541
9/18	L	14-28	Denver	78,176
9/24	W	47-41	at Houston (OT)	57,278
10/1	W	31-10	New England	78,921
10/8	L	14-37	at Indianapolis	58,890
10/16	W	23-20	L.A. Rams	76,231
10/22	W	34- 3	N.Y. Jets	76,811
10/29	W	31-17	Miami	80,208
11/5	L	28-30	at Atlanta	45,267
11/12	W	30- 7	Indianapolis	79,256
11/19	L	24-33	at New England	49,663
11/26	W	24- 7	Cincinnati	80,074
12/4	L	16-17	at Seattle	57,682
12/10	L	19-22	New Orleans	70,037
12/17	L	10-21	at San Francisco	60,927
12/23	W	37- 0	at N.Y. Jets	21,148

(OT) Overtime

Postseason (0-1)

Date	Result		Opponent	Att.
1/6	L	30-34	at Cleveland	78,921

Score by Periods

Bills	59	117	92	135	6	—	409
Opponents	62	44	88	123	0	—	317

Attendance

Home 619,714   Away 405,396   Total 1,025,110
Single-game home record, 80,208 (10-29-89)
Single-season home record, 622,793 (1988)*
*NFL record

1989 Team Statistics

	Bills	Opp.
Total First Downs	334	299
Rushing	136	117
Passing	177	156
Penalty	21	26
Third Down: Made/Att.	86/203	75/213
Third Down: Pct.	42.4	35.2
Fourth Down: Made/Att.	4/8	7/15
Fourth Down: Pct.	50.0	46.7
Total Net Yards	5853	5046
Avg. Per Game	365.8	315.4
Total Plays	1045	1030
Avg. Per Play	5.6	4.9
Net Yards Rushing	2264	1840
Avg. Per Game	141.5	115.0
Total Rushes	532	484
Net Yards Passing	3589	3206
Avg. Per Game	224.3	200.4
Sacked/Yards Lost	35/242	38/289
Gross Yards	3831	3495
Att./Completions	478/281	508/255
Completion Pct.	58.8	50.2
Had Intercepted	20	23
Punts/Avg.	67/38.3	75/38.3
Net Punting Avg.	32.2	32.1
Penalties/Yards Lost	103/831	87/616
Fumbles/Ball Lost	30/21	31/13
Touchdowns	49	34
Rushing	15	15
Passing	32	14
Returns	2	5
Avg. Time of Possession	30:12	29:48

1989 Individual Statistics

Scoring

	TD R	TD P	TD Rt	PAT	FG	Saf	TP
Norwood	0	0	0	46/47	23/30	0	115
Thomas	6	6	0	0/0	0/0	0	72
Reed	0	9	0	0/0	0/0	0	54
Kinnebrew	6	0	0	0/0	0/0	0	36
Harmon	0	4	0	0/0	0/0	0	24
K. Davis	1	2	0	0/0	0/0	0	18
Lofton	0	3	0	0/0	0/0	0	18
Beebe	0	2	0	0/0	0/0	0	12
Kelly	2	0	0	0/0	0/0	0	12
McKeller	0	2	0	0/0	0/0	0	12
Metzelaars	0	2	0	0/0	0/0	0	12
Jackson	0	0	1	0/0	0/0	0	6
Johnson	0	1	0	0/0	0/0	0	6
Kelso	0	0	1	0/0	0/0	0	6
Rolle	0	1	0	0/0	0/0	0	6
Bills	15	32	2	46/48	23/30	0	409
Opponents	15	14	5	33/34	26/37	1	317

Passing

	Att.	Comp.	Yds.	Pct.	TD	Int.	Tkld.	Rate
Kelly	391	228	3130	58.3	25	18	30/216	86.2
Reich	87	53	701	60.9	7	2	4/24	103.7
Johnson	0	0	0	—	0	0	1/2	0.0
Bills	478	281	3831	58.8	32	20	35/242	89.3
Opponents	508	255	3495	50.2	14	23	38/289	62.9

Rushing

	Att.	Yds.	Avg.	LG	TD
Thomas	298	1244	4.2	38	6
Kinnebrew	131	533	4.1	25	6
K. Davis	29	149	5.1	21	1
Kelly	29	137	4.7	19	2
Harmon	17	99	5.8	24	0
Mueller	16	44	2.8	9	0
Reed	2	31	15.5	23	0
Reich	9	30	3.3	9	0
Gelbaugh	1	−3	−3.0	−3	0
Bills	532	2264	4.3	38	15
Opponents	484	1840	3.8	33	15

Receiving

	No.	Yds.	Avg.	LG	TD
Reed	88	1312	14.9	78t	9
Thomas	60	669	11.2	74t	6
Harmon	29	363	12.5	42t	4
Johnson	25	303	12.1	36	1
McKeller	20	341	17.1	39t	2
Metzelaars	18	179	9.9	23	2
Beebe	17	317	18.6	63t	2
Lofton	8	166	20.8	47	3
K. Davis	6	92	15.3	29	2
Kinnebrew	5	60	12.0	18	0
Burkett	3	20	6.7	9	0
Mueller	1	8	8.0	8	0
Rolle	1	1	1.0	1t	1
Bills	281	3831	13.6	78t	32
Opponents	255	3495	13.7	78t	14

Interceptions

	No.	Yds.	Avg.	LG	TD
Kelso	6	101	16.8	43	0
Odomes	5	20	4.0	13	0
L. Smith	2	46	23.0	24	0
Jackson	2	43	21.5	40t	1
Bennett	2	5	2.5	6	0
Drane	1	25	25.0	25	0
Bailey	1	16	16.0	16	0
Still	1	10	10.0	10	0
Sutton	1	3	3.0	3	0
Conlan	1	0	0.0	0	0
Wright	1	0	0.0	0	0
Bills	23	269	11.7	43	1
Opponents	20	364	18.2	80t	2

Punting

	No.	Yds.	Avg.	In 20	LG
Kidd	65	2564	39.4	15	60
Bills	67	2564	38.3	15	60
Opponents	75	2870	38.3	18	59

Punt Returns

	No.	FC	Yds.	Avg.	LG	TD
Sutton, G.B.-Buff.	31	10	273	8.8	26	0
Sutton, Buff.	26	9	231	8.9	26	0
Tucker	6	3	63	10.5	14	0
Johnson	1	0	7	7.0	7	0
Bills	33	12	301	9.1	26	0
Opponents	25	15	227	9.1	25	0

Kickoff Returns

	No.	Yds.	Avg.	LG	TD
Harmon	18	409	22.7	49	0
Beebe	16	353	22.1	85	0
Tucker	10	166	16.6	23	0
K. Davis	3	52	17.3	20	0
Tasker	2	39	19.5	20	0
Rolle	2	20	10.0	14	0
Mueller	1	19	19.0	19	0
Jackson	1	0	0.0	0	0
Bills	53	1058	20.0	85	0
Opponents	75	1187	15.8	40	0

Sacks

	No.
B. Smith	13.0
Talley	6.0
Bennett	5.5
Seals	4.0
Wright	3.0
Radecic	1.5
Burroughs	1.0
Cofield	1.0
Conlan	1.0
Odomes	1.0
Smerlas	1.0
Bills	38.0
Opponents	35.0

1990 Draft Choices

Round	Name	Pos.	College
1.	James Williams	DB	Fresno State
2.	Carwell Gardner	RB	Louisville
3.	Glenn Parker	T	Arizona
4.	Eddie Fuller	RB	Louisiana State
6.	John Nies	P	Arizona
7.	Brent Griffith	G	Minnesota-Duluth
	Brent Collins	LB	Carson-Newman
	Fred De Riggi	NT	Syracuse
8.	Marvcus Patton	LB	UCLA
9.	Clarkston Hines	WR	Duke
10.	Mike Lodish	DT	UCLA
11.	Al Edwards	WR	NW Louisiana

Buffalo Bills 1990 Veteran Roster

No.	Name	Pos.	Ht.	Wt.	Birth-date	NFL Exp.	College	Hometown	How Acq.	'89 Games/ Starts
54	Bailey, Carlton	LB	6-2	237	12/15/64	3	North Carolina	Baltimore, Md.	D9-'88	16/0
75	Ballard, Howard	T	6-6	315	11/3/63	3	Alabama A&M	Ashland, Ala.	D11-'87	16/16
24	Barnes, Lew	WR	5-8	170	12/27/62	3	Oregon	San Diego, Calif.	FA-'90	2/0*
82	Beebe, Don	WR	5-11	177	12/18/64	2	Chadron, Neb.	Sugar Grove, Ill.	D3-'89	14/0
55	Bennett, Cornelius	LB	6-2	235	8/25/66	4	Alabama	Birmingham, Ala.	T(Ind)-'87	12/12
50	Bentley, Ray	LB	6-2	235	11/25/60	5	Central Michigan	Grand Rapids, Mich.	FA-'86	15/15
5	Brady, Kerry	K	6-1	200	8/27/63	2	Hawaii	Vancouver, Wash.	FA-'90	3/0*
61	Burton, Leonard	T	6-3	277	6/18/64	5	South Carolina	Memphis, Tenn.	D3-'86	6/0
90	Cofield, Timmy	LB	6-2	242	5/18/63	5	Elizabeth City State	Murfreesboro, N.C.	W(NYJ)-'89	5/0
58	Conlan, Shane	LB	6-3	235	4/3/64	4	Penn State	Frewsburg, N.Y.	D1-'87	10/9
79	Davis, John	T	6-4	310	8/22/65	4	Georgia Tech	Ellijay, Ga.	FA-'89	16/0
23	Davis, Kenneth	RB	5-10	209	4/10/62	5	Texas Christian	Temple, Tex.	PB(Hou)-'89#	16/0
45	†Drane, Dwight	S	6-2	205	5/6/62	5	Oklahoma	Miami, Fla.	SD1-'84	16/1
85	Franklin, Darryl	WR	5-11	185	2/4/65	2	Washington	Atlanta, Ga.	FA-'89	0*
59	Frerotte, Mitch	G	6-3	280	3/30/63	2	Penn State	Kittanning, Pa.	FA-'88	0*
7	Gilbert, Gale	QB	6-3	210	12/20/61	3	California	Red Bluff, Calif.	FA-'89	0*
22	†Hagy, John	S	5-11	190	12/9/65	3	Texas	Austin, Tex.	D8a-'88	9/0
26	Hale, Chris	CB	5-7	161	1/4/66	2	Southern California	Monrovia, Calif.	D7b-'89	16/0
67	Hull, Kent	C	6-5	275	1/13/61	5	Mississippi State	Greenwood, Miss.	FA-'86	16/16
47	†Jackson, Kirby	CB	5-10	180	2/2/65	4	Mississippi State	Sturgis, Miss.	FA-'87	14/13
12	Kelly, Jim	QB	6-3	218	2/14/60	5	Miami	East Brady, Pa.	D1b-'83	13/13
38	Kelso, Mark	S	5-11	185	7/23/63	5	William & Mary	Pittsburgh, Pa.	FA-'86	16/16
28	†Kinnebrew, Larry	RB	6-2	256	6/11/60	7	Tennessee State	Rome, Ga.	FA-'89	15/10
63	†Lingner, Adam	C	6-4	268	11/2/60	8	Illinois	Rock Island, Ill.	FA-'89	16/0
80	†Lofton, James	WR	6-3	190	7/5/56	13	Stanford	Los Angeles, Calif.	FA-'89	12/2
84	†McKeller, Keith	TE	6-4	245	7/9/64	3	Jacksonville State	Fairfield, Ala.	D9-'87	16/7
74	Mesner, Bruce	NT	6-5	280	3/21/64	4	Maryland	New York, N.Y.	D8-'87	0*
88	†Metzelaars, Pete	TE	6-7	250	5/24/60	9	Wabash	Portage, Mich.	T(Sea)-'85	16/16
36	Mitchell, Devon	S	6-1	198	12/30/62	3	Iowa	Brooklyn, N.Y.	FA-'90	0*
57	Monger, Matt	LB	6-1	240	11/15/61	5	Oklahoma State	Denver, Colo.	FA-'89	9/0
39	†Mueller, Jamie	RB	6-1	230	10/4/64	4	Benedictine	Fairview Park, Ohio	D3b-'87	14/3
11	Norwood, Scott	K	6-0	207	7/17/60	6	James Madison	Alexandria, Va.	FA-'85	16/0
37	Odomes, Nate	CB	5-10	188	8/25/65	4	Wisconsin	Columbus, Ga.	D2a-'87	16/16
94	Pike, Mark	DE	6-4	272	12/27/63	4	Georgia Tech	Villa Hills, Ky.	D7b-'86	16/0
97	Radecic, Scott	LB	6-3	236	6/14/62	7	Penn State	Pittsburgh, Pa.	W(KC)-'87	16/12
83	Reed, Andre	WR	6-1	190	1/29/64	6	Kutztown State	Allentown, Pa.	D4a-'85	16/16
14	†Reich, Frank	QB	6-4	210	12/4/61	6	Maryland	Lebanon, Pa.	D3a-'85	7/3
40	Riddick, Robb	RB	6-0	195	4/26/57	8	Millersville State	Perkasie, Pa.	D9-'81	0*
51	Ritcher, Jim	G	6-3	273	5/21/58	11	North Carolina State	Medina, Ohio	D1-'80	16/16
87	†Rolle, Butch	TE	6-4	245	8/19/64	5	Michigan State	Hallandale, Fla.	D7c-'86	16/1
96	Seals, Leon	DE	6-5	267	1/30/64	4	Jackson State	Baton Rouge, La.	D4b-'87	16/0
78	Smith, Bruce	DE	6-4	280	6/18/63	6	Virginia Tech	Norfolk, Va.	D1a-'85	16/16
30	Smith, Don	RB	5-11	200	10/30/63	4	Mississippi State	Hamilton, Miss.	PB(TB)-'90#	11/0*
46	Smith, Leonard	S	5-11	202	9/2/60	8	McNeese State	Baton Rouge, La.	T(Phx)-'88	15/15
20	Sutton, Mickey	CB-KR	5-9	172	8/28/60	5	Montana	Union City, Calif.	FA-'89	16/0*
56	Talley, Darryl	LB	6-4	235	7/10/60	8	West Virginia	Cleveland, Ohio	D2-'83	16/16
89	Tasker, Steve	WR	5-9	185	4/10/62	6	Northwestern	Leoti, Ky.	W(Hou)-'86	16/0
34	Thomas, Thurman	RB	5-10	198	5/16/66	3	Oklahoma State	Missouri City, Tex.	D2-'88	16/16
69	†Wolford, Will	T	6-5	290	5/18/64	5	Vanderbilt	Louisville, Ky.	D1b-'86	16/16
91	Wright, Jeff	NT	6-2	270	6/13/63	3	Central Missouri State	Lawrence, Kan.	D8b-'88	15/0

* Barnes played 2 games with Kansas City in '89; Brady played 3 games with Buffalo; Franklin, Frerotte, Mesner, and Riddick missed '89 season due to injury; Gilbert last active with Seattle in '86; Mitchell last active with Detroit in '88; D. Smith played 11 games with Tampa Bay; Sutton played 4 games with Green Bay, 12 with Buffalo.

† Option playout; subject to developments.

Plan B unconditional free agent.

Players lost through Plan B (5): RB Ronnie Harmon (SD; 15 games in '89), LB Richard Harvey (NE; 0), WR Flip Johnson (GB; 16), P John Kidd (SD; 16), NT Fred Smerlas (SF; 16).

Also played with Bills in '89—WR Chris Burkett (2 games), CB Derrick Burroughs (3), CB Wayne Davis (6), G Joe Devlin (16), DE Elston Ridgle (1), DE Art Still (16), CB-S-KR Erroll Tucker (4).

Coaching Staff

Head Coach, Marv Levy

Pro Career: Begins fourth full season as Bills head coach. Buffalo won AFC East title in 1989 with 9-7 record and played in AFC Divisional Playoff game against Cleveland. Led Bills to a 12-4 record, the AFC East title, and a berth in the AFC Championship Game in 1988. In first full year in 1987, he led Bills to 7-8 record. Replaced Hank Bullough on November 3, 1986, and compiled a 2-5 record over final seven weeks of season. Previously served as head coach of the Kansas City Chiefs from 1978-82, producing a 31-42 mark. Levy began pro coaching career in 1969 as an assistant with the Philadelphia Eagles. He joined George Allen and the Los Angeles Rams as an assistant one year later and followed Allen to Washington, where he remained with the Redskins through the 1972 season when the Redskins played in Super Bowl VII. He was named head coach of the Montreal Alouettes (CFL) in 1973 and posted a 50-34-4 record and two Grey Cup victories (1974, 1977) in five seasons in Canada. After two seasons away from football, he became head coach of the Chicago Blitz of the USFL in 1984, the team's only year in existence. No pro playing experience. Career record: 62-68.

Background: Running back Coe College 1948-50. Coached at high school level for two years before returning to alma mater in 1953-55. Joined New Mexico staff in 1956 where he served as head coach in 1958-59. Head coach at California from 1960-63 before becoming head coach at William & Mary from 1964-68.

Personal: Born August 3, 1928, Chicago, Ill. Levy was Phi Beta Kappa at Coe College and earned master's degree in English history from Harvard. Marv lives in Orchard Park, N.Y.

Assistant Coaches

Tom Bresnahan, offensive line; born January 21, 1935, Springfield, Mass., lives in Hamburg, N.Y. Tackle Holy Cross 1953-55. No pro playing experience. College coach: Williams 1963-67, Columbia 1968-72, Navy 1973-80. Pro coach: Kansas City Chiefs 1981-82, New York Giants 1983-84, Phoenix Cardinals 1986-88, joined Bills in 1989.

Walt Corey, defensive coordinator, linebackers; born May 9, 1938, Latrobe, Pa., lives in West Seneca, N.Y. Defensive end Miami 1957-59. Pro linebacker Kansas City Chiefs 1960-66. College coach: Utah State 1967-69, Miami 1970-71. Pro coach: Kansas City Chiefs 1971-74, 1978-86, Cleveland Browns 1975-77, joined Bills in 1987.

Bruce DeHaven, special teams; born September 6, 1948, Trousdale, Kan., lives in East Aurora, N.Y. No college or pro playing experience. College coach: Kansas 1979-81, New Mexico State 1982. Pro coach: New Jersey Generals (USFL) 1983, Pittsburgh Maulers (USFL) 1984, Orlando Renegades (USFL) 1985, joined Bills in 1987.

Chuck Dickerson, defensive line; born August 1, 1937, Hammond, Ind., lives in Buffalo, N.Y. Defensive tackle Florida 1955-56, Illinois 1961. Pro defensive lineman Montreal Alouettes (CFL) 1962-64. College coach: Eastern Illinois 1967-70, 1981-82, Minnesota 1983. Pro coach: Toronto Rifles (Continental League) 1964-66, Chicago Fire (WFL) 1974-75, Toronto Argonauts (CFL) 1976-79, Memphis Showboats (USFL) 1984-86, joined Bills in 1987.

Rusty Jones, strength and conditioning; born August 14, 1953, Berwick, Maine, lives in Lakeview, N.Y. No college or pro playing experience. College coach: Springfield 1978-79. Pro coach: Pittsburgh Maulers (USFL) 1983-84, joined Bills in 1985.

Don Lawrence, quality control, tight ends; born June 4, 1937, Cleveland, Ohio, lives in Orchard Park, N.Y. Offensive-defensive lineman Notre Dame 1957-59. Pro offensive-defensive lineman Washington Redskins 1959-61. College coach: Notre Dame 1961-63, Kansas State 1964-65, Cincinnati 1966, Virginia 1970-73 (head coach 1971-73), Texas Christian 1974-75, Missouri 1976-77. Pro coach: British Columbia Lions (CFL) 1978-79, Kansas City Chiefs 1980-82, 1987-88, Buffalo Bills 1983-84, Tampa Bay Buccaneers 1985-86, Winnipeg Blue Bombers (CFL) 1989, rejoined Bills in 1990.

Buffalo Bills 1990 First-Year Roster

Name	Pos.	Ht.	Wt.	Birth-date	College	Hometown	How Acq.
Adams, Michael (1)	CB	5-11	193	4/5/64	Arkansas State	Shelby, Miss.	FA
Aguiar, Louie (1)	P	6-3	210	6/30/66	Utah State	Livermore, Calif.	FA
Collins, Brent	LB	6-1	238	4/27/68	Carson-Newman	New Market, Tenn.	D7b
DeRiggi, Fred	NT	6-2	268	1/15/67	Syracuse	Scranton, Pa.	D7c
Doctor, Sean (1)	RB	6-1	235	7/10/66	Marshall	Buffalo, N.Y.	FA
Doctor, Tom (1)	LB	6-0	235	4/1/65	Canisius	Buffalo, N.Y.	FA-'89
Edwards, Al	WR	5-8	168	5/18/67	N.W. Louisiana	Kenner, La.	D11
Finch, Lonnie (1)	CB-S	6-0	188	10/12/66	Oklahoma	Irving, Tex.	FA
Franklin, Darryl (1)	WR	5-11	185	2/4/65	Washington	Atlanta, Ga.	FA-'89
Fuller, Eddie	RB	5-9	199	6/22/68	Louisiana State	Leesville, La.	D4
Gardner, Carwell	RB	6-2	232	11/27/66	Louisville	Louisville, Ky.	D2
Gerhart, Thomas (1)	S	6-1	200	6/4/65	Ohio University	Lebanon, Pa.	FA
Gicewicz, Rich (1)	TE	6-4	248	12/4/65	Michigan State	Buffalo, N.Y.	FA
Glover, Deval (1)	WR	5-11	184	9/12/66	Syracuse	Troy, N.J.	FA
Griffith, Brent	T	6-6	300	12/14/65	Minnesota-Duluth	Little Falls, Minn.	D7a
Hines, Clarkston	WR	5-11	163	3/21/67	Duke	Jacksonville, Fla.	D9
Hunter, Jeffrey (1)	DE	6-5	285	4/12/66	Albany State	Hephzibah, Ga.	FA
Jarvis, Ralph (1)	DE	6-5	260	6/1/65	Temple	Philadelphia, Pa.	FA
Jaworski, Matt (1)	LB	6-1	227	10/23/67	Colgate	Blasdell, N.Y.	FA
Kolesar, John (1)	WR	5-10	187	4/14/67	Michigan	Westlake, Ohio	D4-'89
Lodish, Mike	NT	6-3	260	8/11/67	UCLA	Birmingham, Mich.	D10
Marshall, Derrell (1)	T	6-4	305	6/9/65	Southern California	Seat Pleasant, Md.	FA
Mims, Carl (1)	CB	5-10	180	10/28/65	Sam Houston State	Gainesville, Tex.	FA
Nelson, Todd (1)	G-T	6-5	290	3/23/66	Wisconsin	Madison, Wis.	FA
Nies, John	P-K	6-2	199	2/13/67	Arizona	Ocean Township, N.J.	D6
Parker, Glenn	T	6-6	301	4/22/66	Arizona	Huntington Beach, Calif.	D3
Patton, Marvcus	LB	6-2	216	5/1/67	UCLA	Lawndale, Calif.	D8
Pritchett, Wes (1)	LB	6-4	234	7/7/66	Notre Dame	Atlanta, Ga.	FA
Smiley, Tim (1)	S	6-0	190	5/11/66	Arkansas State	Wynne, Ark.	FA
Southall, Cornelius (1)	S	6-2	200	5/25/67	Notre Dame	Henrietta, N.Y.	FA
Starr, Eric (1)	RB	5-9	194	2/2/66	North Carolina	Ellenboro, N.C.	FA
Tuten, Rick (1)	P	6-2	218	1/5/65	Florida State	Ocala, Fla.	FA
Williams, James	CB	5-10	172	3/30/67	Fresno State	Coalinga, Calif.	D1

The term NFL Rookie is defined as a player who is in his first season of professional football and has not been on the roster of another professional football team for any regular-season or postseason games. A Rookie is designated by an "R" on NFL rosters. Players who have been active in another professional football league or players who have NFL experience, including either preseason training camp or being on an active roster for fewer than three regular-season or post-season games, are termed NFL First-Year Players. An NFL First-Year Player is designated by a "1" on NFL rosters. Thereafter, a player on an NFL active roster for at least three regular-season or postseason games is credited with an additional year of NFL playing experience.

NOTES

_____

_____

_____

_____

_____

_____

_____

Chuck Lester, defensive assistant; born May 18, 1955, Chicago, Ill., lives in Orchard Park, N.Y. Linebacker Oklahoma 1974. No pro playing experience. College coach: Oklahoma 1982-84. Pro scout: Kansas City Chiefs 1984-87. Pro coach: Joined Bills in 1987.

Ted Marchibroda, quarterbacks, passing-game coordinator; born March 15, 1931, Franklin, Pa., lives in East Aurora, N.Y. Quarterback St. Bonaventure 1950-51, Detroit 1952. Pro quarterback Pittsburgh Steelers 1953, 1955-56, Chicago Cardinals 1957. Pro coach: Washington Redskins 1961-65, 1971-74, Los Angeles Rams 1966-70, Baltimore Colts 1975-79 (head coach), Chicago Bears 1981, Detroit Lions 1982-83, Philadelphia Eagles 1984-85, joined Bills in 1987.

Nick Nicolau, receivers; born May 5, 1933, New York, N.Y., lives in Orchard Park, N.Y. Running back Southern Connecticut 1957-59. No pro playing experience. College coach: Southern Connecticut 1960, Springfield 1961, Bridgeport 1962-69 (head coach 1965-69), Massachusetts 1970, Connecticut 1971-72, Kentucky 1973-75, Kent State 1976. Pro coach: Hamilton Tiger-Cats (CFL) 1977, Montreal Alouettes (CFL) 1978-79, New Orleans Saints 1980, Denver Broncos 1981-87, Los Angeles Raiders 1988, joined Bills in 1989.

Elijah Pitts, running backs; born February 3, 1938, Mayflower, Ark., lives in Orchard Park, N.Y. Running back Philander Smith 1957-60. Pro running back Green Bay Packers 1961-69, 1971, Los Angeles Rams 1970, Chicago Bears 1970, New Orleans Saints 1970. Pro coach: Los Angeles Rams 1974-77, Buffalo Bills 1978-80, Houston Oilers 1981-83, Hamilton Tiger-Cats (CFL) 1984, rejoined Bills in 1985.

Dick Roach, defensive backs; born August 23, 1937, Rapid City, S.D., lives in West Seneca, N.Y. Defensive back Black Hills State 1952-55. No pro playing experience. College coach: Montana State 1966-69, Oregon State 1970, Wyoming 1971-72, Fresno State 1973, Washington State 1974-75. Pro coach: Montreal Alouettes (CFL) 1976-77, Kansas City Chiefs 1978-80, New England Patriots 1981, Michigan Panthers (USFL) 1983-84, Tampa Bay Buccaneers 1985-86, joined Bills in 1987.

CINCINNATI BENGALS

American Football Conference Central Division

Team Colors: Black, Orange, and White

200 Riverfront Stadium
Cincinnati, Ohio 45202
Telephone: (513) 621-3550

Club Officials

President: John Sawyer
General Manager: Paul E. Brown
Assistant General Manager: Michael Brown
Business Manager: Bill Connelly
Director of Public Relations: Allan Heim
Director of Player Personnel: Pete Brown
Accountant: Jay Reis
Ticket Manager: Paul Kelly
Consultant: John Murdough
Trainer: Marv Pollins
Equipment Manager: Tom Gray
Video Director: Al Davis

Stadium: Riverfront Stadium • **Capacity:** 59,755
200 Riverfront Stadium
Cincinnati, Ohio 45202

Playing Surface: AstroTurf-8

Training Camp: Wilmington College
Wilmington, Ohio 45177

1990 Schedule

Preseason

Aug. 11	at Tampa Bay	7:00
Aug. 18	at Atlanta	7:00
Aug. 24	at New England	7:00
Aug. 31	**Detroit**	7:30

Regular Season

Sept. 9	**New York Jets**	4:00
Sept. 16	at San Diego	1:00
Sept. 23	**New England**	1:00
Oct. 1	at Seattle (Monday)	6:00
Oct. 7	at Los Angeles Rams	1:00
Oct. 14	**Houston**	1:00
Oct. 22	at Cleveland (Monday)	9:00
Oct. 28	at Atlanta	8:00
Nov. 4	**New Orleans**	1:00
Nov. 11	**Open Date**	
Nov. 18	**Pittsburgh**	8:00
Nov. 25	**Indianapolis**	1:00
Dec. 2	at Pittsburgh	1:00
Dec. 9	**San Francisco**	1:00
Dec. 16	at Los Angeles Raiders	1:00
Dec. 23	at Houston	12:00
Dec. 30	**Cleveland**	1:00

Bengals Coaching History

(166-167-1)

1968-75	Paul Brown	55-59-1
1976-78	Bill Johnson*	18-15-0
1978-79	Homer Rice	8-19-0
1980-83	Forrest Gregg	34-27-0
1984-89	Sam Wyche	51-47-0

*Resigned after five games in 1978

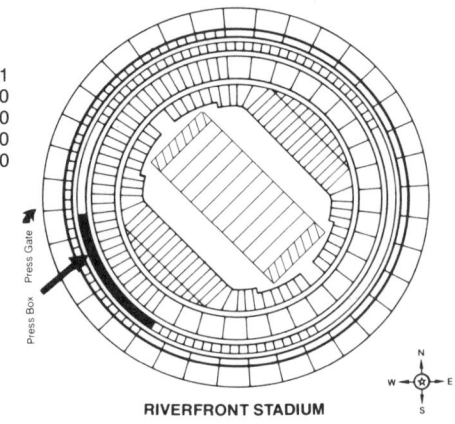

RIVERFRONT STADIUM

Record Holders

Individual Records — Career

Category	Name	Performance
Rushing (Yds.)	Pete Johnson, 1977-1983	5,421
Passing (Yds.)	Ken Anderson, 1971-1986	32,838
Passing (TDs)	Ken Anderson, 1971-1986	197
Receiving (No.)	Isaac Curtis, 1973-1984	420
Receiving (Yds.)	Isaac Curtis, 1973-1984	7,106
Interceptions (No.)	Ken Riley, 1969-1983	63
Punting (Avg.)	Dave Lewis, 1970-73	43.9
Punt Return (Avg.)	Mike Martin, 1983-89	9.9
Kickoff Return (Avg.)	Lemar Parrish, 1970-78	24.7
Field Goals	Jim Breech, 1980-89	184
Touchdowns (Tot.)	Pete Johnson, 1977-1983	70
Points	Jim Breech, 1980-89	875

Individual Records — Single Season

Category	Name	Performance
Rushing (Yds.)	James Brooks, 1989	1,239
Passing (Yds.)	Boomer Esiason, 1986	3,959
Passing (TDs)	Ken Anderson, 1981	29
Receiving (No.)	Dan Ross, 1981	71
Receiving (Yds.)	Eddie Brown, 1988	1,273
Interceptions	Ken Riley, 1976	9
Punting (Avg.)	Dave Lewis, 1970	46.2
Punt Return (Avg.)	Mike Martin, 1984	15.7
Kickoff Return (Avg.)	Lemar Parrish, 1980	30.2
Field Goals	Horst Muhlmann, 1972	27
Touchdowns (Tot.)	Pete Johnson, 1981	16
Points	Jim Breech, 1985	120

Individual Records — Single Game

Category	Name	Performance
Rushing (Yds.)	James Brooks, 12-7-86	163
Passing (Yds.)	Ken Anderson, 11-17-75	447
Passing (TDs)	Boomer Esiason, 12-21-86	5
Receiving (No.)	Tim McGee, 11-9-89	11
Receiving (Yds.)	Eddie Brown, 11-6-88	216
Interceptions	Many times	3
	Last time by David Fulcher, 12-16-89	
Field Goals	Horst Muhlmann, 11-8-70	5
	Horst Muhlmann, 9-24-72	5
	Jim Breech, 11-1-87	5
Touchdowns (Tot.)	Larry Kinnebrew, 10-28-84	4
Points	Larry Kinnebrew, 10-28-84	24

1989 Team Record
Preseason (2-2)

Date	Result		Opponents
8/13	W	24-20	Buffalo
8/19	W	35- 3	at Detroit
8/28	L	10-27	at New Orleans
9/1	L	10-17	at Minnesota
		79-67	

Regular Season (8-8)

Date	Result		Opponents	Att.
9/10	L	14-17	at Chicago	64,730
9/17	W	41-10	Pittsburgh	53,885
9/25	W	21-14	Cleveland	55,996
10/1	W	21-17	at Kansas City	61,165
10/8	W	26-16	at Pittsburgh	52,785
10/15	L	13-20	Miami	58,184
10/22	L	12-23	Indianapolis	57,642
10/29	W	56-23	Tampa Bay	57,225
11/5	L	7-28	at L.A. Raiders	51,080
11/13	L	24-26	at Houston	60,694
11/19	W	42- 7	Detroit	55,720
11/26	L	7-24	at Buffalo	80,074
12/3	W	21- 0	at Cleveland	76,236
12/10	L	17-24	Seattle	54,744
12/17	W	61- 7	Houston	47,510
12/25	L	21-29	at Minnesota	58,829

Score by Periods

Bengals	61	147	98	98	0	—	404
Opponents	50	97	56	82	0	—	285

Attendance
Home 440,906   Away 505,593   Total 946,499
Single-game home record, 60,284 (10-17-71)
Single-season home record, 441,586 (1988)

1989 Team Statistics

	Bengals	Opp.
Total First Downs	348	280
Rushing	136	114
Passing	183	151
Penalty	29	15
Third Down: Made/Att.	100/220	82/209
Third Down: Pct.	45.5	39.2
Fourth Down: Made/Att.	12/24	6/19
Fourth Down: Pct.	50.0	31.6
Total Net Yards	6101	5297
Avg. Per Game	381.3	331.1
Total Plays	1083	997
Avg. Per Play	5.6	5.3
Net Yards Rushing	2483	2162
Avg. Per Game	155.2	135.1
Total Rushes	529	482
Net Yards Passing	3618	3135
Avg. Per Game	226.1	195.9
Sacked/Yards Lost	41/332	33/248
Gross Yards	3950	3383
Att./Completions	513/288	482/256
Completion Pct.	56.1	53.1
Had Intercepted	13	21
Punts/Avg.	65/38.5	75/39.1
Net Punting Avg.	29.9	34.7
Penalties/Yards Lost	85/637	122/1060
Fumbles/Ball Lost	29/19	26/16
Touchdowns	52	32
Rushing	17	9
Passing	32	22
Returns	3	1
Avg. Time of Possession	30:51	29:09

1989 Individual Statistics

Scoring

	TD R	TD P	TD Rt	PAT	FG	Saf	TP
Breech	0	0	0	37/38	12/14	0	73
Brooks	7	2	0	0/0	0/0	0	54
Holman	0	9	0	0/0	0/0	0	54
McGee	0	8	0	0/0	0/0	0	48
Brown	0	6	0	0/0	0/0	0	36
Taylor	3	2	0	0/0	0/0	0	30
Gallery	0	0	0	13/13	2/6	0	19
Ball	3	0	0	0/0	0/0	0	18
Jennings	2	1	0	0/0	0/0	0	18
Martin	0	2	0	0/0	0/0	0	12
Woods	2	0	0	0/0	0/0	0	12
Bussey	0	0	1	0/0	0/0	0	6
Hillary	0	1	0	0/0	0/0	0	6
Smith	0	1	0	0/0	0/0	0	6
Thomas	0	0	1	0/0	0/0	0	6
White	0	0	1	0/0	0/0	0	6
Johnson	0	0	0	0/1	0/0	0	0
Bengals	17	32	3	50/52	14/20	0	404
Opponents	9	22	1	31/32	20/27	1	285

Passing

	Att.	Comp.	Yds.	Pct.	TD	Int.	Tkld.	Rate
Esiason	455	258	3525	56.7	28	11	36/288	92.1
Wilhelm	56	30	425	53.6	4	2	3/17	87.3
Schonert	2	0	0	0.0	0	0	2/27	39.6
Bengals	513	288	3950	56.1	32	13	41/332	91.2
Opponents	482	256	3383	53.1	22	21	33/248	72.6

Rushing

	Att.	Yds.	Avg.	LG	TD
Brooks	221	1239	5.6	65t	7
Ball	98	391	4.0	27	3
Jennings	83	293	3.5	17	2
Esiason	47	278	5.9	24	0
Taylor	30	111	3.7	16	3
Woods	29	94	3.2	12	2
McGee	2	36	18.0	25	0
Wilhelm	6	30	5.0	14	0
Holifield	11	20	1.8	11	0
Hillary	1	-2	-2.0	-2	0
Johnson	1	-7	-7.0	-7	0
Bengals	529	2483	4.7	65t	17
Opponents	482	2162	4.5	92t	9

Receiving

	No.	Yds.	Avg.	LG	TD
McGee	65	1211	18.6	74t	8
Brown	52	814	15.7	46	6
Holman	50	736	14.7	73t	9
Brooks	37	306	8.3	25	2
Hillary	17	162	9.5	17	1
Martin	15	160	10.7	21	2
Kattus	12	93	7.8	16	0
Smith	10	140	14.0	41t	1
Jennings	10	119	11.9	43t	1
Ball	6	44	7.3	15	0
Riggs	5	29	5.8	9	0
Taylor	4	44	11.0	18t	2
Garrett	2	29	14.5	18	0
Holifield	2	18	9.0	14	0
Parker	1	45	45.0	45	0
Bengals	288	3950	13.7	74t	32
Opponents	256	3383	13.2	84t	22

Interceptions

	No.	Yds.	Avg.	LG	TD
Fulcher	8	87	10.9	22	0
Thomas	4	18	4.5	18t	1
Dixon	3	47	15.7	28	0
Billups	2	0	0	0	0
Kelly	1	25	25.0	25	0
White	1	22	22.0	22	0
Carey	1	5	5.0	5	0
Bussey	1	0	0.0	0	0
Bengals	21	204	9.7	28	1
Opponents	13	42	3.2	19	0

Punting

	No.	Yds.	Avg.	In 20	LG
Johnson	61	2446	40.1	14	62
Breech	2	58	29.0	1	32
Bengals	65	2504	38.5	15	62
Opponents	75	2935	39.1	16	57

Punt Returns

	No.	FC	Yds.	Avg.	LG	TD
Martin	15	4	107	7.1	17	0
Smith	12	2	54	4.5	15	0
Hillary	6	4	19	3.2	10	0
Carey	3	2	29	9.7	13	0
Bengals	36	12	209	5.8	17	0
Opponents	33	5	323	9.8	45	0

Kickoff Returns

	No.	Yds.	Avg.	LG	TD
Jennings	26	525	20.2	33	0
Hillary	14	223	15.9	29	0
Carey	6	104	17.3	23	0
Smith	5	65	13.0	19	0
Ball	1	19	19.0	19	0
Taylor	1	5	5.0	5	0
Holifield	1	0	0.0	0	0
Jackson	0	0	—	0	0
Bengals	54	941	17.4	33	0
Opponents	55	1203	21.9	66	0

Sacks

	No.
Buck	6.0
Skow	4.5
Williams	3.5
Krumrie	3.0
Bussey	2.5
Tuatagaloa	2.5
Thomas	2.0
White	2.0
Hammerstein	1.5
McClendon	1.5
Zander	1.5
Kelly	1.0
Wilcots	1.0
Grant	0.5
Bengals	33.0
Opponents	41.0

1990 Draft Choices

Round	Name	Pos.	College
1.	James Francis	LB	Baylor
2.	Harold Green	RB	South Carolina
3.	Bernard Clark	LB	Miami
4.	Mike Brennan	T	Notre Dame
5.	Lynn James	WR	Arizona State
6.	Don Odegard	DB	Nevada-Las Vegas
7.	Craig Ogletree	LB	Auburn
8.	Doug Wellsandt	TE	Washington State
9.	Mitchell Price	DB	Tulane
10.	Eric Crigler	T	Murray State
11.	Tim O'Connor	T	Virginia
12.	Andre Riley	WR	Washington

Cincinnati Bengals 1990 Veteran Roster

No.	Name	Pos.	Ht.	Wt.	Birth-date	NFL Exp.	College	Hometown	How Acq.	'89 Games/ Starts
42	Ball, Eric	RB	6-2	211	7/1/66	2	UCLA	Ypsilanti, Mich.	D2-'89	15/9
35	Barber, Chris	S	6-0	187	11/15/64	3	North Carolina A&T	Winston-Salem, N.C.	FA-'87	8/0
86	Barber, Mike	WR	5-10	172	6/19/67	2	Marshall	Charleston, W. Va.	PB(Phx)-'90#	8/0*
53	Barker, Leo	LB	6-2	227	11/7/59	7	New Mexico State	Cristobal, Panama	D7-'84	16/0
24	†Billups, Lewis	CB	5-11	179	10/10/63	5	North Alabama	Fort Walton Beach, Fla.	D2-'86	16/16
74	Blados, Brian	G	6-5	296	1/11/62	7	North Carolina	Arlington, Va.	D1b-'84	13/10
55	Brady, Ed	LB	6-2	236	6/17/60	7	Illinois	Morris, Ill.	FA-'86	16/0
3	Breech, Jim	K	5-6	161	4/11/56	12	California	Sacramento, Calif.	FA-'89	12/0
21	Brooks, James	RB	5-10	180	12/28/58	10	Auburn	Warner Robins, Ga.	T(SD)-'84	16/14
81	Brown, Eddie	WR	6-0	185	12/17/62	6	Miami	Miami, Fla.	D1-'85	15/15
99	Buck, Jason	DE	6-5	258	7/27/63	4	Brigham Young	St. Anthony, Idaho	D1-'87	16/16
27	Bussey, Barney	S	6-0	206	5/20/62	5	South Carolina State	Lincolnton, Ga.	D5-'84	16/1
34	Carey, Richard	CB	5-9	185	5/6/68	2	Idaho	Seattle, Wash.	FA-'89	7/0
29	Dixon, Rickey	S	5-11	196	12/26/66	3	Oklahoma	Dallas, Tex.	D1-'88	16/0
7	Esiason, Boomer	QB	6-5	215	4/17/61	7	Maryland	East Islip, N.Y.	D2-'84	16/15
33	†Fulcher, David	S	6-3	234	9/28/64	5	Arizona State	Los Angeles, Calif.	D3b-'86	16/16
16	Gelbaugh, Stan	QB	6-3	205	12/4/62	3	Maryland	Hamburg, N.Y.	FA-'90	1/0*
98	Grant, David	NT	6-4	288	9/17/65	4	West Virginia	Belleville, N.J.	D4-'88	16/0
71	†Hammerstein, Mike	DE	6-4	272	3/29/63	4	Michigan	Wapakoneta, Ohio	D3a-'86	15/0
40	Holifield, John	RB	6-0	202	7/14/64	2	West Virginia	Romulus, Mich.	FA-'88	3/0
82	Holman, Rodney	TE	6-3	238	4/20/60	9	Tulane	Ypsilanti, Mich.	D3-'82	16/15
37	Jackson, Robert	S	5-10	186	10/21/58	8	Central Michigan	Allendale, Mich.	FA-'89	14/0
36	Jennings, Stanford	RB	6-1	209	3/12/62	7	Furman	Summerville, S.C.	D3-'84	16/6
68	Jetton, Paul	G	6-4	288	10/6/64	2	Texas	Houston, Tex.	D6-'88	5/2
11	Johnson, Lee	P-K	6-2	200	11/27/61	6	Brigham Young	Conroe, Tex.	FA-'88	16/0
77	Jones, Scott	T	6-5	278	3/20/66	2	Washington	Port Angeles, Wash.	D12-'89	15/0
84	†Kattus, Eric	TE	6-5	241	3/4/63	5	Michigan	Cincinnati, Ohio	D4-'86	16/1
58	†Kelly, Joe	LB	6-2	235	12/11/64	5	Washington	Los Angeles, Calif.	D1-'86	16/16
64	Kozerski, Bruce	C	6-4	287	4/2/62	7	Holy Cross	Plains, Pa.	D9-'84	15/15
69	Krumrie, Tim	NT	6-2	267	5/20/60	8	Wisconsin	Eau Claire, Wis.	D10-'83	16/16
88	Martin, Mike	WR	5-10	181	11/18/60	8	Illinois	Washington, D.C.	D8-'83	12/0
72	McClendon, Skip	DE	6-7	283	4/9/64	4	Arizona State	Detroit, Mich.	D3a-'87	16/5
85	†McGee, Tim	WR	5-10	179	8/7/64	5	Tennessee	Cleveland, Ohio	D1a-'86	16/16
73	Moyer, Ken	T	6-6	292	11/19/66	2	Toledo	Temperance, Mich.	FA-'89	8/0
78	†Muñoz, Anthony	T	6-6	284	8/19/58	11	Southern California	Ontario, Calif.	D1-'80	16/16
23	Palmer, Paul	RB	5-9	181	10/14/64	4	Temple	Potomac, Md.	PB(Dall)-'90#	14/8*
75	Reimers, Bruce	T	6-7	294	9/18/60	7	Iowa State	Humboldt, Iowa	D8-'84	15/15
87	†Riggs, Jim	TE	6-5	245	9/29/63	4	Clemson	Laurinburg, N.C.	D4-'87	10/1
70	Skow, Jim	DE	6-3	243	6/29/63	5	Nebraska	Omaha, Neb.	D3-'86	11/11
83	Smith, Kendal	WR	5-9	189	11/23/65	2	Utah State	Redwood City, Calif.	D7-'89	11/0
20	Taylor, Craig	RB	5-11	224	1/3/66	2	West Virginia	Linden, N.J.	D6-'89	12/0
22	†Thomas, Eric	CB	5-11	181	9/11/64	4	Tulane	Sacramento, Calif.	D2-'87	16/15
96	Tuatagaloa, Natu	DE	6-4	265	5/25/66	2	California	San Rafael, Calif.	D5-'89	14/0
59	Walker, Kevin	LB	6-3	233	12/24/65	3	Maryland	West Milford, N.J.	D3-'88	16/0
63	Walter, Joe	T	6-6	290	6/18/63	6	Texas Tech	Dallas, Tex.	D7a-'85	10/7
51	White, Leon	LB	6-3	237	10/4/63	5	Brigham Young	La Mesa, Calif.	D5-'86	16/16
41	†Wilcots, Solomon	CB	5-11	190	10/9/64	4	Colorado	Rubidoux, Calif.	D8-'87	16/0
4	Wilhelm, Erik	QB	6-3	210	11/19/65	2	Oregon State	Lake Oswego, Ore.	D3-'89	6/0
30	Woods, Ickey	RB	6-2	232	2/28/66	2	Nevada-Las Vegas	Fresno, Calif.	D2-'88	2/2
91	Zander, Carl	LB	6-2	235	3/23/63	6	Tennessee	Mendham, N.J.	D2-'85	16/16

* Barber played 8 games with San Francisco in '89; Gelbaugh played 1 game with Buffalo; Palmer played 14 games with Dallas.

† Option playout; subject to developments.

Plan B unconditional free agent.

Players lost through Plan B (3): WR Ira Hillary (Minn; 16 games in '89), G Max Montoya (Raid; 16), T Rob Woods (KC; 0).

Retired—Reggie Williams, 14-year linebacker, 16 games in '89.

Also played with Bengals in '89—K Jim Gallery (4 games), WR Carl Parker (3), LB Rich Romer (5), QB Turk Schonert (7), NT Dana Wells (1).

COACHING STAFF

Head Coach, Sam Wyche

Pro Career: Bengals finished 8-8 in AFC Central Division in 1989. Wyche led Cincinnati to AFC championship in 1988 with 12-4 regular-season record before coming within 34 seconds of defeating San Francisco (20-16 loss) in Super Bowl XXIII. Became the fifth head coach in Cincinnati history when he was named to lead the Bengals on December 28, 1983. Played quarterback with Bengals 1968-70, Washington Redskins 1971-73, Detroit Lions 1974-75, St. Louis Cardinals 1976, and Buffalo Bills 1977. Quarterback coach with San Francisco 49ers 1979-82. Career record: 51-47.

Background: Attended North Fulton High School in Atlanta and Furman University where he was the quarterback from 1962-65. Assistant coach at South Carolina in 1967. Head coach at Indiana University in 1983.

Personal: Born January 5, 1945, in Atlanta, Ga. Sam and his wife, Jane, have two children—Zak and Kerry. They live in Cincinnati.

Assistant Coaches

Jim Anderson, running backs; born March 27, 1948, Harrisburg, Pa., lives in Cincinnati. Linebacker-defensive end Cal Western (U.S. International) 1969-70. No pro playing experience. College coach: Cal Western 1970-71, Scottsdale Community College 1973, Nevada-Las Vegas 1974-75, Southern Methodist 1977-80, Stanford 1981-83. Pro coach: Joined Bengals in 1984.

Dana Bible, quarterbacks; born October 30, 1953, Erie, Pa., lives in Cincinnati. Defensive back Cincinnati 1972-75. No pro playing experience. College coach: Cincinnati 1976-80, Miami, Ohio 1981-82, 1989, North Carolina State 1983-85, San Diego State 1986-88. Pro coach: Joined Bengals in 1990.

Marv Braden, special teams; born January 25, 1938, Kansas City, Mo., lives in Cincinnati. Linebacker Southwest Missouri State 1956-59. No pro playing experience. College coach: Parsons 1963-66, Northeast Missouri State 1967-68 (head coach), U.S. International 1969-72, Iowa State 1973, Southern Methodist 1974-75, Michigan State 1976. Pro coach: Denver Broncos 1977-80, San Diego Chargers 1981-85, St. Louis-Phoenix Cardinals 1986-89, joined Bengals in 1990.

Bill Johnson, tight ends; born July 14, 1926, Tyler, Tex., lives in Cincinnati. Center Texas A&M 1944-46. Pro center San Francisco 49ers 1948-55. Pro coach: San Francisco 49ers 1956-67, Cincinnati Bengals 1968-78 (head coach 1976-78), Tampa Bay Buccaneers 1979-82, Detroit Lions 1983-84, rejoined Bengals in 1985.

Dick LeBeau, defensive coordinator-defensive backs; born September 9, 1937, London, Ohio, lives in Cincinnati. Halfback Ohio State 1957-59. Pro defensive back Detroit Lions 1959-72. Pro coach: Philadelphia Eagles 1973-75, Green Bay Packers 1976-79, joined Bengals in 1980.

Jim McNally, offensive line-running game; born December 13, 1943, Buffalo, N.Y., lives in Cincinnati. Guard Buffalo 1961-64. No pro playing experience. College coach: Buffalo 1965-70, Marshall 1971-74, Boston College 1975-77, Wake Forest 1978-79. Pro coach: Joined Bengals in 1980.

Dick Selcer, linebackers; born August 22, 1937, Cincinnati, Ohio, lives in Cincinnati. Running back Notre Dame 1955-58. No pro playing experience. College coach: Xavier, Ohio 1962-64, 1970-71 (head coach), Cincinnati 1965-66, Brown 1967-69, Wisconsin 1972-74, Kansas State 1975-77, Southwestern Louisiana 1978-80. Pro coach: Houston Oilers 1981-83, joined Bengals in 1984.

Mike Stock, special teams; born September 29, 1939, Barberton, Ohio, lives in Cincinnati. Fullback Northwestern 1958-60. No pro playing experience. College coach: Northwestern 1961, Buffalo 1966-67, Navy 1968, Notre Dame 1969-75, 1983-86, Wisconsin 1976-77, Eastern Michigan 1978-82 (head coach). Pro coach: Joined Bengals in 1987.

Cincinnati Bengals 1990 First-Year Roster

Name	Pos.	Ht.	Wt.	Birth-date	College	Hometown	How Acq.
Brennan, Mike	T	6-5	282	3/22/67	Notre Dame	Los Angeles, Calif.	D4
Browndyke, David	P-K	6-1	183	4/16/68	Louisiana State	Dallas, Tex.	FA
Chenault, Chris (1)	LB	6-2	240	11/19/65	Kentucky	Lexington, Ky.	D8-'89
Clark, Bernard	LB	6-2	246	1/12/67	Miami	Tampa, Fla.	D3
Clark, David	RB	6-0	211	10/5/68	Dartmouth	Miami, Fla.	FA
Crigler, Eric	T	6-5	295	6/3/67	Murray State	Louisville, Ky.	D10
Egerton, Tim	WR	5-11	165	1/9/66	Delaware State	Plainfield, N.J.	FA
Fitzpatrick, Greg	S	6-2	203	8/7/65	Central State, Ohio	Cleveland, Ohio	FA
Foust, Mike	T	6-5	295	11/13/66	Fresno State	Fresno, Calif.	FA
Francis, James	LB	6-4	250	8/4/68	Baylor	Houston, Tex.	D1
Gaddis, Reggie	DE	6-0	268	7/23/66	Arizona	Pomona, Calif.	FA
Garrett, John (1)	WR	5-11	180	3/2/65	Princeton	Monmouth Beach, N.J.	FA-'89
Green, Anthony	WR	5-11	186	6/12/67	Western Kentucky	Dallas, Tex.	FA
Green, Harold	RB	6-2	218	1/29/68	South Carolina	Ladson, S.C.	D2
Gussman, Gary	K	5-10	180	9/24/65	Miami	Miami, Fla.	FA
Herds, Tyreese	CB	5-11	195	5/9/68	Kansas State	Tampa, Fla.	FA
Hargrove, Larry	CB-KR	5-8	169	11/18/67	Ohio University	Henderson, N.C.	FA
Hodge, David	TE	6-5	235	5/18/67	South Carolina	Simpsonville, S.C.	FA
James, Lynn	WR	6-0	191	1/25/67	Arizona State	Navasota, Tex.	D5
Milberg, Stuart	T	6-5	320	11/25/66	Connecticut	Wilton, Conn.	FA
Murray, Dan	LB	6-1	243	10/20/66	East Stroudsburg	Vernon, N.J.	FA
Myers, Robert	P	6-1	205	9/11/68	Washington State	La Cañada, Calif.	FA
Novacek, Jason	TE	6-3	231	5/13/66	Fresno State	Gothenburg, Neb.	FA
O'Connor, Tim	T	6-6	282	10/16/66	Virginia	Washington, Pa.	D11
Patterson, Craig	NT	6-4	305	7/18/64	Brigham Young	Castle Dale, Utah	FA
Odegard, Don	CB	5-11	177	11/22/66	Nevada-Las Vegas	Kennewick, Wash.	D6
Ogletree, Craig	LB	6-1	231	4/2/68	Auburn	Barnesville, Ga.	D7
Philcox, Todd (1)	QB	6-4	209	9/25/66	Syracuse	Norwalk, Conn.	FA-'89
Price, Mitchell	CB	5-9	185	5/10/67	Tulane	San Antonio, Tex.	D9
Riley, Andre	WR	5-8	174	12/2/66	Washington	Fresno, Calif.	D12
Scrafford, Kirk	G-T	6-6	255	3/16/67	Montana	Billings, Mont.	FA
Segrist, Scott	K	5-9	175	8/8/66	Texas Tech	Lubbock, Tex.	FA
Simpson, John	WR	6-0	172	2/24/66	Baylor	Plano, Tex.	FA
Varano, Rob	WR	6-1	187	7/18/66	Lehigh	Mt. Carmel, Pa.	FA
Wells, Dana (1)	NT	6-1	265	8/5/66	Arizona	Phoenix, Ariz.	D11-'89
Wellsandt, Doug	TE	6-3	250	2/9/67	Washington State	Moses Lake, Wash.	D8
White, Todd	WR-KR	6-0	188	9/15/65	Cal State-Fullerton	Palos Verdes, Calif.	FA
Whiteman, Sean	CB	5-11	185	1/12/68	Syracuse	Clearwater, Fla.	FA

The term NFL Rookie is defined as a player who is in his first season of professional football and has not been on the roster of another professional football team for any regular-season or postseason games. A Rookie is designated by an "R" on NFL rosters. Players who have been active in another professional football league or players who have NFL experience, including either preseason training camp or being on an active roster for fewer than three regular-season or postseason games, are termed NFL First-Year Players. An NFL First-Year Player is designated by a "1" on NFL rosters. Thereafter, a player on an NFL active roster for at least three regular-season or postseason games is credited with an additional year of NFL playing experience.

NOTES

_____

_____

_____

_____

_____

_____

_____

_____

_____

_____

_____

Chuck Studley, linebackers; born January 17, 1929, Maywood, Ill., lives in Cincinnati. Guard Illinois 1949-51. No pro playing experience. College coach: Illinois 1955-59, Massachusetts 1960 (head coach), Cincinnati 1961-68 (head coach). Pro coach: Cincinnati Bengals 1969-78, San Francisco 49ers 1979-82, Houston Oilers 1983 (interim head coach for last 10 games), Miami Dolphins 1984-88, rejoined Bengals in 1989.

Kim Wood, strength; born July 12, 1945, Barrington, Ill., lives in Cincinnati. Running back Wisconsin 1965-68. No pro playing experience. Pro coach: Joined Bengals in 1975.

American Football Conference
Central Division

Team Colors: Seal Brown, Orange, and White

Tower B
Cleveland Stadium
Cleveland, Ohio 44114
Telephone: (216) 696-5555

Club Officials

President and Owner: Arthur B. Modell
Executive Vice President/Legal and
  Administrative: Jim Bailey
Executive Vice President/Football
  Operations: Ernie Accorsi
Vice President/Marketing and Assistant to
  President: David Modell
Vice President/Public Relations: Kevin Byrne
Vice President/Finance: Mike Poplar
Director of Operations: John Lemmo
Director of Security: Ted Chappelle
Treasurer: Mike Srsen
Assistant Directors of Public Relations: Bob Eller,
  Francine Lubera
Player Personnel: Dom Anile, Tom Dimitroff,
  Gary Horton, Mike Lombardi
Head Trainer: Bill Tessendorf
Equipment Manager: Charley Cusick

Stadium: Cleveland Stadium • **Capacity:** 80,098
  West 3rd Street
  Cleveland, Ohio 44114

Playing Surface: Grass

Training Camp: Lakeland Community College
  Mentor, Ohio 44060

1990 Schedule

Preseason
Aug. 4	vs. Chicago at Canton, Ohio	1:00
Aug. 11	at Green Bay	6:00
Aug. 19	**Minnesota**	8:00
Aug. 25	**Washington**	7:00
Sept. 1	at New York Giants	8:00

Regular Season
Sept. 9	**Pittsburgh**	4:00
Sept. 16	at New York Jets	1:00
Sept. 23	**San Diego**	1:00
Sept. 30	at Kansas City	3:00
Oct. 8	at Denver (Monday)	7:00
Oct. 14	at New Orleans	12:00
Oct. 22	**Cincinnati** (Monday)	9:00
Oct. 28	at San Francisco	1:00
Nov. 4	**Buffalo**	1:00
Nov. 11	**Open Date**	
Nov. 18	**Houston**	1:00
Nov. 25	**Miami**	1:00
Dec. 2	**Los Angeles Rams**	1:00
Dec. 9	at Houston	12:00
Dec. 16	**Atlanta**	1:00
Dec. 23	at Pittsburgh	1:00
Dec. 30	at Cincinnati	1:00

Browns Coaching History

(345-227-10)

1950-62	Paul Brown	115-49-5
1963-70	Blanton Collier	79-38-2
1971-74	Nick Skorich	30-26-2
1975-77	Forrest Gregg*	18-23-0
1977	Dick Modzelewski	0-1-0
1978-84	Sam Rutigliano**	47-52-0
1984-88	Marty Schottenheimer	46-31-0
1989	Bud Carson	10-7-1

*Resigned after 13 games in 1977
**Released after eight games in 1984

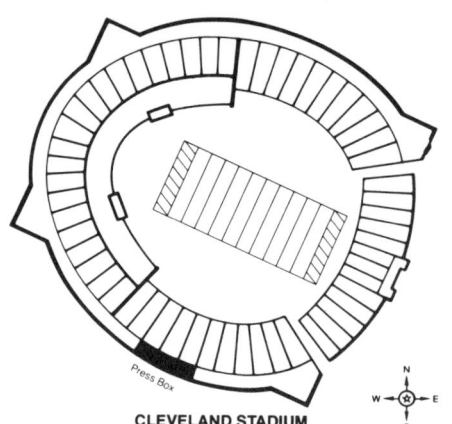

CLEVELAND STADIUM

Record Holders
Individual Records—Career
Category	Name	Performance
Rushing (Yds.)	Jim Brown, 1957-1965	12,312
Passing (Yds.)	Brian Sipe, 1974-1983	23,713
Passing (TDs)	Brian Sipe, 1974-1983	154
Receiving (No.)	Ozzie Newsome, 1978-1989	639
Receiving (Yds.)	Ozzie Newsome, 1978-1989	7,740
Interceptions	Thom Darden, 1972-74, 1976-1981	45
Punting (Avg.)	Horace Gillom, 1950-56	43.8
Punt Return (Avg.)	Greg Pruitt, 1973-1981	11.8
Kickoff Return (Avg.)	Greg Pruitt, 1973-1981	26.3
Field Goals	Lou Groza, 1950-59, 1961-67	234
Touchdowns (Tot.)	Jim Brown, 1957-1965	*126
Points	Lou Groza, 1950-59, 1961-67	1,349

Individual Records—Single Season
Category	Name	Performance
Rushing (Yds.)	Jim Brown, 1963	1,863
Passing (Yds.)	Brian Sipe, 1980	4,132
Passing (TDs)	Brian Sipe, 1980	30
Receiving (No.)	Ozzie Newsome, 1983	89
	Ozzie Newsome, 1984	89
Receiving (Yds.)	Webster Slaughter, 1989	1,236
Interceptions	Thom Darden, 1978	10
Punting (Avg.)	Gary Collins, 1965	46.7
Punt Return (Avg.)	Leroy Kelly, 1965	15.6
Kickoff Return (Avg.)	Billy Reynolds, 1954	29.5
Field Goals	Matt Bahr, 1984	24
	Matt Bahr, 1988	24
Touchdowns (Tot.)	Jim Brown, 1965	21
Points	Jim Brown, 1965	126

Individual Records—Single Game
Category	Name	Performance
Rushing (Yds.)	Jim Brown, 11-24-57	237
	Jim Brown, 11-19-61	237
Passing (Yds.)	Bernie Kosar, 1-3-87	489
Passing (TDs)	Frank Ryan, 12-12-64	5
	Bill Nelsen, 11-2-69	5
	Brian Sipe, 10-7-79	5
Receiving (No.)	Ozzie Newsome, 10-14-84	14
Receiving (Yds.)	Ozzie Newsome, 10-14-84	191
Interceptions	Many times	3
	Last time by Frank Minnifield, 11-22-87	
Field Goals	Don Cockroft, 10-19-75	5
Touchdowns (Tot.)	Dub Jones, 11-25-51	*6
Points	Dub Jones, 11-25-51	36

*NFL Record

1989 Team Record

Preseason (1-4)

Date	Result		Opponents
8/6	L	13-17	vs. Philadelphia
			at London, England
8/12	W	25-24	at Detroit
8/19	L	21-24	Pittsburgh
8/26	L	7-21	at Phoenix
9/2	L	10-27	Tampa Bay
		76-113	

Regular Season (9-6-1)

Date	Result		Opponents	Att.
9/10	W	51- 0	at Pittsburgh	57,928
9/17	W	38-24	N.Y. Jets	73,516
9/25	L	14-21	at Cincinnati	55,996
10/1	W	16-13	Denver	78,637
10/8	L	10-13	at Miami (OT)	58,444
10/15	L	7-17	Pittsburgh	78,840
10/23	W	27- 7	Chicago	78,722
10/29	W	28-17	Houston	78,765
11/5	W	42-31	at Tampa Bay	69,162
11/12	W	17- 7	at Seattle	58,978
11/19	T	10-10	Kansas City (OT)	77,922
11/23	L	10-13	at Detroit	65,624
12/3	L	0-21	Cincinnati	76,236
12/10	L	17-23	at Ind. (OT)	58,550
12/17	W	23-17	Minnesota (OT)	70,777
12/23	W	24-20	at Houston	58,852

(OT) Overtime

Postseason (1-1)

Date	Result		Opponent	Att.
1/6	W	34-30	Buffalo	78,921
1/14	L	21-37	at Denver	76,046

Score by Periods

Browns	48	112	104	64	6	—	334
Opponents	34	67	82	62	9	—	254

Attendance

Home 613,415   Away 483,534   Total 1,096,949
Single-game home record, 85,073 (9-21-70)
Single-season home record, 620,496 (1980)

1989 Team Statistics

	Browns	Opp.
Total First Downs	285	276
Rushing	101	93
Passing	161	161
Penalty	23	22
Third Down: Made/Att.	82/213	82/230
Third Down: Pct.	38.5	35.7
Fourth Down: Made/Att.	1/9	10/16
Fourth Down: Pct.	11.1	62.5
Total Net Yards	5042	4831
Avg. Per Game	315.1	301.9
Total Plays	1011	1031
Avg. Per Play	5.0	4.7
Net Yards Rushing	1609	1670
Avg. Per Game	100.6	104.4
Total Rushes	448	446
Net Yards Passing	3433	3161
Avg. Per Game	214.6	197.6
Sacked/Yards Lost	34/192	45/359
Gross Yards	3625	3520
Att./Completions	529/309	540/269
Completion Pct.	58.4	49.8
Had Intercepted	15	27
Punts/Avg.	97/39.4	94/40.4
Net Punting Avg.	33.8	33.4
Penalties/Yards Lost	128/973	122/985
Fumbles/Ball Lost	23/15	32/11
Touchdowns	41	30
Rushing	14	8
Passing	20	20
Returns	7	2
Avg. Time of Possession	30:26	29:34

1989 Individual Statistics

Scoring

	TD R	TD P	TD Rt	PAT	FG	Saf	TP
Bahr	0	0	0	40/40	16/24	0	88
Metcalf	6	4	0	0/0	0/0	0	60
Slaughter	0	6	0	0/0	0/0	0	36
Manoa	3	2	0	0/0	0/0	0	30
Tillman	0	2	1	0/0	0/0	0	18
Gash	0	0	2	0/0	0/0	0	12
Grayson	0	0	2	0/0	0/0	0	12
Langhorne	0	2	0	0/0	0/0	0	12
K. Jones	1	0	0	0/0	0/0	0	6
Kosar	1	0	0	0/0	0/0	0	6
Mack	1	0	0	0/0	0/0	0	6
Matthews	0	0	1	0/0	0/0	0	6
Middleton	0	1	0	0/0	0/0	0	6
Newsome	0	1	0	0/0	0/0	0	6
Oliphant	1	0	0	0/0	0/0	0	6
Redden	1	0	0	0/0	0/0	0	6
Tennell	0	1	0	0/0	0/0	0	6
Waiters	0	1	0	0/0	0/0	0	6
Wright	0	0	1	0/0	0/0	0	6
Browns	14	20	7	40/40	16/24	0	334
Opponents	8	20	2	29/29	15/28	0	254

Passing

	Att.	Comp.	Yds.	Pct.	TD	Int.	Tkld.	Rate
Kosar	513	303	3533	59.1	18	14	34/192	80.3
Pagel	14	5	60	35.7	1	1	0/0	43.8
Metcalf	2	1	32	50.0	1	0	0/0	135.4
Browns	529	309	3625	58.4	20	15	34/192	80.1
Opponents	540	269	3520	49.8	20	27	45/359	62.3

Rushing

	Att.	Yds.	Avg.	LG	TD
Metcalf	187	633	3.4	43t	6
Manoa	87	289	3.3	22	3
Redden	40	180	4.5	38t	1
K. Jones	43	160	3.7	15	1
Mack	37	130	3.5	12	1
Oliphant	15	97	6.5	21t	1
Kosar	30	70	2.3	23	1
McNeil	2	32	16.0	18	0
Langhorne	5	19	3.8	18	0
Pagel	2	-1	-0.5	4	0
Browns	448	1609	3.6	43t	14
Opponents	446	1670	3.7	39t	8

Receiving

	No.	Yds.	Avg.	LG	TD
Slaughter	65	1236	19.0	97t	6
Langhorne	60	749	12.5	62t	2
Metcalf	54	397	7.4	68t	4
Newsome	29	324	11.2	31	1
Brennan	28	289	10.3	38	0
Manoa	27	241	8.9	32	2
K. Jones	15	126	8.4	36	0
McNeil	10	114	11.4	32	0
Tillman	6	70	11.7	19	2
Redden	6	34	5.7	8	0
Oliphant	3	22	7.3	9	0
Mack	2	7	3.5	4	0
Waiters	1	14	14.0	14t	1
Middleton	1	5	5.0	5t	1
Tennell	1	4	4.0	4t	1
Kosar	1	-7	-7.0	-7	0
Browns	309	3625	11.7	97t	20
Opponents	269	3520	13.1	68	20

Interceptions

	No.	Yds.	Avg.	LG	TD
Wright	9	91	10.1	27t	1
Gash	3	65	21.7	36t	2
M. Johnson	3	43	14.3	23	0
Minnifield	3	29	9.7	25	0
Harper	3	24	8.0	21	0
Grayson	2	25	12.5	14t	1
Matthews	1	25	25.0	25	0
Kramer	1	12	12.0	12	0
Dixon	1	2	2.0	2	0
Lyons	1	0	0.0	0	0
Browns	27	300	11.1	36t	4
Opponents	15	306	20.4	77	1

Punting

	No.	Yds.	Avg.	In 20	LG
Wagner	97	3817	39.4	32	60
Browns	97	3817	39.4	32	60
Opponents	94	3797	40.4	24	57

Punt Returns

	No.	FC	Yds.	Avg.	LG	TD
McNeil	49	15	496	10.1	49	0
Browns	49	15	496	10.1	49	0
Opponents	49	13	418	8.5	27	0

Kickoff Returns

	No.	Yds.	Avg.	LG	TD
Metcalf	31	718	23.2	49	0
Oliphant	5	69	13.8	28	0
McNeil	4	61	15.3	21	0
K. Jones	4	42	10.5	25	0
Braggs	2	20	10.0	18	0
Redden	2	2	1.0	2	0
Joines	1	12	12.0	12	0
E. Johnson	1	8	8.0	8	0
Browns	50	932	18.6	49	0
Opponents	58	1175	20.3	73	0

Sacks

	No.
Baker	7.5
Perry	7.0
Hairston	6.5
Banks	4.0
Blaylock	4.0
Matthews	4.0
Stewart	3.0
Gash	2.0
Gibson	2.0
Charlton	1.0
Grayson	1.0
Harper	1.0
M. Johnson	1.0
Pike	1.0
Browns	45.0
Opponents	34.0

1990 Draft Choices

Round	Name	Pos.	College
2.	Leroy Hoard	RB	Michigan
3.	Anthony Pleasant	DE	Tennessee State
4.	Harlon Barnett	DB	Michigan State
5.	Rob Burnett	DE	Syracuse
6.	Randy Hilliard	DB	N.W. Louisiana
7.	Scott Galbraith	TE	Southern California
8.	Jock Jones	LB	Virginia Tech
9.	Eugene Rowell	WR	Southern Mississippi
10.	Michael Wallace	DB	Jackson State
11.	Clemente Gordon	QB	Grambling
12.	Kerry Simien	WR	Texas A&I

Cleveland Browns 1990 Veteran Roster

No.	Name	Pos.	Ht.	Wt.	Birth-date	NFL Exp.	College	Hometown	How Acq.	'89 Games/ Starts
61	Baab, Mike	C	6-4	270	12/6/59	9	Texas	Fort Worth, Tex.	PB(NE)-'90#	16/16*
9	Bahr, Matt	K	5-10	175	7/6/56	12	Penn State	Langhorne, Pa.	T(SF)-'81	16/0
60	Baker, Al	DE	6-6	280	12/9/56	13	Colorado State	Newark, N.J.	PB(Minn)-'89#	16/16
97	Banks, Robert	DE	6-5	255	12/10/63	3	Notre Dame	Hampton, Va.	PB(Hou)-'89#	15/15
64	Baugh, Tom	C	6-4	290	12/1/63	5	Southern Illinois	Brookridge, Ill.	PB(KC)-'89#	16/0*
24	†Blaylock, Tony	CB	5-10	190	2/21/65	3	Winston-Salem State	Raleigh, N.C.	D4-'88	16/1
77	†Bolden, Rickey	T	6-4	280	9/8/61	7	Southern Methodist	Dallas, Tex.	D4a-'84	6/3
36	Braggs, Stephen	CB	5-9	180	8/29/65	4	Texas	Houston, Tex.	D6-'87	7/0
86	Brennan, Brian	WR	5-10	185	2/15/62	7	Boston College	Bloomfield, Mich.	D4b-'84	14/2
94	Buczkowski, Bob	DT-DE	6-5	260	5/5/64	2	Pittsburgh	Pittsburgh, Pa.	FA-'90	4/0*
58	Charlton, Clifford	LB	6-3	245	2/16/65	3	Florida	Tallahassee, Fla.	D1-'88	15/0
43	Clack, Darryl	RB	5-10	220	10/29/63	5	Arizona State	Widefield, Colo.	FA-'90	8/0*
26	Clayborn, Raymond	CB	6-1	186	1/2/55	14	Texas	Fort Worth, Tex.	PB(NE)-'90#	14/14*
49	Dillahunt, Ellis	S	5-11	196	11/25/64	2	East Carolina	Jacksonville, N.C.	FA-'90	0*
87	Dunn, K.D.	TE	6-3	237	4/28/63	5	Clemson	Decatur, Ga.	FA-'90	1/0*
74	†Farren, Paul	T-G	6-6	270	12/24/60	8	Boston University	Cohasset, Mass.	D12-'83	16/13
69	Fike, Dan	G	6-7	285	6/16/61	6	Florida	Pensacola, Fla.	FA-'85	13/13
30	†Gash, Thane	S	5-11	200	9/1/65	3	East Tennessee State	Hendersonville, N.C.	D7-'88	16/15
16	Gay, Everett	WR	6-2	209	10/23/64	2	Texas	Houston, Tex.	FA-'90	0*
71	Gibson, Tom	DE	6-7	250	12/20/63	2	Northern Arizona	Saugus, Calif.	FA-'89	16/1
56	†Grayson, David	LB	6-2	235	2/27/64	4	Fresno State	San Diego, Calif.	FA-'87	10/10
78	Hairston, Carl	DT	6-2	275	12/15/52	15	Maryland-Eastern Shore	Martinsville, Va.	T(Phil)-'84	16/16
23	Harper, Mark	CB	5-9	185	11/5/61	5	Alcorn State	Memphis, Tenn.	FA-'86	16/2
51	Johnson, Eddie	LB	6-1	225	2/3/59	10	Louisville	Albany, Ga.	D7-'81	16/0
59	†Johnson, Mike	LB	6-1	225	11/26/62	5	Virginia Tech	Hyattsville, Md.	D1b-'84	16/16
95	Jones, Marlon	DE	6-4	260	7/1/64	3	Central State, Ohio	Baltimore, Md.	FA-'87	12/0
66	†Jones, Tony	T	6-5	285	5/24/66	3	Western Carolina	Cannesville, Ga.	FA-'88	9/3
19	Kosar, Bernie	QB	6-5	210	11/25/63	6	Miami	Boardman, Ohio	SD1-'85	16/16
40	Kramer, Kyle	S	6-3	190	1/12/67	2	Bowling Green	Kettering, Ohio	D5a-'89	14/0
88	Langhorne, Reggie	WR	6-2	200	4/7/63	6	Elizabeth City State	Carrollton, Va.	D7-'85	16/15
75	Lucas, Jeff	T	6-7	282	6/30/64	2	West Virginia	Hackensack, N.J.	FA-'90	0*
34	Mack, Kevin	RB	6-0	230	8/9/62	6	Clemson	Kings Mountain, N.C.	SD1-'84	4/1
42	†Manoa, Tim	RB	6-1	240	9/9/64	4	Penn State	Pittsburgh, Pa.	D3a-'87	16/15
57	†Matthews, Clay	LB	6-2	245	3/15/56	13	Southern California	New Trier, Ill.	D1a-'78	16/16
53	McGrew, Lawrence	LB	6-5	233	7/23/57	10	Southern California	Berkeley, Calif.	PB(NE)-'90#	16/16*
21	Metcalf, Eric	RB	5-10	185	1/23/68	2	Texas	Arlington, Va.	D1-'89	16/11
31	†Minnifield, Frank	CB	5-9	180	1/1/60	7	Louisville	Lexington, Ky.	FA-'84	16/16
82	Newsome, Ozzie	TE	6-2	225	3/16/56	13	Alabama	Leighton, Ala.	D1b-'78	16/13
89	Oliphant, Mike	WR-KR	5-9	170	5/19/63	2	Puget Sound	Federal Way, Wash.	T(Wash)-'89	14/0
10	Pagel, Mike	QB	6-2	211	9/13/60	9	Arizona State	Phoenix, Ariz.	T(Ind)-'86	16/0
92	Perry, Michael Dean	DE	6-0	280	8/27/65	3	Clemson	Aiken, S.C.	D2-'88	16/16
75	Pike, Chris	DT	6-8	290	1/13/64	2	Tulsa	Washington, D.C.	T(Phil)-'88	12/0
73	†Rakoczy, Gregg	C	6-6	290	5/18/65	4	Miami	Medford Lakes, N.J.	D2-'87	16/16
35	†Redden, Barry	RB	5-10	219	7/21/60	9	Richmond	Sarasota, Fla.	T(SD)-'89	16/1
52	Rose, Ken	LB	6-1	216	6/9/62	4	Nevada-Las Vegas	Sacramento, Calif.	PB(NYJ)-'90#	15/0*
84	Slaughter, Webster	WR	6-0	170	10/19/64	5	San Diego State	Stockton, Calif.	D2-'86	16/16
71	Smith, Dave	T	6-5	290	12/12/64	2	Southern Illinois	Lansing, Ill.	FA-'90	0*
96	Stewart, Andrew	DE	6-5	265	11/20/65	2	Cincinnati	West Hempstead, N.Y.	D4-'89	16/0
85	Tillman, Lawyer	WR	6-5	230	5/20/66	2	Auburn	Mobile, Ala.	D2-'89	14/1
15	Wagner, Bryan	P	6-2	200	3/28/62	4	Cal State-Northridge	Chula Vista, Calif.	FA-'89	16/0
50	Waiters, Van	LB	6-4	245	2/27/65	3	Indiana	Coral Gables, Fla.	D3-'88	16/5
91	Weston, Rhondy	DT	6-5	275	6/7/66	2	Florida	Belle Glade, Fla.	PB(TB)-'90#	13/2*
27	Wright, Charlie	CB-S	5-10	178	4/5/65	3	Tulsa	Carthage, Mo.	FA-'90	0*
22	†Wright, Felix	S	6-2	195	6/22/59	6	Drake	Carthage, Mo.	FA-'85	16/16

* Baab played 16 games with New England in '89; Baugh played 16 games with Kansas City; Buczkowski played 4 games with Phoenix; Clack played 8 games with Dallas; Clayborn played 14 games with New England; Dillahunt last active with Cincinnati in '88; Dunn played 1 game with N.Y. Jets; Gay active for one game with Tampa Bay but did not play; Lucas last active with Pittsburgh in '87; McGrew played 16 games with New England; Rose played 15 games with N.Y. Jets; Smith last active with Cincinnati in '88; Weston played 13 games with Tampa Bay; C. Wright last active with Tampa Bay in '88.

† Option playout; subject to developments.

#Plan B unconditional free agent.

Players lost through Plan B (5): CB Hanford Dixon (SF; 15 games in '89), RB Keith Jones (Dall; 16), S Robert Lyons (Minn; 9), RB-KR Gerald McNeil (Hou; 16), TE Ron Middleton (Wash; 9).

Also played with Browns in '89—T Mike Graybill (6 games in '89), WR Vernon Joines (4), T Kevin Robbins (1), T Kevin Simons (1), T Daryle Smith (4), TE Derek Tennell (14).

COACHING STAFF

Head Coach, Bud Carson

Pro Career: Begins second year as head coach of the Browns. Became seventh head coach of team on January 27, 1989. Led Browns to AFC Central title and AFC Championship Game in first season. Entered pro coaching ranks as secondary coach of the Pittsburgh Steelers in 1972. Was defensive coordinator there from 1973-77, as Steelers won their first two Super Bowls (IX, X). Joined Los Angeles Rams as defensive coordinator from 1978-81, as Rams played in Super Bowl XIV. Defensive coordinator of Baltimore Colts (1982), Kansas City Chiefs (1983), and New York Jets (1985-88).

Background: Attended Freeport (Pa.) High School. Was an All-Southern defensive back at North Carolina for three seasons. Spent 30 months in the Marines following graduation. Began coaching career at North Carolina (1957-64) and spent one season (1965) at South Carolina. In 1966, he joined Georgia Tech's staff and succeeded Bobby Dodd as head coach the following year, where he compiled a 27-27 record in five years (1967-71). Was a volunteer coach at University of Kansas in 1984.

Personal: Born April 28, 1931, in Freeport, Pa. Bud and his wife, Linda, have four children, Dana, Cliff, Gary, and Cathy, and live in Moreland Hills, Ohio.

Assistant Coaches

Zeke Bratkowski, quarterbacks; born October 20, 1931, Danville, Ill.; lives in Berea, Ohio. Quarterback Georgia 1951-53. Pro quarterback Chicago Bears 1954, 1957-60, Los Angeles Rams 1961-63, Green Bay Packers 1963-68, 1971. Pro coach: Green Bay Packers 1969-70, 1975-81, Chicago Bears 1972-74, Baltimore-Indianapolis Colts 1982-84, New York Jets 1985-89, joined Browns in 1990.

Mike Faulkiner, defensive assistant; born March 27, 1947, Cameron, W. Va., lives in Berea, Ohio. Quarterback-defensive back West Virginia Tech 1967-70. No pro playing experience. College coach: Eastern Illinois 1981. Pro coach: Toronto Argonauts (CFL) 1979, New York Giants (1980), Montreal Alouettes (CFL) 1982, New York Jets 1983-89, joined Browns in 1990.

Hal Hunter, special assistant to head coach; born June 3, 1934, Canonsburg, Pa., lives in Berea, Ohio. Linebacker/guard Pittsburgh 1953-55. No pro playing experience. College coach: Richmond 1958-61, West Virginia 1962-63, Maryland 1964-65, Duke 1966-70, Kentucky 1971-72, Indiana 1973-76, California State (Pa.) 1977-80. Pro coach: Hamilton Tiger-Cats (CFL) 1981, Baltimore/Indianapolis Colts 1982-84 (interim head coach, final game in 1984), Pittsburgh Steelers 1985-88, joined Browns in 1989.

Stan Jones, strength and conditioning; born November 24, 1931, Altoona, Pa., lives in Berea, Ohio. Guard/defensive tackle Maryland 1950-53. Pro guard/defensive tackle Chicago Bears 1954-65, Washington Redskins 1966. Pro coach: Denver Broncos 1967-71; 1976-88, Buffalo Bills 1972-75, joined Browns in 1989.

Paul Lanham, special teams coordinator; born July 31, 1930, Ripley, W. Va., lives in Berea, Ohio. Linebacker Glenville (W. Va.) State. No pro playing experience. College coach: Delaware 1960, Dayton 1961, Colorado State 1962-69, Arkansas 1970-71. Pro coach: St. Louis Cardinals 1972, Washington Redskins 1973-77, 1987-88, Los Angeles Rams 1978-82, Chicago Blitz/Arizona Wranglers (USFL) 1983-84, Detroit Lions 1985-86, joined Browns in 1989.

Richard Mann, receivers; born April 20, 1947, Aliquippa, Pa., lives in Strongsville, Ohio. Wide receiver Arizona State 1966-68. No pro playing experience. College coach: Arizona State 1974-79, Louisville 1980-81. Pro coach: Baltimore/Indianapolis Colts 1982-84, joined Browns in 1985.

Joe Popp, special assistant to head coach; born September 29, 1931, Johnstown, Pa., lives in Berea, Ohio. Lineman Catawba College 1949-52. No pro playing experience. College coach: North Carolina 1962-63, Wake Forest 1964-67, Georgia Tech 1968-72. Pro coach: Chicago Fire (WFL) 1974-75, joined Browns in 1989.

Dan Radakovich, assistant head coach, offensive line; born November 27, 1935, Duquesne, Pa., lives in Berea, Ohio. Center-linebacker Penn State 1954-56. No pro playing experience. College coach: Penn State 1960-69, Cincinnati 1970, Colorado 1972-73, North Carolina State 1982. Pro coach: Pittsburgh Steelers 1971, 1974-77, San Francisco 49ers 1978, Los Angeles Rams 1979-81, Denver Broncos 1983, Minnesota Vikings 1984, New York Jets 1985-88, joined Browns in 1989.

George Sefcik, running backs; born December 27, 1939, Cleveland, Ohio, lives in Westlake, Ohio. Halfback Notre Dame 1959-61. No pro playing experience. College coach: Notre Dame 1963-68, Kentucky 1969-72. Pro coach: Baltimore Colts 1973-74, Cleveland Browns 1975-77, Cincinnati Bengals 1979-83, Green Bay Packers 1984-87, Kansas City Chiefs 1988, rejoined Browns in 1989.

Jim Shofner, offensive coordinator; born December 18, 1935, Grapevine, Tex., lives in Berea, Ohio. Running back Texas Christian 1955-57. Pro defensive back Cleveland Browns 1958-63. College coach: Texas Christian 1964-66, 1974-76 (head coach). Pro coach: San Francisco 49ers 1967-73, 1977, Cleveland Browns 1978-80, Houston Oilers 1981-82, Dallas Cowboys 1983-85, St. Louis/Phoenix Cardinals 1986-89, rejoined Browns in 1990.

Lionel Taylor, special assistant-offense, tight ends; born August 15, 1936, Kansas City, Mo., lives in Berea, Ohio. Flanker New Mexico Highlands 1955-58. Pro wide receiver Chicago Bears 1959, Denver Broncos 1960-66, Houston Oilers 1967-68. College coach: Oregon State 1982-83, Texas Southern 1984-88 (head coach and athletic director). Pro coach: Pittsburgh Steelers 1970-76, Los Angeles Rams 1977-81, joined Browns in 1989.

John Teerlinck, defensive line; born April 9, 1951, Rochester, N.Y., lives in Berea, Ohio. Defensive lineman Western Illinois 1970-73. Pro defensive tackle San Diego Chargers 1974-76. College coach: Iowa Lakes J.C. 1977, Eastern Illinois 1978-79, Illinois 1980-82. Pro coach: Chicago Blitz/Arizona Wranglers (USFL) 1983-84, joined Browns in 1989.

Jim Vechiarella, linebackers; born February 20, 1937, Youngstown, Ohio, lives in Berea, Ohio. Linebacker Youngstown State 1955-57. No pro playing experience. College coach: Youngstown State 1964-74, Southern Illinois 1976-77, Tulane 1978-80. Pro coach: Charlotte Hornets (WFL) 1975, Los Angeles Rams 1981-82, Kansas City Chiefs 1983-85, New York Jets 1986-89, joined Browns in 1990.

Cleveland Browns 1990 First-Year Roster

Name	Pos.	Ht.	Wt.	Birth-date	College	Hometown	How Acq.
Barnett, Harlon	S	5-11	195	1/2/67	Michigan State	Cincinnati, Ohio	D4
Burnett, Rob	DE-NT	6-3	271	8/27/67	Syracuse	Coram, N.Y.	D5
Davis, Anthony	CB	5-10	180	1/10/67	Howard University	Belton, S.C.	FA
Florence, Anthony (1)	CB	6-0	185	12/11/66	Bethune-Cookman	Delray Beach, Fla.	FA
Gainer, Derrick (1)	RB	5-10	220	8/15/66	Florida A&M	Plant City, Fla.	FA
Galbraith, Scott	TE	6-2	257	1/7/67	Southern California	Sacramento, Calif.	D7
Gordon, Clemente	QB	6-2	222	8/14/67	Grambling	Atlanta, Ga.	D11
Graham, Jeff (1)	QB	6-3	196	2/5/66	Long Beach State	Costa Mesa, Calif.	FA
Graybill, Mike (1)	T	6-7	275	10/14/66	Boston University	Hyattsville, Md.	D7-'89
Hilliard, Randy	CB	5-10	162	6/2/67	N.W. Louisiana	Metairie, La.	D6
Hoard, Leroy	RB	5-10	227	5/5/68	Michigan	New Orleans, La.	D2
Jefferson, Ben (1)	T	6-8	345	1/15/66	Maryland	New Rochelle, N.Y.	FA
Joines, Vernon (1)	WR	6-2	200	6/20/65	Maryland	Baltimore, Md.	FA
Jones, Jock	LB	6-2	227	3/13/68	Virginia Tech	Ashland, Va.	D8
Owens, Kerry (1)	LB	6-1	233	7/16/66	Arkansas	Stuttgart, Ark.	FA
Pleasant, Anthony	DE	6-4	250	1/27/67	Tennessee State	Century, Fla.	D3
Robbins, Kevin (1)	G-T	6-4	286	12/12/67	Michigan State	Washington, D.C.	FA-'89
Rowell, Eugene	WR	6-0	184	6/12/68	Southern Mississippi	Auburn, Ala.	D9
Simien, Kerry	WR-KR	5-9	181	12/14/66	Texas A&I	Houston, Tex.	D12
Simons, Kevin (1)	T	6-3	315	4/25/67	Tennessee	Miami, Fla.	FA-'89
Talley, John (1)	TE	6-6	250	12/19/64	West Virginia	Cleveland, Ohio	FA
Tamm, Ralph (1)	G-C	6-3	280	3/11/66	West Chester	Bensalem, Pa.	FA
Tobey, Bryan (1)	RB	6-1	250	4/7/65	Grambling	Hyannis, Mass.	FA
Wallace, Mike	CB	6-0	182	8/28/68	Jackson State	Silvercreek, Miss.	D10
Wilkerson, Gary (1)	CB	6-0	181	10/11/65	Penn State	Sutherland, Va.	D6-'89

The term NFL Rookie is defined as a player who is in his first season of professional football and has not been on the roster of another professional football team for any regular-season or postseason games. A Rookie is designated by an "R" on NFL rosters. Players who have been active in another professional football league or players who have NFL experience, including either preseason training camp or being on an active roster for fewer than three regular-season or postseason games, are termed NFL First-Year Players. An NFL First-Year Player is designated by a "1" on NFL rosters. Thereafter, a player on an NFL active roster for at least three regular-season or postseason games is credited with an additional year of NFL playing experience.

NOTES

DENVER BRONCOS

American Football Conference Western Division

Team Colors: Orange, Royal Blue, and White

13655 East Dove Valley Parkway
Englewood, Colorado 80112
Telephone: (303) 649-9000

Club Officials

President-Chief Executive Officer:
Pat Bowlen
Vice President-Head Coach: Dan Reeves
General Manager: John Beake
Chief Financial Officer-Treasurer:
Robert M. Hurley
Director of Administration: Sandy Waters
Director of Football Operations: Lide Huggins
Director of Player Personnel: Reed Johnson
Director of Media Relations: Jim Saccomano
Ticket Manager: Gail Stuckey
Director of Operations: Bill Harpole
Video Director: Rusty Nail
Director of Player and Community
Relations: Charlie Lee
Equipment Manager: Dan Bill
Trainer: Steve Antonopulos

Stadium: Denver Mile High Stadium •
Capacity: 76,273
1900 West Eliot
Denver, Colorado 80204

Playing Surface: Grass (PAT)

Training Camp: University of Northern Colorado
Greeley, Colorado 80639

1990 Schedule

Preseason
Aug. 4	vs. Seattle at Tokyo	10:00*
Aug. 11	at Indianapolis	7:30
Aug. 20	**San Francisco**	6:00
Aug. 25	at Miami	8:00
Aug. 31	**Phoenix**	7:00

*P.M. Eastern Time

Regular Season
Sept. 9	at Los Angeles Raiders	1:00
Sept. 17	**Kansas City** (Monday)	7:00
Sept. 23	**Seattle**	2:00
Sept. 30	at Buffalo	1:00
Oct. 8	**Cleveland** (Monday)	7:00
Oct. 14	**Pittsburgh**	2:00
Oct. 21	at Indianapolis	12:00
Oct. 28	**Open Date**	
Nov. 4	at Minnesota	7:00
Nov. 11	at San Diego	1:00
Nov. 18	**Chicago**	2:00
Nov. 22	at Detroit (Thanksgiving)	12:30
Dec. 2	**Los Angeles Raiders**	2:00
Dec. 9	at Kansas City	3:00
Dec. 16	**San Diego**	2:00
Dec. 23	at Seattle	5:00
Dec. 30	**Green Bay**	2:00

Broncos Coaching History

(215-227-10)
1960-61	Frank Filchock	7-20-1
1962-64	Jack Faulkner*	9-22-1
1964-66	Mac Speedie**	6-19-1
1966	Ray Malavasi	4-8-0
1967-71	Lou Saban***	20-42-3
1971	Jerry Smith	2-3-0
1972-76	John Ralston	34-33-3
1977-80	Robert (Red) Miller	42-25-0
1981-89	Dan Reeves	91-55-1

*Released after four games in 1964
**Resigned after two games in 1966
***Resigned after nine games in 1971

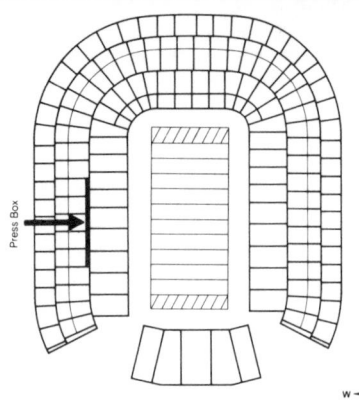

DENVER MILE HIGH STADIUM

Record Holders

Individual Records—Career
Category	Name	Performance
Rushing (Yds.)	Floyd Little, 1967-1975	6,323
Passing (Yds.)	John Elway, 1983-89	21,195
Passing (TDs)	John Elway, 1983-89	120
Receiving (No.)	Lionel Taylor, 1960-66	543
Receiving (Yds.)	Lionel Taylor, 1960-66	6,872
Interceptions	Steve Foley, 1976-1986	44
Punting (Avg.)	Jim Fraser, 1962-64	45.2
Punt Return (Avg.)	Rick Upchurch, 1975-1983	12.1
Kickoff Return (Avg.)	Abner Haynes, 1965-66	26.3
Field Goals	Jim Turner, 1971-79	151
Touchdowns (Tot.)	Floyd Little, 1967-1975	54
Points	Jim Turner, 1971-79	742

Individual Records—Single Season
Category	Name	Performance
Rushing (Yds.)	Otis Armstrong, 1974	1,407
Passing (Yds.)	John Elway, 1985	3,891
Passing (TDs)	Frank Tripucka, 1960	24
Receiving (No.)	Lionel Taylor, 1961	100
Receiving (Yds.)	Steve Watson, 1981	1,244
Interceptions	Goose Gonsoulin, 1960	11
Punting (Avg.)	Jim Fraser, 1963	46.1
Punt Return (Avg.)	Floyd Little, 1967	16.9
Kickoff Return (Avg.)	Bill Thompson, 1969	28.5
Field Goals	Gene Mingo, 1962	27
	David Treadwell, 1989	27
Touchdowns (Tot.)	Sammy Winder, 1986	14
Points	Gene Mingo, 1962	137

Individual Records—Single Game
Category	Name	Performance
Rushing (Yds.)	Otis Armstrong, 12-8-74	183
Passing (Yds.)	Frank Tripucka, 9-15-62	447
Passing (TDs)	Frank Tripucka, 10-28-62	5
	John Elway, 11-18-84	5
Receiving (No.)	Lionel Taylor, 11-29-64	13
	Bobby Anderson, 9-30-73	13
Receiving (Yds.)	Lionel Taylor, 11-27-60	199
Interceptions	Goose Gonsoulin, 9-18-60	*4
	Willie Brown, 11-15-64	*4
Field Goals	Gene Mingo, 10-6-63	5
	Rich Karlis, 11-20-83	5
Touchdowns (Tot.)	Many times	3
	Last time by Gerald Willhite, 11-16-86	
Points	Gene Mingo, 12-10-60	21

*NFL Record

1989 Team Record

Preseason (2-2)

Date	Result		Opponents
8/12	W	17-13	L.A. Rams
8/19	L	17-35	at San Francisco
8/26	W	24-13	Dallas (OT)
9/2	L	34-38	at Indianapolis
		92-107	

Regular Season (11-5)

Date	Result		Opponents	Att.
9/10	W	34-20	Kansas City	74,284
9/18	W	28-14	at Buffalo	78,176
9/24	W	31-21	L.A. Raiders	75,754
10/1	L	13-16	at Cleveland	78,637
10/8	W	16-10	San Diego	75,222
10/15	W	14-3	Indianapolis	74,680
10/22	W	24-21	at Seattle (OT)	62,353
10/29	L	24-28	Philadelphia	75,065
11/5	W	34-7	Pittsburgh	74,739
11/12	W	16-13	at Kansas City	76,245
11/20	W	14-10	at Washington	52,975
11/26	W	41-14	Seattle	75,117
12/3	L	13-16	at L.A. Raid. (OT)	87,560
12/10	L	7-14	N.Y. Giants	63,283
12/16	W	37-0	at Phoenix	56,071
12/24	L	16-19	at San Diego	50,524

(OT) Overtime

Postseason (2-1)

Date	Result		Opponent	Att.
1/7	W	24-23	Pittsburgh	75,477
1/14	W	37-21	Cleveland	76,046
1/28	L	10-55	San Francisco	72,919

Score by Periods

Broncos	84	114	57	104	3	—	362
Opponents	44	53	50	76	3	—	226

Attendance

Home 588,144   Away 542,541   Total 1,130,685
Single-game home record, 76,105 (1-4-87)
Single-season home record, 598,224 (1981)

1989 Team Statistics

	Broncos	Opp.
Total First Downs	308	246
Rushing	125	90
Passing	163	142
Penalty	20	14
Third Down: Made/Att.	111/240	73/216
Third Down: Pct.	46.3	33.8
Fourth Down: Made/Att.	2/9	12/24
Fourth Down: Pct.	22.2	50.0
Total Net Yards	5093	4407
Avg. Per Game	318.3	275.4
Total Plays	1071	977
Avg. Per Play	4.8	4.5
Net Yards Rushing	2092	1580
Avg. Per Game	130.8	98.8
Total Rushes	554	426
Net Yards Passing	3001	2827
Avg. Per Game	187.6	176.7
Sacked/Yards Lost	43/351	47/374
Gross Yards	3352	3201
Att./Completions	474/256	504/268
Completion Pct.	54.0	53.2
Had Intercepted	20	21
Punts/Avg.	80/39.8	84/41.0
Net Punting Avg.	33.7	35.0
Penalties/Yards Lost	83/594	102/823
Fumbles/Ball Lost	26/12	43/22
Touchdowns	40	25
Rushing	15	10
Passing	21	13
Returns	4	2
Avg. Time of Possession	32:17	27:43

1989 Individual Statistics

Scoring

	TD R	TD P	TD Rt	PAT	FG	Saf	TP
Treadwell	0	0	0	39/40	27/33	0	120
Humphrey	7	1	0	0/0	0/0	0	48
Johnson	0	7	0	0/0	0/0	0	42
Bratton	1	3	0	0/0	0/0	0	24
Elway	3	0	0	0/0	0/0	0	18
Sewell	0	3	0	0/0	0/0	0	18
Alexander	2	0	0	0/0	0/0	0	12
Jackson	0	2	0	0/0	0/0	0	12
Kay	0	2	0	0/0	0/0	0	12
Winder	2	0	0	0/0	0/0	0	12
Young	0	2	0	0/0	0/0	0	12
Braxton	0	0	1	0/0	0/0	0	6
Kragen	0	0	1	0/0	0/0	0	6
Mecklenburg	0	0	1	0/0	0/0	0	6
Nattiel	0	1	0	0/0	0/0	0	6
Robbins	0	0	1	0/0	0/0	0	6
Brooks	0	0	0	0/0	0/0	1	2
Broncos	15	21	4	39/40	27/33	1	362
Opponents	10	13	2	25/25	17/27	0	226

Passing

	Att.	Comp.	Yds.	Pct.	TD	Int.	Tkld.	Rate
Elway	416	223	3051	53.6	18	18	35/298	73.7
Kubiak	55	32	284	58.2	2	2	8/53	69.1
Humphrey	2	1	17	50.0	1	0	0/0	118.8
Johnson	1	0	0	0.0	0	0	0/0	39.6
Broncos	474	256	3352	54.0	21	20	43/351	73.7
Opponents	504	268	3201	53.2	13	21	47/374	64.1

Rushing

	Att.	Yds.	Avg.	LG	TD
Humphrey	294	1151	3.9	40	7
Winder	110	351	3.2	16	2
Elway	48	244	5.1	31	3
Alexander	45	146	3.2	11	2
Bratton	30	108	3.6	9	1
Sewell	7	44	6.3	10	0
Kubiak	15	35	2.3	10	0
Jackson	5	13	2.6	8	0
Broncos	554	2092	3.8	40	15
Opponents	426	1580	3.7	24	10

Receiving

	No.	Yds.	Avg.	LG	TD
Johnson	76	1095	14.4	69	7
Jackson	28	446	15.9	49	2
Sewell	25	416	16.6	56	3
Young	22	402	18.3	47	2
Humphrey	22	156	7.1	13	1
Kay	21	197	9.4	20t	2
Mobley	17	200	11.8	36	0
Winder	14	91	6.5	19	0
Nattiel	10	183	18.3	43	1
Bratton	10	69	6.9	17t	3
Alexander	8	84	10.5	28	0
Kelly	3	13	4.3	6	0
Broncos	256	3352	13.1	69	21
Opponents	268	3201	11.9	75t	13

Interceptions

	No.	Yds.	Avg.	LG	TD
Braxton	6	103	17.2	34t	1
Henderson	3	58	19.3	25	0
Atwater	3	34	11.3	30	0
D. Smith	2	78	39.0	50	0
Robbins	2	18	9.0	18t	1
Munford	2	16	8.0	10	0
Corrington	1	8	8.0	8	0
Carrington	1	2	2.0	2	0
Dennison	1	1	1.0	1	0
Broncos	21	318	15.1	50	2
Opponents	20	194	9.7	32t	1

Punting

	No.	Yds.	Avg.	In 20	LG
Horan	77	3111	40.4	24	63
Elway	1	34	34.0	0	34
Kubiak	2	43	21.5	1	29
Broncos	80	3188	39.8	25	63
Opponents	84	3440	41.0	18	64

Punt Returns

	No.	FC	Yds.	Avg.	LG	TD
Bell	21	3	143	6.8	24	0
Johnson	12	6	118	9.8	34	0
Nattiel	9	0	77	8.6	38	0
Woods	2	0	6	3.0	11	0
Carrington	1	0	0	0.0	0	0
Broncos	45	9	344	7.6	38	0
Opponents	28	18	370	13.2	52	0

Kickoff Returns

	No.	Yds.	Avg.	LG	TD
Bell	30	602	20.1	33	0
Carrington	6	152	25.3	68	0
Humphrey	4	86	21.5	29	0
Bratton	2	19	9.5	10	0
Woods	1	17	17.0	17	0
Broncos	43	876	20.4	68	0
Opponents	72	1256	17.4	36	0

Sacks

	No.
Fletcher	12.0
Holmes	9.0
Mecklenburg	7.5
Carreker	5.5
Powers	3.0
Kragen	2.0
Lucas	2.0
Townsend	2.0
Brooks	1.0
Dennison	1.0
Munford	1.0
Broncos	47.0
Opponents	43.0

1990 Draft Choices

Round	Name	Pos.	College
2.	Alton Montgomery	DB	Houston
4.	Jeroy Robinson	LB	Texas A&M
5.	Jeff Davidson	G	Ohio State
	Le-Lo Lang	DB	Washington
6.	Ronnie Haliburton	TE	Louisiana State
7.	Shannon Sharpe	WR	Savannah State
8.	Brad Leggett	C	Southern California
9.	Todd Ellis	QB	South Carolina
10.	James Szymanski	DE	Michigan State
	Anthony Thompson	LB	East Carolina

Denver Broncos 1990 Veteran Roster

No.	Name	Pos.	Ht.	Wt.	Birth-date	NFL Exp.	College	Hometown	How Acq.	'89 Games/Starts
57	Allert, Ty	LB	6-2	238	7/23/63	5	Texas	Rosenberg, Tex.	PB(Phil)-'90#	7/0*
40	Alexander, Jeff	RB	6-0	232	1/15/65	2	Southern University	Baton Rouge, La.	FA-'89	14/6
27	Atwater, Steve	S	6-3	213	10/28/66	2	Arkansas	Chicago, Ill.	D1-'89	16/16
35	Bell, Ken	RB	5-10	190	11/16/64	5	Boston College	Greenwich, Conn.	FA-'86	15/0
54	Bishop, Keith	C-G	6-3	290	3/10/57	10	Baylor	La Jolla, Calif.	D6-'80	14/7
32	Bratton, Melvin	RB	6-1	225	2/2/65	2	Miami	Miami, Fla.	D7-'89	16/3
34	Braxton, Tyrone	CB	5-11	185	12/17/64	4	North Dakota State	Madison, Wis.	D12-'87	16/16
56	†Brooks, Michael	LB	6-1	235	10/2/64	4	Louisiana State	Rustin, La.	D3-'87	16/16
92	Carreker, Alphonso	DE	6-6	272	5/25/62	5	Florida State	Marietta, Ga.	PB(GB)-'89#	16/16
29	Carrington, Darren	CB	6-1	189	10/10/66	2	Northern Arizona	Bronx, N.Y.	D5-'89	16/0
25	†Corrington, Kip	S	6-0	175	4/12/65	2	Texas A&M	Ames, Iowa	T(Det)-'88	16/0
70	Coyle, Eric	T-G	6-2	274	10/26/63	2	Colorado	Longmont, Colo.	FA-'90	0*
58	Curtis, Scott	LB	6-1	230	12/26/64	3	New Hampshire	Lynnfield, Mass.	FA(Phil)-'89#	16/0
55	Dennison, Rick	LB	6-3	220	6/22/58	8	Colorado State	Kalispel, Mont.	FA-'82	15/11
7	Elway, John	QB	6-3	215	6/28/60	8	Stanford	Port Angeles, Wash.	T(Balt)-'83	15/15
85	Embree, Jon	TE	6-3	235	10/15/65	3	Colorado	Englewood, Colo.	FA-'90	0*
73	Fletcher, Simon	LB	6-5	240	2/18/62	6	Houston	Bay City, Tex.	D2b-'85	16/16
69	Hamilton, Darrell	T	6-5	298	5/11/65	2	North Carolina	Washington, D.C.	D3-'89	0*
20	Hampton, Lorenzo	RB	5-11	208	3/12/62	6	Florida	Lake Wales, Fla.	PB(Mia)-'90#	10/0*
36	Haynes, Mark	CB	5-11	195	11/6/58	11	Colorado	Kansas City, Kan.	T(NYG)-'86	14/0
24	Henderson, Wymon	CB	5-9	186	12/15/61	4	Nevada-Las Vegas	North Miami Beach, Fla.	PB(Minn)-'89#	16/15
68	Henke, Brad	DE	6-3	275	4/10/66	2	Arizona	Littleton, Colo.	FA-'89	2/0
90	†Holmes, Ron	DE	6-4	265	8/26/63	6	Washington	Seattle, Wash.	T(TB)-'89	15/8
2	Horan, Mike	P	5-11	190	2/1/59	7	Long Beach State	Orange, Calif.	FA-'86	16/0
26	Humphrey, Bobby	RB	6-1	201	10/11/66	2	Alabama	Birmingham, Ala.	SD1-'89	16/12
80	Jackson, Mark	WR	5-9	180	7/23/63	4	Purdue	Chicago, Ill.	D6b-'86	16/16
81	Johnson, Jason	WR	5-10	178	11/8/65	3	Illinois State	Gary, Ind.	PB(Pitt)-'90#	14/0*
82	Johnson, Vance	WR	5-11	185	3/13/63	6	Arizona	Trenton, N.J.	D2a-'85	16/16
66	†Juriga, Jim	G-T	6-6	275	9/12/64	4	Illinois	Fort Wayne, Ind.	D4-'86	16/16
72	Kartz, Keith	C	6-4	270	5/5/63	4	California	Las Vegas, Nev.	FA-'87	16/16
88	Kay, Clarence	TE	6-2	237	7/30/61	7	Georgia	Seneca, S.C.	D7-'84	16/16
71	†Kragen, Greg	NT	6-3	265	3/4/62	6	Utah State	Chicago, Ill.	FA-'85	14/14
8	Kubiak, Gary	QB	6-0	192	8/15/61	8	Texas A&M	Houston, Tex.	D8-'83	16/1
76	†Lanier, Ken	T	6-3	290	7/8/59	10	Florida State	Columbus, Ohio	D5-'81	16/16
98	Little, David	TE	6-2	226	4/18/61	7	Middle Tennessee State	Selma, Calif.	PB(Phil)-'90#	15/1*
59	Lucas, Tim	LB	6-3	230	4/3/61	4	California	Stockton, Calif.	FA-'87	16/0
97	Mraz, Mark	DE	6-4	260	2/9/65	3	Utah State	Glendora, Calif.	PB(Raid)-'90#	11/0*
96	McCullough, Jake	DE	6-5	270	7/23/65	2	Clemson	Loris, S.C.	D4-'89	10/0
77	Mecklenburg, Karl	LB	6-3	240	9/1/60	8	Minnesota	Edina, Minn.	D12-'83	15/15
89	Mobley, Orson	TE	6-5	259	3/4/63	5	Salem College	Brooksville, Fla.	D6a-'86	12/5
51	†Munford, Marc	LB	6-2	231	2/14/65	4	Nebraska	Lincoln, Neb.	D4-'87	16/6
84	Nattiel, Ricky	WR	5-9	180	1/25/66	4	Florida	Gainesville, Fla.	D1-'87	8/0
60	Perry, Gerald	T	6-6	305	11/12/64	3	Southern University	Columbia, S.C.	D2-'88	16/15
91	Powers, Warren	DE	6-6	287	2/4/65	2	Maryland	Baltimore, Md.	D2b-'89	15/11
74	Provence, Andrew	NT	6-3	270	3/8/61	6	South Carolina	Savannah, Ga.	T(Atl)-'88	0*
48	Robbins, Randy	S	6-2	189	9/14/62	7	Arizona	Casa Grande, Ariz.	D4-'84	16/2
30	Sewell, Steve	RB	6-3	210	4/2/63	6	Oklahoma	San Francisco, Calif.	D1-'85	16/3
49	Smith, Dennis	S	6-3	200	2/3/59	10	Southern California	Santa Monica, Calif.	D1-'81	14/14
65	Smith, Monte	G	6-4	270	4/24/67	2	North Dakota	Madison, Wis.	D9a-'89	14/0
50	Stephens, Rod	LB	6-1	237	6/14/66	2	Georgia Tech	Atlanta, Ga.	PB(SD)-'90#	10/0*
61	Townsend, Andre	DE-NT	6-3	265	10/8/62	7	Mississippi	Chicago, Ill.	D2-'84	13/10
9	Treadwell, David	K	6-1	175	2/27/67	2	Clemson	Columbia, S.C.	T(Phx)-'89	16/0
86	Verhulst, Chris	TE	6-2	249	5/16/66	3	Chico State	Sacramento, Calif.	PB(Hou)-'90#	16/2*
70	White, Robb	DE	6-4	270	5/26/65	3	South Dakota	Aberdeen, S.D.	PB(NYG)-'90#	1/0*
67	Widell, Doug	G	6-4	287	9/23/66	2	Boston College	Hartford, Conn.	D2a-'89	16/10
23	Winder, Sammy	RB	5-11	203	7/15/59	9	Southern Mississippi	Madison, Miss.	D5-'82	16/2
83	Young, Michael	WR	6-1	183	2/21/62	6	UCLA	Hanford, Calif.	PB(Rams)-'89#	16/0

* Allert played 7 games for Philadelphia in '89; Coyle last active with Washington in '88; Embree last active with Rams in '88; Hamilton active for 3 games but did not play; Hampton played 10 games with Miami; J. Johnson played 14 games with Pittsburgh; Little played 15 games with Philadelphia; Mraz played 11 games with L.A. Raiders; Provence last active with Denver in '88; Stephens played 10 games with San Diego; Verhulst played 16 games with Houston; White played 1 game with N.Y. Giants.

† Option playout; subject to developments.

Plan B unconditional free agent.

Players lost through Plan B (4): TE Pat Kelly (NYJ; 16 games in '89), LB Bruce Klostermann (Raid.; 16), C Mike Ruether (Atl; 3), LB Randy Thornton (NYG; 0).

Also played with Broncos in '89—CB Richard Shelton (3 games), WR Chris Woods (1).

Coaching Staff

Head Coach, Dan Reeves

Pro Career: Became ninth head coach in Broncos history on February 28, 1981, after spending entire pro career as both player and coach with Dallas Cowboys. Reeves's Broncos won the AFC Western Division title and AFC championship in 1986, 1987, and 1989, making Denver the only AFC team to reach three Super Bowls during the decade of the 1980s. Denver posted regular-season records of 11-5 (1986), 10-4-1 (1987), and 11-5 (1989) in those championship seasons. Reeves now has played or coached in eight Super Bowls, the most by any single participant in the NFL Championship Game. Led Denver to an 11-5 record in 1985, barely missing a playoff berth. Guided Broncos to AFC West championship with a 13-3 record in 1984, and a 9-7 mark and playoff berth in 1983. His teams were 10-6 in 1981 and 2-7 in 1982. He joined the Cowboys as a free agent running back in 1965 and became a member of the coaching staff in 1970 when he undertook the dual role of player-coach for two seasons. Was Cowboys offensive backfield coach in 1972 and from 1974-76, and became offensive coordinator in 1977. Was an all-purpose running back during his eight seasons as a player, rushing for 1,990 yards and catching 129 passes for 1,693. Career record: 91-55-1.

Background: Quarterback at South Carolina from 1962-64. He was inducted into the school's Hall of Fame in 1978.

Personal: Born January 19, 1944, Rome, Ga. Dan and his wife, Pam, live in Denver and have three children—Dana, Laura, and Lee.

Assistant Coaches

Marvin Bass, special assistant; born August 28, 1919, Norfolk, Va., lives in Denver. Tackle William & Mary 1940-42. No pro playing experience. College coach: William & Mary 1944-48, 1950-51 (head coach), North Carolina 1949, 1953-55, South Carolina 1956-59, 1961-65, Georgia Tech 1960, Richmond 1973. Pro coach: Washington Redskins 1952, Montreal Beavers (Continental League) 1966-67, Montreal Alouettes (CFL) 1968, Buffalo Bills 1969-71, Birmingham Americans (WFL) 1974-75, joined Broncos in 1982.

Barney Chavous, defensive assistant; born March 22, 1951, Aiken, S.C., lives in Denver. Defensive end South Carolina State 1969-72. Pro defensive end Denver Broncos 1973-85. Pro coach: Joined Broncos in 1989.

Mo Forte, running backs; born March 1, 1947, Hannibal, Mo., lives in Denver. Running back Minnesota 1965-68. No pro playing experience. College coach: Minnesota 1970-75, Duke 1976-77, Michigan State 1978-79, Arizona State 1980-81, North Carolina A&T 1982-87 (head coach). Pro coach: Joined Broncos in 1988.

Chan Gailey, quarterbacks/wide receivers; born January 5, 1952, Americus, Ga., lives in Denver. Quarterback Florida 1971-74. No pro playing experience. College coach: Troy State 1976-77, 1983-84 (head coach), Air Force 1978-82. Pro coach: Joined Broncos in 1985.

George Henshaw, offensive line; born January 22, 1948, Richmond, Va., lives in Denver. Defensive tackle West Virginia 1967-69. No pro playing experience. College coach: West Virginia 1970-75, Florida State 1976-82, Alabama 1983-86, Tulsa 1987 (head coach). Pro coach: Joined Broncos in 1988.

Earl Leggett, defensive line; born May 5, 1933, Jacksonville, Fla., lives in Denver. Tackle Hinds J.C. 1953-54, Louisiana State 1955-56. Pro defensive tackle Chicago Bears 1957-65, Los Angeles Rams 1966, New Orleans Saints 1967-68. College coach: Nicholls State 1971, Texas Christian 1972-73. Pro coach: Southern California Sun (WFL) 1974-75, Seattle Seahawks 1976-77, San Francisco 49ers 1978, Los Angeles Raiders 1980-88, joined Broncos in 1989.

Pete Mangurian, tight ends/assistant offensive line; born June 17, 1955, Los Angeles, Calif., lives in Denver. Defensive lineman Louisiana State 1975-78. No pro playing experience. College coach: Southern Methodist 1979-80, New Mexico State 1981, Stanford 1982-83, Louisiana State 1984-87. Pro coach: Joined Broncos in 1988.

Al Miller, strength and conditioning; born August 29, 1947, El Dorado, Ark., lives in Denver. Wide receiver Northeast Louisiana 1966-69. No pro playing experience. College coach: Northwestern Louisiana 1974-78, Mississippi State 1980, Northeast Louisiana 1981, Alabama 1982-84. Pro coach: Joined Broncos in 1985.

Mike Nolan, linebackers; born March 7, 1959, Baltimore, Md., lives in Denver. Safety Oregon 1977-80. No pro playing experience. College coach: Stanford 1982-83, Rice 1984-85, Louisiana State 1986. Pro coach: Joined Broncos in 1987.

Wade Phillips, defensive coordinator; born June 21, 1947, Orange, Tex., lives in Denver. Linebacker Houston 1966-68. No pro playing experience. College coach: Houston 1969, Oklahoma State 1973-74, Kansas 1975. Pro coach: Houston Oilers 1976-80, New Orleans Saints 1981-85 (head coach last four games of 1985), Philadelphia Eagles 1986-88, joined Broncos in 1989.

Harold Richardson, special teams; born September 27, 1944, Houston, Tex., lives in Denver. Tight end Southern Methodist 1964-67. No pro playing experience. College coach: Southern Methodist 1971-72, Oklahoma State 1973-76, Texas Christian 1977-78, North Texas State 1979-80, Colorado State 1986-88. Pro coach: New Orleans Saints 1981-85, joined Broncos in 1989.

Mike Shanahan, quarterbacks; born August 24, 1952, Oak Park, Ill., lives in Denver. Quarterback Eastern Illinois 1970-73. No pro playing experience. College coach: Oklahoma 1975-76, Northern Arizona 1977, Eastern Illinois 1978, Minnesota 1979, Florida 1980-83. Pro coach: Denver Broncos 1984-87, Los Angeles Raiders 1988-89 (head coach), rejoined Broncos in 1989.

Charlie Waters, defensive backs; born September 10, 1948, Miami, Fla., lives in Denver. Safety Clemson 1967-69. Pro safety Dallas Cowboys 1970-81. Pro coach: Joined Broncos in 1988.

Denver Broncos 1990 First-Year Roster

Name	Pos.	Ht.	Wt.	Birth-date	College	Hometown	How Acq.
Allen, Chris	NT	6-5	274	7/10/68	Mesa, Colo.	Englewood, Colo.	FA
Beavers, Scott	G-T	6-4	277	2/17/67	Georgia Tech	Fairburn, Ga.	FA
Brown, Karl	CB-S	6-2	185	5/26/67	Georgia Tech	London, England	FA
Davidson, Jeff	G	6-5	309	10/3/67	Ohio State	Westerville, Ohio	D5a
Ellis, Todd	QB	6-1	208	5/16/67	South Carolina	Greensboro, N.C.	D9
Erney, Scott	QB	6-1	200	12/12/66	Rutgers	Mechanicsburg, Pa.	FA
Ezor, Blake	RB	5-8	181	10/11/66	Michigan State	Las Vegas, Nev.	FA
Goode, Pierre	WR	6-0	175	1/28/67	Alabama	Town Creek, Ala.	FA
Haliburton, Ronnie	TE	6-4	230	4/14/68	Louisiana State	Port Arthur, Tex.	D6
Hegarty, Pat (1)	QB	6-1	195	4/15/67	Texas-El Paso	Buffalo, N.Y.	FA-'89
Henderson, Joe	RB	5-8	178	11/23/67	Clemson	Freehold, N.J.	FA
Howfield, Ian	K	6-2	196	6/6/66	Tennessee	Littleton, Colo.	FA
Husby, John	T-G	6-3	265	3/16/67	Washington State	Bellevue, Wash.	FA
Jelks, Gene	CB-S	5-10	174	1/21/66	Alabama	Gadsden, Ala.	FA
Jones, Tony	WR	5-11	178	1/4/67	Florida	Tallahassee, Fla.	FA
Lang, Le-Lo	CB-S	5-11	185	1/23/67	Washington	Los Angeles, Calif.	D5b
Leggett, Brad	C	6-4	270	1/16/67	Southern California	Vicksburg, Miss.	D8
McFadden, Wes	RB	5-11	203	1/25/67	Clemson	Chester, S.C.	FA
McPhatter, Brian	CB-S	6-2	204	2/22/68	East Carolina	Hope Mills, N.C.	FA
Montgomery, Alton	CB-S	6-0	195	6/16/68	Houston	Griffin, Ga.	D2
Muilenburg, Darrin	T	6-3	286	3/29/68	Colorado	Lakewood, Colo.	FA
Parkinson, Brent	T	6-5	267	5/26/67	Southern California	Canyon Country, Calif.	FA
Robinson, Jeroy	LB	6-1	241	6/6/68	Texas A&M	Houston, Tex.	D4
Sancho, Ron (1)	LB	6-2	235	6/21/65	Louisiana State	New Orleans, La.	FA-'89
Sharpe, Shannon	WR	6-2	225	6/26/68	Savannah State	Glennville, Ga.	D7
Smith, Greg	T	6-7	275	10/18/67	Vanderbilt	Lansing, Mich.	FA
Szymanski, James	DE	6-5	268	9/7/67	Michigan State	Warren, Mich.	D10a
Thompson, Anthony	LB	6-1	227	6/19/67	East Carolina	Stantonsburg, N.C.	D10b
Turner, Vernon	RB	5-8	185	1/6/67	Carson-Newman	Staten Island, N.Y.	FA

The term NFL Rookie is defined as a player who is in his first season of professional football and has not been on the roster of another professional football team for any regular-season or postseason games. A Rookie is designated by an "R" on NFL rosters. Players who have been active in another professional football league or players who have NFL experience, including either preseason training camp or being on an active roster for fewer than three regular-season or postseason games, are termed NFL First-Year Players. An NFL First-Year Player is designated by a "1" on NFL rosters. Thereafter, a player on an NFL active roster for at least three regular-season or postseason games is credited with an additional year of NFL playing experience.

NOTES

_____

_____

_____

_____

_____

_____

_____

_____

**American Football Conference
Central Division**

Team Colors: Columbia Blue, Scarlet,
and White

6910 Fannin Street
Houston, Texas 77030
Telephone: (713) 797-9111

Club Officials

President: K. S. (Bud) Adams, Jr.
Executive Vice President/General Manager:
  Mike Holovak
Executive Vice President/Administration:
  Mike McClure
Executive Assistant to President:
  Thomas S. Smith
Assistant General Manager: Floyd Reese
Director of College Scouting: Dick Corrick
Director of Business Operations: Lewis Mangum
Director of Accounting Services: Marilan Logan
Director of Media Services: Chip Namias
Director of Broadcasting and Marketing:
  Gregg Stengel
Director of Community Affairs and Publications:
  John Keith
Director of Ticket Administration Services:
  Mike Mullis
Assistant Ticket Manager: Ralph Stolarski
Head Trainer: Brad Brown
Assistant Trainer: Don Moseley
Equipment Manager: Gordon Batty
Video Coordinator: Ken Sparacino

Stadium: Astrodome • **Capacity:** 60,502
  Loop 610, Kirby and Fannin Streets
  Houston, Texas 77054

Playing Surface: AstroTurf-8

Training Camp: Blanco Hall
  Southwest Texas State University
  San Marcos, Texas 78666-4616

1990 Schedule

Preseason

Aug. 9	**Detroit**	7:00
Aug. 18	**New York Giants**	7:00
Aug. 26	at Minnesota	12:00
Sept. 1	at Dallas	8:00

Regular Season

Sept. 9	at Atlanta	4:00
Sept. 16	at Pittsburgh	8:00
Sept. 23	**Indianapolis**	12:00
Sept. 30	at San Diego	1:00
Oct. 7	**San Francisco**	12:00
Oct. 14	at Cincinnati	1:00
Oct. 21	**New Orleans**	12:00
Oct. 28	**New York Jets**	12:00
Nov. 4	at Los Angeles Rams	1:00
Nov. 11	**Open Date**	
Nov. 18	at Cleveland	1:00
Nov. 26	**Buffalo** (Monday)	8:00
Dec. 2	at Seattle	1:00
Dec. 9	**Cleveland**	12:00
Dec. 16	at Kansas City	12:00
Dec. 23	**Cincinnati**	12:00
Dec. 30	**Pittsburgh**	7:00

Oilers Coaching History

(200-247-6)

1960-61	Lou Rymkus*	12-7-1
1961	Wally Lemm	10-0-0
1962-63	Frank (Pop) Ivy	17-12-0
1964	Sammy Baugh	4-10-0
1965	Hugh Taylor	4-10-0
1966-70	Wally Lemm	28-40-4
1971	Ed Hughes	4-9-1
1972-73	Bill Peterson**	1-18-0
1973-74	Sid Gillman	8-15-0
1975-80	O.A. (Bum) Phillips	59-38-0
1981-83	Ed Biles***	8-23-0
1983	Chuck Studley	2-8-0
1984-85	Hugh Campbell****	8-22-0
1985-89	Jerry Glanville	35-35-0

*Released after five games in 1961
**Released after five games in 1973
***Resigned after six games in 1983
****Released after 14 games in 1985

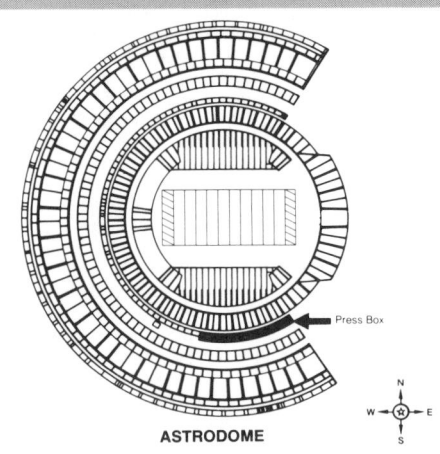

ASTRODOME

Record Holders
Individual Records—Career

Category	Name	Performance
Rushing (Yds.)	Earl Campbell, 1978-1984	8,574
Passing (Yds.)	George Blanda, 1960-66	19,149
Passing (TDs)	George Blanda, 1960-66	165
Receiving (No.)	Charley Hennigan, 1960-66	410
Receiving (Yds.)	Ken Burrough, 1971-1981	6,907
Interceptions	Jim Norton, 1960-68	45
Punting (Avg.)	Jim Norton, 1960-68	42.3
Punt Return (Avg.)	Billy Johnson, 1974-1980	13.2
Kickoff Return (Avg.)	Bobby Jancik, 1962-67	26.4
Field Goals	Tony Zendejas, 1985-89	110
Touchdowns (Tot.)	Earl Campbell, 1978-1984	73
Points	George Blanda, 1960-66	596

Individual Records—Single Season

Category	Name	Performance
Rushing (Yds.)	Earl Campbell, 1980	1,934
Passing (Yds.)	Warren Moon, 1989	3,631
Passing (TDs)	George Blanda, 1961	36
Receiving (No.)	Charley Hennigan, 1964	101
Receiving (Yds.)	Charley Hennigan, 1961	*1,746
Interceptions	Fred Glick, 1963	12
	Mike Reinfeldt, 1979	12
Punting (Avg.)	Jim Norton, 1965	44.2
Punt Return (Avg.)	Billy Johnson, 1977	15.4
Kickoff Return (Avg.)	Ken Hall, 1960	31.2
Field Goals	Tony Zendejas, 1989	25
Touchdowns (Tot.)	Earl Campbell, 1979	19
Points	George Blanda, 1960	115
	Tony Zendejas, 1989	115

Individual Records—Single Game

Category	Name	Performance
Rushing (Yds.)	Billy Cannon, 12-10-61	216
Passing (Yds.)	George Blanda, 10-29-61	464
Passing (TDs)	George Blanda, 11-19-61	*7
Receiving (No.)	Charley Hennigan, 10-13-61	13
Receiving (Yds.)	Charley Hennigan, 10-13-61	272
Interceptions	Many times	3
	Last time by Willie Alexander, 11-14-71	
Field Goals	Skip Butler, 10-12-75	6
Touchdowns (Tot.)	Billy Cannon, 12-10-61	5
Points	Billy Cannon, 12-10-61	30

*NFL Record

1989 Team Record
Preseason (2-2)

Date	Result		Opponents
8/12	L	23-41	at Tampa Bay
8/19	W	26-10	vs. Miami at Jacksonville, Fla.
8/26	W	23-21	vs. L.A. Raiders at Oakland, Calif.
9/2	L	28-30	at Dallas
		100-102	

Regular Season (9-7)

Date	Result		Opponents	Att.
9/10	L	7-38	at Minnesota	54,015
9/17	W	34-27	at San Diego	42,013
9/24	L	41-47	Buffalo (OT)	57,278
10/1	W	39- 7	Miami	53,326
10/8	L	13-23	at New England	59,828
10/15	L	33-28	at Chicago	64,383
10/22	W	27- 0	Pittsburgh	59,091
10/29	L	17-28	at Cleveland	78,765
11/5	W	35-31	Detroit	48,056
11/13	W	26-24	Cincinnati	60,694
11/19	W	23- 7	L.A. Raiders	59,198
11/26	L	0-34	at Kansas City	51,342
12/3	W	23-16	at Pittsburgh	40,541
12/10	W	20-17	Tampa Bay	54,532
12/17	L	7-61	at Cincinnati	47,510
12/23	L	20-24	Cleveland	58,852

(OT) Overtime

Postseason (0-1)

Date	Result		Opponent	Att.
12/31	L	23-26	Pittsburgh (OT)	59,406

Score by Periods

Oilers	50	128	85	102	0	—	365
Opponents	95	106	97	108	6	—	412

Attendance

Home 451,027   Away 438,397   Total 889,424
Single-game home record, 60,694 (11-13-89)
Single-season home record, 451,027 (1989)

1989 Team Statistics

	Oilers	Opp.
Total First Downs	327	314
Rushing	112	119
Passing	185	165
Penalty	30	30
Third Down: Made/Att.	83/203	87/191
Third Down: Pct.	40.9	45.5
Fourth Down: Made/Att.	10/14	10/13
Fourth Down: Pct.	71.4	76.9
Total Net Yards	5427	5211
Avg. Per Game	339.2	325.7
Total Plays	1028	940
Avg. Per Play	5.3	5.5
Net Yards Rushing	1928	1669
Avg. Per Game	120.5	104.3
Total Rushes	495	437
Net Yards Passing	3499	3542
Avg. Per Game	218.7	221.4
Sacked/Yards Lost	37/287	36/277
Gross Yards	3786	3819
Att./Completions	496/295	467/269
Completion Pct.	59.5	57.6
Had Intercepted	16	21
Punts/Avg.	58/41.8	56/37.6
Net Punting Avg.	36.1	34.0
Penalties/Yards Lost	149/1153	109/903
Fumbles/Ball Lost	39/17	25/16
Touchdowns	41	52
Rushing	16	20
Passing	23	28
Returns	2	4
Avg. Time of Possession	31:59	28:01

1989 Individual Statistics

Scoring

	TD R	TD P	TD Rt	PAT	FG	Saf	TP
Zendejas	0	0	0	40/40	25/37	0	115
Hill	0	8	0	0/0	0/0	0	48
Highsmith	4	2	0	0/0	0/0	0	36
Duncan	0	5	0	0/0	0/0	0	30
White	5	0	0	0/0	0/0	0	30
Moon	4	0	0	0/0	0/0	0	24
Givins	0	3	0	0/0	0/0	0	18
Harris	0	2	0	0/0	0/0	0	12
Jeffires	0	2	0	0/0	0/0	0	12
Pinkett	1	1	0	0/0	0/0	0	12
Rozier	2	0	0	0/0	0/0	0	12
Dishman	0	0	1	0/0	0/0	0	6
Seale	0	0	1	0/0	0/0	0	6
McDowell	0	0	0	0/0	0/0	1	2
Oilers	16	23	2	40/41	25/37	2	365
Opponents	20	28	4	49/51	17/21	0	412

Passing

	Att.	Comp.	Yds.	Pct.	TD	Int.	Tkld.	Rate
Moon	464	280	3631	60.3	23	14	35/267	88.9
Carlson	31	15	155	48.4	0	1	2/20	49.8
Zendejas	1	0	0	0.0	0	1	0/0	0.0
Oilers	496	295	3786	59.5	23	16	37/287	85.5
Opponents	467	269	3819	57.6	28	21	36/277	85.4

Rushing

	Att.	Yds.	Avg.	LG	TD
Highsmith	128	531	4.1	25	4
Pinkett	94	449	4.8	60	1
White	104	349	3.4	33	5
Rozier	88	301	3.4	17	2
Moon	70	268	3.8	19	4
Gr. Montgomery	3	17	5.7	11	0
T. Johnson	4	16	4.0	8	0
Duncan	1	0	0.0	0	0
Carlson	3	-3	-1.0	0	0
Oilers	495	1928	3.9	60	16
Opponents	437	1669	3.8	58t	20

Receiving

	No.	Yds.	Avg.	LG	TD
Hill	66	938	14.2	50	8
Givins	55	794	14.4	48	3
Jeffires	47	619	13.2	45t	2
Duncan	43	613	14.3	55	5
Pinkett	31	239	7.7	23	1
Highsmith	18	201	11.2	32	2
Harris	13	202	15.5	36	2
White	6	37	6.2	11	0
Verhulst	4	48	12.0	21	0
Jackson	4	31	7.8	18	0
Rozier	4	28	7.0	8	0
Mrosko	3	28	9.3	14	0
T. Johnson	1	8	8.0	8	0
Oilers	295	3786	12.8	55	23
Opponents	269	3819	14.2	80t	28

Interceptions

	No.	Yds.	Avg.	LG	TD
Brown	5	54	10.8	41	0
Lyles	4	66	16.5	48	0
McDowell	4	65	16.3	21	0
Dishman	4	31	7.8	31	0
Eaton	3	33	11.0	20	0
R. Johnson	1	0	0.0	0	0
Donaldson	0	14	—	14	0
Oilers	21	263	12.5	48	0
Opponents	16	171	10.7	43	0

Punting

	No.	Yds.	Avg.	In 20	LG
Gr. Montgomery	56	2422	43.3	15	63
Oilers	58	2422	41.8	15	63
Opponents	56	2107	37.6	10	55

Punt Returns

	No.	FC	Yds.	Avg.	LG	TD
K. Johnson	19	21	122	6.4	19	0
Oilers	19	21	122	6.4	19	0
Opponents	24	7	191	8.0	28	0

Kickoff Returns

	No.	Yds.	Avg.	LG	TD
K. Johnson	21	372	17.7	39	0
White	17	303	17.8	29	0
Harris	14	331	23.6	63	0
T. Johnson	13	224	17.2	27	0
Mrosko	3	46	15.3	19	0
Williams	2	8	4.0	8	0
Fairs	1	1	1.0	1	0
Lyles	1	0	0.0	0	0
Gl. Montgomery	1	0	0.0	0	0
Verhulst	1	0	0.0	0	0
Oilers	74	1285	17.4	63	0
Opponents	59	1024	17.4	97t	1

Sacks

	No.
Childress	8.5
Fuller	6.5
Jones	6.0
Meads	4.0
Brown	3.0
Fairs	2.5
Lyles	2.0
Gl. Montgomery	1.5
McDowell	1.0
D. Smith	1.0
Oilers	36.0
Opponents	37.0

1990 Draft Choices

Round	Name	Pos.	College
1.	Lamar Lathon	LB	Houston
2.	Jeff Alm	DT	Notre Dame
3.	Willis Peguese	DE	Miami
4.	Eric Still	G	Tennessee
5.	Richard Newbill	LB	Miami
6.	Tony Jones	WR	Texas
7.	Andy Murray	RB	Kentucky
8.	Brett Tucker	DB	Northern Illinois
9.	Pat Coleman	WR	Mississippi
10.	Dee Thomas	DB	Nicholls State
11.	Joey Banes	T	Houston
12.	Reggie Slack	QB	Auburn

Houston Oilers 1990 Veteran Roster

No.	Name	Pos.	Ht.	Wt.	Birth-date	NFL Exp.	College	Hometown	How Acq.	'89 Games/Starts
29	†Allen, Patrick	CB	5-10	182	8/26/61	7	Utah State	Seattle, Wash.	D4b-'84	16/16
31	Arnold, David	S	6-3	210	11/21/66	2	Michigan	Warren, Ohio	PB(Pitt)-'90#	15/0*
33	Bell, Billy	CB	5-10	170	1/16/61	2	Lamar	Dayton, Tex.	FA-'89	4/0
58	Brantley, John	LB	6-2	240	10/23/65	2	Georgia	Wildwood, Fla.	FA-'89	8/0
24	Brown, Steve	CB	5-11	187	3/20/60	8	Oregon	Sacramento, Calif.	D3c-'83	16/16
71	Byrd, Richard	NT	6-4	273	3/20/62	6	Southern Mississippi	Jackson, Miss.	D2b-'85	16/8
67	Camp, Reggie	DE	6-4	270	2/28/61	6	California	Daly City, Calif.	FA-'90	0*
14	†Carlson, Cody	QB	6-3	194	11/5/63	4	Baylor	San Antonio, Tex.	D3-'87	6/0
79	Childress, Ray	NT-DE	6-6	278	10/20/62	6	Texas A&M	Richardson, Tex.	D1a-'85	14/14
77	†Davis, Bruce	T	6-6	315	6/21/56	12	UCLA	Indian Head, Md.	T(Raid)-'87	16/16
28	Dishman, Cris	CB	6-0	178	8/13/65	3	Purdue	Louisville, Ky.	D5a-'88	16/0
80	Duncan, Curtis	WR	5-11	184	1/28/65	4	Northwestern	Detroit, Mich.	D10-'87	16/1
51	†Fairs, Eric	LB	6-3	238	2/17/64	5	Memphis State	Memphis, Tenn.	FA-'86	16/3
88	Ford, Bernard	WR	5-10	171	5/13/66	2	Central Florida	Cordele, Ga.	PB(Dall)-'90#	10/1*
95	Fuller, William	DE	6-3	269	3/8/62	5	North Carolina	Chesapeake, Va.	T(Rams)-'86	15/9
97	Garalczyk, Mark	NT	6-5	272	8/12/64	3	Western Michigan	Fraser, Mich.	PB(NYJ)-'89#	0*
81	Givins, Ernest	WR	5-9	172	9/3/64	5	Louisville	St. Petersburg, Fla.	D2-'86	15/15
59	†Grimsley, John	LB	6-2	238	2/25/62	7	Kentucky	Canton, Ohio	D6a-'84	16/16
83	†Harris, Leonard	WR	5-8	162	11/27/60	5	Texas Tech	McKinney, Tex.	FA-'87	11/0
32	Highsmith, Alonzo	RB	6-1	234	2/28/65	4	Miami	Miami, Fla.	D1a-'87	16/16
85	Hill, Drew	WR	5-9	174	10/5/56	11	Georgia Tech	Newnan, Ga.	T(Rams)-'85	14/12
86	Jackson, Kenny	WR	6-0	183	2/15/62	7	Penn State	South River, N.J.	PB(Phil)-'89#	10/0
84	Jeffires, Haywood	WR	6-2	201	12/12/64	4	North Carolina State	Greensboro, N.C.	D1b-'87	16/4
90	Johnson, Ezra	DE	6-4	255	10/2/55	14	Morris Brown	Shreveport, La.	PB(Ind)-'90#	16/1*
23	Johnson, Richard	CB	6-1	195	9/16/63	6	Wisconsin	Dixmoor, Ill.	D1b-'85	14/0
22	Jones, Quintin	S	5-11	194	7/28/66	2	Pittsburgh	Pompano Beach, Fla.	FA-'90	0*
96	†Jones, Sean	DE	6-7	273	12/19/62	7	Northeastern	Montclair, N.J.	T(Raid)-'88	16/0
27	Kinard, Terry	S	6-1	198	11/24/59	8	Clemson	Sumter, S.C.	PB(NYG)-'90#	16/16*
21	Knight, Leander	CB-S	6-1	196	2/16/63	2	Montclair State	East Orange, N.J.	PB(NYJ)-'90#	13/0*
56	Kozak, Scott	LB	6-3	226	11/28/65	2	Oregon	Colton, Ore.	D2-'89	16/0
93	Lyles, Robert	LB	6-1	230	3/21/61	7	Texas Christian	Los Angeles, Calif.	D5-'84	13/13
78	Maggs, Don	T-G	6-5	285	11/1/61	4	Tulane	Youngstown, Ohio	SD2-'84	16/1
74	Matthews, Bruce	G	6-5	288	8/8/61	8	Southern California	Arcadia, Calif.	D1-'83	16/16
25	McDowell, Bubba	S	6-1	195	11/4/66	2	Miami	Merritt Island, Fla.	D3-'89	16/16
89	McNeil, Gerald	WR-KR	5-8	144	3/27/62	5	Baylor	Killeen, Tex.	PB(Clev)-'90#	16/0*
91	Meads, Johnny	LB	6-2	232	6/25/61	7	Nicholls State	Napoleonville, La.	D3-'84	16/16
94	Montgomery, Glenn	NT	6-0	274	3/31/67	2	Houston	Gretna, La.	D5-'89	15/0
9	Montgomery, Greg	P	6-4	217	10/29/64	3	Michigan State	Red Bank, N.J.	D3-'88	16/0
1	Moon, Warren	QB	6-3	210	11/18/56	7	Washington	Los Angeles, Calif.	FA-'84	16/16
63	Munchak, Mike	G	6-3	284	3/5/60	9	Penn State	Scranton, Pa.	D1-'82	16/16
52	Pennison, Jay	C	6-1	282	9/9/61	5	Nicholls State	Houma, La.	FA-'86	12/12
20	†Pinkett, Allen	RB	5-9	192	1/25/64	5	Notre Dame	Sterling, Va.	D3-'86	16/6
98	Reese, Jerry	NT-DE	6-2	275	7/11/64	2	Kentucky	Hopkinsville, Ky.	FA-'90	0*
66	Robison, Tommy	G-T	6-4	295	11/17/61	3	Texas A&M	Gregory, Tex.	PB(Atl)-'90#	9/3*
30	†Rozier, Mike	RB	5-10	213	3/1/61	6	Nebraska	Camden, N.J.	SD1-'84	12/10
53	Seale, Eugene	LB	5-10	250	6/3/64	4	Lamar	Jasper, Tex.	FA-'87	15/1
54	Smith, Al	LB	6-1	240	11/26/64	4	Utah State	Los Angeles, Calif.	D6a-'87	15/15
99	†Smith, Doug	NT	6-6	286	6/13/59	6	Auburn	Bayboro, N.C.	D2a-'84	15/12
70	Steinkuhler, Dean	T	6-3	287	1/27/61	7	Nebraska	Burr, Neb.	D1-'84	16/16
44	White, Lorenzo	RB	5-11	218	4/12/66	3	Michigan State	Ft. Lauderdale, Fla.	D1-'88	16/0
73	Williams, David	T	6-5	292	6/21/66	2	Florida	Lakeland, Fla.	D1-'89	14/0
69	Williams, Doug	G-T	6-6	295	10/1/62	3	Texas A&M	Cincinnati, Ohio	FA-'90	0*
7	Zendejas, Tony	K	5-8	165	5/15/60	6	Nevada-Reno	Chino, Calif.	T(Wash)-'85	16/0

* Arnold played 15 games with Pittsburgh in '89; Camp last active with Cleveland in '87; Ford played 10 games with Dallas; Garalczyk last active with N.Y. Jets in '88; E. Johnson played 16 games with Indianapolis; Q. Jones last active with Houston in '88; Kinard played 16 games with N.Y. Giants; Knight played 13 games with N.Y. Jets; McNeil played 16 games with Cleveland; Reese last active with Pittsburgh in '88; Robison played 9 games with Atlanta; Do. Williams missed '89 season due to injury.

† Option playout; subject to developments.

Plan B unconditional free agent.

Players lost through Plan B (7): S Jeff Donaldson (KC; 14 games in '89), S Tracy Eaton (Phx; 16), RB Tracy Johnson (Atl; 16), TE Bob Mrosko (NYG; 15), DE Anthony Spears (Dall; 0), TE Chris Verhulst (Den; 16), C George Yarno (GB; 11).

Also played with Oilers in '89—RB Steve Avery (1 game), S Kenny Johnson (16).

COACHING STAFF

Head Coach, Jack Pardee

Pro Career: Named the Oilers' fourteenth head coach on January 9, 1990. Accepted post after serving three years (1987-89) as head coach at University of Houston. While at Houston, Cougars set over 100 NCAA/Southwest Conference records in each of last two years. In 1986, was a scout for the Green Bay Packers. Prior to that, was head coach of successful Houston Gamblers of the USFL from 1984-85 as team led league in total offense and scoring in both seasons. Spent 1982 in private business after serving as defensive coordinator for San Diego Chargers in 1981. That season, Chargers won AFC's Western Division and advanced to AFC Championship Game. From 1978-80, was the head coach of the Washington Redskins, earning NFL Coach of the Year honors in 1979. Was head coach of the Chicago Bears from 1975-77, earning NFC Coach of the Year accolades in 1976 and leading the club in 1977 to its first playoff berth in 14 years. Was general manager/head coach for Florida Blazers of World Football League in 1974, winning division title and advancing to WFL title game. Began coaching career as Redskins' assistant in 1973. Drafted by Los Angeles Rams in second round in 1957 and played 15 seasons at linebacker for Rams (1957-64, 1966-70) and Washington Redskins (1971-72). Was an all-pro selection in 1963 and 1971, and is a member of Rams' all-time fortieth anniversary team. Career record: 44-47.

Background: Played linebacker and fullback in All-America and Academic All-America career for coach Paul "Bear" Bryant at Texas A&M (1953-56). Is a member of the Texas A&M Hall of Fame, National Football Foundation Hall of Fame, College Football Hall of Fame, Texas Sports Hall of Fame, and Senior Bowl Hall of Fame.

Personal: Born April 19, 1936, Exira, Iowa. Jack and his wife, Phyllis, live in Missouri City, Tex., and have two sons, Steven and Ted, and three daughters, Judee, Anne, and Susan.

Assistant Coaches

Jim Eddy, defensive coordinator; born May 2, 1939, Checotah, Okla., lives in Missouri City, Tex. Defensive back/running back New Mexico State (1956-59). No pro playing experience. College coach: New Mexico State 1965-70, Texas-El Paso 1971-72, Houston 1987-89. Pro coach: Saskatchewan Roughriders (CFL) 1974-78 (head coach 1977-78), Hamilton Tiger-Cats (CFL) 1979-80, Montreal Alouettes (CFL) 1981 (head coach), Toronto Argonauts (CFL) 1982-83, Houston Gamblers (USFL) 1984-85, joined Oilers in 1990.

Kevin Gilbride, offensive coordinator; born August 27, 1951, New Haven, Conn., lives in Missouri City, Tex. Quarterback/tight end Southern Connecticut State 1970-73. No pro playing experience. College coach: Idaho State 1974-75, Tufts 1976-77, American International 1978-79, Southern Connecticut State 1980-84 (head coach), East Carolina 1987-88. Pro coach: Ottawa Roughriders (CFL) 1985-86, joined Oilers in 1989.

Frank Novak, running backs; born May 18, 1938, Worcester, Mass., lives in Missouri City, Tex. Quarterback Northern Michigan 1959-61. No pro playing experience. College coach: Northern Michigan 1966-72, East Carolina 1973, Virginia 1974-75, Western Illinois 1976-77, Holy Cross 1978-83, Massachusetts 1986, Missouri 1988. Pro coach: Oklahoma Outlaws (USFL) 1984, Birmingham Stallions (USFL) 1985, joined Oilers in 1989.

Chris Palmer, receivers; born September 23, 1949, Mt. Kisco, N.Y., lives in Missouri City, Tex. Quarterback Southern Connecticut State 1968-71. No pro playing experience. College coach: Connecticut 1972-74, Lehigh 1975, Colgate 1976-82, New Haven 1986-87 (head coach), Boston University 1988-89 (head coach). Pro coach: Montreal Concordes (CFL) 1983, New Jersey Generals (USFL) 1984-85, joined Oilers in 1990.

Richard Smith, special teams-linebackers; born October 17, 1955, Los Angeles, lives in Richmond, Tex. Offensive lineman Rio Hondo (Calif.) J.C. 1975-76, Fresno State 1977-78. No pro playing experience. College coach: Rio Hondo (Calif.) J.C. 1979-80, Cal State-Fullerton 1981-83, California 1984-86, Arizona 1987. Pro coach: Joined Oilers in 1988.

Jim Stanley, defensive line; born June 22, 1934, Dunham, Ky., lives in Houston. Guard/defensive tackle Texas A&M 1954-57. No pro playing experience. College coach: Southern Methodist 1961, Texas-El Paso 1962, Oklahoma State 1963-68, 1972-78 (head coach 1973-78), Navy 1969-70. Pro coach: Winnipeg Blue Bombers (CFL) 1971, New York Giants 1979, Atlanta Falcons 1980-82, Michigan Panthers (USFL) 1983-84 (head coach), Tampa Bay Buccaneers 1986, joined Oilers in 1990.

Pat Thomas, defensive backs; born September 1, 1954, Plano, Tex., lives in Houston. Cornerback Texas A&M 1972-75. Pro cornerback Los Angeles Rams 1976-82. College coach: Houston 1987-89. Pro coach: Houston Gamblers (USFL) 1984-85, joined Oilers in 1990.

Steve Watterson, strength and rehabilitation; born November 27, 1956, Newport, R.I., lives in Sugar Land, Tex. Attended Rhode Island. No college or pro playing experience. Pro coach: Philadelphia Eagles 1984-85 (assistant trainer), joined Oilers in 1986 (elevated to assistant coach in 1988).

Bob Young, offensive line; born September 3, 1942, Marshall, Tex., lives in Houston. Guard Texas 1960-61, Howard Payne 1962-63. Pro guard Denver Broncos 1966-70, Houston Oilers 1971, 1980, St. Louis Cardinals 1972-79, New Orleans Saints 1981. College coach: Houston 1987-89. Pro coach: Houston Gamblers (USFL) 1984-85, joined Oilers in 1990.

Houston Oilers 1990 First-Year Roster

Name	Pos.	Ht.	Wt.	Birth-date	College	Hometown	How Acq.
Alm, Jeff	NT	6-6	273	3/31/68	Notre Dame	Orland Park, Ill.	D2
Banes, Joey	T	6-7	282	4/7/67	Houston	Houston, Tex.	D11
Coleman, Pat	WR	5-7	173	4/8/67	Mississippi	Cleveland, Miss.	D9
Courville, Vince (1)	WR	5-9	170	12/5/59	Rice	Galveston, Tex.	FA
Crawford, Tim (1)	LB	6-4	250	12/17/62	Texas Tech	Houston, Tex.	FA
DiGiacomo, Curt	G	6-4	273	10/24/64	Arizona	Sacramento, Calif.	FA
Gordon, Cedric	WR	6-0	165	11/6/66	Ferris State	Ann Arbor, Mich.	FA
Hartlieb, Chuck (1)	QB	6-1	208	3/12/66	Iowa	Woodstock, Ill.	D12-'89
Jones, Tony	WR	5-7	142	12/30/65	Texas	Grapeland, Tex.	D6
Lathon, Lamar	LB	6-3	250	12/23/67	Houston	Wharton, Tex.	D1
Miotke, Frank (1)	WR	6-0	175	12/22/65	Grand Valley State	Hartland, Mich.	FA
Murray, Andy	RB	6-1	244	4/27/66	Kentucky	Louisville, Ky.	D7
Newbill, Richard	LB	6-1	240	2/8/68	Miami	Clearview, N.J.	D5
Norgard, Erik (1)	C-G	6-1	285	11/4/65	Colorado	Arlington, Wash.	FA
Orlando, Bo (1)	S	5-10	180	4/3/66	West Virginia	Berwick, Pa.	D6-'89
Peguese, Willis	DE	6-4	267	12/18/66	Miami	Miami, Fla.	D3
Perez, Mike	QB	6-2	212	3/7/65	San Jose State	Denver, Colo.	FA
Slack, Reggie	QB	6-1	217	5/2/68	Auburn	Milton, Fla.	D12
Still, Eric	G-T	6-3	279	6/28/67	Tennessee	Germantown, Tenn.	D4
Thomas, Dee	CB-S	5-10	176	11/7/67	Nicholls State	Morgan City, La.	D10
Tucker, Brett	CB-S	5-11	194	9/6/67	Northern Illinois	Sycamore, Ill.	D8

The term NFL Rookie is defined as a player who is in his first season of professional football and has not been on the roster of another professional football team for any regular-season or postseason games. A Rookie is designated by an "R" on NFL rosters. Players who have been active in another professional football league or players who have NFL experience, including either preseason training camp or being on an active roster for fewer than three regular-season or postseason games, are termed NFL First-Year Players. An NFL First-Year Player is designated by a "1" on NFL rosters. Thereafter, a player on an NFL active roster for at least three regular-season or postseason games is credited with an additional year of NFL playing experience.

NOTES

INDIANAPOLIS COLTS

American Football Conference Eastern Division

Team Colors: Royal Blue and White

P. O. Box 535000
Indianapolis, Indiana 46253
Telephone: (317) 297-2658

Club Officials

President-Treasurer: Robert Irsay
Vice President-General Manager: James Irsay
Vice President-General Counsel:
  Michael G. Chernoff
Assistant General Manager: Bob Terpening
Director of Player Personnel: Jack Bushofsky
Controller: Kurt Humphrey
Director of Operations: Pete Ward
Director of Public Relations: Craig Kelley
Ticket Manager: Larry Hall
Assistant Director of Public Relations:
  Rod St. Clair
Purchasing Administrator: David Filar
Equipment Manager: Jon Scott
Assistant Equipment Manager: Chris Matlock
Video Director: Marty Heckscher
Assistant Video Director: John Starliper
Head Trainer: Hunter Smith
Assistant Trainer: Dave Hammer
Team Physician and Orthopedic Surgeon:
  K. Donald Shelbourne
Orthopedic Surgeon: Arthur C. Rettig

Stadium: Hoosier Dome • **Capacity:** 60,127
    100 South Capitol Avenue
    Indianapolis, Indiana 46225

Playing Surface: AstroTurf

Training Camp: Anderson University
    Anderson, Indiana 46011

1990 Schedule

Preseason
Aug. 11	**Denver**	7:30
Aug. 17	at Seattle	7:30
Aug. 27	**Philadelphia**	7:00
Aug. 31	at New Orleans	7:00

Regular Season
Sept. 9	at Buffalo	4:00
Sept. 16	**New England**	12:00
Sept. 23	at Houston	12:00
Sept. 30	at Philadelphia	1:00
Oct. 7	**Kansas City**	12:00
Oct. 14	**Open Date**	
Oct. 21	**Denver**	12:00
Oct. 28	**Miami**	1:00
Nov. 5	**New York Giants** (Monday)	9:00
Nov. 11	at New England	1:00
Nov. 18	**New York Jets**	4:00
Nov. 25	at Cincinnati	1:00
Dec. 2	at Phoenix	2:00
Dec. 9	**Buffalo**	1:00
Dec. 16	at New York Jets	1:00
Dec. 22	**Washington** (Saturday)	8:00
Dec. 30	at Miami	1:00

Colts Coaching History

Baltimore 1953-83
(268-259-7)
1953	Keith Molesworth	3-9-0
1954-62	Weeb Ewbank	61-52-1
1963-69	Don Shula	73-26-4
1970-72	Don McCafferty*	26-11-1
1972	John Sandusky	4-5-0
1973-74	Howard Schnellenberger**	4-13-0
1974	Joe Thomas	2-9-0
1975-79	Ted Marchibroda	41-36-0
1980-81	Mike McCormack	9-23-0
1982-84	Frank Kush***	11-28-1
1984	Hal Hunter	0-1-0
1985-86	Rod Dowhower****	5-24-0
1986-89	Ron Meyer	29-22-0

  *Released after five games in 1972
  **Released after three games in 1974
  ***Resigned after 15 games in 1984
  ****Released after 13 games in 1986

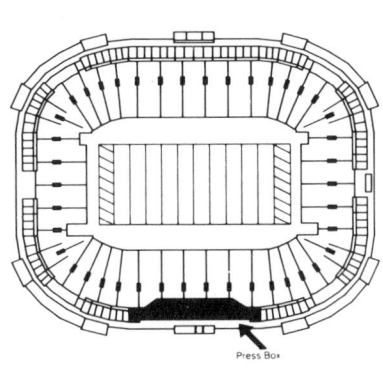

HOOSIER DOME

Record Holders

Individual Records—Career
Category	Name	Performance
Rushing (Yds.)	Lydell Mitchell, 1972-77	5,487
Passing (Yds.)	Johnny Unitas, 1956-1972	39,768
Passing (TDs)	Johnny Unitas, 1956-1972	287
Receiving (No.)	Raymond Berry, 1955-1967	631
Receiving (Yds.)	Raymond Berry, 1955-1967	9,275
Interceptions	Bob Boyd, 1960-68	57
Punting (Avg.)	Rohn Stark, 1982-89	44.1
Punt Return (Avg.)	Wendell Harris, 1964	12.6
Kickoff Return (Avg.)	Jim Duncan, 1969-1971	32.5
Field Goals	Lou Michaels, 1964-69	107
Touchdowns (Tot.)	Lenny Moore, 1956-1967	113
Points	Lenny Moore, 1956-1967	678

Individual Records—Single Season
Category	Name	Performance
Rushing (Yds.)	Eric Dickerson, 1988	1,659
Passing (Yds.)	Johnny Unitas, 1963	3,481
Passing (TDs)	Johnny Unitas, 1959	32
Receiving (No.)	Joe Washington, 1979	82
Receiving (Yds.)	Raymond Berry, 1960	1,298
Interceptions	Tom Keane, 1953	11
Punting (Avg.)	Rohn Stark, 1985	45.9
Punt Return (Avg.)	Clarence Verdin, 1989	12.9
Kickoff Return (Avg.)	Jim Duncan, 1970	35.4
Field Goals	Raul Allegre, 1983	30
Touchdowns (Tot.)	Lenny Moore, 1964	20
Points	Lenny Moore, 1964	120

Individual Records—Single Game
Category	Name	Performance
Rushing (Yds.)	Norm Bulaich, 9-19-71	198
Passing (Yds.)	Johnny Unitas, 9-17-67	401
Passing (TDs)	Gary Cuozzo, 11-14-65	5
	Gary Hogeboom, 10-4-87	5
Receiving (No.)	Lydell Mitchell, 12-15-74	13
	Joe Washington, 9-2-79	13
Receiving (Yds.)	Raymond Berry, 11-10-57	224
Interceptions	Many times	3
	Last time by Leonard Coleman, 10-12-86	
Field Goals	Many times	5
	Last time by Dean Biasucci, 9-25-88	
Touchdowns (Tot.)	Many times	4
	Last time by Eric Dickerson, 10-31-88	
Points	Many times	24
	Last time by Eric Dickerson, 10-31-88	

1989 Team Record
Preseason (4-0)

Date	Result		Opponents
8/12	W	31- 7	at New Orleans
8/19	W	24-23	at Green Bay
8/26	W	30- 0	Tampa Bay
9/2	W	38-34	Denver
		123-64	

Regular Season (8-8)

Date	Result		Opponents	Att.
9/10	L	24-30	San Francisco	60,111
9/17	L	17-31	at L.A. Rams	63,995
9/24	W	13- 9	Atlanta	57,816
10/1	W	17-10	at N.Y. Jets	65,542
10/8	W	37-14	Buffalo	58,890
10/15	L	3-14	at Denver	74,680
10/22	W	23-12	at Cincinnati	57,642
10/29	L	20-23	New Eng. (OT)	59,356
11/5	L	13-19	at Miami	52,680
11/12	L	7-30	at Buffalo	79,256
11/19	W	27-10	N.Y. Jets	58,236
11/26	W	10- 6	San Diego	58,822
12/3	L	16-22	at New England	32,234
12/10	W	23-17	Cleveland (OT)	58,550
12/17	W	42-13	Miami	55,665
12/24	L	6-41	at New Orleans	49,009

(OT) Overtime

Score by Periods

Colts	53	66	53	120	6	—	298
Opponents	67	82	58	91	3	—	301

Attendance
Home 467,446   Away 475,038   Total 942,484
Single-game home record, 61,479 (11-13-83)
Single-season home record, 481,305 (1984)

1989 Team Statistics

	Colts	Opp.
Total First Downs	273	336
Rushing	118	126
Passing	140	192
Penalty	15	18
Third Down: Made/Att.	72/211	95/220
Third Down: Pct.	34.1	43.2
Fourth Down: Made/Att.	7/16	4/10
Fourth Down: Pct.	43.8	40.0
Total Net Yards	4813	5611
Avg. Per Game	300.8	350.7
Total Plays	979	1109
Avg. Per Play	4.9	5.1
Net Yards Rushing	1853	2077
Avg. Per Game	115.8	129.8
Total Rushes	458	507
Net Yards Passing	2960	3534
Avg. Per Game	185.0	220.9
Sacked/Yards Lost	28/174	46/384
Gross Yards	3134	3918
Att./Completions	493/253	556/322
Completion Pct.	51.3	57.9
Had Intercepted	17	21
Punts/Avg.	80/42.4	65/41.6
Net Punting Avg.	32.9	34.5
Penalties/Yards Lost	89/704	103/772
Fumbles/Ball Lost	33/10	34/15
Touchdowns	34	29
Rushing	11	10
Passing	18	15
Returns	5	4
Avg. Time of Possession.	27:15	32:45

1989 Individual Statistics

Scoring

	TD R	TD P	TD Rt	PAT	FG	Saf	TP
Biasucci	0	0	0	31/32	21/27	0	94
Dickerson	7	1	0	0/0	0/0	0	48
Bentley	1	3	1	0/0	0/0	0	30
Brooks	0	4	0	0/0	0/0	0	24
Rison	0	4	0	0/0	0/0	0	24
Beach	0	2	0	0/0	0/0	0	12
Boyer	0	2	0	0/0	0/0	0	12
Trudeau	2	0	0	0/0	0/0	0	12
Verdin	0	1	1	0/0	0/0	0	12
Chandler	1	0	0	0/0	0/0	0	6
R. Dixon	0	0	1	0/0	0/0	0	6
Prior	0	0	1	0/0	0/0	0	6
Pruitt	0	1	0	0/0	0/0	0	6
Taylor	0	0	1	0/0	0/0	0	6
Colts	11	18	5	31/33	21/27	0	298
Opponents	10	15	4	29/29	32/43	1	301

Passing

	Att.	Comp.	Yds.	Pct.	TD	Int.	Tkld.	Rate
Trudeau	362	190	2317	52.5	15	13	20/125	71.3
Chandler	80	39	537	48.8	2	3	3/17	63.4
Ramsey	50	24	280	48.0	1	1	4/26	63.8
Bentley	1	0	0	0.0	0	0	0/0	39.6
Dickerson	0	0	0	—	0	0	1/6	0.0
Colts	493	253	3134	51.3	18	17	28/174	69.1
Opponents	556	322	3918	57.9	15	21	46/384	73.0

Rushing

	Att.	Yds.	Avg.	LG	TD
Dickerson	314	1311	4.2	21t	7
Bentley	75	299	4.0	22	1
Trudeau	35	91	2.6	17	2
Chandler	7	57	8.1	23	1
Hunter	13	47	3.6	11	0
Verdin	4	39	9.8	26	0
Rison	3	18	6.0	18	0
Ramsey	4	5	1.3	3	0
Brooks	2	−3	−1.5	0	0
Stark	1	−11	−11.0	−11	0
Colts	458	1853	4.0	26	11
Opponents	507	2077	4.1	27	10

Receiving

	No.	Yds.	Avg.	LG	TD
Brooks	63	919	14.6	55t	4
Rison	52	820	15.8	61	4
Bentley	52	525	10.1	61	3
Dickerson	30	211	7.0	22	1
Verdin	20	381	19.1	82t	1
Beach	14	87	6.2	17	2
Boyer	11	58	5.3	15	2
Weathers	6	62	10.3	19	0
Pruitt	5	71	14.2	40	1
Colts	253	3134	12.4	82t	18
Opponents	322	3918	12.2	58t	15

Interceptions

	No.	Yds.	Avg.	LG	TD
Taylor	7	225	32.1	80t	1
Prior	6	88	14.7	58t	1
Banks	2	13	6.5	11	0
Young	2	2	1.0	6	0
Daniel	1	34	34.0	34	0
Plummer	1	18	18.0	18	0
Bickett	1	6	6.0	6	0
Ball	1	5	5.0	5	0
Colts	21	391	18.6	80t	2
Opponents	17	345	20.3	92t	2

Punting

	No.	Yds.	Avg.	In 20	LG
Stark	79	3392	42.9	14	64
Colts	80	3392	42.4	14	64
Opponents	65	2702	41.6	19	58

Punt Returns

	No.	FC	Yds.	Avg.	LG	TD
Verdin	23	5	296	12.9	49t	1
Rison	2	2	20	10.0	12	0
C. Washington	1	0	6	6.0	6	0
Prior	0	3	0	—	0	0
Colts	26	10	322	12.4	49t	1
Opponents	51	7	558	10.9	70t	1

Kickoff Returns

	No.	Yds.	Avg.	LG	TD
Verdin	19	371	19.5	29	0
Bentley	17	328	19.3	29	0
Pruitt	12	257	21.4	49	0
Rison	8	150	18.8	30	0
Hunter	4	58	14.5	19	0
Hinnant, Pitt.-Ind.	1	13	13.0	13	0
Colts	60	1164	19.4	49	0
Opponents	63	1208	19.2	48	0

Sacks

	No.
Hand	10.0
E. Johnson	8.5
Bickett	8.0
Thompson	7.0
Herrod	2.0
McDonald	2.0
Young	2.0
Alston	1.0
Armstrong	1.0
Banks	1.0
Benson	1.0
Larson	1.0
Plummer	1.0
Clancy	0.5
Colts	46.0
Opponents	28.0

1990 Draft Choices

Round	Name	Pos.	College
1.	Jeff George	QB	Illinois
2.	Anthony Johnson	RB	Notre Dame
4.	Stacey Simmons	WR	Florida
	Bill Schultz	G	Southern California
	Alan Grant	DB	Stanford
	Pat Cunningham	T	Texas A&M
6.	Tony Walker	LB	Southeast Missouri
7.	James Singletary	LB	East Carolina
8.	Ken Clark	RB	Nebraska
	Harvey Wilson	DB	Southern Univ.
9.	Darvell Huffman	WR	Boston University
11.	Carnel Smith	DE	Pittsburgh
12.	Gene Benhart	QB	Western Illinois
	Dean Brown	G	Notre Dame

Indianapolis Colts 1990 Veteran Roster

No.	Name	Pos.	Ht.	Wt.	Birth-date	NFL Exp.	College	Hometown	How Acq.	'89 Games/Starts
97	†Alston, O'Brien	LB	6-6	241	12/21/65	3	Maryland	New Haven, Conn.	D10-'88	4/4
79	Armstrong, Harvey	NT	6-3	282	12/29/59	7	Southern Methodist	Houston, Tex.	FA-'86	16/16
62	Baldinger, Brian	G	6-4	272	1/7/59	8	Duke	Massapequa Park, N.Y.	FA-'88	16/3
31	Ball, Michael	CB-S	6-0	217	8/5/64	3	Southern University	New Orleans, La.	D4-'88	16/16
51	Banks, Chip	LB	6-4	245	9/18/59	8	Southern California	Augusta, Ga.	T(SD)-'89	10/10
36	†Baylor, John	CB-S	6-0	203	3/5/65	2	Southern Mississippi	Meridian, Miss.	D5-'88	16/8
81	Beach, Pat	TE	6-4	252	12/28/59	8	Washington State	Pullman, Wash.	D6-'82	16/13
95	Benson, Mitchell	NT	6-3	302	5/30/67	2	Texas Christian	Fort Worth, Tex.	D3-'88	16/0
20	Bentley, Albert	RB	5-11	214	8/15/60	6	Miami	Immokalee, Fla.	SD2-'84	16/8
4	†Biasucci, Dean	K	6-0	189	7/25/62	6	Western Carolina	Niagara Falls, N.Y.	FA-'86	16/0
50	Bickett, Duane	LB	6-5	251	12/1/62	6	Southern California	Los Angeles, Calif.	D1-'85	16/16
80	Brooks, Bill	WR	6-0	185	4/6/64	5	Boston University	Milton, Mass.	D4-'86	16/16
71	Call, Kevin	T	6-7	308	11/13/61	7	Colorado State	Boulder, Colo.	D5b-'84	15/15
17	Chandler, Chris	QB	6-4	218	10/12/65	3	Washington	Everett, Wash.	D3-'88	3/3
91	Clancy, Sam	DE	6-7	264	5/29/58	7	Pittsburgh	Pittsburgh, Pa.	PB(Clev)-'89#	16/0
38	Daniel, Eugene	CB	5-11	188	5/4/61	7	Louisiana State	Baton Rouge, La.	D8-'84	15/14
29	Dickerson, Eric	RB	6-3	224	9/2/60	8	Southern Methodist	Sealy, Tex.	T(Rams)-'87	15/14
69	†Dixon, Randy	G	6-3	302	3/12/65	4	Pittsburgh	Clewiston, Fla.	D4-'87	16/16
53	Donaldson, Ray	C	6-3	292	5/17/58	11	Georgia	Rome, Ga.	D2a-'80	16/16
67	Eisenhooth, Stan	T-G	6-5	290	7/8/63	3	Towson State	Wingate, Md.	PB(Sea)-'89#	16/0
37	†Goode, Chris	CB	6-0	195	9/17/63	4	Alabama	Town Creek, Ala.	D10-'87	15/8
78	†Hand, Jon	DE	6-7	301	11/13/63	5	Alabama	Sylacauga, Ala.	D1-'86	16/15
54	†Herrod, Jeff	LB	6-0	246	7/29/66	3	Mississippi	Birmingham, Ala.	D9-'88	15/14
45	Hunter, Ivy Joe	RB	6-0	237	11/16/66	2	Kentucky	Gainesville, Fla.	D7a-'89	16/1
63	Knight, Steve	T	6-4	326	3/13/62	2	Tennessee	Abingdon, Va.	FA-'89	0*
59	Larson, Kurt	LB	6-4	236	2/25/66	2	Michigan State	Waukesha, Wis.	D8-'89	13/0
96	McDonald, Quintus	LB	6-3	240	12/14/66	2	Penn State	Rockingham, N.C.	D6-'89	15/2
73	Moss, Zefross	T	6-6	315	8/17/66	2	Alabama State	Tuscaloosa, Ala.	T(Dall)-'89	16/0
39	Prior, Mike	S	6-0	210	11/14/63	5	Illinois State	Chicago Heights, Ill.	FA-'87	16/16
49	†Pruitt, James	WR	6-3	201	1/29/64	5	Cal State-Fullerton	Los Angeles, Calif.	W(Mia)-'88	16/3
3	Stark, Rohn	P	6-3	203	5/4/59	9	Florida State	Minneapolis, Minn.	D2b-'82	16/0
10	†Strock, Don	QB	6-5	225	11/27/50	17	Virginia Tech	Pottstown, Pa.	FA-'89	0*
27	Taylor, Keith	CB-S	5-11	206	12/21/64	3	Illinois	Pennsauken, N.J.	FA-'88	16/0
99	Thompson, Donnell	DE	6-4	280	10/27/58	10	North Carolina	Lumberton, N.C.	D1b-'81	16/16
10	Trudeau, Jack	QB	6-3	219	9/9/62	5	Illinois	Livermore, Calif.	D2-'86	13/12
83	Verdin, Clarence	WR	5-8	170	6/14/63	5	Southwest Louisiana	New Orleans, La.	T(Wash)-'88	16/7
56	Young, Fredd	LB	6-1	235	11/14/61	7	New Mexico State	Dallas, Tex.	T(Sea)-'88	15/15

* Knight last active with Indianapolis in '88; Strock active for 9 games in '89 but did not play.

† Option playout; subject to developments.

Traded—Tackle Chris Hinton to Atlanta, wide receiver Andre Rison to Atlanta.

#Plan B unconditional free agent.

Players lost through Plan B (8): TE Mark Boyer (NYJ; 16 games in '89), TE John Brandes (Wash; 16), DE Ezra Johnson (Hou; 16), LB Cliff Odom (Mia; 16), CB-S Anthony Parker (NYJ; 1), S Bruce Plummer (SD; 16), G Ben Utt (Atl; 16), CB-S Charles Washington (KC; 16).

Also played with Colts in '89—WR Matt Bouza (2 games), TE Donnie Dee (1), WR Titus Dixon (1), QB Wayne Johnson (active for 4 games but did not play), LB Orlando Lowry (9), LB Dan Murray (2), LB Eric Naposki (1), QB Tom Ramsey (7), LB Ronnie Washington (2), WR Clarence Weathers (4).

COACHING STAFF

Head Coach, Ron Meyer

Pro Career: Named Colts' twelfth head coach on December 1, 1986. Led Colts to AFC Eastern Division championship in 1987 with a 9-6 record. Has won 29 of 51 games with the Colts. Served as head coach of the New England Patriots from 1982-84. Compiled 18-15 regular-season record with one playoff game following the 1982 season. Scout for Dallas Cowboys 1971-72. Career record: 47-38.

Background: Entered coaching ranks at Penn High School in Mishawauka, Indiana, in 1964. Joined staff at Purdue (where he played defensive back 1959-62) in 1965 in charge of the offensive backfield, receivers, and overall passing game. Remained at Purdue through 1970. Named head coach at Nevada-Las Vegas in 1973, directing the Rebels to a three-year 27-8 mark, including an undefeated (11-0) regular season in 1974 before losing in the national semifinals in the NCAA Division II playoffs. Named head coach at Southern Methodist in 1976, where he coached until 1981. The Mustangs had a 34-31-1 record during Meyer's tenure and won the Southwestern Conference championship his final year.

Personal: Born February 17, 1941, in Westerville, Ohio. Ron and his wife, Cindy, live in Indianapolis with their daughters Kathryn and Elizabeth. Ron's sons, Ron, Jr., and Ralph, reside in Dallas.

Assistant Coaches

Leon Burtnett, running backs; born May 30, 1943, Fresno, Calif., lives in Indianapolis. Fullback Southwestern (Kan.) University 1961-65. No pro playing experience. College coach: Montana State 1970, Washington State 1971, Wyoming 1972-73, San Jose State 1974-75, Michigan State 1976, Purdue 1977-86 (head coach 1982-86). Pro coach: Joined Colts in 1987.

George Catavolos, secondary; born May 8, 1945, Chicago, Ill., lives in Indianapolis. Defensive back Purdue 1964-66. No pro playing experience. College coach: Purdue 1967-68, 1971-76, Middle Tennessee State 1969, Louisville 1970, Kentucky 1977-81, Tennessee 1982-83. Pro coach: Joined Colts in 1984.

Milt Jackson, receivers; born October 16, 1943, Groesbeck, Tex., lives in Indianapolis. Defensive back Tulsa 1965-66. Pro defensive back San Francisco 49ers 1967. College coach: Oregon State 1973, Rice 1974, California 1975-76, Oregon 1977-78, UCLA 1979. Pro coach: San Francisco 49ers 1980-82, Buffalo Bills 1983-84, Philadelphia Eagles 1985, Houston Oilers 1986-88, joined Colts in 1989.

Larry Kennan, offensive coordinator; born June 13, 1944, Pomona, Calif., lives in Indianapolis. Quarterback LaVerne College 1962-65. College coach: Colorado 1969-72, Nevada-Las Vegas 1973-75, Southern Methodist 1976-78, Lamar 1979-81. Pro coach: Los Angeles Raiders 1982-87, Denver Broncos 1988, joined Colts in 1989.

Bill Muir, defensive coordinator; born October 26, 1942, Pittsburgh, Pa., lives in Indianapolis. Tackle Susquehanna 1962-64. No pro playing experience. College coach: Susquehanna 1965, Delaware Valley 1966-67, Rhode Island 1970-71, Idaho State 1972-73, Southern Methodist 1976-77. Pro coach: Orlando (Continental Football League) 1968-69, Houston-Shreveport Steamer (WFL) 1975, New England Patriots 1982-84, Detroit Lions 1985-88, joined Colts in 1989.

Dante Scarnecchia, offensive line; born February 15, 1948, Los Angeles, Calif., lives in Indianapolis. Center Taft, Calif., J.C. 1966-67, California Western 1968-69. No pro playing experience. College coach: California Western 1970-72, Iowa State 1973-74, Southern Methodist 1975-76, 1980-81, Pacific 1977-78, Northern Arizona 1979. Pro coach: New England Patriots 1982-88, joined Colts in 1989.

Indianapolis Colts 1990 First-Year Roster

Name	Pos.	Ht.	Wt.	Birth-date	College	Hometown	How Acq.
Ames, Bill	TE	6-5	254	6/24/67	Washington	Spokane, Wash.	FA
Amos, Dale	WR	6-0	178	9/25/66	Franklin & Marshall	Woodbury, N.J.	FA
Barnes, Reggie	RB	5-11	196	2/13/67	N.E. Oklahoma State	Jenks, Okla.	FA
Bell, Jim (1)	RB	6-0	210	6/24/65	Boston College	Claremont, N.H.	FA
Benhart, Gene	QB	6-4	220	1/4/67	Western Illinois	Itasca, Ill.	D12a
Brown, Dean	G-T	6-3	292	9/7/68	Notre Dame	Canton, Ohio	D12b
Clark, Ken	RB	5-9	201	6/11/66	Nebraska	Evergreen, Ala.	D8a
Cunningham, Pat	T	6-6	295	1/4/69	Texas A&M	Los Angeles, Calif.	D4d
Davis, Pat (1)	TE	6-3	284	6/13/66	Syracuse	Trenton, N.J.	FA
Finkelston, Tim	WR	5-10	182	7/25/67	Virginia	Camp Hill, Pa.	FA
Fortune, Chad	TE	6-5	238	12/1/66	Louisville	Valparaiso, Ind.	FA
Freeman, Tim	T	6-4	292	12/16/66	Penn State	Virginia Beach, Va.	FA
George, Jeff	QB	6-4	221	12/8/67	Illinois	Indianapolis, Ind.	D1
Grant, Alan	CB-S	5-10	187	10/1/66	Stanford	Pasadena, Calif.	D4c
Henderson, Joe (1)	RB	6-0	212	4/9/66	Iowa State	Chicago, Ill.	FA
Holloway, Cornell (1)	CB-S	5-11	185	1/30/66	Pittsburgh	Alliance, Ohio	FA
Huffman, Darvell	WR	5-7	158	5/5/67	Boston University	Boston, Mass.	D9
Jackson, Orsorio	CB-S	6-0	194	9/15/68	Tennessee State	Washington, D.C.	FA
Johnson, Anthony	RB	6-0	222	10/25/67	Notre Dame	Indianapolis, Ind.	D2
Johnson, Ricky	RB	6-0	200	3/7/60	Maryland	Liberal, Kan.	FA
Lowery, Doug	DE	6-5	267	4/23/68	DePauw	Plainfield, Ind.	FA
O'Connor, Dwayne	TE	6-3	239	12/17/67	Purdue	Elkhart, Ind.	FA
Rawls, Alfred	RB	5-9	201	12/20/66	Kentucky	Pitts, Ga.	FA
Rider, David	CB-S	6-2	201	9/15/66	New Mexico State	Oakland, Calif.	FA
Riley, Eugene	TE	6-2	227	10/9/66	Ball State	Cincinnati, Ohio	FA
Robinson, Ron	CB-S	6-0	185	5/26/67	Kentucky	Nashville, Tenn.	FA
Schultz, Bill	T	6-5	293	5/1/67	Southern California	Granada Hills, Calif.	D4b
Simmons, Stacey	WR	5-9	183	8/5/68	Florida	Clearwater, Fla.	D4a
Singletary, James	LB	6-2	231	8/17/66	East Carolina	Washington, D.C.	D7
Siragusa, Tony	NT	6-3	296	5/14/67	Pittsburgh	Kenilworth, N.J.	FA
Smith, Carnel	DE	6-2	263	11/13/66	Pittsburgh	Toledo, Ohio	D11
Teeter, Mike	NT-DE	6-2	255	10/14/67	Michigan	Fruitport, Mich.	FA
Tomberlin, Pat	T	6-2	320	1/29/66	Florida State	Jacksonville, Fla.	D4
Vanderbeek, Matt	DE	6-3	241	8/16/67	Michigan State	Holland, Mich.	FA
Vargo, Ron	C	6-1	283	2/9/67	Indiana	Akron, Ohio	FA
Walker, Tony	LB	6-3	235	4/2/68	S.E. Missouri State	Birmingham, Ala.	D6
Williams, Reggie	WR	6-1	190	2/8/66	Pittsburgh	Beaver Falls, Pa.	FA
Wilson, Harvey	CB-S	6-1	191	12/13/68	Southern University	Long Beach, Calif.	D8b
Wright, Bo (1)	RB	5-10	221	9/19/65	Alabama	Mobile, Ala.	FA

The term NFL Rookie is defined as a player who is in his first season of professional football and has not been on the roster of another professional football team for any regular-season or postseason games. A Rookie is designated by an "R" on NFL rosters. Players who have been active in another professional football league or players who have NFL experience, including either preseason training camp or being on an active roster for fewer than three regular-season or postseason games, are termed NFL First-Year Players. An NFL First-Year Player is designated by a "1" on NFL rosters. Thereafter, a player on an NFL active roster for at least three regular-season or postseason games is credited with an additional year of NFL playing experience.

NOTES

_____

_____

_____

_____

_____

_____

_____

_____

_____

_____

_____

Brad Seely, special teams; born September 6, 1956, Vinton, Iowa, lives in Indianapolis. Tackle/guard South Dakota State 1974-77. No pro playing experience. College coach: Colorado State 1980, Southern Methodist 1981, North Carolina State 1982, Pacific 1983, Oklahoma State 1984-88. Pro coach: Joined Colts in 1989.

Rick Venturi, linebackers; born February 23, 1946, Taylorville, Ill., lives in Indianapolis. Quarterback Northwestern 1965-67. No pro playing experience. College coach: Northwestern 1968-72, 1978-80 (head coach), Purdue 1973-76, Illinois 1977. Pro coach: Joined Colts in 1982.

Tom Zupancic, strength and conditioning; born September 14, 1955, Indianapolis, lives in Indianapolis. Defensive tackle-offensive tackle Indiana Central 1975-78. No pro playing experience. Pro coach: Joined Colts in 1984.

American Football Conference Western Division

Team Colors: Red, Gold, and White

One Arrowhead Drive
Kansas City, Missouri 64129
Telephone: (816) 924-9300

Club Officials

Founder: Lamar Hunt
Chairman of the Board: Jack Steadman
President/General Manager and Chief Operating
    Officer: Carl Peterson
Executive Vice President of Administration:
    Tim Connolly
Assistant General Manager: Dennis Thum
Secretary: Jim Seigfreid
Director of Finance/Treasurer:
    Dale Young
Director of Public Relations: Bob Moore
Director of Operations: Bill Dickerson
Director of Sales: Joel Finglass
Director of Development: Ken Blume
Player Personnel Director: Whitey Dovell
Assistant Director of Public Relations:
    Jim Carr
Director of Promotions: Phil Thomas
Community Relations Manager: Brenda Boatright
Ticket Manager: Phil Youtsey
Equipment Manager: Mike Davidson
Assistant Equipment Manager: Albert Veytia
Trainer: Dave Kendall
Assistant Trainer: Bud Epps
Video Coordinator: Mike Dennis
Assistant Video Coordinator: Mike Kirk

Stadium: Arrowhead Stadium • **Capacity:** 78,067
    One Arrowhead Drive
    Kansas City, Missouri 64129

Playing Surface: AstroTurf-8

Training Camp: William Jewell College
    Liberty, Missouri 64068

1990 Schedule

Preseason
Aug. 11	vs. L.A. Rams at Berlin	1:00*
Aug. 18	**New York Jets**	7:00
Aug. 24	at Detroit	7:30
Aug. 31	**Green Bay**	7:00

*P.M. Eastern Time

Regular Season
Sept. 9	**Minnesota**	12:00
Sept. 17	at Denver (Monday)	7:00
Sept. 23	at Green Bay	12:00
Sept. 30	**Cleveland**	3:00
Oct. 7	at Indianapolis	12:00
Oct. 14	**Detroit**	12:00
Oct. 21	at Seattle	1:00
Oct. 28	**Open Date**	
Nov. 4	**Los Angeles Raiders**	12:00
Nov. 11	**Seattle**	12:00
Nov. 18	**San Diego**	12:00
Nov. 25	at Los Angeles Raiders	1:00
Dec. 2	at New England	1:00
Dec. 9	**Denver**	3:00
Dec. 16	**Houston**	12:00
Dec. 23	at San Diego	1:00
Dec. 29	at Chicago (Saturday)	11:30

Chiefs Coaching History

Dallas Texans 1960-62
(218-215-12)
1960-74	Hank Stram	129-79-10
1975-77	Paul Wiggin*	11-24-0
1977	Tom Bettis	1-6-0
1978-82	Marv Levy	31-42-0
1983-86	John Mackovic	30-35-0
1987-88	Frank Gansz	8-22-1
1989	Marty Schottenheimer	8-7-1

*Released after seven games in 1977

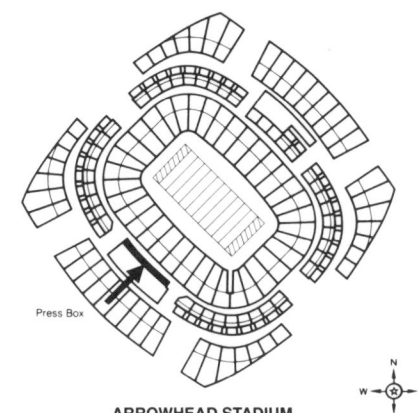

ARROWHEAD STADIUM

Press Box

Record Holders
Individual Records—Career
Category	Name	Performance
Rushing (Yds.)	Ed Podolak, 1969-1977	4,451
Passing (Yds.)	Len Dawson, 1962-1975	28,507
Passing (TDs)	Len Dawson, 1962-1975	237
Receiving (No.)	Henry Marshall, 1976-1987	416
Receiving (Yds.)	Otis Taylor, 1965-1975	7,306
Interceptions	Emmitt Thomas, 1966-1978	58
Punting (Avg.)	Jerrel Wilson, 1963-1977	43.5
Punt Return (Avg.)	J.T. Smith, 1979-1984	10.6
Kickoff Return (Avg.)	Noland Smith, 1967-69	26.8
Field Goals	Jan Stenerud, 1967-1979	279
Touchdowns (Tot.)	Otis Taylor, 1965-1975	60
Points	Jan Stenerud, 1967-1979	1,231

Individual Records—Single Season
Category	Name	Performance
Rushing (Yds.)	Christian Okoye, 1989	1,480
Passing (Yds.)	Bill Kenney, 1983	4,348
Passing (TDs)	Len Dawson, 1964	30
Receiving (No.)	Carlos Carson, 1983	80
Receiving (Yds.)	Carlos Carson, 1983	1,351
Interceptions	Emmitt Thomas, 1974	12
Punting (Avg.)	Jerrel Wilson, 1965	46.0
Punt Return (Avg.)	Abner Haynes, 1960	15.4
Kickoff Return (Avg.)	Dave Grayson, 1962	29.7
Field Goals	Jan Stenerud, 1968	30
	Jan Stenerud, 1970	30
Touchdowns (Tot.)	Abner Haynes, 1962	19
Points	Jan Stenerud, 1968	129

Individual Records—Single Game
Category	Name	Performance
Rushing (Yds.)	Joe Delaney, 11-15-81	193
Passing (Yds.)	Len Dawson, 11-1-64	435
Passing (TDs)	Len Dawson, 11-1-64	6
Receiving (No.)	Ed Podolak, 10-7-73	12
Receiving (Yds.)	Stephone Paige, 12-22-85	309
Interceptions	Bobby Ply, 12-16-62	*4
	Bobby Hunt, 12-4-64	*4
	Deron Cherry, 9-29-85	*4
Field Goals	Many times	5
	Last time by Nick Lowery, 11-13-88	
Touchdowns (Tot.)	Abner Haynes, 11-26-61	5
Points	Abner Haynes, 11-26-61	30

*NFL Record

1989 Team Record
Preseason (1-3)

Date	Result		Opponents
8/12	L	13-23	vs. Minnesota
			at Memphis, Tenn.
8/20	L	3-45	N.Y. Giants
8/27	W	22-17	at Chicago
9/1	L	13-15	N.Y. Jets (OT)
		51-100	

Regular Season (8-7-1)

Date	Result		Opponents	Att.
9/10	L	20-34	at Denver	74,284
9/17	W	24-19	L.A. Raiders	71,741
9/24	L	6-21	at San Diego	40,128
10/1	L	17-21	Cincinnati	61,165
10/8	W	20-16	at Seattle	60,715
10/15	L	14-20	at L.A. Raiders	40,453
10/22	W	36-28	Dallas	76,841
10/29	L	17-23	at Pittsburgh	54,194
11/5	W	20-10	Seattle	54,489
11/12	L	13-16	Denver	76,245
11/19	T	10-10	at Cleveland (OT)	77,922
11/26	W	34- 0	Houston	51,342
12/3	W	26-21	Miami	54,610
12/10	W	21- 3	at Green Bay	56,694
12/17	L	13-20	San Diego	40,623
12/24	W	27-24	at Miami	43,612

(OT) Overtime

Score by Periods

Chiefs	67	137	53	61	0	—	318
Opponents	74	83	47	82	0	—	286

Attendance
Home 487,056   Away 407,874   Total 894,930
Single-game home record, 82,094 (11-5-72)
Single-season home record, 509,291 (1972)

1989 Team Statistics

	Chiefs	Opp.
Total First Downs	304	252
Rushing	120	92
Passing	165	140
Penalty	19	20
Third Down: Made/Att.	88/208	81/211
Third Down: Pct.	42.3	38.4
Fourth Down: Made/Att.	6/9	8/15
Fourth Down: Pct.	66.7	53.3
Total Net Yards	5265	4293
Avg. Per Game	329.1	268.3
Total Plays	1017	952
Avg. Per Play	5.2	4.5
Net Yards Rushing	2227	1766
Avg. Per Game	139.2	110.4
Total Rushes	559	445
Net Yards Passing	3038	2527
Avg. Per Game	189.9	157.9
Sacked/Yards Lost	23/182	36/294
Gross Yards	3220	2821
Att./Completions	435/259	471/236
Completion Pct.	59.5	50.1
Had Intercepted	23	15
Punts/Avg.	67/40.1	82/39.1
Net Punting Avg.	33.8	32.9
Penalties/Yards Lost	116/878	102/797
Fumbles/Ball Lost	32/18	32/18
Touchdowns	35	32
Rushing	18	9
Passing	14	16
Returns	3	7
Avg. Time of Possession	32:35	27:25

1989 Individual Statistics

Scoring

	TD R	TD P	TD Rt	PAT	FG	Saf	TP
Lowery	0	0	0	34/35	24/33	0	106
Okoye	12	0	0	0/0	0/0	0	72
Saxon	3	0	0	0/0	0/0	0	18
Harry	0	2	0	0/0	0/0	0	12
Hayes	0	2	0	0/0	0/0	0	12
Paige	0	2	0	0/0	0/0	0	12
Pelluer	2	0	0	0/0	0/0	0	12
R. Thomas	0	2	0	0/0	0/0	0	12
Carson	0	1	0	0/0	0/0	0	6
Dressel	0	1	0	0/0	0/0	0	6
Gamble	1	0	0	0/0	0/0	0	6
Heard	0	1	0	0/0	0/0	0	6
Maas	0	0	1	0/0	0/0	0	6
Mandley	0	1	0	0/0	0/0	0	6
McNair	0	1	0	0/0	0/0	0	6
Pearson	0	0	1	0/0	0/0	0	6
Roberts	0	1	0	0/0	0/0	0	6
Smith	0	0	1	0/0	0/0	0	6
McGovern	0	0	0	0/0	0/0	1	2
Chiefs	18	14	3	34/35	24/33	1	318
Opponents	9	16	7	31/32	21/26	0	286

Passing

	Att.	Comp.	Yds.	Pct.	TD	Int.	Tkld.	Rate
DeBerg	324	196	2529	60.5	11	16	14/111	75.8
Jaworski	61	36	385	59.0	2	5	1/10	54.3
Pelluer	47	26	301	55.3	1	0	8/61	82.0
Elkins	2	1	5	50.0	0	1	0/0	16.7
Saxon	1	0	0	0.0	0	1	0/0	0.0
Chiefs	435	259	3220	59.5	14	23	23/182	71.2
Opponents	471	236	2821	50.1	16	15	36/294	66.8

Rushing

	Att.	Yds.	Avg.	LG	TD
Okoye	370	1480	4.0	59	12
Saxon	58	233	4.0	19	3
Heard	63	216	3.4	28	0
Pelluer	17	143	8.4	27	2
McNair	23	121	5.3	25	0
Gamble	6	24	4.0	20	1
Harry	1	9	9.0	9	0
Jaworski	4	5	1.3	4	0
Agee	1	3	3.0	3	0
Mandley	2	1	0.5	8	0
DeBerg	14	-8	-0.6	15	0
Chiefs	559	2227	4.0	59	18
Opponents	445	1766	4.0	63t	9

Receiving

	No.	Yds.	Avg.	LG	TD
Paige	44	759	17.3	50	2
Mandley	35	476	13.6	44	1
McNair	34	372	10.9	24	1
Harry	33	430	13.0	25	2
Heard	25	246	9.8	27	1
Weathers, Ind.-K.C.	23	254	11.0	27	0
Weathers, K.C.	17	192	11.3	27	0
Hayes	18	229	12.7	23	2
Saxon	11	86	7.8	18	0
Dressel	9	136	15.1	49t	1
R. Thomas	8	58	7.3	12	2
Roberts	8	55	6.9	25	1
Carson	7	95	13.6	28	1
Worthen	5	69	13.8	21	0
Okoye	2	12	6.0	8	0
Gamble	2	2	1.0	6	0
Carruth	1	3	3.0	3	0
Chiefs	259	3220	12.4	50	14
Opponents	236	2821	12.0	64t	16

Interceptions

	No.	Yds.	Avg.	LG	TD
Lewis	4	37	9.3	22	0
Ross	4	29	7.3	23	0
Cherry	2	27	13.5	27	0
Saleaumua	1	21	21.0	21	0
Snipes	1	16	16.0	16	0
Hill	1	3	3.0	3	0
Ashley	1	0	0.0	0	0
Burruss	1	0	0.0	0	0
Chiefs	15	133	8.9	27	0
Opponents	23	269	11.7	34t	2

Punting

	No.	Yds.	Avg.	In 20	LG
Goodburn	67	2688	40.1	25	54
Chiefs	67	2688	40.1	25	54
Opponents	82	3205	39.1	14	62

Punt Returns

	No.	FC	Yds.	Avg.	LG	TD
Mandley	19	5	151	7.9	19	0
Worthen	19	2	133	7.0	17	0
Barnes	2	0	41	20.5	21	0
Harry	2	0	6	3.0	7	0
Ross	2	0	0	0.0	0	0
Chiefs	44	7	331	7.5	21	0
Opponents	40	10	325	8.1	20	0

Kickoff Returns

	No.	Yds.	Avg.	LG	TD
Copeland	26	466	17.9	36	0
McNair	13	257	19.8	37	0
Worthen	5	113	22.6	27	0
Gamble	3	55	18.3	23	0
Saxon	3	16	5.3	14	0
Saleaumua	1	8	8.0	8	0
Mandley	1	0	0.0	0	0
Chiefs	52	915	17.6	37	0
Opponents	55	1156	21.0	97t	2

Sacks

	No.
D. Thomas	10.0
Smith	7.5
Griffin	6.5
C. Martin	4.0
Saleaumua	2.0
Bell	1.0
Cherry	1.0
Cooper	1.0
Lewis	1.0
Pearson	1.0
Meisner	0.5
Petry	0.5
Chiefs	36.0
Opponents	23.0

1990 Draft Choices

Round	Name	Pos.	College
1.	Percy Snow	LB	Michigan State
2.	Tim Grunhard	C	Notre Dame
4.	Fred Jones	WR	Grambling
5.	Derrick Graham	T	Appalachian State
	Ken Hackemack	T	Texas
6.	Tom Sims	DT	Pittsburgh
7.	Dave Szott	G	Penn State
9.	Michael Owens	RB	Syracuse
10.	Craig Hudson	TE	Wisconsin
11.	Ernest Thompson	RB	Georgia Southern
12.	Tony Jeffery	WR	San Jose State

Kansas City Chiefs 1990 Veteran Roster

No.	Name	Pos.	Ht.	Wt.	Birth-date	NFL Exp.	College	Hometown	How Acq.	'89 Games/ Starts
76	Alt, John	T	6-7	300	5/30/62	7	Iowa	Columbia Heights, Minn.	D1b-'84	16/16
54	Ashley, Walker Lee	LB	6-0	231	7/28/60	7	Penn State	Jersey City, N.J.	PB(Minn)-'89#	16/15
77	Baldinger, Rich	G-T	6-4	292	12/31/59	9	Wake Forest	Long Island, N.Y.	FA-'83	16/8
99	Bell, Mike	DE	6-4	262	8/30/57	10	Colorado State	Wichita, Kan.	D1a-'79	15/6
34	Burruss, Lloyd	S	6-0	205	10/31/57	10	Maryland	Charlottesville, N.C.	D3c-'81	9/1
70	Cannon, Mark	C	6-3	258	6/14/62	7	Texas-Arlington	Austin, Tex.	FA-'89	15/0*
20	Cherry, Deron	S	5-11	202	9/12/59	10	Rutgers	Palmyra, N.J.	FA-'81	15/15
62	Chilton, Gene	C-G	6-3	286	3/27/64	4	Texas	Houston, Tex.	FA-'89	16/0
55	†Cooper, Louis	LB	6-2	238	8/5/63	6	Western Carolina	Marion, S.C.	FA-'85	16/0
25	Copeland, Danny	S-KR	6-2	210	1/24/66	2	Eastern Kentucky	Thomasville, Ga.	FA-'89	16/0
17	DeBerg, Steve	QB	6-3	214	1/9/54	14	San Jose State	Anaheim, Calif.	T(TB)-'88	12/10
42	Donaldson, Jeff	S	6-0	190	4/19/62	7	Colorado	Fort Collins, Colo.	PB(Hou)-'90#	14/14*
75	†Eatman, Irv	T	6-7	298	1/1/61	5	UCLA	Dayton, Ohio	D8-'83	13/13
22	Gamble, Kenny	RB-KR	5-10	204	3/8/65	2	Colgate	Holyoke, Mass.	D10-'88	2/0
2	Goodburn, Kelly	P	6-2	201	4/14/62	4	Emporia State	Cherokee, Iowa	FA-'87	16/0
49	Griffin, James	S	6-2	203	9/7/61	8	Middle Tennessee State	Camilla, Ga.	PB(Det)-'90#	16/1*
98	†Griffin, Leonard	DE	6-4	272	9/22/62	5	Grambling	Lake Providence, La.	D3-'86	16/10
56	†Hackett, Dino	LB	6-3	228	6/28/64	5	Appalachian State	Greensboro, N.C.	D2-'86	13/13
26	Harmon, Kevin	RB	6-0	190	10/26/65	3	Iowa	Queens, N.Y.	PB(Sea)-'90#	4/0*
73	Harris, Michael	C-G	6-4	306	8/30/66	2	Grambling	Shreveport, La.	FA-'89	3/0
86	Harry, Emile	WR	5-11	178	4/5/63	4	Stanford	Los Angeles, Calif.	FA-'86	16/6
85	Hayes, Jonathan	TE	6-5	254	8/11/62	6	Iowa	Pittsburgh, Pa.	D2-'85	16/16
44	†Heard, Herman	RB	5-10	194	11/24/61	7	Southern Colorado	Denver, Colo.	D3-'84	16/10
41	Hill, Willie	S	6-0	200	3/5/63	2	Bishop	Vero Beach, Fla.	FA-'90	0*
7	Jaworski, Ron	QB	6-1	202	3/23/51	16	Youngstown State	Lackawanna, N.Y.	PB(Mia)-'89#	6/3
91	Jones, Rod	TE	6-4	245	3/3/64	4	Washington	Richmond, Calif.	PB(Sea)-'90#	4/0*
3	Karcher, Ken	QB	6-3	205	7/1/63	3	Tulane	Pittsburgh, Pa.	FA-'90	0*
29	Lewis, Albert	CB	6-2	198	10/6/60	8	Grambling	Mansfield, La.	D3-'83	16/16
8	Lowery, Nick	K	6-4	189	5/27/56	11	Dartmouth	Washington, D.C.	FA-'80	16/0
72	†Lutz, David	G-T	6-6	303	12/30/59	8	Georgia Tech	Peachland, N.C.	D2-'83	16/16
63	Maas, Bill	NT-DE	6-5	277	12/19/60	7	Pittsburgh	Newtown Square, Pa.	D1a-'84	10/10
89	†Mandley, Pete	WR	5-10	195	7/29/61	7	Northern Arizona	Mesa, Ariz.	FA-'89	13/12
57	Martin, Chris	LB	6-2	232	12/19/60	8	Auburn	Huntsville, Ala.	FA-'88	16/16
92	McCabe, Jerry	LB	6-2	225	1/25/65	3	Holy Cross	Detroit, Mich.	FA-'90	0*
50	McGovern, Rob	LB	6-2	223	10/1/66	2	Holy Cross	Oradell, N.J.	D10-'89	16/2
48	McNair, Todd	RB-KR	6-1	185	10/7/65	2	Temple	Pennsauken, N.J.	D8b-'89	14/0
69	Meisner, Greg	DE-NT	6-3	271	4/23/59	10	Pittsburgh	New Kensington, Pa.	PB(Rams)-'89#	12/0
68	Morris, Michael	C	6-5	275	2/22/61	3	Northeast Missouri State	Centerville, Iowa	PB(NE)-'90#	11/0*
64	Neville, Tom	G	6-5	300	9/4/61	3	Fresno State	Great Falls, Mont.	FA-'90	0*
9	Nittmo, Bjorn	K	5-11	179	7/26/66	2	Appalachian State	Lomma, Sweden	PB(NYG)-'90#	6/0*
35	Okoye, Christian	RB	6-1	260	8/16/61	4	Azusa Pacific	Enugu, Nigeria	D2-'87	15/14
83	Paige, Stephone	WR	6-2	185	10/15/61	8	Fresno State	Long Beach, Calif.	FA-'83	14/12
24	Pearson, Jayice	CB	5-11	185	8/17/63	5	Washington	Oceanside, Calif.	FA-'86	16/3
11	Pelluer, Steve	QB	6-4	212	7/29/62	7	Washington	Bellevue, Wash.	T(Dall)-'89	5/3
45	Petry, Stan	CB	5-11	175	8/14/66	2	Texas Christian	Manuel, Tex.	D3-'89	16/0
27	Porter, Kevin	S	5-10	219	4/11/66	3	Auburn	Warner Robins, Ga.	D3-'88	16/16
87	Roberts, Alfredo	TE	6-3	246	3/1/65	3	Miami	Hollywood, Fla.	D8-'88	16/2
31	†Ross, Kevin	CB	5-9	182	1/16/62	7	Temple	Paulsboro, N.J.	D7-'84	15/13
97	Saleaumua, Dan	NT	6-0	289	11/11/65	4	Arizona State	San Diego, Calif.	PB(Det)-'89#	16/8
21	†Saxon, James	RB	5-11	215	3/23/66	3	San Jose State	Burton, S.C.	D6-'88	16/2
90	Smith, Neil	DE	6-4	271	4/10/66	3	Nebraska	New Orleans, La.	D1-'88	15/15
52	Snipes, Angelo	LB	6-0	228	1/11/63	4	West Georgia	Atlanta, Ga.	FA-'87	2/0
58	Thomas, Derrick	LB	6-3	234	1/1/67	2	Alabama	Miami, Fla.	D1-'89	16/16
47	Thomas, Johnny	CB-S	5-9	185	8/3/64	3	Baylor	Houston, Tex.	FA-'90	13/0*
81	Thomas, Robb	WR	5-11	171	3/29/66	2	Oregon State	Corvallis, Ore.	D6-'89	8/1
94	Ward, David	LB	6-2	232	3/10/64	3	Southern Arkansas	Helena, Ark.	PB(NE)-'90#	16/0*
19	Ware, Timmie	WR	5-10	175	4/2/63	4	Southern California	Los Angeles, Calif.	PB(Raid)-'90#	13/0*
46	Washington, Charles	CB-S	6-1	208	10/8/66	2	Cameron University	Shreveport, La.	PB(Ind)-'90#	16/0*
53	Webster, Mike	C	6-2	260	3/18/52	17	Wisconsin	Tomahawk, Wis.	PB(Pitt)-'89#	16/16
65	Winters, Frank	C-G	6-3	280	1/23/64	4	Western Illinois	Hampton, Va.	PB(NYG)-'90#	15/0*
84	Worthen, Naz	WR	5-8	177	3/27/66	2	North Carolina State	Jacksonville, Fla.	D3-'89	10/1

* Cannon played 4 games with Green Bay, 11 with Kansas City in '89; Donaldson played 14 games with Houston in '89; Griffin played 16 games with Detroit; Harmon played 4 games with Seattle; Hill last active with Cleveland in '88; Jones played 4 games with Seattle; Karcher last active with Denver in '88; McCabe and Neville missed '89 season due to injury; Morris played 11 games with New England; Nittmo played 6 games with N.Y. Giants; J. Thomas played 13 games with San Diego; Ward played 16 games with New England; Ware played 13 games with L.A. Raiders; Washington played 16 games with Indianapolis; Winters played 15 games with N.Y. Giants.

† Option playout; subject to developments.

Plan B unconditional free agent.

Players lost through Plan B (4): G Mark Adickes (Wash; 16 games in '89), RB Tommie Agee (Dall; 9), LB Stacy Harvey (Mia; 9), WR Clarence Weathers (GB; 11).

Also played with Chiefs in '89—WR-KR Lew Barnes (2 games), RB Paul Ott Carruth (2), WR Carlos Carson (7), DE Bruce Clark (11), TE Chris Dressel (7), S Kenny Hill (8), LB Mike Junkin (5).

COACHING STAFF

Head Coach, Marty Schottenheimer

Pro Career: Begins his second season as Chiefs' head coach after being named seventh head coach in franchise history on January 24, 1989. In 1989, he directed the Chiefs to an 8-7-1 record, only the team's third winning season in the past 16 years. Came to Kansas City after four full seasons with the Cleveland Browns, where he produced four playoff berths, three AFC Central titles, two AFC Championship Game appearances, and consensus AFC coach of the year honors (1986). He has an impressive 48-30-1 regular-season record over the past four years, which stands as the best mark in the AFC over that span. His .603 regular-season winning percentage ranks seventh among active NFL coaches with at least three years experience. He first joined the Browns in 1980 as defensive coordinator after serving as linebackers coach of the Detroit Lions from 1978-79. His first NFL coaching job came with the New York Giants, where he was linebackers coach and defensive coordinator from 1975-77. He served as an assistant coach with the Portland Storm (WFL) in 1974. A seventh-round draft choice of the Buffalo Bills in 1965, he played linebacker with the Bills until 1968 and finished his pro playing career with the Boston Patriots in 1969-70. Career record: 54-38-1.

Background: All-America linebacker at University of Pittsburgh 1962-64. Following retirement from pro football, he worked as a real estate developer in both Miami and Denver from 1971-74.

Personal: Born September 23, 1943, Canonsburg, Pa. Marty and his wife, Patricia, live in Overland Park, Kan., and have one daughter, Kristen, and one son, Brian.

Assistant Coaches

Bruce Arians, running backs; born October 3, 1952, York, Pa., lives in Kansas City. Quarterback Virginia Tech 1971-74. No pro playing experience. College coach: Virginia Tech 1975-77, Mississippi State 1978-80, Alabama 1981-82, Temple 1983-88 (head coach). Pro coach: Joined Chiefs in 1989.

Russ Ball, assistant strength and conditioning; born August 28, 1959, Moberly, Mo., lives in Kansas City. Center Central Missouri State 1977-80. No pro playing experience. College coach: Missouri 1981-88. Pro coach: Joined Chiefs in 1989.

Bill Cowher, defensive coordinator-linebackers; born May 8, 1957, Pittsburgh, Pa., lives in Overland Park, Kan. Linebacker North Carolina State 1975-78. Pro linebacker Cleveland Browns 1980-82, Philadelphia Eagles 1983-84. Pro coach: Cleveland Browns 1985-88, joined Chiefs in 1989.

Tony Dungy, defensive backs; born October 6, 1955, Jackson, Mich., lives in Kansas City. Quarterback Minnesota 1973-76. Pro safety Pittsburgh Steelers 1977-78, San Francisco 49ers 1979. College coach: Minnesota 1980. Pro coach: Pittsburgh Steelers 1981-88, joined Chiefs in 1989.

Jim Erkenbeck, offensive assistant/tight ends; born September 10, 1931, Los Angeles, lives in Mission, Kan. Fullback San Diego State 1949-52. No pro playing experience. College coach: San Diego State 1960-63, Grossmont (Calif.) J.C. 1964-67, Utah State 1968, Washington State 1969-71, California 1972-76. Pro coach: Winnipeg Blue-Bombers (CFL) 1977, Montreal Alouettes (CFL) 1978-81, Calgary Stampeders (CFL) 1982, Philadelphia/Baltimore Stars (USFL) 1983-85, New Orleans Saints 1986, Dallas Cowboys 1987-88, joined Chiefs in 1990.

Howard Mudd, offensive line; born February 10, 1942, Midland, Mich., lives in Kansas City. Guard Hillsdale 1961-63. Pro guard San Francisco 49ers 1964-69, Chicago Bears 1970-71. College coach: California 1972-73. Pro coach: San Diego Chargers 1974-76, San Francisco 49ers 1977, Seattle Seahawks 1978-82, Cleveland Browns 1983-88, joined Chiefs in 1989.

Joe Pendry, offensive coordinator-quarterbacks; born August 5, 1947, Matheny, W. Va., lives in Lakewood, Mo. Tight end West Virginia 1966-67. No pro playing experience. College coach: West Virginia 1967-74, 1976-77, Kansas State 1975, Pittsburgh 1978-79, Michigan State 1980-81. Pro coach: Philadelphia Stars (USFL) 1983, Pittsburgh Maulers (USFL) 1984 (head coach), Cleveland Browns 1985-88, joined Chiefs in 1989.

Tom Pratt, defensive line; born June 21, 1935, Edgerton, Wis., lives in Overland Park, Kan. Linebacker Miami 1953-56. College coach: Miami 1957-59, Southern Mississippi 1960-62. No pro playing experience. Pro coach: Kansas City Chiefs 1963-77, New Orleans Saints 1978-80, Cleveland Browns 1981-88, rejoined Chiefs in 1989.

Dave Redding, strength and conditioning; born June 14, 1952, North Platte, Neb., lives in Kansas City. Defensive end Nebraska 1972-75. No pro playing experience. College coach: Nebraska 1976, Washington State 1977, Missouri 1978-81. Pro coach: Cleveland Browns 1982-88, joined Chiefs in 1989.

Al Saunders, receivers; born February 1, 1947, London, England, lives in Kansas City. Defensive back San Jose State 1966-68. No pro playing experience. College coach: Southern California 1970-71, Missouri 1972, Utah State 1973-75, California 1976-81, Tennessee 1982. Pro coach: San Diego Chargers 1983-88 (head coach 1986-88), joined Chiefs in 1989.

Kurt Schottenheimer, special teams; born October 1, 1949, McDonald, Pa., lives in Kansas City. Defensive back Miami 1969-70. No pro playing experience. College coach: William Patterson 1974, Michigan State 1978-82, Tulane 1983, Louisiana State 1984-85, Notre Dame 1986. Pro coach: Cleveland Browns 1987-88, joined Chiefs in 1989.

Darvin Wallis, special assistant-quality control; born February 14, 1949, Ft. Branch, Ind., lives in Overland Park, Kan. Defensive end Arizona 1970-71. No pro playing experience. College coach: Adams State 1976-77, Tulane 1978-79, Mississippi 1980-81. Pro coach: Cleveland Browns 1982-88, joined Chiefs in 1989.

Kansas City Chiefs 1990 First-Year Roster

Name	Pos.	Ht.	Wt.	Birth-date	College	Hometown	How Acq.
Barker, Bryan (1)	P	6-1	187	6/28/64	Santa Clara	Jacksonville, Fla.	FA
Birden, J.J. (1)	WR	5-9	160	6/16/65	Oregon	Portland, Ore.	FA
Davis, Willie	WR	6-0	159	10/10/67	Central Arkansas	Altheimer, Ark.	FA
Floyd, Norman (1)	CB	6-1	205	2/10/64	South Carolina	Greenville, S.C.	FA
Graham, Derrick	T	6-4	305	3/18/67	Appalachian State	Groveland, Fla.	D5a
Grunhard, Tim	C-G	6-2	292	5/17/68	Notre Dame	Chicago, Ill.	D2
Hackemack, Ken	NT	6-8	298	9/20/67	Texas	Bellville, Tex.	D5b
Huckaby, Howard	WR-KR	5-9	180	8/22/68	Florida A&M	Baton Rouge, La.	FA
Hudson, Craig	LB	6-3	245	5/7/67	Wisconsin	East Aurora, Ill.	FA
Jeffery, Tony	WR	5-10	173	1/11/67	San Jose State	Delano, Calif.	D12
Johnson, Lee	NT	6-0	266	6/9/67	Missouri	Florissant, Mo.	FA
Jones, Bill (1)	RB	5-11	222	9/10/66	Southwest Texas State	Corsicana, Tex.	FA
Jones, Fred	WR	5-11	175	3/6/67	Grambling	Decatur, Ga.	D4
Kiselak, Mike	G	6-3	279	3/9/67	Maryland	North Tarrytown, N.Y.	FA
Lowery, Bren	RB	5-10	197	5/29/67	Maryland	Arlington, Va.	FA
Marts, Lonnie	LB	6-1	225	11/10/68	Tulane	New Orleans, La.	FA
Owens, Michael	RB	5-11	218	4/7/68	Syracuse	Carlisle, Pa.	D9
Rainge, Sherrod	S	6-0	203	7/13/67	Penn State	Brockton, Mass.	FA
Rogers, Tracy (1)	LB	6-2	235	8/13/67	Fresno State	Taft, Calif.	FA
Schonewolf, Rich	NT	6-4	278	12/19/66	Penn State	Philadelphia, Pa.	FA
Shorts, Pete (1)	DE	6-8	278	7/12/66	Illinois State	Vanesville, Wis.	FA
Sims, Tom	NT	6-2	273	4/18/67	Pittsburgh	Detroit, Mich.	D6
Snow, Percy	LB	6-2	244	11/5/67	Michigan State	Canton, Ohio	D1
Szott, David	G	6-4	273	12/12/67	Penn State	Clifton, N.J.	D7
Thomas, Eric	LB	6-0	225	6/19/68	Georgia Tech	Oak Ridge, Tenn.	FA
Thompson, Ernest	RB	6-2	236	3/25/67	Georgia Southern	Louisville, Ga.	D11
Whitaker, Danta (1)	TE	6-4	243	3/14/64	Mississippi Valley State	Atlanta, Ga.	FA
Wolkow, Troy (1)	G	6-4	280	6/25/66	Minnesota	Farmington, Minn.	FA
Woods, Rob (1)	T	6-5	275	10/3/65	Arizona	Hampton, Va.	FA

The term NFL Rookie is defined as a player who is in his first season of professional football and has not been on the roster of another professional football team for any regular-season or postseason games. A Rookie is designated by an "R" on NFL rosters. Players who have been active in another professional football league or players who have NFL experience, including either preseason training camp or being on an active roster for fewer than three regular-season or postseason games, are termed NFL First-Year Players. An NFL First-Year Player is designated by a "1" on NFL rosters. Thereafter, a player on an NFL active roster for at least three regular-season or postseason games is credited with an additional year of NFL playing experience.

NOTES

_____

_____

_____

_____

_____

_____

_____

_____

_____

_____

American Football Conference Western Division

Team Colors: Silver and Black

332 Center Street
El Segundo, California 90245
Telephone: (213) 322-3451

Club Officials

President of the Managing General Partner:
Al Davis
Executive Assistant: Al LoCasale
Player Personnel: Ron Wolf
Pro Football Scout: George Karras
Finance: Gary Huff
Legal Affairs: Jeff Birren, Amy Trask
Senior Executive: John Herrera
Senior Administrator: Morris Bradshaw
Business Manager: Dave Houghton
Administrative Assistant: Mike Madden
Publications: Mike Taylor
Ticket Operations: Peter Eiges
Trainers: George Anderson, H. Rod Martin,
 Todd Sperber
Equipment Manager: Richard Romanski
Assistant Equipment Manager: Bob Romanski

Stadium: Los Angeles Memorial Coliseum •
 Capacity: 92,488
 3911 South Figueroa Street
 Los Angeles, California 90037

Playing Surface: Grass

Training Camp: Radisson Hotel
 Oxnard, California 93030

1990 Schedule

Preseason

Aug. 5	vs. New Orleans at London	1:00*
Aug. 11	at San Francisco	6:00
Aug. 18	**Dallas**	1:00
Aug. 24	at Chicago	7:00
Sept. 1	**San Diego**	1:00

*P.M. Eastern Time

Regular Season

Sept. 9	**Denver**	1:00
Sept. 16	at Seattle	1:00
Sept. 23	**Pittsburgh**	1:00
Sept. 30	**Chicago**	1:00
Oct. 7	at Buffalo	7:30
Oct. 14	**Seattle**	1:00
Oct. 21	at San Diego	1:00
Oct. 28	**Open Date**	
Nov. 4	at Kansas City	12:00
Nov. 11	**Green Bay**	1:00
Nov. 19	at Miami (Monday)	9:00
Nov. 25	**Kansas City**	1:00
Dec. 2	at Denver	2:00
Dec. 10	at Detroit (Monday)	9:00
Dec. 16	**Cincinnati**	1:00
Dec. 22	at Minnesota (Saturday)	3:00
Dec. 30	**San Diego**	1:00

Raiders Coaching History

Oakland 1960-81
(285-171-11)

1960-61	Eddie Erdelatz*	6-10-0
1961-62	Marty Feldman**	2-15-0
1962	Red Conkright	1-8-0
1963-65	Al Davis	23-16-3
1966-68	John Rauch	35-10-1
1969-78	John Madden	112-39-7
1979-87	Tom Flores	91-56-0
1988-89	Mike Shanahan***	8-12-0
1989	Art Shell	7-5-0

*Released after two games in 1961
**Released after five games in 1962
***Released after four games in 1989

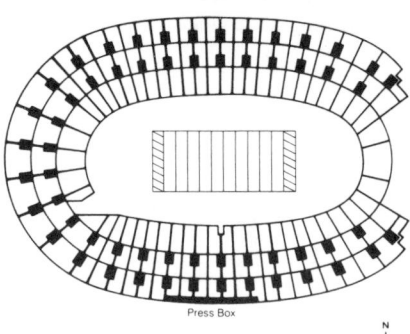

Press Box

MEMORIAL COLISEUM

Record Holders

Individual Records—Career

Category	Name	Performance
Rushing (Yds.)	Marcus Allen, 1982-89	7,275
Passing (Yds.)	Ken Stabler, 1970-79	19,078
Passing (TDs)	Ken Stabler, 1970-79	150
Receiving (No.)	Fred Biletnikoff, 1965-1978	589
Receiving (Yds.)	Fred Biletnikoff, 1965-1978	8,974
Interceptions	Willie Brown, 1967-1978	39
	Lester Hayes, 1977-1986	39
Punting (Avg.)	Ray Guy, 1973-1986	42.5
Punt Return (Avg.)	Claude Gibson, 1963-65	12.6
Kickoff Return (Avg.)	Jack Larscheid, 1960-61	28.4
Field Goals	George Blanda, 1967-1975	156
Touchdowns (Tot.)	Marcus Allen, 1982-89	80
Points	George Blanda, 1967-1975	863

Individual Records—Single Season

Category	Name	Performance
Rushing (Yds.)	Marcus Allen, 1985	1,759
Passing (Yds.)	Ken Stabler, 1979	3,615
Passing (TDs)	Daryle Lamonica, 1969	34
Receiving (No.)	Todd Christensen, 1986	95
Receiving (Yds.)	Art Powell, 1964	1,361
Interceptions	Lester Hayes, 1980	13
Punting (Avg.)	Ray Guy, 1973	45.3
Punt Return (Avg.)	Claude Gibson, 1964	14.4
Kickoff Return (Avg.)	Harold Hart, 1975	30.5
Field Goals	George Blanda, 1973	23
Touchdowns (Tot.)	Marcus Allen, 1984	18
Points	George Blanda, 1968	117

Individual Records—Single Game

Category	Name	Performance
Rushing (Yds.)	Bo Jackson, 11-30-87	221
Passing (Yds.)	Cotton Davidson, 10-25-64	427
Passing (TDs)	Tom Flores, 12-22-63	6
	Daryle Lamonica, 10-19-69	6
Receiving (No.)	Dave Casper, 10-3-76	12
Receiving (Yds.)	Art Powell, 12-22-63	247
Interceptions	Many times	3
	Last time by Charles Phillips, 12-8-75	
Field Goals	Many times	4
	Last time by Jeff Jaeger, 11-12-89	
Touchdowns (Tot.)	Art Powell, 12-22-63	4
	Marcus Allen, 9-24-84	4
Points	Art Powell, 12-22-63	24
	Marcus Allen, 9-24-84	24

1989 Team Record
Preseason (0-4)

Date	Result		Opponents
8/12	L	7-37	San Francisco
8/19	L	20-27	Dallas
8/26	L	21-23	vs. Houston at Oakland, Calif.
9/2	L	38-41	Chicago
		86-128	

Regular Season (8-8)

Date	Result		Opponents	Att.
9/10	W	40-14	San Diego	40,237
9/17	L	19-24	at Kansas City	71,741
9/24	L	21-31	at Denver	75,754
10/1	L	20-24	Seattle	44,319
10/9	W	14- 7	at N.Y. Jets	68,040
10/15	W	20-14	Kansas City	40,453
10/22	L	7-10	at Philadelphia	64,019
10/29	W	37-24	Washington	52,781
11/5	W	28- 7	Cincinnati	51,080
11/12	L	12-14	at San Diego	59,151
11/19	L	7-23	at Houston	59,198
11/26	W	24-21	New England	38,747
12/3	W	16-13	Denver (OT)	87,560
12/10	W	16-14	Phoenix	41,785
12/17	L	17-23	at Seattle	61,076
12/24	L	17-34	at N.Y. Giants	70,306

(OT) Overtime

Score by Periods

Raiders	67	87	91	67	3	—	315
Opponents	77	77	65	78	0	—	297

Attendance
Home 396,962   Away 529,285   Total 926,247
Single-game home record, 90,334 (1-1-84)
Single-season home record, 516,205 (1986)

1989 Team Statistics

	Raiders	Opp.
Total First Downs	259	308
Rushing	93	121
Passing	143	160
Penalty	23	27
Third Down: Made/Att.	67/197	107/225
Third Down: Pct.	34.0	47.6
Fourth Down: Made/Att.	9/13	6/13
Fourth Down: Pct.	69.2	46.2
Total Net Yards	4989	5003
Avg. Per Game	311.8	312.7
Total Plays	912	1045
Avg. Per Play	5.5	4.8
Net Yards Rushing	2038	1940
Avg. Per Game	127.4	121.3
Total Rushes	454	504
Net Yards Passing	2951	3063
Avg. Per Game	184.4	191.4
Sacked/Yards Lost	44/326	35/248
Gross Yards	3277	3311
Att./Completions	414/201	506/277
Completion Pct.	48.6	54.7
Had Intercepted	22	18
Punts/Avg.	67/40.5	72/40.3
Net Punting Avg.	33.9	33.9
Penalties/Yards Lost	132/1105	105/867
Fumbles/Ball Lost	28/12	40/18
Touchdowns	35	36
Rushing	9	15
Passing	21	18
Returns	5	3
Avg. Time of Possession	28:24	31:36

1989 Individual Statistics

Scoring

	TD R	TD P	TD Rt	PAT	FG	Saf	TP
Jaeger	0	0	0	34/34	23/34	0	103
Fernandez	0	9	0	0/0	0/0	0	54
Gault	0	4	0	0/0	0/0	0	24
Jackson	4	0	0	0/0	0/0	0	24
Mueller	2	2	0	0/0	0/0	0	24
Allen	2	0	0	0/0	0/0	0	12
Anderson	0	0	2	0/0	0/0	0	12
Dyal	0	2	0	0/0	0/0	0	12
Junkin	0	2	0	0/0	0/0	0	12
Washington	0	0	2	0/0	0/0	0	12
Alexander	0	1	0	0/0	0/0	0	6
Horton	0	1	0	0/0	0/0	0	6
L. King	0	0	1	0/0	0/0	0	6
Smith	1	0	0	0/0	0/0	0	6
Adams	0	0	0	0/0	0/0	1	2
Raiders	9	21	5	34/35	23/34	1	315
Opponents	15	18	3	36/36	15/21	0	297

Passing

	Att.	Comp.	Yds.	Pct.	TD	Int.	Tkld.	Rate
Beuerlein	217	108	1677	49.8	13	9	22/175	78.4
Schroeder	194	91	1550	46.9	8	13	20/132	60.3
Evans	2	2	50	100.0	0	0	2/19	118.8
Gossett	1	0	0	0.0	0	0	0/0	39.6
Raiders	414	201	3277	48.6	21	22	44/326	70.3
Opponents	506	277	3311	54.7	18	18	35/248	72.0

Rushing

	Att.	Yds.	Avg.	LG	TD
Jackson	173	950	5.5	92t	4
Smith	117	471	4.0	21	1
Allen	69	293	4.2	15	2
Mueller	48	161	3.4	19	2
Porter	13	54	4.2	23	0
Beuerlein	16	39	2.4	10	0
Schroeder	15	38	2.5	19	0
Evans	1	16	16.0	16	0
Fernandez	2	16	8.0	12	0
Raiders	454	2038	4.5	92t	9
Opponents	504	1940	3.8	50t	15

Receiving

	No.	Yds.	Avg.	LG	TD
Fernandez	57	1069	18.8	75t	9
Gault	28	690	24.6	84t	4
Dyal	27	499	18.5	67t	2
Allen	20	191	9.6	26	0
Smith	19	140	7.4	14	0
Mueller	18	240	13.3	29	2
Alexander	15	295	19.7	61	1
Jackson	9	69	7.7	20	0
Horton	4	44	11.0	20	1
Junkin	3	32	10.7	28	2
Brown	1	8	8.0	8	0
Raiders	201	3277	16.3	84t	21
Opponents	277	3311	12.0	51	18

Interceptions

	No.	Yds.	Avg.	LG	TD
Anderson	5	233	46.6	87t	2
Washington	3	46	15.3	32t	1
McDaniel	3	21	7.0	20	0
Benson	2	36	18.0	19	0
Harden	2	1	0.5	1	0
McElroy	2	0	0.0	0	0
Robinson	1	25	25.0	25	0
Raiders	18	362	20.1	87t	3
Opponents	22	298	13.5	41	0

Punting

	No.	Yds.	Avg.	In 20	LG
Gossett	67	2711	40.5	12	60
Raiders	67	2711	40.5	12	60
Opponents	72	2902	40.3	19	74

Punt Returns

	No.	FC	Yds.	Avg.	LG	TD
Adams	19	5	156	8.2	15	0
Edmonds	16	4	168	10.5	20	0
Brown	4	0	43	10.8	29	0
Harden	1	0	11	11.0	11	0
Raiders	40	9	378	9.5	29	0
Opponents	41	9	301	7.3	76t	1

Kickoff Returns

	No.	Yds.	Avg.	LG	TD
Adams	22	425	19.3	37	0
Edmonds	14	271	19.4	43	0
Mueller	5	120	24.0	49	0
Ware	4	86	21.5	29	0
Brown	3	63	21.0	25	0
Smith	2	19	9.5	15	0
Gault	1	16	16.0	16	0
Turk	1	2	2.0	2	0
Junkin	1	0	0.0	0	0
Lee	1	0	0.0	0	0
Raiders	54	1002	18.6	49	0
Opponents	59	1001	17.0	99t	2

Sacks

	No.
Townsend	10.5
Davis	5.5
Long	5.0
Golic	3.5
Wise	3.5
Pickel	3.0
Benson	2.0
McDaniel	1.0
Mraz	0.5
Robinson	0.5
Raiders	35.0
Opponents	44.0

1990 Draft Choices

Round	Name	Pos.	College
1.	Anthony Smith	DE	Arizona
2.	Aaron Wallace	LB	Texas A&M
4.	Torin Dorn	DB	North Carolina
5.	Stan Smagala	DB	Notre Dame
6.	Marcus Wilson	RB	Virginia
7.	Garry Lewis	DB	Alcorn State
8.	Arthur Jimerson	LB	Norfolk State
9.	Leon Perry	RB	Oklahoma
	Ron Lewis	WR	Jackson State
	Myron Jones	RB	Fresno State
12.	Major Harris	QB	West Virginia
	Demetrius Davis	TE	Nevada-Reno

Los Angeles Raiders 1990 Veteran Roster

No.	Name	Pos.	Ht.	Wt.	Birth-date	NFL Exp.	College	Hometown	How Acq.	'89 Games/ Starts
44	†Adams, Stefon	WR	5-10	185	8/11/63	5	East Carolina	High Point, N.C.	D3-'85	14/0
80	†Alexander, Mike	WR	6-3	195	3/19/65	2	Penn State	Piscataway, N.J.	D8-'88	16/0
32	†Allen, Marcus	RB	6-2	205	3/26/60	9	Southern California	San Diego, Calif.	D1-'82	8/5
77	Alzado, Lyle	DE	6-3	265	4/3/49	16	Yankton, S.D.	Brooklyn, N.Y.	FA-'90	0*
33	Anderson, Eddie	S	6-1	200	7/22/63	5	Fort Valley State	Warner Robins, Ga.	FA-'87	15/10
54	Benson, Tom	LB	6-2	240	9/6/61	7	Oklahoma	Ardmore, Tex.	PB(NE)-'89#	16/16
7	†Beuerlein, Steve	QB	6-2	210	3/7/65	3	Notre Dame	Fullerton, Calif.	D4-'87	10/7
24	Brown, Ron	CB	5-11	185	3/31/61	7	Arizona State	Baldwin Park, Calif.	PB(Rams)-'90#	16/0*
81	Brown, Tim	WR	6-0	195	7/22/66	2	Notre Dame	Dallas, Tex.	D1-'88	1/1
59	Burton, Ron	LB	6-1	245	5/2/64	4	North Carolina	Highland Springs, Va.	PB(Phx)-'90#	16/0*
99	Campbell, Joe	DE	6-3	240	12/28/66	3	New Mexico State	Tempe, Ariz.	PB(SD)-'90#	9/0*
29	Carter, Russell	S	6-2	200	2/10/62	7	Southern Methodist	Ardmore, Pa.	T(NYJ)-'88	9/0
23	Crudup, Derrick	RB	6-2	210	2/15/65	2	Oklahoma	Delray Beach, Fla.	FA-'90	4/0
70	Davis, Scott	DE	6-7	275	8/7/65	3	Illinois	Plainfield, Ill.	D1-'88	14/13
84	†Dyal, Mike	TE	6-2	240	5/20/66	2	Texas A&I	Kerrville, Tex.	FA-'88	16/16
50	Ellison, Riki	LB	6-2	225	8/15/60	7	Southern California	Tucson, Ariz.	FA-'90	0*
86	Fernandez, Mervyn	WR	6-3	200	12/29/59	4	San Jose State	San Jose, Calif.	D10-'83	16/13
73	FitzPatrick, James	T	6-7	300	2/1/64	5	Southern California	Beaverton, Ore.	PB(SD)-'90#	13/5*
83	Gault, Willie	WR	6-1	180	9/5/60	8	Tennessee	Griffin, Ga.	T(Chi)-'88	16/16
63	Gesek, John	G	6-5	280	2/18/63	4	Cal State-Sacramento	Danville, Calif.	D10-'87	16/16
79	Golic, Bob	DT	6-2	275	10/26/57	11	Notre Dame	Cleveland, Ohio	PB(Clev)-'89#	16/16
6	Gossett, Jeff	P	6-2	195	1/25/57	9	Eastern Illinois	Charleston, Ill.	T(Hou)-'88	16/0
85	Graddy, Sam	WR	5-10	175	2/10/64	3	Tennessee	Gaffney, S.C.	PB(Den)-'89#	0*
60	Graves, Rory	T	6-6	290	7/21/63	3	Ohio State	Decatur, Ga.	FA-'88	15/15
45	Harden, Mike	S	6-1	195	2/16/59	11	Michigan	Memphis, Tenn.	FA-'89	15/12
22	†Haynes, Mike	CB	6-2	195	7/1/53	15	Arizona State	Los Angeles, Calif.	T(NE)-'83	13/1
61	Hellestrae, Dale	G	6-5	285	7/11/62	4	Southern Methodist	Scottsdale, Ariz.	PB(Buff)-'89#	0*
82	t-Holland, Jamie	WR	6-1	195	2/1/64	4	Ohio State	Wake Forest, N.C.	T(SD)-'90	16/6
88	†Horton, Ethan	TE	6-4	240	12/19/62	4	North Carolina	Kannapolis, N.C.	FA-'89	16/1
98	†Hunley, Ricky	LB	6-2	250	1/11/61	7	Arizona	Petersburg, Va.	FA-'89	12/1
34	Jackson, Bo	RB	6-1	230	11/30/62	4	Auburn	Bessemer, Ala.	D7-'87	11/9
18	Jaeger, Jeff	K	5-11	195	11/26/64	3	Washington	Kent, Wash.	PB(Clev)-'89#	16/0
53	Jordan, Darin	LB	6-1	235	12/4/64	2	Northeastern	Stroughton, Mass.	FA-'90	0*
87	Junkin, Trey	TE	6-2	240	1/23/61	8	Louisiana Tech	Winfield, La.	FA-'85	16/16
92	King, Emanuel	LB	6-4	250	8/15/63	6	Alabama	Leroy, Ala.	PB(Cin)-'89#	16/3
52	†King, Linden	LB	6-4	250	6/28/55	13	Colorado State	Colorado Springs, Colo.	FA-'89	14/13
97	Klostermann, Bruce	LB	6-4	230	4/17/63	4	South Dakota State	Dubuque, Iowa	PB(Den)-'90#	16/0*
25	Land, Dan	CB	6-0	190	7/3/65	2	Albany State	Donalsonville, Ga.	FA-'89	10/0
75	Long, Howie	DE	6-5	270	1/6/60	10	Villanova	Charleston, Mass.	D2-'81	14/10
41	t-McCallum, Napoleon	RB	6-2	215	10/6/63	2	Navy	Milford, Ohio	T(SD)-'90	0*
36	McDaniel, Terry	CB	5-10	175	2/8/65	2	Tennessee	Saginaw, Mich.	D1-'88	16/15
26	†McElroy, Vann	S	6-2	195	1/13/60	9	Baylor	Uvalde, Tex.	D3-'82	7/4
65	Montoya, Max	G	6-5	280	5/12/56	12	UCLA	La Puente, Calif.	PB(Cin)-'90#	16/16*
72	Mosebar, Don	C	6-6	280	9/11/61	8	Southern California	Visalia, Calif.	D1-'83	12/12
42	†Mueller, Vance	RB	6-0	215	5/5/64	5	Occidental	Jackson, Calif.	D4-'86	16/2
43	Patterson, Elvis	CB	5-11	195	10/21/60	7	Kansas	Houston, Tex.	PB(SD)-'90#	16/3*
74	Peat, Todd	T	6-2	310	5/20/64	3	Northern Illinois	Champaign, Ill.	FA-'90	0*
71	Pickel, Bill	DT	6-5	260	11/5/59	8	Rutgers	Brooklyn, N.Y.	D2-'83	16/3
31	†Porter, Kerry	RB	6-1	215	9/23/64	3	Washington State	Vicenza, Italy	FA-'89	16/0
20	†Price, Dennis	CB	6-1	175	6/14/65	3	UCLA	Long Beach, Calif.	D5-'88	5/0
57	Robinson, Jerry	LB	6-2	225	12/18/56	12	UCLA	Santa Rosa, Calif.	T(Phil)-'85	11/11
78	Rother, Tim	T	6-7	275	9/28/65	2	Nebraska	Bellevue, Neb.	D4-'88	16/0
13	†Schroeder, Jay	QB	6-4	215	6/28/61	7	UCLA	Pacific Palisades, Calif.	T(Wash)-'88	11/9
35	†Smith, Steve	RB	6-1	235	8/30/64	4	Penn State	Clinton, Md.	D3-'87	16/16
39	†Strachan, Steve	RB	6-1	225	3/22/63	6	Boston College	Burlington, Mass.	D11-'85	16/0
27	Streeter, George	S	6-1	205	8/28/67	2	Notre Dame	Chicago, Ill.	PB(Chi)-'90#	4/0*
93	†Townsend, Greg	DE	6-3	260	11/3/61	8	Texas Christian	Compton, Calif.	D4-'83	16/12
67	Turk, Dan	C	6-4	270	6/25/62	3	Wisconsin	Milwaukee, Wis.	FA-'89	16/5
48	Washington, Lionel	CB	6-0	185	10/21/60	8	Tulane	New Orleans, La.	T(StL)-'87	16/16
68	Wilkerson, Bruce	T	6-5	285	7/28/64	4	Tennessee	Philadelphia, Tenn.	D2-'87	16/16
90	Wise, Mike	DE	6-7	270	6/5/64	4	California-Davis	Novato, Calif.	D4-'86	16/9
76	Wisniewski, Steve	G	6-4	280	4/7/67	2	Penn State	Houston, Tex.	D2-'89	15/15
66	Wright, Steve	T	6-6	280	4/8/59	8	Northern Illinois	Wayzata, Minn.	FA-'88	16/3

* Alzado last active with Raiders in '85; R. Brown played 16 games with L.A. Rams in '89; Burton played 6 games with Dallas, 10 with Phoenix; Campbell played 9 games with San Diego; Ellison last active with San Francisco in '88; FitzPatrick played 13 games with San Diego; Graddy and Hellestrae missed '89 season due to injury; Jordan last active with Pittsburgh in '88; Klostermann played 16 games with Denver; McCallum last active with Raiders in '86; Montoya played 16 games with Cincinnati; Patterson played 16 games with San Diego; Peat last active with Phoenix in '88; Streeter played 4 games with Chicago.

† Option playout; subject to developments.

Plan B unconditional free agent.

t- Raiders traded for Holland (San Diego), McCallum (San Diego).

Players lost through Plan B (4): RB-KR Bobby Joe Edmonds (Sea; 7 games in '89), C Bill Lewis (Phx; active for 8 games but did not play), DE Mark Mraz (Den; 11), WR Timmy Ware (KC; 13).

Also played with Raiders in '89—LB Joe Costello (2 games), QB Vince Evans (1), DE Pete Koch (4), S Zeph Lee (13), LB Jackie Shipp (3), LB Otis Wilson (1).

COACHING STAFF

Head Coach,
Art Shell

Pro Career: Named ninth head coach in Raiders' history on October 3, 1989. Had been Raiders' offensive line coach for seven years, including 1983 world championship season. He first joined the coaching staff in 1983 after 15 seasons as one of the greatest offensive tackles in pro football history. Came to Raiders in 1968 as third-round draft choice out of Maryland State. Went on to play in 207 league games, including first 156 in a row, and 24 playoff games for the Raiders. Starting left tackle in Super Bowl XI and XV victories. Selected to Pro Bowl eight times—most by any Raiders offensive lineman. Inducted into Pro Football Hall of Fame on August 5, 1989. Also named to state of South Carolina Sports Hall of Fame. Career record: 7-5.

Background: All-America tackle as junior and senior and three-year All-Conference on both offense and defense at Maryland State 1965-1967. Also lettered in basketball.

Personal: Born November 26, 1946, Charleston, S.C. Art and wife, Janice, live in Palos Verdes, California with their sons Arthur III and Christopher.

Assistant Coaches

Dave Adolph, defensive coordinator, linebackers; born June 6, 1937, Akron, Ohio, lives in El Segundo, Calif. Guard-linebacker Akron 1955-58. No pro playing experience. College coach: Akron 1963-64, Connecticut 1965-68, Kentucky 1969-72, Illinois 1973-76, Ohio State 1977-78. Pro coach: Cleveland Browns 1979-84, 1986-88, San Diego Chargers 1985, joined Raiders in 1989.

Fred Biletnikoff, wide receivers; born February 23, 1943, Erie, Pa., lives in El Segundo, Calif. Wide receiver Florida State 1962-64. Pro wide receiver Oakland Raiders 1965-78, Montreal Alouettes (CFL) 1980. College coach: Palomar, Calif., J.C. 1983, Diablo Valley, Calif., J.C. 1984, 1986. Pro coach: Oakland Invaders (USFL) 1985, Arizona Outlaws (USFL) 1986, Calgary Stampeders (CFL) 1987-88, joined Raiders in 1989.

Sam Gruneisen, linebackers; born January 16, 1941, Louisville, Ky., lives in El Segundo, Calif. Tight end-linebacker-kicker Villanova 1959-61. Pro center San Diego Chargers 1962-72, Houston Oilers 1973. College coach: Grossmont, Calif., J.C. 1981, California 1982-83, San Jose State 1986. Pro coach: Los Angeles Express (USFL) 1984-85, joined Raiders in 1987.

Kim Helton, offensive line; born July 28, 1948, Pensacola, Fla., lives in El Segundo, Calif. Center Florida 1967-69. No pro playing experience. College coach: Florida 1972-78, Miami 1979-82. Pro coach: Tampa Bay Buccaneers 1983-86, Houston Oilers 1987-89, joined Raiders in 1990.

Steve Ortmayer, football operations and special teams; born February 13, 1944, Painesville, Ohio, lives in El Segundo, Calif. LaVerne College 1966. No college or pro playing experience. College coach: Colorado 1967-73, Georgia Tech 1974. Pro coach: Kansas City Chiefs 1975-77, Oakland-Los Angeles Raiders 1978-86, San Diego Chargers 1987-89 (Director of Football Operations), rejoined Raiders in 1990.

Terry Robiskie, tight ends; born November 12, 1954, New Orleans, La., lives in Beverly Hills, Calif. Running back Louisiana State 1973-76. Pro running back Oakland Raiders 1977-79, Miami Dolphins 1980-81. Pro coach: Joined Raiders in 1982.

Joe Scannella, offensive backfield; born May 22, 1932, Passaic, N.J., lives in El Segundo, Calif. Quarterback Lehigh 1947-50. Pro safety Saskatchewan Roughriders (CFL) 1951-52. College coach: Cornell 1960, C.W. Post 1963-68 (head coach 1964-68), Vermont 1970-71. Pro coach: Montreal Alouettes (CFL) 1969, 1978-81 (head coach), Oakland Raiders 1972-77, Cleveland Browns 1982-84, rejoined Raiders in 1987.

Los Angeles Raiders 1990 First-Year Roster

Name	Pos.	Ht.	Wt.	Birth-date	College	Hometown	How Acq.
Cormier, Joe (1)	LB	6-6	245	5/3/63	Southern California	Gardena, Calif.	FA
Davis, Demetrius	TE	6-5	225	1/3/67	Nevada-Reno	Vallejo, Calif.	D12
Dorn, Torin	CB	6-0	195	2/29/68	North Carolina	Southfield, Mich.	D4
Francis, Jeff (1)	QB	6-4	220	7/7/66	Tennessee	Mt. Prospect, Ill.	D6-'89
Gilbert, Greg (1)	LB	6-1	220	6/20/67	Alabama	Decatur, Ala.	FA
Harrell, Newt (1)	G	6-5	295	9/17/64	West Texas State	Canyon, Tex.	D10-'88
Harris, Major	QB	6-1	215	2/15/68	West Virginia	Pittsburgh, Pa.	D12
Jimerson, Art	LB	6-3	225	5/12/68	Norfolk State	Chesapeake, Va.	D8
Jones, Myron	RB	5-9	195	2/21/68	Fresno State	Chatsworth, Calif.	D11
Lewis, Garry	CB	5-11	180	8/25/67	Alcorn State	New Orleans, La.	D7
Lewis, Ron	WR	6-1	200	7/31/66	Jackson State	Vicksburg, Miss.	D11
Lloyd, Doug (1)	RB	6-1	220	8/31/65	North Dakota State	Beaver Dam, Wis.	D6-'89
Mitchel, Eric (1)	S	5-11	205	2/13/67	Oklahoma	Pine Bluff, Ark.	FA
Perry, Leon	RB	6-1	230	10/16/66	Oklahoma	Orlando, Fla.	D9
Smith, Anthony	DE	6-3	260	6/28/67	Arizona	Elizabeth City, N.C.	D1
Wallace, Aaron	LB	6-3	240	4/17/67	Texas A&M	Dallas, Tex.	D2
Wilson, Marcus	RB	6-1	205	4/16/68	Virginia	Rochester, N.Y.	D6

The term NFL Rookie is defined as a player who is in his first season of professional football and has not been on the roster of another professional football team for any regular-season or postseason games. A Rookie is designated by an "R" on NFL rosters. Players who have been active in another professional football league or players who have NFL experience, including either preseason training camp or being on an active roster for fewer than three regular-season or postseason games, are termed NFL First-Year Players. An NFL First-Year Player is designated by a "1" on NFL rosters. Thereafter, a player on an NFL active roster for at least three regular-season or postseason games is credited with an additional year of NFL playing experience.

NOTES

Jack Stanton, defensive backs; born June 6, 1938, Bridgeville, Pa., lives in El Segundo, Calif. Running back North Carolina State 1959-60. Pro running back Pittsburgh Steelers 1961, Toronto Argonauts (CFL) 1962-63. College coach: George Washington 1966, North Carolina State 1968-72, Florida State 1973, 1976-83, North Carolina 1974-75, Purdue 1986, New Mexico 1987-88. Pro coach: Atlanta Falcons 1984-85, joined Raiders in 1989.

Bill Urbanik, defensive line; born December 27, 1946, Donora, Pa., lives in El Segundo, Calif. Lineman Ohio State 1965-68. No pro playing experience. College coach: Marshall 1971-73, 1975, Northern Illinois 1976-78, Wake Forest 1979-83. Pro coach: Cincinnati Bengals 1984-88, joined Raiders in 1989.

Tom Walsh, quarterbacks; born April 16, 1949, Vallejo, Calif., lives in Manhattan Beach, Calif. UC-Santa Barbara 1971. No college or pro playing experience. College coach: University of San Diego 1972-76, U.S. International 1979, Murray State 1980, Cincinnati 1981. Pro coach: Joined Raiders in 1982.

Mike White, special projects; born January 4, 1936, Berkeley, Calif., lives in El Segundo, Calif. Offensive end California 1955-57. No pro playing experience. College coach: California 1958-63, 1972-77 (head coach), Stanford 1964-71, Illinois 1980-87 (head coach). Pro coach: San Francisco 49ers 1978-79, joined Raiders in 1990.

MIAMI DOLPHINS

American Football Conference Eastern Division

Team Colors: Aqua, Coral, and White

Joe Robbie Stadium
2269 N.W. 199th Street
Miami, Florida 33056
Telephone: (305) 620-5000

Club Officials

President: Timothy J. Robbie
Executive Vice President: Daniel T. Robbie
Executive Vice President: Janet Robbie
Executive V.P./General Manager:
    Eddie J. Jones
Assistant General Manager: Bryan Wiedmeier
Head Coach: Don Shula
Director of Player Personnel: Charley Winner
Director of Pro Personnel: Monte Clark
Director of College Scouting: Tom Heckert
Director of Media Relations: Harvey Greene
Media Relations Assistants: Scott Stone,
    Fudge Browne
Marketing Director: David Evans
Director of Finance: William T. Duffy
Trainer: Bob Lundy
Equipment Manager: Bob Monica

Stadium: Joe Robbie Stadium •
    Capacity: 73,000
    2269 N.W. 199th Street
    Miami, Florida 33056

Playing Surface: Grass (PAT)

Training Camp: St. Thomas University
    16400-D N.W. 32nd Avenue
    Miami, Florida 33054

1990 Schedule

Preseason
Aug. 11	at Chicago	6:00
Aug. 18	at Philadelphia	7:30
Aug. 25	**Denver**	8:00
Aug. 31	**Minnesota**	8:00

Regular Season
Sept. 9	at New England	4:00
Sept. 16	**Buffalo**	1:00
Sept. 23	at New York Giants	1:00
Sept. 30	at Pittsburgh	1:00
Oct. 7	**New York Jets**	1:00
Oct. 14	**Open Date**	
Oct. 18	**New England** (Thursday)	8:00
Oct. 28	at Indianapolis	1:00
Nov. 4	**Phoenix**	1:00
Nov. 11	at New York Jets	1:00
Nov. 19	**L.A. Raiders** (Monday)	9:00
Nov. 25	at Cleveland	1:00
Dec. 2	at Washington	1:00
Dec. 9	**Philadelphia**	8:00
Dec. 16	**Seattle**	1:00
Dec. 23	at Buffalo	1:00
Dec. 30	**Indianapolis**	1:00

Dolphins Coaching History

(227-145-4)

1966-69	George Wilson	15-39-2
1970-89	Don Shula	212-106-2

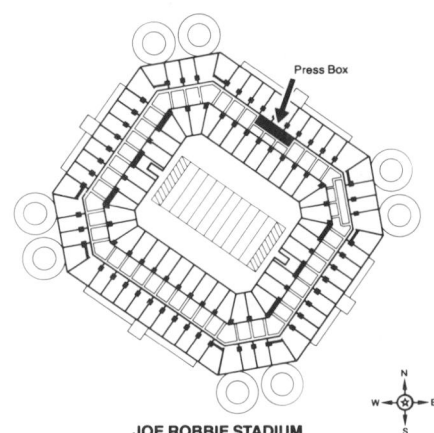

JOE ROBBIE STADIUM

Record Holders
Individual Records—Career

Category	Name	Performance
Rushing (Yds.)	Larry Csonka, 1968-1974, 1979	6,737
Passing (Yds.)	Dan Marino, 1983-89	27,853
Passing (TDs)	Dan Marino, 1983-89	220
Receiving (No.)	Nat Moore, 1974-1986	510
Receiving (Yds.)	Nat Moore, 1974-1986	7,547
Interceptions	Jake Scott, 1970-75	35
Punting (Avg.)	Reggie Roby, 1983-89	43.4
Punt Return (Avg.)	Freddie Solomon, 1975-77	11.4
Kickoff Return (Avg.)	Mercury Morris, 1969-1975	26.5
Field Goals	Garo Yepremian, 1970-78	165
Touchdowns (Tot.)	Nat Moore, 1974-1986	75
Points	Garo Yepremian, 1970-78	830

Individual Records—Single Season

Category	Name	Performance
Rushing (Yds.)	Delvin Williams, 1978	1,258
Passing (Yds.)	Dan Marino, 1984	*5,084
Passing (TDs)	Dan Marino, 1984	*48
Receiving (No.)	Mark Clayton, 1988	86
Receiving (Yds.)	Mark Clayton, 1984	1,389
Interceptions	Dick Westmoreland, 1967	10
Punting (Avg.)	Reggie Roby, 1984	44.7
Punt Return (Avg.)	Freddie Solomon, 1975	12.3
Kickoff Return (Avg.)	Duriel Harris, 1976	32.9
Field Goals	Garo Yepremian, 1971	28
Touchdowns (Tot.)	Mark Clayton, 1984	18
Points	Garo Yepremian, 1971	117

Individual Records—Single Game

Category	Name	Performance
Rushing (Yds.)	Mercury Morris, 9-30-73	197
Passing (Yds.)	Dan Marino, 10-23-88	521
Passing (TDs)	Bob Griese, 11-24-77	6
	Dan Marino, 9-21-86	6
Receiving (No.)	Jim Jensen, 11-6-88	12
Receiving (Yds.)	Mark Duper, 11-10-85	217
Interceptions	Dick Anderson, 12-3-73	*4
Field Goals	Garo Yepremian, 9-26-71	5
Touchdowns (Tot.)	Paul Warfield, 12-15-73	4
Points	Paul Warfield, 12-15-73	24

*NFL Record

1989 Team Record
Preseason (0-4)

Date	Result		Opponents
8/14	L	20-28	Chicago
8/19	L	10-26	vs. Houston at Jacksonville, Fla.
8/25	L	21-35	at Washington
9/1	L	10-20	Philadelphia
		61-109	

Regular Season (8-8)

Date	Result		Opponents	Att.
9/10	L	24-27	Buffalo	54,541
9/17	W	24-10	at New England	57,043
9/24	L	33-40	N.Y. Jets	65,908
10/1	L	7-39	at Houston	53,326
10/8	W	13-10	Cleveland (OT)	58,444
10/15	W	20-13	at Cincinnati	58,184
10/22	W	23-20	Green Bay	56,624
10/29	L	17-31	at Buffalo	80,208
11/5	W	19-13	Indianapolis	52,680
11/12	W	31-23	at N.Y. Jets	65,923
11/19	W	17-14	at Dallas	56,044
11/26	L	14-34	Pittsburgh	59,936
12/3	L	21-26	at Kansas City	54,610
12/10	W	31-10	New England	55,918
12/17	L	13-42	at Indianapolis	55,665
12/24	L	24-27	Kansas City	43,612

(OT) Overtime

Score by Periods

Dolphins	78	96	73	81	3	—	331
Opponents	57	128	77	117	0	—	379

Attendance

Home 447,663   Away 481,003   Total 928,666
Single-game home record, 68,292 (10-23-88)
Single-season home record, 469,277 (1988)

1989 Team Statistics

	Dolphins	Opp.
Total First Downs	310	337
Rushing	88	139
Passing	201	180
Penalty	21	18
Third Down: Made/Att.	101/209	67/194
Third Down: Pct.	48.3	34.5
Fourth Down: Made/Att.	7/14	8/21
Fourth Down: Pct.	50.0	38.1
Total Net Yards	5546	5696
Avg. Per Game	346.6	356.0
Total Plays	1011	1045
Avg. Per Play	5.5	5.5
Net Yards Rushing	1330	2153
Avg. Per Game	83.1	134.6
Total Rushes	400	493
Net Yards Passing	4216	3543
Avg. Per Game	263.5	221.4
Sacked/Yards Lost	10/86	39/268
Gross Yards	4302	3811
Att./Completions	601/331	513/315
Completion Pct.	55.1	61.4
Had Intercepted	25	15
Punts/Avg.	59/41.7	62/39.0
Net Punting Avg.	35.3	31.6
Penalties/Yards Lost	83/614	106/831
Fumbles/Ball Lost	30/16	19/8
Touchdowns	39	43
Rushing	10	19
Passing	26	21
Returns	3	3
Avg. Time of Possession	28:15	31:45

1989 Individual Statistics

Scoring

	TD R	TD P	TD Rt	PAT	FG	Saf	TP
Stoyanovich	0	0	0	38/39	19/26	0	95
Clayton	0	9	0	0/0	0/0	0	54
Jensen	0	6	0	0/0	0/0	0	36
Smith	6	0	0	0/0	0/0	0	36
A. Brown	0	5	0	0/0	0/0	0	30
Edmunds	0	3	0	0/0	0/0	0	18
Logan	0	0	2	0/0	0/0	0	12
Marino	2	0	0	0/0	0/0	0	12
Schwedes	0	1	1	0/0	0/0	0	12
Banks	0	1	0	0/0	0/0	0	6
Davenport	1	0	0	0/0	0/0	0	6
Duper	0	1	0	0/0	0/0	0	6
Stradford	1	0	0	0/0	0/0	0	6
Dolphins	10	26	3	38/39	19/26	1	331
Opponents	19	21	3	42/43	25/33	2	379

Passing

	Att.	Comp.	Yds.	Pct.	TD	Int.	Tkld.	Rate
Marino	550	308	3997	56.0	24	22	10/86	76.9
Secules	50	22	286	44.0	1	3	0/0	44.3
Jensen	1	1	19	100.0	1	0	0/0	158.3
Dolphins	601	331	4302	55.1	26	25	10/86	74.9
Opponents	513	315	3811	61.4	21	15	39/268	85.7

Rushing

	Att.	Yds.	Avg.	LG	TD
Smith	200	659	3.3	25	6
Stradford	66	240	3.6	13	1
Logan	57	201	3.5	14	0
Davenport	14	56	4.0	9	1
Jensen	8	50	6.3	14	0
Hampton	17	47	2.8	9	0
Secules	4	39	9.8	17	0
T. Brown	13	26	2.0	6	0
Faaola	2	10	5.0	5	0
Clayton	3	9	3.0	11	0
Roby	2	0	0.0	0	0
Reaves, Wash.-Mia.	1	−1	−1.0	−1	0
Marino	14	−7	−0.5	2	2
Dolphins	400	1330	3.3	25	10
Opponents	493	2153	4.4	33	19

Receiving

	No.	Yds.	Avg.	LG	TD
Clayton	64	1011	15.8	78t	9
Jensen	61	557	9.1	20	6
Duper	49	717	14.6	41	1
Edmunds	32	382	11.9	30	3
Banks	30	520	17.3	61	1
Stradford	25	233	9.3	32	0
A. Brown	24	410	17.1	48t	5
T. Brown	13	117	9.0	23	0
Hampton	8	25	3.1	12	0
Schwedes	7	174	24.9	65t	1
Smith	7	81	11.6	34	0
Logan	5	34	6.8	11	0
Davenport	3	19	6.3	9	0
Kinchen	1	12	12.0	12	0
Faaola	1	8	8.0	8	0
Hardy	1	2	2.0	2	0
Dolphins	331	4302	13.0	78t	26
Opponents	315	3811	12.1	63t	21

Interceptions

	No.	Yds.	Avg.	LG	TD
Oliver	4	32	8.0	23	0
McNeal	3	−6	−2.0	0	0
Williams	2	43	21.5	24	0
Judson	2	31	15.5	28	0
Thomas	2	4	2.0	4	0
Hobley	1	22	22.0	22	0
Lankford	1	0	0.0	0	0
Dolphins	15	126	8.4	28	0
Opponents	25	335	13.4	48	1

Punting

	No.	Yds.	Avg.	In 20	LG
Roby	58	2458	42.4	18	58
Dolphins	59	2458	41.7	18	58
Opponents	62	2416	39.0	17	63

Punt Returns

	No.	FC	Yds.	Avg.	LG	TD
Schwedes	18	3	210	11.7	70t	1
Stradford	14	5	129	9.2	19	0
Gibson	1	0	−1	−1.0	−1	0
Williams	0	3	0	—	0	0
Dolphins	33	11	338	10.2	70t	1
Opponents	26	13	256	9.8	18	0

Kickoff Returns

	No.	Yds.	Avg.	LG	TD
Logan	24	613	25.5	97t	1
Hampton	17	303	17.8	34	0
Reaves	6	84	14.0	22	0
Schwedes	3	24	8.0	13	0
Faaola	2	30	15.0	17	0
Kinchen	2	26	13.0	17	0
A. Brown	2	9	4.5	9	0
Williams	1	21	21.0	21	0
Davenport	1	19	19.0	19	0
Ahrens	1	10	10.0	10	0
Goode	1	8	8.0	8	0
Brudzinski	1	6	6.0	6	0
Dolphins	61	1153	18.9	97t	1
Opponents	63	1215	19.3	40	0

Sacks

	No.
Cross	10.0
Green	7.5
Sochia	5.0
Bosa	2.0
Kumerow	2.0
Offerdahl	1.5
Ahrens	1.0
Cline	1.0
Frye	1.0
Graf	1.0
Hobley	1.0
Junior	1.0
Krauss	1.0
Lankford	1.0
Thomas	1.0
Williams	1.0
Dolphins	39.0
Opponents	10.0

1990 Draft Choices

Round	Name	Pos.	College
1.	Richmond Webb	T	Texas A&M
2.	Keith Sims	G	Iowa State
3.	Alfred Oglesby	DT	Houston
4.	Scott Mitchell	QB	Utah
	Leroy Holt	RB	Southern California
6.	Sean Vanhorse	DB	Howard
8.	Thomas Woods	WR	Tennessee
9.	Phil Ross	TE	Oregon State
12.	Bobby Harden	DB	Miami

Miami Dolphins 1990 Veteran Roster

No.	Name	Pos.	Ht.	Wt.	Birth-date	NFL Exp.	College	Hometown	How Acq.	'89 Games/ Starts
86	Banks, Fred	WR	5-10	180	5/26/62	5	Liberty	Columbus, Ga.	FA-'87	15/3
97	Bosa, John	DE	6-4	270	1/10/64	4	Boston College	Keene, N.H.	D1-'87	13/3
82	Brown, Andre	WR	6-3	210	8/21/66	2	Miami	Chicago, Ill.	FA-'89	16/0
37	Brown, J.B.	CB	6-0	192	1/5/67	2	Maryland	Fort Washington, Md.	D12-'89	16/0
83	Clayton, Mark	WR	5-9	184	4/8/61	8	Louisville	Indianapolis, Ind.	D8-'83	15/15
91	Cross, Jeff	DE	6-4	270	3/25/66	3	Missouri	Blythe, Calif.	D9-'88	16/16
65	†Dellenbach, Jeff	T-C	6-6	282	2/14/63	6	Wisconsin	Wausau, Wis.	D4b-'85	16/16
74	†Dennis, Mark	T	6-6	290	4/15/65	4	Illinois	Washington, Ill.	D8b-'87	8/1
85	Duper, Mark	WR	5-9	190	1/25/59	9	Northwestern Louisiana	Moreauville, La.	D2-'82	15/14
80	Edmunds, Ferrell	TE	6-6	252	4/16/65	3	Maryland	Danville, Va.	D3-'88	16/16
47	Elder, Donnie	CB	5-9	175	12/13/63	5	Memphis State	Chattanooga, Tenn.	PB(TB)-'90#	16/0*
61	†Foster, Roy	G	6-4	277	5/24/60	9	Southern California	Shawnee Mission, Kan.	D1-'82	16/16
62	Galbreath, Harry	G-C	6-1	275	1/1/65	3	Tennessee	Clarksville, Tenn.	D8a-'88	14/14
79	†Giesler, Jon	T	6-5	275	12/23/56	11	Michigan	Woodville, Ohio	D1-'79	0*
35	Glenn, Kerry	CB	5-9	175	1/3/62	4	Minnesota	East St. Louis, Ill.	PB(NYJ)-90#	14/0*
99	†Graf, Rick	LB	6-5	249	8/29/63	4	Wisconsin	Madison, Wis.	D2a-'87	4/4
55	†Green, Hugh	LB	6-2	228	7/27/59	10	Pittsburgh	Natchez, Miss.	T(TB)-'85	16/16
92	Griggs, David	LB	6-3	239	2/5/67	2	Virginia	Pennsauken, N.J.	FA-'89	5/0
84	†Hardy, Bruce	TE	6-4	236	6/1/56	11	Arizona State	Bingham, Utah	D9-'78	1/0
59	Harvey, Stacy	LB	6-4	245	3/8/65	2	Arizona State	Pasadena, Calif.	PB(KC)-'90#	9/0*
21	Higgs, Mark	RB	5-7	188	4/11/66	3	Kentucky	Owensboro, Ky.	PB(Phil)-'90#	16/1*
29	Hobley, Liffort	S	6-0	202	5/12/62	5	Louisiana State	Shreveport, La.	FA-'87	16/3
11	†Jensen, Jim	WR-RB	6-4	224	11/14/58	10	Boston University	Doylestown, Pa.	D11-'81	16/1
54	Junior, E.J.	LB	6-3	242	12/8/59	10	Alabama	Nashville, Tenn.	PB(Phx)-'89#	16/12
88	†Kinchen, Brian	TE	6-2	232	8/6/65	3	Louisiana State	Baton Rouge, La.	D12-'88	16/0
58	Krauss, Barry	LB	6-3	260	3/17/57	12	Alabama	Pompano Beach, Fla.	W(Clev)-'89	16/12
90	Kumerow, Eric	DE	6-7	268	4/17/65	3	Ohio State	Oak Park, Ill.	D1-'88	12/0
44	Lankford, Paul	CB	6-1	190	6/15/58	9	Penn State	Farmingdale, N.Y.	D3-'82	16/16
20	Logan, Marc	RB	5-11	220	5/9/65	4	Kentucky	Lexington, Ky.	PB(Cin)-'89#	11/4
13	Marino, Dan	QB	6-4	224	9/15/61	8	Pittsburgh	Pittsburgh, Pa.	D1-'83	16/16
22	t-McKyer, Tim	CB	6-1	177	9/5/63	5	Texas-Arlington	Port Arthur, Tex.	T(SF)-'90	7/1
93	Odom, Cliff	LB	6-2	251	8/15/58	10	Texas-Arlington	Beaumont, Tex.	PB(Ind)-90#	16/3*
56	†Offerdahl, John	LB	6-3	240	8/17/64	5	Western Michigan	Fort Atkinson, Wis.	D2-'86	10/8
25	Oliver, Louis	S	6-2	226	3/9/66	2	Florida	Belle Glade, Fla.	D1b-'89	15/13
49	Paige, Tony	RB	5-10	235	10/14/62	7	Virginia Tech	Washington, D.C.	PB(Det)-'90#	16/4*
52	Reichenbach, Mike	LB	6-2	235	9/14/61	7	East Stroudsburg	Bethlehem, Pa.	PB(Phil)-'90#	16/4*
4	Roby, Reggie	P	6-2	246	7/30/61	8	Iowa	East Waterloo, Iowa	D6-'83	16/0
81	†Schwedes, Scott	WR-KR	6-0	182	6/30/65	4	Syracuse	DeWitt, N.Y.	D2b-'87	9/0
9	Secules, Scott	QB	6-3	219	11/8/64	3	Virginia	Centreville, Va.	T(Dall)-'89	15/0
33	Smith, Sammie	RB	6-2	226	5/16/67	2	Florida State	Zellwood, Fla.	D1a-'89	13/12
70	Sochia, Brian	NT	6-3	278	7/21/61	8	Northwestern Oklahoma	Brasher Falls, N.Y.	FA-'86	16/16
18	†Stoudt, Cliff	QB	6-4	218	3/27/55	12	Youngstown State	Oberlin, Ohio	FA-'89	16/15
10	Stoyanovich, Pete	K	5-10	180	4/28/67	2	Indiana	Dearborn Heights, Mich.	D8-'89	16/0
23	†Stradford, Troy	RB	5-9	192	9/11/64	4	Boston College	Linden, N.J.	D4-'89	7/4
24	Thomas, Rodney	CB	5-10	190	12/21/65	3	Brigham Young	Ontario, Calif.	D5-'88	16/2
95	Turner, T.J.	DE	6-4	280	5/16/63	5	Houston	Lufkin, Tex.	D3-'86	14/11
63	Uhlenhake, Jeff	C	6-3	282	1/28/66	2	Ohio State	Newark, Ohio	D5-'89	16/15
26	Williams, Jarvis	S	5-11	198	5/16/65	3	Florida	Palatka, Fla.	D2-'88	16/16
77	Wilson, Karl	DE	6-4	275	3/10/64	4	Louisiana State	Baton Rouge, La.	PB(Phx)-'90#	16/6*

* Elder played 16 games with Tampa Bay in '89; Giesler missed '89 season due to injury; Glenn played 14 games with Tampa Bay; Harvey played 9 games with Kansas City; Higgs played 16 games with Philadelphia; Odom played 16 games with Indianapolis; Paige played 16 games with Detroit; Reichenbach played 16 games with Philadelphia; Wilson played 16 games with Phoenix.

† Option playout; subject to developments.

Plan B unconditional free agent.

t- Dolphins traded for McKyer (San Francisco).

Players lost through Plan B (11): LB Dave Ahrens (Sea; 11 games in '89), RB Tom Brown (Wash; 9), T Louis Cheek (Dall; 13), LB Greg Clark (GB; 16), DE Jackie Cline (Atl; 15), CB Ernest Gibson (NE; 5), RB Lorenzo Hampton (Den; 10), G Greg Johnson (Dall; 0); CB William Judson (Det; 14), T Ronnie Lee (Atl; 15), G Tom Toth (SD; 16).

Also played with Dolphins in '89—LB Bob Brudzinski (10 games in '89), RB Ron Davenport (9), RB Nuu Faaola (10), LB David Frye (11), RB Kerry Goode (1), NT Mike Lambrecht (6), CB Don McNeal (12), G Alvin Powell (2), RB Willard Reeves (2).

COACHING STAFF

Head Coach, Don Shula

Pro Career: Begins his twenty-eighth season as an NFL head coach, and twenty-first with the Dolphins. Miami has won or shared first place in the AFC East in 13 of his 20 years. Has most wins (285) among active NFL coaches and is second only to George Halas's 325. Captured back-to-back NFL championships, defeating Washington 14-7 in Super Bowl VII and Minnesota 24-7 in Super Bowl VIII. Lost to Dallas 24-3 in Super Bowl VI, to Washington 27-17 in Super Bowl XVII, and to San Francisco 38-16 in Super Bowl XIX. His 1972 17-0 club is the only team in NFL history to go undefeated throughout the regular season and postseason. Started his pro playing career with Cleveland Browns as defensive back in 1951. After two seasons with Browns, spent 1953-56 with Baltimore Colts and 1957 with Washington Redskins. Joined Detroit Lions as defensive coach in 1960 and was named head coach of the Colts in 1963. Baltimore had a 13-1 record in 1968 and captured NFL championship before losing to New York Jets in Super Bowl III. Career record: 285-132-6.

Background: Outstanding offensive player at John Carroll University in Cleveland before becoming defensive specialist as a pro. His alma mater gave him doctorate in Humanities in May, 1973. Served as assistant coach at Virginia in 1958 and at Kentucky in 1959.

Personal: Born January 4, 1930, in Painesville, Ohio. Don and his wife, Dorothy, live in Miami Lakes, Fla., and have five children—David, Donna, Sharon, Annie, and Mike. David is Dallas's offensive coordinator and Mike is an assistant coach with Tampa Bay.

Assistant Coaches

George Hill, linebackers; born April 28, 1933, Bay Village, Ohio, lives in Miami. Tackle-fullback Denison 1954-57. No pro playing experience. College coach: Findlay 1959, Denison 1960-64, Cornell 1965, Duke 1966-70, Ohio State 1971-78. Pro coach: Philadelphia Eagles 1979-84, Indianapolis Colts 1985-88, joined Dolphins in 1989.

Tony Nathan, coaches' assistant; born December 14, 1956, Birmingham, Ala., lives in Miami. Running back Alabama 1975-78. Pro running back Miami Dolphins 1979-87. Pro coach: Joined Dolphins in 1988.

Tom Olivadotti, defense; born September 22, 1945, Long Branch, N.J., lives in Cooper City, Fla. Defensive back-wide receiver Upsala 1963-66. No pro playing experience. College coach: Princeton 1975-77, Boston College 1978-79, Miami 1980-83. Pro coach: Cleveland Browns 1985-86, joined Dolphins in 1987.

Mel Phillips, defensive backs; born January 6, 1942, Shelby, N.C., lives in Miami Lakes, Fla. Defensive back-running back North Carolina A&T 1964-65. Pro defensive back San Francisco 49ers 1966-77. Pro coach: Detroit Lions 1980-84, joined Dolphins in 1985.

John Sandusky, assistant head coach, offensive line-run offense; born December 28, 1925, Philadelphia, lives in Hollywood, Fla. Tackle Villanova 1946-49. Pro tackle Cleveland Browns 1950-55, Green Bay Packers 1956. College coach: Villanova 1957-58. Pro coach: Baltimore Colts 1959-72 (head coach 1972), Philadelphia Eagles 1973-75, joined Dolphins in 1976.

Larry Seiple, receivers; born February 14, 1945, Allentown, Pa., lives in Miami Lakes, Fla. Running back-receiver-punter Kentucky 1964-66. Pro punter-tight end-receiver-running back Miami Dolphins 1967-77. College coach: Miami 1978-79. Pro coach: Detroit Lions 1980-84, Tampa Bay Buccaneers 1985-86, joined Dolphins in 1988.

Dan Sekanovich, defensive line; born July 27, 1933, West Hazleton, Pa., lives in Cooper City, Fla. End Tennessee 1951-53. Pro defensive end Montreal Alouettes (CFL) 1954. College coach: Susquehanna 1961-63, Connecticut 1964-67, Pittsburgh 1968, Navy 1969-70, Kentucky 1971-72. Pro coach: Montreal Alouettes (CFL) 1973-76, New York Jets 1977-82, Atlanta Falcons 1983-85, joined Dolphins in 1986.

Gary Stevens, quarterbacks-pass offense; born March 19, 1943, Cleveland, Ohio, lives in Kendall, Fla. Running back John Carroll 1963-65. No pro playing experience. College coach: Louisville 1971-74, Kent State 1975, West Virginia 1976-79, Miami 1980-88. Pro coach: Joined Dolphins in 1989.

Carl Taseff, offensive backs; born September 28, 1928, Cleveland, Ohio, lives in Miami. Back John Carroll 1947-50. Pro defensive back Cleveland Browns 1951, Baltimore Colts 1953-61, Philadelphia Eagles 1961, Buffalo Bills 1962. Pro coach: Boston Patriots 1964, Detroit Lions 1965-66, joined Dolphins in 1970.

Junior Wade, strength-conditioning; born February 2, 1947, Bath, S.C., lives in Miami. South Carolina State 1969. No college or pro playing experience. Pro coach: Joined Dolphins in 1975, coach since 1983.

Mike Westhoff, special teams; born January 10, 1948, Pittsburgh, Pa., lives in Ft. Lauderdale, Fla. Center-linebacker Wichita State 1967-69. No pro playing experience. College coach: Indiana 1974-75, Dayton 1976, Indiana State 1977, Northwestern 1978-80, Texas Christian 1981. Pro coach: Baltimore/Indianapolis Colts 1982-84, Arizona Outlaws (USFL) 1985, joined Dolphins in 1986.

Miami Dolphins 1990 First-Year Roster

Name	Pos.	Ht.	Wt.	Birth-date	College	Hometown	How Acq.
Batiste, Dana (1)	LB	6-0	238	3/22/66	Texas A&M	Spring, Tex.	D9-'89
Brown, Tony (1)	T	6-5	285	7/11/64	Pittsburgh	Stamford, Conn.	FA
Faulkner, Jeff (1)	DE	6-3	270	4/4/64	Southern University	Miami, Fla.	FA
Grant, African (1)	S	6-0	200	8/2/65	Illinois	Englewood, N.J.	FA-'89
Harden, Bobby	S	6-0	192	2/8/67	Miami	Chicago, Ill.	D12
Harris, Walter (1)	DE	6-3	277	9/6/65	Indiana	Detroit, Mich.	FA
Healy, Tim (1)	RB	6-0	226	2/6/67	Delaware	Towson, Md.	FA
Highsmith, Fred (1)	RB	6-2	220	12/7/62	Miami	Jacksonville, Fla.	FA
Holt, Leroy	RB	5-10	236	2/7/67	Southern California	Bernham, Tex.	D5
Jones, Clarence	RB	6-1	205	3/24/65	Army	Washington, D.C.	FA
Limbrick, Garrett (1)	RB	6-2	235	11/16/65	Oklahoma State	Northbrook, Tex.	FA
Martin, Tony (1)	WR	6-0	174	9/5/65	Mesa, Colo.	Miami, Fla.	FA-'89
Mitchell, Scott	QB	6-6	231	1/2/68	Utah	Springville, Utah	D4
Moore, Stevon (1)	CB	5-11	205	2/9/67	Mississippi	Wiggins, Miss.	FA
McGruder, Michael (1)	CB	5-11	180	5/6/62	Kent State	Cleveland Heights, Ohio	FA
Oglesby, Alfred	NT	6-3	271	1/27/67	Houston	Weimer, Tex.	D3
Pettyjohn, Barry (1)	T	6-5	280	3/29/64	Pittsburgh	Cincinnati, Ohio	FA-'89
Popp, Dave (1)	T	6-5	285	10/30/66	Eastern Illinois	Libertyville, Ill.	FA
Reed, Curt	WR	6-3	210	12/3/64	Millikin	McLeansboro, Ill.	FA
Ross, Phil	TE	6-4	221	6/14/67	Oregon State	Seattle, Wash.	D9
Roth, Jeff (1)	NT	6-3	258	4/21/66	Florida	Seminole, Fla.	FA
Searels, Stacy (1)	G-C	6-5	280	5/19/65	Auburn	Trion, Ga.	FA
Sims, Keith	G	6-2	310	6/17/67	Iowa State	Watchung, N.J.	D2
Swarn, George (1)	RB	5-11	230	2/15/64	Miami, Ohio	Cincinnati, Ohio	FA
Vanhorse, Sean	CB	5-10	178	7/22/68	Howard University	Baltimore, Md.	D6
Webb, Richmond	T	6-6	291	1/11/67	Texas A&M	Dallas, Tex.	D1
Weidner, Bert (1)	NT	6-3	275	1/20/66	Kent State	Eden, N.Y.	D11-'89
Woods, Thomas	WR	5-10	174	2/21/65	Tennessee	Gallatin, Tex.	D8
Zdelar, Jim (1)	T	6-5	290	5/24/66	Youngstown State	Youngstown, Ohio	D7

The term NFL Rookie is defined as a player who is in his first season of professional football and has not been on the roster of another professional football team for any regular-season or postseason games. A Rookie is designated by an "R" on NFL rosters. Players who have been active in another professional football league or players who have NFL experience, including either preseason training camp or being on an active roster for fewer than three regular-season or post-season games, are termed NFL First-Year Players. An NFL First-Year Player is designated by a "1" on NFL rosters. Thereafter, a player on an NFL active roster for at least three regular-season or postseason games is credited with an additional year of NFL playing experience.

NOTES

American Football Conference
Eastern Division

Team Colors: Red, White, and Blue

Foxboro Stadium
Route 1
Foxboro, Massachusetts 02035
Telephone: (508) 543-8200

Club Officials

Chairman: Victor K. Kiam II
Vice Chairman: Francis W. Murray
President: William H. Sullivan, Jr.
Vice President: Francis J. (Bucko) Kilroy
General Manager: Patrick J. Sullivan
Vice President-Administration: Robert Durkin
Director of Player Operations: Joe Mendes
Director of Pro Scouting: Bill McPeak
Executive Director of Player Personnel:
    Darryl Stingley
Personnel Scouts: Larry Cook, Charles Garcia,
    Ralph Goldston, Mike Pollom, Ken Sternfeld,
    Bob Teahan
Director of Marketing/Public Relations:
    David J. Wintergrass
Director of Media Relations: Jim Oldham
Media Relations Assistant: Mike Hanson
Box Office Manager: Frank Napoli
Trainer: Ron O'Neil
Equipment Manager: George Luongo
Video Director: Ken Deininger

Stadium: Foxboro Stadium • **Capacity:** 60,794
        Route 1
        Foxboro, Massachusetts 02035

Playing Surface: SuperTurf

Training Camp: Bryant College
        Route 7
        Smithfield, Rhode Island 02917

1990 Schedule

Preseason
Aug. 9	vs. Pittsburgh at Montreal	7:30
Aug. 18	vs. Tampa Bay at Jacksonville	8:00
Aug. 24	**Cincinnati**	7:00
Aug. 31	**Atlanta**	7:30

Regular Season
Sept. 9	**Miami**	4:00
Sept. 16	at Indianapolis	12:00
Sept. 23	at Cincinnati	1:00
Sept. 30	**New York Jets**	4:00
Oct. 7	**Seattle**	1:00
Oct. 14	**Open Date**	
Oct. 18	at Miami (Thursday)	8:00
Oct. 28	**Buffalo**	1:00
Nov. 4	at Philadelphia	1:00
Nov. 11	**Indianapolis**	1:00
Nov. 18	at Buffalo	1:00
Nov. 25	at Phoenix	2:00
Dec. 2	**Kansas City**	1:00
Dec. 9	at Pittsburgh	1:00
Dec. 15	**Washington** (Saturday)	4:00
Dec. 23	at New York Jets	1:00
Dec. 30	**New York Giants**	1:00

Patriots Coaching History

Boston 1960-70
(211-226-9)
1960-61	Lou Saban*	7-12-0
1961-68	Mike Holovak	53-47-9
1969-70	Clive Rush**	5-16-0
1970-72	John Mazur***	9-21-0
1972	Phil Bengtson	1-4-0
1973-78	Chuck Fairbanks****	46-41-0
1978	Hank Bullough-Ron Erhardt#	0-1-0
1979-81	Ron Erhardt	21-27-0
1982-84	Ron Meyer##	18-16-0
1984-89	Raymond Berry	51-41-0

*Released after five games in 1961
**Released after seven games in 1970
***Resigned after nine games in 1972
****Suspended for final regular season game in 1978
#Co-coaches
##Released after eight games in 1984

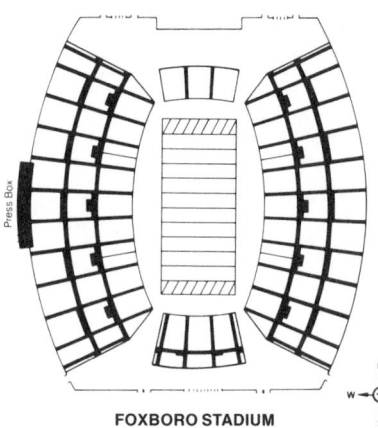

FOXBORO STADIUM

Record Holders
Individual Records — Career
Category	Name	Performance
Rushing (Yds.)	Sam Cunningham, 1973-79, 1981-82	5,453
Passing (Yds.)	Steve Grogan, 1975-1989	26,271
Passing (TDs)	Steve Grogan, 1975-1989	178
Receiving (No.)	Stanley Morgan, 1977-1989	534
Receiving (Yds.)	Stanley Morgan, 1977-1989	10,352
Interceptions	Raymond Clayborn, 1977-1989	36
Punting (Avg.)	Rich Camarillo, 1981-87	42.6
Punt Return (Avg.)	Mack Herron, 1973-75	12.0
Kickoff Return (Avg.)	Horace Ivory, 1977-1981	27.6
Field Goals	Gino Cappelletti, 1960-1970	176
Touchdowns (Tot.)	Stanley Morgan, 1977-1989	68
Points	Gino Cappelletti, 1960-1970	1,130

Individual Records — Single Season
Category	Name	Performance
Rushing (Yds.)	Jim Nance, 1966	1,458
Passing (Yds.)	Vito (Babe) Parilli, 1964	3,465
Passing (TDs)	Vito (Babe) Parilli, 1964	31
Receiving (No.)	Stanley Morgan, 1986	84
Receiving (Yds.)	Stanley Morgan, 1986	1,491
Interceptions	Ron Hall, 1964	11
Punting (Avg.)	Rich Camarillo, 1983	44.6
Punt Return (Avg.)	Mack Herron, 1974	14.8
Kickoff Return (Avg.)	Raymond Clayborn, 1977	31.0
Field Goals	Tony Franklin, 1986	32
Touchdowns (Tot.)	Steve Grogan, 1976	13
	Stanley Morgan, 1979	13
Points	Gino Cappelletti, 1964	155

Individual Records — Single Game
Category	Name	Performance
Rushing (Yds.)	Tony Collins, 9-18-83	212
Passing (Yds.)	Tony Eason, 9-21-86	414
Passing (TDs)	Vito (Babe) Parilli, 11-15-64	5
	Vito (Babe) Parilli, 10-15-67	5
	Steve Grogan, 9-9-79	5
Receiving (No.)	Art Graham, 11-20-66	11
	Tony Collins, 11-29-87	11
Receiving (Yds.)	Stanley Morgan, 11-8-81	182
Interceptions	Many times	3
	Last time by Roland James, 10-23-83	
Field Goals	Gino Cappelletti, 10-4-64	6
Touchdowns (Tot.)	Many times	3
	Last time by Stanley Morgan, 9-21-86	
Points	Gino Cappelletti, 12-18-65	28

1989 Team Record

Preseason (2-2)

Date	Result		Opponents
8/12	L	17-20	N.Y. Giants
8/19	W	17-12	vs. Seattle at St. Louis, Mo.
8/26	W	23- 7	at Atlanta
9/1	L	0-16	Green Bay
		57-55	

Regular Season (5-11)

Date	Result		Opponents	Att.
9/10	W	27-24	at N.Y. Jets	64,541
9/17	L	10-24	Miami	57,043
9/24	L	3-24	Seattle	48,025
10/1	L	10-31	at Buffalo	78,921
10/8	W	23-13	Houston	59,828
10/15	L	15-16	at Atlanta	39,697
10/22	L	20-37	at San Francisco	51,781
10/29	L	23-20	at Ind. (OT)	59,356
11/5	L	26-27	N.Y. Jets	53,366
11/12	L	24-28	New Orleans	47,680
11/19	W	33-24	Buffalo	49,663
11/26	L	21-24	at L.A. Raiders	38,747
12/3	W	22-16	Indianapolis	32,234
12/10	L	10-31	at Miami	55,918
12/17	L	10-28	at Pittsburgh	26,594
12/24	L	20-24	L.A. Rams	27,940

(OT) Overtime

Score by Periods

Patriots	47	66	71	110	3	—	297
Opponents	82	144	58	107	0	—	391

Attendance

Home 375,779   Away 415,555   Total 791,334
Single-game home record, 61,457 (12-5-71)
Single-season home record, 482,572 (1986)

1989 Team Statistics

	Patriots	Opp.
Total First Downs	335	297
Rushing.	114	110
Passing.	187	176
Penalty.	34	11
Third Down: Made/Att.	92/240	72/199
Third Down: Pct.	38.3	36.2
Fourth Down: Made/Att.	10/29	5/12
Fourth Down: Pct.	34.5	41.7
Total Net Yards	5456	5644
Avg. Per Game	341.0	352.8
Total Plays.	1129	975
Avg. Per Play	4.8	5.8
Net Yards Rushing.	1749	1978
Avg. Per Game	109.3	123.6
Total Rushes.	485	495
Net Yards Passing	3707	3666
Avg. Per Game	231.7	229.1
Sacked/Yards Lost	34/265	31/239
Gross Yards	3972	3905
Att./Completions	610/302	449/259
Completion Pct.	49.5	57.7
Had Intercepted	27	16
Punts/Avg.	64/37.4	81/42.1
Net Punting Avg.	31.3	35.2
Penalties/Yards Lost	63/509	111/954
Fumbles/Ball Lost	26/12	22/12
Touchdowns	30	48
Rushing.	12	19
Passing.	17	27
Returns	1	2
Avg. Time of Possession.	30:55	29:05

1989 Individual Statistics

Scoring

	TD R	TD P	TD Rt	PAT	FG	Saf	TP
Davis	0	0	0	13/16	16/23	0	61
Staurovsky	0	0	0	14/14	14/17	0	56
Stephens	7	0	0	0/0	0/0	0	42
C. Jones	0	6	0	0/0	0/0	0	36
Dykes	0	5	0	0/0	0/0	0	30
Fryar	0	3	0	0/0	0/0	0	18
Morgan	0	3	0	0/0	0/0	0	18
Perryman	2	0	0	0/0	0/0	0	12
Allen	1	0	0	0/0	0/0	0	6
Dupard	1	0	0	0/0	0/0	0	6
Egu	1	0	0	0/0	0/0	0	6
Hurst	0	0	1	0/0	0/0	0	6
Patriots	12	17	1	27/30	30/40	0	297
Opponents	19	27	2	46/48	19/26	0	391

Passing

	Att.	Comp.	Yds.	Pct.	TD	Int.	Tkld.	Rate
Grogan	261	133	1697	51.0	9	14	8/64	60.8
Wilson	150	75	1006	50.0	3	5	10/71	64.5
Eason	105	57	761	54.3	4	4	10/78	71.2
Flutie	91	36	493	39.6	2	4	6/52	46.6
Feagles	2	0	0	0.0	0	0	0/0	39.6
Tatupu	1	1	15	100.0	0	0	0/0	118.8
Patriots	610	302	3972	49.5	17	27	34/265	61.3
Opponents	449	259	3905	57.7	27	16	31/239	91.6

Rushing

	Att.	Yds.	Avg.	LG	TD
Stephens	244	833	3.4	35t	7
Perryman	150	562	3.7	18	2
Flutie	16	87	5.4	22	0
Dupard	25	63	2.5	10	1
Allen	11	51	4.6	18	1
Wilson	7	42	6.0	11	0
Tatupu	11	38	3.5	20	0
Egu	3	20	6.7	15t	1
Martin	2	20	10.0	13	0
Grogan	9	19	2.1	7	0
Fryar	2	15	7.5	11	0
C. Jones	1	3	3.0	3	0
Eason	2	-2	-1.0	0	0
Wonsley	2	-2	-1.0	0	0
Patriots	485	1749	3.6	35t	12
Opponents	495	1978	4.0	58t	19

Receiving

	No.	Yds.	Avg.	LG	TD
Sievers	54	615	11.4	46	0
Dykes	49	795	16.2	42	5
C. Jones	48	670	14.0	65t	6
Fryar	29	537	18.5	52	3
Perryman	29	195	6.7	16	0
Morgan	28	486	17.4	55t	3
Stephens	21	207	9.9	37	0
Martin	13	229	17.6	37	0
Dawson	12	101	8.4	17	0
Tatupu	10	54	5.4	11	0
Dupard	6	70	11.7	45	0
Cook	3	13	4.3	5	0
Patriots	302	3972	13.2	65t	17
Opponents	259	3905	15.1	74t	27

Interceptions

	No.	Yds.	Avg.	LG	TD
Hurst	5	31	6.2	16t	1
James	2	50	25.0	28	0
Marion	2	19	9.5	18	0
McSwain	1	18	18.0	18	0
Feggins	1	4	4.0	4	0
Coleman	1	1	1.0	1	0
Clayborn	1	0	0.0	0	0
Rembert	1	0	0.0	0	0
Brown	1	-1	-1.0	-1	0
McGrew	1	-4	-4.0	-4	0
Patriots	16	118	7.4	28	1
Opponents	27	338	12.5	55	2

Punting

	No.	Yds.	Avg.	In 20	LG
Feagles	63	2392	38.0	13	64
Patriots	64	2392	37.4	13	64
Opponents	81	3413	42.1	15	76

Punt Returns

	No.	FC	Yds.	Avg.	LG	TD
Tucker, Buff.-N.E.	19	4	165	8.7	25	0
Tucker, N.E.	13	1	102	7.8	25	0
Martin	19	2	164	8.6	28	0
Fryar	12	1	107	8.9	20	0
Hurst	1	0	6	6.0	6	0
Taylor	0	2	—	—	0	0
Patriots	45	6	379	8.4	28	0
Opponents	38	6	346	9.1	17	0

Kickoff Returns

	No.	Yds.	Avg.	LG	TD
Martin	24	584	24.3	38	0
Tucker, Buff.-N.E.	23	436	19.0	37	0
Tucker, N.E.	13	270	20.8	37	0
Rice	11	242	22.0	46	0
Allen	6	124	20.7	29	0
Wonsley	3	69	23.0	40	0
Taylor	3	52	17.3	22	0
Egu	2	26	13.0	22	0
Hodge	2	19	9.5	11	0
Timpson	2	13	6.5	13	0
Fryar	1	47	47.0	47	0
Rehder	1	14	14.0	14	0
Tatupu	1	2	2.0	2	0
Patriots	69	1462	21.2	47	0
Opponents	61	1199	19.7	60	0

Sacks

	No.
Williams	8.0
Jeter	7.0
McGrew	4.5
Brown	4.0
Sims	3.0
Rembert	2.5
Goad	1.0
Patriots	31.0
Opponents	34.0

1990 Draft Choices

Round	Name	Pos.	College
1.	Chris Singleton	LB	Arizona
	Ray Agnew	DE	North Carolina St.
3.	Tommy Hodson	QB	Louisiana State
	Greg McMurtry	WR	Michigan
5.	Junior Robinson	DB	East Carolina
	Jon Melander	T	Minnesota
	James Gray	RB	Texas Tech
9.	Shawn Bouwens	G	Nebraska Wesleyan
10.	Anthony Landry	RB	Stephen F. Austin
11.	Sean Smith	DE	Georgia Tech
12.	Ventson Donelson	DB	Michigan State
	Blaine Rose	G	Maryland

New England Patriots 1990 Veteran Roster

No.	Name	Pos.	Ht.	Wt.	Birth-date	NFL Exp.	College	Hometown	How Acq.	'89 Games/ Starts
33	Adams, George	RB	6-1	225	12/22/62	6	Kentucky	Lexington, Ky.	PB(NYG)-'90#	14/0*
39	†Allen, Marvin	RB	5-10	208	11/23/65	3	Tulane	Wichita Falls, Tex.	D11-'88	3/0
78	Armstrong, Bruce	T	6-4	284	9/7/65	4	Louisville	Miami, Fla.	D1-'87	16/16
28	†Bowman, Jim	S	6-2	215	10/26/63	6	Central Michigan	Cadillac, Mich.	D2b-'85	13/2
59	Brown, Vincent	LB	6-2	245	1/9/65	3	Mississippi Valley State	Decatur, Ga.	D2-'88	14/10
22	Coleman, Eric	CB	6-0	190	12/27/66	2	Wyoming	Denver, Colo.	D2-'89	8/0
46	Cook, Marv	TE	6-4	234	2/24/66	2	Iowa	West Branch, Iowa	D3a-'89	16/0
87	†Dawson, Lin	TE	6-3	240	6/24/59	9	North Carolina State	Kinston, N.C.	D8b-'81	16/13
67	†Douglas, David	G-C	6-4	280	3/20/63	5	Tennessee	Evansville, Tenn.	PB(Cin)-'89#	5/1
88	Dykes, Hart Lee	WR	6-4	218	9/2/66	2	Oklahoma State	Bay City, Tex.	D1-'89	16/6
66	Fairchild, Paul	G	6-4	270	9/14/61	7	Kansas	Glidden, Iowa	D5-'84	14/14
62	Farrell, Sean	G	6-3	260	5/25/60	9	Penn State	Westhampton, N.Y.	T(TB)-'87	14/14
8	†Feagles, Jeff	P	6-0	198	3/7/66	3	Miami	Scottsdale, Ariz.	FA-'88	16/0
63	†Feehery, Gerry	C	6-2	270	3/9/60	8	Syracuse	Philadelphia, Pa.	FA-'89	0*
80	Fryar, Irving	WR-KR	6-0	200	9/28/62	7	Nebraska	Mt. Holly, N.J.	D1-'84	11/5
76	Gambol, Chris	T	6-6	303	9/4/64	3	Iowa	Oxford, Mich.	PB(Det)-'90#	6/0*
91	Gannon, Chris	DE	6-6	265	1/20/66	2	Southwest Louisiana	Orange Park, Fla.	PB(SD)-'90#	10/1*
43	Gibson, Ernest	CB	5-10	185	10/3/61	7	Furman	Jacksonville, Fla.	PB(Mia)-'90#	5/0*
72	Goad, Tim	NT	6-3	280	2/28/66	3	North Carolina	Claudville, Va.	D4a-'88	16/16
14	†Grogan, Steve	QB	6-4	210	7/24/53	16	Kansas State	Ottawa, Kan.	D5a-'75	7/6
37	Hurst, Maurice	CB	5-10	185	9/17/67	2	Southern University	New Orleans, La.	D4a-'89	16/14
38	†James, Roland	S	6-2	191	2/18/58	11	Tennessee	Xenia, Ohio	D1a-'80	14/14
50	Jarostchuk, Ilia	LB	6-3	236	8/1/64	4	New Hampshire	Utica, N.Y.	PB(Phx)-'90#	16/1*
99	Jeter, Gary	DE	6-4	260	1/24/55	14	Southern California	Cleveland, Ohio	PB(Rams)-'89#	14/0
68	Johnson, Damian	T	6-5	290	12/18/62	5	Kansas State	Great Bend, Kan.	PB(NYG)-'90#	4/4*
83	Jones, Cedric	WR	6-1	184	6/1/60	9	Duke	Weldon, N.C.	D3a-'82	15/12
93	†Jordan, Tim	LB	6-3	226	4/26/64	4	Wisconsin	Madison, Wis.	D4c-'87	9/4
42	Lippett, Ronnie	CB	5-11	180	12/10/60	7	Miami	Sebring, Fla.	D8-'83	0*
91	†Lowry, Orlando	LB	6-4	236	8/14/61	7	Ohio State	Shaker Heights, Ohio	FA-'89	2/0
31	Marion, Fred	S	6-2	191	1/2/59	9	Miami	Gainesville, Fla.	D5-'82	16/16
82	Martin, Sammy	WR-KR	5-11	175	8/21/65	3	Louisiana State	New Orleans, La.	D4b-'88	10/1
23	†McSwain, Rod	CB	6-1	198	1/28/62	7	Clemson	Caroleen, N.C.	T(Atl)-'84	9/4
86	†Morgan, Stanley	WR	5-11	181	2/17/55	14	Tennessee	Easley, S.C.	D1b-'77	10/10
24	Morris, Jamie	RB	5-7	188	6/6/65	3	Michigan	Ayer, Mass.	PB(Wash)-'90#	13/3*
81	Mowatt, Zeke	TE	6-3	240	3/5/61	8	Florida State	Wauchula, Fla.	PB(NYG)-'90#	16/11*
34	†Perryman, Robert	RB	6-1	233	10/16/64	4	Michigan	Bourne, Mass.	D3-'87	16/14
52	Rembert, Johnny	LB	6-3	234	1/19/61	8	Clemson	Arcadia, Fla.	D4-'83	16/16
95	Reynolds, Ed	LB	6-5	242	9/23/61	8	Virginia	Ridgeway, Va.	FA-'83	16/16
51	Scholtz, Bruce	LB	6-6	244	9/26/58	9	Texas	Austin, Tex.	FA-'89	8/2
85	Sievers, Eric	TE	6-4	238	11/9/57	10	Maryland	Arlington, Va.	PB(Rams)-'89#	16/5
77	†Sims, Kenneth	DE	6-5	271	10/31/59	8	Texas	Kosse, Tex.	D1a-'82	15/15
4	†Staurovsky, Jason	K	5-9	170	3/23/63	3	Tulsa	Tulsa, Okla.	FA-'88	7/0
44	Stephens, John	RB	6-1	215	2/23/66	3	Northwestern Louisiana	Springhill, La.	D1-'88	14/12
30	†Tatupu, Mosi	RB	6-0	227	4/26/55	13	Southern California	Honolulu, Hawaii	D8b-'78	14/0
49	Taylor, Kitrick	WR-KR	5-11	190	7/22/64	3	Washington State	Los Angeles, Calif.	FA-'89	4/0
56	Tippett, Andre	LB	6-3	241	12/27/59	8	Iowa	Newark, N.J.	D2b-'82	0*
21	†Tucker, Erroll	CB-KR	5-8	170	7/6/64	3	Utah	Pittsburgh, Pa.	FA-'89	5/0
60	Veris, Garin	DE	6-4	255	2/27/63	5	Stanford	Chillicothe, Ohio	D2a-'85	0*
70	Viaene, David	T	6-5	300	7/14/65	2	Minnesota-Duluth	Appleton, Wis.	FA-'89	16/4
75	Villa, Danny	T	6-5	305	9/21/64	4	Arizona State	Nogales, Ariz.	D5a-'87	15/15
65	White, Bob	C	6-5	273	4/9/63	4	Rhode Island	Lunenburg, Mass.	PB(Dall)-'90#	8/4*
96	Williams, Brent	DE	6-4	275	10/23/64	5	Toledo	Flint, Mich.	D7b-'86	16/16
54	†Williams, Ed	LB	6-4	244	9/8/61	6	Texas	Ector, Tex.	D2-'84	0*
15	†Wilson, Marc	QB	6-5	205	2/15/57	10	Brigham Young	Seattle, Wash.	FA-'89	14/4
35	Wonsley, George	RB	5-10	219	11/23/60	7	Mississippi State	Moss Point, Miss.	FA-'89	5/0

* Adams played 14 games with N.Y. Giants in '89; Feehery active for 3 games but did not play; Gambol played 6 games with Detroit; Gannon played 10 games with San Diego; Gibson played 5 games with Miami; Lippett, Tippett, Veris, and E. Williams missed '89 season due to injury; Jarostchuk played 16 games with Phoenix; Johnson played 4 games with N.Y. Giants; Morris played 13 games with Washington; Mowatt played 16 games with N.Y. Giants; White played 8 games with Dallas.

† Option playout; subject to developments.

Plan B unconditional free agent.

Players lost through Plan B (17): WR Glenn Antrum (NYJ; 1 game in '89), C Mike Baab (Clev; 16), LB Aaron Chubb (GB; 0), CB Raymond Clayborn (Clev; 14) LB Terrence Cooks (Dall; 3), RB Patrick Egu (NYJ; 7), CB Howard Feggins (NYG; 11), NT Milford Hodge (Wash; 16), S Darryl Holmes (Pitt; 13), LB Lawrence McGrew (Clev; 16), NT Emanuel McNeil (NYJ; 1), C Mike Morris (KC; 11), T Tom Rehder (NYJ; 16), CB Rodney Rice (TB; 10), DE Peter Shorts (KC; 1), LB David Ward (KC; 16), C Curtis Wilson (Det; 0).

Also played with Patriots in '89—K Greg Davis (9 games), RB Reggie Dupard (7), QB Tony Eason (3), QB Doug Flutie (5), LB Eric Naposki (1).

COACHING STAFF

Head Coach, Rod Rust

Pro Career: Begins first year as head coach of Patriots. Became tenth head coach of team on February 27, 1990. Was the defensive coordinator of the Montreal Alouettes of the Canadian Football League from 1973-75. Entered NFL coaching ranks in 1976 as linebackers coach of Philadelphia Eagles, a position he held for two seasons. Joined Kansas City Chiefs as defensive coordinator from 1978-82 before taking over the same position with Patriots from 1983-87. His 1985 defensive unit helped the Patriots win the AFC title and play in Super Bowl XX. In 1988, he was defensive coordinator with Kansas City Chiefs and in 1989 was the defensive coordinator of Pittsburgh Steelers.

Background: Attended Franklin High School in Cedar Rapids, Iowa. Played college football at Iowa State from 1947-49. Spent two years in Army before coaching at high school level in Iowa for eight years. He was an assistant coach at New Mexico (1960-62) and Stanford (1963-66) before serving six seasons as head coach at North Texas State (1967-72).

Personal: Born August 2, 1928, in Webster City, Iowa. Rod and his wife, Jean, live in Foxboro, Mass., and have two daughters, Kris and Amy, and two sons, Jeff and George.

Assistant Coaches

Don Blackmon, outside linebackers; born March 14, 1958, Pompano Beach, Fla., lives in Norfolk, Mass. Linebacker Tulsa 1976-80. Pro linebacker New England Patriots 1981-87. Pro coach: Joined Patriots in 1988.

Steve Crosby, special teams; born July 3, 1950, Great Bend, Kan., lives in Foxboro, Mass. Running back Fort Hays State 1969-72. Pro running back New York Giants 1974-76. Pro coach: Miami Dolphins 1977-82, Atlanta Falcons 1983-84, 1986-89, Cleveland Browns 1985, joined Patriots in 1990.

Bobby Grier, offensive backs; born November 10, 1942, Detroit, Mich., lives in Holliston, Mass. Running back Iowa 1961-64. No pro playing experience. College coach: Eastern Michigan 1974-77, Boston College 1978-80. Pro coach: Joined Patriots in 1981 (scout, 1982-83).

Rod Humenuik, offensive line; born June 17, 1938, Detroit, lives in Foxboro, Mass. Guard Southern California 1956-58. Pro guard Winnipeg Blue Bombers (CFL) 1960-62. College coach: Fullerton, Calif., J.C. 1964-65, Southern California 1966-70, Cal State-Northridge 1971-72 (head coach). Pro coach: Toronto Argonauts (CFL) 1973-74, Cleveland Browns 1975-82, Kansas City Chiefs 1983-84, New England Patriots 1985-88, New York Jets 1989, rejoined Patriots in 1990.

Dale Lindsey, defensive line; born January 18, 1943, Bowling Green, Ky., lives in Foxboro, Mass. Linebacker Western Kentucky 1961-64. Pro linebacker Cleveland Browns 1965-73. College coach: Southern Methodist 1988-89. Pro coach: Cleveland Browns 1974, Portland Storm (WFL) 1975, Toronto Argonauts (CFL) 1979-82, Boston Breakers (USFL) 1983, New Jersey Generals (USFL) 1984-85, Green Bay Packers 1986-87, joined Patriots in 1990.

Steve Nelson, inside linebackers; born April 26, 1951, Farmington, Minn., lives in Norfolk, Mass. Linebacker North Dakota State 1970-73. Pro linebacker New England Patriots 1974-87. Pro coach: Joined Patriots in 1990.

John Polonchek, special assistant to head coach; born January 1, 1928, Granastrov, Czechoslovakia, lives in Foxboro, Mass. Running back-defensive back Michigan State 1947-49. No pro playing experience. College coach: Michigan State 1950, 1955-57, Colorado 1959-61. Pro coach: Oakland Raiders 1967-71, Green Bay Packers 1972-74, New England Patriots 1975-81, New Jersey Generals (USFL) 1982-83, Los Angeles Raiders 1984 (scout), rejoined Patriots in 1985.

New England Patriots 1990 First-Year Roster

Name	Pos.	Ht.	Wt.	Birth-date	College	Hometown	How Acq.
Agnew, Ray	DE	6-3	272	12/9/67	North Carolina State	Winston-Salem, N.C.	D1b
Bouwens, Shawn	G	6-4	280	5/26/68	Nebraska Wesleyan	Lincoln, Neb.	D9
Crowley, Pat	G	6-2	284	8/29/67	North Carolina	Hampton Bays, N.Y.	FA
Donelson, Ventson	CB	5-11	180	2/2/68	Michigan State	Rock Island, Ill.	D12a
Drennan, Chris	K	5-9	190	1/26/67	Nebraska	Cypress, Calif.	FA
Gray, James	RB	5-11	200	3/2/67	Texas Tech	Fort Worth, Tex.	D5c
Gregory, Morgan	WR	5-11	185	4/8/68	Nebraska	Denver, Colo.	FA
Hauk, Tim	S	5-11	185	12/20/66	Montana	Big Timbers, Mont.	FA
Hodson, Tommy	QB	6-3	195	1/28/67	Louisiana State	Matthews, La.	D3
Hutson, Brian (1)	S	6-1	198	2/20/65	Mississippi State	Jackson, Miss.	FA
Jackson, Charles	DE	6-4	280	8/4/66	Jackson State	Miami, Fla.	FA
Landry, Anthony	RB	5-9	200	10/28/66	Stephen F. Austin	Jasper, Tex.	D10
McMurtry, Greg	WR	6-2	207	10/15/67	Michigan	Brockton, Mass.	D4
Melander, Jon	T	6-7	280	12/27/66	Minnesota	Fridley, Minn.	D5b
Robinson, Junior	CB	5-9	181	2/3/68	East Carolina	High Point, N.C.	D5a
Rose, Blaine	G	6-5	271	6/13/66	Maryland	Hammondsville, Ohio	D12b
Singleton, Chris	LB	6-2	247	2/20/67	Arizona	Parsippany, N.J.	D1a
Smith, Sean	DE	6-7	280	5/29/67	Georgia Tech	Cincinnati, Ohio	D11
Stephens, Mac	LB	6-3	217	1/21/68	Minnesota	Akron, Ohio	FA
Tardits, Richard (1)	LB	6-2	218	7/30/65	Georgia	Biarritz, France	FA
Warner, Kirk	TE	6-4	225	11/24/67	Georgia	Cochran, Ga.	FA
Williams, Chris	NT	6-3	309	11/23/68	American International	Brockton, Mass.	FA
Zackery, Tony	S	6-2	195	11/20/66	Washington	Seattle, Wash.	FA

The term NFL Rookie is defined as a player who is in his first season of professional football and has not been on the roster of another professional football team for any regular-season or postseason games. A Rookie is designated by an "R" on NFL rosters. Players who have been active in another professional football league or players who have NFL experience, including either preseason training camp or being on an active roster for fewer than three regular-season or post-season games, are termed NFL First-Year Players. An NFL First-Year Player is designated by a "1" on NFL rosters. Thereafter, a player on an NFL active roster for at least three regular-season or postseason games is credited with an additional year of NFL playing experience.

NOTES

_____

_____

_____

_____

_____

_____

_____

_____

_____

Jimmy Raye, offensive coordinator, quarterbacks; born March 26, 1946, Fayetteville, N.C., lives in Foxboro, Mass. Quarterback Michigan State 1965-67. Pro defensive back Philadelphia Eagles 1969. College coach: Michigan State 1971-75, Wyoming 1976. Pro coach: San Francisco 49ers 1977, Detroit Lions 1978-79, Atlanta Falcons 1980-82, 1987-89, Los Angeles Rams 1983-84, Tampa Bay Buccaneers 1985-86, joined Patriots in 1990.

Jerry Simmons, strength and conditioning; born June 15, 1954, Elkhart, Kan., lives in Wrentham, Mass. Linebacker Fort Hays State 1976-77. No pro playing experience. College coach: Fort Hays State 1978, Clemson 1980, Rice 1981-82, Southern California 1983-87. Pro coach: Joined Patriots in 1988.

Charlie Sumner, defensive coordinator, defensive backs; born October 19, 1930, Radford, Va., lives in Foxboro, Mass. Quarterback-running back William & Mary 1952-54. Pro defensive back Chicago Bears 1955-60, Minnesota Vikings 1961-62. Pro coach: Oakland-Los Angeles Raiders 1963-68, 1979-83, 1987-88, Pittsburgh Steelers 1969-72, New England Patriots 1973-78, Oakland Invaders (USFL) 1985 (head coach), rejoined Patriots in 1990.

Richard Wood, receivers; born February 2, 1936, Lanett, Ala., lives in North Attleboro, Mass. Quarterback Auburn 1956-59. Pro quarterback Baltimore Colts 1960-61, San Diego Chargers 1962, Denver Broncos 1962, New York Jets 1963-64, Oakland Raiders 1965, Miami Dolphins 1966. College coach: Georgia 1967-68, Mississippi 1971-73, Auburn 1986. Pro coach: Oakland Raiders 1969-70, Cleveland Browns 1974, New Orleans Saints 1976-77, Atlanta Falcons 1978-82, Philadelphia Eagles 1983, Kansas City Chiefs 1987-88, joined Patriots in 1989.

American Football Conference
Eastern Division

Team Colors: Kelly Green and White

1000 Fulton Avenue
Hempstead, New York 11550
Telephone: (516) 538-6600

Club Officials

Chairman of the Board: Leon Hess
President: Steve Gutman
Vice President & General Manager:
  Dick Steinberg
Pro Personnel Director: Jim Royer
Talent Scouts: Joe Collins, Don Grammer,
  Daryl Gross, Sid Hall, Ron Nay,
  Marv Sunderland
College Scouting Assistant: John Griffin
Director of Public Relations: Frank Ramos
Director of Promotions: Ron Cohen
Public Relations Assistant: Eileen Walker
Public Relations Assistant: Brooks Thomas
Director of Operations: Mike Kensil
Director of Business Relations: Bob Parente
Ticket Manager: Gerry Parravano
Video Director: Jim Pons
Assistant Video Director: John Seiter
Trainer: Bob Reese
Assistant Trainers: Pepper Burruss, Joe Patten
Equipment Manager: Bill Hampton
Assistant Equipment Managers: Bill Hampton, Jr.,
  Mickey Rendine

Stadium: Giants Stadium • **Capacity:** 76,891
  East Rutherford, New Jersey 07073

Playing Surface: AstroTurf

Training Center: 1000 Fulton Avenue
  Hempstead, New York 11550
  (516) 538-6600

1990 Schedule

Preseason
Aug. 11	at Philadelphia	7:30
Aug. 18	at Kansas City	7:00
Aug. 25	at New York Giants	8:00
Aug. 30	at Tampa Bay	7:00

Regular Season
Sept. 9	at Cincinnati	4:00
Sept. 16	**Cleveland**	1:00
Sept. 24	**Buffalo** (Monday)	9:00
Sept. 30	at New England	4:00
Oct. 7	at Miami	1:00
Oct. 14	**San Diego**	1:00
Oct. 21	at Buffalo	1:00
Oct. 28	at Houston	12:00
Nov. 4	**Dallas**	1:00
Nov. 11	**Miami**	1:00
Nov. 18	at Indianapolis	4:00
Nov. 25	**Pittsburgh**	4:00
Dec. 2	at San Diego	1:00
Dec. 9	**Open Date**	
Dec. 16	**Indianapolis**	1:00
Dec. 23	**New England**	1:00
Dec. 30	at Tampa Bay	4:00

Jets Coaching History

New York Titans 1960-62
(200-238-8)
1960-61	Sammy Baugh	14-14-0
1962	Clyde (Bulldog) Turner	5-9-0
1963-73	Weeb Ewbank	73-78-6
1974-75	Charley Winner*	9-14-0
1975	Ken Shipp	1-4-0
1976	Lou Holtz**	3-10-0
1976	Mike Holovak	0-1-0
1977-82	Walt Michaels	41-49-1
1983-89	Joe Walton	54-59-1

*Released after nine games in 1975
**Resigned after 13 games in 1976

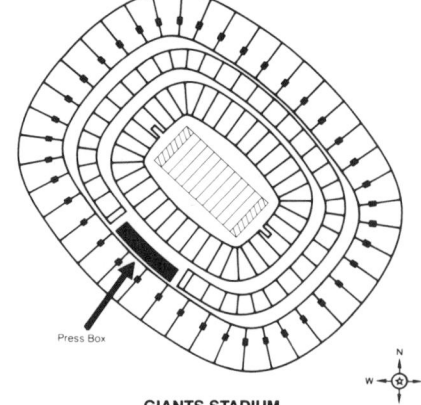

Press Box

GIANTS STADIUM

Record Holders

Individual Records—Career
Category	Name	Performance
Rushing (Yds.)	Freeman McNeil, 1981-89	7,146
Passing (Yds.)	Joe Namath, 1965-1976	27,057
Passing (TDs)	Joe Namath, 1965-1976	170
Receiving (No.)	Don Maynard, 1960-1972	627
Receiving (Yds.)	Don Maynard, 1960-1972	11,732
Interceptions	Bill Baird, 1963-69	34
Punting (Avg.)	Curley Johnson, 1961-68	42.8
Punt Return (Avg.)	Dick Christy, 1961-63	16.2
Kickoff Return (Avg.)	Bobby Humphery, 1984-89	22.8
Field Goals	Pat Leahy, 1974-1989	255
Touchdowns (Tot.)	Don Maynard, 1960-1972	88
Points	Pat Leahy, 1974-1989	1,261

Individual Records—Single Season
Category	Name	Performance
Rushing (Yds.)	Freeman McNeil, 1985	1,331
Passing (Yds.)	Joe Namath, 1967	4,007
Passing (TDs)	Al Dorow, 1960	26
	Joe Namath, 1967	26
Receiving (No.)	Al Toon, 1988	93
Receiving (Yds.)	Don Maynard, 1967	1,434
Interceptions	Dainard Paulson, 1964	12
Punting (Avg.)	Curley Johnson, 1965	45.3
Punt Return (Avg.)	Dick Christy, 1961	21.3
Kickoff Return (Avg.)	Bobby Humphery, 1984	30.7
Field Goals	Jim Turner, 1968	34
Touchdowns (Tot.)	Art Powell, 1960	14
	Don Maynard, 1965	14
	Emerson Boozer, 1972	14
Points	Jim Turner, 1968	145

Individual Records—Single Game
Category	Name	Performance
Rushing (Yds.)	Freeman McNeil, 9-15-85	192
Passing (Yds.)	Joe Namath, 9-24-72	496
Passing (TDs)	Joe Namath, 9-24-72	6
Receiving (No.)	Clark Gaines, 9-21-80	17
Receiving (Yds.)	Don Maynard, 11-17-68	228
Interceptions	Many times	3
	Last time by Erik McMillan, 10-23-88	
Field Goals	Jim Turner, 11-3-68	6
	Bobby Howfield, 12-3-72	6
Touchdowns (Tot.)	Wesley Walker, 9-21-86	4
Points	Jim Turner, 11-3-68	19
	Pat Leahy, 9-16-84	19

1989 Team Record
Preseason (2-2)

Date	Result		Opponents
8/12	L	27-28	vs. Green Bay at Milwaukee
8/20	W	19-10	vs. Philadelphia at Raleigh, N.C.
8/26	L	17-21	at N.Y. Giants
9/1	W	15-13	at Kansas City (OT)
		78-72	

Regular Season (4-12)

Date	Result		Opponents	Att.
9/10	L	24-27	New England	64,541
9/17	L	24-38	at Cleveland	73,516
9/24	W	40-33	at Miami	65,908
10/1	L	10-17	Indianapolis	65,542
10/9	L	7-14	L.A. Raiders	68,040
10/15	L	14-29	at New Orleans	59,521
10/22	L	3-34	at Buffalo	76,811
10/29	L	10-23	San Francisco	62,805
11/5	W	27-26	at New England	53,366
11/12	L	23-31	Miami	65,923
11/19	L	10-27	at Indianapolis	58,236
11/26	W	27- 7	Atlanta	40,429
12/3	W	20-17	at San Diego	38,954
12/10	L	0-13	Pittsburgh	41,037
12/17	L	14-38	at L.A. Rams	53,063
12/23	L	0-37	Buffalo	21,148

(OT) Overtime

Score by Periods

Jets	37	74	60	82	0	—	253
Opponents	53	133	119	106	0	—	411

Attendance
Home 429,465   Away 479,375   Total 908,840
Single-game home record, 74,975 (12-2-84)
Single-season home record, 541,832 (1985)

1989 Team Statistics

	Jets	Opp.
Total First Downs	292	328
Rushing	91	127
Passing	189	178
Penalty	12	23
Third Down: Made/Att.	68/210	82/213
Third Down: Pct.	32.4	38.5
Fourth Down: Made/Att.	7/15	7/16
Fourth Down: Pct.	46.7	43.8
Total Net Yards	5011	5994
Avg. Per Game	313.2	374.6
Total Plays	1032	1059
Avg. Per Play	4.9	5.7
Net Yards Rushing	1596	2136
Avg. Per Game	99.8	133.5
Total Rushes	400	517
Net Yards Passing	3415	3858
Avg. Per Game	213.4	241.1
Sacked/Yards Lost	62/477	28/177
Gross Yards	3892	4035
Att./Completions	570/338	514/282
Completion Pct.	59.3	54.9
Had Intercepted	24	15
Punts/Avg.	87/39.4	69/39.8
Net Punting Avg.	35.5	33.7
Penalties/Yards Lost	116/953	90/675
Fumbles/Ball Lost	32/17	32/9
Touchdowns	30	50
Rushing	11	16
Passing	14	31
Returns	5	3
Avg. Time of Possession	29:16	30:44

1989 Individual Statistics

Scoring

	TD R	TD P	TD Rt	PAT	FG	Saf	TP
Leahy	0	0	0	29/30	14/21	0	71
Vick	5	2	0	0/0	0/0	0	42
Hector	3	2	0	0/0	0/0	0	30
Townsell	0	5	0	0/0	0/0	0	30
McMillan	0	0	3	0/0	0/0	0	18
McNeil	2	1	0	0/0	0/0	0	18
Toon	0	2	0	0/0	0/0	0	12
Burkett	0	1	0	0/0	0/0	0	6
Dressel, K.C.-Jets	0	1	0	0/0	0/0	0	6
Hasty	0	0	1	0/0	0/0	0	6
Neubert	0	1	0	0/0	0/0	0	6
Prokop	1	0	0	0/0	0/0	0	6
Radachowsky	0	0	1	0/0	0/0	0	6
Jets	11	14	5	29/30	14/21	1	253
Opponents	16	31	3	46/50	21/31	1	411

Passing

	Att.	Comp.	Yds.	Pct.	TD	Int.	Tkld.	Rate
O'Brien	477	288	3346	60.4	12	18	50/391	74.3
Eason, N.E.-Jets	141	79	1016	56.0	4	6	17/120	70.5
Eason, Jets	36	22	255	61.1	1	2	7/42	68.6
Ryan	30	15	153	50.0	1	3	2/26	36.5
Mackey	25	11	125	44.0	0	1	3/18	42.9
Malone	2	2	13	100.0	0	0	0/0	93.8
Jets	570	338	3892	59.3	14	24	62/477	70.6
Opponents	514	282	4035	54.9	31	15	28/177	88.5

Rushing

	Att.	Yds.	Avg.	LG	TD
Hector	177	702	4.0	24	3
Vick	112	434	3.9	39t	5
McNeil	80	352	4.4	19t	2
Brown	12	63	5.3	17	0
O'Brien	9	18	2.0	5	0
Prokop	1	17	17.0	17t	1
Epps	1	14	14.0	14	0
Harper	1	3	3.0	3	0
Mackey	2	3	1.5	5	0
Malone	1	0	0.0	0	0
Ryan	1	−1	−1.0	−1	0
Eason, N.E.-Jets	3	−2	−0.7	0	0
Eason, Jets	1	0	0.0	0	0
Burkett	1	−4	−4.0	−4	0
Lageman	1	−5	−5.0	−5	0
Jets	400	1596	4.0	39t	11
Opponents	517	2136	4.1	40t	16

Receiving

	No.	Yds.	Avg.	LG	TD
Toon	63	693	11.0	37t	2
Townsell	45	787	17.5	63t	5
Hector	38	330	8.7	32	2
Vick	34	241	7.1	21	2
McNeil	31	310	10.0	25t	1
Shuler	29	322	11.1	22	0
Neubert	28	302	10.8	35t	1
Burkett, Buff.-Jets	24	298	12.4	30	1
Burkett, Jets	21	278	13.2	30	1
Dressel, K.C.-Jets	12	191	15.9	49t	1
Dressel, Jets	3	55	18.3	43	0
Griggs	9	112	12.4	23	0
Werner	8	115	14.4	36	0
Epps	8	108	13.5	21	0
Walker	8	89	11.1	31	0
Harper	7	127	18.1	48	0
Brown	4	10	2.5	6	0
Dunn	2	13	6.5	8	0
Jets	338	3892	11.5	63t	14
Opponents	282	4035	14.3	78t	31

Interceptions

	No.	Yds.	Avg.	LG	TD
McMillan	6	180	30.0	92t	1
Hasty	5	62	12.4	34t	1
Booty	1	13	13.0	13	0
Mersereau	1	4	4.0	4	0
Gordon	1	2	2.0	2	0
Glenn	1	0	0.0	0	0
Jets	15	261	17.4	92t	2
Opponents	24	282	11.8	87t	2

Punting

	No.	Yds.	Avg.	In 20	LG
Prokop	87	3426	39.4	29	76
Jets	87	3426	39.4	29	76
Opponents	69	2746	39.8	18	59

Punt Returns

	No.	FC	Yds.	Avg.	LG	TD
Townsell	33	12	299	9.1	30	0
Jets	33	12	299	9.1	30	0
Opponents	34	22	257	7.6	49t	1

Kickoff Returns

	No.	Yds.	Avg.	LG	TD
Townsell	34	653	19.2	69	0
Humphery	24	414	17.3	52	0
Epps	9	154	17.1	43	0
Dixon	4	67	16.8	21	0
Nichols	2	9	4.5	7	0
Washington	1	11	11.0	11	0
Byrd	1	1	1.0	1	0
Jets	75	1309	17.5	69	0
Opponents	47	1029	21.9	49	0

Sacks

	No.
Byrd	7.0
Lageman	4.5
Nichols	4.0
Clifton	2.0
Frase	2.0
McMillan	2.0
Stallworth	2.0
Washington	1.5
Gordon	1.0
Lyons	1.0
Glenn	0.5
Mersereau	0.5
Jets	28.0
Opponents	62.0

1990 Draft Choices

Round	Name	Pos.	College
1.	Blair Thomas	RB	Penn State
2.	Reggie Rembert	WR	West Virginia
3.	Tony Stargell	DB	Tennessee State
4.	Troy Taylor	QB	California
5.	Tony Savage	DT	Washington State
	Robert McWright	DB	Texas Christian
6.	Terance Mathis	WR	New Mexico
7.	Dwayne White	G	Alcorn State
	Basil Proctor	LB	West Virginia
8.	Roger Duffy	C	Penn State
9.	Dale Dawkins	WR	Miami
10.	Brad Quast	LB	Iowa
11.	Derrick Kelson	DB	Purdue
12.	Darrell Davis	LB	Texas Christian

New York Jets 1990 Veteran Roster

No.	Name	Pos.	Ht.	Wt.	Birth-date	NFL Exp.	College	Hometown	How Acq.	'89 Games/ Starts
54	†Benson, Troy	LB	6-2	235	7/30/63	5	Pittsburgh	Altoona, Pa.	D5a-'85	16/15
42	†Booty, John	CB-S	6-0	179	10/9/65	3	Texas Christian	Carthage, Tex.	D10-'88	9/1
80	Boyer, Mark	TE	6-4	252	9/16/62	6	Southern California	Huntington Beach, Calif.	PB(Ind)-'90#	16/5*
29	Brown, A.B.	RB	5-9	212	12/4/65	2	West Virginia	Salem, N.J.	D8-'89	16/0
87	Burkett, Chris	WR	6-4	210	8/21/62	6	Jackson State	Collins, Miss.	FA-'89	15/5*
90	Byrd, Dennis	DE	6-5	270	10/5/66	2	Tulsa	Mustang, Okla.	D2-'89	16/0
31	Byrum, Carl	RB	6-0	237	6/29/62	4	Mississippi Valley State	Southaven, Miss.	FA-'90	0*
66	Cadigan, Dave	G-T	6-4	280	4/6/65	3	Southern California	Newport Beach, Calif.	D1-'88	13/4
59	Clifton, Kyle	LB	6-4	236	8/23/62	7	Texas Christian	Bridgeport, Tex.	D3-'84	16/16
61	Criswell, Jeff	T	6-7	290	3/7/64	4	Graceland	Searsboro, Iowa	FA-'88	16/16
49	Curtis, Travis	S	5-10	180	9/27/65	4	West Virginia	Potomac, Md.	PB(Minn)-'90#	16/11*
84	†Dressel, Chris	TE	6-4	245	2/7/61	6	Stanford	Placentia, Calif.	W(KC)-'89	15/0*
11	Eason, Tony	QB	6-4	212	10/8/59	8	Illinois	Walnut Grove, Calif.	W(NE)-'89	5/5*
45	Egu, Patrick	RB	5-11	205	2/20/67	2	Nevada-Reno	Richmond, Calif.	PB(NE)-'90#	7/0*
91	Frase, Paul	DE-DT	6-5	267	5/5/65	3	Syracuse	Barrington, N.H.	D6-'88	16/14
55	Gordon, Alex	LB	6-5	246	9/14/64	4	Cincinnati	Jacksonville, Fla.	D2-'87	16/15
79	†Haight, Mike	G	6-4	281	10/6/62	5	Iowa	Dyersville, Iowa	D1-'86	13/13
40	Hasty, James	CB	6-0	197	5/23/65	3	Washington State	Seattle, Wash.	D3b-'88	16/16
34	†Hector, Johnny	RB	5-11	202	11/26/60	8	Texas A&M	New Iberia, La.	D2-'83	15/9
28	†Howard, Carl	CB-S	6-2	190	9/20/61	7	Rutgers	Irvington, N.J.	FA-'85	15/0
81	Kelly, Pat	TE	6-6	252	10/29/65	3	Syracuse	Webster, N.Y.	PB(Den)-'90#	16/1*
57	Kohlbrand, Joe	LB	6-4	242	3/18/63	6	Miami	Merritt Island, Fla.	PB(NO)-'90#	16/0*
38	Konecny, Mark	RB	6-0	200	4/23/63	3	Alma	Muskegon, Mich.	PB(Phil)-'90#	0*
56	Lageman, Jeff	LB	6-5	250	7/18/67	2	Virginia	Great Falls, Va.	D1-'89	16/15
5	Leahy, Pat	K	6-0	196	3/19/51	17	St. Louis	St. Louis, Mo.	FA-'74	16/0
93	Lyons, Marty	DE-DT	6-5	269	1/15/57	12	Alabama	St. Petersburg, Fla.	D1-'79	10/10
15	Mackey, Kyle	QB	6-3	216	3/2/63	5	East Texas State	Alpine, Tex.	FA-'88	4/1
64	Matich, Trevor	C-G-T	6-4	270	10/9/61	6	Brigham Young	Sacramento, Calif.	PB(Det)-'90#	11/0*
68	McElroy, Reggie	T	6-6	276	3/4/60	8	West Texas State	Beaumont, Tex.	D2-'82	15/15
22	McMillan, Erik	S	6-2	197	5/3/65	3	Missouri	Silver Spring, Md.	D3a-'88	16/16
24	†McNeil, Freeman	RB	5-11	212	4/22/59	10	UCLA	Carson, Calif.	D1-'81	11/7
94	Mersereau, Scott	DT-DE	6-3	280	4/8/65	4	Southern Connecticut	Riverhead, N.Y.	FA-'87	16/15
36	Miano, Rich	S	6-0	200	9/3/62	5	Hawaii	Honolulu, Hawaii	D6b-'85	2/2
72	Miller, Brett	T	6-7	300	10/2/58	8	Iowa	Glendale, Calif.	PB(SD)-'90#	15/11*
51	Mott, Joe	LB	6-4	253	10/6/65	2	Iowa	Tipton, Iowa	D3-'89	16/0
95	Naposki, Eric	LB	6-2	230	12/20/66	2	Connecticut	Eastchester, N.Y.	FA-'90	2/0*
86	Neubert, Keith	TE	6-6	248	9/13/64	2	Nebraska	Fort Atkinson, Wis.	D8-'88	16/2
77	†Nichols, Gerald	DT-DE	6-2	267	2/10/64	4	Florida State	St. Louis, Mo.	D7-'87	16/0
7	O'Brien, Ken	QB	6-4	206	11/27/60	8	California-Davis	Sacramento, Calif.	D1-'83	15/12
17	Parker, Carl	WR	6-2	201	2/5/65	3	Vanderbilt	Valdosta, Ga.	FA-'90	3/0
6	Prokop, Joe	P	6-2	224	7/7/60	5	Cal Poly-Pomona	White Bear Lake, Minn.	FA-'88	16/0
25	Radachowsky, George	S	5-11	195	9/7/62	6	Boston College	Danbury, Conn.	FA-'87	16/2
71	Rehder, Tom	T-G	6-7	280	1/27/65	3	Notre Dame	Santa Maria, Calif.	PB(NE)-'90#	16/0*
82	Shuler, Mickey	TE	6-3	231	8/21/56	13	Penn State	Enola, Pa.	D3-'78	7/7
74	†Singer, Curt	T	6-5	279	11/4/61	4	Tennessee	Aliquippa, Pa.	FA-'89	6/1
96	Stallworth, Ron	DE	6-5	262	2/25/66	2	Auburn	Pensacola, Fla.	D4-'89	16/9
53	†Sweeney, Jim	C	6-4	270	8/8/62	7	Pittsburgh	Pittsburgh, Pa.	D2a-'84	16/16
88	Toon, Al	WR	6-4	205	4/30/63	6	Wisconsin	Newport News, Va.	D1-'85	11/10
83	Townsell, JoJo	WR-KR	5-9	180	11/4/60	6	UCLA	Reno, Nev.	D3-'83	16/16
43	Vick, Roger	RB	6-3	235	8/11/64	4	Texas A&M	Tomball, Tex.	D1-'87	16/10
21	Washington, Brian	S	6-1	220	9/10/65	2	Nebraska	Richmond, Va.	W(Clev)-'89	0*
97	Washington, Marvin	DT-DE	6-6	260	10/22/65	2	Idaho	Dallas, Tex.	D6a-'89	16/0
33	Williams, Terry	CB	5-11	204	10/14/65	3	Bethune-Cookman	Homestead, Fla.	D2-'88	3/0
76	Withycombe, Mike	T-G	6-5	300	11/18/64	3	Fresno State	Lemoore, Calif.	D5-'88	5/1
63	Zawatson, Dave	G-T	6-5	275	4/13/66	2	California	Concord, Calif.	PB(Chi)-'90#	4/0*

* Boyer played 16 games with Indianapolis in '89; Burkett played 2 games with Buffalo; 13 with Jets; Byrum last active with Buffalo in '88; Curtis played 16 games with Minnesota; Dressel played 7 games with Kansas City, 8 with New York Jets; Eason played 3 games with New England, 2 with New York Jets; Egu played 7 games with New England; Kelly played 16 games with Denver; Kohlbrand played 16 games with New Orleans; Konecny missed '89 season due to injury; Matich played 11 games with Detroit; Miller played 15 games with San Diego; Naposki played 1 game with New England, 1 with Indianapolis; Rehder played 16 games with New England; B. Washington last active with Cleveland in '88; Zawatson played 4 games with Chicago.

† Option playout; subject to developments.

Plan B unconditional free agent.

Traded—CB-KR Bobby Humphery to Los Angeles Rams.

Players lost through Plan B (9): LB Adam Bob (TB; 5 games in '89), CB Kerry Glenn (Mia; 14), TE Billy Griggs (Pitt; 4), CB-S Leander Knight (Hou; 13), LB Kevin McArthur (Wash; 9), CB-S Stevon Moore (Mia; 0), LB Ken Rose (Clev; 15), C-G Adam Schreiber (GB; 16), TE Greg Werner (Phil; 10).

Also played with Jets in '89—G Dan Alexander (14 games), WR Sanjay Beach (1), LB Timmy Cofield (6), WR-KR Titus Dixon (3), TE K.D. Dunn (1), WR-KR Phillip Epps (10), RB Nuu Faaola (2), WR-KR Michael Harper (6), QB Mark Malone (1), CB Michael Mitchell (5), QB Pat Ryan (7), WR Wesley Walker (6).

COACHING STAFF

Head Coach, Bruce Coslet

Pro Career: Begins first year as head coach of the Jets. Became eighth full-time head coach of the team on February 6, 1990. Entered pro coaching ranks as tight ends and special teams coach with the San Francisco 49ers in 1980. Joined the Cincinnati Bengals in 1981 as the tight ends and special teams coach and also served in that capacity in 1982. In 1983, was given the added responsibility of the Bengals' passing game. Tutored the Cincinnati receivers in 1984-85 before being named the team's offensive coordinator (1986-89). During that stretch, the Bengals had the NFL's top-rated offense twice (1986 and 1989), and led the AFC in total offense in three of the last four years (1986, 1988, and 1989). Was a key factor in the Bengals' trip to Super Bowl XXIII. Currently is the second youngest head coach in the NFL (two-and-a-half months older than Art Shell of the Raiders). Played tight end for the Cincinnati Bengals 1969-76.

Background: Played tight end at the University of the Pacific from 1965-67.

Personal: Born August 5, 1946, in Oakdale, Calif. Bruce and his wife, Kathy, live in Long Island, and have two children—J.J. and Amy.

Assistant Coaches

Larry Beightol offensive line, born November 21, 1942, Morrisdale, Pa., lives in Long Island. Guard-linebacker Catawba College 1961-63. No pro playing experience. College coach: William & Mary 1968-71, North Carolina State 1972-75, Auburn 1976, Arkansas 1977-78, 1980-82, Louisiana Tech 1979 (head coach). Missouri 1983-84. Pro coach: Atlanta Falcons 1985-86, Tampa Bay Buccaneers 1987-88, San Diego Chargers 1989, joined Jets in 1990.

Kippy Brown, running backs, born March 6, 1955, Sweetwater, Tenn., lives in Long Island. Quarterback Memphis State 1973-77. No pro playing experience. College coach: Memphis State 1978-80, Louisville 1981, Tennessee 1982-89. Pro coach: Joined Jets in 1990.

Pete Carroll, defensive coordinator, born September 15, 1951, San Francisco, Calif., lives in Long Island. Defensive back Pacific 1969-72. No pro playing experience. College coach: Arkansas 1977, Iowa State 1978, Ohio State 1979, North Carolina State 1980-82, Pacific 1983. Pro coach: Buffalo Bills 1984, Minnesota Vikings 1985-89, joined Jets in 1990.

Joe Daniels, quarterbacks, born November 15, 1942, Pittsburgh, Pa., lives in Long Island. Running back Slippery Rock 1961-64. No pro playing experience. College coach: Boston College 1968-77, West Virginia 1978-79, Pittsburgh 1980-82, Akron 1989. Pro coach: Cleveland Browns 1983-84, Buffalo Bills 1986, joined Jets in 1990.

Ed Donatell, defensive assistant, secondary, born February 4, 1957, Akron, Ohio, lives in Long Island. Safety Glenville State 1975-78. No pro playing experience. College coach: Kent State 1979-80, Washington 1981-82, Pacific 1983-85, Idaho 1986-88, Cal State-Fullerton 1989. Pro coach: Joined Jets in 1990.

Foge Fazio, special teams coordinator, born February 22, 1939, Dawmont, W. Va., lives in Long Island. Linebacker-center Pittsburgh 1957-60. Pro linebacker Boston Patriots 1961. College coach: Boston University 1967, Harvard 1968, Pittsburgh 1969-72, 1977-81 (head coach). Cincinnati 1973-76, Notre Dame 1986-87. Pro coach: Atlanta Falcons 1988-89, joined Jets in 1990.

Monte Kiffin, linebackers, born February 29, 1940, Lexington, Neb., lives in Long Island. Defensive end Nebraska 1961-63. Pro defensive end Winnipeg Blue Bombers (CFL) 1965-66. College coach: Nebraska 1965-76, Arkansas 1977-79, North Carolina State 1980-82 (head coach). Pro coach: Green Bay Packers 1983, Buffalo Bills 1984-85, Minnesota Vikings 1985-89, joined Jets in 1990.

New York Jets 1990 First-Year Roster

Name	Pos.	Ht.	Wt.	Birth-date	College	Hometown	How Acq.
Allen, Donnie	WR	6-0	155	5/10/67	Georgia Southern	Macon, Ga.	FA
Antrum, Glenn (1)	WR	5-11	175	2/3/66	Connecticut	Ansonia, Conn.	FA
Baxter, Brad (1)	RB	6-1	231	5/5/67	Alabama State	Slocomb, Ala.	FA-'89
Bell, Grantis (1)	WR-KR	5-9	150	8/11/66	West Virginia	Oakland Park, Fla.	FA
Boone, Randall (1)	S	6-3	196	2/14/68	Georgia Southern	Uvaldo, Ga.	FA
Burman, Jon (1)	T	6-8	300	6/7/66	Illinois	Carmel, Ind.	FA-'89
Davis, Darrell (1)	LB	6-2	255	3/10/66	Texas Christian	Midland, Tex.	D12
Dawkins, Dale	WR	6-1	190	10/30/66	Miami	Vero Beach, Fla.	D9
Douglas, Demetrious	LB	6-2	221	6/8/67	Georgia	College Park, Ga.	FA
Duffy, Roger	C	6-3	285	7/16/67	Penn State	Canton, Ohio	D8
Ebubedike, Victor	RB	6-0	214	1/2/66	Vauxhall, England	London, England	FA
Hall, Michael	CB	6-1	193	1/14/65	New Mexico State	Oklahoma City, Okla.	FA
Kelson, Derrick	CB	6-0	190	5/14/68	Purdue	Warren, Ohio	D11
Mathis, Terance	WR-KR	5-10	170	6/7/67	New Mexico	Stone Mountain, Ga.	D6
Mayes, Michael (1)	CB	5-10	182	8/17/66	Louisiana State	DeRidder, La.	FA
McNeil, Emanuel (1)	NT	6-3	285	6/9/67	Tennessee-Martin	Richmond, Va.	FA
McWright, Robert	CB	5-9	185	11/10/65	Texas Christian	Dallas, Tex.	D5b
Moore, James	WR	5-11	170	5/31/66	Hofstra	Hempstead, N.Y.	FA
Oliver, Jeff (1)	T-G	6-4	292	7/28/65	Boston College	Delhi, N.Y.	FA-'89
Parker, Anthony (1)	CB	5-10	181	2/11/66	Arizona State	Tempe, Ariz.	FA
Proctor, Basil	LB	6-4	230	10/6/66	West Virginia	Miami, Fla.	D7b
Quast, Brad	LB	6-1	245	6/5/68	Iowa	Forest View, Ill.	D10
Rembert, Reggie	WR	6-4	200	12/25/66	West Virginia	Okeechobee, Fla.	D2
Savage, Tony	NT	6-3	295	7/7/67	Washington State	San Francisco, Calif.	D5a
Smith, Irvin (1)	CB-S	5-10	181	3/12/67	Maryland	Poolesville, Md.	FA
Snyder, Brent (1)	QB	6-3	230	6/4/66	Utah State	Joliet, Ill.	FA
Stargell, Tony	CB	5-11	190	8/7/66	Tennessee State	LaGrange, Ga.	D3
Taylor, Troy	QB	6-4	205	4/5/68	California	Sacramento, Calif.	D4
Thomas, Blair	RB	5-10	195	10/7/67	Penn State	Philadelphia, Pa.	D1
Vinson, Phil	WR	6-3	190	1/28/67	New Mexico State	Los Angeles, Calif.	FA
Weaver, Neil	K	5-7	170	9/27/68	Panhandle State	Oklahoma City, Okla.	FA
White, Dwayne	G	6-2	315	2/10/67	Alcorn State	Philadelphia, Pa.	D7a
Williams, Patrick	S	6-2	196	12/17/66	Arkansas	McGeehee, Ark.	FA

The term NFL Rookie is defined as a player who is in his first season of professional football and has not been on the roster of another professional football team for any regular-season or postseason games. A Rookie is designated by an "R" on NFL rosters. Players who have been active in another professional football league or players who have NFL experience, including either preseason training camp or being on an active roster for fewer than three regular-season or postseason games, are termed NFL First-Year Players. An NFL First-Year Player is designated by a "1" on NFL rosters. Thereafter, a player on an NFL active roster for at least three regular-season or postseason games is credited with an additional year of NFL playing experience.

NOTES

_____
_____
_____
_____
_____
_____
_____
_____
_____
_____
_____

Greg Mackrides, strength and conditioning, born July 9, 1954, Philadelphia, Pa., lives in Long Island. No pro playing experience. College coach: Villanova 1985-86, Fairfield 1986-88. 1988 U.S. Olympic Wrestling team 1988, U.S. Pan Am and World touring teams 1986-88. Pro coach: New York Knicks (NBA) 1987-90, joined Jets in 1990.

Chip Myers, receivers, born July 9, 1945, Panama City, Fla., lives in Long Island. Receiver Northwest Oklahoma 1964-66. Pro receiver San Francisco 49ers 1967, Cincinnati Bengals 1969-76. College coach: Illinois 1980-82. Pro coach: Tampa Bay Buccaneers 1983-84, Indianapolis Colts 1985-88, joined Jets in 1990.

Greg Robinson, defensive line, born October 9, 1951, Los Angeles, Calif., lives in Long Island. Linebacker-tight end Pacific 1972-73. No pro playing experience. College coach: Cal State-Fullerton 1977-79, North Carolina State 1980-81, UCLA 1982-89. Pro coach: joined Jets in 1990.

Bob Wylie, offensive assistant, tight ends, born February 16, 1951, Providence, R.I., lives in Long Island. Linebacker Colorado 1969-71. No pro playing experience. College coach: Brown 1980-82, Holy Cross 1983-84, Ohio University 1985-87, Colorado State 1988-89. Pro coach: Joined Jets in 1990.

PITTSBURGH STEELERS

American Football Conference Central Division

Team Colors: Black and Gold

Three Rivers Stadium
300 Stadium Circle
Pittsburgh, Pennsylvania 15212
Telephone: (412) 323-1200

Club Officials

President: Daniel M. Rooney
Vice President: John R. McGinley
Vice President: Arthur J. Rooney, Jr.
Director of Communications: Joe Gordon
Controller: Ralph Meacham
Chief Negotiator/Travel: James A. Boston
Business/Stadium Coordinator: Dan Ferens
Public Relations Director: Dan Edwards
Community Relations Coordinator: Pat Hanlon
Director of Player Personnel: Dick Haley
Director of Pro Personnel and Development:
  Tom Donahoe
College Scouting Coordinator: Tom Modrak
Talent Scout: Bob Schmitz
Talent Scout: Max McCartney
Talent Scout: Charles Bailey
Ticket Sales Manager: Geraldine R. Glenn
Office Manager/Computer: Jim Ellenberger
Trainers: Ralph Berlin, Francis Feld
Equipment Manager: Anthony Parisi

Stadium: Three Rivers Stadium •
  Capacity: 59,000
  300 Stadium Circle
  Pittsburgh, Pennsylvania 15212

Playing Surface: AstroTurf

Training Camp: St. Vincent College
  Latrobe, Pennsylvania 15650

1990 Schedule

Preseason
Aug. 9	vs. New England at Montreal	7:30
Aug. 17	at Washington	8:00
Aug. 25	at Dallas	8:00
Sept. 1	**Philadelphia**	9:00

Regular Season
Sept. 9	at Cleveland	4:00
Sept. 16	**Houston**	8:00
Sept. 23	at Los Angeles Raiders	1:00
Sept. 30	**Miami**	1:00
Oct. 7	**San Diego**	1:00
Oct. 14	at Denver	2:00
Oct. 21	at San Francisco	1:00
Oct. 29	**L.A. Rams** (Monday)	9:00
Nov. 4	**Atlanta**	1:00
Nov. 11	**Open Date**	
Nov. 18	at Cincinnati	8:00
Nov. 25	at New York Jets	4:00
Dec. 2	**Cincinnati**	1:00
Dec. 9	**New England**	1:00
Dec. 16	at New Orleans	12:00
Dec. 23	**Cleveland**	1:00
Dec. 30	at Houston	7:00

Steelers Coaching History

Pittsburgh Pirates 1933-40
(354-395-20)

1933	Forrest (Jap) Douds	3-6-2
1934	Luby DiMelio	2-10-0
1935-36	Joe Bach	10-14-0
1937-39	Johnny Blood (McNally)*	6-19-0
1939-40	Walt Kiesling	3-13-3
1941	Bert Bell**	0-2-0
	Aldo (Buff) Donelli***	0-5-0
1941-44	Walt Kiesling****	13-20-2
1945	Jim Leonard	2-8-0
1946-47	Jock Sutherland	13-10-1
1948-51	Johnny Michelosen	20-26-2
1952-53	Joe Bach	11-13-0
1954-56	Walt Kiesling	14-22-0
1957-64	Raymond (Buddy) Parker	51-47-6
1965	Mike Nixon	2-12-0
1966-68	Bill Austin	11-28-3
1969-89	Chuck Noll	193-140-1

*Released after three games in 1939
**Resigned after two games in 1941
***Released after five games in 1941
****Co-coach with Earle (Greasy) Neale in Philadelphia-
  Pittsburgh merger in 1943 and with Phil Handler in
  Chicago Cardinals-Pittsburgh merger in 1944

Record Holders
Individual Records—Career

Category	Name	Performance
Rushing (Yds.)	Franco Harris, 1972-1983	11,950
Passing (Yds.)	Terry Bradshaw, 1970-1983	27,989
Passing (TDs)	Terry Bradshaw, 1970-1983	212
Receiving (No.)	John Stallworth, 1974-1987	537
Receiving (Yds.)	John Stallworth, 1974-1987	8,723
Interceptions	Mel Blount, 1970-1983	57
Punting (Avg.)	Bobby Joe Green, 1960-61	45.7
Punt Return (Avg.)	Bobby Gage, 1949-1950	14.9
Kickoff Return (Avg.)	Lynn Chandnois, 1950-56	29.6
Field Goals	Gary Anderson, 1982-89	186
Touchdowns (Tot.)	Franco Harris, 1972-1983	100
Points	Gary Anderson, 1982-89	818

Individual Records—Single Season

Category	Name	Performance
Rushing (Yds.)	Franco Harris, 1975	1,246
Passing (Yds.)	Terry Bradshaw, 1979	3,724
Passing (TDs)	Terry Bradshaw, 1978	28
Receiving (No.)	John Stallworth, 1984	80
Receiving (Yds.)	John Stallworth, 1984	1,395
Interceptions	Mel Blount, 1975	11
Punting (Avg.)	Bobby Joe Green, 1961	47.0
Punt Return (Avg.)	Bobby Gage, 1949	16.0
Kickoff Return (Avg.)	Lynn Chandnois, 1952	35.2
Field Goals	Gary Anderson, 1985	33
Touchdowns (Tot.)	Louis Lipps, 1985	15
Points	Gary Anderson, 1985	139

Individual Records—Single Game

Category	Name	Performance
Rushing (Yds.)	John Fuqua, 12-20-70	218
Passing (Yds.)	Bobby Layne, 12-3-58	409
Passing (TDs)	Terry Bradshaw, 11-15-81	5
	Mark Malone, 9-8-85	5
Receiving (No.)	J.R. Wilburn, 10-22-67	12
Receiving (Yds.)	Buddy Dial, 10-22-61	235
Interceptions	Jack Butler, 12-13-53	*4
Field Goals	Gary Anderson, 10-23-88	6
Touchdowns (Tot.)	Ray Mathews, 10-17-54	4
	Roy Jefferson, 11-3-68	4
Points	Ray Mathews, 10-17-54	24
	Roy Jefferson, 11-3-68	24

*NFL Record

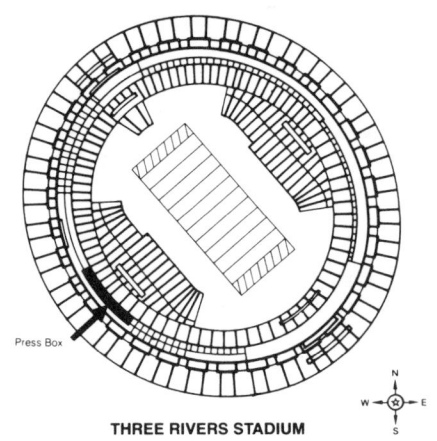

Press Box

THREE RIVERS STADIUM

1989 Team Record
Preseason (2-2)

Date	Result		Opponents
8/12	L	14-21	Washington
8/19	W	24-21	at Cleveland
8/26	L	14-38	at Philadelphia
9/2	W	13-10	at N.Y. Giants
		65-90	

Regular Season (9-7)

Date	Result		Opponents	Att.
9/10	L	0-51	Cleveland	57,928
9/17	L	10-41	at Cincinnati	53,885
9/24	W	27-14	Minnesota	50,744
10/1	W	23- 3	at Detroit	43,804
10/8	L	16-26	Cincinnati	52,785
10/15	W	17- 7	at Cleveland	78,840
10/22	L	0-27	at Houston	59,091
10/29	W	23-17	Kansas City	54,194
11/5	L	7-34	at Denver	74,739
11/12	L	0-20	Chicago	56,505
11/19	W	20-17	San Diego	44,203
11/26	W	34-14	at Miami	59,936
12/3	L	16-23	Houston	40,541
12/10	W	13- 0	at N.Y. Jets	41,037
12/17	W	28-10	New England	26,594
12/24	W	31-22	at Tampa Bay	29,690

Postseason (1-1)

Date	Result		Opponent	Att.
12/31	W	26-23	at Houston (OT)	59,406
1/7	L	23-24	at Denver	75,477

(OT) Overtime

Score by Periods

Steelers	57	91	72	45	0	—	265
Opponents	78	110	60	78	0	—	326

Attendance
Home 383,494   Away 441,022   Total 824,516
Single-game home record, 59,541 (9-30-85)
Single-season home record, 462,567 (1983)

1989 Team Statistics

	Steelers	Opp.
Total First Downs	244	323
Rushing.	106	112
Passing.	117	177
Penalty.	21	34
Third Down: Made/Att.	66/209	106/229
Third Down: Pct.	31.6	46.3
Fourth Down: Made/Att.	6/19	7/20
Fourth Down: Pct.	31.6	35.0
Total Net Yards	3996	5549
Avg. Per Game	249.8	346.8
Total Plays.	955	1077
Avg. Per Play	4.2	5.2
Net Yards Rushing	1818	2008
Avg. Per Game	113.6	125.5
Total Rushes	500	498
Net Yards Passing	2178	3541
Avg. Per Game	136.1	221.3
Sacked/Yards Lost	51/484	31/180
Gross Yards	2662	3721
Att./Completions	404/210	548/290
Completion Pct.	52.0	52.9
Had Intercepted	13	21
Punts/Avg.	83/40.6	69/40.5
Net Punting Avg.	34.1	33.8
Penalties/Yards Lost	116/986	96/785
Fumbles/Ball Lost	32/18	40/21
Touchdowns	29	38
Rushing.	17	16
Passing	10	17
Returns	2	5
Avg. Time of Possession.	28:50	31:10

1989 Individual Statistics

Scoring

	TD R	TD P	TD Rt	PAT	FG	Saf	TP
Anderson	0	0	0	28/28	21/30	0	91
Hoge	8	0	0	0/0	0/0	0	48
Lipps	1	5	0	0/0	0/0	0	36
Worley	5	0	0	0/0	0/0	0	30
Carter	1	3	0	0/0	0/0	0	24
Hill	0	1	0	0/0	0/0	0	6
Mularkey	0	1	0	0/0	0/0	0	6
Wallace	1	0	0	0/0	0/0	0	6
W. Williams	1	0	0	0/0	0/0	0	6
Woodruff	0	0	1	0/0	0/0	0	6
Woodson	0	0	1	0/0	0/0	0	6
Steelers	17	10	2	28/29	21/30	0	265
Opponents	16	17	5	37/38	19/27	2	326

Passing

	Att.	Comp.	Yds.	Pct.	TD	Int.	Tkld.	Rate
Brister	342	187	2365	54.7	9	10	45/452	73.1
Blackledge	60	22	282	36.7	1	3	4/25	36.9
Carter	1	1	15	100	0	0	2/7	118.8
Strom	1	0	0	0.0	0	0	0/0	39.6
Steelers	404	210	2662	52.0	10	13	51/484	67.7
Opponents	548	290	3721	52.9	17	21	31/180	68.8

Rushing

	Att.	Yds.	Avg.	LG	TD
Worley	195	770	3.9	38	5
Hoge	186	621	3.3	31	8
Lipps	13	180	13.8	58t	1
W. Williams	37	131	3.5	13	1
Stone	10	53	5.3	32	0
Brister	27	25	0.9	15	0
Blackledge	9	20	2.2	11	0
Carter	11	16	1.5	7	1
Wallace	5	10	2.0	5	1
Tyrrell	1	3	3.0	3	0
Strom	4	-3	-0.8	0	0
Newsome	2	-8	-4.0	0	0
Steelers	500	1818	3.6	58t	17
Opponents	498	2008	4.0	65t	16

Receiving

	No.	Yds.	Avg.	LG	TD
Lipps	50	944	18.9	79t	5
Carter	38	267	7.0	22t	3
Hoge	34	271	8.0	22	0
Hill	28	455	16.3	53	1
Mularkey	22	326	14.8	34	1
Worley	15	113	7.5	19	0
Stone	7	92	13.1	16	0
W. Williams	6	48	8.0	16	0
Stock	4	74	18.5	27	0
Thompson	4	74	18.5	28	0
O'Shea	1	8	8.0	8	0
Brister	1	-10	-10.0	-10	0
Steelers	210	2662	12.7	79t	10
Opponents	290	3721	12.8	66t	17

Interceptions

	No.	Yds.	Avg.	LG	TD
Woodruff	4	57	14.3	35	0
Everett	3	68	22.7	32	0
Lloyd	3	49	16.3	31	0
Woodson	3	39	13.0	39	0
Little	3	23	7.7	13	0
Griffin	1	15	15.0	15	0
Hall	1	6	6.0	6	0
Hinkle	1	4	4.0	4	0
D. Johnson	1	0	0.0	0	0
Lake	1	0	0.0	0	0
Steelers	21	261	12.4	39	0
Opponents	13	103	7.9	21	1

Punting

	No.	Yds.	Avg.	In 20	LG
Newsome	82	3368	41.1	15	57
Steelers	83	3368	40.6	15	57
Opponents	69	2793	40.5	16	62

Punt Returns

	No.	FC	Yds.	Avg.	LG	TD
Woodson	29	2	207	7.1	20	0
Hill	5	0	22	4.4	12	0
Lipps	4	0	27	6.8	9	0
J. Johnson	2	0	22	11.0	13	0
Steelers	40	2	278	7.0	20	0
Opponents	45	19	361	8.0	42	0

Kickoff Returns

	No.	Yds.	Avg.	LG	TD
Woodson	36	982	27.3	84t	1
Stone	7	173	24.7	73	0
Thompson	4	41	10.3	15	0
J. Williams	4	31	7.8	22	0
J. Johnson	3	43	14.3	19	0
Griffin	1	21	21.0	21	0
Hinnant	1	13	13.0	13	0
Steelers	56	1304	23.3	84t	1
Opponents	53	1096	20.7	42	0

Sacks

	No.
Lloyd	7.0
Willis	6.5
T. Johnson	4.5
G. Williams	3.0
J. Williams	3.0
Jones	2.0
Little	2.0
Lake	1.0
Nickerson	1.0
Olsavsky	1.0
Steelers	31.0
Opponents	51.0

1990 Draft Choices

Round	Name	Pos.	College
1.	Eric Green	TE	Liberty
2.	Kenny Davidson	DE	Louisiana State
3.	Neil O'Donnell	QB	Maryland
	Craig Veasey	DT	Houston
4.	Chris Calloway	WR	Michigan
5.	Barry Foster	RB	Arkansas
6.	Ronald Heard	WR	Bowling Green
7.	Dan Grayson	LB	Washington State
8.	Karl Dunbar	DT	Louisiana State
9.	Gary Jones	DB	Texas A&M
10.	Eddie Miles	LB	Minnesota
11.	Justin Strzelczyk	T	Maine
12.	Richard Bell	RB	Nebraska

Pittsburgh Steelers 1990 Veteran Roster

No.	Name	Pos.	Ht.	Wt.	Birth-date	NFL Exp.	College	Hometown	How Acq.	'89 Games/ Starts
1	Anderson, Gary	K	5-11	180	7/16/59	9	Syracuse	Durban, South Africa	W(Buff)-'82	16/0
60	Blankenship, Brian	G-C	6-1	275	4/7/63	4	Nebraska	Omaha, Neb.	FA-'87	16/7
6	Brister, Bubby	QB	6-3	210	8/15/62	5	Northeast Louisiana	Alexandria, La.	D3-'86	14/14
24	Carter, Rodney	RB	6-0	210	10/30/64	4	Purdue	Elizabeth, N.J.	D7-'86	15/0
63	Dawson, Dermontti	C-G	6-2	275	6/17/65	3	Kentucky	Lexington, Ky.	D2-'88	16/16
27	Everett, Thomas	S	5-9	184	11/21/64	4	Baylor	Daingerfield, Tex.	D4-'87	16/16
68	Freeman, Lorenzo	NT	6-5	298	5/23/64	4	Pittsburgh	East Camden, N.J.	FA-'87	16/0
22	Griffin, Larry	S	6-0	200	1/11/63	5	North Carolina	Chesapeake, Va.	FA-'87	16/1
81	Griggs, Billy	TE	6-3	230	8/4/62	6	Virginia	Pennsauken, N.J.	PB(NYJ)-'90#	5/1*
35	Hall, Delton	CB	6-1	207	1/16/65	4	Clemson	Greensboro, N.C.	D2-'87	16/2
82	Hill, Derek	WR	6-1	193	11/4/67	2	Arizona	Detroit, Mich.	D3-'89	16/8
53	Hinkle, Bryan	LB	6-2	225	6/4/59	9	Oregon	Silverdale, Wash.	D6-'81	13/13
33	Hoge, Merril	RB	6-2	230	1/26/65	4	Idaho State	Pocatello, Idaho	D10-'87	16/16
41	Holmes, Darryl	CB-S	6-2	190	9/6/64	3	Fort Valley State	Warner Robins, Ga.	PB(NE)-'90#	13/0*
62	Ilkin, Tunch	T	6-3	266	9/23/57	11	Indiana State	Highland Park, Ill.	D6-'80	16/16
65	Jackson, John	T	6-6	288	1/4/65	3	Eastern Kentucky	Cincinnati, Ohio	D10-'88	14/12
99	Jenkins, A. J.	LB-DE	6-2	237	4/12/66	2	Cal State-Fullerton	Havelock, N.C.	D9-'89	16/0
44	†Johnson, David	CB	6-0	185	4/14/66	2	Kentucky	Louisville, Ky.	D7-'89	16/0
78	Johnson, Tim	DE-NT	6-3	269	1/29/65	4	Penn State	Sarasota, Fla.	D6a-'87	14/14
97	Jones, Aaron	DE	6-5	257	12/18/66	3	Eastern Kentucky	Apopka, Fla.	D1-'88	16/2
37	Lake, Carnell	S	6-1	205	7/15/67	2	UCLA	Inglewood, Calif.	D2-'89	15/15
51	Lanza, Chuck	C	6-2	260	9/20/64	3	Notre Dame	Germantown, Tenn.	D3-'88	11/0
83	Lipps, Louis	WR	5-10	190	8/9/62	7	Southern Mississippi	Reserve, La.	D1-'84	16/16
50	Little, David	LB	6-1	233	1/3/59	10	Florida	Miami, Fla.	D7-'81	16/16
95	Lloyd, Greg	LB	6-2	222	5/26/65	3	Fort Valley State	Fort Valley, Ga.	D6b-'87	16/16
74	Long, Terry	G	5-11	275	7/21/59	7	East Carolina	Columbia, S.C.	D4b-'84	13/9
84	Mularkey, Mike	TE	6-4	237	11/19/61	8	Florida	Ft. Lauderdale, Fla.	PB(Minn)-'89#	14/14
54	Nickerson, Hardy	LB	6-2	231	9/1/65	4	California	Los Angeles, Calif.	D5-'87	10/8
92	Olsavsky, Jerry	LB	6-1	222	3/29/67	2	Pittsburgh	Youngstown, Ohio	D10-'89	16/8
85	O'Shea, Terry	TE	6-4	236	12/3/66	2	California, Pa.	Pittsburgh, Pa.	FA-'89	16/2
28	Owens, Billy	CB	6-0	198	12/2/65	2	Pittsburgh	Syracuse, N.Y.	FA-'90	0*
71	Ricketts, Tom	T	6-5	298	11/21/65	2	Pittsburgh	Murrysville, Pa.	D1b-'89	12/2
79	Rienstra, John	G	6-5	264	3/22/63	5	Temple	Colorado Springs, Colo.	D1-'86	15/14
97	Romer, Rich	LB	6-3	214	2/27/66	3	Union College	East Greenbush, N.Y.	FA-'90	5/0*
47	Roundtree, Ray	WR	6-0	182	4/19/66	2	Penn State	Aiken, S.C.	FA-'90	0*
40	Shelton, Richard	CB	5-11	186	1/2/66	2	Liberty	Marietta, Ga.	FA-'90	3/0*
80	Stock, Mark	WR	5-11	177	4/27/66	2	Virginia Military	Stone Mountain, Ga.	D6-'89	8/0
20	Stone, Dwight	WR-RB	6-0	190	1/28/64	4	Middle Tennessee State	Florala, Ala.	FA-'87	16/8
90	Stowe, Tyronne	LB	6-1	236	5/30/65	2	Rutgers	Passaic, N.J.	FA-'88	16/0
11	Strom, Rick	QB	6-2	210	3/11/65	2	Georgia Tech	Pittsburgh, Pa.	FA-'89	3/0
87	Thompson, Weegie	WR	6-6	215	3/21/61	7	Florida State	Midlothian, Va.	D4a-'84	16/0
23	Tyrrell, Tim	RB	6-2	215	2/19/61	7	Northern Illinois	Dundee, Ill.	FA-'89	7/0
43	Wallace, Ray	RB	6-0	233	12/3/63	4	Purdue	Indianapolis, Ind.	PB(Hou)-'89#	9/0
98	Williams, Gerald	NT	6-3	279	9/8/63	5	Auburn	Lanett, Ala.	D2-'86	16/16
57	†Williams, Jerrol	LB	6-5	242	7/5/67	2	Purdue	Las Vegas, Nev.	D4-'89	16/3
42	Williams, Warren	RB	6-0	204	7/29/65	3	Miami	Ft. Myers, Fla.	D6-'88	5/2
93	Willis, Keith	DE	6-1	263	7/29/59	8	Northeastern	Newark, N.J.	FA-'82	16/16
49	Woodruff, Dwayne	CB	6-0	195	2/18/57	11	Louisville	New Richmond, Ohio	D6b-'79	16/16
26	Woodson, Rod	CB-KR	6-0	196	3/10/65	4	Purdue	Ft. Wayne, Ind.	D1-'87	15/14
38	Worley, Tim	RB	6-2	228	9/24/66	2	Georgia	Lumberton, N.C.	D1a-'89	15/14
9	Wright, Randy	QB	6-2	203	1/21/61	6	Wisconsin	St. Charles, Ill.	FA-'90	0*

* Griggs played 5 games with N.Y. Jets in '89; Holmes played 13 games with New England; Owens last active with Dallas in '88; Romer played 5 games with Cincinnati; Roundtree last active with Detroit in '88; Shelton played 3 games with Denver; Wright last active with Green Bay in '88.

† Option playout; subject to developments.

Plan B unconditional free agent.

Players lost through Plan B (7): CB David Arnold (Hou; 16 games in '89), WR Jason Johnson (Den; 14), P Harry Newsome (Minn; 16), LB Tracy Simien (NO; 1), LB Vinson Smith (Dall; 0), WR Eric Wilkerson (Det; 1), G-T Craig Wolfley (Minn; 15).

Also played with Steelers in '89—QB Todd Blackledge (3 games), TE Mike Hinnant (5).

COACHING STAFF

Head Coach, Chuck Noll

Pro Career: Became only NFL coach to win four Super Bowls when Steelers defeated Los Angeles Rams 31-19 in Super Bowl XIV. Put together 13 consecutive non-losing seasons and has guided Steelers into postseason play 12 of last 18 years. Led Pittsburgh to consecutive NFL championships twice (1974-75, 1978-79). With 193 career wins, is second among active NFL coaches behind Don Shula (285). Has tenth-highest winning percentage (.579) among active coaches and is fifth among the NFL's all-time winningest coaches with a 193-140-1 career record. Noll is one of only four coaches in NFL history to lead a team for 22 or more consecutive seasons—Curly Lambeau (29), Tom Landry (29), and Steve Owen (23) are the others. Played pro football as guard-linebacker for Cleveland Browns from 1953-59. At age 28, he started coaching career as defensive coach with Los Angeles (San Diego) Chargers in 1960. Left after 1965 season to become defensive backfield coach in Baltimore. Remained with Colts until taking over Pittsburgh as head coach in 1969. Career record: 193-140-1.

Background: Was an all-state star at Benedictine High in Cleveland. Captained the University of Dayton team, playing both tackle and linebacker. He was drafted by the Browns in 1953.

Personal: Born in Cleveland on January 5, 1932. He and his wife, Marianne, live in Pittsburgh and have one son—Chris.

Assistant Coaches

Ron Blackledge, offensive line; born April 15, 1938, Canton, Ohio, lives in Pittsburgh. Tight end-defensive end Bowling Green 1957-59. No pro playing experience. College coach: Ashland 1968-69, Cincinnati 1970-72, Kentucky 1973-75, Princeton 1976, Kent State 1977-81 (head coach 1979-81). Pro coach: Joined Steelers in 1982.

Dave Brazil, defensive coordinator; born March 25, 1936, Detroit, lives in Pittsburgh. No college or pro playing experience. College coach: Holy Cross 1968-69, Tulsa 1970-71, Eastern Michigan 1972-74, Boston College 1978-79, Kent State 1980-82. Pro coach: Detroit Wheel (WFL) 1975, Chicago Fire (WFL) 1976, Kansas City Chiefs 1984-88, joined Steelers in 1989.

John Fox, defensive backs; born February 8, 1955, Virginia Beach, Va., lives in Pittsburgh. Defensive back San Diego State 1975-77. No pro playing experience. College coach: U.S. International 1979, Boise State 1980, Long Beach State 1981, Utah 1982, Kansas 1983, 1985, Iowa State 1984, Pittsburgh 1986-88. Pro coach: Los Angeles Express (USFL) 1985, joined Steelers in 1989.

Joe Greene, defensive line; born September 24, 1946, Temple, Tex., lives in Pittsburgh. Defensive tackle North Texas State 1966-68. Pro defensive tackle Pittsburgh Steelers 1969-81. Inducted into Pro Football Hall of Fame in 1987. Pro coach: Joined Steelers in 1987.

Dick Hoak, offensive backfield; born December 8, 1939, Jeannette, Pa., lives in Greensburg, Pa. Halfback-quarterback Penn State 1958-60. Pro running back Pittsburgh Steelers 1961-70. Pro coach: Joined Steelers in 1972.

Jon Kolb, tight ends, conditioning; born August 30, 1947, Ponca City, Okla., lives in Pittsburgh. Center-linebacker Oklahoma State 1966-68. Pro tackle Pittsburgh Steelers 1969-81. Pro coach: Joined Steelers in 1982.

Dwain Painter, receivers; born February 13, 1942, Monroeville, Pa., lives in Pittsburgh. Quarterback-defensive back Rutgers 1961-64. No pro playing experience. College coach: San Jose State 1971-72, College of San Mateo 1973, Brigham Young 1974-75, UCLA 1976-78, Northern Arizona 1979-81 (head coach), Georgia Tech 1982-85, Texas 1986, Illinois 1987. Pro coach: Joined Steelers in 1988.

George Stewart, special teams; born December 29, 1958, Little Rock, Ark., lives in Pittsburgh. Guard Arkansas 1977-80. No pro playing experience. College coach: Minnesota 1984-85, Notre Dame 1986-88. Pro coach: Joined Steelers in 1989.

Bob Valesente, linebackers; born July 19, 1940, Seneca Falls, N.Y., lives in Pittsburgh. Halfback Ithaca College 1958-61. No pro playing experience. College coach: Cornell 1964-74, Cincinnati 1975-76, Arizona 1977-79, Mississippi State 1980-81, Kansas 1984-87 (head coach 1986-87), Maryland 1988, Pittsburgh 1989. Pro coach: Baltimore Colts 1982-83, joined Steelers in 1990.

Joe Walton, offensive coordinator; born December 15, 1935, Beaver Falls, Pa., lives in Pittsburgh. Tight end-linebacker Pittsburgh 1953-56. Pro tight end Washington Redskins 1957-60, New York Giants 1961-63. Pro coach: New York Giants 1969-73, Washington Redskins 1974-80, New York Jets 1981-89 (head coach 1983-89), joined Steelers in 1990.

Pittsburgh Steelers 1990 First-Year Roster

Name	Pos.	Ht.	Wt.	Birth-date	College	Hometown	How Acq.
Bell, Richard	RB	6-0	196	5/3/67	Nebraska	Altadena, Calif.	D12
Buddenberg, John (1)	T	6-5	275	10/9/65	Akron	Bellaire, Ohio	FA
Calloway, Chris	WR	5-10	181	3/29/68	Michigan	Chicago, Ill.	D4
Cullinane, Gene (1)	C-G	6-4	278	11/10/66	Washburn	Omaha, Neb.	FA
Davidson, Ken	DE	6-5	274	8/17/67	Louisiana State	Shreveport, La.	D2
Dunbar, Karl	DE	6-4	273	5/18/67	Louisiana State	Opelousas, La.	D8
Foster, Barry	RB	5-10	222	12/8/68	Arkansas	Duncanville, Tex.	D5
Fryar, Jeff (1)	T	6-6	290	12/7/64	Indiana	Indianapolis, Ind.	FA
Gouldsby, Mace (1)	NT	6-2	290	8/24/65	San Jose State	San Francisco, Calif.	FA-'89
Grayson, Dan	LB	6-2	239	7/27/67	Washington State	Woodlawn, Wash.	D7
Green, Eric	TE	6-5	274	6/22/67	Liberty	Savannah, Ga.	D1
Haselrig, Carlton (1)	NT	6-1	273	1/22/66	Pittsburgh-Johnstown	Johnstown, Pa.	D12-'89
Heard, Ron	WR	5-10	177	8/20/67	Bowling Green	Detroit, Mich.	D6
Jones, Gary	CB	6-2	203	11/30/67	Texas A&M	Tyler, Tex.	D9
Kirk, Vernon (1)	TE	6-2	245	10/14/66	Pittsburgh	Monongahela, Pa.	FA
Miles, Eddie	LB	6-1	233	9/13/68	Minnesota	Miami, Fla.	D10
O'Donnell, Neil	QB	6-2	217	7/3/66	Maryland	Madison, N.J.	D3a
Pavlik, Michael	G	6-3	285	12/10/66	Virginia Tech	Virginia Beach, Va.	FA
Rutter, Pete	P	6-2	214	11/23/67	Baylor	Katy, Tex.	FA
Stryzinski, Dan (1)	P	6-1	195	5/15/65	Indiana	Indianapolis, Ind.	FA
Strzelczyk, Justin	T	6-5	272	8/18/68	Maine	Seneca, N.Y.	D11
Veasey, Craig	NT	6-2	270	12/25/65	Houston	Clear Lake City, Tex.	D3b
Williams, Marlin (1)	DE	6-3	270	4/12/65	Western Illinois	Tampa, Fla.	FA

The term NFL Rookie is defined as a player who is in his first season of professional football and has not been on the roster of another professional football team for any regular-season or postseason games. A Rookie is designated by an "R" on NFL rosters. Players who have been active in another professional football league or players who have NFL experience, including either preseason training camp or being on an active roster for fewer than three regular-season or post-season games, are termed NFL First-Year Players. An NFL First-Year Player is designated by a "1" on NFL rosters. Thereafter, a player on an NFL active roster for at least three regular-season or postseason games is credited with an additional year of NFL playing experience.

NOTES

_____
_____
_____
_____
_____
_____
_____
_____
_____
_____
_____
_____
_____
_____
_____
_____
_____

SAN DIEGO CHARGERS

American Football Conference Western Division

Team Colors: Navy Blue, White, and Gold

San Diego Jack Murphy Stadium
P.O. Box 20666
San Diego, California 92120
Telephone: (619) 280-2111

Club Officials

Chairman of the Board/President: Alex G. Spanos
Vice Chairman: Dean A. Spanos
General Manager: Bobby Beathard
Director of Administration: Jack E. Teele
Special Assistant to Chairman of the Board:
    Warren B. Jones, Jr.
Assistant General Manager: Dick Daniels
Director of Player Personnel: Billy Devaney
Pro Scouting: Rudy Feldman
Director of Public Relations: Bill Johnston
Business Manager: Pat Curran
Director of Marketing: Rich Israel
Director of Ticket Operations: Joe Scott
Assistant Director of Public Relations:
    Rob Boulware
Chief Financial Officer: Jeremiah T. Murphy
Head Trainer: Keoki Kamau
Equipment Manager: Sid Brooks

Stadium: San Diego Jack Murphy Stadium •
    Capacity: 60,750
    9449 Friars Road
    San Diego, California 92108

Playing Surface: Grass

Training Camp: University of California-
                San Diego
                Third College
                La Jolla, California 92037

1990 Schedule

Preseason
Aug. 11	**Dallas**	7:00
Aug. 18	at Los Angeles Rams	7:00
Aug. 25	**San Francisco**	6:00
Sept. 1	at Los Angeles Raiders	1:00

Regular Season
Sept. 9	at Dallas	3:00
Sept. 16	**Cincinnati**	1:00
Sept. 23	at Cleveland	1:00
Sept. 30	**Houston**	1:00
Oct. 7	at Pittsburgh	1:00
Oct. 14	at New York Jets	1:00
Oct. 21	**Los Angeles Raiders**	1:00
Oct. 28	**Tampa Bay**	1:00
Nov. 4	at Seattle	1:00
Nov. 11	**Denver**	1:00
Nov. 18	at Kansas City	12:00
Nov. 25	**Seattle**	5:00
Dec. 2	**New York Jets**	1:00
Dec. 9	**Open Date**	
Dec. 16	at Denver	2:00
Dec. 23	**Kansas City**	1:00
Dec. 30	at Los Angeles Raiders	1:00

Chargers Coaching History

Los Angeles 1960
(220-217-11)
1960-69	Sid Gillman*	83-51-6
1969-70	Charlie Waller	9-7-3
1971	Sid Gillman**	4-6-0
1971-73	Harland Svare***	7-17-2
1973	Ron Waller	1-5-0
1974-78	Tommy Prothro****	21-39-0
1978-86	Don Coryell#	72-60-0
1986-88	Al Saunders	17-22-0
1989	Dan Henning	6-10-0

*Retired after nine games in 1969
**Resigned after 10 games in 1971
***Resigned after eight games in 1973
****Resigned after four games in 1978
#Resigned after eight games in 1986

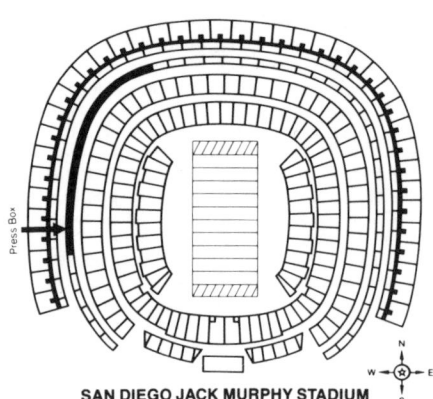

SAN DIEGO JACK MURPHY STADIUM

Record Holders
Individual Records—Career
Category	Name	Performance
Rushing (Yds.)	Paul Lowe, 1960-67	4,963
Passing (Yds.)	Dan Fouts, 1973-1987	43,040
Passing (TDs)	Dan Fouts, 1973-1987	254
Receiving (No.)	Charlie Joiner, 1976-1986	586
Receiving (Yds.)	Lance Alworth, 1962-1970	9,585
Interceptions	Dick Harris, 1960-65	29
Punting (Avg.)	Maury Buford, 1982-84	42.7
Punt Return (Avg.)	Leslie (Speedy) Duncan, 1964-1970	12.3
Kickoff Return (Avg.)	Leslie (Speedy) Duncan, 1964-1970	25.2
Field Goals	Rolf Benirschke, 1977-1986	146
Touchdowns	Lance Alworth, 1962-1970	83
Points	Rolf Benirschke, 1977-1986	766

Individual Records—Single Season
Category	Name	Performance
Rushing (Yds.)	Earnest Jackson, 1984	1,179
Passing (Yds.)	Dan Fouts, 1981	4,802
Passing (TDs)	Dan Fouts, 1981	33
Receiving (No.)	Kellen Winslow, 1980	89
Receiving (Yds.)	Lance Alworth, 1965	1,602
Interceptions	Charlie McNeil, 1961	9
Punting (Avg.)	Dennis Partee, 1969	44.6
Punt Return (Avg.)	Leslie (Speedy) Duncan, 1965	15.5
Kickoff Return (Avg.)	Keith Lincoln, 1962	28.4
Field Goals	Rolf Benirschke, 1980	24
Touchdowns	Chuck Muncie, 1981	19
Points	Rolf Benirschke, 1980	118

Individual Records—Single Game
Category	Name	Performance
Rushing (Yds.)	Gary Anderson, 12-18-88	217
Passing (Yds.)	Dan Fouts, 10-19-80	444
	Dan Fouts, 12-11-82	444
Passing (TDs)	Dan Fouts, 11-22-81	6
Receiving (No.)	Kellen Winslow, 10-7-84	15
Receiving (Yds.)	Wes Chandler, 12-20-82	260
Interceptions	Many times	3
	Last time by Pete Shaw, 11-2-80	
Field Goals	Many times	4
	Last time by Chris Bahr, 12-24-89	
Touchdowns (Tot.)	Kellen Winslow, 11-22-81	5
Points	Kellen Winslow, 11-22-81	30

1989 Team Record
Preseason (2-2)

Date	Result		Opponents
8/13	L	3-20	Dallas
8/19	W	24- 7	at Chicago
8/23	L	14-17	at San Francisco
9/1	W	21-20	Phoenix
		62-64	

Regular Season (6-10)

Date	Result		Opponents	Att.
9/10	L	14-40	at L.A. Raiders	40,237
9/17	L	27-34	Houston	42,013
9/24	W	21- 6	Kansas City	40,128
10/1	W	24-13	at Phoenix	44,201
10/8	L	10-16	at Denver	75,222
10/15	L	16-17	Seattle	50,079
10/22	L	13-20	N.Y. Giants	48,566
10/29	L	7-10	at Seattle	59,691
11/5	W	20-17	Philadelphia	47,019
11/12	W	14-12	L.A. Raiders	59,151
11/19	L	17-20	at Pittsburgh	44,203
11/26	L	6-10	at Indianapolis	58,822
12/3	L	17-20	N.Y. Jets	38,954
12/10	L	21-26	at Washington	47,693
12/17	W	20-13	at Kansas City	40,623
12/24	W	19-16	Denver	50,524

Score by Periods

Chargers	52	43	67	104	0	—	266
Opponents	42	92	67	89	0	—	290

Attendance
Home 376,434   Away 410,692   Total 787,126
Single-game home record, 61,880 (11-29-87)
Single-season home record, 415,626 (1985)

1989 Team Statistics

	Chargers	Opp.
Total First Downs	267	295
Rushing	95	102
Passing	149	172
Penalty	23	21
Third Down: Made/Att.	81/223	81/227
Third Down: Pct.	36.3	35.7
Fourth Down: Made/Att.	6/18	8/13
Fourth Down: Pct.	33.3	61.5
Total Net Yards	4910	4764
Avg. Per Game	306.9	297.8
Total Plays	986	1040
Avg. Per Play	5.0	4.6
Net Yards Rushing	1873	1813
Avg. Per Game	117.1	113.3
Total Rushes	432	479
Net Yards Passing	3037	2951
Avg. Per Game	189.8	184.4
Sacked/Yards Lost	39/254	48/360
Gross Yards	3291	3311
Att./Completions	515/270	513/283
Completion Pct.	52.4	55.2
Had Intercepted	19	25
Punts/Avg.	84/39.5	79/38.6
Net Punting Avg.	32.4	32.9
Penalties/Yards Lost	122/906	93/741
Fumbles/Ball Lost	24/17	21/13
Touchdowns	31	29
Rushing	13	13
Passing	15	15
Returns	3	1
Avg. Time of Possession	28:55	31:05

1989 Individual Statistics

Scoring

	TD R	TD P	TD Rt	PAT	FG	Saf	TP
Bahr	0	0	0	29/30	17/25	0	80
A. Miller	0	10	1	0/0	0/0	0	66
Butts	9	0	0	0/0	0/0	0	54
Spencer	3	0	0	0/0	0/0	0	18
Bernstine	1	1	0	0/0	0/0	0	12
Cox	0	2	0	0/0	0/0	0	12
Glenn	0	0	1	0/0	0/0	0	6
Parker	0	1	0	0/0	0/0	0	6
Smith	0	0	1	0/0	0/0	0	6
Walker	0	1	0	0/0	0/0	0	6
Chargers	13	15	3	29/31	17/25	0	266
Opponents	13	15	1	27/29	29/41	1	290

Passing

	Att.	Comp.	Yds.	Pct.	TD	Int.	Tkld.	Rate
McMahon	318	176	2132	55.3	10	10	28/167	73.5
Tolliver	185	89	1097	48.1	5	8	9/75	57.9
Archer	12	5	62	41.7	0	1	2/12	23.6
Chargers	515	270	3291	52.4	15	19	39/254	66.7
Opponents	513	283	3311	55.2	15	25	48/360	64.4

Rushing

	Att.	Yds.	Avg.	LG	TD
Butts	170	683	4.0	50t	9
Spencer	134	521	3.9	15	3
Nelson, Minn.-S.D.	67	321	4.8	28	0
Nelson, S.D.	36	197	5.5	28	0
McMahon	29	141	4.9	15	0
Bernstine	15	137	9.1	32t	1
Brinson	17	64	3.8	9	0
Holland	6	46	7.7	24	0
A. Miller	4	21	5.3	24	0
Early	1	19	19.0	19	0
Floyd	8	15	1.9	5	0
Archer	2	14	7.0	14	0
Walker	1	9	9.0	9	0
Plummer	1	6	6.0	6	0
Caravello	1	0	0.0	0	0
Tolliver	7	0	0.0	3	0
Chargers	432	1873	4.3	50t	13
Opponents	479	1813	3.8	59	13

Receiving

	No.	Yds.	Avg.	LG	TD
A. Miller	75	1252	16.7	69t	10
Nelson, Minn.-S.D.	38	380	10.0	49	0
Nelson, S.D.	31	314	10.0	49	0
Holland	26	336	12.9	37	0
Walker	24	395	16.5	49	1
Cox	22	200	9.1	24	2
Bernstine	21	222	10.6	36	1
Spencer	18	112	6.2	23	0
Brinson	12	71	5.9	11	0
Early	11	126	11.5	21	0
Caravello	10	95	9.5	37	0
McEwen	7	99	14.1	29	0
Butts	7	21	3.0	8	0
Allen	2	19	9.5	11	0
McConkey, Phx.-S.D.	2	18	9.0	10	0
Parker	2	5	2.5	4	1
Floyd	1	6	6.0	6	0
McMahon	1	4	4.0	4	0
Chargers	270	3291	12.2	69t	15
Opponents	283	3311	11.7	59t	15

Interceptions

	No.	Yds.	Avg.	LG	TD
Byrd	7	38	5.4	22	0
Glenn	4	52	13.0	31	0
Seale	4	47	11.8	25	0
Bennett	3	4	1.3	4	0
Patterson	2	44	22.0	34	0
Lyles	2	28	14.0	28	0
Smith	1	9	9.0	9	0
Figaro	1	2	2.0	2	0
Bayless	1	0	0.0	0	0
Chargers	25	224	9.0	34	0
Opponents	19	179	9.4	40	0

Punting

	No.	Yds.	Avg.	In 20	LG
Ilesic	76	3049	40.1	11	64
Colbert	8	266	33.3	0	46
Chargers	84	3315	39.5	11	64
Opponents	79	3050	38.6	21	63

Punt Returns

	No.	FC	Yds.	Avg.	LG	TD
McConkey, Phx.-S.D.	15	15	124	8.3	20	0
McConkey, S.D.	14	15	111	7.9	20	0
Brinson	11	0	112	10.2	52	0
Walker	6	4	31	5.2	13	0
Usher	3	0	15	5.0	11	0
Allen	2	0	3	1.5	3	0
Figaro	1	0	0	0.0	0	0
Lyles	1	0	0	0.0	0	0
Byrd	0	1	0	—	0	0
Chargers	38	20	272	7.2	52	0
Opponents	43	10	451	10.5	38	0

Kickoff Returns

	No.	Yds.	Avg.	LG	TD
A. Miller	21	533	25.4	91t	1
Holland	29	510	17.6	34	0
Nelson, Minn.-S.D.	14	317	22.6	32	0
Usher	10	159	15.9	26	0
Floyd	3	12	4.0	12	0
McConkey, Phx.-S.D.	2	40	20.0	21	0
Figaro	1	21	21.0	21	0
Chargers	64	1235	19.3	91t	1
Opponents	57	1249	21.9	84t	1

Sacks

	No.
Williams	14.0
O'Neal	12.5
Grossman	10.0
Hinkle	2.5
L. Miller	2.5
Smith	2.5
Bayless	1.0
Glenn	1.0
Lyles	1.0
Phillips	1.0
Chargers	48.0
Opponents	39.0

1990 Draft Choices

Round	Name	Pos.	College
1.	Junior Seau	LB	Southern California
3.	Jeff Mills	LB	Nebraska
	Leo Goeas	G	Hawaii
	Walter Wilson	WR	East Carolina
6.	John Friesz	QB	Idaho
	Frank Cornish	C	UCLA
	David Pool	DB	Carson-Newman
	Derrick Walker	TE	Michigan
7.	Jeff Novak	G	S.W. Texas State
	Joe Staysniak	T	Ohio State
	Nate Lewis	WR	Oregon Tech
	Keith Collins	DB	Appalachian State
8.	J.J. Flannigan	RB	Colorado
9.	Chris Goetz	G	Pittsburgh
10.	Kenny Berry	DB	Miami
11.	Tommie Stowers	TE	Missouri
12.	Elliott Searcy	WR	Southern Univ.

San Diego Chargers 1990 Veteran Roster

No.	Name	Pos.	Ht.	Wt.	Birth-date	NFL Exp.	College	Hometown	How Acq.	'89 Games/Starts
15	†Archer, David	QB	6-2	208	2/15/62	7	Iowa State	Soda Springs, Idaho	FA-'89	16/0
44	Bayless, Martin	S	6-2	212	10/11/62	7	Bowling Green	Dayton, Ohio	T(Buff)-'87	16/16
82	Bernstine, Rod	RB	6-3	238	2/8/65	4	Texas A&M	Bryan, Tex.	D1-'87	5/0
58	†Brandon, David	LB	6-4	230	2/9/65	4	Memphis State	Memphis, Tenn.	T(Buff)-'87	13/0
35	Butts, Marion	RB	6-1	248	8/1/66	2	Florida State	Sylvester, Ga.	D7a-'89	15/5
22	†Byrd, Gill	CB	5-11	198	2/20/61	8	San Jose State	San Francisco, Calif.	D1c-'83	16/16
46	Caravello, Joe	RB	6-3	270	6/6/63	4	Tulane	El Segundo, Calif.	PB(Wash)-'89#	12/9
3	Carney, John	K	5-11	160	4/20/64	2	Notre Dame	West Palm Beach, Fla.	PB(TB)-'90#	1/0*
88	†Cox, Arthur	TE	6-2	277	2/5/61	8	Texas Southern	Plant City, Fla.	FA-'88	16/16
87	Early, Quinn	WR	6-0	190	4/13/65	3	Iowa	Great Neck, N.Y.	D3-'88	6/3
51	†Figaro, Cedric	LB	6-2	250	8/17/66	3	Notre Dame	Lafayette, La.	D6-'88	16/14
25	†Glenn, Vencie	S	6-0	192	10/26/64	5	Indiana State	Terre Haute, Ind.	T(NE)-'86	16/16
92	Grossman, Burt	DE	6-6	270	4/10/67	2	Pittsburgh	Bala-Cynwyd, Pa.	D1-'89	16/16
53	Hall, Courtney	C	6-1	269	8/26/68	2	Rice	Wilmington, Calif.	D2a-'89	16/16
33	Harmon, Ronnie	RB	5-11	200	5/7/64	5	Iowa	Queens, N.Y.	PB(Buff)-'90#	15/2*
93	Hill, Nate	DE	6-4	275	2/21/66	2	Auburn	LaGrange, Ga.	FA-'90	0*
97	†Hinkle, George	DE	6-5	269	3/17/65	3	Arizona	Pacific, Mo.	D11b-'88	14/0
79	Howard, Joey	T	6-5	305	9/14/65	2	Tennessee	Springfield, Ohio	D9-'88	9/2
10	Kidd, John	P	6-3	208	8/22/61	7	Northwestern	Findlay, Ohio	PB(Buff)-'90#	16/0*
24	Lyles, Lester	S	6-3	200	12/27/62	6	Virginia	Washington, D.C.	PB(Phx)-'89#	16/1
31	†McEwen, Craig	RB	6-1	220	12/16/65	4	Utah	Northport, N.Y.	FA-'89	4/3
60	†McKnight, Dennis	C-G	6-3	280	9/12/59	8	Drake	Staten Island, N.Y.	FA-'82	0*
36	Mickles, Joe	RB	5-10	221	12/25/65	2	Mississippi	Birmingham, Ala.	PB(Wash)-'90#	9/0*
83	Miller, Anthony	WR	5-11	185	4/15/65	3	Tennessee	Pasadena, Calif.	D1-'88	16/16
69	Miller, Les	NT	6-7	293	3/1/65	4	Fort Hayes State	Arkansas City, Kan.	FA-'87	14/0
20	Nelson, Darrin	RB	5-9	185	1/2/59	9	Stanford	Downey, Calif.	T(Dall)-'89	15/0*
91	†O'Neal, Leslie	LB	6-4	259	5/7/64	4	Oklahoma State	Little Rock, Ark.	D1a-'86	16/16
85	Parker, Andy	TE	6-5	245	9/8/61	7	Utah	Encinitas, Calif.	PB(Raid)-'89#	10/6
78	Patten, Joel	T	6-7	307	2/7/58	6	Duke	Fairfax, Va.	PB(Ind)-'89#	14/14
75	Phillips, Joe	NT	6-5	275	7/15/63	5	Southern Methodist	Vancouver, Wash.	FA-'87	16/15
23	Plummer, Bruce	S	6-1	203	9/1/64	4	Mississippi State	Bogalusa, La.	PB(Ind)-'90#	16/2*
50	Plummer, Gary	LB	6-2	240	1/26/60	5	California	Fremont, Calif.	FA-'86	16/16
7	Reveiz, Fuad	K	5-11	216	2/24/63	4	Tennessee	Miami, Fla.	FA-'90	0*
65	†Richards, David	G-T	6-4	310	4/11/66	3	UCLA	Dallas, Tex.	D4c-'88	16/16
98	Robinson, Gerald	DE	6-3	262	5/4/63	3	Auburn	Notasulga, Ala.	FA-'89	2/0
64	Rodenhauser, Mark	C	6-5	263	6/1/61	3	Illinois State	Addison, Ill.	PB(Minn)-'90#	16/0*
57	Rolling, Henry	LB	6-2	225	9/8/65	3	Nevada-Reno	Henderson, Nev.	FA-'90	6/0*
45	Sanders, Thomas	RB	5-11	203	1/4/62	6	Texas A&M	Giddings, Tex.	PB(Chi)-'90#	16/0*
30	†Seale, Sam	CB	5-9	185	10/6/62	7	Western State, Colo.	Orange, N.J.	FA-'88	13/12
68	Simmonds, Mike	G	6-4	285	8/12/64	2	Indiana State	Belleville, Ill.	PB(TB)-'90#	5/5*
54	Smith, Billy Ray	LB	6-3	236	8/10/61	8	Arkansas	Plano, Tex.	D1a-'83	16/16
43	†Spencer, Tim	RB	6-1	223	12/10/60	6	Ohio State	St. Clairsville, Ohio	D11b-'83	16/11
76	†Thompson, Broderick	G-T	6-4	295	8/14/60	5	Kansas	Cerritos, Calif.	FA-'87	16/16
11	Tolliver, Billy Joe	QB	6-1	218	2/7/66	2	Texas Tech	Jamestown, N.D.	D2b-'89	5/5
73	Toth, Tom	G	6-5	282	5/23/62	5	Western Michigan	Orland Park, Ill.	PB(Mia)-'90#	16/2*
13	Vlasic, Mark	QB	6-3	206	10/25/63	3	Iowa	Monaca, Pa.	D4-'87	0*
80	Walker, Wayne	WR	5-8	162	12/27/66	2	Texas Tech	Waco, Tex.	FA-'89	13/4
67	Williams, Larry	G	6-5	290	7/3/63	4	Notre Dame	Santa Ana, Calif.	PB(Clev)-'89#	0*
99	Williams, Lee	DE	6-5	271	10/15/62	7	Bethune-Cookman	Ft. Lauderdale, Fla.	SD1-'84	16/16
59	†Woodard, Ken	LB	6-1	220	1/22/60	9	Tuskegee Institute	Detroit, Mich.	FA-'88	16/0
80	Yarber, Eric	WR	5-8	152	9/22/63	2	Idaho	Los Angeles, Calif.	FA-'90	0*

* Carney played 1 game with Tampa Bay in '89; Harmon played 15 games with Buffalo; Hill last active with Miami in '88; Kidd played 16 games with Buffalo; McKnight and Vlasic missed '89 season due to injury; Mickles played 9 games with Washington; Nelson played 5 games with Minnesota; B. Plummer played 16 games with Indianapolis; Reveiz last active with Miami in '88; Rodenhauser played 16 games with Minnesota; Rolling played 6 games with Tampa Bay; Sanders played 16 games with Chicago; Simmonds played 5 games with Tampa Bay; Toth played 16 games with Miami; La. Williams last active with Cleveland in '88; Yarber last active with Washington in '88.

† Option playout; subject to developments.

Traded—RB Gary Anderson to Tampa Bay, WR Jamie Holland and RB Napoleon McCallum to L.A. Raiders.

Retired—Phil McConkey, 7-year wide receiver, 5 games in '89.

Plan B unconditional free agent.

Players lost through Plan B (7); LB Joe Campbell (Raid; 9 games in '89), T James FitzPatrick (Raid; 13), TE Chris Gannon (NE; 10), P Hank Ilesic (Rams; 14), T Brett Miller (NYJ; 14), CB Elvis Patterson (Raid; 16), CB-S Elliot Smith (Den; 2).

Also played with Chargers in '89—WR Anthony Allen (7 games), K Chris Bahr (16), CB Roy Bennett (16), RB Dana Brinson (10), NT Mike Charles (6), P Lewis Colbert (2), S Leonard Coleman (1), LB Jim Collins (13), RB Victor Floyd (6), C Don Macek (2), QB Jim McMahon (12), CB Johnny Thomas (13), WR Darryl Usher (6), TE Mark Walczak (6).

COACHING STAFF

Head Coach, Dan Henning

Pro Career: Begins second season as San Diego's head coach. Named eighth head coach in Chargers' history February 9, 1989, replacing Al Saunders. Previously served as head coach of Atlanta Falcons from 1983-86, producing 22-41-1 record. Henning began his pro coaching career in 1972 as an assistant with Houston Oilers. Also was assistant with New York Jets 1976-78 and Miami Dolphins 1979-80. Served as assistant head coach with Washington Redskins 1981-82 and helped lead Washington to a Super Bowl victory following the 1982 season. Returned to Washington as receivers coach in 1987-88. Played quarterback with Chargers 1964-67. Career record: 28-51-1.

Background: Played quarterback for William & Mary 1960-63. College assistant coach at Florida State 1968-70, 1974, and Virginia Tech 1971-73.

Personal: Born June 21, 1942, Bronx, N.Y. Attended St. Francis Prep in Brooklyn before attending William & Mary. Dan and his wife, Sandy, live in La Mesa, Calif., and have five children—Mary K., Patty, Danny, Terry, and Mike.

Assistant Coaches

Gunther Cunningham, defensive line; born June 19, 1946, Munich, Germany, lives in San Diego. Linebacker Oregon 1965-67. No pro playing experience. College coach: Oregon 1969-71, Arkansas 1972, Stanford 1973-76, California 1977-80. Pro coach: Hamilton Tiger-Cats (CFL) 1981, Indianapolis Colts 1982-84, joined Chargers in 1985.

John Dunn, strength and conditioning; born July 22, 1956, Great Barrington, Mass., lives in San Diego. Guard Penn State 1975-77. No pro playing experience. College coach: Penn State 1978. Pro coach: Washington Redskins 1984-86, Los Angeles Raiders 1987-89, joined Chargers in 1990.

Alex Gibbs, offensive line; born February 11, 1941, Morganton, N.C., lives in San Diego. Running back-defensive back Davidson College 1959-63. No pro playing experience. College coach: Duke 1969-70, Kentucky 1971-72, West Virginia 1973-74, Ohio State 1975-78, Auburn 1979-81, Georgia 1982-83. Pro coach: Denver Broncos 1984-87, Los Angeles Raiders 1988-89, joined Chargers in 1990.

Mike Haluchak, linebackers; born November 28, 1949, Concord, Calif., lives in San Diego. Linebacker Southern California 1967-70. No pro playing experience. College coach: Southern California 1976-77, Cal State-Fullerton 1978, Pacific 1979-80, California 1981, North Carolina State 1982. Pro coach: Oakland Invaders (USFL) 1983-85, joined Chargers in 1986.

Bobby Jackson, running backs; born February 16, 1940, Forsyth, Ga., lives in San Diego. Linebacker-running back Samford (Ga.) 1959-62. No pro playing experience. College coach: Florida State 1965-69, Kansas State 1970-74, Louisville 1975-76, Tennessee 1977-82. Pro coach: Atlanta Falcons 1983-86, joined Chargers in 1987.

Charlie Joiner, receivers; born October 14, 1947, Many, La., lives in San Diego. Wide receiver Grambling 1965-68. Defensive back-wide receiver Houston Oilers 1969-72, Cincinnati Bengals 1972-75, San Diego Chargers 1976-86. Pro coach: Joined Chargers in 1987.

Ron Lynn, defensive coordinator; born December 6, 1944, Youngstown, Ohio, lives in San Diego. Quarterback-defensive back Mount Union (Ohio) 1963-65. No pro playing experience. College coach: Toledo 1966, Mount Union (Ohio) 1967-73, Kent State 1974-76, San Jose State 1977-78, Pacific 1979, California 1980-82. Pro coach: Oakland Invaders (USFL) 1983-85, joined Chargers in 1986.

Joe Madden, defensive assistant; born March 5, 1935, Washington, D.C., lives in San Diego. Back Maryland 1954-56. No pro playing experience. College coach: Mississippi State 1962, Morehead State 1963, Wake Forest 1964-67, Iowa State 1968-71, Kansas State 1972, Pittsburgh 1973-76, Tennessee 1977-79. Pro coach: Detroit Lions 1980-84, Atlanta Falcons 1985-86, joined Chargers in 1989.

San Diego Chargers 1990 First-Year Roster

Name	Pos.	Ht.	Wt.	Birth-date	College	Hometown	How Acq.
Allen, Lee	WR	5-10	165	10/9/67	Idaho	Seattle, Wash.	FA
Belli, Barry (1)	K	5-10	167	8/7/65	Fresno State	Bakersfield, Calif.	FA
Berry, Ken	CB	6-2	185	10/12/66	Miami	Pahokee, Fla.	D10
Brooks, Michael (1)	S	6-0	195	3/12/67	North Carolina State	Greensboro, N.C.	FA-'89
Collins, Keith	CB	5-11	183	2/6/68	Appalachian State	Onslow, N.C.	D7d
Cornish, Frank	C-G	6-4	281	9/24/67	UCLA	Chicago, Ill.	D6b
Davis, Willie	CB	5-10	185	1/6/67	Southern Illinois	Indianapolis, Ind.	FA
Debnam, Derrick	DE	6-2	255	4/18/68	North Carolina	Winston-Salem, N.C.	FA
Dickson, Wayne	LB	6-3	253	11/27/67	Oklahoma	Borger, Tex.	FA
English, Keith (1)	P	6-3	220	3/10/66	Colorado	Greeley, Colo.	FA
Flannigan, J.J.	RB	5-10	195	9/16/68	Colorado	Pomona, Calif.	D8
Floyd, Eric (1)	T	6-5	300	10/28/65	Auburn	Rome, Ga.	FA
Frank, Donald	CB-S	6-0	200	10/24/65	Winston-Salem State	Tarboro, N.C.	FA
Friesz, John	QB	6-4	209	5/19/67	Idaho	Coeur d'Alene, Idaho	D6a
Fuller, Joe (1)	CB	5-11	180	9/25/64	Northern Iowa	Minneapolis, Minn.	FA
Goeas, Leo	T	6-3	280	8/15/66	Hawaii	Honolulu, Ha.	D3b
Goetz, Chris	G	6-2	272	3/13/67	Pittsburgh	Queens, N.Y.	D9
Gunn, Tony	NT	6-5	310	4/5/65	Nevada-Las Vegas	San Diego, Calif.	FA
Jackson, Tim (1)	CB	5-11	192	11/7/65	Nebraska	Dallas, Tex.	FA
Jones, Wendell	WR	5-10	175	12/2/64	Grambling	Monroe, La.	FA
Lewis, Nate	WR	5-11	197	10/19/66	Oregon Tech	Moultrie, Ga.	D7c
Mays, Jerry	RB	5-7	173	12/8/67	Georgia Tech	Thomson, Ga.	FA
Mills, Jeff	LB	6-3	238	10/8/68	Nebraska	Montclair, N.J.	D3a
Moss, Adrian	TE	6-5	254	12/11/66	West Virginia	Cocoa, Fla.	FA
Novak, Jeff	G	6-5	279	7/27/67	S.W. Texas State	Houston, Tex.	D7a
Pool, David	CB	5-9	188	12/20/66	Carson-Newman	Cincinnati, Ohio	D6c
Sale, Ken	LB	6-2	245	5/3/68	Texas-El Paso	Torrance, Calif.	FA
Searcy, Elliott	WR	5-7	173	9/18/67	Southern University	Baton Rouge, La.	D12
Seau, Junior	LB	6-3	243	1/19/69	Southern California	Oceanside, Calif.	D1
Staysniak, Joe	T	6-4	244	6/23/67	Ohio State	Midview, Ohio	D7b
Stowers, Tommie	TE	6-3	225	11/18/66	Missouri	Kansas City, Mo.	D11
Walker, Derrick	TE	6-0	244	6/23/67	Michigan	Chicago Heights, Ill.	D6d
Whelihan, Thomas (1)	K	5-10	198	8/15/66	Missouri	Carrollton, Tex.	FA
Wilson, Walter	WR	5-10	185	10/6/66	East Carolina	Baltimore, Md.	D3c

The term NFL Rookie is defined as a player who is in his first season of professional football and has not been on the roster of another professional football team for any regular-season or postseason games. A Rookie is designated by an "R" on NFL rosters. Players who have been active in another professional football league or players who have NFL experience, including either preseason training camp or being on an active roster for fewer than three regular-season or postseason games, are termed NFL First-Year Players. An NFL First-Year Player is designated by a "1" on NFL rosters. Thereafter, a player on an NFL active roster for at least three regular-season or postseason games is credited with an additional year of NFL playing experience.

NOTES

_____

_____

_____

_____

_____

_____

_____

_____

LeCharls McDaniel, assistant to special teams coordinator; born October 15, 1958, Fort Bragg, N.C., lives in San Diego. Defensive back Cal Poly-SLO 1976-80. Defensive back Washington Redskins 1981-82, New York Giants 1983-84. College coach: Hartnell Community College 1986-88. Pro coach: Joined Chargers in 1989.

Jim Mora, secondary; born November 19, 1961, Los Angeles, lives in San Diego. Defensive back Washington 1980-83. No pro playing experience. College coach: Washington 1984. Pro coach: Joined Chargers in 1989.

Larry Pasquale, special teams coordinator; born April 21, 1941, Brooklyn, N.Y., lives in San Diego. Quarterback Bridgeport 1961-63. No pro playing experience. College coach: Slippery Rock State 1967, Boston University 1968, Navy 1969-70, Massachusetts 1971-75, Idaho State 1976. Pro coach: Montreal Alouettes (CFL) 1977-78, Detroit Lions 1979, New York Jets 1980-89, joined Chargers in 1990.

Jack Reilly, offensive assistant; born May 22, 1945, Boston, Mass., lives in San Diego. Quarterback Washington State 1963, Santa Monica City College 1964, Long Beach State 1965-66. No pro playing experience. College coach: El Camino, Calif., J.C. 1980-84, Utah 1985-89 (head coach). Pro coach: Joined Chargers in 1990.

Ted Tollner, assistant head coach/quarterbacks; born May 29, 1940, San Francisco, lives in San Diego. Quarterback Cal Poly-SLO 1959-61. No pro playing experience. College coach: College of San Mateo 1971-72 (head coach), San Diego State 1973-80, Brigham Young 1981, Southern California 1982-86 (head coach 1983-86). Pro coach: Buffalo Bills 1987-88, joined Chargers in 1989.

Ed White, tight ends; born April 4, 1947, San Diego, Calif., lives in Alpine, Calif. Defensive lineman California 1965-68. Guard-tackle Minnesota 1969-77, San Diego Chargers 1978-85. Pro coach: San Diego Chargers 1986-87, Los Angeles Rams 1988, rejoined the Chargers in 1989.

SEATTLE SEAHAWKS

American Football Conference Western Division

Team Colors: Blue, Green, and Silver

11220 N.E. 53rd Street
Kirkland, Washington 98033
Telephone: (206) 827-9777

Club Officials

Owner: Ken Behring
President/General Manager: Tom Flores
Vice President/Assistant General Manager:
  Chuck Allen
Player Personnel Director: Mike Allman
Vice President/Public Relations: Gary Wright
Publicity Director: Dave Neubert
Community Relations Director: Sandy Gregory
Sales and Marketing Director: Reggie McKenzie
Business Manager: Mickey Loomis
Data Processing Director: Tom Monroe
Ticket Manager: James Nagaoka
Trainer: Jim Whitesel
Equipment Manager: Walt Loeffler

Stadium: Kingdome • **Capacity:** 64,984
  201 South King Street
  Seattle, Washington 98104

Playing Surface: AstroTurf

Training Camp: 11220 N.E. 53rd Street
  Kirkland, Washington 98033

1990 Schedule

Preseason
Aug. 4	vs. Denver at Tokyo	10:00*
Aug. 11	at Phoenix	7:30
Aug. 17	**Indianapolis**	7:30
Aug. 24	**Tampa Bay**	6:00
Aug. 31	at San Francisco	6:00

*P.M. Eastern Time

Regular Season
Sept. 9	at Chicago	12:00
Sept. 16	**Los Angeles Raiders**	1:00
Sept. 23	at Denver	2:00
Oct. 1	**Cincinnati** (Monday)	6:00
Oct. 7	at New England	1:00
Oct. 14	at Los Angeles Raiders	1:00
Oct. 21	**Kansas City**	1:00
Oct. 28	**Open Date**	
Nov. 4	**San Diego**	1:00
Nov. 11	at Kansas City	12:00
Nov. 18	**Minnesota**	1:00
Nov. 25	at San Diego	5:00
Dec. 2	**Houston**	1:00
Dec. 9	vs. Green Bay at Milwaukee	12:00
Dec. 16	at Miami	1:00
Dec. 23	**Denver**	5:00
Dec. 30	**Detroit**	1:00

Seahawks Coaching History
(106-113-0)
1976-82	Jack Patera*	35-59-0
1982	Mike McCormack	4-3-0
1983-89	Chuck Knox	67-51-0

*Released after two games in 1982

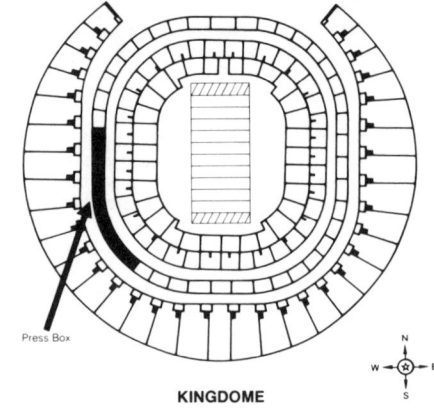

Press Box

KINGDOME

Record Holders
Individual Records—Career
Category	Name	Performance
Rushing (Yds.)	Curt Warner, 1983-89	6,705
Passing (Yds.)	David Krieg, 1980-89	20,585
Passing (TDs)	Dave Krieg, 1980-89	169
Receiving (No.)	Steve Largent, 1976-1989	*819
Receiving (Yds.)	Steve Largent, 1976-1989	*13,089
Interceptions	Dave Brown, 1976-1986	50
Punting (Avg.)	Ruben Rodriguez, 1987-89	40.3
Punt Return (Avg.)	Paul Johns, 1981-84	11.4
Kickoff Return (Avg.)	Bobby Joe Edmonds, 1986-88	22.1
Field Goals	Norm Johnson, 1982-89	136
Touchdowns (Tot.)	Steve Largent, 1976-1989	101
Points	Norm Johnson, 1982-89	708

Individual Records—Single Season
Category	Name	Performance
Rushing (Yds.)	Curt Warner, 1986	1,481
Passing (Yds.)	Dave Krieg, 1984	3,671
Passing (TDs)	Dave Krieg, 1984	32
Receiving (No.)	Steve Largent, 1985	79
Receiving (Yds.)	Steve Largent, 1985	1,287
Interceptions	John Harris, 1981	10
	Kenny Easley, 1984	10
Punting (Avg.)	Herman Weaver, 1980	41.8
Punt Return (Avg.)	Bobby Joe Edmonds, 1987	12.6
Kickoff Return (Avg.)	Al Hunter, 1978	24.1
Field Goals	Norm Johnson, 1986	22
	Norm Johnson, 1988	22
Touchdowns (Tot.)	David Sims, 1978	15
	Sherman Smith, 1979	15
Points	Norm Johnson, 1984	110

Individual Records—Single Game
Category	Name	Performance
Rushing (Yds.)	Curt Warner, 11-27-83	207
Passing (Yds.)	Dave Krieg, 11-20-83	418
Passing (TDs)	Dave Krieg, 12-2-84	5
	Dave Krieg, 9-15-85	5
	Dave Krieg, 11-28-88	5
Receiving (No.)	Steve Largent, 10-18-87	15
Receiving (Yds.)	Steve Largent, 10-18-87	261
Interceptions	Kenny Easley, 9-3-84	3
Field Goals	Norm Johnson, 9-20-87	5
	Norm Johnson, 12-18-88	5
Touchdowns (Tot.)	Daryl Turner, 9-15-85	4
	Curt Warner, 12-11-88	4
Points	Daryl Turner, 9-15-85	24
	Curt Warner, 12-11-88	24

*NFL Record

1989 Team Record
Preseason (3-1)

Date	Result		Opponents
8/11	W	16-10	at Phoenix (OT)
8/19	L	12-17	vs. New England at St. Louis, Mo.
8/25	W	13- 7	Detroit
9/1	W	28-17	San Francisco
		69-51	

Regular Season (7-9)

Date	Result		Opponents	Att.
9/10	L	7-31	at Philadelphia	64,287
9/17	L	24-34	Phoenix	60,444
9/24	W	24- 3	at New England	48,025
10/1	W	24-20	at L.A. Raiders	44,319
10/8	L	16-20	Kansas City	60,715
10/15	W	17-16	at San Diego	50,079
10/22	L	21-24	Denver (OT)	62,353
10/29	W	10- 7	San Diego	59,691
11/5	L	10-20	at Kansas City	54,489
11/12	L	7-17	Cleveland	58,978
11/19	L	3-15	at N.Y. Giants	75,014
11/26	L	14-41	at Denver	75,117
12/4	W	17-16	Buffalo	57,682
12/10	W	24-17	at Cincinnati	54,744
12/17	W	23-17	L.A. Raiders	61,076
12/23	L	0-29	Washington	60,294

(OT) Overtime

Score by Periods

Seahawks	72	60	41	68	0	—	241
Opponents	81	80	86	77	3	—	327

Attendance
Home 481,233   Away 466,074   Total 947,307
Single-game home record, 64,411 (12-15-84)
Single-season home record, 494,103 (1988)

1989 Team Statistics

	Seahawks	Opp.
Total First Downs	290	293
Rushing	86	119
Passing	180	158
Penalty	24	16
Third Down: Made/Att.	85/211	89/213
Third Down: Pct.	40.3	41.8
Fourth Down: Made/Att.	8/17	5/16
Fourth Down: Pct.	47.1	31.3
Total Net Yards	4596	5215
Avg. Per Game	287.3	325.9
Total Plays	1010	997
Avg. Per Play	4.6	5.2
Net Yards Rushing	1392	2118
Avg. Per Game	87.0	132.4
Total Rushes	405	520
Net Yards Passing	3204	3097
Avg. Per Game	200.3	193.6
Sacked/Yards Lost	46/379	32/235
Gross Yards	3583	3332
Att./Completions	559/316	445/252
Completion Pct.	56.5	56.6
Had Intercepted	23	9
Punts/Avg.	76/39.4	74/39.2
Net Punting Avg.	32.9	33.9
Penalties/Yards Lost	79/738	118/809
Fumbles/Ball Lost	43/14	26/13
Touchdowns	28	37
Rushing	5	11
Passing	21	23
Returns	2	3
Avg. Time of Possession	29:20	30:40

1989 Individual Statistics

Scoring

	TD R	TD P	TD Rt	PAT	FG	Saf	TP
N. Johnson	0	0	0	27/27	15/25	0	72
Williams	1	6	0	0/0	0/0	0	42
Blades	0	5	0	0/0	0/0	0	30
Skansi	0	5	0	0/0	0/0	0	30
Warner	3	1	0	0/0	0/0	0	24
Largent	0	3	0	1/1	0/0	0	19
Clark	0	1	0	0/0	0/0	0	6
Fenner	1	0	0	0/0	0/0	0	6
Glasgow	0	0	1	0/0	0/0	0	6
Jefferson	0	0	1	0/0	0/0	0	6
Seahawks	5	21	2	28/28	15/25	0	241
Opponents	11	23	3	35/37	22/32	2	327

Passing

	Att.	Comp.	Yds.	Pct.	TD	Int.	Tkld.	Rate
Krieg	499	286	3309	57.3	21	20	37/289	74.8
Stouffer	59	29	270	49.2	0	3	9/90	40.9
Rodriguez	1	1	4	100.0	0	0	0/0	83.3
Seahawks	559	316	3583	56.5	21	23	46/379	71.3
Opponents	445	252	3332	56.6	23	9	32/235	89.3

Rushing

	Att.	Yds.	Avg.	LG	TD
Warner	194	631	3.3	34	3
Williams	146	499	3.4	21	1
Krieg	40	160	4.0	18	0
Fenner	11	41	3.7	9	1
Harmon	1	24	24.0	24	0
Harris	8	23	2.9	8	0
Stouffer	2	11	5.5	9	0
Blades	1	3	3.0	3	0
Kemp	1	0	0.0	0	0
Rodriguez	1	0	0.0	0	0
Seahawks	405	1392	3.4	34	5
Opponents	520	2118	4.1	38	11

Receiving

	No.	Yds.	Avg.	LG	TD
Blades	77	1063	13.8	60t	5
Williams	76	657	8.6	51t	6
Skansi	39	488	12.5	26	5
Largent	28	403	14.4	33	3
Clark	25	260	10.4	28	1
Warner	23	153	6.7	24	1
Tyler	14	148	10.6	27	0
McNeal	9	147	16.3	48	0
Chadwick, Det.-Sea.	9	104	11.6	19	0
Chadwick, Sea.	8	95	11.9	19	0
Kane	7	94	13.4	20	0
Harris	3	26	8.7	11	0
Fenner	3	23	7.7	9	0
Bouyer	1	9	9.0	9	0
J. Jones	1	8	8.0	8	0
Feasel	1	5	5.0	5	0
Glasgow	1	4	4.0	4	0
Seahawks	316	3583	11.3	60t	21
Opponents	252	3332	13.2	69	23

Interceptions

	No.	Yds.	Avg.	LG	TD
Robinson	5	24	4.8	20	0
Harper	2	15	7.5	15	0
J. Johnson	1	18	18.0	18	0
Comeaux	1	0	0.0	0	0
Seahawks	9	57	6.3	20	0
Opponents	23	248	10.8	30t	2

Punting

	No.	Yds.	Avg.	In 20	LG
Rodriguez	75	2995	39.9	17	59
Seahawks	76	2995	39.4	17	59
Opponents	74	2902	39.2	21	60

Punt Returns

	No.	FC	Yds.	Avg.	LG	TD
Hollis	18	7	164	9.1	21	0
Jefferson	12	10	87	7.3	19	0
Seahawks	30	17	251	8.4	21	0
Opponents	41	12	334	8.1	49	0

Kickoff Returns

	No.	Yds.	Avg.	LG	TD
Jefferson	22	511	23.2	97t	1
Harris	18	334	18.6	25	0
Hollis	15	247	16.5	30	0
Harmon	6	84	14.0	19	0
Clark	1	31	31.0	31	0
McNeal	1	17	17.0	17	0
Woods	1	13	13.0	13	0
Comeaux	1	9	9.0	9	0
Seahawks	65	1246	19.2	97t	1
Opponents	44	814	18.5	37	0

Sacks

	No.
Porter	10.5
Nash	8.0
Bryant	3.5
Green	3.0
Woods	3.0
Hart	2.0
Hunter	1.0
Mitz	1.0
Seahawks	32.0
Opponents	46.0

1990 Draft Choices

Round	Name	Pos.	College
1.	Cortez Kennedy	DT	Miami
2.	Terry Wooden	LB	Syracuse
	Robert Blackmon	DB	Baylor
4.	Chris Warren	RB	Ferrum, Va.
5.	Eric Hayes	DT	Florida State
6.	Ned Bolcar	LB	Notre Dame
7.	Bob Kula	T	Michigan State
8.	Bill Hitchcock	T	Purdue
10.	Robert Morris	DE	Valdosta State
11.	Daryl Reed	DB	Oregon
12.	John Gromos	QB	Vanderbilt

Seattle Seahawks 1990 Veteran Roster

No.	Name	Pos.	Ht.	Wt.	Birth-date	NFL Exp.	College	Hometown	How Acq.	'89 Games/ Starts
50	Ahrens, Dave	LB	6-4	245	12/5/58	10	Wisconsin	Oregon, Wis.	PB(Mia)-'90#	11/8*
65	Bailey, Edwin	G	6-4	273	5/15/59	10	South Carolina State	Savannah, Ga.	D5-'81	16/16
89	Blades, Brian	WR	5-11	184	7/24/65	3	Miami	Ft. Lauderdale, Fla.	D2-'88	16/14
55	Bosworth, Brian	LB	6-2	236	3/9/65	3	Oklahoma	Irving, Tex.	SD1-'87	2/2
8	Bouyer, Willie	WR	6-3	200	9/24/66	2	Michigan State	Detroit, Mich.	FA-'90	1/0*
64	Brilz, Darrick	G	6-3	270	2/14/64	4	Oregon State	Pinole Valley, Calif.	FA-'89	14/0
77	†Bryant, Jeff	DE	6-5	277	5/22/60	9	Clemson	Decatur, Ga.	D1-'82	15/15
59	Cain, Joe	LB	6-1	228	6/11/65	2	Oregon Tech	Compton, Calif.	FA-'89	9/0
88	†Chadwick, Jeff	WR	6-3	190	12/16/60	8	Grand Valley State	Dearborn, Mich.	FA-'89	12/0
84	Clark, Louis	WR	6-0	199	7/3/64	4	Mississippi State	Shannon, Miss.	D10-'87	16/6
53	†Comeaux, Darren	LB	6-1	239	4/15/60	9	Arizona State	San Diego, Calif.	W(SF)-'88	16/13
3	Donnelly, Rick	P	6-0	190	2/17/62	6	Wyoming	Miller Place, N.Y.	PB(Atl)-'90#	0*
31	Edmonds, Bobby Joe	RB	5-11	186	9/26/64	5	Arkansas	St. Louis, Mo.	PB(Raid)-'90#	7/0*
54	†Feasel, Grant	C	6-7	279	6/28/60	6	Abilene Christian	Barstow, Calif.	FA-'87	16/16
44	Fenner, Derrick	RB	6-3	229	4/6/67	2	North Carolina	Oxon Hill, Md.	D10-'89	5/1
90	Franklin, Jethro	DE	6-1	258	10/25/65	2	Fresno State	San Jose, Calif.	FA-'89	7/1
22	Glasgow, Nesby	S	5-10	187	4/15/57	12	Washington	Gardena, Calif.	FA-'88	16/16
79	Green, Jacob	DE	6-3	254	1/21/57	11	Texas A&M	Houston, Tex.	D1-'80	15/14
29	†Harper, Dwayne	CB	5-11	174	3/29/66	3	South Carolina State	Orangeburg, S.C.	D11b-'88	16/13
33	Harris, Elroy	RB	5-9	218	8/18/66	2	Eastern Kentucky	Maitland, Fla.	D3-'89	14/0
63	Hart, Roy	NT	6-1	279	7/10/65	2	South Carolina	Tifton, Ga.	D6-'88	16/1
66	Heck, Andy	T	6-6	291	1/1/67	2	Notre Dame	Fairfax, Va.	D1-'89	16/9
85	Heller, Ron	TE	6-3	236	9/18/63	4	Oregon State	Clark Fork, Idaho	PB(Atl)-'90#	15/13*
23	†Hunter, Patrick	CB	5-11	186	10/24/64	5	Nevada-Reno	San Francisco, Calif.	D3-'86	16/14
26	Jefferson, James	CB	6-1	199	11/18/63	2	Texas A&I	Kingville, Tex.	FA-'89	16/1
24	†Jenkins, Melvin	CB	5-10	182	3/16/62	4	Cincinnati	Jackson, Miss.	FA-'87	16/3
9	Johnson, Norm	K	6-2	197	5/31/60	9	UCLA	Garden Grove, Calif.	FA-'82	16/0
30	Jones, James	RB	6-2	229	3/21/61	8	Florida	Pompano Beach, Fla.	T(Det)-'89	2/0
81	Kane, Tommy	WR	5-11	176	1/14/64	3	Syracuse	Montreal, Canada	D3-'88	5/0
15	†Kemp, Jeff	QB	6-0	201	7/11/59	10	Dartmouth	Bethesda, Md.	T(SF)-'87	9/0
58	Kimmel, Jamie	LB	6-3	235	3/28/62	3	Syracuse	Conklin, N.Y.	FA-'90	0*
17	†Krieg, Dave	QB	6-1	192	10/20/58	11	Milton	Schofield, Wis.	FA-'80	15/14
70	†Mattes, Ron	T	6-6	302	8/8/63	5	Virginia	Shenandoah, Va.	D7-'85	16/8
40	McLemore, Chris	RB	6-1	230	12/31/63	3	Arizona	Las Vegas, Nev.	FA-'90	0*
86	McNeal, Travis	TE	6-3	248	1/10/67	2	Tennessee-Chattanooga	Birmingham, Ala.	D4a-'89	16/6
71	Millard, Bryan	G	6-5	281	12/2/60	7	Texas	Dumas, Tex.	FA-'84	16/16
91	Miller, Darrin	LB	6-1	236	3/24/65	3	Tennessee	Flemington, N.J.	FA-'88	16/0
72	Nash, Joe	NT	6-2	269	10/11/60	9	Boston College	Dorchester, Mass.	FA-'82	16/16
97	Porter, Rufus	LB	6-1	221	5/18/65	3	Southern University	Baton Rouge, La.	FA-'88	16/3
98	Ridgle, Elston	DE	6-5	270	8/24/63	3	Nevada-Reno	Woodland Hills, Calif.	FA-'89	1/0*
41	Robinson, Eugene	S	6-0	186	5/28/63	6	Colgate	Hartford, Conn.	FA-'85	16/14
5	Rodriguez, Ruben	P	6-2	217	3/3/65	4	Arizona	Woodlake, Calif.	D5b-'87	16/0
82	Skansi, Paul	WR	5-11	186	1/11/61	8	Washington	Gig Harbor, Wash.	FA-'85	16/1
11	Stouffer, Kelly	QB	6-3	207	7/6/64	3	Colorado State	Rushville, Neb.	T(Phx)-'88	3/2
56	Tofflemire, Joe	C	6-2	274	7/7/65	2	Arizona	Post Falls, Idaho	D2-'89	0*
87	Tyler, Robert	TE	6-5	257	10/12/65	2	South Carolina State	Salley, N.C.	D8-'88	9/9
32	Williams, John L.	RB	5-11	228	11/23/64	5	Florida	Palatka, Fla.	D1-'86	15/15
57	Woods, Tony	LB	6-4	259	9/11/65	4	Pittsburgh	Newark, N.J.	D1-'87	16/12
92	†Wyman, David	LB	6-2	242	3/31/64	4	Stanford	Reno, Nev.	D2-'87	16/16

* Ahrens played 11 games with Miami in '89; Bouyer played 1 game with Seattle in '89; Donnelly missed '89 season due to injury; Edmonds played 7 games with L.A. Raiders; Heller played 15 games with Atlanta; Kimmel last active with L.A. Raiders in '88; McLemore last active with Raiders in '88; Ridgle played 1 game with Buffalo in '89; Tofflemire active for 16 games but did not play.

† Option playout; subject to developments.

Plan B unconditional free agent.

Retired—Steve Largent, 14-year wide receiver, 10 games in '89; Paul Moyer, 7-year safety, 11 games in '89; Mike Wilson, 12-year tackle, 16 games in '89.

Players lost through Plan B (7): TE Donnie Dee (GB; 3 games in '89), RB Kevin Harmon (KC; 4), LB M. L. Johnson (GB; 13), TE Rod Jones (KC; 4), TE Harper Le Bel (Phil; 16), LB Rod Stephens (Den; 10), RB Curt Warner (L.A. Rams; 16).

Also played with Seahawks in '89—S David Hollis (10 games), S Johnnie Johnson (3), CB-S Thom Kaumeyer (1), LB Vernon Maxwell (9).

COACHING STAFF

Head Coach, Chuck Knox

Pro Career: Named head coach of Seahawks on January 26, 1983, after five seasons as head coach at Buffalo, where he led Bills to AFC East title in 1980. Led Los Angeles Rams to five straight NFC West titles before taking over Bills in 1978. Pro assistant with New York Jets 1963-66, coaching offensive line, before moving to Detroit in 1967. Served Lions in same capacity until named head coach of Rams in 1973. No pro playing experience. Career record: 162-109-1.

Background: Played tackle for Juniata College in Huntingdon, Pa., 1950-53. Was assistant coach at his alma mater in 1954, then spent 1955 season as line coach at Ellwood City High School in Pennsylvania. Moved to Wake Forest as an assistant coach in 1959-60, then Kentucky in 1961-62.

Personal: Born April 27, 1932, Sewickley, Pa. Chuck and his wife, Shirley, live in Bellevue, Wash., and have four children—Chris, Kathy, Colleen, and Chuck.

Assistant Coaches

John Becker, offensive coordinator-receivers; born February 16, 1943, Alexandria, Va., lives in Redmond, Wash. Cal State-Northridge 1965. No college or pro playing experience. College coach: UCLA 1970, New Mexico State 1971, New Mexico 1972-73, Los Angeles Valley J.C. (head coach) 1974-76, Oregon 1977-79. Pro coach: Philadelphia Eagles 1980-83, Buffalo Bills 1984, Indianapolis Colts 1985-88, joined Seahawks in 1989.

Tom Catlin, assistant head coach-defensive coordinator; born September 8, 1931, Ponca City, Okla., lives in Redmond, Wash. Center-linebacker Oklahoma 1950-52. Pro linebacker Cleveland Browns 1953-54, 1957-58, Philadelphia Eagles 1959. College coach: Army 1956. Pro coach: Dallas Texans-Kansas City Chiefs 1960-65, Los Angeles Rams 1966-77, Buffalo Bills 1978-82, joined Seahawks in 1983.

George Dyer, defensive line; born May 4, 1940, Alhambra, Calif., lives in Redmond, Wash. Center-linebacker U.C. Santa Barbara 1961-63. No pro playing experience. College coach: Humboldt State 1964-66, Coalinga, Calif., J.C. 1967 (head coach), Portland State 1968-71, Idaho 1972, San Jose State 1973, Michigan State 1977-79, Arizona State 1980-81. Pro coach: Winnipeg Blue Bombers (CFL) 1974-76, Buffalo Bills 1982, joined Seahawks in 1983.

Chick Harris, offensive backfield; born September 21, 1945, Durham, N.C., lives in Redmond, Wash. Running back Northern Arizona 1966-69. No pro playing experience. College coach: Colorado State 1970-72, Long Beach State 1973-74, Washington 1975-80. Pro coach: Buffalo Bills 1981-82, joined Seahawks in 1983.

Ken Meyer, quarterbacks; born July 14, 1926, Erie, Pa., lives in Bellevue, Wash. Quarterback Denison 1947-50. No pro playing experience. College coach: Denison 1952-57, Wake Forest 1958-59, Florida State 1960-63, Alabama 1963-67, Tulane 1981-82. Pro coach: San Francisco 49ers 1968, 1977 (head coach), New York Jets 1969-72, Los Angeles Rams 1973-76, Chicago Bears 1978-80, joined Seahawks in 1983.

Paul Moyer, staff assistant; born July 26, 1961, Villa Park, Calif., lives in Bellevue, Wash. Safety Fullerton Junior College and Arizona State 1979-82. Pro safety Seattle Seahawks 1983-89. Pro coach: Joined Seahawks in 1990.

Rod Perry, defensive backfield; born September 11, 1953, Fresno, Calif., lives in Kirkland, Wash. Defensive back Fresno City College and Colorado 1971-74. Pro cornerback Los Angeles Rams 1975-82, Cleveland Browns 1983-84. College coach: Columbia University 1985, Fresno City College 1986, Fresno State 1987-88. Pro coach: Joined Seahawks in 1989.

Seattle Seahawks 1990 First-Year Roster

Name	Pos.	Ht.	Wt.	Birth-date	College	Hometown	How Acq.
Andrews, Ricky (1)	LB	6-2	236	4/14/66	Washington	Mililani, Hawaii	FA
Baumann, Charlie (1)	K	6-1	203	8/25/67	West Virginia	Erie, Pa.	FA
Bednarz, Blake	G	6-3	303	9/17/68	Syracuse	Blasdell, N.Y.	FA
Blackmon, Robert	S	6-0	198	5/12/67	Baylor	Van Vleck, Tex.	D3b
Blaylock, Lavent	CB	5-10	180	7/28/66	Indiana State	East St. Louis, Ill.	FA
Bolcar, Ned	LB	6-1	235	1/12/67	Notre Dame	Phillipsburg, N.J.	D6
Brown, Jerry (1)	G	6-4	277	10/8/65	Utah State	Santa Rosa, Calif.	FA
Dodge, Dedrick	S	6-2	180	6/14/67	Florida State	Mulberry, Fla.	FA
Fletcher, Dewayne	CB	6-2	191	9/2/67	Toledo	Flint, Mich.	FA
Garcia, Bobby	G	6-3	253	5/3/67	Miami	Cooper City, Fla.	FA
Gray, Randy	NT	6-6	270	4/3/67	Washington State	Danville, Calif.	FA
Gromos, John	QB	6-5	210	12/9/66	Vanderbilt	Joliet, Ill.	D12
Hayes, Eric	NT	6-3	285	1/12/67	Florida State	Tampa, Fla.	D5
Hitchcock, Bill	T	6-8	308	8/26/65	Purdue	Kirkland, Quebec	D8
Horton, Derek	CB	5-11	184	11/8/67	Oregon	Oakland, Calif.	FA
Jordan, Xavier	LB	6-1	236	8/18/67	Western Kentucky	Atlanta, Ga.	FA
Kaumeyer, Thom (1)	S	5-11	187	3/17/67	Oregon	San Diego, Calif.	FA
Kennedy, Cortez	NT	6-3	293	8/23/68	Miami	Rivercrest, Ark.	D1
Kors, R.J. (1)	S	6-0	195	6/27/66	Long Beach State	Woodland Hills, Calif.	FA
Kula, Bob	T	6-3	282	8/24/67	Michigan State	Birmingham, Mich.	D7
Lee, Alvin	WR	5-10	188	12/6/67	Louisiana State	Beaumont, Tex.	FA
Lindsay, Mike	T	6-7	290	10/20/66	Gardner-Webb	Spartanburg, S.C.	FA
Loville, Derek	RB	5-9	198	7/4/68	Oregon	Pacific, Calif.	FA
McJulian, Paul (1)	P	5-10	190	2/24/65	Jackson State	Chicago, Ill.	FA
Miller, Donald	LB	6-2	223	4/9/64	Idaho State	Chicago, Ill.	FA
Morris, Robert	DE	6-6	265	5/12/68	Valdosta State	Brunswick, Ga.	D10
Murphy, Dave	S	6-0	190	2/16/68	Holy Cross	Walpole, Mass.	FA
Obee, Terry	WR	5-10	182	6/15/68	Oregon	Richmond, Calif.	FA
Oberdorf, Todd	T	6-6	290	1/21/67	Indiana	Fairfield, Ohio	FA
Olson, Rodd	TE	6-4	224	11/27/66	Washington State	Walnut Creek, Calif.	FA
Parquet, Felton	RB	6-0	228	11/12/66	Louisiana State	Destrehan, La.	FA
Reed, Daryl	CB	6-1	186	10/27/67	Oregon	Harbor City, Calif.	D11
Sandusky, Jim (1)	WR	5-10	182	9/1/61	San Diego State	Othello, Wash.	FA-'89
Tanks, Michael	C	6-1	254	8/4/67	Florida State	Decatur, Ga.	FA
Walker, Willie	LB	6-1	243	4/8/67	North Carolina	Bradenton, Fla.	FA
Warren, Chris	RB	6-2	225	1/24/67	Ferrum	Burke, Va.	D4
Watts, Jonathan	S	5-11	203	8/23/67	Western Kentucky	Port Gibson, Miss.	FA
Wheat, Warren (1)	G	6-6	274	5/13/67	Brigham Young	Phoenix, Ariz.	FA-'89
Wooden, Terry	LB	6-3	232	1/14/67	Syracuse	Farmington, Conn.	D2a

The term NFL Rookie is defined as a player who is in his first season of professional football and has not been on the roster of another professional football team for any regular-season or postseason games. A Rookie is designated by an "R" on NFL rosters. Players who have been active in another professional football league or players who have NFL experience, including either preseason training camp or being on an active roster for fewer than three regular-season or postseason games, are termed NFL First-Year Players. An NFL First-Year Player is designated by a "1" on NFL rosters. Thereafter, a player on an NFL active roster for at least three regular-season or postseason games is credited with an additional year of NFL playing experience.

NOTES

_____

_____

_____

_____

_____

_____

_____

Russ Purnell, tight ends-assistant special teams; born June 12, 1948, Chicago, Ill., lives in Bellevue, Wash. Center Orange Coast, Calif., J.C. and Whittier College 1966-69. No pro playing experience. College coach: Whittier 1970-71, Southern California 1982-85. Pro coach: Joined Seahawks in 1986.

Frank Raines, strength and conditioning; born November 29, 1960, Portsmouth, Va., lives in Kirkland, Wash. No college or pro playing experience. Pro coach: Washington Redskins 1986-89, joined Seahawks in 1990.

Kent Stephenson, offensive line; born February 4, 1942, Anita, Iowa, lives in Redmond, Wash. Guardnose tackle Northern Iowa 1962-64. No pro playing experience. College coach: Wayne State 1965-68, North Dakota 1969-71, Southern Methodist 1972-73, Iowa 1974-76, Oklahoma State 1977-78, Kansas 1979-82. Pro coach: Michigan Panthers (USFL) 1983-84, joined Seahawks in 1985.

Rusty Tillman, special teams, assistant linebackers; born February 27, 1948, Beloit, Wis., lives in Bellevue, Wash. Linebacker Northern Arizona 1967-69. Pro linebacker Washington Redskins 1970-77. Pro coach: Joined Seahawks in 1979.

Joe Vitt, special assignments; born August 23, 1954, Camden, N.J., lives in Redmond, Wash. Linebacker Towson State 1973-75. No pro playing experience. Pro coach: Baltimore Colts 1979-81, joined Seahawks in 1982.

THE NFC

National Football Conference
Western Division

Team Colors: Red, Black, White, and Silver

Suwanee Road at I-85
Suwanee, Georgia 30174
Telephone: (404) 945-1111

Club Officials

Chairman of the Board: Rankin M. Smith, Sr.
Executive Vice President: Taylor Smith
Vice President & Chief Financial Officer: Jim Hay
Vice President of Player Personnel:
  Ken Herock
Director of Marketing: Tommy Nobis
Director of Public Relations: Charlie Taylor
Asst. Director of Public Relations: Frank Kleha
Director of Community Relations: Carol Breeding
Director of Ticket Operations: Jack Ragsdale
Asst. Director of Ticket Operations: Luci Bailey
Administrative Assistant/Player Personnel:
  Danny Mock
Talent Scouts: Charley Armey, Bill Baker, Elbert
  Dubenion, Bill Groman
Director of Pro Personnel: Chuck Connor
Controller: Wallace Norman
Trainer: Jerry Rhea
Assistant Trainer: Billy Brooks
Equipment Manager: Whitey Zimmerman
Assistant Equipment Manager: Horace Daniel
Video Director: Tom Atcheson
Assistant Video Director: Mike Gleeson

Stadium: Atlanta-Fulton County Stadium •
    Capacity: 59,643
    521 Capitol Avenue, S.W.
    Atlanta, Georgia 30312

Playing Surface: Grass (PAT)

Training Camp: Suwanee Road at I-85
        Suwanee, Georgia 30174

1990 Schedule

Preseason
Aug. 11	vs. Washington at	
	Chapel Hill, N.C.	7:00
Aug. 18	**Cincinnati**	7:00
Aug. 25	vs. Green Bay at Milwaukee	6:00
Aug. 31	at New England	7:30

Regular Season
Sept. 9	**Houston**	4:00
Sept. 16	at Detroit	1:00
Sept. 23	at San Francisco	1:00
Sept. 30	**Open Date**	
Oct. 7	**New Orleans**	1:00
Oct. 14	**San Francisco**	1:00
Oct. 21	at Los Angeles Rams	1:00
Oct. 28	**Cincinnati**	8:00
Nov. 4	at Pittsburgh	1:00
Nov. 11	at Chicago	12:00
Nov. 18	**Philadelphia**	1:00
Nov. 25	at New Orleans	12:00
Dec. 2	at Tampa Bay	1:00
Dec. 9	**Phoenix**	1:00
Dec. 16	at Cleveland	1:00
Dec. 23	**Los Angeles Rams**	1:00
Dec. 30	**Dallas**	1:00

Falcons Coaching History

(130-221-5)

1966-68	Norb Hecker*	4-26-1
1968-74	Norm Van Brocklin**	37-49-3
1974-76	Marion Campbell***	6-19-0
1976	Pat Peppler	3-6-0
1977-82	Leeman Bennett	47-44-0
1983-86	Dan Henning	22-41-1
1987-89	Marion Campbell****	11-32-0
1989	Jim Hanifan	0-4-0

  *Released after three games in 1968
  **Released after eight games in 1974
  ***Released after five games in 1976
  ****Retired after 12 games in 1989

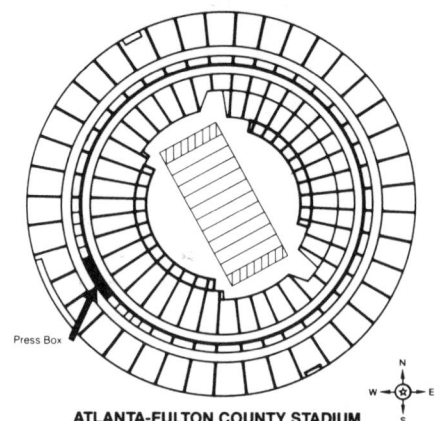

Press Box

N
W — ⊕ — E
S

ATLANTA-FULTON COUNTY STADIUM

Record Holders
Individual Records—Career

Category	Name	Performance
Rushing (Yds.)	Gerald Riggs, 1982-88	6,631
Passing (Yds.)	Steve Bartkowski, 1975-1985	23,468
Passing (TDs)	Steve Bartkowski, 1975-1985	154
Receiving (No.)	Alfred Jenkins, 1975-1983	359
Receiving (Yds.)	Alfred Jenkins, 1975-1983	6,257
Interceptions	Rolland Lawrence, 1973-1980	39
Punting (Avg.)	Rick Donnelly, 1985-89	42.6
Punt Return (Avg.)	Al Dodd, 1973-74	11.8
Kickoff Return (Avg.)	Ron Smith, 1966-67	24.3
Field Goals	Mick Luckhurst, 1981-87	115
Touchdowns (Tot.)	Gerald Riggs, 1982-88	48
Points	Mick Luckhurst, 1981-87	558

Individual Records—Single Season

Category	Name	Performance
Rushing (Yds.)	Gerald Riggs, 1985	1,719
Passing (Yds.)	Steve Bartkowski, 1981	3,830
Passing (TDs)	Steve Bartkowski, 1980	31
Receiving (No.)	William Andrews, 1981	81
Receiving (Yds.)	Alfred Jenkins, 1981	1,358
Interceptions	Scott Case, 1988	10
Punting (Avg.)	Billy Lothridge, 1968	44.3
Punt Return (Avg.)	Gerald Tinker, 1974	13.9
Kickoff Return (Avg.)	Sylvester Stamps, 1987	27.5
Field Goals	Nick Mike-Mayer, 1973	26
Touchdowns (Tot.)	Alfred Jenkins, 1981	13
	Gerald Riggs, 1984	13
Points	Mick Luckhurst, 1981	114

Individual Records—Single Game

Category	Name	Performance
Rushing (Yds.)	Gerald Riggs, 9-2-84	202
Passing (Yds.)	Steve Bartkowski, 11-15-81	416
Passing (TDs)	Randy Johnson, 11-16-69	4
	Steve Bartkowski, 10-19-80	4
	Steve Bartkowski, 10-18-81	4
Receiving (No.)	William Andrews, 11-15-81	15
Receiving (Yds.)	Alfred Jackson, 12-2-84	193
Interceptions	Many times	2
	Last time by Tim Gordon, 11-19-89	
Field Goals	Nick Mike-Mayer, 11-4-73	5
	Tim Mazzetti, 10-30-78	5
Touchdowns (Tot.)	Many times	3
	Last time by Gerald Riggs, 11-17-85	
Points	Many times	18
	Last time by Gerald Riggs, 11-17-85	

1989 Team Record

Preseason (1-3)

Date	Result		Opponents
8/12	L	17-23	at Philadelphia
8/19	L	0-27	at Tampa Bay
8/26	L	7-23	New England
9/1	W	38-17	vs. Buffalo
			at Jacksonville, Fla.

62-90

Regular Season (3-13)

Date	Result		Opponents	Att.
9/10	L	21-31	L.A. Rams	38,708
9/17	W	27-21	Dallas	55,285
9/24	L	9-13	at Indianapolis	57,816
10/1	L	21-23	at Green Bay	54,647
10/8	L	14-26	at L.A. Rams	52,182
10/15	W	16-15	New England	39,697
10/22	L	20-34	at Phoenix	33,894
10/29	L	13-20	at New Orleans	65,153
11/5	W	30-28	Buffalo	45,267
11/12	L	3-45	at San Francisco	59,914
11/19	L	17-26	New Orleans	53,173
11/26	L	7-27	at N.Y. Jets	40,429
12/3	L	10-23	San Francisco	43,128
12/10	L	17-43	at Minnesota	58,116
12/17	L	30-31	Washington	37,501
12/24	L	24-31	Detroit	7,792

Score by Periods

Falcons	43	100	85	51	0	—	279
Opponents	97	118	123	99	0	—	437

Attendance

Home 320,551   Away 422,151   Total 742,702
Single-game home record, 59,257 (10-30-77)
Single-season home record, 442,457 (1980)

1989 Team Statistics

	Falcons	Opp.
Total First Downs	261	336
Rushing	75	156
Passing	173	163
Penalty	13	17
Third Down: Made/Att.	67/206	95/211
Third Down: Pct.	32.5	45.0
Fourth Down: Made/Att.	6/17	7/9
Fourth Down: Pct.	35.3	77.8
Total Net Yards	4669	6025
Avg. Per Game	291.8	376.6
Total Plays	947	1040
Avg. Per Play	4.9	5.8
Net Yards Rushing	1155	2471
Avg. Per Game	72.2	154.4
Total Rushes	318	572
Net Yards Passing	3514	3554
Avg. Per Game	219.6	222.1
Sacked/Yards Lost	51/389	31/183
Gross Yards	3903	3737
Att./Completions	578/312	437/259
Completion Pct.	54.0	59.3
Had Intercepted	12	20
Punts/Avg.	85/40.8	56/41.8
Net Punting Avg.	33/3	34.3
Penalties/Yards Lost	82/671	79/682
Fumbles/Ball Lost	26/11	26/12
Touchdowns	30	49
Rushing	11	26
Passing	17	19
Returns	2	4
Avg. Time of Possession	25:58	34:02

1989 Individual Statistics

Scoring

	TD R	TD P	TD Rt	PAT	FG	Saf	TP
Davis, N.E.-Atl.	0	0	0	25/28	23/34	0	94
Davis, Atl.	0	0	0	12/12	7/11	0	33
McFadden	0	0	0	18/18	15/20	0	63
Jones	6	0	0	0/0	0/0	0	36
Settle	3	2	0	0/0	0/0	0	30
Haynes	0	4	0	0/0	0/0	0	24
Collins	0	3	0	0/0	0/0	0	18
Wilkins	0	3	0	0/0	0/0	0	18
Dixon	0	2	0	0/0	0/0	0	12
Lang	1	1	0	0/0	0/0	0	12
Beckman	0	1	0	0/0	0/0	0	6
Butler	0	0	1	0/0	0/0	0	6
Flowers	1	0	0	0/0	0/0	0	6
Heller	0	1	0	0/0	0/0	0	6
Sanders	0	0	1	0/0	0/0	0	6
Miller	0	0	0	0/0	1/1	0	3
Falcons	11	17	2	30/30	23/32	0	279
Opponents	26	19	4	48/49	31/36	1	437

Passing

	Att.	Comp.	Yds.	Pct.	TD	Int.	Tkld.	Rate
Miller	526	280	3459	53.2	16	10	41/318	76.1
Millen	50	31	432	62.0	1	2	10/71	79.8
Fulhage	1	1	12	100.0	0	0	0/0	116.7
Jones	1	0	0	0.0	0	0	0/0	39.6
Falcons	578	312	3903	54.0	17	12	51/389	76.4
Opponents	437	259	3737	59.3	19	20	31/183	82.5

Rushing

	Att.	Yds.	Avg.	LG	TD
Settle	179	689	3.8	20	3
Jones	52	202	3.9	19	6
Lang	47	176	3.7	22	1
Haynes	4	35	8.8	21	0
Paterra	9	32	3.6	8	0
Flowers	13	24	1.8	4	1
Miller	10	20	2.0	7	0
Fulhage	1	0	0.0	0	0
Millen	1	0	0.0	0	0
Dixon	2	-23	-11.5	0	0
Falcons	318	1155	3.6	22	11
Opponents	572	2471	4.3	38	26

Receiving

	No.	Yds.	Avg.	LG	TD
Collins	58	862	14.9	47	3
Jones	41	396	9.7	46	0
Haynes	40	681	17.0	72t	4
Lang	39	436	11.2	32	1
Settle	39	316	8.1	33	2
Heller	33	324	9.8	30	1
Dixon	25	357	14.3	53t	2
Beckman	11	102	9.3	21	1
Wilkins	8	179	22.4	36	3
Bailey	8	170	21.3	41	0
Paterra	5	42	8.4	20	0
G. Thomas	4	46	11.5	16	0
Sanders	1	-8	-8.0	-8	0
Falcons	312	3903	12.5	72t	17
Opponents	259	3737	14.4	78	19

Interceptions

	No.	Yds.	Avg.	LG	TD
Sanders	5	52	10.4	22	0
Gordon	4	60	15.0	34	0
Cooper	4	54	13.5	38	0
Dimry	2	72	36.0	40	0
Case	2	13	6.5	13	0
Shelley	1	31	31.0	31	0
Zackery	1	3	3.0	3	0
Bruce	1	0	0.0	0	0
Falcons	20	285	14.3	40	0
Opponents	12	85	7.1	27	0

Punting

	No.	Yds.	Avg.	In 20	LG
Fulhage	84	3472	41.3	24	65
Falcons	85	3472	40.8	24	65
Opponents	56	2342	41.8	15	64

Punt Returns

	No.	FC	Yds.	Avg.	LG	TD
Sanders	28	7	307	11.0	68t	1
Jordan	4	0	34	8.5	15	0
Falcons	32	7	341	10.7	68t	1
Opponents	43	20	460	10.7	39	0

Kickoff Returns

	No.	Yds.	Avg.	LG	TD
Sanders	35	725	20.7	72	0
Jones	23	440	19.1	29	0
Paterra	8	129	16.1	31	0
G. Thomas	7	142	20.3	28	0
Jordan	3	27	9.0	13	0
Johnson, N.O.-Atl.	2	34	17.0	19	0
Beckman	2	15	7.5	15	0
Primus	1	16	16.0	16	0
Bruce	1	15	15.0	15	0
Falcons	80	1509	18.9	72	0
Opponents	60	1188	19.8	85	0

Sacks

	No.
Cotton	9.0
Bruce	6.0
Green	5.0
Casillas	2.0
Gann	2.0
Bryan	1.0
Case	1.0
Dimry	1.0
Reid	1.0
B. Thomas	1.0
Taylor	1.0
Tuggle	1.0
Falcons	31.0
Opponents	51.0

1990 Draft Choices

Round	Name	Pos.	College
1.	Steve Broussard	RB	Washington State
2.	Darion Conner	LB	Jackson State
3.	Oliver Barnett	DE	Kentucky
5.	Reggie Redding	TE	Cal State-Fullerton
6.	Mike Pringle	RB	Cal State-Fullerton
8.	Tory Epps	NT	Memphis State
9.	Darrell Jordan	LB	Northern Arizona
10.	Donnie Salum	LB	Arizona
11.	Chris Ellison	DB	Houston
12.	Shawn McCarthy	P	Purdue

Atlanta Falcons 1990 Veteran Roster

No.	Name	Pos.	Ht.	Wt.	Birth-date	NFL Exp.	College	Hometown	How Acq.	'89 Games/Starts
82	†Bailey, Stacey	WR	6-1	163	2/10/60	9	San Jose State	San Rafael, Calif.	D3-'82	15/0
62	Barrows, Scott	G-C	6-3	280	3/31/63	5	West Virginia	Rochester Hills, Mich.	FA-'90	0*
65	†Bingham, Guy	C-G	6-3	260	2/25/58	11	Montana	Aberdeen, Wash.	FA-'89	16/0
70	Bowick, Tony	NT	6-2	265	10/3/66	2	Tennessee-Chattanooga	Dothan, Ala.	D12-'89	12/0
94	Brinson, Dana	WR	5-9	167	4/10/65	2	Nebraska	Valdosta, Ga.	FA-'90	10/0
93	Bruce, Aundray	LB	6-5	248	4/30/66	3	Auburn	Montgomery, Ala.	D1-'88	16/13
77	Bryan, Rick	DE	6-4	265	3/20/62	7	Oklahoma	Coweta, Okla.	D1-'84	2/2
23	Butler, Bobby	CB	5-11	175	5/28/59	10	Florida State	Delray Beach, Fla.	D1-'81	16/11
10	†Campbell, Scott	QB	6-0	195	4/15/62	5	Purdue	Hershey, Pa.	FA-'86	1/0
25	Case, Scott	CB	5-11	178	5/17/62	7	Oklahoma	Edmond, Okla.	D2a-'84	14/8
75	†Casillas, Tony	NT	6-3	280	10/26/63	5	Oklahoma	Norman, Okla.	D1a-'86	16/16
74	†Clayton, Stan	G	6-3	265	1/31/65	3	Penn State	Cherry Hill, N.J.	D10-'88	13/9
98	Cline, Jackie	DE-NT	6-5	280	3/13/60	4	Alabama	McCalla, Ala.	PB(Mia)-'90#	15/2*
85	Collins, Shawn	WR	6-2	207	2/20/67	2	Northern Arizona	San Diego, Calif.	D1b-'89	16/16
51	Cotton, Marcus	LB	6-3	237	8/11/66	3	Southern California	Oakland, Calif.	D2-'88	16/1
5	Davis, Greg	K	5-11	197	10/29/65	4	Citadel	Atlanta, Ga.	FA-'89	6/0
22	Dimry, Charles	CB	6-0	175	1/31/66	3	Nevada-Las Vegas	San Diego, Calif.	D5-'88	16/5
86	Dixon, Floyd	WR	5-9	170	4/9/64	5	Stephen F. Austin	Beaumont, Tex.	D6a-'86	16/5
90	Dixon, Titus	WR	5-6	152	6/15/66	2	Troy State	Clewiston, Fla.	FA-'90	4/0
64	†Dukes, Jamie	G	6-1	285	6/14/64	5	Florida State	Orlando, Fla.	FA-'86	16/16
86	Floyd, Victor	RB	6-1	201	1/24/66	2	Florida State	Pensacola, Fla.	FA-'90	6/0*
79	Fralic, Bill	G	6-5	280	10/31/62	6	Pittsburgh	Penn Hills, Pa.	D1-'85	15/15
17	†Fulhage, Scott	P	5-10	193	11/17/61	4	Kansas State	Beloit, Kan.	FA-'89	16/0
76	Gann, Mike	DE	6-5	270	10/19/63	6	Notre Dame	Lakewood, Colo.	D2-'85	16/16
41	Gordon, Tim	S	6-0	188	5/7/65	4	Tulsa	Ardmore, Okla.	FA-'87	14/13
99	†Green, Tim	LB	6-2	245	12/16/63	5	Syracuse	Liverpool, N.Y.	D1b-'86	16/14
81	Haynes, Michael	WR	6-0	180	12/24/65	3	Northern Arizona	New Orleans, La.	D7-'88	13/11
91	Hinnant, Michael	TE	6-3	258	9/8/66	3	Temple	Washington, D.C.	FA-'90	5/0*
71	t-Hinton, Chris	T-G	6-4	300	7/31/61	6	Northwestern	Chicago, Ill.	T(Ind)-'90	14/14
69	†Hoover, Houston	T-G	6-2	290	6/2/65	3	Jackson State	Yazoo City, Miss.	D6-'88	16/16
68	Hunter, John	T	6-8	296	8/16/65	2	Brigham Young	Northbend, Ore.	FA-'89	4/0
43	Johnson, Tracy	RB	6-0	230	3/13/60	4	Alabama	Kannapolis, N.C.	PB(Hou)-'90#	15/0*
28	Johnson, Undra	RB	5-9	199	1/8/66	2	West Virginia	Ft. Lauderdale, Fla.	FA-'89	1/0
38	Jones, Keith	RB	6-1	210	3/20/66	2	Illinois	Rock Hills, Mo.	D3-'89	14/9
40	Jordan, Brian	S	5-11	202	3/29/67	2	Richmond	Baltimore, Md.	FA-'89	4/0
78	Kenn, Mike	T	6-7	277	2/9/56	13	Michigan	Evanston, Ill.	D1-'78	15/15
33	†Lang, Gene	RB	5-10	206	3/15/62	7	Louisiana State	Pass Christian, Miss.	FA-'88	15/7
90	Lee, Gary	WR	6-1	201	2/12/65	4	Georgia Tech	Warner Robins, Ga.	FA-'90	0*
63	Lee, Ronnie	T	6-3	277	12/24/56	12	Baylor	Tyler, Tex.	PB(Mia)-'90#	15/15*
6	McFadden, Paul	K	5-11	166	9/24/61	7	Youngstown State	Lyndhurst, Ohio	PB(NYG)-'89#	9/0
7	†Millen, Hugh	QB	6-5	216	11/22/63	4	Washington	Seattle, Wash.	FA-'88	5/1
12	Miller, Chris	QB	6-2	200	8/9/65	4	Oregon	Eugene, Ore.	D1-'87	15/15
84	Milling, James	WR	5-9	156	2/14/65	2	Maryland	Winnsboro, S.C.	FA-'90	0*
39	Mitchell, Roland	CB	5-11	180	3/15/64	3	Texas Tech	Bay City, Tex.	FA-'90	3/0*
36	Paterra, Greg	RB	5-11	211	5/11/67	2	Slippery Rock	McKeesport, Pa.	D11-'89	10/0
49	†Primus, James	RB	5-11	196	5/18/64	3	UCLA	San Diego, Calif.	D9-'88	5/0
59	†Rade, John	LB	6-1	240	8/31/60	8	Boise State	Sierra Vista, Ariz.	D8-'83	15/14
95	Reid, Michael	LB	6-2	235	6/25/64	4	Wisconsin	Albany, Ga.	D7-'87	16/3
80	t-Rison, Andre	WR	6-0	191	3/8/67	2	Michigan State	Flint, Mich.	T(Ind)-'90	16/13
56	Ruether, Mike	C	6-4	275	9/20/62	5	Texas	Denver, Colo.	PB(Den)-'90#	3/0*
21	Sanders, Deion	CB	6-0	187	8/9/67	2	Florida State	Ft. Myers, Fla.	D1a-'89	15/10
61	Scully, John	G	6-6	270	8/2/58	9	Notre Dame	Huntington, N.Y.	D4-'81	0*
44	Settle, John	RB	5-9	210	6/2/65	4	Appalachian State	Ruffin, N.C.	FA-'87	15/15
37	†Shelley, Elbert	S	5-11	180	12/24/64	4	Arkansas State	Trumann, Ark.	D11-'87	10/0
67	Taylor, Malcolm	DE	6-6	280	6/20/60	7	Tennessee State	Crystal Springs, Mich.	FA-'89	13/0
53	Thaxton, Galand	LB	6-1	242	10/23/64	2	Wyoming	Denver, Colo.	FA-'89	16/0
72	Thomas, Ben	DE	6-3	275	7/2/61	5	Auburn	Auburn, Ala.	FA-'89	16/13
89	†Thomas, George	WR	5-9	169	7/11/64	2	Nevada-Las Vegas	Riverside, Calif.	D6a-'88	16/0
58	Tuggle, Jessie	LB	5-11	230	2/14/65	4	Valdosta State	Griffin, Ga.	FA-'87	16/16
66	Utt, Ben	G	6-6	293	6/13/59	9	Georgia Tech	Vidalia, Ga.	PB(Ind)-'90#	16/16*
97	Watts, Randy	DE-NT	6-6	279	6/22/63	2	Catawba	Sandersville, Ga.	FA-'90	0*
87	Wilkins, Gary	TE	6-2	235	11/23/63	3	Georgia Tech	West Palm Beach, Fla.	FA-'89	13/1

* Barrows last active with Detroit in '88; Cline played 15 games with Miami in '89; Floyd played 6 games with San Diego; Hinnant played 5 games with Pittsburgh; T. Johnson played 15 games with Houston; G. Lee last active with Detroit in '88; R. Lee played 15 games with Miami; Milling last active with Atlanta in '88; Mitchell played 3 games with Phoenix; Ruether played 3 games with Denver; Utt played 16 games with Indianapolis; Scully last active with Atlanta in '88; Watts last active with Dallas in '87.

† Option playout; subject to developments.

Plan B unconditional free agent.

t- Falcons traded for Hinton (Indianapolis), Rison (Indianapolis).

Players lost through Plan B (6): S Evan Cooper (TB; 16 games in '89), TE Ron Heller (Sea; 15), G Wayne Radloff (SF; 11), G Tommy Robison (Hou; 9), LB Tony Zackery (NE; 1).

Also played with Falcons in '89—TE Brad Beckman (15 games); RB Kenny Flowers (16); NT Curtis Maxey (2); S Robert Moore (16); T Ralph Norwood (11); (9); LB Joel Williams (10).

COACHING STAFF

Head Coach, Jerry Glanville

Pro Career: Named Atlanta's head coach on January 14, 1990, after serving as Houston's head coach since the last two games of the 1985 season. Guided Oilers to three consecutive playoff berths (1987-89). Glanville was the Oilers' defensive coordinator in 1984-85, and has 25 years of coaching experience. He initially coached in the NFL for the Detroit Lions from 1974-76 as the special teams/defense coach. His next NFL position was with the Atlanta Falcons from 1977-82, first serving as defensive backfield/special teams coach before being elevated to defensive coordinator. In 1983, Glanville joined the Buffalo Bills as defensive backfield coach before assuming his duties with the Oilers. Career record: 35-35.

Background: Attended Montana State in 1960 before transferring to Northern Michigan, where he played linebacker from 1961-63. He coached in the Ohio high school system from 1964-66 before accepting an assistant coaching post at Western Kentucky in 1967. From 1968-73, he was an assistant at Georgia Tech, helping the Yellow Jackets to three bowl games.

Personal: Born October 14, 1941, in Detroit, Mich. Jerry and his wife, Brenda, live in Roswell, Ga., with their son, Justin.

Assistant Coaches

Jimmy Carr, secondary; born March 25, 1933, Kayford, W. Va., lives in Atlanta. Running back-defensive back-linebacker Morris Harvey (now Univ. of Charleston, W. Va.) 1951-54. Pro running back-defensive back-linebacker Chicago Cardinals 1955-57, Montreal Alouettes (CFL) 1958, Philadelphia Eagles 1959-63, Washington Redskins 1964-65. Pro coach: Minnesota Vikings 1966-68, 1979-81, Chicago Bears 1969, 1973-74, Philadelphia Eagles 1970-72, Detroit Lions 1975-76, Buffalo Bills 1977, San Francisco 49ers 1978, Denver Gold (USFL) 1983-84, New England Patriots 1985-89, joined Falcons in 1990.

Tim Jorgensen, strength and conditioning; born April 21, 1955, St. Louis, Mo., lives in Snellville, Ga. Guard Southwest Missouri State 1974-76. No pro playing experience. College coach: Southwest Missouri State 1977-78, Alabama 1979, Louisiana State 1980-83. Pro coach: Philadelphia Eagles 1984-86, joined Falcons in 1987.

Bill Kollar, defensive line; born November 12, 1952, Warren, Ohio, lives in Atlanta. Defensive end Montana State 1971-74. Pro defensive end Cincinnati Bengals 1974-76, Tampa Bay Buccaneers 1977-81. College coach: Illinois 1985-87, Purdue 1988-89. Pro coach: Tampa Bay Buccaneers 1984, joined Falcons in 1990.

Wayne McDuffie, offensive line; born December 1, 1944, Hawkinsville, Ga., lives in Atlanta. Offensive-defensive lineman Florida State 1968-71. Pro lineman Norfolk Neptunes (CFL) 1969-70. College coach: New Mexico 1974, Oklahoma State 1975-76, Georgia 1977-81, Florida State 1983-89. Pro coach: Atlanta Falcons 1982, rejoined Falcons in 1990.

Jimmy Robinson, wide receivers; born January 3, 1953, Atlanta, lives in Atlanta. Wide receiver Georgia Tech 1972-74. Pro wide receiver Atlanta Falcons 1975, New York Giants 1976-79, San Francisco 49ers 1980, Denver Broncos 1981. College coach: Georgia Tech 1986-89. Pro coach: Memphis Showboats (USFL) 1984-85, joined the Falcons in 1990.

Tom Rossley, quarterbacks; born August 19, 1946, Painesville, Ohio, lives in Atlanta. Wide receiver Cincinnati 1967-69. No pro playing experience. College coach: Cincinnati 1977, Rice 1978-81, Holy Cross 1986-87, Southern Methodist 1988-89. Pro coach: Montreal Concorde (CFL) 1982-84, San Antonio Gunslingers (USFL) 1985, joined Falcons in 1990.

Keith Rowen, special teams/tight ends; born September 2, 1952, New York, N.Y., lives in Atlanta. Offensive tackle Stanford 1972-74. No pro playing experience. College coach: Stanford 1975-76, Long Beach State 1977-78, Arizona 1979-82. Pro coach: Boston/New Orleans Breakers (USFL) 1983-84, Cleveland Browns 1984, Indianapolis Colts 1985-88, New England Patriots 1989, joined Falcons in 1990.

Ray Sherman, assistant head coach/offense; born November 27, 1951, Berkeley, Calif., lives in Atlanta. Wide receiver Laney, Calif., J.C. 1969-70, Fresno State 1971-72. Pro defensive back Green Bay Packers 1973. College coach: San Jose State 1974, California 1975, 1981, Michigan State 1976-77, Wake Forest 1978-80, Purdue 1982-85, Georgia 1986-87. Pro coach: Houston Oilers 1988-89, joined Falcons in 1990.

Doug Shively, assistant head coach/defense; born March 18, 1938, Lexington, Ky., lives in Atlanta. End Kentucky 1955-58. No pro playing experience. College coach: Virginia Tech 1960-66, Kentucky 1967-70, Clemson 1971-72, North Carolina 1973. Pro coach: New Orleans Saints 1974-76, Atlanta Falcons 1977-82, Arizona Wranglers (USFL) 1983 (head coach), San Diego Chargers 1984, Tampa Bay Buccaneers 1985, Houston Oilers 1986-89, rejoined Falcons in 1990.

Atlanta Falcons 1990 First-Year Roster

Name	Pos.	Ht.	Wt.	Birth-date	College	Hometown	How Acq.
Adams, Scott (1)	T	6-5	275	9/28/66	Georgia	Athens, Ga.	FA
Adleta, John (1)	NT	6-4	280	3/21/66	North Carolina State	Clarksville, Ohio	FA
Barnett, Oliver	NT	6-3	288	4/9/66	Kentucky	Louisville, Ky.	D3
Broussard, Steve	RB	5-7	201	2/22/67	Washington State	Los Angeles, Calif.	D1
Conner, Darion	LB	6-2	256	9/28/67	Jackson State	Prairie Point, Miss.	D2
Ellison, Chris	S	5-10	200	12/20/67	Houston	Dallas, Tex.	D11
Epps, Tory	NT	6-0	280	5/28/67	Memphis State	Uniontown, Pa.	D8
Guidry, Kevin (1)	S	6-0	180	6/16/64	Louisiana State	Lake Charles, La.	FA
Harris, Greg (1)	WR	5-9	157	12/30/65	Troy State	Valdosta, Ga.	FA
Jordan, Darrell	LB	6-3	243	5/17/67	Northern Arizona	Las Vegas, Nev.	D9
Kuipers, Jason (1)	C	6-2	275	2/16/66	Florida State	Winter Haven, Fla.	FA
McCarthy, Shawn	P	6-6	227	2/22/68	Purdue	Fremont, Ohio	D12
Norris, Darron (1)	RB	5-9	195	12/5/66	Texas	Oceanside, Calif.	FA
Norwood, Johnny .	S	6-2	200	5/16/65	Houston	Beaumont, Tex.	FA
Parker, Chris (1)	NT-DE	6-5	285	6/9/66	West Virginia	Allentown, Pa.	FA
Pringle, Mike	RB	5-8	186	10/1/67	Cal State-Fullerton	Los Angeles, Calif.	D6
Redding, Reggie	G-T	6-3	281	9/22/68	Cal State-Fullerton	Cincinnati, Ohio	D5
Renfroe, Gilbert (1)	QB	6-1	195	2/18/63	Tennessee State	Streamwood, Ill.	FA
Ross, Greg	DE-NT	6-3	268	1/11/67	Memphis State	Dyersburg, Tenn.	FA
Royal, Rickey (1)	CB	5-9	187	7/26/66	Arizona	Gainesville, Tex.	FA
Sadowski, Troy (1)	TE	6-5	243	12/8/65	Georgia	Chamblee, Ga.	FA
Salum, Kevin (1)	LB	6-1	233	7/18/66	Arizona	Colorado Springs, Colo.	D10
Simien, Kevin (1)	WR	6-4	202	8/25/66	Fort Hays State	Port Arthur, Tex.	FA
Singer, Paul (1)	QB	6-3	193	3/18/66	Western Illinois	Fort Knox, Kan.	FA

The term NFL Rookie is defined as a player who is in his first season of professional football and has not been on the roster of another professional football team for any regular-season or postseason games. A Rookie is designated by an "R" on NFL rosters. Players who have been active in another professional football league or players who have NFL experience, including either preseason training camp or being on an active roster for fewer than three regular-season or postseason games, are termed NFL First-Year Players. An NFL First-Year Player is designated by a "1" on NFL rosters. Thereafter, a player on an NFL active roster for at least three regular-season or postseason games is credited with an additional year of NFL playing experience.

NOTES

_____

_____

_____

_____

_____

_____

_____

_____

_____

_____

_____

_____

_____

National Football Conference Central Division

Team Colors: Navy Blue, Orange, and White

Corporate Headquarters:
Halas Hall
250 North Washington
Lake Forest, Illinois 60045
Telephone: (708) 295-6600

Club Officials

Chairman of the Board: Edward W. McCaskey
President and Chief Executive Officer: Michael B. McCaskey
Secretary: Virginia H. McCaskey
Vice President-Player Personnel: Bill Tobin
Director of Administration: Tim LeFevour
Director of Community Involvement: Pat McCaskey
Director of Finance: Ted Phillips
Director of Marketing and Communications: Ken Valdiserri
Director of Public Relations: Bryan Harlan
Asst. Director of Public Relations: John Bostrom
Ticket Manager: Gary Christenson
Computer Systems: Greg Gershuny
Video Director: Mitch Friedman
Trainer: Fred Caito
Assistant Trainer: Brian McCaskey
Strength Coordinator: Clyde Emrich
Equipment Manager: Gary Haeger
Assistant Equipment Manager: Tony Medlin
Scouts: Jim Parmer, Rod Graves, Don King, Ken Geiger

Stadium: Soldier Field • **Capacity:** 66,946
425 McFetridge Place
Chicago, Illinois 60605

Playing Surface: Grass

Training Camp: Wisconsin-Platteville
Platteville, Wisconsin 53818

1990 Schedule

Preseason

Aug. 11	**Miami**	6:00
Aug. 18	at Phoenix	7:30
Aug. 24	**Los Angeles Raiders**	7:00
Aug. 30	vs. Buffalo at Columbia, S.C.	8:00

Regular Season

Sept. 9	**Seattle**	12:00
Sept. 16	at Green Bay	12:00
Sept. 23	**Minnesota**	12:00
Sept. 30	at Los Angeles Raiders	1:00
Oct. 7	**Green Bay**	3:00
Oct. 14	**Los Angeles Rams**	6:30
Oct. 21	**Open Date**	
Oct. 28	at Phoenix	2:00
Nov. 4	at Tampa Bay	4:00
Nov. 11	**Atlanta**	12:00
Nov. 18	at Denver	2:00
Nov. 25	at Minnesota	12:00
Dec. 2	**Detroit**	12:00
Dec. 9	at Washington	4:00
Dec. 16	at Detroit	8:00
Dec. 23	**Tampa Bay**	12:00
Dec. 29	**Kansas City** (Saturday)	11:30

Bears Coaching History

Decatur Staleys 1920
Chicago Staleys 1921
(551-352-42)

1920-29	George Halas	84-31-19
1930-32	Ralph Jones	24-10-7
1933-42	George Halas*	89-24-4
1942-45	Hunk Anderson-Luke Johnsos**	23-12-2
1946-55	George Halas	76-43-2
1956-57	John (Paddy) Driscoll	14-10-1
1958-67	George Halas	76-53-6
1968-71	Jim Dooley	20-36-0
1972-74	Abe Gibron	11-30-1
1975-77	Jack Pardee	20-23-0
1978-81	Neill Armstrong	30-35-0
1982-89	Mike Ditka	84-45-0

*Retired after six games to enter U.S. Navy
**Co-coaches

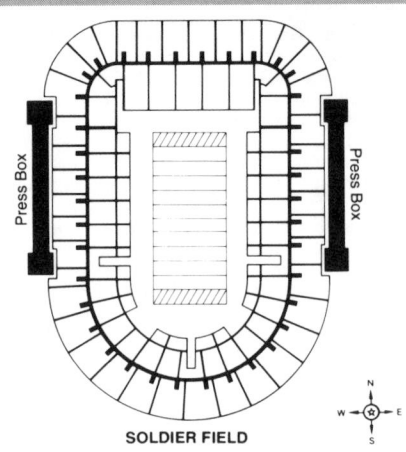

SOLDIER FIELD

Record Holders

Individual Records — Career

Category	Name	Performance
Rushing (Yds.)	Walter Payton, 1975-1987	*16,726
Passing (Yds.)	Sid Luckman, 1939-1950	14,686
Passing (TDs)	Sid Luckman, 1939-1950	137
Receiving (No.)	Walter Payton, 1975-1987	492
Receiving (Yds.)	Johnny Morris, 1958-1967	5,059
Interceptions	Gary Fencik, 1976-1987	38
Punting (Avg.)	George Gulyanics, 1947-1952	44.5
Punt Return (Avg.)	Ray (Scooter) McLean, 1940-47	14.8
Kickoff Return (Avg.)	Gale Sayers, 1965-1971	30.6
Field Goals	Bob Thomas, 1975-1984	128
Touchdowns (Tot.)	Walter Payton, 1975-1987	125
Points	Walter Payton, 1975-1987	750

Individual Records — Single Season

Category	Name	Performance
Rushing (Yds.)	Walter Payton, 1977	1,852
Passing (Yds.)	Bill Wade, 1962	3,172
Passing (TDs)	Sid Luckman, 1943	28
Receiving (No.)	Johnny Morris, 1964	93
Receiving (Yds.)	Johnny Morris, 1964	1,200
Interceptions	Roosevelt Taylor, 1963	9
Punting (Avg.)	Bobby Joe Green, 1963	46.5
Punt Return (Avg.)	Harry Clark, 1943	15.8
Kickoff Return (Avg.)	Gale Sayers, 1967	37.7
Field Goals	Kevin Butler, 1985	31
Touchdowns (Tot.)	Gale Sayers, 1965	**22
Points	Kevin Butler, 1985	**144

Individual Records — Single Game

Category	Name	Performance
Rushing (Yds.)	Walter Payton, 11-20-77	*275
Passing (Yds.)	Johnny Lujack, 12-11-49	468
Passing (TDs)	Sid Luckman, 11-14-43	*7
Receiving (No.)	Jim Keane, 10-23-49	14
Receiving (Yds.)	Harlon Hill, 10-31-54	214
Interceptions	Many times	3
	Last time by Ross Brupbacher, 12-12-76	
Field Goals	Roger LeClerc, 12-3-61	5
	Mac Percival, 10-20-68	5
Touchdowns (Tot.)	Gale Sayers, 12-12-65	*6
Points	Gale Sayers, 12-12-65	36

*NFL Record
**NFL Rookie Record

1989 Team Record
Preseason (2-2)

Date	Result		Opponents
8/14	W	28-20	at Miami
8/19	L	7-24	San Diego
8/26	L	17-22	Kansas City
9/2	W	41-38	at L.A. Raiders
		93-104	

Regular Season (6-10)

Date	Result		Opponents	Att.
9/10	W	17-14	Cincinnati	64,730
9/17	W	38- 7	Minnesota	66,475
9/24	W	47-27	at Detroit	71,418
10/2	W	27-13	Philadelphia	66,625
10/8	L	35-42	at Tampa Bay	72,077
10/15	L	28-33	Houston	64,383
10/23	L	7-27	at Cleveland	78,722
10/29	W	20-10	L.A. Rams	65,506
11/5	L	13-14	at Green Bay	56,556
11/12	W	20- 0	at Pittsburgh	56,505
11/19	L	31-32	Tampa Bay	63,826
11/26	L	14-38	at Washington	50,044
12/3	L	16-27	at Minnesota	60,664
12/10	L	17-27	Detroit	52,650
12/17	L	28-40	Green Bay	44,781
12/24	L	0-26	at San Francisco	60,207

Score by Periods

Bears	40	108	82	128	0	—	358
Opponents	69	111	72	125	0	—	377

Attendance
Home 488,976   Away 506,193   Total 995,169
Single-game home record, 66,475 (9-17-89)
Single-season home record, 495,484 (1986)

1989 Team Statistics

	Bears	Opp.
Total First Downs	302	332
Rushing	136	118
Passing	147	191
Penalty	19	23
Third Down: Made/Att.	94/214	84/207
Third Down: Pct.	43.9	40.6
Fourth Down: Made/Att.	10/18	7/15
Fourth Down: Pct.	55.6	46.7
Total Net Yards	5375	5729
Avg. Per Game	335.9	358.1
Total Plays	1028	1039
Avg. Per Play	5.2	5.5
Net Yards Rushing	2287	1897
Avg. Per Game	142.9	118.6
Total Rushes	516	446
Net Yards Passing	3088	3832
Avg. Per Game	193.0	239.5
Sacked/Yards Lost	28/174	39/247
Gross Yards	3262	4079
Att./Completions	484/267	554/307
Completion Pct.	55.2	55.4
Had Intercepted	25	26
Punts/Avg.	72/39.5	67/39.6
Net Punting Avg.	33.4	34.6
Penalties/Yards Lost	95/846	94/802
Fumbles/Ball Lost	23/17	24/12
Touchdowns	45	43
Rushing	22	21
Passing	21	21
Returns	2	1
Avg. Time of Possession.	31:10	28:50

1989 Individual Statistics

Scoring

	TD R	TD P	TD Rt	PAT	FG	Saf	TP
Anderson	11	4	0	0/0	0/0	0	90
Butler	0	0	0	43/45	15/19	0	88
Muster	5	3	0	0/0	0/0	0	48
Davis	0	3	0	0/0	0/0	0	18
Harbaugh	3	0	0	0/0	0/0	0	18
McKinnon	0	3	0	0/0	0/0	0	18
Thornton	0	3	0	0/0	0/0	0	18
Sanders	0	1	1	0/0	0/0	0	12
Suhey	1	1	0	0/0	0/0	0	12
Boso	0	1	0	0/0	0/0	0	6
Gentry	0	1	0	0/0	0/0	0	6
Green	1	0	0	0/0	0/0	0	6
Morris	0	1	0	0/0	0/0	0	6
Stinson	0	0	1	0/0	0/0	0	6
Tomczak	1	0	0	0/0	0/0	0	6
Bears	22	21	2	43/45	15/19	0	358
Opponents	21	21	1	41/43	26/36	0	377

Passing

	Att.	Comp.	Yds.	Pct.	TD	Int.	Tkld.	Rate
Tomczak	306	156	2058	51.0	16	16	10/68	68.2
Harbaugh	178	111	1204	62.4	5	9	18/106	70.5
Bears	484	267	3262	55.2	21	25	28/174	69.1
Opponents	554	307	4079	55.4	21	26	39/247	72.0

Rushing

	Att.	Yds.	Avg.	LG	TD
Anderson	274	1275	4.7	73	11
Muster	82	327	4.0	20	5
Harbaugh	45	276	6.1	26t	3
Sanders	41	127	3.1	19	0
Gentry	17	106	6.2	29	0
Tomczak	24	71	3.0	18	1
Suhey	20	51	2.6	8	1
Green	5	46	9.2	37t	1
Taylor	2	7	3.5	7	0
Buford	1	6	6.0	6	0
McKinnon	3	5	1.7	3	0
Thornton	1	4	4.0	4	0
Morris	1	-14	-14.0	-14	0
Bears	516	2287	4.4	73	22
Opponents	446	1897	4.3	68t	21

Receiving

	No.	Yds.	Avg.	LG	TD
Anderson	50	434	8.7	49t	4
Gentry	39	463	11.9	79t	1
Muster	32	259	8.1	25	3
Morris	30	486	16.2	58t	1
McKinnon	28	418	14.9	41	3
Davis	26	397	15.3	52t	3
Thornton	24	392	16.3	36t	3
Boso	17	182	10.7	43	1
Suhey	9	73	8.1	22	1
Green	5	48	9.6	21	0
Kozlowski	3	74	24.7	55	0
Sanders	3	28	9.3	16t	1
Waddle	1	8	8.0	8	0
Bears	267	3262	12.2	79t	21
Opponents	307	4079	13.3	97t	21

Interceptions

	No.	Yds.	Avg.	LG	TD
Stinson	4	59	14.8	29t	1
Lynch	3	55	18.3	41	0
Gayle	3	39	13.0	20	0
Woolford	3	0	0.0	0	0
Roper	2	46	23.0	43	0
Jackson	2	16	8.0	16	0
Rivera	2	1	0.5	1	0
Morrissey	2	0	0.0	0	0
Dent	1	30	30.0	30	0
Paul	1	20	20.0	20	0
Duerson	1	2	2.0	2	0
Douglass	1	0	0.0	0	0
Tate	1	0	0.0	0	0
Bears	26	268	10.3	43	1
Opponents	25	182	7.3	53	1

Punting

	No.	Yds.	Avg.	In 20	LG
Buford	72	2844	39.5	21	60
Bears	72	2844	39.5	21	60
Opponents	67	2655	39.6	15	63

Punt Returns

	No.	FC	Yds.	Avg.	LG	TD
Green	16	5	141	8.8	24	0
McKinnon	10	3	67	6.7	17	0
Kozlowski	4	0	-2	-0.5	4	0
Woolford	1	0	12	12.0	12	0
Waddle	1	0	2	2.0	2	0
Bears	32	8	220	6.9	24	0
Opponents	30	5	262	8.7	34	0

Kickoff Returns

	No.	Yds.	Avg.	LG	TD
Gentry	28	667	23.8	63	0
Sanders	23	491	21.3	96t	1
Green	11	239	21.7	37	0
Suhey	6	93	15.5	21	0
Pruitt	2	17	8.5	11	0
Kozlowski	1	12	12.0	12	0
Tate	1	12	12.0	12	0
Chapura	1	8	8.0	8	0
Bears	73	1539	21.1	96t	1
Opponents	68	1375	20.2	62	0

Sacks

	No.
Dent	9.0
McMichael	7.5
Armstrong	5.0
Roper	4.5
Perry	4.0
Chapura	3.0
Hampton	2.0
Rivera	2.0
Singletary	1.0
Woods	1.0
Bears	39.0
Opponents	28.0

1990 Draft Choices

Round	Name	Pos.	College
1.	Mark Carrier	DB	Southern California
2.	Fred Washington	DT	Texas Christian
	Ron Cox	LB	Fresno State
3.	Tim Ryan	DT	Southern California
	Peter Tom Willis	QB	Florida State
4.	Tony Moss	WR	Louisiana State
5.	Pat Chaffey	RB	Oregon State
6.	John Mangum	DB	Alabama
	Bill Anderson	C	Iowa
8.	James Rouse	RB	Arkansas
9.	Johnny Bailey	RB	Texas A&I
10.	Terry Price	DT	Texas A&M
11.	Brent White	DE	Michigan
	Roman Matusz	T	Pittsburgh
12.	Anthony Cooney	DB	Arkansas

Chicago Bears 1990 Veteran Roster

No.	Name	Pos.	Ht.	Wt.	Birth-date	NFL Exp.	College	Hometown	How Acq.	'89 Games/ Starts
35	Anderson, Neal	RB	5-11	210	8/14/64	5	Florida	Graceville, Fla.	D1-'86	16/16
93	Armstrong, Trace	DE	6-4	259	10/5/65	2	Florida	Birmingham, Ala.	D1-'89	15/14
79	Becker, Kurt	G-T	6-5	280	12/22/58	9	Michigan	Aurora, Ill.	PB(Rams)-'90#	2/0*
62	Bortz, Mark	G	6-6	272	2/12/61	8	Iowa	Pardeeville, Wis.	D8-'83	16/16
86	Boso, Cap	TE	6-3	240	9/10/63	4	Illinois	Kansas City, Mo.	FA-'87	16/0
8	Buford, Maury	P	6-0	198	2/18/60	8	Texas Tech	Mt. Pleasant, Tex.	W(GB)-'89	16/0
6	Butler, Kevin	K	6-1	204	7/24/62	6	Georgia	Atlanta, Ga.	D4-'85	16/0
94	Chapura, Dick	DT	6-3	275	6/15/64	3	Missouri	Sarasota, Fla.	D10-'87	16/3
74	†Covert, Jim	T	6-4	278	3/22/60	8	Pittsburgh	Conway, Pa.	D1-'83	15/15
82	Davis, Wendell	WR	5-11	188	1/3/66	3	Louisiana State	Shreveport, La.	D1-'88	14/7
95	Dent, Richard	DE	6-5	268	12/13/60	8	Tennessee State	Atlanta, Ga.	D8-'83	15/15
37	Douglass, Maurice	CB-S	5-11	200	2/12/64	5	Kentucky	Trotwood, Ohio	D8-'86	10/1
22	Duerson, Dave	S	6-1	212	11/28/60	8	Notre Dame	Muncie, Ind.	D3-'83	12/12
68	Dyko, Chris	T	6-6	295	3/16/66	2	Washington State	University, Wash.	D8-'89	8/1
67	Fontenot, Jerry	C-G	6-3	272	11/21/66	2	Texas A&M	Lafayette, La.	D3-'89	16/0
23	Gayle, Shaun	S	5-11	194	3/8/62	7	Ohio State	Hampton, Va.	D10-'84	14/14
29	Gentry, Dennis	WR	5-8	180	2/10/59	9	Baylor	Lubbock, Tex.	D4-'82	16/6
31	Green, Mark	RB	5-11	184	3/22/67	2	Notre Dame	Riverside, Calif.	D5-'89	10/0
99	†Hampton, Dan	DT	6-5	274	9/19/57	12	Arkansas	Oklahoma City, Okla.	D1-'79	4/4
4	Harbaugh, Jim	QB	6-3	204	12/23/63	4	Michigan	Kalamazoo, Mich.	D1-'87	12/5
63	Hilgenberg, Jay	C	6-3	260	3/21/60	10	Iowa	Iowa City, Iowa	FA-'81	16/16
24	†Jackson, Vestee	CB-S	6-0	186	8/14/63	5	Washington	Fresno, Calif.	D2-'86	16/15
92	Johnson, Troy	LB	6-0	236	11/10/64	3	Oklahoma	Houston, Tex.	D5-'88	7/0
53	Jones, Dante	LB	6-1	236	3/23/65	3	Oklahoma	Dallas, Tex.	D2-'88	10/1
88	Kozlowski, Glen	WR	6-1	205	12/31/62	4	Brigham Young	Honolulu, Hawaii	D11-'86	15/0
76	McMichael, Steve	DT	6-2	268	10/17/57	11	Texas	Houston, Tex.	FA-'81	16/16
84	Morris, Ron	WR	6-1	195	11/14/64	4	Southern Methodist	Cooper, Tex.	D2-'87	16/9
51	Morrissey, Jim	LB	6-3	227	12/24/62	6	Michigan State	Flint, Mich.	D11-'85	6/4
25	Muster, Brad	RB	6-3	231	4/11/65	3	Stanford	San Marin, Calif.	D1-'88	16/16
36	Paul, Markus	S	6-2	199	4/1/66	2	Syracuse	Kissimmee, Fla.	D4-'89	16/3
72	Perry, William	DT	6-2	330	12/16/62	6	Clemson	Aiken, S.C.	D1-'85	13/9
52	Pruitt, Mickey	LB	6-1	215	1/10/65	3	Colorado	Chicago, Ill.	FA-'88	14/1
59	Rivera, Ron	LB	6-3	240	1/7/62	7	California	Monterey, Calif.	D2-'84	16/14
55	Roper, John	LB	6-1	228	10/4/65	2	Texas A&M	Yates, Tex.	D2-'89	16/10
50	Singletary, Mike	LB	6-0	230	10/9/58	10	Baylor	Houston, Tex.	D2-'81	16/16
32	Stinson, Lemuel	CB-S	5-9	159	5/10/66	3	Texas Tech	Houston, Tex.	D6-'88	12/4
49	Tate, David	S	6-0	177	11/22/64	3	Colorado	Denver, Colo.	D8-'88	14/4
57	Thayer, Tom	G	6-4	270	8/16/61	6	Notre Dame	Joliet, Ill.	D4-'82	16/16
80	Thornton, James	TE	6-2	242	2/8/65	3	Cal State-Fullerton	Santa Rosa, Calif.	D4-'88	16/16
18	†Tomczak, Mike	QB	6-1	198	10/23/62	6	Ohio State	Calumet City, Ill.	FA-'85	16/11
78	Van Horne, Keith	T	6-6	283	11/6/57	10	Southern California	Mt. Lebanon, Pa.	D1-'81	15/15
73	†Wojciechowski, John	G-T	6-4	270	7/30/63	4	Michigan State	Detroit, Mich.	FA-'87	13/1
21	Woolford, Donnell	CB	5-9	187	1/6/66	2	Clemson	Fayetteville, N.C.	D1a-'89	13/1

* Becker played 2 games with L.A. Rams in '89.

† Option playout; subject to developments.

Plan B unconditional free agent.

Retired—Matt Suhey, 10-year running back, 16 games in '89.

Players lost through Plan B (7): CB-S Lorenzo Lynch (Phx; 16 games in '89), WR Dennis McKinnon (Dall; 16), RB Thomas Sanders (SD; 16), DT John Shannon (SF; 12), CB-S George Streeter (Raiders; 4), DE Tony Woods (NO; 15), T Dave Zawatson (NYJ; 4).

Also played with Bears in '89—LB LaSalle Harper (3 games), LB Steve Hyche (6), RB Brian Taylor (5), WR Tom Waddle (3).

COACHING STAFF

Head Coach, Mike Ditka

Pro Career: Became tenth head coach of Bears on January 20, 1982, after serving nine years as an offensive assistant with Dallas. Led Bears to first Super Bowl title following 15-1 1985 season. Bears shut out New York Giants and Los Angeles Rams in playoffs before routing New England 46-10 in Super Bowl XX. Before a disappointing 6-10 finish in 1989, Ditka led the Bears to five consecutive NFC Central titles. Under his leadership, the Bears qualified for the postseason in five of the past eight seasons and have advanced to the NFC Championship Game on three occasions. Ditka is a 28-year veteran of the NFL as both a player and coach. Had 12-year playing career as a tight end with Chicago (1961-66), Philadelphia (1967-68), and Dallas (1969-72). A first-round draft choice by Chicago in 1961, Ditka was NFL rookie of the year, all-NFL (1961-64), and played in five Pro Bowls (1962-66). He joined Cowboys coaching staff in 1973. In addition to working with Dallas special teams, Ditka coached Cowboys' receivers. During his NFL career, he has been in the playoffs 15 seasons and been a member of five NFC champions and three NFL champions. He became the first tight end to be inducted into the Pro Football Hall of Fame in July, 1988. Career record: 84-45.

Background: Played at Pittsburgh from 1958-60 and was a unanimous All-America his senior year. A two-way performer, he played both tight end and linebacker. He also was one of the nation's leading punters with a 40-plus-yard average over three years.

Personal: Born October 18, 1939, Carnegie, Pa. Mike and his wife, Diana, live in Bannockburn, Ill., and have four children—Michael, Mark, Megan, and Matt.

Assistant Coaches

Steve Kazor, special teams/tight ends; born February 24, 1948, New Kensington, Pa., lives in Vernon Hills, Ill. Nose tackle Westminister College 1967-70. No pro playing experience. College coach: Emporia State 1973 (head coach), Texas-Arlington 1974, Colorado State 1975, Wyoming 1976, Texas 1977-78, Texas-El Paso 1979-80. Pro coach: Joined Bears in 1982.

Greg Landry, offensive coordinator; born December 18, 1946, Nashua, N.H., lives in Libertyville, Ill. Quarterback Massachusetts 1965-67. Pro quarterback Detroit Lions 1968-78, Baltimore Colts 1979-81, Chicago Blitz/Arizona Wranglers (USFL) 1983-84, Chicago Bears 1984. Pro coach: Cleveland Browns 1985, joined Bears in 1986.

Jim LaRue, research and quality control; born August 11, 1925, Clinton, Okla., lives in Libertyville, Ill. Halfback Carson-Newman 1943, Duke 1944-45, Maryland 1947-49. No pro playing experience. College coach: Maryland 1950, Kansas State 1951-54, Houston 1955-56, Southern Methodist 1957-58, Arizona 1959-66 (head coach), Utah 1967-73, Wake Forest 1974-75. Pro coach: Buffalo Bills 1976-77, joined Bears in 1978.

John Levra, defensive line; born October 2, 1937, Arma, Kan., lives in Libertyville, Ill. Guard-linebacker Pittsburg (Kan.) State 1963-65. No pro playing experience. College coach: Stephen F. Austin 1971-74, Kansas 1975-78, North Texas State 1979. Pro coach: British Columbia Lions (CFL) 1980, New Orleans Saints 1981-85, joined Bears in 1986.

David McGinnis, linebackers; born August 7, 1951, Independence, Kan., lives in Lake Forest, Ill. Defensive back Texas Christian 1970-72. No pro playing experience. College coach: Texas Christian 1973-74, 1982, Missouri 1975-77, Indiana State 1978-81, Kansas State 1983-85. Pro coach: Joined Bears in 1986.

Vic Rapp, wide receivers; born December 23, 1935, Marionville, Mo., lives in Rochester, Mich. Running back Southwest Missouri State 1954-57. No pro playing experience. College coach: Arizona 1965-66, Missouri 1967-71. Pro coach: Edmonton Eskimos (CFL) 1972-76, British Columbia Lions (CFL) 1977-82 (head coach), Houston Oilers 1983, Los Angeles Rams 1984, Tampa Bay Buccaneers 1985-86, Detroit Lions 1987, joined Bears in 1989.

Johnny Roland, running backs; born May 21, 1943, Corpus Christi, Tex., lives in Vernon Hills, Ill. Running back Missouri 1963-65. Pro running back St. Louis Cardinals 1966-72, New York Giants 1973. College coach: Notre Dame 1975. Pro coach: Green Bay Packers 1974, Philadelphia Eagles 1976-78, joined Bears in 1983.

Dick Stanfel, offensive line; born July 20, 1927, San Francisco, Calif., lives in Libertyville, Ill. Guard San Francisco 1948-51. Pro guard Detroit Lions 1952-55, Washington Redskins 1956-58. College coach: Notre Dame 1959-62, California 1963. Pro coach: Philadelphia Eagles 1964-70, San Francisco 49ers 1971-75, New Orleans Saints 1976-80 (head coach, 4 games in 1980), joined Bears in 1981.

Vince Tobin, defensive coordinator; born September 29, 1943, in Burlington Junction, Mo., lives in Libertyville, Ill. Defensive back-running back Missouri 1961-64. No pro playing experience. College coach: Missouri 1967-76. Pro coach: British Columbia Lions (CFL) 1977-82, Philadelphia/Baltimore Stars (USFL) 1983-85, joined Bears in 1986.

Zaven Yaralian, defensive backs; born February 5, 1952, Syria, lives in Lake Forest, Ill. Defensive back Nebraska 1972-73. Pro defensive back Green Bay Packers 1974, Philadelphia Bell (WFL) 1975. College coach: Nebraska 1975, Washington State 1976-77, Missouri 1978-83, Florida 1984-87, Colorado 1988-89. Pro coach: Joined Bears in 1990.

Chicago Bears 1990 First-Year Roster

Name	Pos.	Ht.	Wt.	Birth-date	College	Hometown	How Acq.
Anderson, Bill	C	6-3	267	10/8/66	Iowa	Columbia Hgts., Minn.	D8
Bailey, Johnny	RB	5-9	180	3/17/67	Texas A&I	Houston, Tex.	D9
Carrier, Mark	S	6-1	180	4/28/68	Southern California	Lake Charles, La.	D1
Chaffey, Pat	RB	6-1	218	4/19/67	Oregon State	McMinnville, Ore.	D5
Cooney, Anthony	CB-S	6-0	204	2/8/67	Arkansas	Little Rock, Ark.	D12
Cox, Ron	LB	6-2	242	2/27/68	Fresno State	Fresno, Calif.	D2b
Mangum, John	CB-S	5-10	173	3/16/67	Alabama	Magee, Miss.	D6
Matusz, Roman	T	6-4	270	5/10/67	Pittsburgh	Newark, N.J.	D11b
Moss, Tony	WR	5-7	169	6/6/66	Louisiana State	Bossier City, La.	D4
Price, Terry	DT	6-4	272	4/5/68	Texas A&M	Atlanta, Ga.	D10
Rouse, James	RB	6-1	220	12/18/66	Arkansas	Little Rock, Ark.	D8
Ryan, Tim	DT	6-3	268	9/8/67	Southern California	Memphis, Tenn.	D3a
Washington, Fred	DT	6-2	277	7/11/67	Texas Christian	Denison, Tex.	D2a
White, Brent	DE	6-4	254	2/28/67	Michigan	Dayton, Ohio	D11a
Willis, Peter Tom	QB	6-2	188	1/4/67	Florida State	Morris, Ala.	D3b

The term NFL Rookie is defined as a player who is in his first season of professional football and has not been on the roster of another professional football team for any regular-season or postseason games. A Rookie is designated by an "R" on NFL rosters. Players who have been active in another professional football league or players who have NFL experience, including either preseason training camp or being on an active roster for fewer than three regular-season or postseason games, are termed NFL First-Year Players. An NFL First-Year Player is designated by a "1" on NFL rosters. Thereafter, a player on an NFL active roster for at least three regular-season or postseason games is credited with an additional year of NFL playing experience.

NOTES

DALLAS COWBOYS

National Football Conference Eastern Division

Team Colors: Royal Blue, Metallic Silver Blue, and White

Cowboys Center
One Cowboys Parkway
Irving, Texas 75063
Telephone: (214) 556-9900

Club Officials

Owner/President/General Manager:
  Jerry Jones
Director of Player Personnel: Bob Ackles
Director of College Scouting: Dick Mansperger
Director of Pro Personnel: John Wooten
Treasurer: Jack Dixon
Public Relations Directors: Greg Aiello,
  David Pelletier
Administrative Assistant: Bruce Mays
Ticket Manager: Marcia Lavine
Trainers: Kevin O'Neill, Jim Maurer,
  Don Cochren
Equipment Managers: Buck Buchanan, Jerry
  Fowler
Video Directors: Robert Blackwell, Randy Tinsley
Cheerleaders Director: Leslie Haynes

Stadium: Texas Stadium • **Capacity:** 65,024
  Irving, Texas 75062

Playing Surface: Texas Turf

Training Camp: St. Edward's University
  Austin, Texas 78704

1990 Schedule

Preseason
Aug. 11	at San Diego	7:00
Aug. 18	at Los Angeles Raiders	1:00
Aug. 25	**Pittsburgh**	8:00
Sept. 1	**Houston**	8:00

Regular Season
Sept. 9	**San Diego**	3:00
Sept. 16	**New York Giants**	3:00
Sept. 23	at Washington	1:00
Sept. 30	at New York Giants	1:00
Oct. 7	**Tampa Bay**	12:00
Oct. 14	at Phoenix	1:00
Oct. 21	at Tampa Bay	1:00
Oct. 28	**Philadelphia**	12:00
Nov. 4	at New York Jets	1:00
Nov. 11	**San Francisco**	7:00
Nov. 18	at Los Angeles Rams	1:00
Nov. 22	**Washington** (Thanksgiving)	3:00
Dec. 2	**New Orleans**	3:00
Dec. 9	**Open Date**	
Dec. 16	**Phoenix**	12:00
Dec. 23	at Philadelphia	1:00
Dec. 30	at Atlanta	1:00

Cowboys Coaching History

(271-193-6)

1960-88	Tom Landry	270-178-6
1989	Jimmy Johnson	1-15-0

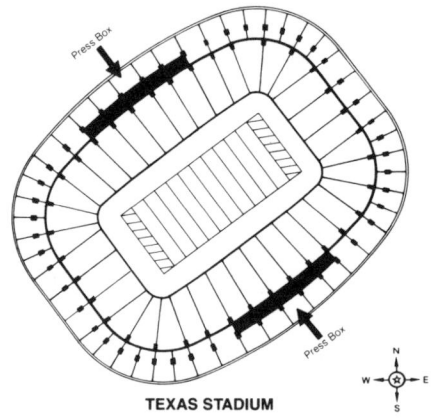

TEXAS STADIUM

Record Holders

Individual Records—Career
Category	Name	Performance
Rushing (Yds.)	Tony Dorsett, 1977-1987	12,036
Passing (Yds.)	Roger Staubach, 1969-1979	22,700
Passing (TDs)	Danny White, 1976-1988	155
Receiving (No.)	Drew Pearson, 1973-1983	489
Receiving (Yds.)	Tony Hill, 1977-1986	7,988
Interceptions	Mel Renfro, 1964-1977	52
Punting (Avg.)	Mike Saxon, 1985-89	40.8
Punt Return (Avg.)	Bob Hayes, 1965-1974	11.1
Kickoff Return (Avg.)	Mel Renfro, 1964-1977	26.4
Field Goals	Rafael Septien, 1978-1986	162
Touchdowns (Tot.)	Tony Dorsett, 1977-1987	86
Points	Rafael Septien, 1978-1986	874

Individual Records—Single Season
Category	Name	Performance
Rushing (Yds.)	Tony Dorsett, 1981	1,646
Passing (Yds.)	Danny White, 1983	3,980
Passing (TDs)	Danny White, 1983	29
Receiving (No.)	Herschel Walker, 1985	76
Receiving (Yds.)	Bob Hayes, 1966	1,232
Interceptions	Everson Walls, 1981	11
Punting (Avg.)	Sam Baker, 1962	45.4
Punt Return (Avg.)	Bob Hayes, 1968	20.8
Kickoff Return (Avg.)	Mel Renfro, 1965	30.0
Field Goals	Rafael Septien, 1981	27
Touchdowns (Tot.)	Dan Reeves, 1966	16
Points	Rafael Septien, 1983	123

Individual Records—Single Game
Category	Name	Performance
Rushing (Yds.)	Tony Dorsett, 12-4-77	206
Passing (Yds.)	Don Meredith, 11-10-63	460
Passing (TDs)	Many times	5
	Last time by Danny White, 10-30-83	
Receiving (No.)	Lance Rentzel, 11-19-67	13
Receiving (Yds.)	Bob Hayes, 11-13-66	246
Interceptions	Herb Adderley, 9-26-71	3
	Lee Roy Jordan, 11-4-73	3
	Dennis Thurman, 12-13-81	3
Field Goals	Roger Ruzek, 12-21-87	5
Touchdowns (Tot.)	Many times	4
	Last time by Duane Thomas, 12-18-71	
Points	Many times	24
	Last time by Duane Thomas, 12-18-71	

1989 Team Record
Preseason (3-1)

Date	Result		Opponents
8/13	W	20- 3	at San Diego
8/19	W	27-20	at L.A. Raiders
8/26	L	21-24	at Denver (OT)
9/2	W	30-20	Houston
		98-75	

Regular Season (1-15)

Date	Result		Opponents	Att.
9/10	L	0-28	at New Orleans	66,977
9/17	L	21-27	at Atlanta	55,285
9/24	L	7-30	Washington	63,200
10/1	L	13-30	N.Y. Giants	51,785
10/8	L	13-31	at Green Bay	56,656
10/15	L	14-31	San Francisco	61,077
10/22	L	28-36	at Kansas City	76,841
10/29	L	10-19	Phoenix	44,431
11/5	W	13- 3	at Washington	53,187
11/12	L	20-24	at Phoenix	49,657
11/19	L	14-17	Miami	56,044
11/23	L	0-27	Philadelphia	54,444
12/3	L	31-35	L.A. Rams	46,100
12/10	L	10-20	at Philadelphia	59,842
12/16	L	0-15	at N.Y. Giants	72,141
12/24	L	10-20	Green Bay	41,265

(OT) Overtime

Score by Periods

Cowboys	47	70	35	52	0	—	204
Opponents	84	118	90	101	0	—	393

Attendance
Home 418,346   Away 490,586   Total 908,932
Single-game home record, 80,259 (11-24-66)
Single-season home record, 511,541 (1981)

1989 Team Statistics

	Cowboys	Opp.
Total First Downs	246	321
Rushing	78	116
Passing	145	183
Penalty	23	22
Third Down: Made/Att.	62/187	106/229
Third Down: Pct.	33.2	46.3
Fourth Down: Made/Att.	8/19	7/12
Fourth Down: Pct.	42.1	58.3
Total Net Yards	4294	5556
Avg. Per Game	268.4	347.3
Total Plays	898	1060
Avg. Per Play	4.8	5.2
Net Yards Rushing	1409	1991
Avg. Per Game	88.1	124.4
Total Rushes	355	543
Net Yards Passing	2885	3565
Avg. Per Game	180.3	222.8
Sacked/Yards Lost	30/239	29/183
Gross Yards	3124	3748
Att./Completions	513/266	488/301
Completion Pct.	51.9	61.7
Had Intercepted	27	7
Punts/Avg.	82/39.8	73/39.9
Net Punting Avg.	34.2	35.3
Penalties/Yards Lost	100/771	102/723
Fumbles/Ball Lost	29/15	22/10
Touchdowns	25	44
Rushing	7	17
Passing	14	21
Returns	4	6
Avg. Time of Possession	25:34	34:26

1989 Individual Statistics

Scoring

	TD R	TD P	TD Rt	PAT	FG	Saf	TP
Zendejas, Phil.-Dall.	0	0	0	33/33	14/24	0	75
Zendejas, Dall.	0	0	0	10/10	5/9	0	25
Ruzek	0	0	0	14/15	5/11	0	29
Dixon	0	2	1	0/0	0/0	0	18
Johnston	0	3	0	0/0	0/0	0	18
Walker	2	1	0	0/0	0/0	0	18
Clack	2	0	0	0/0	0/0	0	12
Folsom	0	2	0	0/0	0/0	0	12
Irvin	0	2	0	0/0	0/0	0	12
Martin	0	2	0	0/0	0/0	0	12
Palmer	2	0	0	0/0	0/0	0	12
Shepard, N.O.-Dall.	0	1	1	0/0	0/0	0	12
Shepard, Dall.	0	1	0	0/0	0/0	0	6
Del Rio	0	0	1	0/0	0/0	0	6
Ford	0	1	0	0/0	0/0	0	6
Holt, Minn.-Dall.	0	0	1	0/0	0/0	0	6
Jeffcoat	0	0	1	0/0	0/0	0	6
Lockhart	0	0	1	0/0	0/0	0	6
Sargent	1	0	0	0/0	0/0	0	6
Cowboys	7	14	4	24/25	10/20	0	204
Opponents	17	21	6	43/44	28/35	1	393

Passing

	Att.	Comp.	Yds.	Pct.	TD	Int.	Tkld.	Rate
Aikman	293	155	1749	52.9	9	18	19/155	55.7
Walsh	219	110	1371	50.2	5	9	11/84	60.5
Saxon	1	1	4	100.0	0	0	0/0	83.3
Cowboys	513	266	3124	51.9	14	27	30/239	57.8
Opponents	488	301	3748	61.7	21	7	29/183	93.9

Rushing

	Att.	Yds.	Avg.	LG	TD
Palmer	112	446	4.0	63t	2
Aikman	38	302	7.9	25	0
Walker	81	246	3.0	20t	2
Johnston	67	212	3.2	13	0
Sargent	20	87	4.4	43	1
Clack	14	40	2.9	17	2
Dixon	3	30	10.0	13	0
Walsh	6	16	2.7	14	0
Tautalatasi	6	15	2.5	6	0
Shepard	3	12	4.0	12	0
Irvin	1	6	6.0	6	0
Saxon	1	1	1.0	1	0
Bates	1	0	0.0	0	0
Scott	2	-4	-2.0	-1	0
Cowboys	355	1409	4.0	63t	7
Opponents	543	1991	3.7	25	17

Receiving

	No.	Yds.	Avg.	LG	TD
Martin	46	644	14.0	46	2
Folsom	28	265	9.5	26	2
Irvin	26	378	14.5	65t	2
Dixon	24	477	19.9	75t	2
Walker	22	261	11.9	52	1
Shepard, N.O.-Dall.	20	304	15.2	37t	1
Shepard, Dall.	18	268	14.9	37t	1
Tautalatasi	17	157	9.2	23	0
Burbage	17	134	7.9	15	0
Palmer	17	93	5.5	13	0
Johnston	16	133	8.3	28	3
Scott	9	63	7.0	12	0
Ford	7	78	11.1	21	1
Sargent	6	50	8.3	21	0
Jennings	6	47	7.8	14	0
Clack	4	69	17.3	44	0
Alexander	1	16	16.0	16	0
Ruzek	1	4	4.0	4	0
Aikman	1	-13	-13.0	-13	0
Cowboys	266	3124	11.7	75t	14
Opponents	301	3748	12.5	79t	21

Interceptions

	No.	Yds.	Avg.	LG	TD
Lockhart	2	14	7.0	12	0
Holt, Minn.-Dall	1	90	90.0	90t	1
Bates	1	18	18.0	18	0
Albritton	1	3	3.0	3	0
Francis	1	2	2.0	2	0
Burton	1	0	0.0	0	0
Horton	1	0	0.0	0	0
Cowboys	7	37	5.3	18	0
Opponents	27	396	14.7	53t	3

Punting

	No.	Yds.	Avg.	In 20	LG
Saxon	79	3233	40.9	19	56
Ruzek	1	28	28.0	0	28
Cowboys	82	3261	39.8	19	56
Opponents	73	2911	39.9	28	58

Punt Returns

	No.	FC	Yds.	Avg.	LG	TD
Shepard, N.O.-Dall	31	2	251	8.1	56t	1
Shepard, Dall.	24	1	160	6.7	17	0
Martin	4	5	32	8.0	12	0
Burbage	3	5	5	1.7	5	0
Cowboys	31	11	197	6.4	17	0
Opponents	38	17	334	8.8	56t	1

Kickoff Returns

	No.	Yds.	Avg.	LG	TD
Dixon	47	1181	25.1	97t	1
Shepard, N.O.-Dall.	27	529	19.6	32	0
Shepard, Dall.	19	394	20.7	32	0
Palmer, Det.-Dall.	11	255	23.2	62	0
Clack	3	56	18.7	24	0
Burbage	3	55	18.3	22	0
Ankrom	2	6	3.0	5	0
Tautalatasi	1	9	9.0	9	0
Chandler	1	8	8.0	8	0
Sargent	1	0	0.0	0	0
Cowboys	77	1709	22.2	97t	1
Opponents	46	853	18.5	34	0

Sacks

	No.
Jeffcoat	11.5
Hamel	3.5
Broughton	3.0
Norton	2.5
Lockhart	2.0
Tolbert	2.0
Horton	1.0
Jones	1.0
Noonan	1.0
Hendrix	0.5
Cowboys	29.0
Opponents	30.0

1990 Draft Choices

Round	Name	Pos.	College
1.	Emmitt Smith	RB	Florida
2.	Alexander Wright	WR	Auburn
3.	Jimmie Jones	DT	Miami
9.	Kenneth Gant	DB	Albany State, Ga.
11.	Dave Harper	LB	Humboldt State

Dallas Cowboys 1990 Veteran Roster

No.	Name	Pos.	Ht.	Wt.	Birth-date	NFL Exp.	College	Hometown	How Acq.	'89 Games/Starts
	Agee, Tommie	RB	6-0	218	2/22/64	3	Auburn	Maplesville, Ala.	PB(KC)-'90#	9/0*
8	Aikman, Troy	QB	6-4	216	11/21/66	2	UCLA	Henryetta, Okla.	D1-'89	11/11
36	Albritton, Vince	S	6-2	214	7/23/62	7	Washington	Oakland, Calif.	FA-'84	16/16
31	Ankrom, Scott	S	6-1	194	1/4/66	2	Texas Christian	San Antonio, Tex.	D12-'89	10/0
40	Bates, Bill	S	6-1	199	6/6/61	8	Tennessee	Knoxville, Tenn.	FA-'83	16/0
79	Broughton, Willie	DT	6-5	275	9/9/64	4	Miami	Fort Pierce, Fla.	FA-'89	16/14
75	Carter, Jon	DT	6-4	273	3/12/65	2	Pittsburgh	Varnardo, La.	FA-'89	13/0
	Cheek, Louis	T	6-6	295	10/6/64	3	Texas A&M	Fairfield, Tex.	PB(Mia)-'90#	13/1*
58	Cooks, Terrence	LB	6-0	230	10/25/66	2	Nicholls State	Napoleonville, La.	PB(NE)-'90#	3/0*
55	Del Rio, Jack	LB	6-4	236	4/4/63	6	Southern California	Castro Valley, Calif.	FA-'89	14/12
86	Dixon, James	WR	5-10	181	2/2/67	2	Houston	Vernon, Tex.	FA-'89	16/7
32	†Flagler, Terrence	RB	6-0	200	9/24/64	4	Clemson	New York, N.Y.	T(SF)-'90	15/0
89	Folsom, Steve	TE	6-5	240	3/21/58	5	Utah	Santa Fe Springs, Calif.	FA-'87	16/16
38	Francis, Ron	CB	5-9	186	4/7/64	4	Baylor	LaMarque, Tex.	D2-'87	15/4
21	Gibson, Antonio	S	6-3	204	7/5/62	5	Cincinnati	Jackson, Miss.	PB(NO)-'90#	16/3*
66	Gogan, Kevin	T	6-7	309	11/2/64	4	Washington	Pacifica, Calif.	D8-'87	13/13
60	Hamel, Dean	DT	6-3	276	7/7/61	6	Tulsa	Warren, Mich.	T(Wash)-'89	16/13
80	Harris, Rod	WR	5-10	183	11/14/66	2	Texas A&M	Dallas, Tex.	PB(NO)-'90#	11/0*
45	Hendrix, Manny	CB	5-10	186	10/20/64	5	Utah	Phoenix, Ariz.	FA-'86	16/3
30	Holt, Issiac	CB	6-2	202	10/4/62	6	Alcorn State	Birmingham, Ala.	T(Minn)-'89	14/1*
20	Horton, Ray	S	5-11	187	4/12/60	8	Washington	Tacoma, Wash.	PB(Cin)-'89#	16/16
99	Howard, David	LB	6-2	230	12/8/61	6	Long Beach State	Long Beach, Calif.	T(Minn)-'89	11/0
88	Irvin, Michael	WR	6-2	202	3/5/66	3	Miami	Fort Lauderdale, Fla.	D1-'88	6/6
77	Jeffcoat, Jim	DE	6-5	256	4/1/61	8	Arizona State	Cliffwood, N.J.	D1-'83	16/16
84	Jennings, Keith	TE	6-4	251	5/19/66	2	Clemson	Summerville, S.C.	D5a-'89	10/0
67	Johnson, Greg	G	6-4	295	12/19/64	2	Oklahoma	Moore, Okla.	PB(Mia)-'90#	0*
91	Johnson, Walter	LB	6-0	240	11/13/63	4	Louisiana Tech	Ferriday, La.	PB(NO)-'90#	15/0*
48	Johnston, Daryl	RB	6-2	234	2/10/66	2	Syracuse	Youngstown, N.Y.	D2-'89	16/10
31	Jones, Keith	RB	5-10	182	2/5/66	2	Nebraska	Omaha, Neb.	PB(Clev)-'90#	16/2*
68	Ker, Crawford	G	6-3	285	5/5/62	6	Florida	Dunedin, Fla.	D3-'85	16/16
15	Laufenberg, Babe	QB	6-3	203	12/5/59	5	Indiana	Encino, Calif.	FA-'89	3/0
56	Lockhart, Eugene	LB	6-2	233	3/8/61	7	Houston	Crockett, Tex.	D6a-'84	16/16
83	Martin, Kelvin	WR	5-9	162	5/14/65	4	Boston College	Jacksonville, Fla.	D4-'87	11/11
85	McKinnon, Dennis	WR	6-1	185	8/22/61	7	Florida State	Quitman, Ga.	PB(Chi)-'90#	16/10*
61	Newton, Nate	G	6-3	318	12/20/61	5	Florida A&M	Orlando, Fla.	FA-'86	16/16
73	Noonan, Danny	DT	6-4	270	7/14/65	4	Nebraska	Lincoln, Neb.	D1-'87	7/5
51	Norton, Ken	LB	6-2	234	9/29/66	3	UCLA	Los Angeles, Calif.	D2-'88	13/13
82	Novacek, Jay	TE	6-4	235	10/24/62	6	Wyoming	Gothenburg, Neb.	PB(Phx)-'90#	16/1*
	Robinson, Lybrant	DE	6-5	250	8/31/64	2	Delaware State	Salisbury, Md.	PB(Wash)-'90#	5/0*
39	Sargent, Broderick	RB	5-11	220	9/16/62	4	Baylor	Waxahachie, Tex.	FA-'89	14/5
4	Saxon, Mike	P	6-3	198	7/10/62	6	San Diego State	Arcadia, Calif.	FA-'85	16/0
35	Scott, Kevin	RB	5-9	177	10/24/63	3	Stanford	Payallup, Wash.	FA-'89#	3/1
94	Shannon, Randy	LB	6-1	221	2/24/66	2	Miami	Miami, Fla.	D11-'89	16/4
87	Shepard, Derrick	WR	5-10	187	1/22/64	3	Oklahoma	Odessa, Tex.	W(NO)-'89	11/8
65	Slaton, Tony	C-G	6-3	280	4/12/61	7	Southern California	Merced, Calif.	PB(Rams)-'90#	15/15*
57	Smith, Vinson	LB	6-2	230	7/3/65	2	East Carolina	Statesville, N.C.	PB(Pitt)-'90#	0*
54	†Solomon, Jesse	LB	6-0	235	11/4/63	5	Florida State	Madison, Fla.	T(Minn)-'89	11/1
70	Stepnoski, Mark	C-G	6-2	269	1/20/67	2	Pittsburgh	Erie, Pa.	D3a-'89	16/4
96	†Stubbs, Daniel	DE	6-4	260	1/3/65	3	Miami	Red Bank, N.J.	T(SF)-'90	16/0
25	Tautalatasi, Junior	RB	5-11	208	3/24/63	5	Washington State	Alameda, Calif.	FA-'89	13/0
92	Tolbert, Tony	DE	6-6	241	12/29/67	2	Texas-El Paso	Englewood, N.J.	D4-'89	16/5
71	†Tuinei, Mark	T	6-5	286	3/31/60	8	Hawaii	Honolulu, Hawaii	FA-'83	16/16
95	†Walen, Mark	DT	6-5	267	3/10/63	3	UCLA	Burlingame, Calif.	D3'-'86	0*
3	Walsh, Steve	QB	6-2	200	12/1/66	2	Miami	St. Paul, Minn.	SD1-'89	8/5
37	Washington, James	S	6-1	196	1/10/65	3	UCLA	Los Angeles, Calif.	PB(Rams)-'90#	8/0*
78	Widell, Dave	T	6-6	292	5/14/65	3	Boston College	Hartford, Conn.	D4-'88	15/2
23	Williams, Robert	CB	5-10	184	10/2/62	4	Baylor	Galveston, Tex.	FA-'87	13/11
6	Zendejas, Luis	K	5-9	179	10/22/61	4	Arizona State	Chino, Calif.	FA-'89	7/0
76	Zimmerman, Jeff	G	6-3	313	1/10/65	3	Florida	Orlando, Fla.	D3-'87	16/1

* Agee played 9 games with Kansas City in '89; Cheek played 13 games with Miami; Cooks played 3 games with New England; Gibson played 16 games with New Orleans; Harris played 11 games with New Orleans; Holt played 5 games with Minnesota, 9 with Dallas; G. Johnson last active with Miami in '88; W. Johnson played 15 games with New Orleans; Jones played 16 games with Cleveland; McKinnon played 16 games with Chicago; Novacek played 16 games with Phoenix; Robinson played 5 games with Washington; Slaton played 15 games with L.A. Rams; V. Smith last active with Atlanta in '88; Walen missed '89 season due to injury; Washington played 8 games with L.A. Rams.

† Option playout; subject to developments.

Plan B unconditional free agent.

Players lost through Plan B (4): WR Cornell Burbage (Minn; 10 games in '89), WR Bernard Ford (Hou; 10); RB Paul Palmer (Cin; 9), C Bob White (NE; 8).

Also played with Cowboys in '89—WR Ray Alexander (2 games), CB-S Eric Brown (1), LB Ron Burton (6), TE Thornton Chandler (6), RB Darryl Clack (8), LB Garry Cobb (3), LB Onzy Elam (1), LB Steve Hendrickson (4), CB-S Tim Jackson (1), RB Undra Johnson (active for 1 game but did not play), DE Ed Jones (16), NT Kevin Lilly (1), C Tom Rafferty (12), K Roger Ruzek (9), DT Sean Smith (2), LB Ken Tippins (6), RB Herschel Walker (5).

COACHING STAFF

Head Coach,
Jimmy Johnson

Pro Career: Named second head coach in Cowboys' history on February 25, 1989. Youngest head coach in the NFC. No pro playing experience.

Background: All-Southwest Conference defensive lineman on Arkansas's 1964 undefeated national championship team. Began coaching career in 1965 at Louisiana Tech. Moved on as an assistant at Wichita State 1967, Iowa State 1968-69, Oklahoma 1970-72, Arkansas 1973-76, and Pittsburgh 1977-78. Head coach at Oklahoma State from 1979-83. Compiled 52-9 (.853) record in five seasons as head coach at the University of Miami. Under Johnson, the Hurricanes won the national championship in 1987 and 34 of 36 games from 1986-88. Career collegiate record: 81-34-3.

Personal: Born July 16, 1943, Port Arthur, Tex. Jimmy lives in Irving, Tex., and has two sons, Brent and Chad.

Assistant Coaches

Hubbard Alexander, wide receivers; born February 14, 1939, Winston-Salem, N.C., lives in Irving, Tex. Center Tennessee State 1958-61. No pro playing experience. College coach: Tennessee State 1962-63, Vanderbilt 1974-78, Miami 1979-88. Pro coach: Joined Cowboys in 1989.

Joe Avezzano, special teams; born November 17, 1943, Yonkers, N.Y., lives in Irving, Tex. Guard Florida State 1961-65. Pro center Boston Patriots 1966. College coach: Florida State 1968, Iowa State 1969-72, Pittsburgh 1973-76, Tennessee 1977-79, Oregon State 1980-84 (head coach), Texas 1985-88. Pro coach: Joined Cowboys in 1990.

Joe Brodsky, running backs; born June 9, 1934, Miami, Fla., lives in Irving, Tex. Fullback/linebacker Florida 1953-56. No pro playing experience. College coach: Miami 1978-88. Pro coach: Joined Cowboys in 1989.

Dave Campo, defensive assistant; born July 18, 1947, New London, Conn., lives in Coppell, Tex. Defensive back Central Connecticut State 1967-70. No pro playing experience. College coach: Central Connecticut State 1971-72, Albany State 1973, Bridgeport 1974, Pittsburgh 1975, Washington State 1976, Boise State 1977-79, Oregon State 1980, Weber State 1981-82, Iowa State 1983, Syracuse 1984-86, Miami 1987-88. Pro coach: Joined Cowboys in 1989.

Butch Davis, defensive line; born November 17, 1951, Tahlequah, Okla., lives in Coppell, Tex. Defensive end Arkansas 1971-74. No pro playing experience. College coach: Oklahoma State 1979-83, Miami 1984-88. Pro coach: Joined Cowboys in 1989.

Steve Hoffman, kickers, research and development; born September 8, 1958, Camden, N.J., lives in Irving, Tex. Quarterback-running back-wide receiver Dickinson College 1979-82. Pro punter Washington Federals (USFL) 1983. College coach: Miami 1985-87. Pro coach: Joined Cowboys in 1989.

Alan Lowry, tight ends; born November 21, 1950, Irving, Tex., lives in Roanoke, Tex. Defensive back-quarterback Texas 1970-72. No pro playing experience. College coach: Virginia Tech 1974, Wyoming 1975, Texas 1976-81. Pro coach: Joined Cowboys in 1982.

Dick Nolan, defensive backs; born March 26, 1932, Pittsburgh, Pa., lives in Roanoke, Tex. Offensive-defensive back Maryland 1951-53. Pro defensive back New York Giants 1954-57, 1959-61, St. Louis Cardinals 1958, Dallas Cowboys 1962 (player-coach). Pro coach: Dallas Cowboys 1963-67, San Francisco 49ers 1968-75 (head coach), New Orleans Saints 1977-80 (head coach), Houston Oilers 1981, rejoined Cowboys in 1982.

Dave Shula, offensive coordinator/quarterbacks; born May 28, 1959, Lexington, Ky., lives in Coppell, Tex. Wide receiver Dartmouth 1978-80. Pro wide receiver Baltimore Colts 1981. Pro coach: Miami Dolphins 1982-88, joined Cowboys in 1989.

Dave Wannstedt, defensive coordinator/linebackers; born May 21, 1952, Pittsburgh, Pa., lives in Coppell, Tex. Offensive tackle Pittsburgh 1970-73. No pro playing experience. College coach: Pittsburgh 1975-78, Oklahoma State 1979-82, Southern California 1983-85, Miami 1986-88. Pro coach: Joined Cowboys in 1989.

Mike Woicik, strength and conditioning; born September 26, 1956, Westwood, Mass., lives in Irving, Tex. Boston College 1974-78. No college or pro playing experience. College coach: Springfield 1978-80, Syracuse 1980-89. Pro coach: Joined Cowboys in 1990.

Tony Wise, offensive line; born December 28, 1951, Albany, N.Y., lives in Coppell, Tex. Offensive lineman Ithaca College 1971-72. No pro playing experience. College coach: Albany State 1973, Bridgeport 1974, Central Connecticut State 1975, Washington State 1976, Pittsburgh 1977-78, Oklahoma State 1979-83, Syracuse 1984, Miami 1985-88. Pro coach: Joined Cowboys in 1989.

Dallas Cowboys 1990 First-Year Roster

Name	Pos.	Ht.	Wt.	Birth-date	College	Hometown	How Acq.
Brinkley, Lester (1)	DE	6-6	270	5/13/65	Mississippi	Drew, Tex.	FA
Burnice, Karl (1)	T	6-8	317	12/16/67	Oregon Tech	Cleveland, Miss.	FA
Crockett, Willis (1)	LB	6-3	221	8/25/66	Georgia Tech	Douglas, Ga.	D5b-'89
Delaney, Jarrod (1)	WR	6-1	205	12/1/66	Texas Christian	Houston, Tex.	FA
Ervin, Corris (1)	CB-S	5-11	176	8/30/66	Central Florida	Vineland, N.J.	FA
Franks, Dave (1)	G	6-4	290	2/7/66	Connecticut	Waterbury, Conn.	FA
Gant, Kenneth	CB	5-11	178	4/18/67	Albany State	Lakeland, Fla.	FA
Harper, Dave	LB	6-1	220	5/5/66	Humboldt State	Eureka, Calif.	D11
Henry, Charles (1)	TE	6-4	230	4/18/64	Miami	St. Petersburg, Fla.	FA
Huebner, Tom	TE	6-6	250	10/17/66	Pittsburgh	Pittsburgh, Pa.	FA
Jokisch, Paul (1)	TE	6-7	248	1/4/64	Michigan	Birmingham, Mich.	FA
Jones, Jimmie	DT	6-4	284	1/9/66	Miami	Okeechobee, Fla.	D3
McNair, Fred	QB	6-1	220	12/11/68	Alcorn State	Mt. Olive, Miss.	FA
Mull, Curt	T	6-5	282	9/17/67	Georgia	Longwood, Fla.	FA
Sims, Tim	CB	6-0	205	6/1/66	Miami	Belle Glade, Fla.	FA
Smagala, Stan	CB	5-10	184	4/6/68	Notre Dame	Burbank, Ill.	D5
Smith, Emmitt	RB	5-9	199	5/15/69	Florida	Escambia, Fla.	D1
Spears, Anthony (1)	NT	6-5	260	11/4/65	Portland State	Pittsburg, Calif.	FA
Stumon, Greg (1)	LB	6-0	236	5/26/63	Southern Arkansas	Plain Dealing, La.	FA
Warner, Mark	T	6-7	290	12/21/67	Canisius	Cato, N.Y.	FA
Williams, Mike (1)	WR	5-10	177	10/9/66	Northeastern	Golden's Bridge, N.Y.	FA
Willis, Ken	K	5-11	190	10/6/66	Kentucky	Owensboro, Ky.	FA
Wright, Alexander	WR	6-0	187	7/19/67	Auburn	Albany, Ga.	D2

The term NFL Rookie is defined as a player who is in his first season of professional football and has not been on the roster of another professional football team for any regular-season or postseason games. A Rookie is designated by an "R" on NFL rosters. Players who have been active in another professional football league or players who have NFL experience, including either preseason training camp or being on an active roster for fewer than three regular-season or postseason games, are termed NFL First-Year Players. An NFL First-Year Player is designated by a "1" on NFL rosters. Thereafter, a player on an NFL active roster for at least three regular-season or postseason games is credited with an additional year of NFL playing experience.

NOTES

_____

_____

_____

_____

_____

_____

_____

_____

_____

_____

_____

_____

_____

_____

_____

National Football Conference Central Division

Team Colors: Honolulu Blue and Silver

**Pontiac Silverdome
1200 Featherstone Road — Box 4200
Pontiac, Michigan 48057
Telephone: (313) 335-4131**

Club Officials

President-Owner: William Clay Ford
Executive Vice President-CEO:
 Chuck Schmidt
Vice President/Player Personnel:
 Jerome R. Vainisi
Director of Player Personnel: Joe Bushofsky
Scouts: Dirk Dierking, Allen Hughes, Ron Hughes,
 Scott McEwen, Jim Owens, Jerry Neri,
 John Trump
Director of Public Relations: Bill Keenist
Director of Player Relations: Otis Canty
Accountant/Travel Coordinator: Tom Lesnau
Video Director: Steve Hermans
Director of Communications: Tim Pendell
Assistant Director of Public Relations:
 Wayne B. Moss
Ticket Manager: Fred Otto
Trainer: Kent Falb
Strength and Conditioning: Bert Hill
Equipment Manager: Dan Jaroshewich

Stadium: Pontiac Silverdome • Capacity: 80,500
 1200 Featherstone Road
 Pontiac, Michigan 48057

Playing Surface: AstroTurf

Training Camp: Pontiac Silverdome
 Pontiac, Michigan 48057

1990 Schedule

Preseason
Aug. 9	at Houston	7:00
Aug. 17	**Buffalo**	7:30
Aug. 24	**Kansas City**	7:30
Aug. 31	at Cincinnati	7:30

Regular Season
Sept. 9	**Tampa Bay**	1:00
Sept. 16	**Atlanta**	1:00
Sept. 23	at Tampa Bay	8:00
Sept. 30	**Green Bay**	1:00
Oct. 7	at Minnesota	12:00
Oct. 14	at Kansas City	12:00
Oct. 21	**Open Date**	
Oct. 28	at New Orleans	12:00
Nov. 4	**Washington**	1:00
Nov. 11	**Minnesota**	1:00
Nov. 18	at New York Giants	1:00
Nov. 22	**Denver** (Thanksgiving)	12:30
Dec. 2	at Chicago	12:00
Dec. 10	**L.A. Raiders** (Monday)	9:00
Dec. 16	**Chicago**	8:00
Dec. 22	at Green Bay (Saturday)	11:30
Dec. 30	at Seattle	1:00

Lions Coaching History

**Portsmouth Spartans 1930-33
(375-388-32)**

1930	Hal (Tubby) Griffen	5-6-3
1931-36	George (Potsy) Clark	49-20-6
1937-38	Earl (Dutch) Clark	14-8-0
1939	Elmer (Gus) Henderson	6-5-0
1940	George (Potsy) Clark	5-5-1
1941-42	Bill Edwards*	4-9-1
1942	John Karcis	0-8-0
1943-47	Charles (Gus) Dorais	20-31-2
1948-50	Alvin (Bo) McMillin	12-24-0
1951-56	Raymond (Buddy) Parker	50-24-2
1957-64	George Wilson	55-45-6
1965-66	Harry Gilmer	10-16-2
1967-72	Joe Schmidt	43-35-7
1973	Don McCafferty	6-7-1
1974-76	Rick Forzano**	15-17-0
1976-77	Tommy Hudspeth	11-13-0
1978-84	Monte Clark	43-63-1
1985-88	Darryl Rogers***	18-40-0
1988-89	Wayne Fontes	9-12-0

*Released after three games in 1942
**Resigned after four games in 1976
***Released after 11 games in 1988.

Record Holders
Individual Records—Career
Category	Name	Performance
Rushing (Yds.)	Billy Sims, 1980-84	5,106
Passing (Yds.)	Bobby Layne, 1950-58	15,710
Passing (TDs)	Bobby Layne, 1950-58	118
Receiving (No.)	Charlie Sanders, 1968-1977	336
Receiving (Yds.)	Gail Cogdill, 1960-68	5,220
Interceptions	Dick LeBeau, 1959-1972	62
Punting (Avg.)	Yale Lary, 1952-53, 1956-1964	44.3
Punt Return (Avg.)	Jack Christiansen, 1951-58	12.8
Kickoff Return (Avg.)	Pat Studstill, 1961-67	25.7
Field Goals	Eddie Murray, 1980-89	212
Touchdowns (Tot.)	Billy Sims, 1980-84	47
Points	Eddie Murray, 1980-89	943

Individual Records—Single Season
Category	Name	Performance
Rushing (Yds.)	Barry Sanders, 1989	1,470
Passing (Yds.)	Gary Danielson, 1980	3,223
Passing (TDs)	Bobby Layne, 1951	26
Receiving (No.)	James Jones, 1984	77
Receiving (Yds.)	Pat Studstill, 1966	1,266
Interceptions	Don Doll, 1950	12
	Jack Christiansen, 1953	12
Punting (Avg.)	Yale Lary, 1963	48.9
Punt Return (Avg.)	Jack Christiansen, 1952	21.5
Kickoff Return (Avg.)	Tom Watkins, 1965	34.4
Field Goals	Eddie Murray, 1980	27
Touchdowns (Tot.)	Billy Sims, 1980	16
Points	Doak Walker, 1950	128

Individual Records—Single Game
Category	Name	Performance
Rushing (Yds.)	Bob Hoernschemeyer, 11-23-50	198
Passing (Yds.)	Bobby Layne, 11-5-50	374
Passing (TDs)	Gary Danielson, 12-9-78	5
Receiving (No.)	Cloyce Box, 12-3-50	12
	James Jones, 9-28-86	12
Receiving (Yds.)	Cloyce Box, 12-3-50	302
Interceptions	Don Doll, 10-23-49	*4
Field Goals	Garo Yepremian, 11-13-66	6
Touchdowns (Tot.)	Cloyce Box, 12-3-50	4
Points	Cloyce Box, 12-3-50	24

*NFL Record

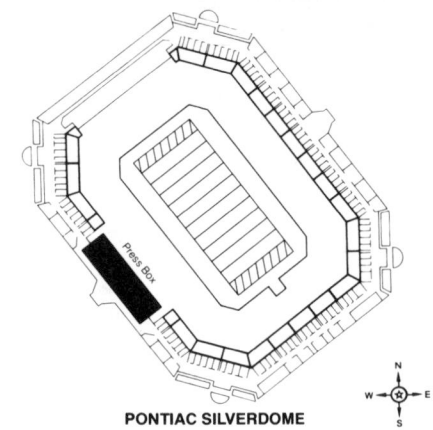

PONTIAC SILVERDOME

1989 Team Record
Preseason (0-4)

Date	Result		Opponents
8/12	L	25-34	Cleveland
8/19	L	3-35	Cincinnati
8/26	L	7-13	at Seattle
9/2	L	14-24	at L.A. Rams

Regular Season (7-9)

Date	Result		Opponents	Att.
9/10	L	13-16	Phoenix	36,735
9/17	L	14-24	at N.Y. Giants	76,021
9/24	L	27-47	Chicago	71,418
10/1	L	3-23	Pittsburgh	43,804
10/8	L	17-24	at Minnesota	55,380
10/15	W	17-16	at Tampa Bay	46,225
10/22	L	7-20	Minnesota	51,579
10/29	L	20-23	at Green Bay (OT)	53,731
11/5	L	31-35	at Houston	48,056
11/12	W	31-22	Green Bay	44,324
11/19	L	7-42	at Cincinnati	55,720
11/23	W	13-10	Cleveland	65,624
12/3	W	21-14	New Orleans	38,550
12/10	W	27-17	at Chicago	52,650
12/17	W	33-7	Tampa Bay	40,362
12/24	W	31-24	at Atlanta	7,792

(OT) Overtime

Score by Periods

Lions	68	108	65	71	0	—	312
Opponents	29	156	89	87	3	—	364

Attendance
Home 392,296 Away 395,575 Total 787,871
Single-game home record, 80,444 (12-20-81)
Single-season home record, 622,593 (1980)

1989 Team Statistics

	Lions	Opp.
Total First Downs	274	314
Rushing	117	98
Passing	139	189
Penalty	18	27
Third Down: Made/Att.	63/189	83/220
Third Down: Pct.	33.3	37.7
Fourth Down: Made/Att.	8/13	10/14
Fourth Down: Pct.	61.5	71.4
Total Net Yards	4992	5537
Avg. Per Game	312.0	346.1
Total Plays	928	1064
Avg. Per Play	5.4	5.2
Net Yards Rushing	2053	1621
Avg. Per Game	128.3	101.3
Total Rushes	421	454
Net Yards Passing	2939	3916
Avg. Per Game	183.7	244.8
Sacked/Yards Lost	57/343	40/277
Gross Yards	3282	4193
Att./Completions	450/229	570/370
Completion Pct.	50.9	64.9
Had Intercepted	24	16
Punts/Avg.	83/42.6	80/41.2
Net Punting Avg.	36.0	31.8
Penalties/Yards Lost	121/977	107/993
Fumbles/Ball Lost	37/24	28/16
Touchdowns	36	42
Rushing	23	18
Passing	11	19
Returns	2	5
Avg. Time of Possession	26:14	33:46

1989 Individual Statistics

Scoring

	TD R	TD P	TD Rt	PAT	FG	Saf	TP
Murray	0	0	0	36/36	20/21	0	96
B. Sanders	14	0	0	0/0	0/0	0	84
R. Johnson	0	8	0	0/0	0/0	0	48
Gagliano	4	0	0	0/0	0/0	0	24
Peete	4	0	0	0/0	0/0	0	24
Clark	0	2	0	0/0	0/0	0	12
Hipple	1	0	0	0/0	0/0	0	6
Holmes	0	0	1	0/0	0/0	0	6
Phillips	0	1	0	0/0	0/0	0	6
White	0	0	1	0/0	0/0	0	6
Lions	23	11	2	36/36	20/21	0	312
Opponents	18	19	5	41/42	23/33	1	364

Passing

	Att.	Comp.	Yds.	Pct.	TD	Int.	Tkld.	Rate
Gagliano	232	117	1671	50.4	6	12	25/153	61.2
Peete	195	103	1479	52.8	5	9	27/164	67.0
Hipple	18	7	90	38.9	0	3	5/26	15.7
Long	5	2	42	40.0	0	0	0/0	70.4
Lions	450	229	3282	50.9	11	24	57/343	60.8
Opponents	570	370	4193	64.9	19	16	40/277	86.2

Rushing

	Att.	Yds.	Avg.	LG	TD
B. Sanders	280	1470	5.3	34	14
Gagliano	41	192	4.7	19	4
Peete	33	148	4.5	14t	4
Paige	30	105	3.5	16	0
Painter	15	64	4.3	9	0
R. Johnson	12	38	3.2	14	0
Gray	3	22	7.3	14	0
Hipple	2	11	5.5	10	1
L. Brown	1	3	3.0	3	0
Long	3	2	0.7	6	0
McDonald	1	-2	-2.0	-2	0
Lions	421	2053	4.9	34	23
Opponents	454	1621	3.6	53t	18

Receiving

	No.	Yds.	Avg.	LG	TD
R. Johnson	70	1091	15.6	75t	8
Clark	41	748	18.2	69	2
Phillips	30	352	11.7	55t	1
Stanley	24	304	12.7	37	0
B. Sanders	24	282	11.8	46	0
Mobley	13	158	12.2	30	0
McDonald	12	138	11.5	24	0
Ford	5	56	11.2	37	0
Painter	3	41	13.7	27	0
Gray	2	47	23.5	30	0
T. Johnson	2	29	14.5	22	0
Paige	2	27	13.5	15	0
Chadwick	1	9	9.0	9	0
Lions	229	3282	14.3	75t	11
Opponents	370	4193	11.3	69t	19

Interceptions

	No.	Yds.	Avg.	LG	TD
Holmes	6	77	12.8	36	1
J. Williams	5	15	3.0	9	0
Gibson	1	10	10.0	10	0
Crockett	1	5	5.0	5	0
Noga	1	0	0.0	0	0
Taylor	1	0	0.0	0	0
White	1	0	0.0	0	0
Lions	16	107	6.7	36	1
Opponents	24	447	18.6	90t	3

Punting

	No.	Yds.	Avg.	In 20	LG
Arnold	82	3538	43.1	14	64
Lions	83	3538	42.6	14	64
Opponents	80	3293	41.2	22	58

Punt Returns

	No.	FC	Yds.	Avg.	LG	TD
Stanley	36	5	496	13.8	74	0
Gray	11	2	76	6.9	15	0
Woods	0	1	0	—	0	0
Lions	47	8	572	12.2	74	0
Opponents	46	12	373	8.1	30	0

Kickoff Returns

	No.	Yds.	Avg.	LG	TD
Gray	24	640	26.7	57	0
Palmer	11	255	23.2	62	0
Stanley	9	95	10.6	19	0
B. Sanders	5	118	23.6	43	0
Alexander	5	100	20.0	25	0
Woods	2	28	14.0	15	0
Dallafior	2	13	6.5	13	0
Painter	1	14	14.0	14	0
Crockett	1	8	8.0	8	0
Griffin	1	1	1.0	1	0
Miller	0	0	—	0	0
Lions	61	1272	20.9	62	0
Opponents	65	1037	16.0	99t	1

Sacks

	No.
Ball	9.0
Cofer	9.0
E. Williams	5.5
Spielman	5.0
J. Williams	4.0
Brooks	2.0
Jamison	2.0
McNorton	1.0
Peete	1.0
White	1.0
Griffin	0.5
Lions	40.0
Opponents	57.0

1990 Draft Choices

Round	Name	Pos.	College
1.	Andre Ware	QB	Houston
2.	Dan Owens	DE	Southern California
3.	Marc Spindler	DE	Pittsburgh
4.	Rob Hinckley	LB	Stanford
	Chris Oldham	DB	Oregon
5.	Jeff Campbell	WR	Colorado
6.	Maurice Henry	LB	Kansas State
7.	Tracy Hayworth	LB	Tennessee
8.	Willie Green	WR	Mississippi
	Roman Fortin	G	San Diego State
9.	Jack Linn	T	West Virginia
10.	Bill Miller	WR	Illinois State
11.	Reginald Warnsley	RB	So. Mississippi
12.	Robert Claiborne	WR	San Diego State

Detroit Lions 1990 Veteran Roster

No.	Name	Pos.	Ht.	Wt.	Birth-date	NFL Exp.	College	Hometown	How Acq.	'89 Games/Starts
32	Alexander, Bruce	CB	5-9	169	9/17/65	2	Stephen F. Austin	Lufkin, Tex.	FA-'89	8/1
65	Andolsek, Eric	G	6-2	286	8/22/66	3	Louisiana State	Thibodaux, La.	D5-'88	16/16
6	Arnold, Jim	P	6-3	211	1/31/61	8	Vanderbilt	Dalton, Ga.	FA-'86	16/0
93	Ball, Jerry	NT	6-1	298	12/15/64	4	Southern Methodist	Beaumont, Tex.	D3-'87	16/16
36	Blades, Bennie	S	6-1	221	9/3/66	3	Miami	Ft. Lauderdale, Fla.	D1-'88	16/16
97	Brooks, Kevin	DE-NT	6-6	278	2/9/63	6	Michigan	Detroit, Mich.	FA-'89	15/15
75	Brown, Lomas	T	6-4	287	3/30/63	6	Florida	Miami, Fla.	D1-'85	16/16
95	†Brown, Mark	LB	6-2	240	7/18/61	8	Purdue	Inglewood, Calif.	W(Mia)-'89	6/3
50	Caston, Toby	LB	6-1	243	7/17/65	4	Louisiana State	Monroe, La.	PB(Hou)-'89#	16/0
82	Clark, Robert	WR	5-11	173	8/8/65	3	North Carolina Central	Richmond, Va.	PB(NO)-'89#	16/16
30	Cocroft, Sherman	S	6-1	190	8/29/61	5	San Jose State	Watsonville, Calif.	PB(TB)-'90#	10/2*
55	Cofer, Michael	LB	6-5	244	4/7/60	8	Tennessee	Knoxville, Tenn.	D3-'83	15/7
39	Crockett, Ray	CB	5-9	181	11/5/67	2	Baylor	Duncanville, Tex.	D4-'89	16/0
67	Dallafior, Ken	G-C	6-4	279	8/26/59	6	Minnesota	Madison Heights, Mich.	PB(SD)-'89#	16/11
79	Duckens, Mark	DE	6-4	270	3/4/65	2	Arizona State	Wichita, Kan.	PB(NYG)-'90#	15/0*
77	Ferguson, Keith	DE	6-5	276	4/3/59	10	Ohio State	Miami, Fla.	W(SD)-'85	4/1
80	Ford, John	WR	6-2	204	7/31/66	2	Virginia	Belle Glade, Fla.	D2-'89	7/1
14	†Gagliano, Bob	QB	6-3	196	9/5/58	6	Utah State	Glendale, Calif.	FA-'89	11/7
98	Gibson, Dennis	LB	6-2	243	2/8/64	4	Iowa State	Ankeny, Iowa	D8-'87	6/6
53	Glover, Kevin	C-G	6-2	282	6/17/63	6	Maryland	Upper Marlboro, Md.	D2-'85	16/16
23	Gray, Mel	WR-KR	5-9	162	3/16/61	5	Purdue	Williamsburg, Va.	PB(NO)-'89#	10/1
62	Green, Curtis	DE-NT	6-3	273	6/3/57	10	Alabama State	Quincy, Fla.	D2-'81	16/0
89	Greer, Terry	WR	6-1	192	9/27/57	5	Alabama State	Memphis, Tenn.	PB(SF)-'90#	11/0*
58	Jamison, George	LB	6-2	228	9/30/62	4	Cincinnati	Bridgeton, N.J.	SD2-'84	11/6
84	Johnson, Richard	WR	5-6	184	10/19/61	2	Colorado	San Pedro, Calif.	FA-'89	16/15
57	Jones, Victor	LB	6-2	240	10/19/66	3	Virginia Tech	Rockville, Md.	FA-'89	11/9
49	Judson, William	CB	6-1	192	3/26/59	9	South Carolina State	Atlanta, Ga.	PB(Mia)-'90#	14/14*
90	Karpinski, Keith	LB	6-3	225	10/12/66	2	Penn State	Hamtramck, Mich.	D11-'89	16/0
83	Matthews, Aubrey	WR	5-7	165	9/15/62	5	Delta State	Jacksonville, Fla.	PB(GB)-'90#	13/3*
29	McNorton, Bruce	CB	5-10	175	2/28/59	9	Georgetown, Ky.	Daytona Beach, Fla.	D4-'82	8/0
25	Miller, Chuckie	CB-S	5-10	180	5/9/65	2	UCLA	Aniston, Ala.	FA-'90	0*
44	Miller, John	S	6-1	195	6/22/66	2	Michigan State	Farmington, Mich.	FA-'89	9/0
3	Murray, Eddie	K	5-10	180	8/29/56	11	Tulane	Victoria, British Columbia	D7-'80	16/0
51	†Noga, Niko	LB	6-1	235	3/2/62	7	Hawaii	Honolulu, Hawaii	FA-'89	14/1
26	Painter, Carl	RB	5-9	188	5/10/64	3	Hampton Institute	Norfolk, Va.	D6-'88	15/0
9	Peete, Rodney	QB	6-0	193	3/16/66	2	Southern California	Tucson, Ariz.	D6-'89	8/8
96	Pete, Lawrence	NT	6-0	282	1/18/66	2	Nebraska	Wichita, Kan.	D5-'89	16/0
24	Phillips, Jason	WR	5-7	168	10/11/66	2	Houston	Houston, Tex.	D10-'89	16/6
31	Richard, Gary	CB	5-10	176	10/9/65	2	Missouri	Denver, Colo.	FA-'90	0*
73	Salem, Harvey	T-G	6-6	289	1/15/61	8	California	El Cerrito, Calif.	T(Hou)-'86	10/8
20	Sanders, Barry	RB	5-8	203	7/16/68	2	Oklahoma State	Wichita, Kan.	D1-'89	15/13
64	†Sanders, Eric	T-G	6-7	286	10/22/58	10	Nevada-Reno	Reno, Nev.	W(Atl)-'86	16/7
54	Spielman, Chris	LB	6-0	244	10/11/65	3	Ohio State	Canton, Ohio	D2a-'88	16/16
21	†Taylor, Terry	CB	5-10	191	7/18/61	7	Southern Illinois	Warren, Ohio	T(Sea)-'89	15/15
60	Utley, Mike	G-T	6-6	279	12/20/65	2	Washington State	Seattle, Wash.	D3-'89	5/5
28	Welch, Herb	S	5-11	180	1/12/61	6	UCLA	Watchung, N.J.	PB(Wash)-'90#	9/0*
35	White, William	CB-S	5-10	191	2/19/66	3	Ohio State	Lima, Ohio	D4-'88	15/15
4	Williams, Byron	WR	6-2	185	10/31/60	3	Texas-Arlington	Texarkana, Tex.	FA-'90	0*
76	†Williams, Eric	DE	6-4	286	2/24/62	7	Washington State	Stockton, Calif.	D3a-'84	16/16
59	†Williams, Jimmy	LB	6-3	225	11/15/60	9	Nebraska	Washington, D.C.	D1-'82	16/16

* Cocroft played 10 games with Tampa Bay in '89; Duckens played 15 games with N.Y. Giants; Greer played 11 games with San Francisco; Judson played 14 games with Miami; Matthews played 13 games with Green Bay; C. Miller last active with Indianapolis in '88; Richard last active with Green Bay in '88; Welch played 9 games with Washington; B. Williams last active with N.Y. Giants in '86.

† Option playout; subject to developments.

Plan B unconditional free agent.

Traded—QB Chuck Long to L.A. Rams.

Players lost through Plan B (9): DE James Cribbs (GB; 7 games in '89), T Chris Gambol (NE; 6), S James Griffin (KC; 16), CB Jerry Holmes (GB; 16), C Trevor Matich (Jets; 11), G-T Joe Milinichik (Rams; 15), RB Tony Paige (Mia; 16), WR Walter Stanley (Wash; 14), WR Michael Williams (Hou; 1).

Also played with Lions in '89—CB Michael Brim (2 games), WR Jeff Chadwick (1), DE Byron Darby (1), QB Eric Hipple (1), WR Troy Johnson (9), WR Keith McDonald (6), WR Stacey Mobley (10), RB Paul Palmer (5), CB Jerry Woods (2).

COACHING STAFF

Head Coach,
Wayne Fontes

Pro Career: Became Lions' seventeenth head coach on December 22, 1988, after serving five weeks as interim head coach. Fontes led the Lions to a 2-3 record during that span and to a 7-9 record in 1989, including five straight season-ending wins. He began his fourth season (1988) in Detroit as the team's defensive coordinator and secondary coach, following a nine-year stint with the Tampa Bay Buccaneers. A former defensive back with the New York Jets, Fontes advanced from secondary coach to defensive coordinator to assistant head coach of the Buccaneers during his years at Tampa Bay. As a player with the Jets, his brief pro career was cut short by a broken leg after two seasons (1963-64). However, his 83-yard interception return against Houston (12-15-63) did stand as the Jets' team record until it was broken last season by Erik McMillan's 93-yarder. Career record: 9-12.

Background: A former two-sport star (football and baseball) at Michigan State, Fontes earned all-Big Ten honors at defensive back for the Spartans. He earned his bachelor's degree in education and biological science and later earned his master's degree in administration, all from Michigan State. After directing the freshman team at Michigan State in 1965, Fontes became defensive backfield coach at Dayton in 1968. He also served in the same capacity at Iowa (1969-71) and Southern California (1972-75).

Personal: Born February 17, 1939, New Bedford, Mass. Fontes and his wife, Evelyn, live in Rochester Hills, Mich., and have three children: Mike, Scott, and Kim.

Assistant Coaches

Don Clemons, administrative assistant; born February 15, 1954, Newark, N.J., lives in Rochester, Mich. Defensive end Muehlenberg College 1973-76. No pro playing experience. College coach: Kutztown State 1977-78, New Mexico 1979, Arizona State 1980-84. Pro coach: Detroit Lions 1985-87, rejoined Lions in 1989.

Darrel "Mouse" Davis, offensive passing assistant; born September 6, 1932, Palouse, Wash., lives in Lake Orion, Mich. Quarterback Western Oregon State 1952-55. No pro playing experience. College coach: Portland State 1974-80 (head coach 1975-80). Pro coach: Toronto Argonauts (CFL) 1982-83, Houston Gamblers (USFL) 1984, Denver Gold (USFL) 1985, joined Lions in 1989.

Len Fontes, defensive backs; born March 8, 1938, New Bedford, Mass., lives in Pontiac, Mich. Defensive back Ohio State 1958-59. No pro playing experience. College coach: Eastern Michigan 1968, Dayton 1969-72, Navy 1973, Miami 1974-79. Pro coach: Cleveland Browns 1980-82, New York Giants 1983-88, joined Lions in 1990.

Frank Gansz, special teams; born November 22, 1938, Altoona, Pa., lives in Auburn Hills, Mich. Center-linebacker Navy 1957-59. No pro playing experience. College coach: Air Force 1964, Colgate 1968, Navy 1969, Oklahoma State 1973, 1975, Army 1974, UCLA 1976-77. Pro coach: San Francisco 49ers 1978, Cincinnati Bengals 1979-80, Kansas City Chiefs 1981-82, 1986-88 (head coach 1987-88), joined Lions in 1989.

June Jones, quarterbacks, receivers; born February 19, 1953, Portland, Ore., lives in Lake Orion, Mich. Quarterback Hawaii 1973-74, Portland State 1975-76. Pro quarterback Atlanta Falcons 1977-81, Toronto Argonauts (CFL) 1982. College coach: Hawaii 1983. Pro coach: Toronto Argonauts (CFL) 1982, Houston Gamblers (USFL) 1984, Denver Gold (USFL) 1985, Houston Oilers 1987-88, joined Lions in 1989.

Lamar Leachman, defensive line; born August 7, 1934, Cartersville, Ga., lives in Pontiac, Mich. Center-linebacker Tennessee 1952-55. No pro playing experience. College coach: Richmond 1966-67, Georgia Tech 1968-71, Memphis State 1972, South Carolina 1973. Pro coach: New York Stars (WFL) 1974, Toronto Argonauts (CFL) 1975-77, Montreal Alouettes (CFL) 1978-79, New York Giants 1980-89, joined Lions in 1990.

Dave Levy, running backs; born October 25, 1932, Carrollton, Mo., lives in Lake Orion, Mich. Guard UCLA 1952-53. No pro playing experience. College coach: UCLA 1954, Long Beach City College 1955, Southern California 1960-75. Pro coach: San Diego Chargers 1980-88, joined Lions in 1989.

Billie Matthews, defensive backs; born March 15, 1930, Houston, Tex., lives in Rochester, Mich. Quarterback Southern University 1948-51. No pro playing experience. College coach: Kansas 1970, UCLA 1971-78. Pro coach: San Francisco 49ers 1979-82, Philadelphia Eagles 1983-84, Indianapolis Colts 1985-86, Kansas City Chiefs 1987-88, joined Lions in 1989.

Herb Paterra, inside linebackers; born November 8, 1940, Glassport, Pa., lives in Rochester Hills, Mich. Offensive guard-linebacker Michigan State 1960-62. Pro linebacker Buffalo Bills 1963-64, Hamilton Tiger-Cats (CFL) 1965-68. College coach: Michigan State 1969-71, Wyoming 1972-74. Pro coach: Charlotte Hornets (WFL) 1974, Hamilton Tiger-Cats (CFL) 1978-79, Los Angeles Rams 1980-82, Edmonton Eskimos (CFL) 1983, Green Bay Packers 1984-85, Buffalo Bills 1986, Tampa Bay Buccaneers 1987-88, joined Lions in 1989.

Charlie Sanders, tight ends; born August 25, 1946, Greensboro, N.C., lives in Rochester, Mich. Tight end Minnesota 1966-67. Pro tight end Detroit Lions 1968-77. Pro coach: Joined Lions in 1989.

Jerry Wampfler, offensive line; born August 6, 1932, New Philadelphia, Ohio, lives in Lake Orion, Mich. Tackle Miami, Ohio 1951-54. No pro playing experience. College coach: Presbyterian 1955, Miami, Ohio 1963-65, Notre Dame 1966-69, Colorado State 1970-72 (head coach). Pro coach: Philadelphia Eagles 1973-75, 1979-83, Buffalo Bills 1976-77, New York Giants 1978, Green Bay Packers 1984-87, San Diego Chargers 1988, joined Lions in 1989.

Woody Widenhofer, defensive coordinator, outside linebackers; born January 20, 1943, Riverview, Mich., lives in Rochester Hills, Mich. Linebacker Missouri 1961-64. No pro playing experience. College coach: Michigan State 1969-70, Eastern Michigan 1971, Minnesota 1972, Missouri 1985-88 (head coach). Pro coach: Pittsburgh Steelers 1973-83, Oklahoma Outlaws (USFL) 1984 (head coach), joined Lions in 1989.

Detroit Lions 1990 First-Year Roster

Name	Pos.	Ht.	Wt.	Birth-date	College	Hometown	How Acq.
Broady, Tim (1)	CB-S	6-0	210	2/20/66	Murray State	Madisonville, Ky.	FA
Campbell, Jeff	WR	5-8	167	3/29/68	Colorado	Vail, Colo.	D5
Claiborne, Robert	WR	5-10	175	7/10/67	San Diego State	New Orleans, La.	D12
Dawson, Ken	RB	6-0	230	8/15/66	Appalachian State	Norfolk, Va.	FA
Farr, Mike	WR	5-10	192	8/8/67	UCLA	Birmingham, Mich.	FA
Fortin, Roman	T	6-5	270	2/26/67	San Diego State	Columbus, Ga.	D8b
Green, Willie	WR	6-2	179	4/2/66	Mississippi	Clarke, Ga.	D8a
Hayworth, Tracy	LB-DE	6-3	250	12/18/67	Tennessee	Franklin, Tenn.	D7
Henry, Maurice	RB	5-11	220	3/12/67	Kansas State	Salina, Kan.	D6
Hinckley, Rob	LB	6-4	241	7/19/67	Stanford	Walnut Creek, Calif.	D4a
Linn, Jack	G	6-5	278	6/10/67	West Virginia	Rochester, Pa.	D9
Oldham, Chris	CB	5-9	183	10/26/68	Oregon	Sacramento, Calif.	D4b
Marlatt, Pat (1)	DE	6-5	270	5/3/66	West Virginia State	Alexandria, Va.	FA
Miller, Bill	WR	5-10	180	6/28/67	Illinois State	Fort Wayne, Ind.	D10
Owens, Dan	DE	6-3	268	3/16/67	Southern California	Whittier, Calif.	D2
Smith, Davis	WR	5-4	150	3/27/67	Texas Southern	New Orleans, La.	FA
Spindler, Marc	NT	6-5	277	11/28/69	Pittsburgh	West Scranton, Pa.	D3
Ware, Andre	QB	6-2	205	7/31/68	Houston	Dickinson, Tex.	D1
Warnsley, Reginald	RB	5-10	225	4/5/68	Southern Mississippi	Laurel, Miss.	D11
Wilkerson, Eric (1)	RB	5-9	185	12/19/66	Kent State	Cleveland, Ohio	FA
Wilson, Curtis	C	6-3	290	10/30/65	Missouri	Chillicothe, Mo.	FA

The term NFL Rookie is defined as a player who is in his first season of professional football and has not been on the roster of another professional football team for any regular-season or postseason games. A Rookie is designated by an "R" on NFL rosters. Players who have been active in another professional football league or players who have NFL experience, including either preseason training camp or being on an active roster for fewer than three regular-season or postseason games, are termed NFL First-Year Players. An NFL First-Year Player is designated by a "1" on NFL rosters. Thereafter, a player on an NFL active roster for at least three regular-season or postseason games is credited with an additional year of NFL playing experience.

NOTES

_____

_____

_____

_____

_____

_____

_____

_____

_____

_____

_____

_____

National Football Conference
Central Division

Team Colors: Dark Green, Gold, and White

1265 Lombardi Avenue
P.O. Box 10628
Green Bay, Wisconsin 54307-0628
Telephone: (414) 496-5700

Club Officials

Chairman of the Board: Robert J. Parins
President, CEO: Bob Harlan
Vice President: John Fabry
Secretary: Peter M. Platten III
Treasurer: Phil Hendrickson
Executive Vice President, Football Operations:
  Tom Braatz
Executive Assistant to the President:
  Phil Pionek
Executive Director of Public Relations:
  Lee Remmel
Director of Marketing/Community Relations:
  Jeff Cieply
Asst. Director of Public Relations: Jeff Blumb
Green Bay Ticket Director: Mark Wagner
Milwaukee Ticket Director: Marge Paget
Controller: Dick Blasczyk
Video Director: Al Treml
Trainer: Domenic Gentile
Equipment Manager: Bob Noel

Stadium: Lambeau Field • **Capacity:** 59,543
    P.O. Box 10628
    1265 Lombardi Avenue
    Green Bay, Wisconsin 54307-0628
    Milwaukee County Stadium •
    Capacity: 56,051
    Highway I-94
    Milwaukee, Wisconsin 53214

Playing Surfaces: Grass

Training Camp: St. Norbert College
    West DePere, Wisconsin 54115

1990 Schedule

Preseason
Aug. 11	**Cleveland**	6:00
Aug. 18	vs. New Orleans at	
	Madison, Wis.	1:00
Aug. 25	vs. Atlanta at Milwaukee	6:00
Aug. 31	at Kansas City	7:00

Regular Season
Sept. 9	**Los Angeles Rams**	12:00
Sept. 16	**Chicago**	12:00
Sept. 23	**Kansas City**	12:00
Sept. 30	at Detroit	1:00
Oct. 7	at Chicago	3:00
Oct. 14	at Tampa Bay	1:00
Oct. 21	**Open Date**	
Oct. 28	**Minnesota** at Milwaukee	12:00
Nov. 4	**San Francisco**	12:00
Nov. 11	at Los Angeles Raiders	1:00
Nov. 18	at Phoenix	2:00
Nov. 25	**Tampa Bay** at Milwaukee	12:00
Dec. 2	at Minnesota	7:00
Dec. 9	**Seattle** at Milwaukee	12:00
Dec. 16	at Philadelphia	4:00
Dec. 22	**Detroit** (Saturday)	11:30
Dec. 30	at Denver	2:00

Packers Coaching History
(479-391-36)

1921-49	Earl (Curly) Lambeau	212-106-21
1950-53	Gene Ronzani*	14-31-1
1953	Hugh Devore- Ray (Scooter) McLean**	0-2-0
1954-57	Lisle Blackbourn	17-31-0
1958	Ray (Scooter) McLean	1-10-1
1959-67	Vince Lombardi	98-30-4
1968-70	Phil Bengtson	20-21-1
1971-74	Dan Devine	25-28-4
1975-83	Bart Starr	53-77-3
1984-87	Forrest Gregg	25-37-1
1988-89	Lindy Infante	14-18-0

*Released after 10 games in 1953
**Co-coaches

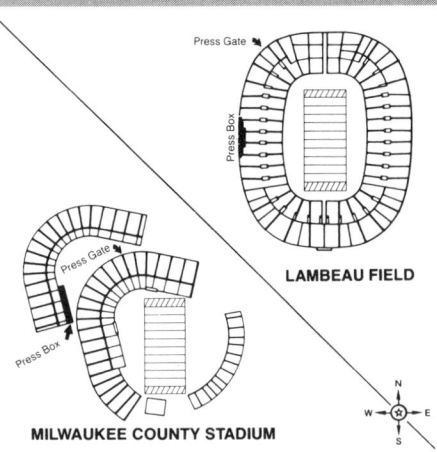

LAMBEAU FIELD

MILWAUKEE COUNTY STADIUM

Record Holders
Individual Records — Career

Category	Name	Performance
Rushing (Yds.)	Jim Taylor, 1958-1966	8,207
Passing (Yds.)	Bart Starr, 1956-1971	23,718
Passing (TDs)	Bart Starr, 1956-1971	152
Receiving (No.)	James Lofton, 1978-1986	530
Receiving (Yds.)	James Lofton, 1978-1986	9,656
Interceptions	Bobby Dillon, 1952-59	52
Punting (Avg.)	Dick Deschaine, 1955-57	42.6
Punt Return (Avg.)	Billy Grimes, 1950-52	13.2
Kickoff Return (Avg.)	Travis Williams, 1967-1970	26.7
Field Goals	Chester Marcol, 1972-1980	120
Touchdowns (Tot.)	Don Hutson, 1935-1945	105
Points	Don Hutson, 1935-1945	823

Individual Records — Single Season

Category	Name	Performance
Rushing (Yds.)	Jim Taylor, 1962	1,407
Passing (Yds.)	Lynn Dickey, 1983	4,458
Passing (TDs)	Lynn Dickey, 1983	32
Receiving (No.)	Don Hutson, 1942	74
Receiving (Yds.)	Sterling Sharpe, 1989	1,423
Interceptions	Irv Comp, 1943	10
Punting (Avg.)	Jerry Norton, 1963	44.7
Punt Return (Avg.)	Billy Grimes, 1950	19.1
Kickoff Return (Avg.)	Travis Williams, 1967	41.1
Field Goals	Chester Marcol, 1972	33
Touchdowns (Tot.)	Jim Taylor, 1962	19
Points	Paul Hornung, 1960	*176

Individual Records — Single Game

Category	Name	Performance
Rushing (Yds.)	Jim Taylor, 12-3-61	186
Passing (Yds.)	Lynn Dickey, 10-12-80	418
Passing (TDs)	Many times	5
	Last time by Lynn Dickey, 9-4-83	
Receiving (No.)	Don Hutson, 11-22-42	14
Receiving (Yds.)	Bill Howton, 10-21-56	257
Interceptions	Bobby Dillon, 11-26-53	*4
	Willie Buchanon, 9-24-78	*4
Field Goals	Many times	4
	Last time by Chris Jacke, 12-17-89	
Touchdowns (Tot.)	Paul Hornung, 12-12-65	5
Points	Paul Hornung, 10-8-61	33

*NFL Record

1989 Team Record
Preseason (3-1)

Date	Result		Opponents
8/12	W	28-27	vs. N.Y. Jets
			at Milwaukee
8/19	L	23-24	Indianapolis
8/26	W	27-24	vs. Buffalo
			at Madison, Wis.
9/1	W	16- 0	at New England
		94-75	

Regular Season (10-6)

Date	Result		Opponents	Att.
9/10	L	21-23	Tampa Bay	55,650
9/17	W	35-34	New Orleans	55,809
9/24	L	38-41	at L.A. Rams	57,701
10/1	W	23-21	Atlanta	54,647
10/8	W	31-13	Dallas	56,656
10/15	L	14-26	at Minnesota	62,075
10/22	L	20-23	at Miami	56,624
10/29	W	23-20	Detroit (OT)	53,731
11/5	W	14-13	Chicago	56,556
11/12	L	22-31	at Detroit	44,324
11/19	W	21-17	at San Francisco	62,219
11/26	W	20-19	Minnesota	55,592
12/3	W	17-16	at Tampa Bay	58,120
12/10	L	3-21	Kansas City	56,694
12/17	W	40-28	at Chicago	44,781
12/24	W	20-10	at Dallas	41,265

(OT) Overtime

Score by Periods

Packers	71	74	89	125	3	—	362
Opponents	77	157	70	52	0	—	356

Attendance
Home 445,335   Away 426,809   Total 872,144
Single-game home record, 56,895 (11-3-85, Lambeau Field), 56,258 (9-28-80, Milwaukee County Stadium)
Single-season home record, 445,335 (1989)

1989 Team Statistics

	Packers	Opp.
Total First Downs	342	307
Rushing	114	116
Passing	207	179
Penalty	21	12
Third Down: Made/Att.	93/204	86/191
Third Down: Pct.	45.6	45.0
Fourth Down: Made/Att.	8/12	5/6
Fourth Down: Pct.	66.7	83.3
Total Net Yards	5780	5347
Avg. Per Game	361.3	334.2
Total Plays	1045	970
Avg. Per Play	5.5	5.5
Net Yards Rushing	1732	2008
Avg. Per Game	108.3	125.5
Total Rushes	397	460
Net Yards Passing	4048	3339
Avg. Per Game	253.0	208.7
Sacked/Yards Lost	48/277	34/214
Gross Yards	4325	3553
Att./Completions	600/354	476/302
Completion Pct.	59.0	63.4
Had Intercepted	20	25
Punts/Avg.	66/40.6	65/40.7
Net Punting Avg.	31.0	35.9
Penalties/Yards Lost	81/666	105/851
Fumbles/Ball Lost	35/13	28/15
Touchdowns	42	41
Rushing	13	15
Passing	27	22
Returns	2	4
Avg. Time of Possession	30:21	29:39

1989 Individual Statistics

Scoring

	TD R	TD P	TD Rt	PAT	FG	Saf	TP
Jacke	0	0	0	42/42	22/28	0	108
Sharpe	0	12	1	0/0	0/0	0	78
Fullwood	5	0	0	0/0	0/0	0	30
Majkowski	5	0	0	0/0	0/0	0	30
West	0	5	0	0/0	0/0	0	30
Fontenot	1	3	0	0/0	0/0	0	24
Bland	0	1	1	0/0	0/0	0	12
Kemp	0	2	0	0/0	0/0	0	12
Query	0	2	0	0/0	0/0	0	12
Didier	0	1	0	0/0	0/0	0	6
Haddix	0	1	0	0/0	0/0	0	6
Woodside	1	0	0	0/0	0/0	0	6
Workman	1	0	0	0/0	0/0	0	6
Packers	13	27	2	42/42	22/28	1	362
Opponents	15	22	4	39/41	23/30	1	356

Passing

	Att.	Comp.	Yds.	Pct.	TD	Int.	Tkld.	Rate
Majkowski	599	353	4318	58.9	27	20	47/268	82.3
Dilweg	1	1	7	100.0	0	0	0/0	95.8
Fontenot	0	0	0	—	0	0	1/9	0.0
Packers	600	354	4325	59.0	27	20	48/277	82.4
Opponents	476	302	3553	63.4	22	25	34/214	79.6

Rushing

	Att.	Yds.	Avg.	LG	TD
Fullwood	204	821	4.0	38	5
Majkowski	75	358	4.8	20	5
Woodside	46	273	5.9	68t	1
Haddix	44	135	3.1	10	0
Fontenot	17	69	4.1	19	1
Kemp	5	43	8.6	14	0
Sharpe	2	25	12.5	26	0
Workman	4	8	2.0	3	1
Packers	397	1732	4.4	68t	13
Opponents	460	2008	4.4	73	15

Receiving

	No.	Yds.	Avg.	LG	TD
Sharpe	90	1423	15.8	79t	12
Woodside	59	527	8.9	33	0
Kemp	48	611	12.7	39	2
Fontenot	40	372	9.3	38t	3
Query	23	350	15.2	45	2
West	22	269	12.2	31	5
Fullwood	19	214	11.3	67	0
Matthews	18	200	11.1	25	0
Haddix	15	111	7.4	23	1
Bland	11	164	14.9	46t	1
Didier	7	71	10.1	24t	1
Spagnola	2	13	6.5	14	0
Packers	354	4325	12.2	79t	27
Opponents	302	3553	11.8	61	22

Interceptions

	No.	Yds.	Avg.	LG	TD
D. Brown	6	12	2.0	12	0
Murphy	3	31	10.3	20	0
Stills	3	20	6.7	12	0
Stephen	2	16	8.0	8	0
Lee	2	10	5.0	10	0
Noble	2	10	5.0	10	0
Dent	1	53	53.0	53	0
Pitts	1	37	37.0	37	0
Holland	1	26	26.0	26	0
Cecil	1	16	16.0	16	0
Anderson	1	1	1.0	1	0
Greene	1	0	0.0	0	0
Jakes	1	0	0.0	0	0
Packers	25	232	9.3	53	0
Opponents	20	321	16.1	81t	2

Punting

	No.	Yds.	Avg.	In 20	LG
Bracken	66	2682	40.6	17	63
Packers	66	2682	40.6	17	63
Opponents	65	2644	40.7	17	55

Punt Returns

	No.	FC	Yds.	Avg.	LG	TD
Query	30	7	247	8.2	15	0
Sutton	5	1	42	8.4	17	0
Pitts	0	1	0	—	0	0
Packers	35	9	289	8.3	17	0
Opponents	30	11	416	13.9	74	0

Kickoff Returns

	No.	Yds.	Avg.	LG	TD
Workman	33	547	16.6	46	0
Bland	13	256	19.7	37	0
Fullwood	11	243	22.1	35	0
Query	6	125	20.8	28	0
Woodside	2	38	19.0	23	0
Fontenot	2	30	15.0	20	0
Didier	1	0	0.0	0	0
Mandarich	1	0	0.0	0	0
Stephen	0	0	—	0	0
Packers	69	1239	18.0	46	0
Opponents	63	1389	22.0	90	0

Sacks

	No.
Harris	19.5
R. Brown	3.0
Greene	2.0
Noble	2.0
Winter	2.0
Hall	1.0
Murphy	1.0
Nelson	1.0
Stephen	1.0
Weddington	1.0
Patterson	0.5
Packers	34.0
Opponents	48.0

1990 Draft Choices

Round	Name	Pos.	College
1.	Tony Bennett	LB	Mississippi
	Darrell Thompson	RB	Minnesota
2.	LeRoy Butler	DB	Florida State
3.	Bobby Houston	LB	North Carolina St.
4.	Jackie Harris	TE	N.E. Louisiana
5.	Charles Wilson	WR	Memphis State
6.	Bryce Paup	LB	Northern Iowa
7.	Lester Archambeau	DE	Stanford
8.	Roger Brown	DB	Virginia Tech
9.	Kirk Baumgartner	QB	Wis.-Stephens Pt.
10.	Jerome Martin	DB	Western Kentucky
11.	Harry Jackson	RB	St. Cloud, Minn.
12.	Kirk Maggio	P	UCLA

Green Bay Packers 1990 Veteran Roster

No.	Name	Pos.	Ht.	Wt.	Birth-date	NFL Exp.	College	Hometown	How Acq.	'89 Games/Starts
67	Ard, Billy	G	6-3	270	3/12/59	10	Wake Forest	Watchung, N.J.	PB(NYG)-'89#	15/0
76	Ariey, Mike	T	6-5	285	3/12/64	2	San Diego State	Bakersfield, Calif.	PB(NYG)-'89#	1/0
83	Bland, Carl	WR	5-11	182	8/17/61	7	Virginia Union	Richmond, Va.	PB(Det)-'89#	16/0
61	Boyarsky, Jerry	NT	6-3	290	5/15/59	10	Pittsburgh	Scranton, Pa.	FA-'87	13/0
17	Bracken, Don	P	6-1	211	2/16/62	6	Michigan	Thermopolis, Wyo.	FA-'85	16/0
62	Brock, Matt	DE	6-4	267	1/14/66	2	Oregon	San Diego, Calif.	D3a-'89	7/0
32	Brown, Dave	CB	6-1	197	1/16/53	16	Michigan	Akron, Ohio	T(Sea)-'89	16/16
93	†Brown, Robert	DE	6-2	267	5/21/60	9	Virginia Tech	Edenton, N.C.	D4-'82	16/16
51	Bush, Blair	C	6-3	272	11/25/56	13	Washington	Palos Verdes, Calif.	PB(Sea)-'89#	16/15
63	Campen, James	C-G	6-3	270	6/11/64	4	Tulane	Sacramento, Calif.	PB(NO)-'89#	15/1
26	†Cecil, Chuck	S	6-0	184	11/8/64	3	Arizona	San Diego, Calif.	D4b-'88	9/0
55	Clark, Greg	LB	6-1	234	3/5/65	3	Arizona State	Torrance, Calif.	PB(Mia)-'90#	16/4*
92	Cribbs, James	DE	6-3	269	7/10/66	2	Memphis State	Memphis, Tenn.	PB(Det)-'90#	8/0*
60	†Croston, David	T	6-5	280	11/10/63	2	Iowa	Sioux City, Iowa	D3a-'87	0*
49	Dee, Donnie	TE	6-4	252	3/17/65	3	Tulsa	Kansas City, Mo.	PB(Sea)-'90#	5/2*
56	Dent, Burnell	LB	6-1	236	3/16/63	5	Tulane	St. Rose, La.	D6-'86	16/2
80	Didier, Clint	TE	6-5	240	4/4/59	9	Portland State	Pasco, Wash.	FA-'88	16/4
8	Dilweg, Anthony	QB	6-3	215	3/28/65	2	Duke	Bethesda, Md.	D3b-'89	1/0
99	Dorsey, John	LB	6-2	243	8/31/60	6	Connecticut	Leonardtown, Md.	D4-'84	0*
94	Fears, Willie	DE-NT	6-5	285	6/4/64	2	Arkansas-Pine Bluff	Barton, Ark.	FA-'90	0*
27	†Fontenot, Herman	RB	6-0	206	9/12/63	6	Louisiana State	Beaumont, Tex.	T(Clev)-'89	16/0
30	Frazier, Paul	RB	5-8	196	11/12/67	2	Northwestern Louisiana	Coushatta, La.	PB(NO)-'90#	15/0*
21	†Fullwood, Brent	RB	5-11	209	10/10/63	4	Auburn	St. Cloud, Fla.	D1-'87	15/15
23	†Greene, Tiger	S	6-0	194	2/15/62	6	Western Carolina	Hendersonville, N.C.	FA-'86	16/0
35	Haddix, Michael	RB	6-2	227	12/27/61	8	Mississippi State	Walnut, Miss.	PB(Phil)-'89#	16/1
72	Hall, Mark	DE	6-4	285	8/21/65	2	Southwestern Louisiana	Patterson, La.	D7-'89	7/0
65	†Hallstrom, Ron	G	6-6	290	6/11/59	9	Iowa	Moline, Ill.	D1-'82	16/16
97	Harris, Tim	LB	6-5	235	9/10/64	5	Memphis State	Birmingham, Ala.	D4a-'86	16/16
48	Harris, William	TE	6-5	254	2/10/65	3	Bishop, Tex.	Houston, Tex.	PB(TB)-'90#	16/1*
5	Hatcher, Dale	P	6-3	240	4/15/63	6	Clemson	Cheraw, S.C.	PB(Rams)-'90#	16/0*
50	Holland, Johnny	LB	6-2	221	3/11/65	4	Texas A&M	Hempstead, Tex.	D2-'87	16/15
44	Holmes, Jerry	CB	6-2	175	12/22/57	9	West Virginia	Hampton, Va.	PB(Det)-'90#	16/16*
13	Jacke, Chris	K	6-0	197	3/12/66	2	Texas-El Paso	Richardson, Tex.	D6-'89	16/0
24	Jakes, Van	CB	6-0	190	5/10/61	7	Kent State	Buffalo, N.Y.	PB(NO)-'89#	16/4
88	Johnson, Flip	WR	5-10	183	7/13/63	3	McNeese State	Beaumont, Tex.	PB(Buff)-'90#	16/5*
53	Johnson, M.L.	LB	6-2	229	1/26/64	4	Hawaii	Los Angeles, Calif.	PB(Sea)-'90#	12/8*
81	Kemp, Perry	WR	5-11	170	12/31/61	4	California State, Pa.	Canonsburg, Pa.	FA-'88	14/13
10	Kiel, Blair	QB	6-0	214	11/29/61	6	Notre Dame	Columbus, Ind.	FA-'89	0*
22	Lee, Mark	CB	5-11	189	3/20/58	11	Washington	Hanford, Calif.	D2-'80	12/10
7	†Majkowski, Don	QB	6-2	197	2/25/64	4	Virginia	DePew, N.Y.	D10-'87	16/16
77	Mandarich, Tony	T	6-5	300	9/23/66	2	Michigan State	Oakville, Canada	D1-'89	14/0
47	Martin, Tracy	WR	6-2	205	12/4/64	2	North Dakota	Minneapolis, Minn.	FA-'90	0*
98	Miller, Shawn	DE	6-4	255	3/14/61	7	Utah State	Ogden, Utah	PB(Rams)-'90#	16/11*
57	Moran, Rich	G	6-2	275	3/19/62	6	San Diego State	Pleasanton, Calif.	D3-'85	16/16
37	†Murphy, Mark	S	6-2	201	4/22/58	9	West Liberty	Canton, Ohio	FA-'84	16/16
79	†Nelson, Bob	NT	6-4	275	3/3/59	4	Miami	Baltimore, Md.	FA-'88	16/16
91	†Noble, Brian	LB	6-3	252	9/6/62	6	Arizona State	Anaheim, Calif.	D5-'85	16/16
6	Norseth, Mike	QB	6-2	205	8/22/64	3	Kansas	La Crescenta, Calif.	PB(Clev)-'90#	0*
96	Patterson, Shawn	DE	6-5	261	6/13/64	3	Arizona State	Tempe, Ariz.	D2-'88	6/6
28	†Pitts, Ron	CB	5-10	175	10/14/62	5	UCLA	Orchard Park, N.Y.	FA-'88	14/2
85	Query, Jeff	WR-KR	5-11	165	3/7/67	2	Millikin	Forsyth, Ill.	D5a-'89	16/0
75	†Ruettgers, Ken	T	6-5	280	8/20/62	6	Southern California	Bakersfield, Calif.	D1-'85	16/16
84	Sharpe, Sterling	WR	5-11	202	4/6/65	3	South Carolina	Glenville, Ga.	D1-'88	16/16
89	Spagnola, John	TE	6-4	242	8/1/57	11	Yale	Bethlehem, Pa.	PB(Sea)-'89#	6/0
54	Stephen, Scott	LB	6-2	232	6/18/64	4	Arizona State	Los Angeles, Calif.	D3b-'87	16/2
70	Uecker, Keith	G-T	6-5	284	6/29/60	7	Auburn	Hollywood, Fla.	W(Den)-'84	0*
73	†Veingrad, Alan	T	6-5	277	7/24/63	4	East Texas State	Miami, Fla.	FA-'86	16/16
87	Weathers, Clarence	WR	5-9	180	1/10/62	8	Delaware State	Fort Pierce, Fla.	PB(KC)-'90#	11/0*
52	Weddington, Mike	LB	6-4	245	10/9/60	5	Oklahoma	Temple, Tex.	FA-'86	15/0
86	West, Ed	TE	6-1	243	8/2/61	7	Auburn	Leighton, Ala.	FA-'84	13/12
68	†Winter, Blaise	DE-NT	6-3	275	1/31/62	6	Syracuse	Blauvelt, N.Y.	T(SD)-'88	16/10
33	†Woodside, Keith	RB	5-11	203	7/29/64	3	Texas A&M	Vidalia, La.	D3-'88	16/16
46	Workman, Vince	RB	5-10	193	5/9/68	2	Ohio State	Dublin, Ohio	D5b-'89	15/0
64	Yarno, George	C-G	6-2	270	8/12/57	10	Washington State	Spokane, Wash.	PB(Hou)-'90#	11/3*

* Clark played 16 games with Miami in '89; Cribbs played 8 games with Detroit; Croston, Dorsey, and Uecker missed '89 season due to injury; Dee played 1 game with Indianapolis, 4 with Seattle; Fears last active with Cincinnati in '87; Frazier played 15 games with New Orleans; W. Harris played 16 games with Tampa Bay; Hatcher played 16 games with L.A. Rams; Holmes played 16 games with Detroit; F. Johnson played 16 games with Buffalo; M.L. Johnson played 12 games with Seattle; Kiel was active for 9 games, but did not play; Martin last active with N.Y. Jets in '88; Miller played 16 games with L.A. Rams; Norseth last active with Cincinnati in '88; Weathers played 11 games with Kansas City; Yarno played 11 games with Houston.

† Option playout; subject to developments.

Plan B unconditional free agent.

Players lost through Plan B (2): WR Aubrey Matthews (Det; 13 games in '89), CB-S Ken Stills (Minn; 16).

Also played with Packers in '89—LB John Anderson (14 games in '89), C Mark Cannon (15), CB-S Michael McGruder (2), CB Mickey Sutton (3).

COACHING STAFF

Head Coach,
Lindy Infante

Pro Career: Named Packers' head coach on February 3, 1988, after serving as offensive coordinator of Cleveland Browns in 1986-87. In that two-year span the Browns won more games (22) than any other team in the AFC. Was previously head coach of the Jacksonville Bulls (USFL) in 1984-85, compiling a 15-21 record. Earlier had been quarterback/receivers coach of the Cincinnati Bengals in 1980-81 and offensive coordinator in 1982, helping Bengals gain Super Bowl XVI berth in 1981 and compile the best record in the NFL over the 1981-82 seasons (19-6). Began pro coaching career with Charlotte Hornets (WFL) in 1975, later moving into the NFL with the New York Giants in 1978. Career record: 14-18.

Background: Running back and defensive back at University of Florida (1960-62), winning second-team All-Southeastern Conference honors as senior, when he also was a team captain. Entered coaching at Miami High School (1965). College assistant at Florida 1966-71, Memphis State 1972-74, and Tulane 1976, 1979.

Personal: Born May 27, 1940, in Miami, Fla. Attended Miami High School. He and his wife, Stephanie, live in Green Bay and have two sons, Brett, 18, and Brad, 17.

Assistant Coaches

Greg Blache, defensive line; born March 9, 1949, New Orleans, La., lives in Green Bay. No college or pro playing experience. College coach: Notre Dame 1973-75, 1981-83, Tulane 1976-80, Southern University 1986, Kansas 1987. Pro coach: Jacksonville Bulls (USFL) 1984-85, joined Packers in 1988.

Hank Bullough, defensive coordinator; born January 24, 1934, Scranton, Pa., lives in Green Bay. Offensive guard Michigan State 1952-54. Pro offensive guard Green Bay Packers 1955, 1958. College coach: Michigan State 1959-69. Pro coach: Baltimore Colts 1970-72, New England Patriots 1973-79, Cincinnati Bengals 1980-83, Pittsburgh Maulers (USFL) 1984-85, Buffalo Bills 1985-86 (compiled 4-17 record as head coach from October 1, 1985, through November 3, 1986), joined Packers in 1988.

Joe B. Clark, general offensive assistant; born December 22, 1932, Los Angeles, Calif., lives in Green Bay. Quarterback Santa Clara 1951-52. No pro playing experience. College coach: Wooster College 1958-59, Detroit 1960-64, Tulane 1965-70, Memphis State 1974, Nicholls State 1981-83, Southeastern Louisiana 1985, Southern University 1986. Pro coach: Charlotte Hornets (WFL) 1975, Jacksonville Bulls (USFL) 1984-85, joined Packers in 1988.

Charlie Davis, offensive line; born August 7, 1944, San Diego, Calif., lives in Green Bay. Linebacker San Diego City College 1961, UCLA 1962-64. No pro playing experience. College coach: San Francisco State 1967-70, Xavier 1971-73, Ball State 1974-75, Tulane 1976-80. Pro coach: Jacksonville Bulls (USFL) 1984-85, Cleveland Browns 1986-87, joined Packers in 1988.

Buddy Geis, receivers; born September 16, 1946, Altoona, Pa., lives in Green Bay. Running back Lock Haven State 1967-69. No pro playing experience. College coach: Arizona 1973-76, Tulane 1977-82, Memphis State 1986-87. Pro coach: Jacksonville Bulls (USFL) 1984-85, joined Packers in 1988.

Dick Jauron, defensive backfield; born October 7, 1950, Swampscott, Mass., lives in Green Bay. Defensive back Yale 1970-72. Pro defensive back Detroit Lions 1973-77, Cincinnati Bengals 1978-80. Pro coach: Buffalo Bills 1985, joined Packers in 1986.

Virgil Knight, strength-conditioning; born January 30, 1948, Clarksville, Ark., lives in Green Bay. Tight end Northeastern Oklahoma 1968-70. No pro playing experience. College coach: Arkansas Tech 1975-78, Florida 1979-80, Auburn 1981-83. Pro coach: Joined Packers in 1984.

Green Bay Packers 1990 First-Year Roster

Name	Pos.	Ht.	Wt.	Birth-date	College	Hometown	How Acq.
Aeilts, Rick	TE	6-3	235	12/13/65	S.E. Missouri State	Champaign, Ill.	FA
Affholter, Erik (1)	WR	5-11	181	4/10/66	Southern California	Agoura, Calif.	D4-'89
Archambeau, Lester	DE	6-4	253	6/27/67	Stanford	Montville, N.J.	D7
Avery, Steve (1)	RB	6-2	230	8/18/66	Northern Michigan	Brookfield, Wis.	FA
Baumgartner, Kirk	QB	6-2	203	11/3/67	Wis.-Stevens Point	Colby, Wis.	D9
Bennett, Tony	LB	6-1	234	7/1/67	Mississippi	Alligator, Miss.	D1a
Brown, Roger	CB	6-2	203	12/16/66	Virginia Tech	Baltimore, Md.	D8
Butler, LeRoy	CB	5-11	193	7/19/68	Florida State	Jacksonville, Fla.	D2
Champion, Tony	WR	6-1	180	3/19/63	Tennessee-Martin	Humboldt, Tenn.	FA
Chubb, Aaron (1)	LB	6-5	235	8/17/66	Georgia	Rockmart, Ga.	FA
Harris, Jackie	TE	6-3	231	1/4/68	N.E. Louisiana State	Pine Bluff, Ark.	D4
Houston, Bobby	LB	6-1	230	10/26/67	North Carolina State	Hyattsville, Md.	D3
Jackson, Harry	RB	5-10	223	3/15/68	St. Cloud	Minneapolis, Minn.	D11
Kirby, Scott (1)	T	6-6	284	8/7/66	Arizona State	Pinelles, Fla.	FA
Maggio, Kirk	P	6-0	158	9/18/67	UCLA	Towson, Md.	D12
Martin, Jerome	S	6-0	210	2/3/68	Western Kentucky	Tallahassee, Fla.	D10
Paup, Bryce	LB	6-4	238	2/29/68	Northern Iowa	Scranton, Iowa	D6
Shiver, Stan	S	6-2	209	5/18/66	Florida State	Tifton, Ga.	FA
Shulman, Brian	P	5-10	184	4/20/66	Auburn	Brentwood, Tenn.	FA
Stell, Damon	RB	5-10	196	9/8/66	Oklahoma	Oklahoma City, Okla.	FA
Thompson, Darrell	RB	6-0	219	11/23/67	Minnesota	Rochester, Minn.	D1b
Wilson, Charles	WR	5-9	178	7/1/68	Memphis State	Godby, Fla.	D5
Woods, Jerry (1)	S	5-10	191	2/13/66	Northern Michigan	Racine, Wis.	FA
Wright, Charles	G	6-4	280	10/31/66	Florida	San Clemente, Calif.	FA

The term NFL Rookie is defined as a player who is in his first season of professional football and has not been on the roster of another professional football team for any regular-season or postseason games. A Rookie is designated by an "R" on NFL rosters. Players who have been active in another professional football league or players who have NFL experience, including either preseason training camp or being on an active roster for fewer than three regular-season or post-season games, are termed NFL First-Year Players. An NFL First-Year Player is designated by a "1" on NFL rosters. Thereafter, a player on an NFL active roster for at least three regular-season or postseason games is credited with an additional year of NFL playing experience.

NOTES

_____

_____

_____

_____

_____

_____

_____

_____

_____

_____

_____

_____

_____

_____

_____

Dick Moseley, outside linebackers; born August 1, 1933, Detroit, Mich., lives in Green Bay. Running back-defensive back Eastern Michigan 1953-55. No pro playing experience. College coach: Eastern Michigan 1968-70, Wichita State 1971, Minnesota 1972-78, Colorado 1979-81. Pro coach: New Jersey Generals (USFL) 1982, Pittsburgh Maulers (USFL) 1983, Buffalo Bills 1984-85, Chicago Bruisers (Arena Football) 1987, joined Packers in 1988.

Willie Peete, offensive backfield; born July 14, 1937, Mesa, Ariz., lives in Green Bay. Tight end-defensive end Arizona 1956-59. No pro playing experience. College coach: Arizona 1960-62, 1971-82. Pro coach: Kansas City Chiefs 1983-86, joined Packers in 1987.

Howard Tippett, special teams; born September 23, 1938, Tallassee, Ala., lives in Green Bay. Quarterback/safety East Tennessee State 1956-58. No pro playing experience. College coach: Tulane 1963-65, West Virginia 1966, 1970-71, Houston 1967-69, Washington State 1976, UCLA 1980, Illinois 1987. Pro coach: Jacksonville Express (WFL) 1974-75, Tampa Bay Buccaneers 1981-86, joined Packers in 1988.

LOS ANGELES RAMS

National Football Conference Western Division

Team Colors: Royal Blue, Gold, and White

Business Address:
2327 West Lincoln Avenue
Anaheim, California 92801
Telephone: (714) 535-7267

Ticket Office:
Anaheim Stadium
1900 State College Boulevard
Anaheim, California 92806
Telephone: (714) 937-6767

Club Officials

President: Georgia Frontiere
Executive Vice President: John Shaw
Vice President-General Counsel: Jay Zygmunt
Vice President-Media and Community Relations:
  Marshall Klein
Administrator, Football Operations: Jack Faulkner
Director of Operations: Dick Beam
General Counsel: Steve Novak
Director of Player Personnel: John Math
Administrative Assistant/Consultant:
  Paul (Tank) Younger
Administration: Jack Youngblood
Director of Administration: Barbara Robinson
Director of Promotions/Sales: Pete Donovan
Director of Public Relations: John Oswald
Assistant Director of Public Relations: Dennis
  Bickmeier
Trainers: George Menefee, Jim Anderson,
  Garrett Giemont, Blynn DeNiro
Equipment Managers: Don Hewitt, Todd Hewitt

Stadium: Anaheim Stadium • **Capacity:** 69,008
  Anaheim, California 92806

Playing Surface: Grass

Training Camp: California-Irvine
  Irvine, California 92717

1990 Schedule

Preseason
Aug. 11	vs. Kansas City at Berlin	1:00*
Aug. 18	**San Diego**	7:00
Aug. 25	**Phoenix**	7:00
Aug. 31	at Washington	8:00

*P.M. Eastern Time

Regular Season
Sept. 9	at Green Bay	12:00
Sept. 16	at Tampa Bay	1:00
Sept. 23	**Philadelphia**	1:00
Sept. 30	**Open Date**	
Oct. 7	**Cincinnati**	1:00
Oct. 14	at Chicago	6:30
Oct. 21	**Atlanta**	1:00
Oct. 29	at Pittsburgh (Monday)	9:00
Nov. 4	**Houston**	1:00
Nov. 11	**New York Giants**	1:00
Nov. 18	**Dallas**	1:00
Nov. 25	at San Francisco	1:00
Dec. 2	at Cleveland	1:00
Dec. 9	**New Orleans**	1:00
Dec. 17	**San Francisco** (Monday)	6:00
Dec. 23	at Atlanta	1:00
Dec. 31	at New Orleans (Monday)	7:00

Rams Coaching History

Cleveland 1937-45
(388-312-20)

1937-38	Hugo Bezdek*	1-13-0
1938	Art Lewis	4-4-0
1939-42	Earl (Dutch) Clark	16-26-2
1944	Aldo (Buff) Donelli	4-6-0
1945-46	Adam Walsh	16-5-1
1947	Bob Snyder	6-6-0
1948-49	Clark Shaughnessy	14-8-3
1950-52	Joe Stydahar**	19-9-0
1952-54	Hamp Pool	23-11-2
1955-59	Sid Gillman	28-32-1
1960-62	Bob Waterfield***	9-24-1
1962-65	Harland Svare	14-31-3
1966-70	George Allen	49-19-4
1971-72	Tommy Prothro	14-12-2
1973-77	Chuck Knox	57-20-1
1978-82	Ray Malavasi	43-36-0
1983-89	John Robinson	71-50-0

*Released after three games in 1938
**Resigned after one game in 1952
***Resigned after eight games in 1962

Record Holders

Individual Records—Career
Category	Name	Performance
Rushing (Yds.)	Eric Dickerson, 1983-87	7,245
Passing (Yds.)	Roman Gabriel, 1962-1972	22,223
Passing (TDs)	Roman Gabriel, 1962-1972	154
Receiving (No.)	Tom Fears, 1948-1956	400
Receiving (Yds.)	Elroy (Crazylegs) Hirsch, 1949-1957	6,289
Interceptions	Ed Meador, 1959-1970	46
Punting (Avg.)	Danny Villanueva, 1960-64	44.2
Punt Return (Avg.)	Henry Ellard, 1983-89	11.4
Kickoff Return (Avg.)	Tom Wilson, 1956-1961	27.1
Field Goals	Mike Lansford, 1982-89	143
Touchdowns (Tot.)	Eric Dickerson, 1983-87	58
Points	Mike Lansford, 1982-89	702

Individual Records—Single Season
Category	Name	Performance
Rushing (Yds.)	Eric Dickerson, 1984	*2,105
Passing (Yds.)	Jim Everett, 1989	4,310
Passing (TDs)	Jim Everett, 1988	31
Receiving (No.)	Henry Ellard, 1988	86
Receiving (Yds.)	Elroy (Crazylegs) Hirsch, 1951	1,425
Interceptions	Dick (Night Train) Lane, 1952	*14
Punting (Avg.)	Danny Villanueva, 1962	45.5
Punt Return (Avg.)	Woodley Lewis, 1952	18.5
Kickoff Return (Avg.)	Verda (Vitamin T) Smith, 1950	33.7
Field Goals	David Ray, 1973	30
Touchdowns (Tot.)	Eric Dickerson, 1983	20
Points	David Ray, 1973	130

Individual Records—Single Game
Category	Name	Performance
Rushing (Yds.)	Eric Dickerson, 1-4-86	248
Passing (Yds.)	Norm Van Brocklin, 9-28-51	*554
Passing (TDs)	Many times	5
	Last time by Jim Everett, 9-25-88	
Receiving (No.)	Tom Fears, 12-3-50	*18
Receiving (Yds.)	Willie Anderson, 11-26-89	*336
Interceptions	Many times	3
	Last time by Pat Thomas, 10-7-79	
Field Goals	Bob Waterfield, 12-9-51	5
Touchdowns (Tot.)	Bob Shaw, 12-11-49	4
	Elroy (Crazylegs) Hirsch, 9-28-51	4
	Harold Jackson, 10-14-73	4
Points	Bob Shaw, 12-11-49	24
	Elroy (Crazylegs) Hirsch, 9-28-51	24
	Harold Jackson, 10-14-73	24

*NFL Record

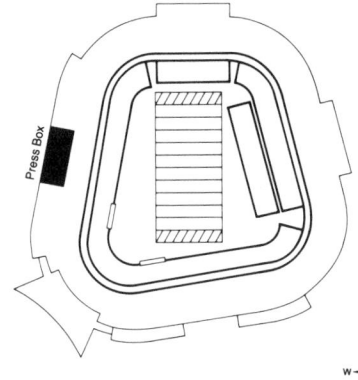

ANAHEIM STADIUM

Press Box

N W E S

1989 Team Record
Preseason (4-1)

Date	Result		Opponents
8/5	W	16-13	vs. San Francisco (OT) at Tokyo, Japan
8/12	L	13-17	at Denver
8/21	W	23-20	Phoenix
8/26	W	24-14	Minnesota
9/2	W	24-14	Detroit
		100-78	

Regular Season (11-5)

Date	Result		Opponents	Att.
9/10	W	31-21	at Atlanta	38,708
9/17	W	31-17	Indianapolis	63,995
9/24	W	41-38	Green Bay	57,701
10/1	W	13-12	at San Francisco	64,250
10/8	W	26-14	Atlanta	52,182
10/16	L	20-23	at Buffalo	76,231
10/22	L	21-40	New Orleans	57,567
10/29	L	10-20	at Chicago	65,506
11/5	L	21-23	at Minnesota (OT)	59,600
11/12	W	31-10	N.Y. Giants	65,127
11/19	W	37-14	Phoenix	53,176
11/26	W	20-17	at New Orleans (OT)	64,274
12/3	W	35-31	at Dallas	46,100
12/11	L	27-30	San Francisco	67,959
12/17	W	38-14	N.Y. Jets	53,063
12/24	W	24-20	at New England	27,940

Postseason (2-1)

Date	Result		Opponent	Att.
12/31	W	21- 7	at Philadelphia	65,479
1/7	W	19-13	at N.Y. Giants (OT)	76,526
1/14	L	3-30	at San Francisco	65,634

(OT) Overtime

Score by Periods

Rams	122	124	61	116	3	—	426
Opponents	50	87	83	122	2	—	344

Attendance
Home 470,770   Away 442,609   Total 913,379
Single-game home record, 67,037 (12-23-84)
Single-season home record, 500,403 (1980)

1989 Team Statistics

	Rams	Opp.
Total First Downs	321	306
Rushing	107	101
Passing	197	181
Penalty	17	24
Third Down: Made/Att.	87/215	81/215
Third Down: Pct.	40.5	37.7
Fourth Down: Made/Att.	9/15	6/13
Fourth Down: Pct.	60.0	46.2
Total Net Yards	6042	5567
Avg. Per Game	377.6	347.9
Total Plays	1027	1023
Avg. Per Play	5.9	5.4
Net Yards Rushing	1909	1543
Avg. Per Game	119.3	96.4
Total Rushes	472	404
Net Yards Passing	4133	4024
Avg. Per Game	258.3	251.5
Sacked/Yards Lost	32/236	42/278
Gross Yards	4369	4302
Att./Completions	523/308	577/345
Completion Pct.	58.9	59.8
Had Intercepted	18	21
Punts/Avg.	74/38.3	81/41.5
Net Punting Avg.	32.1	34.7
Penalties/Yards Lost	102/823	93/798
Fumbles/Ball Lost	26/11	38/15
Touchdowns	51	38
Rushing	19	13
Passing	29	24
Returns	3	1
Avg. Time of Possession	30:35	29:25

1989 Individual Statistics

Scoring

	TD R	TD P	TD Rt	PAT	FG	Saf	TP
Lansford	0	0	0	51/51	23/30	0	120
Bell	15	0	0	0/0	0/0	0	90
Ellard	0	8	0	0/0	0/0	0	48
Anderson	0	5	0	0/0	0/0	0	30
Johnson	0	5	0	0/0	0/0	0	30
McGee	1	4	0	0/0	0/0	0	30
A. Cox	0	3	0	0/0	0/0	0	18
Delpino	1	1	0	0/0	0/0	0	12
Holohan	0	2	0	0/0	0/0	0	12
Ro. Brown	0	1	0	0/0	0/0	0	6
Everett	1	0	0	0/0	0/0	0	6
Gary	1	0	0	0/0	0/0	0	6
Gray	0	0	1	0/0	0/0	0	6
Newsome	0	0	1	0/0	0/0	0	6
Stewart	0	0	1	0/0	0/0	0	6
S. Smith, Dall-TB-Rams	0	0	0	0/0	0/0	1	2
Rams	19	29	3	51/51	23/30	0	426
Opponents	13	24	1	36/38	26/29	1	344

Passing

	Att.	Comp.	Yds.	Pct.	TD	Int.	Tkld.	Rate
Everett	518	304	4310	58.7	29	17	29/214	90.6
Herrmann	5	4	59	80.0	0	1	3/22	76.3
Rams	523	308	4369	58.9	29	18	32/236	90.1
Opponents	577	345	4302	59.8	24	21	42/278	81.7

Rushing

	Att.	Yds.	Avg.	LG	TD
Bell	272	1137	4.2	47	15
Delpino	78	368	4.7	32t	1
Gary	37	163	4.4	18	1
McGee	21	99	4.7	15	1
Green	26	73	2.8	9	0
Everett	25	31	1.2	13t	1
Ro. Brown	6	27	4.5	12	0
Ellard	2	10	5.0	6	0
Holohan	1	3	3.0	3	0
Hatcher	1	0	0.0	0	0
Anderson	1	-1	-1.0	-1	0
Herrmann	2	-1	-0.5	0	0
Rams	472	1909	4.0	47	19
Opponents	404	1543	3.8	40	13

Receiving

	No.	Yds.	Avg.	LG	TD
Ellard	70	1382	19.7	53	8
Holohan	51	510	10.0	31	2
Anderson	44	1146	26.0	78t	5
McGee	37	303	8.2	25	4
Delpino	34	334	9.8	25	1
Johnson	25	148	5.9	22	5
A. Cox	20	340	17.0	51t	3
Bell	19	85	4.5	14	0
Ro. Brown	5	113	22.6	39t	1
Gary	2	13	6.5	8	0
Green	1	-5	-5.0	-5	0
Rams	308	4369	14.2	78t	29
Opponents	345	4302	12.5	95t	24

Interceptions

	No.	Yds.	Avg.	LG	TD
Gray	6	48	8.0	27t	1
Irvin	3	43	14.3	18	0
Stewart	2	76	38.0	41t	1
Strickland	2	56	28.0	29	0
Hicks	2	27	13.5	27	0
Newsome	1	81	81.0	81t	1
Stams	1	20	20.0	20	0
Henley	1	10	10.0	10	0
Owens	1	4	4.0	4	0
Wilcher	1	4	4.0	4	0
Miller	1	3	3.0	3	0
Rams	21	372	17.7	81t	3
Opponents	18	207	11.5	42	0

Punting

	No.	Yds.	Avg.	In 20	LG
Hatcher	73	2834	38.8	15	54
Rams	74	2834	38.3	15	54
Opponents	81	3364	41.5	14	57

Punt Returns

	No.	FC	Yds.	Avg.	LG	TD
Henley	28	19	266	9.5	25	0
Hicks	4	3	39	9.8	15	0
Ellard	2	0	20	10.0	10	0
Irvin	1	2	7	7.0	7	0
Rams	35	24	332	9.5	25	0
Opponents	34	20	315	9.3	68t	1

Kickoff Returns

	No.	Yds.	Avg.	LG	TD
Ro. Brown	47	968	20.6	74	0
Delpino	17	334	19.6	30	0
McDonald	2	22	11.0	12	0
Gary	1	4	4.0	4	0
Rams	67	1328	19.8	74	0
Opponents	84	1633	19.4	47	0

Sacks

	No.
Greene	16.5
Wilcher	5.0
Piel	4.0
Faryniarz	3.0
Reed	3.0
Wright	3.0
Bethune	2.0
B. Smith	2.0
Strickland	2.0
Miller	1.0
S. Smith, Dall-TB-Rams	1.0
Jerue	0.5
Rams	42.0
Opponents	32.0

1990 Draft Choices

Round	Name	Pos.	College
1.	Bern Brostek	C	Washington
2.	Pat Terrell	DB	Notre Dame
3.	Latin Berry	RB	Oregon
6.	Tim Stallworth	WR	Washington State
7.	Kent Elmore	P	Tennessee
8.	Ray Savage	LB	Virginia
	Elbert Crawford	C	Arkansas
9.	Tony Lomack	WR	Florida
10.	Steve Bates	DE	James Madison
11.	Bill Goldberg	DT	Georgia
12.	David Lang	RB	Northern Arizona

Los Angeles Rams 1990 Veteran Roster

No.	Name	Pos.	Ht.	Wt.	Birth-date	NFL Exp.	College	Hometown	How Acq.	'89 Games/ Starts
83	Anderson, Willie	WR	6-0	172	3/7/65	3	UCLA	Paulsboro, N.J.	D2b-'88	16/13
42	Bell, Greg	RB	5-10	210	8/1/62	7	Notre Dame	Columbus, Ohio	T(Buff)-'87	16/15
57	Bethune, George	LB	6-4	240	3/30/67	2	Alabama	Ft. Walton Beach, Fla.	D7-'89	16/0
88	Carter, Pat	TE	6-4	250	8/1/66	3	Florida State	Sarasota, Fla.	T(Det)-'89	16/0
84	Cox, Aaron	WR	5-9	178	3/13/65	3	Arizona State	Los Angeles, Calif.	D1b-'88	16/3
72	Cox, Robert	T	6-5	285	12/30/63	5	UCLA	Dublin, Calif.	D6-'86	16/2
14	Craig, Paco	WR	5-10	170	2/2/65	2	UCLA	Riverside, Calif.	FA-'90	0*
39	Delpino, Robert	RB	6-0	205	11/2/65	3	Missouri	Dodge City, Kan.	D5a-'88	16/1
80	Ellard, Henry	WR	5-11	182	7/21/61	8	Fresno State	Fresno, Calif.	D2-'83	14/12
11	Everett, Jim	QB	6-5	212	1/3/63	5	Purdue	Albuquerque, N.M.	T(Hou)-'86	16/16
51	†Faryniarz, Brett	LB	6-3	235	7/23/65	3	San Diego State	Sacramento, Calif.	FA-'88	16/0
43	Gary, Cleveland	RB	6-0	226	5/4/66	2	Miami	Indiantown, Fla.	D1b-'89	10/0
25	Gray, Jerry	CB	6-0	185	12/2/62	6	Texas	Lubbock, Tex.	D1-'85	16/16
30	Green, Gaston	RB	5-11	192	8/1/66	3	UCLA	Gardena, Calif.	D1a-'88	6/1
91	†Greene, Kevin	LB	6-3	250	7/31/62	6	Auburn	Granite City, Ill.	D5-'85	16/16
70	Hawkins, Bill	DT	6-6	268	5/9/66	2	Miami	Miami, Fla.	D1a-'89	13/1
20	Henley, Darryl	CB	5-9	170	10/30/66	2	UCLA	LaVerne, Calif.	D2c-'89	15/0
9	Herrmann, Mark	QB	6-4	202	1/9/59	10	Purdue	Carmel, Ind.	FA-'88	3/0
28	Hicks, Clifford	CB	5-10	188	8/18/64	4	Oregon	San Diego, Calif.	D3-'87	15/6
81	†Holohan, Pete	TE	6-4	232	7/25/59	10	Notre Dame	Liverpool, N.Y.	T(SD)-'88	16/6
48	t-Humphery, Bobby	CB-KR	5-10	180	8/23/61	7	New Mexico State	Lubbock, Tex.	T(NYJ)-'90	16/16
8	Ilesic, Hank	P	6-1	210	9/7/59	2	No College	Mississauga, Canada	PB(SD)-'90#	14/0*
31	Jackson, Alfred	CB	6-0	177	7/10/67	2	San Diego State	Tulare, Calif.	D5-'89	7/0
86	†Johnson, Damone	TE	6-4	250	3/2/62	5	Cal Poly-SLO	Santa Monica, Calif.	D6-'85	16/16
52	Kelm, Larry	LB	6-4	240	11/29/64	4	Texas A&M	Corpus Christi, Tex.	D4-'87	7/6
1	Lansford, Mike	K	6-0	190	7/20/58	9	Washington	Arcadia, Calif.	FA-'82	16/0
16	t-Long, Chuck	QB	6-4	221	2/18/63	5	Iowa	Wheaton, Ill.	T(Det)-'90	1/0
67	Love, Duval	G	6-3	287	6/24/63	6	UCLA	Fountain Valley, Calif.	D10-'85	15/1
90	McDonald, Mike	LB	6-1	235	6/22/58	6	Southern California	Burbank, Calif.	FA-'88	16/0
24	McGee, Buford	RB	6-0	210	8/16/60	7	Mississippi	Durant, Miss.	T(SD)-'87	16/13
71	Milinichik, Joe	G	6-5	275	3/30/63	4	North Carolina State	Macungie, Pa.	PB(Det)-'90#	15/1*
66	Newberry, Tom	G	6-2	285	12/20/62	5	Wisconsin-LaCrosse	Onalaska, Wis.	D2-'86	16/16
26	Newman, Anthony	S	6-0	199	11/25/65	3	Oregon	Beaverton, Ore.	D2a-'88	15/1
22	Newsome, Vince	S	6-1	185	1/22/61	8	Washington	Vacaville, Calif.	D4-'83	16/16
58	Owens, Mel	LB	6-2	240	12/7/58	10	Michigan	Detroit, Mich.	D1-'81	16/11
75	Pankey, Irv	T	6-5	295	2/15/58	11	Penn State	Aberdeen, Pa.	D2-'80	14/14
95	Piel, Mike	DT	6-4	263	9/21/65	2	Illinois	El Toro, Calif.	D3-'88	13/6
93	†Reed, Doug	DE	6-3	265	7/16/60	7	San Diego State	San Diego, Calif.	D4-'83	11/11
78	Slater, Jackie	T	6-4	285	5/27/54	15	Jackson State	Meridian, Miss.	D3-'76	16/16
96	Smith, Brian	LB-DT	6-6	242	4/23/66	2	Auburn	Opelika, Ala.	D2b-'89	3/0
56	Smith, Doug	C	6-3	272	11/25/56	13	Bowling Green	Columbus, Ohio	FA-'78	16/16
97	Smith, Sean	DT	6-4	275	3/27/65	4	Grambling	Bogalusa, La.	FA-'89	2/1
50	Stams, Frank	LB	6-2	240	7/17/65	2	Notre Dame	Akron, Ohio	D2a-'89	16/3
23	†Stewart, Michael	S	6-0	195	7/12/65	4	Fresno State	Bakersfield, Calif.	D8-'87	16/15
53	Strickland, Fred	LB	6-2	250	8/15/66	3	Purdue	Lakeland, N.J.	D2c-'88	12/12
21	Warner, Curt	RB	5-11	205	3/18/61	8	Penn State	Wyoming, W. Va.	PB(Sea)-'90#	16/15*
54	Wilcher, Mike	LB	6-3	245	3/20/60	8	North Carolina	Washington, D.C.	D2-'83	16/16
99	†Wright, Alvin	NT	6-2	285	2/5/61	5	Jacksonville State	Wedonee, Ala.	FA-'86	16/16

* Craig last active with Detroit in '88; Ilesic played 14 games with San Diego in '89; Milinichik played 15 games with Detroit; Warner played 16 games with Seattle.

† Option playout; subject to developments.

Plan B unconditional free agent.

t- Rams traded for Humphery (N.Y. Jets), Long (Detroit).

Players lost through Plan B (6); G Kurt Becker (Chi; 2 games), WR-KR Ron Brown (Raid; 16), P Dale Hatcher (GB; 16), DT Shawn Miller (GB; 16), G Tony Slaton (Dall; 15), S James Washington (Dall; 9).

Also played with Rams in '89—LB Richard Brown (13 games); QB Steve Dils (active for 1 game but did not play); CB LeRoy Irvin (13), LB Mark Jerue (6).

COACHING STAFF

Head Coach,
John Robinson

Pro Career: Enters his eighth season as Rams head coach. In 1989, he guided the team to its sixth playoff appearance in seven seasons. Led the Rams to a 13-6 record in 1989, including playoff wins over Philadelphia (21-7) and New York Giants (19-13) before losing to San Francisco in NFC Championship Game. He is the winningest coach in club history with 71 victories and has won 10 or more games in six different seasons with the Rams. Became seventeenth head coach in club history on February 14, 1983. Arrived with 23 years of experience, including one on the professional level with the Raiders in 1975. No pro playing experience. Career record: 71-50.

Background: Played end at Oregon 1955-58. Began coaching career with his alma mater from 1960-71. Became an assistant at Southern California from 1972-74. Returned as head coach in 1976 before resigning after the 1982 season. Compiled seven-year .819 winning percentage at Southern California with 67 wins, 14 losses, and 2 ties.

Personal: Born July 25, 1935, Chicago, Ill. John lives in Yorba Linda, Calif.

Assistant Coaches

Larry Brooks, assistant defensive line; born June 10, 1950, Prince George, Va., lives in Fountain Valley, Calif. Defensive tackle Virginia State 1968-71. Pro defensive tackle Los Angeles Rams 1972-82. Pro coach: Joined Rams in 1983.

Dick Coury, quarterbacks; born September 29, 1929, Athens, Ohio, lives in Anaheim, Calif. No college or pro playing experience. College coach: Southern California 1965-67, Cal State-Fullerton 1968-70 (head coach). Pro coach: Denver Broncos 1971-73, Portland Storm (WFL) 1974 (head coach), San Diego Chargers 1975, Philadelphia Eagles 1976-81, Boston/Portland Breakers (USFL) 1983-85 (head coach), joined Rams in 1986.

Artie Gigantino, assistant linebackers coach; born June 14, 1951, Edison, N.J., lives in Anaheim, Calif. Linebacker Bridgeport 1969-72. No pro playing experience. College coach: California 1973-78, Southern California 1979-86. Pro coach: Joined Rams in 1987.

Marv Goux, defensive line; born September 8, 1932, Santa Barbara, Calif., lives in Long Beach, Calif. Linebacker Southern California 1952, 1954-55. No pro playing experience. College coach: Southern California 1957-82. Pro coach: Joined Rams in 1983.

Gil Haskell, running backs; born September 24, 1943, San Francisco, lives in Diamond Bar, Calif. Defensive back San Francisco State 1961, 1963-65. No pro playing experience. College coach: Southern California 1978-82. Pro coach: Joined Rams in 1983.

Hudson Houck, offensive line; born January 7, 1943, Los Angeles, lives in Newport Beach, Calif. Center Southern California 1962-64. No pro playing experience. College coach: Southern California 1970-72, 1976-82, Stanford 1973-75. Pro coach: Joined Rams in 1983.

Jairo Penaranda, special teams; born June 15, 1958, Barranquilla, Colombia, lives in Burbank, Calif. Fullback UCLA 1978-80. Pro fullback Los Angeles Rams 1981, Oakland Invaders (USFL) 1983, Memphis Showboats (USFL) 1984, Philadelphia Eagles 1985. College coach: Southern California 1987-88. Pro coach: Memphis Showboats (USFL) 1984-85, joined Rams in 1990.

Steve Shafer, defensive backs; born December 8, 1940, Glendale, Calif., lives in Laguna Niguel, Calif. Quarterback-defensive back Utah State 1961-62. Pro defensive back British Columbia Lions (CFL) 1963-67. College coach: San Mateo, Calif., J.C. 1968-74 (head coach 1973-74), San Diego State 1975-82. Pro coach: Joined Rams in 1983.

Los Angeles Rams 1990 First-Year Roster

Name	Pos.	Ht.	Wt.	Birth-date	College	Hometown	How Acq.
Adams, Theo	T	6-5	265	4/24/66	Hawaii	Honolulu, Hawaii	FA
Ashe, Richard (1)	TE	6-4	260	3/14/67	Humboldt State	Moreno Valley, Calif.	FA
Bates, Stephen	DE	6-4	249	6/28/66	James Madison	Pittsburgh, Pa.	D10
Barry, Latin	CB	5-10	196	1/13/67	Oregon	Lakeview Terrace, Calif.	D3
Brostek, Bern	C	6-3	300	9/11/66	Washington	Honolulu, Hawaii	D1
Bruno, Anthony	DE	6-5	278	11/24/65	Cal State-Hayward	Monterey, Calif.	FA
Crawford, Elbert	C	6-3	280	6/20/66	Arkansas	Chicago, Ill.	D8b
Elmore, Kent	P	6-2	180	4/27/67	Tennessee	Apopka, Fla.	D7
Faison, Derrick	WR	6-4	200	8/24/67	Howard University	Lake City, S.C.	FA
Farr, Mel, Jr. (1)	RB	6-0	223	8/12/66	UCLA	Birmingham, Mich.	FA-'89
Flenoid, Bobby	CB	5-10	178	8/17/67	Long Beach State	Berkeley, Calif.	FA
Gilbreath, Monty	WR	5-8	175	10/24/68	San Diego State	Woodland Hills, Calif.	FA
Goldberg, Bill	NT	6-3	266	12/27/66	Georgia	Tulsa, Okla.	D11
Gray, Terry	T	6-2	280	5/25/68	Baylor	Spring, Tex.	FA
Henley, Thomas (1)	WR	5-11	180	7/28/65	Stanford	La Verne, Calif.	FA
Hord, Randall	NT	6-4	253	12/20/67	Southern California	Riverside, Calif.	FA
Kane, Michael	RB	5-10	195	8/28/65	Cal State-Northridge	La Canada, Calif.	FA
Knudson, Gary (1)	TE	6-4	242	5/6/66	Arizona State	Edmonds, Wash.	FA
Lang, David	RB	5-11	201	3/28/67	Northern Arizona	San Bernardino, Calif.	D12
Leggett, Jerry (1)	LB	6-4	266	8/23/65	Cal State-Fullerton	Meridian, Miss.	FA
Lomack, Tony	WR	5-8	180	4/27/68	Florida	Tallahassee, Fla.	D9
Lossow, Rodney (1)	C	6-3	273	8/26/65	Wisconsin	Minneapolis, Minn.	FA
Manu, Tony (1)	LB	6-0	245	2/5/68	Idaho State	Edwards, Calif.	FA
Mickel, Jeff (1)	G	6-6	300	8/4/66	Eastern Washington	Edmonds, Wash.	FA
Mitchell, Mario (1)	CB-S	5-10	180	12/23/66	San Diego State	Compton, Calif.	FA
Messner, Mark (1)	LB	6-2	256	12/19/65	Michigan	Detroit, Mich.	D6b-'89
Ortega, David	LB	6-1	238	12/20/66	California	Santa Fe Springs, Calif.	FA
Parker, Chris (1)	QB	6-1	195	12/19/64	Cal State-Northridge	San Bernardino, Calif.	FA
Pellum, William	WR	5-10	170	10/31/66	Washington State	Palm Springs, Calif.	FA
Sargent, Anthony (1)	WR	5-9	172	12/1/66	Wyoming	Los Angeles, Calif.	FA
Savage, Ray	LB	6-1	245	1/3/68	Virginia	Hampton, Va.	D8a
Stallworth, Tim	WR	5-10	180	8/26/66	Washington State	Pacoima, Calif.	D6
Taylor, Gene (1)	WR	6-3	192	11/12/62	Fresno State	Richmond, Calif.	FA
Terrell, Pat	S	6-0	195	3/18/68	Notre Dame	Memphis, Tenn.	D2
Whittingham, Fred	RB	5-10	200	3/16/67	Brigham Young	Orange, Calif.	FA
Yniguez, Paul	C	6-3	275	11/21/67	Kansas State	La Mirada, Calif.	FA

The term NFL Rookie is defined as a player who is in his first season of professional football and has not been on the roster of another professional football team for any regular-season or postseason games. A Rookie is designated by an "R" on NFL rosters. Players who have been active in another professional football league or players who have NFL experience, including either preseason training camp or being on an active roster for fewer than three regular-season or postseason games, are termed NFL First-Year Players. An NFL First-Year Player is designated by a "1" on NFL rosters. Thereafter, a player on an NFL active roster for at least three regular-season or postseason games is credited with an additional year of NFL playing experience.

NOTES

_____

_____

_____

_____

_____

_____

_____

_____

_____

_____

_____

Fritz Shurmur, defensive coordinator; born July 15, 1932, Riverview, Mich., lives in Diamond Bar, Calif. Center Albion 1951-53. No pro playing experience. College coach: Albion 1956-61, Wyoming 1962-74 (head coach 1971-74). Pro coach: Detroit Lions 1975-77, New England Patriots 1978-81, joined Rams in 1982.

Norval Turner, tight ends-wide receivers; born May 17, 1952, Martinez, Calif., lives in Huntington Beach, Calif. Quarterback Oregon 1972-74. No pro playing experience. College coach: Oregon 1975, Southern California 1976-84. Pro coach: Joined Rams in 1985.

Fred Whittingham, linebackers coach; born February 4, 1942, Boston, Mass., lives in Santa Ana, Calif. Linebacker Cal Poly-SLO 1960-62. Pro linebacker Los Angeles Rams 1964, Philadelphia Eagles 1965-66, 1971, New Orleans Saints 1967-68, Dallas Cowboys 1969-70. College coach: Brigham Young 1973-81. Pro coach: Joined Rams in 1982.

Ernie Zampese, offensive coordinator; born March 12, 1936, Santa Barbara, Calif., lives in El Toro, Calif. Halfback Southern California 1956-58. No pro playing experience. College coach: Hancock, Calif., J.C. 1962-65, Cal Poly-SLO 1966, San Diego State 1967-75. Pro coach: San Diego Chargers 1976, 1979-86, New York Jets 1977-78 (scout), joined Rams in 1987.

MINNESOTA VIKINGS

National Football Conference Central Division

Team Colors: Purple, Gold, and White

9520 Viking Drive
Eden Prairie, Minnesota 55344
Telephone: (612) 828-6500

Club Officers

Chairman of the Board: John Skoglund
President: Wheelock Whitney
Senior Vice President: Jack Steele
Senior Vice President and Treasurer:
   Jaye F. Dyer
Secretary: Sheldon Kaplan
Executive Vice President: Mike Lynn

Club Officials

General Manager: Mike Lynn
Assistant G.M./Administration: Jeff Diamond
Assistant G.M./Football: Bob Hollway
Director of Finance: Harley Peterson
Ticket Manager: Harry Randolph
Director of Football Operations: Jerry Reichow
Director of Player Personnel: Frank Gilliam
Head Scout: Ralph Kohl
Assistant Head Scout: Don Deisch
Regional Scout: John Carson
Regional Scout: Conrad Cardano
Director of Public Relations: Merrill Swanson
Director of Communications and Community
   Relations: Kernal Buhler
Assistant Public Relations Director:
   Daniel Endy
Trainer: Fred Zamberletti
Equipment Manager: Dennis Ryan

Stadium: Hubert H. Humphrey Metrodome •
   Capacity: 63,000
   500 11th Avenue So.
   Minneapolis, Minnesota 55415

Playing Surface: AstroTurf

Training Camp: Mankato State University
   Mankato, Minnesota 56001

1990 Schedule

Preseason
Aug. 11	**New Orleans**	7:00
Aug. 19	at Cleveland	8:00
Aug. 26	**Houston**	12:00
Aug. 31	at Miami	8:00

Regular Season
Sept. 9	at Kansas City	12:00
Sept. 16	**New Orleans**	3:00
Sept. 23	at Chicago	12:00
Sept. 30	**Tampa Bay**	12:00
Oct. 7	**Detroit**	12:00
Oct. 15	at Philadelphia (Monday)	9:00
Oct. 21	**Open Date**	
Oct. 28	vs. Green Bay at Milw.	12:00
Nov. 4	**Denver**	7:00
Nov. 11	at Detroit	1:00
Nov. 18	at Seattle	1:00
Nov. 25	**Chicago**	12:00
Dec. 2	**Green Bay**	7:00
Dec. 9	at New York Giants	1:00
Dec. 16	at Tampa Bay	1:00
Dec. 22	**L.A. Raiders** (Saturday)	3:00
Dec. 30	**San Francisco**	12:00

Vikings Coaching History

(241-200-9)

1961-66	Norm Van Brocklin	29-51-4
1967-83	Bud Grant	161-99-5
1984	Les Steckel	3-13-0
1985	Bud Grant	7-9-0
1986-89	Jerry Burns	41-28-0

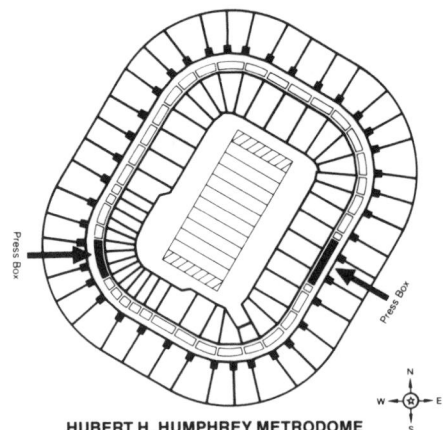

HUBERT H. HUMPHREY METRODOME

Record Holders

Individual Records — Career
Category	Name	Performance
Rushing (Yds.)	Chuck Foreman, 1973-79	5,879
Passing (Yds.)	Fran Tarkenton, 1961-66, 1972-78	33,098
Passing (TDs)	Fran Tarkenton, 1961-66, 1972-78	239
Receiving (No.)	Ahmad Rashad, 1976-1982	400
Receiving (Yds.)	Sammy White, 1976-1985	5,925
Interceptions	Paul Krause, 1968-1979	53
Punting (Avg.)	Bobby Walden, 1964-67	42.9
Punt Return (Avg.)	Tommy Mason, 1961-66	10.4
Kickoff Return (Avg.)	Bob Reed, 1962-63	27.1
Field Goals	Fred Cox, 1963-1977	282
Touchdowns (Tot.)	Bill Brown, 1962-1974	76
Points	Fred Cox, 1963-1977	1,365

Individual Records — Single Season
Category	Name	Performance
Rushing (Yds.)	Chuck Foreman, 1976	1,155
Passing (Yds.)	Tommy Kramer, 1981	3,912
Passing (TDs)	Tommy Kramer, 1981	26
Receiving (No.)	Rickey Young, 1978	88
Receiving (Yds.)	Anthony Carter, 1988	1,225
Interceptions	Paul Krause, 1975	10
Punting (Avg.)	Bobby Walden, 1964	46.4
Punt Return (Avg.)	Leo Lewis, 1987	12.5
Kickoff Return (Avg.)	John Gilliam, 1972	26.3
Field Goals	Rich Karlis, 1989	31
Touchdowns (Tot.)	Chuck Foreman, 1975	22
Points	Chuck Foreman, 1975	132

Individual Records — Single Game
Category	Name	Performance
Rushing (Yds.)	Chuck Foreman, 10-24-76	200
Passing (Yds.)	Tommy Kramer, 11-2-86	490
Passing (TDs)	Joe Kapp, 9-28-69	*7
Receiving (No.)	Rickey Young, 12-16-79	15
Receiving (Yds.)	Sammy White, 11-7-76	210
Interceptions	Many times	3
	Last time by Willie Teal, 11-28-82	
Field Goals	Rich Karlis, 11-5-89	#7
Touchdowns (Tot.)	Chuck Foreman, 12-20-75	4
	Ahmad Rashad, 9-2-79	4
Points	Chuck Foreman, 12-20-75	24
	Ahmad Rashad, 9-2-79	24

*NFL Record
#Ties NFL Record

1989 Team Record

Preseason (3-1)

Date	Result		Opponents
8/12	W	23-13	vs. Kansas City at Memphis, Tenn.
8/21	W	24-13	Washington
8/26	L	14-24	at L.A. Rams
9/1	W	17-10	Cincinnati
		78-60	

Regular Season (10-6)

Date	Result		Opponents	Att.
9/10	W	38- 7	Houston	54,015
9/17	L	7-38	at Chicago	66,475
9/24	L	14-27	at Pittsburgh	50,744
10/1	W	17- 3	Tampa Bay	54,817
10/8	W	24-17	Detroit	55,380
10/15	W	26-14	Green Bay	62,075
10/22	W	20- 7	at Detroit	51,579
10/30	L	14-24	at N.Y. Giants	76,041
11/5	W	23-21	L.A. Rams (OT)	59,600
11/12	W	24-10	at Tampa Bay	56,271
11/19	L	9-10	at Philadelphia	65,944
11/26	L	19-20	at Green Bay	55,592
12/3	W	27-16	Chicago	60,664
12/10	W	43-17	Atlanta	58,116
12/17	L	17-23	at Cleveland (OT)	70,777
12/25	W	29-21	Cincinnati	58,829

(OT) Overtime

Postseason (0-1)

Date	Result		Opponent	Att.
1/6	L	13-41	at San Francisco	64,918

Score by Periods

Vikings	80	139	80	50	2	—	351
Opponents	54	47	55	113	6	—	275

Attendance

Home 463,496   Away 493,423   Total 956,919
Single-game home record, 62,851 (10-19-86)
Single-season home record, 464,902 (1983)

1989 Team Statistics

	Vikings	Opp.
Total First Downs	326	266
Rushing	126	100
Passing	172	140
Penalty	28	26
Third Down: Made/Att.	73/215	78/233
Third Down: Pct.	34.0	33.5
Fourth Down: Made/Att.	11/16	16/25
Fourth Down: Pct.	68.8	64.0
Total Net Yards	5255	4184
Avg. Per Game	328.4	261.5
Total Plays	1053	1021
Avg. Per Play	5.0	4.1
Net Yards Rushing	2066	1683
Avg. Per Game	129.1	105.2
Total Rushes	514	462
Net Yards Passing	3189	2501
Avg. Per Game	199.3	156.3
Sacked/Yards Lost	40/279	71/502
Gross Yards	3468	3003
Att./Completions	499/272	488/252
Completion Pct.	54.5	51.6
Had Intercepted	19	18
Punts/Avg.	72/39.8	95/40.6
Net Punting Avg.	33.4	34.6
Penalties/Yards Lost	119/974	116/903
Fumbles/Ball Lost	28/14	29/18
Touchdowns	36	34
Rushing	12	14
Passing	17	18
Returns	7	2
Avg. Time of Possession	30:40	29:20

1989 Individual Statistics

Scoring

	TD R	TD P	TD Rt	PAT	FG	Saf	TP
Karlis	0	0	0	27/28	31/39	0	120
Walker, Dall.-Minn.	7	2	1	0/0	0/0	0	60
Walker, Minn.	5	1	1	0/0	0/0	0	42
Fenney	4	2	0	0/0	0/0	0	36
Carter	0	4	0	0/0	0/0	0	24
Jordan	0	3	0	0/0	0/0	0	18
Anderson	2	0	0	0/0	0/0	0	12
Gustafson	0	2	0	0/0	0/0	0	12
Novoselsky	0	2	0	0/0	0/0	0	12
Garcia	0	0	0	8/8	1/5	0	11
Merriweather	0	0	1	0/0	0/0	1	8
Holt	0	0	1	0/0	0/0	0	6
Ingram	0	1	0	0/0	0/0	0	6
Jones	0	1	0	0/0	0/0	0	6
Lewis	0	1	0	0/0	0/0	0	6
Millard	0	0	1	0/0	0/0	0	6
Newton	0	0	1	0/0	0/0	0	6
Rutland	0	0	1	0/0	0/0	0	6
Thomas	0	0	1	0/0	0/0	0	6
Wilson	1	0	0	0/0	0/0	0	6
Berry	0	0	0	0/0	0/0	1	2
Vikings	12	17	7	35/36	32/44	2	351
Opponents	14	18	2	32/33	13/21	0	275

Passing

	Att.	Comp.	Yds.	Pct.	TD	Int.	Tkld.	Rate
Wilson	362	194	2543	53.6	9	12	27/194	70.5
Kramer	136	77	906	56.6	7	7	12/75	72.7
Dozier	1	1	19	100.0	1	0	0/0	158.3
Rice	0	0	0	—	0	0	1/10	0.0
Vikings	499	272	3468	54.5	17	19	40/279	72.0
Opponents	488	252	3003	51.6	18	18	71/502	67.7

Rushing

	Att.	Yds.	Avg.	LG	TD
Walker, Dall.-Minn.	250	915	3.7	47	7
Walker, Minn.	169	669	4.0	47	5
Fenney	151	588	3.9	25	4
Dozier	46	207	4.5	38	0
Anderson	52	189	3.6	14	2
Wilson	32	132	4.1	23	1
Nelson	31	124	4.0	24	0
Clark, Phx.-Minn.	20	99	5.0	14	0
Clark, Minn.	10	57	5.7	14	0
Jones	1	37	37.0	37	0
Rice	6	25	4.2	10	0
Carter	3	18	6.0	17	0
Lewis	1	11	11.0	11	0
Kramer	12	9	0.8	5	0
Vikings	514	2066	4.0	47	12
Opponents	462	1683	3.6	37t	14

Receiving

	No.	Yds.	Avg.	LG	TD
Carter	65	1066	16.4	50	4
Jones	42	694	16.5	50	1
Walker, Dall.-Minn.	40	423	10.6	52	2
Walker, Minn.	18	162	9.0	24	1
Jordan	35	506	14.5	34	3
Fenney	30	254	8.5	26	2
Anderson	20	193	9.7	18	0
Dozier	14	148	10.6	30	0
Gustafson	14	144	10.3	22	2
Lewis	12	148	12.3	28t	1
Nelson	7	52	7.4	11	0
Ingram	5	47	9.4	21	1
Rice	4	29	7.3	14	0
Novoselsky	4	11	2.8	6	2
Clark	2	14	7.0	12	0
Vikings	272	3468	12.8	50	17
Opponents	252	3003	11.9	65t	18

Interceptions

	No.	Yds.	Avg.	LG	TD
Browner	5	70	14.0	34	0
Merriweather	3	29	9.7	15t	1
Rutland	2	7	3.5	7	0
Lee	2	0	0.0	0	0
Holt	1	90	90.0	90t	1
Millard	1	48	48.0	48	0
Edwards	1	18	18.0	18	0
Dusbabek	1	2	2.0	2	0
Fullington	1	0	0.0	0	0
Studwell	1	0	0.0	0	0
Vikings	18	264	14.7	90t	2
Opponents	19	138	7.3	39t	2

Punting

	No.	Yds.	Avg.	In 20	LG
Scribner	72	2864	39.8	16	55
Vikings	72	2864	39.8	16	55
Opponents	95	3859	40.6	28	61

Punt Returns

	No.	FC	Yds.	Avg.	LG	TD
Lewis	44	27	446	10.1	65	0
Carter	1	0	2	2.0	2	0
Vikings	45	27	448	10.0	65	0
Opponents	32	7	300	9.4	26	0

Kickoff Returns

	No.	Yds.	Avg.	LG	TD
Nelson	14	317	22.6	32	0
Walker	13	374	28.8	93t	1
Dozier	12	258	21.5	63	0
Anderson	5	75	15.0	36	0
Lewis	2	30	15.0	15	0
Clark, Phx.-Minn.	2	6	3.0	6	0
Clark, Minn.	1	6	6.0	6	0
Carter	1	19	19.0	19	0
Curtis	1	18	18.0	18	0
Rice	1	13	13.0	13	0
Fenney	1	12	12.0	12	0
Vikings	51	1122	22.0	93t	1
Opponents	68	1287	18.9	44	0

Sacks

	No.
Doleman	21.0
Millard	18.0
Noga	11.5
Thomas	9.0
Merriweather	3.5
Berry	3.0
Clarke	2.0
Browner	1.0
Strauthers	1.0
Studwell	1.0
Vikings	71.0
Opponents	40.0

1990 Draft Choices

Round	Name	Pos.	College
3.	Mike Jones	TE	Texas A&M
	Marion Hobby	DE	Tennessee
4.	Alonzo Hampton	DB	Pittsburgh
5.	Reggie Thornton	WR	Bowling Green
	Cedric Smith	RB	Florida
7.	John Levelis	LB	C.W. Post
8.	Craig Schlichting	DE	Wyoming
9.	Terry Allen	RB	Clemson
10.	Pat Newman	WR	Utah State
	Donald Smith	DB	Liberty
12.	Ron Goetz	LB	Minnesota

Minnesota Vikings 1990 Veteran Roster

No.	Name	Pos.	Ht.	Wt.	Birth-date	NFL Exp.	College	Hometown	How Acq.	'89 Games/ Starts
46	Anderson, Alfred	RB	6-1	219	8/4/61	6	Baylor	Waco, Tex.	D3-'84	11/8
50	Berry, Ray	LB	6-2	230	10/28/63	4	Baylor	Abilene, Tex.	D2-'87	16/10
68	Blair, Paul	T	6-4	280	8/3/63	3	Oklahoma State	Edmund, Okla.	FA-'90	0*
53	Braxton, David	LB	6-1	232	5/26/65	2	Wake Forest	Omaha, Neb.	D2-'89	3/0
44	†Brim, Michael	CB	6-0	186	1/23/66	3	Virginia Union	Danville, Va.	FA-'89	7/0
47	Browner, Joey	S	6-2	212	5/15/60	8	Southern California	Warren, Ohio	D1-'83	16/16
19	†Burbage, Cornell	WR	5-10	189	2/22/65	4	Kentucky	Lexington, Ky.	PB(Dall)-'90#	10/1*
81	†Carter, Anthony	WR	5-11	166	9/17/60	6	Michigan	Riviera Beach, Fla.	T(Mia)-'85	16/16
33	†Clark, Jessie	RB	6-0	223	1/3/60	8	Arkansas	Phoenix, Ariz.	FA-'89	14/0*
71	†Clarke, Ken	DT	6-2	281	8/28/56	12	Syracuse	Savannah, Ga.	FA-'89	11/0
56	Doleman, Chris	DE	6-5	250	10/16/61	6	Pittsburgh	York, Pa.	D1-'85	16/16
42	†Dozier, D.J.	RB	6-0	198	9/21/65	4	Penn State	Virginia Beach, Va.	D1-'87	8/1
59	Dusbabek, Mark	LB	6-3	230	6/23/64	2	Minnesota	Faribault, Minn.	FA-'89	16/1
31	Fenney, Rick	RB	6-1	240	12/7/64	4	Washington	Everett, Wash.	D8-'87	16/8
62	†Foote, Chris	C	6-4	265	12/2/56	8	Southern California	Boulder, Colo.	T(NYG)-'87	16/0
29	Fullington, Darrell	S	6-1	183	4/17/64	3	Miami	New Smyrna Beach, Fla.	D5-'87	16/2
51	†Galvin, John	LB	6-3	226	7/9/65	2	Boston College	Lowell, Mass.	PB(NYJ)-'89#	0*
16	†Gannon, Rich	QB	6-3	197	12/20/65	4	Delaware	Philadelphia, Pa.	T(NE)-'87	0*
80	†Gustafson, Jim	WR	6-1	181	3/16/61	5	St. Thomas, Minn.	Minneapolis, Minn.	FA-'85	16/0
74	Habib, Brian	T	6-7	282	12/2/64	2	Washington	Ellensburg, Wash.	D10-'89	16/0
89	Hillary, Ira	WR	5-11	190	11/13/62	4	South Carolina	Edgefield, S.C.	PB(Cin)-'90#	16/1*
82	†Hilton, Carl	TE	6-3	232	2/28/64	4	Houston	Galveston, Tex.	D7-'86	1/0
72	†Huffman, David	G	6-6	283	4/4/57	10	Notre Dame	Dallas, Tex.	FA-'85	16/3
86	Ingram, Darryl	TE	6-2	230	5/2/66	2	California	Lubbock, Tex.	D4-'89	16/2
76	Irwin, Tim	T	6-6	289	12/13/58	10	Tennessee	Knoxville, Tenn.	D3-'81	16/16
84	Jones, Hassan	WR	6-0	195	7/2/64	5	Florida State	Clearwater, Fla.	D5-'86	16/13
83	Jordan, Steve	TE	6-3	236	1/10/61	9	Brown	Phoenix, Ariz.	D7-'82	16/15
69	Kalis, Todd	G	6-5	269	6/10/65	3	Arizona State	Phoenix, Ariz.	D4-'88	16/0
3	†Karlis, Rich	K	6-0	180	5/23/59	9	Cincinnati	Salem, Ohio	FA-'89	13/0
77	Knight, Shawn	DT-DE	6-6	280	6/4/64	4	Brigham Young	Provo, Utah	PB(Phx)-'90#	7/1*
39	Lee, Carl	CB	5-11	184	4/6/61	8	Marshall	South Charleston, W.Va.	D7-'83	16/16
87	†Lewis, Leo	WR	5-8	171	9/17/56	9	Missouri	Columbia, Mo.	FA-'81	16/0
63	†Lowdermilk, Kirk	C	6-3	263	4/10/63	6	Ohio State	Salem, Ohio	D3a-'85	16/16
49	Lyons, Robert	S	6-1	195	5/16/66	2	Akron	Wheeling, W.Va.	PB(Clev)-'90#	9/0*
78	Marrone, Doug	C-G	6-5	295	7/25/64	3	Syracuse	Bronx, N.Y.	PB(NO)-'90#	3/0*
79	Martin, Doug	DE	6-3	270	5/22/57	10	Washington	Fairfield, Calif.	D1-'80	7/1
64	McDaniel, Randall	G	6-3	268	12/19/64	3	Arizona State	Avondale, Ariz.	D1-'88	14/13
26	McMillian, Audray	CB	6-0	190	8/13/62	5	Houston	Carthage, Tex.	PB(Hou)-'89#	16/2
57	Merriweather, Mike	LB	6-2	221	11/26/60	8	Pacific	Vallejo, Calif.	T(Pitt)-'89	16/16
75	Millard, Keith	DT	6-6	260	3/18/62	6	Washington State	Pullman, Wash.	D1-'84	15/15
18	Newsome, Harry	P	6-0	188	1/25/63	6	Wake Forest	Cheraw, S.C.	PB(Pitt)-'90#	0*
85	Novoselsky, Brent	TE	6-2	238	1/8/66	3	Pennsylvania	Skokie, Ill.	FA-'89	15/3
99	Noga, Al	DT	6-1	245	9/16/66	3	Hawaii	Honolulu, Hawaii	D3-'88	16/15
52	Rasmussen, Randy	C-G	6-1	254	9/27/60	6	Minnesota	Minneapolis, Minn.	FA-'87	7/0
36	Rice, Allen	RB	5-10	203	4/5/62	7	Baylor	Houston, Tex.	D5-'84	4/0
48	†Rutland, Reggie	S	6-1	195	6/20/64	4	Georgia Tech	East Point, Ga.	D4-'87	16/16
12	Salisbury, Sean	QB	6-5	215	3/9/63	3	Southern California	Escondido, Calif.	FA-'90	0*
17	Schillinger, Andy	WR	5-11	186	11/22/64	2	Miami, Ohio	Avon Lake, Ohio	PB(Phx)-'90#	0*
60	Schreiber, Adam	C-G	6-4	285	2/20/62	7	Texas	Huntsville, Ala.	PB(NYJ)-'90#	15/0*
13	†Scribner, Bucky	P	6-0	205	7/11/60	5	Kansas	Lawrence, Kan.	FA-'87	16/0
27	Stills, Ken	S	5-10	196	9/6/63	6	Wisconsin	Oceanside, Calif.	PB(GB)-'90#	16/16*
94	Strauthers, Thomas	DE	6-4	265	4/6/61	7	Jackson State	Brookhaven, Miss.	PB(Det)-'89#	12/0
55	Studwell, Scott	LB	6-2	228	8/27/54	14	Illinois	Evansville, Ind.	D9-'77	16/16
97	Thomas, Henry	DT	6-2	268	1/12/65	4	Louisiana State	Houston, Tex.	D3-'87	14/14
34	Walker, Herschel	RB	6-1	226	3/3/62	5	Georgia	Wrightsville, Ga.	T(Dall)-'89	16/14*
11	Wilson, Wade	QB	6-3	208	2/1/59	10	East Texas State	Commerce, Tex.	D8-'81	14/12
73	Wolfley, Craig	G-T	6-1	270	5/19/58	11	Syracuse	Buffalo, N.Y.	PB(Pitt)-'90#	15/4*
65	Zimmerman, Gary	T	6-6	277	12/13/61	5	Oregon	Fullerton, Calif.	T(NYG)-'86	16/16

* Blair last active with Chicago in '88; Burbage played 10 games with Dallas in '89; Clark played 11 games with Phoenix, 3 with Minnesota; Galvin and Schillinger missed '89 season due to injury; Gannon active for 13 games but did not play; Hillary played 16 games with Cincinnati; Knight played 7 games with Phoenix; Lyons played 9 games with Cleveland; Marrone played 3 games with New Orleans; Newsome played 16 games with Pittsburgh; Salisbury last active with Indianapolis in '88; Schreiber played 15 games with N.Y. Jets; Stills played 16 games with Green Bay; Walker played 5 games with Dallas, 11 games with Minnesota; Wolfley played 15 games with Pittsburgh.

† Option playout; subject to developments.

Plan B unconditional free agent.

Players lost through Plan B (3): S Travis Curtis (NYJ; 16 games in '89), S Brad Edwards (Wash; 9), C Mark Rodenhauser (SD; 16).

Also played with Vikings in '89—C John Adickes (1 game), RB Rick Bayless (1), K Teddy Garcia (3), CB Issiac Holt (5), QB Tommy Kramer (8), RB Darrin Nelson (5), DT Tim Newton (9), CB Daryl Smith (5), LB Jesse Solomon (4).

COACHING STAFF

Head Coach,
Jerry Burns

Pro Career: Named fourth head coach in Vikings' history on January 6, 1986. Served as Vikings' assistant head coach and offensive coordinator under Bud Grant in 1985. Since his arrival in Minnesota as offensive coordinator in 1968, became known as an innovator and was credited with popularizing such changes as the one-back offense and short passing game. Has coached in six Super Bowls. Directed Vikings' offense in Super Bowls IV, VIII, IX, and XI, and coached defensive backs for Vince Lombardi on Green Bay's Super Bowl champions in Super Bowls I and II. He coached with the Packers in 1966-67 before joining the Vikings in 1968. No pro playing experience. Career record: 41-28.

Background: Quarterback at Michigan 1949-50. Began coaching career at Hawaii in 1951 as backfield coach for football team and head baseball coach. Moved to Whittier (Calif.) College in 1952 as backfield coach before returning to native Detroit in 1953 as head football coach at St. Mary's of Redford High School. Assistant coach at Iowa from 1954-60 before being named Hawkeyes head coach in 1961. Iowa was 16-27-2 in five seasons under Burns.

Personal: Born January 24, 1927, in Detroit, Mich. Graduated from Michigan with bachelor of science degree in physical education. Jerry and his wife, Marlyn, live in Eden Prairie, Minn., and have five children—Michael, Erin, Kelly, Kathy, and Kerry.

Assistant Coaches

Tom Batta, tight ends-special teams; born October 6, 1942, Youngstown, Ohio, lives in Bloomington, Minn. Offensive-defensive lineman Kent State 1961-63. No pro playing experience. College coach: Akron 1973, Colorado 1974-78, Kansas 1979-82, North Carolina State 1983. Pro coach: Joined Vikings in 1984.

Maxie Baughan, linebackers; born August 3, 1938, Forkland, Ala., lives in Eden Prairie, Minn. Center-linebacker Georgia Tech 1956-60. Pro linebacker Philadelphia Eagles 1960-65, Los Angeles Rams 1966-70, Washington Redskins 1971, 1974. College coach: Georgia Tech 1972-73; Cornell 1983-88 (head coach). Pro coach: Baltimore Colts 1975-79, Detroit Lions 1980-82, joined the Vikings in 1990.

Jerry Brown, defensive backs; born September 28, 1949, Kent, Ohio, lives in Eden Prairie, Minn. Defensive back Northwestern 1969-72. No pro playing experience. College coach: Eastern Illinois 1977-79, Cal State-Fullerton 1980-87. Pro coach: Joined Vikings in 1988.

John Brunner, running backs; born September 6, 1937, Perkasie, Pa., lives in Eden Prairie, Minn. Running back Maryland 1955-56, East Stroudsburg State 1958-59. No pro playing experience. College coach: Villanova 1967-69, Temple 1970-73, 1976-79, Princeton 1974-75. Pro coach: Detroit Lions 1980-82, Green Bay Packers 1983, Tampa Bay Buccaneers 1984, New England Patriots 1985-86 (scout), joined Vikings in 1987.

John Michels, offensive line; born February 15, 1931, Philadelphia, Pa., lives in Bloomington, Minn. Guard Tennessee 1949-52. Pro guard Philadelphia Eagles 1953, 1956, Winnipeg Blue Bombers (CFL) 1957. College coach: Texas A&M 1958. Pro coach: Winnipeg Blue Bombers (CFL) 1959-66, joined Vikings in 1967.

Tom Moore, assistant head coach/offense; born November 7, 1938, Owatanna, Minn., lives in Bloomington, Minn. Quarterback Iowa 1957-60. No pro playing experience. College coach: Iowa 1961-62, Dayton 1965-68, Wake Forest 1969, Georgia Tech 1970-71, Minnesota 1972-73, 1975-76. Pro coach: New York Stars (WFL) 1974, Pittsburgh Steelers 1977-89, joined Vikings in 1990.

Floyd Peters, defensive coordinator; born May 21, 1936, Council Bluffs, Iowa, lives in Bloomington, Minn. Defensive tackle-guard San Francisco State 1954-57. Pro defensive lineman Baltimore Colts 1958, Cleveland Browns 1959-62, Detroit Lions 1963, Philadelphia Eagles 1964-69, Washington Redskins 1970 (player/coach). Pro scout: Miami Dolphins 1971-73. Pro coach: New York Giants 1974-75, San Francisco 49ers 1976-77, Detroit Lions 1978-81, St. Louis Cardinals 1982-85, joined Vikings in 1986.

Dick Rehbein, wide receivers; born November 22, 1955, Green Bay, Wis., lives in Edina, Minn. Center Ripon 1973-77. No pro playing experience. Pro coach: Green Bay Packers 1979-83, Los Angeles Express (USFL) 1984, joined Vikings in 1984.

Bob Schnelker, offensive coordinator; born October 17, 1928, Galion, Ohio, lives in Eden Prairie, Minn. Tight end Bowling Green 1946-49. Pro tight end Cleveland Browns 1953, New York Giants 1954-59, Minnesota Vikings 1961, Pittsburgh Steelers 1961. Pro coach: Los Angeles Rams 1963-65, Green Bay Packers 1966-71, 1982-85, San Diego Chargers 1972-73, Miami Dolphins 1974, Kansas City Chiefs 1975-77, Detroit Lions 1978-81, joined Vikings in 1986.

Marc Trestman, administrative assistant to head coach, backs; born January 15, 1956, Minneapolis, Minn., lives in Eden Prairie, Minn. Quarterback Minnesota 1975-77, Moorhead (Minn.) State 1978. Pro quarterback Minnesota Vikings 1979. College coach: Miami 1981-84. Pro coach: Minnesota Vikings 1985-86, Tampa Bay Buccaneers 1987, Cleveland Browns 1988-89, rejoined Vikings in 1990.

Paul Wiggin, defensive line; born November 18, 1934, Modesto, Calif., lives in Eden Prairie, Minn. Offensive-defensive tackle Stanford 1953-56. Pro defensive end Cleveland Browns 1957-67. College coach: Stanford 1980-83 (head coach). Pro coach: San Francisco 49ers 1968-74, Kansas City Chiefs 1975-77 (head coach), New Orleans Saints 1978-79, joined Vikings in 1985.

Minnesota Vikings 1990 First-Year Roster

Name	Pos.	Ht.	Wt.	Birth-date	College	Hometown	How Acq.
Allen, Terry	RB	5-10	210	2/21/68	Clemson	Homer, Ga.	D9
Becker, Chris (1)	P	6-1	192	9/6/66	Texas Christian	Taylor, Tex.	FA
Campbell, Jim	K	6-3	220	5/17/67	Eastern Kentucky	Williamsburg, Ky.	FA
Eilers, Pat	S	5-11	193	9/3/66	Notre Dame	St. Paul, Minn.	FA
Gaiters, Chris	WR	5-11	187	12/12/67	Minnesota	Zanesville, Ohio	FA
Goetz, Ron	LB	6-3	236	2/8/68	Minnesota	Waconia, Minn.	D12
Hampton, Alonzo	CB	5-10	197	1/19/67	Pittsburgh	Denver, Colo.	D4
Hobby, Marion	DE	6-4	277	11/7/66	Tennessee	Birmingham, Ala.	D3b
Johnson, Ken (1)	S	6-2	197	9/14/66	Florida A&M	Thomaston, Ga.	FA
Jones, Mike	TE	6-3	255	11/10/66	Texas A&M	Bridgeport, Conn.	D3a
Levelis, John	LB	6-1	235	4/19/67	C.W. Post	Lindenhurst, N.Y.	D7
Newman, Pat	WR	5-11	189	9/10/68	Utah State	San Diego, Calif.	D10
Schlichting, Craig	DE	6-5	257	2/20/67	Wyoming	Spring Lake Park, Minn.	D8
Smith, Cedric	RB	5-10	223	5/27/68	Florida	Enterprise, Ala.	D5b
Smith, Donald	CB	5-11	186	2/21/68	Liberty	Danville, Va.	D10
Thornton, Reggie	WR	5-11	165	9/26/67	Bowling Green	Detroit, Mich.	D5a
Williams, Wayne (1)	RB	5-10	197	8/13/67	Florida	Titusville, Fla.	FA
Woodson, Shawn (1)	LB	6-2	226	8/12/66	James Madison	Buckingham, Va.	FA

The term NFL Rookie is defined as a player who is in his first season of professional football and has not been on the roster of another professional football team for any regular-season or postseason games. A Rookie is designated by an "R" on NFL rosters. Players who have been active in another professional football league or players who have NFL experience, including either preseason training camp or being on an active roster for fewer than three regular-season or postseason games, are termed NFL First-Year Players. An NFL First-Year Player is designated by a "1" on NFL rosters. Thereafter, a player on an NFL active roster for at least three regular-season or postseason games is credited with an additional year of NFL playing experience.

NOTES

_____

_____

_____

_____

_____

_____

_____

_____

_____

_____

_____

_____

NEW ORLEANS SAINTS

National Football Conference Western Division

Team Colors: Old Gold, Black, and White

1500 Poydras Street
New Orleans, Louisiana 70112
Telephone: (504) 733-0255

Club Officials

Owner/General Partner: Tom Benson
President/General Manager: Jim Finks
Vice President/Administration: Jim Miller
Business Manager/Controller: Bruce Broussard
Director of Player Personnel: Bill Kuharich
Director of Marketing: Greg Suit
Assistant Director of Marketing: Bill Ferrante
Director of Media Relations: Rusty Kasmiersky
Assistant Director of Media Relations: Neal Gulkis
Director of Travel/Entertainment: Barra Birrcher
Player Personnel Scouts: Bill Baker, Hamp Cook,
   Hokie Gajan, Tom Marino, Carmen Piccone
Ticket Manager: Sandy King
Trainer: Dean Kleinschmidt
Equipment Manager: Dan Simmons
Video Director: Albert Aucoin

Stadium: Louisiana Superdome •
   Capacity: 69,065
   1500 Poydras Street
   New Orleans, Louisiana 70112

Playing Surface: AstroTurf

Training Camp: University of Wisconsin-LaCrosse
   LaCrosse, Wisconsin 54601

1990 Schedule

Preseason
Aug. 5	vs. L.A. Raiders at London .	1:00*
Aug. 11	at Minnesota	7:00
Aug. 18	vs. Green Bay at Madison, Wis.	1:00
Aug. 25	**Buffalo**	7:00
Aug. 31	**Indianapolis**	7:00

*P.M. Eastern Time

Regular Season
Sept. 10	**San Francisco** (Monday)	8:00
Sept. 16	at Minnesota	3:00
Sept. 23	**Phoenix**	12:00
Sept. 30	**Open Date**	
Oct. 7	at Atlanta	1:00
Oct. 14	**Cleveland**	12:00
Oct. 21	at Houston	12:00
Oct. 28	**Detroit**	12:00
Nov. 4	at Cincinnati	1:00
Nov. 11	**Tampa Bay**	12:00
Nov. 18	at Washington	1:00
Nov. 25	**Atlanta**	12:00
Dec. 2	at Dallas	3:00
Dec. 9	at Los Angeles Rams	1:00
Dec. 16	**Pittsburgh**	12:00
Dec. 23	at San Francisco	1:00
Dec. 31	**L.A. Rams** (Monday)	7:00

Saints Coaching History

(121-213-5)

1967-70	Tom Fears*	13-34-2
1970-72	J.D. Roberts	7-25-3
1973-75	John North**	11-23-0
1975	Ernie Hefferle	1-7-0
1976-77	Hank Stram	7-21-0
1978-80	Dick Nolan***	15-29-0
1980	Dick Stanfel	1-3-0
1981-85	O.A. (Bum) Phillips****	27-42-0
1985	Wade Phillips	1-3-0
1986-89	Jim Mora	38-26-0

*Released after seven games in 1970
**Released after six games in 1975
***Released after 12 games in 1980
****Resigned after 12 games in 1985

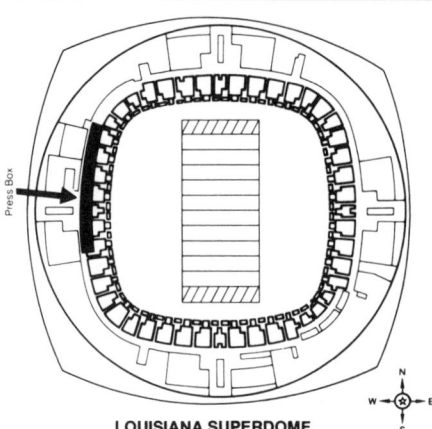

LOUISIANA SUPERDOME

Record Holders

Individual Records—Career
Category	Name	Performance
Rushing (Yds.)	George Rogers, 1981-84	4,267
Passing (Yds.)	Archie Manning, 1971-1982	21,734
Passing (TDs)	Archie Manning, 1971-1982	115
Receiving (No.)	Dan Abramowicz, 1967-1973	309
Receiving (Yds.)	Dan Abramowicz, 1967-1973	4,875
Interceptions	Dave Waymer, 1980-89	37
Punting (Avg.)	Tom McNeill, 1967-69	42.3
Punt Return (Avg.)	Mel Gray, 1986-88	13.4
Kickoff Return (Avg.)	Walter Roberts, 1967	26.3
Field Goals	Morten Andersen, 1982-89	171
Touchdowns (Tot.)	Dan Abramowicz, 1967-1973	37
	Dalton Hilliard, 1986-89	37
Points	Morten Andersen, 1982-89	760

Individual Records—Single Season
Category	Name	Performance
Rushing (Yds.)	George Rogers, 1981	1,674
Passing (Yds.)	Archie Manning, 1980	3,716
Passing (TDs)	Archie Manning, 1980	23
Receiving (No.)	Eric Martin, 1988	85
Receiving (Yds.)	Eric Martin, 1989	1,090
Interceptions	Dave Whitsell, 1967	10
Punting (Avg.)	Brian Hansen, 1984	43.8
Punt Return (Avg.)	Mel Gray, 1987	14.7
Kickoff Return (Avg.)	Don Shy, 1969	27.9
Field Goals	Morten Andersen, 1985	31
Touchdowns (Tot.)	Dalton Hilliard, 1989	18
Points	Morten Andersen, 1987	121

Individual Records—Single Game
Category	Name	Performance
Rushing (Yds.)	George Rogers, 9-4-83	206
Passing (Yds.)	Archie Manning, 12-7-80	377
Passing (TDs)	Billy Kilmer, 11-2-69	6
Receiving (No.)	Tony Galbreath, 9-10-78	14
Receiving (Yds.)	Wes Chandler, 9-2-79	205
Interceptions	Tommy Myers, 9-3-78	3
	Dave Waymer, 10-6-85	3
	Reggie Sutton, 10-18-87	3
Field Goals	Morten Andersen, 12-1-85	5
	Morten Andersen, 11-15-87	5
Touchdowns (Tot.)	Many times	3
	Last time by Dalton Hilliard, 10-22-89	
Points	Many times	18
	Last time by Dalton Hilliard, 10-22-89	

1989 Team Record
Preseason (1-3)

Date	Result		Opponents
8/12	L	7-31	Indianapolis
8/19	L	7-10	at Buffalo
8/28	W	27-10	Cincinnati
9/1	L	21-26	Washington
		62-77	

Regular Season (9-7)

Date	Result		Opponents	Att.
9/10	W	28- 0	Dallas	
9/17	L	34-35	at Green Bay	55,809
9/24	L	10-20	at Tampa Bay	44,053
10/1	L	14-16	Washington	64,358
10/8	L	20-24	San Francisco	60,488
10/15	W	29-14	N.Y. Jets	59,521
10/22	W	40-21	at L.A. Rams	57,567
10/29	W	20-13	Atlanta	65,153
11/6	L	13-31	at San Francisco	60,667
11/12	W	28-24	at New England	47,680
11/19	W	26-17	at Atlanta	53,173
11/26	L	17-20	L.A. Rams (OT)	64,274
12/3	L	14-21	at Detroit	38,550
12/10	W	22-19	at Buffalo	70,037
12/18	W	30-20	Philadelphia	59,218
12/24	W	41- 6	Indianapolis	49,009

(OT) Overtime

Score by Periods

Saints	105	123	60	98	0	—	386
Opponents	27	96	89	86	3	—	301

Attendance
Home 488,998   Away 427,536   Total 916,534
Single-game home record, 70,940 (11-4-79)
Single-season home record, 531,156 (1988)

1989 Team Statistics

	Saints	Opp.
Total First Downs	304	293
Rushing	108	79
Passing	167	198
Penalty.	29	16
Third Down: Made/Att.	89/207	82/216
Third Down: Pct.	43.0	38.0
Fourth Down: Made/Att.	5/10	8/17
Fourth Down: Pct.	50.0	47.1
Total Net Yards	5328	5186
Avg. Per Game.	333.0	324.1
Total Plays.	999	997
Avg. Per Play	5.3	5.2
Net Yards Rushing	1948	1326
Avg. Per Game.	121.8	82.9
Total Rushes	502	373
Net Yards Passing	3380	3860
Avg. Per Game.	211.3	241.3
Sacked/Yards Lost	36/271	47/362
Gross Yards	3651	4222
Att./Completions	461/284	577/320
Completion Pct.	61.6	55.5
Had Intercepted	19	21
Punts/Avg.	71/39.1	75/39.4
Net Punting Avg.	34.2	33.2
Penalties/Yards Lost	90/676	105/850
Fumbles/Ball Lost	28/12	35/18
Touchdowns	46	35
Rushing	19	10
Passing	23	23
Returns	4	2
Avg. Time of Possession.	33:43	26:17

1989 Individual Statistics

Scoring

	TD R	TD P	TD Rt	PAT	FG	Saf	TP
Hilliard	13	5	0	0/0	0/0	0	108
Andersen	0	0	0	44/45	20/29	0	104
E. Martin	0	8	0	0/0	0/0	0	48
Brenner	0	4	0	0/0	0/0	0	24
Hill	0	4	0	0/0	0/0	0	24
Jordan	3	0	0	0/0	0/0	0	18
Cook	0	0	1	0/0	0/0	0	6
Fourcade	1	0	0	0/0	0/0	0	6
Frazier	1	0	0	0/0	0/0	0	6
Heyward	1	0	0	0/0	0/0	0	6
Maxie	0	0	1	0/0	0/0	0	6
Morse	0	0	1	0/0	0/0	0	6
Shepard	0	0	1	0/0	0/0	0	6
Tice	0	1	0	0/0	0/0	0	6
Turner	0	1	0	0/0	0/0	0	6
Forde	0	0	0	0/0	0/0	1	2
Warren	0	0	0	0/0	0/0	1	2
Saints	19	23	4	44/46	20/29	3	386
Opponents	10	23	2	34/35	19/24	0	301

Passing

	Att.	Comp.	Yds.	Pct.	TD	Int.	Tkld.	Rate
Hebert	353	222	2686	62.9	15	15	22/171	82.7
Fourcade	107	61	930	57.0	7	4	13/96	92.0
Hilliard	1	1	35	100.0	1	0	0/0	158.3
Hill	0	0	0	0.0	0	0	1/4	0.0
Saints	461	284	3651	61.6	23	19	36/271	85.9
Opponents	577	320	4222	55.5	23	21	47/362	76.9

Rushing

	Att.	Yds.	Avg.	LG	TD
Hilliard	344	1262	3.7	40	13
Heyward	49	183	3.7	15	1
Jordan	38	179	4.7	32	3
Frazier	25	112	4.5	21	1
Fourcade	14	91	6.5	14	1
Hebert	25	87	3.5	11	0
Morse	2	43	21.5	39	0
Turner	2	8	4.0	6	0
Winslow	1	0	0.0	0	0
Hill	1	−7	−7.0	−7	0
Perriman	1	−10	−10.0	−10	0
Saints	502	1948	3.9	40	19
Opponents	373	1326	3.6	38	10

Receiving

	No.	Yds.	Avg.	LG	TD
E. Martin	68	1090	16.0	53t	8
Hilliard	52	514	9.9	54t	5
Hill	48	636	13.3	46	4
Brenner	34	398	11.7	30t	4
Turner	22	279	12.7	54t	1
Perriman	20	356	17.8	47	0
Heyward	13	69	5.3	12	0
Tice	9	98	10.9	23	1
Scales	8	89	11.1	26	0
Jordan	4	53	13.3	17	0
Frazier	3	25	8.3	22	0
Shepard	2	36	18.0	23	0
Cook	1	8	8.0	8	0
Saints	284	3651	12.9	54t	23
Opponents	320	4222	13.2	75t	23

Interceptions

	No.	Yds.	Avg.	LG	TD
Waymer	6	66	11.0	42	0
Massey	5	26	5.2	22	0
Cook	3	81	27.0	63t	1
Maxie	3	41	13.7	26t	1
Mack	2	0	0.0	0	0
Swilling	1	14	14.0	14	0
Atkins	1	−2	−2.0	−2	0
Saints	21	226	10.8	63t	2
Opponents	19	265	13.9	40	1

Punting

	No.	Yds.	Avg.	In 20	LG
Barnhardt	55	2179	39.6	17	56
Winslow	16	595	37.2	4	50
Saints	71	2774	39.1	21	56
Opponents	75	2956	39.4	15	63

Punt Returns

	No.	FC	Yds.	Avg.	LG	TD
Harris	27	7	196	7.3	20	0
Morse	10	1	29	2.9	16	0
Shepard	7	1	91	13.0	56t	1
Hill	7	0	41	5.9	13	0
Perriman	1	0	10	10.0	10	0
Turner	1	0	7	7.0	7	0
Massey	0	0	54	—	54	0
Saints	53	9	428	8.1	57	1
Opponents	35	16	244	7.0	28	0

Kickoff Returns

	No.	Yds.	Avg.	LG	TD
Harris	19	378	19.9	39	0
Atkins	12	245	20.4	32	0
Morse	10	278	27.8	99t	1
Frazier	8	157	19.6	29	0
Shepard	8	135	16.9	24	0
U. Johnson	2	34	17.0	19	0
Phillips	1	24	24.0	24	0
Hilliard	1	20	20.0	20	0
Hill	1	13	13.0	13	0
Scales	1	0	0.0	0	0
Saints	63	1284	20.4	99t	1
Opponents	55	983	17.9	72	0

Sacks

	No.
Swilling	16.5
Warren	9.5
Jackson	7.5
Wilks	4.0
Mills	3.0
W. Martin	2.5
Cook	1.0
Geathers	1.0
V. Johnson	1.0
Mack	1.0
Saints	47.0
Opponents	36.0

1990 Draft Choices

Round	Name	Pos.	College
1.	Renaldo Turnbull	DE	West Virginia
2.	Vince Buck	DB	Central State, Ohio
3.	Joel Smeenge	DE	Western Michigan
4.	DeMond Winston	LB	Vanderbilt
5.	Charles Arbuckle	TE	UCLA
6.	Mike Buck	QB	Maine
	James Williams	LB	Mississippi State
7.	Scott Hough	G	Maine
8.	Gerry Gdowski	QB	Nebraska
	Derrick Carr	DE	Bowling Green
9.	Broderick Graves	RB	Winston-Salem St.
	Lonnie Brockman	LB	West Virginia
10.	Gary Cooper	WR	Clemson
	Ernest Spears	DB	Southern California
11.	Webbie Burnett	NT	Western Kentucky
12.	Chris Port	G	Duke

New Orleans Saints 1990 Veteran Roster

No.	Name	Pos.	Ht.	Wt.	Birth-date	NFL Exp.	College	Hometown	How Acq.	'89 Games/ Starts
7	Andersen, Morten	K	6-2	221	8/19/60	9	Michigan State	Indianapolis, Ind.	D4-'82	16/0
28	†Atkins, Gene	S	6-1	200	11/22/64	4	Florida A&M	Tallahassee, Fla.	D7-'87	14/12
6	†Barnhardt, Tommy	P	6-2	207	6/11/63	4	North Carolina	China Grove, N.C.	FA-'89	11/0
85	Brenner, Hoby	TE	6-5	245	6/2/59	10	Southern California	Fullerton, Calif.	D3b-'81	16/16
67	†Brock, Stan	T	6-6	292	6/8/58	11	Colorado	Beaverton, Ore.	D1-'80	16/16
41	†Cook, Toi	CB	5-11	188	12/3/64	4	Stanford	Van Nuys, Calif.	D8-'87	16/14
79	†Derby, Glenn	T	6-6	290	6/27/64	2	Wisconsin	Oconomowoc, Wis.	FA-'89	3/0
72	†Dombrowski, Jim	T	6-5	298	10/19/63	5	Virginia	Williamsville, N.Y.	D1-'86	16/16
63	Edelman, Brad	G	6-6	270	9/3/60	9	Missouri	Creve Coeur, Mo.	D2-'82	8/8
52	†Forde, Brian	LB	6-3	225	11/1/63	3	Washington State	Montreal, Canada	D7-'88	16/1
11	Fourcade, John	QB	6-1	215	10/11/60	4	Mississippi	Marrero, La.	FA-'87	13/3
74	Haverdink, Kevin	T	6-5	285	10/20/65	2	Western Michigan	Hamilton, Mich.	D5-'89	16/7
3	†Hebert, Bobby	QB	6-4	215	8/19/60	6	Northwestern Louisiana	Cut Off, La.	FA-'85	14/13
34	Heyward, Craig	RB	5-11	260	9/26/66	3	Pittsburgh	Passaic, N.J.	D1-'88	16/6
61	Hilgenberg, Joel	C-G	6-2	252	7/10/62	7	Iowa	Iowa City, Iowa	D4-'84	16/13
87	†Hill, Lonzell	WR	5-11	189	9/25/65	4	Washington	Stockton, Calif.	D2-'87	16/12
21	Hilliard, Dalton	RB	5-8	204	1/21/64	5	Louisiana State	Patterson, La.	D2-'86	16/16
57	†Jackson, Rickey	LB	6-2	243	3/20/58	10	Pittsburgh	Pahokee, Fla.	D2-'81	14/14
53	Johnson, Vaughan	LB	6-3	235	3/24/62	5	North Carolina State	Morehead City, N.C.	SD1-'84	16/16
89	†Jones, Mike	WR	5-11	180	4/14/62	7	Tennessee State	Chattanooga, Tenn.	FA-'89	3/0
23	Jordan, Buford	RB	6-0	223	6/26/62	5	McNeese State	Iota, La.	FA-'86	11/7
60	Korte, Steve	C	6-2	271	1/15/60	8	Arkansas	Littleton, Colo.	D2-'83	5/4
24	†Mack, Milton	CB	5-11	182	9/20/63	4	Alcorn State	Jackson, Miss.	D5-'87	16/4
84	Martin, Eric	WR	6-1	207	11/8/61	6	Louisiana State	Van Vleck, Tex.	D7-'85	16/16
93	Martin, Wayne	DE	6-5	275	10/26/65	2	Arkansas	Cherry Valley, Ark.	D1-'89	16/0
40	Massey, Robert	CB	5-10	182	2/17/67	2	North Carolina Central	Charlotte, N.C.	D2-'89	16/16
39	†Maxie, Brett	S	6-2	194	1/13/62	6	Texas Southern	Dallas, Tex.	FA-'85	16/2
36	Mayes, Rueben	RB	5-11	200	6/6/63	4	Washington State	N. Battleford, Saskatchewan	D3a-'86	0*
51	Mills, Sam	LB	5-9	225	6/3/59	5	Montclair State	Long Branch, N.J.	FA-'86	16/15
35	†Morse, Bobby	RB	5-10	213	10/3/65	3	Michigan State	Muskegon, Mich.	FA-'89	11/0
80	Perriman, Brett	WR	5-9	180	10/10/65	3	Miami	Miami, Fla.	D2-'88	14/1
43	Phillips, Kim	CB	5-9	188	10/28/66	2	North Texas State	New Boston, Tex.	D3-'89	5/0
83	Scales, Greg	TE	6-4	253	5/9/66	3	Wake Forest	Winston-Salem, N.C.	D5a-'88	14/4
56	†Swilling, Pat	LB	6-3	242	10/25/64	5	Georgia Tech	Toccoa, Ga.	D3b-'86	16/15
82	Tice, John	TE	6-5	249	6/22/60	8	Maryland	Central Islip, N.Y.	D3a-'83	15/2
54	Toles, Alvin	LB	6-1	234	3/23/63	5	Tennessee	Forsythe, Ga.	D1-'85	0*
65	†Trapilo, Steve	G	6-5	281	9/20/64	4	Boston College	Dorchester, Mass.	D4-'87	16/16
88	Turner, Floyd	WR	5-11	188	5/29/66	2	Northwestern Louisiana	Mansfield, La.	D6-'89	13/0
94	Wilks, Jim	NT	6-5	275	3/12/58	10	San Diego State	Pasadena, Calif.	D12-'81	16/15
18	†Wilson, Dave	QB	6-3	206	4/27/59	9	Illinois	Anaheim, Calif.	SD1-'81	0*
69	Woods, Tony	DE	6-4	274	3/14/66	2	Oklahoma	Colorado Springs, Colo.	PB(Chi)-'90#	15/2*

* Mayes and Toles missed '89 season due to injury; Wilson active for 15 games but did not play in '89; Woods played 15 games with Chicago in '89.

† Option playout; subject to developments.

Plan B unconditional free agent.

Players lost through Plan B (10): RB Paul Frazier (GB; 15 games in '89); DE James Geathers (Wash; 15); S Antonio Gibson (Dall; 16); WR Rod Harris (Dall; 11); LB Walter Johnson (Dall; 15); LB Joe Kohlbrand (NYJ; 16); G Doug Marrone (Minn; 1); NT Pat Swoopes (Wash; 15); G Jeff Walker (Phx; 13); S Dave Waymer (SF; 16).

Also played with Saints in '89—LB James Haynes (3 games), RB Undra Johnson (5), CB Michael Mayes (2), CB Calvin Nicholson (1), WR Derrick Shepard (4), DE Michael Simmons (1), S Bennie Thompson (2), DE Frank Warren (16), P George Winslow (5).

COACHING STAFF

Head Coach,
Jim Mora

Pro Career: Begins fifth year as an NFL coach, after leading Saints to third straight winning season in 1989 with a 9-7 mark. Was named 1987 NFL coach of the year after leading Saints to a 12-4 record and the team's first playoff appearance. Came to New Orleans following a three-year career as the winningest coach in USFL history as head coach of the Philadelphia/Baltimore Stars. Directed Stars to championship game in each of his three seasons and won league championship in 1984 and 1985. He won USFL coach of the year honors following the 1984 season. Mora began his pro coaching career in 1978 as defensive line coach of the Seattle Seahawks. In 1982, he became defensive coordinator of the New England Patriots and played a vital role in the Patriots' march to the playoffs that year. No pro playing experience. Career record: 38-26.

Background: Played tight end and defensive end at Occidental College. Assistant coach at Occidental 1960-63 and head coach 1964-67. Linebacker coach at Stanford on a staff that included former Eagles head coach Dick Vermeil. Defensive assistant at Colorado 1968-73. Linebacker coach under Vermeil at UCLA 1974. Defensive coordinator at Washington 1975-77. Received bachelor's degree in physical education from Occidental in 1957. Also holds master's degree in education from Southern California.

Personal: Born May 24, 1935, in Glendale, Calif. Jim and his wife, Connie, live in Metairie, La., and have three sons—Michael, Stephen, and Jim, defensive backs coach for the San Diego Chargers.

Assistant Coaches

Paul Boudreau, offensive line; born December 30, 1949, Somerville, Mass., lives in Destrehan, La. Guard Boston College 1971-73. No pro playing experience. College coach: Boston College 1974-76, Maine 1977-78, Dartmouth 1979-81, Navy 1983. Pro coach: Edmonton Eskimos (CFL) 1983-86, joined Saints in 1987.

Dom Capers, defensive backs; born August 7, 1950, Cambridge, Ohio, lives in Destrehan, La. Defensive back Mount Union College 1968-71. No pro playing experience. College coach: Hawaii 1975-76, San Jose State 1977, California 1978-79, Tennessee 1980-81, Ohio State 1982-83. Pro coach: Philadelphia/Baltimore Stars (USFL) 1984-85, joined Saints in 1986.

Vic Fangio, outside linebackers; born August 22, 1958, Dunmore, Pa., lives in Destrehan, La. Defensive back East Stroudsburg 1976-78. No pro playing experience. College coach: North Carolina 1983. Pro coach: Philadelphia/Baltimore Stars (USFL) 1984-85, joined Saints in 1986.

Joe Marciano, tight ends-special teams; born February 10, 1954, Scranton, Pa., lives in Kenner, La. Quarterback Temple 1972-75. No pro playing experience. College coach: East Stroudsburg 1977, Rhode Island 1978-79, Villanova 1980, Penn State 1981, Temple 1982. Pro coach: Philadelphia/Baltimore Stars (USFL) 1983-85, joined Saints in 1986.

Russell Paternostro, strength and conditioning; born July 21, 1940, New Orleans, La., lives in Covington, La. San Diego State. No college or pro playing experience. Pro coach: Joined Saints in 1981.

John Pease, defensive line; born October 14, 1943, Pittsburgh, Pa., lives in Kenner, La. Wingback Utah 1963-64. No pro playing experience. College coach: Fullerton, Calif., J.C. 1970-73, Long Beach State 1974-76, Utah 1977, Washington 1978-83. Pro coach: Philadelphia/Baltimore Stars (USFL) 1983-85, joined Saints in 1986.

Steve Sidwell, defensive coordinator-inside linebackers; born August 30, 1944, Winfield, Kan., lives in Destrehan, La. Linebacker Colorado 1962-65. No pro playing experience. College coach: Colorado 1966-73, Nevada-Las Vegas 1974-75, Southern Methodist 1976-81. Pro coach: New England Patriots 1982-84, Indianapolis Colts 1985, joined Saints in 1986.

New Orleans Saints 1990 First-Year Roster

Name	Pos.	Ht.	Wt.	Birth-date	College	Hometown	How Acq.
Alphin, Gerald (1)	WR	6-3	220	5/21/64	Kansas State	St. Louis, Mo.	FA
Arbuckle, Charles	TE	6-2	238	9/13/68	UCLA	Houston, Tex.	D5
Brockman, Lonnie	LB	6-3	230	3/14/68	West Virginia	Pittsburgh, Pa.	D9b
Buck, Mike	QB	6-3	227	4/22/67	Maine	Long Island City, N.Y.	D6a
Buck, Vince	CB	6-0	198	1/12/67	Central State, Ohio	Owensboro, Ky.	D2
Burnett, Webbie	NT	6-2	277	11/7/67	Western Kentucky	Pensacola, Fla.	D11
Carr, Derrick	DE	6-5	259	1/30/67	Bowling Green	Detroit, Mich.	D8b
Cooper, Gary	WR	6-1	190	12/14/66	Clemson	Ambridge, Pa.	D10a
Cooper, Richard (1)	T	6-4	285	11/1/64	Tennessee	Memphis, Tenn.	FA-'89
Fenerty, Gill (1)	RB	6-0	205	8/24/63	Holy Cross	New Orleans, La.	FA
Garrett, Jason (1)	QB	6-0	196	3/28/66	Princeton	Chagrin, Ohio	FA-'89
Gdowski, Gerry	QB	6-0	192	8/9/67	Nebraska	Fremont, Neb.	D8a
Graves, Broderick	RB	5-11	194	4/7/68	Winston-Salem State	Charlotte, N.C.	D9a
Griffin, Willie (1)	NT	6-3	280	3/24/68	Nebraska	Monrovia, Calif.	FA
Hough, Scott	G-T	6-4	282	5/14/66	Maine	Newton, Mass.	D7
King, Thomas (1)	S	6-1	190	3/31/66	S.W. Louisiana	Winnfield, La.	FA
Lindstrom, Eric (1)	LB	6-3	235	5/27/66	Boston College	Weymouth, Mass.	FA
Nicholson, Calvin (1)	CB	5-9	183	7/9/67	Oregon State	Inglewood, Calif.	D11-'89
Port, Chris	T	6-5	290	11/2/67	Duke	Wanaque, N.J.	D12
Simien, Tracy (1)	LB	6-1	245	5/21/67	Texas Christian	Sweeny, Tex.	FA
Simmons, Michael (1)	DE	6-4	269	11/14/65	Mississippi State	Eupora, Miss.	FA-'89
Smeenge, Joel	DE	6-5	250	4/1/68	Western Michigan	Grand Rapids, Mich.	D3
Spears, Ernest	S	5-11	192	11/6/67	Southern California	Oceanside, Calif.	D10b
Thompson, Bennie (1)	S	6-0	200	2/10/63	Grambling	New Orleans, La.	FA-'89
Turnbull, Renaldo	DE	6-4	248	1/5/66	West Virginia	St. Thomas, Virgin Is.	D1
Wheeler, Todd (1)	C	6-4	269	7/25/67	Georgia	Lindale, Ga.	FA-'89
Williams, James	LB	6-0	230	10/10/68	Mississippi State	North Natchez, Miss.	D6b
Winston, DeMond	LB	6-2	239	9/14/68	Vanderbilt	Lansing, Mich.	D4

The term NFL Rookie is defined as a player who is in his first season of professional football and has not been on the roster of another professional football team for any regular-season or postseason games. A Rookie is designated by an "R" on NFL rosters. Players who have been active in another professional football league or players who have NFL experience, including either preseason training camp or being on an active roster for fewer than three regular-season or postseason games, are termed NFL First-Year Players. An NFL First-Year Player is designated by a "1" on NFL rosters. Thereafter, a player on an NFL active roster for at least three regular-season or postseason games is credited with an additional year of NFL playing experience.

NOTES

Jim Skipper, running backs; born January 23, 1949, Breaux Bridge, La., lives in Kenner, La. Defensive back Whittier College 1971-72. No pro playing experience. College coach: Cal Poly-Pomona 1974-76, San Jose State 1977-78, Pacific 1979, Oregon 1980-82. Pro coach: Philadelphia/Baltimore Stars (USFL) 1983-85, joined Saints in 1986.

Carl Smith, offensive coordinator-quarterbacks; born April 26, 1948, Wasco, Calif., lives in Kenner, La. Defensive back Cal Poly-SLO 1968-70. No pro playing experience. College coach: Cal Poly-SLO 1971, Colorado 1972-73, Southwestern Louisiana 1974-78, Lamar 1979-81, North Carolina State 1982. Pro coach: Philadelphia/Baltimore Stars (USFL) 1983-85, joined Saints in 1986.

Steve Walters, wide receivers; born June 16, 1948, Jonesboro, Ark., lives in Destrehan, La. Quarterback-defensive back Arkansas 1967-70. No pro playing experience. College coach: Tampa 1973, Northeast Louisiana 1974-75, Morehead State 1976, Tulsa 1977-78, Memphis State 1979, Southern Methodist 1980-81, Alabama 1985. Pro coach: New England Patriots 1982-84, joined Saints in 1986.

National Football Conference Eastern Division

Team Colors: Blue, Red, and White

Giants Stadium
East Rutherford, New Jersey 07073
Telephone: (201) 935-8111

Club Officials

President: Wellington T. Mara
Vice President-Treasurer: Timothy J. Mara
Vice President-Secretary: Raymond J. Walsh
Vice President-General Manager: George Young
Assistant General Manager: Harry Hulmes
Controller: John Pasquali
Director of Player Personnel: Tom Boisture
Director of Pro Personnel: Tim Rooney
Director of Media Services: Ed Croke
Director of Promotions: Tom Power
Director of Special Projects: Victor Del Guercio
Box Office Treasurer: Jim Gleason
Head Trainer: Ronnie Barnes
Assistant Trainers: John Johnson, Mike Ryan
Equipment Manager: Ed Wagner, Jr.

Stadium: Giants Stadium • **Capacity:** 77,152
East Rutherford, New Jersey 07073

Playing Surface: AstroTurf

Training Camp: Fairleigh Dickinson-Madison
Florham Park, N.J. 07932

1990 Schedule

Preseason
Aug. 13	at Buffalo	8:00
Aug. 18	at Houston	7:00
Aug. 25	**New York Jets**	8:00
Sept. 1	**Cleveland**	8:00

Regular Season
Sept. 9	**Philadelphia**	8:00
Sept. 16	at Dallas	3:00
Sept. 23	**Miami**	1:00
Sept. 30	**Dallas**	1:00
Oct. 7	**Open Date**	
Oct. 14	at Washington	4:00
Oct. 21	**Phoenix**	4:00
Oct. 28	**Washington**	4:00
Nov. 5	at Indianapolis (Monday)	9:00
Nov. 11	at Los Angeles Rams	1:00
Nov. 18	**Detroit**	1:00
Nov. 25	at Philadelphia	1:00
Dec. 3	at San Francisco (Monday)	6:00
Dec. 9	**Minnesota**	1:00
Dec. 15	**Buffalo** (Saturday)	12:30
Dec. 23	at Phoenix	2:00
Dec. 30	at New England	1:00

Giants Coaching History

(464-387-32)
1925	Bob Folwell	8-4-0
1926	Joe Alexander	8-4-1
1927-28	Earl Potteiger	15-8-3
1929-30	LeRoy Andrews*	24-5-1
1930	Benny Friedman	2-0-0
1931-53	Steve Owen	153-108-17
1954-60	Jim Lee Howell	54-29-4
1961-68	Allie Sherman	57-54-4
1969-73	Alex Webster	29-40-1
1974-76	Bill Arnsparger**	7-28-0
1976-78	John McVay	14-23-0
1979-82	Ray Perkins	24-35-0
1983-89	Bill Parcells	69-49-1

*Released after 15 games in 1930
**Released after seven games in 1976

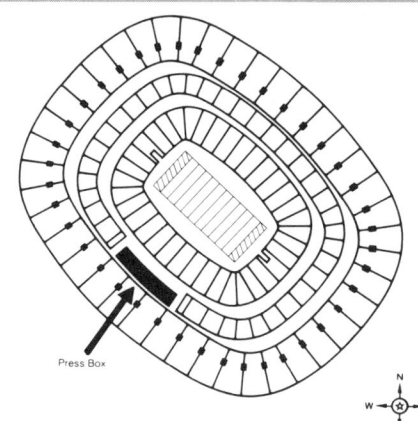

Press Box

GIANTS STADIUM

Record Holders
Individual Records—Career
Category	Name	Performance
Rushing (Yds.)	Joe Morris, 1982-88	5,296
Passing (Yds.)	Phil Simms, 1979-1989	26,235
Passing (TDs)	Charlie Conerly, 1948-1961	173
Receiving (No.)	Joe Morrison, 1959-1972	395
Receiving (Yds.)	Frank Gifford, 1952-1960, 1962-64	5,434
Interceptions	Emlen Tunnell, 1948-1958	74
Punting (Avg.)	Don Chandler, 1956-1964	43.8
Punt Return (Avg.)	Dave Meggett, 1989	12.7
Kickoff Return (Avg.)	Rocky Thompson, 1971-72	27.2
Field Goals	Pete Gogolak, 1966-1974	126
Touchdowns (Tot.)	Frank Gifford, 1952-1960, 1962-64	78
Points	Pete Gogolak, 1966-1974	646

Individual Records—Single Season
Category	Name	Performance
Rushing (Yds.)	Joe Morris, 1986	1,516
Passing (Yds.)	Phil Simms, 1984	4,044
Passing (TDs)	Y.A. Tittle, 1963	36
Receiving (No.)	Earnest Gray, 1983	78
Receiving (Yds.)	Homer Jones, 1967	1,209
Interceptions	Otto Schnellbacher, 1951	11
	Jim Patton, 1958	11
Punting (Avg.)	Don Chandler, 1959	46.6
Punt Return (Avg.)	Merle Hapes, 1942	15.5
Kickoff Return (Avg.)	John Salscheider, 1949	31.6
Field Goals	Ali Haji-Sheikh, 1983	*35
Touchdowns (Tot.)	Joe Morris, 1985	21
Points	Ali Haji-Sheikh, 1983	127

Individual Records—Single Game
Category	Name	Performance
Rushing (Yds.)	Gene Roberts, 11-12-50	218
Passing (Yds.)	Phil Simms, 10-13-85	513
Passing (TDs)	Y.A. Tittle, 10-28-62	*7
Receiving (No.)	Mark Bavaro, 10-13-85	12
Receiving (Yds.)	Del Shofner, 10-28-62	269
Interceptions	Many times	3
	Last time by Terry Kinard, 9-27-87	
Field Goals	Joe Danelo, 10-18-81	6
Touchdowns (Tot.)	Ron Johnson, 10-2-72	4
	Earnest Gray, 9-7-80	4
Points	Ron Johnson, 10-2-72	24
	Earnest Gray, 9-7-80	24

*NFL Record

1989 Team Record
Preseason (3-1)

Date	Result		Opponents
8/12	W	20-17	at New England
8/20	W	45- 7	at Kansas City
8/26	W	21-17	N.Y. Jets
9/2	L	10-13	Pittsburgh
		96-54	

Regular Season (12-4)

Date	Result		Opponents	Att.
9/11	W	27-24	at Washington	54,160
9/17	W	24-14	Detroit	76,021
9/24	W	35- 7	Phoenix	75,742
10/1	W	30-13	at Dallas	51,785
10/8	L	19-21	at Philadelphia	65,688
10/15	W	20-17	Washington	76,245
10/22	W	20-13	at San Diego	48,566
10/30	W	24-14	Minnesota	76,041
11/5	W	20-13	at Phoenix	46,588
11/12	L	10-31	at L.A. Rams	65,127
11/19	W	15- 3	Seattle	75,014
11/27	L	24-34	at San Francisco	63,461
12/3	L	17-24	Philadelphia	74,809
12/10	W	14- 7	at Denver	63,283
12/16	W	15- 0	Dallas	72,141
12/24	W	34-17	L.A. Raiders	70,306

Postseason (0-1)

Date	Result		Opponent	Att.
1/7	L	13-19	L.A. Rams (OT)	76,526

(OT) Overtime

Score by Periods

Giants	77	83	100	88	0	—	348
Opponents	55	66	38	93	0	—	252

Attendance
Home 596,319   Away 458,658   Total 1,054,977
Single-game home record, 76,633 (1-11-87)
Single-season home record, 596,319 (1989)

1989 Team Statistics

	Giants	Opp.
Total First Downs	298	266
Rushing	118	90
Passing	157	159
Penalty	23	17
Third Down: Made/Att.	102/232	79/205
Third Down: Pct.	44.0	38.5
Fourth Down: Made/Att.	17/22	4/17
Fourth Down: Pct.	77.3	23.5
Total Net Yards	4963	4664
Avg. Per Game	310.2	291.5
Total Plays	1046	946
Avg. Per Play	4.7	4.9
Net Yards Rushing	1889	1539
Avg. Per Game	118.1	96.2
Total Rushes	556	421
Net Yards Passing	3074	3125
Avg. Per Game	192.1	195.3
Sacked/Yards Lost	46/281	39/302
Gross Yards	3355	3427
Att./Completions	444/248	486/273
Completion Pct.	55.9	56.2
Had Intercepted	16	22
Punts/Avg.	70/43.1	74/40.1
Net Punting Avg.	37.8	30.8
Penalties/Yards Lost	83/675	109/800
Fumbles/Ball Lost	30/14	38/15
Touchdowns	37	30
Rushing	17	10
Passing	17	16
Returns	3	4
Avg. Time of Possession	32:23	27:37

1989 Individual Statistics

Scoring

	TD R	TD P	TD Rt	PAT	FG	Saf	TP
Anderson	14	0	·0	0/0	0/0	0	84
Allegre	0	0	0	23/24	20/26	0	83
Nittmo	0	0	0	12/13	9/12	0	39
Meggett	0	4	1	0/0	0/0	0	30
Turner	0	4	0	0/0	0/0	0	24
Bavaro	0	3	0	0/0	0/0	0	18
Baker	0	2	0	0/0	0/0	0	12
Hostetler	2	0	0	0/0	0/0	0	12
Banks	0	1	0	0/0	0/0	0	6
Cross	0	1	0	0/0	0/0	0	6
Ingram	0	1	0	0/0	0/0	0	6
P. Johnson	0	0	1	0/0	0/0	0	6
Kinard	0	0	1	0/0	0/0	0	6
Manuel	0	1	0	0/0	0/0	0	6
Simms	1	0	0	0/0	0/0	0	6
Marshall	0	0	0	0/0	0/0	1	2
Reasons	0	0	0	0/0	0/0	1	2
Giants	17	17	3	35/37	29/38	2	348
Opponents	10	16	4	30/30	14/21	0	252

Passing

	Att.	Comp.	Yds.	Pct.	TD	Int.	Tkld.	Rate
Simms	405	228	3061	56.3	14	14	40/244	77.6
Hostetler	39	20	294	51.3	3	2	6/37	80.5
Giants	444	248	3355	55.9	17	16	46/281	77.9
Opponents	486	273	3427	56.2	16	22	39/302	70.4

Rushing

	Att.	Yds.	Avg.	LG	TD
Anderson	325	1023	3.1	36t	14
Tillman	79	290	3.7	19	0
Carthon	57	153	2.7	18	0
Simms	32	141	4.4	15	1
Meggett	28	117	4.2	18	0
Hostetler	11	71	6.5	19t	2
Rouson	11	51	4.6	9	0
Adams	9	29	3.2	8	0
Turner	2	11	5.5	14	0
Reasons	1	2	2.0	2	0
Ingram	1	1	1.0	1	0
Giants	556	1889	3.4	36t	17
Opponents	421	1539	3.7	44	10

Receiving

	No.	Yds.	Avg.	LG	TD
Turner	38	467	12.3	44	4
Meggett	34	531	15.6	62t	4
Manuel	33	539	16.3	49	1
Anderson	28	268	9.6	26	0
Mowatt	27	288	10.7	31	0
Bavaro	22	278	12.6	29	3
Ingram	17	290	17.1	41t	1
Carthon	15	132	8.8	18	0
Baker	13	255	19.6	39t	2
Rouson	7	121	17.3	39	0
Cross	6	107	17.8	27	1
Robinson	4	41	10.3	16	0
Adams	2	7	3.5	10	0
Banks	1	22	22.0	22t	1
Tillman	1	9	9.0	9	0
Giants	248	3355	13.5	62t	17
Opponents	273	3427	12.6	71t	16

Interceptions

	No.	Yds.	Avg.	LG	TD
Kinard	5	135	27.0	58t	1
P. Johnson	3	60	20.0	39t	1
P. Williams	3	14	4.7	14	0
Guyton	2	27	13.5	14	0
S. White	2	18	9.0	18	0
Collins	2	12	6.0	12	0
A. White	2	8	4.0	9	0
Reasons	1	40	40.0	40	0
DeOssie	1	10	10.0	10	0
Banks	1	6	6.0	6	0
Giants	22	330	15.0	58t	2
Opponents	16	240	15.0	60t	2

Punting

	No.	Yds.	Avg.	In 20	LG
Landeta	70	3019	43.1	19	71
Giants	70	3019	43.1	19	71
Opponents	74	2964	40.1	15	91

Punt Returns

	No.	FC	Yds.	Avg.	LG	TD
Meggett	46	14	582	12.7	76t	1
Giants	46	14	582	12.7	76t	1
Opponents	29	15	236	8.1	23	0

Kickoff Returns

	No.	Yds.	Avg.	LG	TD
Meggett	27	577	21.4	43	0
Ingram	22	332	15.1	29	0
Rouson	1	17	17.0	17	0
Collins	1	0	0.0	0	0
Giants	51	926	18.2	43	0
Opponents	73	1306	17.9	63	0

Sacks

	No.
Taylor	15.0
Marshall	9.5
Howard	5.5
Banks	4.0
Collins	1.0
Cooks	1.0
Cox	1.0
P. Johnson	1.0
Reasons	1.0
Giants	39.0
Opponents	46.0

1990 Draft Choices

Round	Name	Pos.	College
1.	Rodney Hampton	RB	Georgia
2.	Mike Fox	DT	West Virginia
3.	Greg Mark	DE	Miami
4.	David Whitmore	DB	Stephen F. Austin
5.	Craig Kupp	QB	Pacific Lutheran
7.	Aaron Emanuel	RB	Southern California
8.	Barry Voorhees	T	Cal St.-Northridge
9.	Clint James	DE	Louisiana State
10.	Otis Moore	DT	Clemson
11.	Tim Downing	DE	Washington State
12.	Matt Stover	K	Louisiana Tech

New York Giants 1990 Veteran Roster

No.	Name	Pos.	Ht.	Wt.	Birth-date	NFL Exp.	College	Hometown	How Acq.	'89 Games/ Starts
2	Allegre, Raul	K	5-10	167	6/15/59	8	Texas	Torreon, Mexico	FA-'86	10/0
24	†Anderson, Ottis	RB	6-2	225	11/19/57	12	Miami	West Palm Beach, Fla.	T(StL)-'86	16/16
85	Baker, Stephen	WR	5-8	160	8/30/64	4	Fresno State	San Antonio, Tex.	D3-'87	15/4
58	Banks, Carl	LB	6-4	235	8/29/62	7	Michigan State	Flint, Mich.	D1-'84	16/16
89	Bavaro, Mark	TE	6-4	245	4/28/63	6	Notre Dame	Danvers, Mass.	D4-'85	7/7
44	†Carthon, Maurice	RB	6-1	225	4/24/61	6	Arkansas State	Osceola, Ark.	FA-'85	16/10
25	†Collins, Mark	CB	5-10	190	1/16/64	5	Cal State-Fullerton	San Bernardino, Calif.	D2-'86	16/16
98	Cooks, Johnie	LB	6-4	251	11/23/58	9	Mississippi State	Leland, Miss.	FA-'88	16/13
87	Cross, Howard	TE	6-5	245	8/8/67	2	Alabama	Huntsville, Ala.	D6-'89	16/4
99	DeOssie, Steve	LB	6-2	248	11/22/62	7	Boston College	Tacoma, Wash.	FA-'89	9/3
77	†Dorsey, Eric	DE	6-5	280	8/5/64	5	Notre Dame	McLean, Va.	D1-'86	2/2
76	Elliott, John	T	6-7	305	4/1/65	3	Michigan	Lake Ronkonkoma, N.Y.	D2-'88	13/11
26	Feggins, Howard	CB	5-10	190	5/6/65	3	North Carolina-Charlotte	South Hill, Va.	PB(NE)-'90#	11/0*
29	Guyton, Myron	S	6-1	205	8/26/67	2	Eastern Kentucky	Metcalf, Ga.	D8-'89	16/15
15	Hostetler, Jeff	QB	6-3	212	4/22/61	6	West Virginia	Johnston, Pa.	D3-'84	16/1
74	†Howard, Erik	NT	6-4	268	11/12/64	5	Washington State	San Jose, Calif.	D2a-'86	16/16
82	Ingram, Mark	WR	5-10	188	8/23/65	4	Michigan State	Rockford, Ill.	D1-'87	16/3
47	Jackson, Greg	S	6-1	200	8/20/66	2	Louisiana State	Hialeah, Fla.	D3a-'89	16/1
54	†Jiles, Dwayne	LB	6-4	245	11/23/61	6	Texas Tech	Linden, Tex.	FA-'89	9/0
52	Johnson, Pepper	LB	6-3	248	6/29/64	5	Ohio State	Detroit, Mich.	D2b-'86	14/4
61	Kratch, Bob	G	6-3	288	1/6/66	2	Iowa	Mahwah, N.J.	D3-'89	4/1
5	†Landeta, Sean	P	6-0	200	1/6/62	5	Towson State	Baltimore, Md.	FA-'85	16/0
86	Manuel, Lionel	WR	5-11	180	4/13/62	7	Pacific	La Puente, Calif.	D7-'84	16/12
70	Marshall, Leonard	DE	6-3	285	10/22/61	8	Louisiana State	Franklin, La.	D2-'83	16/16
30	Meggett, David	RB-KR	5-7	180	4/3/66	2	Towson State	Charleston, S.C.	D5-'89	16/2
60	Moore, Eric	T	6-5	290	1/21/65	3	Indiana	Berkeley, Mo.	D1-'88	16/13
20	†Morris, Joe	RB	5-7	195	9/15/60	9	Syracuse	Ayer, Mass.	D2-'82	0*
80	Mrosko, Bob	TE	6-5	270	11/13/65	2	Penn State	Cleveland, Ohio	PB(Hou)-'90#	15/14*
65	Oates, Bart	C	6-3	265	12/16/58	6	Brigham Young	Albany, Ga.	FA-'85	16/16
55	†Reasons, Gary	LB	6-4	234	2/18/62	7	Northwestern Louisiana	Cowely, Tex.	D4a-'84	16/12
72	Riesenberg, Doug	T	6-5	275	7/22/65	4	California	Moscow, Idaho	D6a-'87	16/16
66	Roberts, William	T	6-5	280	8/5/62	6	Ohio State	Miami, Fla.	D1a-'84	16/16
81	†Robinson, Stacy	WR	5-11	186	2/19/62	6	North Dakota State	St. Paul, Minn.	D2-'85	6/0
22	†Rouson, Lee	RB	6-1	222	10/18/62	6	Colorado	Greensboro, N.C.	D8-'85	16/0
11	Simms, Phil	QB	6-3	214	11/3/56	11	Morehead State	Louisville, Ky.	D1-'79	15/15
56	Taylor, Lawrence	LB	6-3	243	2/4/59	10	North Carolina	Williamsburg, Va.	D1-'81	16/15
21	Thompson, Reyna	CB	6-0	193	8/28/63	5	Baylor	Dallas, Tex.	PB(Mia)-'89#	16/0
34	Tillman, Lewis	RB	6-0	195	4/16/66	2	Jackson State	Oklahoma City, Okla.	D4-'89	16/0
83	Turner, Odessa	WR	6-3	205	10/12/64	4	Northwestern Louisiana	Monroe, La.	D4-'87	13/10
73	Washington, John	DE	6-4	275	2/20/63	5	Oklahoma State	Houston, Tex.	D3-'86	16/14
36	White, Adrian	S	6-0	200	4/6/64	4	Florida	Orange Park, Fla.	D2-'87	15/0
39	White, Sheldon	CB-S	5-11	188	3/1/65	3	Miami, Ohio	Dayton, Ohio	D3-'88	16/1
59	Williams, Brian	C-G	6-5	300	6/8/66	2	Minnesota	Mt. Lebanon, Pa.	D1-'89	14/4
23	Williams, Perry	CB	6-2	203	5/12/61	7	North Carolina State	Hamlet, N.C.	D7-'83	16/16

* Feggins played 11 games with Denver in '89; Morris missed '89 season due to injury; Mrosko played 15 games with Houston.

† Option playout; subject to developments.

Plan B unconditional free agent.

Retired—Karl Nelson, 6-year tackle, 0 games in '89.

Players lost through Plan B (10): RB George Adams (NE; 14 games in '89), S Greg Cox (SF; 16), DE Mark Duckens (Det; 15), G Damian Johnson (NE; 4), S Terry Kinard (Hou; 16), TE Zeke Mowatt (NE; 16), K Bjorn Nittmo (KC; 6), QB Jeff Rutledge (Wash; 1), DE Robb White (Den; 15), C Frank Winters (KC; 15).

Also played with Giants in '89—LB Ricky Shaw (7 games).

COACHING STAFF

Head Coach,
Bill Parcells

Pro Career: Became twelfth head coach in New York Giants history on December 15, 1982. Led Giants to Super Bowl XXI victory over Denver 39-20 after Wild Card playoff berths in both 1984 and 1985. Parcells begins eighth campaign as head coach after spending two seasons as the Giants' defensive coordinator and linebacker coach. Started pro coaching career in 1980 as linebacker coach with New England Patriots. Career record: 69-49-1.

Background: Linebacker at Wichita State 1961-63. College assistant Hastings (Neb.) 1964, Wichita State 1965, Army 1966-69, Florida State 1970-72, Vanderbilt 1973-74, Texas Tech 1975-77, Air Force 1978 (head coach).

Personal: Born August 22, 1941, Englewood, N.J. Bill and his wife, Judy, live in Upper Saddle River, N.J., and have three daughters—Suzy, Jill, and Dallas.

Assistant Coaches

Bill Belichick, defensive coordinator/secondary; born April 16, 1952, Nashville, Tenn., lives in Chatham, N.J. Center-tight end Wesleyan 1972-74. No pro playing experience. Pro coach: Baltimore Colts 1975, Detroit Lions 1976-77, Denver Broncos 1978, joined Giants in 1979.

Tom Coughlin, receivers; born August 31, 1946, Waterloo, N.Y., lives in Sparta, N.J. Halfback Syracuse 1965-67. No pro playing experience. College coach: Rochester Tech 1969-73 (head coach), Syracuse 1974-80, Boston College 1981-83. Pro coach: Philadelphia Eagles 1984-85, Green Bay Packers 1986-87, joined Giants in 1988.

Romeo Crennel, defensive line; born June 18, 1947, Lynchburg, Va., lives in Montvale, N.J. Defensive lineman Western Kentucky 1966-69. No pro playing experience. College coach: Western Kentucky 1970-74, Texas Tech 1975-77, Mississippi 1978-79, Georgia Tech 1980. Pro coach: Joined Giants in 1981.

Ron Erhardt, offensive coordinator; born February 27, 1932, Mandan, N.D., lives in Wykoff, N.J. Quarterback Jamestown (N.D.) College 1951-54. No pro playing experience. College coach: North Dakota State 1963-72 (head coach 1966-72). Pro coach: New England Patriots 1973-81 (head coach 1979-81), joined Giants in 1982.

Al Groh, linebackers; born July 13, 1944, New York City, lives in Randolph, N.J. Defensive end Virginia 1964-67. No pro playing experience. College coach: Army 1968-69, Virginia 1970-72, North Carolina 1973-77, Air Force 1978-79, Texas Tech 1980, Wake Forest 1981-86 (head coach), South Carolina 1988. Pro coach: Atlanta Falcons 1987, joined Giants in 1989.

Ray Handley, running backs; born October 8, 1944, Artesia, N.M., lives in West Orange, N.J. Running back Stanford 1963-65. No pro playing experience. College coach: Stanford 1967, 1971-74, 1979-83, Army 1968-69, Air Force 1975-78. Pro coach: Joined Giants in 1984.

Fred Hoaglin, offensive line; born January 28, 1944, Alliance, Ohio, lives in Sparta, N.J. Center Pittsburgh 1962-65. Pro center Cleveland Browns 1966-72, Baltimore Colts 1973, Houston Oilers 1974-75, Seattle Seahawks 1976. Pro coach: Detroit Lions 1978-84, joined Giants in 1985.

Johnny Parker, strength and conditioning; born February 1, 1947, Greenville, S.C., lives in Montvale, N.J. Graduate of Mississippi, master's degree from Delta State University. No college or pro playing experience. College coach: South Carolina 1974-76, Indiana 1977-79, Louisiana State 1980, Mississippi 1981-83. Pro coach: Joined Giants in 1984.

Mike Pope, tight ends; born March 15, 1942, Monroe, N.C., lives in River Vale, N.J. Quarterback Lenoir Rhyne 1962-64. No pro playing experience. College coach: Florida State 1970-74, Texas Tech 1975-77, Mississippi 1978-82. Pro coach: Joined Giants in 1983.

New York Giants 1990 First-Year Roster

Name	Pos.	Ht.	Wt.	Birth-date	College	Hometown	How Acq.
Abrams, Bobby	LB	6-3	230	4/12/67	Michigan	Detroit, Mich.	FA
Apolskis, Richard	G	6-3	288	1/6/67	Arkansas	Houston, Tex.	FA
Barlow, Gary	G	6-4	281	3/26/67	Pacific	Tracy, Calif.	FA
Baur, Frank	QB	6-4	220	7/5/66	Lafayette	Wilkes-Barre, Pa.	FA
Boysaw, Greg	CB-S	6-1	207	12/11/66	Illinois	Urbana, Ill.	FA
Brown, Roy	G	6-4	270	10/27/67	Virginia	Urbana, Ohio	FA
Bryant, Win	NT	6-3	274	11/7/66	Nicholls State	Miami, Fla.	FA
Cunningham, Ed	T	6-8	295	5/10/66	Texas	Wichita Falls, Kan.	FA
Dennis, Mark	LB	6-1	238	10/25/67	Central Michigan	Windsor, Canada	FA
Downing, Tim	DE	6-5	260	4/9/67	Washington State	Chico, Calif.	D11
Doyen, William	T	6-8	328	12/19/64	West Virginia Tech	Queens, N.Y.	FA
Emanuel, Aaron	RB	6-2	225	1/10/67	Southern California	Palmdale, Calif.	D7
Fishback, Joe	CB-S	5-11	198	11/29/87	Carson-Newman	Knoxville, Tenn.	FA
Fox, Mike	DE	6-6	275	8/5/67	West Virginia	Akron, Ohio	D2
Greene, Terrance	CB-S	6-3	210	4/26/67	DePaul	Flint, Mich.	FA
Grider, David	NT	6-3	290	1/7/67	Northeast Oklahoma	Muskogee, Okla.	FA
Hampton, Rodney	RB	5-11	215	4/3/69	Georgia	Houston, Tex.	D1
Holmes, Jeffrey	CB-S	6-2	212	8/8/67	Azusa Pacific	Los Angeles, Calif.	FA
James, Clint	DE	6-6	270	4/17/67	Louisiana State	New Orleans, La.	D9
Kupp, Craig	QB	6-4	215	4/14/67	Pacific Lutheran	Sunnyside, Wash.	D5
Kyles, Troy	WR	6-0	180	8/13/68	Howard University	Lorain, Ohio	FA
Lang, Bruce	WR	6-0	184	1/25/66	Fairmont State	Tampa, Fla.	FA
Lindsey, Michael	LB	6-1	240	1/30/66	Southern University	New Orleans, La.	FA
Lock, Andy	T	6-3	275	9/16/67	Missouri	Carrollton, Mo.	FA
Mark, Greg	DE	6-2	252	7/7/67	Miami	Pennsauken, N.J.	D3
Millington, Sean	RB	6-2	225	2/1/68	Simon-Fraser	Vancouver, Canada	FA
Molander, Scooter (1)	QB	6-2	200	10/26/66	Colorado State	Colorado Springs, Colo.	FA
Moore, Otis	NT	6-4	270	4/26/67	Clemson	Augusta, Ga.	D10
Ng, Philip	WR	6-0	185	7/7/66	Lafayette	San Francisco, Calif.	FA
Riddick, Michael	WR	6-3	195	1/7/68	Delaware State	Plainfield, N.J.	FA
Robinson, Chad	LB	6-3	230	6/18/67	Brigham Young	Provo, Utah	FA
Sanders, Terrance	DE	6-6	330	8/18/67	Grambling	Detroit, Mich.	FA
Seay, Clarence	WR	5-9	170	8/11/67	Texas-El Paso	El Paso, Tex.	FA
Smith, Billy (1)	P	5-11	190	9/30/66	Tenn.-Chattanooga	St. Louis, Mo.	FA
Stover, Matt	K	5-11	178	1/27/68	Louisiana Tech	Dallas, Tex.	D12
Thorson, Chad	LB	6-2	243	7/6/67	Wheaton	Columbus, Ohio	FA
Vines, Kenneth	C	6-4	285	5/3/67	Central State, Ohio	Baltimore, Md.	FA
Voorhees, Barry	G	6-5	290	12/7/63	Cal State-Northridge	Goleta, Calif.	D8
Whitmore, David	S	6-0	235	7/6/67	Stephen F. Austin	Daingerfield, Tex.	D4

The term NFL Rookie is defined as a player who is in his first season of professional football and has not been on the roster of another professional football team for any regular-season or postseason games. A Rookie is designated by an "R" on NFL rosters. Players who have been active in another professional football league or players who have NFL experience, including either preseason training camp or being on an active roster for fewer than three regular-season or postseason games, are termed NFL First-Year Players. An NFL First-Year Player is designated by a "1" on NFL rosters. Thereafter, a player on an NFL active roster for at least three regular-season or postseason games is credited with an additional year of NFL playing experience.

NOTES

_____
_____
_____
_____
_____
_____
_____
_____
_____
_____
_____
_____
_____

Mike Sweatman, special teams; born October 23, 1946, Kansas City, Mo., lives in Wayne, N.J. Linebacker Kansas 1964-67. No pro playing experience. College coach: Kansas 1973-74, 1979-82, Tulsa 1977-78, Tennessee 1983. Pro coach: Minnesota Vikings 1984, joined Giants in 1985.

PHILADELPHIA EAGLES

National Football Conference Eastern Division

Team Colors: Kelly Green, Silver, and White

**Veterans Stadium
Broad Street and Pattison Avenue
Philadelphia, Pennsylvania 19148
Telephone: (215) 463-2500**

Club Officials

Owner: Norman Braman
President-Chief Operating Officer: Harry Gamble
Vice President-Chief Financial Officer: Mimi Box
Vice President-Marketing and Development:
  Decker Uhlhorn
Asst. to the President: George Azar, Patrick Forte
Director of Player Personnel: Joe Woolley
Asst. to Director of Player Personnel:
  Tom Gamble
Director of Public Relations: Ron Howard
Asst. Director of Public Relations: Rich Burg
Asst. Director of Marketing: Suzi Braman
Associate Directors of Sales and Marketing:
  Jim Gallagher, Leslie Stephenson
Director of Administration: Vicki Chatley
Ticket Manager: Leo Carlin
Director of Penthouse Sales: Lou Scheinfeld
Asst. Director of Penthouse Sales: Ken Iman
Trainer: Otho Davis
Asst. Trainer: David Price
Player Relations Consultant: Lem Burnham, Ph.D.
Equipment Manager: Rusty Sweeney
Video Director: Mike Dougherty

Stadium: Veterans Stadium •
  Capacity: 65,356
  Broad Street and Pattison Avenue
  Philadelphia, Pennsylvania 19148

Playing Surface: AstroTurf-8

Training Camp: West Chester University
  West Chester, Pennsylvania
  19382

1990 Schedule

Preseason
Aug. 11	**New York Jets**	7:30
Aug. 18	**Miami**	7:30
Aug. 27	at Indianapolis	7:00
Sept. 1	at Pittsburgh	9:00

Regular Season
Sept. 9	at New York Giants	8:00
Sept. 16	**Phoenix**	1:00
Sept. 23	at Los Angeles Rams	1:00
Sept. 30	**Indianapolis**	1:00
Oct. 7	**Open Date**	
Oct. 15	**Minnesota** (Monday)	9:00
Oct. 21	at Washington	1:00
Oct. 28	at Dallas	12:00
Nov. 4	**New England**	1:00
Nov. 12	**Washington** (Monday)	9:00
Nov. 18	at Atlanta	1:00
Nov. 25	**New York Giants**	1:00
Dec. 2	at Buffalo	1:00
Dec. 9	at Miami	8:00
Dec. 16	**Green Bay**	4:00
Dec. 23	**Dallas**	1:00
Dec. 29	at Phoenix (Saturday)	2:00

Eagles Coaching History
(323-407-24)
1933-35	Lud Wray	9-21-1
1936-40	Bert Bell	10-44-2
1941-50	Earle (Greasy) Neale*	66-44-5
1951	Alvin (Bo) McMillin**	2-0-0
1951	Wayne Millner	2-8-0
1952-55	Jim Trimble	25-20-3
1956-57	Hugh Devore	7-16-1
1958-60	Lawrence (Buck) Shaw	20-16-1
1961-63	Nick Skorich	15-24-3
1964-68	Joe Kuharich	28-41-1
1969-71	Jerry Williams***	7-22-2
1971-72	Ed Khayat	8-15-2
1973-75	Mike McCormack	16-25-1
1976-82	Dick Vermeil	57-51-0
1983-85	Marion Campbell****	17-29-1
1985	Fred Bruney	1-0-0
1986-89	Buddy Ryan	33-31-1

*Co-coach with Walt Kiesling in Philadelphia-Pittsburgh
  merger in 1943
**Retired after two games in 1951
***Released after three games in 1971
****Released after 15 games in 1985

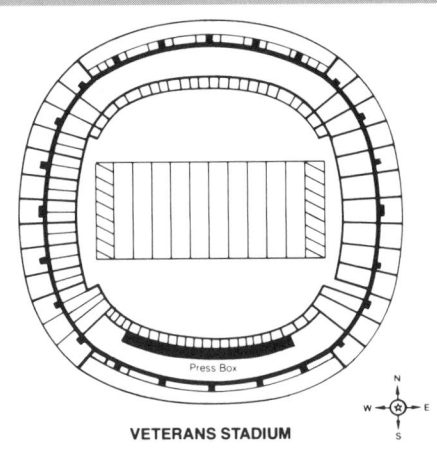

VETERANS STADIUM

Record Holders
Individual Records—Career
Category	Name	Performance
Rushing (Yds.)	Wilbert Montgomery, 1977-1984	6,538
Passing (Yds.)	Ron Jaworski, 1977-1986	26,963
Passing (TDs)	Ron Jaworski, 1977-1986	175
Receiving (No.)	Harold Carmichael, 1971-1983	589
Receiving (Yds.)	Harold Carmichael, 1971-1983	8,978
Interceptions	Bill Bradley, 1969-1976	34
Punting (Avg.)	Joe Muha, 1946-1950	42.9
Punt Return (Avg.)	Steve Van Buren, 1944-1951	13.9
Kickoff Return (Avg.)	Steve Van Buren, 1944-1951	26.7
Field Goals	Paul McFadden, 1984-87	91
Touchdowns (Tot.)	Harold Carmichael, 1971-1983	79
Points	Bobby Walston, 1951-1962	881

Individual Records—Single Season
Category	Name	Performance
Rushing (Yds.)	Wilbert Montgomery, 1979	1,512
Passing (Yds.)	Randall Cunningham, 1988	3,808
Passing (TDs)	Sonny Jurgensen, 1961	32
Receiving (No.)	Keith Jackson, 1988	81
Receiving (Yds.)	Mike Quick, 1983	1,409
Interceptions	Bill Bradley, 1971	11
Punting (Avg.)	Joe Muha, 1948	47.2
Punt Return (Avg.)	Steve Van Buren, 1944	15.3
Kickoff Return (Avg.)	Al Nelson, 1972	29.1
Field Goals	Paul McFadden, 1984	30
Touchdowns (Tot.)	Steve Van Buren, 1945	18
Points	Paul McFadden, 1984	116

Individual Records—Single Game
Category	Name	Performance
Rushing (Yds.)	Steve Van Buren, 11-27-49	205
Passing (Yds.)	Bobby Thomason, 11-18-53	437
Passing (TDs)	Adrian Burk, 10-17-54	*7
Receiving (No.)	Don Looney, 12-1-40	14
Receiving (Yds.)	Tommy McDonald, 12-10-60	237
Interceptions	Russ Craft, 9-24-50	*4
Field Goals	Tom Dempsey, 11-12-72	6
Touchdowns (Tot.)	Many times	4
	Last time by Wilbert Montgomery, 10-7-79	
Points	Bobby Walston, 10-17-54	25

*NFL Record

1989 Team Record
Preseason (4-1)

Date	Result		Opponents
8/6	W	17-13	vs. Cleveland at London, England
8/12	W	23-17	Atlanta
8/20	L	10-19	vs. N.Y. Jets at Raleigh, N.C.
8/26	W	38-14	Pittsburgh
9/2	W	20-10	at Miami
		108-73	

Regular Season (11-5)

Date	Result		Opponents	Att.
9/10	W	31- 7	Seattle	64,287
9/17	W	42-37	at Washington	53,493
9/24	L	28-38	San Francisco	66,042
10/2	L	13-27	at Chicago	66,625
10/8	W	21-19	N.Y. Giants	65,688
10/15	W	17- 5	at Phoenix	42,620
10/22	W	10- 7	L.A. Raiders	64,019
10/29	W	28-24	at Denver	75,065
11/5	L	17-20	at San Diego	47,019
11/12	L	3-10	Washington	65,443
11/19	W	10- 9	Minnesota	65,944
11/23	W	27- 0	at Dallas	54,444
12/3	W	24-17	at N.Y. Giants	74,809
12/10	W	20-10	Dallas	59,842
12/18	L	20-30	at New Orleans	59,218
12/24	W	31-14	Phoenix	43,287

Postseason (0-1)

Date	Result		Opponent	Att.
12/31	L	7-21	L.A. Rams	65,479

Score by Periods

Eagles	61	91	84	106	0	—	342
Opponents	74	74	47	79	0	—	274

Attendance
Home 494,552   Away 473,293   Total 967,845
Single-game home record, 72,111 (11-1-81)
Single-season home record, 557,325 (1980)

1989 Team Statistics

	Eagles	Opp.
Total First Downs	321	281
Rushing	120	81
Passing	171	171
Penalty	30	29
Third Down: Made/Att.	97/246	79/217
Third Down: Pct.	39.4	36.4
Fourth Down: Made/Att.	6/13	5/15
Fourth Down: Pct.	46.2	33.3
Total Net Yards	5320	4894
Avg. Per Game	332.5	305.9
Total Plays	1123	1017
Avg. Per Play	4.7	4.8
Net Yards Rushing	2208	1605
Avg. Per Game	138.0	100.3
Total Rushes	540	426
Net Yards Passing	3112	3289
Avg. Per Game	194.5	205.6
Sacked/Yards Lost	45/343	62/424
Gross Yards	3455	3713
Att./Completions	538/294	529/258
Completion Pct.	54.6	48.8
Had Intercepted	16	30
Punts/Avg.	87/39.0	85/42.0
Net Punting Avg.	35.3	35.5
Penalties/Yards Lost	114/938	118/956
Fumbles/Ball Lost	43/16	44/26
Touchdowns	40	33
Rushing	14	6
Passing	23	26
Returns	3	1
Avg. Time of Possession	30:43	29:17

1989 Individual Statistics

Scoring

	TD R	TD P	TD Rt	PAT	FG	Saf	TP
Ruzek, Dall.-Phil.	0	0	0	28/29	13/22	0	67
Ruzek, Phil.	0	0	0	14/14	8/11	0	38
Carter	0	11	0	0/0	0/0	0	66
Zendejas	0	0	0	23/23	9/15	0	50
Byars	5	0	0	0/0	0/0	0	30
Cunningham	4	0	0	0/0	0/0	0	24
Jackson	0	3	0	0/0	0/0	0	18
Toney	3	0	0	0/0	0/0	0	18
DeLine	0	0	0	3/3	3/7	0	12
Garrity	0	2	0	0/0	0/0	0	12
Giles	0	2	0	0/0	0/0	0	12
Quick	0	2	0	0/0	0/0	0	12
Sherman	2	0	0	0/0	0/0	0	12
Carson, K.C.-Phil.	0	1	0	0/0	0/0	0	6
Drummond	0	1	0	0/0	0/0	0	6
Everett	0	0	1	0/0	0/0	0	6
Johnson	0	1	0	0/0	0/0	0	6
Little	0	1	0	0/0	0/0	0	6
Simmons	0	0	1	0/0	0/0	0	6
Waters	0	0	1	0/0	0/0	0	6
Harris	0	0	0	0/0	0/0	1	2
Eagles	14	23	3	40/40	20/33	1	342
Opponents	6	26	1	30/33	14/26	2	274

Passing

	Att.	Comp.	Yds.	Pct.	TD	Int.	Tkld.	Rate
Cunningham	532	290	3400	54.5	21	15	45/343	75.5
Cavanaugh	5	3	33	60.0	1	1	0/0	79.6
Ruzek	1	1	22	100.0	1	0	0/0	158.3
Eagles	538	294	3455	54.6	23	16	45/343	76.2
Opponents	529	258	3713	48.8	26	30	62/424	64.7

Rushing

	Att.	Yds.	Avg.	LG	TD
Cunningham	104	621	6.0	51	4
Toney	172	582	3.4	44	3
Byars	133	452	3.4	16t	5
Higgs	49	184	3.8	13	0
Sherman	40	177	4.4	37	2
Drummond	32	127	4.0	16	0
Reichenbach	1	30	30.0	30	0
Teltschik	1	23	23.0	23	0
Carter	2	16	8.0	11	0
Runager	2	5	2.5	5	0
Johnson	1	3	3.0	3	0
Cavanaugh	2	−3	−1.5	0	0
Carson	1	−9	−9.0	−9	0
Eagles	540	2208	4.1	51	14
Opponents	426	1605	3.8	58	6

Receiving

	No.	Yds.	Avg.	LG	TD
Byars	68	721	10.6	60	0
Jackson	63	648	10.3	33	3
Carter	45	605	13.4	42	11
Johnson	20	295	14.8	34	1
Toney	19	124	6.5	15	0
Drummond	17	180	10.6	21	1
Giles	16	225	14.1	66t	2
Quick	13	228	17.5	40	2
Garrity	13	209	16.1	31	2
Carson, K.C.-Phil.	8	107	13.4	28	1
Carson, Phil.	1	12	12.0	12	0
Sherman	8	85	10.6	17	0
Williams	4	32	8.0	11	0
Higgs	3	9	3.0	8	0
Edwards	2	74	37.0	66	0
Little	2	8	4.0	7	1
Ruzek, Dall.-Phil.	1	4	4.0	4	0
Eagles	294	3455	11.8	66t	23
Opponents	258	3713	14.4	80t	26

Interceptions

	No.	Yds.	Avg.	LG	TD
Allen	8	38	4.8	18	0
Everett	4	64	16.0	30t	1
Frizzell	4	58	14.5	27	0
Jenkins	4	58	14.5	22	0
Evans	3	23	7.7	15	0
Harris	2	18	9.0	11	0
Simmons	1	60	60.0	60t	1
Golic	1	23	23.0	23	0
Waters	1	20	20.0	20	0
Bell	1	13	13.0	13	0
Joyner	1	0	0.0	0	0
Eagles	30	375	12.5	60t	2
Opponents	16	147	9.2	37	0

Punting

	No.	Yds.	Avg.	In 20	LG
Cunningham	6	319	53.2	3	91
Teltschik	57	2246	39.4	12	58
Tuten	7	256	36.6	1	45
Runager	17	568	33.4	5	52
Ruzek, Dall.-Phil.	1	28	28.0	0	28
Eagles	87	3389	39.0	21	91
Opponents	85	3571	42.0	19	71

Punt Returns

	No.	FC	Yds.	Avg.	LG	TD
Williams	30	7	267	8.9	24	0
Edwards	7	5	64	9.1	28	0
Eagles	37	12	331	8.9	28	0
Opponents	37	21	215	5.8	16	0

Kickoff Returns

	No.	Yds.	Avg.	LG	TD
Higgs	16	293	18.3	30	0
Williams	14	249	17.8	28	0
Sherman	13	222	17.1	45	0
Edwards	3	23	7.7	11	0
Little	2	14	7.0	12	0
Byars	1	27	27.0	27	0
Eagles	49	828	16.9	45	0
Opponents	60	1307	21.8	93t	1

Sacks

	No.
Simmons	15.5
White	11.0
Brown	10.5
Pitts	7.0
Joyner	5.0
Hopkins	3.5
Golic	3.0
Evans	2.0
Harris	2.0
Frizzell	1.5
Waters	1.0
Eagles	62.0
Opponents	45.0

1990 Draft Choices

Round	Name	Pos.	College
1.	Ben Smith	DB	Georgia
2.	Mike Bellamy	WR	Illinois
3.	Fred Barnett	WR	Arkansas State
5.	Calvin Williams	WR	Purdue
6.	Kevin Thompson	DB	Oklahoma
7.	Terry Strouf	T	Wis.-LaCrosse
8.	Curt Dykes	T	Oregon
9.	Cecil Gray	DT	North Carolina
10.	Orlando Adams	DT	Jacksonville State
11.	John Hudson	C	Auburn
	Tyrone Watson	WR	Tennessee State
12.	Judd Garrett	RB	Princeton

Philadelphia Eagles 1990 Veteran Roster

No.	Name	Pos.	Ht.	Wt.	Birth-date	NFL Exp.	College	Hometown	How Acq.	'89 Games/ Starts
72	†Alexander, David	C-T	6-3	282	7/28/64	4	Tulsa	Broken Arrow, Okla.	D5-'87	16/16
21	Allen, Eric	CB	5-10	188	11/22/65	3	Arizona State	San Diego, Calif.	D2-'88	15/15
49	Bell, Todd	S	6-1	215	11/28/58	9	Ohio State	Middletown, Ohio	FA-'88	4/4
99	Brown, Jerome	DT	6-2	295	2/4/65	4	Miami	Brooksville, Fla.	D1-'87	16/16
41	†Byars, Keith	RB	6-1	238	10/14/63	5	Ohio State	Dayton, Ohio	D1-'86	16/15
80	Carter, Cris	WR	6-3	198	11/25/65	4	Ohio State	Middletown, Ohio	SD4-'87	16/15
6	Cavanaugh, Matt	QB	6-2	210	10/27/56	13	Pittsburgh	Youngstown, Ohio	T(SF)-'86	9/0
12	Cunningham, Randall	QB	6-4	203	3/27/63	6	Nevada-Las Vegas	Santa Barbara, Calif.	D2-'85	16/16
78	Darwin, Matt	T	6-4	275	3/11/63	5	Texas A&M	Spring, Tex.	D4-'86	15/12
36	Drummond, Robert	RB	6-1	205	6/21/67	2	Syracuse	Jamesville, N.Y.	D3a-'89	16/1
84	Edwards, Anthony	WR-KR	5-11	195	5/26/66	2	New Mexico Highlands	Casa Grande, Ariz.	FA-'89	9/0
56	†Evans, Byron	LB	6-2	235	2/23/64	4	Arizona	Phoenix, Ariz.	D4-'87	16/16
33	Frizzell, William	CB-S	6-3	206	9/8/62	7	North Carolina Central	Greenville, N.C.	FA-'86	16/0
86	†Garrity, Gregg	WR	5-10	175	11/24/60	7	Penn State	Bradford Woods, Pa.	W(Pitt)-'84	9/0
83	†Giles, Jimmie	TE	6-3	245	11/8/54	14	Alcorn State	Greenville, Miss.	FA-'89	16/5
90	Golic, Mike	DT	6-5	275	12/12/62	5	Notre Dame	Cleveland, Ohio	FA-'87	16/0
54	Hager, Britt	LB	6-1	222	2/20/66	2	Texas	Odessa, Tex.	D3b-'89	16/0
95	Harris, Al	LB	6-5	265	12/31/56	11	Arizona State	Bangor, Maine	PB(Chi)-'89#	16/16
73	†Heller, Ron	T	6-6	280	8/25/62	7	Penn State	East Meadow, N.Y.	T(Sea)-'88	16/16
34	†Hoage, Terry	S	6-3	201	4/11/62	7	Georgia	Huntsville, Tex.	FA-'86	6/0
48	†Hopkins, Wes	S	6-1	215	9/26/61	7	Southern Methodist	Birmingham, Ala.	D2a-'83	16/15
88	Jackson, Keith	TE	6-2	250	4/19/65	3	Oklahoma	Little Rock, Ark.	D1-'88	14/12
46	†Jenkins, Izel	CB	5-10	191	5/27/64	3	North Carolina State	Wilson, N.C.	D11-'88	16/13
85	Johnson, Ron	WR	6-3	190	9/21/58	6	Long Beach State	Monterey, Calif.	FA-'88	14/9
31	Jones, Tyrone	S	6-4	223	11/9/66	2	Arkansas State	Ruston, La.	FA-'89	3/0
59	Joyner, Seth	LB	6-2	248	11/18/64	5	Texas-El Paso	Spring Valley, N.Y.	D8-'86	14/14
94	†Kaufusi, Steve	DE-DT	6-4	274	10/17/63	2	Brigham Young	Salt Lake City, Utah	D12-'88	16/0
87	Le Bel, Harper	TE	6-4	251	7/14/63	2	Colorado State	Sherman Oaks, Calif.	PB(Sea)-'90#	16/0*
37	Lilly, Sammy	CB	5-9	178	2/12/65	2	Georgia Tech	Augusta, Ga.	FA-'89	15/0
74	Pitts, Mike	DT	6-5	277	9/25/60	8	Alabama	Baltimore, Md.	T(Atl)-'87	16/16
82	Quick, Mike	WR	6-2	195	5/14/59	9	North Carolina State	Richmond, N.C.	D1-'82	6/5
66	Reeves, Ken	T-G	6-5	270	10/4/61	6	Texas A&M	Pittsburg, Tex.	D6-'86	14/3
50	†Rimington, Dave	C-G	6-3	285	5/22/60	8	Nebraska	Omaha, Neb.	FA-'88	6/1
7	†Ruzek, Roger	K	6-1	195	12/17/60	4	Weber State	San Francisco, Calif.	FA-'89	14/0*
79	Schad, Mike	G	6-5	290	10/2/63	3	Queens College, Canada	Bellville, Ontario	PB(Rams)-'89#	16/16
51	Shaw, Ricky	LB	6-4	240	7/28/65	3	Oklahoma State	Fayetteville, N.C.	FA-'89	15/0*
23	Sherman, Heath	RB-KR	6-0	190	3/27/67	2	Texas A&I	El Campo, Tex.	D6-'89	15/1
96	Simmons, Clyde	DE	6-6	275	8/4/64	5	Western Carolina	Wilmington, N.C.	D9-'86	16/16
68	†Singletary, Reggie	G-T	6-3	285	1/17/64	4	North Carolina State	Whiteville, N.C.	FA-'89	1/0
52	Small, Jessie	LB	6-3	239	11/30/66	2	Eastern Kentucky	Boston, Ga.	D2-'89	16/1
65	Solt, Ron	G	6-3	288	5/19/62	6	Maryland	Wilkes Barre, Pa.	T(Ind)-'88	13/12
61	†Tamburello, Ben	G-C	6-3	278	9/9/64	3	Auburn	Birmingham, Ala.	D3-'87	16/4
10	Teltschik, John	P	6-2	210	3/8/64	5	Texas	Kerrville, Tex.	W(Chi)-'86	10/0
25	†Toney, Anthony	RB	6-0	227	9/23/62	5	Texas A&M	Salinas, Calif.	D2a-'86	14/14
20	Waters, Andre	S	5-11	199	3/10/62	7	Cheyney State	Pahokee, Fla.	FA-'84	16/13
47	Werner, Greg	TE	6-4	236	10/21/66	2	DePauw	Greenfield, Ind.	PB(NYJ)-'90#	10/0*
92	White, Reggie	DE	6-5	285	12/19/61	6	Tennessee	Chattanooga, Tenn.	SD1-'85	16/16

* Le Bel played 16 games with Seattle in '89; Ruzek played 9 games with Dallas, 5 with Philadelphia; Shaw played 7 games with N.Y. Giants; Werner played 10 games with N.Y. Jets.

† Option playout; subject to developments.

Plan B unconditional free agent.

Players lost through Plan B (6): LB Ty Allert (Den; 7 games in '89), CB Eric Everett (TB; 16), RB Mark Higgs (Mia; 15), TE David Little (Den; 16), LB Mike Reichenbach (Mia; 16), P Rick Tuten (Buff; 2).

Also played with Eagles in '89—WR Carlos Carson (6 games), K Steve DeLine (3), S Alan Dial (1), LB Dwayne Jiles (1), P Max Runager (4), WR Henry Williams (13), K Luis Zendejas (8).

COACHING STAFF

Head Coach, Buddy Ryan

Pro Career: Ryan led the Eagles to back-to-back playoff appearances in 1988 and 1989. During that span, Ryan's club compiled a 21-11 regular-season record and captured the NFC Eastern Division title in 1988 with a 10-6 mark. Ryan was named head coach of the Eagles on January 29, 1986, after eight seasons as the defensive coordinator of the Chicago Bears. An NFL assistant coach for 18 years, Ryan has been on the staffs of three Super Bowl teams: Jets, 1968; Vikings, 1976; and Bears, 1985. He served as defensive line coach under Bud Grant with the Minnesota Vikings in 1976-77 before joining Chicago. From 1968-75, he was on the defensive staff of the New York Jets under coach Weeb Ewbank. In Ryan's eight seasons as defensive coordinator with Chicago, his defenses ranked among the NFL's top 10 six times. He devised the "46 defense" with its multiple variations of alignments and coverages. Career record: 33-31-1.

Background: Ryan was a four-year letterman at Oklahoma State from 1952-55 as an offensive guard. While serving in the U.S. Army in Korea, Ryan played on the Fourth Army championship team in Japan. He served as an assistant at the University of Buffalo from 1961-65, Vanderbilt 1966, and the University of the Pacific 1967. Ryan has a master's degree in education from Middle Tennessee State.

Personal: Born James Ryan on February 17, 1934, Frederick, Okla. Buddy and his wife, Joan, live in Cherry Hill, N.J., and have three sons: Jimmy, Jr., Rex, and Robert.

Assistant Coaches

Dave Atkins, offensive backfield; born May 18, 1949, Victoria, Tex., lives in Marlton, N.J. Running back Texas-El Paso 1970-72. Pro running back San Francisco 49ers 1973, Honolulu Hawaiians (WFL) 1974, San Diego Chargers 1975. College coach: Texas-El Paso 1979-80, San Diego State 1981-85. Pro coach: Joined Eagles in 1986.

Tom Bettis, defensive backs; born March 17, 1933, Chicago, Ill., lives in Marlton, N.J. Linebacker-guard Purdue 1952-54. Linebacker Green Bay Packers 1955-61, Pittsburgh Steelers 1962, Chicago Bears 1963. Pro coach: Chicago Bears 1964-65 (scout), Kansas City Chiefs 1966-77, 1988, St. Louis Cardinals 1978-84, Cleveland Browns 1985, Houston Oilers 1986-87, joined Eagles in 1989.

Lew Carpenter, receivers; born January 12, 1932, Hayti, Mo. Running back-end Arkansas 1950-52. Pro running back-defensive back-end Detroit Lions 1953-55, Cleveland Browns 1957-58, Green Bay Packers 1959-63. College coach: Southwest Texas State 1989. Pro coach: Minnesota Vikings 1964-66, Atlanta Falcons 1967-68, Washington Redskins 1969-70, St. Louis Cardinals 1971-72, Houston Oilers 1973-74, Green Bay Packers 1975-85, Detroit Lions 1986-88, joined Eagles in 1990.

Jeff Fisher, defensive coordinator/linebackers; born February 25, 1958, Culver City, Calif., lives in Voorhees, N.J. Defensive back Southern California 1978-80. Pro defensive back-punt returner Chicago Bears 1981-85. Pro coach: Joined Eagles in 1986.

Dale Haupt, defensive line; born April 12, 1929, Manitowoc, Wis., lives in Cherry Hill, N.J. Defensive lineman-linebacker Wyoming 1950-53. No pro playing experience. College coach: Tennessee 1960-63, Iowa State 1964-65, Richmond 1966-71, North Carolina State 1972-76, Duke 1977. Pro coach: Chicago Bears 1978-85, joined Eagles in 1986.

Ronnie Jones, strength and conditioning/assistant linebackers; born October 17, 1955, Dumas, Tex., lives in Cherry Hill, N.J. Running back Northwestern State (Okla.) 1974-77. College coach: Northeastern State (Okla.) 1979-83, Tulsa 1984, Arizona State 1985-86. Pro coach: Joined Eagles in 1987.

Philadelphia Eagles 1990 First-Year Roster

Name	Pos.	Ht.	Wt.	Birth-date	College	Hometown	How Acq.
Adams, Orlando	DT	6-0	303	8/6/67	Jacksonville State	East Point, Ga.	D10
Bailey, David (1)	DE	6-4	240	9/3/65	Oklahoma State	Stillwater, Okla.	FA-'89
Barnett, Fred	WR	6-0	203	6/17/66	Arkansas State	Gunnison, Miss.	D3
Bellamy, Mike	WR	6-0	195	6/28/66	Illinois	Chicago, Ill.	D2
Berardelli, Paul (1)	G-C	6-2	276	11/19/67	Villanova	Scranton, Pa.	FA-'89
Dial, Alan (1)	S	6-1	188	2/2/65	UCLA	Anniston, Ala.	FA-'88
Dykes, Curt	T	6-3	274	12/27/67	Oregon	Hemet, Calif.	D8
Gabbard, Steve (1)	T	6-4	275	7/19/66	Florida State	Charlotte, N.C.	FA-'89
Garrett, Judd	RB	6-1	205	6/25/67	Princeton	Monmouth Beach, N.J.	D12
Gray, Cecil	DT	6-4	264	2/16/68	North Carolina	Norfolk, Va.	D9
Hudson, John	C	6-2	265	1/29/68	Auburn	Memphis, Tenn.	D11a
Porter, Mark (1)	K	6-0	190	12/3/65	Kansas State	Salinas, Kan.	FA
Salmon, David	P	6-4	220	5/16/65	North Carolina State	Raleigh, N.C.	FA
Sherman, Paul	G-T	6-5	315	9/5/67	East Tennessee State	Millington, Tenn.	FA
Smith, Ben	S	5-11	183	5/14/67	Georgia	Warner Robins, Ga.	D1
Strouf, Terry	T	6-2	285	10/1/66	Wisconsin-LaCrosse	Ojibwa, Wis.	D7
Thompson, Kevin	S	5-10	190	4/17/66	Oklahoma	Houston, Tex.	D6
Vaughn, Willie	WR	5-11	205	6/7/67	Kansas	Kansas City, Mo.	FA
Watson, Tyrone	WR	6-4	210	2/10/67	Tennessee State	Dawson, Ga.	D11b
Williams, Calvin	WR	5-11	181	3/3/67	Purdue	Baltimore, Md.	D5

The term NFL Rookie is defined as a player who is in his first season of professional football and has not been on the roster of another professional football team for any regular-season or postseason games. A Rookie is designated by an "R" on NFL rosters. Players who have been active in another professional football league or players who have NFL experience, including either preseason training camp or being on an active roster for fewer than three regular-season or postseason games, are termed NFL First-Year Players. An NFL First-Year Player is designated by a "1" on NFL rosters. Thereafter, a player on an NFL active roster for at least three regular-season or postseason games is credited with an additional year of NFL playing experience.

NOTES

Rich Kotite, offensive coordinator/quarterbacks; born October 13, 1942. Brooklyn, N.Y., lives in Philadelphia. End Wagner 1963-65. Pro tight end New York Giants 1967, 1969-72. Pittsburgh Steelers 1968. College coach: Tennessee-Chattanooga 1973-76. Pro coach: New Orleans Saints 1977, Cleveland Browns 1978-82, New York Jets 1983-89, joined Eagles in 1990.

Dan Neal, assistant offensive line; born August 30, 1949, Corbin, Ky., lives in Cherry Hill, N.J. Center Kentucky 1970-72. Pro center Baltimore Colts 1973-74, Chicago Bears 1975-83. Pro coach: Joined Eagles in 1986.

Al Roberts, special teams; born January 6, 1944, Fresno, Calif., lives in Marlton, N.J. Running back Washington 1964-65, Puget Sound 1967-68. No pro playing experience. College coach: Washington 1977-82, Purdue 1986, Wyoming 1987. Pro coach: Los Angeles Express (USFL) 1983-84, Houston Oilers 1984-85, joined Eagles in 1988.

Bill Walsh, offensive line; born September 8, 1927, Phillipsburg, N.J., lives in Marlton, N.J. Center Notre Dame 1945-48. Pro center Pittsburgh Steelers 1949-54. College coach: Notre Dame 1955-58, Kansas State 1959. Pro coach: Dallas Texans-Kansas City Chiefs 1960-74, Atlanta Falcons 1975-82, Houston Oilers 1983-86, joined Eagles in 1987.

PHOENIX CARDINALS

National Football Conference Eastern Division

Team Colors: Cardinal Red, Black, and White

P.O. Box 888
Phoenix, Arizona 85001-0888
Telephone: (602) 967-1010

Club Officials

President: William V. Bidwill
Executive Vice President: Joe Rhein
Vice President/General Manager: Larry Wilson
Vice President/Administration: Curt Mosher
Vice President/Communications: Terry Bledsoe
Secretary and General Counsel:
  Thomas J. Guilfoil
Treasurer: Charley Schlegel
Counsel: Bob Wallace
Director of Pro Personnel: Erik Widmark
Director of Player Personnel: George Boone
Public Relations Director: Paul Jensen
Media Coordinator: Greg Gladysiewski
Director of Community Relations: Adele Harris
Director of Marketing: Joe Castor
Ticket Manager: Steve Walsh
Trainer: John Omohundro
Assistant Trainers: Jim Shearer, Jeff Herndon
Equipment Manager: Mark Ahlemeier
Assistant Equipment Manager: Steve Christensen

Stadium: Sun Devil Stadium • **Capacity:** 72,000
    Fifth Street
    Tempe, Arizona 85287

Playing Surface: Grass

Training Camp: Northern Arizona University
    Flagstaff, Arizona 86011

1990 Schedule

Preseason

Aug. 11	**Seattle**	7:30
Aug. 18	**Chicago**	7:30
Aug. 25	at Los Angeles Rams	7:00
Aug. 31	at Denver	7:00

Regular Season

Sept. 9	at Washington	1:00
Sept. 16	at Philadelphia	1:00
Sept. 23	at New Orleans	12:00
Sept. 30	**Washington**	5:00
Oct. 7	**Open Date**	
Oct. 14	**Dallas**	1:00
Oct. 21	at New York Giants	4:00
Oct. 28	**Chicago**	2:00
Nov. 4	at Miami	1:00
Nov. 11	at Buffalo	1:00
Nov. 18	**Green Bay**	2:00
Nov. 25	**New England**	2:00
Dec. 2	**Indianapolis**	2:00
Dec. 9	at Atlanta	1:00
Dec. 16	at Dallas	12:00
Dec. 23	**New York Giants**	2:00
Dec. 29	**Philadelphia** (Saturday)	2:00

Cardinals Coaching History

Chicago 1920-59
St. Louis 1960-87
(366-482-39)

1920-22	John (Paddy) Driscoll	17-8-4
1923-24	Arnold Horween	13-8-1
1925-26	Norman Barry	16-8-2
1927	Guy Chamberlin	3-7-1
1928	Fred Gillies	1-5-0
1929	Dewey Scanlon	6-6-1
1930	Ernie Nevers	5-6-2
1931	LeRoy Andrews*	0-1-0
1931	Ernie Nevers	5-3-0
1932	Jack Chevigny	2-6-2
1933-34	Paul Schissler	6-15-1
1935-38	Milan Creighton	16-26-4
1939	Ernie Nevers	1-10-0
1940-42	Jimmy Conzelman	8-22-3
1943-45	Phil Handler**	1-29-0
1946-48	Jimmy Conzelman	27-10-0
1949	Phil Handler-Buddy Parker***	2-4-0
1949	Raymond (Buddy) Parker	4-1-1
1950-51	Earl (Curly) Lambeau****	7-15-0
1951	Phil Handler-Cecil Isbell#	1-1-0
1952	Joe Kuharich	4-8-0
1953-54	Joe Stydahar	3-20-1
1955-57	Ray Richards	14-21-1
1958-61	Frank (Pop) Ivy##	17-29-2
1961	Chuck Drulis-Ray Prochaska-Ray Willsey###	2-0-0
1962-65	Wally Lemm	27-26-3
1966-70	Charley Winner	35-30-5
1971-72	Bob Hollway	8-18-2
1973-77	Don Coryell	42-29-1
1978-79	Bud Wilkinson####	9-20-0
1979	Larry Wilson	2-1-0
1980-85	Jim Hanifan	39-50-1
1986-89	Gene Stallings@	23-34-1
1989	Hank Kuhlmann	0-5-0

*Resigned after one game in 1931
**Co-coach with Walt Kiesling in Chicago Cardinals-Pittsburgh merger in 1944
***Co-coaches for first six games in 1949
****Resigned after 10 games in 1951
#Co-coaches
##Resigned after 12 games in 1961
###Co-coaches
####Released after 13 games in 1979
@Released after 11 games in 1989

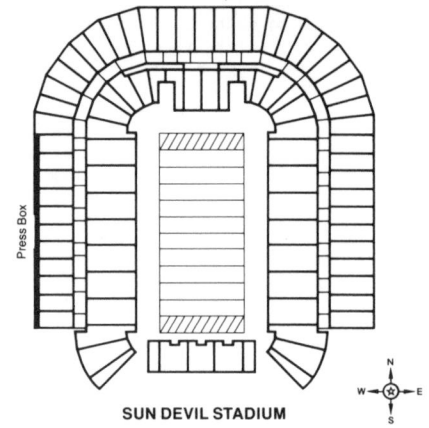

SUN DEVIL STADIUM

Record Holders

Individual Records — Career

Category	Name	Performance
Rushing (Yds.)	Ottis Anderson, 1979-1986	7,999
Passing (Yds.)	Jim Hart, 1966-1983	34,639
Passing (TDs)	Jim Hart, 1966-1983	209
Receiving (No.)	Jackie Smith, 1963-1977	480
Receiving (Yds.)	Jackie Smith, 1963-1977	7,918
Interceptions	Larry Wilson, 1960-1972	52
Punting (Avg.)	Jerry Norton, 1959-1961	44.9
Punt Return (Avg.)	Charley Trippi, 1947-1955	13.7
Kickoff Return (Avg.)	Ollie Matson, 1952, 1954-58	28.5
Field Goals	Jim Bakken, 1962-1978	282
Touchdowns (Tot.)	Roy Green, 1979-1989	62
Points	Jim Bakken, 1962-1978	1,380

Individual Records — Single Season

Category	Name	Performance
Rushing (Yds.)	Ottis Anderson, 1979	1,605
Passing (Yds.)	Neil Lomax, 1984	4,614
Passing (TDs)	Charley Johnson, 1963	28
	Neil Lomax, 1984	28
Receiving (No.)	J.T. Smith, 1987	91
Receiving (Yds.)	Roy Green, 1984	1,555
Interceptions	Bob Nussbaumer, 1949	12
Punting (Avg.)	Jerry Norton, 1960	45.6
Punt Return (Avg.)	John (Red) Cochran, 1949	20.9
Kickoff Return (Avg.)	Ollie Matson, 1958	35.5
Field Goals	Jim Bakken, 1967	27
Touchdowns (Tot.)	John David Crow, 1962	17
Points	Jim Bakken, 1967	117
	Neil O'Donoghue, 1984	117

Individual Records — Single Game

Category	Name	Performance
Rushing (Yds.)	John David Crow, 12-18-60	203
Passing (Yds.)	Neil Lomax, 12-16-84	468
Passing (TDs)	Jim Hardy, 10-2-50	6
	Charley Johnson, 9-26-65	6
	Charley Johnson, 11-2-69	6
Receiving (No.)	Sonny Randle, 11-4-62	16
Receiving (Yds.)	Sonny Randle, 11-4-62	256
Interceptions	Bob Nussbaumer, 11-13-49	*4
	Jerry Norton, 11-20-60	*4
Field Goals	Jim Bakken, 9-24-67	*7
Touchdowns (Tot.)	Ernie Nevers, 11-28-29	*6
Points	Ernie Nevers, 11-28-29	*40

*NFL Record

1989 Team Record
Preseason (1-3)

Date	Result		Opponents
8/11	L	10-16	Seattle (OT)
8/21	L	20-23	at L.A. Rams
8/26	W	21- 7	Cleveland
9/1	L	20-21	at San Diego
		71-67	

Regular Season (5-11)

Date	Result		Opponents	Att.
910	W	16-13	at Detroit	36,735
9/17	W	34-24	at Seattle	60,444
9/24	L	7-35	at N.Y. Giants	75,742
10/1	L	13-24	San Diego	44,201
10/8	L	28-30	at Washington	53,335
10/15	L	5-17	Philadelphia	42,620
10/22	W	34-20	Atlanta	33,894
10/29	W	19-10	at Dallas	44,431
11/5	L	13-20	N.Y. Giants	46,588
11/12	W	24-20	Dallas	49,657
11/19	L	14-37	at L.A. Rams	53,176
11/26	L	13-14	Tampa Bay	33,297
12/3	L	10-29	Washington	38,870
12/10	L	14-16	at L.A. Raiders	41,785
12/16	L	0-37	Denver	56,071
12/24	L	14-31	at Philadelphia	43,287

(OT) Overtime

Score by Periods

Cardinals	43	76	51	88	0	—	258
Opponents	68	99	90	120	0	—	377

Attendance
Home 345,198   Away 408,935   Total 754,133
Single-game home record, 67,139 (9-12-88)
Single-season home record, 472,937 (1988)

1989 Team Statistics

	Cardinals	Opp.
Total First Downs	262	329
Rushing	83	113
Passing	157	185
Penalty	22	31
Third Down: Made/Att.	87/220	104/238
Third Down: Pct.	39.5	43.7
Fourth Down: Made/Att.	4/14	9/11
Fourth Down: Pct.	28.6	81.8
Total Net Yards	4641	5877
Avg. Per Game	290.1	367.3
Total Plays	986	1100
Avg. Per Play	4.7	5.3
Net Yards Rushing	1361	2302
Avg. Per Game	85.1	143.9
Total Rushes	407	539
Net Yards Passing	3280	3575
Avg. Per Game	205.0	223.4
Sacked/Yards Lost	56/379	30/219
Gross Yards	3659	3794
Att./Completions	523/279	531/286
Completion Pct.	53.3	53.9
Had Intercepted	30	16
Punts/Avg.	82/43.6	76/41.5
Net Punting Avg.	37.6	33.8
Penalties/Yards Lost	113/856	106/916
Fumbles/Ball Lost	24/14	18/11
Touchdowns	29	41
Rushing	10	12
Passing	17	24
Returns	2	5
Avg. Time of Possession	28:27	31:33

1989 Individual Statistics

Scoring

	TD R	TD P	TD Rt	PAT	FG	Saf	TP
Del Greco	0	0	0	28/29	18/26	0	82
Green	0	7	0	0/0	0/0	0	42
Ferrell	6	0	0	0/0	0/0	0	36
J. Smith	0	5	0	0/0	0/0	0	30
Jones	0	3	0	0/0	0/0	0	18
Jordan	2	0	0	0/0	0/0	0	12
Hogeboom	1	0	0	0/0	0/0	0	6
Holmes	0	1	0	0/0	0/0	0	6
McDonald	0	0	1	0/0	0/0	0	6
Novacek	0	1	0	0/0	0/0	0	6
Wolfley	1	0	0	0/0	0/0	0	6
Zordich	0	0	1	0/0	0/0	0	6
Wilson	0	0	0	0/0	0/0	1	2
Cardinals	10	17	2	28/29	18/26	1	258
Opponents	12	24	5	40/41	29/40	2	377

Passing

	Att.	Comp.	Yds.	Pct.	TD	Int.	Tkld.	Rate
Hogeboom	364	204	2591	56.0	14	19	40/266	69.5
Tupa	134	65	973	48.5	3	9	14/94	52.2
Rosenbach	22	9	95	40.9	0	1	2/19	35.2
Awalt	1	0	0	0.0	0	1	0/0	0.0
Camarillo	1	1	0	100.0	0	0	0/0	79.2
Sikahema	1	0	0	0.0	0	0	0/0	39.6
Cardinals	523	279	3659	53.3	17	30	56/379	62.6
Opponents	531	286	3794	53.9	24	16	30/219	79.2

Rushing

	Att.	Yds.	Avg.	LG	TD
Ferrell	149	502	3.4	44t	6
Jordan	83	211	2.5	15	2
S. Mitchell	43	165	3.8	14	0
Sikahema	38	145	3.8	27	0
Hogeboom	27	89	3.3	15	1
Tupa	15	75	5.0	13	0
Clark	10	42	4.2	9	0
Wolfley	13	36	2.8	5t	1
Baker	20	31	1.6	6	0
Rosenbach	6	26	4.3	8	0
J. Smith	2	21	10.5	11	0
Jones	1	18	18.0	18	0
Cardinals	407	1361	3.3	44t	10
Opponents	539	2302	4.3	51	12

Receiving

	No.	Yds.	Avg.	LG	TD
J. Smith	62	778	12.5	31	5
Jones	45	838	18.6	72t	3
Green	44	703	16.0	59t	7
Awalt	33	360	10.9	28	0
Sikahema	23	245	10.7	37	0
Novacek	23	225	9.8	30	1
Ferrell	18	122	6.8	25	0
Holmes	13	271	20.8	77t	1
Jordan	6	20	3.3	8	0
Wolfley	5	38	7.6	22	0
Baker	2	18	9.0	9	0
McConkey	2	18	9.0	10	0
S. Mitchell	1	10	10.0	10	0
Usher	1	8	8.0	8	0
Reeves	1	5	5.0	5	0
Cardinals	279	3659	13.1	77t	17
Opponents	286	3794	13.3	75t	24

Interceptions

	No.	Yds.	Avg.	LG	TD
McDonald	7	170	24.3	53t	1
Mack	4	15	3.8	9	0
Downs	1	37	37.0	37	0
Young	1	32	32.0	32	0
Zordich	1	16	16.0	16t	1
Wahler	1	5	5.0	5	0
Burton, Dall.-Phx.	1	0	0.0	0	0
Carter	1	0	0.0	0	0
Cardinals	16	275	17.2	53t	2
Opponents	30	327	10.9	59t	3

Punting

	No.	Yds.	Avg.	In 20	LG
Tupa	6	280	46.7	2	51
Camarillo	76	3298	43.4	21	58
Cardinals	82	3578	43.6	23	58
Opponents	76	3155	41.5	22	64

Punt Returns

	No.	FC	Yds.	Avg.	LG	TD
Sikahema	37	13	433	11.7	53	0
Usher, S.D.-Phx.	4	0	25	6.3	11	0
Usher, Phx.	1	0	10	10.0	10	0
Jones	1	0	13	13.0	13	0
McConkey	1	0	13	13.0	13	0
Cardinals	40	13	469	11.7	53	0
Opponents	46	18	371	8.1	20	0

Kickoff Returns

	No.	Yds.	Avg.	LG	TD
Sikahema	43	874	20.3	52	0
Usher, S.D.-Phx.	27	506	18.7	33	0
Usher, Phx.	17	347	20.4	33	0
Baker	11	245	22.3	33	0
Jones	7	124	17.7	27	0
McConkey	2	40	20.0	21	0
Carr	1	15	15.0	15	0
Reeves	1	5	5.0	5	0
Clark	1	0	0.0	0	0
Cardinals	83	1650	19.9	52	0
Opponents	57	1193	20.9	49	0

Sacks

	No.
Harvey	7.0
Galloway	5.5
Nunn	5.0
Saddler	3.5
Bell	2.0
Clasby	2.0
Hill	1.0
Mack	1.0
Wahler	1.0
Wilson	1.0
Zordich	1.0
Cardinals	30.0
Opponents	56.0

1990 Draft Choices

Round	Name	Pos.	College
2.	Anthony Thompson	RB	Indiana
3.	Ricky Proehl	WR	Wake Forest
4.	Travis Davis	DT	Michigan State
5.	Larry Centers	RB	Stephen F. Austin
6.	Tyrone Shavers	WR	Lamar
7.	Johnny Johnson	RB	San Jose State
8.	Mickey Washington	DB	Texas A&M
9.	David Bavaro	LB	Syracuse
10.	Dave Elle	TE	South Dakota
11.	Dempsey Norman	WR	St. Francis, Ill.
12.	Donnie Riley	RB	Central Michigan
	Ken McMichel	DB	Oklahoma

Phoenix Cardinals 1990 Veteran Roster

No.	Name	Pos.	Ht.	Wt.	Birth-date	NFL Exp.	College	Hometown	How Acq.	'89 Games/ Starts
80	†Awalt, Robert	TE	6-5	244	4/9/64	4	San Diego State	Sacramento, Calif.	D3a-'87	16/15
44	Baker, Tony	RB	5-10	190	6/11/64	4	East Carolina	High Point, N.C.	FA-'89	10/2
55	†Bell, Anthony	LB	6-3	235	7/2/64	5	Michigan State	Miami, Fla.	D1-'86	16/15
71	Bostic, Joe	G	6-3	276	4/20/57	11	Clemson	Greensboro, N.C.	D3-'79	0*
16	†Camarillo, Rich	P	5-11	185	11/29/59	10	Washington	Pico Rivera, Calif.	FA-'89	15/0
45	Carr, Lydell	RB	6-1	228	5/27/65	2	Oklahoma	Enid, Okla.	PB(NO)-'89#	5/0
41	Carter, Carl	CB	5-11	189	3/7/64	5	Texas Tech	Fort Worth, Tex.	D4-'86	15/15
79	†Clasby, Bob	DT	6-5	276	9/28/60	5	Notre Dame	Milton, Mass.	FA-'86	4/4
17	Del Greco, Al	K	5-10	198	3/2/62	7	Auburn	Coral Gables, Fla.	FA-'87	16/0
21	Eaton, Tracey	S	6-1	190	7/19/65	3	Portland State	Medford, Ore.	PB(Hou)-'90#	16/2*
65	Galloway, David	DE	6-3	259	2/16/59	9	Florida	Brandon, Fla.	D2-'82	12/11
81	Green, Roy	WR	6-0	194	6/30/57	12	Henderson State	Magnolia, Ark.	D1-'80	12/12
73	Hadd, Gary	DT	6-4	278	10/19/65	3	Minnesota	Burnsville, Minn.	PB(Det)-'89#	10/4
56	Harvey, Ken	LB	6-2	230	5/6/65	3	California	Austin, Tex.	D1-'88	16/16
5	Hogeboom, Gary	QB	6-4	207	8/21/58	11	Central Michigan	Grand Rapids, Mich.	PB(Ind)-'89#	14/13
83	Holmes, Don	WR	5-10	177	4/1/61	5	Mesa, Colo.	Grand Junction, Colo.	W(Ind)-'86	15/1
53	Jax, Garth	LB	6-2	229	9/16/63	5	Florida State	Houston, Tex.	PB(Dall)-'89#	16/0
86	Jones, Ernie	WR	5-11	191	12/15/64	3	Indiana	Elkhart, Ind.	D7-'88	15/10
32	†Jordan, Tony	RB	6-2	220	5/5/65	3	Kansas State	Rochester, N.Y.	D5b-'88	13/8
57	†Kauahi, Kani	C	6-2	270	9/6/59	8	Hawaii	Honolulu, Hawaii	PB(GB)-'89#	16/2
70	†Kennard, Derek	C-G	6-3	309	9/9/62	5	Nevada-Reno	Stockton, Calif.	SD2-'84	14/14
52	Kirk, Randy	LB	6-2	231	12/27/64	4	San Diego State	San Jose, Calif.	PB(SD)-'89#	6/0
51	Lewis, Bill	C	6-7	275	7/12/63	5	Nebraska	Sioux City, Iowa	PB(Raid)-'90#	0*
29	Lynch, Lorenzo	CB	5-9	199	4/6/63	3	Cal State-Sacramento	Oakland, Calif.	PB(Chi)-'90#	16/2*
47	†Mack, Cedric	CB	6-0	185	9/14/60	8	Baylor	Freeport, Tex.	D2-'83	16/16
46	†McDonald, Tim	CB-S	6-2	209	1/6/65	4	Southern California	Fresno, Calif.	D2-'87	16/16
54	McKenzie, Reggie	LB	6-1	242	2/8/63	5	Tennessee	Knoxville, Tenn.	PB(Raid)-'89#	0*
30	Mitchell, Stump	RB	5-9	194	3/15/59	10	Citadel	St. Mary's, Ga.	D9-'81	3/3
78	†Nunn, Freddie Joe	DE	6-4	250	4/9/62	6	Mississippi	Louisville, Miss.	D1-'85	12/6
89	Reeves, Walter	TE	6-3	249	12/15/65	2	Auburn	Eufaula, Ala.	D2-'89	16/3
63	Robbins, Tootie	T	6-5	307	6/2/58	9	East Carolina	Windsor, N.C.	D4-'82	9/9
3	Rosenbach, Timm	QB	6-2	210	10/27/66	2	Washington State	Pullman, Wash.	SD1-'89	2/1
72	†Saddler, Rod	DE	6-5	280	9/26/65	4	Texas A&M	Atlanta, Ga.	D4-'87	15/15
67	Sharpe, Luis	T	6-4	260	6/16/60	9	UCLA	Detroit, Mich.	D1-'82	14/14
36	†Sikahema, Vai	RB-KR	5-9	184	8/29/62	5	Brigham Young	American Samoa	D10-'86	16/2
84	Smith, J.T.	WR	6-2	187	10/29/55	13	North Texas State	Leonard, Tex.	FA-'85	9/8
61	Smith, Lance	T-G	6-2	278	11/1/63	6	Louisiana State	Kannapolis, N.C.	D3-'85	16/16
27	Taylor, Jay	CB	5-9	170	11/8/67	2	San Jose State	San Diego, Calif.	D6-'89	16/2
19	Tupa, Tom	QB-P	6-4	220	9/6/66	3	Ohio State	Brecksville, Ohio	D3-'88	13/2
23	Turner, Marcus	CB-S	6-0	191	1/13/66	2	UCLA	Long Beach, Calif.	W(Den)-'89	14/2
66	Wahler, Jim	DT	6-3	268	7/29/66	2	UCLA	San Jose, Calif.	D4-'89	13/11
60	Walker, Jeff	T	6-4	295	1/22/63	4	Memphis State	Jonesboro, Ark.	PB(NO)-'90#	13/0*
68	Wolf, Joe	T-G	6-5	279	12/28/66	2	Boston College	Allentown, Pa.	D1b-'89	16/15
24	†Wolfley, Ron	RB	6-0	222	10/14/62	6	West Virginia	Orchard Park, N.Y.	D4-'85	16/1
43	Young, Lonnie	CB-S	6-1	191	7/18/63	6	Michigan State	Flint, Mich.	D12-'85	10/9
38	Zordich, Mike	CB-S	5-11	197	10/12/63	4	Penn State	Youngstown, Ohio	PB(NYJ)-'89#	16/7

* Bostic and McKenzie missed '89 season due to injury; Eaton played 16 games with Houston in '89; Lewis active for 9 games with L.A. Raiders but did not play; Lynch played 16 games with Chicago; Walker played 13 games with New Orleans.

† Option playout; subject to developments.

Plan B unconditional free agent.

Retired—Neil Lomax, 8-year quarterback, 0 games in '89.

Players lost through Plan B (8): WR Mike Barber (Cin; 0 games in '89), LB Ron Burton (Raid; 10), T Scott Dill (TB; 16), LB Ilia Jarostchuk (NE; 16), DT Shawn Knight (Minn; 7), TE Jay Novacek (Dall; 16), WR Andy Schillinger (Minn; 0), DE Karl Wilson (Mia; 15).

Also played with Cardinals in '89—CB Michael Adams (3 games), DE Bob Buczkowski (4), RB Jessie Clark (11), RB Earl Ferrell (15), DE Freddie Gilbert (2), CB Kevin Guidry (3), WR Phil McConkey (6), CB Roland Mitchell (3), G Todd Peat (4), T Mark Traynowicz (2), WR Daryl Usher (7).

COACHING STAFF

Head Coach,
Joe Bugel

Pro Career: Named head coach on February 7, 1990. Became thirty-first head coach in the history of the franchise dating back to 1920. Assistant head coach-offense under Joe Gibbs with Washington Redskins from 1981-89. Tutored the famous "Hogs" as Redskins' offensive line coach during his tenure with Washington. The Redskins reached the play-offs five times in nine seasons, posting an 11-3 (.786) postseason record. He won three NFL championships and four division titles in that span. Four Redskin offensive linemen earned Pro Bowl recognition under Bugel's tutelage—Jeff Bostic, Russ Grimm, Joe Jacoby, and Mark May. Coached Houston Oilers' offensive line from 1977-80 when team set rushing and passing records (1980). He began his professional coaching career with the Detroit Lions in 1975-76.

Background: Offensive guard at Western Kentucky (1960-62). He served as an assistant coach at Western Kentucky (1964-68), Navy (1969), Iowa State (1973), and Ohio State (1974).

Personal: Born March 10, 1940, in Pittsburgh, Pa. Joe and wife, Brenda, live in Phoenix, and have three daughters—Angie, Holly, and Jennifer.

Assistant Coaches

Ted Cottrell, defensive line; born June 13, 1947, Chester, Pa., lives in Phoenix. Linebacker Delaware Valley College 1966-68. Pro linebacker Atlanta Falcons 1969-70, Winnipeg Blue Bombers (CFL) 1971. College coach: Rutgers 1973-80, 1983. Pro coach: Kansas City Chiefs 1981-82, New Jersey Generals (USFL) 1983-84, Buffalo Bills 1986-89, joined Phoenix in 1990.

Bobby Hammond, running backs; born February 20, 1952, Orangeburg, S.C., lives in Phoenix. Running back Morgan State 1973-75. Pro running back New York Giants 1976-79, Washington Redskins 1979-80. Pro coach: New York Jets 1983-89, joined Phoenix in 1990.

Jim Johnson, defensive secondary; born May 26, 1941, Maywood, Ill., lives in Phoenix. Quarterback Missouri 1959-62. Pro tight end Buffalo Bills 1963-64. College coach: Missouri Southern 1967-68 (head coach), Drake 1969-72, Indiana 1973-76, Notre Dame 1977-80. Pro coach: Oklahoma Outlaws (USFL) 1984, Jacksonville Bulls (USFL) 1985, joined Phoenix in 1986.

Tom Lovat, offensive line; born December 28, 1938, Bingham, Utah, lives in Phoenix. Guard-linebacker Utah 1958-60. No pro playing experience. College coach: Utah 1967, 1972-76 (head coach 1974-76), Idaho State 1968-70, Stanford 1977-79, Wyoming 1989. Pro coach: Saskatchewan Roughriders (CFL) 1971, Green Bay Packers 1980, St. Louis Cardinals 1981-84, Indianapolis Colts 1985-88, joined Phoenix in 1990.

Mike Murphy, defensive assistant/quality control; born September 25, 1944, New York, N.Y., lives in Phoenix. Guard-linebacker Huron, S.D., College 1962-65. No pro playing experience. College coach: Vermont 1970-73, Idaho State 1974-76, Western Illinois 1977-78. Pro coach: Saskatchewan Roughriders (CFL) 1979-83, Chicago Blitz (USFL) 1984, Detroit Lions 1985-89, joined Phoenix in 1990.

Joe Pascale, defensive coordinator; born April 4, 1946, New York, N.Y., lives in Phoenix. Linebacker Connecticut 1963-66. No pro playing experience. College coach: Connecticut 1967-68, Rhode Island 1969-73, Idaho State 1974-76 (head coach 1976), Princeton 1977-79. Pro coach: Montreal Alouettes (CFL) 1980-81, Ottawa Rough Riders (CFL) 1982-83, New Jersey Generals (USFL) 1984-85, joined Phoenix in 1986.

Ted Plumb, receivers; born August 20, 1939, Reno, Nev., lives in Phoenix. Wide receiver Baylor 1960-61. Pro wide receiver Buffalo Bills 1962. College coach: Cerritos, J.C. 1966-67, Texas Christian 1968-70, Tulsa 1971, Kansas 1972-73. Pro coach: New York Giants 1974-76, Atlanta Falcons 1977-79, Chicago Bears 1980-85, Philadelphia Eagles 1986-89, joined Phoenix in 1990.

Phoenix Cardinals 1990 First-Year Roster

Name	Pos.	Ht.	Wt.	Birth-date	College	Hometown	How Acq.
Applewhite, Mike	DE-DT	6-2	256	4/7/66	East Carolina	Henderson, N.C.	FA
Bavaro, David	LB	6-0	231	3/27/67	Syracuse	Danvers, Mass.	D9
Blair, Stanley (1)	CB	6-0	190	4/4/64	S.E. Oklahoma State	Pine Bluff, Ark.	FA
Brandom, John	G	6-2	273	8/4/66	Arizona	Napa, Calif.	FA
Burch, John (1)	RB	5-10	200	4/4/66	Tennessee-Martin	St. Augustine, Fla.	D8-'89
Centers, Larry	RB	5-10	203	6/1/68	Stephen F. Austin	Tatum, Tex.	D5
Davis, Bob	LB	6-0	236	1/25/69	Brigham Young	West Palm Beach, Fla.	D4
Davis, Travis	DT	6-1	274	5/10/66	Michigan State	Warren, Ohio	D10
Elle, David	TE	6-4	241	10/14/66	South Dakota	Yankton, S.D.	FA
Field, Amod	WR	5-11	181	10/11/67	Montclair State	Passaic, N.J.	FA
Hess, Bill (1)	WR	5-9	172	2/6/66	Utah	Orefield, Pa.	FA
Jackson, James	DE-DT	6-1	280	10/30/65	Northern Arizona	Rockford, Ill.	FA
Jackson, John	WR	5-10	170	1/2/67	Southern California	Brooklyn, N.Y.	FA
Johnson, Johnny	RB	6-2	212	6/11/68	San Jose State	Santa Clara, Calif.	D7
Johnson, Mike	QB	6-1	185	5/2/67	Akron	Los Angeles, Calif.	FA
Jones, DeWaine	RB	5-10	200	12/14/67	Wyoming	Colorado Springs, Colo.	FA
Jorden, Tim (1)	TE	6-3	233	10/30/66	Indiana	Lakewood, Ohio	FA-'89
Lawrence, Oliver	LB	6-1	243	11/9/67	Louisiana State	Monroe, La.	FA
Lyle, Win	K	5-9	170	3/13/68	Auburn	Florence, Ala.	FA
Mathis, Jeff	DE-DT	6-1	279	5/18/67	Georgia Tech	Atlanta, Ga.	FA
McMichel, Ken	LB	6-0	208	6/4/67	Oklahoma	Indianapolis, Ind.	D12b
Nicholl, Kevin	K	5-10	184	8/1/68	Central Michigan	Mt. Clemens, Mich.	FA
Norman, Dempsey	WR	5-7	175	2/7/66	St. Francis	Chicago, Ill.	D11
Osborne, Eldonta	LB	6-0	215	8/12/67	Louisiana Tech	Jonesboro, La.	FA
Pfeifer, Mike	T	6-6	318	8/9/66	Kentucky	Louisville, Ky.	FA
Proehl, Ricky	WR	5-10	181	3/7/68	Wake Forest	Belle Mead, N.J.	D3
Prouty, Lance	T-G	6-5	292	11/23/66	South Dakota State	Norwalk, Conn.	FA
Riley, Donnie	CB	5-9	205	10/2/66	Central Michigan	Grand Rapids, Mich.	D12a
Shavers, Tyrone	WR	6-2	205	7/14/67	Lamar	Texarkana, Tex.	D6
Smith, Dennis	TE	6-0	224	2/14/67	Utah	Los Angeles, Calif.	FA
Smith, Vernice (1)	G-T	6-2	280	10/24/65	Florida A&M	Orlando, Fla.	FA-'89
Thompson, Anthony	RB	5-11	207	4/8/67	Indiana	Terre Haute, Ind.	D2
Washington, Mickey	CB	5-9	187	7/8/68	Texas A&M	Galveston, Tex.	D8
Waters, Preston	CB	5-9	185	8/8/68	West Virginia	Miami, Fla.	FA

The term NFL Rookie is defined as a player who is in his first season of professional football and has not been on the roster of another professional football team for any regular-season or postseason games. A Rookie is designated by an "R" on NFL rosters. Players who have been active in another professional football league or players who have NFL experience, including either preseason training camp or being on an active roster for fewer than three regular-season or post-season games, are termed NFL First-Year Players. An NFL First-Year Player is designated by a "1" on NFL rosters. Thereafter, a player on an NFL active roster for at least three regular-season or postseason games is credited with an additional year of NFL playing experience.

NOTES

_____

_____

_____

_____

_____

_____

_____

_____

_____

Jerry Rhome, offensive coordinator; born March 6, 1942, Dallas, Tex., lives in Phoenix. Quarterback Southern Methodist 1960-61, Tulsa 1963-64. Pro quarterback Dallas Cowboys 1965-68, Cleveland Browns 1969, Houston Oilers 1970, Los Angeles Rams 1971-72. College coach: Tulsa 1973-75. Pro coach: Seattle Seahawks 1976-82, Washington Redskins 1983-87, San Diego Chargers 1988, Dallas Cowboys 1989, joined Phoenix in 1990.

Pete Rodriguez, special teams; born July 25, 1940, Chicago, Ill., lives in Phoenix. Guard-linebacker Denver University 1959-60, Western State, Colo. 1961-63. No pro playing experience. College coach: Western State, Colo. 1964, Arizona 1968-69, Western Illinois 1970-73, 1979-82 (head coach), Florida State 1974-75, Iowa State 1976-78, Northern Iowa 1986. Pro coach: Michigan Panthers (USFL) 1983-84, Denver Gold (USFL) 1985, Jacksonville Bulls (USFL) 1986, Ottawa Rough Riders (CFL) 1987, Los Angeles Raiders 1988-89, joined Phoenix in 1990.

Bob Rogucki, strength and conditioning; born September 27, 1953, Clarksburg, W. Va., lives in Phoenix. No college or pro playing experience. College coach: Penn State 1981, Weber State 1982, Army 1983-89, joined Phoenix in 1990.

SAN FRANCISCO 49ERS

National Football Conference Western Division

Team Colors: Forty Niners Gold and Scarlet

4949 Centennial Boulevard
Santa Clara, California 95054
Telephone: (408) 562-4949

Club Officials

Owner/President: Edward J. DeBartolo, Jr.
Executive Vice President-Front Office/
   League Relations: Carmen Policy
Vice President-Football Administration:
   John McVay
Vice President-Business Operations & C.F.O:
   Keith Simon
Administrative Assistant: Dwight Clark
Administrative Assistant: Norb Hecker
Director of Pro Scouting: Allan Webb
Director of College Scouting: Tony Razzano
Director of Public Relations: Jerry Walker
Director of Publications: Rodney Knox
Director of Marketing/Promotions:
   Laurie Albrecht
Coordinator of Football Operations: Neal Dahlen
Ticket Manager: Ken Dargel
Director of Stadium Operations:
   Murlan (Mo) Fowell
Video Director: Robert Yanagi
Trainer: Lindsy McLean
Equipment Manager: Bronco Hinek

Stadium: Candlestick Park • **Capacity:** 65,729
   San Francisco, California 94124

Playing Surface: Grass

Training Camp: Sierra Community College
   Rocklin, California 95677

1990 Schedule

Preseason

Aug. 11	**Los Angeles Raiders**	6:00
Aug. 20	at Denver	6:00
Aug. 25	at San Diego	6:00
Aug. 31	**Seattle**	6:00

Regular Season

Sept. 10	at New Orleans (Monday)	8:00
Sept. 16	**Washington**	1:00
Sept. 23	**Atlanta**	1:00
Sept. 30	**Open Date**	
Oct. 7	at Houston	12:00
Oct. 14	at Atlanta	1:00
Oct. 21	**Pittsburgh**	1:00
Oct. 28	**Cleveland**	1:00
Nov. 4	at Green Bay	12:00
Nov. 11	at Dallas	7:00
Nov. 18	**Tampa Bay**	1:00
Nov. 25	**Los Angeles Rams**	1:00
Dec. 3	**New York Giants** (Monday)	6:00
Dec. 9	at Cincinnati	1:00
Dec. 17	at L.A. Rams (Monday)	6:00
Dec. 23	**New Orleans**	1:00
Dec. 30	at Minnesota	12:00

49ers Coaching History

(299-265-13)

1950-54	Lawrence (Buck) Shaw	33-25-2
1955	Norman (Red) Strader	4-8-0
1956-58	Frankie Albert	19-17-1
1959-63	Howard (Red) Hickey*	27-27-1
1963-67	Jack Christiansen	26-38-3
1968-75	Dick Nolan	56-56-5
1976	Monte Clark	8-6-0
1977	Ken Meyer	5-9-0
1978	Pete McCulley**	1-8-0
1978	Fred O'Connor	1-6-0
1979-88	Bill Walsh	102-63-1
1989	George Seifert	17-2-0

*Resigned after three games in 1963
**Released after nine games in 1978

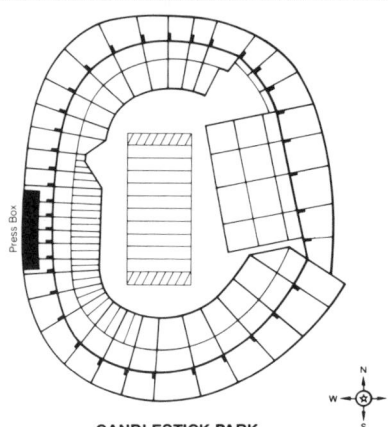

CANDLESTICK PARK

Record Holders

Individual Records — Career

Category	Name	Performance
Rushing (Yds.)	Joe Perry, 1950-1960, 1963	7,344
Passing (Yds.)	John Brodie, 1957-1973	31,548
Passing (TDs)	Joe Montana, 1979-1989	216
Receiving (No.)	Dwight Clark, 1979-1987	506
Receiving (Yds.)	Dwight Clark, 1979-1987	6,750
Interceptions	Ronnie Lott, 1981-89	48
Punting (Avg.)	Tommy Davis, 1959-1969	44.7
Punt Return (Avg.)	Manfred Moore, 1974-75	14.7
Kickoff Return (Avg.)	Abe Woodson, 1958-1964	29.4
Field Goals	Ray Wersching, 1977-1987	190
Touchdowns (Tot.)	Jerry Rice, 1985-89	70
Points	Ray Wersching, 1977-1987	979

Individual Records — Single Season

Category	Name	Performance
Rushing (Yds.)	Roger Craig, 1988	1,502
Passing (Yds.)	Joe Montana, 1983	3,910
Passing (TDs)	Joe Montana, 1987	31
Receiving (No.)	Roger Craig, 1985	92
Receiving (Yds.)	Jerry Rice, 1986	1,570
Interceptions	Dave Baker, 1960	10
	Ronnie Lott, 1986	10
Punting (Avg.)	Tommy Davis, 1965	45.8
Punt Return (Avg.)	Dana McLemore, 1982	22.3
Kickoff Return (Avg.)	Joe Arenas, 1953	34.4
Field Goals	Mike Cofer, 1989	29
Touchdowns (Tot.)	Jerry Rice, 1987	23
Points	Jerry Rice, 1987	138

Individual Records — Single Game

Category	Name	Performance
Rushing (Yds.)	Delvin Williams, 10-31-76	194
Passing (Yds.)	Joe Montana, 12-11-89	458
Passing (TDs)	John Brodie, 11-23-65	5
	Steve Spurrier, 11-19-72	5
	Joe Montana, 10-6-85	5
	Joe Montana, 9-24-89	5
Receiving (No.)	Many times	12
	Last time by Roger Craig, 12-1-86	
Receiving (Yds.)	Jerry Rice, 12-9-85	241
Interceptions	Dave Baker, 12-4-60	*4
Field Goals	Ray Wersching, 10-16-83	6
Touchdowns (Tot.)	Billy Kilmer, 10-15-61	4
Points	Gordy Soltau, 10-27-51	26

*NFL Record

1989 Team Record

Preseason (3-2)

Date	Result		Opponents
8/5	L	13-16	vs. L.A. Rams at Tokyo, Japan
8/12	W	37- 7	at L.A. Raiders
8/19	W	35-17	Denver
8/23	W	17-14	San Diego
9/1	L	17-28	Seattle
		119-82	

Regular Season (14-2)

Date	Result		Opponents	Att.
9/10	W	30-24	at Indianapolis	60,111
9/17	W	20-16	at Tampa Bay	64,087
9/24	W	38-28	at Philadelphia	66,042
10/1	L	12-13	L.A. Rams	64,250
10/8	W	24-20	at New Orleans	60,488
10/15	W	31-14	at Dallas	61,077
10/22	W	37-20	New England	51,781
10/29	W	23-10	at N.Y. Jets	62,805
11/6	W	31-13	New Orleans	60,667
11/12	W	45- 3	Atlanta	59,914
11/19	L	17-21	Green Bay	62,219
11/27	W	34-24	N.Y. Giants	63,461
12/3	W	23-10	at Atlanta	43,128
12/11	W	30-27	at L.A. Rams	67,959
12/17	W	21-10	Buffalo	60,927
12/24	W	26- 0	Chicago	60,207

Postseason (3-0)

Date	Result		Opponent	Att.
1/6	W	41-13	Minnesota	64,918
1/14	W	30- 3	L.A. Rams	65,634
1/28	W	55-10	Denver	72,919

Score by Periods

49ers	67	137	64	174	0	—	442
Opponents	59	77	53	64	0	—	253

Attendance

Home 483,426   Away 485,697   Total 969,123
Single-game home record, 64,250 (10-1-89)
Single-season home record, 483,426 (1989)

1989 Team Statistics

	49ers	Opp.
Total First Downs	350	283
Rushing	124	76
Passing	209	178
Penalty	17	29
Third Down: Made/Att.	80/190	76/210
Third Down: Pct.	42.1	36.2
Fourth Down: Made/Att.	6/9	9/19
Fourth Down: Pct.	66.7	47.4
Total Net Yards	6268	4618
Avg. Per Game	391.8	288.6
Total Plays	1021	979
Avg. Per Play	6.1	4.7
Net Yards Rushing	1966	1383
Avg. Per Game	122.9	86.4
Total Rushes	493	372
Net Yards Passing	4302	3235
Avg. Per Game	268.9	202.2
Sacked/Yards Lost	45/282	43/333
Gross Yards	4584	3568
Att./Completions	483/339	564/316
Completion Pct.	70.2	56.0
Had Intercepted	11	21
Punts/Avg.	56/39.8	74/38.9
Net Punting Avg.	31.2	32.0
Penalties/Yards Lost	109/922	75/581
Fumbles/Ball Lost	32/14	34/16
Touchdowns	51	26
Rushing	14	9
Passing	35	15
Returns	2	2
Avg. Time of Possession	31:45	28:15

1989 Individual Statistics

Scoring

	TD R	TD P	TD Rt	PAT	FG	Saf	TP
Cofer	0	0	0	49/51	29/36	0	136
Rice	0	17	0	0/0	0/0	0	102
Taylor	0	10	0	0/0	0/0	0	60
Craig	6	1	0	0/0	0/0	0	42
Jones	0	4	0	0/0	0/0	0	24
Montana	3	0	0	0/0	0/0	0	18
Rathman	1	1	0	0/0	0/0	0	12
Young	2	0	0	0/0	0/0	0	12
Flagler	1	0	0	0/0	0/0	0	6
Haley	0	0	1	0/0	0/0	0	6
Henderson	1	0	0	0/0	0/0	0	6
Jackson	0	0	1	0/0	0/0	0	6
Walls	0	1	0	0/0	0/0	0	6
Wilson	0	1	0	0/0	0/0	0	6
49ers	14	35	2	49/51	29/36	0	442
Opponents	9	15	2	26/26	23/31	1	253

Passing

	Att.	Comp.	Yds.	Pct.	TD	Int.	Tkld.	Rate
Montana	386	271	3521	70.2	26	8	33/198	112.4
Young	92	64	1001	69.6	8	3	12/84	120.8
Bono	5	4	62	80.0	1	0	0/0	157.9
49ers	483	339	4584	70.2	35	11	45/282	114.8
Opponents	564	316	3568	56.0	15	21	43/333	68.5

Rushing

	Att.	Yds.	Avg.	LG	TD
Craig	271	1054	3.9	27	6
Rathman	79	305	3.9	13	1
Montana	49	227	4.6	19	3
Flagler	33	129	3.9	29t	1
Young	38	126	3.3	22	2
Sydney	9	56	6.2	18	0
Rice	5	33	6.6	17	0
Henderson	7	30	4.3	11t	1
Taylor	1	6	6.0	6	0
Helton	1	0	0.0	0	0
49ers	493	1966	4.0	29t	14
Opponents	372	1383	3.7	23	9

Receiving

	No.	Yds.	Avg.	LG	TD
Rice	82	1483	18.1	68t	17
Rathman	73	616	8.4	36	1
Taylor	60	1077	18.0	95t	10
Craig	49	473	9.7	44	1
Jones	40	500	12.5	36t	4
Wilson	9	103	11.4	19	1
Sydney	9	71	7.9	13	0
Flagler	6	51	8.5	30	0
Walls	4	16	4.0	9	1
Henderson	3	130	43.3	78	0
Williams	3	38	12.7	17	0
Greer	1	26	26.0	26	0
49ers	339	4584	13.5	95t	35
Opponents	316	3568	11.3	65t	15

Interceptions

	No.	Yds.	Avg.	LG	TD
Lott	5	34	6.8	28	0
Brooks	3	31	10.3	19	0
Wright	2	37	18.5	23	0
Jackson	2	35	17.5	19	0
Griffin	2	6	3.0	3	0
Turner	1	42	42.0	42	0
Holmoe	1	23	23.0	23	0
McKyer	1	18	18.0	18	0
Romanowski	1	13	13.0	13	0
Pollard	1	12	12.0	12	0
Millen	1	10	10.0	10	0
DeLong	1	1	1.0	1	0
49ers	21	262	12.5	42	0
Opponents	11	140	12.7	35	0

Punting

	No.	Yds.	Avg.	In 20	LG
Helton	55	2226	40.5	13	56
49ers	56	2226	39.8	13	56
Opponents	74	2875	38.9	18	57

Punt Returns

	No.	FC	Yds.	Avg.	LG	TD
Taylor	36	20	417	11.6	37	0
Griffin	1	0	9	9.0	9	0
Greer	1	0	3	3.0	3	0
Romanowski	1	0	0	0.0	0	0
49ers	39	20	429	11.0	37	0
Opponents	35	4	361	10.3	22	0

Kickoff Returns

	No.	Yds.	Avg.	LG	TD
Flagler	32	643	20.1	41	0
Tillman	10	206	20.6	60	0
Sydney	3	16	5.3	16	0
Taylor	2	51	25.5	27	0
Henderson	2	21	10.5	13	0
Greer	1	17	17.0	17	0
Jackson	1	0	0.0	0	0
49ers	51	954	18.7	60	0
Opponents	76	1435	18.9	37	0

Sacks

	No.
Haley	10.5
Holt	10.5
Fagan	7.0
Stubbs	4.5
Roberts	3.5
Kugler	3.0
Brooks	1.0
Romanowski	1.0
Walter	1.0
49ers	43.0
Opponents	45.0

1990 Draft Choices

Round	Name	Pos.	College
1.	Dexter Carter	RB	Florida State
2.	Dennis Brown	DT	Washington
	Eric Davis	DB	Jacksonville State
3.	Ronald Lewis	WR	Florida State
4.	Dean Caliguire	C	Pittsburgh
6.	Frank Pollack	T	Northern Arizona
8.	Dwight Pickens	WR	Fresno State
9.	Odell Haggins	DT	Florida State
10.	Martin Harrison	DE	Washington
11.	Anthony Shelton	DB	Tennessee State

San Francisco 49ers 1990 Veteran Roster

No.	Name	Pos.	Ht.	Wt.	Birth-date	NFL Exp.	College	Hometown	How Acq.	'89 Games/ Starts
67	Aronson, Doug	G	6-4	278	8/14/64	2	San Diego State	So. San Francisco, Calif.	FA-'90	0*
79	†Barton, Harris	T	6-4	280	4/19/64	4	North Carolina	Atlanta, Ga.	D1a-'87	16/16
13	Bono, Steve	QB	6-4	215	5/11/62	6	UCLA	Norristown, Pa.	FA-'89	1/0
65	†Bregel, Jeff	G	6-4	280	5/1/64	4	Southern California	Granada Hills, Calif.	D2-'87	3/3
31	†Brooks, Chet	S	5-11	191	1/1/66	3	Texas A&M	Dallas, Tex.	D11-'88	15/15
64	†Burt, Jim	NT	6-1	270	6/7/59	10	Miami	Waldwick, N.J.	FA-'89	8/3
95	Carter, Michael	NT	6-2	285	10/29/60	7	Southern Methodist	Dallas, Tex.	D5a-'84	8/8
6	†Cofer, Mike	K	6-1	190	2/19/62	3	North Carolina State	Charlotte, N.C.	FA-'88	16/0
69	Collie, Bruce	G-T	6-6	275	6/27/62	6	Texas-Arlington	San Antonio, Tex.	D5-'85	16/15
38	Cox, Greg	S	6-0	217	1/6/65	3	San Jose State	San Jose, Calif.	PB(NYG)-'90#	16/0*
33	Craig, Roger	RB	6-0	224	7/10/60	8	Nebraska	Davenport, Iowa	D2-'83	16/16
68	Cully, Dave	T	6-7	275	6/15/64	2	Utah	La Mirada, Calif.	FA-'89	2/0
59	DeLong, Keith	LB	6-2	235	8/14/67	2	Tennessee	Knoxville, Tenn.	D1-'89	15/0
28	Dixon, Hanford	CB	6-0	185	12/25/58	10	Southern Mississippi	Lakewood, Ohio	PB(Clev)-'90#	15/15*
75	†Fagan, Kevin	DE	6-4	265	4/25/63	4	Miami	Lake Worth, Fla.	D4c-'86	16/15
55	†Fahnhorst, Jim	LB	6-4	230	11/8/58	7	Minnesota	St. Cloud, Minn.	FA-'84	7/7
98	†Goss, Antonio	LB	6-4	228	8/11/66	2	North Carolina	Pelham, Ga.	D6-'86	8/0
29	Griffin, Don	CB	6-0	176	3/17/64	5	Middle Tennessee State	Randleman, N.C.	D12a-'89	16/16
94	†Haley, Charles	LB-DE	6-5	230	1/6/64	5	James Madison	Campbell County, Va.	D4a-'86	16/16
65	Hamilton, Steve	DE	6-4	275	9/29/61	5	East Carolina	Williamsville, N.Y.	FA-'90	0*
9	†Helton, Barry	P	6-3	205	1/2/66	3	Colorado	Simla, Colo.	D4-'88	16/0
30	Henderson, Keith	RB	6-1	220	8/4/66	2	Georgia	Cartersville, Ga.	D3-'89	6/0
56	Hendrickson, Steve	LB	6-0	245	8/30/66	2	California	Napa, Calif.	D6-'89	11/0
78	Holt, Pierce	DE	6-4	280	1/1/62	3	Angelo State	Houston, Tex.	D2b-'88	16/11
4	Horne, Greg	P	6-0	190	11/22/64	3	Arkansas	Russellville, Ark.	FA-'90	0*
40	Jackson, Johnny	S	6-1	204	1/11/67	2	Houston	Harlingen, Tex.	D5a-'89	16/2
84	Jones, Brent	TE	6-4	230	2/12/63	4	Santa Clara	San Jose, Calif.	FA-'87	16/16
57	Kennedy, Sam	LB	6-3	235	7/10/64	2	San Jose State	Aptos, Calif.	FA-'90	0*
60	Lockett, Danny	LB	6-2	250	7/11/64	3	Arizona	Fort Valley, Ga.	FA-'90	0*
42	Lott, Ronnie	S	6-0	200	5/8/59	10	Southern California	Rialto, Calif.	D1-'81	11/11
62	McIntyre, Guy	G	6-3	265	2/17/61	7	Georgia	Thomasville, Ga.	D3-'84	16/13
54	†Millen, Matt	LB	6-2	245	3/12/58	11	Penn State	Whitehall, Pa.	FA-'89	15/9
16	Montana, Joe	QB	6-2	195	6/11/56	12	Notre Dame	New Eagle, Pa.	D3-'79	13/13
77	Paris, Bubba	T	6-6	306	10/6/60	8	Michigan	Louisville, Ky.	D2-'82	16/16
26	Pollard, Darryl	CB	5-11	187	5/11/65	4	Weber State	Foster City, Calif.	FA-'88	16/14
57	Radloff, Wayne	C	6-5	277	5/17/61	6	Georgia	Lawrenceville, Ga.	PB(Atl)-'90#	11/3*
44	Rathman, Tom	RB	6-1	232	10/7/62	5	Nebraska	Grand Island, Neb.	D3a-'86	16/16
80	Rice, Jerry	WR	6-2	200	10/13/62	6	Mississippi Valley State	Crawford, Miss.	D1-'85	16/16
91	Roberts, Larry	DE	6-3	275	6/2/63	5	Alabama	Dothan, Ala.	D2-'86	15/5
53	Romanowski, Bill	LB	6-4	231	4/2/66	3	Boston College	Vernon, Conn.	D3-'88	16/4
61	Sapolu, Jesse	C	6-4	260	3/10/61	5	Hawaii	Honolulu, Hawaii	D11-'83	16/16
71	Shannon, John	DE	6-3	270	1/18/65	3	Kentucky	Highland Park, Ill.	PB(Chi)-'90#	12/1*
88	Sherrard, Mike	WR	6-2	187	6/21/63	2	UCLA	Los Angeles, Calif.	PB(Dall)-'89#	0*
72	Smerlas, Fred	NT	6-4	291	4/8/57	12	Boston College	Waltham, Mass.	PB(Buff)-'90#	16/16*
32	Swoope, Craig	S	6-2	210	2/3/64	4	Illinois	Ft. Pierce, Fla.	FA-'90	0*
24	Sydney, Harry	RB	6-0	217	6/26/59	4	Kansas	Fayetteville, N.C.	FA-'87	7/0
66	Tausch, Terry	G	6-4	278	2/5/59	9	Texas	Plano, Tex.	PB(Minn)-'89#	9/0
82	Taylor, John	WR	6-1	185	3/31/62	4	Delaware State	Pennsauken, N.J.	D3c-'86	15/15
47	Tennell, Derek	TE	6-5	248	2/12/64	4	UCLA	West Covina, Calif.	FA-'90	14/3*
60	†Thomas, Chuck	C	6-3	280	12/24/60	5	Oklahoma	Houston, Tex.	FA-'87	16/0
23	Tillman, Spencer	RB	5-11	206	4/21/64	4	Oklahoma	Houston, Tex.	PB(Hou)-'89#	15/0
58	†Turner, Keena	LB	6-2	222	10/22/58	11	Purdue	Chicago, Ill.	D2-'80	13/12
74	Wallace, Steve	T	6-5	276	12/27/64	5	Auburn	Atlanta, Ga.	D4b-'86	16/1
89	Walls, Wesley	TE	6-5	246	2/26/66	2	Mississippi	Pontotic, Miss.	D2-'89	16/0
99	Walter, Michael	LB	6-3	238	11/30/60	8	Oregon	Eugene, Ore.	FA-'84	16/16
51	Washington, Chris	LB	6-4	240	3/6/62	6	Iowa State	Tampa, Fla.	PB(TB)-'89#	0*
43	Waymer, Dave	S	6-1	188	7/1/58	11	Notre Dame	Mooresville, N.C.	PB(NO)-'90#	16/16*
81	Williams, Jamie	TE	6-4	245	2/25/60	8	Nebraska	Houston, Tex.	PB(Hou)-'89#	3/0
85	Wilson, Mike	WR	6-3	215	12/19/58	10	Washington State	Los Angeles, Calif.	FA-'81	16/1
21	†Wright, Eric	CB	6-1	185	4/18/59	9	Missouri	St. Louis, Mo.	D2b-'81	11/1
8	Young, Steve	QB	6-2	200	10/11/61	6	Brigham Young	Salt Lake City, Utah	T(TB)-'87	10/3

* Aronson last active with Cincinnati in '87; Cox played 16 games with N.Y. Giants in '89; Dixon played 15 games with Cleveland; Hamilton, Sherrard, and Washington missed '89 season due to injury; Horne last active with Cincinnati in '87; Kennedy last active with San Francisco in '88; Lockett last active with Detroit in '87; Radloff played 11 games with Atlanta; Shannon played 12 games with Chicago; Smerlas played 16 games with Buffalo; Tennell played 14 games with Cleveland; Waymer played 16 games with New Orleans.

† Option playout; subject to developments.

Plan B unconditional free agent.

Retired—Tom Holmoe, 7-year safety, 7 games in '89; Pete Kugler, 7-year defensive end, 14 games in '89; Jeff Stover, 8-year defensive end, 0 games in '89.

Traded—RB Terrence Flagler to Dallas, DE Danny Stubbs to Dallas.

Players lost through Plan B (1): WR Terry Greer (Det; 11 games in '89).

Also played with 49ers in '89—WR Mike Barber (8 games), NT Kevin Lilly (1), NT Rollin Putzier (11), CB Mike Richardson (3).

COACHING STAFF

Head Coach, George Seifert

Pro Career: Named 49ers' head coach January 26, 1989, after serving as team's defensive coordinator since 1983. Immediately earned a place in NFL history, winning a record 17 games his first year and becoming only the second rookie head coach to lead his team to a Super Bowl title (Don McCafferty of Baltimore—1970—was the first). Joined 49ers as secondary coach in 1980. In only his second season in the pro ranks, San Francisco posted the number-two defense in the league and won the Super Bowl XVI title, despite three rookies starting in the defensive backfield. Appointed the team's defensive coordinator in 1983. Finished 1987 with the top-ranked defense in the NFL and a 13-2 record. In 1988, San Francisco's defense ranked third en route to the Super Bowl XXIII title. Then, in his first year as head coach, the 49ers won Super Bowl XXIV. No pro playing experience. Career record: 17-2.

Background: Linebacker at University of Utah (1960-62). Served a six-month tour of duty with the U.S. Army following graduation from Utah. Returned to Utah as a graduate assistant in 1964. Named head coach at Westminster College in Salt Lake City in 1965. Assistant at Iowa (1966), Oregon (1967-71), and Stanford (1972-74). Left Stanford to become head coach at Cornell University (1975-76). Joined Bill Walsh's staff at Stanford in 1977 and helped the Cardinal to a two-year mark of 17-7, including victories in the Sun and Bluebonnet Bowls. Received BA in zoology and masters in physical education from San Jose State in 1963.

Personal: Born January 22, 1940, in San Francisco, Calif. He and his wife, Linda, have two children—Eve and Jason—and live in Sunnyvale, Calif.

Assistant Coaches

Jerry Attaway, conditioning; born January 3, 1946, Susanville, Calif., lives in San Jose, Calif. Defensive back Yuba, Calif., J.C. 1964-65, Cal-Davis 1967. No pro playing experience. College coach: Cal-Davis 1970-71, Idaho 1972-74, Utah State 1975-77, Southern California 1978-82. Pro coach: Joined 49ers in 1983.

Tommy Hart, defensive assistant; born November 11, 1944, Macon, Ga., lives in Redwood City, Calif. Offensive guard/defensive end Morris Brown 1964-68. Pro defensive end San Francisco 49ers 1968-77, Chicago Bears 1978-79, New Orleans Saints 1980. Pro coach: Joined 49ers in 1982.

Mike Holmgren, offensive coordinator/quarterbacks; born June 15, 1948, San Francisco, Calif., lives in San Jose, Calif. Quarterback Southern California 1966-69. No pro playing experience. College coach: San Francisco State 1981, Brigham Young 1982-85. Pro coach: Joined 49ers in 1986.

Al Lavan, running backs; born September 13, 1946, Pierce, Fla., lives in San Jose, Calif. Defensive back Colorado State 1965-67. Pro defensive back Philadelphia Eagles 1968, Atlanta Falcons 1969-70. College coach: Colorado State 1972, Louisville 1973, Iowa State 1974, Georgia Tech 1977-78, Stanford 1979. Pro coach: Atlanta Falcons 1975-76, Dallas Cowboys 1980-88, joined 49ers in 1989.

Sherman Lewis, receivers; born June 29, 1942, Louisville, Ky., lives in Sunnyvale, Calif. Running back Michigan State 1961-63. Pro running back Toronto Argonauts (CFL) 1964-65, New York Jets 1966. College coach: Michigan State 1969-82. Pro coach: Joined 49ers in 1983.

John Marshall, defensive line; born October 2, 1945, Arroyo Grande, Calif., lives in Pleasanton, Calif. Linebacker Washington State 1964. No pro playing experience. College coach: Oregon 1970-76, Southern California 1977-79. Pro coach: Green Bay Packers 1980-82, Atlanta Falcons 1983-85, Indianapolis Colts 1986-88, joined 49ers in 1989.

Bobb McKittrick, offensive line; born December 29, 1935, Baker, Ore., lives in San Mateo, Calif. Guard Oregon State 1955-57. No pro playing experience. College coach: Oregon State 1961-64, UCLA 1965-70. Pro coach: Los Angeles Rams 1971-72, San Diego Chargers 1974-78, joined 49ers in 1979.

Bill McPherson, defensive coordinator; born October 24, 1931, Santa Clara, Calif., lives in San Jose, Calif. Tackle Santa Clara 1950-52. No pro playing experience. College coach: Santa Clara 1963-74, UCLA 1975-77. Pro coach: Philadelphia Eagles 1978, joined 49ers in 1979.

Ray Rhodes, defensive backfield; born October 20, 1950, Mexia, Tex., lives in Fremont, Calif. Running back-wide receiver Texas Christian 1969-70, Tulsa 1972-73. Pro defensive back New York Giants 1974-79, San Francisco 49ers 1980. Pro coach: Joined 49ers in 1981.

Lynn Stiles, special teams/tight ends; born April 12, 1941, Kermit, Tex., lives in Sunnyvale, Calif. Guard Utah 1961-62. No pro playing experience. College coach: Utah 1963-65, Iowa 1966-70, UCLA 1971-75, San Jose State 1976-78 (head coach). Pro coach: Philadelphia Eagles 1979-85, joined 49ers in 1987.

Bob Zeman, linebackers; born February 22, 1937, Wheaton, Ill., lives in Boulder Creek, Calif. Fullback/halfback Wisconsin 1957-59. Pro defensive back Los Angeles/San Diego Chargers 1960-61, 1965-66, Denver Broncos 1962-63. College coach: Northwestern 1968-69, Wisconsin 1970. Pro coach: Oakland Raiders 1971-77, 1984-86, Denver Broncos 1978-82, Buffalo Bills 1983, joined 49ers in 1989.

San Francisco 49ers 1990 First-Year Roster

Name	Pos.	Ht.	Wt.	Birth-date	College	Hometown	How Acq.
Beach, Sanjay (1)	WR	6-1	190	2/21/66	Colorado State	Freeport, N.Y.	FA
Brown, Dennis	DE	6-4	290	11/6/67	Washington	Long Beach, Calif.	D2a
Bynum, Reggie (1)	WR	6-1	190	2/10/64	Oregon State	San Jose, Calif.	FA
Caliguire, Dean	C	6-2	282	3/2/67	Pittsburgh	Pittsburgh, Pa.	D4a
Carter, Dexter	RB	5-9	170	9/15/67	Florida State	Appling County, Ga.	D1
Davis, Eric	WR	5-11	178	1/28/68	Jacksonville State	Anniston, Ala.	D2b
Dillard, Rodney (1)	LB	6-3	230	6/30/65	Arizona State	St. Petersburg, Fla.	FA
Edeen, David (1)	DE	6-4	280	5/23/66	Wyoming	Cheyenne, Wy.	FA
Haggins, Odell	NT	6-2	255	2/27/67	Florida State	Bartow, Fla.	D9
Harrison, Martin	LB-DE	6-5	240	9/20/67	Washington	Bellevue, Wash.	D10
Knox, Tyreese (1)	RB	6-0	212	7/3/65	Nebraska	Daly City, Calif.	FA
Lewis, Kevin (1)	CB	5-10	180	11/14/66	N.W. Louisiana	New Orleans, La.	FA
Lewis, Ronald	WR	5-11	173	3/25/68	Florida State	Jacksonville, Fla.	D3a
Nedved, Jeff (1)	WR	5-8	167	11/2/64	Cal State-Hayward	San Jose, Calif.	FA-'89
Pickens, Dwight	WR	5-10	170	5/18/66	Fresno State	Los Angeles, Calif.	D8
Pollack, Frank	T	6-4	277	11/5/67	Northern Arizona	Phoenix, Ariz.	D6
Shelton, Anthony	S	5-11	195	9/4/67	Tennessee State	Fayetteville, Tenn.	D11a
Shepherd, Mark	DE	6-4	272	9/23/67	Arkansas	Monroe, La.	FA
Siglar, Ricky (1)	T	6-7	296	6/14/66	San Jose State	Albuquerque, N.M.	FA-'89
Slater, Brian (1)	WR	6-4	200	5/15/66	Washington	Lake Stevens, Wash.	FA
Stephenson, Jeff (1)	LB	6-4	240	12/14/65	St. Cloud State	Minneapolis, Minn.	FA-'89
Turner, Lafayette	S	6-1	206	9/24/66	Texas A&M	Dallas, Tex.	FA
Weir, Robert (1)	NT	6-3	270	2/4/61	Southern Methodist	Dallas, Tex.	FA
Wiese, Brett (1)	G-C	6-4	280	8/6/66	Washington	Issaquah, Wash.	FA
Wyatt, Greg	QB	6-3	195	2/15/67	Northern Arizona	Phoenix, Ariz.	FA
Young, Todd	TE	6-5	257	2/2/67	Penn State	Tempe, Ariz.	FA

The term NFL Rookie is defined as a player who is in his first season of professional football and has not been on the roster of another professional football team for any regular-season or postseason games. A Rookie is designated by an "R" on NFL rosters. Players who have been active in another professional football league or players who have NFL experience, including either preseason training camp or being on an active roster for fewer than three regular-season or postseason games, are termed NFL First-Year Players. An NFL First-Year Player is designated by a "1" on NFL rosters. Thereafter, a player on an NFL active roster for at least three regular-season or postseason games is credited with an additional year of NFL playing experience.

NOTES

National Football Conference Central Division

Team Colors: Florida Orange, White, and Red

One Buccaneer Place
Tampa, Florida 33607
Telephone: (813) 870-2700

Club Officials

Owner-President: Hugh F. Culverhouse
Vice President: Joy Culverhouse
Vice President-Head Coach: Ray Perkins
Vice President-Treasurer: Gay Culverhouse
Vice President: Steve Story
Secretary: Jo Alexander
Assistant to the President: Phil Krueger
Director of Player Personnel: Jerry Angelo
Director of Pro Personnel: Ruston Webster
Director of Ticket Operations: Terry Wooten
Director of Public Relations: Rick Odioso
Dir. of Marketing & Advertising: Fred Doremus
Dir. of Corp. & Community Relations: Jane Pince
Asst. Director-Public Relations: Cheryl Harden
Media Relations Assistant: Mark Schiefelbein
Administrative Assistant: Paul Royak
College Personnel: James Harris, Tim Ruskell
Accountant: Pat Smith
Trainer: Chris Smith
Assistant Trainer: Joe Joe Petrone
Equipment Manager: Frank Pupello
Assistant Equipment Manager: Carl Melchior
Video Director: Dave Levy
Assistant Video Director: Mike Perkins

Stadium: Tampa Stadium • **Capacity:** 74,315
North Dale Mabry
Tampa, Florida 33607

Playing Surface: Grass

Training Camp: University of Tampa
401 W. Kennedy Boulevard
Tampa, Florida 33606

1990 Schedule

Preseason
Aug. 11	**Cincinnati**	7:00
Aug. 18	vs. N.E. at Jacksonville	8:00
Aug. 24	at Seattle	6:00
Aug. 30	**New York Jets**	7:00

Regular Season
Sept. 9	at Detroit	1:00
Sept. 16	**Los Angeles Rams**	1:00
Sept. 23	**Detroit**	8:00
Sept. 30	at Minnesota	12:00
Oct. 7	at Dallas	12:00
Oct. 14	**Green Bay**	1:00
Oct. 21	**Dallas**	1:00
Oct. 28	at San Diego	1:00
Nov. 4	**Chicago**	4:00
Nov. 11	at New Orleans	12:00
Nov. 18	at San Francisco	1:00
Nov. 25	vs. Green Bay at Milw.	1:00
Dec. 2	**Atlanta**	1:00
Dec. 9	**Open Date**	
Dec. 16	**Minnesota**	1:00
Dec. 23	at Chicago	12:00
Dec. 30	**New York Jets**	4:00

Buccaneers Coaching History

(63-152-1)
1976-84	John McKay	45-91-1
1985-86	Leeman Bennett	4-28-0
1987-89	Ray Perkins	14-33-0

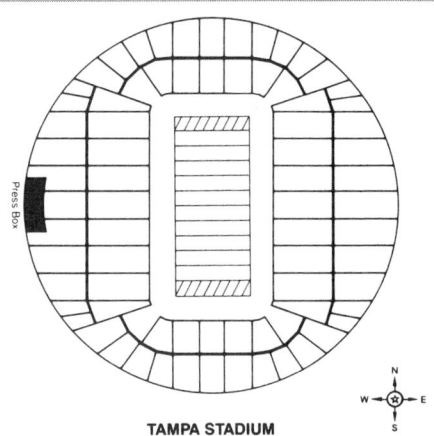

TAMPA STADIUM

Record Holders

Individual Records—Career
Category	Name	Performance
Rushing (Yds.)	James Wilder, 1981-89	5,957
Passing (Yds.)	Doug Williams, 1978-1982	12,648
Passing (TDs)	Doug Williams, 1978-1982	73
Receiving (No.)	James Wilder, 1981-89	430
Receiving (Yds.)	Kevin House, 1980-86	4,928
Interceptions	Cedric Brown, 1977-1984	29
Punting (Avg.)	Frank Garcia, 1983-87	41.1
Punt Return (Avg.)	Bobby Futrell, 1986-89	8.3
Kickoff Ret. (Avg.)	Isaac Hagins, 1976-1980	21.9
Field Goals	Donald Igwebuike, 1985-89	94
Touchdowns (Tot.)	James Wilder, 1981-89	46
Points	Donald Igwebuike, 1985-89	416

Individual Records—Single Season
Category	Name	Performance
Rushing (Yds.)	James Wilder, 1984	1,544
Passing (Yds.)	Doug Williams, 1981	3,563
Passing (TDs)	Doug Williams, 1980	20
	Vinny Testaverde, 1989	20
Receiving (No.)	James Wilder, 1984	85
Receiving (Yds.)	Kevin House, 1981	1,176
Interceptions	Cedric Brown, 1981	9
Punting (Avg.)	Larry Swider, 1981	42.7
Punt Return (Avg.)	Willie Drewrey, 1989	11.0
Kickoff Return (Avg.)	Isaac Hagins, 1977	23.5
Field Goals	Donald Igwebuike, 1985	22
	Donald Igwebuike, 1989	22
Touchdowns (Tot.)	James Wilder, 1984	13
Points	Donald Igwebuike, 1989	99

Individual Records—Single Game
Category	Name	Performance
Rushing (Yds.)	James Wilder, 11-6-83	219
Passing (Yds.)	Doug Williams, 11-16-80	486
Passing (TDs)	Steve DeBerg, 9-13-87	5
Receiving (No.)	James Wilder, 9-15-85	13
Receiving (Yds.)	Mark Carrier, 12-6-87	212
Interceptions	Many times	2
	Last time by Harry Hamilton, 10-1-89	
Field Goals	Bill Capece, 1-2-83	4
	Bill Capece, 10-30-83	4
	Donald Igwebuike, 11-24-85	4
	Donald Igwebuike, 11-19-89	4
Touchdowns	Jimmie Giles, 10-20-85	4
Points	Jimmie Giles, 10-20-85	24

1989 Team Record

Preseason (3-1)

Date	Result		Opponents
8/12	W	41-23	Houston
8/19	W	27- 0	Atlanta
8/26	L	0-30	at Indianapolis
9/2	W	27-10	at Cleveland
		95-63	

Regular Season (5-11)

Date	Result		Opponents	Att.
9/10	W	23-21	at Green Bay	55,650
9/17	L	16-20	San Francisco	64,087
9/24	W	20-10	New Orleans	44,053
10/1	L	3-17	at Minnesota	54,817
10/8	W	42-35	Chicago	72,077
10/15	L	16-17	Detroit	46,225
10/22	L	28-32	at Washington	53,862
10/29	L	23-56	at Cincinnati	57,225
11/5	L	31-42	Cleveland	69,162
11/12	L	10-24	Minnesota	56,271
11/19	W	32-31	at Chicago	63,826
11/26	W	14-13	at Phoenix	33,297
12/3	L	16-17	Green Bay	58,120
12/10	L	17-20	at Houston	54,532
12/17	L	7-33	at Detroit	40,362
12/24	L	22-31	Pittsburgh	29,690

Score by Periods

Buccaneers	58	92	42	128	0	—	320
Opponents	79	144	86	110	0	—	419

Attendance

Home 439,685   Away 413,571   Total 853,256
Single-game home record, 72,077 (10-8-89)
Single-season home record, 545,980 (1979)

1989 Team Statistics

	Buccaneers	Opp.
Total First Downs	288	317
Rushing	84	115
Passing	174	170
Penalty	30	32
Third Down: Made/Att.	95/230	87/208
Third Down: Pct.	41.3	41.8
Fourth Down: Made/Att.	7/13	10/17
Fourth Down: Pct.	53.8	58.8
Total Net Yards	4842	5460
Avg. Per Game	302.6	341.3
Total Plays	1025	1027
Avg. Per Play	4.7	5.3
Net Yards Rushing	1507	2023
Avg. Per Game	94.2	126.4
Total Rushes	412	479
Net Yards Passing	3335	3437
Avg. Per Game	208.4	214.8
Sacked/Yards Lost	43/331	33/222
Gross Yards	3666	3659
Att./Completions	570/302	515/301
Completion Pct.	53.0	58.4
Had Intercepted	28	21
Punts/Avg.	86/38.5	69/40.3
Net Punting Avg.	32.1	31.4
Penalties/Yards Lost	104/881	109/869
Fumbles/Ball Lost	21/9	30/18
Touchdowns	36	51
Rushing	10	18
Passing	23	29
Returns	3	4
Avg. Time of Possession	29:55	30:05

1989 Individual Statistics

Scoring

	TD R	TD P	TD Rt	PAT	FG	Saf	TP
Igwebuike	0	0	0	33/35	22/28	0	99
Carrier	0	9	0	0/0	0/0	0	54
Tate	8	1	0	0/0	0/0	0	54
Hill	0	5	0	0/0	0/0	0	30
Wilder	0	3	0	0/0	0/0	0	18
Hall	0	2	0	0/0	0/0	0	12
Howard	1	1	0	0/0	0/0	0	12
Reynolds	0	0	2	0/0	0/0	0	12
Davis	0	0	1	0/0	0/0	0	6
Drewrey	0	1	0	0/0	0/0	0	6
W. Harris	0	1	0	0/0	0/0	0	6
Stamps	1	0	0	0/0	0/0	0	6
Cocroft	0	0	0	0/0	0/0	1	2
S. Smith	0	0	0	0/0	0/0	1	2
Mohr	0	0	0	1/1	0/0	0	1
Buccaneers	10	23	3	34/36	22/28	2	320
Opponents	18	29	4	51/51	20/24	1	419

Passing

	Att.	Comp.	Yds.	Pct.	TD	Int.	Tkld.	Rate
Testaverde	480	258	3133	53.8	20	22	38/294	68.9
Ferguson	90	44	533	48.9	3	6	5/37	50.8
Buccaneers	570	302	3666	53.0	23	28	43/331	66.0
Opponents	515	301	3659	58.4	29	21	33/222	82.2

Rushing

	Att.	Yds.	Avg.	LG	TD
Tate	167	589	3.5	48	8
Howard	108	357	3.3	15	1
Wilder	70	244	3.5	14	0
Stamps	29	141	4.9	21t	1
Testaverde	25	139	5.6	16	0
D. Smith	7	37	5.3	17	0
Ferguson	4	6	1.5	7	0
Peebles	2	-6	-3.0	1	0
Buccaneers	412	1507	3.7	48	10
Opponents	479	2023	4.2	59t	18

Receiving

	No.	Yds.	Avg.	LG	TD
Carrier	86	1422	16.5	78t	9
Hill	50	673	13.5	53	5
Wilder	36	335	9.3	27	3
Hall	30	331	11.0	32	2
Howard	30	188	6.3	18	1
Stamps	15	82	5.5	21	0
Drewrey	14	157	11.2	18	1
Peebles	11	180	16.4	32	0
W. Harris	11	102	9.3	21	1
Tate	11	75	6.8	19	1
D. Smith	7	110	15.7	44	0
Mitchell	1	11	11.0	11	0
Buccaneers	302	3666	12.1	78t	23
Opponents	301	3659	12.2	79t	29

Interceptions

	No.	Yds.	Avg.	LG	TD
Hamilton	6	70	11.7	30	0
Robinson	6	44	7.3	16	0
Reynolds	5	87	17.4	68t	1
O. Harris	1	19	19.0	19	0
Davis	1	13	13.0	13t	1
Futrell	1	1	1.0	1	0
Elder	1	0	0.0	0	0
Buccaneers	21	234	11.1	68t	2
Opponents	28	240	8.6	39	2

Punting

	No.	Yds.	Avg.	In 20	LG
Mohr	84	3311	39.4	10	58
Buccaneers	86	3311	38.5	10	58
Opponents	69	2781	40.3	14	60

Punt Returns

	No.	FC	Yds.	Avg.	LG	TD
Drewrey	20	2	220	11.0	55	0
Futrell	12	2	76	6.3	15	0
Buccaneers	32	4	296	9.3	55	0
Opponents	54	12	492	9.1	65	0

Kickoff Returns

	No.	Yds.	Avg.	LG	TD
Elder	40	685	17.1	30	0
Stamps	9	145	16.1	36	0
Howard	5	82	16.4	19	0
Futrell	4	58	14.5	22	0
Wilder	2	42	21.0	23	0
Drewrey	1	26	26.0	26	0
Pillow	1	17	17.0	17	0
Buccaneers	62	1055	17.0	36	0
Opponents	55	1143	20.8	72	0

Sacks

	No.
Murphy	6.0
Moss	5.5
Goff	4.0
Davis	3.0
Jarvis	3.0
Robinson	2.5
Thomas	2.0
Weston	2.0
Cannon	1.0
Lee	1.0
Randle	1.0
S. Smith	1.0
Seals	1.0
Buccaneers	33.0
Opponents	43.0

1990 Draft Choices

Round	Name	Pos.	College
1.	Keith McCants	LB	Alabama
2.	Reggie Cobb	RB	Tennessee
4.	Jesse Anderson	TE	Mississippi State
	Tony Mayberry	C	Wake Forest
5.	Ian Beckles	G	Indiana
6.	Derrick Douglas	RB	Louisiana Tech
7.	Donnie Gardner	DE	Kentucky
9.	Terry Cook	DE	Fresno State
10.	Mike Busch	TE	Iowa State
11.	Terry Anthony	WR	Florida State
12.	Todd Hammel	QB	Stephen F. Austin

Tampa Bay Buccaneers 1990 Veteran Roster

No.	Name	Pos.	Ht.	Wt.	Birth-date	NFL Exp.	College	Hometown	How Acq.	'89 Games/ Starts
40	†Anderson, Gary	RB	6-1	190	4/18/61	5	Arkansas	Columbia, Mo.	T(SD)-'90	0*
56	Anno, Sam	LB	6-2	235	1/26/65	4	Southern California	Santa Monica, Calif.	PB(Minn)-'89#	16/0
75	Bax, Carl	G	6-4	290	1/5/66	2	Missouri	St. Charles, Mo.	D8-'89	6/4
55	Bob, Adam	LB	6-3	255	10/30/67	2	Texas A&M	Lafayette, La.	PB(NYJ)-'90#	5/0*
69	Bruhin, John	G	6-3	285	12/9/64	3	Tennessee	Knoxville, Tenn.	D4b-'88	9/8
78	Cannon, John	DE	6-5	265	7/30/60	9	William & Mary	Long Branch, N.J.	D3-'82	16/3
88	†Carrier, Mark	WR	6-0	185	10/28/65	4	Nicholls State	Church Point, La.	D3-'87	16/15
53	Coleman, Sidney	LB	6-2	250	1/14/64	3	Southern Mississippi	Gulfport, Miss.	FA-'88	4/0
21	Cooper, Evan	CB-S	5-11	195	6/28/62	7	Michigan	Miami, Fla.	PB(Atl)-'90#	16/13*
79	†Davis, Reuben	DE	6-4	285	5/7/65	3	North Carolina	Greensboro, N.C.	D9-'88	16/15
76	Dill, Scott	T	6-5	285	4/5/66	3	Memphis State	Birmingham, Ala.	PB(Phx)-'90#	16/0*
87	Drewrey, Willie	WR	5-7	170	4/28/63	6	West Virginia	Burlington, N.J.	PB(Hou)-'89#	16/0
42	Everett, Eric	CB-S	5-10	170	7/13/66	3	Texas Tech	Daingerfield, Tex.	PB(Phil)-'90#	15/1*
36	Futrell, Bobby	CB-S	5-11	190	8/4/62	5	Elizabeth City State	Ahoskie, N.C.	FA-'86	16/1
94	Goff, Robert	DE	6-3	270	10/2/65	3	Auburn	Bradenton, Fla.	D4a-'88	12/12
65	Graham, Dan	C	6-2	270	5/10/65	2	Northern Illinois	Wheaton, Ill.	FA-'88	0*
60	Grimes, Randy	C	6-4	275	7/20/60	8	Baylor	Tyler, Tex.	D2-'83	16/16
74	Gruber, Paul	T	6-5	290	2/24/65	3	Wisconsin	Prairie du Sac, Wis.	D1-'88	16/16
45	Haddix, Wayne	RB	6-1	205	7/23/65	3	Liberty	Middleton, Tenn.	FA-'90	0*
82	Hall, Ron	TE	6-4	245	3/15/64	4	Hawaii	Escondido, Calif.	D4b-'87	16/15
39	Hamilton, Harry	S	6-0	195	11/29/62	7	Penn State	Nanticoke, Pa.	FA-'88	13/13
20	Harris, Odie	CB-S	6-0	190	4/1/66	3	Sam Houston State	Bryan, Tex.	FA-'88	16/2
84	†Hill, Bruce	WR	6-0	180	2/29/64	4	Arizona State	Lancaster, Calif.	D4c-'87	16/16
43	Howard, William	RB	6-0	240	6/2/64	3	Tennessee	Lima, Ohio	D5-'88	16/12
1	Igwebuike, Donald	K	5-9	190	12/27/60	6	Clemson	Anambra, Nigeria	D10-'85	16/0
95	Jarvis, Curt	NT	6-2	270	1/28/65	3	Alabama	Gardendale, Ala.	D7a-'87	14/12
22	†Jones, Rod	CB-S	6-0	185	3/31/64	5	Southern Methodist	Dallas, Tex.	D1-'86	16/16
38	Lawson, Jamie	RB	5-10	240	10/2/65	2	Nicholls State	Raceland, La.	D5-'89	5/0
97	†Lee, Shawn	NT	6-2	285	10/24/66	3	North Alabama	Brooklyn, N.Y.	D6-'88	15/3
99	†Marve, Eugene	LB	6-2	240	8/14/60	9	Saginaw Valley State	Flint, Mich.	T(Buff)-'88	16/16
73	McHale, Tom	G	6-4	280	2/25/63	4	Cornell	Gaithersburg, Md.	FA-'87	15/10
41	Mitchell, Alvin	RB	6-0	235	8/20/64	2	Auburn	Venice, Fla.	FA-'89	5/0
5	Mohr, Chris	P	6-4	220	5/11/66	2	Alabama	Thomson, Ga.	D6-'89	16/0
58	†Moss, Winston	LB	6-3	235	12/24/65	4	Miami	Miami, Fla.	D2b-'87	16/16
59	†Murphy, Kevin	LB	6-2	235	9/8/63	5	Oklahoma	Plano, Tex.	D2-'86	16/16
57	Najarian, Pete	LB	6-2	235	12/22/63	3	Minnesota	Minneapolis, Minn.	FA-'88	12/0
96	Newton, Tim	NT	6-0	275	3/23/63	6	Florida	Orlando, Fla.	FA-'90	9/2*
86	Parks, Jeff	TE	6-4	245	9/14/64	4	Auburn	Gardendale, Ala.	FA-'88	0*
83	Peebles, Danny	WR	5-11	180	4/30/66	2	North Carolina State	Raleigh, N.C.	D3-'89	13/1
80	†Pillow, Frank	WR	5-10	170	3/11/65	3	Tennessee State	Nashville, Tenn.	D11-'88	3/0
54	Randle, Ervin	LB	6-1	250	10/12/62	6	Baylor	Hearne, Tex.	D3-'85	16/16
29	†Reynolds, Ricky	CB-S	5-11	190	1/19/65	4	Washington State	Sacramento, Calif.	D2a-'87	16/15
31	Rice, Rodney	CB-S	5-8	180	6/18/66	2	Brigham Young	Atwater, Calif.	PB(NE)-'90#	10/0*
30	Robinson, Mark	S	5-11	200	9/13/62	7	Penn State	Silver Spring, Md.	T(KC)-'88	15/15
24	Stamps, Sylvester	RB	5-7	180	2/24/61	6	Jackson State	Vicksburg, Miss.	PB(Atl)-'89#	10/1
70	†Swayne, Harry	T	6-5	270	2/2/65	4	Rutgers	Philadelphia, Pa.	D7b-'87	16/0
34	Tate, Lars	RB	6-2	215	2/2/66	3	Georgia	Indianapolis, Ind.	D2-'88	15/14
72	†Taylor, Rob	T	6-6	290	11/14/60	5	Northwestern	Fairmont, Ohio	FA-'86	16/16
14	Testaverde, Vinny	QB	6-5	215	11/13/63	4	Miami	Elmont, N.Y.	D1-'87	14/14
51	Thomas, Broderick	LB	6-4	245	2/20/67	2	Nebraska	Houston, Tex.	D1-'89	16/0
23	Williams, Keith	RB	5-10	175	9/30/64	2	Southwest Missouri	Texarkana, Ark.	FA-'90	0*

* Anderson last active with San Diego in '88; Bob played 5 games with N.Y. Jets in '89; Cooper played 16 games with Atlanta; Dill played 16 games with Phoenix; Everett played 15 games with Philadelphia; Graham active for 16 games with Tampa Bay but did not play; Haddix last active with N.Y. Giants in '88; Newton played 9 games with Minnesota; Parks last active with Tampa Bay in '88; Rice played in 10 games with New England; Williams last active with Atlanta in '87.

† Option playout; subject to developments.

Plan B unconditional free agent.

Players lost through Plan B (8): K John Carney (SD; 1 game in '89), S Sherman Cocroft (Det; 10), CB-S Donnie Elder (Mia; 16), TE William Harris (GB; 16), G Mike Simmonds (SD; 5), RB Don Smith (Buff; 11), DE Rhondy Weston (Clev; 12), RB James Wilder (Wash; 15).

Also played with Buccaneers in '89—QB Kerwin Bell (active for 4 games but did not play), T Mark Cooper (6), QB Joe Ferguson (5), WR Everett Gay (1), DE Sean Smith (3), TE Jackie Walker (14).

COACHING STAFF

Head Coach,
Ray Perkins

Pro Career: Named third head coach in Tampa Bay Buccaneers' history on December 31, 1986. Previous head coaching experience in the NFL came with New York Giants where he compiled a 24-35 record between 1979 and 1982. Perkins built the Giants into a playoff team by 1981, his third season. It marked the Giants' first playoff appearance in 18 years. Perkins worked five years as an assistant in the NFL, spending 1974-77 as receivers coach with New England Patriots and 1978 as offensive coordinator with San Diego Chargers. Drafted by the Baltimore Colts in the seventh round of the 1967 draft, and played five seasons there. Career record: 38-68.

Background: Bear Bryant's hand-picked successor at University of Alabama, where he compiled a 32-15-1 record between 1983-86, including three bowl game victories. College receiver at Alabama 1964-66 and All-America as a senior. College assistant at Mississippi State (1973).

Personal: Born November 6, 1941, in Mt. Olive, Mississippi. Ray and his wife, Carolyn, live in Tampa and have two sons—Tony and Mike.

Assistant Coaches

John Bobo, offensive line; born February 18, 1958, Alapaha, Ga., lives in Tampa. Tight end-defensive end Maryville 1976-79. No pro playing experience. College coach: Alabama 1985-86. Pro coach: Joined Buccaneers in 1987.

Tommy Brasher, defensive line; born December 30, 1940, El Dorado, Ark., lives in Tampa. Linebacker Arkansas 1961-63. No pro playing experience. College coach: Arkansas 1970, Virginia Tech 1971-73, Northeast Louisiana 1974, 1976, Southern Methodist 1977-81. Pro coach: Shreveport Steamer (WFL) 1975, New England Patriots 1982-84, Philadelphia Eagles 1985, Atlanta Falcons 1986-89, joined Buccaneers in 1990.

Fred Bruney, assistant head coach, defensive coordinator; born December 30, 1931, Martin's Ferry, Ohio, lives in Tampa. Back Ohio State 1949-52. Pro defensive back San Francisco 49ers 1953-56, Pittsburgh Steelers 1957, Washington Redskins 1958, Boston Patriots 1960-62. College coach: Ohio State 1959. Pro coach: Boston Patriots 1963, Philadelphia Eagles 1964-68, 1977-85, Atlanta Falcons 1969-76, 1986-89, joined Buccaneers in 1990.

Joel Collier, offensive assistant; born December 25, 1963, Buffalo, N.Y., lives in Tampa. Linebacker Northern Colorado 1983-86. No pro playing experience. College coach: Northern Colorado 1987, Syracuse 1988-89. Pro coach: Joined Buccaneers in 1990.

Sylvester Croom, running backs; born September 25, 1954, Tuscaloosa, Ala., lives in Tampa. Center Alabama 1971-74. Pro center New Orleans Saints 1975. College coach: Alabama 1976-86. Pro coach: Joined Buccaneers in 1987.

Jeff Fitzgerald, defensive assistant; born April 18, 1960, Burbank, Calif., lives in Tampa. No college or pro playing experience. College coach: Cincinnati 1985, Alabama 1986-89. Pro coach: Joined Buccaneers in 1990.

Kent Johnson, strength and conditioning; born February 21, 1956, Mexia, Tex., lives in Tampa. Defensive back Stephen F. Austin 1974-77. No pro playing experience. College coach: Northeast Louisiana 1979, Northwestern State (La.) 1980-81, Alabama 1983-86. Pro coach: Joined Buccaneers in 1987.

Joe Kines, outside linebackers; born July 13, 1944, Piedmont, Ala., lives in Tampa. Linebacker Jacksonville (Ala.) State 1963-65. No pro playing experience. College coach: Jacksonville State 1966, 1972-76, Clemson 1977-78, Florida 1979-84, Alabama 1985-86. Pro coach: Joined Buccaneers in 1987.

Tampa Bay Buccaneers 1990 First-Year Roster

Name	Pos.	Ht.	Wt.	Birth-date	College	Hometown	How Acq.
Anderson, Jesse	TE	6-2	245	5/8/67	Mississippi State	West Point, Miss.	D4a
Anthony, Terry	WR	6-0	200	3/9/68	Florida State	Daytona Beach, Fla.	D11
Beckles, Ian	G	6-1	295	7/20/67	Indiana	Montreal, Canada	D5
Blackmon, Terry	CB-S	5-9	170	12/21/65	Texas A&I	Van Vleck, Tex.	FA
Busch, Mike	TE	6-4	250	7/7/68	Iowa State	Donahue, Iowa	D10
Carlson, Jeff (1)	QB	6-3	215	5/23/66	Weber State	Garden Grove, Calif.	FA
Cheattom, Carlo (1)	CB-S	5-11	190	3/18/67	Auburn	Muscle Shoals, Ala.	FA
Citizen, Tony	RB	5-9	210	5/25/66	McNeese State	Church Point, La.	FA
Cobb, Reggie	RB	6-0	225	7/7/68	Tennessee	Knoxville, Tenn.	D2
Cook, Terry	DE	6-3	270	4/29/64	Fresno State	Duarte, Calif.	D9
DeWitt, Ken	RB	5-9	180	12/20/66	N.W. Louisiana	Mansfield, La.	FA
Douglas, Derrick	RB	5-10	205	8/10/68	Louisiana Tech	Shreveport, La.	D6
Duncan, Herb (1)	WR	6-0	185	12/18/65	Northern Arizona	San Diego, Calif.	D11b-'89
Fleming, Terry	LB	6-1	230	12/10/66	Mississippi College	Mobile, Ala.	FA
Ford, Chris	WR	6-1	185	5/20/67	Lamar	Houston, Tex.	FA
Gardner, Donnie	DE	6-4	265	2/17/68	Kentucky	Louisville, Ky.	D7
Goods, Bennie	LB	6-3	255	2/20/68	Alcorn State	Pattison, Miss.	FA
Greene, A.J. (1)	CB-S	5-9	175	6/24/66	Wake Forest	Hendersonville, N.C.	FA
Hammel, Todd	QB	6-1	205	12/7/66	Stephen F. Austin	Durant, Okla.	D12
Harvey, John (1)	RB	5-11	185	12/28/66	Texas-El Paso	Spring Valley, N.Y.	FA-'89
Hegdale, Steve (1)	T	6-5	290	10/24/65	Tulsa	McAlister, Tex.	FA-'89
Mayberry, Tony	C	6-4	285	12/8/67	Wake Forest	Springfield, Va.	D4b
McCants, Keith	LB	6-3	255	11/19/68	Alabama	Mobile, Ala.	D1
Perkins, Bruce	RB	6-2	230	8/14/67	Arizona State	Waterloo, Iowa	FA
Roland, Benji (1)	NT	6-4	270	4/4/67	Auburn	Eastman, Ga.	FA
Royals, Mark (1)	P	6-5	215	6/22/64	Appalachian State	Mathews, Va.	FA
Seals, Ray (1)	NT	6-3	270	6/17/65	No college	Syracuse, N.Y.	FA-'88
Smith, David	QB	6-0	185	4/30/65	Alabama	Gadsden, Ala.	FA
Thomas, Stevie	WR	6-1	195	7/24/67	Bethune-Cookman	St. Petersburg, Fla.	FA
Thompson, Shelton	DE	6-3	280	1/9/67	Florida State	Lakeland, Fla.	FA
Watts, Carl	G	6-3	260	5/30/67	North Carolina	Hampton, Va.	FA

The term NFL Rookie is defined as a player who is in his first season of professional football and has not been on the roster of another professional football team for any regular-season or postseason games. A Rookie is designated by an "R" on NFL rosters. Players who have been active in another professional football league or players who have NFL experience, including either preseason training camp or being on an active roster for fewer than three regular-season or post-season games, are termed NFL First-Year Players. An NFL First-Year Player is designated by a "1" on NFL rosters. Thereafter, a player on an NFL active roster for at least three regular-season or postseason games is credited with an additional year of NFL playing experience.

NOTES

_____

_____

_____

_____

_____

_____

_____

_____

_____

_____

_____

_____

_____

_____

Mike Shula, quarterbacks; born June 3, 1965, Baltimore, Md., lives in Tampa. Quarterback Alabama 1984-86. Pro quarterback Tampa Bay Buccaneers 1987. Pro coach: Joined Buccaneers in 1988.

Rodney Stokes, special teams; born February 3, 1953, Brookhaven, Miss., lives in Tampa. Linebacker Delta State 1976-77. No pro playing experience. College coach: Alabama 1983-86. Pro coach: Joined Buccaneers in 1987.

Richard Williamson, assistant head coach, receivers; born April 13, 1941, Fort Deposit, Ala., lives in Tampa. Receiver Alabama 1959-62. No pro playing experience. College coach: Alabama 1963-67, 1970-71, Arkansas 1968-69, 1972-74, Memphis State 1975-80 (head coach). Pro coach: Kansas City Chiefs 1983-86, joined Buccaneers in 1987.

National Football Conference
Eastern Division

Team Colors: Burgundy and Gold

Redskin Park
P.O. Box 17247
Dulles International Airport
Washington, D.C. 20041
Telephone: (703) 471-9100

Club Officials

Chairman of the Board-CEO: Jack Kent Cooke
Executive Vice President: John Kent Cooke
Secretary: Stuart Haney
Controller: Gregory Dillon
Board of Directors: Jack Kent Cooke, John Kent
   Cooke, James Lacher, William A. Shea, Esq.
General Manager: Charles Casserly
Assistant General Manager: Bobby Mitchell
Director of Pro Scouting: Joe Mack
Director of Pro Player Personnel: Kirk Mee
Director of College Scouting: George Saimes
Scouts: Jerry Fauls, Chuck Banker, Gene Bates
V.P./Communications: Charlie Dayton
Dir. of Marketing/Stadium Operations: Paul Denfeld
Director of Information: Jamie Crittenberger
Director of Media Relations: Mike McCall
Video Director: Donnie Schoenmann
Assistant Video Director: Hugh McPhillips
Ticket Manager: Sue Barton
Asst. Ticket Mgrs.: Larry Desautels, Tony Lyman
Head Trainer: Bubba Tyer
Assistant Trainers: Al Bellamy, Kevin Bastin
Equipment Manager: Jay Brunetti
Asst. Equipment Manager: Jim Knight

Stadium: RFK Stadium • **Capacity:** 55,672
   East Capitol Street
   Washington, D.C. 20003

Playing Surface: Grass

Training Camp: Dickinson College
   Carlisle, Pennsylvania 17013
   (717) 245-1140

1990 Schedule

Preseason
Aug. 11	vs. Atl. at Chapel Hill, N.C.	7:00
Aug. 17	**Pittsburgh**	8:00
Aug. 25	at Cleveland	7:00
Aug. 31	**Los Angeles Rams**	8:00

Regular Season
Sept. 9	**Phoenix**	1:00
Sept. 16	at San Francisco	1:00
Sept. 23	**Dallas**	1:00
Sept. 30	at Phoenix	5:00
Oct. 7	**Open Date**	
Oct. 14	**New York Giants**	4:00
Oct. 21	**Philadelphia**	1:00
Oct. 28	at New York Giants	4:00
Nov. 4	at Detroit	1:00
Nov. 12	at Philadelphia (Monday)	9:00
Nov. 18	**New Orleans**	1:00
Nov. 22	at Dallas (Thanksgiving)	3:00
Dec. 2	**Miami**	1:00
Dec. 9	**Chicago**	4:00
Dec. 15	at New England (Saturday)	4:00
Dec. 22	at Indianapolis (Saturday)	8:00
Dec. 30	**Buffalo**	1:00

Redskins Coaching History

Boston 1932-36
(408-348-26)

1932	Lud Wray	4-4-2
1933-34	William (Lone Star) Dietz	11-11-2
1935	Eddie Casey	2-8-1
1936-42	Ray Flaherty	56-23-3
1943	Arthur (Dutch) Bergman	7-4-1
1944-45	Dudley DeGroot	14-6-1
1946-48	Glen (Turk) Edwards	16-18-1
1949	John Whelchel*	3-3-1
1949-51	Herman Ball**	4-16-0
1951	Dick Todd	5-4-0
1952-53	Earl (Curly) Lambeau	10-13-1
1954-58	Joe Kuharich	26-32-2
1959-60	Mike Nixon	4-18-2
1961-65	Bill McPeak	21-46-3
1966-68	Otto Graham	17-22-3
1969	Vince Lombardi	7-5-2
1970	Bill Austin	6-8-0
1971-77	George Allen	69-35-1
1978-80	Jack Pardee	24-24-0
1981-89	Joe Gibbs	102-48-0

*Released after seven games in 1949
**Released after three games in 1951

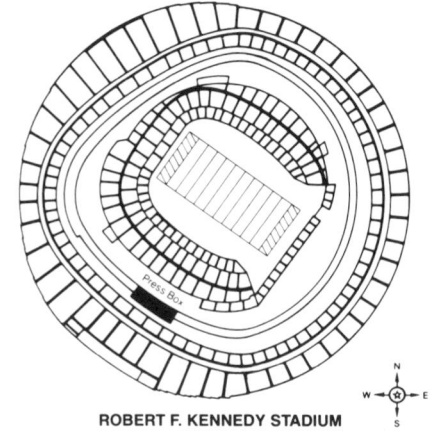

ROBERT F. KENNEDY STADIUM

Record Holders
Individual Records—Career

Category	Name	Performance
Rushing (Yds.)	John Riggins, 1976-79, 1981-85	7,472
Passing (Yds.)	Joe Theismann, 1974-1985	25,206
Passing (TDs)	Sonny Jurgensen, 1964-1974	209
Receiving (No.)	Art Monk, 1980-89	662
Receiving (Yds.)	Art Monk, 1980-89	9,165
Interceptions	Brig Owens, 1966-1977	36
Punting (Avg.)	Sammy Baugh, 1937-1952	*45.1
Punt Return (Avg.)	Johnny Williams, 1952-53	12.8
Kickoff Return (Avg.)	Bobby Mitchell, 1962-68	28.5
Field Goals	Mark Moseley, 1974-1986	263
Touchdowns (Tot.)	Charley Taylor, 1964-1977	90
Points	Mark Moseley, 1974-1986	1,206

Individual Records—Single Season

Category	Name	Performance
Rushing (Yds.)	John Riggins, 1983	1,347
Passing (Yds.)	Jay Schroeder, 1986	4,109
Passing (TDs)	Sonny Jurgensen, 1967	31
Receiving (No.)	Art Monk, 1984	*106
Receiving (Yds.)	Bobby Mitchell, 1963	1,436
Interceptions	Dan Sandifer, 1948	13
Punting (Avg.)	Sammy Baugh, 1940	*51.4
Punt Return (Avg.)	Johnny Williams, 1952	15.3
Kickoff Return (Avg.)	Mike Nelms, 1981	29.7
Field Goals	Mark Moseley, 1983	33
Touchdowns (Tot.)	John Riggins, 1983	*24
Points	Mark Moseley, 1983	161

Individual Records—Single Game

Category	Name	Performance
Rushing (Yds.)	Gerald Riggs, 9-17-89	221
Passing (Yds.)	Sammy Baugh, 10-31-43	446
Passing (TDs)	Sammy Baugh, 10-31-43	6
	Sammy Baugh, 11-23-47	6
Receiving (No.)	Art Monk, 12-15-85	13
	Kelvin Bryant, 12-7-86	13
Receiving (Yds.)	Anthony Allen, 10-4-87	255
Interceptions	Sammy Baugh, 11-14-43	*4
	Dan Sandifer, 10-31-48	*4
Field Goals	Many times	5
	Last time by Mark Moseley, 10-26-80	
Touchdowns (Tot.)	Dick James, 12-17-61	4
	Larry Brown, 12-4-73	4
Points	Dick James, 12-17-61	24
	Larry Brown, 12-4-73	24

*NFL Record

1989 Team Record
Preseason (4-1)

Date	Result		Opponents
8/5	W	31-6	vs. Buffalo
			at Canton, Ohio
8/12	W	21-14	at Pittsburgh
8/21	L	13-24	at Minnesota
8/25	W	35-21	Miami
9/1	W	26-21	at New Orleans
		126-86	

Regular Season (10-6)

Date	Result		Opponents	Att.
9/11	L	24-27	N.Y. Giants	54,160
9/17	L	37-42	Philadelphia	53,493
9/24	W	30- 7	at Dallas	63,200
10/1	W	16-14	at New Orleans	64,358
10/8	W	30-28	Phoenix	53,335
10/15	L	17-20	at N.Y. Giants	76,245
10/22	W	32-28	Tampa Bay	53,862
10/29	L	24-37	at L.A. Raiders	52,781
11/5	L	3-13	Dallas	53,187
11/12	W	10- 3	at Philadelphia	65,443
11/20	L	10-14	Denver	52,975
11/26	W	38-14	Chicago	50,044
12/3	W	29-10	at Phoenix	38,870
12/10	W	26-21	San Diego	47,693
12/17	W	31-30	at Atlanta	37,501
12/23	W	29- 0	at Seattle	60,294

Score by Periods

Redskins	80	82	127	97	0	—	386
Opponents	76	99	47	86	0	—	308

Attendance
Home 418,749   Away 458,692   Total 877,441
Single-game home record, 55,750 (11-10-85)
Single-season home record, 434,854 (1986)

1989 Team Statistics

	Redskins	Opp.
Total First Downs	338	274
Rushing	101	72
Passing	217	177
Penalty	20	25
Third Down: Made/Att.	105/240	77/202
Third Down: Pct.	43.8	38.1
Fourth Down: Made/Att.	10/19	4/11
Fourth Down: Pct.	52.6	36.4
Total Net Yards	6253	4915
Avg. Per Game	390.8	307.2
Total Plays	1116	954
Avg. Per Play	5.6	5.2
Net Yards Rushing	1904	1344
Avg. Per Game	119.0	84.0
Total Rushes	514	384
Net Yards Passing	4349	3571
Avg. Per Game	271.8	223.2
Sacked/Yards Lost	21/127	40/304
Gross Yards	4476	3875
Att./Completions	581/337	530/277
Completion Pct.	58.0	52.3
Had Intercepted	17	27
Punts/Avg.	63/42.3	76/40.1
Net Punting Avg.	33.3	34.5
Penalties/Yards Lost	105/881	98/796
Fumbles/Ball Lost	32/20	24/15
Touchdowns	42	38
Rushing	14	9
Passing	24	25
Returns	4	4
Avg. Time of Possession	32:58	27:02

1989 Individual Statistics

Scoring

	TD R	TD P	TD Rt	PAT	FG	Saf	TP
Lohmiller	0	0	0	41/41	29/40	0	128
Byner	7	2	0	0/0	0/0	0	54
Clark	0	9	0	0/0	0/0	0	54
Monk	0	8	0	0/0	0/0	0	48
Riggs	4	0	0	0/0	0/0	0	24
Sanders	0	4	0	0/0	0/0	0	24
Morris	2	0	0	0/0	0/0	0	12
Coleman	0	0	1	0/0	0/0	0	6
Dupard, N.E.-Wash.	1	0	0	0/0	0/0	0	6
Howard	0	0	1	0/0	0/0	0	6
A. Johnson	0	0	1	0/0	0/0	0	6
Rypien	1	0	0	0/0	0/0	0	6
Walton	0	0	1	0/0	0/0	0	6
Warren	0	1	0	0/0	0/0	0	6
Manley	0	0	0	0/0	0/0	1	2
Stokes	0	0	0	0/0	0/0	1	2
Redskins	14	24	4	41/42	29/40	3	386
Opponents	9	25	4	38/38	14/23	0	308

Passing

	Att.	Comp.	Yds.	Pct.	TD	Int.	Tkld.	Rate
Rypien	476	280	3768	58.8	22	13	16/108	88.1
Williams	93	51	585	54.8	1	3	2/10	64.1
Humphries	10	5	91	50.0	1	1	3/9	75.4
Byner	1	0	0	0.0	0	0	0/0	39.6
Sanders	1	1	32	100.0	0	0	0/0	118.8
Redskins	581	337	4476	58.0	24	17	21/127	84.1
Opponents	530	277	3875	52.3	25	27	40/304	70.6

Rushing

	Att.	Yds.	Avg.	LG	TD
Riggs	201	834	4.1	58	4
Byner	134	580	4.3	24	7
Morris	124	336	2.7	12t	2
Dupard, N.E.-Wash.	37	111	3.0	19	1
Dupard, Wash.	12	48	4.0	19	0
Rypien	26	56	2.2	15	1
Clark	2	19	9.5	11	0
Sanders	4	19	4.8	13	0
Humphries	5	10	2.0	9	0
Monk	3	8	2.7	14	0
Coleman	1	−1	−1.0	−1	0
Reaves	1	−1	−1.0	−1	0
Williams	1	−4	−4.0	−4	0
Redskins	514	1904	3.7	58	14
Opponents	384	1344	3.5	73t	9

Receiving

	No.	Yds.	Avg.	LG	TD
Monk	86	1186	13.8	60t	8
Sanders	80	1138	14.2	68	4
Clark	79	1229	15.6	80t	9
Byner	54	458	8.5	27	2
Warren	15	167	11.1	25	1
Morris	8	65	8.1	17	0
Riggs	7	67	9.6	13	0
Dupard, N.E.-Wash.	6	70	11.7	45	0
J. Johnson	4	84	21.0	39	0
Orr	3	80	26.7	48	0
Tice	1	2	2.0	2	0
Redskins	337	4476	13.3	80t	24
Opponents	277	3875	14.0	72t	25

Interceptions

	No.	Yds.	Avg.	LG	TD
A. Johnson	4	94	23.5	59t	1
Walton	4	58	14.5	29t	1
B. Davis	4	40	10.0	15	0
Bowles	3	25	8.3	25	0
Wilburn	3	13	4.3	13	0
Coleman	2	24	12.0	24t	1
Grant	2	0	0.0	0	0
Green	2	0	0.0	0	0
Marshall	1	18	18.0	18	0
W. Davis	1	11	11.0	11	0
Gouveia	1	1	1.0	1	0
Redskins	27	284	10.5	59t	3
Opponents	17	229	13.5	45t	1

Punting

	No.	Yds.	Avg.	In 20	LG
Mojsiejenko	62	2663	43.0	21	74
Redskins	63	2663	42.3	21	74
Opponents	76	3047	40.1	22	59

Punt Returns

	No.	FC	Yds.	Avg.	LG	TD
Howard	21	18	200	9.5	38	0
Sanders	2	2	12	6.0	7	0
Green	1	0	11	11.0	11	0
B. Davis	1	0	3	3.0	3	0
Mayhew	1	0	0	0.0	0	0
Redskins	26	20	226	8.7	38	0
Opponents	34	5	383	11.3	53	0

Kickoff Returns

	No.	Yds.	Avg.	LG	TD
Howard	21	522	24.9	99t	1
A. Johnson	24	504	21.0	38	0
Sanders	9	134	14.9	29	0
Mandeville	1	10	10.0	10	0
Branch	1	6	6.0	6	0
Gouveia	1	0	0.0	0	0
Orr	1	0	0.0	0	0
Redskins	58	1176	20.3	99t	1
Opponents	74	1532	20.7	96t	1

Sacks

	No.
Mann	10.0
Manley	9.0
Coleman	4.0
Marshall	4.0
Caldwell	3.5
Grant	3.5
Stokes	3.0
Koch	2.0
Bowles	1.0
Redskins	40.0
Opponents	21.0

1990 Draft Choices

Round	Name	Pos.	College
2.	Andre Collins	LB	Penn State
3.	Mohammed Elewonibi	G	Brigham Young
4.	Cary Conklin	QB	Washington
	Rico Labbe	DB	Boston College
5.	Brian Mitchell	RB	S.W. Louisiana
6.	Kent Wells	DT	Nebraska
9.	Tim Moxley	G	Ohio State
10.	D'Juan Francisco	DB	Notre Dame
	Thomas Rayam	DT	Alabama
11.	Jon Leverenz	LB	Minnesota

Washington Redskins 1990 Veteran Roster

No.	Name	Pos.	Ht.	Wt.	Birth-date	NFL Exp.	College	Hometown	How Acq.	'89 Games/ Starts
61	Adickes, Mark	G	6-4	275	4/22/61	5	Baylor	Richardson, Tex.	PB(KC)-'90#	16/11*
56	†Bonner, Brian	LB	6-2	225	10/9/65	2	Minnesota	Minneapolis, Minn.	FA-'88	6/0
53	†Bostic, Jeff	C	6-2	260	9/18/58	11	Clemson	Greensboro, N.C.	FA-'80	16/16
23	†Bowles, Todd	S	6-2	203	11/18/63	5	Temple	Elizabeth, N.J.	FA-'86	16/16
29	Branch, Reggie	RB	5-11	235	10/22/62	6	East Carolina	Sanford, Fla.	FA-'86	10/0
46	Brandes, John	TE	6-2	250	4/2/64	4	Cameron University	Fort Riley, Kan.	PB(Ind)-'90#	16/11*
67	Brown, Ray	T	6-5	280	12/12/62	9	Arkansas State	Marion, Ark.	FA-'89	7/0
38	Brown, Tom	RB	6-1	228	11/20/64	2	Pittsburgh	Ridgeway, Pa.	PB(Mia)-'90#	16/0*
24	Bryant, Kelvin	RB	6-2	195	9/26/60	4	North Carolina	Tarboro, N.C.	D7-'86	0*
21	Byner, Earnest	RB	5-10	215	9/15/62	7	East Carolina	Milledgeville, Ga.	T(Clev)-'89	16/13
50	†Caldwell, Ravin	LB	6-3	229	8/4/63	4	Arkansas	Fort Smith, Ark.	D5-'86	15/13
84	Clark, Gary	WR	5-9	173	5/1/62	6	James Madison	Dublin, Va.	FA-'85	15/12
51	†Coleman, Monte	LB	6-2	230	11/4/57	12	Central Arkansas	Pine Bluff, Ark.	D11-'79	15/3
34	Davis, Brian	CB	6-2	190	8/31/63	4	Nebraska	Phoenix, Ariz.	D2a-'87	15/9
26	†Davis, Wayne	CB	5-11	180	7/17/63	6	Indiana State	Mt. Healthy, Ohio	FA-'89	8/0
25	Dupard, Reggie	RB	5-11	205	10/30/63	5	Southern Methodist	New Orleans, La.	FA-'89	7/0
27	Edwards, Brad	S	6-2	196	3/22/66	3	South Carolina	Fayetteville, N.C.	PB(Minn)-'90#	9/1*
97	Geathers, James	DE	6-7	290	6/26/60	6	Wichita State	Georgetown, S.C.	PB(NO)-'90#	15/15*
54	Gouveia, Kurt	LB	6-1	227	9/14/64	4	Brigham Young	Waianae, Hawaii	D8-'86	15/1
77	†Grant, Darryl	DT	6-1	275	11/22/59	10	Rice	San Antonio, Tex.	D9-'81	16/16
28	Green, Darrell	CB	5-8	170	2/15/60	8	Texas A&I	Houston, Tex.	D1-'83	7/7
68	Grimm, Russ	G	6-3	275	5/2/59	10	Pittsburgh	Southmoreland, Pa.	D3-'81	12/9
59	Harbour, Dave	C	6-4	265	10/23/65	3	Illinois	Naperville, Ill.	FA-'88	16/0
75	Hodge, Milford	DT	6-3	278	3/11/61	5	Washington State	San Francisco, Calif.	PB(NE)-'90#	16/1*
80	†Howard, Joe	WR	5-8	170	12/21/62	3	Notre Dame	Washington, D.C.	FA-'89	15/0
16	Humphries, Stan	QB	6-2	223	4/14/65	2	Northeastern Louisiana	Shreveport, La.	D6-'88	2/0
66	Jacoby, Joe	T	6-7	310	7/6/59	10	Louisville	Louisville, Ky.	FA-'81	10/10
47	Johnson, A.J.	CB	5-8	176	6/22/67	2	Southwest Texas State	San Antonio, Tex.	D6-'89	16/8
88	Johnson, Jimmie	TE	6-2	246	10/6/66	2	Howard University	Augusta, Ga.	D12a-'89	16/0
74	†Koch, Markus	DE	6-5	275	2/13/63	5	Boise State	Ontario, Canada	D2a-'85	10/7
79	Lachey, Jim	T	6-6	290	6/4/63	6	Ohio State	St. Henry, Ohio	T(Raid)-'88	14/14
8	Lohmiller, Chip	K	6-3	213	7/16/66	3	Minnesota	Springfield, Mo.	D2-'88	16/0
71	Mann, Charles	DE	6-6	270	4/12/61	8	Nevada-Reno	Sacramento, Calif.	D3-'83	16/16
91	Manusky, Greg	LB	6-1	242	8/12/66	3	Colgate	Wyoming, Pa.	FA-'88	16/7
58	Marshall, Wilber	LB	6-1	230	4/18/62	7	Florida	Titusville, Fla.	FA-'88	16/6
73	May, Mark	G-T	6-6	295	11/2/59	10	Pittsburgh	Oneonta, N.Y.	D1-'81	9/9
35	Mayhew, Martin	CB	5-8	172	10/8/65	2	Florida State	Tallahassee, Fla.	FA-'89	16/7
57	McArthur, Kevin	LB	6-2	250	5/11/63	5	Lamar	Lake Charles, La.	PB(NYJ)-'90#	9/1*
63	McKenzie, Raleigh	C-G	6-2	270	2/8/63	6	Tennessee	Knoxville, Tenn.	D11-'85	15/8
48	Middleton, Ron	TE	6-2	255	7/17/65	5	Auburn	Atmore, Ala.	PB(Clev)-'90#	9/0*
62	Mitz, Alonzo	DE	6-3	275	6/5/63	5	Florida	Fort Pierce, Fla.	FA-'90	12/3*
2	Mojsiejenko, Ralf	P	6-3	212	1/28/63	6	Michigan State	Bridgman, Mich.	T(SD)-'89	16/0
81	Monk, Art	WR	6-3	209	12/5/57	11	Syracuse	White Plains, N.Y.	D1-'80	16/12
87	Orr, Terry	TE	6-3	227	9/27/61	5	Texas	Abilene, Tex.	D10-'85	16/1
37	†Riggs, Gerald	RB	6-1	232	11/6/60	9	Arizona State	Las Vegas, Nev.	T(Atl)-'89	12/7
99	Rocker, Tracy	DT	6-3	288	4/9/66	2	Auburn	Atlanta, Ga.	D3-'89	16/10
10	Rutledge, Jeff	QB	6-1	195	1/22/57	12	Alabama	Birmingham, Ala.	PB(NYG)-'90#	1/0*
11	Rypien, Mark	QB	6-4	234	10/2/62	4	Washington State	Spokane, Wash.	D6-'86	14/14
83	Sanders, Ricky	WR	5-11	180	8/30/62	5	Southwest Texas State	Temple, Tex.	T(NE)-'86	16/12
69	Schlereth, Mark	G	6-3	285	1/25/66	2	Idaho	Anchorage, Alaska	D10-'89	6/6
76	Simmons, Ed	T	6-5	300	12/31/63	4	Eastern Washington	Stockton, Calif.	D6b-'87	16/8
89	Stanley, Walter	WR	5-9	180	11/5/62	6	Mesa, Colo.	Chicago, Ill.	PB(Det)-'90#	14/12*
60	Stokes, Fred	DE	6-3	262	3/14/64	4	Georgia Southern	Vidalia, Ga.	FA-'89	16/5
64	Swoopes, Pat	DT	6-3	280	3/4/64	3	Mississippi State	Bradshaw, Miss.	PB(NO)-'90#	15/0*
86	Tice, Mike	TE	6-7	247	2/2/59	10	Maryland	Central Islip, N.Y.	FA-'89	16/5
31	Vaughn, Clarence	S	6-0	202	7/17/64	4	Northern Illinois	Chicago, Ill.	D8-'87	16/4
40	Walton, Alvin	S	6-0	180	3/14/64	5	Kansas	Banning, Calif.	D3-'86	13/12
85	†Warren, Don	TE	6-4	242	5/5/56	12	San Diego State	Covina, Calif.	D4-'79	15/15
82	Whisenhunt, Ken	TE	6-3	240	2/28/62	5	Georgia Tech	Augusta, Ga.	FA-'89	0*
32	Wilder, James	RB	6-3	225	5/12/58	10	Missouri	Sikeston, Mo.	PB(TB)-'90#	15/4*

* Adickes played 16 games with Kansas City in '89; Brandes played 16 games with Indianapolis; T. Brown played 9 games with Miami; Bryant and Whisenhunt missed '89 season due to injury; Edwards played 9 games with Minnesota; Geathers played 15 games with New Orleans; Hodge played 16 games with New England; McArthur played 9 games with N.Y. Jets; Middleton played 9 games with Cleveland; Mitz played 12 games with Seattle; Rutledge played 1 game with N.Y. Giants; Stanley played 14 games with Detroit; Swoopes played 15 games with New Orleans; Wilder played 15 games with Tampa Bay.

† Option playout; subject to developments.

Plan B unconditional free agent.

Retired—Neal Olkewicz, 11-year linebacker, 9 games in '89.

Players lost through Plan B (6): WR Carl Harry (Hou; 1 game in '89), RB Joe Mickles (SD; 9), RB Jamie Morris (NE; 12); DE Lybrant Robinson (Dall; 5), G Ralph Tamm (Clev; 0); S Herb Welch (Det; 9).

Also played with Redskins in '89—LB Don Graham (1 game), S Chris Mandeville (1), DE Dexter Manley (10), RB Willard Reaves (1), DT Mike Stensrud (8), CB Barry Wilburn (8), QB Doug Williams (4).

COACHING STAFF

Head Coach,
Joe Gibbs

Pro Career: Enters tenth season as Redskins' all-time leader in wins. Picked up 100th coaching victory in 26-21 squeaker over San Diego in Week 14, becoming the seventh fastest NFL coach to reach that plateau. Has led Redskins to two Super Bowl titles and three Super Bowl appearances during 1980's. Washington has appeared in postseason play five of last eight seasons under Gibbs. Named head coach on January 13, 1981, after spending eight years as an NFL assistant coach and nine seasons on the collegiate level. Came to Redskins from San Diego Chargers, where he was offensive coordinator in 1979 and 1980. Prior to that, he was offensive coordinator for the Tampa Bay Buccaneers in 1978 and offensive backfield coach for the St. Louis Cardinals from 1973-77. While he was with San Diego, the Chargers won the AFC West title and led the NFL in passing two straight years. No pro playing experience. Career record: 102-48.

College: Played tight end, linebacker, and guard under Don Coryell at San Diego State in 1961 and 1962 after spending two years at Cerritos, Calif., J.C. 1959-60. Started college coaching career at San Diego State 1964-66, followed by Florida State 1967-68, Southern California 1969-70, and Arkansas 1971-72.

Personal: Born November 25, 1940, in Mocksville, N.C. Graduated from Santa Fe Springs, Calif., High School. Two-time national racquetball champion and ranked second in the over-35 category in 1978. He and his wife, Pat, live in Vienna, Va., and have two sons—J.D. and Coy.

Assistant Coaches

Don Breaux, running backs; born August 3, 1940, Jennings, La., lives in Centreville, Va. Quarterback McNeese State 1959-61. Pro quarterback Denver Broncos 1963, San Diego Chargers 1964-65. College coach: Florida State 1966-67, Arkansas 1968-71, 1977-80, Florida 1973-74, Texas 1975-76. Pro coach: Joined Redskins in 1981.

Jack Burns, quarterbacks; born January 3, 1949, Tampa, Fla., lives in Herndon, Va. Safety Florida 1967-71. No pro playing experience. College coach: Florida 1971-73, 1975, Louisville 1974, 1985-88, Texas 1976, Vanderbilt 1977-78, Auburn 1979-80. Pro scout: Tampa Bay Bandits (USFL) 1981-83. Pro coach: Joined Redskins in 1989.

Bobby DePaul, administrative assistant; born January 29, 1963, Cheverly, Md., lives in Bowie, Md. Linebacker Maryland 1982-83. No pro playing experience. College coach: Catholic University 1986-88. Pro coach: Joined Redskins in 1989.

Rod Dowhower, offensive assistant, passing game; born April 15, 1943, Ord, Nebraska, lives in Ashburn, Va. Quarterback San Diego State 1963-65. No pro playing experience. College coach: San Diego State 1966-72, UCLA 1974-75, Boise State 1976, Stanford 1977-79 (head coach 1979). Pro coach: St. Louis Cardinals 1973, 1982-84, Denver Broncos 1980-81, Indianapolis Colts 1985-86 (head coach), Atlanta Falcons 1987-89, joined Redskins in 1990.

Jim Hanifan, offensive line; born September 21, 1933, Compton, Calif., lives in Reston, Va. Tight end California 1952-54. Pro tight end Toronto Argonauts (CFL) 1955. College coach: Glendale, Calif., J.C. 1964-66, Utah 1967-70, California 1971-72, San Diego State 1972-73. Pro coach: St. Louis Cardinals 1974-85 (head coach 1980-85), Atlanta Falcons 1987-89 (interim head coach last four games of 1989), joined Redskins in 1990.

Larry Peccatiello, defensive coordinator; born December 21, 1935, Newark, N.J., lives in Warrenton, Va. Receiver William & Mary 1955-58. No pro playing experience. College coach: William & Mary 1961-68, Navy 1969-70, Rice 1971. Pro coach: Houston Oilers 1972-75, Seattle Seahawks 1976-80, joined Redskins in 1981.

Washington Redskins 1990 First-Year Roster

Name	Pos.	Ht.	Wt.	Birth-date	College	Hometown	How Acq.
Adams, Tim	DT	6-4	280	3/16/66	Brigham Young	Cimarron, Kan.	FA
Andrews, Romel	DT	6-4	262	7/4/63	Tennessee-Martin	Ripley, Tenn.	FA
Cherry, Marcus	WR	5-9	183	2/14/67	Boston College	Washington, D.C.	FA
Collins, Andre	LB	6-1	230	5/4/68	Penn State	Cinnaminson, N.J.	D2
Conklin, Cary	QB	6-4	215	2/29/68	Washington	Yakima, Wash.	D4a
Crossman, Dan	CB-S	5-11	185	1/17/67	Pittsburgh	Pottstown, Pa.	FA
Dunn, Chris (1)	LB	6-3	235	2/1/66	Cal Poly-SLO	Whittier, Calif.	FA
Durden, John	T	6-6	294	8/2/67	Florida	Alachua, Fla.	FA
Elewonibi, Mohammed	G	6-4	282	12/16/65	Brigham Young	Kamloops, Canada	D3
Fagan, Jay	G	6-3	280	4/15/67	Montana	Missoula, Mont.	FA
Forsythe, Byron	C	6-3	270	12/27/66	Houston	Spring, Tex.	FA
Francisco, D'Juan	CB	5-10	185	2/5/67	Notre Dame	Cincinnati, Ohio	D10a
Glaser, Doug	T	6-6	295	5/24/68	Nebraska	Balch Springs, Tex.	FA
Hobbs, Steve (1)	WR	5-11	195	11/14/65	North Alabama	Mendenhall, Miss.	FA
Labbe, Rico	S	6-0	210	6/16/67	Boston College	Rockville, Md.	D4b
Leverenz, Jon	LB	6-2	230	8/29/67	Minnesota	Ankeny, Iowa	D11
Mitchell, Brian	RB	5-10	195	8/18/68	S.W. Louisiana	Plaquemine, La.	D5
Moxley, Tim	G	6-7	320	3/6/67	Ohio State	Columbus, Ohio	D9
Rayam, Thomas	DE	6-6	285	1/3/68	Alabama	Orlando, Fla.	D10b
Searcy, George	RB	5-11	210	11/22/68	East Tennessee State	Jacksonville, Fla.	FA
Smith, Paul	WR	5-8	185	5/21/67	Houston	Houston, Tex.	FA
Vladic, Larry	CB-S	6-0	192	6/28/68	Oregon State	Diamond Bar, Calif.	FA
Waddle, Percy	WR	6-0	180	9/13/67	Texas A&M	Columbus, Tex.	FA
Wells, Kent	DT	6-4	295	7/25/67	Nebraska	Lincoln, Neb.	D6
Wolfolk, Kevin	LB	6-1	225	2/6/67	Portland State	Ft. Washington, Md.	FA

The term NFL Rookie is defined as a player who is in his first season of professional football and has not been on the roster of another professional football team for any regular-season or postseason games. A Rookie is designated by an "R" on NFL rosters. Players who have been active in another professional football league or players who have NFL experience, including either preseason training camp or being on an active roster for fewer than three regular-season or post-season games, are termed NFL First-Year Players. An NFL First-Year Player is designated by a "1" on NFL rosters. Thereafter, a player on an NFL active roster for at least three regular-season or postseason games is credited with an additional year of NFL playing experience.

NOTES

_____
_____
_____
_____
_____
_____
_____
_____
_____
_____

Richie Petitbon, assistant head coach-defense; born April 18, 1938, New Orleans, La., lives in Vienna, Va. Quarterback-defensive back Tulane 1955-58. Pro defensive back Chicago Bears 1959-67, Los Angeles Rams 1969-70, Washington Redskins 1971-73. Pro coach: Houston Oilers 1974-77, joined Redskins in 1978.

Dan Riley, conditioning; born October 19, 1949, Syracuse, N.Y., lives in Herndon, Va. No college or pro playing experience. College coach: Army 1973-76, Penn State 1977-81. Pro coach: Joined Redskins in 1982.

Wayne Sevier, special teams; born July 3, 1941, San Diego, Calif., lives in Broad Run, Va. Quarterback Chaffey, Calif., J.C. 1960, San Diego State 1961-62. No pro playing experience. College coach: California Western 1968-69. Pro coach: St. Louis Cardinals 1974-75, Atlanta Falcons 1976, San Diego Chargers 1979-80, 1987-88, Washington Redskins 1981-86, rejoined Redskins in 1989.

Warren Simmons, tight ends; born February 25, 1942, Poughkeepsie, N.Y., lives in Centreville, Va. Center San Diego State 1963-65. No pro playing experience. College coach: Cal State-Fullerton 1972-75, Cerritos, Calif., J.C. 1976-80. Pro coach: Joined Redskins in 1981.

Charley Taylor, wide receivers; born September 28, 1942, Grand Prairie, Tex., lives in Reston, Va. Running back Arizona State 1961-63. Pro running back-wide receiver Washington Redskins 1964-76. Pro coach: Joined Redskins in 1982.

Emmitt Thomas, defensive backs; born June 4, 1943, Angleton, Tex., lives in Reston, Va. Quarterback-wide receiver Bishop (Tex.) College 1963-65. Pro defensive back Kansas City Chiefs 1966-78. College coach: Central Missouri State 1979-80. Pro coach: St. Louis Cardinals 1981-85, joined Redskins in 1986.

LaVern Torgeson, defensive line; born February 28, 1929, LaCrosse, Wash., lives in Fairfax, Va. Center-linebacker Washington State 1948-50. Pro linebacker Detroit Lions 1951-54, Washington Redskins 1955-58. Pro coach: Washington Redskins 1959-61, 1971-77, Pittsburgh Steelers 1962-68, Los Angeles Rams 1969-70, 1978-80, rejoined Redskins in 1981.

1989 SEASON IN REVIEW

Trades

1989 Interconference Trades

Punter **Monte Robbins** from Washington to New England for a draft choice (4/26).

Kicker **David Treadwell** from Phoenix to Denver for a draft choice (5/30).

Defensive tackle **Kevin Brooks** from Dallas to Denver for a draft choice (7/10).

Tackle **Daryle Smith** from Dallas to Seattle for a draft choice (7/25).

Tackle **Curt Singer** from Detroit to Seattle for a draft choice (7/29).

Guard **Winford Hood** from Denver to Phoenix for a draft choice (8/4).

Center **Kevin Thomas** from Seattle to Phoenix for a draft choice (8/5).

Quarterback **Scott Secules** from Dallas to Miami for a draft choice (8/7).

Wide receiver **Gary Lee** from Detroit to Denver for a draft choice (8/8).

Tackle **Darryl Haley** from Green Bay to Cleveland for a draft choice (8/12).

Defensive tackle **Chuck Ehin** from Indianapolis to Dallas for a draft choice (8/22).

Tackle **Zefross Moss** from Dallas to Indianapolis for a draft choice (8/22).

Punter **Ralf Mojsiejenko** from San Diego to Washington for a draft choice (8/30).

Running back **James Jones** from Detroit to Seattle for defensive back **Terry Taylor** (8/31).

Center **Guy Bingham** from the New York Jets to Atlanta for a draft choice (9/4).

Defensive end **Ron Holmes** from Tampa Bay to Denver for a draft choice (9/6).

Quarterback **Steve Pelluer** from Dallas to Kansas City for a draft choice (10/17).

Running back **Darrin Nelson** from Dallas to San Diego for a draft choice (10/17).

1990 Interconference Trades

Atlanta's first- and fourth-round choices in 1990 to Indianapolis for the Colts' fifth-round choice in 1990 and first-round choice in 1991. Indianapolis selected quarterback **Jeff George** (Illinois) and wide receiver **Stacey Simmons** (Florida). Atlanta selected tight end **Reggie Redding** (Cal State-Fullerton) (4/22).

Tackle **Chris Hinton** and wide receiver **Andre Rison** from Indianapolis to Atlanta for past considerations (4/22).

San Diego's fourth-round choice in 1990 from the Los Angeles Raiders to San Francisco for the 49ers' fourth- and fifth-round choices in 1990. San Francisco selected center **Dean Caliguire** (Pittsburgh). The Los Angeles Raiders sent both San Francisco choices to Washington to complete a 1988 trade (4/22).

Running back **Gary Anderson** from San Diego to Tampa Bay for the Buccaneers' third-round choice in 1990 and third-round choice in 1991. San Diego selected linebacker **Jeff Mills** (Nebraska) (4/22).

Minnesota's first-round choice in 1990 and San Francisco's third-round choice in 1990 from Dallas to Pittsburgh for the Steelers' first-round choice in 1990. Dallas selected running back **Emmitt Smith** (Florida). Pittsburgh selected tight end **Eric Green** (Liberty) and defensive tackle **Craig Veasey** (Houston) (4/22).

Denver's third-round choice in 1990, Miami's fifth-round choice in 1990, and Dallas's seventh-round choice in 1990 from Dallas to New England for Seattle's third-round choice in 1990 and the Patriots' sixth- and eighth-round choices in 1990. Dallas selected defensive end **Jimmie Jones** (Miami) and traded New England's sixth-round choice to San Diego and eighth-round choice to the Los Angeles Raiders. New England selected wide receiver **Greg McMurtry** (Michigan), running back **James Gray** (Texas Tech), and traded Dallas's seventh-round choice to Buffalo (4/22).

New England's fourth-round choice in 1990 to Washington for Dallas's fifth-round choice in 1990 and Atlanta's fifth-round choice in 1990. Washington selected quarterback **Cary Conklin** (Washington). New England selected defensive back **Junior Robinson** (East Carolina) and traded Atlanta's fifth-round choice to Denver (4/22).

New York Jets defensive back-kick returner **Bobby Humphery** to the Los Angeles Rams for Rams' fifth-round choice in 1990. The Jets selected defensive back **Robert McWright** (Texas Christian) (4/22).

The Los Angeles Raiders traded the rights to defensive back **Stan Smagala** (Notre Dame) to Dallas for Minnesota's sixth-round choice, New England's eighth-round choice, Seattle's ninth-round choice, Indianapolis's tenth-round choice, and San Francisco's eleventh-round choice, all in 1990. The Los Angeles Raiders' traded Minnesota's sixth-round choice to New Orleans and Indianapolis's tenth-round choice to Denver, and selected linebacker **Arthur Jimerson** (Norfolk State), running back **Leon Perry** (Oklahoma), and running back **Myron Jones** (Fresno State) (4/23).

New Orleans's fourth-round choice in 1991 to the Los Angeles Raiders for Minnesota's sixth-round choice in 1990 and the Raiders' eighth-, ninth-, tenth-, and eleventh-round choices in 1990. New Orleans selected linebacker **James Williams** (Mississippi State), quarterback **Gerry Gdowski** (Nebraska), running back **Broderick Graves** (Winston-Salem State), wide receiver **Gary Cooper** (Clemson), and nose tackle **Webbie Burnett** (Western Kentucky) (4/23).

San Diego's third-round choice in 1991 to Dallas for the Cowboys' sixth-round choice, New England's sixth-round choice, and the New York Giants' sixth-round choice, all in 1990. San Diego selected quarterback **John Friesz** (Idaho), center **Frank Cornish** (UCLA), and tight end **Derrick Walker** (Michigan) (4/23).

San Francisco's fifth-round choice in 1990 from Washington to Miami for the Dolphins' tenth-round choice in 1990 and fourth-round choice in 1991. Miami selected running back **Leroy Holt** (Southern California). Washington selected defensive back **D'Juan Francisco** (Notre Dame) (4/23).

The Los Angeles Raiders' seventh-round choice in 1990 and Minnesota's eleventh-round choice in 1990 from the Raiders to Chicago for the Bears' seventh-round choice in 1990. Los Angeles selected defensive back **Garry Lewis** (Alcorn State). Chicago selected tackle **Bill Anderson** (Iowa) and tackle **Roman Matusz** (Pittsburgh) (4/23).

Cornerback **Tim McKyer** from San Francisco to Miami for the Dolphins' eleventh-round choice in 1990 and second-round choice in 1991. San Francisco selected defensive back **Anthony Shelton** (Tennessee State) (4/23).

1989 AFC Trades

Tackle **Bill Contz** from Denver to Indianapolis for a draft choice (8/21).

Running back **Barry Redden** from San Diego to Cleveland for a draft choice (9/4).

Linebacker **Chip Banks** from San Diego to Indianapolis for a draft choice (10/17).

1990 AFC Trades

Seattle's first-round choice in 1990, Indianapolis's first-round choice in 1990, and Seattle's third-round choice in 1990 and fourth-round choice in 1991 to New England for the Patriots' first- and second-round choices in 1990. Seattle selected defensive tackle **Cortez Kennedy** (Miami) and linebacker **Terry Wooden** (Syracuse). New England selected linebacker **Chris Singleton** (Arizona), defensive end **Ray Agnew** (North Carolina State), and traded Seattle's third-round choice to Dallas (4/22).

Atlanta's fifth-round choice in 1990 from New England to Denver for the Broncos' fourth-round choice in 1991. Denver selected guard **Jeff Davidson** (Ohio State) (4/22).

Dallas' seventh-round choice in 1990 and New England's seventh-round choice in 1990 from New England to Buffalo for the Bills' twelfth-round choice in 1990 and fourth-round choice in 1991. Buffalo selected guard **Brent Griffith** (Minnesota-Duluth) and linebacker **Brent Collins** (Carson-Newman). New England selected guard **Blaine Rose** (Maryland) (4/23).

Indianapolis's tenth-round choice in 1990 from the Los Angeles Raiders to Denver for the Broncos' eleventh-round choice in 1990. Denver selected defensive end **James Szymanski** (Michigan State). The Los Angeles Raiders selected wide receiver **Ron Lewis** (Jackson State) (4/23).

Cleveland's fifth-round choice in 1991 to Miami for the Dolphins' seventh-round choice in 1990. Cleveland selected tight end **Scott Galbraith** (Southern California) (4/23).

1989 NFC Trades

Linebacker **Steve DeOssie** from Dallas to New York Giants for a draft choice (5/12).

Tight end **Pat Carter** from Detroit to the Los Angeles Rams for a draft choice (8/18).

Defensive tackle **Dean Hamel** from Washington to Dallas for a draft choice (8/30).

Running back **Herschel Walker** from Dallas to Minnesota for linebackers **Jesse Solomon** and **David Howard,** running back **Darrin Nelson,** defensive back **Issiac Holt,** defensive end **Alex Stewart,** and a draft choice (10/13).

1990 NFC Trades

Running back **Terrence Flagler,** defensive end **Daniel Stubbs,** and San Francisco's third- and eleventh-round choices in 1990 to Dallas for Minnesota's second-round choice in 1990 and Kansas City's third-round choice in 1990. San Francisco selected defensive tackle **Dennis Brown** (Washington) and wide receiver **Ron Lewis** (Florida State). Dallas traded San Francisco's third-round choice to Pittsburgh and San Francisco's eleventh-round choice to the Los Angeles Raiders (4/23).

1989 PRESEASON STANDINGS

American Football Conference

Eastern Division

	W	L	T	Pct.	Pts.	OP
Indianapolis	4	0	0	1.000	123	64
New England	2	2	0	.500	57	55
N.Y. Jets	2	2	0	.500	78	72
Buffalo*	1	4	0	.200	77	127
Miami	0	4	0	.000	61	109

Central Division

	W	L	T	Pct.	Pts.	OP
Cincinnati	2	2	0	.500	79	67
Houston	2	2	0	.500	100	102
Pittsburgh	2	2	0	.500	65	90
Cleveland***	1	4	0	.250	76	113

Western Division

	W	L	T	Pct.	Pts.	OP
Seattle	3	1	0	.750	69	51
Denver	2	2	0	.500	92	107
San Diego	2	2	0	.500	62	64
Kansas City	1	3	0	.250	55	100
L.A. Raiders	0	4	0	.000	86	128

*Includes Hall of Fame Game
**Includes American Bowl '89 in Tokyo
***Includes American Bowl '89 in London

National Football Conference

Eastern Division

	W	L	T	Pct.	Pts.	OP
Philadel.***	4	1	0	.800	108	73
Washington*	4	1	0	.800	126	86
Dallas	3	1	0	.750	98	75
N.Y. Giants	3	1	0	.750	96	54
Phoenix	1	3	0	.250	71	67

Central Division

	W	L	T	Pct.	Pts.	OP
Green Bay	3	1	0	.750	94	75
Minnesota	3	1	0	.750	78	60
Tampa Bay	3	1	0	.750	95	63
Chicago	2	2	0	.500	93	104
Detroit	0	4	0	.000	48	97

Western Division

	W	L	T	Pct.	Pts.	OP
L.A. Rams**	4	1	0	.800	100	78
San Fran.**	3	2	0	.600	119	82
New Orleans	1	3	0	.250	62	77
Atlanta	1	3	0	.250	62	90

AFC Preseason Results—Team By Team

Eastern Division

Buffalo (1-4)

6	Washgtn (HOF)	31
20	Cincinnati	24
10	*New Orleans	7
24	Green Bay	27
17	Atlanta	38
77		127

Indianapolis (4-0)

31	New Orleans	7
24	Green Bay	23
30	*Tampa Bay	0
38	*Denver	34
123		64

Miami (0-4)

20	*Chicago	28
10	Houston	26
21	Washington	35
10	*Philadelphia	20
61		109

New England (2-2)

17	*N.Y. Giants	20
17	Seattle	12
23	Atlanta	7
0	*Green Bay	16
57		55

N.Y. Jets (2-2)

27	Green Bay	28
19	Philadelphia	10
17	N.Y. Giants	21
15	Kansas City (OT)	13
78		72

Central Division

Cincinnati (2-2)

24	*Buffalo	20
35	Detroit	3
10	New Orleans	27
10	Minnesota	17
79		67

Cleveland (1-4)

13	Philadelphia (ABL)	17
25	Detroit	24
21	*Pittsburgh	24
7	Phoenix	21
10	*Tampa Bay	27
76		113

Houston (2-2)

23	Tampa Bay	41
26	Miami	10
23	L.A. Raiders	21
28	Dallas	30
100		102

Pittsburgh (2-2)

14	*Washington	21
24	Cleveland	21
14	Philadelphia	38
13	N.Y. Giants	10
65		90

Western Division

Denver (2-2)

17	*L.A. Rams	13
17	San Francisco	35
24	*Dallas	21
34	Indianapolis	38
92		107

Kansas City (1-3)

13	Minnesota	23
7	*N.Y. Giants	45
22	Chicago	17
13	*N.Y. Jets (OT)	15
55		100

L.A. Raiders (0-4)

7	*San Francisco	37
20	*Dallas	27
21	Houston	23
38	*Chicago	41
86		128

San Diego (2-2)

3	*Dallas	20
24	Chicago	7
14	San Francisco	17
21	*Phoenix	20
62		64

Seattle (3-1)

16	Phoenix	10
12	New England	17
13	*Detroit	7
28	*San Francisco	17
69		51

NFC Preseason Results—Team By Team

Eastern Division

Dallas (3-1)

20	San Diego	3
27	L.A. Raiders	20
21	Denver	24
30	*Houston	28
98		75

N.Y. Giants (3-1)

20	New England	17
45	Kansas City	7
21	*N.Y. Jets	17
10	*Pittsburgh	13
96		54

Philadelphia (4-1)

17	Cleveland (ABL)	13
23	*Atlanta	17
10	N.Y. Jets	19
38	*Pittsburgh	14
20	Miami	10
108		73

Phoenix (1-3)

10	*Seattle	16
20	L.A. Rams	23
21	*Cleveland	7
20	San Diego	21
71		67

Washington (4-1)

31	Buffalo (HOF)	6
21	Pittsburgh	14
13	Minnesota	24
35	*Miami	21
26	New Orleans	21
126		86

Central Division

Chicago (2-2)

28	Miami	20
7	*San Diego	24
17	*Kansas City	22
41	L.A. Raiders	38
93		104

Detroit (0-4)

24	*Cleveland	25
3	*Cincinnati	35
7	Seattle	13
14	L.A. Rams	24
48		97

Green Bay (3-1)

28	N.Y. Jets	27
23	*Indianapolis	24
27	Buffalo	24
16	New England	0
94		75

Minnesota (3-1)

23	Kansas City	13
24	*Washington	13
14	L.A. Rams	24
17	*Cincinnati	10
78		60

Tampa Bay (3-1)

41	*Houston	23
27	*Atlanta	0
0	Indianapolis	30
27	Cleveland	10
95		63

Western Division

Atlanta (1-3)

17	Philadelphia	23
0	Tampa Bay	27
7	*New England	23
38	Buffalo	17
62		90

L.A. Rams (4-1)

16	S.F. (OT) (ABJ)	13
13	Denver	17
23	*Phoenix	20
24	*Minnesota	14
24	*Detroit	14
100		78

New Orleans (1-3)

7	*Indianapolis	31
7	Buffalo	10
27	*Cincinnati	10
21	*Washington	26
62		77

San Francisco (3-2)

13	Rams (OT) (ABJ)	16
37	L.A. Raiders	7
35	*Denver	17
17	*San Diego	14
17	Seattle	28
119		82

*denotes home game
(OT) denotes overtime
(HOF) denotes Hall of Fame Game
(ABL) denotes American Bowl Game in London
(ABJ) denotes American Bowl Game in Japan

143

American Football Conference

Eastern Division

	W	L	T	Pct.	Pts.	OP
Buffalo	9	7	0	.563	409	317
Indianapolis	8	8	0	.500	298	301
Miami	8	8	0	.500	331	379
New England	5	11	0	.313	297	391
N.Y. Jets	4	12	0	.250	253	411

Central Division

	W	L	T	Pct.	Pts.	OP
Cleveland	9	6	1	.594	334	254
Houston*	9	7	0	.563	365	412
Pittsburgh*	9	7	0	.563	265	326
Cincinnati	8	8	0	.500	404	285

Western Division

	W	L	T	Pct.	Pts.	OP
Denver	11	5	0	.688	362	226
Kansas City	8	7	1	.531	318	286
L.A. Raiders	8	8	0	.500	315	297
Seattle	7	9	0	.438	241	327
San Diego	6	10	0	.375	266	290

National Football Conference

Eastern Division

	W	L	T	Pct.	Pts.	OP
N.Y. Giants	12	4	0	.750	348	252
Philadelphia*	11	5	0	.688	342	274
Washington	10	6	0	.625	386	308
Phoenix	5	11	0	.313	258	377
Dallas	1	15	0	.063	204	393

Central Division

	W	L	T	Pct.	Pts.	OP
Minnesota	10	6	0	.625	351	275
Green Bay	10	6	0	.625	362	356
Detroit	7	9	0	.438	312	364
Chicago	6	10	0	.375	358	377
Tampa Bay	5	11	0	.313	320	419

Western Division

	W	L	T	Pct.	Pts.	OP
San Francisco	14	2	0	.875	442	253
L.A. Rams*	11	5	0	.688	426	344
New Orleans	9	7	0	.563	386	301
Atlanta	3	13	0	.188	279	437

Wild Card qualifiers for playoffs

Indianapolis finished ahead of Miami in AFC East because of better conference record (7-5 vs. 6-8). Houston finished ahead of Pittsburgh in AFC Central because of head-to-head sweep (2-0). Minnesota finished ahead of Green Bay in NFC Central because of better division record (6-2 vs. 5-3).

First-Round Playoffs

AFC.........................Pittsburgh 26, Houston 23 (OT), December 31, at Houston
NFC.........................L.A. Rams 21, Philadelphia 7, December 31, at Philadelphia

Divisional Playoffs

AFC................................Cleveland 34, Buffalo 30, January 6, at Cleveland
Denver 24, Pittsburgh 23, January 7, at Denver
NFC....................San Francisco 41, Minnesota 13, January 6, at San Francisco
L.A. Rams 19, N.Y. Giants 13 (OT), January 7, at New York

Championship Games

AFC.........................Denver 37, Cleveland 21, January 14, at Denver
NFC.........................San Francisco 30, L.A. Rams 3, January 14, at San Francisco
SUPER BOWL XXIV San Francisco 55, Denver 10, January 28, at Louisiana Superdome, New Orleans, Louisiana

AFC-NFC PRO BOWL . NFC 27, AFC 21, February 4, at Aloha Stadium, Honolulu, Hawaii

AFC Season Records—Team by Team

BUFFALO (9-7)

27	at Miami	24
14	*Denver	28
47	at Houston (OT)	41
31	*New England	10
14	at Indianapolis	37
23	*L.A. Rams	20
34	*N.Y. Jets	3
31	*Miami	17
28	at Atlanta	30
30	*Indianapolis	7
24	at New England	33
24	*Cincinnati	7
16	at Seattle	17
19	*New Orleans	22
10	at San Francisco	21
37	at New York Jets	0
409		**317**

CINCINNATI (8-8)

14	at Chicago	17
41	*Pittsburgh	10
21	*Cleveland	14
21	at Kansas City	17
26	at Pittsburgh	16
13	*Miami	20
12	*Indianapolis	23
56	*Tampa Bay	23
7	at L.A. Raiders	28
24	at Houston	26
42	*Detroit	7
7	at Buffalo	24
21	at Cleveland	0
17	*Seattle	24
61	*Houston	7
21	at Minnesota	29
404		**285**

CLEVELAND (9-6-1)

51	at Pittsburgh	0
38	*New York Jets	24
14	at Cincinnati	21
16	*Denver	13
10	at Miami (OT)	13
7	*Pittsburgh	17
27	*Chicago	7
28	*Houston	17
42	at Tampa Bay	31
17	at Seattle	7
10	*Kansas City (OT)	10
10	at Detroit	13
0	*Cincinnati	21
17	at Indianapolis (OT)	23
23	*Minnesota (OT)	17
24	at Houston	20
334		**254**

DENVER (11-5)

34	*Kansas City	20
28	at Buffalo	14
31	*L.A. Raiders	21
13	at Cleveland	16
16	*San Diego	10
14	*Indianapolis	3
24	at Seattle (OT)	21
24	*Philadelphia	28
34	*Pittsburgh	7
16	at Kansas City	13
14	at Washington	10
41	*Seattle	14
13	at L.A. Raiders (OT)	16
7	*N.Y. Giants	14
37	at Phoenix	0
16	at San Diego	19
362		**226**

HOUSTON (9-7)

7	at Minnesota	38
34	at San Diego	27
41	*Buffalo (OT)	47
39	*Miami	7
13	at New England	23
33	at Chicago	28
27	*Pittsburgh	0
17	at Cleveland	28
35	*Detroit	31
26	*Cincinnati	24
23	*L.A. Raiders	7
0	at Kansas City	34
23	at Pittsburgh	16
20	*Tampa Bay	17
7	at Cincinnati	61
20	*Cleveland	24
365		**412**

INDIANAPOLIS (8-8)

24	*San Francisco	30
17	at L.A. Rams	31
13	*Atlanta	9
17	at N.Y. Jets	10
37	*Buffalo	14
3	at Denver	14
23	at Cincinnati	12
20	*New England (OT)	23
13	at Miami	19
7	at Buffalo	30
27	*N.Y. Jets	10
10	*San Diego	6
16	at New England	22
23	*Cleveland (OT)	17
42	*Miami	13
6	at New Orleans	41
298		**301**

KANSAS CITY (8-7-1)

20	at Denver	34
24	*L.A. Raiders	19
6	at San Diego	21
17	*Cincinnati	21
20	at Seattle	16
14	at L.A. Raiders	20
36	*Dallas	28
17	at Pittsburgh	23
20	*Seattle	10
13	*Denver	16
10	at Cleveland (OT)	10
34	*Houston	0
26	*Miami	21
21	at Green Bay	3
13	*San Diego	20
27	at Miami	24
318		**286**

L.A. RAIDERS (8-8)

40	*San Diego	14
19	at Kansas City	24
21	at Denver	31
20	*Seattle	24
14	at N.Y. Jets	7
20	*Kansas City	14
7	at Philadelphia	10
37	*Washington	24
28	*Cincinnati	7
12	at San Diego	14
7	at Houston	23
24	*New England	21
16	*Denver (OT)	13
16	*Phoenix	14
17	at Seattle	23
17	at N.Y. Giants	34
315		**297**

MIAMI (8-8)

24	*Buffalo	27
24	at New England	10
33	*N.Y. Jets	40
7	at Houston	39
13	*Cleveland (OT)	10
20	at Cincinnati	13
23	*Green Bay	20
17	at Buffalo	31
19	*Indianapolis	13
31	at N.Y. Jets	23
17	at Dallas	14
14	*Pittsburgh	34
21	at Kansas City	26
31	*New England	10
13	at Indianapolis	42
24	*Kansas City	27
331		**379**

NEW ENGLAND (5-11)

27	at N.Y. Jets	24
10	*Miami	24
3	*Seattle	24
10	at Buffalo	31
23	*Houston	13
15	at Atlanta	16
20	at San Francisco	37
23	at Indianapolis (OT)	20
26	*N.Y. Jets	27
24	*New Orleans	28
33	*Buffalo	24
21	at L.A. Raiders	24
22	*Indianapolis	16
10	at Miami	31
10	at Pittsburgh	28
20	*L.A. Rams	24
297		**391**

N.Y. JETS (4-12)

24	*New England	27
24	at Cleveland	38
40	at Miami	33
10	*Indianapolis	17
7	*L.A. Raiders	14
14	at New Orleans	29
3	at Buffalo	34
10	*San Francisco	23
27	at New England	26
23	*Miami	31
10	at Indianapolis	27
27	*Atlanta	7
20	at San Diego	17
0	*Pittsburgh	13
14	at L.A. Rams	38
0	*Buffalo	37
253		**411**

PITTSBURGH (9-7)

0	*Cleveland	51
10	at Cincinnati	41
27	*Minnesota	14
23	at Detroit	3
16	*Cincinnati	26
17	at Cleveland	7
0	at Houston	27
23	*Kansas City	17
7	at Denver	34
0	*Chicago	20
20	*San Diego	17
34	at Miami	14
16	*Houston	23
13	at N.Y. Jets	0
28	*New England	10
31	at Tampa Bay	22
265		**326**

SAN DIEGO (6-10)

14	at L.A. Raiders	40
27	*Houston	34
21	*Kansas City	6
24	at Phoenix	13
10	at Denver	16
16	*Seattle	17
13	*N.Y. Giants	20
7	at Seattle	10
20	*Philadelphia	17
14	*L.A. Raiders	12
17	at Pittsburgh	20
6	at Indianapolis	10
17	*N.Y. Jets	20
21	at Washington	26
20	at Kansas City	13
19	*Denver	16
266		**290**

SEATTLE (7-9)

7	at Philadelphia	31
24	*Phoenix	34
24	at New England	3
24	at L.A. Raiders	20
16	*Kansas City	20
17	at San Diego	16
21	*Denver (OT)	24
10	*San Diego	7
10	at Kansas City	20
7	*Cleveland	17
3	at N.Y. Giants	15
14	at Denver	41
17	*Buffalo	16
24	at Cincinnati	17
23	*L.A. Raiders	17
0	*Washington	29
241		**327**

* denotes home game
(OT) denotes overtime

NFC Season Records—Team by Team

ATLANTA (3-13)

21	*L.A. Rams	31
27	*Dallas	21
9	at Indianapolis	13
21	at Green Bay	23
14	at L.A. Rams	26
16	*New England	15
20	at Phoenix	34
13	at New Orleans	20
30	*Buffalo	28
3	at San Francisco	45
17	*New Orleans	26
7	at N.Y. Jets	27
10	*San Francisco	23
17	at Minnestoa	43
30	*Washington	31
24	*Detroit	31
279		437

CHICAGO (6-10)

17	*Cincinnati	14
38	*Minnesota	7
47	at Detroit	27
27	*Philadelphia	13
35	at Tampa Bay	42
28	*Houston	33
7	at Cleveland	27
20	*L.A. Rams	10
13	at Green Bay	14
20	at Pittsburgh	0
31	*Tampa Bay	32
14	at Washington	38
16	at Minnesota	27
17	*Detroit	27
28	*Green Bay	40
0	at San Francisco	26
358		377

DALLAS (1-15)

0	at New Orleans	28
21	at Atlanta	27
7	*Washington	30
13	*N.Y. Giants	30
13	at Green Bay	31
14	*San Francisco	31
28	at Kansas City	36
10	*Phoenix	19
13	at Washington	3
20	at Phoenix	24
14	*Miami	17
0	*Philadelphia	27
31	*L.A. Rams	35
10	at Philadelphia	20
0	at N.Y. Giants	15
10	*Green Bay	20
204		393

DETROIT (7-9)

13	*Phoenix	16
14	at N.Y. Giants	24
27	*Chicago	47
3	*Pittsburgh	23
17	at Minnesota	24
17	at Tampa Bay	16
7	*Minnesota	20
20	at Green Bay	
	(OT)	23
31	at Houston	35
31	*Green Bay	22
7	at Cincinnati	42
13	*Cleveland	10
21	*New Orleans	14
27	at Chicago	17
33	*Tampa Bay	7
31	at Atlanta	24
312		364

GREEN BAY (10-6)

21	*Tampa Bay	23
35	*New Orleans	34
38	at L.A. Rams	41
23	*Atlanta	21
31	*Dallas	13
14	at Minnesota	26
20	at Miami	23
23	*Detroit (OT)	20
14	*Chicago	13
22	at Detroit	31
21	at San Francisco	17
20	*Minnesota	19
17	at Tampa Bay	16
3	*Kansas City	21
40	at Chicago	28
20	at Dallas	10
362		356

L.A. RAMS (11-5)

31	at Atlanta	21
31	*Indianapolis	17
41	*Green Bay	38
13	at San Francisco	12
26	*Atlanta	14
20	at Buffalo	23
21	*New Orleans	40
10	at Chicago	20
21	at Minnesota (OT)	23
31	*N.Y. Giants	10
37	*Phoenix	14
20	at New Orleans	
	(OT)	17
35	at Dallas	31
27	*San Francisco	30
38	*N.Y. Jets	14
24	at New England	20
426		344

MINNESOTA (10-6)

38	*Houston	7
7	at Chicago	38
14	at Pittsburgh	27
17	*Tampa Bay	3
24	*Detroit	17
26	*Green Bay	14
20	at Detroit	7
14	at N.Y. Giants	24
23	*L.A. Rams (OT)	21
24	at Tampa Bay	10
9	at Philadelphia	10
19	at Green Bay	20
27	*Chicago	16
43	*Atlanta	17
17	at Cleveland (OT)	23
29	*Cincinnati	21
351		275

NEW ORLEANS (9-7)

28	*Dallas	0
34	at Green Bay	35
10	at Tampa Bay	20
14	*Washington	16
20	*San Francisco	24
29	*N.Y. Jets	14
40	at L.A. Rams	21
20	*Atlanta	13
13	at San Francisco	31
28	at New England	24
26	at Atlanta	17
17	*L.A. Rams (OT)	20
14	at Detroit	21
22	at Buffalo	19
30	*Philadelphia	20
41	*Indianapolis	6
386		301

N.Y. GIANTS (12-4)

27	at Washington	24
24	*Detroit	14
35	*Phoenix	7
30	at Dallas	13
19	at Philadelphia	21
20	*Washington	17
20	at San Diego	13
24	*Minnesota	14
20	at Phoenix	13
10	at L.A. Rams	31
15	*Seattle	3
24	at San Francisco	34
17	*Philadelphia	24
14	at Denver	7
15	*Dallas	0
34	*L.A. Raiders	17
348		252

PHILADELPHIA (11-5)

31	*Seattle	7
42	at Washington	37
28	*San Francisco	38
13	at Chicago	27
21	*N.Y. Giants	19
17	at Phoenix	5
10	*L.A. Raiders	7
28	at Denver	24
17	at San Diego	20
3	*Washington	10
10	*Minnesota	9
27	at Dallas	0
24	at N.Y. Giants	17
20	*Dallas	10
20	at New Orleans	30
31	*Phoenix	14
342		274

PHOENIX (5-11)

16	at Detroit	13
34	at Seattle	24
7	at N.Y. Giants	35
13	*San Diego	24
28	at Washington	30
5	*Philadelphia	17
34	*Atlanta	20
19	at Dallas	10
13	*N.Y. Giants	20
24	*Dallas	20
14	at L.A. Rams	37
13	*Tampa Bay	14
10	*Washington	29
14	at L.A. Raiders	16
0	*Denver	37
14	at Philadelphia	31
258		377

SAN FRANCISCO (14-2)

30	at Indianapolis	24
20	at Tampa Bay	16
38	at Philadelphia	28
12	*L.A. Rams	13
24	at New Orleans	20
31	at Dallas	14
37	*New England	20
23	at N.Y. Jets	10
31	*New Orleans	13
45	*Atlanta	3
17	*Green Bay	21
34	*N.Y. Giants	24
23	at Atlanta	10
30	at L.A. Rams	27
21	*Buffalo	10
26	*Chicago	0
442		253

TAMPA BAY (5-11)

23	at Green Bay	21
16	*San Francisco	20
20	*New Orleans	10
3	at Minnesota	17
42	*Chicago	35
16	*Detroit	17
28	at Washington	32
23	at Cincinnati	56
31	*Cleveland	42
10	*Minnesota	24
32	at Chicago	31
14	at Phoenix	13
16	*Green Bay	17
17	at Houston	20
7	at Detroit	33
22	*Pittsburgh	31
320		419

WASHINGTON (10-6)

24	*N.Y. Giants	27
37	*Philadelphia	42
30	at Dallas	7
16	at New Orleans	14
30	*Phoenix	28
17	at N.Y. Giants	20
32	*Tampa Bay	28
24	at L.A. Raiders	37
3	*Dallas	13
10	at Philadelphia	3
10	*Denver	14
38	*Chicago	14
29	at Phoenix	10
26	*San Diego	21
31	at Atlanta	30
29	at Seattle	0
386		308

* denotes home game
(OT) denotes overtime

Attendances as they appear in the following, and in the club-by-club sections starting on page 26, are turnstile counts and not paid attendance. Paid attendance totals are on page 203.

First Week Summaries

Standings

American Football Conference

Eastern Division

	W	L	T	Pct.	Pts.	OP
Buffalo	1	0	0	1.000	27	24
New England	1	0	0	1.000	27	24
Indianapolis	0	1	0	.000	24	30
Miami	0	1	0	.000	24	27
N.Y. Jets	0	1	0	.000	24	27

Central Division

	W	L	T	Pct.	Pts.	OP
Cleveland	1	0	0	1.000	51	0
Cincinnati	0	1	0	1.000	14	17
Houston	0	1	0	.000	7	38
Pittsburgh	0	1	0	.000	0	51

Western Division

	W	L	T	Pct.	Pts.	OP
Denver	1	0	0	1.000	34	20
L.A. Raiders	1	0	0	1.000	40	14
Kansas City	0	1	0	.000	20	34
San Diego	0	1	0	.000	14	40
Seattle	0	1	0	.000	7	31

National Football Conference

Eastern Division

	W	L	T	Pct.	Pts.	OP
N.Y. Giants	1	0	0	1.000	27	24
Philadelphia	1	0	0	1.000	31	7
Phoenix	1	0	0	1.000	16	13
Dallas	0	1	0	.000	0	28
Washington	0	1	0	.000	24	27

Central Division

	W	L	T	Pct.	Pts.	OP
Chicago	1	0	0	1.000	17	14
Minnesota	1	0	0	1.000	38	7
Tampa Bay	1	0	0	1.000	23	21
Detroit	0	1	0	.000	13	16
Green Bay	0	1	0	.000	21	23

Western Division

	W	L	T	Pct.	Pts.	OP
L.A. Rams	1	0	0	1.000	31	21
New Orleans	1	0	0	1.000	28	0
San Francisco	1	0	0	1.000	30	24
Atlanta	0	1	0	.000	21	31

Sunday, September 10

Buffalo 27, Miami 24—at Joe Robbie Stadium, attendance 54,541. Jim Kelly's two-yard touchdown run as time expired gave the Bills their fifth straight victory over the Dolphins. Trailing 24-13, Kelly hit Flip Johnson with a 26-yard touchdown pass to narrow the score to 24-20 with 2:50 remaining. Nate Odomes's interception set up the Bills' winning drive. Kelly's scoring run was his first NFL rushing touchdown.

Buffalo	3	0	10	14	—	27
Miami	0	10	7	7	—	24

Buff — FG Norwood 34
Mia — Stradford 1 run (Stoyanovich kick)
Mia — FG Stoyanovich 29
Buff — Kinnebrew 2 run (Norwood kick)
Mia — Logan 2 blocked punt return (Stoyanovich kick)
Buff — FG Norwood 37
Mia — A. Brown 8 pass from Marino (Stoyanovich kick)
Buff — Johnson 26 pass from Kelly (Norwood kick)
Buff — Kelly 2 run (Norwood kick)

Chicago 17, Cincinnati 14—at Soldier Field, attendance 64,730. Mike Tomczak's fourth-quarter 20-yard scoring pass to James Thornton lifted the Bears over the defending AFC champion Bengals. Trailing 14-7 in third quarter, Dennis Gentry's 51-yard kickoff return set up Kevin Butler's 29-yard field goal. Tomczak's game-winning touchdown pass to Thornton capped a 95-yard drive. Neal Anderson rushed for a career-high 146 yards on 21 carries for the Bears. Chicago extended its consecutive opening-day victory streak to six.

Cincinnati	7	0	7	0	—	14
Chicago	0	7	3	7	—	17

Cin — Brooks 4 pass from Esiason (Gallery kick)
Chi — Tomczak 11 run (Butler kick)
Cin — Woods 5 run (Gallery kick)
Chi — FG Butler 29
Chi — Thornton 20 pass from Tomczak (Butler kick)

Cleveland 51, Pittsburgh 0—at Three Rivers Stadium, attendance 57,982. Cleveland's defense turned three turnovers into scores and recorded six sacks en route to a 51-0 shutout of the Steelers. David Grayson scored on a 28-yard fumble recovery and returned an interception 14 yards for a touchdown for the Browns. Clay Matthews also returned a fumble three yards for a score. Tim Manoa had touchdown runs of three and two yards. With his performance, Grayson was named AFC Defensive Player of the Week. The loss was the Steelers' worst since a 54-7 defeat to Green Bay in 1951.

Cleveland	17	13	14	7	—	51
Pittsburgh	0	0	0	0	—	0

Clev — Matthews 3 fumble recovery return (Bahr kick)
Clev — FG Bahr 27
Clev — Grayson 28 fumble recovery return (Bahr kick)
Clev — FG Bahr 20
Clev — Manoa 3 run (Bahr kick)
Clev — FG Bahr 27
Clev — Manoa 2 run (Bahr kick)
Clev — Grayson 14 interception return (Bahr kick)
Clev — Oliphant 21 run (Bahr kick)

New Orleans 28, Dallas 0—at Louisiana Superdome, attendance 66,977. Derrick Shepard returned a punt 56 yards for a touchdown as the Saints spoiled Cowboys head coach Jimmy Johnson's NFL debut. Touchdown runs by Dalton Hilliard (four yards) and Craig Heyward (one), and Shepard's punt return gave New Orleans a 21-0 halftime lead. The Saints, who had a 44:02 to 15:58 time-of-possession advantage, held the Cowboys to 20 yards rushing. The game was only the fourth shutout in the Cowboys' history and their first since a 44-0 loss to Chicago on November 17, 1985.

Dallas	0	0	0	0	—	0
New Orleans	7	14	0	7	—	28

NO — Hilliard 4 run (Andersen kick)
NO — Heyward 1 run (Andersen kick)
NO — Shepard 56 punt return (Andersen kick)
NO — Frazier 1 run (Andersen kick)

Minnesota 38, Houston 7—at Metrodome, attendance 54,015. Anthony Carter caught seven passes for 123 yards and a touchdown to help the Vikings down the Oilers. Wade Wilson connected on a 32-yard touchdown pass to Carter and a two-yard pass to Steve Jordan in the first quarter to give the Vikings a 14-7 lead. Rick Fenney's one-yard scoring run and Teddy Garcia's 35-yard field goal put Minnesota ahead 24-7 at halftime. The Vikings' defense accounted for seven sacks. It was the first opening day loss for the Oilers since 1984.

Houston	7	0	0	0	—	7
Minnesota	14	10	7	7	—	38

Hou — Highsmith 1 run (Zendejas kick)
Minn — Carter 32 pass from Wilson (Garcia kick)
Minn — Jordan 2 pass from Wilson (Garcia kick)
Minn — Fenney 1 run (Garcia kick)
Minn — FG Garcia 35
Minn — Fenney 3 run (Garcia kick)
Minn — Anderson 2 run (Garcia kick)

Denver 34, Kansas City 20—at Mile High Stadium, attendance 74,284. The Broncos turned four Chiefs turnovers into 24 points to defeat Kansas City. Following David Treadwell's 41-yard field goal, Denver jumped to a 17-0 first-quarter lead on Tyrone Braxton's 34-yard interception returned for a touchdown and Sammy Winder's two-yard run which was set up by Greg Kragen's fumble recovery. Kansas City narrowed the Broncos lead to 27-20 in the fourth quarter, but Randy Robbins's score on an 18-yard interception return sealed the win for Denver.

Kansas City	0	10	3	7	—	20
Denver	17	0	7	10	—	34

Den — FG Treadwell 41
Den — Braxton 34 interception return (Treadwell kick)
Den — Winder 2 run (Treadwell kick)
KC — FG Lowery 41
KC — Gamble 1 run (Lowery kick)
KC — FG Lowery 23
Den — Sewell 9 pass from Elway (Treadwell kick)
Den — FG Treadwell 29
KC — Carson 5 pass from DeBerg (Lowery kick)
Den — Robbins 18 interception return (Treadwell kick)

Los Angeles Rams 31, Atlanta 21—at Atlanta-Fulton County Stadium, attendance 38,708. Jim Everett threw for one touchdown and ran for another as the Rams defeated the Falcons. Falcons rookie Deion Sanders returned a punt 68 yards for a score midway through the first quarter, but Mike Lansford's 23-yard field goal, plus Greg Bell's two-yard scoring run and Everett's 46-yard pass to Henry Ellard, gave the Rams a 17-14 halftime advantage. Everett also scored on a 13-yard keeper and Bell added an eight-yard touchdown run in the second half.

L.A. Rams	3	14	7	7	—	31
Atlanta	7	7	0	7	—	21

Atl — Sanders 68 punt return (McFadden kick)
Rams — FG Lansford 23
Rams — Bell 2 run (Lansford kick)
Atl — Dixon 53 pass from Miller (McFadden kick)
Rams — Ellard 46 pass from Everett (Lansford kick)
Rams — Everett 13 run (Lansford kick)
Rams — Bell 8 run (Lansford kick)
Atl — Haynes 33 pass from Miller (McFadden kick)

New England 27, New York Jets 24—at Giants Stadium, attendance 64,541. Reggie Dupard's four-yard touchdown run with 1:55 remaining lifted the Patriots over the Jets. New England built a commanding 21-0 halftime lead on Tony Eason's touchdown passes to Irving Fryar (20 yards) and Stanley Morgan (30), and John Stephens's one-yard run. New York battled back to score 24 points in the second half, but Eason led a 38-yard drive to set up Dupard's winning touchdown run.

New England	7	14	0	6	—	27
N.Y. Jets	0	0	17	7	—	24

NE — Fryar 20 pass from Eason (Davis kick)
NE — Morgan 30 pass from Eason (Davis kick)
NE — Stephens 1 run (Davis kick)
NYJ — Vick 1 pass from O'Brien (Leahy kick)
NYJ — FG Leahy 40
NYJ — Prokop 17 run (Leahy kick)
NYJ — Townsell 48 pass from O'Brien (Leahy kick)
NE — Dupard 4 run (kick failed)

Phoenix 16, Detroit 13—at Pontiac Silverdome, attendance 36,735. Al Del Greco's 33-yard field goal with 13 seconds left in the game led the Cardinals over the Lions. Del Greco had two second-quarter field goals which gave Phoenix a 6-3 edge, but rookie Barry Sanders ran three yards for a touchdown to put the Lions ahead 10-6 in the third quarter. Gary Hogeboom connected with Roy Green on a 15-yard touchdown pass, but Eddie Murray's 23-yard field goal tied the game 13-13 midway through the fourth quarter.

Phoenix	0	6	0	10	—	16
Detroit	3	0	7	3	—	13

Det — FG Murray 30
Phx — FG Del Greco 29
Phx — FG Del Greco 23
Det — Sanders 3 run (Murray kick)
Phx — Green 15 pass from Hogeboom (Del Greco kick)
Det — FG Murray 23
Phx — FG Del Greco 33

Los Angeles Raiders 40, San Diego 14—at Memorial Coliseum, attendance 40,237. Steve Beuerlein came off the bench and threw for two touchdowns as the Raiders easily beat the Chargers. Beuerlein replaced starting quarterback Jay Schroeder in the first quarter and led a 78-yard drive capped by Mervyn Fernandez's four-yard scoring reception. Marcus Allen added a one-yard touchdown run which gave Los Angeles a 21-7 halftime lead. Willie Gault's four receptions for 131 yards included a 39-yard scoring pass from Beuerlein in the third quarter.

San Diego	7	0	7	0	—	14
L.A. Raiders	7	14	7	12	—	40

Raiders — Mueller 26 pass from Schroeder (Jaeger kick)
SD — Butts 50 run (Bahr kick)
Raiders — Fernandez 4 pass from Beuerlein (Jaeger kick)
Raiders — Allen 1 run (Jaeger kick)
Raiders — Gault 39 pass from Beuerlein (Jaeger kick)
SD — Butts 1 run (Bahr kick)
Raiders — FG Jaeger 22
Raiders — Safety, Floyd tackled in end zone
Raiders — Mueller 1 run (Jaeger kick)

San Francisco 30, Indianapolis 24—at Hoosier Dome, attendance 60,111. Roger Craig carried 24 times for 131 yards and two touchdowns as the 49ers overcame the Colts. Joe Montana put the game out of reach when he connected with Jerry Rice on a 58-yard scoring pass in the fourth quarter to put the 49ers ahead 30-17. Mike Cofer added field goals of 38, 26, and 31 yards for San Francisco. The Colts' Eric Dickerson rushed for 106 yards to become only the seventh player in NFL history to reach the 10,000-yard mark (10,021).

San Francisco	3	10	10	7	—	30
Indianapolis	3	7	0	14	—	24

SF — FG Cofer 38
Ind — FG Biasucci 31
SF — Craig 1 run (Cofer kick)
Ind — Brooks 22 pass from Chandler (Biasucci kick)
SF — FG Cofer 26
SF — Craig 4 run (Cofer kick)
SF — FG Cofer 31
Ind — Chandler 1 run (Biasucci kick)
SF — Rice 58 pass from Montana (Cofer kick)
Ind — Bentley recovered blocked punt in end zone (Biasucci kick)

Philadelphia 31, Seattle 7—at Veterans Stadium, attendance 64,287. Randall Cunningham threw scoring passes to Cris Carter and Mike Quick to lead the Eagles past the Seahawks. Philadelphia's defense had three interceptions, three sacks, and a blocked punt (by Andre Waters) which set up Anthony Toney's one-yard touchdown run in the first quarter. Luis Zendejas kicked a 24-yard field goal and Cunningham hit Carter for an eight-yard scoring pass to put Philadelphia ahead 17-7 at halftime. Cunningham also connected with Quick on an eight-yard touchdown pass in the third quarter. Eric Everett completed the Eagles' scoring with a 30-yard interception return for a score late in the fourth quarter.

Seattle	7	0	0	0	—	7
Philadelphia	7	10	7	7	—	31

Phil — Toney 1 run (Zendejas kick)
Sea — Largent 23 pass from Krieg (N. Johnson kick)
Phil — FG Zendejas 24

Phil —Carter 8 pass from Cunningham (Zendejas kick)
Phil —Quick 8 pass from Cunningham (Zendejas kick)
Phil —Everett 30 interception return (Zendejas kick)

Tampa Bay 23, Green Bay 21—at Lambeau Field, attendance 55,650. Lars Tate ran for two second-quarter touchdowns as the Buccaneers edged the Packers. Tampa Bay jumped to a 20-7 halftime lead on Tate's scoring runs of two and one yards, and Vinny Testaverde's nine-yard pass to William Howard. Green Bay narrowed the deficit to 20-14 on Don Majkowski's 11-yard pass to Ed West, but Mark Robinson's interception with less than five minutes remaining ended the Packers' final drive.

Tampa Bay	0	20	3	0	—	23
Green Bay	7	0	7	7	—	21

GB —Fullwood 3 run (Jacke kick)
TB —Tate 2 run (Igwebuike kick)
TB —Tate 1 run (Igwebuike kick)
TB —Howard 9 pass from Testaverde (kick failed)
GB —West 11 pass from Majkowski (Jacke kick)
TB —FG Igwebuike 52
GB —Bland fumble recovery in end zone (Jacke kick)

Monday, September 11

New York Giants 27, Washington 24—at Robert F. Kennedy Stadium, attendance 54,160. Raul Allegre's 52-yard field goal with six seconds remaining gave the Giants a 27-24 victory over the Redskins. New York jumped to a 14-3 halftime advantage on Phil Simms's scoring passes to Odessa Turner (30 yards) and Dave Meggett (62). The Giants extended the lead to 21-10 in the fourth quarter, but Mark Rypien's six-yard touchdown pass to Art Monk and Monte Coleman's 24-yard interception returned for a score put the Redskins ahead 24-21. Allegre's 32-yard field goal with 2:17 remaining tied the game.

N.Y. Giants	7	7	0	13	—	27
Washington	0	3	7	14	—	24

NYG —Turner 30 pass from Simms (Allegre kick)
NYG —Meggett 62 pass from Simms (Allegre kick)
Wash —FG Lohmiller 24
Wash —Sanders 48 pass from Rypien (Lohmiller kick)
NYG —Anderson 14 run (Allegre kick)
Wash —Monk 6 pass from Rypien (Lohmiller kick)
Wash —Coleman 24 interception return (Lohmiller kick)
NYG —FG Allegre 32
NYG —FG Allegre 52

Second Week Summaries

Standings

American Football Conference

Eastern Division

	W	L	T	Pct.	Pts.	OP
Buffalo	1	1	0	.500	41	52
Miami	1	1	0	.500	48	37
New England	1	1	0	.500	37	48
Indianapolis	0	2	0	.000	41	61
N.Y. Jets	0	2	0	.000	48	65
Central Division						
Cleveland	2	0	0	1.000	89	24
Cincinnati	1	1	0	.500	55	27
Houston	1	1	0	.500	41	65
Pittsburgh	0	2	0	.000	10	92
Western Division						
Denver	2	0	0	1.000	62	34
Kansas City	1	1	0	.500	44	53
L.A. Raiders	1	1	0	.500	59	38
San Diego	0	2	0	.000	41	74
Seattle	0	2	0	.000	31	65

National Football Conference

Eastern Division

	W	L	T	Pct.	Pts.	OP
N.Y. Giants	2	0	0	1.000	51	38
Philadelphia	2	0	0	1.000	73	44
Phoenix	2	0	0	1.000	50	37
Dallas	0	2	0	.000	21	55
Washington	0	2	0	.000	61	69
Central Division						
Chicago	2	0	0	1.000	55	21
Green Bay	1	1	0	.500	56	57
Minnesota	1	1	0	.500	45	45
Tampa Bay	1	1	0	.500	39	41
Detroit	0	2	0	.000	27	40
Western Division						
L.A. Rams	2	0	0	1.000	62	38
San Francisco	2	0	0	1.000	50	40
Atlanta	1	1	0	.500	48	52
New Orleans	1	1	0	.500	62	35

Sunday, September 17

Atlanta 27, Dallas 21—at Atlanta-Fulton County Stadium, attendance 55,825. Kenny Flowers and John Settle each ran for second-half touchdowns as the Falcons rallied to defeat the Cowboys. Trailing 21-10 at halftime, Paul McFadden kicked a 38-yard field goal and Chris Miller led a 75-yard drive, capped by Flowers's one-yard touchdown run, to narrow the score to 21-20. Miller then drove the Falcons 59 yards to Settle's four-yard scoring run midway through the fourth quarter.

Dallas	14	7	0	0	—	21
Atlanta	7	3	10	7	—	27

Dall —Irvin 65 pass from Aikman (Ruzek kick)
Atl —Butler 29 fumble recovery return (McFadden kick)
Dall —Walker 4 run (Ruzek kick)
Atl —FG McFadden 28
Dall —Walker 20 run (Ruzek kick)
Atl —FG McFadden 38
Atl —Flowers 1 run (McFadden kick)
Atl —Settle 4 run (McFadden kick)

New York Giants 24, Detroit 14—at Giants Stadium, attendance 76,021. Phil Simms's fourth-quarter 24-yard touchdown pass to Mark Bavaro helped the Giants defeat the Lions. Detroit led 14-3 in the third quarter on Bob Gagliano's 71-yard scoring bomb to Richard Johnson and Barry Sanders's four-yard run. New York came back in the third quarter on Ottis Anderson's 11-yard run for a score and Simms's nine-yard touchdown pass to Odessa Turner. Lawrence Taylor's fumble recovery set up Simms's decisive pass to Bavaro. Taylor was named NFC Defensive Player of the Week for his performance.

Detroit	0	7	7	0	—	14
N.Y. Giants	3	0	14	7	—	24

NYG —FG Allegre 49
Det —Johnson 71 pass from Gagliano (Murray kick)
Det —B. Sanders 4 run (Murray kick)
NYG —Anderson 11 run (Allegre kick)
NYG —Turner 9 pass from Simms (Allegre kick)
NYG —Bavaro 24 pass from Simms (Allegre kick)

Houston 34, San Diego 27—at San Diego Jack Murphy Stadium, attendance 42,013. Warren Moon threw two touchdown passes and ran for another to lead the Oilers past the Chargers. San Diego led 14-3 in the second quarter, but Moon hit Ernest Givins for a 14-yard touchdown pass and then scored on a one-yard keeper. Tony Zendejas's 32-yard field goal as time expired in the first half gave Houston a 20-14 lead. The Oilers' final scoring came on Al Smith's fumble recovery which set up Moon's five-yard touchdown pass to Drew Hill and Alonzo Highsmith's 16-yard touchdown run.

Houston	3	17	14	0	—	34
San Diego	7	7	0	13	—	27

Hou —FG Zendejas 24
SD —Miller 63 pass from McMahon (Bahr kick)
SD —Butts 1 run (Bahr kick)
Hou —Givins 14 pass from Moon (Zendejas kick)
Hou —Moon 1 run (Zendejas kick)
Hou —FG Zendejas 32
Hou —Hill 5 pass from Moon (Zendejas kick)
Hou —Highsmith 16 run (Zendejas kick)
SD —Butts 1 run (pass failed)
SD —Miller 10 pass from McMahon (Bahr kick)

Los Angeles Rams 31, Indianapolis 17—at Anaheim Stadium, attendance 63,995. Jim Everett and Henry Ellard connected for three touchdown passes as the Rams defeated the Colts. Everett, who completed 28 of 35 for 368 yards, found Ellard on scoring passes of 29, 17, and 6 yards. Greg Bell added a two-yard touchdown run late in the fourth quarter. Eric Dickerson, who played for the Rams from 1983-87, made his first return to Anaheim Stadium since he was traded to the Colts in 1987, and ran for 116 yards on 21 carries and caught five passes for 45 yards.

Indianapolis	3	14	0	0	—	17
L.A. Rams	10	7	7	7	—	31

Rams —FG Lansford 40
Ind —FG Biasucci 19
Rams —Ellard 29 pass from Everett (Lansford kick)
Ind —Verdin 82 pass from Chandler (Biasucci kick)
Ind —Dickerson 2 run (Biasucci kick)
Rams —Ellard 17 pass from Everett (Lansford kick)
Rams —Ellard 6 pass from Everett (Lansford kick)
Rams —Bell 2 run (Lansford kick)

Kansas City 24, Los Angeles Raiders 19—at Arrowhead Stadium, attendance 71,741. Christian Okoye's one-yard run for a touchdown midway through the fourth quarter lifted the Chiefs over the Raiders. Kansas City held a 17-16 edge at halftime on Steve DeBerg's 49-yard scoring pass to Chris Dressel, Okoye's eight-yard run, and Nick Lowery's 47-yard field goal. Los Angeles went ahead 19-16 on Jeff Jaeger's 40-yard field goal, but DeBerg led an 87-yard drive to set up Okoye's winning run.

L.A. Raiders	6	10	3	0	—	19
Kansas City	7	10	0	7	—	24

Raiders —Fernandez 25 pass from Schroeder (kick failed)
KC —Dressel 49 pass from DeBerg (Lowery kick)
Raiders —Junkin 3 pass from Schroeder (Jaeger kick)
KC —FG Lowery 47
Raiders —FG Jaeger 39
KC —Okoye 8 run (Lowery kick)
Raiders —FG Jaeger 40
KC —Okoye 1 run (Lowery kick)

Miami 24, New England 10—at Sullivan Stadium, attendance 57,043. Dan Marino threw three touchdown passes as the Dolphins broke a seven-game losing streak to the Patriots. Marino completed a pair of touchdown passes to Jim Jensen (16 and 10 yards) and also had a 15-yard scoring toss to Mark Clayton. The Dolphins' offense extended their NFL record to 14 straight games without allowing a quarterback sack. Marino's three touchdown passes gave him 200 in 89 career games. The fastest a player had reached 200 previously was in 121 games by Johnny Unitas. Marino was named AFC Offensive Player of the Week.

Miami	17	7	0	0	—	24
New England	0	0	3	7	—	10

Mia —Clayton 15 pass from Marino (Stoyanovich kick)
Mia —Jensen 16 pass from Marino (Stoyanovich kick)
Mia —FG Stoyanovich 31
Mia —Jensen 10 pass from Marino (Stoyanovich kick)
NE —FG Davis 28
NE —Dykes 6 pass from Eason (Davis kick)

Chicago 38, Minnesota 7—at Soldier Field, attendance 66,475. Neal Anderson ran for two touchdowns and caught a third as the Bears easily beat the Vikings. Mike Tomczak opened the Bears' scoring with a 24-yard touchdown pass to Anderson in the first quarter. Shaun Gayle's interception set up Anderson's two-yard touchdown run in the fourth quarter. Anderson then scored on a 13-yard run, and, 17 seconds later, Lemuel Stinson returned an interception 29 yards for a touchdown. Mark Green's 37-yard run completed the scoring. The Bears' defense held the Vikings to 67 yards rushing.

Minnesota	0	7	0	0	—	7
Chicago	7	3	0	28	—	38

Chi —Anderson 24 pass from Tomczak (Butler kick)
Minn —Gustafson 4 pass from Wilson (Garcia kick)
Chi —FG Butler 40
Chi —Anderson 2 run (Butler kick)
Chi —Anderson 13 run (Butler kick)
Chi —Stinson 29 interception return (Butler kick)
Chi —Green 37 run (Butler kick)

Green Bay 35, New Orleans 34—at Lambeau Field, attendance 55,809. Don Majkowski's three-yard touchdown pass to Sterling Sharpe with 1:26 remaining lifted the Packers over the Saints. New Orleans jumped out to a 24-7 halftime lead, but Green Bay narrowed the score to 31-28 on two Majkowski touchdown passes to Ed West (three and 17 yards) and Brent Fullwood's four-yard run. The Saints went ahead 34-28 on Morten Andersen's 32-yard field goal, but Majkowski led an 80-yard drive to set up Sharpe's game-winning reception.

New Orleans	14	10	0	10	—	34
Green Bay	0	7	14	14	—	35

NO —Hill 32 pass from Hebert (Andersen kick)
NO —Hilliard 3 run (Andersen kick)
NO —Brenner 1 pass from Hebert (Andersen kick)
GB —Fullwood 1 run (Jacke kick)
NO —FG Andersen 38
GB —Fullwood 4 run (Jacke kick)
GB —West 3 pass from Majkowski (Jacke kick)
NO —Hill 24 pass from Hebert (Andersen kick)
GB —West 17 pass from Majkowski (Jacke kick)
NO —FG Andersen 32
GB —Sharpe 3 pass from Majkowski (Jacke kick)

Cleveland 38, New York Jets 24—at Cleveland Stadium, attendance 73,516. Bernie Kosar threw three touchdown passes as the Browns defeated the Jets. Cleveland took a 21-14 lead in the third quarter when Kosar hit Tim Manoa with a six-yard scoring pass. Kosar also completed touchdown passes to Ozzie Newsome (4 yards) and Webster Slaughter (35). The Browns' defense had four interceptions, including one by Thane Gash, which he returned 36 yards for a score in the second quarter.

N.Y. Jets	0	7	10	7	—	24
Cleveland	0	14	14	10	—	38

NYJ —Vick 39 run (Leahy kick)
Clev —Slaughter 35 pass from Kosar (Bahr kick)
Clev —Gash 36 interception return (Bahr kick)
NYJ —Townsell 49 pass from O'Brien (Leahy kick)
Clev —Manoa 6 pass from Kosar (Bahr kick)
NYJ —FG Leahy 36
Clev —Jones 9 run (Bahr kick)
NYJ —McNeil 1 run (Leahy kick)
Clev —Newsome 4 pass from Kosar (Bahr kick)
Clev —FG Bahr 21

Philadelphia 42, Washington 37—at Robert F. Kennedy Stadium, attendance 53,493. Randall Cunningham threw three fourth-quarter touchdown passes to rally the Eagles past the Redskins. Washington held a commanding 30-14 lead at halftime behind Mark Rypien's touchdown passes to Earnest Byner (11 yards) and Gary Clark (80, 5). But Cunningham, who completed 34 of 46 attempts for 447 yards, threw five-yard touchdown passes to Keith Jackson and Cris Carter and a two-yard pass to Mike Quick to narrow the score to 37-35. Al Harris then recovered a fumble for the Eagles and lateraled to Wes Hopkins, who returned the ball 77 yards to set up Cunningham's four-yard game-winning pass to Jackson.

Philadelphia	7	7	7	21	— 42
Washington	20	10	0	7	— 37

Wash —Clark 80 pass from Rypien (kick failed)
Wash —Riggs 41 run (Lohmiller kick)
Wash —Byner 11 pass from Rypien (Lohmiller kick)
Phil —Jackson 17 pass from Cunningham (Zendejas kick)
Wash —Clark 5 pass from Rypien (Lohmiller kick)
Phil —Toney 3 run (Zendejas kick)
Wash —FG Lohmiller 25
Phil —Jackson 5 pass from Cunningham (Zendejas kick)
Phil —Carter 5 pass from Cunningham (Zendejas kick)
Wash —Monk 43 pass from Rypien (Lohmiller kick)
Phil —Quick 2 pass from Cunningham (Zendejas kick)
Phil —Jackson 4 pass from Cunningham (Zendejas kick)

Phoenix 34, Seattle 24—at Kingdome, attendance 60,444. Gary Hogeboom passed for four touchdowns, including three to wide receiver Roy Green, to help the Cardinals past the Seahawks. Green, who had eight catches for 166 yards, had scoring receptions of 51, 6, and 59 yards. Tony Jordan ran one yard for a touchdown in the first quarter and Hogeboom hit J.T. Smith with a 25-yard scoring pass in third quarter to complete the Cardinals' scoring. Seattle wide receiver Brian Blades had nine receptions for 146 yards and a touchdown (five yards).

Phoenix	13	0	7	14	— 34
Seattle	0	7	7	10	— 24

Phx —Green 51 pass from Hogeboom (kick failed)
Phx —Jordan 1 run (Del Greco kick)
Sea —Skansi 3 pass from Krieg (N. Johnson kick)
Phx —Smith 25 pass from Hogeboom (Del Greco kick)
Sea —Skansi 17 pass from Krieg (N. Johnson kick)
Phx —Green 6 pass from Hogeboom (Del Greco kick)
Sea —FG N. Johnson 39
Phx —Green 59 pass from Hogeboom (Del Greco kick)
Sea —Blades 5 pass from Krieg (N. Johnson kick)

Cincinnati 41, Pittsburgh 10—at Riverfront Stadium, attendance 53,885. Boomer Esiason completed 19 of 35 passes for 328 yards and two touchdowns as the Bengals easily defeated the Steelers. The Bengals took a 20-3 halftime advantage on Jim Gallery's 26- and 47-yard field goals, Eddie Brown's 27-yard scoring reception, and Ickey Woods's one-yard run. Stanford Jennings scored two touchdowns in the second half on a one-yard run and a 43-yard scoring reception from Esiason. The Bengals' defense registered six sacks.

Pittsburgh	3	0	7	0	— 10
Cincinnati	3	17	7	14	— 41

Cin —FG Gallery 26
Pitt —FG Anderson 38
Cin —Brown 27 pass from Esiason (Gallery kick)
Cin —FG Gallery 47
Cin —Woods 1 run (Gallery kick)
Pitt —Hill 7 pass from Brister (Anderson kick)
Cin —Jennings 1 run (Gallery kick)
Cin —Brooks 2 run (Gallery kick)
Cin —Jennings 43 pass from Esiason (Gallery kick)

San Francisco 20, Tampa Bay 16—at Tampa Stadium, attendance 64,087. Joe Montana ran four yards for a touchdown with 40 seconds remaining in the game as the 49ers rallied to defeat the Buccaneers. The first three quarters were limited to all field goals as Donald Igwebuike kicked three for the Buccaneers (23, 44, and 37 yards) and Mike Cofer booted two for the 49ers (47 and 32). Jerry Rice then gave the 49ers a 13-9 lead on a two-yard touchdown reception from Montana midway through fourth quarter. The Buccaneers came right back to take a 16-13 lead on Vinny Testaverde's 18-yard scoring pass to Mark Carrier. Montana's decisive scoring run capped a 53-yard drive.

San Francisco	0	6	0	14	— 20
Tampa Bay	3	0	6	7	— 16

TB —FG Igwebuike 23
SF —FG Cofer 47
SF —FG Cofer 32
TB —FG Igwebuike 44
TB —FG Igwebuike 37
SF —Rice 2 pass from Montana (Cofer kick)
TB —Carrier 18 pass from Testaverde (Igwebuike kick)
SF —Montana 4 run (Cofer kick)

Monday, September 18

Denver 28, Buffalo 14—at Rich Stadium, attendance 78,176. Denver's defense recorded three sacks, three interceptions, and a safety as the Broncos beat the Bills. Denver jumped to a 18-0 halftime lead on Michael Brooks's safety as he tackled Jamie Mueller in the end zone, David Treadwell's three field goals (22, 33, and 46 yards), and John Elway's 19-yard yard scoring pass to Vance Johnson. Denver sealed the win in the second half on Treadwell's 24-yard field goal and Bobby Humphrey's five-yard yard scoring run.

Denver	5	13	3	7	— 28
Buffalo	0	0	7	7	— 14

Den —Safety, Brooks tackled Mueller in end zone
Den —FG Treadwell 22
Den —FG Treadwell 33
Den —V. Johnson 19 pass from Elway (Treadwell kick)
Den —FG Treadwell 46
Den —FG Treadwell 24
Buff —Kinnebrew 1 run (Norwood kick)
Buff —Harmon 20 pass from Kelly (Norwood kick)
Den —Humphrey 5 run (Treadwell kick)

Third Week Summaries

Standings

American Football Conference

Eastern Division

	W	L	T	Pct.	Pts.	OP
Buffalo	2	1	0	.667	88	93
Indianapolis	1	2	0	.333	54	70
Miami	1	2	0	.333	81	77
New England	1	2	0	.333	40	72
N.Y. Jets	1	2	0	.333	88	98
Central Division						
Cincinnati	2	1	0	.667	76	41
Cleveland	2	1	0	.667	103	45
Houston	1	2	0	.333	82	112
Pittsburgh	1	2	0	.333	37	106
Western Division						
Denver	3	0	0	1.000	93	55
Kansas City	1	2	0	.333	50	74
L.A. Raiders	1	2	0	.333	80	69
San Diego	1	2	0	.333	62	80
Seattle	1	2	0	.333	55	68

National Football Conference

Eastern Division

	W	L	T	Pct.	Pts.	OP
N.Y. Giants	3	0	0	1.000	86	45
Philadelphia	2	1	0	.667	101	82
Phoenix	2	1	0	.667	57	72
Washington	1	2	0	.333	91	76
Dallas	0	3	0	.000	28	85
Central Division						
Chicago	3	0	0	1.000	102	48
Tampa Bay	2	1	0	.667	59	51
Green Bay	1	2	0	.333	94	98
Minnesota	1	2	0	.333	59	72
Detroit	0	3	0	.000	54	87
Western Division						
L.A. Rams	3	0	0	1.000	103	76
San Francisco	3	0	0	1.000	88	68
Atlanta	1	2	0	.333	57	65
New Orleans	1	2	0	.333	72	55

Sunday, September 24

Indianapolis 13, Atlanta 9—at Hoosier Dome, attendance 57,816. Dean Biasucci kicked two field goals and Jack Trudeau ran for a touchdown as the Colts downed the Falcons. Atlanta led 9-0 in the third quarter on three Paul McFadden field goals (19, 34, and 27 yards). Biasucci's 25- and 29-yard field goals cut the Falcons' lead to 9-6 late in the third quarter. Chris Miller's fumble set up Trudeau's one-yard scoring run on the first play of the fourth quarter.

Atlanta	3	3	3	0	— 9
Indianapolis	0	0	6	7	— 13

Atl —FG McFadden 19
Atl —FG McFadden 34
Atl —FG McFadden 27
Ind —FG Biasucci 25
Ind —FG Biasucci 29
Ind —Trudeau 1 run (Biasucci kick)

Buffalo 47, Houston 41—at Astrodome, attendance 57,278. Jim Kelly's 28-yard touchdown pass to Andre Reed 8:42 into overtime gave the Bills a 47-41 victory over the Oilers. Buffalo led 34-24 in the fourth quarter, but Warren Moon hit Ernest Givins with a 26-yard scoring pass and Lorenzo White ran one yard for a touchdown to put Houston ahead 38-34. Kelly then fired a 26-yard touchdown pass to Thurman Thomas as the Bills recaptured the lead 41-38. Tony Zendejas's 52-yard field goal with three seconds remaining sent the game into overtime. Kelly, who completed 17 of 29 passes for 363 yards and five touchdowns, was named AFC Offensive Player of the Week.

Buffalo	10	10	7	14	6	— 47
Houston	7	3	14	17	0	— 41

Buff —FG Norwood 43
Hou —Moon 1 run (Zendejas kick)
Buff —Thomas 6 pass from Kelly (Norwood kick)
Buff —FG Norwood 26
Hou —FG Zendejas 26
Buf —Kelso 76 blocked field goal return (Norwood kick)
Buff —Beebe 63 pass from Kelly (Norwood kick)
Hou —Highsmith 4 run (Zendejas kick)
Hou —Dishman 7 blocked punt return (Zendejas kick)
Buff —Reed 78 pass from Kelly (Norwood kick)
Hou —Givins 26 pass from Moon (Zendejas kick)
Hou —White 1 run (Zendejas kick)
Buff —Thomas 26 pass from Kelly (Norwood kick)
Hou —FG Zendejas 52
Buff —Reed 28 pass from Kelly

Chicago 47, Detroit 27—at Pontiac Silverdome, attendance 71,418. Mike Tomczak threw for 302 yards and two touchdowns as the Bears defeated the Lions for the tenth consecutive time. Chicago's Neal Anderson, who carried 16 times for 116 yards, had a 53-yard touchdown run in the third quarter. Kevin Butler converted on all four field goal attempts from 21, 22, 25, and 32 yards. Anderson's backfield mate, Brad Muster, ran six yards for a score and also caught a three-yard touchdown pass from Tomczak.

Chicago	10	10	13	14	— 47
Detroit	0	13	7	7	— 27

Chi —FG Butler 21
Chi —Muster 6 run (Butler kick)
Det —Sanders 3 run (Murray kick)
Chi —McKinnon 40 pass from Tomczak (Butler kick)
Det —FG Murray 40
Chi —FG Butler 22
Det —FG Murray 48
Chi —Anderson 53 run (Butler kick)
Det —Gagliano 1 run (Murray kick)
Chi —FG Butler 25
Chi —FG Butler 32
Chi —Muster 3 pass from Tomczak (Butler kick)
Chi —Harbaugh 1 run (Butler kick)
Det —Gagliano 1 run (Murray kick)

Los Angeles Rams 41, Green Bay 38—at Anaheim Stadium, attendance 57,701. Greg Bell ran 28 times for 221 yards and two touchdowns to help the Rams overcome the Packers. Los Angeles took a 38-7 lead in the first half on Jim Everett's scoring passes to Buford McGee (four yards), Damone Johnson (four), Bell's scoring runs (one and 45 yards), Vince Newsome's 81-yard interception returned for a score, and Mike Lansford's 39-yard field goal. Green Bay came alive in the second half to score 24 consecutive points, but Lansford's 45-yard field goal increased the Rams lead to 41-31. Green Bay running back Brent Fullwood ran one yard for a touchdown to narrow the margin to 41-38, but the Rams held on for the win.

Green Bay	0	7	21	10	— 38
L.A. Rams	10	28	0	3	— 41

Rams —FG Lansford 39
Rams —Bell 1 run (Lansford kick)
GB —Majkowski 8 run (Jacke kick)
Rams —McGee 4 pass from Everett (Lansford kick)
Rams —Newsome 81 interception return (Lansford kick)
Rams —Bell 45 run (Lansford kick)
Rams —Johnson 4 pass from Everett (Lansford kick)
GB —Sharpe 18 pass from Majkowski (Jacke kick)
GB —Fullwood 11 run (Jacke kick)
GB —West 1 pass from Majkowski (Jacke kick)
GB —FG Jacke 43
Rams —FG Lansford 45
GB —Fullwood 1 run (Jacke kick)

San Diego 21, Kansas City 6—at San Diego Jack Murphy Stadium, attendance 40,128. Rod Bernstine ran for one touchdown and caught another as the Chargers defeated the Chiefs for their first win of the season. Vencie Glenn's interception set up Tim Spencer's nine-yard run to give San Diego a 7-6 halftime edge. Jim McMahon capped a 74-yard, 11-play drive with a one-yard touchdown toss to Bernstine. Bernstine's 32-yard scoring run put the game out of reach with 3:31 to play.

Kansas City	3	3	0	0	— 6
San Diego	7	0	7	7	— 21

SD —Spencer 9 run (Bahr kick)
KC —FG Lowery 23
KC —FG Lowery 31
SD —Bernstine 1 pass from McMahon (Bahr kick)
SD —Bernstine 32 run (Bahr kick)

Denver 31, Los Angeles Raiders 21—at Mile High Stadium, attendance 75,754. John Elway and Mark Jackson combined for two touchdowns to help the Broncos defeat the Raiders. Elway ran 29 yards for a score and connected with Jackson on touchdown passes of 46 and 11 yards as Denver took a commanding 28-0 halftime advantage. David Treadwell's 38-yard field goal in the fourth quarter provided all the scoring the Broncos needed. Denver's defense was outstanding, recording three sacks, three interceptions, and three fumble recoveries.

L.A. Raiders	0	0	7	14	— 21
Denver	21	7	0	3	— 31

Den —Elway 29 run (Treadwell kick)
Den —Alexander 1 run (Treadwell kick)
Den —Jackson 46 pass from Elway (Treadwell kick)
Den —Jackson 11 pass from Elway (Treadwell kick)
Raiders —Washington 22 interception return (Jaeger kick)
Raiders —Fernandez 75 pass from Schroeder (Jaeger kick)
Raiders —L. King 15 fumble recovery return (Jaeger kick)
Den —FG Treadwell 38

Pittsburgh 27, Minnesota 14—at Three Rivers Stadium, attendance 50,744. Merril Hoge ran two yards for a touchdown to help lead the Steelers past the Vikings for their first win of the season. With the score deadlocked 14-14 in the second quarter, Hoge's touchdown run put Pittsburgh ahead 21-14 at halftime. Gary Anderson kicked fourth-quarter field goals from 38 and 44 yards, which completed the scoring. The Steelers' defense accounted for five sacks and two interceptions.

Minnesota	7	7	0	0	— 14
Pittsburgh	7	14	0	6	— 27

Pitt —Mularkey 15 pass from Brister (G. Anderson kick)
Minn —Wilson 1 run (Garcia kick)
Pitt —Worley 8 run (G. Anderson kick)
Minn —Thomas 27 fumble recovery return (Garcia kick)
Pitt —Hoge 2 run (G. Anderson kick)
Pitt —FG G. Anderson 38
Pitt —FG G. Anderson 44

Tampa Bay 20, New Orleans 10—at Tampa Stadium, attendance 44,053. Vinny Testaverde threw a touchdown pass to Ron Hall and Lars Tate ran for a score as the Buccaneers broke a six-game losing streak against the Saints. Tate's five-yard touchdown run in the third quarter broke a 10-10 halftime tie and put the Buccaneers ahead for good. Donald Igwebuike's second field goal of the day, a 37-yarder in the fourth quarter, assured the win. Mark Carrier had five receptions for 120 yards for Tampa Bay.

New Orleans	7	3	0	0	— 10
Tampa Bay	0	10	7	3	— 20

NO —Hilliard 1 run (Andersen kick)
TB —FG Igwebuike 34
TB —Hall 11 pass from Testaverde (Igwebuike kick)
NO —FG Andersen 33
TB —Tate 5 run (Igwebuike kick)
TB —FG Igwebuike 37

New York Jets 40, Miami 33—at Joe Robbie Stadium, attendance 65,908. Ken O'Brien threw three second-half touchdown passes as the Jets rallied to beat the Dolphins for their first victory of the season. After trailing 20-12 at halftime, O'Brien's 37-yard touchdown pass to Al Toon narrowed the deficit to 23-19 in the third quarter. The Jets trailed 33-26 in the fourth quarter before Johnny Hector scored on a one-yard run to tie the score 33-33, and less than two minutes later, O'Brien threw an 11-yard scoring pass to Roger Vick for the game-winning score.

N.Y. Jets	3	9	7	21	— 40
Miami	7	13	10	3	— 33

NYJ —FG Leahy 32
Mia —Edmunds 8 pass from Marino (Stoyanovich kick)
Mia —Edmunds 19 pass from Jensen (kick failed)
NYJ —Radachowsky 78 blocked field goal return (Leahy kick)
NYJ —Safety, punt snapped out of end zone
Mia —Banks 43 pass from Marino (Stoyanovich kick)
Mia —FG Stoyanovich 21
NYJ —Toon 37 pass from O'Brien (Leahy kick)
Mia —Clayton 14 pass from Marino (Stoyanovich kick)
NYJ —Hector 23 pass from O'Brien (Leahy kick)
Mia —FG Stoyanovich 20
NYJ —Hector 1 run (Leahy kick)
NYJ —Vick 11 pass from O'Brien (Leahy kick)

New York Giants 35, Phoenix 7—at Giants Stadium, attendance 75,742. Raul Allegre kicked four field goals and the Giants' defense registered five sacks, four interceptions, and two fumble recoveries en route to victory over the Cardinals. The Giants took a 14-0 first-quarter lead on Phil Simms's 39-yard scoring pass to Stephen Baker and Terry Kinard's 58-yard interception return for a touchdown. New York led 20-0 at halftime after Allegre kicked two field goals (22 and 38 yards) in the second quarter. The Giants completed their scoring on two more field goals by Allegre, Ottis Anderson's 36-yard run for a score, and a safety when Gary Reasons tackled Gary Hogeboom in the end zone. Hogeboom's 21-yard touchdown pass to J. T. Smith prevented the shutout.

Phoenix	0	0	0	7	— 7
N.Y. Giants	14	6	5	10	— 35

NYG —Baker 39 pass from Simms (Allegre kick)
NYG —Kinard 58 interception return (Allegre kick)
NYG —FG Allegre 22
NYG —FG Allegre 38
NYG —FG Allegre 32
NYG —Safety, Reasons tackled Hogeboom in end zone
NYG —Anderson 36 run (Allegre kick)
NYG —FG Allegre 32
Phx —J. Smith 21 pass from Hogeboom (Del Greco kick)

San Francisco 38, Philadelphia 28—at Veterans Stadium, attendance 66,042. Joe Montana threw four touchdown passes in the fourth quarter to rally the 49ers over the Eagles. Trailing 28-17 with 6:03 remaining, Montana cut the Eagles' lead to 28-24 with an eight-yard touchdown throw to Tom Rathman. Montana then led a three-play drive capped by his 25-yard scoring pass to Brent Jones to go ahead 31-28. Ronnie Lott's interception set up Jerry Rice's 33-yard scoring reception from Montana with 2:02 left in the game. Montana, who was 25 of 34 for 428 yards, was named NFC Offensive Player of the Week.

San Francisco	7	3	0	28	— 38
Philadelphia	9	3	6	10	— 28

SF —Rice 68 pass from Montana (Cofer kick)
Phil —Sherman 2 run (Zendejas kick)
Phil —Safety, Harris tackled Montana in end zone
Phil —FG Zendejas 35
SF —FG Cofer 32
Phil —FG Zendejas 35
Phil —FG Zendejas 44
Phil —FG Zendejas 20
SF —Taylor 70 pass from Montana (Cofer kick)
Phil —Giles 3 pass from Cunningham (Zendejas kick)
SF —Rathman 8 pass from Montana (Cofer kick)
SF —Jones 25 pass from Montana (Cofer kick)
SF —Rice 33 pass from Montana (Cofer kick)

Seattle 24, New England 3—at Sullivan Stadium, attendance 48,025. Dave Krieg completed touchdown passes in the second quarter to three different receivers to lead the Seahawks past the Patriots. Krieg hit Louis Clark (27 yards), Paul Skansi (19), and John L. Williams (10). Norm Johnson added a 23-yard field goal in the third quarter to finish Seattle's scoring.

Seattle	0	21	3	0	— 24
New England	3	0	0	0	— 3

NE —FG Davis 35
Sea —Clark 27 pass from Krieg (N. Johnson kick)
Sea —Skansi 19 pass from Krieg (N. Johnson kick)
Sea —Williams 10 pass from Krieg (N. Johnson kick)
Sea —FG N. Johnson 23

Washington 30, Dallas 7—at Texas Stadium, attendance 53,200. Earnest Byner ran for a touchdown and Chip Lohmiller added three field goals as the Redskins downed the Cowboys. Washington jumped to a 14-7 first-quarter lead on Alvin Walton's 29-yard interception return for a touchdown and Byner's 12-yard scoring run. Lohmiller kicked field goals of 26, 37, and 33 yards. Jamie Morris, who carried 26 times for 100 yards, scored the Redskins' final touchdown on a 12-yard run in the fourth quarter.

Washington	14	3	3	10	— 30
Dallas	7	0	0	0	— 7

Wash —Walton 29 interception return (Lohmiller kick)
Dall —Jeffcoat 77 fumble recovery return (Ruzek kick)
Wash —Byner 12 run (Lohmiller kick)
Wash —FG Lohmiller 26
Wash —FG Lohmiller 37
Wash —Morris 12 run (Lohmiller kick)
Wash —FG Lohmiller 33

Monday, September 25

Cincinnati 21, Cleveland 14—at Riverfront Stadium, attendance 55,996. Boomer Esiason passed for three touchdowns as the Bengals beat the division-rival Browns. Esiason's pair of scoring passes to Rodney Holman (eight, 16 yards) tied the game at halftime 14-14. His 19-yard touchdown pass to James Brooks provided the only scoring in the second half. Cornerback Eric Thomas preserved the victory when he deflected Bernie Kosar's fourth-down pass into the end zone with 1:41 remaining in the game.

Cleveland	0	14	0	0	— 14
Cincinnati	0	14	7	0	— 21

Cin —Holman 8 pass from Esiason (Gallery kick)
Clev —Metcalf 5 pass from Kosar (Bahr kick)
Cin —Holman 16 pass from Esiason (Gallery kick)
Clev —Manoa 6 pass from Kosar (Bahr kick)
Cin —Brooks 19 pass from Esiason (Gallery kick)

Fourth Week Summaries

Standings

American Football Conference

Eastern Division

	W	L	T	Pct.	Pts.	OP
Buffalo	3	1	0	.750	119	103
Indianapolis	2	2	0	.500	71	80
Miami	1	3	0	.250	88	116
New England	1	3	0	.250	50	103
N.Y. Jets	1	3	0	.250	98	115

Central Division

	W	L	T	Pct.	Pts.	OP
Cincinnati	3	1	0	.750	97	58
Cleveland	3	1	0	.750	119	58
Houston	2	2	0	.500	121	119
Pittsburgh	2	2	0	.500	60	109

Western Division

	W	L	T	Pct.	Pts.	OP
Denver	3	1	0	.750	106	71
San Diego	2	2	0	.500	86	93
Seattle	2	2	0	.500	79	88
Kansas City	1	3	0	.250	67	95
L.A. Raiders	1	3	0	.250	100	93

National Football Conference

Eastern Division

	W	L	T	Pct.	Pts.	OP
N.Y. Giants	4	0	0	1.000	116	58
Philadelphia	2	2	0	.500	114	109
Phoenix	2	2	0	.500	70	96
Washington	2	2	0	.500	107	90
Dallas	0	4	0	.000	41	115

Central Division

	W	L	T	Pct.	Pts.	OP
Chicago	4	0	0	1.000	129	61
Green Bay	2	2	0	.500	117	119
Minnesota	2	2	0	.500	76	75
Tampa Bay	2	2	0	.500	62	68
Detroit	0	4	0	.000	57	110

Western Division

	W	L	T	Pct.	Pts.	OP
L.A. Rams	4	0	0	1.000	116	88
San Francisco	3	1	0	.750	100	81
Atlanta	1	3	0	.250	78	88
New Orleans	1	3	0	.250	86	71

Sunday, October 1

Green Bay 23, Atlanta 21—at Milwaukee County Stadium, attendance 54,647. Chris Jacke's 22-yard field goal with 1:42 remaining in the game gave the Packers a win over the Falcons. Trailing 21-6 in the fourth quarter, Sterling Sharpe recovered a fumble by teammate Jeff Query and ran five yards for a touchdown. Don Majkowski's 37-yard scoring pass to Herman Fontenot narrowed the margin to 21-20. Jacke's winning field goal capped a 13-play drive. Jacke also kicked 35- and 52-yard field goals in the second quarter.

Atlanta	7	7	7	0	— 21
Green Bay	0	6	0	17	— 23

Atl —Beckman 3 pass from Millen (McFadden kick)
GB —FG Jacke 35
Atl —Settle 1 run (McFadden kick)
GB —FG Jacke 52
Atl —Lang 10 run (McFadden kick)
GB —Sharpe 5 run with recovered fumble (Jacke kick)
GB —Fontenot 37 pass from Majkowski (Jacke kick)
GB —FG Jacke 22

Cincinnati 21, Kansas City 17—at Arrowhead Stadium, attendance 60,165. Leon White ran 22 yards for a touchdown with a fourth-quarter recovered fumble to give the Bengals a 21-17 victory over the Chiefs. Kansas City running back Christian Okoye, who had 25 carries for 101 yards, gave the Chiefs a 10-0 second quarter lead on an 11-yard scoring run. Seventeen-year NFL veteran quarterback Ron Jaworski's five-yard touchdown pass to rookie Robb Thomas put Kansas City ahead 17-7 before Cincinnati rookie Eric Ball's two-yard run closed the margin to 17-14 at halftime.

Cincinnati	0	14	0	7	— 21
Kansas City	3	14	0	0	— 17

KC —FG Lowery 23
KC —Okoye 11 run (Lowery kick)
Cin —McGee 40 pass from Esiason (Gallery kick)
KC —R. Thomas 5 pass from Jaworski (Lowery kick)
Cin —Ball 2 run (Gallery kick)
Cin —White 22 fumble recovery return (Gallery kick)

Cleveland 16, Denver 13—at Cleveland Stadium, attendance 78,637. Matt Bahr's 48-yard field goal as time ran out lifted the Browns over the Broncos. Cleveland led 10-3 at halftime on Bernie Kosar's nine-yard touchdown pass to Webster Slaughter and Bahr's 36-yard field goal. Bahr added a 48-yard field goal in the third quarter, but David Treadwell's 26-yard field goal and John Elway's seven-yard scoring pass to Vance Johnson tied the game 13-13 with less than four minutes remaining. The Browns' victory ended a 10-game, 15-year losing streak to the Broncos.

Denver	0	3	3	7	— 13
Cleveland	7	3	3	3	— 16

Clev —Slaughter 9 pass from Kosar (Bahr kick)
Den —FG Treadwell 21
Clev —FG Bahr 36
Clev —FG Bahr 48
Den —FG Treadwell 26
Den —Johnson 7 pass from Elway (Treadwell kick)
Clev —FG Bahr 48

Indianapolis 17, New York Jets 10—at Giants Stadium, attendance 65,542. Clarence Verdin returned a punt 49 yards for a score as the Colts rallied to defeat the Jets. Trailing 10-0, Jack Trudeau's 55-yard scoring bomb to Bill Brooks cut New York's advantage to 10-7 in the third quarter. Dean Biasucci's 38-yard field goal in the fourth quarter tied the game 10-10. Less than two minutes later, Verdin's punt return gave Indianapolis the go-ahead score. Brooks had seven receptions for 159 yards. The Jets' Erik McMillan returned an interception in the first quarter 92 yards for a score.

Indianapolis	0	0	7	10	— 17
N.Y. Jets	7	3	0	0	— 10

NYJ —McMillan 92 interception return (Leahy kick)
NYJ —FG Leahy 26
Ind —Brooks 55 pass from Trudeau (Biasucci kick)
Ind —FG Biasucci 38
Ind —Verdin 49 punt return (Biasucci kick)

Los Angeles Rams 13, San Francisco 12—at Candlestick Park, attendance 64,250. Mike Lansford's 26-yard field goal with two seconds remaining knocked the 49ers from the undefeated ranks. Los Angeles held a 10-9 edge on Lansford's 40-yard field goal and Jim Everett's 65-yard scoring strike to Willie Anderson. San Francisco went ahead in the fourth quarter 12-10 on a 17-yard field goal by Mike Cofer. After a 49ers turnover, Everett led the Rams on a nine-play, 72-yard drive to set up Lansford's winning kick. Los Angeles lifted its record to 4-0 for the second consecutive season.

L.A. Rams	3	7	0	3	—	13
San Francisco	6	3	0	3	—	12

SF —FG Cofer 26
Rams —FG Lansford 40
SF —FG Cofer 32
Rams —Anderson 65 pass from Everett (Lansford kick)
SF —FG Cofer 41
SF —FG Cofer 17
Rams —FG Lansford 26

Houston 39, Miami 7—at Astrodome, attendance 53,326. Warren Moon completed 19 of 23 passes for 254 yards and two touchdowns as the Oilers easily beat the Dolphins. Moon connected on touchdown passes to Allen Pinkett (two yards) and Curtis Duncan (25). Pinkett also scored on a 10-yard run and Alonzo Highsmith ran for a three-yard touchdown. Tony Zendejas added field goals for the Oilers of 32, 40, and 32 yards. Houston's defense held quarterback Dan Marino to a career-low 103 yards passing. Miami avoided being shut out late in the fourth quarter when Marc Logan returned a kickoff 97 yards for a touchdown.

Miami	0	0	0	7	—	7
Houston	2	17	6	14	—	39

Hou —Safety, Roby fumble out of end zone
Hou —FG Zendejas 32
Hou —Highsmith 3 run (Zendejas kick)
Hou —Pinkett 2 pass from Moon (Zendejas kick)
Hou —FG Zendejas 40
Hou —FG Zendejas 32
Hou —Duncan 25 pass from Moon (Zendejas kick)
Hou —Pinkett 10 run (Zendejas kick)
Mia —Logan 97 kickoff return (Stoyanovich kick)

Buffalo 31, New England 10—at Rich Stadium, attendance 78,921. Thurman Thomas ran for one touchdown and caught another to help the Bills top the Patriots. Thomas, who gained 204 total yards, scored on a four-yard run in the first quarter and a 74-yard reception from Jim Kelly in the fourth period. Kelly's two other touchdown passes were to Keith McKeller (39 yards) and Pete Metzelaars (eight). Bills wide receiver Andre Reed had four catches for 114 yards.

New England	3	0	7	0	—	10
Buffalo	7	17	0	7	—	31

NE —FG Davis 35
Buff —Thomas 4 run (Norwood kick)
Buff —McKeller 39 pass from Kelly (Norwood kick)
Buff —Metzelaars 8 pass from Kelly (Norwood kick)
Buff —FG Norwood 36
NE —Jones 20 pass from Flutie (Davis kick)
Buff —Thomas 74 pass from Kelly (Norwood kick)

New York Giants 30, Dallas 13—at Texas Stadium, attendance 51,785. Phil Simms threw two touchdown passes and Raul Allegre kicked three field goals to lead the Giants over the Cowboys. Simms's scoring throws went to Dave Meggett (33 yards) and Mark Bavaro (13). Allegre connected on field goals of 37, 32, and 27 yards. Ottis Anderson added a one-yard run for a score. Dallas quarterback Steve Walsh replaced injured Troy Aikman and threw a 27-yard touchdown pass to Herschel Walker in the fourth quarter. The victory gave the Giants a 4-0 record for the first time since 1968.

N.Y. Giants	3	17	7	3	—	30
Dallas	0	6	0	7	—	13

NYG—FG Allegre 37
Dall —FG Ruzek 19
NYG—Anderson 1 run (Allegre kick)
Dall —FG Ruzek 33
NYG—Meggett 33 pass from Simms (Allegre kick)
NYG—FG Allegre 32
NYG—Bavaro 13 pass from Simms (Allegre kick)
NYG—FG Allegre 27
Dall —Walker 27 pass from Walsh (Ruzek kick)

Pittsburgh 23, Detroit 3—at Pontiac Silverdome, attendance 43,804. Bubby Brister threw a touchdown pass and the Steelers' defense registered three sacks, two interceptions, and two fumble recoveries in their victory over the Lions. Pittsburgh took a 10-3 halftime lead on Brister's 48-yard touchdown pass to Louis Lipps and Gary Anderson's 20-yard field goal. Interceptions by Larry Griffin, which set up Rodney Carter's one-yard touchdown run, and Dwayne Woodruff, which set up Ray Wallace's two-yard scoring run, put the Steelers ahead 23-3. Brister, who completed a team-record 15 straight passes, was named AFC Offensive Player of the Week.

Pittsburgh	0	10	7	6	—	23
Detroit	3	0	0	0	—	3

Det —FG Murray 37
Pitt —Lipps 48 pass from Brister (Anderson kick)
Pitt —FG Anderson 20
Pitt —Carter 1 run (Anderson kick)
Pitt —Wallace 2 run (pass failed)

San Diego 24, Phoenix 13—at Sun Devil Stadium, attendance 44,201. Billy Ray Smith returned a fumble 15 yards for a score in the fourth quarter to highlight the Chargers' win over the Cardinals. San Diego, which trailed 13-7 entering the final period, rallied for 17 points on Marion Butts's two-yard touchdown run, Smith's fumble recovery returned for a touchdown, and Chris Bahr's 37-yard field goal.

San Diego	0	0	7	17	—	24
Phoenix	0	3	10	0	—	13

Phx —FG Del Greco 36
Phx —FG Del Greco 33
SD —Miller 16 pass from McMahon (Bahr kick)
Phx —Green 59 pass from Hogeboom (Del Greco kick)
SD —Butts 2 run (Bahr kick)
SD —B. Smith 15 fumble recovery return (Bahr kick)
SD —FG Bahr 37

Seattle 24, Los Angeles Raiders 20—at Memorial Coliseum, attendance 44,319. Curt Warner carried 21 times for 102 yards and a touchdown to lead the Seahawks over the Raiders. Seattle took a 7-0 first-quarter lead on Dave Krieg's 14-yard scoring strike to John L. Williams, but Los Angeles tallied 17 consecutive points to take a 17-7 lead. Warner ran six yards for a touchdown and Krieg hit Brian Blades with a 19-yard touchdown pass to put Seattle ahead 21-17. Jeff Jaeger's 28-yard field goal brought the Raiders to within one point at 21-20, but Norm Johnson's 48-yard field goal with 1:15 remaining sealed the Seahawks' victory.

Seattle	7	0	0	17	—	24
L.A. Raiders	0	10	7	3	—	20

Sea —Williams 14 pass from Krieg (N. Johnson kick)
Raiders —FG Jaeger 45
Raiders —Washington 37 fumble recovery return (Jaeger kick)
Raiders —Fernandez 36 pass from Schroeder (Jaeger kick)
Sea —Warner 6 run (N. Johnson kick)
Sea —Blades 19 pass from Krieg (N. Johnson kick)
Raiders —FG Jaeger 28
Sea —FG N. Johnson 48

Minnesota 17, Tampa Bay 3—at Metrodome, attendance 54,817. Tommy Kramer threw two touchdown passes and the Vikings' defense limited the Buccaneers to 82 yards passing en route to victory. Kramer connected with Anthony Carter on a 12-yard touchdown strike and Rich Karlis kicked a 20-yard field goal as Minnesota took a 10-3 halftime lead. Leo Lewis completed Minnesota's scoring, catching a 28-yard pass from Kramer. The Vikings held a 36:04 to 23:56 time-of-possession advantage over the Buccaneers.

Tampa Bay	0	3	0	0	—	3
Minnesota	0	10	7	0	—	17

Minn —Carter 12 pass from Kramer (Karlis kick)
Minn —FG Karlis 20
TB —FG Igwebuike 44
Minn —Lewis 28 pass from Kramer (Karlis kick)

Washington 16, New Orleans 14—at Louisiana Superdome, attendance 46,358. Chip Lohmiller kicked three field goals and Gerald Riggs ran for a touchdown to help the Redskins edge the Saints. Trailing 14-3 in the third quarter, Lohmiller's 19-yard field goal and Riggs's nine-yard scoring run narrowed the score to 14-13. Dave Harbour's recovery of a muffed Saints punt early in the fourth quarter set up Lohmiller's decisive 18-yard field goal.

Washington	3	0	10	3	—	16
New Orleans	7	7	0	0	—	14

Wash —FG Lohmiller 48
NO —Hill 11 pass from Hebert (Andersen kick)
NO —Hilliard 3 run (Andersen kick)
Wash —FG Lohmiller 19
Wash —Riggs 9 run (Lohmiller kick)
Wash —FG Lohmiller 18

Monday, October 2

Chicago 27, Philadelphia 13—at Soldier Field, attendance 66,625. Mike Tomczak threw three touchdown passes and the Bears' defense accounted for four sacks and four interceptions to down the Eagles. Tomczak threw for first-quarter scores to Dennis McKinnon (14 yards) and Matt Suhey (one). Neal Anderson added a two-yard touchdown run in the second quarter to give Chicago a 20-3 lead it never relinquished. Philadelphia cut the score to 20-13 on Gregg Garrity's 24-yard scoring reception from Randall Cunningham and Luis Zendejas's 36-yard field goal, but Tomczak's third touchdown pass, a 36-yarder to James Thornton, was too much for the Eagles to overcome.

Phildelphia	0	0	3	10	—	13
Chicago	0	13	7	7	—	27

Chi —McKinnon 14 pass from Tomczak (Butler kick)
Chi —Suhey 1 pass from Tomczak (kick failed)
Phil —FG Zendejas 47
Chi —Anderson 2 run (Butler kick)
Phil —Garrity 24 pass from Cunningham (Zendejas kick)
Phil —FG Zendejas 19
Chi —Thornton 36 pass from Tomczak (Butler kick)

Fifth Week Summaries

Standings

American Football Conference

Eastern Division

	W	L	T	Pct.	Pts.	OP
Buffalo	3	2	0	.600	133	140
Indianapolis	3	2	0	.600	108	94
Miami	2	3	0	.400	101	126
New England	2	3	0	.400	73	116
N.Y. Jets	1	4	0	.200	105	129
Central Division						
Cincinnati	4	1	0	.800	123	74
Cleveland	3	2	0	.600	129	71
Houston	2	3	0	.400	134	142
Pittsburgh	2	3	0	.400	76	135
Western Division						
Denver	4	1	0	.800	122	81
Kansas City	2	3	0	.400	87	111
L.A. Raiders	2	3	0	.400	114	100
San Diego	2	3	0	.400	96	109
Seattle	2	3	0	.400	95	108

National Football Conference

Eastern Division

	W	L	T	Pct.	Pts.	OP
N.Y. Giants	4	1	0	.800	135	79
Philadelphia	3	2	0	.600	135	128
Washington	3	2	0	.600	137	118
Phoenix	2	3	0	.400	98	126
Dallas	0	5	0	.000	54	146
Central Division						
Chicago	4	1	0	.800	164	103
Green Bay	3	2	0	.600	148	132
Minnesota	3	2	0	.600	100	92
Tampa Bay	3	2	0	.600	104	103
Detroit	0	5	0	.000	74	134
Western Division						
L.A. Rams	5	0	0	1.000	142	102
San Francisco	4	1	0	.800	124	101
Atlanta	1	4	0	.200	92	114
New Orleans	1	4	0	.200	106	95

Sunday, October 8

Los Angeles 26, Atlanta 14—at Anaheim Stadium, attendance 52,182. The Rams remained the NFL's only unbeaten team as Jim Everett completed 16 of 28 attempts for 290 yards and two touchdowns to lead Los Angeles over Atlanta. The Rams jumped to a 20-7 halftime advantage on Everett's scoring strikes to Pete Holohan (13 yards) and Robert Delpino (nine), and a pair of Mike Lansford field goals (48 and 35 yards). Lansford added field goals of 27 and 42 yards in the third quarter to complete the Rams' scoring. Henry Ellard had eight receptions for 165 yards for the Rams.

Atlanta	7	0	7	0	—	14
L.A. Rams	10	10	6	0	—	26

Rams —Holohan 13 pass from Everett (Lansford kick)
Atl —Collins 9 pass from Miller (McFadden kick)
Rams —FG Lansford 48
Rams —Delpino 9 pass from Everett (Lansford kick)
Rams —FG Lansford 35
Rams —FG Lansford 27
Atl —Jones 3 run (McFadden kick)
Rams —FG Lansford 42

Indianapolis 37, Buffalo 14—at Hoosier Dome, attendance 58,890. Eric Dickerson ran for two touchdowns and the Colts' defense recorded four sacks, four interceptions, and two forced fumbles to help Indianapolis defeat Buffalo. The Colts took a 20-0 halftime lead as Dickerson and Jack Trudeau each scored on one-yard runs in the first quarter and Dean Biasucci kicked 32- and 46-yard field goals in the second quarter. Biasucci added a 25-yarder in the third quarter. Dickerson ran four yards for a touchdown and Keith Taylor returned an interception 80 yards for a touchdown in the fourth quarter to complete the Colts' scoring. Buffalo's Frank Reich came off the bench to replace injured Bills quarterback Jim Kelly and threw a 17-yard touchdown pass to Kenneth Davis in the fourth quarter.

Buffalo	0	0	7	7	—	14
Indianapolis	14	6	3	14	—	37

Ind —Dickerson 1 run (Biasucci kick)
Ind —Trudeau 1 run (Biasucci kick)
Ind —FG Biasucci 32
Ind —FG Biasucci 46
Ind —FG Biasucci 25
Buff —Reed 16 pass from Kelly (Norwood kick)
Ind —Dickerson 4 run (Biasucci kick)
Buff —K. Davis 17 pass from Reich (Norwood kick)
Ind —Taylor 80 interception return (Biasucci kick)

Tampa Bay 42, Chicago 35—at Tampa Stadium, attendance 72,077. Vinny Testaverde threw three touchdown passes to lead the Buccaneers past the Bears for the first time in 13 games. Testaverde connected with Mark Carrier (11 yards), William Harris (three), and Bruce Hill (22) in the first half, and Lars Tate had a pair of scoring runs (16 and four yards) in the second half to finish Tampa Bay's scoring. The loss knocked Chicago from the undefeated ranks. The entire Tampa Bay offensive unit was named NFC Co-Players of the Week.

Chicago	0	14	7	14	—	35
Tampa Bay	14	14	0	14	—	42

TB — Carrier 11 pass from Testaverde (Igwebuike kick)
TB — Howard 1 run (Igwebuike kick)
TB — Harris 3 pass from Testaverde (Igwebuike kick)
Chi — Anderson 5 run (Butler kick)
TB — Hill 22 pass from Testaverde (Igwebuike kick)
Chi — Anderson 1 run (Butler kick)
Chi — Sanders 16 pass from Tomczak (Butler kick)
TB — Tate 16 run (Igwebuike kick)
TB — Tate 4 run (Mohr run)
Chi — Harbaugh 26 run (Butler kick)
Chi — Anderson 1 run (Butler kick)

Cincinnati 26, Pittsburgh 16—at Three Rivers Stadium, attendance 52,785. Boomer Esiason led a pair of 80-yard drives for scores and threw a seven-yard touchdown pass to Mike Martin as the Bengals downed the Steelers. Cincinnati took a 13-10 halftime edge on Jim Breech's field goals of 24 and 27 yards and Martin's scoring reception. James Brooks, who carried 17 times for 127 yards, had touchdown runs of 13 and 65 yards in the fourth quarter to seal the win.

Cincinnati	0	13	0	13	—	26
Pittsburgh	7	3	3	3	—	16

Pitt — Carter 22 pass from Brister (Anderson kick)
Cin — FG Breech 24
Cin — FG Breech 27
Pitt — FG Anderson 24
Cin — Martin 7 pass from Esiason (Breech kick)
Pitt — FG Anderson 40
Cin — Brooks 13 run (kick failed)
Pitt — FG Anderson 34
Cin — Brooks 65 run (Breech kick)

Miami 13, Cleveland 10—at Joe Robbie Stadium, attendance 58,444. Pete Stoyanovich's 35-yard field goal 6:28 into overtime gave the Dolphins a victory over the Browns. Miami led 10-3 at halftime on Stoyanovich's 43-yard field goal and Dan Marino's 35-yard touchdown pass to Mark Duper. Cleveland tied the game on Matt Bahr's 50-yard field goal and Eric Metcalf's eight-yard run for a score to cap an 80-yard drive. Marino passed for 234 yards to set a team career yardage record with 25,101 yards and become the twenty-fifth NFL quarterback to throw for 25,000 yards.

Cleveland	0	3	7	0	0	—	10
Miami	3	7	0	0	3	—	13

Mia — FG Stoyanovich 43
Mia — Duper 35 pass from Marino (Stoyanovich kick)
Clev — FG Bahr 50
Clev — Metcalf 8 run (Bahr kick)
Mia — FG Stoyanovich 35

Green Bay 31, Dallas 13—at Lambeau Field, attendance 56,656. Don Majkowski threw four touchdown passes, including two to Herman Fontenot, as the Packers defeated the winless Cowboys. Majkowski, who completed 21 of 32 passes for 313 yards, threw touchdowns to Fontenot (seven yards) and Sterling Sharpe (79) in the first half. Majkowski found Fontenot for a 38-yard touchdown pass and Perry Kemp for a four-yard score in the second half. Sharpe finished the day with six catches for 132 yards.

Dallas	6	7	0	0	—	13
Green Bay	10	7	7	7	—	31

Dall — Irvin 5 pass from Walsh (kick blocked)
GB — FG Jacke 26
GB — Fontenot 7 pass from Majkowski (Jacke kick)
Dall — Lockhart 40 fumble recovery return (Ruzek kick)
GB — Sharpe 79 pass from Majkowski (Jacke kick)
GB — Fontenot 38 pass from Majkowski (Jacke kick)
GB — Kemp 4 pass from Majkowski (Jacke kick)

Minnesota 24, Detroit 17—at Metrodome, attendance 55,380. Mike Merriweather and Issiac Holt each returned interceptions for touchdowns as the Vikings held on to defeat the Lions. Minnesota scored all 24 of its points in the second quarter on Rich Karlis's 22-yard field goal, interception returns by Merriweather (15 yards) and Holt (90), and Brent Novoselsky's two-yard scoring reception from Tommy Kramer. Defensive tackle Keith Millard had three sacks and returned an interception 48 yards to earn NFC Defensive Player of the Week honors.

Detroit	7	3	0	7	—	17
Minnesota	0	24	0	0	—	24

Det — Hipple 1 run (Murray kick)
Minn — FG Karlis 22
Minn — Merriweather 15 interception return (Karlis kick)
Minn — Holt 90 interception return (Karlis kick)
Minn — Novoselsky 2 pass from Kramer (Karlis kick)
Det — FG Murray 50
Det — Gagliano 1 run (Murray kick)

New England 23, Houston 13—at Sullivan Stadium, attendance 59,828. John Stephens ran for a score and Greg Davis kicked three field goals as the Patriots beat the Oilers to end a three-game losing streak. New England took a 10-3 halftime lead on Davis's 30-yard field goal and Marvin Allen's one-yard run for a score. Davis added 34- and 43-yard field goals and Stephens scored on an 11-yard run in the second half to finish the Patriots' scoring.

Houston	0	3	0	10	—	13
New England	10	0	10	3	—	23

NE — FG Davis 30
NE — Allen 1 run (Davis kick)
Hou — FG Zendejas 46
NE — FG Davis 34
NE — Stephens 11 run (Davis kick)
Hou — FG Zendejas 22
NE — FG Davis 43
Hou — Hill 20 pass from Moon (Zendejas kick)

Kansas City 20, Seattle 16—at Kingdome, attendance 60,715. Christian Okoye carried 30 times for 156 yards and a touchdown as the Chiefs rallied to defeat the Seahawks. Seattle led 16-3 at halftime, but Okoye's 13-yard touchdown run narrowed the score to 16-10 in the third quarter. Kansas City took the lead for good in the fourth quarter on Nick Lowery's 25-yard field goal and Ron Jaworski's two-yard scoring pass to Alfredo Roberts. Okoye was named AFC Offensive Player of the Week.

Kansas City	3	0	7	10	—	20
Seattle	7	9	0	0	—	16

Sea — Jefferson 97 kickoff return (N. Johnson kick)
KC — FG Lowery 39
Sea — FG N. Johnson 37
Sea — FG N. Johnson 26
Sea — FG N. Johnson 37
KC — Okoye 13 run (Lowery kick)
KC — FG Lowery 25
KC — Roberts 2 pass from Jaworski (Lowery kick)

San Francisco 24, New Orleans 20—at Louisiana Superdome, attendance 60,488. Joe Montana threw three touchdown passes in the second half to rally the 49ers past the Saints. New Orleans jumped out to a 17-3 lead, but Jerry Rice, who had seven receptions for 149 yards, scored on a 60-yard reception from Joe Montana to trim the margin to 17-10 entering the fourth quarter. Montana then hit John Taylor with a 21-yard touchdown pass to tie the game 17-17. Morten Andersen's 39-yard field goal moved the Saints ahead 20-17, but Montana's second touchdown pass to Taylor (32 yards) won the game for the 49ers.

San Francisco	0	3	7	14	—	24
New Orleans	0	10	7	3	—	20

SF — FG Cofer 41
NO — Brenner 2 pass from Hebert (Andersen kick)
NO — FG Andersen 49
NO — Hilliard 19 pass from Hebert (Andersen kick)
SF — Rice 60 pass from Montana (Cofer kick)
SF — Taylor 21 pass from Montana (Cofer kick)
NO — FG Andersen 39
SF — Taylor 32 pass from Montana (Cofer kick)

Philadelphia 21, New York Giants 19—at Veterans Stadium, attendance 65,688. Randall Cunningham ran for two touchdowns and led an 81-yard drive for another as the Eagles knocked the Giants from the undefeated ranks. New York held a 19-14 lead in the fourth quarter on four Raul Allegre field goals (25, 41, 45, and 24 yards) and Jeff Hostetler's 22-yard touchdown pass to Carl Banks on a fake field goal. Cunningham, who scored on runs of five and one yards, hit three different receivers in the 81-yard game-winning march to set up Anthony Toney's two-yard touchdown run for the go-ahead score with 1:18 remaining.

N.Y. Giants	3	10	0	6	—	19
Philadelphia	0	7	0	14	—	21

NYG — FG Allegre 25
NYG — Banks 22 pass from Hostetler (Allegre kick)
Phil — Cunningham 5 run (Zendejas kick)
NYG — FG Allegre 41
NYG — FG Allegre 45
Phil — Cunningham 1 run (Zendejas kick)
NYG — FG Allegre 24
Phil — Toney 2 run (Zendejas kick)

Washington 30, Phoenix 28—at Robert F. Kennedy Stadium, attendance 55,692. Mark Rypien threw two scoring passes in the fourth quarter to lead the Redskins' comeback victory over the Cardinals. Washington built a 13-0 lead on a pair of Chip Lohmiller field goals (22 and 32 yards) and Earnest Byner's two-yard scoring pass from Rypien, but Phoenix scored two touchdowns for a 14-13 halftime lead. After Phoenix went ahead 21-13 in the fourth quarter, Washington rallied for 17 straight points on Lohmiller's 37-yard field goal and Rypien's touchdown passes to Art Monk (12 yards) and Gary Clark (23). The Cardinals narrowed the score to 30-28 on Gary Hogeboom's 17-yard scoring throw to J.T. Smith (his third receiving touchdown of the game) with 14 seconds left.

Phoenix	0	14	7	7	—	28
Washington	10	3	0	17	—	30

Wash — FG Lohmiller 22
Wash — Byner 2 pass from Rypien (Lohmiller kick)
Wash — FG Lohmiller 32
Phx — Smith 7 pass from Hogeboom (Del Greco kick)
Phx — Smith 20 pass from Hogeboom (Del Greco kick)
Phx — Ferrell 44 run (Del Greco kick)
Wash — FG Lohmiller 37
Wash — Monk 12 pass from Rypien (Lohmiller kick)
Wash — Clark 23 pass from Rypien (Lohmiller kick)
Phx — Smith 17 pass from Hogeboom (Del Greco kick)

Denver 16, San Diego 10—at Mile High Stadium, attendance 75,222. Rookie Bobby Humphrey ran for 102 yards and a touchdown in his first NFL start to help the Broncos defeat the Chargers. Denver took a 6-3 halftime lead on two David Treadwell field goals (18 and 46 yards). Marion Butts's two-yard scoring run in the third quarter put San Diego ahead 10-6. The Broncos narrowed the score to 10-9 on Treadwell's 27-yard field goal before Humphrey scored the game-winning touchdown on a 17-yard run.

San Diego	3	0	7	0	—	10
Denver	0	6	0	10	—	16

SD — FG Bahr 39
Den — FG Treadwell 46
Den — FG Treadwell 18
SD — Butts 2 run (Bahr kick)
Den — FG Treadwell 27
Den — Humphrey 17 run (Treadwell kick)

Monday, October 9

Los Angeles Raiders 14, New York Jets 7—at Giants Stadium, attendance 68,040. Eddie Anderson returned an interception 87 yards for a score as the Raiders defeated the Jets 14-7 to give Art Shell a victory in his head coaching debut. After a scoreless first half, Jay Schroeder threw a 73-yard scoring bomb to Mervyn Fernandez to put Los Angeles ahead 7-0. Roger Vick ran one yard for a touchdown late in the third quarter to tie the game 7-7. Shell was named to succeed Mike Shanahan on October 3.

L.A. Raiders	0	0	7	7	—	14
N.Y. Jets	0	0	7	0	—	7

Raiders — Fernandez 73 pass from Schroeder (Jaeger kick)
NYJ — Vick 1 run (Leahy kick)
Raiders — Anderson 87 interception return (Jaeger kick)

Sixth Week Summaries

Standings

American Football Conference

Eastern Division

	W	L	T	Pct.	Pts.	OP
Buffalo	4	2	0	.667	156	160
Indianapolis	3	3	0	.500	111	108
Miami	3	3	0	.500	121	139
New England	2	4	0	.333	88	132
N.Y. Jets	1	5	0	.167	119	158

Central Division

	W	L	T	Pct.	Pts.	OP
Cincinnati	4	2	0	.667	136	94
Cleveland	3	3	0	.500	136	88
Houston	3	3	0	.500	167	170
Pittsburgh	3	3	0	.500	93	142

Western Division

	W	L	T	Pct.	Pts.	OP
Denver	5	1	0	.833	136	84
L.A. Raiders	3	3	0	.500	134	114
Seattle	3	3	0	.500	112	124
Kansas City	2	4	0	.333	101	131
San Diego	2	4	0	.333	112	126

National Football Conference

Eastern Division

	W	L	T	Pct.	Pts.	OP
N.Y. Giants	5	1	0	.833	155	96
Philadelphia	4	2	0	.667	152	133
Washington	3	3	0	.500	154	138
Phoenix	2	4	0	.333	103	143
Dallas	0	6	0	.000	68	177

Central Division

	W	L	T	Pct.	Pts.	OP
Chicago	4	2	0	.667	192	136
Minnesota	4	2	0	.667	126	106
Green Bay	3	3	0	.500	162	158
Tampa Bay	3	3	0	.500	120	120
Detroit	1	5	0	.167	91	150

Western Division

	W	L	T	Pct.	Pts.	OP
L.A. Rams	5	1	0	.833	162	125
San Francisco	5	1	0	.833	155	115
Atlanta	2	4	0	.333	108	129
New Orleans	2	4	0	.333	135	109

Sunday, October 15

Detroit 17, Tampa Bay 16—at Tampa Stadium, attendance 46,225. Rookie Rodney Peete ran five yards for the game-winning score with 23 seconds remaining as the Lions captured their first victory of the season. Trailing 10-3 in the third quarter, Peete threw a 33-yard touchdown pass to Robert Clark to tie the game. Tampa Bay got the lead back behind Donald Igwebuike's two field goals (33 and 34 yards). Peete led the Lions on a 76-yard, eight-play drive to set up his winning touchdown run. He was named NFC Offensive Player of the Week for his performance.

Detroit	3	0	7	7	—	17
Tampa Bay	0	10	3	3	—	16

Det — FG Murray 28
TB — Reynolds 68 interception return (Igwebuike kick)
TB — FG Igwebuike 27
Det — Clark 33 pass from Peete (Murray kick)
TB — FG Igwebuike 34
TB — FG Igwebuike 33
Det — Peete 5 run (Murray kick)

Minnesota 26, Green Bay 14—at Metrodome, attendance 62,075. Herschel Walker, making his Vikings debut, ran for 148 yards on 18 carries to help Minnesota down the Packers. Rick Fenney had an outstanding game as well, running for an eight-yard touchdown and scoring on an eight-yard reception from Tommy Kramer. Kramer also connected with Jim Gustafson on a six-yard touchdown pass. Keith Millard recorded four of the Vikings' eight sacks.

Green Bay	7	0	0	7	—	14
Minnesota	0	17	9	0	—	26

GB —Fontenot 1 run (Jacke kick)
Minn —FG Karlis 28
Minn —Fenney 8 run (Karlis kick)
Minn —Gustafson 6 pass from Kramer (Karlis kick)
Minn —Fenney 8 pass from Kramer (Karlis kick)
Minn —Safety, Berry tackled Majkowski in end zone
GB —Bland 46 pass from Majkowski (Jacke kick)

Houston 33, Chicago 28—at Soldier Field, attendance 64,383. Lorenzo White ran 12 yards for a score with 1:46 remaining to rally the Oilers past the Bears. Warren Moon, who threw touchdown passes to Drew Hill (42 yards) and Haywood Jeffires (45), scored on a one-yard keeper to narrow Chicago's lead to 28-26 late in the fourth quarter. Moon, who completed 16 of 26 passes for 317 yards, was named AFC Offensive Player of the Week.

Houston	0	10	9	14	—	33
Chicago	0	14	7	7	—	28

Chi —Anderson 6 pass from Tomczak (Butler kick)
Hou —FG Zendejas 27
Hou —Hill 42 pass from Moon (Zendejas kick)
Chi —Anderson 1 run (Butler kick)
Hou —FG Zendejas 19
Chi —Gentry 79 pass from Tomczak (Butler kick)
Hou —Jeffires 45 pass from Moon (kick failed)
Chi —Thornton 7 pass from Tomczak (Butler kick)
Hou —Moon 1 run (Zendejas kick)
Hou —White 12 run (Zendejas kick)

Denver 14, Indianapolis 3—at Mile High Stadium, attendance 74,600. Sammy Winder and Bobby Humphrey each ran for touchdowns to lead the Broncos past the Colts. Humphrey gave Denver a 7-3 halftime lead when he scored on a two-yard run early in the second quarter. Winder completed the Broncos' scoring with a one-yard touchdown run late in the fourth quarter. Denver's defense held Colts running back Eric Dickerson to 35 yards on 13 carries and limited the Colts to 128 yards total offense.

Indianapolis	3	0	0	0	—	3
Denver	0	7	0	7	—	14

Ind —FG Biasucci 55
Den —Humphrey 2 run (Treadwell kick)
Den —Winder 1 run (Treadwell kick)

Los Angeles Raiders 20, Kansas City 14—at Memorial Coliseum, attendance 40,453. Bo Jackson, playing in his first game of the season, ran for 85 yards and a touchdown as the Raiders downed the Chiefs. Jackson scored on a two-yard run and Jeff Jaeger kicked a 24-yard field goal to put Los Angeles ahead 10-7 at halftime. Jaeger then added a career-long 50-yard field goal in the third quarter and Vance Mueller ran six yards for a touchdown to complete the Raiders' scoring.

Kansas City	7	0	0	7	—	14
L.A. Raiders	3	7	3	7	—	20

KC —Okoye 2 run (Lowery kick)
Raiders —FG Jaeger 24
Raiders —Jackson 2 run (Jaeger kick)
Raiders —FG Jaeger 50
Raiders —Mueller 6 run (Jaeger kick)
KC —R. Thomas 11 pass from DeBerg (Lowery kick)

Miami 20, Cincinnati 13—at Riverfront Stadium, attendance 58,184. Dan Marino and Ron Davenport each ran for touchdowns to help the Dolphins defeat the Bengals. Trailing 13-3 in the third quarter, Marino ran for a one-yard touchdown. It was Marino's first rushing score since December 7, 1987, when he scored on a one-yard bootleg. Pete Stoyanovich kicked a 33-yard field goal to tie the game at 13-13, before Davenport ran five yards for the decisive touchdown late in the fourth quarter. The loss ended the Bengals' 12-game winning streak at Riverfront Stadium.

Miami	0	3	7	10	—	20
Cincinnati	10	3	0	0	—	13

Cin —FG Breech 20
Cin —Holman 38 pass from Esiason (Breech kick)
Mia —FG Stoyanovich 29
Cin —FG Breech 22
Mia —Marino 1 run (Stoyanovich kick)
Mia —FG Stoyanovich 33
Mia —Davenport 5 run (Stoyanovich kick)

Atlanta 16, New England 15—at Atlanta-Fulton County Stadium, attendance 39,697. Paul McFadden kicked a 22-yard field goal with five seconds remaining as the Falcons edged the Patriots. The victory helped Atlanta snap a three-game losing streak. The Falcons cut the Patriots' lead to 15-13 at halftime on McFadden's pair of 30-yard field goals and Keith Jones's one-yard run for a score. Quarterback Chris Miller led Atlanta on a 67-yard, 11-play drive to set up McFadden's winning kick.

New England	6	9	0	0	—	15
Atlanta	3	10	0	3	—	16

NE —FG Davis 52
Atl —FG McFadden 30
NE —FG Davis 32
NE —FG Davis 32
Atl —FG McFadden 30
NE —Jones 15 pass from Flutie (kick failed)
Atl —Jones 1 run (McFadden kick)
Atl —FG McFadden 22

New Orleans 29, New York Jets 14—at Louisiana Superdome, attendance 59,521. Bobby Hebert threw for three touchdowns to help the Saints defeat the Jets. New Orleans took a 13-7 halftime lead on Morten Andersen's two field goals (42 and 29 yards) and Hebert's three-yard scoring pass to Lonzell Hill. James Geathers's fumble recovery in the third quarter set up Hebert's second touchdown pass of the day, a four-yarder to Eric Martin. Hebert combined with Martin again on a 53-yard scoring pass early in the fourth quarter to put the game away.

N.Y. Jets	0	7	0	7	—	14
New Orleans	6	7	7	9	—	29

NO —FG Andersen 42
NO —FG Andersen 29
NYJ —Hasty 34 interception return (Leahy kick)
NO —Hill 3 pass from Hebert (Andersen kick)
NO —Martin 4 pass from Hebert (Andersen kick)
NO —Safety, Schreiber holding penalty in end zone
NO —Martin 53 pass from Hebert (Andersen kick)
NYJ —McMillan 74 fumble recovery return (Leahy kick)

Philadelphia 17, Phoenix 5—at Sun Devil Stadium, attendance 42,620. Randall Cunningham and Cris Carter combined for two touchdown passes as the Eagles defeated the Cardinals. Cunningham connected with Carter on a two-yard scoring pass and then led a 75-yard, third-quarter drive capped by his 40-yard scoring throw to Carter. The Eagles increased their lead on Luis Zendejas's 42-yard field goal in the fourth quarter.

Philadelphia	0	0	14	3	—	17
Phoenix	0	5	0	0	—	5

Phx —Safety, Wilson tackled Toney in end zone
Phx —FG Del Greco 41
Phil —Carter 2 pass from Cunningham (Zendejas kick)
Phil —Carter 40 pass from Cunningham (Zendejas kick)
Phil —FG Zendejas 42

Pittsburgh 17, Cleveland 7—at Cleveland Stadium, attendance 78,840. Warren Williams's one-yard touchdown run in the fourth quarter helped the Steelers upend the Browns. Pittsburgh broke a seven-game losing streak to Cleveland, which included a 51-0 loss to the Browns on September 10, as their defense accounted for four interceptions and seven turnovers. Todd Blackledge threw a 14-yard touchdown pass to Rodney Carter in the third quarter for the Steelers. Dwight Stone's 73-yard kickoff return set up Williams's scoring run.

Pittsburgh	3	0	7	7	—	17
Cleveland	0	0	0	7	—	7

Pitt —FG Anderson 49
Pitt —Carter 14 pass from Blackledge (Anderson kick)
Clev —Metcalf 2 run (Bahr kick)
Pitt —Williams 1 run (Anderson kick)

San Francisco 31, Dallas 14—at Texas Stadium, attendance 61,077. Steve Young, replacing injured starting quarterback Joe Montana, threw two touchdown passes, and Roger Craig ran for another as the 49ers downed the winless Cowboys to earn their fifth road victory of the season. With the score deadlocked at 14-14 in the fourth quarter, Young completed an eight-yard touchdown pass to Jerry Rice. Mike Cofer added a 31-yard field goal and Craig ran one yard for a touchdown to complete the scoring.

San Francisco	0	7	7	17	—	31
Dallas	0	7	7	0	—	14

SF —Jones 36 pass from Young (Cofer kick)
Dall —Martin 32 pass from Walsh (Ruzek kick)
SF —Jackson 75 blocked field goal return (Cofer kick)
Dall —Clack 1 run (Ruzek kick)
SF —Rice 8 pass from Young (Cofer kick)
SF —FG Cofer 31
SF —Craig 1 run (Cofer kick)

Seattle 17, San Diego 16—at San Diego Jack Murphy Stadium, attendance 50,079. The Seahawks blocked an extra-point attempt late in the fourth quarter to edge the Chargers. Seattle took a 17-10 third-quarter lead on John L. Williams's six-yard scoring reception. San Diego drove 82 yards on 10 plays late in the fourth quarter to set up Marion Butts's two-yard touchdown run. The Chargers' attempt to tie the game was thwarted when Chris Bahr's extra-point try was blocked by Jeff Bryant.

Seattle	10	0	7	0	—	17
San Diego	7	3	0	6	—	16

SD —Cox 3 pass from McMahon (Bahr kick)
Sea —Warner 1 run (N. Johnson kick)
Sea —FG N. Johnson 50
SD —FG Bahr 29
Sea —Williams 6 pass from Krieg (N. Johnson kick)
SD —Butts 2 run (kick blocked)

New York Giants 20, Washington 17—at Giants Stadium, attendance 76,245. Phil Simms threw two fourth-quarter touchdown passes to lead the Giants over the Redskins. Trailing 10-6 entering in the fourth quarter, Simms threw a 12-yard scoring pass to Mark Bavaro and then hit Odessa Turner with a 25-yard scoring pass to give the Giants a 20-10 lead. Mark Rypien threw a five-yard touchdown pass to Art Monk to narrow the score late in the fourth quarter to 20-17, but the Giants held on for the victory.

Washington	0	3	7	7	—	17
N.Y. Giants	3	0	3	14	—	20

NYG —FG Allegre 33
Wash —FG Lohmiller 37
NYG —FG Allegre 49
Wash —Sanders 29 pass from Rypien (Lohmiller kick)
NYG —Bavaro 12 pass from Simms (Allegre kick)
NYG —Turner 25 pass from Simms (Allegre kick)
Wash —Monk 5 pass from Rypien (Lohmiller kick)

Monday, October 16

Buffalo 23, Los Angeles Rams 20—at Rich Stadium, attendance 76,231. Frank Reich hit Andre Reed with an eight-yard touchdown pass with 16 seconds remaining as the Bills knocked the Rams from the undefeated ranks. Scott Norwood kicked field goals from 38, 37, and 40 yards, but Buffalo still trailed the Rams 13-9 in the fourth quarter. Reich, making his first NFL start for the injured Jim Kelly, threw a one-yard scoring pass to Thurman Thomas for a 16-13 Buffalo edge, but Jim Everett responded with a 78-yard touchdown bomb to Flipper Anderson to give the Rams a 20-16 lead with 1:22 remaining. Reich's scoring pass to Reed capped a 64-yard drive.

L.A. Rams	7	0	3	10	—	20
Buffalo	0	6	0	17	—	23

Rams —McGee 3 pass from Everett (Lansford kick)
Buff —FG Norwood 38
Buff —FG Norwood 47
Rams —FG Lansford 34
Buff —FG Norwood 40
Rams —FG Lansford 36
Buff —Thomas 1 pass from Reich (Norwood kick)
Rams —Anderson 78 pass from Everett (Lansford kick)
Buff —Reed 8 pass from Reich (Norwood kick)

Seventh Week Summaries

Standings

American Football Conference

Eastern Division

	W	L	T	Pct.	Pts.	OP
Buffalo	5	2	0	.714	190	163
Indianapolis	4	3	0	.571	134	120
Miami	4	3	0	.571	144	159
New England	2	5	0	.286	108	169
N.Y. Jets	1	6	0	.143	122	192

Central Division

	W	L	T	Pct.	Pts.	OP
Cincinnati	4	3	0	.571	148	117
Cleveland	4	3	0	.571	163	95
Houston	4	3	0	.571	194	170
Pittsburgh	3	4	0	.429	93	169

Western Division

	W	L	T	Pct.	Pts.	OP
Denver	6	1	0	.857	160	105
Kansas City	3	4	0	.429	137	159
L.A. Raiders	3	4	0	.429	141	124
Seattle	3	4	0	.429	133	148
San Diego	2	5	0	.286	125	146

National Football Conference

Eastern Division

	W	L	T	Pct.	Pts.	OP
N.Y. Giants	6	1	0	.857	175	109
Philadelphia	5	2	0	.714	162	140
Washington	4	3	0	.571	186	166
Phoenix	3	4	0	.429	137	163
Dallas	0	7	0	.000	96	213

Central Division

	W	L	T	Pct.	Pts.	OP
Minnesota	5	2	0	.714	146	113
Chicago	4	3	0	.571	199	163
Green Bay	3	4	0	.429	182	181
Tampa Bay	3	4	0	.429	148	152
Detroit	1	6	0	.143	98	170

Western Division

	W	L	T	Pct.	Pts.	OP
San Francisco	6	1	0	.857	192	135
L.A. Rams	5	2	0	.714	183	165
New Orleans	3	4	0	.429	175	130
Atlanta	2	5	0	.286	128	163

Sunday, October 22

Phoenix 34, Atlanta 20—at Sun Devil Stadium, attendance 33,894. Earl Ferrell ran for three touchdowns to power the Cardinals over the Falcons. Ferrell had two scoring runs in the first quarter from one and six yards, and Ron Wolfley added a five-yard run to put Phoenix ahead 21-6 at halftime. The Cardinals increased their lead in the second half on a pair of Al Del Greco field goals from 50 and 22 yards and Ferrell's third touchdown run of the day, a three-yarder.

Atlanta	0	6	7	7	— 20
Phoenix	14	7	3	10	— 34

Phx —Ferrell 1 run (Del Greco kick)
Phx —Ferrell 6 run (Del Greco kick)
Atl —FG McFadden 37
Phx —Wolfley 5 run (Del Greco kick)
Atl —FG McFadden 37
Phx —FG Del Greco 50
Atl —K. Jones 14 run (McFadden kick)
Phx —Ferrell 3 run (Del Greco kick)
Atl —Settle 16 pass from Miller (McFadden kick)
Phx —FG Del Greco 22

Kansas City 36, Dallas 28—at Arrowhead Stadium, attendance 76,841. Christian Okoye ran for 170 yards and two touchdowns to help the Chiefs past the Cowboys. Kansas City jumped to a 27-14 first-half lead on Okoye scoring runs of two and 13 yards, James Saxon's four-yard touchdown run, and a pair of Nick Lowery field goals (43 and 27 yards). Rob McGovern blocked a punt out of the end zone for a safety and Steve Pelluer scored on a five-yard keeper in the third quarter to complete the Chiefs' scoring.

Dallas	7	7	0	14	— 28
Kansas City	14	13	9	0	— 36

KC —Okoye 2 run (Lowery kick)
Dall —Palmer 63 run (Ruzek kick)
KC —Okoye 13 run (Lowery kick)
KC —Saxon 4 run (Lowery kick)
Dall —Dixon 97 kickoff return (Ruzek kick)
KC —FG Lowery 43
KC —FG Lowery 27
KC —Safety, McGovern blocked punt out of end zone
KC —Pelluer 5 run (Lowery kick)
Dall —Clack 1 run (Ruzek kick)
Dall —Folsom 4 pass from Walsh (Ruzek kick)

Denver 24, Seattle 21—at Kingdome, attendance 62,353. David Treadwell's 27-yard field goal 7:46 into overtime gave the Broncos a 24-21 come-from-behind win over the Seahawks. Trailing 14-0 in the third quarter, Denver tied the game on Bobby Humphrey's one-yard touchdown run and John Elway's two-yard scoring pass to Clarence Kay. Dave Krieg connected with Paul Skansi on a 24-yard touchdown pass to give Seattle the lead 21-14, but Elway hit Vance Johnson for a 54-yard scoring pass with 2:19 remaining to send the game into overtime.

Denver	0	0	7	14	3	— 24
Seattle	7	7	0	7	0	— 21

Sea —Williams 4 run (N. Johnson kick)
Sea —Williams 6 pass from Krieg (N. Johnson kick)
Den —Humphrey 1 run (Treadwell kick)
Den —Kay 2 pass from Elway (Treadwell kick)
Sea —Skansi 24 pass from Krieg (N. Johnson kick)
Den —V. Johnson 54 pass from Elway (Treadwell kick)
Den —FG Treadwell 27

Miami 23, Green Bay 20—at Joe Robbie Stadium, attendance 56,624. Pete Stoyanovich's 33-yard field goal with six seconds remaining lifted the Dolphins over the Packers. Miami led 20-6 in the third quarter on Dan Marino touchdown passes to Jim Jensen (seven yards) and Mark Clayton (24), and Stoyanovich's 36- and 21-yard field goals. Don Majkowski combined with Sterling Sharpe on a pair of scoring passes in the fourth quarter (22 and 10 yards) to tie the game with 53 seconds left. Marino then marched the Dolphins 58 yards to set up Stoyanovich's winning field goal.

Green Bay	3	3	0	14	— 20
Miami	7	3	7	6	— 23

Mia —Jensen 7 pass from Marino (Stoyanovich kick)
GB —FG Jacke 44
GB —FG Jacke 21
Mia —FG Stoyanovich 36
Mia —Clayton 24 pass from Marino (Stoyanovich kick)
Mia —FG Stoyanovich 21
GB —Sharpe 22 pass from Majkowski (Jacke kick)
GB —Sharpe 10 pass from Majkowski (Jacke kick)
Mia —FG Stoyanovich 33

Indianapolis 23, Cincinnati 12—at Riverfront Stadium, attendance 57,642. The Colts turned two turnovers into 14 points en route to a 23-12 victory over the Bengals. Trailing 12-9, Indianapolis's Duane Bickett recovered a fumble with 2:07 left in the game to set up Jack Trudeau's three-yard scoring pass to Albert Bentley. Keith Taylor's interception with 1:22 remaining set up Eric Dickerson's game-clinching 21-yard touchdown run. Dickerson finished the day with 31 carries for 152 yards.

Indianapolis	0	3	6	14	— 23
Cincinnati	6	3	0	3	— 12

Cin —FG Breech 30
Cin —FG Breech 29
Cin —FG Breech 23
Ind —FG Biasucci 27
Ind —B. Brooks 2 pass from Trudeau (kick failed)
Cin —FG Breech 21
Ind —Bentley 3 pass from Trudeau (Biasucci kick)
Ind —Dickerson 21 run (Biasucci kick)

Philadelphia 10, Los Angeles Raiders 7—at Veterans Stadium, attendance 64,019. The Eagles' defense had four sacks and two interceptions which set up 10 points as Philadelphia held on to defeat the Raiders. After a scoreless first half, Izel Jenkins's interception late in the third quarter led to Randall Cunningham's one-yard scramble for a score. Byron Evans's interception set up Luis Zendejas's 34-yard field goal which proved to be decisive. Steve Beuerlein's 24-yard touchdown pass to Willie Gault in the fourth quarter prevented the shutout.

L.A. Raiders	0	0	0	7	— 7
Philadelphia	0	0	10	0	— 10

Phil —Cunningham 1 run (Zendejas kick)
Phil —FG Zendejas 34
Raiders —Gault 24 pass from Beuerlein (Jaeger kick)

Minnesota 20, Detroit 7—at Pontiac Silverdome, attendance 51,579. The Vikings' defense accounted for eight sacks, two interceptions, and three fumble recoveries to lead Minnesota past Detroit. The Vikings took a 13-0 halftime lead on Rich Karlis's pair of 40-yard field goals and Herschel Walker's one-yard run for a touchdown. Joey Browner's third-quarter interception set up Alfred Anderson's four-yard scoring run to finish the Vikings' scoring.

Minnesota	3	10	7	0	— 20
Detroit	0	0	0	7	— 7

Minn —FG Karlis 40
Minn —FG Karlis 40
Minn —Walker 1 run (Karlis kick)
Minn —Anderson 4 run (Karlis kick)
Det —Peete 2 run (Murray kick)

San Francisco 37, New England 20—at Stanford Stadium, attendance 70,000. Steve Young, who came off the bench to replace Joe Montana, threw three touchdown passes as the 49ers defeated the Patriots. Young connected with Wesley Walls on a one-yard scoring toss to help put San Francisco ahead 17-10 at halftime. Young then hit Jerry Rice (50 yards) and John Taylor (43) in the second half for scores. Roger Craig added a three-yard touchdown run late in the fourth quarter to complete the 49ers' scoring. The game, originally scheduled for Candlestick Park, was moved to Stanford Stadium in Palo Alto following the Bay Area earthquake on October 17.

New England	0	10	7	3	— 20
San Francisco	0	17	7	13	— 37

NE —Morgan 55 pass from Grogan (Davis kick)
SF —Rice 3 pass from Montana (Cofer kick)
SF —FG Cofer 23
NE —FG Davis 49
SF —Walls 1 pass from Young (Cofer kick)
NE —Morgan 19 pass from Grogan (Davis kick)
SF —Rice 50 pass from Young (Cofer kick)
NE —FG Davis 21
SF —Taylor 43 pass from Young (Cofer kick)
SF —Craig 3 run (kick failed)

New Orleans 40, Los Angeles Rams 21—at Anaheim Stadium, attendance 57,567. Bobby Hebert completed three touchdown passes as the Saints handed the Rams their second straight loss. New Orleans took a 19-7 halftime lead on Dalton Hilliard's 20-yard reception and two-yard run, and Morten Andersen's 39- and 27-yard field goals. Hebert then hit Floyd Turner (54 yards) and Eric Martin (37) for touchdown passes in the third quarter. Hilliard, who also scored on a seven-yard run in the fourth quarter to finish the Saints' scoring, was named NFC Offensive Player of the Week.

New Orleans	10	9	14	7	— 40
L.A. Rams	7	0	7	7	— 21

NO —Hilliard 20 pass from Hebert (Andersen kick)
NO —FG Andersen 39
Rams —Ellard 3 pass from Everett (Lansford kick)
NO —Hilliard 2 run (kick failed)
NO —FG Andersen 27
NO —Turner 54 pass from Hebert (Andersen kick)
NO —E. Martin 37 pass from Hebert (Andersen kick)
Rams —Johnson 1 pass from Everett (Lansford kick)
NO —Hilliard 7 run (Andersen kick)
Rams —Johnson 3 pass from Everett (Lansford kick)

New York Giants 20, San Diego 13—at San Diego Jack Murphy Stadium, attendance 48,566. Ottis Anderson scored on a pair of four-yard touchdown runs in the second half as the Giants defeated the Chargers. Anderson, who carried 27 times for 96 yards, ran for his first score midway through the third quarter to put New York ahead 13-3. He added his second touchdown run in the fourth quarter to increase the score to 20-6. San Diego's Vencie Glenn returned a fumble 81 yards for a touchdown, the longest in Chargers history.

N.Y. Giants	3	3	7	7	— 20
San Diego	0	3	3	7	— 13

NYG —FG Allegre 21
SD —FG Bahr 26
NYG —FG Allegre 40
NYG —Anderson 4 run (Allegre kick)
SD —FG Bahr 30
NYG —Anderson 4 run (Allegre kick)
SD —Glenn 81 fumble recovery return (Bahr kick)

Buffalo 34, New York Jets 3—at Rich Stadium, attendance 76,811. Frank Reich threw three touchdown passes as the Bills easily defeated the Jets. Reich hit Andre Reed for a 20-yard touchdown pass in the third quarter and added scoring passes to Ronnie Harmon (12 yards) and Kenneth Davis (seven) in the fourth quarter. Scott Norwood also kicked field goals of 38 and 27 yards for the Bills. Buffalo's defense recorded five sacks and forced three turnovers.

N.Y. Jets	0	0	3	0	— 3
Buffalo	3	10	7	14	— 34

Buff —FG Norwood 38
Buff —Thomas 3 run (Norwood kick)
Buff —FG Norwood 27
Buff —Reed 20 pass from Reich (Norwood kick)
NYJ —FG Leahy 41
Buff —Harmon 12 pass from Reich (Norwood kick)
Buff —K. Davis 7 pass from Reich (Norwood kick)

Houston 27, Pittsburgh 0—at Astrodome, attendance 59,091. Warren Moon completed 17 of 29 passes for 229 yards and three touchdowns to lead the Oilers past the Steelers. Moon threw first-half touchdowns to Alonzo Highsmith (three and five yards) and Curtis Duncan (51). Tony Zendejas's 51-yard field goal completed the Oilers' scoring. The victory was Houston's first shutout since December 20, 1980, when the team defeated the Steelers 6-0.

Pittsburgh	0	0	0	0	— 0
Houston	7	17	3	0	— 27

Hou —Highsmith 3 pass from Moon (Zendejas kick)
Hou —FG Zendejas 41
Hou —Duncan 51 pass from Moon (Zendejas kick)
Hou —Highsmith 5 pass from Moon (Zendejas kick)
Hou —FG Zendejas 51

Washington 32, Tampa Bay 28—at Robert F. Kennedy Stadium, attendance 52,862. Mark Rypien combined with Gary Clark for two touchdown passes as the Redskins outdistanced the Buccaneers. Washington took a 29-7 third-quarter lead on Rypien scoring passes of 10 and seven yards to Clark, Gerald Riggs's six-yard run, Dexter Manley's safety, and Chip Lohmiller's field goals of 33 and 42 yards. Vinny Testaverde then threw touchdown passes to Lars Tate (10 yards) and Bruce Hill (20) to narrow the score to 29-21. After Lohmiller kicked a 29-yard field goal to give Washington a 32-21 lead, Testaverde hit Mark Carrier for a four-yard score.

Tampa Bay	7	0	0	21	— 28
Washington	0	12	17	3	— 32

TB —Reynolds 33 blocked punt return (Igwebuike kick)
Wash —FG Lohmiller 33
Wash —Safety, Manley tackled Testaverde in end zone
Wash —Clark 7 pass from Rypien (Lohmiller kick)
Wash —Clark 10 pass from Rypien (Lohmiller kick)
Wash —FG Lohmiller 42
Wash —Riggs 6 run (Lohmiller kick)
TB —Tate 10 pass from Testaverde (Igwebuike kick)
TB —Hill 20 pass from Testaverde (Igwebuike kick)
Wash —FG Lohmiller 29
TB —Carrier 4 pass from Testaverde (Igwebuike kick)

Monday, October 23

Cleveland 27, Chicago 7—at Cleveland Stadium, attendance 78,722. Rookie Eric Metcalf caught a touchdown pass and ran for a score as the Browns handed the Bears their third straight defeat. It was the first time since 1981 that Chicago had lost three consecutive games. Metcalf scored on a three-yard reception from Bernie Kosar in the first quarter and had a seven-yard scoring run in the third quarter. Matt Bahr added field goals of 31 and 35 yards for Cleveland. Webster Slaughter had six receptions for a career-high 186 yards for the Browns, including a club-record 97-yard touchdown catch from Kosar.

Chicago	0	0	0	7	— 7
Cleveland	7	0	10	10	— 27

Clev —Metcalf 3 pass from Kosar (Bahr kick)
Clev —FG Bahr 31
Clev —Metcalf 7 run (Bahr kick)
Clev —Slaughter 97 pass from Kosar (Bahr kick)
Chi —Davis 5 pass from Harbaugh (Butler kick)
Clev —FG Bahr 35

Eighth Week Summaries

Standings

American Football Conference

Eastern Division

	W	L	T	Pct.	Pts.	OP
Buffalo	6	2	0	.750	221	180
Indianapolis	4	4	0	.500	154	143
Miami	4	4	0	.500	161	190
New England	3	5	0	.375	131	189
N.Y. Jets	1	7	0	.125	132	215

Central Division

Cincinnati	5	3	0	.625	204	140
Cleveland	5	3	0	.625	191	112
Houston	4	4	0	.500	211	198
Pittsburgh	4	4	0	.500	116	186

Western Division

Denver	6	2	0	.750	184	133
L.A. Raiders	4	4	0	.500	178	148
Seattle	4	4	0	.500	143	155
Kansas City	3	5	0	.375	154	182
San Diego	2	6	0	.250	132	156

National Football Conference

Eastern Division

	W	L	T	Pct.	Pts.	OP
N.Y. Giants	7	1	0	.875	199	123
Philadelphia	6	2	0	.750	190	164
Phoenix	4	4	0	.500	156	173
Washington	4	4	0	.500	210	203
Dallas	0	8	0	.000	106	232

Central Division

Chicago	5	3	0	.625	219	173
Minnesota	5	3	0	.625	160	137
Green Bay	4	4	0	.500	205	201
Tampa Bay	3	5	0	.375	171	208
Detroit	1	7	0	.125	118	193

Western Division

San Francisco	7	1	0	.875	215	145
L.A. Rams	5	3	0	.625	193	185
New Orleans	4	4	0	.500	195	143
Atlanta	2	6	0	.250	141	183

Sunday, October 29

New Orleans 20, Atlanta 13—at Louisiana Superdome, attendance 65,153. Dalton Hilliard's one-yard touchdown run with 2:12 remaining lifted the Saints over the Falcons. New Orleans took a 10-0 halftime lead on Hilliard's 21-yard scoring reception from Bobby Hebert in the first quarter and Morten Andersen's 32-yard field goal. Andersen added a 44-yard field goal, but Paul McFadden's 41- and 48-yard field goals and Chris Miller's 18-yard touchdown pass to Shawn Collins tied the game 13-13. Pat Swilling, who registered three sacks and forced two fumbles, was named NFC Defensive Player of the Week.

Atlanta	0	0	10	3	— 13
New Orleans	7	3	3	7	— 20

NO —Hilliard 21 pass from Hebert (Andersen kick)
NO —FG Andersen 32
Atl —Collins 18 pass from Miller (McFadden kick)
NO —FG Andersen 44
Atl —FG McFadden 41
Atl —FG McFadden 48
NO —Hilliard 1 run (Andersen kick)

Green Bay 23, Detroit 20—at Milwaukee County Stadium, attendance 53,731. Chris Jacke's 38-yard field goal 2:14 into overtime gave the Packers a 23-20 victory over the Lions. Green Bay led 20-10 after three quarters on Don Majkowski's touchdown passes of four yards to Jeff Query and two yards to Sterling Sharpe, and Jacke's pair of field goals (49 and 21 yards). Detroit tied the game in the fourth quarter on Eddie Murray's 46-yard field goal and Rodney Peete's 14-yard touchdown run. Packers safety Mark Murphy's interception on the first play of overtime set up Jacke's winning field goal.

Detroit	7	3	0	10	0	— 20
Green Bay	3	7	10	0	3	— 23

GB —FG Jacke 49
Det —Johnson 6 pass from Peete (Murray kick)
Det —FG Murray 42
GB —Query 4 pass from Majkowski (Jacke kick)
GB —FG Jacke 21
GB —Sharpe 2 pass from Majkowski (Jacke kick)
Det —FG Murray 46
Det —Peete 14 run (Murray kick)
GB —FG Jacke 38

Cleveland 28, Houston 17—at Cleveland Stadium, attendance 78,765. Bernie Kosar hit Webster Slaughter on two scoring bombs as the Browns beat the Oilers. Trailing 10-0 in the third quarter, Kosar scored on a five-yard run, then hit Slaughter on an 80-yard flea-flicker touchdown pass to put Cleveland ahead 14-10. Mike Rozier ran one yard for a touchdown as Houston regained the lead 17-14. Kosar then connected with Slaughter on a 77-yard touchdown pass to give the Browns the lead for good. Running back Eric Metcalf's 32-yard touchdown pass to Reggie Langhorne in the fourth quarter put the game out of reach. Slaughter, who finished the game with four receptions for a career-high 184 yards, was named AFC Offensive Player of the Week.

Houston	7	3	7	0	— 17
Cleveland	0	0	21	7	— 28

Hou —Jeffires 13 pass from Moon (Zendejas kick)
Hou —FG Zendejas 23
Clev —Kosar 5 run (Bahr kick)
Clev —Slaughter 80 pass from Kosar (Bahr kick)
Hou —Rozier 1 run (Zendejas kick)
Clev —Slaughter 77 pass from Kosar (Bahr kick)
Clev —Langhorne 32 pass from Metcalf (Bahr kick)

Pittsburgh 23, Kansas City 17—at Three Rivers Stadium, attendance 54,194. Bubby Brister and Louis Lipps combined for two touchdown passes to lead the Steelers over the Chiefs. Pittsburgh jumped to a 16-3 halftime lead on three Gary Anderson field goals (41, 47, and 29 yards) and Brister's 16-yard first scoring pass to Lipps. Kansas City went ahead 17-16 in the third quarter on Bill Maas's four-yard fumble recovery and Pete Mandley's eight-yard scoring pass from Steve DeBerg. Pittsburgh came right back on Brister's 64-yard touchdown pass to Lipps. Lipps caught seven passes for 130 yards, while Kansas City wide receiver Stephone Paige caught seven for 163 yards.

Kansas City	0	3	14	0	— 17
Pittsburgh	10	6	7	0	— 23

Pitt —FG Anderson 41
Pitt —Lipps 16 pass from Brister (Anderson kick)
Pitt —FG Anderson 47
Pitt —FG Anderson 29
KC —FG Lowery 50
KC —Mandley 8 pass from DeBerg (Lowery kick)
KC —Maas 4 fumble recovery return (Lowery kick)
Pitt —Lipps 64 pass from Brister (Anderson kick)

Chicago 20, Los Angeles Rams 10—at Anaheim Stadium, attendance 65,506. Jim Harbaugh, who replaced Mike Tomczak at quarterback for Chicago in the second quarter, ran one yard for a touchdown to help the Bears down the Rams. After the teams exchanged field goals in the first half, Brad Muster ran one yard for a score in the third quarter to put Chicago ahead 10-3. Harbaugh then scrambled one yard for a touchdown and Kevin Butler kicked a 46-yard field goal (his one-hundredth career field goal) to complete the Bears' scoring. Los Angeles, which started the season with five consecutive wins, suffered its third straight loss.

L.A. Rams	0	3	0	7	— 10
Chicago	0	3	7	10	— 20

Rams —FG Lansford 45
Chi —FG Butler 35
Chi —Muster 1 run (Butler kick)
Chi —Harbaugh 1 run (Butler kick)
Rams —Bell 1 run (Lansford kick)
Chi —FG Butler 46

Buffalo 31, Miami 17—at Rich Stadium, attendance 80,208. Thurman Thomas and Larry Kinnebrew combined for 269 yards rushing as the Bills defeated the Dolphins to win their third straight game. Thomas, who had 148 yards on 27 carries, scored on a 30-yard run in the second quarter. Kinnebrew, who finished the day with 21 carries for 121 yards, scored on a one-yard run in the second period. Frank Reich also threw a 63-yard touchdown bomb to Don Beebe in the first half. Scott Norwood added a 45-yard field goal and Kirby Jackson returned an interception 40 yards for a score in the second half to finish Buffalo's scoring. Jeff Wright's sack of Dan Marino ended the Dolphins' NFL-record 19-game streak without allowing a sack.

Miami	3	0	7	7	— 17
Buffalo	0	21	0	10	— 31

Mia —FG Stoyanovich 45
Buff —Kinnebrew 1 run (Norwood kick)
Buff —Thomas 30 run (Norwood kick)
Buff —Beebe 63 pass from Reich (Norwood kick)
Mia —Clayton 44 pass from Marino (Stoyanovich kick)
Buff —FG Norwood 45
Buff —Jackson 40 interception return (Norwood kick)
Mia —A. Brown 44 pass from Secules (Stoyanovich kick)

New England 23, Indianapolis 20—at Hoosier Dome, attendance 59,356. Greg Davis's 51-yard field goal with 9:57 elapsed in overtime gave the Patriots a 23-20 win over the Colts. Trailing 17-13 late in the fourth quarter, John Stephens ran one yard for a touchdown to put New England ahead 20-17. Dean Biasucci's 39-yard field goal with 51 seconds remaining sent the game into overtime. Davis also hit on field goals of 47 and 48 yards.

New England	3	0	7	10	3	— 23
Indianapolis	10	0	0	10	0	— 20

NE —FG Davis 47
Ind —Rison 22 pass from Trudeau (Biasucci kick)
Ind —FG Biasucci 32
NE —Jones 8 pass from Grogan (Davis kick)
NE —FG Davis 48
Ind —Boyer 7 pass from Trudeau (Biasucci kick)
NE —Stephens 1 run (Davis kick)
Ind —FG Biasucci 39
NE —FG Davis 51

Philadelphia 28, Denver 24—at Mile High Stadium, attendance 75,065. Keith Byars ran for two touchdowns, including a one-yard scoring run with 5:25 left, to rally the Eagles over the Broncos. Philadelphia led 14-7 at halftime on Byars's 16-yard touchdown run and Randall Cunningham's five-yard scoring pass to Cris Carter. The Eagles increased their lead to 21-7 on Cunningham's 66-yard touchdown bomb to Jimmie Giles. Denver responded with 17 unanswered points, but William Frizzell's fumble recovery set up Byars's winning run.

Philadelphia	14	0	7	7	— 28
Denver	0	7	10	7	— 24

Phil —Byars 16 run (Zendejas kick)
Phil —Carter 5 pass from Cunningham (Zendejas kick)
Den —Elway 10 run (Treadwell kick)
Phil —Giles 66 pass from Cunningham (Zendejas kick)
Den —Johnson 13 pass from Elway (Treadwell kick)
Den —FG Treadwell 18
Den —Bratton 4 pass from Elway (Treadwell kick)
Phil —Byars 1 run (Zendejas kick)

Phoenix 19, Dallas 10—at Texas Stadium, attendance 44,431. Al Del Greco kicked four field goals as the Cardinals handed the Cowboys their eighth straight loss. Del Greco field goals of 40 and 25 yards in the first quarter gave Phoenix a 6-3 halftime edge. Mike Zordich then returned an interception 16 yards for a touchdown in the third quarter to put the Cardinals ahead 13-3. Tim McDonald's interception in the fourth quarter set up Del Greco's 31-yard field goal. He also kicked a 42-yarder with 1:23 remaining.

Phoenix	6	0	7	6	— 19
Dallas	0	3	0	7	— 10

Phx —FG Del Greco 40
Phx —FG Del Greco 25
Dall —FG Ruzek 37
Phx —Zordich 16 interception return (Del Greco kick)
Phx —FG Del Greco 31
Dall —Sheppard 37 pass from Walsh (Ruzek kick)
Phx —FG Del Greco 42

Seattle 10, San Diego 7—at Kingdome, attendance 59,691. Dave Krieg's 21-yard touchdown pass to Brian Blades with 40 seconds remaining lifted the Seahawks over the Chargers. Norm Johnson's 27-yard field goal in the first quarter was the only scoring in the game until San Diego's Jim McMahon hit Arthur Cox with a 14-yard scoring pass with less than three minutes left to give San Diego a 7-3 lead. Seattle then drove 71 yards in eight plays capped by Krieg's winning touchdown pass. San Diego's defense registered five sacks.

San Diego	0	0	0	7	— 7
Seattle	3	0	0	7	— 10

Sea —FG N. Johnson 27
SD —Cox 14 pass from McMahon (Bahr kick)
Sea —Blades 21 pass from Krieg (N. Johnson kick)

San Francisco 23, New York Jets 10—at Giants Stadium, attendance 62,805. Jerry Rice caught one touchdown pass and Mike Cofer kicked three field goals to help the 49ers defeat the Jets. San Francisco took a 20-7 lead on Steve Young's (starting in place of injured Joe Montana) 10-yard scoring pass to Brent Jones, Steve Bono's (who replaced the injured Young) 45-yard pass to Rice, and Cofer's field goals from 25 and 41 yards. Cofer also had a 40-yard field goal in the second half to complete the 49ers' scoring.

San Francisco	7	13	3	0	— 23
N.Y. Jets	0	7	3	0	— 10

SF —Jones 10 pass from Young (Cofer kick)
NYJ —McMillan 45 fumble recovery return (Leahy kick)
SF —Rice 45 pass from Bono (Cofer kick)
SF —FG Cofer 25
SF —FG Cofer 41
NYJ —FG Leahy 34
SF —FG Cofer 40

Cincinnati 56, Tampa Bay 23—at Riverfront Stadium, attendance 57,225. Boomer Esiason tied his club record by throwing five touchdown passes to lead the Bengals over the Buccaneers. Esiason threw two scoring passes to both Rodney Holman (one and nine yards) and Eddie Brown (eight and 18), and also hit Tim McGee (14) for another score. Rookie Erik Wilhelm replaced Esiason in the fourth quarter and connected with McGee on a 46-yard touchdown bomb. James Brooks carried 17 times for 131 yards for Cincinnati.

Tampa Bay	7	9	0	7	— 23
Cincinnati	7	14	21	14	— 56

TB —Hill 3 pass from Testaverde (Igwebuike kick)
Cin —Holman 1 pass from Esiason (Breech kick)
Cin —Ball 1 run (Breech kick)
TB —Safety, Esiason ran out of end zone
TB —Carrier 17 pass from Testaverde (Igwebuike kick)
Cin —Brown 8 pass from Esiason (Breech kick)
Cin —Brooks 4 run (Breech kick)
Cin —McGee 14 pass from Esiason (Breech kick)
Cin —Holman 9 pass from Esiason (Breech kick)
Cin —Brown 18 pass from Esiason (Breech kick)
Cin —McGee 46 pass from Wilhelm (Breech kick)
TB —Hill 2 pass from Testaverde (Igwebuike kick)

Los Angeles Raiders 37, Washington 24—at Memorial Coliseum, attendance 52,781. Steve Beuerlein made his first start of the season and threw two touchdown passes to lead the Raiders over the Redskins. Beuerlein connected with Mervyn Fernandez for two scoring passes (18 and eight yards) in the first quarter to give Los Angeles a 14-0 lead. Bo Jackson, who ran for 144 yards on 19 carries for the Raiders, scored on a 73-yard run to give the Raiders a 24-10 lead. Jeff Jaeger then kicked two field goals (29 and 37 yards) to put the game out of reach. Joe Howard's 99-yard first-quarter kickoff return for a touchdown was the Redskins first since 1978.

Washington	7	3	7	7	— 24
L.A. Raiders	14	3	20	0	— 37

Raiders — Fernandez 18 pass from Beuerlein (Jaeger kick)
Raiders — Fernandez 8 pass from Beuerlein (Jaeger kick)
Wash — Howard 99 kickoff return (Lohmiller kick)
Raiders — FG Jaeger 26
Wash — FG Lohmiller 43
Raiders — Jackson 73 run (Jaeger kick)
Raiders — FG Jaeger 29
Raiders — FG Jaeger 37
Raiders — Anderson 45 interception return (Jaeger kick)
Wash — Clark 27 pass from Rypien (Lohmiller kick)
Wash — Sanders 14 pass from Humphries (Lohmiller kick)

Monday, October 30

New York Giants 24, Minnesota 14—at Giants Stadium, attendance 76,041. Pepper Johnson returned an interception for a score and New York's defense had six sacks to lead the Giants past the Vikings. Johnson's 37-yard interception return for a touchdown tied the game 7-7 in the third quarter. The Giants then scored 17 unanswered points within a 2:25 span on Jeff Hostetler's 11-yard scoring pass to Lionel Manuel, Ottis Anderson's two-yard touchdown run, and Raul Allegre's 39-yard field goal to put the game away. New York's defense had six sacks and held Vikings running back Herschel Walker to 68 yards rushing.

Minnesota	7	0	0	7	— 14
N.Y. Giants	0	0	17	7	— 24

Minn — Walker 8 pass from Kramer (Karlis kick)
NYG — P. Johnson 39 interception return (Allegre kick)
NYG — FG Allegre 39
NYG — Manuel 11 pass from Hostetler (Allegre kick)
NYG — Anderson 2 run (Allegre kick)
Minn — Fenney 1 run (Karlis kick)

Ninth Week Summaries

Standings

American Football Conference

Eastern Division

	W	L	T	Pct.	Pts.	OP
Buffalo	6	3	0	.667	249	210
Miami	5	4	0	.556	180	203
Indianapolis	4	5	0	.444	167	162
New England	3	6	0	.333	157	216
N.Y. Jets	2	7	0	.222	159	241

Central Division

	W	L	T	Pct.	Pts.	OP
Cleveland	6	3	0	.667	233	143
Cincinnati	5	4	0	.556	211	168
Houston	5	4	0	.556	246	229
Pittsburgh	4	5	0	.444	123	220

Western Division

	W	L	T	Pct.	Pts.	OP
Denver	7	2	0	.778	218	140
L.A. Raiders	5	4	0	.556	206	155
Kansas City	4	5	0	.444	174	192
Seattle	4	5	0	.444	153	175
San Diego	3	6	0	.333	152	173

National Football Conference

Eastern Division

	W	L	T	Pct.	Pts.	OP
N.Y. Giants	8	1	0	.889	219	136
Philadelphia	6	3	0	.667	207	184
Phoenix	4	5	0	.444	169	193
Washington	4	5	0	.444	213	216
Dallas	1	8	0	.111	119	235

Central Division

	W	L	T	Pct.	Pts.	OP
Minnesota	6	3	0	.667	183	158
Chicago	5	4	0	.556	232	187
Green Bay	5	4	0	.556	219	214
Tampa Bay	3	6	0	.333	202	250
Detroit	1	8	0	.111	149	228

Western Division

	W	L	T	Pct.	Pts.	OP
San Francisco	8	1	0	.889	246	158
L.A. Rams	5	4	0	.556	214	208
New Orleans	4	5	0	.444	208	174
Atlanta	3	6	0	.333	171	211

Sunday, November 5

Atlanta 30, Buffalo 28—at Atlanta-Fulton County Stadium, attendance 45,267. Paul McFadden's 50-yard field goal with two seconds remaining lifted the Falcons over the Bills. Atlanta trailed 21-20 late in the fourth quarter, but Keith Jones ran three yards for a touchdown to give the Falcons a 27-21 lead. Buffalo regained the lead when Don Beebe's 85-yard kickoff return set up Larry Kinnebrew's one-yard touchdown run with 29 seconds remaining. Chris Miller's 41-yard pass to Stacey Bailey set up McFadden's game-winning kick.

Buffalo	7	0	14	7	— 28
Atlanta	0	3	17	10	— 30

Buff — Lofton 6 pass from Kelly (Norwood kick)
Atl — FG McFadden 54
Atl — Jones 1 run (McFadden kick)
Buff — McKeller 11 pass from Kelly (Norwood kick)
Atl — Dixon 26 pass from Miller (McFadden kick)
Atl — FG McFadden 26
Buff — Thomas 2 run (Norwood kick)
Atl — Jones 3 run (McFadden kick)
Buff — Kinnebrew 1 run (Norwood kick)
Atl — FG McFadden 50

Green Bay 14, Chicago 13—at Lambeau Field, attendance 56,556. Don Majkowski connected with Sterling Sharpe on a 14-yard touchdown pass with 32 seconds remaining to give the Packers a 14-13 win over the Bears. Majkowski hit Clint Didier with a 24-yard scoring pass early in the first quarter to put Green Bay ahead 7-0, but Chicago scored 13 unanswered points on Kevin Butler's 25- and 37-yard field goals and Brad Muster's two-yard touchdown run. Majkowski's game-winning touchdown throw was called back when the on-field officials ruled Majkowski stepped over the line of scrimmage before throwing the ball. However, Replay Official Bill Parkinson ruled the ball was behind the line of scrimmage before Majkowski threw, which gave the Packers a touchdown and the victory.

Chicago	3	0	10	0	— 13
Green Bay	7	0	0	7	— 14

GB — Didier 24 pass from Majkowski (Jacke kick)
Chi — FG Butler 25
Chi — FG Butler 37
Chi — Muster 2 run (Butler kick)
GB — Sharpe 14 pass from Majkowski (Jacke kick)

Los Angeles Raiders 28, Cincinnati 7—at Memorial Coliseum, attendance 51,080. Bo Jackson scored on a team-record 92-yard run to highlight the Raiders' victory over the Bengals. Los Angeles took a 21-0 halftime lead on Jackson's 92- and two-yard runs, and Jay Schroeder's 25-yard touchdown pass to Vance Mueller. Willie Gault had two receptions for 147 yards, including an 84-yard touchdown reception from Schroeder in the third quarter. Erik Wilhelm, who replaced Boomer Esiason, threw a 34-yard touchdown pass to Tim McGee to prevent the shutout.

Cincinnati	0	0	0	7	— 7
L.A. Raiders	14	7	7	0	— 28

Raiders — Jackson 7 run (Jaeger kick)
Raiders — Jackson 92 run (Jaeger kick)
Raiders — Mueller 25 pass from Schroeder (Jaeger kick)
Raiders — Gault 84 pass from Schroeder (Jaeger kick)
Cin — McGee 34 pass from Wilhelm (Breech kick)

Cleveland 42, Tampa Bay 31—at Tampa Stadium, attendance 69,162. Felix Wright and Thane Gash each returned interceptions for touchdowns to lead the Browns past the Buccaneers. Cleveland jumped to a 35-17 lead on Bernie Kosar touchdown passes to Eric Metcalf (24 yards) and Lawyer Tillman (seven), Wright's 27-yard interception return, and Gash's 15-yard interception return. Gash's return came 19 seconds after Wright's. Kosar also hit Derek Tennell with a four-yard touchdown pass. Metcalf, who finished with 17 carries for 87 yards and seven receptions for 50 yards, scored on a 43-yard run in the fourth quarter to complete Cleveland's scoring.

Cleveland	7	28	0	7	— 42
Tampa Bay	7	10	7	7	— 31

TB — Tate 1 run (Igwebuike kick)
Clev — Metcalf 24 pass from Kosar (Bahr kick)
Clev — Tillman 7 pass from Kosar (Bahr kick)
Clev — Wright 27 interception return (Bahr kick)
Clev — Gash 15 interception return (Bahr kick)
TB — Wilder 9 pass from Testaverde (Igwebuike kick)
Clev — Tennell 4 pass from Kosar (Bahr kick)
TB — FG Igwebuike 53
TB — Wilder 9 pass from Testaverde (Igwebuike kick)
Clev — Metcalf 43 run (Bahr kick)
TB — Tate 1 run (Igwebuike kick)

Houston 35, Detroit 31—at Astrodome, attendance 48,056. Warren Moon completed two touchdown passes as the Oilers rallied from a 10-point deficit to defeat the Lions. Trailing 24-14 in the third quarter, Moon threw a six-yard touchdown pass to Ernest Givins and followed with a seven-yarder to Drew Hill. Moon, who completed 30 of 38 passes for 345 yards, ran two yards for a score late in the fourth quarter to put the game out of reach. Detroit running back Barry Sanders ran 14 yards for a touchdown to narrow the score, but Houston recovered the ensuing onside kick and ran out the clock to win.

Detroit	7	10	7	7	— 31
Houston	7	7	14	7	— 35

Det — Sanders 1 run (Murray kick)
Hou — White 1 run (Zendejas kick)
Det — Clark 16 pass from Peete (Murray kick)
Hou — Rozier 1 run (Zendejas kick)
Det — FG Murray 47
Det — White 20 fumble recovery return (Murray kick)
Hou — Givins 6 pass from Moon (Zendejas kick)
Hou — Hill 7 pass from Moon (Zendejas kick)
Hou — Moon 2 run (Zendejas kick)
Det — Sanders 14 run (Murray kick)

Miami 19, Indianapolis 13—at Joe Robbie Stadium, attendance 52,680. Dan Marino threw touchdown passes to Mark Clayton (13 yards) and Andre Brown (10) as the Dolphins defeated the Colts. Pete Stoyanovich also kicked an 18-yard field goal in the first quarter for Miami. Sammie Smith gained 123 yards on 23 carries to become the first Dolphin to rush for over 100 yards since Troy Stradford (120 yards on 12/7/87 vs. New York Jets).

Indianapolis	3	0	0	10		— 13
Miami	3	9	7	0		— 19

Mia — FG Stoyanovich 18
Ind — FG Biasucci 36
Mia — Clayton 13 pass from Marino (Stoyanovich kick)
Mia — Safety, ball snapped out of end zone
Mia — A. Brown 10 pass from Marino (Stoyanovich kick)
Ind — FG Biasucci 33
Ind — Rison 7 pass from Trudeau (Biasucci kick)

Minnesota 23, Los Angeles Rams 21—at Metrodome, attendance 59,600. Mike Merriweather blocked a punt out of the end zone for a safety 2:14 into overtime as the Vikings downed the Rams. The score marked the first time since the overtime rule was adopted in 1974 that a game was decided in overtime by a safety. Minnesota's Rich Karlis accounted for all 21 of the Vikings' points in regulation by kicking seven field goals (20, 24, 22, 25, 29, 36, and 40 yards) to tie an NFL record set by Jim Bakken of the Cardinals on September 24, 1967.

L.A. Rams	7	0	0	14	0	— 21
Minnesota	3	9	6	3	2	— 23

Minn — FG Karlis 20
Rams — Bell 1 run (Lansford kick)
Minn — FG Karlis 24
Minn — FG Karlis 22
Minn — FG Karlis 25
Minn — FG Karlis 29
Minn — FG Karlis 36
Rams — Ellard 6 pass from Everett (Lansford kick)
Rams — Bell 1 run (Lansford kick)
Minn — FG Karlis 40
Minn — Safety, Merriweather blocked punt out of end zone

New York Giants 20, Phoenix 13—at Sun Devil Stadium, attendance 46,588. Jeff Hostetler ran for two touchdowns and threw for another to lead the Giants past the Cardinals. Hostetler, starting for injured Phil Simms, ran 19 yards for a touchdown and connected with Stephen Baker on a 35-yard scoring pass to put New York ahead 14-3 at halftime. Hostetler also added a three-yard run in the second half to complete the Giants' scoring. New York's defense recorded six sacks, while the offense held a 38:10 to 21:50 time-of-possession advantage.

N.Y. Giants	7	7	6	0	— 20
Phoenix	3	0	7	3	— 13

NYG — Hostetler 19 run (Allegre kick)
Phx — FG Del Greco 37
NYG — S. Baker 35 pass from Hostetler (Allegre kick)
Phx — Hogeboom 5 run (Del Greco kick)
NYG — Hostetler 3 run (kick failed)
Phx — FG Del Greco 46

New York Jets 27, New England 26—at Sullivan Stadium, attendance 53,366. Pat Leahy kicked a 23-yard field goal on the final play of the game as the Jets edged the Patriots. New York led 24-12 in the fourth quarter on a pair of Ken O'Brien touchdown passes, to JoJo Townsell (35 yards) and Chris Burkett (29), Freeman McNeil's 19-yard run, and Leahy's 18-yard field goal. Patriots quarterback Marc Wilson threw scoring passes of 65 yards to Cedric Jones and 11 yards to Hart Lee Dykes to move New England ahead 26-24 with 1:03 remaining. O'Brien, who completed 22 of 29 passes for 386 yards, was named AFC Offensive Player of the Week.

N.Y. Jets	7	7	3	10	— 27
New England	3	0	6	17	— 26

NYJ — McNeil 19 run (Leahy kick)
NE — FG Davis 47
NYJ — Townsell 35 pass from O'Brien (Leahy kick)
NE — Stephens 35 run (kick failed)
NYJ — FG Leahy 18
NE — FG Davis 26
NYJ — Burkett 29 pass from O'Brien (Leahy kick)
NE — Jones 65 pass from Wilson (Davis kick)
NE — Dykes 11 pass from Wilson (Davis kick)
NYJ — FG Leahy 23

San Diego 20, Philadelphia 17—at San Diego Jack Murphy Stadium, attendance 47,019. Chris Bahr kicked a 49-yard field goal with four seconds remaining as the Chargers defeated the Eagles to snap a four-game losing streak. San Diego took a 17-7 fourth-quarter lead on Jim McMahon's two touchdown passes to Anthony Miller (six and 69 yards) and Bahr's 23-yard field goal. Philadelphia tied the game 17-17 on Steve DeLine's 43-yard field goal and Keith Byars's three-yard run for a score. Leslie O'Neal had three-and-a-half sacks and was named AFC Defensive Player of the Week.

Philadelphia	0	7	0	10	— 17
San Diego	7	0	10	3	— 20

SD — Miller 6 pass from McMahon (Bahr kick)
Phil — Garrity 4 pass from Cunningham (DeLine kick)
SD — FG Bahr 23
SD — Miller 69 pass from McMahon (Bahr kick)
Phil — FG DeLine 43
Phil — Byars 3 run (DeLine kick)
SD — FG Bahr 49

Denver 34, Pittsburgh 7—at Mile High Stadium, attendance 74,739. John Elway threw one touchdown pass and ran for another as the Broncos easily beat the Steelers. Bobby Humphrey's 105 yards rushing included a 22-yard touchdown run in the first quarter and a 12-yard scoring run in the fourth quarter. Elway hit Vance Johnson on a 44-yard touchdown pass and ran two yards for a touchdown after Pittsburgh punter Harry Newsome was tackled at the Steelers' 2-yard line. David Treadwell added two 26-yard field goals for Denver.

Pittsburgh	0	7	0	0	—	7
Denver	10	3	7	14	—	34

Den —Humphrey 22 run (Treadwell kick)
Den —FG Treadwell 26
Pitt —Carter 15 pass from Brister (Anderson kick)
Den —FG Treadwell 26
Den —Johnson 44 pass from Elway (Treadwell kick)
Den —Elway 2 run (Treadwell kick)
Den —Humphrey 12 run (Treadwell kick)

Kansas City 20, Seattle 10—at Arrowhead Stadium, attendance 54,488. Christian Okoye ran for 126 yards on 37 carries, including an eight-yard touchdown run, to lead the Chiefs past the Seahawks. Kansas City took a 17-10 lead in the first half on Okoye's touchdown run, quarterback Steve Pelluer's 10-yard scoring run, and Nick Lowery's 34-yard field goal. Louis Cooper's fumble recovery set up Lowery's 33-yard field goal for the only scoring in the second half. The Chiefs, who also defeated the Seahawks 20-16 on October 8, completed their first season sweep of AFC West rival Seattle since 1981.

Seattle	7	3	0	0	—	10
Kansas City	7	10	0	3	—	20

Sea —Glasgow 38 fumble recovery return (N. Johnson kick)
KC —Okoye 8 run (Lowery kick)
KC —Pelluer 10 run (Lowery kick)
KC —FG Lowery 34
Sea —FG N. Johnson 18
KC —FG Lowery 33

Dallas 13, Washington 3—at Robert F. Kennedy Stadium, attendance 53,187. Paul Palmer rushed 18 times for 110 yards as the Cowboys downed the Redskins for their first victory of the season. The game also marked the first win for Dallas under rookie head coach Jimmy Johnson. The Cowboys broke a 3-3 tie in the third quarter on Palmer's two-yard run. Roger Ruzek, who kicked a 20-yard field goal in the first quarter, added a 43-yarder to complete Dallas's scoring. Ruzek's fourth-quarter field goal was set up by Bill Bates's interception.

Dallas	0	3	7	3	—	13
Washington	0	0	3	0	—	3

Dall —FG Ruzek 20
Wash —FG Lohmiller 35
Dall —Palmer 2 run (Ruzek kick)
Dall —FG Ruzek 43

Monday, November 6

San Francisco 31, New Orleans 13—at Candlestick Park, attendance 60,667. Joe Montana completed 22 of 31 passes for 302 yards and three touchdowns as the 49ers defeated the Saints. Montana threw all three of his touchdowns in the first half on passes to Jerry Rice (32 and two yards) and John Taylor (46) to put San Francisco ahead 21-10. Montana also scrambled three yards for a score in the fourth quarter. Rice's two touchdown receptions lifted his career total to 60, breaking the team record of 59, set by Gene Washington.

New Orleans	7	3	3	0	—	13
San Francisco	7	14	3	7	—	31

SF —Rice 32 pass from Montana (Cofer kick)
NO —Hilliard 1 run (Andersen kick)
SF —Rice 2 pass from Montana (Cofer kick)
NO —FG Andersen 39
SF —Taylor 46 pass from Montana (Cofer kick)
NO —FG Andersen 23
SF —FG Cofer 44
SF —Montana 3 run (Cofer kick)

Tenth Week Summaries

Standings

American Football Conference

Eastern Division

	W	L	T	Pct.	Pts.	OP
Buffalo	7	3	0	.700	279	217
Miami	6	4	0	.600	211	226
Indianapolis	4	6	0	.400	174	192
New England	3	7	0	.300	181	244
N.Y. Jets	2	8	0	.200	182	272

Central Division

	W	L	T	Pct.	Pts.	OP
Cleveland	7	3	0	.700	250	150
Houston	6	4	0	.600	272	253
Cincinnati	5	5	0	.500	235	194
Pittsburgh	4	6	0	.400	123	240

Western Division

	W	L	T	Pct.	Pts.	OP
Denver	8	2	0	.800	234	153
L.A. Raiders	5	5	0	.500	218	169
Kansas City	4	6	0	.400	187	208
San Diego	4	6	0	.400	166	185
Seattle	4	6	0	.400	160	192

National Football Conference

Eastern Division

	W	L	T	Pct.	Pts.	OP
N.Y. Giants	8	2	0	.800	229	167
Philadelphia	6	4	0	.600	210	194
Phoenix	5	5	0	.500	193	213
Washington	5	5	0	.500	223	219
Dallas	1	9	0	.100	139	259

Central Division

	W	L	T	Pct.	Pts.	OP
Minnesota	7	3	0	.700	207	168
Chicago	6	4	0	.600	252	187
Green Bay	5	5	0	.500	241	245
Tampa Bay	3	7	0	.300	212	274
Detroit	2	8	0	.200	180	250

Western Division

	W	L	T	Pct.	Pts.	OP
San Francisco	9	1	0	.900	291	161
L.A. Rams	6	4	0	.600	245	218
New Orleans	5	5	0	.500	236	198
Atlanta	3	7	0	.300	174	256

Sunday, November 12

San Francisco 45, Atlanta 3—at Candlestick Park, attendance 59,914. Joe Montana threw three touchdown passes and ran for another as the 49ers rolled over the Falcons. San Francisco took a commanding 28-3 halftime lead on Montana's one-yard run and his touchdown passes to Jerry Rice (38 yards) and John Taylor (two), and Charles Haley's three-yard fumble return for a score. Montana found Rice again with an 11-yard touchdown completion in the third quarter. Atlanta quarterback Chris Miller, replacing injured kicker Paul McFadden, kicked a 23-yard field goal in the second quarter for the Falcons' only points.

Atlanta	0	3	0	0	—	3
San Francisco	7	21	10	7	—	45

SF —Montana 1 run (Cofer kick)
Atl —FG Miller 23
SF —Rice 38 pass from Montana (Cofer kick)
SF —Haley 3 fumble recovery return (Cofer kick)
SF —Taylor 2 pass from Montana (Cofer kick)
SF —Rice 11 pass from Montana (Cofer kick)
SF —FG Cofer 18
SF —Henderson 11 run (Cofer kick)

Chicago 20, Pittsburgh 0—at Three Rivers Stadium, attendance 56,505. Jim Harbaugh completed a touchdown pass and Chicago's defense forced six turnovers as the Bears blanked the Steelers to end a three-game losing streak. Chicago scored all its points in the first half on Neal Anderson's two-yard run, Harbaugh's 20-yard touchdown pass to Brad Muster, and Kevin Butler's field goals from 39 and 35 yards.

Chicago	7	13	0	0	—	20
Pittsburgh	0	0	0	0	—	0

Chi —N. Anderson 2 run (Butler kick)
Chi —FG Butler 39
Chi —Muster 20 pass from Harbaugh (Butler kick)
Chi —FG Butler 35

Cleveland 17, Seattle 7—at Kingdome, attendance 58,978. Bernie Kosar completed a 17-yard scoring pass to Lawyer Tillman to lead the Browns past the Seahawks for their fourth straight victory. Felix Wright's interception set up Kosar's touchdown pass to Tillman. Tim Manoa opened Cleveland's scoring with a one-yard run in the second quarter. Clay Matthews returned an interception 25 yards to set up Matt Bahr's 29-yard field goal with 3:25 remaining to put the game out of reach.

Cleveland	0	7	7	3	—	17
Seattle	7	0	0	0	—	7

Sea —Blades 8 pass from Krieg (N. Johnson kick)
Clev —Manoa 1 run (Bahr kick)
Clev —Tillman 17 pass from Kosar (Bahr kick)
Clev —FG Bahr 29

Phoenix 24, Dallas 20—at Sun Devil Stadium, attendance 49,657. Tom Tupa's 72-yard touchdown pass to Ernie Jones with 58 seconds remaining lifted the Cardinals over the Cowboys. Trailing 13-7 in the fourth quarter, Tupa fired a 38-yard scoring pass to Jones and Al Del Greco kicked a 45-yard field goal to put Phoenix ahead 17-13. Troy Aikman's 75-yard scoring bomb to James Dixon with 1:43 remaining gave Dallas a 20-17 lead. Tim McDonald, whose two interceptions included a 53-yarder for a touchdown, was named NFC Defensive Player of the Week.

Dallas	3	10	0	7	—	20
Phoenix	0	7	0	17	—	24

Dall —FG Zendejas 32
Dall —FG Zendejas 29
Phx —McDonald 53 interception return (Del Greco kick)
Dall —Martin 5 pass from Aikman (Zendejas kick)
Phx —FG Del Greco 45
Phx —Jones 38 pass from Tupa (Del Greco kick)
Dall —Dixon 75 pass from Aikman (Zendejas kick)
Phx —Jones 72 pass from Tupa (Del Greco kick)

Denver 16, Kansas City 13—at Arrowhead Stadium, attendance 76,245. David Treadwell kicked a 26-yard field goal with one second remaining to give the Broncos a 16-13 victory over the Chiefs. Denver took a 13-6 fourth-quarter lead on Greg Kragen's 17-yard fumble recovery return for a touchdown and Treadwell's pair of field goals (18 and 27 yards). Steve Pelluer tied the game with less than six minutes remaining with a three-yard scoring pass to Emile Harry. John Elway led a 10-play, 71-yard march to set up Treadwell's decisive kick.

Denver	3	7	3	3	—	16
Kansas City	0	6	0	7	—	13

Den —FG Treadwell 18
KC —FG Lowery 39
Den —Kragen 17 fumble recovery return (Treadwell kick)
KC —FG Lowery 42
Den —FG Treadwell 27
KC —Harry 5 pass from Pelluer (Lowery kick)
Den —FG Treadwell 26

Detroit 31, Green Bay 22—at Pontiac Silverdome, attendance 44,324. Rodney Peete combined with Richard Johnson on two touchdown passes as the Lions defeated the Packers. Detroit built a 24-3 halftime lead on Peete's scoring throws to Johnson (17 and eight yards), Eddie Murray's 45-yard field goal, and Jerry Holmes's 23-yard interception return for a score. Green Bay narrowed the scoring margin to 24-20 in the fourth quarter, but Barry Sanders's one-yard touchdown run sealed Detroit's victory.

Green Bay	0	3	14	5	—	22
Detroit	3	21	0	7	—	31

Det —FG Murray 45
Det —Johnson 17 pass from Peete (Murray kick)
Det —Johnson 8 pass from Peete (Murray kick)
GB —FG Jacke 34
Det —Holmes 23 interception return (Murray kick)
GB —Haddix 6 pass from Majkowski (Jacke kick)
GB —Workman 1 run (Jacke kick)
GB —FG Jacke 40
Det —Sanders 1 run (Murray kick)
GB —Safety, Peete ran out of end zone

Buffalo 30, Indianapolis 7—at Rich Stadium, attendance 79,256. Jim Kelly threw three touchdown passes, including two to Andre Reed, as the Bills beat the Colts. Buffalo took a 27-0 lead on Kelly's eight-yard touchdown pass to Thurman Thomas, Scott Norwood's two field goals (42 and 40 yards), and Kelly's two scoring passes to Reed (32 and three yards). The Bills held a 41:14 to 18:46 time-of-possession advantage.

Indianapolis	0	0	0	7	—	7
Buffalo	13	14	0	3	—	30

Buff —Thomas 8 pass from Kelly (Norwood kick)
Buff —FG Norwood 42
Buff —FG Norwood 40
Buff —Reed 32 pass from Kelly (Norwood kick)
Buff —Reed 3 pass from Kelly (Norwood kick)
Buff —FG Norwood 32
Ind —Dixon recovered fumble in end zone (Biasucci kick)

Miami 31, New York Jets 23—at Giants Stadium, attendance 65,923. Dan Marino threw three touchdown passes to rally the Dolphins past the Jets. Marino connected on an eight-yard touchdown pass to Andre Brown in the first half. He then came back in the third quarter and completed scoring passes to Mark Clayton (78 yards) and Scott Schwedes (65). Sammie Smith also added a two-yard touchdown run in the third period to put the Dolphins, who trailed 20-10 at halftime, ahead 31-20. Miami's Pete Stoyanovich kicked a 59-yard field goal in the second quarter, the third longest in NFL history.

Miami	0	10	21	0	—	31
N.Y. Jets	3	17	0	3	—	23

NYJ —FG Leahy 38
NYJ —FG Leahy 20
NYJ —Vick 26 run (Leahy kick)
Mia —FG Stoyanovich 59
NYJ —McNeil 25 pass from O'Brien (Leahy kick)
Mia —A. Brown 8 pass from Marino (Stoyanovich kick)
Mia —Clayton 78 pass from Marino (Stoyanovich kick)
Mia —Schwedes 65 pass from Marino (Stoyanovich kick)
Mia —S. Smith 2 run (Stoyanovich kick)
NYJ —FG Leahy 22

Minnesota 24, Tampa Bay 10—at Tampa Stadium, attendance 56,271. Reggie Rutland returned a fumble 27 yards for a touchdown to help the Vikings defeat the Buccaneers. Minnesota built a 17-0 lead in the first quarter on Wade Wilson's three-yard scoring pass to Steve Jordan, Rutland's fumble recovery for a score, and Rich Karlis's 41-yard field goal. Herschel Walker ran one yard for a touchdown in the second half to finish Minnesota's scoring. The Vikings' defense registered seven sacks, including three by Chris Doleman.

Minnesota	17	0	0	7	—	24
Tampa Bay	0	3	0	7	—	10

Minn —FG Karlis 41
Minn —Rutland 27 fumble recovery return (Karlis kick)
Minn —Jordan 3 pass from Wilson (Karlis kick)
TB —FG Igwebuike 22
TB —Wilder 5 pass from Testaverde (Igwebuike kick)
Minn —Walker 1 run (Karlis kick)

New Orleans 28, New England 24—at Sullivan Stadium, attendance 47,680. Dalton Hilliard carried 28 times for 106 yards and two touchdowns to lead the Saints past the Patriots. New Orleans took a commanding 28-10 lead at halftime as Hilliard ran for two scores (three and 10 yards), Bobby Hebert completed a one-yard touchdown pass to Hoby Brenner, and Brett Maxie returned an interception 26 yards. The victory gave the Saints their tenth straight win against AFC opponents.

New Orleans	7	21	0	0	— 28
New England	0	10	0	14	— 24

NO — Hilliard 3 run (Andersen kick)
NO — Brenner 1 pass from Hebert (Andersen kick)
NO — Maxie 26 interception return (Andersen kick)
NO — Hilliard 10 run (Andersen kick)
NE — Perryman 1 run (Staurovsky kick)
NE — FG Staurovsky 44
NE — Dykes 13 pass from Grogan (Staurovsky kick)
NE — Perryman 3 run (Staurovsky kick)

Los Angeles Rams 31, New York Giants 10—at Anaheim Stadium, attendance 65,127. Jim Everett completed two scoring passes and Greg Bell ran for two touchdowns as the Rams downed the Giants to end a four-game losing streak. The Rams took a commanding 24-3 halftime lead on Everett's touchdown passes to Aaron Cox (five yards) and Willie Anderson (21). Greg Bell also had scoring runs of one and two yards for Los Angeles. The Rams' defense had four sacks and limited the Giants to six yards rushing. Everett, who completed a club-record 18 consecutive passes, was named NFC Offensive Player of the Week.

N.Y. Giants	0	3	0	7	— 10
L.A. Rams	10	14	7	0	— 31

Rams — FG Lansford 44
Rams — Bell 1 run (Lansford kick)
NYG — FG Allegre 22
Rams — A. Cox 51 pass from Everett (Lansford kick)
Rams — Anderson 21 pass from Everett (Lansford kick)
Rams — Bell 2 run (Lansford kick)
NYG — Anderson 1 run (Allegre kick)

Washington 10, Philadelphia 3—at Veterans Stadium, attendance 65,443. Earnest Byner ran one yard for a touchdown as the Redskins outscored the Eagles to snap a two-game losing streak. Washington took a 3-0 first-quarter lead on Tracy Rocker's fumble recovery which set up Chip Lohmiller's 34-yard field goal. The Redskins finished their scoring on Byner's run. Dexter Manley's three sacks included a tackle of Randall Cunningham on fourth down with 1:36 remaining in the game to end the Eagles' final threat.

Washington	3	7	0	0	— 10
Philadelphia	0	3	0	0	— 3

Wash — FG Lohmiller 34
Wash — Byner 1 run (Lohmiller kick)
Phil — FG DeLine 49

San Diego 14, Los Angeles Raiders 12—at San Diego Jack Murphy Stadium, attendance 59,151. Anthony Miller returned a kickoff 91 yards for a score to highlight the Chargers' win over the Raiders. Los Angeles led 12-0 midway through the third quarter on four Jeff Jaeger field goals (23, 36, 33, and 32 yards). Miller's kickoff return narrowed the deficit to 12-7. Cedric Figaro's fourth-quarter fumble recovery at the Raiders' 23-yard line set up Tim Spencer's five-yard game-winning touchdown run.

L.A. Raiders	3	6	3	0	— 12
San Diego	0	0	7	7	— 14

Raiders — FG Jaeger 23
Raiders — FG Jaeger 36
Raiders — FG Jaeger 33
Raiders — FG Jaeger 32
SD — A. Miller 91 kickoff return (Bahr kick)
SD — Spencer 5 run (Bahr kick)

Monday, November 13

Houston 26, Cincinnati 24—at Astrodome, attendance 60,694. Tony Zendejas kicked four field goals, including a game-winning 28-yarder as time expired, as the Oilers edged the Bengals. Zendejas's 32-, 42-, and 37-yard field goals and Eugene Seale's recovery of a blocked punt in the end zone put Houston ahead 16-14 in the fourth quarter. Jim Breech's 38-yard field goal gave the Bengals a 24-23 advantage with 7:33 remaining. Oilers quarterback Warren Moon guided his team 70 yards to set up Zendejas's winning kick.

Cincinnati	0	14	0	10	— 24
Houston	0	7	6	13	— 26

Cin — Brooks 58 run (Breech kick)
Hou — Seale recovered blocked punt in end zone (Zendejas kick)
Cin — Taylor 1 run (Breech kick)
Hou — FG Zendejas 32
Hou — FG Zendejas 42
Hou — FG Zendejas 47
Cin — Holman 73 pass from Esiason (Breech kick)
Hou — Harris 23 pass from Moon (Zendejas kick)
Cin — FG Breech 38
Hou — FG Zendejas 28

Eleventh Week Summaries

Standings

American Football Conference

Eastern Division	W	L	T	Pct.	Pts.	OP
Buffalo	7	4	0	.636	303	250
Miami	7	4	0	.636	228	240
Indianapolis	5	6	0	.455	201	202
New England	4	7	0	.364	214	268
N.Y. Jets	2	9	0	.182	192	299
Central Division						
Cleveland	7	3	1	.682	260	160
Houston	7	4	0	.636	295	260
Cincinnati	6	5	0	.545	277	201
Pittsburgh	5	6	0	.455	143	257
Western Division						
Denver	9	2	0	.818	248	163
L.A. Raiders	5	6	0	.455	225	192
Kansas City	4	6	1	.409	197	218
San Diego	4	7	0	.364	183	205
Seattle	4	7	0	.364	163	207

National Football Conference

Eastern Division	W	L	T	Pct.	Pts.	OP
N.Y. Giants	9	2	0	.818	244	170
Philadelphia	7	4	0	.636	220	203
Phoenix	5	6	0	.455	207	250
Washington	5	6	0	.455	233	233
Dallas	1	10	0	.091	153	276
Central Division						
Minnesota	7	4	0	.636	216	178
Chicago	6	5	0	.545	283	219
Green Bay	6	5	0	.545	262	262
Tampa Bay	4	7	0	.364	244	305
Detroit	2	9	0	.182	187	292
Western Division						
San Francisco	9	2	0	.818	308	182
L.A. Rams	7	4	0	.636	282	232
New Orleans	6	5	0	.545	262	215
Atlanta	3	8	0	.273	191	282

Sunday, November 19

New England 33, Buffalo 24—at Sullivan Stadium, attendance 49,663. Maurice Hurst returned an interception for a score to highlight the Patriots' victory over the Bills. Trailing 24-13 in the fourth quarter, New England quarterback Steve Grogan connected with Hart Lee Dykes for a 14-yard touchdown pass and Jason Staurovsky kicked a 34-yard field goal to narrow the score to 24-23 with 3:06 remaining. Hurst then returned an interception 16 yards for a score to give the Patriots a 30-24 lead. Staurovsky, who kicked two field goals in the first quarter (34 and 24 yards) added a 38-yard field goal with 13 seconds left to put the game out of reach.

Buffalo	7	3	0	14	— 24
New England	0	6	7	20	— 33

Buff — Thomas 3 run (Norwood kick)
NE — FG Staurovsky 34
NE — FG Staurovsky 24
Buff — FG Norwood 31
NE — Egu 15 run (Staurovsky kick)
Buff — Kinnebrew 1 run (Norwood kick)
Buff — Thomas 25 pass from Kelly (Norwood kick)
NE — Dykes 14 pass from Grogan (Staurovsky kick)
NE — FG Staurovsky 34
NE — Hurst 16 interception return (Staurovsky kick)
NE — FG Staurovsky 38

Cincinnati 42, Detroit 7—at Riverfront Stadium, attendance 55,720. Boomer Esiason completed 30 of 39 passes for 399 yards and three touchdowns as the Bengals easily defeated the Lions. Cincinnati exploded for 28 points in the second quarter on Esiason's scoring passes to Tim McGee (17 yards) and Craig Taylor (one), Taylor's three-yard run for a touchdown, and Barney Bussey's recovery of a blocked punt in the end zone for a touchdown. Esiason then connected with Mike Martin for a 15-yard touchdown throw in the second half and backup quarterback Erik Wilhelm finished the Bengals' scoring with a 41-yard pass to Kendal Smith. McGee finished the day with 11 receptions for a career-high 194 yards. Esiason and McGee were named co-AFC Offensive Players of the Week.

Detroit	7	0	0	0	— 7
Cincinnati	0	28	7	7	— 42

Det — Sanders 2 run (Murray kick)
Cin — McGee 17 pass from Esiason (Breech kick)
Cin — Taylor 3 run (Breech kick)
Cin — Taylor 1 pass from Esiason (Breech kick)
Cin — Bussey blocked punt recovery in end zone (Breech kick)
Cin — Martin 15 pass from Esiason (Breech kick)
Cin — Smith 41 pass from Wilhelm (Breech kick)

Green Bay 21, San Francisco 17—at Candlestick Park, attendance 62,219. Don Majkowski ran for two touchdowns as the Packers defeated the 49ers. Majkowski opened the scoring with a two-yard run midway through the first quarter. He increased his streak of 13 straight games with a scoring pass when he hit Sterling Sharpe with a four-yard pass to help Green Bay to a 14-14 halftime tie. Majkowski's second scoring run, an eight-yarder in the fourth quarter, capped the Packers' scoring. Mike Cofer's 44-yard field goal with 7:43 remaining closed the margin to 21-17 but San Francisco could not overtake the Packers.

Green Bay	7	7	0	7	— 21
San Francisco	7	7	0	3	— 17

GB — Majkowski 2 run (Jacke kick)
SF — Craig 4 pass from Montana (Cofer kick)
GB — Sharpe 4 pass from Majkowski (Jacke kick)
SF — Rice 9 pass from Montana (Cofer kick)
GB — Majkowski 8 run (Jacke kick)
SF — FG Cofer 44

Kansas City 10, Cleveland 10—at Cleveland Stadium, attendance 77,922. The Chiefs and the Browns played to only the thirteenth tie since overtime was adopted in 1974. Matt Bahr's 40-yard field goal in the second quarter provided the only scoring in the first half. Neil Smith gave the Chiefs the lead 7-3 when he recovered Mike Oliphant's fumble in the end zone for a touchdown. Eric Metcalf's one-yard run for a score put Cleveland ahead 10-7, but Nick Lowery's 41-yard field goal with 3:48 remaining tied the game. Lowery missed a 31-yard attempt with four seconds remaining in regulation and a 47-yarder in overtime that would have provided Kansas City with the victory.

Kansas City	0	0	7	3	0	— 10
Cleveland	0	3	7	0	0	— 10

Clev — FG Bahr 40
KC — Smith 3 fumble recovery return (Lowery kick)
Clev — Metcalf 1 run (Bahr kick)
KC — FG Lowery 41

Houston 23, Los Angeles Raiders 7—at Astrodome, attendance 59,198. Warren Moon threw two touchdown passes as the Oilers beat the Raiders. Houston took a 17-7 halftime lead on Moon's touchdown pass to Curtis Duncan, Tony Zendejas's 20-yard field goal, and Moon's 11-yard scoring pass to Leonard Harris, which was set up by Tracy Eaton's interception. Zendejas added field goals of 20 and 46 yards in the second half for the Oilers.

L.A. Raiders	0	7	0	0	— 7
Houston	7	10	3	3	— 23

Hou — Duncan 25 pass from Moon (Zendejas kick)
Raiders — Dyal 22 pass from Beuerlein (Jaeger kick)
Hou — FG Zendejas 20
Hou — Harris 11 pass from Moon (Zendejas kick)
Hou — FG Zendejas 20
Hou — FG Zendejas 46

Miami 17, Dallas 14—at Texas Stadium, attendance 58,738. Dan Marino and Andre Brown combined on a touchdown pass to highlight the Dolphins' victory over the Cowboys. Pete Stoyanovich kicked a 23-yard field goal to trim the Cowboys lead to 14-10 and Marino fired a 48-yard scoring pass to Brown on the last play of the first half. After a scoreless third period, Liffort Hobley's interception set up Sammie Smith's decisive one-yard touchdown run in the fourth quarter.

Miami	0	10	0	7	— 17
Dallas	7	7	0	0	— 14

Dall — Sargent 1 run (Zendejas kick)
Mia — FG Stoyanovich 23
Dall — Johnston 6 pass from Aikman (Zendejas kick)
Mia — A. Brown 48 pass from Marino (Stoyanovich kick)
Mia — Smith 1 run (Stoyanovich kick)

Philadelphia 10, Minnesota 9—at Veterans Stadium, attendance 65,944. Randall Cunningham found Cris Carter with a three-yard scoring pass with 2:32 remaining in the game as the Eagles came back to beat the Vikings. Minnesota's Herschel Walker returned the opening kickoff 93 yards for a score, but Rich Karlis missed the extra point. Karlis kicked a 49-yard field goal in the third quarter to give the Vikings a 9-3 lead.

Minnesota	6	0	3	0	— 9
Philadelphia	3	0	0	7	— 10

Minn — Walker 93 kickoff return (kick failed)
Phil — FG DeLine 34
Minn — FG Karlis 49
Phil — Carter 3 pass from Cunningham (DeLine kick)

New Orleans 26, Atlanta 17—at Atlanta Fulton County Stadium, attendance 53,173. Dalton Hilliard ran for a career-high 158 yards and one touchdown as the Saints handed the Falcons their first loss at home this season. Hilliard ran 22 yards for a touchdown and Brian Forde blocked a punt out of the end zone for a safety to put New Orleans ahead 12-10 in the third quarter. Buford Jordan scored on a pair of runs (two and one yard) in the fourth quarter to put the game away. Pat Swilling accounted for three-and-a-half sacks and was named NFC Defensive Player of the Week.

New Orleans	3	0	9	14	— 26
Atlanta	3	7	7	0	— 17

Atl — FG Davis 45
NO — FG Andersen 33
Atl — Settle 27 pass from Miller (Davis kick)
NO — Hilliard 22 run (Andersen kick)
NO — Safety, Forde blocked punt out of end zone

Atl —Wilkins 19 pass from Miller (Davis kick)
NO —Jordan 2 run (Andersen kick)
NO —Jordan 1 run (Andersen kick)

Los Angeles Rams 37, Phoenix 14—at Anaheim Stadium, attendance 53,176. Jim Everett connected with Henry Ellard for two touchdown passes to help the Rams overtake the Cardinals. Everett, who completed 15 of 24 passes for 308 yards, hit Ellard on scoring strikes of 49 and 42 yards. Mike Lansford kicked three field goals (27, 23, and 40 yards) for Los Angeles. The Rams opened the scoring on Michael Stewart's 41-yard interception return for a score en route to a 24-0 halftime advantage. Los Angeles' defense registered five sacks.

Phoenix	0	0	7	7	— 14
L.A. Rams	14	10	3	10	— 37

Rams —Stewart 41 interception return (Lansford kick)
Rams —Ellard 49 pass from Everett (Lansford kick)
Rams —Delpino 32 run (Lansford kick)
Rams —FG Lansford 27
Rams —FG Lansford 23
Phx —Holmes 77 pass from Tupa (Del Greco kick)
Rams —FG Lansford 40
Rams —Ellard 42 pass from Everett (Lansford kick)
Phx —Jordan 1 run (Del Greco kick)

Pittsburgh 20, San Diego 17—at Three Rivers Stadium, attendance 44,203. Bubby Brister led Pittsburgh on a 91-yard drive capped by Merril Hoge's one-yard scoring run with 6:17 to play as the Steelers defeated the Chargers. Jim McMahon's touchdown passes to Anthony Miller (20 and 19 yards), and Chris Bahr's 27-yard field goal gave San Diego a 17-13 third-quarter lead. Pittsburgh's special teams also contributed to the victory as Gary Anderson kicked field goals of 49 and 28 yards and Rod Woodson returned a kickoff 84 yards for a score.

San Diego	0	7	10	0	— 17
Pittsburgh	3	3	7	7	— 20

Pitt —FG Anderson 49
SD —A. Miller 20 pass from McMahon (Bahr kick)
Pitt —FG Anderson 28
SD —FG Bahr 27
Pitt —Woodson 84 kickoff return (Anderson kick)
SD —A. Miller 19 pass from McMahon (Bahr kick)
Pitt —Hoge 1 run (Anderson kick)

New York Giants 15, Seattle 3—at Giants Stadium, attendance 75,014. Phil Simms connected with Howard Cross on a 16-yard touchdown pass on the game's opening series and Bjorn Nittmo kicked two field goals as the Giants handed the Seahawks their third consecutive loss. New York extended its 7-0 halftime lead in the third quarter to 15-0 on Nittmo's pair of 32-yard field goals and a safety by Leonard Marshall. Norm Johnson's 42-yard field goal in the fourth quarter prevented the shutout.

Seattle	0	0	0	3	— 3
N.Y. Giants	7	0	8	0	— 15

NYG —Cross 16 pass from Simms (Nittmo kick)
NYG —FG Nittmo 32
NYG —Safety, Stouffer fumbled ball out of end zone
NYG —FG Nittmo 32
Sea —FG Johnson 42

Tampa Bay 32, Chicago 31—at Soldier Field, attendance 63,826. Donald Igwebuike kicked four field goals, including a 28-yarder as time expired, to lift the Buccaneers over the Bears. Leading 10-3 at halftime, Tampa Bay extended its advantage to 29-17 on Igwebuike's two field goals (22 and 29 yards), Lars Tate's 15-yard touchdown run, and Vinny Testaverde's 78-yard touchdown bomb to Mark Carrier. Chicago went ahead 30-29 on two Mike Tomczak scoring passes, just 50 seconds apart, to Wendell Davis (26 and 52 yards) in the fourth quarter. Tampa Bay also defeated Chicago 42-35 on October 8 to give the team its first-ever season sweep of the Bears.

Tampa Bay	10	0	3	19	— 32
Chicago	0	3	7	21	— 31

TB —FG Igwebuike 26
TB —Davis 13 interception return (Igwebuike kick)
Chi —FG Butler 40
TB —FG Igwebuike 22
Chi —Anderson 59 run (Butler kick)
TB —Tate 15 run (Igwebuike kick)
TB —FG Igwebuike 29
Chi —Morris 58 pass from Tomczak (Butler kick)
TB —Carrier 78 pass from Testaverde (kick failed)
Chi —Davis 26 pass from Tomczak (Butler kick)
Chi —Davis 52 pass from Tomczak (Butler kick)
TB —FG Igwebuike 28

Indianapolis 27, New York Jets 10—at Hoosier Dome, attendance 58,236. Eric Dickerson carried 31 times for 131 yards and a touchdown to lead the Colts over the Jets. Indianapolis took a 20-3 halftime advantage on a one-yard scoring run by Albert Bentley, Dean Biasucci's 45- and 31-yard field goals, and Jack Trudeau's one-yard pass to Pat Beach. Dickerson added a one-yard scoring run in the third quarter to put the game away.

N.Y. Jets	0	3	0	7	— 10
Indianapolis	3	17	7	0	— 27

Ind —FG Biasucci 45
Ind —Bentley 1 run (Biasucci kick)
NYJ —FG Leahy 46
Ind —Beach 1 pass from Trudeau (Biasucci kick)
Ind —FG Biasucci 31
Ind —Dickerson 1 run (Biasucci kick)
NYJ —Townsell 23 pass from Ryan (Leahy kick)

Monday, November 20

Denver 14, Washington 10—at R.F.K. Stadium, attendance 52,975. Gary Kubiak, starting for John Elway, who was sidelined with a virus, threw two touchdown passes to lead the Broncos over the Redskins. Denver tied the game 7-7 in the first quarter when Kubiak connected with Melvin Bratton for a one-yard scoring pass. Kubiak then hit Ricky Nattiel with a five-yard scoring pass in the second quarter to give Denver a 14-7 lead. Chip Lohmiller kicked a 32-yard field goal in the third quarter to cut the Broncos lead to 14-10, but the Redskins could get no closer. Denver rookie running back Bobby Humphrey carried 31 times for 110 yards, his third 100-yard game of the season.

Denver	7	7	0	0	— 14
Washington	7	0	3	0	— 10

Wash —Morris 8 run (Lohmiller kick)
Den —Bratton 1 pass from Kubiak (Treadwell kick)
Den —Nattiel 5 pass from Kubiak (Treadwell kick)
Wash —FG Lohmiller 32

Twelfth Week Summaries

Standings

American Football Conference

Eastern Division	W	L	T	Pct.	Pts.	OP
Buffalo	8	4	0	.667	327	257
Miami	7	5	0	.583	242	274
Indianapolis	6	6	0	.500	211	208
New England	4	8	0	.333	235	292
N.Y. Jets	3	9	0	.250	219	306
Central Division						
Cleveland	7	4	1	.625	270	173
Houston	7	5	0	.583	295	294
Cincinnati	6	6	0	.500	284	225
Pittsburgh	6	6	0	.500	177	271
Western Division						
Denver*	10	2	0	.833	289	177
L.A. Raiders	6	6	0	.500	249	213
Kansas City	5	6	1	.458	231	218
San Diego	4	8	0	.333	189	215
Seattle	4	8	0	.333	177	248

National Football Conference

Eastern Division	W	L	T	Pct.	Pts.	OP
N.Y. Giants	9	3	0	.750	268	204
Philadelphia	8	4	0	.667	247	203
Washington	6	6	0	.500	271	247
Phoenix	5	7	0	.417	220	264
Dallas	1	11	0	.083	153	303
Central Division						
Green Bay	7	5	0	.583	282	281
Minnesota	7	5	0	.583	235	198
Chicago	6	6	0	.500	297	257
Tampa Bay	5	7	0	.417	258	318
Detroit	3	9	0	.250	200	302
Western Division						
San Francisco	10	2	0	.833	342	206
L.A. Rams	8	4	0	.667	302	249
New Orleans	6	6	0	.500	279	235
Atlanta	3	9	0	.250	198	309

**Clinched Division Title*

Thursday, November 23

Detroit 13, Cleveland 10—at Pontiac Silverdome, attendance 65,624. Barry Sanders carried 28 times for 145 yards to help the Lions record a Thanksgiving Day victory over the Browns. Detroit tied Cleveland 10-10 at halftime on Eddie Murray's 39-yard field goal and Bob Gagliano's 27-yard scoring pass to Richard Johnson. Murray's 35-yard field goal in the third quarter proved decisive. Sanders raised his season rushing total to 1,016 yards to become the first Lions player since Billy Sims (1,040 in 1983) to rush for more than 1,000 yards.

Cleveland	0	10	0	0	— 10
Detroit	0	10	3	0	— 13

Det —FG Murray 39
Clev —FG Bahr 35
Det —Johnson 27 pass from Gagliano (Murray kick)
Clev —Redden 38 run (Bahr kick)
Det —FG Murray 35

Philadelphia 27, Dallas 0—at Texas Stadium, attendance 54,444. Randall Cunningham and Cris Carter combined for two touchdowns as the Eagles blanked the Cowboys. Philadelphia took a 10-0 halftime advantage on Cunningham's six-yard scoring pass to Carter and Roger Ruzek's 36-yard field goal. The Eagles put the game out of reach in the third quarter as Cunningham found Carter on an 18-yard touchdown pass and Keith Byars ran one yard for a score. Ruzek, who played with Dallas earlier in the season, added a 38-yard field goal in the fourth quarter to complete Philadelphia's scoring.

Philadelphia	0	10	14	3	— 27
Dallas	0	0	0	0	— 0

Phil —Carter 6 pass from Cunningham (Ruzek kick)
Phil —FG Ruzek 36
Phil —Carter 18 pass from Cunningham (Ruzek kick)
Phil —Byars 1 run (Ruzek kick)
Phil —FG Ruzek 38

Sunday, November 26

New York Jets 27, Atlanta 7—at Giants Stadium, attendance 40,429. Johnny Hector ran for two touchdowns to help the Jets defeat the Falcons for their first home victory of the season. New York took a 17-0 halftime lead on Pat Leahy's 28-yard field goal, Hector's first of two one-yard scoring runs, and Al Toon's 12-yard touchdown pass from Ken O'Brien.

Atlanta	0	0	7	0	— 7
N.Y. Jets	3	14	10	0	— 27

NYJ —FG Leahy 28
NYJ —Hector 1 run (Leahy kick)
NYJ —Toon 12 pass from O'Brien (Leahy kick)
NYJ —FG Leahy 46
Atl —Wilkins 16 pass from Miller (Davis kick)
NYJ —Hector 1 run (Leahy kick)

Washington 38, Chicago 14—at R.F.K. Stadium, attendance 50,044. Mark Rypien threw for a career-high 401 yards and four touchdowns as the Redskins overcame the Bears. Washington jumped to a 14-0 second-quarter lead on Rypien's scoring passes to Don Warren (three yards) and Gary Clark (five). Chicago came back to tie the score 14-14 at halftime on Thomas Sanders's 96-yard kickoff return for a touchdown and Mike Tomczak's 12-yard scoring pass to Dennis McKinnon. The Redskins put the game away in the second half on Rypien's two touchdown passes to Art Monk (18 and nine yards), Chip Lohmiller's 28-yard field goal, and Earnest Byner's four-yard run.

Chicago	0	14	0	0	— 14
Washington	0	14	10	14	— 38

Wash —Warren 3 pass from Rypien (Lohmiller kick)
Wash —Clark 5 pass from Rypien (Lohmiller kick)
Chi —T. Sanders 96 kickoff return (Butler kick)
Chi —McKinnon 12 pass from Tomczak (Butler kick)
Wash —FG Lohmiller 28
Wash —Monk 18 pass from Rypien (Lohmiller kick)
Wash —Monk 9 pass from Rypien (Lohmiller kick)
Wash —Byner 4 run (Lohmiller kick)

Buffalo 24, Cincinnati 7—at Rich Stadium, attendance 80,074. Jim Kelly completed touchdown passes to three different receivers as the Bills defeated the Bengals. Buffalo jumped to a 10-0 halftime lead on Scott Norwood's 24-yard field goal and Kelly's 19-yard touchdown pass to Andre Reed. Kelly then threw scoring passes in the second half to Ronnie Harmon (42 yards) and Butch Rolle (one) to finish the Bills' scoring. Bills running back Thurman Thomas (26 carries for 100 yards) and Bengals running back James Brooks (20 for 105) each went over the 1,000-yard rushing mark for the season.

Cincinnati	0	0	7	0	— 7
Buffalo	3	7	7	7	— 24

Buff —FG Norwood 24
Buff —Reed 19 pass from Kelly (Norwood)
Buff —Harmon 42 pass from Kelly (Norwood kick)
Cin —Jennings 5 run (Breech kick)
Buff —Rolle 1 pass from Kelly (Norwood kick)

Kansas City 34, Houston 0—at Arrowhead Stadium, attendance 51,342. James Saxon and Christian Okoye each ran for touchdowns as the Chiefs shut out the Oilers. Kansas City took a commanding 20-0 halftime lead on Nick Lowery's pair of field goals (31 and 34 yards), Saxon's scored on a one-yard run, and Jayice Pearson's one-yard blocked punt return for a touchdown. Steve DeBerg threw a seven-yard touchdown pass to Jonathan Hayes and Okoye ran 17 yards for a score in the second half to complete the Chief's scoring. Okoye became the first Kansas City player since Joe Delaney in 1981 to rush for more than 1,000 yards in a season (1,043).

Houston	0	0	0	0	— 0
Kansas City	10	10	7	7	— 34

KC —FG Lowery 31
KC —Saxon 4 run (Lowery kick)
KC —FG Lowery 34
KC —Pearson 1 blocked punt return (Lowery kick)
KC —Hayes 7 pass from DeBerg (Lowery)
KC —Okoye 17 run (Lowery kick)

Green Bay 20, Minnesota 19—at Milwaukee County Stadium, attendance 55,592. Don Majkowski threw two touchdown passes to Sterling Sharpe as the Packers edged the Vikings to gain a share of first place with Minnesota in the NFC Central. Green Bay led 10-6 at halftime on Chris Jacke's 36-yard field goal and Majkowski's 34-yard scoring pass to Sharpe. Minnesota came back to take the lead 16-13 in the third quarter on Rich Karlis's third field goal of the game and Herschel Walker's six-yard run. But Majkowski's 9-yard scoring pass to Sharpe put the game away. Sharpe finished the day with 10 receptions for 157 yards.

Minnesota	3	3	10	3	— 19
Green Bay	3	7	3	7	— 20

GB —FG Jacke 36
Minn —FG Karlis 19
GB —Sharpe 34 pass from Majkowski (Jacke kick)
Minn —FG Karlis 34
Minn —FG Karlis 27
Minn —Walker 6 run (Karlis kick)
GB —FG Jacke 42

GB —Sharpe 9 pass from Majkowski (Jacke kick)
Minn —FG Karlis 19

Los Angeles Raiders 24, New England 21—at Memorial Coliseum, attendance 38,747. Jeff Jaeger's 32-yard field goal with 5:57 remaining in the game lifted the Raiders over the Patriots. Steve Beuerlein threw touchdown passes to Mike Alexander (12 yards) and Mervyn Fernandez (13) to help Los Angeles to a 14-14 tie at halftime. Steve Smith then ran 11 yards for a touchdown to put Los Angeles ahead 21-14, but Steve Grogan fired a 34-yard scoring pass to Hart Lee Dykes to re-tie the game 21-21. Beuerlein led the Raiders on a 53-yard, 13-play march to set up Jaeger's game-winning field goal.

New England	0	14	7	0	— 21
L.A. Raiders	7	7	7	3	— 24

Raiders —Alexander 12 pass Beuerlein (Jaeger kick)
NE —C. Jones 1 pass from Grogan (Staurovsky kick)
NE —Fryar 49 pass from Grogan (Staurovsky kick)
Raiders —Fernandez 13 pass from Beuerlein (Jaeger kick)
Raiders —Smith 11 run (Jaeger kick)
NE —Dykes 34 pass from Grogan (Staurovsky kick)
Raiders —FG Jaeger 32

Pittsburgh 34, Miami 14—at Joe Robbie Stadium, attendance 59,936. Merril Hoge ran for three scores to lead Pittsburgh past Miami. The game was played in a torrential downpour. The Dolphins jumped to a 14-0 first-quarter lead, but the Steelers turned three turnovers into points on Hoge's one-yard run, Dwayne Woodruff's 21-yard fumble recovery return for a touchdown, and Gary Anderson's 27-yard field goal. Hoge added scoring runs of five and one yards in the third quarter.

Pittsburgh	0	17	17	0	— 34
Miami	14	0	0	0	— 14

Mia —Smith 1 run (Stoyanovich kick)
Mia —Clayton 66 pass from Marino (Stoyanovich kick)
Pitt —Hoge 1 run (Anderson kick)
Pitt —Woodruff 21 run with lateral after Lake 2 fumble recovery return (Anderson kick)
Pitt —FG Anderson 27
Pitt —Hoge 5 run (Anderson kick)
Pitt —FG Anderson 42
Pitt —Hoge 1 run (Anderson kick)

Indianapolis 10, San Diego 6—at Hoosier Dome, attendance 58,822. Jack Trudeau hit Bill Brooks on a 25-yard touchdown pass with 1:54 remaining in the game as the Colts defeated the Chargers. San Diego's Chris Bahr (33 yards) and Indianapolis' Dean Biasucci (22) traded field goals for a 3-3 halftime deadlock. Bahr then connected on a 38-yard field goal to put San Diego ahead 6-3 late in the fourth quarter before Trudeau threw the game-winning pass to Brooks.

San Diego	0	3	0	3	— 6
Indianapolis	0	3	0	7	— 10

SD —FG Bahr 33
Ind —FG Biasucci 22
SD —FG Bahr 38
Ind —Brooks 25 pass from Trudeau (Biasucci kick)

Denver 41, Seattle 14—at Mile High Stadium, attendance 75,117. John Elway threw four touchdown passes as the Broncos downed the Seahawks to clinch their fourth division title of the 1980s. Denver jumped to a commanding 38-0 halftime lead on Elway's scoring passes to Vance Johnson (four and 10 yards), Steve Sewell (32), and Michael Young (nine), Bobby Humphrey's four-yard run, and David Treadwell's 30-yard field goal. Steve Largent's 31-yard scoring reception lifted his career touchdown total to 99, tying Don Hutson's NFL record. Johnson finished the day with six receptions for 154 yards and was named AFC Offensive Player of the Week.

Seattle	0	0	7	7	— 14
Denver	14	24	0	3	— 41

Den —Johnson 4 pass from Elway (Treadwell kick)
Den —Humphrey 4 run (Treadwell kick)
Den —FG Treadwell 30
Den —Johnson 10 pass from Elway (Treadwell kick)
Den —Sewell 32 pass from Elway (Treadwell kick)
Den —Young 9 pass from Elway (Treadwell kick)
Sea —Fenner 5 run (N. Johnson kick)
Den —FG Treadwell 45
Sea —Largent 31 pass from Krieg (N. Johnson kick)

Tampa Bay 14, Phoenix 13—at Sun Devil Stadium, attendance 33,297. Vinny Testaverde threw a five-yard touchdown pass to Mark Carrier with five seconds remaining as the Buccaneers downed the Cardinals. Tampa Bay opened the scoring in the second quarter on Testaverde's five-yard scoring pass to Bruce Hill. Phoenix then scored 13 unanswered points on Earl Ferrell's one-yard touchdown run and a pair of Al Del Greco field goals (21 and 28 yards). Testaverde's game-winning pass capped a 14-play, 82-yard drive.

Tampa Bay	0	7	0	7	— 14
Phoenix	0	10	3	0	— 13

TB —Hill 5 pass from Testaverde (Igwebuike kick)
Phx —Ferrell 1 run (Del Greco kick)
Phx —FG Del Greco 21
Phx —FG Del Greco 28
TB —Carrier 5 pass from Testaverde (Igwebuike kick)

Los Angeles Rams 20, New Orleans 17—at Louisiana Superdome, attendance 64,274. Willie Anderson caught 15 passes for an NFL-record 336 yards as the Rams defeated the Saints in overtime. Trailing New Orleans 17-3 in the fourth quarter, the Rams sent the game into overtime when Buford McGee ran five yards for a touchdown and Jim Everett connected with Anderson on a 15-yard touchdown pass. Mike Lansford's 31-yard field goal 6:36 into overtime gave Los Angeles the win. Anderson, who broke Kansas City wide receiver Stephone Paige's 1985 record of 309 receiving yards, was named NFC Offensive Player of the Week.

L.A. Rams	0	3	0	14	3	— 20
New Orleans	7	3	7	0	0	— 17

NO —Martin 19 pass from Hebert (Andersen kick)
NO —FG Andersen 36
Rams —FG Lansford 32
NO —Martin 35 pass from Hebert (Andersen kick)
Rams —McGee 5 run (Lansford kick)
Rams —Anderson 15 pass from Everett (Andersen kick)
Rams —FG Lansford 31

Monday, November 27

San Francisco 34, New York Giants 24—at Candlestick Park, attendance 63,471. Joe Montana completed three touchdown passes, including two to Jerry Rice, as the 49ers downed the Giants to remain atop the NFC West. Montana broke a 7-7 tie in the first quarter with a four-yard touchdown pass to Rice. San Francisco took a commanding 24-10 halftime lead on Montana's 17-yard scoring pass to Brent Jones and Mike Cofer's 44-yard field goal. New York battled back and tied the game 24-24 on Phil Simms's scoring passes to David Meggett (53 yards) and Odessa Turner (seven). But Cofer's 45-yard field goal in the fourth quarter broke the tie and Tom Rathman's one-yard touchdown run with 1:08 remaining sealed the victory.

N.Y. Giants	7	3	7	7	— 24
San Francisco	14	10	0	10	— 34

SF —Taylor 4 pass from Montana (Cofer kick)
NYG —Anderson 2 run (Nittmo kick)
SF —Rice 4 pass from Montana (Cofer kick)
SF —FG Cofer 44
SF —Jones 17 pass from Montana (Cofer kick)
NYG —FG Nittmo 39
NYG —Meggett 53 pass from Simms (Nittmo kick)
NYG —Turner 7 pass from Simms (Nittmo kick)
SF —FG Cofer 45
SF —Rathman 1 run (Cofer kick)

Thirteenth Week Summaries

Standings

American Football Conference

Eastern Division	W	L	T	Pct.	Pts.	OP
Buffalo	8	5	0	.615	343	274
Miami	7	6	0	.538	263	300
Indianapolis	6	7	0	.462	227	230
New England	5	8	0	.385	257	308
N.Y. Jets	4	9	0	.308	239	323
Central Division						
Houston	8	5	0	.615	318	310
Cleveland	7	5	1	.577	270	194
Cincinnati	7	6	0	.538	305	225
Pittsburgh	6	7	0	.462	193	294
Western Division						
Denver*	10	3	0	.769	302	193
L.A. Raiders	7	6	0	.538	265	226
Kansas City	6	6	1	.500	257	239
Seattle	5	8	0	.385	194	264
San Diego	4	9	0	.308	206	235

National Football Conference

Eastern Division	W	L	T	Pct.	Pts.	OP
N.Y. Giants	9	4	0	.692	285	228
Philadelphia	9	4	0	.692	271	220
Washington	7	6	0	.538	300	257
Phoenix	5	8	0	.385	230	293
Dallas	1	12	0	.077	184	338
Central Division						
Green Bay	8	5	0	.615	299	297
Minnesota	8	5	0	.615	262	214
Chicago	6	7	0	.462	313	284
Tampa Bay	5	8	0	.385	274	335
Detroit	4	9	0	.308	221	316
Western Division						
San Francisco	11	2	0	.846	365	216
L.A. Rams	9	4	0	.692	337	280
New Orleans	6	7	0	.462	293	256
Atlanta	3	10	0	.231	208	332

**Clinched Division Title*

Sunday, December 3

Cincinnati 21, Cleveland 0—at Cleveland Stadium, attendance 76,236. Boomer Esiason threw two touchdown passes as the Bengals blanked the Browns. James Brooks gave Cincinnati a 7-0 halftime lead on a one-yard touchdown run early in the second quarter. The Bengals put the game away in the third quarter on Esiason's scoring passes to Tim McGee (38 yards) and Rodney Holman (nine). Leon White's interception set up McGee's touchdown and Carl Zander's fumble recovery set up Holman's score. The Browns had not been shut out at home since November 17, 1977, when they fell to the Raiders 7-0.

Cincinnati	0	7	14	0	— 21
Cleveland	0	0	0	0	— 0

Cin —Brooks 1 run (Breech kick)
Cin —McGee 38 pass from Esiason (Breech kick)
Cin —Holman 9 pass from Esiason (Breech kick)

Los Angeles Raiders 16, Denver 13—at Memorial Coliseum, attendance 87,560. Jeff Jaeger kicked a 26-yard field goal 7:02 into overtime to lift the Raiders over the Broncos. With the Raiders trailing 13-6, Steve Beuerlein threw a 67-yard scoring pass to Mike Dyal midway through the fourth quarter to send the game into overtime. Los Angeles moved from their 29-yard line to Denver's nine-yard line to set up Jaeger's winning kick.

Denver	0	10	0	3	0	— 13
L.A. Raiders	3	0	3	7	3	— 16

Raiders —FG Jaeger 37
Den —FG Treadwell 34
Den —Bratton 5 run (Treadwell kick)
Raiders —FG Jaeger 46
Den —FG Treadwell 35
Raiders —Dyal 67 pass from Beuerlein (Jaeger kick)
Raiders —FG Jaeger 26

Green Bay 17, Tampa Bay 16—at Tampa Stadium, attendance 58,120. Chris Jacke's 47-yard field goal as time expired gave the Packers a 17-16 victory over the Buccaneers. Green Bay took a 14-13 fourth quarter lead on two scoring passes to Sterling Sharpe (21 and 55 yards). Donald Igwebuike's 36-yard field goal with 1:35 remaining put Tampa Bay ahead 16-14. Jacke's game-winning kick capped a 12-play, 52-yard drive. Sharpe finished with eight receptions for 169 yards. The win moved the Packers into a first-place tie with Minnesota in the NFC Central.

Green Bay	7	0	0	10	— 17
Tampa Bay	0	3	3	10	— 16

GB —Sharpe 21 pass from Majkowski (Jacke kick)
TB —FG Igwebuike 49
TB —FG Igwebuike 40
TB —Stamps 21 run (Igwebuike kick)
GB —Sharpe 55 pass from Majkowski (Bracken kick)
TB —FG Igwebuike 36
GB —FG Jacke 47

Houston 23, Pittsburgh 16—at Three Rivers Stadium, attendance 40,541. Lorenzo White's one-yard touchdown run with 21 seconds remaining gave the Oilers a 23-16 win over the Steelers and moved them into first place in the AFC Central. Houston led 14-10 at halftime on Warren Moon's scoring passes to Curtis Duncan (18 yards) and Drew Hill (27). Pittsburgh kicker Gary Anderson kicked two second half-field goals to tie the game 16-16, but Moon completed a 37-yard pass to Haywood Jeffires to set up White's winning touchdown.

Houston	0	14	2	7	— 23
Pittsburgh	3	7	3	3	— 16

Pitt —FG Anderson 18
Pitt —Hoge 4 run (Anderson kick)
Hou —Duncan 18 pass from Moon (Zendejas kick)
Hou —Hill 27 pass from Moon (Zendejas kick)
Pitt —FG Anderson 37
Hou —Safety, McDowell tackled Newsome in end zone
Pitt —FG Anderson 18
Hou —White 1 run (Zendejas kick)

New England 22, Indianapolis 16—at Sullivan Stadium, attendance 32,234. John Stephens rushed for 124 yards, including a 10-yard touchdown run with 25 seconds remaining as the Patriots outlasted the Colts. Indianapolis took a 16-15 fourth-quarter lead on Jack Trudeau's eight-year scoring pass to Eric Dickerson, but the Patriots came right back and won the game on Stephens's decisive run. Dickerson's 80 yards rushing put him over the 1,000-yard mark (1,013) for an NFL-record seventh straight season. Jason Staurovsky kicked five field goals (44, 37, 24, 50, and 23 yards) for New England, and his seven attempts tied the club record set by Gino Cappelletti in 1969.

Indianapolis	0	3	7	6	— 16
New England	6	0	3	13	— 22

NE —FG Staurovsky 44
NE —FG Staurovsky 37
Ind —FG Biasucci 18
NE —FG Staurovsky 24
Ind —Benson 9 pass from Trudeau (Biasucci kick)
NE —FG Staurovsky 50
NE —FG Staurovsky 23
Ind —Dickerson 8 pass from Trudeau (kick failed)
NE —Stephens 10 run (Staurovsky kick)

Los Angeles Rams 35, Dallas 31—at Texas Stadium, attendance 46,100. Jim Everett completed four touchdown passes, including two to Aaron Cox, as the Rams rallied to defeat the Cowboys. After the Rams led 14-10 at halftime, Dallas took a 31-21 lead midway through the fourth quarter on Troy Aikman's scoring passes to James Dixon (35 yards), Steve Folsom (five), and Bernard Ford (10). Everett then hit Ron Brown with a 35-yard touchdown pass and completed a 23-yarder to Cox for the game-winning touchdown.

L.A. Rams	14	0	7	14	—	35
Dallas	0	10	7	14	—	31

Rams —Johnson 1 pass from Everett (Lansford kick)
Rams —Bell 1 run (Lansford kick)
Dall —Johnston 9 pass from Aikman (Zendejas kick)
Dall —FG Zendejas 47
Rams —Cox 18 pass from Everett (Lansford kick)
Dall —Dixon 35 pass from Aikman (Zendejas kick)
Dall —Folsom 5 pass from Aikman (Zendejas kick)
Dall —Ford 10 pass from Aikman (Zendejas kick)
Rams —Brown 35 pass from Everett (Lansford kick)
Rams —Cox 23 pass from Everett (Lansford kick)

Kansas City 26, Miami 21—at Arrowhead Stadium, attendance 54,610. Christian Okoye and Stephone Paige combined for 281 yards as the Chiefs defeated the Dolphins. Kansas City took a 16-0 halftime lead on Okoye's three-yard run, Steve DeBerg's 38-yard scoring pass to Paige, and Nick Lowery's 34-yard field goal. Miami's Dan Marino threw three touchdown passes in the second half, but DeBerg's eight-yard scoring pass to Herman Heard put the game out of reach. Okoye's 148-yard rushing effort gave him 1,191 yards for the season, breaking the Chiefs' single-season rushing record of 1,121, set by Joe Delaney in 1981.

Miami	0	0	7	14	—	21
Kansas City	13	3	3	7	—	26

KC —Okoye 3 run (kick failed)
KC —Paige 38 pass from DeBerg (Lowery kick)
KC —FG Lowery 34
Mia —Jensen 8 pass from Marino (Stoyanovich kick)
KC —FG Lowery 28
Mia —Clayton 15 pass from Marino (Stoyanovich kick)
KC —Heard 8 pass from DeBerg (Lowery kick)
Mia —Jensen 9 pass from Marino (Stoyanovich kick)

Detroit 21, New Orleans 14—at Pontiac Silverdome, attendance 38,550. Richard Johnson caught eight passes for a career-high 248 yards to help the Lions down the Saints. The teams played to a 14-14 halftime tie as Detroit's Rodney Peete and Barry Sanders scored on six- and three-yard runs, respectively, and New Orleans' Dalton Hilliard ran one yard for a score and Bobby Morse returned a kickoff 99 yards for a touchdown. Bob Gagliano came off the bench in the third quarter to replace an injured Peete and connected with Johnson on the 75-yard game-winning pass.

New Orleans	0	14	0	0	—	14
Detroit	7	7	7	0	—	21

Det —Peete 6 run (Murray kick)
NO —Hilliard 1 run (Andersen kick)
Det —Sanders 3 run (Murray kick)
NO —Morse 99 kickoff return (Andersen kick)
Det —Johnson 75 pass from Gagliano (Murray kick)

New York Jets 20, San Diego 17—at San Diego Jack Murphy Stadium, attendance 38,954. Roger Vick ran for two touchdowns in the fourth quarter to lead the Jets over the Chargers. New York jumped to a 7-0 first-quarter lead on Ken O'Brien's nine-yard scoring pass to Johnny Hector. San Diego took a 10-7 advantage on Marion Butts's 40-yard run and Chris Bahr's 39-yard field goal. Vick had a one-yard scoring run midway through the fourth quarter and, less than two minutes later, added a 14-yard dash for the decisive touchdown.

N.Y. Jets	7	0	0	13	—	20
San Diego	0	7	3	7	—	17

NYJ —Hector 9 pass from O'Brien (Leahy kick)
SD —Butts 40 run (Bahr kick)
SD —FG Bahr 39
NYJ —Vick 1 run (Leahy kick)
NYJ —Vick 14 run (kick failed)
SD —A. Miller 8 pass from Tolliver (Bahr kick)

Philadelphia 24, New York Giants 17—at Giants Stadium, attendance 74,809. Philadelphia's defense converted three takeaways into points as the Eagles defeated New York to move into a first-place tie with the Giants in the NFC East. Philadelphia took a 14-0 lead in the first 10 minutes of the game on Andre Waters's three-yard fumble recovery return for a touchdown and Clyde Simmons's 60-yard interception return for a score. Roger Ruzek kicked a 35-yard field goal to give the Eagles a 17-7 halftime lead. The Giants tied the game in the third quarter 17-17 on Bjorn Nittmo's 38-yard field goal and Ottis Anderson's one-yard run, but Keith Byars's two-yard touchdown run in the fourth quarter proved decisive.

Philadelphia	14	3	0	7	—	24
N.Y. Giants	7	0	10	0	—	17

Phil —Waters 3 fumble recovery return (Ruzek kick)
Phil —Simmons 60 interception return (Ruzek kick)
NYG —Ingram 41 pass from Simms (Nittmo kick)
Phil —FG Ruzek 35
NYG —FG Nittmo 38
NYG —Anderson 1 run (Nittmo kick)
Phil —Byars 2 run (Ruzek kick)

San Francisco 23, Atlanta 10—at Atlanta-Fulton County Stadium, attendance 43,128. Steve Young accounted for two second-half touchdowns as the 49ers handed the Falcons their second home loss of the season. Young, who replaced the injured Joe Montana at the end of the first half for San Francisco, connected with John Taylor on a 38-yard scoring pass and ran one yard for a touchdown to put the 49ers ahead 20-10 in the fourth quarter. Mike Cofer kicked three field goals (35, 23, and 27 yards) for San Francisco, while Taylor had five receptions for 162 yards.

San Francisco	6	0	7	10	—	23
Atlanta	0	10	0	0	—	10

SF —FG Cofer 35
SF —FG Cofer 23
Atl —FG Davis 46
Atl —Heller 28 pass from Miller (Davis kick)
SF —Taylor 38 pass from Young (Cofer kick)
SF —Young 1 run (Cofer kick)
SF —FG Cofer 27

Washington 29, Phoenix 10—at Sun Devil Stadium, attendance 38,870. Gerald Riggs and Earnest Byner each scored on one-yard runs as the Redskins defeated the Cardinals. Riggs's one-yard scoring run in the third quarter broke a 10-10 halftime tie. Washington increased its lead in the second half to 29-10 on A.J. Johnson's 59-yard interception return for a score, Chip Lohmiller's 24-yard field goal, and a safety. Johnson also recorded two interceptions and was named NFC Defensive Player of the Week.

Washington	3	7	14	5	—	29
Phoenix	0	10	0	0	—	10

Wash —FG Lohmiller 29
Wash —Byner 1 run (Lohmiller kick)
Phx —FG Del Greco 27
Phx —Ferrell 1 run (Del Greco kick)
Wash —Riggs 1 run (Lohmiller kick)
Wash —Johnson 59 interception return (Lohmiller kick)
Wash —FG Lohmiller 24
Wash —Safety, Tupa intentional grounding penalty in end zone

Minnesota 27, Chicago 16—at Metrodome, attendance 60,664. Wade Wilson completed two scoring passes to help the Vikings past the Bears and into a first-place tie with Green Bay for the NFC Central lead. Minnesota jumped to a 17-3 halftime lead on Herschel Walker's one-yard touchdown run. Wilson's 46-yard touchdown pass to Hassan Jones, and Rich Karlis's 51-yard field goal. Wilson also threw a 24-yard touchdown pass to Anthony Carter in the second half and Karlis added a 45-yard field goal to put the game away.

Chicago	3	0	7	6	—	16
Minnesota	7	10	7	3	—	27

Chi —FG Butler 33
Minn —Walker 1 run (Karlis kick)
Minn —Jones 46 pass from Wilson (Karlis kick)
Minn —FG Karlis 51
Chi —Boso 3 pass from Tomczak (Butler kick)
Minn —Carter 24 pass from Wilson (Karlis kick)
Chi —Suhey 1 run (kick blocked)
Minn —FG Karlis 45

Monday, December 4

Seattle 17, Buffalo 16—at Kingdome, attendance 57,682. Dave Krieg threw a 51-yard scoring pass to John L. Williams in the fourth quarter as the Seahawks rallied to defeat the Bills and break a four-game losing streak. With the score tied 10-10 at halftime, Buffalo kicker Scott Norwood kicked two field goals (40 and 43 yards) to put the Bills ahead 16-10 in the third quarter. Krieg's 298 yards passing moved him past the 20,000-yard career mark (20,117).

Buffalo	0	10	6	0	—	16
Seattle	10	0	0	7	—	17

Sea —FG N. Johnson 29
Sea —Warner 1 run (Largent run)
Buff —Reed 61 pass from Kelly (Norwood kick)
Buff —FG Norwood 32
Buff —FG Norwood 40
Buff —FG Norwood 43
Sea —Williams 51 pass from Krieg (N. Johnson kick)

Fourteenth Week Summaries

Standings

American Football Conference

Eastern Division

	W	L	T	Pct.	Pts.	OP
Buffalo	8	6	0	.571	362	296
Miami	8	6	0	.571	294	310
Indianapolis	7	7	0	.500	250	247
New England	5	9	0	.357	267	339
N.Y. Jets	4	10	0	.286	239	336

Central Division

Houston	9	5	0	.643	338	327
Cleveland	7	6	1	.536	287	217
Cincinnati	7	7	0	.500	322	249
Pittsburgh	7	7	0	.500	206	294

Western Division

Denver*	10	4	0	.714	309	207
L.A. Raiders	8	6	0	.571	281	240
Kansas City	7	6	1	.536	278	242
Seattle	6	8	0	.429	218	281
San Diego	4	10	0	.286	227	261

National Football Conference

Eastern Division

	W	L	T	Pct.	Pts.	OP
N.Y. Giants	10	4	0	.714	299	235
Philadelphia	10	4	0	.714	291	230
Washington	8	6	0	.571	326	278
Phoenix	5	9	0	.357	244	309
Dallas	1	13	0	.071	194	358

Central Division

Minnesota	9	5	0	.643	305	231
Green Bay	8	6	0	.571	302	318
Chicago	6	8	0	.429	330	311
Tampa Bay	5	9	0	.357	291	355
Detroit	5	9	0	.357	248	333

Western Division

San Francisco*	12	2	0	.857	395	243
L.A. Rams	9	5	0	.643	364	310
New Orleans	7	7	0	.500	315	275
Atlanta	3	11	0	.214	225	375

**Clinched Division Title*

Sunday, December 10

Minnesota 43, Atlanta 17—at Metrodome, attendance 58,116. Chris Doleman had four sacks and forced two fumbles which led to touchdowns to lead the Vikings' win over the Falcons. Minnesota jumped out to a 20-10 halftime lead on Wade Wilson's two-yard scoring pass to Darryl Ingram, running back D.J. Dozier's 19-yard pass to Anthony Carter, and Rich Karlis's two field goals (21 and 39 yards). Doleman's first forced fumble was returned 21 yards for a score by defensive tackle Keith Millard. Doleman's second forced fumble was returned five yards for a touchdown by Tim Newton late in the third quarter. Karlis added field goals of 29 and 19 yards in the fourth quarter. Doleman was named NFC Defensive Player of the Week.

Atlanta	3	7	7	0	—	17
Minnesota	7	13	17	6	—	43

Minn —Ingram 2 pass from Wilson (Karlis kick)
Atl —FG Davis 26
Minn —FG Karlis 21
Atl —Wilkins 26 pass from Miller (Davis kick)
Minn —Carter 19 pass from Dozier (Karlis kick)
Minn —FG Karlis 39
Atl —Collins 17 pass from Miller (Davis kick)
Minn —Millard 31 fumble recovery return (Karlis kick)
Minn —FG Karlis 26
Minn —Newton 5 fumble recovery return (Karlis kick)
Minn —FG Karlis 29
Minn —FG Karlis 19

Indianapolis 23, Cleveland 17—at Hoosier Dome, attendance 58,550. Mike Prior's 58-yard interception return for a touchdown 10:54 into overtime lifted the Colts over the Browns. Indianapolis scored first on Jack Trudeau's 51-yard touchdown pass to Andre Rison in the first quarter. Cleveland countered with 17 unanswered points on Eric Metcalf's 12-yard run, Lawyer Tillman's recovered blocked punt in the end zone, and Matt Bahr's 48-yard field goal. The Colts tied the game on Dean Biasucci's 35-yard field goal and Tom Ramsey's one-yard completion to Pat Beach. Bahr missed a 39-yard field goal with 25 seconds left in regulation that would have won the game. Prior also had a fumble recovery and seven tackles and was named AFC Defensive Player of the Week.

Cleveland	0	10	7	0	0	—	17
Indianapolis	7	0	3	7	6	—	23

Ind —Rison 51 pass from Trudeau (Biasucci kick)
Clev —Metcalf 12 run (Bahr kick)
Clev —FG Bahr 48
Clev —Tillman recovered blocked punt in end zone (Bahr kick)
Ind —FG Biasucci 35
Ind —Beach 1 pass from Ramsey (Biasucci kick)
Ind —Prior 58 interception return

Philadelphia 20, Dallas 10—at Veterans Stadium, attendance 66,769. Cris Carter had two touchdown receptions to lead the Eagles' 20-10 win over the Cowboys. After a scoreless first quarter, Carter scored on a four-yard reception from Randall Cunningham to cap a 75-yard drive. Philadelphia increased its lead to 17-3 at halftime on a 13-yard pass from Matt Cavanaugh to Carter on a fake field goal play and Roger Ruzek's 29-yard field goal. Ruzek added a field goal of 46 yards for the Eagles in the second half.

Dallas	0	3	7	0	—	10
Philadelphia	0	17	3	0	—	20

Phil —Carter 4 pass from Cunningham (Ruzek kick)
Phil —Carter 13 pass from Cavanaugh (Ruzek kick)
Dall —FG Zendejas 47
Phil —FG Ruzek 29
Phil —FG Ruzek 46
Dall —Johnston 18 pass from Aikman (Zendejas kick)

Detroit 27, Chicago 17—at Soldier Field, attendance 52,650. Barry Sanders ran for 120 yards and two touchdowns as the Lions ended a 10-game losing streak to the Bears. Detroit scored 17 points in the second quarter on touchdown runs by Bob Gagliano (14 yards) and Sanders (18), and Eddie Murray's 45-yard field goal. Sanders's second scoring run, a three-yarder, and Murray's 28-yard field goal completed the Lions' scoring. The loss knocked Chicago out of playoff contention for the first time since 1983.

Detroit	0	17	7	3	— 27
Chicago	3	7	0	7	— 17

Chi — FG Butler 22
Det — Gagliano 14 run (Murray kick)
Det — B. Sanders 18 run (Murray kick)
Chi — Muster 11 run (Butler kick)
Det — FG Murray 45
Det — B. Sanders 3 run (Murray kick)
Det — FG Murray 28
Chi — Anderson 1 run (Butler kick)

Kansas City 21, Green Bay 3—at Lambeau Field, attendance 56,694. Christian Okoye rushed a club-record 38 times for 131 yards and a touchdown to power the Chiefs over the Packers. Kansas City scored all its points in the second period on scoring passes from Steve DeBerg to Jonathan Hayes (11 yards) and Emile Harry (12), and Okoye's three-yard run. Green Bay managed only a 25-yard field goal by Chris Jacke in the second quarter. The Chiefs' defense recorded four sacks, one interception, and held the Packers to only four second-half first downs.

Kansas City	0	21	0	0	— 21
Green Bay	0	3	0	0	— 3

KC — Hayes 11 pass from DeBerg (Lowery kick)
GB — FG Jacke 25
KC — Okoye 3 run (Lowery kick)
KC — Harry 12 pass from DeBerg (Lowery kick)

New Orleans 22, Buffalo 19—at Rich Stadium, attendance 70,037. John Fourcade, making his first NFL start since 1987, threw for 302 yards and two touchdowns to lift the Saints over the Bills. Fourcade's two touchdown passes came in the first quarter on completions to John Tice (12 yards) and Dalton Hilliard (54). Buffalo went ahead 19-16 in the third quarter, but Morten Andersen tied the game with a 26-yard field goal. Toi Cook returned an interception to the Bills' 15-yard line to set up Andersen's game-winning 22-yard field goal.

New Orleans	13	3	3	3	— 22
Buffalo	0	12	7	0	— 19

NO — Tice 12 pass from Fourcade (kick failed)
NO — Hilliard 54 pass from Fourcade (Andersen kick)
Buff — Lofton 42 pass from Kelly (kick failed)
NO — FG Andersen 31
Buff — FG Norwood 43
Buff — FG Norwood 48
Buff — Metzelaars 2 pass from Kelly (Norwood kick)
NO — FG Andersen 26
NO — FG Andersen 22

New York Giants 14, Denver 7—at Mile High Stadium, attendance 63,283. David Meggett scored on a 57-yard touchdown pass to highlight the Giants' victory over the Broncos in a game that was played during a snowstorm. Ottis Anderson's three-yard run in the second quarter opened the scoring for the Giants. Meggett's punt return to the Broncos' 36-yard line set up Anderson's touchdown run. The Giants' defense halted two Denver scoring drives in the final two minutes of the game. Denver avoided being shut out on John Elway's 32-yard scoring pass to Michael Young.

N.Y. Giants	0	14	0	0	— 14
Denver	0	0	0	7	— 7

NYG — Anderson 3 run (Nittmo kick)
NYG — Meggett 57 pass from Simms (Nittmo kick)
Den — Young 32 pass from Elway (Treadwell kick)

Los Angeles Raiders 16, Phoenix 14—at Memorial Coliseum, attendance 41,785. Marcus Allen's one-yard scoring dive with 40 seconds remaining gave the Raiders a 16-14 comeback win over the Cardinals. Los Angeles led 9-7 in the fourth quarter on three Jeff Jaeger field goals (25, 30, and 48 yards), but Gary Hogeboom's two-yard touchdown completion to Jay Novacek put Phoenix ahead 14-9. Allen, appearing in his first game since October 9, capped a 46-yard, 13-play drive with his game-winning run.

Phoenix	0	7	0	7	— 14
L.A. Raiders	0	6	3	7	— 16

Raiders — FG Jaeger 25
Phx — Jones 35 pass from Hogeboom (Del Greco kick)
Raiders — FG Jaeger 30
Raiders — FG Jaeger 48
Phx — Novacek 2 pass from Hogeboom (Del Greco kick)
Raiders — Allen 1 run (Jaeger kick)

Pittsburgh 13, New York Jets 0—at Giants Stadium, attendance 41,037. Tim Worley ran for a touchdown and Gary Anderson kicked two field goals as the Steelers downed the Jets to record their first shutout in four years. Pittsburgh took a 7-0 halftime lead on rookie Worley's 35-yard touchdown run. Anderson completed the Steelers' scoring with field goals of 42 and 45 yards. Pittsburgh linebacker Greg Lloyd led the defense with an interception and a sack. The Steelers' last shutout was a 20-0 win over Houston on September 22, 1985.

Pittsburgh	7	0	0	6	— 13
N.Y. Jets	0	0	0	0	— 0

Pitt — Worley 35 run (Anderson kick)
Pitt — FG Anderson 42
Pitt — FG Anderson 45

Washington 26, San Diego 21—at R.F.K. Stadium, attendance 47,693. Mark Rypien threw two touchdown passes and Chip Lohmiller kicked four field goals to lead the Redskins past the Chargers. Trailing 14-7 in the third quarter, Lohmiller kicked three field goals (38, 31, and 32 yards) to put Washington ahead 16-14. The Redskins increased their lead in the fourth quarter on Rypien's 33-yard touchdown pass to Gary Clark and Lohmiller's 28-yard field goal. Art Monk's nine catches gave him 651 career receptions, moving him into third place on the NFL's all-time receiving list. The victory was the 100th of Joe Gibbs's career.

San Diego	14	0	0	7	— 21
Washington	0	7	9	10	— 26

SD — A. Miller 25 pass from Tolliver (Bahr kick)
SD — Walker 5 pass from Tolliver (Bahr kick)
Wash — Sanders 45 pass from Rypien (Lohmiller kick)
Wash — FG Lohmiller 38
Wash — FG Lohmiller 31
Wash — FG Lohmiller 32
SD — Butts 10 run (Bahr kick)
Wash — Clark 33 pass from Rypien (Lohmiller kick)
Wash — FG Lohmiller 28

Seattle 24, Cincinnati 17—at Riverfront Stadium, attendance 54,744. Dave Krieg's one-yard touchdown pass to Curt Warner with 3:51 to play gave the Seahawks the win over the Bengals. Trailing 10-7 in the third quarter, Norm Johnson kicked a 48-yard field goal and Krieg completed a 60-yard scoring pass to Brian Blades for a 17-10 lead. Cincinnati's Eric Thomas returned an interception 18 yards for a touchdown to tie the game with 9:39 remaining. Steve Largent's 10-yard scoring reception in the second quarter gave him 100 for his career, breaking the NFL record of 99 he shared with Don Hutson.

Seattle	0	7	10	7	— 24
Cincinnati	7	3	0	7	— 17

Cin — McGee 21 pass from Esiason (Breech kick)
Cin — FG Breech 24
Sea — Largent 10 pass from Krieg (N. Johnson kick)
Sea — FG N. Johnson 48
Sea — Blades 60 pass from Krieg (N. Johnson kick)
Cin — Thomas 18 interception return (Breech kick)
Sea — Warner 1 pass from Krieg (N. Johnson kick)

Houston 20, Tampa Bay 17—at Astrodome, attendance 54,532. Warren Moon completed two touchdown passes as the Oilers defeated the Buccaneers to remain in playoff contention. Houston took a 20-3 halftime lead as Moon completed scoring passes to Drew Hill (12 yards) and Curtis Duncan (16), and Tony Zendejas kicked a pair of field goals (30 and 37 yards). Safety Bubba McDowell's fumble recovery at the Houston 21 with 1:18 remaining sealed the win.

Tampa Bay	3	0	7	7	— 17
Houston	3	17	0	0	— 20

Hou — FG Zendejas 30
TB — FG Igwebuike 21
Hou — D. Hill 12 pass from Moon (Zendejas kick)
Hou — FG Zendejas 37
Hou — Duncan 16 pass from Moon (Zendejas kick)
TB — Drewrey 6 pass from Testaverde (Igwebuike kick)
TB — Hall 24 pass from Testaverde (Igwebuike kick)

Miami 31, New England 10—at Joe Robbie Stadium, attendance 62,127. Sammie Smith ran for three touchdowns as the Dolphins downed the Patriots to remain in playoff contention. Smith had one- and seven-yard scoring runs in the first half and added a two-yarder in the fourth quarter. Dan Marino, who completed 21 of 32 passes for 300 yards, also scored on a one-yard run at the end of the first half.

New England	3	0	7	0	— 10
Miami	7	14	0	10	— 31

Mia — S. Smith 1 run (Stoyanovich kick)
NE — FG Staurovsky 36
Mia — S. Smith 7 run (Stoyanovich kick)
Mia — Marino 1 run (Stoyanovich kick)
NE — Stephens 1 run (Staurovsky kick)
Mia — Smith 2 run (Stoyanovich kick)
Mia — FG Stoyanovich 23

Monday, December 11

San Francisco 30, Los Angeles Rams 27—at Anaheim Stadium, attendance 68,936. Joe Montana and John Taylor combined for two touchdown passes to lift the 49ers over the Rams. Down 17-0 in the first quarter, San Francisco's Mike Cofer kicked a 19-yard field goal and Montana threw a 92-yard scoring bomb to Taylor to close out the half trailing 17-14. The Rams answered with Jim Everett's 13-yard scoring pass to Buford McGee and Mike Lansford's 22-yard field goal to put them ahead 27-14. But Montana countered with scoring passes to Mike Wilson (seven yards) and Taylor (96). Roger Craig's one-yard scoring run gave the 49ers the victory. Taylor, who caught 11 passes for a club-record 286 yards, was the first player in NFL history to have two 90-yard scoring plays in a single game. He was named NFC Offensive Player of the Week.

San Francisco	0	10	0	20	— 30
L.A. Rams	17	0	7	3	— 27

Rams — Bell 3 run (Lansford kick)
Rams — Johnson 4 pass from Everett (Lansford kick)
Rams — FG Lansford 25
SF — FG Cofer 19
SF — Taylor 92 pass from Montana (Cofer kick)
Rams — McGee 13 pass from Everett (Lansford kick)
Rams — FG Lansford 22
SF — Wilson 7 pass from Montana (Cofer kick)
SF — Taylor 96 pass from Montana (kick failed)
SF — Craig 1 run (Cofer kick)

Fifteenth Week Summaries

Standings

American Football Conference

Eastern Division

	W	L	T	Pct.	Pts.	OP
Buffalo	8	7	0	.533	372	317
Indianapolis	8	7	0	.533	292	260
Miami	8	7	0	.533	307	352
New England	5	10	0	.333	277	367
N.Y. Jets	4	11	0	.267	253	374

Central Division

	W	L	T	Pct.	Pts.	OP
Houston	9	6	0	.600	345	388
Cleveland	8	6	1	.567	310	234
Cincinnati	8	7	0	.533	383	256
Pittsburgh	8	7	0	.533	234	304

Western Division

	W	L	T	Pct.	Pts.	OP
Denver*	11	4	0	.733	346	207
L.A. Raiders	8	7	0	.533	298	263
Kansas City	7	7	1	.500	291	262
Seattle	7	8	0	.467	241	298
San Diego	5	10	0	.333	247	274

National Football Conference

Eastern Division

	W	L	T	Pct.	Pts.	OP
N.Y. Giants**	11	4	0	.733	314	235
Philadelphia	10	5	0	.667	311	260
Washington	9	6	0	.600	357	308
Phoenix	5	10	0	.333	244	346
Dallas	1	14	0	.067	194	373

Central Division

	W	L	T	Pct.	Pts.	OP
Green Bay	9	6	0	.600	342	346
Minnesota	9	6	0	.600	322	254
Chicago	6	9	0	.400	358	351
Detroit	6	9	0	.400	281	340
Tampa Bay	5	10	0	.333	298	388

Western Division

	W	L	T	Pct.	Pts.	OP
San Francisco*	13	2	0	.867	416	253
L.A. Rams	10	5	0	.667	402	324
New Orleans	8	7	0	.533	345	295
Atlanta	3	12	0	.214	255	406

**Clinched Division Title*
***Clinched Playoff Position*

Saturday, December 16

New York Giants 15, Dallas 0—at Giants Stadium, attendance 72,141. Bjorn Nittmo kicked three field goals as the Giants downed the Cowboys to earn a playoff berth for the first time in three years. With the Giants leading 3-0, Dwayne Giles blocked a punt to set up Nittmo's second field goal, a 33-yarder, in the first quarter. Ottis Anderson, who finished the day with 91 yards on 25 carries, scored on a one-yard run in the third quarter to put the game away. The Giants, who held a commanding 41:59 to 18:01 time-of-possession advantage, limited the Cowboys to 108 total yards on offense.

Dallas	0	0	0	0	— 0
N.Y. Giants	6	3	6	0	— 15

NYG — FG Nittmo 33
NYG — FG Nittmo 22
NYG — FG Nittmo 26
NYG — Anderson 1 run (kick blocked)

Denver 37, Phoenix 0—at Sun Devil Stadium, attendance 56,071. John Elway completed two touchdown passes and Bobby Humphrey rushed for 128 yards as the Broncos shut out the Cardinals. The victory gave the Broncos the home-field advantage throughout the playoffs. Denver jumped out to a 20-0 lead in the first half on Karl Mecklenburg's 23-yard fumble recovery return for a score, Elway's 14-yard touchdown pass to Steve Sewell, and David Treadwell's 38- and 33-yard field goals. Humphrey, who became the first Denver rookie to surpass 1,000 yards (1,100) rushing, also threw a 17-yard touchdown pass to Melvin Bratton in the third quarter. Elway's 20-yard scoring pass to Clarence Kay and Treadwell's 35-yard field goal finished the Broncos' scoring.

Denver	7	13	14	3	— 37
Phoenix	0	0	0	0	— 0

Den — Mecklenburg 23 fumble recovery return (Treadwell kick)
Den — FG Treadwell 38
Den — Sewell 14 pass from Elway (Treadwell kick)
Den — FG Treadwell 33
Den — Bratton 17 pass from Humphrey (Treadwell kick)

Den — Kay 20 pass to Elway (Treadwell kick)
Den — FG Treadwell 35

Sunday, December 17

San Francisco 21, Buffalo 10—at Candlestick Park, attendance 60,927. Steve Young threw for one touchdown and ran for another to lead the 49ers over the Bills. Leading 7-3 in the fourth quarter, San Francisco put the game away on Young's two-yard scoring run and Young's eight-yard touchdown pass to Jerry Rice. Roger Craig, who carried 25 times for 105 yards and a touchdown, reached the 1,000-yard mark (1,023) for the third time in his career.

Buffalo	3	0	0	7	—	10
San Francisco	0	0	7	14	—	21

Buff — FG Norwood 23
SF — Craig 1 run (Cofer kick)
SF — Young 2 run (Cofer kick)
SF — Rice 8 pass from Young (Cofer kick)
Buff — Kelly 1 run (Norwood kick)

Green Bay 40, Chicago 28—at Soldier Field, attendance 44,781. Don Majkowski threw for one touchdown and ran for two others as the Packers kept their playoff hopes alive by downing the Bears. Green Bay led 24-14 at halftime on scoring runs by Keith Woodside (68 yards) and Majkowski (17), Perry Kemp's 27-yard touchdown reception from Majkowski, and Chris Jacke's 19-yard field goal. The Packers put the game away in the second half on Jacke's three field goals (44, 23, and 21 yards) and Majkowski's one-yard run. The Bears dropped their fifth straight game for the first time since 1978.

Green Bay	14	10	6	10	—	40
Chicago	7	7	14	0	—	28

GB — Woodside 68 run (Jacke kick)
Chi — Muster 3 pass from Harbaugh (Butler kick)
GB — Kemp 27 pass from Majkowski (Jacke kick)
Chi — Anderson 21 pass from Harbaugh (Butler kick)
GB — FG Jacke 19
GB — Majkowski 17 run (Jacke kick)
GB — FG Jacke 44
Chi — Anderson 49 pass from Harbaugh (Butler kick)
GB — FG Jacke 23
Chi — Muster 4 run (Butler kick)
GB — Majkowski 1 run (Jacke kick)
GB — FG Jacke 21

Cincinnati 61, Houston 7—at Riverfront Stadium, attendance 47,510. Boomer Esiason threw four touchdown passes as the Bengals posted the largest margin of victory in team history with a 61-7 defeat of the Oilers. Cincinnati took a 31-0 halftime lead on Esiason's two scoring passes to Eddie Brown (22 and 35 yards) and one to Rodney Holman (five), James Brooks's 14-yard run for a touchdown, and Jim Breech's 27-yard field goal. Esiason, who completed 20 of 27 passes for 326 yards, also found Tim McGee with a 74-yard scoring bomb in the third quarter. The Bengals held the Oilers to just 14 first downs and 186 offensive yards.

Houston	0	0	0	7	—	7
Cincinnati	21	10	21	9	—	61

Cin — Brown 22 pass from Esiason (Breech kick)
Cin — Brooks 14 run (Breech kick)
Cin — Brown 35 pass from Esiason (Breech kick)
Cin — Holman 5 pass from Esiason (Breech kick)
Cin — FG Breech 27
Cin — Taylor 5 run (Breech kick)
Cin — McGee 74 pass from Esiason (Breech kick)
Cin — Ball 5 run (Breech kick)
Hou — White 1 run (Zendejas kick)
Cin — Hillary 10 pass from Wilhelm (kick failed)
Cin — FG Breech 30

Indianapolis 42, Miami 13—at Hoosier Dome, attendance 55,665. Jack Trudeau completed four touchdown passes and Eric Dickerson ran for two more scores as the Colts easily beat the Dolphins. With the Colts clinging to a 14-13 edge at halftime, Dickerson ran one yard for a touchdown and Trudeau hit James Pruitt for a five-yard touchdown to go ahead 28-13 in the third quarter. Indianapolis put the game away in the fourth quarter when Trudeau found Albert Bentley on a six-yard touchdown and Dickerson added a two-yard run. Trudeau was named AFC Offensive Player of the Week.

Miami	10	3	0	0	—	13
Indianapolis	7	7	14	14	—	42

Mia — FG Stoyanovich 43
Mia — Schwedes 70 punt return (Stoyanovich kick)
Ind — Rison 6 pass from Trudeau (Biasucci kick)
Mia — FG Stoyanovich 47
Ind — Boyer 1 pass from Trudeau (Biasucci kick)
Ind — Dickerson 1 run (Biasucci kick)
Ind — Pruitt 5 pass from Trudeau (Biasucci kick)
Ind — Bentley 6 pass from Trudeau (Biasucci kick)
Ind — Dickerson 2 run (Biasucci kick)

Cleveland 23, Minnesota 17—at Cleveland Stadium, attendance 70,777. Mike Pagel completed a 14-yard touchdown pass to linebacker Van Waiters on a fake field goal play 9:30 into overtime to lift the Browns over the Vikings. Cleveland took a 14-10 lead in the third quarter on Bernie Kosar's five-yard touchdown pass to Ron Middleton and a 62-yard scoring bomb to Reggie Langhorne. Minnesota came back to lead 17-14 with 3:37 to play as Tommy Kramer found Steve Jordan with a two-yard pass. Matt Bahr's 32-yard field goal with 24 seconds remaining in regulation sent the game into overtime.

Minnesota	0	3	7	7	0	—	17
Cleveland	0	0	14	3	6	—	23

Minn — FG Karlis 44
Clev — Middleton 5 pass from Kosar (Bahr kick)
Minn — Walker 26 run (Karlis kick)
Clev — Langhorne 62 pass from Kosar (Bahr kick)
Minn — Jordan 2 pass from Kramer (Karlis kick)
Clev — FG Bahr 32
Clev — Waiters 14 pass from Pagel

Pittsburgh 28, New England 10—at Three Rivers Stadium, attendance 26,594. Tim Worley ran for 104 yards and a touchdown to help the Steelers defeat the Patriots. Pittsburgh took a 14-3 lead at halftime on Worley's eight-yard scoring run and Merril Hoge's one-yard touchdown. The Steelers went ahead 21-3 in the third quarter as Greg Lloyd's fumble recovery led to Louis Lipps's 58-yard touchdown.

New England	3	0	0	7	—	10
Pittsburgh	7	7	7	7	—	28

Pitt — Worley 8 run (Anderson kick)
NE — FG Staurovsky 20
Pitt — Hoge 1 run (Anderson kick)
Pitt — Lipps 58 run (Anderson kick)
Pitt — Hoge 2 run (Anderson kick)
NE — C. Jones 12 pass from Wilson (Staurovsky kick)

Los Angeles Rams 38, New York Jets 14—at Anaheim Stadium, attendance 53,063. Jim Everett threw for 273 yards and two touchdowns as the Rams defeated the Jets. Los Angeles jumped to a 28-7 halftime advantage as Everett completed scoring passes to Pete Holohan (25 yards) and Willie Anderson (43) and Greg Bell ran for two scores (one and five yards). The Rams increased their lead in the second half on Mike Lansford's 37-yard field goal and Cleveland Gary's five-yard touchdown run. Los Angeles's defense registered seven sacks and had three fumble recoveries.

N.Y. Jets	7	0	0	7	—	14
L.A. Rams	7	21	0	10	—	38

Rams — Holohan 25 pass from Everett (Lansford kick)
NYJ — Townsell 63 pass from Eason (Leahy kick)
Rams — Bell 1 run (Lansford kick)
Rams — Anderson 43 pass from Everett (Lansford kick)
Rams — Bell 5 run (Lansford kick)
Rams — FG Lansford 37
Rams — Gary 5 run (Lansford kick)
NYJ — Neubert 35 pass from O'Brien (Leahy kick)

San Diego 20, Kansas City 13—at Arrowhead Stadium, attendance 40,623. Rookie Marion Butts rushed a club-record 39 times for 176 yards as the Chargers defeated the Chiefs. After Kansas City scored 13 consecutive points, San Diego came back to score 20 unanswered points on Billy Joe Tolliver's scoring passes to Andy Parker (one yard) and Anthony Miller (five), and a pair of Chris Bahr field goals (43 and 20 yards). Roy Bennett's interception in the end zone with 19 seconds remaining ended the Chiefs' final scoring threat.

San Diego	0	7	3	10	—	20
Kansas City	0	13	0	0	—	13

KC — FG Lowery 36
KC — FG Lowery 30
KC — McNair 11 pass from DeBerg (Lowery kick)
SD — Parker 1 pass from Tolliver (Bahr kick)
SD — FG Bahr 43
SD — A. Miller 5 pass from Tolliver (Bahr kick)
SD — FG Bahr 20

Detroit 33, Tampa Bay 7—at Pontiac Silverdome, attendance 40,362. Barry Sanders carried 21 times for 104 yards and a touchdown to lead the Lions past the Buccaneers. Detroit led 24-0 at halftime on Bob Gagliano's scoring passes to Richard Johnson (two yards) and Jason Phillips (55), Eddie Murray's first of four field goals (33 yards), and Sanders's four-yard run. Murray added field goals from 43, 35, and 36 yards in the second half to complete the Lions' scoring. Sanders's 1,312 yards for the season broke Detroit's rookie record of 1,308, set by Billy Sims in 1980.

Tampa Bay	0	0	0	7	—	7
Detroit	14	10	3	6	—	33

Det — Johnson 2 pass from Gagliano (Murray kick)
Det — Phillips 55 pass from Gagliano (Murray kick)
Det — FG Murray 33
Det — Sanders 4 run (Murray kick)
Det — FG Murray 43
Det — FG Murray 35
Det — FG Murray 36
TB — Carrier 69 pass from Ferguson (Igwebuike kick)

Washington 31, Atlanta 30—at Atlanta-Fulton County Stadium, attendance 37,501. Mark Rypien threw for one touchdown and ran for another as the Redskins rallied to defeat the Falcons. Trailing 27-10 in the third quarter, Rypien hit Art Monk with a 60-yard touchdown bomb, Earnest Byner ran one yard for a score, and Rypien scored on a nine-yard keeper to put Washington ahead 31-27. Monk, who also scored on a 34-yard reception from Doug Williams in the first quarter, finished the day with six receptions for 131 yards.

Washington	3	7	21	0	—	31
Atlanta	3	24	3	0	—	30

Atl — FG Davis 33
Wash — FG Lohmiller 37
Wash — Monk 34 pass from Williams (Lohmiller kick)
Atl — Haynes 72 pass from Miller (Davis kick)
Atl — Haynes 17 pass from Miller (Davis kick)
Atl — FG Davis 24
Atl — Settle 3 run (Davis kick)
Wash — Monk 60 pass from Rypien (Lohmiller kick)
Wash — Byner 1 run (Lohmiller kick)
Wash — Rypien 9 run (Lohmiller kick)
Atl — FG Davis 32

Seattle 23, Los Angeles Raiders 17—at Kingdome, attendance 61,076. Dave Krieg passed for two touchdowns as the Seahawks defeated the Raiders. Seattle took a 13-3 halftime lead on Krieg's five-yard scoring pass to Paul Skansi, and Norm Johnson's field goals from 29 and 25 yards. Krieg's 13-yard touchdown pass to John L. Williams and Johnson's field goal from 43 yards completed the Seahawks' scoring. Williams ended the day with 12 receptions for 129 yards.

L.A. Raiders	3	0	14	0	—	17
Seattle	7	6	7	3	—	23

Sea — Skansi 5 pass from Krieg (N. Johnson kick)
Raiders — FG Jaeger 19
Sea — FG N. Johnson 29
Sea — FG N. Johnson 25
Raiders — Gault 36 pass from Beuerlein (Jaeger kick)
Raiders — Junkin 1 pass from Beuerlein (Jaeger kick)
Sea — J. Williams 13 pass from Krieg (N. Johnson kick)
Sea — FG N. Johnson 43

Monday, December 19

New Orleans 30, Philadelphia 20—at Louisiana Superdome, attendance 68,561. John Fourcade threw three touchdown passes, including two to Eric Martin, to lift the Saints past the Eagles. New Orleans went ahead 16-10 at halftime as Fourcade hit Martin on a 17-yard touchdown pass and Dalton Hilliard on a 35-yard score, and Frank Warren, who registered three sacks for the game, tackled Randall Cunningham in the end zone for a safety. Philadelphia scored 10 third-quarter points to take a 20-16 lead, but Fourcade's 20-yard touchdown pass to Martin, and Buford Jordan's one-yard scoring run in the fourth quarter put the game away.

Philadelphia	0	10	10	0	—	20
New Orleans	7	9	0	14	—	30

NO — Martin 17 pass from Fourcade (Andersen kick)
NO — Hilliard 35 pass from Fourcade (Andersen kick)
Phil — Johnson 13 pass from Cunningham (Ruzek kick)
Phil — FG Ruzek 21
NO — Safety, Warren tackled Cunningham in end zone
Phil — Little 1 pass from Cunningham (Ruzek kick)
Phil — FG Ruzek 19
NO — Martin 20 pass from Fourcade (Andersen kick)
NO — Jordan 1 run (Andersen kick)

Sixteenth Week Summaries

Standings

American Football Conference

Eastern Division

	W	L	T	Pct.	Pts.	OP
Buffalo*	9	7	0	.563	409	317
Indianapolis	8	8	0	.500	298	301
Miami	8	8	0	.500	331	379
New England	5	11	0	.313	297	391
N.Y. Jets	4	12	0	.250	253	411

Central Division

	W	L	T	Pct.	Pts.	OP
Cleveland*	9	6	1	.594	334	254
Houston*	9	7	0	.563	365	412
Pittsburgh*	9	7	0	.563	265	326
Cincinnati	8	8	0	.500	404	285

Western Division

	W	L	T	Pct.	Pts.	OP
Denver*	11	5	0	.688	362	226
Kansas City	8	7	1	.531	318	286
L.A. Raiders	8	8	0	.500	315	297
Seattle	7	9	0	.438	241	327
San Diego	6	10	0	.375	266	290

National Football Conference

Eastern Division

	W	L	T	Pct.	Pts.	OP
N.Y. Giants*	12	4	0	.750	348	252
Philadelphia*	11	5	0	.688	342	274
Washington	10	6	0	.625	386	308
Phoenix	5	11	0	.313	258	377
Dallas	1	15	0	.063	204	393

Central Division

	W	L	T	Pct.	Pts.	OP
Minnesota*	10	6	0	.625	351	275
Green Bay	10	6	0	.625	362	356
Detroit	7	9	0	.438	312	364
Chicago	6	10	0	.375	358	377
Tampa Bay	5	11	0	.313	320	419

Western Division

San Francisco*	14	2	0	.875	442	253
L.A. Rams*	11	5	0	.688	426	344
New Orleans	9	7	0	.563	386	301
Atlanta	3	13	0	.188	279	437

**Denotes playoff team*

Indianapolis finished ahead of Miami in AFC East because of better conference record (7-5 vs. 6-8). Houston finished ahead of Pittsburgh in AFC Central because of head-to-head sweep (2-0). Minnesota finished ahead of Green Bay in NFC Central because of better division record (6-2 vs. 5-3).

Saturday, December 23

Buffalo 37, N.Y. Jets 0—at Giants Stadium, attendance 21,148. Jim Kelly threw two touchdown passes as the Bills blanked the Jets to earn their second straight AFC East title. Larry Kinnebrew's one-yard scoring run and Scott Norwood's 26-yard field goal put Buffalo ahead 10-0 at halftime. Kelly then completed scoring passes of 18 yards to James Lofton and 25 yards to Ronnie Harmon to put the game out of reach. Thurman Thomas's three-yard scoring run and Kenneth Davis's 17-yard touchdown run completed the scoring. It was the largest margin of victory in Bills history.

Buffalo	3	7	20	7	— 37
N.Y. Jets	0	0	0	0	— 0

Buff —FG Norwood 26
Buff —Kinnebrew 1 run (Norwood kick)
Buff —Lofton 18 pass from Kelly (kick failed)
Buff —Harmon 25 pass from Kelly (Norwood kick)
Buff —Thomas 3 run (Norwood kick)
Buff —K. Davis 17 run (Norwood kick)

Washington 29, Seattle 0—at Kingdome, attendance 60,294. Gary Clark caught nine passes for 149 yards and a touchdown to help the Redskins defeat the Seahawks. Mark Rypien fired a 44-yard scoring pass to Clark in the third quarter to increase Washington's lead to 20-0. Earnest Byner had two touchdowns (two and eight yards) among 19 carries for 63 yards. Seattle's Steve Largent caught two passes for 41 yards in his final NFL game after a record-setting 14-year career.

Washington	10	3	16	0	— 29
Seattle	0	0	0	0	— 0

Wash —FG Lohmiller 29
Wash —Byner 2 run (Lohmiller kick)
Wash —FG Lohmiller 27
Wash —Clark 44 pass from Rypien (Lohmiller kick)
Wash —Safety, Stokes tackled Krieg in end zone
Wash —Byner 8 run (Lohmiller kick)

Cleveland 24, Houston 20—at Astrodome, attendance 58,342. Kevin Mack's four-yard touchdown run with 39 seconds remaining lifted the Browns to their fourth AFC Central Division title in five years. Cleveland took a 17-0 second-quarter lead on Bernie Kosar's touchdown passes to Eric Metcalf (68 yards) and Webster Slaughter (40), and Matt Bahr's 32-yard field goal. Houston came back, scoring 20 unanswered points on Warren Moon scoring throws to Drew Hill (nine and 27 yards), and Tony Zendejas's field goals of 30 and 37 yards. Moon finished with 414 yards passing on 32 completions in 51 attempts, with two touchdowns and one interception.

Cleveland	10	7	0	7	— 24
Houston	0	3	7	10	— 20

Clev —FG Bahr 32
Clev —Metcalf 68 pass from Kosar (Bahr kick)
Clev —Slaughter 40 pass from Kosar (Bahr kick)
Hou —FG Zendejas 30
Hou —Hill 9 pass from Moon (Zendejas kick)
Hou —FG Zendejas 37
Hou —Hill 27 pass from Moon (Zendejas kick)
Clev —Mack 4 run (Bahr kick)

Sunday, December 24

San Francisco 26, Chicago 0—at Candlestick Park, attendance 58,829. Joe Montana threw for a touchdown and Mike Cofer kicked four field goals as the 49ers shut out the Bears. San Francisco jumped out to a 16-0 halftime lead as Montana connected with Jerry Rice for a 29-yard scoring pass and Cofer kicked three field goals (29, 24, and 36 yards). Cofer then added a 47-yard field goal and Terrence Flagler ran 29 yards for a touchdown in the second half. Montana finished the season with a 112.4 passer rating, surpassing Milt Plum's NFL record of 110.4, set in 1960.

Chicago	0	0	0	0	— 0
San Francisco	3	13	3	7	— 26

SF —FG Cofer 29
SF —FG Cofer 24
SF —Rice 29 pass from Montana (Cofer kick)
SF —FG Cofer 36
SF —FG Cofer 47
SF —Flagler 29 run (Cofer kick)

San Diego 19, Denver 16—at San Diego Jack Murphy Stadium, attendance 50,524. Chris Bahr's 45-yard field goal as time expired lifted the Chargers over the Broncos. San Diego trailed Denver 10-9 in the fourth quarter when Tim Spencer ran one yard for a score to put the Chargers ahead 16-10. Denver tied the game 16-16 with 35 seconds remaining on Jeff Alexander's one-yard run for a touchdown. Bahr's winning field goal concluded a 45-yard drive. The Chargers' defense forced three turnovers and recorded seven sacks.

Denver	0	7	3	6	— 16
San Diego	0	6	3	10	— 19

SD —FG Bahr 22
Den —Humphrey 12 pass from Elway (Treadwell kick)
SD —FG Bahr 41
SD —FG Bahr 53
Den —FG Treadwell 24
SD —Spencer 1 run (Bahr kick)
Den —Alexander 1 run (kick failed)
SD —FG Bahr 45

Detroit 31, Atlanta 24—at Atlanta-Fulton County Stadium, attendance 7,092. Barry Sanders ran for 158 yards and three touchdowns to pace the Lions' win over the Falcons. Detroit led 14-10 at the half on Bob Gagliano's 34-yard scoring pass to Richard Johnson, and Sanders's 25-yard scoring run. Sanders added two more touchdown runs (17 and 18 yards) in the second half. The Lions finished with five straight victories, their longest winning streak since 1970. Sanders concluded his rookie season with 1,470 yards rushing, breaking the club record of 1,437 set by Billy Sims in 1981. Johnson had seven receptions for 135 yards.

Detroit	7	7	10	7	— 31
Atlanta	0	10	0	14	— 24

Det —Johnson 34 pass from Gagliano (Murray kick)
Atl —FG Davis 25
Det —Sanders 25 run (Murray kick)
Atl —Lang 9 pass from Miller (Davis kick)
Det —FG Murray 39
Det —Sanders 17 run (Murray kick)
Det —Sanders 18 run (Murray kick)
Atl —Jones 1 run (Davis kick)
Atl —Haynes 6 pass from Miller (Davis kick)

Green Bay 20, Dallas 10—at Texas Stadium, attendance 41,265. Don Majkowski completed two touchdown passes as the Packers downed the Cowboys. Majkowski hit Jeff Query for a 14-yard touchdown and Chris Jacke kicked a 28-yard field goal to give Green Bay a 10-3 halftime lead. Dallas tied the game midway through the third quarter on Jack Del Rio's 57-yard fumble recovery returned for a score. Majkowski broke the tie with a five-yard touchdown pass to Ed West and put the game out of reach late in the fourth quarter on Chris Jacke's 24-yard field goal. Green Bay finished the season with a 10-6 record, its best mark since a 10-4 finish in 1972.

Green Bay	3	7	7	3	— 20
Dallas	3	0	7	0	— 10

GB —FG Jacke 28
Dall —FG Zendejas 41
GB —Query 14 pass from Majkowski (Jacke kick)
Dall —Del Rio 57 fumble recovery return (Zendejas kick)
GB —West 5 pass from Majkowski (Jacke kick)
GB —FG Jacke 24

New Orleans 41, Indianapolis 6—at Louisiana Superdome, attendance 49,009. John Fourcade threw for two touchdowns and ran for a third as the Saints knocked the Colts out of the playoffs. New Orleans built a 10-6 lead in the first half on Morten Andersen's 21-yard field goal and Fourcade's three-yard touchdown pass to Eric Martin. The Saints blanked the Colts in the second half while scoring 31 unanswered points on Fourcade's 30-yard touchdown pass to Hoby Brenner and Fourcade's two-yard keeper. Andersen added a 29-yard field goal and Toi Cook returned an interception 63 yards for a touchdown to finish New Orleans's scoring.

Indianapolis	0	6	0	0	— 6
New Orleans	3	7	7	24	— 41

NO —FG Andersen 21
Ind —FG Biasucci 41
NO —Martin 3 pass from Fourcade (Andersen kick)
Ind —FG Biasucci 24
NO —Hilliard 7 run (Andersen kick)
NO —Brenner 30 pass from Fourcade (Andersen kick)
NO —Fourcade 2 run (Andersen kick)
NO —FG Andersen 29
NO —Cook 63 interception return (Andersen kick)

Kansas City 27, Miami 24—at Joe Robbie Stadium, attendance 43,612. Nick Lowery kicked a 41-yard field goal with 1:31 remaining to lift the Chiefs past Miami. Kansas City scored 21 second-quarter points on Steve DeBerg's 20-yard touchdown pass to Stephone Paige and scoring runs by James Saxon (six yards) and Christian Okoye (one). Miami tied the game 24-24 late in the fourth quarter but the Chiefs moved 44 yards in nine plays to set up Lowery's game-winning field goal. The loss knocked the Dolphins out of the playoffs.

Kansas City	0	21	3	3	— 27
Miami	7	7	0	10	— 24

Mia —Jensen 4 pass from Marino (Stoyanovich kick)
KC —Paige 20 pass from DeBerg (Lowery kick)
Mia —Edmunds 3 pass from Marino (Stoyanovich kick)
KC —Saxon 6 run (Lowery kick)
KC —Okoye 1 run (Lowery kick)
KC —FG Lowery 19
Mia —FG Stoyanovich 22
Mia —Clayton 7 pass from Marino (Stoyanovich kick)
KC —FG Lowery 41

New York Giants 34, Los Angeles Raiders 17—at Giants Stadium, attendance 70,306. Ottis Anderson ran for two touchdowns and Dave Meggett returned a punt for a score as the Giants clinched the NFC Eastern Division title for the first time since 1986. New York took an early 7-0 lead in the first quarter on Meggett's 76-yard punt return for a touchdown. Anderson's one-yard scoring run in the second quarter helped the Giants to a 17-17 halftime tie. Anderson (one yard) and Phil Simms (three) had scoring runs in the second half. Anderson, who rushed for 74 yards, lifted his season total to 1,023 yards, his first 1,000-rushing season since 1984.

L.A. Raiders	7	10	0	0	— 17
N.Y. Giants	7	10	10	7	— 34

NYG —Meggett 76 punt return (Nittmo kick)
Raiders —Horton 1 pass from Beuerlein (Jaeger kick)
Raiders —Fernandez 30 pass from Beuerlein (Jaeger kick)
NYG —Anderson 1 run (Nittmo kick)
Raiders —FG Jaeger 42
NYG —FG Nittmo 28
NYG —Anderson 1 run (Nittmo kick)
NYG —FG Nittmo 21
NYG —Simms 3 run (Nittmo kick)

Los Angeles Rams 24, New England 20—at Sullivan Stadium, attendance 27,940. Greg Bell ran for 210 yards and a touchdown as the Rams rallied to defeat the Patriots and earn an NFC Wild Card berth. Los Angeles jumped to a 17-3 lead in the third quarter on Mike Lansford's 19-yard field goal, Jerry Gray's 27-yard interception return for a score, and Jim Everett's seven-yard scoring pass to Buford McGee. New England rallied to take a 20-17 advantage in the fourth quarter, but Bell's three-yard scoring run with 1:55 left in the game gave the Rams the victory.

L.A. Rams	3	7	7	7	— 24
New England	0	3	7	10	— 20

Rams —FG Lansford 19
Rams —Gray 27 interception return (Lansford kick)
NE —FG Staurovsky 44
Rams —McGee 7 pass from Everett (Lansford kick)
NE —Fryar 47 pass from Grogan (Staurovsky kick)
NE —Stephens 4 run (Staurovsky kick)
NE —FG Staurovsky 48
Rams —Bell 3 run (Lansford kick)

Pittsburgh 31, Tampa Bay 22—at Tampa Stadium, attendance 29,690. Louis Lipps had four receptions for 137 yards, including two touchdown receptions, as the Steelers beat the Buccaneers. Pittsburgh jumped to a 24-10 lead on Bubby Brister's scoring throws to Lipps (79 and 12 yards), Tim Worley's one-yard run, and a 32-yard field goal by Gary Anderson. Rod Woodson's 72-yard kickoff return to the Buccaneers' 17-yard line set up Worley's second touchdown run in the third quarter. Woodson also had a 12-yard interception return to set up Gary Anderson's 32-yard field goal.

Pittsburgh	7	17	7	0	— 31
Tampa Bay	7	3	3	9	— 22

Pitt —Worley 1 run (Anderson kick)
TB —Carrier 7 pass from Ferguson (Igwebuike kick)
Pitt —Lipps 79 pass from Brister (Anderson kick)
TB —FG Igwebuike 45
Pitt —Lipps 12 pass from Brister (Anderson kick)
Pitt —FG Anderson 32
TB —FG Igwebuike 24
Pitt —Worley 1 run (Anderson kick)
TB —Safety, Cocroft blocked punt out of end zone
TB —Carrier 39 pass from Ferguson (Igwebuike kick)

Philadelphia 31, Phoenix 14—at Veterans Stadium, attendance 43,287. Randall Cunningham ran for one touchdown and threw for another as the Eagles defeated the Cardinals to gain a Wild Card playoff berth. Philadelphia took a 21-14 halftime lead on Cunningham's 14-yard run, a 22-yard pass on a fake field goal from Eagles kicker Roger Ruzek to Cris Carter, and Cunningham's four-yard completion to Robert Drummond. Ruzek's 39-yard field goal and Heath Sherman's seven-yard scoring run completed the Eagles' scoring.

Phoenix	7	7	0	0	— 14
Philadelphia	7	14	3	7	— 31

Phx —Green 6 pass from Hogeboom (Del Greco kick)
Phil —Cunningham 14 run (Ruzek kick)
Phil —Carter 22 pass from Ruzek (Ruzek kick)
Phil —Drummond 4 pass from Cunningham (Ruzek kick)
Phx —Green 36 pass from Hogeboom (Del Greco kick)
Phil —FG Ruzek 39
Phil —Sherman 7 run (Ruzek kick)

Monday, December 25

Minnesota 29, Cincinnati 21—at Metrodome, attendance 58,829. Rich Karlis kicked five field goals and Minnesota's defense produced six turnovers as the Vikings downed the Bengals to clinch the NFC Central Division title and knock Cincinnati out of the playoffs. Karlis kicked all five field goals in the first half and Rick Fenney grabbed an 11-yard pass from Wade Wilson to help Minnesota to a 22-7 halftime lead. The Bengals narrowed the score to

22-21 in the fourth quarter, but Wade Wilson's one-yard scoring completion to Brent Novoselsky with 4:17 to play sealed the win. Chris Doleman recorded three of the Vikings' six sacks.

Cincinnati	0	7	7	7	— 21
Minnesota	6	16	0	7	— 29

Minn — FG Karlis 31
Minn — FG Karlis 37
Minn — FG Karlis 22
Minn — Fenney 11 pass from Wilson (Karlis kick)
Minn — FG Karlis 42
Cin — Brown 34 pass from Esiason (Breech kick)
Minn — FG Karlis 24
Cin — Holman 65 pass from Esiason (Breech kick)
Cin — Taylor 18 pass from Esiason (Breech kick)
Minn — Novoselsky 1 pass from Wilson (Karlis kick)

Seventeenth Week Summaries

Sunday, December 31, 1989
AFC First-Round Playoff Game

Pittsburgh 26, Houston 23—at Astrodome, attendance 59,406. Gary Anderson kicked a 50-yard field goal 3:26 into overtime to cap the Steelers' 26-23 comeback win over the Oilers and earn Pittsburgh its first playoff victory since 1984. The Steelers, despite being outgained by Houston 380 to 289 total yards, led the game for more than three quarters. Rookie running back Tim Worley converted a fourth-and-one play into a nine-yard touchdown run and Anderson kicked field goals of 25, 30, and 48 yards for a 16-9 fourth-quarter lead. Houston's Warren Moon tied the score with an 18-yard touchdown pass to Ernest Givins and gave the Oilers their only lead, 23-16, when he found Givins on a nine-yard scoring pass with six minutes to play. Pittsburgh's Bubby Brister countered with an 82-yard, 11-play drive capped by Merril Hoge's one-yard touchdown plunge with 46 seconds remaining. Anderson's extra point tied the score and sent the game into overtime. The Steelers won the extra period coin toss but were forced to punt. Rod Woodson recovered Lorenzo White's fumble on the Oilers' first play in overtime to set up Anderson's decisive field goal. Hoge became the first Steelers player to gain 100 yards (17 carries for 100 yards) in a postseason game since Franco Harris in 1978. Moon completed 29 of 48 passes for 315 yards and two touchdowns, including 11 to Givins for 136 yards and both scores.

Pittsburgh	7	3	3	10	3	— 26
Houston	0	6	3	14	0	— 23

Pitt — Worley 9 run (Anderson kick)
Hou — FG Zendejas 26
Hou — FG Zendejas 35
Pitt — FG Anderson 25
Hou — FG Zendejas 26
Pitt — FG Anderson 30
Pitt — FG Anderson 48
Hou — Givins 18 pass from Moon (Zendejas kick)
Hou — Givins 9 pass from Moon (Zendejas kick)
Pitt — Hoge 2 run (Anderson kick)
Pitt — FG Anderson 50

Sunday, December 31, 1989
NFC First-Round Playoff Game

Los Angeles 21, Philadelphia 7—at Veterans Stadium, attendance 65,479. The Los Angeles Rams captured the NFC First-Round Playoff with a 21-7 victory over Philadelphia. The Rams jumped to a 14-0 lead midway through the opening quarter on Jim Everett touchdown passes of 39 yards to Henry Ellard and four yards to Damone Johnson. Greg Bell rushed 27 times for 124 yards for the Rams, including a seven-yard scoring run in the fourth period. Everett completed 18 of 33 passes for 281 yards and two touchdowns, with two interceptions. Los Angeles held advantages in time of possession (33:38 to 26:22) and yards (409 to 306). Kevin Greene had two sacks and a fumble recovery for Los Angeles.

L.A. Rams	14	0	0	7	— 21
Philadelphia	0	0	0	7	— 7

Rams — Ellard 39 pass from Everett (Lansford kick)
Rams — Johnson 4 pass from Everett (Lansford kick)
Phil — Toney 1 run (Ruzek kick)
Rams — Bell 7 run (Lansford kick)

Eighteenth Week Summaries

Saturday, January 6, 1990
AFC Divisional Playoff Game

Cleveland 34, Buffalo 30—at Cleveland Stadium, attendance 78,921. Clay Matthews's interception at the Cleveland 1-yard line with three seconds to play helped the Browns preserve a 34-30 win over the Bills and earn a berth in the AFC Championship Game for the third time in four years. Buffalo scored on its sixth offensive play of the game when Andre Reed and Jim Kelly combined on a 72-yard pass play. Cleveland's Bernie Kosar countered with touchdown passes of 52 yards to Webster Slaughter and three yards to Ron Middleton for a 17-14 halftime lead. Cleveland extended its lead to 24-14 on Kosar's 44-yard touchdown pass to Slaughter following an interception by Mark Harper. The Bills cut their deficit to three points as Mark Kelso's fumble recovery at the Cleveland 21 set up Kelly's six-yard scoring pass to Thurman Thomas. Cleveland rookie Eric Metcalf returned the ensuing kickoff 90 yards for a touchdown, the first such play in Browns' postseason history. After the teams swapped field goals, Kelly hit Thomas on a three-yard touchdown pass. However, the extra point failed. Thomas tied an NFL postseason record with 13 receptions for 150 yards, while Kelly set a club playoff mark with 405 yards passing on 28 completions in 54 attempts, with four touchdowns and two interceptions. Kosar completed 20 of 29 passes for 251 yards. Slaughter gained 114 yards on three receptions.

Buffalo	7	7	7	9	— 30
Cleveland	3	14	14	3	— 34

Buff — Reed 72 pass from Kelly (Norwood kick)
Clev — FG Bahr 45
Clev — Slaughter 52 pass from Kosar (Bahr kick)
Buff — Lofton 33 pass from Kelly (Norwood kick)
Clev — Middleton 3 pass from Kosar (Bahr kick)
Clev — Slaughter 44 pass from Kosar (Bahr kick)
Buff — Thomas 6 pass from Kelly (Norwood kick)
Clev — Metcalf 90 kickoff return (Bahr kick)
Buff — FG Norwood 30
Clev — FG Bahr 47
Buff — Thomas 3 pass from Kelly (kick failed)

Saturday, January 6, 1990
NFC Divisional Playoff Game

San Francisco 41, Minnesota 13—at Candlestick Park, attendance 64,918. Defending Super Bowl champion and 1989 NFC West titlist San Francisco gained its fourth NFC Championship Game berth of the decade with a 41-13 victory over NFC Central champion Minnesota. Joe Montana threw four touchdown passes in the first half to lead San Francisco to a 27-3 advantage at intermission. Montana finished with 17 completions in 24 attempts for 241 yards, and the four touchdowns. Roger Craig carried 18 times for 125 yards and one touchdown. Jerry Rice caught six passes for 114 yards and two touchdowns. Ronnie Lott set a club playoff record when he returned an interception 58 yards for a score. Minnesota's 71 sacks during the regular season were the second highest total in NFL history. However, San Francisco did not allow a sack in its victory.

Minnesota	3	0	3	7	— 13
San Francisco	7	20	0	14	— 41

Minn — FG Karlis 38
SF — Rice 72 pass from Montana (Cofer kick)
SF — Jones 8 pass from Montana (Cofer kick)
SF — Taylor 8 pass from Montana (kick failed)
SF — Rice 13 pass from Montana (Cofer kick)
Minn — FG Karlis 44
SF — Lott 58 interception return (Cofer kick)
SF — Craig 4 run (Cofer kick)
Minn — Fenney 3 run (Karlis kick)

Sunday, January 7, 1990
AFC Divisional Playoff Game

Denver 24, Pittsburgh 23—at Mile High Stadium, attendance 75,477. Melvin Bratton scored on a one-yard run with 2:27 to play and David Treadwell added the extra point to give the Broncos a 24-23 win. Denver trailed until that point. Pittsburgh jumped out to a 10-0 advantage on Gary Anderson's first of three field goals (32 yards), and Merril Hoge's seven-yard run. Denver's Bratton scored on a one-yard plunge, but Louis Lipps put the Steelers back on top by 10 with a nine-yard touchdown catch from Bubby Brister. Tyrone Braxton recovered a fumble at the Steelers' 37-yard line early in the third quarter. One play later, John Elway completed a 37-yard touchdown pass to Vance Johnson to tie the score 17-17. Anderson's field goals of 35 and 32 yards gave the Steelers a 23-17 lead, but Elway marched the Broncos 71 yards in nine plays for the winning score. Randy Robbins's fumble recovery at the Pittsburgh 18-yard line with 2:02 remaining sealed the win. Hoge gained 120 yards on 16 carries for the Steelers. Mark Jackson had five receptions for 111 yards for the Broncos.

Pittsburgh	3	14	3	3	— 23
Denver	0	10	7	7	— 24

Pitt — FG Anderson 32
Pitt — Hoge 7 run (Anderson kick)
Den — Bratton 1 run (Treadwell kick)
Pitt — Lipps 9 pass from Brister (Anderson kick)
Den — FG Treadwell 43
Den — Johnson 37 pass from Elway (Treadwell kick)
Pitt — FG Anderson 35
Pitt — FG Anderson 32
Den — Bratton 1 run (Treadwell kick)

Sunday, January 7, 1990
NFC Divisional Playoff Game

Los Angeles Rams 19, New York 13—at Giants Stadium, attendance 76,526. The Wild Card entry Los Angeles Rams gained their first NFC Championship Game berth since 1985 with a 19-13 overtime win over the NFC East champion New York Giants. The Giants took a 6-0 lead on Raul Allegre's field goals of 34 and 41 yards. The Rams gained a 7-6 edge on Willie Anderson's 20-yard touchdown catch with 17 seconds remaining in the first half. New York regained the lead with 1:57 remaining in the third period when Ottis Anderson scored on a two-yard run. The Rams tied the game with 3:01 left in regulation on Mike Lansford's 22-yard field goal. In the overtime, the Rams took the kickoff and scored on Jim Everett's 30-yard scoring pass to Anderson 1:06 into the extra period. Everett completed 25 of 44 passes for 315 yards. Los Angeles's Henry Ellard produced his first 100-yard postseason game with eight catches for 125 yards.

L.A. Rams	0	7	0	6	6	— 19
N.Y. Giants	6	0	7	0	0	— 13

NYG — FG Allegre 35
NYG — FG Allegre 41
Rams — Anderson 20 pass from Everett (Lansford kick)
NYG — Anderson 2 run (Allegre kick)
Rams — FG Lansford 31
Rams — FG Lansford 22
Rams — Anderson 30 pass from Everett

Nineteenth Week Summaries

Sunday, January 14, 1990
AFC Championship Game

Denver 37, Cleveland 21—at Mile High Stadium, attendance 76,046. The AFC West champion Denver Broncos advanced to their third Super Bowl in the past four seasons by defeating the AFC Central titlist Cleveland Browns 37-21. Denver eclipsed or tied 17 team postseason records and exceeded or equalled 11 more individual marks. John Elway completed 20 of 36 passes for 385 yards and three touchdowns. He also led all rushers with 39 yards on five carries. Elway's 385 passing yards and 424 yards total offense were team records. Elway's 70-yard touchdown pass to Michael Young gave the Broncos a 10-0 halftime lead. Young hauled in a 53-yard pass in the third quarter to set up Orson Mobley's five-yard scoring catch for a 17-7 Denver lead. After Sammy Winder extended the Broncos' advantage to 24-7 on a seven-yard run, Cleveland closed the gap to three points by scoring a pair of touchdowns within a 2:11 span. Denver countered by scoring on three of its four fourth-quarter drives. The Broncos' defense limited the Browns to 256 total yards and deflected six Kosar passes.

Cleveland	0	0	21	0	— 21
Denver	3	7	14	13	— 37

Den — FG Treadwell 29
Den — Young 70 pass from Elway (Treadwell kick)
Clev — Brennan 27 pass from Kosar (Bahr kick)
Den — Mobley 5 pass from Elway (Treadwell kick)
Den — Winder 7 run (Treadwell kick)
Clev — Brennan 10 pass from Kosar (Bahr kick)
Clev — Manoa 2 run (Bahr kick)
Den — Winder 39 pass from Elway (Treadwell kick)
Den — FG Treadwell 34
Den — FG Treadwell 31

Sunday, January 14, 1990
NFC Championship Game

San Francisco 30, Los Angeles Rams 3—at Candlestick Park, attendance 65,634. NFC Western Division champion San Francisco gained its fourth Super Bowl berth by dominating the Los Angeles Rams 30-3 in the NFC title game. The 49ers won Super Bowls XVI, XIX, and XXIII. The Rams took a 3-0 lead on Mike Lansford's 23-yard field goal on their first offensive series, but they were held in check the rest of the game. San Francisco amassed 29 first downs compared to Los Angeles's nine; 442 yards to 156; and a time-of-possession advantage of 39:48 to 20:12. San Francisco's Joe Montana completed 26 of 30 passes for 262 yards and two touchdowns. Montana's 31 career postseason touchdown passes surpassed the previous NFL record of 30 by Terry Bradshaw. San Francisco built a 21-3 halftime lead on touchdown catches of 20 yards by Brent Jones and 18 yards by John Taylor, plus a one-yard scoring run by Roger Craig, who gained 93 yards on 23 carries. In the second half, Mike Cofer added field goals of 28, 36, and 25 yards. Montana distributed his passes to eight different receivers. Jerry Rice had six catches for 55 yards and Tom Rathman had six receptions for 48 yards. The 49ers' defense collected interceptions by Tim McKyer, Ronnie Lott, and Keena Turner.

L.A. Rams	3	0	0	0	— 3
San Francisco	0	21	3	6	— 30

Rams — FG Lansford 23
SF — Jones 20 pass from Montana (Cofer kick)
SF — Craig 1 run (Cofer kick)
SF — Taylor 18 pass from Montana (Cofer kick)
SF — FG Cofer 28
SF — FG Cofer 36
SF — FG Cofer 25

Twentieth Week Summary

Sunday, January 28, 1990
Super Bowl XXIV
New Orleans, Louisiana

San Francisco 55, Denver 10—at Louisiana Superdome, New Orleans, Louisiana, attendance 72,919. NFC titlist San Francisco won its fourth Super Bowl championship with a 55-10 victory over AFC champion Denver. The 49ers, who also won Super Bowls XVI, XIX, and XXIII, tied the Pittsburgh Steelers for most Super Bowl victories. The Steelers captured Super Bowls IX, X, XIII, and XIV. San Francisco's 55 points broke the previous Super Bowl scoring mark of 46 points by Chicago in 1986. San Francisco tallied touchdowns on four of its six first-half possessions to hold a 27-3 lead at intermission. The 49ers first half scoring drives were lengthy and time-consuming (10 plays for 66 yards, 10 for 54 yards, 14 for 69 yards, and five for 59 yards). Interceptions by Michael Walter and Chet Brooks ended the Broncos' first two possessions of the second half. Joe Montana was named Super Bowl most valuable player for a record third time. Montana completed 22 of 29 passes for 297 yards and a Super Bowl-record five touchdowns (old record: four, Terry Bradshaw, Pittsburgh, 1979, and Doug Williams, Washington, 1988). Jerry Rice, Super Bowl XXIII most valuable player, caught seven passes for 148 yards and a Super Bowl record three touchdowns. The 49ers' domination included first downs (28 to 12), net yards (461 to 167), and time of possession (39:31 to 20:39).

San Francisco	13	14	14	14	—	55
Denver	3	0	7	0	—	10

SF — Rice 20 pass from Montana (Cofer kick)
Den — FG Treadwell 42
SF — Jones 7 pass from Montana (kick failed)
SF — Rathman 1 run (Cofer kick)
SF — Rice 38 pass from Montana (Cofer kick)
SF — Rice 28 pass from Montana (Cofer kick)
SF — Taylor 35 pass from Montana (Cofer kick)
Den — Elway run 3 (Treadwell kick)
SF — Rathman 3 run (Cofer kick)
SF — Craig 1 run (Cofer kick)

Twenty-First Week Summary
Sunday, February 4, 1990
AFC-NFC Pro Bowl
Honolulu, Hawaii

NFC 27, AFC 21 — at Aloha Stadium, Honolulu, Hawaii, attendance 50,445. The NFC captured its second straight Pro Bowl as the defense accounted for a pair of touchdowns and forced five turnovers before the eleventh consecutive sellout crowd at Aloha Stadium. The AFC held a 7-6 halftime edge on a one-yard run by Christian Okoye of the Chiefs, but the NFC rallied with 21 unanswered points in the third quarter. Dave Meggett of the Giants began the comeback on an 11-yard touchdown reception from the Eagles' Randall Cunningham. The Rams' Jerry Gray followed with a 51-yard interception return for a score and the Vikings' Keith Millard added an eight-yard fumble return for a touchdown four minutes later to give the NFC a commanding 27-7 lead. Seattle's Dave Krieg rallied the AFC with a five-yard touchdown pass to Miami's Ferrell Edmunds. Cleveland's Mike Johnson then returned an interception 22 yards for a score to pull the AFC to within six points 27-21. Gray, who was credited with seven tackles, was voted the Dan McGuire Award as player of the game. Krieg led all quarterbacks by completing 15 of 23 passes for 148 yards and one touchdown. Buffalo's Thurman Thomas topped all receivers with five catches for 47 yards, while Indianapolis's Eric Dickerson led all rushers with 46 yards on 15 carries. The win gave the NFC a 12-8 advantage in Pro Bowl games since 1970.

NFC	3	3	21	0	—	27
AFC	0	7	0	14	—	21

NFC — FG Murray 23
NFC — FG Murray 41
AFC — Okoye 1 run (Treadwell kick)
NFC — Meggett 11 pass from Cunningham (Murray kick)
NFC — Gray 51 interception return (Murray kick)
NFC — Millard 8 fumble recovery return (Murray kick)
AFC — Edmunds 5 pass from Krieg (Treadwell kick)
AFC — Johnson 22 interception return (Treadwell kick)

1989 ALL-PRO TEAMS

1989 PFWA All-Pro Team
Selected by the Professional Football Writers of America
Offense
Jerry Rice, San Francisco . . . . Wide Receiver
Sterling Sharpe, Green Bay . . . . Wide Receiver
Keith Jackson, Philadelphia. . . . . Tight End
Anthony Muñoz, Cincinnati . . . . Tackle
Gary Zimmerman, Minnesota . . . . Tackle
Tom Newberry, Los Angeles Rams. . . . . Guard
Mike Munchak, Houston. . . . . Guard
Jay Hilgenberg, Chicago . . . . Center
Joe Montana, San Francisco . . . . Quarterback
Christian Okoye, Kansas City . . . . Running Back
Barry Sanders, Detroit . . . . Running Back
Eddie Murray, Detroit . . . . Kicker
Rod Woodson, Pittsburgh. . . . . Kick Returner

Defense
Chris Doleman, Minnesota . . . . Defensive End
Reggie White, Philadelphia. . . . . Defensive End
Michael Dean Perry, Cleveland . . . . Defensive Tackle
Keith Millard, Minnesota . . . . Defensive Tackle
Tim Harris, Green Bay . . . . Outside Linebacker
Lawrence Taylor, New York Giants . . . . Outside Linebacker
Mike Singletary, Chicago . . . . Inside Linebacker
Jerry Gray, Los Angeles Rams . . . . Cornerback
Albert Lewis, Kansas City . . . . Cornerback
David Fulcher, Cincinnati . . . . Safety
Ronnie Lott, San Francisco . . . . Safety
Sean Landeta, New York Giants . . . . Punter
Dave Meggett, New York Giants . . . . Punt Returner

1989 Associated Press All-Pro Team
Offense
Jerry Rice, San Francisco . . . . Wide Receiver
Sterling Sharpe, Green Bay . . . . Wide Receiver
Keith Jackson, Philadelphia . . . . Tight End
Anthony Muñoz, Cincinnati . . . . Tackle
Jim Lachey, Washington. . . . . Tackle
Tom Newberry, Los Angeles Rams. . . . . Guard
Bruce Matthews, Houston . . . . Guard
Jay Hilgenberg, Chicago . . . . Center
Joe Montana, San Francisco . . . . Quarterback
Christian Okoye, Kansas City . . . . Running Back
Barry Sanders, Detroit . . . . Running Back
Mike Cofer, San Francisco . . . . Kicker

Defense
Chris Doleman, Minnesota . . . . Defensive End
Reggie White, Philadelphia. . . . . Defensive End
Michael Dean Perry, Cleveland . . . . Defensive Tackle
Keith Millard, Minnesota . . . . Defensive Tackle
Tim Harris, Green Bay . . . . Outside Linebacker
Lawrence Taylor, New York Giants . . . . Outside Linebacker
Mike Singletary, Chicago. . . . . Inside Linebacker
Eric Allen, Philadelphia. . . . . Cornerback
Albert Lewis, Kansas City . . . . Cornerback
David Fulcher, Cincinnati . . . . Safety
Ronnie Lott, San Francisco . . . . Safety
Sean Landeta, New York Giants. . . . . Punter

1989 All-NFL Team
Selected by the Associated Press and Professional Football Writers of America
Offense
Jerry Rice, San Francisco (AP, PFWA) . . . . Wide Receiver
Sterling Sharpe, Green Bay (AP, PFWA). Wide Receiver
Keith Jackson, Philadelphia (AP, PFWA) . . . . Tight End
Anthony Muñoz, Cincinnati (AP, PFWA) . . . . Tackle
Jim Lachey, Washington (AP) . . . . Tackle
Gary Zimmerman, Minnesota (PFWA) . . . . Tackle
Tom Newberry, Los Angeles Rams (AP, PFWA) . . . . Guard
Bruce Matthews, Houston (AP). . . . . Guard
Mike Munchak, Houston (PFWA) . . . . Guard
Jay Hilgenberg, Chicago (AP, PFWA) . . . . Center
Joe Montana, San Francisco (AP, PFWA) . . . . Quarterback
Christian Okoye, Kansas City (AP, PFWA) . . . . Running Back
Barry Sanders, Detroit (AP, PFWA). . . . . Running Back

Defense
Chris Doleman, Minnesota (AP, PFWA). Defensive End
Reggie White, Philadelphia (AP, PFWA) . . . . Defensive End
Michael Dean Perry, Cleveland (AP, PFWA). . . . . Defensive Tackle
Keith Millard, Minnesota (AP, PFWA) . . . . Defensive Tackle
Tim Harris, Green Bay (AP, PFWA) . . . . Outside Linebacker
Lawrence Taylor, New York Giants (AP, PFWA) . . . . Outside Linebacker
Mike Singletary, Chicago (AP, PFWA) . . . . Inside Linebacker
Albert Lewis, Kansas City (AP, PFWA). . . . . Cornerback
Eric Allen, Philadelphia (AP) . . . . Cornerback
Jerry Gray, Los Angeles Rams (PFWA) . . . . Cornerback
David Fulcher, Cincinnati (AP, PFWA) . . . . Safety
Ronnie Lott, San Francisco (AP, PFWA). . . . . Safety

Specialists
Eddie Murray, Detroit (PFWA) . . . . Kicker
Mike Cofer, San Francisco (AP) . . . . Kicker
Sean Landeta, New York Giants (AP, PFWA) . . . . Punter
Rod Woodson, Pittsburgh (PFWA) . . . . Kick Returner
Dave Meggett, New York Giants (PFWA). . . . . Punt Returner

1989 UPI All-AFC Team
Selected by United Press International
Offense
Andre Reed, Buffalo. . . . . Wide Receiver
Webster Slaughter, Cleveland . . . . Wide Receiver
Rodney Holman, Cincinnati . . . . Tight End
Anthony Muñoz, Cincinnati . . . . Tackle
Chris Hinton, Indianapolis . . . . Tackle
Bruce Matthews, Houston . . . . Guard
Mike Munchak, Houston. . . . . Guard
Kent Hull, Buffalo . . . . Center
Warren Moon, Houston . . . . Quarterback
Christian Okoye, Kansas City . . . . Running Back
Thurman Thomas, Buffalo. . . . . Running Back
David Treadwell, Denver . . . . Kicker

Defense
Bruce Smith, Buffalo . . . . Defensive End
Lee Williams, San Diego . . . . Defensive End
Michael Dean Perry, Cleveland . . . . Defensive Tackle
Derrick Thomas, Kansas City . . . . Outside Linebacker
Leslie O'Neal, San Diego. . . . . Outside Linebacker
Karl Mecklenburg, Denver . . . . Inside Linebacker
Mike Johnson, Cleveland . . . . Inside Linebacker
Albert Lewis, Kansas City . . . . Cornerback
Frank Minnifield, Cleveland . . . . Cornerback
Erik McMillan, New York Jets. . . . . Safety
David Fulcher, Cincinnati . . . . Safety
Greg Montgomery, Houston . . . . Punter

1989 UPI All-NFC Team

Selected by United Press International

Offense

Jerry Rice, San Francisco	Wide Receiver
Sterling Sharpe, Green Bay	Wide Receiver
Keith Jackson, Philadelphia	Tight End
Jim Lachey, Washington	Tackle
Paul Gruber, Tampa Bay	Tackle
Tom Newberry, Los Angeles Rams	Guard
Bill Fralic, Atlanta	Guard
Jay Hilgenberg, Chicago	Center
Joe Montana, San Francisco	Quarterback
Barry Sanders, Detroit	Running Back
Neal Anderson, Chicago	Running Back
Mike Cofer, San Francisco	Kicker

Defense

Reggie White, Philadelphia	Defensive End
Chris Doleman, Minnesota	Defensive End
Keith Millard, Minnesota	Defensive Tackle
Tim Harris, Green Bay	Outside Linebacker
Lawrence Taylor, New York Giants	Outside Linebacker
Mike Singletary, Chicago	Inside Linebacker
Vaughan Johnson, New Orleans	Inside Linebacker
Eric Allen, Philadelphia	Cornerback
Don Griffin, San Francisco	Cornerback
Ronnie Lott, San Francisco	Safety
Tim McDonald, Phoenix	Safety
Sean Landeta, New York Giants	Punter

1989 PFWA All-Rookie Team

Selected by Professional Football Writers of America

Offense

Andre Rison, Indianapolis	Wide Receiver
Shawn Collins, Atlanta	Wide Receiver
Travis McNeal, Seattle	Tight End
Andy Heck, Seattle	Tackle
Kevin Haverdink, New Orleans	Tackle
Steve Wisniewski, Los Angeles Raiders	Guard
Joe Wolf, Phoenix	Guard
Courtney Hall, San Diego	Center
Troy Aikman, Dallas	Quarterback
Barry Sanders, Detroit	Running Back
Bobby Humphrey, Denver	Running Back
Chris Jacke, Green Bay	Kicker

Defense

Burt Grossman, San Diego	Defensive End
Trace Armstrong, Chicago	Defensive End
Bill Hawkins, Los Angeles Rams	Defensive Tackle
Tracy Rocker, Washington	Defensive Tackle
Derrick Thomas, Kansas City	Outside Linebacker
Jeff Lageman, New York Jets	Outside Linebacker
Jerry Olsavsky, Pittsburgh	Inside Linebacker
Robert Massey, New Orleans	Cornerback
Deion Sanders, Atlanta	Cornerback
Carnell Lake, Pittsburgh	Safety
Steve Atwater, Denver	Safety
Chris Mohr, Tampa Bay	Punter

1989 UPI All-Rookie Team

Selected by United Press International

Offense

Shawn Collins, Atlanta	Wide Receiver
Andre Rison, Indianapolis	Wide Receiver
Howard Cross, New York Giants	Tight End
Kevin Haverdink, New Orleans	Tackle
Andy Heck, Seattle	Tackle
Steve Wisniewski, Los Angeles Raiders	Guard
Joe Wolf, Phoenix	Guard
Courtney Hall, San Diego	Center
Troy Aikman, Dallas	Quarterback
Bobby Humphrey, Denver	Running Back
Barry Sanders, Detroit	Running Back
Chris Jacke, Green Bay	Kicker
James Dixon, Dallas	Kick Returner
Dave Meggett, New York Giants	Punt Returner

Defense

Trace Armstrong, Chicago	Defensive End
Burt Grossman, San Diego	Defensive End
Tracy Rocker, Washington	Defensive Tackle
John Roper, Chicago	Outside Linebacker
Derrick Thomas, Kansas City	Outside Linebacker
Eric Hill, Phoenix	Inside Linebacker
Jerry Olsavsky, Pittsburgh	Inside Linebacker
Maurice Hurst, New England	Cornerback
Donnell Woolford, Chicago	Cornerback
Steve Atwater, Denver	Safety
Louis Oliver, Miami	Safety
Chris Mohr, Tampa Bay	Punter

1989 Professional Football Awards

	NFL	AFC	NFC
Professional Football Writers of America			
Most Valuable Player	Joe Montana		
Rookie of the Year	Barry Sanders		
Coach of the Year		Chuck Noll	Lindy Infante
Associated Press			
Most Valuable Player	Joe Montana		
Offensive Player of the Year	Joe Montana		
Defensive Player of the Year	Keith Millard		
Rookie of the Year—Offense	Barry Sanders		
Rookie of the Year—Defense	Derrick Thomas		
Coach of the Year	Lindy Infante		
United Press International			
Offensive Player of the Year		Christian Okoye	Joe Montana
Defensive Player of the Year		Michael Dean Perry	Keith Millard
Coach of the Year		Dan Reeves	Lindy Infante
The Sporting News			
Player of the Year	Joe Montana		
Rookie of the Year	Barry Sanders		
Coach of the Year	Lindy Infante		
Football News			
Player of the Year		Warren Moon	Joe Montana
Coach of the Year		Dan Reeves	Lindy Infante
Pro Football Weekly			
Offensive Player of the Year	Joe Montana		
Defensive Player of the Year	Keith Millard		
Rookie of the Year-Offense	Barry Sanders		
Rookie of the Year-Defense	Derrick Thomas		
Coach of the Year	George Seifert		
Football Digest			
Player of the Year	Joe Montana		
Rookie of the Year-Offense	Barry Sanders		
Rookie of the Year-Defense	Steve Atwater		
Coach of the Year	George Seifert		
Maxwell Club			
Player of the Year (Bert Bell Trophy)	Joe Montana		
Super Bowl XXIV Most Valuable Player			
	Joe Montana		
AFC-NFC Pro Bowl			
Player of the Game (Dan McGuire Award)	Jerry Gray		

AFC-NFC Players of the Week:

	AFC Offense	**AFC Defense**	**NFC Offense**	**NFC Defense**
Week 1	QB Jim Kelly, Buff.	LB David Grayson, Clev.	QB Vinny Testaverde, T.B.	DT Dan Hampton, Chi.
Week 2	QB Dan Marino, Mia.	LB Derrick Thomas, K.C.	QB Randall Cunningham, Phil.	LB Lawrence Taylor, NYG
Week 3	QB Jim Kelly, Buff.	CB Gill Byrd, S.D.	QB Joe Montana, S.F.	S Vince Newsome, Rams
Week 4	QB Bubby Brister, Pitt.	S David Fulcher, Cin.	QB Mike Tomczak, Chi.	LB Tim Harris, G.B.
Week 5	RB Christian Okoye, K.C.	S Louis Oliver, Mia.	Buccaneers Offense	DT Keith Millard, Minn.
Week 6	QB Warren Moon, Hou.	S Carnell Lake, Pitt.	QB Rodney Peete, Det.	DT Jerome Brown, Phil.
Week 7	QB John Elway, Den.	S Keith Taylor, Ind.	RB Dalton Hilliard, N.O.	LB Mike Merriweather, Minn.
Week 8	WR Webster Slaughter, Clev.	S Eddie Anderson, Raiders	QB Don Majkowski, G.B.	LB Pat Swilling, N.O.
Week 9	QB Ken O'Brien, NYJ	DE Leslie O'Neal, S.D.	K Rich Karlis, Minn.	LB Lawrence Taylor, NYG
Week 10	QB Dan Marino, Mia.	NT Greg Kragen, Den.	QB Jim Everett, Rams	S Tim McDonald, Phx.
Week 11	QB Boomer Esiason, Cin. & WR Tim McGee, Cin.	DE Brent Williams, N.E.	WR Henry Ellard, Rams	LB Pat Swilling, N.O.
Week 12	WR Vance Johnson, Den.	DE Leonard Griffin, K.C.	WR Willie Anderson, Rams	DE Pierce Holt, S.F.
Week 13	TE Mike Dyal, Raiders	S David Fulcher, Cin.	WR Richard Johnson, Det.	CB A.J. Johnson, Wash.
Week 14	WR Steve Largent, Sea.	S Mike Prior, Ind.	WR John Taylor, S.F.	DE Chris Doleman, Minn.
Week 15	QB Jack Trudeau, Ind.	S David Fulcher, Cin.	QB Mark Rypien, Wash.	LB Brett Faryniarz, Rams
Week 16	WR Louis Lipps, Pitt.	LB Leslie O'Neal, S.D.	RB Greg Bell, Rams	DE Chris Doleman, Minn.

AFC-NFC Players of the Month:

	AFC Offense	**AFC Defense**	**NFC Offense**	**NFC Defense**
Sept.	QB Jim Kelly, Buff.	LB Mike Johnson, Clev.	RB Neal Anderson, Chi.	LB Lawrence Taylor, NYG
Oct.	WR Webster Slaughter, Clev.	S Dennis Smith, Den.	QB Bobby Hebert, N.O.	DT Keith Millard, Minn.
Nov.	WR Anthony Miller, S.D.	LB Karl Mecklenburg, Den.	QB Joe Montana, S.F.	LB Tim Harris, G.B.
Dec.	RB John L. Williams, Sea.	S David Fulcher, Cin.	RB Barry Sanders, Det.	DE Chris Doleman, Minn.

Ten Best Rushing Performances, 1989

	Attempts	Yards	TD
1. Gerald Riggs Washington vs. Philadelphia, September 17	29	221	1
Greg Bell L.A. Rams vs. Green Bay, September 24	28	221	2
3. Greg Bell L.A. Rams vs. New England, December 24	26	210	1
4. Barry Sanders Detroit vs. Green Bay, October 29	30	184	0
5. Marion Butts San Diego vs. Kansas City, December 17	39	176	0
6. Christian Okoye Kansas City vs. Dallas, October 22	33	170	2
7. Bo Jackson L.A. Raiders vs. Cincinnati, November 5	13	159	2
8. Dalton Hilliard New Orleans vs. Atlanta, November 19	29	158	1
Barry Sanders Detroit vs. Atlanta, December 24	20	158	3
10. Christian Okoye Kansas City vs. Seattle, October 8	30	156	1

100-Yard Rushing Performances, 1989

First Week
Neal Anderson, Chicago	146 yards vs. Cincinnati
Roger Craig, San Francisco	131 yards vs. Indianapolis
Greg Bell, L.A. Rams	128 yards vs. Atlanta
Gerald Riggs, Washington	111 yards vs. N.Y. Giants
Eric Dickerson, Indianapolis	106 yards vs. San Francisco

Second Week
Gerald Riggs, Washington	221 yards vs. Philadelphia
Brent Fullwood, Green Bay	125 yards vs. New Orleans
Eric Dickerson, Indianapolis	116 yards vs. L.A. Rams
James Brooks, Cincinnati	113 yards vs. Pittsburgh

Third Week
Greg Bell, L.A. Rams	221 yards vs. Green Bay
Barry Sanders, Detroit	126 yards vs. Chicago
Neal Anderson, Chicago	116 yards vs. Detroit
Christian Okoye, Kansas City	112 yards vs. San Diego
Jamie Morris, Washington	100 yards vs. Dallas

Fourth Week
Thurman Thomas, Buffalo	105 yards vs. New England
Curt Warner, Seattle	102 yards vs. L.A. Raiders
Christian Okoye, Kansas City	101 yards vs. Cincinnati

Fifth Week
Christian Okoye, Kansas City	156 yards vs. Seattle
James Brooks, Cincinnati	127 yards vs. Pittsburgh
Brent Fullwood, Green Bay	119 yards vs. Dallas
Lars Tate, Tampa Bay	112 yards vs. Chicago
Bobby Humphrey, Denver	102 yards vs. San Diego
Earnest Byner, Washington	100 yards vs. Phoenix

Sixth Week
Herschel Walker, Minnesota	148 yards vs. Green Bay
Thurman Thomas, Buffalo	105 yards vs. L.A. Rams
Ottis Anderson, N.Y. Giants	101 yards vs. Washington

Seventh Week
Christian Okoye, Kansas City	170 yards vs. Dallas
Eric Dickerson, Indianapolis	152 yards vs. Cincinnati

Eighth Week
Barry Sanders, Detroit	184 yards vs. Green Bay
Thurman Thomas, Buffalo	148 yards vs. Miami
Bo Jackson, L.A. Raiders	144 yards vs. Washington
James Brooks, Cincinnati	131 yards vs. Tampa Bay
Larry Kinnebrew, Buffalo	121 yards vs. Miami
Christian Okoye, Kansas City	101 yards vs. Pittsburgh

Ninth Week
Bo Jackson, L.A. Raiders	159 yards vs. Cincinnati
Christian Okoye, Kansas City	126 yards vs. Seattle
Sammie Smith, Miami	123 yards vs. Indianapolis
Paul Palmer, Dallas	110 yards vs. Washington
Bobby Humphrey, Denver	105 yards vs. Pittsburgh

Tenth Week
James Brooks, Cincinnati	141 yards vs. Houston
Thurman Thomas, Buffalo	127 yards vs. Indianapolis
Roger Craig, San Francisco	109 yards vs. Atlanta
Dalton Hilliard, New Orleans	106 yards vs. New England
Bo Jackson, L.A. Raiders	103 yards vs. San Diego

Eleventh Week
Dalton Hilliard, New Orleans	158 yards vs. Atlanta
Eric Dickerson, Indianapolis	131 yards vs. N.Y. Jets
John Stephens, New England	126 yards vs. Buffalo
Barry Sanders, Detroit	114 yards vs. Cincinnati
Bobby Humphrey, Denver	110 yards vs. Washington
Neal Anderson, Chicago	100 yards vs. Tampa Bay

Twelfth Week
Barry Sanders, Detroit	145 yards vs. Cleveland
Dalton Hilliard, New Orleans	112 yards vs. L.A. Rams
James Brooks, Cincinnati	105 yards vs. Buffalo
Thurman Thomas, Buffalo	100 yards vs. Cincinnati

Thirteenth Week
Christian Okoye, Kansas City	148 yards vs. Miami
Bobby Humphrey, Denver	125 yards vs. L.A. Raiders
John Stephens, New England	124 yards vs. Indianapolis
Lorenzo White, Houston	115 yards vs. Pittsburgh
Johnny Hector, N.Y. Jets	106 yards vs. San Diego
Tim Worley, Pittsburgh	103 yards vs. Houston

Fourteenth Week
Eric Dickerson, Indianapolis	137 yards vs. Cleveland
Christian Okoye, Kansas City	131 yards vs. Green Bay
Barry Sanders, Detroit	120 yards vs. Chicago
Bo Jackson, L.A. Raiders	114 yards vs. Phoenix

Fifteenth Week
Marion Butts, San Diego	176 yards vs. Kansas City
Bobby Humphrey, Denver	128 yards vs. Phoenix
Neal Anderson, Chicago	119 yards vs. Green Bay
Keith Woodside, Green Bay	116 yards vs. Chicago
Eric Dickerson, Indianapolis	107 yards vs. Miami
Roger Craig, San Francisco	105 yards vs. Buffalo
Barry Sanders, Detroit	104 yards vs. Tampa Bay
Tim Worley, Pittsburgh	104 yards vs. New England

Sixteenth Week
Greg Bell, L.A. Rams	210 yards vs. New England
Barry Sanders, Detroit	158 yards vs. Atlanta

Times 100 or More (74)
Okoye, 8; Sanders, 7; Dickerson, 6; Brooks, Humphrey, Thomas, 5; N. Anderson, Jackson, 4; Bell, Craig, Hilliard, 3; Fullwood, Riggs, Stephens, Worley, 2.

Ten Best Passing Yardage Performances, 1989

	Att.	Comp.	Yards	TD
1. Joe Montana San Francisco vs. L.A. Rams, December 11	42	30	458	3
2. Jim Everett L.A. Rams vs. New Orleans, November 26	51	29	454	1
3. Randall Cunningham Philadelphia vs. Washington, September 17	46	34	447	5
4. Joe Montana San Francisco vs. Philadelphia, Sept. 24	34	24	428	5
5. Dan Marino Miami vs. N.Y. Jets, September 24	55	33	427	3
6. Warren Moon Houston vs. Cleveland, December 23	51	32	414	2
7. Randall Cunningham Philadelphia vs. Chicago, October 2	62	32	401	1
Mark Rypien Washington vs. Chicago, November 26	47	30	401	4
9. Boomer Esiason Cincinnati vs. Detroit, November 19	39	30	399	3
10. Jim McMahon San Diego vs. Houston, September 17	45	27	389	2

300-Yard Passing Performances, 1989

First Week
Mark Rypien, Washington — 349 yards vs. N.Y. Giants
Second Week
Randall Cunningham, Phil. — 447 yards vs. Washington
Jim McMahon, San Diego — 389 yards vs. Houston
Jim Everett, L.A. Rams — 368 yards vs. Indianapolis
Don Majkowski, Green Bay — 354 yards vs. New Orleans
Bob Gagliano, Detroit — 344 yards vs. N.Y. Giants
Tony Eason, New England — 341 yards vs. Miami
Boomer Esiason, Cincinnati — 328 yards vs. Pittsburgh
Third Week
Joe Montana, San Francisco — 428 yards vs. Philadelphia
Dan Marino, Miami — 427 yards vs. N.Y. Jets
Jim Kelly, Buffalo — 363 yards vs. Houston
Warren Moon, Houston — 338 yards vs. Buffalo
Don Majkowski, Green Bay — 335 yards vs. L.A. Rams
Ken O'Brien, N.Y. Jets — 329 yards vs. Miami
Mike Tomczak, Chicago — 302 yards vs. Detroit
Fourth Week
Randall Cunningham, Phil. — 401 yards vs. Chicago
Fifth Week
Chris Miller, Atlanta — 340 yards vs. L.A. Rams
Ken O'Brien, N.Y. Jets — 338 yards vs. L.A. Raiders
Mark Rypien, Washington — 333 yards vs. Phoenix
Don Majkowski, Green Bay — 313 yards vs. Dallas
Bobby Hebert, New Orleans — 308 yards vs. San Francisco
Sixth Week
Warren Moon, Houston — 317 yards vs. Chicago
Seventh Week
John Elway, Denver — 344 yards vs. Seattle
Dan Marino, Miami — 333 yards vs. Green Bay
Vinny Testaverde, Tampa Bay — 311 yards vs. Washington
Eighth Week
Don Majkowski, Green Bay — 367 yards vs. Detroit
Mark Rypien, Washington — 364 yards vs. L.A. Raiders
Steve Grogan, New England — 355 yards vs. Indianapolis
Steve DeBerg, Kansas City — 338 yards vs. Pittsburgh
Vinny Testaverde, Tampa Bay — 336 yards vs. Cincinnati
Dave Krieg, Seattle — 311 yards vs. San Diego
Ninth Week
Ken O'Brien, N.Y. Jets — 386 yards vs. New England
Vinny Testaverde, Tampa Bay — 370 yards vs. Cleveland
Warren Moon, Houston — 345 yards vs. Detroit
Joe Montana, San Francisco — 302 yards vs. New Orleans
Tenth Week
Troy Aikman, Dallas — 379 yards vs. Phoenix
Dan Marino, Miami — 359 yards vs. N.Y. Jets
Don Majkowski, Green Bay — 357 yards vs. Detroit

Eleventh Week
Boomer Esiason, Cincinnati — 399 yards vs. Detroit
Jim Kelly, Buffalo — 356 yards vs. New England
Joe Montana, San Francisco — 325 yards vs. Green Bay
Jim Everett, L.A. Rams — 308 yards vs. Phoenix
Twelfth Week
Jim Everett, L.A. Rams — 454 yards vs. New Orleans
Mark Rypien, Washington — 401 yards vs. Chicago
Phil Simms, N.Y. Giants — 326 yards vs. San Francisco
Wade Wilson, Minnesota — 309 yards vs. Green Bay
Thirteenth Week
Jim Everett, L.A. Rams — 341 yards vs. Dallas
Don Majkowski, Green Bay — 331 yards vs. Tampa Bay
Fourteenth Week
Joe Montana, San Francisco — 458 yards vs. L.A. Rams
Bernie Kosar, Cleveland — 353 yards vs. Indianapolis
Billy Joe Tolliver, San Diego — 350 yards vs. Washington
Vinny Testaverde, Tampa Bay — 328 yards vs. Houston
John Fourcade, New Orleans — 302 yards vs. Buffalo
Mark Rypien, Washington — 302 yards vs. San Diego
Dan Marino, Miami — 300 yards vs. New England
Fifteenth Week
Boomer Esiason, Cincinnati — 326 yards vs. Houston
Chris Miller, Atlanta — 310 yards vs. Washington
Randall Cunningham, Phil. — 306 yards vs. New Orleans
Sixteenth Week
Warren Moon, Houston — 414 yards vs. Cleveland
Boomer Esiason, Cincinnati — 367 yards vs. Minnesota
Dan Marino, Miami — 339 yards vs. Kansas City
Chris Miller, Atlanta — 334 yards vs. Detroit
Steve Grogan, New England — 313 yards vs. L.A. Rams
Billy Joe Tolliver, San Diego — 305 yards vs. Denver
Wade Wilson, Minnesota — 303 yards vs. Cincinnati

Times 300 or More (65)

Majkowski, 6; Marino, Rypien, 5; Esiason, Everett, Montana, Moon, Testaverde, 4; Cunningham, Miller, O'Brien, 3; Grogan, Kelly, Tolliver, Wilson, 2.

Ten Best Receiving Performances, 1989

	No.	Yds.	TD
1. Willie Anderson L.A. Rams vs. New Orleans, November 26	15	336	1
2. John Taylor San Francisco vs. L.A. Rams, December 11	11	286	2
3. Richard Johnson Detroit vs. New Orleans, December 3	8	248	1
4. Henry Ellard L.A. Rams vs. Indianapolis, September 17	12	230	3
5. James Dixon Dallas vs. Phoenix, November 12	6	203	1
6. Tim McGee Cincinnati vs. Detroit, November 19	11	194	1
7. Michael Haynes Atlanta vs. Washington, December 17	6	190	2
8. Webster Slaughter Cleveland vs. Chicago, October 23	8	186	1
9. Webster Slaughter Cleveland vs. Houston, October 29	4	184	2
10. Richard Johnson Detroit vs. N.Y. Giants, September 17	9	172	1

100-Yard Receiving Performances, 1989
(Number in parentheses is receptions.)

First Week
Jerry Rice, San Francisco — 163 yards (6) vs. Indianapolis
Cedric Jones, New England — 148 yards (8) vs. N.Y. Jets
Ricky Sanders, Washington — 143 yards (6) vs. N.Y. Giants
Mike Quick, Philadelphia — 140 yards (6) vs. Seattle
Willie Gault, L.A. Raiders — 131 yards (4) vs. San Diego
Anthony Carter, Minnesota — 123 yards (7) vs. Houston
J.T. Smith, Phoenix — 121 yards (10) vs. Detroit
Gary Clark, Washington — 101 yards (6) vs. N.Y. Giants

Second Week
Henry Ellard, L.A. Rams — 230 yards (12) vs. Indianapolis
Richard Johnson, Detroit — 172 yards (9) vs. N.Y. Giants
Roy Green, Phoenix — 166 yards (8) vs. Seattle
Anthony Miller, San Diego — 162 yards (7) vs. Houston
Andre Reed, Buffalo — 157 yards (13) vs. Denver
Gary Clark, Washington — 153 yards (4) vs. Philadelphia
Brian Blades, Seattle — 146 yards (9) vs. Phoenix
Keith Byars, Philadelphia — 130 yards (8) vs. Washington
Keith Jackson, Philadelphia — 126 yards (12) vs. Washington
Louis Lipps, Pittsburgh — 122 yards (5) vs. Cincinnati
Jerry Rice, San Francisco — 122 yards (8) vs. Tampa Bay
Michael Irvin, Dallas — 115 yards (5) vs. Atlanta
Sterling Sharpe, Green Bay — 107 yards (8) vs. New Orleans
J.T. Smith, Phoenix — 104 yards (7) vs. Seattle
Tim McGee, Cincinnati — 100 yards (6) vs. Pittsburgh

Third Week
Jerry Rice, San Francisco — 164 yards (6) vs. Philadelphia
Sterling Sharpe, Green Bay — 164 yards (8) vs. L.A. Rams
Al Toon, N.Y. Jets — 159 yards (10) vs. Miami
John Taylor, San Francisco — 136 yards (6) vs. Philadelphia
Andre Reed, Buffalo — 135 yards (5) vs. Houston
Mervyn Fernandez, L.A. Raiders — 124 yards (4) vs. Denver
Mark Carrier, Tampa Bay — 120 yards (5) vs. New Orleans
Art Monk, Washington — 114 yards (6) vs. Dallas
Mark Duper, Miami — 113 yards (6) vs. N.Y. Jets

Fourth Week
Bill Brooks, Indianapolis — 159 yards (7) vs. N.Y. Jets
Vance Johnson, Denver — 145 yards (5) vs. Cleveland
Shawn Collins, Atlanta — 126 yards (5) vs. Green Bay
Louis Lipps, Pittsburgh — 126 yards (7) vs. Detroit
Robert Clark, Detroit — 124 yards (6) vs. Pittsburgh
J.T. Smith, Phoenix — 123 yards (11) vs. San Diego
Andre Reed, Buffalo — 114 yards (4) vs. New England
Brian Blades, Seattle — 113 yards (7) vs. L.A. Raiders
Cris Carter, Philadelphia — 113 yards (8) vs. Chicago
Mervyn Fernandez, L.A. Raiders — 113 yards (7) vs. Seattle
Willie Anderson, L.A. Rams — 112 yards (4) vs. San Francisco

Fifth Week
Henry Ellard, L.A. Rams — 165 yards (8) vs. Atlanta
Jerry Rice, San Francisco — 149 yards (7) vs. New Orleans
Sterling Sharpe, Green Bay — 132 yards (6) vs. Dallas
Ernest Givins, Houston — 128 yards (5) vs. New England
J.T. Smith, Phoenix — 114 yards (8) vs. Washington
Bill Brooks, Indianapolis — 111 yards (5) vs. Buffalo
Bruce Hill, Tampa Bay — 107 yards (6) vs. Chicago
Mark Carrier, Tampa Bay — 105 yards (6) vs. Chicago
Art Monk, Washington — 102 yards (8) vs. Phoenix

Sixth Week
Ernie Jones, Phoenix — 144 yards (8) vs. Philadelphia
Eric Martin, New Orleans — 131 yards (5) vs. N.Y. Jets
Mark Duper, Miami — 129 yards (5) vs. Cincinnati
Drew Hill, Houston — 128 yards (5) vs. Chicago
Anthony Miller, San Diego — 116 yards (7) vs. Seattle
Dennis Gentry, Chicago — 110 yards (6) vs. Houston
Andre Reed, Buffalo — 106 yards (8) vs. L.A. Rams
Webster Slaughter, Cleveland — 106 yards (7) vs. Pittsburgh

Seventh Week
Webster Slaughter, Cleveland — 186 yards (8) vs. Chicago
Michael Young, Denver — 137 yards (6) vs. Seattle
Eric Martin, New Orleans — 116 yards (5) vs. L.A. Rams
Jerry Rice, San Francisco — 112 yards (6) vs. New England
Mark Carrier, Tampa Bay — 106 yards (8) vs. Washington
Tom Rathman, San Francisco — 103 yards (11) vs. New England
Irving Fryar, New England — 102 yards (5) vs. San Francisco

Eighth Week
Webster Slaughter, Cleveland — 184 yards (4) vs. Houston
Stephone Paige, Kansas City — 163 yards (7) vs. Pittsburgh
Ricky Sanders, Washington — 158 yards (12) vs. L.A. Raiders
Vance Johnson, Denver — 148 yards (9) vs. Philadelphia
Gary Clark, Washington — 145 yards (8) vs. L.A. Raiders
Louis Lipps, Pittsburgh — 130 yards (7) vs. Kansas City
Andre Rison, Indianapolis — 129 yards (6) vs. New England
Tim McGee, Cincinnati — 127 yards (5) vs. Tampa Bay
Bruce Hill, Tampa Bay — 125 yards (7) vs. Cincinnati
Mark Clayton, Miami — 122 yards (7) vs. Buffalo
Brian Blades, Seattle — 117 yards (10) vs. San Diego
Eric Sievers, New England — 113 yards (7) vs. Indianapolis
Andre Brown, Miami — 105 yards (5) vs. Buffalo
Sterling Sharpe, Green Bay — 105 yards (7) vs. Detroit
Mark Carrier, Tampa Bay — 100 yards (7) vs. Cincinnati
Henry Ellard, L.A. Rams — 100 yards (5) vs. Chicago

Ninth Week
Willie Gault, L.A. Raiders — 147 yards (2) vs. Cincinnati
Robert Clark, Detroit — 141 yards (6) vs. Houston
Anthony Miller, San Diego — 129 yards (5) vs. Philadelphia
Cedric Jones, New England — 127 yards (6) vs. N.Y. Jets
James Wilder, Tampa Bay — 107 yards (8) vs. Cleveland
Drew Hill, Houston — 101 yards (9) vs. Detroit
Andre Reed, Buffalo — 100 yards (5) vs. Atlanta

Tenth Week
James Dixon, Dallas — 203 yards (6) vs. Phoenix
Ernie Jones, Phoenix — 139 yards (3) vs. Dallas
Mark Clayton, Miami — 125 yards (4) vs. N.Y. Jets
Louis Lipps, Pittsburgh — 112 yards (4) vs. Chicago
Scott Schwedes, Miami — 107 yards (3) vs. N.Y. Jets
Robert Awalt, Phoenix — 105 yards (6) vs. Dallas
Hart Lee Dykes, New England — 105 yards (5) vs. New Orleans

Eleventh Week
Tim McGee, Cincinnati — 194 yards (11) vs. Detroit
Mark Carrier, Tampa Bay — 164 yards (6) vs. Chicago
Henry Ellard, L.A. Rams — 163 yards (5) vs. Phoenix
Andre Rison, Indianapolis — 108 yards (5) vs. N.Y. Jets
Andre Reed, Buffalo — 107 yards (6) vs. New England
Jerry Rice, San Francisco — 106 yards (9) vs. Green Bay
Anthony Miller, San Diego — 104 yards (7) vs. Pittsburgh
Mervyn Fernandez, L.A. Raiders — 102 yards (5) vs. Houston

Twelfth Week

Willie Anderson, L.A. Rams	336 yards (15)	vs. New Orleans
Sterling Sharpe, Green Bay	157 yards (10)	vs. Minnesota
Vance Johnson, Denver	154 yards (6)	vs. Seattle
Art Monk, Washington	152 yards (9)	vs. Chicago
Gary Clark, Washington	124 yards (8)	vs. Chicago
Brian Blades, Seattle	122 yards (8)	vs. Denver
Jerry Rice, San Francisco	117 yards (7)	vs. N.Y. Giants
Stephone Paige, Kansas City	114 yards (7)	vs. Houston
Eric Martin, New Orleans	107 yards (5)	vs. L.A. Rams
Anthony Carter, Minnesota	103 yards (6)	vs. Green Bay
Bill Brooks, Indianapolis	101 yards (8)	vs. San Diego

Thirteenth Week

Richard Johnson, Detroit	248 yards (8)	vs. New Orleans
Sterling Sharpe, Green Bay	169 yards (8)	vs. Tampa Bay
John Taylor, San Francisco	162 yards (5)	vs. Atlanta
Mike Dyal, L.A. Raiders	134 yards (4)	vs. Denver
Stephone Paige, Kansas City	133 yards (7)	vs. Miami
Mark Clayton, Miami	128 yards (9)	vs. Kansas City
Lionel Manuel, N.Y. Giants	126 yards (4)	vs. Philadelphia
Roy Green, Phoenix	116 yards (8)	vs. Washington
Hart Lee Dykes, New England	114 yards (6)	vs. Indianapolis
Mark Carrier, Tampa Bay	104 yards (7)	vs. Green Bay
Aaron Cox, L.A. Rams	103 yards (5)	vs. Dallas

Fourteenth Week

John Taylor, San Francisco	286 yards (11)	vs. L.A. Rams
Anthony Miller, San Diego	152 yards (8)	vs. Washington
Webster Slaughter, Cleveland	152 yards (6)	vs. Indianapolis
Mark Carrier, Tampa Bay	135 yards (10)	vs. Houston
Andre Rison, Indianapolis	135 yards (5)	vs. Cleveland
Fred Banks, Miami	119 yards (6)	vs. New England
Mervyn Fernandez, L.A. Raiders	119 yards (5)	vs. Phoenix
Eric Sievers, New England	117 yards (6)	vs. Miami
Tim McGee, Cincinnati	109 yards (7)	vs. Seattle
Brian Blades, Seattle	107 yards (6)	vs. Cincinnati
Wayne Walker, San Diego	105 yards (7)	vs. Washington
Mark Clayton, Miami	102 yards (6)	vs. New England
Eric Martin, New Orleans	100 yards (4)	vs. Buffalo

Fifteenth Week

Michael Haynes, Atlanta	190 yards (6)	vs. Washington
Ricky Sanders, Washington	167 yards (7)	vs. Atlanta
Tim McGee, Cincinnati	147 yards (6)	vs. Houston
Reggie Langhorne, Cleveland	140 yards (6)	vs. Minnesota
Mark Carrier, Tampa Bay	131 yards (4)	vs. Detroit
Art Monk, Washington	131 yards (6)	vs. Atlanta
Hart Lee Dykes, New England	130 yards (10)	vs. Pittsburgh
John L. Williams, Seattle	129 yards (12)	vs. L.A. Raiders
Eric Martin, New Orleans	120 yards (9)	vs. Philadelphia
Jason Phillips, Detroit	115 yards (10)	vs. Tampa Bay
Andre Reed, Buffalo	115 yards (10)	vs. San Francisco
Keith Byars, Philadelphia	109 yards (6)	vs. New Orleans
Eddie Brown, Cincinnati	107 yards (6)	vs. Houston

Sixteenth Week

Gary Clark, Washington	149 yards (9)	vs. Seattle
Drew Hill, Houston	141 yards (10)	vs. Cleveland
Louis Lipps, Pittsburgh	137 yards (4)	vs. Tampa Bay
Richard Johnson, Detroit	135 yards (7)	vs. Atlanta
Mervyn Fernandez, L.A. Raiders	125 yards (6)	vs. N.Y. Giants
Anthony Carter, Minnesota	118 yards (7)	vs. Cincinnati
Henry Ellard, L.A. Rams	111 yards (4)	vs. New England
Eddie Brown, Cincinnati	109 yards (6)	vs. Minnesota
Hart Lee Dykes, New England	108 yards (8)	vs. L.A. Rams
Mark Clayton, Miami	102 yards (6)	vs. Kansas City
Mark Carrier, Tampa Bay	101 yards (6)	vs. Pittsburgh
Jerry Rice, San Francisco	101 yards (4)	vs. Chicago

Times 100 or More (165)

Carrier, 9; Rice, 8; Reed, 7; Sharpe, 6; Blades, G. Clark, Clayton, Ellard, Fernandez, Lipps, Martin, McGee, Miller, 5; Dykes, Monk, Slaughter, J.T. Smith, 4; Brooks, Carter, B. Hill, R. Johnson, V. Johnson, Paige, Rison, Sanders, Taylor, 3; Anderson, Brown, Byars, R. Clark, Duper, Gault, Green, C. Jones, E. Jones, Sievers, 2.

American Football Conference Offense

	Buff.	Cin.	Clev.	Den.	Hou.	Ind.	K.C.	Raid.	Mia.	N.E.	N.Y.J.	Pitt.	S.D.	Sea.
First Downs	334	348	285	308	327	273	304	259	310	335	292	244	267	290
Rushing	136	136	101	125	112	118	120	93	88	114	91	106	95	86
Passing	177	183	161	163	185	140	165	143	201	187	189	117	149	180
Penalty	21	29	23	20	30	15	19	23	21	34	12	21	23	24
Rushes	532	529	448	554	495	458	559	454	400	485	400	500	432	405
Net Yds. Gained	2264	2483	1609	2092	1928	1853	2227	2038	1330	1749	1596	1818	1873	1392
Avg. Gain	4.3	4.7	3.6	3.8	3.9	4.0	4.0	4.5	3.3	3.6	4.0	3.6	4.3	3.4
Avg. Yds. per Game	141.5	155.2	100.6	130.8	120.5	115.8	139.2	127.4	83.1	109.3	99.8	113.6	117.1	87.0
Passes Attempted	478	513	529	474	496	493	435	414	601	610	570	404	515	559
Completed	281	288	309	256	295	253	259	201	331	302	338	210	270	316
% Completed	58.8	56.1	58.4	54.0	59.5	51.3	59.5	48.6	55.1	49.5	59.3	52.0	52.4	56.5
Total Yds. Gained	3831	3950	3625	3352	3786	3134	3220	3277	4302	3972	3892	2662	3291	3583
Times Sacked	35	41	34	43	37	28	23	44	10	34	62	51	39	46
Yds. Lost	242	332	192	351	287	174	182	326	86	265	477	484	254	379
Net Yds. Gained	3589	3618	3433	3001	3499	2960	3038	2951	4216	3707	3415	2178	3037	3204
Avg. Yds. per Game	224.3	226.1	214.6	187.6	218.7	185.0	189.9	184.4	263.5	231.7	213.4	136.1	189.8	200.3
Net Yds. per Pass Play	7.00	6.53	6.10	5.80	6.56	5.68	6.63	6.44	6.90	5.76	5.40	4.79	5.48	5.30
Yds. Gained per Comp.	13.63	13.72	11.73	13.09	12.83	12.39	12.43	16.30	13.00	13.15	11.51	12.68	12.19	11.34
Combined Net Yds. Gained	5853	6101	5042	5093	5427	4813	5265	4989	5546	5456	5011	3996	4910	4596
% Total Yds. Rushing	38.7	40.7	31.9	41.1	35.5	38.5	42.3	40.8	24.0	32.1	31.8	45.5	38.1	30.3
% Total Yds. Passing	61.3	59.3	68.1	58.9	64.5	61.5	57.7	59.2	76.0	67.9	68.2	54.5	61.9	69.7
Avg. Yds. per Game	365.8	381.3	315.1	318.3	339.2	300.8	329.1	311.8	346.6	341.0	313.2	249.8	306.9	287.3
Ball Control Plays	1045	1083	1011	1071	1028	979	1017	912	1011	1129	1032	955	986	1010
Avg. Yds. per Play	5.6	5.6	5.0	4.8	5.3	4.9	5.2	5.5	5.5	4.8	4.9	4.2	5.0	4.6
Avg. Time of Poss.	30:12	30:51	30:26	32:17	31:59	27:15	32:35	28:24	28:15	30:55	29:16	28:50	28:55	29:20
Third Down Efficiency	42.4	45.5	38.5	46.3	40.9	34.1	42.3	34.0	48.3	38.3	32.4	31.6	36.3	40.3
Had Intercepted	20	13	15	20	16	17	23	22	25	27	24	13	19	23
Yds. Opp. Returned	364	42	306	194	171	345	269	298	335	338	282	103	179	248
Ret. by Opp. for TD	2	0	1	1	0	2	2	0	1	2	2	1	0	2
Punts	67	65	97	80	58	80	67	67	59	64	87	83	84	76
Yds. Punted	2564	2504	3817	3188	2422	3392	2688	2711	2458	2392	3426	3368	3315	2995
Avg. Yds. per Punt	38.3	38.5	39.4	39.8	41.8	42.4	40.1	40.5	41.7	37.4	39.4	40.6	39.5	39.4
Punt Returns	33	36	49	45	19	26	44	40	33	45	33	40	38	30
Yds. Returned	301	209	496	344	122	322	331	378	338	379	299	278	272	251
Avg. Yds. per Return	9.1	5.8	10.1	7.6	6.4	12.4	7.5	9.5	10.2	8.4	9.1	7.0	7.2	8.4
Returned for TD	0	0	0	0	0	1	0	1	0	0	0	0	0	0
Kickoff Returns	53	54	50	43	74	60	52	54	61	69	75	56	64	65
Yds. Returned	1058	941	932	876	1285	1164	915	1002	1153	1462	1309	1304	1235	1246
Avg. Yds. per Return	20.0	17.4	18.6	20.4	17.4	19.4	17.6	18.6	18.9	21.2	17.5	23.3	19.3	19.2
Returned for TD	0	0	0	0	0	0	0	0	1	0	0	1	1	1
Fumbles	30	29	23	26	39	33	32	28	30	26	32	32	24	43
Lost	21	19	15	12	17	10	18	12	16	12	17	18	17	14
Out of Bounds	2	0	1	1	3	2	2	3	2	2	0	1	1	5
Own Rec. for TD	0	0	0	0	0	1	0	0	0	0	0	0	0	0
Opp. Rec. by	13	16	11	22	16	15	18	18	8	12	8	21	12	13
Opp. Rec. for TD	0	1	2	2	0	0	2	2	0	0	2	1	2	1
Penalties	103	85	128	83	149	89	116	132	83	63	116	116	122	79
Yds. Penalized	831	637	973	594	1153	704	878	1105	614	509	953	986	906	738
Total Points Scored	409	404	334	362	365	298	318	315	331	297	253	265	266	241
Total TDs	49	52	41	40	41	34	35	35	39	30	30	29	31	28
TDs Rushing	15	17	14	15	16	11	18	9	10	12	11	17	13	5
TDs Passing	32	32	20	21	23	18	14	21	26	17	14	10	15	21
TDs on Ret. and Rec.	2	3	7	4	2	5	3	5	3	1	5	2	3	2
Extra Points	46	50	40	39	40	31	34	34	38	27	29	28	29	28
Safeties	0	0	0	1	2	0	1	1	1	0	1	0	0	0
Field Goals Made	23	14	16	27	25	21	24	23	19	30	14	21	17	15
Field Goals Attempted	30	20	24	33	37	27	33	34	26	40	21	30	25	25
% Successful	76.7	70.0	66.7	81.8	67.6	77.8	72.7	67.6	73.1	75.0	66.7	70.0	68.0	60.0

American Football Conference Defense

	Buff.	Cin.	Clev.	Den.	Hou.	Ind.	K.C.	Raid.	Mia.	N.E.	N.Y.J.	Pitt.	S.D.	Sea.
First Downs	299	280	276	246	314	336	252	308	337	297	328	323	295	293
Rushing	117	114	93	90	119	126	92	121	139	110	127	112	102	119
Passing	156	151	161	142	165	192	140	160	180	176	178	177	172	158
Penalty	26	15	22	14	30	18	20	27	18	11	23	34	21	16
Rushes	484	482	446	426	437	507	445	504	493	495	517	498	479	520
Net Yds. Gained	1840	2162	1670	1580	1669	2077	1766	1940	2153	1978	2136	2008	1813	2118
Avg. Gain	3.8	4.5	3.7	3.7	3.8	4.1	4.0	3.8	4.4	4.0	4.1	4.0	3.8	4.1
Avg. Yds. per Game	115.0	135.1	104.4	98.8	104.3	129.8	110.4	121.3	134.6	123.6	133.5	125.5	113.3	132.4
Passes Attempted	508	482	540	504	467	556	471	506	513	449	514	548	513	445
Completed	255	256	269	268	269	322	236	277	315	259	282	290	283	252
% Completed	50.2	53.1	49.8	53.2	57.6	57.9	50.1	54.7	61.4	57.7	54.9	52.9	55.2	56.6
Total Yds. Gained	3495	3383	3520	3201	3819	3918	2821	3311	3811	3905	4035	3721	3311	3332
Times Sacked	38	33	45	47	36	46	36	35	39	31	28	31	48	32
Yds. Lost	289	248	359	374	277	384	294	248	268	239	177	180	360	235
Net Yds. Gained	3206	3135	3161	2827	3542	3534	2527	3063	3543	3666	3858	3541	2951	3097
Avg. Yds. per Game	200.4	195.9	197.6	176.7	221.4	220.9	157.9	191.4	221.4	229.1	241.1	221.3	184.4	193.6
Net Yds. per Pass Play	5.87	6.09	5.40	5.13	7.04	5.87	4.98	5.66	6.42	7.64	7.12	6.12	5.26	6.49
Yds. Gained per Comp.	13.71	13.21	13.09	11.94	14.20	12.17	11.95	11.95	12.10	15.08	14.31	12.83	11.70	13.22
Combined Net Yds. Gained	5046	5297	4831	4407	5211	5611	4293	5003	5696	5644	5994	5549	4764	5215
% Total Yds. Rushing	36.5	40.8	34.6	35.9	32.0	37.0	41.1	38.8	37.8	35.0	35.6	36.2	38.1	40.6
% Total Yds. Passing	63.5	59.2	65.4	64.1	68.0	63.0	58.9	61.2	62.2	65.0	64.4	63.8	61.9	59.4
Avg. Yds. per Game	315.4	331.1	301.9	275.4	325.7	350.7	268.3	312.7	356.0	352.8	374.6	346.8	297.8	325.9
Ball Control Plays	1030	997	1031	977	940	1109	952	1045	1045	975	1059	1077	1040	997
Avg. Yds. per Play	4.9	5.3	4.7	4.5	5.5	5.1	4.5	4.8	5.5	5.8	5.7	5.2	4.6	5.2
Avg. Time of Poss.	29:48	29:09	29:34	27:43	28:01	32:45	27:25	31:36	31:45	29:05	30:44	31:10	31:05	30:40
Third Down Efficiency	35.2	39.2	35.7	33.8	45.5	43.2	38.4	47.6	34.5	36.2	38.5	46.3	35.7	41.8
Intercepted by	23	21	27	21	21	21	15	18	15	16	15	21	25	9
Yds. Returned by	269	204	300	318	263	391	133	362	126	118	261	261	224	57
Returned for TD	1	1	4	2	0	2	0	3	0	1	2	0	0	0
Punts	75	75	94	84	56	65	82	72	62	81	69	69	79	74
Yds. Punted	2870	2935	3797	3440	2107	2702	3205	2902	2416	3413	2746	2793	3050	2902
Avg. Yds. per Punt	38.3	39.1	40.4	41.0	37.6	41.6	39.1	40.3	39.0	42.1	39.8	40.5	38.6	39.2
Punt Returns	25	33	49	28	24	51	40	41	26	38	34	45	43	41
Yds. Returned	227	323	418	370	191	558	325	301	256	346	257	361	451	334
Avg. Yds. per Return	9.1	9.8	8.5	13.2	8.0	10.9	8.1	7.3	9.8	9.1	7.6	8.0	10.5	8.1
Returned for TD	0	0	0	0	0	1	0	1	0	0	1	0	0	0
Kickoff Returns	75	55	58	72	59	63	55	59	63	61	47	53	57	44
Yds. Returned	1187	1203	1175	1256	1024	1208	1156	1001	1215	1199	1029	1096	1249	814
Avg. Yds. per Return	15.8	21.9	20.3	17.4	17.4	19.2	21.0	17.0	19.3	19.7	21.9	20.7	21.9	18.5
Returned for TD	0	0	0	0	1	0	2	2	0	0	0	0	1	0
Fumbles	31	26	32	43	25	34	32	40	19	22	32	40	21	26
Lost	13	16	11	22	16	15	18	18	8	12	9	21	13	13
Out of Bounds	1	1	2	4	1	1	1	0	2	1	4	2	1	4
Own Rec. for TD	1	0	0	0	1	0	0	0	0	0	0	0	0	0
Opp. Rec. by	21	19	15	12	17	10	18	12	16	12	17	17	17	14
Opp. Rec. for TD	0	0	1	1	0	0	3	0	1	0	0	4	0	1
Penalties	87	122	122	102	109	103	102	105	106	111	90	96	93	118
Yds. Penalized	616	1060	985	823	903	772	797	867	831	954	675	785	741	809
Total Points Scored	317	285	254	226	412	301	286	297	379	391	411	326	290	327
Total TDs	34	32	30	25	52	29	32	36	43	48	50	38	29	37
TDs Rushing	15	9	8	10	20	10	9	15	19	19	16	16	13	11
TDs Passing	14	22	20	13	28	15	16	18	21	27	31	17	15	23
TDs on Ret. and Rec.	5	1	2	2	4	4	7	3	3	2	3	5	1	3
Extra Points	33	31	29	25	49	29	31	36	42	46	46	37	27	35
Safeties	1	1	0	0	0	1	0	0	2	0	1	2	1	2
Field Goals Made	26	20	15	17	17	32	21	15	25	19	21	19	29	22
Field Goals Attempted	37	27	28	27	21	43	26	21	33	26	31	27	41	32
% Successful	70.3	74.1	53.6	63.0	81.0	74.4	80.8	71.4	75.8	73.1	67.7	70.4	70.7	68.8

National Football Conference Offense

	Atl.	Chi.	Dall.	Det.	G.B.	Rams	Minn.	N.O.	N.Y.G.	Phil.	Phx.	S.F.	T.B.	Wash.
First Downs	261	302	246	274	342	321	326	304	298	321	262	350	288	338
Rushing	75	136	78	117	114	107	126	108	118	120	83	124	84	101
Passing	173	147	145	139	207	197	172	167	157	171	157	209	174	217
Penalty	13	19	23	18	21	17	28	29	23	30	22	17	30	20
Rushes	318	516	355	421	397	472	514	502	556	540	407	493	412	514
Net Yds. Gained	1155	2287	1409	2053	1732	1909	2066	1948	1889	2208	1361	1966	1507	1904
Avg. Gain	3.6	4.4	4.0	4.9	4.4	4.0	4.0	3.9	3.4	4.1	3.3	4.0	3.7	3.7
Avg. Yds. per Game	72.2	142.9	88.1	128.3	108.3	119.3	129.1	121.8	118.1	138.0	85.1	122.9	94.2	119.0
Passes Attempted	578	484	513	450	600	523	499	461	444	538	523	483	570	581
Completed	312	267	266	229	354	308	272	284	248	294	279	339	302	337
% Completed	54.0	55.2	51.9	50.9	59.0	58.9	54.5	61.6	55.9	54.6	53.3	70.2	53.0	58.0
Total Yds. Gained	3903	3262	3124	3282	4325	4369	3468	3651	3355	3455	3659	4584	3666	4476
Times Sacked	51	28	30	57	48	32	40	36	46	45	56	45	43	21
Yds. Lost	389	174	239	343	277	236	279	271	281	343	379	282	331	127
Net Yds. Gained	3514	3088	2885	2939	4048	4133	3189	3380	3074	3112	3280	4302	3335	4349
Avg. Yds. per Game	219.6	193.0	180.3	183.7	253.0	258.3	199.3	211.3	192.1	194.5	205.0	268.9	208.4	271.8
Net Yds. per Pass Play	5.59	6.03	5.31	5.80	6.25	7.45	5.92	6.80	6.27	5.34	5.66	8.15	5.44	7.22
Yds. Gained per Comp.	12.51	12.22	11.74	14.33	12.22	14.19	12.75	12.86	13.53	11.75	13.11	13.52	12.14	13.28
Combined Net Yds. Gained	4669	5375	4294	4992	5780	6042	5255	5328	4963	5320	4641	6268	4842	6253
% Total Yds. Rushing	24.7	42.5	32.8	41.1	30.0	31.6	39.3	36.6	38.1	41.5	29.3	31.4	31.1	30.4
% Total Yds. Passing	75.3	57.5	67.2	58.9	70.0	68.4	60.7	63.4	61.9	58.5	70.7	68.6	68.9	69.6
Avg. Yds. per Game	291.8	335.9	268.4	312.0	361.3	377.6	328.4	333.0	310.2	332.5	290.1	391.8	302.6	390.8
Ball Control Plays	947	1028	898	928	1045	1027	1053	999	1046	1123	986	1021	1025	1116
Avg. Yds. per Play	4.9	5.2	4.8	5.4	5.5	5.9	5.0	5.3	4.7	4.7	4.7	6.1	4.7	5.6
Avg. Time of Poss.	25:58	31:10	25:34	26:14	30:21	30:35	30:40	33:43	32:23	30:43	28:27	31:45	29:55	32:58
Third Down Efficiency	32.5	43.9	33.2	33.3	45.6	40.5	34.0	43.0	44.0	39.4	39.5	42.1	41.3	43.8
Had Intercepted	12	25	27	24	20	18	19	19	16	16	30	11	28	17
Yds. Opp. Returned	85	182	396	447	321	207	138	265	240	147	327	140	240	229
Ret. by Opp. for TD	0	1	3	3	2	0	2	1	2	0	3	0	2	1
Punts	85	72	82	83	66	74	72	71	70	87	82	56	86	63
Yds. Punted	3472	2844	3261	3538	2682	2834	2864	2774	3019	3389	3578	2226	3311	2663
Avg. Yds. per Punt	40.8	39.5	39.8	42.6	40.6	38.3	39.8	39.1	43.1	39.0	43.6	39.8	38.5	42.3
Punt Returns	32	32	31	47	35	35	45	53	46	37	40	39	32	26
Yds. Returned	341	220	197	572	289	332	448	428	582	331	469	429	296	226
Avg. Yds. per Return	10.7	6.9	6.4	12.2	8.3	9.5	10.0	8.1	12.7	8.9	11.7	11.0	9.3	8.7
Returned for TD	1	0	0	0	0	0	0	1	1	0	0	0	0	0
Kickoff Returns	80	73	77	61	69	67	51	63	51	49	83	51	62	58
Yds. Returned	1509	1539	1709	1272	1239	1328	1122	1284	926	828	1650	954	1055	1176
Avg. Yds. per Return	18.9	21.1	22.2	20.9	18.0	19.8	22.0	20.4	18.2	16.9	19.9	18.7	17.0	20.3
Returned for TD	0	1	1	0	0	0	1	1	0	0	0	0	0	1
Fumbles	26	23	29	37	35	26	28	28	30	43	24	32	21	32
Lost	11	17	15	24	13	11	14	12	14	16	14	14	9	20
Out of Bounds	0	1	1	3	3	4	2	1	0	4	0	5	2	0
Own Rec. for TD	0	0	0	1	2	0	0	0	0	0	0	0	0	0
Opp. Rec. by	12	12	10	16	15	15	18	18	15	26	11	16	18	15
Opp. Rec. for TD	1	0	3	0	0	0	4	0	0	1	0	1	0	0
Penalties	82	95	100	121	81	102	119	90	83	114	113	109	104	105
Yds. Penalized	671	846	771	977	666	823	974	676	675	938	856	922	881	881
Total Points Scored	279	358	204	312	362	426	351	386	348	342	258	442	320	386
Total TDs	30	45	25	36	42	51	36	46	37	40	29	51	36	42
TDs Rushing	11	22	7	23	13	19	12	19	17	14	10	14	10	14
TDs Passing	17	21	14	11	27	29	17	23	17	23	17	35	23	24
TDs on Ret. and Rec.	2	2	4	2	2	3	7	4	3	3	2	2	3	4
Extra Points	30	43	24	36	42	51	35	44	35	40	28	49	34	41
Safeties	0	0	0	0	1	0	2	3	2	1	1	0	2	3
Field Goals Made	23	15	10	20	22	23	32	20	29	20	18	29	22	29
Field Goals Attempted	32	19	20	21	28	30	44	29	38	33	26	36	28	40
% Successful	71.9	78.9	50.0	95.2	78.6	76.7	72.7	69.0	76.3	60.6	69.2	80.6	78.6	72.5

National Football Conference Defense

	Atl.	Chi.	Dall.	Det.	G.B.	Rams	Minn.	N.O.	N.Y.G.	Phil.	Phx.	S.F.	T.B.	Wash.
First Downs	336	332	321	314	307	306	266	293	266	281	329	283	317	274
Rushing	156	118	116	98	116	101	100	79	90	81	113	76	115	72
Passing	163	191	183	189	179	181	140	198	159	171	185	178	170	177
Penalty	17	23	22	27	12	24	26	16	17	29	31	29	32	25
Rushes	572	446	543	454	460	404	462	373	421	426	539	372	479	384
Net Yds. Gained	2471	1897	1991	1621	2008	1543	1683	1326	1539	1605	2302	1383	2023	1344
Avg. Gain	4.3	4.3	3.7	3.6	4.4	3.8	3.6	3.6	3.7	3.8	4.3	3.7	4.2	3.5
Avg. Yds. per Game	154.4	118.6	124.4	101.3	125.5	96.4	105.2	82.9	96.2	100.3	143.9	86.4	126.4	84.0
Passes Attempted	437	554	488	570	476	577	488	577	486	529	531	564	515	530
Completed	259	307	301	370	302	345	252	320	273	258	286	316	301	277
% Completed	59.3	55.4	61.7	64.9	63.4	59.8	51.6	55.5	56.2	48.8	53.9	56.0	58.4	52.3
Total Yds. Gained	3737	4079	3748	4193	3553	4302	3003	4222	3427	3713	3794	3568	3659	3875
Times Sacked	31	39	29	40	34	42	71	47	39	62	30	43	33	40
Yds. Lost	183	247	183	277	214	278	502	362	302	424	219	333	222	304
Net Yds. Gained	3554	3832	3565	3916	3339	4024	2501	3860	3125	3289	3575	3235	3437	3571
Avg. Yds. per Game	222.1	239.5	222.8	244.8	208.7	251.5	156.3	241.3	195.3	205.6	223.4	202.2	214.8	223.2
Net Yds. per Pass Play	7.59	6.46	6.90	6.42	6.55	6.50	4.47	6.19	5.95	5.57	6.37	5.33	6.27	6.26
Yds. Gained per Comp.	14.43	13.29	12.45	11.33	11.76	12.47	11.92	13.19	12.55	14.39	13.27	11.29	12.16	13.99
Combined Net Yds. Gained	6025	5729	5556	5537	5347	5567	4184	5186	4664	4894	5877	4618	5460	4915
% Total Yds. Rushing	41.0	33.1	35.8	29.3	37.6	27.7	40.2	25.6	33.0	32.8	39.2	29.9	37.1	27.3
% Total Yds. Passing	59.0	66.9	64.2	70.7	62.4	72.3	59.8	74.4	67.0	67.2	60.8	70.1	62.9	72.7
Avg. Yds. per Game	376.6	358.1	347.3	346.1	334.2	347.9	261.5	324.1	291.5	305.9	367.3	288.6	341.3	307.2
Ball Control Plays	1040	1039	1060	1064	970	1023	1021	997	946	1017	1100	979	1027	954
Avg. Yds. per Play	5.8	5.5	5.2	5.2	5.5	5.4	4.1	5.2	4.9	4.8	5.3	4.7	5.3	5.2
Avg. Time of Poss.	34:02	28:50	34:26	33:46	29:39	29:25	29:20	26:17	27:37	29:17	31:33	28:15	30:05	27:02
Third Down Efficiency	45.0	40.6	46.3	37.7	45.0	37.7	33.5	38.0	38.5	36.4	43.7	36.2	41.8	38.1
Intercepted by	20	26	7	16	25	21	18	21	22	30	16	21	21	27
Yds. Returned by	285	268	37	107	232	372	264	226	330	375	275	262	234	284
Returned for TD	0	1	0	1	0	3	2	2	2	2	2	0	2	3
Punts	56	67	73	80	65	81	95	75	74	85	76	74	69	76
Yds. Punted	2342	2655	2911	3293	2644	3364	3859	2956	2964	3571	3155	2875	2781	3047
Avg. Yds. per Punt	41.8	39.6	39.9	41.2	40.7	41.5	40.6	39.4	40.1	42.0	41.5	38.9	40.3	40.1
Punt Returns	43	30	38	46	30	34	32	35	29	37	46	35	54	34
Yds. Returned	460	262	334	373	416	315	300	244	236	215	371	361	492	383
Avg. Yds. per Return	10.7	8.7	8.8	8.1	13.9	9.3	9.4	7.0	8.1	5.8	8.1	10.3	9.1	11.3
Returned for TD	0	0	1	0	0	1	0	0	0	0	0	0	0	0
Kickoff Returns	60	68	46	65	63	84	68	55	73	60	57	76	55	74
Yds. Returned	1188	1375	853	1037	1389	1633	1287	983	1306	1307	1193	1435	1143	1532
Avg. Yds. per Return	19.8	20.2	18.5	16.0	22.0	19.4	18.9	17.9	17.9	21.8	20.9	18.9	20.8	20.7
Returned for TD	0	0	0	1	0	0	0	0	0	1	0	0	0	1
Fumbles	26	24	22	28	28	38	29	35	38	44	18	34	30	24
Lost	12	12	10	16	15	15	18	18	15	26	11	16	18	15
Out of Bounds	2	1	0	1	2	2	3	3	3	2	3	0	3	1
Own Rec. for TD	1	0	0	0	0	0	0	0	0	0	0	0	1	0
Opp. Rec. by	11	17	15	24	13	11	14	11	14	16	14	14	9	20
Opp. Rec. for TD	3	0	1	0	2	0	0	1	2	0	2	1	1	1
Penalties	79	94	102	107	105	93	116	105	109	118	106	75	109	98
Yds. Penalized	682	802	723	993	851	798	903	850	800	956	916	581	869	796
Total Points Scored	437	377	393	364	356	344	275	301	252	274	377	253	419	308
Total TDs	49	43	44	42	41	38	34	35	30	33	41	26	51	38
TDs Rushing	26	21	17	18	15	13	14	10	10	6	12	9	18	9
TDs Passing	19	21	21	19	22	24	18	23	16	26	24	15	29	25
TDs on Ret. and Rec.	4	1	6	5	4	1	2	2	4	1	5	2	4	4
Extra Points	48	41	43	41	39	36	32	34	30	30	40	26	51	38
Safeties	1	0	1	1	1	1	0	0	0	2	2	1	1	0
Field Goals Made	31	26	28	23	23	26	13	19	14	14	29	23	20	14
Field Goals Attempted	36	36	35	33	30	29	21	24	21	26	40	31	24	23
% Successful	86.1	72.2	80.0	69.7	76.7	89.7	61.9	79.2	66.7	53.8	72.5	74.2	83.3	60.9

AFC, NFC, and NFL Summary

	AFC Offense Total	AFC Offense Average	AFC Defense Total	AFC Defense Average	NFC Offense Total	NFC Offense Average	NFC Defense Total	NFC Defense Average	NFL Total	NFL Average
First Downs	4176	298.3	4184	298.9	4233	302.4	4225	301.8	8409	300.3
Rushing	1521	108.6	1581	112.9	1491	106.5	1431	102.2	3012	107.6
Passing	2340	167.1	2308	164.9	2432	173.7	2464	176.0	4772	170.4
Penalty	315	22.5	295	21.1	310	22.1	330	23.6	625	22.3
Rushes	6651	475.1	6733	480.9	6417	458.4	6335	452.5	13,068	466.7
Net Yds. Gained	26,252	1875.1	26,910	1922.1	25,394	1813.9	24,736	1766.9	51,646	1844.5
Avg. Gain	—	3.9	—	4.0	—	4.0	—	3.9	—	4.0
Avg. Yds. per Game	—	117.2	—	120.1	—	113.4	—	110.4	—	115.3
Passes Attempted	7091	506.5	7016	501.1	7247	517.6	7322	523.0	14,338	512.1
Completed	3909	279.2	3833	273.8	4091	292.2	4167	297.6	8000	285.7
% Completed	—	55.1	—	54.6	—	56.5	—	56.9	—	55.8
Total Yds. Gained	49,877	3562.6	49,583	3541.6	52,579	3755.6	52,873	3776.6	102,456	3659.1
Times Sacked	527	37.6	525	37.5	578	41.3	580	41.4	1105	39.5
Yds. Lost	4031	287.9	2932	280.9	3951	282.2	4050	289.3	7982	285.1
Net Yds. Gained	45,846	3274.7	45,651	3260.8	48,628	3473.4	48,823	3487.4	94,474	3374.1
Avg. Yds. per Game	—	204.7	—	203.8	—	217.1	—	218.0	—	210.9
Net Yds. per Pass Play	—	6.02	—	6.05	—	6.21	—	6.18	—	6.12
Yds. Gained per Comp.	—	12.76	—	12.94	—	12.85	—	12.69	—	12.81
Combined Net Yds. Gained	72,098	5149.9	72,561	5182.9	74,022	5287.3	73,559	5254.2	146,120	5218.6
% Total Yds. Rushing	—	36.4	—	37.1	—	34.3	—	33.6	—	35.3
% Total Yds. Passing	—	63.6	—	62.9	—	65.7	—	66.4	—	64.7
Avg. Yds. per Game	—	321.9	—	323.9	—	330.5	—	328.4	—	326.2
Ball Control Plays	14,269	1019.2	14,274	1019.6	14,242	1017.3	14,237	1016.9	28,511	1018.3
Avg. Yds. per Play	—	5.1	—	5.1	—	5.2	—	5.2	—	5.1
Third Down Efficiency	—	39.4	—	39.4	—	39.9	—	39.9	—	39.7
Interceptions	268	19.1	277	19.8	291	20.8	282	20.1	559	20.0
Yds. Returned	3287	234.8	3474	248.1	3551	253.6	3364	240.3	6838	244.2
Returned for TD	16	1.1	16	1.1	20	1.4	20	1.4	36	1.3
Punts	1034	73.9	1037	74.1	1049	74.9	1046	74.7	2083	74.4
Yds. Punted	41,240	2945.7	41,278	2948.4	42,455	3032.5	42,417	3029.8	83,695	2989.1
Avg. Yds. per Punt	—	39.9	—	39.8	—	40.5	—	40.6	—	40.2
Punt Returns	511	36.5	518	37.0	530	37.9	523	37.4	1041	37.2
Yds. Returned	4320	308.6	4718	337.0	5160	368.6	4762	340.1	9480	338.6
Avg. Yds. per Return	—	8.5	—	9.1	—	9.7	—	9.1	—	9.1
Returned for TD	2	0.1	3	0.2	3	0.2	2	0.1	5	0.2
Kickoff Returns	830	59.3	821	58.6	895	63.9	904	64.6	1725	61.6
Yds. Returned	15,882	1134.4	15,812	1129.4	17,591	1256.5	17,661	1261.5	33,473	1195.5
Avg. Yds. per Return	—	19.1	—	19.3	—	19.7	—	19.5	—	19.4
Returned for TD	4	0.3	6	0.4	5	0.4	3	0.2	9	0.3
Fumbles	427	30.5	423	30.2	414	29.6	418	29.9	841	30.0
Lost	218	15.6	205	14.6	204	14.6	217	15.5	422	15.1
Out of Bounds	25	1.8	25	1.8	26	1.9	26	1.9	51	1.8
Own Rec. for TD	1	0.1	2	0.1	3	0.2	2	0.1	4	0.1
Opp. Rec.	203	14.5	217	15.5	217	15.5	203	14.5	420	15.0
Opp. Rec. for TD	15	1.1	11	0.8	10	0.7	14	1.0	25	0.9
Penalties	1464	104.6	1466	104.7	1418	101.3	1416	101.1	2882	102.9
Yds. Penalized	11,581	827.2	11,618	829.9	11,557	825.5	11,520	822.9	23,138	826.4
Total Points Scored	4458	318.4	4502	321.6	4774	341.0	4730	337.9	9232	329.7
Total TDs	514	36.7	515	36.8	546	39.0	545	38.9	1060	37.9
TDs Rushing	183	13.1	190	13.6	205	14.6	198	14.1	388	13.9
TDs Passing	284	20.3	280	20.0	298	21.3	302	21.6	582	20.8
TDs on Ret. and Rec.	47	3.4	45	3.2	43	3.1	45	3.2	90	3.2
Extra Points	493	35.2	496	35.4	532	38.0	529	37.8	1025	36.6
Safeties	7	0.5	11	0.8	15	1.1	11	0.8	22	0.8
Field Goals Made	289	20.6	298	21.3	312	22.3	303	21.6	601	21.5
Field Goals Attempted	405	28.9	420	30.0	424	30.3	409	29.2	829	29.6
% Successful	—	71.4	—	71.0	—	73.6	—	74.1	—	72.5

Club Leaders

	Offense	Defense
First Downs	S.F. 350	Den. 246
Rushing	Chi., Buff., & Cin. 136	Wash. 72
Passing	Wash. 217	K.C. & Minn. 140
Penalty	N.E. 34	N.E. 11
Rushes	K.C. 559	S.F. 372
Net Yds. Gained	Cin. 2483	N.O. 1326
Avg. Gain	Det. 4.9	Wash. 3.5
Passes Attempted	N.E. 610	Atl. 437
Completed	G.B. 354	K.C. 236
% Completed	S.F. 70.2	Phil. 48.8
Total Yds. Gained	S.F. 4584	K.C. 2821
Times Sacked	Mia. 10	Minn. 71
Yds. Lost	Mia. 86	Minn. 502
Net Yds. Gained	Wash. 4349	Minn. 2501
Net Yds. per Pass Play	S.F. 8.15	Minn. 4.47
Yds. Gained per Comp.	Raiders 16.30	Det. 11.33
Combined Net Yds. Gained	S.F. 6268	Minn. 4184
% Total Yds. Rushing	Pitt. 45.5	N.O. 25.6
% Total Yds. Passing	Mia. 76.0	K.C. 58.9
Ball Control Plays	N.E. 1129	Hou. 940
Avg. Yds. per Play	S.F. 6.13	Minn. 4.10
Avg. Time of Poss.	N.O. 33:43	—
Third Down Efficiency	Mia. 48.3	Minn. 33.5
Interceptions	—	Phil. 30
Yds. Returned	—	Ind. 391
Returned for TD	—	Clev. 4
Punts	Clev. 97	—
Yds. Punted	Clev. 3817	—
Avg. Yds. per Punt	Phoe. 43.6	—
Punt Returns	N.O. 53	Hou. 24
Yds. Returned	N.Y.G. 582	Hou. 191
Avg. Yds. per Return	N.Y.G. 12.7	Phil. 5.8
Returned for TD	Five with 1	—
Kickoff Returns	Phoe. 83	Sea. 44
Yds. Returned	Dall. 1709	Sea. 814
Avg. Yds. per Return	Pitt. 23.3	Buff. 15.8
Returned for TD	Nine with 1	—
Total Points Scored	S.F. 442	Den. 226
Total TDs	Cin. 52	Den. 25
TDs Rushing	Det. 23	Phil. 6
TDs Passing	S.F. 35	Den. 13
TDs on Ret. and Rec.	Clev. & Minn. 7	Five with 1
Extra Points	Rams 51	Den. 25
Safeties	N.O. & Wash. 3	—
Field Goals Made	Minn. 32	Minn. 13
Field Goals Attempted	Minn. 44	Four with 21
% Successful	Det. 95.2	Clev. 53.6

National Football League
Club Rankings by Yards

	Offense			Defense		
Team	Total	Rush	Pass	Total	Rush	Pass
Atlanta	24	28	9	28	28	19
Buffalo	5	3	8	11	14	10
Chicago	10	2	19	25	15	24
Cincinnati	3	*1	7	15	26	8
Cleveland	16	21	11	7	10	9
Dallas	27	24	27	20	18	20
Denver	15	6	23	3	6	3
Detroit	18	8	26	18	8	27
Green Bay	6	20	5	16	19T	13
Houston	9	12	10	13	9	17
Indianapolis	23	17	24	22	22	15
Kansas City	13	4	21	2	12	2
Los Angeles Raiders	19	9	25	10	16	5
Los Angeles Rams	4	13	4	21	5	28
Miami	7	27	3	24	25	18
Minnesota	14	7	17	*1	11	*1
New England	8	19	6	23	17	23
New Orleans	11	11	13	12	*1	26
New York Giants	20	15	20	5	4	7
New York Jets	17	22	12	27	24	25
Philadelphia	12	5	18	8	7	12
Phoenix	25	26	15	26	27	22
Pittsburgh	28	18	28	19	19T	16
San Diego	21	16	22	6	13	4
San Francisco	*1	10	2	4	3	11
Seattle	26	25	16	14	23	6
Tampa Bay	22	23	14	17	21	14
Washington	2	14	*1	9	2	21

*—League leader

T—Tied for position

AFC Takeaways/Giveaways

	Takeaways			Giveaways			Net Diff.
	Int.	Fum.	Total	Int.	Fum.	Total	
Denver	21	22	43	20	12	32	11
Pittsburgh	21	21	42	13	18	31	11
Indianapolis	21	15	36	17	10	27	9
Cleveland	27	11	38	15	15	30	8
Cincinnati	21	16	37	13	19	32	5
Houston	21	16	37	16	17	33	4
Los Angeles Raiders	18	18	36	22	12	34	2
San Diego	25	13	38	19	17	36	2
Buffalo	23	13	36	20	21	41	− 5
Kansas City	15	18	33	23	18	41	− 8
New England	16	12	28	27	12	39	−11
Seattle	9	13	22	23	14	37	−15
New York Jets	15	9	24	24	17	41	−17
Miami	15	8	23	25	16	41	−18

NFC Takeaways/Giveaways

	Takeaways			Giveaways			Net Diff.
	Int.	Fum.	Total	Int.	Fum.	Total	
Philadelphia	30	26	56	16	16	32	24
San Francisco	21	16	37	11	14	25	12
Atlanta	20	12	32	12	11	23	9
New Orleans	21	18	39	19	12	31	8
New York Giants	22	15	37	16	14	30	7
Green Bay	25	15	40	20	13	33	7
Los Angeles Rams	21	15	36	18	11	29	7
Washington	27	15	42	17	20	37	5
Minnesota	18	18	36	19	14	33	3
Tampa Bay	21	18	39	28	9	37	2
Chicago	26	12	38	25	17	42	− 4
Detroit	16	16	32	24	24	48	−16
Phoenix	16	11	27	30	14	44	−17
Dallas	7	10	17	27	15	42	−25

Scoring

Points
NFC: 136—Mike Cofer, San Francisco
AFC: 120—David Treadwell, Denver

Touchdowns
NFC: 18—Dalton Hilliard, New Orleans
AFC: 12—Christian Okoye, Kansas City
12—Thurman Thomas, Buffalo

Extra Points
NFC: 51—Mike Lansford, L.A. Rams
AFC: 46—Scott Norwood, Buffalo

Field Goals
NFC: 31—Rich Karlis, Minnesota
AFC: 27—David Treadwell, Denver

Field Goal Attempts
NFC: 40—Chip Lohmiller, Washington
AFC: 37—Tony Zendejas, Houston

Longest Field Goal
AFC: 59—Pete Stoyanovich, Miami at N.Y. Jets, November 12
NFC: 54—Paul McFadden, Atlanta vs. Buffalo, November 5

Most Points, Game
NFC: 21—Rich Karlis, Minnesota vs. L.A. Rams, November 5
(7 FG) (OT)
AFC: 18—Merril Hoge, Pittsburgh at Miami, November 26 (3 TD)
18—Sammie Smith, Miami vs. New England, December 10
(3 TD)

Team Leaders, Points
AFC: BUFFALO: 115, Scott Norwood; CINCINNATI: 73, Jim Breech; CLEVELAND: 88, Matt Bahr; DENVER: 120, David Treadwell; HOUSTON: 115, Tony Zendejas; INDIANAPOLIS: 94, Dean Biasucci; KANSAS CITY: 106, Nick Lowery; L.A. RAIDERS: 103, Jeff Jaeger; MIAMI: 95, Pete Stoyanovich; NEW ENGLAND: 61, Greg Davis; N.Y. JETS: 71, Pat Leahy; PITTSBURGH: 91, Gary Anderson; SAN DIEGO: 80, Chris Bahr; SEATTLE: 72, Norm Johnson.
NFC: ATLANTA: 63, Paul McFadden; CHICAGO: 90, Neal Anderson; DALLAS: 29, Roger Ruzek; DETROIT: 96, Eddie Murray; GREEN BAY: 108, Chris Jacke; L.A. RAMS: 120, Mike Lansford; MINNESOTA: 120, Rich Karlis; NEW ORLEANS: 108, Dalton Hilliard; N.Y. GIANTS: 84, Ottis Anderson; PHILADELPHIA: 66, Cris Carter; PHOENIX: 82, Al Del Greco; SAN FRANCISCO: 136, Mike Cofer; TAMPA BAY: 99, Donald Igwebuike; WASHINGTON: 128, Chip Lohmiller.

Team Champions
NFC: 442—San Francisco
AFC: 409—Buffalo

AFC Scoring—Team

	TD	TDR	TDP	TD Misc.	PAT	PAT Att.	FG	FG Att.	SAF	TP
Buffalo	49	15	32	2	46	48	23	30	0	409
Cincinnati	52	17	32	3	50	52	14	20	0	404
Houston	41	16	23	2	40	41	25	37	2	365
Denver	40	15	21	4	39	40	27	33	1	362
Cleveland	41	14	20	7	40	40	16	24	0	334
Miami	39	10	26	3	38	39	19	26	1	331
Kansas City	35	18	14	3	34	34	25	33	1	318
L.A. Raiders	35	9	21	5	34	35	23	34	0	315
Indianapolis	34	11	18	5	31	33	21	27	0	298
New England	30	12	17	1	27	30	30	40	0	297
San Diego	31	13	15	3	29	31	17	25	0	266
Pittsburgh	29	17	10	2	28	29	21	30	0	265
N.Y. Jets	30	11	14	5	29	30	14	21	1	253
Seattle	28	5	21	2	28	28	15	25	0	241
AFC Total	514	183	284	47	493	511	289	405	7	4458
AFC Average	36.7	13.1	20.3	3.4	35.2	36.5	20.6	28.9	0.5	318.4

NFC Scoring—Team

	TD	TDR	TDP	TD Misc.	PAT	PAT Att.	FG	FG Att.	SAF	TP
San Francisco	51	14	35	2	49	51	29	36	0	442
L.A. Rams	51	19	29	3	51	51	23	30	0	426
New Orleans	46	19	23	4	44	46	20	29	3	386
Washington	42	14	24	4	41	42	29	40	3	386
Green Bay	42	13	27	2	42	42	22	28	1	362
Chicago	45	22	21	2	43	45	15	19	0	358
Minnesota	36	12	17	7	35	36	32	44	2	351
N.Y. Giants	37	17	17	3	35	37	29	38	2	348
Philadelphia	40	14	23	3	40	40	20	33	1	342
Tampa Bay	36	10	23	3	34	36	22	28	2	320
Detroit	36	23	11	2	36	36	20	21	0	312
Atlanta	30	11	17	2	30	30	23	32	0	279

	TD	TDR	TDP	TD Misc.	PAT	PAT Att.	FG	FG Att.	SAF	TP
Phoenix	29	10	17	2	28	29	18	26	1	258
Dallas	25	7	14	4	24	25	10	20	0	204
NFC Total	546	205	298	43	532	546	312	424	15	4774
NFC Average	39.0	14.6	21.3	3.1	38.0	39.0	22.3	30.3	1.1	341.0
League Total	1060	388	582	90	1025	1057	601	829	22	9232
League Avg.	37.9	13.9	20.8	3.2	36.6	37.8	21.5	29.6	0.8	329.7

NFL Top 10 Scorers —Touchdowns

	TD	TDR	TDP	TD Misc.	TP
Hilliard, Dalton, New Orleans	18	13	5	0	108
Rice, Jerry, San Francisco	17	0	17	0	102
Anderson, Neal, Chicago	15	11	4	0	90
Bell, Greg, L.A. Rams	15	15	0	0	90
Anderson, Ottis, N.Y. Giants	14	14	0	0	84
Sanders, Barry, Detroit	14	14	0	0	84
Sharpe, Sterling, Green Bay	13	0	12	1	78
Okoye, Christian, Kansas City	12	12	0	0	72
Thomas, Thurman, Buffalo	12	6	6	0	72
Carter, Cris, Philadelphia	11	0	11	0	66
Miller, Anthony, San Diego	11	0	10	1	66

NFL Top 10 Scorers — Kicking

	PAT	PAT Att.	FG	FG Att.	TP
Cofer, Mike, San Francisco	49	51	29	36	136
Lohmiller, Chip, Washington	41	41	29	40	128
Karlis, Rich, Minnesota	27	28	31	39	120
Lansford, Mike, L.A. Rams	51	51	23	30	120
Treadwell, David, Denver	39	40	27	33	120
Norwood, Scott, Buffalo	46	47	23	30	115
Zendejas, Tony, Houston	40	40	25	37	115
Jacke, Chris, Green Bay	42	42	22	28	108
Lowery, Nick, Kansas City	34	35	24	33	106
Andersen, Morten, New Orleans	44	45	20	29	104

AFC Scoring—Individual

Kickers	PAT	PAT Att.	FG	FG Att.	TP
Treadwell, David, Denver	39	40	27	33	120
Norwood, Scott, Buffalo	46	47	23	30	115
Zendejas, Tony, Houston	40	40	25	37	115
Lowery, Nick, Kansas City	34	35	24	33	106
Jaeger, Jeff, L.A. Raiders	34	34	23	34	103
Stoyanovich, Pete, Miami	38	39	19	26	95
Biasucci, Dean, Indianapolis	31	32	21	27	94
Anderson, Gary, Pittsburgh	28	28	21	30	91
Bahr, Matt, Cleveland	40	40	16	24	88
Bahr, Chris, San Diego	29	30	17	25	80
Breech, Jim, Cincinnati	37	38	12	14	73
Johnson, Norm, Seattle	27	27	15	25	72
Leahy, Pat, N.Y. Jets	29	30	14	21	71
Staurovsky, Jason, New England	14	14	14	17	56
Gallery, Jim, Cincinnati	13	13	2	6	19
Johnson, Lee, Cincinnati	0	1	0	0	0

Non-Kickers	TD	TDR	TDP	TD Misc.	TP
Okoye, Christian, Kansas City	12	12	0	0	72
Thomas, Thurman, Buffalo	12	6	6	0	72
Miller, Anthony, San Diego	11	0	10	1	66
Metcalf, Eric, Cleveland	10	6	4	0	60
Brooks, James, Cincinnati	9	7	2	0	54
Butts, Marion, San Diego	9	9	0	0	54
Clayton, Mark, Miami	9	0	9	0	54
Fernandez, Mervyn, L.A. Raiders	9	0	9	0	54
Holman, Rodney, Cincinnati	9	0	9	0	54
Reed, Andre, Buffalo	9	0	9	0	54
Dickerson, Eric, Indianapolis	8	7	1	0	48
Hill, Drew, Houston	8	0	8	0	48
Hoge, Merril, Pittsburgh	8	8	0	0	48
Humphrey, Bobby, Denver	8	7	1	0	48
McGee, Tim, Cincinnati	8	0	8	0	48
Johnson, Vance, Denver	7	0	7	0	42
Stephens, John, New England	7	7	0	0	42
Vick, Roger, N.Y. Jets	7	5	2	0	42
Williams, John L., Seattle	7	1	6	0	42
Brown, Eddie, Cincinnati	6	0	6	0	36
Highsmith, Alonzo, Houston	6	4	2	0	36
Jensen, Jim, Miami	6	0	6	0	36
Jones, Cedric, New England	6	0	6	0	36
Kinnebrew, Larry, Buffalo	6	6	0	0	36
Lipps, Louis, Pittsburgh	6	1	5	0	36

	TD	TDR	TDP	TD Misc.	TP
Slaughter, Webster, Cleveland	6	0	6	0	36
Smith, Sammie, Miami	6	6	0	0	36
Bentley, Albert, Indianapolis	5	1	3	1	30
Blades, Brian, Seattle	5	0	5	0	30
Brown, Andre, Miami	5	0	5	0	30
Duncan, Curtis, Houston	5	0	5	0	30
Dykes, Hart Lee, New England	5	0	5	0	30
Hector, Johnny, N.Y. Jets	5	3	2	0	30
Manoa, Tim, Cleveland	5	3	2	0	30
Skansi, Paul, Seattle	5	0	5	0	30
Taylor, Craig, Cincinnati	5	3	2	0	30
Townsell, JoJo, N.Y. Jets	5	0	5	0	30
White, Lorenzo, Houston	5	5	0	0	30
Worley, Tim, Pittsburgh	5	5	0	0	30
Bratton, Mel, Denver	4	1	3	0	24
Brooks, Bill, Indianapolis	4	0	4	0	24
Carter, Rodney, Pittsburgh	4	1	3	0	24
Gault, Willie, L.A. Raiders	4	0	4	0	24
Harmon, Ronnie, Buffalo	4	0	4	0	24
Jackson, Bo, L.A. Raiders	4	4	0	0	24
Moon, Warren, Houston	4	4	0	0	24
Mueller, Vance, L.A. Raiders	4	2	2	0	24
Rison, Andre, Indianapolis	4	0	4	0	24
Warner, Curt, Seattle	4	3	1	0	24
Largent, Steve, Seattle	3	0	3	0	#19
Ball, Eric, Cincinnati	3	3	0	0	18
Davis, Kenneth, Buffalo	3	1	2	0	18
Edmunds, Ferrell, Miami	3	0	3	0	18
Elway, John, Denver	3	3	0	0	18
Fryar, Irving, New England	3	0	3	0	18
Givins, Ernest, Houston	3	0	3	0	18
Jennings, Stanford, Cincinnati	3	2	1	0	18
Lofton, James, Buffalo	3	0	3	0	18
McMillan, Erik, N.Y. Jets	3	0	0	3	18
McNeil, Freeman, N.Y. Jets	3	2	1	0	18
Morgan, Stanley, New England	3	0	3	0	18
Saxon, James, Kansas City	3	3	0	0	18
Sewell, Steve, Denver	3	0	3	0	18
Spencer, Tim, San Diego	3	3	0	0	18
Tillman, Lawyer, Cleveland	3	0	2	1	18
Alexander, Jeff, Denver	2	2	0	0	12
Allen, Marcus, L.A. Raiders	2	2	0	0	12
Anderson, Eddie, L.A. Raiders	2	0	0	2	12
Beach, Pat, Indianapolis	2	0	2	0	12
Beebe, Don, Buffalo	2	0	2	0	12
Bernstine, Rod, San Diego	2	1	1	0	12
Boyer, Mark, Indianapolis	2	0	2	0	12
Cox, Arthur, San Diego	2	0	2	0	12
Dyal, Mike, L.A. Raiders	2	0	2	0	12
Gash, Thane, Cleveland	2	0	0	2	12
Grayson, Dave, Cleveland	2	0	0	2	12
Harris, Leonard, Houston	2	0	2	0	12
Harry, Emile, Kansas City	2	0	2	0	12
Hayes, Jonathan, Kansas City	2	0	2	0	12
Jackson, Mark, Denver	2	0	2	0	12
Jeffires, Haywood, Houston	2	0	2	0	12
Junkin, Trey, L.A. Raiders	2	0	2	0	12
Kay, Clarence, Denver	2	0	2	0	12
Kelly, Jim, Buffalo	2	2	0	0	12
Langhorne, Reggie, Cleveland	2	0	2	0	12
Logan, Marc, Miami	2	0	0	2	12
Marino, Dan, Miami	2	2	0	0	12
Martin, Mike, Cincinnati	2	0	2	0	12
McKeller, Keith, Buffalo	2	0	2	0	12
Metzelaars, Pete, Buffalo	2	0	2	0	12
Paige, Stephone, Kansas City	2	0	2	0	12
Pelluer, Steve, Kansas City	2	2	0	0	12
Perryman, Bob, New England	2	2	0	0	12
Pinkett, Allen, Houston	2	1	1	0	12
Rozier, Mike, Houston	2	2	0	0	12
Schwedes, Scott, Miami	2	0	1	1	12
Thomas, Robb, Kansas City	2	0	2	0	12
Toon, Al, N.Y. Jets	2	0	2	0	12
Trudeau, Jack, Indianapolis	2	2	0	0	12
Verdin, Clarence, Indianapolis	2	0	1	1	12
Washington, Lionel, L.A. Raiders	2	0	0	2	12
Winder, Sammy, Denver	2	2	0	0	12
Woods, Ickey, Cincinnati	2	2	0	0	12
Young, Mike, Denver	2	0	2	0	12
Alexander, Mike, L.A. Raiders	1	0	1	0	6
Allen, Marvin, New England	1	1	0	0	6
Banks, Fred, Miami	1	0	1	0	6
Braxton, Tyrone, Denver	1	0	0	1	6
Burkett, Chris, N.Y. Jets	1	0	1	0	6
Bussey, Barney, Cincinnati	1	0	0	1	6
Carson, Carlos, Kansas City	1	0	1	0	6
Chandler, Chris, Indianapolis	1	1	0	0	6
Clark, Louis, Seattle	1	0	1	0	6

	TD	TDR	TDP	TD Misc.	TP
Davenport, Ron, Miami	1	1	0	0	6
Dishman, Chris, Houston	1	0	0	1	6
Dixon, Randy, Indianapolis	1	0	0	1	6
Dressel, Chris, Kansas City	1	0	1	0	6
Dupard, Reggie, New England	1	1	0	0	6
Duper, Mark, Miami	1	0	1	0	6
Egu, Patrick, New England	1	1	0	0	6
Fenner, Derrick, Seattle	1	1	0	0	6
Gamble, Kenny, Kansas City	1	1	0	0	6
Glasgow, Nesby, Seattle	1	0	0	1	6
Glenn, Vencie, San Diego	1	0	0	1	6
Hasty, James, N.Y. Jets	1	0	0	1	6
Heard, Herman, Kansas City	1	0	1	0	6
Hill, Derek, Pittsburgh	1	0	1	0	6
Hillary, Ira, Cincinnati	1	0	1	0	6
Horton, Ethan, L.A. Raiders	1	0	1	0	6
Hurst, Maurice, New England	1	0	0	1	6
Jackson, Kirby, Buffalo	1	0	0	1	6
Jefferson, James, Seattle	1	0	0	1	6
Johnson, Flip, Buffalo	1	0	1	0	6
Jones, Keith, Cleveland	1	1	0	0	6
Kelso, Mark, Buffalo	1	0	0	1	6
King, Linden, L.A. Raiders	1	0	0	1	6
Kosar, Bernie, Cleveland	1	1	0	0	6
Kragen, Greg, Denver	1	0	0	1	6
Maas, Bill, Kansas City	1	0	0	1	6
Mack, Kevin, Cleveland	1	1	0	0	6
Mandley, Pete, Kansas City	1	0	1	0	6
Matthews, Clay, Cleveland	1	0	0	1	6
McNair, Todd, Kansas City	1	0	1	0	6
Mecklenburg, Karl, Denver	1	0	0	1	6
Middleton, Ron, Cleveland	1	0	1	0	6
Mularkey, Mike, Pittsburgh	1	0	1	0	6
Nattiel, Ricky, Denver	1	0	1	0	6
Neubert, Keith, N.Y. Jets	1	0	1	0	6
Newsome, Ozzie, Cleveland	1	0	1	0	6
Oliphant, Mike, Cleveland	1	1	0	0	6
Parker, Andy, San Diego	1	0	1	0	6
Pearson, J.C., Kansas City	1	0	0	1	6
Prior, Mike, Indianapolis	1	0	0	1	6
Prokop, Joe, N.Y. Jets	1	1	0	0	6
Pruitt, James, Indianapolis	1	0	1	0	6
Radachowsky, George, N.Y. Jets	1	0	0	1	6
Redden, Barry, Cleveland	1	1	0	0	6
Robbins, Randy, Denver	1	0	0	1	6
Roberts, Alfredo, Kansas City	1	0	1	0	6
Rolle, Butch, Buffalo	1	0	1	0	6
Seale, Eugene, Houston	1	0	0	1	6
Smith, Billy Ray, San Diego	1	0	0	1	6
Smith, Kendal, Cincinnati	1	0	1	0	6
Smith, Neil, Kansas City	1	0	0	1	6
Smith, Steve, L.A. Raiders	1	1	0	0	6
Stradford, Troy, Miami	1	1	0	0	6
Taylor, Keith, Indianapolis	1	0	0	1	6
Tennell, Derek, Cleveland	1	0	1	0	6
Thomas, Eric, Cincinnati	1	0	0	1	6
Waiters, Van, Cleveland	1	0	1	0	6
Walker, Wayne, San Diego	1	0	1	0	6
Wallace, Ray, Pittsburgh	1	1	0	0	6
White, Leon, Cincinnati	1	0	0	1	6
Williams, Warren, Pittsburgh	1	1	0	0	6
Woodruff, Dwayne, Pittsburgh	1	0	0	1	6
Woodson, Rod, Pittsburgh	1	0	0	1	6
Wright, Felix, Cleveland	1	0	0	1	6
Adams, Stefon, L.A. Raiders	0	0	0	0	*2
Brooks, Michael, Denver	0	0	0	0	*2
McDowell, Bubba, Houston	0	0	0	0	*2
McGovern, Rob, Kansas City	0	0	0	0	*2

#indicates extra point scored.
*indicates safety scored.

NFC Scoring—Individual

Kickers	PAT	PAT Att.	FG	FG Att.	TP
Cofer, Mike, San Francisco	49	51	29	36	136
Lohmiller, Chip, Washington	41	41	29	40	128
Karlis, Rich, Minnesota	27	28	31	39	120
Lansford, Mike, L.A. Rams	51	51	23	30	120
Jacke, Chris, Green Bay	42	42	22	28	108
Andersen, Morten, New Orleans	44	45	20	29	104
Igwebuike, Donald, Tampa Bay	33	35	22	28	99
Murray, Eddie, Detroit	36	36	20	21	96
Davis, Greg, New England-Atlanta	25	28	23	34	94
Butler, Kevin, Chicago	43	45	15	19	88
Allegre, Raul, N.Y. Giants	23	24	20	26	83
Del Greco, Al, Phoenix	28	29	18	26	82
Zendejas, Luis, Philadelphia-Dallas	33	33	14	24	75
Ruzek, Roger, Dallas-Philadelphia	28	29	13	22	67

Kickers	PAT	PAT Att.	FG	FG Att.	TP
McFadden, Paul, Atlanta	18	18	15	20	63
Nittmo, Bjorn, N.Y. Giants	12	13	9	12	39
DeLine, Steve, Philadelphia	3	3	3	7	12
Garcia, Teddy, Minnesota	8	8	1	5	11
Miller, Chris, Atlanta	0	0	1	1	3

Non-Kickers	TD	TDR	TDP	TD Misc.	TP
Hilliard, Dalton, New Orleans	18	13	5	0	108
Rice, Jerry, San Francisco	17	0	17	0	102
Anderson, Neal, Chicago	15	11	4	0	90
Bell, Greg, L.A. Rams	15	15	0	0	90
Anderson, Ottis, N.Y. Giants	14	14	0	0	84
Sanders, Barry, Detroit	14	14	0	0	84
Sharpe, Sterling, Green Bay	13	0	12	1	78
Carter, Cris, Philadelphia	11	0	11	0	66
Taylor, John, San Francisco	10	0	10	0	60
Walker, Herschel, Dallas-Minnesota	10	7	2	1	60
Byner, Earnest, Washington	9	7	2	0	54
Carrier, Mark, Tampa Bay	9	0	9	0	54
Clark, Gary, Washington	9	0	9	0	54
Tate, Lars, Tampa Bay	9	8	1	0	54
Ellard, Henry, L.A. Rams	8	0	8	0	48
Johnson, Richard, Detroit	8	0	8	0	48
Martin, Eric, New Orleans	8	0	8	0	48
Monk, Art, Washington	8	0	8	0	48
Muster, Brad, Chicago	8	5	3	0	48
Craig, Roger, San Francisco	7	6	1	0	42
Green, Roy, Phoenix	7	0	7	0	42
Fenney, Rick, Minnesota	6	4	2	0	36
Ferrell, Earl, Phoenix	6	6	0	0	36
Jones, Keith, Atlanta	6	6	0	0	36
Anderson, Willie, L.A. Rams	5	0	5	0	30
Byars, Keith, Philadelphia	5	5	0	0	30
Fullwood, Brent, Green Bay	5	5	0	0	30
Hill, Bruce, Tampa Bay	5	0	5	0	30
Johnson, Damone, L.A. Rams	5	0	5	0	30
Majkowski, Don, Green Bay	5	5	0	0	30
McGee, Buford, L.A. Rams	5	1	4	0	30
Meggett, Dave, N.Y. Giants	5	0	4	1	30
Settle, John, Atlanta	5	3	2	0	30
Smith, J.T., Phoenix	5	0	5	0	30
West, Ed, Green Bay	5	0	5	0	30
Brenner, Hoby, New Orleans	4	0	4	0	24
Carter, Anthony, Minnesota	4	0	4	0	24
Cunningham, Randall, Philadelphia	4	4	0	0	24
Fontenot, Herman, Green Bay	4	1	3	0	24
Gagliano, Bob, Detroit	4	4	0	0	24
Haynes, Michael, Atlanta	4	0	4	0	24
Hill, Lonzell, New Orleans	4	0	4	0	24
Jones, Brent, San Francisco	4	0	4	0	24
Peete, Rodney, Detroit	4	4	0	0	24
Riggs, Gerald, Washington	4	4	0	0	24
Sanders, Ricky, Washington	4	0	4	0	24
Turner, Odessa, N.Y. Giants	4	0	4	0	24
Bavaro, Mark, N.Y. Giants	3	0	3	0	18
Collins, Shawn, Atlanta	3	0	3	0	18
Cox, Aaron, L.A. Rams	3	0	3	0	18
Davis, Wendell, Chicago	3	0	3	0	18
Dixon, James, Dallas	3	0	2	1	18
Harbaugh, Jim, Chicago	3	3	0	0	18
Jackson, Keith, Philadelphia	3	0	3	0	18
Johnston, Daryl, Dallas	3	0	3	0	18
Jones, Ernie, Phoenix	3	0	3	0	18
Jordan, Buford, New Orleans	3	3	0	0	18
Jordan, Steve, Minnesota	3	0	3	0	18
McKinnon, Dennis, Chicago	3	0	3	0	18
Montana, Joe, San Francisco	3	3	0	0	18
Thornton, James, Chicago	3	0	3	0	18
Toney, Anthony, Philadelphia	3	3	0	0	18
Wilder, James, Tampa Bay	3	0	3	0	18
Wilkins, Gary, Atlanta	3	0	3	0	18
Anderson, Alfred, Minnesota	2	2	0	0	12
Baker, Stephen, N.Y. Giants	2	0	2	0	12
Bland, Carl, Green Bay	2	0	1	1	12
Clack, Darryl, Dallas	2	2	0	0	12
Clark, Robert, Detroit	2	0	2	0	12
Delpino, Robert, L.A. Rams	2	1	1	0	12
Dixon, Floyd, Atlanta	2	0	2	0	12
Folsom, Steve, Dallas	2	0	2	0	12
Garrity, Gregg, Philadelphia	2	0	2	0	12
Giles, Jimmie, Philadelphia	2	0	2	0	12
Gustafson, Jim, Minnesota	2	0	2	0	12
Hall, Ron, Tampa Bay	2	0	2	0	12
Holohan, Pete, L.A. Rams	2	0	2	0	12
Hostetler, Jeff, N.Y. Giants	2	2	0	0	12
Howard, William, Tampa Bay	2	1	1	0	12
Irvin, Michael, Dallas	2	0	2	0	12
Jordan, Tony, Phoenix	2	2	0	0	12

	TD	TDR	TDP	TD Misc.	TP
Kemp, Perry, Green Bay	2	0	2	0	12
Lang, Gene, Atlanta	2	1	1	0	12
Martin, Kelvin, Dallas	2	0	2	0	12
Morris, Jamie, Washington	2	2	0	0	12
Novoselsky, Brent, Minnesota	2	0	2	0	12
Palmer, Paul, Dallas	2	2	0	0	12
Query, Jeff, Green Bay	2	0	2	0	12
Quick, Mike, Philadelphia	2	0	2	0	12
Rathman, Tom, San Francisco	2	1	1	0	12
Reynolds, Ricky, Tampa Bay	2	0	0	2	12
Sanders, Thomas, Chicago	2	0	1	1	12
Shepard, Derrick, New Orleans-Dallas	2	0	1	1	12
Sherman, Heath, Philadelphia	2	2	0	0	12
Suhey, Matt, Chicago	2	1	1	0	12
Young, Steve, San Francisco	2	2	0	0	12
Merriweather, Mike, Minnesota	1	0	0	1	*8
Banks, Carl, N.Y. Giants	1	0	1	0	6
Beckman, Brad, Atlanta	1	0	1	0	6
Boso, Cap, Chicago	1	0	1	0	6
Brown, Ron, L.A. Rams	1	0	1	0	6
Butler, Bobby, Atlanta	1	0	0	1	6
Coleman, Monte, Washington	1	0	0	1	6
Cook, Toi, New Orleans	1	0	0	1	6
Cross, Howard, N.Y. Giants	1	0	1	0	6
Davis, Reuben, Tampa Bay	1	0	0	1	6
Del Rio, Jack, Dallas	1	0	0	1	6
Didier, Clint, Green Bay	1	0	1	0	6
Drewrey, Willie, Tampa Bay	1	0	1	0	6
Drummond, Robert, Philadelphia	1	0	1	0	6
Everett, Eric, Philadelphia	1	0	0	1	6
Everett, Jim, L.A. Rams	1	1	0	0	6
Flagler, Terrence, San Francisco	1	1	0	0	6
Flowers, Kenny, Atlanta	1	1	0	0	6
Ford, Bernard, Dallas	1	0	1	0	6
Fourcade, John, New Orleans	1	1	0	0	6
Frazier, Paul, New Orleans	1	1	0	0	6
Gary, Cleveland, L.A. Rams	1	1	0	0	6
Gentry, Dennis, Chicago	1	0	1	0	6
Gray, Jerry, L.A. Rams	1	0	0	1	6
Green, Mark, Chicago	1	1	0	0	6
Haddix, Michael, Green Bay	1	0	1	0	6
Haley, Charles, San Francisco	1	0	0	1	6
Harris, William, Tampa Bay	1	0	1	0	6
Heller, Ron, Atlanta	1	0	1	0	6
Henderson, Keith, San Francisco	1	1	0	0	6
Heyward, Craig, New Orleans	1	1	0	0	6
Hipple, Eric, Detroit	1	1	0	0	6
Hogeboom, Gary, Phoenix	1	1	0	0	6
Holmes, Don, Phoenix	1	0	1	0	6
Holmes, Jerry, Detroit	1	0	0	1	6
Holt, Issiac, Minnesota	1	0	0	1	6
Howard, Joe, Washington	1	0	0	1	6
Ingram, Darryl, Minnesota	1	0	1	0	6
Ingram, Mark, N.Y. Giants	1	0	1	0	6
Jackson, Johnny, San Francisco	1	0	0	1	6
Jeffcoat, Jim, Dallas	1	0	0	1	6
Johnson, A.J., Washington	1	0	0	1	6
Johnson, Pepper, N.Y. Giants	1	0	0	1	6
Johnson, Ron, Philadelphia	1	0	1	0	6
Jones, Hassan, Minnesota	1	0	1	0	6
Kinard, Terry, N.Y. Giants	1	0	0	1	6
Lewis, Leo, Minnesota	1	0	1	0	6
Little, David, Philadelphia	1	0	1	0	6
Lockhart, Eugene, Dallas	1	0	0	1	6
Manuel, Lionel, N.Y. Giants	1	0	1	0	6
Maxie, Brett, New Orleans	1	0	0	1	6
McDonald, Tim, Phoenix	1	0	0	1	6
Millard, Keith, Minnesota	1	0	0	1	6
Morris, Ron, Chicago	1	0	1	0	6
Morse, Bobby, New Orleans	1	0	0	1	6
Newsome, Vince, L.A. Rams	1	0	0	1	6
Newton, Tim, Minnesota	1	0	0	1	6
Novacek, Jay, Phoenix	1	0	1	0	6
Phillips, Jason, Detroit	1	0	1	0	6
Rutland, Reggie, Minnesota	1	0	0	1	6
Rypien, Mark, Washington	1	1	0	0	6
Sanders, Deion, Atlanta	1	0	0	1	6
Sargent, Broderick, Dallas	1	1	0	0	6
Simmons, Clyde, Philadelphia	1	0	0	1	6
Simms, Phil, N.Y. Giants	1	1	0	0	6
Stamps, Sylvester, Tampa Bay	1	1	0	0	6
Stewart, Michael, L.A. Rams	1	0	0	1	6
Stinson, Lemuel, Chicago	1	0	0	1	6
Thomas, Henry, Minnesota	1	0	0	1	6
Tice, John, New Orleans	1	0	1	0	6
Tomczak, Mike, Chicago	1	1	0	0	6
Turner, Floyd, New Orleans	1	0	1	0	6
Walls, Wesley, San Francisco	1	0	1	0	6

	TD	TDR	TDP	TD Misc.	TP
Walton, Alvin, Washington	1	0	0	1	6
Warren, Don, Washington	1	0	1	0	6
Waters, Andre, Philadelphia	1	0	0	1	6
White, William, Detroit	1	0	0	1	6
Wilson, Mike, San Francisco	1	0	1	0	6
Wilson, Wade, Minnesota	1	1	0	0	6
Wolfley, Ron, Phoenix	1	1	0	0	6
Woodside, Keith, Green Bay	1	1	0	0	6
Workman, Vince, Green Bay	1	1	0	0	6
Zordich, Mike, Phoenix	1	0	0	1	6
Berry, Ray, Minnesota	0	0	0	0	*2
Cocroft, Sherman, Tampa Bay	0	0	0	0	*2
Forde, Brian, New Orleans	0	0	0	0	*2
Harris, Al, Philadelphia	0	0	0	0	*2
Manley, Dexter, Washington	0	0	0	0	*2
Marshall, Leonard, N.Y. Giants	0	0	0	0	*2
Reasons, Gary, N.Y. Giants	0	0	0	0	*2
Smith, Sean, Tampa Bay	0	0	0	0	*2
Stokes, Fred, Washington	0	0	0	0	*2
Warren, Frank, New Orleans	0	0	0	0	*2
Wilson, Karl, Phoenix	0	0	0	0	*2
Mohr, Chris, Tampa Bay	0	0	0	0	#1

*indicates safety scored.
#indicates extra point scored.

Field Goals

Best Percentage
NFC: .952—Eddie Murray, Detroit
AFC: .824—Jason Staurovsky, New England
Made
NFC: 31—Rich Karlis, Minnesota
AFC: 27—David Treadwell, Denver
Attempts
NFC: 40—Chip Lohmiller, Washington
AFC: 37—Tony Zendejas, Houston
Longest
AFC: 59—Pete Stoyanovich, Miami
NFC: 54—Paul McFadden, Atlanta
Average Yards Made
NFC: 38.5—Eddie Murray, Detroit
AFC: 36.3—Scott Norwood, Buffalo

AFC Field Goals—Team

	FG	FG Att.	Pct.	Long
Denver	27	33	.818	46
Indianapolis	21	27	.778	55
Buffalo	23	30	.767	48
New England	30	40	.750	52
Miami	19	26	.731	59
Kansas City	24	33	.727	50
Cincinnati	14	20	.700	47
Pittsburgh	21	30	.700	49
San Diego	17	25	.680	53
L.A. Raiders	23	34	.676	50
Houston	25	37	.676	52
Cleveland	16	24	.667	50
N.Y. Jets	14	21	.667	46
Seattle	15	25	.600	50
AFC Totals	289	405	—	59
AFC Average	20.6	28.9	.714	—

NFC Field Goals—Team

	FG	FG Att.	Pct.	Long
Detroit	20	21	.952	50
San Francisco	29	36	.806	47
Chicago	15	19	.789	46
Green Bay	22	28	.786	52
Tampa Bay	22	28	.786	53
L.A. Rams	23	30	.767	48
N.Y. Giants	29	38	.763	52
Minnesota	32	44	.727	51
Washington	29	40	.725	48
Atlanta	23	32	.719	54
Phoenix	18	26	.692	50
New Orleans	20	29	.690	49
Philadelphia	20	33	.606	49
Dallas	10	20	.500	47
NFC Totals	312	424	—	54
NFC Average	22.3	30.3	.736	—
League Totals	601	829	—	59
League Average	21.5	29.6	.725	—

AFC Field Goals—Individual

	1-19	20-29	30-39	40-49	50 & Over	Totals	Avg. Yds. Att.	Avg. Yds. Made	Avg. Yds. Miss	Long
Staurovsky, Jason, New England	0-0 —	4-4 1.000	5-7 .714	4-5 .800	1-1 1.000	14-17 .824	35.9	35.7	37.0	50
Treadwell, David, Denver	3-3 1.000	13-14 .929	8-8 1.000	3-7 .429	0-1 .000	27-33 .818	31.8	29.4	43.0	46
Biasucci, Dean, Indianapolis	2-2 1.000	6-6 1.000	9-10 .900	3-5 .600	1-4 .250	21-27 .778	40.0	32.5	48.2	55
Norwood, Scott, Buffalo	0-0 —	5-6 .833	8-9 .889	10-15 .667	0-0 —	23-30 .767	37.1	36.3	39.6	48
Stoyanovich, Pete, Miami	1-1 1.000	8-8 1.000	5-6 .833	4-8 .500	1-3 .333	19-26 .731	35.7	32.2	45.4	59
Lowery, Nick, Kansas City	1-1 1.000	6-6 1.000	10-14 .714	6-9 .667	1-3 .333	24-33 .727	35.9	33.9	41.3	50
Anderson, Gary, Pittsburgh	2-2 1.000	5-5 1.000	5-8 .625	9-15 .600	0-0 —	21-30 .700	37.6	35.3	42.8	49
Bahr, Chris, San Diego	0-0 —	6-6 1.000	6-9 .667	4-6 .667	1-4 .250	17-25 .680	37.7	34.9	43.6	53
Jaeger, Jeff, L.A. Raiders	1-1 1.000	8-10 .800	8-9 .889	5-12 .417	1-2 .500	23-34 .676	35.9	33.4	41.2	50
Zendejas, Tony, Houston	1-1 1.000	8-9 .889	9-14 .643	5-11 .455	2-2 1.000	25-37 .676	35.0	33.0	39.1	52
Bahr, Matt, Cleveland	0-0 —	5-5 1.000	6-8 .750	4-9 .444	1-2 .500	16-24 .667	37.9	34.9	43.8	50
Leahy, Pat, N.Y. Jets	1-1 1.000	6-7 .857	3-4 .750	4-8 .500	0-1 .000	14-21 .667	34.7	31.4	41.3	46
Johnson, Norm, Seattle	1-1 1.000	6-7 .857	3-4 .750	4-8 .500	1-5 .200	15-25 .600	38.6	34.7	44.5	50
Non-Qualifiers (Less than 15 attempts)										
Breech, Jim, Cincinnati	0-0 —	9-9 1.000	3-4 .750	0-1 .000	0-0 —	12-14 .857	28.4	26.3	41.5	38
Gallery, Jim, Cincinnati	0-0 —	1-1 1.000	0-1 .000	1-4 .250	0-0 —	2-6 .333	40.2	36.5	42.0	47
AFC Totals	13-13 1.000	99-106 .934	94-124 .758	71-132 .538	12-30 .400	289-405 .714	36.0	33.5	42.3	59
League Totals	27-27 1.000	204-216 .944	199-252 .790	150-273 .549	21-61 .344	601-829 .725	36.0	33.5	42.7	59

Leader based on percentage, minimum 16 field goal attempts.

NFC Field Goals — Individual

	1-19	20-29	30-39	40-49	50 & Over	Totals	Avg. Yds. Att.	Avg. Yds. Made	Avg. Yds. Miss	Long
Murray, Eddie	0-0	3-3	8-9	8-8	1-1	20-21	38.2	38.5	34.0	50
Detroit	—	1.000	.889	1.000	1.000	.952				
Cofer, Mike	3-3	8-8	8-9	10-15	0-1	29-36	35.1	33.0	43.9	47
San Francisco	1.000	1.000	.889	.667	.000	.806				
Karlis, Rich	3-3	14-15	5-6	8-12	1-3	31-39	33.7	31.1	43.6	51
Minnesota	1.000	.933	.833	.667	.333	.795				
Butler, Kevin	0-0	6-6	6-7	3-5	0-1	15-19	34.5	32.1	43.5	46
Chicago	—	1.000	.857	.600	.000	789				
Igwebuike, Donald	0-0	9-9	6-6	5-10	2-3	22-28	37.3	34.5	47.2	53
Tampa Bay	—	1.000	1.000	.500	.667	.786				
Jacke, Chris	1-1	9-9	4-6	7-9	1-3	22-28	35.6	33.4	43.8	52
Green Bay	1.000	1.000	.667	.778	.333	.786				
Allegre, Raul	0-0	6-6	8-9	5-9	1-2	20-26	37.0	34.6	45.0	52
N.Y. Giants	—	1.000	.889	.556	.500	.769				
Lansford, Mike	1-1	7-8	7-7	8-10	0-4	23-30	36.5	33.9	44.9	48
L.A. Rams	1.000	.875	1.000	.800	.000	.767				
McFadden, Paul,	1-1	4-4	6-7	2-6	2-2	15-20	37.0	34.7	43.6	54
Atlanta	1.000	1.000	.857	.333	1.000	.750				
Lohmiller, Chip,	2-2	11-11	13-15	3-11	0-1	29-40	34.7	31.3	43.5	48
Washington	1.000	1.000	.867	.273	.000	.725				
Del Greco, Al,	0-0	7-7	5-6	5-11	1-2	18-26	37.1	33.8	44.4	50
Phoenix	—	1.000	.833	.455	.500	.692				
Andersen, Morten,	0-0	7-8	10-11	3-6	0-4	20-29	36.9	33.2	45.1	49
New Orleans	—	.875	.909	.500	.000	.690				
Davis, Greg,	0-0	6-6	8-12	7-14	2-2	23-34	38.1	36.6	41.3	52
New England-Atlanta	—	1.000	.667	.500	1.000	.676				
Ruzek, Roger,	2-2	3-4	6-10	2-5	0-1	13-22	34.3	31.9	37.8	46
Dallas-Philadelphia	1.000	.750	.600	.400	.000	.591				
Zendejas, Luis,	1-1	3-3	4-6	6-12	0-2	14-24	38.3	35.4	42.5	47
Philadelphia-Dallas	1.000	1.000	.667	.500	.000	.583				
Non-Qualifiers (Less than 15 attempts)										
Miller, Chris,	0-0	1-1	0-0	0-0	0-0	1-1	25.0	25.0	0.0	25
Atlanta	—	1.000	—	—	—	1.000				
Nittmo, Bjorn,	0-0	4-5	5-5	0-2	0-0	9-12	32.7	30.1	40.3	39
N.Y. Giants	—	.800	1.000	.000	—	.750				
DeLine, Steve,	0-0	0-0	1-2	2-5	0-0	3-7	42.4	42.0	42.8	49
Philadelphia	—	—	.500	.400	—	.429				
Garcia, Teddy,	0-0	0-0	1-4	0-0	0-1	1-5	38.0	35.0	38.8	35
Minnesota	—	—	.250	—	.000	.200				
NFC Totals	14-14	105-110	105-128	79-141	9-31	312-424	36.0	33.5	43.1	54
	1.000	.955	.820	.560	.290	.736				
League Totals	27-27	204-216	199-252	150-273	21-61	601-829	36.0	33.5	42.7	59
	1.000	.944	.790	.549	.344	.725				

Leader based on percentage, minimum 16 field goal attempts.

Rushing

Individual Champions
AFC: 1,480—Christian Okoye, Kansas City
NFC: 1,470—Barry Sanders, Detroit

Most Yards, Game
NFC: 221—Gerald Riggs, Washington vs. Philadelphia, September 17
(29 attempts, 1 TD)
Greg Bell, L.A. Rams vs. Green Bay, September 24
(28 attempts, 2 TD)
AFC: 176—Marion Butts, San Diego at Kansas City, December 17
(39 attempts)

Longest:
AFC: 92—Bo Jackson, L.A. Raiders vs. Cincinnati, November 5 (TD)
NFC: 73—Neal Anderson, Chicago vs. Green Bay, December 17

Attempts
AFC: 370—Christian Okoye, Kansas City
NFC: 344—Dalton Hilliard, New Orleans

Most Attempts, Game
AFC: 39—Marion Butts, San Diego at Kansas City, December 17
(176 yards)
NFC: 38—Jamie Morris, Washington at Philadelphia, November 12
(88 yards)

Yards Per Attempt
NFC: 6.0—Randall Cunningham, Philadelphia
AFC: 5.6—James Brooks, Cincinnati

Touchdowns
NFC: 15—Greg Bell, L.A. Rams
AFC: 12—Christian Okoye, Kansas City

Team Leaders, Yards
AFC: BUFFALO: 1,244, Thurman Thomas; CINCINNATI: 1,239, James Brooks; CLEVELAND: 633, Eric Metcalf; DENVER: 1,151, Bobby Humphrey; HOUSTON: 531, Alonzo Highsmith; INDIANAPOLIS: 1,311, Eric Dickerson; KANSAS CITY: 1,480, Christian Okoye; L.A. RAIDERS: 950, Bo Jackson; MIAMI: 659, Sammie Smith; NEW ENGLAND: 833, John Stephens; N.Y. JETS: 702, Johnny Hector; PITTSBURGH: 770, Tim Worley; SAN DIEGO: 683, Marion Butts; SEATTLE: 631, Curt Warner.
NFC: ATLANTA: 689, John Settle; CHICAGO: 1,275, Neal Anderson; DAL-LAS: 446, Paul Palmer; DETROIT: 1,470, Barry Sanders; GREEN BAY: 821, Brent Fullwood; L.A. RAMS: 1,137, Greg Bell; MINNESOTA: 669, Herschel Walker; NEW ORLEANS: 1,262, Dalton Hilliard; N.Y. GIANTS: 1,023, Ottis Anderson; PHILADELPHIA: 621, Randall Cunningham; PHOENIX: 502, Earl Ferrell; SAN FRANCISCO: 1,054, Roger Craig; TAMPA BAY: 589, Lars Tate; WASHINGTON: 834, Gerald Riggs.

Team Champions
AFC: 2,483—Cincinnati
NFC: 2,287—Chicago

AFC Rushing—Team

	Att.	Yards	Avg.	Long	TD
Cincinnati	529	2483	4.7	65t	17
Buffalo	532	2264	4.3	38	15
Kansas City	559	2227	4.0	59	18
Denver	554	2092	3.8	40	15
L.A. Raiders	454	2038	4.5	92t	9
Houston	495	1928	3.9	60	16
San Diego	432	1873	4.3	50t	13
Indianapolis	458	1853	4.0	26	11
Pittsburgh	500	1818	3.6	58t	17
New England	485	1749	3.6	35t	12
Cleveland	448	1609	3.6	43t	14
N.Y. Jets	400	1596	4.0	39t	11
Seattle	405	1392	3.4	34	5
Miami	400	1330	3.3	25	10
AFC Total	6,651	26,252	—	92t	183
AFC Average	475.1	1875.1	3.9	—	13.1

NFC Rushing—Team

	Att.	Yards	Avg.	Long	TD
Chicago	516	2287	4.4	73	22
Philadelphia	540	2208	4.1	51	14
Minnesota	514	2066	4.0	47	12
Detroit	421	2053	4.9	34	23
San Francisco	493	1966	4.0	29t	14
New Orleans	502	1948	3.9	40	19
L.A. Rams	472	1909	4.0	47	19
Washington	514	1904	3.7	58	14
N.Y. Giants	556	1889	3.4	36t	17
Green Bay	397	1732	4.4	68t	13
Tampa Bay	412	1507	3.7	48	10
Dallas	355	1409	4.0	63t	7

	Att.	Yards	Avg.	Long	TD
Phoenix	407	1361	3.3	44t	10
Atlanta	318	1155	3.6	22	11
NFC Total	6,417	25,394	—	73	205
NFC Average	458.4	1813.9	4.0	—	14.6
League Total	13,068	51,646	—	92t	388
League Average	466.7	1844.5	4.0	—	13.9

NFL Top 10 Rushers

	Att.	Yards	Avg.	Long	TD
Okoye, Christian, Kansas City	370	1480	4.0	59	12
Sanders, Barry, Detroit	280	1470	5.3	34	14
Dickerson, Eric, Indianapolis	314	1311	4.2	21t	7
Anderson, Neal, Chicago	274	1275	4.7	73	11
Hilliard, Dalton, New Orleans	344	1262	3.7	40	13
Thomas, Thurman, Buffalo	298	1244	4.2	38	6
Brooks, James, Cincinnati	221	1239	5.6	65t	7
Humphrey, Bobby, Denver	294	1151	3.9	40	7
Bell, Greg, L.A. Rams	272	1137	4.2	47	15
Craig, Roger, San Francisco	271	1054	3.9	27	6

AFC Rushing—Individual

	Att.	Yards	Avg.	Long	TD
Okoye, Christian, Kansas City	370	1480	4.0	59	12
Dickerson, Eric, Indianapolis	314	1311	4.2	21t	7
Thomas, Thurman, Buffalo	298	1244	4.2	38	6
Brooks, James, Cincinnati	221	1239	5.6	65t	7
Humphrey, Bobby, Denver	294	1151	3.9	40	7
Jackson, Bo, L.A. Raiders	173	950	5.5	92t	4
Stephens, John, New England	244	833	3.4	35t	7
Worley, Tim, Pittsburgh	195	770	3.9	38	5
Hector, Johnny, N.Y. Jets	177	702	4.0	24	3
Butts, Marion, San Diego	170	683	4.0	50t	9
Smith, Sammie, Miami	200	659	3.3	25	6
Metcalf, Eric, Cleveland	187	633	3.4	43t	6
Warner, Curt, Seattle	194	631	3.3	34	3
Hoge, Merril, Pittsburgh	186	621	3.3	31	8
Perryman, Bob, New England	150	562	3.7	18	2
Kinnebrew, Larry, Buffalo	131	533	4.1	25	6
Highsmith, Alonzo, Houston	128	531	4.1	25	4
Spencer, Tim, San Diego	134	521	3.9	15	3
Williams, John L., Seattle	146	499	3.4	21	1
Smith, Steve, L.A. Raiders	117	471	4.0	21	1
Pinkett, Allen, Houston	94	449	4.8	60	1
Vick, Roger, N.Y. Jets	112	434	3.9	39t	5
Ball, Eric, Cincinnati	98	391	4.0	27	3
McNeil, Freeman, N.Y. Jets	80	352	4.4	19t	2
Winder, Sammy, Denver	110	351	3.2	16	2
White, Lorenzo, Houston	104	349	3.4	33	5
Nelson, Darrin, Minnesota-San Diego	67	321	4.8	28	0
Rozier, Mike, Houston	88	301	3.4	17	2
Bentley, Albert, Indianapolis	75	299	4.0	22	1
Allen, Marcus, L.A. Raiders	69	293	4.2	15	2
Jennings, Stanford, Cincinnati	83	293	3.5	17	2
Manoa, Tim, Cleveland	87	289	3.3	22	3
Esiason, Boomer, Cincinnati	47	278	5.9	24	0
Moon, Warren, Houston	70	268	3.8	19	4
Elway, John, Denver	48	244	5.1	31	3
Stradford, Troy, Miami	66	240	3.6	13	1
Saxon, James, Kansas City	58	233	4.0	19	3
Heard, Herman, Kansas City	63	216	3.4	28	0
Logan, Marc, Miami	57	201	3.5	14	0
Lipps, Louis, Pittsburgh	13	180	13.8	58t	1
Redden, Barry, Cleveland	40	180	4.5	38t	1
Mueller, Vance, L.A. Raiders	48	161	3.4	19	2
Jones, Keith, Cleveland	43	160	3.7	15	1
Krieg, Dave, Seattle	40	160	4.0	18	0
Davis, Kenneth, Buffalo	29	149	5.1	21	1
Alexander, Jeff, Denver	45	146	3.2	11	2
Pelluer, Steve, Kansas City	17	143	8.4	27	2
McMahon, Jim, San Diego	29	141	4.9	15	0
Bernstine, Rod, San Diego	15	137	9.1	32t	1
Kelly, Jim, Buffalo	29	137	4.7	19	2
Williams, Warren, Pittsburgh	37	131	3.5	13	1
Mack, Kevin, Cleveland	37	130	3.5	12	1
McNair, Todd, Kansas City	23	121	5.3	25	0
Taylor, Craig, Cincinnati	30	111	3.7	16	3
Bratton, Mel, Denver	30	108	3.6	9	1
Harmon, Ronnie, Buffalo	17	99	5.8	24	0
Oliphant, Mike, Cleveland	15	97	6.5	21t	1
Woods, Ickey, Cincinnati	29	94	3.2	12	2
Trudeau, Jack, Indianapolis	35	91	2.6	17	2
Flutie, Doug, New England	16	87	5.4	22	0
Kosar, Bernie, Cleveland	30	70	2.3	23	1
Brinson, Dana, San Diego	17	64	3.8	9	0
Brown, Anthony, N.Y. Jets	12	63	5.3	17	0
Chandler, Chris, Indianapolis	7	57	8.1	23	1
Davenport, Ron, Miami	14	56	4.0	9	1
Porter, Kerry, L.A. Raiders	13	54	4.2	23	0
Stone, Dwight, Pittsburgh	10	53	5.3	32	0
Allen, Marvin, New England	11	51	4.6	18	1
Jensen, Jim, Miami	8	50	6.3	14	0
Hampton, Lorenzo, Miami	17	47	2.8	9	0
Hunter, Ivy Joe, Indianapolis	13	47	3.6	11	0
Holland, Jamie, San Diego	6	46	7.7	24	0
Mueller, Jamie, Buffalo	16	44	2.8	9	0
Sewell, Steve, Denver	7	44	6.3	10	0
Wilson, Marc, New England	7	42	6.0	11	0
Fenner, Derrick, Seattle	11	41	3.7	9	1
Beuerlein, Steve, L.A. Raiders	16	39	2.4	10	0
Secules, Scott, Miami	4	39	9.8	17	0
Verdin, Clarence, Indianapolis	4	39	9.8	26	0
Schroeder, Jay, L.A. Raiders	15	38	2.5	19	0
Tatupu, Mosi, New England	11	38	3.5	20	0
McGee, Tim, Cincinnati	2	36	18.0	25	0
Kubiak, Gary, Denver	15	35	2.3	10	0
McNeil, Gerald, Cleveland	2	32	16.0	18	0
Reed, Andre, Buffalo	2	31	15.5	23	0
Reich, Frank, Buffalo	9	30	3.3	9	0
Wilhelm, Erik, Cincinnati	6	30	5.0	14	0
Brown, Tom, Miami	13	26	2.0	6	0
Brister, Bubby, Pittsburgh	27	25	0.9	15	0
Gamble, Kenny, Kansas City	6	24	4.0	20	1
Harmon, Kevin, Seattle	1	24	24.0	24	0
Harris, Elroy, Seattle	8	23	2.9	8	0
Miller, Anthony, San Diego	4	21	5.3	24	0
Blackledge, Todd, Pittsburgh	9	20	2.2	11	0
Egu, Patrick, New England	3	20	6.7	15t	1
Holifield, John, Cincinnati	11	20	1.8	11	0
Martin, Sammy, New England	2	20	10.0	13	0
Early, Quinn, San Diego	1	19	19.0	19	0
Grogan, Steve, New England	9	19	2.1	7	0
Langhorne, Reggie, Cleveland	5	19	3.8	18	0
O'Brien, Ken, N.Y. Jets	9	18	2.0	5	0
Rison, Andre, Indianapolis	3	18	6.0	18	0
Montgomery, Greg, Houston	3	17	5.7	11	0
Prokop, Joe, N.Y. Jets	1	17	17.0	17t	1
Carter, Rodney, Pittsburgh	11	16	1.5	7	1
Evans, Vince, L.A. Raiders	1	16	16.0	16	0
Fernandez, Mervyn, L.A. Raiders	2	16	8.0	12	0
Johnson, Tracy, Houston	4	16	4.0	8	0
Floyd, Victor, San Diego	8	15	1.9	5	0
Fryar, Irving, New England	2	15	7.5	11	0
Archer, David, San Diego	2	14	7.0	14	0
Epps, Phillip, N.Y. Jets	1	14	14.0	14	0
Jackson, Mark, Denver	5	13	2.6	8	0
Stouffer, Kelly, Seattle	2	11	5.5	9	0
Faaola, Nuu, Miami	2	10	5.0	5	0
Wallace, Ray, Pittsburgh	5	10	2.0	5	1
Clayton, Mark, Miami	3	9	3.0	11	0
Harry, Emile, Kansas City	1	9	9.0	9	0
Walker, Wayne, San Diego	1	9	9.0	9	0
Plummer, Gary, San Diego	1	6	6.0	6	0
Jaworski, Ron, Kansas City	4	5	1.3	4	0
Ramsey, Tom, Indianapolis	4	5	1.3	3	0
Agee, Tommie, Kansas City	1	3	3.0	3	0
Blades, Brian, Seattle	1	3	3.0	3	0
Harper, Michael, N.Y. Jets	1	3	3.0	3	0
Jones, Cedric, New England	1	3	3.0	3	0
Mackey, Kyle, N.Y. Jets	2	3	1.5	5	0
Tyrrell, Tim, Pittsburgh	1	3	3.0	3	0
Mandley, Pete, Kansas City	2	1	0.5	8	0
Caravello, Joe, San Diego	1	0	0.0	0	0
Duncan, Curtis, Houston	1	0	0.0	0	0
Kemp, Jeff, Seattle	1	0	0.0	0	0
Malone, Mark, N.Y. Jets	1	0	0.0	0	0
Roby, Reggie, Miami	2	0	0.0	0	0
Rodriguez, Ruben, Seattle	1	0	0.0	0	0
Tolliver, Billy Joe, San Diego	7	0	0.0	3	0
Pagel, Mike, Cleveland	2	−1	−0.5	4	0
Ryan, Pat, N.Y. Jets	1	−1	−1.0	−1	0
Eason, Tony, New England-N.Y. Jets	3	−2	−0.7	0	0
Hillary, Ira, Cincinnati	1	−2	−2.0	−2	0
Wonsley, George, New England	2	−2	−1.0	0	0
Brooks, Bill, Indianapolis	2	−3	−1.5	0	0
Carlson, Cody, Houston	3	−3	−1.0	0	0
Gelbaugh, Stan, Buffalo	1	−3	−3.0	−3	0
Strom, Rick, Pittsburgh	4	−3	−0.8	0	0
Burkett, Chris, N.Y. Jets	1	−4	−4.0	−4	0
Lageman, Jeff, N.Y. Jets	1	−5	−5.0	−5	0
Johnson, Lee, Cincinnati	1	−7	−7.0	−7	0
Marino, Dan, Miami	14	−7	−0.5	2	2
DeBerg, Steve, Kansas City	14	−8	−0.6	15	0
Newsome, Harry, Pittsburgh	2	−8	−4.0	0	0
Stark, Rohn, Indianapolis	1	−11	−11.0	−11	0

t indicates touchdown.
Leader based on most yards gained.

NFC Rushing—Individual

	Att.	Yards	Avg.	Long	TD
Sanders, Barry, Detroit	280	1470	5.3	34	14
Anderson, Neal, Chicago	274	1275	4.7	73	11
Hilliard, Dalton, New Orleans	344	1262	3.7	40	13
Bell, Greg, L.A. Rams	272	1137	4.2	47	15
Craig, Roger, San Francisco	271	1054	3.9	27	6
Anderson, Ottis, N.Y. Giants	325	1023	3.1	36t	14
Walker, Herschel, Dallas-Minnesota	250	915	3.7	47	7
Riggs, Gerald, Washington	201	834	4.1	58	4
Fullwood, Brent, Green Bay	204	821	4.0	38	5
Settle, John, Atlanta	179	689	3.8	20	3
Cunningham, Randall, Philadelphia	104	621	6.0	51	4
Tate, Lars, Tampa Bay	167	589	3.5	48	8
Fenney, Rick, Minnesota	151	588	3.9	25	4
Toney, Anthony, Philadelphia	172	582	3.4	44	3
Byner, Earnest, Washington	134	580	4.3	24	7
Ferrell, Earl, Phoenix	149	502	3.4	44t	6
Byars, Keith, Philadelphia	133	452	3.4	16t	5
Palmer, Paul, Dallas	112	446	4.0	63t	2
Delpino, Robert, L.A. Rams	78	368	4.7	32t	1
Majkowski, Don, Green Bay	75	358	4.8	20	5
Howard, William, Tampa Bay	108	357	3.3	15	1
Morris, Jamie, Washington	124	336	2.7	12t	2
Muster, Brad, Chicago	82	327	4.0	20	5
Rathman, Tom, San Francisco	79	305	3.9	13	1
Aikman, Troy, Dallas	38	302	7.9	25	0
Tillman, Lewis, N.Y. Giants	79	290	3.7	19	0
Harbaugh, Jim, Chicago	45	276	6.1	26t	3
Woodside, Keith, Green Bay	46	273	5.9	68t	1
Wilder, James, Tampa Bay	70	244	3.5	14	0
Montana, Joe, San Francisco	49	227	4.6	19	3
Johnston, Daryl, Dallas	67	212	3.2	13	0
Jordan, Tony, Phoenix	83	211	2.5	15	2
Dozier, D.J., Minnesota	46	207	4.5	38	0
Jones, Keith, Atlanta	52	202	3.9	19	6
Gagliano, Bob, Detroit	41	192	4.7	19	4
Anderson, Alfred, Minnesota	52	189	3.6	14	2
Higgs, Mark, Philadelphia	49	184	3.8	13	0
Heyward, Craig, New Orleans	49	183	3.7	15	1
Jordan, Buford, New Orleans	38	179	4.7	32	3
Sherman, Heath, Philadelphia	40	177	4.4	37	2
Lang, Gene, Atlanta	47	176	3.7	22	1
Mitchell, Stump, Phoenix	43	165	3.8	14	0
Gary, Cleveland, L.A. Rams	37	163	4.4	18	1
Carthon, Maurice, N.Y. Giants	57	153	2.7	18	0
Peete, Rodney, Detroit	33	148	4.5	14t	4
Sikahema, Vai, Phoenix	38	145	3.8	27	0
Simms, Phil, N.Y. Giants	32	141	4.4	15	1
Stamps, Sylvester, Tampa Bay	29	141	4.9	21t	1
Testaverde, Vinny, Tampa Bay	25	139	5.6	16	0
Haddix, Michael, Green Bay	44	135	3.1	10	0
Wilson, Wade, Minnesota	32	132	4.1	23	1
Flagler, Terrence, San Francisco	33	129	3.9	29t	1
Drummond, Robert, Philadelphia	32	127	4.0	16	0
Sanders, Thomas, Chicago	41	127	3.1	19	0
Young, Steve, San Francisco	38	126	3.3	22	2
Meggett, Dave, N.Y. Giants	28	117	4.2	18	0
Frazier, Paul, New Orleans	25	112	4.5	21	1
Dupard, Reggie, New England-Wash.	37	111	3.0	19	1
Gentry, Dennis, Chicago	17	106	6.2	29	0
Paige, Tony, Detroit	30	105	3.5	16	0
Clark, Jessie, Phoenix-Minnesota	20	99	5.0	14	0
McGee, Buford, L.A. Rams	21	99	4.7	15	1
Fourcade, John, New Orleans	14	91	6.5	14	1
Hogeboom, Gary, Phoenix	27	89	3.3	15	1
Hebert, Bobby, New Orleans	25	87	3.5	11	0
Sargent, Broderick, Dallas	20	87	4.4	43	1
Tupa, Tom, Phoenix	15	75	5.0	13	0
Green, Gaston, L.A. Rams	26	73	2.8	9	0
Hostetler, Jeff, N.Y. Giants	11	71	6.5	19t	2
Tomczak, Mike, Chicago	24	71	3.0	18	1
Fontenot, Herman, Green Bay	17	69	4.1	19	1
Painter, Carl, Detroit	15	64	4.3	9	0
Rypien, Mark, Washington	26	56	2.2	15	1
Sydney, Harry, San Francisco	9	56	6.2	18	0
Rouson, Lee, N.Y. Giants	11	51	4.6	9	0
Suhey, Matt, Chicago	20	51	2.6	8	1
Green, Mark, Chicago	5	46	9.2	37t	1
Kemp, Perry, Green Bay	5	43	8.6	14	0
Morse, Bobby, New Orleans	2	43	21.5	39	0
Clack, Darryl, Dallas	14	40	2.9	17	2
Johnson, Richard, Detroit	12	38	3.2	14	0
Jones, Hassan, Minnesota	1	37	37.0	37	0
Smith, Don, Tampa Bay	7	37	5.3	17	0
Wolfley, Ron, Phoenix	13	36	2.8	5t	1
Haynes, Michael, Atlanta	4	35	8.8	21	0
Rice, Jerry, San Francisco	5	33	6.6	17	0
Paterra, Greg, Atlanta	9	32	3.6	8	0
Baker, Tony, Phoenix	20	31	1.6	6	0

	Att.	Yards	Avg.	Long	TD
Everett, Jim, L.A. Rams	25	31	1.2	13t	1
Dixon, James, Dallas	3	30	10.0	13	0
Henderson, Keith, San Francisco	7	30	4.3	11t	1
Reichenbach, Mike, Philadelphia	1	30	30.0	30	0
Adams, George, N.Y. Giants	9	29	3.2	8	0
Brown, Ron, L.A. Rams	6	27	4.5	12	0
Rosenbach, Timm, Phoenix	6	26	4.3	8	0
Rice, Allen, Minnesota	6	25	4.2	10	0
Sharpe, Sterling, Green Bay	2	25	12.5	26	0
Flowers, Kenny, Atlanta	13	24	1.8	4	1
Teltschik, John, Philadelphia	1	23	23.0	23	0
Gray, Mel, Detroit	3	22	7.3	14	0
Smith, J.T., Phoenix	2	21	10.5	11	0
Miller, Chris, Atlanta	10	20	2.0	7	0
Clark, Gary, Washington	2	19	9.5	11	0
Sanders, Ricky, Washington	4	19	4.8	13	0
Carter, Anthony, Minnesota	3	18	6.0	17	0
Jones, Ernie, Phoenix	1	18	18.0	18	0
Carter, Cris, Philadelphia	2	16	8.0	11	0
Walsh, Steve, Dallas	6	16	2.7	14	0
Tautalatasi, Junior, Dallas	6	15	2.5	6	0
Shepard, Derrick, Dallas	3	12	4.0	12	0
Hipple, Eric, Detroit	2	11	5.5	10	1
Lewis, Leo, Minnesota	1	11	11.0	11	0
Turner, Odessa, N.Y. Giants	2	11	5.5	14	0
Ellard, Henry, L.A. Rams	2	10	5.0	6	0
Humphries, Stan, Washington	5	10	2.0	9	0
Kramer, Tommy, Minnesota	12	9	0.8	5	0
Monk, Art, Washington	3	8	2.7	14	0
Turner, Floyd, New Orleans	2	8	4.0	6	0
Workman, Vince, Green Bay	4	8	2.0	3	1
Taylor, Brian, Chicago	2	7	3.5	7	0
Buford, Maury, Chicago	1	6	6.0	6	0
Ferguson, Joe, Tampa Bay	4	6	1.5	7	0
Irvin, Michael, Dallas	1	6	6.0	6	0
Taylor, John, San Francisco	1	6	6.0	6	0
McKinnon, Dennis, Chicago	3	5	1.7	3	0
Runager, Max, Philadelphia	2	5	2.5	5	0
Thornton, James, Chicago	1	4	4.0	4	0
Brown, Lomas, Detroit	1	3	3.0	3	0
Holohan, Pete, L.A. Rams	1	3	3.0	3	0
Johnson, Ron, Philadelphia	1	3	3.0	3	0
Long, Chuck, Detroit	3	2	0.7	6	0
Reasons, Gary, N.Y. Giants	1	2	2.0	2	0
Ingram, Mark, N.Y. Giants	1	1	1.0	1	0
Saxon, Mike, Dallas	1	1	1.0	1	0
Bates, Bill, Dallas	1	0	0.0	0	0
Fulhage, Scott, Atlanta	1	0	0.0	0	0
Hatcher, Dale, L.A. Rams	1	0	0.0	0	0
Helton, Barry, San Francisco	1	0	0.0	0	0
Millen, Hugh, Atlanta	1	0	0.0	0	0
Winslow, George, New Orleans	1	0	0.0	0	0
Anderson, Willie, L.A. Rams	1	−1	−1.0	−1	0
Coleman, Monte, Washington	1	−1	−1.0	−1	0
Herrmann, Mark, L.A. Rams	2	−1	−0.5	0	0
Reaves, Willard, Washington	1	−1	−1.0	−1	0
McDonald, Keith, Detroit	1	−2	−2.0	−2	0
Cavanaugh, Matt, Philadelphia	2	−3	−1.5	0	0
Scott, Kevin, Dallas	2	−4	−2.0	−1	0
Williams, Doug, Washington	1	−4	−4.0	−4	0
Peebles, Danny, Tampa Bay	2	−6	−3.0	1	0
Hill, Lonzell, New Orleans	1	−7	−7.0	−7	0
Carson, Carlos, Philadelphia	1	−9	−9.0	−9	0
Perriman, Brett, New Orleans	1	−10	−10.0	−10	0
Morris, Ron, Chicago	1	−14	−14.0	−14	0
Dixon, Floyd, Atlanta	2	−23	−11.5	0	0

t indicates touchdown.
Leader based on most yards gained.

Passing

Individual Champions (Rating Points)
NFC: 112.4—Joe Montana, San Francisco
AFC: 92.1—Boomer Esiason, Cincinnati

Completion Percentage
NFC: 70.2—Joe Montana, San Francisco
AFC: 60.5—Steve DeBerg, Kansas City

Attempts
NFC: 599—Don Majkowski, Green Bay
AFC: 550—Dan Marino, Miami

Completions
NFC: 353—Don Majkowski, Green Bay
AFC: 308—Dan Marino, Miami

Yards
NFC: 4,318—Don Majkowski, Green Bay
AFC: 3,997—Dan Marino, Miami

Most Yards, Game
NFC: 458—Joe Montana, San Francisco at L.A. Rams, December 11 (30-42, 3 TD)
AFC: 427—Dan Marino, Miami vs. N.Y. Jets, September 24 (33-55, 3 TD)

Longest

AFC: 97—Bernie Kosar (to Webster Slaughter), Cleveland vs. Chicago, October 23 (TD)

NFC: 95—Joe Montana (to John Taylor), San Francisco at L.A. Rams, December 11 (TD)

Yards Per Attempt

NFC: 9.12—Joe Montana, San Francisco

AFC: 8.01—Jim Kelly, Buffalo

Touchdown Passes

NFC: 29—Jim Everett, L.A. Rams

AFC: 28—Boomer Esiason, Cincinnati

Most Touchdown Passes, Game

AFC: 5—Jim Kelly, Buffalo at Houston, September 24 (17-29, 363 yards) (OT)

—Boomer Esiason, Cincinnati vs. Tampa Bay, October 29 (17-28, 197 yards)

NFC: 5—Randall Cunningham, Philadelphia at Washington, September 17 (34-46, 447 yards)

—Joe Montana, San Francisco at Philadelphia, September 24 (25-34, 428 yards)

Lowest Interception Percentage

NFC: 1.9—Chris Miller, Atlanta

AFC: 2.4—Boomer Esiason, Cincinnati

Team Champions

NFC: 4,349—Washington

AFC: 4,216—Miami

AFC Passing —Team

	Att.	Comp.	Pct. Comp.	Gross Yards	Tkd.	Yards Lost	Net Yards	TD	Pct. TD	Long	Int.	Pct. Int.	Avg. Yds. Att.	Avg. Yds. Comp.
Miami	601	331	55.1	4302	10	86	4216	26	4.3	78t	25	4.2	7.16	13.00
New England	610	302	49.5	3972	34	265	3707	17	2.8	65t	27	4.4	6.51	13.15
Cincinnati	513	288	56.1	3950	41	332	3618	32	6.2	74t	13	2.5	7.70	13.72
Buffalo	478	281	58.8	3831	35	242	3589	32	6.7	78t	20	4.2	8.01	13.63
Houston	496	295	59.5	3786	37	287	3499	23	4.6	55	16	3.2	7.63	12.83
Cleveland	529	309	58.4	3625	34	192	3433	20	3.8	97t	15	2.8	6.85	11.73
N.Y. Jets	570	338	59.3	3892	62	477	3415	14	2.5	63t	24	4.2	6.83	11.51
Seattle	559	316	56.5	3583	46	379	3204	21	3.8	60t	23	4.1	6.41	11.34
Kansas City	435	259	59.5	3220	23	182	3038	14	3.2	50	23	5.3	7.40	12.43
San Diego	515	270	52.4	3291	39	254	3037	15	2.9	69t	19	3.7	6.39	12.19
Denver	474	256	54.0	3352	43	351	3001	21	4.4	69	20	4.2	7.07	13.09
Indianapolis	493	253	51.3	3134	28	174	2960	18	3.7	82t	17	3.4	6.36	12.39
L.A. Raiders	414	201	48.6	3277	44	326	2951	21	5.1	84t	22	5.3	7.92	16.30
Pittsburgh	404	210	52.0	2662	51	484	2178	10	2.5	79t	13	3.2	6.59	12.68
AFC Total	7091	3909	—	49877	527	4031	45846	284	—	97t	277	—	—	—
AFC Average	506.5	279.2	55.1	3562.6	37.6	287.9	3274.7	20.3	4.0	—	19.8	3.9	7.03	12.76

NFC Passing —Team

	Att.	Comp.	Pct. Comp.	Gross Yards	Tkd.	Yards Lost	Net Yards	TD	Pct. TD	Long	Int.	Pct. Int.	Avg. Yds. Att.	Avg. Yds. Comp.
Washington	581	337	58.0	4476	21	127	4349	24	4.1	80t	17	2.9	7.70	13.28
San Francisco	483	339	70.2	4584	45	282	4302	35	7.2	95t	11	2.3	9.49	13.52
L.A. Rams	523	308	58.9	4369	32	236	4133	29	5.5	78t	18	3.4	8.35	14.19
Green Bay	600	354	59.0	4325	48	277	4048	27	4.5	79t	20	3.3	7.21	12.22
Atlanta	578	312	54.0	3903	51	389	3514	17	2.9	72t	12	2.1	6.75	12.51
New Orleans	461	284	61.6	3651	36	271	3380	23	5.0	54t	19	4.1	7.92	12.86
Tampa Bay	570	302	53.0	3666	43	331	3335	23	4.0	78t	28	4.9	6.43	12.14
Phoenix	523	279	53.3	3659	56	379	3280	17	3.3	77t	30	5.7	7.00	13.11
Minnesota	499	272	54.5	3468	40	279	3189	17	3.4	50	19	3.8	6.95	12.75
Philadelphia	538	294	54.6	3455	45	343	3112	23	4.3	66t	16	3.0	6.42	11.75
Chicago	484	267	55.2	3262	28	174	3088	21	4.3	79t	25	5.2	6.74	12.22
N.Y. Giants	444	248	55.9	3355	46	281	3074	17	3.8	62t	16	3.6	7.56	13.53
Detroit	450	229	50.9	3282	57	343	2939	11	2.4	75t	24	5.3	7.29	14.33
Dallas	513	266	51.9	3124	30	239	2885	14	2.7	75t	27	5.3	6.09	11.74
NFC Total	7247	4091	—	52579	578	3951	48628	298	—	95t	282	—	—	—
NFC Average	517.6	292.2	56.5	3755.6	41.3	282.2	3473.4	21.3	4.1	—	20.1	3.9	7.26	12.85
League Total	14338	8000	—	102456	1105	7982	94474	582	—	97t	559	—	—	—
League Average	512.1	285.7	55.8	3659.1	39.5	285.1	3374.1	20.8	4.1	—	20.0	3.9	7.15	12.81

Leader based on net yards.

NFL Top 10 Individual Qualifiers

	Att.	Comp.	Pct. Comp.	Yards	Avg. Gain	TD	Pct. TD	Long	Int.	Pct. Int.	Rating Points
Montana, Joe, San Francisco	386	271	70.2	3521	9.12	26	6.7	95t	8	2.1	112.4
Esiason, Boomer, Cincinnati	455	258	56.7	3525	7.75	28	6.2	74t	11	2.4	92.1
Everett, Jim, L.A. Rams	518	304	58.7	4310	8.32	29	5.6	78t	17	3.3	90.6
Moon, Warren, Houston	464	280	60.3	3631	7.83	23	5.0	55	14	3.0	88.9
Rypien, Mark, Washington	476	280	58.8	3768	7.92	22	4.6	80t	13	2.7	88.1
Kelly, Jim, Buffalo	391	228	58.3	3130	8.01	25	6.4	78t	18	4.6	86.2
Hebert, Bobby, New Orleans	353	222	62.9	2686	7.61	15	4.2	54t	15	4.2	82.7
Majkowski, Don, Green Bay	599	353	58.9	4318	7.21	27	4.5	79t	20	3.3	82.3
Kosar, Bernie, Cleveland	513	303	59.1	3533	6.89	18	3.5	97t	14	2.7	80.3
Simms, Phil, N.Y. Giants	405	228	56.3	3061	7.56	14	3.5	62t	14	3.5	77.6

AFC Passing — Individual Qualifiers

	Att.	Comp.	Pct. Comp.	Yards	Avg. Gain	TD	Pct. TD	Long	Int.	Pct. Int.	Rating Points
Esiason, Boomer, Cincinnati	455	258	56.7	3525	7.75	28	6.2	74t	11	2.4	92.1
Moon, Warren, Houston	464	280	60.3	3631	7.83	23	5.0	55	14	3.0	88.9
Kelly, Jim, Buffalo	391	228	58.3	3130	8.01	25	6.4	78t	18	4.6	86.2
Kosar, Bernie, Cleveland	513	303	59.1	3533	6.89	18	3.5	97t	14	2.7	80.3
Marino, Dan, Miami	550	308	56.0	3997	7.27	24	4.4	78t	22	4.0	76.9
DeBerg, Steve, Kansas City	324	196	60.5	2529	7.81	11	3.4	50	16	4.9	75.8
Krieg, Dave, Seattle	499	286	57.3	3309	6.63	21	4.2	60t	20	4.0	74.8
O'Brien, Ken, N.Y. Jets	477	288	60.4	3346	7.01	12	2.5	57	18	3.8	74.3

	Att.	Comp.	Pct. Comp.	Yards	Avg. Gain	TD	Pct. TD	Long	Int.	Pct. Int.	Rating Points
Elway, John, Denver	416	223	53.6	3051	7.33	18	4.3	69	18	4.3	73.7
McMahon, Jim, San Diego	318	176	55.3	2132	6.70	10	3.1	69t	10	3.1	73.5
Brister, Bubby, Pittsburgh	342	187	54.7	2365	6.92	9	2.6	79t	10	2.9	73.1
Trudeau, Jack, Indianapolis	362	190	52.5	2317	6.40	15	4.1	71	13	3.6	71.3
Grogan, Steve, New England	261	133	51.0	1697	6.50	9	3.4	55t	14	5.4	60.8

Non-qualifiers	Att.	Comp.	Pct. Comp.	Yards	Avg. Gain	TD	Pct. TD	Long	Int.	Pct. Int.	Rating Points
Reich, Frank, Buffalo	87	53	60.9	701	8.06	7	8.0	63t	2	2.3	103.7
Wilhelm, Erik, Cincinnati	56	30	53.6	425	7.59	4	7.1	46t	2	3.6	87.3
Pelluer, Steve, Kansas City	47	26	55.3	301	6.40	1	2.1	24	0	0.0	82.0
Beuerlein, Steve, L.A. Raiders	217	108	49.8	1677	7.73	13	6.0	67t	9	4.1	78.4
Eason, Tony, New England-N.Y. Jets	141	79	56.0	1016	7.21	4	2.8	63t	6	4.3	70.5
Kubiak, Gary, Denver	55	32	58.2	284	5.16	2	3.6	22	2	3.6	69.1
Wilson, Marc, New England	150	75	50.0	1006	6.71	3	2.0	65t	5	3.3	64.5
Ramsey, Tom, Indianapolis	50	24	48.0	280	5.60	1	2.0	47	1	2.0	63.8
Chandler, Chris, Indianapolis	80	39	48.8	537	6.71	2	2.5	82t	3	3.8	63.4
Schroeder, Jay, L.A. Raiders	194	91	46.9	1550	7.99	8	4.1	84t	13	6.7	60.3
Tolliver, Billy Joe, San Diego	185	89	48.1	1097	5.93	5	2.7	49	8	4.3	57.9
Jaworski, Ron, Kansas City	61	36	59.0	385	6.31	2	3.3	32	5	8.2	54.3
Carlson, Cody, Houston	31	15	48.4	155	5.00	0	0.0	23	1	3.2	49.8
Flutie, Doug, New England	91	36	39.6	493	5.42	2	2.2	36	4	4.4	46.6
Secules, Scott, Miami	50	22	44.0	286	5.72	1	2.0	44t	3	6.0	44.3
Pagel, Mike, Cleveland	14	5	35.7	60	4.29	1	7.1	18	1	7.1	43.8
Mackey, Kyle, N.Y. Jets	25	11	44.0	125	5.00	0	0.0	22	1	4.0	42.9
Stouffer, Kelly, Seattle	59	29	49.2	270	4.58	0	0.0	29	3	5.1	40.9
Blackledge, Todd, Pittsburgh	60	22	36.7	282	4.70	1	1.7	30	3	5.0	36.9
Ryan, Pat, N.Y. Jets	30	15	50.0	153	5.10	1	3.3	25	3	10.0	36.5
Archer, David, San Diego	12	5	41.7	62	5.17	0	0.0	17	1	8.3	23.6

Less than 10 attempts	Att.	Comp.	Pct. Comp.	Yards	Avg. Gain	TD	Pct. TD	Long	Int.	Pct. Int.	Rating Points
Bentley, Albert, Indianapolis	1	0	0.0	0	0.00	0	0.0	0	0	0.0	39.6
Carter, Rodney, Pittsburgh	1	1	100.0	15	15.00	0	0.0	15	0	0.0	118.8
Dickerson, Eric, Indianapolis	0	0	—	0	—	0	—	0	0	—	0.0
Elkins, Mike, Kansas City	2	1	50.0	5	2.50	0	0.0	5	1	50.0	16.7
Evans, Vince, L.A. Raiders	2	2	100.0	50	25.00	0	0.0	40	0	0.0	118.8
Feagles, Jeff, New England	2	0	0.0	0	0.00	0	0.0	0	0	0.0	39.6
Gossett, Jeff, L.A. Raiders	1	0	0.0	0	0.00	0	0.0	0	0	0.0	39.6
Humphrey, Bobby, Denver	2	1	50.0	17	8.50	1	50.0	17t	0	0.0	118.8
Jensen, Jim, Miami	1	1	100.0	19	19.00	1	100.0	19t	0	0.0	158.3
Johnson, Flip, Buffalo	0	0	—	0	—	0	—	0	0	—	0.0
Johnson, Vance, Denver	1	0	0.0	0	0.00	0	0.0	0	0	0.0	39.6
Malone, Mark, N.Y. Jets	2	2	100.0	13	6.50	0	0.0	11	0	0.0	93.8
Metcalf, Eric, Cleveland	2	1	50.0	32	16.00	1	50.0	32t	0	0.0	135.4
Rodriguez, Ruben, Seattle	1	1	100.0	4	4.00	0	0.0	4	0	0.0	83.3
Saxon, James, Kansas City	1	0	0.0	0	0.00	0	0.0	0	1	100.0	0.0
Schonert, Turk, Cincinnati	2	0	0.0	0	0.00	0	0.0	0	0	0.0	39.6
Strom, Rick, Pittsburgh	1	0	0.0	0	0.00	0	0.0	0	0	0.0	39.6
Tatupu, Mosi, New England	1	1	100.0	15	15.00	0	0.0	15	0	0.0	118.8
Zendejas, Tony, Houston	1	0	0.0	0	0.00	0	0.0	0	1	100.0	0.0

t indicates touchdown.
Leader based on rating points, minimum 224 attempts.

NFC Passing — Individual Qualifiers

	Att.	Comp.	Pct. Comp.	Yards	Avg. Gain	TD	Pct. TD	Long	Int.	Pct. Int.	Rating Points
Montana, Joe, San Francisco	386	271	70.2	3521	9.12	26	6.7	95t	8	2.1	112.4
Everett, Jim, L.A. Rams	518	304	58.7	4310	8.32	29	5.6	78t	17	3.3	90.6
Rypien, Mark, Washington	476	280	58.8	3768	7.92	22	4.6	80t	13	2.7	88.1
Hebert, Bobby, New Orleans	353	222	62.9	2686	7.61	15	4.2	54t	15	4.2	82.7
Majkowski, Don, Green Bay	599	353	58.9	4318	7.21	27	4.5	79t	20	3.3	82.3
Simms, Phil, N.Y. Giants	405	228	56.3	3061	7.56	14	3.5	62t	14	3.5	77.6
Miller, Chris, Atlanta	526	280	53.2	3459	6.58	16	3.0	72t	10	1.9	76.1
Cunningham, Randall, Philadelphia	532	290	54.5	3400	6.39	21	3.9	66t	15	2.8	75.5
Wilson, Wade, Minnesota	362	194	53.6	2543	7.02	9	2.5	50	12	3.3	70.5
Hogeboom, Gary, Phoenix	364	204	56.0	2591	7.12	14	3.8	59t	19	5.2	69.5
Testaverde, Vinny, Tampa Bay	480	258	53.8	3133	6.53	20	4.2	78t	22	4.6	68.9
Tomczak, Mike, Chicago	306	156	51.0	2058	6.73	16	5.2	79t	16	5.2	68.2
Gagliano, Bob, Detroit	232	117	50.4	1671	7.20	6	2.6	75t	12	5.2	61.2
Aikman, Troy, Dallas	293	155	52.9	1749	5.97	9	3.1	75t	18	6.1	55.7

Non-qualifiers	Att.	Comp.	Pct. Comp.	Yards	Avg. Gain	TD	Pct. TD	Long	Int.	Pct. Int.	Rating Points
Young, Steve, San Francisco	92	64	69.6	1001	10.88	8	8.7	50t	3	3.3	120.8
Fourcade, John, New Orleans	107	61	57.0	930	8.69	7	6.5	54t	4	3.7	92.0
Hostetler, Jeff, N.Y. Giants	39	20	51.3	294	7.54	3	7.7	35t	2	5.1	80.5
Millen, Hugh, Atlanta	50	31	62.0	432	8.64	1	2.0	47	2	4.0	79.8
Humphries, Stan, Washington	10	5	50.0	91	9.10	1	10.0	39	1	10.0	75.4
Kramer, Tommy, Minnesota	136	77	56.6	906	6.66	7	5.1	39	7	5.1	72.7
Harbaugh, Jim, Chicago	178	111	62.4	1204	6.76	5	2.8	49t	9	5.1	70.5
Peete, Rodney, Detroit	195	103	52.8	1479	7.58	5	2.6	69	9	4.6	67.0
Williams, Doug, Washington	93	51	54.8	585	6.29	1	1.1	46	3	3.2	64.1
Walsh, Steve, Dallas	219	110	50.2	1371	6.26	5	2.3	46	9	4.1	60.5
Tupa, Tom, Phoenix	134	65	48.5	973	7.26	3	2.2	77t	9	6.7	52.2
Ferguson, Joe, Tampa Bay	90	44	48.9	533	5.92	3	3.3	69t	6	6.7	50.8
Rosenbach, Timm, Phoenix	22	9	40.9	95	4.32	0	0.0	24	1	4.5	35.2
Hipple, Eric, Detroit	18	7	38.9	90	5.00	0	0.0	30	3	16.7	15.7

Less than 10 attempts

Less than 10 attempts	Att.	Comp.	Pct. Comp.	Yards	Avg. Gain	TD	Pct. TD	Long	Int.	Pct. Int.	Rating Points
Awalt, Robert, Phoenix	1	0	0.0	0	0.00	0	0.0	0	1	100.0	0.0
Bono, Steve, San Francisco	5	4	80.0	62	12.40	1	20.0	45t	0	0.0	157.9
Byner, Earnest, Washington	1	0	0.0	0	0.00	0	0.0	0	0	0.0	39.6
Camarillo, Rich, Phoenix	1	1	100.0	0	0.00	0	0.0	0	0	0.0	79.2
Cavanaugh, Matt, Philadelphia	5	3	60.0	33	6.60	1	20.0	13t	1	20.0	79.6
Dilweg, Anthony, Green Bay	1	1	100.0	7	7.00	0	0.0	7	0	0.0	95.8
Dozier, D. J., Minnesota	1	1	100.0	19	19.00	1	100.0	19t	0	0.0	158.3
Fontenot, Herman, Green Bay	0	0	—	0	—	0	—	0	0	—	0.0
Fulhage, Scott, Atlanta	1	1	100.0	12	12.00	0	0.0	12	0	0.0	116.7
Herrmann, Mark, L.A. Rams	5	4	80.0	59	11.80	0	0.0	23	1	20.0	76.3
Hill, Lonzell, New Orleans	0	0	—	0	—	0	—	0	0	—	0.0
Hilliard, Dalton, New Orleans	1	1	100.0	35	35.00	1	100.0	35t	0	0.0	158.3
Jones, Keith, Atlanta	1	0	0.0	0	0.00	0	0.0	0	0	0.0	39.6
Long, Chuck, Detroit	5	2	40.0	42	8.40	0	0.0	37	0	0.0	70.4
Rice, Allen, Minnesota	0	0	—	0	—	0	—	0	0	—	0.0
Ruzek, Roger, Philadelphia	1	1	100.0	22	22.00	1	100.0	22t	0	0.0	158.3
Sanders, Ricky, Washington	1	1	100.0	32	32.00	0	0.0	32	0	0.0	118.8
Saxon, Mike, Dallas	1	1	100.0	4	4.00	0	0.0	4	0	0.0	83.3
Sikahema, Vai, Phoenix	1	0	0.0	0	0.00	0	0.0	0	0	0.0	39.6

t indicates touchdown.
Leader based on rating points, minimum 224 attempts.

Pass Receiving

Individual Champions
NFC: 90—Sterling Sharpe, Green Bay
AFC: 88—Andre Reed, Buffalo

Most Receptions, Game
NFC: 15—Willie Anderson, L.A. Rams at New Orleans, November 26 (336 yards, 1 TD) (OT)
AFC: 13—Andre Reed, Buffalo vs. Denver, September 18 (157 yards)

Yards
NFC: 1483—Jerry Rice, San Francisco
AFC: 1312—Andre Reed, Buffalo

Most Yards, Game
NFC: 336—Willie Anderson, L.A. Rams at New Orleans, November 26 (15 receptions, 1 TD) (OT)
AFC: 194—Tim McGee, Cincinnati vs. Detroit, November 19 (11 receptions, 1 TD)

Longest
AFC: 97—Webster Slaughter (from Bernie Kosar) Cleveland vs. Chicago, October 23 (TD)
NFC: 95—John Taylor (from Joe Montana) San Francisco at L.A. Rams, December 11 (TD)

Yards Per Reception
NFC: 26.0—Willie Anderson, L.A. Rams
AFC: 19.0—Webster Slaughter, Cleveland

Touchdowns
NFC: 17—Jerry Rice, San Francisco
AFC: 10—Anthony Miller, San Diego

Team Leaders, Receptions
AFC: BUFFALO: 88, Andre Reed; CINCINNATI: 65, Tim McGee; CLEVELAND: 65, Webster Slaughter; DENVER: 76, Vance Johnson; HOUSTON: 66, Drew Hill; INDIANAPOLIS: 63, Bill Brooks; KANSAS CITY: 44, Stephone Paige; L.A. RAIDERS: 57, Mervyn Fernandez; MIAMI: 64, Mark Clayton; NEW ENGLAND: 54, Eric Sievers; N.Y. JETS: 63, Al Toon; PITTSBURGH: 50, Louis Lipps; SAN DIEGO: 75, Anthony Miller; SEATTLE: 77, Brian Blades.
NFC: ATLANTA: 58, Shawn Collins; CHICAGO: 50, Neal Anderson; DALLAS: 46, Kelvin Martin; DETROIT: 70, Richard Johnson; GREEN BAY: 90, Sterling Sharpe; L.A. RAMS: 70, Henry Ellard; MINNESOTA: 65, Anthony Carter; NEW ORLEANS: 68, Eric Martin; N.Y. GIANTS: 38, Odessa Turner; PHILADELPHIA: 68, Keith Byars; PHOENIX: 62, J.T. Smith; SAN FRANCISCO: 82, Jerry Rice; TAMPA BAY: 86, Mark Carrier; WASHINGTON: 86, Art Monk.

NFL Top 10 Pass Receivers

	No.	Yards	Avg.	Long	TD
Sharpe, Sterling, Green Bay	90	1423	15.8	79t	12
Reed, Andre, Buffalo	88	1312	14.9	78t	9
Carrier, Mark, Tampa Bay	86	1422	16.5	78t	9
Monk, Art, Washington	86	1186	13.8	60t	8
Rice, Jerry, San Francisco	82	1483	18.1	68t	17
Sanders, Ricky, Washington	80	1138	14.2	68	4
Clark, Gary, Washington	79	1229	15.6	80t	9
Blades, Brian, Seattle	77	1063	13.8	60t	6
Johnson, Vance, Denver	76	1095	14.4	69	7
Williams, John L., Seattle	76	657	8.6	51t	6

NFL Top 10 Pass Receivers By Yards

	Yards	No.	Avg.	Long	TD
Rice, Jerry, San Francisco	1483	82	18.1	68t	17
Sharpe, Sterling, Green Bay	1423	90	15.8	79t	12
Carrier, Mark, Tampa Bay	1422	86	16.5	78t	9
Ellard, Henry, L.A. Rams	1382	70	19.7	53	8
Reed, Andre, Buffalo	1312	88	14.9	78t	9
Miller, Anthony, San Diego	1252	75	16.7	69t	10

Slaughter, Webster, Cleveland	1236	65	19.0	97t	6
Clark, Gary, Washington	1229	79	15.6	80t	9
McGee, Tim, Cincinnati	1211	65	18.6	74t	8
Monk, Art, Washington	1186	86	13.8	60t	8

AFC Pass Receiving—Individual

	No.	Yards	Avg.	Long	TD
Reed, Andre, Buffalo	88	1312	14.9	78t	9
Blades, Brian, Seattle	77	1063	13.8	60t	5
Johnson, Vance, Denver	76	1095	14.4	69	7
Williams, John L., Seattle	76	657	8.6	51t	6
Miller, Anthony, San Diego	75	1252	16.7	69t	10
Hill, Drew, Houston	66	938	14.2	50	8
Slaughter, Webster, Cleveland	65	1236	19.0	97t	6
McGee, Tim, Cincinnati	65	1211	18.6	74t	8
Clayton, Mark, Miami	64	1011	15.8	78t	9
Brooks, Bill, Indianapolis	63	919	14.6	55t	4
Toon, Al, N.Y. Jets	63	693	11.0	37t	2
Jensen, Jim, Miami	61	557	9.1	20	6
Langhorne, Reggie, Cleveland	60	749	12.5	62t	2
Thomas, Thurman, Buffalo	60	669	11.2	74t	6
Fernandez, Mervyn, L.A. Raiders	57	1069	18.8	75t	9
Givins, Ernest, Houston	55	794	14.4	48	3
Sievers, Eric, New England	54	615	11.4	46	0
Metcalf, Eric, Cleveland	54	397	7.4	68t	4
Rison, Andre, Indianapolis	52	820	15.8	61	4
Brown, Eddie, Cincinnati	52	814	15.7	46	6
Bentley, Albert, Indianapolis	52	525	10.1	61	3
Lipps, Louis, Pittsburgh	50	944	18.9	79t	5
Holman, Rodney, Cincinnati	50	736	14.7	73t	9
Dykes, Hart Lee, New England	49	795	16.2	42	5
Duper, Mark, Miami	49	717	14.6	41	1
Jones, Cedric, New England	48	670	14.0	65t	6
Jeffires, Haywood, Houston	47	619	13.2	45t	2
Townsell, JoJo, N.Y. Jets	45	787	17.5	63t	5
Paige, Stephone, Kansas City	44	759	17.3	50	2
Duncan, Curtis, Houston	43	613	14.3	55	5
Skansi, Paul, Seattle	39	488	12.5	26	5
Nelson, Darrin, Minnesota-San Diego	38	380	10.0	49	0
Hector, Johnny, N.Y. Jets	38	330	8.7	32	2
Carter, Rodney, Pittsburgh	38	267	7.0	22t	3
Brooks, James, Cincinnati	37	306	8.3	25	2
Mandley, Pete, Kansas City	35	476	13.6	44	1
McNair, Todd, Kansas City	34	372	10.9	24	1
Hoge, Merril, Pittsburgh	34	271	8.0	22	0
Vick, Roger, N.Y. Jets	34	241	7.1	21	2
Harry, Emile, Kansas City	33	430	13.0	25	2
Edmunds, Ferrell, Miami	32	382	11.9	30	3
McNeil, Freeman, N.Y. Jets	31	310	10.0	25t	1
Pinkett, Allen, Houston	31	239	7.7	23	1
Banks, Fred, Miami	30	520	17.3	61	1
Dickerson, Eric, Indianapolis	30	211	7.0	22	1
Fryar, Irving, New England	29	537	18.5	52	3
Harmon, Ronnie, Buffalo	29	363	12.5	42t	4
Newsome, Ozzie, Cleveland	29	324	11.2	31	1
Shuler, Mickey, N.Y. Jets	29	322	11.1	22	0
Perryman, Bob, New England	29	195	6.7	16	0
Gault, Willie, L.A. Raiders	28	690	24.6	84t	4
Morgan, Stanley, New England	28	486	17.4	55t	3
Hill, Derek, Pittsburgh	28	455	16.3	53	1
Jackson, Mark, Denver	28	446	15.9	49	2
Largent, Steve, Seattle	28	403	14.4	33	3
Neubert, Keith, N.Y. Jets	28	302	10.8	35t	1

	No.	Yards	Avg.	Long	TD
Brennan, Brian, Cleveland	28	289	10.3	38	0
Dyal, Mike, L.A. Raiders	27	499	18.5	67t	2
Manoa, Tim, Cleveland	27	241	8.9	32	2
Holland, Jamie, San Diego	26	336	12.9	37	0
Sewell, Steve, Denver	25	416	16.6	56	3
Johnson, Flip, Buffalo	25	303	12.1	36	1
Clark, Louis, Seattle	25	260	10.4	28	1
Heard, Herman, Kansas City	25	246	9.8	27	1
Stradford, Troy, Miami	25	233	9.3	32	0
Brown, Andre, Miami	24	410	17.1	48t	5
Walker, Wayne, San Diego	24	395	16.5	49	1
Burkett, Chris, Buffalo-N.Y. Jets	24	298	12.4	30	1
Weathers, Clarence, Indianapolis-K.C.	23	254	11.0	27	0
Warner, Curt, Seattle	23	153	6.7	24	1
Young, Mike, Denver	22	402	18.3	47	2
Mularkey, Mike, Pittsburgh	22	326	14.8	34	1
Cox, Arthur, San Diego	22	200	9.1	24	2
Humphrey, Bobby, Denver	22	156	7.1	13	1
Bernstine, Rod, San Diego	21	222	10.6	36	1
Stephens, John, New England	21	207	9.9	37	0
Kay, Clarence, Denver	21	197	9.4	20t	2
Verdin, Clarence, Indianapolis	20	381	19.1	82t	1
McKeller, Keith, Buffalo	20	341	17.1	39t	2
Allen, Marcus, L.A. Raiders	20	191	9.6	26	0
Smith, Steve, L.A. Raiders	19	140	7.4	14	0
Mueller, Vance, L.A. Raiders	18	240	13.3	29	2
Hayes, Jonathan, Kansas City	18	229	12.7	23	2
Highsmith, Alonzo, Houston	18	201	11.2	32	2
Metzelaars, Pete, Buffalo	18	179	9.9	23	2
Spencer, Tim, San Diego	18	112	6.2	23	0
Beebe, Don, Buffalo	17	317	18.6	63t	2
Mobley, Orson, Denver	17	200	11.8	36	0
Hillary, Ira, Cincinnati	17	162	9.5	17	1
Alexander, Mike, L.A. Raiders	15	295	19.7	61	1
Martin, Mike, Cincinnati	15	160	10.7	21	2
Jones, Keith, Cleveland	15	126	8.4	36	0
Worley, Tim, Pittsburgh	15	113	7.5	19	0
Tyler, Robert, Seattle	14	148	10.6	27	0
Winder, Sammy, Denver	14	91	6.5	19	0
Beach, Pat, Indianapolis	14	87	6.2	17	2
Martin, Sammy, New England	13	229	17.6	37	0
Harris, Leonard, Houston	13	202	15.5	36	2
Brown, Tom, Miami	13	117	9.0	23	0
Dressel, Chris, Kansas City-N.Y. Jets	12	191	15.9	49t	1
Dawson, Lin, New England	12	101	8.4	17	0
Kattus, Eric, Cincinnati	12	93	7.8	16	0
Brinson, Dana, San Diego	12	71	5.9	11	0
Early, Quinn, San Diego	11	126	11.5	21	0
Saxon, James, Kansas City	11	86	7.8	18	0
Boyer, Mark, Indianapolis	11	58	5.3	15	2
Nattiel, Ricky, Denver	10	183	18.3	43	1
Smith, Kendal, Cincinnati	10	140	14.0	41t	1
Jennings, Stanford, Cincinnati	10	119	11.9	43t	1
McNeil, Gerald, Cleveland	10	114	11.4	32	0
Caravello, Joe, San Diego	10	95	9.5	37	0
Bratton, Mel, Denver	10	69	6.9	17t	3
Tatupu, Mosi, New England	10	54	5.4	11	0
McNeal, Travis, Seattle	9	147	16.3	48	0
Griggs, Billy, N.Y. Jets	9	112	12.4	23	0
Chadwick, Jeff, Detroit-Seattle	9	104	11.6	19	0
Jackson, Bo, L.A. Raiders	9	69	7.7	20	0
Lofton, James, Buffalo	8	166	20.8	47	3
Werner, Greg, N.Y. Jets	8	115	14.4	36	0
Epps, Phillip, N.Y. Jets	8	108	13.5	21	0
Walker, Wesley, N.Y. Jets	8	89	11.1	31	0
Alexander, Jeff, Denver	8	84	10.5	28	0
Thomas, Robb, Kansas City	8	58	7.3	12	2
Roberts, Alfredo, Kansas City	8	55	6.9	25	1
Hampton, Lorenzo, Miami	8	25	3.1	12	0
Schwedes, Scott, Miami	7	174	24.9	65t	1
Harper, Michael, N.Y. Jets	7	127	18.1	48	0
McEwen, Craig, San Diego	7	99	14.1	29	0
Kane, Tommy, Seattle	7	94	13.4	20	0
Stone, Dwight, Pittsburgh	7	92	13.1	16	0
Smith, Sammy, Miami	7	81	11.6	34	0
Butts, Marion, San Diego	7	21	3.0	8	0
Davis, Kenneth, Buffalo	6	92	15.3	29	2
Dupard, Reggie, New England	6	70	11.7	45	0
Tillman, Lawyer, Cleveland	6	70	11.7	19	2
Williams, Warren, Pittsburgh	6	48	8.0	16	0
Ball, Eric, Cincinnati	6	44	7.3	15	0
White, Lorenzo, Houston	6	37	6.2	11	0
Redden, Barry, Cleveland	6	34	5.7	8	0
Pruitt, James, Indianapolis	5	71	14.2	40	1
Worthen, Naz, Kansas City	5	69	13.8	21	0
Kinnebrew, Larry, Buffalo	5	60	12.0	18	0
Logan, Marc, Miami	5	34	6.8	11	0
Riggs, Jim, Cincinnati	5	29	5.8	9	0
Stock, Mark, Pittsburgh	4	74	18.5	27	0

	No.	Yards	Avg.	Long	TD
Thompson, Weegie, Pittsburgh	4	74	18.5	28	0
Verhulst, Chris, Houston	4	48	12.0	21	0
Horton, Ethan, L.A. Raiders	4	44	11.0	20	1
Taylor, Craig, Cincinnati	4	44	11.0	18t	2
Jackson, Kenny, Houston	4	31	7.8	18	0
Rozier, Mike, Houston	4	28	7.0	8	0
Brown, Anthony, N.Y. Jets	4	10	2.5	6	0
Junkin, Trey, L.A. Raiders	3	32	10.7	28	2
Mrosko, Bob, Houston	3	28	9.3	14	0
Harris, Elroy, Seattle	3	26	8.7	11	0
Fenner, Derrick, Seattle	3	23	7.7	9	0
Oliphant, Mike, Cleveland	3	22	7.3	9	0
Davenport, Ron, Miami	3	19	6.3	9	0
Cook, Marv, New England	3	13	4.3	5	0
Kelly, Pat, Denver	3	13	4.3	6	0
Garrett, John, Cincinnati	2	29	14.5	18	0
Allen, Anthony, San Diego	2	19	9.5	11	0
Holifield, John, Cincinnati	2	18	9.0	14	0
Dunn, K.D., N.Y. Jets	2	13	6.5	8	0
Okoye, Christian, Kansas City	2	12	6.0	8	0
Mack, Kevin, Cleveland	2	7	3.5	4	0
Parker, Andy, San Diego	2	5	2.5	4	1
Gamble, Kenny, Kansas City	2	2	1.0	6	0
Parker, Carl, Cincinnati	1	45	45.0	45	0
Waiters, Van, Cleveland	1	14	14.0	14t	1
Kinchen, Brian, Miami	1	12	12.0	12	0
Buoyer, Willie, Seattle	1	9	9.0	9	0
Brown, Tim, L.A. Raiders	1	8	8.0	8	0
Faaola, Nuu, Miami	1	8	8.0	8	0
Johnson, Tracy, Houston	1	8	8.0	8	0
Jones, James, Seattle	1	8	8.0	8	0
Mueller, Jamie, Buffalo	1	8	8.0	8	0
O'Shea, Terry, Pittsburgh	1	8	8.0	8	0
Floyd, Victor, San Diego	1	6	6.0	6	0
Feasel, Grant, Seattle	1	5	5.0	5	0
Middleton, Ron, Cleveland	1	5	5.0	5t	1
Glasgow, Nesby, Seattle	1	4	4.0	4	0
McMahon, Jim, San Diego	1	4	4.0	4	0
Tennell, Derek, Cleveland	1	4	4.0	4t	1
Carruth, Paul Ott, Kansas City	1	3	3.0	3	0
Hardy, Bruce, Miami	1	2	2.0	2	0
Rolle, Butch, Buffalo	1	1	1.0	1t	1
Kosar, Bernie, Cleveland	1	−7	−7.0	−7	0
Brister, Bubby, Pittsburgh	1	−10	−10.0	−10	0

t indicates touchdown.
Leader based on most passes caught.

NFC Pass Receiving—Individual

	No.	Yards	Avg.	Long	TD
Sharpe, Sterling, Green Bay	90	1423	15.8	79t	12
Carrier, Mark, Tampa Bay	86	1422	16.5	78t	9
Monk, Art, Washington	86	1186	13.8	60t	8
Rice, Jerry, San Francisco	82	1483	18.1	68t	17
Sanders, Ricky, Washington	80	1138	14.2	68	4
Clark, Gary, Washington	79	1229	15.6	80t	9
Rathman, Tom, San Francisco	73	616	8.4	36	1
Ellard, Henry, L.A. Rams	70	1382	19.7	53	8
Johnson, Richard, Detroit	70	1091	15.6	75t	8
Martin, Eric, New Orleans	68	1090	16.0	53t	8
Byars, Keith, Philadelphia	68	721	10.6	60	0
Carter, Anthony, Minnesota	65	1066	16.4	50	4
Jackson, Keith, Philadelphia	63	648	10.3	33	3
Smith, J.T., Phoenix	62	778	12.5	31	5
Taylor, John, San Francisco	60	1077	18.0	95t	10
Woodside, Keith, Green Bay	59	527	8.9	33	0
Collins, Shawn, Atlanta	58	862	14.9	47	3
Byner, Earnest, Washington	54	458	8.5	27	2
Hilliard, Dalton, New Orleans	52	514	9.9	54t	5
Holohan, Pete, L.A. Rams	51	510	10.0	31	2
Hill, Bruce, Tampa Bay	50	673	13.5	53	5
Anderson, Neal, Chicago	50	434	8.7	49t	4
Craig, Roger, San Francisco	49	473	9.7	44	1
Hill, Lonzell, New Orleans	48	636	13.3	46	4
Kemp, Perry, Green Bay	48	611	12.7	39	2
Martin, Kelvin, Dallas	46	644	14.0	46	2
Jones, Ernie, Phoenix	45	838	18.6	72t	3
Carter, Cris, Philadelphia	45	605	13.4	42	11
Anderson, Willie, L.A. Rams	44	1146	26.0	78t	5
Green, Roy, Phoenix	44	703	16.0	59t	7
Jones, Hassan, Minnesota	42	694	16.5	50	1
Clark, Robert, Detroit	41	748	18.2	69	2
Jones, Keith, Atlanta	41	396	9.7	46	0
Haynes, Michael, Atlanta	40	681	17.0	72t	4
Jones, Brent, San Francisco	40	500	12.5	36t	4
Walker, Herschel, Dallas-Minnesota	40	423	10.6	52	2
Fontenot, Herman, Green Bay	40	372	9.3	38t	3
Gentry, Dennis, Chicago	39	463	11.9	79t	1
Lang, Gene, Atlanta	39	436	11.2	32	1

	No.	Yards	Avg.	Long	TD
Settle, John, Atlanta	39	316	8.1	33	2
Turner, Odessa, N.Y. Giants	38	467	12.3	44	4
McGee, Buford, L.A. Rams	37	303	8.2	25	4
Wilder, James, Tampa Bay	36	335	9.3	27	3
Jordan, Steve, Minnesota	35	506	14.5	34	3
Meggett, Dave, N.Y. Giants	34	531	15.6	62t	4
Brenner, Hoby, New Orleans	34	398	11.7	30t	4
Delpino, Robert, L.A. Rams	34	334	9.8	25	1
Manuel, Lionel, N.Y. Giants	33	539	16.3	49	1
Awalt, Robert, Phoenix	33	360	10.9	28	0
Heller, Ron, Atlanta	33	324	9.8	30	1
Muster, Brad, Chicago	32	259	8.1	25	3
Morris, Ron, Chicago	30	486	16.2	58t	1
Phillips, Jason, Detroit	30	352	11.7	55t	1
Hall, Ron, Tampa Bay	30	331	11.0	32	2
Fenney, Rick, Minnesota	30	254	8.5	26	2
Howard, William, Tampa Bay	30	188	6.3	18	1
McKinnon, Dennis, Chicago	28	418	14.9	41	3
Anderson, Ottis, N.Y. Giants	28	268	9.6	26	0
Folsom, Steve, Dallas	28	265	9.5	26	2
Mowatt, Zeke, N.Y. Giants	27	288	10.7	31	0
Davis, Wendell, Chicago	26	397	15.3	52t	3
Irvin, Michael, Dallas	26	378	14.5	65t	2
Dixon, Floyd, Atlanta	25	357	14.3	53t	2
Johnson, Damone, L.A. Rams	25	148	5.9	22	5
Dixon, James, Dallas	24	477	19.9	75t	2
Thornton, James, Chicago	24	392	16.3	36t	3
Stanley, Walter, Detroit	24	304	12.7	37	0
Sanders, Barry, Detroit	24	282	11.8	46	0
Query, Jeff, Green Bay	23	350	15.2	45	2
Sikahema, Vai, Phoenix	23	245	10.7	37	0
Novacek, Jay, Phoenix	23	225	9.8	30	1
Turner, Floyd, New Orleans	22	279	12.7	54t	1
Bavaro, Mark, N.Y. Giants	22	278	12.6	29	3
West, Ed, Green Bay	22	269	12.2	31	5
Perriman, Brett, New Orleans	20	356	17.8	47	0
Cox, Aaron, L.A. Rams	20	340	17.0	51t	3
Shepard, Derrick, New Orleans-Dallas	20	304	15.2	37t	1
Johnson, Ron, Philadelphia	20	295	14.8	34	1
Anderson, Alfred, Minnesota	20	193	9.7	18	0
Fullwood, Brent, Green Bay	19	214	11.3	67	0
Toney, Anthony, Philadelphia	19	124	6.5	15	0
Bell, Greg, L.A. Rams	19	85	4.5	14	0
Matthews, Aubrey, Green Bay	18	200	11.1	25	0
Ferrell, Earl, Phoenix	18	122	6.8	25	0
Ingram, Mark, N.Y. Giants	17	290	17.1	41t	1
Boso, Cap, Chicago	17	182	10.7	43	1
Drummond, Robert, Philadelphia	17	180	10.6	21	1
Tautalatasi, Junior, Dallas	17	157	9.2	23	0
Burbage, Cornell, Dallas	17	134	7.9	15	0
Palmer, Paul, Dallas	17	93	5.5	13	0
Giles, Jimmie, Philadelphia	16	225	14.1	66t	2
Johnston, Daryl, Dallas	16	133	8.3	28	3
Warren, Don, Washington	15	167	11.1	25	1
Carthon, Maurice, N.Y. Giants	15	132	8.8	18	0
Haddix, Michael, Green Bay	15	111	7.4	23	1
Stamps, Sylvester, Tampa Bay	15	82	5.5	21	0
Drewrey, Willie, Tampa Bay	14	157	11.2	18	1
Dozier, D.J., Minnesota	14	148	10.6	30	0
Gustafson, Jim, Minnesota	14	144	10.3	22	2
Holmes, Don, Phoenix	13	271	20.8	77t	1
Baker, Stephen, N.Y. Giants	13	255	19.6	39t	2
Quick, Mike, Philadelphia	13	228	17.5	40	2
Garrity, Gregg, Philadelphia	13	209	16.1	31	2
Mobley, Stacey, Detroit	13	158	12.2	30	0
Heyward, Craig, New Orleans	13	69	5.3	12	0
Lewis, Leo, Minnesota	12	148	12.3	28t	1
McDonald, Keith, Detroit	12	138	11.5	24	0
Peebles, Danny, Tampa Bay	11	180	16.4	32	0
Bland, Carl, Green Bay	11	164	14.9	46t	1
Beckman, Brad, Atlanta	11	102	9.3	21	1
Harris, William, Tampa Bay	11	102	9.3	21	1
Tate, Lars, Tampa Bay	11	75	6.8	19	1
Wilson, Mike, San Francisco	9	103	11.4	19	1
Tice, John, New Orleans	9	98	10.9	23	1
Suhey, Matt, Chicago	9	73	8.1	22	1
Sydney, Harry, San Francisco	9	71	7.9	13	0
Scott, Kevin, Dallas	9	63	7.0	12	0
Wilkins, Gary, Atlanta	8	179	22.4	36	3
Bailey, Stacey, Atlanta	8	170	21.3	41	0
Carson, Carlos, Kansas City-Philadelphia	8	107	13.4	28	1
Scales, Greg, New Orleans	8	89	11.1	26	0
Sherman, Heath, Philadelphia	8	85	10.6	17	0
Morris, Jamie, Washington	8	65	8.1	17	0
Rouson, Lee, N.Y. Giants	7	121	17.3	39	0
Smith, Don, Tampa Bay	7	110	15.7	44	0
Ford, Bernard, Dallas	7	78	11.1	21	1
Didier, Clint, Green Bay	7	71	10.1	24t	1
Riggs, Gerald, Washington	7	67	9.6	13	0

	No.	Yards	Avg.	Long	TD
Cross, Howard, N.Y. Giants	6	107	17.8	27	1
Flagler, Terrence, San Francisco	6	51	8.5	30	0
Sargent, Broderick, Dallas	6	50	8.3	21	0
Jennings, Keith, Dallas	6	47	7.8	14	0
Jordan, Tony, Phoenix	6	20	3.3	8	0
Brown, Ron, L.A. Rams	5	113	22.6	39t	1
Ford, John, Detroit	5	56	11.2	37	0
Green, Mark, Chicago	5	48	9.6	21	0
Ingram, Darryl, Minnesota	5	47	9.4	21	1
Paterra, Greg, Atlanta	5	42	8.4	20	0
Wolfley, Ron, Phoenix	5	38	7.6	22	0
Johnson, Jimmy, Washington	4	84	21.0	39	0
Clack, Darryl, Dallas	4	69	17.3	44	0
Jordan, Buford, New Orleans	4	53	13.3	17	0
Thomas, George, Atlanta	4	46	11.5	16	0
Robinson, Stacy, N.Y. Giants	4	41	10.3	16	0
Williams, Henry, Philadelphia	4	32	8.0	11	0
Rice, Allen, Minnesota	4	29	7.3	14	0
Walls, Wesley, San Francisco	4	16	4.0	9	1
Novoselsky, Brent, Minnesota	4	11	2.8	6	2
Henderson, Keith, San Francisco	3	130	43.3	78	0
Orr, Terry, Washington	3	80	26.7	48	0
Kozlowski, Glen, Chicago	3	74	24.7	55	0
Painter, Carl, Detroit	3	41	13.7	27	0
Williams, Jamie, San Francisco	3	38	12.7	17	0
Sanders, Thomas, Chicago	3	28	9.3	16t	1
Frazier, Paul, New Orleans	3	25	8.3	22	0
Higgs, Mark, Philadelphia	3	9	3.0	8	0
Edwards, Anthony, Philadelphia	2	74	37.0	66	0
Gray, Mel, Detroit	2	47	23.5	30	0
Johnson, Troy, Detroit	2	29	14.5	22	0
Paige, Tony, Detroit	2	27	13.5	15	0
Baker, Tony, Phoenix	2	18	9.0	9	0
McConkey, Phil, Phoenix	2	18	9.0	10	0
Clark, Jessie, Minnesota	2	14	7.0	12	0
Gary, Cleveland, L.A. Rams	2	13	6.5	8	0
Spagnola, John, Green Bay	2	13	6.5	14	0
Little, David, Philadelphia	2	8	4.0	7	1
Adams, George, N.Y. Giants	2	7	3.5	10	0
Greer, Terry, San Francisco	1	26	26.0	26	0
Banks, Carl, N.Y. Giants	1	22	22.0	22t	1
Alexander, Ray, Dallas	1	16	16.0	16	0
Mitchell, Alvin, Tampa Bay	1	11	11.0	11	0
Mitchell, Stump, Phoenix	1	10	10.0	10	0
Tillman, Lewis, N.Y. Giants	1	9	9.0	9	0
Cook, Toi, New Orleans	1	8	8.0	8	0
Usher, Darryl, Phoenix	1	8	8.0	8	0
Waddle, Tom, Chicago	1	8	8.0	8	0
Reeves, Walter, Phoenix	1	5	5.0	5	0
Ruzek, Roger, Dallas	1	4	4.0	4	0
Tice, Mike, Washington	1	2	2.0	2	0
Green, Gaston, L.A. Rams	1	−5	−5.0	−5	0
Sanders, Deion, Atlanta	1	−8	−8.0	−8	0
Aikman, Troy, Dallas	1	−13	−13.0	−13	0

t indicates touchdown.
Leader based on most passes caught.

Interceptions

Individual Champions
AFC: 9—Felix Wright, Cleveland
NFC: 8—Eric Allen, Philadelphia

Most Interceptions, Game
AFC: 3—David Fulcher, Cincinnati at Kansas City, October 1 (38 yards)
3—David Fulcher, Cincinnati vs. Houston, December 17 (22 yards)
NFC: 2—By 19 players

Yards
AFC: 233—Eddie Anderson, L.A. Raiders
NFC: 170—Tim McDonald, Phoenix

Longest
AFC: 92—Erik McMillan, N.Y. Jets. vs. Indianapolis, October 1 (TD)
NFC: 90—Issiac Holt, Minnesota vs. Detroit, October 8 (TD)

Touchdowns
AFC: 2—Eddie Anderson, L.A. Raiders
2—Thane Gash, Cleveland
NFC: 1—By 20 players

Team Leaders, Interceptions
AFC: BUFFALO: 6, Mark Kelso; CINCINNATI: 8, David Fulcher; CLEVELAND: 9, Felix Wright; DENVER: 6, Tyrone Braxton; HOUSTON: 5, Steve Brown; INDIANAPOLIS: 7, Keith Taylor; KANSAS CITY: 7, Albert Lewis, Kevin Ross; L.A. RAIDERS: 5, Eddie Anderson; MIAMI: 4, Louis Oliver; NEW ENGLAND: 5, Maurice Hurst; N.Y. JETS: 6, Erik McMillan; PITTSBURGH: 4, Dwayne Woodruff; SAN DIEGO: 7, Gill Byrd; SEATTLE: 5, Eugene Robinson.

NFC: ATLANTA: 5, Deion Sanders; CHICAGO: 4, Lemuel Stinson; DALLAS: 2, Eugene Lockhart; DETROIT: 6, Jerry Holmes; GREEN BAY: 6, Dave Brown; L.A. RAMS: 6, Jerry Gray; MINNESOTA: 5, Joey Browner; NEW ORLEANS: 6, David Waymer; N.Y. GIANTS: 5, Terry Kinard; PHILADELPHIA: 8, Eric Allen; PHOENIX: 7, Tim McDonald; SAN

FRANCISCO: 5, Ronnie Lott; TAMPA BAY: 6, Harry Hamilton, Mark Robinson; WASHINGTON: 4, Brian Davis, A.J. Johnson, Alvin Walton.

Team Champions
NFC: 30—Philadelphia
AFC: 27—Cleveland

AFC Interceptions—Team

	No.	Yards	Avg.	Long	TD
Cleveland	27	300	11.1	36t	4
San Diego	25	224	9.0	34	0
Buffalo	23	269	11.7	43	1
Indianapolis	21	391	18.6	80t	2
Denver	21	318	15.1	50	2
Houston	21	263	12.5	48	0
Pittsburgh	21	261	12.4	39	0
Cincinnati	21	204	9.7	28	1
L.A. Raiders	18	362	20.1	87t	3
New England	16	118	7.4	28	1
N.Y. Jets	15	261	17.4	92t	2
Kansas City	15	133	8.9	27	0
Miami	15	126	8.4	28	0
Seattle	9	57	6.3	20	0
AFC Total	277	3474	—	92t	16
AFC Average	19.8	248.1	12.5	—	1.1

NFC Interceptions—Team

	No.	Yards	Avg.	Long	TD
Philadelphia	30	375	12.5	60t	2
Washington	27	284	10.5	59t	3
Chicago	26	268	10.3	43	1
Green Bay	25	232	9.3	53	0
N.Y. Giants	22	330	15.0	58t	2
L.A. Rams	21	372	17.7	81t	3
San Francisco	21	262	12.5	42	0
Tampa Bay	21	234	11.1	68t	2
New Orleans	21	226	10.8	63t	2
Atlanta	20	285	14.3	40	0
Minnesota	18	264	14.7	90t	2
Phoenix	16	275	17.2	53t	2
Detroit	16	107	6.7	36	1
Dallas	7	37	5.3	18	0
NFC Total	282	3364	—	90t	20
NFC Average	20.1	240.3	11.9	—	1.4
League Total	559	6838	—	92t	36
League Average	20.0	244.2	12.2	—	1.3

NFL Top 10 Interceptors

	No.	Yards	Avg.	Long	TD
Wright, Felix, Cleveland	9	91	10.1	27t	1
Fulcher, David, Cincinnati	8	87	10.9	22	0
Allen, Eric, Philadelphia	8	38	4.8	18	0
Taylor, Keith, Indianapolis	7	225	32.1	80t	1
McDonald, Tim, Phoenix	7	170	24.3	53t	1
Byrd, Gill, San Diego	7	38	5.4	22	0
McMillan, Erik, N.Y. Jets	6	180	30.0	92t	1
Braxton, Tyrone, Denver	6	103	17.2	34t	1
Kelso, Mark, Buffalo	6	101	16.8	43	0
Prior, Mike, Indianapolis	6	88	14.7	58t	1
Holmes, Jerry, Detroit	6	77	12.8	36	1
Hamilton, Harry, Tampa Bay	6	70	11.7	30	0
Waymer, Dave, New Orleans	6	66	11.0	42	0
Gray, Jerry, L.A. Rams	6	48	8.0	27t	1
Robinson, Mark, Tampa Bay	6	44	7.3	16	0
Brown, Dave, Green Bay	6	12	2.0	12	0

AFC Interceptions—Individual

	No.	Yards	Avg.	Long	TD
Wright, Felix, Cleveland	9	91	10.1	27t	1
Fulcher, David, Cincinnati	8	87	10.9	22	0
Taylor, Keith, Indianapolis	7	225	32.1	80t	1
Byrd, Gill, San Diego	7	38	5.4	22	0
McMillan, Erik, N.Y. Jets	6	180	30.0	92t	1
Braxton, Tyrone, Denver	6	103	17.2	34t	1
Kelso, Mark, Buffalo	6	101	16.8	43	0
Prior, Mike, Indianapolis	6	88	14.7	58t	1
Anderson, Eddie, L.A. Raiders	5	233	46.6	87t	2
Hasty, James, N.Y. Jets	5	62	12.4	34t	1
Brown, Steve, Houston	5	54	10.8	41	0
Hurst, Maurice, New England	5	31	6.2	16t	1
Robinson, Eugene, Seattle	5	24	4.8	20	0
Odomes, Nate, Buffalo	5	20	4.0	13	0
Lyles, Robert, Houston	4	66	16.5	48	0
McDowell, Bubba, Houston	4	65	16.3	21	0
Woodruff, Dwayne, Pittsburgh	4	57	14.3	35	0
Glenn, Vencie, San Diego	4	52	13.0	31	0
Seale, Sam, San Diego	4	47	11.8	25	0

	No.	Yards	Avg.	Long	TD
Lewis, Albert, Kansas City	4	37	9.3	22	0
Oliver, Louis, Miami	4	32	8.0	23	0
Dishman, Cris, Houston	4	31	7.8	31	0
Ross, Kevin, Kansas City	4	29	7.3	23	0
Thomas, Eric, Cincinnati	4	18	4.5	18t	1
Everett, Thomas, Pittsburgh	3	68	22.7	32	0
Gash, Thane, Cleveland	3	65	21.7	36t	2
Henderson, Wymon, Denver	3	58	19.3	25	0
Lloyd, Greg, Pittsburgh	3	49	16.3	31	0
Dixon, Rickey, Cincinnati	3	47	15.7	28	0
Washington, Lionel, L.A. Raiders	3	46	15.3	32t	1
Johnson, Mike, Cleveland	3	43	14.3	23	0
Woodson, Rod, Pittsburgh	3	39	13.0	39	0
Atwater, Steve, Denver	3	34	11.3	30	0
Eaton, Tracey, Houston	3	33	11.0	20	0
Minnifield, Frank, Cleveland	3	29	9.7	25	0
Little, David, Pittsburgh	3	23	7.7	13	0
McDaniel, Terry, L.A. Raiders	3	21	7.0	20	0
Harper, Mark, Cleveland	3	8	2.7	8	0
Bennett, Roy, San Diego	3	4	1.3	4	0
McNeal, Don, Miami	3	−6	−2.0	0	0
Smith, Dennis, Denver	2	78	39.0	50	0
James, Roland, New England	2	50	25.0	28	0
Smith, Leonard, Buffalo	2	46	23.0	24	0
Patterson, Elvis, San Diego	2	44	22.0	34	0
Jackson, Kirby, Buffalo	2	43	21.5	40t	1
Williams, Jarvis, Miami	2	43	21.5	24	0
Benson, Thomas, L.A. Raiders	2	36	18.0	19	0
Judson, William, Miami	2	31	15.5	28	0
Lyles, Lester, San Diego	2	28	14.0	28	0
Cherry, Deron, Kansas City	2	27	13.5	27	0
Grayson, Dave, Cleveland	2	25	12.5	14t	1
Marion, Fred, New England	2	19	9.5	18	0
Robbins, Randy, Denver	2	18	9.0	18t	1
Munford, Marc, Denver	2	16	8.0	10	0
Harper, Dwayne, Seattle	2	15	7.5	15	0
Banks, Chip, Indianapolis	2	13	6.5	11	0
Bennett, Cornelius, Buffalo	2	5	2.5	6	0
Thomas, Rodney, Miami	2	4	2.0	4	0
Young, Fredd, Indianapolis	2	2	1.0	6	0
Harden, Mike, L.A. Raiders	2	1	0.5	1	0
Billups, Lewis, Cincinnati	2	0	0.0	0	0
McElroy, Vann, L.A. Raiders	2	0	0.0	0	0
Daniel, Eugene, Indianapolis	1	34	34.0	34	0
Drane, Dwight, Buffalo	1	25	25.0	25	0
Kelly, Joe, Cincinnati	1	25	25.0	25	0
Matthews, Clay, Cleveland	1	25	25.0	25	0
Robinson, Jerry, L.A. Raiders	1	25	25.0	25	0
Hobley, Liffort, Miami	1	22	22.0	22	0
White, Leon, Cincinnati	1	22	22.0	22	0
Saleaumua, Dan, Kansas City	1	21	21.0	21	0
Johnson, Johnnie, Seattle	1	18	18.0	18	0
McSwain, Rod, New England	1	18	18.0	18	0
Plummer, Bruce, Indianapolis	1	18	18.0	18	0
Bailey, Carlton, Buffalo	1	16	16.0	16	0
Snipes, Angelo, Kansas City	1	16	16.0	16	0
Griffin, Larry, Pittsburgh	1	15	15.0	15	0
Booty, John, N.Y. Jets	1	13	13.0	13	0
Kramer, Kyle, Cleveland	1	12	12.0	12	0
Still, Art, Buffalo	1	10	10.0	10	0
Smith, Billy Ray, San Diego	1	9	9.0	9	0
Corrington, Kip, Denver	1	8	8.0	8	0
Bickett, Duane, Indianapolis	1	6	6.0	6	0
Hall, Delton, Pittsburgh	1	6	6.0	6	0
Ball, Michael, Indianapolis	1	5	5.0	5	0
Carey, Richard, Cincinnati	1	5	5.0	5	0
Feggins, Howard, New England	1	4	4.0	4	0
Hinkle, Bryan, Pittsburgh	1	4	4.0	4	0
Mersereau, Scott, N.Y. Jets	1	4	4.0	4	0
Hill, Kenny, Kansas City	1	3	3.0	3	0
Sutton, Mickey, Buffalo	1	3	3.0	3	0
Carrington, Darren, Denver	1	2	2.0	2	0
Dixon, Hanford, Cleveland	1	2	2.0	2	0
Figaro, Cedric, San Diego	1	2	2.0	2	0
Gordon, Alex, N.Y. Jets	1	2	2.0	2	0
Coleman, Eric, New England	1	1	1.0	1	0
Dennison, Rick, Denver	1	1	1.0	1	0
Ashley, Walker Lee, Kansas City	1	0	0.0	0	0
Bayless, Martin, San Diego	1	0	0.0	0	0
Burruss, Lloyd, Kansas City	1	0	0.0	0	0
Bussey, Barney, Cincinnati	1	0	0.0	0	0
Clayborn, Raymond, New England	1	0	0.0	0	0
Comeaux, Darren, Seattle	1	0	0.0	0	0
Conlan, Shane, Buffalo	1	0	0.0	0	0
Glenn, Kerry, N.Y. Jets	1	0	0.0	0	0
Johnson, David, Pittsburgh	1	0	0.0	0	0
Johnson, Richard, Houston	1	0	0.0	0	0
Lake, Carnell, Pittsburgh	1	0	0.0	0	0
Lankford, Paul, Miami	1	0	0.0	0	0

	No.	Yards	Avg.	Long	TD
Lyons, Robert, Cleveland	1	0	0.0	0	0
Rembert, Johnny, New England	1	0	0.0	0	0
Wright, Jeff, Buffalo	1	0	0.0	0	0
Brown, Vincent, New England	1	−1	−1.0	−1	0
McGrew, Larry, New England	1	−4	−4.0	−4	0
Donaldson, Jeff, Houston	0	14	—	14	0

t indicates touchdown.
Leader based on most interceptions.

NFC Interceptions—Individual

	No.	Yards	Avg.	Long	TD
Allen, Eric, Philadelphia	8	38	4.8	18	0
McDonald, Tim, Phoenix	7	170	24.3	53t	1
Holmes, Jerry, Detroit	6	77	12.8	36	1
Hamilton, Harry, Tampa Bay	6	70	11.7	30	0
Waymer, Dave, New Orleans	6	66	11.0	42	0
Gray, Jerry, L.A. Rams	6	48	8.0	27t	1
Robinson, Mark, Tampa Bay	6	44	7.3	16	0
Brown, Dave, Green Bay	6	12	2.0	12	0
Kinard, Terry, N.Y. Giants	5	135	27.0	58t	1
Reynolds, Ricky, Tampa Bay	5	87	17.4	68t	1
Browner, Joey, Minnesota	5	70	14.0	34	0
Sanders, Deion, Atlanta	5	52	10.4	22	0
Lott, Ronnie, San Francisco	5	34	6.8	28	0
Massey, Robert, New Orleans	5	26	5.2	22	0
Williams, Jimmy, Detroit	5	15	3.0	9	0
Johnson, AJ, Washington	4	94	23.5	59t	1
Everett, Eric, Philadelphia	4	64	16.0	30t	1
Gordon, Tim, Atlanta	4	60	15.0	34	0
Stinson, Lemuel, Chicago	4	59	14.8	29t	1
Frizzell, William, Philadelphia	4	58	14.5	27	0
Jenkins, Izel, Philadelphia	4	58	14.5	22	0
Walton, Alvin, Washington	4	58	14.5	29t	1
Cooper, Evan, Atlanta	4	54	13.5	38	0
Davis, Brian, Washington	4	40	10.0	15	0
Mack, Cedric, Phoenix	4	15	3.8	9	0
Cook, Toi, New Orleans	3	81	27.0	63t	1
Johnson, Pepper, N.Y. Giants	3	60	20.0	39t	1
Lynch, Lorenzo, Chicago	3	55	18.3	41	0
Irvin, LeRoy, L.A. Rams	3	43	14.3	18	0
Maxie, Brett, New Orleans	3	41	13.7	26t	1
Gayle, Shaun, Chicago	3	39	13.0	20	0
Brooks, Chet, San Francisco	3	31	10.3	19	0
Murphy, Mark, Green Bay	3	31	10.3	20	0
Merriweather, Mike, Minnesota	3	29	9.7	15t	1
Bowles, Todd, Washington	3	25	8.3	25	0
Evans, Byron, Philadelphia	3	23	7.7	15	0
Stills, Ken, Green Bay	3	20	6.7	12	0
Williams, Perry, N.Y. Giants	3	14	4.7	14	0
Wilburn, Barry, Washington	3	13	4.3	13	0
Woolford, Donnell, Chicago	3	0	0.0	0	0
Stewart, Michael, L.A. Rams	2	76	38.0	41t	1
Dimry, Charles, Atlanta	2	72	36.0	40	0
Strickland, Fred, L.A. Rams	2	56	28.0	29	0
Roper, John, Chicago	2	46	23.0	43	0
Wright, Eric, San Francisco	2	37	18.5	23	0
Jackson, Johnny, San Francisco	2	35	17.5	19	0
Guyton, Myron, N.Y. Giants	2	27	13.5	14	0
Hicks, Cliff, L.A. Rams	2	27	13.5	27	0
Coleman, Monte, Washington	2	24	12.0	24t	1
Harris, Al, Philadelphia	2	18	9.0	11	0
White, Sheldon, N.Y. Giants	2	18	9.0	18	0
Jackson, Vestee, Chicago	2	16	8.0	16	0
Stephen, Scott, Green Bay	2	16	8.0	8	0
Lockhart, Eugene, Dallas	2	14	7.0	12	0
Case, Scott, Atlanta	2	13	6.5	13	0
Collins, Mark, N.Y. Giants	2	12	6.0	12	0
Lee, Mark, Green Bay	2	10	5.0	10	0
Noble, Brian, Green Bay	2	10	5.0	10	0
White, Adrian, N.Y. Giants	2	8	4.0	9	0
Rutland, Reggie, Minnesota	2	7	3.5	7	0
Griffin, Don, San Francisco	2	6	3.0	3	0
Rivera, Ron, Chicago	2	1	0.5	1	0
Grant, Darryl, Washington	2	0	0.0	0	0
Green, Darrell, Washington	2	0	0.0	0	0
Lee, Carl, Minnesota	2	0	0.0	0	0
Mack, Milton, New Orleans	2	0	0.0	0	0
Morrissey, Jim, Chicago	2	0	0.0	0	0
Holt, Issiac, Minnesota	1	90	90.0	90t	1
Newsome, Vince, L.A. Rams	1	81	81.0	81t	1
Simmons, Clyde, Philadelphia	1	60	60.0	60t	1
Dent, Burnell, Green Bay	1	53	53.0	53	0
Millard, Keith, Minnesota	1	48	48.0	48	0
Turner, Keena, San Francisco	1	42	42.0	42	0
Reasons, Gary, N.Y. Giants	1	40	40.0	40	0
Downs, Michael, Phoenix	1	37	37.0	37	0
Pitts, Ron, Green Bay	1	37	37.0	37	0
Young, Lonnie, Phoenix	1	32	32.0	32	0

	No.	Yards	Avg.	Long	TD
Shelley, Elbert, Atlanta	1	31	31.0	31	0
Dent, Richard, Chicago	1	30	30.0	30	0
Holland, Johnny, Green Bay	1	26	26.0	26	0
Golic, Mike, Philadelphia	1	23	23.0	23	0
Holmoe, Tom, San Francisco	1	23	23.0	23	0
Paul, Markus, Chicago	1	20	20.0	20	0
Stams, Frank, L.A. Rams	1	20	20.0	20	0
Waters, Andre, Philadelphia	1	20	20.0	20	0
Harris, Odie, Tampa Bay	1	19	19.0	19	0
Bates, Bill, Dallas	1	18	18.0	18	0
Edwards, Brad, Minnesota	1	18	18.0	18	0
Marshall, Wilber, Washington	1	18	18.0	18	0
McKyer, Tim, San Francisco	1	18	18.0	18	0
Cecil, Chuck, Green Bay	1	16	16.0	16	0
Zordich, Mike, Phoenix	1	16	16.0	16t	1
Swilling, Pat, New Orleans	1	14	14.0	14	0
Bell, Todd, Philadelphia	1	13	13.0	13	0
Davis, Reuben, Tampa Bay	1	13	13.0	13t	1
Romanowski, Bill, San Francisco	1	13	13.0	13	0
Pollard, Darryl, San Francisco	1	12	12.0	12	0
Davis, Wayne, Washington	1	11	11.0	11	0
DeOssie, Steve, N.Y. Giants	1	10	10.0	10	0
Gibson, Dennis, Detroit	1	10	10.0	10	0
Henley, Darryl, L.A. Rams	1	10	10.0	10	0
Millen, Matt, San Francisco	1	10	10.0	10	0
Banks, Carl, N.Y. Giants	1	6	6.0	6	0
Crockett, Ray, Detroit	1	5	5.0	5	0
Wahler, Jim, Phoenix	1	5	5.0	5	0
Owens, Mel, L.A. Rams	1	4	4.0	4	0
Wilcher, Mike, L.A. Rams	1	4	4.0	4	0
Albritton, Vince, Dallas	1	3	3.0	3	0
Miller, Shawn, L.A. Rams	1	3	3.0	3	0
Zackery, Tony, Atlanta	1	3	3.0	3	0
Duerson, Dave, Chicago	1	2	2.0	2	0
Dusbabek, Mark, Minnesota	1	2	2.0	2	0
Francis, Ron, Dallas	1	2	2.0	2	0
Anderson, John, Green Bay	1	1	1.0	1	0
DeLong, Keith, San Francisco	1	1	1.0	1	0
Futrell, Bobby, Tampa Bay	1	1	1.0	1	0
Gouveia, Kurt, Washington	1	1	1.0	1	0
Bruce, Aundray, Atlanta	1	0	0.0	0	0
Burton, Ron, Dallas	1	0	0.0	0	0
Carter, Carl, Phoenix	1	0	0.0	0	0
Douglass, Maurice, Chicago	1	0	0.0	0	0
Elder, Donnie, Tampa Bay	1	0	0.0	0	0
Fullington, Darrell, Minnesota	1	0	0.0	0	0
Greene, Tiger, Green Bay	1	0	0.0	0	0
Horton, Ray, Dallas	1	0	0.0	0	0
Jakes, Van, Green Bay	1	0	0.0	0	0
Joyner, Seth, Philadelphia	1	0	0.0	0	0
Noga, Niko, Detroit	1	0	0.0	0	0
Studwell, Scott, Minnesota	1	0	0.0	0	0
Tate, David, Chicago	1	0	0.0	0	0
Taylor, Terry, Detroit	1	0	0.0	0	0
White, William, Detroit	1	0	0.0	0	0
Atkins, Gene, New Orleans	1	−2	−2.0	−2	0

t indicates touchdown.
Leader based on most interceptions.

Punting

Average Yards Per Punt
NFC: 43.4—Rich Camarillo, Phoenix
AFC: 43.3—Greg Montgomery, Houston

Net Average Yards Per Punt
NFC: 37.8—Sean Landeta, N.Y. Giants
AFC: 36.1—Greg Montgomery, Houston

Longest
NFC: 91—Randall Cunningham, Philadelphia at N.Y. Giants, December 3
AFC: 76—Joe Prokop, N.Y. Jets at New England, November 5

Punts
AFC: 97—Bryan Wagner, Cleveland
NFC: 84—Scott Fulhage, Atlanta
84—Chris Mohr, Tampa Bay

Punts, Game
AFC: 12—Bryan Wagner, Cleveland vs. Kansas City, November 19 (463 yards)
NFC: 11—Bucky Scribner, Minnesota at Cleveland, December 17 (378 yards) (OT)

Team Champions
NFC: 43.6—Phoenix
AFC: 42.4—Indianapolis

AFC Punting—Team

	Net Punts	Gross Yards	Long	Gross Avg.	TB	Blk.	Opp. Ret.	Ret. Yards	In 20	Net Avg.
Indianapolis	80	3392	64	42.4	10	1	51	558	14	32.9
Houston	58	2422	63	41.8	7	2	24	191	15	36.1
Miami	59	2458	58	41.7	6	1	26	256	18	35.3
Pittsburgh	83	3368	57	40.6	9	1	45	361	15	34.1
L.A. Raiders	67	2711	60	40.5	7	0	41	301	12	33.9
Kansas City	67	2688	54	40.1	5	0	40	325	25	33.8
Denver	80	3188	63	39.8	6	0	28	370	25	33.7
San Diego	84	3315	64	39.5	7	0	43	451	11	32.4
Seattle	76	2995	59	39.4	8	1	41	334	17	32.9
N.Y. Jets	87	3426	76	39.4	4	0	34	257	29	35.5
Cleveland	97	3817	60	39.4	6	0	49	418	32	33.8
Cincinnati	65	2504	62	38.5	12	2	33	323	15	29.9
Buffalo	67	2564	60	38.3	9	2	25	227	15	32.2
New England	64	2392	64	37.4	2	1	38	346	13	31.3
AFC Total	1,034	41,240	76	—	98	11	518	4,718	256	—
AFC Average	73.9	2,945.7	—	39.9	7.0	0.8	37.0	337.0	18.3	33.4

NFC Punting—Team

	Net Punts	Gross Yards	Long	Gross Avg.	TB	Blk.	Opp. Ret.	Ret. Yards	In 20	Net Avg.
Phoenix	82	3578	58	43.6	6	0	46	371	23	37.6
N.Y. Giants	70	3019	71	43.1	7	0	29	236	19	37.8
Detroit	83	3538	64	42.6	9	1	46	373	14	36.0
Washington	63	2663	74	42.3	9	1	34	383	21	33.3
Atlanta	85	3472	65	40.8	9	1	43	460	24	33.3
Green Bay	66	2682	63	40.6	11	0	30	416	17	31.0
Minnesota	72	2864	55	39.8	8	0	32	300	16	33.4
Dallas	82	3261	56	39.8	6	2	38	334	19	34.2
San Francisco	56	2226	56	39.8	6	1	35	361	13	31.2
Chicago	72	2844	60	39.5	9	0	30	262	21	33.4
New Orleans	71	2774	56	39.1	5	0	35	244	21	34.2
Philadelphia	87	3389	91	39.0	5	0	37	215	21	35.3
Tampa Bay	86	3311	58	38.5	3	2	54	492	10	32.1
L.A. Rams	74	2834	54	38.3	7	1	34	315	15	32.1
NFC Total	1,049	42,455	91	—	100	9	523	4,762	254	—
NFC Average	74.9	3,032.5	—	40.5	7.1	0.6	37.4	340.1	18.1	34.0
League Total	2,083	83,695	91	—	198	20	1,041	9,480	510	—
League Average	74.4	2,989.1	—	40.2	7.1	0.7	37.2	338.6	18.2	33.7

NFL Top 10 Punters

	Net Punts	Gross Yards	Long	Gross Avg.	Total Punts	TB	Blk.	Opp. Ret.	Ret. Yards	In 20	Net Avg.
Camarillo, Rich, Phoenix	76	3298	58	43.4	76	6	0	42	330	21	37.5
Montgomery, Greg, Houston	56	2422	63	43.3	58	7	2	24	191	15	36.1
Arnold, Jim, Detroit	82	3538	64	43.1	83	9	1	46	373	14	36.0
Landeta, Sean, N.Y. Giants	70	3019	71	43.1	70	7	0	29	236	19	37.8
Mojsiejenko, Ralf, Washington	62	2663	74	43.0	63	9	1	34	383	21	33.3
Stark, Rohn, Indianapolis	79	3392	64	42.9	80	10	1	51	558	14	32.9
Roby, Reggie, Miami	58	2458	58	42.4	59	6	1	26	256	18	35.3
Fulhage, Scott, Atlanta	84	3472	65	41.3	85	9	1	43	460	24	33.3
Newsome, Harry, Pittsburgh	82	3368	57	41.1	83	9	1	45	361	15	34.1
Saxon, Mike, Dallas	79	3233	56	40.9	81	6	2	37	334	19	34.3

AFC Punting—Individual

	Net Punts	Gross Yards	Long	Gross Avg.	Total Punts	TB	Blk.	Opp. Ret.	Ret. Yards	In 20	Net Avg.
Montgomery, Greg, Houston	56	2422	63	43.3	58	7	2	24	191	15	36.1
Stark, Rohn, Indianapolis	79	3392	64	42.9	80	10	1	51	558	14	32.9
Roby, Reggie, Miami	58	2458	58	42.4	59	6	1	26	256	18	35.3
Newsome, Harry, Pittsburgh	82	3368	57	41.1	83	9	1	45	361	15	34.1
Gossett, Jeff, L.A. Raiders	67	2711	60	40.5	67	7	0	41	301	12	33.9
Horan, Mike, Denver	77	3111	63	40.4	77	5	0	28	370	24	34.3
Goodburn, Kelly, Kansas City	67	2688	54	40.1	67	5	0	40	325	25	33.8
Ilesic, Hank, San Diego	76	3049	64	40.1	76	7	0	39	408	11	32.9
Johnson, Lee, Cincinnati	61	2446	62	40.1	63	11	2	33	323	14	30.2
Rodriguez, Ruben, Seattle	75	2995	59	39.9	76	8	1	41	334	17	32.9
Kidd, John, Buffalo	65	2564	60	39.4	67	9	2	25	227	15	32.2
Prokop, Joe, N.Y. Jets	87	3426	76	39.4	87	4	0	34	257	29	35.5
Wagner, Bryan, Cleveland	97	3817	60	39.4	97	6	0	49	418	32	33.8
Feagles, Jeff, New England	63	2392	64	38.0	64	2	1	38	346	13	31.3
Non-Qualifiers											
Colbert, Lewis, San Diego	8	266	46	33.3	8	0	0	4	43	0	27.9
Breech, Jim, Cincinnati	2	58	32	29.0	2	1	0	0	0	1	19.0
Kubiak, Gary, Denver	2	43	29	21.5	2	0	0	0	0	1	21.5
Elway, John, Denver	1	34	34	34.0	1	1	0	0	0	0	14.0

Leader based on gross average, minimum 40 punts.

NFC Punting—Individual

	Net Punts	Gross Yards	Long	Gross Avg.	Total Punts	TB	Blk.	Opp. Ret.	Ret. Yards	In 20	Net Avg.
Camarillo, Rich, Phoenix	76	3298	58	43.4	76	6	0	42	330	21	37.5
Arnold, Jim, Detroit	82	3538	64	43.1	83	9	1	46	373	14	36.0
Landeta, Sean, N.Y. Giants	70	3019	71	43.1	70	7	0	29	236	19	37.8
Mojsiejenko, Ralf, Washington	62	2663	74	43.0	63	9	1	34	383	21	33.3
Fulhage, Scott, Atlanta	84	3472	65	41.3	85	9	1	43	460	24	33.3
Saxon, Mike, Dallas	79	3233	56	40.9	81	6	2	37	334	19	34.3
Bracken, Don, Green Bay	66	2682	63	40.6	66	11	0	30	416	17	31.0
Helton, Barry, San Francisco	55	2226	56	40.5	56	6	1	35	361	13	31.2
Scribner, Bucky, Minnesota	72	2864	55	39.8	72	8	0	32	300	16	33.4
Barnhardt, Tommy, New Orleans	55	2179	56	39.6	55	4	0	28	174	17	35.0
Buford, Maury, Chicago	72	2844	60	39.5	72	9	0	30	262	21	33.4
Mohr, Chris, Tampa Bay	84	3311	58	39.4	86	3	2	54	492	10	32.1
Teltschik, John, Philadelphia	57	2246	58	39.4	57	3	0	29	175	12	35.3
Hatcher, Dale, L.A. Rams	73	2834	54	38.8	74	7	1	34	315	15	32.1
Non-Qualifiers											
Runager, Max, Philadelphia	17	568	52	33.4	17	1	0	6	30	5	30.5
Winslow, George, New Orleans	16	595	50	37.2	16	1	0	7	70	4	31.6
Tuten, Rick, Philadelphia	7	256	45	36.6	7	1	0	1	1	1	33.6
Cunningham, Randall, Philadelphia	6	319	91	53.2	6	0	0	1	9	3	51.7
Tupa, Tom, Phoenix	6	280	51	46.7	6	0	0	4	41	2	39.8
Ruzek, Roger, Dallas	1	28	28	28.0	1	0	0	1	0	0	28.0

Leader based on gross average, minimum 40 punts.

Punt Returns

Yards Per Return
NFC: 13.8—Walter Stanley, Detroit
AFC: 12.9—Clarence Verdin, Indianapolis
Yards
NFC: 582—Dave Meggett, N.Y. Giants
AFC: 496—Gerald McNeil, Cleveland
Yards, Game
NFC: 114—Dave Meggett, N.Y. Giants vs. L.A. Raiders, December 24
(5 returns)
AFC: 103—Gerald McNeil, Cleveland at Indianapolis, December 10
(5 returns) (OT)
Longest
NFC: 76—Dave Meggett, N.Y. Giants vs. L.A. Raiders, December 24 (TD)
AFC: 70—Scott Schwedes, Miami at Indianapolis, December 17 (TD)
Returns
AFC: 49—Gerald McNeil, Cleveland
NFC: 46—Dave Meggett, N.Y. Giants
Returns, Game
AFC: 8—Phil McConkey, San Diego at Indianapolis, November 26
(75 yards)
NFC: 7—Walter Stanley, Detroit vs. New Orleans, December 3 (53 yards)
Fair Catches
NFC: 27—Leo Lewis, Minnesota
AFC: 21—Kenny Johnson, Houston
Touchdowns
AFC: 1—Scott Schwedes, Miami
1—Clarence Verdin, Indianapolis
NFC: 1—Dave Meggett, N.Y. Giants
1—Deion Sanders, Atlanta
1—Derrick Shepard, New Orleans
Team Champion
NFC: 12.7—N.Y. Giants
AFC: 12.4—Indianapolis

AFC Punt Returns—Team

	No.	FC	Yards	Avg.	Long	TD
Indianapolis	26	10	322	12.4	49t	1
Miami	33	11	338	10.2	70t	1
Cleveland	49	15	496	10.1	49	0
L.A. Raiders	40	9	378	9.5	29	0
Buffalo	33	12	301	9.1	26	0
N.Y. Jets	33	12	299	9.1	30	0
New England	45	6	379	8.4	28	0
Seattle	30	17	251	8.4	21	0
Denver	45	9	344	7.6	38	0
Kansas City	44	7	331	7.5	21	0
San Diego	38	20	272	7.2	52	0
Pittsburgh	40	2	278	7.0	20	0
Houston	19	21	122	6.4	19	0
Cincinnati	36	12	209	5.8	17	0
AFC Total	511	163	4,320	—	70t	2
AFC Average	36.5	11.6	308.6	8.5	—	0.1

NFC Punt Returns—Team

	No.	FC	Yards	Avg.	Long	TD
N.Y. Giants	46	14	582	12.7	76t	1
Detroit	47	8	572	12.2	74	0
Phoenix	40	13	469	11.7	53	0
San Francisco	39	20	429	11.0	37	0
Atlanta	32	7	341	10.7	68t	1
Minnesota	45	27	448	10.0	65	0
L.A. Rams	35	24	332	9.5	25	0
Tampa Bay	32	4	296	9.3	55	0
Philadelphia	37	12	331	8.9	28	0
Washington	26	20	226	8.7	38	0
Green Bay	35	9	289	8.3	17	0
New Orleans	53	9	428	8.1	57	1
Chicago	32	8	220	6.9	24	0
Dallas	31	11	197	6.4	17	0
NFC Total	530	186	5,160	—	76t	3
NFC Average	37.9	13.3	368.6	9.7	—	0.2
League Total	1,041	349	9480	—	76t	5
League Average	37.2	12.5	338.6	9.1	—	0.2

NFL Top 10 Punt Returners

	No.	FC	Yards	Avg.	Long	TD
Stanley, Walter, Detroit	36	5	496	13.8	74	0
Verdin, Clarence, Indianapolis	23	5	296	12.9	49t	1
Meggett, Dave, N.Y. Giants	46	14	582	12.7	76t	1
Sikahema, Vai, Phoenix	37	13	433	11.7	53	0
Taylor, John, San Francisco	36	20	417	11.6	37	0
Drewrey, Willie, Tampa Bay	20	2	220	11.0	55	0
Sanders, Deion, Atlanta	28	7	307	11.0	68t	1
Lewis, Leo, Minnesota	44	27	446	10.1	65	0
McNeil, Gerald, Cleveland	49	15	496	10.1	49	0
Howard, Joe, Washington	21	18	200	9.5	38	0

AFC Punt Returns—Individual

	No.	FC	Yards	Avg.	Long	TD
Verdin, Clarence, Indianapolis	23	5	296	12.9	49t	1
McNeil, Gerald, Cleveland	49	15	496	10.1	49	0
Townsell, JoJo, N.Y. Jets	33	12	299	9.1	30	0
Sutton, Mickey, G.B.-Buffalo	31	10	273	8.8	26	0
Woodson, Rod, Pittsburgh	29	2	207	7.1	20	0
Bell, Ken, Denver	21	3	143	6.8	24	0
Non-Qualifiers						
Tucker, Erroll, Buffalo-N.E.	19	4	165	8.7	25	0
Martin, Sammy, New England	19	2	164	8.6	28	0
Adams, Stefon, L.A. Raiders	19	5	156	8.2	15	0
Mandley, Pete, Kansas City	19	2	151	7.9	19	0
Worthen, Naz, Kansas City	19	5	133	7.0	17	0
Johnson, Kenny, Houston	19	21	122	6.4	19	0
Schwedes, Scott, Miami	18	3	210	11.7	70t	1
Hollis, David, Seattle	18	7	164	9.1	21	0
Edmonds, Bobby Joe, Raiders	16	4	168	10.5	20	0
McConkey, Phil, Phoenix-S.D.	15	15	124	8.3	20	0
Martin, Mike, Cincinnati	15	4	107	7.1	17	0
Stradford, Troy, Miami	14	5	129	9.2	19	0
Johnson, Vance, Denver	12	6	118	9.8	34	0
Fryar, Irving, New England	12	1	107	8.9	20	0
Jefferson, James, Seattle	12	10	87	7.3	19	0
Smith, Kendal, Cincinnati	12	2	54	4.5	15	0
Brinson, Dana, San Diego	11	0	112	10.2	52	0
Nattiel, Ricky, Denver	9	0	77	8.6	38	0
Walker, Wayne, San Diego	6	4	31	5.2	13	0
Hillary, Ira, Cincinnati	6	4	19	3.2	10	0
Hill, Derek, Pittsburgh	5	0	22	4.4	12	0
Brown, Tim, L.A. Raiders	4	0	43	10.8	29	0
Lipps, Louis, Pittsburgh	4	0	27	6.8	9	0
Carey, Richard, Cincinnati	3	2	29	9.7	13	0
Barnes, Lew, Kansas City	2	0	41	20.5	21	0
Johnson, Jason, Pittsburgh	2	0	22	11.0	13	0
Rison, Andre, Indianapolis	2	2	20	10.0	12	0
Harry, Emile, Kansas City	2	0	6	3.0	7	0
Woods, Chris, Denver	2	0	6	3.0	11	0
Allen, Anthony, San Diego	2	0	3	1.5	3	0
Ross, Kevin, Kansas City	2	0	0	0.0	0	0
Harden, Mike, L.A. Raiders	1	0	11	11.0	11	0
Johnson, Flip, Buffalo	1	0	7	7.0	7	0
Hurst, Maurice, New England	1	0	6	6.0	6	0
Washington, Charles, Indianapolis	1	0	6	6.0	6	0
Carrington, Darren, Denver	1	0	0	0.0	0	0
Figaro, Cedric, San Diego	1	0	0	0.0	0	0
Lyles, Lester, San Diego	1	0	0	0.0	0	0
Gibson, Ernest, Miami	1	0	−1	−1.0	−1	0
Byrd, Gill, San Diego	0	1	0	—	0	0
Prior, Mike, Indianapolis	0	3	0	—	0	0
Taylor, Kitrick, New England	0	2	0	—	0	0
Williams, Jarvis, Miami	0	3	0	—	0	0

t indicates touchdown.
Leader based on average return, minimum 20 returns.

NFC Punt Returns—Individual

	No.	FC	Yards	Avg.	Long	TD
Stanley, Walter, Detroit	36	5	496	13.8	74	0
Meggett, Dave, N.Y. Giants	46	14	582	12.7	76t	1
Sikahema, Vai, Phoenix	37	13	433	11.7	53	0
Taylor, John, San Francisco	36	20	417	11.6	37	0
Drewrey, Willie, Tampa Bay	20	2	220	11.0	55	0
Sanders, Deion, Atlanta	28	7	307	11.0	68t	1
Lewis, Leo, Minnesota	44	27	446	10.1	65	0
Howard, Joe, Washington	21	18	200	9.5	38	0
Henley, Darryl, L.A. Rams	28	19	266	9.5	25	0
Williams, Henry, Philadelphia	30	7	267	8.9	24	0
Query, Jeff, Green Bay	30	7	247	8.2	15	0
Shepard, Derrick, N.O.-Dallas	31	2	251	8.1	56t	1
Harris, Rod, New Orleans	27	7	196	7.3	20	0
Non-Qualifiers						
Green, Mark, Chicago	16	5	141	8.8	24	0
Futrell, Bobby, Tampa Bay	12	2	76	6.3	15	0
Gray, Mel, Detroit	11	2	76	6.9	15	0
McKinnon, Dennis, Chicago	10	3	67	6.7	17	0
Morse, Bobby, New Orleans	10	1	29	2.9	16	0
Edwards, Anthony, Philadelphia	7	5	64	9.1	28	0
Hill, Lonzell, New Orleans	7	0	41	5.9	13	0
Hicks, Cliff, L.A. Rams	4	3	39	9.8	15	0
Jordan, Brian, Atlanta	4	0	34	8.5	15	0
Martin, Kelvin, Dallas	4	5	32	8.0	12	0

	No.	FC	Yards	Avg.	Long	TD
Usher, Darryl, San Diego-Phoenix	4	0	25	6.3	11	0
Kozlowski, Glen, Chicago	4	0	−2	−0.5	4	0
Burbage, Cornell, Dallas	3	5	5	1.7	5	0
Ellard, Henry, L.A. Rams	2	0	20	10.0	10	0
Sanders, Ricky, Washington	2	2	12	6.0	7	0
Jones, Ernie, Phoenix	1	0	13	13.0	13	0
Woolford, Donnell, Chicago	1	0	12	12.0	12	0
Green, Darrell, Washington	1	0	11	11.0	11	0
Perriman, Brett, New Orleans	1	0	10	10.0	10	0
Griffin, Don, San Francisco	1	0	9	9.0	9	0
Irvin, LeRoy, L.A. Rams	1	2	7	7.0	7	0
Turner, Floyd, New Orleans	1	0	7	7.0	7	0
Davis, Brian, Washington	1	0	3	3.0	3	0
Greer, Terry, San Francisco	1	0	3	3.0	3	0
Carter, Anthony, Minnesota	1	0	2	2.0	2	0
Waddle, Tom, Chicago	1	0	2	2.0	2	0
Mayhew, Martin, Washington	1	0	0	0.0	0	0
Romanowski, Bill, San Francisco	1	0	0	0.0	0	0
Massey, Robert, New Orleans	0	0	54	—	54	0
Pitts, Ron, Green Bay	0	1	0	—	0	0
Woods, Jerry, Detroit	0	1	0	—	0	0

t indicates touchdown.

Leader based on average return, minimum 20 returns.

Kickoff Returns

Yards Per Return
  AFC: 27.3—Rod Woodson, Pittsburgh
  NFC: 26.7—Mel Gray, Detroit
Yards
  NFC: 1,181—James Dixon, Dallas
  AFC: 982—Rod Woodson, Pittsburgh
Yards, Game
  NFC: 186—James Dixon, Dallas at Green Bay, October 8 (5 returns)
  AFC: 168—James Jefferson, Seattle vs. Kansas City, October 8
      (5 returns)
Longest
  NFC: 99—Joe Howard, Washington at L.A. Raiders, October 29 (TD)
      99—Bobby Morse, New Orleans at Detroit, December 3 (TD)
  AFC: 97—Marc Logan, Miami at Houston, October 1 (TD)
      97—James Jefferson, Seattle vs. Kansas City, October 8 (TD)
Returns
  NFC: 47—Ron Brown, L.A. Rams
      47—James Dixon, Dallas
  AFC: 36—Rod Woodson, Pittsburgh
Returns, Game
  NFC: 7—Darryl Usher, Phoenix at L.A. Rams, November 19 (145 yards)
  AFC: 6—Leonard Harris, Houston at Minnesota, September 10
      (142 yards)
      6—Erroll Tucker, New England at Miami, December 10 (118 yards)
      6—Albert Bentley, Indianapolis at New Orleans, December 24
      (110 yards)
Touchdowns
  AFC: 1—Marc Logan, Miami
      1—James Jefferson, Seattle
      1—Anthony Miller, San Diego
      1—Rod Woodson, Pittsburgh
  NFC: 1—James Dixon, Dallas
      1—Joe Howard, Washington
      1—Bobby Morse, New Orleans
      1—Thomas Sanders, Chicago
      1—Herschel Walker, Minnesota
Team Champion
  AFC: 23.3—Pittsburgh
  NFC: 22.2—Dallas

AFC Kickoff Returns—Team

	No.	Yards	Avg.	Long	TD
Pittsburgh	56	1304	23.3	84t	1
New England	69	1462	21.2	47	0
Denver	43	876	20.4	68	0
Buffalo	53	1058	20.0	85	0
Indianapolis	60	1164	19.4	49	0
San Diego	64	1235	19.3	91t	1
Seattle	65	1246	19.2	97t	1
Miami	61	1153	18.9	97t	1
Cleveland	50	932	18.6	49	0
L.A. Raiders	54	1002	18.6	49	0
Kansas City	52	915	17.6	37	0
N.Y. Jets	75	1309	17.5	69	0
Cincinnati	54	941	17.4	33	0
Houston	74	1285	17.4	63	0
AFC Total	830	15,882	—	97t	4
AFC Average	59.3	1,134.4	19.1	—	0.3

NFC Kickoff Returns—Team

	No.	Yards	Avg.	Long	TD
Dallas	77	1709	22.2	97t	1
Minnesota	51	1122	22.0	93t	1
Chicago	73	1539	21.1	96t	1
Detroit	61	1272	20.9	62	0
New Orleans	63	1284	20.4	99t	1
Washington	58	1176	20.3	99t	1
Phoenix	83	1650	19.9	52	0
L.A. Rams	67	1328	19.8	74	0
Atlanta	80	1509	18.9	72	0
San Francisco	51	954	18.7	60	0
N.Y. Giants	51	926	18.2	43	0
Green Bay	69	1239	18.0	46	0
Tampa Bay	62	1055	17.0	36	0
Philadelphia	49	828	16.9	45	0
NFC Total	895	17,591	—	99t	5
NFC Average	63.0	1,256.5	19.7	—	0.4
League Total	1,725	33,473	—	99t	9
League Average	61.6	1,195.5	19.4	—	0.3

NFL Top 10 Kickoff Returners

	No.	Yards	Avg.	Long	TD
Woodson, Rod, Pittsburgh	36	982	27.3	84t	1
Gray, Mel, Detroit	24	640	26.7	57	0
Logan, Marc, Miami	24	613	25.5	97t	1
Miller, Anthony, San Diego	21	533	25.4	91t	1
Dixon, James, Dallas	47	1181	25.1	97t	1
Howard, Joe, Washington	21	522	24.9	99t	1
Martin, Sammy, New England	24	584	24.3	38	0
Gentry, Dennis, Chicago	28	667	23.8	63	0
Jefferson, James, Seattle	22	511	23.2	97t	1
Metcalf, Eric, Cleveland	31	718	23.2	49	0

AFC Kickoff Returns—Individual

	No.	Yards	Avg.	Long	TD
Woodson, Rod, Pittsburgh	36	982	27.3	84t	1
Logan, Marc, Miami	24	613	25.5	97t	1
Miller, Anthony, San Diego	21	533	25.4	91t	1
Martin, Sammy, New England	24	584	24.3	38	0
Jefferson, James, Seattle	22	511	23.2	97t	1
Metcalf, Eric, Cleveland	31	718	23.2	49	0
Jennings, Stanford, Cincinnati	26	525	20.2	33	0
Bell, Ken, Denver	30	602	20.1	33	0
Adams, Stefon, L.A. Raiders	22	425	19.3	37	0
Townsell, JoJo, N.Y. Jets	34	653	19.2	69	0
Tucker, Erroll, Buffalo-New England	23	436	19.0	37	0
Copeland, Danny, Kansas City	26	466	17.9	36	0
Johnson, Kenny, Houston	21	372	17.7	39	0
Holland, Jamie, San Diego	29	510	17.6	34	0
Humphery, Bobby, N.Y. Jets	24	414	17.3	52	0

Non-Qualifiers

	No.	Yards	Avg.	Long	TD
Verdin, Clarence, Indianapolis	19	371	19.5	29	0
Harmon, Ronnie, Buffalo	18	409	22.7	49	0
Harris, Elroy, Seattle	18	334	18.6	25	0
Bentley, Albert, Indianapolis	17	328	19.3	29	0
Hampton, Lorenzo, Miami	17	303	17.8	34	0
White, Lorenzo, Houston	17	303	17.8	29	0
Beebe, Don, Buffalo	16	353	22.1	85	0
Hollis, David, Seattle	15	247	16.5	30	0
Harris, Leonard, Houston	14	331	23.6	63	0
Edmonds, Bobby Joe, L.A. Raiders	14	271	19.4	43	0
Hillary, Ira, Cincinnati	14	223	15.9	29	0
McNair, Todd, Kansas City	13	257	19.8	37	0
Johnson, Tracy, Houston	13	224	17.2	27	0
Pruitt, James, Indianapolis	12	257	21.4	49	0
Rice, Rodney, New England	11	242	22.0	46	0
Epps, Phillip, N.Y. Jets	9	154	17.1	43	0
Rison, Andre, Indianapolis	8	150	18.8	30	0
Stone, Dwight, Pittsburgh	7	173	24.7	73	0
Carrington, Darren, Denver	6	152	25.3	68	0
Allen, Marvin, New England	6	124	20.7	29	0
Carey, Richard, Cincinnati	6	104	17.3	23	0
Harmon, Kevin, Seattle	6	84	14.0	19	0
Reaves, Willard, Miami	6	84	14.0	22	0
Mueller, Vance, L.A. Raiders	5	120	24.0	49	0
Worthen, Naz, Kansas City	5	113	22.6	27	0
Oliphant, Mike, Cleveland	5	69	13.8	28	0
Smith, Kendal, Cincinnati	5	65	13.0	19	0
Humphrey, Bobby, Denver	4	86	21.5	29	0
Ware, Timmie, L.A. Raiders	4	86	21.5	29	0
Dixon, Titus, N.Y. Jets	4	67	16.8	21	0
McNeil, Gerald, Cleveland	4	61	15.3	21	0
Hunter, Ivy Joe, Indianapolis	4	58	14.5	19	0
Jones, Keith, Cleveland	4	42	10.5	25	0

	No.	Yards	Avg.	Long	TD
Thompson, Weegie, Pittsburgh	4	41	10.3	15	0
Williams, Jerrol, Pittsburgh	4	31	7.8	22	0
Wonsley, George, New England	3	69	23.0	40	0
Brown, Tim, L.A. Raiders	3	63	21.0	25	0
Gamble, Kenny, Kansas City	3	55	18.3	23	0
Davis, Kenneth, Buffalo	3	52	17.3	20	0
Taylor, Kitrick, New England	3	52	17.3	22	0
Mrosko, Bob, Houston	3	46	15.3	19	0
Johnson, Jason, Pittsburgh	3	43	14.3	19	0
Schwedes, Scott, Miami	3	24	8.0	13	0
Saxon, James, Kansas City	3	16	5.3	14	0
Floyd, Victor, San Diego	3	12	4.0	12	0
Tasker, Steve, Buffalo	2	39	19.5	20	0
Faaola, Nuu, Miami	2	30	15.0	17	0
Egu, Patrick, New England	2	26	13.0	22	0
Kinchen, Brian, Miami	2	26	13.0	17	0
Braggs, Stephen, Cleveland	2	20	10.0	18	0
Rolle, Butch, Buffalo	2	20	10.0	14	0
Bratton, Mel, Denver	2	19	9.5	10	0
Hodge, Milford, New England	2	19	9.5	11	0
Smith, Steve, L.A. Raiders	2	19	9.5	15	0
Timpson, Michael, New England	2	13	6.5	13	0
Brown, Andre, Miami	2	9	4.5	9	0
Nichols, Gerald, N.Y. Jets	2	9	4.5	7	0
Williams, David, Houston	2	8	4.0	8	0
Redden, Barry, Cleveland	2	2	1.0	2	0
Fryar, Irving, New England	1	47	47.0	47	0
Clark, Louis, Seattle	1	31	31.0	31	0
Figaro, Cedric, San Diego	1	21	21.0	21	0
Griffin, Larry, Pittsburgh	1	21	21.0	21	0
Williams, Jarvis, Miami	1	21	21.0	21	0
Ball, Eric, Cincinnati	1	19	19.0	19	0
Davenport, Ron, Miami	1	19	19.0	19	0
Mueller, Jamie, Buffalo	1	19	19.0	19	0
McNeal, Travis, Seattle	1	17	17.0	17	0
Woods, Chris, Denver	1	17	17.0	17	0
Gault, Willie, L.A. Raiders	1	16	16.0	16	0
Rehder, Tom, New England	1	14	14.0	14	0
Hinnant, Mike, Pittsburgh	1	13	13.0	13	0
Woods, Tony, Seattle	1	13	13.0	13	0
Joines, Vernon, Cleveland	1	12	12.0	12	0
Washington, Marvin, N.Y. Jets	1	11	11.0	11	0
Ahrens, Dave, Miami	1	10	10.0	10	0
Comeaux, Darren, Seattle	1	9	9.0	9	0
Goode, Kerry, Miami	1	8	8.0	8	0
Johnson, Eddie, Cleveland	1	8	8.0	8	0
Saleaumua, Dan, Kansas City	1	8	8.0	8	0
Brudzinski, Bob, Miami	1	6	6.0	6	0
Taylor, Craig, Cincinnati	1	5	5.0	5	0
Tatupu, Mosi, New England	1	2	2.0	2	0
Turk, Dan, L.A. Raiders	1	2	2.0	2	0
Byrd, Dennis, N.Y. Jets	1	1	1.0	1	0
Fairs, Eric, Houston	1	1	1.0	1	0
Holifield, John, Cincinnati	1	0	0.0	0	0
Jackson, Kirby, Buffalo	1	0	0.0	0	0
Junkin, Trey, L.A. Raiders	1	0	0.0	0	0
Lee, Zeph, L.A. Raiders	1	0	0.0	0	0
Lyles, Robert, Houston	1	0	0.0	0	0
Mandley, Pete, Kansas City	1	0	0.0	0	0
Montgomery, Glenn, Houston	1	0	0.0	0	0
Verhulst, Chris, Houston	1	0	0.0	0	0
Jackson, Robert, Cincinnati	0*	0	—	0	0

t indicates touchdown.

* indicates fair catch.

Leader based on average return, minimum 20 returns.

NFC Kickoff Returns—Individual

	No.	Yards	Avg.	Long	TD
Gray, Mel, Detroit	24	640	26.7	57	0
Dixon, James, Dallas	47	1181	25.1	97t	1
Howard, Joe, Washington	21	522	24.9	99t	1
Gentry, Dennis, Chicago	28	667	23.8	63	0
Meggett, Dave, N.Y. Giants	27	577	21.4	43	0
Sanders, Thomas, Chicago	23	491	21.3	96t	1
Johnson, A.J., Washington	24	504	21.0	38	0
Sanders, Deion, Atlanta	35	725	20.7	72	0
Brown, Ron, L.A. Rams	47	968	20.6	74	0
Sikahema, Vai, Phoenix	43	874	20.3	52	0
Flagler, Terrence, San Francisco	32	643	20.1	41	0
Shepard, Derrick, New Orleans-Dallas	27	529	19.6	32	0
Jones, Keith, Atlanta	23	440	19.1	29	0
Usher, Darryl, San Diego-Phoenix	27	506	18.7	33	0
Elder, Donnie, Tampa Bay	40	685	17.1	30	0
Workman, Vince, Green Bay	33	547	16.6	46	0
Ingram, Mark, N.Y. Giants	22	332	15.1	29	0

Non-Qualifiers

	No.	Yards	Avg.	Long	TD
Harris, Rod, New Orleans	19	378	19.9	39	0
Delpino, Robert, L.A. Rams	17	334	19.6	30	0

	No.	Yards	Avg.	Long	TD
Higgs, Mark, Philadelphia	16	293	18.3	30	0
Nelson, Darrin, Minnesota	14	317	22.6	32	0
Williams, Henry, Philadelphia	14	249	17.8	28	0
Walker, Herschel, Minnesota	13	374	28.8	93t	1
Bland, Carl, Green Bay	13	256	19.7	37	0
Sherman, Heath, Philadelphia	13	222	17.1	45	0
Dozier, D.J., Minnesota	12	258	21.5	63	0
Atkins, Gene, New Orleans	12	245	20.4	32	0
Palmer, Paul, Detroit	11	255	23.2	62	0
Baker, Tony, Phoenix	11	245	22.3	33	0
Fullwood, Brent, Green Bay	11	243	22.1	35	0
Green, Mark, Chicago	11	239	21.7	37	0
Morse, Bobby, New Orleans	10	278	27.8	99t	1
Tillman, Spencer, San Francisco	10	206	20.6	60	0
Stamps, Sylvester, Tampa Bay	9	145	16.1	36	0
Sanders, Ricky, Washington	9	134	14.9	29	0
Stanley, Walter, Detroit	9	95	10.6	19	0
Frazier, Paul, New Orleans	8	157	19.6	29	0
Paterra, Greg, Atlanta	8	129	16.1	31	0
Thomas, George, Atlanta	7	142	20.3	28	0
Jones, Ernie, Phoenix	7	124	17.7	27	0
Query, Jeff, Green Bay	6	125	20.8	28	0
Suhey, Matt, Chicago	6	93	15.5	21	0
Sanders, Barry, Detroit	5	118	23.6	43	0
Alexander, Bruce, Detroit	5	100	20.0	25	0
Howard, William, Tampa Bay	5	82	16.4	19	0
Anderson, Alfred, Minnesota	5	75	15.0	36	0
Futrell, Bobby, Tampa Bay	4	58	14.5	22	0
Clack, Darryl, Dallas	3	56	18.7	24	0
Burbage, Cornell, Dallas	3	55	18.3	22	0
Jordan, Brian, Atlanta	3	27	9.0	13	0
Edwards, Anthony, Philadelphia	3	23	7.7	11	0
Sydney, Harry, San Francisco	3	16	5.3	16	0
Taylor, John, San Francisco	2	51	25.5	27	0
Wilder, James, Tampa Bay	2	42	21.0	23	0
McConkey, Phil, Phoenix	2	40	20.0	21	0
Woodside, Keith, Green Bay	2	38	19.0	23	0
Johnson, Undra, New Orleans	2	34	17.0	19	0
Fontenot, Herman, Green Bay	2	30	15.0	20	0
Lewis, Leo, Minnesota	2	30	15.0	15	0
Woods, Jerry, Detroit	2	28	14.0	15	0
McDonald, Mike, L.A. Rams	2	22	11.0	12	0
Henderson, Keith, San Francisco	2	21	10.5	13	0
Pruitt, Mickey, Chicago	2	17	8.5	11	0
Beckman, Brad, Atlanta	2	15	7.5	15	0
Little, David, Philadelphia	2	14	7.0	12	0
Dallafior, Ken, Detroit	2	13	6.5	13	0
Ankrom, Scott, Dallas	2	6	3.0	5	0
Clark, Jessie, Phoenix-Minnesota	2	6	3.0	6	0
Byars, Keith, Philadelphia	1	27	27.0	27	0
Drewrey, Willie, Tampa Bay	1	26	26.0	26	0
Phillips, Kim, New Orleans	1	24	24.0	24	0
Hilliard, Dalton, New Orleans	1	20	20.0	20	0
Carter, Anthony, Minnesota	1	19	19.0	19	0
Curtis, Travis, Minnesota	1	18	18.0	18	0
Greer, Terry, San Francisco	1	17	17.0	17	0
Pillow, Frank, Tampa Bay	1	17	17.0	17	0
Rouson, Lee, N.Y. Giants	1	17	17.0	17	0
Primus, James, Atlanta	1	16	16.0	16	0
Bruce, Aundray, Atlanta	1	15	15.0	15	0
Carr, Lydell, Phoenix	1	15	15.0	15	0
Painter, Carl, Detroit	1	14	14.0	14	0
Hill, Lonzell, New Orleans	1	13	13.0	13	0
Rice, Allen, Minnesota	1	13	13.0	13	0
Fenney, Rick, Minnesota	1	12	12.0	12	0
Kozlowski, Glen, Chicago	1	12	12.0	12	0
Tate, David, Chicago	1	12	12.0	12	0
Mandeville, Chris, Washington	1	10	10.0	10	0
Tautalatasi, Junior, Dallas	1	9	9.0	9	0
Chandler, Thornton, Dallas	1	8	8.0	8	0
Chapura, Dick, Chicago	1	8	8.0	8	0
Crockett, Ray, Detroit	1	8	8.0	8	0
Branch, Reggie, Washington	1	6	6.0	6	0
Reeves, Walter, Phoenix	1	5	5.0	5	0
Gary, Cleveland, L.A. Rams	1	4	4.0	4	0
Griffin, James, Detroit	1	1	1.0	1	0
Collins, Mark, N.Y. Giants	1	0	0.0	0	0
Didier, Clint, Green Bay	1	0	0.0	0	0
Gouveia, Kurt, Washington	1	0	0.0	0	0
Jackson, Johnny, San Francisco	1	0	0.0	0	0
Mandarich, Tony, Green Bay	1	0	0.0	0	0
Orr, Terry, Washington	1	0	0.0	0	0
Sargent, Broderick, Dallas	1	0	0.0	0	0
Scales, Greg, New Orleans	1	0	0.0	0	0
Miller, John, Detroit	0*	0	—	0	0
Stephen, Scott, Green Bay	0*	0	—	0	0

t indicates touchdown.

* indicates fair catch.

Leader based on average return, minimum 20 returns.

Fumbles

Most Fumbles
- AFC: 18—Dave Krieg, Seattle
- NFC: 17—Randall Cunningham, Philadelphia

Most Fumbles, Game
- AFC: 6—Dave Krieg, Seattle at Kansas City, November 5
- NFC: 4—Mark Rypien, Washington at L.A. Raiders, October 29

Own Fumbles Recovered
- AFC: 9—Dave Krieg, Seattle
- NFC: 6—Don Majkowski, Green Bay

Most Own Fumbles Recovered, Game
- AFC: 3—Dave Krieg, Seattle at Kansas City, November 5
- NFC: 2—William Howard, Tampa Bay vs. San Francisco, September 17
- 2—Steve Walsh, Dallas vs. San Francisco, October 15
- 2—Earnest Byner, Washington at L.A. Raiders, October 29
- 2—Chris Miller, Atlanta vs. San Francisco, December 3
- 2—Dave Meggett, N.Y. Giants vs. L.A. Raiders, December 24
- 2—Jim Everett, L.A. Rams at New England, December 24

Opponents' Fumbles Recovered
- AFC: 5—Nesby Glasgow, Seattle
- 5—Carnell Lake, Pittsburgh
- 5—Dan Saleamua, Kansas City
- NFC: 5—Chris Doleman, Minnesota
- 5—James Geathers, New Orleans

Most Opponents' Fumbles Recovered, Game
- AFC: 2—Dave Grayson, Cleveland at Pittsburgh, 2—September 10
- 2—Billy Ray Smith, San Diego at Phoenix, October 1
- 2—Carnell Lake, Pittsburgh vs. San Diego, November 19
- 2—Joe Kelly, Cincinnati vs. Detroit, November 19
- 2—Dan Saleamua, Kansas City vs. Miami, December 3
- NFC: 2—James Geathers, New Orleans vs. N.Y. Jets, October 15
- 2—Michael Stewart, L.A. Rams at Buffalo, October 16
- 2—Bill Romanowski, San Francisco at N.Y. Jets, October 29
- 2—Brett Faryniarz, L.A. Rams vs. N.Y. Jets, December 17

Yards
- AFC: 119—Erik McMillan, N.Y. Jets
- NFC: 77—Wes Hopkins, Philadelphia
- 77—Jim Jeffcoat, Dallas

Longest
- AFC: 81—Vencie Glenn, San Diego vs. N.Y. Giants, October 22 (TD)
- NFC: 77—Al Harris (0) to Wes Hopkins (77), Philadelphia at Washington, September 17
- 77—Jim Jeffcoat, Dallas vs. Washington, September 24 (TD)

AFC Fumbles—Team

	Fum.	Own Rec.	Fum. *O.B.	TD	Opp. Rec.	TD	Yds.	Tot. Rec.
Cleveland	23	7	1	0	11	2	42	18
San Diego	24	6	1	0	12	2	79	18
Denver	26	13	1	0	22	2	92	35
New England	26	12	2	0	12	0	40	24
L.A. Raiders	28	13	3	0	18	2	65	31
Cincinnati	29	10	0	0	16	1	75	26
Buffalo	30	7	2	0	13	0	13	20
Miami	30	12	2	0	8	0	-1	20
N.Y. Jets	32	15	0	0	8	2	113	23
Kansas City	32	12	2	0	18	2	-26	30
Pittsburgh	32	13	1	0	21	1	17	34
Indianapolis	33	21	2	1	15	0	1	36
Houston	39	19	3	0	16	0	-57	35
Seattle	43	24	5	0	13	1	-6	37
AFC Total	427	184	25	1	203	15	447	387
AFC Average	30.5	13.1	1.8	0.1	14.5	1.1	31.9	27.6

NFC Fumbles—Team

	Fum.	Own Rec.	Fum. *O.B.	TD	Opp. Rec.	TD	Yds.	Tot. Rec.
Tampa Bay	21	10	2	0	18	0	4	28
Chicago	23	5	1	0	12	0	16	17
Phoenix	24	10	0	0	11	0	-3	21
Atlanta	26	15	0	0	12	1	23	27
L.A. Rams	26	11	4	0	15	0	2	26
Minnesota	28	12	2	0	18	4	93	30
New Orleans	28	15	1	0	18	0	-38	33
Dallas	29	13	1	0	10	3	161	23
N.Y. Giants	30	16	0	0	15	0	15	31
San Francisco	32	13	5	0	16	1	1	29
Washington	32	12	0	0	15	0	12	27
Green Bay	35	19	3	2	15	0	72	34
Detroit	37	10	3	1	16	0	84	26
Philadelphia	43	23	4	0	26	1	161	49
NFC Total	414	184	26	3	217	10	603	401
NFC Average	29.6	13.1	1.9	0.2	15.5	0.7	43.1	28.6
League Total	841	368	51	4	420	25	1050	788
League Average	30.0	13.1	1.8	0.1	15.0	0.9	37.5	28.1

*indicates fumbled out of bounds.
Yards includes aborted plays, own recoveries, and opponents' recoveries.

AFC Fumbles—Individual

	Fum.	Own Rec.	Opp. Rec.	Yds.	Tot. Rec.
Adams, Stefon, L.A. Raiders	2	1	0	0	1
Adickes, Mark, Kansas City	0	1	0	0	1
Alexander, Dan, N.Y. Jets	0	1	0	0	1
Allen, Marcus, L.A. Raiders	2	0	0	0	0
Allen, Marvin, New England	0	0	1	0	1
Allen, Patrick, Houston	0	1	0	0	1
Atwater, Steve, Denver	0	0	1	29	1
Baab, Mike, New England	0	1	0	0	1
Bahr, Chris, San Diego	0	1	0	0	1
Bailey, Edwin, Seattle	0	1	0	0	1
Baldinger, Brian, Indianapolis	0	1	0	0	1
Ball, Eric, Cincinnati	3	0	0	0	0
Banker, Ted, Cleveland	0	1	0	-1	1
Banks, Chip, Indianapolis	0	0	1	0	1
Banks, Fred, Miami	1	1	0	0	1
Banks, Robert, Cleveland	0	0	2	0	2
Bayless, Martin, San Diego	0	0	1	0	1
Beach, Pat, Indianapolis	1	0	0	0	0
Beebe, Don, Buffalo	1	0	0	0	0
Bell, Ken, Denver	5	4	1	0	5
Bennett, Cornelius, Buffalo	0	0	2	5	2
Benson, Thomas, L.A. Raiders	0	0	2	0	2
Bentley, Albert, Indianapolis	3	3	0	7	3
Beuerlein, Steve, L.A. Raiders	6	3	0	-8	3
Bickett, Duane, Indianapolis	0	0	3	2	3
Blackledge, Todd, Pittsburgh	3	0	0	0	0
Blades, Brian, Seattle	3	1	0	0	1
Boyer, Mark, Indianapolis	1	1	0	0	1
Braxton, Tyrone, Denver	0	0	2	35	2
Brennan, Brian, Cleveland	1	1	0	0	1
Brinson, Dana, San Diego	3	0	0	0	0
Brister, Bubby, Pittsburgh	4	1	0	0	1
Brooks, Bill, Indianapolis	1	0	0	0	0
Brooks, James, Cincinnati	9	1	0	0	1
Brooks, Michael, Denver	0	0	2	0	2
Brown, Andre, Miami	1	1	0	0	1
Brown, Tim, L.A. Raiders	1	0	0	0	0
Brown, Tom, Miami	1	1	0	0	1
Brown, Vincent, New England	0	0	2	0	2
Buck, Jason, Cincinnati	0	0	1	0	1
Burroughs, Derrick, Buffalo	0	0	1	0	1
Butts, Marion, San Diego	2	1	0	0	1
Byrd, Richard, Houston	0	0	2	0	2
Call, Kevin, Indianapolis	0	1	0	0	1
Caravello, Joe, San Diego	0	1	0	0	1
Carey, Richard, Cincinnati	1	1	0	0	1
Carlson, Cody, Houston	1	1	0	-6	1
Carrington, Darren, Denver	1	0	0	0	0
Cherry, Deron, Kansas City	0	0	2	0	2
Childress, Ray, Houston	0	0	1	0	1
Clancy, Sam, Indianapolis	0	0	3	0	3
Clark, Greg, Miami	0	0	1	0	1
Clark, Louis, Seattle	1	0	0	0	1
Clayton, Mark, Miami	1	0	0	0	0
Clifton, Kyle, N.Y. Jets	0	0	1	0	1
Comeaux, Darren, Seattle	0	0	1	0	1
Cooper, Louis, Kansas City	0	0	1	6	1
Copeland, Danny, Kansas City	1	1	0	0	1
Criswell, Jeff, N.Y. Jets	0	1	0	0	1
Daniel, Eugene, Indianapolis	0	0	1	5	1
Davis, Kenneth, Buffalo	2	0	0	0	0
Davis, Scott, L.A. Raiders	0	0	1	0	1
DeBerg, Steve, Kansas City	4	3	0	-26	3
Dennison, Rick, Denver	0	0	1	0	1
Dickerson, Eric, Indianapolis	10	0	0	0	0
Dishman, Cris, Houston	0	0	1	0	1
Dixon, Randy, Indianapolis	0	1	0	0	1
Dixon, Titus, N.Y. Jets	1	0	0	0	0
Donaldson, Ray, Indianapolis	1	1	0	-22	1
Dressel, Chris, Kansas City	1	0	0	0	0
Duncan, Curtis, Houston	1	0	0	0	0
Dupard, Reggie, New England	1	0	0	0	0
Dykes, Hart Lee, New England	3	1	0	0	1
Eason, Tony, New England-N.Y. Jets	3	0	0	0	0
Eatman, Irv, Kansas City	0	1	0	0	1
Edmunds, Ferrell, Miami	1	1	0	0	1
Egu, Patrick, New England	1	1	0	0	1
Elway, John, Denver	9	2	0	-4	2
Esiason, Boomer, Cincinnati	8	2	0	-4	2
Evans, Vince, L.A. Raiders	1	0	0	0	0
Everett, Thomas, Pittsburgh	1	0	1	21	1
Fairs, Eric, Houston	0	0	2	0	2
Farren, Paul, Cleveland	0	1	0	0	1
Feagles, Jeff, New England	1	1	0	0	1
Feasel, Grant, Seattle	0	1	0	0	1
Fernandez, Mervyn, L.A. Raiders	3	0	0	0	0
Figaro, Cedric, San Diego	0	0	1	0	1

	Fum.	Own Rec.	Opp. Rec.	Yds.	Tot. Rec.
Fletcher, Simon, Denver	0	0	1	0	1
Floyd, Victor, San Diego	1	0	0	0	0
Flutie, Doug, New England	1	0	0	0	0
Fryar, Irving, New England	2	0	0	0	0
Fulcher, David, Cincinnati	0	0	4	0	4
Galbreath, Harry, Miami	0	1	0	0	1
Gannon, Chris, San Diego	0	0	1	0	1
Gash, Thane, Cleveland	0	0	1	15	1
Givins, Ernest, Houston	0	0	1	0	1
Glasgow, Nesby, Seattle	0	0	5	38	5
Glenn, Vencie, San Diego	0	0	1	81	1
Gordon, Alex, N.Y. Jets	0	0	1	0	1
Grayson, Dave, Cleveland	0	0	2	31	2
Green, Hugh, Miami	0	0	2	0	2
Green, Jacob, Seattle	0	0	1	0	1
Griffin, Larry, Pittsburgh	0	0	1	0	1
Grimsley, John, Houston	0	0	1	3	1
Grogan, Steve, New England	3	2	0	0	2
Hackett, Dino, Kansas City	0	0	1	0	1
Hall, Courtney, San Diego	1	0	0	−29	0
Hall, Delton, Pittsburgh	0	0	1	0	1
Hammerstein, Mike, Cincinnati	0	0	1	0	1
Hampton, Lorenzo, Miami	1	0	0	0	0
Hand, Jon, Indianapolis	0	0	2	7	2
Harden, Mike, L.A. Raiders	0	0	3	22	3
Harmon, Ronnie, Buffalo	2	0	0	0	0
Harper, Dwayne, Seattle	0	0	1	0	1
Harper, Mark, Cleveland	0	0	1	0	1
Harper, Michael, N.Y. Jets	0	0	1	0	1
Harris, Elroy, Seattle	1	0	0	0	0
Harris, Leonard, Houston	1	0	0	0	0
Harry, Emile, Kansas City	1	0	0	0	0
Hasty, James, N.Y. Jets	1	0	2	2	2
Hayes, Jonathan, Kansas City	1	0	0	0	0
Heard, Herman, Kansas City	2	0	0	0	0
Heck, Andy, Seattle	0	1	0	0	1
Hector, Johnny, N.Y. Jets	1	0	0	0	0
Henderson, Wymon, Denver	1	0	0	0	0
Highsmith, Alonzo, Houston	6	2	0	0	2
Hill, Derek, Pittsburgh	2	0	0	0	0
Hill, Drew, Houston	1	1	0	5	1
Hill, Kenny, Kansas City	0	0	1	0	1
Hillary, Ira, Cincinnati	1	0	0	0	0
Hinkle, Bryan, Pittsburgh	0	0	1	0	1
Hinton, Chris, Indianapolis	0	2	0	0	2
Hobley, Liffort, Miami	0	0	1	12	1
Hoge, Merril, Pittsburgh	2	2	0	0	2
Holifield, John, Cincinnati	1	0	0	0	0
Hollis, David, Seattle	1	0	0	0	0
Howard, Joey, San Diego	0	1	0	0	1
Hull, Kent, Buffalo	0	2	0	0	2
Humphery, Bobby, N.Y. Jets	4	4	0	0	4
Humphrey, Bobby, Denver	4	3	0	0	3
Hunley, Ricky, L.A. Raiders	0	1	0	0	1
Jackson, Bo, L.A. Raiders	1	0	0	0	0
Jackson, Kirby, Buffalo	0	0	1	0	1
Jackson, Mark, Denver	1	0	0	−8	0
Jackson, Robert, Cincinnati	0	1	0	0	1
James, Roland, New England	0	0	1	7	1
Jaworski, Ron, Kansas City	2	2	0	−7	2
Jefferson, James, Seattle	3	2	1	0	3
Jenkins, Mel, Seattle	0	0	1	0	1
Jennings, Stanford, Cincinnati	1	0	0	0	0
Johnson, Ezra, Indianapolis	0	0	1	0	1
Johnson, Jason, Pittsburgh	1	1	0	0	1
Johnson, Kenny, Houston	4	1	2	0	3
Johnson, M.L., Seattle	0	0	2	0	2
Johnson, Tracy, Houston	1	0	0	0	0
Jones, Cedric, New England	1	2	0	4	2
Jones, Keith, Cleveland	1	1	0	0	1
Jones, Sean, Houston	0	0	2	0	2
Jones, Tony, Cleveland	0	1	0	0	1
Jordan, Tim, New England	0	0	1	0	1
Kay, Clarence, Denver	0	1	0	0	1
Kelly, Jim, Buffalo	6	3	0	−6	3
Kelly, Joe, Cincinnati	0	0	3	23	3
Kelso, Mark, Buffalo	0	0	2	0	2
Kemp, Jeff, Seattle	1	0	0	−3	0
Kinchen, Brian, Miami	2	0	0	−35	0
King, Linden, L.A. Raiders	0	0	3	15	3
Kinnebrew, Larry, Buffalo	3	0	0	0	0
Kosar, Bernie, Cleveland	2	2	0	−1	2
Kozak, Scott, Houston	0	0	1	0	1
Kozerski, Bruce, Cincinnati	0	1	0	0	1
Kragen, Greg, Denver	0	0	4	17	4
Krieg, Dave, Seattle	18	9	0	−20	9
Krumrie, Tim, Cincinnati	0	0	1	9	1
Kubiak, Gary, Denver	2	1	0	0	1
Lake, Carnell, Pittsburgh	0	1	5	2	6
Langhorne, Reggie, Cleveland	3	0	0	0	0
Largent, Steve, Seattle	0	1	0	0	1
LeBel, Harper, Seattle	1	0	0	−25	0
Lee, Zeph, L.A. Raiders	1	0	0	0	0
Lipps, Louis, Pittsburgh	2	1	0	0	1
Little, David, Pittsburgh	0	1	1	0	2
Lloyd, Greg, Pittsburgh	1	0	3	0	3
Logan, Marc, Miami	1	2	0	−1	2
Long, Howie, L.A. Raiders	0	0	1	0	1
Lutz, Dave, Kansas City	0	1	0	0	1
Lyles, Lester, San Diego	1	0	1	0	1
Maas, Bill, Kansas City	0	0	2	4	2
Mack, Kevin, Cleveland	1	0	0	0	0
Mackey, Kyle, N.Y. Jets	1	0	0	0	0
Maggs, Don, Houston	0	3	0	0	3
Malone, Mark, N.Y. Jets	1	0	0	−4	0
Mandley, Pete, Kansas City	1	0	0	0	0
Manoa, Tim, Cleveland	2	0	0	0	0
Marino, Dan, Miami	7	0	0	−4	0
Marion, Fred, New England	0	0	1	0	1
Martin, Chris, Kansas City	0	0	3	0	3
Martin, Mike, Cincinnati	1	1	0	0	1
Martin, Sammy, New England	1	0	0	0	0
Matthews, Bruce, Houston	2	0	1	−29	1
Matthews, Clay, Cleveland	1	0	2	−2	2
Maxwell, Vernon, Seattle	0	0	1	0	1
McClendon, Skip, Cincinnati	0	0	1	0	1
McConkey, Phil, San Diego	1	0	0	0	0
McDowell, Bubba, Houston	1	0	1	0	1
McGrew, Larry, New England	0	0	1	0	1
McKeller, Keith, Buffalo	1	0	0	0	0
McMahon, Jim, San Diego	3	1	0	0	1
McMillan, Erik, N.Y. Jets	0	0	2	119	2
McNair, Todd, Kansas City	1	0	0	0	0
McNeil, Freeman, N.Y. Jets	1	0	0	0	0
Mecklenburg, Karl, Denver	0	0	4	23	4
Metcalf, Eric, Cleveland	5	0	0	0	0
Millard, Bryan, Seattle	0	1	0	4	1
Miller, Anthony, San Diego	1	0	0	0	0
Miller, Darrin, Seattle	0	1	0	0	1
Miller, Les, San Diego	0	0	1	0	1
Minnifield, Frank, Cleveland	0	0	1	0	1
Montgomery, Greg, Houston	1	0	0	0	0
Moon, Warren, Houston	11	6	0	−13	6
Mueller, Jamie, Buffalo	1	0	0	0	0
Mueller, Vance, L.A. Raiders	0	0	1	0	1
Munford, Marc, Denver	0	0	1	0	1
Munoz, Anthony, Cincinnati	0	2	0	0	2
Nattiel, Ricky, Denver	2	0	0	0	0
Nelson, Darrin, San Diego	1	0	0	0	0
Neubert, Keith, N.Y. Jets	2	1	0	0	1
Newsome, Harry, Pittsburgh	1	1	0	−13	1
O'Brien, Ken, N.Y. Jets	10	4	0	−4	4
Okoye, Christian, Kansas City	8	0	0	0	0
Oliphant, Mike, Cleveland	3	0	0	0	0
O'Neal, Leslie, San Diego	0	0	2	10	2
Paige, Stephone, Kansas City	3	1	0	0	1
Patterson, Elvis, San Diego	0	0	1	0	1
Pelluer, Steve, Kansas City	2	1	0	−8	1
Pennison, Jay, Houston	2	1	0	−17	1
Perry, Gerald, Denver	0	1	0	0	1
Perry, Michael Dean, Cleveland	0	0	2	0	2
Perryman, Bob, New England	2	1	0	0	1
Pike, Mark, Buffalo	0	0	1	0	1
Pinkett, Allen, Houston	1	0	0	0	0
Plummer, Bruce, Indianapolis	0	0	1	0	1
Plummer, Gary, San Diego	0	0	1	0	1
Porter, Kerry, L.A. Raiders	0	0	1	0	1
Prior, Mike, Indianapolis	0	0	1	10	1
Pruitt, James, Indianapolis	2	0	0	0	0
Ramsey, Tom, Indianapolis	1	1	0	0	1
Redden, Barry, Cleveland	2	0	0	0	0
Reed, Andre, Buffalo	4	0	0	0	0
Reich, Frank, Buffalo	2	0	0	0	0
Rembert, Johnny, New England	0	0	1	27	1
Reynolds, Ed, New England	0	0	1	0	1
Rice, Rodney, New England	0	0	1	0	1
Rienstra, John, Pittsburgh	0	1	0	0	1
Rison, Andre, Indianapolis	1	0	0	0	0
Robbins, Randy, Denver	0	0	1	0	1
Robinson, Eugene, Seattle	1	1	0	0	1
Robinson, Jerry, L.A. Raiders	1	0	0	0	0
Roby, Reggie, Miami	0	2	0	0	2
Rodriguez, Ruben, Seattle	0	1	0	0	1
Ross, Kevin, Kansas City	1	0	0	0	0
Rozier, Mike, Houston	4	0	0	0	0
Saleaumua, Dan, Kansas City	0	0	5	2	5

	Fum.	Own Rec.	Opp. Rec.	Yds.	Tot. Rec.
Saxon, James, Kansas City	2	0	0	0	0
Schroeder, Jay, L.A. Raiders	6	2	0	0	2
Schwedes, Scott, Miami	3	2	0	0	2
Seals, Leon, Buffalo	0	0	1	0	1
Sievers, Eric, New England	1	0	0	0	0
Slaughter, Webster, Cleveland	2	0	0	0	0
Smith, Al, Houston	0	0	1	0	1
Smith, Billy Ray, San Diego	0	0	2	23	2
Smith, Dennis, Denver	0	1	2	0	3
Smith, Kendal, Cincinnati	1	0	0	0	0
Smith, Leonard, Buffalo	0	0	2	14	2
Smith, Neil, Kansas City	0	0	2	3	2
Smith, Sammie, Miami	6	0	0	0	0
Smith, Steve, L.A. Raiders	2	1	0	0	1
Spencer, Tim, San Diego	3	0	0	0	0
Stephens, John, New England	3	1	0	0	1
Stone, Dwight, Pittsburgh	2	1	0	0	1
Stouffer, Kelly, Seattle	3	1	0	0	1
Stowe, Tyronne, Pittsburgh	0	0	2	3	2
Stradford, Troy, Miami	4	1	0	0	1
Strom, Rick, Pittsburgh	1	0	0	−18	0
Sutton, Mickey, Green Bay-Buffalo	2	0	1	0	1
Thomas, Derrick, Kansas City	0	0	1	0	1
Thomas, Eric, Cincinnati	0	0	1	0	1
Thomas, Robb, Kansas City	1	0	0	0	0
Thomas, Rodney, Miami	0	0	2	46	2
Thomas, Thurman, Buffalo	7	2	0	0	2
Thompson, Donnell, Indianapolis	0	0	2	0	2
Timpson, Michael, New England	1	0	0	0	0
Tolliver, Billy Joe, San Diego	4	1	0	−6	1
Townsell, JoJo, N.Y. Jets	4	3	0	0	3
Townsend, Andre, Denver	0	0	2	0	2
Townsend, Greg, L.A. Raiders	0	0	1	0	1
Trudeau, Jack, Indianapolis	10	7	0	−5	7
Tucker, Erroll, New England	2	2	0	0	2
Turk, Dan, L.A. Raiders	1	0	0	−8	0
Turner, T.J., Miami	0	0	2	0	2
Tyrrell, Tim, Pittsburgh	0	0	1	0	1
Uhlenhake, Jeff, Miami	1	0	0	−19	0
Usher, Darryl, San Diego	1	0	0	0	0
Verdin, Clarence, Indianapolis	1	2	0	−5	2
Vick, Roger, N.Y. Jets	4	1	0	0	1
Walker, Kevin, Cincinnati	0	0	1	0	1
Walker, Wayne, San Diego	2	0	0	0	0
Ware, Timmie, L.A. Raiders	1	0	0	0	0
Warner, Curt, Seattle	7	2	0	0	2
Washington, Lionel, L.A. Raiders	0	0	3	44	3
Washington, Marvin, N.Y. Jets	0	0	1	0	1
Weathers, Clarence, Indianapolis	1	1	0	2	1
White, Leon, Cincinnati	0	0	2	22	2
White, Lorenzo, Houston	2	1	0	0	1
Wilhelm, Erik, Cincinnati	2	1	0	0	1
Wilkerson, Bruce, L.A. Raiders	0	2	0	0	2
Williams, Brent, New England	0	0	2	2	2
Williams, Gerald, Pittsburgh	0	0	1	0	1
Williams, John L., Seattle	2	1	0	0	1
Williams, Warren, Pittsburgh	0	1	0	0	1
Wilson, Marc, New England	2	0	0	0	0
Winder, Sammy, Denver	1	0	0	0	0
Wise, Mike, L.A. Raiders	0	0	2	0	2
Wisniewski, Steve, L.A. Raiders	0	3	0	0	3
Woodruff, Dwayne, Pittsburgh	0	0	1	21	1
Woods, Ickey, Cincinnati	1	0	0	0	0
Woods, Tony, Seattle	1	0	0	0	0
Woodson, Rod, Pittsburgh	3	1	3	1	4
Worley, Tim, Pittsburgh	9	1	0	0	1
Worthen, Naz, Kansas City	1	1	0	0	1
Wright, Jeff, Buffalo	0	0	2	0	2
Yarno, George, Houston	0	1	0	0	1
Zander, Carl, Cincinnati	0	0	1	25	1
Zendejas, Tony, Houston	0	1	0	0	1

Yards include aborted plays, own recoveries, and opponents' recoveries.
Touchdowns: Erik McMillan, N.Y. Jets 2; Randy Dixon, Indianapolis; Nesby Glasgow, Seattle; Vencie Glenn, San Diego; Dave Grayson, Cleveland; Linden King, L.A. Raiders; Greg Kragen, Denver; Bill Maas, Kansas City; Clay Matthews, Cleveland; Karl Mecklenburg, Denver; Billy Ray Smith, San Diego; Neil Smith, Kansas City; Lionel Washington, L.A. Raiders; Leon White, Cincinnati; Dwayne Woodruff, Pittsburgh.
Includes both offensive and defensive recoveries for touchdowns.

NFC Fumbles—Individual

	Fum.	Own Rec.	Opp. Rec.	Yds.	Tot. Rec.
Aikman, Troy, Dallas	6	3	0	0	3
Albritton, Vince, Dallas	0	0	1	0	1
Alexander, David, Philadelphia	1	1	0	−4	1
Allen, Eric, Philadelphia	1	0	0	7	0
Anderson, Alfred, Minnesota	3	1	0	0	1
Anderson, Neal, Chicago	5	0	0	0	0
Anderson, Ottis, N.Y. Giants	2	0	0	0	0
Ankrom, Scott, Dallas	1	1	0	0	1
Armstrong, Trace, Chicago	0	0	1	0	1
Atkins, Gene, New Orleans	1	1	1	0	2
Baker, Tony, Phoenix	1	0	0	0	0
Ball, Jerry, Detroit	0	0	3	0	3
Banks, Carl, N.Y. Giants	0	0	1	0	1
Beckman, Brad, Atlanta	0	0	1	0	1
Bell, Greg, L.A. Rams	7	1	0	0	1
Bell, Todd, Philadelphia	0	0	1	0	1
Bethune, George, L.A. Rams	0	0	1	0	1
Blades, Bennie, Detroit	0	0	1	0	1
Bland, Carl, Green Bay	0	2	1	4	3
Bortz, Mark, Chicago	0	1	0	0	1
Bowles, Todd, Washington	0	0	1	0	1
Branch, Reggie, Washington	0	0	1	0	1
Brenner, Hoby, New Orleans	1	0	0	0	0
Brock, Stan, New Orleans	0	1	0	0	1
Brooks, Chet, San Francisco	0	0	1	0	1
Brooks, Kevin, Detroit	1	0	1	3	1
Brown, Jerome, Philadelphia	0	0	2	17	2
Brown, Lomas, Detroit	0	1	0	0	1
Brown, Richard, L.A. Rams	0	0	2	0	2
Brown, Ron, L.A. Rams	3	0	0	0	0
Buczkowski, Bob, Phoenix	0	0	1	0	1
Bush, Blair, Green Bay	0	1	0	0	1
Butler, Bobby, Atlanta	0	0	1	29	1
Byars, Keith, Philadelphia	4	4	0	6	4
Byner, Earnest, Washington	2	2	0	0	2
Carrier, Mark, Tampa Bay	1	0	0	0	0
Carter, Anthony, Minnesota	0	1	0	0	1
Carter, Cris, Philadelphia	1	1	0	0	1
Carthon, Maurice, N.Y. Giants	1	0	0	0	0
Casillas, Tony, Atlanta	0	0	3	0	3
Cavanaugh, Matt, Philadelphia	1	0	0	0	0
Clack, Darryl, Dallas	1	1	0	0	1
Clark, Gary, Washington	1	0	0	0	0
Clark, Jessie, Phoenix-Minnesota	2	2	0	0	2
Clark, Robert, Detroit	2	0	0	0	0
Clayton, Stan, Atlanta	0	1	0	0	1
Cocroft, Sherman, Tampa Bay	0	0	1	0	1
Coleman, Monte, Washington	1	0	1	0	1
Collins, Mark, N.Y. Giants	0	0	2	8	2
Cook, Toi, New Orleans	1	0	0	0	0
Covert, Jim, Chicago	0	1	0	0	1
Cox, Aaron, L.A. Rams	1	1	1	4	2
Craig, Roger, San Francisco	4	1	0	0	1
Crockett, Ray, Detroit	0	0	1	0	1
Cross, Howard, N.Y. Giants	1	0	0	0	0
Cunningham, Randall, Philadelphia	17	4	0	−6	4
Davis, Reuben, Tampa Bay	0	0	2	0	2
Del Rio, Jack, Dallas	0	0	2	57	2
Delpino, Robert, L.A. Rams	1	0	0	0	0
Dent, Richard, Chicago	0	0	2	0	2
Dill, Scott, Phoenix	0	1	0	0	1
Dixon, James, Dallas	4	1	0	0	1
Doleman, Chris, Minnesota	0	0	5	7	5
Dombrowski, Jim, New Orleans	0	1	0	0	1
Dorsey, Eric, N.Y. Giants	0	0	1	0	1
Douglass, Maurice, Chicago	0	0	1	0	1
Dozier, D.J., Minnesota	2	2	0	0	2
Drummond, Robert, Philadelphia	0	1	0	0	1
Dusbabek, Mark, Minnesota	0	0	2	0	2
Edwards, Anthony, Philadelphia	2	1	0	0	1
Elder, Donnie, Tampa Bay	2	1	0	0	1
Evans, Byron, Philadelphia	0	0	3	21	3
Everett, Jim, L.A. Rams	4	4	0	−1	4
Fagan, Kevin, San Francisco	0	0	2	0	2
Faryniarz, Brett, L.A. Rams	0	0	2	0	2
Fenney, Rick, Minnesota	0	0	1	0	1
Ferguson, Joe, Tampa Bay	1	0	0	0	0
Ferrell, Earl, Phoenix	2	0	0	0	0
Flagler, Terrence, San Francisco	5	1	0	0	1
Fontenot, Herman, Green Bay	0	1	1	0	2
Fontenot, Jerry, Chicago	0	0	1	0	1
Forde, Brian, New Orleans	0	0	1	0	1
Fourcade, John, New Orleans	2	2	0	0	2
Frazier, Paul, New Orleans	1	0	0	0	0
Frizzell, William, Philadelphia	0	0	3	12	3
Fulhage, Scott, Atlanta	1	1	0	−20	1
Fullwood, Brent, Green Bay	6	1	0	0	1
Futrell, Bobby, Tampa Bay	1	1	0	0	1
Gagliano, Bob, Detroit	3	2	0	−1	2
Gary, Cleveland, L.A. Rams	1	0	0	0	0
Gayle, Shaun, Chicago	0	0	2	11	2

	Fum.	Own Rec.	Opp. Rec.	Yds.	Tot. Rec.
Geathers, James, New Orleans	0	0	5	0	5
Gentry, Dennis, Chicago	1	0	0	0	0
Gibson, Antonio, New Orleans	1	0	2	0	2
Gibson, Dennis, Detroit	0	0	3	−4	3
Giles, Jimmie, Philadelphia	0	0	1	0	1
Goff, Robert, Tampa Bay	0	0	1	0	1
Golic, Mike, Philadelphia	0	0	0	8	0
Goss, Antonio, San Francisco	0	0	1	0	1
Grant, Darryl, Washington	0	0	1	0	1
Gray, Jerry, L.A. Rams	0	0	1	0	1
Green, Darrell, Washington	1	1	0	0	1
Green, Gaston, L.A. Rams	1	0	0	0	0
Green, Roy, Phoenix	2	0	0	0	0
Green, Tim, Atlanta	1	1	1	5	2
Greene, Kevin, L.A. Rams	0	0	2	0	2
Greene, Tiger, Green Bay	1	0	1	0	1
Greer, Terry, San Francisco	1	0	0	0	0
Griffin, Don, San Francisco	0	0	1	0	1
Guyton, Myron, N.Y. Giants	0	0	3	4	3
Haddix, Michael, Green Bay	2	0	0	0	0
Hager, Britt, Philadelphia	0	0	2	9	2
Haley, Charles, San Francisco	0	0	1	3	1
Hall, Ron, Tampa Bay	0	1	0	0	1
Hamilton, Harry, Tampa Bay	0	0	1	0	1
Harbaugh, Jim, Chicago	2	0	0	0	0
Harbour, Dave, Washington	0	0	1	0	1
Harris, Al, Philadelphia	0	0	2	0	2
Harris, Rod, New Orleans	4	1	0	0	1
Harris, Tim, Green Bay	0	0	3	0	3
Hebert, Bobby, New Orleans	2	0	0	0	0
Heller, Ron, Atlanta	1	0	0	0	0
Helton, Barry, San Francisco	1	1	0	−13	1
Henderson, Keith, San Francisco	1	0	1	0	1
Hendrix, Manny, Dallas	0	0	1	0	1
Henley, Darryl, L.A. Rams	1	1	0	0	1
Herrmann, Mark, L.A. Rams	2	0	0	−2	0
Heyward, Craig, New Orleans	2	1	0	0	1
Higgs, Mark, Philadelphia	3	1	0	0	1
Hilgenberg, Joel, New Orleans	1	1	0	−37	1
Hill, Bruce, Tampa Bay	2	0	0	0	0
Hill, Eric, Phoenix	0	0	1	0	1
Hill, Lonzell, New Orleans	1	0	0	0	0
Hilliard, Dalton, New Orleans	7	2	0	0	2
Hogeboom, Gary, Phoenix	5	1	0	−4	1
Holland, Johnny, Green Bay	0	0	3	0	3
Holohan, Pete, L.A. Rams	1	0	0	0	0
Holt, Pierce, San Francisco	0	0	1	0	1
Hopkins, Wes, Philadelphia	0	0	3	77	3
Hostetler, Jeff, N.Y. Giants	2	1	0	0	1
Howard, Erik, N.Y. Giants	0	0	1	0	1
Howard, Joe, Washington	2	0	0	0	0
Howard, William, Tampa Bay	2	2	0	4	2
Humphries, Stan, Washington	1	1	0	0	1
Ingram, Mark, N.Y. Giants	2	2	0	0	2
Irvin, Michael, Dallas	0	0	1	0	1
Jackson, Greg, N.Y. Giants	0	0	1	0	1
Jackson, Johnny, San Francisco	0	0	1	0	1
Jackson, Keith, Philadelphia	1	0	0	0	0
Jackson, Vestee, Chicago	0	0	1	0	1
Jarvis, Curt, Tampa Bay	0	0	1	0	1
Jeffcoat, Jim, Dallas	0	0	3	77	3
Jiles, Dwayne, N.Y. Giants	0	0	1	0	1
Johnson, Pepper, N.Y. Giants	0	0	1	0	1
Johnson, Richard, Detroit	3	0	0	0	0
Johnson, Ron, Philadelphia	2	0	0	0	0
Johnson, Vaughan, New Orleans	0	0	1	−1	1
Johnston, Daryl, Dallas	3	0	0	0	0
Jones, Ernie, Phoenix	3	1	0	0	1
Jones, Hassan, Minnesota	2	0	0	0	0
Jones, Victor, Detroit	0	0	2	0	2
Jordan, Brian, Atlanta	1	1	1	0	2
Jordan, Steve, Minnesota	1	0	0	0	0
Jordan, Tony, Phoenix	4	0	0	0	0
Kelm, Larry, L.A. Rams	0	0	1	0	1
Kemp, Perry, Green Bay	3	1	0	0	1
Kinard, Terry, N.Y. Giants	0	0	1	4	1
Knight, Shawn, Phoenix	0	0	1	0	1
Kozlowski, Glen, Chicago	1	0	0	0	0
Kramer, Tommy, Minnesota	1	0	0	−7	0
Lachey, Jim, Washington	0	0	1	0	1
Lang, Gene, Atlanta	1	1	0	0	1
Lewis, Leo, Minnesota	4	2	0	0	2
Little, David, Philadelphia	1	0	0	−14	0
Lockhart, Eugene, Dallas	0	0	2	40	2
Lowdermilk, Kirk, Minnesota	0	1	0	0	1
Majkowski, Don, Green Bay	15	6	0	−13	6
Mann, Charles, Washington	0	0	2	0	2
Manuel, Lionel, N.Y. Giants	0	1	0	0	1

	Fum.	Own Rec.	Opp. Rec.	Yds.	Tot. Rec.
Manusky, Greg, Washington	0	0	1	0	1
Marshall, Wilber, Washington	0	0	2	6	2
Martin, Eric, New Orleans	1	1	0	0	1
Martin, Wayne, New Orleans	0	0	2	0	2
Marve, Eugene, Tampa Bay	0	0	1	0	1
Maxie, Brett, New Orleans	0	0	1	0	1
May, Mark, Washington	0	2	0	0	2
Mayhew, Martin, Washington	1	0	0	0	0
McDonald, Tim, Phoenix	0	0	1	1	1
McGee, Buford, L.A. Rams	2	0	0	0	0
McGruder, Michael, Green Bay	0	1	0	0	1
McKinnon, Dennis, Chicago	3	1	0	0	1
McMichael, Steve, Chicago	0	0	1	0	1
Meggett, Dave, N.Y. Giants	8	3	0	0	3
Merriweather, Mike, Minnesota	0	0	1	0	1
Millard, Keith, Minnesota	0	0	1	31	1
Millen, Hugh, Atlanta	2	1	0	−11	1
Millen, Matt, San Francisco	0	0	3	2	3
Miller, Chris, Atlanta	13	5	0	−3	5
Miller, John, Detroit	0	0	1	0	1
Mills, Sam, New Orleans	0	0	1	0	1
Mojsiejenko, Ralf, Washington	0	0	1	0	1
Monk, Art, Washington	2	0	0	0	0
Montana, Joe, San Francisco	9	3	0	−3	3
Moore, Eric, N.Y. Giants	0	2	1	0	3
Moore, Robert, Atlanta	0	0	1	0	1
Moran, Rich, Green Bay	0	1	0	0	1
Morris, Jamie, Washington	3	0	0	0	0
Morris, Ron, Chicago	1	0	0	0	0
Morse, Bobby, New Orleans	0	1	0	0	1
Mowatt, Zeke, N.Y. Giants	1	1	0	0	1
Murphy, Kevin, Tampa Bay	0	0	2	0	2
Murphy, Mark, Green Bay	0	0	1	0	1
Muster, Brad, Chicago	2	0	0	0	0
Najarian, Peter, Tampa Bay	0	0	1	0	1
Nelson, Bob, Green Bay	0	0	1	0	1
Newsome, Vince, L.A. Rams	0	0	1	0	1
Newton, Tim, Minnesota	0	0	1	5	1
Noble, Brian, Green Bay	0	0	1	0	1
Noga, Al, Minnesota	0	0	1	0	1
Novacek, Jay, Phoenix	0	0	1	0	1
Nunn, Freddie Joe, Phoenix	0	0	1	0	1
Oates, Bart, N.Y. Giants	1	0	0	0	0
Paige, Tony, Detroit	1	1	0	0	1
Painter, Carl, Detroit	1	0	0	0	0
Palmer, Paul, Dallas	3	0	0	0	0
Pankey, Irv, L.A. Rams	0	1	0	0	1
Paris, Bubba, San Francisco	0	1	0	0	1
Paterra, Greg, Atlanta	2	0	0	0	0
Peebles, Danny, Tampa Bay	1	1	0	1	1
Peete, Rodney, Detroit	9	3	0	0	3
Perry, William, Chicago	0	0	2	5	2
Phillips, Jason, Detroit	1	1	0	0	1
Piel, Mike, L.A. Rams	0	1	0	0	1
Pitts, Mike, Philadelphia	0	0	2	0	2
Query, Jeff, Green Bay	1	0	1	0	1
Rade, John, Atlanta	1	0	2	14	2
Rathman, Tom, San Francisco	1	2	0	12	2
Reed, Doug, L.A. Rams	0	0	1	0	1
Reeves, Ken, Philadelphia	0	1	0	0	1
Reeves, Walter, Phoenix	0	0	1	2	1
Reichenbach, Mike, Philadelphia	0	0	1	0	1
Reynolds, Ricky, Tampa Bay	0	0	2	0	2
Rice, Allen, Minnesota	0	1	0	0	1
Riesenberg, Doug, N.Y. Giants	0	2	0	0	2
Riggs, Gerald, Washington	3	0	0	0	0
Rivera, Ron, Chicago	0	0	1	0	1
Roberts, Larry, San Francisco	0	0	1	0	1
Robinson, Mark, Tampa Bay	0	0	3	0	3
Rocker, Tracy, Washington	0	0	1	0	1
Rolling, Henry, Tampa Bay	0	0	1	0	1
Romanowski, Bill, San Francisco	1	0	2	0	2
Roper, John, Chicago	1	0	0	0	0
Rosenbach, Timm, Phoenix	2	1	0	0	1
Rouson, Lee, N.Y. Giants	0	1	0	0	1
Ruettgers, Ken, Green Bay	0	2	0	0	2
Runager, Max, Philadelphia	0	1	0	0	1
Rutland, Reggie, Minnesota	0	0	2	27	2
Ruzek, Roger, Philadelphia	0	1	0	0	1
Rypien, Mark, Washington	14	2	0	0	2
Sanders, Barry, Detroit	10	0	0	0	0
Sanders, Deion, Atlanta	2	1	0	0	1
Sanders, Thomas, Chicago	2	0	0	0	0
Sargent, Broderick, Dallas	1	0	0	0	0
Schlereth, Mark, Washington	0	1	0	0	1
Settle, John, Atlanta	1	1	0	0	1
Sharpe, Luis, Phoenix	0	1	0	3	1
Sharpe, Sterling, Green Bay	1	1	0	5	1

	Fum.	Own Rec.	Opp. Rec.	Yds.	Tot. Rec.
Shepard, Derrick, New Orleans-Dallas	2	0	0	0	0
Sherman, Heath, Philadelphia	4	3	0	0	3
Sikahema, Vai, Phoenix	2	3	0	0	3
Simms, Phil, N.Y. Giants	9	3	0	-1	3
Smith, Don, Tampa Bay	1	0	0	0	0
Smith, Lance, Phoenix	0	0	1	0	1
Spielman, Chris, Detroit	0	0	2	31	2
Stamps, Sylvester, Tampa Bay	2	1	1	0	2
Stanley, Walter, Detroit	5	1	0	0	1
Stephen, Scott, Green Bay	0	0	1	76	1
Stepnoski, Mark, Dallas	0	3	0	0	3
Stewart, Michael, L.A. Rams	1	0	3	4	3
Stokes, Fred, Washington	0	1	1	6	2
Streeter, George, Chicago	0	1	0	0	1
Strickland, Fred, L.A. Rams	0	1	0	-3	1
Studwell, Scott, Minnesota	0	0	2	0	2
Suhey, Matt, Chicago	1	0	0	0	0
Swilling, Pat, New Orleans	0	0	1	0	1
Sydney, Harry, San Francisco	1	0	0	0	0
Tate, Lars, Tampa Bay	2	0	0	0	0
Tautalatasi, Junior, Dallas	3	2	0	1	2
Taylor, Jay, Phoenix	0	0	1	1	1
Taylor, John, San Francisco	3	0	0	0	0
Taylor, Terry, Detroit	0	0	1	35	1
Testaverde, Vinny, Tampa Bay	4	2	0	0	2
Thomas, Ben, Atlanta	0	0	1	9	1
Thomas, Henry, Minnesota	0	0	3	37	3
Thornton, James, Chicago	2	0	0	0	0
Tice, John, New Orleans	0	1	0	0	1
Tillman, Lewis, N.Y. Giants	1	0	0	0	0
Tillman, Spencer, San Francisco	0	1	0	0	1
Tomczak, Mike, Chicago	2	0	0	0	0
Toney, Anthony, Philadelphia	4	3	0	-3	3
Tuggle, Jessie, Atlanta	0	1	0	0	1
Tupa, Tom, Phoenix	2	1	0	-6	1
Turner, Floyd, New Orleans	1	2	1	0	3
Turner, Marcus, Phoenix	0	0	1	0	1
Turner, Odessa, N.Y. Giants	1	0	0	0	0
Van Horne, Keith, Chicago	0	1	0	0	1
Vaughn, Clarence, Washington	0	0	1	0	1
Wahler, Jim, Phoenix	0	0	1	0	1
Walker, Herschel, Dallas-Minnesota	7	0	0	0	0
Walls, Wesley, San Francisco	1	1	0	0	1
Walsh, Steve, Dallas	3	2	0	-14	2
Walter, Mike, San Francisco	0	0	1	0	1
Walton, Alvin, Washington	1	1	0	0	1
Warren, Don, Washington	0	1	0	0	1
Warren, Frank, New Orleans	0	0	1	0	1
Washington, James, L.A. Rams	0	1	0	0	1
Washington, John, N.Y. Giants	0	0	2	0	2
Waters, Andre, Philadelphia	0	0	3	21	3
Waymer, Dave, New Orleans	0	0	1	0	1
Weddington, Mike, Green Bay	0	0	1	0	1
Weston, Rhondy, Tampa Bay	0	0	1	0	1
White, Bob, Dallas	1	0	0	0	0
White, Reggie, Philadelphia	0	0	1	10	1
White, William, Detroit	0	1	0	20	1
Wilcher, Mike, L.A. Rams	1	0	0	0	0
Wilder, James, Tampa Bay	2	1	0	0	1
Wilkins, Gary, Atlanta	0	1	0	0	1
Williams, Henry, Philadelphia	1	2	1	0	3
Williams, Jimmy, Detroit	0	0	1	0	1
Williams, Perry, N.Y. Giants	1	0	0	0	0
Wilson, Mike, San Francisco	2	1	0	0	1
Wilson, Wade, Minnesota	5	2	0	-7	2
Winslow, George, New Orleans	1	0	0	0	0
Woods, Jerry, Detroit	1	0	0	0	0
Woodside, Keith, Green Bay	4	1	0	0	1
Workman, Vince, Green Bay	1	1	0	0	1
Young, Steve, San Francisco	2	1	0	0	1
Zackery, Tony, Atlanta	0	0	1	0	1

Yards include aborted plays, own recoveries, and opponents' recoveries.
Touchdowns: Carl Bland, Green Bay; Bobby Butler, Atlanta; Jack Del Rio, Dallas; Charles Haley, San Francisco; Jim Jeffcoat, Dallas; Eugene Lockhart, Dallas; Keith Millard, Minnesota; Tim Newton, Minnesota; Reggie Rutland, Minnesota; Sterling Sharpe, Green Bay, Henry Thomas, Minnesota; Andre Waters, Philadelphia; William White, Detroit.
Includes both offensive and defensive recoveries for touchdowns.

Sacks

Individual Champions
NFC: 21.0—Chris Doleman, Minnesota
AFC: 14.0—Lee Williams, San Diego

Most Sacks, Game
NFC: 4.0—Tim Harris, Green Bay vs. Atlanta, October 1
4.0—Keith Millard, Minnesota vs. Green Bay, October 15
4.0—Pierce Holt, San Francisco vs. N.Y. Giants, November 27
4.0—Chris Doleman, Minnesota vs. Cincinnati, December 25
AFC: 3.5—Greg Townsend, L.A. Raiders vs. Washington, October 29
3.5—Leslie O'Neal, San Diego vs. Philadelphia, November 5

Team Champions
NFC: 71—Minnesota
AFC: 48—San Diego

AFC Sacks—Team

	Sacks	Yards
San Diego	48	360
Denver	47	374
Indianapolis	46	384
Cleveland	45	359
Miami	39	268
Buffalo	38	289
Kansas City	36	294
Houston	36	277
L.A. Raiders	35	248
Cincinnati	33	248
Seattle	32	235
New England	31	239
Pittsburgh	31	180
N.Y. Jets	28	177
AFC Total	525	3,932
AFC Average	37.5	280.9

NFC Sacks—Team

	Sacks	Yards
Minnesota	71	502
Philadelphia	62	424
New Orleans	47	362
San Francisco	43	333
L.A. Rams	42	278
Washington	40	304
Detroit	40	277
N.Y. Giants	39	302
Chicago	39	247
Green Bay	34	214
Tampa Bay	33	222
Atlanta	31	183
Phoenix	30	219
Dallas	29	183
NFC Total	580	4,050
NFC Average	41.4	289.3
League Total	1,105	7,982
League Average	39.5	285.1

NFL Top 10 Individual Leaders in Sacks

	Total		Total
Doleman, Chris, Minnesota	21.0	Simmons, Clyde, Philadelphia	15.5
Harris, Tim, Green Bay	19.5	Taylor, Lawrence, N.Y. Giants	15.0
Millard, Keith, Minnesota	18.0	Williams, Lee, San Diego	14.0
Greene, Kevin, L.A. Rams	16.5	Smith, Bruce, Buffalo	13.0
Swilling, Pat, New Orleans	16.5	O'Neal, Leslie, San Diego	12.5

AFC Sacks—Individual

Name	
Williams, Lee, San Diego	14.0
Smith, Bruce, Buffalo	13.0
O'Neal, Leslie, San Diego	12.5
Fletcher, Simon, Denver	12.0
Porter, Rufus, Seattle	10.5
Townsend, Greg, L.A. Raiders	10.5
Cross, Jeff, Miami	10.0
Grossman, Burt, San Diego	10.0
Hand, Jon, Indianapolis	10.0
Thomas, Derrick, Kansas City	10.0
Holmes, Ron, Denver	9.0
Childress, Ray, Houston	8.5
Johnson, Ezra, Indianapolis	8.5
Bickett, Duane, Indianapolis	8.0
Nash, Joe, Seattle	8.0
Williams, Brent, New England	8.0
Baker, Al, Cleveland	7.5
Green, Hugh, Miami	7.5
Mecklenburg, Karl, Denver	7.5
Byrd, Dennis, N.Y. Jets	7.0
Jeter, Gary, New England	7.0
Lloyd, Greg, Pittsburgh	7.0
Perry, Michael Dean, Cleveland	7.0
Thompson, Donnell, Indianapolis	7.0
Fuller, William, Houston	6.5
Griffin, Leonard, Kansas City	6.5
Hairston, Carl, Cleveland	6.5
Smith, Neil, Kansas City	6.5
Willis, Keith, Pittsburgh	6.5
Buck, Jason, Cincinnati	6.0
Jones, Sean, Houston	6.0
Talley, Darryl, Buffalo	6.0
Bennett, Cornelius, Buffalo	5.5
Carreker, Alphonso, Denver	5.5
Davis, Scott, L.A. Raiders	5.5
Long, Howie, L.A. Raiders	5.0
Sochia, Brian, Miami	5.0
Johnson, Tim, Pittsburgh	4.5
Lageman, Jeff, N.Y. Jets	4.5
McGrew, Larry, New England	4.5
Skow, Jim, Cincinnati	4.5
Banks, Robert, Cleveland	4.0
Blaylock, Anthony, Cleveland	4.0
Brown, Vincent, New England	4.0
Martin, Chris, Kansas City	4.0
Matthews, Clay, Cleveland	4.0
Meads, Johnny, Houston	4.0
Nichols, Gerald, N.Y. Jets	4.0
Seals, Leon, Buffalo	4.0
Bryant, Jeff, Seattle	3.5
Golic, Bob, L.A. Raiders	3.5
Williams, Reggie, Cincinnati	3.5
Wise, Mike, L.A. Raiders	3.5
Brown, Steve, Houston	3.0
Green, Jacob, Seattle	3.0
Krumrie, Tim, Cincinnati	3.0
Pickel, Bill, L.A. Raiders	3.0
Powers, Warren, Denver	3.0
Sims, Kenneth, New England	3.0
Stewart, Andrew, Cleveland	3.0
Williams, Gerald, Pittsburgh	3.0
Williams, Jerrol, Pittsburgh	3.0
Woods, Tony, Seattle	3.0
Wright, Jeff, Buffalo	3.0
Bussey, Barney, Cincinnati	2.5
Fairs, Eric, Houston	2.5
Hinkle, George, San Diego	2.5
Miller, Les, San Diego	2.5
Rembert, Johnny, New England	2.5
Smith, Billy Ray, San Diego	2.5
Tuatagaloa, Natu, Cincinnati	2.5
Benson, Thomas, L.A. Raiders	2.0
Bosa, John, Miami	2.0
Clifton, Kyle, N.Y. Jets	2.0
Frase, Paul, N.Y. Jets	2.0
Gash, Thane, Cleveland	2.0
Gibson, Tom, Cleveland	2.0
Hart, Roy, Seattle	2.0
Herrod, Jeff, Indianapolis	2.0
Jones, Aaron, Pittsburgh	2.0
Kragen, Greg, Denver	2.0
Kumerow, Eric, Miami	2.0
Little, David, Pittsburgh	2.0
Lucas, Tim, Denver	2.0
Lyles, Robert, Houston	2.0
McDonald, Quintus, Indianapolis	2.0
McMillan, Erik, N.Y. Jets	2.0
Saleaumua, Dan, Kansas City	2.0
Stallworth, Ron, N.Y. Jets	2.0
Thomas, Eric, Cincinnati	2.0
Townsend, Andre, Denver	2.0
White, Leon, Cincinnati	2.0
Young, Fredd, Indianapolis	2.0
Hammerstein, Mike, Cincinnati	1.5
McClendon, Skip, Indianapolis	1.5
Montgomery, Glenn, Houston	1.5
Offerdahl, John, Miami	1.5
Radecic, Scott, Buffalo	1.5
Washington, Marvin, N.Y. Jets	1.5
Zander, Carl, Cincinnati	1.5
Ahrens, Dave, Miami	1.0
Alston, O'Brien, Indianapolis	1.0
Armstrong, Harvey, Indianapolis	1.0
Banks, Chip, Indianapolis	1.0
Bayless, Martin, San Diego	1.0
Bell, Mike, Kansas City	1.0
Brooks, Michael, Denver	1.0
Burroughs, Derrick, Buffalo	1.0
Charlton, Clifford, Cleveland	1.0
Cherry, Deron, Kansas City	1.0
Cline, Jackie, Miami	1.0
Cofield, Tim, Buffalo	1.0
Conlan, Shane, Buffalo	1.0
Cooper, Louis, Kansas City	1.0
Dennison, Rick, Denver	1.0
Frye, David, Miami	1.0
Glenn, Vencie, San Diego	1.0
Goad, Tim, New England	1.0
Gordon, Alex, N.Y. Jets	1.0
Graf, Rick, Miami	1.0
Grayson, Dave, Cleveland	1.0
Harper, Mark, Cleveland	1.0
Hobley, Liffort, Miami	1.0
Hunter, Patrick, Seattle	1.0
Johnson, Mike, Cleveland	1.0
Junior, E.J., Miami	1.0
Kelly, Joe, Cincinnati	1.0
Krauss, Barry, Miami	1.0
Lake, Carnell, Pittsburgh	1.0
Lankford, Paul, Miami	1.0
Larson, Kurt, Indianapolis	1.0
Lewis, Albert, Kansas City	1.0
Lyles, Lester, San Diego	1.0
Lyons, Marty, N.Y. Jets	1.0
McDaniel, Terry, L.A. Raiders	1.0
McDowell, Bubba, Houston	1.0
Mitz, Alonzo, Seattle	1.0
Munford, Marc, Denver	1.0
Nickerson, Hardy, Pittsburgh	1.0
Odomes, Nate, Buffalo	1.0
Olsavsky, Jerry, Pittsburgh	1.0
Pearson, Jayice, Kansas City	1.0
Phillips, Joe, San Diego	1.0
Pike, Chris, Cleveland	1.0
Plummer, Bruce, Indianapolis	1.0
Smerlas, Fred, Buffalo	1.0
Smith, Doug, Houston	1.0
Thomas, Rodney, Miami	1.0
Wilcots, Solomon, Cincinnati	1.0
Williams, Jarvis, Miami	1.0
Clancy, Sam, Indianapolis	0.5
Glenn, Kerry, N.Y. Jets	0.5
Grant, David, Cincinnati	0.5
Meisner, Greg, Kansas City	0.5
Mersereau, Scott, N.Y. Jets	0.5
Mraz, Mark, L.A. Raiders	0.5
Petry, Stan, Kansas City	0.5
Robinson, Jerry, L.A. Raiders	0.5

NFC Sacks—Individual

Name	
Doleman, Chris, Minnesota	21.0
Harris, Tim, Green Bay	19.5
Millard, Keith, Minnesota	18.0
Greene, Kevin, L.A. Rams	16.5
Swilling, Pat, New Orleans	16.5
Simmons, Clyde, Philadelphia	15.5
Taylor, Lawrence, N.Y. Giants	15.0
Jeffcoat, Jim, Dallas	11.5
Noga, Al, Minnesota	11.5
White, Reggie, Philadelphia	11.0
Brown, Jerome, Philadelphia	10.5
Haley, Charles, San Francisco	10.5
Holt, Pierce, San Francisco	10.5
Mann, Charles, Washington	10.0
Marshall, Leonard, N.Y. Giants	9.5
Warren, Frank, New Orleans	9.5
Ball, Jerry, Detroit	9.0
Cofer, Mike, Detroit	9.0
Cotton, Marcus, Atlanta	9.0
Dent, Richard, Chicago	9.0
Manley, Dexter, Washington	9.0
Thomas, Henry, Minnesota	9.0
Jackson, Rickey, New Orleans	7.5
McMichael, Steve, Chicago	7.5
Fagan, Kevin, San Francisco	7.0
Harvey, Ken, Phoenix	7.0
Pitts, Mike, Philadelphia	7.0
Bruce, Aundray, Atlanta	6.0
Murphy, Kevin, Tampa Bay	6.0
Galloway, David, Phoenix	5.5
Howard, Erik, N.Y. Giants	5.5
Moss, Winston, Tampa Bay	5.5
Williams, Eric, Detroit	5.5
Armstrong, Trace, Chicago	5.0
Green, Tim, Atlanta	5.0
Nunn, Freddie Joe, Phoenix	5.0
Spielman, Chris, Detroit	5.0
Wilcher, Mike, L.A. Rams	5.0
Joyner, Seth, Philadelphia	4.5
Roper, John, Chicago	4.5
Stubbs, Danny, San Francisco	4.5
Banks, Carl, N.Y. Giants	4.0
Coleman, Monte, Washington	4.0
Goff, Robert, Tampa Bay	4.0
Marshall, Wilber, Washington	4.0
Perry, William, Chicago	4.0
Piel, Mike, L.A. Rams	4.0
Wilks, Jim, New Orleans	4.0
Williams, Jimmy, Detroit	4.0
Caldwell, Ravin, Washington	3.5
Grant, Darryl, Washington	3.5
Hamel, Dean, Dallas	3.5
Hopkins, Wes, Philadelphia	3.5
Merriweather, Mike, Minnesota	3.5
Roberts, Larry, San Francisco	3.5
Saddler, Rod, Phoenix	3.5
Berry, Ray, Minnesota	3.0
Broughton, Willie, Dallas	3.0
Brown, Robert, Green Bay	3.0
Chapura, Dick, Chicago	3.0
Davis, Reuben, Tampa Bay	3.0
Faryniarz, Brett, L.A. Rams	3.0
Golic, Mike, Philadelphia	3.0
Jarvis, Curt, Tampa Bay	3.0
Kugler, Pete, San Francisco	3.0
Mills, Sam, New Orleans	3.0
Reed, Doug, L.A. Rams	3.0
Stokes, Fred, Washington	3.0
Wright, Alvin, L.A. Rams	3.0
Harris, Al, Philadelphia	2.5
Martin, Wayne, New Orleans	2.5
Norton, Ken, Dallas	2.5
Robinson, Mark, Tampa Bay	2.5
Bell, Anthony, Phoenix	2.0
Bethune, George, L.A. Rams	2.0
Brooks, Kevin, Detroit	2.0
Casillas, Tony, Atlanta	2.0
Clarke, Ken, Minnesota	2.0
Clasby, Bob, Phoenix	2.0
Evans, Byron, Philadelphia	2.0
Gann, Mike, Atlanta	2.0
Greene, Tiger, Green Bay	2.0
Hampton, Dan, Chicago	2.0
Jamison, George, Detroit	2.0
Koch, Markus, Washington	2.0
Lockhart, Eugene, Dallas	2.0
Noble, Brian, Green Bay	2.0
Rivera, Ron, Chicago	2.0
Smith, Brian, L.A. Rams	2.0
Strickland, Fred, L.A. Rams	2.0
Thomas, Broderick, Tampa Bay	2.0
Tolbert, Tony, Dallas	2.0
Weston, Rhondy, Tampa Bay	2.0
Winter, Blaise, Green Bay	2.0
Frizzell, William, Philadelphia	1.5
Bowles, Todd, Washington	1.0
Brooks, Chet, San Francisco	1.0
Browner, Joey, Minnesota	1.0
Bryan, Rick, Atlanta	1.0
Cannon, John, Tampa Bay	1.0
Case, Scott, Atlanta	1.0
Collins, Mark, N.Y. Giants	1.0
Cook, Toi, New Orleans	1.0
Cooks, Johnie, N.Y. Giants	1.0
Cox, Greg, N.Y. Giants	1.0
Dimry, Charles, Atlanta	1.0
Geathers, James, New Orleans	1.0
Hall, Mark, Green Bay	1.0
Hill, Eric, Phoenix	1.0
Horton, Ray, Dallas	1.0
Johnson, Pepper, N.Y. Giants	1.0
Johnson, Vaughan, New Orleans	1.0
Jones, Ed, Dallas	1.0
Lee, Shawn, Tampa Bay	1.0
Mack, Cedric, Phoenix	1.0
Mack, Milton, New Orleans	1.0
McNorton, Bruce, Detroit	1.0
Miller, Shawn, L.A. Rams	1.0
Murphy, Mark, Green Bay	1.0
Nelson, Bob, Green Bay	1.0
Noonan, Danny, Dallas	1.0
Pete, Lawrence, Detroit	1.0
Randle, Ervin, Tampa Bay	1.0
Reasons, Gary, N.Y. Giants	1.0
Reid, Michael, Atlanta	1.0
Romanowski, Bill, San Francisco	1.0
Seals, Ray, Tampa Bay	1.0
Singletary, Mike, Chicago	1.0
Smith, Sean, Tampa Bay	1.0
Stephen, Scott, Green Bay	1.0
Strauthers, Tom, Minnesota	1.0
Studwell, Scott, Minnesota	1.0
Taylor, Malcolm, Atlanta	1.0
Thomas, Ben, Atlanta	1.0
Tuggle, Jessie, Atlanta	1.0
Wahler, Jim, Phoenix	1.0
Walter, Mike, San Francisco	1.0
Waters, Andre, Philadelphia	1.0
Weddington, Mike, Green Bay	1.0
White, William, Detroit	1.0
Wilson, Karl, Phoenix	1.0
Woods, Tony, Chicago	1.0
Zordich, Michael, Phoenix	1.0
Griffin, James, Detroit	0.5
Hendrix, Manny, Dallas	0.5
Jerue, Mark, L.A. Rams	0.5
Patterson, Shawn, Green Bay	0.5

1989 NFL Paid Attendance Breakdown

	Games	Attendance	Average
AFC Preseason	7	378,397	54,057
NFC Preseason	8	394,699	49,337
AFC-NFC Preseason, Interconference	44	2,315,009	52,614
NFL Preseason Total	**59**	**3,088,105**	**52,341**
AFC Regular Season	86	5,369,302	62,434
NFC Regular Season	86	5,083,185	59,107
AFC-NFC Regular Season, Interconference	52	3,173,175	61,023
NFL Regular Season Total	**224**	**13,625,662**	**60,829**
AFC First-Round Playoff	1		
(Pittsburgh-Houston)		59,406	
AFC Divisional Playoffs	2		
(Buffalo-Cleveland)		78,921	
(Pittsburgh-Denver)		75,477	
AFC Championship Game	1		
(Cleveland-Denver)		76,046	
NFC First-Round Playoff	1		
(Los Angeles Rams-Philadelphia)		65,479	
NFC Divisional Playoffs	2		
(Los Angeles Rams-New York Giants)		76,526	
(Minnesota-San Francisco)		64,918	
NFC Championship Game	1		
(Los Angeles Rams-San Francisco)		65,634	
Super Bowl XXIV at New Orleans, Louisiana	1		
(San Francisco-Denver)		72,919	
AFC-NFC Pro Bowl at Honolulu, Hawaii	1	50,445	
NFL Postseason Total	**10**	**685,771**	**68,577**
NFL All Games	**293**	**17,399,538**	**59,384**

One Million Plus Club

During the 1989 season, nine teams drew a combined home and away paid attendance of over one million. The Denver Broncos drew an NFL-leading 1,152,315 fans in 1989.

Team	Total Paid Home Attendance	Total Paid Visiting Attendance	Total Paid Attendance
Denver	598,930	553,385	1,152,315
Cleveland	625,240	503,743	1,128,983
N.Y. Jets	603,520	501,240	1,104,760
Buffalo	626,399	474,551	1,100,950
N.Y. Giants	607,611	482,901	1,090,512
Chicago	528,225	522,133	1,050,358
San Francisco	511,854	514,136	1,025,990
Philadelphia	525,485	488,249	1,013,734
Minnesota	491,559	516,499	1,008,058

INSIDE THE NUMBERS

Comparison of Joe Montana's Career Statistics With Hall of Fame Quarterbacks Whose Careers Ended Since 1945

Passing

	Att.	Comp.	Pct.	Yds.	Avg.	Lng.	TD	Pct.	Int.	Pct.	Rating
Joe Montana	4059	2593	63.9	31,054	7.65	96t	216	5.3	107	2.6	94.0
Sammy Baugh	2995	1693	56.5	21,886	7.31	86t	187	6.2	203	6.8	72.0
George Blanda	4007	1911	47.7	26,920	6.72	95t	236	5.9	277	6.9	60.8
Terry Bradshaw	3901	2025	51.9	27,989	7.17	90t	212	5.4	210	5.4	70.9
Len Dawson	3741	2136	57.1	28,711	7.67	92t	239	6.4	183	4.9	82.6
Otto Graham	1565	872	55.7	13,499	8.63	81t	88	5.6	94	6.0	78.1
Arnie Herber*	1175	481	40.9	8,041	6.84	92t	78	6.6	106	9.0	49.3
Sonny Jurgensen	4262	2433	57.1	32,224	7.56	99t	255	6.0	189	4.4	82.8
Bobby Layne	3700	1814	49.0	26,768	7.23	97t	196	5.3	243	6.6	63.4
Sid Luckman	1744	904	51.8	14,686	8.42	86t	137	7.9	132	7.6	75.0
Joe Namath	3762	1886	50.1	27,663	7.35	91	173	4.6	220	5.8	65.6
Bart Starr	3149	1808	57.4	24,718	7.85	91t	152	4.8	138	4.4	80.5
Roger Staubach	2958	1685	57.0	22,700	7.67	91t	153	5.2	109	3.7	83.4
Fran Tarkenton	6467	3686	57.0	47,003	7.27	89t	342	5.3	266	4.1	80.4
Y.A. Tittle	3817	2118	55.5	28,339	7.42	78t	212	5.6	221	5.8	73.8
Johnny Unitas	5186	2830	54.6	40,239	7.76	89t	290	5.6	253	4.9	78.2
Norm Van Brocklin	2895	1553	53.6	23,611	8.16	91t	173	6.0	178	6.1	75.3
Bob Waterfield	1617	814	50.3	11,849	7.33	91t	97	6.0	128	7.9	61.6

Rushing

	Yrs.	Last Year	G	Att.	Yds.	Avg.	Lng.	TD
Joe Montana	11	1989	151	371	1405	3.8	21	19
Sammy Baugh	16	1952	165	324	325	1.0	41t	9
George Blanda	26	1975	340	135	344	2.5	19	9
Terry Bradshaw	14	1983	168	444	2257	5.1	39	32
Len Dawson	19	1975	211	294	1293	4.4	43	9
Otto Graham	6	1955	72	306	682	2.2	36	33
Arnie Herber*	13	1945	x	250	116	0.5	x	2
Sonny Jurgensen	18	1974	218	181	492	2.7	33	15
Bobby Layne	15	1962	175	611	2451	4.0	36	25
Sid Luckman	12	1950	128	204	−239	−1.2	40t	4
Joe Namath	13	1977	140	71	140	2.0	39	7
Bart Starr	16	1971	196	247	1308	5.3	39	15
Roger Staubach	11	1979	131	410	2264	5.5	33	20
Fran Tarkenton	18	1978	246	675	3674	5.4	52t	32
Y.A. Tittle	15	1964	178	291	999	3.4	45	33
Johnny Unitas	18	1973	211	450	1777	3.9	34	13
Norm Van Brocklin	12	1960	140	102	40	0.4	16	11
Bob Waterfield	8	1952	91	75	21	0.3	25	13

*statistics do not include 1930-31 seasons.   xUnavailable.

Joe Montana's Game-by-Game Postseason Career

Date	Game	Opponent	Att.	Comp.	Pct.	Yds.	Avg.	TD	Int.	Rating
Jan. 3, 1982	NFC Divisional Playoff	N.Y. Giants	31	20	64.5	304	9.81	2	1	104.8
Jan. 10, 1982	NFC Championship Game	Dallas	35	22	62.9	286	8.17	3	3	81.4
Jan. 24, 1982	Super Bowl XVI	Cincinnati	22	14	63.6	157	7.14	1	0	100.0
Dec. 31, 1983	NFC Divisional Playoff	Detroit	31	18	58.1	201	6.48	1	1	74.8
Jan. 8, 1984	NFC Championship Game	Washington	48	27	56.3	347	7.23	3	1	91.2
Dec. 29, 1984	NFC Divisional Playoff	N.Y. Giants	39	25	64.1	309	7.92	3	3	82.1
Jan. 6, 1985	NFC Championship Game	Chicago	34	18	52.9	233	6.85	1	2	60.0
Jan. 20, 1985	Super Bowl XIX	Miami	35	24	68.6	331	9.46	3	0	127.2
Dec. 29, 1985	NFC First-Round Game	N.Y. Giants	47	26	55.3	296	6.30	0	1	65.6
Jan. 4, 1987	NFC Divisional Playoff	N.Y. Giants	15	8	53.3	98	6.53	0	2	34.2
Jan. 9, 1988	NFC Divisional Playoff	Minnesota	26	12	46.2	109	4.19	0	1	42.0
Jan. 1, 1989	NFC Divisional Playoff	Minnesota	27	16	59.3	178	6.59	3	1	100.5
Jan. 8, 1989	NFC Championship Game	Chicago	27	17	63.0	288	10.67	3	0	136.0
Jan. 22, 1989	Super Bowl XXIII	Cincinnati	36	23	63.9	357	9.92	2	0	115.2
Jan. 6, 1990	NFC Divisional Playoff	Minnesota	24	17	70.8	241	10.04	4	0	142.5
Jan. 14, 1990	NFC Championship Game	L.A. Rams	30	26	86.7	262	8.73	2	0	125.3
Jan. 28, 1990	Super Bowl XXIV	Denver	29	22	75.9	297	10.24	5	0	147.6
Totals (17 games)			536	335	62.5	4294	8.01	36	16	97.5

All-Time Rankings of Players in Four Categories That Determine NFL Passer Rating

Minimum: 1500 Attempts

Completion Percentage

	Pct.	Att.	Comp.
Joe Montana	63.88	4059	2593
Ken Stabler	59.85	3793	2270
Danny White	59.69	2950	1761
Ken O'Brien	59.63	2467	1471
Dan Marino	59.56	3650	2174
Ken Anderson	59.31	4475	2654
Jim Kelly	59.24	1742	1032
Dan Fouts	58.83	5604	3297
Tony Eason	58.46	1536	898
Bernie Kosar	58.45	1940	1134

Touchdown Percentage

	Pct.	Att.	TD
Sid Luckman	7.86	1744	137
Frank Ryan	6.99	2133	149
Len Dawson	6.39	3741	239
Daryle Lamonica	6.31	2601	164
Sammy Baugh	6.24	2995	187
Charley Conerly	6.11	2833	173
Dan Marino	6.03	3650	220
Bob Waterfield	6.00	1617	97
Earl Morrall	5.99	2689	161
Sonny Jurgensen	5.98	4262	255

Average Yards Per Pass

	Avg.	Att.	Yards
Otto Graham	8.63	1565	13,499
Sid Luckman	8.42	1744	14,686

	Avg.	Att.	Yards
Norm Van Brocklin	8.16	2895	23,611
Boomer Esiason	8.03	2285	18,350
Ed Brown	7.85	1987	15,600
Bart Starr	7.85	3149	24,718
Johnny Unitas	7.76	5186	40,239
Earl Morrall	7.74	2689	20,809
Dan Fouts	7.68	5604	43,040
Len Dawson	7.67	3741	28,711

Interception Percentage

	Pct.	Att.	Int.
Bernie Kosar	2.42	1940	47
Joe Montana	2.64	4059	107
Ken O'Brien	2.76	2467	68
Neil Lomax	2.85	3153	90
Randall Cunningham	3.24	1788	58
Tony Eason	3.26	1536	50
Roman Gabriel	3.31	4498	149
Boomer Esiason	3.33	2285	76
Dan Marino	3.42	3650	125
Bill Kenney	3.54	2430	86

Teams That Finished In First Place In Their Division the Season After Finishing in Last Place

Season	Team	Record	Previous Season
1967	Houston	9-4-1	*3-11
1968	Minnesota	8-6	3-8-3
1970	Cincinnati	8-6	4-9-1
1970	San Francisco	10-3-1	4-8-2
1972	Green Bay	10-4	4-8-2
1975	Baltimore	10-4	2-12
1979	Tampa Bay	10-6	5-11
1981	Cincinnati	12-4	6-10
1987	Indianapolis	9-6	3-13
1988	Cincinnati	12-4	4-11

*tied for last place

Records of NFL Teams in 1980s

AFC	W - L - T	Pct.	Division Titles	Playoff Berths	Postseason Record	Super Bowl Record
Miami	94-57-1	.622	4	5	6-5	0-2
Denver	93-58-1	.615	4	5	6-5	0-3
L.A. Raiders	89-63-0	.586	2	5	8-3	2-0
Cleveland	83-68-1	.549	5	7	3-7	0-0
Cincinnati	81-71-0	.533	2	3	4-3	0-2
New England	78-74-0	.513	1	3	3-3	0-1
Seattle	78-74-0	.513	1	4	3-4	0-0
Pittsburgh	77-75-0	.507	2	4	2-4	0-0
N.Y. Jets	73-77-2	.487	0	4	3-4	0-0
San Diego	72-80-0	.474	2	3	3-3	0-0
Buffalo	69-83-0	.454	3	4	2-4	0-0
Kansas City	66-84-2	.441	0	1	0-1	0-0
Houston	62-90-0	.408	0	4	2-4	0-0
Indianapolis	54-97-1	.359	1	1	0-1	0-0

NFC	W - L - T	Pct.	Division Titles	Playoff Berths	Postseason Record	Super Bowl Record
San Francisco	104-47-1	.688	7	8	13-4	4-0
Washington	97-55-0	.638	3	5	11-3	2-1
Chicago	92-60-0	.605	5	5	5-4	1-0
L.A. Rams	86-66-0	.566	1	7	4-7	0-0
N.Y. Giants	81-70-1	.536	2	5	6-4	1-0
Dallas	79-73-0	.520	2	5	5-5	0-0
Minnesota	77-75-0	.507	2	5	4-5	0-0
Philadelphia	76-74-2	.507	2	4	2-4	0-1
New Orleans	67-85-0	.441	0	1	0-1	0-0
Green Bay	65-84-3	.438	0	1	1-1	0-0
Phoenix	62-88-2	.414	0	1	0-1	0-0
Detroit	61-90-1	.405	1	2	0-2	0-0
Atlanta	57-94-1	.378	1	2	0-2	0-0
Tampa Bay	45-106-1	.299	1	2	0-2	0-0

Indianapolis totals include Baltimore, 1980-83
L.A. Raiders totals include Oakland, 1980-81
Phoenix totals include St. Louis, 1980-87

In 1982, due to players' strike, the divisional format was abandoned. (L.A. Raiders and Washington won regular-season conference titles, not included in "Division Titles" totals listed above. Sixteen teams were awarded playoff berths, included in totals listed above.)

Home Records Since 1980

AFC	W - L - T	Pct.	NFC	W - L - T	Pct.
Denver	58-19-0	.753	Chicago	54-22-0	.711
Miami	53-21-1	.713	Washington	52-23-0	.693
L.A. Raiders	49-27-0	.645	San Francisco	49-27-0	.645
Cleveland	46-28-1	.620	Minnesota	48-29-0	.623
Cincinnati	47-29-0	.618	L.A. Rams	46-30-0	.605

AFC	W - L - T	Pct.	NFC	W - L - T	Pct.
New England	47-29-0	.618	N.Y. Giants	46-31-0	.597
Pittsburgh	46-29-0	.613	Dallas	44-32-0	.579
Seattle	46-31-0	.597	Philadelphia	41-35-1	.539
Buffalo	45-32-0	.584	Detroit	37-38-1	.493
Kansas City	42-32-0	.573	Green Bay	37-38-1	.493
Houston	42-34-0	.553	New Orleans	35-41-0	.461
San Diego	41-34-0	.547	Phoenix	34-40-1	.460
N.Y. Jets	38-37-1	.507	Atlanta	30-46-1	.396
Indianapolis	29-46-1	.388	Tampa Bay	29-46-1	.388

Road Records Since 1980

AFC	W - L - T	Pct.	NFC	W - L - T	Pct.
Miami	41-36-0	.532	San Francisco	55-20-1	.730
L.A. Raiders	40-36-0	.526	Washington	45-32-0	.584
Cleveland	37-40-0	.481	L.A. Rams	40-36-0	.526
Denver	35-39-1	.473	Chicago	38-38-0	.500
N.Y. Jets	35-40-1	.467	N.Y. Giants	35-39-1	.473
Cincinnati	34-42-0	.447	Philadelphia	35-39-1	.473
Seattle	32-43-0	.427	Dallas	35-41-0	.461
New England	31-45-0	.408	New Orleans	32-44-0	.421
Pittsburgh	31-46-0	.403	Minnesota	29-46-0	.387
San Diego	31-46-0	.403	Green Bay	28-46-2	.382
Indianapolis	25-51-0	.329	Phoenix	28-48-1	.370
Buffalo	24-51-0	.320	Atlanta	27-48-0	.360
Kansas City	23-52-2	.312	Detroit	24-52-0	.316
Houston	20-56-0	.263	Tampa Bay	16-60-0	.211

Records by Months Since 1980

AFC	Sept. W - L - T	Oct. W - L - T	Nov. W - L - T	*Dec. W - L - T	Total W - L - T	Pct.
Miami	24-12	21-17-1	24-18	25-10	94-57-1	.622
Denver	22-13-1	28-11	26-15	17-19	93-58-1	.615
L.A. Raiders	22-14	23-16	23-18	21-15	89-63-0	.586
Cleveland	18-18	22-17	25-16-1	18-17	83-68-1	.549
Cincinnati	16-19	21-19	22-20	22-13	81-71-0	.533
New England	16-20	23-16	21-21	18-17	78-74-0	.513
Seattle	18-18	22-17	19-23	19-16	78-74-0	.513
Pittsburgh	17-18	21-19	22-20	17-18	77-75-0	.507
N.Y. Jets	19-17	19-18-2	22-21	13-21	73-77-2	.487
San Diego	19-17	12-27	23-19	18-17	72-80-0	.474
Buffalo	19-17	20-19	20-22	10-25	69-83-0	.454
Kansas City	17-19	16-22-1	13-28-1	20-15	66-84-2	.441
Houston	13-23	15-24	19-23	15-20	62-90-0	.408
Indianapolis	10-26	17-22	13-29	14-20-1	54-97-1	.359

NFC	Sept. W - L - T	Oct. W - L - T	Nov. W - L - T	*Dec. W - L - T	Total W - L - T	Pct.
San Francisco	25-11	25-13-1	26-15	28-8	104-47-1	.688
Washington	18-18	25-14	27-16	27-7	97-55-0	.638
Chicago	22-14	24-15	27-15	19-16	92-60-0	.605
L.A. Rams	23-13	22-17	23-19	18-17	86-66-0	.566
N.Y. Giants	19-17	19-19-1	21-20	22-14	81-70-1	.536
Dallas	25-11	19-20	22-21	13-21	79-73-0	.520
Minnesota	22-14	17-22	22-21	16-18	77-75-0	.507
Philadelphia	17-19	25-14	19-22-1	15-19-1	76-74-2	.507
New Orleans	15-21	17-22	21-21	14-21	67-85-0	.441
Green Bay	9-26-1	17-21-1	20-22	19-15-1	65-84-3	.438
Phoenix	14-22	17-21-1	17-26	14-19-1	62-88-2	.414
Detroit	15-21	15-24	17-25-1	14-20	61-90-1	.405
Atlanta	17-19	12-26-1	17-25	11-24	57-94-1	.378
Tampa Bay	11-25	8-30-1	16-26	10-25	45-106-1	.299

Indianapolis totals include Baltimore, 1980-83
L.A. Raiders totals include Oakland, 1980-81
Phoenix totals include St. Louis, 1980-87

*Includes one game for each team played during January.

Takeaways/Giveaways in 1980s

	Takeaways			Giveaways			Net
AFC	Int.	Fum.	Total	Int.	Fum.	Total	Diff.
Seattle	215	186	401	196	156	352	49
Cincinnati	194	149	343	166	135	301	42
Kansas City	228	158	386	187	160	347	39
Denver	216	169	385	204	145	349	36
Pittsburgh	240	144	384	212	154	366	18
New England	187	156	343	210	134	344	− 1
Cleveland	202	129	331	176	158	334	− 3
N.Y. Jets	197	139	336	181	158	339	− 3
Miami	198	140	338	201	141	342	− 4
Indianapolis	164	162	326	200	135	335	− 9
L.A. Raiders	197	152	349	228	170	398	−49
Houston	171	152	323	220	160	380	−57
San Diego	186	158	344	235	175	410	−66
Buffalo	170	151	321	220	177	397	−76

Takeaways / Giveaways

NFC	Int.	Fum.	Total	Int.	Fum.	Total	Net Diff.
San Francisco	227	145	372	145	134	279	93
Philadelphia	218	161	379	176	143	319	60
Minnesota	214	169	383	215	123	338	45
Washington	229	143	372	176	155	331	41
Atlanta	191	151	342	182	148	330	12
L.A. Rams	210	155	365	192	165	357	8
Chicago	220	141	361	201	162	363	− 2
N.Y. Giants	194	154	348	197	155	352	− 4
Dallas	224	155	379	228	158	386	− 7
New Orleans	189	152	341	211	153	364	− 23
Green Bay	199	173	372	245	158	403	− 31
Tampa Bay	188	160	348	221	158	379	− 31
Detroit	191	147	338	207	164	371	− 33
Phoenix	165	141	306	192	158	350	− 44

High and Low Single-Game Yardage Totals in 1980s

Most Total Yards, Game
- 661   San Diego vs. Cincinnati, Dec. 20, 1982
- 621   Cincinnati vs. N.Y. Jets, Dec. 21, 1986
- 597   N.Y. Jets vs. Miami, Nov. 27, 1988
- 594   Chicago vs. Green Bay, Dec. 7, 1980
- 593   San Diego vs. L.A. Raiders, Nov. 10, 1985 (OT)

Fewest Total Yards, Game
- 24   Chicago vs. Detroit, Nov. 22, 1981
- 53   Pittsburgh vs. Cleveland, Sept. 10, 1989
- 57   New England vs. N.Y. Jets, Sept. 19, 1982
- 60   Detroit vs. Minnesota, Nov. 24, 1988
- 65   Tampa Bay vs. Green Bay, Dec. 1, 1985
- 65   Seattle vs. New England, Dec. 4, 1988

Most Yards Rushing, Game
- 356   L.A. Raiders vs. Seattle, Nov. 30, 1987
- 354   Dallas vs. Baltimore, Dec. 6, 1981
- 343   Pittsburgh vs. N.Y. Jets, Sept. 20, 1981
- 330   St. Louis vs. New Orleans, Oct. 5, 1980
- 330   Detroit vs. L.A. Rams, Sept. 7, 1980

Fewest Yards Rushing, Game
- 0   Buffalo vs. Chicago, Oct. 2, 1988
- 1   Tampa Bay vs. Washington, Oct. 22, 1989
- 2   New England vs. New Orleans, Nov. 30, 1986
- 6   N.Y. Giants vs. L.A. Rams, Nov. 12, 1989
- 8   N.Y. Giants vs. L.A. Rams, Sept. 30, 1984

Most Yards Passing, Game
- 521   Miami vs. N.Y. Jets, Oct. 23, 1988
- 506   L.A. Rams vs. Chicago, Dec. 26, 1982
- 494   San Diego vs. Seattle, Sept. 15, 1985
- 486   San Diego vs. Cincinnati, Dec. 20, 1982
- 486   Tampa Bay vs. Minnesota, Nov. 16, 1980

Fewest Yards Passing, Game
- − 22   Atlanta vs. Chicago, Nov. 24, 1985
- − 20   Chicago vs. Detroit, Nov. 22, 1981
- − 13   Cincinnati vs. San Diego, Oct. 4, 1987
- − 12   St. Louis vs. Washington, Dec. 21, 1980
- − 4   Houston vs. Cincinnati, Oct. 4, 1981
- − 4   New England vs. N.Y. Jets, Sept. 19, 1982

NFL Individual Leaders From 1980 Through 1989

Points
- 1006, Nick Lowery
- 943, Ed Murray
- 904, Pat Leahy
- 897, Chris Bahr
- 875, Jim Breech

Touchdowns
- 86, Eric Dickerson
- 80, Marcus Allen
- 70, Steve Largent
- 70, Jerry Rice
- 66, James Brooks

Field Goals
- 225, Nick Lowery
- 212, Ed Murray
- 186, Gary Anderson
- 180, Pat Leahy
- 179, Chris Bahr

Rushes
- 2450, Eric Dickerson
- 2290, Walter Payton
- 2188, Tony Dorsett
- 1943, Ottis Anderson
- 1788, Gerald Riggs

Rushing Yards
- 11,226, Eric Dickerson
- 9800, Walter Payton
- 9300, Tony Dorsett
- 7712, Ottis Anderson
- 7465, Gerald Riggs

Rushing TDs
- 82, Eric Dickerson
- 63, Marcus Allen
- 62, John Riggins
- 61, Ottis Anderson
- 55, Curt Warner

Passes
- 4036, Joe Montana
- 3650, Dan Marino
- 3599, Dan Fouts
- 3393, Phil Simms
- 3153, Neil Lomax

Completions
- 2580, Joe Montana
- 2174, Dan Marino
- 2156, Dan Fouts
- 1846, Phil Simms
- 1817, Neil Lomax

Passing Yards
- 30,958, Joe Montana
- 28,301, Dan Marino
- 27,853, Dan Marino
- 24,492, Phil Simms
- 22,771, Neil Lomax

TD Passes
- 220, Dan Marino
- 215, Joe Montana
- 172, Dan Fouts
- 169, Dave Krieg
- 152, Danny White

Receptions
- 662, Art Monk
- 595, Steve Largent
- 546, Ozzie Newsome
- 516, Kellen Winslow
- 507, James Lofton

Reception Yards
- 9465, James Lofton
- 9336, Steve Largent
- 9165, Art Monk
- 8087, Stanley Morgan
- 7684, Roy Green

Receiving TDs
- 69, Steve Largent
- 66, Jerry Rice
- 63, Mark Clayton
- 62, Roy Green
- 60, Mike Quick

Interceptions
- 48, Ronnie Lott
- 46, Dave Brown
- 44, John Harris
- 44, Everson Walls
- 43, Deron Cherry

Sacks (since 1982)
- 104, Lawrence Taylor
- 91, Dexter Manley
- 81, Richard Dent
- 81, Reggie White
- 79, Jacob Green

Coaches in the 1980s

Highest Won-Lost Percentage (Minimum 50 Games)
- .669   Joe Gibbs, Washington (91-45)
- .665   Bill Walsh, San Francisco (90-45-1)
- .658   Mike Ditka, Chicago (79-41)
- .629   Dan Reeves, Denver (85-50-1)
- .622   Don Shula, Miami (94-57-1)

Most Super Bowls Won
- 3   Bill Walsh, San Francisco
- 2   Tom Flores, L.A. Raiders
- 2   Joe Gibbs, Washington
- 1   Mike Ditka, Chicago
- 1   Bill Parcells, N.Y. Giants
- 1   George Seifert, San Francisco

All-Time Records of Current NFL Teams

Buffalo Bills

Season	All Games W	L	T	Home Games W	L	T	Road Games W	L	T
1960	5	8	1	3	4		2	4	1
1961	6	8		2	5		4	3	
1962	7	6	1	3	3	1	4	3	
1963	7	6	1	4	2	1	3	4	
1964	12	2		6	1		6	1	
1965	10	3	1	5	2		5	1	1
1966	9	4	1	4	2	1	5	2	
1967	4	10		2	5		2	5	
1968	1	12	1	1	6		0	6	1
1969	4	10		4	3		0	7	
1970	3	10	1	1	6		2	4	1
1971	1	13		1	6		0	7	
1972	4	9	1	2	4	1	2	5	
1973	9	5		5	2		4	3	
1974	9	5		5	2		4	3	
1975	8	6		3	4		5	2	
1976	2	12		1	6		1	6	
1977	3	11		1	6		2	5	
1978	5	11		4	4		1	7	
1979	7	9		3	5		4	4	
1980	11	5		6	2		5	3	
1981	10	6		7	1		3	5	
1982	4	5		4	1		0	4	
1983	8	8		3	5		5	3	
1984	2	14		2	6		0	8	
1985	2	14		2	6		0	8	
1986	4	12		3	5		1	7	
1987	7	8		4	4		3	4	
1988	12	4		8	0		4	4	
1989	9	7		6	2		3	5	
Total	185	243	8	105	110	4	80	133	4

Cincinnati Bengals

Season	All Games W	L	T	Home Games W	L	T	Road Games W	L	T
1968	3	11		2	5		1	6	
1969	4	9	1	4	3		0	6	1
1970	8	6		5	2		3	4	
1971	4	10		3	4		1	6	
1972	8	6		4	3		4	3	
1973	10	4		7	0		3	4	
1974	7	7		4	3		3	4	
1975	11	3		6	1		5	2	
1976	10	4		6	1		4	3	
1977	8	6		5	2		3	4	
1978	4	12		3	5		1	7	
1979	4	12		4	4		0	8	
1980	6	10		3	5		3	5	
1981	12	4		8	0		4	4	
1982	7	2		4	0		3	2	
1983	7	9		4	4		3	5	
1984	8	8		5	3		3	5	
1985	7	9		5	3		2	6	
1986	10	6		6	2		4	4	
1987	4	11		1	7		3	4	
1988	12	4		8	0		4	4	
1989	8	8		5	3		3	5	
Total	162	161	1	100	62		62	99	1

Cleveland Browns

Season	All Games W	L	T	Home Games W	L	T	Road Games W	L	T
1950	10	2		5	1		5	1	
1951	11	1		6	0		5	1	
1952	8	4		4	2		4	2	
1953	11	1		6	0		5	1	
1954	9	3		5	1		4	2	
1955	9	2	1	5	1		4	1	1
1956	5	7		1	5		4	2	
1957	9	2	1	6	0		3	2	1
1958	9	3		4	2		5	1	
1959	7	5		3	3		4	2	
1960	8	3	1	4	2		4	1	1
1961	8	5	1	4	3		4	2	1
1962	7	6	1	4	2	1	3	4	
1963	10	4		5	2		5	2	
1964	10	3	1	5	1	1	5	2	
1965	11	3		5	2		6	1	
1966	9	5		5	2		4	3	

Season	All Games W	L	T	Home Games W	L	T	Road Games W	L	T
1967	9	5		6	1		3	4	
1968	10	4		5	2		5	2	
1969	10	3	1	5	1	1	5	2	
1970	7	7		4	3		3	4	
1971	9	5		4	3		5	2	
1972	10	4		4	3		6	1	
1973	7	5	2	5	1	1	2	4	1
1974	4	10		3	4		1	6	
1975	3	11		3	4		0	7	
1976	9	5		6	1		3	4	
1977	6	8		2	5		4	3	
1978	8	8		5	3		3	5	
1979	9	7		5	3		4	4	
1980	11	5		6	2		5	3	
1981	5	11		3	5		2	6	
1982	4	5		2	2		2	3	
1983	9	7		6	2		3	5	
1984	5	11		2	6		3	5	
1985	8	8		5	3		3	5	
1986	12	4		6	2		6	2	
1987	10	5		5	2		5	3	
1988	10	6		6	2		4	4	
1989	9	6	1	5	2	1	4	4	
Total	335	209	10	180	91	5	155	118	5

Denver Broncos

Season	All Games W	L	T	Home Games W	L	T	Road Games W	L	T
1960	4	9	1	2	4	1	2	5	
1961	3	11		2	5		1	6	
1962	7	7		3	4		4	3	
1963	2	11	1	2	5		0	6	1
1964	2	11	1	2	4	1	0	7	
1965	4	10		2	5		2	5	
1966	4	10		3	4		1	6	
1967	3	11		1	6		2	5	
1968	5	9		3	4		2	5	
1969	5	8	1	4	2	1	1	6	
1970	5	8	1	3	3	1	2	5	
1971	4	9	1	2	4	1	2	5	
1972	5	9		3	4		2	5	
1973	7	5	2	3	3	1	4	2	1
1974	7	6	1	3	3	1	4	3	
1975	6	8		5	2		1	6	
1976	9	5		6	1		3	4	
1977	12	2		6	1		6	1	
1978	10	6		6	2		4	4	
1979	10	6		6	2		4	4	
1980	8	8		4	4		4	4	
1981	10	6		8	0		2	6	
1982	2	7		1	4		1	3	
1983	9	7		6	2		3	5	
1984	13	3		7	1		6	2	
1985	11	5		6	2		5	3	
1986	11	5		7	1		4	4	
1987	10	4	1	7	1		3	3	1
1988	8	8		6	2		2	6	
1989	11	5		6	2		5	3	
Total	207	219	10	125	87	7	82	132	3

Houston Oilers

Season	All Games W	L	T	Home Games W	L	T	Road Games W	L	T
1960	10	4		6	1		4	3	
1961	10	3	1	6	1		4	2	1
1962	11	3		6	1		5	2	
1963	6	8		4	3		2	5	
1964	4	10		3	4		1	6	
1965	4	10		3	4		1	6	
1966	3	11		3	4		0	7	
1967	9	4	1	5	2		4	2	1
1968	7	7		3	4		4	3	
1969	6	6	2	4	2	1	2	4	1
1970	3	10	1	1	6		2	4	1
1971	4	9	1	3	3	1	1	6	
1972	1	13		1	6		0	7	
1973	1	13		0	7		1	6	
1974	7	7		3	4		4	3	
1975	10	4		5	2		5	2	
1976	5	9		3	4		2	5	
1977	8	6		5	2		3	4	
1978	10	6		5	3		5	3	
1979	11	5		6	2		5	3	
1980	11	5		6	2		5	3	
1981	7	9		5	3		2	6	
1982	1	8		1	4		0	4	
1983	2	14		2	6		0	8	
1984	3	13		2	6		1	7	
1985	5	11		4	4		1	7	
1986	5	11		4	4		1	7	

Season	All Games W	L	T	Home Games W	L	T	Road Games W	L	T
1987	9	6		5	2		4	4	
1988	10	6		7	1		3	5	
1989	9	7		6	2		3	5	
Total	192	238	6	117	99	2	75	139	4

Indianapolis Colts*

Season	All Games W	L	T	Home Games W	L	T	Road Games W	L	T
1944	2	8		1	3		1	5	
1945	3	6	1	2	2	1	1	4	
1946	2	8	1	1	5		1	3	1
1947	4	7	1	2	3	1	2	4	
1948	3	9		2	4		1	5	
1949	1	10	1	0	5	1	1	5	
1950	7	5		5	1		2	4	
1951	1	9	2	0	3	1	1	6	1
1952	1	11		1	4		0	7	
1953	3	9		2	4		1	5	
1954	3	9		2	4		1	5	
1955	5	6	1	4	1	1	1	5	
1956	5	7		4	2		1	5	
1957	7	5		4	2		3	3	
1958	9	3		6	0		3	3	
1959	9	3		4	2		5	1	
1960	6	6		4	2		2	4	
1961	8	6		5	2		3	4	
1962	7	7		3	4		4	3	
1963	8	6		4	3		4	3	
1964	12	2		7	1		5	1	
1965	10	3	1	5	2		5	1	1
1966	9	5		5	2		4	3	
1967	11	1	2	6	0	1	5	1	1
1968	13	1		6	1		7	0	
1969	8	5	1	4	2	1	4	3	
1970	11	2	1	5	1	1	6	1	
1971	10	4		5	2		5	2	
1972	5	9		2	5		3	4	
1973	4	10		3	4		1	6	
1974	2	12		0	7		2	5	
1975	10	4		5	2		5	2	
1976	11	3		6	1		5	2	
1977	10	4		6	1		4	3	
1978	5	11		2	6		3	5	
1979	5	11		3	5		2	6	
1980	7	9		2	6		5	3	
1981	2	14		1	7		1	7	
1982	0	8	1	0	3	1	0	5	
1983	7	9		3	5		4	4	
1984	4	12		2	6		2	6	
1985	5	11		4	4		1	7	
1986	3	13		1	7		2	6	
1987	9	6		4	4		5	2	
1988	9	7		6	2		3	5	
1989	8	8		6	2		2	6	
Total	284	324	13	155	144	9	129	180	4

*includes Boston Yanks (1944-48), New York Bulldogs (1949), New York Yanks (1950-51), Dallas Texans (1952), and Baltimore Colts (1953-83).

Kansas City Chiefs*

Season	All Games W	L	T	Home Games W	L	T	Road Games W	L	T
1960	8	6		5	2		3	4	
1961	6	8		4	3		2	5	
1962	11	3		6	1		5	2	
1963	5	7	2	4	3		1	4	2
1964	7	7		4	3		3	4	
1965	7	5	2	5	2		2	3	2
1966	11	2	1	4	2	1	7	0	
1967	9	5		4	3		5	2	
1968	12	2		6	1		6	1	
1969	11	3		6	1		5	2	
1970	7	5	2	4	1	2	3	4	
1971	10	3	1	7	0		3	3	1
1972	8	6		3	4		5	2	
1973	7	5	2	5	1	1	2	4	1
1974	5	9		1	6		4	3	
1975	5	9		3	4		2	5	
1976	5	9		1	6		4	3	
1977	2	12		1	6		1	6	
1978	4	12		3	5		1	7	
1979	7	9		3	5		4	4	
1980	8	8		3	5		5	3	
1981	9	7		5	3		4	4	
1982	3	6		2	2		1	4	
1983	6	10		5	3		1	7	
1984	8	8		5	3		3	5	
1985	6	10		5	3		1	7	
1986	10	6		6	2		4	4	
1987	4	11		3	4		1	7	

Season	All Games W	L	T	Home Games W	L	T	Road Games W	L	T
1988	4	11	1	4	4		0	7	1
1989	8	7	1	5	3		3	4	1
Total	213	211	12	122	91	4	91	120	8

*includes Dallas Texans (1960-62).

Los Angeles Raiders*

Season	All Games W	L	T	Home Games W	L	T	Road Games W	L	T
1960	6	8		3	4		3	4	
1961	2	12		1	6		1	6	
1962	1	13		1	6		0	7	
1963	10	4		6	1		4	3	
1964	5	7	2	5	2		0	5	2
1965	8	5	1	5	2		3	3	1
1966	8	5	1	3	3	1	5	2	
1967	13	1		7	0		6	1	
1968	12	2		6	1		6	1	
1969	12	1	1	7	0		5	1	1
1970	8	4	2	6	1		2	3	2
1971	8	4	2	5	1	1	3	3	1
1972	10	3	1	5	1	1	5	2	
1973	9	4	1	5	2		4	2	1
1974	12	2		6	1		6	1	
1975	11	3		6	1		5	2	
1976	13	1		7	0		6	1	
1977	11	3		6	1		5	2	
1978	9	7		4	4		5	3	
1979	9	7		6	2		3	5	
1980	11	5		6	2		5	3	
1981	7	9		4	4		3	5	
1982	8	1		4	0		4	1	
1983	12	4		6	2		6	2	
1984	11	5		6	2		5	3	
1985	12	4		7	1		5	3	
1986	8	8		3	5		5	3	
1987	5	10		3	5		2	5	
1988	7	9		3	5		4	4	
1989	8	8		7	1		1	7	
Total	266	159	11	149	66	3	117	93	8

*includes Oakland Raiders (1960-81).

Miami Dolphins

Season	All Games W	L	T	Home Games W	L	T	Road Games W	L	T
1966	3	11		2	5		1	6	
1967	4	10		4	3		0	7	
1968	5	8	1	1	5	1	4	3	
1969	3	10	1	2	4	1	1	6	
1970	10	4		6	1		4	3	
1971	10	3	1	6	1		4	2	1
1972	14	0		7	0		7	0	
1973	12	2		7	0		5	2	
1974	11	3		7	0		4	3	
1975	10	4		5	2		5	2	
1976	6	8		3	4		3	4	
1977	10	4		6	1		4	3	
1978	11	5		7	1		4	4	
1979	10	6		6	2		4	4	
1980	8	8		5	3		3	5	
1981	11	4	1	6	1	1	5	3	
1982	7	2		4	0		3	2	
1983	12	4		7	1		5	3	
1984	14	2		7	1		7	1	
1985	12	4		8	0		4	4	
1986	8	8		4	4		4	4	
1987	8	7		4	3		4	4	
1988	6	10		4	4		2	6	
1989	8	8		4	4		4	4	
Total	213	135	4	122	50	3	91	85	1

New England Patriots*

Season	All Games W	L	T	Home Games W	L	T	Road Games W	L	T
1960	5	9		3	4		2	5	
1961	9	4	1	4	2	1	5	2	
1962	9	4	1	6	1		3	3	1
1963	7	6	1	5	1	1	2	5	
1964	10	3	1	4	2	1	6	1	
1965	4	8	2	1	4	2	3	4	
1966	8	4	2	4	2	1	4	2	1
1967	3	10	1	2	4		1	6	1
1968	4	10		2	5		2	5	
1969	4	10		2	5		2	5	
1970	2	12		1	6		1	6	
1971	6	8		5	2		1	6	
1972	3	11		2	5		1	6	
1973	5	9		3	4		2	5	
1974	7	7		3	4		4	3	
1975	3	11		2	5		1	6	
1976	11	3		6	1		5	2	
1977	9	5		6	1		3	4	

Season	All Games			Home Games			Road Games		
	W	L	T	W	L	T	W	L	T
1978	11	5		5	3		6	2	
1979	9	7		6	2		3	5	
1980	10	6		6	2		4	4	
1981	2	14		2	6		0	8	
1982	5	4		3	1		2	3	
1983	8	8		5	3		3	5	
1984	9	7		5	3		4	4	
1985	11	5		7	1		4	4	
1986	11	5		4	4		7	1	
1987	8	7		5	3		3	4	
1988	9	7		7	1		2	6	
1989	5	11		3	5		2	6	
Total	207	220	9	119	92	6	88	128	3

*includes Boston Patriots (1960-70).

New York Jets*

Season	All Games			Home Games			Road Games		
	W	L	T	W	L	T	W	L	T
1960	7	7		3	4		4	3	
1961	7	7		5	2		2	5	
1962	5	9		2	5		3	4	
1963	5	8	1	4	2	1	1	6	
1964	5	8	1	5	1	1	0	7	
1965	5	8	1	3	3	1	2	5	
1966	6	6	2	4	3		2	3	2
1967	8	5	1	4	2	1	4	3	
1968	11	3		6	1		5	2	
1969	10	4		5	2		5	2	
1970	4	10		2	5		2	5	
1971	6	8		4	3		2	5	
1972	7	7		4	3		3	4	
1973	4	10		2	4		2	6	
1974	7	7		3	4		4	3	
1975	3	11		1	6		2	5	
1976	3	11		2	5		1	6	
1977	3	11		1	6		2	5	
1978	8	8		4	4		4	4	
1979	8	8		6	2		2	6	
1980	4	12		2	6		2	6	
1981	10	5	1	6	2		4	3	1
1982	6	3		3	1		3	2	
1983	7	9		2	6		5	3	
1984	7	9		3	5		4	4	
1985	11	5		7	1		4	4	
1986	10	6		5	3		5	3	
1987	6	9		4	4		2	5	
1988	8	7	1	5	2	1	3	5	
1989	4	12		1	6		3	5	
Total	195	233	8	108	104	5	87	129	3

*includes New York Titans (1960-62).

Pittsburgh Steelers*

Season	All Games			Home Games			Road Games		
	W	L	T	W	L	T	W	L	T
1933	3	6	2	2	3		1	3	2
1934	2	10		1	5		1	5	
1935	4	8		2	5		2	3	
1936	6	6		4	1		2	5	
1937	4	7		2	4		2	3	
1938	2	9		0	5		2	4	
1939	1	9	1	1	4		0	5	1
1940	2	7	2	1	2	2	1	5	
1941	1	9	1	1	4		0	5	1
1942	7	4		3	2		4	2	
1945	2	8		1	4		1	4	
1946	5	5	1	4	1		1	4	1
1947	8	4		5	1		3	3	
1948	4	8		4	2		0	6	
1949	6	5	1	3	2	1	3	3	
1950	6	6		2	4		4	2	
1951	4	7	1	1	4	1	3	3	
1952	5	7		2	4		3	3	
1953	6	6		3	3		3	3	
1954	5	7		4	2		1	5	
1955	4	8		3	2		1	6	
1956	5	7		3	3		2	4	
1957	6	6		4	2		2	4	
1958	7	4	1	5	1		2	3	1
1959	6	5	1	3	2	1	3	3	
1960	5	6	1	4	2		1	4	1
1961	6	8		4	3		2	5	
1962	9	5		4	3		5	2	
1963	7	4	3	5	0	2	2	4	1
1964	5	9		2	5		3	4	
1965	2	12		1	6		1	6	
1966	5	8	1	3	3	1	2	5	
1967	4	9	1	1	6		3	3	1
1968	2	11	1	1	6		1	5	1
1969	1	13		1	6		0	7	
1970	5	9		4	3		1	6	
1971	6	8		5	2		1	6	
1972	11	3		7	0		4	3	
1973	10	4		7	1		3	3	
1974	10	3	1	5	2		5	1	1
1975	12	2		6	1		6	1	
1976	10	4		6	1		4	3	
1977	9	5		6	1		3	4	
1978	14	2		7	1		7	1	
1979	12	4		8	0		4	4	
1980	9	7		6	2		3	5	
1981	8	8		5	3		3	5	
1982	6	3		4	0		2	3	
1983	10	6		4	4		6	2	
1984	9	7		6	2		3	5	
1985	7	9		5	3		2	6	
1986	6	10		4	4		2	6	
1987	8	7		4	3		4	4	
1988	5	11		4	4		1	7	
1989	9	7		4	4		5	3	
Total	333	372	19	197	153	8	136	219	11

*includes Pittsburgh Pirates (1933-40).

San Diego Chargers*

Season	All Games			Home Games			Road Games		
	W	L	T	W	L	T	W	L	T
1960	10	4		5	2		5	2	
1961	12	2		6	1		6	1	
1962	4	10		3	4		1	6	
1963	11	3		6	1		5	2	
1964	8	5	1	4	3		4	2	1
1965	9	2	3	4	1	2	5	1	1
1966	7	6	1	5	2		2	4	1
1967	8	5	1	5	2	1	3	3	
1968	9	5		4	3		5	2	
1969	8	6		5	2		3	4	
1970	5	6	3	2	3	2	3	3	1
1971	6	8		6	1		0	7	
1972	4	9	1	2	5		2	4	1
1973	2	11	1	2	5		0	6	1
1974	5	9		3	4		2	5	
1975	2	12		1	6		1	6	
1976	6	8		3	4		3	4	
1977	7	7		3	4		4	3	
1978	9	7		5	3		4	4	
1979	12	4		7	1		5	3	
1980	11	5		6	2		5	3	
1981	10	6		5	3		5	3	
1982	6	3		3	1		3	2	
1983	6	10		4	4		2	6	
1984	7	9		4	4		3	5	
1985	8	8		6	2		2	6	
1986	4	12		2	6		2	6	
1987	8	7		4	3		4	4	
1988	6	10		3	5		3	5	
1989	6	10		4	4		2	6	
Total	216	209	11	122	91	5	94	118	6

*includes Los Angeles Chargers (1960).

Seattle Seahawks

Season	All Games			Home Games			Road Games		
	W	L	T	W	L	T	W	L	T
1976	2	12		1	6		1	6	
1977	5	9		3	4		2	5	
1978	9	7		5	3		4	4	
1979	9	7		5	3		4	4	
1980	4	12		0	8		4	4	
1981	6	10		5	3		1	7	
1982	4	5		3	2		1	3	
1983	9	7		5	3		4	4	
1984	12	4		7	1		5	3	
1985	8	8		5	3		3	5	
1986	10	6		7	1		3	5	
1987	9	6		6	2		3	4	
1988	9	7		5	3		4	4	
1989	7	9		3	5		4	4	
Total	103	109		60	47		43	62	

Atlanta Falcons

Season	All Games			Home Games			Road Games		
	W	L	T	W	L	T	W	L	T
1966	3	11		1	6		2	5	
1967	1	12	1	1	5	1	0	7	
1968	2	12		1	6		1	6	
1969	6	8		4	3		2	5	
1970	4	8	2	3	4		1	4	2
1971	7	6	1	4	3		3	3	1
1972	7	7		4	3		3	4	
1973	9	5		4	3		5	2	
1974	3	11		2	5		1	6	
1975	4	10		3	4		1	6	
1976	4	10		3	4		1	6	
1977	7	7		4	3		3	4	
1978	9	7		7	1		2	6	
1979	6	10		3	5		3	5	
1980	12	4		6	2		6	2	
1981	7	9		4	4		3	5	
1982	5	4		2	3		3	1	
1983	7	9		4	4		3	5	
1984	4	12		2	6		2	6	
1985	4	12		3	5		1	7	
1986	7	8	1	2	5	1	5	3	
1987	3	12		2	6		1	6	
1988	5	11		2	6		3	5	
1989	3	13		3	5		0	8	
Total	129	218	5	74	101	2	55	117	3

Chicago Bears*

Season	All Games			Home Games			Road Games		
	W	L	T	W	L	T	W	L	T
1920	10	1	2	6	0	1	4	1	1
1921	9	1	1	9	1	1	0	0	
1922	9	3		7	1		2	2	
1923	9	2	1	7	1	1	2	1	
1924	6	1	4	5	0	3	1	1	1
1925	9	5	3	7	1	1	2	4	2
1926	12	1	3	10	0	2	2	1	1
1927	9	3	2	7	1	1	2	2	1
1928	7	5	1	6	3		1	2	1
1929	4	9	2	1	5	2	3	4	
1930	9	4	1	5	2	1	4	2	
1931	8	5		6	3		2	2	
1932	7	1	6	6	1	1	1	0	5
1933	10	2	1	6	0		4	2	1
1934	13	0		5	0		8	0	
1935	6	4	2	1	2	2	5	2	
1936	9	3		3	1		6	2	
1937	9	1	1	4	1		5	0	1
1938	6	5		2	3		4	2	
1939	8	3		4	1		4	2	
1940	8	3		5	0		3	3	
1941	10	1		5	1		5	0	
1942	11	0		6	0		5	0	
1943	8	1	1	5	0		3	1	1
1944	6	3	1	4	0	1	2	3	
1945	3	7		2	3		1	4	
1946	8	2	1	4	1	1	4	1	
1947	8	4		4	2		4	2	
1948	10	2		5	1		5	1	
1949	9	3		5	1		4	2	
1950	9	3		6	0		3	3	
1951	7	5		3	3		4	2	
1952	5	7		3	3		2	4	
1953	3	8	1	1	4	1	2	4	
1954	8	4		4	2		4	2	
1955	8	4		5	1		3	3	
1956	9	2	1	6	0		3	2	1
1957	5	7		2	4		3	3	
1958	8	4		5	1		3	3	
1959	8	4		4	2		4	2	
1960	5	6	1	4	2		1	4	1
1961	8	6		5	2		3	4	
1962	9	5		4	3		5	2	
1963	11	1	2	6	0	1	5	1	1
1964	5	9		2	5		3	4	
1965	9	5		5	2		4	3	
1966	5	7	2	4	1	2	1	6	
1967	7	6	1	3	3	1	4	3	
1968	7	7		2	5		5	2	
1969	1	13		1	6		0	7	
1970	6	8		3	4		3	4	
1971	6	8		4	3		2	5	
1972	4	9	1	1	5	1	3	4	
1973	3	11		1	6		2	5	
1974	4	10		4	3		0	7	
1975	4	10		3	4		1	6	
1976	7	7		4	3		3	4	
1977	9	5		5	2		4	3	
1978	7	9		4	4		3	5	
1979	10	6		6	2		4	4	
1980	7	9		5	3		2	6	
1981	6	10		4	4		2	6	
1982	3	6		2	2		1	4	
1983	8	8		5	3		3	5	
1984	10	6		6	2		4	4	
1985	15	1		8	0		7	1	
1986	14	2		7	1		7	1	
1987	11	4		6	2		5	2	

Season	All Games W	L	T	Home Games W	L	T	Road Games W	L	T
1988	12	4		7	1		5	3	
1989	6	10		4	4		2	6	
Total	539	341	42	316	143	24	223	198	18

*includes Decatur Staleys (1920) and Chicago Staleys (1921).

Dallas Cowboys

Season	All Games W	L	T	Home Games W	L	T	Road Games W	L	T
1960	0	11	1	0	6		0	5	1
1961	4	9	1	2	4	1	2	5	
1962	5	8	1	2	4	1	3	4	
1963	4	10		3	4	1	1	6	
1964	5	8	1	2	4	1	3	4	
1965	7	7		5	2		2	5	
1966	10	3	1	6	1		4	2	1
1967	9	5		5	2		4	3	
1968	12	2		5	2		7	0	
1969	11	2	1	6	0	1	5	2	
1970	10	4		6	1		4	3	
1971	11	3		6	1		5	2	
1972	10	4		5	2		5	2	
1973	10	4		6	1		4	3	
1974	8	6		5	2		3	4	
1975	10	4		5	2		5	2	
1976	11	3		6	1		5	2	
1977	12	2		6	1		6	1	
1978	12	4		7	1		5	3	
1979	11	5		6	2		5	3	
1980	12	4		8	0		4	4	
1981	12	4		8	0		4	4	
1982	6	3		3	2		3	1	
1983	12	4		6	2		6	2	
1984	9	7		5	3		4	4	
1985	10	6		7	1		3	5	
1986	7	9		3	5		4	4	
1987	7	8		3	4		4	4	
1988	3	13		1	7		2	6	
1989	1	15		0	8		1	7	
Total	251	177	6	138	75	4	113	102	2

Detroit Lions*

Season	All Games W	L	T	Home Games W	L	T	Road Games W	L	T
1930	5	6	3	5	1	2	0	5	1
1931	11	3		8	0		3	3	
1932	6	2	4	3	0	2	3	2	2
1933	6	5		4	1		2	4	
1934	10	3		6	2		4	1	
1935	7	3	2	5	0	1	2	3	1
1936	8	4		5	1		3	3	
1937	7	4		4	2		3	2	
1938	7	4		4	3		3	1	
1939	6	5		4	2		2	3	
1940	5	5	1	3	3		2	2	1
1941	4	6	1	3	2		1	4	1
1942	0	11		0	7		0	4	
1943	3	6	1	2	2	1	1	4	
1944	6	3	1	4	2		2	1	1
1945	7	3		4	1		3	2	
1946	1	10		1	5		0	5	
1947	3	9		2	4		1	5	
1948	2	10		2	4		0	6	
1949	4	8		2	4		2	4	
1950	6	6		4	2		2	4	
1951	7	4	1	3	3	1	4	1	
1952	9	3		6	1		3	2	
1953	10	2		5	1		5	1	
1954	9	2	1	5	0	1	4	2	
1955	3	9		3	4		0	5	
1956	9	3		5	1		4	2	
1957	8	4		5	1		3	3	
1958	4	7	1	2	4		2	3	1
1959	3	8	1	2	4		1	4	1
1960	7	5		5	1		2	4	
1961	8	5	1	2	5		6	0	1
1962	11	3		7	0		4	3	
1963	5	8	1	3	3	1	2	5	
1964	7	5	2	3	3	1	4	2	1
1965	6	7	1	2	4	1	4	3	
1966	4	9	1	3	4		1	5	1
1967	5	7	2	3	4		2	3	2
1968	4	8	2	1	4	2	3	4	
1969	9	4	1	5	2		4	2	1
1970	10	4		6	1		4	3	
1971	7	6	1	3	4		4	2	1
1972	8	5	1	5	2		3	3	1
1973	6	7	1	4	3		2	4	1
1974	7	7		4	3		3	4	
1975	7	7		4	3		3	4	
1976	6	8		5	2		1	6	
1977	6	8		5	2		1	6	
1978	7	9		5	3		2	6	
1979	2	14		2	6		0	8	
1980	9	7		6	2		3	5	
1981	8	8		7	1		1	7	
1982	4	5		2	3		2	2	
1983	9	7		6	2		3	5	
1984	4	11	1	2	5	1	2	6	
1985	7	9		6	2		1	7	
1986	5	11		1	7		4	4	
1987	4	11		1	6		3	5	
1988	4	12		2	6		2	6	
1989	7	9		4	4		3	5	
Total	369	384	32	226	163	14	143	221	18

*includes Portsmouth Spartans (1930-33).

Green Bay Packers

Season	All Games W	L	T	Home Games W	L	T	Road Games W	L	T
1921	3	2	1	2	1		1	1	1
1922	4	3	3	4	1	1	0	2	2
1923	7	2	1	4	2	1	3	0	
1924	7	4		5	0		2	4	
1925	8	5		6	0		2	5	
1926	7	3	3	4	1	2	3	2	1
1927	7	2	1	6	1		1	1	1
1928	6	4	3	2	2	2	4	2	1
1929	12	0	1	5	0		7	0	1
1930	10	3	1	6	0		4	3	1
1931	12	2		8	0		4	2	
1932	10	3	1	5	0	1	5	3	
1933	5	7	1	3	2	1	2	5	
1934	7	6		4	2		3	4	
1935	8	4		5	2		3	2	
1936	10	1	1	5	1		5	0	1
1937	7	4		3	2		4	2	
1938	8	3		4	2		4	1	
1939	9	2		4	1		5	1	
1940	6	4	1	4	2		2	2	1
1941	10	1		4	1		6	0	
1942	8	2	1	4	1		4	1	1
1943	7	2	1	2	1	1	5	1	
1944	8	2		5	0		3	2	
1945	6	4		4	1		2	3	
1946	6	5		2	3		4	2	
1947	6	5	1	4	2		2	3	1
1948	3	9		2	4		1	5	
1949	2	10		1	5		1	5	
1950	3	9		3	3		0	6	
1951	3	9		2	4		1	5	
1952	6	6		3	3		3	3	
1953	2	9	1	1	5		1	4	1
1954	4	8		2	4		2	4	
1955	6	6		5	1		1	5	
1956	4	8		2	4		2	4	
1957	3	9		1	5		2	4	
1958	1	10	1	1	4	1	0	6	
1959	7	5		4	2		3	3	
1960	8	4		4	2		4	2	
1961	11	3		6	1		5	2	
1962	13	1		7	0		6	1	
1963	11	2	1	6	1		5	1	1
1964	8	5	1	4	3		4	2	1
1965	10	3	1	6	1		4	2	1
1966	12	2		6	1		6	1	
1967	9	4	1	4	2	1	5	2	
1968	6	7	1	2	5		4	2	1
1969	8	6		5	2		3	4	
1970	6	8		4	3		2	5	
1971	4	8	2	3	3	1	1	5	1
1972	10	4		4	3		6	1	
1973	5	7	2	3	2	2	2	5	
1974	6	8		4	3		2	5	
1975	4	10		3	4		1	6	
1976	5	9		4	3		1	6	
1977	4	10		2	5		2	5	
1978	8	7	1	5	2	1	3	5	
1979	5	11		4	4		1	7	
1980	5	10	1	4	4		1	6	1
1981	8	8		4	4		4	4	
1982	5	3	1	3	1		2	2	1
1983	8	8		5	3		3	5	
1984	8	8		5	3		3	5	
1985	8	8		5	3		3	5	
1986	4	12		1	7		3	5	
1987	5	9	1	2	5	1	3	4	
1988	4	12		2	6		2	6	
1989	10	6		6	2		4	4	
Total	466	386	36	264	163	16	202	223	20

Los Angeles Rams*

Season	All Games W	L	T	Home Games W	L	T	Road Games W	L	T
1937	1	10		0	5		1	5	
1938	4	7		2	2		2	5	
1939	5	5	1	3	2	1	2	3	
1940	4	6	1	3	1	1	1	5	
1941	2	9		1	4		1	5	
1942	5	6		3	2		2	4	
1944	4	6		1	2		3	4	
1945	9	1		4	0		5	1	
1946	6	4	1	3	2		3	2	1
1947	6	6		3	3		3	3	
1948	6	5	1	3	2	1	3	3	
1949	8	2	2	5	1		3	1	2
1950	9	3		5	1		4	2	
1951	8	4		5	2		3	2	
1952	9	3		5	1		4	2	
1953	8	3	1	5	1		3	2	1
1954	6	5	1	3	2	1	3	3	
1955	8	3	1	5	1		3	2	1
1956	4	8		4	2		0	6	
1957	6	6		5	1		1	5	
1958	8	4		4	2		4	2	
1959	2	10		0	6		2	4	
1960	4	7	1	2	3	1	2	4	
1961	4	10		4	3		0	7	
1962	1	12	1	0	7		1	5	1
1963	5	9		3	4		2	5	
1964	5	7	2	3	2	2	2	5	
1965	4	10		3	4		1	6	
1966	8	6		5	2		3	4	
1967	11	1	2	5	1	1	6	0	1
1968	10	3	1	5	2		5	1	1
1969	11	3		5	2		6	1	
1970	9	4	1	3	3	1	6	1	
1971	8	5	1	4	2	1	4	3	
1972	6	7	1	4	3		2	4	1
1973	12	2		7	0		5	2	
1974	10	4		6	1		4	3	
1975	12	2		6	1		6	1	
1976	10	3	1	5	2		5	1	1
1977	10	4		7	0		3	4	
1978	12	4		6	2		6	2	
1979	9	7		4	4		5	3	
1980	11	5		6	2		5	3	
1981	6	10		4	4		2	6	
1982	2	7		1	4		1	3	
1983	9	7		5	3		4	4	
1984	10	6		5	3		5	3	
1985	11	5		6	2		5	3	
1986	10	6		6	2		4	4	
1987	6	9		3	4		3	5	
1988	10	6		6	2		4	4	
1989	11	5		6	2		5	3	
Total	375	292	20	205	123	10	170	169	10

*includes Cleveland Rams (1937-42, 1944-45).

Minnesota Vikings

Season	All Games W	L	T	Home Games W	L	T	Road Games W	L	T
1961	3	11		3	4		0	7	
1962	2	11	1	1	5	1	1	6	
1963	5	8	1	3	4		2	4	1
1964	8	5	1	4	3		4	2	1
1965	7	7		2	5		5	2	
1966	4	9	1	2	5		2	4	1
1967	3	8	3	1	4	2	2	4	1
1968	8	6		4	3		4	3	
1969	12	2		7	0		5	2	
1970	12	2		7	0		5	2	
1971	11	3		5	2		6	1	
1972	7	7		3	4		4	3	
1973	12	2		7	0		5	2	
1974	10	4		4	3		6	1	
1975	12	2		7	0		5	2	
1976	11	2	1	6	0	1	5	2	
1977	9	5		5	2		4	3	
1978	8	7	1	5	3		3	4	1
1979	7	9		4	4		3	5	
1980	9	7		5	3		4	4	
1981	7	9		5	3		2	6	
1982	5	4		4	1		1	3	
1983	8	8		5	3		3	5	
1984	3	13		2	6		1	7	
1985	7	9		4	4		3	5	
1986	9	7		5	3		4	4	
1987	8	7		5	2		3	5	
1988	11	5		7	1		4	4	
1989	10	6		8	0		2	6	
Total	228	185	9	129	79	4	99	106	5

New Orleans Saints

Season	All Games W	L	T	Home Games W	L	T	Road Games W	L	T
1967	3	11		2	5		1	6	
1968	4	9	1	3	4		1	5	1
1969	5	9		3	4		2	5	
1970	2	11	1	2	5		0	6	1
1971	4	8	2	2	4	1	2	4	1
1972	2	11	1	2	5		0	6	1
1973	5	9		5	2		0	7	
1974	5	9		4	3		1	6	
1975	2	12		2	5		0	7	
1976	4	10		2	5		2	5	
1977	3	11		2	5		1	6	
1978	7	9		3	5		4	4	
1979	8	8		3	5		5	3	
1980	1	15		0	8		1	7	
1981	4	12		2	6		2	6	
1982	4	5		2	3		2	2	
1983	8	8		5	3		3	5	
1984	7	9		3	5		4	4	
1985	5	11		3	5		2	6	
1986	7	9		4	4		3	5	
1987	12	3		6	1		6	2	
1988	10	6		5	3		5	3	
1989	9	7		5	3		4	4	
Total	121	212	5	70	98	1	51	114	4

New York Giants

Season	All Games W	L	T	Home Games W	L	T	Road Games W	L	T
1925	8	4		7	2		1	2	
1926	8	4	1	5	2	1	3	2	
1927	11	1	1	7	1		4	0	1
1928	4	7	2	1	2	2	3	5	
1929	13	1	1	7	1		6	0	1
1930	13	4		6	2		7	2	
1931	7	6	1	4	2	1	3	4	
1932	4	6	2	3	2	1	1	4	1
1933	11	3		7	0		4	3	
1934	8	5		5	1		3	4	
1935	9	3		4	2		5	1	
1936	5	6	1	3	3	1	2	3	
1937	6	3	2	4	2	1	2	1	1
1938	8	2	1	6	1		2	1	1
1939	9	1	1	6	0		3	1	1
1940	6	4	1	4	3		2	1	1
1941	8	3		5	2		3	1	
1942	5	5	1	3	2	1	2	3	
1943	6	3	1	4	2		2	1	1
1944	8	1	1	5	1		3	0	1
1945	3	6	1	2	4		1	2	1
1946	7	3	1	5	1	1	2	2	
1947	2	8	2	2	3	1	0	5	1
1948	4	8		2	4		2	4	
1949	6	6		2	4		4	2	
1950	10	2		5	1		5	1	
1951	9	2	1	5	1		4	1	1
1952	7	5		2	4		5	1	
1953	3	9		2	4		1	5	
1954	7	5		4	2		3	3	
1955	6	5	1	4	1	1	2	4	
1956	8	3	1	4	1	1	4	2	
1957	7	5		3	3		4	2	
1958	9	3		5	1		4	2	
1959	10	2		5	1		5	1	
1960	6	4	2	1	3	2	5	1	
1961	10	3	1	4	2	1	6	1	
1962	12	2		6	1		6	1	
1963	11	3		5	2		6	1	
1964	2	10	2	2	5		0	5	2
1965	7	7		3	4		4	3	
1966	1	12	1	1	6		0	6	1
1967	7	7		5	2		2	5	
1968	7	7		3	4		4	3	
1969	6	8		5	2		1	6	
1970	9	5		5	2		4	3	
1971	4	10		1	6		3	4	
1972	8	6		4	3		4	3	
1973	2	11	1	2	4	1	0	7	
1974	2	12		0	7		2	5	
1975	5	9		2	5		3	4	
1976	3	11		3	4		0	7	
1977	5	9		3	4		2	5	
1978	6	10		5	3		1	7	
1979	6	10		4	4		2	6	
1980	4	12		2	6		2	6	
1981	9	7		4	4		5	3	
1982	4	5		2	3		2	2	
1983	3	12	1	1	7		2	5	1
1984	9	7		6	2		3	5	
1985	10	6		6	2		4	4	

(continued)

Season	All Games W	L	T	Home Games W	L	T	Road Games W	L	T
1986	14	2		8	0		6	2	
1987	6	9		5	3		1	6	
1988	10	6		5	3		5	3	
1989	12	4		7	1		5	3	
Total	455	370	32	258	172	16	197	198	16

Philadelphia Eagles

Season	All Games W	L	T	Home Games W	L	T	Road Games W	L	T
1933	3	5	1	2	3	1	1	2	
1934	4	7		2	4		2	3	
1935	2	9		0	5		2	4	
1936	1	11		1	6		0	5	
1937	2	8	1	0	5	1	2	3	
1938	5	6		2	3		3	3	
1939	1	9	1	1	3	1	0	6	
1940	1	10		1	4		0	6	
1941	2	8	1	1	4	1	1	4	
1942	2	9		0	5		2	4	
1944	7	1	2	3	1	2	4	0	
1945	7	3		6	0		1	3	
1946	6	5		3	2		3	3	
1947	8	4		6	1		2	3	
1948	9	2	1	6	0		3	2	1
1949	11	1		6	0		5	1	
1950	6	6		2	4		4	2	
1951	4	8		1	5		3	3	
1952	7	5		4	2		3	3	
1953	7	4	1	5	0	1	2	4	
1954	7	4	1	5	1		2	3	1
1955	4	7	1	4	2		0	5	1
1956	3	8	1	2	3	1	1	5	
1957	4	8		3	3		1	5	
1958	2	9	1	2	4		0	5	1
1959	6	5		4	1		2	4	
1960	10	2		5	1		5	1	
1961	10	4		5	2		5	2	
1962	3	10	1	2	5		1	5	1
1963	2	10	2	1	5	1	1	5	1
1964	6	8		3	4		3	4	
1965	5	9		2	5		3	4	
1966	9	5		5	2		4	3	
1967	6	7	1	5	2		1	5	1
1968	2	12		1	6		1	6	
1969	4	9	1	2	5		2	4	1
1970	3	10	1	3	3	1	0	7	
1971	6	7	1	3	4		3	3	1
1972	2	11	1	0	6	1	2	5	
1973	5	8	1	4	3		1	5	1
1974	7	7		5	2		2	5	
1975	4	10		2	5		2	5	
1976	4	10		2	5		2	5	
1977	5	9		4	3		1	6	
1978	9	7		5	3		4	4	
1979	11	5		5	3		6	2	
1980	12	4		7	1		5	3	
1981	10	6		6	2		4	4	
1982	3	6		1	4		2	2	
1983	5	11		1	7		4	4	
1984	6	9	1	5	3		1	6	1
1985	7	9		4	4		3	5	
1986	5	10	1	2	5	1	3	5	
1987	7	8		4	4		3	4	
1988	10	6		5	3		5	3	
1989	11	5		6	2		5	3	
Total	310	396	23	177	180	12	133	216	11

Phoenix Cardinals*

Season	All Games W	L	T	Home Games W	L	T	Road Games W	L	T
1920	6	2	2	5	1	1	1	1	1
1921	3	3	2	3	3	1	0	0	1
1922	8	3		8	3		0	0	
1923	8	4		8	3		0	1	
1924	5	4	1	5	3	1	0	1	
1925	11	2	1	11	2		0	0	1
1926	5	6	1	3	3		2	3	1
1927	3	7	1	2	3	1	1	4	
1928	1	5		1	1		0	4	
1929	6	6	1	3	2		3	4	1
1930	5	6	2	3	2		2	4	2
1931	5	4		3	0		2	4	
1932	2	6	2	1	2	1	1	4	1
1933	1	9	1	0	4	1	1	5	
1934	5	6		2	2		3	4	
1935	6	4	2	2	2		4	2	2
1936	3	8	1	3	1	1	0	7	
1937	5	5	1	1	3		4	2	1
1938	2	9		1	4		1	5	
1939	1	10		0	4		1	6	
1940	2	7	2	2	1	1	0	6	1
1941	3	7	1	0	3	1	3	4	
1942	3	8		2	2		1	6	
1943	0	10		0	3		0	7	
1945	1	9		0	3		1	6	
1946	6	5		2	2		4	3	
1947	9	3		5	0		4	3	
1948	11	1		5	1		6	0	
1949	6	5	1	2	3	1	4	2	
1950	5	7		3	3		2	4	
1951	3	9		1	5		2	4	
1952	4	8		2	4		2	4	
1953	1	10	1	0	5	1	1	5	
1954	2	10		2	4		0	6	
1955	4	7	1	3	2	1	1	5	
1956	7	5		4	2		3	3	
1957	3	9		0	6		3	3	
1958	2	9	1	1	4	1	1	5	
1959	2	10		2	4		0	6	
1960	6	5	1	3	2	1	3	3	
1961	7	7		3	4		4	3	
1962	4	9	1	2	4	1	2	5	
1963	9	5		3	4		6	1	
1964	9	3	2	4	1	1	5	2	1
1965	5	9		2	5		3	4	
1966	8	5	1	5	1	1	3	4	
1967	6	7	1	3	3	1	3	4	
1968	9	4	1	4	2	1	5	2	
1969	4	9	1	3	4		1	5	1
1970	8	5	1	6	1		2	4	1
1971	4	9	1	1	5		3	4	
1972	4	9	1	2	5		2	4	1
1973	4	9	1	2	4	1	2	5	
1974	10	4		5	2		5	2	
1975	11	3		6	1		5	2	
1976	10	4		6	1		4	3	
1977	7	7		4	3		3	4	
1978	6	10		3	5		3	5	
1979	5	11		3	5		2	6	
1980	5	11		2	6		3	5	
1981	7	9		5	3		2	6	
1982	5	4		1	3		4	1	
1983	8	7	1	4	3	1	4	4	
1984	9	7		5	3		4	4	
1985	5	11		4	4		1	7	
1986	4	11	1	3	5		1	6	1
1987	7	8		4	3		3	5	
1988	7	9		4	4		3	5	
1989	5	11		2	6		3	5	
Total	363	470	39	205	207	22	158	263	17

*includes Chicago Cardinals (1920-59) and St. Louis Cardinals (1960-87).

San Francisco 49ers

Season	All Games W	L	T	Home Games W	L	T	Road Games W	L	T
1950	3	9		3	3		0	6	
1951	7	4	1	5	1		2	3	1
1952	7	5		3	3		4	2	
1953	9	3		5	1		4	2	
1954	7	4	1	4	2		3	2	1
1955	4	8		2	4		2	4	
1956	5	6	1	3	3		2	3	1
1957	8	4		5	1		3	3	
1958	6	6		4	2		2	4	
1959	7	5		4	2		3	3	
1960	7	5		3	3		4	2	
1961	7	6	1	5	1	1	2	5	
1962	6	8		1	6		5	2	
1963	2	12		2	5		0	7	
1964	4	10		3	4		1	6	
1965	7	6	1	4	2	1	3	4	
1966	6	6	2	4	2	1	2	4	1
1967	7	7		3	4		4	3	
1968	7	6	1	3	3	1	4	3	
1969	4	8	2	3	3	1	1	5	1
1970	10	3	1	5	1	1	5	2	
1971	9	5		4	3		5	2	
1972	8	5	1	4	2	1	4	3	
1973	5	9		3	4		2	5	
1974	6	8		3	4		3	4	
1975	5	9		2	5		3	4	
1976	8	6		4	3		4	3	
1977	5	9		3	4		2	5	
1978	2	14		2	6		0	8	
1979	2	14		2	6		0	8	
1980	6	10		4	4		2	6	
1981	13	3		7	1		6	2	
1982	3	6		0	5		3	1	

Season	All Games W	L	T	Home Games W	L	T	Road Games W	L	T
1983	10	6		4	4		6	2	
1984	15	1		7	1		8	0	
1985	10	6		5	3		5	3	
1986	10	5	1	6	2		4	3	1
1987	13	2		6	1		7	1	
1988	10	6		4	4		6	2	
1989	14	2		6	2		8	0	
Total	284	257	13	150	120	7	134	137	6

Tampa Bay Buccaneers

Season	All Games W	L	T	Home Games W	L	T	Road Games W	L	T
1976	0	14		0	7		0	7	
1977	2	12		1	6		1	6	
1978	5	11		3	5		2	6	
1979	10	6		5	3		5	3	
1980	5	10	1	2	5	1	3	5	
1981	9	7		6	2		3	5	
1982	5	4		4	1		1	3	
1983	2	14		1	7		1	7	
1984	6	10		6	2		0	8	
1985	2	14		2	6		0	8	
1986	2	14		1	7		1	7	
1987	4	11		2	5		2	6	
1988	5	11		3	5		2	6	
1989	5	11		2	6		3	5	
Total	62	149	1	38	67	1	24	82	

Washington Redskins*

Season	All Games W	L	T	Home Games W	L	T	Road Games W	L	T
1932	4	4	2	2	3	1	2	1	1
1933	5	5	2	4	2		1	3	2
1934	6	6		4	3		2	3	
1935	2	8	1	2	5		0	3	1
1936	7	5		4	3		3	2	
1937	8	3		4	2		4	1	
1938	6	3	2	3	1	1	3	2	1
1939	8	2	1	5	0	1	3	2	
1940	9	2		6	0		3	2	
1941	6	5		4	2		2	3	
1942	10	1		5	1		5	0	
1943	6	3	1	4	2		2	1	1
1944	6	3	1	4	2		2	1	1
1945	8	2		6	0		2	2	
1946	5	5	1	3	2	1	2	3	
1947	4	8		4	2		0	6	
1948	7	5		4	2		3	3	
1949	4	7	1	3	3		1	4	1
1950	3	9		1	5		2	4	
1951	5	7		2	4		3	3	
1952	4	8		1	5		3	3	
1953	6	5	1	3	3		3	2	1
1954	3	9		3	3		0	6	
1955	8	4		3	3		5	1	
1956	6	6		4	2		2	4	
1957	5	6	1	2	3	1	3	3	
1958	4	7	1	3	2	1	1	5	
1959	4	8		2	4		2	4	
1960	1	9	2	1	4	1	0	5	1
1961	1	12	1	1	6		0	6	1
1962	5	7	2	3	4		2	3	2
1963	3	11		1	6		2	5	
1964	6	8		4	3		2	5	
1965	6	8		3	4		3	4	
1966	7	7		4	3		3	4	
1967	5	6	3	2	4	1	3	2	2
1968	5	9		3	4		2	5	
1969	7	5	2	4	2	1	3	3	1
1970	6	8		4	3		2	5	
1971	9	4	1	4	2	1	5	2	
1972	11	3		6	1		5	2	
1973	10	4		7	0		3	4	
1974	10	4		6	1		4	3	
1975	8	6		5	2		3	4	
1976	10	4		5	2		5	2	
1977	9	5		5	2		4	3	
1978	8	8		5	3		3	5	
1979	10	6		6	2		4	4	
1980	6	10		4	4		2	6	
1981	8	8		5	3		3	5	
1982	8	1		3	1		5	0	
1983	14	2		7	1		7	1	
1984	11	5		7	1		4	4	
1985	10	6		5	3		5	3	
1986	12	4		7	1		5	3	
1987	11	4		6	1		5	3	
1988	7	9		4	4		3	5	
1989	10	6		4	4		6	2	
Total	393	335	26	226	150	10	167	185	16

*includes Boston Braves (1932) and Boston Redskins (1933-36).

Records for Each Current NFL Team for Most Points in a Game (Regular Season Only)

Note: When the record has been achieved more than once, only the most recent game is shown; summaries are listed in alphabetical order by conference. Bold face indicates team holding record.

BUFFALO BILLS
September 18, 1966, at Buffalo

Miami.................. 3 7 0 14 — 24
Buffalo .... 21 27 3 10 — 61
TDs: Buff—Bobby Burnett 2, Butch Byrd 2, Jack Spikes 2, Bobby Crockett, Jack Kemp; Mia—Dave Kocourek, Bo Roberson, John Roderick. TD Passes: Buff—Jack Kemp, Daryle Lamonica; Mia—George Wilson 3. FGs: Buff—Booth Lusteg; Mia—Gene Mingo.

CINCINNATI BENGALS
December 17, 1989, at Cincinnati

Houston .... 0 0 0 7 — 7
Cincinnati .... 21 10 21 9 — 61
TDs: Cin—Eddie Brown 2, Eric Ball, James Brooks, Ira Hillary, Rodney Holman, Tim McGee, Craig Taylor; Hou—Lorenzo White. TD Passes: Cin—Boomer Esiason 4, Erik Wilhelm. FGs: Cin—Jim Breech 2.

CLEVELAND BROWNS
November 7, 1954, at Cleveland

Washington .... 0 3 0 0 — 3
Cleveland............. 13 14 21 14 — 62
TDs: Clev—Darrell Brewster 2, Mo Bassett, Ken Gorgal, Otto Graham, Dub Jones, Dante Lavelli, Curley Morrison. TD Passes: Clev—George Ratterman 3, Otto Graham. FGs: Clev—Lou Groza 2; Wash—Vic Janowicz.

DENVER BRONCOS
October 6, 1963, at Denver

San Diego .... 13 7 0 14 — 34
Denver .... 3 14 9 24 — 50
TDs: Den—Lionel Taylor 2, Goose Gonsoulin, Gene Prebola, Donnie Stone; SD—Keith Lincoln 2, Lance Alworth, Paul Lowe, Jacque MacKinnon. TD Passes: Den—John McCormick 3; SD—Tobin Rote 3, John Hadl 2. FGs: Den—Gene Mingo 5.

HOUSTON OILERS
October 14, 1962, at Houston

New York Titans .... 3 7 7 0 — 17
Houston................ 14 21 14 7 — 56
TDs: Hou—Bill Groman, 2, Bob McLeod 2, Dave Smith 2, Willard Dewveall, Charley Hennigan; NY—Dick Christy, Ed Cooke. TD Passes: Hou—George Blanda 6, Jacky Lee. FGs: NY—Bill Shockley.

INDIANAPOLIS COLTS
December 12, 1976, at Baltimore

Buffalo.................. 3 3 7 7 — 20
Baltimore Colts .... 7 13 28 10 — 58
TDs: Balt—Roger Carr, Raymond Chester, Glenn Doughty, Roosevelt Leaks, Derrel Luce, Lydell Mitchell, Howard Stevens; Buff—Bob Chandler, O.J. Simpson. TD Passes: Balt—Bert Jones 3; Buff—Gary Marangi. FGs: Balt—Toni Linhart 3; Buff—George Jakowenko 2.

KANSAS CITY CHIEFS
September 7, 1963, at Denver

Kansas City .... 14 14 21 10 — 59
Denver .... 0 7 0 0 — 7
TDs: KC—Chris Burford 2, Frank Jackson 2, Dave Grayson, Abner Haynes, Sherrill Headrick, Curtis McClinton; Den—Lionel Taylor. TD Passes: KC—Len Dawson 4, Curtis McClinton; Den—Mickey Slaughter. FG: KC—Tommy Brooker.

LOS ANGELES RAIDERS
December 22, 1963, at Oakland

Houston .... 7 21 14 0 — 49
Oakland Raiders .... 7 28 7 10 — 52
TDs: Oak—Art Powell 4, Clem Daniels, Claude Gibson, Ken Herock; Hou—Willard Dewveall 2, Dave Smith 2, Charley Hennigan, Bob McLeod, Charley Tolar. TD Passes: Oak—Tom Flores 6; Hou—George Blanda 5. FG: Oak—Mike Mercer.

MIAMI DOLPHINS
November 24, 1977, at St. Louis

Miami .... 14 14 20 7 — 55
St. Louis .... 7 0 0 7 — 14
TDs: Mia—Nat Moore 3, Gary Davis, Duriel Harris, Leroy Harris, Benny Malone, Andre Tillman; StL—Ike Harris, Terry Metcalf. TD Passes: Mia—Bob Griese 6; StL—Jim Hart.

NEW ENGLAND PATRIOTS
September 9, 1979, at New England

New York Jets .... 3 0 0 0 — 3
New England .... 14 21 7 14 — 56
TDs: NE—Harold Jackson 3, Stanley Morgan 2, Allan Clark, Andy Johnson, Don Westbrook. TD Passes: NE—Steve Grogan 5, Tom Owen. FG: NYJ—Pat Leahy.

NEW YORK JETS
November 17, 1985, at New York

Tampa Bay .... 14 7 0 7 — 28
New York Jets .... 17 24 14 7 — 62
TDs: NYJ—Mickey Shuler 3, Johnny Hector 2, Tony Paige, Al Toon, Wesley Walker; TB—James Wilder 2, Kevin House, Calvin Magee. TD Passes: NYJ—Ken O'Brien 5; TB—Steve DeBerg 2. FGs: NYJ—Pat Leahy 2.

PITTSBURGH STEELERS
November 30, 1952, at Pittsburgh

New York Giants .... 0 0 7 0 — 7
Pittsburgh .... 14 14 7 28 — 63
TDs: Pitt—Lynn Chandnois 2, Dick Hensley 2, Jack Butler, George Hays, Ray Mathews, Ed Modzelewski, Elbie Nickel; NYG—Bill Stribling. TD Passes: Pitt—Jim Finks 4, Gary Kerkorian; NYG—Tom Landry.

SAN DIEGO CHARGERS
December 22, 1963, at San Diego

Denver .... 7 10 3 0 — 20
San Diego .... 10 16 10 22 — 58
TDs: SD—Paul Lowe 2, Chuck Allen, Bobby Jackson, Dave Kocourek, Keith Lincoln, Jacque MacKinnon; Den—Billy Joe, Donnie Stone. TD Passes: SD—John Hadl, Tobin Rote; Den—Don Breaux. FGs: SD—George Blair 3; Den—Gene Mingo 2.

SEATTLE SEAHAWKS
October 30, 1977, at Seattle

Buffalo................. 3 0 7 7 — 17
Seattle .... 14 28 7 7 — 56
TDs: Sea—Steve Largent 2, Duke Fergerson, Al Hunter, David Sims, Sherman Smith, Don Testerman, Jim Zorn; Buff—Joe Ferguson, John Kimbrough. TD Passes: Sea—Jim Zorn 4; Buff—Joe Ferguson. FG: Buff—Carson Long.

ATLANTA FALCONS
September 16, 1973, at New Orleans

Atlanta .... 0 24 21 17 — 62
New Orleans .... 0 0 7 0 — 7
TDs: Atl—Ken Burrow 2, Eddie Ray 2, Wes Chesson, Tom Hayes, Art Malone, Joe Profit; NO—Bill Butler. TD Passes: Atl—Dick Shiner 3, Bob Lee; NO—Archie Manning. FGs: Atl—Nick Mike-Mayer.

CHICAGO BEARS
December 7, 1980, at Chicago

Green Bay .... 0 7 0 0 — 7
Chicago .... 0 28 13 20 — 61
TDs: Chi—Walter Payton 3, Brian Baschnagel, Robin Earl, Roland Harper, Willie McClendon, Len Walterscheid, Rickey Watts; GB—James Lofton. TD Passes: Chi—Vince Evans 3; GB—Lynn Dickey.

DALLAS COWBOYS
October 12, 1980, at Dallas

San Francisco .... 0 7 0 7 — 14
Dallas .... 14 24 14 7 — 59
TDs: Dall—Drew Pearson 3, Ron Springs 2, Tony Dorsett, Billy Joe DuPree, Robert Newhouse; SF—Dwight Clark 2. TD Passes: Dall—Danny White 4; SF—Steve DeBerg 2. FG: Dall—Rafael Septien.

DETROIT LIONS
October 26, 1952, at Green Bay

Detroit .... 14 14 14 10 — 52
Green Bay .... 7 3 7 0 — 17
TDs: Det—Jug Girard 2, Bob Hoernschemeyer 2, Jack Christiansen, Jim Smith, Bill Swiacki; GB—Billy Howton, Jim Keane. TD Passes: Det—Bobby Layne 3; GB—Babe Parilli, Tobin Rote. FGs: Det—Pat Harder; GB—Bill Reichardt.

GREEN BAY PACKERS
October 7, 1945, at Milwaukee

Detroit .... 0 7 7 7 — 21
Green Bay .... 0 41 9 7 — 57
TDs: GB—Don Hutson 4, Charley Brock, Irv Comp, Ted Fritsch, Clyde Goodnight; Det—Chuck Fenen-

bock, John Greene, Bob Westfall. TD Passes: GB—Tex McKay 4, Lou Brock, Irv Comp; Det—Dave Ryan.

LOS ANGELES RAMS
October 22, 1950, at Los Angeles

Baltimore	13	0	7	7	— 27
Los Angeles	21	14	14	21	— 70

TDs: LA—Bob Boyd 2, Vitamin T. Smith 2, Tom Fears, Elroy (Crazylegs) Hirsch, Dick Hoerner, Ralph Pasquariello, Dan Towler, Bob Waterfield; Balt—Chet Mutryn 2, Adrian Burk, Billy Stone. TD Passes: LA—Norm Van Brocklin 2, Bob Waterfield 2, Glenn Davis; Balt—Adrian Burk 3.

MINNESOTA VIKINGS
October 18, 1970, at Minnesota

Dallas	3	3	0	7	— 13
Minnesota	14	20	17	3	— 54

TDs: Minn—Clint Jones 2, Ed Sharockman 2, John Beasley, Dave Osborn; Dall—Calvin Hill. TD Pass: Minn—Gary Cuozzo. FGs: Minn—Fred Cox 4; Dall—Mike Clark 2.

NEW ORLEANS SAINTS
November 21, 1976, at Seattle

New Orleans	3	17	28	3	— 51
Seattle	6	0	7	14	— 27

TDs: NO—Bobby Douglass 2, Tony Galbreath, Chuck Muncie, Tom Myers, Elex Price; Sea—Sherman Smith 2, Steve Largent, Jim Zorn. TD Pass: Sea—Bill Munson. FGs: NO—Rich Szaro 3.

NEW YORK GIANTS
November 26, 1972, at New York

Philadelphia	3	7	0	0	— 10
New York Giants	14	24	10	14	— 62

TDs: NYG—Don Herrmann 2, Ron Johnson 2, Bob Tucker 2, Randy Johnson; Phil—Harold Jackson. TD Passes: NYG—Norm Snead 3, Randy Johnson 2; Phil—John Reaves. FGs: NYG—Pete Gogolak 2; Phil—Tom Dempsey.

PHILADELPHIA EAGLES
November 6, 1934, at Philadelphia

Cincinnati Reds	0	0	0	0	— 0
Philadelphia	26	6	12	20	— 64

TDs: Phil—Joe Carter 3, Swede Hanson 3, Marvin Ellstrom, Roger Kirkman, Ed Matesic, Ed Storm. TD Passes: Phil—Ed Matesic 2, Albert Weiner 2, Marvin Elstrom.

ST. LOUIS CARDINALS
November 13, 1949, at New York

Chicago Cardinals	7	31	14	13	— 65
New York Bulldogs	7	0	6	7	— 20

TDs: Chi—Red Cochran 2, Pat Harder 2, Bill Dewell, Mel Kutner, Bob Ravensburg, Vic Schwall, Charlie Trippi; NY—Joe Golding, Frank Muehlheuser, Johnny Rauch. TD Passes: Chi—Paul Christman 3, Jim Hardy 3; NY—Bobby Layne. FG: Chi—Pat Harder.

SAN FRANCISCO 49ERS
September 19, 1965, at San Francisco

Chicago	3	0	0	21	— 24
San Francisco	0	24	21	7	— 52

TDs: SF—Bernie Casey 2, John David Crow, Charlie Krueger, Gary Lewis, Dave Parks, Ken Willard; Chi—Charlie Bivins 2, Andy Livingston. TD Passes: SF—John Brodie 4; Chi—Rudy Bukich 2. FGs: SF—Tommy Davis; Chi—Roger LeClerc.

TAMPA BAY BUCCANEERS
September 13, 1987, at Tampa Bay

Atlanta	0	3	0	7	— 10
Tampa Bay	14	13	7	14	— 48

TDs: TB—Gerald Carter 2, Cliff Austin, Steve Bartalo, Mark Carrier, Phil Freeman, Calvin Magee; Atl—Stacey Bailey. TD Passes: TB—Steve DeBerg 5; Atl—Scott Campbell. FG: Atl—Mick Luckhurst.

WASHINGTON REDSKINS
November 27, 1966, at Washington

New York Giants	0	14	14	13	— 41
Washington	13	21	14	24	— 72

TDs: Wash—A. D. Whitfield 3, Brig Owens 2, Charley Taylor 2, Rickie Harris, Joe Don Looney, Bobby Mitchell; NYG—Allen Jacobs, Homer Jones, Dan Lewis, Joe Morrison, Aaron Thomas, Gary Wood. TD Passes: Wash—Sonny Jurgensen 3; NYG—Gary Wood 2, Tom Kennedy. FG: Wash—Charlie Gogolak.

NFL Games In Which a Team Has Scored 60 or More Points

(Home team in capitals)

Regular Season

WASHINGTON 72, New York Giants 41	November 27, 1966
LOS ANGELES RAMS 70, Baltimore 27	October 22, 1950
Chicago Cardinals 65, NEW YORK BULLDOGS 20	November 13, 1949
LOS ANGELES RAMS 65, Detroit 24	October 29, 1950
PHILADELPHIA 64, Cincinnati 0	November 6, 1934
CHICAGO CARDINALS 63, New York Giants 35	October 17, 1948
AKRON 62, Oorang 0	October 29, 1922
PITTSBURGH 62, New York Giants 7	November 30, 1952
CLEVELAND 62, New York Giants 14	December 6, 1953
CLEVELAND 62, Washington 3	November 7, 1954
NEW YORK GIANTS 62, Philadelphia 10	November 26, 1972
ATLANTA 62, NEW ORLEANS 7	September 16, 1973
NEW YORK JETS 62, Tampa Bay 28	November 17, 1985
CHICAGO 61, San Francisco 20	December 12, 1965
Cincinnati 61, HOUSTON 17	December 17, 1972
CHICAGO 61, Green Bay 7	December 7, 1980
CINCINNATI 61, Houston 7	December 17, 1989
ROCK ISLAND 60, Evansville 0	October 15, 1922
CHICAGO CARDINALS 60, Rochester 0	October 7, 1923

Postseason

Chicago Bears 73, WASHINGTON 0	December 8, 1940

Youngest and Oldest Regular Starters in NFL in 1989

Minimum: 8 Games Started

Five Youngest Regular Starters

	Birthdate	Games Started	Position
Courtney Hall, San Diego	8/26/68	16	C
Barry Sanders, Detroit	7/16/68	13	RB
Eric Metcalf, Cleveland	1/23/68	11	RB
Derek Hill, Pittsburgh	11/4/67	8	WR
Maurice Hurst, New England	9/17/67	14	CB

Five Oldest Regular Starters

	Birthdate	Games Started	Position
Ed Jones, Dallas	2/23/51	10	DE
Mike Webster, Kansas City	3/18/52	16	C
Carl Hairston, Cleveland	12/15/52	16	DE
Dave Brown, Green Bay	1/16/53	16	CB
Steve DeBerg, Kansas City	1/19/54	10	QB

Youngest and Oldest Regular Starters By Position

Minimum: 8 Games Started

	Youngest	Oldest
QB	11/21/66 Troy Aikman, Dall.	1/19/54 Steve DeBerg, K.C.
RB	7/16/68 Barry Sanders, Det.	1/19/57 Ottis Anderson, Giants
WR	11/4/67 Derek Hill, Pitt.	9/28/54 Steve Largent, Sea.
TE	5/20/66 Mike Dyal, Raiders	3/16/56 Ozzie Newsome, Clev.
C	8/26/68 Courtney Hall, S.D.	3/18/52 Mike Webster, K.C.
G	4/7/67 Steve Wisniewski, Raiders	2/23/54 Joe Devlin, Buff.
T	1/1/67 Andy Heck, Sea.	5/27/54 Jackie Slater, Rams
DE	4/10/67 Burt Grossman, S.D.	2/23/51 Ed Jones, Dall.
DT	7/29/66 Jim Wahler, Phx.	12/15/52 Carl Hairston, Clev.
LB	7/18/67 Jeff Lageman, Jets	8/27/54 Scott Studwell, Minn.
CB	9/17/67 Maurice Hurst, N.E.	1/16/53 Dave Brown, G.B.
S	8/26/67 Myron Guyton, Giants	4/15/57 Nesby Glasgow, Sea.

NFL by the Numbers

0 Field goal attempts of less than 20 yards were missed by NFL kickers last season. They went 27-for-27 from that range.

2.14 Career rate of touchdown passes per game by Dan Marino, highest in NFL history.

2.42 Career rate of interceptions per 100 passes by Bernie Kosar, lowest rate by any quarterback in NFL history.

3 Teams that have not won a division title since the 1970 merger of the AFL and the NFL: Houston, New Orleans, New York Jets.

4 Consecutive post-season games in which John Taylor has caught a touchdown pass. NFL record: eight consecutive games by John Stallworth.

6 Consecutive opening-day victories recorded by both the Chicago Bears and the New England Patriots, the longest active streaks of that type in the NFL.

7 Great players of the past to be inducted into the Pro Football Hall of Fame on August 4: Buck Buchanon, Bob Griese, Franco Harris, Ted Hendricks, Jack Lambert, Tom Landry, Bob St. Clair.

8 Consecutive seasons that the Dolphins have allowed the fewest sacks in the NFL. No other team ever led for more than three years in succession.

10 Players selected from the University of Southern California in the 1990 draft, the most from any college.

11 Post-season touchdowns by Jerry Rice, the highest total among active players.

13 Total of tie games played in NFL in 16 seasons since sudden death overtime was enacted for regular-season games.

17 Weeks over which NFL teams will each play 16 regular-season games in the 1990 season.

18 Field goals of 50+ yards by Nick Lowery, the most by an kicker in NFL history.

20 Post-season games won by Dallas Cowboys, most by any team in NFL history.

25 Interceptions by Ronnie Lott over the past four seasons, the most by any NFL player.

58 Games of 100+ yards rushing by Eric Dickerson, tied with Jim Brown for second place in NFL history. Walter Payton, with 77 such games, holds NFL record.

62 Career interceptions by Dave Brown, the most among active players and tied for fifth place in NFL history.

77.3 Career field goal percentage of Nick Lowery, the best by any kicker (with 100 field goals) in NFL history.

86 Regular-season starts won by Joe Montana, the most by any active NFL quarterback.

94.0 Career pass rating by Joe Montana, highest in NFL history.

99.2 Career extra-point percentage of Gary Anderson, second-best in NFL history. He would need to make his next 89 attempts to break Tommy Davis's NFL record of 99.4 percent.

104 Sacks by Lawrence Taylor, the most by any NFL player since 1982 (when they were first compiled).

149 Consecutive games by Jim Breech scoring at least one point, just two games shy of Fred Cox's NFL record.

194 Consecutive games by San Francisco without being shut out, longest streak by any NFL team.

269 Games won by Don Shula in regular-season play, just 50 short of George Halas's NFL record.

1006 Points scored by Nick Lowery during 1980s, most by any player.

1968 Year of birth for Courtney Hall of San Diego, the youngest regular starter in the NFL last season.

Eric Dickerson's Career Rushing vs. Each Opponent

Opponent	Games	Rushes	Yards	Yards Per Rush	Yards Per Game	TD
Atlanta	9	179	852	4.8	94.7	9
Buffalo	6	138	547	4.0	91.2	3
Chicago	4	115	482	4.2	120.5	5
Cincinnati	2	53	241	4.5	120.5	2
Cleveland	5	109	492	4.5	98.4	2
Dallas	2	49	244	5.0	122.0	1
Denver	2	34	194	5.7	97.0	4
Detroit	2	54	329	6.1	164.5	4
Green Bay	4	95	426	4.5	106.5	2
Houston	4	105	609	5.8	152.3	4
Indianapolis	1	25	121	4.8	121.0	1
Kansas City	1	26	68	2.6	68.0	1
L.A. Raiders	1	25	98	3.9	98.0	0
L.A. Rams	1	21	116	5.5	116.0	1
Miami	6	154	780	5.1	130.0	6
Minnesota	3	73	217	3.0	72.3	1
New England	7	165	616	3.7	88.0	3
New Orleans	9	192	907	4.7	100.8	6
N.Y. Giants	3	77	312	4.1	104.0	1
N.Y. Jets	7	153	620	4.1	88.6	6
Philadelphia	2	45	161	3.6	80.5	0
Phoenix	3	79	525	6.6	175.0	4
Pittsburgh	1	23	49	2.1	49.0	0
San Diego	4	105	452	4.3	113.0	0
San Francisco	9	170	832	4.9	92.4	3
Seattle	1	31	150	4.8	150.0	3
Tampa Bay	5	143	749	5.2	149.8	10
Washington	1	12	37	3.1	37.0	0
Totals	105	2450	11,226	4.6	106.9	82

Phoenix totals include three games vs. St. Louis.

Roger Craig's Career Rushing vs. Each Opponent

Opponent	Games	Rushes	Yards	Yards Per Rush	Yards Per Game	TD
Atlanta	14	182	962	5.3	68.7	6
Buffalo	2	40	152	3.8	76.0	1
Chicago	5	46	176	3.8	35.2	0
Cincinnati	2	24	69	2.9	34.5	0
Cleveland	2	22	71	3.2	35.5	2
Dallas	3	41	186	4.5	62.0	2
Denver	2	48	260	5.4	130.0	0
Detroit	3	42	185	4.4	61.7	1
Green Bay	3	34	128	3.8	42.7	0
Houston	2	24	99	4.1	49.5	1
Indianapolis	2	26	153	5.9	76.5	2
Kansas City	1	15	55	3.7	55.0	1
L.A. Raiders	2	27	92	3.4	46.0	0
L.A. Rams	14	222	949	4.3	67.8	9
Miami	2	29	154	5.3	77.0	2
Minnesota	5	71	247	3.5	49.4	3
New England	3	56	206	3.7	68.7	2
New Orleans	14	186	765	4.1	54.6	5
N.Y. Giants	4	57	235	4.1	58.8	0
N.Y. Jets	3	42	190	4.5	63.3	2
Philadelphia	4	50	186	3.7	46.5	0
Phoenix	4	51	277	5.4	69.3	2
Pittsburgh	2	16	45	2.8	22.5	0
San Diego	1	17	87	5.1	87.0	2
Seattle	2	36	161	4.5	80.5	0
Tampa Bay	5	76	295	3.9	59.0	6
Washington	4	65	240	3.7	60.0	0
Totals	110	1545	6625	4.3	60.2	49

Phoenix totals include three games vs. St. Louis.

Joe Montana's Career Passing vs. Each Opponent

Opponent	Games	Att.	Cmp.	Pct.	Yards	Avg. Gain	TD	Int.	Sacked
Atlanta	19	483	314	65.0	3562	7.37	28	15	26/182
Buffalo	2	64	43	67.2	381	5.95	2	0	6/46
Chicago	7	162	90	55.6	1023	6.31	5	4	20/144
Cincinnati	3	115	71	61.7	738	6.42	7	5	7/60
Cleveland	3	103	71	68.9	818	7.94	6	4	5/40
Dallas	4	89	57	64.0	824	9.26	8	2	5/39
Denver	4	106	58	54.7	779	7.35	4	3	6/50
Detroit	5	120	74	61.7	713	5.94	2	2	9/55
Green Bay	4	109	79	72.5	853	7.83	4	2	8/50
Houston	3	107	75	70.1	846	7.91	7	3	3/13
Indianapolis	1	26	15	57.7	233	8.96	1	0	3/29
Kansas City	2	69	43	62.3	488	7.07	2	2	3/16
L.A. Raiders	4	96	51	53.1	659	6.86	4	1	11/92
L.A. Rams	21	626	409	65.3	5178	8.27	34	12	42/283
Miami	2	30	19	63.3	267	8.90	1	0	3/22
Minnesota	4	84	56	66.7	741	8.82	9	2	5/24
New England	4	108	69	63.9	791	7.32	6	2	6/39
New Orleans	19	465	288	61.9	3494	7.51	30	13	32/199
N.Y. Giants	7	181	120	66.3	1283	7.09	9	3	7/38
N.Y. Jets	3	79	48	60.8	538	6.81	3	3	3/17
Philadelphia	3	54	35	64.8	546	10.11	5	2	9/52
Phoenix	6	141	95	67.4	1389	9.85	13	5	7/53
Pittsburgh	3	120	80	66.7	762	6.35	3	6	2/17
San Diego	3	68	45	66.2	627	9.22	6	2	2/13
Seattle	3	62	37	59.7	539	8.69	6	4	3/17
Tampa Bay	7	219	153	69.9	1630	7.44	6	5	10/67
Washington	5	173	98	56.6	1352	7.82	5	5	9/84
Totals	151	4059	2593	63.9	31,054	7.65	216	107	252/1741

L.A. Raiders totals include one game vs. Oakland
Phoenix totals include six games vs. St. Louis

Phil Simms's Career Passing vs. Each Opponent

Opponent	Games	Att.	Cmp.	Pct.	Yards	Avg. Gain	TD	Int.	Sacked
Atlanta	4	116	66	56.9	910	7.84	4	3	12/81
Chicago	1	28	15	53.6	181	6.46	1	0	8/53
Cincinnati	1	62	40	64.5	513	8.27	1	2	7/70
Cleveland	1	37	23	62.2	289	7.81	1	2	4/22
Dallas	18	473	237	50.1	3773	7.98	29	30	48/362
Denver	3	78	43	55.1	519	6.65	1	1	8/64
Detroit	3	94	65	69.1	765	8.14	4	0	11/73
Green Bay	5	156	97	62.2	1302	8.35	11	4	16/111
Houston	1	24	13	54.2	234	9.75	2	1	0/0
Indianapolis	1	14	7	50.0	67	4.79	1	4	3/19
Kansas City	3	82	42	51.2	587	7.16	5	5	7/52
L.A. Raiders	2	55	31	56.4	408	7.42	2	2	5/39
L.A. Rams	6	209	112	53.6	1352	6.47	6	6	24/196
Minnesota	2	39	25	64.1	310	7.95	1	2	3/22
New Orleans	5	155	90	58.1	1011	6.52	5	7	13/88
N.Y. Jets	4	135	78	57.8	928	6.87	5	2	21/167
Philadelphia	15	459	232	50.5	3284	7.15	16	15	48/349
Phoenix	15	434	218	50.2	2843	6.55	28	10	43/270
Pittsburgh	1	16	10	62.5	106	6.63	1	1	3/24
San Diego	3	99	54	54.5	667	6.74	1	4	8/72
San Francisco	6	226	129	57.1	1649	7.30	8	8	27/178
Seattle	3	78	43	55.1	487	6.24	3	5	9/59
Tampa Bay	6	177	101	57.1	960	5.42	5	5	17/189
Washington	15	412	209	50.7	3090	7.50	17	20	51/391
Totals	124	3658	1980	54.1	26,235	7.17	156	137	396/2951

Indianapolis totals include one game vs. Baltimore
Phoenix totals include 12 games vs. St. Louis

Dan Marino's Career Passing vs. Each Opponent

Opponent	Games	Att.	Cmp.	Pct.	Yards	Avg. Gain	TD	Int.	Sacked
Atlanta	1	40	20	50.0	303	7.58	2	4	0/0
Buffalo	13	444	287	64.6	3433	7.73	25	21	14/129
Cincinnati	3	103	60	58.3	745	7.23	4	1	4/30
Cleveland	3	122	71	58.2	933	7.65	7	5	0/0
Dallas	3	115	66	57.4	860	7.48	6	3	4/36
Denver	1	43	25	58.1	390	9.07	3	0	3/25
Detroit	1	44	23	52.3	247	5.61	2	2	1/8
Green Bay	3	114	76	66.7	939	8.24	9	5	1/5
Houston	5	140	78	55.7	998	7.13	8	7	2/9
Indianapolis	14	457	273	59.7	3541	7.75	26	6	10/75
Kansas City	3	119	69	58.0	815	6.85	8	3	2/20
L.A. Raiders	4	142	80	56.3	1021	7.19	10	5	5/49
L.A. Rams	2	84	54	64.3	682	8.12	7	2	1/4
Minnesota	1	37	20	54.1	264	7.14	2	3	0/0
New England	13	445	248	55.7	2949	6.63	19	22	7/64
New Orleans	2	63	39	61.9	391	6.21	4	1	1/6
N.Y. Jets	12	473	284	60.0	4026	8.51	37	17	14/87
Philadelphia	2	73	45	61.6	622	8.52	4	2	3/31
Phoenix	1	36	24	66.7	429	11.92	3	0	1/9
Pittsburgh	5	147	93	63.3	1158	7.88	8	8	0/0

Opponent	Games	Att.	Cmp.	Pct.	Yards	Avg. Gain	TD	Int.	Sacked
San Diego	3	122	77	63.1	957	7.84	6	1	4/29
San Francisco	2	75	42	56.0	495	6.60	3	4	3/29
Tampa Bay	2	85	54	63.5	568	6.68	5	1	0/0
Washington	2	78	43	55.1	704	9.03	8	1	0/0
Totals	103	3650	2174	59.6	27,853	7.63	220	125	83/670

Indianapolis totals include two games vs. Baltimore.
Phoenix totals include one game vs. St. Louis.

John Elway's Career Passing vs. Each Opponent

Opponent	Games	Att.	Cmp.	Pct.	Yards	Avg. Gain	TD	Int.	Sacked
Atlanta	2	64	35	54.7	526	8.22	4	2	4/26
Buffalo	3	81	40	49.4	518	6.40	4	2	6/51
Chicago	3	53	27	50.9	388	7.32	3	3	3/25
Cincinnati	2	47	30	63.8	355	7.55	4	1	2/13
Cleveland	4	108	58	53.7	859	7.95	7	3	5/43
Dallas	1	24	12	50.0	200	8.33	3	0	1/2
Detroit	2	52	32	61.5	456	8.77	2	1	4/40
Green Bay	2	68	41	60.3	386	5.68	0	4	1/4
Houston	1	35	17	48.6	256	7.31	3	3	2/15
Indianapolis	5	153	77	50.3	998	6.52	4	2	13/103
Kansas City	12	368	193	52.4	2273	6.18	6	23	21/154
L.A. Raiders	12	348	193	55.5	2272	6.53	13	16	28/249
L.A. Rams	2	74	39	52.7	501	6.77	5	2	3/24
Miami	1	37	18	48.6	250	6.76	0	1	3/24
Minnesota	2	58	38	65.5	463	7.98	7	1	4/30
New England	4	140	75	53.6	917	6.55	6	4	6/35
New Orleans	2	79	46	58.2	519	6.57	4	2	4/35
N.Y. Giants	2	94	52	55.3	628	6.68	1	2	3/19
N.Y. Jets	1	28	13	46.4	145	5.18	0	1	5/27
Philadelphia	3	84	44	52.4	567	6.75	4	5	13/104
Phoenix	1	29	20	69.0	247	8.52	2	2	2/14
Pittsburgh	4	108	60	55.6	756	7.00	5	4	8/64
San Diego	13	398	218	54.8	2583	6.49	8	16	30/203
San Francisco	2	81	41	50.6	425	5.25	3	3	5/43
Seattle	13	424	226	53.3	3425	8.08	21	11	28/219
Washington	1	35	20	57.1	282	8.06	1	0	3/23
Totals	100	3070	1665	54.2	21,195	6.90	120	114	207/1589

Boomer Esiason's Career Passing vs. Each Opponent

Opponent	Games	Att.	Cmp.	Pct.	Yards	Avg. Gain	TD	Int.	Sacked
Atlanta	2	32	15	46.9	168	5.25	0	0	2/0
Buffalo	5	106	60	56.6	840	7.92	5	3	5/42
Chicago	2	66	32	48.5	396	6.00	2	4	6/56
Cleveland	11	256	135	52.7	1805	7.05	8	9	15/119
Dallas	2	54	31	57.4	470	8.70	6	0	2/9
Denver	1	30	21	70.0	306	10.20	2	1	1/4
Detroit	2	66	43	65.2	566	8.58	3	2	2/3
Green Bay	1	24	15	62.5	207	8.63	3	0	3/24
Houston	11	321	190	59.2	2801	8.73	18	13	21/144
Indianapolis	2	57	31	54.4	405	7.11	2	2	6/55
Kansas City	4	121	67	55.4	940	7.77	5	3	7/71
L.A. Raiders	3	63	37	58.7	525	8.33	3	0	4/37
Miami	2	61	34	55.7	422	6.16	2	1	4/52
Minnesota	2	79	48	60.8	619	7.84	4	4	7/62
New England	4	124	66	53.2	967	7.80	7	6	4/36
New Orleans	2	43	18	41.9	171	3.98	2	2	6/58
N.Y. Giants	1	24	15	62.5	193	8.04	3	0	4/36
N.Y. Jets	5	117	65	55.6	1099	9.39	10	4	12/83
Philadelphia	1	32	20	62.5	363	11.34	4	1	1/10
Phoenix	2	38	24	63.2	356	9.37	4	1	3/22
Pittsburgh	11	316	186	58.9	2718	8.60	16	11	20/185
San Diego	2	63	36	57.1	498	7.90	5	2	7/57
San Francisco	1	29	14	48.3	180	6.21	1	1	3/16
Seattle	3	77	44	57.1	594	7.71	2	2	7/56
Tampa Bay	1	28	17	60.7	197	7.04	5	0	1/1
Washington	2	58	32	55.2	544	9.38	4	2	4/39
Totals	85	2285	1296	56.7	18,350	8.03	126	76	155/1277

Phoenix totals include one game vs. St. Louis.

Jerry Rice's Career Receiving vs. Each Opponent

Opponent	Games	Rec.	Yards	Yards Per Rec.	Yards Per Game	TD
Atlanta	9	35	579	16.5	64.3	7
Buffalo	1	3	46	15.3	46.0	1
Chicago	4	19	299	15.7	74.8	5
Cincinnati	1	4	86	21.5	86.0	2
Cleveland	1	7	126	18.0	126.0	3
Dallas	2	9	139	15.4	69.5	1
Denver	2	7	145	20.7	72.5	0
Detroit	2	3	38	12.7	19.0	0
Green Bay	3	17	245	14.4	81.7	3
Houston	1	7	77	11.0	77.0	1
Indianapolis	2	12	335	27.9	167.5	4

Opponent	Games	Rec.	Yards	Yards Per Rec.	Yards Per Game	TD
Kansas City	1	1	19	19.0	19.0	0
L.A. Raiders	2	8	155	19.4	77.5	0
L.A. Rams	10	40	814	20.4	81.4	6
Miami	1	3	76	25.3	76.0	2
Minnesota	3	12	233	19.4	77.7	2
New England	2	10	147	14.7	73.5	2
New Orleans	10	46	804	17.5	80.4	6
N.Y. Giants	3	20	312	15.6	104.0	3
N.Y. Jets	2	10	192	19.2	96.0	1
Philadelphia	2	9	234	26.0	117.0	3
Phoenix	2	7	193	27.6	96.5	3
Pittsburgh	1	8	106	13.3	106.0	1
San Diego	1	6	171	28.5	171.0	2
Seattle	2	8	205	25.6	102.5	3
Tampa Bay	3	20	279	14.0	93.0	4
Washington	3	15	309	20.6	103.0	1
Totals	76	346	6364	18.4	83.7	66

Phoenix totals include one game vs. St. Louis.

Starting Records of Active NFL Quarterbacks
Minimum: 10 starts

	W-L-T	Pct.
Don Strock	16-6	.727
Jim McMahon	50-22	.694
Joe Montana	86-38	.694
Mike Tomczak	20-9	.690
Jay Schroeder	32-16	.667
John Elway	64-33-1	.658
Doug Flutie	9-5	.643
Bernie Kosar	39-23-1	.637
Chris Chandler	10-6	.625
Wade Wilson	24-15	.615
Dan Marino	62-39	.614
Jeff Kemp	13-8-1	.614
Dave Krieg	57-37	.606
Jim Everett	29-19	.604
Mark Rypien	12-8	.600
Marc Wilson	27-18	.600
Phil Simms	71-50	.587
Turk Schonert	7-5	.583
Bobby Hebert	29-21	.580
Pat Ryan	11-8	.579
Randall Cunningham	30-22-1	.575
Steve Grogan	74-57	.565
Tony Eason	29-24	.547
Boomer Esiason	42-35	.545
Steve Beuerlein	8-7	.533
Todd Blackledge	15-14	.517
Don Majkowski	15-14-1	.517
Ron Jaworski	72-69-1	.511
Ken O'Brien	35-35-1	.500
Eric Hipple	28-29	.491
Jim Kelly	28-29	.491
Tommy Kramer	54-56	.491
Gary Hogeboom	18-19	.486
Doug Williams	38-42-1	.475
Joe Ferguson	79-92	.462
Cliff Stoudt	9-11	.450
Warren Moon	35-49	.417
Bubby Brister	12-17	.414
Dave Wilson	12-19	.387
Jack Trudeau	12-21	.364
Steve Young	10-18	.357
Mike Pagel	17-33-1	.343
Steve Pelluer	9-19-1	.328
Vinny Testaverde	10-23	.303
Steve DeBerg	30-70-1	.302
Chris Miller	8-22	.267
Chuck Long	4-17	.190
Mark Herrmann	2-9	.182
Troy Aikman	0-11	.000

Individual NFL Leaders Over Last 2 Seasons, Last 3 Seasons, Last 4 Seasons

Last 2 Seasons	Last 3 Seasons	Last 4 Seasons
Points		
257 Mike Cofer	335 Morten Andersen	443 Morten Andersen
244 Scott Norwood	324 Nick Lowery	420 Rich Karlis
237 Mike Lansford	321 Tony Zendejas	415 Tony Zendejas
229 Tony Zendejas	316 Rich Karlis	409 Mike Lansford
225 Rich Karlis	305 Scott Norwood	396 Jerry Rice
225 Chip Lohmiller		

Last 2 Seasons / Last 3 Seasons / Last 4 Seasons

Touchdowns

Last 2 Seasons	Last 3 Seasons	Last 4 Seasons
33 Greg Bell	50 Jerry Rice	66 Jerry Rice
27 Neal Anderson	34 Greg Bell	40 Greg Bell
27 Jerry Rice	33 Neal Anderson	40 Mark Clayton
24 Dalton Hilliard	32 Dalton Hilliard	40 Eric Dickerson
23 James Brooks	30 Mark Clayton	39 Herschel Walker
23 Mark Clayton		39 Curt Warner
23 Eric Dickerson		

Field Goals

Last 2 Seasons	Last 3 Seasons	Last 4 Seasons
56 Mike Cofer	74 Morten Andersen	100 Morten Andersen
55 Scott Norwood	72 Rich Karlis	92 Gary Anderson
54 Rich Karlis	71 Gary Anderson	92 Rich Karlis
51 Nick Lowery	70 Dean Biasucci	89 Nick Lowery
49 Gary Anderson	70 Nick Lowery	89 Tony Zendejas

Rushes

Last 2 Seasons	Last 3 Seasons	Last 4 Seasons
702 Eric Dickerson	985 Eric Dickerson	1,389 Eric Dickerson
611 Herschel Walker	820 Herschel Walker	1,013 Curt Warner
581 Roger Craig	796 Roger Craig	1,000 Roger Craig
560 Greg Bell	694 Curt Warner	971 Herschel Walker
548 Dalton Hilliard	671 Dalton Hilliard	860 Gerald Riggs

Rushing Yards

Last 2 Seasons	Last 3 Seasons	Last 4 Seasons
2,970 Eric Dickerson	4,258 Eric Dickerson	6,079 Eric Dickerson
2,556 Roger Craig	3,371 Roger Craig	4,201 Roger Craig
2,429 Herschel Walker	3,320 Herschel Walker	4,122 Curt Warner
2,381 Neal Anderson	2,967 Neal Anderson	4,057 Herschel Walker
2,349 Greg Bell	2,641 Curt Warner	3,547 James Brooks

Rushing TDs

Last 2 Seasons	Last 3 Seasons	Last 4 Seasons
31 Greg Bell	31 Greg Bell	38 Eric Dickerson
23 Neal Anderson	27 Eric Dickerson	35 Greg Bell
22 Ottis Anderson	26 Neal Anderson	34 Curt Warner
21 Eric Dickerson	25 Dalton Hilliard	32 Johnny Hector
18 Dalton Hilliard	24 Johnny Hector	31 Herschel Walker

Passes

Last 2 Seasons	Last 3 Seasons	Last 4 Seasons
1,156 Dan Marino	1,600 Dan Marino	2,223 Dan Marino
1,092 Randall Cunningham	1,498 Randall Cunningham	1,826 John Elway
1,035 Jim Everett	1,337 Jim Everett	1,776 Ken O'Brien
946 Vinny Testaverde	1,322 John Elway	1,752 Boomer Esiason
935 Don Majkowski	1,294 Ken O'Brien	1,742 Jim Kelly

Completions

Last 2 Seasons	Last 3 Seasons	Last 4 Seasons
662 Dan Marino	925 Dan Marino	1,303 Dan Marino
612 Jim Everett	814 Randall Cunningham	1,058 Ken O'Brien
591 R. Cunningham	775 Joe Montana	1,032 Jim Kelly
531 Don Majkowski	774 Jim Everett	1,010 Bernie Kosar
524 Ken O'Brien	758 Ken O'Brien	1,001 John Elway

Passing Yards

Last 2 Seasons	Last 3 Seasons	Last 4 Seasons
8,431 Dan Marino	11,676 Dan Marino	16,422 Dan Marino
8,274 Jim Everett	10,418 Boomer Esiason	14,377 Boomer Esiason
7,208 Randall Cunningham	10,338 Jim Everett	13,043 John Elway
7,097 Boomer Esiason	9,994 Randall Cunningham	12,901 Jim Kelly
6,510 Jim Kelly	9,558 John Elway	12,310 Bernie Kosar

TD Passes

Last 2 Seasons	Last 3 Seasons	Last 4 Seasons
60 Jim Everett	78 Dan Marino	122 Dan Marino
56 Boomer Esiason	75 Joe Montana	96 Boomer Esiason
52 Dan Marino	72 Boomer Esiason	83 Dave Krieg
45 R. Cunningham	70 Jim Everett	83 Joe Montana
44 Joe Montana	68 Randall Cunningham	81 Jim Kelly

Receptions

Last 2 Seasons	Last 3 Seasons	Last 4 Seasons
159 Andre Reed	236 J.T. Smith	316 J.T. Smith
158 Art Monk	224 Al Toon	309 Al Toon
156 Henry Ellard	216 Andre Reed	297 Jerry Rice
156 Al Toon	211 Jerry Rice	272 Roger Craig
153 Eric Martin	207 Henry Ellard	269 Art Monk
153 Ricky Sanders		269 Andre Reed

Reception Yards

Last 2 Seasons	Last 3 Seasons	Last 4 Seasons
2,796 Henry Ellard	3,867 Jerry Rice	5,437 Jerry Rice
2,789 Jerry Rice	3,595 Henry Ellard	4,452 Gary Clark
2,392 Mark Carrier	3,213 Anthony Carter	4,180 Drew Hill
2,291 Anthony Carter	3,187 Gary Clark	4,066 Mark Clayton
2,286 Ricky Sanders	3,068 Drew Hill	4,042 Henry Ellard

Receiving TDs

Last 2 Seasons	Last 3 Seasons	Last 4 Seasons
26 Jerry Rice	48 Jerry Rice	63 Jerry Rice
23 Mark Clayton	30 Mark Clayton	40 Mark Clayton
18 Henry Ellard	24 Drew Hill	30 Gary Clark
18 Drew Hill	23 Gary Clark	29 Drew Hill
17 Cris Carter	22 Eric Martin	27 Eric Martin
		27 Andre Reed

Interceptions

Last 2 Seasons	Last 3 Seasons	Last 4 Seasons
14 Gill Byrd	19 Mark Kelso	25 Ronnie Lott
14 Erik McMillan	18 Felix Wright	23 Dave Waymer
14 Felix Wright	16 Joey Browner	21 Deron Cherry
13 Eric Allen	16 David Fulcher	21 Felix Wright
13 David Fulcher	16 Barry Wilburn	20 Joey Browner
13 Mark Kelso		20 David Fulcher

Sacks

Last 2 Seasons	Last 3 Seasons	Last 4 Seasons
33 Kevin Greene	50 Reggie White	68 Reggie White
33 Tim Harris	42.5 Lawrence Taylor	63 Lawrence Taylor
30.5 Lawrence Taylor	40 Chris Doleman	51 Bruce Smith
29 Chris Doleman	40 Tim Harris	48 Tim Harris
29 Reggie White	39.5 Kevin Greene	48 Lee Williams

NFL Team Leaders Over Last 2 Seasons, Last 3 Seasons, Last 4 Seasons

Highest Won-Lost Percentage

Last 2 Seasons	Last 3 Seasons	Last 4 Seasons
.750 San Francisco	.787 San Francisco	.754 San Francisco
.688 N.Y. Giants	.660 New Orleans	.683 Cleveland
.656 Buffalo	.628 Cleveland	.667 N.Y. Giants
.656 L.A. Rams	.628 Denver	.659 Cleveland
.656 Minnesota	.617 Chicago	.643 Denver
.656 Philadelphia	.617 Minnesota	

Most Points

Last 2 Seasons	Last 3 Seasons	Last 4 Seasons
852 Cincinnati	1,270 San Francisco	1,644 San Francisco
833 L.A. Rams	1,150 L.A. Rams	1,546 Cincinnati
811 San Francisco	1,137 Cincinnati	1,491 Minnesota
789 Houston	1,134 Houston	1,478 Washington
757 Minnesota	1,120 New Orleans	1,459 L.A. Rams

Most Total Yards

Last 2 Seasons	Last 3 Seasons	Last 4 Seasons
12,168 San Francisco	18,155 San Francisco	24,237 San Francisco
12,158 Cincinnati	17,535 Cincinnati	24,025 Cincinnati
11,932 Washington	17,529 Washington	23,130 Washington
11,850 L.A. Rams	16,805 Miami	23,129 Miami
11,267 Miami	16,501 L.A. Rams	21,439 Denver

Most Rushing Yards

Last 2 Seasons	Last 3 Seasons	Last 4 Seasons
5,193 Cincinnati	7,357 Cincinnati	9,890 Cincinnati
4,606 Chicago	6,726 San Francisco	9,260 Chicago
4,489 San Francisco	6,560 Chicago	8,712 San Francisco
4,397 Buffalo	6,245 Indianapolis	8,466 L.A. Rams
4,177 Houston	6,237 Buffalo	8,413 Pittsburgh

Most Passing Yards

Last 2 Seasons	Last 3 Seasons	Last 4 Seasons
8,732 Miami	12,608 Miami	17,387 Miami
8,485 Washington	11,980 Washington	15,849 Washington
7,938 L.A. Rams	11,429 San Francisco	15,525 San Francisco
7,679 San Francisco	10,513 St. L./Phoenix	14,135 Cincinnati
7,333 Green Bay	10,492 L.A. Rams	14,068 Cleveland

Fewest Turnovers

Last 2 Seasons	Last 3 Seasons	Last 4 Seasons
51 San Francisco	77 San Francisco	106 San Francisco
57 Indianapolis	91 Cincinnati	116 Cleveland
57 N.Y. Giants	91 Indianapolis	120 Philadelphia
58 Philadelphia	91 New Orleans	125 Minnesota
59 Cincinnati	92 Cleveland	127 Cincinnati

Fewest Points Allowed

Last 2 Seasons	Last 3 Seasons	Last 4 Seasons
508 Minnesota	781 Cleveland	1,047 San Francisco
542 Cleveland	800 San Francisco	1,061 Chicago
547 San Francisco	843 Minnesota	1,091 Cleveland
554 Buffalo	854 Indianapolis	1,104 N.Y. Giants
556 N.Y. Giants	859 Buffalo	1,116 Minnesota

Fewest Total Yards Allowed

Last 2 Seasons	Last 3 Seasons	Last 4 Seasons
8,275 Minnesota	13,099 Minnesota	18,111 Minnesota
9,193 San Francisco	13,288 San Francisco	18,168 San Francisco
9,319 Kansas City	13,862 Cleveland	18,434 Chicago
9,598 Cleveland	14,304 Cleveland	19,131 Cleveland
9,624 Buffalo	14,408 N.Y. Giants	19,165 N.Y. Giants

Fewest Rushing Yards Allowed

Last 2 Seasons	Last 3 Seasons	Last 4 Seasons
2,971 San Francisco	4,582 San Francisco	6,099 Chicago
3,089 Washington	4,636 Chicago	6,137 San Francisco
3,105 New Orleans	4,655 New Orleans	6,214 New Orleans
3,223 Chicago	4,768 Washington	6,350 N.Y. Giants
3,229 L.A. Rams	4,900 Philadelphia	6,573 Washington

Fewest Passing Yards Allowed

Last 2 Seasons	Last 3 Seasons	Last 4 Seasons
4,961 Kansas City	8,090 Minnesota	11,306 Minnesota
4,990 Minnesota	8,267 Kansas City	11,462 Kansas City
5,760 Denver	8,556 Denver	11,852 Denver
5,930 Buffalo	8,706 San Francisco	11,995 Green Bay
6,008 Cleveland	8,784 Buffalo	12,031 San Francisco

Most Opponents' Turnovers

Last 2 Seasons	Last 3 Seasons	Last 4 Seasons
100 Philadelphia	148 Philadelphia	184 Philadelphia
89 Minnesota	126 Minnesota	168 Minnesota
81 Green Bay	123 Green Bay	162 New Orleans
79 Houston	119 Denver	162 San Francisco
75 Pittsburgh	119 New Orleans	155 Green Bay
75 San Francisco	119 Pittsburgh	

Longest Streaks in NFL History

Games Played

282	Jim Marshall	1960-79
240	Mick Tingelhoff	1962-78
234	Jim Bakken	1962-78

Games Scoring

151	Fred Cox	1963-73
149	Jim Breech	1980-89 (current)
133	Garo Yepremian	1970-79

Games Scoring Touchdowns

18	Lenny Moore	1963-65
14	O.J. Simpson	1975
13	John Riggins	1982-83
	Jerry Rice	1986-87

Extra Points

234	Tommy Davis	1959-65
221	Jim Turner	1967-74
202	Gary Anderson	1983-88

Games Scoring Field Goals

31	Fred Cox	1968-70
28	Jim Turner	1970-72
23	Morten Andersen	1986-88

Field Goals

24	Kevin Butler	1988-89
23	Mark Moseley	1981-82
22	Pat Leahy	1985-86

100-Yard Rushing Games

11	Marcus Allen	1985-86
9	Walter Payton	1985
7	O.J. Simpson	1972-73
	Earl Campbell	1979

Games Rushing For Touchdowns

13	John Riggins	1982-83
	George Rogers	1985-86
11	Lenny Moore	1963-64
10	Greg Bell	1988-89

Passes Completed

22	Joe Montana	1987
20	Ken Anderson	1983
18	Steve DeBerg	1982
	Lynn Dickey	1983
	Joe Montana	1984
	Don Majkowski	1989

300-Yard Passing Games

5	Joe Montana	1982
4	Dan Fouts	1979
	Bill Kenney	1983

Games Passing For Touchdowns

47	Johnny Unitas	1956-60
30	Dan Marino	1985-87
28	Dave Krieg	1983-85

Passes Without Interception

294	Bart Starr	1964-65
211	Ken O'Brien	1987-88
208	Milt Plum	1959-60

Games With Receptions

177	Steve Largent	1977-89
150	Ozzie Newsome	1979-89
127	Harold Carmichael	1972-80

100-Yard Receiving Games

7	Charley Hennigan	1961
	Bill Groman	1961
6	Raymond Berry	1960
	Pat Studstill	1966
5	Elroy (Crazylegs) Hirsch	1951
	Bob Boyd	1954
	Terry Barr	1963
	Lance Alworth	1966

Games With Touchdown Receptions

13	Jerry Rice	1986-87
11	Elroy (Crazylegs) Hirsch	1950-51
	Buddy Dial	1959-60
9	Lance Alworth	1963

Games With Interceptions

8	Tom Morrow	1962-63
7	Paul Krause	1964
	Larry Wilson	1966
	Ben Davis	1968

Punts Without A Block

623	Dave Jennings	1976-83
619	Ray Guy	1979-86
578	Bobby Walden	1964-72

Records of Teams on Opening Day, 1933-89

AFC	W	L	T	Pct.	Longest W Strk.	Longest L Strk.	Current Streak
Denver	18	11	1	.621	3	4	W-1
L.A. Raiders	18	12	0	.600	5	5	W-3
San Diego	18	12	0	.600	6	4	L-3
Cleveland	23	17	0	.575	5	5	W-2
Houston	16	14	0	.533	4	3	L-1
Pittsburgh	27	24	4	.529	4	3	L-1
Cincinnati	11	11	0	.500	4	4	L-1
Kansas City	15	15	0	.500	5	4	L-2
New England	15	15	0	.500	6	3	W-6
Indianapolis	22	23	1	.489	8	6	L-6
Miami	10	13	1	.435	4	5	L-5
N.Y. Jets	13	17	0	.433	3	5	L-2
Buffalo	11	19	0	.367	3	5	W-2
Seattle	4	10	0	.286	3	8	L-1

NFC	W	L	T	Pct.	Longest W Strk.	Longest L Strk.	Current Streak
Dallas	22	7	1	.759	17	3	L-3
Minnesota	17	11	1	.607	4	2	W-1
N.Y. Giants	31	22	4	.585	3	3	W-2
Chicago	32	24	1	.571	7	6	W-6
L.A. Rams	29	23	0	.558	5	6	W-2
Detroit	30	25	2	.545	7	4	L-1
Atlanta	13	11	0	.542	5	3	L-3
Green Bay	28	26	3	.519	5	6	L-5
Washington	27	26	4	.509	6	5	L-1
San Francisco	18	21	1	.462	4	3	W-2
Phoenix	25	30	1	.455	6	6	W-1
Philadelphia	22	33	1	.400	5	9	W-2
Tampa Bay	5	9	0	.357	3	5	W-1
New Orleans	5	18	0	.217	1	6	W-1

Note: All tied games occurred prior to 1972, when calculation of ties in percentages as half-win, half-loss was begun.

Records of All NFL Teams for 1989 in Each Category of Games:

AFC	Status at Halftime			Status After 3 Quarters		
	Leading	Tied	Trailing	Leading	Tied	Trailing
Buffalo	7-3	0-1	2-3	7-2	0-1	2-4
Cincinnati	6-4	1-1	1-3	6-3	1-1	1-4
Cleveland	6-1-1	1-2	2-3	9-1-1	0-1	0-4
Denver	10-2	0-0	1-3	9-2	0-0	2-3
Houston	6-1	0-0	3-6	7-0	0-0	2-7
Indianapolis	3-1	1-1	4-6	3-1	2-1	3-6
Kansas City	7-2	0-0	1-5-1	6-2	0-0	2-5-1
L.A. Raiders	4-2	2-2	2-4	5-3	2-0	1-5
Miami	5-2	0-0	3-6	5-2	1-0	2-6
New England	3-1	0-1	2-9	3-1	1-1	1-9
N.Y. Jets	2-2	1-1	1-9	2-1	0-1	2-10
Pittsburgh	8-0	0-0	1-7	8-0	0-1	1-6
San Diego	1-2	1-3	4-5	2-3	0-1	4-6
Seattle	3-2	2-1	2-6	5-2	0-0	2-7

NFC	Leading	Tied	Trailing	Leading	Tied	Trailing
Atlanta	0-5	0-0	3-8	0-3	0-0	3-10
Chicago	4-1	2-1	0-8	5-2	0-0	1-8
Dallas	1-3	0-1	0-11	1-3	0-1	0-11
Detroit	4-2	2-1	1-6	6-1	0-0	1-8
Green Bay	6-0	2-0	2-6	5-0	1-0	4-6
L.A. Rams	9-2	1-1	1-2	10-2	0-0	1-3
Minnesota	10-3	0-0	0-3	10-2	0-0	0-4
New Orleans	8-4	0-2	1-1	6-4	1-0	2-3
N.Y. Giants	8-1	2-0	2-3	11-1	0-1	1-2
Philadelphia	6-1	1-1	4-3	7-2	1-0	3-3
Phoenix	4-5	0-1	1-5	3-3	0-0	2-8
San Francisco	8-0	1-1	5-1	9-0	1-1	4-1
Tampa Bay	3-1	1-0	1-10	4-2	0-0	1-9
Washington	4-1	2-1	4-4	8-2	0-0	2-4
Totals	146-54-1	23-23	54-146-1	162-50-1	11-11	50-162-1

Trailing at Halftime

	1981-89	1989 ONLY
Home Teams	197-549-3 (.265)	26-60-0 (.302)
Road Teams	183-792-4 (.189)	28-86-1 (.248)
All Teams	380-1341-7 (.222)	54-146-1 (.271)

Trailing After 3 Quarters

	1981-89	1989 ONLY
Home Teams	164-606-2 (.214)	26-63-0 (.292)
Road Teams	150-870-5 (.149)	24-99-1 (.198)
All Teams	314-1476-7 (.177)	50-162-1 (.237)

Oldest Individual Single-Season or Single-Game Records in NFL Record & Fact Book

Regular-Season Records That Have Not Been Surpassed or Tied

Most Points, Game—40, Ernie Nevers, Chi. Cardinals vs. Chi. Bears, Nov. 28, 1929 (6-td, 4-pat)

Most Touchdowns Rushing, Game—6, Ernie Nevers, Chi. Cardinals vs. Chi. Bears, Nov. 28, 1929

Highest Average Gain, Rushing, Season (Qualifiers)—9.94, Beattie Feathers, Chi. Bears, 1934 (101-1,004)

Highest Punting Average, Season (Qualifiers)—51.40, Sammy Baugh, Washington, 1940 (35-1,799)

Highest Punting Average, Game (minimum: 4 punts)—61.75, Bob Cifers, Detroit vs. Chi. Bears, Nov. 24, 1946 (4-247)

Highest Average Gain, Pass Receptions, Season (minimum: 24 receptions)—32.58, Don Currivan, Boston, 1947 (24-782)

Highest Average Gain, Passing, Game (minimum: 20 passes)—18.58, Sammy Baugh, Washington vs. Boston, Oct. 31, 1948 (24-446)

Most Touchdowns, Fumble Recoveries, Game—2, Fred (Dippy) Evans, Chi. Bears vs. Washington, Nov. 28, 1948

Most Yards Gained, Intercepted Passes, Rookie, Season—301, Don Doll, Detroit, 1949

Most Passes Had Intercepted, Game—8, Jim Hardy, Chi. Cardinals vs. Philadelphia, Sept. 24, 1950

Highest Average Gain, Rushing, Game (minimum: 10 attempts)—17.09, Marion Motley, Cleveland vs. Pittsburgh, Oct. 29, 1950 (11-188)

Most Yards Gained, Kickoff Returns, Game—294, Wally Triplett, Detroit vs. Los Angeles, Oct. 29, 1950

Highest Kickoff Return Average, Game (minimum: 3 returns)—73.50, Wally Triplett, Detroit vs. Los Angeles, Oct. 29, 1950 (4-294)

Most Pass Receptions, Game—18, Tom Fears, Los Angeles vs. Green Bay, Dec. 3, 1950

Highest Punt Return Average, Season (Qualifiers)—23.00, Herb Rich, Baltimore, 1950 (12-276)

Highest Punt Return Average, Rookie, Season (Qualifiers)—23.00, Herb Rich, Baltimore, 1950 (12-276)

Most Yards Passing, Game—554, Norm Van Brocklin, Los Angeles vs. N.Y. Yanks, Sept. 28, 1951

Most Touchdowns, Punt Returns, Rookie, Season—4, Jack Christiansen, Detroit, 1951

Most Interceptions By, Season—14, Dick (Night Train) Lane, Los Angeles, 1952

Most Interceptions By, Rookie, Season—14, Dick (Night Train) Lane, Los Angeles, 1952

Highest Average Gain, Passing, Season (Qualifiers)—11.17, Tommy O'Connell, Cleveland, 1957 (110-1,229)

Most Points, Season—176, Paul Hornung, Green Bay, 1960 (15-td, 41-pat, 15-fg)

Most Yards Gained, Pass Receptions, Rookie, Season—1,473, Bill Groman, Houston, 1960

Largest Trades in NFL History

(Based on number of players or draft choices involved)

15—March 26, 1953—T Mike McCormack, DT Don Colo, LB Tom Catlin, DB John Petitbon, and G Herschell Forester from Baltimore to Cleveland for DB Don Shula, DB Bert Rechichar, DB Carl Taseff, LB Ed Sharkey, E Gern Nagler, QB Harry Agganis, T Dick Batten, T Stu Sheets, G Art Spinney, and G Elmer Willhoite.

15—January 28, 1971—LB Marlin McKeever, first- and third-round choices in 1971, and third-, fourth-, sixth-, and seventh-round choices in 1972 from Washington to the Los Angeles Rams for LB Maxie Baughan, LB Jack Pardee, LB Myron Pottios, RB Jeff Jordan, G John Wilbur, DT Diron Talbert, and a fifth-round choice in 1971.

12—June 13, 1952—Selection rights to Les Richter from the Dallas Texans to the Los Angeles Rams for RB Dick Hoerner, DB Tom Keane, DB George Sims, C Joe Reid, HB Billy Baggett, T Jack Halliday, FB Dick McKissack, LB Vic Vasicek, E Richard Wilkins, C Aubrey Phillips, and RB Dave Anderson.

10—March 23, 1959—Ollie Matson from the Chicago Cardinals to the Los Angeles Rams for T Frank Fuller, DE Glenn Holtzman, T Ken Panfil, DT Art Hauser, E John Tracey, FB Larry Hickman, HB Don Brown, the Rams second-round choice in 1960, and a player to be delivered during the 1959 training camp.

10—October 31, 1987—RB Eric Dickerson from the Los Angeles Rams to Indianapolis. The rights to LB Cornelius Bennett from Indianapolis to Buffalo. Indianapolis running back Owen Gill and the Colts' first- and second-round choices in 1988 and second-round choice in 1989, plus Bills running back Greg Bell and Buffalo's first-round choice in 1988 and first- and second-round choices in 1989 to the Rams.

Retired Uniform Numbers in NFL

AFC

Buffalo:	None	
Cincinnati:	Bob Johnson	54
Cleveland:	Otto Graham	14
	Jim Brown	32
	Ernie Davis	45
	Don Fleming	46
	Lou Groza	76
Denver:	Frank Tripucka	18
	Floyd Little	44
Houston:	Earl Campbell	34
	Jim Norton	43
	Elvin Bethea	65
Indianapolis:	Johnny Unitas	19
	Buddy Young	22
	Lenny Moore	24
	Art Donovan	70
	Jim Parker	77
	Raymond Berry	82
	Gino Marchetti	89
Kansas City:	Len Dawson	16
	Abner Haynes	28
	Stone Johnson	33
	Mack Lee Hill	36
	Bobby Bell	78
Los Angeles Raiders:	None	
Miami:	Bob Griese	12
New England:	Gino Cappelletti	20
	Steve Nelson	57
	Jim Hunt	79
	Bob Dee	89
New York Jets:	Joe Namath	12
	Don Maynard	13
Pittsburgh:	None	
San Diego:	Dan Fouts	14
Seattle:	"Fans/the twelfth man"	12

NFC

Atlanta:	William Andrews	31
	Jeff Van Note	57
	Tommy Nobis	60
Chicago:	Bronko Nagurski	3
	George McAfee	5
	Willie Galimore	28
	Walter Payton	34
	Brian Piccolo	41
	Sid Luckman	42
	Bill Hewitt	56
	Bill George	61
	Bulldog Turner	66
	Red Grange	77
Dallas:	None	
Detroit:	Dutch Clark	7
	Bobby Layne	22
	Doak Walker	37
	Joe Schmidt	56
	Chuck Hughes	85
	Charlie Sanders	88
Green Bay:	Tony Canadeo	3
	Don Hutson	14
	Bart Starr	15
	Ray Nitschke	66
Los Angeles Rams:	Bob Waterfield	7
	Merlin Olsen	74
Minnesota:	Fran Tarkenton	10
New Orleans:	Jim Taylor	31
	Doug Atkins	81
New York Giants:	Ray Flaherty	1
	Mel Hein	7
	Y. A. Tittle	14
	Al Blozis	32
	Joe Morrison	40
	Charlie Conerly	42
	Ken Strong	50
Philadelphia:	Steve Van Buren	15
	Tom Brookshier	40
	Pete Retzlaff	44
	Chuck Bednarik	60
	Al Wistert	70
Phoenix:	Larry Wilson	8
	Stan Mauldin	77
	J. V. Cain	88
	Marshall Goldberg	99
San Francisco:	John Brodie	12
	Joe Perry	34
	Jimmy Johnson	37
	Hugh McElhenny	39
	Charlie Krueger	70
	Leo Nomellini	73
	Dwight Clark	87
Tampa Bay:	Lee Roy Selmon	63
Washington:	Sammy Baugh	33

1989 NFL Score by Quarters

AFC Offense

	1	2	3	4	OT	PTS
Buffalo	59	117	92	135	6	409
Cincinnati	61	147	98	98	0	404
Houston	50	128	85	102	0	365
Denver	84	114	57	104	3	362
Cleveland	48	112	104	64	6	334
Miami	78	96	73	81	3	331
Kansas City	67	137	53	61	0	318
L.A. Raiders	67	87	91	67	3	315
Indianapolis	53	66	53	120	6	298
New England	47	66	71	110	3	297
San Diego	52	43	67	104	0	266
Pittsburgh	57	91	72	45	0	265
N.Y. Jets	37	74	60	82	0	253
Seattle	72	60	41	68	0	241

NFC Offense

	1	2	3	4	OT	PTS
San Francisco	67	137	64	174	0	442
L.A. Rams	122	124	61	116	3	426
New Orleans	105	123	60	98	0	386
Washington	80	82	127	97	0	386
Green Bay	71	74	89	125	3	362
Chicago	40	108	82	128	0	358
Minnesota	80	139	80	50	2	351
N.Y. Giants	77	83	100	88	0	348
Philadelphia	61	91	84	106	0	342
Tampa Bay	58	92	42	128	0	320
Detroit	68	108	65	71	0	312
Atlanta	43	100	85	51	0	279
Phoenix	43	76	51	88	0	258
Dallas	47	70	35	52	0	204

AFC Defense

	1	2	3	4	OT	PTS
Denver	44	53	50	76	3	226
Cleveland	34	67	82	62	9	254
Cincinnati	50	97	56	82	0	285
Kansas City	74	83	47	82	0	286
San Diego	42	92	67	89	0	290
L.A. Raiders	77	77	65	78	0	297
Indianapolis	67	82	58	91	3	301
Buffalo	62	44	88	123	0	317
Pittsburgh	78	110	60	78	0	326
Seattle	81	80	86	77	3	327
Miami	57	128	77	117	0	379
New England	82	144	58	107	0	391
N.Y. Jets	53	133	119	106	0	411
Houston	95	106	97	108	6	412

NFC Defense

	1	2	3	4	OT	PTS
N.Y. Giants	55	66	38	93	0	252
San Francisco	59	77	53	64	0	253
Philadelphia	74	74	47	79	0	274
Minnesota	54	47	55	113	6	275
New Orleans	27	96	89	86	3	301
Washington	76	99	47	86	0	308
L.A. Rams	50	87	83	122	2	344
Green Bay	77	157	70	52	0	356
Detroit	29	156	89	87	3	364
Chicago	69	111	72	125	0	377
Phoenix	68	99	90	120	0	377
Dallas	84	118	90	101	0	393
Tampa Bay	79	144	86	110	0	419
Atlanta	97	118	123	99	0	437

NFL TOTALS

	1	2	3	4	OT	PTS
	1794	2745	2042	2613	38	9232

Team Leaders

Offense

	Most Scored	Fewest Scored
1st Quarter	122, L.A. Rams	37, N.Y. Jets
2nd Quarter	147, Cincinnati	43, San Diego
3rd Quarter	127, Washington	35, Dallas
4th Quarter	174, San Francisco	45, Pittsburgh

Defense

	Most Allowed	Fewest Allowed
1st Quarter	97, Atlanta	27, New Orleans
2nd Quarter	157, Green Bay	44, Buffalo
3rd Quarter	123, Atlanta	38, N.Y. Giants
4th Quarter	125, Chicago	52, Green Bay

Greatest Comebacks in NFL History (Most Points Overcome To Win Game)

Regular-Season Games

From 28 points behind to win:
December 7, 1980, at San Francisco

New Orleans	14	21	0	0	0 —	35
San Francisco	0	7	14	14	3 —	38

NO —Harris 33 pass from Manning (Ricardo kick)
NO —Childs 21 pass from Manning (Ricardo kick)
NO —Holmes 1 run (Ricardo kick)
SF —Solomon 57 punt return (Wersching kick)
NO —Holmes 1 run (Ricardo kick)
NO —Harris 41 pass from Manning (Ricardo kick)
SF —Montana 1 run (Wersching kick)
SF —Clark 71 pass from Montana (Wersching kick)
SF —Solomon 14 pass from Montana (Wersching kick)
SF —Elliott 7 run (Wersching kick)
SF —FG Wersching 36

	N.O.	S.F.
First Downs	27	24
Total Yards	519	430
Yards Rushing	143	176
Yards Passing	376	254
Turnovers	3	0

From 25 points behind to win:
November 8, 1987, at St. Louis

Tampa Bay	7	7	14	0 —	28
St. Louis	0	3	0	28 —	31

TB —Carrier 5 pass from DeBerg (Igwebuike kick)
TB —Carter 3 pass from DeBerg (Igwebuike kick)
StL —FG Gallery 31
TB —Smith 34 pass from DeBerg (Igwebuike kick)
TB —Smith 3 run (Igwebuike kick)
StL —Awalt 4 pass from Lomax (Gallery kick)
StL —Noga 23 fumble recovery (Gallery kick)
StL —J. Smith 11 pass from Lomax (Gallery kick)
StL —J. Smith 17 pass from Lomax (Gallery kick)

	T.B.	St.L.
First Downs	26	26
Total Yards	377	415
Yards Rushing	83	137
Yards Passing	294	278
Turnovers	1	2

From 24 points behind to win:
October 27, 1946, at Washington

Philadelphia	0	0	14	14 —	28
Washington	10	14	0	0 —	24

Wash—Rosato 2 run (Poillon kick)
Wash—FG Poillon 28
Wash—Rosato 4 run (Poillon kick)
Wash—Lapka recovered fumble in end zone (Poillon kick)
Phil —Steele 1 run (Lio kick)
Phil —Pritchard 45 pass from Thompson (Lio kick)
Phil —Steinke 7 pass from Thompson (Lio kick)
Phil —Ferrante 30 pass from Thompson (Lio kick)

	Phil.	Wash.
First Downs	14	8
Total Yards	262	127
Yards Rushing	34	66
Yards Passing	228	61
Turnovers	6	3

From 24 points behind to win:
October 20, 1957, at Detroit

Baltimore	7	14	6	0 —	27
Detroit	0	3	7	21 —	31

Balt —Mutscheller 15 pass from Unitas (Rechichar kick)
Det —FG Martin 47
Balt —Moore 72 pass from Unitas (Rechichar kick)
Balt —Mutscheller 52 pass from Unitas (Rechichar kick)
Balt —Moore 4 pass from Unitas (kick failed)
Det —Junker 14 pass from Rote (Layne kick)
Det —Cassady 26 pass from Layne (Layne kick)
Det —Johnson 1 run (Layne kick)
Det —Cassady 29 pass from Layne (Layne kick)

	Balt.	Det.
First Downs	15	20
Total Yards	322	369
Yards Rushing	117	178
Yards Passing	205	191
Turnovers	6	4

From 24 points behind to win:
October 25, 1959, at Chicago

Philadelphia	0	0	21	7	— 28
Chi. Cardinals	7	10	7	0	— 24

Chi —Crow 10 pass from Roach (Conrad kick)
Chi —J. Hill 77 blocked field goal return (Conrad kick)
Chi —FG Conrad 15
Chi —Lane 37 interception return (Conrad kick)
Phil —Barnes 1 run (Walston kick)
Phil —McDonald 29 pass from Van Brocklin (Walston kick)
Phil —Barnes 2 run (Walston kick)
Phil —McDonald 22 pass from Van Brocklin (Walston kick)

	Phil.	Chi.
First Downs	22	14
Total Yards	399	313
Yards Rushing	168	163
Yards Passing	231	150
Turnovers	2	6

From 24 points behind to win:
October 23, 1960, at Denver

Boston	10	7	7	0	— 24
Denver	0	0	14	17	— 31

Bos —FG Cappelletti 12
Bos —Colclough 10 pass from Songin (Cappelletti kick)
Bos —Wells 6 pass from Songin (Cappelletti kick)
Bos —Miller 47 pass from Songin (Cappelletti kick)
Den —Carmichael 21 pass from Tripucka (Mingo kick)
Den —Jessup 19 pass from Tripucka (Mingo kick)
Den —Carmichael 35 lateral from Taylor, pass from Tripucka (Mingo kick)
Den —Taylor 8 pass from Tripucka (Mingo kick)
Den —FG Mingo 9

	Bos.	Den.
First Downs	19	16
Total Yards	434	326
Yards Rushing	211	65
Yards Passing	223	261
Turnovers	7	4

From 24 points behind to win:
December 15, 1974, at Miami

New England	21	3	0	3	— 27
Miami	0	17	7	10	— 34

NE —Hannah recovered fumble in end zone (J. Smith kick)
NE —Sanders 23 interception return (J. Smith kick)
NE —Herron 4 pass from Plunkett (J. Smith kick)
NE —FG J. Smith 46
Mia —Nottingham 1 run (Yepremian kick)
Mia —Baker 37 pass from Morrall (Yepremian kick)
Mia —FG Yepremian 28
Mia —Baker 46 pass from Morrall (Yepremian kick)
NE —FG J. Smith 34
Mia —Nottingham 2 run (Yepremian kick)
Mia —FG Yepremian 40

	N.E.	Mia.
First Downs	18	18
Total Yards	333	333
Yards Rushing	114	61
Yards Passing	219	272
Turnovers	3	4

From 24 points behind to win:
December 4, 1977, at Minnesota

San Francisco	0	10	14	3	— 27
Minnesota	0	0	7	21	— 28

SF —Delvin Williams 2 run (Wersching kick)
SF —FG Wersching 31
SF —Dave Williams 80 kickoff return (Wersching kick)
SF —Delvin Williams 5 run (Wersching kick)
Minn —McClanahan 15 pass from Lee (Cox kick)
Minn —Rashad 8 pass from Kramer (Cox kick)
Minn —Tucker 9 pass from Kramer (Cox kick)
SF —FG Wersching 31
Minn —S. White 69 pass from Kramer (Cox kick)

	S.F.	Minn.
First Downs	19	18
Total Yards	243	309
Yards Rushing	196	52
Yards Passing	47	257
Turnovers	2	5

From 24 points behind to win:
September 23, 1979, at Denver

Seattle	10	10	14	0	— 34
Denver	0	10	21	6	— 37

Sea —FG Herrera 28
Sea —Doornink 5 run (Herrera kick)
Den —FG Turner 27
Sea —Doornink 5 run (Herrera kick)
Den —Armstrong 2 run (Turner kick)
Sea —FG Herrera 22
Sea —McCullum 13 pass from Zorn (Herrera kick)
Sea —Smith 1 run (Herrera kick)
Den —Studdard 2 pass from Morton (Turner kick)
Den —Moses 11 pass from Morton (Turner kick)
Den —Upchurch 35 pass from Morton (Turner kick)
Den —Lytle 1 run (kick failed)

	Sea.	Den.
First Downs	22	23
Total Yards	350	344
Yards Rushing	153	90
Yards Passing	197	254
Turnovers	4	3

From 24 points behind to win:
September 23, 1979, at Cincinnati

Houston	0	10	17	0	3	— 30
Cincinnati	14	10	0	3	0	— 27

Cin —Johnson 1 run (Bahr kick)
Cin —Alexander 2 run (Bahr kick)
Cin —Johnson 1 run (Bahr kick)
Cin —FG Bahr 52
Hou —Burrough 35 pass from Pastorini (Fritsch kick)
Hou —FG Fritsch 33
Hou —Campbell 8 run (Fritsch kick)
Hou —Caster 22 pass from Pastorini (Fritsch kick)
Hou —FG Fritsch 47
Cin —FG Bahr 55
Hou —FG Fritsch 29

	Hou.	Cin.
First Downs	19	21
Total Yards	361	265
Yards Rushing	177	165
Yards Passing	184	100
Turnovers	3	2

From 24 points behind to win:
November 22, 1982, at Los Angeles

San Diego	10	14	0	0	— 24
L.A. Raiders	0	7	14	7	— 28

SD —FG Benirschke 19
SD —Scales 29 pass from Fouts (Benirschke kick)
SD —Muncie 2 run (Benirschke kick)
SD —Muncie 1 run (Benirschke kick)
Raiders —Christensen 1 pass from Plunkett (Bahr kick)
Raiders —Allen 3 run (Bahr kick)
Raiders —Allen 6 run (Bahr kick)
Raiders —Hawkins 1 run (Bahr kick)

	S.D.	Raiders
First Downs	26	23
Total Yards	411	326
Yards Rushing	72	181
Yards Passing	339	145
Turnovers	4	2

From 24 points behind to win:
September 26, 1988, at Denver

L.A. Raiders	0	0	14	13	3	— 30
Denver	7	17	0	3	0	— 27

Den —Dorsett 1 run (Karlis kick)
Den —Dorsett 1 run (Karlis kick)
Den —Sewell 7 pass from Elway (Karlis kick)
Den —FG Karlis 39
Raiders —Smith 40 pass from Schroeder (Bahr kick)
Raiders —Smith 42 pass from Schroeder (Bahr kick)
Raiders —FG Bahr 28
Raiders —Allen 4 run (Bahr kick)
Den —FG Karlis 25
Raiders —FG Bahr 44
Raiders —FG Bahr 35

	Raiders	Den.
First Downs	20	23
Total Yards	363	398
Yards Rushing	128	189
Yards Passing	235	209
Turnovers	1	5

Postseason Games

From 20 points behind to win:
Western Conference Playoff Game
December 22, 1957, at San Francisco

Detroit	0	7	14	10	— 31
San Francisco	14	10	3	0	— 27

SF —Owens 34 pass from Tittle (Soltau kick)
SF —McElhenny 47 pass from Tittle (Soltau kick)
Det—Junker 4 pass from Rote (Martin kick)
SF —Wilson 12 pass from Tittle (Soltau kick)
SF —FG Soltau 25
SF —FG Soltau 10
Det—Tracy 2 run (Martin kick)
Det—Tracy 58 run (Martin kick)
Det—Gedman 3 run (Martin kick)
Det—FG Martin 14

	Det.	S.F.
First Downs	22	20
Total Yards	324	351
Yards Rushing	129	127
Yards Passing	195	224
Turnovers	5	4

From 18 points behind to win:
NFC Divisional Playoff Game
December 23, 1972, at San Francisco

Dallas	3	10	0	17	— 30
San Francisco	7	14	7	0	— 28

SF —Washington 97 kickoff return (Gossett kick)
Dall—FG Fritsch 37
SF —Schreiber 1 run (Gossett kick)
SF —Schreiber 1 run (Gossett kick)
Dall—FG Fritsch 45
Dall—Alworth 28 pass from Morton (Fritsch kick)
SF —Schreiber 1 run (Gossett kick)
Dall—FG Fritsch 27
Dall—Parks 20 pass from Staubach (Fritsch kick)
Dall—Sellers 10 pass from Staubach (Fritsch kick)

	Dall.	S.F.
First Downs	22	13
Total Yards	402	255
Yards Rushing	165	105
Yards Passing	237	150
Turnovers	5	3

From 18 points behind to win:
AFC Divisional Playoff Game
January 4, 1986, at Miami

Cleveland	7	7	7	0	— 21
Miami	3	0	14	7	— 24

Mia —FG Reveiz 51
Clev—Newsome 16 pass from Kosar (Bahr kick)
Clev—Byner 21 run (Bahr kick)
Clev—Byner 66 run (Bahr kick)
Mia —Moore 6 pass from Marino (Reveiz kick)
Mia —Davenport 31 run (Reveiz kick)
Mia —Davenport 1 run (Reveiz kick)

	Clev.	Mia.
First Downs	17	20
Total Yards	313	330
Yards Rushing	251	92
Yards Passing	62	238
Turnovers	1	1

From 14 points behind to win:
NFC Divisional Playoff Game
January 3, 1981, at Philadelphia

Minnesota	7	7	2	0	— 16
Philadelphia	0	7	14	10	— 31

Minn —S. White 30 pass from Kramer (Danmeier kick)
Minn —Brown 1 run (Danmeier kick)
Phil —Carmichael 9 pass from Jaworski (Franklin kick)
Phil —Montgomery 8 run (Franklin kick)
Minn —Safety, Jaworski tackled in end zone by Martin and Blair
Phil —Montgomery 5 run (Franklin kick)
Phil —FG Franklin 33
Phil —Harrington 2 run (Franklin kick)

	Minn.	Phil.
First Downs	14	24
Total Yards	215	305
Yards Rushing	36	126
Yards Passing	179	179
Turnovers	8	3

From 14 points behind to win:
NFC Divisional Playoff Game
January 4, 1981, at Atlanta

Dallas	3	7	0	20	— 30
Atlanta	10	7	7	3	— 27

Atl —FG Mazzetti 38
Atl —Jenkins 60 pass from Bartkowski (Mazzetti kick)
Dall —FG Septien 38
Dall —DuPree 5 pass from D. White (Septien kick)
Atl —Cain 1 run (Mazzetti kick)
Atl —Andrews 5 pass from Bartkowski (Mazzetti kick)
Dall —Newhouse 1 run (Septien kick)
Atl —FG Mazzetti 34
Dall —D. Pearson 14 pass from D. White (Septien kick)
Dall —D. Pearson 23 pass from D. White (pass failed)

	Dall.	Atl.
First Downs	22	18
Total Yards	422	371
Yards Rushing	112	86
Yards Passing	310	283
Turnovers	2	2

From 14 points behind to win:
NFC Divisional Playoff Game
January 10, 1988, at Chicago

Washington	0	14	7	0	— 21
Chicago	7	7	3	0	— 17

Chi —Thomas 2 run (Butler kick)
Chi —Morris 14 pass from McMahon (Butler kick)
Wash —Rogers 3 run (Haji-Sheikh kick)
Wash —Didier 18 pass from Williams (Haji-Sheikh kick)
Wash —Green 52 punt return (Haji-Sheikh kick)
Chi —FG Butler 25

	Wash.	Chi.
First Downs	17	15
Total Yards	272	280
Yards Rushing	72	110
Yards Passing	200	170
Turnovers	2	3

Records of NFL Divisions in Out-of-Division Games 1978-89

Since 1978, teams in a five-team division have been scheduled for eight games against out-of-division opponents; teams in a four-team division have been scheduled for 10 such games. These charts indicate the annual records for each division's teams in games against teams from other divisions:

AFC East

	W	L	T	Pct.	Pos.
1978.	20	20	0	.500	4T
1979.	19	21	0	.475	4
1980.	20	20	0	.500	3
1981.	16	24	0	.400	6
1982.	10	10	1	.500	3T
1983.	22	18	0	.550	2T
1984.	16	24	0	.400	4
1985.	21	19	0	.475	3
1986.	16	24	0	.400	5
1987.	18	17	0	.514	3T
1988.	24	15	1	.613	2
1989.	14	26	0	.350	6
Totals.	216	238	2	.476	5

AFC Central

	W	L	T	Pct.	Pos.
1978.	24	16	0	.600	1
1979.	24	16	0	.600	2
1980.	25	15	0	.625	1
1981.	20	20	0	.500	3
1982.	10	10	0	.500	3T
1983.	16	24	0	.400	5
1984.	13	27	0	.325	5
1985.	15	25	0	.375	6
1986.	21	19	0	.525	4
1987.	19	17	0	.528	2
1988.	25	15	0	.625	1
1989.	23	16	1	.588	2
Totals.	235	220	1	.516	3

AFC West

	W	L	T	Pct.	Pos.
1978.	21	19	0	.525	2T
1979.	27	13	0	.675	1
1980.	22	18	0	.550	2
1981.	22	18	0	.550	2
1982.	12	11	0	.522	2
1983.	22	18	0	.550	2T
1984.	31	9	0	.775	1
1985.	25	15	0	.625	1
1986.	23	17	0	.575	1T
1987.	17	19	1	.473	5
1988.	14	25	1	.363	6
1989.	20	19	1	.513	3
Totals.	256	201	3	.560	1

NFC East

	W	L	T	Pct.	Pos.
1978	21	19	0	.525	2T
1979	23	17	0	.575	3
1980	19	21	0	.475	4
1981	26	14	0	.650	1
1982	13	6	0	.684	1
1983	23	17	0	.575	1
1984	24	15	1	.613	2
1985	22	18	0	.550	2
1986	23	17	0	.575	1T
1987	18	17	0	.514	3T
1988	17	23	0	.425	4
1989	19	21	0	.475	4
Totals	248	205	1	.547	2

NFC Central

	W	L	T	Pct.	Pos.
1978	16	24	0	.400	6
1979	14	26	0	.350	5
1980	16	24	0	.400	6
1981	18	22	0	.450	4T
1982	12	12	1	.500	3T
1983	15	25	0	.375	6
1984	11	28	1	.288	6
1985	19	21	0	.475	4
1986	14	26	0	.350	6
1987	14	24	1	.372	6
1988	16	24	0	.400	5
1989	18	22	0	.450	5
Totals	183	278	3	.398	6

NFC West

	W	L	T	Pct.	Pos.
1978	18	22	0	.450	5
1979	13	27	0	.325	6
1980	18	22	0	.450	5
1981	18	22	0	.450	4T
1982	7	15	0	.318	6
1983	22	18	0	.550	2T
1984	24	16	0	.600	3
1985	18	22	0	.450	5
1986	23	17	0	.575	1T
1987	23	15	0	.605	1
1988	23	17	0	.575	3
1989	25	15	0	.625	1
Totals	232	228	0	.504	4

Composite Standings for 12 Seasons

	W	L	T	Pct.
AFC West	256	201	3	.560
NFC East	248	205	1	.547
AFC Central	235	220	1	.516
NFC West	232	228	0	.504
AFC East	216	238	2	.476
NFC Central	183	278	3	.398

Records of NFL Teams Since 1970 AFL-NFL Merger

AFC	W - L - T	Pct.	Division Titles	Playoff Berths	Post-season Record	Super Bowl Record
Miami	198- 96-2	.672	9	12	14-10	2-3
L.A. Raiders	189-101-6	.649	8	12	16-9	3-0
Pittsburgh	176-119-1	.596	9	12	16-8	4-0
Denver	168-122-6	.578	6	8	8-8	0-4
Cleveland	155-138-3	.529	6	9	3-9	0-0
Cincinnati	155-141-0	.524	4	6	4-6	0-2
New England	144-152-0	.486	2	5	3-5	0-1
Seattle*	103-109-0	.486	1	4	3-4	0-0
San Diego	130-161-5	.448	3	4	3-4	0-0
Kansas City	126-163-7	.438	1	2	0-2	0-0
Indianapolis	127-167-2	.432	5	6	4-5	1-0
N.Y. Jets	126-168-2	.429	0	4	3-4	0-0
Houston	122-172-2	.416	0	6	6-6	0-0
Buffalo	120-174-2	.409	3	5	2-5	0-0

NFC	W - L - T	Pct.	Division Titles	Playoff Berths	Post-season Record	Super Bowl Record
Washington	188-107-1	.637	4	10	13-8	2-2
L.A. Rams	184-108-4	.628	8	14	10-14	0-1
Dallas	184-112-0	.622	9	14	19-12	2-3
Minnesota	176-118-2	.598	10	13	11-13	0-3
San Francisco	164-129-3	.559	10	11	15-7	4-0
Chicago	152-143-1	.515	5	7	5-6	1-0
Philadelphia	132-158-6	.456	2	6	3-6	0-1
Phoenix	131-159-6	.453	2	3	0-3	0-0
N.Y. Giants	131-163-2	.446	2	5	6-4	1-0
Detroit	127-165-4	.436	1	3	0-3	0-0
Green Bay	122-166-8	.426	1	2	1-2	0-0
Atlanta	117-175-4	.402	1	3	1-3	0-0
New Orleans	109-183-4	.375	0	1	0-1	0-0
Tampa Bay*	62-149-1	.295	2	3	1-3	0-0

*entered NFL in 1976.
Indianapolis totals include Baltimore, 1970-83
L.A. Raiders totals include Oakland, 1970-81
Phoenix totals include St. Louis, 1970-87

Tie games before 1972 are not calculated in won-lost percentage.

In 1982, due to players' strike, the divisional format was abandoned. (L.A. Raiders and Washington won regular-season conference titles, not included in "Division Titles" totals listed above. Sixteen teams were awarded playoff berths, included in totals listed above.)

Longest Winning Streaks Since 1970

Regular-season games

16	Miami, 1971-73	(1 in 1971, 14 in 1972, 1 in 1973)
16	Miami, 1983-84	(5 in 1983, 11 in 1984)
14	Oakland, 1976-77	(10 in 1976, 4 in 1977)
13	Chicago, 1984-85	(1 in 1984, 12 in 1985)
13	Minnesota, 1974-75	(3 in 1974, 10 in 1975)
11	Pittsburgh, 1975	
11	Baltimore, 1975-76	(9 in 1975, 2 in 1976)
10	Miami, 1973	
10	Pittsburgh, 1976-77	(9 in 1976, 1 in 1977)
10	Denver, 1984	

NFL Playoff Appearances by Seasons

Team	Number of Seasons in Playoffs
Cleveland	22
Los Angeles Rams	22
New York Giants	21
Chicago	18
Dallas	18
Washington	16
Los Angeles Raiders	15
Minnesota	15
Green Bay	13
Pittsburgh	13
Miami	12
San Francisco	12
Houston	11
Indianapolis	11
Philadelphia	10
Buffalo	9
San Diego	9
Denver	8
Detroit	8
Cincinnati	6
Kansas City	6
New England	6
New York Jets	6
Phoenix	5
Seattle	4
Atlanta	3
Tampa Bay	3
New Orleans	1

Teams in Super Bowl Contention, 1978-89

	With 3 Weeks to Play	With 2 Weeks to Play	With 1 Week to Play
1989	21	18	17
1988	21	18	15
1987	19	19	15
1986	19	17	14
1985	21	18	13
1984	18	14	13
1983	24	19	15
1982	20	17	12
1981	21	20	16
1980	20	14	12
1979	19	15	13
1978	20	17	12

Games Decided by 7 Points or Less and 3 Points or Less (1970-89)

	Games Decided by 7 Points or Less	Games Decided by 3 Points or Less
1970	58 of 182 (31.9%)	32 of 182 (17.6%)
1971	77 of 182 (42.3%)	34 of 182 (18.7%)
1972	71 of 182 (39.0%)	38 of 182 (20.9%)
1973	60 of 182 (32.9%)	28 of 182 (15.4%)
1974	91 of 182 (50.0%)	36 of 182 (19.8%)
1975	64 of 182 (35.1%)	35 of 182 (19.2%)
1976	72 of 196 (36.7%)	37 of 196 (18.9%)
1977	87 of 196 (44.3%)	35 of 196 (17.9%)
1978	108 of 224 (48.2%)	49 of 224 (21.9%)
1979	104 of 224 (46.4%)	51 of 224 (22.8%)
1980	108 of 224 (48.2%)	58 of 224 (25.9%)
1981	89 of 224 (39.7%)	59 of 224 (26.3%)
1982	60 of 126 (47.6%)	31 of 126 (24.6%)
1983	106 of 224 (47.3%)	54 of 224 (24.1%)
1984	96 of 224 (42.9%)	59 of 224 (26.3%)
1985	87 of 224 (38.8%)	38 of 224 (17.0%)
1986	106 of 224 (47.3%)	47 of 224 (21.0%)
1987	98 of 210 (46.7%)	40 of 210 (19.0%)
1988	113 of 224 (50.4%)	62 of 224 (27.7%)
1989	107 of 224 (47.8%)	55 of 224 (24.6%)

1989 Records of Teams in Close Games

AFC	Overall Record	Decided by 7 Pts. or Less	Decided By 3 Pts. or Less
Buffalo	9-7	3-3	2-3
Cincinnati	8-8	2-4	0-2
Cleveland	9-6-1	3-4-1	1-2-1
Denver	11-5	4-5	2-3
Houston	9-7	6-2	2-0
Indianapolis	8-8	4-4	0-1
Kansas City	8-7-1	4-5-1	1-1-1
L.A. Raiders	8-8	5-5	3-2
Miami	8-8	5-4	3-2
New England	5-11	3-5	2-3
N.Y. Jets	4-12	3-3	2-1
Pittsburgh	9-7	2-1	1-0
San Diego	6-10	4-9	3-4
Seattle	7-9	6-2	3-1

NFC	Overall Record	Decided by 7 Pts. or Less	Decided By 3 Pts. or Less
Atlanta	3-13	3-5	2-2
Chicago	6-10	1-4	1-2
Dallas	1-15	0-4	0-1
Detroit	7-9	4-4	2-2
Green Bay	10-6	7-3	6-3
L.A. Rams	11-5	5-3	3-3
Minnesota	10-6	2-3	1-2
New Orleans	9-7	3-5	1-3
N.Y. Giants	12-4	5-2	2-1
Philadelphia	11-5	6-2	3-1
Phoenix	5-11	2-4	1-3
San Francisco	14-2	4-2	1-1
Tampa Bay	5-11	4-5	3-3
Washington	10-6	6-4	3-2

Super Bowl Champions Who Did Not Make Playoffs The Following Year

Washington—Super Bowl XXII champions did not make playoffs in the 1988 season.

N.Y. Giants—Super Bowl XXI champions did not make playoffs in the 1987 season.

San Francisco—Super Bowl XVI champions did not make playoffs in the 1982 season.

Oakland—Super Bowl XV champions did not make playoffs in the 1981 season.

Pittsburgh—Super Bowl XIV champions did not make playoffs in the 1980 season.

Kansas City—Super Bowl IV champions did not make playoffs in the 1970 season.

Green Bay—Super Bowl II champions did not make playoffs in the 1968 season.

HISTORY

The Professional Football Hall of Fame is located in Canton, Ohio, site of the organizational meeting on September 17, 1920, from which the National Football League evolved. The NFL recognized Canton as the Hall of Fame site on April 27, 1961. Canton area individuals, foundations, and companies donated almost $400,000 in cash and services to provide funds for the construction of the original two-building complex, which was dedicated on September 7, 1963. The original Hall of Fame complex was almost doubled in size with the completion of a $620,000 expansion project that was dedicated on May 10, 1971. A second expansion project was completed on November 20, 1978. It now features four exhibition areas and a theater twice the size of the original one.

The Hall represents the sport of pro football in many ways—through four large and colorful exhibition galleries, in the twin enshrinement halls, with numerous fan-participation electronic devices, a research library, and an NFL gift shop.

In recent years, the Pro Football Hall of Fame has become an extremely popular tourist attraction. At the end of 1989, a total of 4,653,883 fans had visited the Pro Football Hall of Fame.

New members of the Pro Football Hall of Fame are elected annually by a 30-member National Board of Selectors, made up of media representatives from every league city, one at-large representative, and the president of the Pro Football Writers of America. Between four and seven new members are elected each year. An affirmative vote of approximately 80 percent is needed for election.

Any fan may nominate any eligible player or contributor simply by writing to the Pro Football Hall of Fame. Players must be retired five years to be eligible, while a coach need only to be retired with no time limit specified. Contributors (administrators, owners, et al.) may be elected while they are still active.

The charter class of 17 enshrinees was elected in 1963 and the honor roll now stands at 155 with the election of a seven-man class in 1990. That class consists of Buck Buchanan, Bob Griese, Franco Harris, Ted Hendricks, Jack Lambert, Tom Landry, and Bob St. Clair.

Roster of Members

HERB ADDERLEY
Defensive back. 6-1, 200. Born in Philadelphia, Pennsylvania, June 8, 1939. Michigan State. Inducted in 1980. 1961-69 Green Bay Packers, 1970-72 Dallas Cowboys.

LANCE ALWORTH
Wide receiver. 6-0, 184. Born in Houston, Texas, August 3, 1940. Arkansas. Inducted in 1978. 1962-70 San Diego Chargers, 1971-72 Dallas Cowboys.

DOUG ATKINS
Defensive end. 6-8, 275. Born in Humboldt, Tennessee, May 8, 1930. Tennessee. Inducted in 1982. 1953-54 Cleveland Browns, 1955-66 Chicago Bears, 1967-69 New Orleans Saints.

MORRIS (RED) BADGRO
End. 6-0, 190. Born in Orilla, Washington, December 1, 1902. Southern California. Inducted in 1981. 1927 New York Yankees, 1930-35 New York Giants, 1936 Brooklyn Dodgers.

CLIFF BATTLES
Halfback. 6-1, 201. Born in Akron, Ohio, May 1, 1910. Died April 28, 1981. West Virginia Wesleyan. Inducted in 1968. 1932 Boston Braves, 1933-36 Boston Redskins, 1937 Washington Redskins.

SAMMY BAUGH
Quarterback. 6-2, 180. Born in Temple, Texas, March 17, 1914. Texas Christian. Inducted in 1963. 1937-52 Washington Redskins.

CHUCK BEDNARIK
Center-linebacker. 6-3, 230. Born in Bethlehem, Pennsylvania, May 1, 1925. Pennsylvania. Inducted in 1967. 1949-62 Philadelphia Eagles.

BERT BELL
Team owner. Commissioner. Born in Philadelphia, Pennsylvania, February 25, 1895. Died October 11, 1959. Pennsylvania. Inducted in 1963.

1933-40 Philadelphia Eagles, 1941-42 Pittsburgh Steelers, 1943 Phil-Pitt, 1944-46 Pittsburgh Steelers. Commissioner, 1946-59.

BOBBY BELL
Linebacker. 6-4, 225. Born in Shelby, North Carolina, June 17, 1940. Minnesota. Inducted in 1983. 1963-74 Kansas City Chiefs.

RAYMOND BERRY
End. 6-2, 187. Born in Corpus Christi, Texas, February 27, 1933. Southern Methodist. Inducted in 1973. 1955-67 Baltimore Colts.

CHARLES W. BIDWILL, SR.
Team owner. Born in Chicago, Illinois, September 16, 1895. Died April 19, 1947. Loyola of Chicago. Inducted in 1967. 1933-43 Chicago Cardinals, 1944 Card-Pitt, 1945-47 Chicago Cardinals.

FRED BILETNIKOFF
Wide receiver. 6-1, 190. Born in Erie, Pennsylvania, February 23, 1943. Florida State. Inducted in 1988. 1965-78 Oakland Raiders.

GEORGE BLANDA
Quarterback-kicker. 6-2, 215. Born in Youngwood, Pennsylvania, September 17, 1927. Kentucky. Inducted in 1981. 1949-58 Chicago Bears, 1950 Baltimore Colts, 1960-66 Houston Oilers, 1967-75 Oakland Raiders.

MEL BLOUNT
Cornerback. 6-3, 205. Born in Vidalia, Georgia, April 10, 1948. Southern University. Inducted in 1989. 1970-83 Pittsburgh Steelers.

TERRY BRADSHAW
Quarterback. 6-3, 210. Born in Shreveport, Louisiana, September 2, 1948. Louisiana Tech. Inducted in 1989. 1970-83 Pittsburgh Steelers.

JIM BROWN
Fullback. 6-2, 232. Born in St. Simons, Georgia, February 17, 1936.

Syracuse. Inducted in 1971. 1957-65 Cleveland Browns.

PAUL BROWN
Coach. Born in Norwalk, Ohio, September 7, 1908. Miami, Ohio. Inducted in 1967. 1946-49 Cleveland Browns (AAFC), 1950-62 Cleveland Browns, 1968-75 Cincinnati Bengals.

ROOSEVELT BROWN
Tackle. 6-3, 255. Born in Charlottesville, Virginia, October 20, 1932. Morgan State. Inducted in 1975. 1953-65 New York Giants.

WILLIE BROWN
Defensive back. 6-1, 210. Born in Yazoo City, Mississippi, December 2, 1940. Grambling. Inducted in 1984. 1963-66 Denver Broncos, 1967-78 Oakland Raiders.

BUCK BUCHANAN
Defensive tackle. 6-7, 274. Born in Gainesville, Alabama, September 10, 1940. Grambling. Inducted in 1990. 1963-75 Kansas City Chiefs.

DICK BUTKUS
Linebacker. 6-3, 245. Born in Chicago, Illinois, December 9, 1942. Illinois. Inducted in 1979. 1965-73 Chicago Bears.

TONY CANADEO
Halfback. 5-11, 195. Born in Chicago, Illinois, May 5, 1919. Gonzaga. Inducted in 1974. 1941-44, 1946-52 Green Bay Packers.

JOE CARR
NFL president. Born in Columbus, Ohio, October 22, 1880. Died May 20, 1939. Did not attend college. Inducted in 1963. President, 1921-39 National Football League.

GUY CHAMBERLIN
End. Coach. 6-2, 210. Born in Blue Springs, Nebraska, January 16, 1894. Died April 4, 1967. Nebraska. Inducted in 1965. 1920 Decatur Staleys, 1921 Chicago Staleys, player-coach 1922-23 Canton Bulldogs, 1924 Cleveland Bulldogs, 1925-26 Frankford Yellow Jackets, 1927 Chicago Cardinals.

JACK CHRISTIANSEN
Defensive back. 6-1, 185. Born in Sublette, Kansas, December 20, 1928. Died June 29, 1986. Colorado State. Inducted in 1970. 1951-58 Detroit Lions.

EARL (DUTCH) CLARK
Quarterback. 6-0, 185. Born in Fowler, Colorado, October 11, 1906. Died August 5, 1978. Colorado College. Inducted in 1963. 1931-32 Portsmouth Spartans, 1934-38 Detroit Lions.

GEORGE CONNOR
Tackle-linebacker. 6-3, 240. Born in Chicago, Illinois, January 21, 1925. Holy Cross, Notre Dame. Inducted in 1975. 1948-55 Chicago Bears.

JIMMY CONZELMAN
Quarterback. Coach. Team owner. 6-0, 180. Born in St. Louis, Missouri, March 6, 1898. Died July 31, 1970. Washington, Missouri. Inducted in 1964. 1920 Decatur Staleys, 1921-22 Rock Island, Ill., Independents, 1923-24 Milwaukee Badgers; owner-

coach, 1925-26 Detroit Panthers; player-coach 1927-29, coach 1930 Providence Steam Roller; coach, 1940-42 Chicago Cardinals, 1946-48 Chicago Cardinals.

LARRY CSONKA
Running back. 6-3, 235. Born in Stow, Ohio, December 25, 1946. Syracuse. Inducted in 1987. Miami Dolphins 1968-74, 1979, New York Giants 1976-78.

WILLIE DAVIS
Defensive end. 6-3, 245. Born in Lisbon, Louisiana, July 24, 1934. Grambling. Inducted in 1981. 1958-59 Cleveland Browns, 1960-69 Green Bay Packers.

LEN DAWSON
Quarterback. 6-0, 190. Born in Alliance, Ohio, June 20, 1935. Purdue. Inducted in 1987. Pittsburgh Steelers 1957-59, Cleveland Browns 1960-61, Dallas Texans 1962, Kansas City Chiefs 1963-75.

MIKE DITKA
Tight end. 6-3, 225. Born in Carnegie, Pennsylvania, October 18, 1939. Pittsburgh. Inducted in 1988. 1961-66 Chicago Bears, 1967-68 Philadelphia Eagles, 1969-72 Dallas Cowboys.

ART DONOVAN
Defensive tackle. 6-3, 265. Born in Bronx, New York, June 5, 1925. Boston College. Inducted in 1968. 1950 Baltimore Colts, 1951 New York Yanks, 1952 Dallas Texans, 1953-61 Baltimore Colts.

JOHN (PADDY) DRISCOLL
Quarterback. 5-11, 160. Born in Evanston, Illinois, January 11, 1896. Died June 29, 1968. Northwestern. Inducted in 1965. 1920 Decatur Staleys, 1920-25 Chicago Cardinals, 1926-29 Chicago Bears. Coach, 1956-57 Chicago Bears.

BILL DUDLEY
Halfback. 5-10, 176. Born in Bluefield, Virginia, December 24, 1921. Virginia. Inducted in 1966. 1942, 1945-46 Pittsburgh Steelers, 1947-49 Detroit Lions, 1950-51, 1953 Washington Redskins.

GLEN (TURK) EDWARDS
Tackle. 6-2, 260. Born in Mold, Washington, September 28, 1907. Died January 12, 1973. Washington State. Inducted in 1969. 1932 Boston Braves, 1933-36 Boston Redskins, 1937-40 Washington Redskins.

WEEB EWBANK
Coach. Born in Richmond, Indiana, May 6, 1907. Miami, Ohio. Inducted in 1978. 1954-62 Baltimore Colts, 1963-73 New York Jets.

TOM FEARS
End. 6-2, 215. Born in Los Angeles, California, December 3, 1923. Santa Clara, UCLA. Inducted in 1970. 1948-56 Los Angeles Rams.

RAY FLAHERTY
End. Coach. Born in Spokane, Washington, September 1, 1904. Gonzaga. Inducted in 1976. 1926 Los Angeles Wildcats (AFL), 1927-28 New York Yankees, 1928-29, 1931-35 New York Giants. Coach, 1936 Boston Red-

skins, 1937-42 Washington Redskins, 1946-48 New York Yankees (AAFC), 1949 Chicago Hornets (AAFC).

LEN FORD
End. 6-5, 260. Born in Washington, D.C., February 18, 1926. Died March 14, 1972. Michigan. Inducted in 1976. 1948-49 Los Angeles Dons (AAFC), 1950-57 Cleveland Browns, 1958 Green Bay Packers.

DAN FORTMANN
Guard. 6-0, 207. Born in Pearl River, New York, April 11, 1916. Colgate. Inducted in 1965. 1936-43 Chicago Bears.

FRANK GATSKI
Center. 6-3, 240. Born in Farmington, West Virginia, March 18, 1922. Marshall, Auburn. Inducted in 1985. 1946-49 Cleveland Browns (AAFC), 1950-56 Cleveland Browns, 1957 Detroit Lions.

BILL GEORGE
Linebacker. 6-2, 230. Born in Waynesburg, Pennsylvania, October 27, 1930. Died September 30, 1982. Wake Forest. Inducted in 1974. 1952-65 Chicago Bears, 1966 Los Angeles Rams.

FRANK GIFFORD
Halfback. 6-1, 195. Born in Santa Monica, California, August 16, 1930. Southern California. Inducted in 1977. 1952-60, 1962-64 New York Giants.

SID GILLMAN
Coach. Born in Minneapolis, Minnesota, October 26, 1911. Ohio State. Inducted in 1983. 1955-59 Los Angeles Rams, 1960 Los Angeles Chargers, 1961-69 San Diego Chargers, 1973-74 Houston Oilers.

OTTO GRAHAM
Quarterback. 6-1, 195. Born in Waukegan, Illinois, December 6, 1921. Northwestern. Inducted in 1965. 1946-49 Cleveland Browns (AAFC), 1950-55 Cleveland Browns.

HAROLD (RED) GRANGE
Halfback. 6-0, 185. Born in Forksville, Pennsylvania, June 13, 1903. Illinois. Inducted in 1963. 1925 Chicago Bears, 1926 New York Yankees (AFL), 1927 New York Yankees, 1929-34 Chicago Bears.

JOE GREENE
Defensive tackle. 6-4, 260. Born in Temple, Texas, September 24, 1946. North Texas State. Inducted in 1987. 1969-81 Pittsburgh Steelers.

FORREST GREGG
Tackle. 6-4, 250. Born in Birthright, Texas, October 18, 1933. Southern Methodist. Inducted in 1977. 1956, 1958-70 Green Bay Packers, 1971 Dallas Cowboys.

BOB GRIESE
Quarterback. 6-1, 190. Born in Evansville, Indiana, February 3, 1945. Purdue. Inducted in 1990. 1967-80 Miami Dolphins.

LOU GROZA
Tackle-kicker. 6-3, 250. Born in Martin's Ferry, Ohio, January 25, 1924. Ohio State. Inducted in 1974. 1946-49 Cleveland Browns (AAFC), 1950-59, 1961-67 Cleveland Browns.

JOE GUYON
Halfback. 6-1, 180. Born in Mahnomen, Minnesota, November 26, 1892. Died November 27, 1971. Carlisle, Georgia Tech. Inducted in 1966. 1920 Canton Bulldogs, 1921 Cleveland Indians, 1922-23 Oorang Indians, 1924 Rock Island, Ill., Independents, 1924-25 Kansas City Cowboys, 1927 New York Giants.

GEORGE HALAS
End. Coach. Team owner. Born in Chicago, Illinois, February 2, 1895. Died October 31, 1983. Illinois. Inducted in 1963. 1920 Decatur Staleys, 1921 Chicago Staleys, 1922-29 Chicago Bears; coach, 1933-42, 1946-55, 1958-67 Chicago Bears.

JACK HAM
Linebacker. 6-1, 225. Born in Johnstown, Pennsylvania, December 23, 1948. Penn State. Inducted in 1988. 1971-82 Pittsburgh Steelers.

FRANCO HARRIS
Running back. 6-2, 225. Born in Fort Dix, New Jersey, March 7, 1950. Penn State. Inducted in 1990. 1972-83 Pittsburgh Steelers, 1984 Seattle Seahawks.

ED HEALEY
Tackle. 6-3, 220. Born in Indian Orchard, Massachusetts, December 28, 1894. Died December 9, 1978. Dartmouth. Inducted in 1964. 1920-22 Rock Island, Ill., Independents, 1922-27 Chicago Bears.

MEL HEIN
Center. 6-2, 225. Born in Redding, California, August 22, 1909. Washington State. Inducted in 1963. 1931-45 New York Giants.

TED HENDRICKS
Linebacker. 6-7, 235. Born in Guatemala City, Guatemala, November 1, 1947. Miami. Inducted in 1990. 1969-73 Baltimore Colts, 1974 Green Bay Packers, 1975-81 Oakland Raiders, 1982-83 Los Angeles Raiders.

WILBUR (PETE) HENRY
Tackle. 6-0, 250. Born in Mansfield, Ohio, October 31, 1897. Died February 7, 1952. Washington & Jefferson. Inducted in 1963. 1920-23, 1925-26 Canton Bulldogs, 1927 New York Giants, 1927-28 Pottsville Maroons.

ARNIE HERBER
Quarterback. 6-1, 200. Born in Green Bay, Wisconsin, April 2, 1910. Died October 14, 1969. Wisconsin, Regis College. Inducted in 1966. 1930-40 Green Bay Packers, 1944-45 New York Giants.

BILL HEWITT
End. 5-11, 191. Born in Bay City, Michigan, October 8, 1909. Died January 14, 1947. Michigan. Inducted in 1971. 1932-36 Chicago Bears, 1937-39 Philadelphia Eagles, 1943 Phil-Pitt.

CLARKE HINKLE
Fullback. 5-11, 201. Born in Toronto, Ohio, April 10, 1909. Died November 9, 1988. Bucknell. Inducted in 1964. 1932-41 Green Bay Packers.

ELROY (CRAZYLEGS) HIRSCH
Halfback-end. 6-2, 190. Born in Wausau, Wisconsin, June 17, 1923. Wisconsin, Michigan. Inducted in 1968. 1946-48 Chicago Rockets (AAFC), 1949-57 Los Angeles Rams.

PAUL HORNUNG
Halfback. 6-2, 220. Born in Louisville, Kentucky, December 23, 1935. Notre Dame. Inducted in 1986. 1957-62, 1964-66 Green Bay Packers.

KEN HOUSTON
Safety. 6-3, 198. Born in Lufkin, Texas, November 12, 1944. Prairie View A&M. Inducted in 1986. 1967-72 Houston Oilers, 1973-80 Washington Redskins.

CAL HUBBARD
Tackle. 6-5, 250. Born in Keytesville, Missouri, October 31, 1900. Died October 17, 1977. Centenary, Geneva. Inducted in 1963. 1927-28 New York Giants, 1929-33, 1935 Green Bay Packers, 1936 New York Giants, 1936 Pittsburgh Pirates.

SAM HUFF
Linebacker. 6-1, 230. Born in Morgantown, West Virginia, October 4, 1934. West Virginia. Inducted in 1982. 1956-63 New York Giants, 1964-67, 1969 Washington Redskins.

LAMAR HUNT
Team owner. Born in El Dorado, Arkansas, August 2, 1932. Southern Methodist. Inducted in 1972. 1960-62 Dallas Texans, 1963-90 Kansas City Chiefs.

DON HUTSON
End. 6-1, 180. Born in Pine Bluff, Arkansas, January 31, 1913. Alabama. Inducted in 1963. 1935-45 Green Bay Packers.

JOHN HENRY JOHNSON
Fullback. 6-2, 225. Born in Waterproof, Louisiana, November 24, 1929. St. Mary's, Arizona State. Inducted in 1987. San Francisco 49ers 1954-56, Detroit Lions 1957-59, Pittsburgh Steelers 1960-65, Houston Oilers 1966.

DAVID (DEACON) JONES
Defensive end. 6-5, 250. Born in Eatonville, Florida, December 9, 1938. Mississippi Vocational. Inducted in 1980. 1961-71 Los Angeles Rams, 1972-73 San Diego Chargers, 1974 Washington Redskins.

SONNY JURGENSEN
Quarterback. 6-0, 203. Born in Wilmington, North Carolina, August 23, 1934. Duke. Inducted in 1983. 1957-63 Philadelphia Eagles, 1964-74 Washington Redskins.

WALT KIESLING
Guard. Coach. 6-2, 245. Born in St. Paul, Minnesota, March 27, 1903. Died March 2, 1962. St. Thomas (Minnesota). Inducted in 1966. 1926-27 Duluth Eskimos, 1928 Pottsville Maroons, 1929-33 Chicago Cardinals, 1934 Chicago Bears, 1935-36 Green Bay Packers, 1937-38 Pittsburgh Pirates; coach, 1939-42 Pittsburgh Steelers; co-coach, 1943 Phil-Pitt, 1944 Card-Pitt; coach, 1954-56 Pittsburgh Steelers.

FRANK (BRUISER) KINARD
Tackle. 6-1, 210. Born in Pelahatchie, Mississippi, October 23, 1914. Died September 7, 1985. Mississippi. Inducted in 1971. 1938-44 Brooklyn Dodgers-Tigers, 1946-47 New York Yankees (AAFC).

EARL (CURLY) LAMBEAU
Coach. Born in Green Bay, Wiscon-

sin, April 9, 1898. Died June 1, 1965. Notre Dame. Inducted in 1963. 1919-49 Green Bay Packers, 1950-51 Chicago Cardinals, 1952-53 Washington Redskins.

JACK LAMBERT
Linebacker. 6-4, 220. Born in Mantua, Ohio, July 8, 1952. Kent State. Inducted in 1990. 1974-84 Pittsburgh Steelers.

TOM LANDRY
Coach. Born in Mission, Texas, September 11, 1924. Texas. Inducted in 1990. 1960-88 Dallas Cowboys.

DICK (NIGHT TRAIN) LANE
Defensive back. 6-2, 210. Born in Austin, Texas, April 16, 1928. Scottsbluff Junior College. Inducted in 1974. 1952-53 Los Angeles Rams, 1954-59 Chicago Cardinals, 1960-65 Detroit Lions.

JIM LANGER
Center. 6-2, 255. Born in Little Falls, Minnesota, May 16, 1948. South Dakota State. Inducted in 1987. Miami Dolphins 1970-79, Minnesota Vikings 1980-81.

WILLIE LANIER
Linebacker. 6-1, 245. Born in Clover, Virginia, August 21, 1945. Morgan State. Inducted in 1986. 1967-77 Kansas City Chiefs.

YALE LARY
Defensive back-punter. 5-11, 189. Born in Fort Worth, Texas, November 24, 1930. Texas A&M. Inducted in 1979. 1952-53, 1956-64 Detroit Lions.

DANTE LAVELLI
End. 6-0, 199. Born in Hudson, Ohio, February 23, 1923. Ohio State. Inducted in 1975. 1946-49 Cleveland Browns (AAFC), 1950-56 Cleveland Browns.

BOBBY LAYNE
Quarterback. 6-2, 190. Born in Santa Anna, Texas, December 19, 1926. Died December 1, 1986. Texas. Inducted in 1967. 1948 Chicago Bears, 1949 New York Bulldogs, 1950-58 Detroit Lions, 1958-62 Pittsburgh Steelers.

ALPHONSE (TUFFY) LEEMANS
Fullback. 6-0, 200. Born in Superior, Wisconsin, November 12, 1912. Died January 19, 1979. George Washington. Inducted in 1978. 1936-43 New York Giants.

BOB LILLY
Defensive tackle. 6-5, 260. Born in Olney, Texas, July 26, 1939. Texas Christian. Inducted in 1980. 1961-74 Dallas Cowboys.

VINCE LOMBARDI
Coach. Born in Brooklyn, New York, June 11, 1913. Died September 3, 1970. Fordham. Inducted in 1971. 1959-67 Green Bay Packers, 1969 Washington Redskins.

SID LUCKMAN
Quarterback. 6-0, 195. Born in Brooklyn, New York, November 21, 1916. Columbia. Inducted in 1965. 1939-50 Chicago Bears.

ROY (LINK) LYMAN
Tackle. 6-2, 252. Born in Table Rock, Nebraska, November 30, 1898. Died December 16, 1972. Nebraska. In-

ducted in 1964. 1922-23, 1925 Canton Bulldogs, 1924 Cleveland Bulldogs, 1925 Frankford Yellow Jackets, 1926-28, 1930-31, 1933-34 Chicago Bears.

TIM MARA
Team owner. Born in New York, New York, July 29, 1887. Died February 17, 1959. Did not attend college. Inducted in 1963. 1925-59 New York Giants.

GINO MARCHETTI
Defensive end. 6-4, 245. Born in Smithers, West Virginia, January 2, 1927. San Francisco. Inducted in 1972. 1952 Dallas Texans, 1953-64, 1966 Baltimore Colts.

GEORGE PRESTON MARSHALL
Team owner. Born in Grafton, West Virginia, October 11, 1897. Died August 9, 1969. Randolph-Macon. Inducted in 1963. 1932 Boston Braves, 1933-36 Boston Redskins, 1937-69 Washington Redskins.

OLLIE MATSON
Halfback. 6-2, 220. Born in Trinity, Texas, May 1, 1930. San Francisco. Inducted in 1972. 1952, 1954-58 Chicago Cardinals, 1959-62 Los Angeles Rams, 1963 Detroit Lions, 1964-66 Philadelphia Eagles.

DON MAYNARD
Wide receiver. 6-1, 175. Born in Crosbyton, Texas, January 25, 1935. Texas Western. Inducted in 1987. New York Giants 1958, New York Titans 1960-62, New York Jets 1963-72, St. Louis Cardinals 1973.

GEORGE McAFEE
Halfback. 6-0, 177. Born in Ironton, Ohio, March 13, 1918. Duke. Inducted in 1966. 1940-41, 1945-50 Chicago Bears.

MIKE McCORMACK
Tackle. 6-4, 248. Born in Chicago, Illinois, June 21, 1930. Kansas. Inducted in 1984. 1951 New York Yanks, 1954-62 Cleveland Browns.

HUGH McELHENNY
Halfback. 6-1, 198. Born in Los Angeles, California, December 31, 1928. Washington. Inducted in 1970. 1952-60 San Francisco 49ers, 1961-62 Minnesota Vikings, 1963 New York Giants, 1964 Detroit Lions.

JOHNNY BLOOD (McNALLY)
Halfback. 6-0, 185. Born in New Richmond, Wisconsin, November 27, 1903. Died November 28, 1985. St. John's (Minnesota). Inducted in 1963. 1925-26 Milwaukee Badgers, 1926-27 Duluth Eskimos, 1928 Pottsville Maroons, 1929-33 Green Bay Packers, 1934 Pittsburgh Pirates, 1935-36 Green Bay Packers; player-coach, 1937-39 Pittsburgh Pirates.

MIKE MICHALSKE
Guard. 6-0, 209. Born in Cleveland, Ohio, April 24, 1903. Died October 26, 1983. Penn State. Inducted in 1964. 1926 New York Yankees (AFL), 1927-28 New York Yankees, 1929-35, 1937 Green Bay Packers.

WAYNE MILLNER
End. 6-0, 191. Born in Roxbury, Massachusetts, January 31, 1913. Died November 19, 1976. Notre Dame. Inducted in 1968. 1936 Boston Redskins, 1937-41, 1945 Washington Redskins.

BOBBY MITCHELL
Running back-wide receiver. 6-0, 195. Born in Hot Springs, Arkansas, June 6, 1935. Illinois. Inducted in 1983. 1958-61 Cleveland Browns, 1962-68 Washington Redskins.

RON MIX
Tackle. 6-4, 250. Born in Los Angeles, California, March 10, 1938. Southern California. Inducted in 1979. 1960 Los Angeles Chargers, 1961-69 San Diego Chargers, 1971 Oakland Raiders.

LENNY MOORE
Back. 6-1, 198. Born in Reading, Pennsylvania, November 25, 1933. Penn State. Inducted in 1975. 1956-67 Baltimore Colts.

MARION MOTLEY
Fullback. 6-1, 238. Born in Leesburg, Georgia, June 5, 1920. South Carolina State, Nevada. Inducted in 1968. 1946-49 Cleveland Browns (AAFC), 1950-53 Cleveland Browns, 1955 Pittsburgh Steelers.

GEORGE MUSSO
Guard-tackle. 6-2, 270. Born in Collinsville, Illinois. April 8, 1910. Millikin. Inducted in 1982. 1933-44 Chicago Bears.

BRONKO NAGURSKI
Fullback. 6-2, 225. Born in Rainy River, Ontario, Canada, November 3, 1908. Died January 9, 1990. Minnesota. Inducted in 1963. 1930-37, 1943 Chicago Bears.

JOE NAMATH
Quarterback. 6-2, 200. Born in Beaver Falls, Pennsylvania, May 31, 1943. Alabama. Inducted in 1985. 1965-76 New York Jets, 1977 Los Angeles Rams.

EARLE (GREASY) NEALE
Coach. Born in Parkersburg, West Virginia, November 5, 1891. Died November 2, 1973. West Virginia Wesleyan. Inducted in 1969. 1941-42, 1944-50 Philadelphia Eagles; co-coach, Phil-Pitt 1943.

ERNIE NEVERS
Fullback. 6-1, 205. Born in Willow River, Minnesota, June 11, 1903. Died May 3, 1976. Stanford. Inducted in 1963. 1926-27 Duluth Eskimos, 1929-31 Chicago Cardinals.

RAY NITSCHKE
Linebacker. 6-3, 235. Born in Elmwood Park, Illinois, December 29, 1936. Illinois. Inducted in 1978. 1958-72 Green Bay Packers.

LEO NOMELLINI
Defensive tackle. 6-3, 250. Born in Lucca, Italy, June 19, 1924. Minnesota. Inducted in 1969. 1950-63 San Francisco 49ers.

MERLIN OLSEN
Defensive tackle. 6-5, 270. Born in Logan, Utah, September 15, 1940. Utah State. Inducted in 1982. 1962-76 Los Angeles Rams.

JIM OTTO
Center. 6-2, 255. Born in Wausau, Wisconsin, January 5, 1938. Miami. Inducted in 1980. 1960-74 Oakland Raiders.

STEVE OWEN
Tackle. Coach. 6-0, 235. Born in Cleo Springs, Oklahoma, April 21, 1898. Died May 17, 1964. Phillips. Inducted in 1966. 1924-25 Kansas City Cowboys, 1926-30 New York Giants; coach, 1931-53 New York Giants.

ALAN PAGE
Defensive tackle. 6-4, 225. Born in Canton, Ohio, August 7, 1945. Inducted in 1988. 1967-78 Minnesota Vikings, 1978-81 Chicago Bears.

CLARENCE (ACE) PARKER
Quarterback. 5-11, 168. Born in Portsmouth, Virginia, May 17, 1912. Duke. Inducted in 1972. 1937-41 Brooklyn Dodgers, 1945 Boston Yanks, 1946 New York Yankees (AAFC).

JIM PARKER
Guard-tackle. 6-3, 273. Born in Macon, Georgia, April 3, 1934. Ohio State. Inducted in 1973. 1957-67 Baltimore Colts.

JOE PERRY
Fullback. 6-0, 200. Born in Stevens, Arkansas, January 22, 1927. Compton Junior College. Inducted in 1969. 1948-49 San Francisco 49ers (AAFC), 1950-60, 1963 San Francisco 49ers, 1961-62 Baltimore Colts.

PETE PIHOS
End. 6-1, 210. Born in Orlando, Florida, October 22, 1923. Indiana. Inducted in 1970. 1947-55 Philadelphia Eagles.

HUGH (SHORTY) RAY
Supervisor of officials 1938-56. Born in Highland Park, Illinois, September 21, 1884. Died September 16, 1956. Illinois. Inducted in 1966.

DAN REEVES
Team owner. Born in New York, New York, June 30, 1912. Died April 15, 1971. Georgetown. Inducted in 1967. 1941-45 Cleveland Rams, 1946-71 Los Angeles Rams.

JIM RINGO
Center. 6-1, 235. Born in Orange, New Jersey, November 21, 1931. Syracuse. Inducted in 1981. 1953-63 Green Bay Packers, 1964-67 Philadelphia Eagles.

ANDY ROBUSTELLI
Defensive end. 6-0, 230. Born in Stamford, Connecticut, December 6, 1925. Arnold College. Inducted in 1971. 1951-55 Los Angeles Rams, 1956-64 New York Giants.

ART ROONEY
Team owner. Born in Coulterville, Pennsylvania, January 27, 1901. Died August 25, 1988. Georgetown, Duquesne. Inducted in 1964. 1933-40 Pittsburgh Pirates, 1941-42, 1945-88 Pittsburgh Steelers, 1943 Phil-Pitt, 1944 Card-Pitt.

PETE ROZELLE
Commissioner. Born in South Gate, California, March 1, 1926. San Francisco. Inducted in 1985. Commissioner 1960-89.

BOB ST. CLAIR
Tackle. 6-9, 265. Born in San Francisco, California, February 18, 1931. San Francisco, Tulsa. Inducted in 1990. 1953-63 San Francisco 49ers.

GALE SAYERS
Running back. 6-0, 200. Born in Wichita, Kansas, May 30, 1943.

Kansas. Inducted in 1977. 1965-71 Chicago Bears.

JOE SCHMIDT
Linebacker. 6-0, 222. Born in Pittsburgh, Pennsylvania, January 19, 1932. Pittsburgh. Inducted in 1973. 1953-65 Detroit Lions.

ART SHELL
Tackle. 6-5, 285. Born in Charleston, South Carolina, November 25, 1946. Maryland State-Eastern Shore. Inducted in 1989. 1968-81 Oakland Raiders, 1982 Los Angeles Raiders.

O.J. SIMPSON
Running back. 6-1, 212. Born in San Francisco, California, July 9, 1947. Southern California. Inducted in 1985. 1969-77 Buffalo Bills, 1978-79 San Francisco 49ers.

BART STARR
Quarterback. 6-1, 200. Born in Montgomery, Alabama, January 9, 1934. Alabama. Inducted in 1977. 1956-71 Green Bay Packers.

ROGER STAUBACH
Quarterback. 6-3, 202. Born in Cincinnati, Ohio, February 5, 1942. Navy. Inducted in 1985. 1969-79 Dallas Cowboys.

ERNIE STAUTNER
Defensive tackle. 6-2, 235. Born in Prinzing-by-Cham, Bavaria, Germany, April 20, 1925. Boston College. Inducted in 1969. 1950-63 Pittsburgh Steelers.

KEN STRONG
Halfback. 5-11, 210. Born in New Haven, Connecticut, August 6, 1906. Died October 5, 1979. New York University. Inducted in 1967. 1929-32 Staten Island Stapletons, 1933-35, 1939, 1944-47 New York Giants, 1936-37 New York Yanks (AFL).

JOE STYDAHAR
Tackle. 6-4, 230. Born in Kaylor, Pennsylvania, March 3, 1912. Died March 23, 1977. West Virginia. Inducted in 1967. 1936-42, 1945-46 Chicago Bears.

FRAN TARKENTON
Quarterback. 6-0, 185. Born in Richmond, Virginia, February 3, 1940. Georgia. Inducted in 1986. 1961-66, 1972-78 Minnesota Vikings, 1967-71 New York Giants.

CHARLEY TAYLOR
Running back-wide receiver. 6-3, 210. Born in Grand Prairie, Texas, September 28, 1941. Arizona State. Inducted in 1984. 1964-75, 1977 Washington Redskins.

JIM TAYLOR
Fullback. 6-0, 216. Born in Baton Rouge, Louisiana, September 20, 1935. Louisiana State. Inducted in 1976. 1958-66 Green Bay Packers, 1967 New Orleans Saints.

JIM THORPE
Halfback. 6-1, 190. Born in Prague, Oklahoma, May 28, 1888. Died March 28, 1953. Carlisle. Inducted in 1963. 1915-17, 1919-20, 1926 Canton Bulldogs, 1921 Cleveland Indians, 1922-23 Oorang Indians, 1924 Rock Island, Ill., Independents, 1925 New York Giants, 1928 Chicago Cardinals.

Y.A. TITTLE
Quarterback. 6-0, 200. Born in Marshall, Texas, October 24, 1926. Louisiana State. Inducted in 1971. 1948-49 Baltimore Colts (AAFC), 1950 Baltimore Colts, 1951-60 San Francisco 49ers, 1961-64 New York Giants.

GEORGE TRAFTON
Center. 6-2, 235. Born in Chicago, Illinois, December 6, 1896. Died September 5, 1971. Notre Dame. Inducted in 1964. 1920 Decatur Staleys, 1921 Chicago Staleys, 1922-32 Chicago Bears.

CHARLEY TRIPPI
Halfback. 6-0, 185. Born in Pittston, Pennsylvania, December 14, 1922. Georgia. Inducted in 1968. 1947-55 Chicago Cardinals.

EMLEN TUNNELL
Safety. 6-1, 200. Born in Bryn Mawr, Pennsylvania, March 29, 1925. Died July 23, 1975. Toledo, Iowa. Inducted in 1967. 1948-58 New York Giants, 1959-61 Green Bay Packers.

CLYDE (BULLDOG) TURNER
Center. 6-2, 235. Born in Sweetwater, Texas, November 10, 1919. Hardin-Simmons. Inducted in 1966. 1940-52 Chicago Bears.

JOHNNY UNITAS
Quarterback. 6-1, 195. Born in Pittsburgh, Pennsylvania, May 7, 1933. Louisville. Inducted in 1979. 1956-72 Baltimore Colts, 1973 San Diego Chargers.

GENE UPSHAW
Guard. 6-5, 255. Born in Robstown, Texas, August 15, 1945. Texas A & I. Inducted in 1987. Oakland Raiders 1967-81.

NORM VAN BROCKLIN
Quarterback. 6-1, 190. Born in Eagle Butte, South Dakota, March 15, 1926. Died May 2, 1983. Oregon. Inducted in 1971. 1949-57 Los Angeles Rams, 1958-60 Philadelphia Eagles.

STEVE VAN BUREN
Halfback. 6-1, 200. Born in La Ceiba, Honduras, December 28, 1920. Louisiana State. Inducted in 1965. 1944-51 Philadelphia Eagles.

DOAK WALKER
Halfback. 5-10, 172. Born in Dallas, Texas, January 1, 1927. Southern Methodist. Inducted in 1986. 1950-55 Detroit Lions.

PAUL WARFIELD
Wide receiver. 6-0, 188. Born in Warren, Ohio, November 28, 1942. Ohio State. Inducted in 1983. 1964-69, 1976-77 Cleveland Browns, 1970-74 Miami Dolphins.

BOB WATERFIELD
Quarterback. 6-2, 200. Born in Elmira, New York, July 26, 1920. Died March 25, 1983. UCLA. Inducted in 1965. 1945 Cleveland Rams, 1946-52 Los Angeles Rams.

ARNIE WEINMEISTER
Defensive tackle. 6-4, 235. Born in Rhein, Saskatchewan, Canada, March 23, 1923. Washington. Inducted in 1984. 1948-49 New York Yankees (AAFC), 1950-53 New York Giants.

BILL WILLIS
Guard. 6-2, 215. Born in Columbus, Ohio, October 5, 1921. Ohio State. Inducted in 1977. 1946-49 Cleveland Browns (AAFC), 1950-53 Cleveland Browns.

LARRY WILSON
Safety. 6-0, 190. Born in Rigby, Idaho, March 24, 1938. Utah. Inducted in 1978. 1960-72 St. Louis Cardinals.

ALEX WOJCIECHOWICZ
Center. 6-0, 235. Born in South River, New Jersey, August 12, 1915. Fordham. Inducted in 1968. 1938-46 Detroit Lions, 1946-50 Philadelphia Eagles.

WILLIE WOOD
Safety. 5-10, 190. Born in Washington, D.C., December 23, 1936. Southern California. Inducted in 1989. 1960-71 Green Bay Packers.

1869 Rutgers and Princeton played a college soccer football game, the first ever, November 6. The game used modified London Football Association rules. During the next seven years, rugby gained favor with the major eastern schools over soccer, and modern football began to develop from rugby.

1876 At the Massasoit convention, the first rules for American football were written. Walter Camp, who would become known as "the father of American football," first became involved with the game.

1892 In an era in which football was a major attraction of local athletic clubs, an intense competition between two Pittsburgh-area clubs, the Allegheny Athletic Association (AAA) and the Pittsburgh Athletic Club (PAC), led to the making of the first professional football player. Former Yale All-America guard William (Pudge) Heffelfinger was paid $500 by the AAA to play in a game against the PAC, becoming the first person to be paid to play football, November 12. The AAA won the game 4-0 when Heffelfinger picked up a PAC fumble and ran 35 yards for a touchdown.

1893 The Pittsburgh Athletic Club signed one of its players, probably halfback Grant Dibert, to the first known pro football contract, which covered all of the PAC's games for the year.

1895 John Brallier became the first football player to openly turn pro, accepting $10 and expenses to play for the Latrobe YMCA against the Jeannette Athletic Club.

1896 The Allegheny Athletic Association team fielded the first completely professional team for its abbreviated two-game season.

1897 The Latrobe Athletic Association football team went entirely professional, becoming the first team to play a full season with only professionals.

1898 A touchdown was changed from four points to five.

1899 Chris O'Brien formed a neighborhood team, which played under the name the Morgan Athletic Club, on the south side of Chicago. The team later became known as the Normals, then the Racine (for a street in Chicago) Cardinals, the Chicago Cardinals, the St. Louis Cardinals, and, in 1988, the Phoenix Cardinals. The team remains the oldest continuing operation in pro football.

1900 William C. Temple took over the team payments for the Duquesne Country and Athletic Club, becoming the first known individual club owner.

1902 Baseball's Philadelphia Athletics, managed by Connie Mack, and the Philadelphia Phillies formed professional football teams, joining the Pittsburgh Stars in the first attempt at a pro football league, named the National Football League. The Athletics won the first night football game ever played, 39-0 over Kanaweola AC at Elmira, New York, November 21.

All three teams claimed the pro championship for the year, but the league president, Dave Berry, named the Stars the champions. Pitcher Rube Waddell was with the Athletics, and pitcher Christy Mathewson a fullback for Pittsburgh.

The first World Series of pro football, actually a five-team tournament, was played among a team made up of players from both the Athletics and the Phillies, but simply named "New York;" the New York Knickerbockers; the Syracuse AC; the Warlow AC; and the Orange (New Jersey) AC at New York's original Madison Square Garden. New York and Syracuse played the first indoor football game before 3,000, December 28. Syracuse, with Glen (Pop) Warner at guard, won 6-0 and went on to win the tournament.

1903 The Franklin (Pa.) Athletic Club won the second and last World Series of pro football over the Oreos AC of Asbury Park, New Jersey; the Watertown Red and Blacks; and the Orange AC.

Pro football was popularized in Ohio when the Massillon Tigers, a strong amateur team, hired four Pittsburgh pros to play in the season-ending game against Akron. At the same time, pro football declined in the Pittsburgh area, and the emphasis on the pro game moved west from Pennsylvania to Ohio.

1904 A field goal was changed from five points to four.

Ohio had at least seven pro teams, with Massillon winning the Ohio Independent Championship, that is, the pro title. Talk surfaced about forming a state-wide league to end spiraling salaries brought about by constant bidding for players and to write universal rules for the game. The feeble attempt to start the league failed.

Halfback Charles Follis signed a contract with the Shelby AC, making him the first-known black pro football player.

1905 The Canton AC, later to become known as the Bulldogs, became a professional team. Massillon again won the Ohio League championship.

1906 The forward pass was legalized. The first authenticated pass completion in a pro game came on October 27, when George (Peggy) Parratt of Massillon threw a completion to Dan (Bullet) Riley in a victory over a combined Benwood-Moundsville team.

Archrivals Canton and Massillon, the two best pro teams in America, played twice, with Canton winning the first game but Massillon winning the second and the Ohio League championship. A betting scandal and the financial disaster wrought upon the two clubs by paying huge salaries caused a temporary decline in interest in pro football in the two cities and, somewhat, through Ohio.

1909 A field goal dropped from four points to three.

1912 A touchdown was increased from five points to six.

Jack Cusack revived a strong pro team in Canton.

1913 Jim Thorpe, a former football and track star at the Carlisle Indian School (Pa.) and a double gold medal winner at the 1912 Olympics in Stockholm, played for the Pine Village Pros in Indiana.

1915 Massillon again fielded a major team, reviving the old rivalry with Canton. Cusack signed Thorpe to play for Canton for $250 a game.

1916 With Thorpe and former Carlisle teammate Pete Calac starring, Canton went 9-0-1, won the Ohio League championship, and was acclaimed the pro football champion.

1917 Despite an upset by Massillon, Canton again won the Ohio League championship.

1919 Canton again won the Ohio League championship, despite the team having been turned over from Cusack to Ralph Hay. Thorpe and Calac were joined in the backfield by Joe Guyon.

Earl (Curly) Lambeau and George Calhoun organized the Green Bay Packers. Lambeau's employer at the Indian Packing Company provided $500 for equipment and allowed the team to use the company field for practices. The Packers went 10-1.

1920 Pro football was in a state of confusion due to three major problems: dramatically rising salaries; players continually jumping from one team to another following the highest offer; and the use of college players still enrolled in school. A league in which all the members would follow the same rules seemed the answer. An organizational meeting, at which the Akron Pros, Canton Bulldogs, Cleveland Indians, and Dayton Triangles were represented, was held in Canton, Ohio, August 20. This meeting resulted in the formation of the American Professional Football Conference.

A second organizational meeting was held in Canton, September 17. The teams were from four states—Akron, Canton, Cleveland, and Dayton from Ohio; the Hammond Pros and Muncie Flyers from Indiana; the Rochester Jeffersons from New York; and the Rock Island Independents, Decatur Staleys, and Racine Cardinals from Illinois. The name of the league was changed to the American Professional Football Association. Hoping to capitalize on his fame, the members elected Thorpe president; Stanley Cofall of Cleveland was elected vice president. A membership fee of $100 per team was charged to give an appearance of respectability, but no team ever paid it. Scheduling was left up to the teams, and there was a wide variation both in the overall number of games played and in the number played against APFA member teams.

Four other teams—the Buffalo All-Americans, Chicago Tigers, Columbus Panhandles, and Detroit Heralds—joined the league sometime during the year. On September 26, the first game featuring an APFA team was played at Rock Island's Douglas Park. A crowd of 800 watched the Independents defeat the St. Paul Ideals 48-0. A week later, October 3, the first game matching two APFA teams was held. At Triangle Park, Dayton defeated Columbus 14-0, with Lou Partlow of Dayton scoring the first touchdown in a game between Association teams. The same day, Rock Island defeated Muncie 45-0.

By the beginning of December, most of the teams in the APFA had abandoned their hopes for a championship, and some of them, including the Chicago Tigers and the Detroit Heralds, had finished their seasons, disbanded, and had their franchises canceled by the Association. Four teams—Akron, Buffalo, Canton, and Decatur—still had championship as-

pirations, but a series of late-season games among them left Akron as the only undefeated team in the Association. At one of these games, Akron sold tackle Bob Nash to Buffalo for $300 and five percent of the gate receipts—the first APFA player deal.

1921 At the league meeting in Akron, April 30, the championship of the 1920 season was awarded to the Akron Pros. The APFA was reorganized, with Joe Carr of the Columbus Panhandles named president and Carl Storck of Dayton secretary-treasurer. Carr moved the Association's headquarters to Columbus, drafted a league constitution and by-laws, gave teams territorial rights, restricted player movements, developed membership criteria for the franchises, and issued standings for the first time, so that the APFA would have a clear champion.

The Association's membership increased to 22 teams, including the Green Bay Packers, who were awarded to John Clair of the Acme Packing Company.

Thorpe moved from Canton to the Cleveland Indians, but he was hurt early in the season and played very little.

A.E. Staley turned the Decatur Staleys over to player-coach George Halas, who moved the team to Cubs Park in Chicago. Staley paid Halas $5,000 to keep the name "Staleys" for one more year. Halas made halfback Ed (Dutch) Sternaman his partner.

The Staleys claimed the APFA championship with a 9-1-1 record, as did Buffalo at 9-1-2. Carr ruled in favor of the Staleys, giving Halas his first championship.

1922 After admitting the use of players who had college eligibility remaining during the 1921 season, Clair and the Green Bay management withdrew from the APFA, January 28. Curly Lambeau promised to obey league rules and then used $50 of his own money to buy back the franchise. Bad weather and low attendance plagued the Packers, and Lambeau went broke, but local merchants arranged a $2,500 loan for the club. A public non-profit corporation was set up to operate the team, with Lambeau as head coach and manager.

The American Professional Football Association changed its name to the National Football League, June 24. The Chicago Staleys became the Chicago Bears.

The NFL fielded 18 teams, including the new Oorang Indians of Marion, Ohio, an all-Indian team featuring Thorpe, Joe Guyon, and Pete Calac, and sponsored by the Oorang dog kennels.

Canton, led by player-coach Guy Chamberlin and tackles Link Lyman and Wilbur (Pete) Henry, emerged as the league's first true powerhouse, going 10-0-2.

1923 For the first time, all of the franchises considered to be part of the NFL fielded teams. Thorpe played first for Oorang, then for the Toledo Maroons. Against the Bears, Thorpe fumbled, and Halas picked up the ball and returned it 98 yards for a touchdown, a record that would last until 1972.

Canton had its second consecutive undefeated season, going 11-0-1 for the NFL title.

1924 The league had 18 franchises, including new ones in Kansas City, Kenosha, and Frankford, a section of Philadelphia. League champion Canton, successful on the field but not at the box office, was purchased by the owner of the Cleveland franchise, who kept the Canton franchise inactive, while using the best players for his Cleveland team, which he renamed the Bulldogs. Cleveland won the title with a 7-1-1 record.

1925 Five new franchises were admitted to the NFL—the New York Giants, who were awarded to Tim Mara and Billy Gibson for $500; the Detroit Panthers, featuring Jimmy Conzelman as owner, coach, and tailback; the Providence Steam Roller; a new Canton Bulldogs team; and the Pottsville Maroons, who had been perhaps the most successful independent pro team. The NFL established its first player limit, at 16 players.

Late in the season, the NFL made its greatest coup in gaining national recognition. Shortly after the University of Illinois season ended in November, All-America halfback Harold (Red) Grange signed a contract to play with the Chicago Bears. On Thanksgiving Day, a crowd of 36,000—the largest in pro football history—watched Grange and the Bears play the Chicago Cardinals to a scoreless tie at Wrigley Field. At the beginning of December, the Bears left on a barnstorming tour that saw them play eight games in 12 days, in St. Louis, Philadelphia, New York City, Washington, Boston, Pittsburgh, Detroit, and Chicago. A crowd of 73,000 watched the game against the Giants at the Polo Grounds, helping assure the future of the troubled NFL franchise in New York. The Bears then played nine more games in the South and West, including a game in Los Angeles, in which 75,000 fans watched them defeat the Los Angeles Tigers in the Los Angeles Memorial Coliseum.

Pottsville and the Chicago Cardinals were the top contenders for the league title, with Pottsville winning a late-season meeting 21-7. Pottsville scheduled a game against a team of former Notre Dame players for Shibe Park in Philadelphia. Frankford lodged a protest not only because the game was in Frankford's "protected territory," but because it was being played the same day as a Yellow Jackets home game. Carr gave three different notices forbidding Pottsville to play the game, but Pottsville played anyway, December 12. That day, Carr fined the club, suspended it from all rights and privileges (including the right to play for the NFL championship), and returned its franchise to the league. The Cardinals, who ended the season with the best record in the league, were named the 1925 champions.

1926 Grange's manager, C.C. Pyle, told the Bears that Grange wouldn't play for them unless he was paid a five-figure salary and given one-third ownership of the team. The Bears refused. Pyle leased Yankee Stadium in New York City, then petitioned for an NFL franchise. After he was refused, he started the first American Football League. It lasted one season and included Grange's New York Yankees and eight other teams. The AFL champion Philadelphia Quakers

played a December game against the New York Giants, seventh in the NFL, and the Giants won 31-0. At the end of the season, the AFL folded.

Halas pushed through a rule that prohibited any team from signing a player whose college class had not graduated.

The NFL grew to 22 teams, including the Duluth Eskimos, who signed All-America fullback Ernie Nevers of Stanford, giving the league a gate attraction to rival Grange. The 15-member Eskimos, dubbed the "Iron Men of the North," played 29 exhibition and league games, 28 on the road, and Nevers played in all but 29 minutes of them.

Frankford edged the Bears for the championship, despite Halas having obtained John (Paddy) Driscoll from the Cardinals. On December 4, the Yellow Jackets scored in the final two minutes to defeat the Bears 7-6 and move ahead of them in the standings.

1927 At a special meeting in Cleveland, April 23, Carr decided to secure the NFL's future by eliminating the financially weaker teams and consolidating the quality players onto a limited number of more successful teams. The new-look NFL dropped to 12 teams, and the center of gravity of the league left the Midwest, where the NFL had started, and began to emerge in the large cities of the East. One of the new teams was Grange's New York Yankees, but Grange suffered a knee injury and the Yankees finished in the middle of the pack. The NFL championship was won by the cross-town rival New York Giants, who posted 10 shutouts in 13 games.

1928 Grange and Nevers both retired from pro football, and Duluth disbanded, as the NFL was reduced to only 10 teams. The Providence Steam Roller of Jimmy Conzelman and Pearce Johnson won the championship, playing in the Cycledrome, a 10,000-seat oval that had been built for bicycle races.

1929 Chris O'Brien sold the Chicago Cardinals to David Jones, July 27.

The NFL added a fourth official, the field judge, July 28.

Grange and Nevers returned to the NFL. Nevers scored six rushing touchdowns and four extra points as the Cardinals beat Grange's Bears 40-6, November 28. The 40 points set a record that remains the NFL's oldest.

Providence became the first NFL team to host a game at night under floodlights, against the Cardinals, November 3.

The Packers added back Johnny Blood (McNally), tackle Cal Hubbard, and guard Mike Michalske, and won their first NFL championship, edging the Giants, who featured quarterback Benny Friedman.

1930 Dayton, the last of the NFL's original franchises, was purchased by John Dwyer, moved to Brooklyn, and renamed the Dodgers. The Portsmouth, Ohio, Spartans entered the league.

The Packers edged the Giants for the title, but the most improved team was the Bears. Halas retired as a player and replaced himself as coach of the Bears with Ralph Jones, who refined the T-formation by introducing wide ends and a halfback in motion. Jones also introduced rookie All-America fullback-tackle Bronko

Nagurski.

The Giants defeated a team of former Notre Dame players coached by Knute Rockne 22-0 before 55,000 at the Polo Grounds, December 14. The proceeds went to the New York Unemployment Fund to help those suffering because of the Great Depression, and the easy victory helped give the NFL credibility with the press and the public.

1931 The NFL decreased to 10 teams, and halfway through the season the Frankford franchise folded. Carr fined the Bears, Packers, and Portsmouth $1,000 each for using players whose college classes had not graduated.

The Packers won an unprecedented third consecutive title, beating out the Spartans, who were led by rookie backs Earl (Dutch) Clark and Glenn Presnell.

1932 George Preston Marshall, Vincent Bendix, Jay O'Brien, and M. Dorland Doyle were awarded a franchise for Boston, July 9. Despite the presence of two rookies—halfback Cliff Battles and tackle Glen (Turk) Edwards—the new team, named the Braves, lost money and Marshall was left as the sole owner at the end of the year.

NFL membership dropped to eight teams, the lowest in history. Official statistics were kept for the first time. The Bears and the Spartans finished the season in the first-ever tie for first place. After the season finale, the league office arranged for the first playoff game in NFL history. The game was moved indoors to Chicago Stadium because of bitter cold and heavy snow. The arena allowed only an 80-yard field that came right to the walls. The goal posts were moved from the end lines to the goal lines and, for safety, inbounds lines or hashmarks where the ball would be put in play were drawn 10 yards from the walls that butted against the sidelines. The Bears won 9-0, December 18, scoring the winning touchdown on a two-yard pass from Nagurski to Grange. The Spartans claimed Nagurski's pass was thrown from less than five yards behind the line of scrimmage, violating the existing passing rule, but the play stood.

1933 The NFL, which long had followed the rules of college football, made a number of significant changes from the college game for the first time and began to independently develop rules serving its needs and the style of play it preferred. The innovations from the 1932 championship game—inbounds line or hashmarks and goal posts on the goal lines—were adopted. Also the forward pass was legalized from anywhere behind the line of scrimmage, February 25.

Marshall and Halas pushed through a proposal that divided the NFL into two divisions, with the winners to meet in an annual championship game, July 8.

Three new franchises joined the league—the Pittsburgh Pirates of Art Rooney, the Philadelphia Eagles of Bert Bell and Lud Wray, and the Cincinnati Reds. The Staten Island Stapletons suspended operations for a year, but never returned to the league.

Halas bought out Sternaman, became sole owner of the Bears, and reinstated himself as head coach. Marshall changed the name of the

Boston Braves to the Redskins. David Jones sold the Chicago Cardinals to Charles W. Bidwill.

In the first NFL Championship Game scheduled before the season, the Western Division champion Bears defeated the Eastern Division champion Giants 23-21 at Wrigley Field, December 17.

1934 G.A. (Dick) Richards purchased the Portsmouth Spartans, moved them to Detroit, and renamed them the Lions.

Professional football gained new prestige when the Bears were matched against the best college football players in the first Chicago College All-Star Game, August 31. The game ended in a scoreless tie before 79,432 at Soldier Field.

The Cincinnati Reds lost their first eight games, then were suspended from the league for defaulting on payments. The St. Louis Gunners, an independent team, joined the NFL by buying the Cincinnati franchise and went 1-2 the last three weeks.

Rookie Beattie Feathers of the Bears became the NFL's first 1,000-yard rusher, gaining 1,004 on 101 carries. The Thanksgiving Day game between the Bears and the Lions became the first NFL game broadcast nationally, with Graham McNamee the announcer for CBS radio.

In the championship game, on an extremely cold and icy day at the Polo Grounds, the Giants trailed the Bears 13-3 in the third quarter before changing to basketball shoes for better footing. The Giants won 30-13 in what has come to be known as the "Sneakers Game," December 9.

The player waiver rule was adopted, December 10.

1935 The NFL adopted Bert Bell's proposal to hold an annual draft of college players, to begin in 1936, with teams selecting in an inverse order of finish, May 19. The inbounds line or hashmarks were moved nearer the center of the field, 15 yards from the sidelines.

All-America end Don Hutson of Alabama joined Green Bay. The Lions defeated the Giants 26-7 in the NFL Championship Game, December 15.

1936 There were no franchise transactions for the first year since the formation of the NFL. It also was the first year in which all member teams played the same number of games.

The Eagles made University of Chicago halfback and Heisman Trophy winner Jay Berwanger the first player ever selected in the NFL draft, February 8. The Eagles traded his rights to the Bears, but Berwanger never played pro football. The first player selected to actually sign was the number-two pick, Riley Smith of Alabama, who was selected by Boston.

A rival league was formed, and it became the second to call itself the American Football League. The Boston Shamrocks were its champions.

Due to poor attendance, Marshall, the owner of the host team, moved the Championship Game from Boston to the Polo Grounds in New York. Green Bay defeated the Redskins 21-6, December 13.

1937 Homer Marshman was granted a Cleveland franchise, named the Rams, February 12. Marshall moved the Redskins to Washington, D.C., February 13. The Redskins signed TCU All-America tailback Sammy Baugh, who led them to a 28-21 victory over the Bears in the NFL Championship Game, December 12.

The Los Angeles Bulldogs had an 8-0 record to win the AFL title, but then the two-year-old league folded.

1938 At the suggestion of Halas, Hugh (Shorty) Ray became a technical advisor on rules and officiating to the NFL. A new rule called for a 15-yard penalty for roughing the passer.

Rookie Byron (Whizzer) White of the Pittsburgh Pirates led the NFL in rushing. The Giants defeated the Packers 23-17 for the NFL title, December 11.

Marshall, *Los Angeles Times* sports editor Bill Henry, and promoter Tom Gallery established the Pro Bowl game between the NFL champion and a team of pro all-stars.

1939 The New York Giants defeated the Pro All-Stars 13-10 in the first Pro Bowl, at Wrigley Field, Los Angeles, January 15.

Carr, NFL president since 1921, died in Columbus, May 20. Carl Storck was named acting president, May 25.

An NFL game was televised for the first time when NBC broadcast the Brooklyn Dodgers-Philadelphia Eagles game from Ebbets Field to approximately 1,000 sets then in New York.

Green Bay defeated New York 27-0 in the NFL Championship Game, December 10 at Milwaukee. NFL attendance exceeded one million in a season for the first time, reaching 1,071,200.

1940 A six-team rival league, the third to call itself the American Football League, was formed, and the Columbus Bullies won its championship.

Halas's Bears, with additional coaching by Clark Shaughnessy of Stanford, defeated the Redskins 73-0 in the NFL Championship Game, December 8. The game, which was the most decisive victory in NFL history, popularized the Bears' T-formation with a man-in-motion. It was the first championship carried on network radio, broadcast by Red Barber to 120 stations of the Mutual Broadcasting System, which paid $2,500 for the rights.

Art Rooney sold the Pittsburgh franchise to Alexis Thompson, December 9, then bought part interest in the Philadelphia Eagles.

1941 Elmer Layden was named the first Commissioner of the NFL, March 1; Storck, the acting president, resigned, April 5. NFL headquarters were moved to Chicago.

Bell and Rooney traded the Eagles to Thompson for the Pirates, then renamed their new team the Steelers. Homer Marshman sold the Rams to Daniel F. Reeves and Fred Levy, Jr.

The league by-laws were revised to provide for playoffs in case there were ties in division races, and sudden-death overtimes in case a playoff game was tied after four quarters. An official *NFL Record Manual* was published for the first time.

Columbus again won the championship of the AFL, but the two-year-old league then folded.

The Bears and the Packers finished in a tie for the Western Division championship, setting up the first divisional playoff game in league history. The Bears won 33-14, then defeated the Giants 37-9 for the NFL championship, December 21.

1942 Players departing for service in World War II depleted the rosters of

NFL teams. Halas left the Bears in midseason to join the Navy, and Luke Johnsos and Heartley (Hunk) Anderson served as co-coaches as the Bears went 11-0 in the regular season. The Redskins defeated the Bears 14-6 in the NFL Championship Game, December 13.

1943 The Cleveland Rams, with co-owners Reeves and Levy in the service, were granted permission to suspend operations for one season, April 6. Levy transferred his stock in the team to Reeves, April 16.

The NFL adopted free substitution, April 7. The league also made the wearing of helmets mandatory and approved a 10-game schedule for all teams.

Philadelphia and Pittsburgh were granted permission to merge for one season, June 19. The team, known as Phil-Pitt (and called the Steagles by fans), divided home games between the two cities, and Earle (Greasy) Neale of Philadelphia and Walt Kiesling of Pittsburgh served as co-coaches. The merger automatically dissolved the last day of the season, December 5.

Ted Collins was granted a franchise for Boston, to become active in 1944.

Sammy Baugh led the league in passing, punting, and interceptions. He led the Redskins to a tie with the Giants for the Eastern Division title, and then to a 28-0 victory in a divisional playoff game. The Bears beat the Redskins 41-21 in the NFL Championship Game, December 26.

1944 Collins, who had wanted a franchise in Yankee Stadium in New York, named his new team in Boston the Yanks. Cleveland resumed operations. The Brooklyn Dodgers changed their name to the Tigers.

Coaching from the bench was legalized, April 20.

The Cardinals and the Steelers were granted permission to merge for one year under the name Card-Pitt, April 21. Phil Handler of the Cardinals and Walt Kiesling of the Steelers served as co-coaches. The merger automatically dissolved the last day of the season, December 3.

In the NFL Championship Game, Green Bay defeated the New York Giants 14-7, December 17.

1945 The inbounds lines or hash-marks were moved from 15 yards away from the sidelines to nearer the center of the field—20 yards from the sidelines.

Brooklyn and Boston merged into a team that played home games in both cities and was known simply as "The Yanks." The team was coached by former Boston head coach Herb Kopf. In December, the Brooklyn franchise withdrew from the NFL to join the new All-America Football Conference; all the players on its active and reserve lists were assigned to The Yanks, who once again became the Boston Yanks.

Halas rejoined the Bears late in the season after service with the U.S. Navy. Although Halas took over much of the coaching duties, Anderson and Johnsos remained the coaches of record throughout the season.

Steve Van Buren of Philadelphia led the NFL in rushing, kickoff returns, and scoring.

After the Japanese surrendered ending World War II, a count showed that the NFL service roster, limited to men who had played in league games,

totaled 638, 21 of whom had died in action.

Rookie quarterback Bob Waterfield led Cleveland to a 15-14 victory over Washington in the NFL Championship Game, December 16.

1946 The contract of Commissioner Layden was not renewed, and Bert Bell, the co-owner of the Steelers, replaced him, January 11. Bell moved the league headquarters from Chicago to the Philadelphia suburb of Bala Cynwyd.

Free substitution was withdrawn and substitutions were limited to no more than three men at a time. Forward passes were made automatically incomplete upon striking the goal posts, January 11.

The NFL took on a truly national appearance for the first time when Reeves was granted permission by the league to move his NFL champion Rams to Los Angeles.

The rival All-America Football Conference began play with eight teams. The Cleveland Browns, coached by Paul Brown, won the AAFC's first championship, defeating the New York Yankees 14-9.

Bill Dudley of the Steelers led the NFL in rushing, interceptions, and punt returns, and won the league's most valuable player award.

Backs Frank Filchock and Merle Hapes of the Giants were questioned about an attempt by a New York man to fix the championship game with the Bears. Bell suspended Hapes but allowed Filchock to play; he played well, but Chicago won 24-14, December 15.

1947 The NFL added a fifth official, the back judge.

A bonus choice was made for the first time in the NFL draft. One team each year would select the special choice before the first round began. The Chicago Bears won a lottery and the rights to the first choice and drafted back Bob Fenimore of Oklahoma A&M.

The Cleveland Browns again won the AAFC title, defeating the New York Yankees 14-3.

Charles Bidwill, Sr., owner of the Cardinals, died April 19, but his wife and sons retained ownership of the team. On December 28, the Cardinals won the NFL Championship Game 28-21 over the Philadelphia Eagles, who had beaten Pittsburgh 21-0 in a playoff.

1948 Plastic helmets were prohibited. A flexible artificial tee was permitted at the kickoff. Officials other than the referee were equipped with whistles, not horns, January 14.

Fred Mandel sold the Detroit Lions to a syndicate headed by D. Lyle Fife, January 15.

Halfback Fred Gehrke of the Los Angeles Rams painted horns on the Rams' helmets, the first modern helmet emblems in pro football.

The Cleveland Browns won their third straight championship in the AAFC, going 14-0 and then defeating the Buffalo Bills 49-7.

In a blizzard, the Eagles defeated the Cardinals 7-0 in the NFL Championship Game, December 19.

1949 Alexis Thompson sold the champion Eagles to a syndicate headed by James P. Clark, January 15. The Boston Yanks became the New York Bulldogs, sharing the Polo Grounds with the Giants.

Free substitution was adopted for one year, January 20.

The NFL had two 1,000-yard rushers in the same season for the first time—Steve Van Buren of Philadelphia and Tony Canadeo of Green Bay.

The AAFC played its season with a one-division, seven-team format. On December 9, Bell announced a merger agreement in which three AAFC franchises—Cleveland, San Francisco, and Baltimore—would join the NFL in 1950. The Browns won their fourth consecutive AAFC title, defeating the 49ers 21-7, December 11.

In a heavy rain, the Eagles defeated the Rams 14-0 in the NFL Championship Game, December 18.

1950 Unlimited free substitution was restored, opening the way for the era of two platoons and specialization in pro football, January 20.

Curly Lambeau, founder of the franchise and Green Bay's head coach since 1921, resigned under fire, February 1.

The name National Football League was restored after about three months as the National-American Football League. The American and National conferences were created to replace the Eastern and Western divisions, March 3.

The New York Bulldogs became the Yanks and divided the players of the former AAFC Yankees with the Giants. A special allocation draft was held in which the 13 teams drafted the remaining AAFC players, with special consideration for Baltimore, which received 15 choices compared to 10 for other teams.

The Los Angeles Rams became the first NFL team to have all of its games—both home and away—televised. The Washington Redskins followed the Rams in arranging to televise their games; other teams made deals to put selected games on television.

In the first game of the season, former AAFC champion Cleveland defeated NFL champion Philadelphia 35-10. For the first time, deadlocks occurred in both conferences and playoffs were necessary. The Browns defeated the Giants in the American and the Rams defeated the Bears in the National. Cleveland defeated Los Angeles 30-28 in the NFL Championship Game, December 24.

1951 The Pro Bowl game, dormant since 1942, was revived under a new format matching the all-stars of each conference at the Los Angeles Memorial Coliseum. The American Conference defeated the National Conference 28-27, January 14.

Abraham Watner returned the Baltimore franchise and its player contracts back to the NFL for $50,000. Baltimore's former players were made available for drafting at the same time as college players, January 18.

A rule was passed that no tackle, guard, or center would be eligible to catch a forward pass, January 18.

The Rams reversed their television policy and televised only road games.

The NFL Championship Game was televised coast-to-coast for the first time, December 23. The DuMont Network paid $75,000 for the rights to the game, in which the Rams defeated the Browns 24-17.

1952 Ted Collins sold the New York Yanks' franchise back to the NFL, January 19. A new franchise was awarded to a group in Dallas after it purchased the assets of the Yanks, January 24. The new Texans went 1-11, with the owners turning the franchise back to the league in midseason. For the last five games of the season, the commissioner's office operated the Texans as a road team, using Hershey, Pennsylvania, as a home base. At the end of the season the franchise was cancelled, the last time an NFL team failed.

The Pittsburgh Steelers abandoned the Single-Wing for the T-formation, the last pro team to do so.

The Detroit Lions won their first NFL championship in 17 years, defeating the Browns 17-7 in the title game, December 28.

1953 A Baltimore group headed by Carroll Rosenbloom was granted a franchise and was awarded the holdings of the defunct Dallas organization, January 23. The team, named the Colts, put together the largest trade in league history, acquiring 10 players from Cleveland in exchange for five.

The names of the American and National conferences were changed to the Eastern and Western conferences, January 24.

Jim Thorpe died, March 28.

Mickey McBride, founder of the Cleveland Browns, sold the franchise to a syndicate headed by Dave R. Jones, June 10.

The NFL policy of blacking out home games was upheld by Judge Allan K. Grim of the U.S. District Court in Philadelphia, November 12.

The Lions again defeated the Browns in the NFL Championship Game, winning 17-16, December 27.

1954 The Canadian Football League began a series of raids on NFL teams, signing quarterback Eddie LeBaron and defensive end Gene Brito of Washington and defensive tackle Arnie Weinmeister of the Giants, among others.

Fullback Joe Perry of the 49ers became the first player in league history to gain 1,000 yards rushing in consecutive seasons.

Cleveland defeated Detroit 56-10 in the NFL Championship Game, December 26.

1955 The sudden-death overtime rule was used for the first time in a preseason game between the Rams and Giants at Portland, Oregon, August 28. The Rams won 23-17 three minutes into overtime.

A rule change declared the ball dead immediately if the ball carrier touched the ground with any part of his body except his hands or feet while in the grasp of an opponent.

The NFL Players Association was founded.

The Baltimore Colts made an 80-cent phone call to Johnny Unitas and signed him as a free agent. Another quarterback, Otto Graham, played his last game as the Browns defeated the Rams 38-14 in the NFL Championship Game, December 26. Graham had quarterbacked the Browns to 10 championship-game appearances in 10 years.

NBC replaced DuMont as the network for the title game, paying a rights fee of $100,000.

1956 Grabbing an opponent's facemask (other than the ball carrier) was made illegal. Using radio receivers to communicate with players on the field was prohibited. A natural leather ball with white end stripes replaced

the white ball with black stripes for night games.

The Giants moved from the Polo Grounds to Yankee Stadium.

Halas retired as coach of the Bears, and was replaced by Paddy Driscoll.

CBS became the first network to broadcast some NFL regular-season games to selected television markets across the nation.

The Giants routed the Bears 47-7 in the NFL Championship Game, December 30.

1957 Pete Rozelle was named general manager of the Rams. Anthony J. Morabito, founder and co-owner of the 49ers, died of a heart attack during a game against the Bears at Kezar Stadium, October 28. An NFL-record crowd of 102,368 saw the 49ers-Rams game at the Los Angeles Memorial Coliseum, November 10.

The Lions came from 20 points down to post a 31-27 playoff victory over the 49ers, December 22. Detroit defeated Cleveland 59-14 in the NFL Championship Game, December 29.

1958 The bonus selection in the draft was eliminated, January 29. The last selection was quarterback King Hill of Rice by the Chicago Cardinals.

Halas reinstated himself as coach of the Bears.

Jim Brown of Cleveland gained an NFL record 1,527 yards rushing. In a divisional playoff game, the Giants held Brown to eight yards and defeated Cleveland 10-0.

Baltimore, coached by Weeb Ewbank, defeated the Giants 23-17 in the first sudden-death overtime in an NFL Championship Game, December 28. The game ended when Colts fullback Alan Ameche scored on a one-yard touchdown run after 8:15 of overtime.

1959 Vince Lombardi was named head coach of the Green Bay Packers, January 28. Tim Mara, the cofounder of the Giants, died, February 17.

Lamar Hunt of Dallas announced his intentions to form a second pro football league. The first meeting was held in Chicago, August 14, and consisted of Hunt representing Dallas; Bob Howsam, Denver; K.S. (Bud) Adams, Houston; Barron Hilton, Los Angeles; Max Winter and Bill Boyer, Minneapolis; and Harry Wismer, New York City. They made plans to begin play in 1960.

The new league was named the American Football League, August 22. Buffalo, owned by Ralph Wilson, became the seventh franchise, October 28. Boston, owned by William H. Sullivan, became the eighth team, November 22. The first AFL draft, lasting 33 rounds, was held, November 22. Joe Foss was named AFL Commissioner, November 30. An additional draft of 20 rounds was held by the AFL, December 2.

NFL Commissioner Bert Bell died of a heart attack suffered at Franklin Field, Philadelphia, during the last two minutes of a game between the Eagles and the Steelers, October 11. Treasurer Austin Gunsel was named president in the office of the commissioner, October 14.

The Colts again defeated the Giants in the NFL Championship Game, 31-16, December 27.

1960 Pete Rozelle was elected NFL Commissioner as a compromise choice on the twenty-third ballot, Jan-

uary 26. Rozelle moved the league offices to New York City.

Hunt was elected AFL president for 1960, January 26. Minneapolis withdrew from the AFL, January 27, and the same ownership was given an NFL franchise for Minnesota (to start in 1961), January 28. Dallas received an NFL franchise for 1960, January 28. Oakland received an AFL franchise, January 30.

The AFL adopted the two-point option on points after touchdown, January 28. A "no-tampering" verbal pact, relative to players' contracts, was agreed to between the NFL and AFL, February 9.

The NFL owners voted to allow the transfer of the Chicago Cardinals to St. Louis, March 13.

The AFL signed a five-year television contract with ABC, June 9.

The Boston Patriots defeated the Buffalo Bills 28-7 before 16,000 at Buffalo in the first AFL preseason game, July 30. The Denver Broncos defeated the Patriots 13-10 before 21,597 at Boston in the first AFL regular-season game, September 9.

Philadelphia defeated Green Bay 17-13 in the NFL Championship Game, December 26.

1961 The Houston Oilers defeated the Los Angeles Chargers 24-16 before 32,183 in the first AFL Championship Game, January 1.

Detroit defeated Cleveland 17-16 in the first Playoff Bowl, or Bert Bell Benefit Bowl, between second-place teams in each conference in Miami, January 7.

End Willard Dewveall of the Bears played out his option and joined the Oilers, becoming the first player to deliberately move from one league to the other, January 14.

Ed McGah, Wayne Valley, and Robert Osborne bought out their partners in the ownership of the Raiders, January 17. The Chargers were transferred to San Diego, February 10. Dave R. Jones sold the Browns to a group headed by Arthur B. Modell, March 22. The Howsam brothers sold the Broncos to a group headed by Calvin Kunz and Gerry Phipps, May 26.

NBC was awarded a two-year contract for radio and television rights to the NFL Championship Game for $615,000 annually, $300,000 of which was to go directly into the NFL Player Benefit Plan, April 5.

Canton, Ohio, where the league that became the NFL was formed in 1920, was chosen as the site of the Pro Football Hall of Fame, April 27. Dick McCann, a former Redskins executive, was named executive director.

A bill legalizing single-network television contracts by professional sports leagues was introduced in Congress by Representative Emanuel Celler. It passed the House and Senate and was signed into law by President John F. Kennedy, September 30.

Houston defeated San Diego 10-3 for the AFL championship, December 24. Green Bay won its first NFL championship since 1944, defeating the New York Giants 37-0, December 31.

1962 The Western Division defeated the Eastern Division 47-27 in the first AFL All-Star Game, played before 20,973 in San Diego, January 7.

Both leagues prohibited grabbing any player's facemask. The AFL vot-

ed to make the scoreboard clock the official timer of the game.

The NFL entered into a single-network agreement with CBS for telecasting all regular-season games for $4,650,000 annually, January 10.

Judge Roszel Thompson of the U.S. District Court in Baltimore ruled against the AFL in its antitrust suit against the NFL, May 21. The AFL had charged the NFL with monopoly and conspiracy in areas of expansion, television, and player signings. The case lasted two and a half years, the trial two months.

McGah and Valley acquired controlling interest in the Raiders, May 24. The AFL assumed financial responsibility for the New York Titans, November 8. With Commissioner Rozelle as referee, Daniel F. Reeves regained the ownership of the Rams, outbidding his partners in sealed-envelope bidding for the team, November 27.

The Dallas Texans defeated the Oilers 20-17 for the AFL championship at Houston after 17 minutes, 54 seconds of overtime on a 25-yard field goal by Tommy Brooker, December 23. The game lasted a record 77 minutes, 54 seconds.

Judge Edward Weinfeld of the U.S. District Court in New York City upheld the legality of the NFL's television blackout within a 75-mile radius of home games and denied an injunction that would have forced the championship game between the Giants and the Packers to be televised in the New York City area, December 28. The Packers beat the Giants 16-7 for the NFL title, December 30.

1963 The Dallas Texans transferred to Kansas City, becoming the Chiefs, February 8. The New York Titans were sold to a five-man syndicate headed by David (Sonny) Werblin, March 28. Weeb Ewbank became the Titans' new head coach and the team's name was changed to the Jets, April 15. They began play in Shea Stadium.

NFL Properties, Inc., was founded to serve as the licensing arm of the NFL.

Rozelle indefinitely suspended Green Bay halfback Paul Hornung and Detroit defensive tackle Alex Karras for placing bets on their own teams and on other NFL games; he also fined five other Detroit players $2,000 each for betting on one game in which they did not participate, and the Detroit Lions Football Company $2,000 on each of two counts for failure to report information promptly and for lack of sideline supervision.

Paul Brown, head coach of the Browns since their inception, was fired and replaced by Blanton Collier. Don Shula replaced Weeb Ewbank as head coach of the Colts.

The AFL allowed the Jets and Raiders to select players from other franchises in hopes of giving the league more competitive balance, May 11.

NBC was awarded exclusive network broadcasting rights for the 1963 AFL Championship Game for $926,000, May 23.

The Pro Football Hall of Fame was dedicated at Canton, Ohio, September 7.

The U.S. Fourth Circuit Court of Appeals reaffirmed the lower court's finding for the NFL in the $10-million suit brought by the AFL, ending three and a half years of litigation, November 21.

Jim Brown of Cleveland rushed for an NFL single-season record 1,863 yards.

Boston defeated Buffalo 26-8 in the first divisional playoff game in AFL history, December 28. The Chargers defeated the Patriots in the AFL Championship Game, January 5.

The Bears defeated the Giants 14-10 in the NFL Championship Game, a record sixth and last title for Halas in his thirty-sixth season as the Bears' coach, December 29.

1964 The Chargers defeated the Patriots in the AFL Championship Game, January 5.

William Clay Ford, the Lions' president since 1961, purchased the team, January 10. A group representing the late James P. Clark sold the Eagles to a group headed by Jerry Wolman, January 21. Carroll Rosenbloom, the majority owner of the Colts since 1953, acquired complete ownership of the team, January 23.

CBS submitted the winning bid of $14.1 million per year for the NFL regular-season television rights for 1964 and 1965, January 24. CBS acquired the rights to the championship games for 1964 and 1965 for $1.8 million per game, April 17.

The AFL signed a five-year, $36-million television contract with NBC to begin with the 1965 season, assuring each team approximately $900,000 a year from television rights, January 29.

Hornung and Karras were reinstated by Rozelle, March 16.

Pete Gogolak of Cornell signed a contract with Buffalo, becoming the first soccer-style kicker in pro football.

Buffalo defeated San Diego 20-7 in the AFL Championship Game, December 26. Cleveland defeated Baltimore 27-0 in the NFL Championship Game, December 27.

1965 The NFL teams pledged not to sign college seniors until completion of all their games, including bowl games, and empowered the Commissioner to discipline the clubs up to as much as the loss of an entire draft list for a violation of the pledge, February 15.

The NFL added a sixth official, the line judge, February 19. The color of the officials' penalty flags was changed from white to bright gold, April 5.

Atlanta was awarded an NFL franchise for 1966, with Rankin Smith, Sr., as owner, June 30. Miami was awarded an AFL franchise for 1966, with Joe Robbie and Danny Thomas as owners, August 16.

Green Bay defeated Baltimore 13-10 in sudden-death overtime in a Western Conference playoff game. Don Chandler kicked a 25-yard field goal for the Packers after 13 minutes, 39 seconds of overtime, December 26. The Packers then defeated the Browns 23-12 in the NFL Championship Game, January 2.

In the AFL Championship Game, the Bills again defeated the Chargers, 23-0, December 26.

CBS acquired the rights to the NFL regular-season games in 1966 and 1967, with an option for 1968, for $18.8 million per year, December 29.

1966 The AFL-NFL war reached its peak, as the leagues spent a combined $7 million to sign their 1966 draft choices. The NFL signed 75 percent of its 232 draftees, the AFL

46 percent of its 181. Of the 111 common draft choices, 79 signed with the NFL, 28 with the AFL, and 4 went unsigned.

The rights to the 1966 and 1967 NFL Championship Games were sold to CBS for $2 million per game, February 14.

Foss resigned as AFL Commissioner, April 7. Al Davis, the head coach and general manager of the Raiders, was named to replace him, April 8.

Goal posts offset from the goal line, painted bright yellow, and with uprights 20 feet above the crossbar were made standard in the NFL, May 16.

A series of secret meetings regarding a possible AFL-NFL merger were held in the spring between Hunt of Kansas City and Tex Schramm of Dallas. Rozelle announced the merger, June 8. Under the agreement, the two leagues would combine to form an expanded league with 24 teams, to be increased to 26 in 1968 and to 28 by 1970 or soon thereafter. All existing franchises would be retained, and no franchises would be transferred outside their metropolitan areas. While maintaining separate schedules through 1969, the leagues agreed to play an annual AFL-NFL World Championship Game beginning in January, 1967, and to hold a combined draft, also beginning in 1967. Preseason games would be held between teams of each league starting in 1967. Official regular-season play would start in 1970 when the two leagues would officially merge to form one league with two conferences. Rozelle was named Commissioner of the expanded league setup.

Davis rejoined the Raiders, and Milt Woodard was named president of the AFL, July 25.

The St. Louis Cardinals moved into newly constructed Busch Memorial Stadium.

Barron Hilton sold the Chargers to a group headed by Eugene Klein and Sam Schulman, August 25.

Congress approved the AFL-NFL merger, passing legislation exempting the agreement itself from antitrust action, October 21.

New Orleans was awarded an NFL franchise to begin play in 1967, November 1. John Mecom, Jr., of Houston was designated majority stockholder and president of the franchise, December 15.

The NFL was realigned for the 1967-69 seasons into the Capitol and Century Divisions in the Eastern Conference and the Central and Coastal Divisions in the Western Conference, December 2. New Orleans and the New York Giants agreed to switch divisions in 1968 and return to the 1967 alignment in 1969.

The rights to the Super Bowl for four years were sold to CBS and NBC for $9.5 million, December 13.

1967 Green Bay earned the right to represent the NFL in the first AFL-NFL World Championship Game by defeating Dallas 34-27, January 1. The same day, Kansas City defeated Buffalo 31-7 to represent the AFL. The Packers defeated the Chiefs 35-10 before 61,946 fans at the Los Angeles Memorial Coliseum in the first game between AFL and NFL teams, January 15. The winning players' share for the Packers was $15,000 each, and the losing players' share for the Chiefs was $7,500 each. The

game was televised by both CBS and NBC.

The "sling-shot" goal post and a six-foot-wide border around the field were made standard in the NFL, February 22.

Baltimore made Bubba Smith, a Michigan State defensive lineman, the first choice in the first combined AFL-NFL draft, March 14.

The AFL awarded a franchise to begin play in 1968 to Cincinnati, May 24. A group with Paul Brown as part owner, general manager, and head coach, was awarded the Cincinnati franchise, September 27.

Arthur B. Modell, the president of the Cleveland Browns, was elected president of the NFL, May 28.

An AFL team defeated an NFL team for the first time, when Denver beat Detroit 13-7 in a preseason game, August 5.

Green Bay defeated Dallas 21-17 for the NFL championship on a last-minute one-yard quarterback sneak by Bart Starr in 13-below-zero temperature at Green Bay, December 31. The same day, Oakland defeated Houston 40-7 for the AFL championship.

1968 Green Bay defeated Oakland 33-14 in Super Bowl II at Miami, January 14. The game had the first $3-million gate in pro football history.

Vince Lombardi resigned as head coach of the Packers, but remained as general manager, January 28.

Werblin sold his shares in the Jets to his partners Don Lillis, Leon Hess, Townsend Martin, and Phil Iselin, May 21. Lillis assumed the presidency of the club, but then died July 23. Iselin was appointed president, August 6.

Halas retired for the fourth and last time as head coach of the Bears, May 27.

The Oilers left Rice Stadium for the Astrodome and became the first NFL team to play its home games in a domed stadium.

The movie "Heidi" became a footnote in sports history when NBC didn't show the last 1:05 of the Jets-Raiders game in order to permit the children's special to begin on time. The Raiders scored two touchdowns in the last 42 seconds to win 43-32, November 17.

Ewbank became the first coach to win titles in both the NFL and AFL when his Jets defeated the Raiders 27-23 for the AFL championship, December 29. The same day, Baltimore defeated Cleveland 34-0.

1969 The AFL established a playoff format for the 1969 season, with the winner in one division playing the runner-up in the other, January 11.

An AFL team won the Super Bowl for the first time, as the Jets defeated the Colts 16-7 at Miami, January 12 in Super Bowl III. The title "Super Bowl" was recognized by the NFL for the first time.

Vince Lombardi became part owner, executive vice-president, and head coach of the Washington Redskins, Feb. 7.

Wolman sold the Eagles to Leonard Tose, May 1.

Baltimore, Cleveland, and Pittsburgh agreed to join the AFL teams to form the 13-team American Football Conference of the NFL in 1970, May 17. The NFL also agreed on a playoff format that would include one "wild-card" team per conference — the second-place team with the best

record.

Monday Night Football was signed for 1970. ABC acquired the rights to televise 13 NFL regular-season Monday night games in 1970, 1971, and 1972.

George Preston Marshall, president emeritus of the Redskins, died at 72, August 9.

The NFL marked its fiftieth year by the wearing of a special patch by each of the 16 teams.

1970 Kansas City defeated Minnesota 23-7 in Super Bowl IV at New Orleans, January 11. The gross receipts of approximately $3.8 million were the largest ever for a one-day sports event.

Four-year television contracts, under which CBS would televise all NFC games and NBC all AFC games (except Monday night games) and the two would divide televising the Super Bowl and AFC-NFC Pro Bowl games, were announced, January 26.

Art Modell resigned as president of the NFL, March 12. Milt Woodard resigned as president of the AFL, March 13. Lamar Hunt was elected president of the AFC and George Halas was elected president of the NFC, March 19.

The merged 26-team league adopted rules changes putting names on the backs of players' jerseys, making a point after touchdown worth only one point, and making the scoreboard clock the official timing device of the game, March 18.

The Players Negotiating Committee and the NFL Players Association announced a four-year agreement guaranteeing approximately $4,535,000 annually to player pension and insurance benefits, August 3. The owners also agreed to contribute $250,000 annually to improve or implement items such as disability payments, widows' benefits, maternity benefits, and dental benefits. The agreement also provided for increased preseason game and per diem payments, averaging approximately $2.6 million annually.

The Pittsburgh Steelers moved into Three Rivers Stadium. The Cincinnati Bengals moved to Riverfront Stadium.

Lombardi died of cancer at 57, September 3.

Tom Dempsey of New Orleans kicked a game-winning NFL-record 63-yard field goal against Detroit, November 8.

1971 Baltimore defeated Dallas 16-13 on Jim O'Brien's 32-yard field goal with five seconds to go in Super Bowl V at Miami, January 17. The NBC telecast was viewed in an estimated 23,980,000 homes, the largest audience ever for a one-day sports event.

The NFC defeated the AFC 27-6 in the first AFC-NFC Pro Bowl at Los Angeles, January 24.

The Boston Patriots changed their name to the New England Patriots, March 25. Their new stadium, Schaefer Stadium, was dedicated in a 20-14 preseason victory over the Giants.

The Philadelphia Eagles left Franklin Field and played their games at the new Veterans Stadium.

The San Francisco 49ers left Kezar Stadium and moved their games to Candlestick Park.

Daniel F. Reeves, the president and general manager of the Rams, died at 58, April 15.

The Dallas Cowboys moved from

the Cotton Bowl into their new home, Texas Stadium, October 24.

Miami defeated Kansas City 27-24 in sudden-death overtime in an AFC Divisional Playoff Game, December 25. Garo Yepremian kicked a 37-yard field goal for the Dolphins after 22 minutes, 40 seconds of overtime, as the game lasted 82 minutes, 40 seconds overall, making it the longest game in history.

1972 Dallas defeated Miami 24-3 in Super Bowl VI at New Orleans, January 16. The CBS telecast was viewed in an estimated 27,450,000 homes, the top-rated one-day telecast ever.

The inbounds lines or hashmarks were moved nearer the center of the field, 23 yards, 1 foot, 9 inches from the sidelines, March 23. The method of determining won-lost percentage in standings changed. Tie games, previously not counted in the standings, were made equal to a half-game won and a half-game lost, May 24.

Robert Irsay purchased the Los Angeles Rams and transferred ownership of the club to Carroll Rosenbloom in exchange for the Baltimore Colts, July 13.

William V. Bidwill purchased the stock of his brother Charles (Stormy) Bidwill to become the sole owner of the St. Louis Cardinals, September 2.

The National District Attorneys Association endorsed the position of professional leagues in opposing proposed legalization of gambling on professional team sports, September 28.

Franco Harris's "Immaculate Reception" gave the Steelers their first postseason win ever, 13-7 over the Raiders, December 23.

1973 Rozelle announced that all Super Bowl VII tickets were sold and that the game would be telecast in Los Angeles, the site of the game, on an experimental basis, January 3.

Miami defeated Washington 14-7 in Super Bowl VII at Los Angeles, completing a 17-0 season, the first perfect-record regular-season and postseason mark in NFL history, January 14. The NBC telecast was viewed by approximately 75 million people.

The AFC defeated the NFC 33-28 in the Pro Bowl in Dallas, the first time since 1942 that the game was played outside Los Angeles, January 21.

A jersey numbering system was adopted, April 5: 1-19 for quarterbacks and specialists, 20-49 for running backs and defensive backs, 50-59 for centers and linebackers, 60-79 for defensive linemen and interior offensive linemen other than centers, and 80-89 for wide receivers and tight ends. Players who had been in the NFL in 1972 could continue to use old numbers.

NFL Charities, a non-profit organization, was created to derive an income from monies generated from NFL Properties' licensing of NFL trademarks and team names, June 26. NFL Charities was set up to support education and charitable activities and to supply economic support to persons formerly associated with professional football who were no longer able to support themselves.

Congress adopted experimental legislation (for three years) requiring any NFL game that had been declared a sellout 72 hours prior to kickoff to be made available for local televising, September 14. The legislation provided for an annual review to be made by the Federal Communications Commission.

The Buffalo Bills moved their home games from War Memorial Stadium to Rich Stadium in nearby Orchard Park. The Giants tied the Eagles 23-23 in the final game in Yankee Stadium, September 23. The Giants played the rest of their home games at the Yale Bowl in New Haven, Connecticut.

A rival league, the World Football League, was formed and was reported in operation, October 2. It had plans to start play in 1974.

O.J. Simpson of Buffalo became the first player to rush for more than 2,000 yards in a season, gaining 2,003.

1974 Miami defeated Minnesota 24-7 in Super Bowl VIII at Houston, the second consecutive Super Bowl championship for the Dolphins, January 13. The CBS telecast was viewed by approximately 75 million people.

Rozelle was given a 10-year contract effective January 1, 1973, February 27.

Tampa Bay was awarded a franchise to begin operation in 1976, April 24.

Sweeping rules changes were adopted to add action and tempo to games: one sudden-death overtime period was added for preseason and regular-season games; the goal posts were moved from the goal line to the end lines; kickoffs were moved from the 40- to the 35-yard line; after missed field goals from beyond the 20, the ball was to be returned to the line of scrimmage; restrictions were placed on members of the punting team to open up return possibilities; roll-blocking and cutting of wide receivers was eliminated; the extent of downfield contact a defender could have with an eligible receiver was restricted; the penalties for offensive holding, illegal use of the hands, and tripping were reduced from 15 to 10 yards; wide receivers blocking back toward the ball within three yards of the line of scrimmage were prevented from blocking below the waist, April 25.

The Toronto Northmen of the WFL signed Larry Csonka, Jim Kiick, and Paul Warfield of Miami, March 31.

Seattle was awarded an NFL franchise to begin play in 1976, June 4. Lloyd W. Nordstrom, president of the Seattle Seahawks, and Hugh Culverhouse, president of the Tampa Bay Buccaneers, signed franchise agreements, December 5.

The Birmingham Americans defeated the Florida Blazers 22-21 in the WFL World Bowl, winning the league championship, December 5.

1975 Pittsburgh defeated Minnesota 16-6 in Super Bowl IX at New Orleans, the Steelers' first championship since entering the NFL in 1933. The NBC telecast was viewed by approximately 78 million people.

The divisional winners with the highest won-loss percentage were made the home team for the divisional playoffs, and the surviving winners with the highest percentage made home teams for the championship games, June 26.

Referees were equipped with wireless microphones for all preseason, regular-season, and playoff games.

The Lions moved to the new Pontiac Silverdome. The Giants played their home games in Shea Stadium. The Saints moved into the Louisiana Superdome.

The World Football League folded, October 22.

1976 Pittsburgh defeated Dallas 21-17 in Super Bowl X in Miami. The Steelers joined Green Bay and Miami as the only teams to win two Super Bowls; the Cowboys became the first wild-card team to play in the Super Bowl. The CBS telecast was viewed by an estimated 80 million people, the largest television audience in history.

Lloyd Nordstrom, the president of the Seahawks, died at 66, January 20. His brother Elmer succeeded him as majority representative of the team.

The owners awarded Super Bowl XII, to be played on January 15, 1978, to New Orleans. They also adopted the use of two 30-second clocks for all games, visible to both players and fans to note the official time between the ready-for-play signal and snap of the ball, March 16.

A veteran player allocation was held to stock the Seattle and Tampa Bay franchises with 39 players each, March 30-31. In the college draft, Seattle and Tampa Bay each received eight extra choices, April 8-9.

The Giants moved into new Giants Stadium in East Rutherford, New Jersey.

The Steelers defeated the College All-Stars in a storm-shortened Chicago College All-Star Game, the last of the series, July 23. St. Louis defeated San Diego 20-10 in a preseason game before 38,000 in Korakuen Stadium, Tokyo, in the first NFL game outside of North America, August 16.

1977 Oakland defeated Minnesota 32-14 before a record crowd of 100,421 in Super Bowl XI at Pasadena, January 9. The paid attendance was a pro record 103,438. The NBC telecast was viewed by 81.9 million people, the largest ever to view a sports event. The victory was the fifth consecutive for the AFC in the Super Bowl.

The NFL Players Association and the NFL Management Council ratified a collective bargaining agreement extending until 1982, covering five football seasons while continuing the pension plan—including years 1974, 1975, and 1976—with contributions totaling more than $55 million. The total cost of the agreement was estimated at $107 million. The agreement called for a college draft at least through 1986; contained a no-strike, no-suit clause; established a 43-man active player limit; reduced pension vesting to four years; provided for increases in minimum salaries and preseason and postseason pay; improved insurance, medical, and dental benefits; modified previous practices in player movement and control; and reaffirmed the NFL Commissioner's disciplinary authority. Additionally, the agreement called for the NFL member clubs to make payments totaling $16 million the next 10 years to settle various legal disputes, February 25.

The San Francisco 49ers were sold to Edward J. DeBartolo, Jr., March 28.

A 16-game regular season, 4-game preseason was adopted to begin in 1978, March 29. A second wild card team was adopted for the playoffs beginning in 1978, with the wild card teams to play each other and the winners advancing to a round of eight postseason series.

The Seahawks were permanently aligned in the AFC Western Division and the Buccaneers in the NFC Central Division, March 31.

The owners awarded Super Bowl XIII, to be played on January 21, 1979, to Miami to be played in the Orange Bowl; Super Bowl XIV, to be played January 20, 1980, was awarded to Pasadena, to be played in the Rose Bowl, June 14.

Rules changes were adopted to open up the passing game and to cut down on injuries. Defenders were permitted to make contact with eligible receivers only once; the head slap was outlawed; offensive linemen were prohibited from thrusting their hands to an opponent's neck, face, or head; and wide receivers were prohibited from clipping, even in the legal clipping zone.

Rozelle negotiated contracts with the three television networks to televise all NFL regular-season and postseason games, plus selected preseason games, for four years beginning with the 1978 season. ABC was awarded yearly rights to 16 Monday night games, four prime-time games, the AFC-NFC Pro Bowl, and the Hall of Fame games. CBS received the rights to all NFC regular-season and postseason games (except those in the ABC package) and to Super Bowls XIV and XVI. NBC received the rights to all AFC regular-season and postseason games (except those in the ABC package) and to Super Bowls XIII and XV. Industry sources considered it the largest single television package ever negotiated, October.

Chicago's Walter Payton set a single-game rushing record with 275 yards (40 carries) against Minnesota, November 20.

1978 Dallas defeated Denver 27-10 in Super Bowl XII, held indoors for the first time, at the Louisiana Superdome in New Orleans, January 15. The CBS telecast was viewed by more than 102 million people, meaning the game was watched by more viewers than any other show of any kind in the history of television. Dallas's victory was the first for the NFC in six years.

According to a Louis Harris Sports Survey, 70 percent of the nation's sports fans said they followed football, compared to 54 percent who followed baseball. Football increased its lead as the country's favorite, 26 percent to 16 percent for baseball, January 19.

A seventh official, the side judge, was added to the officiating crew, March 14.

The NFL continued a trend toward opening up the game. Rules changes permitted a defender to maintain contact with a receiver within five yards of the line of scrimmage, but restricted contact beyond that point. The pass-blocking rule was interpreted to permit the extending of arms and open hands, March 17.

A study on the use of instant replay as an officiating aid was made during seven nationally televised preseason games.

The NFL played for the first time in Mexico City, with the Saints defeating the Eagles 14-7 in a preseason game, August 5.

Bolstered by the expansion of the

regular-season schedule from 14 to 16 weeks, NFL paid attendance exceeded 12 million (12,771,800) for the first time. The per-game average of 57,017 was the third-highest in league history and the most since 1973.

1979 Pittsburgh defeated Dallas 35-31 in Super Bowl XIII at Miami to become the first team ever to win three Super Bowls, January 21. The NBC telecast was viewed in 35,090,000 homes, by an estimated 96.6 million fans.

The owners awarded three future Super Bowl sites: Super Bowl XV to the Louisiana Superdome in New Orleans, to be played on January 25, 1981; Super Bowl XVI to the Pontiac Silverdome in Pontiac, Michigan, to be played on January 24, 1982; and Super Bowl XVII to Pasadena's Rose Bowl, to be played on January 30, 1983, March 13.

NFL rules changes emphasized additional player safety. The changes prohibited players on the receiving team from blocking below the waist during kickoffs, punts, and field-goal attempts; prohibited the wearing of torn or altered equipment and exposed pads that could be hazardous; extended the zone in which there could be no crackback blocks; and instructed officials to quickly whistle a play dead when a quarterback was clearly in the grasp of a tackler, March 16.

Rosenbloom, the president of the Rams, drowned at 72, April 2. His widow, Georgia, assumed control of the club.

1980 Pittsburgh defeated the Los Angeles Rams 31-19 in Super Bowl XIV at Pasadena to become the first team to win four Super Bowls, January 20. The game was viewed in a record 35,330,000 homes.

The AFC-NFC Pro Bowl, won 37-27 by the NFC, was played before 48,060 fans at Aloha Stadium in Honolulu, Hawaii. It was the first time in the 30-year history of the Pro Bowl that the game was played in a non-NFL city.

Rules changes placed greater restrictions on contact in the area of the head, neck, and face. Under the heading of "personal foul," players were prohibited from directly striking, swinging, or clubbing on the head, neck, or face. Starting in 1980, a penalty could be called for such contact whether or not the initial contact was made below the neck area.

CBS, with a record bid of $12 million, won the national radio rights to 26 NFL regular-season games and all 10 postseason games for the 1980-83 seasons.

The Los Angeles Rams moved their home games to Anaheim Stadium in nearby Orange County, California.

The Oakland Raiders joined the Los Angeles Coliseum Commission's antitrust suit against the NFL. The suit contended the league violated antitrust laws in declining to approve a proposed move by the Raiders from Oakland to Los Angeles.

NFL regular-season attendance of nearly 13.4 million set a record for the third year in a row. The average paid attendance for the 224-game 1980 regular season was 59,787, the highest in the league's 61-year history. NFL games in 1980 were played before 92.4 percent of total stadium capacity.

Television ratings in 1980 were the second-best in NFL history, trailing only the combined ratings of the 1976 season. All three networks posted gains, and NBC's 15.0 rating was its best ever. CBS and ABC had their best ratings since 1977, with 15.3 and 20.8 ratings, respectively. CBS Radio reported a record audience of 7 million for Monday night and special games.

1981 Oakland defeated Philadelphia 27-10 in Super Bowl XV at the Louisiana Superdome in New Orleans, to become the first wild card team to win a Super Bowl, January 25.

Edgar F. Kaiser, Jr., purchased the Denver Broncos from Gerald and Allan Phipps, February 26.

The owners adopted a disaster plan for re-stocking a team should the club be involved in a fatal accident, March 20.

The owners awarded Super Bowl XVIII to Tampa to be played in Tampa Stadium on January 22, 1984, June 3.

A CBS-New York Times poll showed that 48 percent of sports fans preferred football to 31 percent for baseball.

The NFL teams hosted 167 representatives from 44 predominantly black colleges during training camps for a total of 289 days. The program was adopted for renewal during each training camp period.

NFL regular-season attendance—13.6 million for an average of 60,745—set a record for the fourth year in a row. It also was the first time the per-game average exceeded 60,000. NFL games in 1981 were played before 93.8 percent of total stadium capacity.

ABC and CBS set all-time rating highs. ABC finished with a 21.7 rating and CBS with a 17.5 rating. NBC was down slightly to 13.9.

1982 San Francisco defeated Cincinnati 26-21 in Super Bowl XVI at the Pontiac Silverdome, in the first Super Bowl held in the North, January 24. The CBS telecast achieved the highest rating of any televised sports event ever, 49.1 with a 73.0 share. The game was viewed by a record 110.2 million fans. CBS Radio reported a record 14 million listeners for the game.

The NFL signed a five-year contract with the three television networks (ABC, CBS, and NBC) to televise all NFL regular-season and postseason games starting with the 1982 season.

The owners awarded the 1983, 1984, and 1985 AFC-NFC Pro Bowls to Honolulu's Aloha Stadium.

A jury ruled against the NFL in the antitrust trial brought by the Los Angeles Coliseum Commission and the Oakland Raiders, May 7. The verdict cleared the way for the Raiders to move to Los Angeles, where they defeated Green Bay 24-3 in their first preseason game, August 29.

The 1982 season was reduced from a 16-game schedule to 9 as the result of a 57-day players' strike. The strike was called by the NFLPA at 12:00 midnight on Monday, September 20, following the Green Bay at New York Giants game. Play resumed November 21-22 following ratification of the Collective Bargaining Agreement by NFL owners, November 17 in New York.

Under the Collective Bargaining Agreement, which was to run through the 1986 season, the NFL draft was

extended through 1992 and the veteran free-agent system was left basically unchanged. A minimum salary schedule for years of experience was established; training camp and postseason pay were increased; players' medical, insurance, and retirement benefits were increased; and a severance-pay system was introduced to aid in career transition, a first in professional sports.

Despite the players' strike, the average paid attendance in 1982 was 58,472, the fifth-highest in league history.

The owners awarded the sites of two Super Bowls, December 14: Super Bowl XIX, to be played on January 20, 1985, to Stanford University Stadium in Palo Alto, California, with San Francisco as host team; and Super Bowl XX, to be played on January 26, 1986, to the Louisiana Superdome in New Orleans.

1983 Because of the shortened season, the NFL adopted a format of 16 teams competing in a Super Bowl Tournament for the 1982 playoffs. The NFC's number-one seed, Washington, defeated the AFC's number-two seed, Miami, 27-17 in Super Bowl XVII at the Rose Bowl in Pasadena, January 30. The Redskins' victory marked only the second time the NFC had won consecutive Super Bowls.

Super Bowl XVII was the second-highest rated television program of all time, giving the NFL a sweep of the top 10 live programs in television history. The game was viewed in more than 40 million homes, the largest ever for a live telecast.

Halas, the owner of the Bears and the last surviving member of the NFL's second organizational meeting, died at 88, October 31.

1984 The Los Angeles Raiders defeated Washington 38-9 in Super Bowl XVIII at Tampa Stadium, January 22. The game achieved a 46.4 rating and 71.0 share.

An 11-man group headed by H.R. (Bum) Bright purchased the Dallas Cowboys from Clint Murchison, Jr., March 20. Club president Tex Schramm was designated as managing general partner.

Patrick Bowlen purchased a majority interest in the Denver Broncos from Edgar Kaiser, Jr., March 21.

The Colts relocated to Indianapolis, March 28. Their new home became the Hoosier Dome.

The owners awarded two Super Bowl sites at their May 23-25 meetings: Super Bowl XXI, to be played on January 25, 1987, to the Rose Bowl in Pasadena; and Super Bowl XXII, to be played on January 31, 1988, to San Diego Jack Murphy Stadium.

The New York Jets moved their home games to Giants Stadium in East Rutherford, New Jersey.

Alex G. Spanos purchased a majority interest in the San Diego Chargers from Eugene V. Klein, August 28.

Houston defeated Pittsburgh 23-20 to mark the one-hundredth overtime game in regular-season play since overtime was adopted in 1974, December 2.

On the field, many all-time records were set: Dan Marino of Miami passed for 5,084 yards and 48 touchdowns; Eric Dickerson of the Los Angeles Rams rushed for 2,105 yards; Art Monk of Washington caught 106 passes; and Walter Payton of Chicago broke Jim Brown's career rushing

mark, finishing the season with 13,309 yards.

According to a CBS Sports/New York Times survey, 53 percent of the nation's sports fans said they most enjoyed watching football, compared to 18 percent for baseball, December 2-4.

NFL paid attendance exceeded 13 million for the fifth consecutive complete regular season when 13,398,112, an average of 59,813, attended games. The figure was the second-highest in league history. Teams averaged 42.4 points per game, the second-highest total since the 1970 merger.

1985 San Francisco defeated Miami 38-16 in Super Bowl XIX at Stanford Stadium in Palo Alto, California, January 20. The game was viewed on television by more people than any other live event in history. President Ronald Reagan, who took his second oath of office before tossing the coin for the game, was one of 115,936,000 viewers. The game drew a 46.4 rating and a 63.0 share. In addition, 6 million people watched the Super Bowl in the United Kingdom and a similar number in Italy. Super Bowl XIX had a direct economic impact of $113.5 million on the San Francisco Bay area.

NBC Radio and the NFL entered into a two-year agreement granting NBC the radio rights to a 37-game package in each of the 1985-86 seasons, March 6. The package included 27 regular-season games and 10 postseason games.

The owners awarded two Super Bowl sites at their annual meeting, March 10-15: Super Bowl XXIII, to be played on January 22, 1989, to the proposed Dolphins Stadium in Miami; and Super Bowl XXIV, to be played on January 28, 1990, to the Louisiana Superdome in New Orleans.

Norman Braman, in partnership with Edward Leibowitz, bought the Philadelphia Eagles from Leonard Tose, April 29.

Bruce Smith, a Virginia Tech defensive lineman selected by Buffalo, was the first player chosen in the fiftieth NFL draft, April 30.

A group headed by Tom Benson, Jr., was approved to purchase the New Orleans Saints from John W. Mecom, Jr., June 3.

The NFL owners adopted a resolution calling for a series of overseas preseason games, beginning in 1986, with one game to be played in England/Europe and/or one game in Japan each year. The game would be a fifth preseason game for the clubs involved and all arrangements and selection of the clubs would be under the control of the Commissioner, May 23.

The league-wide conversion to videotape from movie film for coaching study was approved.

Commissioner Rozelle was authorized to extend the commitment to Honolulu's Aloha Stadium for the AFC-NFC Pro Bowl for 1988, 1989, and 1990, October 15.

The NFL set a single-weekend paid attendance record when 902,657 tickets were sold for the weekend of October 27-28.

A Louis Harris poll in December revealed that pro football remained the sport most followed by Americans. Fifty-nine percent of those surveyed followed pro football, compared with 54 percent who followed baseball.

The Chicago-Miami Monday game had the highest rating, 29.6, and share, 46.0, of any prime-time game in NFL history, December 2. The game was viewed in more than 25 million homes.

The NFL showed a ratings increase on all three networks for the season, gaining 4 percent on NBC, 10 on CBS, and 16 on ABC.

1986 Chicago defeated New England 46-10 in Super Bowl XX at the Louisiana Superdome, January 26. The Patriots had earned the right to play the Bears by becoming the first wild card team to win three consecutive games on the road. The NBC telecast replaced the final episode of M*A*S*H as the most-viewed television program in history, with an audience of 127 million viewers, according to A.C. Nielsen figures. In addition to drawing a 48.3 rating and a 70 percent share in the United States, Super Bowl XX was televised to 59 foreign countries and beamed via satellite to the QE II. An estimated 300 million Chinese viewed a tape delay of the game in March. NBC Radio figures indicated an audience of 10 million for the game.

Super Bowl XX injected more than $100 million into the New Orleans-area economy, and fans spent $250 per day and a record $17.69 per person on game day.

The owners adopted limited use of instant replay as an officiating aid, prohibited players from wearing or otherwise displaying equipment, apparel, or other items that carry commercial names, names of organizations, or personal messages of any type, March 11.

After an 11-week trial, a jury in U.S. District Court in New York awarded the United States Football League one dollar in its $1.7 billion antitrust suit against the NFL. The jury rejected all of the USFL's television-related claims, which were the self-proclaimed "heart" of the USFL's case, July 29.

Chicago defeated Dallas 17-6 at Wembley Stadium in London in the first American Bowl. The game drew a sellout crowd of 82,699 and the NBC national telecast in this country produced a 12.4 rating and 36 percent share, making it the second-highest-rated daytime preseason game and highest daytime preseason television audience ever with 10,650,000 viewers, August 3.

Monday Night Football became the longest-running prime-time series in the history of the ABC network.

Instant replay was used to reverse two plays in 31 preseason games. During the regular season, 374 plays were closely reviewed by replay officials, leading to 38 reversals in 224 games. Eighteen plays were closely reviewed by instant replay in 10 postseason games with three reversals.

1987 The New York Giants defeated Denver 39-20 in Super Bowl XXI and captured their first NFL title since 1956. The game, played in Pasadena's Rose Bowl, drew a sellout crowd of 101,063. According to A.C. Nielsen figures, the CBS broadcast of the game was viewed in the U.S. on television by 122,640,000 people, making the telecast the second most-watched television show of all-time behind Super Bowl XX. The game was watched live or on tape in 55 foreign countries and NBC Radio's broadcast of the game was

heard by a record 10.1 million people.

The NFL set an all-time paid attendance mark of 17,304,463 for all games, including preseason, regular-season, and postseason. Average regular-season game attendance (60,663) exceeded the 60,000 figure for only the second time in league history.

New three-year TV contracts with ABC, CBS, and NBC were announced for 1987-89 at the NFL annual meeting in Maui, Hawaii, March 15. Commissioner Rozelle and Broadcast Committee Chairman Art Modell also announced a three-year contract with ESPN to televise a mini-series of 13 prime-time games each season. The ESPN contract was the first with a cable network. However, NFL games on ESPN also were scheduled for regular television in the city of the visiting team and in the home city if the game was sold out 72 hours in advance.

Owners also voted to continue in effect for one year the instant replay system used during the 1986 season.

A special payment program was adopted to benefit nearly 1,000 former NFL players who participated in the League before the current Bert Bell NFL Pension Plan was created and made retroactive to the 1959 season. Players covered by the new program spent at least five years in the League and played all or part of their career prior to 1959. Each vested player would receive $60 per month for each year of service in the League for life.

Possible sites for Super Bowl XXV were reduced to five locations by the NFL Super Bowl XXV Site Selection Committee: Anaheim Stadium, Los Angeles Memorial Coliseum, Joe Robbie Stadium, San Diego Jack Murphy Stadium, and Tampa Stadium.

NFL and CBS Radio jointly announced agreement granting CBS the radio rights to a 40-game package in each of the next three NFL seasons, 1987-89, April 7.

NFL owners awarded Super Bowl XXV, to be played on January 27, 1991, to Tampa Stadium, May 20.

Over 400 former NFL players from the pre-1959 era received their first payments from NFL owners, July 1.

The NFL's debut on ESPN produced the two highest-rated and most-watched sports programs in basic cable history. The Chicago at Miami game on August 16 drew an 8.9 rating in 3.81 million homes. Those records fell two weeks later when the Los Angeles Raiders at Dallas game achieved a 10.2 cable rating in 4.36 million homes.

Fifty-eight preseason games drew a record paid attendance of 3,116,870.

The 1987 season was reduced from a 16-game season to 15 as the result of a 24-day players' strike. The strike was called by the NFLPA on Tuesday, September 22, following the New England at New York Jets game. Games scheduled for the third weekend were cancelled but the games of weeks four, five, and six were played with replacement teams. Striking players returned for the seventh week of the season, October 25.

In a three-team deal involving 10 players and/or draft choices, the Los Angeles Rams traded running back Eric Dickerson to the Indianapolis

Colts for six draft choices and two players. Buffalo obtained the rights to linebacker Cornelius Bennett from Indianapolis, sending Greg Bell and three draft choices to the Rams. The Colts added Owen Gill and three draft choices of their own to complete the deal with the Rams, October 31.

The Chicago at Minnesota game became the highest rated and most-watched sports program in basic cable history when it drew a 14.4 cable rating in 6.5 million homes, December 6.

Instant replay was used to reverse eight plays in 52 preseason games. During the strike-shortened 210-game regular season, 490 plays were closely reviewed by replay officials, leading to 57 reversals. Eighteen plays were closely reviewed by instant replay in 10 postseason games, with three reversals.

1988 Washington defeated Denver 42-10 in Super Bowl XXII to earn a second victory this decade in the NFL Championship Game. The game, played for the first time in San Diego Jack Murphy Stadium, drew a sellout crowd of 73,302. According to A.C. Nielsen figures, the ABC broadcast of the game was viewed in the U.S. on television by 115,000,000 people. The game was seen live or on tape in 60 foreign countries, including the People's Republic of China, and CBS's radio broadcast of the game was heard by 13.7 million people.

A total of 811 players shared in the postseason pool of $16.9 million, the most ever distributed in a single season.

In a unanimous 3-0 decision, the 2nd Circuit Court of Appeals in New York upheld the verdict of the jury that in July, 1986, had awarded the United States Football League one dollar in its $1.7 billion antitrust suit against the NFL. In a 91-page opinion, Judge Ralph K. Winter said the USFL sought "through court decree the success it failed to gain among football fans," March 10.

By a 23-5 margin, owners voted to continue the instant replay system for the third consecutive season with the Instant Replay Official to be assigned to a regular seven-man, on-the-field crew. At the NFL annual meeting in Phoenix, Arizona, a 45-second clock was also approved to replace the 30-second clock. For a normal sequence of plays, the interval between plays was changed to 45 seconds from the time the ball is signaled dead until it is snapped on the succeeding play.

NFL owners approved the transfer of the Cardinals' franchise from St. Louis to Phoenix; approved two Supplemental Drafts each year—one prior to training camp and one prior to the regular season; and voted to initiate an annual series of games in Japan/Asia as early as the 1989 preseason, March 14-18.

The NFL Annual Selection Meeting returned to a separate two-day format and for the first time originated on a Sunday. ESPN drew a 3.6 rating during their seven-hour coverage of the draft, which was viewed in 1.6 million homes, April 24-25.

Art Rooney, founder and owner of the Steelers, died at 87, August 25.

Paid and average attendance of 934,271 and 66,734 at 14 games on October 16-17 set single weekend records.

Commissioner Rozelle announced that two teams would play a preseason game as part of the American Bowl series on August 6, 1989, in the Korakuen Tokyo Dome in Japan, December 16.

NFL regular-season paid attendance of 13,535,335 and the average of 60,427 was the third highest all-time. Buffalo set an NFL team single-season, in-house attendance mark of 622,793.

1989 San Francisco defeated Cincinnati 20-16 in Super Bowl XXIII. The game, played for the first time at Joe Robbie Stadium in Miami, was attended by a sellout crowd of 75,129. NBC's telecast of the game was watched by an estimated 110,780,000 viewers, according to A.C. Nielsen, making it the sixth most-watched program in television history. The game was seen live or on tape in 60 foreign countries, including an estimated 300 million in China. The CBS Radio broadcast of the game was heard by 11.2 million people.

Commissioner Rozelle announced his retirement, pending the naming of a successor, March 22 at the NFL annual meeting at Palm Desert, California.

Following the announcement, AFC president Lamar Hunt and NFC president Wellington Mara announced the formation of a six-man search committee composed of Art Modell, Robert Parins, Dan Rooney, and Ralph Wilson. Hunt and Mara served as co-chairmen.

By a 24-4 margin, owners voted to continue the instant replay system for the fourth straight season. A strengthened policy regarding anabolic steroids and masking agents was announced by Commissioner Rozelle. NFL clubs called for strong disciplinary measures in cases of feigned injuries and adopted a joint proposal by the Long-Range Planning and Finance committees regarding player personnel rules, March 19-23.

Two hundred twenty-nine unconditional free agents signed with new teams under management's Plan B system, April 1.

Jerry Jones purchased a majority interest in the Dallas Cowboys from H.R. (Bum) Bright, April 18.

Tex Schramm was named president of the new World League of American Football to work with a six-man committee of Dan Rooney, chairman; Norman Braman, Lamar Hunt, Victor Kiam, Mike Lynn, and Bill Walsh, April 18.

NFL and CBS Radio jointly announced agreement extending CBS's radio rights to an annual 40-game package through the 1994 season, April 18.

NFL owners awarded Super Bowl XXVI, to be played on January 26, 1992, to Minneapolis, May 24.

As of opening day, September 10, of the 229 Plan B free agents, 111 were active and 23 others were on teams' reserve lists. Ninety-two others were waived and three retired.

Art Shell was named head coach of the Los Angeles Raiders making him the NFL's first black head coach since Fritz Pollard coached the Akron Pros in 1921, October 3.

The site of the New England Patriots at San Francisco 49ers game scheduled for Candlestick Park on October 22 was switched to Stanford Stadium in the aftermath of the Bay

Area Earthquake of October 17. The change was announced on October 19.

Paul Tagliabue became the seventh chief executive of the NFL on October 26 when he was chosen to succeed Commissioner Pete Rozelle on the sixth ballot of a three-day meeting in Cleveland, Ohio.

In all, 12 ballots were required to select Tagliabue. Two were conducted at a meeting in Chicago on July 6, and four at a meeting in Dallas on October 10-11. On the twelfth ballot, with Seattle absent, Tagliabue received more than the 19 affirmative votes required for election from among the 27 clubs present.

The transfer from Commissioner Rozelle to Commissioner Tagliabue took place at 12:01 A.M. on Sunday, November 5.

NFL Charities donated $1 million through United Way to benefit Bay Area earthquake victims, November 6.

NFL paid attendance of 17,399,538 was the highest total in league history. This included a total of 13,625,662 for an average of 60,829—both NFL records—for the 224-game regular season.

1990 San Francisco defeated Denver 55-10 in Super Bowl XXIV at the Louisiana Superdome, January 28. San Francisco joined Pittsburgh as the NFL's only teams to win four Super Bowls.

The NFL announced revisions in its 1990 Draft eligibility rules. College juniors became eligible but must renounce their collegiate football eligibility before applying for the NFL Draft, February 16.

Commissioner Tagliabue announced NFL teams will play their 16-game schedule over 17 weeks in 1990 and 1991 and 16 games over 18 weeks in 1992 and 1993, February 27.

The NFL revised its playoff format to include two additional Wild Card teams (one per conference).

Commissioner Tagliabue and Broadcast Committee Chairman Art Modell announced a four-year contract with Turner Broadcasting to televise nine Sunday-night games.

New four-year TV agreements were ratified for 1990-93 for ABC, CBS, NBC, ESPN, and TNT at the NFL annual meeting in Orlando, Florida, March 12. The contracts totaled $3.6 billion, the largest in TV history.

The NFL announced plans to expand its American Bowl series of preseason games. In addition to games in London and Tokyo, American Bowl games were scheduled for Berlin, Germany, and Montreal, Canada, in 1990.

For the fifth straight year, NFL owners voted to continue a limited system of Instant Replay. Beginning in 1990, the replay official will have a two-minute time limit to make a decision. The vote was 21-7, March 12.

NFL owners awarded Super Bowl XXVII to be played in 1993, to Phoenix, March 13.

Commissioner Tagliabue announced the formation of a Committee on Expansion and Realignment, March 13. He also named a Player Advisory Council, comprised of 12 former NFL players, March 14.

184 Plan B unconditional free agents signed with new teams, April 2.

Commissioner Tagliabue appoint-ed Dr. John Lombardo as the League's Drug Advisor for anabolic steroids, April 25 and named Dr. Lawrence Brown as the League's Advisor for Drugs of Abuse, May 17.

NFL owners awarded Super Bowl XXVIII, to be played in 1994, to the proposed Georgia Dome, May 23.

NFL COMMISSIONERS AND PRESIDENTS*

1920 . . . . Jim Thorpe, President
1921-39 . . . . Joe Carr, President
1939-41 . . . . . Carl Storck, President
1941-46 . . . . Elmer Layden, Commissioner
1946-59 . . . Bert Bell, Commissioner
1960-89 . . . . Pete Rozelle, Commissioner
1989-present . . . . Paul Tagliabue, Commissioner

*NFL treasurer Austin Gunsel served as president in the office of the commissioner following the death of Bert Bell (Oct. 11, 1959) until the election of Pete Rozelle (Jan. 26, 1960).

1989

American Conference

Eastern Division

	W	L	T	Pct.	Pts.	OP
Buffalo	9	7	0	.563	409	317
Indianapolis	8	8	0	.500	298	301
Miami	8	8	0	.500	331	379
New England	5	11	0	.313	297	391
N.Y. Jets	4	12	0	.250	253	411

Central Division

	W	L	T	Pct.	Pts.	OP
Cleveland	9	6	1	.594	334	254
Houston*	9	7	0	.563	365	412
Pittsburgh*	9	7	0	.563	265	326
Cincinnati	8	8	0	.500	404	285

Western Division

	W	L	T	Pct.	Pts.	OP
Denver	11	5	0	.688	362	226
Kansas City	8	7	1	.531	318	286
L.A. Raiders	8	8	0	.500	315	297
Seattle	7	9	0	.438	241	327
San Diego	6	10	0	.375	266	290

National Conference

Eastern Division

	W	L	T	Pct.	Pts.	OP
N.Y. Giants	12	4	0	.750	348	252
Philadelphia*	11	5	0	.688	342	274
Washington	10	6	0	.625	386	308
Phoenix	5	11	0	.313	258	377
Dallas	1	15	0	.063	204	393

Central Division

	W	L	T	Pct.	Pts.	OP
Minnesota	10	6	0	.625	351	275
Green Bay	10	6	0	.625	362	356
Detroit	7	9	0	.438	312	364
Chicago	6	10	0	.375	358	377
Tampa Bay	5	11	0	.313	320	419

Western Division

	W	L	T	Pct.	Pts.	OP
San Francisco	14	2	0	.875	442	253
L.A. Rams*	11	5	0	.688	426	344
New Orleans	9	7	0	.563	386	301
Atlanta	3	13	0	.188	279	437

Wild Card qualifiers for playoffs

Indianapolis finished ahead of Miami in AFC East because of better conference record (7-5 vs. 6-8). Houston finished ahead of Pittsburgh in AFC Central because of head-to-head sweep (2-0). Minnesota finished ahead of Green Bay in NFC Central because of better division record (6-2 vs. 5-3).

First round playoff: Pittsburgh 26, HOUSTON 23 (OT)
Divisional playoffs: CLEVELAND 34, Buffalo 30; DENVER 24, Pittsburgh 23
AFC championship: DENVER 37, Cleveland 21
First round playoff: L.A. Rams 21, PHILADELPHIA 7
Divisional playoffs: L.A. Rams 19, N.Y. GIANTS 13 (OT);
   SAN FRANCISCO 41, Minnesota 13
NFC championship: SAN FRANCISCO 30, L.A. Rams 3
Super Bowl XXIV: San Francisco (NFC) 55, Denver (AFC) 10 at Louisiana Superdome, New Orleans, Louisiana

In the Past Standings section, home teams in playoff games are indicated by capital letters.

1988

American Conference

Eastern Division

	W	L	T	Pct.	Pts.	OP
Buffalo	12	4	0	.750	329	237
Indianapolis	9	7	0	.563	354	315
New England	9	7	0	.563	250	284
N.Y. Jets	8	7	1	.531	372	354
Miami	6	10	0	.375	319	380

Central Division

	W	L	T	Pct.	Pts.	OP
Cincinnati	12	4	0	.750	448	329
Cleveland*	10	6	0	.625	304	288
Houston*	10	6	0	.625	424	365
Pittsburgh	5	11	0	.313	336	421

Western Division

	W	L	T	Pct.	Pts.	OP
Seattle	9	7	0	.563	339	329
Denver	8	8	0	.500	327	352
L.A. Raiders	7	9	0	.438	325	369
San Diego	6	10	0	.375	231	332
Kansas City	4	11	1	.281	254	320

National Conference

Eastern Division

	W	L	T	Pct.	Pts.	OP
Philadelphia	10	6	0	.625	379	319
N.Y. Giants	10	6	0	.625	359	304
Washington	7	9	0	.438	345	387
Phoenix	7	9	0	.438	344	398
Dallas	3	13	0	.188	265	381

Central Division

	W	L	T	Pct.	Pts.	OP
Chicago	12	4	0	.750	312	215
Minnesota*	11	5	0	.688	406	233
Tampa Bay	5	11	0	.313	261	350
Detroit	4	12	0	.250	220	313
Green Bay	4	12	0	.250	240	315

Western Division

	W	L	T	Pct.	Pts.	OP
San Francisco	10	6	0	.625	369	294
L.A. Rams*	10	6	0	.625	407	293
New Orleans	10	6	0	.625	312	283
Atlanta	5	11	0	.313	244	315

Wild Card qualifiers for playoffs

Indianapolis finished second in AFC East on basis of better record versus common opponents (7-5) over New England (6-6). Cleveland gained first AFC Wild Card position based on better division record (4-2) over Houston (3-3). Philadelphia finished first in NFC East on basis of head-to-head sweep over New York Giants. Washington finished third in NFC East on basis of better division record (4-4) over Phoenix (3-5). Detroit finished fourth in NFC Central on basis of head-to-head sweep over Green Bay. San Francisco finished first in NFC West based on better head-to-head record (3-1) over Los Angeles Rams (2-2) and New Orleans (1-3). Los Angeles Rams finished second in NFC West on basis of better division record (4-2) over New Orleans (3-3) and earned Wild Card position based on better conference record (8-4) over New York Giants (9-5) and New Orleans (6-6).

First round playoff: Houston 24, CLEVELAND 23
Divisional playoffs: CINCINNATI 21, Seattle 13; BUFFALO 17, Houston 10
AFC championship: CINCINNATI 21, Buffalo 10
First round playoff: MINNESOTA 28, Los Angeles Rams 17
Divisional playoffs: CHICAGO 20, Philadelphia 12; SAN FRANCISCO 34, Minnesota 9
NFC championship: San Francisco 28, CHICAGO 3
Super Bowl XXIII: San Francisco (NFC) 20, Cincinnati (AFC) 16 at Joe Robbie Stadium, Miami, Florida

1987

American Conference

Eastern Division

	W	L	T	Pct.	Pts.	OP
Indianapolis	9	6	0	.600	300	238
New England	8	7	0	.533	320	293
Miami	8	7	0	.533	362	335
Buffalo	7	8	0	.467	270	305
N.Y. Jets	6	9	0	.400	334	360

Central Division

	W	L	T	Pct.	Pts.	OP
Cleveland	10	5	0	.667	390	239
Houston*	9	6	0	.600	345	349
Pittsburgh	8	7	0	.533	285	299
Cincinnati	4	11	0	.267	285	370

Western Division

	W	L	T	Pct.	Pts.	OP
Denver	10	4	1	.700	379	288
Seattle*	9	6	0	.600	371	314
San Diego	8	7	0	.533	253	317
L.A. Raiders	5	10	0	.333	301	289
Kansas City	4	11	0	.267	273	388

National Conference

Eastern Division

	W	L	T	Pct.	Pts.	OP
Washington	11	4	0	.733	379	285
Dallas	7	8	0	.467	340	348
St. Louis	7	8	0	.467	362	368
Philadelphia	7	8	0	.467	337	380
N.Y. Giants	6	9	0	.400	280	312

Central Division

	W	L	T	Pct.	Pts.	OP
Chicago	11	4	0	.733	356	282
Minnesota*	8	7	0	.533	336	335
Green Bay	5	9	1	.367	255	300
Tampa Bay	4	11	0	.267	286	360
Detroit	4	11	0	.267	269	384

Western Division

	W	L	T	Pct.	Pts.	OP
San Francisco	13	2	0	.867	459	253
New Orleans*	12	3	0	.800	422	283
L.A. Rams	6	9	0	.400	317	361
Atlanta	3	12	0	.200	205	436

Wild Card qualifiers for playoffs

Houston gained first AFC Wild Card position on better conference record (7-4) over Seattle (5-6).

First round playoff: HOUSTON 23, Seattle 20 (OT)
Divisional playoffs: CLEVELAND 38, Indianapolis 21
   DENVER 34, Houston 10
AFC championship: DENVER 38, Cleveland 33
First round playoff: Minnesota 44, NEW ORLEANS 10
Divisional playoffs: Minnesota 36, SAN FRANCISCO 24
   Washington 21, CHICAGO 17
NFC championship: WASHINGTON 17, Minnesota 10
Super Bowl XXII: Washington (NFC) 42, Denver (AFC) 10, at San Diego Jack Murphy Stadium, San Diego, Calif.
Note: 1987 regular season was reduced from 16 to 15 games for each team due to players' strike.

1986

American Conference

Eastern Division

	W	L	T	Pct.	Pts.	OP
New England	11	5	0	.688	412	307
N.Y. Jets*	10	6	0	.625	364	386
Miami	8	8	0	.500	430	405
Buffalo	4	12	0	.250	287	348
Indianapolis	3	13	0	.188	229	400

Central Division

	W	L	T	Pct.	Pts.	OP
Cleveland	12	4	0	.750	391	310
Cincinnati	10	6	0	.625	409	394
Pittsburgh	6	10	0	.375	307	336
Houston	5	11	0	.313	274	329

Western Division

	W	L	T	Pct.	Pts.	OP
Denver	11	5	0	.688	378	327
Kansas City*	10	6	0	.625	358	326
Seattle	10	6	0	.625	366	293
L.A. Raiders	8	8	0	.500	323	346
San Diego	4	12	0	.250	335	396

National Conference

Eastern Division

	W	L	T	Pct.	Pts.	OP
N.Y. Giants	14	2	0	.875	371	236
Washington*	12	4	0	.750	368	296
Dallas	7	9	0	.438	346	337
Philadelphia	5	10	1	.344	256	312
St. Louis	4	11	1	.281	218	351

Central Division

	W	L	T	Pct.	Pts.	OP
Chicago	14	2	0	.875	352	187
Minnesota	9	7	0	.563	398	273
Detroit	5	11	0	.313	277	326
Green Bay	4	12	0	.250	254	418
Tampa Bay	2	14	0	.125	239	473

Western Division

	W	L	T	Pct.	Pts.	OP
San Francisco	10	5	1	.656	374	247
L.A. Rams*	10	6	0	.625	309	267
Atlanta	7	8	1	.469	280	280
New Orleans	7	9	0	.438	288	287

Wild Card qualifiers for playoffs

New York Jets gained first AFC Wild Card position on better conference record (8-4) over Kansas City (9-5), Seattle (7-5), and Cincinnati (7-5). Kansas City gained second Wild Card position based on better conference record (9-5) over Seattle (7-5) and Cincinnati (7-5).

First round playoff: NEW YORK JETS 35, Kansas City 15
Divisional playoffs: CLEVELAND 23, New York Jets 20 (OT)
   DENVER 22, New England 17
AFC championship: Denver 23, CLEVELAND 20 (OT)
First round playoff: WASHINGTON 19, Los Angeles Rams 7
Divisional playoffs: Washington 27, CHICAGO 13
   NEW YORK GIANTS 49, San Francisco 3
NFC championship: NEW YORK GIANTS 17, Washington 0
Super Bowl XXI: New York Giants (NFC) 39, Denver (AFC) 20, at Rose Bowl, Pasadena, Calif.

1985

American Conference

Eastern Division

	W	L	T	Pct.	Pts.	OP
Miami	12	4	0	.750	428	320
N.Y. Jets*	11	5	0	.688	393	264
New England*	11	5	0	.688	362	290
Indianapolis	5	11	0	.313	320	386
Buffalo	2	14	0	.125	200	381

Central Division

	W	L	T	Pct.	Pts.	OP
Cleveland	8	8	0	.500	287	294
Cincinnati	7	9	0	.438	441	437
Pittsburgh	7	9	0	.438	379	355
Houston	5	11	0	.313	284	412

Western Division

	W	L	T	Pct.	Pts.	OP
L.A. Raiders	12	4	0	.750	354	308
Denver	11	5	0	.688	380	329
Seattle	8	8	0	.500	349	303
San Diego	8	8	0	.500	467	435
Kansas City	6	10	0	.375	317	360

National Conference

Eastern Division

	W	L	T	Pct.	Pts.	OP
Dallas	10	6	0	.625	357	333
N.Y. Giants*	10	6	0	.625	399	283
Washington	10	6	0	.625	297	312
Philadelphia	7	9	0	.438	286	310
St. Louis	5	11	0	.313	278	414

Central Division

	W	L	T	Pct.	Pts.	OP
Chicago	15	1	0	.938	456	198
Green Bay	8	8	0	.500	337	355
Minnesota	7	9	0	.438	346	359
Detroit	7	9	0	.438	307	366
Tampa Bay	2	14	0	.125	294	448

Western Division

	W	L	T	Pct.	Pts.	OP
L.A. Rams	11	5	0	.688	340	277
San Francisco*	10	6	0	.625	411	263
New Orleans	5	11	0	.313	294	401
Atlanta	4	12	0	.250	282	452

*Wild Card qualifiers for playoffs

New York Jets gained first AFC Wild Card position on better conference record (9-3) over New England (8-4) and Denver (8-4). New England gained second AFC Wild Card position based on better record vs. common opponents (4-2) than Denver (3-3). Dallas won NFC Eastern Division title based on better record (4-0) vs. New York Giants (1-3) and Washington (1-3). New York Giants gained first NFC Wild Card position based on better conference record (8-4) over San Francisco (7-5) and Washington (6-6). San Francisco gained second NFC Wild Card position based on head-to-head victory over Washington.

First round playoff: New England 26, NEW YORK JETS 14
Divisional playoffs: MIAMI 24, Cleveland 21;
   New England 27, LOS ANGELES RAIDERS 20
AFC championship: New England 31, MIAMI 14
First round playoff: NEW YORK GIANTS 17, San Francisco 3
Divisional playoffs: LOS ANGELES RAMS 20, Dallas 0;
   CHICAGO 21, New York Giants 0
NFC championship: CHICAGO 24, Los Angeles Rams 0
Super Bowl XX: Chicago (NFC) 46, New England (AFC) 10, at Louisiana Superdome,
   New Orleans, La.

1984

American Conference

Eastern Division

	W	L	T	Pct.	Pts.	OP
Miami	14	2	0	.875	513	298
New England	9	7	0	.563	362	352
N.Y. Jets	7	9	0	.438	332	364
Indianapolis	4	12	0	.250	239	414
Buffalo	2	14	0	.125	250	454

Central Division

	W	L	T	Pct.	Pts.	OP
Pittsburgh	9	7	0	.563	387	310
Cincinnati	8	8	0	.500	339	339
Cleveland	5	11	0	.313	250	297
Houston	3	13	0	.188	240	437

Western Division

	W	L	T	Pct.	Pts.	OP
Denver	13	3	0	.813	353	241
Seattle*	12	4	0	.750	418	282
L.A. Raiders*	11	5	0	.688	368	278
Kansas City	8	8	0	.500	314	324
San Diego	7	9	0	.438	394	413

National Conference

Eastern Division

	W	L	T	Pct.	Pts.	OP
Washington	11	5	0	.688	426	310
N.Y. Giants*	9	7	0	.563	299	301
St. Louis	9	7	0	.563	423	345
Dallas	9	7	0	.563	308	308
Philadelphia	6	9	1	.406	278	320

Central Division

	W	L	T	Pct.	Pts.	OP
Chicago	10	6	0	.625	325	248
Green Bay	8	8	0	.500	390	309
Tampa Bay	6	10	0	.375	335	380
Detroit	4	11	1	.281	283	408
Minnesota	3	13	0	.188	276	484

Western Division

	W	L	T	Pct.	Pts.	OP
San Francisco	15	1	0	.938	475	227
L.A. Rams*	10	6	0	.625	346	316
New Orleans	7	9	0	.438	298	361
Atlanta	4	12	0	.250	281	382

*Wild Card qualifiers for playoffs

New York Giants clinched Wild Card berth based on 3-1 record vs. St. Louis's 2-2 and Dallas's 1-3. St. Louis finished ahead of Dallas based on better division record (5-3 to 3-5).

First round playoff: SEATTLE 13, Los Angeles Raiders 7
Divisional playoffs: MIAMI 31, Seattle 10; Pittsburgh 24, DENVER 17
AFC championship: MIAMI 45, Pittsburgh 28
First round playoff: New York Giants 16, LOS ANGELES RAMS 13
Divisional playoffs: SAN FRANCISCO 21, New York Giants 10;
   Chicago 23, WASHINGTON 19
NFC championship: SAN FRANCISCO 23, Chicago 0
Super Bowl XIX: San Francisco (NFC) 38, Miami (AFC) 16, at Stanford Stadium,
   Stanford, Calif.

1983

American Conference

Eastern Division

	W	L	T	Pct.	Pts.	OP
Miami	12	4	0	.750	389	250
New England	8	8	0	.500	274	289
Buffalo	8	8	0	.500	283	351
Baltimore	7	9	0	.438	264	354
N.Y. Jets	7	9	0	.438	313	331

Central Division

	W	L	T	Pct.	Pts.	OP
Pittsburgh	10	6	0	.625	355	303
Cleveland	9	7	0	.563	356	342
Cincinnati	7	9	0	.438	346	302
Houston	2	14	0	.125	288	460

Western Division

	W	L	T	Pct.	Pts.	OP
L.A. Raiders	12	4	0	.750	442	338
Seattle*	9	7	0	.563	403	397
Denver*	9	7	0	.563	302	327
San Diego	6	10	0	.375	358	462
Kansas City	6	10	0	.375	386	367

National Conference

Eastern Division

	W	L	T	Pct.	Pts.	OP
Washington	14	2	0	.875	541	332
Dallas*	12	4	0	.750	479	360
St. Louis	8	7	1	.531	374	428
Philadelphia	5	11	0	.313	233	322
N.Y. Giants	3	12	1	.219	267	347

Central Division

	W	L	T	Pct.	Pts.	OP
Detroit	9	7	0	.563	347	286
Green Bay	8	8	0	.500	429	439
Chicago	8	8	0	.500	311	301
Minnesota	8	8	0	.500	316	348
Tampa Bay	2	14	0	.125	241	380

Western Division

	W	L	T	Pct.	Pts.	OP
San Francisco	10	6	0	.625	432	293
L.A. Rams*	9	7	0	.563	361	344
New Orleans	8	8	0	.500	319	337
Atlanta	7	9	0	.438	370	389

*Wild Card qualifiers for playoffs

Seattle and Denver gained Wild Card berths over Cleveland because of their victories over the Browns.

First round playoff: SEATTLE 31, Denver 7
Divisional playoffs: Seattle 27, MIAMI 20; LOS ANGELES RAIDERS 38, Pittsburgh 10
AFC championship: LOS ANGELES RAIDERS 30, Seattle 14
First round playoff: Los Angeles Rams 24, DALLAS 17
Divisional playoffs: SAN FRANCISCO 24, Detroit 23; WASHINGTON 51, L.A. Rams 7
NFC championship: WASHINGTON 24, San Francisco 21
Super Bowl XVIII: Los Angeles Raiders (AFC) 38, Washington (NFC) 9, at Tampa Stadium,
   Tampa, Fla.

1982

American Conference

	W	L	T	Pct.	Pts.	OP
L.A. Raiders	8	1	0	.889	260	200
Miami	7	2	0	.778	198	131
Cincinnati	7	2	0	.778	232	177
Pittsburgh	6	3	0	.667	204	146
San Diego	6	3	0	.667	288	221
N.Y. Jets	6	3	0	.667	245	166
New England	5	4	0	.556	143	157
Cleveland	4	5	0	.444	140	182
Buffalo	4	5	0	.444	150	154
Seattle	4	5	0	.444	127	147
Kansas City	3	6	0	.333	176	184
Denver	2	7	0	.222	148	226
Houston	1	8	0	.111	136	245
Baltimore	0	8	1	.056	113	236

National Conference

	W	L	T	Pct.	Pts.	OP
Washington	8	1	0	.889	190	128
Dallas	6	3	0	.667	226	145
Green Bay	5	3	1	.611	226	169
Minnesota	5	4	0	.556	187	198
Atlanta	5	4	0	.556	183	199
St. Louis	5	4	0	.556	135	170
Tampa Bay	5	4	0	.556	158	178
Detroit	4	5	0	.444	181	176
New Orleans	4	5	0	.444	129	160
N.Y. Giants	4	5	0	.444	164	160
San Francisco	3	6	0	.333	209	206
Chicago	3	6	0	.333	141	174
Philadelphia	3	6	0	.333	191	195
L.A. Rams	2	7	0	.222	200	250

As the result of a 57-day players' strike, the 1982 NFL regular season schedule was reduced from 16 weeks to 9. At the conclusion of the regular season, the NFL conducted a 16-team postseason Super Bowl Tournament. Eight teams from each conference were seeded 1-8 based on their records during the season.

Miami finished ahead of Cincinnati based on better conference record (6-1 to 6-2). Pittsburgh won common games tie-breaker with San Diego (3-1 to 2-1) after New York Jets were eliminated from three-way tie based on conference record (Pittsburgh and San Diego 5-3 vs. Jets 2-3). Cleveland finished ahead of Buffalo and Seattle based on better conference record (4-3 to 3-3 to 3-5). Minnesota (4-1), Atlanta (4-3), St. Louis (5-4), Tampa Bay (3-3) seeds were determined by best won-lost record in conference games. Detroit finished ahead of New Orleans and the New York Giants based on better conference record (4-4 to 3-5 to 3-5).

First round playoff: MIAMI 28, New England 13
   LOS ANGELES RAIDERS 27, Cleveland 10
   New York Jets 44, CINCINNATI 17
   San Diego 31, PITTSBURGH 28
Second round playoff: New York Jets 17, LOS ANGELES RAIDERS 14
   MIAMI 34, San Diego 13
AFC championship: MIAMI 14, New York Jets 0
First round playoff: WASHINGTON 31, Detroit 7
   GREEN BAY 41, St. Louis 16
   MINNESOTA 30, Atlanta 24
   DALLAS 30, Tampa Bay 17
Second round playoff: WASHINGTON 21, Minnesota 7
   DALLAS 37, Green Bay 26
NFC championship: WASHINGTON 31, Dallas 17
Super Bowl XVII: Washington (NFC) 27, Miami (AFC) 17, at Rose Bowl, Pasadena, Calif.

1981

American Conference

Eastern Division
	W	L	T	Pct.	Pts.	OP
Miami	11	4	1	.719	345	275
N.Y. Jets*	10	5	1	.656	355	287
Buffalo*	10	6	0	.625	311	276
Baltimore	2	14	0	.125	259	533
New England	2	14	0	.125	322	370

Central Division
	W	L	T	Pct.	Pts.	OP
Cincinnati	12	4	0	.750	421	304
Pittsburgh	8	8	0	.500	356	297
Houston	7	9	0	.438	281	355
Cleveland	5	11	0	.313	276	375

Western Division
	W	L	T	Pct.	Pts.	OP
San Diego	10	6	0	.625	478	390
Denver	10	6	0	.625	321	289
Kansas City	9	7	0	.563	343	290
Oakland	7	9	0	.438	273	343
Seattle	6	10	0	.375	322	388

National Conference

Eastern Division
	W	L	T	Pct.	Pts.	OP
Dallas	12	4	0	.750	367	277
Philadelphia*	10	6	0	.625	368	221
N.Y. Giants*	9	7	0	.563	295	257
Washington	8	8	0	.500	347	349
St. Louis	7	9	0	.438	315	408

Central Division
	W	L	T	Pct.	Pts.	OP
Tampa Bay	9	7	0	.563	315	268
Detroit	8	8	0	.500	397	322
Green Bay	8	8	0	.500	324	361
Minnesota	7	9	0	.438	325	369
Chicago	6	10	0	.375	253	324

Western Division
	W	L	T	Pct.	Pts.	OP
San Francisco	13	3	0	.813	357	250
Atlanta	7	9	0	.438	426	355
Los Angeles	6	10	0	.375	303	351
New Orleans	4	12	0	.250	207	378

*Wild Card qualifiers for playoffs

San Diego won AFC Western title over Denver on the basis of a better division record (6-2 to 5-3). Buffalo won a Wild Card playoff berth over Denver as the result of a 9-7 victory in head-to-head competition.

First round playoff: Buffalo 31, NEW YORK JETS 27
Divisional playoffs: San Diego 41, MIAMI 38 (OT); CINCINNATI 28, Buffalo 21
AFC championship: CINCINNATI 27, San Diego 7
First round playoff: New York Giants 27, PHILADELPHIA 21
Divisional playoffs: DALLAS 38, Tampa Bay 0; SAN FRANCISCO 38, New York Giants 24
NFC championship: SAN FRANCISCO 28, Dallas 27
Super Bowl XVI: San Francisco (NFC) 26, Cincinnati (AFC) 21, at Silverdome, Pontiac, Mich.

1980

American Conference

Eastern Division
	W	L	T	Pct.	Pts.	OP
Buffalo	11	5	0	.688	320	260
New England	10	6	0	.625	441	325
Miami	8	8	0	.500	266	305
Baltimore	7	9	0	.438	355	387
N.Y. Jets	4	12	0	.250	302	395

Central Division
	W	L	T	Pct.	Pts.	OP
Cleveland	11	5	0	.688	357	310
Houston*	11	5	0	.688	295	251
Pittsburgh	9	7	0	.563	352	313
Cincinnati	6	10	0	.375	244	312

Western Division
	W	L	T	Pct.	Pts.	OP
San Diego	11	5	0	.688	418	327
Oakland*	11	5	0	.688	364	306
Kansas City	8	8	0	.500	319	336
Denver	8	8	0	.500	310	323
Seattle	4	12	0	.250	291	408

National Conference

Eastern Division
	W	L	T	Pct.	Pts.	OP
Philadelphia	12	4	0	.750	384	222
Dallas*	12	4	0	.750	454	311
Washington	6	10	0	.375	261	293
St. Louis	5	11	0	.313	299	350
N.Y. Giants	4	12	0	.250	249	425

Central Division
	W	L	T	Pct.	Pts.	OP
Minnesota	9	7	0	.563	317	308
Detroit	9	7	0	.563	334	272
Chicago	7	9	0	.438	304	264
Tampa Bay	5	10	1	.344	271	341
Green Bay	5	10	1	.344	231	371

Western Division
	W	L	T	Pct.	Pts.	OP
Atlanta	12	4	0	.750	405	272
Los Angeles*	11	5	0	.688	424	289
San Francisco	6	10	0	.375	320	415
New Orleans	1	15	0	.063	291	487

*Wild Card qualifiers for playoffs

Philadelphia won division title over Dallas on the basis of best net points in division games (plus 84 net points to plus 50). Minnesota won division title because of a better conference record than Detroit (8-4 to 9-5). Cleveland won division title because of a better conference record than Houston (8-4 to 7-5). San Diego won division title over Oakland on the basis of best net points in division games (plus 60 net points to plus 37).

First round playoff: OAKLAND 27, Houston 7
Divisional playoffs: SAN DIEGO 20, Buffalo 14; Oakland 14, CLEVELAND 12
AFC championship: Oakland 34, SAN DIEGO 27
First round playoff: DALLAS 34, Los Angeles 13
Divisional playoffs: PHILADELPHIA 31, Minnesota 16; Dallas 30, ATLANTA 27
NFC championship: PHILADELPHIA 20, Dallas 7
Super Bowl XV: Oakland (AFC) 27, Philadelphia (NFC) 10, at Louisiana Superdome, New Orleans, La.

1979

American Conference

Eastern Division
	W	L	T	Pct.	Pts.	OP
Miami	10	6	0	.625	341	257
New England	9	7	0	.563	411	326
N.Y. Jets	8	8	0	.500	337	383
Buffalo	7	9	0	.438	268	279
Baltimore	5	11	0	.313	271	351

Central Division
	W	L	T	Pct.	Pts.	OP
Pittsburgh	12	4	0	.750	416	262
Houston*	11	5	0	.688	362	331
Cleveland	9	7	0	.563	359	352
Cincinnati	4	12	0	.250	337	421

Western Division
	W	L	T	Pct.	Pts.	OP
San Diego	12	4	0	.750	411	246
Denver*	10	6	0	.625	289	262
Seattle	9	7	0	.563	378	372
Oakland	9	7	0	.563	365	337
Kansas City	7	9	0	.438	238	262

National Conference

Eastern Division
	W	L	T	Pct.	Pts.	OP
Dallas	11	5	0	.688	371	313
Philadelphia*	11	5	0	.688	339	282
Washington	10	6	0	.625	348	295
N.Y. Giants	6	10	0	.375	237	323
St. Louis	5	11	0	.313	307	358

Central Division
	W	L	T	Pct.	Pts.	OP
Tampa Bay	10	6	0	.625	273	237
Chicago*	10	6	0	.625	306	249
Minnesota	7	9	0	.438	259	337
Green Bay	5	11	0	.313	246	316
Detroit	2	14	0	.125	219	365

Western Division
	W	L	T	Pct.	Pts.	OP
Los Angeles	9	7	0	.563	323	309
New Orleans	8	8	0	.500	370	360
Atlanta	6	10	0	.375	300	388
San Francisco	2	14	0	.125	308	416

*Wild Card qualifiers for playoffs

Dallas won division title because of a better conference record than Philadelphia (10-2 to 9-3). Tampa Bay won division title because of a better division record than Chicago (6-2 to 5-3). Chicago won a Wild Card berth over Washington on the basis of best net points in all games (plus 57 net points to plus 53).

First round playoff: HOUSTON 13, Denver 7
Divisional playoffs: Houston 17, SAN DIEGO 14; PITTSBURGH 34, Miami 14
AFC championship: PITTSBURGH 27, Houston 13
First round playoff: PHILADELPHIA 27, Chicago 17
Divisional playoffs: TAMPA BAY 24, Philadelphia 17; Los Angeles 21, DALLAS 19
NFC championship: Los Angeles 9, TAMPA BAY 0
Super Bowl XIV: Pittsburgh (AFC) 31, Los Angeles (NFC) 19, at Rose Bowl, Pasadena, Calif.

1978

American Conference

Eastern Division
	W	L	T	Pct.	Pts.	OP
New England	11	5	0	.688	358	286
Miami*	11	5	0	.688	372	254
N.Y. Jets	8	8	0	.500	359	364
Buffalo	5	11	0	.313	302	354
Baltimore	5	11	0	.313	239	421

Central Division
	W	L	T	Pct.	Pts.	OP
Pittsburgh	14	2	0	.875	356	195
Houston*	10	6	0	.625	283	298
Cleveland	8	8	0	.500	334	356
Cincinnati	4	12	0	.250	252	284

Western Division
	W	L	T	Pct.	Pts.	OP
Denver	10	6	0	.625	282	198
Oakland	9	7	0	.563	311	283
Seattle	9	7	0	.563	345	358
San Diego	9	7	0	.563	355	309
Kansas City	4	12	0	.250	243	327

National Conference

Eastern Division
	W	L	T	Pct.	Pts.	OP
Dallas	12	4	0	.750	384	208
Philadelphia*	9	7	0	.563	270	250
Washington	8	8	0	.500	273	283
St. Louis	6	10	0	.375	248	296
N.Y. Giants	6	10	0	.375	264	298

Central Division
	W	L	T	Pct.	Pts.	OP
Minnesota	8	7	1	.531	294	306
Green Bay	8	7	1	.531	249	269
Detroit	7	9	0	.438	290	300
Chicago	7	9	0	.438	253	274
Tampa Bay	5	11	0	.313	241	259

Western Division
	W	L	T	Pct.	Pts.	OP
Los Angeles	12	4	0	.750	316	245
Atlanta*	9	7	0	.563	240	290
New Orleans	7	9	0	.438	281	298
San Francisco	2	14	0	.125	219	350

*Wild Card qualifiers for playoffs

New England won division title on the basis of a better division record than Miami (6-2 to 5-3). Minnesota won division title because of a better head-to-head record against Green Bay (1-0-1).

First round playoff: Houston 17, MIAMI 9
Divisional playoffs: Houston 31, NEW ENGLAND 14; PITTSBURGH 33, Denver 10
AFC championship: PITTSBURGH 34, Houston 5
First round playoff: ATLANTA 14, Philadelphia 13
Divisional playoffs: DALLAS 27, Atlanta 20; LOS ANGELES 34, Minnesota 10
NFC championship: Dallas 28, LOS ANGELES 0
Super Bowl XIII: Pittsburgh (AFC) 35, Dallas (NFC) 31, at Orange Bowl. Miami, Fla.

1977
American Conference
Eastern Division
	W	L	T	Pct.	Pts.	OP
Baltimore	10	4	0	.714	295	221
Miami	10	4	0	.714	313	197
New England	9	5	0	.643	278	217
N.Y. Jets	3	11	0	.214	191	300
Buffalo	3	11	0	.214	160	313

Central Division
	W	L	T	Pct.	Pts.	OP
Pittsburgh	9	5	0	.643	283	243
Houston	8	6	0	.571	299	230
Cincinnati	8	6	0	.571	238	235
Cleveland	6	8	0	.429	269	267

Western Division
	W	L	T	Pct.	Pts.	OP
Denver	12	2	0	.857	274	148
Oakland*	11	3	0	.786	351	230
San Diego	7	7	0	.500	222	205
Seattle	5	9	0	.357	282	373
Kansas City	2	12	0	.143	225	349

National Conference
Eastern Division
	W	L	T	Pct.	Pts.	OP
Dallas	12	2	0	.857	345	212
Washington	9	5	0	.643	196	189
St. Louis	7	7	0	.500	272	287
Philadelphia	5	9	0	.357	220	207
N.Y. Giants	5	9	0	.357	181	265

Central Division
	W	L	T	Pct.	Pts.	OP
Minnesota	9	5	0	.643	231	227
Chicago*	9	5	0	.643	255	253
Detroit	6	8	0	.429	183	252
Green Bay	4	10	0	.286	134	219
Tampa Bay	2	12	0	.143	103	223

Western Division
	W	L	T	Pct.	Pts.	OP
Los Angeles	10	4	0	.714	302	146
Atlanta	7	7	0	.500	179	129
San Francisco	5	9	0	.357	220	260
New Orleans	3	11	0	.214	232	336

*Wild Card qualifier for playoffs
Baltimore won division title on the basis of a better conference record than Miami (9-3 to 8-4). Chicago won a Wild Card berth over Washington on the basis of best net points in conference games (plus 48 net points to plus 4).
Divisional playoffs: DENVER 34, Pittsburgh 21; Oakland 37, BALTIMORE 31 (OT).
AFC championship: DENVER 20, Oakland 17
Divisional playoffs: DALLAS 37, Chicago 7; Minnesota 14, LOS ANGELES 7
NFC championship: DALLAS 23, Minnesota 6
Super Bowl XII: Dallas (NFC) 27, Denver (AFC) 10, at Louisiana Superdome, New Orleans, La.

1976
American Conference
Eastern Division
	W	L	T	Pct.	Pts.	OP
Baltimore	11	3	0	.786	417	246
New England*	11	3	0	.786	376	236
Miami	6	8	0	.429	263	264
N.Y. Jets	3	11	0	.214	169	383
Buffalo	2	12	0	.143	245	363

Central Division
	W	L	T	Pct.	Pts.	OP
Pittsburgh	10	4	0	.714	342	138
Cincinnati	10	4	0	.714	335	210
Cleveland	9	5	0	.643	267	287
Houston	5	9	0	.357	222	273

Western Division
	W	L	T	Pct.	Pts.	OP
Oakland	13	1	0	.929	350	237
Denver	9	5	0	.643	315	206
San Diego	6	8	0	.429	248	285
Kansas City	5	9	0	.357	290	376
Tampa Bay	0	14	0	.000	125	412

National Conference
Eastern Division
	W	L	T	Pct.	Pts.	OP
Dallas	11	3	0	.786	296	194
Washington*	10	4	0	.714	291	217
St. Louis	10	4	0	.714	309	267
Philadelphia	4	10	0	.286	165	286
N.Y. Giants	3	11	0	.214	170	250

Central Division
	W	L	T	Pct.	Pts.	OP
Minnesota	11	2	1	.821	305	176
Chicago	7	7	0	.500	253	216
Detroit	6	8	0	.429	262	220
Green Bay	5	9	0	.357	218	299

Western Division
	W	L	T	Pct.	Pts.	OP
Los Angeles	10	3	1	.750	351	190
San Francisco	8	6	0	.571	270	190
Atlanta	4	10	0	.286	172	312
New Orleans	4	10	0	.286	253	346
Seattle	2	12	0	.143	229	429

*Wild Card qualifier for playoffs
Baltimore won division title on the basis of a better division record than New England (7-1 to 6-2). Pittsburgh won division title because of a two-game sweep over Cincinnati. Washington won Wild Card berth over St. Louis because of a two-game sweep over Cardinals.
Divisional playoffs: OAKLAND 24, New England 21; Pittsburgh 40, BALTIMORE 14
AFC championship: OAKLAND 24, Pittsburgh 7
Divisional playoffs: MINNESOTA 35, Washington 20; Los Angeles 14, DALLAS 12
NFC championship: MINNESOTA 24, Los Angeles 13
Super Bowl XI: Oakland (AFC) 32, Minnesota (NFC) 14, at Rose Bowl, Pasadena, Calif.

1975
American Conference
Eastern Division
	W	L	T	Pct.	Pts.	OP
Baltimore	10	4	0	.714	395	269
Miami	10	4	0	.714	357	222
Buffalo	8	6	0	.571	420	355
New England	3	11	0	.214	258	358
N.Y. Jets	3	11	0	.214	258	433

Central Division
	W	L	T	Pct.	Pts.	OP
Pittsburgh	12	2	0	.857	373	162
Cincinnati*	11	3	0	.786	340	246
Houston	10	4	0	.714	293	226
Cleveland	3	11	0	.214	218	372

Western Division
	W	L	T	Pct.	Pts.	OP
Oakland	11	3	0	.786	375	255
Denver	6	8	0	.429	254	307
Kansas City	5	9	0	.357	282	341
San Diego	2	12	0	.143	189	345

National Conference
Eastern Division
	W	L	T	Pct.	Pts.	OP
St. Louis	11	3	0	.786	356	276
Dallas*	10	4	0	.714	350	268
Washington	8	6	0	.571	325	276
N.Y. Giants	5	9	0	.357	216	306
Philadelphia	4	10	0	.286	225	302

Central Division
	W	L	T	Pct.	Pts.	OP
Minnesota	12	2	0	.857	377	180
Detroit	7	7	0	.500	245	262
Chicago	4	10	0	.286	191	379
Green Bay	4	10	0	.286	226	285

Western Division
	W	L	T	Pct.	Pts.	OP
Los Angeles	12	2	0	.857	312	135
San Francisco	5	9	0	.357	255	286
Atlanta	4	10	0	.286	240	289
New Orleans	2	12	0	.143	165	360

*Wild Card qualifier for playoffs
Baltimore won division title on the basis of a two-game sweep over Miami.
Divisional playoffs: PITTSBURGH 28, Baltimore 10; OAKLAND 31, Cincinnati 28
AFC championship: PITTSBURGH 16, Oakland 10
Divisional playoffs: LOS ANGELES 35, St. Louis 23; Dallas 17, MINNESOTA 14
NFC championship: Dallas 37, LOS ANGELES 7
Super Bowl X: Pittsburgh (AFC) 21, Dallas (NFC) 17, at Orange Bowl, Miami, Fla.

1974
American Conference
Eastern Division
	W	L	T	Pct.	Pts.	OP
Miami	11	3	0	.786	327	216
Buffalo*	9	5	0	.643	264	244
New England	7	7	0	.500	348	289
N.Y. Jets	7	7	0	.500	279	300
Baltimore	2	12	0	.143	190	329

Central Division
	W	L	T	Pct.	Pts.	OP
Pittsburgh	10	3	1	.750	305	189
Cincinnati	7	7	0	.500	283	259
Houston	7	7	0	.500	236	282
Cleveland	4	10	0	.286	251	344

Western Division
	W	L	T	Pct.	Pts.	OP
Oakland	12	2	0	.857	355	228
Denver	7	6	1	.536	302	294
Kansas City	5	9	0	.357	233	293
San Diego	5	9	0	.357	212	285

National Conference
Eastern Division
	W	L	T	Pct.	Pts.	OP
St. Louis	10	4	0	.714	285	218
Washington*	10	4	0	.714	320	196
Dallas	8	6	0	.571	297	235
Philadelphia	7	7	0	.500	242	217
N.Y. Giants	2	12	0	.143	195	299

Central Division
	W	L	T	Pct.	Pts.	OP
Minnesota	10	4	0	.714	310	195
Detroit	7	7	0	.500	256	270
Green Bay	6	8	0	.429	210	206
Chicago	4	10	0	.286	152	279

Western Division
	W	L	T	Pct.	Pts.	OP
Los Angeles	10	4	0	.714	263	181
San Francisco	6	8	0	.429	226	236
New Orleans	5	9	0	.357	166	263
Atlanta	3	11	0	.214	111	271

*Wild Card qualifier for playoffs
St. Louis won division title because of a two-game sweep over Washington.
Divisional playoffs: OAKLAND 28, Miami 26; PITTSBURGH 32, Buffalo 14
AFC championship: Pittsburgh 24, OAKLAND 13
Divisional playoffs: MINNESOTA 30, St. Louis 14; LOS ANGELES 19, Washington 10
NFC championship: MINNESOTA 14, Los Angeles 10
Super Bowl IX: Pittsburgh (AFC) 16, Minnesota (NFC) 6, at Tulane Stadium, New Orleans, La.

1973
American Conference
Eastern Division
	W	L	T	Pct.	Pts.	OP
Miami	12	2	0	.857	343	150
Buffalo	9	5	0	.643	259	230
New England	5	9	0	.357	258	300
Baltimore	4	10	0	.286	226	341
N.Y. Jets	4	10	0	.286	240	306

Central Division
	W	L	T	Pct.	Pts.	OP
Cincinnati	10	4	0	.714	286	231
Pittsburgh*	10	4	0	.714	347	210
Cleveland	7	5	2	.571	234	255
Houston	1	13	0	.071	199	447

Western Division
	W	L	T	Pct.	Pts.	OP
Oakland	9	4	1	.679	292	175
Denver	7	5	2	.571	354	296
Kansas City	7	5	2	.571	231	192
San Diego	2	11	1	.179	188	386

National Conference
Eastern Division
	W	L	T	Pct.	Pts.	OP
Dallas	10	4	0	.714	382	203
Washington*	10	4	0	.714	325	198
Philadelphia	5	8	1	.393	310	393
St. Louis	4	9	1	.321	286	365
N.Y. Giants	2	11	1	.179	226	362

Central Division
	W	L	T	Pct.	Pts.	OP
Minnesota	12	2	0	.857	296	168
Detroit	6	7	1	.464	271	247
Green Bay	5	7	2	.429	202	259
Chicago	3	11	0	.214	195	334

Western Division
	W	L	T	Pct.	Pts.	OP
Los Angeles	12	2	0	.857	388	178
Atlanta	9	5	0	.643	318	224
New Orleans	5	9	0	.357	163	312
San Francisco	5	9	0	.357	262	319

*Wild Card qualifier for playoffs
Cincinnati won division title on the basis of a better conference record than Pittsburgh (8-3 to 7-4). Dallas won division title on the basis of a better point differential vs. Washington (net 13 points).
Divisional playoffs: OAKLAND 33, Pittsburgh 14; MIAMI 34, Cincinnati 16
AFC championship: MIAMI 27, Oakland 10
Divisional playoffs: MINNESOTA 27, Washington 20; DALLAS 27, Los Angeles 16
NFC championship: Minnesota 27, DALLAS 10
Super Bowl VIII: Miami (AFC) 24, Minnesota (NFC) 7, at Rice Stadium, Houston, Tex.

1972
American Conference
Eastern Division
	W	L	T	Pct.	Pts.	OP
Miami	14	0	0	1.000	385	171
N.Y. Jets	7	7	0	.500	367	324
Baltimore	5	9	0	.357	235	252
Buffalo	4	9	1	.321	257	377
New England	3	11	0	.214	192	446

Central Division
	W	L	T	Pct.	Pts.	OP
Pittsburgh	11	3	0	.786	343	175
Cleveland*	10	4	0	.714	268	249
Cincinnati	8	6	0	.571	299	229
Houston	1	13	0	.071	164	380

Western Division
	W	L	T	Pct.	Pts.	OP
Oakland	10	3	1	.750	365	248
Kansas City	8	6	0	.571	287	254
Denver	5	9	0	.357	325	350
San Diego	4	9	1	.321	264	344

National Conference
Eastern Division
	W	L	T	Pct.	Pts.	OP
Washington	11	3	0	.786	336	218
Dallas*	10	4	0	.714	319	240
N.Y. Giants	8	6	0	.571	331	247
St. Louis	4	9	1	.321	193	303
Philadelphia	2	11	1	.179	145	352

Central Division
	W	L	T	Pct.	Pts.	OP
Green Bay	10	4	0	.714	304	226
Detroit	8	5	1	.607	339	290
Minnesota	7	7	0	.500	301	252
Chicago	4	9	1	.321	225	275

Western Division
	W	L	T	Pct.	Pts.	OP
San Francisco	8	5	1	.607	353	249
Atlanta	7	7	0	.500	269	274
Los Angeles	6	7	1	.464	291	286
New Orleans	2	11	1	.179	215	361

*Wild Card qualifier for playoffs
Divisional playoffs: PITTSBURGH 13, Oakland 7; MIAMI 20, Cleveland 14
AFC championship: Miami 21, PITTSBURGH 17
Divisional playoffs: Dallas 30, SAN FRANCISCO 28; WASHINGTON 16, Green Bay 3
NFC championship: WASHINGTON 26, Dallas 3
Super Bowl VII: Miami (AFC) 14, Washington (NFC) 7, at Memorial Coliseum, Los Angeles, Calif.

1971
American Conference
Eastern Division
	W	L	T	Pct.	Pts.	OP
Miami	10	3	1	.769	315	174
Baltimore*	10	4	0	.714	313	140
New England	6	8	0	.429	238	325
N.Y. Jets	6	8	0	.429	212	299
Buffalo	1	13	0	.071	184	394

Central Division
	W	L	T	Pct.	Pts.	OP
Cleveland	9	5	0	.643	285	273
Pittsburgh	6	8	0	.429	246	292
Houston	4	9	1	.308	251	330
Cincinnati	4	10	0	.286	284	265

Western Division
	W	L	T	Pct.	Pts.	OP
Kansas City	10	3	1	.769	302	208
Oakland	8	4	2	.667	344	278
San Diego	6	8	0	.429	311	341
Denver	4	9	1	.308	203	275

National Conference
Eastern Division
	W	L	T	Pct.	Pts.	OP
Dallas	11	3	0	.786	406	222
Washington*	9	4	1	.692	276	190
Philadelphia	6	7	1	.462	221	302
St. Louis	4	9	1	.308	231	279
N.Y. Giants	4	10	0	.286	228	362

Central Division
	W	L	T	Pct.	Pts.	OP
Minnesota	11	3	0	.786	245	139
Detroit	7	6	1	.538	341	286
Chicago	6	8	0	.429	185	276
Green Bay	4	8	2	.333	274	298

Western Division
	W	L	T	Pct.	Pts.	OP
San Francisco	9	5	0	.643	300	216
Los Angeles	8	5	1	.615	313	260
Atlanta	7	6	1	.538	274	277
New Orleans	4	8	2	.333	266	347

Wild Card qualifier for playoffs

Divisional playoffs: Miami 27, KANSAS CITY 24 (OT); Baltimore 20, CLEVELAND 3
AFC championship: MIAMI 21, Baltimore 0
Divisional playoffs: Dallas 20, MINNESOTA 12; SAN FRANCISCO 24, Washington 20
NFC championship: DALLAS 14, San Francisco 3
Super Bowl VI: Dallas (NFC) 24, Miami (AFC) 3, at Tulane Stadium, New Orleans, La.

1970
American Conference
Eastern Division
	W	L	T	Pct.	Pts.	OP
Baltimore	11	2	1	.846	321	234
Miami*	10	4	0	.714	297	228
N.Y. Jets	4	10	0	.286	255	286
Buffalo	3	10	1	.231	204	337
Boston Patriots	2	12	0	.143	149	361

Central Division
	W	L	T	Pct.	Pts.	OP
Cincinnati	8	6	0	.571	312	255
Cleveland	7	7	0	.500	286	265
Pittsburgh	5	9	0	.357	210	272
Houston	3	10	1	.231	217	352

Western Division
	W	L	T	Pct.	Pts.	OP
Oakland	8	4	2	.667	300	293
Kansas City	7	5	2	.583	272	244
San Diego	5	6	3	.455	282	278
Denver	5	8	1	.385	253	264

National Conference
Eastern Division
	W	L	T	Pct.	Pts.	OP
Dallas	10	4	0	.714	299	221
N.Y. Giants	9	5	0	.643	301	270
St. Louis	8	5	1	.615	325	228
Washington	6	8	0	.429	297	314
Philadelphia	3	10	1	.231	241	332

Central Division
	W	L	T	Pct.	Pts.	OP
Minnesota	12	2	0	.857	335	143
Detroit*	10	4	0	.714	347	202
Chicago	6	8	0	.429	256	261
Green Bay	6	8	0	.429	196	293

Western Division
	W	L	T	Pct.	Pts.	OP
San Francisco	10	3	1	.769	352	267
Los Angeles	9	4	1	.692	325	202
Atlanta	4	8	2	.333	206	261
New Orleans	2	11	1	.154	172	347

Wild Card qualifier for playoffs

Divisional playoffs: BALTIMORE 17, Cincinnati 0; OAKLAND 21, Miami 14
AFC championship: BALTIMORE 27, Oakland 17
Divisional playoffs: DALLAS 5, Detroit 0; San Francisco 17, MINNESOTA 14
NFC championship: Dallas 17, SAN FRANCISCO 10
Super Bowl V: Baltimore (AFC) 16, Dallas (NFC) 13, at Orange Bowl, Miami, Fla.

1969 NFL
Eastern Conference
Capitol Division
	W	L	T	Pct.	Pts.	OP
Dallas	11	2	1	.846	369	223
Washington	7	5	2	.583	307	319
New Orleans	5	9	0	.357	311	393
Philadelphia	4	9	1	.308	279	377

Century Division
	W	L	T	Pct.	Pts.	OP
Cleveland	10	3	1	.769	351	300
N.Y. Giants	6	8	0	.429	264	298
St. Louis	4	9	1	.308	314	389
Pittsburgh	1	13	0	.071	218	404

Western Conference
Coastal Division
	W	L	T	Pct.	Pts.	OP
Los Angeles	11	3	0	.786	320	243
Baltimore	8	5	1	.615	279	268
Atlanta	6	8	0	.429	276	268
San Francisco	4	8	2	.333	277	319

Central Division
	W	L	T	Pct.	Pts.	OP
Minnesota	12	2	0	.857	379	133
Detroit	9	4	1	.692	259	188
Green Bay	8	6	0	.571	269	221
Chicago	1	13	0	.071	210	339

Conference championships: Cleveland 38, DALLAS 14; MINNESOTA 23, Los Angeles 20
NFL championship: MINNESOTA 27, Cleveland 7
Super Bowl IV: Kansas City (AFL) 23, Minnesota (NFL) 7, at Tulane Stadium, New Orleans, La.

1969 AFL
Eastern Division
	W	L	T	Pct.	Pts.	OP
N.Y. Jets	10	4	0	.714	353	269
Houston	6	6	2	.500	278	279
Boston Patriots	4	10	0	.286	266	316
Buffalo	4	10	0	.286	230	359
Miami	3	10	1	.231	233	332

Western Division
	W	L	T	Pct.	Pts.	OP
Oakland	12	1	1	.923	377	242
Kansas City	11	3	0	.786	359	177
San Diego	8	6	0	.571	288	276
Denver	5	8	1	.385	297	344
Cincinnati	4	9	1	.308	280	367

Divisional Playoffs: Kansas City 13, N.Y. JETS 6; OAKLAND 56, Houston 7
AFL championship: Kansas City 17, OAKLAND 7

1968 NFL
Eastern Conference
Capitol Division
	W	L	T	Pct.	Pts.	OP
Dallas	12	2	0	.857	431	186
N.Y. Giants	7	7	0	.500	294	325
Washington	5	9	0	.357	249	358
Philadelphia	2	12	0	.143	202	351

Century Division
	W	L	T	Pct.	Pts.	OP
Cleveland	10	4	0	.714	394	273
St. Louis	9	4	1	.692	325	289
New Orleans	4	9	1	.308	246	327
Pittsburgh	2	11	1	.154	244	397

Western Conference
Coastal Division
	W	L	T	Pct.	Pts.	OP
Baltimore	13	1	0	.929	402	144
Los Angeles	10	3	1	.769	312	200
San Francisco	7	6	1	.538	303	310
Atlanta	2	12	0	.143	170	389

Central Division
	W	L	T	Pct.	Pts.	OP
Minnesota	8	6	0	.571	282	242
Chicago	7	7	0	.500	250	333
Green Bay	6	7	1	.462	281	227
Detroit	4	8	2	.333	207	241

Conference championships: CLEVELAND 31, Dallas 20; BALTIMORE 24, Minnesota 14
NFL championship: Baltimore 34, CLEVELAND 0
Super Bowl III: N.Y. Jets (AFL) 16, Baltimore (NFL) 7, at Orange Bowl, Miami, Fla.

1968 AFL
Eastern Division
	W	L	T	Pct.	Pts.	OP
N.Y. Jets	11	3	0	.786	419	280
Houston	7	7	0	.500	303	248
Miami	5	8	1	.385	276	355
Boston Patriots	4	10	0	.286	229	406
Buffalo	1	12	1	.077	199	367

Western Division
	W	L	T	Pct.	Pts.	OP
Oakland	12	2	0	.857	453	233
Kansas City	12	2	0	.857	371	170
San Diego	9	5	0	.643	382	310
Denver	5	9	0	.357	255	404
Cincinnati	3	11	0	.214	215	329

Western Division playoff: OAKLAND 41, Kansas City 6
AFL championship: N.Y. JETS 27, Oakland 23

1967 NFL
Eastern Conference
Capitol Division
	W	L	T	Pct.	Pts.	OP
Dallas	9	5	0	.643	342	268
Philadelphia	6	7	1	.462	351	409
Washington	5	6	3	.455	347	353
New Orleans	3	11	0	.214	233	379

Century Division
	W	L	T	Pct.	Pts.	OP
Cleveland	9	5	0	.643	334	297
N.Y. Giants	7	7	0	.500	369	379
St. Louis	6	7	1	.462	333	356
Pittsburgh	4	9	1	.308	281	320

Western Conference
Coastal Division
	W	L	T	Pct.	Pts.	OP
Los Angeles	11	1	2	.917	398	196
Baltimore	11	1	2	.917	394	198
San Francisco	7	7	0	.500	273	337
Atlanta	1	12	1	.077	175	422

Central Division
	W	L	T	Pct.	Pts.	OP
Green Bay	9	4	1	.692	332	209
Chicago	7	6	1	.538	239	218
Detroit	5	7	2	.417	260	259
Minnesota	3	8	3	.273	233	294

Los Angeles won division title on the basis of advantage in points (58-34) in two games vs. Baltimore.

Conference championships: DALLAS 52, Cleveland 14; GREEN BAY 28, Los Angeles 7
NFL championship: GREEN BAY 21, Dallas 17
Super Bowl II: Green Bay (NFL) 33, Oakland (AFL) 14, at Orange Bowl, Miami, Fla.

1967 AFL
Eastern Division
	W	L	T	Pct.	Pts.	OP
Houston	9	4	1	.692	258	199
N.Y. Jets	8	5	1	.615	371	329
Buffalo	4	10	0	.286	237	285
Miami	4	10	0	.286	219	407
Boston Patriots	3	10	1	.231	280	389

Western Division
	W	L	T	Pct.	Pts.	OP
Oakland	13	1	0	.929	468	233
Kansas City	9	5	0	.643	408	254
San Diego	8	5	1	.615	360	352
Denver	3	11	0	.214	256	409

AFL championship: OAKLAND 40, Houston 7

1966 NFL
Eastern Conference
	W	L	T	Pct.	Pts.	OP
Dallas	10	3	1	.769	445	239
Cleveland	9	5	0	.643	403	259
Philadelphia	9	5	0	.643	326	340
St. Louis	8	5	1	.615	264	265
Washington	7	7	0	.500	351	355
Pittsburgh	5	8	1	.385	316	347
Atlanta	3	11	0	.214	204	437
N.Y. Giants	1	12	1	.077	263	501

Western Conference
	W	L	T	Pct.	Pts.	OP
Green Bay	12	2	0	.857	335	163
Baltimore	9	5	0	.643	314	226
Los Angeles	8	6	0*	.571	289	212
San Francisco	6	6	2	.500	320	325
Chicago	5	7	2	.417	234	272
Detroit	4	9	1	.308	206	317
Minnesota	4	9	1	.308	292	304

NFL championship: Green Bay 34, DALLAS 27
Super Bowl I: Green Bay (NFL) 35, Kansas City (AFL) 10, at Memorial Coliseum, Los Angeles, Calif.

1966 AFL
Eastern Division
	W	L	T	Pct.	Pts.	OP
Buffalo	9	4	1	.692	358	255
Boston Patriots	8	4	2	.677	315	283
N.Y. Jets	6	6	2	.500	322	312
Houston	3	11	0	.214	335	396
Miami	3	11	0	.214	213	362

Western Division
	W	L	T	Pct.	Pts.	OP
Kansas City	11	2	1	.846	448	276
Oakland	8	5	1	.615	315	288
San Diego	7	6	1	.538	335	284
Denver	4	10	0	.286	196	381

AFL championship: Kansas City 31, BUFFALO 7

1965 NFL
Eastern Conference
	W	L	T	Pct.	Pts.	OP
Cleveland	11	3	0	.786	363	325
Dallas	7	7	0	.500	325	280
N.Y. Giants	7	7	0	.500	270	338
Washington	6	8	0	.429	257	301
Philadelphia	5	9	0	.357	363	359
St. Louis	5	9	0	.357	296	309
Pittsburgh	2	12	0	.143	202	397

Western Conference
	W	L	T	Pct.	Pts.	OP
Green Bay	10	3	1	.769	316	224
Baltimore	10	3	1	.769	389	284
Chicago	9	5	0	.643	409	275
San Francisco	7	6	1	.538	421	402
Minnesota	7	7	0	.500	383	403
Detroit	6	7	1	.462	257	295
Los Angeles	4	10	0	.286	269	328

Western Conference playoff: GREEN BAY 13, Baltimore 10 (OT)
NFL championship: GREEN BAY 23, Cleveland 12

1965 AFL

Eastern Division

	W	L	T	Pct.	Pts.	OP
Buffalo	10	3	1	.769	313	226
N.Y. Jets	5	8	1	.385	285	303
Boston Patriots	4	8	2	.333	244	302
Houston	4	10	0	.286	298	429

Western Division

	W	L	T	Pct.	Pts.	OP
San Diego	9	2	3	.818	340	227
Oakland	8	5	1	.615	298	239
Kansas City	7	5	2	.583	322	285
Denver	4	10	0	.286	303	392

AFL championship: Buffalo 23, SAN DIEGO 0

1964 NFL

Eastern Conference

	W	L	T	Pct.	Pts.	OP
Cleveland	10	3	1	.769	415	293
St. Louis	9	3	2	.750	357	331
Philadelphia	6	8	0	.429	312	313
Washington	6	8	0	.429	307	305
Dallas	5	8	1	.385	250	289
Pittsburgh	5	9	0	.357	253	315
N.Y. Giants	2	10	2	.167	241	399

Western Conference

	W	L	T	Pct.	Pts.	OP
Baltimore	12	2	0	.857	428	225
Green Bay	8	5	1	.615	342	245
Minnesota	8	5	1	.615	355	296
Detroit	7	5	2	.583	280	260
Los Angeles	5	7	2	.417	283	339
Chicago	5	9	0	.357	260	379
San Francisco	4	10	0	.286	236	330

NFL championship: CLEVELAND 27, Baltimore 0

1964 AFL

Eastern Division

	W	L	T	Pct.	Pts.	OP
Buffalo	12	2	0	.857	400	242
Boston Patriots	10	3	1	.769	365	297
N.Y. Jets	5	8	1	.385	278	315
Houston	4	10	0	.286	310	355

Western Division

	W	L	T	Pct.	Pts.	OP
San Diego	8	5	1	.615	341	300
Kansas City	7	7	0	.500	366	306
Oakland	5	7	2	.417	303	350
Denver	2	11	1	.154	240	438

AFL championship: BUFFALO 20, San Diego 7

1963 NFL

Eastern Conference

	W	L	T	Pct.	Pts.	OP
N.Y. Giants	11	3	0	.786	448	280
Cleveland	10	4	0	.714	343	262
St. Louis	9	5	0	.643	341	283
Pittsburgh	7	4	3	.636	321	295
Dallas	4	10	0	.286	305	378
Washington	3	11	0	.214	279	398
Philadelphia	2	10	2	.167	242	381

Western Conference

	W	L	T	Pct.	Pts.	OP
Chicago	11	1	2	.917	301	144
Green Bay	11	2	1	.846	369	206
Baltimore	8	6	0	.571	316	285
Detroit	5	8	1	.385	326	265
Minnesota	5	8	1	.385	309	390
Los Angeles	5	9	0	.357	210	350
San Francisco	2	12	0	.143	198	391

NFL championship: CHICAGO 14, N.Y. Giants 10

1963 AFL

Eastern Division

	W	L	T	Pct.	Pts.	OP
Boston Patriots	7	6	1	.538	327	257
Buffalo	7	6	1	.538	304	291
Houston	6	8	0	.429	302	372
N.Y. Jets	5	8	1	.385	249	399

Western Division

	W	L	T	Pct.	Pts.	OP
San Diego	11	3	0	.786	399	256
Oakland	10	4	0	.714	363	288
Kansas City	5	7	2	.417	347	263
Denver	2	11	1	.154	301	473

Eastern Division playoff: Boston 26, BUFFALO 8
AFL championship: SAN DIEGO 51, Boston 10

1962 NFL

Eastern Conference

	W	L	T	Pct.	Pts.	OP
N.Y. Giants	12	2	0	.857	398	283
Pittsburgh	9	5	0	.643	312	363
Cleveland	7	6	1	.538	291	257
Washington	5	7	2	.417	305	376
Dallas Cowboys	5	8	1	.385	398	402
St. Louis	4	9	1	.308	287	361
Philadelphia	3	10	1	.231	282	356

Western Conference

	W	L	T	Pct.	Pts.	OP
Green Bay	13	1	0	.929	415	148
Detroit	11	3	0	.786	315	177
Chicago	9	5	0	.643	321	287
Baltimore	7	7	0	.500	293	288
San Francisco	6	8	0	.429	282	331
Minnesota	2	11	1	.154	254	410
Los Angeles	1	12	1	.077	220	334

NFL championship: Green Bay 16, N.Y. GIANTS 7

1962 AFL

Eastern Division

	W	L	T	Pct.	Pts.	OP
Houston	11	3	0	.786	387	270
Boston Patriots	9	4	1	.692	346	295
Buffalo	7	6	1	.538	309	272
N.Y. Titans	5	9	0	.357	278	423

Western Division

	W	L	T	Pct.	Pts.	OP
Dallas Texans	11	3	0	.786	389	233
Denver	7	7	0	.500	353	334
San Diego	4	10	0	.286	314	392
Oakland	1	13	0	.071	213	370

AFL championship: Dallas Texans 20, HOUSTON 17 (OT)

1961 NFL

Eastern Conference

	W	L	T	Pct.	Pts.	OP
N.Y. Giants	10	3	1	.769	368	220
Philadelphia	10	4	0	.714	361	297
Cleveland	8	5	1	.615	319	270
St. Louis	7	7	0	.500	279	267
Pittsburgh	6	8	0	.429	295	287
Dallas Cowboys	4	9	1	.308	236	380
Washington	1	12	1	.077	174	392

Western Conference

	W	L	T	Pct.	Pts.	OP
Green Bay	11	3	0	.786	391	223
Detroit	8	5	1	.615	270	258
Baltimore	8	6	0	.571	302	307
Chicago	8	6	0	.571	326	302
San Francisco	7	6	1	.538	346	272
Los Angeles	4	10	0	.286	263	333
Minnesota	3	11	0	.214	285	407

NFL championship: GREEN BAY 37, N.Y. Giants 0

1961 AFL

Eastern Division

	W	L	T	Pct.	Pts.	OP
Houston	10	3	1	.769	513	242
Boston Patriots	9	4	1	.692	413	313
N.Y. Titans	7	7	0	.500	301	390
Buffalo	6	8	0	.429	294	342

Western Division

	W	L	T	Pct.	Pts.	OP
San Diego	12	2	0	.857	396	219
Dallas Texans	6	8	0	.429	334	343
Denver	3	11	0	.214	251	432
Oakland	2	12	0	.143	237	458

AFL championship: Houston 10, SAN DIEGO 3

1960 NFL

Eastern Conference

	W	L	T	Pct.	Pts.	OP
Philadelphia	10	2	0	.833	321	246
Cleveland	8	3	1	.727	362	217
N.Y. Giants	6	4	2	.600	271	261
St. Louis	6	5	1	.545	288	230
Pittsburgh	5	6	1	.455	240	275
Washington	1	9	2	.100	178	309

Western Conference

	W	L	T	Pct.	Pts.	OP
Green Bay	8	4	0	.667	332	209
Detroit	7	5	0	.583	239	212
San Francisco	7	5	0	.583	208	205
Baltimore	6	6	0	.500	288	234
Chicago	5	6	1	.455	194	299
L.A. Rams	4	7	1	.364	265	297
Dallas Cowboys	0	11	1	.000	177	369

NFL championship: PHILADELPHIA 17, Green Bay 13

1960 AFL

Eastern Conference

	W	L	T	Pct.	Pts.	OP
Houston	10	4	0	.714	379	285
N.Y. Titans	7	7	0	.500	382	399
Buffalo	5	8	1	.385	296	303
Boston	5	9	0	.357	286	349

Western Conference

	W	L	T	Pct.	Pts.	OP
L.A. Chargers	10	4	0	.714	373	336
Dallas Texans	8	6	0	.571	362	253
Oakland	6	8	0	.429	319	388
Denver	4	9	1	.308	309	393

AFL championship: HOUSTON 24, L.A. Chargers 16

1959

Eastern Conference

	W	L	T	Pct.	Pts.	OP
N.Y. Giants	10	2	0	.833	284	170
Cleveland	7	5	0	.583	270	214
Philadelphia	7	5	0	.583	268	278
Pittsburgh	6	5	1	.545	257	216
Washington	3	9	0	.250	185	350
Chi. Cardinals	2	10	0	.167	234	324

Western Conference

	W	L	T	Pct.	Pts.	OP
Baltimore	9	3	0	.750	374	251
Chi. Bears	8	4	0	.667	252	196
Green Bay	7	5	0	.583	248	246
San Francisco	7	5	0	.583	255	237
Detroit	3	8	1	.273	203	275
Los Angeles	2	10	0	.167	242	315

NFL championship: BALTIMORE 31, N.Y. Giants 16

1958

Eastern Conference

	W	L	T	Pct.	Pts.	OP
N.Y. Giants	9	3	0	.750	246	183
Cleveland	9	3	0	.750	302	217
Pittsburgh	7	4	1	.636	261	230
Washington	4	7	1	.364	214	268
Chi. Cardinals	2	9	1	.182	261	356
Philadelphia	2	9	1	.182	235	306

Western Conference

	W	L	T	Pct.	Pts.	OP
Baltimore	9	3	0	.750	381	203
Chi. Bears	8	4	0	.667	298	230
Los Angeles	8	4	0	.667	344	278
San Francisco	6	6	0	.500	257	324
Detroit	4	7	1	.364	261	276
Green Bay	1	10	1	.091	193	382

Eastern Conference playoff: N.Y. GIANTS 10, Cleveland 0
NFL championship: Baltimore 23, N.Y. GIANTS 17 (OT)

1957

Eastern Conference

	W	L	T	Pct.	Pts.	OP
Cleveland	9	2	1	.818	269	172
N.Y. Giants	7	5	0	.583	254	211
Pittsburgh	6	6	0	.500	161	178
Washington	5	6	1	.455	251	230
Philadelphia	4	8	0	.333	173	230
Chi. Cardinals	3	9	0	.250	200	299

Western Conference

	W	L	T	Pct.	Pts.	OP
Detroit	8	4	0	.667	251	231
San Francisco	8	4	0	.667	260	264
Baltimore	7	5	0	.583	303	235
Los Angeles	6	6	0	.500	307	278
Chi. Bears	5	7	0	.417	203	211
Green Bay	3	9	0	.250	218	311

Western Conference playoff: Detroit 31, SAN FRANCISCO 27
NFL championship: DETROIT 59, Cleveland 14

1956

Eastern Conference

	W	L	T	Pct.	Pts.	OP
N.Y. Giants	8	3	1	.727	264	197
Chi. Cardinals	7	5	0	.583	240	182
Washington	6	6	0	.500	183	225
Cleveland	5	7	0	.417	167	177
Pittsburgh	5	7	0	.417	217	250
Philadelphia	3	8	1	.273	143	215

Western Conference

	W	L	T	Pct.	Pts.	OP
Chi. Bears	9	2	1	.818	363	246
Detroit	9	3	0	.750	300	188
San Francisco	5	6	1	.455	233	284
Baltimore	5	7	0	.417	270	322
Green Bay	4	8	0	.333	264	342
Los Angeles	4	8	0	.333	291	307

NFL championship: N.Y. GIANTS 47, Chi. Bears 7

1955

Eastern Conference

	W	L	T	Pct.	Pts.	OP
Cleveland	9	2	1	.818	349	218
Washington	8	4	0	.667	246	222
N.Y. Giants	6	5	1	.545	267	223
Chi. Cardinals	4	7	1	.364	224	252
Philadelphia	4	7	1	.364	248	231
Pittsburgh	4	8	0	.333	195	285

Western Conference

	W	L	T	Pct.	Pts.	OP
Los Angeles	8	3	1	.727	260	231
Chi. Bears	8	4	0	.667	294	251
Green Bay	6	6	0	.500	258	276
Baltimore	5	6	1	.455	214	239
San Francisco	4	8	0	.333	216	298
Detroit	3	9	0	.250	230	275

NFL championship: Cleveland 38, LOS ANGELES 14

1954

Eastern Conference

	W	L	T	Pct.	Pts.	OP
Cleveland	9	3	0	.750	336	162
Philadelphia	7	4	1	.636	284	230
N.Y. Giants	7	5	0	.583	293	184
Pittsburgh	5	7	0	.417	219	263
Washington	3	9	0	.250	207	432
Chi. Cardinals	2	10	0	.167	183	347

Western Conference

	W	L	T	Pct.	Pts.	OP
Detroit	9	2	1	.818	337	189
Chi. Bears	8	4	0	.667	301	279
San Francisco	7	4	1	.636	313	251
Los Angeles	6	5	1	.545	314	285
Green Bay	4	8	0	.333	234	251
Baltimore	3	9	0	.250	131	279

NFL championship: CLEVELAND 56, Detroit 10

1953

Eastern Conference

	W	L	T	Pct.	Pts.	OP
Cleveland	11	1	0	.917	348	162
Philadelphia	7	4	1	.636	352	215
Washington	6	5	1	.545	208	215
Pittsburgh	6	6	0	.500	211	263
N.Y. Giants	3	9	0	.250	179	277
Chi. Cardinals	1	10	1	.091	190	337

Western Conference

	W	L	T	Pct.	Pts.	OP
Detroit	10	2	0	.833	271	205
San Francisco	9	3	0	.750	372	237
Los Angeles	8	3	1	.727	366	236
Chi. Bears	3	8	1	.273	218	262
Baltimore	3	9	0	.250	182	350
Green Bay	2	9	1	.182	200	338

NFL championship: DETROIT 17, Cleveland 16

1952

American Conference

	W	L	T	Pct.	Pts.	OP
Cleveland	8	4	0	.667	310	213
N.Y. Giants	7	5	0	.583	234	231
Philadelphia	7	5	0	.583	252	271
Pittsburgh	5	7	0	.417	300	273
Chi. Cardinals	4	8	0	.333	172	221
Washington	4	8	0	.333	240	287

National Conference

	W	L	T	Pct.	Pts.	OP
Detroit	9	3	0	.750	344	192
Los Angeles	9	3	0	.750	349	234
San Francisco	7	5	0	.583	285	221
Green Bay	6	6	0	.500	295	312
Chi. Bears	5	7	0	.417	245	326
Dallas Texans	1	11	0	.083	182	427

National Conference playoff: DETROIT 31, Los Angeles 21
NFL championship: Detroit 17, CLEVELAND 7

1951

American Conference

	W	L	T	Pct.	Pts.	OP
Cleveland	11	1	0	.917	331	152
N.Y. Giants	9	2	1	.818	254	161
Washington	5	7	0	.417	183	296
Pittsburgh	4	7	1	.364	183	235
Philadelphia	4	8	0	.333	234	264
Chi. Cardinals	3	9	0	.250	210	287

National Conference

	W	L	T	Pct.	Pts.	OP
Los Angeles	8	4	0	.667	392	261
Detroit	7	4	1	.636	336	259
San Francisco	7	4	1	.636	255	205
Chi. Bears	7	5	0	.583	286	282
Green Bay	3	9	0	.250	254	375
N.Y. Yanks	1	9	2	.100	241	382

NFL championship: LOS ANGELES 24, Cleveland 17

1950

American Conference

	W	L	T	Pct.	Pts.	OP
Cleveland	10	2	0	.833	310	144
N.Y. Giants	10	2	0	.833	268	150
Philadelphia	6	6	0	.500	254	141
Pittsburgh	6	6	0	.500	180	195
Chi. Cardinals	5	7	0	.417	233	287
Washington	3	9	0	.250	232	326

National Conference

	W	L	T	Pct.	Pts.	OP
Los Angeles	9	3	0	.750	466	309
Chi. Bears	9	3	0	.750	279	207
N.Y. Yanks	7	5	0	.583	366	367
Detroit	6	6	0	.500	321	285
Green Bay	3	9	0	.250	244	406
San Francisco	3	9	0	.250	213	300
Baltimore	1	11	0	.083	213	462

American Conference playoff: CLEVELAND 8, N.Y. Giants 3
National Conference playoff: LOS ANGELES 24, Chi. Bears 14
NFL championship: CLEVELAND 30, Los Angeles 28

1949

Eastern Division

	W	L	T	Pct.	Pts.	OP
Philadelphia	11	1	0	.917	364	134
Pittsburgh	6	5	1	.545	224	214
N.Y. Giants	6	6	0	.500	287	298
Washington	4	7	1	.364	268	339
N.Y. Bulldogs	1	10	1	.091	153	365

Western Division

	W	L	T	Pct.	Pts.	OP
Los Angeles	8	2	2	.800	360	239
Chi. Bears	9	3	0	.750	332	218
Chi. Cardinals	6	5	1	.545	360	301
Detroit	4	8	0	.333	237	259
Green Bay	2	10	0	.167	114	329

NFL championship: Philadelphia 14, LOS ANGELES 0

1948

Eastern Division

	W	L	T	Pct.	Pts.	OP
Philadelphia	9	2	1	.818	376	156
Washington	7	5	0	.583	291	287
N.Y. Giants	4	8	0	.333	297	388
Pittsburgh	4	8	0	.333	200	243
Boston	3	9	0	.250	174	372

Western Division

	W	L	T	Pct.	Pts.	OP
Chi. Cardinals	11	1	0	.917	395	226
Chi. Bears	10	2	0	.833	375	151
Los Angeles	6	5	1	.545	327	269
Green Bay	3	9	0	.250	154	290
Detroit	2	10	0	.167	200	407

NFL championship: PHILADELPHIA 7, Chi. Cardinals 0

1947

Eastern Division

	W	L	T	Pct.	Pts.	OP
Philadelphia	8	4	0	.667	308	242
Pittsburgh	8	4	0	.667	240	259
Boston	4	7	1	.364	168	256
Washington	4	8	0	.333	295	367
N.Y. Giants	2	8	2	.200	190	309

Western Division

	W	L	T	Pct.	Pts.	OP
Chi. Cardinals	9	3	0	.750	306	231
Chi. Bears	8	4	0	.667	363	241
Green Bay	6	5	1	.545	274	210
Los Angeles	6	6	0	.500	259	214
Detroit	3	9	0	.250	231	305

Eastern Division playoff: Philadelphia 21, PITTSBURGH 0
NFL championship: CHI. CARDINALS 28, Philadelphia 21

1946

Eastern Division

	W	L	T	Pct.	Pts.	OP
N.Y. Giants	7	3	1	.700	236	162
Philadelphia	6	5	0	.545	231	220
Washington	5	5	1	.500	171	191
Pittsburgh	5	5	1	.500	136	117
Boston	2	8	1	.200	189	273

Western Division

	W	L	T	Pct.	Pts.	OP
Chi. Bears	8	2	1	.800	289	193
Los Angeles	6	4	1	.600	277	257
Green Bay	6	5	0	.545	148	158
Chi. Cardinals	6	5	0	.545	260	198
Detroit	1	10	0	.091	142	310

NFL championship: Chi. Bears 24, N.Y. GIANTS 14

1945

Eastern Division

	W	L	T	Pct.	Pts.	OP
Washington	8	2	0	.800	209	121
Philadelphia	7	3	0	.700	272	133
N.Y. Giants	3	6	1	.333	179	198
Boston	3	6	1	.333	123	211
Pittsburgh	2	8	0	.200	79	220

Western Division

	W	L	T	Pct.	Pts.	OP
Cleveland	9	1	0	.900	244	136
Detroit	7	3	0	.700	195	194
Green Bay	6	4	0	.600	258	173
Chi. Bears	3	7	0	.300	192	235
Chi. Cardinals	1	9	0	.100	98	228

NFL championship: CLEVELAND 15, Washington 14

1944

Eastern Division

	W	L	T	Pct.	Pts.	OP
N.Y. Giants	8	1	1	.889	206	75
Philadelphia	7	1	2	.875	267	131
Washington	6	3	1	.667	169	180
Boston	2	8	0	.200	82	233
Brooklyn	0	10	0	.000	69	166

Western Division

	W	L	T	Pct.	Pts.	OP
Green Bay	8	2	0	.800	238	141
Chi. Bears	6	3	1	.667	258	172
Detroit	6	3	1	.667	216	151
Cleveland	4	6	0	.400	188	224
Card-Pitt	0	10	0	.000	108	328

NFL championship: Green Bay 14, N.Y. GIANTS 7

1943

Eastern Division

	W	L	T	Pct.	Pts.	OP
Washington	6	3	1	.667	229	137
N.Y. Giants	6	3	1	.667	197	170
Phil-Pitt	5	4	1	.556	225	230
Brooklyn	2	8	0	.200	65	234

Western Division

	W	L	T	Pct.	Pts.	OP
Chi. Bears	8	1	1	.889	303	157
Green Bay	7	2	1	.778	264	172
Detroit	3	6	1	.333	178	218
Chi. Cardinals	0	10	0	.000	95	238

Eastern Division playoff: Washington 28, N.Y. GIANTS 0
NFL championship: CHI. BEARS 41, Washington 21

1942

Eastern Division

	W	L	T	Pct.	Pts.	OP
Washington	10	1	0	.909	227	102
Pittsburgh	7	4	0	.636	167	119
N.Y. Giants	5	5	1	.500	155	139
Brooklyn	3	8	0	.273	100	168
Philadelphia	2	9	0	.182	134	239

Western Division

	W	L	T	Pct.	Pts.	OP
Chi. Bears	11	0	0	1.000	376	84
Green Bay	8	2	1	.800	300	215
Cleveland	5	6	0	.455	150	207
Chi. Cardinals	3	8	0	.273	98	209
Detroit	0	11	0	.000	38	263

NFL championship: WASHINGTON 14, Chi. Bears 6

1941

Eastern Division

	W	L	T	Pct.	Pts.	OP
N.Y. Giants	8	3	0	.727	238	114
Brooklyn	7	4	0	.636	158	127
Washington	6	5	0	.545	176	174
Philadelphia	2	8	1	.200	119	218
Pittsburgh	1	9	1	.100	103	276

Western Division

	W	L	T	Pct.	Pts.	OP
Chi. Bears	10	1	0	.909	396	147
Green Bay	10	1	0	.909	258	120
Detroit	4	6	1	.400	121	195
Chi. Cardinals	3	7	1	.300	127	197
Cleveland	2	9	0	.182	116	244

Western Division playoff: CHI. BEARS 33, Green Bay 14
NFL championship: CHI. BEARS 37, N.Y. Giants 9

1940

Eastern Division

	W	L	T	Pct.	Pts.	OP
Washington	9	2	0	.818	245	142
Brooklyn	8	3	0	.727	186	120
N.Y. Giants	6	4	1	.600	131	133
Pittsburgh	2	7	2	.222	60	178
Philadelphia	1	10	0	.091	111	211

Western Division

	W	L	T	Pct.	Pts.	OP
Chi. Bears	8	3	0	.727	238	152
Green Bay	6	4	1	.600	238	155
Detroit	5	5	1	.500	138	153
Cleveland	4	6	1	.400	171	191
Chi. Cardinals	2	7	2	.222	139	222

NFL championship: Chi. Bears 73, WASHINGTON 0

1939

Eastern Division

	W	L	T	Pct.	Pts.	OP
N.Y. Giants	9	1	1	.900	168	85
Washington	8	2	1	.800	242	94
Brooklyn	4	6	1	.400	108	219
Philadelphia	1	9	1	.100	105	200
Pittsburgh	1	9	1	.100	114	216

Western Division

	W	L	T	Pct.	Pts.	OP
Green Bay	9	2	0	.818	233	153
Chi. Bears	8	3	0	.727	298	157
Detroit	6	5	0	.545	145	150
Cleveland	5	5	1	.500	195	164
Chi. Cardinals	1	10	0	.091	84	254

NFL championship: GREEN BAY 27, N.Y. Giants 0

1938

Eastern Division

	W	L	T	Pct.	Pts.	OP
N.Y. Giants	8	2	1	.800	194	79
Washington	6	3	2	.667	148	154
Brooklyn	4	4	3	.500	131	161
Philadelphia	5	6	0	.455	154	164
Pittsburgh	2	9	0	.182	79	169

Western Division

	W	L	T	Pct.	Pts.	OP
Green Bay	8	3	0	.727	223	118
Detroit	7	4	0	.636	119	108
Chi. Bears	6	5	0	.545	194	148
Cleveland	4	7	0	.364	131	215
Chi. Cardinals	2	9	0	.182	111	168

NFL championship: N.Y. GIANTS 23, Green Bay 17

1937

Eastern Division

	W	L	T	Pct.	Pts.	OP
Washington	8	3	0	.727	195	120
N.Y. Giants	6	3	2	.667	128	109
Pittsburgh	4	7	0	.364	122	145
Brooklyn	3	7	1	.300	82	174
Philadelphia	2	8	1	.200	86	177

Western Division

	W	L	T	Pct.	Pts.	OP
Chi. Bears	9	1	1	.900	201	100
Green Bay	7	4	0	.636	220	122
Detroit	7	4	0	.636	180	105
Chi. Cardinals	5	5	1	.500	135	165
Cleveland	1	10	0	.091	75	207

NFL championship: Washington 28, CHI. BEARS 21

1936

Eastern Division

	W	L	T	Pct.	Pts.	OP
Boston	7	5	0	.583	149	110
Pittsburgh	6	6	0	.500	98	187
N.Y. Giants	5	6	1	.455	115	163
Brooklyn	3	8	1	.273	92	161
Philadelphia	1	11	0	.083	51	206

Western Division

	W	L	T	Pct.	Pts.	OP
Green Bay	10	1	1	.909	248	118
Chi. Bears	9	3	0	.750	222	94
Detroit	8	4	0	.667	235	102
Chi. Cardinals	3	8	1	.273	74	143

NFL championship: Green Bay 21, Boston 6, at Polo Grounds, N.Y.

1935

Eastern Division

	W	L	T	Pct.	Pts.	OP
N.Y. Giants	9	3	0	.750	180	96
Brooklyn	5	6	1	.455	90	141
Pittsburgh	4	8	0	.333	100	209
Boston	2	8	1	.200	65	123
Philadelphia	2	9	0	.182	60	179

Western Division

	W	L	T	Pct.	Pts.	OP
Detroit	7	3	2	.700	191	111
Green Bay	8	4	0	.667	181	96
Chi. Bears	6	4	2	.600	192	106
Chi. Cardinals	6	4	2	.600	99	97

NFL championship: DETROIT 26, N.Y. Giants 7
One game between Boston and Philadelphia was canceled.

1934

Eastern Division

	W	L	T	Pct.	Pts.	OP
N.Y. Giants	8	5	0	.615	147	107
Boston	6	6	0	.500	107	94
Brooklyn	4	7	0	.364	61	153
Philadelphia	4	7	0	.364	127	85
Pittsburgh	2	10	0	.167	51	206

Western Division

	W	L	T	Pct.	Pts.	OP
Chi. Bears	13	0	0	1.000	286	86
Detroit	10	3	0	.769	238	59
Green Bay	7	6	0	.538	156	112
Chi. Cardinals	5	6	0	.455	80	84
St. Louis	1	2	0	.333	27	61
Cincinnati	0	8	0	.000	10	243

NFL championship: N.Y. GIANTS 30, Chi. Bears 13

1933

Eastern Division

	W	L	T	Pct.	Pts.	OP
N.Y. Giants	11	3	0	.786	244	101
Brooklyn	5	4	1	.556	93	54
Boston	5	5	2	.500	103	97
Philadelphia	3	5	1	.375	77	158
Pittsburgh	3	6	2	.333	67	208

NFL championship: CHI. BEARS 23, N.Y. Giants 21

1932

	W	L	T	Pct.
Chicago Bears	7	1	6	.875
Green Bay Packers	10	3	1	.769
Portsmouth Spartans	6	2	4	.750
Boston Braves	4	4	2	.500
New York Giants	4	6	2	.400
Brooklyn Dodgers	3	9	0	.250
Chicago Cardinals	2	6	2	.250
Staten Island Stapletons	2	7	3	.222

Chicago Bears and Portsmouth finished regularly scheduled games tied for first place. Bears won playoff game, which counted in standing, 9-0.

1931

	W	L	T	Pct.
Green Bay Packers	12	2	0	.857
Portsmouth Spartans	11	3	0	.786
Chicago Bears	8	5	0	.615
Chicago Cardinals	5	4	0	.556
New York Giants	7	6	1	.538
Providence Steam Roller	4	4	3	.500
Staten Island Stapletons	4	6	1	.400
Cleveland Indians	2	8	0	.200
Brooklyn Dodgers	2	12	0	.143
Frankford Yellow Jackets	1	6	1	.143

1930

	W	L	T	Pct.
Green Bay Packers	10	3	1	.769
New York Giants	13	4	0	.765
Chicago Bears	9	4	1	.692
Brooklyn Dodgers	7	4	1	.636
Providence Steam Roller	6	4	1	.600
Staten Island Stapletons	5	5	2	.500
Chicago Cardinals	5	6	2	.455
Portsmouth Spartans	5	6	3	.455
Frankford Yellow Jackets	4	13	1	.222
Minneapolis Red Jackets	1	7	1	.125
Newark Tornadoes	1	10	1	.091

1929

	W	L	T	Pct.
Green Bay Packers	12	0	1	1.000
New York Giants	13	1	1	.929
Frankford Yellow Jackets	9	4	5	.692
Chicago Cardinals	6	6	1	.500
Boston Bulldogs	4	4	0	.500
Orange Tornadoes	3	4	4	.429
Staten Island Stapletons	3	4	3	.429
Providence Steam Roller	4	6	2	.400
Chicago Bears	4	9	2	.308
Buffalo Bisons	1	7	1	.125
Minneapolis Red Jackets	1	9	0	.100
Dayton Triangles	0	6	0	.000

1928

	W	L	T	Pct.
Providence Steam Roller	8	1	2	.889
Frankford Yellow Jackets	11	3	2	.786
Detroit Wolverines	7	2	1	.778
Green Bay Packers	6	4	3	.600
Chicago Bears	7	5	1	.583
New York Giants	4	7	2	.364
New York Yankees	4	8	1	.333
Pottsville Maroons	2	8	0	.200
Chicago Cardinals	1	5	0	.167
Dayton Triangles	0	7	0	.000

1927

	W	L	T	Pct.
New York Giants	11	1	1	.917
Green Bay Packers	7	2	1	.778
Chicago Bears	9	3	2	.750
Cleveland Bulldogs	8	4	1	.667
Providence Steam Roller	8	5	1	.615
New York Yankees	7	8	1	.467
Frankford Yellow Jackets	6	9	3	.400
Pottsville Maroons	5	8	0	.385
Chicago Cardinals	3	7	1	.300
Dayton Triangles	1	6	1	.143
Duluth Eskimos	1	8	0	.111
Buffalo Bisons	0	5	0	.000

Western Division

	W	L	T	Pct.	Pts.	OP
Chi. Bears	10	2	1	.833	133	82
Portsmouth	6	5	0	.545	128	87
Green Bay	5	7	1	.417	170	107
Cincinnati	3	6	1	.333	38	110
Chi. Cardinals	1	9	1	.100	52	101

1926

	W	L	T	Pct.
Frankford Yellow Jackets	14	1	1	.933
Chicago Bears	12	1	3	.923
Pottsville Maroons	10	2	1	.833
Kansas City Cowboys	8	3	0	.727
Green Bay Packers	7	3	3	.700
Los Angeles Buccaneers	6	3	1	.667
New York Giants	8	4	1	.667
Duluth Eskimos	6	5	3	.545
Buffalo Rangers	4	4	2	.500
Chicago Cardinals	5	6	1	.455
Providence Steam Roller	5	7	1	.417
Detroit Panthers	4	6	2	.400
Hartford Blues	3	7	0	.300
Brooklyn Lions	3	8	0	.273
Milwaukee Badgers	2	7	0	.222
Akron Pros	1	4	3	.200
Dayton Triangles	1	4	1	.200
Racine Tornadoes	1	4	0	.200
Columbus Tigers	1	6	0	.143
Canton Bulldogs	1	9	3	.100
Hammond Pros	0	4	0	.000
Louisville Colonels	0	4	0	.000

1925

	W	L	T	Pct.
Chicago Cardinals	11	2	1	.846
Pottsville Maroons	10	2	0	.833
Detroit Panthers	8	2	2	.800
New York Giants	8	4	0	.667
Akron Indians	4	2	2	.667
Frankford Yellow Jackets	13	7	0	.650
Chicago Bears	9	5	3	.643
Rock Island Independents	5	3	3	.625
Green Bay Packers	8	5	0	.615
Providence Steam Roller	6	5	1	.545
Canton Bulldogs	4	4	0	.500
Cleveland Bulldogs	5	8	1	.385
Kansas City Cowboys	2	5	1	.286
Hammond Pros	1	4	0	.250
Buffalo Bisons	1	6	2	.143
Duluth Kelleys	0	3	0	.000
Rochester Jeffersons	0	6	1	.000
Milwaukee Badgers	0	6	0	.000
Dayton Triangles	0	7	1	.000
Columbus Tigers	0	9	0	.000

1924

	W	L	T	Pct.
Cleveland Bulldogs	7	1	1	.875
Chicago Bears	6	1	4	.857
Frankford Yellow Jackets	11	2	1	.846
Duluth Kelleys	5	1	0	.833
Rock Island Independents	6	2	2	.750
Green Bay Packers	7	4	0	.636
Racine Legion	4	3	3	.571
Chicago Cardinals	5	4	1	.556
Buffalo Bisons	6	5	0	.545
Columbus Tigers	4	4	0	.500
Hammond Pros	2	2	1	.500
Milwaukee Badgers	5	8	0	.385
Akron Indians	2	6	0	.333
Dayton Triangles	2	6	0	.333
Kansas City Blues	2	7	0	.222
Kenosha Maroons	0	5	1	.000
Minneapolis Marines	0	6	0	.000
Rochester Jeffersons	0	7	0	.000

1923

	W	L	T	Pct.
Canton Bulldogs	11	0	1	1.000
Chicago Bears	9	2	1	.818
Green Bay Packers	7	2	1	.778
Milwaukee Badgers	7	2	3	.778
Cleveland Indians	3	1	3	.750
Chicago Cardinals	8	4	0	.667
Duluth Kelleys	4	3	0	.571
Columbus Tigers	5	4	1	.556
Buffalo All-Americans	4	4	3	.500
Racine Legion	4	4	2	.500
Toledo Maroons	2	3	2	.400
Rock Island Independents	2	3	3	.400
Minneapolis Marines	2	5	2	.286
St. Louis All-Stars	1	4	2	.200
Hammond Pros	1	5	1	.167
Dayton Triangles	1	6	1	.143
Akron Indians	1	6	0	.143
Oorang Indians	1	10	0	.091
Rochester Jeffersons	0	2	0	.000
Louisville Brecks	0	3	0	.000

1922

	W	L	T	Pct.
Canton Bulldogs	10	0	2	1.000
Chicago Bears	9	3	0	.750
Chicago Cardinals	8	3	0	.727
Toledo Maroons	5	2	2	.714
Rock Island Independents	4	2	1	.667
Racine Legion	6	4	1	.600
Dayton Triangles	4	3	1	.571
Green Bay Packers	4	3	3	.571
Buffalo All-Americans	5	4	1	.556
Akron Pros	3	5	2	.375
Milwaukee Badgers	2	4	3	.333
Oorang Indians	2	6	0	.250
Minneapolis Marines	1	3	0	.250
Louisville Brecks	1	3	0	.250
Evansville Crimson Giants	0	3	0	.000
Rochester Jeffersons	0	4	1	.000
Hammond Pros	0	5	1	.000
Columbus Panhandles	0	7	0	.000

1921

	W	L	T	Pct.
Chicago Staleys	9	1	1	.900
Buffalo All-Americans	9	1	2	.900
Akron Pros	8	3	1	.727
Canton Bulldogs	5	2	3	.714
Rock Island Independents	4	2	1	.667
Evansville Crimson Giants	3	2	0	.600
Green Bay Packers	3	2	1	.600
Dayton Triangles	4	4	1	.500
Chicago Cardinals	3	3	2	.500
Rochester Jeffersons	2	3	0	.400
Cleveland Indians	3	5	0	.375
Washington Senators	1	2	0	.333
Cincinnati Celts	1	3	0	.250
Hammond Pros	1	3	1	.250
Minneapolis Marines	1	3	1	.250
Detroit Heralds	1	5	1	.167
Columbus Panhandles	1	8	0	.111
Tonawanda Kardex	0	1	0	.000
Muncie Flyers	0	2	0	.000
Louisville Brecks	0	2	0	.000
New York Giants	0	2	0	.000

1920

	W	L	T	Pct.
Akron Pros	8	0	3	1.000
Decatur Staleys	10	1	2	.909
Buffalo All-Americans	9	1	1	.900
Chicago Cardinals	6	2	2	.750
Rock Island Independents	6	2	2	.750
Dayton Triangles	5	2	2	.714
Rochester Jeffersons	6	3	2	.667
Canton Bulldogs	7	4	2	.636
Detroit Heralds	2	3	3	.400
Cleveland Tigers	2	4	2	.333
Chicago Tigers	2	5	1	.286
Hammond Pros	2	5	0	.286
Columbus Panhandles	2	6	2	.250
Muncie Flyers	0	1	0	.000

RS = REGULAR SEASON
PS = POSTSEASON

ATLANTA vs. BUFFALO
RS: Falcons lead series, 3-2
1973—Bills, 17-6 (A)
1977—Bills, 3-0 (B)
1980—Falcons, 30-14 (B)
1983—Falcons, 31-14 (A)
1989—Falcons, 30-28 (A)
(Points—Falcons 97, Bills 76)

ATLANTA vs. CHICAGO
RS: Falcons lead series, 9-6
1966—Bears, 23-6 (C)
1967—Bears, 23-14 (A)
1968—Falcons, 16-13 (C)
1969—Falcons, 48-31 (A)
1970—Bears, 23-14 (A)
1972—Falcons, 37-21 (C)
1973—Falcons, 46-6 (A)
1974—Falcons, 13-10 (A)
1976—Falcons, 10-0 (C)
1977—Falcons, 16-10 (A)
1978—Bears, 13-7 (C)
1980—Falcons, 28-17 (A)
1983—Falcons, 20-17 (C)
1985—Bears, 36-0 (C)
1986—Bears, 13-10 (A)
(Points—Falcons 285, Bears 256)

ATLANTA vs. CINCINNATI
RS: Bengals lead series, 5-1
1971—Falcons, 9-6 (C)
1975—Bengals, 21-14 (A)
1978—Bengals, 37-7 (C)
1981—Bengals, 30-28 (A)
1984—Bengals, 35-14 (C)
1987—Bengals, 16-10 (A)
(Points—Bengals 145, Falcons 82)

ATLANTA vs. CLEVELAND
RS: Browns lead series, 7-1
1966—Browns, 49-17 (A)
1968—Browns, 30-7 (C)
1971—Falcons, 31-14 (C)
1976—Browns, 20-17 (A)
1978—Browns, 24-16 (A)
1981—Browns, 28-17 (C)
1984—Browns, 23-7 (A)
1987—Browns, 38-3 (C)
(Points—Browns 226, Falcons 115)

ATLANTA vs. DALLAS
RS: Cowboys lead series, 7-4
PS: Cowboys lead series, 2-0
1966—Cowboys, 47-14 (A)
1967—Cowboys, 37-7 (D)
1969—Cowboys, 24-17 (A)
1970—Cowboys, 13-0 (A)
1974—Cowboys, 24-0 (A)
1976—Falcons, 17-10 (A)
1978—*Cowboys, 27-20 (D)
1980—*Cowboys, 30-27 (A)
1985—Cowboys, 24-10 (D)
1986—Falcons, 37-35 (A)
1987—Falcons, 21-10 (D)
1988—Cowboys, 26-20 (D)
1989—Falcons 27-21 (A)
(Points—Cowboys 328, Falcons 217)
*NFC Divisional Playoff

ATLANTA vs. DENVER
RS: Broncos lead series, 4-3
1970—Broncos, 24-10 (D)
1972—Falcons, 23-20 (A)
1975—Falcons, 35-21 (A)
1979—Broncos, 20-17 (A) OT
1982—Falcons, 34-27 (D)
1985—Broncos, 44-28 (A)
1988—Broncos, 30-14 (D)
(Points—Broncos 186, Falcons 161)

ATLANTA vs. DETROIT
RS: Lions lead series, 15-5
1966—Lions, 28-10 (D)
1967—Lions, 24-3 (D)
1968—Lions, 24-7 (A)
1969—Lions, 27-21 (D)
1971—Lions, 41-38 (D)
1972—Lions, 26-23 (A)
1973—Lions, 31-6 (D)
1975—Lions, 17-14 (A)
1976—Lions, 24-10 (D)
1977—Falcons, 17-6 (A)
1978—Falcons, 14-0 (A)
1979—Lions, 24-23 (D)
1980—Falcons, 43-28 (A)
1983—Falcons, 30-14 (D)
1984—Lions, 27-24 (A) OT
1985—Lions, 28-27 (A)
1986—Falcons, 20-6 (D)
1987—Lions, 30-13 (A)
1988—Lions, 31-17 (D)
1989—Lions, 31-24 (A)
(Points—Lions 467, Falcons 384)

ATLANTA vs. GREEN BAY
RS: Packers lead series, 9-7
1966—Packers, 56-3 (Mil)
1967—Packers, 23-0 (Mil)
1968—Packers, 38-7 (A)
1969—Packers, 28-10 (GB)
1970—Packers, 27-24 (GB)
1971—Falcons, 28-21 (A)
1972—Falcons, 10-9 (Mil)
1974—Falcons, 10-3 (A)
1975—Packers, 22-13 (GB)
1976—Packers, 24-20 (A)
1979—Falcons, 25-7 (A)
1981—Falcons, 31-17 (GB)
1982—Packers, 38-7 (A)
1983—Falcons, 47-41 (A) OT
1988—Falcons, 20-0 (A)
1989—Packers, 23-21 (Mil)
(Points—Packers 377, Falcons 276)

ATLANTA vs. HOUSTON
RS: Falcons lead series, 4-2
1972—Falcons, 20-10 (A)
1976—Oilers, 20-14 (H)
1978—Falcons, 20-14 (A)
1981—Falcons, 31-27 (H)
1984—Falcons, 42-10 (A)
1987—Oilers, 37-33 (H)
(Points—Falcons 160, Oilers 118)

ATLANTA vs. *INDIANAPOLIS
RS: Colts lead series, 10-0
1966—Colts, 19-7 (A)
1967—Colts, 38-31 (B)
       Colts, 49-7 (A)
1968—Colts, 28-20 (A)
       Colts, 44-0 (B)
1969—Colts, 21-14 (A)
       Colts, 13-6 (B)
1974—Colts, 17-7 (A)
1986—Colts, 28-23 (A)
1989—Colts, 13-9 (I)
(Points—Colts 270, Falcons 124)
*Franchise in Baltimore prior to 1984

ATLANTA vs. KANSAS CITY
RS: Chiefs lead series, 2-0
1972—Chiefs, 17-14 (A)
1985—Chiefs, 38-10 (KC)
(Points—Chiefs 55, Falcons 24)

ATLANTA vs. *L.A. RAIDERS
RS: Raiders lead series, 4-2
1971—Falcons, 24-13 (A)
1975—Raiders, 37-34 (O) OT
1979—Raiders, 50-19 (O)
1982—Raiders, 38-14 (A)
1985—Raiders, 34-24 (A)
1988—Raiders, 12-6 (LA)
(Points—Raiders 178, Falcons 127)
*Franchise in Oakland prior to 1982

ATLANTA vs. L.A. RAMS
RS: Rams lead series, 34-10-2
1966—Rams, 19-14 (A)
1967—Rams, 31-3 (A)
       Rams, 20-3 (LA)
1968—Rams, 27-14 (LA)
       Rams, 17-10 (A)
1969—Rams, 17-7 (LA)
       Rams, 38-6 (A)
1970—Tie, 10-10 (LA)
       Rams, 17-7 (A)
1971—Tie, 20-20 (LA)
       Rams, 24-16 (A)
1972—Falcons, 31-3 (A)
       Rams, 20-7 (LA)
1973—Rams, 31-0 (A)
       Falcons, 15-13 (A)
1974—Rams, 21-0 (LA)
       Rams, 30-7 (A)
1975—Rams, 22-7 (LA)
       Rams, 16-7 (A)
1976—Rams, 30-14 (A)
       Rams, 59-0 (LA)
1977—Falcons, 17-6 (A)
       Rams, 23-7 (LA)
1978—Rams, 10-0 (LA)
       Falcons, 15-7 (A)
1979—Rams, 20-14 (LA)
       Rams, 34-13 (A)
1980—Falcons, 13-10 (A)
       Rams, 20-17 (LA) OT
1981—Rams, 37-35 (A)
       Rams, 21-16 (LA)
1982—Falcons, 34-17 (A)
1983—Rams, 27-21 (LA)
       Rams, 36-13 (A)
1984—Rams, 30-28 (LA)
       Rams, 24-10 (A)
1985—Rams, 17-6 (LA)
       Falcons, 30-14 (A)
1986—Rams, 26-14 (A)
       Rams, 14-7 (LA)

1987—Falcons, 24-20 (A)
       Rams, 33-0 (LA)
1988—Rams, 33-0 (A)
       Rams, 22-7 (LA)
1989—Rams, 31-21 (A)
       Rams, 26-14 (LA)
(Points—Rams 1,029, Falcons 588)

ATLANTA vs. MIAMI
RS: Dolphins lead series, 4-1
1970—Dolphins, 20-7 (A)
1974—Dolphins, 42-7 (M)
1980—Dolphins, 20-17 (A)
1983—Dolphins, 31-24 (M)
1986—Falcons, 20-14 (M)
(Points—Dolphins 127, Falcons 75)

ATLANTA vs. MINNESOTA
RS: Vikings lead series, 10-6
PS: Vikings lead series, 1-0
1966—Falcons, 20-13 (M)
1967—Falcons, 21-20 (A)
1968—Vikings, 47-7 (M)
1969—Falcons, 10-3 (A)
1970—Vikings, 37-7 (A)
1971—Vikings, 24-7 (M)
1973—Falcons, 20-14 (A)
1974—Vikings, 23-10 (M)
1975—Vikings, 38-0 (M)
1977—Vikings, 14-7 (A)
1980—Vikings, 24-23 (M)
1982—*Vikings, 30-24 (M)
1984—Vikings, 27-20 (M)
1985—Falcons, 14-13 (M)
1987—Vikings, 24-13 (M)
1989—Vikings, 43-17 (M)
(Points—Vikings 424, Falcons 251)
*NFC First Round Playoff

ATLANTA vs. NEW ENGLAND
RS: Series tied, 3-3
1972—Patriots, 21-20 (NE)
1977—Patriots, 16-10 (A)
1980—Falcons, 37-21 (NE)
1983—Falcons, 24-13 (A)
1986—Patriots, 25-17 (NE)
1989—Falcons, 16-15 (A)
(Points—Falcons 124, Patriots 111)

ATLANTA vs. NEW ORLEANS
RS: Falcons lead series, 24-17
1967—Saints, 27-24 (NO)
1969—Falcons, 45-17 (A)
1970—Falcons, 14-3 (NO)
       Falcons, 32-14 (A)
1971—Falcons, 28-6 (A)
       Falcons, 24-20 (NO)
1972—Falcons, 21-14 (NO)
       Falcons, 36-20 (A)
1973—Falcons, 62-7 (NO)
       Falcons, 14-10 (A)
1974—Saints, 14-13 (NO)
       Saints, 13-3 (A)
1975—Falcons, 14-7 (A)
       Saints, 23-7 (NO)
1976—Saints, 30-0 (NO)
       Falcons, 23-20 (A)
1977—Saints, 21-20 (NO)
       Falcons, 35-7 (A)
1978—Falcons, 20-17 (NO)
       Falcons, 20-17 (A)
1979—Falcons, 40-34 (NO) OT
       Saints, 37-6 (A)
1980—Falcons, 41-14 (NO)
       Falcons, 31-13 (A)
1981—Falcons, 27-0 (A)
       Falcons, 41-10 (NO)
1982—Falcons, 35-0 (A)
       Saints, 35-6 (NO)
1983—Saints, 19-17 (A)
       Saints, 27-10 (NO)
1984—Falcons, 36-28 (NO)
       Saints, 17-13 (A)
1985—Falcons, 31-24 (NO)
       Falcons, 16-10 (NO)
1986—Falcons, 31-10 (NO)
       Saints, 14-9 (A)
1987—Saints, 38-0 (A)
1988—Saints, 29-21 (A)
       Saints, 10-9 (NO)
1989—Saints, 20-13 (NO)
       Saints, 26-17 (A)
(Points—Falcons 905, Saints 722)

ATLANTA vs. N.Y. GIANTS
RS: Series tied, 6-6
1966—Falcons, 27-16 (NY)
1968—Falcons, 24-21 (A)
1971—Giants, 21-17 (A)
1974—Falcons, 14-7 (New Haven)
1977—Falcons, 17-3 (A)
1978—Falcons, 23-20 (A)
1979—Giants, 24-3 (NY)

1981—Giants, 27-24 (A) OT
1982—Falcons, 16-14 (NY)
1983—Giants, 16-13 (A) OT
1984—Giants, 19-7 (A)
1988—Giants, 23-16 (A)
(Points—Giants 211, Falcons 201)

ATLANTA vs. N.Y. JETS
RS: Jets lead series, 3-2
1973—Falcons, 28-20 (NY)
1980—Jets, 14-7 (A)
1983—Jets, 27-21 (NY)
1986—Jets, 28-14 (A)
1989—Jets, 27-7 (NY)
(Points—Jets 110, Falcons 83)

ATLANTA vs. PHILADELPHIA
RS: Eagles lead series, 7-6-1
PS: Falcons lead series, 1-0
1966—Eagles, 23-10 (A)
1967—Eagles, 38-7 (A)
1969—Falcons, 27-3 (P)
1970—Tie, 13-13 (P)
1973—Falcons, 44-27 (P)
1976—Falcons, 14-13 (A)
1978—*Falcons, 14-13 (A)
1979—Falcons, 14-10 (P)
1980—Falcons, 20-17 (P)
1981—Eagles, 16-13 (P)
1983—Eagles, 28-24 (P)
1984—Falcons, 26-10 (A)
1985—Eagles, 23-17 (P) OT
1986—Eagles, 16-0 (A)
1988—Falcons, 27-24 (P)
(Points—Eagles 275, Falcons 269)
*NFC First Round Playoff

ATLANTA vs. *PHOENIX
RS: Cardinals lead series, 8-4
1966—Falcons, 16-10 (A)
1968—Cardinals, 17-12 (StL)
1971—Cardinals, 26-9 (A)
1973—Falcons, 32-10 (A)
1975—Cardinals, 23-20 (StL)
1978—Cardinals, 42-21 (StL)
1980—Falcons, 33-27 (StL) OT
1981—Falcons, 41-20 (A)
1982—Cardinals, 23-20 (A)
1986—Falcons, 33-13 (A)
1987—Cardinals, 34-21 (A)
1989—Cardinals, 34-20 (P)
(Points—Cardinals 301, Falcons 256)
*Franchise in St. Louis prior to 1988

ATLANTA vs. PITTSBURGH
RS: Steelers lead series, 7-1
1966—Steelers, 57-33 (A)
1968—Steelers, 41-21 (A)
1970—Falcons, 27-16 (A)
1974—Steelers, 24-17 (P)
1978—Steelers, 31-7 (P)
1981—Steelers, 34-20 (A)
1984—Steelers, 35-10 (P)
1987—Steelers, 28-12 (A)
(Points—Steelers 266, Falcons 147)

ATLANTA vs. SAN DIEGO
RS: Falcons lead series, 2-1
1973—Falcons, 41-0 (SD)
1979—Falcons, 28-26 (SD)
1988—Chargers, 10-7 (A)
(Points—Falcons 76, Chargers 36)

ATLANTA vs. SAN FRANCISCO
RS: 49ers lead series, 27-18-1
1966—49ers, 44-7 (A)
1967—49ers, 38-7 (SF)
       49ers, 34-28 (A)
1968—49ers, 28-13 (SF)
       49ers, 14-12 (A)
1969—49ers, 24-12 (A)
       Falcons, 21-7 (SF)
1970—Falcons, 21-20 (A)
       49ers, 24-20 (SF)
1971—Falcons, 20-17 (A)
       49ers, 24-3 (SF)
1972—49ers, 49-14 (A)
       49ers, 20-0 (SF)
1973—49ers, 13-9 (A)
       Falcons, 17-3 (SF)
1974—49ers, 16-10 (A)
       Falcons, 27-0 (SF)
1975—Falcons, 17-3 (SF)
       Falcons, 31-9 (A)
1976—49ers, 15-0 (SF)
       Falcons, 21-16 (A)
1977—Falcons, 7-0 (SF)
       49ers, 10-3 (A)
1978—Falcons, 20-17 (SF)
       Falcons, 21-10 (A)
1979—49ers, 20-15 (SF)
       Falcons, 31-21 (A)
1980—Falcons, 20-17 (SF)
       Falcons, 35-10 (A)
1981—Falcons, 34-17 (A)

49ers, 17-14 (SF)
1982—Falcons, 17-7 (SF)
1983—49ers, 24-20 (SF)
  Falcons, 28-24 (A)
1984—49ers, 14-5 (SF)
  49ers, 35-17 (A)
1985—49ers, 35-16 (SF)
  49ers, 38-17 (A)
1986—Tie, 10-10 (A) OT
  49ers, 20-0 (SF)
1987—49ers, 25-17 (A)
  49ers, 35-7 (SF)
1988—Falcons, 34-17 (SF)
  49ers, 13-3 (A)
1989—49ers, 45-3 (SF)
  49ers, 23-10 (A)
(Points—49ers 937, Falcons 699)

ATLANTA vs. SEATTLE
RS: Seahawks lead series, 4-0
1976—Seahawks, 30-13 (S)
1979—Seahawks, 31-28 (A)
1985—Seahawks, 30-26 (S)
1988—Seahawks, 31-20 (A)
(Points—Seahawks 122, Falcons 87)

ATLANTA vs. TAMPA BAY
RS: Series tied, 4-4
1977—Falcons, 17-0 (TB)
1978—Buccaneers, 14-9 (TB)
1979—Falcons, 17-14 (A)
1981—Buccaneers, 24-23 (TB)
1984—Buccaneers, 23-6 (TB)
1986—Falcons, 23-20 (TB) OT
1987—Buccaneers, 48-10 (TB)
1988—Falcons, 17-10 (A)
(Points—Buccaneers 153, Falcons 122)

ATLANTA vs. WASHINGTON
RS: Redskins lead series, 10-3-1
1966—Redskins, 33-20 (W)
1967—Tie, 20-20 (A)
1969—Redskins, 27-20 (W)
1972—Redskins, 24-13 (W)
1975—Redskins, 30-27 (A)
1977—Redskins, 10-6 (W)
1978—Falcons, 20-17 (A)
1979—Redskins, 16-7 (A)
1980—Falcons, 10-6 (A)
1983—Redskins, 37-21 (A)
1984—Redskins, 27-14 (W)
1985—Redskins, 44-10 (A)
1987—Falcons, 21-20 (A)
1989—Redskins, 31-30 (A)
(Points—Redskins 342, Falcons 239)

BUFFALO vs. ATLANTA
RS: Falcons lead series, 3-2;
See Atlanta vs. Buffalo

BUFFALO vs. CHICAGO
RS: Bears lead series, 3-1
1970—Bears, 31-13 (C)
1974—Bills, 16-6 (B)
1979—Bears, 7-0 (B)
1988—Bears, 24-3 (C)
(Points—Bears 68, Bills 32)

BUFFALO vs. CINCINNATI
RS: Bengals lead series, 9-6
PS: Bengals lead series, 2-0
1968—Bengals, 34-23 (C)
1969—Bills, 16-13 (B)
1970—Bengals, 43-14 (B)
1973—Bengals, 16-13 (B)
1975—Bengals, 33-24 (C)
1978—Bills, 5-0 (B)
1979—Bills, 51-24 (B)
1980—Bills, 14-0 (C)
1981—Bengals, 27-24 (C) OT
  *Bengals, 28-21 (C)
1983—Bills, 10-6 (C)
1984—Bengals, 52-21 (C)
1985—Bengals, 23-17 (B)
1986—Bengals, 36-33 (C) OT
1988—Bengals, 35-21 (C)
  **Bengals, 21-10 (C)
1989—Bills, 24-7 (B)
(Points—Bengals 398, Bills 341)
*AFC Divisional Playoff
**AFC Championship

BUFFALO vs. CLEVELAND
RS: Browns lead series, 7-2
PS: Browns lead series, 1-0
1972—Browns, 27-10 (C)
1974—Bills, 15-10 (C)
1977—Browns, 27-16 (B)
1978—Browns, 41-20 (C)
1981—Bills, 22-13 (B)
1984—Browns, 13-10 (B)
1985—Browns, 17-7 (C)
1986—Browns, 21-17 (B)
1987—Browns, 27-21 (C)
1989—*Browns, 34-30 (C)
(Points—Browns 230, Bills 168)
*AFC Divisional Playoff

BUFFALO vs. DALLAS
RS: Cowboys lead series, 3-1
1971—Cowboys, 49-37 (B)
1976—Cowboys, 17-10 (D)
1981—Cowboys, 27-14 (D)
1984—Bills, 14-3 (B)
(Points—Cowboys 96, Bills 75)

BUFFALO vs. DENVER
RS: Bills lead series, 14-10-1
1960—Broncos, 27-21 (B)
  Tie, 38-38 (D)
1961—Broncos, 22-10 (B)
  Bills, 23-10 (D)
1962—Broncos, 23-20 (B)
  Bills, 45-38 (D)
1963—Bills, 30-28 (D)
  Bills, 27-17 (B)
1964—Bills, 30-13 (B)
  Bills, 30-19 (D)
1965—Bills, 30-15 (D)
  Bills, 31-13 (B)
1966—Bills, 38-21 (B)
1967—Bills, 17-16 (B)
  Broncos, 21-20 (B)
1968—Broncos, 34-32 (D)
1969—Bills, 41-28 (B)
1970—Broncos, 25-10 (B)
1975—Bills, 38-14 (B)
1977—Broncos, 26-6 (D)
1979—Broncos, 19-16 (B)
1981—Bills, 9-7 (B)
1984—Broncos, 37-7 (B)
1987—Bills, 21-14 (B)
1989—Broncos, 28-14 (B)
(Points—Bills 604, Broncos 553)

BUFFALO vs. DETROIT
RS: Series tied, 1-1-1
1972—Tie, 21-21 (B)
1976—Lions, 27-14 (D)
1979—Bills, 20-17 (D)
(Points—Lions 65, Bills 55)

BUFFALO vs. GREEN BAY
RS: Bills lead series, 3-1
1974—Bills, 27-7 (GB)
1979—Bills, 19-12 (B)
1982—Packers, 33-21 (Mil)
1988—Bills, 28-0 (B)
(Points—Bills 95, Packers 52)

BUFFALO vs. HOUSTON
RS: Oilers lead series, 18-11
PS: Bills lead series, 1-0
1960—Bills, 25-24 (B)
  Oilers, 31-23 (H)
1961—Bills, 22-12 (H)
  Oilers, 28-16 (B)
1962—Oilers, 28-23 (B)
  Oilers, 17-14 (H)
1963—Oilers, 31-20 (B)
  Oilers, 28-14 (H)
1964—Bills, 48-17 (H)
  Bills, 24-10 (B)
1965—Oilers, 19-17 (B)
  Bills, 29-18 (H)
1966—Bills, 27-20 (B)
  Bills, 42-20 (H)
1967—Oilers, 20-3 (B)
  Oilers, 10-3 (H)
1968—Oilers, 30-7 (H)
  Oilers, 35-6 (H)
1969—Oilers, 17-3 (B)
  Oilers, 28-14 (H)
1971—Oilers, 20-14 (B)
1974—Oilers, 21-9 (B)
1976—Oilers, 13-3 (B)
1978—Oilers, 17-10 (H)
1983—Bills, 30-13 (B)
1985—Bills, 20-0 (B)
1986—Oilers, 16-7 (H)
1987—Bills, 34-30 (H)
1988—*Bills, 17-10 (B)
1989—Bills, 47-41 (H) OT
(Points—Oilers 624, Bills 571)
*AFC Divisional Playoff

BUFFALO vs. INDIANAPOLIS
RS: Series tied, 19-19-1
1970—Tie, 17-17 (Balt)
  Colts, 20-14 (Buff)
1971—Bills, 43-0 (Buff)
  Colts, 24-0 (Balt)
1972—Colts, 17-0 (Buff)
  Colts, 35-7 (Balt)
1973—Bills, 31-13 (Buff)
  Bills, 24-17 (Balt)
1974—Bills, 6-0 (Buff)
1975—Bills, 38-31 (Balt)
  Colts, 42-35 (Buff)
1976—Colts, 31-13 (Buff)
  Colts, 58-20 (Balt)
1977—Colts, 17-14 (Balt)
  Colts, 31-13 (Buff)
1978—Bills, 24-17 (Balt)
  Bills, 21-14 (Balt)
1979—Bills, 31-13 (Balt)
  Colts, 14-13 (Buff)
1980—Colts, 17-12 (Buff)
  Colts, 28-24 (Balt)
1981—Bills, 35-3 (Balt)
  Bills, 23-17 (Buff)
1982—Bills, 20-0 (Buff)
1983—Bills, 28-23 (Buff)
  Bills, 30-7 (Balt)
1984—Colts, 31-17 (I)
  Bills, 21-15 (Buff)
1985—Colts, 49-17 (I)
  Bills, 21-9 (Buff)
1986—Bills, 24-13 (Buff)
  Colts, 24-14 (I)
1987—Colts, 47-6 (Buff)
  Bills, 27-3 (I)
1988—Bills, 34-23 (Buff)
  Colts, 17-14 (I)
1989—Colts, 37-14 (I)
  Bills, 30-7 (Buff)
(Points—Colts 838, Bills 759)
*Franchise in Baltimore prior to 1984

BUFFALO vs. *KANSAS CITY
RS: Bills lead series, 15-11-1
PS: Chiefs lead series, 1-0
1960—Texans, 45-28 (B)
  Texans, 24-7 (D)
1961—Bills, 27-24 (B)
  Bills, 30-20 (D)
1962—Texans, 41-21 (D)
  Bills, 23-14 (B)
1963—Tie, 27-27 (B)
  Bills, 35-26 (KC)
1964—Bills, 34-17 (B)
  Bills, 35-22 (KC)
1965—Bills, 23-7 (KC)
  Bills, 34-25 (B)
1966—Chiefs, 42-20 (B)
  Bills, 29-14 (KC)
  **Chiefs, 31-7 (B)
1967—Chiefs, 23-13 (KC)
1968—Chiefs, 18-7 (B)
1969—Chiefs, 29-7 (B)
  Chiefs, 22-19 (KC)
1971—Chiefs, 22-9 (KC)
1973—Bills, 23-14 (B)
1976—Bills, 50-17 (B)
1978—Bills, 28-13 (B)
  Chiefs, 14-10 (KC)
1982—Bills, 14-9 (B)
1983—Bills, 14-9 (KC)
1986—Chiefs, 20-17 (B)
  Bills, 17-14 (KC)
(Points—Chiefs 608, Bills 603)
*Franchise in Dallas prior to 1963 and known as Texans
**AFL Championship

BUFFALO vs. *L.A. RAIDERS
RS: Raiders lead series, 13-12
1960—Bills, 38-9 (B)
  Raiders, 20-7 (O)
1961—Bills, 31-22 (B)
  Bills, 26-21 (O)
1962—Bills, 14-6 (B)
  Bills, 10-6 (O)
1963—Raiders, 35-17 (O)
  Bills, 12-0 (B)
1964—Bills, 23-20 (B)
  Raiders, 16-13 (O)
1965—Bills, 17-12 (B)
  Bills, 17-14 (O)
1966—Bills, 31-10 (O)
1967—Raiders, 24-20 (B)
  Raiders, 28-21 (O)
1968—Raiders, 48-6 (B)
  Raiders, 13-10 (O)
1969—Raiders, 50-21 (O)
1972—Raiders, 28-16 (O)
1974—Bills, 21-20 (B)
1977—Raiders, 34-13 (O)
1980—Bills, 24-7 (B)
1983—Raiders, 27-24 (B)
1987—Raiders, 34-21 (LA)
1988—Bills, 37-21 (B)
(Points—Raiders 534, Bills 481)
*Franchise in Oakland prior to 1982

BUFFALO vs. L.A. RAMS
RS: Rams lead series, 3-2
1970—Rams, 19-0 (B)
1974—Rams, 19-14 (LA)
1980—Bills, 10-7 (B) OT
1983—Rams, 41-17 (LA)
1989—Bills, 23-20 (B)
(Points—Rams 106, Bills 64)

BUFFALO vs. MIAMI
RS: Dolphins lead series, 34-13-1
1966—Bills, 58-24 (B)
  Bills, 29-0 (M)
1967—Bills, 35-13 (B)
  Dolphins, 17-14 (M)
1968—Tie, 14-14 (M)
  Dolphins, 21-17 (B)
1969—Dolphins, 24-6 (M)
  Bills, 28-3 (B)
1970—Dolphins, 33-14 (B)
  Dolphins, 45-7 (M)
1971—Dolphins, 29-14 (B)
  Dolphins, 34-0 (M)
1972—Dolphins, 24-23 (M)
  Dolphins, 30-16 (B)
1973—Dolphins, 27-6 (M)
  Dolphins, 17-0 (B)
1974—Dolphins, 24-16 (B)
  Dolphins, 35-28 (M)
1975—Dolphins, 35-30 (M)
  Bills, 31-21 (M)
1976—Dolphins, 30-21 (B)
  Dolphins, 45-27 (M)
1977—Dolphins, 13-0 (B)
  Dolphins, 31-14 (M)
1978—Dolphins, 31-24 (B)
  Dolphins, 25-24 (B)
1979—Dolphins, 9-7 (B)
  Dolphins, 17-7 (M)
1980—Bills, 17-7 (B)
  Dolphins, 17-14 (M)
1981—Bills, 31-21 (B)
  Dolphins, 16-6 (M)
1982—Dolphins, 9-7 (B)
  Dolphins, 27-10 (M)
1983—Dolphins, 12-0 (B)
  Bills, 38-35 (B) OT
1984—Dolphins, 21-17 (B)
  Dolphins, 38-7 (M)
1985—Dolphins, 23-14 (B)
  Dolphins, 28-0 (M)
1986—Dolphins, 27-14 (M)
  Dolphins, 34-24 (B)
1987—Bills, 34-31 (M) OT
  Bills, 27-0 (B)
1988—Bills, 9-6 (B)
  Bills, 31-6 (M)
1989—Bills, 27-24 (M)
  Bills, 31-17 (B)
(Points—Dolphins 1,080, Bills 858)

BUFFALO vs. MINNESOTA
RS: Vikings lead series, 4-2
1971—Vikings, 19-0 (B)
1975—Vikings, 35-13 (B)
1979—Vikings, 10-3 (M)
1982—Bills, 23-22 (B)
1985—Vikings, 27-20 (B)
1988—Bills, 13-10 (B)
(Points—Vikings 123, Bills 72)

BUFFALO vs. *NEW ENGLAND
RS: Patriots lead series, 32-26-1
PS: Patriots lead series, 1-0
1960—Bills, 13-0 (Bos)
  Bills, 38-14 (Buff)
1961—Patriots, 23-21 (Buff)
  Patriots, 52-21 (Bos)
1962—Tie, 28-28 (Buff)
  Patriots, 21-10 (Bos)
1963—Bills, 28-21 (Buff)
  Patriots, 17-7 (Bos)
  **Patriots, 26-8 (Buff)
1964—Patriots, 36-28 (Buff)
  Bills, 24-14 (Bos)
1965—Bills, 24-7 (Buff)
  Bills, 23-7 (Bos)
1966—Patriots, 20-10 (Buff)
  Patriots, 14-3 (Bos)
1967—Patriots, 23-0 (Buff)
  Bills, 44-16 (Bos)
1968—Patriots, 16-7 (Buff)
  Patriots, 23-6 (Bos)
1969—Bills, 23-16 (Buff)
  Patriots, 35-21 (Bos)
1970—Bills, 45-10 (Bos)
  Patriots, 14-10 (Buff)
1971—Patriots, 38-33 (NE)
  Bills, 27-20 (Buff)
1972—Bills, 38-14 (Buff)
  Bills, 27-24 (NE)
1973—Bills, 31-13 (NE)
  Bills, 37-13 (Buff)
1974—Bills, 30-28 (Buff)
  Bills, 29-28 (NE)
1975—Bills, 45-31 (Buff)
  Bills, 34-14 (NE)
1976—Patriots, 26-22 (Buff)
  Patriots, 20-10 (NE)
1977—Bills, 24-14 (NE)
  Patriots, 20-7 (Buff)
1978—Patriots, 14-10 (Buff)
  Patriots, 26-24 (NE)
1979—Patriots, 26-6 (Buff)
  Bills, 16-13 (NE) OT
1980—Bills, 31-13 (Buff)
  Patriots, 24-2 (NE)
1981—Bills, 20-17 (Buff)
  Bills, 19-10 (NE)
1982—Patriots, 30-19 (NE)
1983—Patriots, 31-0 (Buff)
  Patriots, 21-7 (NE)
1984—Bills, 21-17 (Buff)
  Patriots, 38-10 (NE)

1985—Patriots, 17-14 (Buff)
 Patriots, 14-3 (NE)
1986—Patriots, 23-3 (Buff)
 Patriots, 22-19 (NE)
1987—Patriots, 14-7 (NE)
 Patriots, 13-7 (Buff)
1988—Bills, 16-14 (NE)
 Bills, 23-20 (Buff)
1989—Bills, 31-10 (Buff)
 Patriots, 33-24 (NE)
(Points—Patriots 1,220, Bills 1,164)
*Franchise in Boston prior to 1971
**Division Playoff

BUFFALO vs. NEW ORLEANS
RS: Series tied, 2-2
1973—Saints, 13-0 (NO)
1980—Bills, 35-26 (NO)
1983—Bills, 27-21 (B)
1989—Saints, 22-19 (B)
(Points—Saints 82, Bills 81)

BUFFALO vs. N.Y. GIANTS
RS: Series tied, 2-2
1970—Giants, 20-6 (NY)
1975—Giants, 17-14 (B)
1978—Bills, 41-17 (B)
1987—Bills, 6-3 (B) OT
(Points—Bills 67, Giants 57)

BUFFALO vs. *N.Y. JETS
RS: Bills lead series, 30-28
PS: Bills lead series, 1-0
1960—Titans, 27-3 (NY)
 Titans, 17-13 (B)
1961—Bills, 41-31 (B)
 Titans, 21-14 (NY)
1962—Titans, 17-6 (B)
 Bills, 20-3 (NY)
1963—Bills, 45-14 (B)
 Bills, 19-10 (NY)
1964—Bills, 34-24 (B)
 Bills, 20-7 (NY)
1965—Bills, 33-21 (B)
 Jets, 14-12 (NY)
1966—Bills, 33-23 (NY)
 Bills, 14-3 (B)
1967—Bills, 20-17 (B)
 Jets, 20-10 (NY)
1968—Bills, 37-35 (B)
 Jets, 25-21 (NY)
1969—Jets, 33-19 (B)
 Jets, 16-6 (NY)
1970—Bills, 34-31 (B)
 Bills, 10-6 (NY)
1971—Jets, 28-17 (NY)
 Jets, 20-7 (B)
1972—Jets, 41-24 (B)
 Jets, 41-3 (NY)
1973—Bills, 9-7 (B)
 Bills, 34-14 (NY)
1974—Bills, 16-12 (B)
 Jets, 20-10 (NY)
1975—Bills, 42-14 (B)
 Bills, 24-23 (NY)
1976—Jets, 17-14 (NY)
 Jets, 19-14 (B)
1977—Jets, 24-19 (B)
 Bills, 14-10 (NY)
1978—Jets, 21-20 (B)
 Jets, 45-14 (NY)
1979—Bills, 46-31 (B)
 Bills, 14-12 (NY)
1980—Bills, 20-10 (B)
 Bills, 31-24 (NY)
1981—Bills, 31-0 (B)
 Jets, 33-14 (NY)
 **Bills, 31-27 (NY)
1983—Bills, 34-10 (B)
 Bills, 24-17 (NY)
1984—Jets, 28-26 (B)
 Jets, 21-17 (NY)
1985—Jets, 42-3 (NY)
 Jets, 27-7 (B)
1986—Jets, 28-24 (B)
 Jets, 14-13 (NY)
1987—Jets, 31-28 (B)
 Bills, 17-14 (NY)
1988—Bills, 37-14 (NY)
 Bills, 9-6 (B) OT
1989—Bills, 34-3 (B)
 Bills, 37-0 (NY)
Points—Bills 1,218, Jets, 1,187)
*Jets known as Titans prior to 1963
**AFC First Round Playoff

BUFFALO vs. PHILADELPHIA
RS: Eagles lead series, 4-1
1973—Bills, 27-26 (B)
1981—Eagles, 20-14 (B)
1984—Eagles, 27-17 (B)
1985—Eagles, 21-17 (P)
1987—Eagles, 17-7 (P)
(Points—Eagles 111, Bills 82)

BUFFALO vs. *PHOENIX
RS: Cardinals lead series, 3-2
1971—Cardinals, 28-23 (B)

1975—Bills, 32-14 (StL)
1981—Cardinals, 24-0 (StL)
1984—Cardinals, 37-7 (StL)
1986—Bills, 17-10 (B)
(Points—Cardinals 113, Bills 79)
*Franchise in St. Louis prior to 1988

BUFFALO vs. PITTSBURGH
RS: Series tied, 5-5
PS: Steelers lead series, 1-0
1970—Steelers, 23-10 (P)
1972—Steelers, 38-21 (B)
1974—*Steelers, 32-14 (P)
1975—Bills, 30-21 (P)
1978—Steelers, 28-17 (B)
1979—Steelers, 28-0 (P)
1980—Bills, 28-13 (B)
1982—Bills, 13-0 (B)
1985—Steelers, 30-24 (P)
1986—Bills, 16-12 (B)
1988—Bills, 36-28 (B)
(Points—Steelers 253, Bills 209)
*AFC Divisional Playoff

BUFFALO vs. *SAN DIEGO
RS: Chargers lead series, 16-7-2
PS: Bills lead series, 2-1
1960—Chargers, 24-10 (B)
 Bills, 32-3 (LA)
1961—Chargers, 19-11 (B)
 Chargers, 28-10 (SD)
1962—Bills, 35-10 (B)
 Bills, 40-20 (SD)
1963—Chargers, 14-10 (SD)
 Chargers, 23-13 (B)
1964—Bills, 30-3 (B)
 Bills, 27-24 (SD)
 **Bills, 20-7 (B)
1965—Chargers, 34-3 (B)
 Tie, 20-20 (SD)
 **Bills, 23-0 (SD)
1966—Chargers, 27-7 (SD)
 Tie, 17-17 (B)
1967—Chargers, 37-17 (B)
1968—Chargers, 21-6 (B)
1969—Chargers, 45-6 (SD)
1971—Chargers, 20-3 (SD)
1973—Chargers, 34-7 (SD)
1976—Chargers, 34-13 (B)
1979—Chargers, 27-19 (SD)
1980—Bills, 26-24 (SD)
 ***Chargers, 20-14 (SD)
1981—Bills, 28-27 (SD)
1985—Chargers, 14-9 (B)
 Chargers, 40-7 (SD)
(Points—Chargers 616, Bills 463)
*Franchise in Los Angeles prior to 1961
**AFL Championship
***AFC Divisional Playoff

BUFFALO vs. SAN FRANCISCO
RS: Series tied, 2-2
1972—Bills, 27-20 (B)
1980—Bills, 18-13 (SF)
1983—49ers, 23-10 (B)
1989—49ers, 21-10 (SF)
(Points—49ers 77, Bills 65)

BUFFALO vs. SEATTLE
RS: Seahawks lead series, 3-1
1977—Seahawks, 56-17 (S)
1984—Seahawks, 31-28 (S)
1988—Bills, 13-3 (S)
1989—Seahawks, 17-16 (S)
(Points—Seahawks 107, Bills 74)

BUFFALO vs. TAMPA BAY
RS: Buccaneers lead series, 4-1
1976—Bills, 14-9 (TB)
1978—Buccaneers, 31-10 (TB)
1982—Buccaneers, 24-23 (TB)
1986—Buccaneers, 34-28 (TB)
1988—Buccaneers, 10-5 (B)
(Points—Buccaneers 108, Bills 80)

BUFFALO vs. WASHINGTON
RS: Redskins lead series, 3-2
1972—Bills, 24-17 (W)
1977—Redskins, 10-0 (B)
1981—Bills, 21-14 (B)
1984—Redskins, 41-14 (W)
1987—Redskins, 27-7 (B)
(Points—Redskins 109, Bills 66)

CHICAGO vs. ATLANTA
RS: Falcons lead series, 9-6;
See Atlanta vs. Chicago

CHICAGO vs. BUFFALO
RS: Bears lead series, 3-1;
See Buffalo vs. Chicago

CHICAGO vs. CINCINNATI
RS: Series tied, 2-2
1972—Bengals, 13-3 (Chi)
1980—Bengals, 17-14 (Chi) OT
1986—Bears, 44-7 (Cin)
1989—Bears, 17-14 (Chi)
(Points—Bears 78, Bengals 51)

CHICAGO vs. CLEVELAND
RS: Browns lead series, 7-3

1951—Browns, 42-21 (Cle)
1954—Browns, 39-10 (Chi)
1960—Browns, 42-0 (Cle)
1961—Bears, 17-14 (Chi)
1967—Browns, 24-0 (Cle)
1969—Browns, 28-24 (Chi)
1972—Bears, 17-0 (Cle)
1980—Browns, 27-21 (Cle)
1986—Bears, 41-31 (Chi)
1989—Browns, 27-7 (Cle)
(Points—Browns 274, Bears 158)

CHICAGO vs. DALLAS
RS: Cowboys lead series, 7-6
PS: Cowboys lead series, 1-0
1960—Bears, 17-7 (C)
1962—Bears, 34-33 (D)
1964—Cowboys, 24-10 (C)
1968—Cowboys, 34-3 (C)
1971—Bears, 23-19 (C)
1973—Cowboys, 20-17 (C)
1976—Cowboys, 31-21 (C)
1977—*Cowboys, 37-7 (C)
1979—Cowboys, 24-20 (D)
1981—Cowboys, 10-9 (C)
1984—Cowboys, 23-14 (C)
1985—Bears, 44-0 (D)
1986—Bears, 24-10 (D)
1988—Bears, 17-7 (C)
(Points—Cowboys 279, Bears 260)
*NFC Divisional Playoff

CHICAGO vs. DENVER
RS: Series tied, 4-4
1971—Broncos, 6-3 (D)
1973—Bears, 33-14 (D)
1976—Broncos, 28-14 (C)
1978—Broncos, 16-7 (D)
1981—Bears, 35-24 (D)
1983—Bears, 31-14 (C)
1984—Bears, 27-0 (C)
1987—Broncos, 31-29 (D)
(Points—Bears 179, Broncos 133)

CHICAGO vs. *DETROIT
RS: Bears lead series, 70-45-5
1930—Spartans, 7-6 (P)
 Bears, 14-6 (C)
1931—Bears, 9-6 (C)
 Spartans, 3-0 (P)
1932—Tie, 13-13 (C)
 Tie, 7-7 (P)
 Bears, 9-0 (C)
1933—Bears, 17-14 (C)
 Bears, 17-7 (P)
1934—Bears, 19-16 (D)
 Bears, 10-7 (C)
1935—Tie, 20-20 (C)
 Lions, 14-2 (D)
1936—Bears, 12-10 (C)
 Lions, 13-7 (D)
1937—Bears, 28-20 (C)
 Bears, 13-0 (D)
1938—Lions, 13-7 (C)
 Lions, 14-7 (D)
1939—Lions, 10-0 (C)
 Bears, 23-13 (D)
1940—Bears, 7-0 (C)
 Lions, 17-14 (D)
1941—Bears, 49-0 (C)
 Bears, 24-7 (D)
1942—Bears, 16-0 (C)
 Bears, 42-0 (D)
1943—Bears, 27-21 (D)
 Bears, 35-14 (C)
1944—Tie, 21-21 (C)
 Lions, 41-21 (D)
1945—Lions, 16-10 (D)
 Lions, 35-28 (D)
1946—Bears, 42-6 (C)
 Bears, 45-24 (D)
1947—Bears, 33-24 (C)
 Bears, 34-14 (D)
1948—Bears, 28-0 (C)
 Bears, 42-14 (D)
1949—Bears, 27-24 (C)
 Bears, 28-7 (D)
1950—Bears, 35-21 (C)
 Bears, 6-3 (C)
1951—Bears, 28-23 (D)
 Lions, 41-28 (D)
1952—Bears, 24-23 (C)
 Lions, 45-21 (D)
1953—Lions, 20-16 (D)
 Lions, 13-7 (C)
1954—Lions, 48-23 (D)
 Bears, 28-24 (C)
1955—Bears, 24-14 (C)
 Bears, 21-20 (D)
1956—Lions, 42-10 (C)
 Bears, 38-21 (D)
1957—Lions, 27-7 (D)
 Lions, 21-13 (C)
1958—Bears, 20-7 (D)
 Bears, 21-16 (C)
1959—Bears, 24-14 (C)

Bears, 25-14 (C)
1960—Bears, 28-7 (C)
 Lions, 36-0 (D)
1961—Bears, 31-17 (D)
 Lions, 16-15 (C)
1962—Lions, 17-14 (C)
 Bears, 3-0 (C)
1963—Bears, 37-21 (D)
 Bears, 24-14 (C)
1964—Lions, 10-0 (C)
 Bears, 27-24 (D)
1965—Bears, 38-10 (C)
 Bears, 17-10 (D)
1966—Lions, 14-3 (D)
 Tie, 10-10 (C)
1967—Bears, 14-3 (C)
 Bears, 27-13 (D)
1968—Lions, 42-0 (D)
 Lions, 28-10 (C)
1969—Lions, 13-7 (D)
 Lions, 20-3 (C)
1970—Lions, 28-14 (D)
 Lions, 16-10 (C)
1971—Bears, 28-23 (D)
 Lions, 28-3 (C)
1972—Lions, 38-24 (D)
 Lions, 14-0 (C)
1973—Lions, 30-7 (C)
 Lions, 40-7 (D)
1974—Bears, 17-9 (C)
 Lions, 34-17 (D)
1975—Lions, 27-7 (D)
 Bears, 25-21 (C)
1976—Bears, 10-3 (C)
 Lions, 14-10 (D)
1977—Bears, 30-20 (C)
 Bears, 31-14 (D)
1978—Bears, 19-0 (D)
 Lions, 21-17 (C)
1979—Bears, 35-7 (D)
 Lions, 20-0 (D)
1980—Bears, 24-7 (C)
 Bears, 23-17 (D) OT
1981—Lions, 48-17 (D)
 Lions, 23-7 (C)
1982—Lions, 17-10 (C)
 Bears, 20-17 (C)
1983—Lions, 31-17 (D)
 Lions, 38-17 (C)
1984—Bears, 16-14 (C)
 Bears, 30-13 (D)
1985—Bears, 24-3 (C)
 Bears, 37-17 (D)
1986—Bears, 13-7 (C)
 Bears, 16-13 (D)
1987—Bears, 30-10 (C)
 Bears, 24-7 (D)
1988—Bears, 24-7 (D)
 Bears, 13-12 (C)
1989—Bears, 47-27 (D)
 Lions, 27-17 (C)
(Points—Bears 2,262, Lions 2,009)
*Franchise in Portsmouth prior to 1934
and known as the Spartans

CHICAGO vs. GREEN BAY
RS: Bears lead series, 75-57-6
PS: Bears lead series, 1-0
1921—Staleys, 20-0 (C)
1923—Bears, 3-0 (GB)
1924—Bears, 3-0 (C)
1925—Packers, 14-10 (GB)
 Bears, 21-0 (C)
1926—Tie, 6-6 (GB)
 Bears, 19-13 (C)
 Tie, 3-3 (C)
1927—Bears, 7-6 (GB)
 Bears, 14-6 (C)
1928—Tie, 12-12 (GB)
 Packers, 16-6 (C)
 Packers, 6-0 (C)
1929—Packers, 23-0 (GB)
 Packers, 14-0 (C)
 Packers, 25-0 (C)
1930—Packers, 7-0 (GB)
 Packers, 13-12 (C)
 Bears, 21-0 (C)
1931—Packers, 7-0 (GB)
 Packers, 6-2 (C)
 Bears, 7-6 (C)
1932—Tie, 0-0 (GB)
 Packers, 2-0 (C)
 Bears, 9-0 (C)
1933—Bears, 14-7 (GB)
 Bears, 10-7 (C)
 Bears, 7-6 (C)
1934—Bears, 24-10 (GB)
 Bears, 27-14 (C)
1935—Packers, 7-0 (GB)
 Packers, 17-14 (C)
1936—Bears, 30-3 (GB)
 Packers, 21-10 (C)
1937—Bears, 14-2 (GB)
 Packers, 24-14 (C)
1938—Bears, 2-0 (GB)

249

Packers, 24-17 (C)
1939—Packers, 21-16 (GB)
Bears, 30-27 (C)
1940—Bears, 41-10 (GB)
Bears, 14-7 (C)
1941—Bears, 25-17 (GB)
Packers, 16-14 (C)
**Bears, 33-14 (C)
1942—Packers, 44-28 (GB)
Bears, 38-7 (C)
1943—Tie, 21-21 (GB)
Bears, 21-7 (C)
1944—Packers, 42-28 (GB)
Bears, 21-0 (C)
1945—Packers, 31-21 (GB)
Bears, 28-24 (C)
1946—Bears, 30-7 (GB)
Bears, 10-7 (C)
1947—Packers, 29-20 (GB)
Bears, 20-17 (C)
1948—Packers, 45-7 (GB)
Bears, 7-6 (C)
1949—Bears, 17-0 (GB)
Bears, 24-3 (C)
1950—Packers, 31-21 (GB)
Bears, 28-14 (C)
1951—Bears, 31-20 (GB)
Bears, 24-13 (C)
1952—Bears, 24-14 (GB)
Packers, 41-28 (C)
1953—Bears, 17-13 (GB)
Tie, 21-21 (C)
1954—Bears, 10-3 (GB)
Bears, 28-23 (C)
1955—Packers, 24-3 (GB)
Bears, 52-31 (C)
1956—Bears, 37-21 (GB)
Bears, 38-14 (C)
1957—Packers, 21-17 (GB)
Bears, 21-14 (C)
1958—Bears, 34-20 (GB)
Bears, 24-10 (C)
1959—Packers, 9-6 (GB)
Bears, 28-17 (C)
1960—Bears, 17-14 (GB)
Packers, 41-13 (C)
1961—Packers, 24-0 (GB)
Packers, 31-28 (C)
1962—Packers, 49-0 (GB)
Packers, 38-7 (C)
1963—Bears, 10-3 (GB)
Bears, 26-7 (C)
1964—Packers, 23-12 (GB)
Packers, 17-3 (C)
1965—Packers, 23-14 (GB)
Bears, 31-10 (C)
1966—Packers, 17-0 (GB)
Packers, 13-6 (C)
1967—Packers, 13-10 (GB)
Packers, 17-13 (C)
1968—Packers, 13-10 (GB)
Packers, 28-27 (C)
1969—Packers, 17-0 (GB)
Packers, 21-3 (C)
1970—Packers, 20-19 (GB)
Bears, 35-17 (C)
1971—Packers, 17-14 (C)
Packers, 31-10 (GB)
1972—Packers, 20-17 (GB)
Packers, 23-17 (C)
1973—Bears, 31-17 (GB)
Packers, 21-0 (C)
1974—Bears, 10-9 (C)
Packers, 20-3 (Mil)
1975—Bears, 27-14 (C)
Packers, 28-7 (GB)
1976—Bears, 24-13 (C)
Bears, 16-10 (GB)
1977—Bears, 26-0 (GB)
Bears, 21-10 (C)
1978—Packers, 24-14 (GB)
Bears, 14-0 (C)
1979—Bears, 6-3 (C)
Bears, 15-14 (GB)
1980—Packers, 12-6 (GB) OT
Bears, 61-7 (C)
1981—Packers, 16-9 (C)
Packers, 21-17 (GB)
1983—Packers, 31-28 (GB)
Bears, 23-21 (C)
1984—Bears, 9-7 (GB)
Packers, 20-14 (C)
1985—Bears, 23-7 (C)
Bears, 16-10 (GB)
1986—Bears, 25-12 (GB)
Bears, 12-10 (C)
1987—Bears, 26-24 (GB)
Bears, 23-10 (C)
1988—Bears, 24-6 (GB)
Bears, 16-0 (C)
1989—Packers, 14-13 (GB)
Packers, 40-28 (C)
(Points—Bears 2,350, Packers 2,044)

*Bears known as Staleys prior to 1922
**Division Playoff
CHICAGO vs. HOUSTON
RS: Oilers lead series, 3-2
1973—Bears, 35-14 (C)
1977—Oilers, 47-0 (H)
1980—Oilers, 10-6 (C)
1986—Bears, 20-7 (H)
1989—Oilers, 33-28 (C)
(Points—Oilers 111, Bears 89)
CHICAGO vs. *INDIANAPOLIS
RS: Colts lead series, 21-15
1953—Colts, 13-9 (B)
Colts, 16-14 (C)
1954—Bears, 28-9 (C)
Bears, 28-13 (B)
1955—Colts, 23-17 (B)
Bears, 38-10 (C)
1956—Colts, 28-21 (B)
Bears, 58-27 (C)
1957—Colts, 21-10 (B)
Colts, 29-14 (C)
1958—Bears, 51-38 (B)
Colts, 17-0 (C)
1959—Bears, 26-21 (B)
Colts, 21-7 (C)
1960—Colts, 42-7 (B)
Colts, 24-20 (C)
1961—Bears, 24-10 (C)
Bears, 21-20 (B)
1962—Bears, 35-15 (C)
Bears, 57-0 (B)
1963—Bears, 10-3 (C)
Bears, 17-7 (B)
1964—Colts, 52-0 (B)
Colts, 40-24 (C)
1965—Bears, 26-21 (C)
Bears, 13-0 (B)
1966—Bears, 27-17 (C)
Colts, 21-16 (B)
1967—Colts, 24-3 (C)
1968—Colts, 28-7 (B)
1969—Colts, 24-21 (C)
1970—Colts, 21-20 (B)
1975—Colts, 35-7 (C)
1983—Colts, 22-19 (B) OT
1985—Bears, 17-10 (C)
1988—Bears, 17-13 (I)
(Points—Colts 753, Bears 711)
*Franchise in Baltimore prior to 1984
CHICAGO vs. KANSAS CITY
RS: Bears lead series, 3-1
1973—Chiefs, 19-7 (KC)
1977—Bears, 28-27 (C)
1981—Bears, 16-13 (KC) OT
1987—Bears, 31-28 (C)
(Points—Chiefs 87, Bears 82)
CHICAGO vs. *L.A. RAIDERS
RS: Series tied, 3-3
1972—Raiders, 28-21 (O)
1976—Raiders, 28-27 (O)
1978—Raiders, 25-19 (C) OT
1981—Bears, 23-6 (O)
1984—Bears, 17-6 (C)
1987—Bears, 6-3 (LA)
(Points—Bears 113, Raiders 96)
*Franchise in Oakland prior to 1982
CHICAGO vs. *L.A. RAMS
RS: Bears lead series, 43-28-3
PS: Series tied, 1-1
1937—Bears, 20-2 (Clev)
Bears, 15-7 (C)
1938—Rams, 14-7 (C)
Bears, 23-21 (Clev)
1939—Bears, 30-21 (Clev)
Bears, 35-21 (C)
1940—Bears, 21-14 (Clev)
Bears, 47-25 (C)
1941—Bears, 48-21 (Clev)
Bears, 31-13 (C)
1942—Bears, 21-7 (Clev)
Bears, 47-0 (C)
1944—Rams, 19-7 (Clev)
Bears, 28-21 (C)
1945—Rams, 17-0 (Clev)
Rams, 41-21 (C)
1946—Tie, 28-28 (C)
Bears, 27-21 (LA)
1947—Bears, 41-21 (LA)
Rams, 17-14 (C)
1948—Bears, 42-21 (C)
Bears, 21-6 (LA)
1949—Rams, 31-16 (C)
Rams, 27-24 (LA)
1950—Bears, 24-20 (LA)
Bears, 24-14 (C)
**Rams, 24-14 (LA)
1951—Rams, 42-17 (C)
1952—Rams, 31-7 (LA)
Rams, 40-24 (C)
1953—Rams, 38-24 (LA)
Bears, 24-21 (C)
1954—Rams, 42-38 (LA)

Bears, 24-13 (C)
1955—Bears, 31-20 (LA)
Bears, 24-3 (C)
1956—Bears, 35-24 (LA)
Bears, 30-21 (C)
1957—Bears, 34-26 (C)
Bears, 16-10 (LA)
1958—Bears, 31-10 (C)
Rams, 41-35 (LA)
1959—Bears, 28-21 (C)
Bears, 26-21 (LA)
1960—Bears, 34-27 (C)
Tie, 24-24 (LA)
1961—Bears, 21-17 (LA)
Bears, 28-24 (C)
1962—Bears, 27-23 (LA)
Bears, 30-14 (C)
1963—Bears, 52-14 (LA)
Bears, 6-0 (C)
1964—Bears, 38-17 (C)
Bears, 34-24 (LA)
1965—Rams, 30-28 (LA)
Bears, 31-6 (C)
1966—Rams, 31-17 (LA)
Bears, 17-10 (C)
1967—Bears, 28-17 (C)
1968—Bears, 17-16 (LA)
1969—Rams, 9-7 (C)
1971—Rams, 17-3 (LA)
1972—Tie, 13-13 (C)
1973—Rams, 26-0 (C)
1975—Rams, 38-10 (LA)
1976—Rams, 20-12 (LA)
1977—Bears, 24-23 (C)
1979—Bears, 27-23 (C)
1981—Bears, 24-7 (C)
1982—Bears, 34-26 (LA)
1983—Rams, 21-14 (LA)
1984—Rams, 29-13 (LA)
1985—***Bears, 24-0 (C)
1986—Rams, 20-17 (C)
1988—Rams, 23-3 (LA)
1989—Bears, 20-10 (C)
(Points—Bears 1,764, Rams 1,554)
*Franchise in Cleveland prior to 1946
**Conference Playoff
***NFC Championship
CHICAGO vs. MIAMI
RS: Dolphins lead series, 4-1
1971—Dolphins, 34-3 (M)
1975—Dolphins, 46-13 (C)
1979—Dolphins, 31-16 (M)
1985—Dolphins, 38-24 (M)
1988—Bears, 34-7 (C)
(Points—Dolphins 156, Bears 90)
CHICAGO vs. MINNESOTA
RS: Vikings lead series, 29-26-2
1961—Vikings, 37-13 (M)
Bears, 52-35 (C)
1962—Bears, 13-0 (M)
Bears, 31-30 (C)
1963—Bears, 28-7 (M)
Tie, 17-17 (C)
1964—Bears, 34-28 (M)
Vikings, 41-14 (C)
1965—Bears, 45-37 (M)
Vikings, 24-17 (C)
1966—Bears, 13-10 (M)
Bears, 41-28 (C)
1967—Bears, 17-7 (M)
Tie, 10-10 (C)
1968—Bears, 27-17 (M)
Bears, 26-24 (C)
1969—Vikings, 31-0 (C)
Vikings, 31-14 (M)
1970—Vikings, 24-0 (C)
Vikings, 16-13 (M)
1971—Bears, 20-17 (M)
Vikings, 27-10 (C)
1972—Bears, 13-10 (C)
Vikings, 23-10 (M)
1973—Vikings, 22-13 (M)
Vikings, 31-13 (M)
1974—Vikings, 11-7 (M)
Vikings, 17-0 (C)
1975—Vikings, 28-3 (M)
Vikings, 13-9 (C)
1976—Vikings, 20-19 (M)
Bears, 14-13 (C)
1977—Vikings, 22-16 (M) OT
Bears, 10-7 (C)
1978—Vikings, 24-20 (C)
Vikings, 17-14 (M)
1979—Bears, 26-7 (C)
Vikings, 30-27 (M)
1980—Vikings, 34-14 (C)
Vikings, 13-7 (M)
1981—Vikings, 24-21 (M)
Bears, 10-9 (C)
1982—Vikings, 35-7 (M)
1983—Vikings, 23-14 (C)
Bears, 19-13 (M)
1984—Bears, 16-7 (C)

Bears, 34-3 (M)
1985—Bears, 33-24 (M)
Bears, 27-9 (C)
1986—Bears, 23-0 (C)
Vikings, 23-7 (M)
1987—Bears, 27-7 (C)
Bears, 30-24 (M)
1988—Vikings, 31-7 (C)
Vikings, 28-27 (M)
1989—Bears, 38-7 (C)
Vikings, 27-16 (M)
(Points—Vikings 1,134, Bears 1,046)
CHICAGO vs. NEW ENGLAND
RS: Patriots lead series, 3-2
PS: Bears lead series, 1-0
1973—Patriots, 13-10 (C)
1979—Patriots, 27-7 (C)
1982—Bears, 26-13 (C)
1985—Bears, 20-7 (C)
*Bears, 46-10 (New Orleans)
1988—Patriots, 30-7 (NE)
(Points—Bears 116, Patriots 110)
*Super Bowl XX
CHICAGO vs. NEW ORLEANS
RS: Bears lead series, 7-5
1968—Bears, 23-17 (NO)
1970—Bears, 24-3 (NO)
1971—Bears, 35-14 (C)
1973—Saints, 21-16 (NO)
1974—Bears, 24-10 (C)
1975—Bears, 42-17 (NO)
1977—Saints, 42-24 (C)
1980—Bears, 22-3 (C)
1982—Saints, 10-0 (C)
1983—Saints, 34-31 (NO) OT
1984—Bears, 20-7 (C)
1987—Saints, 19-17 (C)
(Points—Bears 278, Saints 197)
CHICAGO vs. N.Y. GIANTS
RS: Bears lead series, 23-14-2
PS: Bears lead series, 5-2
1925—Bears, 19-7 (NY)
Giants, 9-0 (C)
1926—Bears, 7-0 (C)
1927—Giants, 13-7 (NY)
1928—Giants, 13-0 (C)
1929—Giants, 26-14 (C)
Giants, 34-0 (NY)
Giants, 14-9 (C)
1930—Giants, 12-0 (C)
Bears, 12-0 (NY)
1931—Bears, 6-0 (C)
Bears, 12-6 (NY)
Giants, 25-6 (C)
1932—Bears, 28-8 (NY)
Bears, 6-0 (C)
1933—Bears, 14-10 (C)
Giants, 3-0 (NY)
*Bears, 23-21 (C)
1934—Bears, 27-7 (C)
Bears, 10-9 (NY)
*Giants, 30-13 (NY)
1935—Bears, 20-3 (NY)
Giants, 3-0 (C)
1936—Bears, 25-7 (NY)
1937—Tie, 3-3 (C)
1939—Giants, 16-13 (NY)
1940—Bears, 37-21 (NY)
1941—*Bears, 37-9 (C)
1942—Bears, 26-7 (NY)
1943—Bears, 56-7 (NY)
1946—Giants, 14-0 (C)
*Bears, 24-14 (NY)
1948—Bears, 35-14 (C)
1949—Giants, 35-28 (NY)
1956—Tie, 17-17 (NY)
*Giants, 47-7 (NY)
1962—Giants, 26-24 (C)
1963—*Bears, 14-10 (C)
1965—Bears, 35-14 (NY)
1967—Bears, 34-7 (C)
1969—Giants, 28-24 (NY)
1970—Bears, 24-16 (NY)
1974—Bears, 16-13 (C)
1977—Bears, 12-9 (NY) OT
1985—**Bears, 21-0 (C)
1987—Bears, 34-19 (C)
(Points—Bears 792, Giants 593)
*NFL Championship
**NFC Divisional Playoff
CHICAGO vs. N.Y. JETS
RS: Bears lead series, 2-1
1974—Jets, 23-21 (C)
1979—Bears, 23-13 (C)
1985—Bears, 19-6 (NY)
(Points—Bears 63, Jets 42)
CHICAGO vs. PHILADELPHIA
RS: Bears lead series, 22-3-1
PS: Series tied, 1-1
1933—Tie, 3-3 (P)
1935—Bears, 39-0 (P)
1936—Bears, 17-0 (P)
Bears, 28-7 (P)

1938—Bears, 28-6 (P)
1939—Bears, 27-14 (C)
1941—Bears, 49-14 (P)
1942—Bears, 45-14 (C)
1944—Bears, 28-7 (P)
1946—Bears, 21-14 (C)
1947—Bears, 40-7 (C)
1948—Eagles, 12-7 (P)
1949—Bears, 38-21 (C)
1955—Bears, 17-10 (C)
1961—Eagles, 16-14 (P)
1963—Bears, 16-7 (C)
1968—Bears, 29-16 (P)
1970—Bears, 20-16 (C)
1972—Bears, 21-12 (P)
1975—Bears, 15-13 (C)
1979—*Eagles, 27-17 (P)
1980—Eagles, 17-14 (P)
1983—Bears, 7-6 (P)
        Bears, 17-14 (C)
1986—Bears, 13-10 (C) OT
1987—Bears, 35-3 (P)
1988—**Bears, 20-12 (C)
1989—Bears, 27-13 (C)
(Points—Bears 652, Eagles 311)
*NFC First Round Playoff
**NFC Divisional Playoff
CHICAGO vs. **PHOENIX
RS: Bears lead series, 50-25-6
(NP denotes Normal Park;
Wr denotes Wrigley Field;
Co denotes Comiskey Park;
So denotes Soldier Field;
all Chicago)
1920—Cardinals, 7-6 (NP)
        Staleys, 10-0 (Wr)
1921—Tie, 0-0 (Wr)
1922—Cardinals, 6-0 (Co)
        Cardinals, 9-0 (Co)
1923—Bears, 3-0 (Wr)
1924—Bears, 6-0 (Wr)
        Bears, 21-0 (Co)
1925—Cardinals, 9-0 (Co)
        Tie, 0-0 (Wr)
1926—Bears, 16-0 (Wr)
        Bears, 10-0 (So)
        Tie, 0-0 (Wr)
1927—Bears, 9-0 (NP)
        Cardinals, 3-0 (Wr)
1928—Bears, 15-0 (NP)
        Bears, 34-0 (Wr)
1929—Tie, 0-0 (Wr)
        Cardinals, 40-6 (Co)
1930—Bears, 32-6 (Co)
        Bears, 6-0 (Wr)
1931—Bears, 26-13 (Wr)
        Bears, 18-7 (Wr)
1932—Tie, 0-0 (Wr)
        Bears, 34-0 (Wr)
1933—Bears, 12-9 (Wr)
        Bears, 22-6 (Wr)
1934—Bears, 20-0 (Wr)
        Bears, 17-6 (Wr)
1935—Tie, 7-7 (Wr)
        Bears, 13-0 (Wr)
1936—Bears, 7-3 (Wr)
        Cardinals, 14-7 (Wr)
1937—Bears, 16-7 (Wr)
        Bears, 42-28 (Wr)
1938—Bears, 16-13 (So)
        Bears, 34-28 (Wr)
1939—Bears, 44-7 (Wr)
        Bears, 48-7 (Wr)
1940—Cardinals, 21-7 (Co)
        Bears, 31-23 (Wr)
1941—Bears, 53-7 (Wr)
        Bears, 34-24 (Co)
1942—Bears, 41-14 (Wr)
        Bears, 21-7 (Co)
1943—Bears, 20-0 (Wr)
        Bears, 35-24 (Co)
1945—Cardinals, 16-7 (Wr)
        Bears, 28-20 (Co)
1946—Bears, 34-17 (Co)
        Cardinals, 35-28 (Wr)
1947—Cardinals, 31-7 (Co)
        Cardinals, 30-21 (Wr)
1948—Bears, 28-17 (Co)
        Cardinals, 24-21 (Wr)
1949—Bears, 17-7 (Co)
        Bears, 52-21 (Wr)
1950—Bears, 27-6 (Wr)
        Cardinals, 20-10 (Co)
1951—Cardinals, 28-14 (Co)
        Cardinals, 24-14 (Wr)
1952—Cardinals, 21-10 (Co)
        Bears, 10-7 (Wr)
1953—Cardinals, 24-17 (Wr)
1954—Bears, 29-7 (Co)
1955—Cardinals, 53-14 (Co)
1956—Bears, 10-3 (Wr)
1957—Bears, 14-6 (Co)
1958—Bears, 30-14 (Wr)

1959—Bears, 31-7 (So)
1965—Bears, 34-13 (Wr)
1966—Cardinals, 24-17 (StL)
1967—Bears, 30-3 (Wr)
1969—Cardinals, 20-17 (StL)
1972—Bears, 27-10 (StL)
1975—Cardinals, 34-20 (StL)
1977—Cardinals, 16-13 (StL)
1978—Bears, 17-10 (So)
1979—Bears, 42-6 (So)
1982—Cardinals, 10-7 (So)
1984—Cardinals, 38-21 (StL)
(Points—Bears 1,517, Cardinals 977)
*Franchise in Decatur prior to 1921; Bears
known as Staleys prior to 1922
**Franchise in St. Louis prior to 1988
and in Chicago prior to 1960
CHICAGO vs. *PITTSBURGH
RS: Bears lead series, 15-4-1
1934—Bears, 28-0 (P)
1935—Bears, 23-7 (P)
1936—Bears, 27-9 (P)
        Bears, 26-6 (C)
1937—Bears, 7-0 (P)
1939—Bears, 32-0 (P)
1941—Bears, 34-7 (C)
1945—Bears, 28-7 (P)
1947—Bears, 49-7 (C)
1949—Bears, 30-21 (C)
1958—Steelers, 24-10 (P)
1959—Steelers, 27-21 (C)
1963—Tie, 17-17 (P)
1967—Steelers, 41-13 (P)
1969—Bears, 38-7 (C)
1971—Bears, 17-15 (C)
1975—Steelers, 34-3 (P)
1980—Steelers, 38-3 (P)
1986—Bears, 13-10 (C) OT
1989—Bears, 20-0 (P)
(Points—Bears 445, Steelers 271)
*Steelers known as Pirates prior to 1941
CHICAGO vs. SAN DIEGO
RS: Chargers lead series, 4-1
1970—Chargers, 20-7 (C)
1974—Chargers, 28-21 (SD)
1978—Chargers, 40-7 (C)
1981—Bears, 20-17 (C) OT
1984—Chargers, 20-7 (SD)
(Points—Chargers 125, Bears 62)
CHICAGO vs. SAN FRANCISCO
RS: Bears lead series, 25-24-1
PS: 49ers lead series, 2-0
1950—Bears, 32-20 (SF)
        Bears, 17-0 (C)
1951—Bears, 13-7 (C)
1952—49ers, 40-16 (C)
        Bears, 20-17 (SF)
1953—49ers, 35-28 (C)
        49ers, 24-14 (SF)
1954—49ers, 31-24 (C)
        Bears, 31-27 (SF)
1955—49ers, 20-19 (C)
        Bears, 34-23 (SF)
1956—Bears, 31-7 (C)
        Bears, 38-21 (SF)
1957—49ers, 21-17 (C)
        49ers, 21-17 (SF)
1958—Bears, 28-6 (C)
        Bears, 27-14 (SF)
1959—49ers, 20-17 (SF)
        Bears, 14-3 (C)
1960—Bears, 27-10 (C)
        49ers, 25-7 (SF)
1961—Bears, 31-0 (C)
        49ers, 41-31 (SF)
1962—Bears, 30-14 (C)
        Bears, 34-27 (C)
1963—49ers, 20-14 (SF)
        Bears, 27-7 (C)
1964—49ers, 31-21 (C)
        Bears, 23-21 (C)
1965—49ers, 52-24 (SF)
        Bears, 61-20 (C)
1966—Tie, 30-30 (C)
        49ers, 41-14 (SF)
1967—Bears, 28-14 (SF)
1968—Bears, 27-19 (C)
1969—49ers, 42-21 (SF)
1970—Bears, 37-16 (C)
1971—49ers, 13-0 (SF)
1972—49ers, 34-21 (C)
1974—49ers, 34-0 (C)
1975—49ers, 31-3 (SF)
1976—Bears, 19-12 (SF)
1978—Bears, 16-13 (SF)
1979—Bears, 28-27 (SF)
1981—49ers, 28-17 (SF)
1983—Bears, 13-3 (C)
1984—*49ers, 23-0 (SF)
1985—Bears, 26-10 (C)
1987—49ers, 41-0 (SF)
1988—Bears, 10-9 (C)
        *49ers, 28-3 (C)

1989—49ers, 26-0 (SF)
(Points—49ers 1,147, Bears 1,052)
*NFC Championship
CHICAGO vs. SEATTLE
RS: Seahawks lead series, 4-1
1976—Bears, 34-7 (S)
1978—Seahawks, 31-29 (C)
1982—Seahawks, 20-14 (S)
1984—Seahawks, 38-9 (S)
1987—Seahawks, 34-21 (C)
(Points—Seahawks 130, Bears 107)
CHICAGO vs. TAMPA BAY
RS: Bears lead series, 18-6
1977—Bears, 10-0 (TB)
1978—Buccaneers, 33-19 (TB)
        Bears, 14-3 (C)
1979—Buccaneers, 17-13 (C)
        Bears, 14-0 (TB)
1980—Bears, 23-0 (C)
        Bears, 14-13 (TB)
1981—Bears, 28-17 (C)
        Buccaneers, 20-10 (TB)
1982—Buccaneers, 26-23 (TB) OT
1983—Bears, 17-10 (C)
        Bears, 27-0 (TB)
1984—Bears, 34-14 (C)
        Bears, 44-9 (TB)
1985—Bears, 38-28 (C)
        Bears, 27-19 (TB)
1986—Bears, 23-3 (TB)
        Bears, 48-14 (C)
1987—Bears, 20-3 (C)
        Bears, 27-26 (TB)
1988—Bears, 28-10 (C)
        Bears, 27-15 (TB)
1989—Buccaneers, 42-35 (TB)
        Buccaneers, 32-31 (C)
(Points—Bears 594, Buccaneers 354)
CHICAGO vs. *WASHINGTON
RS: Bears lead series, 18-10-1
PS: Redskins lead series, 4-3
1932—Tie, 7-7 (B)
1933—Bears, 7-0 (C)
        Redskins, 10-0 (B)
1934—Bears, 21-0 (B)
1935—Bears, 30-14 (B)
1936—Bears, 26-0 (B)
1937—**Redskins, 28-21 (C)
1938—Bears, 31-7 (C)
1940—Redskins, 7-3 (W)
        **Bears, 73-0 (W)
1941—Bears, 35-21 (C)
1942—**Redskins, 14-6 (W)
1943—Redskins, 21-7 (W)
        **Bears, 41-21 (C)
1945—Redskins, 28-21 (W)
1946—Bears, 24-20 (C)
1947—Bears, 56-20 (W)
1948—Bears, 48-13 (C)
1949—Bears, 31-21 (W)
1951—Bears, 27-0 (W)
1953—Bears, 27-24 (W)
1957—Redskins, 14-3 (C)
1964—Redskins, 27-20 (W)
1968—Redskins, 38-28 (W)
1971—Bears, 16-15 (C)
1974—Redskins, 42-0 (W)
1976—Bears, 33-7 (C)
1978—Bears, 14-10 (W)
1980—Bears, 35-21 (C)
1981—Redskins, 24-7 (C)
1984—***Bears, 23-19 (W)
1985—Bears, 45-10 (C)
1986—***Redskins, 27-13 (C)
1987—***Redskins, 21-17 (C)
1988—Bears, 34-14 (W)
1989—Redskins, 38-14 (W)
(Points—Bears 844, Redskins 603)
*Franchise in Boston prior to 1937 and
known as Braves prior to 1933
**NFL Championship
***NFC Divisional Playoff

────────────────────

CINCINNATI vs. ATLANTA
RS: Bengals lead series, 5-1;
See Atlanta vs. Cincinnati
CINCINNATI vs. BUFFALO
RS: Bengals lead series, 9-6
PS: Bengals lead series, 2-0;
See Buffalo vs. Cincinnati
CINCINNATI vs. CHICAGO
RS: Series tied, 2-2;
See Chicago vs. Cincinnati
CINCINNATI vs. CLEVELAND
RS: Bengals lead series, 20-19
1970—Browns, 30-27 (Cle)
        Bengals, 14-10 (Cin)
1971—Browns, 27-24 (Cin)
        Browns, 31-27 (Cle)
1972—Browns, 27-6 (Cin)
        Browns, 27-24 (Cin)
1973—Browns, 17-10 (Cle)
        Bengals, 34-17 (Cin)

1974—Bengals, 33-7 (Cin)
        Bengals, 34-24 (Cle)
1975—Bengals, 24-17 (Cin)
        Browns, 35-23 (Cle)
1976—Bengals, 45-24 (Cle)
        Bengals, 21-6 (Cin)
1977—Browns, 13-3 (Cin)
        Bengals, 10-7 (Cle)
1978—Bengals, 13-10 (Cle) OT
        Bengals, 48-16 (Cin)
1979—Browns, 28-27 (Cle)
        Bengals, 16-12 (Cin)
1980—Browns, 31-7 (Cle)
        Browns, 27-24 (Cin)
1981—Browns, 20-17 (Cin)
        Bengals, 41-21 (Cle)
1982—Bengals, 23-10 (Cin)
1983—Browns, 17-7 (Cle)
        Bengals, 28-21 (Cin)
1984—Bengals, 12-9 (Cin)
        Bengals, 20-17 (Cle) OT
1985—Bengals, 27-10 (Cin)
        Browns, 24-6 (Cle)
1986—Bengals, 30-13 (Cle)
        Browns, 34-3 (Cin)
1987—Browns, 34-0 (Cin)
        Browns, 38-24 (Cle)
1988—Bengals, 24-17 (Cin)
        Browns, 23-16 (Cle)
1989—Bengals, 21-14 (Cin)
        Bengals, 21-0 (Cle)
(Points—Bengals 811, Browns 768)
CINCINNATI vs. DALLAS
RS: Series tied, 2-2
1973—Cowboys, 38-10 (D)
1979—Cowboys, 38-13 (D)
1985—Bengals, 50-24 (C)
1988—Bengals, 38-24 (D)
(Points—Cowboys 124, Bengals 111)
CINCINNATI vs. DENVER
RS: Broncos lead series, 9-6
1968—Bengals, 24-10 (C)
        Broncos, 10-7 (D)
1969—Broncos, 30-23 (C)
        Broncos, 27-16 (D)
1971—Bengals, 24-10 (C)
1972—Bengals, 21-10 (C)
1973—Broncos, 28-10 (D)
1975—Bengals, 17-16 (D)
1976—Bengals, 17-7 (C)
1977—Broncos, 24-13 (C)
1979—Broncos, 10-0 (D)
1981—Bengals, 38-21 (C)
1983—Broncos, 24-17 (D)
1984—Broncos, 20-17 (D)
1986—Broncos, 34-28 (D)
(Points—Broncos 281, Bengals 272)
CINCINNATI vs. DETROIT
RS: Bengals lead series, 3-2
1970—Lions, 38-3 (D)
1974—Lions, 23-19 (C)
1983—Bengals, 17-9 (C)
1986—Bengals, 24-17 (D)
1989—Bengals, 42-7 (C)
(Points—Bengals 105, Lions 94)
CINCINNATI vs. GREEN BAY
RS: Bengals lead series, 4-2
1971—Packers, 20-17 (GB)
1976—Bengals, 28-7 (C)
1977—Bengals, 17-7 (Mil)
1980—Packers, 14-9 (GB)
1983—Bengals, 34-14 (C)
1986—Bengals, 34-28 (Mil)
(Points—Bengals 139, Packers 90)
CINCINNATI vs. HOUSTON
RS: Bengals lead series, 23-18-1
1968—Oilers, 27-17 (C)
1969—Tie, 31-31 (H)
1970—Oilers, 20-13 (C)
        Bengals, 30-20 (H)
1971—Oilers, 10-6 (H)
        Bengals, 28-13 (C)
1972—Bengals, 30-7 (C)
        Bengals, 61-17 (H)
1973—Bengals, 24-10 (C)
        Bengals, 27-24 (H)
1974—Oilers, 34-21 (C)
        Oilers, 20-3 (H)
1975—Bengals, 21-19 (H)
        Bengals, 23-19 (C)
1976—Bengals, 27-7 (H)
        Bengals, 31-27 (C)
1977—Bengals, 13-10 (C) OT
        Oilers, 21-16 (H)
1978—Bengals, 28-13 (C)
        Oilers, 17-10 (H)
1979—Oilers, 30-27 (C) OT
        Oilers, 42-21 (H)
1980—Bengals, 13-10 (C)
        Oilers, 23-3 (H)
1981—Bengals, 17-10 (H)
        Bengals, 34-21 (C)
1982—Bengals, 27-6 (C)

251

Bengals, 35-27 (H)
1983—Bengals, 55-14 (H)
   Bengals, 38-10 (C)
1984—Bengals, 13-3 (C)
   Bengals, 31-13 (H)
1985—Oilers, 44-27 (H)
   Bengals, 45-27 (C)
1986—Bengals, 31-28 (C)
   Oilers, 32-28 (H)
1987—Oilers, 31-29 (C)
   Oilers, 21-17 (H)
1988—Bengals, 44-21 (C)
   Oilers, 41-6 (H)
1989—Oilers, 26-24 (H)
   Bengals, 61-7 (C)
(Points—Bengals 1,076, Oilers 863)

CINCINNATI vs.*INDIANAPOLIS
RS: Series tied, 5-5
PS: Colts lead series, 1-0
1970—**Colts, 17-0 (B)
1972—Colts, 20-19 (C)
1974—Bengals, 24-14 (B)
1976—Colts, 28-27 (B)
1979—Colts, 38-28 (B)
1980—Bengals, 34-33 (C)
1981—Bengals, 41-19 (B)
1982—Bengals, 20-17 (B)
1983—Colts, 34-31 (C)
1987—Bengals, 23-21 (I)
1989—Colts, 23-12 (C)
(Points—Colts 264, Bengals 259)
*Franchise in Baltimore prior to 1984
**AFC Divisional Playoff

CINCINNATI vs. KANSAS CITY
RS: Chiefs lead series, 10-9
1968—Chiefs, 13-3 (KC)
   Chiefs, 16-9 (C)
1969—Bengals, 24-19 (C)
   Chiefs, 42-22 (KC)
1970—Chiefs, 27-19 (C)
1972—Bengals, 23-16 (KC)
1973—Bengals, 14-6 (C)
1974—Bengals, 33-6 (C)
1976—Bengals, 27-24 (KC)
1977—Bengals, 27-7 (KC)
1978—Chiefs, 24-23 (C)
1979—Bengals, 10-7 (C)
1980—Bengals, 20-6 (KC)
1983—Chiefs, 20-15 (KC)
1984—Chiefs, 27-22 (C)
1986—Chiefs, 24-14 (KC)
1987—Bengals, 30-27 (C) OT
1988—Chiefs, 31-28 (KC)
1989—Bengals, 21-17 (KC)
(Points—Bengals 381, Chiefs 362)

CINCINNATI vs. *L.A. RAIDERS
RS: Raiders lead series, 12-5
PS: Raiders lead series, 1-0
1968—Raiders, 31-10 (O)
   Raiders, 34-0 (C)
1969—Bengals, 31-17 (C)
   Raiders, 37-17 (O)
1970—Bengals, 31-21 (C)
1971—Raiders, 31-27 (O)
1972—Bengals, 20-14 (C)
1974—Bengals, 30-27 (O)
1975—Bengals, 14-10 (C)
   **Raiders, 31-28 (O)
1976—Raiders, 35-20 (O)
1978—Raiders, 34-21 (C)
1980—Raiders, 28-17 (O)
1982—Bengals, 31-17 (C)
1983—Raiders, 20-10 (C)
1985—Raiders, 13-6 (LA)
1988—Bengals, 45-21 (LA)
1989—Bengals, 28-7 (LA)
(Points—Raiders 458, Bengals 356)
*Franchise in Oakland prior to 1982
**AFC Divisional Playoff

CINCINNATI vs. L.A. RAMS
RS: Bengals lead series, 3-2
1972—Rams, 15-12 (LA)
1976—Bengals, 20-12 (C)
1978—Bengals, 20-19 (LA)
1981—Bengals, 24-10 (C)
1984—Rams, 24-14 (C)
(Points—Bengals 90, Rams 80)

CINCINNATI vs. MIAMI
RS: Dolphins lead series, 8-3
PS: Dolphins lead series, 1-0
1968—Dolphins, 24-22 (C)
   Bengals, 38-21 (M)
1969—Bengals, 27-21 (C)
1971—Bengals, 23-13 (C)
1973—*Dolphins, 34-16 (M)
1974—Dolphins, 24-3 (M)
1977—Bengals, 23-17 (C)
1978—Bengals, 21-0 (M)
1980—Dolphins, 17-16 (M)
1983—Dolphins, 38-14 (M)
1987—Dolphins, 20-14 (C)
1989—Dolphins, 20-13 (C)
(Points—Dolphins 280, Bengals 199)

*AFC Divisional Playoff

CINCINNATI vs. MINNESOTA
RS: Series tied, 3-3
1973—Bengals, 27-0 (C)
1977—Vikings, 42-10 (M)
1980—Bengals, 14-0 (C)
1983—Vikings, 20-14 (M)
1986—Bengals, 24-20 (C)
1989—Vikings, 29-21 (M)
(Points—Vikings 111, Bengals 110)

CINCINNATI vs. *NEW ENGLAND
RS: Patriots lead series, 7-4
1968—Patriots, 33-14 (B)
1969—Patriots, 25-14 (C)
1970—Bengals, 45-7 (C)
1972—Bengals, 31-7 (NE)
1975—Bengals, 27-10 (C)
1978—Patriots, 10-3 (C)
1979—Bengals, 20-14 (C)
1984—Patriots, 20-14 (NE)
1985—Patriots, 34-23 (NE)
1986—Patriots, 31-7 (NE)
1988—Patriots, 27-21 (NE)
(Points—Bengals 237, Patriots 200)
*Franchise in Boston prior to 1971

CINCINNATI vs. NEW ORLEANS
RS: Series tied, 3-3
1970—Bengals, 26-6 (C)
1975—Bengals, 21-0 (NO)
1978—Saints, 20-18 (C)
1981—Saints, 17-7 (NO)
1984—Bengals, 24-21 (NO)
1987—Saints, 41-24 (C)
(Points—Bengals 120, Saints 105)

CINCINNATI vs. N. Y. GIANTS
RS: Bengals lead series, 3-0
1972—Bengals, 13-10 (C)
1977—Bengals, 30-13 (C)
1985—Bengals, 35-30 (C)
(Points—Bengals 78, Giants 53)

CINCINNATI vs. N. Y. JETS
RS: Jets lead series, 7-5
PS: Jets lead series, 1-0
1968—Jets, 27-14 (NY)
1969—Jets, 21-7 (C)
   Jets, 40-7 (NY)
1971—Jets, 35-21 (NY)
1973—Bengals, 20-14 (C)
1975—Bengals, 42-3 (NY)
1981—Bengals, 31-30 (NY)
1982—*Jets, 44-17 (C)
1984—Jets, 43-23 (NY)
1985—Jets, 29-20 (C)
1986—Bengals, 52-21 (C)
1987—Jets, 27-20 (NY)
1988—Bengals, 36-19 (C)
(Points—Jets 353, Bengals 310)
*AFC First Round Playoff

CINCINNATI vs. PHILADELPHIA
RS: Bengals lead series, 5-0
1971—Bengals, 37-14 (C)
1975—Bengals, 31-0 (P)
1979—Bengals, 37-13 (C)
1982—Bengals, 18-14 (P)
1988—Bengals, 28-24 (P)
(Points—Bengals 151, Eagles 65)

CINCINNATI vs. *PHOENIX
RS: Bengals lead series, 3-1
1973—Bengals, 42-24 (C)
1979—Bengals, 34-28 (C)
1985—Cardinals, 41-27 (StL)
1988—Bengals, 21-14 (C)
(Points—Bengals 124, Cardinals 107)
*Franchise in St. Louis prior to 1988

CINCINNATI vs. PITTSBURGH
RS: Steelers lead series, 20-19
1970—Steelers, 21-10 (P)
   Bengals, 34-7 (C)
1971—Steelers, 21-10 (P)
   Steelers, 21-13 (C)
1972—Bengals, 15-10 (C)
   Steelers, 40-17 (P)
1973—Bengals, 19-7 (C)
   Steelers, 20-13 (P)
1974—Bengals, 17-10 (C)
   Steelers, 27-3 (P)
1975—Steelers, 30-24 (C)
   Steelers, 35-14 (P)
1976—Steelers, 23-6 (P)
   Steelers, 7-3 (C)
1977—Steelers, 20-14 (P)
   Bengals, 17-10 (C)
1978—Steelers, 28-3 (P)
   Steelers, 7-6 (P)
1979—Bengals, 34-10 (C)
   Steelers, 37-17 (P)
1980—Bengals, 30-28 (C)
   Bengals, 17-16 (P)
1981—Bengals, 34-7 (C)
   Bengals, 17-10 (P)
1982—Steelers, 26-20 (P) OT
1983—Steelers, 24-14 (C)
   Bengals, 23-10 (P)

1984—Steelers, 38-17 (P)
   Bengals, 22-20 (C)
1985—Bengals, 37-24 (P)
   Bengals, 26-21 (C)
1986—Bengals, 24-22 (C)
   Steelers, 30-9 (P)
1987—Steelers, 23-20 (P)
   Steelers, 30-16 (P)
1988—Bengals, 17-12 (P)
   Bengals, 42-7 (C)
1989—Bengals, 41-10 (C)
   Bengals, 26-16 (P)
(Points—Steelers 765, Bengals 741)

CINCINNATI vs. SAN DIEGO
RS: Chargers lead series, 11-7
PS: Bengals lead series, 1-0
1968—Chargers, 29-13 (SD)
   Chargers, 31-10 (C)
1969—Bengals, 34-20 (C)
   Chargers, 21-14 (SD)
1970—Bengals, 17-14 (SD)
1971—Bengals, 31-0 (C)
1973—Bengals, 20-13 (SD)
1974—Chargers, 20-17 (C)
1975—Bengals, 47-17 (C)
1977—Chargers, 24-3 (SD)
1978—Chargers, 22-13 (SD)
1979—Chargers, 26-24 (C)
1980—Chargers, 31-14 (C)
1981—Bengals, 40-17 (SD)
   *Bengals, 27-7 (C)
1982—Chargers, 50-34 (SD)
1985—Chargers, 44-41 (C)
1987—Chargers, 10-9 (C)
1988—Bengals, 27-10 (C)
(Points—Bengals 435, Chargers 406)
*AFC Championship

CINCINNATI vs. SAN FRANCISCO
RS: 49ers lead series, 4-1
PS: 49ers lead series, 2-0
1974—Bengals, 21-3 (SF)
1978—49ers, 28-12 (SF)
1981—49ers, 21-3 (C)
   *49ers, 26-21 (Detroit)
1984—49ers, 23-17 (SF)
1987—49ers, 27-26 (C)
1988—**49ers, 20-16 (Miami)
(Points—49ers 148, Bengals 116)
*Super Bowl XVI
**Super Bowl XXIII

CINCINNATI vs. SEATTLE
RS: Bengals lead series, 5-3
PS: Bengals lead series, 1-0
1977—Bengals, 42-20 (C)
1981—Bengals, 27-21 (C)
1982—Bengals, 24-10 (C)
1984—Seahawks, 26-6 (C)
1985—Seahawks, 28-24 (C)
1986—Bengals, 34-7 (C)
1987—Bengals, 17-10 (S)
1988—*Bengals, 21-13 (C)
1989—Seahawks, 24-17 (C)
(Points—Bengals 212, Seahawks 159)
*AFC Divisional Playoff

CINCINNATI vs. TAMPA BAY
RS: Bengals lead series, 3-1
1976—Bengals, 21-0 (C)
1980—Buccaneers, 17-12 (C)
1983—Bengals, 23-17 (TB)
1989—Bengals, 56-23 (C)
(Points—Bengals 112, Buccaneers 57)

CINCINNATI vs. WASHINGTON
RS: Redskins lead series, 3-2
1970—Bengals, 20-0 (W)
1974—Bengals, 28-17 (C)
1979—Redskins, 28-14 (W)
1985—Redskins, 27-24 (W)
1988—Bengals, 20-17 (C) OT
(Points—Redskins 109, Bengals 86)

CLEVELAND vs. ATLANTA
RS: Browns lead series, 7-1;
See Atlanta vs. Cleveland

CLEVELAND vs. BUFFALO
RS: Browns lead series, 7-2
PS: Browns lead series, 1-0;
See Buffalo vs. Cleveland

CLEVELAND vs. CHICAGO
RS: Browns lead series, 7-3;
See Chicago vs. Cleveland

CLEVELAND vs. CINCINNATI
RS: Bengals lead series, 20-19;
See Cincinnati vs. Cleveland

CLEVELAND vs. DALLAS
RS: Browns lead series, 14-8
PS: Browns lead series, 2-1
1960—Browns, 48-7 (D)
1961—Browns, 25-7 (C)
   Browns, 38-17 (D)
1962—Browns, 19-10 (C)
   Cowboys, 45-21 (D)
1963—Browns, 41-24 (D)
   Browns, 27-17 (C)

1964—Browns, 27-6 (C)
   Browns, 20-16 (D)
1965—Browns, 23-17 (C)
   Browns, 24-17 (D)
1966—Browns, 30-21 (C)
   Cowboys, 26-14 (D)
1967—Cowboys, 21-14 (C)
   *Cowboys, 52-14 (D)
1968—Cowboys, 28-7 (C)
   *Browns, 31-20 (C)
1969—Browns, 42-10 (C)
   *Browns, 38-14 (D)
1970—Cowboys, 6-2 (C)
1974—Cowboys, 41-17 (D)
1979—Browns, 26-7 (C)
1982—Cowboys, 31-14 (D)
1985—Cowboys, 20-7 (D)
1988—Browns, 24-21 (C)
(Points—Browns 593, Cowboys 501)
*Conference Championship

CLEVELAND vs. DENVER
RS: Broncos lead series, 9-4
PS: Broncos lead series, 3-0
1970—Browns, 27-13 (C)
1971—Broncos, 27-0 (C)
1972—Browns, 27-20 (C)
1974—Browns, 23-21 (C)
1975—Broncos, 16-15 (D)
1976—Broncos, 44-13 (D)
1978—Broncos, 19-7 (C)
1980—Broncos, 19-16 (C)
1981—Broncos, 23-20 (D) OT
1983—Broncos, 27-6 (D)
1984—Broncos, 24-14 (C)
1986—*Broncos, 23-20 (C) OT
1987—*Broncos, 38-33 (D)
1988—Broncos, 30-7 (D)
1989—Browns, 16-13 (C)
   *Broncos, 37-21 (D)
(Points—Broncos 394, Browns 265)
*AFC Championship

CLEVELAND vs. DETROIT
RS: Lions lead series, 10-3
PS: Lions lead series, 3-1
1952—Lions, 17-6 (D)
   *Lions, 17-7 (C)
1953—Lions, 17-16 (D)
1954—Lions, 14-10 (C)
   *Browns, 56-10 (C)
1957—Lions, 20-7 (D)
   *Lions, 59-14 (D)
1958—Lions, 30-10 (C)
1963—Lions, 38-10 (D)
1964—Browns, 37-21 (D)
1967—Lions, 31-14 (D)
1969—Lions, 28-21 (C)
1970—Lions, 41-24 (D)
1975—Lions, 21-10 (D)
1983—Browns, 31-26 (D)
1986—Browns, 24-21 (D)
1989—Lions, 13-10 (D)
(Points—Lions 424, Browns 307)
*NFL Championship

CLEVELAND vs. GREEN BAY
RS: Packers lead series, 7-5
PS: Packers lead series, 1-0
1953—Browns, 27-0 (C)
1955—Browns, 41-10 (C)
1956—Browns, 24-7 (Mil)
1961—Packers, 49-17 (C)
1964—Packers, 28-21 (Mil)
1965—*Packers, 23-12 (GB)
1966—Packers, 21-20 (C)
1967—Packers, 55-7 (Mil)
1969—Browns, 20-7 (C)
1972—Packers, 26-10 (C)
1980—Packers, 26-21 (C)
1983—Packers, 35-21 (Mil)
1986—Packers, 17-14 (C)
(Points—Packers 299, Browns 260)
*NFL Championship

CLEVELAND vs. HOUSTON
RS: Browns lead series, 26-13
PS: Oilers lead series, 1-0
1970—Browns, 28-14 (C)
   Browns, 21-10 (H)
1971—Browns, 31-0 (C)
   Browns, 37-24 (H)
1972—Browns, 23-17 (C)
   Browns, 20-0 (C)
1973—Browns, 42-13 (C)
   Browns, 23-13 (H)
1974—Browns, 20-7 (C)
   Oilers, 28-24 (H)
1975—Oilers, 40-10 (C)
   Oilers, 21-10 (H)
1976—Browns, 21-7 (H)
   Browns, 13-10 (C)
1977—Browns, 24-23 (C)
   Oilers, 19-15 (H)
1978—Oilers, 16-13 (C)
   Oilers, 14-10 (H)
1979—Oilers, 31-10 (H)

Browns, 14-7 (C)
1980—Oilers, 16-7 (C)
Browns, 17-14 (H)
1981—Oilers, 9-3 (C)
Oilers, 17-13 (H)
1982—Browns, 20-14 (H)
1983—Browns, 25-19 (C) OT
Oilers, 34-27 (H)
1984—Browns, 27-10 (C)
Browns, 27-20 (H)
1985—Browns, 21-6 (H)
Browns, 28-21 (C)
1986—Browns, 23-20 (H)
Browns, 13-10 (C) OT
1987—Oilers, 15-10 (C)
Browns, 40-7 (H)
1988—Oilers, 24-17 (H)
Browns, 28-23 (C)
*Oilers, 24-23 (C)
1989—Browns, 28-17 (C)
Browns, 24-20 (H)
(Points—Browns 830, Oilers 654)
*AFC First Round Playoff

CLEVELAND vs. *INDIANAPOLIS
RS: Browns lead series, 11-5
PS: Series tied, 2-2
1956—Colts, 21-7 (C)
1959—Browns, 38-31 (B)
1962—Colts, 36-14 (C)
1964—**Browns, 27-0 (C)
1968—Browns, 30-20 (B)
**Colts, 34-0 (C)
1971—Browns, 14-13 (B)
***Colts, 20-3 (C)
1973—Browns, 24-14 (C)
1975—Colts, 21-7 (B)
1978—Browns, 45-24 (B)
1979—Browns, 13-10 (C)
1980—Browns, 28-27 (B)
1981—Browns, 42-28 (C)
1983—Browns, 41-23 (C)
1986—Browns, 24-9 (I)
1987—Colts, 9-7 (C)
***Browns, 38-21 (C)
1988—Browns, 23-17 (C)
1989—Colts, 23-17 (I) OT
(Points—Browns 442, Colts 401)
*Franchise in Baltimore prior to 1984
**NFL Championship
***AFC Divisional Playoff

CLEVELAND vs. KANSAS CITY
RS: Browns lead series, 6-5-2
1971—Chiefs, 13-7 (KC)
1972—Chiefs, 31-7 (C)
1973—Tie, 20-20 (KC)
1975—Browns, 40-14 (C)
1976—Chiefs, 39-14 (KC)
1977—Browns, 44-7 (C)
1978—Chiefs, 17-3 (KC)
1979—Browns, 27-24 (KC)
1980—Browns, 20-13 (C)
1984—Chiefs, 10-6 (KC)
1986—Browns, 20-7 (C)
1988—Browns, 6-3 (KC)
1989—Tie, 10-10 (C) OT
(Points—Browns 224, Chiefs 208)

CLEVELAND vs. *L.A. RAIDERS
RS: Raiders lead series, 8-2
PS: Raiders lead series, 2-0
1970—Raiders, 23-20 (O)
1971—Raiders, 34-20 (C)
1973—Browns, 7-3 (O)
1974—Raiders, 40-24 (C)
1975—Raiders, 38-17 (O)
1977—Raiders, 26-10 (C)
1979—Raiders, 19-14 (O)
1980—**Raiders, 14-12 (C)
1982—***Raiders, 27-10 (LA)
1985—Raiders, 21-20 (C)
1986—Raiders, 27-14 (LA)
1987—Raiders, 24-17 (LA)
(Points—Raiders 289, Browns 192)
*Franchise in Oakland prior to 1982
**AFC Divisional Playoff
***AFC First Round Playoff

CLEVELAND vs. L.A. RAMS
RS: Browns lead series, 7-6
PS: Browns lead series, 2-1
1950—*Browns, 30-28 (C)
1951—Browns, 38-23 (LA)
*Rams, 24-17 (LA)
1952—Browns, 37-7 (C)
1955—*Browns, 38-14 (LA)
1957—Browns, 45-31 (C)
1958—Browns, 30-27 (LA)
1963—Browns, 20-6 (C)
1965—Rams, 42-7 (LA)
1968—Rams, 24-6 (C)
1973—Rams, 30-17 (LA)
1977—Browns, 9-0 (C)
1978—Browns, 30-19 (C)
1981—Rams, 27-16 (LA)
1984—Rams, 20-17 (LA)

1987—Browns, 30-17 (C)
(Points—Browns 378, Rams 348)
*NFL Championship

CLEVELAND vs. MIAMI
RS: Browns lead series, 4-3
PS: Dolphins lead series, 2-0
1970—Browns, 28-0 (M)
1972—*Dolphins, 20-14 (M)
1973—Dolphins, 17-9 (C)
1976—Browns, 17-13 (C)
1979—Browns, 30-24 (C) OT
1985—*Dolphins, 24-21 (M)
1986—Browns, 26-16 (C)
1988—Dolphins, 38-31 (M)
1989—Dolphins, 13-10 (M) OT
(Points—Browns 186, Dolphins 165)
*AFC Divisional Playoff

CLEVELAND vs. MINNESOTA
RS: Vikings lead series, 6-3
PS: Vikings lead series, 1-0
1965—Vikings, 27-17 (C)
1967—Browns, 14-10 (C)
1969—Vikings, 51-3 (M)
*Vikings, 27-7 (M)
1973—Vikings, 26-3 (M)
1975—Vikings, 42-10 (C)
1980—Vikings, 28-23 (M)
1983—Vikings, 27-21 (C)
1986—Browns, 23-20 (M)
1989—Browns, 23-17 (C) OT
(Points—Vikings 275, Browns 144)
*NFL Championship

CLEVELAND vs. NEW ENGLAND
RS: Browns lead series, 7-2
1971—Browns, 27-7 (C)
1974—Browns, 21-14 (NE)
1977—Browns, 30-27 (C) OT
1980—Patriots, 34-17 (NE)
1982—Browns, 10-7 (C)
1983—Browns, 30-0 (NE)
1984—Patriots, 17-16 (C)
1985—Browns, 24-20 (C)
1987—Browns, 20-10 (NE)
(Points—Browns 195, Patriots 136)

CLEVELAND vs. NEW ORLEANS
RS: Browns lead series, 8-2
1967—Browns, 42-7 (NO)
1968—Browns, 24-10 (NO)
Browns, 35-17 (C)
1969—Browns, 27-17 (NO)
1971—Browns, 21-17 (NO)
1975—Browns, 17-16 (C)
1978—Browns, 24-16 (NO)
1981—Browns, 20-17 (C)
1984—Saints, 16-14 (C)
1987—Saints, 28-21 (NO)
(Points—Browns 245, Saints 161)

CLEVELAND vs. N.Y. GIANTS
RS: Browns lead series, 25-15-2
PS: Series tied, 1-1
1950—Giants, 6-0 (C)
Giants, 17-13 (NY)
*Browns, 8-3 (C)
1951—Browns, 14-13 (C)
Browns, 10-0 (NY)
1952—Browns, 17-9 (C)
Giants, 37-34 (NY)
1953—Browns, 7-0 (NY)
Browns, 62-14 (C)
1954—Browns, 24-14 (C)
Browns, 16-7 (NY)
1955—Browns, 24-14 (C)
Tie, 35-35 (NY)
1956—Giants, 21-9 (C)
Browns, 24-7 (NY)
1957—Browns, 6-3 (C)
Browns, 34-28 (NY)
1958—Browns, 21-17 (C)
Giants, 13-10 (NY)
*Giants, 10-0 (NY)
1959—Giants, 10-6 (C)
Giants, 48-7 (NY)
1960—Giants, 17-13 (C)
Browns, 48-34 (NY)
1961—Giants, 37-21 (C)
Tie, 7-7 (NY)
1962—Browns, 17-7 (C)
Giants, 17-13 (NY)
1963—Browns, 35-24 (NY)
Giants, 33-6 (C)
1964—Browns, 42-20 (C)
Browns, 52-20 (NY)
1965—Browns, 38-14 (NY)
Browns, 34-21 (C)
1966—Browns, 28-7 (NY)
Browns, 49-40 (C)
1967—Browns, 38-34 (NY)
Browns, 24-14 (C)
1968—Browns, 45-10 (C)
1969—Browns, 28-17 (C)
Giants, 27-14 (NY)
1973—Browns, 12-10 (C)
1977—Browns, 21-7 (NY)

1985—Browns, 35-33 (NY)
(Points—Browns 985, Giants 792)
*Conference Playoff

CLEVELAND vs. N.Y. JETS
RS: Browns lead series, 8-4
PS: Browns lead series, 1-0
1970—Browns, 31-21 (N)
1972—Browns, 26-10 (NY)
1976—Browns, 38-17 (C)
1978—Browns, 37-34 (C) OT
1979—Browns, 25-22 (NY) OT
1980—Browns, 17-14 (C)
1981—Jets, 14-13 (C)
1983—Browns, 10-7 (C)
1984—Jets, 24-20 (C)
1985—Jets, 37-10 (NY)
1986—*Browns, 23-20 (C) OT
1988—Jets, 23-3 (C)
1989—Browns, 38-24 (C)
(Points—Browns 291, Jets 267)
*AFC Divisional Playoff

CLEVELAND vs. PHILADELPHIA
RS: Browns lead series, 30-11-1
1950—Browns, 35-10 (P)
Browns, 13-7 (C)
1951—Browns, 20-17 (C)
Browns, 24-9 (NY)
1952—Browns, 49-7 (P)
Eagles, 28-20 (C)
1953—Browns, 37-13 (C)
Eagles, 42-27 (P)
1954—Eagles, 28-10 (C)
Browns, 6-0 (C)
1955—Browns, 21-17 (C)
Eagles, 33-17 (P)
1956—Browns, 16-0 (P)
Browns, 17-14 (C)
1957—Browns, 24-7 (C)
Eagles, 17-7 (P)
1958—Browns, 28-14 (C)
Browns, 21-14 (P)
1959—Browns, 28-7 (C)
Browns, 28-21 (P)
1960—Browns, 41-24 (P)
Eagles, 31-29 (C)
1961—Eagles, 27-20 (P)
Browns, 45-24 (C)
1962—Eagles, 35-7 (P)
Tie, 14-14 (C)
1963—Browns, 37-7 (C)
Browns, 23-17 (P)
1964—Browns, 28-20 (P)
Browns, 38-24 (C)
1965—Browns, 35-17 (P)
Browns, 38-34 (C)
1966—Browns, 27-7 (C)
Eagles, 33-21 (P)
1967—Eagles, 28-24 (C)
1968—Browns, 47-13 (C)
1969—Browns, 27-20 (P)
1972—Browns, 27-17 (P)
1976—Browns, 24-3 (C)
1979—Browns, 24-19 (P)
1982—Eagles, 24-21 (C)
1988—Browns, 19-3 (C)
(Points—Browns 1,064, Eagles 746)

CLEVELAND vs. *PHOENIX
RS: Browns lead series, 31-10-3
1950—Browns, 34-24 (Cle)
Browns, 10-7 (Chi)
1951—Browns, 34-17 (Chi)
Browns, 49-28 (Cle)
1952—Browns, 28-13 (Cle)
Browns, 10-0 (Chi)
1953—Browns, 27-7 (Chi)
Browns, 27-16 (Cle)
1954—Browns, 31-7 (Cle)
Browns, 35-3 (Chi)
1955—Browns, 26-20 (Chi)
Browns, 35-24 (Cle)
1956—Cardinals, 9-7 (Chi)
Cardinals, 24-7 (Cle)
1957—Browns, 17-7 (Chi)
Browns, 31-0 (Cle)
1958—Browns, 35-28 (Cle)
Browns, 38-24 (Chi)
1959—Browns, 34-7 (Chi)
Browns, 17-7 (Cle)
1960—Browns, 28-27 (Cle)
Tie, 17-17 (StL)
1961—Browns, 20-17 (Cle)
Browns, 21-10 (StL)
1962—Browns, 34-7 (Cle)
Browns, 38-14 (Cle)
1963—Cardinals, 20-14 (Cle)
Browns, 24-10 (StL)
1964—Tie, 33-33 (Cle)
Cardinals, 28-19 (StL)
1965—Cardinals, 49-13 (StL)
Browns, 27-24 (StL)
1966—Cardinals, 34-28 (Cle)
Browns, 38-10 (StL)
1967—Browns, 20-16 (Cle)

Browns, 20-16 (StL)
1968—Cardinals, 27-21 (Cle)
Cardinals, 27-16 (StL)
1969—Tie, 21-21 (Cle)
Browns, 27-21 (StL)
1974—Cardinals, 29-7 (Cle)
1979—Browns, 38-20 (StL)
1985—Cardinals, 27-24 (Cle) OT
1988—Browns, 29-21 (P)
(Points—Browns 1,109, Cardinals 797)
*Franchise in St. Louis prior to 1988,
and in Chicago prior to 1960

CLEVELAND vs. PITTSBURGH
RS: Browns lead series, 48-32
1950—Browns, 30-17 (P)
Browns, 45-7 (C)
1951—Browns, 17-0 (C)
Browns, 28-0 (P)
1952—Browns, 21-20 (P)
Browns, 29-28 (C)
1953—Browns, 34-16 (C)
Browns, 20-16 (P)
1954—Steelers, 55-27 (P)
Browns, 42-7 (C)
1955—Browns, 41-14 (C)
Browns, 30-7 (P)
1956—Browns, 14-10 (P)
Steelers, 24-16 (C)
1957—Browns, 23-12 (P)
Browns, 24-0 (C)
1958—Browns, 45-12 (C)
Browns, 27-10 (C)
1959—Steelers, 17-7 (P)
Steelers, 21-20 (C)
1960—Browns, 28-20 (C)
Steelers, 14-10 (P)
1961—Browns, 30-28 (C)
Steelers, 17-13 (C)
1962—Browns, 41-14 (P)
Browns, 35-14 (C)
1963—Browns, 35-23 (C)
Steelers, 9-7 (P)
1964—Steelers, 23-7 (C)
Browns, 30-17 (P)
1965—Browns, 24-19 (C)
Browns, 42-21 (P)
1966—Browns, 41-10 (C)
Steelers, 16-6 (P)
1967—Browns, 21-10 (C)
Browns, 34-14 (P)
1968—Browns, 31-24 (C)
Browns, 45-24 (P)
1969—Browns, 42-31 (C)
Browns, 24-3 (P)
1970—Browns, 15-7 (C)
Steelers, 28-9 (P)
1971—Browns, 27-17 (C)
Steelers, 26-9 (P)
1972—Browns, 26-24 (C)
Steelers, 30-0 (P)
1973—Steelers, 33-6 (P)
Browns, 21-16 (C)
1974—Steelers, 20-16 (P)
Steelers, 26-16 (C)
1975—Steelers, 42-6 (C)
Steelers, 31-17 (P)
1976—Steelers, 31-14 (P)
Browns, 18-16 (C)
1977—Steelers, 28-14 (C)
Steelers, 35-31 (P)
1978—Steelers, 15-9 (P) OT
Steelers, 34-14 (C)
1979—Steelers, 51-35 (P)
Steelers, 33-30 (P) OT
1980—Browns, 27-26 (C)
Steelers, 16-13 (P)
1981—Steelers, 13-7 (P)
Steelers, 32-10 (C)
1982—Browns, 10-9 (C)
Steelers, 37-21 (P)
1983—Browns, 44-17 (P)
Browns, 30-17 (C)
1984—Browns, 20-10 (C)
Steelers, 23-20 (P)
1985—Browns, 17-7 (C)
Steelers, 10-9 (P)
1986—Browns, 27-24 (P)
Browns, 37-31 (C) OT
1987—Browns, 34-10 (C)
Browns, 19-13 (P)
1988—Browns, 23-9 (P)
Browns, 27-7 (C)
1989—Browns, 51-0 (P)
Steelers, 17-7 (C)
(Points—Browns 1,845, Steelers 1,542)

CLEVELAND vs. SAN DIEGO
RS: Chargers lead series, 6-5-1
1970—Chargers, 27-10 (C)
1972—Browns, 21-17 (SD)
1973—Tie, 16-16 (C)
1974—Chargers, 36-35 (SD)
1976—Browns, 21-17 (C)
1977—Chargers, 37-14 (SD)

1981—Chargers, 44-14 (C)
1982—Chargers, 30-13 (C)
1983—Browns, 30-24 (SD) OT
1985—Browns, 21-7 (SD)
1986—Browns, 47-17 (C)
1987—Chargers, 27-24 (SD) OT
(Points—Chargers 299, Browns 266)

CLEVELAND vs. SAN FRANCISCO
RS: Browns lead series, 8-5
1950—Browns, 34-14 (C)
1951—49ers, 24-10 (SF)
1953—Browns, 23-21 (C)
1955—Browns, 38-3 (SF)
1959—49ers, 21-20 (C)
1962—Browns, 13-10 (SF)
1968—Browns, 33-21 (SF)
1970—49ers, 34-31 (SF)
1974—Browns, 7-0 (C)
1978—Browns, 24-7 (C)
1981—Browns, 15-12 (SF)
1984—49ers, 41-7 (C)
1987—49ers, 38-24 (SF)
(Points—Browns 279, 49ers 246)

CLEVELAND vs. SEATTLE
RS: Seahawks lead series, 8-3
1977—Seahawks, 20-19 (S)
1978—Seahawks, 47-24 (S)
1979—Seahawks, 29-24 (C)
1980—Browns, 27-3 (S)
1981—Seahawks, 42-21 (S)
1982—Browns, 21-7 (S)
1983—Seahawks, 24-9 (C)
1984—Seahawks, 33-0 (S)
1985—Seahawks, 31-13 (C)
1988—Seahawks, 16-10 (C)
1989—Browns, 17-7 (S)
(Points—Seahawks 259, Browns 185)

CLEVELAND vs. TAMPA BAY
RS: Browns lead series, 4-0
1976—Browns, 24-7 (TB)
1980—Browns, 34-27 (TB)
1983—Browns, 20-0 (C)
1989—Browns, 42-31 (TB)
(Points—Browns 120, Buccaneers 65)

CLEVELAND vs. WASHINGTON
RS: Browns lead series, 32-8-1
1950—Browns, 20-14 (C)
　　　Browns, 45-21 (W)
1951—Browns, 45-0 (C)
1952—Browns, 19-15 (C)
　　　Browns, 48-24 (W)
1953—Browns, 30-14 (W)
　　　Browns, 27-3 (C)
1954—Browns, 62-3 (C)
　　　Browns, 34-14 (W)
1955—Redskins, 27-17 (C)
　　　Browns, 24-14 (W)
1956—Redskins, 20-9 (W)
　　　Redskins, 20-17 (C)
1957—Browns, 21-17 (C)
　　　Tie, 30-30 (W)
1958—Browns, 20-10 (W)
　　　Browns, 21-14 (C)
1959—Browns, 34-7 (C)
　　　Browns, 31-17 (W)
1960—Browns, 31-10 (W)
　　　Browns, 27-16 (C)
1961—Browns, 31-7 (C)
　　　Browns, 17-6 (W)
1962—Redskins, 17-16 (C)
　　　Redskins, 17-9 (W)
1963—Browns, 37-14 (C)
　　　Browns, 27-20 (W)
1964—Browns, 27-13 (W)
　　　Browns, 34-24 (C)
1965—Browns, 17-7 (W)
　　　Browns, 24-16 (C)
1966—Browns, 38-14 (W)
　　　Browns, 14-3 (C)
1967—Browns, 42-37 (C)
1968—Browns, 24-21 (W)
1969—Browns, 27-23 (C)
1971—Browns, 20-13 (W)
1975—Redskins, 23-7 (C)
1979—Redskins, 13-9 (C)
1985—Redskins, 14-7 (C)
1988—Browns, 17-13 (W)
(Points—Browns 1,056, Redskins 625)

DALLAS vs. ATLANTA
RS: Cowboys lead series, 7-4
PS: Cowboys lead series, 2-0;
See Atlanta vs. Dallas

DALLAS vs. BUFFALO
RS: Cowboys lead series, 3-1;
See Buffalo vs. Dallas

DALLAS vs. CHICAGO
RS: Cowboys lead series, 7-6
PS: Cowboys lead series, 1-0;
See Chicago vs. Dallas

DALLAS vs. CINCINNATI
RS: Series tied, 2-2;
See Cincinnati vs. Dallas

DALLAS vs. CLEVELAND
RS: Browns lead series, 14-8
PS: Browns lead series, 2-1;
See Cleveland vs. Dallas

DALLAS vs. DENVER
RS: Series tied, 2-2
PS: Cowboys lead series, 1-0
1973—Cowboys, 22-10 (Den)
1977—Cowboys, 14-6 (Dal)
　　　*Cowboys, 27-10 (New Orleans)
1980—Broncos, 41-20 (Den)
1986—Broncos, 29-14 (Den)
(Points—Cowboys 97, Broncos 96)
*Super Bowl XII

DALLAS vs. DETROIT
RS: Cowboys lead series, 6-4
PS: Cowboys lead series, 1-0
1960—Lions, 23-14 (Det)
1963—Cowboys, 17-14 (Dal)
1968—Cowboys, 59-13 (Dal)
1970—*Cowboys, 5-0 (Dal)
1972—Cowboys, 28-24 (Det)
1975—Cowboys, 36-10 (Det)
1977—Cowboys, 37-0 (Dal)
1981—Lions, 27-24 (Det)
1985—Lions, 26-21 (Det)
1986—Cowboys, 31-7 (Det)
1987—Lions, 27-17 (Det)
(Points—Cowboys 289, Lions 171)
*NFC Divisional Playoff

DALLAS vs. GREEN BAY
RS: Packers lead series, 8-4
PS: Packers lead series, 2-1
1960—Packers, 41-7 (GB)
1964—Packers, 45-21 (GB)
1965—Packers, 13-3 (Mil)
1966—*Packers, 34-27 (D)
1967—*Packers, 21-17 (GB)
1968—Packers, 28-17 (D)
1970—Cowboys, 16-3 (D)
1972—Packers, 16-13 (Mil)
1975—Packers, 19-17 (D)
1978—Cowboys, 42-14 (Mil)
1980—Cowboys, 28-7 (Mil)
1982—**Cowboys, 37-26 (D)
1984—Cowboys, 20-6 (D)
1989—Packers, 31-13 (GB)
　　　Packers, 20-10 (D)
(Points—Packers 324, Cowboys 288)
*NFL Championship
**NFC Second Round Playoff

DALLAS vs. HOUSTON
RS: Cowboys lead series, 4-2
1970—Cowboys, 52-10 (D)
1974—Cowboys, 10-0 (H)
1979—Oilers, 30-24 (D)
1982—Cowboys, 37-7 (H)
1985—Cowboys, 17-10 (H)
1988—Oilers, 25-17 (D)
(Points—Cowboys 157, Oilers 82)

DALLAS vs. *INDIANAPOLIS
RS: Cowboys lead series, 6-2
PS: Colts lead series, 1-0
1960—Colts, 45-7 (D)
1967—Colts, 23-17 (B)
1969—Cowboys, 27-10 (D)
1970—**Colts, 16-13 (Miami)
1972—Cowboys, 21-0 (B)
1976—Cowboys, 30-27 (D)
1978—Cowboys, 38-0 (D)
1981—Cowboys, 37-13 (B)
1984—Cowboys, 22-3 (D)
(Points—Cowboys 212, Colts 137)
*Franchise in Baltimore prior to 1984
**Super Bowl V

DALLAS vs. KANSAS CITY
RS: Series tied, 2-2
1970—Cowboys, 27-16 (KC)
1975—Chiefs, 34-31 (D)
1983—Cowboys, 41-21 (D)
1989—Chiefs, 36-28 (KC)
(Points—Cowboys 127, Chiefs 107)

DALLAS vs. *L.A. RAIDERS
RS: Raiders lead series, 3-1
1974—Raiders, 27-23 (O)
1980—Cowboys, 19-13 (O)
1983—Raiders, 40-38 (D)
1986—Raiders, 17-13 (D)
(Points—Raiders 97, Cowboys 93)
*Franchise in Oakland prior to 1982

DALLAS vs. L.A. RAMS
RS: Rams lead series, 8-7
PS: Series tied, 4-4
1960—Rams, 38-13 (D)
1962—Cowboys, 27-17 (LA)
1967—Rams, 35-13 (D)
1969—Rams, 24-23 (LA)
1971—Cowboys, 28-21 (D)
1973—Rams, 37-31 (LA)
　　　*Cowboys, 27-16 (D)
1975—Cowboys, 18-7 (D)
　　　**Cowboys, 37-7 (LA)
1976—*Rams, 14-12 (D)

1978—Rams, 27-14 (LA)
　　　**Cowboys, 28-0 (LA)
1979—Cowboys, 30-6 (D)
　　　*Rams, 21-19 (D)
1980—Rams, 38-14 (LA)
　　　***Cowboys, 34-13 (D)
1981—Cowboys, 29-17 (D)
1983—***Rams, 24-17 (D)
1984—Cowboys, 20-13 (LA)
1985—*Rams, 20-0 (LA)
1986—Rams, 29-10 (LA)
1987—Cowboys, 29-21 (LA)
1989—Rams, 35-31 (D)
(Points—Cowboys 504, Rams 480)
*NFC Divisional Playoff
**NFC Championship
***NFC First Round Playoff

DALLAS vs. MIAMI
RS: Dolphins lead series, 5-1
PS: Cowboys lead series, 1-0
1971—*Cowboys, 24-3 (New Orleans)
1973—Dolphins, 14-7 (D)
1978—Dolphins, 23-16 (M)
1981—Cowboys, 28-27 (D)
1984—Dolphins, 28-21 (M)
1987—Dolphins, 20-14 (D)
1989—Dolphins, 17-14 (D)
(Points—Dolphins 132, Cowboys 124)
*Super Bowl VI

DALLAS vs. MINNESOTA
RS: Cowboys lead series, 7-6
PS: Cowboys lead series, 3-1
1961—Cowboys, 21-7 (D)
　　　Cowboys, 28-0 (M)
1966—Cowboys, 28-17 (D)
1968—Cowboys, 20-7 (M)
1970—Vikings, 54-13 (M)
1971—*Cowboys, 20-12 (M)
1973—**Vikings, 27-10 (D)
1974—Vikings, 23-21 (D)
1975—*Cowboys, 17-14 (M)
1977—Cowboys, 16-10 (M) OT
　　　**Cowboys, 23-6 (D)
1978—Vikings, 21-10 (D)
1979—Cowboys, 36-20 (M)
1982—Vikings, 31-27 (M)
1983—Cowboys, 37-24 (M)
1987—Vikings, 44-38 (D) OT
1988—Vikings, 43-3 (D)
(Points—Cowboys 368, Vikings 360)
*NFC Divisional Playoff
**NFC Championship

DALLAS vs. NEW ENGLAND
RS: Cowboys lead series, 6-0
1971—Cowboys, 44-21 (D)
1975—Cowboys, 34-31 (NE)
1978—Cowboys, 17-10 (D)
1981—Cowboys, 35-21 (NE)
1984—Cowboys, 20-17 (D)
1987—Cowboys, 23-17 (NE) OT
(Points—Cowboys 173, Patriots 117)

DALLAS vs. NEW ORLEANS
RS: Cowboys lead series, 11-3
1967—Cowboys, 14-10 (D)
　　　Cowboys, 27-10 (NO)
1968—Cowboys, 17-3 (NO)
1969—Cowboys, 21-17 (NO)
　　　Cowboys, 33-17 (D)
1971—Saints, 24-14 (NO)
1973—Cowboys, 40-3 (D)
1976—Cowboys, 24-6 (NO)
1978—Cowboys, 27-7 (D)
1982—Cowboys, 21-7 (D)
1983—Cowboys, 21-20 (D)
1984—Cowboys, 30-27 (D) OT
1988—Saints, 20-17 (NO)
1989—Saints, 28-0 (NO)
(Points—Cowboys 306, Saints 199)

DALLAS vs. N.Y. GIANTS
RS: Cowboys lead series, 35-18-2
1960—Tie, 31-31 (NY)
1961—Giants, 31-10 (NY)
　　　Cowboys, 17-16 (NY)
1962—Giants, 41-10 (D)
　　　Giants, 41-31 (NY)
1963—Giants, 37-21 (NY)
　　　Giants, 34-27 (D)
1964—Tie, 13-13 (D)
　　　Cowboys, 31-21 (NY)
1965—Cowboys, 31-2 (D)
　　　Cowboys, 38-20 (NY)
1966—Cowboys, 52-7 (D)
　　　Cowboys, 17-7 (NY)
1967—Cowboys, 38-24 (NY)
1968—Giants, 27-21 (D)
　　　Cowboys, 28-10 (NY)
1969—Cowboys, 25-3 (D)
1970—Cowboys, 28-10 (D)
　　　Giants, 23-20 (NY)
1971—Cowboys, 20-13 (D)
　　　Cowboys, 42-14 (NY)
1972—Cowboys, 23-14 (NY)
　　　Giants, 23-3 (D)

1973—Cowboys, 45-28 (D)
　　　Cowboys, 23-10 (New Haven)
1974—Giants, 14-6 (D)
　　　Cowboys, 21-7 (New Haven)
1975—Cowboys, 13-7 (NY)
　　　Cowboys, 14-3 (D)
1976—Cowboys, 24-14 (NY)
　　　Cowboys, 9-3 (D)
1977—Cowboys, 41-21 (D)
　　　Cowboys, 24-10 (NY)
1978—Cowboys, 34-24 (NY)
　　　Cowboys, 24-3 (D)
1979—Cowboys, 16-14 (NY)
　　　Cowboys, 28-7 (D)
1980—Cowboys, 24-3 (D)
　　　Giants, 38-35 (NY)
1981—Cowboys, 18-10 (D)
　　　Giants, 13-10 (NY) OT
1983—Cowboys, 28-13 (D)
　　　Cowboys, 38-20 (NY)
1984—Cowboys, 28-7 (NY)
　　　Giants, 19-7 (D)
1985—Cowboys, 30-29 (NY)
　　　Cowboys, 28-21 (D)
1986—Cowboys, 31-28 (D)
　　　Giants, 17-14 (NY)
1987—Cowboys, 16-14 (NY)
　　　Cowboys, 33-24 (D)
1988—Giants, 12-10 (D)
　　　Giants, 29-21 (NY)
1989—Giants, 30-13 (D)
　　　Giants, 15-0 (NY)
(Points—Cowboys 1,262, Giants 990)

DALLAS vs. N.Y. JETS
RS: Cowboys lead series, 4-0
1971—Cowboys, 52-10 (D)
1975—Cowboys, 31-21 (NY)
1978—Cowboys, 30-7 (NY)
1987—Cowboys, 38-24 (NY)
(Points—Cowboys 151, Jets 62)

DALLAS vs. PHILADELPHIA
RS: Cowboys lead series, 36-22
PS: Eagles lead series, 1-0
1960—Eagles, 27-25 (D)
1961—Eagles, 43-7 (D)
　　　Eagles, 35-13 (P)
1962—Cowboys, 41-19 (D)
　　　Eagles, 28-14 (P)
1963—Cowboys, 24-21 (P)
　　　Cowboys, 27-20 (D)
1964—Eagles, 17-14 (D)
　　　Eagles, 24-14 (P)
1965—Eagles, 35-24 (D)
　　　Cowboys, 21-19 (P)
1966—Cowboys, 56-7 (D)
　　　Eagles, 24-23 (P)
1967—Eagles, 21-14 (P)
　　　Cowboys, 38-17 (D)
1968—Cowboys, 45-13 (P)
　　　Cowboys, 34-14 (D)
1969—Cowboys, 38-7 (P)
　　　Cowboys, 49-14 (D)
1970—Cowboys, 17-7 (P)
　　　Cowboys, 21-17 (D)
1971—Cowboys, 42-7 (P)
　　　Cowboys, 20-7 (D)
1972—Cowboys, 28-6 (D)
　　　Cowboys, 28-7 (P)
1973—Eagles, 30-16 (P)
　　　Cowboys, 31-10 (D)
1974—Eagles, 13-10 (P)
　　　Cowboys, 31-24 (D)
1975—Cowboys, 20-17 (D)
　　　Cowboys, 27-17 (P)
1976—Cowboys, 27-7 (D)
　　　Cowboys, 26-7 (P)
1977—Cowboys, 16-10 (P)
　　　Cowboys, 24-14 (D)
1978—Cowboys, 14-7 (D)
　　　Cowboys, 31-13 (P)
1979—Eagles, 31-21 (D)
　　　Cowboys, 24-17 (P)
1980—Eagles, 17-10 (P)
　　　Cowboys, 35-27 (D)
　　　*Eagles, 20-7 (P)
1981—Cowboys, 17-14 (P)
　　　Cowboys, 21-10 (D)
1982—Cowboys, 24-20 (D)
1983—Cowboys, 37-7 (D)
　　　Cowboys, 27-20 (P)
1984—Cowboys, 23-17 (D)
　　　Cowboys, 26-10 (P)
1985—Eagles, 16-14 (D)
　　　Cowboys, 34-17 (P)
1986—Cowboys, 17-14 (D)
　　　Eagles, 23-21 (D)
1987—Cowboys, 41-22 (D)
　　　Eagles, 37-20 (D)
1988—Eagles, 24-23 (P)
　　　Eagles, 23-7 (D)
1989—Eagles, 27-0 (D)
　　　Eagles, 20-10 (P)

(Points—Cowboys 1,402, Eagles 1,065)
*NFC Championship
DALLAS vs. *PHOENIX
RS: Cowboys lead series, 33-21-1
1960—Cardinals, 12-10 (StL)
1961—Cardinals, 31-17 (D)
Cardinals, 31-13 (StL)
1962—Cardinals, 28-24 (D)
Cardinals, 52-20 (StL)
1963—Cardinals, 34-7 (D)
Cowboys, 28-24 (StL)
1964—Cardinals, 16-6 (D)
Cowboys, 31-13 (StL)
1965—Cardinals, 20-13 (StL)
Cowboys, 27-13 (D)
1966—Tie, 10-10 (StL)
Cowboys, 31-17 (D)
1967—Cowboys, 46-21 (D)
1968—Cowboys, 27-10 (StL)
1969—Cowboys, 24-3 (D)
1970—Cardinals, 20-7 (StL)
Cardinals, 38-0 (D)
1971—Cowboys, 16-13 (StL)
Cowboys, 31-12 (D)
1972—Cowboys, 33-24 (D)
Cowboys, 27-6 (StL)
1973—Cowboys, 45-10 (D)
Cowboys, 30-3 (StL)
1974—Cardinals, 31-28 (StL)
Cowboys, 17-14 (D)
1975—Cowboys, 37-31 (D) OT
Cardinals, 31-17 (StL)
1976—Cardinals, 21-17 (StL)
Cowboys, 19-14 (D)
1977—Cowboys, 30-24 (StL)
Cardinals, 24-17 (D)
1978—Cowboys, 21-12 (D)
Cowboys, 24-21 (StL) OT
1979—Cowboys, 22-21 (StL)
Cowboys, 22-13 (D)
1980—Cowboys, 27-24 (StL)
Cowboys, 31-21 (D)
1981—Cowboys, 30-17 (D)
Cardinals, 20-17 (StL)
1982—Cowboys, 24-7 (StL)
1983—Cowboys, 34-17 (StL)
Cowboys, 35-17 (D)
1984—Cardinals, 31-20 (D)
Cowboys, 24-17 (StL)
1985—Cardinals, 21-10 (StL)
Cowboys, 35-17 (D)
1986—Cowboys, 31-7 (StL)
Cowboys, 37-6 (D)
1987—Cardinals, 24-13 (StL)
Cowboys, 21-16 (D)
1988—Cowboys, 17-14 (P)
Cardinals, 16-10 (D)
1989—Cowboys, 19-10 (D)
Cardinals, 24-20 (P)
(Points—Cowboys 1,240, Cardinals 1,053)
*Franchise in St. Louis prior to 1988
DALLAS vs. PITTSBURGH
RS: Series tied, 11-11
PS: Steelers lead series, 2-0
1960—Steelers, 35-28 (D)
1961—Cowboys, 27-24 (D)
Steelers, 37-7 (P)
1962—Steelers, 30-28 (D)
Cowboys, 42-27 (P)
1963—Steelers, 27-21 (P)
Steelers, 24-19 (D)
1964—Steelers, 23-17 (P)
Cowboys, 17-14 (D)
1965—Steelers, 22-13 (P)
Cowboys, 24-17 (D)
1966—Cowboys, 52-21 (D)
Cowboys, 20-7 (P)
1967—Cowboys, 24-21 (P)
1968—Cowboys, 28-7 (D)
1969—Cowboys, 10-7 (P)
1972—Cowboys, 17-13 (D)
1975—*Steelers, 21-17 (Miami)
1977—Steelers, 28-13 (P)
1978—**Steelers, 35-31 (Miami)
1979—Steelers, 14-3 (P)
1982—Cowboys, 36-28 (D)
1985—Cowboys, 27-13 (D)
1988—Steelers, 24-21 (P)
(Points—Cowboys 534, Steelers 527)
*Super Bowl X
**Super Bowl XIII
DALLAS vs. SAN DIEGO
RS: Cowboys lead series, 3-1
1972—Cowboys, 34-28 (SD)
1980—Cowboys, 42-31 (D)
1983—Chargers, 24-23 (SD)
1986—Cowboys, 24-21 (SD)
(Points—Cowboys 123, Chargers 104)
DALLAS vs. SAN FRANCISCO
RS: 49ers lead series, 8-5-1
PS: Cowboys lead series, 3-1
1960—49ers, 26-14 (D)
1963—49ers, 31-24 (SF)

1965—Cowboys, 39-31 (D)
1967—49ers, 24-16 (SF)
1969—Tie, 24-24 (D)
1970—Cowboys, 17-10 (SF)
1971—*Cowboys, 14-3 (D)
1972—49ers, 31-10 (D)
**Cowboys, 30-28 (SF)
1974—Cowboys, 20-14 (D)
1977—Cowboys, 42-35 (D)
1979—Cowboys, 21-13 (SF)
1980—Cowboys, 59-14 (D)
1981—49ers, 45-14 (SF)
*49ers, 28-27 (SF)
1983—49ers, 42-17 (SF)
1985—49ers, 31-16 (SF)
1989—49ers, 31-14 (D)
(Points—49ers 461, Cowboys 418)
*NFC Championship
**NFC Divisional Playoff
DALLAS vs. SEATTLE
RS: Cowboys lead series, 3-1
1976—Cowboys, 28-13 (S)
1980—Cowboys, 51-7 (D)
1983—Cowboys, 35-10 (S)
1986—Seahawks, 31-14 (D)
(Points—Cowboys 128, Seahawks 61)
DALLAS vs. TAMPA BAY
RS: Cowboys lead series, 4-0
PS: Cowboys lead series, 2-0
1977—Cowboys, 23-7 (D)
1980—Cowboys, 28-17 (D)
1981—*Cowboys, 38-0 (D)
1982—Cowboys, 14-9 (D)
**Cowboys, 30-17 (D)
1983—Cowboys, 27-24 (D) OT
(Points—Cowboys 160, Buccaneers 74)
*NFC Divisional Playoff
**NFC First Round Playoff
DALLAS vs. WASHINGTON
RS: Cowboys lead series, 33-23-2
PS: Redskins lead series, 2-0
1960—Redskins, 26-14 (W)
1961—Tie, 28-28 (D)
Redskins, 34-24 (W)
1962—Tie, 35-35 (D)
Cowboys, 38-10 (W)
1963—Redskins, 21-17 (W)
Cowboys, 35-20 (D)
1964—Cowboys, 24-18 (D)
Redskins, 28-16 (W)
1965—Cowboys, 27-7 (D)
Redskins, 34-31 (W)
1966—Cowboys, 31-30 (W)
Redskins, 34-31 (D)
1967—Cowboys, 17-14 (W)
Redskins, 27-20 (D)
1968—Cowboys, 44-24 (W)
Cowboys, 29-20 (D)
1969—Cowboys, 41-28 (W)
Cowboys, 20-10 (D)
1970—Cowboys, 45-21 (W)
Cowboys, 34-0 (D)
1971—Redskins, 20-16 (D)
Cowboys, 13-0 (W)
1972—Redskins, 24-20 (W)
Cowboys, 34-24 (D)
*Redskins, 26-3 (W)
1973—Redskins, 14-7 (W)
Cowboys, 27-7 (D)
1974—Redskins, 28-21 (W)
Cowboys, 24-23 (D)
1975—Redskins, 30-24 (W) OT
Cowboys, 31-10 (D)
1976—Cowboys, 20-7 (W)
Redskins, 27-14 (D)
1977—Cowboys, 34-16 (D)
Cowboys, 14-7 (W)
1978—Redskins, 9-5 (W)
Cowboys, 37-10 (D)
1979—Redskins, 34-20 (D)
Cowboys, 35-34 (D)
1980—Cowboys, 17-3 (W)
Cowboys, 14-10 (D)
1981—Cowboys, 26-10 (W)
Cowboys, 24-10 (D)
1982—Cowboys, 24-10 (W)
*Redskins, 31-17 (W)
1983—Cowboys, 31-30 (W)
Redskins, 31-10 (D)
1984—Redskins, 34-14 (W)
Redskins, 30-28 (D)
1985—Cowboys, 44-14 (D)
Cowboys, 13-7 (W)
1986—Cowboys, 30-6 (D)
Redskins, 41-14 (W)
1987—Redskins, 13-7 (D)
Redskins, 24-20 (W)
1988—Redskins, 35-17 (D)
Cowboys, 24-17 (W)
1989—Redskins, 30-7 (D)
Cowboys, 13-3 (W)
(Points—Cowboys 1,394, Redskins 1,208)
*NFC Championship

DENVER vs. ATLANTA
RS: Broncos lead series, 4-3;
See Atlanta vs. Denver
DENVER vs. BUFFALO
RS: Bills lead series, 14-10-1;
See Buffalo vs. Denver
DENVER vs. CHICAGO
RS: Series tied, 4-4;
See Chicago vs. Denver
DENVER vs. CINCINNATI
RS: Broncos lead series, 9-6;
See Cincinnati vs. Denver
DENVER vs. CLEVELAND
RS: Broncos lead series, 9-4
PS: Broncos lead series, 3-0;
See Cleveland vs. Denver
DENVER vs. DALLAS
RS: Series tied, 2-2
PS: Cowboys lead series, 1-0;
See Dallas vs. Denver
DENVER vs. DETROIT
RS: Broncos lead series, 4-2
1971—Lions, 24-20 (Den)
1974—Broncos, 31-27 (Det)
1978—Lions, 17-14 (Det)
1981—Broncos, 27-21 (Den)
1984—Broncos, 28-7 (Det)
1987—Broncos, 34-0 (Den)
(Points—Broncos 154, Lions 96)
DENVER vs. GREEN BAY
RS: Broncos lead series, 3-1-1
1971—Packers, 34-13 (Mil)
1975—Broncos, 23-13 (D)
1978—Broncos, 16-3 (D)
1984—Broncos, 17-14 (D)
1987—Tie, 17-17 (Mil) OT
(Points—Broncos 86, Packers 81)
DENVER vs. HOUSTON
RS: Oilers lead series, 18-10-1
PS: Series tied, 1-1
1960—Oilers, 45-25 (D)
Oilers, 20-10 (H)
1961—Oilers, 55-14 (D)
Oilers, 45-14 (H)
1962—Broncos, 20-10 (D)
Oilers, 34-17 (H)
1963—Oilers, 20-14 (H)
Oilers, 33-24 (D)
1964—Oilers, 38-17 (D)
Oilers, 34-15 (H)
1965—Oilers, 28-17 (D)
Broncos, 31-21 (H)
1966—Oilers, 45-7 (H)
Broncos, 40-38 (D)
1967—Oilers, 10-6 (H)
Oilers, 20-18 (D)
1968—Oilers, 38-17 (H)
1969—Oilers, 24-21 (H)
Tie, 20-20 (D)
1970—Oilers, 31-21 (H)
1972—Oilers, 30-17 (D)
1973—Broncos, 48-20 (H)
1974—Broncos, 37-14 (D)
1976—Oilers, 17-3 (H)
1977—Broncos, 24-14 (H)
1979—*Oilers, 13-7 (H)
1980—Oilers, 20-16 (D)
1983—Broncos, 26-14 (H)
1985—Broncos, 31-20 (D)
1987—Oilers, 40-10 (D)
**Broncos, 34-10 (D)
(Points—Oilers 797, Broncos 645)
*AFC First Round Playoff
**AFC Divisional Playoff
DENVER vs. *INDIANAPOLIS
RS: Broncos lead series, 7-2
1974—Broncos, 17-6 (B)
1977—Broncos, 27-13 (D)
1978—Colts, 7-6 (B)
1981—Broncos, 28-10 (D)
1983—Broncos, 17-10 (B)
Broncos, 21-19 (D)
1985—Broncos, 15-10 (I)
1988—Colts, 55-23 (D)
1989—Broncos, 14-3 (D)
(Points—Broncos 168, Colts 133)
*Franchise in Baltimore prior to 1984
DENVER vs. *KANSAS CITY
RS: Chiefs lead series, 35-24
1960—Texans, 17-14 (D)
Texans, 34-7 (Da)
1961—Texans, 19-12 (D)
Texans, 49-21 (Da)
1962—Texans, 24-3 (D)
Texans, 17-10 (Da)
1963—Chiefs, 59-7 (D)
Chiefs, 52-21 (KC)
1964—Broncos, 33-27 (D)
Chiefs, 49-39 (KC)
1965—Chiefs, 31-23 (D)
Chiefs, 45-35 (KC)
1966—Chiefs, 37-10 (KC)

Chiefs, 56-10 (D)
1967—Chiefs, 52-9 (KC)
Chiefs, 38-24 (D)
1968—Chiefs, 34-2 (KC)
Chiefs, 30-7 (D)
1969—Chiefs, 26-13 (D)
Chiefs, 31-17 (KC)
1970—Broncos, 26-13 (D)
Chiefs, 16-0 (KC)
1971—Chiefs, 16-3 (D)
Chiefs, 28-10 (KC)
1972—Chiefs, 45-24 (D)
Chiefs, 24-21 (KC)
1973—Chiefs, 16-14 (KC)
Broncos, 14-10 (D)
1974—Broncos, 17-14 (KC)
Chiefs, 42-34 (D)
1975—Broncos, 37-33 (D)
Chiefs, 26-13 (KC)
1976—Broncos, 35-26 (KC)
Broncos, 17-16 (D)
1977—Broncos, 23-7 (D)
Broncos, 14-7 (KC)
1978—Broncos, 23-17 (KC) OT
Broncos, 24-3 (D)
1979—Broncos, 24-10 (KC)
Broncos, 20-3 (D)
1980—Chiefs, 23-17 (D)
Chiefs, 31-14 (KC)
1981—Chiefs, 28-14 (KC)
Broncos, 16-13 (D)
1982—Chiefs, 37-16 (D)
1983—Broncos, 27-24 (D)
Chiefs, 48-17 (KC)
1984—Broncos, 21-0 (D)
Chiefs, 16-13 (KC)
1985—Broncos, 30-10 (KC)
Broncos, 14-13 (D)
1986—Broncos, 38-17 (D)
Chiefs, 37-10 (KC)
1987—Broncos, 26-17 (KC)
Broncos, 20-17 (D)
1988—Chiefs, 20-13 (KC)
Broncos, 17-11 (D)
1989—Broncos, 34-20 (D)
Broncos, 16-13 (KC)
(Points—Chiefs 1,494, Broncos 1,083)
*Franchise in Dallas prior to 1963 and known as Texans
DENVER vs. *L.A. RAIDERS
RS: Raiders lead series, 39-18-2
PS: Broncos lead series, 1-0
1960—Broncos, 31-14 (O)
Raiders, 48-10 (O)
1961—Raiders, 33-19 (D)
Raiders, 27-24 (D)
1962—Broncos, 44-7 (D)
Broncos, 23-6 (O)
1963—Raiders, 26-10 (D)
Raiders, 35-31 (O)
1964—Raiders, 40-7 (O)
Tie, 20-20 (D)
1965—Raiders, 28-20 (D)
Raiders, 24-13 (O)
1966—Raiders, 17-3 (D)
Raiders, 28-10 (O)
1967—Raiders, 51-0 (O)
Raiders, 21-17 (D)
1968—Raiders, 43-7 (D)
Raiders, 33-27 (O)
1969—Raiders, 24-14 (D)
Raiders, 41-10 (O)
1970—Raiders, 35-23 (O)
Raiders, 24-19 (D)
1971—Raiders, 27-16 (D)
Raiders, 21-13 (O)
1972—Broncos, 30-23 (O)
Raiders, 37-20 (O)
1973—Tie, 23-23 (D)
Raiders, 21-17 (O)
1974—Raiders, 28-17 (D)
Broncos, 20-17 (O)
1975—Broncos, 42-17 (D)
Raiders, 17-10 (O)
1976—Raiders, 17-10 (D)
Raiders, 19-6 (O)
1977—Broncos, 30-7 (D)
Raiders, 24-14 (O)
**Broncos, 20-17 (D)
1978—Broncos, 14-6 (D)
Broncos, 21-6 (O)
1979—Broncos, 27-3 (O)
Raiders, 14-10 (D)
1980—Raiders, 9-3 (O)
Raiders, 24-21 (D)
1981—Broncos, 9-7 (D)
Broncos, 17-0 (O)
1982—Raiders, 27-10 (LA)
1983—Raiders, 22-7 (D)
Raiders, 22-20 (LA)
1984—Broncos, 16-13 (D)
Broncos, 22-19 (LA) OT
1985—Raiders, 31-28 (LA) OT

255

Raiders, 17-14 (D) OT
1986—Broncos, 38-36 (D)
    Broncos, 21-10 (LA)
1987—Broncos, 30-14 (D)
    Broncos, 23-17 (LA)
1988—Raiders, 30-27 (D) OT
    Raiders, 21-20 (LA)
1989—Broncos, 31-21 (D)
    Raiders, 16-13 (LA) (OT)
(Points—Raiders 1,371, Broncos 1,066)
*Franchise in Oakland prior to 1982
**AFC Championship

DENVER vs. L.A. RAMS
RS: Series tied, 3-3
1972—Broncos, 16-10 (LA)
1974—Rams, 17-10 (D)
1979—Rams, 13-9 (D)
1982—Broncos, 27-24 (LA)
1985—Rams, 20-16 (LA)
1988—Broncos, 35-24 (D)
(Points—Broncos 113, Rams 108)

DENVER vs. MIAMI
RS: Dolphins lead series, 5-2-1
1966—Dolphins, 24-7 (M)
    Broncos, 17-7 (D)
1967—Dolphins, 35-21 (M)
1968—Broncos, 21-14 (D)
1969—Dolphins, 27-24 (M)
1971—Tie, 10-10 (D)
1975—Dolphins, 14-13 (M)
1985—Dolphins, 30-26 (D)
(Points—Dolphins 161, Broncos 139)

DENVER vs. MINNESOTA
RS: Vikings lead series, 3-2
1972—Vikings, 23-20 (D)
1978—Vikings, 12-9 (M) OT
1981—Broncos, 19-17 (D)
1984—Broncos, 42-21 (D)
1987—Vikings, 34-27 (M)
(Points—Broncos 117, Vikings 107)

DENVER vs. *NEW ENGLAND
RS: Broncos lead series, 14-12
PS: Broncos lead series, 1-0
1960—Broncos, 13-10 (B)
    Broncos, 31-24 (D)
1961—Patriots, 45-17 (B)
    Patriots, 28-24 (D)
1962—Patriots, 41-16 (B)
    Patriots, 33-29 (D)
1963—Broncos, 14-10 (D)
    Patriots, 40-21 (B)
1964—Patriots, 39-10 (D)
    Patriots, 12-7 (B)
1965—Broncos, 27-10 (B)
    Patriots, 28-20 (D)
1966—Patriots, 24-10 (D)
    Broncos, 17-10 (B)
1967—Broncos, 26-21 (D)
1968—Patriots, 20-17 (D)
    Broncos, 35-14 (B)
1969—Broncos, 35-7 (D)
1972—Broncos, 45-21 (D)
1976—Patriots, 38-14 (NE)
1979—Broncos, 45-10 (D)
1980—Patriots, 23-14 (NE)
1984—Broncos, 26-19 (D)
1986—Broncos, 27-20 (D)
    **Broncos, 22-17 (D)
1987—Broncos, 31-20 (D)
1988—Broncos, 21-10 (D)
(Points—Broncos 614, Patriots 594)
*Franchise in Boston prior to 1971
**AFC Divisional Playoff

DENVER vs. NEW ORLEANS
RS: Broncos lead series, 4-1
1970—Broncos, 31-6 (NO)
1974—Broncos, 33-17 (D)
1979—Broncos, 10-3 (D)
1985—Broncos, 34-23 (D)
1988—Saints, 42-0 (NO)
(Points—Broncos 108, Saints 91)

DENVER vs. N.Y. GIANTS
RS: Giants lead series, 3-2
PS: Giants lead series, 1-0
1972—Giants, 29-17 (NY)
1976—Broncos, 14-13 (NY)
1980—Broncos, 14-9 (NY)
1986—Giants, 19-16 (NY)
    *Giants, 39-20 (Pasadena)
1989—Giants, 14-7 (D)
(Points—Giants 123, Broncos 88)
*Super Bowl XXI

DENVER vs. *N.Y. JETS
RS: Jets lead series, 11-10-1
1960—Titans, 28-24 (NY)
    Titans, 30-27 (D)
1961—Titans, 35-28 (NY)
    Broncos, 27-10 (D)
1962—Broncos, 32-10 (NY)
    Titans, 46-45 (D)
1963—Tie, 35-35 (NY)
    Jets, 14-9 (D)
1964—Jets, 30-6 (NY)

Broncos, 20-16 (D)
1965—Broncos, 16-13 (D)
    Jets, 45-10 (NY)
1966—Jets, 16-7 (D)
1967—Jets, 38-24 (D)
    Broncos, 33-24 (NY)
1968—Broncos, 21-13 (NY)
1969—Broncos, 21-19 (D)
1973—Broncos, 40-28 (NY)
1976—Broncos, 46-3 (D)
1978—Jets, 31-28 (D)
1980—Broncos, 31-24 (D)
1986—Jets, 22-10 (NY)
(Points—Broncos 540, Jets 530)
*Jets known as Titans prior to 1963

DENVER vs. PHILADELPHIA
RS: Eagles lead series, 4-2
1971—Eagles, 17-16 (P)
1975—Eagles, 25-10 (D)
1980—Eagles, 27-6 (P)
1983—Eagles, 13-10 (D)
1986—Broncos, 33-7 (P)
1989—Eagles, 28-24 (D)
(Points—Broncos 114, Eagles 102)

DENVER vs. *PHOENIX
RS: Broncos lead series, 2-0-1
1973—Tie, 17-17 (StL)
1977—Broncos, 7-0 (D)
1989—Broncos, 37-0 (P)
(Points—Broncos 61, Cardinals 17)
*Franchise in St. Louis prior to 1988

DENVER vs. PITTSBURGH
RS: Broncos lead series, 8-4-1
PS: Series tied, 2-2
1970—Broncos, 16-13 (D)
1971—Broncos, 22-10 (P)
1973—Broncos, 23-13 (P)
1974—Tie, 35-35 (D) OT
1975—Steelers, 20-9 (P)
1977—Broncos, 21-7 (D)
    *Broncos, 34-21 (D)
1978—Steelers, 21-17 (D)
    *Steelers, 33-10 (P)
1979—Steelers, 42-7 (D)
1983—Broncos, 14-10 (P)
1984—*Steelers, 24-17 (D)
1985—Broncos, 31-23 (P)
1986—Broncos, 21-10 (P)
1988—Steelers, 39-21 (P)
1989—Broncos, 34-7 (D)
    *Broncos, 24-23 (D)
(Points—Broncos 356, Steelers 351)
*AFC Divisional Playoff

DENVER vs. *SAN DIEGO
RS: Broncos lead series, 30-29-1
1960—Chargers, 23-19 (D)
    Chargers, 41-33 (LA)
1961—Chargers, 37-0 (D)
    Chargers, 19-16 (D)
1962—Broncos, 30-21 (D)
    Broncos, 23-20 (SD)
1963—Broncos, 50-34 (D)
    Chargers, 58-20 (SD)
1964—Chargers, 42-14 (SD)
    Chargers, 31-20 (D)
1965—Chargers, 34-31 (SD)
    Chargers, 33-21 (D)
1966—Chargers, 24-17 (SD)
    Broncos, 20-17 (D)
1967—Chargers, 38-21 (D)
    Chargers, 24-20 (SD)
1968—Chargers, 55-24 (SD)
    Chargers, 47-23 (D)
1969—Broncos, 13-0 (D)
    Chargers, 45-24 (SD)
1970—Broncos, 24-21 (SD)
    Tie, 17-17 (D)
1971—Broncos, 20-16 (D)
    Chargers, 45-17 (SD)
1972—Chargers, 37-14 (SD)
    Broncos, 38-13 (D)
1973—Broncos, 30-19 (D)
    Broncos, 42-28 (SD)
1974—Broncos, 27-7 (D)
    Chargers, 17-0 (SD)
1975—Broncos, 27-17 (SD)
    Broncos, 13-10 (D) OT
1976—Broncos, 26-0 (D)
    Chargers, 17-0 (SD)
1977—Broncos, 17-14 (SD)
    Broncos, 17-9 (D)
1978—Broncos, 27-14 (D)
    Chargers, 23-0 (SD)
1979—Broncos, 7-0 (D)
    Chargers, 17-7 (SD)
1980—Chargers, 30-13 (D)
    Broncos, 20-13 (SD)
1981—Chargers, 42-24 (D)
    Chargers, 34-17 (SD)
1982—Chargers, 23-3 (D)
    Chargers, 30-20 (SD)
1983—Broncos, 14-6 (D)
    Chargers, 31-7 (SD)

1984—Broncos, 16-13 (SD)
    Broncos, 16-13 (D)
1985—Chargers, 30-10 (SD)
    Broncos, 30-24 (D) OT
1986—Broncos, 31-14 (SD)
    Chargers, 9-3 (D)
1987—Broncos, 31-17 (SD)
    Broncos, 24-0 (D)
1988—Broncos, 34-3 (D)
    Broncos, 12-0 (SD)
1989—Broncos, 16-10 (D)
    Chargers, 19-16 (SD)
(Points—Chargers 1,313, Broncos 1,198)
*Franchise in Los Angeles prior to 1961

DENVER vs. SAN FRANCISCO
RS: Broncos lead series, 4-2
PS: 49ers lead series, 1-0
1970—49ers, 19-14 (SF)
1973—49ers, 36-34 (D)
1979—Broncos, 38-28 (SF)
1982—Broncos, 24-21 (D)
1985—Broncos, 17-16 (D)
1988—Broncos, 16-13 (SF) OT
1989—*49ers, 55-10 (New Orleans)
(Points—49ers 188, Broncos 153)
*Super Bowl XXIV

DENVER vs. SEATTLE
RS: Broncos lead series, 15-10
PS: Seahawks lead series, 1-0
1977—Broncos, 24-13 (S)
1978—Broncos, 28-7 (D)
    Broncos, 20-17 (S) OT
1979—Broncos, 37-34 (D)
    Seahawks, 28-23 (S)
1980—Broncos, 36-20 (D)
    Broncos, 25-17 (S)
1981—Seahawks, 13-10 (S)
    Broncos, 23-13 (D)
1982—Seahawks, 17-10 (D)
    Seahawks, 13-11 (S)
1983—Seahawks, 27-19 (S)
    Broncos, 38-27 (D)
    *Seahawks, 31-7 (S)
1984—Seahawks, 27-24 (S)
    Broncos, 31-14 (S)
1985—Broncos, 13-10 (D) OT
    Broncos, 27-24 (S)
1986—Broncos, 20-13 (D)
    Seahawks, 41-16 (S)
1987—Broncos, 40-17 (D)
    Seahawks, 28-21 (S)
1988—Seahawks, 21-14 (S)
    Seahawks, 42-14 (S)
1989—Broncos, 24-21 (S) OT
    Broncos, 41-14 (D)
(Points—Broncos 596, Seahawks 549)
*AFC First Round Playoff

DENVER vs. TAMPA BAY
RS: Broncos lead series, 2-0
1976—Broncos, 48-13 (D)
1981—Broncos, 24-7 (TB)
(Points—Broncos 72, Buccaneers 20)

DENVER vs. WASHINGTON
RS: Broncos lead series, 3-2
PS: Redskins lead series, 1-0
1970—Redskins, 19-3 (D)
1974—Redskins, 30-3 (W)
1980—Broncos, 20-17 (D)
1986—Broncos, 31-30 (D)
1987—*Redskins, 42-10 (San Diego)
1989—Broncos, 14-10 (W)
(Points—Redskins 148, Broncos 81)
*Super Bowl XXII

DETROIT vs. ATLANTA
RS: Lions lead series, 14-5;
See Atlanta vs. Detroit

DETROIT vs. BUFFALO
RS: Series tied, 1-1-1;
See Buffalo vs. Detroit

DETROIT vs. CHICAGO
RS: Bears lead series, 70-45-5;
See Chicago vs. Detroit

DETROIT vs. CINCINNATI
RS: Bengals lead series, 3-2;
See Cincinnati vs. Detroit

DETROIT vs. CLEVELAND
RS: Lions lead series, 10-3
PS: Lions lead series, 3-1;
See Cleveland vs. Detroit

DETROIT vs. DALLAS
RS: Cowboys lead series, 6-4
PS: Cowboys lead series, 1-0;
See Dallas vs. Detroit

DETROIT vs. DENVER
RS: Broncos lead series, 4-2;
See Denver vs. Detroit

*DETROIT vs. GREEN BAY
RS: Packers lead series, 60-52-7
1930—Packers, 47-13 (GB)
    Tie, 6-6 (P)
1932—Packers, 15-10 (GB)
    Spartans, 19-0 (P)

1933—Packers, 17-0 (GB)
    Spartans, 7-0 (P)
1934—Lions, 3-0 (GB)
    Packers, 3-0 (D)
1935—Packers, 13-9 (GB)
    Packers, 31-7 (GB)
    Lions, 20-10 (D)
1936—Packers, 20-18 (GB)
    Packers, 26-17 (D)
1937—Packers, 26-6 (GB)
    Packers, 14-13 (D)
1938—Lions, 17-7 (GB)
    Packers, 28-7 (D)
1939—Packers, 26-7 (GB)
    Packers, 12-7 (D)
1940—Lions, 23-14 (GB)
    Packers, 50-7 (D)
1941—Packers, 23-0 (GB)
    Packers, 24-7 (D)
1942—Packers, 38-7 (Mil)
    Packers, 28-7 (D)
1943—Packers, 35-14 (GB)
    Packers, 27-6 (D)
1944—Packers, 27-6 (GB)
    Packers, 14-0 (D)
1945—Packers, 57-21 (Mil)
    Lions, 14-3 (D)
1946—Packers, 10-7 (Mil)
    Packers, 9-0 (D)
1947—Packers, 34-17 (GB)
    Packers, 35-14 (D)
1948—Packers, 33-21 (GB)
    Lions, 24-20 (D)
1949—Packers, 16-14 (GB)
    Lions, 21-7 (D)
1950—Lions, 45-7 (GB)
    Lions, 24-21 (D)
1951—Lions, 24-17 (GB)
    Lions, 52-35 (D)
1952—Lions, 52-17 (GB)
    Lions, 48-24 (D)
1953—Lions, 14-7 (GB)
    Lions, 34-15 (D)
1954—Lions, 21-17 (GB)
    Lions, 28-24 (D)
1955—Packers, 20-17 (GB)
    Lions, 24-10 (D)
1956—Lions, 20-16 (GB)
    Packers, 24-20 (D)
1957—Lions, 24-14 (GB)
    Lions, 18-6 (D)
1958—Tie, 13-13 (GB)
    Lions, 24-14 (D)
1959—Packers, 28-10 (GB)
    Packers, 24-17 (D)
1960—Packers, 28-9 (GB)
    Lions, 23-10 (D)
1961—Lions, 17-13 (Mil)
    Packers, 17-9 (D)
1962—Packers, 9-7 (GB)
    Lions, 26-14 (D)
1963—Packers, 31-10 (Mil)
    Tie, 13-13 (D)
1964—Packers, 14-10 (D)
    Packers, 30-7 (GB)
1965—Packers, 31-21 (GB)
    Lions, 12-7 (GB)
1966—Packers, 23-14 (GB)
    Packers, 31-7 (D)
1967—Tie, 17-17 (GB)
    Packers, 27-17 (D)
1968—Lions, 23-17 (GB)
    Tie, 14-14 (D)
1969—Packers, 28-17 (D)
    Lions, 16-10 (GB)
1970—Lions, 40-0 (D)
    Lions, 20-0 (D)
1971—Lions, 31-28 (D)
    Tie, 14-14 (Mil)
1972—Packers, 24-23 (D)
    Packers, 33-7 (GB)
1973—Tie, 13-13 (GB)
    Lions, 34-0 (D)
1974—Packers, 21-19 (Mil)
    Lions, 19-17 (D)
1975—Lions, 30-16 (Mil)
    Lions, 13-10 (D)
1976—Packers, 24-14 (GB)
    Lions, 27-6 (D)
1977—Lions, 10-6 (D)
    Packers, 10-9 (GB)
1978—Lions, 13-7 (D)
    Packers, 35-14 (Mil)
1979—Packers, 24-16 (Mil)
    Packers, 18-13 (D)
1980—Lions, 29-7 (Mil)
    Lions, 24-3 (D)
1981—Lions, 31-27 (D)
    Packers, 31-17 (GB)
1982—Lions, 30-10 (GB)
    Lions, 27-24 (D)
1983—Lions, 38-14 (D)
    Lions, 23-20 (Mil) OT

1984—Packers, 41-9 (GB)
    Lions, 31-28 (D)
1985—Packers, 43-10 (GB)
    Packers, 26-23 (D)
1986—Lions, 21-14 (GB)
    Packers, 44-40 (D)
1987—Lions, 19-16 (GB) OT
    Packers, 34-33 (D)
1988—Lions, 19-9 (Mil)
    Lions, 30-14 (D)
1989—Packers, 23-20 (Mil) OT
    Lions, 31-22 (D)
(Points—Packers 2,304, Lions 2,112)
*Franchise in Portsmouth prior to 1934
and known as the Spartans
DETROIT vs. HOUSTON
RS: Oilers lead series, 3-2
1971—Lions, 31-7 (H)
1975—Oilers, 24-8 (H)
1983—Oilers, 27-17 (H)
1986—Lions, 24-13 (D)
1989—Oilers, 35-31 (H)
(Points—Lions 111, Oilers 106)
DETROIT vs. *INDIANAPOLIS
RS: Colts lead series, 17-16-2
1953—Lions, 27-17 (B)
    Lions, 17-7 (D)
1954—Lions, 35-0 (D)
    Lions, 27-3 (B)
1955—Colts, 28-13 (B)
    Lions, 24-14 (D)
1956—Lions, 31-14 (B)
    Lions, 27-3 (D)
1957—Colts, 34-14 (B)
    Lions, 31-27 (D)
1958—Colts, 28-15 (B)
    Colts, 40-14 (D)
1959—Colts, 21-9 (B)
    Colts, 31-24 (D)
1960—Lions, 30-17 (D)
    Lions, 20-15 (B)
1961—Lions, 16-15 (B)
    Colts, 17-14 (D)
1962—Lions, 29-20 (B)
    Lions, 21-14 (D)
1963—Colts, 25-21 (D)
    Colts, 24-21 (B)
1964—Colts, 34-0 (D)
    Lions, 31-14 (B)
1965—Colts, 31-7 (B)
    Tie, 24-24 (D)
1966—Colts, 45-14 (B)
    Lions, 20-14 (D)
1967—Colts, 41-7 (B)
1968—Colts, 27-10 (D)
1969—Tie, 17-17 (B)
1973—Colts, 29-27 (D)
1977—Lions, 13-10 (B)
1980—Colts, 10-9 (D)
1985—Colts, 14-6 (I)
(Points—Colts 724, Lions 665)
*Franchise in Baltimore prior to 1984
DETROIT vs. KANSAS CITY
RS: Series tied, 3-3
1971—Lions, 32-21 (D)
1975—Chiefs, 24-21 (KC) OT
1980—Chiefs, 20-17 (KC)
1981—Lions, 27-10 (D)
1987—Chiefs, 27-20 (D)
1988—Lions, 7-6 (KC)
(Points—Lions 124, Chiefs 108)
DETROIT vs. *L.A. RAIDERS
RS: Raiders lead series, 4-2
1970—Lions, 28-14 (D)
1974—Raiders, 35-13 (O)
1978—Raiders, 29-17 (O)
1981—Lions, 16-0 (D)
1984—Raiders, 24-3 (D)
1987—Raiders, 27-7 (LA)
(Points—Raiders 129, Lions 84)
*Franchise in Oakland prior to 1982
DETROIT vs. *L.A. RAMS
RS: Rams lead series, 39-33-1
PS: Lions lead series, 1-0
1937—Lions, 28-0 (C)
    Lions, 27-7 (D)
1938—Rams, 21-17 (C)
    Lions, 6-0 (D)
1939—Lions, 15-7 (D)
    Rams, 14-3 (C)
1940—Lions, 6-0 (D)
    Rams, 24-0 (C)
1941—Lions, 17-7 (D)
    Lions, 14-0 (C)
1942—Rams, 14-0 (D)
    Rams, 27-7 (C)
1944—Rams, 20-17 (D)
    Lions, 26-14 (C)
1945—Rams, 28-21 (D)
1946—Rams, 35-14 (LA)
    Rams, 41-20 (D)
1947—Rams, 27-13 (D)
    Rams, 28-17 (LA)

1948—Rams, 44-7 (LA)
    Rams, 34-27 (D)
1949—Rams, 27-24 (LA)
    Rams, 21-10 (D)
1950—Rams, 30-28 (D)
    Rams, 65-24 (LA)
1951—Rams, 27-21 (D)
    Lions, 24-22 (LA)
1952—Lions, 17-14 (LA)
    Lions, 24-16 (D)
    **Lions, 31-21 (D)
1953—Rams, 31-19 (D)
    Rams, 37-24 (LA)
1954—Lions, 21-3 (D)
    Lions, 27-24 (LA)
1955—Lions, 17-10 (D)
    Rams, 24-13 (LA)
1956—Lions, 24-21 (D)
    Lions, 16-7 (LA)
1957—Lions, 10-7 (D)
    Rams, 35-17 (LA)
1958—Rams, 42-28 (D)
    Lions, 41-24 (LA)
1959—Lions, 17-7 (LA)
    Lions, 23-17 (D)
1960—Rams, 48-35 (LA)
    Lions, 12-10 (D)
1961—Lions, 14-13 (LA)
    Lions, 28-10 (LA)
1962—Lions, 13-10 (D)
    Lions, 12-3 (LA)
1963—Lions, 23-2 (LA)
    Rams, 28-21 (D)
1964—Tie, 17-17 (LA)
    Lions, 37-17 (D)
1965—Lions, 20-0 (D)
    Lions, 31-7 (LA)
1966—Rams, 14-7 (D)
    Rams, 23-3 (LA)
1967—Rams, 31-7 (D)
1968—Rams, 10-7 (LA)
1969—Lions, 28-0 (D)
1970—Lions, 28-23 (LA)
1971—Rams, 21-13 (D)
1972—Lions, 34-17 (LA)
1974—Rams, 16-13 (LA)
1975—Rams, 20-0 (D)
1976—Lions, 20-17 (D)
1980—Lions, 41-20 (LA)
1981—Rams, 20-13 (LA)
1982—Lions, 19-14 (LA)
1983—Rams, 21-10 (LA)
1986—Rams, 14-10 (LA)
1987—Rams, 37-16 (D)
1988—Rams, 17-10 (LA)
(Points—Rams 1,434, Lions 1,334)
*Franchise in Cleveland prior to 1946
**Conference Playoff
DETROIT vs. MIAMI
RS: Dolphins lead series, 2-1
1973—Dolphins, 34-7 (M)
1979—Dolphins, 28-10 (D)
1985—Lions, 31-21 (D)
(Points—Dolphins 83, Lions 48)
DETROIT vs. MINNESOTA
RS: Vikings lead series, 37-18-2
1961—Lions, 37-10 (M)
    Lions, 13-7 (D)
1962—Lions, 17-6 (M)
    Lions, 37-23 (D)
1963—Lions, 28-10 (D)
    Vikings, 34-31 (M)
1964—Lions, 24-20 (M)
    Tie, 23-23 (D)
1965—Lions, 31-29 (M)
    Vikings, 29-7 (D)
1966—Lions, 32-31 (M)
    Vikings, 28-16 (D)
1967—Tie, 10-10 (M)
    Lions, 14-3 (D)
1968—Vikings, 24-10 (M)
    Vikings, 13-6 (D)
1969—Vikings, 24-10 (M)
    Vikings, 27-0 (D)
1970—Vikings, 30-17 (D)
    Vikings, 24-20 (M)
1971—Vikings, 16-13 (D)
    Vikings, 29-10 (M)
1972—Vikings, 34-10 (D)
    Vikings, 16-14 (M)
1973—Vikings, 23-9 (D)
    Vikings, 28-7 (M)
1974—Vikings, 7-6 (D)
    Lions, 20-16 (M)
1975—Vikings, 25-19 (M)
    Lions, 17-10 (D)
1976—Vikings, 10-9 (D)
    Vikings, 31-23 (M)
1977—Vikings, 14-7 (M)
    Vikings, 30-21 (D)
1978—Vikings, 17-7 (M)
    Lions, 45-14 (D)
1979—Vikings, 13-10 (D)

    Vikings, 14-7 (M)
1980—Lions, 27-7 (D)
    Vikings, 34-0 (M)
1981—Vikings, 26-24 (M)
    Lions, 45-7 (D)
1982—Vikings, 34-31 (D)
1983—Vikings, 20-17 (M)
    Lions, 13-2 (D)
1984—Vikings, 29-28 (D)
    Lions, 16-14 (M)
1985—Vikings, 16-13 (M)
    Lions, 41-21 (D)
1986—Lions, 13-10 (M)
    Vikings, 24-10 (D)
1987—Vikings, 34-19 (M)
    Vikings, 17-14 (D)
1988—Vikings, 44-17 (M)
    Vikings, 23-0 (D)
1989—Vikings, 24-17 (M)
    Vikings, 20-7 (D)
(Points—Vikings 1,161, Lions 989)
DETROIT vs. NEW ENGLAND
RS: Series tied, 2-2
1971—Lions, 34-7 (NE)
1976—Lions, 30-10 (D)
1979—Patriots, 24-17 (NE)
1985—Patriots, 23-6 (NE)
(Points—Lions 87, Patriots 64)
DETROIT vs. NEW ORLEANS
RS: Series tied, 5-5-1
1968—Tie, 20-20 (D)
1970—Saints, 19-17 (NO)
1972—Lions, 27-14 (D)
1973—Saints, 20-13 (NO)
1974—Lions, 19-14 (D)
1976—Saints, 17-16 (NO)
1977—Lions, 23-19 (D)
1979—Saints, 17-7 (NO)
1980—Lions, 24-13 (D)
1988—Saints, 22-14 (D)
1989—Lions, 21-14 (D)
(Points—Lions 201, Saints 189)
DETROIT vs. N.Y. GIANTS
RS: Lions lead series, 17-14-1
PS: Lions lead series, 1-0
1930—Giants, 19-6 (P)
1931—Spartans, 14-6 (P)
    Giants, 14-0 (NY)
1932—Spartans, 7-0 (P)
    Spartans, 6-0 (NY)
1933—Spartans, 17-7 (P)
    Giants, 13-10 (NY)
1934—Lions, 9-0 (D)
1935—**Lions, 26-7 (D)
1936—Giants, 14-7 (NY)
    Lions, 38-0 (D)
1937—Lions, 17-0 (NY)
1939—Lions, 18-14 (D)
1941—Giants, 20-13 (NY)
1943—Tie, 0-0 (D)
1945—Giants, 35-14 (NY)
1947—Lions, 35-7 (D)
1949—Lions, 45-21 (NY)
1953—Lions, 27-16 (NY)
1955—Giants, 24-19 (D)
1958—Giants, 19-17 (D)
1962—Giants, 17-14 (NY)
1964—Lions, 26-3 (D)
1967—Lions, 30-7 (NY)
1969—Lions, 24-0 (D)
1972—Lions, 30-16 (D)
1974—Lions, 20-19 (D)
1976—Giants, 24-10 (NY)
1982—Giants, 13-6 (D)
1983—Lions, 15-9 (D)
1988—Giants, 30-10 (NY)
    Giants, 13-10 (D) OT
1989—Giants, 24-14 (NY)
(Points—Lions 554, Giants 411)
*Franchise in Portsmouth prior to 1934
and known as the Spartans
**NFL Championship
DETROIT vs. N.Y. JETS
RS: Jets lead series, 3-2
1972—Lions, 37-20 (D)
1979—Jets, 31-10 (NY)
1982—Jets, 28-13 (D)
1985—Lions, 31-20 (D)
1988—Jets, 17-10 (D)
(Points—Jets 116, Lions 101)
DETROIT vs. PHILADELPHIA
RS: Lions lead series, 12-9-2
1933—Spartans, 25-0 (P)
1934—Lions, 10-0 (D)
1935—Lions, 35-0 (D)
1936—Lions, 23-0 (D)
1938—Eagles, 21-7 (D)
1940—Lions, 21-0 (P)
1941—Lions, 21-17 (D)
1945—Lions, 28-24 (D)
1948—Eagles, 45-21 (P)
1949—Eagles, 22-14 (D)
1951—Lions, 28-10 (P)
1954—Tie, 13-13 (D)

1957—Lions, 27-16 (P)
1960—Eagles, 28-10 (P)
1961—Eagles, 27-24 (D)
1965—Lions, 35-28 (P)
1968—Eagles, 12-0 (D)
1971—Eagles, 23-20 (D)
1974—Eagles, 28-17 (P)
1977—Lions, 17-13 (D)
1979—Eagles, 44-7 (D)
1984—Tie, 23-23 (P) OT
1986—Lions, 13-11 (P)
(Points—Lions 439, Eagles 405)
*Franchise in Portsmouth prior to 1934
and known as the Spartans
DETROIT vs. **PHOENIX
RS: Lions lead series, 25-16-5
1930—Tie, 0-0 (P)
    Cardinals, 23-0 (C)
1931—Cardinals, 20-19 (C)
1932—Tie, 7-7 (P)
1933—Spartans, 7-6 (P)
1934—Lions, 6-0 (P)
    Lions, 17-13 (C)
1935—Tie, 10-10 (C)
    Lions, 7-6 (C)
1936—Lions, 39-0 (D)
    Lions, 14-7 (C)
1937—Lions, 16-7 (C)
    Lions, 16-7 (C)
1938—Lions, 10-0 (C)
    Lions, 7-3 (C)
1939—Lions, 21-3 (D)
    Lions, 17-3 (C)
1940—Tie, 0-0 (Buffalo)
    Lions, 43-14 (C)
1941—Tie, 14-14 (C)
    Lions, 21-3 (D)
1942—Cardinals, 13-0 (C)
    Cardinals, 7-0 (D)
1943—Lions, 35-17 (D)
    Lions, 7-0 (C)
1945—Lions, 10-0 (C)
    Lions, 26-0 (D)
1946—Cardinals, 34-14 (C)
    Cardinals, 36-14 (D)
1947—Cardinals, 45-21 (C)
    Cardinals, 17-7 (D)
1948—Cardinals, 56-20 (C)
    Cardinals, 28-14 (D)
1949—Lions, 24-7 (C)
    Cardinals, 42-19 (D)
1959—Lions, 45-21 (D)
1961—Lions, 45-14 (StL)
1967—Cardinals, 38-28 (StL)
1969—Lions, 20-0 (D)
1970—Lions, 16-3 (D)
1973—Lions, 20-16 (StL)
1975—Cardinals, 24-13 (D)
1978—Cardinals, 21-14 (StL)
1980—Lions, 20-7 (D)
    Cardinals, 24-23 (StL)
1989—Cardinals, 16-13 (D)
(Points—Lions 759, Cardinals 642)
*Franchise in St. Louis prior to 1988
and known as the Spartans
**Franchise in St. Louis prior to 1988
and in Chicago prior to 1960
DETROIT vs. *PITTSBURGH
RS: Lions lead series, 13-10-1
1934—Lions, 40-7 (D)
1936—Lions, 28-3 (D)
1937—Lions, 7-3 (D)
1938—Lions, 16-7 (D)
1940—Pirates, 10-7 (D)
1942—Steelers, 35-7 (D)
1946—Lions, 17-7 (D)
1947—Steelers, 17-10 (P)
1948—Lions, 17-14 (D)
1949—Steelers, 14-7 (P)
1950—Lions, 10-7 (D)
1952—Lions, 31-6 (P)
1953—Lions, 38-21 (D)
1955—Lions, 31-28 (P)
1956—Lions, 45-7 (D)
1959—Tie, 10-10 (P)
1962—Lions, 45-7 (D)
1966—Steelers, 17-3 (P)
1967—Steelers, 24-14 (D)
1969—Steelers, 16-13 (P)
1973—Steelers, 24-10 (P)
1983—Lions, 45-3 (D)
1986—Steelers, 27-17 (P)
1989—Steelers, 23-3 (P)
(Points—Lions 471, Steelers 337)
*Steelers known as Pirates prior to 1941
DETROIT vs. SAN DIEGO
RS: Lions lead series, 3-2
1972—Lions, 34-20 (D)
1977—Lions, 20-0 (D)
1978—Lions, 31-14 (D)
1981—Chargers, 28-23 (SD)
1984—Chargers, 27-24 (SD)
(Points—Lions 132, Chargers 89)

DETROIT vs. SAN FRANCISCO
RS: Lions lead series, 25-23-1
PS: Series tied, 1-1
1950—Lions, 24-7 (D)
　　　49ers, 28-27 (SF)
1951—49ers, 20-10 (D)
　　　49ers, 21-17 (SF)
1952—49ers, 17-3 (SF)
　　　49ers, 28-0 (D)
1953—Lions, 24-21 (D)
　　　Lions, 14-10 (SF)
1954—49ers, 37-31 (SF)
　　　Lions, 48-7 (D)
1955—49ers, 27-24 (D)
　　　49ers, 38-21 (SF)
1956—Lions, 20-17 (D)
　　　Lions, 17-13 (SF)
1957—49ers, 35-31 (SF)
　　　Lions, 31-10 (D)
　　　*Lions, 31-27 (SF)
1958—49ers, 24-21 (SF)
　　　Lions, 35-21 (D)
1959—49ers, 34-13 (D)
　　　49ers, 33-7 (SF)
1960—49ers, 14-10 (D)
　　　Lions, 24-0 (SF)
1961—49ers, 49-0 (D)
　　　Tie, 20-20 (SF)
1962—Lions, 45-24 (D)
　　　Lions, 38-24 (SF)
1963—Lions, 26-3 (D)
　　　Lions, 45-7 (SF)
1964—Lions, 26-17 (SF)
　　　Lions, 24-7 (D)
1965—49ers, 27-21 (D)
　　　49ers, 17-14 (SF)
1966—49ers, 27-24 (D)
　　　49ers, 41-14 (D)
1967—Lions, 45-3 (SF)
1968—49ers, 14-7 (D)
1969—Lions, 26-14 (SF)
1970—Lions, 28-7 (D)
1971—49ers, 31-27 (SF)
1973—Lions, 30-20 (D)
1974—Lions, 17-13 (D)
1975—Lions, 28-17 (SF)
1977—49ers, 28-7 (SF)
1978—Lions, 33-14 (D)
1980—Lions, 17-13 (D)
1981—Lions, 24-17 (D)
1983—**49ers, 24-23 (SF)
1984—49ers, 30-27 (D)
1985—Lions, 23-21 (D)
1988—49ers, 20-13 (SF)
(Points—Lions 1,155, 49ers 1,038)
*Conference Playoff
**NFC Divisional Playoff
DETROIT vs. SEATTLE
RS: Seahawks lead series, 3-1
1976—Lions, 41-14 (S)
1978—Seahawks, 28-16 (S)
1984—Seahawks, 38-17 (S)
1987—Seahawks, 37-14 (D)
(Points—Seahawks 117, Lions 88)
DETROIT vs. TAMPA BAY
RS: Lions lead series, 13-11
1977—Lions, 16-7 (D)
1978—Lions, 15-7 (TB)
　　　Lions, 34-23 (D)
1979—Buccaneers, 31-16 (TB)
　　　Buccaneers, 16-14 (D)
1980—Lions, 24-10 (TB)
　　　Lions, 27-14 (D)
1981—Buccaneers, 28-10 (TB)
　　　Buccaneers, 20-17 (D)
1982—Buccaneers, 23-21 (TB)
1983—Lions, 11-0 (TB)
　　　Lions, 23-20 (D)
1984—Buccaneers, 21-17 (TB)
　　　Lions, 13-7 (D) OT
1985—Lions, 30-9 (D)
　　　Buccaneers, 19-16 (TB) OT
1986—Buccaneers, 24-20 (D)
　　　Lions, 38-17 (TB)
1987—Buccaneers, 31-27 (D)
　　　Lions, 20-10 (TB)
1988—Buccaneers, 23-20 (D)
　　　Buccaneers, 21-10 (TB)
1989—Lions, 17-16 (TB)
　　　Lions, 33-7 (D)
(Points—Lions 489, Buccaneers 404)
***DETROIT vs. **WASHINGTON**
RS: Redskins lead series, 19-8
PS: Redskins lead series, 1-0
1932—Spartans, 10-0 (P)
1933—Spartans, 13-0 (B)
1934—Lions, 24-0 (D)
1935—Lions, 17-7 (B)
　　　Lions, 14-0 (D)
1938—Redskins, 7-5 (D)
1939—Redskins, 31-7 (W)
1940—Redskins, 20-14 (D)
1942—Redskins, 15-3 (D)

1943—Redskins, 42-20 (W)
1946—Redskins, 17-16 (W)
1947—Lions, 38-21 (D)
1948—Redskins, 46-21 (W)
1951—Lions, 35-17 (D)
1956—Redskins, 18-17 (W)
1965—Lions, 14-10 (D)
1968—Redskins, 14-3 (W)
1970—Redskins, 31-10 (W)
1973—Redskins, 20-0 (D)
1976—Redskins, 20-7 (W)
1978—Redskins, 21-19 (D)
1979—Redskins, 27-24 (D)
1981—Redskins, 33-31 (W)
1982—***Redskins, 31-7 (W)
1983—Redskins, 38-17 (W)
1984—Redskins, 28-14 (D)
1985—Redskins, 24-3 (W)
1987—Redskins, 20-13 (W)
(Points—Redskins 558, Lions 416)
*Franchise in Portsmouth prior to 1934 and known as the Spartans.
**Franchise in Boston prior to 1937
***NFC First Round Playoff

GREEN BAY vs. ATLANTA
RS: Packers lead series, 9-7;
See Atlanta vs. Green Bay
GREEN BAY vs. BUFFALO
RS: Bills lead series, 3-1;
See Buffalo vs. Green Bay
GREEN BAY vs. CHICAGO
RS: Bears lead series, 75-57-6
PS: Bears lead series, 1-0;
See Chicago vs. Green Bay
GREEN BAY vs. CINCINNATI
RS: Bengals lead series, 4-2;
See Cincinnati vs. Green Bay
GREEN BAY vs. CLEVELAND
RS: Packers lead series, 7-5
PS: Packers lead series, 1-0;
See Cleveland vs. Green Bay
GREEN BAY vs. DALLAS
RS: Packers lead series, 8-4
PS: Packers lead series, 2-1;
See Dallas vs. Green Bay
GREEN BAY vs. DENVER
RS: Broncos lead series, 3-1-1;
See Denver vs. Green Bay
GREEN BAY vs. DETROIT
RS: Packers lead series, 60-52-7;
See Detroit vs. Green Bay
GREEN BAY vs. HOUSTON
RS: Oilers lead series, 3-2
1972—Packers, 23-10 (H)
1977—Oilers, 16-10 (GB)
1980—Oilers, 22-3 (GB)
1983—Packers, 41-38 (H) OT
1986—Oilers, 31-3 (GB)
(Points—Oilers 117, Packers 80)
GREEN BAY vs. *INDIANAPOLIS
RS: Colts lead series, 18-17-1
PS: Packers lead series, 1-0
1953—Packers, 37-14 (GB)
　　　Packers, 35-24 (B)
1954—Packers, 7-6 (B)
　　　Packers, 24-13 (Mil)
1955—Colts, 24-20 (Mil)
　　　Colts, 14-10 (B)
1956—Packers, 38-33 (Mil)
　　　Colts, 28-21 (B)
1957—Colts, 45-17 (Mil)
　　　Packers, 24-21 (B)
1958—Colts, 24-17 (Mil)
　　　Colts, 56-0 (B)
1959—Colts, 38-21 (B)
　　　Colts, 28-24 (Mil)
1960—Packers, 35-21 (GB)
　　　Colts, 38-24 (B)
1961—Packers, 45-7 (GB)
　　　Colts, 45-21 (B)
1962—Packers, 17-6 (B)
　　　Packers, 17-13 (GB)
1963—Packers, 31-20 (GB)
　　　Packers, 34-20 (B)
1964—Colts, 21-20 (GB)
　　　Colts, 24-21 (B)
1965—Packers, 20-17 (Mil)
　　　Packers, 42-27 (B)
　　　**Packers, 13-10 (GB) OT
1966—Packers, 24-3 (Mil)
　　　Packers, 14-10 (B)
1967—Colts, 13-10 (B)
1968—Colts, 16-3 (B)
1969—Colts, 14-6 (B)
1970—Colts, 13-10 (Mil)
1974—Packers, 20-13 (B)
1982—Tie, 20-20 (B) OT
1985—Colts, 37-10 (I)
1988—Colts, 20-13 (GB)
(Points—Colts 796, Packers 765)
*Franchise in Baltimore prior to 1984
**Conference Playoff

GREEN BAY vs. KANSAS CITY
RS: Chiefs lead series, 2-1-1
PS: Packers lead series, 1-0
1966—*Packers, 35-10 (Los Angeles)
1973—Tie, 10-10 (Mil)
1977—Chiefs, 20-10 (KC)
1987—Packers, 23-3 (KC)
1989—Chiefs, 21-3 (GB)
(Points—Packers 81, Chiefs 64)
*Super Bowl I
GREEN BAY vs. *L.A. RAIDERS
RS: Raiders lead series, 5-0
PS: Packers lead series, 1-0
1967—**Packers, 33-14 (Miami)
1972—Raiders, 20-14 (GB)
1976—Raiders, 18-14 (O)
1978—Raiders, 28-3 (GB)
1984—Raiders, 28-7 (LA)
1987—Raiders, 20-0 (GB)
(Points—Raiders 128, Packers 71)
*Franchise in Oakland prior to 1982
**Super Bowl II
GREEN BAY vs. *L.A. RAMS
RS: Rams lead series, 41-33-2
PS: Packers lead series, 1-0
1937—Packers, 35-10 (C)
　　　Packers, 35-7 (GB)
1938—Packers, 26-17 (GB)
　　　Packers, 28-7 (C)
1939—Rams, 27-24 (GB)
　　　Packers, 7-6 (C)
1940—Packers, 31-14 (GB)
　　　Tie, 13-13 (C)
1941—Packers, 24-7 (Mil)
　　　Packers, 17-14 (C)
1942—Packers, 45-28 (GB)
　　　Packers, 30-12 (C)
1944—Packers, 30-21 (GB)
　　　Packers, 42-7 (C)
1945—Packers, 27-14 (GB)
　　　Rams, 20-7 (C)
1946—Rams, 21-17 (Mil)
　　　Rams, 38-17 (LA)
1947—Packers, 17-14 (Mil)
　　　Packers, 30-10 (LA)
1948—Packers, 16-0 (GB)
　　　Rams, 24-10 (LA)
1949—Rams, 48-7 (GB)
　　　Rams, 35-7 (LA)
1950—Rams, 45-14 (Mil)
　　　Rams, 51-14 (LA)
1951—Rams, 28-0 (Mil)
　　　Rams, 42-14 (LA)
1952—Rams, 30-28 (Mil)
　　　Rams, 45-27 (LA)
1953—Rams, 38-20 (Mil)
　　　Rams, 33-17 (LA)
1954—Packers, 35-17 (Mil)
　　　Rams, 35-27 (LA)
1955—Packers, 30-28 (Mil)
　　　Rams, 31-17 (LA)
1956—Packers, 42-17 (Mil)
　　　Rams, 49-21 (LA)
1957—Rams, 31-27 (Mil)
　　　Rams, 42-17 (LA)
1958—Rams, 20-7 (GB)
　　　Rams, 34-20 (LA)
1959—Rams, 45-6 (Mil)
　　　Packers, 38-20 (LA)
1960—Rams, 33-31 (Mil)
　　　Packers, 35-21 (LA)
1961—Packers, 35-17 (GB)
　　　Packers, 24-17 (LA)
1962—Packers, 41-10 (Mil)
　　　Packers, 20-17 (LA)
1963—Packers, 42-10 (GB)
　　　Packers, 31-14 (LA)
1964—Rams, 27-17 (Mil)
　　　Tie, 24-24 (LA)
1965—Packers, 6-3 (Mil)
　　　Rams, 21-10 (LA)
1966—Packers, 24-13 (GB)
　　　Packers, 27-23 (LA)
1967—Rams, 27-24 (LA)
　　　**Packers, 28-7 (Mil)
1968—Rams, 16-14 (Mil)
1969—Rams, 34-21 (LA)
1970—Rams, 31-21 (GB)
1971—Rams, 30-13 (LA)
1973—Rams, 24-7 (LA)
1974—Packers, 17-6 (Mil)
1975—Rams, 22-5 (LA)
1977—Rams, 24-6 (Mil)
1978—Rams, 31-14 (LA)
1980—Rams, 51-21 (GB)
1981—Rams, 35-23 (LA)
1982—Packers, 35-23 (Mil)
1983—Packers, 27-24 (Mil)
1984—Packers, 31-6 (Mil)
1985—Rams, 34-17 (LA)
1988—Rams, 34-7 (GB)
1989—Rams, 41-38 (LA)
(Points—Rams 1,858, Packers 1,686)

*Franchise in Cleveland prior to 1946
**Conference Championship
GREEN BAY vs. MIAMI
RS: Dolphins lead series, 6-0
1971—Dolphins, 27-6 (Mia)
1975—Dolphins, 31-7 (GB)
1979—Dolphins, 27-7 (Mia)
1985—Dolphins, 34-24 (GB)
1988—Dolphins, 24-17 (Mia)
1989—Dolphins, 23-20 (Mia)
(Points—Dolphins 166, Packers 81)
GREEN BAY vs. MINNESOTA
RS: Packers lead series, 29-27-1
1961—Packers, 33-7 (GB)
　　　Packers, 28-10 (Mil)
1962—Packers, 34-7 (GB)
　　　Packers, 48-21 (Minn)
1963—Packers, 37-28 (Minn)
　　　Packers, 28-7 (GB)
1964—Vikings, 24-23 (GB)
　　　Packers, 42-13 (Minn)
1965—Packers, 38-13 (Minn)
　　　Packers, 24-19 (GB)
1966—Vikings, 20-17 (GB)
　　　Packers, 28-16 (Minn)
1967—Vikings, 10-7 (Mil)
　　　Packers, 30-27 (Minn)
1968—Vikings, 26-13 (GB)
　　　Vikings, 14-10 (Minn)
1969—Vikings, 19-7 (GB)
　　　Vikings, 9-7 (Minn)
1970—Packers, 13-10 (Mil)
　　　Vikings, 10-3 (Minn)
1971—Vikings, 24-13 (GB)
　　　Vikings, 3-0 (Minn)
1972—Vikings, 27-13 (GB)
　　　Packers, 23-7 (Minn)
1973—Vikings, 11-3 (Minn)
　　　Vikings, 31-7 (GB)
1974—Vikings, 32-17 (GB)
　　　Packers, 19-7 (Minn)
1975—Vikings, 28-17 (GB)
　　　Vikings, 24-3 (Minn)
1976—Vikings, 17-10 (Mil)
　　　Vikings, 20-9 (Minn)
1977—Vikings, 19-7 (Minn)
　　　Vikings, 13-6 (GB)
1978—Vikings, 21-7 (Minn)
　　　Tie, 10-10 (GB) OT
1979—Vikings, 27-21 (Minn) OT
　　　Packers, 19-7 (Mil)
1980—Vikings, 16-3 (GB)
　　　Packers, 25-13 (Minn)
1981—Vikings, 30-13 (Mil)
　　　Packers, 35-23 (Minn)
1982—Packers, 26-7 (Mil)
1983—Vikings, 20-17 (GB) OT
　　　Packers, 29-21 (Minn)
1984—Packers, 45-17 (Mil)
　　　Vikings, 38-14 (Minn)
1985—Packers, 20-17 (Minn)
　　　Packers, 27-17 (Mil)
1986—Vikings, 42-7 (Minn)
　　　Vikings, 32-6 (GB)
1987—Packers, 23-16 (Mil)
　　　Packers, 16-10 (Minn)
1988—Packers, 34-14 (Minn)
　　　Packers, 18-6 (GB)
1989—Vikings, 26-14 (Minn)
　　　Packers, 20-19 (GB)
(Points—Packers 1,103, Vikings 985)
GREEN BAY vs. NEW ENGLAND
RS: Series tied, 2-2
1973—Patriots, 33-24 (NE)
1979—Packers, 27-14 (GB)
1985—Patriots, 26-20 (NE)
1988—Packers, 45-3 (Mil)
(Points—Packers 116, Patriots 76)
GREEN BAY vs. NEW ORLEANS
RS: Packers lead series, 11-4
1968—Packers, 29-7 (Mil)
1971—Saints, 29-21 (Mil)
1972—Packers, 30-20 (NO)
1973—Packers, 30-10 (Mil)
1975—Saints, 20-19 (NO)
1976—Packers, 32-27 (NO)
1977—Packers, 24-20 (NO)
1978—Packers, 28-17 (Mil)
1979—Packers, 28-19 (Mil)
1981—Packers, 35-7 (NO)
1984—Packers, 23-13 (NO)
1985—Packers, 38-14 (Mil)
1986—Saints, 24-10 (NO)
1987—Saints, 33-24 (NO)
1989—Packers, 35-34 (GB)
(Points—Packers 406, Saints 294)
GREEN BAY vs. N.Y. GIANTS
RS: Packers lead series, 21-19-2
PS: Packers lead series, 4-1
1928—Giants, 6-0 (NY)
　　　Packers, 7-0 (NY)
1929—Packers, 20-6 (NY)
1930—Packers, 14-7 (GB)

Giants, 13-6 (NY)
1931—Packers, 27-7 (GB)
Packers, 14-10 (NY)
1932—Packers, 13-0 (GB)
Giants, 6-0 (NY)
1933—Packers, 10-7 (Mil)
Giants, 17-6 (NY)
1934—Packers, 20-6 (Mil)
Giants, 17-3 (NY)
1935—Packers, 16-7 (GB)
1936—Packers, 26-14 (NY)
1937—Giants, 10-0 (Mil)
1938—Giants, 15-3 (NY)
*Giants, 23-17 (NY)
1939—*Packers, 27-0 (Mil)
1940—Packers, 7-3 (NY)
1942—Tie, 21-21 (NY)
1943—Packers, 35-21 (NY)
1944—Giants, 24-0 (NY)
*Packers, 14-7 (NY)
1945—Packers, 23-14 (NY)
1947—Tie, 24-24 (NY)
1948—Giants, 49-3 (Mil)
1949—Giants, 30-10 (GB)
1952—Packers, 17-3 (NY)
1957—Giants, 31-17 (GB)
1959—Giants, 20-3 (NY)
1961—Packers, 20-17 (Mil)
*Packers, 37-0 (GB)
1962—*Packers, 16-7 (NY)
1967—Packers, 48-21 (NY)
1969—Packers, 20-10 (Mil)
1971—Giants, 42-40 (GB)
1973—Packers, 16-14 (New Haven)
1975—Packers, 40-14 (Mil)
1980—Giants, 27-21 (NY)
1981—Packers, 27-14 (NY)
Packers, 26-24 (Mil)
1982—Packers, 27-19 (NY)
1983—Giants, 27-3 (NY)
1985—Packers, 23-20 (GB)
1986—Giants, 55-24 (NY)
1987—Giants, 20-10 (NY)
(Points—Packers 794, Giants 756)
*NFL Championship

GREEN BAY vs. N.Y. JETS
RS: Jets lead series, 4-1
1973—Packers, 23-7 (Mil)
1979—Jets, 27-22 (GB)
1981—Jets, 28-3 (NY)
1982—Jets, 15-13 (NY)
1985—Jets, 24-3 (Mil)
(Points—Jets 101, Packers 64)

GREEN BAY vs. PHILADELPHIA
RS: Packers lead series, 18-4
PS: Eagles lead series, 1-0
1933—Packers, 35-9 (GB)
Packers, 10-0 (P)
1934—Packers, 19-6 (GB)
1935—Packers, 13-6 (P)
1937—Packers, 37-7 (Mil)
1939—Packers, 23-16 (P)
1940—Packers, 27-20 (Mil)
1942—Packers, 7-0 (P)
1946—Packers, 19-7 (P)
1947—Eagles, 28-14 (P)
1951—Packers, 37-24 (GB)
1952—Packers, 12-10 (Mil)
1954—Packers, 37-14 (P)
1958—Packers, 38-35 (GB)
1960—*Eagles, 17-13 (P)
1962—Packers, 49-0 (P)
1968—Packers, 30-13 (GB)
1970—Packers, 30-17 (Mil)
1974—Eagles, 36-14 (P)
1976—Packers, 28-13 (GB)
1978—Eagles, 10-3 (P)
1979—Eagles, 21-10 (GB)
1987—Packers, 16-10 (GB) OT
(Points—Packers 521, Eagles 319)
*NFL Championship

GREEN BAY vs. *PHOENIX
RS: Packers lead series, 38-21-4
PS: Packers lead series, 1-0
1921—Tie, 3-3 (C)
1922—Cardinals, 16-3 (C)
1924—Cardinals, 3-0 (C)
1925—Cardinals, 9-6 (C)
1926—Cardinals, 13-7 (GB)
Packers, 3-0 (C)
1927—Packers, 13-0 (GB)
Tie, 6-6 (C)
1928—Packers, 20-0 (GB)
1929—Packers, 9-2 (GB)
Packers, 7-6 (C)
Packers, 12-0 (C)
1930—Packers, 14-0 (GB)
Cardinals, 13-6 (C)
1931—Packers, 26-7 (GB)
Cardinals, 21-13 (C)
1932—Packers, 15-7 (GB)
Packers, 19-9 (C)
1933—Packers, 14-6 (C)

1934—Packers, 15-0 (GB)
Cardinals, 9-0 (Mil)
Cardinals, 6-0 (C)
1935—Cardinals, 7-6 (GB)
Cardinals, 3-0 (Mil)
Cardinals, 9-7 (C)
1936—Packers, 10-7 (GB)
Packers, 24-0 (Mil)
Tie, 0-0 (C)
1937—Cardinals, 14-7 (GB)
Packers, 34-13 (Mil)
1938—Packers, 28-7 (Mil)
Packers, 24-22 (Buffalo)
1939—Packers, 14-10 (GB)
Packers, 27-20 (Mil)
1940—Packers, 31-6 (Mil)
Packers, 28-7 (C)
1941—Packers, 14-13 (Mil)
Packers, 17-9 (GB)
1942—Packers, 17-13 (C)
Packers, 55-24 (GB)
1943—Packers, 28-7 (C)
Packers, 35-14 (Mil)
1945—Packers, 33-14 (GB)
1946—Packers, 19-7 (C)
Cardinals, 24-6 (GB)
1947—Cardinals, 14-10 (GB)
Cardinals, 21-20 (C)
1948—Cardinals, 17-7 (Mil)
Cardinals, 42-7 (C)
1949—Cardinals, 39-17 (Mil)
Cardinals, 41-21 (C)
1955—Packers, 31-14 (GB)
1956—Packers, 24-21 (C)
1962—Packers, 17-0 (Mil)
1963—Packers, 30-7 (StL)
1967—Packers, 31-23 (StL)
1969—Packers, 45-28 (GB)
1971—Tie, 16-16 (StL)
1973—Packers, 25-21 (GB)
1976—Cardinals, 29-0 (StL)
1982—**Packers, 41-16 (GB)
1984—Packers, 24-23 (GB)
1985—Cardinals, 43-28 (StL)
1988—Packers, 26-17 (P)
(Points—Packers 1,095, Cardinals 818)
*Franchise in St. Louis prior to 1988, and in Chicago prior to 1960
**NFC First Round Playoff

GREEN BAY vs. *PITTSBURGH
RS: Packers lead series, 16-11
1933—Packers, 47-0 (GB)
1935—Packers, 27-0 (GB)
Packers, 34-14 (P)
1936—Packers, 42-10 (Mil)
1938—Packers, 20-0 (GB)
1940—Packers, 24-3 (Mil)
1941—Packers, 54-7 (P)
1942—Packers, 24-21 (Mil)
1946—Packers, 17-7 (GB)
1947—Steelers, 18-17 (Mil)
1948—Steelers, 38-7 (P)
1949—Steelers, 30-7 (Mil)
1951—Packers, 35-33 (Mil)
Steelers, 28-7 (P)
1953—Packers, 31-14 (P)
1954—Steelers, 21-20 (GB)
1957—Packers, 27-10 (P)
1960—Packers, 19-13 (P)
1963—Packers, 33-14 (Mil)
1965—Packers, 41-9 (P)
1967—Steelers, 24-17 (GB)
1969—Packers, 38-34 (P)
1970—Packers, 20-12 (P)
1975—Steelers, 16-13 (Mil)
1980—Steelers, 22-20 (P)
1983—Steelers, 25-21 (GB)
1986—Steelers, 27-3 (P)
(Points—Packers 648, Steelers 467)
*Steelers known as Pirates prior to 1941

GREEN BAY vs. SAN DIEGO
RS: Packers lead series, 3-1
1970—Packers, 22-20 (SD)
1974—Packers, 34-0 (GB)
1978—Packers, 24-3 (SD)
1984—Chargers, 34-28 (GB)
(Points—Packers 108, Chargers 57)

GREEN BAY vs. SAN FRANCISCO
RS: 49ers lead series, 24-21-1
1950—Packers, 25-21 (GB)
49ers, 30-14 (SF)
1951—49ers, 31-19 (SF)
1952—49ers, 24-14 (SF)
1953—49ers, 37-7 (Mil)
49ers, 48-14 (SF)
1954—49ers, 23-17 (Mil)
49ers, 35-0 (SF)
1955—Packers, 27-21 (Mil)
Packers, 28-7 (SF)
1956—49ers, 17-16 (GB)
49ers, 38-20 (SF)
1957—49ers, 24-14 (Mil)
49ers, 27-20 (SF)

1958—49ers, 33-12 (Mil)
49ers, 48-21 (SF)
1959—Packers, 21-20 (GB)
Packers, 36-14 (SF)
1960—Packers, 41-14 (Mil)
Packers, 13-0 (SF)
1961—Packers, 30-10 (GB)
49ers, 22-21 (SF)
1962—Packers, 31-13 (Mil)
Packers, 31-21 (SF)
1963—Packers, 28-10 (Mil)
Packers, 21-17 (SF)
1964—Packers, 24-14 (Mil)
49ers, 24-14 (SF)
1965—Packers, 27-10 (GB)
Tie, 24-24 (SF)
1966—49ers, 21-20 (SF)
Packers, 20-7 (Mil)
1967—Packers, 13-0 (GB)
1968—49ers, 27-20 (SF)
1969—Packers, 14-7 (GB)
1970—49ers, 26-10 (SF)
1972—Packers, 34-24 (Mil)
1973—49ers, 20-6 (SF)
1974—49ers, 7-6 (GB)
1976—49ers, 26-14 (GB)
1977—Packers, 16-14 (Mil)
1980—Packers, 23-16 (Mil)
1981—49ers, 13-3 (Mil)
1986—49ers, 31-17 (Mil)
1987—49ers, 23-12 (GB)
1989—Packers, 21-17 (SF)
(Points—49ers 956, Packers 879)

GREEN BAY vs. SEATTLE
RS: Packers lead series, 3-2
1976—Packers, 27-20 (Mil)
1978—Packers, 45-28 (Mil)
1981—Packers, 34-24 (GB)
1984—Seahawks, 30-24 (Mil)
1987—Seahawks, 24-13 (S)
(Points—Packers 143, Seahawks 126)

GREEN BAY vs. TAMPA BAY
RS: Packers lead series, 11-10-1
1977—Packers, 13-0 (TB)
1978—Packers, 9-7 (GB)
Packers, 17-7 (TB)
1979—Buccaneers, 21-10 (GB)
Buccaneers, 21-3 (TB)
1980—Tie, 14-14 (TB) OT
Buccaneers, 20-17 (Mil)
1981—Buccaneers, 21-10 (GB)
Buccaneers, 37-3 (TB)
1983—Packers, 55-14 (GB)
Packers, 12-9 (TB) OT
1984—Buccaneers, 30-27 (TB) OT
Packers, 27-14 (GB)
1985—Packers, 21-0 (GB)
Packers, 20-17 (TB)
1986—Packers, 31-7 (Mil)
Packers, 21-7 (TB)
1987—Buccaneers, 23-17 (Mil)
1988—Buccaneers, 13-10 (GB)
Buccaneers, 27-24 (TB)
1989—Buccaneers, 23-21 (GB)
Packers, 17-16 (TB)
(Points—Packers 399, Buccaneers 347)

GREEN BAY vs. *WASHINGTON
RS: Packers lead series, 13-12-1
PS: Series tied, 1-1
1932—Packers, 21-0 (B)
1933—Tie, 7-7 (GB)
Redskins, 20-7 (B)
1934—Packers, 10-0 (B)
1936—Packers, 31-2 (GB)
Packers, 7-3 (B)
**Packers, 21-6 (New York)
1937—Redskins, 14-6 (W)
1939—Redskins, 24-14 (Mil)
1941—Packers, 22-17 (W)
1943—Redskins, 33-7 (Mil)
1946—Packers, 20-7 (W)
1947—Packers, 27-10 (W)
1948—Redskins, 23-7 (W)
1949—Redskins, 30-0 (W)
1950—Packers, 35-21 (Mil)
1952—Packers, 35-20 (Mil)
1958—Redskins, 37-21 (W)
1959—Packers, 21-0 (W)
1968—Packers, 27-7 (W)
1972—Packers, 21-16 (W)
***Redskins, 16-3 (W)
1974—Redskins, 17-6 (GB)
1977—Redskins, 10-9 (W)
1979—Redskins, 38-21 (W)
1983—Packers, 48-47 (GB)
1986—Redskins, 16-7 (GB)
1988—Redskins, 20-17 (Mil)
(Points—Packers 483, Redskins 456)
*Franchise in Boston prior to 1937 and known as Braves prior to 1933
**NFL Championship
***NFC Divisional Playoff

HOUSTON vs. ATLANTA
RS: Falcons lead series, 4-2;
See Atlanta vs. Houston

HOUSTON vs. BUFFALO
RS: Oilers lead series, 18-11
PS: Bills lead series, 1-0;
See Buffalo vs. Houston

HOUSTON vs. CHICAGO
RS: Oilers lead series, 3-2;
See Chicago vs. Houston

HOUSTON vs. CINCINNATI
RS: Bengals lead series, 23-18-1;
See Cincinnati vs. Houston

HOUSTON vs. CLEVELAND
RS: Browns lead series, 26-13
PS: Oilers lead series, 1-0;
See Cleveland vs. Houston

HOUSTON vs. DALLAS
RS: Cowboys lead series, 4-2;
See Dallas vs. Houston

HOUSTON vs. DENVER
RS: Oilers lead series, 18-10-1
PS: Series tied, 1-1;
See Denver vs. Houston

HOUSTON vs. DETROIT
RS: Oilers lead series, 3-2;
See Detroit vs. Houston

HOUSTON vs. GREEN BAY
RS: Oilers lead series, 3-2;
See Green Bay vs. Houston

HOUSTON vs. *INDIANAPOLIS
RS: Colts lead series, 6-5
1970—Colts, 24-20 (H)
1973—Colts, 31-27 (B)
1976—Colts, 38-14 (B)
1979—Oilers, 28-16 (B)
1980—Oilers, 21-16 (H)
1983—Colts, 20-10 (B)
1984—Colts, 35-21 (H)
1985—Colts, 34-16 (I)
1986—Oilers, 31-17 (H)
1987—Colts, 51-27 (I)
1988—Oilers, 17-14 (I) OT
(Points—Colts 292, Oilers 236)
*Franchise in Baltimore prior to 1984

HOUSTON vs. *KANSAS CITY
RS: Chiefs lead series, 21-13
PS: Chiefs lead series, 1-0
1960—Oilers, 20-10 (H)
Texans, 24-0 (D)
1961—Texans, 26-21 (D)
Oilers, 38-7 (H)
1962—Texans, 31-7 (H)
Oilers, 14-6 (D)
**Texans, 20-17 (H) OT
1963—Chiefs, 28-7 (KC)
Oilers, 28-7 (H)
1964—Chiefs, 28-7 (KC)
Chiefs, 28-19 (H)
1965—Chiefs, 52-21 (KC)
Oilers, 38-36 (H)
1966—Chiefs, 48-23 (KC)
Oilers, 25-20 (H)
1967—Chiefs, 24-19 (KC)
1968—Chiefs, 26-21 (H)
Chiefs, 24-10 (KC)
1969—Chiefs, 24-0 (H)
1970—Chiefs, 24-9 (KC)
1971—Chiefs, 20-16 (H)
1973—Chiefs, 38-14 (KC)
1974—Chiefs, 17-7 (H)
1975—Oilers, 17-13 (KC)
1977—Oilers, 34-20 (H)
1978—Oilers, 20-17 (KC)
1979—Oilers, 20-6 (H)
1980—Chiefs, 21-20 (KC)
1981—Chiefs, 23-10 (KC)
1983—Chiefs, 13-10 (H) OT
1984—Oilers, 17-16 (KC)
1985—Oilers, 23-20 (H)
1986—Chiefs, 27-13 (KC)
1988—Oilers, 7-6 (H)
1989—Chiefs, 34-0 (KC)
(Points—Chiefs 784, Oilers 572)
*Franchise in Dallas prior to 1963 and known as Texans
**AFL Championship

HOUSTON vs. *L.A. RAIDERS
RS: Raiders lead series, 19-12
PS: Raiders lead series, 3-0
1960—Oilers, 37-22 (O)
Raiders, 14-13 (H)
1961—Oilers, 55-0 (H)
Raiders, 47-16 (O)
1962—Oilers, 28-20 (H)
Oilers, 32-17 (H)
1963—Raiders, 24-13 (H)
Raiders, 52-49 (O)
1964—Raiders, 42-28 (H)
Raiders, 20-10 (O)
1965—Raiders, 21-17 (O)
Raiders, 33-21 (H)
1966—Oilers, 31-0 (H)

Raiders, 38-23 (O)
1967—Raiders, 19-7 (H)
    **Raiders, 40-7 (O)
1968—Raiders, 24-15 (H)
1969—Raiders, 21-17 (O)
    ***Raiders, 56-7 (O)
1971—Raiders, 41-21 (O)
1972—Raiders, 34-0 (H)
1973—Raiders, 17-6 (H)
1975—Oilers, 27-26 (O)
1976—Raiders, 14-13 (H)
1977—Raiders, 34-29 (O)
1978—Raiders, 21-17 (O)
1979—Oilers, 31-17 (H)
1980—****Raiders, 27-7 (O)
1981—Oilers, 17-16 (H)
1983—Raiders, 20-6 (LA)
1984—Raiders, 24-14 (H)
1986—Raiders, 28-17 (H)
1988—Oilers, 38-35 (H)
1989—Oilers, 23-7 (H)
(Points—Raiders 826, Oilers 737)
*Franchise in Oakland prior to 1982
**AFL Championship
***Inter-Divisional Playoff
****AFC First Round Playoff

HOUSTON vs. L.A. RAMS
RS: Rams lead series, 3-2
1973—Rams, 31-26 (H)
1978—Rams, 10-6 (H)
1981—Oilers, 27-20 (LA)
1984—Rams, 27-16 (LA)
1987—Oilers, 20-16 (H)
(Points—Rams 104, Oilers 95)

HOUSTON vs. MIAMI
RS: Series tied, 10-10
PS: Oilers lead series, 1-0
1966—Dolphins, 20-13 (H)
    Dolphins, 29-28 (M)
1967—Oilers, 17-14 (H)
    Oilers, 41-10 (M)
1968—Oilers, 24-10 (M)
    Dolphins, 24-7 (H)
1969—Oilers, 22-10 (H)
    Oilers, 32-7 (M)
1970—Dolphins, 20-10 (H)
1972—Dolphins, 34-13 (M)
1975—Oilers, 20-19 (H)
1977—Oilers, 27-7 (H)
1978—Oilers, 35-30 (H)
    *Oilers, 17-9 (M)
1979—Oilers, 9-6 (M)
1981—Dolphins, 16-10 (H)
1983—Dolphins, 24-17 (H)
1984—Dolphins, 28-10 (H)
1985—Oilers, 26-23 (H)
1986—Dolphins, 28-7 (M)
1989—Oilers, 39-7 (H)
(Points—Oilers 404, Dolphins 395)
*AFC First Round Playoff

HOUSTON vs. MINNESOTA
RS: Vikings lead series, 3-2
1974—Vikings, 51-10 (M)
1980—Oilers, 20-16 (H)
1983—Vikings, 34-14 (M)
1986—Oilers, 23-10 (H)
1989—Vikings, 38-7 (M)
(Points—Vikings 149, Oilers 74)

HOUSTON vs. *NEW ENGLAND
RS: Patriots lead series, 16-13-1
PS: Oilers lead series, 1-0
1960—Oilers, 24-10 (B)
    Oilers, 37-21 (H)
1961—Tie, 31-31 (B)
    Oilers, 27-15 (H)
1962—Patriots, 34-21 (H)
    Oilers, 21-17 (H)
1963—Patriots, 45-3 (B)
    Patriots, 46-28 (H)
1964—Patriots, 25-24 (H)
    Patriots, 34-17 (H)
1965—Patriots, 31-10 (H)
    Patriots, 42-14 (H)
1966—Patriots, 27-21 (B)
    Patriots, 38-14 (H)
1967—Patriots, 18-7 (B)
    Oilers, 27-6 (H)
1968—Oilers, 16-0 (B)
    Oilers, 45-17 (H)
1969—Patriots, 24-0 (B)
    Oilers, 27-23 (H)
1971—Patriots, 28-20 (NE)
1973—Patriots, 32-0 (H)
1975—Oilers, 7-0 (NE)
1978—Oilers, 26-23 (NE)
    **Oilers, 31-14 (NE)
1980—Oilers, 38-34 (H)
1981—Patriots, 38-10 (NE)
1982—Patriots, 29-21 (NE)
1987—Patriots, 21-7 (H)
1988—Oilers, 31-6 (H)
1989—Patriots, 23-13 (NE)
(Points—Patriots 731, Oilers 639)

*Franchise in Boston prior to 1971
**AFC Divisional Playoff

HOUSTON vs. NEW ORLEANS
RS: Saints lead series, 3-2-1
1971—Tie, 13-13 (H)
1976—Oilers, 31-26 (NO)
1978—Oilers, 17-12 (NO)
1981—Saints, 27-24 (H)
1984—Saints, 27-10 (H)
1987—Saints, 24-10 (NO)
(Points—Saints 129, Oilers 105)

HOUSTON vs. N.Y. GIANTS
RS: Giants lead series, 3-0
1973—Giants, 34-14 (NY)
1982—Giants, 17-14 (NY)
1985—Giants, 35-14 (NY)
(Points—Giants 86, Oilers 42)

HOUSTON vs. *N.Y. JETS
RS: Oilers lead series, 15-11-1
1960—Oilers, 27-21 (H)
    Oilers, 42-28 (NY)
1961—Oilers, 49-13 (H)
    Oilers, 48-21 (NY)
1962—Oilers, 56-17 (H)
    Oilers, 44-10 (NY)
1963—Oilers, 31-27 (H)
    Jets, 24-17 (NY)
1964—Oilers, 24-21 (NY)
    Oilers, 33-17 (H)
1965—Oilers, 27-21 (H)
    Jets, 41-14 (NY)
1966—Jets, 52-13 (NY)
    Oilers, 24-0 (H)
1967—Tie, 28-28 (NY)
1968—Jets, 20-14 (H)
    Jets, 26-7 (NY)
1969—Jets, 26-17 (NY)
    Jets, 34-26 (H)
1972—Oilers, 26-20 (H)
1974—Oilers, 27-22 (NY)
1977—Oilers, 20-0 (H)
1979—Oilers, 27-24 (H) OT
1980—Jets, 31-28 (NY) OT
1981—Jets, 33-17 (NY)
1984—Oilers, 31-20 (H)
1988—Jets, 45-3 (NY)
(Points—Oilers 717, Jets 645)
*Jets known as Titans prior to 1963

HOUSTON vs. PHILADELPHIA
RS: Eagles lead series, 4-0
1972—Eagles, 18-17 (H)
1979—Eagles, 26-20 (H)
1982—Eagles, 35-14 (P)
1988—Eagles, 32-23 (P)
(Points—Eagles 111, Oilers 74)

HOUSTON vs. *PHOENIX
RS: Cardinals lead series, 3-2
1970—Cardinals, 44-0 (StL)
1974—Cardinals, 31-27 (H)
1979—Cardinals, 24-17 (H)
1985—Oilers, 20-10 (StL)
1988—Oilers, 38-20 (H)
(Points—Cardinals 129, Oilers 102)
*Franchise in St. Louis prior to 1988

HOUSTON vs. PITTSBURGH
RS: Steelers lead series, 25-14
PS: Steelers lead series, 3-0
1970—Oilers, 19-7 (H)
    Steelers, 7-3 (H)
1971—Steelers, 23-16 (P)
    Oilers, 29-3 (H)
1972—Steelers, 24-7 (P)
    Steelers, 9-3 (H)
1973—Steelers, 36-7 (H)
    Steelers, 33-7 (P)
1974—Steelers, 13-7 (H)
    Oilers, 13-10 (P)
1975—Steelers, 24-17 (P)
    Steelers, 32-9 (H)
1976—Steelers, 32-16 (P)
    Steelers, 21-0 (H)
1977—Oilers, 27-10 (H)
    Steelers, 27-10 (P)
1978—Oilers, 24-17 (P)
    Steelers, 13-3 (H)
    *Steelers, 34-5 (P)
1979—Steelers, 38-7 (P)
    Oilers, 20-17 (H)
    *Steelers, 27-13 (P)
1980—Steelers, 31-17 (P)
    Oilers, 6-0 (H)
1981—Steelers, 26-13 (H)
    Oilers, 21-20 (H)
1982—Steelers, 24-10 (H)
1983—Steelers, 40-28 (H)
    Steelers, 17-10 (P)
1984—Steelers, 35-7 (P)
    Oilers, 23-20 (H) OT
1985—Steelers, 20-0 (P)
    Steelers, 30-7 (H)
1986—Steelers, 22-16 (H) OT
    Steelers, 21-10 (P)
1987—Oilers, 23-3 (P)

Oilers, 24-16 (H)
1988—Oilers, 34-14 (P)
    Steelers, 37-34 (H)
1989—Oilers, 27-0 (H)
    Oilers, 23-16 (P)
    **Steelers, 26-23 (H)
(Points—Steelers 875, Oilers 618)
*AFC Championship
**AFC First Round Playoff

HOUSTON vs. *SAN DIEGO
RS: Chargers lead series, 17-11-1
PS: Oilers lead series, 3-0
1960—Oilers, 38-28 (H)
    Chargers, 24-21 (LA)
    **Oilers, 24-16 (H)
1961—Chargers, 34-24 (SD)
    Oilers, 33-13 (H)
    **Oilers, 10-3 (SD)
1962—Oilers, 42-17 (SD)
    Oilers, 33-27 (H)
1963—Chargers, 27-0 (SD)
    Chargers 20-14 (H)
1964—Chargers, 27-21 (SD)
    Chargers, 20-17 (H)
1965—Chargers, 31-14 (SD)
    Chargers, 37-26 (H)
1966—Chargers, 28-22 (H)
1967—Chargers, 13-3 (SD)
    Oilers, 24-17 (H)
1968—Chargers, 30-14 (SD)
1969—Chargers, 21-17 (H)
1970—Tie, 31-31 (SD)
1971—Oilers, 49-33 (H)
1972—Chargers, 34-20 (SD)
1974—Oilers, 21-14 (H)
1975—Oilers, 33-17 (H)
1976—Chargers, 30-27 (SD)
1978—Chargers, 45-24 (H)
1979—***Oilers, 17-14 (SD)
1984—Chargers, 31-14 (SD)
1985—Oilers, 37-35 (H)
1986—Chargers, 27-0 (SD)
1987—Oilers, 33-18 (H)
1989—Oilers, 34-27 (SD)
(Points—Chargers 789, Oilers 737)
*Franchise in Los Angeles prior to 1961
**AFL Championship
***AFC Divisional Playoff

HOUSTON vs. SAN FRANCISCO
RS: 49ers lead series, 4-2
1970—49ers, 30-20 (H)
1975—Oilers, 27-13 (SF)
1978—Oilers, 20-19 (H)
1981—49ers, 28-6 (SF)
1984—49ers, 34-21 (H)
1987—49ers, 27-20 (SF)
(Points—49ers 151, Oilers 114)

HOUSTON vs. SEATTLE
RS: Series tied, 3-3
PS: Oilers lead series, 1-0
1977—Oilers, 22-10 (H)
1979—Seahawks, 34-14 (S)
1980—Seahawks, 26-7 (H)
1981—Oilers, 35-17 (H)
1982—Oilers, 23-21 (H)
1987—*Oilers, 23-20 (H) OT
1988—Seahawks, 27-24 (S)
(Points—Seahawks 155, Oilers 148)
*AFC First Round Playoff

HOUSTON vs. TAMPA BAY
RS: Oilers lead series, 3-1
1976—Oilers, 20-0 (H)
1980—Oilers, 20-14 (H)
1983—Buccaneers, 33-24 (TB)
1989—Oilers, 20-17 (H)
(Points—Oilers 84, Buccaneers 64)

HOUSTON vs. WASHINGTON
RS: Oilers lead series, 3-2
1971—Redskins, 22-13 (W)
1975—Oilers, 13-10 (H)
1979—Oilers, 29-27 (W)
1985—Redskins, 16-13 (W)
1988—Oilers, 41-17 (H)
(Points—Oilers 109, Redskins 92)

INDIANAPOLIS vs. ATLANTA
RS: Colts lead series, 10-0;
See Atlanta vs. Indianapolis
INDIANAPOLIS vs. BUFFALO
RS: Series tied, 19-19-1;
See Buffalo vs. Indianapolis
INDIANAPOLIS vs. CHICAGO
RS: Colts lead series, 21-15;
See Chicago vs. Indianapolis
INDIANAPOLIS vs. CINCINNATI
RS: Series tied, 5-5
PS: Colts lead series, 1-0;
See Cincinnati vs. Indianapolis
INDIANAPOLIS vs. CLEVELAND
RS: Browns lead series, 11-5
PS: Series tied, 2-2;
See Cleveland vs. Indianapolis
INDIANAPOLIS vs. DALLAS

RS: Cowboys lead series, 6-2
PS: Colts lead series, 1-0;
See Dallas vs. Indianapolis
INDIANAPOLIS vs. DENVER
RS: Broncos lead series, 7-2;
See Denver vs. Indianapolis
INDIANAPOLIS vs. DETROIT
RS: Colts lead series, 17-16-2;
See Detroit vs. Indianapolis
INDIANAPOLIS vs. GREEN BAY
RS: Colts lead series, 17-16
PS: Packers lead series, 1-0;
See Green Bay vs. Indianapolis
INDIANAPOLIS vs. HOUSTON
RS: Colts lead series, 6-5;
See Houston vs. Indianapolis

*INDIANAPOLIS vs. KANSAS CITY
RS: Chiefs lead series, 6-3
1970—Chiefs, 44-24 (B)
1972—Chiefs, 24-10 (KC)
1975—Colts, 28-14 (B)
1977—Colts, 17-6 (KC)
1979—Chiefs, 14-0 (KC)
    Chiefs, 10-7 (B)
1980—Colts, 31-24 (KC)
    Chiefs, 38-28 (B)
1985—Chiefs, 20-7 (KC)
(Points—Chiefs 194, Colts 152)
*Franchise in Baltimore prior to 1984

*INDIANAPOLIS vs **L.A. RAIDERS
RS: Raiders lead series, 3-2
PS: Series tied, 1-1
1970—***Colts, 27-17 (B)
1971—Colts, 37-14 (O)
1973—Raiders, 34-21 (B)
1975—Raiders, 31-20 (B)
1977—****Raiders, 37-31 (B) OT
1984—Raiders, 21-7 (LA)
1986—Colts, 30-24 (LA)
(Points—Raiders 178, Colts 173)
*Franchise in Baltimore prior to 1984
**Franchise in Oakland prior to 1982
***AFC Championship
****AFC Divisional Playoff

*INDIANAPOLIS vs. L.A. RAMS
RS: Colts lead series, 20-16-2
1953—Rams, 21-13 (B)
    Rams, 45-2 (LA)
1954—Rams, 48-0 (B)
    Colts, 22-21 (LA)
1955—Tie, 17-17 (B)
    Rams, 20-14 (LA)
1956—Colts, 56-21 (B)
    Rams, 31-7 (LA)
1957—Colts, 31-14 (B)
    Rams, 37-21 (LA)
1958—Colts, 34-7 (B)
    Rams, 30-28 (LA)
1959—Colts, 35-21 (B)
    Rams, 45-26 (LA)
1960—Colts, 31-17 (B)
    Rams, 10-3 (LA)
1961—Colts, 27-24 (B)
    Rams, 34-17 (LA)
1962—Colts, 30-27 (B)
    Colts, 14-2 (LA)
1963—Rams, 17-16 (LA)
    Colts, 19-16 (B)
1964—Colts, 35-20 (B)
    Colts, 24-7 (LA)
1965—Colts, 35-20 (B)
    Colts, 20-17 (LA)
1966—Colts, 17-3 (LA)
    Rams, 23-7 (B)
1967—Tie, 24-24 (B)
    Rams, 34-10 (LA)
1968—Colts, 27-10 (B)
    Colts, 28-24 (LA)
1969—Rams, 27-20 (B)
    Colts, 13-7 (LA)
1971—Colts, 24-17 (B)
1975—Rams, 24-13 (LA)
1986—Rams, 24-7 (I)
1989—Rams, 31-17 (LA)
(Points—Rams 818, Colts 803)
*Franchise in Baltimore prior to 1984

*INDIANAPOLIS vs. MIAMI
RS: Dolphins lead series, 27-13
PS: Dolphins lead series, 1-0
1970—Colts, 35-0 (B)
    Dolphins, 34-17 (M)
1971—Dolphins, 17-14 (M)
    Colts, 14-3 (B)
    **Dolphins, 21-0 (M)
1972—Dolphins, 23-0 (M)
    Dolphins, 16-0 (B)
1973—Dolphins, 44-0 (M)
    Colts, 16-3 (B)
1974—Dolphins, 17-7 (M)
    Dolphins, 17-16 (B)
1975—Colts, 33-17 (B)
    Colts, 10-7 (B) OT
1976—Colts, 28-14 (B)

Colts, 17-16 (M)
1977—Colts, 45-28 (B)
     Dolphins, 17-6 (M)
1978—Dolphins, 42-0 (B)
     Dolphins, 26-8 (M)
1979—Dolphins, 19-0 (M)
     Dolphins, 28-24 (B)
1980—Colts, 30-17 (M)
     Dolphins, 24-14 (B)
1981—Dolphins, 31-28 (B)
     Dolphins, 27-10 (M)
1982—Dolphins, 24-20 (M)
     Dolphins, 34-7 (B)
1983—Dolphins, 21-7 (B)
     Dolphins, 37-0 (M)
1984—Dolphins, 44-7 (M)
     Dolphins, 35-17 (I)
1985—Dolphins, 30-13 (M)
     Dolphins, 34-20 (I)
1986—Dolphins, 30-10 (M)
     Dolphins, 17-13 (I)
1987—Dolphins, 23-10 (I)
     Colts, 40-21 (M)
1988—Colts, 15-13 (I)
     Colts, 31-28 (M)
1989—Dolphins, 19-13 (M)
     Colts, 42-13 (I)
(Points—Dolphins 931, Colts 637)
*Franchise in Baltimore prior to 1984
**AFC Championship
INDIANAPOLIS vs. MINNESOTA
RS: Colts lead series, 11-6-1
PS: Colts lead series, 1-0
1961—Colts, 34-33 (B)
     Vikings, 28-20 (M)
1962—Colts, 34-7 (M)
     Colts, 42-17 (B)
1963—Colts, 37-34 (M)
     Colts, 41-10 (B)
1964—Vikings, 34-24 (M)
     Colts, 17-14 (B)
1965—Colts, 35-16 (B)
     Colts, 41-21 (M)
1966—Colts, 38-23 (M)
     Colts, 20-17 (B)
1967—Tie, 20-20 (M)
1968—Colts, 21-9 (B)
     **Colts, 24-14 (B)
1969—Vikings, 52-14 (M)
1971—Vikings, 10-3 (M)
1982—Vikings, 13-10 (M)
1988—Vikings, 12-3 (M)
(Points—Colts 478, Vikings 384)
*Franchise in Baltimore prior to 1984
**Conference Championship
INDIANAPOLIS vs. **NEW ENGLAND
RS: Patriots lead series, 22-17
1970—Colts, 14-6 (Bos)
     Colts, 27-3 (Balt)
1971—Colts, 23-3 (NE)
     Patriots, 21-17 (Balt)
1972—Colts, 24-17 (NE)
     Colts, 31-0 (Balt)
1973—Patriots, 24-16 (NE)
     Colts, 18-13 (Balt)
1974—Patriots, 42-3 (NE)
     Patriots, 27-17 (Balt)
1975—Patriots, 21-10 (NE)
     Colts, 34-21 (Balt)
1976—Colts, 27-13 (NE)
     Patriots, 21-14 (Balt)
1977—Patriots, 17-3 (NE)
     Colts, 30-24 (Balt)
1978—Patriots, 34-27 (NE)
     Patriots, 35-14 (Balt)
1979—Colts, 31-26 (NE)
     Patriots, 50-21 (NE)
1980—Patriots, 37-21 (Balt)
     Patriots, 47-21 (NE)
1981—Colts, 29-28 (NE)
     Colts, 23-21 (Balt)
1982—Patriots, 24-13 (Balt)
1983—Colts, 29-23 (NE) OT
     Colts, 12-7 (B)
1984—Patriots, 50-17 (I)
     Patriots, 16-10 (NE)
1985—Patriots, 34-15 (NE)
     Patriots, 38-31 (I)
1986—Patriots, 33-3 (NE)
     Patriots, 30-21 (I)
1987—Colts, 30-16 (I)
     Patriots, 24-0 (NE)
1988—Patriots, 21-17 (NE)
     Colts, 24-21 (I)
1989—Patriots, 23-20 (I) OT
     Patriots, 22-16 (NE)
(Points—Patriots 926, Colts 760)
*Franchise in Baltimore prior to 1984
**Franchise in Boston prior to 1971
INDIANAPOLIS vs. NEW ORLEANS
RS: Colts lead series, 3-2
1967—Colts, 30-10 (B)
1969—Colts, 30-10 (NO)

1973—Colts, 14-10 (B)
1986—Saints, 17-14 (I)
1989—Saints, 41-6 (NO)
(Points—Colts 94, Saints 88)
INDIANAPOLIS vs. N. Y. GIANTS
RS: Colts lead series, 5-3
PS: Colts lead series, 2-0
1954—Colts, 20-14 (B)
1955—Giants, 17-7 (NY)
1958—Giants, 24-21 (NY)
     **Colts, 23-17 (NY) OT
1959—**Colts, 31-16 (B)
1963—Giants, 37-28 (B)
1968—Colts, 26-0 (NY)
1971—Colts, 31-7 (NY)
1975—Colts, 21-0 (NY)
1979—Colts, 31-7 (NY)
(Points—Colts 239, Giants 139)
*Franchise in Baltimore prior to 1984
**NFL Championship
INDIANAPOLIS vs. N. Y. JETS
RS: Colts lead series, 21-18
PS: Jets lead series, 1-0
1968—**Jets 16-7 (Miami)
1970—Colts, 29-22 (NY)
     Colts, 35-20 (B)
1971—Colts, 22-0 (B)
     Colts, 14-13 (NY)
1972—Jets, 44-34 (B)
     Jets, 24-20 (NY)
1973—Jets, 34-10 (B)
     Jets, 20-17 (NY)
1974—Colts, 35-20 (NY)
     Jets, 45-38 (B)
1975—Colts, 45-28 (NY)
     Colts, 52-19 (B)
1976—Colts, 20-0 (NY)
     Colts, 33-16 (B)
1977—Colts, 20-12 (NY)
     Colts, 33-12 (B)
1978—Jets, 33-10 (B)
     Jets, 24-16 (NY)
1979—Colts, 10-8 (B)
     Jets, 30-17 (NY)
1980—Colts, 17-14 (NY)
     Colts, 35-21 (B)
1981—Jets, 41-14 (B)
     Jets, 25-0 (NY)
1982—Jets, 37-0 (NY)
1983—Colts, 17-14 (NY)
     Jets, 10-6 (B)
1984—Jets, 23-14 (I)
     Jets, 9-5 (NY)
1985—Jets, 25-20 (NY)
     Jets, 35-17 (I)
1986—Jets, 26-7 (I)
     Jets, 31-16 (NY)
1987—Colts, 6-0 (I)
     Colts, 19-14 (NY)
1988—Colts, 38-14 (I)
     Jets, 34-16 (NY)
1989—Colts, 17-10 (NY)
     Colts, 27-10 (I)
(Points—Jets 829, Colts 812)
*Franchise in Baltimore prior to 1984
**Super Bowl III
INDIANAPOLIS vs. PHILADELPHIA
RS: Series tied, 5-5
1953—Eagles, 45-14 (P)
1965—Colts, 34-24 (B)
1967—Colts, 38-6 (P)
1969—Colts, 24-20 (B)
1970—Colts, 29-10 (B)
1974—Eagles, 30-10 (P)
1978—Eagles, 17-14 (B)
1981—Eagles, 38-13 (P)
1983—Colts, 22-21 (P)
1984—Eagles, 16-7 (P)
(Points—Eagles 227, Colts 205)
*Franchise in Baltimore prior to 1984
INDIANAPOLIS vs. **PHOENIX
RS: Cardinals lead series, 5-4
1961—Colts, 16-0 (B)
1964—Colts, 47-27 (B)
1968—Colts, 27-0 (B)
1972—Cardinals, 10-3 (B)
1976—Cardinals, 24-17 (StL)
1978—Colts, 30-17 (StL)
1980—Cardinals, 17-10 (B)
1981—Cardinals, 35-24 (B)
1984—Cardinals, 34-33 (I)
(Points—Colts 207, Cardinals 164)
*Franchise in Baltimore prior to 1984
**Franchise in St. Louis prior to 1988
INDIANAPOLIS vs. PITTSBURGH
RS: Steelers lead series, 8-4
PS: Steelers lead series, 2-0
1957—Steelers, 19-13 (B)
1968—Colts, 41-7 (P)
1971—Colts, 34-21 (B)
1974—Steelers, 30-0 (B)
1975—**Steelers, 28-10 (P)

1976—***Steelers, 40-14 (B)
1977—Colts, 31-21 (B)
1978—Steelers, 35-13 (P)
1979—Steelers, 17-13 (P)
1980—Steelers, 20-17 (B)
1983—Steelers, 24-13 (B)
1984—Steelers, 17-16 (I)
1985—Steelers, 45-3 (P)
1987—Steelers, 21-7 (P)
(Points—Steelers 344, Colts 226)
*Franchise in Baltimore prior to 1984
**AFC Divisional Playoff
INDIANAPOLIS vs. SAN DIEGO
RS: Chargers lead series, 6-5
1970—Colts, 16-14 (SD)
1972—Chargers, 23-20 (B)
1976—Colts, 37-21 (SD)
1981—Chargers, 43-14 (B)
1982—Chargers, 44-26 (SD)
1984—Chargers, 38-10 (I)
1986—Chargers, 17-3 (I)
1987—Chargers, 16-13 (I)
     Colts, 20-7 (SD)
1988—Colts, 16-0 (SD)
1989—Colts, 10-6 (I)
(Points—Chargers 229, Colts 185)
*Franchise in Baltimore prior to 1984
INDIANAPOLIS vs. SAN FRANCISCO
RS: Colts lead series, 21-16
1953—49ers, 38-21 (B)
     49ers, 45-14 (SF)
1954—Colts, 17-13 (B)
     49ers, 10-7 (SF)
1955—Colts, 26-14 (B)
     49ers, 35-24 (SF)
1956—Colts, 20-17 (B)
     49ers, 30-17 (SF)
1957—Colts, 27-21 (B)
     49ers, 17-13 (SF)
1958—Colts, 35-27 (B)
     49ers, 21-12 (SF)
1959—Colts, 45-14 (B)
     Colts, 34-14 (SF)
1960—49ers, 30-22 (B)
     49ers, 34-10 (SF)
1961—Colts, 20-17 (B)
     Colts, 27-24 (SF)
1962—49ers, 21-13 (B)
     Colts, 22-3 (SF)
1963—Colts, 20-14 (SF)
     Colts, 20-3 (B)
1964—Colts, 37-7 (B)
     Colts, 14-3 (SF)
1965—Colts, 27-24 (B)
     Colts, 34-28 (SF)
1966—Colts, 36-14 (B)
     Colts, 30-14 (SF)
1967—Colts, 41-7 (B)
     Colts, 26-9 (SF)
1968—Colts, 27-10 (B)
     Colts, 42-14 (SF)
1969—49ers, 24-21 (B)
     49ers, 20-17 (SF)
1972—49ers, 24-21 (SF)
1986—49ers, 35-14 (SF)
1989—49ers, 30-24 (I)
(Points—Colts 874, 49ers 728)
*Franchise in Baltimore prior to 1984
INDIANAPOLIS vs. SEATTLE
RS: Colts lead series, 2-0
1977—Colts, 29-14 (S)
1978—Colts, 17-14 (S)
(Points—Colts 46, Seahawks 28)
*Franchise in Baltimore prior to 1984
INDIANAPOLIS vs. TAMPA BAY
RS: Colts lead series, 4-1
1976—Colts, 42-17 (B)
1979—Buccaneers, 29-26 (B) OT
1985—Colts, 31-23 (TB)
1987—Colts, 24-6 (I)
1988—Colts, 35-31 (I)
(Points—Colts 158, Buccaneers 106)
*Franchise in Baltimore prior to 1984
INDIANAPOLIS vs. WASHINGTON
RS: Colts lead series, 15-6
1953—Colts, 27-17 (B)
1954—Redskins, 24-21 (W)
1955—Redskins, 14-13 (B)
1956—Colts, 19-17 (B)
1957—Colts, 21-17 (W)
1958—Colts, 35-10 (B)
1959—Redskins, 27-24 (W)
1960—Colts, 20-0 (B)
1961—Colts, 27-6 (W)
1962—Colts, 34-21 (B)
1963—Colts, 36-20 (W)
1964—Colts, 45-17 (B)
1965—Colts, 38-7 (W)
1966—Colts, 37-10 (B)
1967—Colts, 17-13 (W)
1969—Colts, 41-17 (B)
1973—Redskins, 22-14 (W)
1977—Colts, 10-3 (B)

1978—Colts, 21-17 (B)
1981—Redskins, 38-14 (W)
1984—Redskins, 35-7 (I)
(Points—Colts 521, Redskins 352)
*Franchise in Baltimore prior to 1984

KANSAS CITY vs. ATLANTA
RS: Chiefs lead series, 2-0;
See Atlanta vs. Kansas City
KANSAS CITY vs. BUFFALO
RS: Bills lead series, 15-11-1
PS: Chiefs lead series, 1-0;
See Buffalo vs. Kansas City
KANSAS CITY vs. CHICAGO
RS: Bears lead series, 3-1;
See Chicago vs. Kansas City
KANSAS CITY vs. CINCINNATI
RS: Chiefs lead series, 10-9;
See Cincinnati vs. Kansas City
KANSAS CITY vs. CLEVELAND
RS: Browns lead series, 6-5-2;
See Cleveland vs. Kansas City
KANSAS CITY vs. DALLAS
RS: Series tied, 2-2;
See Dallas vs. Kansas City
KANSAS CITY vs. DENVER
RS: Chiefs lead series, 35-24;
See Denver vs. Kansas City
KANSAS CITY vs. DETROIT
RS: Series tied, 3-3;
See Detroit vs. Kansas City
KANSAS CITY vs. GREEN BAY
RS: Chiefs lead series, 2-1-1
PS: Packers lead series, 1-0;
See Green Bay vs. Kansas City
KANSAS CITY vs. HOUSTON
RS: Chiefs lead series, 21-13
PS: Chiefs lead series, 1-0;
See Houston vs. Kansas City
KANSAS CITY vs. INDIANAPOLIS
RS: Chiefs lead series, 6-3;
See Indianapolis vs. Kansas City
KANSAS CITY vs. **L.A. RAIDERS
RS: Raiders lead series, 34-23-2
PS: Series tied, 1-1
1960—Texans, 34-16 (O)
     Raiders, 20-19 (D)
1961—Texans, 42-35 (O)
     Raiders, 43-11 (D)
1962—Texans, 26-16 (O)
     Texans, 35-7 (D)
1963—Raiders, 10-7 (O)
     Raiders, 22-7 (KC)
1964—Chiefs, 21-9 (O)
     Chiefs, 42-7 (KC)
1965—Raiders, 37-10 (O)
     Chiefs, 14-7 (KC)
1966—Chiefs, 32-10 (O)
     Raiders, 34-13 (KC)
1967—Raiders, 23-21 (O)
     Raiders, 44-22 (KC)
1968—Chiefs, 24-10 (KC)
     Raiders, 38-21 (O)
     ***Raiders, 41-6 (O)
1969—Chiefs, 27-24 (KC)
     Raiders, 10-6 (O)
     ****Chiefs, 17-7 (O)
1970—Tie, 17-17 (KC)
     Raiders, 20-6 (O)
1971—Tie, 20-20 (O)
     Chiefs, 16-14 (KC)
1972—Chiefs, 27-14 (KC)
     Raiders, 26-3 (O)
1973—Chiefs, 16-3 (KC)
     Raiders, 37-7 (O)
1974—Raiders, 27-7 (O)
     Raiders, 7-6 (KC)
1975—Chiefs, 42-10 (KC)
     Raiders, 28-20 (O)
1976—Raiders, 24-21 (KC)
     Raiders, 21-10 (O)
1977—Raiders, 37-28 (KC)
     Raiders, 21-20 (O)
1978—Raiders, 28-6 (O)
     Raiders, 20-10 (KC)
1979—Chiefs, 35-7 (KC)
     Chiefs, 24-21 (O)
1980—Raiders, 27-14 (KC)
     Chiefs, 31-17 (O)
1981—Chiefs, 27-0 (KC)
     Chiefs, 28-17 (O)
1982—Raiders, 21-16 (KC)
1983—Raiders, 21-20 (LA)
     Raiders, 28-20 (KC)
1984—Raiders, 22-20 (KC)
     Raiders, 17-7 (LA)
1985—Chiefs, 36-20 (KC)
     Raiders, 19-10 (LA)
1986—Raiders, 24-17 (KC)
     Chiefs, 20-17 (LA)
1987—Raiders, 35-17 (LA)
     Chiefs, 16-10 (KC)
1988—Raiders, 27-17 (KC)

Raiders, 17-10 (LA)
1989—Chiefs, 24-19 (KC)
Raiders, 20-14 (LA)
(Points—Raiders 1,221, Chiefs 1,191)
*Franchise in Dallas prior to 1963 and known as Texans
**Franchise in Oakland prior to 1982
***Division Playoff
****AFL Championship

KANSAS CITY vs. L.A. RAMS
RS: Rams lead series, 3-0
1973—Rams, 23-13 (KC)
1982—Rams, 20-14 (LA)
1985—Rams, 16-0 (LA)
(Points—Rams 59, Chiefs 27)

KANSAS CITY vs. MIAMI
RS: Chiefs lead series, 9-6
PS: Dolphins lead series, 1-0
1966—Chiefs, 34-16 (KC)
Chiefs, 19-18 (M)
1967—Chiefs, 24-0 (M)
Chiefs, 41-0 (KC)
1968—Chiefs, 48-3 (M)
1969—Chiefs, 17-10 (KC)
1971—*Dolphins, 27-24 (KC) OT
1972—Dolphins, 20-10 (KC)
1974—Dolphins, 9-3 (M)
1976—Chiefs, 20-17 (M) OT
1981—Dolphins, 17-7 (KC)
1983—Dolphins, 14-6 (M)
1985—Dolphins, 31-0 (M)
1987—Dolphins, 42-0 (M)
1989—Chiefs, 26-21 (KC)
Chiefs, 27-24 (M)
(Points—Chiefs 306, Dolphins 269)
*AFC Divisional Playoff

KANSAS CITY vs. MINNESOTA
RS: Vikings lead series, 2-1
PS: Chiefs lead series, 1-0
1969—*Chiefs, 23-7 (New Orleans)
1970—Vikings, 27-10 (M)
1974—Vikings, 35-15 (KC)
1981—Chiefs, 10-6 (M)
(Points—Vikings 75, Chiefs 58)
*Super Bowl IV

*KANSAS CITY vs. **NEW ENGLAND
RS: Chiefs lead series, 11-7-3
1960—Patriots, 42-14 (B)
Texans, 34-0 (D)
1961—Patriots, 18-17 (D)
Patriots, 28-21 (B)
1962—Texans, 42-28 (D)
Texans, 27-7 (B)
1963—Tie, 24-24 (B)
Chiefs, 35-3 (KC)
1964—Patriots, 24-7 (B)
Patriots, 31-24 (KC)
1965—Chiefs, 27-17 (KC)
Tie, 10-10 (B)
1966—Chiefs, 43-24 (B)
Tie, 27-27 (KC)
1967—Chiefs, 33-10 (B)
1968—Chiefs, 31-17 (KC)
1969—Chiefs, 31-0 (B)
1970—Chiefs, 23-10 (KC)
1973—Chiefs, 10-7 (NE)
1977—Patriots, 21-17 (NE)
1981—Patriots, 33-17 (NE)
(Points—Chiefs 514, Patriots 381)
*Franchise located in Dallas prior to 1963 and known as Texans
**Franchise in Boston prior to 1971

KANSAS CITY vs. NEW ORLEANS
RS: Series tied, 2-2
1972—Chiefs, 20-17 (NO)
1976—Saints, 27-17 (KC)
1982—Chiefs, 27-17 (NO)
1985—Chiefs, 47-27 (NO)
(Points—Chiefs 101, Saints 98)

KANSAS CITY vs. N.Y. GIANTS
RS: Giants lead series, 5-1
1974—Giants, 33-27 (KC)
1978—Giants, 26-10 (NY)
1979—Giants, 21-17 (KC)
1983—Chiefs, 38-17 (KC)
1984—Giants, 28-27 (NY)
1988—Giants, 28-12 (NY)
(Points—Giants 153, Chiefs 131)

*KANSAS CITY vs. **N.Y. JETS
RS: Chiefs lead series, 13-12-1
PS: Series tied, 1-1
1960—Titans, 37-35 (D)
Titans, 41-35 (NY)
1961—Titans, 28-7 (NY)
Texans, 35-24 (D)
1962—Texans, 20-17 (D)
Texans, 52-31 (NY)
1963—Jets, 17-0 (NY)
Chiefs, 48-0 (KC)
1964—Jets, 27-14 (NY)
Chiefs, 24-7 (KC)
1965—Chiefs, 14-10 (NY)
Jets, 13-10 (KC)

1966—Chiefs, 32-24 (NY)
1967—Chiefs, 42-18 (KC)
Chiefs, 21-7 (NY)
1968—Jets, 20-19 (KC)
1969—Chiefs, 34-16 (NY)
***Chiefs, 13-6 (NY)
1971—Jets, 13-10 (NY)
1974—Chiefs, 24-16 (KC)
1975—Jets, 30-24 (KC)
1982—Chiefs, 37-13 (KC)
1984—Jets, 17-16 (KC)
Jets, 28-7 (NY)
1986—****Jets, 35-15 (NY)
1987—Jets, 16-9 (KC)
1988—Tie, 17-17 (NY)
Chiefs, 38-34 (KC)
(Points—Chiefs 652, Jets 562)
*Franchise in Dallas prior to 1963 and known as Texans
**Jets known as Titans prior to 1963
***Inter-Divisional Playoff
****AFC First Round Playoff

KANSAS CITY vs. PHILADELPHIA
RS: Eagles lead series, 1-0
1972—Eagles, 21-20 (KC)

KANSAS CITY vs. *PHOENIX
RS: Chiefs lead series, 3-1-1
1970—Tie, 6-6 (KC)
1974—Chiefs, 17-13 (StL)
1980—Chiefs, 21-13 (StL)
1983—Chiefs, 38-14 (KC)
1986—Cardinals, 23-14 (StL)
(Points—Chiefs 96, Cardinals 69)
*Franchise in St. Louis prior to 1988

KANSAS CITY vs. PITTSBURGH
RS: Steelers lead series, 12-5
1970—Chiefs, 31-14 (P)
1971—Chiefs, 38-16 (M)
1972—Steelers, 16-7 (P)
1974—Steelers, 34-24 (KC)
1975—Steelers, 28-3 (P)
1976—Steelers, 45-0 (KC)
1978—Steelers, 27-24 (P)
1979—Steelers, 30-3 (KC)
1980—Steelers, 21-16 (P)
1981—Chiefs, 37-33 (P)
1982—Steelers, 35-14 (P)
1984—Chiefs, 37-27 (P)
1985—Steelers, 36-28 (KC)
1986—Chiefs, 24-19 (P)
1987—Steelers, 17-16 (KC)
1988—Steelers, 16-10 (P)
1989—Steelers, 23-17 (P)
(Points—Steelers 437, Chiefs 329)

*KANSAS CITY vs. **SAN DIEGO
RS: Chargers lead series, 31-27-1
1960—Chargers, 21-20 (LA)
Texans, 17-0 (D)
1961—Chargers, 26-10 (D)
Chargers, 24-14 (SD)
1962—Chargers, 32-28 (SD)
Texans, 26-17 (D)
1963—Chargers, 24-10 (SD)
Chargers, 38-17 (KC)
1964—Chargers, 28-14 (KC)
Chiefs, 49-6 (SD)
1965—Tie, 10-10 (SD)
Chiefs, 31-7 (KC)
1966—Chiefs, 24-14 (KC)
Chiefs, 27-17 (SD)
1967—Chargers, 45-31 (SD)
Chargers, 17-16 (KC)
1968—Chiefs, 27-20 (KC)
Chiefs, 40-3 (SD)
1969—Chiefs, 27-9 (SD)
Chiefs, 27-3 (KC)
1970—Chiefs, 26-14 (KC)
Chargers, 31-13 (SD)
1971—Chargers, 21-14 (SD)
Chiefs, 31-10 (KC)
1972—Chiefs, 26-14 (SD)
Chargers, 27-17 (KC)
1973—Chiefs, 19-0 (SD)
Chiefs, 33-6 (KC)
1974—Chiefs, 24-14 (SD)
Chargers, 14-7 (KC)
1975—Chiefs, 12-10 (SD)
Chargers, 28-20 (KC)
1976—Chargers, 30-16 (KC)
Chiefs, 23-20 (SD)
1977—Chargers, 23-7 (KC)
Chiefs, 21-16 (SD)
1978—Chargers, 29-23 (SD) OT
Chiefs, 23-0 (KC)
1979—Chargers, 20-14 (KC)
Chargers, 28-7 (SD)
1980—Chiefs, 24-7 (KC)
Chargers, 20-7 (SD)
1981—Chargers, 42-31 (SD)
Chargers, 22-20 (SD)
1982—Chiefs, 19-12 (KC)
1983—Chargers, 17-14 (SD)
Chargers, 41-38 (SD)

1984—Chiefs, 31-13 (KC)
Chiefs, 42-21 (SD)
1985—Chargers, 31-20 (SD)
Chiefs, 38-34 (KC)
1986—Chiefs, 42-41 (KC)
Chiefs, 24-23 (SD)
1987—Chiefs, 20-13 (KC)
Chargers, 42-21 (SD)
1988—Chargers, 24-23 (KC)
Chargers, 24-13 (SD)
1989—Chargers, 21-6 (SD)
Chargers, 20-13 (KC)
(Points—Chiefs 1,270, Chargers 1,201)
*Franchise in Dallas prior to 1963 and known as Texans
**Franchise in Los Angeles prior to 1961

KANSAS CITY vs. SAN FRANCISCO
RS: 49ers lead series, 3-1
1971—Chiefs, 26-17 (SF)
1975—49ers, 20-3 (KC)
1982—49ers, 26-13 (KC)
1985—49ers, 31-3 (SF)
(Points—49ers 94, Chiefs 45)

KANSAS CITY vs. SEATTLE
RS: Chiefs lead series, 13-10
1977—Seahawks, 34-31 (KC)
1978—Seahawks, 13-10 (KC)
Seahawks, 23-19 (S)
1979—Chiefs, 24-6 (S)
Chiefs, 37-21 (KC)
1980—Seahawks, 17-16 (KC)
Chiefs, 31-30 (S)
1981—Chiefs, 20-14 (S)
Chiefs, 40-13 (KC)
1983—Chiefs, 17-13 (KC)
Seahawks, 51-48 (S) OT
1984—Seahawks, 45-0 (S)
Chiefs, 34-7 (KC)
1985—Chiefs, 28-7 (KC)
Seahawks, 24-6 (S)
1986—Seahawks, 23-17 (S)
Chiefs, 27-7 (KC)
1987—Seahawks, 43-14 (S)
Chiefs, 41-20 (KC)
1988—Seahawks, 31-10 (S)
Chiefs, 27-24 (KC)
1989—Chiefs, 20-16 (S)
Chiefs, 20-10 (KC)
(Points—Chiefs 537, Seahawks 492)

KANSAS CITY vs. TAMPA BAY
RS: Chiefs lead series, 4-2
1976—Chiefs, 28-19 (TB)
1978—Buccaneers, 30-13 (KC)
1979—Buccaneers, 3-0 (TB)
1981—Chiefs, 19-10 (KC)
1984—Chiefs, 24-20 (KC)
1986—Chiefs, 27-20 (KC)
(Points—Chiefs 111, Buccaneers 102)

KANSAS CITY vs. WASHINGTON
RS: Chiefs lead series, 2-1
1971—Chiefs, 27-20 (KC)
1976—Chiefs, 33-30 (W)
1983—Redskins, 27-12 (W)
(Points—Redskins 77, Chiefs 72)

L.A. RAIDERS vs. ATLANTA
RS: Raiders lead series, 4-2;
See Atlanta vs. L.A. Raiders

L.A. RAIDERS vs. BUFFALO
RS: Raiders lead series, 13-12;
See Buffalo vs. L.A. Raiders

L.A. RAIDERS vs. CHICAGO
RS: Series tied, 3-3;
See Chicago vs. L.A. Raiders

L.A. RAIDERS vs. CINCINNATI
RS: Raiders lead series, 12-5
PS: Raiders lead series, 1-0;
See Cincinnati vs. L.A. Raiders

L.A. RAIDERS vs. CLEVELAND
RS: Raiders lead series, 8-2
PS: Raiders lead series, 2-0;
See Cleveland vs. L.A. Raiders

L.A. RAIDERS vs. DALLAS
RS: Raiders lead series, 3-1;
See Dallas vs. L.A. Raiders

L.A. RAIDERS vs. DENVER
RS: Raiders lead series, 39-18-2
PS: Broncos lead series, 1-0;
See Denver vs. L.A. Raiders

L.A. RAIDERS vs. DETROIT
RS: Raiders lead series, 4-2;
See Detroit vs. L.A. Raiders

L.A. RAIDERS vs. GREEN BAY
RS: Raiders lead series, 5-0
PS: Packers lead series, 1-0;
See Green Bay vs. L.A. Raiders

L.A. RAIDERS vs. HOUSTON
RS: Raiders lead series, 19-12
PS: Raiders lead series, 3-0;
See Houston vs. L.A. Raiders

L.A. RAIDERS vs. INDIANAPOLIS
RS: Raiders lead series, 3-2
PS: Series tied, 1-1;

See Indianapolis vs. L.A. Raiders

L.A. RAIDERS vs. KANSAS CITY
RS: Raiders lead series, 34-23-2
PS: Series tied, 1-1;
See Kansas City vs. L.A. Raiders

*L.A. RAIDERS vs. L.A. RAMS
RS: Raiders lead series, 4-2
1972—Rams, 45-17 (O)
1977—Rams, 20-14 (LA)
1979—Raiders, 24-17 (LA)
1982—Raiders, 37-31 (LA Raiders)
1985—Raiders, 16-6 (LA Rams)
1988—Rams, 22-17 (LA Raiders)
(Points—Raiders 153, Rams 113)
*Franchise in Oakland prior to 1982

*L.A. RAIDERS vs. MIAMI
RS: Raiders lead series, 13-3-1
PS: Raiders lead series, 2-1
1966—Raiders, 23-14 (M)
Raiders, 21-10 (O)
1967—Raiders, 31-17 (O)
1968—Raiders, 47-21 (M)
1969—Raiders, 20-17 (O)
Tie, 20-20 (M)
1970—Dolphins, 20-13 (M)
**Raiders, 21-14 (O)
1973—Raiders, 12-7 (O)
***Dolphins, 27-10 (M)
1974—**Raiders, 28-26 (O)
1975—Raiders, 31-21 (M)
1978—Dolphins, 23-6 (M)
1979—Raiders, 13-3 (O)
1980—Raiders, 16-10 (O)
1981—Raiders, 33-17 (M)
1983—Raiders, 27-14 (LA)
1984—Raiders, 45-34 (M)
1986—Raiders, 30-28 (M)
1988—Dolphins, 24-14 (LA)
(Points—Raiders 461, Dolphins 367)
*Franchise in Oakland prior to 1982
**AFC Divisional Playoff
***AFC Championship

*L.A. RAIDERS vs. MINNESOTA
RS: Raiders lead series, 4-2
PS: Raiders lead series, 1-0
1973—Vikings, 24-16 (M)
1976—**Raiders, 32-14 (Pasadena)
1977—Raiders, 35-13 (O)
1978—Raiders, 27-20 (O)
1981—Raiders, 36-10 (O)
1984—Raiders, 23-20 (LA)
1987—Vikings, 31-20 (M)
(Points—Raiders 189, Vikings 132)
*Franchise in Oakland prior to 1982
**Super Bowl XI

*L.A. RAIDERS vs. **NEW ENGLAND
RS: Series tied, 12-12-1
PS: Series tied, 1-1
1960—Raiders, 27-14 (O)
Patriots, 34-28 (B)
1961—Patriots, 20-17 (B)
Patriots, 35-21 (O)
1962—Patriots, 26-16 (B)
Raiders, 20-0 (O)
1963—Patriots, 20-14 (O)
Patriots, 20-14 (B)
1964—Patriots, 17-14 (O)
Tie, 43-43 (B)
1965—Raiders, 24-10 (B)
Raiders, 30-21 (O)
1966—Patriots, 24-21 (B)
1967—Raiders, 35-7 (O)
Raiders, 48-14 (B)
1968—Raiders, 41-10 (O)
1969—Raiders, 38-23 (B)
1971—Patriots, 20-6 (NE)
1974—Raiders, 41-26 (O)
1976—Patriots, 48-17 (NE)
***Raiders, 24-21 (O)
1978—Patriots, 21-14 (O)
1981—Raiders, 27-17 (O)
1985—Raiders, 35-20 (NE)
***Patriots, 27-20 (LA)
1987—Patriots, 26-23 (NE)
1989—Raiders, 24-21 (LA)
(Points—Raiders 682, Patriots 585)
*Franchise in Oakland prior to 1982
**Franchise in Boston prior to 1971
***AFC Divisional Playoff

*L.A. RAIDERS vs. NEW ORLEANS
RS: Raiders lead series, 3-1-1
1971—Tie, 21-21 (NO)
1975—Raiders, 48-10 (O)
1979—Raiders, 42-35 (NO)
1985—Raiders, 23-13 (LA)
1988—Saints, 20-6 (NO)
(Points—Raiders 140, Saints 99)
*Franchise in Oakland prior to 1982

*L.A. RAIDERS vs. N.Y. GIANTS
RS: Raiders lead series, 3-2
1973—Raiders, 42-0 (O)
1980—Raiders, 33-17 (NY)
1983—Raiders, 27-12 (LA)

1986—Giants, 14-9 (LA)
1989—Giants, 34-17 (NY)
(Points—Raiders 128, Giants 77)
*Franchise in Oakland prior to 1982

*L.A. RAIDERS vs. **N.Y. JETS
RS: Raiders lead series, 13-9-2
PS: Jets lead series, 2-0
1960—Raiders, 28-27 (NY)
    Titans, 31-28 (O)
1961—Titans, 14-6 (O)
    Titans, 23-12 (NY)
1962—Titans, 28-17 (O)
    Titans, 31-21 (NY)
1963—Jets, 10-7 (NY)
    Raiders, 49-26 (O)
1964—Jets, 35-13 (NY)
    Raiders, 35-26 (O)
1965—Tie, 24-24 (NY)
    Raiders, 24-14 (O)
1966—Raiders, 24-21 (NY)
    Tie, 28-28 (O)
1967—Jets, 27-14 (NY)
    Raiders, 38-29 (O)
1968—Raiders, 43-32 (O)
    ***Jets, 27-23 (NY)
1969—Raiders, 27-14 (NY)
1970—Raiders, 14-13 (NY)
1972—Raiders, 24-16 (O)
1977—Raiders, 28-27 (NY)
1979—Jets, 28-19 (NY)
1982—****Jets, 17-14 (LA)
1985—Raiders, 31-0 (LA)
1989—Raiders, 14-7 (NY)
(Points—Raiders 605, Jets 575)
*Franchise in Oakland prior to 1982
**Jets known as Titans prior to 1963
***AFL Championship
****AFC Second Round Playoff

*L.A. RAIDERS vs. PHILADELPHIA
RS: Eagles lead series, 3-2
PS: Raiders lead series, 1-0
1971—Raiders, 34-10 (O)
1976—Raiders, 26-7 (P)
1980—Eagles, 10-7 (P)
    **Raiders, 27-10 (NO)
1986—Eagles, 33-27 (LA) OT
1989—Eagles, 10-7 (P)
(Points—Raiders 128, Eagles 80)
*Franchise in Oakland prior to 1982
**Super Bowl XV

*L.A. RAIDERS vs. **PHOENIX
RS: Raiders lead series, 2-1
1973—Raiders, 17-10 (StL)
1983—Cardinals, 34-24 (LA)
1989—Raiders, 16-14 (LA)
(Points—Cardinals 58, Raiders 57)
*Franchise in Oakland prior to 1982
**Franchise in St. Louis prior to 1988

*L.A. RAIDERS vs. PITTSBURGH
RS: Raiders lead series, 6-3
PS: Series tied, 3-3
1970—Raiders, 31-14 (O)
1972—Steelers, 34-28 (P)
    **Steelers, 13-7 (P)
1973—Steelers, 17-9 (O)
    **Raiders, 33-14 (O)
1974—Raiders, 17-0 (P)
    ***Steelers, 24-13 (O)
1975—***Steelers, 16-10 (P)
1976—Raiders, 31-28 (O)
    ***Raiders, 24-7 (O)
1977—Raiders, 16-7 (P)
1980—Raiders, 45-34 (P)
1981—Raiders, 30-27 (O)
1983—**Raiders, 38-10 (LA)
1984—Steelers, 13-7 (LA)
(Points—Raiders 339, Steelers 258)
*Franchise in Oakland prior to 1982
**AFC Divisional Playoff
***AFC Championship

*L.A. RAIDERS vs. **SAN DIEGO
RS: Raiders lead series, 37-21-2
PS: Raiders lead series, 1-0
1960—Chargers, 52-28 (LA)
    Chargers, 41-17 (O)
1961—Chargers, 44-0 (SD)
    Chargers, 41-10 (O)
1962—Chargers, 42-33 (O)
    Chargers, 31-21 (SD)
1963—Raiders, 34-33 (SD)
    Raiders, 41-27 (O)
1964—Chargers, 31-17 (O)
    Raiders, 21-20 (SD)
1965—Chargers, 17-6 (O)
    Chargers, 24-14 (SD)
1966—Chargers, 29-20 (SD)
    Raiders, 41-19 (O)
1967—Chargers, 51-10 (O)
    Raiders, 41-21 (SD)
1968—Chargers, 23-14 (O)
    Raiders, 34-27 (SD)
1969—Chargers, 24-12 (SD)
    Raiders, 21-16 (O)

1970—Tie, 27-27 (SD)
    Raiders, 20-17 (O)
1971—Raiders, 34-0 (SD)
    Raiders, 34-33 (O)
1972—Tie, 17-17 (O)
    Raiders, 21-19 (SD)
1973—Raiders, 27-17 (SD)
    Raiders, 31-3 (O)
1974—Raiders, 14-10 (SD)
    Raiders, 17-10 (O)
1975—Raiders, 6-0 (SD)
    Raiders, 25-0 (O)
1976—Raiders, 27-17 (SD)
    Raiders, 24-0 (O)
1977—Raiders, 24-0 (O)
    Chargers, 12-7 (SD)
1978—Chargers, 21-20 (SD)
    Chargers, 27-23 (O)
1979—Chargers, 30-10 (SD)
    Raiders, 45-22 (O)
1980—Chargers, 30-24 (SD) OT
    Raiders, 38-24 (O)
    ***Raiders, 34-27 (SD)
1981—Chargers, 55-21 (O)
    Chargers, 23-10 (SD)
1982—Raiders, 28-24 (LA)
    Raiders, 41-34 (SD)
1983—Raiders, 42-10 (SD)
    Raiders, 30-14 (LA)
1984—Raiders, 33-30 (SD)
    Raiders, 44-37 (SD)
1985—Raiders, 34-21 (LA)
    Chargers, 40-34 (SD) OT
1986—Raiders, 17-13 (LA)
    Raiders, 37-31 (SD) OT
1987—Chargers, 23-17 (LA)
    Chargers, 16-14 (SD)
1988—Raiders, 24-13 (LA)
    Raiders, 13-3 (SD)
1989—Raiders, 40-14 (LA)
    Chargers, 14-12 (SD)
(Points—Raiders 1,529, Chargers 1,337)
*Franchise in Oakland prior to 1982
**Franchise in Los Angeles prior to 1961
***AFC Championship

*L.A. RAIDERS vs. SAN FRANCISCO
RS: Raiders lead series, 4-2
1970—49ers, 38-7 (O)
1974—Raiders, 35-24 (SF)
1979—Raiders, 23-10 (O)
1982—Raiders, 23-17 (SF)
1985—49ers, 34-10 (LA)
1988—Raiders, 9-3 (SF)
(Points—49ers 126, Raiders 107)
*Franchise in Oakland prior to 1982

*L.A. RAIDERS vs. SEATTLE
RS: Seahawks lead series, 14-10
PS: Series tied, 1-1
1977—Raiders, 44-7 (O)
1978—Seahawks, 27-7 (S)
    Seahawks, 17-16 (O)
1979—Seahawks, 27-10 (S)
    Seahawks, 29-24 (O)
1980—Raiders, 33-14 (O)
    Raiders, 19-17 (S)
1981—Raiders, 20-10 (O)
    Raiders, 32-31 (S)
1982—Raiders, 28-23 (LA)
1983—Seahawks, 38-36 (S)
    Seahawks, 34-21 (LA)
    **Raiders, 30-14 (LA)
1984—Raiders, 28-14 (LA)
    Seahawks, 17-14 (S)
    ***Seahawks, 13-7 (S)
1985—Seahawks, 33-3 (S)
    Raiders, 13-3 (LA)
1986—Raiders, 14-10 (LA)
    Seahawks, 37-0 (S)
1987—Seahawks, 35-13 (S)
    Raiders, 37-14 (LA)
1988—Seahawks, 35-27 (S)
    Seahawks, 43-37 (LA)
1989—Seahawks, 24-20 (LA)
    Seahawks, 23-17 (S)
(Points—Seahawks 589, Raiders 550)
*Franchise in Oakland prior to 1982
**AFC Championship
***AFC First Round Playoff

*L.A. RAIDERS vs. TAMPA BAY
RS: Raiders lead series, 2-0
1976—Raiders, 49-16 (O)
1981—Raiders, 18-16 (O)
(Points—Raiders 67, Buccaneers 32)
*Franchise in Oakland prior to 1982

*L.A. RAIDERS vs. WASHINGTON
RS: Raiders lead series, 4-2
PS: Raiders lead series, 1-0
1970—Raiders, 34-20 (O)
1975—Raiders, 26-23 (W) OT
1980—Raiders, 24-21 (O)
1983—Redskins, 37-35 (W)
    **Raiders, 38-9 (Tampa)
1986—Redskins, 10-6 (W)

1989—Raiders, 37-24 (LA)
(Points—Raiders 200, Redskins 144)
*Franchise in Oakland prior to 1982
**Super Bowl XVIII

L.A. RAMS vs. ATLANTA
RS: Rams lead series, 34-10-2;
See Atlanta vs. L.A. Rams
L.A. RAMS vs. BUFFALO
RS: Rams lead series, 3-2;
See Buffalo vs. L.A. Rams
L.A. RAMS vs. CHICAGO
RS: Bears lead series, 43-28-3
PS: Series tied, 1-1;
See Chicago vs. L.A. Rams
L.A. RAMS vs. CINCINNATI
RS: Bengals lead series, 3-2;
See Cincinnati vs. L.A. Rams
L.A. RAMS vs. CLEVELAND
RS: Browns lead series, 7-6
PS: Browns lead series, 2-1;
See Cleveland vs. L.A. Rams
L.A. RAMS vs. DALLAS
RS: Rams lead series, 8-7
PS: Series tied, 4-4;
See Dallas vs. L.A. Rams
L.A. RAMS vs. DENVER
RS: Series tied, 3-3;
See Denver vs. L.A. Rams
L.A. RAMS vs. DETROIT
RS: Rams lead series, 39-33-1
PS: Lions lead series, 1-0;
See Detroit vs. L.A. Rams
L.A. RAMS vs. GREEN BAY
RS: Rams lead series, 41-33-2
PS: Packers lead series, 1-0;
See Green Bay vs. L.A. Rams
L.A. RAMS vs. HOUSTON
RS: Rams lead series, 3-2;
See Houston vs. L.A. Rams
L.A. RAMS vs. INDIANAPOLIS
RS: Colts lead series, 20-16-2;
See Indianapolis vs. L.A. Rams
L.A. RAMS vs. KANSAS CITY
RS: Rams lead series, 3-0;
See Kansas City vs. L.A. Rams
L.A. RAMS VS. L.A. RAIDERS
RS: Raiders lead series, 4-2;
See L.A. Raiders vs. L.A. Rams
L.A. RAMS vs. MIAMI
RS: Dolphins lead series, 4-1
1971—Dolphins, 20-14 (LA)
1976—Rams, 31-28 (M)
1980—Dolphins, 35-14 (LA)
1983—Dolphins, 30-14 (M)
1986—Dolphins 37-31 (LA) OT
(Points—Dolphins 150, Rams 104)
L.A. RAMS vs. MINNESOTA
RS: Vikings lead series, 13-11-2
PS: Vikings lead series, 5-1
1961—Rams, 31-17 (LA)
    Vikings, 42-21 (M)
1962—Vikings, 38-14 (LA)
    Tie, 24-24 (M)
1963—Rams, 27-24 (LA)
    Vikings, 21-13 (M)
1964—Rams, 22-13 (LA)
    Vikings, 34-13 (M)
1965—Vikings, 38-35 (LA)
    Vikings, 24-13 (M)
1966—Vikings, 35-7 (M)
    Rams, 21-6 (LA)
1967—Rams, 39-3 (LA)
1968—Rams, 31-3 (M)
1969—Vikings, 20-13 (LA)
    *Vikings, 23-20 (M)
1970—Vikings, 13-3 (M)
1972—Vikings, 45-41 (LA)
1973—Vikings, 10-9 (M)
1974—Rams, 20-17 (LA)
    **Vikings, 14-10 (M)
1976—Tie, 10-10 (M) OT
    **Vikings, 24-13 (M)
1977—Rams, 35-3 (LA)
    ***Vikings, 14-7 (LA)
1978—Rams, 34-17 (M)
    ***Rams, 34-10 (LA)
1979—Rams, 27-21 (LA) OT
1985—Rams, 13-10 (LA)
1987—Vikings, 21-16 (LA)
1988—****Vikings, 28-17 (M)
1989—Vikings, 23-21 (M) OT
(Points—Rams 654, Vikings 645)
*Conference Championship
**NFC Championship
***NFC Divisional Playoff
****NFC First Round Playoff
L.A. RAMS vs. NEW ENGLAND
RS: Patriots lead series, 3-2
1974—Patriots, 20-14 (NE)
1980—Rams, 17-14 (NE)
1983—Patriots, 21-7 (LA)
1986—Patriots, 30-28 (LA)

1989—Rams, 24-20 (NE)
(Points—Patriots 105, Rams 90)
L.A. RAMS vs. NEW ORLEANS
RS: Rams lead series, 26-14
1967—Rams, 27-13 (NO)
1969—Rams, 36-17 (LA)
1970—Rams, 30-17 (NO)
    Rams, 34-16 (LA)
1971—Saints, 24-20 (NO)
    Rams, 45-28 (LA)
1972—Rams, 34-14 (LA)
    Saints, 19-16 (NO)
1973—Rams, 29-7 (LA)
    Rams, 24-13 (NO)
1974—Rams, 24-0 (LA)
    Saints, 20-7 (NO)
1975—Rams, 38-14 (LA)
    Rams, 14-7 (NO)
1976—Rams, 16-10 (NO)
    Rams, 33-14 (LA)
1977—Rams, 14-7 (LA)
    Saints, 27-26 (NO)
1978—Rams, 26-20 (NO)
    Saints, 10-3 (LA)
1979—Rams, 35-17 (NO)
    Saints, 29-14 (LA)
1980—Rams, 45-31 (LA)
    Rams, 27-7 (NO)
1981—Saints, 23-17 (NO)
    Saints, 21-13 (LA)
1983—Rams, 30-27 (NO)
    Rams, 26-24 (NO)
1984—Rams, 28-10 (NO)
    Rams, 34-21 (LA)
1985—Rams, 28-10 (LA)
    Saints, 29-3 (NO)
1986—Saints, 6-0 (NO)
    Rams, 26-13 (LA)
1987—Saints, 37-10 (NO)
    Saints, 31-14 (LA)
1988—Rams, 12-10 (NO)
    Saints, 14-10 (LA)
1989—Saints, 40-21 (LA)
    Rams, 20-17 (NO) OT
(Points—Rams 909, Saints 714)

*L.A. RAMS vs. N.Y. GIANTS
RS: Rams lead series, 18-7
PS: Series tied, 1-1
1938—Giants, 28-0 (NY)
1940—Rams, 13-0 (NY)
1941—Giants, 49-14 (NY)
1945—Rams, 21-17 (NY)
1946—Rams, 31-21 (NY)
1947—Rams, 34-10 (LA)
1948—Rams, 52-37 (NY)
1953—Rams, 21-7 (LA)
1954—Rams, 17-16 (NY)
1959—Giants, 23-21 (LA)
1961—Giants, 24-14 (NY)
1966—Rams, 55-14 (LA)
1968—Rams, 24-21 (LA)
1970—Rams, 31-3 (NY)
1973—Rams, 40-6 (LA)
1976—Rams, 24-10 (LA)
1978—Rams, 20-17 (NY)
1979—Giants, 20-14 (LA)
1980—Rams, 28-7 (NY)
1981—Giants, 10-7 (NY)
1983—Rams, 16-6 (LA)
1984—Rams, 33-12 (LA)
    **Giants, 16-13 (LA)
1985—Giants, 24-19 (NY)
1988—Rams, 45-31 (NY)
1989—Rams, 31-10 (LA)
    ***Rams, 19-13 (NY) OT
(Points—Rams 657, Giants 452)
*Franchise in Cleveland prior to 1946
**NFC First Round Playoff
***NFC Divisional Playoff
L.A. RAMS vs. N.Y. JETS
RS: Rams lead series, 4-2
1970—Rams, 31-20 (LA)
1974—Rams, 20-13 (NY)
1980—Rams, 38-13 (LA)
1983—Jets, 27-24 (NY) OT
1986—Rams, 17-3 (NY)
1989—Rams, 38-14 (LA)
(Points—Rams 157, Jets 101)
*L.A. RAMS vs. PHILADELPHIA
RS: Rams lead series, 15-10-1
PS: Series tied, 1-1
1937—Rams, 21-3 (P)
1939—Rams, 35-13 (Colorado Springs)
1940—Rams, 21-13 (C)
1942—Rams, 24-14 (Akron)
1944—Eagles, 26-13 (P)
1945—Eagles, 28-14 (P)
1946—Eagles, 25-14 (LA)
1947—Eagles, 14-7 (P)
1948—Tie, 28-28 (LA)
1949—Eagles, 38-14 (P)
    **Eagles, 14-0 (LA)
1950—Eagles, 56-20 (P)

263

1955—Rams, 23-21 (P)
1956—Rams, 27-7 (LA)
1957—Rams, 17-13 (LA)
1959—Eagles, 23-20 (P)
1964—Rams, 20-10 (LA)
1967—Rams, 33-17 (LA)
1969—Rams, 23-17 (P)
1972—Rams, 34-3 (P)
1975—Rams, 42-3 (P)
1977—Rams, 20-0 (LA)
1978—Rams, 16-14 (P)
1983—Eagles, 13-9 (P)
1985—Rams, 17-6 (P)
1986—Eagles, 34-20 (P)
1988—Eagles, 30-24 (P)
1989—***Rams, 21-7 (P)
(Points—Rams 577, Eagles 490)
*Franchise in Cleveland prior to 1946
**NFL Championship
***NFC First Round Playoff

*L.A. RAMS vs. **PHOENIX
RS: Rams lead series, 22-16-2
PS: Rams lead series, 1-0
1937—Cardinals, 6-0 (Clev)
    Cardinals, 13-7 (Chi)
1938—Cardinals, 7-6 (Clev)
    Cardinals, 31-17 (Chi)
1939—Rams, 24-0 (Chi)
    Rams, 14-0 (Clev)
1940—Rams, 26-14 (Clev)
    Cardinals, 17-7 (Chi)
1941—Rams, 10-6 (Clev)
    Cardinals, 7-0 (Chi)
1942—Cardinals, 7-0 (Clev)
    Rams, 7-3 (Clev)
1945—Rams, 21-0 (Clev)
    Rams, 35-21 (Chi)
1946—Cardinals, 34-10 (Chi)
    Rams, 17-14 (LA)
1947—Rams, 27-7 (LA)
    Cardinals, 17-10 (Chi)
1948—Cardinals, 27-22 (LA)
    Cardinals, 27-24 (Chi)
1949—Tie, 28-28 (Chi)
    Cardinals, 31-27 (LA)
1951—Rams, 45-21 (LA)
1953—Tie, 24-24 (Chi)
1954—Rams, 28-17 (LA)
1958—Rams, 20-14 (Chi)
1960—Cardinals, 43-21 (LA)
1965—Rams, 27-3 (StL)
1968—Rams, 24-13 (StL)
1970—Rams, 34-13 (LA)
1972—Cardinals, 24-14 (StL)
1975—***Rams, 35-23 (LA)
1976—Cardinals, 30-28 (LA)
1979—Rams, 21-0 (LA)
1980—Rams, 21-13 (StL)
1984—Rams, 16-13 (StL)
1985—Rams, 46-14 (LA)
1986—Rams, 16-10 (StL)
1987—Rams, 27-24 (StL)
1988—Cardinals, 41-27 (LA)
1989—Rams, 37-14 (LA)
(Points—Rams 850, Cardinals 671)
*Franchise in Cleveland prior to 1946
**Franchise in St. Louis prior to 1988
and in Chicago prior to 1960
***NFC Divisional Playoff

*L.A. RAMS vs. **PITTSBURGH
RS: Rams lead series, 13-3-2
PS: Steelers lead series, 1-0
1938—Rams, 13-7 (New Orleans)
1939—Tie, 14-14 (C)
1941—Rams, 17-14 (Akron)
1947—Rams, 48-7 (P)
1948—Rams, 31-14 (LA)
1949—Tie, 7-7 (P)
1952—Rams, 28-14 (LA)
1955—Rams, 27-26 (LA)
1956—Steelers, 30-13 (P)
1961—Rams, 24-14 (LA)
1964—Rams, 26-14 (P)
1968—Rams, 45-10 (LA)
1971—Rams, 23-14 (P)
1975—Rams, 10-3 (LA)
1978—Rams, 10-7 (LA)
1979—***Steelers, 31-19 (Pasadena)
1981—Steelers, 24-0 (P)
1984—Steelers, 24-14 (P)
1987—Rams, 31-21 (LA)
(Points—Rams 400, Steelers 295)
*Franchise in Cleveland prior to 1946
**Steelers known as Pirates prior to 1941
***Super Bowl XIV

L.A. RAMS vs. SAN DIEGO
RS: Series tied, 2-2
1970—Rams, 37-10 (LA)
1975—Rams, 13-10 (SD) OT
1979—Chargers, 40-16 (LA)
1988—Chargers, 38-24 (LA)
(Points—Chargers 98, Rams 90)

L.A. RAMS vs. SAN FRANCISCO

RS: Rams lead series, 47-31-2
PS: 49ers lead series, 1-0
1950—Rams, 35-14 (SF)
    Rams, 28-21 (LA)
1951—49ers, 44-17 (SF)
    Rams, 23-16 (LA)
1952—Rams, 35-9 (LA)
    Rams, 34-21 (SF)
1953—49ers, 31-30 (SF)
    49ers, 31-27 (LA)
1954—Tie, 24-24 (LA)
    Rams, 42-34 (SF)
1955—Rams, 23-14 (SF)
    Rams, 27-14 (LA)
1956—49ers, 33-30 (SF)
    Rams, 30-6 (LA)
1957—49ers, 23-20 (SF)
    Rams, 37-24 (LA)
1958—Rams, 33-3 (SF)
    Rams, 56-7 (LA)
1959—49ers, 34-0 (SF)
    49ers, 24-16 (LA)
1960—49ers, 13-9 (SF)
    Rams, 23-7 (LA)
1961—49ers, 35-0 (SF)
    Rams, 17-7 (LA)
1962—Rams, 28-14 (SF)
    49ers, 24-17 (LA)
1963—Rams, 28-21 (LA)
    Rams, 21-17 (SF)
1964—Rams, 42-14 (LA)
    49ers, 28-7 (SF)
1965—49ers, 45-21 (LA)
    49ers, 30-27 (SF)
1966—Rams, 34-3 (LA)
    49ers, 21-13 (SF)
1967—49ers, 27-24 (LA)
    Rams, 17-7 (SF)
1968—Rams, 24-10 (LA)
    Tie, 20-20 (SF)
1969—Rams, 27-21 (SF)
    Rams, 41-30 (LA)
1970—49ers, 20-6 (LA)
    Rams, 30-13 (SF)
1971—Rams, 20-13 (SF)
    Rams, 17-6 (LA)
1972—Rams, 31-7 (LA)
    Rams, 26-16 (SF)
1973—Rams, 40-20 (SF)
    Rams, 31-13 (LA)
1974—Rams, 37-14 (LA)
    Rams, 15-13 (SF)
1975—Rams, 23-14 (SF)
    49ers, 24-23 (LA)
1976—49ers, 16-0 (LA)
    Rams, 23-3 (SF)
1977—Rams, 34-14 (LA)
    Rams, 23-10 (SF)
1978—Rams, 27-10 (LA)
    Rams, 31-28 (SF)
1979—Rams, 27-24 (LA)
    Rams, 26-20 (SF)
1980—Rams, 48-26 (LA)
    Rams, 31-17 (SF)
1981—49ers, 20-17 (LA)
    49ers, 33-31 (SF)
1982—49ers, 30-24 (LA)
    Rams, 21-20 (SF)
1983—Rams, 10-7 (SF)
    49ers, 45-35 (LA)
1984—49ers, 33-0 (LA)
    49ers, 19-16 (SF)
1985—49ers, 28-14 (LA)
    Rams, 27-20 (SF)
1986—Rams, 16-13 (LA)
    49ers, 24-14 (SF)
1987—49ers, 31-10 (LA)
    49ers, 48-0 (SF)
1988—49ers, 24-21 (LA)
    Rams, 38-16 (SF)
1989—Rams, 13-12 (SF)
    49ers, 30-27 (LA)
    *49ers, 30-3 (SF)
(Points—Rams 1,897, 49ers 1,661)
*NFC Championship

L.A. RAMS vs. SEATTLE
RS: Rams lead series, 4-0
1976—Rams, 45-6 (LA)
1979—Rams, 24-0 (S)
1985—Rams, 35-24 (S)
1988—Rams, 31-10 (LA)
(Points—Rams 135, Seahawks 40)

L.A. RAMS vs. TAMPA BAY
RS: Rams lead series, 6-2
PS: Rams lead series, 1-0
1977—Rams, 31-0 (LA)
1978—Rams, 26-23 (LA)
1979—Buccaneers, 21-6 (TB)
    *Rams, 9-0 (TB)
1980—Buccaneers, 10-9 (TB)
1984—Rams, 34-33 (TB)
1985—Rams, 31-27 (TB)
1986—Rams, 26-20 (LA) OT

1987—Rams, 35-3 (LA)
(Points—Rams 207, Buccaneers 137)
*NFC Championship

*L.A. RAMS vs. WASHINGTON
RS: Redskins lead series, 13-4-1
PS: Series tied, 2-2
1937—Redskins, 16-7 (C)
1938—Redskins, 37-13 (W)
1941—Redskins, 17-13 (W)
1942—Redskins, 33-14 (W)
1944—Redskins, 14-10 (W)
1945—**Rams, 15-14 (C)
1948—Rams, 41-13 (W)
1949—Rams, 53-27 (W)
1951—Redskins, 31-21 (W)
1962—Rams, 20-14 (W)
1963—Redskins, 37-14 (LA)
1967—Tie, 28-28 (LA)
1969—Rams, 24-13 (W)
1971—Redskins, 38-24 (LA)
1974—Redskins, 23-17 (LA)
    ***Rams, 19-10 (LA)
1977—Redskins, 17-14 (W)
1981—Redskins, 30-7 (LA)
1983—Redskins, 42-20 (LA)
    ***Redskins, 51-7 (W)
1986—****Redskins, 19-7 (W)
1987—Rams, 30-26 (W)
(Points—Redskins 556, Rams 412)
*Franchise in Cleveland prior to 1946
**NFL Championship
***NFC Divisional Playoff
****NFC First Round Playoff

MIAMI vs. ATLANTA
RS: Dolphins lead series, 4-1;
See Atlanta vs. Miami
MIAMI vs. BUFFALO
RS: Dolphins lead series, 34-13-1;
See Buffalo vs. Miami
MIAMI vs. CHICAGO
RS: Dolphins lead series, 4-1;
See Chicago vs. Miami
MIAMI vs. CINCINNATI
RS: Dolphins lead series, 8-3
PS: Dolphins lead series, 1-0;
See Cincinnati vs. Miami
MIAMI vs. CLEVELAND
RS: Browns lead series, 4-3
PS: Dolphins lead series, 2-0;
See Cleveland vs. Miami
MIAMI vs. DALLAS
RS: Dolphins lead series, 5-1
PS: Cowboys lead series, 1-0;
See Dallas vs. Miami
MIAMI vs. DENVER
RS: Dolphins lead series, 5-2-1;
See Denver vs. Miami
MIAMI vs. DETROIT
RS: Dolphins lead series, 2-1;
See Detroit vs. Miami
MIAMI vs. GREEN BAY
RS: Dolphins lead series, 6-0;
See Green Bay vs. Miami
MIAMI vs. HOUSTON
RS: Series tied, 10-10
PS: Oilers lead series, 1-0;
See Houston vs. Miami
MIAMI vs. INDIANAPOLIS
RS: Dolphins lead series, 27-13
PS: Dolphins lead series, 1-0;
See Indianapolis vs. Miami
MIAMI vs. KANSAS CITY
RS: Chiefs lead series, 9-6
PS: Dolphins lead series, 1-0;
See Kansas City vs. Miami
MIAMI vs. L.A. RAIDERS
RS: Raiders lead series, 13-3-1
PS: Raiders lead series, 2-1;
See L.A. Raiders vs. Miami
MIAMI vs. L.A. RAMS
RS: Dolphins lead series, 4-1;
See L.A. Rams vs. Miami
MIAMI vs. MINNESOTA
RS: Dolphins lead series, 4-1
PS: Dolphins lead series, 1-0
1972—Dolphins, 16-14 (Minn)
1973—*Dolphins, 24-7 (Houston)
1976—Vikings, 29-7 (Mia)
1979—Dolphins, 27-12 (Minn)
1982—Dolphins, 22-14 (Mia)
1988—Dolphins, 24-7 (Mia)
(Points—Dolphins 120, Vikings 83)
*Super Bowl VIII
MIAMI vs. *NEW ENGLAND
RS: Dolphins lead series, 26-20
PS: Series tied, 1-1
1966—Patriots, 20-14 (M)
1967—Patriots, 41-10 (B)
    Dolphins, 41-32 (M)
1968—Dolphins, 34-10 (B)
    Dolphins, 38-7 (M)
1969—Dolphins, 17-16 (B)

Patriots, 38-23 (Tampa)
1970—Patriots, 27-14 (B)
    Dolphins, 37-20 (M)
1971—Dolphins, 41-3 (M)
    Patriots, 34-13 (NE)
1972—Dolphins, 52-0 (M)
    Dolphins, 37-21 (NE)
1973—Dolphins, 44-23 (M)
    Dolphins, 30-14 (NE)
1974—Patriots, 34-24 (NE)
    Dolphins, 34-27 (M)
1975—Dolphins, 22-14 (NE)
    Dolphins, 20-7 (M)
1976—Patriots, 30-14 (NE)
    Dolphins, 10-3 (M)
1977—Dolphins, 17-5 (M)
    Patriots, 14-10 (NE)
1978—Patriots, 33-24 (NE)
    Dolphins, 23-3 (M)
1979—Dolphins, 28-13 (NE)
    Dolphins, 39-24 (M)
1980—Patriots, 34-0 (NE)
    Dolphins, 16-13 (M) OT
1981—Dolphins, 30-27 (NE) OT
    Dolphins, 24-14 (M)
1982—Patriots, 3-0 (NE)
    **Dolphins, 28-13 (M)
1983—Dolphins, 34-24 (M)
    Patriots, 17-6 (NE)
1984—Dolphins, 28-7 (M)
    Dolphins, 44-24 (NE)
1985—Dolphins, 17-13 (NE)
    Dolphins, 30-27 (M)
    ***Patriots, 31-14 (M)
1986—Patriots, 34-7 (NE)
    Patriots, 34-27 (M)
1987—Patriots, 28-21 (NE)
    Patriots, 24-10 (M)
1988—Patriots, 21-10 (NE)
    Patriots, 6-3 (M)
1989—Dolphins, 24-10 (NE)
    Dolphins, 31-10 (M)
(Points—Dolphins 1,095, Patriots 946)
*Franchise in Boston prior to 1971
**AFC First Round Playoff
***AFC Championship
MIAMI vs. NEW ORLEANS
RS: Dolphins lead series, 4-1
1970—Dolphins, 21-10 (M)
1974—Dolphins, 21-0 (NO)
1980—Dolphins, 21-16 (M)
1983—Saints, 17-7 (NO)
1986—Dolphins, 31-27 (NO)
(Points—Dolphins 101, Saints 70)
MIAMI vs. N.Y. GIANTS
RS: Dolphins lead series, 1-0
1972—Dolphins, 23-13 (NY)
MIAMI vs. N.Y. JETS
RS: Dolphins lead series, 24-23-1
PS: Dolphins lead series, 1-0
1966—Jets, 19-14 (M)
    Jets, 30-13 (NY)
1967—Jets, 29-7 (NY)
    Jets, 33-14 (M)
1968—Jets, 35-17 (NY)
    Jets, 31-7 (M)
1969—Jets, 34-31 (NY)
    Jets, 27-9 (M)
1970—Dolphins, 20-6 (NY)
    Dolphins, 16-10 (M)
1971—Jets, 14-10 (M)
    Dolphins, 30-14 (NY)
1972—Dolphins, 27-17 (NY)
    Dolphins, 28-24 (M)
1973—Dolphins, 31-3 (M)
    Dolphins, 24-14 (NY)
1974—Dolphins, 21-17 (M)
    Jets, 17-14 (NY)
1975—Dolphins, 43-0 (NY)
    Dolphins, 27-7 (M)
1976—Dolphins, 16-0 (M)
    Dolphins, 27-7 (NY)
1977—Dolphins, 21-17 (M)
    Dolphins, 14-10 (NY)
1978—Jets, 33-20 (NY)
    Jets, 24-13 (M)
1979—Jets, 33-27 (NY)
    Jets, 27-24 (M)
1980—Jets, 17-14 (NY)
    Jets, 24-17 (M)
1981—Tie, 28-28 (M) OT
    Jets, 16-15 (NY)
1982—Dolphins, 45-28 (NY)
    Dolphins, 20-19 (M)
    *Dolphins, 14-0 (M)
1983—Dolphins, 32-14 (M)
    Dolphins, 34-14 (NY)
1984—Dolphins, 31-17 (M)
    Dolphins, 28-17 (M)
1985—Jets, 23-7 (NY)
    Dolphins, 21-17 (M)
1986—Jets, 51-45 (NY) OT
    Dolphins, 45-3 (M)

264

1987—Jets, 37-31 (NY) OT
   Dolphins, 37-28 (M)
1988—Jets, 44-30 (M)
   Jets, 38-34 (NY)
1989—Jets, 40-33 (M)
   Dolphins, 31-23 (NY)
(Points—Dolphins 1,157, Jets 1,030)
*AFC Championship
MIAMI vs. PHILADELPHIA
RS: Dolphins lead series, 4-2
1970—Eagles, 24-17 (P)
1975—Dolphins, 24-16 (M)
1978—Eagles, 17-3 (P)
1981—Dolphins, 13-10 (M)
1984—Dolphins, 24-23 (P)
1987—Dolphins, 28-10 (P)
(Points—Dolphins 109, Eagles 100)
MIAMI vs. *PHOENIX
RS: Dolphins lead series, 5-0
1972—Dolphins, 31-10 (M)
1977—Dolphins, 55-14 (StL)
1978—Dolphins, 24-10 (M)
1981—Dolphins, 20-7 (StL)
1984—Dolphins, 36-28 (StL)
(Points—Dolphins 166, Cardinals 69)
*Franchise in St. Louis prior to 1988
MIAMI vs. PITTSBURGH
RS: Dolphins lead series, 6-4
PS: Dolphins lead series, 2-1
1971—Dolphins, 24-21 (M)
1972—*Dolphins, 21-17 (P)
1973—Dolphins, 30-26 (M)
1976—Steelers, 14-3 (P)
1979—**Steelers, 34-14 (P)
1980—Steelers, 23-10 (P)
1981—Dolphins, 30-10 (M)
1984—Dolphins, 31-7 (P)
   *Dolphins, 45-28 (M)
1985—Dolphins, 24-20 (M)
1987—Dolphins, 35-24 (M)
1988—Steelers, 40-24 (P)
1989—Steelers, 34-14 (M)
(Points—Dolphins 305, Steelers 298)
*AFC Championship
**AFC Divisional Playoff
MIAMI vs. SAN DIEGO
RS: Chargers lead series, 8-5
PS: Series tied, 1-1
1966—Chargers, 44-10 (SD)
1967—Chargers, 24-0 (SD)
   Dolphins, 41-24 (M)
1968—Chargers, 34-28 (SD)
1969—Chargers, 21-14 (M)
1972—Dolphins, 24-10 (M)
1974—Dolphins, 28-21 (SD)
1977—Chargers, 14-13 (M)
1978—Dolphins, 28-21 (SD)
1980—Chargers, 27-24 (M) OT
1981—*Chargers, 41-38 (M) OT
1982—**Dolphins, 34-13 (M)
1984—Chargers, 34-28 (SD) OT
1986—Chargers, 50-28 (SD)
1988—Dolphins, 31-28 (M)
(Points—Chargers 406, Dolphins 369)
*AFC Divisional Playoff
**AFC Second Round Playoff
MIAMI vs. SAN FRANCISCO
RS: Dolphins lead series, 4-1
PS: 49ers lead series, 1-0
1973—Dolphins, 21-13 (M)
1977—Dolphins, 19-15 (SF)
1980—Dolphins, 17-13 (M)
1983—Dolphins, 20-17 (SF)
1984—*49ers, 38-16 (Stanford)
1986—49ers, 31-16 (M)
(Points—49ers 127, Dolphins 109)
*Super Bowl XIX
MIAMI vs. SEATTLE
RS: Dolphins lead series, 2-1
PS: Series tied, 1-1
1977—Dolphins, 31-13 (M)
1979—Dolphins, 19-10 (M)
1983—*Seahawks, 27-20 (M)
1984—*Dolphins, 31-10 (M)
1987—Seahawks, 24-20 (S)
(Points—Dolphins 121, Seahawks 84)
*AFC Divisional Playoff
MIAMI vs. TAMPA BAY
RS: Dolphins lead series, 3-1
1976—Dolphins, 23-20 (TB)
1982—Buccaneers, 23-17 (TB)
1985—Dolphins, 41-38 (M)
1988—Dolphins, 17-14 (TB)
(Points—Dolphins 98, Buccaneers 95)
MIAMI vs. WASHINGTON
RS: Dolphins lead series, 4-1
PS: Series tied, 1-1
1972—*Dolphins, 14-7 (Los Angeles)
1974—Redskins, 20-17 (W)
1978—Dolphins, 16-0 (W)
1981—Dolphins, 13-10 (M)
1982—**Redskins, 27-17 (Pasadena)
1984—Dolphins, 35-17 (W)

1987—Dolphins, 23-21 (M)
(Points—Dolphins 135, Redskins 102)
*Super Bowl VII
**Super Bowl XVII

MINNESOTA vs. ATLANTA
RS: Vikings lead series, 10-6
PS: Vikings lead series, 1-0;
See Atlanta vs. Minnesota
MINNESOTA vs. BUFFALO
RS: Vikings lead series, 4-2;
See Buffalo vs. Minnesota
MINNESOTA vs. CHICAGO
RS: Vikings lead series, 29-26-2;
See Chicago vs. Minnesota
MINNESOTA vs. CINCINNATI
RS: Series tied, 3-3;
See Cincinnati vs. Minnesota
MINNESOTA vs. CLEVELAND
RS: Vikings lead series, 6-3
PS: Vikings lead series, 1-0;
See Cleveland vs. Minnesota
MINNESOTA vs. DALLAS
RS: Cowboys lead series, 7-6
PS: Cowboys lead series, 3-1;
See Dallas vs. Minnesota
MINNESOTA vs. DENVER
RS: Vikings lead series, 3-2;
See Denver vs. Minnesota
MINNESOTA vs. DETROIT
RS: Vikings lead series, 37-18-2;
See Detroit vs. Minnesota
MINNESOTA vs. GREEN BAY
RS: Packers lead series, 29-27-1;
See Green Bay vs. Minnesota
MINNESOTA vs. HOUSTON
RS: Vikings lead series, 3-2;
See Houston vs. Minnesota
MINNESOTA vs. INDIANAPOLIS
RS: Colts lead series, 11-6-1
PS: Colts lead series, 1-0;
See Indianapolis vs. Minnesota
MINNESOTA vs. KANSAS CITY
RS: Vikings lead series, 2-1
PS: Chiefs lead series, 1-0;
See Kansas City vs. Minnesota
MINNESOTA vs. L.A. RAIDERS
RS: Raiders lead series, 4-2
PS: Raiders lead series, 1-0;
See L.A. Raiders vs. Minnesota
MINNESOTA vs. L.A. RAMS
RS: Vikings lead series, 13-11-2
PS: Vikings lead series, 5-1;
See L.A. Rams vs. Minnesota
MINNESOTA vs. MIAMI
RS: Dolphins lead series, 4-1
PS: Dolphins lead series, 1-0;
See Miami vs. Minnesota
MINNESOTA vs. *NEW ENGLAND
RS: Series tied, 2-2
1970—Vikings, 35-14 (B)
1974—Patriots, 17-14 (M)
1979—Patriots, 27-23 (NE)
1988—Vikings, 36-6 (M)
(Points—Vikings 108, Patriots 64)
*Franchise in Boston prior to 1971
MINNESOTA vs. NEW ORLEANS
RS: Vikings lead series, 10-4
PS: Vikings lead series, 1-0
1968—Saints, 20-17 (NO)
1970—Vikings, 26-0 (M)
1971—Vikings, 23-10 (NO)
1972—Vikings, 37-6 (M)
1974—Vikings, 29-9 (M)
1975—Vikings, 20-7 (NO)
1976—Vikings, 40-9 (NO)
1978—Saints, 31-24 (NO)
1980—Vikings, 23-20 (M)
1981—Vikings, 20-10 (M)
1983—Saints, 17-16 (NO)
1985—Saints, 30-23 (M)
1986—Vikings, 33-17 (M)
1987—*Vikings, 44-10 (NO)
1988—Vikings, 45-3 (M)
(Points—Vikings 420, Saints 199)
*NFC First Round Playoff
MINNESOTA vs. N.Y. GIANTS
RS: Vikings lead series, 6-3
1964—Vikings, 30-21 (NY)
1965—Vikings, 40-14 (M)
1967—Vikings, 27-24 (M)
1969—Giants, 24-23 (NY)
1971—Vikings, 17-10 (NY)
1973—Vikings, 31-7 (New Haven)
1976—Vikings, 24-7 (M)
1986—Giants, 22-20 (M)
1989—Giants, 24-14 (NY)
(Points—Vikings 226, Giants 153)
MINNESOTA vs. N.Y. JETS
RS: Jets lead series, 3-1
1970—Jets, 20-10 (NY)
1975—Vikings, 29-21 (M)
1979—Jets, 14-7 (NY)

1982—Jets 42-14 (M)
(Points—Jets 97, Vikings 60)
MINNESOTA vs. PHILADELPHIA
RS: Vikings lead series, 10-4
PS: Eagles lead series, 1-0
1962—Vikings, 31-21 (M)
1963—Vikings, 34-13 (P)
1968—Vikings, 24-17 (P)
1971—Vikings, 13-0 (P)
1973—Vikings, 28-21 (M)
1976—Vikings, 31-12 (P)
1978—Vikings, 28-27 (M)
1980—Eagles, 42-7 (M)
   *Eagles, 31-16 (P)
1981—Vikings, 35-23 (M)
1984—Eagles, 19-17 (P)
1985—Vikings, 28-23 (P)
   Eagles, 37-35 (M)
1988—Vikings, 23-21 (M)
1989—Eagles, 10-9 (P)
(Points—Vikings 359, Eagles 317)
*NFC Divisional Playoff
MINNESOTA vs. *PHOENIX
RS: Cardinals lead series, 7-2
PS: Vikings lead series, 1-0
1963—Cardinals, 56-14 (M)
1967—Cardinals, 34-24 (M)
1969—Vikings, 27-10 (StL)
1972—Cardinals, 19-17 (M)
1974—Vikings, 28-24 (StL)
   **Vikings, 30-14 (M)
1977—Cardinals, 27-7 (M)
1979—Cardinals, 37-7 (StL)
1981—Cardinals, 30-17 (StL)
1983—Cardinals, 41-31 (StL)
(Points—Cardinals 292, Vikings 202)
*Franchise in St. Louis prior to 1988
**NFC Divisional Playoff
MINNESOTA vs. PITTSBURGH
RS: Vikings lead series, 6-4
PS: Steelers lead series, 1-0
1962—Steelers, 39-31 (P)
1964—Vikings, 30-10 (M)
1967—Vikings, 41-27 (P)
1969—Vikings, 52-14 (M)
1972—Vikings, 23-10 (P)
1974—*Steelers, 16-6 (New Orleans)
1976—Vikings, 17-6 (M)
1980—Steelers, 23-17 (M)
1983—Vikings, 17-14 (P)
1986—Vikings, 31-7 (M)
1989—Steelers, 27-14 (P)
(Points—Vikings 266, Steelers 206)
*Super Bowl IX
MINNESOTA vs. SAN DIEGO
RS: Series tied, 3-3
1971—Chargers, 30-14 (SD)
1975—Vikings, 28-13 (M)
1978—Chargers, 13-7 (M)
1981—Vikings, 33-31 (SD)
1984—Chargers, 42-13 (M)
1985—Vikings, 21-17 (M)
(Points—Chargers 146, Vikings 116)
MINNESOTA vs. SAN FRANCISCO
RS: Vikings lead series, 14-12-1
PS: 49ers lead series, 3-1
1961—49ers, 38-24 (M)
   49ers, 38-28 (SF)
1962—49ers, 21-7 (SF)
   49ers, 35-12 (M)
1963—Vikings, 24-20 (SF)
   Vikings, 45-14 (M)
1964—Vikings, 27-22 (SF)
   Vikings, 24-7 (M)
1965—Vikings, 42-41 (SF)
   49ers, 45-24 (M)
1966—Tie, 20-20 (SF)
   Vikings, 28-3 (SF)
1967—49ers, 27-21 (M)
1968—Vikings, 30-20 (M)
1969—Vikings, 10-7 (M)
1970—*49ers, 17-14 (M)
1971—49ers, 13-9 (M)
1972—49ers, 20-17 (SF)
1973—Vikings, 17-13 (SF)
1975—Vikings, 27-17 (M)
1976—Vikings, 20-16 (SF)
1977—Vikings, 28-27 (M)
1979—Vikings, 28-22 (M)
1983—49ers, 48-17 (M)
1984—49ers, 51-7 (SF)
1985—Vikings, 28-21 (M)
1986—Vikings, 27-24 (SF) OT
1987—*Vikings, 36-24 (SF)
1988—49ers, 24-21 (SF)
   *49ers, 34-9 (SF)
1989—*49ers, 41-13 (SF)
(Points—Vikings 774, Vikings 680)
*NFC Divisional Playoff
MINNESOTA vs. SEATTLE
RS: Seahawks lead series, 3-1
1976—Vikings, 27-21 (M)
1978—Seahawks, 29-28 (S)

1984—Seahawks, 20-12 (M)
1987—Seahawks, 28-17 (S)
(Points—Seahawks 98, Vikings 84)
MINNESOTA vs. TAMPA BAY
RS: Vikings lead series, 18-6
1977—Vikings, 9-3 (TB)
1978—Buccaneers, 16-10 (M)
   Vikings, 24-7 (TB)
1979—Buccaneers, 12-10 (M)
   Vikings, 23-22 (TB)
1980—Vikings, 38-30 (M)
   Vikings, 21-10 (TB)
1981—Buccaneers, 21-13 (TB)
   Vikings, 25-10 (M)
1982—Vikings, 17-10 (M)
1983—Vikings, 19-16 (TB) OT
   Buccaneers, 17-12 (M)
1984—Buccaneers, 35-31 (TB)
   Vikings, 27-24 (M)
1985—Vikings, 31-16 (TB)
   Vikings, 26-7 (M)
1986—Vikings, 23-10 (TB)
   Vikings, 45-13 (M)
1987—Buccaneers, 20-10 (TB)
   Vikings, 23-17 (M)
1988—Vikings, 14-13 (M)
   Vikings, 49-20 (TB)
1989—Vikings, 17-3 (M)
   Vikings, 24-10 (TB)
(Points—Vikings 541, Buccaneers 362)
MINNESOTA vs. WASHINGTON
RS: Redskins lead series, 5-3
PS: Series tied, 2-2
1968—Vikings, 27-14 (M)
1970—Vikings, 19-10 (W)
1972—Redskins, 24-21 (M)
1973—*Vikings, 27-20 (M)
1975—Redskins, 31-30 (W)
1976—*Vikings, 35-20 (M)
1980—Vikings, 39-14 (W)
1982—**Redskins, 21-7 (W)
1984—Redskins, 31-17 (M)
1986—Redskins, 44-38 (W) OT
1987—Redskins, 27-24 (M) OT
   ***Redskins, 17-10 (W)
(Points—Vikings 294, Redskins 273)
*NFC Divisional Playoff
**NFC Second Round Playoff
***NFC Championship

NEW ENGLAND vs. ATLANTA
RS: Series tied, 3-3;
See Atlanta vs. New England
NEW ENGLAND vs. BUFFALO
RS: Patriots lead series, 32-26-1
PS: Patriots lead series, 1-0;
See Buffalo vs. New England
NEW ENGLAND vs. CHICAGO
RS: Patriots lead series, 3-2
PS: Bears lead series, 1-0;
See Chicago vs. New England
NEW ENGLAND vs. CINCINNATI
RS: Patriots lead series, 7-4;
See Cincinnati vs. New England
NEW ENGLAND vs. CLEVELAND
RS: Browns lead series, 7-2;
See Cleveland vs. New England
NEW ENGLAND vs. DALLAS
RS: Cowboys lead series, 6-0;
See Dallas vs. New England
NEW ENGLAND vs. DENVER
RS: Broncos lead series, 14-12
PS: Broncos lead series, 1-0;
See Denver vs. New England
NEW ENGLAND vs. DETROIT
RS: Series tied, 2-2;
See Detroit vs. New England
NEW ENGLAND vs. GREEN BAY
RS: Series tied, 2-2;
See Green Bay vs. New England
NEW ENGLAND vs. HOUSTON
RS: Patriots lead series, 16-13-1
PS: Oilers lead series, 1-0;
See Houston vs. New England
NEW ENGLAND vs. INDIANAPOLIS
RS: Patriots lead series, 22-17;
See Indianapolis vs. New England
NEW ENGLAND vs. KANSAS CITY
RS: Chiefs lead series, 11-7-3;
See Kansas City vs. New England
NEW ENGLAND vs. L.A. RAIDERS
RS: Series tied, 12-12-1
PS: Series tied, 1-1;
See L.A. Raiders vs. New England
NEW ENGLAND vs. L.A. RAMS
RS: Patriots lead series, 3-2;
See L.A. Rams vs. New England
NEW ENGLAND vs. MIAMI
RS: Dolphins lead series, 26-20
PS: Series tied, 1-1;
See Miami vs. New England
NEW ENGLAND vs. MINNESOTA
RS: Series tied, 2-2;

265

See Minnesota vs. New England

NEW ENGLAND vs. NEW ORLEANS
RS: Patriots lead series, 5-1
1972—Patriots, 17-10 (NO)
1976—Patriots, 27-6 (NE)
1980—Patriots, 38-27 (NO)
1983—Patriots, 7-0 (NE)
1986—Patriots, 21-20 (NO)
1989—Saints, 28-24 (NE)
(Points—Patriots 134, Saints 91)

*NEW ENGLAND vs. N.Y. GIANTS
RS: Giants lead series, 2-1
1970—Giants, 16-0 (B)
1974—Giants, 28-20 (New Haven)
1987—Giants, 17-10 (NY)
(Points—Giants 53, Patriots 38)
Franchise in Boston prior to 1971

*NEW ENGLAND vs. **N.Y. JETS
RS: Jets lead series, 32-26-1
PS: Patriots lead series, 1-0
1960—Patriots, 28-24 (NY)
Patriots, 38-21 (B)
1961—Titans, 21-20 (B)
Titans, 37-30 (NY)
1962—Patriots, 43-14 (NY)
Patriots, 24-17 (B)
1963—Patriots, 38-14 (B)
Jets, 31-24 (NY)
1964—Patriots, 26-10 (B)
Jets, 35-14 (NY)
1965—Jets, 30-20 (B)
Patriots, 27-23 (NY)
1966—Tie, 24-24 (B)
Jets, 38-28 (NY)
1967—Jets, 30-23 (NY)
Jets, 29-24 (B)
1968—Jets, 47-31 (Birmingham)
Jets, 48-14 (NY)
1969—Jets, 23-14 (B)
Jets, 23-17 (NY)
1970—Jets, 31-21 (B)
Jets, 17-3 (NY)
1971—Patriots, 20-0 (NE)
Jets, 13-6 (NY)
1972—Jets, 41-13 (NE)
Jets, 34-10 (NY)
1973—Jets, 9-7 (NE)
Jets, 33-13 (NY)
1974—Patriots, 24-0 (NY)
Jets, 21-16 (NE)
1975—Jets, 36-7 (NY)
Jets, 30-28 (NE)
1976—Patriots, 41-7 (NE)
Patriots, 38-24 (NY)
1977—Jets, 30-27 (NY)
Patriots, 24-13 (NE)
1978—Patriots, 55-21 (NE)
Patriots, 19-17 (NY)
1979—Patriots, 56-3 (NE)
Jets, 27-26 (NY)
1980—Patriots, 21-11 (NY)
Patriots, 34-21 (NE)
1981—Jets, 28-24 (NY)
Jets, 17-6 (NE)
1982—Jets, 31-7 (NE)
1983—Patriots, 23-13 (NE)
Jets, 26-3 (NY)
1984—Patriots, 28-21 (NY)
Patriots, 30-20 (NE)
1985—Patriots, 20-13 (NE)
Jets, 16-13 (NY) OT
***Patriots, 26-14 (NY)
1986—Patriots, 20-6 (NY)
Jets, 31-24 (NE)
1987—Jets, 43-24 (NY)
Patriots, 42-20 (NE)
1988—Jets, 28-3 (NE)
Patriots, 14-13 (NY)
1989—Patriots, 27-24 (NY)
Jets, 27-26 (NE)
(Points—Patriots 1,401, Jets 1,344)
Franchise in Boston prior to 1971
*Jets known as Titans prior to 1963
***AFC First Round Playoff

NEW ENGLAND vs. PHILADELPHIA
RS: Eagles lead series, 4-2
1973—Eagles, 24-23 (P)
1977—Patriots, 14-6 (NE)
1978—Patriots, 24-14 (NE)
1981—Eagles, 13-3 (P)
1984—Eagles, 27-17 (P)
1987—Eagles, 34-31 (NE) OT
(Points—Eagles 118, Patriots 112)

*NEW ENGLAND vs. **PHOENIX
RS: Cardinals lead series, 4-1
1970—Cardinals, 31-0 (StL)
1975—Cardinals, 24-17 (StL)
1978—Cardinals, 16-6 (StL)
1981—Cardinals, 27-20 (NE)
1984—Cardinals, 33-10 (NE)
(Points—Cardinals 121, Patriots 63)
Franchise in Boston prior to 1971
*Franchise in St. Louis prior to 1988

NEW ENGLAND vs. PITTSBURGH
RS: Steelers lead series, 6-3
1972—Steelers, 33-3 (P)
1974—Steelers, 21-17 (NE)
1976—Patriots, 30-27 (P)
1979—Steelers, 16-13 (NE) OT
1981—Steelers, 27-21 (P) OT
1982—Steelers, 37-14 (P)
1983—Patriots, 28-23 (P)
1986—Patriots, 34-0 (P)
1989—Steelers, 28-10 (P)
(Points—Steelers 212, Patriots 170)

*NEW ENGLAND vs. **SAN DIEGO
RS: Patriots lead series, 13-11-2
PS: Chargers lead series, 1-0
1960—Patriots, 35-0 (LA)
Chargers, 45-16 (B)
1961—Chargers, 38-27 (B)
Patriots, 41-0 (SD)
1962—Patriots, 24-20 (B)
Patriots, 20-14 (SD)
1963—Chargers, 17-13 (SD)
Chargers, 7-6 (B)
***Chargers, 51-10 (SD)
1964—Patriots, 33-28 (SD)
Chargers, 26-17 (B)
1965—Tie, 10-10 (B)
Patriots, 22-6 (SD)
1966—Chargers, 24-0 (SD)
Patriots, 35-17 (B)
1967—Chargers, 28-14 (SD)
Tie, 31-31 (SD)
1968—Chargers, 27-17 (B)
1969—Chargers, 13-10 (B)
Chargers, 28-18 (SD)
1970—Chargers, 16-14 (B)
1973—Patriots, 30-14 (NE)
1975—Patriots, 33-19 (SD)
1977—Patriots, 24-20 (SD)
1978—Patriots, 28-23 (NE)
1979—Patriots, 27-21 (NE)
1983—Patriots, 37-21 (NE)
(Points—Patriots 592, Chargers 564)
Franchise in Boston prior to 1971
*Franchise in Los Angeles prior to 1961
***AFL Championship

NEW ENGLAND vs. SAN FRANCISCO
RS: 49ers lead series, 5-1
1971—49ers, 27-10 (SF)
1975—Patriots, 24-16 (NE)
1980—49ers, 21-17 (SF)
1983—49ers, 33-13 (NE)
1986—49ers, 29-24 (NE)
1989—49ers, 37-20 (SF)
(Points—49ers 163, Patriots 108)

NEW ENGLAND vs. SEATTLE
RS: Patriots lead series, 6-3
1977—Patriots, 31-0 (NE)
1980—Patriots, 37-31 (S)
1982—Patriots, 16-0 (S)
1983—Seahawks, 24-6 (S)
1984—Patriots, 38-23 (NE)
1985—Patriots, 20-13 (S)
1986—Seahawks, 38-31 (NE)
1988—Patriots, 13-7 (NE)
1989—Seahawks, 24-3 (NE)
(Points—Patriots 195, Seahawks 160)

NEW ENGLAND vs. TAMPA BAY
RS: Patriots lead series, 3-0
1976—Patriots, 31-14 (TB)
1985—Patriots, 32-14 (TB)
1988—Patriots, 10-7 (NE) OT
(Points—Patriots 73, Buccaneers 35)

NEW ENGLAND vs. WASHINGTON
RS: Redskins lead series, 3-1
1972—Patriots, 24-23 (NE)
1978—Redskins, 16-14 (NE)
1981—Redskins, 24-22 (W)
1984—Redskins, 26-10 (NE)
(Points—Redskins 89, Patriots 70)

NEW ORLEANS vs. ATLANTA
RS: Falcons lead series, 24-17;
See Atlanta vs. New Orleans

NEW ORLEANS vs. BUFFALO
RS: Series tied, 2-2;
See Buffalo vs. New Orleans

NEW ORLEANS vs. CHICAGO
RS: Bears lead series, 7-5;
See Chicago vs. New Orleans

NEW ORLEANS vs. CINCINNATI
RS: Series tied, 3-3;
See Cincinnati vs. New Orleans

NEW ORLEANS vs. CLEVELAND
RS: Browns lead series, 8-2;
See Cleveland vs. New Orleans

NEW ORLEANS vs. DALLAS
RS: Cowboys lead series, 11-3;
See Dallas vs. New Orleans

NEW ORLEANS vs. DENVER
RS: Broncos lead series, 4-1;
See Denver vs. New Orleans

NEW ORLEANS vs. DETROIT

RS: Series tied, 5-5-1;
See Detroit vs. New Orleans

NEW ORLEANS vs. GREEN BAY
RS: Packers lead series, 11-4;
See Green Bay vs. New Orleans

NEW ORLEANS vs. HOUSTON
RS: Saints lead series, 3-2-1;
See Houston vs. New Orleans

NEW ORLEANS vs. INDIANAPOLIS
RS: Colts lead series, 3-2;
See Indianapolis vs. New Orleans

NEW ORLEANS vs. KANSAS CITY
RS: Series tied, 2-2;
See Kansas City vs. New Orleans

NEW ORLEANS vs. L.A. RAIDERS
RS: Raiders lead series, 3-1-1;
See L.A. Raiders vs. New Orleans

NEW ORLEANS vs. L.A. RAMS
RS: Rams lead series, 26-14;
See L.A. Rams vs. New Orleans

NEW ORLEANS vs. MIAMI
RS: Dolphins lead series, 4-1;
See Miami vs. New Orleans

NEW ORLEANS vs. MINNESOTA
RS: Vikings lead series, 10-4
PS: Vikings lead series, 1-0;
See Minnesota vs. New Orleans

NEW ORLEANS vs. NEW ENGLAND
RS: Patriots lead series, 5-1;
See New England vs. New Orleans

NEW ORLEANS vs. N.Y. GIANTS
RS: Giants lead series, 8-6
1967—Giants, 27-21 (NY)
1968—Giants, 38-21 (NY)
1969—Saints, 25-24 (NY)
1970—Saints, 14-10 (NO)
1972—Giants, 45-21 (NY)
1975—Giants, 28-14 (NO)
1978—Saints, 28-17 (NO)
1979—Saints, 24-14 (NO)
1981—Giants, 20-7 (NY)
1984—Saints, 10-3 (NY)
1985—Giants, 21-13 (NO)
1986—Giants, 20-17 (NY)
1987—Saints, 23-14 (NO)
1988—Saints, 13-12 (NO)
(Points—Giants 294, Saints 250)

NEW ORLEANS vs. N.Y. JETS
RS: Jets lead series, 4-2
1972—Jets, 18-17 (NY)
1977—Jets, 16-13 (NO)
1980—Saints, 21-20 (NY)
1983—Jets, 31-28 (NO)
1986—Jets, 28-23 (NY)
1989—Saints, 29-14 (NO)
(Points—Saints 131, Jets 127)

NEW ORLEANS vs. PHILADELPHIA
RS: Eagles lead series, 9-7
1967—Saints, 31-24 (NO)
Eagles, 48-21 (P)
1968—Eagles, 29-17 (P)
1969—Eagles, 13-10 (P)
Saints, 26-17 (NO)
1972—Saints, 21-3 (NO)
1974—Saints, 14-10 (NO)
1977—Eagles, 28-7 (P)
1978—Eagles, 24-17 (NO)
1979—Eagles, 26-14 (NO)
1980—Eagles, 34-21 (NO)
1981—Eagles, 31-14 (NO)
1983—Saints, 20-17 (P) OT
1985—Saints, 23-21 (NO)
1987—Eagles, 27-17 (P)
1989—Saints, 30-20 (NO)
(Points—Eagles 372, Saints 303)

NEW ORLEANS vs. *PHOENIX
RS: Cardinals lead series, 10-5
1967—Cardinals, 31-20 (StL)
1968—Cardinals, 21-20 (NO)
Cardinals, 31-17 (StL)
1969—Saints, 51-42 (StL)
1970—Cardinals, 24-17 (StL)
1974—Saints, 14-0 (NO)
1977—Cardinals, 49-31 (StL)
1980—Cardinals, 40-7 (NO)
1981—Cardinals, 30-3 (StL)
1982—Cardinals, 21-7 (NO)
1983—Saints, 28-17 (NO)
1984—Saints, 34-24 (NO)
1985—Cardinals, 28-16 (StL)
1986—Saints, 16-7 (StL)
1987—Cardinals, 24-19 (StL)
(Points—Cardinals 389, Saints 300)
Franchise in St. Louis prior to 1988

NEW ORLEANS vs. PITTSBURGH
RS: Saints lead series, 5-4
1967—Saints, 14-10 (NO)
1968—Saints, 16-12 (P)
Saints, 24-14 (NO)
1969—Saints, 27-24 (NO)
1974—Steelers, 28-7 (NO)
1978—Steelers, 20-14 (NO)
1981—Steelers, 20-6 (NO)

1984—Saints, 27-24 (NO)
1987—Saints, 20-16 (P)
(Points—Steelers 172, Saints 151)

NEW ORLEANS vs. SAN DIEGO
RS: Chargers lead series, 3-1
1973—Chargers, 17-14 (SD)
1977—Chargers, 14-0 (S)
1979—Chargers, 35-0 (NO)
1988—Saints, 23-17 (SD)
(Points—Chargers 83, Saints 37)

NEW ORLEANS vs. SAN FRANCISCO
RS: 49ers lead series, 28-11-2
1967—49ers, 27-13 (SF)
1969—Saints, 43-38 (NO)
1970—Tie, 20-20 (SF)
49ers, 38-27 (NO)
1971—49ers, 38-20 (NO)
Saints, 26-20 (SF)
1972—49ers, 37-2 (SF)
Tie, 20-20 (SF)
1973—49ers, 40-0 (SF)
Saints, 16-10 (NO)
1974—49ers, 17-13 (NO)
49ers, 35-21 (SF)
1975—49ers, 35-21 (SF)
49ers, 16-6 (NO)
1976—49ers, 33-3 (SF)
49ers, 27-7 (NO)
1977—49ers, 10-7 (NO) OT
49ers, 20-17 (SF)
1978—Saints, 14-7 (SF)
Saints, 24-13 (NO)
1979—Saints, 30-21 (SF)
Saints, 31-20 (NO)
1980—49ers, 26-23 (NO)
49ers, 38-35 (SF) OT
1981—Saints, 21-14 (SF)
49ers, 21-17 (NO)
1982—Saints, 23-20 (SF)
1983—49ers, 32-13 (NO)
49ers, 27-0 (SF)
1984—49ers, 30-20 (SF)
49ers, 35-3 (NO)
1985—Saints, 20-17 (SF)
49ers, 31-19 (NO)
1986—49ers, 26-17 (SF)
Saints, 23-10 (NO)
1987—49ers, 24-22 (NO)
Saints, 26-24 (SF)
1988—49ers, 34-33 (NO)
49ers, 30-17 (SF)
1989—49ers, 24-20 (NO)
49ers, 31-13 (SF)
(Points—49ers 1,043, Saints 739)

NEW ORLEANS vs. SEATTLE
RS: Series tied, 2-2
1976—Saints, 51-27 (S)
1979—Seahawks, 38-24 (S)
1985—Seahawks, 27-3 (NO)
1988—Saints, 20-19 (S)
(Points—Seahawks 111, Saints 98)

NEW ORLEANS vs. TAMPA BAY
RS: Saints lead series, 8-4
1977—Buccaneers, 33-14 (NO)
1978—Saints, 17-10 (TB)
1979—Saints, 42-14 (TB)
1981—Buccaneers, 31-14 (NO)
1982—Buccaneers, 13-10 (NO)
1983—Saints, 24-21 (TB)
1984—Saints, 17-13 (NO)
1985—Saints, 20-13 (NO)
1986—Saints, 38-7 (NO)
1987—Saints, 44-34 (NO)
1988—Saints, 13-9 (NO)
1989—Buccaneers, 20-10 (TB)
(Points—Saints 263, Buccaneers 218)

NEW ORLEANS vs. WASHINGTON
RS: Redskins lead series, 10-4
1967—Redskins, 30-10 (NO)
Saints, 30-14 (W)
1968—Saints, 37-17 (NO)
1969—Redskins, 26-20 (NO)
Redskins, 17-14 (W)
1971—Redskins, 24-14 (W)
1973—Saints, 19-3 (NO)
1975—Redskins, 41-3 (W)
1979—Saints, 14-10 (W)
1980—Redskins, 22-14 (W)
1982—Redskins, 27-10 (NO)
1986—Redskins, 14-6 (NO)
1988—Redskins, 27-24 (W)
1989—Redskins, 16-14 (NO)
(Points—Redskins 288, Saints 229)

N.Y. GIANTS vs. ATLANTA
RS: Series tied, 6-6;
See Atlanta vs. N.Y. Giants

N.Y. GIANTS vs. BUFFALO
RS: Series tied, 2-2;
See Buffalo vs. N.Y. Giants

N.Y. GIANTS vs. CHICAGO
RS: Bears lead series, 23-14-2
PS: Bears lead series, 5-2;

See Chicago vs. N.Y. Giants

N.Y. GIANTS vs. CINCINNATI
RS: Bengals lead series, 3-0;
See Cincinnati vs. N.Y. Giants

N.Y. GIANTS vs. CLEVELAND
RS: Browns lead series, 25-15-2
PS: Series tied, 1-1;
See Cleveland vs. N.Y. Giants

N.Y. GIANTS vs. DALLAS
RS: Cowboys lead series, 35-18-2;
See Dallas vs. N.Y. Giants

N.Y. GIANTS vs. DENVER
RS: Giants lead series, 3-2
PS: Giants lead series, 1-0;
See Denver vs. N.Y. Giants

N.Y. GIANTS vs. DETROIT
RS: Lions lead series, 17-14-1
PS: Lions lead series, 1-0;
See Detroit vs. N.Y. Giants

N.Y. GIANTS vs. GREEN BAY
RS: Packers lead series, 21-19-2
PS: Packers lead series, 4-1;
See Green Bay vs. N.Y. Giants

N.Y. GIANTS vs. HOUSTON
RS: Giants lead series, 3-0;
See Houston vs. N.Y. Giants

N.Y. GIANTS vs. INDIANAPOLIS
RS: Colts lead series, 5-3
PS: Colts lead series, 2-0;
See Indianapolis vs. N.Y. Giants

N.Y. GIANTS vs. KANSAS CITY
RS: Giants lead series, 5-1;
See Kansas City vs. N.Y. Giants

N.Y. GIANTS vs. L.A. RAIDERS
RS: Raiders lead series, 3-2;
See L.A. Raiders vs. N.Y. Giants

N.Y. GIANTS vs. L.A. RAMS
RS: Rams lead series, 18-7
PS: Series tied, 1-1;
See L.A. Rams vs. N.Y. Giants

N.Y. GIANTS vs. MIAMI
RS: Dolphins lead series, 1-0;
See Miami vs. N.Y. Giants

N.Y. GIANTS vs. MINNESOTA
RS: Vikings lead series, 6-3;
See Minnesota vs. N.Y. Giants

N.Y. GIANTS vs. NEW ENGLAND
RS: Giants lead series, 2-1;
See New England vs. N.Y. Giants

N.Y. GIANTS vs. NEW ORLEANS
RS: Giants lead series, 8-6;
See New Orleans vs. N.Y. Giants

N.Y. GIANTS vs. N.Y. JETS
RS: Series tied, 3-3
1970—Giants, 22-10 (NYJ)
1974—Jets, 26-20 (New Haven) OT
1981—Jets, 26-7 (NYG)
1984—Giants, 20-10 (NYJ)
1987—Giants, 20-7 (NYG)
1988—Jets, 27-21 (NYJ)
(Points—Giants 110, Jets 106)

N.Y. GIANTS vs. PHILADELPHIA
RS: Giants lead series, 59-49-2
PS: Giants lead series, 1-0
1933—Giants, 56-0 (NY)
        Giants, 20-14 (P)
1934—Giants, 17-0 (NY)
        Eagles, 6-0 (P)
1935—Giants, 10-0 (NY)
        Giants, 21-14 (P)
1936—Eagles, 10-7 (P)
        Giants, 21-17 (NY)
1937—Giants, 16-7 (P)
        Giants, 21-0 (NY)
1938—Eagles, 14-10 (P)
        Giants, 17-7 (NY)
1939—Giants, 13-3 (P)
        Giants, 27-10 (NY)
1940—Giants, 20-14 (P)
        Giants, 17-7 (NY)
1941—Giants, 24-0 (P)
        Giants, 16-0 (NY)
1942—Giants, 35-17 (NY)
        Giants, 14-0 (P)
1944—Eagles, 24-17 (NY)
        Tie, 21-21 (P)
1945—Eagles, 38-17 (P)
        Giants, 28-21 (NY)
1946—Eagles, 24-14 (P)
        Giants, 45-17 (NY)
1947—Eagles, 23-0 (P)
        Eagles, 41-24 (NY)
1948—Eagles, 45-0 (P)
        Eagles, 35-14 (NY)
1949—Eagles, 24-3 (NY)
        Eagles, 17-3 (P)
1950—Giants, 7-3 (NY)
        Giants, 9-7 (P)
1951—Giants, 26-24 (NY)
        Giants, 23-7 (P)
1952—Giants, 31-7 (P)
        Eagles, 14-10 (NY)
1953—Eagles, 30-7 (NY)

Giants, 37-28 (NY)
1954—Giants, 27-14 (NY)
        Eagles, 29-14 (P)
1955—Eagles, 27-17 (P)
        Giants, 31-7 (NY)
1956—Giants, 20-3 (NY)
        Giants, 21-7 (P)
1957—Giants, 24-20 (P)
        Giants, 13-0 (NY)
1958—Giants, 27-24 (P)
        Giants, 24-10 (NY)
1959—Eagles, 49-21 (P)
        Giants, 24-7 (NY)
1960—Eagles, 17-10 (NY)
        Eagles, 31-23 (P)
1961—Giants, 38-21 (NY)
        Giants, 28-24 (P)
1962—Giants, 29-13 (P)
        Giants, 19-14 (NY)
1963—Giants, 37-14 (P)
        Giants, 42-14 (NY)
1964—Eagles, 38-7 (P)
        Eagles, 23-17 (NY)
1965—Giants, 16-14 (P)
        Giants, 35-27 (NY)
1966—Eagles, 35-17 (P)
        Eagles, 31-3 (NY)
1967—Giants, 44-7 (NY)
1968—Giants, 34-25 (P)
        Giants, 7-6 (NY)
1969—Eagles, 23-20 (NY)
1970—Giants, 30-23 (NY)
        Eagles, 23-20 (P)
1971—Eagles, 23-7 (P)
        Eagles, 41-28 (NY)
1972—Giants, 27-12 (P)
        Giants, 62-10 (NY)
1973—Tie, 23-23 (NY)
        Eagles, 20-16 (P)
1974—Eagles, 35-7 (P)
        Eagles, 20-7 (New Haven)
1975—Eagles, 23-14 (P)
        Eagles, 13-10 (NY)
1976—Eagles, 20-7 (P)
        Eagles, 10-0 (NY)
1977—Eagles, 28-10 (NY)
        Eagles, 17-14 (P)
1978—Eagles, 19-17 (NY)
        Eagles, 20-3 (P)
1979—Eagles, 23-17 (P)
        Eagles, 17-13 (NY)
1980—Eagles, 35-3 (NY)
        Eagles, 31-16 (NY)
1981—Eagles, 24-10 (NY)
        Giants, 20-10 (P)
        *Giants, 27-21 (P)
1982—Giants, 23-7 (NY)
        Giants, 26-24 (P)
1983—Eagles, 17-13 (NY)
        Giants, 23-0 (P)
1984—Giants, 28-27 (NY)
        Eagles, 24-10 (P)
1985—Giants, 21-0 (NY)
        Giants, 16-10 (P) OT
1986—Giants, 35-3 (NY)
        Giants, 17-14 (P)
1987—Giants, 20-17 (P)
        Giants, 23-20 (NY) OT
1988—Eagles, 24-13 (P)
        Eagles, 23-17 (NY) OT
1989—Eagles, 21-19 (P)
        Giants, 24-17 (NY)
(Points—Giants 2,142, Eagles 1,954)
*NFC First Round Playoff

N.Y. GIANTS vs. *PHOENIX
RS: Giants lead series, 59-33-2
1926—Giants, 20-0 (NY)
1927—Giants, 28-7 (NY)
1929—Giants, 24-21 (NY)
1930—Giants, 25-12 (NY)
        Giants, 13-7 (C)
1935—Cardinals, 14-13 (NY)
1936—Giants, 14-6 (NY)
1938—Giants, 6-0 (NY)
1939—Giants, 17-7 (NY)
1941—Cardinals, 10-7 (NY)
1942—Giants, 21-7 (NY)
1943—Giants, 24-13 (NY)
1946—Giants, 28-24 (NY)
1947—Giants, 35-31 (NY)
1948—Cardinals, 63-35 (NY)
1949—Giants, 41-38 (C)
1950—Cardinals, 17-3 (C)
        Giants, 51-21 (NY)
1951—Giants, 28-17 (NY)
        Giants, 10-0 (C)
1952—Cardinals, 24-23 (NY)
        Giants, 28-6 (C)
1953—Giants, 21-7 (NY)
        Giants, 23-20 (C)
1954—Giants, 41-10 (C)
        Giants, 31-17 (NY)
1955—Cardinals, 28-17 (C)

Giants, 10-0 (NY)
1956—Cardinals, 35-27 (C)
        Giants, 23-10 (NY)
1957—Giants, 27-14 (NY)
        Giants, 28-21 (C)
1958—Giants, 37-7 (Buffalo)
        Cardinals, 23-6 (C)
1959—Giants, 9-3 (NY)
        Giants, 30-20 (Minn)
1960—Giants, 35-14 (StL)
        Cardinals, 20-13 (NY)
1961—Giants, 21-10 (NY)
        Giants, 24-9 (StL)
1962—Giants, 31-14 (StL)
        Giants, 31-28 (NY)
1963—Giants, 38-21 (StL)
        Cardinals, 24-17 (NY)
1964—Giants, 34-17 (NY)
        Tie, 10-10 (StL)
1965—Giants, 14-10 (NY)
        Giants, 28-15 (StL)
1966—Cardinals, 24-19 (StL)
        Cardinals, 20-17 (NY)
1967—Giants, 37-20 (StL)
        Giants, 37-14 (NY)
1968—Cardinals, 28-21 (NY)
1969—Cardinals, 42-17 (StL)
        Giants, 49-6 (NY)
1970—Giants, 35-17 (NY)
        Giants, 34-17 (StL)
1971—Giants, 21-20 (StL)
        Cardinals, 24-7 (NY)
1972—Giants, 27-21 (NY)
        Giants, 13-7 (StL)
1973—Cardinals, 35-27 (StL)
        Giants, 24-13 (New Haven)
1974—Cardinals, 23-21 (New Haven)
        Cardinals, 26-14 (StL)
1975—Cardinals, 26-14 (StL)
        Cardinals, 20-13 (NY)
1976—Cardinals, 27-21 (StL)
        Cardinals, 17-14 (NY)
1977—Cardinals, 28-0 (StL)
        Giants, 27-7 (NY)
1978—Cardinals, 20-10 (StL)
        Giants, 17-0 (NY)
1979—Cardinals, 27-14 (NY)
        Cardinals, 29-20 (StL)
1980—Giants, 41-35 (StL)
        Cardinals, 23-7 (NY)
1981—Giants, 34-14 (NY)
        Giants, 20-10 (StL)
1982—Cardinals, 24-21 (StL)
1983—Tie, 20-20 (StL) OT
        Cardinals, 10-6 (NY)
1984—Giants, 16-10 (NY)
        Cardinals, 31-21 (StL)
1985—Giants, 27-17 (NY)
        Giants, 34-3 (StL)
1986—Giants, 13-6 (StL)
        Giants, 27-7 (NY)
1987—Giants, 30-7 (NY)
        Cardinals, 27-24 (StL)
1988—Cardinals, 24-17 (P)
        Giants, 44-7 (NY)
1989—Giants, 35-7 (NY)
        Giants, 20-13 (P)
(Points—Giants 2,136, Cardinals 1,616)
*Franchise in St. Louis prior to 1988
and in Chicago prior to 1960

N.Y. GIANTS vs. *PITTSBURGH
RS: Giants lead series, 41-26-3
1933—Giants, 23-2 (P)
        Giants, 27-3 (NY)
1934—Giants, 14-12 (P)
        Giants, 17-7 (NY)
1935—Giants, 42-7 (P)
        Giants, 13-0 (NY)
1936—Pirates, 10-7 (P)
1937—Giants, 10-7 (P)
        Giants, 17-0 (NY)
1938—Giants, 27-14 (P)
        Pirates, 13-10 (NY)
1939—Giants, 14-7 (P)
        Giants, 23-7 (NY)
1940—Tie, 10-10 (P)
        Giants, 12-0 (NY)
1941—Giants, 37-10 (P)
        Giants, 28-7 (NY)
1942—Steelers, 13-10 (NY)
        Steelers, 17-9 (P)
1945—Giants, 34-6 (P)
        Steelers, 21-7 (NY)
1946—Giants, 17-14 (P)
        Giants, 7-0 (NY)
1947—Steelers, 38-21 (NY)
        Steelers, 24-7 (P)
1948—Giants, 34-27 (NY)
        Steelers, 38-28 (P)
1949—Steelers, 28-7 (P)
        Steelers, 21-17 (NY)
1950—Giants, 18-7 (P)
        Steelers, 17-6 (NY)

1951—Tie, 13-13 (P)
        Giants, 14-0 (NY)
1952—Steelers, 63-7 (P)
1953—Steelers, 24-14 (P)
        Steelers, 14-10 (NY)
1954—Giants, 30-6 (P)
        Giants, 24-3 (NY)
1955—Steelers, 30-23 (P)
1956—Steelers, 19-17 (NY)
        Giants, 38-10 (P)
        Giants, 17-14 (P)
1957—Giants, 35-0 (NY)
        Steelers, 21-10 (P)
1958—Giants, 17-6 (NY)
        Steelers, 31-10 (P)
1959—Giants, 21-16 (P)
        Steelers, 14-9 (NY)
1960—Giants, 19-17 (P)
        Giants, 27-24 (NY)
1961—Giants, 17-14 (P)
        Giants, 42-21 (NY)
1962—Giants, 31-27 (P)
        Steelers, 20-17 (NY)
1963—Steelers, 31-0 (P)
        Giants, 33-17 (NY)
1964—Steelers, 27-24 (P)
        Steelers, 44-17 (NY)
1965—Giants, 23-13 (P)
        Giants, 35-10 (NY)
1966—Tie, 34-34 (P)
        Steelers, 47-28 (NY)
1967—Giants, 27-24 (P)
        Giants, 28-20 (NY)
1968—Giants, 34-20 (P)
1969—Giants, 10-7 (NY)
        Giants, 21-17 (P)
1971—Steelers, 17-13 (P)
1976—Steelers, 27-0 (NY)
1985—Steelers, 28-10 (NY)
(Points—Giants 1,370, Steelers 1,159)
*Steelers known as Pirates prior to 1941

N.Y. GIANTS vs. SAN DIEGO
RS: Giants lead series, 4-2
1971—Giants, 35-17 (NY)
1975—Giants, 35-24 (NY)
1980—Chargers, 44-7 (SD)
1983—Chargers, 41-34 (NY)
1986—Giants, 20-7 (NY)
1989—Giants, 20-13 (SD)
(Points—Giants 151, Chargers 146)

N.Y. GIANTS vs. SAN FRANCISCO
RS: Giants lead series, 10-8
PS: Series tied, 2-2
1952—Giants, 23-14 (NY)
1956—Giants, 38-21 (SF)
1957—49ers, 27-17 (NY)
1960—Giants, 21-19 (SF)
1963—Giants, 48-14 (NY)
1968—49ers, 26-10 (NY)
1972—Giants, 23-17 (SF)
1975—Giants, 26-23 (SF)
1977—Giants, 20-17 (NY)
1978—Giants, 27-10 (NY)
1979—Giants, 32-16 (NY)
1980—49ers, 12-0 (SF)
1981—49ers, 17-10 (SF)
        *49ers, 38-24 (SF)
1984—Giants, 31-10 (NY)
        *49ers, 21-10 (SF)
1985—**Giants, 17-3 (SF)
1986—Giants, 21-17 (SF)
        *Giants, 49-3 (NY)
1987—49ers, 41-21 (NY)
1988—49ers, 20-17 (NY)
1989—49ers, 34-24 (SF)
(Points—Giants 488, 49ers 441)
*NFC Divisional Playoff
**NFC First Round Playoff

N.Y. GIANTS vs. SEATTLE
RS: Giants lead series, 4-2
1976—Giants, 28-16 (NY)
1980—Giants, 27-21 (S)
1981—Giants, 32-0 (S)
1983—Seahawks, 17-12 (NY)
1986—Seahawks, 17-12 (S)
1989—Giants, 15-3 (NY)
(Points—Giants 126, Seahawks 74)

N.Y. GIANTS vs. TAMPA BAY
RS: Giants lead series, 6-3
1977—Giants, 10-0 (TB)
1978—Giants, 19-13 (TB)
        Giants, 17-14 (NY)
1979—Giants, 17-14 (NY)
        Buccaneers, 31-3 (TB)
1980—Buccaneers, 30-13 (TB)
1984—Giants, 17-14 (NY)
        Buccaneers, 20-17 (TB)
1985—Giants, 22-20 (NY)
(Points—Buccaneers 156, Giants 135)

N.Y. GIANTS vs. *WASHINGTON
RS: Giants lead series, 64-47-3
PS: Series tied, 1-1
1932—Braves, 14-6 (B)

Tie, 0-0 (NY)
1933—Redskins, 21-20 (B)
    Giants, 7-0 (NY)
1934—Giants, 16-13 (B)
    Giants, 3-0 (NY)
1935—Giants, 20-12 (B)
    Giants, 17-6 (NY)
1936—Giants, 7-0 (B)
    Redskins, 14-0 (NY)
1937—Redskins, 13-3 (NY)
    Redskins, 49-14 (NY)
1938—Giants, 10-7 (W)
    Giants, 36-0 (NY)
1939—Tie, 0-0 (W)
    Giants, 9-7 (NY)
1940—Redskins, 21-7 (W)
    Giants, 21-7 (NY)
1941—Giants, 17-10 (W)
    Giants, 20-13 (NY)
1942—Giants, 14-7 (W)
    Redskins, 14-7 (NY)
1943—Giants, 14-10 (NY)
    Giants, 31-7 (W)
    **Redskins, 28-0 (NY)
1944—Giants, 16-13 (NY)
    Giants, 31-0 (W)
1945—Redskins, 24-14 (NY)
    Redskins, 17-0 (W)
1946—Redskins, 24-14 (W)
    Giants, 31-0 (NY)
1947—Redskins, 28-20 (NY)
    Giants, 35-10 (NY)
1948—Redskins, 41-10 (W)
    Redskins, 28-21 (NY)
1949—Giants, 45-35 (W)
    Giants, 23-7 (NY)
1950—Giants, 21-17 (W)
    Giants, 24-21 (NY)
1951—Giants, 35-14 (W)
    Giants, 28-14 (NY)
1952—Giants, 14-10 (W)
    Redskins, 27-17 (NY)
1953—Redskins, 13-9 (W)
    Redskins, 24-21 (NY)
1954—Giants, 51-21 (W)
    Giants, 24-7 (NY)
1955—Giants, 35-7 (NY)
    Giants, 27-20 (W)
1956—Redskins, 33-7 (W)
    Giants, 28-14 (NY)
1957—Giants, 24-20 (W)
    Redskins, 31-14 (NY)
1958—Giants, 21-14 (W)
    Giants, 30-0 (NY)
1959—Giants, 45-14 (NY)
    Giants, 24-10 (W)
1960—Tie, 24-24 (NY)
    Giants, 17-3 (W)
1961—Giants, 24-21 (W)
    Giants, 53-0 (NY)
1962—Giants, 49-34 (W)
    Giants, 42-24 (W)
1963—Giants, 24-14 (W)
    Giants, 44-14 (NY)
1964—Giants, 13-10 (NY)
    Redskins, 36-21 (W)
1965—Redskins, 23-7 (NY)
    Giants, 27-10 (W)
1966—Giants, 13-10 (NY)
    Redskins, 72-41 (W)
1967—Redskins, 38-34 (W)
1968—Giants, 48-21 (NY)
    Giants, 13-10 (W)
1969—Redskins, 20-14 (W)
1970—Giants, 35-33 (NY)
    Giants, 27-24 (W)
1971—Redskins, 30-3 (NY)
    Redskins, 23-7 (W)
1972—Redskins, 23-16 (NY)
    Redskins, 27-13 (W)
1973—Redskins, 21-3 (New Haven)
    Redskins, 27-24 (W)
1974—Redskins, 13-10 (New Haven)
    Redskins, 24-3 (W)
1975—Redskins, 49-13 (W)
    Redskins, 21-13 (NY)
1976—Redskins, 19-17 (W)
    Giants, 12-9 (NY)
1977—Giants, 20-17 (NY)
    Giants, 17-6 (W)
1978—Giants, 17-6 (NY)
    Redskins, 16-13 (W) OT
1979—Redskins, 27-0 (W)
    Giants, 14-6 (NY)
1980—Redskins, 23-21 (NY)
    Redskins, 16-13 (W)
1981—Giants, 17-7 (W)
    Redskins, 30-27 (NY) OT
1982—Redskins, 27-17 (NY)
    Redskins, 15-14 (W)
1983—Redskins, 33-17 (NY)
    Redskins, 31-22 (W)
1984—Redskins, 30-14 (W)

Giants, 37-13 (NY)
1985—Giants, 17-3 (NY)
    Redskins, 23-21 (W)
1986—Giants, 27-20 (NY)
    Giants, 24-14 (W)
    ***Giants, 17-0 (NY)
1987—Redskins, 38-12 (NY)
    Redskins, 23-19 (W)
1988—Giants, 27-20 (NY)
    Giants, 24-23 (W)
1989—Giants, 27-24 (W)
    Giants, 20-17 (NY)
(Points—Giants 2,277, Redskins 2,066)
*Franchise in Boston prior to 1937 and known as Braves prior to 1933
**Division Playoff
***NFC Championship

N.Y. JETS vs. ATLANTA
RS: Jets lead series, 3-2;
See Atlanta vs. N.Y. Jets
N.Y. JETS vs. BUFFALO
RS: Bills lead series, 30-28
PS: Bills lead series, 1-0;
See Buffalo vs. N.Y. Jets
N.Y. JETS vs. CHICAGO
RS: Bears lead series, 2-1;
See Chicago vs. N.Y. Jets
N.Y. JETS vs. CINCINNATI
RS: Jets lead series, 7-5
PS: Jets lead series, 1-0;
See Cincinnati vs. N.Y. Jets
N.Y. JETS vs. CLEVELAND
RS: Browns lead series, 8-4
PS: Browns lead series, 1-0;
See Cleveland vs. N.Y. Jets
N.Y. JETS vs. DALLAS
RS: Cowboys lead series, 4-0;
See Dallas vs. N.Y. Jets
N.Y. JETS vs. DENVER
RS: Jets lead series, 11-10-1;
See Denver vs. N.Y. Jets
N.Y. JETS vs. DETROIT
RS: Jets lead series, 3-2;
See Detroit vs. N.Y. Jets
N.Y. JETS vs. GREEN BAY
RS: Jets lead series, 4-1;
See Green Bay vs. N.Y. Jets
N.Y. JETS vs. HOUSTON
RS: Oilers lead series, 15-11-1;
See Houston vs. N.Y. Jets
N.Y. JETS vs. INDIANAPOLIS
RS: Colts lead series, 21-18
PS: Jets lead series, 1-0;
See Indianapolis vs. N.Y. Jets
N.Y. JETS vs. KANSAS CITY
RS: Chiefs lead series, 13-12-1
PS: Series tied, 1-1;
See Kansas City vs. N.Y. Jets
N.Y. JETS vs. L.A. RAIDERS
RS: Raiders lead series, 13-9-2
PS: Jets lead series, 2-0;
See L.A. Raiders vs. N.Y. Jets
N.Y. JETS vs. L.A. RAMS
RS: Rams lead series, 4-2;
See L.A. Rams vs. N.Y. Jets
N.Y. JETS vs. MIAMI
RS: Dolphins lead series, 24-23-1
PS: Dolphins lead series, 1-0;
See Miami vs. N.Y. Jets
N.Y. JETS vs. MINNESOTA
RS: Jets lead series, 3-1;
See Minnesota vs. N.Y. Jets
N.Y. JETS vs. NEW ENGLAND
RS: Jets lead series, 32-26-1
PS: Patriots lead series, 1-0;
See New England vs. N.Y. Jets
N.Y. JETS vs. NEW ORLEANS
RS: Jets lead series, 4-2;
See New Orleans vs. N.Y. Jets
N.Y. JETS vs. N.Y. GIANTS
RS: Series tied, 3-3;
See N.Y. Giants vs. N.Y. Jets
N.Y. JETS vs. PHILADELPHIA
RS: Eagles lead series, 4-0
1973—Eagles, 24-23 (P)
1977—Eagles, 27-0 (P)
1978—Eagles, 17-9 (P)
1987—Eagles, 38-27 (NY)
(Points—Eagles 106, Jets 59)
N.Y. JETS vs. *PHOENIX
RS: Cardinals lead series, 2-1
1971—Cardinals, 17-10 (StL)
1975—Cardinals 37-6 (NY)
1978—Jets, 23-10 (NY)
(Points—Cardinals 64, Jets 39)
*Franchise in St. Louis prior to 1988
N.Y. JETS vs. PITTSBURGH
RS: Steelers lead series, 10-1
1970—Steelers, 21-17 (P)
1973—Steelers, 26-14 (P)
1975—Steelers, 20-7 (NY)
1977—Steelers, 23-20 (NY)

1978—Steelers, 28-17 (NY)
1981—Steelers, 38-10 (P)
1983—Steelers, 34-7 (NY)
1984—Steelers, 23-17 (NY)
1986—Steelers, 45-24 (NY)
1988—Jets, 24-20 (NY)
1989—Steelers, 13-0 (P)
(Points—Steelers 291, Jets 157)
*N.Y. JETS vs. **SAN DIEGO
RS: Chargers lead series, 14-8-1
1960—Chargers, 21-7 (NY)
    Chargers, 50-43 (LA)
1961—Chargers, 25-10 (NY)
    Chargers, 48-13 (SD)
1962—Chargers, 40-14 (SD)
    Titans, 23-3 (NY)
1963—Chargers, 24-20 (SD)
    Chargers, 53-7 (NY)
1964—Tie, 17-17 (NY)
    Chargers, 38-3 (SD)
1965—Chargers, 34-9 (NY)
    Chargers, 38-7 (SD)
1966—Jets, 17-16 (NY)
    Chargers, 42-27 (SD)
1967—Jets, 42-31 (SD)
1968—Jets, 23-20 (NY)
    Jets, 37-15 (SD)
1969—Chargers, 34-27 (SD)
1971—Chargers, 49-21 (SD)
1974—Jets, 27-14 (NY)
1975—Chargers, 24-16 (SD)
1983—Jets, 41-29 (NY)
1989—Jets, 20-17 (SD)
(Points—Chargers 682, Jets 471)
*Jets known as Titans prior to 1963
**Franchise in Los Angeles prior to 1961
N.Y. JETS vs. SAN FRANCISCO
RS: 49ers lead series, 5-1
1971—49ers, 24-21 (NY)
1976—49ers, 17-6 (SF)
1980—49ers, 37-27 (NY)
1983—Jets, 27-13 (SF)
1986—49ers, 24-10 (SF)
1989—49ers, 23-10 (NY)
(Points—49ers 138, Jets 101)
N.Y. JETS vs. SEATTLE
RS: Seahawks lead series, 7-3
1977—Seahawks, 17-0 (NY)
1978—Seahawks, 24-17 (NY)
1979—Seahawks, 30-7 (S)
1980—Seahawks, 27-17 (NY)
1981—Seahawks, 19-3 (NY)
    Seahawks, 27-23 (S)
1983—Seahawks, 17-10 (NY)
1985—Jets, 17-14 (NY)
1986—Jets, 38-7 (S)
1987—Jets, 30-14 (NY)
(Points—Seahawks 196, Jets 162)
N.Y. JETS vs. TAMPA BAY
RS: Jets lead series, 3-1
1976—Jets, 34-0 (NY)
1982—Jets, 32-17 (NY)
1984—Buccaneers, 41-21 (TB)
1985—Jets, 62-28 (NY)
(Points—Jets 149, Buccaneers 86)
N.Y. JETS vs. WASHINGTON
RS: Redskins lead series, 4-0
1972—Redskins, 35-17 (NY)
1976—Redskins, 37-16 (NY)
1978—Redskins, 23-3 (W)
1987—Redskins, 17-16 (W)
(Points—Redskins 112, Jets 52)

PHILADELPHIA vs. ATLANTA
RS: Eagles lead series, 7-6-1
PS: Falcons lead series, 1-0;
See Atlanta vs. Philadelphia
PHILADELPHIA vs. BUFFALO
RS: Eagles lead series, 4-1
See Buffalo vs. Philadelphia
PHILADELPHIA vs. CHICAGO
RS: Bears lead series, 22-3-1
PS: Series tied, 1-1;
See Chicago vs. Philadelphia
PHILADELPHIA vs. CINCINNATI
RS: Bengals lead series, 5-0;
See Cincinnati vs. Philadelphia
PHILADELPHIA vs. CLEVELAND
RS: Browns lead series, 30-11-1;
See Cleveland vs. Philadelphia
PHILADELPHIA vs. DALLAS
RS: Cowboys lead series, 36-22
PS: Eagles lead series, 1-0;
See Dallas vs. Philadelphia
PHILADELPHIA vs. DENVER
RS: Eagles lead series, 4-2;
See Denver vs. Philadelphia
PHILADELPHIA vs. DETROIT
RS: Lions lead series, 12-9-2;
See Detroit vs. Philadelphia
PHILADELPHIA vs. GREEN BAY
RS: Packers lead series, 18-4
PS: Eagles lead series, 1-0;

See Green Bay vs. Philadelphia
PHILADELPHIA vs. HOUSTON
RS: Eagles lead series, 4-0;
See Houston vs. Philadelphia
PHILADELPHIA vs. INDIANAPOLIS
RS: Series tied, 5-5;
See Indianapolis vs. Philadelphia
PHILADELPHIA vs. KANSAS CITY
RS: Eagles lead series, 1-0;
See Kansas City vs. Philadelphia
PHILADELPHIA vs. L.A. RAIDERS
RS: Eagles lead series, 3-2
PS: Raiders lead series, 1-0;
See L.A. Raiders vs. Philadelphia
PHILADELPHIA vs. L.A. RAMS
RS: Rams lead series, 15-10-1
PS: Series tied, 1-1;
See L.A. Rams vs. Philadelphia
PHILADELPHIA vs. MIAMI
RS: Dolphins lead series, 4-2;
See Miami vs. Philadelphia
PHILADELPHIA vs. MINNESOTA
RS: Vikings lead series, 10-4
PS: Eagles lead series, 1-0;
See Minnesota vs. Philadelphia
PHILADELPHIA vs. NEW ENGLAND
RS: Eagles lead series, 4-2;
See New England vs. Philadelphia
PHILADELPHIA vs. NEW ORLEANS
RS: Eagles lead series, 9-7;
See New Orleans vs. Philadelphia
PHILADELPHIA vs. N.Y. GIANTS
RS: Giants lead series, 59-49-2
PS: Giants lead series, 1-0;
See N.Y. Giants vs. Philadelphia
PHILADELPHIA vs. N.Y. JETS
RS: Eagles lead series, 4-0;
See N.Y. Jets vs. Philadelphia
PHILADELPHIA vs. *PHOENIX
RS: Cardinals lead series, 41-38-5
PS: Series tied, 1-1
1935—Cardinals, 12-3 (C)
1936—Cardinals, 13-0 (C)
1937—Tie, 6-6 (P)
1938—Eagles, 7-0 (Erie, Pa.)
1941—Eagles, 21-14 (P)
1945—Eagles, 21-6 (P)
1947—Cardinals, 45-21 (P)
    **Cardinals, 28-21 (C)
1948—Cardinals, 21-14 (P)
    **Eagles, 7-0 (P)
1949—Eagles, 28-3 (P)
1950—Eagles, 45-7 (C)
    Cardinals, 14-10 (P)
1951—Eagles, 17-14 (C)
1952—Eagles, 10-7 (P)
    Cardinals, 28-22 (C)
1953—Eagles, 56-17 (C)
    Eagles, 38-0 (P)
1954—Eagles, 35-16 (C)
    Eagles, 30-14 (P)
1955—Tie, 24-24 (C)
    Eagles, 27-3 (P)
1956—Cardinals, 20-6 (P)
    Cardinals, 28-17 (C)
1957—Eagles, 38-21 (C)
    Cardinals, 31-27 (P)
1958—Tie, 21-21 (P)
    Eagles, 49-21 (P)
1959—Eagles, 28-24 (Minn)
    Eagles, 27-17 (P)
1960—Eagles, 31-27 (P)
    Eagles, 20-6 (StL)
1961—Cardinals, 30-27 (P)
    Eagles, 20-7 (StL)
1962—Cardinals, 27-21 (P)
    Cardinals, 45-35 (StL)
1963—Cardinals, 28-24 (P)
    Cardinals, 38-14 (StL)
1964—Cardinals, 38-13 (P)
    Cardinals, 36-34 (StL)
1965—Eagles, 34-27 (P)
    Eagles, 28-24 (StL)
1966—Cardinals, 16-13 (StL)
    Cardinals, 41-10 (P)
1967—Cardinals, 48-14 (StL)
1968—Cardinals, 45-17 (P)
1969—Cardinals, 34-30 (StL)
1970—Cardinals, 35-20 (P)
    Cardinals, 23-14 (StL)
1971—Eagles, 37-20 (StL)
    Eagles, 19-7 (P)
1972—Tie, 6-6 (P)
    Cardinals, 24-23 (StL)
1973—Cardinals, 34-23 (P)
    Eagles, 27-24 (StL)
1974—Cardinals, 7-3 (P)
    Cardinals, 13-3 (P)
1975—Cardinals, 31-20 (StL)
    Cardinals, 24-23 (P)
1976—Cardinals, 33-14 (StL)
    Cardinals, 17-14 (P)
1977—Cardinals, 21-17 (P)

Cardinals, 21-16 (StL)
1978—Cardinals, 16-10 (P)
Eagles, 14-10 (StL)
1979—Eagles, 24-20 (StL)
Eagles, 16-13 (P)
1980—Cardinals, 24-14 (StL)
Eagles, 17-3 (P)
1981—Eagles, 52-10 (StL)
Eagles, 38-0 (P)
1982—Cardinals, 23-20 (P)
1983—Cardinals, 14-11 (P)
Cardinals, 31-7 (StL)
1984—Cardinals, 34-14 (P)
Cardinals, 17-16 (StL)
1985—Eagles, 30-7 (P)
Eagles, 24-14 (StL)
1986—Cardinals, 13-10 (StL)
Tie, 10-10 (P) OT
1987—Eagles, 28-23 (StL)
Cardinals, 31-19 (P)
1988—Eagles, 31-21 (P)
Eagles, 23-17 (Phoe)
1989—Eagles, 17-5 (Phoe)
Eagles, 31-14 (P)
(Points—Eagles 1,820, Cardinals 1,698)
*Franchise in St. Louis prior to 1988
and in Chicago prior to 1960
**NFL Championship

PHILADELPHIA vs. *PITTSBURGH
RS: Eagles lead series, 42-25-3
PS: Eagles lead series, 1-0
1933—Eagles, 25-6 (Phila)
1934—Eagles, 17-0 (Pitt)
Pirates, 9-7 (Phila)
1935—Pirates, 17-7 (Phila)
Eagles, 17-6 (Pitt)
1936—Pirates, 17-0 (Pitt)
Pirates, 6-0 (Johnstown, Pa.)
1937—Pirates, 27-14 (Pitt)
Pirates, 16-7 (Pitt)
1938—Eagles, 27-7 (Buffalo)
Eagles, 14-7 (Charleston, W. Va.)
1939—Eagles, 17-14 (Phila)
Pirates, 24-12 (Pitt)
1940—Pirates, 7-3 (Pitt)
Eagles, 7-0 (Phila)
1941—Eagles, 10-7 (Pitt)
Tie, 7-7 (Phila)
1942—Eagles, 24-14 (Phila)
Steelers, 14-0 (Phila)
1945—Eagles, 45-3 (Pitt)
Eagles, 30-6 (Phila)
1946—Steelers, 10-7 (Pitt)
Eagles, 10-7 (Phila)
1947—Steelers, 35-24 (Pitt)
Eagles, 21-0 (Phila)
**Eagles, 21-0 (Pitt)
1948—Eagles, 34-7 (Pitt)
Eagles, 17-0 (Phila)
1949—Eagles, 38-7 (Pitt)
Eagles, 34-17 (Phila)
1950—Eagles, 17-10 (Phila)
Steelers, 9-7 (Phila)
1951—Eagles, 34-13 (Pitt)
Steelers, 17-13 (Phila)
1952—Eagles, 31-25 (Pitt)
Eagles, 26-21 (Phila)
1953—Eagles, 23-17 (Phila)
Eagles, 35-7 (Pitt)
1954—Eagles, 24-22 (Phila)
Steelers, 17-7 (Pitt)
1955—Steelers, 13-7 (Pitt)
Eagles, 24-0 (Phila)
1956—Eagles, 35-21 (Phila)
Eagles, 14-7 (Phila)
1957—Steelers, 6-0 (Pitt)
Eagles, 7-6 (Phila)
1958—Steelers, 24-3 (Pitt)
Steelers, 31-24 (Phila)
1959—Eagles, 28-24 (Phila)
Steelers, 31-0 (Pitt)
1960—Eagles, 34-7 (Phila)
Steelers, 27-21 (Pitt)
1961—Eagles, 21-16 (Phila)
Eagles, 35-24 (Pitt)
1962—Steelers, 13-7 (Pitt)
Steelers, 26-17 (Phila)
1963—Tie, 21-21 (Phila)
Tie, 20-20 (Pitt)
1964—Eagles, 21-7 (Phila)
Eagles, 34-10 (Pitt)
1965—Steelers, 20-14 (Phila)
Eagles, 47-13 (Pitt)
1966—Eagles, 31-14 (Pitt)
Eagles, 27-23 (Phila)
1967—Eagles, 34-24 (Phila)
1968—Steelers, 6-3 (Pitt)
1969—Eagles, 41-27 (Phila)
1970—Eagles, 30-20 (Phila)
1974—Steelers, 27-0 (Pitt)
1979—Eagles, 17-14 (Phila)
1988—Eagles, 27-26 (Pitt)
(Points—Eagles 1,357, Steelers 993)

*Steelers known as Pirates prior to 1941
**Division Playoff

PHILADELPHIA vs. SAN DIEGO
RS: Chargers lead series, 3-2
1974—Eagles, 13-7 (SD)
1980—Chargers, 22-21 (SD)
1985—Chargers, 20-14 (SD)
1986—Eagles, 23-7 (P)
1989—Chargers, 20-17 (SD)
(Points—Eagles 88, Chargers 76)

PHILADELPHIA vs. SAN FRANCISCO
RS: 49ers lead series, 11-4-1
1951—Eagles, 21-14 (P)
1953—49ers, 31-21 (SF)
1956—Tie, 10-10 (P)
1958—49ers, 30-24 (P)
1959—49ers, 24-14 (SF)
1964—Eagles, 28-24 (P)
1966—Eagles, 35-34 (SF)
1967—49ers, 28-27 (P)
1969—Eagles, 14-13 (SF)
1971—49ers, 31-3 (P)
1973—49ers, 38-28 (SF)
1975—Eagles, 27-17 (P)
1983—Eagles, 22-17 (SF)
1984—49ers, 21-9 (P)
1985—49ers, 24-13 (SF)
1989—49ers, 38-28 (P)
(Points—49ers 399, Eagles 319)

PHILADELPHIA vs. SEATTLE
RS: Eagles lead series, 3-1
1976—Eagles, 27-10 (P)
1980—Eagles, 27-20 (S)
1986—Seahawks, 24-20 (S)
1989—Eagles, 31-7 (P)
(Points—Eagles 105, Seahawks 61)

PHILADELPHIA vs. TAMPA BAY
RS: Eagles lead series, 3-0
PS: Buccaneers lead series, 1-0
1977—Eagles, 13-3 (P)
1979—*Buccaneers, 24-17 (TB)
1981—Eagles, 20-10 (P)
1988—Eagles, 41-14 (TB)
(Points—Eagles 91, Buccaneers 51)
*NFC Divisional Playoff

PHILADELPHIA vs. *WASHINGTON
RS: Redskins lead series, 63-41-5
1934—Eagles, 6-0 (B)
Redskins, 14-7 (P)
1935—Eagles, 7-6 (B)
1936—Redskins, 26-3 (P)
Redskins, 17-7 (B)
1937—Eagles, 14-0 (W)
Redskins, 10-7 (P)
1938—Redskins, 26-23 (P)
Redskins, 20-14 (W)
1939—Redskins, 7-0 (P)
Redskins, 7-6 (W)
1940—Redskins, 34-17 (P)
Redskins, 13-6 (W)
1941—Redskins, 21-17 (P)
Redskins, 20-14 (W)
1942—Redskins, 14-10 (P)
Redskins, 30-27 (W)
1944—Tie, 31-31 (P)
Eagles, 37-7 (W)
1945—Redskins, 24-14 (W)
Eagles, 16-0 (P)
1946—Eagles, 28-24 (W)
Redskins, 27-10 (P)
1947—Eagles, 45-42 (P)
Eagles, 38-14 (W)
1948—Eagles, 45-0 (W)
Eagles, 42-21 (P)
1949—Eagles, 49-14 (P)
Eagles, 44-21 (W)
1950—Eagles, 35-3 (P)
Eagles, 33-0 (W)
1951—Redskins, 27-23 (P)
Eagles, 35-21 (W)
1952—Eagles, 38-20 (P)
Redskins, 27-21 (W)
1953—Tie, 21-21 (P)
Redskins, 10-0 (W)
1954—Eagles, 49-21 (W)
Eagles, 41-33 (P)
1955—Eagles, 31-30 (P)
Redskins, 34-21 (W)
1956—Eagles, 13-9 (P)
Redskins, 19-17 (W)
1957—Eagles, 21-12 (P)
Redskins, 42-7 (W)
1958—Redskins, 24-14 (P)
Redskins, 20-0 (W)
1959—Eagles, 30-23 (P)
Eagles, 34-14 (W)
1960—Eagles, 19-13 (P)
Eagles, 38-28 (W)
1961—Eagles, 14-7 (P)
Eagles, 27-24 (W)
1962—Redskins, 27-21 (P)
Eagles, 37-14 (W)
1963—Eagles, 37-24 (W)

Redskins, 13-10 (P)
1964—Redskins, 35-20 (W)
Redskins, 21-10 (P)
1965—Redskins, 23-21 (W)
Eagles, 21-14 (P)
1966—Redskins, 27-13 (P)
Eagles, 37-28 (W)
1967—Eagles, 35-24 (P)
Tie, 35-35 (W)
1968—Redskins, 17-14 (W)
Redskins, 16-10 (P)
1969—Tie, 28-28 (W)
Redskins, 34-29 (P)
1970—Redskins, 33-21 (P)
Redskins, 24-6 (W)
1971—Tie, 7-7 (W)
Redskins, 20-13 (P)
1972—Redskins, 14-0 (W)
Redskins, 23-7 (P)
1973—Redskins, 28-7 (P)
Redskins, 38-20 (W)
1974—Redskins, 27-20 (P)
Redskins, 26-7 (W)
1975—Eagles, 26-10 (P)
Eagles, 26-3 (W)
1976—Redskins, 20-17 (P) OT
Redskins, 24-0 (W)
1977—Redskins, 23-17 (W)
Redskins, 17-14 (P)
1978—Redskins, 35-30 (W)
Eagles, 17-10 (P)
1979—Eagles, 28-17 (P)
Redskins, 17-7 (W)
1980—Eagles, 24-14 (W)
Eagles, 24-0 (W)
1981—Eagles, 36-13 (P)
Redskins, 15-13 (W)
1982—Redskins, 37-34 (P) OT
Redskins, 13-9 (W)
1983—Redskins, 23-13 (P)
Redskins, 28-24 (W)
1984—Redskins, 20-0 (W)
Eagles, 16-10 (P)
1985—Eagles, 19-6 (W)
Redskins, 17-12 (P)
1986—Redskins, 41-14 (W)
Redskins, 21-14 (P)
1987—Redskins, 34-24 (W)
Eagles, 31-27 (P)
1988—Redskins, 17-10 (W)
Redskins, 20-19 (P)
1989—Eagles, 42-37 (W)
Redskins, 10-3 (P)
(Points—Eagles 2,208, Redskins 2,178)
*Franchise in Boston prior to 1937

PHOENIX vs. ATLANTA
RS: Cardinals lead series, 8-4;
See Atlanta vs. Phoenix
PHOENIX vs. BUFFALO
RS: Cardinals lead series, 3-2;
See Buffalo vs. Phoenix
PHOENIX vs. CHICAGO
RS: Bears lead series, 50-25-6;
See Chicago vs. Phoenix
PHOENIX vs. CINCINNATI
RS: Bengals lead series, 3-1;
See Cincinnati vs. Phoenix
PHOENIX vs. CLEVELAND
RS: Browns lead series, 31-10-3;
See Cleveland vs. Phoenix
PHOENIX vs. DALLAS
RS: Cowboys lead series, 33-21-1;
See Dallas vs. Phoenix
PHOENIX vs. DENVER
RS: Broncos lead series, 2-0-1;
See Denver vs. Phoenix
PHOENIX vs. DETROIT
RS: Lions lead series, 25-16-5;
See Detroit vs. Phoenix
PHOENIX vs. GREEN BAY
RS: Packers lead series, 38-21-4
PS: Packers lead series, 1-0;
See Green Bay vs. Phoenix
PHOENIX vs. HOUSTON
RS: Cardinals lead series, 3-2;
See Houston vs. Phoenix
PHOENIX vs. INDIANAPOLIS
RS: Cardinals lead series, 5-4;
See Indianapolis vs. Phoenix
PHOENIX vs. KANSAS CITY
RS: Chiefs lead series, 3-1-1;
See Kansas City vs. Phoenix
PHOENIX vs. L.A. RAIDERS
RS: Raiders lead series, 2-1;
See L.A. Raiders vs. Phoenix
PHOENIX vs. L.A. RAMS
RS: Rams lead series, 22-16-2
PS: Rams lead series, 1-0;
See L.A. Rams vs. Phoenix
PHOENIX vs. MIAMI
RS: Dolphins lead series, 5-0;
See Miami vs. Phoenix

PHOENIX vs. MINNESOTA
RS: Cardinals lead series, 7-2
PS: Vikings lead series, 1-0;
See Minnesota vs. Phoenix
PHOENIX vs. NEW ENGLAND
RS: Cardinals lead series, 4-1;
See New England vs. Phoenix
PHOENIX vs. NEW ORLEANS
RS: Cardinals lead series, 10-5;
See New Orleans vs. Phoenix
PHOENIX vs. N.Y. GIANTS
RS: Giants lead series, 59-33-2;
See N.Y. Giants vs. Phoenix
PHOENIX vs. N.Y. JETS
RS: Cardinals lead series, 2-1;
See N.Y. Jets vs. Phoenix
PHOENIX vs. PHILADELPHIA
RS: Cardinals lead series, 41-38-5
PS: Series tied, 1-1;
See Philadelphia vs. Phoenix
***PHOENIX vs. **PITTSBURGH**
RS: Steelers lead series, 29-21-3
1933—Pirates, 14-13 (C)
1935—Pirates, 17-13 (P)
1936—Cardinals, 14-6 (C)
1937—Cardinals, 13-7 (P)
1939—Cardinals, 10-0 (P)
1940—Tie, 7-7 (P)
1942—Steelers, 19-3 (P)
1945—Steelers, 23-0 (P)
1946—Steelers, 14-7 (P)
1948—Cardinals, 24-7 (C)
1950—Steelers, 28-17 (C)
Steelers, 28-7 (P)
1951—Steelers, 28-14 (C)
1952—Steelers, 34-28 (C)
Steelers, 17-14 (P)
1953—Steelers, 31-28 (P)
Steelers, 21-17 (C)
1954—Cardinals, 17-14 (C)
Steelers, 20-17 (P)
1955—Steelers, 14-7 (P)
Cardinals, 27-13 (C)
1956—Steelers, 14-7 (P)
Cardinals, 38-27 (C)
1957—Steelers, 29-20 (P)
Steelers, 27-2 (C)
1958—Steelers, 27-20 (C)
Steelers, 38-21 (P)
1959—Cardinals, 45-24 (C)
Steelers, 35-20 (P)
1960—Steelers, 27-14 (P)
Cardinals, 38-7 (StL)
1961—Steelers, 30-27 (P)
Cardinals, 20-0 (StL)
1962—Steelers, 26-17 (StL)
Steelers, 19-7 (P)
1963—Steelers, 23-10 (P)
Cardinals, 24-23 (StL)
1964—Cardinals, 34-30 (StL)
Cardinals, 21-20 (P)
1965—Cardinals, 20-7 (P)
Cardinals, 21-17 (P)
1966—Steelers, 30-9 (P)
Cardinals, 6-3 (StL)
1967—Cardinals, 28-14 (P)
Tie, 14-14 (StL)
1968—Tie, 28-28 (StL)
Cardinals, 20-10 (P)
1969—Cardinals, 27-14 (P)
Cardinals, 47-10 (StL)
1972—Steelers, 25-19 (StL)
1979—Steelers, 24-21 (StL)
1985—Steelers, 23-10 (P)
1988—Cardinals, 31-14 (Phoe)
(Points—Steelers 1,021, Cardinals 983)
*Franchise in St. Louis prior to 1988
and in Chicago prior to 1960
**Steelers known as Pirates prior to 1941
***PHOENIX vs. SAN DIEGO**
RS: Chargers lead series, 4-1
1971—Chargers, 20-17 (SD)
1976—Chargers, 43-24 (SD)
1983—Chargers, 44-14 (SD)
1987—Chargers, 28-24 (SD)
1989—Chargers, 24-13 (P)
(Points—Chargers 129, Cardinals 122)
*Franchise in St. Louis prior to 1988
***PHOENIX vs. SAN FRANCISCO**
RS: Series tied, 8-8
1951—Cardinals, 27-21 (SF)
1957—Cardinals, 20-10 (SF)
1962—49ers, 24-17 (SF)
1964—Cardinals, 23-13 (SF)
1968—49ers, 35-17 (SF)
1971—49ers, 26-14 (St)
1974—Cardinals, 34-9 (SF)
1976—Cardinals, 23-20 (StL) OT
1978—Cardinals, 16-10 (StL)
1979—Cardinals, 13-10 (StL)
1980—49ers, 24-21 (SF) OT
1982—49ers, 31-20 (StL)
1983—49ers, 42-27 (StL)

1986—49ers, 43-17 (SF)
1987—49ers, 34-28 (SF)
1988—Cardinals, 24-23 (P)
(Points—49ers 375, Cardinals 341)
*Franchise in St. Louis prior to 1988
and in Chicago prior to 1960
PHOENIX vs. SEATTLE
RS: Cardinals lead series, 3-0
1976—Cardinals, 30-24 (S)
1983—Cardinals, 33-28 (StL)
1989—Cardinals, 34-24 (S)
(Points—Cardinals 97, Seahawks 76)
*Franchise in St. Louis prior to 1988
PHOENIX vs. TAMPA BAY
RS: Cardinals lead series, 6-4
1977—Buccaneers, 17-7 (TB)
1981—Buccaneers, 20-10 (TB)
1983—Cardinals, 34-27 (TB)
1985—Buccaneers, 16-0 (TB)
1986—Cardinals, 30-19 (TB)
          Cardinals, 21-17 (StL)
1987—Cardinals, 31-28 (StL)
          Cardinals, 31-14 (TB)
1988—Cardinals, 30-24 (TB)
1989—Buccaneers, 14-13 (P)
(Points—Cardinals 207, Buccaneers 196)
*Franchise in St. Louis prior to 1988
PHOENIX vs. **WASHINGTON
RS: Redskins lead series, 56-33-2;
1932—Cardinals, 9-0 (B)
          Braves, 8-6 (C)
1933—Redskins, 10-0 (C)
          Tie, 0-0 (B)
1934—Redskins, 9-0 (B)
1935—Cardinals, 6-0 (B)
1936—Redskins, 13-10 (B)
1937—Cardinals, 21-14 (W)
1939—Redskins, 28-7 (W)
1940—Redskins, 28-21 (W)
1942—Redskins, 28-0 (W)
1943—Redskins, 13-7 (W)
1945—Redskins, 24-21 (W)
1947—Redskins, 45-21 (W)
1949—Cardinals, 38-7 (C)
1950—Cardinals, 38-28 (W)
1951—Redskins, 7-3 (C)
          Redskins, 20-17 (W)
1952—Redskins, 23-7 (C)
          Cardinals, 17-6 (W)
1953—Redskins, 24-13 (C)
          Redskins, 28-17 (W)
1954—Cardinals, 38-16 (C)
          Redskins, 37-20 (W)
1955—Cardinals, 24-10 (W)
          Redskins, 31-0 (C)
1956—Cardinals, 31-3 (W)
          Redskins, 17-14 (C)
1957—Redskins, 37-14 (C)
          Cardinals, 44-14 (W)
1958—Cardinals, 37-10 (C)
          Redskins, 45-31 (W)
1959—Cardinals, 49-21 (C)
          Redskins, 23-14 (W)
1960—Cardinals, 44-7 (StL)
          Cardinals, 26-14 (W)
1961—Cardinals, 24-0 (W)
          Cardinals, 38-24 (StL)
1962—Redskins, 24-14 (W)
          Tie, 17-17 (StL)
1963—Cardinals, 21-7 (W)
          Cardinals, 24-20 (StL)
1964—Cardinals, 23-17 (W)
          Cardinals, 38-24 (StL)
1965—Cardinals, 37-16 (W)
          Redskins, 24-20 (StL)
1966—Cardinals, 23-7 (W)
          Redskins, 26-20 (W)
1967—Cardinals, 27-21 (W)
1968—Cardinals, 41-14 (StL)
1969—Redskins, 33-17 (W)
1970—Cardinals, 27-17 (StL)
          Redskins, 28-27 (W)
1971—Cardinals, 24-17 (StL)
          Redskins, 20-0 (W)
1972—Cardinals, 24-10 (W)
          Redskins, 33-3 (StL)
1973—Cardinals, 34-27 (StL)
          Redskins, 31-13 (W)
1974—Redskins, 17-10 (W)
          Cardinals, 23-20 (StL)
1975—Cardinals, 27-17 (W)
          Cardinals, 20-17 (StL) OT
1976—Redskins, 20-10 (W)
          Redskins, 16-10 (StL)
1977—Redskins, 24-14 (W)
          Redskins, 26-20 (StL)
1978—Redskins, 28-10 (StL)
          Cardinals, 27-17 (W)
1979—Redskins, 17-7 (StL)
          Redskins, 30-28 (W)
1980—Redskins, 23-0 (W)
          Redskins, 31-7 (StL)
1981—Cardinals, 40-30 (StL)

Redskins, 42-21 (W)
1982—Redskins, 12-7 (StL)
          Redskins, 28-0 (W)
1983—Redskins, 38-14 (StL)
          Redskins, 45-7 (W)
1984—Cardinals, 26-24 (StL)
          Redskins, 29-27 (W)
1985—Redskins, 27-10 (W)
          Redskins, 27-16 (StL)
1986—Redskins, 28-21 (W)
          Redskins, 20-17 (StL)
1987—Redskins, 28-21 (W)
          Redskins, 34-17 (StL)
1988—Cardinals, 30-21 (P)
          Redskins, 33-17 (W)
1989—Redskins, 30-28 (W)
          Redskins, 29-10 (P)
(Points—Redskins 1,957, Cardinals 1,719)
*Franchise in St. Louis prior to 1988
and in Chicago prior to 1960
**Franchise in Boston prior to 1937 and
known as Braves prior to 1933

PITTSBURGH vs. ATLANTA
RS: Falcons lead series, 7-1;
See Atlanta vs. Pittsburgh
PITTSBURGH vs. BUFFALO
RS: Series tied, 5-5
PS: Steelers lead series, 1-0;
See Buffalo vs. Pittsburgh
PITTSBURGH vs. CHICAGO
RS: Bears lead series, 15-4-1;
See Chicago vs. Pittsburgh
PITTSBURGH vs. CINCINNATI
RS: Steelers lead series, 20-19;
See Cincinnati vs. Pittsburgh
PITTSBURGH vs. CLEVELAND
RS: Browns lead series, 48-32;
See Cleveland vs. Pittsburgh
PITTSBURGH vs. DALLAS
RS: Series tied, 11-11
PS: Steelers lead series, 2-0;
See Dallas vs. Pittsburgh
PITTSBURGH vs. DENVER
RS: Broncos lead series, 8-4-1
PS: Series tied, 2-2;
See Denver vs. Pittsburgh
PITTSBURGH vs. DETROIT
RS: Lions lead series, 13-10-1;
See Detroit vs. Pittsburgh
PITTSBURGH vs. GREEN BAY
RS: Packers lead series, 16-11;
See Green Bay vs. Pittsburgh
PITTSBURGH vs. HOUSTON
RS: Steelers lead series, 25-14
PS: Steelers lead series, 3-0;
See Houston vs. Pittsburgh
PITTSBURGH vs. INDIANAPOLIS
RS: Steelers lead series, 8-4
PS: Steelers lead series, 2-0;
See Indianapolis vs. Pittsburgh
PITTSBURGH vs. KANSAS CITY
RS: Steelers lead series, 12-5;
See Kansas City vs. Pittsburgh
PITTSBURGH vs. L.A. RAIDERS
RS: Raiders lead series, 6-3
PS: Series tied, 3-3;
See L.A. Raiders vs. Pittsburgh
PITTSBURGH vs. L.A. RAMS
RS: Rams lead series, 13-3-2
PS: Steelers lead series, 1-0;
See L.A. Rams vs. Pittsburgh
PITTSBURGH vs. MIAMI
RS: Dolphins lead series, 6-4
PS: Dolphins lead series, 2-1;
See Miami vs. Pittsburgh
PITTSBURGH vs. MINNESOTA
RS: Vikings lead series, 6-4
PS: Steelers lead series, 1-0;
See Minnesota vs. Pittsburgh
PITTSBURGH vs. NEW ENGLAND
RS: Steelers lead series, 6-3;
See New England vs. Pittsburgh
PITTSBURGH vs. NEW ORLEANS
RS: Saints lead series, 5-4;
See New Orleans vs. Pittsburgh
PITTSBURGH vs. N.Y. GIANTS
RS: Giants lead series, 41-26-3;
See N.Y. Giants vs. Pittsburgh
PITTSBURGH vs. N.Y. JETS
RS: Steelers lead series, 10-1;
See N.Y. Jets vs. Pittsburgh
PITTSBURGH vs. PHILADELPHIA
RS: Eagles lead series, 42-25-3
PS: Eagles lead series, 1-0;
See Philadelphia vs. Pittsburgh
PITTSBURGH vs. PHOENIX
RS: Steelers lead series, 29-21-3;
See Phoenix vs. Pittsburgh
PITTSBURGH vs. SAN DIEGO
RS: Steelers lead series, 10-4
PS: Chargers lead series, 1-0
1971—Steelers, 21-17 (P)

1972—Steelers, 24-2 (SD)
1973—Steelers, 38-21 (P)
1975—Steelers, 37-0 (SD)
1976—Steelers, 23-0 (P)
1977—Steelers, 10-9 (SD)
1979—Chargers, 35-7 (SD)
1980—Chargers, 26-17 (SD)
1982—*Chargers, 31-28 (P)
1983—Steelers, 26-3 (P)
1984—Steelers, 52-24 (P)
1985—Chargers, 54-44 (SD)
1987—Steelers, 20-16 (SD)
1988—Chargers, 20-14 (SD)
1989—Steelers, 20-17 (P)
(Points—Steelers 381, Chargers 275)
*AFC First Round Playoff
PITTSBURGH vs. SAN FRANCISCO
RS: Steelers lead series, 7-6
1951—49ers, 28-24 (P)
1952—49ers, 24-7 (SF)
1954—49ers, 31-3 (SF)
1958—49ers, 23-20 (SF)
1961—Steelers, 20-10 (SF)
1965—49ers, 27-17 (SF)
1968—49ers, 45-28 (P)
1973—Steelers, 37-14 (SF)
1977—Steelers, 27-0 (P)
1978—Steelers, 24-7 (SF)
1981—49ers, 17-14 (P)
1984—Steelers, 20-17 (SF)
1987—Steelers, 30-17 (P)
(Points—Steelers 288, 49ers 243)
PITTSBURGH vs. SEATTLE
RS: Steelers lead series, 4-3
1977—Steelers, 30-20 (P)
1978—Steelers, 21-10 (P)
1981—Seahawks, 24-21 (S)
1982—Seahawks, 16-0 (S)
1983—Steelers, 27-21 (S)
1986—Seahawks, 30-0 (S)
1987—Steelers, 13-9 (P)
(Points—Seahawks 130, Steelers 112)
PITTSBURGH vs. TAMPA BAY
RS: Steelers lead series, 4-0
1976—Steelers, 42-0 (P)
1980—Steelers, 24-21 (TB)
1983—Steelers, 17-12 (P)
1989—Steelers, 31-22 (TB)
(Points—Steelers 114, Buccaneers 55)
PITTSBURGH vs. **WASHINGTON
RS: Redskins lead series, 41-27-3
1933—Redskins, 21-6 (P)
          Pirates, 16-14 (B)
1934—Redskins, 7-0 (P)
          Redskins, 39-0 (B)
1935—Pirates, 6-0 (P)
          Redskins, 13-3 (B)
1936—Pirates, 10-0 (P)
          Redskins, 30-0 (B)
1937—Redskins, 34-20 (W)
          Pirates, 21-13 (P)
1938—Redskins, 7-0 (P)
          Redskins, 15-0 (W)
1939—Redskins, 44-14 (W)
          Redskins, 21-14 (P)
1940—Redskins, 40-10 (P)
          Redskins, 37-10 (W)
1941—Redskins, 24-20 (P)
          Redskins, 23-3 (W)
1942—Redskins, 28-14 (W)
          Redskins, 14-0 (P)
1945—Redskins, 14-0 (W)
          Redskins, 24-0 (W)
1946—Tie, 14-14 (W)
          Steelers, 14-7 (P)
1947—Redskins, 27-26 (W)
          Steelers, 21-14 (P)
1948—Redskins, 17-14 (W)
          Steelers, 10-7 (P)
1949—Redskins, 27-14 (P)
          Redskins, 27-14 (W)
1950—Steelers, 26-7 (W)
          Redskins, 24-7 (P)
1951—Redskins, 22-7 (P)
          Steelers, 20-10 (W)
1952—Redskins, 28-24 (P)
          Steelers, 24-23 (W)
1953—Redskins, 17-9 (P)
          Steelers, 14-13 (W)
1954—Steelers, 37-7 (P)
          Redskins, 17-14 (W)
1955—Redskins, 23-14 (P)
          Redskins, 28-17 (W)
1956—Steelers, 30-13 (P)
          Steelers, 23-0 (W)
1957—Steelers, 28-7 (P)
          Redskins, 10-3 (W)
1958—Steelers, 24-16 (P)
          Tie, 14-14 (W)
1959—Redskins, 23-17 (P)
          Steelers, 27-6 (W)
1960—Tie, 27-27 (W)
          Steelers, 22-10 (P)

1961—Steelers, 20-0 (P)
          Steelers, 30-14 (P)
1962—Steelers, 23-21 (P)
          Steelers, 27-24 (W)
1963—Steelers, 38-27 (P)
          Steelers, 34-28 (W)
1964—Redskins, 30-0 (P)
          Steelers, 14-7 (W)
1965—Redskins, 31-3 (P)
          Redskins, 35-14 (W)
1966—Redskins, 33-27 (P)
          Redskins, 24-10 (W)
1967—Redskins, 15-10 (P)
1968—Redskins, 16-13 (W)
1969—Redskins, 14-7 (P)
1973—Steelers, 21-16 (P)
1979—Steelers, 38-7 (P)
1985—Redskins, 30-23 (P)
1988—Redskins, 30-29 (W)
(Points—Redskins 1,349, Steelers 1,103)
*Steelers known as Pirates prior to 1941
**Franchise in Boston prior to 1937

SAN DIEGO vs. ATLANTA
RS: Falcons lead series, 2-1;
See Atlanta vs. San Diego
SAN DIEGO vs. BUFFALO
RS: Chargers lead series, 16-7-2
PS: Bills lead series, 2-1;
See Buffalo vs. San Diego
SAN DIEGO vs. CHICAGO
RS: Chargers lead series, 4-1;
See Chicago vs. San Diego
SAN DIEGO vs. CINCINNATI
RS: Chargers lead series, 11-7
PS: Bengals lead series, 1-0;
See Cincinnati vs. San Diego
SAN DIEGO vs. CLEVELAND
RS: Chargers lead series, 6-5-1;
See Cleveland vs. San Diego
SAN DIEGO vs. DALLAS
RS: Cowboys lead series, 3-1;
See Dallas vs. San Diego
SAN DIEGO vs. DENVER
RS: Broncos lead series, 30-29-1;
See Denver vs. San Diego
SAN DIEGO vs. DETROIT
RS: Lions lead series, 3-2;
See Detroit vs. San Diego
SAN DIEGO vs. GREEN BAY
RS: Packers lead series, 3-1;
See Green Bay vs. San Diego
SAN DIEGO vs. HOUSTON
RS: Chargers lead series, 17-11-1
PS: Oilers lead series, 3-0;
See Houston vs. San Diego
SAN DIEGO vs. INDIANAPOLIS
RS: Chargers lead series, 6-5;
See Indianapolis vs. San Diego
SAN DIEGO vs. KANSAS CITY
RS: Chargers lead series, 31-27-1;
See Kansas City vs. San Diego
SAN DIEGO vs. L.A. RAIDERS
RS: Raiders lead series, 37-21-2
PS: Raiders lead series, 1-0;
See L.A. Raiders vs. San Diego
SAN DIEGO vs. L.A. RAMS
RS: Series tied, 2-2;
See L.A. Rams vs. San Diego
SAN DIEGO vs. MIAMI
RS: Chargers lead series, 8-5
PS: Series tied, 1-1;
See Miami vs. San Diego
SAN DIEGO vs. MINNESOTA
RS: Series tied, 3-3;
See Minnesota vs. San Diego
SAN DIEGO vs. NEW ENGLAND
RS: Patriots lead series, 13-11-2
PS: Chargers lead series, 1-0;
See New England vs. San Diego
SAN DIEGO vs. NEW ORLEANS
RS: Chargers lead series, 3-1;
See New Orleans vs. San Diego
SAN DIEGO vs. N.Y. GIANTS
RS: Giants lead series, 4-2;
See N.Y. Giants vs. San Diego
SAN DIEGO vs. N.Y. JETS
RS: Chargers lead series, 14-8-1;
See N.Y. Jets vs. San Diego
SAN DIEGO vs. PHILADELPHIA
RS: Chargers lead series, 3-2;
See Philadelphia vs. San Diego
SAN DIEGO vs. PHOENIX
RS: Chargers lead series, 4-1;
See Phoenix vs. San Diego
SAN DIEGO vs. PITTSBURGH
RS: Steelers lead series, 10-4
PS: Chargers lead series, 1-0;
See Pittsburgh vs. San Diego
SAN DIEGO vs. SAN FRANCISCO
RS: Chargers lead series, 3-2
1972—49ers, 34-3 (SF)
1976—Chargers, 13-7 (SD) OT

1979—Chargers, 31-9 (SD)
1982—Chargers, 41-37 (SF)
1988—49ers, 48-10 (SD)
(Points—49ers 135, Chargers 98)
SAN DIEGO vs. SEATTLE
RS: Seahawks lead series, 12-10
1977—Chargers, 30-28 (S)
1978—Chargers, 24-20 (S)
Chargers, 37-10 (SD)
1979—Chargers, 33-16 (S)
Chargers, 20-10 (SD)
1980—Chargers, 34-13 (S)
Chargers, 21-14 (SD)
1981—Chargers, 24-10 (SD)
Seahawks, 44-23 (S)
1983—Seahawks, 34-31 (S)
Chargers, 28-21 (SD)
1984—Seahawks, 31-17 (S)
Seahawks, 24-0 (SD)
1985—Seahawks, 49-35 (SD)
Seahawks, 26-21 (S)
1986—Seahawks, 33-7 (S)
Seahawks, 34-24 (SD)
1987—Seahawks, 34-3 (S)
1988—Chargers, 17-6 (SD)
Seahawks, 17-14 (S)
1989—Seahawks, 17-16 (SD)
Seahawks, 10-7 (S)
(Points—Seahawks 501, Chargers 466)
SAN DIEGO vs. TAMPA BAY
RS: Chargers lead series, 3-0
1976—Chargers, 23-0 (TB)
1981—Chargers, 24-23 (TB)
1987—Chargers, 17-13 (TB)
(Points—Chargers 64, Buccaneers 36)
SAN DIEGO vs. WASHINGTON
RS: Redskins lead series, 5-0
1973—Redskins, 38-0 (W)
1980—Redskins, 40-17 (W)
1983—Redskins, 27-24 (SD)
1986—Redskins, 30-27 (SD)
1989—Redskins, 26-21 (W)
(Points—Redskins 161, Chargers 89)

SAN FRANCISCO vs. ATLANTA
RS: 49ers lead series, 27-18-1;
See Atlanta vs. San Francisco
SAN FRANCISCO vs. BUFFALO
RS: Series tied, 2-2;
See Buffalo vs. San Francisco
SAN FRANCISCO vs. CHICAGO
RS: Bears lead series, 25-24-1
PS: 49ers lead series, 2-0;
See Chicago vs. San Francisco
SAN FRANCISCO vs. CINCINNATI
RS: 49ers lead series, 4-1
PS: 49ers lead series, 2-0;
See Cincinnati vs. San Francisco
SAN FRANCISCO vs. CLEVELAND
RS: Browns lead series, 8-5;
See Cleveland vs. San Francisco
SAN FRANCISCO vs. DALLAS
RS: 49ers lead series, 8-5-1
PS: Cowboys lead series, 3-1;
See Dallas vs. San Francisco
SAN FRANCISCO vs. DENVER
RS: Broncos lead series, 4-2
PS: 49ers lead series, 1-0;
See Denver vs. San Francisco
SAN FRANCISCO vs. DETROIT
RS: Lions lead series, 25-23-1
PS: Series tied, 1-1;
See Detroit vs. San Francisco
SAN FRANCISCO vs. GREEN BAY
RS: 49ers lead series, 24-21-1;
See Green Bay vs. San Francisco
SAN FRANCISCO vs. HOUSTON
RS: 49ers lead series, 4-2;
See Houston vs. San Francisco
SAN FRANCISCO vs. INDIANAPOLIS
RS: Colts lead series, 21-16;
See Indianapolis vs. San Francisco
SAN FRANCISCO vs. KANSAS CITY
RS: 49ers lead series, 3-1;
See Kansas City vs. San Francisco
SAN FRANCISCO vs. L.A RAIDERS
RS: Raiders lead series, 4-2;
See L.A. Raiders vs. San Francisco
SAN FRANCISCO vs. L.A. RAMS
RS: Rams lead series, 47-31-2
PS: 49ers lead series, 1-0;
See L.A. Rams vs. San Francisco
SAN FRANCISCO vs. MIAMI
RS: Dolphins lead series, 4-1
PS: 49ers lead series, 1-0;
See Miami vs. San Francisco
SAN FRANCISCO vs. MINNESOTA
RS: Vikings lead series, 14-12-1
PS: 49ers lead series, 3-1;
See Minnesota vs. San Francisco
SAN FRANCISCO vs. NEW ENGLAND
RS: 49ers lead series, 5-1;
See New England vs. San Francisco

SAN FRANCISCO vs. NEW ORLEANS
RS: 49ers lead series, 28-11-2;
See New Orleans vs. San Francisco
SAN FRANCISCO vs. N.Y. GIANTS
RS: Giants lead series, 10-8
PS: Series tied, 2-2;
See N.Y. Giants vs. San Francisco
SAN FRANCISCO vs. N.Y. JETS
RS: 49ers lead series, 5-1;
See N.Y. Jets vs. San Francisco
SAN FRANCISCO vs. PHILADELPHIA
RS: 49ers lead series, 11-4-1;
See Philadelphia vs. San Francisco
SAN FRANCISCO vs. PHOENIX
RS: Series tied, 8-8;
See Phoenix vs. San Francisco
SAN FRANCISCO vs. PITTSBURGH
RS: Steelers lead series, 7-6;
See Pittsburgh vs. San Francisco
SAN FRANCISCO vs. SAN DIEGO
RS: Chargers lead series, 3-2;
See San Diego vs. San Francisco
SAN FRANCISCO vs. SEATTLE
RS: 49ers lead series, 3-1
1976—49ers, 37-21 (S)
1979—Seahawks, 35-24 (SF)
1985—49ers, 19-6 (SF)
1988—49ers, 38-7 (S)
(Points—49ers 118, Seahawks 69)
SAN FRANCISCO vs. TAMPA BAY
RS: 49ers lead series, 8-1
1977—49ers, 20-10 (SF)
1978—49ers, 6-3 (SF)
1979—49ers, 23-7 (SF)
1980—Buccaneers, 24-23 (SF)
1983—49ers, 35-21 (SF)
1984—49ers, 24-17 (SF)
1986—49ers, 31-7 (TB)
1987—49ers, 24-10 (TB)
1989—49ers, 20-16 (TB)
(Points—49ers 206, Buccaneers 115)
SAN FRANCISCO vs. WASHINGTON
RS: 49ers lead series, 8-6-1
PS: Series tied, 1-1
1952—49ers, 23-17 (W)
1954—49ers, 41-7 (SF)
1955—Redskins, 7-0 (W)
1961—49ers, 35-3 (SF)
1967—Redskins, 31-28 (W)
1969—Tie, 17-17 (SF)
1970—49ers, 26-17 (SF)
1971—*49ers, 24-20 (SF)
1973—Redskins, 33-9 (W)
1976—Redskins, 24-21 (SF)
1978—Redskins, 38-20 (W)
1981—49ers, 30-17 (W)
1983—**Redskins, 24-21 (W)
1984—49ers, 37-31 (SF)
1985—49ers, 35-8 (W)
1986—Redskins, 14-6 (W)
1988—49ers, 37-21 (W)
(Points—49ers 410, Redskins 329)
*NFC Divisional Playoff
**NFC Championship

SEATTLE vs. ATLANTA
RS: Seahawks lead series, 4-0;
See Atlanta vs. Seattle
SEATTLE vs. BUFFALO
RS: Seahawks lead series, 3-1;
See Buffalo vs. Seattle
SEATTLE vs. CHICAGO
RS: Seahawks lead series, 4-1;
See Chicago vs. Seattle
SEATTLE vs. CINCINNATI
RS: Bengals lead series, 5-3
PS: Bengals lead series, 1-0;
See Cincinnati vs. Seattle
SEATTLE vs. CLEVELAND
RS: Seahawks lead series, 8-3;
See Cleveland vs. Seattle
SEATTLE vs. DALLAS
RS: Cowboys lead series, 3-1;
See Dallas vs. Seattle
SEATTLE vs. DENVER
RS: Broncos lead series, 15-10
PS: Seahawks lead series, 1-0;
See Denver vs. Seattle
SEATTLE vs. DETROIT
RS: Seahawks lead series, 3-1;
See Detroit vs. Seattle
SEATTLE vs. GREEN BAY
RS: Packers lead series, 3-2;
See Green Bay vs. Seattle
SEATTLE vs. HOUSTON
RS: Series tied, 3-3
PS: Oilers lead series, 1-0;
See Houston vs. Seattle
SEATTLE vs. INDIANAPOLIS
RS: Colts lead series, 2-0;
See Indianapolis vs. Seattle
SEATTLE vs. KANSAS CITY
RS: Chiefs lead series, 13-10;

See Kansas City vs. Seattle
SEATTLE vs. L.A. RAIDERS
RS: Seahawks lead series, 14-10
PS: Series tied, 1-1;
See L.A. Raiders vs. Seattle
SEATTLE vs. L.A. RAMS
RS: Rams lead series, 4-0;
See L.A. Rams vs. Seattle
SEATTLE vs. MIAMI
RS: Dolphins lead series, 2-1
PS: Series tied, 1-1;
See Miami vs. Seattle
SEATTLE vs. MINNESOTA
RS: Seahawks lead series, 3-1;
See Minnesota vs. Seattle
SEATTLE vs. NEW ENGLAND
RS: Patriots lead series, 6-3;
See New England vs. Seattle
SEATTLE vs. NEW ORLEANS
RS: Series tied, 2-2;
See New Orleans vs. Seattle
SEATTLE vs. N.Y. GIANTS
RS: Giants lead series, 4-2;
See N.Y. Giants vs. Seattle
SEATTLE vs. N.Y. JETS
RS: Seahawks lead series, 7-3;
See N.Y. Jets vs. Seattle
SEATTLE vs. PHILADELPHIA
RS: Eagles lead series, 3-1;
See Philadelphia vs. Seattle
SEATTLE vs. PHOENIX
Cardinals lead series, 3-0;
See Phoenix vs. Seattle
SEATTLE vs. PITTSBURGH
RS: Steelers lead series, 4-3;
See Pittsburgh vs. Seattle
SEATTLE vs. SAN DIEGO
RS: Seahawks lead series, 12-10;
See San Diego vs. Seattle
SEATTLE vs. SAN FRANCISCO
RS: 49ers lead series, 3-1;
See San Francisco vs. Seattle
SEATTLE vs. TAMPA BAY
RS: Seahawks lead series, 2-0
1976—Seahawks, 13-10 (TB)
1977—Seahawks, 30-23 (S)
(Points—Seahawks 43, Buccaneers 33)
SEATTLE vs. WASHINGTON
RS: Redskins lead series, 4-1
1976—Redskins, 31-7 (W)
1980—Seahawks, 14-0 (S)
1983—Redskins, 27-17 (S)
1986—Redskins, 19-14 (W)
1989—Redskins, 29-0 (S)
(Points—Redskins 106, Seahawks 52)

TAMPA BAY vs. ATLANTA
RS: Series tied, 4-4;
See Atlanta vs. Tampa Bay
TAMPA BAY vs. BUFFALO
RS: Buccaneers lead series, 4-1;
See Buffalo vs. Tampa Bay
TAMPA BAY vs. CHICAGO
RS: Bears lead series, 18-6;
See Chicago vs. Tampa Bay
TAMPA BAY vs. CINCINNATI
RS: Bengals lead series, 3-1;
See Cincinnati vs. Tampa Bay
TAMPA BAY vs. CLEVELAND
RS: Browns lead series, 4-0;
See Cleveland vs. Tampa Bay
TAMPA BAY vs. DALLAS
RS: Cowboys lead series, 4-0
PS: Cowboys lead series, 2-0;
See Dallas vs. Tampa Bay
TAMPA BAY vs. DENVER
RS: Broncos lead series, 2-0;
See Denver vs. Tampa Bay
TAMPA BAY vs. DETROIT
RS: Lions lead series, 13-11;
See Detroit vs. Tampa Bay
TAMPA BAY vs. GREEN BAY
RS: Packers lead series, 11-10-1;
See Green Bay vs. Tampa Bay
TAMPA BAY vs. HOUSTON
RS: Oilers lead series, 3-1;
See Houston vs. Tampa Bay
TAMPA BAY vs. INDIANAPOLIS
RS: Colts lead series, 4-1;
See Indianapolis vs. Tampa Bay
TAMPA BAY vs. KANSAS CITY
RS: Chiefs lead series, 4-2;
See Kansas City vs. Tampa Bay
TAMPA BAY vs. L.A RAIDERS
RS: Raiders lead series, 2-0;
See L.A. Raiders vs. Tampa Bay
TAMPA BAY vs. L.A. RAMS
RS: Rams lead series, 6-2
PS: Rams lead series, 1-0;
See L.A. Rams vs. Tampa Bay
TAMPA BAY vs. MIAMI
RS: Dolphins lead series, 3-1;
See Miami vs. Tampa Bay

TAMPA BAY vs. MINNESOTA
RS: Vikings lead series, 18-6;
See Minnesota vs. Tampa Bay
TAMPA BAY vs. NEW ENGLAND
RS: Patriots lead series, 3-0;
See New England vs. Tampa Bay
TAMPA BAY vs. NEW ORLEANS
RS: Saints lead series, 8-4;
See New Orleans vs. Tampa Bay
TAMPA BAY vs. N.Y. GIANTS
RS: Giants lead series, 6-3;
See N.Y. Giants vs. Tampa Bay
TAMPA BAY vs. N.Y. JETS
RS: Jets lead series, 3-1;
See N.Y. Jets vs. Tampa Bay
TAMPA BAY vs. PHILADELPHIA
RS: Eagles lead series, 3-0
PS: Buccaneers lead series, 1-0;
See Philadelphia vs. Tampa Bay
TAMPA BAY vs. PHOENIX
RS: Cardinals lead series, 6-4
See Phoenix vs. Tampa Bay
TAMPA BAY vs. PITTSBURGH
RS: Steelers lead series, 4-0;
See Pittsburgh vs. Tampa Bay
TAMPA BAY vs. SAN DIEGO
RS: Chargers lead series, 3-0;
See San Diego vs. Tampa Bay
TAMPA BAY vs. SAN FRANCISCO
RS: 49ers lead series, 8-1;
See San Francisco vs. Tampa Bay
TAMPA BAY vs. SEATTLE
RS: Seahawks lead series, 2-0;
See Seattle vs. Tampa Bay
TAMPA BAY vs. WASHINGTON
RS: Redskins lead series, 3-0
1977—Redskins, 10-0 (TB)
1982—Redskins, 21-13 (TB)
1989—Redskins, 32-28 (W)
(Points—Redskins 63, Buccaneers 41)

WASHINGTON vs. ATLANTA
RS: Redskins lead series, 10-3-1;
See Atlanta vs. Washington
WASHINGTON vs. BUFFALO
RS: Redskins lead series, 3-2;
See Buffalo vs. Washington
WASHINGTON vs. CHICAGO
RS: Bears lead series, 18-10-1
PS: Redskins lead series, 4-3;
See Chicago vs. Washington
WASHINGTON vs. CINCINNATI
RS: Redskins lead series, 3-2;
See Cincinnati vs. Washington
WASHINGTON vs. CLEVELAND
RS: Browns lead series, 32-8-1;
See Cleveland vs. Washington
WASHINGTON vs. DALLAS
RS: Cowboys lead series, 33-23-2
PS: Redskins lead series, 2-0;
See Dallas vs. Washington
WASHINGTON vs. DENVER
RS: Broncos lead series, 3-2
PS: Redskins lead series, 1-0;
See Denver vs. Washington
WASHINGTON vs. DETROIT
RS: Redskins lead series, 19-8
PS: Redskins lead series, 1-0;
See Detroit vs. Washington
WASHINGTON vs. GREEN BAY
RS: Packers lead series, 13-12-1
PS: Series tied, 1-1;
See Green Bay vs. Washington
WASHINGTON vs. HOUSTON
RS: Oilers lead series, 3-2;
See Houston vs. Washington
WASHINGTON vs. INDIANAPOLIS
RS: Colts lead series, 15-6;
See Indianapolis vs. Washington
WASHINGTON vs. KANSAS CITY
RS: Chiefs lead series, 2-1;
See Kansas City vs. Washington
WASHINGTON vs. L.A. RAIDERS
RS: Raiders lead series, 4-2
PS: Raiders lead series, 1-0;
See L.A. Raiders vs. Washington
WASHINGTON vs. L.A. RAMS
RS: Redskins lead series, 13-4-1
PS: Series tied, 2-2;
See L.A. Rams vs. Washington
WASHINGTON vs. MIAMI
RS: Dolphins lead series, 4-1
PS: Series tied, 1-1;
See Miami vs. Washington
WASHINGTON vs. MINNESOTA
RS: Redskins lead series, 5-3
PS: Series tied, 2-2;
See Minnesota vs. Washington
WASHINGTON vs. NEW ENGLAND
RS: Redskins lead series, 3-1;
See New England vs. Washington
WASHINGTON vs. NEW ORLEANS
RS: Redskins lead series, 10-4;

See New Orleans vs. Washington
WASHINGTON vs. N.Y. GIANTS
RS: Redskins lead series, 62-49-3
PS: Series tied, 1-1;
See N.Y. Giants vs. Washington
WASHINGTON vs. N.Y. JETS
RS: Redskins lead series, 4-0;
See N.Y. Jets vs. Washington
WASHINGTON vs. PHILADELPHIA
RS: Redskins lead series, 63-41-5;
See Philadelphia vs. Washington
WASHINGTON vs. PHOENIX
RS: Redskins lead series, 56-33-2;
See Phoenix vs. Washington
WASHINGTON vs. PITTSBURGH
RS: Redskins lead series, 41-27-3;
See Pittsburgh vs. Washington
WASHINGTON vs. SAN DIEGO
RS: Redskins lead series, 5-0;
See San Diego vs. Washington
WASHINGTON vs. SAN FRANCISCO
RS: 49ers lead series, 8-6-1
PS: Series tied, 1-1;
See San Francisco vs. Washington
WASHINGTON vs. SEATTLE
RS: Redskins lead series, 4-1;
See Seattle vs. Washington
WASHINGTON vs. TAMPA BAY
RS: Redskins lead series, 3-0;
See Tampa Bay vs. Washington

SUPER BOWL SUMMARIES

Results

Season	Date	Winner (Share)	Loser (Share)	Score	Site	Attendance
XXIV	1-28-90	San Francisco ($36,000)	Denver ($18,000)	55-10	New Orleans	72,919
XXIII	1-22-89	San Francisco ($36,000)	Cincinnati ($18,000)	20-16	Miami	75,129
XXII	1-31-88	Washington ($36,000)	Denver ($18,000)	42-10	San Diego	73,302
XXI	1-25-87	N.Y. Giants ($36,000)	Denver ($18,000)	39-20	Pasadena	101,063
XX	1-26-86	Chicago ($36,000)	New England ($18,000)	46-10	New Orleans	73,818
XIX	1-20-85	San Francisco ($36,000)	Miami ($18,000)	38-16	Stanford	84,059
XVIII	1-22-84	L.A. Raiders ($36,000)	Washington ($18,000)	38-9	Tampa	72,920
XVII	1-30-83	Washington ($36,000)	Miami ($18,000)	27-17	Pasadena	103,667
XVI	1-24-82	San Francisco ($18,000)	Cincinnati ($9,000)	26-21	Pontiac	81,270
XV	1-25-81	Oakland ($18,000)	Philadelphia ($9,000)	27-10	New Orleans	76,135
XIV	1-20-80	Pittsburgh ($18,000)	Los Angeles ($9,000)	31-19	Pasadena	103,985
XIII	1-21-79	Pittsburgh ($18,000)	Dallas ($9,000)	35-31	Miami	79,484
XII	1-15-78	Dallas ($18,000)	Denver ($9,000)	27-10	New Orleans	75,583
XI	1-9-77	Oakland ($15,000)	Minnesota ($7,500)	32-14	Pasadena	103,438
X	1-18-76	Pittsburgh ($15,000)	Dallas ($7,500)	21-17	Miami	80,187
IX	1-12-75	Pittsburgh ($15,000)	Minnesota ($7,500)	16-6	New Orleans	80,997
VIII	1-13-74	Miami ($15,000)	Minnesota ($7,500)	24-7	Houston	71,882
VII	1-14-73	Miami ($15,000)	Washington ($7,500)	14-7	Los Angeles	90,182
VI	1-16-72	Dallas ($15,000)	Miami ($7,500)	24-3	New Orleans	81,023
V	1-17-71	Baltimore ($15,000)	Dallas ($7,500)	16-13	Miami	79,204
IV	1-11-70	Kansas City ($15,000)	Minnesota ($7,500)	23-7	New Orleans	80,562
III	1-12-69	N.Y. Jets ($15,000)	Baltimore ($7,500)	16-7	Miami	75,389
II	1-14-68	Green Bay ($15,000)	Oakland ($7,500)	33-14	Miami	75,546
I	1-15-67	Green Bay ($15,000)	Kansas City ($7,500)	35-10	Los Angeles	61,946

Super Bowl Composite Standings

	W	L	Pct.	Pts.	OP
Pittsburgh Steelers	4	0	1.000	103	73
San Francisco 49ers	4	0	1.000	139	63
Green Bay Packers	2	0	1.000	68	24
Chicago Bears	1	0	1.000	46	10
New York Giants	1	0	1.000	39	20
New York Jets	1	0	1.000	16	7
Oakland/L.A. Raiders	3	1	.750	111	66
Washington Redskins	2	2	.500	85	79
Baltimore Colts	1	1	.500	23	29
Kansas City Chiefs	1	1	.500	33	42
Dallas Cowboys	2	3	.400	112	85
Miami Dolphins	2	3	.400	74	103
Los Angeles Rams	0	1	.000	19	31
New England Patriots	0	1	.000	10	46
Philadelphia Eagles	0	1	.000	10	27
Cincinnati Bengals	0	2	.000	37	46
Denver Broncos	0	4	.000	50	163
Minnesota Vikings	0	4	.000	34	95

Super Bowl Most Valuable Players

Super Bowl I — QB Bart Starr, Green Bay
Super Bowl II — QB Bart Starr, Green Bay
Super Bowl III — QB Joe Namath, New York Jets
Super Bowl IV — QB Len Dawson, Kansas City
Super Bowl V — LB Chuck Howley, Dallas
Super Bowl VI — QB Roger Staubach, Dallas
Super Bowl VII — S Jake Scott, Miami
Super Bowl VIII — RB Larry Csonka, Miami
Super Bowl IX — RB Franco Harris, Pittsburgh
Super Bowl X — WR Lynn Swann, Pittsburgh
Super Bowl XI — WR Fred Biletnikoff, Oakland
Super Bowl XII — DT Randy White and DE Harvey Martin, Dallas
Super Bowl XIII — QB Terry Bradshaw, Pittsburgh
Super Bowl XIV — QB Terry Bradshaw, Pittsburgh
Super Bowl XV — QB Jim Plunkett, Oakland
Super Bowl XVI — QB Joe Montana, San Francisco
Super Bowl XVII — RB John Riggins, Washington
Super Bowl XVIII — RB Marcus Allen, Los Angeles Raiders
Super Bowl XIX — QB Joe Montana, San Francisco
Super Bowl XX — DE Richard Dent, Chicago
Super Bowl XXI — QB Phil Simms, New York Giants
Super Bowl XXII — QB Doug Williams, Washington
Super Bowl XXIII — WR Jerry Rice, San Francisco
Super Bowl XXIV — QB Joe Montana, San Francisco

Super Bowl XXIV

Louisiana Superdome, New Orleans, Louisiana   January 28, 1990
Attendance: 72,919

SAN FRANCISCO 55, DENVER 10—NFC titlist San Francisco won its fourth Super Bowl championship with a 55-10 victory over AFC champion Denver. The 49ers, who also won Super Bowls XVI, XIX, and XXIII, tied the Pittsburgh Steelers for most Super Bowl victories. The Steelers captured Super Bowls IX, X, XIII, and XIV. San Francisco's 55 points broke the previous Super Bowl scoring mark of 46 points by Chicago in Super Bowl XX. San Francisco scored touchdowns on four of its six first-half possessons to hold a 27-3 lead at halftime. The 49ers' first half scoring drives were lengthy and time-consuming (10 plays for 66 yards, 10 for 54, 14 for 69, and 5 for 59). Interceptions by Michael Walter and Chet Brooks ended the Broncos' first two possessions of the second half. San Francisco quarterback Joe Montana was named the Super Bowl most valuable player for a record third time. Montana completed 22 of 29 passes for 297 yards and a Super Bowl-record five touchdowns (old record: four; Terry Bradshaw, Pittsburgh, Super Bowl XIII, and Doug Williams, Washington, Super Bowl XXII). Jerry Rice, Super Bowl XXIII most valuable player, caught seven passes for 148 yards and three touchdowns. The 49ers' domination included first downs (28 to 12), net yards (461 to 167), and time of possession (39:31 to 20:29).

San Francisco (55)	Offense	Denver (10)
John Taylor	WR	Vance Johnson
Bubba Paris	LT	Gerald Perry
Guy McIntyre	LG	Jim Juriga
Jesse Sapolu	C	Keith Kartz
Bruce Collie	RG	Doug Widell
Harris Barton	RT	Ken Lanier
Brent Jones	TE	Orson Mobley
Jerry Rice	WR	Mark Jackson
Joe Montana	QB	John Elway
Roger Craig	RB	Steve Sewell
Tom Rathman	RB	Bobby Humphrey
	Defense	
Pierce Holt	LE	Alphonso Carreker
Michael Carter	NT	Greg Kragen
Kevin Fagan	RE	Ron Holmes
Charles Haley	LOLB	Michael Brooks
Matt Millen	LILB	Rick Dennison
Michael Walter	RILB	Karl Mecklenburg
Keena Turner	ROLB	Simon Fletcher
Darryl Pollard	LCB	Tyrone Braxton
Don Griffin	RCB	Wymon Henderson
Chet Brooks	SS	Dennis Smith
Ronnie Lott	FS	Steve Atwater

Substitutions

San Francisco—Offense: K—Mike Cofer. P—Barry Helton. QB—Steve Young. RB—Terrence Flager, Harry Sydney, Spencer Tillman. WR—Mike Sherrard, Mike Wilson. TE—Wesley Walls, Jamie Williams. C—Chuck Thomas. G—Terry Tausch. T—Steve Wallace. Defense: E—Larry Roberts, Danny Stubbs. NT—Jim Burt, Pete Kugler. LB—Keith DeLong, Steve Hendrickson, Bill Romanowski. CB—Tim McKyer, Eric Wright. S—Johnny Jackson. DNP: None.

Denver—Offense: K—David Treadwell. P—Mike Horan. QB—Gary Kubiak. RB—Ken Bell, Melvin Bratton, Sammy Winder. WR—Ricky Nattiel, Mike Young. TE—Paul Green, Clarence Kay. C—Keith Bishop. G—Monte Smith. Defense: E—Warren Powers, Andre Townsend. NT—Brad Henke. LB—Scott Curtis, Bruce Klostermann, Tim Lucas, Marc Munford. CB—Darren Carrington, Mark Haynes. S—Kip Corrington, Randy Robbins. DNP: None

Officials

Referee—Dick Jorgensen. Umpire—Hendi Ancich. Line Judge—Ron Blum. Head Linesman—Earnie Frantz. Back Judge—Al Jury. Field Judge—Don

Orr. Side Judge—Gerry Austin. Replay Official—Al Sabato.

Scoring

San Francisco (NFC)	13	14	14	14	— 55
Denver (AFC)	3	0	7	0	— 10

SF —Rice 20 pass from Montana (Cofer kick)
Den—FG Treadwell 42
SF —Jones 7 pass from Montana (kick failed)
SF —Rathman 1 run (Cofer kick)
SF —Rice 38 pass from Montana (Cofer kick)
SF —Rice 28 pass from Montana (Cofer kick)
SF —Taylor 35 pass from Montana (Cofer kick)
Den—Elway 3 run (Treadwell kick)
SF —Rathman 3 run (Cofer kick)
SF —Craig 1 run (Cofer kick)

Team Statistics

	San Francisco	Denver
Total First Downs	28	12
First Downs Rushing	14	5
First Downs Passing	14	6
First Downs Penalty	0	1
Total Net Yardage	461	167
Total Offensive Plays	77	52
Average Gain per Offensive Play	6.0	3.2
Rushes	44	17
Yards Gained Rushing (net)	144	64
Average Yards per Rush	3.3	3.8
Passes Attempted	32	29
Passes Completed	24	11
Had Intercepted	0	2
Tackled Attempting to Pass	1	6
Yards Lost Attempting to Pass	0	33
Yards Gained Passing (net)	317	103
Punts	4	6
Average Distance	39.5	38.5
Punt Returns	3	2
Punt Return Yardage	38	11
Kickoff Returns	3	9
Kickoff Return Yardage	49	196
Interception Return Yardage	42	0
Total Return Yardage	129	207
Fumbles	0	3
Own Fumbles Recovered	0	1
Opponents Fumbles Recovered	2	0
Penalties	4	0
Yards Penalized	38	0
Total Points Scored	55	10
Touchdowns Rushing	3	1
Touchdowns Passing	5	0
Touchdowns Returns	0	0
Extra Points	7	1
Field Goals	0	1
Field Goals Attempted	0	1
Safeties	0	0
Third Down Efficiency	8/15	3/11
Fourth Down Efficiency	2/2	0/0
Time of Possession	39:31	20:29

Individual Statistics

Rushing

San Fran.	No.	Yds.	LG	TD
Craig	20	69	18	1
Rathman	11	38	18	2
Montana	2	15	10	0
Flagler	6	14	10	0
Young	4	6	11	0
Sydney	1	2	2	0

Denver	No.	Yds.	LG	TD
Humphrey	12	61	34	0
Elway	4	8	3	1
Winder	1	−5	−5	0

Passing

San Fran.	Att.	Comp.	Yds.	TD	Int.
Montana	29	22	297	5	0
Young	3	2	20	0	0

Denver	Att.	Comp.	Yds.	TD	Int.
Elway	26	10	108	0	2
Kubiak	3	1	28	0	0

Receiving

San Fran.	No.	Yds.	LG	TD
Rice	7	148	38	3
Craig	5	34	12	0
Rathman	4	43	18	0
Taylor	3	49	35	1
Sherrard	1	13	13	0
Walls	1	9	9	0
Jones	1	7	7	1
Sydney	1	7	7	0
Williams	1	7	7	0

Denver	No.	Yds.	LG	TD
Humphrey	3	38	27	0
Sewell	2	22	12	0
Johnson	2	21	13	0
Nattiel	1	28	28	0
Bratton	1	14	14	0
Winder	1	7	7	0
Kay	1	6	6	0

Interceptions

San Fran.	No.	Yds.	LG	TD
Brooks	1	38	38	0
Walter	1	4	4	0

Denver	No.	Yds.	LG	TD
None				

Punting

San Fran.	No.	Avg.	LG	Blk.
Helton	4	39.5	47	0

Denver	No.	Avg.	LG	Blk.
Horan	6	38.5	43	0

Punt Returns

San Fran.	No.	FC	Yds.	LG	TD
Taylor	3	2	38	17	0

Denver	No.	FC	Yds.	LG	TD
Johnson	2	1	11	7	0

Kickoff Returns

San Fran.	No.	Yds.	LG	TD
Flagler	3	49	22	0

Denver	No.	Yds.	LG	TD
Carrington	6	146	39	0
Bell	2	41	24	0
Bratton	1	9	9	0

Super Bowl XXIII

Joe Robbie Stadium, Miami, Florida — January 22, 1989
Attendance: 75,129

SAN FRANCISCO 20, CINCINNATI 16—NFC champion San Francisco captured its third Super Bowl of the 1980s by defeating AFC champion Cincinnati 20-16. The 49ers, who also won Super Bowls XVI and XIX, are the first NFC team to win three Super Bowls. Pittsburgh with four Super Bowl titles (IX, X, XIII, and XIV) and the Oakland/Los Angeles Raiders with three (XI, XV, and XVIII) lead AFC franchises. Even though San Francisco held an advantage in total net yards (453 to 229), the 49ers found themselves trailing the Bengals late in the game. With the score tied 13-13, Cincinnati took a 16-13 lead on Jim Breech's 40-yard field goal with 3:20 remaining. It was Breech's third field goal of the day and came after successful earlier attempts of 34 and 43 yards. The 49ers started their winning drive at their own 8-yard line. Over the next 11 plays, San Francisco covered 92 yards with the decisive score coming on a 10-yard pass from quarterback Joe Montana to wide receiver John Taylor with 34 seconds remaining. At halftime, the score was 3-3, which represented the first time in Super Bowl history the score was tied at intermission. After the teams traded third-period field goals, the Bengals jumped ahead 13-6 on Stanford Jennings's 93-yard kickoff return for a touchdown with 34 seconds remaining in the quarter. The 49ers didn't waste any time coming back as they covered 85 yards in four plays, concluding with Montana's 14-yard scoring pass to Rice 57 seconds into the final stanza. Rice was named the game's most valuable player after compiling 11 catches for a Super Bowl record 215 yards. Montana completed 23 of 36 passes for a Super Bowl record 357 yards and two touchdowns.

Scoring

Cincinnati (AFC)	0	3	10	3	— 16
San Francisco (NFC)	3	0	3	14	— 20

SF —FG Cofer 41
Cin—FG Breech 34
Cin—FG Breech 43
SF —FG Cofer 32
Cin—Jennings 93 kickoff return (Breech kick)
SF —Rice 14 pass from Montana (Cofer kick)
Cin—FG Breech 40
SF —Taylor 10 pass from Montana (Cofer kick)

Super Bowl XXII

San Diego Jack Murphy Stadium, San Diego, California — January 31, 1988
Attendance: 73,302

WASHINGTON 42, DENVER 10—NFC champion Washington won Super Bowl XXII and its second NFL championship of the 1980s with a 42-10 decision over AFC champion Denver. The Redskins, who also won Super Bowl XVII, enjoyed a record-setting second quarter en route to the victory. The Broncos broke in front 10-0 when quarterback John Elway threw a 56-yard touchdown pass to wide receiver Ricky Nattiel on the Broncos' first play from scrimmage. Following a Washington punt, Denver's Rich Karlis kicked a 24-yard field goal to cap a six-play, 61-yard scoring drive. The Redskins then erupted for 35 points on five straight possessions in the second period and coasted thereafter. The 35 points established an NFL postseason mark for most points scored in a period, bettering the previous total of 21 by San Francisco in Super Bowl XIX and Chicago in Super Bowl XX. Redskins quarterback Doug Williams led the second-period explosion by throwing a Super Bowl record-tying four touchdown passes, including 80- and 50-yarders to wide receiver Ricky Sanders, a 27-yarder to wide receiver Gary Clark, and an 8-yarder to tight end Clint Didier. Washington scored five touchdowns in 18 plays with total time of possession of only 5:47. Overall, Williams completed 18 of 29 passes for 340 yards and was named the game's most valuable player. His pass-yardage total eclipsed the previous Super Bowl record of 331 yards by Joe Montana of San Francisco in Super Bowl XIX. Sanders ended with 193 yards on eight catches, breaking the previous Super Bowl yardage record of 161 yards by Lynn Swann of Pittsburgh in Game X. Rookie running back Timmy Smith was the game's leading rusher with 22 carries for a Super Bowl record 204 yards, breaking the previous mark of 191 yards by Marcus Allen of the Raiders in Game XVIII. Smith also scored twice on runs of 58 and 4 yards. Washington's six touchdowns and 602 total yards gained also set Super Bowl records. Redskins cornerback Barry Wilburn had two of the team's three interceptions, and strong safety Alvin Walton had two of Washington's five sacks.

Washington (NFC)	0	35	0	7	— 42
Denver (AFC)	10	0	0	0	— 10

Den —Nattiel 56 pass from Elway (Karlis kick)
Den —FG Karlis 24
Wash—Sanders 80 pass from Williams (Haji-Sheikh kick)
Wash—Clark 27 pass from Williams (Haji-Sheikh kick)
Wash—Smith 58 run (Haji-Sheikh kick)
Wash—Sanders 50 pass from Williams (Haji-Sheikh kick)
Wash—Didier 8 pass from Williams (Haji-Sheikh kick)
Wash—Smith 4 run (Haji-Sheikh kick)

Super Bowl XXI

Rose Bowl, Pasadena, California — January 25, 1987
Attendance: 101,063

NEW YORK GIANTS 39, DENVER 20—The NFC champion New York Giants captured their first NFL title since 1956 when they downed the AFC champion Denver Broncos, 39-20, in Super Bowl XXI. The victory marked the NFC's fifth NFL title in the past six seasons. The Broncos, behind the passing of quarterback John Elway, who was 13 of 20 for 187 yards in the first half, held a 10-9 lead at intermission, the narrowest halftime margin in Super Bowl history. Denver's Rich Karlis opened the scoring with a Super Bowl record-tying 48-yard field goal. New York drove 78 yards in nine plays on the next series to take a 7-3 lead on quarterback Phil Simms's six-yard touchdown pass to tight end Zeke Mowatt. The Broncos came right back with a 58-yard scoring drive on six plays capped by Elway's four-yard touchdown run. The only scoring in the second period was the sack of Elway in the end zone by defensive end George Martin for a New York safety. The Giants produced a key defensive stand early in the second quarter when the Broncos had a first down at the New York one-yard line, but failed to score on three running plays and Karlis's 23-yard missed field-goal attempt. The Giants took command of the game in the third period en route to a 30-point second half, the most ever scored in one half of Super Bowl play. New York took the lead for good on tight end Mark Bavaro's 13-yard touchdown catch 4:52 into the third period. The nine-play, 63-yard scoring drive included the successful conversion of a fourth down and one play on the New York 46-yard line. Denver was limited to only two net yards on seven offensive plays in the third period. Simms set Super Bowl records for most consecutive completions (10) and highest completion percentage (88 percent on 22 completions in 25 attempts). He also passed for 268 yards and three touchdowns and was named the game's most valuable player. New York running back Joe Morris was the game's leading rusher with 20 carries for 67 yards. Denver wide receiver Vance Johnson led all receivers with five catches for 121 yards. The Giants defeated their three playoff opponents by a cumulative total of 82 points (New York 105, opponents 23), the largest such margin by a Super Bowl winner.

Denver (AFC)	10	0	0	10	— 20
N.Y. Giants (NFC)	7	2	17	13	— 39

Den —FG Karlis 48
NYG—Mowatt 6 pass from Simms (Allegre kick)
Den —Elway 4 run (Karlis kick)
NYG—Safety, Martin tackled Elway in end zone
NYG—Bavaro 13 pass from Simms (Allegre kick)
NYG—FG Allegre 21
NYG—Morris 1 run (Allegre kick)
NYG—McConkey 6 pass from Simms (Allegre kick)
Den —FG Karlis 28
NYG—Anderson 2 run (kick failed)
Den —V. Johnson 47 pass from Elway (Karlis kick)

Super Bowl XX

Louisiana Superdome, New Orleans, Louisiana   January 26, 1986
Attendance: 73,818

CHICAGO 46, NEW ENGLAND 10—The NFC champion Chicago Bears, seeking their first NFL title since 1963, scored a Super Bowl-record 46 points in downing AFC champion New England 46-10 in Super Bowl XX. The previous record for most points in a Super Bowl was 38, shared by San Francisco in XIX and the Los Angeles Raiders in XVIII. The Bears' league-leading defense tied the Super Bowl record for sacks (7) and limited the Patriots to a record-low seven yards rushing. New England took the quickest lead in Super Bowl history when Tony Franklin kicked a 36-yard field goal with 1:19 elapsed in the first period. The score came about because of Larry McGrew's fumble recovery at the Chicago 19-yard line. However, the Bears rebounded for a 23-3 first-half lead, while building a yardage advantage of 237 total yards to New England's minus 19. Running back Matt Suhey rushed eight times for 37 yards, including an 11-yard touchdown run, and caught one pass for 24 yards in the first half. After the Patriots first drive of the second half ended with a punt to the Bears' 4-yard line, Chicago marched 96 yards in nine plays with quarterback Jim McMahon's one-yard scoring run capping the drive. McMahon became the first quarterback in Super Bowl history to rush for a pair of touchdowns. The Bears completed their scoring via a 28-yard interception return by reserve cornerback Reggie Phillips, a one-yard run by defensive tackle/fullback William Perry, and a safety when defensive end Henry Waechter tackled Patriots quarterback Steve Grogan in the end zone. Bears defensive end Richard Dent became the fourth defender to be named the game's most valuable player after contributing 1½ sacks. The Bears' victory margin of 36 points was the largest in Super Bowl history, bettering the previous mark of 29 by the Los Angeles Raiders when they topped Washington 38-9 in Game XVIII. McMahon completed 12 of 20 passes for 256 yards before leaving the game in the fourth period with a wrist injury. The NFL's all-time leading rusher, Bears running back Walter Payton, carried 22 times for 61 yards. Wide receiver Willie Gault caught four passes for 129 yards, the fourth-most receiving yards in a Super Bowl. Chicago coach Mike Ditka became the second man (Tom Flores of Raiders was the other) who played in a Super Bowl and coached a team to a victory in the game.

Chicago (NFC)	13	10	21	2	— 46
New England (AFC)	3	0	0	7	— 10

NE —FG Franklin 36
Chi—FG Butler 28
Chi—FG Butler 24
Chi—Suhey 11 run (Butler kick)
Chi—McMahon 2 run (Butler kick)
Chi—FG Butler 24
Chi—McMahon 1 run (Butler kick)
Chi—Phillips 28 interception return (Butler kick)
Chi—Perry 1 run (Butler kick)
NE —Fryar 8 pass from Grogan (Franklin kick)
Chi—Safety, Waechter tackled Grogan in end zone

Super Bowl XIX

Stanford Stadium, Stanford, California   January 20, 1985
Attendance: 84,059

SAN FRANCISCO 38, MIAMI 16—The San Francisco 49ers captured their second Super Bowl title with a dominating offense and a defense that tamed Miami's explosive passing attack. The Dolphins held a 10-7 lead at the end of the first period, which represented the most points scored by two teams in an opening quarter of a Super Bowl. However, the 49ers used excellent field position in the second period to build a 28-16 halftime lead. Running back Roger Craig set a Super Bowl record by scoring three touchdowns on pass receptions of 8 and 16 yards and a run of 2 yards. San Francisco's Joe Montana was voted the game's most valuable player. He joined Green Bay's Bart Starr and Pittsburgh's Terry Bradshaw as the only two-time Super Bowl most valuable players. Montana completed 24 of 35 passes for a Super Bowl-record 331 yards and three touchdowns, and rushed five times for 59 yards, including a six-yard touchdown. Craig had 58 yards on 15 carries and caught seven passes for 77 yards. Wendell Tyler rushed 13 times for 65 yards and had four catches for 70 yards. Dwight Clark had six receptions for 77 yards, while Russ Francis had five for 60. San Francisco's 537 total net yards bettered the previous Super Bowl record of 429 yards by Oakland in Super Bowl XI. The 49ers also held a time of possession advantage over the Dolphins of 37:11 to 22:49.

Miami (AFC)	10	6	0	0	— 16
San Francisco (NFC)	7	21	10	0	— 38

Mia—FG von Schamann 37
SF —Monroe 33 pass from Montana (Wersching kick)
Mia—D. Johnson 2 pass from Marino (von Schamann kick)
SF —Craig 8 pass from Montana (Wersching kick)
SF —Montana 6 run (Wersching kick)
SF —Craig 2 run (Wersching kick)
Mia—FG von Schamann 31
Mia—FG von Schamann 30
SF —FG Wersching 27
SF —Craig 16 pass from Montana (Wersching kick)

Super Bowl XVIII

Tampa Stadium, Tampa, Florida   January 22, 1984
Attendance: 72,920

LOS ANGELES RAIDERS 38, WASHINGTON 9—The Los Angeles Raiders dominated the Washington Redskins from the beginning in Super Bowl XVIII and achieved the most lopsided victory in Super Bowl history, surpassing Green Bay's 35-10 win over Kansas City in Super Bowl I. The Raiders took a 7-0 lead 4:52 into the game when Derrick Jensen blocked a Jeff Hayes punt and recovered it in the end zone for a touchdown. With 9:14 remaining in the first half, Raiders quarterback Jim Plunkett threw a 12-yard touchdown pass to wide receiver Cliff Branch to complete a three-play, 65-yard drive. Washington cut the Raiders' lead to 14-3 on a 24-yard field goal by Mark Moseley. With seven seconds left in the first half, Raiders linebacker Jack Squirek intercepted a Joe Theismann pass at the Redskins' 5-yard line and ran it in for a touchdown to give Los Angeles a 21-3 halftime lead. In the third period, running back Marcus Allen, who rushed for a Super Bowl record 191 yards on 20 carries, increased the Raiders' lead to 35-9 on touchdown runs of 5 and 74 yards, the latter erasing the previous Super Bowl record of 58 yards set by Baltimore's Tom Matte in Game III. Allen was named the game's most valuable player. The victory over Washington raised Raiders coach Tom Flores's playoff record to 8-1, including a 27-10 win against Philadelphia in Super Bowl XV. The 38 points scored by the Raiders was the highest total by a Super Bowl team. The previous high was 35 points by Green Bay in Game I and Pittsburgh in Game XIII.

Washington (NFC)	0	3	6	0	— 9
L.A. Raiders (AFC)	7	14	14	3	— 38

Raiders—Jensen recovered blocked punt in end zone (Bahr kick)
Raiders—Branch 12 pass from Plunkett (Bahr kick)
Wash —FG Moseley 24
Raiders—Squirek 5 interception return (Bahr kick)
Wash —Riggins 1 run (kick blocked)
Raiders—Allen 5 run (Bahr kick)
Raiders—Allen 74 run (Bahr kick)
Raiders—FG Bahr 21

Super Bowl XVII

Rose Bowl, Pasadena, California   January 30, 1983
Attendance: 103,667

WASHINGTON 27, MIAMI 17—Fullback John Riggins's Super Bowl record 166 yards on 38 carries sparked Washington to a 27-17 victory over AFC champion Miami. It was Riggins's fourth straight 100-yard rushing game during the playoffs, also a record. The win marked Washington's first NFL title since 1942, and was only the second time in Super Bowl history NFC teams scored consecutive victories (Green Bay did it in Super Bowls I and II and San Francisco won Super Bowl XVI). The Redskins, under second-year head coach Joe Gibbs, used a balanced offense that accounted for 400 total yards (a Super Bowl record 276 yards rushing and 124 passing), second in Super Bowl history to 429 yards by Oakland in Super Bowl XI. The Dolphins built a 17-10 halftime lead on a 76-yard touchdown pass from quarterback David Woodley to wide receiver Jimmy Cefalo 6:49 into the first period, a 20-yard field goal by Uwe von Schamann with 6:00 left in the half, and a Super Bowl record 98-yard kickoff return by Fulton Walker with 1:38 remaining. Washington had tied the score at 10-10 with 1:51 left on a four-yard touchdown pass from Joe Theismann to wide receiver Alvin Garrett. Mark Moseley started the Redskins' scoring with a 31-yard field goal early in the second period, and added a 20-yarder midway through the third period to cut the Dolphins' lead to 17-13. Riggins, who was voted the game's most valuable player, gave Washington its first lead of the game with 10:01 left when he ran 43 yards off left tackle for a touchdown on a fourth-and-one situation. Wide receiver Charlie Brown caught a six-yard scoring pass from Theismann with 1:55 left to complete the scoring. The Dolphins managed only 176 yards (142 in first half). Theismann completed 15 of 23 passes for 143 yards, two touchdowns, and had two interceptions. For Miami, Woodley was 4 of 14 for 97 yards, with one touchdown, and one interception. Don Strock was 0 for 3 in relief.

Miami (AFC)	7	10	0	0	— 17
Washington (NFC)	0	10	3	14	— 27

Mia —Cefalo 76 pass from Woodley (von Schamann kick)
Wash—FG Moseley 31
Mia —FG von Schamann 20
Wash—Garrett 4 pass from Theismann (Moseley kick)
Mia —Walker 98 kickoff return (von Schamann kick)
Wash—FG Moseley 20
Wash—Riggins 43 run (Moseley kick)
Wash—Brown 6 pass from Theismann (Moseley kick)

Super Bowl XVI

Pontiac Silverdome, Pontiac, Michigan   January 24, 1982
Attendance: 81,270

SAN FRANCISCO 26, CINCINNATI 21—Ray Wersching's Super Bowl record-tying four field goals and Joe Montana's controlled passing helped lift the San Francisco 49ers to their first NFL championship with a 26-21 victory over Cincinnati. The 49ers built a game-record 20-0 halftime lead via Montana's one-yard touchdown run, which capped an 11-play, 68-yard drive; fullback Earl Cooper's 11-yard scoring pass from Montana, which climaxed a Super Bowl record 92-yard drive on 12 plays; and Wersching's 22- and 26-yard field goals. The Bengals rebounded in the second half, closing the gap to 20-14 on quarterback Ken Anderson's five-yard run and Dan Ross's four-yard reception from Anderson, who established Super Bowl passing records for completions (25) and completion percentage (73.5 percent on 25 of 34). Wersching added early fourth-period field goals of 40 and 23 yards to increase the 49ers' lead to 26-14. The Bengals managed to score on an Anderson-to-Ross three-yard pass with only 16 seconds remaining. Ross set a Super Bowl record with 11 receptions for 104 yards. Montana, the game's most valuable player, completed 14 of 22 passes for 157 yards. Cincinnati compiled 356 yards to San Francisco's 275, which marked the first time in Super Bowl history that the team that gained the most yards from scrimmage lost the game.

San Francisco (NFC)	7	13	0	6	— 26
Cincinnati (AFC)	0	0	7	14	— 21

SF —Montana 1 run (Wersching kick)
SF —Cooper 11 pass from Montana (Wersching kick)
SF —FG Wersching 22
SF —FG Wersching 26
Cin —Anderson 5 run (Breech kick)
Cin —Ross 4 pass from Anderson (Breech kick)
SF —FG Wersching 40
SF —FG Wersching 23
Cin —Ross 3 pass from Anderson (Breech kick)

Super Bowl XV

Louisiana Superdome, New Orleans, Louisiana   January 25, 1981
Attendance: 76,135

OAKLAND 27, PHILADELPHIA 10—Jim Plunkett threw three touchdown passes, including an 80-yarder to Kenny King, as the Raiders became the first wild card team to win the Super Bowl. Plunkett's touchdown bomb to King—the longest play in Super Bowl history—gave Oakland a decisive 14-0 lead with nine seconds left in the first period. Linebacker Rod Martin had set up Oakland's first touchdown, a two-yard reception by Cliff Branch, with a 17-yard interception return to the Eagles' 30 yard line. The Eagles never recovered from that early deficit, managing only a Tony Franklin field goal (30 yards) and an eight-yard touchdown pass from Ron Jaworski to Keith Krepfle the rest of the game. Plunkett, who became a starter in the sixth game of the season, completed 13 of 21 for 261 yards and was named the game's most valuable player. Oakland won 9 of 11 games with Plunkett starting, but that was good enough only for second place in the AFC West, although they tied division winner San Diego with an 11-5 record. The Raiders, who had previously won Super Bowl XI over Minnesota, had to win three playoff games to get to the championship game. Oakland defeated Houston 27-7 at home followed by road victories over Cleveland, 14-12 and San Diego, 34-27. Oakland's Mark van Eeghen was the game's leading rusher with 75 yards on 18 carries. Philadelphia's Wilbert Montgomery led all receivers with six receptions for 91 yards. Branch had five for 67 yards and Harold Carmichael of Philadelphia five for 83. Martin finished the game with three interceptions, a Super Bowl record.

Oakland (AFC)	14	0	10	3	— 27
Philadelphia (NFC)	0	3	0	7	— 10

Oak—Branch 2 pass from Plunkett (Bahr kick)
Oak—King 80 pass from Plunkett (Bahr kick)
Phil—FG Franklin 30
Oak—Branch 29 pass from Plunkett (Bahr kick)
Oak—FG Bahr 46
Phil—Krepfle 8 pass from Jaworski (Franklin kick)
Oak—FG Bahr 35

Super Bowl XIV

Rose Bowl, Pasadena, California   January 20, 1980
Attendance: 103,985

PITTSBURGH 31, LOS ANGELES 19—Terry Bradshaw completed 14 of 21 passes for 309 yards and set two passing records as the Steelers became the first team to win four Super Bowls. Despite three interceptions by the Rams, Bradshaw kept his poise and brought the Steelers from behind twice in the second half. Trailing 13-10 at halftime, Pittsburgh went ahead 17-13 when Bradshaw hit Lynn Swann with a 47-yard touchdown pass after 2:48 of the third quarter. On the Rams' next possession Vince Ferragamo, who completed 15 of 25 passes for 212 yards, responded with a 50-yard pass to Billy Waddy that moved Los Angeles from its own 26 to the Steelers' 24. On the following play, Lawrence McCutcheon connected with Ron Smith on a halfback option pass that gave the Rams a 19-17 lead. On Pittsburgh's initial possession of the final period, Bradshaw threw a 73-yard scoring pass to John Stallworth to put the Steelers in front to stay, 24-19. Franco Harris scored on a one-yard run later in the quarter to seal the verdict. A 45-yard pass from Bradshaw to Stallworth was the key play in the drive to Harris's score. Bradshaw, the game's most valuable player for the second straight year, set career Super Bowl records for most touchdown passes (nine) and most passing yards (932). Larry Anderson gave the Steelers excellent field position throughout the game with five kickoff returns for a record 162 yards.

Los Angeles (NFC)	7	6	6	0	— 19
Pittsburgh (AFC)	3	7	7	14	— 31

Pitt—FG Bahr 41
LA —Bryant 1 run (Corral kick)
Pitt—Harris 1 run (Bahr kick)
LA —FG Corral 31
LA —FG Corral 45
Pitt—Swann 47 pass from Bradshaw (Bahr kick)
LA —Smith 24 pass from McCutchen (kick failed)
Pitt—Stallworth 73 pass from Bradshaw (Bahr kick)
Pitt—Harris 1 run (Bahr kick)

Super Bowl XIII

Orange Bowl, Miami, Florida   January 21, 1979
Attendance: 79,484

PITTSBURGH 35, DALLAS 31—Terry Bradshaw threw a record four touchdown passes to lead the Steelers to victory. The Steelers became the first team to win three Super Bowls, mostly because of Bradshaw's accurate arm. Bradshaw, voted the game's most valuable player, completed 17 of 30 passes for 318 yards, a personal high. Four of those passes were for touchdowns—two to John Stallworth and the third, with 26 seconds remaining in the second period, to Rocky Bleier for a 21-14 halftime lead. The Cowboys scored twice before intermission on Roger Staubach's 39-yard pass to Tony Hill and a 37-yard fumble return by linebacker Mike Hegman, who stole the ball from Bradshaw. The Steelers broke open the contest with two touchdowns in a span of 19 seconds midway through the final period. Franco Harris rambled 22 yards up the middle to give the Steelers a 28-17 lead with 7:10 left. Pittsburgh got the ball right back when Randy White fumbled the kickoff and Dennis Winston recovered for the Steelers. On first down, Bradshaw fired his fourth touchdown pass, an 18-yarder to Lynn Swann to boost the Steelers' lead to 35-17 with 6:51 to play. The Cowboys refused to let the Steelers run away with the contest. Staubach connected with Billy Joe DuPree on a seven-yard scoring pass with 2:27 left. Then the Cowboys recovered an onside kick and Staubach took them in for another score, passing four yards to Butch Johnson with 22 seconds remaining. Bleier recovered another onside kick left to seal the victory for the Steelers.

Pittsburgh (AFC)	7	14	0	14	— 35
Dallas (NFC)	7	7	3	14	— 31

Pitt —Stallworth 28 pass from Bradshaw (Gerela kick)
Dall—Hill 39 pass from Staubach (Septien kick)
Dall—Hegman 37 fumble recovery return (Septien kick)
Pitt —Stallworth 75 pass from Bradshaw (Gerela kick)
Pitt —Bleier 7 pass from Bradshaw (Gerela kick)
Dall—FG Septien 27
Pitt —Harris 22 run (Gerela kick)
Pitt —Swann 18 pass from Bradshaw (Gerela kick)
Dall—DuPree 7 pass from Staubach (Septien kick)
Dall—B. Johnson 4 pass from Staubach (Septien kick)

Super Bowl XII

Louisiana Superdome, New Orleans, Louisiana   January 15, 1978
Attendance: 75,583

DALLAS 27, DENVER 10—The Cowboys evened their Super Bowl record at 2-2 by defeating Denver before a sellout crowd of 75,583, plus 102,010,000 television viewers, the largest audience ever to watch a sporting event. Dallas converted two interceptions into 10 points and Efren Herrera added a 43-yard field goal for a 13-0 halftime advantage. In the third period Craig Morton engineered a drive to the Cowboys' 30 and Jim Turner's 47-yard field goal made the score 13-3. After an exchange of punts, Butch Johnson made a spectacular diving catch in the end zone to complete a 45-yard pass from Roger Staubach and put the Cowboys ahead 20-3. Following Rick Upchurch's 67-yard kickoff return, Norris Weese guided the Broncos to a touchdown to cut the Dallas lead to 20-10. Dallas clinched the victory when running back Robert Newhouse threw a 29-yard touchdown pass to Golden Richards with 7:04 remaining in the game. It was the first pass thrown by Newhouse since 1975. Harvey Martin and Randy White, who were named co-most valuable players, led the Cowboys' defense, which recovered four fumbles and intercepted four passes.

Dallas (NFC)	10	3	7	7	—	27
Denver (AFC)	0	0	10	0	—	10

Dall—Dorsett 3 run (Herrera kick)
Dall—FG Herrera 35
Dall—FG Herrera 43
Den—FG Turner 47
Dall—Johnson 45 pass from Staubach (Herrera kick)
Den—Lytle 1 run (Turner kick)
Dall—Richards 29 pass from Newhouse (Herrera kick)

Super Bowl XI

Rose Bowl, Pasadena, California   January 9, 1977
Attendance: 103,438

OAKLAND 32, MINNESOTA 14—The Raiders won their first NFL championship before a record Super Bowl crowd plus 81 million television viewers, the largest audience ever to watch a sporting event. The Raiders gained a record-breaking 429 yards, including running back Clarence Davis's 137 yards rushing. Wide receiver Fred Biletnikoff made four key receptions, which earned him the game's most valuable player trophy. Oakland scored on three successive possessions in the second quarter to build a 16-0 halftime lead. Errol Mann's 24-yard field goal opened the scoring, then the AFC champions put together drives of 64 and 35 yards, scoring on a one-yard pass from Ken Stabler to Dave Casper and a one-yard run by Pete Banaszak. The Raiders increased their lead to 19-0 on a 40-yard field goal in the third quarter, but Minnesota responded with a 12-play, 68-yard drive late in the period, with Fran Tarkenton passing eight yards to wide receiver Sammy White to cut the deficit to 19-7. Two fourth-quarter interceptions clinched the title for the Raiders. One set up Banaszak's second touchdown run, the other resulted in cornerback Willie Brown's Super Bowl record 75-yard interception return.

Oakland (AFC)	0	16	3	13	—	32
Minnesota (NFC)	0	0	7	7	—	14

Oak—FG Mann 24
Oak—Casper 1 pass from Stabler (Mann kick)
Oak—Banaszak 1 run (kick failed)
Oak—FG Mann 40
Minn—S. White 8 pass from Tarkenton (Cox kick)
Oak—Banaszak 2 run (Mann kick)
Oak—Brown 75 interception return (kick failed)
Minn—Voigt 13 pass from Lee (Cox kick)

Super Bowl X

Orange Bowl, Miami, Florida   January 18, 1976
Attendance: 80,187

PITTSBURGH 21, DALLAS 17—The Steelers won the Super Bowl for the second year in a row on Terry Bradshaw's 64-yard touchdown pass to Lynn Swann and an aggressive defense that snuffed out a late rally by the Cowboys with an end-zone interception on the final play of the game. In the fourth quarter, Pittsburgh ran on fourth down and gave up the ball on the Cowboys' 39 with 1:22 to play. Roger Staubach ran and passed for two first downs but his last desperation pass was picked off by Glen Edwards. Dallas's scoring was the result of two touchdown passes by Staubach, one to Drew Pearson for 29 yards and the other to Percy Howard for 34 yards. Toni Fritsch had a 36-yard field goal. The Steelers scored on two touchdown passes by Bradshaw, one to Randy Grossman for seven yards and the long bomb to Swann. Roy Gerela had 36- and 18-yard field goals. Reggie Harrison blocked a punt through the end zone for a safety. Swann set a Super Bowl record by gaining 161 yards on his four receptions.

Dallas (NFC)	7	3	0	7	—	17
Pittsburgh (AFC)	7	0	0	14	—	21

Dall—D. Pearson 29 pass from Staubach (Fritsch kick)
Pitt—Grossman 7 pass from Bradshaw (Gerela kick)
Dall—FG Fritsch 36
Pitt—Safety, Harrison blocked Hoopes's punt through end zone
Pitt—FG Gerela 36
Pitt—FG Gerela 18
Pitt—Swann 64 pass from Bradshaw (kick failed)
Dall—P. Howard 34 pass from Staubach (Fritsch kick)

Super Bowl IX

Tulane Stadium, New Orleans, Louisiana   January 12, 1975
Attendance: 80,997

PITTSBURGH 16, MINNESOTA 6—AFC champion Pittsburgh, in its initial Super Bowl appearance, and NFC champion Minnesota, making a third bid for its first Super Bowl title, struggled through a first half in which the only score was produced by the Steelers' defense when Dwight White downed Vikings' quarterback Fran Tarkenton in the end zone for a safety 7:49 into the second period. The Steelers forced another break and took advantage on the second half kickoff when Minnesota's Bill Brown fumbled and Marv Kellum recovered for Pittsburgh on the Vikings' 30. After Rocky Bleier failed to gain on first down, Franco Harris carried three consecutive times for 24 yards, a loss of 3, and a nine-yard touchdown and a 9-0 lead. Though its offense was completely stymied by Pittsburgh's defense, Minnesota managed to move into a threatening position after 4:27 of the final period when Matt Blair blocked Bobby Walden's punt and Terry Brown recovered the ball in the end zone for a touchdown. Fred Cox's kick failed and the Steelers led 9-6. Pittsburgh wasted no time putting the victory away. The Steelers took the ensuing kickoff and marched 66 yards in 11 plays, climaxed by Terry Bradshaw's four-yard scoring pass to Larry Brown with 3:31 left. Pittsburgh's defense permitted Minnesota only 119 yards total

offense, including a Super Bowl low of 17 yards rushing. The Steelers, meanwhile, gained 333 yards, including Harris's record 158 yards on 34 carries.

Pittsburgh (AFC)	0	2	7	7	—	16
Minnesota (NFC)	0	0	0	6	—	6

Pitt—Safety, White downed Tarkenton in end zone
Pitt—Harris 9 run (Gerela kick)
Minn—T. Brown recovered blocked punt in end zone (kick failed)
Pitt—L. Brown 4 pass from Bradshaw (Gerela kick)

Super Bowl VIII

Rice Stadium, Houston, Texas   January 13, 1974
Attendance: 71,882

MIAMI 24, MINNESOTA 7—The defending NFL champion Dolphins, representing the AFC for the third straight year, scored the first two times they had possession on marches of 62 and 56 yards in the first period while the Miami defense limited the Vikings to only six plays. Larry Csonka climaxed the initial 10-play drive with a five-yard touchdown bolt through right guard after 5:27 had elapsed. Four plays later, Miami began another 10-play scoring drive, which ended with Jim Kiick bursting one yard through the middle for another touchdown after 13:38 of the period. Garo Yepremian added a 28-yard field goal midway in the second period for a 17-0 Miami lead. Minnesota then drove from its 20 to a second-and-two situation on the Miami 7 yard line with 1:18 left in the half. But on two plays, Miami limited Oscar Reed to one yard. On fourth-and-one from the 6, Reed went over right tackle, but Dolphins middle linebacker Nick Buoniconti jarred the ball loose and Jake Scott recovered for Miami to halt the Minnesota threat. The Vikings were unable to muster enough offense in the second half to threaten the Dolphins. Csonka rushed 33 times for a Super Bowl record 145 yards. Bob Griese of Miami completed six of seven passes for 73 yards.

Minnesota (NFC)	0	0	0	7	—	7
Miami (AFC)	14	3	7	0	—	24

Mia—Csonka 5 run (Yepremian kick)
Mia—Kiick 1 run (Yepremian kick)
Mia—FG Yepremian 28
Mia—Csonka 2 run (Yepremian kick)
Minn—Tarkenton 4 run (Cox kick)

Super Bowl VII

Memorial Coliseum, Los Angeles, California   January 14, 1973
Attendance: 90,182

MIAMI 14, WASHINGTON 7—The Dolphins played virtually perfect football in the first half as their defense permitted the Redskins to cross midfield only once and their offense turned good field position into two touchdowns. On its third possession, Miami opened its first scoring drive from the Dolphins' 37 yard line. An 18-yard pass from Bob Griese to Paul Warfield preceded by three plays Griese's 28-yard touchdown pass to Howard Twilley. After Washington moved from its 17 to the Miami 48 with two minutes remaining in the first half, Dolphins linebacker Nick Buoniconti intercepted a Billy Kilmer pass at the Miami 41 and returned it to the Washington 27. Jim Kiick ran for three yards, Larry Csonka for three, Griese passed to Jim Mandich for 19, and Kiick gained one to the 1 yard line. With 18 seconds left until intermission, Kiick scored from the 1. Washington's only touchdown came with 2:07 left in the game and resulted from a blocked field goal attempt and fumble by Garo Yepremian, with the Redskins' Mike Bass picking the ball out of the air and running 49 yards for the score. Jake Scott, who had two interceptions, including one three yards into the end zone that he returned 55 yards, was voted the game's most valuable player.

Miami (AFC)	7	7	0	0	—	14
Washington (NFC)	0	0	0	7	—	7

Mia—Twilley 28 pass from Griese (Yepremian kick)
Mia—Kiick 1 run (Yepremian kick)
Wash—Bass 49 fumble recovery return (Knight kick)

Super Bowl VI

Tulane Stadium, New Orleans, Louisiana   January 16, 1972
Attendance: 81,023

DALLAS 24, MIAMI 3—The Cowboys rushed for a record 252 yards and their defense limited the Dolphins to a low of 185 yards while not permitting a touchdown for the first time in Super Bowl history. Dallas converted Chuck Howley's recovery of Larry Csonka's first fumble of the season into a 3-0 advantage and led at halftime 10-3. After Dallas received the second-half kickoff, Duane Thomas led a 71-yard march in eight plays for a 17-3 margin. Howley intercepted Bob Griese's pass at the 50 and returned it to the Miami 9 early in the fourth period, and three plays later Roger Staubach passed seven yards to Mike Ditka for the final touchdown. Thomas rushed for 95 yards and Walt Garrison gained 74. Staubach, voted the game's most valuable player, completed 12 of 19 passes for 119 yards and two touchdowns.

Dallas (NFC)	3	7	7	7	—	24
Miami (AFC)	0	3	0	0	—	3

Dall—FG Clark 9
Dall—Alworth 7 pass from Staubach (Clark kick)
Mia—FG Yepremian 31
Dall—D. Thomas 3 run (Clark kick)
Dall—Ditka 7 pass from Staubach (Clark kick)

Super Bowl V

Orange Bowl, Miami, Florida   January 17, 1971
Attendance: 79,204

BALTIMORE 16, DALLAS 13—A 32-yard field goal by first-year kicker Jim O'Brien brought the Baltimore Colts a victory over the Dallas Cowboys in the final five seconds of Super Bowl V. The game between the champions of the AFC and NFC was played on artificial turf for the first time. Dallas led 13-6 at the half but interceptions by Rick Volk and Mike Curtis set up a Baltimore touchdown and O'Brien's decisive kick in the fourth period. Earl Morrall relieved an injured Johnny Unitas late in the first half, although Unitas completed the Colts' only scoring pass. It caromed off receiver Eddie Hinton's fingertips, off Dallas defensive back Mel Renfro, and finally settled into the grasp of John Mackey, who went 45 yards to score on a 75-yard play.

Baltimore (AFC)	0	6	0	10	— 16
Dallas (NFC)	3	10	0	0	— 13

Dall—FG Clark 14
Dall—FG Clark 30
Balt—Mackey 75 pass from Unitas (kick blocked)
Dall—Thomas 7 pass from Morton (Clark kick)
Balt—Nowatzke 2 run (O'Brien kick)
Balt—FG O'Brien 32

Super Bowl IV

Tulane Stadium, New Orleans, Louisiana   January 11, 1970
Attendance: 80,562

KANSAS CITY 23, MINNESOTA 7—The AFL squared the Super Bowl at two games apiece with the NFL, building a 16-0 halftime lead behind Len Dawson's superb quarterbacking and a powerful defense. Dawson, the fourth consecutive quarterback to be chosen the Super Bowl's top player, called an almost flawless game, completing 12 of 17 passes and hitting Otis Taylor on a 46-yard play for the final Chiefs touchdown. The Kansas City defense limited Minnesota's strong rushing game to 67 yards and had three interceptions and two fumble recoveries. The crowd of 80,562 set a Super Bowl record, as did the gross receipts of $3,817,872.69.

Minnesota (NFL)	0	0	7	0	— 7
Kansas City (AFL)	3	13	7	0	— 23

KC —FG Stenerud 48
KC —FG Stenerud 32
KC —FG Stenerud 25
KC —Garrett 5 run (Stenerud kick)
Minn—Osborn 4 run (Cox kick)
KC —Taylor 46 pass from Dawson (Stenerud kick)

Super Bowl III

Orange Bowl, Miami, Florida   January 12, 1969
Attendance: 75,389

NEW YORK JETS 16, BALTIMORE 7—Jets quarterback Joe Namath "guaranteed" victory on the Thursday before the game, then went out and led the AFL to its first Super Bowl victory over a Baltimore team that had lost only once in 16 games all season. Namath, chosen the outstanding player, completed 17 of 28 passes for 206 yards and directed a steady attack that dominated the NFL champions after the Jets' defense had intercepted Colts quarterback Earl Morrall three times in the first half. The Jets had 337 total yards, including 121 yards rushing by Matt Snell. Johnny Unitas, who had missed most of the season with a sore elbow, came off the bench and led Baltimore to its only touchdown late in the fourth quarter after New York led 16-0.

New York Jets (AFL)	0	7	6	3	— 16
Baltimore (NFL)	0	0	0	7	— 7

NYJ—Snell 4 run (Turner kick)
NYJ—FG Turner 32
NYJ—FG Turner 30
NYJ—FG Turner 9
Balt—Hill 1 run (Michaels kick)

Super Bowl II

Orange Bowl, Miami, Florida   January 14, 1968
Attendance: 75,546

GREEN BAY 33, OAKLAND 14—Green Bay, after winning its third consecutive NFL championship, won the Super Bowl title for the second straight year 33-14 over the AFL champion Raiders in a game that drew the first $3-million gate in football history. Bart Starr again was chosen the game's most valuable player as he completed 13 of 24 passes for 202 yards and one touchdown and directed a Packers attack that was in control all the way after building a 16-7 halftime lead. Don Chandler kicked four field goals and all-pro cornerback Herb Adderley capped the Green Bay scoring with a 60-yard run with an interception. The game marked the last for Vince Lombardi as Packers coach, ending nine years at Green Bay in which he won six Western Conference championships, five NFL championships, and two Super Bowls.

Green Bay (NFL)	3	13	10	7	— 33
Oakland (AFL)	0	7	0	7	— 14

GB —FG Chandler 39
GB —FG Chandler 20
GB —Dowler 62 pass from Starr (Chandler kick)
Oak—Miller 23 pass from Lamonica (Blanda kick)
GB —FG Chandler 43
GB —Anderson 2 run (Chandler kick)
GB —FG Chandler 31
GB —Adderley 60 interception return (Chandler kick)
Oak—Miller 23 pass from Lamonica (Blanda kick)

Super Bowl I

Memorial Coliseum, Los Angeles, California   January 15, 1967
Attendance: 61,946

GREEN BAY 35, KANSAS CITY 10—The Green Bay Packers opened the Super Bowl series by defeating Kansas City's American Football League champions 35-10 behind the passing of Bart Starr, the receiving of Max McGee, and a key interception by all-pro safety Willie Wood. Green Bay broke open the game with three second-half touchdowns, the first of which was set up by Wood's 50-yard return of an interception to the Chiefs' 5 yard line. McGee, filling in for ailing Boyd Dowler after having caught only four passes all season, caught seven from Starr for 138 yards and two touchdowns. Elijah Pitts ran for two other scores. The Chiefs' 10 points came in the second quarter, the only touchdown on a seven-yard pass from Len Dawson to Curtis McClinton. Starr completed 16 of 23 passes for 250 yards and two touchdowns and was chosen the most valuable player. The Packers collected $15,000 per man and the Chiefs $7,500—the largest single-game shares in the history of team sports.

Kansas City (AFL)	0	10	0	0	— 10
Green Bay (NFL)	7	7	14	7	— 35

GB—McGee 37 pass from Starr (Chandler kick)
KC—McClinton 7 pass from Dawson (Mercer kick)
GB—Taylor 14 run (Chandler kick)
KC—FG Mercer 31
GB—Pitts 5 run (Chandler kick)
GB—McGee 13 pass from Starr (Chandler kick)
GB—Pitts 1 run (Chandler kick)

AFC Championship Game
Includes AFL Championship Games (1960-69)

Results

Season	Date	Winner (Share)	Loser (Share)	Score	Site	Attendance
1989	Jan. 14	Denver ($18,000)	Cleveland ($18,000)	37-21	Denver	76,046
1988	Jan. 8	Cincinnati ($18,000)	Buffalo ($18,000)	21-10	Cincinnati	59,747
1987	Jan. 17	Denver ($18,000)	Cleveland ($18,000)	38-33	Denver	76,197
1986	Jan. 11	Denver ($18,000)	Cleveland ($18,000)	23-20*	Cleveland	79,973
1985	Jan. 12	New England ($18,000)	Miami ($18,000)	31-14	Miami	75,662
1984	Jan. 6	Miami ($18,000)	Pittsburgh ($18,000)	45-28	Miami	76,029
1983	Jan. 8	L.A. Raiders ($18,000)	Seattle ($18,000)	30-14	Los Angeles	91,445
1982	Jan. 23	Miami ($18,000)	N.Y. Jets ($18,000)	14-0	Miami	67,396
1981	Jan. 10	Cincinnati ($9,000)	San Diego ($9,000)	27-7	Cincinnati	46,302
1980	Jan. 11	Oakland ($9,000)	San Diego ($9,000)	34-27	San Diego	52,675
1979	Jan. 6	Pittsburgh ($9,000)	Houston ($9,000)	27-13	Pittsburgh	50,475
1978	Jan. 7	Pittsburgh ($9,000)	Houston ($9,000)	34-5	Pittsburgh	50,725
1977	Jan. 1	Denver ($9,000)	Oakland ($9,000)	20-17	Denver	75,044
1976	Dec. 26	Oakland ($8,500)	Pittsburgh ($5,500)	24-7	Oakland	53,821
1975	Jan. 4	Pittsburgh ($8,500)	Oakland ($5,500)	16-10	Pittsburgh	50,609
1974	Dec. 29	Pittsburgh ($8,500)	Oakland ($5,500)	24-13	Oakland	53,800
1973	Dec. 30	Miami ($8,500)	Oakland ($5,500)	27-10	Miami	79,325
1972	Dec. 31	Miami ($8,500)	Pittsburgh ($5,500)	21-17	Pittsburgh	50,845
1971	Jan. 2	Miami ($8,500)	Baltimore ($5,500)	21-0	Miami	76,622
1970	Jan. 3	Baltimore ($8,500)	Oakland ($5,500)	27-17	Baltimore	54,799
1969	Jan. 4	Kansas City ($7,755)	Oakland ($6,252)	17-7	Oakland	53,564
1968	Dec. 29	N.Y. Jets ($7,007)	Oakland ($5,349)	27-23	New York	62,627
1967	Dec. 31	Oakland ($6,321)	Houston ($4,996)	40-7	Oakland	53,330
1966	Jan. 1	Kansas City ($5,309)	Buffalo ($3,799)	31-7	Buffalo	42,080
1965	Dec. 26	Buffalo ($5,189)	San Diego ($3,447)	23-0	San Diego	30,361
1964	Dec. 26	Buffalo ($2,668)	San Diego ($1,738)	20-7	Buffalo	40,242
1963	Jan. 5	San Diego ($2,498)	Boston ($1,596)	51-10	San Diego	30,127
1962	Dec. 23	Dallas ($2,206)	Houston ($1,471)	20-17*	Houston	37,981
1961	Dec. 24	Houston ($1,792)	San Diego ($1,111)	10-3	San Diego	29,556
1960	Jan. 1	Houston ($1,025)	L.A. Chargers ($718)	24-16	Houston	32,183

*Sudden death overtime.

AFC Championship Game
Composite Standings

	W	L	Pct.	Pts.	OP
Denver Broncos	4	0	1.000	118	91
Kansas City Chiefs*	3	0	1.000	68	31
Cincinnati Bengals	2	0	1.000	48	17
Miami Dolphins	5	1	.833	142	86
Pittsburgh Steelers	4	3	.571	153	131
Baltimore Colts	1	1	.500	27	38
Buffalo Bills	2	2	.500	60	59
New England Patriots**	1	1	.500	41	65
New York Jets	1	1	.500	27	37
Oakland/L.A. Raiders	4	7	.364	225	213
Houston Oilers	2	4	.333	76	140
San Diego Chargers***	1	6	.143	111	148
Seattle Seahawks	0	1	.000	14	30
Cleveland Browns	0	3	.000	74	98

*One game played when franchise was in Dallas (Texans). (Won 20-17)
**One game played when franchise was in Boston. (Lost 51-10)
***One game played when franchise was in Los Angeles. (Lost 24-16)

1989 American Football Conference Championship Game

Mile High Stadium, Denver, Colorado   January 14, 1990
Attendance: 76,046

DENVER 37, CLEVELAND 21 — The AFC West champion Denver Broncos advanced to their third Super Bowl in the past four seasons by defeating the AFC Central titlist Cleveland Browns 37-21. Denver eclipsed or tied 17 team postseason records and equaled or exceeded 11 more individual marks. John Elway completed 20 of 36 passes for 385 yards and three touchdowns. He also led all rushers with 39 yards on five carries. Elway's 385 passing yards and 424 yards total offense were team records. Elway's 70-yard touchdown pass to Michael Young gave the Broncos a 10-0 halftime lead. Young hauled in a 53-yard pass in the third quarter to set up Orson Mobley's five-yard scoring catch for a 17-7 Denver lead. After Sammy Winder extended the Broncos' advantage to 24-7 on a seven-yard run, Cleveland closed the gap to three points by scoring a pair of touchdowns within a 2:11 span. Denver countered by scoring on three of its four fourth-quarter drives. The Broncos' defense limited the Browns to 256 total yards and deflected six Bernie Kosar passes.

Cleveland (21)	Offense	Denver (37)
Reggie Langhorne	WR	Vance Johnson
Paul Farren	LT	Gerald Perry
Ted Banker	LG	Jim Juriga
Gregg Rakoczy	C	Keith Kartz
Tony Jones	RG	Doug Widell
Cody Risien	RT	Ken Lanier
Ozzie Newsome	TE	Pat Kelly
Webster Slaughter	WR	Mark Jackson
Bernie Kosar	QB	John Elway
Kevin Mack	RB	Melvin Bratton
Eric Metcalf	RB	Bobby Humphrey
	Defense	
Al Baker	LE	Alphonso Carreker
Carl Hairston	LT-NT	Greg Kragen
Michael Dean Perry	RT-RE	Ron Holmes
Robert Banks	RE-LOLB	Michael Brooks
Clay Matthews	LLB-LILB	Rick Dennison
Mike Johnson	MLB-RILB	Karl Mecklenburg
David Grayson	RLB-ROLB	Simon Fletcher
Frank Minnifield	LCB	Tyrone Braxton
Hanford Dixon	RCB	Wymon Henderson
Felix Wright	SS	Dennis Smith
Thane Gash	FS	Steve Atwater

Substitutions

Cleveland—Offense: K—Matt Bahr. P—Bryan Wagner. QB—Mike Pagel. RB—Keith Jones, Tim Manoa, Mike Oliphant, Barry Redden. WR—Brian Brennan, Gerald McNeil, Lawyer Tillman. TE—Ron Middleton. C—Tom Baugh. G—Rickey Bolden. Defense: E—Andrew Stewart. T—Tom Gibson, Chris Pike. LB—Clifford Charlton, Eddie Johnson, Van Waiters. CB—Mark Harper. S—Kyle Kramer, Robert Lyons. DNP: CB—Tony Blaylock.
Denver—Offense: K—David Treadwell. P—Mike Horan. QB—Gary Kubiak. RB—Ken Bell, Steve Sewell, Sammy Winder. WR—Ricky Nattiel, Michael Young. TE—Clarence Kay, Orson Mobley. C—Keith Bishop. G—Monte Smith. Defense: E—Warren Powers, Andre Townsend. NT—Brad Henke. LB—Scott Curtis, Bruce Klostermann, Tim Lucas, Marc Munford. CB—Darren Carrington, Mark Haynes. S—Kip Corrington, Randy Robbins. DNP: None.

Officials

Referee—Dick Hantak. Umpire—Art Demmas. Line Judge—Bill Reynolds. Head Linesman—Dale Williams. Back Judge—Paul Baetz. Field Judge—Jack Vaughn. Side Judge—Nate Jones. Replay Official—Chuck Heberling.

Scoring

Cleveland	0	0	21	0 — 21	
Denver	3	7	14	13 — 37	

Den — FG Treadwell 39
Den — Young 70 pass from Elway (Treadwell kick)
Clev — Brennan 27 pass from Kosar (Bahr kick)
Den — Mobley 5 pass from Elway (Treadwell kick)
Den — Winder 7 run (Treadwell kick)
Clev — Brennan 10 pass from Kosar (Bahr kick)
Clev — Manoa 2 run (Bahr kick)
Den — Winder 39 pass from Elway (Treadwell kick)
Den — FG Treadwell 34
Den — FG Treadwell 31

Team Statistics

	Cleveland	Denver
Total First Downs	14	22
First Downs Rushing	3	6
First Downs Passing	11	14
First Downs Penalty	0	2
Total Net Yardage	256	497
Total Offensive Plays	62	76
Average Gain per Offensive Play	4.1	6.5
Rushes	14	39
Yards Gained Rushing (net)	66	120
Average Yards per Rush	4.7	3.1
Passes Attempted	44	36
Passes Completed	19	20
Had Intercepted	3	0
Tackled Attempting to Pass	4	1
Yards Lost Attempting to Pass	20	8
Yards Gained Passing (net)	190	377
Punts	8	5
Average Distance	42.3	46.4
Punt Returns	1	4
Punt Return Yardage	7	36
Kickoff Returns	7	0
Kickoff Return Yardage	130	0
Interception Return Yardage	0	14
Total Return Yardage	137	50
Fumbles	3	2
Own Fumbles Recovered	3	0
Opponents Fumbles Recovered	2	0
Penalties	8	1
Yards Penalized	55	5

Total Points Scored	21	37
Touchdowns Rushing	1	1
Touchdowns Passing	2	3
Touchdowns Returns	0	0
Extra Points	3	4
Field Goals	0	3
Field Goals Attempted	0	4
Safeties	0	0
Third Down Efficiency	3/13	9/18
Fourth Down Efficiency	0/1	0/0
Time of Possession	23:07	36:53

Individual Statistics

Rushing

Cleveland	No.	Yds.	LG	TD
Mack	6	36	19	0
Kosar	2	22	16	0
Manoa	2	5	3	1
Metcalf	3	4	2	0
Langhorne	1	−1	−1	0
Denver	No.	Yds.	LG	TD
Elway	5	39	25	0
Winder	21	37	9	1
Humphrey	8	23	9	0
Sewell	4	17	12	0
Bratton	1	4	4	0

Passing

Cleveland	Att.	Comp.	Yds.	TD	Int.
Kosar	44	19	210	2	3
Denver	Att.	Comp.	Yds.	TD	Int.
Elway	36	20	385	3	0

Receiving

Cleveland	No.	Yds.	LG	TD
Langhorne	5	78	27	0
Brennan	5	58	27	2
Slaughter	3	36	16	0
Mack	2	8	5	0
Metcalf	2	7	4	0
Tillman	1	15	15	0
Manoa	1	8	8	0

Denver	No.	Yds.	LG	TD
Johnson	7	91	23	0
Sewell	3	55	43	0
Young	2	123	70	1
Winder	2	39	39	1
Jackson	2	25	13	0
Mobley	2	22	17	1
Humphrey	1	23	23	0
Bratton	1	7	7	0

Interceptions

Cleveland	No.	Yds.	LG	TD
None				
Denver	No.	Yds.	LG	TD
D. Smith	2	13	9	0
Corrington	1	1	1	0

Punting

Cleveland	No.	Avg.	LG	Blk.
Wagner	8	42.3	52	0
Denver	No.	Avg.	LG	Blk.
Horan	5	46.4	61	0

Punt Returns

Cleveland	No.	FC	Yds.	LG	TD
McNeil	1	1	7	7	0
Denver	No.	FC	Yds.	LG	TD
Johnson	4	0	36	11	0

Kickoff Returns

Cleveland	No.	Yds.	LG	TD
Metcalf	6	118	28	0
K. Jones	1	12	12	0
Denver	No.	Yds.	LG	TD
None				

NFC Championship Game

Includes NFL Championship Games (1933-69)

Results

Season	Date	Winner (Share)	Loser (Share)	Score	Site	Attendance
1989	Jan. 14	San Francisco ($18,000)	L.A. Rams ($18,000)	30-3	San Francisco	65,634
1988	Jan. 8	San Francisco ($18,000)	Chicago ($18,000)	28-3	Chicago	66,946
1987	Jan. 17	Washington ($18,000)	Minnesota ($18,000)	17-10	Washington	55,212
1986	Jan. 11	New York Giants ($18,000)	Washington ($18,000)	17-0	New York	76,891
1985	Jan. 12	Chicago ($18,000)	L.A. Rams ($18,000)	24-0	Chicago	66,030
1984	Jan. 6	San Francisco ($18,000)	Chicago ($18,000)	23-0	San Francisco	61,336
1983	Jan. 8	Washington ($18,000)	San Francisco ($18,000)	24-21	Washington	55,363
1982	Jan. 22	Washington ($18,000)	Dallas ($18,000)	31-17	Washington	55,045
1981	Jan. 10	San Francisco ($9,000)	Dallas ($9,000)	28-27	San Francisco	60,525
1980	Jan. 11	Philadelphia ($9,000)	Dallas ($9,000)	20-7	Philadelphia	71,522
1979	Jan. 6	Los Angeles ($9,000)	Tampa Bay ($9,000)	9-0	Tampa Bay	72,033
1978	Jan. 7	Dallas ($9,000)	Los Angeles ($9,000)	28-0	Los Angeles	71,086
1977	Jan. 1	Dallas ($9,000)	Minnesota ($9,000)	23-6	Dallas	64,293
1976	Dec. 26	Minnesota ($8,500)	Los Angeles ($5,500)	24-13	Minnesota	48,379
1975	Jan. 4	Dallas ($8,500)	Los Angeles ($5,500)	37-7	Los Angeles	88,919
1974	Dec. 29	Minnesota ($8,500)	Los Angeles ($5,500)	14-10	Minnesota	48,444
1973	Dec. 30	Minnesota ($8,500)	Dallas ($5,500)	27-10	Dallas	64,422
1972	Dec. 31	Washington ($8,500)	Dallas ($5,500)	26-3	Washington	53,129
1971	Jan. 2	Dallas ($8,500)	San Francisco ($5,500)	14-3	Dallas	63,409
1970	Jan. 3	Dallas ($8,500)	San Francisco ($5,500)	17-10	San Francisco	59,364
1969	Jan. 4	Minnesota ($7,930)	Cleveland ($5,118)	27-7	Minnesota	46,503
1968	Dec. 29	Baltimore ($9,306)	Cleveland ($5,963)	34-0	Cleveland	78,410
1967	Dec. 31	Green Bay ($7,950)	Dallas ($5,299)	21-17	Green Bay	50,861
1966	Jan. 1	Green Bay ($9,813)	Dallas ($6,527)	34-27	Dallas	74,152
1965	Jan. 2	Green Bay ($7,819)	Cleveland ($5,288)	23-12	Green Bay	50,777
1964	Dec. 27	Cleveland ($8,052)	Baltimore ($5,571)	27-0	Cleveland	79,544
1963	Dec. 29	Chicago ($5,899)	New York ($4,218)	14-10	Chicago	45,801
1962	Dec. 30	Green Bay ($5,888)	New York ($4,166)	16-7	New York	64,892
1961	Dec. 31	Green Bay ($5,195)	New York ($3,339)	37-0	Green Bay	39,029
1960	Dec. 26	Philadelphia ($5,116)	Green Bay ($3,105)	17-13	Philadelphia	67,325
1959	Dec. 27	Baltimore ($4,674)	New York ($3,083)	31-16	Baltimore	57,545
1958	Dec. 28	Baltimore ($4,718)	New York ($3,111)	23-17*	New York	64,185
1957	Dec. 29	Detroit ($4,295)	Cleveland ($2,750)	59-14	Detroit	55,263
1956	Dec. 30	New York ($3,779)	Chi. Bears ($2,485)	47-7	New York	56,836
1955	Dec. 26	Cleveland ($3,508)	Los Angeles ($2,316)	38-14	Los Angeles	85,693
1954	Dec. 26	Cleveland ($2,478)	Detroit ($1,585)	56-10	Cleveland	43,827
1953	Dec. 27	Detroit ($2,424)	Cleveland ($1,654)	17-16	Detroit	54,577

1952	Dec. 28	Detroit ($2,274)	Cleveland ($1,712)	17-7	Cleveland	50,934
1951	Dec. 23	Los Angeles ($2,108)	Cleveland ($1,483)	24-17	Los Angeles	57,522
1950	Dec. 24	Cleveland ($1,113)	Los Angeles ($686)	30-28	Cleveland	29,751
1949	Dec. 18	Philadelphia ($1,094)	Los Angeles ($739)	14-0	Los Angeles	27,980
1948	Dec. 19	Philadelphia ($1,540)	Chi. Cardinals ($874)	7-0	Philadelphia	36,309
1947	Dec. 28	Chi. Cardinals ($1,132)	Philadelphia ($754)	28-21	Chicago	30,759
1946	Dec. 15	Chi. Bears ($1,975)	New York ($1,295)	24-14	New York	58,346
1945	Dec. 16	Cleveland ($1,469)	Washington ($902)	15-14	Cleveland	32,178
1944	Dec. 17	Green Bay ($1,449)	New York ($814)	14-7	New York	46,016
1943	Dec. 26	Chi. Bears ($1,146)	Washington ($765)	41-21	Chicago	34,320
1942	Dec. 13	Washington ($965)	Chi. Bears ($637)	14-6	Washington	36,006
1941	Dec. 21	Chi. Bears ($430)	New York ($288)	37-9	Chicago	13,341
1940	Dec. 8	Chi. Bears ($873)	Washington ($606)	73-0	Washington	36,034
1939	Dec. 10	Green Bay ($703.97)	New York ($455.57)	27-0	Milwaukee	32,279
1938	Dec. 11	New York ($504.45)	Green Bay ($368.81)	23-17	New York	48,120
1937	Dec. 12	Washington ($225.90)	Chi. Bears ($127.78)	28-21	Chicago	15,870
1936	Dec. 13	Green Bay ($250)	Boston ($180)	21-6	New York	29,545
1935	Dec. 15	Detroit ($313.35)	New York ($200.20)	26-7	Detroit	15,000
1934	Dec. 9	New York ($621)	Chi. Bears ($414.02)	30-13	New York	35,059
1933	Dec. 17	Chi. Bears ($210.34)	New York ($140.22)	23-21	Chicago	26,000

*Sudden death overtime.

NFC Championship Game
Composite Standings

	W	L	Pct.	Pts.	OP
Green Bay Packers	8	2	.800	223	116
Philadelphia Eagles	4	1	.800	79	48
Baltimore Colts	3	1	.750	88	60
Detroit Lions*	4	2	.667	129	109
Minnesota Vikings	4	2	.667	108	80
San Francisco 49ers	4	3	.571	143	88
Washington Redskins**	6	5	.545	181	245
Chicago Bears	7	6	.536	286	245
Phoenix Cardinals***	1	1	.500	28	28
Dallas Cowboys	5	7	.417	227	213
Cleveland Browns	4	7	.364	224	253
New York Giants	4	11	.267	225	309
Los Angeles Rams****	3	9	.250	123	270
Tampa Bay Buccaneers	0	1	.000	0	9

*One game played when franchise was in Portsmouth. (Lost 9-0)
**One game played when franchise was in Boston. (Lost 21-6)
***Both games played when franchise was in Chicago. (Won 28-21, lost 7-0)
****One game played when franchise was in Cleveland. (Won 15-14)

1989 National Football Conference Championship Game

Candlestick Park, San Francisco, California   January 14, 1990
Attendance: 65,634

SAN FRANCISCO 49ERS 30, LOS ANGELES RAMS 3—NFC Western Division champion San Francisco gained its fourth Super Bowl berth by dominating the Los Angeles Rams 30-3 in the NFC title game. The Rams took a 3-0 lead on Mike Lansford's 23-yard field goal on their first offensive series, but they were held in check the rest of the game. San Francisco had 29 first downs to Los Angeles's nine; 442 yards to 156; and a time-of-possession advantage of 39:48 to 20:12. San Francisco's Joe Montana completed 26 of 30 passes for 262 yards and two touchdowns. Montana's 31 career postseason touchdown passes surpassed the previous NFL record of 30 by Terry Bradshaw. San Francisco built a 21-3 halftime lead on touchdown catches of 20 yards by Brent Jones and 18 yards by John Taylor, plus a one-yard scoring run by Roger Craig, who gained 93 yards on 23 carries. In the second half, Mike Cofer added field goals of 28, 36, and 25 yards. Montana distributed his passes to eight different receivers. Jerry Rice had six catches for 55 yards and Tom Rathman had six receptions for 48 yards. The 49ers' defense collected interceptions by Tim McKyer, Ronnie Lott, and Keena Turner.

L.A. Rams (3)	Offense	San Francisco (30)
Willie Anderson	WR	John Taylor
Irv Pankey	LT	Bubba Paris
Tom Newberry	LG	Guy McIntyre
Doug Smith	C	Jesse Sapolu
Duval Love	RG	Bruce Collie
Jackie Slater	RT	Harris Barton
Pete Holohan	TE	Brent Jones
Henry Ellard	WR	Jerry Rice
Jim Everett	QB	Joe Montana
Buford McGee	RB	Roger Craig
Greg Bell	RB	Tom Rathman

	Defense	
Shawn Miller	LE	Pierce Holt
Alvin Wright	NT	Pete Kugler
Mike Piel	RE	Kevin Fagan
Kevin Greene	LOLB	Charles Haley
Larry Kelm	LILB	Matt Millen
Fred Strickland	RILB	Michael Walter
Mike Wilcher	ROLB	Keena Turner
Jerry Gray	LCB	Darryl Pollard
LeRoy Irvin	RCB	Don Griffin
Michael Stewart	SS	Chet Brooks
James Washington	FS	Ronnie Lott

Substitutions

L.A. Rams—Offense: K—Mike Lansford. P—Dale Hatcher. RB—Robert Delpino, Mel Farr, Cleveland Gary. WR—Aaron Cox. TE—Pat Carter, Damone Johnson. KR—Ron Brown. G—Tony Slaton. T—Robert Cox. Defense: NT—Sean Smith. LB—George Bethune, Brett Faryniarz, Mike McDonald, Mark Messner, Mel Owens, Frank Stams. CB—Darryl Henley, Alfred Jackson. S—Johnnie Johnson. DNP: QB—Mark Herrmann. S—Vince Newsome.
San Francisco—Offense: K—Mike Cofer. P—Barry Helton. QB—Steve Young. RB—Terrence Flagler, Keith Henderson, Spencer Tillman. WR—Mike Sherrard, Mike Wilson. TE—Wesley Walls, Jamie Williams. C—Chuck Thomas. G—Terry Tausch. T—Steve Wallace. Defense: E—Larry Roberts, Danny Stubbs. NT—Jim Burt, Michael Carter. LB—Keith DeLong, Steve Hendrickson, Bill Romanowski. CB—Tim McKyer, Eric Wright. S—Johnny Jackson. DNP: None.

Officials

Referee—Jerry Markbreit. Umpire—Rex Stuart. Line Judge—Ron DeSouza. Head Linesman—Earnie Frantz. Back Judge—Tom Sifferman. Field Judge—Bob Wortman. Side Judge—Tom Fincken. Replay Official—Tom Kelleher.

Scoring

L.A. Rams	3	0	0	0	— 3
San Francisco	0	21	3	6	— 30

Rams —FG Lansford 23
SF —Jones 20 pass from Montana (Cofer kick)
SF —Craig 1 run (Cofer kick)
SF —Taylor 18 pass from Montana (Cofer kick)
SF —FG Cofer 28
SF —FG Cofer 36
SF —FG Cofer 25

Team Statistics

	L.A. Rams	San Francisco
Total First Downs	9	29
First Downs Rushing	0	12
First Downs Passing	9	16
First Downs Penalty	0	1
Total Net Yardage	156	442
Total Offensive Plays	47	76
Average Gain per Offensive Play	3.3	5.8
Rushes	10	44
Yards Gained Rushing (net)	26	179
Average Yards per Rush	2.6	4.1
Passes Attempted	36	31
Passes Completed	16	27
Had Intercepted	3	0
Tackled Attempting to Pass	1	1
Yards Lost Attempting to Pass	11	5
Yards Gained Passing (net)	130	263
Punts	7	2
Average Distance	31.4	31.0

Punt Returns	1	1
Punt Return Yardage	10	2
Kickoff Returns	6	2
Kickoff Return Yardage	146	35
Interception Return Yardage	0	56
Total Return Yardage	156	93
Fumbles	1	3
Own Fumbles Recovered	1	1
Opponents Fumbles Recovered	2	0
Penalties	1	4
Yards Penalized	10	40
Total Points Scored	3	30
Touchdowns Rushing	0	1
Touchdowns Passing	0	2
Touchdowns Returns	0	0
Extra Points	0	3
Field Goals	1	3
Field Goals Attempted	1	4
Safeties	0	0
Third Down Efficiency	3/12	7/13
Fourth Down Efficiency	0/0	0/0
Time of Possession	20:12	39:48

Individual Statistics

Rushing

L.A. Rams	No.	Yds.	LG	TD
Bell	8	20	5	0
Delpino	1	3	3	0
Gary	1	3	3	0

San Francisco	No.	Yds.	LG	TD
Craig	23	93	13	1
Rathman	10	63	17	0
Flagler	8	19	12	0
Montana	1	4	4	0
Henderson	1	1	1	0
Young	1	−1	−1	0

Passing

L.A. Rams	Att.	Comp.	Yds.	TD	Int.
Everett	36	16	141	0	3

San Fran.	Att.	Comp.	Yds.	TD	Int.
Montana	30	26	262	2	0
Young	1	1	6	0	0

Receiving

L.A. Rams	No.	Yds.	LG	TD
McGee	7	53	17	0
Holohan	3	26	18	0
Bell	2	23	18	0
Ellard	2	18	12	0
Anderson	1	14	14	0
D. Johnson	1	7	7	0

San Fran.	No.	Yds.	LG	TD
Rice	6	55	19	0
Rathman	6	48	13	0
Jones	4	46	20	1
Taylor	4	45	18	1
Craig	3	40	16	0
Sherrard	2	21	15	0
Wilson	1	7	7	0
Williams	1	6	6	0

Interceptions

L.A. Rams	No.	Yds.	LG	TD
None				

San Fran.	No.	Yds.	LG	TD
McKyer	1	27	27	0
Turner	1	15	15	0
Lott	1	14	14	0

Punting

L.A. Rams	No.	Avg.	LG	Blk.
Hatcher	7	31.4	41	0

San Fran.	No.	Avg.	LG	Blk.
Helton	2	31.0	36	0

Punt Returns

L.A. Rams	No.	FC	Yds.	LG	TD
Irvin	1	0	10	10	0

San Fran.	No.	FC	Yds.	LG	TD
Taylor	1	4	2	2	0

Kickoff Returns

L.A. Rams	No.	Yds.	LG	TD
Delpino	4	95	46	0
Brown	2	51	27	0

San Fran.	No.	Yds.	LG	TD
Flagler	1	19	19	0
Tillman	1	16	16	0

AFC Divisional Playoffs

Includes Second-Round Playoff Games (1982), AFC Inter-Divisional Games (1969), and special playoff games to break ties for AFL Division Championships (1963, 1968)

Results

Season	Date	Winner (Share)	Loser (Share)	Score	Site	Attendance
1989	Jan. 7	Denver ($10,000)	Pittsburgh ($10,000)	24-23	Denver	75,477
	Jan. 6	Cleveland ($10,000)	Buffalo ($10,000)	34-30	Cleveland	78,921
1988	Jan. 1	Buffalo ($10,000)	Houston ($10,000)	17-10	Buffalo	79,532
	Dec. 31	Cincinnati ($10,000)	Seattle ($10,000)	21-13	Cincinnati	58,560
1987	Jan. 10	Denver ($10,000)	Houston ($10,000)	34-10	Denver	75,440
	Jan. 9	Cleveland ($10,000)	Indianapolis ($10,000)	38-21	Cleveland	79,372
1986	Jan. 4	Denver ($10,000)	New England ($10,000)	22-17	Denver	75,262
	Jan. 3	Cleveland ($10,000)	N.Y. Jets ($10,000)	23-20*	Cleveland	79,720
1985	Jan. 5	New England ($10,000)	L.A. Raiders ($10,000)	27-20	Los Angeles	87,163
	Jan. 4	Miami ($10,000)	Cleveland ($10,000)	24-21	Miami	74,667
1984	Dec. 30	Pittsburgh ($10,000)	Denver ($10,000)	24-17	Denver	74,981
	Dec. 29	Miami ($10,000)	Seattle ($10,000)	31-10	Miami	73,469
1983	Jan. 1	L.A. Raiders ($10,000)	Pittsburgh ($10,000)	38-10	Los Angeles	90,380
	Dec. 31	Seattle ($10,000)	Miami ($10,000)	27-20	Miami	74,136
1982	Jan. 16	Miami ($10,000)	San Diego ($10,000)	34-13	Miami	71,383
	Jan. 15	N.Y. Jets ($10,000)	L.A. Raiders ($10,000)	17-14	Los Angeles	90,038
1981	Jan. 3	Cincinnati ($5,000)	Buffalo ($5,000)	28-21	Cincinnati	55,420
	Jan. 2	San Diego ($5,000)	Miami ($5,000)	41-38*	Miami	73,735
1980	Jan. 4	Oakland ($5,000)	Cleveland ($5,000)	14-12	Cleveland	78,245
	Jan. 3	San Diego ($5,000)	Buffalo ($5,000)	20-14	San Diego	52,253
1979	Dec. 30	Pittsburgh ($5,000)	Miami ($5,000)	34-14	Pittsburgh	50,214
	Dec. 29	Houston ($5,000)	San Diego ($5,000)	17-14	San Diego	51,192
1978	Dec. 31	Houston ($5,000)	New England ($5,000)	31-14	New England	60,735
	Dec. 30	Pittsburgh ($5,000)	Denver ($5,000)	33-10	Pittsburgh	50,230
1977	Dec. 24	Oakland ($5,000)	Baltimore ($5,000)	37-31	Baltimore	59,925
	Dec. 24	Denver ($5,000)	Pittsburgh ($5,000)	34-21	Denver	75,059
1976	Dec. 19	Pittsburgh ($)	Baltimore ($)	40-14	Baltimore	59,296
	Dec. 18	Oakland ($)	New England ($)	24-21	Oakland	53,050
1975	Dec. 28	Oakland ($)	Cincinnati ($)	31-28	Oakland	53,030
	Dec. 27	Pittsburgh ($)	Baltimore ($)	28-10	Pittsburgh	49,557
1974	Dec. 22	Pittsburgh ($)	Buffalo ($)	32-14	Pittsburgh	49,841
	Dec. 21	Oakland ($)	Miami ($)	28-26	Oakland	53,023
1973	Dec. 23	Miami ($)	Cincinnati ($)	34-16	Miami	78,928
	Dec. 22	Oakland ($)	Pittsburgh ($)	33-14	Oakland	52,646
1972	Dec. 24	Miami ($)	Cleveland ($)	20-14	Miami	78,916
	Dec. 23	Pittsburgh ($)	Oakland ($)	13-7	Pittsburgh	50,327
1971	Dec. 26	Baltimore ($)	Cleveland ($)	20-3	Cleveland	70,734
	Dec. 25	Miami ($)	Kansas City ($)	27-24*	Kansas City	45,822
1970	Dec. 27	Oakland ($)	Miami ($)	21-14	Oakland	52,594
	Dec. 26	Baltimore ($)	Cincinnati ($)	17-0	Baltimore	49,694
1969	Dec. 21	Oakland ($)	Houston ($)	56-7	Oakland	53,539
	Dec. 20	Kansas City ($)	N.Y. Jets ($)	13-6	New York	62,977
1968	Dec. 22	Oakland ($)	Kansas City ($)	41-6	Oakland	53,605
1963	Dec. 28	Boston ($)	Buffalo ($)	26-8	Buffalo	33,044

*Sudden Death Overtime.

$ Players received 1/14 of annual salary for playoff appearances.

1989 AFC Divisional Playoffs

Cleveland Stadium, Cleveland, Ohio January 6, 1990
Attendance: 78,921

CLEVELAND 34, BUFFALO 30—Clay Matthews's interception at the Cleveland 1-yard line with three seconds to play helped the Browns preserve a 34-30 win over the Bills and earn a berth in the AFC Championship Game for the third time in four years. Buffalo scored on its sixth play of the game when Jim Kelly and Andre Reed combined on a 72-yard pass play. Cleveland's Bernie Kosar countered with touchdown passes of 52 yards to Webster Slaughter and three yards to Ron Middleton for a 17-14 halftime lead. Cleveland extended its lead to 24-14 on Kosar's 44-yard touchdown pass to Slaughter following an interception by Mark Harper. The Bills cut the deficit to three points as Mark Kelso's fumble recovery at the Cleveland 21 set up Kelly's six-yard scoring pass to Thurman Thomas. Cleveland rookie Eric Metcalf returned the ensuing kickoff 90 yards for a touchdown, the first such play in Browns' postseason history. After the teams swapped field goals, Kelly hit Thomas for a three-yard touchdown pass. However, the extra point failed. Thomas tied an NFL postseason record with 13 receptions for 150 yards, while Kelly set a club playoff mark with 405 yards passing on 28 of 54 with four touchdowns and two interceptions. Kosar completed 20 of 29 passes for 251 yards. Slaughter gained 114 yards on three receptions.

Buffalo	7	7	7	9	—	30
Cleveland	3	14	14	3	—	34

Buff—Reed 72 pass from Kelly (Norwood kick)
Clev—FG Bahr 45
Clev—Slaughter 52 pass from Kosar (Bahr kick)
Buff—Lofton 33 pass from Kelly (Norwood kick)
Clev—Middleton 3 pass from Kosar (Bahr kick)
Clev—Slaughter 44 pass from Kosar (Bahr kick)
Buff—Thomas 6 pass from Kelly (Norwood kick)
Clev—Metcalf 90 kickoff return (Bahr kick)
Buff—FG Norwood 30
Clev—FG Bahr 47
Buff—Thomas 3 pass from Kelly (kick failed)

Mile High Stadium, Denver, Colorado January 7, 1990
Attendance: 75,477

DENVER 24, PITTSBURGH 23—Melvin Bratton scored on a one-yard run with 2:27 to play and David Treadwell added the extra point to give the Broncos a 24-23 win. Pittsburgh jumped out to a 10-0 advantage on Gary Anderson's first of three field goals (32 yards) and Merril Hoge's seven-yard run. Denver's Bratton scored on a one-yard plunge, but Louis Lipps put the Steelers' lead back to 10 with a nine-yard touchdown catch from Bubby Brister. Tyrone Braxton recovered a fumble at the Steelers' 37-yard line early in the third quarter. One play later, John Elway completed a 37-yard touchdown pass to Vance Johnson to tie the score 17-17. Anderson's field goals of 35 and 32 yards put the Steelers back on top, but Elway marched the Broncos 71 yards in nine plays for the winning score. Randy Robbins's fumble recovery at the Pittsburgh 18-yard line with 2:02 remaining sealed the win. Hoge gained 120 yards on 16 carries for the Broncos. Mark Jackson had five receptions for 111 yards for the Broncos.

Pittsburgh	3	14	3	3	—	23
Denver	0	10	7	7	—	24

Pitt—FG Anderson 32
Pitt—Hoge 7 run (Anderson kick)
Den—Bratton 1 run (Treadwell kick)
Pitt—Lipps 9 pass from Brister (Anderson kick)
Den—FG Treadwell 43
Den—Johnson 37 pass from Elway (Treadwell kick)
Pitt—FG Anderson 35
Pitt—FG Anderson 32
Den—Bratton 1 run (Treadwell kick)

NFC Divisional Playoffs

Includes Second-Round Playoff Games (1982), NFL Conference Championship Games (1967-69), and special playoff games to break ties for NFL Division or Conference Championships (1941, 1943, 1947, 1950, 1952, 1957, 1958, 1965)

Results

Season	Date	Winner (Share)	Loser (Share)	Score	Site	Attendance
1989	Jan. 7	L.A. Rams ($10,000)	N.Y. Giants ($10,000)	19-13*	East Rutherford	76,526
	Jan. 6	San Francisco ($10,000)	Minnesota ($10,000)	41-13	San Francisco	64,918
1988	Jan. 1	San Francisco ($10,000)	Minnesota ($10,000)	34-9	San Francisco	61,848
	Dec. 31	Chicago ($10,000)	Philadelphia ($10,000)	20-12	Chicago	65,534
1987	Jan. 10	Washington ($10,000)	Chicago ($10,000)	21-17	Chicago	65,268
	Jan. 9	Minnesota ($10,000)	San Francisco ($10,000)	36-24	San Francisco	63,008
1986	Jan. 4	N.Y. Giants ($10,000)	San Francisco ($10,000)	49-3	East Rutherford	75,691
	Jan. 3	Washington ($10,000)	Chicago ($10,000)	27-13	Chicago	65,524
1985	Jan. 5	Chicago ($10,000)	N.Y. Giants ($10,000)	21-0	Chicago	65,670
	Jan. 4	L.A. Rams ($10,000)	Dallas ($10,000)	20-0	Anaheim	66,581
1984	Dec. 30	Chicago ($10,000)	Washington ($10,000)	23-19	Washington	55,431
	Dec. 29	San Francisco ($10,000)	N.Y. Giants ($10,000)	21-10	San Francisco	60,303
1983	Jan. 1	Washington ($10,000)	L.A. Rams ($10,000)	51-7	Washington	54,440
	Dec. 31	San Francisco ($10,000)	Detroit ($10,000)	24-23	San Francisco	59,979
1982	Jan. 16	Dallas ($10,000)	Green Bay ($10,000)	37-26	Dallas	63,972
	Jan. 15	Washington ($10,000)	Minnesota ($10,000)	21-7	Washington	54,593
1981	Jan. 3	San Francisco ($5,000)	N.Y. Giants ($5,000)	38-24	San Francisco	58,360
	Jan. 2	Dallas ($5,000)	Tampa Bay ($5,000)	38-0	Dallas	64,848
1980	Jan. 4	Dallas ($5,000)	Atlanta ($5,000)	30-27	Atlanta	59,793
	Jan. 3	Philadelphia ($5,000)	Minnesota ($5,000)	31-16	Philadelphia	70,178
1979	Dec. 30	Los Angeles ($5,000)	Dallas ($5,000)	21-19	Dallas	64,792
	Dec. 29	Tampa Bay ($5,000)	Philadelphia ($5,000)	24-17	Tampa Bay	71,402
1978	Dec. 31	Los Angeles ($5,000)	Minnesota ($5,000)	34-10	Los Angeles	70,436
	Dec. 30	Dallas ($5,000)	Atlanta ($5,000)	27-20	Dallas	63,406
1977	Dec. 26	Dallas ($5,000)	Chicago ($5,000)	37-7	Dallas	63,260
	Dec. 26	Minnesota ($5,000)	Los Angeles ($5,000)	14-7	Los Angeles	70,203
1976	Dec. 19	Los Angeles ($)	Dallas ($)	14-12	Dallas	63,283
	Dec. 18	Minnesota ($)	Washington ($)	35-20	Minnesota	47,466
1975	Dec. 28	Dallas ($)	Minnesota ($)	17-14	Minnesota	48,050
	Dec. 27	Los Angeles ($)	St. Louis ($)	35-23	Los Angeles	73,459
1974	Dec. 22	Los Angeles ($)	Washington ($)	19-10	Los Angeles	77,925
	Dec. 21	Minnesota ($)	St. Louis ($)	30-14	Minnesota	48,150
1973	Dec. 23	Dallas ($)	Los Angeles ($)	27-16	Dallas	63,272
	Dec. 22	Minnesota ($)	Washington ($)	27-20	Minnesota	48,040
1972	Dec. 24	Washington ($)	Green Bay ($)	16-3	Washington	52,321
	Dec. 23	Dallas ($)	San Francisco ($)	30-28	San Francisco	59,746
1971	Dec. 26	San Francisco ($)	Washington ($)	24-20	San Francisco	45,327
	Dec. 25	Dallas ($)	Minnesota ($)	20-12	Minnesota	47,307
1970	Dec. 27	San Francisco ($)	Minnesota ($)	17-14	Minnesota	45,103
	Dec. 26	Dallas ($)	Detroit ($)	5-0	Dallas	69,613
1969	Dec. 28	Cleveland ($)	Dallas ($)	38-14	Dallas	69,321
	Dec. 27	Minnesota ($)	Los Angeles ($)	23-20	Minnesota	47,900
1968	Dec. 22	Baltimore ($)	Minnesota ($)	24-14	Baltimore	60,238
	Dec. 21	Cleveland ($)	Dallas ($)	31-20	Cleveland	81,497
1967	Dec. 24	Dallas ($)	Cleveland ($)	52-14	Dallas	70,786
	Dec. 23	Green Bay ($)	Los Angeles ($)	28-7	Milwaukee	49,861
1965	Dec. 26	Green Bay ($)	Baltimore ($)	13-10*	Green Bay	50,484
1958	Dec. 21	N.Y. Giants (#)	Cleveland (#)	10-0	New York	61,274
1957	Dec. 22	Detroit (#)	San Francisco (#)	31-27	San Francisco	60,118

1952	Dec. 21	Detroit (#)	Los Angeles (#)	31-21	Detroit	47,645
1950	Dec. 17	Los Angeles (#)	Chicago Bears (#)	24-14	Los Angeles	83,501
	Dec. 17	Cleveland (#)	N.Y. Giants (#)	8-3	Cleveland	33,054
1947	Dec. 21	Philadelphia (#)	Pittsburgh (#)	21-0	Pittsburgh	35,729
1943	Dec. 19	Washington (+)	N.Y. Giants (+)	28-0	New York	42,800
1941	Dec. 14	Chicago Bears (+)	Green Bay (+)	33-14	Chicago	43,425

*Sudden Death Overtime.
$ Players received 1/14 of annual salary for playoff appearances.
# Players received 1/12 of annual salary for playoff appearances.
+ Players received 1/10 of annual salary for playoff appearances.

1989 NFC Divisional Playoffs

Candlestick Park, San Francisco, California   January 6, 1990
Attendance: 64,918
SAN FRANCISCO 41, MINNESOTA 13—Defending Super Bowl champion and 1989 NFC West titlist San Francisco gained its fifth NFC Championship Game of the decade with a 41-13 victory over NFC Central champion Minnesota. Joe Montana threw four touchdown passes in the first half to lead San Francisco to a 27-3 advantage at intermission. Montana finished with 17 completions in 24 attempts for 241 yards and four touchdowns. Roger Craig carried 18 times for 125 yards and one touchdown. Jerry Rice caught six passes for 114 yards and two touchdowns. Ronnie Lott set a club playoff record when he returned an interception 58 yards for a score. Minnesota's 71 sacks during the regular season were the second highest total in NFL history; however, San Francisco did not allow a sack.

Minnesota	3	0	3	7 — 13
San Francisco	7	20	0	14 — 41

Minn — FG Karlis 38
SF — Rice 72 pass from Montana (Cofer kick)
SF — Jones 8 pass from Montana (Cofer kick)
SF — Taylor 8 pass from Montana (kick failed)
SF — Rice 13 pass from Montana (Cofer kick)
Minn — FG Karlis 44
SF — Lott 58 interception return (Cofer kick)
SF — Craig 4 run (Cofer kick)
Minn — Fenney 3 run (Karlis kick)

Giants Stadium, East Rutherford, New Jersey   January 7, 1990
Attendance: 76,526
LOS ANGELES RAMS 19, NEW YORK GIANTS 13—The Wild Card entry Los Angeles Rams gained their first NFC Championship Game berth since 1985 with a 19-13 overtime win over the NFC East champion New York Giants. The Giants took a 6-0 lead on Raul Allegre's field goals of 35 and 41 yards. The Rams gained a 7-6 edge on Willie Anderson's 20-yard touchdown catch with 17 seconds remaining in the first half. New York regained the lead with 1:57 remaining in the third period when Ottis Anderson scored on a two-yard run. The Rams tied the game with 3:01 left in regulation on Mike Lansford's 22-yard field goal. In the overtime, the Rams took the kickoff and scored on Jim Everett's 30-yard scoring pass to Anderson 1:06 into the extra period. Everett completed 25 of 44 passes for 315 yards. Los Angeles's Henry Ellard produced his first 100-yard postseason game with eight catches for 125 yards.

L.A. Rams	0	7	0	6	6 — 19
N.Y. Giants	6	0	7	0	0 — 13

NYG — FG Allegre 35
NYG — FG Allegre 41
Rams — W. Anderson 20 pass from Everett (Lansford kick)
NYG — O. Anderson 2 run (Allegre kick)
Rams — FG Lansford 31
Rams — FG Lansford 22
Rams — W. Anderson 30 pass from Everett (no PAT attempted)

AFC First-Round Playoff Games

Results

Season	Date	Winner (Share)	Loser (Share)	Score	Site	Attendance
1989	Dec. 31	Pittsburgh ($6,000)	Houston ($6,000)	26-23*	Houston	59,406
1988	Dec. 26	Houston ($6,000)	Cleveland ($6,000)	24-23	Cleveland	75,896
1987	Jan. 3	Houston ($6,000)	Seattle ($6,000)	23-20*	Houston	50,519
1986	Dec. 28	N.Y. Jets ($6,000)	Kansas City ($6,000)	35-15	East Rutherford	75,210
1985	Dec. 28	New England ($6,000)	N.Y. Jets ($6,000)	26-14	East Rutherford	75,945
1984	Dec. 22	Seattle ($6,000)	L.A. Raiders ($6,000)	13-7	Seattle	62,049
1983	Dec. 24	Seattle ($6,000)	Denver ($6,000)	31-7	Seattle	64,275
1982	Jan. 9	N.Y. Jets ($6,000)	Cincinnati ($6,000)	44-17	Cincinnati	57,560
	Jan. 9	San Diego ($6,000)	Pittsburgh ($6,000)	31-28	Pittsburgh	53,546
	Jan. 8	L.A. Raiders ($6,000)	Cleveland ($6,000)	27-10	Los Angeles	56,555
	Jan. 8	Miami ($6,000)	New England ($6,000)	28-13	Miami	68,842
1981	Dec. 27	Buffalo ($3,000)	N.Y. Jets ($3,000)	31-27	New York	57,050
1980	Dec. 28	Oakland ($3,000)	Houston ($3,000)	27-7	Oakland	53,333
1979	Dec. 23	Houston ($3,000)	Denver ($3,000)	13-7	Houston	48,776
1978	Dec. 24	Houston ($3,000)	Miami ($3,000)	17-9	Miami	72,445

*Sudden death overtime.

1989 AFC First-Round Playoff Game

Astrodome, Houston, Texas   December 31, 1989
Attendance: 59,406
PITTSBURGH 26, HOUSTON 23—Pittsburgh's Gary Anderson kicked a 50-yard field goal 3:26 into overtime to cap the Steelers' 26-23 comeback win over the Oilers and earn their first playoff victory since 1984. Pittsburgh, despite being outgained by Houston 380 to 289 total yards, led the game for over three quarters. Pittsburgh took a 16-9 fourth-quarter lead on running back Tim Worley's nine-yard touchdown run and Anderson's field goals of 25, 30, and 48 yards. Houston's Warren Moon tied the score with an 18-yard touchdown pass to Ernest Givins and gave the Oilers their only lead, 23-16, when he found Givins on a nine-yard scoring pass with six minutes to play. Pittsburgh's Bubby Brister countered with an 82-yard, 11-play drive capped by Merril Hoge's two-yard touchdown plunge with 46 seconds remaining. Anderson's extra point tied the score and sent the game into overtime. The Steelers won the extra period coin toss but were forced to punt. Rod Woodson recovered Lorenzo White's fumble on the Oilers' first play in overtime to set up Anderson's decisive field goal. Hoge became the first Steeler to gain 100 yards (17 carries for 100 yards) in a postseason game since Franco Harris in 1978. Moon completed 29 of 48 passes for 315 yards and two touchdowns, including 11 to Givins for 136 yards and both scores.

Pittsburgh	7	3	3	10	3 — 26
Houston	0	6	3	14	0 — 23

Pitt — Worley 9 run (Anderson kick)
Hou — FG Zendejas 26
Hou — FG Zendejas 35
Pitt — FG Anderson 25
Hou — FG Zendejas 26
Pitt — FG Anderson 30
Pitt — FG Anderson 48
Hou — Givins 18 pass from Moon (Zendejas kick)
Hou — Givins 9 pass from Moon (Zendejas kick)
Pitt — Hoge 2 run (Anderson kick)
Pitt — FG Anderson 50

NFC First-Round Playoff Games

Results

Season	Date	Winner (Share)	Loser (Share)	Score	Site	Attendance
1989	Dec. 31	L.A. Rams ($6,000)	Philadelphia ($6,000)	21-7	Philadelphia	65,479
1988	Dec. 26	Minnesota ($6,000)	L.A. Rams ($6,000)	28-17	Minnesota	61,204
1987	Jan. 3	Minnesota ($6,000)	New Orleans ($6,000)	44-10	New Orleans	68,546
1986	Dec. 28	Washington ($6,000)	L.A. Rams ($6,000)	19-7	Washington	54,567
1985	Dec. 29	N.Y. Giants ($6,000)	San Francisco ($6,000)	17-3	East Rutherford	75,131
1984	Dec. 23	N.Y. Giants ($6,000)	L.A. Rams ($6,000)	16-3	Anaheim	67,037
1983	Dec. 26	L.A. Rams ($6,000)	Dallas ($6,000)	24-17	Dallas	62,118
1982	Jan. 9	Dallas ($6,000)	Tampa Bay ($6,000)	30-17	Dallas	65,042
	Jan. 9	Minnesota ($6,000)	Atlanta ($6,000)	30-24	Minnesota	60,560
	Jan. 8	Green Bay ($6,000)	St. Louis ($6,000)	41-16	Green Bay	54,282
	Jan. 8	Washington ($6,000)	Detroit ($6,000)	31-7	Washington	55,045
1981	Dec. 27	N.Y. Giants ($3,000)	Philadelphia ($3,000)	27-21	Philadelphia	71,611
1980	Dec. 28	Dallas ($3,000)	Los Angeles ($3,000)	34-13	Dallas	63,052
1979	Dec. 23	Philadelphia ($3,000)	Chicago ($3,000)	27-17	Philadelphia	69,397
1978	Dec. 24	Atlanta ($3,000)	Philadelphia ($3,000)	14-13	Atlanta	59,403

1989 NFC First-Round Playoff Game

Veterans Stadium, Philadelphia, Pennsylvania   December 31, 1989
Attendance: 65,479

LOS ANGELES RAMS 21, PHILADELPHIA 7—The Los Angeles Rams captured the NFC First-Round Playoff with a 21-7 victory over Philadelphia. The Rams jumped to a 14-0 lead midway through the opening quarter on a pair of Jim Everett touchdown passes of 39 yards to Henry Ellard and four yards to Damone Johnson. Greg Bell rushed 27 times for 124 yards for the Rams, including a seven-yard scoring run in the fourth period. Everett completed 18 of 33 passes for 281 yards and two touchdowns, with two interceptions. Los Angeles held advantages in time of possession (33:38 to 26:22) and yards (409 to 306). Kevin Greene had two sacks and a fumble recovery for Los Angeles.

L.A. Rams	14	0	0	7 — 21
Philadelphia	0	0	0	7 — 7

Rams—Ellard 39 pass from Everett (Lansford kick)
Rams—Johnson 4 pass from Everett (Lansford kick)
Phil —Toney 1 run (Ruzek kick)
Rams—Bell 7 run (Lansford kick)

AFC-NFC Pro Bowl At A Glance (1971-1990)
NFC leads series, 12-8

Results

Year	Date	Winner (Share)	Loser (Share)	Score	Site	Attendance
1990	Feb. 4	NFC ($10,000)	AFC ($5,000)	27-21	Honolulu	50,445
1989	Jan. 29	NFC ($10,000)	AFC ($5,000)	34-3	Honolulu	50,113
1988	Feb. 7	AFC ($10,000)	NFC ($5,000)	15-6	Honolulu	50,113
1987	Feb. 1	AFC ($10,000)	NFC ($5,000)	10-6	Honolulu	50,101
1986	Feb. 2	NFC ($10,000)	AFC ($5,000)	28-24	Honolulu	50,101
1985	Jan. 27	AFC ($10,000)	NFC ($5,000)	22-14	Honolulu	50,385
1984	Jan. 29	NFC ($10,000)	AFC ($5,000)	45-3	Honolulu	50,445
1983	Feb. 6	NFC ($10,000)	AFC ($5,000)	20-19	Honolulu	49,883
1982	Jan. 31	AFC ($5,000)	NFC ($2,500)	16-13	Honolulu	50,402
1981	Feb. 1	NFC ($5,000)	AFC ($2,500)	21-7	Honolulu	50,360
1980	Jan. 27	NFC ($5,000)	AFC ($2,500)	37-27	Honolulu	49,800
1979	Jan. 29	NFC ($5,000)	AFC ($2,500)	13-7	Los Angeles	46,281
1978	Jan. 23	NFC ($5,000)	AFC ($2,500)	14-13	Tampa	51,337
1977	Jan. 17	AFC ($2,000)	NFC ($1,500)	24-14	Seattle	64,752
1976	Jan. 26	NFC ($2,000)	AFC ($1,500)	23-20	New Orleans	30,546
1975	Jan. 20	NFC ($2,000)	AFC ($1,500)	17-10	Miami	26,484
1974	Jan. 20	AFC ($2,000)	NFC ($1,500)	15-13	Kansas City	66,918
1973	Jan. 21	AFC ($2,000)	NFC ($1,500)	33-28	Irving	37,091
1972	Jan. 23	AFC ($2,000)	NFC ($1,500)	26-13	Los Angeles	53,647
1971	Jan. 24	NFC ($2,000)	AFC ($1,500)	27-6	Los Angeles	48,222

1990 AFC-NFC Pro Bowl

Aloha Stadium, Honolulu, Hawaii   February 4, 1990
Attendance: 50,445

NFC 27, AFC 21—The NFC captured its second straight Pro Bowl as the defense accounted for a pair of touchdowns and forced five turnovers before the eleventh consecutive sellout crowd at Aloha Stadium. The AFC held a 7-6 halftime edge on a one-yard scoring run by Christian Okoye of the Chiefs. The NFC then rallied with 21 unanswered points in the third quarter. Dave Meggett of the Giants began the comeback with an 11-yard touchdown reception from Philadelphia's Randall Cunningham. The Rams' Jerry Gray followed with a 51-yard interception return for a score and the Vikings' Keith Millard added an eight-yard fumble return for a touchdown four minutes later to give the NFC a commanding 27-7 lead. Seattle's Dave Krieg rallied the AFC with a five-yard touchdown pass to Miami's Ferrell Edmunds. Cleveland's Mike Johnson then returned an interception 22 yards for a score to pull the AFC to within six points 27-21. Gray, who was credited with seven tackles, was voted the Dan McGuire Award as player of the game. Krieg led all quarterbacks by completing 15 of 23 for 148 yards and one touchdown. Buffalo's Thurman Thomas topped all receivers with five catches for 47 yards, while Indianapolis's Eric Dickerson led all rushers with 46 yards on 15 carries. The win gave the NFC a 12-8 advantage in Pro Bowl games since 1971.

NFC (27)		AFC (21)
	Offense	
Jerry Rice (San Francisco)	WR	Andre Reed (Buffalo)
Gary Zimmerman (Minnesota)	LT	Anthony Muñoz (Cincinnati)
Randall McDaniel (Minnesota)	LG	Mike Munchak (Houston)
Jay Hilgenberg (Chicago)	C	Ray Donaldson (Indianapolis)
Guy McIntyre (San Francisco)	RG	Bruce Matthews (Houston)
Jackie Slater (L.A. Rams)	RT	Chris Hinton (Indianapolis)
Keith Jackson (Philadelphia)	TE	Rodney Holman (Cincinnati)
Sterling Sharpe (Green Bay)	WR	Webster Slaughter (Cleveland)
Randall Cunningham (Philadelphia)	QB	Warren Moon (Houston)
Barry Sanders (Detroit)	RB	Christian Okoye (Kansas City)
Ron Wolfley (Phoenix)	RB	James Brooks (Cincinnati)
	Defense	
Reggie White (Philadelphia)	LE	Lee Williams (San Diego)
Keith Millard (Minnesota)	NT	Michael Dean Perry (Cleveland)
Chris Doleman (Minnesota)	RE	Bruce Smith (Buffalo)
Tim Harris (Green Bay)	LOLB	Clay Matthews (Cleveland)
Chris Spielman (Detroit)	LILB	John Offerdahl (Miami)
Mike Singletary (Chicago)	RILB	Shane Conlan (Buffalo)
Lawrence Taylor (N.Y. Giants)	ROLB	Derrick Thomas (Kansas City)
Carl Lee (Minnesota)	LCB	Albert Lewis (Kansas City)
Jerry Gray (L.A. Rams)	RCB	Frank Minnifield (Cleveland)
Joey Browner (Minnesota)	SS	David Fulcher (Cincinnati)
Ronnie Lott (San Francisco)	FS	Erik McMillan (N.Y. Jets)

Substitutions

NFC—Offense: K—Eddie Murray (Detroit). P—Rich Camarillo (Phoenix). QB—Mark Rypien (Washington). RB—Brent Fullwood (Green Bay), Dalton Hilliard (New Orleans). WR—Mark Carrier (Tampa Bay), Henry Ellard (L.A. Rams). TE—Steve Jordan (Minnesota). KR—Dave Meggett (N.Y. Giants). C—Doug Smith (L.A. Rams). G—Bill Fralic (Atlanta). T—Luis Sharpe (Phoenix). Defense: E—Charles Mann (Washington). NT—Jerry Ball (Detroit). LB—Kevin Greene (L.A. Rams), Vaughan Johnson (New Orleans), Pat Swilling (New Orleans). CB—Eric Allen (Philadelphia). S—Tim McDonald (Phoenix). DNP—Roger Craig (San Francisco).
AFC—Offense: K—David Treadwell (Denver). P—Reggie Roby (Miami). QB—Dave Krieg (Seattle). RB—Eric Dickerson (Indianapolis), Thurman

Thomas (Buffalo). WR—Brian Blades (Seattle), Anthony Miller (San Diego). TE—Ferrell Edmunds (Miami). KR—Rod Woodson (Pittsburgh). C—Kent Hull (Buffalo). G—Max Montoya (Cincinnati). T—Tunch Ilkin (Pittsburgh). ST—Rufus Porter (Seattle). Defense: E—Howie Long (L.A. Raiders). NT—Greg Kragen (Denver). LB—Mike Johnson (Cleveland), Leslie O'Neal (San Diego), Johnny Rembert (New England). CB—Kevin Ross (Kansas City). S—Dennis Smith (Denver). DNP—None.

Head Coaches

NFC—John Robinson (L.A. Rams)
AFC—Bud Carson (Cleveland)

Officials

Referee—Johnny Grier. Umpire—Gordon Wells. Line Judge—Ray Dodez. Head Linesman—Sid Semon. Back Judge—Don Wedge. Field Judge—John Robison. Side Judge—Gil Mace.

Scoring

NFC	3	3	21	0	— 27
AFC	0	7	0	14	— 21

NFC—FG Murray 23
NFC—FG Murray 41
AFC—Okoye 1 run (Treadwell kick)
NFC—Meggett 11 pass from Cunningham (Murray kick)
NFC—Gray 51 interception return (Murray kick)
NFC—Millard 8 fumble recovery return (Murray kick)
AFC—Edmunds 5 pass from Krieg (Treadwell kick)
AFC—M. Johnson 22 interception return (Treadwell kick)

Team Statistics

	NFC	AFC
Total First Downs	14	18
First Downs Rushing	3	7
First Downs Passing	8	8
First Downs Penalty	3	3
Total Net Yardage	220	248
Total Offensive Plays	57	69
Average Gain per Offensive Play	3.9	3.6
Rushes	26	31
Yards Gained Rushing (net)	83	103
Average Yards per Rush	3.2	3.3
Passes Attempted	29	35
Passes Completed	13	20
Passes Had Intercepted	4	2
Tackled Attempting to Pass	2	3
Yards Lost Attempting to Pass	25	23
Yards Gained Passing (net)	137	145
Punts	3	4
Average Distance	49.3	46.0
Punt Returns	4	3
Punt Return Yardage	43	23
Kickoff Returns	3	6
Kickoff Return Yardage	60	140
Interception Return Yardage	51	22
Total Return Yardage	154	185
Fumbles	1	4
Own Fumbles Recovered	1	1
Opponents Fumbles Recovered	3	0
Penalties	9	9

	NFC	AFC
Yards Penalized	42	61
Total Points Scored	27	21
Touchdowns	3	3
Touchdowns Rushing	0	1
Touchdowns Passing	1	1
Touchdowns Returns	2	1
Extra Points	3	3
Field Goals	2	0
Field Goals Attempted	3	0
Safeties	0	0
Third Down Efficiency	4/13	6/14
Fourth Down Efficiency	0/0	1/1
Time of Possession	29:05	30:55

Individual Statistics

Rushing

NFC	No.	Yds.	LG	TD
Sanders	13	41	8	0
Hilliard	9	28	7	0
Cunningham	3	12	9	0
Meggett	1	2	2	0

AFC	No.	Yds.	LG	TD
Dickerson	15	46	7	0
Okoye	6	23	11	1
Krieg	3	15	17	0
Moon	2	7	6	0
Thomas	2	7	12	0
Brooks	3	5	3	0

Passing

NFC	Att.	Comp.	Yds.	TD	Int.
Cunningham	19	9	97	1	1
Rypien	10	4	65	0	3

AFC	Att.	Comp.	Yds.	TD	Int.
Krieg	23	15	148	1	0
Moon	12	5	20	0	2

Receiving

NFC	No.	Yds.	LG	TD
Rice	4	40	11	0
Sanders	3	24	18	0
Carrier	2	35	31	0
Meggett	2	18	11	1
Jordan	1	37	37	0
Wolfley	1	8	8	0

AFC	No.	Yds.	LG	TD
Thomas	5	47	16	0
Miller	5	24	8	0
Dickerson	4	21	7	0
Holman	1	34	34	0
Reed	1	19	19	0
Blades	1	8	8	0
Slaughter	1	8	8	0
Edmunds	1	5	5	1
Okoye	1	2	2	0

Interceptions

NFC	No.	Yds.	LG	TD
Gray	1	51	51	1
Harris	1	0	0	0

AFC	No.	Yds.	LG	TD
Fulcher	2	10	10	0
Matthews	1	27	27	0
Johnson	1	22	22	1

Punting

NFC	No.	Avg.	LG	Blk.
Camarillo	3	49.3	53	0

AFC	No.	Avg.	LG	Blk.
Roby	4	46.0	52	0

Punt Returns

NFC	No.	FC	Yds.	LG	TD
Meggett	4	0	43	24	0

AFC	No.	FC	Yds.	LG	TD
Woodson	3	0	23	12	0

Kickoff Returns

NFC	No.	Yds.	LG	TD
S. Sharpe	2	37	21	0
Meggett	1	23	23	0

AFC	No.	Yds.	LG	TD
Woodson	3	79	31	0
Thomas	3	61	37	0

1989 AFC-NFC Pro Bowl

Aloha Stadium, Honolulu, Hawaii   January 29, 1989
Attendance: 50,113

NFC 34, AFC 3—The NFC scored 34 unanswered points to snap a two-game losing streak to the AFC before the tenth straight sellout crowd in Honolulu's Aloha Stadium. Bills kicker Scott Norwood provided the AFC's only points on a 38-yard field goal 6:23 into the game. Touchdown runs by Dallas's Herschel Walker (four yards) and Atlanta's John Settle (one) brought the NFC a 14-3 halftime lead. Walker added a seven-yard scoring run, the Saints' Morten Andersen kicked field goals of 27 and 51 yards, and Los Angeles Rams' wide receiver Henry Ellard caught an eight-yard scoring pass from Minnesota quarterback Wade Wilson in the second half to complete the scoring. Chicago running back Neal Anderson and Philadelphia quarterback Randall Cunningham, who were both appearing in their first Pro Bowl, also played major roles in the NFC's victory. Anderson rushed 13 times for 85 yards and had two receptions for 17. Cunningham, who was voted the game's outstanding player, completed 10 of 14 passes for 63 yards and rushed for 49 yards. The NFC, which had five takeaways, outgained the AFC 355 yards to 167 and held a time-of-possession advantage of 35:18 to 24:42. Houston quarterback Warren Moon completed 13 of 20 passes for 134 yards for the AFC. The win gave the NFC an 11-8 advantage in Pro Bowl games.

AFC	3	0	0	0 — 3
NFC	7	7	10	10 — 34

AFC—FG Norwood 38
NFC—Walker 4 run (Andersen kick)
NFC—Settle 1 run (Andersen kick)
NFC—FG Andersen 27
NFC—Walker 7 run (Andersen kick)
NFC—FG Andersen 51
NFC—Ellard 8 pass from Wilson (Andersen kick)

1988 AFC-NFC Pro Bowl

Aloha Stadium, Honolulu, Hawaii   February 7, 1988
Attendance: 50,113

AFC 15, NFC 6—Led by a tenacious pass rush, the AFC defeated the NFC for the second consecutive year, 15-6, before the ninth straight sellout crowd in Honolulu's Aloha Stadium. Buffalo quarterback Jim Kelly scored the game's lone touchdown on a one-yard run for a 7-6 halftime lead. Colts kicker Dean Biasucci added field goals from 37 and 30 yards to complete the AFC's scoring. Saints kicker Morten Andersen had 25- and 36-yard field goals to account for the NFC's points. AFC defenders held the NFC to 213 yards and recorded eight sacks. Bills defensive end Bruce Smith, who had five tackles and two sacks, was voted the game's outstanding player. Oilers running back Mike Rozier led all rushers with 49 yards on nine carries. Jets wide receiver Al Toon had five receptions for 75 yards. The AFC generated 341 yards total offense and held a time-of-possession advantage of 34:14 to 25:46. By winning, the AFC cut the NFC's lead in the Pro Bowl series to 10-8.

NFC	0	6	0	0 — 6
AFC	0	7	6	2 — 15

NFC—FG Andersen 25
AFC—Kelly 1 run (Biasucci kick)
NFC—FG Andersen 36
AFC—FG Biasucci 37
AFC—FG Biasucci 30
AFC—Safety, Montana forced out of end zone

1987 AFC-NFC Pro Bowl

Aloha Stadium, Honolulu, Hawaii   February 1, 1987
Attendance: 50,101

AFC 10, NFC 6—The AFC defeated the NFC, 10-6, in the lowest-scoring game in AFC-NFC Pro Bowl history. The AFC took a 10-0 halftime lead on Broncos quarterback John Elway's 10-yard touchdown pass to Raiders tight end Todd Christensen and Patriots kicker Tony Franklin's 26-yard field goal. The AFC defense made the lead stand up by forcing the NFC to settle for a pair of field goals from 38 and 19 yards by Saints kicker Morten Andersen after the NFC had first downs at the AFC 31-, 7-, 16-, 15-, 5-, and 7-yard lines. Both AFC scores were set up by fumble recoveries by Seahawks linebacker Fredd Young and Dolphins linebacker John Offerdahl, respectively. Eagles defensive end Reggie White, who tied a Pro Bowl record with four sacks and also contributed seven solo tackles, was voted the game's outstanding player. The AFC victory cut the NFC's lead in the Pro Bowl series to 10-7.

AFC	7	3	0	0 — 10
NFC	0	0	3	3 — 6

AFC—Christensen 10 pass from Elway (Franklin kick)
AFC—FG Franklin 26
NFC—FG Andersen 38
NFC—FG Andersen 19

1986 AFC-NFC Pro Bowl

Aloha Stadium, Honolulu, Hawaii   February 2, 1986
Attendance: 50,101

NFC 28, AFC 24—New York Giants quarterback Phil Simms brought the NFC back from a 24-7 halftime deficit to a 28-24 win over the AFC. Simms, who completed 15 of 27 passes for 212 yards and three touchdowns, was named the most valuable player of the game. The AFC had taken its first-half lead behind a two-yard run by Los Angeles Raiders running back Marcus Allen, who also threw a 51-yard scoring pass to San Diego wide receiver Wes Chandler, an 11-yard touchdown catch by Pittsburgh wide receiver Louis Lipps, and a 34-yard field goal by Steelers kicker Gary Anderson. Minnesota's Joey Browner accounted for the NFC's only score before halftime on a 48-yard touchdown interception return. After intermission, the NFC blanked the AFC while scoring three touchdowns via a 15-yard catch by Washington wide receiver Art Monk, a 2-yard reception by Dallas tight end Doug Cosbie, and a 15-yard catch by Tampa Bay tight end Jimmie Giles with 2:47 remaining in the game. The victory gave the NFC a 10-6 Pro Bowl record vs. the AFC.

NFC	0	7	7	14 — 28
AFC	7	17	0	0 — 24

AFC—Allen 2 run (Anderson kick)
NFC—Browner 48 interception return (Andersen kick)
AFC—Chandler 51 pass from Allen (Anderson kick)
AFC—FG Anderson 34
AFC—Lipps 11 pass from O'Brien (Anderson kick)
NFC—Monk 15 pass from Simms (Andersen kick)
NFC—Cosbie 2 pass from Simms (Andersen kick)
NFC—Giles 15 pass from Simms (Andersen kick)

1985 AFC-NFC Pro Bowl

Aloha Stadium, Honolulu, Hawaii   January 27, 1985
Attendance: 50,385

AFC 22, NFC 14—Defensive end Art Still of the Kansas City Chiefs recovered a fumble and returned it 83 yards for a touchdown to clinch the AFC's victory over the NFC. Still's touchdown came in the fourth period with the AFC trailing 14-12 and was one of several outstanding defensive plays in a Pro Bowl dominated by two record-breaking defenses. Both teams combined for a Pro Bowl-record 17 sacks, including four by New York Jets defensive end Mark Gastineau, who was named the game's outstanding player. The AFC's first score came on a safety when Gastineau tackled running back Eric Dickerson of the Los Angeles Rams in the end zone. The AFC's second score, a six-yard pass from Miami's Dan Marino to Los Angeles Raiders running back Marcus Allen, was set up by a partial block of a punt by Seahawks linebacker Fredd Young. The NFC leads the series 9-6.

AFC	0	9	0	13 — 22
NFC	0	0	7	7 — 14

AFC—Safety, Gastineau tackled Dickerson in end zone
AFC—Allen 6 pass from Marino (Johnson kick)
NFC—Lofton 13 pass from Montana (Stenerud kick)

NFC—Payton 1 run (Stenerud kick)
AFC—FG Johnson 33
AFC—Still 83 fumble recovery return (Johnson kick)
AFC—FG Johnson 22

1984 AFC-NFC Pro Bowl

Aloha Stadium, Honolulu, Hawaii   January 29, 1984
Attendance: 50,445

NFC 45, AFC 3—The NFC won its sixth Pro Bowl in the last seven seasons, 45-3 over the AFC. The NFC was led by the passing of most valuable player Joe Theismann of Washington, who completed 21 of 27 passes for 242 yards and three touchdowns. Theismann set Pro Bowl records for completions and touchdown passes. The NFC established Pro Bowl marks for most points scored and fewest points allowed. Running back William Andrews of Atlanta had six carries for 43 yards and caught four passes for 49 yards, including scoring receptions of 16 and 2 yards. Los Angeles Rams rookie Eric Dickerson gained 46 yards on 11 carries, including a 14-yard touchdown run, and had 45 yards on five catches. Rams safety Nolan Cromwell had a 44-yard interception return for a touchdown early in the third period to give the NFC a commanding 24-3 lead. Green Bay wide receiver James Lofton caught an eight-yard touchdown pass, while tight end teammate Paul Coffman had a six-yard scoring catch.

NFC	3	14	14	14 —	45
AFC	0	3	0	0 —	3

NFC—FG Haji-Sheikh 23
NFC—Andrews 16 pass from Theismann (Haji-Sheikh kick)
NFC—Andrews 2 pass from Montana (Haji-Sheikh kick)
AFC—FG Anderson 43
NFC—Cromwell 44 interception return (Haji-Sheikh kick)
NFC—Lofton 8 pass from Theismann (Haji-Sheikh kick)
NFC—Coffman 6 pass from Theismann (Haji-Sheikh kick)
NFC—Dickerson 14 run (Haji-Sheikh kick)

1983 AFC-NFC Pro Bowl

Aloha Stadium, Honolulu, Hawaii   February 6, 1983
Attendance: 49,883

NFC 20, AFC 19—Danny White threw an 11-yard touchdown pass to John Jefferson with 35 seconds remaining to give the NFC a 20-19 victory over the AFC. White, who completed 14 of 26 passes for 162 yards, kept the winning 65-yard drive alive with a 14-yard completion to Jefferson on a fourth-and-seven play at the AFC 25. The AFC was ahead 12-10 at halftime and increased the lead to 19-10 in the third period, when Marcus Allen scored on a one-yard run. Dan Fouts, who attempted 30 passes, set Pro Bowl records for most completions (17) and yards (274). John Stallworth was the AFC's leading receiver with seven catches for 67 yards. William Andrews topped the NFC with five receptions for 48 yards. Fouts and Jefferson were voted co-winners of the player of the game award.

AFC	9	3	7	0 —	19
NFC	0	10	0	10 —	20

AFC—Walker 34 pass from Fouts (Benirschke kick)
AFC—Safety, Still tackled Theismann in end zone
NFC—Andrews 3 run (Moseley kick)
NFC—FG Moseley 35
AFC—FG Benirschke 29
AFC—Allen 1 run (Benirschke kick)
NFC—FG Moseley 41
NFC—Jefferson 11 pass from D. White (Moseley kick)

1982 AFC-NFC Pro Bowl

Aloha Stadium, Honolulu, Hawaii   January 31, 1982
Attendance: 50,402

AFC 16, NFC 13—Nick Lowery kicked a 23-yard field goal with three seconds remaining to give the AFC a 16-13 victory over the NFC. Lowery's kick climaxed a 69-yard drive directed by quarterback Dan Fouts. The NFC gained a 13-13 tie with 2:43 to go when Tony Dorsett ran four yards for a touchdown. In the drive to the game-winning field goal, Fouts completed three passes, including a 23-yarder to San Diego teammate Kellen Winslow that put the ball on the NFC's 5-yard line. Two plays later, Lowery kicked the field goal. Winslow, who caught six passes for 86 yards, was named co-player of the game along with NFC defensive end Lee Roy Selmon.

NFC	0	6	0	7 —	13
AFC	0	0	13	3 —	16

NFC—Giles 4 pass from Montana (kick blocked)
AFC—Muncie 2 run (kick failed)
AFC—Campbell 1 run (Lowery kick)
NFC—Dorsett 4 run (Septien kick)
AFC—FG Lowery 23

1981 AFC-NFC Pro Bowl

Aloha Stadium, Honolulu, Hawaii   February 1, 1981
Attendance: 50,360

NFC 21, AFC 7—Ed Murray kicked four field goals and Steve Bartkowski fired a 55-yard scoring pass to Alfred Jenkins to lead the NFC to its fourth straight victory over the AFC and a 7-4 edge in the series. Murray was named the game's most valuable player and missed tying Garo Yepremian's Pro Bowl record of five field goals when a 37-yard attempt hit the crossbar with 22 seconds remaining. The AFC's only score came on a nine-yard pass from Brian Sipe to Stanley Morgan in the second period. Bartkowski completed 9 of 21 for 173 yards, while Sipe connected on 10 of 15 for 142 yards. Ottis Anderson led

all rushers with 70 yards on 10 carries. Earl Campbell, the NFL's leading rusher in 1980, was limited to 24 yards on eight attempts.

AFC	0	7	0	0 —	7
NFC	3	6	0	12 —	21

NFC—FG Murray 31
AFC—Morgan 9 pass from Sipe (J. Smith kick)
NFC—FG Murray 31
NFC—FG Murray 34
NFC—Jenkins 55 pass from Bartkowski (Murray kick)
NFC—FG Murray 36
NFC—Safety, Shell called for holding in end zone

1980 AFC-NFC Pro Bowl

Aloha Stadium, Honolulu, Hawaii   January 27, 1980
Attendance: 49,800

NFC 37, AFC 27—Running back Chuck Muncie ran for two touchdowns and threw a 25-yard option pass for another score to give the NFC its third consecutive victory over the AFC. Muncie, who was selected the game's most valuable player, snapped a 3-3 tie on a one-yard touchdown run at 1:41 of the second quarter, then scored on an 11-yard run in the fourth quarter for the NFC's final touchdown. Two scoring records were set in the game—37 points by the NFC, eclipsing the 33 by the AFC in 1973, and the 64 points by both teams, surpassing the 61 scored in 1973.

NFC	3	20	7	7 —	37
AFC	3	7	10	7 —	27

NFC—FG Moseley 37
AFC—FG Fritsch 19
NFC—Muncie 1 run (Moseley kick)
AFC—Pruitt 1 pass from Bradshaw (Fritsch kick)
NFC—D. Hill 13 pass from Manning (kick failed)
NFC—T. Hill 25 pass from Muncie (Moseley kick)
NFC—Henry 86 punt return (Moseley kick)
AFC—Campbell 2 run (Fritsch kick)
AFC—FG Fritsch 29
NFC—Muncie 11 run (Moseley kick)
AFC—Campbell 1 run (Fritsch kick)

1979 AFC-NFC Pro Bowl

Memorial Coliseum, Los Angeles, California   January 29, 1979
Attendance: 46,281

NFC 13, AFC 7—Roger Staubach completed 9 of 15 passes for 125 yards, including the winning touchdown on a 19-yard strike to Dallas Cowboys teammate Tony Hill in the third period. The winning drive began at the AFC's 45 yard line after a shanked punt. Staubach hit Ahmad Rashad with passes of 15 and 17 yards to set up Hill's decisive catch. The victory gave the NFC a 5-4 advantage in Pro Bowl games. Rashad, who accounted for 89 yards on five receptions, was named the player of the game. The AFC led 7-6 at halftime on Bob Griese's eight-yard scoring toss to Steve Largent late in the second quarter. Largent finished the game with five receptions for 75 yards. The NFC scored first as Archie Manning marched his team 70 yards in 11 plays, capped by Wilbert Montgomery's two-yard touchdown run. The AFC's Earl Campbell was the game's leading rusher with 66 yards on 12 carries.

AFC	0	7	0	0 —	7
NFC	0	6	7	0 —	13

NFC—Montgomery 2 run (kick failed)
AFC—Largent 8 pass from Griese (Yepremian kick)
NFC—T. Hill 19 pass from Staubach (Corral kick)

1978 AFC-NFC Pro Bowl

Tampa Stadium, Tampa, Florida   January 23, 1978
Attendance: 51,337

NFC 14, AFC 13—Walter Payton, the NFL's leading rusher in 1977, sparked a second-half comeback to give the NFC a 14-13 win and tie the series between the two conferences at four victories each. Payton, who was the game's most valuable player, gained 77 yards on 13 carries and scored the tying touchdown on a one-yard burst with 7:37 left in the game. Efren Herrera kicked the winning extra point. The AFC dominated the first half of the game, taking a 13-0 lead on field goals of 21 and 39 yards by Toni Linhart and a 10-yard touchdown pass from Ken Stabler to Oakland teammate Cliff Branch. On the NFC's first possession of the second half, Pat Haden put together the first touchdown drive after Eddie Brown returned Ray Guy's punt to the AFC 46-yard line. Haden connected on all four of his passes on that drive, finally hitting Terry Metcalf with a four-yard scoring toss. The NFC continued to rally and, with Jim Hart at quarterback, moved 63 yards in 12 plays for the go-ahead score. During the winning drive, Hart completed five of six passes for 38 yards and Payton picked up 20 more on the ground.

AFC	3	10	0	0 —	13
NFC	0	0	7	7 —	14

AFC—FG Linhart 21
AFC—Branch 10 pass from Stabler (Linhart kick)
AFC—FG Linhart 39
NFC—Metcalf 4 pass from Haden (Herrera kick)
NFC—Payton 1 run (Herrera kick)

1977 AFC-NFC Pro Bowl

Kingdome, Seattle, Washington   January 17, 1977
Attendance: 64,752

AFC 24, NFC 14—O. J. Simpson's three-yard touchdown burst at 7:03 of the first quarter gave the AFC a lead it would not surrender, the victory breaking a two-game NFC win streak and giving the American Conference stars a 4-3 series lead. The AFC took a 17-7 lead midway through the second period on the first of two Ken Anderson touchdown passes, a 12-yarder to Charlie Joiner. But the NFC mounted a 73-yard drive capped by Lawrence McCutcheon's one-yard touchdown plunge to pull within three of the AFC, 17-14, at the half. Following a scoreless third quarter, player of the game Mel Blount thwarted a possible NFC score when he intercepted Jim Hart's pass in the end zone. Less than three minutes later, Blount again picked off a Hart pass, returning it 16 yards to the NFC 27. That set up Anderson's 27-yard touchdown strike to Cliff Branch for the final score.

NFC	0	14	0	0 —	14
AFC	10	7	0	7 —	24

AFC—Simpson 3 run (Linhart kick)
AFC—FG Linhart 31
NFC—Thomas 15 run (Bakken kick)
AFC—Joiner 12 pass from Anderson (Linhart kick)
NFC—McCutcheon 1 run (Bakken kick)
AFC—Branch 27 pass from Anderson (Linhart kick)

1976 AFC-NFC Pro Bowl
Superdome, New Orleans, Louisiana   January 26, 1976
Attendance: 30,546

NFC 23, AFC 20—Mike Boryla, a late substitute who did not enter the game until 5:39 remained, lifted the National Football Conference to a 23-20 victory over the American Football Conference with two touchdown passes in the final minutes. It was the second straight NFC win, squaring the series at 3-3. Until Boryla started firing the ball the AFC was in control, leading 13-0 at the half. Boryla entered the game after Billy Johnson had raced 90 yards with a punt to make the score 20-9 in favor of the AFC. He floated a 14-yard pass to Terry Metcalf and later fired an eight-yarder to Mel Gray for the winner.

AFC	0	13	0	7 —	20
NFC	0	0	9	14 —	23

AFC—FG Stenerud 20
AFC—FG Stenerud 35
AFC—Burrough 64 pass from Pastorini (Stenerud kick)
NFC—FG Bakken 42
NFC—Foreman 4 pass from Hart (kick blocked)
AFC—Johnson 90 punt return (Stenerud kick)
NFC—Metcalf 14 pass from Boryla (Bakken kick)
NFC—Gray 8 pass from Boryla (Bakken kick)

1975 AFC-NFC Pro Bowl
Orange Bowl, Miami, Florida   January 20, 1975
Attendance: 26,484

NFC 17, AFC 10—Los Angeles quarterback James Harris, who took over the NFC offense after Jim Hart of St. Louis suffered a laceration above his right eye in the second period, threw a pair of touchdown passes early in the fourth period to pace the NFC to its second victory in the five-game Pro Bowl series. The NFC win snapped a three-game AFC victory string. Harris, who was named the player of the game, connected with St. Louis's Mel Gray for an eight-yard touchdown 2:03 into the final period. One minute and 24 seconds later, following a recovery by Washington's Ken Houston of a fumble by Franco Harris of Pittsburgh, Harris tossed another eight-yard scoring pass to Washington's Charley Taylor for the decisive points.

NFC	0	3	0	14 —	17
AFC	0	0	10	0 —	10

NFC—FG Marcol 33
AFC—Warfield 32 pass from Griese (Gerela kick)
AFC—FG Gerela 33
NFC—Gray 8 pass from J. Harris (Marcol kick)
NFC—Taylor 8 pass from J. Harris (Marcol kick)

1974 AFC-NFC Pro Bowl
Arrowhead Stadium, Kansas City, Missouri   January 20, 1974
Attendance: 66,918

AFC 15, NFC 13—Miami's Garo Yepremian kicked his fifth consecutive field goal without a miss from the 42-yard line with 21 seconds remaining to give the AFC its third straight victory since the NFC won the inaugural game following the 1970 season. The field goal by Yepremian, who was voted the game's outstanding player, offset a 21-yard field goal by Atlanta's Nick Mike-Mayer that had given the NFC a 13-12 advantage with 1:41 remaining. The only touchdown in the game was scored by the NFC on a 14-yard pass from Philadelphia's Roman Gabriel to Lawrence McCutcheon of the Los Angeles Rams.

NFC	0	10	0	3 —	13
AFC	3	3	3	6 —	15

AFC—FG Yepremian 16
NFC—FG Mike-Mayer 27
NFC—McCutcheon 14 pass from Gabriel (Mike-Mayer kick)
AFC—FG Yepremian 37
AFC—FG Yepremian 27
AFC—FG Yepremian 41
NFC—FG Mike-Mayer 21
AFC—FG Yepremian 42

1973 AFC-NFC Pro Bowl
Texas Stadium, Irving, Texas   January 21, 1973
Attendance: 37,091

AFC 33, NFC 28—Paced by the rushing and receiving of player of the game O.J. Simpson, the AFC erased a 14-0 first period deficit and built a command-

ing 33-14 lead midway through the fourth period before the NFC managed two touchdowns in the final minute of play. Simpson rushed for 112 yards and caught three passes for 58 more to gain unanimous recognition in the balloting for player of the game. John Brockington scored three touchdowns for the NFC.

AFC	0	10	10	13 —	33
NFC	14	0	0	14 —	28

NFC—Brockington 1 run (Marcol kick)
NFC—Brockington 3 pass from Kilmer (Marcol kick)
AFC—Simpson 7 run (Gerela kick)
AFC—FG Gerela 18
AFC—FG Gerela 22
AFC—Hubbard 11 run (Gerela kick)
AFC—O. Taylor 5 pass from Lamonica (kick failed)
AFC—Bell 12 interception return (Gerela kick)
NFC—Brockington 1 run (Marcol kick)
NFC—Kwalick 12 pass from Snead (Marcol kick)

1972 AFC-NFC Pro Bowl
Memorial Coliseum, Los Angeles, California   January 23, 1972
Attendance: 53,647

AFC 26, NFC 13—Four field goals by Jan Stenerud of Kansas City, including a 6-6 tie-breaker from 48 yards, helped lift the AFC from a 6-0 deficit to a 19-6 advantage early in the fourth period. The AFC defense picked off three interceptions. Stenerud was selected as the outstanding offensive player and his Kansas City teammate, linebacker Willie Lanier, was the game's outstanding defensive player.

AFC	0	3	13	10 —	26
NFC	0	6	0	7 —	13

NFC—Grim 50 pass from Landry (kick failed)
AFC—FG Stenerud 25
AFC—FG Stenerud 23
AFC—FG Stenerud 48
AFC—Morin 5 pass from Dawson (Stenerud kick)
AFC—FG Stenerud 42
NFC—V. Washington 2 run (Knight kick)
AFC—F. Little 6 run (Stenerud kick)

1971 AFC-NFC Pro Bowl
Memorial Coliseum, Los Angeles, California   January 24, 1971
Attendance: 48,222

NFC 27, AFC 6—Mel Renfro of Dallas broke open the first meeting between the American Football Conference and National Football Conference all-star teams as he returned a pair of punts 82 and 56 yards for touchdowns in the final period to provide the NFC with a 27-6 victory over the AFC. Renfro was voted the game's outstanding back and linebacker Fred Carr of Green Bay the outstanding lineman.

AFC	0	3	3	0 —	6
NFC	0	3	10	14 —	27

AFC—FG Stenerud 37
NFC—FG Cox 13
NFC—Osborn 23 pass from Brodie (Cox kick)
NFC—FG Cox 35
AFC—FG Stenerud 16
NFC—Renfro 82 punt return (Cox kick)
NFC—Renfro 56 punt return (Cox kick)

Pro Bowl All-Time Results

Date	Result	Site (attendance)	Honored players
Jan. 15, 1939	New York Giants 13, Pro All-Stars 10	Wrigley Field, Los Angeles (20,000)	
Jan. 14, 1940	Green Bay 16, NFL All-Stars 7	Gilmore Stadium, Los Angeles (18,000)	
Dec. 29, 1940	Chicago Bears 28, NFL All-Stars 14	Gilmore Stadium, Los Angeles (21,624)	
Jan. 4, 1942	Chicago Bears 35, NFL All-Stars 24	Polo Grounds, New York (17,725)	
Dec. 27, 1942	NFL All-Stars 17, Washington 14	Shibe Park, Philadelphia (18,671)	
Jan. 14, 1951	American Conf. 28, National Conf. 27	Los Angeles Memorial Coliseum (53,676)	Otto Graham, Cleveland, player of the game
Jan. 12, 1952	National Conf. 30, American Conf. 13	Los Angeles Memorial Coliseum (19,400)	Dan Towler, Los Angeles, player of the game
Jan. 10, 1953	National Conf. 27, American Conf. 7	Los Angeles Memorial Coliseum (34,208)	Don Doll, Detroit, player of the game
Jan. 17, 1954	East 20, West 9	Los Angeles Memorial Coliseum (44,214)	Chuck Bednarik, Philadelphia, player of the game
Jan. 16, 1955	West 26, East 19	Los Angeles Memorial Coliseum (43,972)	Billy Wilson, San Francisco, player of the game
Jan. 15, 1956	East 31, West 30	Los Angeles Memorial Coliseum (37,867)	Ollie Matson, Chi. Cardinals, player of the game
Jan. 13, 1957	West 19, East 10	Los Angeles Memorial Coliseum (44,177)	Bert Rechichar, Baltimore, outstanding back Ernie Stautner, Pittsburgh, outstanding lineman
Jan. 12, 1958	West 26, East 7	Los Angeles Memorial Coliseum (66,634)	Hugh McElhenny, San Francisco, outstanding back Gene Brito, Washington, outstanding lineman
Jan. 11, 1959	East 28, West 21	Los Angeles Memorial Coliseum (72,250)	Frank Gifford, N.Y. Giants, outstanding back Doug Atkins, Chi. Bears, outstanding lineman
Jan. 17, 1960	West 38, East 21	Los Angeles Memorial Coliseum (56,876)	Johnny Unitas, Baltimore, outstanding back Gene (Big Daddy) Lipscomb, Baltimore, outstanding lineman
Jan. 15, 1961	West 35, East 31	Los Angeles Memorial Coliseum (62,971)	Johnny Unitas, Baltimore, outstanding back Sam Huff, N.Y. Giants, outstanding lineman
Jan. 7, 1962	AFL West 47, East 27	Balboa Stadium, San Diego (20,973)	Cotton Davidson, Dallas Texans, player of the game
Jan. 14, 1962	NFL West 31, East 30	Los Angeles Memorial Coliseum (57,409)	Jim Brown, Cleveland, outstanding back Henry Jordan, Green Bay, outstanding lineman
Jan. 13, 1963	AFL West 21, East 14	Balboa Stadium, San Diego (27,641)	Curtis McClinton, Dallas Texans, outstanding offensive player Earl Faison, San Diego, outstanding defensive player
Jan. 13, 1963	NFL East 30, West 20	Los Angeles Memorial Coliseum (61,374)	Jim Brown, Cleveland, outstanding back Gene (Big Daddy) Lipscomb, Pittsburgh, outstanding lineman
Jan. 12, 1964	NFL West 31, East 17	Los Angeles Memorial Coliseum (67,242)	Johnny Unitas, Baltimore, player of the game Gino Marchetti, Baltimore, outstanding lineman
Jan. 19, 1964	AFL West 27, East 24	Balboa Stadium, San Diego (20,016)	Keith Lincoln, San Diego, outstanding offensive player Archie Matsos, Oakland, outstanding defensive player
Jan. 10, 1965	NFL West 34, East 14	Los Angeles Memorial Coliseum (60,598)	Fran Tarkenton, Minnesota, outstanding back Terry Barr, Detroit, outstanding lineman
Jan. 16, 1965	AFL West 38, East 14	Jeppesen Stadium, Houston (15,446)	Keith Lincoln, San Diego, outstanding offensive player Willie Brown, Denver, outstanding defensive player
Jan. 15, 1966	AFL All-Stars 30, Buffalo 19	Rice Stadium, Houston (35,572)	Joe Namath, N.Y. Jets, most valuable player, offense Frank Buncom, San Diego, most valuable player, defense
Jan. 15, 1966	NFL East 36, West 7	Los Angeles Memorial Coliseum (60,124)	Jim Brown, Cleveland, outstanding back Dale Meinert, St. Louis, outstanding lineman
Jan. 21, 1967	AFL East 30, West 23	Oakland-Alameda County Coliseum (18,876)	Babe Parilli, Boston, outstanding offensive player Verlon Biggs, N.Y. Jets, outstanding defensive player
Jan. 22, 1967	NFL East 20, West 10	Los Angeles Memorial Coliseum (15,062)	Gale Sayers, Chicago, outstanding back Floyd Peters, Philadelphia, outstanding lineman
Jan. 21, 1968	AFL East 25, West 24	Gator Bowl, Jacksonville, Fla. (40,103)	Joe Namath and Don Maynard, N.Y. Jets, out. off. players Leslie (Speedy) Duncan, San Diego, out. def. player
Jan. 21, 1968	NFL West 38, East 20	Los Angeles Memorial Coliseum (53,289)	Gale Sayers, Chicago, outstanding back Dave Robinson, Green Bay, outstanding lineman
Jan. 19, 1969	AFL West 38, East 25	Gator Bowl, Jacksonville, Fla. (41,058)	Len Dawson, Kansas City, outstanding offensive player George Webster, Houston, outstanding defensive player
Jan. 19, 1969	NFL West 10, East 7	Los Angeles Memorial Coliseum (32,050)	Roman Gabriel, Los Angeles, outstanding back Merlin Olsen, Los Angeles, outstanding lineman
Jan. 17, 1970	AFL West 26, East 3	Astrodome, Houston (30,170)	John Hadl, San Diego, player of the game
Jan. 18, 1970	NFL West 16, East 13	Los Angeles Memorial Coliseum (57,786)	Gale Sayers, Chicago, outstanding back George Andrie, Dallas, outstanding lineman
Jan. 24, 1971	NFC 27, AFC 6	Los Angeles Memorial Coliseum (48,222)	Mel Renfro, Dallas, outstanding back Fred Carr, Green Bay, outstanding lineman
Jan. 23, 1972	AFC 26, NFC 13	Los Angeles Memorial Coliseum (53,647)	Jan Stenerud, Kansas City, outstanding offensive player Willie Lanier, Kansas City, outstanding defensive player
Jan. 21, 1973	AFC 33, NFC 28	Texas Stadium, Irving (37,091)	O.J. Simpson, Buffalo, player of the game
Jan. 20, 1974	AFC 15, NFC 13	Arrowhead Stadium, Kansas City (66,918)	Garo Yepremian, Miami, player of the game
Jan. 20, 1975	NFC 17, AFC 10	Orange Bowl, Miami (26,484)	James Harris, Los Angeles, player of the game
Jan. 26, 1976	NFC 23, AFC 20	Louisiana Superdome, New Orleans (30,546)	Billy Johnson, Houston, player of the game
Jan. 17, 1977	AFC 24, NFC 14	Kingdome, Seattle (64,752)	Mel Blount, Pittsburgh, player of the game
Jan. 23, 1978	NFC 14, AFC 13	Tampa Stadium (51,337)	Walter Payton, Chicago, player of the game
Jan. 29, 1979	NFC 13, AFC 7	Los Angeles Memorial Coliseum (46,281)	Ahmad Rashad, Minnesota, player of the game
Jan. 27, 1980	NFC 37, AFC 27	Aloha Stadium, Honolulu (49,800)	Chuck Muncie, New Orleans, player of the game
Feb. 1, 1981	NFC 21, AFC 7	Aloha Stadium, Honolulu (50,360)	Eddie Murray, Detroit, player of the game
Jan. 31, 1982	AFC 16, NFC 13	Aloha Stadium, Honolulu (50,402)	Kellen Winslow, San Diego, and Lee Roy Selmon, Tampa Bay, players of the game
Feb. 6, 1983	NFC 20, AFC 19	Aloha Stadium, Honolulu (49,883)	Dan Fouts, San Diego, and John Jefferson, Green Bay, players of the game
Jan. 29, 1984	NFC 45, AFC 3	Aloha Stadium, Honolulu (50,445)	Joe Theismann, Washington, player of the game
Jan. 27, 1985	AFC 22, NFC 14	Aloha Stadium, Honolulu (50,385)	Mark Gastineau, N.Y. Jets, player of the game
Feb. 2, 1986	NFC 28, AFC 24	Aloha Stadium, Honolulu (50,101)	Phil Simms, N.Y. Giants, player of the game
Feb. 1, 1987	AFC 10, NFC 6	Aloha Stadium, Honolulu (50,101)	Reggie White, Philadelphia, player of the game
Feb. 7, 1988	AFC 15, NFC 6	Aloha Stadium, Honolulu (50,113)	Bruce Smith, Buffalo, player of the game
Jan. 29, 1989	NFC 34, AFC 3	Aloha Stadium, Honolulu (50,113)	Randall Cunningham, Philadelphia, player of the game
Feb. 4, 1990	NFC 27, AFC 21	Aloha Stadium, Honolulu (50,445)	Jerry Gray, L.A. Rams, player of the game

Chicago All-Star Game

Pro teams won 31, lost 9, and tied 2. The game was discontinued after 1976.

Year	Date	Winner	Loser	Attendance
1976*	July 23	Pittsburgh 24	All-Stars 0	52,895
1975	Aug. 1	Pittsburgh 21	All-Stars 14	54,103
1974		No game was played		
1973	July 27	Miami 14	All-Stars 3	54,103
1972	July 28	Dallas 20	All-Stars 7	54,162
1971	July 30	Baltimore 24	All-Stars 17	52,289
1970	July 31	Kansas City 24	All-Stars 3	69,940
1969	Aug. 1	N.Y. Jets 26	All-Stars 24	74,208
1968	Aug. 2	Green Bay 34	All-Stars 17	69,917
1967	Aug. 4	Green Bay 27	All-Stars 0	70,934
1966	Aug. 5	Green Bay 38	All-Stars 0	72,000
1965	Aug. 6	Cleveland 24	All-Stars 16	68,000
1964	Aug. 7	Chicago 28	All-Stars 17	65,000
1963	Aug. 2	All-Stars 20	Green Bay 17	65,000
1962	Aug. 3	Green Bay 42	All-Stars 20	65,000
1961	Aug. 4	Philadelphia 28	All-Stars 14	66,000
1960	Aug. 12	Baltimore 32	All-Stars 7	70,000
1959	Aug. 14	Baltimore 29	All-Stars 0	70,000
1958	Aug. 15	All-Stars 35	Detroit 19	70,000
1957	Aug. 9	N.Y. Giants 22	All-Stars 12	75,000
1956	Aug. 10	Cleveland 26	All-Stars 0	75,000
1955	Aug. 12	All-Stars 30	Cleveland 27	75,000
1954	Aug. 13	Detroit 31	All-Stars 6	93,470
1953	Aug. 14	Detroit 24	All-Stars 10	93,818
1952	Aug. 15	Los Angeles 10	All-Stars 7	88,316
1951	Aug. 17	Cleveland 33	All-Stars 0	92,180
1950	Aug. 11	All-Stars 17	Philadelphia 7	88,885
1949	Aug. 12	Philadelphia 38	All-Stars 0	93,780
1948	Aug. 20	Chi. Cardinals 28	All-Stars 0	101,220
1947	Aug. 22	All-Stars 16	Chi. Bears 0	105,840
1946	Aug. 23	All-Stars 16	Los Angeles 0	97,380
1945	Aug. 30	Green Bay 19	All-Stars 7	92,753
1944	Aug. 30	Chi. Bears 24	All-Stars 21	48,769
1943	Aug. 25	All-Stars 27	Washington 7	48,471
1942	Aug. 28	Chi. Bears 21	All-Stars 0	101,100
1941	Aug. 28	Chi. Bears 37	All-Stars 13	98,203
1940	Aug. 29	Green Bay 45	All-Stars 28	84,567
1939	Aug. 30	N.Y. Giants 9	All-Stars 0	81,456
1938	Aug. 31	All-Stars 28	Washington 16	74,250
1937	Sept. 1	All-Stars 6	Green Bay 0	84,560
1936	Sept. 3	All-Stars 7	Detroit 7 (tie)	76,000
1935	Aug. 29	Chi. Bears 5	All-Stars 0	77,450
1934	Aug. 31	Chi. Bears 0	All-Stars 0 (tie)	79,432

*Game shortened due to thunderstorms.

NFL Playoff Bowl

Western Conference won 8, Eastern Conference won 2.
All games played at Miami's Orange Bowl.

1970	Los Angeles Rams 31, Dallas Cowboys 0
1969	Dallas Cowboys 17, Minnesota Vikings 13
1968	Los Angeles Rams 30, Cleveland Browns 6
1967	Baltimore Colts 20, Philadelphia Eagles 14
1966	Baltimore Colts 35, Dallas Cowboys 3
1965	St. Louis Cardinals 24, Green Bay Packers 17
1964	Green Bay Packers 40, Cleveland Browns 23
1963	Detroit Lions 17, Pittsburgh Steelers 10
1962	Detroit Lions 28, Philadelphia Eagles 10
1961	Detroit Lions 17, Cleveland Browns 16

Pro Football Hall of Fame Game

1962	New York Giants 21, St. Louis Cardinals 21
1963	Pittsburgh Steelers 16, Cleveland Browns 7
1964	Baltimore Colts 48, Pittsburgh Steelers 17
1965	Washington Redskins 20, Detroit Lions 3
1966	No game
1967	Philadelphia Eagles 28, Cleveland Browns 13
1968	Chicago Bears 30, Dallas Cowboys 24
1969	Green Bay Packers 38, Atlanta Falcons 24
1970	New Orleans Saints 14, Minnesota Vikings 13
1971	Los Angeles Rams (NFC) 17, Houston Oilers (AFC) 6
1972	Kansas City Chiefs (AFC) 23, New York Giants (NFC) 17
1973	San Francisco 49ers (NFC) 20, New England Patriots (AFC) 7
1974	St. Louis Cardinals (NFC) 21, Buffalo Bills (AFC) 13
1975	Washington Redskins (NFC) 17, Cincinnati Bengals (AFC) 9
1976	Denver Broncos (AFC) 10, Detroit Lions (NFC) 7
1977	Chicago Bears (NFC) 20, New York Jets (AFC) 6
1978	Philadelphia Eagles (NFC) 17, Miami Dolphins (AFC) 3
1979	Oakland Raiders (AFC) 20, Dallas Cowboys (NFC) 13
1980*	San Diego Chargers (AFC) 0, Green Bay Packers (NFC) 0
1981	Cleveland Browns (AFC) 24, Atlanta Falcons (NFC) 10
1982	Minnesota Vikings (NFC) 30, Baltimore Colts (AFC) 14
1983	Pittsburgh Steelers (AFC) 27, New Orleans Saints (NFC) 14
1984	Seattle Seahawks (AFC) 38, Tampa Bay Buccaneers (NFC) 0
1985	New York Giants (NFC) 21, Houston Oilers (AFC) 20
1986	New England Patriots (AFC) 21, St. Louis Cardinals (NFC) 16
1987	San Francisco 49ers (NFC) 20, Kansas City Chiefs (AFC) 7
1988	Cincinnati Bengals (AFC) 14, Los Angeles Rams (NFC) 7
1989	Washington Redskins (NFC) 31, Buffalo Bills (AFC) 6

*Game called with 5:29 remaining due to severe thunder & lightning.

NFL International Games

Date	Site	Teams
Aug. 12, 1950	Ottawa, Canada	N.Y. Giants 20, Ottawa Roughriders 6
Aug. 11, 1951	Ottawa, Canada	N.Y. Giants 38, Ottawa Roughriders 6
Aug. 5, 1959	Toronto, Canada	Chi. Cardinals 55, Tor. Argonauts 26
Aug. 6, 1960	Toronto, Canada	Pittsburgh 43, Toronto Argonauts 16
Aug. 15, 1960	Toronto, Canada	Chicago Bears 16, N.Y. Giants 7
Aug. 2, 1961	Toronto, Canada	St. Louis 36, Toronto Argonauts 7
Aug. 5, 1961	Montreal, Canada	Chi. Bears 34, Montreal Allouettes 16
Aug. 8, 1961	Hamilton, Canada	Hamilton Tiger-Cats 38, Buffalo 21
Aug. 11, 1969	Montreal, Canada	Pittsburgh 17, N.Y. Giants 13
Aug. 25, 1969	Montreal, Canada	Detroit 22, Boston Patriots 9
Aug. 16, 1976	Tokyo, Japan	St. Louis 20, San Diego 10
Aug. 5, 1978	Mexico City, Mexico	New Orleans 14, Philadelphia 7
Aug. 6, 1983	London, England	Minnesota 28, St. Louis 10
Aug. 3, 1986	London, England	Chicago Bears 17, Dallas 6
Aug. 9, 1987	London, England	L.A. Rams 28, Denver 27
July 31, 1988	London, England	Miami 27, San Francisco 21
Aug. 14, 1988	Goteborg, Sweden	Minnesota 28, Chicago 21
Aug. 18, 1988	Montreal, Canada	N.Y. Jets 11, Cleveland 7
Aug. 5, 1989	Tokyo, Japan	L.A. Rams 16, San Francisco 13 (OT)
Aug. 6, 1989	London, England	Philadelphia 17, Cleveland 13

AFC VS. NFC (REGULAR SEASON), 1970-1989

	1970	1971	1972	1973	1974	1975	1976	1977	1978	1979	1980	1981	1982	1983	1984	1985	1986	1987	1988	1989	Totals
Miami	2-1	3-0	3-0	3-0	2-1	3-0	0-2	2-0	3-1	4-0	4-0	3-1	1-1	3-1	4-0	3-1	2-2	3-0	3-1	2-0	53-12
L.A. Raiders	1-2	1-1-1	3-0	2-1	3-0	3-0	3-0	1-1	4-0	4-0	2-2	2-2	3-0	2-2	3-1	3-1	1-3	2-2	1-3	2-2	46-23-1
Pittsburgh	0-3	1-2	2-1	3-0	3-0	2-1	1-1	2-0	3-1	3-1	4-0	3-1	1-0	2-2	3-1	1-3	2-2	2-2	1-3	3-1	42-25
Cincinnati	1-2	1-2	2-1	2-1	2-1	3-0	2-0	2-1	2-2	2-2	2-2	2-2	1-0	3-1	2-2	2-2	3-1	1-2	4-0	2-2	41-26
Denver	2-2	1-3	1-3	0-3-1	2-2	2-1	2-0	1-1	2-2	3-1	3-1	3-1	2-1	0-2	3-1	3-1	3-1	2-1-1	3-1	2-2	40-30-2
Seattle								1-0	3-1	3-1	1-3	0-2	1-0	1-3	4-0	2-2	3-1	4-0	1-3	0-4	24-20
Cleveland	0-3	2-1	1-2	1-2	1-2	1-3	2-0	1-1	4-0	3-1	3-1	3-1	0-2	2-2	1-3	1-3	2-2	2-2	4-0	3-1	37-32
San Diego	1-2	2-1	0-3	1-2	1-2	0-3	2-0	1-1	2-2	3-1	2-2	2-2	1-0	2-2	4-0	1-1	0-4	2-0	2-2	2-2	31-32
Kansas City	0-2-1	2-1	2-1	1-1-1	1-2	2-1	1-1	1-1	0-2	0-2	2-0	2-2	0-3	2-2	1-1	2-2	1-1	1-2	0-2	2-0	23-29-2
Indianapolis	3-0	2-1	0-3	2-1	1-2	2-1	0-2	1-1	2-2	1-1	1-1	0-4	0-1-1	2-0	0-4	3-1	1-3	1-0	2-2	1-3	25-33-1
New England	0-3	0-3	3-0	2-1	3-0	1-2	1-1	2-0	2-2	3-1	1-3	0-4	0-1	2-2	0-4	3-1	3-1	0-3	2-2	0-4	28-38
N.Y. Jets	2-1	0-3	1-2	0-3	2-1	0-3	0-2	1-1	1-3	3-1	1-3	2-0	4-0	3-1	0-2	2-2	2-2	0-4	2-0	1-3	27-37
Houston	0-3	0-2-1	0-3	0-3	0-3	3-0	2-0	2-0	2-2	2-2	4-0	1-3	0-3	1-3	0-4	1-3	2-2	2-2	3-1	3-1	28-40-1
Buffalo	0-3	0-3	2-0-1	2-1	2-1	1-2	0-2	1-1	1-1	2-2	3-1	1-3	1-2	1-3	1-3	0-2	1-1	1-2	2-2	1-3	23-38-1
Tampa Bay							0-1														0-1
TOTALS	12-27-1	15-23-2	20-19-1	19-19-2	23-17	23-17	16-12	19-9	31-21	36-16	33-19	24-28	15-14-1	26-26	26-26	27-25	26-26	23-22-1	30-22	24-28	468-416-8

NFC VS. AFC (REGULAR SEASON), 1970-1989

	1970	1971	1972	1973	1974	1975	1976	1977	1978	1979	1980	1981	1982	1983	1984	1985	1986	1987	1988	1989	Totals
Dallas	3-0	3-0	3-0	2-1	2-1	2-1	2-0	1-1	3-1	1-3	3-1	4-0	2-1	2-2	2-2	3-1	1-3	2-1	0-4	0-2	41-25
Philadelphia	2-1	1-2	2-1	2-1	2-1	0-3	0-2	1-1	3-1	2-2	3-1	3-1	2-1	1-1	3-1	1-1	2-2	3-1	2-2	3-1	38-27
Washington	2-1	1-2	1-2	2-1	2-1	1-2	1-1	1-1	2-2	2-2	1-3	2-2		4-0	3-1	4-0	3-1	2-1	1-3	2-2	37-28
L.A. Rams	2-1	1-2	1-2	3-0	3-1	3-0	1-1	2-0	2-2	2-2	2-2	1-3	1-2	1-3	3-1	3-1	2-2	1-2	2-2	3-1	39-30
San Francisco	4-0	2-1	2-1	1-2	0-3	1-2	1-1	0-2	1-3	0-4	2-2	3-1	1-3	2-2	3-1	3-1	4-0	3-1	2-2	4-0	39-32
Minnesota	2-1	2-1	1-2	2-1	2-1	4-0	2-0	1-1	1-3	1-3	1-3	1-3	1-3	4-0	0-4	2-0	1-3	2-1	2-2	2-2	34-34
N.Y. Giants	3-0	1-2	1-2	1-2	1-2	2-1	0-2	0-2	1-1	1-1	1-3	1-1	1-0	0-4	2-0	2-2	3-1	2-1	1-1	4-0	28-28
Phoenix	2-0-1	2-1	1-2	0-2-1	2-1	2-1	1-1	0-2	0-4	1-3	1-1	3-1		3-1	3-1	2-2	1-1	0-1	1-3	1-3	26-31-2
Chicago	1-2	1-2	1-2	2-2	0-3	0-3	0-2	1-1	0-4	2-2	0-4	4-0	1-1	1-1	2-2	3-1	4-0	2-2	3-1	2-2	30-37
Detroit	3-0	4-0	2-0-1	0-3	1-2	1-2	2-0	2-0	2-2	0-4	0-2	2-2	0-1	1-3	0-4	2-2	1-3	0-4	1-1	1-3	25-38-1
New Orleans	0-3	0-1-2	0-3	1-2	0-3	0-3	1-2	0-2	1-3	0-4	1-3	2-2	1-0	1-3	3-1	0-4	1-3	4-0	4-0	4-0	24-42-2
Atlanta	1-2	3-0	2-2	2-1	0-3	1-2	0-2	0-2	1-3	1-3	2-2	1-3	1-1	3-1	1-3	0-4	1-3	0-4	1-3	2-2	23-46
Green Bay	2-1	2-1	2-1	1-1-1	2-1	0-3	0-2	0-3	2-2	1-3	1-3	1-1	1-1-1	2-2	0-4	0-4	1-3	1-2-1	1-3	0-2	20-43-3
Tampa Bay								0-1	2-0	2-0	1-3	0-4	2-1	1-3	1-1	0-4	1-1	0-2	1-3	0-4	11-27
Seattle							1-0														1-0
TOTALS	27-12-1	23-15-2	19-20-1	19-19-2	17-23	17-23	12-16	9-19	21-31	16-36	19-33	28-24	14-15-1	26-26	26-26	25-27	26-26	22-23-1	22-30	28-24	416-468-8

1989 Interconference Games
(Home Team in capital letters)

NFC 28, AFC 24

AFC Victories

INDIANAPOLIS 13, Atlanta 9

PITTSBURGH 27, Minnesota 14

Pittsburgh 23, DETROIT 3

San Diego 24, PHOENIX 13

Houston 33, CHICAGO 28

BUFFALO 23, Los Angeles Rams 20

KANSAS CITY 36, Dallas 28

MIAMI 23, Green Bay 20

CLEVELAND 27, Chicago 7

CINCINNATI 56, Tampa Bay 23

LOS ANGELES RAIDERS 37, Washington 24

Cleveland 42, TAMPA BAY 31

HOUSTON 35, Detroit 31

SAN DIEGO 20, Philadelphia 17

CINCINNATI 42, Detroit 7

Miami 17, DALLAS 14

Denver 14, WASHINGTON 10

NEW YORK JETS 27, Atlanta 10

Kansas City 21, GREEN BAY 3

LOS ANGELES RAIDERS 16, Phoenix 14

HOUSTON 20, Tampa Bay 17

Denver 37, PHOENIX 0

CLEVELAND 23, Minnesota 17

Pittsburgh 31, TAMPA BAY 22

NFC Victories

CHICAGO 17, Cincinnati 14

MINNESOTA 38, Houston 7

San Francisco 30, INDIANAPOLIS 24

PHILADELPHIA 31, Seattle 7

LOS ANGELES RAMS 31, Indianapolis 17

Phoenix 34, SEATTLE 24

ATLANTA 16, New England 15

NEW ORLEANS 29, New York Jets 14

PHILADELPHIA 10, Los Angeles Raiders 7

SAN FRANCISCO 37, New England 20

New York Giants 20, SAN DIEGO 17

Philadelphia 28, DENVER 24

San Francisco 23, NEW YORK JETS 10

ATLANTA 30, Buffalo 28

Chicago 20, PITTSBURGH 0

New Orleans 28, NEW ENGLAND 24

NEW YORK GIANTS 15, Seattle 3

DETROIT 13, Cleveland 10

New Orleans 22, BUFFALO 19

New York Giants 14, DENVER 7

WASHINGTON 26, San Diego 21

SAN FRANCISCO 21, Buffalo 10

LOS ANGELES RAMS 38, New York Jets 14

Washington 29, SEATTLE 0

NEW ORLEANS 41, Indianapolis 6

NEW YORK GIANTS 34, Los Angeles Raiders 17

Los Angeles Rams 24, NEW ENGLAND 20

MINNESOTA 29, Cincinnati 21

Regular Season Interconference Records, 1970-1989

American Football Conference

Eastern Division	W	L	T	Pct.
Miami	53	12	0	.815
Indianapolis	25	33	1	.432
New England	28	38	0	.424
New York Jets	27	37	0	.422
Buffalo	23	38	1	.379

Central Division				
Pittsburgh	42	25	0	.627
Cincinnati	41	26	0	.612
Cleveland	37	32	0	.536
Houston	28	40	1	.413

Western Division				
Los Angeles Raiders	46	23	1	.657
Denver	40	30	2	.556
Seattle	24	20	0	.545
San Diego	31	32	0	.492
Kansas City	23	29	2	.462

National Football Conference

Eastern Division	W	L	T	Pct.
Dallas	41	25	0	.621
Philadelphia	38	27	0	.585
Washington	37	28	0	.569
New York Giants	28	28	0	.500
Phoenix	26	31	2	.458

Central Division				
Minnesota	34	34	0	.500
Chicago	30	37	0	.448
Detroit	25	38	1	.405
Green Bay	20	43	3	.326
Tampa Bay	11	27	0	.289

Western Division				
Los Angeles Rams	39	30	0	.565
San Francisco	39	32	0	.549
New Orleans	24	42	2	.368
Atlanta	23	46	0	.333

Interconference Victories, 1970-1989

	Regular Season				Preseason		
	AFC	NFC	Tie		AFC	NFC	Tie
1970	12	27	1	1970	21	28	1
1971	15	23	2	1971	28	28	3
1972	20	19	1	1972	27	25	4
1973	19	19	2	1973	23	35	2
1974	23	17	0	1974	35	25	0
1975	23	17	0	1975	30	26	1
1976	16	12	0	1976	30	31	0
1977	19	9	0	1977	38	25	0
1978	31	21	0	1978	20	19	0
1979	36	16	0	1979	25	18	0
1980	33	19	0	1980	22	20	1
1981	24	28	0	1981	18	19	0
1982	15	14	1	1982	25	16	0
1983	26	26	0	1983	15	24	0
1984	26	26	0	1984	16	19	0
1985	27	25	0	1985	10	22	1
1986	26	26	0	1986	22	17	0
1987	23	22	1	1987	22	22	0
1988	30	22	0	1988	23	16	1
1989	24	28	0	1989	16	27	0
Total	468	416	8	Total	466	462	14

Monday Night Football, 1970–1989

(Home Team in capitals, games listed in chronological order.)

1989
New York Giants 27, WASHINGTON 24
Denver 28, BUFFALO 14
CINCINNATI 21, Cleveland 14
CHICAGO 27, Philadelphia 13
Los Angeles Raiders 14, NEW YORK JETS 7
BUFFALO 23, Los Angeles Rams 20
CLEVELAND 27, Chicago 7
NEW YORK GIANTS 24, Minnesota 14
SAN FRANCISCO 31, New Orleans 13
HOUSTON 26, Cincinnati 24
Denver 14, WASHINGTON 10
SAN FRANCISCO 34, New York Giants 24
SEATTLE 17, Buffalo 16
San Francisco 30, LOS ANGELES RAMS 27
NEW ORLEANS 30, Philadelphia 20
MINNESOTA 29, Cincinnati 21

1988
NEW YORK GIANTS 27, Washington 20
Dallas 17, PHOENIX 14
CLEVELAND 23, Indianapolis 17
Los Angeles Raiders 30, DENVER 27 (OT)
NEW ORLEANS 20, Dallas 17
PHILADELPHIA 24, New York Giants 13
Buffalo 37, NEW YORK JETS 14
CHICAGO 10, San Francisco 9
INDIANAPOLIS 55, Denver 23
HOUSTON 24, Cleveland 17
Buffalo 31, MIAMI 6
SAN FRANCISCO 37, Washington 21
SEATTLE 35, Los Angeles Raiders 27
LOS ANGELES RAMS 23, Chicago 3
MIAMI 38, Cleveland 31
MINNESOTA 28, Chicago 27

1987
CHICAGO 34, New York Giants 19
NEW YORK JETS 43, New England 24
San Francisco 41, NEW YORK GIANTS 21
DENVER 30, Los Angeles Raiders 14
Washington 13, DALLAS 7
CLEVELAND 30, Los Angeles Rams 17
MINNESOTA 34, Denver 27
DALLAS 33, New York Giants 24
NEW YORK JETS 30, Seattle 14
DENVER 31, Chicago 29
Los Angeles Rams 30, WASHINGTON 26
Los Angeles Raiders 37, SEATTLE 14
MIAMI 37, New York Jets 28
SAN FRANCISCO 41, Chicago 0
Dallas 29, LOS ANGELES RAMS 21
New England 24, MIAMI 10

1986
DALLAS 31, New York Giants 28
Denver 21, PITTSBURGH 10
Chicago 25, GREEN BAY 12
Dallas 31, ST. LOUIS 7
SEATTLE 33, San Diego 7
CINCINNATI 24, Pittsburgh 22
NEW YORK JETS 22, Denver 10
NEW YORK GIANTS 27, Washington 20
Los Angeles Rams 20, CHICAGO 17
CLEVELAND 26, Miami 16
WASHINGTON 14, San Francisco 6
MIAMI 45, New York Jets 3
New York Giants 21, SAN FRANCISCO 17
SEATTLE 37, Los Angeles Raiders 0
Chicago 16, DETROIT 13
New England 34, MIAMI 27

1985
DALLAS 44, Washington 14
CLEVELAND 17, Pittsburgh 7
Los Angeles Rams 35, SEATTLE 24
Cincinnati 37, PITTSBURGH 24
WASHINGTON 27, St. Louis 10
NEW YORK JETS 23, Miami 7
CHICAGO 23, Green Bay 7
LOS ANGELES RAIDERS 34, San Diego 21
ST. LOUIS 21, Dallas 10
DENVER 17, San Francisco 16
WASHINGTON 23, New York Giants 21
SAN FRANCISCO 19, Seattle 6
MIAMI 30, Chicago 24

Los Angeles Rams 27, SAN FRANCISCO 20
MIAMI 30, New England 27
L.A. Raiders 16, L.A. RAMS 6

1984
Dallas 20, LOS ANGELES RAMS 13
SAN FRANCISCO 37, Washington 31
Miami 21, BUFFALO 17
LOS ANGELES RAIDERS 33, San Diego 30
PITTSBURGH 38, Cincinnati 17
San Francisco 31, NEW YORK GIANTS 10
DENVER 17, Green Bay 14
Los Angeles Rams 24, ATLANTA 10
Seattle 24, SAN DIEGO 0
WASHINGTON 27, Atlanta 14
SEATTLE 17, Los Angeles Raiders 14
NEW ORLEANS 27, Pittsburgh 24
MIAMI 28, New York Jets 17
SAN DIEGO 20, Chicago 7
Los Angeles Raiders 24, DETROIT 3
MIAMI 28, Dallas 21

1983
Dallas 31, WASHINGTON 30
San Diego 17, KANSAS CITY 14
LOS ANGELES RAIDERS 27, Miami 14
NEW YORK GIANTS 27, Green Bay 3
New York Jets 34, BUFFALO 10
Pittsburgh 24, CINCINNATI 14
GREEN BAY 48, Washington 47
ST. LOUIS 20, New York Giants 20 (OT)
Washington 27, SAN DIEGO 24
DETROIT 15, New York Giants 9
Los Angeles Rams 36, ATLANTA 13
New York Jets 31, NEW ORLEANS 28
MIAMI 38, Cincinnati 14
DETROIT 13, Minnesota 2
Green Bay 12, TAMPA BAY 9 (OT)
SAN FRANCISCO 42, Dallas 17

1982
Pittsburgh 36, DALLAS 28
Green Bay 27, NEW YORK GIANTS 19
LOS ANGELES RAIDERS 28, San Diego 24
TAMPA BAY 23, Miami 17
New York Jets 28, DETROIT 13
Dallas 37, HOUSTON 7
SAN DIEGO 50, Cincinnati 34
MIAMI 27, Buffalo 10
MINNESOTA 31, Dallas 27

1981
San Diego 44, CLEVELAND 14
Oakland 36, MINNESOTA 10
Dallas 35, NEW ENGLAND 21
Los Angeles 24, CHICAGO 7
PHILADELPHIA 16, Atlanta 13
BUFFALO 31, Miami 21
DETROIT 48, Chicago 17
PITTSBURGH 26, Houston 13
DENVER 19, Minnesota 17
DALLAS 27, Buffalo 14
SEATTLE 44, San Diego 23
ATLANTA 31, Minnesota 30
MIAMI 13, Philadelphia 10
OAKLAND 30, Pittsburgh 27
LOS ANGELES 21, Atlanta 16
SAN DIEGO 23, Oakland 10

1980
Dallas 17, WASHINGTON 3
Houston 16, CLEVELAND 7
PHILADELPHIA 35, New York Giants 3
NEW ENGLAND 23, Denver 14
CHICAGO 23, Tampa Bay 0
DENVER 20, Washington 17
Oakland 45, PITTSBURGH 34
NEW YORK JETS 17, Miami 14
CLEVELAND 27, Chicago 21
HOUSTON 38, New England 34
Oakland 19, SEATTLE 17
Los Angeles 27, NEW ORLEANS 7
OAKLAND 9, Denver 3
MIAMI 16, New England 13 (OT)
LOS ANGELES 38, Dallas 14
SAN DIEGO 26, Pittsburgh 17

1979
Pittsburgh 16, NEW ENGLAND 13 (OT)
Atlanta 14, PHILADELPHIA 10
WASHINGTON 27, New York Giants 0
CLEVELAND 26, Dallas 7
GREEN BAY 27, New England 14
OAKLAND 13, Miami 3
NEW YORK JETS 14, Minnesota 7
PITTSBURGH 42, Denver 7
Seattle 31, ATLANTA 28
Houston 9, MIAMI 6
Philadelphia 31, DALLAS 21
LOS ANGELES 20, Atlanta 14
SEATTLE 30, New York Jets 7
Oakland 42, NEW ORLEANS 35
HOUSTON 20, Pittsburgh 17
SAN DIEGO 17, Denver 7

1978
DALLAS 38, Baltimore 0
MINNESOTA 12, Denver 9 (OT)
Baltimore 34, NEW ENGLAND 27
Minnesota 24, CHICAGO 20
WASHINGTON 9, Dallas 5
MIAMI 21, Cincinnati 0
DENVER 16, Chicago 7
Houston 24, PITTSBURGH 17
ATLANTA 15, Los Angeles 7
BALTIMORE 21, Washington 17
Oakland 34, CINCINNATI 21
HOUSTON 35, Miami 30
Pittsburgh 24, SAN FRANCISCO 7
SAN DIEGO 40, Chicago 7
Cincinnati 20, LOS ANGELES 19
MIAMI 23, New England 3

1977
PITTSBURGH 27, San Francisco 0
CLEVELAND 30, New England 27 (OT)
Oakland 37, KANSAS CITY 28
CHICAGO 24, Los Angeles 23
PITTSBURGH 20, Cincinnati 14
LOS ANGELES 35, Minnesota 3
ST. LOUIS 28, New York Giants 0
BALTIMORE 10, Washington 3
St. Louis 24, DALLAS 17
WASHINGTON 10, Green Bay 9
OAKLAND 34, Buffalo 13
MIAMI 17, Baltimore 6
Dallas 42, SAN FRANCISCO 35

1976
Miami 30, BUFFALO 21
Oakland 24, KANSAS CITY 21
Washington 20, PHILADELPHIA 17 (OT)
MINNESOTA 17, Pittsburgh 6
San Francisco 16, LOS ANGELES 0
NEW ENGLAND 41, New York Jets 7
WASHINGTON 20, St. Louis 10
BALTIMORE 38, Houston 14
CINCINNATI 20, Los Angeles 12
DALLAS 17, Buffalo 10
Baltimore 17, MIAMI 16
SAN FRANCISCO 20, Minnesota 16
OAKLAND 35, Cincinnati 20

1975
Oakland 31, MIAMI 21
DENVER 23, Green Bay 13
Dallas 36, DETROIT 10
WASHINGTON 27, St. Louis 17
New York Giants 17, BUFFALO 14
Minnesota 13, CHICAGO 9
Los Angeles 42, PHILADELPHIA 3
Kansas City 34, DALLAS 31
CINCINNATI 33, Buffalo 24
Pittsburgh 32, HOUSTON 9
MIAMI 20, New England 7
OAKLAND 17, Denver 10
SAN DIEGO 24, New York Jets 16

1974
BUFFALO 21, Oakland 20
PHILADELPHIA 13, Dallas 10
WASHINGTON 30, Denver 3
MIAMI 21, New York Jets 17
DETROIT 17, San Francisco 13
CHICAGO 10, Green Bay 9
PITTSBURGH 24, Atlanta 17
Los Angeles 15, SAN FRANCISCO 13
Minnesota 28, ST. LOUIS 24

Kansas City 42, DENVER 34
Pittsburgh 28, NEW ORLEANS 7
MIAMI 24, Cincinnati 3
Washington 23, LOS ANGELES 17

1973
GREEN BAY 23, New York Jets 7
DALLAS 40, New Orleans 3
DETROIT 31, Atlanta 6
WASHINGTON 14, Dallas 7
Miami 17, CLEVELAND 9
DENVER 23, Oakland 23
BUFFALO 23, Kansas City 14
PITTSBURGH 21, Washington 16
KANSAS CITY 19, Chicago 7
ATLANTA 20, Minnesota 14
SAN FRANCISCO 20, Green Bay 6
MIAMI 30, Pittsburgh 26
LOS ANGELES 40, New York Giants 6

1972
Washington 24, MINNESOTA 21

Kansas City 20, NEW ORLEANS 17
New York Giants 27, PHILADELPHIA 12
Oakland 34, HOUSTON 0
Green Bay 24, DETROIT 23
CHICAGO 13, Minnesota 10
DALLAS 28, Detroit 24
Baltimore 24, NEW ENGLAND 17
Cleveland 21, SAN DIEGO 17
WASHINGTON 24, Atlanta 13
MIAMI 31, St. Louis 10
Los Angeles 26, SAN FRANCISCO 16
OAKLAND 24, New York Jets 16

1971
Minnesota 16, DETROIT 13
ST. LOUIS 17, New York Jets 10
Oakland 34, CLEVELAND 20
DALLAS 20, New York Giants 13
KANSAS CITY 38, Pittsburgh 16
MINNESOTA 10, Baltimore 3
GREEN BAY 14, Detroit 14
BALTIMORE 24, Los Angeles 17

SAN DIEGO 20, St. Louis 17
ATLANTA 28, Green Bay 21
MIAMI 34, Chicago 3
Kansas City 26, SAN FRANCISCO 17
Washington 38, LOS ANGELES 24

1970
CLEVELAND 31, New York Jets 21
Kansas City 44, BALTIMORE 24
DETROIT 28, Chicago 14
Green Bay 22, SAN DIEGO 20
OAKLAND 34, Washington 20
MINNESOTA 13, Los Angeles 3
PITTSBURGH 21, Cincinnati 10
Baltimore 13, GREEN BAY 10
St. Louis 38, DALLAS 0
PHILADELPHIA 23, New York Giants 20
Miami 20, ATLANTA 7
Cleveland 21, HOUSTON 10
Detroit 28, LOS ANGELES 23

Monday Night Won-Lost Records, 1970-1989

	Total	1989	1988	1987	1986	1985	1984	1983	1982	1981	1980	1979	1978	1977	1976	1975	1974	1973	1972	1971	1970
Buffalo	6-11	1-2	2-0				0-1	0-1	0-1	1-1				0-1	0-2	0-2	1-0	1-0			
Cincinnati	6-12	1-2			1-0	1-0	0-1	0-2	0-1				1-2	0-1	1-1	1-0	0-1				0-1
Cleveland	11-7	1-1	1-2	1-0	1-0	1-0				0-1	1-1	1-0		1-0				0-1	1-0	0-1	2-0
Denver	11-12-1	2-0	0-2	2-1	1-1	1-0	1-0			1-0	1-2	0-2	1-1				1-1	0-2	0-0-1		
Houston	8-6	1-0	1-0						0-1	0-1	2-0	2-0	2-0		0-1	0-1			0-1		0-1
Indianapolis	9-5		1-1										2-1	1-1	2-0				1-0	1-1	1-1
Kansas City	7-4							0-1						0-1	0-1	1-0	1-0	1-1	1-0	2-0	1-0
L.A. Raiders	27-6-1	1-0	1-1	1-1	0-1	2-0	2-1	1-0	1-0	2-1	3-0	2-0	1-0	2-0	2-0	2-0	0-1	0-0-1	2-0	1-0	1-0
Miami	24-14		1-1	1-1	1-2	2-1	3-0	1-1	1-1	1-1	1-1	0-2	2-1	1-0	1-1	1-1	2-0	2-0	1-0	1-0	1-0
New England	4-12			1-1	1-0	0-1				0-1	1-2	0-2	0-2	0-1	1-0	0-1		0-1			
New York Jets	9-13	0-1	0-1	2-1	1-1	1-0	0-1	2-0	1-0		1-0	1-1		0-1	0-1	0-1	0-1	0-1	0-1	0-1	0-1
Pittsburgh	14-13				0-2	0-2	1-1	1-0	1-0	1-1	0-2	2-1	1-1	2-0	0-1	1-0	2-0	1-1		0-1	1-0
San Diego	10-9				0-1	0-1	1-2	1-1	1-1	2-1	1-0	1-0	1-0			1-0		0-1	1-0	0-1	
Seattle	9-5	1-0	1-0	0-2	2-0	0-2	2-0			1-0	0-1	2-0									
Atlanta	5-11						0-2	0-1		1-2		1-2	1-0				0-1	1-1	0-1	1-0	0-1
Chicago	10-18	1-1	1-2	1-2	2-1	1-1	0-1				0-2	1-1		0-3	1-0		0-1	1-0	0-1	1-0	0-1
Dallas	19-16		1-1	2-1	2-0	1-1	1-1	1-1	1-2	2-0	1-1	0-2	1-1	1-1	1-0	1-1	0-1	1-1	1-0	1-0	0-1
Detroit	7-7-1				0-1		0-1	2-0	0-1	1-0						0-1	1-0	1-0	0-2	0-1-1	2-0
Green Bay	7-10-1				0-1	0-1	0-1	2-1	1-0			1-0		0-1		0-1	0-1	1-1	1-0	0-1-1	1-1
L.A. Rams	17-16	0-2	1-0	1-2	1-0	2-1	1-1	1-0		2-0	2-0	1-0	0-2	1-1	0-2	1-0	1-1	1-0	1-0	0-2	0-2
Minnesota	12-11	1-1	1-0	1-0				0-1	1-0	0-3		0-1	2-0	0-1	1-1	1-0	1-0	0-1	0-2	2-0	1-0
New Orleans	3-7	1-1	1-0				1-0	0-1			0-1	0-1					0-1	0-1	0-1		
New York Giants	8-16-1	2-1	1-1	0-3	2-1	0-1	0-1	1-1-1	0-1		0-1	0-1		0-1		1-0		0-1	1-0	0-1	0-1
Philadelphia	6-7	0-2	1-0								1-1	1-0	1-1			0-1	0-1	1-0	0-1		1-0
Phoenix	5-8-1		0-1		0-1	1-1		0-0-1					2-0	0-1	0-1	0-1		0-1	1-1	1-0	
San Francisco	13-12	3-0	1-1	2-0	0-2	1-2	2-0	1-0					0-1	0-2	2-0		0-2	1-0	0-1	0-1	
Tampa Bay	1-2							0-1	1-0		0-1										
Washington	18-16	0-2	0-2	1-1	1-1	2-1	1-1	1-2			0-2	1-0	1-1	1-1	2-0	1-0	2-0	1-1	2-0	1-0	0-1

Monday Night Syndrome

1989

Of the 15 winning teams:	14 won the next week	Of the 30 NFL teams:	24 won the next week
	1 lost the next week		6 lost the next week
	0 tied the next week		0 tied the next week
Of the 15 losing teams:	10 won the next week		
	5 lost the next week		
	0 tied the next week		

1970-1989

Of the 274 winning teams:	159 won the next week	Of the 554 NFL teams:	311 won the next week
	112 lost the next week		239 lost the next week
	3 tied the next week		4 tied the next week
Of the 274 losing teams:	147 won the next week		
	126 lost the next week		
	1 tied the next week		
Of the 6 tying teams:	5 won the next week		
	1 lost the next week		
	0 tied the next week		

Thursday-Sunday Night Football, 1974-1989

(Home Team in capitals, games listed in chronological order.)

1989
Dallas 13, WASHINGTON 3 (Sun.)
SAN DIEGO 14, Los Angeles Raiders 12 (Sun.)
INDIANAPOLIS 27, New York Jets 10 (Sun.)
Los Angeles Rams 20, NEW ORLEANS 17 (Sun.)
MINNESOTA 27, Chicago 16 (Sun.)
MIAMI 31, New England 10 (Sun.)
SEATTLE 23, Los Angeles Raiders 17 (Sun.)
Cleveland 24, HOUSTON 20 (Sat.)

1988
HOUSTON 41, Washington 17 (Sun.)
Los Angeles Raiders 13, SAN DIEGO 3 (Sun.)
Minnesota 34, DALLAS 3 (Sun.)
New England 6, MIAMI 3 (Sun.)
New York Giants 13, NEW ORLEANS 12 (Sun.)
Pittsburgh 37, HOUSTON 34 (Sun.)
SEATTLE 42, Denver 14 (Sun.)
Los Angeles Rams 38, SAN FRANCISCO 16 (Sun.)

1987
NEW YORK GIANTS 17, New England 10 (Sun.)
SAN DIEGO 16, Los Angeles Raiders 14 (Sun.)
Miami 20, DALLAS 14 (Sun.)
SAN FRANCISCO 38, Cleveland 24 (Sun.)
Chicago 30, MINNESOTA 24 (Sun.)
SEATTLE 28, Denver 21 (Sun.)
MIAMI 23, Washington 21 (Sun.)
SAN FRANCISCO 48, Los Angeles Rams 0 (Sun.)

1986
New England 20, NEW YORK JETS 6 (Thur.)
Cincinnati 30, CLEVELAND 13 (Thur.)
Los Angeles Raiders 37, SAN DIEGO 31 (OT) (Thur.)
LOS ANGELES RAMS 29, Dallas 10 (Sun.)
SAN FRANCISCO 24, Los Angeles Rams 14 (Fri.)

1985
KANSAS CITY 36, Los Angeles Raiders 20 (Thur.)
Chicago 33, MINNESOTA 24 (Thur.)
Dallas 30, NEW YORK GIANTS 29 (Sun.)
SAN DIEGO 54, Pittsburgh 44 (Sun.)
Denver 27, SEATTLE 24 (Fri.)

1984
Pittsburgh 23, NEW YORK JETS 17 (Thur.)
Denver 24, CLEVELAND 14 (Sun.)
DALLAS 30, New Orleans 27 (Sun.)
Washington 31, MINNESOTA 17 (Thur.)
SAN FRANCISCO 19, Los Angeles Rams 16 (Fri.)

1983
San Francisco 48, MINNESOTA 17 (Thur.)
CLEVELAND 17, Cincinnati 7 (Thur.)
Los Angeles Raiders 40, DALLAS 38 (Sun.)
Los Angeles Raiders 42, SAN DIEGO 10 (Thur.)
MIAMI 34, New York Jets 14 (Fri.)

1982
BUFFALO 23, Minnesota 22 (Thur.)
SAN FRANCISCO 30, Los Angeles Rams 24 (Thur.)
ATLANTA 17, San Francisco 7 (Sun.)

1981
MIAMI 30, Pittsburgh 10 (Thur.)
Philadelphia 20, BUFFALO 14 (Thur.)
DALLAS 29, Los Angeles 17 (Sun.)
HOUSTON 17, Cleveland 13 (Thur.)

1980
TAMPA BAY 10, Los Angeles 9 (Thur.)
DALLAS 42, San Diego 31 (Sun.)
San Diego 27, MIAMI 24 (OT) (Thur.)
HOUSTON 6, Pittsburgh 0 (Thur.)

1979
Los Angeles 13, DENVER 9 (Thur.)
DALLAS 30, Los Angeles 6 (Sun.)
OAKLAND 45, San Diego 22 (Thur.)
MIAMI 39, New England 24 (Thur.)

1978
New England 21, OAKLAND 14 (Sun.)
Minnesota 21, DALLAS 10 (Thur.)
LOS ANGELES 10, Pittsburgh 7 (Sun.)
Denver 21, OAKLAND 6 (Sun.)

1977
Minnesota 30, DETROIT 21 (Sat.)

1976
Los Angeles 20, DETROIT 17 (Sat.)

1975
LOS ANGELES 10, Pittsburgh 3 (Sat.)

1974
OAKLAND 27, Dallas 23 (Sat.)

History of Overtime Games

Preseason

Aug. 28, 1955	Los Angeles 23, New York Giants 17, at Portland, Oregon
Aug. 24, 1962	Denver 27, Dallas Texans 24, at Fort Worth, Texas
Aug. 10, 1974	San Diego 20, New York Jets 14, at San Diego
Aug. 17, 1974	Pittsburgh 33, Philadelphia 30, at Philadelphia
Aug. 17, 1974	Dallas 19, Houston 13, at Dallas
Aug. 17, 1974	Cincinnati 13, Atlanta 7, at Atlanta
Sept. 6, 1974	Buffalo 23, New York Giants 17, at Buffalo
Aug. 9, 1975	Baltimore 23, Denver 20, at Denver
Aug. 30, 1975	New England 20, Green Bay 17, at Milwaukee
Sept. 13, 1975	Minnesota 14, San Diego 14, at San Diego
Aug. 1, 1976	New England 13, New York Giants 7, at New England
Aug. 2, 1976	Kansas City 9, Houston 3, at Kansas City
Aug. 20, 1976	New Orleans 26, Baltimore 20, at Baltimore
Sept. 4, 1976	Dallas 26, Houston 20, at Dallas
Aug. 13, 1977	Seattle 23, Dallas 17, at Seattle
Aug. 28, 1977	New England 13, Pittsburgh 10, at New England
Aug. 28, 1977	New York Giants 24, Buffalo 21, at East Rutherford, N.J.
Aug. 2, 1979	Seattle 12, Minnesota 9, at Minnesota
Aug. 4, 1979	Los Angeles 20, Oakland 14, at Los Angeles
Aug. 24, 1979	Denver 20, New England 17, at Denver
Aug. 23, 1980	Tampa Bay 20, Cincinnati 14, at Tampa Bay
Aug. 5, 1981	San Francisco 27, Seattle 24, at Seattle
Aug. 29, 1981	New Orleans 20, Detroit 17, at New Orleans
Aug. 28, 1982	Miami 17, Kansas City 17, at Kansas City
Sept. 3, 1982	Miami 16, New York Giants 13, at Miami
Aug. 6, 1983	L.A. Raiders 26, San Francisco 23, at Los Angeles
Aug. 6, 1983	Atlanta 13, Washington 10, at Atlanta
Aug. 13, 1983	St. Louis 27, Chicago 24, at St. Louis
Aug. 18, 1983	New York Jets 20, Cincinnati 17, at Cincinnati
Aug. 27, 1983	Chicago 20, Kansas City 17, at Chicago
Aug. 11, 1984	Pittsburgh 20, Philadelphia 17, at Pittsburgh
Aug. 9, 1985	Buffalo 10, Detroit 10, at Pontiac, Mich.
Aug. 10, 1985	Minnesota 16, Miami 13, at Miami
Aug. 17, 1985	Dallas 27, San Diego 24, at San Diego
Aug. 24, 1985	N.Y. Giants 34, N.Y. Jets 31, at East Rutherford, N.J.
Aug. 15, 1986	Washington 27, Pittsburgh 24, at Washington
Aug. 15, 1986	Detroit 30, Seattle 27, at Detroit
Aug. 23, 1986	Los Angeles Rams 20, San Diego 17, at Anaheim
Aug. 30, 1986	Minnesota 23, Indianapolis 20, at Indianapolis
Aug. 23, 1987	Philadelphia 19, New England 13, at New England
Sept. 5, 1987	Cleveland 30, Green Bay 24, at Milwaukee
Sept. 6, 1987	Kansas City 13, St. Louis 10, at Memphis, Tenn.
Aug. 11, 1988	Seattle 16, Detroit 13, at Detroit
Aug. 19, 1988	Miami 16, Denver 13, at Miami
Aug. 20, 1988	Houston 20, Los Angeles Rams 17, at Anaheim
Aug. 21, 1988	Minnesota 19, Phoenix 16, at Phoenix
Aug. 5, 1989	Los Angeles Rams 16, San Francisco 13, at Tokyo, Japan
Aug. 26, 1989	Denver 24, Dallas 21, at Denver
Sept. 1, 1989	N.Y. Jets 15, Kansas City 13, at Kansas City

Regular Season

Sept. 22, 1974—Pittsburgh 35, Denver 35, at Denver; Steelers win toss. Gilliam's pass intercepted and returned by Rowser to Denver's 42. Turner misses 41-yard field goal. Walden punts and Greer returns to Broncos' 39. Van Heusen punts and Edwards returns to Steelers' 16. Game ends with Steelers on own 26.

Nov. 10, 1974—New York Jets 26, New York Giants 20, at New Haven, Conn.; Giants win toss. Gogolak misses 42-yard field goal. Namath passes to Boozer for five yards and touchdown at 6:53.

Sept. 28, 1975—Dallas 37, St. Louis 31, at Dallas; Cardinals win toss. Hart's pass intercepted and returned by Jordan to Cardinals' 37. Staubach passes to DuPree for three yards and touchdown at 7:53.

Oct. 12, 1975—Los Angeles 13, San Diego 10, at San Diego; Chargers win toss. Partee punts to Rams' 14. Dempsey kicks 22-yard field goal at 9:27.

Nov. 2, 1975—Washington 30, Dallas 24, at Washington; Cowboys win toss. Staubach's pass intercepted and returned by Houston to Cowboys' 35. Kilmer runs one yard for touchdown at 6:34.

Nov. 16, 1975—St. Louis 20, Washington 17, at St. Louis; Cardinals win toss. Bakken kicks 37-yard field goal at 7:00.

Nov. 23, 1975—Kansas City 24, Detroit 21, at Kansas City; Lions win toss. Chiefs take over on downs at own 38. Stenerud kicks 26-yard field goal at 6:44.

Nov. 23, 1975—Oakland 26, Washington 23, at Washington; Redskins win toss. Bragg punts to Raiders' 42. Blanda kicks 27-yard field goal at 7:13.

Nov. 30, 1975—Denver 13, San Diego 10, at Denver; Broncos win toss. Turner kicks 25-yard field goal at 4:13.

Nov. 30, 1975—Oakland 37, Atlanta 34, at Oakland; Falcons win toss. James punts to Raiders' 16. Guy punts and Herron returns to Falcons' 41. Nick Mike-Mayer misses 45-yard field goal. Guy punts into Falcons' end zone. James punts to Raiders' 39. Blanda kicks 36-yard field goal at 15:00.

Dec. 14, 1975—Baltimore 10, Miami 7, at Baltimore; Dolphins win toss. Seiple punts to Colts' 4. Linhart kicks 31-yard field goal at 12:44.

Sept. 19, 1976—Minnesota 10, Los Angeles 10, at Minnesota; Vikings win toss. Tarkenton's pass intercepted by Monte Jackson and returned to Minnesota 16. Allen blocks Dempsey's 30-yard field goal attempt, ball rolls into end zone for touchback. Clabo punts and Scribner returns to Rams' 20. Rusty Jackson punts to Vikings' 35. Tarkenton's pass intercepted by Kay at Rams' 1, no return. Game ends with Rams on own 3.

***Sept. 27, 1976—Washington 20, Philadelphia 17,** at Philadelphia; Eagles win toss. Jones punts and E. Brown loses one yard on return to Redskins' 40. Bragg punts 51 yards into end zone for touchback. Jones punts and E. Brown returns to Redskins' 42. Bragg punts and Marshall returns to Eagles' 41. Boryla's pass intercepted by Dusek at Redskins' 37, no return. Bragg punts and Bradley returns. Philadelphia holding penalty moves ball back to Eagles' 8. Boryla pass intercepted by E. Brown and returned to Eagles' 22. Moseley kicks 29-yard field goal at 12:49.

Oct. 17, 1976—Kansas City 20, Miami 17, at Miami; Chiefs win toss. Wilson punts into end zone for touchback. Bulaich fumbles into Kansas City end zone, Collier recovers for touchback. Stenerud kicks 34-yard field goal at 14:48.

Oct. 31, 1976—St. Louis 23, San Francisco 20, at St. Louis; Cardinals win toss. Joyce punts and Leonard fumbles on return, Jones recovers at 49ers' 43. Bakken kicks 21-yard field goal at 6:42.

Dec. 5, 1976—San Diego 13, San Francisco 7, at San Diego; Chargers win toss. Morris runs 13 yards for touchdown at 5:12.

Sept. 18, 1977—Dallas 16, Minnesota 10, at Minnesota; Vikings win toss. Dallas starts on Vikings' 47 after a punt early in the overtime period. Staubach scores seven plays later on a four-yard run at 6:14.

***Sept. 26, 1977—Cleveland 30, New England 27,** at Cleveland; Browns win toss. Sipe throws a 22-yard pass to Logan at Patriots' 19. Cockroft kicks 35-yard field goal at 4:45.

Oct. 16, 1977—Minnesota 22, Chicago 16, at Minnesota; Bears win toss. Parsons punts 53 yards to Vikings' 18. Minnesota drives to Bears' 11. On a first-and-10, Vikings fake a field goal and holder Krause hits Voigt with a touchdown pass at 6:45.

Oct. 30, 1977—Cincinnati 13, Houston 10, at Cincinnati; Bengals win toss. Bahr kicks a 22-yard field goal at 5:51.

Nov. 13, 1977—San Francisco 10, New Orleans 7, at New Orleans; Saints win toss. Saints fail to move ball and Blanchard punts to 49ers' 41. Wersching kicks a 33-yard field goal at 6:33.

Dec. 18, 1977—Chicago 12, New York Giants 9, at East Rutherford, N.J.; Giants win toss. The ball changes hands eight times before Thomas kicks a 28-yard field goal at 14:51.

Sept. 10, 1978—Cleveland 13, Cincinnati 10, at Cleveland; Browns win toss. Collins returns kickoff 41 yards to Browns' 47. Cockroft kicks 27-yard field goal at 4:30.

***Sept. 11, 1978—Minnesota 12, Denver 9,** at Minnesota; Vikings win toss. Danmeier kicks 44-yard field goal at 2:56.

Sept. 24, 1978—Pittsburgh 15, Cleveland 9, at Pittsburgh; Steelers win toss. Cunningham scores on a 37-yard "gadget" pass from Bradshaw at 3:43. Steelers start winning drive on their 21.

Sept. 24, 1978—Denver 23, Kansas City 17, at Kansas City; Broncos win toss. Dilts punts to Kansas City. Chiefs advance to Broncos' 40 where Reed fails to make first down on fourth-and-one situation. Broncos march downfield. Preston scores two-yard touchdown at 10:28.

Oct. 1, 1978—Oakland 25, Chicago 19, at Chicago; Bears win toss. Both teams punt on first possession. On Chicago's second offensive series, Colzie intercepts Avellini's pass and returns it to Bears' 3. Three plays later, Whittington runs two yards for a touchdown at 5:19.

Oct. 15, 1978—Dallas 24, St. Louis 21, at St. Louis; Cowboys win toss. Dallas drives from its 23 into field goal range. Septien kicks 27-yard field goal at 3:28.

Oct. 29, 1978—Denver 20, Seattle 17, at Seattle; Broncos win toss. Ball changes hands four times before Turner kicks 18-yard field goal at 12:59.

Nov. 12, 1978—San Diego 29, Kansas City 23, at San Diego; Chiefs win toss. Fouts hits Jefferson for decisive 14-yard touchdown pass on the last play (15:00) of overtime period.

Nov. 12, 1978—Washington 16, New York Giants 13, at Washington; Redskins win toss. Moseley kicks winning 45-yard field goal at 8:32 after missing first down field goal attempt of 35 yards at 4:50.

Nov. 26, 1978—Green Bay 10, Minnesota 10, at Green Bay; Packers win toss. Both teams have possession of the ball four times.

Dec. 9, 1978—Cleveland 37, New York Jets 34, at Cleveland; Browns win toss. Cockroft kicks 22-yard field goal at 3:07.

Sept. 2, 1979—Atlanta 40, New Orleans 34, at New Orleans; Falcons win toss. Bartkowski's pass intercepted by Myers and returned to Falcons' 46. Erxleben punts to Falcons' 4. James punts to Chandler on Saints' 43. Erxleben punts and Ryckman returns to Falcons' 28. James punts and Chandler returns to Saints' 36. Erxleben retrieves punt snap on Saints' 1 and attempts pass. Mayberry intercepts and returns six yards for touchdown at 8:22.

Sept. 2, 1979—Cleveland 25, New York Jets 22, at New York; Jets win toss. Leahy's 43-yard field goal attempt goes wide right at 4:41. Evans's punt blocked by Dykes is recovered by Newton. Ramsey punts into end zone for touchback. Evans punts and Harper returns to Jets' 24. Robinson's pass intercepted by Davis and returned 33 yards to Jets' 31. Cockroft kicks 27-yard field goal at 14:45.

***Sept. 3, 1979—Pittsburgh 16, New England 13,** at Foxboro; Patriots win toss. Hare punts to Swann at Steelers' 31. Bahr kicks 41-yard field goal at 5:10.

Sept. 9, 1979—Tampa Bay 29, Baltimore 26, at Baltimore; Colts win toss. Landry fumbles, recovered by Kollar at Colts' 14. O'Donoghue kicks 31-yard, first-down field goal at 1:41.

Sept. 16, 1979—Denver 20, Atlanta 17, at Atlanta; Broncos win toss. Broncos march 65 yards to Falcons' 7. Turner kicks 24-yard field goal at 6:15.

Sept. 23, 1979—Houston 30, Cincinnati 27, at Cincinnati; Oilers win toss. Parsley punts and Lusby returns to Bengals' 33. Bahr's 32-yard field goal attempt is wide right at 8:05. Parsley's punt downed on Bengals' 5. McInally punts and Ellender returns to Bengals' 42. Fritsch's third down, 29-yard field goal attempt hits left upright and bounces through at 14:28.

Sept. 23, 1979—Minnesota 27, Green Bay 21, at Minnesota; Vikings win toss. Kramer throws 50-yard touchdown pass to Rashad at 3:18.

Oct. 28, 1979—Houston 27, New York Jets 24, at Houston; Oilers win toss. Oilers march 58 yards to Jets' 18. Fritsch kicks 35-yard field goal at 5:10.

Nov. 18, 1979—Cleveland 30, Miami 24, at Cleveland; Browns win toss. Sipe passes 39 yards to Rucker for touchdown at 1:59.

Nov. 25, 1979—Pittsburgh 33, Cleveland 30, at Pittsburgh; Browns win toss. Sipe's pass intercepted by Blount on Steelers' 4. Bradshaw pass intercepted by Bolton on Browns' 12. Evans punts and Bell returns to Steelers' 17. Bahr kicks 37-yard field goal at 14:51.

Nov. 25, 1979—Buffalo 16, New England 13, at Foxboro; Patriots win toss. Hare's punt downed on Bills' 38. Jackson punts and Morgan returns to Patriots' 20. Grogan's pass intercepted by Haslett and returned to Bills' 42. Ferguson's 51-yard pass to Butler sets up N. Mike-Mayer's 29-yard field goal at 9:15.

Dec. 2, 1979—Los Angeles 27, Minnesota 21, at Los Angeles; Rams win toss. Clark punts and Miller returns to Vikings' 25. Kramer's pass intercepted by Brown and returned to Rams' 40. Cromwell, holding for 22-yard field goal attempt, runs around left end untouched for winning score at 6:53.

Sept. 7, 1980—Green Bay 12, Chicago 6, at Green Bay; Bears win toss. Parsons punts and Nixon returns 16 yards. Five plays later, Marcol returns own blocked field goal attempt 24 yards for touchdown at 6:00.

Sept. 14, 1980—San Diego 30, Oakland 24, at San Diego; Raiders win toss. Pastorini's first-down pass intercepted by Edwards. Millen intercepts Fouts' first-down pass and returns to San Diego 46. Bahr's 50-yard field goal attempt partially blocked by Williams and recovered on Chargers' 32. Eight plays later, Fouts throws 24-yard touchdown pass to Jefferson at 8:09.

Sept. 14, 1980—San Francisco 24, St. Louis 21, at San Francisco; Cardinals win toss. Swider punts and Robinson returns to 49ers' 32. San Francisco drives 52 yards to St. Louis 16, where Wersching kicks 33-yard field goal at 4:12.

Oct. 12, 1980—Green Bay 14, Tampa Bay 14, at Tampa Bay; Packers win toss. Teams trade punts twice. Lee returns second Tampa Bay punt to Green Bay 42. Dickey completes three passes to Buccaneers' 18, where Birney's 36-yard field goal attempt is wide right as time expires.

Nov. 9, 1980—Atlanta 33, St. Louis 27, at St. Louis; Falcons win toss. Strong runs 21 yards for touchdown at 4:20.

#**Nov. 20, 1980—San Diego 27, Miami 24,** at Miami; Chargers win toss. Partridge punts into end zone, Dolphins take over on their own 20. Woodley's pass for Nathan intercepted by Lowe and returned 28 yards to Dolphins' 12. Benirschke kicks 28-yard field goal at 7:14.

Nov. 23, 1980—New York Jets 31, Houston 28, at New York; Jets win toss. Leahy kicks 38-yard field goal at 3:58.

Nov. 27, 1980—Chicago 23, Detroit 17, at Detroit; Bears win toss. Williams returns kickoff 95 yards for touchdown at 0:21.

Dec. 7, 1980—Buffalo 10, Los Angeles 7, at Buffalo; Rams win toss. Corral punts and Hooks returns to Bills' 34. Ferguson's 30-yard pass to Lewis sets up N. Mike-Mayer's 30-yard field goal at 5:14.

Dec. 7, 1980—San Francisco 38, New Orleans 35, at San Francisco; Saints win toss. Erxleben's punt downed by Hardy on 49ers' 27. Wersching kicks 36-yard field goal at 7:40.

***Dec. 8, 1980—Miami 16, New England 13,** at Miami; Dolphins win toss. Von Schamann kicks 23-yard field goal at 3:20.

Dec. 14, 1980—Cincinnati 17, Chicago 14, at Chicago; Bengals win toss. Breech kicks 28-yard field goal at 4:23.

Dec. 21, 1980—Los Angeles 20, Atlanta 17, at Los Angeles; Rams win toss. Corral's punt downed at Rams' 37. James punts into end zone for touchback. Corral's punt downed on Falcons' 17. Bartkowski fumbles when hit by Harris, recovered by Delaney. Corral kicks 23-yard field goal on first play of possession at 7:00.

Sept. 27, 1981—Cincinnati 27, Buffalo 24, at Cincinnati; Bills win toss. Cater punts into end zone for touchback. Bengals drive to the Bills' 10 where Breech kicks 28-yard field goal at 9:33.

Sept. 27, 1981—Pittsburgh 27, New England 21, at Pittsburgh; Patriots win toss. Hubach punts and Smith returns five yards to midfield. Four plays later Bradshaw throws 24-yard touchdown pass to Swann at 3:19.

Oct. 4, 1981—Miami 28, New York Jets 28, at Miami; Jets win toss. Teams trade punts twice. Leahy's 48-yard field goal attempt is wide right as time expires.

Oct. 25, 1981—New York Giants 27, Atlanta 24, at Atlanta; Giants win toss. Jennings' punt goes out of bounds at New York 47. Bright returns Atlanta punt to Giants' 14. Woerner fair catches punt at own 28. Andrews fumbles on first play, recovered by Van Pelt. Danelo kicks 40-yard field goal four plays later at 9:20.

Oct. 25, 1981—Chicago 20, San Diego 17, at Chicago; Bears win toss. Teams trade punts. Bears' second punt returned by Brooks to Chargers' 33. Fouts pass intercepted by Fencik and returned 32 yards to San Diego 27. Roveto kicks 27-yard field goal seven plays later at 9:30.

Nov. 8, 1981—Chicago 16, Kansas City 13, at Kansas City; Bears win toss. Teams trade punts. Kansas City takes over on downs on its own 38. Fuller's fumble recovered by Harris on Chicago 36. Roveto's 37-yard field goal wide, but Chiefs penalized for leverage. Roveto's 22-yard field goal attempt three plays later is good at 13:07.

Nov. 8, 1981—Denver 23, Cleveland 20, at Denver; Browns win toss. D. Smith recovers Hill's fumble at Denver 48. Morton's 33-yard pass to Upchurch and six-yard run by Preston set up Steinfort's 30-yard field goal at 4:10.

Nov. 8, 1981—Miami 30, New England 27, at New England; Dolphins win toss. Orosz punts and Morgan returns six yards to New England 26. Grogan's pass intercepted by Brudzinski who returns 19 yards to Patriots' 26. Von Schamann kicks 30-yard field goal on first down at 7:09.

Nov. 15, 1981—Washington 30, New York Giants 27, at New York; Giants win toss. Nelms returns Giants' punt 26 yards to New York 47. Five plays later Moseley kicks 48-yard field goal at 3:44.

Dec. 20, 1981—New York Giants 13, Dallas 10, at New York; Cowboys win toss and kick off. Jennings punts to Dallas 40. Taylor recovers Dorsett's fumble on second down. Danelo's 33-yard field goal attempt hits right upright and bounces back. White's pass for Pearson intercepted by Hunt and returned seven yards to Dallas 24. Four plays later Danelo kicks 35-yard field goal at 6:19.

Sept. 12, 1982—Washington 37, Philadelphia 34, at Philadelphia; Redskins win toss. Theismann completes five passes for 63 yards to set up Moseley's 26-yard field goal at 4:47.

Sept. 19, 1982—Pittsburgh 26, Cincinnati 20, at Pittsburgh; Bengals win toss. Anderson's pass intended for Kreider intercepted by Woodruff and returned 30 yards to Cincinnati 2. Bradshaw completes two-yard touchdown pass to Stallworth on first down at 1:08.

Dec. 19, 1982—Baltimore 20, Green Bay 20, at Baltimore; Packers win toss. K. Anderson intercepts Dickey's first-down pass and returns to Packers' 42. Miller's 44-yard field goal attempt blocked by G. Lewis. Teams trade punts before Stenerud's 47-yard field goal attempt is wide right. Teams trade punts again before time expires in Colts possession.

Jan. 2, 1983—Tampa Bay 26, Chicago 23, at Tampa Bay; Bears win toss. Parsons punts to T. Bell at Buccaneers' 40. Capece kicks 33-yard field goal at 3:14.

Sept. 4, 1983—Baltimore 29, New England 23, at New England; Patriots win toss. Cooks runs 52 yards with fumble recovery three plays into overtime at 0:30.

Sept. 4, 1983—Green Bay 41, Houston 38, at Houston; Packers win toss. Stenerud kicks 42-yard field goal at 5:55.

Sept. 11, 1983—New York Giants 16, Atlanta 13, at Atlanta; Giants win toss. Dennis returns kickoff 54 yards to Atlanta 41. Haji-Sheikh kicks 30-yard field goal at 3:38.

Sept. 18, 1983—New Orleans 34, Chicago 31, at New Orleans; Bears win toss. Parsons punts and Groth returns five yards to New Orleans 34. Stabler pass intercepted by Schmidt at Chicago 47. Parsons punt downed by Gentry at New Orleans 2. Stabler gains 36 yards in four passes; Wilson 38 in six carries. Andersen kicks 41-yard field goal at 10:57.

Sept. 18, 1983—Minnesota 19, Tampa Bay 16, at Tampa; Vikings win toss. Coleman punts and Bell returns eight yards to Tampa Bay 47. Capece's 33-yard field goal attempt sails wide at 7:26. Dils and Young combine for 48-yard gain to Tampa Bay 27. Ricardo kicks 42-yard field goal at 9:27.

Sept. 25, 1983—Baltimore 22, Chicago 19, at Baltimore; Colts win toss. Allegre kicks 33-yard field goal nine plays later at 4:51.

Sept. 25, 1983—Cleveland 30, San Diego 24, at San Diego; Browns win toss. Walker returns kickoff 33 yards to Cleveland 37. Sipe completes 48-yard touchdown pass to Holt four plays later at 1:53.

Sept. 25, 1983—New York Jets 27, Los Angeles Rams 24, at New York; Jets win toss. Ramsey punts to Irvin who returns to 25 but penalty puts Rams on own 13. Holmes 30-yard interception return sets up Leahy's 26-yard field goal at 3:22.

Oct. 9, 1983—Buffalo 38, Miami 35, at Miami; Dolphins win toss. Von Schamann's 52-yard field goal attempt goes wide at 12:36. Cater punts to Clayton who loses 11 to own 13. Von Schamann's 43-yard field goal attempt sails wide at 5:15. Danelo kicks 36-yard field goal nine plays later at 13:58.

Oct. 9, 1983—Dallas 27, Tampa Bay 24, at Dallas; Cowboys win toss. Septien's 51-yard field goal attempt goes wide but Buccaneers penalized for roughing kicker. Septien kicks 42-yard field goal at 4:38.

Oct. 23, 1983—Kansas City 13, Houston 10, at Houston; Chiefs win toss. Lowery kicks 41-yard field goal 13 plays later at 7:41.

Oct. 23, 1983—Minnesota 20, Green Bay 17, at Green Bay; Packers win toss. Scribner's punt downed on Vikings' 42. Ricardo kicks 32-yard field goal eight plays later at 5:05.

***Oct. 24, 1983—New York Giants 20, St. Louis 20,** at St. Louis; Cardinals win toss. Teams trade punts before O'Donoghue's 44-yard field goal attempt is wide left. Jennings' punt returned by Bird to St. Louis 21. Lomax pass intercepted by Haynes who loses six yards to New York 33. Jennings' punt downed on St. Louis 17. O'Donoghue's 19-yard field goal attempt is wide right. Rutledge's pass intercepted by L. Washington who returns 25 yards to New York 25. O'Donoghue's 42-yard field goal attempt is wide right. Rutledge's pass intercepted by W. Smith at St. Louis 33 to end game.

Oct. 30, 1983—Cleveland 25, Houston 19, at Cleveland; Oilers win toss. Teams trade punts. Nielsen's pass intercepted by Whitwell who returns to Houston 20. Green runs 20 yards for touchdown on first down at 6:34.

Nov. 20, 1983—Detroit 23, Green Bay 20, at Milwaukee; Packers win toss. Scribner punts and Jenkins returns 14 yards to Green Bay 45. Murray's 33-yard field goal attempt is wide left at 9:32. Whitehurst's pass intercepted by Watkins and returned to Green Bay 27. Murray kicks 37-yard field goal four plays later at 8:30.

Nov. 27, 1983—Atlanta 47, Green Bay 41, at Atlanta; Packers win toss. K. Johnson returns interception 31 yards for touchdown at 2:13.

Nov. 27, 1983—Seattle 51, Kansas City 48, at Seattle; Seahawks win toss. Dixon's 47-yard kickoff return sets up N. Johnson's 42-yard field goal at 1:36.

Dec. 11, 1983—New Orleans 20, Philadelphia 17, at Philadelphia; Eagles win toss. Runager punts to Groth who fair catches on New Orleans 32. Stabler completes two passes for 36 yards to Goodlow to set up Andersen's 50-yard field goal at 5:30.

***Dec. 12, 1983—Green Bay 12, Tampa Bay 9,** at Tampa; Packers win toss. Stenerud kicks 23-yard field goal 11 plays later at 4:07.

Sept. 9, 1984—Detroit 27, Atlanta 24, at Atlanta; Lions win toss. Murray kicks 48-yard field goal nine plays later at 5:06.

Sept. 30, 1984—Tampa Bay 30, Green Bay 27, at Tampa; Packers win toss. Scribner punts 44 yards to Tampa Bay 2. Epps returns Garcia's punt three yards to Green Bay 27. Scribner's punt downed on Buccaneers' 33. Ariri kicks 46-yard field goal 11 plays later at 10:32.

Oct. 14, 1984—Detroit 13, Tampa Bay 7, at Detroit; Buccaneers win toss. Tampa Bay drives to Lions' 39 before Wilder fumbles. Five plays later Danielson hits Thompson with 37-yard touchdown pass at 4:34.

Oct. 21, 1984—Dallas 30, New Orleans 27, at Dallas; Cowboys win toss. Septien kicks 41-yard field goal eight plays later at 3:42.

Oct. 28, 1984—Denver 22, Los Angeles Raiders 19, at Los Angeles; Raiders win toss. Hawkins fumble recovered by Foley at Denver 7. Teams trade punts. Karlis' 42-yard field goal attempt is wide left. Teams trade punts. Wilson pass intercepted by R. Jackson at Los Angeles 45, returned 23 yards to Los Angeles 22. Karlis kicks 35-yard field goal two plays later at 15:00.

Nov. 4, 1984—Philadelphia 23, Detroit 23, at Detroit; Lions win toss. Lions drive to Eagles' 3 in eight plays. Murray's 21-yard field goal attempt hits right upright and bounces back. Jaworski's pass intercepted by Watkins at Detroit 5.

Teams trade punts. Cooper returns Black's punt five yards to Eagles' 14. Time expires four plays later with Eagles on own 21.

Nov. 18, 1984—San Diego 34, Miami 28, at San Diego; Chargers win toss. McGee scores eight plays later on a 25-yard run at 3:17.

Dec. 2, 1984—Cincinnati 20, Cleveland 17, at Cleveland; Browns win toss. Simmons returns Cox's punt 30 yards to Cleveland 35. Breech kicks 35-yard field goal seven plays later at 4:34.

Dec. 2, 1984—Houston 23, Pittsburgh 20, at Houston; Oilers win toss. Cooper kicks 30-yard field goal 16 plays later at 5:53.

Sept. 8, 1985—St. Louis 27, Cleveland 24, at Cleveland; Cardinals win toss. O'Donoghue kicks 35-yard field goal nine plays later at 5:27.

Sept. 29, 1985—New York Giants 16, Philadelphia 10, at Philadelphia; Eagles win toss. Jaworski's pass tipped by Quick and intercepted by Patterson who returns 29 yards for touchdown at 0:55.

Oct. 20, 1985—Denver 13, Seattle 10, at Denver; Seahawks win toss. Teams trade punts twice. Krieg's pass intercepted by Hunter and returned to Seahawks' 15. Karlis kicks 24-yard field goal four plays later at 9:19.

Nov. 10, 1985—Philadelphia 23, Atlanta 17, at Philadelphia; Falcons win toss. Donnelly's 62-yard punt goes out of bounds at Eagles' 1. Jaworski completes 99-yard touchdown pass to Quick two plays later at 1:49.

Nov. 10, 1985—San Diego 40, Los Angeles Raiders 34, at San Diego; Chargers win toss. James scores on 17-yard run seven plays later at 3:44.

Nov. 17, 1985—Denver 30, San Diego 24, at Denver; Chargers win toss. Thomas' 40-yard field goal attempt blocked by Smith and returned 60 yards by Wright for touchdown at 4:45.

Nov. 24, 1985—New York Jets 16, New England 13, at New York; Jets win toss. Teams trade punts twice. Patriots' second punt returned 46 yards by Sohn to Patriots' 15. Leahy kicks 32-yard field goal one play later at 10:05.

Nov. 24, 1985—Tampa Bay 19, Detroit 16, at Tampa; Lions win toss. Teams trade punts. Lions' punt downed on Buccaneers' 38. Igwebuike kicks 24-yard field goal 11 plays later at 12:31.

Nov. 24, 1985—Los Angeles Raiders 31, Denver 28, at Los Angeles; Raiders win toss. Bahr kicks 32-yard field goal six plays later at 2:42.

Dec. 8, 1985—Los Angeles Raiders 17, Denver 14, at Denver; Broncos win toss. Teams trade punts twice. Elway's fumble recovered by Townsend at Broncos' 8. Bahr kicks 26-yard field goal one play later at 4:55.

Sept. 14, 1986—Chicago 13, Philadelphia 10, at Chicago; Eagles win toss. Crawford's fumble of kickoff recovered by Jackson at Eagles' 35. Butler kicks 23-yard field goal 10 plays later at 5:56.

Sept. 14, 1986—Cincinnati 36, Buffalo 33, at Cincinnati; Bills win toss. Zander intercepts Kelly's first-down pass and returns it to Bills' 17. Breech kicks 20-yard field goal two plays later at 0:56.

Sept. 21, 1986—New York Jets 51, Miami 45, at New York; Jets win toss. O'Brien completes 43-yard touchdown pass to Walker five plays later at 2:35.

Sept. 28, 1986—Pittsburgh 22, Houston 16, at Houston; Oilers win toss. Johnson's punt returned 41 yards by Woods to Oilers' 15. Abercrombie scores on three-yard run three plays later at 2:35.

Sept. 28, 1986—Atlanta 23, Tampa Bay 20, at Tampa; Falcons win toss. Teams trade punts. Luckhurst kicks 34-yard field goal 10 plays later at 12:35.

Oct. 5, 1986—Los Angeles Rams 26, Tampa Bay 20, at Anaheim; Rams win toss. Dickerson scores four plays later on 42-yard run at 2:16.

Oct. 12, 1986—Minnesota 27, San Francisco 24, at San Francisco; Vikings win toss. C. Nelson kicks 28-yard field goal nine plays later at 4:27.

Oct. 19, 1986—San Francisco 10, Atlanta 10, at Atlanta; Falcons win toss. Teams trade punts twice. Donnelly punts to 49ers' 27. The following play Wilson recovers Rice's fumble at 49ers' 46 as time expires.

Nov. 2, 1986—Washington 44, Minnesota 38, at Washington; Redskins win toss. Schroeder completes 38-yard touchdown pass to Clark four plays later at 1:46.

Nov. 20, 1986—Los Angeles Raiders 37, San Diego 31, at San Diego; Raiders win toss. Teams trade punts. Allen scores five plays later on 28-yard run at 8:33.

Nov. 23, 1986—Cleveland 37, Pittsburgh 31, at Cleveland; Browns win toss. Teams trade punts. Six plays later Kosar hits Slaughter with 36-yard touchdown pass at 6:37.

Nov. 30, 1986—Chicago 13, Pittsburgh 10, at Chicago; Bears win toss and kick off. Newsome's punt returned by Barnes to Chicago 49. Butler kicks 42-yard field goal five plays later at 3:55.

Nov. 30, 1986—Philadelphia 33, Los Angeles Raiders 27, at Los Angeles; Eagles win toss. Teams trade punts. Long recovers Cunningham's fumble at Philadelphia 42. Waters returns Allen's fumble 81 yards to Los Angeles 4. Cunningham scores on one-yard run two plays later at 6:53.

Nov. 30, 1986—Cleveland 13, Houston 10, at Cleveland; Oilers win toss and kick off. Gossett punts to Houston 39. Luck's pass intercepted by Minnifield at Cleveland 21. Gossett punts to Houston 34. Luck's pass intercepted by Minnifield at Cleveland 43 who returns 20 yards to Houston 37. Moseley kicks 29-yard field goal nine plays later at 14:44.

Dec. 7, 1986—St. Louis 10, Philadelphia 10, at Philadelphia; Cardinals win toss. White blocks Schubert's 40-yard field goal attempt. Teams trade punts. McFadden's 43-yard field goal attempt is wide left. Schubert's 37-yard field goal attempt is wide right. Cavanaugh's pass intercepted by Carter and returned to Eagles' 48 to end game.

Dec. 14, 1986—Miami 37, Los Angeles Rams 31, at Anaheim; Dolphins win toss. Marino completes 20-yard touchdown pass to Duper six plays later at 3:04.

Sept. 20, 1987—Denver 17, Green Bay 17, at Green Bay; Packers win toss. Del Greco's 47-yard field goal attempt is short. Teams trade punts. Elway intercepted by Noble who returns 10 yards to Green Bay 34. Davis fumbles on next play and Smith recovers. Two plays later, Karlis's 40-yard field goal attempt is wide left. Time expires two plays later with Packers on own 23.

Oct. 11, 1987—Detroit 19, Green Bay 16, at Green Bay; Lions win toss. Prindle's 42-yard field goal attempt is wide left. Packers punt downed on Detroit 17. Prindle kicks 31-yard field goal 16 plays later at 12:26.

Oct. 18, 1987—New York Jets 37, Miami 31, at New York; Jets win toss. Teams trade punts. Ryan intercepted by Hooper at Jets' 47 who returns 11 yards. Mackey intercepted by Haslett at Jets' 37 who returns 9 yards. Jets punt. Mackey intercepted by Radachowsky who returns 45 yards to Miami 24. Ryan completes eight-yard touchdown pass to Hunter five plays later at 14:26.

Oct. 18, 1987—Green Bay 16, Philadelphia 10, at Green Bay; Packers win toss. Hargrove scores on seven-yard run 10 plays later at 5:04.

Oct. 18, 1987—Buffalo 6, New York Giants 3, at Buffalo; Bills win toss. Schlopy's 28-yard field goal attempt is wide left. Teams trade punts. Rutledge intercepted by Clark who returns 23 yards to Buffalo 40. Schlopy kicks 27-yard field goal nine plays later at 14:41.

Oct. 25, 1987—Buffalo 34, Miami 31, at Miami; Bills win toss. Norwood kicks 27-yard field goal seven plays later at 4:12.

Nov. 1, 1987—San Diego 27, Cleveland 24, at San Diego; Browns win toss. Kosar intercepted by Glenn who returns 20 yards to Browns' 25. Abbott kicks 33-yard field goal three plays later at 2:16.

Nov. 15, 1987—Dallas 23, New England 17, at New England; Cowboys win toss. Walker scores on 60-yard run four plays later at 1:50.

Nov. 26, 1987—Minnesota 44, Dallas 38, at Dallas; Vikings win toss. Coleman's punt downed by Hilton at Cowboys' 37. White intercepted by Studwell who returns 12 yards to Vikings' 37. D. Nelson scores on 24-yard run seven plays later at 7:51.

Nov. 29, 1987—Philadelphia 34, New England 31, at New England; Patriots win toss. Ramsey intercepted by Joyner who returns 29 yards to Eagles' 32. Fryar fair catches Teltschik's punt at Patriots' 13. Franklin's 46-yard field goal attempt is short. McFadden's 39-yard field goal attempt is wide left. Tatupu fumbles on next play and Cobb recovers. McFadden kicks 38-yard field goal four plays later at 12:16.

Dec. 6, 1987—New York Giants 23, Philadelphia 20, at New York; Giants win toss and kick off. Teams trade punts twice. Teltschik's punt is returned 16 yards by McConkey to Eagles' 33. Three plays later, Allegre's 50-yard field goal attempt is blocked by Joyner and returned 25 yards by Hoage to Eagles' 30. McConkey returns Teltschik's punt four yards to Giants' 44. Allegre kicks 28-yard field goal four plays later at 10:42.

Dec. 6, 1987—Cincinnati 30, Kansas City 27, at Cincinnati; Bengals win toss. Teams trade punts. Breech kicks 32-yard field goal 16 plays later at 9:44.

Dec. 26, 1987—Washington 27, Minnesota 24, at Minnesota; Redskins win toss. Haji-Sheikh kicks 26-yard field goal six plays later at 2:09.

Sept. 4, 1988—Houston 17, Indianapolis 14, at Indianapolis; Colts win toss. Dickerson fumble recovered by Odom who returns six yards to Colts' 42. Zendejas kicks 35-yard field goal six plays later at 3:51.

***Sept. 26, 1988—Los Angeles Raiders 30, Denver 27,** at Denver; Broncos win toss. Teams trade punts twice. Elway intercepted by Lee who returns 20 yards to Broncos' 31. Bahr kicks 35-yard field goal four plays later at 12:35.

Oct. 2, 1988—New York Jets 17, Kansas City 17, at New York; Chiefs win toss. Chiefs punt goes into end zone for touchback. Leahy's 44-yard field goal attempt is wide right. Chiefs punt is returned by Townsell to Jets' 26. Burruss recovers McNeil's fumble at Chiefs' 11. DeBerg intercepted by Humphery at Jets' 49. Three plays later, time expires.

Oct. 9, 1988—Denver 16, San Francisco 13, at San Francisco; Broncos win toss and kick off. Young intercepted by Haynes at Broncos' 32. Denver punt downed at 49ers' 5. Young intercepted by Wilson who returns seven yards to 49ers' 5. Karlis kicks 22-yard field goal two plays later at 8:11.

Oct. 30, 1988—New York Giants 13, Detroit 10, at Detroit; Lions win toss. James's fumble recovered by Taylor at Lions' 22. Three plays later, McFadden kicks 33-yard field goal at 1:13.

Nov. 20, 1988—Buffalo 9, New York Jets 6, at Buffalo; Jets win toss. Vick's fumble recovered by Bennett at Bills' 32. Norwood kicks 30-yard field goal five plays later at 3:47.

Nov. 20, 1988—Philadelphia 23, New York Giants 17, at New York; Eagles win toss. Philadelphia's punt goes into end zone for touchback. Hostetler intercepted by Hoage who returns 11 yards to Giants' 41. Six plays later, Zendejas's 30-yard field-goal attempt is blocked and ball is recovered behind line of scrimmage by Eagles' Simmons, who runs 15 yards for touchdown at 3:09.

Dec. 11, 1988—New England 10, Tampa Bay 7, at New England; Buccaneers win toss and kick off. Staurovsky kicks 27-yard field goal six plays later at 3:08.

Dec. 17, 1988—Cincinnati 20, Washington 17, at Cincinnati; Bengals win toss. Cincinnati's punt returned by Oliphant to Redskins' 16. Grant recovers Williams's fumble at Redskins' 17. Breech kicks 20-yard field goal three plays later at 7:01.

Sept. 24, 1989—Buffalo 47, Houston 41, at Houston; Oilers win toss. Johnson returns Brady's kickoff 17 yards to Oilers' 19. Oilers drive to Buffalo 25, Zendejas's 37-yard field goal blocked, but Bills offsides and Zendejas's second attempt is wide left. Bills' ball and Kelly completes series of passes, including 28-yard game-winner to Andre Reed, at 8:42.

Oct. 8, 1989—Miami 13, Cleveland 10, at Miami; Browns win toss. Metcalf returns Stoyanovich's kickoff 20 yards to Browns' 28. Browns drive ball 46 yards in eight plays; Bahr wide left on 44-yard field goal attempt. Dolphins ball. Browns called for pass interference on Marino pass to Banks at Cleveland 47. Two plays later, Banks's 20-yard reception at Browns' 23 sets up winning 35-yard field goal by Stoyanovich at 6:23.

Oct. 22, 1989—Denver 24, Seattle 21, at Seattle; Seahawks win toss. Treadwell's 56-yard kickoff returned 18 yards by Jefferson to Seahawks' 27. Seahawks drive to Broncos' 22 in 10 plays, but Johnson's 40-yard field goal attempt wide left. Smith intercepts a Krieg pass and returns it 28 yards to Seahawks' 10. Treadwell kicks winning 27-yard field goal at 7:46.

Oct. 29, 1989—New England 23, Indianapolis 20, at Indianapolis; Patriots win toss. Biasucci kickoff returned 13 yards to Patriots' 23 by Martin. Holding penalty brings ball back to Patriots' 13. After six plays, Feagles punt returned 11 yards by Verdin to Colts' 28. Six plays later, Colts punt to Martin at Patriots' 12. Grogan completes three straight passes to Patriots' 44. Five consecutive runs put New England on Colts' 33. Davis kicks a 51-yard winning field goal for Patriots at 9:46.

Oct. 29, 1989—Green Bay 23, Detroit 20, at Milwaukee; Lions win toss. Sanders touchback on Jacke kickoff. On first play, Murphy intercepts Lions' Peete and returns it three yards to Packers' 26. Fullwood gains five yards on three plays to set up Jacke's 38-yard field goal at 2:14.

Nov. 5, 1989—Minnesota 23, L.A. Rams 21, at Minneapolis; Rams win toss. Karlis's kick returned 18 yards by Delpino to Rams' 19. Drive stops at Rams' 28. Merriweather blocks Hatcher's punt at 12. Ball rolls out of end zone for safety.

Nov. 19, 1989—Cleveland 10, Kansas City 10, at Cleveland; Browns win toss. Browns punt three times; Chiefs twice; before Kansas City's Lowery misses 47-yard field goal with 17 seconds remaining in overtime. Kosar's pass intercepted as time expired.

Nov. 26, 1989—Los Angeles Rams 20, New Orleans 17, at New Orleans; Saints win toss. Lansford's kickoff returned 27 yards to Saints' 30. After four plays, Barnhardt punts to Rams' 15. Saints penalized 35 yards for interference to Rams' 43. Three plays later, Everett hits Anderson with 14-yard pass to Saints' 40, then 26-yarder to put Rams in field goal position. Lansford kicks 31-yard field goal at 6:38.

Dec. 3, 1989—Los Angeles Raiders 16, Denver 13, at Los Angeles; Broncos win toss. Bell returns Jaeger kickoff 14 yards to Broncos' 18. Broncos penalized for illegal block to Broncos' 9. Elway completes three passes for two first downs. On third and eight Elway sacked for 10-yard loss. Horan punts, Adams calls for fair catch at Raiders' 29. Dyal's 26-yard reception moves Raiders to Denver 43. Raiders move ball 34 yards in three plays to set up Jaeger's 26-yard field goal at 7:02.

Dec. 10, 1989—Indianapolis 23, Cleveland 17, at Indianapolis; Browns win toss. Teams trade punts. McNeil returns Colts' punt 42 yards to 42. Seven plays later, Bahr misses 35-yard field goal attempt. Three plays later, Stark punts and McNeil returns ball to 50-yard line. Two plays later, Prior intercepts Kosar's pass at Colts' 42 and returns it 58 yards for touchdown at 10:54.

Dec. 17, 1989—Cleveland 23, Minnesota 17, at Cleveland; Browns win toss. Browns punt to Vikings' 18. Six plays later Vikings punt to Browns' 22. Nine plays later, Bahr lines up to attempt 31-yard field goal. Holder Pagel takes snap and passes 14 yards to Waiters for touchdown at 9:30.

*indicates Monday night game
#indicates Thursday night game

Postseason

Dec. 28, 1958·—Baltimore 23, New York Giants 17, at New York; Giants win toss. Maynard returns kickoff to Giants' 20. Chandler punts and Taseff returns one yard to Colts' 20. Colts win at 8:15 on a one-yard run by Ameche.

Dec. 23, 1962—Dallas Texans 20, Houston Oilers 17, at Houston; Texans win toss and kick off. Jancik returns kickoff to Oilers' 33. Norton punts and Jackson makes fair catch on Texans' 22. Wilson punts and Jancik makes fair catch on Oilers' 45. Robinson intercepts Blanda's pass and returns 13 yards to Oilers' 47. Wilson's punt rolls dead at Oilers' 12. Hull intercepts Blanda's pass and returns 23 yards to midfield. Texans win at 17:54 on a 25-yard field goal by Brooker.

Dec. 26, 1965—Green Bay 13, Baltimore 10, at Green Bay; Packers win toss. Moore returns kickoff to Packers' 22. Chandler punts and Haymond returns nine yards to Colts' 41. Gilburg punts and Wood makes fair catch at Packers' 21. Chandler punts and Haymond returns one yard to Colts' 41. Michaels misses 47-yard field goal. Packers win at 13:39 on 25-yard field goal by Chandler.

Dec. 25, 1971—Miami 27, Kansas City 24, at Kansas City; Chiefs win toss. Podolak, after a lateral from Buchanan, returns kickoff to Chiefs' 46. Stenerud's 42-yard field goal is blocked. Seiple punts and Podolak makes fair catch at Chiefs' 17. Wilson punts and Scott returns 18 yards to Dolphins' 39. Yepremian misses 62-yard field goal. Scott intercepts Dawson's pass and returns 15 yards to Dolphins' 46. Seiple punts and Podolak loses one yard to Chiefs' 15. Wilson punts and Scott makes fair catch on Dolphins' 30. Dolphins win at 22:40 on a 37-yard field goal by Yepremian.

Dec. 24, 1977—Oakland 37, Baltimore 31, at Baltimore; Colts win toss. Raiders start on own 42 following a punt late in the first overtime. Oakland works way into field goal range on Stabler's 19-yard pass to Branch at Colts' 26. Four plays later, on the second play of the second overtime, Stabler hits Casper with a 10-yard touchdown pass at 15:43.

Jan. 2, 1982—San Diego 41, Miami 38, at Miami; Chargers win toss. San Diego drives from its 13 to Miami 8. On second-and-goal, Benirschke misses 27-yard field goal attempt wide left at 9:15. Miami has the ball twice and San Diego twice more before the Dolphins get their third possession. Miami drives from the San Diego 46 to Chargers' 17 and on fourth-and-two, von Schamann's 34-yard field goal attempt is blocked by San Diego's Winslow after 11:27. Fouts then completes four of five passes, including a 39-yarder to Joiner that puts the ball on Dolphins' 10. On first down, Benirschke kicks a 29-yard field goal at 13:52. San Diego's winning drive covered 74 yards in six plays.

Jan. 3, 1987—Cleveland 23, New York Jets 20, at Cleveland; Jets win toss. Jets' punt downed at Browns' 26. Moseley's 23-yard field goal attempt is wide right. Teams trade punts. Jets' second punt downed at Browns' 31. First overtime period expires eight plays later with Browns in possession at Jets' 42. Moseley kicks 27-yard field goal four plays into second overtime at 17:02.

Jan. 11, 1987—Denver 23, Cleveland 20, at Cleveland; Browns win toss. Broncos hold Browns on four downs. Browns' punt returned four yards to Denver's 25. Elway completes 22- and 28-yard passes to set up Karlis's 33-yard field goal nine plays into drive at 5:38.

Jan. 3, 1988—Houston 23, Seattle 20, at Houston; Seahawks win toss. Rodriguez punts to K. Johnson who returns one yard to Houston 15. Zendejas kicks 32-yard field goal 12 plays later at 8:05.

Dec. 31, 1989—Pittsburgh 26, Houston 23, at Houston; Steelers win toss. Steelers punt to Oilers. Oilers' fumble recovered by Woodson and returned three yards. Four plays and 13 yards later, Anderson kicks a 50-yard field goal at 3:26.

Jan. 7, 1990—Los Angeles Rams 19, New York Giants 13, at New York; Rams win toss. Everett completes two passes to move ball to Giants' 48. White

called for pass interference; ball spotted on Giants' 25. Everett hits Anderson with a 30-yard touchdown pass at 1:06.

NFL Postseason Overtime Games (By Length of Game)

Dec. 25, 1971	Miami 27, KANSAS CITY 24	82:40
Dec. 23, 1962	Dallas Texans 20, HOUSTON 17	77:54
Jan. 3, 1987	CLEVELAND 23, New York Jets 20	77:02
Dec. 24, 1977	Oakland 37, BALTIMORE 31	75:43
Jan. 2, 1982	San Diego 41, MIAMI 38	73:52
Dec. 26, 1965	GREEN BAY 13, Baltimore 10	73:39
Dec. 28, 1958	Baltimore 23, N.Y. GIANTS 17	68:15
Jan. 3, 1988	HOUSTON 23, Seattle 20	68:05
Jan. 11, 1987	Denver 23, CLEVELAND 20	65:38
Dec. 31, 1989	Pittsburgh 26, HOUSTON 23	63:26
Jan. 7, 1990	Los Angeles Rams 19, N.Y. GIANTS 13	61:06

Home team in CAPS

Overtime Won-Lost Records, 1974-1989 (Regular Season)

AFC	W	L	T
Buffalo	7	2	0
Cincinnati	7	3	0
Cleveland	10	8	1
Denver	10	5	2
Houston	4	8	0
Indianapolis	4	3	1
Kansas City	3	5	2
Los Angeles Raiders	8	4	0
Miami	4	9	1
New England	2	10	0
New York Jets	6	4	2
Pittsburgh	6	3	1
San Diego	7	6	0
Seattle	1	3	0

NFC	W	L	T
Atlanta	4	7	1
Chicago	6	7	0
Dallas	6	3	0
Detroit	4	5	1
Green Bay	5	6	4
Los Angeles Rams	5	4	1
Minnesota	8	5	2
New Orleans	2	5	0
New York Giants	6	6	1
Philadelphia	4	7	2
Phoenix	3	4	2
San Francisco	3	4	1
Tampa Bay	4	7	1
Washington	7	3	0

Overtime Games By Year (Regular Season)

1989-11		1981-10	
1988- 9		1980-13	
1987-13		1979-12	
1986-16		1978-11	
1985-10		1977- 6	
1984- 9		1976- 5	
1983-19		1975- 9	
1982- 4		1974- 2	

Overtime Game Summary—1974-1989

There have been 159 overtime games in regular-season play since the rule was adopted in 1974 (11 this season). Breakdown follows:

114 (11 times in 1989) times both teams had at least one possession (72%)

45 (0) times the team which won the toss drove for winning score (30 FG, 15 TD) (28%)

77 (2) times the team which won the toss won the game (48%)

69 (8) times the team which lost the toss won the game (43%)

99 (6) games were decided by a field goal (62%)

46 (3) games were decided by a touchdown (29%)

1 (1) game was decided by a safety (.6%)

13 (1) games ended tied (8%). Last time: Nov. 19, 1989, Cleveland 10, Kansas City 10, at Cleveland

Most Overtime Games, Season

5 Green Bay Packers, 1983
4 Denver Broncos, 1985
4 Cleveland Browns, 1989
3 By many teams, last time: Green Bay Packers, New England Patriots, Philadelphia Eagles, 1987

Longest Consecutive Game Streaks Without Overtime (current)

56 games Atlanta Falcons (last OT game, 10/19/86 vs. San Francisco)
50 games Chicago Bears (last OT game, 11/30/86 vs. Pittsburgh)
50 games Pittsburgh Steelers (last OT game, 11/30/86 vs. Chicago)

Shortest Overtime Games

0:21 Chicago 23, Detroit 17; 11/27/80—Initial overtime kickoff return for a touchdown.
0:30 Baltimore 29, New England 23; 9/4/83
0:55 New York Giants 16, Philadelphia 10; 9/29/85

Longest Overtime Games (All Postseason Games)

22:40 Miami 27, Kansas City 24; 12/25/71
17:54 Dallas Texans 20, Houston 17; 12/23/62
17:02 Cleveland 23, New York Jets 20; 1/3/87

There have been 11 postseason overtime games dating back to 1958. Ten times, both teams had at least one possession. Last postseason overtime: Los Angeles Rams 19, New York Giants 13, 1/7/90.

Overtime Scoring Summary

99 were decided by a field goal

19 were decided by a touchdown pass

16 were decided by a touchdown run

 4 were decided by interceptions (Atlanta 40, New Orleans 34, 9/2/79; Atlanta 47, Green Bay 41, 11/27/83; New York Giants 16, Philadelphia 10, 9/29/85; Indianapolis 23, Cleveland 17, 12/10/89)

 2 were decided on a fake field goal/touchdown pass (Minnesota 22, Chicago 16, 10/16/77; Cleveland 23, Minnesota 17, 12/17/89)

 1 was decided by a kickoff return (Chicago 23, Detroit 17, 11/27/80)

 1 was decided by a fumble recovery (Baltimore 29, New England 23, 9/4/83)

 1 was decided on a fake field goal/touchdown run (Los Angeles Rams 27, Minnesota 21, 12/2/79)

 1 was decided on a blocked field goal (Denver 30, San Diego 24, 11/17/85)

 1 was decided on a blocked field goal/recovery by kicker (Green Bay 12, Chicago 6, 9/7/80)

 1 was decided on a blocked field goal/recovery by kicking team (Philadelphia 23, New York Giants 17, 11/20/88)

 1 was decided by a safety (Minnesota 23, Los Angeles Rams 21, 11/5/89)

13 ended tied

Overtime Records

Longest Touchdown Pass

99 Yards—Ron Jaworski to Mike Quick, Philadelphia 23, Atlanta 17 (11/10/85)
50 Yards—Tommy Kramer to Ahmad Rashad, Minnesota 27, Green Bay 21 (9/23/79)
48 Yards—Brian Sipe to Harry Holt, Cleveland 30, San Diego 24 (9/23/83)

Longest Touchdown Run

60 Yards—Herschel Walker, Dallas 23, New England 17 (11/15/87)
42 Yards—Eric Dickerson, Los Angeles Rams 26, Tampa Bay 20 (10/5/86)
28 Yards—Marcus Allen, Los Angeles Raiders 37, San Diego 31 (11/20/86)

Longest Field Goal

51 Yards—Greg Davis, New England 23, Indianapolis 20 (10/29/89)
50 Yards—Morten Andersen, New Orleans 20, Philadelphia 17 (12/11/83)
48 Yards—Eddie Murray, Detroit 27, Atlanta 24 (9/9/84);
           Mark Moseley, Washington 30, New York Giants 27 (11/15/81)

Longest Touchdown Plays

99 Yards—(Pass) Ron Jaworski to Mike Quick, Philadelphia 23, Atlanta 17 (11/10/85)
60 Yards—(Blocked field goal return) Louis Wright, Denver 30, San Diego 24 (11/17/85)
           (Run) Herschel Walker, Dallas 23, New England 17 (11/15/87)
58 Yards—(Interception return) Mike Prior, Indianapolis 23, Cleveland 17 (12/10/89)

NFL Paid Attendance

Year	Regular Season	Average	Postseason	Super Bowl
1989#	13,625,662 (224 games)	#60,829	685,771 (10)	72,919
1988	13,539,848 (224 games)	60,446	658,317 (10)	75,129
1987*	11,406,166 (210 games)	54,315	656,977 (10)	73,302
1986	13,588,551 (224 games)	60,663	734,002 (10)	101,063
1985	13,345,047 (224 games)	59,567	710,768 (10)	73,818
1984	13,398,112 (224 games)	59,813	665,194 (10)	84,059
1983	13,277,222 (224 games)	59,273	675,513 (10)	72,932
1982**	7,367,438 (126 games)	58,472	1,033,153 (16)	103,667
1981	13,606,990 (224 games)	60,745	637,763 (10)	81,270
1980	13,392,230 (224 games)	59,787	624,430 (10)	75,500
1979	13,182,039 (224 games)	58,848	630,326 (10)	103,985
1978	12,771,800 (224 games)	57,017	624,388 (10)	79,641
1977	11,018,632 (196 games)	56,218	534,925 (8)	75,804
1976	11,070,543 (196 games)	56,482	492,884 (8)	103,438
1975	10,213,193 (182 games)	56,116	475,919 (8)	80,187
1974	10,236,322 (182 games)	56,244	438,664 (8)	80,997
1973	10,730,933 (182 games)	58,961	525,433 (8)	71,882
1972	10,445,827 (182 games)	57,395	483,345 (8)	90,182
1971	10,076,035 (182 games)	55,363	483,891 (8)	81,023
1970	9,533,333 (182 games)	52,381	458,493 (8)	79,204
1969	6,096,127 (112 games) NFL	54,430	162,279 (3)	80,562
	2,843,373 (70 games) AFL	40,620	167,088 (3)	
1968	5,882,313 (112 games) NFL	52,521	215,902 (3)	75,377
	2,635,004 (70 games) AFL	37,643	114,438 (2)	
1967	5,938,924 (112 games) NFL	53,026	166,208 (3)	75,546
	2,295,697 (63 games) AFL	36,439	53,330 (1)	
1966	5,337,044 (105 games) NFL	50,829	74,152 (1)	†61,946
	2,160,369 (63 games) AFL	34,291	42,080 (1)	
1965	4,634,021 (98 games) NFL	47,286	100,304 (2)	
	1,782,384 (56 games) AFL	31,828	30,361 (1)	
1964	4,563,049 (98 games) NFL	46,562	79,544 (1)	
	1,447,875 (56 games) AFL	25,855	40,242 (1)	
1963	4,163,643 (98 games) NFL	42,486	45,801 (1)	
	1,208,697 (56 games) AFL	21,584	63,171 (2)	
1962	4,003,421 (98 games) NFL	40,851	64,892 (1)	
	1,147,302 (56 games) AFL	20,487	37,981 (1)	
1961	3,986,159 (98 games) NFL	40,675	39,029 (1)	
	1,002,657 (56 games) AFL	17,904	29,556 (1)	
1960	3,128,296 (78 games) NFL	40,106	67,325 (1)	
	926,156 (56 games) AFL	16,538	32,183 (1)	
1959	3,140,000 (72 games)	43,617	57,545 (1)	
1958	3,006,124 (72 games)	41,752	123,659 (2)	
1957	2,836,318 (72 games)	39,393	119,579 (2)	
1956	2,551,263 (72 games)	35,434	56,836 (1)	
1955	2,521,836 (72 games)	35,026	85,693 (1)	
1954	2,190,571 (72 games)	30,425	43,827 (1)	
1953	2,164,585 (72 games)	30,064	54,577 (1)	
1952	2,052,126 (72 games)	28,502	97,507 (2)	
1951	1,913,019 (72 games)	26,570	57,522 (1)	
1950	1,977,753 (78 games)	25,356	136,647 (3)	
1949	1,391,735 (60 games)	23,196	27,980 (1)	
1948	1,525,243 (60 games)	25,421	36,309 (1)	
1947	1,837,437 (60 games)	30,624	66,268 (2)	
1946	1,732,135 (55 games)	31,493	58,346 (1)	
1945	1,270,401 (50 games)	25,408	32,178 (1)	
1944	1,019,649 (50 games)	20,393	46,016 (1)	
1943	969,128 (40 games)	24,228	71,315 (2)	
1942	887,920 (55 games)	16,144	36,006 (1)	
1941	1,108,615 (55 games)	20,157	55,870 (2)	
1940	1,063,025 (55 games)	19,328	36,034 (1)	
1939	1,071,200 (55 games)	19,476	32,279 (1)	
1938	937,197 (55 games)	17,040	48,120 (1)	
1937	963,039 (55 games)	17,510	15,878 (1)	
1936	816,007 (54 games)	15,111	29,545 (1)	
1935	638,178 (53 games)	12,041	15,000 (1)	
1934	492,684 (60 games)	8,211	35,059 (1)	

Record

*Players' 24-day strike reduced 224-game schedule to 210 games.

**Players' 57-day strike reduced 224-game schedule to 126 games.

†Only Super Bowl that did not sell out.

NFL's 10 Biggest Attendance Weekends

(Paid Count)

Weekend	Games	Attendance
October 16-17, 1988	14	934,211
October 29-30, 1989	14	915,401
October 27-28, 1985	14	902,128
October 12-13, 1980	14	898,223
September 23-24, 1984	14	894,402
November 11-12, 1979	14	890,972
October 8-9, 1989	14	888,271
September 17-18, 1989	14	888,264
September 16, 19-20, 1983	14	886,323
September 11-12, 1988	14	885,815

NFL's 10 Highest Scoring Weekends

Point Total	Date	Weekend
761	October 16-17, 1983	7th
736	October 25-26, 1987	7th
732	November 9-10, 1980	10th
725	November 24, 27-28, 1983	13th
714	September 17-18, 1989	2nd
711	November 26, 29-30, 1987	12th
710	November 28, December 1-2, 1985	13th
696	October 2-3, 1983	5th
693	September 24-25, 1989	3rd
676	September 21-22, 1980	3rd

Top 10 Televised Sports Events

(Based on A.C. Nielsen Figures)

Program	Date	Network	Share	Rating
Super Bowl XVI	1/24/82	CBS	73.0	49.1
Super Bowl XVII	1/30/83	NBC	69.0	48.6
Super Bowl XX	1/26/86	NBC	70.0	48.3
Super Bowl XII	1/15/78	CBS	67.0	47.2
Super Bowl XIII	1/21/79	NBC	74.0	47.1
Super Bowl XVIII	1/22/84	CBS	71.0	46.4
Super Bowl XIX	1/20/85	ABC	63.0	46.4
Super Bowl XIV	1/20/80	CBS	67.0	46.3
Super Bowl XXI	1/25/87	CBS	66.0	45.8
Super Bowl XI	1/9/77	NBC	73.0	44.4

Ten Most Watched TV Programs & Estimated Total Number of Viewers

(Based on A.C. Nielsen Figures)

Program	Date	Network	*Total Viewers
Super Bowl XX	Jan. 26, 1986	NBC	127,000,000
Super Bowl XXI	Jan. 25, 1987	CBS	122,640,000
M*A*S*H (Special)	Feb. 28, 1983	CBS	121,624,000
Super Bowl XIX	Jan. 20, 1985	ABC	115,936,000
Super Bowl XXII	Jan. 31, 1988	ABC	115,000,000
Super Bowl XXIII	Jan. 22, 1989	NBC	110,800,000
Super Bowl XVI	Jan. 24, 1982	CBS	110,230,000
Super Bowl XVII	Jan. 30, 1983	NBC	109,040,000
Super Bowl XXIV	Jan. 28, 1990	CBS	109,000,000
Super Bowl XII	Jan. 15, 1978	CBS	102,010,000

*Watched some portion of the broadcast

NUMBER-ONE DRAFT CHOICES

Season	Team	Player	Position	College
1990	Indianapolis	Jeff George	QB	Illinois
1989	Dallas	Troy Aikman	QB	UCLA
1988	Atlanta	Aundray Bruce	LB	Auburn
1987	Tampa Bay	Vinny Testaverde	QB	Miami
1986	Tampa Bay	Bo Jackson	RB	Auburn
1985	Buffalo	Bruce Smith	DE	Virginia Tech
1984	New England	Irving Fryar	WR	Nebraska
1983	Baltimore	John Elway	QB	Stanford
1982	New England	Kenneth Sims	DT	Texas
1981	New Orleans	George Rogers	RB	South Carolina
1980	Detroit	Billy Sims	RB	Oklahoma
1979	Buffalo	Tom Cousineau	LB	Ohio State
1978	Houston	Earl Campbell	RB	Texas
1977	Tampa Bay	Ricky Bell	RB	Southern California
1976	Tampa Bay	Lee Roy Selmon	DE	Oklahoma
1975	Atlanta	Steve Bartkowski	QB	California
1974	Dallas	Ed Jones	DE	Tennessee State
1973	Houston	John Matuszak	DE	Tampa
1972	Buffalo	Walt Patulski	DE	Notre Dame
1971	New England	Jim Plunkett	QB	Stanford
1970	Pittsburgh	Terry Bradshaw	QB	Louisiana Tech
1969	Buffalo (AFL)	O. J. Simpson	RB	Southern California
1968	Minnesota	Ron Yary	T	Southern California
1967	Baltimore	Bubba Smith	DT	Michigan State
1966	Atlanta	Tommy Nobis	LB	Texas
	Miami (AFL)	Jim Grabowski	RB	Illinois
1965	New York Giants	Tucker Frederickson	RB	Auburn
	Houston (AFL)	Lawrence Elkins	E	Baylor
1964	San Francisco	Dave Parks	E	Texas Tech
	Boston (AFL)	Jack Concannon	QB	Boston College
1963	Los Angeles	Terry Baker	QB	Oregon State
	Kansas City (AFL)	Buck Buchanan	DT	Grambling
1962	Washington	Ernie Davis	RB	Syracuse
	Oakland (AFL)	Roman Gabriel	QB	North Carolina State
1961	Minnesota	Tommy Mason	RB	Tulane
	Buffalo (AFL)	Ken Rice	G	Auburn
1960	Los Angeles	Billy Cannon	RB	Louisiana State
	(AFL had no formal first pick)			
1959	Green Bay	Randy Duncan	QB	Iowa
1958	Chicago Cardinals	King Hill	QB	Rice
1957	Green Bay	Paul Hornung	HB	Notre Dame
1956	Pittsburgh	Gary Glick	DB	Colorado A&M
1955	Baltimore	George Shaw	QB	Oregon
1954	Cleveland	Bobby Garrett	QB	Stanford
1953	San Francisco	Harry Babcock	E	Georgia
1952	Los Angeles	Bill Wade	QB	Vanderbilt
1951	New York Giants	Kyle Rote	HB	Southern Methodist
1950	Detroit	Leon Hart	E	Notre Dame
1949	Philadelphia	Chuck Bednarik	C	Pennsylvania
1948	Washington	Harry Gilmer	QB	Alabama
1947	Chicago Bears	Bob Fenimore	HB	Oklahoma A&M
1946	Boston	Frank Dancewicz	QB	Notre Dame
1945	Chicago Cardinals	Charley Trippi	HB	Georgia
1944	Boston	Angelo Bertelli	QB	Notre Dame
1943	Detroit	Frank Sinkwich	HB	Georgia
1942	Pittsburgh	Bill Dudley	HB	Virginia
1941	Chicago Bears	Tom Harmon	HB	Michigan
1940	Chicago Cardinals	George Cafego	HB	Tennessee
1939	Chicago Cardinals	Ki Aldrich	C	Texas Christian
1938	Cleveland	Corbett Davis	FB	Indiana
1937	Philadelphia	Sam Francis	FB	Nebraska
1936	Philadelphia	Jay Berwanger	HB	Chicago

Note: From 1947 through 1958, the first selection in the draft was a Bonus pick, awarded to the winner of a random draw. That club, in turn, forfeited its last-round draft choice. The winner of the Bonus choice was eliminated from future draws. The system was abolished after 1958, by which time all clubs had received a Bonus choice.

If club had no first-round selection, first player drafted is listed with round in parentheses.

Atlanta Falcons

Year	Player, College, Position
1966	Tommy Nobis, Texas, LB
	Randy Johnson, Texas A&I, QB
1967	Leo Carroll, San Diego State, DE (2)
1968	Claude Humphrey, Tennessee State, DE
1969	George Kunz, Notre Dame, T
1970	John Small, Citadel, LB
1971	Joe Profit, Northeast Louisiana, RB
1972	Clarence Ellis, Notre Dame, DB
1973	Greg Marx, Notre Dame, DT (2)
1974	Gerald Tinker, Kent State, WR (2)
1975	Steve Bartkowski, California, QB
1976	Bubba Bean, Texas A&M, RB
1977	Warren Bryant, Kentucky, T
	Wilson Faumuina, San Jose State, DT
1978	Mike Kenn, Michigan, T
1979	Don Smith, Miami, DE
1980	Junior Miller, Nebraska, TE
1981	Bobby Butler, Florida State, DB
1982	Gerald Riggs, Arizona State, RB
1983	Mike Pitts, Alabama, DE
1984	Rick Bryan, Oklahoma, DT
1985	Bill Fralic, Pittsburgh, T
1986	Tony Casillas, Oklahoma, NT
	Tim Green, Syracuse, LB
1987	Chris Miller, Oregon, QB
1988	Aundray Bruce, Auburn, LB
1989	Deion Sanders, Florida State, DB
	Shawn Collins, Northern Arizona, WR
1990	Steve Broussard, Washington State, RB

Buffalo Bills

Year	Player, College, Position
1960	Richie Lucas, Penn State, QB
1961	Ken Rice, Auburn, T
1962	Ernie Davis, Syracuse, RB
1963	Dave Behrman, Michigan State, C
1964	Carl Eller, Minnesota, DE
1965	Jim Davidson, Ohio State, T
1966	Mike Dennis, Mississippi, RB
1967	John Pitts, Arizona State, S
1968	Haven Moses, San Diego State, WR
1969	O.J. Simpson, Southern California, RB
1970	Al Cowlings, Southern California, DE
1971	J. D. Hill, Arizona State, WR
1972	Walt Patulski, Notre Dame, DE
1973	Paul Seymour, Michigan, TE
	Joe DeLamielleure, Michigan State, G
1974	Reuben Gant, Oklahoma State, TE
1975	Tom Ruud, Nebraska, LB
1976	Mario Clark, Oregon, DB
1977	Phil Dokes, Oklahoma State, DT
1978	Terry Miller, Oklahoma State, RB
1979	Tom Cousineau, Ohio State, LB
	Jerry Butler, Clemson, WR
1980	Jim Ritcher, North Carolina State, C
1981	Booker Moore, Penn State, RB
1982	Perry Tuttle, Clemson, WR
1983	Tony Hunter, Notre Dame, TE
	Jim Kelly, Miami, QB
1984	Greg Bell, Notre Dame, RB
1985	Bruce Smith, Virginia Tech, DE
	Derrick Burroughs, Memphis State, DB
1986	Ronnie Harmon, Iowa, RB
	Will Wolford, Vanderbilt, T
1987	Shane Conlan, Penn State, LB
1988	Thurman Thomas, Oklahoma State, RB (2)
1989	Don Beebe, Chadron, Neb., WR (3)
1990	James Williams, Fresno State, DB

Chicago Bears

Year	Player, College, Position
1936	Joe Stydahar, West Virginia, T
1937	Les McDonald, Nebraska, E
1938	Joe Gray, Oregon State, B
1939	Sid Luckman, Columbia, QB
	Bill Osmanski, Holy Cross, B
1940	Clyde (Bulldog) Turner, Hardin-Simmons, C
1941	Tom Harmon, Michigan, B
1942	Frankie Albert, Stanford, B
1943	Bob Steber, Missouri, B
1944	Ray Evans, Kansas, B
1945	Don Lund, Michigan, B
1946	Johnny Lujack, Notre Dame, QB
1947	Bob Fenimore, Oklahoma State, B
	Don Kindt, Wisconsin, B
1948	Bobby Layne, Texas, QB
	Max Bumgardner, Texas, E
1949	Dick Harris, Texas, C
1950	Chuck Hunsinger, Florida, B
	Fred Morrison, Ohio State, B
1951	Bob Williams, Notre Dame, B
	Billy Stone, Bradley, B
	Gene Schroeder, Virginia, E
1952	Jim Dooley, Miami, B
1953	Billy Anderson, Compton (Calif.) J.C., B
1954	Stan Wallace, Illinois, B
1955	Ron Drzewiecki, Marquette, B
1956	Menan (Tex) Schriewer, Texas, E
1957	Earl Leggett, Louisiana State, T
1958	Chuck Howley, West Virginia, G
1959	Don Clark, Ohio State, B
1960	Roger Davis, Syracuse, G
1961	Mike Ditka, Pittsburgh, E
1962	Ronnie Bull, Baylor, RB
1963	Dave Behrman, Michigan State, C
1964	Dick Evey, Tennessee, DT
1965	Dick Butkus, Illinois, LB
	Gale Sayers, Kansas, RB
	Steve DeLong, Tennessee, T
1966	George Rice, Louisiana State, DT
1967	Loyd Phillips, Arkansas, DE
1968	Mike Hull, Southern California, RB
1969	Rufus Mayes, Ohio State, T
1970	George Farmer, UCLA, WR (3)
1971	Joe Moore, Missouri, RB
1972	Lionel Antoine, Southern Illinois, T
	Craig Clemons, Iowa, DB
1973	Wally Chambers, Eastern Kentucky, DE
1974	Waymond Bryant, Tennessee State, LB
	Dave Gallagher, Michigan, DT
1975	Walter Payton, Jackson State, RB
1976	Dennis Lick, Wisconsin, T
1977	Ted Albrecht, California, T
1978	Brad Shearer, Texas, DT (3)
1979	Dan Hampton, Arkansas, DT
	Al Harris, Arizona State, DE
1980	Otis Wilson, Louisville, LB
1981	Keith Van Horne, Southern California, T
1982	Jim McMahon, Brigham Young, QB
1983	Jim Covert, Pittsburgh, T
	Willie Gault, Tennessee, WR
1984	Wilber Marshall, Florida, LB
1985	William Perry, Clemson, DT
1986	Neal Anderson, Florida, RB
1987	Jim Harbaugh, Michigan, QB
1988	Brad Muster, Stanford, RB
	Wendell Davis, Louisiana State, WR
1989	Donnell Woolford, Clemson, DB
	Trace Armstrong, Florida, DE
1990	Mark Carrier, Southern California, DB

Cincinnati Bengals

Year	Player, College, Position
1968	Bob Johnson, Tennessee, C
1969	Greg Cook, Cincinnati, QB
1970	Mike Reid, Penn State, DT
1971	Vernon Holland, Tennessee State, T
1972	Sherman White, California, DE
1973	Isaac Curtis, San Diego State, WR
1974	Bill Kollar, Montana State, DT
1975	Glenn Cameron, Florida, LB
1976	Billy Brooks, Oklahoma, WR
	Archie Griffin, Ohio State, RB
1977	Eddie Edwards, Miami, DT
	Wilson Whitley, Houston, DT
	Mike Cobb, Michigan State, TE
1978	Ross Browner, Notre Dame, DT
	Blair Bush, Washington, C
1979	Jack Thompson, Washington State, QB
	Charles Alexander, Louisiana State, RB
1980	Anthony Muñoz, Southern California, T
1981	David Verser, Kansas, WR
1982	Glen Collins, Mississippi State, DE
1983	Dave Rimington, Nebraska, C
1984	Ricky Hunley, Arizona, LB
	Pete Koch, Maryland, DE
	Brian Blados, North Carolina, T
1985	Eddie Brown, Miami, WR
	Emanuel King, Alabama, LB
1986	Joe Kelly, Washington, LB
	Tim McGee, Tennessee, WR
1987	Jason Buck, Brigham Young, DE
1988	Rickey Dixon, Oklahoma, DB
1989	Eric Ball, UCLA, RB (2)
1990	James Francis, Baylor, LB

Cleveland Browns

Year	Player, College, Position
1950	Ken Carpenter, Oregon State, B
1951	Ken Konz, Louisiana State, B
1952	Bert Rechichar, Tennessee, DB
	Harry Agganis, Boston U., QB
1953	Doug Atkins, Tennessee, DE
1954	Bobby Garrett, Stanford, QB
	John Bauer, Illinois, G
1955	Kurt Burris, Oklahoma, C
1956	Preston Carpenter, Arkansas, B
1957	Jim Brown, Syracuse, RB
1958	Jim Shofner, Texas Christian, DB
1959	Rich Kreitling, Illinois, DE
1960	Jim Houston, Ohio State, DE
1961	Bobby Crespino, Mississippi, TE
1962	Gary Collins, Maryland, WR
	Leroy Jackson, Western Illinois, RB
1963	Tom Hutchinson, Kentucky, WR
1964	Paul Warfield, Ohio State, WR
1965	James Garcia, Purdue, T (2)
1966	Milt Morin, Massachusetts, TE
1967	Bob Matheson, Duke, LB
1968	Marvin Upshaw, Trinity, Tex., DT-DE
1969	Ron Johnson, Michigan, RB
1970	Mike Phipps, Purdue, QB
	Bob McKay, Texas, T
1971	Clarence Scott, Kansas State, CB
1972	Thom Darden, Michigan, DB
1973	Steve Holden, Arizona State, WR
	Pete Adams, Southern California, T (2)
1974	Billy Corbett, Johnson C. Smith, T (2)
1975	Mack Mitchell, Houston, DE
1976	Mike Pruitt, Purdue, RB
1977	Robert Jackson, Texas A&M, LB
1978	Clay Matthews, Southern California, LB
	Ozzie Newsome, Alabama, TE
1979	Willis Adams, Houston, WR
1980	Charles White, Southern California, RB
1981	Hanford Dixon, Southern Mississippi, DB
1982	Chip Banks, Southern California, LB
1983	Ron Brown, Arizona State, WR (2)
1984	Don Rogers, UCLA, DB
1985	Greg Allen, Florida State, RB (2)
1986	Webster Slaughter, San Diego State, WR (2)
1987	Mike Junkin, Duke, LB
1988	Clifford Charlton, Florida, LB
1989	Eric Metcalf, Texas, RB
1990	Leroy Hoard, Michigan, RB (2)

Dallas Cowboys

Year	Player, College, Position
1960	None
1961	Bob Lilly, Texas Christian, DT
1962	Sonny Gibbs, Texas Christian, QB (2)
1963	Lee Roy Jordan, Alabama, LB
1964	Scott Appleton, Texas, DT
1965	Craig Morton, California, QB
1966	John Niland, Iowa, G
1967	Phil Clark, Northwestern, DB (3)
1968	Dennis Homan, Alabama, WR
1969	Calvin Hill, Yale, RB
1970	Duane Thomas, West Texas State, RB
1971	Tody Smith, Southern California, DE
1972	Bill Thomas, Boston College, RB
1973	Billy Joe DuPree, Michigan State, TE
1974	Ed (Too Tall) Jones, Tennessee State, DE
	Charley Young, North Carolina State, RB
1975	Randy White, Maryland, LB
	Thomas Henderson, Langston, LB

Year	Player, College, Position
1976	Aaron Kyle, Wyoming, DB
1977	Tony Dorsett, Pittsburgh, RB
1978	Larry Bethea, Michigan State, DE
1979	Robert Shaw, Tennessee, C
1980	Bill Roe, Colorado, LB (3)
1981	Howard Richards, Missouri, T
1982	Rod Hill, Kentucky State, DB
1983	Jim Jeffcoat, Arizona State, DE
1984	Billy Cannon, Jr., Texas A&M, LB
1985	Kevin Brooks, Michigan, DE
1986	Mike Sherrard, UCLA, WR
1987	Danny Noonan, Nebraska, DT
1988	Michael Irvin, Miami, WR
1989	Troy Aikman, UCLA, QB
1990	Emmitt Smith, Florida, RB

Denver Broncos

Year	Player, College, Position
1960	Roger LeClerc, Trinity, Conn., C
1961	Bob Gaiters, New Mexico State, RB
1962	Merlin Olsen, Utah State, DT
1963	Kermit Alexander, UCLA, CB
1964	Bob Brown, Nebraska, T
1965	Dick Butkus, Illinois, LB (2)
1966	Jerry Shay, Purdue, DT
1967	Floyd Little, Syracuse, RB
1968	Curley Culp, Arizona State, DE (2)
1969	Grady Cavness, Texas-El Paso, DB (2)
1970	Bob Anderson, Colorado, RB
1971	Marv Montgomery, Southern California, T
1972	Riley Odoms, Houston, TE
1973	Otis Armstrong, Purdue, RB
1974	Randy Gradishar, Ohio State, LB
1975	Louis Wright, San Jose State, DB
1976	Tom Glassic, Virginia, G
1977	Steve Schindler, Boston College, G
1978	Don Latimer, Miami, DT
1979	Kelvin Clark, Nebraska, T
1980	Rulon Jones, Utah State, DE (2)
1981	Dennis Smith, Southern California, DB
1982	Gerald Willhite, San Jose State, RB
1983	Chris Hinton, Northwestern, G
1984	Andre Townsend, Mississippi, DE (2)
1985	Steve Sewell, Oklahoma, RB
1986	Jim Juriga, Illinois, T (4)
1987	Ricky Nattiel, Florida, WR
1988	Ted Gregory, Syracuse, NT
1989	Steve Atwater, Arkansas, DB
1990	Alton Montgomery, Houston, DB (2)

Detroit Lions

Year	Player, College, Position
1936	Sid Wagner, Michigan State, G
1937	Lloyd Cardwell, Nebraska, B
1938	Alex Wojciechowicz, Fordham, C
1939	John Pingel, Michigan State, B
1940	Doyle Nave, Southern California, B
1941	Jim Thomason, Texas A&M, B
1942	Bob Westfall, Michigan, B
1943	Frank Sinkwich, Georgia, B
1944	Otto Graham, Northwestern, B
1945	Frank Szymanski, Notre Dame, C
1946	Bill Dellastatious, Missouri, B
1947	Glenn Davis, Army, B
1948	Y. A. Tittle, Louisiana State, B
1949	John Rauch, Georgia, B
1950	Leon Hart, Notre Dame, E
	Joe Watson, Rice, C
1951	Dick Stanfel, San Francisco, G (2)
1952	Yale Lary, Texas A&M, B (3)
1953	Harley Sewell, Texas, G
1954	Dick Chapman, Rice, T
1955	Dave Middleton, Auburn, B
1956	Hopalong Cassady, Ohio State, B
1957	Bill Glass, Baylor, G
1958	Alex Karras, Iowa, T
1959	Nick Pietrosante, Notre Dame, B
1960	John Robinson, Louisiana State, S
1961	Danny LaRose, Missouri, T (2)
1962	John Hadl, Kansas, QB
1963	Daryl Sanders, Ohio State, T
1964	Pete Beathard, Southern California, QB
1965	Tom Nowatzke, Indiana, RB
1966	Nick Eddy, Notre Dame, RB (2)
1967	Mel Farr, UCLA, RB
1968	Greg Landry, Massachusetts, QB

	Earl McCullouch, Southern California, WR
1969	Altie Taylor, Utah State, RB (2)
1970	Steve Owens, Oklahoma, RB
1971	Bob Bell, Cincinnati, DT
1972	Herb Orvis, Colorado, DE
1973	Ernie Price, Texas A&I, DE
1974	Ed O'Neil, Penn State, LB
1975	Lynn Boden, South Dakota State, G
1976	James Hunter, Grambling, DB
	Lawrence Gaines, Wyoming, RB
1977	Walt Williams, New Mexico State, DB (2)
1978	Luther Bradley, Notre Dame, DB
1979	Keith Dorney, Penn State, T
1980	Billy Sims, Oklahoma, RB
1981	Mark Nichols, San Jose State, WR
1982	Jimmy Williams, Nebraska, LB
1983	James Jones, Florida, RB
1984	David Lewis, California, TE
1985	Lomas Brown, Florida, T
1986	Chuck Long, Iowa, QB
1987	Reggie Rogers, Washington, DE
1988	Bennie Blades, Miami, DB
1989	Barry Sanders, Oklahoma State, RB
1990	Andre Ware, Houston, QB

Green Bay Packers

Year	Player, College, Position
1936	Russ Letlow, San Francisco, G
1937	Eddie Jankowski, Wisconsin, B
1938	Cecil Isbell, Purdue, B
1939	Larry Buhler, Minnesota, B
1940	Harold Van Every, Minnesota, B
1941	George Paskvan, Wisconsin, B
1942	Urban Odson, Minnesota, T
1943	Dick Wildung, Minnesota, T
1944	Merv Pregulman, Michigan, G
1945	Walt Schlinkman, Texas Tech, B
1946	Johnny (Strike) Strzykalski, Marquette, B
1947	Ernie Case, UCLA, B
1948	Earl (Jug) Girard, Wisconsin, B
1949	Stan Heath, Nevada, B
1950	Clayton Tonnemaker, Minnesota, C
1951	Bob Gain, Kentucky, T
1952	Babe Parilli, Kentucky, QB
1953	Al Carmichael, Southern California, B
1954	Art Hunter, Notre Dame, T
	Veryl Switzer, Kansas State, B
1955	Tom Bettis, Purdue, G
1956	Jack Losch, Miami, B
1957	Paul Hornung, Notre Dame, B
	Ron Kramer, Michigan, E
1958	Dan Currie, Michigan State, C
1959	Randy Duncan, Iowa, B
1960	Tom Moore, Vanderbilt, RB
1961	Herb Adderley, Michigan State, CB
1962	Earl Gros, Louisiana State, RB
1963	Dave Robinson, Penn State, LB
1964	Lloyd Voss, Nebraska, DT
1965	Donny Anderson, Texas Tech, RB
	Lawrence Elkins, Baylor, E
1966	Jim Grabowski, Illinois, RB
	Gale Gillingham, Minnesota, T
1967	Bob Hyland, Boston College, C
	Don Horn, San Diego State, QB
1968	Fred Carr, Texas-El Paso, LB
	Bill Lueck, Arizona, G
1969	Rich Moore, Villanova, DT
1970	Mike McCoy, Notre Dame, DT
	Rich McGeorge, Elon, TE
1971	John Brockington, Ohio State, RB
1972	Willie Buchanon, San Diego State, DB
	Jerry Tagge, Nebraska, QB
1973	Barry Smith, Florida State, WR
1974	Barty Smith, Richmond, RB
1975	Bill Bain, Southern California, G (2)
1976	Mark Koncar, Colorado, T
1977	Mike Butler, Kansas, DE
	Ezra Johnson, Morris Brown, DE
1978	James Lofton, Stanford, WR
	John Anderson, Michigan, LB
1979	Eddie Lee Ivery, Georgia Tech, RB
1980	Bruce Clark, Penn State, DE
	George Cumby, Oklahoma, LB
1981	Rich Campbell, California, QB
1982	Ron Hallstrom, Iowa, G
1983	Tim Lewis, Pittsburgh, DB
1984	Alphonso Carreker, Florida State, DE
1985	Ken Ruettgers, Southern California, T
1986	Kenneth Davis, Texas Christian, RB (2)

1987	Brent Fullwood, Auburn, RB
1988	Sterling Sharpe, South Carolina, WR
1989	Tony Mandarich, Michigan State, T
1990	Tony Bennett, Mississippi, LB
	Darrell Thompson, Minnesota, RB

Houston Oilers

Year	Player, College, Position
1960	Billy Cannon, Louisiana State, RB
1961	Mike Ditka, Pittsburgh, E
1962	Ray Jacobs, Howard Payne, DT
1963	Danny Brabham, Arkansas, LB
1964	Scott Appleton, Texas, DT
1965	Lawrence Elkins, Baylor, WR
1966	Tommy Nobis, Texas, LB
1967	George Webster, Michigan State, LB
	Tom Regner, Notre Dame, G
1968	Mac Haik, Mississippi, WR (2)
1969	Ron Pritchard, Arizona State, LB
1970	Doug Wilkerson, N. Carolina Central, G
1971	Dan Pastorini, Santa Clara, QB
1972	Greg Sampson, Stanford, DE
1973	John Matuszak, Tampa, DE
	George Amundson, Iowa State, RB
1974	Steve Manstedt, Nebraska, LB (4)
1975	Robert Brazile, Jackson State, LB
	Don Hardeman, Texas A&I, RB
1976	Mike Barber, Louisiana Tech, TE (2)
1977	Morris Towns, Missouri, T
1978	Earl Campbell, Texas, RB
1979	Mike Stensrud, Iowa State, DE (2)
1980	Angelo Fields, Michigan State, T (2)
1981	Michael Holston, Morgan State, WR (3)
1982	Mike Munchak, Penn State, G
1983	Bruce Matthews, Southern California, T
1984	Dean Steinkuhler, Nebraska, T
1985	Ray Childress, Texas A&M, DE
	Richard Johnson, Wisconsin, DB
1986	Jim Everett, Purdue, QB
1987	Alonzo Highsmith, Miami, RB
	Haywood Jeffires, North Carolina St., WR
1988	Lorenzo White, Michigan State, RB
1989	David Williams, Florida, T
1990	Lamar Lathon, Houston, LB

Indianapolis Colts

Year	Player, College, Position
1953	Billy Vessels, Oklahoma, B
1954	Cotton Davidson, Baylor, B
1955	George Shaw, Oregon, B
	Alan Ameche, Wisconsin, FB
1956	Lenny Moore, Penn State, B
1957	Jim Parker, Ohio State, G
1958	Lenny Lyles, Louisville, B
1959	Jackie Burkett, Auburn, C
1960	Ron Mix, Southern California, T
1961	Tom Matte, Ohio State, RB
1962	Wendell Harris, Louisiana State, S
1963	Bob Vogel, Ohio State, T
1964	Marv Woodson, Indiana, CB
1965	Mike Curtis, Duke, LB
1966	Sam Ball, Kentucky, T
1967	Bubba Smith, Michigan State, DT
	Jim Detwiler, Michigan, RB
1968	John Williams, Minnesota, G
1969	Eddie Hinton, Oklahoma, WR
1970	Norman Bulaich, Texas Christian, RB
1971	Don McCauley, North Carolina, RB
	Leonard Dunlap, North Texas State, DB
1972	Tom Drougas, Oregon, T
1973	Bert Jones, Louisiana State, QB
	Joe Ehrmann, DT, Syracuse
1974	John Dutton, Nebraska, DE
	Roger Carr, Louisiana Tech, WR
1975	Ken Huff, North Carolina, G
1976	Ken Novak, Purdue, DT
1977	Randy Burke, Kentucky, WR
1978	Reese McCall, Auburn, TE
1979	Barry Krauss, Alabama, LB
1980	Curtis Dickey, Texas A&M, RB
	Derrick Hatchett, Texas, DB
1981	Randy McMillan, Pittsburgh, RB
	Donnell Thompson, North Carolina, DT
1982	Johnie Cooks, Mississippi State, LB
	Art Schlichter, Ohio State, QB
1983	John Elway, Stanford, QB
1984	Leonard Coleman, Vanderbilt, DB
	Ron Solt, Maryland, G

Year	Player, College, Position
1985	Duane Bickett, Southern California, LB
1986	Jon Hand, Alabama, DE
1987	Cornelius Bennett, Alabama, LB
1988	Chris Chandler, Washington, QB (3)
1989	Andre Rison, Michigan State, WR
1990	Jeff George, Illinois, QB

Kansas City Chiefs

Year	Player, College, Position
1960	Don Meredith, Southern Methodist, QB
1961	E.J. Holub, Texas Tech, C
1962	Ronnie Bull, Baylor, RB
1963	Buck Buchanan, Grambling, DT
	Ed Budde, Michigan State, G
1964	Pete Beathard, Southern California, QB
1965	Gale Sayers, Kansas, RB
1966	Aaron Brown, Minnesota, DE
1967	Gene Trosch, Miami, DE-DT
1968	Mo Moorman, Texas A&M, G
	George Daney, Texas-El Paso, G
1969	Jim Marsalis, Tennessee State, CB
1970	Sid Smith, Southern California, T
1971	Elmo Wright, Houston, WR
1972	Jeff Kinney, Nebraska, RB
1973	Gary Butler, Rice, TE (2)
1974	Woody Green, Arizona State, RB
1975	Elmore Stephens, Kentucky, TE (2)
1976	Rod Walters, Iowa, G
1977	Gary Green, Baylor, DB
1978	Art Still, Kentucky, DE
1979	Mike Bell, Colorado State, DE
	Steve Fuller, Clemson, QB
1980	Brad Budde, Southern California, G
1981	Willie Scott, South Carolina, TE
1982	Anthony Hancock, Tennessee, WR
1983	Todd Blackledge, Penn State, QB
1984	Bill Maas, Pittsburgh, DT
	John Alt, Iowa, T
1985	Ethan Horton, North Carolina, RB
1986	Brian Jozwiak, West Virginia, T
1987	Paul Palmer, Temple, RB
1988	Neil Smith, Nebraska, DE
1989	Derrick Thomas, Alabama, LB
1990	Percy Snow, Michigan State, LB

Los Angeles Raiders

Year	Player, College, Position
1960	Dale Hackbart, Wisconsin, CB
1961	Joe Rutgens, Illinois, DT
1962	Roman Gabriel, North Carolina State, QB
1963	George Wilson, Alabama, RB (6)
1964	Tony Lorick, Arizona State, RB
1965	Harry Schuh, Memphis State, T
1966	Rodger Bird, Kentucky, S
1967	Gene Upshaw, Texas A&I, G
1968	Eldridge Dickey, Tennessee State, QB
1969	Art Thoms, Syracuse, DT
1970	Raymond Chester, Morgan State, TE
1971	Jack Tatum, Ohio State, S
1972	Mike Siani, Villanova, WR
1973	Ray Guy, Southern Mississippi, P
1974	Henry Lawrence, Florida A&M, T
1975	Neal Colzie, Ohio State, DB
1976	Charles Philyaw, Texas Southern, DT (2)
1977	Mike Davis, Colorado, DB (2)
1978	Dave Browning, Washington, DE (2)
1979	Willie Jones, Florida State, DE (2)
1980	Marc Wilson, Brigham Young, QB
1981	Ted Watts, Texas Tech, DB
	Curt Marsh, Washington, T
1982	Marcus Allen, Southern California, RB
1983	Don Mosebar, Southern California, T
1984	Sean Jones, Northeastern, DE (2)
1985	Jessie Hester, Florida State, WR
1986	Bob Buczkowski, Pittsburgh, DE
1987	John Clay, Missouri, T
1988	Tim Brown, Notre Dame, WR
	Terry McDaniel, Tennessee, DB
	Scott Davis, Illinois, DE
1989	Jeff Francis, Tennessee, QB (6)
1990	Anthony Smith, Arizona, DE

Los Angeles Rams

Year	Player, College, Position
1937	Johnny Drake, Purdue, B
1938	Corbett Davis, Indiana, B
1939	Parker Hall, Mississippi, B
1940	Ollie Cordill, Rice, B
1941	Rudy Mucha, Washington, C
1942	Jack Wilson, Baylor, B
1943	Mike Holovak, Boston College, B
1944	Tony Butkovich, Illinois, B
1945	Elroy (Crazylegs) Hirsch, Wisconsin, B
1946	Emil Sitko, Notre Dame, B
1947	Herman Wedemeyer, St. Mary's, Calif., B
1948	Tom Keane, West Virginia, B (2)
1949	Bobby Thomason, Virginia Military, B
1950	Ralph Pasquariello, Villanova, B
	Stan West, Oklahoma, G
1951	Bud McFadin, Texas, G
1952	Bill Wade, Vanderbilt, QB
	Bob Carey, Michigan State, E
1953	Donn Moomaw, UCLA, C
	Ed Barker, Washington State, E
1954	Ed Beatty, Cincinnati, C
1955	Larry Morris, Georgia Tech, C
1956	Joe Marconi, West Virginia, B
	Charles Horton, Vanderbilt, B
1957	Jon Arnett, Southern California, B
	Del Shofner, Baylor, E
1958	Lou Michaels, Kentucky, T
	Jim Phillips, Auburn, E
1959	Dick Bass, Pacific, B
	Paul Dickson, Baylor, T
1960	Billy Cannon, Louisiana State, RB
1961	Marlin McKeever, Southern California, E-LB
1962	Roman Gabriel, North Carolina State, QB
	Merlin Olsen, Utah State, DT
1963	Terry Baker, Oregon State, QB
	Rufus Guthrie, Georgia Tech, G
1964	Bill Munson, Utah State, QB
1965	Clancy Williams, Washington State, CB
1966	Tom Mack, Michigan, G
1967	Willie Ellison, Texas Southern, RB (2)
1968	Gary Beban, UCLA, QB (2)
1969	Larry Smith, Florida, RB
	Jim Seymour, Notre Dame, WR
	Bob Klein, Southern California, TE
1970	Jack Reynolds, Tennessee, LB
1971	Isiah Robertson, Southern, LB
	Jack Youngblood, Florida, DE
1972	Jim Bertelsen, Texas, RB (2)
1973	Cullen Bryant, Colorado, DB (2)
1974	John Cappelletti, Penn State, RB
1975	Mike Fanning, Notre Dame, DT
	Dennis Harrah, Miami, T
	Doug France, Ohio State, T
1976	Kevin McLain, Colorado State, LB
1977	Bob Brudzinski, Ohio State, LB
1978	Elvis Peacock, Oklahoma, RB
1979	George Andrews, Nebraska, LB
	Kent Hill, Georgia Tech, T
1980	Johnnie Johnson, Texas, DB
1981	Mel Owens, Michigan, LB
1982	Barry Redden, Richmond, RB
1983	Eric Dickerson, Southern Methodist, RB
1984	Hal Stephens, East Carolina, DE (5)
1985	Jerry Gray, Texas, DB
1986	Mike Schad, Queen's University, Canada, T
1987	Donald Evans, Winston-Salem, DE (2)
1988	Gaston Green, UCLA, RB
	Aaron Cox, Arizona State, WR
1989	Bill Hawkins, Miami, DE
	Cleveland Gary, Miami, RB
1990	Bern Brostek, Washington, C

Miami Dolphins

Year	Player, College, Position
1966	Jim Grabowski, Illinois, RB
	Rick Norton, Kentucky, QB
1967	Bob Griese, Purdue, QB
1968	Larry Csonka, Syracuse, RB
	Doug Crusan, Indiana, T
1969	Bill Stanfill, Georgia, DE
1970	Jim Mandich, Michigan, TE (2)
1971	Otto Stowe, Iowa State, WR (2)
1972	Mike Kadish, Notre Dame, DT
1973	Chuck Bradley, Oregon, C (2)
1974	Donald Reese, Jackson State, DE
1975	Darryl Carlton, Tampa, T
1976	Larry Gordon, Arizona State, LB
	Kim Bokamper, San Jose State, LB
1977	A.J. Duhe, Louisiana State, DT
1978	Guy Benjamin, Stanford, QB (2)
1979	Jon Giesler, Michigan, T
1980	Don McNeal, Alabama, DB
1981	David Overstreet, Oklahoma, RB
1982	Roy Foster, Southern California, G
1983	Dan Marino, Pittsburgh, QB
1984	Jackie Shipp, Oklahoma, LB
1985	Lorenzo Hampton, Florida, RB
1986	John Offerdahl, Western Michigan, LB (2)
1987	John Bosa, Boston College, DE
1988	Eric Kumerow, Ohio State, DE
1989	Sammie Smith, Florida State, RB
	Louis Oliver, Florida, DB
1990	Richmond Webb, Texas A&M, T

Minnesota Vikings

Year	Player, College, Position
1961	Tommy Mason, Tulane, RB
1962	Bill Miller, Miami, WR (3)
1963	Jim Dunaway, Mississippi, T
1964	Carl Eller, Minnesota, DE
1965	Jack Snow, Notre Dame, WR
1966	Jerry Shay, Purdue, DT
1967	Clint Jones, Michigan State, RB
	Gene Washington, Michigan State, WR
	Alan Page, Notre Dame, DT
1968	Ron Yary, Southern California, T
1969	Ed White, California, G (2)
1970	John Ward, Oklahoma State, DT
1971	Leo Hayden, Ohio State, RB
1972	Jeff Siemon, Stanford, LB
1973	Chuck Foreman, Miami, RB
1974	Fred McNeill, UCLA, LB
	Steve Riley, Southern California, T
1975	Mark Mullaney, Colorado State, DE
1976	James White, Oklahoma State, DT
1977	Tommy Kramer, Rice, QB
1978	Randy Holloway, Pittsburgh, DE
1979	Ted Brown, North Carolina State, RB
1980	Doug Martin, Washington, DT
1981	Mardye McDole, Mississippi State, WR (2)
1982	Darrin Nelson, Stanford, RB
1983	Joey Browner, Southern California, DB
1984	Keith Millard, Washington State, DE
1985	Chris Doleman, Pittsburgh, LB
1986	Gerald Robinson, Auburn, DE
1987	D.J. Dozier, Penn State, RB
1988	Randall McDaniel, Arizona State, G
1989	David Braxton, Wake Forest, LB (2)
1990	Mike Jones, Texas A&M, TE (3)

New England Patriots

Year	Player, College, Position
1960	Ron Burton, Northwestern, RB
1961	Tommy Mason, Tulane, RB
1962	Gary Collins, Maryland, WR
1963	Art Graham, Boston College, WR
1964	Jack Concannon, Boston College, QB
1965	Jerry Rush, Michigan State, DE
1966	Karl Singer, Purdue, T
1967	John Charles, Purdue, S
1968	Dennis Byrd, North Carolina State, DE
1969	Ron Sellers, Florida State, WR
1970	Phil Olsen, Utah State, DE
1971	Jim Plunkett, Stanford, QB
1972	Tom Reynolds, San Diego State, WR (2)
1973	John Hannah, Alabama, G
	Sam Cunningham, Southern California, RB
	Darryl Stingley, Purdue, WR
1974	Steve Corbett, Boston College, G (2)
1975	Russ Francis, Oregon, TE
1976	Mike Haynes, Arizona State, DB
	Pete Brock, Colorado, C
	Tim Fox, Ohio State, DB
1977	Raymond Clayborn, Texas, DB
	Stanley Morgan, Tennessee, WR
1978	Bob Cryder, Alabama, G
1979	Rick Sanford, South Carolina, DB
1980	Roland James, Tennessee, DB
	Vagas Ferguson, Notre Dame, RB
1981	Brian Holloway, Stanford, T
1982	Kenneth Sims, Texas, DT
	Lester Williams, Miami, DT
1983	Tony Eason, Illinois, QB
1984	Irving Fryar, Nebraska, WR
1985	Trevor Matich, Brigham Young, C
1986	Reggie Dupard, Southern Methodist, RB
1987	Bruce Armstrong, Louisville, T
1988	John Stephens, Northwestern St., La., RB

1989	Hart Lee Dykes, Oklahoma State, WR
1990	Chris Singleton, Arizona, LB
	Ray Agnew, North Carolina State, DE

New Orleans Saints

Year	Player, College, Position
1967	Les Kelley, Alabama, RB
1968	Kevin Hardy, Notre Dame, DE
1969	John Shinners, Xavier, G
1970	Ken Burrough, Texas Southern, WR
1971	Archie Manning, Mississippi, QB
1972	Royce Smith, Georgia, G
1973	Derland Moore, Oklahoma, DE (2)
1974	Rick Middleton, Ohio State, LB
1975	Larry Burton, Purdue, WR
	Kurt Schumacher, Ohio State, T
1976	Chuck Muncie, California, RB
1977	Joe Campbell, Maryland, DE
1978	Wes Chandler, Florida, WR
1979	Russell Erxleben, Texas, P-K
1980	Stan Brock, Colorado, T
1981	George Rogers, South Carolina, RB
1982	Lindsay Scott, Georgia, WR
1983	Steve Korte, Arkansas, G (2)
1984	James Geathers, Wichita State, DE
1985	Alvin Toles, Tennessee, LB
1986	Jim Dombrowski, Virginia, T
1987	Shawn Knight, Brigham Young, DT
1988	Craig Heyward, Pittsburgh, RB
1989	Wayne Martin, Arkansas, DE
1990	Renaldo Turnbull, West Virginia, DE

New York Giants

Year	Player, College, Position
1936	Art Lewis, Ohio U., T
1937	Ed Widseth, Minnesota, T
1938	George Karamatic, Gonzaga, B
1939	Walt Neilson, Arizona, B
1940	Grenville Lansdell, Southern California, B
1941	George Franck, Minnesota, B
1942	Merle Hapes, Mississippi, B
1943	Steve Filipowicz, Fordham, B
1944	Billy Hillenbrand, Indiana, B
1945	Elmer Barbour, Wake Forest, B
1946	George Connor, Notre Dame, T
1947	Vic Schwall, Northwestern, B
1948	Tony Minisi, Pennsylvania, B
1949	Paul Page, Southern Methodist, B
1950	Travis Tidwell, Auburn, B
1951	Kyle Rote, Southern Methodist, B
	Jim Spavital, Oklahoma A&M, B
1952	Frank Gifford, Southern California, B
1953	Bobby Marlow, Alabama, B
1954	Ken Buck, Pacific, C (2)
1955	Joe Heap, Notre Dame, B
1956	Henry Moore, Arkansas, B (2)
1957	Sam DeLuca, South Carolina, T (2)
1958	Phil King, Vanderbilt, B
1959	Lee Grosscup, Utah, B
1960	Lou Cordileone, Clemson, G
1961	Bruce Tarbox, Syracuse, G (2)
1962	Jerry Hillebrand, Colorado, LB
1963	Frank Lasky, Florida, T (2)
1964	Joe Don Looney, Oklahoma, RB
1965	Tucker Frederickson, Auburn, RB
1966	Francis Peay, Missouri, T
1967	Louis Thompson, Alabama, DT (4)
1968	Dick Buzin, Penn State, T (2)
1969	Fred Dryer, San Diego State, DE
1970	Jim Files, Oklahoma, LB
1971	Rocky Thompson, West Texas State, WR
1972	Eldridge Small, Texas A&I, DB
	Larry Jacobson, Nebraska, DE
1973	Brad Van Pelt, Michigan State, LB (2)
1974	John Hicks, Ohio State, G
1975	Al Simpson, Colorado State, T (2)
1976	Troy Archer, Colorado, DE
1977	Gary Jeter, Southern California, DT
1978	Gordon King, Stanford, T
1979	Phil Simms, Morehead State, QB
1980	Mark Haynes, Colorado, DB
1981	Lawrence Taylor, North Carolina, LB
1982	Butch Woolfolk, Michigan, RB
1983	Terry Kinard, Clemson, DB
1984	Carl Banks, Michigan State, LB
	William Roberts, Ohio State, T
1985	George Adams, Kentucky, RB

1986	Eric Dorsey, Notre Dame, DE
1987	Mark Ingram, Michigan State, WR
1988	Eric Moore, Indiana, T
1989	Brian Williams, Minnesota, C-G
1990	Rodney Hampton, Georgia, RB

New York Jets

Year	Player, College, Position
1960	George Izo, Notre Dame, QB
1961	Tom Brown, Minnesota, G
1962	Sandy Stephens, Minnesota, QB
1963	Jerry Stovall, Louisiana State, S
1964	Matt Snell, Ohio State, RB
1965	Joe Namath, Alabama, QB
	Tom Nowatzke, Indiana, RB
1966	Bill Yearby, Michigan, DT
1967	Paul Seiler, Notre Dame, T
1968	Lee White, Weber State, RB
1969	Dave Foley, Ohio State, T
1970	Steve Tannen, Florida, CB
1971	John Riggins, Kansas, RB
1972	Jerome Barkum, Jackson State, WR
	Mike Taylor, Michigan, LB
1973	Burgess Owens, Miami, DB
1974	Carl Barzilauskas, Indiana, DT
1975	Anthony Davis, Southern California, RB (2)
1976	Richard Todd, Alabama, QB
1977	Marvin Powell, Southern California, T
1978	Chris Ward, Ohio State, T
1979	Marty Lyons, Alabama, DE
1980	Johnny (Lam) Jones, Texas, WR
1981	Freeman McNeil, UCLA, RB
1982	Bob Crable, Notre Dame, LB
1983	Ken O'Brien, Cal-Davis, QB
1984	Russell Carter, Southern Methodist, DB
	Ron Faurot, Arkansas, DE
1985	Al Toon, Wisconsin, WR
1986	Mike Haight, Iowa, T
1987	Roger Vick, Texas A&M, RB
1988	Dave Cadigan, Southern California, T
1989	Jeff Lageman, Virginia, LB
1990	Blair Thomas, Penn State, RB

Philadelphia Eagles

Year	Player, College, Position
1936	Jay Berwanger, Chicago, B
1937	Sam Francis, Nebraska, B
1938	Jim McDonald, Ohio State, B
1939	Davey O'Brien, Texas Christian, B
1940	George McAfee, Duke, B
1941	Art Jones, Richmond, B (2)
1942	Pete Kmetovic, Stanford, B
1943	Joe Muha, Virginia Military, B
1944	Steve Van Buren, Louisiana State, B
1945	John Yonaker, Notre Dame, E
1946	Leo Riggs, Southern California, B
1947	Neill Armstrong, Oklahoma A&M, E
1948	Clyde (Smackover) Scott, Arkansas, B
1949	Chuck Bednarik, Pennsylvania, C
	Frank Tripucka, Notre Dame, B
1950	Harry (Bud) Grant, Minnesota, E
1951	Ebert Van Buren, Louisiana State, B
	Chet Mutryn, Xavier, B
1952	Johnny Bright, Drake, B
1953	Al Conway, Army, B (2)
1954	Neil Worden, Notre Dame, B
1955	Dick Bielski, Maryland, B
1956	Bob Pellegrini, Maryland, C
1957	Clarence Peaks, Michigan State, B
1958	Walt Kowalczyk, Michigan State, B
1959	J.D. Smith, Rice, B
1960	Ron Burton, Northwestern, RB
1961	Art Baker, Syracuse, RB
1962	Pete Case, Georgia, G (2)
1963	Ed Budde, Michigan State, G
1964	Bob Brown, Nebraska, T
1965	Ray Rissmiller, Georgia, T (2)
1966	Randy Beisler, Indiana, DE
1967	Harry Jones, Arkansas, RB
1968	Tim Rossovich, Southern California, DE
1969	Leroy Keyes, Purdue, RB
1970	Steve Zabel, Oklahoma, TE
1971	Richard Harris, Grambling, DE
1972	John Reaves, Florida, QB
1973	Jerry Sisemore, Texas, T
	Charle Young, Southern California, TE
1974	Mitch Sutton, Kansas, DT (3)

1975	Bill Capraun, Miami, T (7)
1976	Mike Smith, Florida, DE (4)
1977	Skip Sharp, Kansas, DB (5)
1978	Reggie Wilkes, Georgia Tech, LB (3)
1979	Jerry Robinson, UCLA, LB
1980	Roynell Young, Alcorn State, DB
1981	Leonard Mitchell, Houston, DE
1982	Mike Quick, North Carolina State, WR
1983	Michael Haddix, Mississippi State, RB
1984	Kenny Jackson, Penn State, WR
1985	Kevin Allen, Indiana, T
1986	Keith Byars, Ohio State, RB
1987	Jerome Brown, Miami, DT
1988	Keith Jackson, Oklahoma, TE
1989	Jessie Small, Eastern Kentucky, LB (2)
1990	Ben Smith, Georgia, DB

Phoenix Cardinals

Year	Player, College, Position
1936	Jim Lawrence, Texas Christian, B
1937	Ray Buivid, Marquette, B
1938	Jack Robbins, Arkansas, B
1939	Charles (Ki) Aldrich, Texas Christian, C
1940	George Cafego, Tennessee, B
1941	John Kimbrough, Texas A&M, B
1942	Steve Lach, Duke, B
1943	Glenn Dobbs, Tulsa, B
1944	Pat Harder, Wisconsin, B
1945	Charley Trippi, Georgia, B
1946	Dub Jones, Louisiana State, B
1947	DeWitt (Tex) Coulter, Army, T
1948	Jim Spavital, Oklahoma A&M, B
1949	Bill Fischer, Notre Dame, G
1950	Jack Jennings, Ohio State, T (2)
1951	Jerry Groom, Notre Dame, C
1952	Ollie Matson, San Francisco, B
1953	Johnny Olszewski, California, B
1954	Lamar McHan, Arkansas, B
1955	Max Boydston, Oklahoma, E
1956	Joe Childress, Auburn, B
1957	Jerry Tubbs, Oklahoma, C
1958	King Hill, Rice, B
	John David Crow, Texas A&M, B
1959	Bill Stacy, Mississippi State, B
1960	George Izo, Notre Dame, QB
1961	Ken Rice, Auburn, B
1962	Fate Echols, Northwestern, DT
	Irv Goode, Kentucky, C
1963	Jerry Stovall, Louisiana State, S
	Don Brumm, Purdue, DE
1964	Ken Kortas, Louisville, DT
1965	Joe Namath, Alabama, QB
1966	Carl McAdams, Oklahoma, LB
1967	Dave Williams, Washington, WR
1968	MacArthur Lane, Utah State, RB
1969	Roger Wehrli, Missouri, DB
1970	Larry Stegent, Texas A&M, RB
1971	Norm Thompson, Utah, CB
1972	Bobby Moore, Oregon, RB-WR
1973	Dave Butz, Purdue, DT
1974	J.V. Cain, Colorado, TE
1975	Tim Gray, Texas A&M, DB
1976	Mike Dawson, Arizona, DT
1977	Steve Pisarkiewicz, Missouri, QB
1978	Steve Little, Arkansas, K
	Ken Greene, Washington State, DB
1979	Ottis Anderson, Miami, RB
1980	Curtis Greer, Michigan, DE
1981	E. J. Junior, Alabama, LB
1982	Luis Sharpe, UCLA, T
1983	Leonard Smith, McNeese State, DB
1984	Clyde Duncan, Tennessee, WR
1985	Freddie Joe Nunn, Mississippi, LB
1986	Anthony Bell, Michigan State, LB
1987	Kelly Stouffer, Colorado State, QB
1988	Ken Harvey, California, LB
1989	Eric Hill, Louisiana State, LB
	Joe Wolf, Boston College, G
1990	Anthony Thompson, Indiana, RB (2)

Pittsburgh Steelers

Year	Player, College, Position
1936	Bill Shakespeare, Notre Dame, B
1937	Mike Basrak, Duquesne, C
1938	Byron (Whizzer) White, Colorado, B
1939	Bill Patterson, Baylor, B (3)
1940	Kay Eakin, Arkansas, B

1941	Chet Gladchuk, Boston College, C (2)
1942	Bill Dudley, Virginia, B
1943	Bill Daley, Minnesota, B
1944	Johnny Podesto, St. Mary's, Calif., B
1945	Paul Duhart, Florida, B
1946	Felix (Doc) Blanchard, Army, B
1947	Hub Bechtol, Texas, E
1948	Dan Edwards, Georgia, E
1949	Bobby Gage, Clemson, B
1950	Lynn Chandnois, Michigan State, B
1951	Butch Avinger, Alabama, B
1952	Ed Modzelewski, Maryland, B
1953	Ted Marchibroda, St. Bonaventure, B
1954	Johnny Lattner, Notre Dame, B
1955	Frank Varrichione, Notre Dame, T
1956	Gary Glick, Colorado A&M, B
	Art Davis, Mississippi State, B
1957	Len Dawson, Purdue, B
1958	Larry Krutko, West Virginia, B (2)
1959	Tom Barnett, Purdue, B (8)
1960	Jack Spikes, Texas Christian, RB
1961	Myron Pottios, Notre Dame, LB (2)
1962	Bob Ferguson, Ohio State, RB
1963	Frank Atkinson, Stanford, T (8)
1964	Paul Martha, Pittsburgh, S
1965	Roy Jefferson, Utah, WR (2)
1966	Dick Leftridge, West Virginia, RB
1967	Don Shy, San Diego State, RB (2)
1968	Mike Taylor, Southern California, T
1969	Joe Greene, North Texas State, DT
1970	Terry Bradshaw, Louisiana Tech, QB
1971	Frank Lewis, Grambling, WR
1972	Franco Harris, Penn State, RB
1973	J.T. Thomas, Florida State, DB
1974	Lynn Swann, Southern California, WR
1975	Dave Brown, Michigan, DB
1976	Bennie Cunningham, Clemson, TE
1977	Robin Cole, New Mexico, LB
1978	Ron Johnson, Eastern Michigan, DB
1979	Greg Hawthorne, Baylor, RB
1980	Mark Malone, Arizona State, QB
1981	Keith Gary, Oklahoma, DE
1982	Walter Abercrombie, Baylor, RB
1983	Gabriel Rivera, Texas Tech, DT
1984	Louis Lipps, Southern Mississippi, WR
1985	Darryl Sims, Wisconsin, DE
1986	John Rienstra, Temple, G
1987	Rod Woodson, Purdue, DB
1988	Aaron Jones, Eastern Kentucky, DE
1989	Tim Worley, Georgia, RB
	Tom Ricketts, Pittsburgh, T
1990	Eric Green, Liberty, TE

San Diego Chargers

Year	Player, College, Position
1960	Monty Stickles, Notre Dame, E
1961	Earl Faison, Indiana, DE
1962	Bob Ferguson, Ohio State, RB
1963	Walt Sweeney, Syracuse, G
1964	Ted Davis, Georgia Tech, LB
1965	Steve DeLong, Tennessee, DE
1966	Don Davis, Cal State-Los Angeles, DT
1967	Ron Billingsley, Wyoming, DE
1968	Russ Washington, Missouri, DT
	Jimmy Hill, Texas A&I, DB
1969	Marty Domres, Columbia, QB
	Bob Babich, Miami, Ohio, LB
1970	Walker Gillette, Richmond, WR
1971	Leon Burns, Long Beach State, RB
1972	Pete Lazetich, Stanford, DE (2)
1973	Johnny Rodgers, Nebraska, WR
1974	Bo Matthews, Colorado, RB
	Don Goode, Kansas, LB
1975	Gary Johnson, Grambling, DT
	Mike Williams, Louisiana State, DB
1976	Joe Washington, Oklahoma, RB
1977	Bob Rush, Memphis State, C
1978	John Jefferson, Arizona State, WR
1979	Kellen Winslow, Missouri, TE
1980	Ed Luther, San Jose State, QB (4)
1981	James Brooks, Auburn, RB
1982	Hollis Hall, Clemson, DB (7)
1983	Billy Ray Smith, Arkansas, LB
	Gary Anderson, Arkansas, WR
	Gill Byrd, San Jose State, DB
1984	Mossy Cade, Texas, DB
1985	Jim Lachey, Ohio State, G
1986	Leslie O'Neal, Oklahoma State, DE
	James FitzPatrick, Southern California, T

1987	Rod Bernstine, Texas A&M, TE
1988	Anthony Miller, Tennessee, WR
1989	Burt Grossman, Pittsburgh, DE
1990	Junior Seau, Southern California, LB

San Francisco 49ers

Year	Player, College, Position
1950	Leo Nomellini, Minnesota, T
1951	Y.A. Tittle, Louisiana State, B
1952	Hugh McElhenny, Washington, B
1953	Harry Babcock, Georgia, E
	Tom Stolhandske, Texas, E
1954	Bernie Faloney, Maryland, B
1955	Dickie Moegle, Rice, B
1956	Earl Morrall, Michigan State, B
1957	John Brodie, Stanford, B
1958	Jim Pace, Michigan, B
	Charlie Krueger, Texas A&M, T
1959	Dave Baker, Oklahoma, B
	Dan James, Ohio State, C
1960	Monty Stickles, Notre Dame, E
1961	Jimmy Johnson, UCLA, CB
	Bernie Casey, Bowling Green, WR
	Bill Kilmer, UCLA, QB
1962	Lance Alworth, Arkansas, WR
1963	Kermit Alexander, UCLA, CB
1964	Dave Parks, Texas Tech, WR
1965	Ken Willard, North Carolina, RB
	George Donnelly, Illinois, DB
1966	Stan Hindman, Mississippi, DE
1967	Steve Spurrier, Florida, QB
	Cas Banaszek, Northwestern, T
1968	Forrest Blue, Auburn, C
1969	Ted Kwalick, Penn State, TE
	Gene Washington, Stanford, WR
1970	Cedrick Hardman, North Texas State, DE
	Bruce Taylor, Boston U., DB
1971	Tim Anderson, Ohio State, DB
1972	Terry Beasley, Auburn, WR
1973	Mike Holmes, Texas Southern, DB
1974	Wilbur Jackson, Alabama, RB
	Bill Sandifer, UCLA, DT
1975	Jimmy Webb, Mississippi State, DT
1976	Randy Cross, UCLA, C (2)
1977	Elmo Boyd, Eastern Kentucky, WR (3)
1978	Ken MacAfee, Notre Dame, TE
	Dan Bunz, Cal State-Long Beach, LB
1979	James Owens, UCLA, WR (2)
1980	Earl Cooper, Rice, RB
	Jim Stuckey, Clemson, DT
1981	Ronnie Lott, Southern California, DB
1982	Bubba Paris, Michigan, T (2)
1983	Roger Craig, Nebraska, RB (2)
1984	Todd Shell, Brigham Young, LB
1985	Jerry Rice, Mississippi Valley State, WR
1986	Larry Roberts, Alabama, DE (2)
1987	Harris Barton, North Carolina, T
	Terrence Flagler, Clemson, RB
1988	Danny Stubbs, Miami, DE (2)
1989	Keith DeLong, Tennessee, LB
1990	Dexter Carter, Florida State, RB

Seattle Seahawks

Year	Player, College, Position
1976	Steve Niehaus, Notre Dame, DT
1977	Steve August, Tulsa, G
1978	Keith Simpson, Memphis State, DB
1979	Manu Tuiasosopo, UCLA, DT
1980	Jacob Green, Texas A&M, DE
1981	Ken Easley, UCLA, DB
1982	Jeff Bryant, Clemson, DE
1983	Curt Warner, Penn State, RB
1984	Terry Taylor, Southern Illinois, DB
1985	Owen Gill, Iowa, RB (2)
1986	John L. Williams, Florida, RB
1987	Tony Woods, Pittsburgh, LB
1988	Brian Blades, Miami, WR (2)
1989	Andy Heck, Notre Dame, T
1990	Cortez Kennedy, Miami, DT

Tampa Bay Buccaneers

Year	Player, College, Position
1976	Lee Roy Selmon, Oklahoma, DT
1977	Ricky Bell, Southern California, RB
1978	Doug Williams, Grambling, QB
1979	Greg Roberts, Oklahoma, G (2)

1980	Ray Snell, Wisconsin, G
1981	Hugh Green, Pittsburgh, LB
1982	Sean Farrell, Penn State, G
1983	Randy Grimes, Baylor, C (2)
1984	Keith Browner, Southern California, LB (2)
1985	Ron Holmes, Washington, DE
1986	Bo Jackson, Auburn, RB
	Roderick Jones, Southern Methodist, DB
1987	Vinny Testaverde, Miami, QB
1988	Paul Gruber, Wisconsin, T
1989	Broderick Thomas, Nebraska, LB
1990	Keith McCants, Alabama, LB

Washington Redskins

Year	Player, College, Position
1936	Riley Smith, Alabama, B
1937	Sammy Baugh, Texas Christian, B
1938	Andy Farkas, Detroit, B
1939	I.B. Hale, Texas Christian, T
1940	Ed Boell, New York U., B
1941	Forest Evashevski, Michigan, B
1942	Orban (Spec) Sanders, Texas, B
1943	Jack Jenkins, Missouri, B
1944	Mike Micka, Colgate, B
1945	Jim Hardy, Southern California, B
1946	Cal Rossi, UCLA, B*
1947	Cal Rossi, UCLA, B
1948	Harry Gilmer, Alabama, B
	Lowell Tew, Alabama, B
1949	Rob Goode, Texas A&M, B
1950	George Thomas, Oklahoma, B
1951	Leon Heath, Oklahoma, B
1952	Larry Isbell, Baylor, B
1953	Jack Scarbath, Maryland, B
1954	Steve Meilinger, Kentucky, E
1955	Ralph Guglielmi, Notre Dame, B
1956	Ed Vereb, Maryland, B
1957	Don Bosseler, Miami, B
1958	Mike Sommer, George Washington, B (2)
1959	Don Allard, Boston College, B
1960	Richie Lucas, Penn State, QB
1961	Norman Snead, Wake Forest, QB
	Joe Rutgens, Illinois, DT
1962	Ernie Davis, Syracuse, RB
1963	Pat Richter, Wisconsin, TE
1964	Charley Taylor, Arizona State, RB-WR
1965	Bob Breitenstein, Tulsa, T (2)
1966	Charlie Gogolak, Princeton, K
1967	Ray McDonald, Idaho, RB
1968	Jim Smith, Oregon, DB
1969	Eugene Epps, Texas-El Paso, DB (2)
1970	Bill Brundige, Colorado, DT (2)
1971	Cotton Speyrer, Texas, WR (2)
1972	Moses Denson, Maryland State, RB (8)
1973	Charles Cantrell, Lamar, G (5)
1974	Jon Keyworth, Colorado, TE (6)
1975	Mike Thomas, Nevada-Las Vegas, RB (6)
1976	Mike Hughes, Baylor, G (5)
1977	Duncan McColl, Stanford, DE (4)
1978	Tony Green, Florida, RB (6)
1979	Don Warren, San Diego State, TE (4)
1980	Art Monk, Syracuse, WR
1981	Mark May, Pittsburgh, T
1982	Vernon Dean, San Diego State, DB (2)
1983	Darrell Green, Texas A&I, DB
1984	Bob Slater, Oklahoma, DT (2)
1985	Tory Nixon, San Diego State, DB (2)
1986	Markus Koch, Boise State, DE (2)
1987	Brian Davis, Nebraska, DB (2)
1988	Chip Lohmiller, Minnesota, K (2)
1989	Tracy Rocker, Auburn, DT (3)
1990	Andre Collins, Penn State, LB (2)

Choice lost due to ineligibility.

RECORDS

Compiled by Elias Sports Bureau

The following records reflect all available official information on the National Football League from its formation in 1920 to date. Also included are all applicable records from the American Football League, 1960-69.

Individual Records

Service

Most Seasons

26 George Blanda, Chi. Bears, 1949, 1950-58; Baltimore, 1950; Houston, 1960-66; Oakland, 1967-75
21 Earl Morrall, San Francisco, 1956; Pittsburgh, 1957-58; Detroit, 1958-64; N.Y. Giants, 1965-67; Baltimore, 1968-71; Miami, 1972-76
20 Jim Marshall, Cleveland, 1960; Minnesota, 1961-79

Most Seasons, One Club

19 Jim Marshall, Minnesota, 1961-79
18 Jim Hart, St. Louis, 1966-83
 Jeff Van Note, Atlanta, 1969-86
17 Lou Groza, Cleveland, 1950-59, 1961-67
 Johnny Unitas, Baltimore, 1956-72
 John Brodie, San Francisco, 1957-73
 Jim Bakken, St. Louis, 1962-78
 Mick Tingelhoff, Minnesota, 1962-78

Most Games Played, Career

340 George Blanda, Chi. Bears, 1949, 1950-58; Baltimore, 1950; Houston, 1960-66; Oakland, 1967-75
282 Jim Marshall, Cleveland, 1960; Minnesota, 1961-79
263 Jan Stenerud, Kansas City, 1967-79; Green Bay, 1980-83; Minnesota, 1984-85

Most Consecutive Games Played, Career

282 Jim Marshall, Cleveland, 1960; Minnesota, 1961-79
240 Mick Tingelhoff, Minnesota, 1962-78
234 Jim Bakken, St. Louis, 1962-78

Most Seasons, Coach

40 George Halas, Chi. Bears, 1920-29, 1933-42, 1946-55, 1958-67
33 Earl (Curly) Lambeau, Green Bay, 1921-49; Chi. Cardinals, 1950-51; Washington, 1952-53
29 Tom Landry, Dallas, 1960-88

Scoring

Most Seasons Leading League

5 Don Hutson, Green Bay, 1940-44
 Gino Cappelletti, Boston, 1961, 1963-66
3 Earl (Dutch) Clark, Portsmouth, 1932; Detroit, 1935-36
 Pat Harder, Chi. Cardinals, 1947-49
 Paul Hornung, Green Bay, 1959-61
2 Jack Manders, Chi. Bears, 1934, 1937
 Gordy Soltau, San Francisco, 1952-53
 Doak Walker, Detroit, 1950, 1955
 Gene Mingo, Denver, 1960, 1962
 Jim Turner, N.Y. Jets, 1968-69
 Fred Cox, Minnesota, 1969-70
 Chester Marcol, Green Bay, 1972, 1974
 John Smith, New England, 1979-80

Most Consecutive Seasons Leading League

5 Don Hutson, Green Bay, 1940-44
4 Gino Cappelletti, Boston, 1963-66
3 Pat Harder, Chi. Cardinals, 1947-49
 Paul Hornung, Green Bay, 1959-61

Points

Most Points, Career

2,002 George Blanda, Chi. Bears, 1949, 1950-58; Baltimore, 1950; Houston, 1960-66; Oakland, 1967-75 (9-td, 943-pat, 335-fg)
1,699 Jan Stenerud, Kansas City, 1967-79; Green Bay, 1980-83; Minnesota, 1984-85 (580-pat, 373-fg)
1,439 Jim Turner, N.Y. Jets, 1964-70; Denver, 1971-79 (1-td, 521-pat, 304-fg)

Most Points, Season

176 Paul Hornung, Green Bay, 1960 (15-td, 41-pat, 15-fg)
161 Mark Moseley, Washington, 1983 (62-pat, 33-fg)
155 Gino Cappelletti, Boston, 1964 (7-td, 38-pat, 25-fg)

Most Points, No Touchdowns, Season

161 Mark Moseley, Washington, 1983 (62-pat, 33-fg)
145 Jim Turner, N.Y. Jets, 1968 (43-pat, 34-fg)
144 Kevin Butler, Chicago, 1985 (51-pat, 31-fg)

Most Seasons, 100 or More Points

7 Jan Stenerud, Kansas City, 1967-71; Green Bay, 1981, 1983
 Nick Lowery, Kansas City, 1981, 1983-86, 1988-89
6 Gino Cappelletti, Boston, 1961-66
 George Blanda, Houston, 1960-61; Oakland, 1967-69, 1973
 Bruce Gossett, Los Angeles, 1966-67, 1969; San Francisco, 1970-71, 1973
5 Lou Michaels, Pittsburgh, 1962; Baltimore, 1964-65, 1967-68
 Tony Franklin, Philadelphia, 1979, 1981; New England, 1984-86
 Rich Karlis, Denver, 1984-86, 1988; Minnesota, 1989
 Morten Andersen, New Orleans, 1985-89

Most Points, Rookie, Season

144 Kevin Butler, Chicago, 1985 (51-pat, 31-fg)
132 Gale Sayers, Chicago, 1965 (22-td)
128 Doak Walker, Detroit, 1950 (11-td, 38-pat, 8-fg)
 Cookie Gilchrist, Buffalo, 1962 (15-td, 14-pat, 8-fg)
 Chester Marcol, Green Bay, 1972 (29-pat, 33-fg)

Most Points, Game

40 Ernie Nevers, Chi. Cardinals vs. Chi. Bears, Nov. 28, 1929 (6-td, 4-pat)
36 Dub Jones, Cleveland vs. Chi. Bears, Nov. 25, 1951 (6-td)
 Gale Sayers, Chicago vs. San Francisco, Dec. 12, 1965 (6-td)
33 Paul Hornung, Green Bay vs. Baltimore, Oct. 8, 1961 (4-td, 6-pat, 1-fg)

Most Consecutive Games Scoring

151 Fred Cox, Minnesota, 1963-73
149 Jim Breech, Oakland, 1979; Cincinnati, 1980-89 (current)
133 Garo Yepremian, Miami, 1970-78; New Orleans, 1979

Touchdowns

Most Seasons Leading League

8 Don Hutson, Green Bay, 1935-38, 1941-44
3 Jim Brown, Cleveland, 1958-59, 1963
 Lance Alworth, San Diego, 1964-66
2 By many players

Most Consecutive Seasons Leading League

4 Don Hutson, Green Bay, 1935-38, 1941-44
3 Lance Alworth, San Diego, 1964-66
2 By many players

Most Touchdowns, Career

126 Jim Brown, Cleveland, 1957-65 (106-r, 20-p)
125 Walter Payton, Chicago, 1975-87 (110-r, 15-p)
116 John Riggins, N.Y. Jets, 1971-75; Washington, 1976-79, 1981-85 (104-r, 12-p)

Most Touchdowns, Season

24 John Riggins, Washington, 1983 (24-r)
23 O.J. Simpson, Buffalo, 1975 (16-r, 7-p)
 Jerry Rice, San Francisco, 1987 (1-r, 22-p)
22 Gale Sayers, Chicago, 1965 (14-r, 6-p, 2-ret)
 Chuck Foreman, Minnesota, 1975 (13-r, 9-p)

Most Touchdowns, Rookie, Season

22 Gale Sayers, Chicago, 1965 (14-r, 6-p, 2-ret)
20 Eric Dickerson, L.A. Rams, 1983 (18-r, 2-p)
16 Billy Sims, Detroit, 1980 (13-r, 3-p)

Most Touchdowns, Game

6 Ernie Nevers, Chi. Cardinals vs. Chi. Bears, Nov. 28, 1929 (6-r)
 Dub Jones, Cleveland vs. Chi. Bears, Nov. 25, 1951 (4-r, 2-p)
 Gale Sayers, Chicago vs. San Francisco, Dec. 12, 1965 (4-r, 1-p, 1-ret)
5 Bob Shaw, Chi. Cardinals vs. Baltimore, Oct. 2, 1950 (5-p)
 Jim Brown, Cleveland vs. Baltimore, Nov. 1, 1959 (5-r)
 Abner Haynes, Dall. Texans vs. Oakland, Nov. 26, 1961 (4-r, 1-p)
 Billy Cannon, Houston vs. N.Y. Titans, Dec. 10, 1961 (3-r, 2-p)
 Cookie Gilchrist, Buffalo vs. N.Y. Jets, Dec. 8, 1963 (5-r)
 Paul Hornung, Green Bay vs. Baltimore, Dec. 12, 1965 (3-r, 2-p)
 Kellen Winslow, San Diego vs. Oakland, Nov. 22, 1981 (5-p)
4 By many players

Most Consecutive Games Scoring Touchdowns

18 Lenny Moore, Baltimore, 1963-65
14 O.J. Simpson, Buffalo, 1975
13 John Riggins, Washington, 1982-83
 Jerry Rice, San Francisco, 1986-87

Points After Touchdown

Most Seasons Leading League

8 George Blanda, Chi. Bears, 1956; Houston, 1961-62; Oakland, 1967-69, 1972, 1974
4 Bob Waterfield, Cleveland, 1945; Los Angeles, 1946, 1950, 1952
3 Earl (Dutch) Clark, Portsmouth, 1932; Detroit, 1935-36
 Jack Manders, Chi. Bears, 1933-35
 Don Hutson, Green Bay, 1941-42, 1945

Most Points After Touchdown Attempted, Career

959 George Blanda, Chi. Bears, 1949, 1950-58; Baltimore, 1950; Houston, 1960-66; Oakland, 1967-75
657 Lou Groza, Cleveland, 1950-59, 1961-67
601 Jan Stenerud, Kansas City, 1967-79; Green Bay, 1980-83; Minnesota, 1984-85

Most Points After Touchdown Attempted, Season

70 Uwe von Schamann, Miami, 1984
65 George Blanda, Houston, 1961
63 Mark Moseley, Washington, 1983

Most Points After Touchdown Attempted, Game

10 Charlie Gogolak, Washington vs. N.Y. Giants, Nov. 27, 1966
9 Pat Harder, Chi. Cardinals vs. N.Y. Giants, Oct. 17, 1948; vs. N.Y. Bulldogs, Nov. 13, 1949
 Bob Waterfield, Los Angeles vs. Baltimore, Oct. 22, 1950
 Bob Thomas, Chicago vs. Green Bay, Dec. 7, 1980
8 By many players

Most Points After Touchdown, Career

943 George Blanda, Chi. Bears, 1949, 1950-58; Baltimore, 1950; Houston, 1960-66; Oakland, 1967-75
641 Lou Groza, Cleveland, 1950-59, 1961-67
580 Jan Stenerud, Kansas City, 1967-79; Green Bay, 1980-83; Minnesota, 1984-85

Most Points After Touchdown, Season

66 Uwe von Schamann, Miami, 1984
64 George Blanda, Houston, 1961
62 Mark Moseley, Washington, 1983

Most Points After Touchdown, Game

9 Pat Harder, Chi. Cardinals vs. N.Y. Giants, Oct. 17, 1948
 Bob Waterfield, Los Angeles vs. Baltimore, Oct. 22, 1950
 Charlie Gogolak, Washington vs. N.Y. Giants, Nov. 27, 1966
8 By many players

Most Consecutive Points After Touchdown

234 Tommy Davis, San Francisco, 1959-65
221 Jim Turner, N.Y. Jets, 1967-70; Denver, 1971-74
202 Gary Anderson, Pittsburgh, 1983-88

Highest Points After Touchdown Percentage, Career (200 points after touchdown)

99.43 Tommy Davis, San Francisco, 1959-69 (350-348)
99.24 Gary Anderson, Pittsburgh, 1982-89 (262-260)
99.12 Nick Lowery, New England, 1978; Kansas City, 1980-89 (341-338)

Most Points After Touchdown, No Misses, Season

56 Danny Villanueva, Dallas, 1966
 Ray Wersching, San Francisco, 1984
54 Mike Clark, Dallas, 1968
 George Blanda, Oakland, 1968
53 Pat Harder, Chi. Cardinals, 1948

Most Points After Touchdown, No Misses, Game

9 Pat Harder, Chi. Cardinals vs. N.Y. Giants, Oct. 17, 1948
 Bob Waterfield, Los Angeles vs. Baltimore, Oct. 22, 1950
8 By many players

Field Goals

Most Seasons Leading League

    5   Lou Groza, Cleveland, 1950, 1952-54, 1957
    4   Jack Manders, Chi. Bears, 1933-34, 1936-37
         Ward Cuff, N.Y. Giants, 1938-39, 1943; Green Bay, 1947
         Mark Moseley, Washington, 1976-77, 1979, 1982
    3   Bob Waterfield, Los Angeles, 1947, 1949, 1951
         Gino Cappelletti, Boston, 1961, 1963-64
         Fred Cox, Minnesota, 1965, 1969-70
         Jan Stenerud, Kansas City, 1967, 1970, 1975

Most Consecutive Seasons Leading League

    3   Lou Groza, Cleveland, 1952-54
    2   By many players

Most Field Goals Attempted, Career

    638   George Blanda, Chi. Bears, 1949, 1950-58; Baltimore, 1950; Houston, 1960-66; Oakland, 1967-75
    558   Jan Stenerud, Kansas City, 1967-79; Green Bay, 1980-83; Minnesota, 1984-85
    488   Jim Turner, N.Y. Jets, 1964-70; Denver, 1971-79

Most Field Goals Attempted, Season

    49   Bruce Gossett, Los Angeles, 1966
         Curt Knight, Washington, 1971
    48   Chester Marcol, Green Bay, 1972
    47   Jim Turner, N.Y. Jets, 1969
         David Ray, Los Angeles, 1973
         Mark Moseley, Washington, 1983

Most Field Goals Attempted, Game

    9   Jim Bakken, St. Louis vs. Pittsburgh, Sept. 24, 1967
    8   Lou Michaels, Pittsburgh vs. St. Louis, Dec. 2, 1962
         Garo Yepremian, Detroit vs. Minnesota, Nov. 13, 1966
         Jim Turner, N.Y. Jets vs. Buffalo, Nov. 3, 1968
    7   By many players

Most Field Goals, Career

    373   Jan Stenerud, Kansas City, 1967-79; Green Bay, 1980-83; Minnesota, 1984-85
    335   George Blanda, Chi. Bears, 1949, 1950-58; Baltimore, 1950; Houston, 1960-66; Oakland, 1967-75
    304   Jim Turner, N.Y. Jets, 1964-70; Denver, 1971-79

Most Field Goals, Season

    35   Ali Haji-Sheikh, N.Y. Giants, 1983
    34   Jim Turner, N.Y. Jets, 1968
    33   Chester Marcol, Green Bay, 1972
         Mark Moseley, Washington, 1983
         Gary Anderson, Pittsburgh, 1985

Most Field Goals, Rookie, Season

    35   Ali Haji-Sheikh, N.Y. Giants, 1983
    33   Chester Marcol, Green Bay, 1972
    31   Kevin Butler, Chicago, 1985

Most Field Goals, Game

    7   Jim Bakken, St. Louis vs. Pittsburgh, Sept. 24, 1967
         Rich Karlis, Minnesota vs. L.A. Rams, Nov. 5, 1989 (OT)
    6   Gino Cappelletti, Boston vs. Denver, Oct. 4, 1964
         Garo Yepremian, Detroit vs. Minnesota, Nov. 13, 1966
         Jim Turner, N.Y. Jets vs. Buffalo, Nov. 3, 1968
         Tom Dempsey, Philadelphia vs. Houston, Nov. 12, 1972
         Bobby Howfield, N.Y. Jets vs. New Orleans, Dec. 3, 1972
         Jim Bakken, St. Louis vs. Atlanta, Dec. 9, 1973
         Joe Danelo, N.Y. Giants vs. Seattle, Oct. 18, 1981
         Ray Wersching, San Francisco vs. New Orleans, Oct. 16, 1983
         Gary Anderson, Pittsburgh vs. Denver, Oct. 23, 1988
    5   By many players

Most Field Goals, One Quarter

    4   Garo Yepremian, Detroit vs. Minnesota, Nov. 13, 1966 (second quarter)
         Curt Knight, Washington vs. N.Y. Giants, Nov. 15, 1970 (second quarter)
         Roger Ruzek, Dallas vs. N.Y. Giants, Nov. 2, 1987 (fourth quarter)
    3   By many players

Most Consecutive Games Scoring Field Goals

    31   Fred Cox, Minnesota, 1968-70
    28   Jim Turner, N.Y. Jets, 1970; Denver, 1971-72
    23   Morten Andersen, New Orleans, 1986-88

Most Consecutive Field Goals

    24   Kevin Butler, Chicago, 1988-89
    23   Mark Moseley, Washington, 1981-82
    22   Pat Leahy, N.Y. Jets, 1985-86

Longest Field Goal

    63   Tom Dempsey, New Orleans vs. Detroit, Nov. 8, 1970
    60   Steve Cox, Cleveland vs. Cincinnati, Oct. 21, 1984
    59   Tony Franklin, Philadelphia vs. Dallas, Nov. 12, 1979
         Pete Stoyanovich, Miami vs. N.Y. Jets, Nov. 12, 1989

Highest Field Goal Percentage, Career (100 field goals)

    77.32   Nick Lowery, New England, 1978; Kansas City, 1980-89 (291-225)
    77.03   Morten Andersen, New Orleans, 1982-89 (222-171)
    76.86   Gary Anderson, Pittsburgh, 1982-89 (242-186)

Highest Field Goal Percentage, Season (Qualifiers)

    95.24   Mark Moseley, Washington, 1982 (21-20)
            Ed Murray, Detroit, 1988 (21-20)
            Ed Murray, Detroit, 1989 (21-20)
    91.67   Jan Stenerud, Green Bay, 1981 (24-22)
    88.89   Nick Lowery, Kansas City, 1985 (27-24)
            Dean Biasucci, Indianapolis, 1987 (27-24)

Most Field Goals, No Misses, Game

    7   Rich Karlis, Minnesota vs. L.A. Rams, Nov. 5, 1989 (OT)
    6   Gino Cappelletti, Boston vs. Denver, Oct. 4, 1964
         Joe Danelo, N.Y. Giants vs. Seattle, Oct. 18, 1981
         Ray Wersching, San Francisco vs. New Orleans, Oct. 16, 1983
         Gary Anderson, Pittsburgh vs. Denver, Oct. 23, 1988
    5   By many players

Most Field Goals, 50 or More Yards, Career

    18   Nick Lowery, New England, 1978; Kansas City, 1980-89
    17   Jan Stenerud, Kansas City, 1967-79; Green Bay, 1980-83; Minnesota, 1984-85
    14   Ed Murray, Detroit, 1980-89

Most Field Goals, 50 or More Yards, Season

    6   Dean Biasucci, Indianapolis, 1988
    5   Fred Steinfort, Denver, 1980

         Norm Johnson, Seattle, 1986
    4   Horst Muhlmann, Cincinnati, 1970
         Mark Moseley, Washington, 1977
         Nick Lowery, Kansas City, 1980
         Raul Allegre, Baltimore, 1983

Most Field Goals, 50 or More Yards, Game

    2   Jim Martin, Detroit vs. Baltimore, Oct. 23, 1960
         Tom Dempsey, New Orleans vs. Los Angeles, Dec. 6, 1970
         Chris Bahr, Cincinnati vs. Houston, Sept. 23, 1979
         Nick Lowery, Kansas City vs. Seattle, Sept. 14, 1980
         Mark Moseley, Washington vs. New Orleans, Oct. 26, 1980
         Fred Steinfort, Denver vs. Seattle, Dec. 21, 1980
         Mick Luckhurst, Atlanta vs. Denver, Dec. 5, 1982
         Morten Andersen, New Orleans vs. Philadelphia, Dec. 11, 1983
         Mick Luckhurst, Atlanta vs. L.A. Rams, Oct. 7, 1984
         Paul McFadden, Philadelphia vs. Detroit, Nov. 4, 1984
         Nick Lowery, Kansas City vs. New Orleans, Sept. 8, 1985
         Pat Leahy, N.Y. Jets vs. New England, Oct. 20, 1985
         Tony Zendejas, Houston vs. San Diego, Nov. 24, 1985
         Norm Johnson, Seattle vs. L.A. Raiders, Dec. 8, 1986
         Raul Allegre, N.Y. Giants vs. Philadelphia, Nov. 15, 1987
         Nick Lowery, Kansas City vs. Detroit, Nov. 26, 1987
         Dean Biasucci, Indianapolis vs. Miami, Sept. 25, 1988
         Paul McFadden, Atlanta vs. Buffalo, Nov. 5, 1989

Safeties

Most Safeties, Career

    4   Ted Hendricks, Baltimore, 1969-73; Green Bay, 1974; Oakland, 1975-81; L.A. Raiders, 1982-83
         Doug English, Detroit, 1975-79, 1981-85
    3   Bill McPeak, Pittsburgh, 1949-57
         Charlie Krueger, San Francisco, 1959-73
         Ernie Stautner, Pittsburgh, 1950-63
         Jim Katcavage, N.Y. Giants, 1956-68
         Roger Brown, Detroit, 1960-66; Los Angeles, 1967-69
         Bruce Maher, Detroit, 1960-67; N.Y. Giants, 1968-69
         Ron McDole, St. Louis, 1961; Houston, 1962; Buffalo, 1963-70; Washington, 1971-78
         Alan Page, Minnesota, 1967-78; Chicago, 1979-81
         Lyle Alzado, Denver, 1971-78; Cleveland, 1979-81; L.A. Raiders, 1982-85
         Rulon Jones, Denver, 1980-88
         Steve McMichael, New England, 1980; Chicago, 1981-89
    2   By many players

Most Safeties, Season

    2   Tom Nash, Green Bay, 1932
         Roger Brown, Detroit, 1962
         Ron McDole, Buffalo, 1964
         Alan Page, Minnesota, 1971
         Fred Dryer, Los Angeles, 1973
         Benny Barnes, Dallas, 1973
         James Young, Houston, 1977
         Tom Hannon, Minnesota, 1981
         Doug English, Detroit, 1983
         Don Blackmon, New England, 1985
         Timothy Harris, Green Bay, 1988

Most Safeties, Game

    2   Fred Dryer, Los Angeles vs. Green Bay, Oct. 21, 1973

Rushing

Most Seasons Leading League

    8   Jim Brown, Cleveland, 1957-61, 1963-65
    4   Steve Van Buren, Philadelphia, 1945, 1947-49
         O.J. Simpson, Buffalo, 1972-73, 1975-76
         Eric Dickerson, L.A. Rams, 1983-84, 1986; Indianapolis, 1988
    3   Earl Campbell, Houston, 1978-80

Most Consecutive Seasons Leading League

    5   Jim Brown, Cleveland, 1957-61
    3   Steve Van Buren, Philadelphia, 1947-49
         Jim Brown, Cleveland, 1963-65
         Earl Campbell, Houston, 1978-80
    2   Bill Paschal, N.Y. Giants, 1943-44
         Joe Perry, San Francisco, 1953-54
         Jim Nance, Boston, 1966-67
         Leroy Kelly, Cleveland, 1967-68
         O.J. Simpson, Buffalo, 1972-73; 1975-76
         Eric Dickerson, L.A. Rams, 1983-84

Attempts

Most Seasons Leading League

    6   Jim Brown, Cleveland, 1958-59, 1961, 1963-65
    4   Steve Van Buren, Philadelphia, 1947-50
         Walter Payton, Chicago, 1976-79
    3   Cookie Gilchrist, Buffalo, 1963-64; Denver, 1965
         Jim Nance, Boston, 1966-67, 1969
         O.J. Simpson, Buffalo, 1973-75
         Eric Dickerson, L.A. Rams, 1983, 1986; Indianapolis, 1988

Most Consecutive Seasons Leading League

    4   Steve Van Buren, Philadelphia, 1947-50
         Walter Payton, Chicago, 1976-79
    3   Jim Brown, Cleveland, 1963-65
         Cookie Gilchrist, Buffalo, 1963-64; Denver, 1965
         O.J. Simpson, Buffalo, 1973-75
    2   By many players

Most Attempts, Career

    3,838   Walter Payton, Chicago, 1975-87
    2,949   Franco Harris, Pittsburgh, 1972-83; Seattle, 1984
    2,936   Tony Dorsett, Dallas, 1977-87; Denver, 1988

Most Attempts, Season

    407   James Wilder, Tampa Bay, 1984
    404   Eric Dickerson, L.A. Rams, 1986
    397   Gerald Riggs, Atlanta, 1985

Most Attempts, Rookie, Season
- 390   Eric Dickerson, L.A. Rams, 1983
- 378   George Rogers, New Orleans, 1981
- 335   Curt Warner, Seattle, 1983

Most Attempts, Game
- 45   Jamie Morris, Washington vs. Cincinnati, Dec. 17, 1988 (OT)
- 43   Butch Woolfolk, N.Y. Giants vs. Philadelphia, Nov. 20, 1983
-      James Wilder, Tampa Bay vs. Green Bay, Sept. 30, 1984 (OT)
- 42   James Wilder, Tampa Bay vs. Pittsburgh, Oct. 30, 1983

Yards Gained
Most Yards Gained, Career
- 16,726   Walter Payton, Chicago, 1975-87
- 12,739   Tony Dorsett, Dallas, 1977-87; Denver, 1988
- 12,312   Jim Brown, Cleveland, 1957-65

Most Seasons, 1,000 or More Yards Rushing
- 10   Walter Payton, Chicago, 1976-81, 1983-86
- 8   Franco Harris, Pittsburgh, 1972, 1974-79, 1983
-    Tony Dorsett, Dallas, 1977-81, 1983-85
- 7   Jim Brown, Cleveland, 1958-61, 1963-65
-    Eric Dickerson, L.A. Rams, 1983-86; L.A. Rams-Indianapolis, 1987; Indianapolis, 1988-89

Most Consecutive Seasons, 1,000 or More Yards Rushing
- 7   Eric Dickerson, L.A. Rams, 1983-86; L.A. Rams-Indianapolis, 1987; Indianapolis, 1988-89
- 6   Franco Harris, Pittsburgh, 1974-79
-    Walter Payton, Chicago, 1976-81
- 5   Jim Taylor, Green Bay, 1960-64
-    O.J. Simpson, Buffalo, 1972-76
-    Tony Dorsett, Dallas, 1977-81

Most Yards Gained, Season
- 2,105   Eric Dickerson, L.A. Rams, 1984
- 2,003   O.J. Simpson, Buffalo, 1973
- 1,934   Earl Campbell, Houston, 1980

Most Yards Gained, Rookie, Season
- 1,808   Eric Dickerson, L.A. Rams, 1983
- 1,674   George Rogers, New Orleans, 1981
- 1,605   Ottis Anderson, St. Louis, 1979

Most Yards Gained, Game
- 275   Walter Payton, Chicago vs. Minnesota, Nov. 20, 1977
- 273   O.J. Simpson, Buffalo vs. Detroit, Nov. 25, 1976
- 250   O.J. Simpson, Buffalo vs. New England, Sept. 16, 1973

Most Games, 200 or More Yards Rushing, Career
- 6   O.J. Simpson, Buffalo, 1969-77; San Francisco, 1978-79
- 4   Jim Brown, Cleveland, 1957-65
-    Earl Campbell, Houston, 1978-84; New Orleans, 1984-85
- 3   Eric Dickerson, L.A. Rams, 1983-87; Indianapolis, 1987-89

Most Games, 200 or More Yards Rushing, Season
- 4   Earl Campbell, Houston, 1980
- 3   O.J. Simpson, Buffalo, 1973
- 2   Jim Brown, Cleveland, 1963
-    O.J. Simpson, Buffalo, 1976
-    Walter Payton, Chicago, 1977
-    Eric Dickerson, L.A. Rams, 1984
-    Greg Bell, L.A. Rams, 1989

Most Consecutive Games, 200 or More Yards Rushing
- 2   O.J. Simpson, Buffalo, 1973, 1976
-    Earl Campbell, Houston, 1980

Most Games, 100 or More Yards Rushing, Career
- 77   Walter Payton, Chicago, 1975-87
- 58   Jim Brown, Cleveland, 1957-65
-    Eric Dickerson, L.A. Rams, 1983-87; Indianapolis, 1987-89
- 47   Franco Harris, Pittsburgh, 1972-83; Seattle, 1984

Most Games, 100 or More Yards Rushing, Season
- 12   Eric Dickerson, L.A. Rams, 1984
- 11   O.J. Simpson, Buffalo, 1973
-    Earl Campbell, Houston, 1979
-    Marcus Allen, L.A. Raiders, 1985
-    Eric Dickerson, L.A. Rams, 1986
- 10   Walter Payton, Chicago, 1977, 1985
-    Earl Campbell, Houston, 1980

Most Consecutive Games, 100 or More Yards Rushing
- 11   Marcus Allen, L.A. Raiders, 1985-86
- 9   Walter Payton, Chicago, 1985
- 7   O.J. Simpson, Buffalo, 1972-73
-    Earl Campbell, Houston, 1979

Longest Run From Scrimmage
- 99   Tony Dorsett, Dallas vs. Minnesota, Jan. 3, 1983 (TD)
- 97   Andy Uram, Green Bay vs. Chi. Cardinals, Oct. 8, 1939 (TD)
-    Bob Gage, Pittsburgh vs. Chi. Bears, Dec. 4, 1949 (TD)
- 96   Jim Spavital, Baltimore vs. Green Bay, Nov. 5, 1950 (TD)
-    Bob Hoernschemeyer, Detroit vs. N.Y. Yanks, Nov. 23, 1950 (TD)

Average Gain
Highest Average Gain, Career (700 attempts)
- 5.22   Jim Brown, Cleveland, 1957-65 (2,359-12,312)
- 5.14   Eugene (Mercury) Morris, Miami, 1969-75; San Diego, 1976 (804-4,133)
- 5.00   Gale Sayers, Chicago, 1965-71 (991-4,956)

Highest Average Gain, Season (Qualifiers)
- 9.94   Beattie Feathers, Chi. Bears, 1934 (101-1,004)
- 6.87   Bobby Douglass, Chicago, 1972 (141-968)
- 6.78   Dan Towler, Los Angeles, 1951 (126-854)

Highest Average Gain, Game (10 attempts)
- 17.09   Marion Motley, Cleveland vs. Pittsburgh, Oct. 29, 1950 (11-188)
- 16.70   Bill Grimes, Green Bay vs. N.Y. Yanks, Oct. 8, 1950 (10-167)
- 16.57   Bobby Mitchell, Cleveland vs. Washington, Nov. 15, 1959 (14-232)

Touchdowns
Most Seasons Leading League
- 5   Jim Brown, Cleveland, 1957-59, 1963, 1965
- 4   Steve Van Buren, Philadelphia, 1945, 1947-49
- 3   Abner Haynes, Dall. Texans, 1960-62
-    Cookie Gilchrist, Buffalo, 1962-64

-    Paul Lowe, L.A. Chargers, 1960; San Diego, 1961, 1965
-    Leroy Kelly, Cleveland, 1966-68

Most Consecutive Seasons Leading League
- 3   Steve Van Buren, Philadelphia, 1947-49
-    Jim Brown, Cleveland, 1957-59
-    Abner Haynes, Dall. Texans, 1960-62
-    Cookie Gilchrist, Buffalo, 1962-64
-    Leroy Kelly, Cleveland, 1966-68

Most Touchdowns, Career
- 110   Walter Payton, Chicago, 1975-87
- 106   Jim Brown, Cleveland, 1957-65
- 104   John Riggins, N.Y. Jets, 1971-75; Washington, 1976-79, 1981-85

Most Touchdowns, Season
- 24   John Riggins, Washington, 1983
- 21   Joe Morris, N.Y. Giants, 1985
- 19   Jim Taylor, Green Bay, 1962
-    Earl Campbell, Houston, 1979
-    Chuck Muncie, San Diego, 1981

Most Touchdowns, Rookie, Season
- 18   Eric Dickerson, L.A. Rams, 1983
- 15   Ickey Woods, Cincinnati, 1988
- 14   Gale Sayers, Chicago, 1965
-    Barry Sanders, Detroit, 1989

Most Touchdowns, Game
- 6   Ernie Nevers, Chi. Cardinals vs. Chi. Bears, Nov. 28, 1929
- 5   Jim Brown, Cleveland vs. Baltimore, Nov. 1, 1959
-    Cookie Gilchrist, Buffalo vs. N.Y. Jets, Dec. 8, 1963
- 4   By many players

Most Consecutive Games Rushing for Touchdowns
- 13   John Riggins, Washington, 1982-83
-    George Rogers, Washington, 1985-86
- 11   Lenny Moore, Baltimore, 1963-64
- 10   Greg Bell, L.A. Rams, 1988-89

Passing
Most Seasons Leading League
- 6   Sammy Baugh, Washington, 1937, 1940, 1943, 1945, 1947, 1949
- 4   Len Dawson, Dall. Texans, 1962; Kansas City, 1964, 1966, 1968
-    Roger Staubach, Dallas, 1971, 1973, 1978-79
-    Ken Anderson, Cincinnati, 1974-75, 1981-82
- 3   Arnie Herber, Green Bay, 1932, 1934, 1936
-    Norm Van Brocklin, Los Angeles, 1950, 1952, 1954
-    Bart Starr, Green Bay, 1962, 1964, 1966

Most Consecutive Seasons Leading League
- 2   Cecil Isbell, Green Bay, 1941-42
-    Milt Plum, Cleveland, 1960-61
-    Ken Anderson, Cincinnati, 1974-75, 1981-82
-    Roger Staubach, Dallas, 1978-79

Pass Rating
Highest Pass Rating, Career (1,500 attempts)
- 94.0   Joe Montana, San Francisco, 1979-89
- 89.3   Dan Marino, Miami, 1983-89
- 87.3   Boomer Esiason, Cincinnati, 1984-89

Highest Pass Rating, Season (Qualifiers)
- 112.4   Joe Montana, San Francisco, 1989
- 110.4   Milt Plum, Cleveland, 1960
- 109.9   Sammy Baugh, Washington, 1945

Highest Pass Rating, Rookie, Season (Qualifiers)
- 96.0   Dan Marino, Miami, 1983
- 88.2   Greg Cook, Cincinnati, 1969
- 84.0   Charlie Conerly, N.Y. Giants, 1948

Attempts
Most Seasons Leading League
- 4   Sammy Baugh, Washington, 1937, 1943, 1947-48
-    Johnny Unitas, Baltimore, 1957, 1959-61
-    George Blanda, Chi. Bears, 1953; Houston, 1963-65
- 3   Arnie Herber, Green Bay, 1932, 1934, 1936
-    Sonny Jurgensen, Washington, 1966-67, 1969
-    Dan Marino, Miami, 1984, 1986, 1988
- 2   By many players

Most Consecutive Seasons Leading League
- 3   Johnny Unitas, Baltimore, 1959-61
-    George Blanda, Houston, 1963-65
- 2   By many players

Most Passes Attempted, Career
- 6,467   Fran Tarkenton, Minnesota, 1961-66, 1972-78; N.Y. Giants, 1967-71
- 5,604   Dan Fouts, San Diego, 1973-87
- 5,186   Johnny Unitas, Baltimore, 1956-72; San Diego, 1973

Most Passes Attempted, Season
- 623   Dan Marino, Miami, 1986
- 609   Dan Fouts, San Diego, 1981
- 606   Dan Marino, Miami, 1988

Most Passes Attempted, Rookie, Season
- 439   Jim Zorn, Seattle, 1976
- 417   Jack Trudeau, Indianapolis, 1986
- 375   Norm Snead, Washington, 1961

Most Passes Attempted, Game
- 68   George Blanda, Houston vs. Buffalo, Nov. 1, 1964
- 66   Chris Miller, Atlanta vs. Detroit, Dec. 24, 1989
- 62   Joe Namath, N.Y. Jets vs. Baltimore, Oct. 18, 1970
-    Steve Dils, Minnesota vs. Tampa Bay, Sept. 5, 1981
-    Phil Simms, N.Y. Giants vs. Cincinnati, Oct. 13, 1985
-    Randall Cunningham, Philadelphia vs. Chicago, Oct. 2, 1989

Completions
Most Seasons Leading League
- 5   Sammy Baugh, Washington, 1937, 1943, 1945, 1947-48
- 4   George Blanda, Chi. Bears, 1953; Houston, 1963-65
-    Sonny Jurgensen, Philadelphia, 1961; Washington, 1966-67, 1969
-    Dan Marino, Miami, 1984-86, 1988
- 3   Arnie Herber, Green Bay, 1932, 1934, 1936

Johnny Unitas, Baltimore, 1959-60, 1963
John Brodie, San Francisco, 1965, 1968, 1970
Fran Tarkenton, Minnesota, 1975-76, 1978

Most Consecutive Seasons Leading League
3   George Blanda, Houston, 1963-65
    Dan Marino, Miami, 1984-86
2   By many players

Most Passes Completed, Career
3,686   Fran Tarkenton, Minnesota, 1961-66, 1972-78; N.Y. Giants, 1967-71
3,297   Dan Fouts, San Diego, 1973-87
2,830   Johnny Unitas, Baltimore, 1956-72; San Diego, 1973

Most Passes Completed, Season
378   Dan Marino, Miami, 1986
362   Dan Marino, Miami, 1984
360   Dan Fouts, San Diego, 1981

Most Passes Completed, Rookie, Season
208   Jim Zorn, Seattle, 1976
204   Jack Trudeau, Indianapolis, 1986
183   Jeff Komlo, Detroit, 1979

Most Passes Completed, Game
42   Richard Todd, N.Y. Jets vs. San Francisco, Sept. 21, 1980
40   Ken Anderson, Cincinnati vs. San Diego, Dec. 20, 1982
     Phil Simms, N.Y. Giants vs. Cincinnati, Oct. 13, 1985
39   Dan Marino, Miami vs. Buffalo, Nov. 16, 1986

Most Consecutive Passes Completed
22   Joe Montana, San Francisco vs. Cleveland (5), Nov. 29, 1987; vs. Green Bay (17), Dec. 6, 1987
20   Ken Anderson, Cincinnati vs. Houston, Jan. 2, 1983
18   Steve DeBerg, Denver vs. L.A. Rams (17), Dec. 12, 1982; vs. Kansas City (1), Dec. 19, 1982
     Lynn Dickey, Green Bay vs. Houston, Sept. 4, 1983
     Joe Montana, San Francisco vs. L.A. Rams (13), Oct. 28, 1984; vs. Cincinnati (5), Nov. 4, 1984
     Dan Majkowski, Green Bay vs. New Orleans, Sept. 18, 1989

Completion Percentage
Most Seasons Leading League
8   Len Dawson, Dall. Texans, 1962; Kansas City, 1964-69, 1975
7   Sammy Baugh, Washington, 1940, 1942-43, 1945, 1947-49
5   Joe Montana, San Francisco, 1980-81, 1985, 1987, 1989

Most Consecutive Seasons Leading League
6   Len Dawson, Kansas City, 1964-69
3   Sammy Baugh, Washington, 1947-49
    Otto Graham, Cleveland, 1953-55
    Milt Plum, Cleveland, 1959-61
2   By many players

Highest Completion Percentage, Career (1,500 attempts)
63.88   Joe Montana, San Francisco, 1979-89 (4,059-2,593)
59.85   Ken Stabler, Oakland, 1970-79; Houston, 1980-81; New Orleans, 1982-84 (3,793-2,270)
59.69   Danny White, Dallas, 1976-88 (2,950-1,761)

Highest Completion Percentage, Season (Qualifiers)
70.55   Ken Anderson, Cincinnati, 1982 (309-218)
70.33   Sammy Baugh, Washington, 1945 (182-128)
70.21   Joe Montana, San Francisco, 1989 (386-271)

Highest Completion Percentage, Rookie, Season (Qualifiers)
58.45   Dan Marino, Miami, 1983 (296-173)
57.14   Jim McMahon, Chicago, 1982 (269-181)
56.07   Fran Tarkenton, Minnesota, 1961 (280-157)

Highest Completion Percentage, Game (20 attempts)
90.91   Ken Anderson, Cincinnati vs. Pittsburgh, Nov. 10, 1974 (22-20)
90.48   Lynn Dickey, Green Bay vs. New Orleans, Dec. 13, 1981 (21-19)
87.50   Danny White, Dallas vs. Philadelphia, Nov. 6, 1983 (24-21)

Yards Gained
Most Seasons Leading League
5   Sonny Jurgensen, Philadelphia, 1961-62; Washington, 1966-67, 1969
4   Sammy Baugh, Washington, 1937, 1940, 1947-48
    Johnny Unitas, Baltimore, 1957, 1959-60, 1963
    Dan Fouts, San Diego, 1979-82
    Dan Marino, Miami, 1984-86, 1988
3   Arnie Herber, Green Bay, 1932, 1934, 1936
    Sid Luckman, Chi. Bears, 1943, 1945-46
    John Brodie, San Francisco, 1965, 1968, 1970
    John Hadl, San Diego, 1965, 1968, 1971
    Joe Namath, N.Y. Jets, 1966-67, 1972

Most Consecutive Seasons Leading League
4   Dan Fouts, San Diego, 1979-82
3   Dan Marino, Miami, 1984-86
2   By many players

Most Yards Gained, Career
47,003   Fran Tarkenton, Minnesota, 1961-66, 1972-78; N.Y. Giants, 1967-71
43,040   Dan Fouts, San Diego, 1973-87
40,239   Johnny Unitas, Baltimore, 1956-72; San Diego, 1973

Most Seasons, 3,000 or More Yards Passing
6   Dan Fouts, San Diego, 1979-81, 1984-86
    Dan Marino, Miami, 1984-89
    Joe Montana, San Francisco, 1981, 1983-85, 1987, 1989
5   Sonny Jurgensen, Philadelphia, 1961-62; Washington, 1966-67, 1969
    Tommy Kramer, Minnesota, 1979-81, 1985-86
    John Elway, Denver, 1985-89
    Boomer Esiason, Cincinnati, 1985-89
    Phil Simms, N.Y. Giants, 1984-86, 1988-89
4   Brian Sipe, Cleveland, 1979-81, 1983
    Ron Jaworski, Philadelphia, 1980-81, 1983, 1985
    Danny White, Dallas, 1980-81, 1983, 1985
    Neil Lomax, St. Louis, 1984-85, 1987; Phoenix, 1988

Most Yards Gained, Season
5,084   Dan Marino, Miami, 1984
4,802   Dan Fouts, San Diego, 1981
4,746   Dan Marino, Miami, 1986

Most Yards Gained, Rookie, Season
2,571   Jim Zorn, Seattle, 1976

2,507   Dennis Shaw, Buffalo, 1970
2,337   Norm Snead, Washington, 1961
Most Yards Gained, Game
554   Norm Van Brocklin, Los Angeles vs. N.Y. Yanks, Sept. 28, 1951
521   Dan Marino, Miami vs. N.Y. Jets, Oct. 23, 1988
513   Phil Simms, N.Y. Giants vs. Cincinnati, Oct. 13, 1985

Most Games, 400 or More Yards Passing, Career
10   Dan Marino, Miami, 1983-89
6   Dan Fouts, San Diego, 1973-87
5   Sonny Jurgensen, Philadelphia, 1957-63; Washington, 1964-74
    Joe Montana, San Francisco, 1979-89

Most Games, 400 or More Yards Passing, Season
4   Dan Marino, Miami, 1984
3   Dan Marino, Miami, 1986
2   George Blanda, Houston, 1961
    Sonny Jurgensen, Philadelphia, 1961
    Joe Namath, N.Y. Jets, 1972
    Dan Fouts, San Diego, 1982
    Dan Fouts, San Diego, 1985
    Phil Simms, N.Y. Giants, 1985
    Ken O'Brien, N.Y. Jets, 1986
    Bernie Kosar, Cleveland, 1986
    Dan Marino, Miami, 1988
    Randall Cunningham, Philadelphia, 1989
    Joe Montana, San Francisco, 1989

Most Consecutive Games, 400 or More Yards Passing
2   Dan Fouts, San Diego, 1982
    Dan Marino, Miami, 1984
    Phil Simms, N.Y. Giants, 1985

Most Games, 300 or More Yards Passing, Career
51   Dan Fouts, San Diego, 1973-87
37   Dan Marino, Miami, 1983-89
30   Joe Montana, San Francisco, 1979-89

Most Games, 300 or More Yards Passing, Season
9   Dan Marino, Miami, 1984
8   Dan Fouts, San Diego, 1980
7   Dan Fouts, San Diego, 1981, 1985
    Bill Kenney, Kansas City, 1983
    Neil Lomax, St. Louis, 1984

Most Consecutive Games, 300 or More Yards Passing, Season
5   Joe Montana, San Francisco, 1982
4   Dan Fouts, San Diego, 1979
    Bill Kenney, Kansas City, 1983
3   By many players

Longest Pass Completion (All TDs except as noted)
99   Frank Filchock (to Farkas), Washington vs. Pittsburgh, Oct. 15, 1939
     George Izo (to Mitchell), Washington vs. Cleveland, Sept. 15, 1963
     Karl Sweetan (to Studstill), Detroit vs. Baltimore, Oct. 16, 1966
     Sonny Jurgensen (to Allen), Washington vs. Chicago, Sept. 15, 1968
     Jim Plunkett (to Branch), L.A. Raiders vs. Washington, Oct. 2, 1983
     Ron Jaworski (to Quick), Philadelphia vs. Atlanta, Nov. 10, 1985
98   Doug Russell (to Tinsley), Chi. Cardinals vs. Cleveland, Nov. 27, 1938
     Ogden Compton (to Lane), Chi. Cardinals vs. Green Bay, Nov. 13, 1955
     Bill Wade (to Farrington), Chicago Bears vs. Detroit, Oct. 8, 1961
     Jacky Lee (to Dewveall), Houston vs. San Diego, Nov. 25, 1962
     Earl Morrall (to Jones), N.Y. Giants vs. Pittsburgh, Sept. 11, 1966
     Jim Hart (to Moore), St. Louis vs. Los Angeles, Dec. 10, 1972 (no TD)
97   Pat Coffee (to Tinsley), Chi. Cardinals vs. Chi. Bears, Dec. 5, 1937
     Bobby Layne (to Box), Detroit vs. Green Bay, Nov. 26, 1953
     George Shaw (to Tarr), Denver vs. Boston, Sept. 21, 1962
     Bernie Kosar (to Slaughter), Cleveland vs. Chicago, Oct. 23, 1989

Average Gain
Most Seasons Leading League
7   Sid Luckman, Chi. Bears, 1939-43, 1946-47
3   Arnie Herber, Green Bay, 1932, 1934, 1936
    Norm Van Brocklin, Los Angeles, 1950, 1952, 1954
    Len Dawson, Dall. Texans, 1962; Kansas City, 1966, 1968
    Bart Starr, Green Bay, 1966-68

Most Consecutive Seasons Leading League
5   Sid Luckman, Chi. Bears, 1939-43
3   Bart Starr, Green Bay, 1966-68
2   Bernie Masterson, Chi. Bears, 1937-38
    Sid Luckman, Chi. Bears, 1946-47
    Johnny Unitas, Baltimore, 1964-65
    Terry Bradshaw, Pittsburgh, 1977-78
    Steve Grogan, New England, 1980-81

Highest Average Gain, Career (1,500 attempts)
8.63   Otto Graham, Cleveland, 1950-55 (1,565-13,499)
8.42   Sid Luckman, Chi. Bears, 1939-50 (1,744-14,686)
8.16   Norm Van Brocklin, Los Angeles, 1949-57; Philadelphia, 1958-60 (2,895-23,611)

Highest Average Gain, Season (Qualifiers)
11.17   Tommy O'Connell, Cleveland, 1957 (110-1,229)
10.86   Sid Luckman, Chi. Bears, 1943 (202-2,194)
10.55   Otto Graham, Cleveland, 1953 (258-2,722)

Highest Average Gain, Rookie, Season (Qualifiers)
9.411   Greg Cook, Cincinnati, 1969 (197-1,854)
9.409   Bob Waterfield, Cleveland, 1945 (171-1,609)
8.36   Zeke Bratkowski, Chi. Bears, 1954 (130-1,087)

Highest Average Gain, Game (20 attempts)
18.58   Sammy Baugh, Washington vs. Boston, Oct. 31, 1948 (24-446)
18.50   Johnny Unitas, Baltimore vs. Atlanta, Nov. 12, 1967 (20-370)
17.71   Joe Namath, N.Y. Jets vs. Baltimore, Sept. 24, 1972 (28-496)

Touchdowns
Most Seasons Leading League
4   Johnny Unitas, Baltimore, 1957-60
    Len Dawson, Dall. Texans, 1962; Kansas City, 1963, 1965-66
3   Arnie Herber, Green Bay, 1932, 1934, 1936
    Sid Luckman, Chi. Bears, 1943, 1945-46
    Y.A. Tittle, San Francisco, 1955; N.Y. Giants, 1962-63
    Dan Marino, Miami, 1984-86

2 By many players

Most Consecutive Seasons Leading League
4 Johnny Unitas, Baltimore, 1957-60
3 Dan Marino, Miami, 1984-86
2 By many players

Most Touchdown Passes, Career
342 Fran Tarkenton, Minnesota, 1961-66, 1972-78; N.Y. Giants, 1967-71
290 Johnny Unitas, Baltimore, 1956-72; San Diego, 1973
255 Sonny Jurgensen, Philadelphia, 1957-63; Washington, 1964-74

Most Touchdown Passes, Season
48 Dan Marino, Miami, 1984
44 Dan Marino, Miami, 1986
36 George Blanda, Houston, 1961
Y.A. Tittle, N.Y. Giants, 1963

Most Touchdown Passes, Rookie, Season
22 Charlie Conerly, N.Y. Giants, 1948
20 Dan Marino, Miami, 1983
19 Jim Plunkett, New England, 1971

Most Touchdown Passes, Game
7 Sid Luckman, Chi. Bears vs. N.Y. Giants, Nov. 14, 1943
Adrian Burk, Philadelphia vs. Washington, Oct. 17, 1954
George Blanda, Houston vs. N.Y. Titans, Nov. 19, 1961
Y.A. Tittle, N.Y. Giants vs. Washington, Oct. 28, 1962
Joe Kapp, Minnesota vs. Baltimore, Sept. 28, 1969
6 By many players. Last time: Tommy Kramer, Minnesota vs. Green Bay, Sept. 28, 1986

Most Games, Four or More Touchdown Passes, Career
17 Johnny Unitas, Baltimore, 1956-72; San Diego, 1973
16 Dan Marino, Miami, 1983-89
13 George Blanda, Chi. Bears, 1949, 1950-58; Baltimore, 1950; Houston, 1960-66; Oakland, 1967-75

Most Games, Four or More Touchdown Passes, Season
6 Dan Marino, Miami, 1984
5 Dan Marino, Miami, 1986
4 George Blanda, Houston, 1961
Vince Ferragamo, Los Angeles, 1980

Most Consecutive Games, Four or More Touchdown Passes
4 Dan Marino, Miami, 1984
2 By many players

Most Consecutive Games, Touchdown Passes
47 Johnny Unitas, Baltimore, 1956-60
30 Dan Marino, Miami, 1985-87
28 Dave Krieg, Seattle, 1983-85

Had Intercepted

Most Consecutive Passes Attempted, None Intercepted
294 Bart Starr, Green Bay, 1964-65
211 Ken O'Brien, N.Y. Jets, 1987-88
208 Milt Plum, Cleveland, 1959-60

Most Passes Had Intercepted, Career
277 George Blanda, Chi. Bears, 1949, 1950-58; Baltimore, 1950; Houston, 1960-66; Oakland, 1967-75
268 John Hadl, San Diego, 1962-72; Los Angeles, 1973-74; Green Bay, 1974-75; Houston, 1976-77
266 Fran Tarkenton, Minnesota, 1961-66, 1972-78; N.Y. Giants, 1967-71

Most Passes Had Intercepted, Season
42 George Blanda, Houston, 1962
35 Vinny Testaverde, Tampa Bay, 1988
34 Frank Tripucka, Denver, 1960

Most Passes Had Intercepted, Game
8 Jim Hardy, Chi. Cardinals vs. Philadelphia, Sept. 24, 1950
7 Parker Hall, Cleveland vs. Green Bay, Nov. 8, 1942
Frank Sinkwich, Detroit vs. Green Bay, Oct. 24, 1943
Bob Waterfield, Los Angeles vs. Green Bay, Oct. 17, 1948
Zeke Bratkowski, Chicago vs. Baltimore, Oct. 2, 1960
Tommy Wade, Pittsburgh vs. Philadelphia, Dec. 12, 1965
Ken Stabler, Oakland vs. Denver, Oct. 16, 1977
Steve DeBerg, Tampa Bay vs. San Francisco, Sept. 7, 1986
6 By many players

Most Attempts, No Interceptions, Game
60 Davey O'Brien, Philadelphia vs. Washington, Dec. 1, 1940
57 Joe Montana, San Francisco vs. Atlanta, Oct. 6, 1985
54 Dan Marino, Miami vs. Buffalo, Nov. 16, 1986

Lowest Percentage, Passes Had Intercepted

Most Seasons Leading League, Lowest Percentage, Passes Had Intercepted
5 Sammy Baugh, Washington, 1940, 1942, 1944-45, 1947
3 Charlie Conerly, N.Y. Giants, 1950, 1956, 1959
Bart Starr, Green Bay, 1962, 1964, 1966
Roger Staubach, Dallas, 1971, 1977, 1979
Ken Anderson, Cincinnati, 1972, 1981-82
Ken O'Brien, N.Y. Jets, 1985, 1987-88
2 By many players

Lowest Percentage, Passes Had Intercepted, Career (1,500 attempts)
2.42 Bernie Kosar, Cleveland, 1985-89 (1,940-47)
2.64 Joe Montana, San Francisco, 1979-89 (4,059-107)
2.76 Ken O'Brien, N.Y. Jets, 1984-89 (2,467-68)

Lowest Percentage, Passes Had Intercepted, Season (Qualifiers)
0.66 Joe Ferguson, Buffalo, 1976 (151-1)
1.16 Steve Bartkowski, Atlanta, 1983 (432-5)
1.20 Bart Starr, Green Bay, 1966 (251-3)

Lowest Percentage, Passes Had Intercepted, Rookie, Season (Qualifiers)
2.03 Dan Marino, Miami, 1983 (296-6)
2.10 Gary Wood, N.Y. Giants, 1964 (143-3)
2.82 Bernie Kosar, Cleveland, 1985 (248-7)

Times Sacked

Times Sacked has been compiled since 1963.

Most Times Sacked, Career
483 Fran Tarkenton, Minnesota, 1961-66, 1972-78; N.Y. Giants, 1967-71
405 Craig Morton, Dallas, 1965-74; N.Y. Giants, 1974-76; Denver, 1977-82
398 Ken Anderson, Cincinnati, 1971-86

Most Times Sacked, Season
72 Randall Cunningham, Philadelphia, 1986
62 Ken O'Brien, N.Y. Jets, 1985
61 Neil Lomax, St. Louis, 1985

Most Times Sacked, Game
12 Bert Jones, Baltimore vs. St. Louis, Oct. 26, 1980
Warren Moon, Houston vs. Dallas, Sept. 29, 1985
11 Charley Johnson, St. Louis vs. N.Y. Giants, Nov. 1, 1964
Bart Starr, Green Bay vs. Detroit, Nov. 7, 1965
Jack Kemp, Buffalo vs. Oakland, Oct. 15, 1967
Bob Berry, Atlanta vs. St. Louis, Nov. 24, 1968
Greg Landry, Detroit vs. Dallas, Oct. 6, 1975
Ron Jaworski, Philadelphia vs. St. Louis, Dec. 18, 1983
Paul McDonald, Cleveland vs. Kansas City, Sept. 30, 1984
Archie Manning, Minnesota vs. Chicago, Oct. 28, 1984
Steve Pelluer, Dallas vs. San Diego, Nov. 16, 1986
Randall Cunningham, Philadelphia vs. L.A. Raiders, Nov. 30, 1986 (OT)
David Norrie, N.Y. Jets vs. Dallas, Oct. 4, 1987
10 By many players

Pass Receiving

Most Seasons Leading League
8 Don Hutson, Green Bay, 1936-37, 1939, 1941-45
5 Lionel Taylor, Denver, 1960-63, 1965
3 Tom Fears, Los Angeles, 1948-50
Pete Pihos, Philadelphia, 1953-55
Billy Wilson, San Francisco, 1954, 1956-57
Raymond Berry, Baltimore, 1958-60
Lance Alworth, San Diego, 1966, 1968-69

Most Consecutive Seasons Leading League
5 Don Hutson, Green Bay, 1941-45
4 Lionel Taylor, Denver, 1960-63
3 Tom Fears, Los Angeles, 1948-50
Pete Pihos, Philadelphia, 1953-55
Raymond Berry, Baltimore, 1958-60

Most Pass Receptions, Career
819 Steve Largent, Seattle, 1976-89
750 Charlie Joiner, Houston, 1969-72; Cincinnati, 1972-75; San Diego, 1976-86
662 Art Monk, Washington, 1980-89

Most Seasons, 50 or More Pass Receptions
10 Steve Largent, Seattle, 1976, 1978-81, 1983-87
7 Raymond Berry, Baltimore, 1958-62, 1965-66
Art Powell, N.Y. Titans, 1960-62; Oakland, 1963-66
Lance Alworth, San Diego, 1963-69
Charley Taylor, Washington, 1964, 1966-67, 1969, 1973-75
Charlie Joiner, San Diego, 1976, 1979-81, 1983-85
Wes Chandler, New Orleans, 1979-80; New Orleans-San Diego, 1981; San Diego, 1983-86
Dwight Clark, San Francisco, 1980-86
James Lofton, Green Bay, 1979-81, 1983-86
Kellen Winslow, San Diego, 1980-84, 1986-87
Art Monk, Washington, 1980-81, 1984-86, 1988-89
6 Lionel Taylor, Denver, 1960-65
Bobby Mitchell, Washington, 1962-67
Ahmad Rashad, Minnesota, 1976-81
Ozzie Newsome, Cleveland, 1979-81, 1983-85

Most Pass Receptions, Season
106 Art Monk, Washington, 1984
101 Charley Hennigan, Houston, 1964
100 Lionel Taylor, Denver, 1961

Most Pass Receptions, Rookie, Season
83 Earl Cooper, San Francisco, 1980
81 Keith Jackson, Philadelphia, 1988
72 Bill Groman, Houston, 1960

Most Pass Receptions, Game
18 Tom Fears, Los Angeles vs. Green Bay, Dec. 3, 1950
17 Clark Gaines, N.Y. Jets vs. San Francisco, Sept. 21, 1980
16 Sonny Randle, St. Louis vs. N.Y. Giants, Nov. 4, 1962

Most Consecutive Games, Pass Receptions
177 Steve Largent, Seattle, 1977-89
150 Ozzie Newsome, Cleveland, 1979-89
127 Harold Carmichael, Philadelphia, 1972-80

Yards Gained

Most Seasons Leading League
7 Don Hutson, Green Bay, 1936, 1938-39, 1941-44
3 Raymond Berry, Baltimore, 1957, 1959-60
Lance Alworth, San Diego, 1965-66, 1968
2 By many players

Most Consecutive Seasons Leading League
4 Don Hutson, Green Bay, 1941-44
2 By many players

Most Yards Gained, Career
13,089 Steve Largent, Seattle, 1976-89
12,146 Charlie Joiner, Houston, 1969-72; Cincinnati, 1972-75; San Diego, 1976-86
11,834 Don Maynard, N.Y. Giants, 1958; N.Y. Jets, 1960-72; St. Louis, 1973

Most Seasons, 1,000 or More Yards, Pass Receiving
8 Steve Largent, Seattle, 1978-81, 1983-86
7 Lance Alworth, San Diego, 1963-69
5 Art Powell, N.Y. Titans, 1960, 1962; Oakland, 1963-64, 1966
Don Maynard, N.Y. Jets, 1960, 1962, 1965, 1967-68
James Lofton, Green Bay, 1980-81, 1983-85

Most Yards Gained, Season
1,746 Charley Hennigan, Houston, 1961
1,602 Lance Alworth, San Diego, 1965
1,570 Jerry Rice, San Francisco, 1986

Most Yards Gained, Rookie, Season
1,473 Bill Groman, Houston, 1960
1,231 Bill Howton, Green Bay, 1952
1,131 Bill Brooks, Indianapolis, 1986

Most Yards Gained, Game
336 Willie Anderson, L.A. Rams vs. New Orleans, Nov. 26, 1989 (OT)

309 Stephone Paige, Kansas City vs. San Diego, Dec. 22, 1985
303 Jim Benton, Cleveland vs. Detroit, Nov. 22, 1945

Most Games, 200 or More Yards Pass Receiving, Career
5 Lance Alworth, San Diego, 1962-70; Dallas, 1971-72
4 Don Hutson, Green Bay, 1935-45
  Charley Hennigan, Houston, 1960-66
3 Don Maynard, N.Y. Giants, 1958; N.Y. Jets, 1960-72; St. Louis, 1973
  Wes Chandler, New Orleans, 1978-81; San Diego, 1981-87; San Francisco, 1988

Most Games, 200 or More Yards Pass Receiving, Season
3 Charley Hennigan, Houston, 1961
2 Don Hutson, Green Bay, 1942
  Gene Roberts, N.Y. Giants, 1949
  Lance Alworth, San Diego, 1963
  Don Maynard, N.Y. Jets, 1968

Most Games, 100 or More Yards Pass Receiving, Career
50 Don Maynard, N.Y. Giants, 1958; N.Y. Jets, 1960-72; St. Louis, 1973
41 Lance Alworth, San Diego, 1962-70; Dallas, 1971-72
40 Steve Largent, Seattle, 1976-89

Most Games, 100 or More Yards Pass Receiving, Season
10 Charley Hennigan, Houston, 1961
9 Elroy (Crazylegs) Hirsch, Los Angeles, 1951
  Bill Groman, Houston, 1960
  Lance Alworth, San Diego, 1965
  Don Maynard, N.Y. Jets, 1967
  Stanley Morgan, New England, 1986
  Mark Carrier, Tampa Bay, 1989
8 Charley Hennigan, Houston, 1964
  Lance Alworth, San Diego, 1967
  Mark Duper, Miami, 1986
  Jerry Rice, San Francisco, 1989

Most Consecutive Games, 100 or More Yards Pass Receiving
7 Charley Hennigan, Houston, 1961
  Bill Groman, Houston, 1961
6 Raymond Berry, Baltimore, 1960
  Pat Studstill, Detroit, 1966
5 Elroy (Crazylegs) Hirsch, Los Angeles, 1951
  Bob Boyd, Los Angeles, 1954
  Terry Barr, Detroit, 1963
  Lance Alworth, San Diego, 1966

Longest Pass Reception (All TDs except as noted)
99 Andy Farkas (from Filchock), Washington vs. Pittsburgh, Oct. 15, 1939
  Bobby Mitchell (from Izo), Washington vs. Cleveland, Sept. 15, 1963
  Pat Studstill (from Sweetan), Detroit vs. Baltimore, Oct. 16, 1966
  Gerry Allen (from Jurgensen), Washington vs. Chicago, Sept. 15, 1968
  Cliff Branch (from Plunkett), L.A. Raiders vs. Washington, Oct. 2, 1983
  Mike Quick (from Jaworski), Philadelphia vs. Atlanta, Nov. 10, 1985
98 Gaynell Tinsley (from Russell), Chi. Cardinals vs. Cleveland, Nov. 17, 1938
  Dick (Night Train) Lane (from Compton), Chi. Cardinals vs. Green Bay, Nov. 13, 1955
  John Farrington (from Wade), Chicago vs. Detroit, Oct. 8, 1961
  Willard Dewveall (from Lee), Houston vs. San Diego, Nov. 25, 1962
  Homer Jones (from Morrall), N.Y. Giants vs. Pittsburgh, Sept. 11, 1966
  Bobby Moore (from Hart), St. Louis vs. Los Angeles, Dec. 10, 1972 (no TD)
97 Gaynell Tinsley (from Coffee), Chi. Cardinals vs. Chi. Bears, Dec. 5, 1937
  Cloyce Box (from Layne), Detroit vs. Green Bay, Nov. 26, 1953
  Jerry Tarr (from Shaw), Denver vs. Boston, Sept. 21, 1962
  Webster Slaughter (from Kosar), Cleveland vs. Chicago, Oct. 23, 1989

Average Gain
Highest Average Gain, Career (200 receptions)
22.26 Homer Jones, N.Y. Giants, 1964-69; Cleveland, 1970 (224-4,986)
20.83 Buddy Dial, Pittsburgh, 1959-63; Dallas, 1964-66 (261-5,436)
20.75 Willie Gault, Chicago, 1983-87; L.A. Raiders, 1988-89 (228-4732)

Highest Average Gain, Season (24 receptions)
32.58 Don Currivan, Boston, 1947 (24-782)
31.44 Bucky Pope, Los Angeles, 1964 (25-786)
28.60 Bobby Duckworth, San Diego, 1984 (25-715)

Highest Average Gain, Game (3 receptions)
60.67 Bill Groman, Houston vs. Denver, Nov. 20, 1960 (3-182)
  Homer Jones, N.Y. Giants vs. Washington, Dec. 12, 1965 (3-182)
60.33 Don Currivan, Boston vs. Washington, Nov. 30, 1947 (3-181)
59.67 Bobby Duckworth, San Diego vs. Chicago, Dec. 3, 1984 (3-179)

Touchdowns
Most Seasons Leading League
9 Don Hutson, Green Bay, 1935-38, 1940-44
3 Lance Alworth, San Diego, 1964-66
  Jerry Rice, San Francisco, 1986-87, 1989
2 By many players

Most Consecutive Seasons Leading League
5 Don Hutson, Green Bay, 1940-44
4 Don Hutson, Green Bay, 1935-38
3 Lance Alworth, San Diego, 1964-66

Most Touchdowns, Career
100 Steve Largent, Seattle, 1976-89
99 Don Hutson, Green Bay, 1935-45
88 Don Maynard, N.Y. Giants, 1958; N.Y. Jets, 1960-72; St. Louis, 1973

Most Touchdowns, Season
22 Jerry Rice, San Francisco, 1987
18 Mark Clayton, Miami, 1984
17 Don Hutson, Green Bay, 1942
  Elroy (Crazylegs) Hirsch, Los Angeles, 1951
  Bill Groman, Houston, 1961
  Jerry Rice, San Francisco, 1989

Most Touchdowns, Rookie, Season
13 Bill Howton, Green Bay, 1952
  John Jefferson, San Diego, 1979
12 Harlon Hill, Chi. Bears, 1954
  Bill Groman, Houston, 1960
  Mike Ditka, Chicago, 1961
  Bob Hayes, Dallas, 1965
10 Bill Swiacki, N.Y. Giants, 1948

Bucky Pope, Los Angeles, 1964
Sammy White, Minnesota, 1976
Daryl Turner, Seattle, 1984

Most Touchdowns, Game
5 Bob Shaw, Chi. Cardinals vs. Baltimore, Oct. 2, 1950
  Kellen Winslow, San Diego vs. Oakland, Nov. 22, 1981
4 By many players. Last time: Wesley Walker, N.Y. Jets vs. Miami, Sept. 21, 1986 (OT)

Most Consecutive Games, Touchdowns
13 Jerry Rice, San Francisco, 1986-87
11 Elroy (Crazylegs) Hirsch, Los Angeles, 1950-51
  Buddy Dial, Pittsburgh, 1959-60
9 Lance Alworth, San Diego, 1963

Interceptions By
Most Seasons Leading League
3 Everson Walls, Dallas, 1981-82, 1985
2 Dick (Night Train) Lane, Los Angeles, 1952; Chi. Cardinals, 1954
  Jack Christiansen, Detroit, 1953, 1957
  Milt Davis, Baltimore, 1957, 1959
  Dick Lynch, N.Y. Giants, 1961, 1963
  Johnny Robinson, Kansas City, 1966, 1970
  Bill Bradley, Philadelphia, 1971-72
  Emmitt Thomas, Kansas City, 1969, 1974

Most Interceptions By, Career
81 Paul Krause, Washington, 1964-67; Minnesota, 1968-79 .
79 Emlen Tunnell, N.Y. Giants, 1948-58; Green Bay, 1959-61
68 Dick (Night Train) Lane, Los Angeles, 1952-53; Chi. Cardinals, 1954-59; Detroit, 1960-65

Most Interceptions By, Season
14 Dick (Night Train) Lane, Los Angeles, 1952
13 Dan Sandifer, Washington, 1948
  Orban (Spec) Sanders, N.Y. Yanks, 1950
  Lester Hayes, Oakland, 1980
12 By nine players

Most Interceptions By, Rookie, Season
14 Dick (Night Train) Lane, Los Angeles, 1952
13 Dan Sandifer, Washington, 1948
12 Woodley Lewis, Los Angeles, 1950
  Paul Krause, Washington, 1964

Most Interceptions By, Game
4 Sammy Baugh, Washington vs. Detroit, Nov. 14, 1943
  Dan Sandifer, Washington vs. Boston, Oct. 31, 1948
  Don Doll, Detroit vs. Chi. Cardinals, Oct. 23, 1949
  Bob Nussbaumer, Chi. Cardinals vs. N.Y. Bulldogs, Nov. 13, 1949
  Russ Craft, Philadelphia vs. Chi. Cardinals, Sept. 24, 1950
  Bobby Dillon, Green Bay vs. Detroit, Nov. 26, 1953
  Jack Butler, Pittsburgh vs. Washington, Dec. 13, 1953
  Austin (Goose) Gonsoulin, Denver vs. Buffalo, Sept. 18, 1960
  Jerry Norton, St. Louis vs. Washington, Nov. 20, 1960; vs. Pittsburgh, Nov. 26, 1961
  Dave Baker, San Francisco vs. L.A. Rams, Dec. 4, 1960
  Bobby Ply, Dall. Texans vs. San Diego, Dec. 16, 1962
  Bobby Hunt, Kansas City vs. Houston, Oct. 4, 1964
  Willie Brown, Denver vs. N.Y. Jets, Nov. 15, 1964
  Dick Anderson, Miami vs. Pittsburgh, Dec. 3, 1973
  Willie Buchanon, Green Bay vs. San Diego, Sept. 24, 1978
  Deron Cherry, Kansas City vs. Seattle, Sept. 29, 1985

Most Consecutive Games, Passes Intercepted By
8 Tom Morrow, Oakland, 1962-63
7 Paul Krause, Washington, 1964
  Larry Wilson, St. Louis, 1966
  Ben Davis, Cleveland, 1968
6 Dick (Night Train) Lane, Chi. Cardinals, 1954-55
  Will Sherman, Los Angeles, 1954-55
  Jim Shofner, Cleveland, 1960
  Paul Krause, Minnesota, 1968
  Willie Williams, N.Y. Giants, 1968
  Kermit Alexander, San Francisco, 1968-69
  Mel Blount, Pittsburgh, 1975
  Eric Harris, Kansas City, 1980
  Lester Hayes, Oakland, 1980
  Barry Wilburn, Washington, 1987

Yards Gained
Most Seasons Leading League
2 Dick (Night Train) Lane, Los Angeles, 1952; Chi. Cardinals, 1954
  Herb Adderley, Green Bay, 1965, 1969
  Dick Anderson, Miami, 1968, 1970

Most Yards Gained, Career
1,282 Emlen Tunnell, N.Y. Giants, 1948-58; Green Bay, 1959-61
1,207 Dick (Night Train) Lane, Los Angeles, 1952-53; Chi. Cardinals, 1954-59; Detroit, 1960-65
1,185 Paul Krause, Washington, 1964-67; Minnesota, 1968-79

Most Yards Gained, Season
349 Charlie McNeil, San Diego, 1961
301 Don Doll, Detroit, 1949
298 Dick (Night Train) Lane, Los Angeles, 1952

Most Yards Gained, Rookie, Season
301 Don Doll, Detroit, 1949
298 Dick (Night Train) Lane, Los Angeles, 1952
275 Woodley Lewis, Los Angeles, 1950

Most Yards Gained, Game
177 Charlie McNeil, San Diego vs. Houston, Sept. 24, 1961
167 Dick Jauron, Detroit vs. Chicago, Nov. 18, 1973
151 Tom Myers, New Orleans vs. Minnesota, Sept. 3, 1978
  Mike Haynes, L.A. Raiders vs. Miami, Dec. 2, 1984

Longest Return (All TDs)
103 Vencie Glenn, San Diego vs. Denver, Nov. 29, 1987
102 Bob Smith, Detroit vs. Chi. Bears, Nov. 24, 1949
  Erich Barnes, N.Y. Giants vs. Dall. Cowboys, Oct. 15, 1961
  Gary Barbaro, Kansas City vs. Seattle, Dec. 11, 1977
  Louis Breeden, Cincinnati vs. San Diego, Nov. 8, 1981

101 Richie Petitbon, Chicago vs Los Angeles, Dec. 9, 1962
    Henry Carr, N.Y. Giants vs. Los Angeles, Nov. 13, 1966
    Tony Greene, Buffalo vs. Kansas City, Oct. 3, 1976
    Tom Pridemore, Atlanta vs. San Francisco, Sept. 20, 1981

Touchdowns

Most Touchdowns, Career
- 9 Ken Houston, Houston, 1967-72; Washington, 1973-80
- 7 Herb Adderley, Green Bay, 1961-69; Dallas, 1970-72
    Erich Barnes, Chi. Bears, 1958-60; N.Y. Giants, 1961-64; Cleveland, 1965-70
    Lem Barney, Detroit, 1967-77
- 6 Tom Janik, Denver, 1963-64; Buffalo, 1965-68; Boston, 1969-70; New England, 1971
    Miller Farr, Denver, 1965; San Diego, 1965-66; Houston, 1967-69; St. Louis, 1970-72; Detroit, 1973
    Bobby Bell, Kansas City, 1963-74

Most Touchdowns, Season
- 4 Ken Houston, Houston, 1971
    Jim Kearney, Kansas City, 1972
- 3 Dick Harris, San Diego, 1961
    Dick Lynch, N.Y. Giants, 1963
    Herb Adderley, Green Bay, 1965
    Lem Barney, Detroit, 1967
    Miller Farr, Houston, 1967
    Monte Jackson, Los Angeles, 1976
    Rod Perry, Los Angeles, 1978
    Ronnie Lott, San Francisco, 1981
    Lloyd Burruss, Kansas City, 1986
- 2 By many players

Most Touchdowns, Rookie, Season
- 3 Lem Barney, Detroit, 1967
    Ronnie Lott, San Francisco, 1981
- 2 By many players

Most Touchdowns, Game
- 2 Bill Blackburn, Chi. Cardinals vs. Boston, Oct. 24, 1948
    Dan Sandifer, Washington vs. Boston, Oct. 31, 1948
    Bob Franklin, Cleveland vs. Chicago, Dec. 11, 1960
    Bill Stacy, St. Louis vs. Dall. Cowboys, Nov. 5, 1961
    Jerry Norton, St. Louis vs. Pittsburgh, Nov. 26, 1961
    Miller Farr, Houston vs. Buffalo, Dec. 7, 1968
    Ken Houston, Houston vs. San Diego, Dec. 19, 1971
    Jim Kearney, Kansas City vs. Denver, Oct. 1, 1972
    Lemar Parrish, Cincinnati vs. Houston, Dec. 17, 1972
    Dick Anderson, Miami vs. Pittsburgh, Dec. 3, 1973
    Prentice McCray, New England vs. N.Y. Jets, Nov. 21, 1976
    Kenny Johnson, Atlanta vs. Green Bay, Nov. 27, 1983 (OT)
    Mike Kozlowski, Miami vs. N.Y. Jets, Dec. 16, 1983
    Dave Brown, Seattle vs. Kansas City, Nov. 4, 1984
    Lloyd Burruss, Kansas City vs. San Diego, Oct. 19, 1986

Punting

Most Seasons Leading League
- 4 Sammy Baugh, Washington, 1940-43
    Jerrel Wilson, Kansas City, 1965, 1968, 1972-73
- 3 Yale Lary, Detroit, 1959, 1961, 1963
    Jim Fraser, Denver, 1962-64
    Ray Guy, Oakland, 1974-75, 1977
    Rohn Stark, Baltimore, 1983; Indianapolis, 1985-86
- 2 By many players

Most Consecutive Seasons Leading League
- 4 Sammy Baugh, Washington, 1940-43
- 3 Jim Fraser, Denver, 1962-64
- 2 By many players

Punts

Most Punts, Career
- 1,154 Dave Jennings, N.Y. Giants, 1974-84; N.Y. Jets, 1985-87
- 1,083 John James, Atlanta, 1972-81; Detroit, 1982, Houston, 1982-84
- 1,072 Jerrel Wilson, Kansas City, 1963-77; New England, 1978

Most Punts, Season
- 114 Bob Parsons, Chicago, 1981
- 109 John James, Atlanta, 1978
- 108 John Teltschik, Philadelphia, 1986

Most Punts, Rookie, Season
- 108 John Teltschik, Philadelphia, 1986
- 99 Lewis Colbert, Kansas City, 1986
- 96 Mike Connell, San Francisco, 1978
    Chris Norman, Denver, 1984

Most Punts, Game
- 15 John Teltschik, Philadelphia vs. N.Y. Giants, Dec. 6, 1987 (OT)
- 14 Dick Nesbitt, Chi. Cardinals vs. Chi. Bears, Nov. 30, 1933
    Keith Molesworth, Chi. Bears vs. Green Bay, Dec. 10, 1933
    Sammy Baugh, Washington vs. Philadelphia, Nov. 5, 1939
    Carl Kinscherf, N.Y. Giants vs. Detroit, Nov. 7, 1943
    George Taliaferro, N.Y. Yanks vs. Los Angeles, Sept. 28, 1951
- 12 By many players. Last time: Bryan Wagner, Cleveland vs. Kansas City, Nov. 19, 1989 (OT)

Longest Punt
- 98 Steve O'Neal, N.Y. Jets vs. Denver, Sept. 21, 1969
- 94 Joe Lintzenich, Chi. Bears vs. N.Y. Giants, Nov. 16, 1931
- 91 Randall Cunningham, Philadelphia vs. N.Y. Giants, Dec. 3, 1989

Average Yardage

Highest Average, Punting, Career (300 punts)
- 45.10 Sammy Baugh, Washington, 1937-52 (338-15,245)
- 44.68 Tommy Davis, San Francisco, 1959-69 (511-22,833)
- 44.29 Yale Lary, Detroit, 1952-53, 1956-64 (503-22,279)

Highest Average, Punting, Season (Qualifiers)
- 51.40 Sammy Baugh, Washington, 1940 (35-1,799)
- 48.94 Yale Lary, Detroit, 1963 (35-1,713)
- 48.73 Sammy Baugh, Washington, 1941 (30-1,462)

Highest Average, Punting, Rookie, Season (Qualifiers)
- 46.40 Bobby Walden, Minnesota, 1964 (72-3,341)

46.22 Dave Lewis, Cincinnati, 1970 (79-3,651)
45.92 Frank Sinkwich, Detroit, 1943 (12-551)

Highest Average, Punting, Game (4 punts)
- 61.75 Bob Cifers, Detroit vs. Chi. Bears, Nov. 24, 1946 (4-247)
- 61.60 Roy McKay, Green Bay vs. Chi. Cardinals, Oct. 28, 1945 (5-308)
- 59.40 Sammy Baugh, Washington vs. Detroit, Oct. 27, 1940 (5-297)

Punts Had Blocked

Most Consecutive Punts, None Blocked
- 623 Dave Jennings, N.Y. Giants, 1976-83
- 619 Ray Guy, Oakland, 1979-81; L.A. Raiders, 1982-86
- 578 Bobby Walden, Minnesota, 1964-67; Pittsburgh, 1968-72

Most Punts Had Blocked, Career
- 14 Herman Weaver, Detroit, 1970-76; Seattle, 1977-80
- 12 Jerrel Wilson, Kansas City, 1963-77; New England, 1978
    Tom Blanchard, N.Y. Giants, 1971-73; New Orleans, 1974-78; Tampa Bay, 1979-81
- 11 David Lee, Baltimore, 1966-78

Most Punts Had Blocked, Season
- 6 Harry Newsome, Pittsburgh, 1988
- 3 By many players

Punt Returns

Most Seasons Leading League
- 3 Les (Speedy) Duncan, San Diego, 1965-66; Washington, 1971
    Rick Upchurch, Denver, 1976, 1978, 1982
- 2 Dick Christy, N.Y. Titans, 1961-62
    Claude Gibson, Oakland, 1963-64
    Billy Johnson, Houston, 1975, 1977

Punt Returns

Most Punt Returns, Career
- 282 Billy Johnson, Houston, 1974-80; Atlanta, 1982-87; Washington, 1988
- 264 J. T. Smith, Washington, 1978; Kansas City, 1978-84; St. Louis, 1985-87; Phoenix, 1988-89
- 258 Emlen Tunnell, N.Y. Giants, 1948-58; Green Bay, 1959-61

Most Punt Returns, Season
- 70 Danny Reece, Tampa Bay, 1979
- 62 Fulton Walker, Miami-L.A. Raiders, 1985
- 58 J. T. Smith, Kansas City, 1979
    Greg Pruitt, L.A. Raiders, 1983
    Leo Lewis, Minnesota, 1988

Most Punt Returns, Rookie, Season
- 57 Lew Barnes, Chicago, 1986
- 54 James Jones, Dallas, 1980
- 53 Louis Lipps, Pittsburgh, 1984

Most Punt Returns, Game
- 11 Eddie Brown, Washington vs. Tampa Bay, Oct. 9, 1977
- 10 Theo Bell, Pittsburgh vs. Buffalo, Dec. 16, 1979
    Mike Nelms, Washington vs. New Orleans, Dec. 26, 1982
- 9 Rodger Bird, Oakland vs. Denver, Sept. 10, 1967
    Ralph McGill, San Francisco vs. Atlanta, Oct. 29, 1972
    Ed Podolak, Kansas City vs. San Diego, Nov. 10, 1974
    Anthony Leonard, San Francisco vs. New Orleans, Oct. 17, 1976
    Butch Johnson, Dallas vs. Buffalo, Nov. 15, 1976
    Larry Marshall, Philadelphia vs. Tampa Bay, Sept. 18, 1977
    Nesby Glasgow, Baltimore vs. Kansas City, Sept. 2, 1979
    Mike Nelms, Washington vs. St. Louis, Dec. 21, 1980
    Leon Bright, N.Y. Giants vs. Philadelphia, Dec. 11, 1982
    Pete Shaw, N.Y. Giants vs. Philadelphia, Nov. 20, 1983
    Cleotha Montgomery, L.A. Raiders vs. Detroit, Dec. 10, 1984
    Phil McConkey, N.Y. Giants vs. Philadelphia, Dec. 6, 1987 (OT)

Fair Catches

Most Fair Catches, Career
- 102 Willie Wood, Green Bay, 1960-71
- 99 Phil McConkey, N.Y. Giants, 1984-88; Green Bay, 1986; San Diego, 1989
- 76 Bobby Bryant, Minnesota, 1968-80

Most Fair Catches, Season
- 27 Leo Lewis, Minnesota, 1989
- 25 Mark Konecny, Philadelphia, 1988
    Phil McConkey, N.Y. Giants, 1988
- 24 Ken Graham, San Diego, 1969

Most Fair Catches, Game
- 7 Lem Barney, Detroit vs. Chicago, Nov. 21, 1976
    Bobby Morse, Philadelphia vs. Buffalo, Dec. 27, 1987
- 6 Jake Scott, Miami vs. Buffalo, Dec. 20, 1970
    Greg Pruitt, L.A. Raiders vs. Seattle, Oct. 7, 1984
    Phil McConkey, San Diego vs. Kansas City, Dec. 17, 1989
- 5 By many players

Yards Gained

Most Seasons Leading League
- 3 Alvin Haymond, Baltimore, 1965-66; Los Angeles, 1969
- 2 Bill Dudley, Pittsburgh, 1942, 1946
    Emlen Tunnell, N.Y. Giants, 1951-52
    Dick Christy, N.Y. Titans, 1961-62
    Claude Gibson, Oakland, 1963-64
    Rodger Bird, Oakland, 1966-67
    J. T. Smith, Kansas City, 1979-80
    Vai Sikahema, St. Louis, 1986-87

Most Yards Gained, Career
- 3,317 Billy Johnson, Houston, 1974-80; Atlanta, 1982-87; Washington, 1988
- 3,008 Rick Upchurch, Denver, 1975-83
- 2,730 J. T. Smith, Washington, 1978; Kansas City, 1978-84; St. Louis, 1985-87; Phoenix, 1988-89

Most Yards Gained, Season
- 692 Fulton Walker, Miami-L.A. Raiders, 1985
- 666 Greg Pruitt, L.A. Raiders, 1983
- 656 Louis Lipps, Pittsburgh, 1984

Most Yards Gained, Rookie, Season
- 656 Louis Lipps, Pittsburgh, 1984

655 Neal Colzie, Oakland, 1975
608 Mike Haynes, New England, 1976

Most Yards Gained, Game
207 LeRoy Irvin, Los Angeles vs. Atlanta, Oct. 11, 1981
205 George Atkinson, Oakland vs. Buffalo, Sept. 15, 1968
184 Tom Watkins, Detroit vs. San Francisco, Oct. 6, 1963

Longest Punt Return (All TDs)
98 Gil LeFebvre, Cincinnati vs. Brooklyn, Dec. 3, 1933
    Charlie West, Minnesota vs. Washington, Nov. 3, 1968
    Dennis Morgan, Dallas vs. St. Louis, Oct. 13, 1974
97 Greg Pruitt, L.A. Raiders vs. Washington, Oct. 2, 1983
96 Bill Dudley, Washington vs. Pittsburgh, Dec. 3, 1950

Average Yardage
Highest Average, Career (75 returns)
12.78 George McAfee, Chi. Bears, 1940-41, 1945-50 (112-1,431)
12.75 Jack Christiansen, Detroit, 1951-58 (85-1,084)
12.55 Claude Gibson, San Diego, 1961-62; Oakland, 1963-65 (110-1,381)

Highest Average, Season (Qualifiers)
23.00 Herb Rich, Baltimore, 1950 (12-276)
21.47 Jack Christiansen, Detroit, 1952 (15-322)
21.28 Dick Christy, N.Y. Titans, 1961 (18-383)

Highest Average, Rookie, Season (Qualifiers)
23.00 Herb Rich, Baltimore, 1950 (12-276)
20.88 Jerry Davis, Chi. Cardinals, 1948 (16-334)
20.73 Frank Sinkwich, Detroit, 1943 (11-228)

Highest Average, Game (3 returns)
47.67 Chuck Latourette, St. Louis vs. New Orleans, Sept. 29, 1968 (3-143)
47.33 Johnny Roland, St. Louis vs. Philadelphia, Oct. 2, 1966 (3-142)
45.67 Dick Christy, N.Y. Titans vs. Denver, Sept. 24, 1961 (3-137)

Touchdowns
Most Touchdowns, Career
8 Jack Christiansen, Detroit, 1951-58
   Rick Upchurch, Denver, 1975-83
6 Billy Johnson, Houston, 1974-80; Atlanta, 1982-87; Washington, 1988
5 Emlen Tunnell, N.Y. Giants, 1948-58; Green Bay, 1959-61

Most Touchdowns, Season
4 Jack Christiansen, Detroit, 1951
   Rick Upchurch, Denver, 1976
3 Emlen Tunnell, N.Y. Giants, 1951
   Billy Johnson, Houston, 1975
   LeRoy Irvin, Los Angeles, 1981
2 By many players

Most Touchdowns, Rookie, Season
4 Jack Christiansen, Detroit, 1951
2 By six players

Most Touchdowns, Game
2 Jack Christiansen, Detroit vs. Los Angeles, Oct. 14, 1951; vs. Green Bay, Nov. 22, 1951
   Dick Christy, N.Y. Titans vs. Denver, Sept. 24, 1961
   Rick Upchurch, Denver vs. Cleveland, Sept. 26, 1976
   LeRoy Irvin, Los Angeles vs. Atlanta, Oct. 11, 1981
   Vai Sikahema, St. Louis vs. Tampa Bay, Dec. 21, 1986

Kickoff Returns
Most Seasons Leading League
3 Abe Woodson, San Francisco, 1959, 1962-63
2 Lynn Chandnois, Pittsburgh, 1951-52
   Bobby Jancik, Houston, 1962-63
   Travis Williams, Green Bay, 1967; Los Angeles, 1971

Kickoff Returns
Most Kickoff Returns, Career
275 Ron Smith, Chicago, 1965, 1970-72; Atlanta, 1966-67; Los Angeles, 1968-69; San Diego, 1973; Oakland, 1974
243 Bruce Harper, N.Y. Jets, 1977-84
194 Steve Odom, Green Bay, 1974-79; N.Y. Giants, 1979

Most Kickoff Returns, Season
60 Drew Hill, Los Angeles, 1981
55 Bruce Harper, N.Y. Jets, 1978, 1979
   David Turner, Cincinnati, 1979
   Stump Mitchell, St. Louis, 1981
53 Eddie Payton, Minnesota, 1980
   Buster Rhymes, Minnesota, 1985

Most Kickoff Returns, Rookie, Season
55 Stump Mitchell, St. Louis, 1981
53 Buster Rhymes, Minnesota, 1985
50 Nesby Glasgow, Baltimore, 1979
   Dino Hall, Cleveland, 1979

Most Kickoff Returns, Game
9 Noland Smith, Kansas City vs. Oakland, Nov. 23, 1967
   Dino Hall, Cleveland vs. Pittsburgh, Oct. 7, 1979
   Paul Palmer, Kansas City vs. Seattle, Sept. 20, 1987
8 George Taliaferro, N.Y. Yanks vs. N.Y. Giants, Dec. 3, 1950
   Bobby Jancik, Houston vs. Boston, Dec. 8, 1963; vs. Oakland, Dec. 22, 1963
   Mel Renfro, Dallas vs. Green Bay, Nov. 29, 1964
   Willie Porter, Boston vs. N.Y. Jets, Sept. 22, 1968
   Keith Moody, Buffalo vs. Seattle, Oct. 30, 1977
   Brian Baschnagel, Chicago vs. Houston, Nov. 6, 1977
   Bruce Harper, N.Y. Jets vs. New England, Oct. 29, 1978; vs. New England, Sept. 9, 1979
   Dino Hall, Cleveland vs. Pittsburgh, Nov. 25, 1979
   Terry Metcalf, Washington vs. St. Louis, Sept. 20, 1981
   Harlan Huckleby, Green Bay vs. Washington, Oct. 17, 1983
   Gary Ellerson, Green Bay vs. St. Louis, Sept. 29, 1985
   Bobby Humphery, N.Y. Jets vs. Cincinnati, Dec. 21, 1986
   Bobby Joe Edmonds, Seattle vs. L.A. Raiders, Nov. 30, 1987
   Joe Cribbs, Miami vs. Pittsburgh, Dec. 18, 1988
7 By many players

Yards Gained
Most Seasons Leading League
3 Bruce Harper, N.Y. Jets, 1977-79
2 Marshall Goldberg, Chi. Cardinals, 1941-42
   Woodley Lewis, Los Angeles, 1953-54
   Al Carmichael, Green Bay, 1956-57
   Timmy Brown, Philadelphia, 1961, 1963
   Bobby Jancik, Houston, 1963, 1966
   Ron Smith, Atlanta, 1966-67

Most Yards Gained, Career
6,922 Ron Smith, Chicago, 1965, 1970-72; Atlanta, 1966-67; Los Angeles, 1968-69; San Diego, 1973; Oakland, 1974
5,538 Abe Woodson, San Francisco, 1958-64; St. Louis, 1965-66
5,407 Bruce Harper, N.Y. Jets, 1977-84

Most Yards Gained, Season
1,345 Buster Rhymes, Minnesota, 1985
1,317 Bobby Jancik, Houston, 1963
1,314 Dave Hampton, Green Bay, 1971

Most Yards Gained, Rookie, Season
1,345 Buster Rhymes, Minnesota, 1985
1,292 Stump Mitchell, St. Louis, 1981
1,245 Odell Barry, Denver, 1964

Most Yards Gained, Game
294 Wally Triplett, Detroit vs. Los Angeles, Oct. 29, 1950
247 Timmy Brown, Philadelphia vs. Dallas, Nov. 6, 1966
244 Noland Smith, Kansas City vs. San Diego, Oct. 15, 1967

Longest Kickoff Return (All TDs)
106 Al Carmichael, Green Bay vs. Chi. Bears, Oct. 7, 1956
    Noland Smith, Kansas City vs. Denver, Dec. 17, 1967
    Roy Green, St. Louis vs. Dallas, Oct. 21, 1979
105 Frank Seno, Chi. Cardinals vs. N.Y. Giants, Oct. 20, 1946
    Ollie Matson, Chi. Cardinals vs. Washington, Oct. 14, 1956
    Abe Woodson, San Francisco vs. Los Angeles, Nov. 8, 1959
    Timmy Brown, Philadelphia vs. Cleveland, Sept. 17, 1961
    Jon Arnett, Los Angeles vs. Detroit, Oct. 29, 1961
    Eugene (Mercury) Morris, Miami vs. Cincinnati, Sept. 14, 1969
    Travis Williams, Los Angeles vs. New Orleans, Dec. 5, 1971
104 By many players

Average Yardage
Highest Average, Career (75 returns)
30.56 Gale Sayers, Chicago, 1965-71 (91-2,781)
29.57 Lynn Chandnois, Pittsburgh, 1950-56 (92-2,720)
28.69 Abe Woodson, San Francisco, 1958-64; St. Louis, 1965-66 (193-5,538)

Highest Average, Season (Qualifiers)
41.06 Travis Williams, Green Bay, 1967 (18-739)
37.69 Gale Sayers, Chicago, 1967 (16-603)
35.50 Ollie Matson, Chi. Cardinals, 1958 (14-497)

Highest Average, Rookie, Season (Qualifiers)
41.06 Travis Williams, Green Bay, 1967 (18-739)
33.08 Tom Moore, Green Bay, 1960 (12-397)
32.88 Duriel Harris, Miami, 1976 (17-559)

Highest Average, Game (3 returns)
73.50 Wally Triplett, Detroit vs. Los Angeles, Oct. 29, 1950 (4-294)
67.33 Lenny Lyles, San Francisco vs. Baltimore, Dec. 18, 1960 (3-202)
65.33 Ken Hall, Houston vs. N.Y. Titans, Oct. 23, 1960 (3-196)

Touchdowns
Most Touchdowns, Career
6 Ollie Matson, Chi. Cardinals, 1952, 1954-58; L.A. Rams, 1959-62; Detroit, 1963; Philadelphia, 1964
   Gale Sayers, Chicago, 1965-71
   Travis Williams, Green Bay, 1967-70; Los Angeles, 1971
5 Bobby Mitchell, Cleveland, 1958-61; Washington, 1962-68
   Abe Woodson, San Francisco, 1958-64; St. Louis, 1965-66
   Timmy Brown, Green Bay, 1959; Philadelphia, 1960-67; Baltimore, 1968
4 Cecil Turner, Chicago, 1968-73
   Ron Brown, L.A. Rams, 1984-89

Most Touchdowns, Season
4 Travis Williams, Green Bay, 1967
   Cecil Turner, Chicago, 1970
3 Verda (Vitamin T) Smith, Los Angeles, 1950
   Abe Woodson, San Francisco, 1963
   Gale Sayers, Chicago, 1967
   Raymond Clayborn, New England, 1977
   Ron Brown, L.A. Rams, 1985
2 By many players

Most Touchdowns, Rookie, Season
4 Travis Williams, Green Bay, 1967
3 Raymond Clayborn, New England, 1977
2 By seven players

Most Touchdowns, Game
2 Timmy Brown, Philadelphia vs. Dallas, Nov. 6, 1966
   Travis Williams, Green Bay vs. Cleveland, Nov. 12, 1967
   Ron Brown, L.A. Rams vs. Green Bay, Nov. 24, 1985

Combined Kick Returns
Most Combined Kick Returns, Career
510 Ron Smith, Chicago, 1965, 1970-72; Atlanta, 1966-67; Los Angeles, 1968-69; San Diego, 1973; Oakland, 1974 (p-235, k-275)
426 Bruce Harper, N.Y. Jets, 1977-84 (p-183, k-243)
423 Alvin Haymond, Baltimore, 1964-67; Philadelphia, 1968; Los Angeles, 1969-71; Washington, 1972; Houston, 1973 (p-253, k-170)

Most Combined Kick Returns, Season
100 Larry Jones, Washington, 1975 (p-53, k-47)
97 Stump Mitchell, St. Louis, 1981 (p-42, k-55)
94 Nesby Glasgow, Baltimore, 1979 (p-44, k-50)

Most Combined Kick Returns, Game
13 Stump Mitchell, St. Louis vs. Atlanta, Oct. 18, 1981 (p-6, k-7)
12 Mel Renfro, Dallas vs. Green Bay, Nov. 29, 1964 (p-4, k-8)
   Larry Jones, Washington vs. Dallas, Dec. 13, 1975 (p-6, k-6)
   Eddie Brown, Washington vs. Tampa Bay, Oct. 9, 1977 (p-11, k-1)

Yards Gained
Most Yards Returned, Career
8,710　Ron Smith, Chicago, 1965, 1970-72; Atlanta, 1966-67; Los Angeles, 1968-69;
San Diego, 1973; Oakland, 1974 (p-1,788, k-6,922)
7,191　Bruce Harper, N.Y. Jets, 1977-84 (p-1,784, k-5,407)
6,740　Les (Speedy) Duncan, San Diego, 1964-70; Washington, 1971-74
(p-2,201, k-4,539)
Most Yards Returned, Season
1,737　Stump Mitchell, St. Louis, 1981 (p-445, k-1,292)
1,658　Bruce Harper, N.Y. Jets, 1978 (p-378, k-1,280)
1,591　Mike Nelms, Washington, 1981 (p-492, k-1,099)
Most Yards Returned, Game
294　Wally Triplett, Detroit vs. Los Angeles, Oct. 29, 1950 (k-294)
Woodley Lewis, Los Angeles vs. Detroit, Oct. 18, 1953 (p-120, k-174)
289　Eddie Payton, Detroit vs. Minnesota, Dec. 17, 1977 (p-105, k-184)
282　Les (Speedy) Duncan, San Diego vs. N.Y. Jets, Nov. 24, 1968 (p-102, k-180)

Touchdowns
Most Touchdowns, Career
9　Ollie Matson, Chi. Cardinals, 1952, 1954-58; Los Angeles, 1959-62;
Detroit, 1963; Philadelphia, 1964-66 (p-3, k-6)
8　Jack Christiansen, Detroit, 1951-58 (p-8)
Bobby Mitchell, Cleveland, 1958-61; Washington, 1962-68 (p-3, k-5)
Gale Sayers, Chicago, 1965-71 (p-2, k-6)
Rick Upchurch, Denver, 1975-83 (p-8)
Billy Johnson, Houston, 1974-80; Atlanta, 1982-87; Washington, 1988 (p-6, k-2)
7　Abe Woodson, San Francisco, 1958-64; St. Louis, 1965-66 (p-2, k-5)
Most Touchdowns, Season
4　Jack Christiansen, Detroit, 1951 (p-4)
Emlen Tunnell, N.Y. Giants, 1951 (p-3, k-1)
Gale Sayers, Chicago, 1967 (p-1, k-3)
Travis Williams, Green Bay, 1967 (k-4)
Cecil Turner, Chicago, 1970 (k-4)
Billy Johnson, Houston, 1975 (p-3, k-1)
Rick Upchurch, Denver, 1976 (p-4)
3　Verda (Vitamin T) Smith, Los Angeles, 1950 (k-3)
Abe Woodson, San Francisco, 1963 (k-3)
Raymond Clayborn, New England, 1977 (k-3)
Billy Johnson, Houston, 1977 (p-2, k-1)
LeRoy Irvin, Los Angeles, 1981 (p-3)
Ron Brown, L.A. Rams, 1985 (k-3)
2　By many players
Most Touchdowns, Game
2　Jack Christiansen, Detroit vs. Los Angeles, Oct. 14, 1951 (p-2); vs. Green Bay,
Nov. 22, 1951 (p-2)
Jim Patton, N.Y. Giants vs. Washington, Oct. 30, 1955 (p-1, k-1)
Bobby Mitchell, Cleveland vs. Philadelphia, Nov. 23, 1958 (p-1, k-1)
Dick Christy, N.Y. Titans vs. Denver, Sept. 24, 1961 (p-2)
Al Frazier, Denver vs. Boston, Dec. 3, 1961 (p-1, k-1)
Timmy Brown, Philadelphia vs. Dallas, Nov. 6, 1966 (k-2)
Travis Williams, Green Bay vs. Cleveland, Nov. 12, 1967 (k-2); vs. Pittsburgh,
Nov. 2, 1969 (p-1, k-1)
Gale Sayers, Chicago vs. San Francisco, Dec. 3, 1967 (p-1, k-1)
Rick Upchurch, Denver vs. Cleveland, Sept. 26, 1976 (p-2)
Eddie Payton, Detroit vs. Minnesota, Dec. 17, 1977 (p-1, k-1)
LeRoy Irvin, Los Angeles vs. Atlanta, Oct. 11, 1981 (p-2)
Ron Brown, L.A. Rams vs. Green Bay, Nov. 24, 1985 (k-2)
Vai Sikahema, St. Louis vs. Tampa Bay, Dec. 21, 1986 (p-2)

Fumbles
Most Fumbles, Career
106　Dan Fouts, San Diego, 1973-87
105　Roman Gabriel, Los Angeles, 1962-72; Philadelphia, 1973-77
95　Johnny Unitas, Baltimore, 1956-72; San Diego, 1973
Most Fumbles, Season
18　Dave Krieg, Seattle, 1989
17　Dan Pastorini, Houston, 1973
Warren Moon, Houston, 1984
Randall Cunningham, Philadelphia, 1989
16　Don Meredith, Dallas, 1964
Joe Cribbs, Buffalo, 1980
Steve Fuller, Kansas City, 1980
Paul McDonald, Cleveland, 1984
Phil Simms, N.Y. Giants, 1985
Most Fumbles, Game
7　Len Dawson, Kansas City vs. San Diego, Nov. 15, 1964
6　Sam Etcheverry, St. Louis vs. N.Y. Giants, Sept. 17, 1961
Dave Krieg, Seattle vs. Kansas City, Nov. 5, 1989
5　Paul Christman, Chi. Cardinals vs. Green Bay, Nov. 10, 1946
Charlie Conerly, N.Y. Giants vs. San Francisco, Dec. 1, 1957
Jack Kemp, Buffalo vs. Houston, Oct. 29, 1967
Roman Gabriel, Philadelphia vs. Oakland, Nov. 21, 1976
Randall Cunningham, Philadelphia vs. L.A. Raiders, Nov. 30, 1986 (OT)
Willie Totten, Buffalo vs. Indianapolis, Oct. 4, 1987
Dave Walter, Cincinnati vs. Seattle, Oct. 11, 1987

Fumbles Recovered
Most Fumbles Recovered, Career, Own and Opponents'
43　Fran Tarkenton, Minnesota, 1961-66, 1972-78; N.Y. Giants, 1967-71 (43 own)
38　Jack Kemp, Pittsburgh, 1957; L.A. Chargers, 1960; San Diego, 1961-62;
Buffalo, 1962-67, 1969 (38 own)
Dan Fouts, San Diego, 1973-87 (37 own, 1 opp)
37　Roman Gabriel, Los Angeles, 1962-72; Philadelphia, 1973-77 (37 own)
Most Fumbles Recovered, Season, Own and Opponents'
9　Don Hultz, Minnesota, 1963 (9 opp)
Dave Krieg, Seattle, 1989 (9 own)
8　Paul Christman, Chi. Cardinals, 1945 (8 own)
Joe Schmidt, Detroit, 1955 (8 opp)
Bill Butler, Minnesota, 1963 (8 own)

Kermit Alexander, San Francisco, 1965 (4 own, 4 opp)
Jack Lambert, Pittsburgh, 1976 (1 own, 7 opp)
Danny White, Dallas, 1981 (8 own)
Dan Marino, Miami, 1988 (7 own, 1 opp)
7　By many players
Most Fumbles Recovered, Game, Own and Opponents'
4　Otto Graham, Cleveland vs. N.Y. Giants, Oct. 25, 1953 (4 own)
Sam Etcheverry, St. Louis vs. N.Y. Giants, Sept. 17, 1961 (4 own)
Roman Gabriel, Los Angeles vs. San Francisco, Oct. 12, 1969 (4 own)
Joe Ferguson, Buffalo vs. Miami, Sept. 18, 1977 (4 own)
Randall Cunningham, Philadelphia vs. L.A. Raiders, Nov. 30, 1986 (OT) (4
own)
3　By many players

Own Fumbles Recovered
Most Own Fumbles Recovered, Career
43　Fran Tarkenton, Minnesota, 1961-66, 1972-78; N.Y. Giants, 1967-71
38　Jack Kemp, Pittsburgh, 1957; L.A. Chargers, 1960; San Diego, 1961-62;
Buffalo, 1962-67, 1969
37　Roman Gabriel, Los Angeles, 1962-72; Philadelphia, 1973-77
Dan Fouts, San Diego, 1973-87
Most Own Fumbles Recovered, Season
9　Dave Krieg, Seattle, 1989
8　Paul Christman, Chi. Cardinals, 1945
Bill Butler, Minnesota, 1963
Danny White, Dallas, 1981
7　By many players
Most Own Fumbles Recovered, Game
4　Otto Graham, Cleveland vs. N.Y. Giants, Oct. 25, 1953
Sam Etcheverry, St. Louis vs. N.Y. Giants, Sept. 17, 1961
Roman Gabriel, Los Angeles vs. San Francisco, Oct. 12, 1969
Joe Ferguson, Buffalo vs. Miami, Sept. 18, 1977
Randall Cunningham, Philadelphia vs. L.A. Raiders, Nov. 30, 1986 (OT)
3　By many players

Opponents' Fumbles Recovered
Most Opponents' Fumbles Recovered, Career
29　Jim Marshall, Cleveland, 1960; Minnesota, 1961-79
25　Dick Butkus, Chicago, 1965-73
23　Carl Eller, Minnesota, 1964-78; Seattle, 1979
Reggie Williams, Cincinnati, 1976-89
Most Opponents' Fumbles Recovered, Season
9　Don Hultz, Minnesota, 1963
8　Joe Schmidt, Detroit, 1955
7　Alan Page, Minnesota, 1970
Jack Lambert, Pittsburgh, 1976
Ray Childress, Houston, 1988
Most Opponents' Fumbles Recovered, Game
3　Corwin Clatt, Chi. Cardinals vs. Detroit, Nov. 6, 1949
Vic Sears, Philadelphia vs. Green Bay, Nov. 2, 1952
Ed Beatty, San Francisco vs. Los Angeles, Oct. 7, 1956
Ron Carroll, Houston vs. Cincinnati, Oct. 27, 1974
Maurice Spencer, New Orleans vs. Atlanta, Oct. 10, 1976
Steve Nelson, New England vs. Philadelphia, Oct. 8, 1978
Charles Jackson, Kansas City vs. Pittsburgh, Sept. 6, 1981
Willie Buchanon, San Diego vs. Denver, Sept. 27, 1981
Joey Browner, Minnesota vs. San Francisco, Sept. 8, 1985
Ray Childress, Houston vs. Washington, Oct. 30, 1988
2　By many players

Yards Returning Fumbles
Longest Fumble Run (All TDs)
104　Jack Tatum, Oakland vs. Green Bay, Sept. 24, 1972 (opp)
98　George Halas, Chi. Bears vs. Oorang Indians, Marion, Ohio, Nov. 4, 1923
(opp)
97　Chuck Howley, Dallas vs. Atlanta, Oct. 2, 1966 (opp)

Touchdowns
Most Touchdowns, Career (Total)
4　Bill Thompson, Denver, 1969-81
3　Ralph Heywood, Detroit, 1947-48; Boston, 1948; N.Y. Bulldogs, 1949
Leo Sugar, Chi. Cardinals, 1954-59; St. Louis, 1960; Philadelphia, 1961; Detroit,
1962
Bud McFadin, Los Angeles, 1952-56; Denver, 1960-63; Houston, 1964-65
Doug Cline, Houston, 1960-66; San Diego, 1966
Bob Lilly, Dall. Cowboys, 1961-74
Chris Hanburger, Washington, 1965-78
Lemar Parrish, Cincinnati, 1970-77; Washington, 1978-81; Buffalo, 1982
Paul Krause, Washington, 1964-67; Minnesota, 1968-79
Brad Dusek, Washington, 1974-81
David Logan, Tampa Bay, 1979-86; Green Bay, 1987
Thomas Howard, Kansas City, 1977-83; St. Louis, 1984-85
2　By many players
Most Touchdowns, Season (Total)
2　Harold McPhail, Boston, 1934
Harry Ebding, Detroit, 1937
John Morelli, Boston, 1944
Frank Maznicki, Boston, 1947
Fred (Dippy) Evans, Chi. Bears, 1948
Ralph Heywood, Boston, 1948
Art Tait, N.Y. Yanks, 1951
John Dwyer, Los Angeles, 1952
Leo Sugar, Chi. Cardinals, 1957
Doug Cline, Houston, 1961
Jim Bradshaw, Pittsburgh, 1964
Royce Berry, Cincinnati, 1970
Ahmad Rashad, Buffalo, 1974
Tim Gray, Kansas City, 1977
Charles Phillips, Oakland, 1978
Kenny Johnson, Atlanta, 1981
George Martin, N.Y. Giants, 1981
Del Rodgers, Green Bay, 1982
Mike Douglass, Green Bay, 1983

Shelton Robinson, Seattle, 1983
Erik McMillan, N.Y. Jets, 1989

Most Touchdowns, Career (Own recovered)
2   Ken Kavanaugh, Chi. Bears, 1940-41, 1945-50
    Mike Ditka, Chicago, 1961-66; Philadelphia, 1967-68; Dallas, 1969-72
    Gail Cogdill, Detroit, 1960-68; Baltimore, 1968; Atlanta, 1969-70
    Ahmad Rashad, St. Louis, 1972-73; Buffalo, 1974; Minnesota, 1976-82
    Jim Mitchell, Atlanta, 1969-79
    Drew Pearson, Dallas, 1973-83
    Del Rodgers, Green Bay, 1982, 1984; San Francisco, 1987-88

Most Touchdowns, Season (Own recovered)
2   Ahmad Rashad, Buffalo, 1974
    Del Rodgers, Green Bay, 1982
1   By many players

Most Touchdowns, Career (Opponents' recovered)
3   Leo Sugar, Chi. Cardinals, 1954-59; St. Louis, 1960; Philadelphia, 1961; Detroit, 1962
    Doug Cline, Houston, 1960-66; San Diego, 1966
    Bud McFadin, Los Angeles, 1952-56; Denver, 1960-63; Houston, 1964-65
    Bob Lilly, Dall. Cowboys, 1961-74
    Chris Hanburger, Washington, 1965-78
    Paul Krause, Washington, 1964-67; Minnesota, 1968-79
    Lemar Parrish, Cincinnati, 1970-77; Washington, 1978-81; Buffalo, 1982
    Bill Thompson, Denver, 1969-81
    Brad Dusek, Washington, 1974-81
    David Logan, Tampa Bay, 1979-86; Green Bay, 1987
    Thomas Howard, Kansas City, 1977-83; St. Louis, 1984-85
2   By many players

Most Touchdowns, Season (Opponents' recovered)
2   Harold McPhail, Boston, 1934
    Harry Ebding, Detroit, 1937
    John Morelli, Boston, 1944
    Frank Maznicki, Boston, 1947
    Fred (Dippy) Evans, Chi. Bears, 1948
    Ralph Heywood, Boston, 1948
    Art Tait, N.Y. Yanks, 1951
    John Dwyer, Los Angeles, 1952
    Leo Sugar, Chi. Cardinals, 1957
    Doug Cline, Houston, 1961
    Jim Bradshaw, Pittsburgh, 1964
    Royce Berry, Cincinnati, 1970
    Tim Gray, Kansas City, 1977
    Charles Phillips, Oakland, 1978
    Kenny Johnson, Atlanta, 1981
    George Martin, N.Y. Giants, 1981
    Mike Douglass, Green Bay, 1983
    Shelton Robinson, Seattle, 1983
    Erik McMillan, N.Y. Jets, 1989

Most Touchdowns, Game (Opponents' recovered)
2   Fred (Dippy) Evans, Chi. Bears vs. Washington, Nov. 28, 1948

Combined Net Yards Gained
Rushing, receiving, interception returns, punt returns, kickoff returns, and fumble returns
Most Seasons Leading League
5   Jim Brown, Cleveland, 1958-61, 1964
3   Cliff Battles, Boston, 1932-33; Washington, 1937
    Gale Sayers, Chicago, 1965-67
    Eric Dickerson, L.A. Rams, 1983-84, 1986
2   By many players

Most Consecutive Seasons Leading League
4   Jim Brown, Cleveland, 1958-61
3   Gale Sayers, Chicago, 1965-67
2   Cliff Battles, Boston, 1932-33
    Charley Trippi, Chi. Cardinals, 1948-49
    Timmy Brown, Philadelphia, 1962-63
    Floyd Little, Denver, 1967-68
    James Brooks, San Diego, 1981-82
    Eric Dickerson, L.A. Rams, 1983-84

Attempts
Most Attempts, Career
4,368   Walter Payton, Chicago, 1975-87
3,351   Tony Dorsett, Dallas, 1977-87; Denver, 1988
3,281   Franco Harris, Pittsburgh, 1972-83; Seattle, 1984
Most Attempts, Season
496   James Wilder, Tampa Bay, 1984
449   Marcus Allen, L.A. Raiders, 1985
442   Eric Dickerson, L.A. Rams, 1983
Most Attempts, Rookie, Season
442   Eric Dickerson, L.A. Rams, 1983
395   George Rogers, New Orleans, 1981
390   Joe Cribbs, Buffalo, 1980
Most Attempts, Game
48   James Wilder, Tampa Bay vs. Pittsburgh, Oct. 30, 1983
47   James Wilder, Tampa Bay vs. Green Bay, Sept. 30, 1984 (OT)
46   Gerald Riggs, Atlanta vs. L.A. Rams, Nov. 17, 1985

Yards Gained
Most Yards Gained, Career
21,803   Walter Payton, Chicago, 1975-87
16,326   Tony Dorsett, Dallas, 1977-87; Denver, 1988
15,459   Jim Brown, Cleveland, 1957-65
Most Yards Gained, Season
2,535   Lionel James, San Diego, 1985
2,462   Terry Metcalf, St. Louis, 1975
2,444   Mack Herron, New England, 1974
Most Yards Gained, Rookie, Season
2,317   Tim Brown, L.A. Raiders, 1988
2,272   Gale Sayers, Chicago, 1965
2,212   Eric Dickerson, L.A. Rams, 1983
Most Yards Gained, Game
373   Billy Cannon, Houston vs. N.Y. Titans, Dec. 10, 1961

---

345   Lionel James, San Diego vs. L.A. Raiders, Nov. 10, 1985 (OT)
341   Timmy Brown, Philadelphia vs. St. Louis, Dec. 16, 1962

Sacks
Sacks have been compiled since 1982.
Most Sacks, Career
104   Lawrence Taylor, N.Y. Giants, 1982-89
91   Dexter Manley, Washington, 1982-89
81   Richard Dent, Chicago, 1983-89
    Reggie White, Philadelphia, 1985-89
Most Sacks, Season
22   Mark Gastineau, N.Y. Jets, 1984
21   Reggie White, Philadelphia, 1987
    Chris Doleman, Minnesota, 1989
20.5   Lawrence Taylor, N.Y. Giants, 1986
Most Sacks, Rookie, Season
12.5   Leslie O'Neal, San Diego, 1986
12   Charles Haley, San Francisco, 1986
11   Vernon Maxwell, Baltimore, 1983
Most Sacks, Game
6   Fred Dean, San Francisco vs. New Orleans, Nov. 13, 1983
5.5   William Gay, Detroit vs. Tampa Bay, Sept. 4, 1983
5   Howie Long, L.A. Raiders vs. Washington, Oct. 2, 1983
    Randy Holloway, Minnesota vs. Atlanta, Sept. 16, 1984
    Jim Jeffcoat, Dallas vs. Washington, Nov. 10, 1985
    Leslie O'Neal, San Diego vs. Dallas, Nov. 16, 1986
    Gary Jeter, L.A. Rams vs. L.A. Raiders, Sept. 18, 1988

Miscellaneous
Longest Return of Missed Field Goal (All TDs)
101   Al Nelson, Philadelphia vs. Dallas, Sept. 26, 1971
100   Al Nelson, Philadelphia vs. Cleveland, Dec. 11, 1966
    Ken Ellis, Green Bay vs. N.Y. Giants, Sept. 19, 1971
99   Jerry Williams, Los Angeles vs. Green Bay, Dec. 16, 1951
    Carl Taseff, Baltimore vs. Los Angeles, Dec. 12, 1959
    Timmy Brown, Philadelphia vs. St. Louis, Sept. 16, 1962

Team Records

Championships
Most Seasons League Champion
11   Green Bay, 1929-31, 1936, 1939, 1944, 1961-62, 1965-67
9   Chi. Bears, 1921, 1932-33, 1940-41, 1943, 1946, 1963, 1985
5   N.Y. Giants, 1927, 1934, 1938, 1956, 1986
Most Consecutive Seasons League Champion
3   Green Bay, 1929-31
    Green Bay, 1965-67
2   Canton, 1922-23
    Chi. Bears, 1932-33
    Chi. Bears, 1940-41
    Philadelphia, 1948-49
    Detroit, 1952-53
    Cleveland, 1954-55
    Baltimore, 1958-59
    Houston, 1960-61
    Green Bay, 1961-62
    Buffalo, 1964-65
    Miami, 1972-73
    Pittsburgh, 1974-75
    Pittsburgh, 1978-79
    San Francisco, 1988-89
Most Times Finishing First, Regular Season (Since 1933)
18   Clev. Browns, 1950-55, 1957, 1964-65, 1967-69, 1971, 1980, 1985-87, 1989
16   N.Y. Giants, 1933-35, 1938-39, 1941, 1944, 1946, 1956, 1958-59, 1961-63, 1986, 1989
15   Clev./L.A. Rams, 1945, 1949-51, 1955, 1967, 1969, 1973-79, 1985
    Chi. Bears, 1933-34, 1937, 1940-43, 1946, 1956, 1963, 1984-88
Most Consecutive Times Finishing First, Regular Season (Since 1933)
7   Los Angeles, 1973-79
6   Cleveland, 1950-55
    Dallas, 1966-71
    Minnesota, 1973-78
    Pittsburgh, 1974-79
5   Oakland, 1972-76
    Chicago, 1984-88

Games Won
Most Consecutive Games Won
17   Chi. Bears, 1933-34
16   Chi. Bears, 1941-42
    Miami, 1971-73
    Miami, 1983-84
15   L.A. Chargers/San Diego, 1960-61
Most Consecutive Games Without Defeat
25   Canton, 1921-23 (won 22, tied 3)
24   Chi. Bears, 1941-43 (won 23, tied 1)
23   Green Bay, 1928-30 (won 21, tied 2)
Most Games Won, Season
15   San Francisco, 1984
    Chicago, 1985
14   Miami, 1972
    Pittsburgh, 1978
    Washington, 1983
    Miami, 1984
    Chicago, 1986
    N.Y. Giants, 1986
    San Francisco, 1989
13   Chi. Bears, 1934
    Green Bay, 1962
    Oakland, 1967
    Baltimore, 1968

Oakland, 1976
San Francisco, 1981
Denver, 1984
San Francisco, 1987

Most Consecutive Games Won, Season
14 Miami, 1972
13 Chi. Bears, 1934
12 Minnesota, 1969
Chicago, 1985

Most Consecutive Games Won, Start of Season
14 Miami, 1972, entire season
13 Chi. Bears, 1934, entire season
12 Chicago, 1985

Most Consecutive Games Won, End of Season
14 Miami, 1972, entire season
13 Chi. Bears, 1934, entire season
11 Chi. Bears, 1942, entire season
Cleveland, 1951

Most Consecutive Games Without Defeat, Season
14 Miami, 1972 (won 14)
13 Chi. Bears, 1926 (won 11, tied 2)
Green Bay, 1929 (won 12, tied 1)
Chi. Bears, 1934 (won 13)
Baltimore, 1967 (won 11, tied 2)
12 Canton, 1922 (won 10, tied 2)
Canton, 1923 (won 11, tied 1)
Minnesota, 1969 (won 12)
Chicago, 1985 (won 12)

Most Consecutive Games Without Defeat, Start of Season
14 Miami, 1972 (won 14), entire season
13 Chi. Bears, 1926 (won 11, tied 2)
Green Bay, 1929 (won 12, tied 1), entire season
Chi. Bears, 1934 (won 13), entire season
Baltimore, 1967 (won 11, tied 2)
12 Canton, 1922 (won 10, tied 2), entire season
Canton, 1923 (won 11, tied 1), entire season
Chicago, 1985 (won 12)

Most Consecutive Games Without Defeat, End of Season
14 Miami, 1972 (won 14), entire season
13 Green Bay, 1929 (won 12, tied 1), entire season
Chi. Bears, 1934 (won 13), entire season
12 Canton, 1922 (won 10, tied 2), entire season
Canton, 1923 (won 11, tied 1), entire season

Most Consecutive Home Games Won
27 Miami, 1971-74
20 Green Bay, 1929-32
18 Oakland, 1968-70
Dallas, 1979-81

Most Consecutive Home Games Without Defeat
30 Green Bay, 1928-33 (won 27, tied 3)
27 Miami, 1971-74 (won 27)
23 Chi. Bears, 1923-25 (won 19, tied 6)

Most Consecutive Road Games Won
11 L.A. Chargers/San Diego, 1960-61
San Francisco, 1987-88
10 Chi. Bears, 1941-42
Dallas, 1968-69
New Orleans, 1987-88
San Francisco, 1988-89
9 Chi. Bears, 1933-34
Kansas City, 1966-67
Oakland, 1967-68
Oakland, 1974-75
Pittsburgh, 1974-75
Oakland, 1976-77
Washington, 1981-83
San Francisco, 1983-84

Most Consecutive Road Games Without Defeat
13 Chi. Bears, 1941-43 (won 12, tied 1)
12 Green Bay, 1928-30 (won 10, tied 2)
11 L.A. Chargers/San Diego, 1960-61 (won 11)
Los Angeles, 1966-68 (won 10, tied 1)
San Francisco, 1987-88 (won 11)

Most Shutout Games Won or Tied, Season (Since 1932)
7 Chi. Bears, 1932 (won 4, tied 3)
Green Bay, 1932 (won 6, tied 1)
Detroit, 1934 (won 7)
5 Chi. Cardinals, 1934 (won 5)
N.Y. Giants, 1944 (won 5)
Pittsburgh, 1976 (won 5)
4 By many teams

Most Consecutive Shutout Games Won or Tied (Since 1932)
7 Detroit, 1934 (won 7)
3 Chi. Bears, 1932 (tied 3)
Green Bay, 1932 (won 3)
New York, 1935 (won 3)
St. Louis, 1970 (won 3)
Pittsburgh, 1976 (won 3)
2 By many teams

Games Lost

Most Consecutive Games Lost
26 Tampa Bay, 1976-77
19 Chi. Cardinals, 1942-43, 1945
Oakland, 1961-62
18 Houston, 1972-73

Most Consecutive Games Without Victory
26 Tampa Bay, 1976-77 (lost 26)
23 Rochester, 1922-25 (lost 21, tied 2)
Washington, 1960-61 (lost 20, tied 3)
19 Dayton, 1927-29 (lost 18, tied 1)
Chi. Cardinals, 1942-43, 1945 (lost 19)
Oakland, 1961-62 (lost 19)

Most Games Lost, Season
15 New Orleans, 1980
Dallas, 1989
14 Tampa Bay, 1976
San Francisco, 1978
Detroit, 1979
San Francisco, 1979
Baltimore, 1981
New England, 1981
Houston, 1983
Tampa Bay, 1983
Buffalo, 1984
Buffalo, 1985
Tampa Bay, 1985
Tampa Bay, 1986
13 By many teams

Most Consecutive Games Lost, Season
14 Tampa Bay, 1976
New Orleans, 1980
Baltimore, 1981
13 Oakland, 1962
Indianapolis, 1986
12 Tampa Bay, 1977

Most Consecutive Games Lost, Start of Season
14 Tampa Bay, 1976, entire season
New Orleans, 1980
13 Oakland, 1962
Indianapolis, 1986
12 Tampa Bay, 1977

Most Consecutive Games Lost, End of Season
14 Tampa Bay, 1976, entire season
13 Pittsburgh, 1969
11 Philadelphia, 1936
Detroit, 1942, entire season
Houston, 1972

Most Consecutive Games Without Victory, Season
14 Tampa Bay, 1976, entire season
New Orleans, 1980
Baltimore, 1981
13 Washington, 1961
Oakland, 1962
Indianapolis, 1986
12 Dall. Cowboys, 1960, entire season
Tampa Bay, 1977

Most Consecutive Games Without Victory, Start of Season
14 Tampa Bay, 1976, entire season
New Orleans, 1980
13 Washington, 1961
Oakland, 1962
Indianapolis, 1986
12 Dall. Cowboys, 1960, entire season
Tampa Bay, 1977

Most Consecutive Games Without Victory, End of Season
14 Tampa Bay, 1976, entire season
13 Pittsburgh, 1969
12 Dall. Cowboys, 1960, entire season

Most Consecutive Home Games Lost
14 Dallas, 1988-89 (current)
13 Houston, 1972-73
Tampa Bay, 1976-77
11 Oakland, 1961-62
Los Angeles, 1961-63

Most Consecutive Home Games Without Victory
14 Dallas, 1988-89 (lost 14) (current)
13 Houston, 1972-73 (lost 13)
Tampa Bay, 1976-77 (lost 13)
12 Philadelphia, 1936-38 (lost 11, tied 1)

Most Consecutive Road Games Lost
23 Houston, 1981-84
22 Buffalo, 1983-86
19 Tampa Bay, 1983-85

Most Consecutive Road Games Without Victory
23 Houston, 1981-84 (lost 23)
22 Buffalo, 1983-86 (lost 22)
19 Tampa Bay, 1983-85 (lost 19)

Most Shutout Games Lost or Tied, Season (Since 1932)
6 Cincinnati, 1934 (lost 6)
Pittsburgh, 1934 (lost 6)
Philadelphia, 1936 (lost 6)
Tampa Bay, 1977 (lost 6)
5 Boston, 1932 (lost 4, tied 1)
N.Y. Giants, 1932 (lost 4, tied 1)
Boston, 1933 (lost 4, tied 1)
Cincinnati, 1933 (lost 4, tied 1)
Brooklyn, 1934 (lost 5)
Brooklyn, 1942 (lost 5)
Detroit, 1942 (lost 5)
Tampa Bay, 1976 (lost 5)
4 By many teams

Most Consecutive Shutout Games Lost or Tied (Since 1932)
6 Brooklyn, 1942-43 (lost 6)
4 Chi. Bears, 1932 (lost 1, tied 3)
Philadelphia, 1936 (lost 4)
3 Chi. Cardinals, 1934 (lost 3), 1938 (lost 3)
Brooklyn, 1935 (lost 3), 1937 (lost 3)
Oakland, 1981 (lost 3)

Tie Games

Most Tie Games, Season
6 Chi. Bears, 1932
5 Frankford, 1929
4 Chi. Bears, 1924

Orange, 1929
Portsmouth, 1932
Most Consecutive Tie Games
  3 Chi. Bears, 1932
  2 By many teams

Scoring
Most Seasons Leading League
  9 Chi. Bears, 1934-35, 1939, 1941-43, 1946-47, 1956
  6 Green Bay, 1932, 1936-38, 1961-62
     L.A. Rams, 1950-52, 1957, 1967, 1973
  5 Oakland, 1967-69, 1974, 1977
     Dall. Cowboys, 1966, 1968, 1971, 1978, 1980
     San Diego, 1963, 1965, 1981-82, 1985
     San Francisco, 1953, 1965, 1970, 1987, 1989
Most Consecutive Seasons Leading League
  3 Green Bay, 1936-38
     Chi. Bears, 1941-43
     Los Angeles, 1950-52
     Oakland, 1967-69

Points
Most Points, Season
  541 Washington, 1983
  513 Houston, 1961
      Miami, 1984
  479 Dallas, 1983
Fewest Points, Season (Since 1932)
  37 Cincinnati/St. Louis, 1934
  38 Cincinnati, 1933
     Detroit, 1942
  51 Pittsburgh, 1934
     Philadelphia, 1936
Most Points, Game
  72 Washington vs. N.Y. Giants, Nov. 27, 1966
  70 Los Angeles vs. Baltimore, Oct. 22, 1950
  65 Chi. Cardinals vs. N.Y. Bulldogs, Nov. 13, 1949
     Los Angeles vs. Detroit, Oct. 29, 1950
Most Points, Both Teams, Game
  113 Washington (72) vs. N.Y. Giants (41), Nov. 27, 1966
  101 Oakland (52) vs. Houston (49), Dec. 22, 1963
  99 Seattle (51) vs. Kansas City (48), Nov. 27, 1983 (OT)
Fewest Points, Both Teams, Game
  0 In many games. Last time: N.Y. Giants vs. Detroit, Nov. 7, 1943
Most Points, Shutout Victory, Game
  64 Philadelphia vs. Cincinnati, Nov. 6, 1934
  62 Akron vs. Oorang, Oct. 29, 1922
  60 Rock Island vs. Evansville, Oct. 15, 1922
     Chi. Cardinals vs. Rochester, Oct. 7, 1923
Fewest Points, Shutout Victory, Game
  2 Green Bay vs. Chi. Bears, Oct. 16, 1932
    Chi. Bears vs. Green Bay, Sept. 18, 1938
Most Points Overcome to Win Game
  28 San Francisco vs. New Orleans, Dec. 7, 1980 (OT) (trailed 7-35, won 38-35)
  25 St. Louis vs. Tampa Bay, Nov. 8, 1987 (trailed 3-28, won 31-28)
  24 Philadelphia vs. Washington, Oct. 27, 1946 (trailed 0-24, won 28-24)
     Detroit vs. Baltimore, Oct. 20, 1957 (trailed 3-27, won 31-27)
     Philadelphia vs. Chi. Cardinals, Oct. 25, 1959 (trailed 0-24, won 28-24)
     Denver vs. Boston, Oct. 23, 1960 (trailed 0-24, won 31-24)
     Miami vs. New England, Dec. 15, 1974 (trailed 0-24, won 34-27)
     Minnesota vs. San Francisco, Dec. 4, 1977 (trailed 0-24, won 28-27)
     Denver vs. Seattle, Sept. 23, 1979 (trailed 10-34, won 37-34)
     Houston vs. Cincinnati, Sept. 23, 1979 (OT) (trailed 0-24, won 30-27)
     L.A. Raiders vs. San Diego, Nov. 22, 1982 (trailed 0-24, won 28-24)
     L.A. Raiders vs. Denver, Sept. 26, 1988 (OT) (trailed 0-24, won 30-27)
Most Points Overcome to Tie Game
  31 Denver vs. Buffalo, Nov. 27, 1960 (trailed 7-38, tied 38-38)
  28 Los Angeles vs. Philadelphia, Oct. 3, 1948 (trailed 0-28, tied 28-28)
Most Points, Each Half
1st: 49 Green Bay vs. Tampa Bay, Oct. 2, 1983
    48 Buffalo vs. Miami, Sept. 18, 1966
    45 Green Bay vs. Cleveland, Nov. 12, 1967
       Indianapolis vs. Denver, Oct. 31, 1988
2nd: 49 Chi. Bears vs. Philadelphia, Nov. 30, 1941
    48 Chi. Cardinals vs. Baltimore, Oct. 2, 1950
       N.Y. Giants vs. Baltimore, Nov. 19, 1950
    45 Cincinnati vs. Houston, Dec. 17, 1972
Most Points, Both Teams, Each Half
1st: 70 Houston (35) vs. Oakland (35), Dec. 22, 1963
    62 N.Y. Jets (41) vs. Tampa Bay (21), Nov. 17, 1985
    59 St. Louis (31) vs. Philadelphia (28), Dec. 16, 1962
2nd: 65 Washington (38) vs. N.Y. Giants (27), Nov. 27, 1966
    62 L.A. Raiders (31) vs. San Diego (31), Jan. 2, 1983
    58 New England (37) vs. Baltimore (21), Nov. 23, 1980
       N.Y. Jets (37) vs. New England (21), Sept. 21, 1987
Most Points, One Quarter
  41 Green Bay vs. Detroit, Oct. 7, 1945 (second quarter)
     Los Angeles vs. Detroit, Oct. 29, 1950 (third quarter)
  37 Los Angeles vs. Green Bay, Sept. 21, 1980 (second quarter)
  35 Chi. Cardinals vs. Boston, Oct. 24, 1948 (third quarter)
     Green Bay vs. Cleveland, Nov. 12, 1967 (first quarter)
     Green Bay vs. Tampa Bay, Oct. 2, 1983 (second quarter)
Most Points, Both Teams, One Quarter
  49 Oakland (28) vs. Houston (21), Dec. 22, 1963 (second quarter)
  48 Green Bay (41) vs. Detroit (7), Oct. 7, 1945 (second quarter)
     Los Angeles (41) vs. Detroit (7), Oct. 29, 1950 (third quarter)
  47 St. Louis (27) vs. Philadelphia (20), Dec. 13, 1964 (second quarter)
Most Points, Each Quarter
1st: 35 Green Bay vs. Cleveland, Nov. 12, 1967
    31 Buffalo vs. Kansas City, Sept. 13, 1964
    28 By six teams
2nd: 41 Green Bay vs. Detroit, Oct. 7, 1945
    37 Los Angeles vs. Green Bay, Sept. 21, 1980

    35 Green Bay vs. Tampa Bay, Oct. 2, 1983
3rd: 41 Los Angeles vs. Detroit, Oct. 29, 1950
    35 Chi. Cardinals vs. Boston, Oct. 24, 1948
    28 By nine teams
4th: 31 Oakland vs. Denver, Dec. 17, 1960
       Oakland vs. San Diego, Dec. 8, 1963
       Atlanta vs. Green Bay, Sept. 13, 1981
    28 By many teams
Most Points, Both Teams, Each Quarter
1st: 42 Green Bay (35) vs. Cleveland (7), Nov. 12, 1967
    35 Dall. Texans (21) vs. N.Y. Titans (14), Nov. 11, 1962
       Dallas (28) vs. Philadelphia (7), Oct. 19, 1969
       Kansas City (21) vs. Seattle (14), Dec. 11, 1977
    34 Los Angeles (21) vs. Baltimore (13), Oct. 22, 1950
       Oakland (21) vs. Atlanta (13), Nov. 30, 1975
2nd: 49 Oakland (28) vs. Houston (21), Dec. 22, 1963
    48 Green Bay (41) vs. Detroit (7), Oct. 7, 1945
    47 St. Louis (27) vs. Philadelphia (20), Dec. 13, 1964
3rd: 48 Los Angeles (41) vs. Detroit (7), Oct. 29, 1950
    42 Washington (28) vs. Philadelphia (14), Oct. 1, 1955
    41 Green Bay (21) vs. N.Y. Yanks (20), Oct. 8, 1950
4th: 42 Chi. Cardinals (28) vs. Philadelphia (14), Dec. 7, 1947
       Green Bay (28) vs. Chi. Bears (14), Nov. 6, 1955
       N.Y. Jets (28) vs. Boston (14), Oct. 27, 1968
       Pittsburgh (21) vs. Cleveland (21), Oct. 18, 1969
    41 Baltimore (27) vs. New England (14), Sept. 18, 1978
       New England (27) vs. Baltimore (14), Nov. 23, 1980
    40 Chicago (21) vs. Tampa Bay (19), Nov. 19, 1989
Most Consecutive Games Scoring
  274 Cleveland, 1950-71
  218 Dallas, 1970-85
  217 Oakland, 1966-81

Touchdowns
Most Seasons Leading League, Touchdowns
  13 Chi. Bears, 1932, 1934-35, 1939, 1941-44, 1946-48, 1956, 1965
  7 Dall. Cowboys, 1966, 1968, 1971, 1973, 1977-78, 1980
  6 Oakland, 1967-69, 1972, 1974, 1977
     San Diego, 1965, 1979, 1981-82, 1985
Most Consecutive Seasons Leading League, Touchdowns
  4 Chi. Bears, 1941-44
     Los Angeles, 1949-52
  3 Chi. Bears, 1946-48
     Baltimore, 1957-59
     Oakland, 1967-69
  2 By many teams
Most Touchdowns, Season
  70 Miami, 1984
  66 Houston, 1961
  64 Los Angeles, 1950
Fewest Touchdowns, Season (Since 1932)
  3 Cincinnati, 1933
  4 Cincinnati/St. Louis, 1934
  5 Detroit, 1942
Most Touchdowns, Game
  10 Philadelphia vs. Cincinnati, Nov. 6, 1934
     Los Angeles vs. Baltimore, Oct. 22, 1950
     Washington vs. N.Y. Giants, Nov. 27, 1966
  9 Chi. Cardinals vs. Rochester, Oct. 7, 1923
     Chi. Cardinals vs. N.Y. Giants, Oct. 17, 1948
     Chi. Cardinals vs. N.Y. Bulldogs, Nov. 13, 1949
     Los Angeles vs. Detroit, Oct. 29, 1950
     Pittsburgh vs. N.Y. Giants, Nov. 30, 1952
     Chicago vs. San Francisco, Dec. 12, 1965
     Chicago vs. Green Bay, Dec. 7, 1980
  8 By many teams.
Most Touchdowns, Both Teams, Game
  16 Washington (10) vs. N.Y. Giants (6), Nov. 27, 1966
  14 Chi. Cardinals (9) vs. N.Y. Giants (5), Oct. 17, 1948
     Los Angeles (10) vs. Baltimore (4), Oct. 22, 1950
     Houston (7) vs. Oakland (7), Dec. 22, 1963
  13 New Orleans (7) vs. St. Louis (6), Nov. 2, 1969
     Kansas City (7) vs. Seattle (6), Nov. 27, 1983 (OT)
     San Diego (8) vs. Pittsburgh (5), Dec. 8, 1985
     N.Y. Jets (7) vs. Miami (6), Sept. 21, 1986 (OT)
Most Consecutive Games Scoring Touchdowns
  166 Cleveland, 1957-69
  97 Oakland, 1966-73
  96 Kansas City, 1963-70

Points After Touchdown
Most Points After Touchdown, Season
  66 Miami, 1984
  65 Houston, 1961
  62 Washington, 1983
Fewest Points After Touchdown, Season
  2 Chi. Cardinals, 1933
  3 Cincinnati, 1933
     Pittsburgh, 1934
  4 Cincinnati/St. Louis, 1934
Most Points After Touchdown, Game
  10 Los Angeles vs. Baltimore, Oct. 22, 1950
  9 Chi. Cardinals vs. N.Y. Giants, Oct. 17, 1948
     Pittsburgh vs. N.Y. Giants, Nov. 30, 1952
     Washington vs. N.Y. Giants, Nov. 27, 1966
  8 By many teams
Most Points After Touchdown, Both Teams, Game
  14 Chi. Cardinals (9) vs. N.Y. Giants (5), Oct. 17, 1948
     Houston (7) vs. Oakland (7), Dec. 22, 1963
     Washington (9) vs. N.Y. Giants (5), Nov. 27, 1966
  13 Los Angeles (10) vs. Baltimore (3), Oct. 22, 1950
  12 In many games

Field Goals

Most Seasons Leading League, Field Goals
11 Green Bay, 1935-36, 1940-43, 1946-47, 1955, 1972, 1974
7 Washington, 1945, 1956, 1971, 1976-77, 1979, 1982
N.Y. Giants, 1933, 1937, 1939, 1941, 1944, 1959, 1983
5 Portsmouth/Detroit, 1932-33, 1937-38, 1980

Most Consecutive Seasons Leading League, Field Goals
4 Green Bay, 1940-43
3 Cleveland, 1952-54
2 By many teams

Most Field Goals Attempted, Season
49 Los Angeles, 1966
Washington, 1971
48 Green Bay, 1972
47 N.Y. Jets, 1969
Los Angeles, 1973
Washington, 1983

Fewest Field Goals Attempted, Season (Since 1938)
0 Chi. Bears, 1944
2 Cleveland, 1939
Card-Pitt, 1944
Boston, 1946
Chi. Bears, 1947
3 Chi. Bears, 1945
Cleveland, 1945

Most Field Goals Attempted, Game
9 St. Louis vs. Pittsburgh, Sept. 24, 1967
8 Pittsburgh vs. St. Louis, Dec. 2, 1962
Detroit vs. Minnesota, Nov. 13, 1966
N.Y. Jets vs. Buffalo, Nov. 3, 1968
7 By many teams

Most Field Goals Attempted, Both Teams, Game
11 St. Louis (6) vs. Pittsburgh (5), Nov. 13, 1966
Washington (6) vs. Chicago (5), Nov. 14, 1971
Green Bay (6) vs. Detroit (5), Sept. 29, 1974
Washington (6) vs. N.Y. Giants (5), Nov. 14, 1976
10 Denver (5) vs. Boston (5), Nov. 11, 1962
Boston (7) vs. San Diego (3), Sept. 20, 1964
Buffalo (7) vs. Houston (3), Dec. 5, 1965
St. Louis (7) vs. Atlanta (3), Dec. 11, 1966
Boston (7) vs. Buffalo (3), Sept. 24, 1967
Detroit (7) vs. Minnesota (3), Sept. 20, 1971
Washington (7) vs. Houston (3), Oct. 10, 1971
Green Bay (5) vs. St. Louis (5), Dec. 5, 1971
Kansas City (7) vs. Buffalo (3), Dec. 19, 1971
Kansas City (5) vs. San Diego (5), Oct. 29, 1972
Minnesota (6) vs. Chicago (4), Sept. 23, 1973
Cleveland (7) vs. Denver (3), Oct. 19, 1975
Cleveland (5) vs. Denver (5), Oct. 5, 1980
9 In many games

Most Field Goals, Season
35 N.Y. Giants, 1983
34 N.Y. Jets, 1968
33 Green Bay, 1972
Washington, 1983
Pittsburgh, 1985
New Orleans, 1987

Fewest Field Goals, Season (Since 1932)
0 Boston, 1932, 1935
Chi. Cardinals, 1932, 1945
Green Bay, 1932, 1944
N.Y. Giants, 1932
Brooklyn, 1944
Card-Pitt, 1944
Chi. Bears, 1944, 1947
Boston, 1946
Baltimore, 1950
Dallas, 1952

Most Field Goals, Game
7 St. Louis vs. Pittsburgh, Sept. 24, 1967
Minnesota vs. L.A. Rams, Nov. 5, 1989 (OT)
6 Boston vs. Denver, Oct. 4, 1964
Detroit vs. Minnesota, Nov. 13, 1966
N.Y. Jets vs. Buffalo, Nov. 3, 1968
Philadelphia vs. Houston, Nov. 12, 1972
N.Y. Jets vs. New Orleans, Dec. 3, 1972
St. Louis vs. Atlanta, Dec. 9, 1973
N.Y. Giants vs. Seattle, Oct. 18, 1981
San Francisco vs. New Orleans, Oct. 16, 1983
Pittsburgh vs. Denver, Oct. 23, 1988
5 By many teams

Most Field Goals, Both Teams, Game
8 Cleveland (4) vs. St. Louis (4), Sept. 20, 1964
Chicago (5) vs. Philadelphia (3), Oct. 20, 1968
Washington (5) vs. Chicago (3), Nov. 14, 1971
Kansas City (5) vs. Buffalo (3), Dec. 19, 1971
Detroit (4) vs. Green Bay (4), Sept. 29, 1974
Cleveland (5) vs. Denver (3), Oct. 19, 1975
New England (4) vs. San Diego (4), Nov. 9, 1975
San Francisco (6) vs. New Orleans (2), Oct. 16, 1983
Seattle (5) vs. L.A. Raiders (3), Dec. 18, 1988
7 In many games

Most Consecutive Games Scoring Field Goals
31 Minnesota, 1968-70
22 San Francisco, 1988-89
21 San Francisco, 1970-72
New Orleans, 1987-88

Safeties

Most Safeties, Season
4 Detroit, 1962
3 By many teams

Most Safeties, Game
3 L.A. Rams vs. N.Y. Giants, Sept. 30, 1984
2 Cincinnati vs. Chi. Cardinals, Nov. 19, 1933
Detroit vs. Brooklyn, Dec. 1, 1935
N.Y. Giants vs. Pittsburgh, Sept. 17, 1950
N.Y. Giants vs. Washington, Nov. 5, 1961
Chicago vs. Pittsburgh, Nov. 9, 1969
Dallas vs. Philadelphia, Nov. 19, 1972
Los Angeles vs. Green Bay, Oct. 21, 1973
Oakland vs. San Diego, Oct. 26, 1975
Denver vs. Seattle, Jan. 2, 1983
New Orleans vs. Cleveland, Sept. 13, 1987
Buffalo vs. Denver, Nov. 8, 1987

Most Safeties, Both Teams, Game
3 L.A. Rams (3) vs. N.Y. Giants (0), Sept. 30, 1984
2 Chi. Bears (1) vs. San Francisco (1), Oct. 19, 1952
Cincinnati (1) vs. Los Angeles (1), Oct. 22, 1972
Atlanta (1) vs. Detroit (1), Oct. 5, 1980
Houston (1) vs. Philadelphia (1), Oct. 2, 1988
(Also see previous record)

First Downs

Most Seasons Leading League
9 Chi. Bears, 1935, 1939, 1941, 1943, 1945, 1947-49, 1955
7 San Diego, 1965, 1969, 1980-83, 1985
6 L.A. Rams, 1946, 1950-51, 1954, 1957, 1973

Most Consecutive Seasons Leading League
4 San Diego, 1980-83
3 Chi. Bears, 1947-49
2 By many teams

Most First Downs, Season
387 Miami, 1984
380 San Diego, 1985
379 San Diego, 1981

Fewest First Downs, Season
51 Cincinnati, 1933
64 Pittsburgh, 1935
67 Philadelphia, 1937

Most First Downs, Game
39 N.Y. Jets vs. Miami, Nov. 27, 1988
38 Los Angeles vs. N.Y. Giants, Nov. 13, 1966
37 Green Bay vs. Philadelphia, Nov. 11, 1962

Fewest First Downs, Game
0 N.Y. Giants vs. Green Bay, Oct. 1, 1933
Pittsburgh vs. Boston, Oct. 29, 1933
Philadelphia vs. Detroit, Sept. 20, 1935
N.Y. Giants vs. Washington, Sept. 27, 1942
Denver vs. Houston, Sept. 3, 1966

Most First Downs, Both Teams, Game
62 San Diego (32) vs. Seattle (30), Sept. 15, 1985
59 Miami (31) vs. Buffalo (28), Oct. 9, 1983 (OT)
Seattle (33) vs. Kansas City (26), Nov. 27, 1983 (OT)
N.Y. Jets (32) vs. Miami (27), Sept. 21, 1986 (OT)
N.Y. Jets (39) vs. Miami (20), Nov. 27, 1988
58 Los Angeles (30) vs. Chi. Bears (28), Oct. 24, 1954
Denver (34) vs. Kansas City (24), Nov. 18, 1974
Atlanta (35) vs. New Orleans (23), Sept. 2, 1979 (OT)
Pittsburgh (36) vs. Cleveland (22), Nov. 25, 1979 (OT)
San Diego (34) vs. Miami (24), Nov. 18, 1984 (OT)
Cincinnati (32) vs. San Diego (26), Sept. 22, 1985

Fewest First Downs, Both Teams, Game
5 N.Y. Giants (0) vs. Green Bay (5), Oct. 1, 1933

Most First Downs, Rushing, Season
181 New England, 1978
177 Los Angeles, 1973
176 Chicago, 1985

Fewest First Downs, Rushing, Season
36 Cleveland, 1942
Boston, 1944
39 Brooklyn, 1943
40 Philadelphia, 1940
Detroit, 1945

Most First Downs, Rushing, Game
25 Philadelphia vs. Washington, Dec. 2, 1951
21 Cleveland vs. Philadelphia, Dec. 13, 1959
Los Angeles vs. New Orleans, Nov. 25, 1973
Pittsburgh vs. Kansas City, Nov. 7, 1976
New England vs. Denver, Nov. 28, 1976
Oakland vs. Green Bay, Sept. 17, 1978
20 By eight teams

Fewest First Downs, Rushing, Game
0 By many teams. Last time: Tampa Bay vs. Washington, Oct. 22, 1989

Most First Downs, Passing, Season
259 San Diego, 1985
250 Miami, 1986
244 San Diego, 1980

Fewest First Downs, Passing, Season
18 Pittsburgh, 1941
23 Brooklyn, 1942
N.Y. Giants, 1944
24 N.Y. Giants, 1943

Most First Downs, Passing, Game
29 N.Y. Giants vs. Cincinnati, Oct. 13, 1985
27 San Diego vs. Seattle, Sept. 15, 1985
26 Miami vs. Cleveland, Dec. 12, 1988

Fewest First Downs, Passing, Game
0 By many teams. Last time: Houston vs. Kansas City, Oct. 9, 1988

Most First Downs, Penalty, Season
42 Chicago, 1987
41 Denver, 1986
39 Seattle, 1978

Fewest First Downs, Penalty, Season
  2 Brooklyn, 1940
  4 Chi. Cardinals, 1940
     N.Y. Giants, 1942, 1944
     Washington, 1944
     Cleveland, 1952
     Kansas City, 1969
  5 Brooklyn, 1939
     Chi. Bears, 1939
     Detroit, 1953
     Los Angeles, 1953
     Houston, 1982
Most First Downs, Penalty, Game
  11 Denver vs. Houston, Oct. 6, 1985
   9 Chi. Bears vs. Cleveland, Nov. 25, 1951
      Baltimore vs. Pittsburgh, Oct. 30, 1977
      N.Y. Jets vs. Houston, Sept. 18, 1988
   8 Philadelphia vs. Detroit, Dec. 2, 1979
      Cincinnati vs. N.Y. Jets, Oct. 6, 1985
      Buffalo vs. Houston, Sept. 20, 1987
Fewest First Downs, Penalty, Game
   0 By many teams

Net Yards Gained Rushing and Passing
Most Seasons Leading League
  12 Chi. Bears, 1932, 1934-35, 1939, 1941-44, 1947, 1949, 1955-56
   7 San Diego, 1963, 1965, 1980-83, 1985
   6 L.A. Rams, 1946, 1950-51, 1954, 1957, 1973
      Baltimore, 1958-60, 1964, 1967, 1976
      Dall. Cowboys, 1966, 1968-69, 1971, 1974, 1977
Most Consecutive Seasons Leading League
   4 Chi. Bears, 1941-44
      San Diego, 1980-83
   3 Baltimore, 1958-60
      Houston, 1960-62
      Oakland, 1968-70
   2 By many teams
Most Yards Gained, Season
  6,936 Miami, 1984
  6,744 San Diego, 1981
  6,535 San Diego, 1985
Fewest Yards Gained, Season
  1,150 Cincinnati, 1933
  1,443 Chi. Cardinals, 1934
  1,486 Chi. Cardinals, 1933
Most Yards Gained, Game
  735 Los Angeles vs. N.Y. Yanks, Sept. 28, 1951
  683 Pittsburgh vs. Chi. Cardinals, Dec. 13, 1958
  682 Chi. Bears vs. N.Y. Giants, Nov. 14, 1943
Fewest Yards Gained, Game
   -7 Seattle vs. Los Angeles, Nov. 4, 1979
   -5 Denver vs. Oakland, Sept. 10, 1967
   14 Chi. Cardinals vs. Detroit, Sept. 15, 1940
Most Yards Gained, Both Teams, Game
  1,133 Los Angeles (636) vs. N.Y. Yanks (497), Nov. 19, 1950
  1,102 San Diego (661) vs. Cincinnati (441), Dec. 20, 1982
  1,087 St. Louis (589) vs. Philadelphia (498), Dec. 16, 1962
Fewest Yards Gained, Both Teams, Game
   30 Chi. Cardinals (14) vs. Detroit (16), Sept. 15, 1940
  136 Chi. Cardinals (50) vs. Green Bay (86), Nov. 18, 1934
  154 N.Y. Giants (51) vs. Washington (103), Dec. 11, 1960
Most Consecutive Games, 400 or More Yards Gained
  11 San Diego, 1982-83
   6 Houston, 1961-62
      San Diego, 1981
      San Francisco, 1987
   5 Chi. Bears, 1947
      Philadelphia, 1953
      Chi. Bears, 1955
      Oakland, 1968
      New England, 1981
      Cincinnati, 1986
Most Consecutive Games, 300 or More Yards Gained
  29 Los Angeles, 1949-51
  26 Miami, 1983-85
  19 Cleveland, 1978-79
      San Diego, 1980-82
      San Francisco, 1988-89

Rushing
Most Seasons Leading League
  16 Chi. Bears, 1932, 1934-35, 1939-42, 1951, 1955-56, 1968, 1977, 1983-86
   6 Cleveland, 1958-59, 1963, 1965-67
   5 Buffalo, 1962, 1964, 1973, 1975, 1982
Most Consecutive Seasons Leading League
   4 Chi. Bears, 1939-42, 1983-86
   3 Detroit, 1936-38
      San Francisco, 1952-54
      Cleveland, 1965-67
   2 By many teams
Most Rushing Attempts, Season
  681 Oakland, 1977
  674 Chicago, 1984
  671 New England, 1978
Fewest Rushing Attempts, Season
  211 Philadelphia, 1982
  219 San Francisco, 1982
  225 Houston, 1982
Most Rushing Attempts, Game
  72 Chi. Bears vs. Brooklyn, Oct. 20, 1935
  70 Chi. Cardinals vs. Green Bay, Dec. 5, 1948
  69 Chi. Cardinals vs. Green Bay, Dec. 6, 1936

Kansas City vs. Cincinnati, Sept. 3, 1978
Fewest Rushing Attempts, Game
   6 Chi. Cardinals vs. Boston, Oct. 29, 1933
   7 Oakland vs. Buffalo, Oct. 15, 1963
      Houston vs. N.Y. Giants, Dec. 8, 1985
   8 Denver vs. Oakland, Dec. 17, 1960
      Buffalo vs. St. Louis, Sept. 9, 1984
Most Rushing Attempts, Both Teams, Game
  108 Chi. Cardinals (70) vs. Green Bay (38), Dec. 5, 1948
  105 Oakland (62) vs. Atlanta (43), Nov. 30, 1975 (OT)
  103 Kansas City (53) vs. San Diego (50), Nov. 12, 1978 (OT)
Fewest Rushing Attempts, Both Teams, Game
   36 Cincinnati (16) vs. Chi. Bears (20), Sept. 30, 1934
   37 Atlanta (18) vs. San Francisco (19), Oct. 6, 1985
   38 N.Y. Jets (13) vs. Buffalo (25), Nov. 8, 1964

Yards Gained
Most Yards Gained Rushing, Season
  3,165 New England, 1978
  3,088 Buffalo, 1973
  2,986 Kansas City, 1978
Fewest Yards Gained Rushing, Season
  298 Philadelphia, 1940
  467 Detroit, 1946
  471 Boston, 1944
Most Yards Gained Rushing, Game
  426 Detroit vs. Pittsburgh, Nov. 4, 1934
  423 N.Y. Giants vs. Baltimore, Nov. 19, 1950
  420 Boston vs. N.Y. Giants, Oct. 8, 1933
Fewest Yards Gained Rushing, Game
  -53 Detroit vs. Chi. Cardinals, Oct. 17, 1943
  -36 Philadelphia vs. Chi. Bears, Nov. 19, 1939
  -33 Phil-Pitt vs. Brooklyn, Oct. 2, 1943
Most Yards Gained Rushing, Both Teams, Game
  595 Los Angeles (371) vs. N.Y. Yanks (224), Nov. 18, 1951
  574 Chi. Bears (396) vs. Pittsburgh (178), Oct. 10, 1934
  557 Chi. Bears (406) vs. Green Bay (151), Nov. 6, 1955
Fewest Yards Gained Rushing, Both Teams, Game
  -15 Detroit (-53) vs. Chi. Cardinals (38), Oct. 17, 1943
    4 Detroit (-10) vs. Chi. Cardinals (14), Sept. 15, 1940
   63 Chi. Cardinals (-1) vs. N.Y. Giants (64), Oct. 18, 1953

Average Gain
Highest Average Gain, Rushing, Season
  5.74 Cleveland, 1963
  5.65 San Francisco, 1954
  5.56 San Diego, 1963
Lowest Average Gain, Rushing, Season
  0.94 Philadelphia, 1940
  1.45 Boston, 1944
  1.55 Pittsburgh, 1935

Touchdowns
Most Touchdowns, Rushing, Season
  36 Green Bay, 1962
  33 Pittsburgh, 1976
  30 Chi. Bears, 1941
      New England, 1978
      Washington, 1983
Fewest Touchdowns, Rushing, Season
   1 Brooklyn, 1934
   2 Chi. Cardinals, 1933
      Cincinnati, 1933
      Pittsburgh, 1934
      Philadelphia, 1935
      Philadelphia, 1936
      Philadelphia, 1937
      Philadelphia, 1938
      Pittsburgh, 1940
      Philadelphia, 1972
   3 By many teams
Most Touchdowns, Rushing, Game
   7 Los Angeles vs. Atlanta, Dec. 4, 1976
   6 By many teams
Most Touchdowns, Rushing, Both Teams, Game
   8 Los Angeles (6) vs. N.Y. Yanks (2), Nov. 18, 1951
      Cleveland (6) vs. Los Angeles (2), Nov. 24, 1957
   7 In many games

Passing
Attempts
Most Passes Attempted, Season
  709 Minnesota, 1981
  662 San Diego, 1984
  645 Miami, 1986
Fewest Passes Attempted, Season
  102 Cincinnati, 1933
  106 Boston, 1933
  120 Detroit, 1937
Most Passes Attempted, Game
  68 Houston vs. Buffalo, Nov 1, 1964
  66 Atlanta vs. Detroit, Dec. 24, 1989
  65 San Diego vs. Kansas City, Oct. 19, 1986
Fewest Passes Attempted, Game
   0 Green Bay vs. Portsmouth, Oct. 8, 1933
      Detroit vs. Cleveland, Sept. 10, 1937
      Pittsburgh vs. Brooklyn, Nov. 16, 1941
      Pittsburgh vs. Los Angeles, Nov. 13, 1949
      Cleveland vs. Philadelphia, Dec. 3, 1950
Most Passes Attempted, Both Teams, Game
  104 Miami (55) vs. N.Y. Jets (49), Oct. 18, 1987 (OT)
  102 San Francisco (57) vs. Atlanta (45), Oct. 6, 1985

100 Tampa Bay (54) vs. Kansas City (46), Oct. 28, 1984
    San Francisco (60) vs. Washington (40), Nov. 17, 1986
    Philadelphia (62) vs. Chicago (38), Oct. 2, 1989
Fewest Passes Attempted, Both Teams, Game
    4 Chi. Cardinals (1) vs. Detroit (3), Nov. 3, 1935
      Detroit (0) vs. Cleveland (4), Sept. 10, 1937
    6 Chi. Cardinals (2) vs. Detroit (4), Sept. 15, 1940
    8 Brooklyn (2) vs. Philadelphia (6), Oct. 1, 1939

Completions
Most Passes Completed, Season
    401 San Diego, 1984
    392 Miami, 1986
    386 San Diego, 1985
Fewest Passes Completed, Season
    25 Cincinnati, 1933
    33 Boston, 1933
    34 Chi. Cardinals, 1934
      Detroit, 1934
Most Passes Completed, Game
    42 N.Y. Jets vs. San Francisco, Sept. 21, 1980
    40 Cincinnati vs. San Diego, Dec. 20, 1982
      Dallas vs. Detroit, Sept. 15, 1985
      N.Y. Giants vs. Cincinnati, Oct. 13, 1985
    39 Miami vs. Buffalo, Nov. 16, 1986
Fewest Passes Completed, Game
    0 By many teams. Last time: Buffalo vs. N.Y. Jets, Sept. 29, 1974
Most Passes Completed, Both Teams, Game
    68 San Francisco (37) vs. Atlanta (31), Oct. 6, 1985
    66 Cincinnati (40) vs. San Diego (26), Dec. 20, 1982
    65 San Diego (33) vs. San Francisco (32), Dec. 11, 1982
      San Diego (37) vs. Miami (28), Nov. 18, 1984 (OT)
Fewest Passes Completed, Both Teams, Game
    1 Chi. Cardinals (0) vs. Philadelphia (1), Nov. 8, 1936
      Detroit (0) vs. Cleveland (1), Sept. 10, 1937
      Chi. Cardinals (0) vs. Detroit (1), Sept. 15, 1940
      Brooklyn (0) vs. Pittsburgh (1), Nov. 29, 1942
    2 Chi. Cardinals (0) vs. Detroit (2), Nov. 3, 1935
      Buffalo (0) vs. N.Y. Jets (2), Sept. 29, 1974
    3 Brooklyn (1) vs. Philadelphia (2), Oct. 1, 1939

Yards Gained
Most Seasons Leading League, Passing Yardage
    10 San Diego, 1965, 1968, 1971, 1978-83, 1985
    8 Chi. Bears, 1932, 1939, 1941, 1943, 1945, 1949, 1954, 1964
      Washington, 1938, 1940, 1944, 1947-48, 1967, 1974, 1989
    6 Clev. Browns, 1951, 1953-55, 1959-60
      Dall. Texans/Kansas City, 1962, 1964, 1966-69
      San Francisco, 1952, 1957-58, 1965, 1981, 1983
Most Consecutive Seasons Leading League, Passing Yardage
    6 San Diego, 1978-83
    4 Green Bay, 1934-37
    3 Miami, 1986-88
Most Yards Gained, Passing, Season
    5,018 Miami, 1984
    4,870 San Diego, 1985
    4,779 Miami, 1986
Fewest Yards Gained, Passing, Season
    302 Chi. Cardinals, 1934
    357 Cincinnati, 1933
    459 Boston, 1934
Most Yards Gained, Passing, Game
    554 Los Angeles vs. N.Y. Yanks, Sept. 28, 1951
    530 Minnesota vs. Baltimore, Sept. 28, 1969
    521 Miami vs. N.Y. Jets, Oct. 23, 1988
Fewest Yards Gained, Passing, Game
    −53 Denver vs. Oakland, Sept. 10, 1967
    −52 Cincinnati vs. Houston, Oct. 31, 1971
    −39 Atlanta vs. San Francisco, Oct. 23, 1976
Most Yards Gained, Passing, Both Teams, Game
    884 N.Y. Jets (449) vs. Miami (435), Sept. 21, 1986 (OT)
    883 San Diego (486) vs. Cincinnati (397), Dec. 20, 1982
    849 Minnesota (471) vs. Washington (378), Nov. 2, 1986 (OT)
Fewest Yards Gained, Passing, Both Teams, Game
    −11 Green Bay (−10) vs. Dallas (−1), Oct. 24, 1965
    1 Chi. Cardinals (0) vs. Philadelphia (1), Nov. 8, 1936
    7 Brooklyn (0) vs. Pittsburgh (7), Nov. 29, 1942

Times Sacked
Most Seasons Leading League, Fewest Times Sacked
    9 Miami, 1973, 1982-89
    4 San Diego, 1963-64, 1967-68
      San Francisco, 1964-65, 1970-71
    3 N.Y. Jets, 1965-66, 1968
      Houston, 1961-62, 1978
      St. Louis, 1974-76
Most Consecutive Seasons Leading League, Fewest Times Sacked
    8 Miami, 1982-89
    3 St. Louis, 1974-76
    2 By many teams
Most Times Sacked, Season
    104 Philadelphia, 1986
    72 Philadelphia, 1987
    70 Atlanta, 1968
Fewest Times Sacked, Season
    7 Miami, 1988
    8 San Francisco, 1970
      St. Louis, 1975
    9 N.Y. Jets, 1966
Most Times Sacked, Game
    12 Pittsburgh vs. Dallas, Nov. 20, 1966
      Baltimore vs. St. Louis, Oct. 26, 1980
      Detroit vs. Chicago, Dec. 16, 1984

Houston vs. Dallas, Sept. 29, 1985
    11 St. Louis vs. N.Y. Giants, Nov. 1, 1964
      Los Angeles vs. Baltimore, Nov. 22, 1964
      Denver vs. Buffalo, Dec. 13, 1964
      Green Bay vs. Detroit, Nov. 7, 1965
      Buffalo vs. Oakland, Oct. 15, 1967
      Denver vs. Oakland, Nov. 5, 1967
      Atlanta vs. St. Louis, Nov. 24, 1968
      Detroit vs. Dallas, Oct. 6, 1975
      Philadelphia vs. St. Louis, Dec. 18, 1983
      Cleveland vs. Kansas City, Sept. 30, 1984
      Minnesota vs. Chicago, Oct. 28, 1984
      Atlanta vs. Cleveland, Nov. 18, 1984
      Dallas vs. San Diego, Nov. 16, 1986
      Philadelphia vs. Detroit, Nov. 16, 1986
      Philadelphia vs. L.A. Raiders, Nov. 30, 1986 (OT)
      L.A. Raiders vs. Seattle, Dec. 8, 1986
      N.Y. Jets vs. Dallas, Oct. 4, 1987
      Philadelphia vs. Chicago, Oct. 4, 1987
    10 By many teams
Most Times Sacked, Both Teams, Game
    18 Green Bay (10) vs. San Diego (8), Sept. 24, 1978
    17 Buffalo (10) vs. N.Y. Titans (7), Nov. 23, 1961
      Pittsburgh (12) vs. Dallas (5), Nov. 20, 1966
      Atlanta (9) vs. Philadelphia (8), Dec. 16, 1984
      Philadelphia (11) vs. L.A. Raiders (6), Nov. 30, 1986 (OT)
    16 Los Angeles (11) vs. Baltimore (5), Nov. 22, 1964
      Buffalo (11) vs. Oakland (5), Oct. 15, 1967

Completion Percentage
Most Seasons Leading League, Completion Percentage
    11 Washington, 1937, 1939-40, 1942-45, 1947-48, 1969-70
    8 San Francisco, 1952, 1957-58, 1965, 1981, 1983, 1987, 1989
    7 Green Bay, 1936, 1941, 1961-62, 1964, 1966, 1968
Most Consecutive Seasons Leading League, Completion Percentage
    4 Washington, 1942-45
      Kansas City, 1966-69
    3 Cleveland, 1953-55
    2 By many teams
Highest Completion Percentage, Season
    70.65 Cincinnati, 1982 (310-219)
    70.19 San Francisco, 1989 (483-339)
    64.27 San Francisco, 1987 (501-322)
Lowest Completion Percentage, Season
    22.9 Philadelphia, 1936 (170-39)
    24.5 Cincinnati, 1933 (102-25)
    25.0 Pittsburgh, 1941 (168-42)

Touchdowns
Most Touchdowns, Passing, Season
    49 Miami, 1984
    48 Houston, 1961
    46 Miami, 1986
Fewest Touchdowns, Passing, Season
    0 Cincinnati, 1933
      Pittsburgh, 1945
    1 Boston, 1932
      Boston, 1933
      Chi. Cardinals, 1934
      Cincinnati/St. Louis, 1934
      Detroit, 1942
    2 Chi. Cardinals, 1932
      Stapleton, 1932
      Chi. Cardinals, 1935
      Brooklyn, 1936
      Pittsburgh, 1942
Most Touchdowns, Passing, Game
    7 Chi. Bears vs. N.Y. Giants, Nov. 14, 1943
      Philadelphia vs. Washington, Oct. 17, 1954
      Houston vs. N.Y. Titans, Nov. 19, 1961
      Houston vs. N.Y. Titans, Oct. 14, 1962
      N.Y. Giants vs. Washington, Oct. 28, 1962
      Minnesota vs. Baltimore, Sept. 28, 1969
      San Diego vs. Oakland, Nov. 22, 1981
    6 By many teams.
Most Touchdowns, Passing, Both Teams, Game
    12 New Orleans (6) vs. St. Louis (6), Nov. 2, 1969
    11 N.Y. Giants (7) vs. Washington (4), Oct. 28, 1962
      Oakland (6) vs. Houston (5), Dec. 22, 1963
    10 Miami (6) vs. N.Y. Jets (4), Sept. 21, 1986 (OT)

Passes Had Intercepted
Most Passes Had Intercepted, Season
    48 Houston, 1962
    45 Denver, 1961
    41 Card-Pitt, 1944
Fewest Passes Had Intercepted, Season
    5 Cleveland, 1960
      Green Bay, 1966
    6 Green Bay, 1964
      St. Louis, 1982
    7 Los Angeles, 1969
Most Passes Had Intercepted, Game
    9 Detroit vs. Green Bay, Oct. 24, 1943
      Pittsburgh vs. Philadelphia, Dec. 12, 1965
    8 Green Bay vs. N.Y. Giants, Nov. 21, 1948
      Chi. Cardinals vs. Philadelphia, Sept. 24, 1950
      N.Y. Yanks vs. N.Y. Giants, Dec. 16, 1951
      Denver vs. Houston, Dec. 2, 1962
      Chi. Bears vs. Detroit, Sept. 22, 1968
      Baltimore vs. N.Y. Jets, Sept. 23, 1973
    7 By many teams. Last time: Green Bay vs. New Orleans, Sept. 14, 1986

Most Passes Had Intercepted, Both Teams, Game
```
13  Denver (8) vs. Houston (5), Dec. 2, 1962
11  Philadelphia (7) vs. Boston (4), Nov. 3, 1935
    Boston (6) vs. Pittsburgh (5), Dec. 1, 1935
    Cleveland (7) vs. Green Bay (4), Oct. 30, 1938
    Green Bay (7) vs. Detroit (4), Oct. 20, 1940
    Detroit (7) vs. Chi. Bears (4), Nov. 22, 1942
    Detroit (7) vs. Cleveland (4), Nov. 26, 1944
    Chi. Cardinals (8) vs. Philadelphia (3), Sept. 24, 1950
    Washington (7) vs. N.Y. Giants (4), Dec. 8, 1963
    Pittsburgh (9) vs. Philadelphia (2), Dec 12, 1965
10  In many games
```

Punting
Most Seasons Leading League (Average Distance)
```
 7  Denver, 1962-64, 1966-67, 1982, 1988
 6  Washington, 1940-43, 1945, 1958
    Kansas City, 1968, 1971-73, 1979, 1984
 4  L.A. Rams, 1946, 1949, 1955-56
    Baltimore/Indianapolis, 1966, 1969, 1983, 1985
```
Most Consecutive Seasons Leading League (Average Distance)
```
 4  Washington, 1940-43
 3  Cleveland, 1950-52
    Denver, 1962-64
    Kansas City, 1971-73
```
Most Punts, Season
```
114  Chicago, 1981
113  Boston, 1934
     Brooklyn, 1934
112  Boston, 1935
```
Fewest Punts, Season
```
23  San Diego, 1982
31  Cincinnati, 1982
32  Chi. Bears, 1941
```
Most Punts, Game
```
17  Chi. Bears vs. Green Bay, Oct. 22, 1933
    Cincinnati vs. Pittsburgh, Oct. 22, 1933
16  Cincinnati vs. Portsmouth, Sept. 17, 1933
    Chi. Cardinals vs. Chi. Bears, Nov. 30, 1933; vs. Detroit, Sept. 15, 1940
```
Fewest Punts, Game
```
 0  By many teams. Last time: Green Bay vs. Chicago, Dec. 17, 1989
```
Most Punts, Both Teams, Game
```
31  Chi. Bears (17) vs. Green Bay (14), Oct. 22, 1933
    Cincinnati (17), vs. Pittsburgh (14), Oct. 22, 1933
29  Chi. Cardinals (15) vs. Cincinnati (14), Nov. 12, 1933
    Chi. Cardinals (16) vs. Chi. Bears (13), Nov. 30, 1933
    Chi. Cardinals (16) vs. Detroit (13), Sept. 15, 1940
```
Fewest Punts, Both Teams, Game
```
 1  Dall. Cowboys (0) vs. Cleveland (1), Dec. 3, 1961
    Chicago (0) vs. Detroit (1), Oct. 1, 1972
    San Francisco (0) vs. N.Y. Giants (1), Oct. 15, 1972
    Green Bay (0) vs. Buffalo (1), Dec. 5, 1982
    Miami (0) vs. Buffalo (1), Oct. 12, 1986
    Green Bay (0) vs. Chicago (1), Dec. 17, 1989
 2  In many games
```

Average Yardage
Highest Average Distance, Punting, Season
```
47.6  Detroit, 1961 (56-2,664)
47.0  Pittsburgh, 1961 (73-3,431)
46.9  Pittsburgh, 1953 (80-3,752)
```
Lowest Average Distance, Punting, Season
```
32.7  Card-Pitt, 1944 (60-1,964)
33.8  Cincinnati, 1986 (59-1,996)
33.9  Detroit, 1969 (74-2,510)
```

Punt Returns
Most Seasons Leading League (Average Return)
```
 8  Detroit, 1943-45, 1951-52, 1962, 1966, 1969
 7  Chi. Cardinals/St. Louis, 1948-49, 1955-56, 1959, 1986-87
 5  Cleveland, 1958, 1960, 1964-65, 1967
    Green Bay, 1950, 1953-54, 1961, 1972
    Dall. Texans/Kansas City, 1960, 1968, 1970, 1979-80
```
Most Consecutive Seasons Leading League (Average Return)
```
 3  Detroit, 1943-45
 2  By many teams
```
Most Punt Returns, Season
```
71  Pittsburgh, 1976
    Tampa Bay, 1979
    L.A. Raiders, 1985
67  Pittsburgh, 1974
    Los Angeles, 1978
    L.A. Raiders, 1984
65  San Francisco, 1976
```
Fewest Punt Returns, Season
```
12  Baltimore, 1981
    San Diego, 1982
14  Los Angeles, 1961
    Philadelphia, 1962
    Baltimore, 1982
15  Houston, 1960
    Washington, 1960
    Oakland, 1961
    N.Y. Giants, 1969
    Philadelphia, 1973
    Kansas City, 1982
```
Most Punt Returns, Game
```
12  Philadelphia vs. Cleveland, Dec. 3, 1950
11  Chi. Bears vs. Chi. Cardinals, Oct. 8, 1950
    Washington vs. Tampa Bay, Oct. 9, 1977
10  Philadelphia vs. N.Y. Giants, Nov. 26, 1950
    Philadelphia vs. Tampa Bay, Sept. 18, 1977
```

```
    Pittsburgh vs. Buffalo, Dec. 16, 1979
    Washington vs. New Orleans, Dec. 26, 1982
```
Most Punt Returns, Both Teams, Game
```
17  Philadelphia (12) vs. Cleveland (5), Dec. 3, 1950
16  N.Y. Giants (9) vs. Philadelphia (7), Dec. 12, 1954
    Washington (11) vs. Tampa Bay (5), Oct. 9, 1977
15  Detroit (8) vs. Cleveland (7), Sept. 27, 1942
    Los Angeles (8) vs. Baltimore (7), Nov. 27, 1966
    Pittsburgh (8) vs. Houston (7), Dec. 1, 1974
    Philadelphia (10) vs. Tampa Bay (5), Sept. 18, 1977
    Baltimore (9) vs. Kansas City (6), Sept. 2, 1979
    Washington (10) vs. New Orleans (5), Dec. 26, 1982
    L.A. Raiders (8) vs. Cleveland (7), Nov. 16, 1986
```

Fair Catches
Most Fair Catches, Season
```
34  Baltimore, 1971
32  San Diego, 1969
30  St. Louis, 1967
    Minnesota, 1971
```
Fewest Fair Catches, Season
```
 0  San Diego, 1975
    New England, 1976
    Tampa Bay, 1976
    Pittsburgh, 1977
    Dallas, 1982
 1  Cleveland, 1974
    San Francisco, 1975
    Kansas City, 1976
    St. Louis, 1976
    San Diego, 1976
    L.A. Rams, 1982
    St. Louis, 1982
    Tampa Bay, 1982
 2  By many teams
```
Most Fair Catches, Game
```
 7  Minnesota vs. Dallas, Sept. 25, 1966
    Detroit vs. Chicago, Nov. 21, 1976
    Philadelphia vs. Buffalo, Dec. 27, 1987
 6  By many teams
```

Yards Gained
Most Yards, Punt Returns, Season
```
785  L.A. Raiders, 1985
781  Chi. Bears, 1948
774  Pittsburgh, 1974
```
Fewest Yards, Punt Returns, Season
```
27  St. Louis, 1965
35  N.Y. Giants, 1965
37  New England, 1972
```
Most Yards, Punt Returns, Game
```
231  Detroit vs. San Francisco, Oct. 6, 1963
225  Oakland vs. Buffalo, Sept. 15, 1968
219  Los Angeles vs. Atlanta, Oct. 11, 1981
```
Most Yards, Punt Returns, Both Teams, Game
```
282  Los Angeles (219) vs. Atlanta (63), Oct. 11, 1981
245  Detroit (231) vs. San Francisco (14), Oct. 6, 1963
244  Oakland (225) vs. Buffalo (19), Sept. 15, 1968
```

Average Yards Returning Punts
Highest Average, Punt Returns, Season
```
20.2  Chi. Bears, 1941 (27-546)
19.1  Chi. Cardinals, 1948 (35-669)
18.2  Chi. Cardinals, 1949 (30-546)
```
Lowest Average, Punt Returns, Season
```
1.2  St. Louis, 1965 (23-27)
1.5  N.Y. Giants, 1965 (24-35)
1.7  Washington, 1970 (27-45)
```

Touchdowns Returning Punts
Most Touchdowns, Punt Returns, Season
```
 5  Chi. Cardinals, 1959
 4  Chi. Cardinals, 1948
    Detroit, 1951
    N.Y. Giants, 1951
    Denver, 1976
 3  Washington, 1941
    Detroit, 1952
    Pittsburgh, 1952
    Houston, 1975
    Los Angeles, 1981
```
Most Touchdowns, Punt Returns, Game
```
 2  Detroit vs. Los Angeles, Oct. 14, 1951
    Detroit vs. Green Bay, Nov. 22, 1951
    Chi. Cardinals vs. Pittsburgh, Nov. 1, 1959
    Chi. Cardinals vs. N.Y. Giants, Nov. 22, 1959
    N.Y. Titans vs. Denver, Sept. 24, 1961
    Denver vs. Cleveland, Sept. 26, 1976
    Los Angeles vs. Atlanta, Oct. 11, 1981
    St. Louis vs. Tampa Bay, Dec. 21, 1986
```
Most Touchdowns, Punt Returns, Both Teams, Game
```
 2  Philadelphia (1) vs. Washington (1), Nov. 9, 1952
    Kansas City (1) vs. Buffalo (1), Sept. 11, 1966
    Baltimore (1) vs. New England (1), Nov. 18, 1979
    L.A. Raiders (1) vs. Philadelphia (1), Nov. 30, 1986 (OT)
    (Also see previous record)
```

Kickoff Returns
Most Seasons Leading League (Average Return)
```
 7  Washington, 1942, 1947, 1962-63, 1973-74, 1981
 6  Chicago Bears, 1943, 1948, 1958, 1966, 1972, 1985
 5  N.Y. Giants, 1944, 1946, 1949, 1951, 1953
```

Most Consecutive Seasons Leading League (Average Return)
- 3 Denver, 1965-67
- 2 By many teams

Most Kickoff Returns, Season
- 88 New Orleans, 1980
- 86 Minnesota, 1984
- 84 Baltimore, 1981

Fewest Kickoff Returns, Season
- 17 N.Y. Giants, 1944
- 20 N.Y. Giants, 1941, 1943
-       Chi. Bears, 1942
- 23 Washington, 1942

Most Kickoff Returns, Game
- 12 N.Y. Giants vs. Washington, Nov. 27, 1966
- 10 By many teams

Most Kickoff Returns, Both Teams, Game
- 19 N.Y. Giants (12) vs. Washington (7), Nov. 27, 1966
- 18 Houston (10) vs. Oakland (8), Dec. 22, 1963
- 17 Washington (9) vs. Green Bay (8), Oct. 17, 1983
-       San Diego (9) vs. Pittsburgh (8), Dec. 8, 1985
-       Detroit (9) vs. Green Bay (8), Nov. 27, 1986
-       L.A. Raiders (9) vs. Seattle (8), Dec. 18, 1988

Yards Gained
Most Yards, Kickoff Returns, Season
- 1,973 New Orleans, 1980
- 1,824 Houston, 1963
- 1,801 Denver, 1963

Fewest Yards, Kickoff Returns, Season
- 282 N.Y. Giants, 1940
- 381 Green Bay, 1940
- 424 Chicago, 1963

Most Yards, Kickoff Returns, Game
- 362 Detroit vs. Los Angeles, Oct. 29, 1950
- 304 Chi. Bears vs. Green Bay, Nov. 9, 1952
- 295 Denver vs. Boston, Oct. 4, 1964

Most Yards, Kickoff Returns, Both Teams, Game
- 560 Detroit (362) vs. Los Angeles (198), Oct. 29, 1950
- 453 Washington (236) vs. Philadelphia (217), Sept. 28, 1947
- 447 N.Y. Giants (236) vs. Cleveland (211), Dec. 4, 1966

Average Yardage
Highest Average, Kickoff Returns, Season
- 29.4 Chicago, 1972 (52-1,528)
- 28.9 Pittsburgh, 1952 (39-1,128)
- 28.2 Washington, 1962 (61-1,720)

Lowest Average, Kickoff Returns, Season
- 16.3 Chicago, 1963 (26-424)
- 16.4 Chicago, 1983 (58-953)
- 16.5 San Diego, 1961 (39-642)

Touchdowns
Most Touchdowns, Kickoff Returns, Season
- 4 Green Bay, 1967
-      Chicago, 1970
- 3 Los Angeles, 1950
-      Chi. Cardinals, 1954
-      San Francisco, 1963
-      Denver, 1966
-      Chicago, 1967
-      New England, 1977
-      L.A. Rams, 1985
- 2 By many teams

Most Touchdowns, Kickoff Returns, Game
- 2 Chi. Bears vs. Green Bay, Sept. 22, 1940
-      Chi. Bears vs. Green Bay, Nov. 9, 1952
-      Philadelphia vs. Dallas, Nov. 6, 1966
-      Green Bay vs. Cleveland, Nov. 12, 1967
-      L.A. Rams vs. Green Bay, Nov. 24, 1985

Most Touchdowns, Kickoff Returns, Both Teams, Game
- 2 Washington (1) vs. Philadelphia (1), Nov. 1, 1942
-      Washington (1) vs. Philadelphia (1), Sept. 28, 1947
-      Los Angeles (1) vs. Detroit (1), Oct. 29, 1950
-      N.Y. Yanks (1) vs. N.Y. Giants (1), Nov. 4, 1951 (consecutive)
-      Baltimore (1) vs. Chi. Bears (1), Oct. 4, 1958
-      Buffalo (1) vs. Boston (1), Nov. 3, 1962
-      Pittsburgh (1) vs. Dallas (1), Oct. 30, 1966
-      St. Louis (1) vs. Washington (1), Sept. 23, 1973 (consecutive)
-      Atlanta (1) vs. San Francisco (1), Dec. 20, 1987 (consecutive)
-      Houston (1) vs. Pittsburgh (1), Dec. 4, 1988
-      (Also see previous record)

Fumbles
Most Fumbles, Season
- 56 Chi. Bears, 1938
-      San Francisco, 1978
- 54 Philadelphia, 1946
- 51 New England, 1973

Fewest Fumbles, Season
- 8 Cleveland, 1959
- 11 Green Bay, 1944
- 12 Brooklyn, 1934
-      Detroit, 1943
-      Cincinnati, 1982
-      Minnesota, 1982

Most Fumbles, Game
- 10 Phil-Pitt vs. New York, Oct. 9, 1943
-      Detroit vs. Minnesota, Nov. 12, 1967
-      Kansas City vs. Houston, Oct. 12, 1969
-      San Francisco vs. Detroit, Dec. 17, 1978
- 9 Philadelphia vs. Green Bay, Oct. 13, 1946
-      Kansas City vs. San Diego, Nov. 15, 1964
-      N.Y. Giants vs. Buffalo, Oct. 20, 1975

-      St. Louis vs. Washington, Oct. 25, 1976
-      San Diego vs. Green Bay, Sept. 24, 1978
-      Pittsburgh vs. Cincinnati, Oct. 14, 1979
-      Cleveland vs. Seattle, Dec. 20, 1981
- 8 By many teams. Last time: Seattle vs. Kansas City, Nov. 5, 1989

Most Fumbles, Both Teams, Game
- 14 Chi. Bears (7) vs. Cleveland (7), Nov. 24, 1940
-      St. Louis (8) vs. N.Y. Giants (6), Sept. 17, 1961
-      Kansas City (10) vs. Houston (4), Oct. 12, 1969
- 13 Washington (8) vs. Pittsburgh (5), Nov. 14, 1937
-      Philadelphia (7) vs. Boston (6), Dec. 8, 1946
-      N.Y. Giants (7) vs. Washington (6), Nov. 5, 1950
-      Kansas City (9) vs. San Diego (4), Nov. 15, 1964
-      Buffalo (7) vs. Denver (6), Dec. 13, 1964
-      N.Y. Jets (7) vs. Houston (6), Sept. 12, 1965
-      Houston (8) vs. Pittsburgh (5), Dec. 9, 1973
-      St. Louis (9) vs. Washington (4), Oct. 25, 1976
-      Cleveland (9) vs. Seattle (4), Dec. 20, 1981
-      Green Bay (7) vs. Detroit (6), Oct. 6, 1985
- 12 In many games

Fumbles Lost
Most Fumbles Lost, Season
- 36 Chi. Cardinals, 1959
- 31 Green Bay, 1952
- 29 Chi. Cardinals, 1946
-      Pittsburgh, 1950

Fewest Fumbles Lost, Season
- 3 Philadelphia, 1938
-      Minnesota, 1980
- 4 San Francisco, 1960
-      Kansas City, 1982
- 5 Chi. Cardinals, 1943
-      Detroit, 1943
-      N.Y. Giants, 1943
-      Cleveland, 1959
-      Minnesota, 1982

Most Fumbles Lost, Game
- 8 St. Louis vs. Washington, Oct. 25, 1976
- 7 Cincinnati vs. Buffalo, Nov. 30, 1969
-      Cleveland vs. Seattle, Dec. 20, 1981
- 6 By many teams. Last time: L.A. Rams vs. New England, Dec. 11, 1983

Fumbles Recovered
Most Fumbles Recovered, Season, Own and Opponents'
- 58 Minnesota, 1963 (27 own, 31 opp)
- 51 Chi. Bears, 1938 (37 own, 14 opp)
-      San Francisco, 1978 (24 own, 27 opp)
- 50 Philadelphia, 1987 (23 own, 27 opp)

Fewest Fumbles Recovered, Season, Own and Opponents'
- 9 San Francisco, 1982 (5 own, 4 opp)
- 11 Cincinnati, 1982 (5 own, 6 opp)
- 13 Baltimore, 1967 (5 own, 8 opp)
-      N.Y. Jets, 1967 (7 own, 6 opp)
-      Philadelphia, 1968 (6 own, 7 opp)
-      Miami, 1973 (5 own, 8 opp)
-      Chicago, 1982 (6 own, 7 opp)
-      Denver, 1982 (6 own, 7 opp)
-      Miami, 1982 (5 own, 8 opp)
-      N.Y. Giants, 1982 (7 own, 6 opp)

Most Fumbles Recovered, Game, Own and Opponents'
- 10 Denver vs. Buffalo, Dec. 13, 1964 (5 own, 5 opp)
-      Pittsburgh vs. Houston, Dec. 9, 1973 (5 own, 5 opp)
-      Washington vs. St. Louis, Oct. 25, 1976 (2 own, 8 opp)
- 9 St. Louis vs. N.Y. Giants, Sept. 17, 1961 (6 own, 3 opp)
-      Houston vs. Cincinnati, Oct. 27, 1974 (4 own, 5 opp)
-      Kansas City vs. Dallas, Nov. 10, 1975 (4 own, 5 opp)
-      Green Bay vs. Detroit, Oct. 6, 1985 (5 own, 4 opp)
- 8 By many teams

Most Own Fumbles Recovered, Season
- 37 Chi. Bears, 1938
- 28 Pittsburgh, 1987
- 27 Philadelphia, 1946
-      Minnesota, 1963

Fewest Own Fumbles Recovered, Season
- 2 Washington, 1958
- 3 Detroit, 1956
-      Cleveland, 1959
-      Houston, 1982
- 4 By many teams

Most Opponents' Fumbles Recovered, Season
- 31 Minnesota, 1963
- 29 Cleveland, 1951
- 28 Green Bay, 1946
-      Houston, 1977
-      Seattle, 1983

Fewest Opponents' Fumbles Recovered, Season
- 3 Los Angeles, 1974
- 4 Philadelphia, 1944
-      San Francisco, 1982
- 5 Baltimore, 1982

Most Opponents' Fumbles Recovered, Game
- 8 Washington vs. St. Louis, Oct. 25, 1976
- 7 Buffalo vs. Cincinnati, Nov. 30, 1969
-      Seattle vs. Cleveland, Dec. 20, 1981
- 6 By many teams. Last time: New England vs. L.A. Rams, Dec. 11, 1983

Touchdowns
Most Touchdowns, Fumbles Recovered, Season, Own and Opponents'
- 5 Chi. Bears, 1942 (1 own, 4 opp)
-      Los Angeles, 1952 (1 own, 4 opp)
-      San Francisco, 1965 (1 own, 4 opp)
-      Oakland, 1978 (2 own, 3 opp)

        4   Chi. Bears, 1948 (1 own, 3 opp)
            Boston, 1948 (4 opp)
            Denver, 1979 (1 own, 3 opp)
            Atlanta, 1981 (1 own, 3 opp)
            Denver, 1984 (4 opp)
            St. Louis, 1987 (4 opp)
            Minnesota, 1989 (4 opp)
        3   By many teams

Most Touchdowns, Own Fumbles Recovered, Season
        2   Chi. Bears, 1953
            New England, 1973
            Buffalo, 1974
            Denver, 1975
            Oakland, 1978
            Green Bay, 1982
            New Orleans, 1983
            Cleveland, 1986
            Green Bay, 1989

Most Touchdowns, Opponents' Fumbles Recovered, Season
        4   Detroit, 1937
            Chi. Bears, 1942
            Boston, 1948
            Los Angeles, 1952
            San Francisco, 1965
            Denver, 1984
            St. Louis, 1987
            Minnesota, 1989
        3   By many teams

Most Touchdowns, Fumbles Recovered, Game, Own and Opponents'
        2   By many teams

Most Touchdowns, Own Fumbles Recovered, Game
        1   By many teams

Most Touchdowns, Opponents' Fumbles Recovered, Game
        2   Detroit vs. Cleveland, Nov. 7, 1937
            Philadelphia vs. N.Y. Giants, Sept. 25, 1938
            Chi. Bears vs. Washington, Nov. 28, 1948
            N.Y. Giants vs. Pittsburgh, Sept. 17, 1950
            Cleveland vs. Dall. Cowboys, Dec. 3, 1961
            Cleveland vs. N.Y. Giants, Oct. 25, 1964
            Green Bay vs. Dallas, Nov. 26, 1964
            San Francisco vs. Detroit, Nov. 14, 1965
            Oakland vs. Buffalo, Dec. 24, 1967
            N.Y. Giants vs. Green Bay, Sept. 19, 1971
            Washington vs. San Diego, Sept. 16, 1973
            New Orleans vs. San Francisco, Oct. 19, 1975
            Cincinnati vs. Pittsburgh, Oct. 14, 1979
            Atlanta vs. Detroit, Oct. 5, 1980
            Kansas City vs. Oakland, Oct. 5, 1980
            New England vs. Baltimore, Nov. 23, 1980
            Denver vs. Green Bay, Oct. 15, 1984
            Miami vs. Kansas City, Oct. 11, 1987
            St. Louis vs. New Orleans, Oct. 11, 1987
            Minnesota vs. Atlanta, Dec. 10, 1989

Turnovers
(Number of times losing the ball on interceptions and fumbles.)
Most Turnovers, Season
       63   San Francisco, 1978
       58   Chi. Bears, 1947
            Pittsburgh, 1950
            N.Y. Giants, 1983
       57   Green Bay, 1950
            Houston, 1962, 1963
            Pittsburgh, 1965
Fewest Turnovers, Season
       12   Kansas City, 1982
       14   N.Y. Giants, 1943
            Cleveland, 1959
       16   San Francisco, 1960
            Cincinnati, 1982
            St. Louis, 1982
            Washington, 1982
Most Turnovers, Game
       12   Detroit vs. Chi. Bears, Nov. 22, 1942
            Chi. Cardinals vs. Philadelphia, Sept. 24, 1950
            Pittsburgh vs. Philadelphia, Dec. 12, 1965
       11   San Diego vs. Green Bay, Sept. 24, 1978
       10   Washington vs. N.Y. Giants, Dec. 4, 1938
            Pittsburgh vs. Green Bay, Nov. 23, 1941
            Detroit vs. Green Bay, Oct. 24, 1943
            Chi. Cardinals vs. Green Bay, Nov. 10, 1946
            Chi. Cardinals vs. N.Y. Giants, Nov. 2, 1952
            Minnesota vs. Detroit, Dec. 9, 1962
            Houston vs. Oakland, Sept. 7, 1963
            Washington vs. N.Y. Giants, Dec. 8, 1963
            Chicago vs. Detroit, Sept. 22, 1968
            St. Louis vs. Washington, Oct. 25, 1975
            N.Y. Jets vs. New England, Nov. 21, 1976
            San Francisco vs. Dallas, Oct. 12, 1980
            Cleveland vs. Seattle, Dec. 20, 1981
            Detroit vs. Denver, Oct. 7, 1984
Most Turnovers, Both Teams, Game
       17   Detroit (12) vs. Chi. Bears (5), Nov. 22, 1942
            Boston (9) vs. Philadelphia (8), Dec. 8, 1946
       16   Chi. Cardinals (12) vs. Philadelphia (4), Sept. 24, 1950
            Chi. Cardinals (8) vs. Chi. Bears (8), Dec. 7, 1958
            Minnesota (10) vs. Detroit (6), Dec. 9, 1962
            Houston (9) vs. Kansas City (7), Oct. 12, 1969
       15   Philadelphia (8) vs. Chi. Cardinals (7), Oct. 3, 1954
            Denver (9) vs. Houston (6), Dec. 2, 1962
            Washington (10) vs. N.Y. Giants (5), Dec. 8, 1963
            St. Louis (9) vs. Kansas City (6), Oct. 2, 1983

Penalties
Most Seasons Leading League, Fewest Penalties
       11   Miami, 1968, 1976-84, 1986
        9   Pittsburgh, 1946-47, 1950-52, 1954, 1963, 1965, 1968
        6   Boston/New England, 1962, 1964-65, 1973, 1987, 1989
Most Consecutive Seasons Leading League, Fewest Penalties
        9   Miami, 1976-84
        3   Pittsburgh, 1950-52
        2   By many teams
Most Seasons Leading League, Most Penalties
       16   Chi. Bears, 1941-44, 1946-49, 1951, 1959-61, 1963, 1965, 1968, 1976
        7   Oakland/L.A. Raiders, 1963, 1966, 1968-69, 1975, 1982, 1984
        6   L.A. Rams, 1950, 1952, 1962, 1969, 1978, 1980
Most Consecutive Seasons Leading League, Most Penalties
        4   Chi. Bears, 1941-44, 1946-49
        3   Chi. Cardinals, 1954-56
            Chi. Bears, 1959-61
Fewest Penalties, Season
       19   Detroit, 1937
       21   Boston, 1935
       24   Philadelphia, 1936
Most Penalties, Season
      149   Houston, 1989
      144   Buffalo, 1983
      143   L.A. Raiders, 1984
Fewest Penalties, Game
        0   By many teams. Last time: Dallas vs. Washington, Nov. 5, 1989
Most Penalties, Game
       22   Brooklyn vs. Green Bay, Sept. 17, 1944
            Chi. Bears vs. Philadelphia, Nov. 26, 1944
       21   Cleveland vs. Chi. Bears, Nov. 25, 1951
       20   Tampa Bay vs. Seattle, Oct. 17, 1976
Fewest Penalties, Both Teams, Game
        0   Brooklyn vs. Pittsburgh, Oct. 28, 1934
            Brooklyn vs. Boston, Sept. 28, 1936
            Cleveland vs. Chi. Bears, Oct. 9, 1938
            Pittsburgh vs. Philadelphia, Nov. 10, 1940
Most Penalties, Both Teams, Game
       37   Cleveland (21) vs. Chi. Bears (16), Nov. 25, 1951
       35   Tampa Bay (20) vs. Seattle (15), Oct. 17, 1976
       33   Brooklyn (22) vs. Green Bay (11), Sept. 17, 1944

Yards Penalized
Most Seasons Leading League, Fewest Yards Penalized
       11   Miami, 1967-68, 1973, 1977-84
        8   Boston/Washington, 1935, 1953-54, 1956-58, 1970, 1985
        7   Pittsburgh, 1946-47, 1950, 1952, 1962, 1965, 1968
Most Consecutive Seasons Leading League, Fewest Yards Penalized
        8   Miami, 1977-84
        3   Washington, 1956-58
            Boston, 1964-66
        2   By many teams
Most Seasons Leading League, Most Yards Penalized
       15   Chi. Bears, 1935, 1937, 1939-44, 1946-47, 1949, 1951, 1961-62, 1968
        7   Oakland/L.A. Raiders, 1963-64, 1968-69, 1975, 1982, 1984
        6   Buffalo, 1962, 1967, 1970, 1972, 1981, 1983
Most Consecutive Seasons Leading League, Most Yards Penalized
        6   Chi. Bears, 1939-44
        3   Cleveland, 1976-78
        2   By many teams
Fewest Yards Penalized, Season
      139   Detroit, 1937
      146   Philadelphia, 1937
      159   Philadelphia, 1936
Most Yards Penalized, Season
    1,274   Oakland, 1969
    1,239   Baltimore, 1979
    1,209   L.A. Raiders, 1984
Fewest Yards Penalized, Game
        0   By many teams. Last time: Dallas vs. Washington, Nov. 5, 1989
Most Yards Penalized, Game
      209   Cleveland vs. Chi. Bears, Nov. 25, 1951
      190   Tampa Bay vs. Seattle, Oct. 17, 1976
      189   Houston vs. Buffalo, Oct. 31, 1965
Fewest Yards Penalized, Both Teams, Game
        0   Brooklyn vs. Pittsburgh, Oct. 28, 1934
            Brooklyn vs. Boston, Sept. 28, 1936
            Cleveland vs. Chi. Bears, Oct. 9, 1938
            Pittsburgh vs. Philadelphia, Nov. 10, 1940
Most Yards Penalized, Both Teams, Game
      374   Cleveland (209) vs. Chi. Bears (165), Nov. 25, 1951
      310   Tampa Bay (190) vs. Seattle (120), Oct. 17, 1976
      309   Green Bay (184) vs. Boston (125), Oct. 21, 1945

Defense

Scoring
Most Seasons Leading League, Fewest Points Allowed
        9   Chi. Bears, 1932, 1936-37, 1942, 1948, 1963, 1985-86, 1988
        8   N.Y. Giants, 1935, 1938-39, 1941, 1944, 1958-59, 1961
        6   Cleveland, 1951, 1953-57
Most Consecutive Seasons Leading League, Fewest Points Allowed
        5   Cleveland, 1953-57
        3   Buffalo, 1964-66
            Minnesota, 1969-71
        2   By many teams
Fewest Points Allowed, Season (Since 1932)
       44   Chi. Bears, 1932
       54   Brooklyn, 1933
       59   Detroit, 1934
Most Points Allowed, Season
      533   Baltimore, 1981

501 N.Y. Giants, 1966
487 New Orleans, 1980
Fewest Touchdowns Allowed, Season (Since 1932)
6 Chi. Bears, 1932
Brooklyn, 1933
7 Detroit, 1934
8 Green Bay, 1932
Most Touchdowns Allowed, Season
68 Baltimore, 1981
66 N.Y. Giants, 1966
63 Baltimore, 1950

First Downs

Fewest First Downs Allowed Season
77 Detroit, 1935
79 Boston, 1935
82 Washington, 1937
Most First Downs Allowed, Season
406 Baltimore, 1981
371 Seattle, 1981
366 Green Bay, 1983
Fewest First Downs Allowed, Rushing, Season
35 Chi. Bears, 1942
40 Green Bay, 1939
41 Brooklyn, 1944
Most First Downs Allowed, Rushing, Season
179 Detroit, 1985
178 New Orleans, 1980
175 Seattle, 1981
Fewest First Downs Allowed, Passing, Season
33 Chi. Bears, 1943
34 Pittsburgh, 1941
Washington, 1943
35 Detroit, 1940
Philadelphia, 1940, 1944
Most First Downs Allowed, Passing, Season
218 San Diego, 1985
216 San Diego, 1981
N.Y. Jets, 1986
214 Baltimore, 1981
Fewest First Downs Allowed, Penalty, Season
1 Boston, 1944
3 Philadelphia, 1940
Pittsburgh, 1945
Washington, 1957
4 Cleveland, 1940
Green Bay, 1943
N.Y. Giants, 1943
Most First Downs Allowed, Penalty, Season
48 Houston, 1985
46 Houston, 1986
43 L.A. Raiders, 1984

Net Yards Allowed Rushing and Passing

Most Seasons Leading League, Fewest Yards Allowed
8 Chi. Bears, 1942-43, 1948, 1958, 1963, 1984-86
6 N.Y. Giants, 1938, 1940-41, 1951, 1956, 1959
5 Boston/Washington, 1935-37, 1939, 1946
Philadelphia, 1944-45, 1949, 1953, 1981
Minnesota, 1969-70, 1975, 1988-89
Most Consecutive Seasons Leading League, Fewest Yards Allowed
3 Boston/Washington, 1935-37
Chicago, 1984-86
2 By many teams
Fewest Yards Allowed, Season
1,539 Chi. Cardinals, 1934
1,703 Chi. Bears, 1942
1,789 Brooklyn, 1933
Most Yards Allowed, Season
6,793 Baltimore, 1981
6,403 Green Bay, 1983
6,352 Minnesota, 1984

Rushing

Most Seasons Leading League, Fewest Yards Allowed
10 Chi. Bears, 1937, 1939, 1942, 1946, 1949, 1963, 1984-85, 1987-88
7 Detroit, 1938, 1950, 1952, 1962, 1970, 1980-81
6 Dallas, 1966-69, 1972, 1978
Most Consecutive Seasons Leading League, Fewest Yards Allowed
4 Dallas, 1966-69
2 By many teams
Fewest Yards Allowed, Rushing, Season
519 Chi. Bears, 1942
558 Philadelphia, 1944
762 Pittsburgh, 1982
Most Yards Allowed, Rushing, Season
3,228 Buffalo, 1978
3,106 New Orleans, 1980
3,010 Baltimore, 1978
Fewest Touchdowns Allowed, Rushing, Season
2 Detroit, 1934
Dallas, 1968
Minnesota, 1971
3 By many teams
Most Touchdowns Allowed, Rushing, Season
36 Oakland, 1961
31 N.Y. Giants, 1980
Tampa Bay, 1986
30 Baltimore, 1981

Passing

Most Seasons Leading League, Fewest Yards Allowed
8 Green Bay, 1947-48, 1962, 1964-68
7 Washington, 1939, 1942, 1945, 1952-53, 1980, 1985
6 Chi. Bears, 1938, 1943-44, 1958, 1960, 1963
Minnesota, 1969-70, 1972, 1975-76, 1989
Most Consecutive Seasons Leading League, Fewest Yards Allowed
5 Green Bay, 1964-68
2 By many teams
Fewest Yards Allowed, Passing, Season
545 Philadelphia, 1934
558 Portsmouth, 1933
585 Chi. Cardinals, 1934
Most Yards Allowed, Passing, Season
4,389 N.Y. Jets, 1986
4,311 San Diego, 1981
4,293 San Diego, 1985
Fewest Touchdowns Allowed, Passing, Season
1 Portsmouth, 1932
Philadelphia, 1934
2 Brooklyn, 1933
Chi. Bears, 1934
3 Chi. Bears, 1932
Green Bay, 1932
Green Bay, 1934
Chi. Bears, 1936
New York, 1939
New York, 1944
Most Touchdowns Allowed, Passing, Season
40 Denver, 1963
38 St. Louis, 1969
37 Washington, 1961
Baltimore, 1981

Sacks

Most Seasons Leading League
5 Oakland/L.A. Raiders, 1966-68, 1982, 1986
4 Boston/New England, 1961, 1963, 1977, 1979
Dallas, 1966, 1968-69, 1978
3 Dallas/Kansas City, 1960, 1965, 1969
San Francisco, 1967, 1972, 1976
L.A. Rams, 1968, 1970, 1988
Most Consecutive Seasons Leading League
3 Oakland, 1966-68
2 Dallas, 1968-69
Most Sacks, Season
72 Chicago, 1984
71 Minnesota, 1989
70 Chicago, 1987
Fewest Sacks, Season
11 Baltimore, 1982
12 Buffalo, 1982
13 Baltimore, 1981
Most Sacks, Game
12 Dallas vs. Pittsburgh, Nov. 20, 1966
St. Louis vs. Baltimore, Oct. 26, 1980
Chicago vs. Detroit, Dec. 16, 1984
Dallas vs. Houston, Sept. 29, 1985
11 N.Y. Giants vs. St. Louis, Nov. 1, 1964
Baltimore vs. Los Angeles, Nov. 22, 1964
Buffalo vs. Denver, Dec. 13, 1964
Detroit vs. Green Bay, Nov. 7, 1965
Oakland vs. Buffalo, Oct. 15, 1967
Oakland vs. Denver, Nov. 5, 1967
St. Louis vs. Atlanta, Nov. 24, 1968
Dallas vs. Detroit, Oct. 6, 1975
St. Louis vs. Philadelphia, Dec. 18, 1983
Kansas City vs. Cleveland, Sept. 30, 1984
Chicago vs. Minnesota, Oct. 28, 1984
Cleveland vs. Atlanta, Nov. 18, 1984
Detroit vs. Philadelphia, Nov. 16, 1986
San Diego vs. Dallas, Nov. 16, 1986
L.A. Raiders vs. Philadelphia, Nov. 30, 1986 (OT)
Seattle vs. L.A. Raiders, Dec. 8, 1986
Chicago vs. Philadelphia, Oct. 4, 1987
Dallas vs. N.Y. Jets, Oct. 4, 1987
10 By many teams
Most Opponents Yards Lost Attempting to Pass, Season
666 Oakland, 1967
583 Chicago, 1984
573 San Francisco, 1976
Fewest Opponents Yards Lost Attempting to Pass, Season
75 Green Bay, 1956
77 N.Y. Bulldogs, 1949
78 Green Bay, 1958

Interceptions By

Most Seasons Leading League
9 N.Y. Giants, 1933, 1937-39, 1944, 1948, 1951, 1954, 1961
8 Green Bay, 1940, 1942-43, 1947, 1955, 1957, 1962, 1965
7 Chi. Bears, 1935-36, 1941-42, 1946, 1963, 1985
Most Consecutive Seasons Leading League
5 Kansas City, 1966-70
3 N.Y. Giants, 1937-39
2 By many teams
Most Passes Intercepted By, Season
49 San Diego, 1961
42 Green Bay, 1943
41 N.Y. Giants, 1951
Fewest Passes Intercepted By, Season
3 Houston, 1982
5 Baltimore, 1982

6 Houston, 1972
St. Louis, 1982

Most Passes Intercepted By, Game
9 Green Bay vs. Detroit, Oct. 24, 1943
Philadelphia vs. Pittsburgh, Dec. 12, 1965
8 N.Y. Giants vs. Green Bay, Nov. 21, 1948
Philadelphia vs. Chi. Cardinals, Sept. 24, 1950
N.Y. Giants vs. N.Y. Yanks, Dec. 16, 1951
Houston vs. Denver, Dec. 2, 1962
Detroit vs. Chicago, Sept. 22, 1968
N.Y. Jets vs. Baltimore, Sept. 23, 1973
7 By many teams. Last time: New Orleans vs. Green Bay, Sept. 14, 1986

Most Consecutive Games, One or More Interceptions By
46 L.A. Chargers/San Diego, 1960-63
37 Detroit, 1960-63
36 Boston, 1944-47

Most Yards Returning Interceptions, Season
929 San Diego, 1961
712 Los Angeles, 1952
697 Seattle, 1984

Fewest Yards Returning Interceptions, Season
5 Los Angeles, 1959
37 Dallas, 1989
42 Philadelphia, 1982

Most Yards Returning Interceptions, Game
325 Seattle vs. Kansas City, Nov. 4, 1984
314 Los Angeles vs. San Francisco, Oct. 18, 1964
245 Houston vs. N.Y. Jets, Oct. 15, 1967

Most Touchdowns, Returning Interceptions, Season
9 San Diego, 1961
7 Seattle, 1984
6 Cleveland, 1960
Green Bay, 1966
Detroit, 1967
Houston, 1967

Most Touchdowns Returning Interceptions, Game
4 Seattle vs. Kansas City, Nov. 4, 1984
3 Baltimore vs. Green Bay, Nov. 5, 1950
Cleveland vs. Chicago, Dec. 11, 1960
Philadelphia vs. Pittsburgh, Dec. 12, 1965
Baltimore vs. Pittsburgh, Sept. 29, 1968
Buffalo vs. N.Y. Jets, Sept. 29, 1968
Houston vs. San Diego, Dec. 19, 1971
Cincinnati vs. Houston, Dec. 17, 1972
Tampa Bay vs. New Orleans, Dec. 11, 1977
2 By many teams

Most Touchdowns Returning Interceptions, Both Teams, Game
4 Philadelphia (3) vs. Pittsburgh (1), Dec. 12, 1965
Seattle (4) vs. Kansas City (0), Nov. 4, 1984
3 Los Angeles (2) vs. Detroit (1), Nov. 1, 1953
Cleveland (2) vs. N.Y. Giants (1), Dec. 18, 1960
Pittsburgh (2) vs. Cincinnati (1), Oct. 10, 1983
Kansas City (2) vs. San Diego (1), Oct. 19, 1986
(Also see previous record)

Punt Returns
Fewest Opponents Punt Returns, Season
7 Washington, 1962
San Diego, 1982
10 Buffalo, 1982
11 Boston, 1962

Most Opponents Punt Returns, Season
71 Tampa Bay, 1976, 1977
69 N.Y. Giants, 1953
68 Cleveland, 1974

Fewest Yards Allowed, Punt Returns, Season
22 Green Bay, 1967
34 Washington, 1962
39 Cleveland, 1959
Washington, 1972

Most Yards Allowed, Punt Returns, Season
932 Green Bay, 1949
913 Boston, 1947
906 New Orleans, 1974

Lowest Average Allowed, Punt Returns, Season
1.20 Chi. Cardinals, 1954 (46-55)
1.22 Cleveland, 1959 (32-39)
1.55 Chi. Cardinals, 1953 (44-68)

Highest Average Allowed, Punt Returns, Season
18.6 Green Bay, 1949 (50-932)
18.0 Cleveland, 1977 (31-558)
17.9 Boston, 1960 (20-357)

Most Touchdowns Allowed, Punt Returns, Season
4 New York, 1959
3 Green Bay, 1949
Chi. Cardinals, 1951
Los Angeles, 1951
Washington, 1952
Dallas, 1952
Pittsburgh, 1959
N.Y. Jets, 1968
Cleveland, 1977
Atlanta, 1986
Tampa Bay, 1986
2 By many teams

Kickoff Returns
Fewest Opponents Kickoff Returns, Season
10 Brooklyn, 1943
15 Detroit, 1942
Brooklyn, 1944

18 Cleveland, 1941
Boston, 1944

Most Opponents Kickoff Returns, Season
91 Washington, 1983
89 New England, 1980
88 San Diego, 1981

Fewest Yards Allowed, Kickoff Returns, Season
225 Brooklyn, 1943
293 Brooklyn, 1944
361 Seattle, 1982

Most Yards Allowed, Kickoff Returns, Season
2,045 Kansas City, 1966
1,827 Chicago, 1985
1,816 N.Y. Giants, 1963

Lowest Average Allowed, Kickoff Returns, Season
14.3 Cleveland, 1980 (71-1,018)
15.0 Seattle, 1982 (24-361)
15.8 Buffalo, 1987 (43-679)

Highest Average Allowed, Kickoff Returns, Season
29.5 N.Y. Jets, 1972 (47-1,386)
29.4 Los Angeles, 1950 (48-1,411)
29.1 New England, 1971 (49-1,427)

Most Touchdowns Allowed, Kickoff Returns, Season
3 Minnesota, 1963, 1970
Dallas, 1966
Detroit, 1980
Pittsburgh, 1986
2 By many teams

Fumbles
Fewest Opponents Fumbles, Season
11 Cleveland, 1956
Baltimore, 1982
13 Los Angeles, 1956
Chicago, 1960
Cleveland, 1963
Cleveland, 1965
Detroit, 1967
San Diego, 1969
14 Baltimore, 1970
Oakland, 1975
Buffalo, 1982
St. Louis, 1982
San Francisco, 1982

Most Opponents Fumbles, Season
50 Minnesota, 1963
San Francisco, 1978
48 N.Y. Giants, 1980
N.Y. Jets, 1986
47 N.Y. Giants, 1977
Seattle, 1984

Turnovers
(Number of times losing the ball on interceptions and fumbles.)
Fewest Opponents Turnovers, Season
11 Baltimore, 1982
13 San Francisco, 1982
15 St. Louis, 1982

Most Opponents Turnovers, Season
66 San Diego, 1961
63 Seattle, 1984
61 Washington, 1983

Most Opponents Turnovers, Game
12 Chi. Bears vs. Detroit, Nov. 22, 1942
Philadelphia vs. Chi. Cardinals, Sept. 24, 1950
Philadelphia vs. Pittsburgh, Dec. 12, 1965
11 Green Bay vs. San Diego, Sept. 24, 1978
10 N.Y. Giants vs. Washington, Dec. 4, 1938
Green Bay vs. Pittsburgh, Nov. 23, 1941
Green Bay vs. Detroit, Oct. 24, 1943
Green Bay vs. Chi. Cardinals, Nov. 10, 1946
N.Y. Giants vs. Chi. Cardinals, Nov. 2, 1952
Detroit vs. Minnesota, Dec. 9, 1962
Oakland vs. Houston, Sept. 7, 1963
N.Y. Giants vs. Washington, Dec. 8, 1963
Detroit vs. Chicago, Sept. 22, 1968
Washington vs. St. Louis, Oct. 25, 1976
New England vs. N.Y. Jets, Nov. 21, 1976
Dallas vs. San Francisco, Oct. 12, 1980
Seattle vs. Cleveland, Dec. 20, 1981
Denver vs. Detroit, Oct. 7, 1984

OUTSTANDING PERFORMERS

1,000 Yards Rushing in a Season

Year	Player, Team	Att.	Yards	Avg.	Long	TD
1989	Christian Okoye, Kansas City	370	1,480	4.0	59	12
	*Barry Sanders, Detroit	280	1,470	5.3	34	14
	Eric Dickerson, Indianapolis[7]	314	1,311	4.2	21	7
	Neal Anderson, Chicago[2]	274	1,275	4.7	73	11
	Dalton Hilliard, New Orleans	344	1,262	3.7	40	13
	Thurman Thomas, Buffalo	298	1,244	4.2	38	6
	James Brooks, Cincinnati[2]	221	1,239	5.6	65	7
	*Bobby Humphrey, Denver	294	1,151	3.9	40	7
	Greg Bell, L.A. Rams[3]	272	1,137	4.2	47	15
	Roger Craig, San Francisco[3]	271	1,054	3.9	27	6
	Ottis Anderson, N.Y. Giants[6]	325	1,023	3.1	36	14
1988	Eric Dickerson, Indianapolis[6]	388	1,659	4.3	41	14
	Herschel Walker, Dallas	361	1,514	4.2	38	5
	Roger Craig, San Francisco[2]	310	1,502	4.8	46	9
	Greg Bell, L.A. Rams[2]	288	1,212	4.2	44	16
	*John Stephens, New England	297	1,168	3.9	52	4
	Gary Anderson, San Diego	225	1,119	5.0	36	3
	Neal Anderson, Chicago	249	1,106	4.4	80	12
	Joe Morris, N.Y. Giants[3]	307	1,083	3.5	27	5
	*Ickey Woods, Cincinnati	203	1,066	5.3	56	15
	Curt Warner, Seattle[4]	266	1,025	3.9	29	10
	John Settle, Atlanta	232	1,024	4.4	62	7
	Mike Rozier, Houston	251	1,002	4.0	28	10
1987	Charles White, L.A. Rams	324	1,374	4.2	58	11
	Eric Dickerson, L.A. Rams-Indianapolis[5]	283	1,288	4.6	57	6
1986	Eric Dickerson, L.A. Rams[4]	404	1,821	4.5	42	11
	Joe Morris, N.Y. Giants[2]	341	1,516	4.4	54	14
	Curt Warner, Seattle[3]	319	1,481	4.6	60	13
	*Rueben Mayes, New Orleans	286	1,353	4.7	50	8
	Walter Payton, Chicago[10]	321	1,333	4.2	41	8
	Gerald Riggs, Atlanta[3]	343	1,327	3.9	31	9
	George Rogers, Washington[4]	303	1,203	4.0	42	18
	James Brooks, Cincinnati	205	1,087	5.3	56	5
1985	Marcus Allen, L.A. Raiders[3]	390	1,759	4.6	61	11
	Gerald Riggs, Atlanta[2]	397	1,719	4.3	50	10
	Walter Payton, Chicago[9]	324	1,551	4.8	40	9
	Joe Morris, N.Y. Giants	294	1,336	4.5	65	21
	Freeman McNeil, N.Y. Jets[2]	294	1,331	4.5	69	3
	Tony Dorsett, Dallas[8]	305	1,307	4.3	60	7
	James Wilder, Tampa Bay[2]	365	1,300	3.6	28	10
	Eric Dickerson, L.A. Rams[3]	292	1,234	4.2	43	12
	Craig James, New England	263	1,227	4.7	65	5
	*Kevin Mack, Cleveland	222	1,104	5.0	61	7
	Curt Warner, Seattle[2]	291	1,094	3.8	38	8
	George Rogers, Washington[3]	231	1,093	4.7	35	7
	Roger Craig, San Francisco	214	1,050	4.9	62	9
	Earnest Jackson, Philadelphia[2]	282	1,028	3.6	59	5
	Stump Mitchell, St. Louis	183	1,006	5.5	64	7
	Earnest Byner, Cleveland	244	1,002	4.1	36	8
1984	Eric Dickerson, L.A. Rams[2]	379	2,105	5.6	66	14
	Walter Payton, Chicago[8]	381	1,684	4.4	72	11
	James Wilder, Tampa Bay	407	1,544	3.8	37	13
	Gerald Riggs, Atlanta	353	1,486	4.2	57	13
	Wendell Tyler, San Francisco[3]	246	1,262	5.1	40	7
	John Riggins, Washington[5]	327	1,239	3.8	24	14
	Tony Dorsett, Dallas[7]	302	1,189	3.9	31	6
	Earnest Jackson, San Diego	296	1,179	4.0	32	8
	Ottis Anderson, St. Louis[5]	289	1,174	4.1	24	6
	Marcus Allen, L.A. Raiders[2]	275	1,168	4.2	52	13
	Sammy Winder, Denver	296	1,153	3.9	24	4
	*Greg Bell, Buffalo	262	1,100	4.2	85	7
	Freeman McNeil, N.Y. Jets	229	1,070	4.7	53	5
1983	*Eric Dickerson, L.A. Rams	390	1,808	4.6	85	18
	William Andrews, Atlanta[4]	331	1,567	4.7	27	7
	*Curt Warner, Seattle	335	1,449	4.3	60	13
	Walter Payton, Chicago[7]	314	1,421	4.5	49	6
	John Riggins, Washington[4]	375	1,347	3.6	44	24
	Tony Dorsett, Dallas[6]	289	1,321	4.6	77	8
	Earl Campbell, Houston[5]	322	1,301	4.0	42	12
	Ottis Anderson, St. Louis[4]	296	1,270	4.3	43	5
	Mike Pruitt, Cleveland[4]	293	1,184	4.0	27	10
	George Rogers, New Orleans[2]	256	1,144	4.5	76	5
	Joe Cribbs, Buffalo[3]	263	1,131	4.3	45	3
	Curtis Dickey, Baltimore	254	1,122	4.4	56	4
	Tony Collins, New England	219	1,049	4.8	50	10
	Billy Sims, Detroit[3]	220	1,040	4.7	41	7
	Marcus Allen, L.A. Raiders	266	1,014	3.8	19	9
	Franco Harris, Pittsburgh[8]	279	1,007	3.6	19	5
1981	*George Rogers, New Orleans	378	1,674	4.4	79	13
	Tony Dorsett, Dallas[5]	342	1,646	4.8	75	4
	Billy Sims, Detroit[2]	296	1,437	4.9	51	13
	Wilbert Montgomery, Philadelphia[3]	286	1,402	4.9	41	8
	Ottis Anderson, St. Louis[3]	328	1,376	4.2	28	9
	Earl Campbell, Houston[4]	361	1,376	3.8	43	10
	William Andrews, Atlanta[3]	289	1,301	4.5	29	10
	Walter Payton, Chicago[6]	339	1,222	3.6	39	6
	Chuck Muncie, San Diego[2]	251	1,144	4.6	73	19
	*Joe Delaney, Kansas City	234	1,121	4.8	82	3
	Mike Pruitt, Cleveland[3]	247	1,103	4.5	21	7
	Joe Cribbs, Buffalo[2]	257	1,097	4.3	35	3
	Pete Johnson, Cincinnati	274	1,077	3.9	39	12
	Wendell Tyler, Los Angeles[2]	260	1,074	4.1	69	12
	Ted Brown, Minnesota	274	1,063	3.9	34	6
1980	Earl Campbell, Houston[3]	373	1,934	5.2	55	13
	Walter Payton, Chicago[5]	317	1,460	4.6	69	6
	Ottis Anderson, St. Louis[2]	301	1,352	4.5	52	9
	William Andrews, Atlanta[2]	265	1,308	4.9	33	4
	*Billy Sims, Detroit	313	1,303	4.2	52	13
	Tony Dorsett, Dallas[4]	278	1,185	4.3	56	11
	*Joe Cribbs, Buffalo	306	1,185	3.9	48	11
	Mike Pruitt, Cleveland[2]	249	1,034	4.2	56	6
1979	Earl Campbell, Houston[2]	368	1,697	4.6	61	19
	Walter Payton, Chicago[4]	369	1,610	4.4	43	14
	*Ottis Anderson, St. Louis	331	1,605	4.8	76	8
	Wilbert Montgomery, Philadelphia[2]	338	1,512	4.5	62	9
	Mike Pruitt, Cleveland	264	1,294	4.9	77	9
	Ricky Bell, Tampa Bay	283	1,263	4.5	49	7
	Chuck Muncie, New Orleans	238	1,198	5.0	69	11
	Franco Harris, Pittsburgh[7]	267	1,186	4.4	71	11
	John Riggins, Washington[3]	260	1,153	4.4	66	9
	Wendell Tyler, Los Angeles	218	1,109	5.1	63	9
	Tony Dorsett, Dallas[3]	250	1,107	4.4	41	6
	*William Andrews, Atlanta	239	1,023	4.3	23	3
1978	*Earl Campbell, Houston	302	1,450	4.8	81	13
	Walter Payton, Chicago[3]	333	1,395	4.2	76	11
	Tony Dorsett, Dallas[2]	290	1,325	4.6	63	7
	Delvin Williams, Miami[2]	272	1,258	4.6	58	8
	Wilbert Montgomery, Philadelphia	259	1,220	4.7	47	9
	Terdell Middleton, Green Bay	284	1,116	3.9	76	11
	Franco Harris, Pittsburgh[6]	310	1,082	3.5	37	8
	Mark van Eeghen, Oakland[3]	270	1,080	4.0	34	9
	*Terry Miller, Buffalo	238	1,060	4.5	60	7
	Tony Reed, Kansas City	206	1,053	5.1	62	5
	John Riggins, Washington[2]	248	1,014	4.1	31	5
1977	Walter Payton, Chicago[2]	339	1,852	5.5	73	14
	Mark van Eeghen, Oakland[2]	324	1,273	3.9	27	7
	Lawrence McCutcheon, Los Angeles[4]	294	1,238	4.2	48	7
	Franco Harris, Pittsburgh[5]	300	1,162	3.9	61	11
	Lydell Mitchell, Baltimore[3]	301	1,159	3.9	64	3
	Chuck Foreman, Minnesota[3]	270	1,112	4.1	51	6
	Greg Pruitt, Cleveland[3]	236	1,086	4.6	78	3
	Sam Cunningham, New England	270	1,015	3.8	31	4
	*Tony Dorsett, Dallas	208	1,007	4.8	84	12
1976	O.J. Simpson, Buffalo[5]	290	1,503	5.2	75	8
	Walter Payton, Chicago	311	1,390	4.5	60	13
	Delvin Williams, San Francisco	248	1,203	4.9	80	7
	Lydell Mitchell, Baltimore[2]	289	1,200	4.2	43	5
	Lawrence McCutcheon, Los Angeles[3]	291	1,168	4.0	40	9
	Chuck Foreman, Minnesota[2]	278	1,155	4.2	46	13
	Franco Harris, Pittsburgh[4]	289	1,128	3.9	30	14
	Mike Thomas, Washington	254	1,101	4.3	28	5
	Rocky Bleier, Pittsburgh	220	1,036	4.7	28	5
	Mark van Eeghen, Oakland	233	1,012	4.3	21	3
	Otis Armstrong, Denver[2]	247	1,008	4.1	31	5
	Greg Pruitt, Cleveland[2]	209	1,000	4.8	64	4
1975	O.J. Simpson, Buffalo[4]	329	1,817	5.5	88	16
	Franco Harris, Pittsburgh[3]	262	1,246	4.8	36	10
	Lydell Mitchell, Baltimore	289	1,193	4.1	70	11
	Jim Otis, St. Louis	269	1,076	4.0	30	5
	Chuck Foreman, Minnesota	280	1,070	3.8	31	13
	Greg Pruitt, Cleveland	217	1,067	4.9	50	8
	John Riggins, N.Y. Jets	238	1,005	4.2	42	8
	Dave Hampton, Atlanta	250	1,002	4.0	22	5
1974	Otis Armstrong, Denver	263	1,407	5.3	43	9
	*Don Woods, San Diego	227	1,162	5.1	56	7
	O.J. Simpson, Buffalo[3]	270	1,125	4.2	41	3
	Lawrence McCutcheon, Los Angeles[2]	236	1,109	4.7	23	3
	Franco Harris, Pittsburgh[2]	208	1,006	4.8	54	5
1973	O.J. Simpson, Buffalo[2]	332	2,003	6.0	80	12
	John Brockington, Green Bay[3]	265	1,144	4.3	53	3
	Calvin Hill, Dallas[2]	273	1,142	4.2	21	6
	Lawrence McCutcheon, Los Angeles	210	1,097	5.2	37	2
	Larry Csonka, Miami[3]	219	1,003	4.6	25	5
1972	O.J. Simpson, Buffalo	292	1,251	4.3	94	6
	Larry Brown, Washington[2]	285	1,216	4.3	38	8
	Ron Johnson, N.Y. Giants[2]	298	1,182	4.0	35	9
	Larry Csonka, Miami[2]	213	1,117	5.2	45	6
	Marv Hubbard, Oakland	219	1,100	5.0	39	4
	*Franco Harris, Pittsburgh	188	1,055	5.6	75	10
	Calvin Hill, Dallas	245	1,036	4.2	26	6
	Mike Garrett, San Diego[2]	272	1,031	3.8	41	6
	John Brockington, Green Bay[2]	274	1,027	3.7	30	8
	Eugene (Mercury) Morris, Miami	190	1,000	5.3	33	12
1971	Floyd Little, Denver	284	1,133	4.0	40	6
	*John Brockington, Green Bay	216	1,105	5.1	52	4
	Larry Csonka, Miami	195	1,051	5.4	28	7
	Steve Owens, Detroit	246	1,035	4.2	23	8
	Willie Ellison, Los Angeles	211	1,000	4.7	80	4
1970	Larry Brown, Washington	237	1,125	4.7	75	5
	Ron Johnson, N.Y. Giants	263	1,027	3.9	68	8
1969	Gale Sayers, Chicago[2]	236	1,032	4.4	28	8
1968	Leroy Kelly, Cleveland[3]	248	1,239	5.0	65	16
	*Paul Robinson, Cincinnati	238	1,023	4.3	87	8
1967	Jim Nance, Boston[2]	269	1,216	4.5	53	7
	Leroy Kelly, Cleveland[2]	235	1,205	5.1	42	11
	Hoyle Granger, Houston	236	1,194	5.1	67	6
	Mike Garrett, Kansas City	236	1,087	4.6	58	9
1966	Jim Nance, Boston	299	1,458	4.9	65	11
	Gale Sayers, Chicago	229	1,231	5.4	58	8
	Leroy Kelly, Cleveland	209	1,141	5.5	70	15
	Dick Bass, Los Angeles[2]	248	1,090	4.4	50	8
1965	Jim Brown, Cleveland[7]	289	1,544	5.3	67	17
	Paul Lowe, San Diego[2]	222	1,121	5.0	59	7
1964	Jim Brown, Cleveland[6]	280	1,446	5.2	71	7
	Jim Taylor, Green Bay[5]	235	1,169	5.0	84	12
	John Henry Johnson, Pittsburgh[2]	235	1,048	4.5	45	7

Year	Player, Team	Att.	Yards	Avg.	Long	TD
1963	Jim Brown, Cleveland[5]	291	1,863	6.4	80	12
	Clem Daniels, Oakland	215	1,099	5.1	74	3
	Jim Taylor, Green Bay[4]	248	1,018	4.1	40	9
	Paul Lowe, San Diego	177	1,010	5.7	66	8
1962	Jim Taylor, Green Bay[3]	272	1,474	5.4	51	19
	John Henry Johnson, Pittsburgh	251	1,141	4.5	40	7
	*Cookie Gilchrist, Buffalo	214	1,096	5.1	44	13
	Abner Haynes, Dall. Texans	221	1,049	4.7	71	13
	Dick Bass, Los Angeles	196	1,033	5.3	57	6
	Charlie Tolar, Houston	244	1,012	4.1	25	7
1961	Jim Brown, Cleveland[4]	305	1,408	4.6	38	8
	Jim Taylor, Green Bay[2]	243	1,307	5.4	53	15
1960	Jim Brown, Cleveland[3]	215	1,257	5.8	71	9
	Jim Taylor, Green Bay	230	1,101	4.8	32	11
	John David Crow, St. Louis	183	1,071	5.9	57	6
1959	Jim Brown, Cleveland[2]	290	1,329	4.6	70	14
	J. D. Smith, San Francisco	207	1,036	5.0	73	10
1958	Jim Brown, Cleveland	257	1,527	5.9	65	17
1956	Rick Casares, Chi. Bears	234	1,126	4.8	68	12
1954	Joe Perry, San Francisco[2]	173	1,049	6.1	58	8
1953	Joe Perry, San Francisco	192	1,018	5.3	51	10
1949	Steve Van Buren, Philadelphia[2]	263	1,146	4.4	41	11
	Tony Canadeo, Green Bay	208	1,052	5.1	54	4
1947	Steve Van Buren, Philadelphia	217	1,008	4.6	45	13
1934	*Beattie Feathers, Chi. Bears	101	1,004	9.9	82	8

**First year in the league.*

200 Yards Rushing in a Game

Date	Player, Team, Opponent	Att.	Yards	TD
Dec. 24, 1989	Greg Bell, L.A. Rams vs. New England	26	210	1
Sept. 24, 1989	Greg Bell, L.A. Rams vs. Green Bay	28	221	2
Sept. 17, 1989	Gerald Riggs, Washington vs. Philadelphia	29	221	1
Dec. 18, 1988	Gary Anderson, San Diego vs. Kansas City	34	217	1
Nov. 30, 1987	*Bo Jackson, L.A. Raiders vs. Seattle	18	221	2
Nov. 15, 1987	Charles White, L.A. Rams vs. St. Louis	34	213	1
Dec. 7, 1986	Rueben Mayes, New Orleans vs. Miami	28	203	2
Oct. 5, 1986	Eric Dickerson, L.A. Rams vs. Tampa Bay (OT)	30	207	2
Dec. 21, 1985	George Rogers, Washington vs. St. Louis	34	206	1
Dec. 21, 1985	Joe Morris, N.Y. Giants vs. Pittsburgh	36	202	3
Dec. 9, 1984	Eric Dickerson, L.A. Rams vs. Houston	27	215	2
Nov. 18, 1984	*Greg Bell, Buffalo vs. Dallas	27	206	1
Nov. 4, 1984	Eric Dickerson, L.A. Rams vs. St. Louis	21	208	0
Sept. 2, 1984	Gerald Riggs, Atlanta vs. New Orleans	35	202	2
Nov. 27, 1983	*Curt Warner, Seattle vs. Kansas City (OT)	32	207	3
Nov. 6, 1983	James Wilder, Tampa Bay vs. Minnesota	31	219	1
Sept. 18, 1983	Tony Collins, New England vs. N.Y. Jets	23	212	3
Sept. 4, 1983	George Rogers, New Orleans vs. St. Louis	24	206	2
Dec. 21, 1980	Earl Campbell, Houston vs. Minnesota	29	203	1
Nov. 16, 1980	Earl Campbell, Houston vs. Chicago	31	206	0
Oct. 26, 1980	Earl Campbell, Houston vs. Cincinnati	27	202	2
Oct. 19, 1980	Earl Campbell, Houston vs. Tampa Bay	33	203	0
Nov. 26, 1978	*Terry Miller, Buffalo vs. N.Y. Giants	21	208	2
Dec. 4, 1977	*Tony Dorsett, Dallas vs. Philadelphia	23	206	2
Nov. 20, 1977	Walter Payton, Chicago vs. Minnesota	40	275	1
Oct. 30, 1977	Walter Payton, Chicago vs. Green Bay	23	205	2
Dec. 5, 1976	O.J. Simpson, Buffalo vs. Miami	24	203	1
Nov. 25, 1976	O.J. Simpson, Buffalo vs. Detroit	29	273	2
Oct. 24, 1976	Chuck Foreman, Minnesota vs. Philadelphia	28	200	2
Dec. 14, 1975	Greg Pruitt, Cleveland vs. Kansas City	26	214	3
Sept. 28, 1975	O.J. Simpson, Buffalo vs. Pittsburgh	28	227	1
Dec. 16, 1973	O.J. Simpson, Buffalo vs. N.Y. Jets	34	200	1
Dec. 9, 1973	O.J. Simpson, Buffalo vs. New England	22	219	1
Sept. 16, 1973	O.J. Simpson, Buffalo vs. New England	29	250	2
Dec. 5, 1971	Willie Ellison, Los Angeles vs. New Orleans	26	247	1
Dec. 20, 1970	John (Frenchy) Fuqua, Pittsburgh vs. Philadelphia	20	218	2
Nov. 3, 1968	Gale Sayers, Chicago vs. Green Bay	24	205	0
Oct. 30, 1966	Jim Nance, Boston vs. Oakland	38	208	2
Oct. 10, 1964	John Henry Johnson, Pittsburgh vs. Cleveland	30	200	3
Dec. 8, 1963	Cookie Gilchrist, Buffalo vs. N.Y. Jets	36	243	5
Nov. 3, 1963	Jim Brown, Cleveland vs. Philadelphia	28	223	1
Oct. 20, 1963	Clem Daniels, Oakland vs. N.Y. Jets	27	200	2
Sept. 22, 1963	Jim Brown, Cleveland vs. Dallas	20	232	2
Dec. 10, 1961	Billy Cannon, Houston vs. N.Y. Titans	25	216	3
Nov. 19, 1961	Jim Brown, Cleveland vs. Philadelphia	34	237	4
Dec. 18, 1960	John David Crow, St. Louis vs. Pittsburgh	24	203	0
Nov. 15, 1959	Bobby Mitchell, Cleveland vs. Washington	14	232	3
Nov. 24, 1957	*Jim Brown, Cleveland vs. Los Angeles	31	237	4
Dec. 16, 1956	*Tom Wilson, Los Angeles vs. Green Bay	23	223	0
Nov. 22, 1953	Dan Towler, Los Angeles vs. Baltimore	14	205	1
Nov. 12, 1950	Gene Roberts, N.Y. Giants vs. Chi. Cardinals	26	218	2
Nov. 27, 1949	Steve Van Buren, Philadelphia vs. Pittsburgh	27	205	0
Oct. 8, 1933	Cliff Battles, Boston vs. N.Y. Giants	16	215	1

**First year in the league.*

Times 200 or More

53 times by 35 players . . . Simpson 6; Brown, Campbell 4; Bell, Dickerson 3; Payton, Riggs, Rogers 2.

4,000 Yards Passing in a Season

Year	Player, Team	Att.	Comp.	Pct.	Yards	TD	Int.
1989	Don Majkowski, Green Bay	599	353	58.9	4,318	27	20
	Jim Everett, L.A. Rams	518	304	58.7	4,310	29	17
1988	Dan Marino, Miami[4]	606	354	58.4	4,434	28	23
1986	Dan Marino, Miami[3]	623	378	60.7	4,746	44	23
	Jay Schroeder, Washington	541	276	51.0	4,109	22	22
1985	Dan Marino, Miami[2]	567	336	59.3	4,137	30	21
1984	Dan Marino, Miami	564	362	64.2	5,084	48	17
	Neil Lomax, St. Louis	560	345	61.6	4,614	28	16
	Phil Simms, N.Y. Giants	533	286	53.7	4,044	22	18
1983	Lynn Dickey, Green Bay	484	289	59.7	4,458	32	29
	Bill Kenney, Kansas City	603	346	57.4	4,348	24	18
1981	Dan Fouts, San Diego[3]	609	360	59.1	4,802	33	17
1980	Dan Fouts, San Diego[2]	589	348	59.1	4,715	30	24
	Brian Sipe, Cleveland	554	337	60.8	4,132	30	14
1979	Dan Fouts, San Diego	530	332	62.6	4,082	24	24
1967	Joe Namath, N.Y. Jets	491	258	52.5	4,007	26	28

400 Yards Passing in a Game

Date	Player, Team, Opponent	Att.	Comp.	Yards	TD
Dec. 23, 1989	Warren Moon, Houston vs. Cleveland	51	32	414	2
Dec. 11, 1989	Joe Montana, San Francisco vs. L.A. Rams	42	30	458	3
Nov. 26, 1989	Jim Everett, L.A. Rams vs. New Orleans (OT)	51	29	454	1
Nov. 26, 1989	Mark Rypien, Washington vs. Chicago	47	30	401	4
Oct. 2, 1989	Randall Cunningham, Philadelphia vs. Chicago	62	32	401	1
Sept. 24, 1989	Joe Montana, San Francisco vs. Philadelphia	34	25	428	5
Sept. 24, 1989	Dan Marino, Miami vs. N.Y. Jets	55	33	427	3
Sept. 17, 1989	Randall Cunningham, Phil. vs. Washington	46	34	447	5
Dec. 18, 1988	Dave Krieg, Seattle at L.A. Raiders	32	19	410	4
Dec. 12, 1988	Dan Marino, Miami vs. Cleveland	50	30	404	4
Oct. 23, 1988	Dan Marino, Miami vs. N.Y. Jets	60	35	521	3
Oct. 16, 1988	Vinny Testaverde, Tampa Bay at Indianapolis	42	25	469	2
Sept. 11, 1988	Doug Williams, Washington vs. Pittsburgh	52	30	430	2
Nov. 29, 1987	Tom Ramsey, New England vs. Philadelphia	53	34	402	3
Nov. 22, 1987	Boomer Esiason, Cincinnati vs. Pittsburgh	53	30	409	0
Sept. 20, 1987	Neil Lomax, St. Louis vs. San Diego	61	32	457	3
Dec. 21, 1986	Boomer Esiason, Cincinnati vs. N.Y. Jets	30	23	425	5
Dec. 14, 1986	Dan Marino, Miami vs. L.A. Rams (OT)	46	29	403	5
Nov. 23, 1986	Bernie Kosar, Cleveland vs. Pittsburgh (OT)	46	28	414	2
Nov. 17, 1986	Joe Montana, San Francisco vs. Washington	60	33	441	0
Nov. 16, 1986	Dan Marino, Miami vs. Buffalo	54	39	404	4
Nov. 10, 1986	Bernie Kosar, Cleveland vs. Miami	50	32	401	0
Nov. 2, 1986	Tommy Kramer, Minnesota vs. Washington (OT)	35	20	490	4
Nov. 2, 1986	Ken O'Brien, N.Y. Jets vs. Seattle	32	26	431	4
Oct. 27, 1986	Jay Schroeder, Washington vs. N.Y. Giants	40	22	420	1
Oct. 12, 1986	Steve Grogan, New England vs. N.Y. Jets	42	23	401	3
Sept. 21, 1986	Ken O'Brien, N.Y. Jets vs. Miami (OT)	43	29	479	4
Sept. 21, 1986	Dan Marino, Miami vs. N.Y. Jets (OT)	50	30	448	6
Sept. 21, 1986	Tony Eason, New England vs. Seattle	45	26	414	3
Dec. 20, 1985	John Elway, Denver vs. Seattle	42	24	432	1
Nov. 10, 1985	Dan Fouts, San Diego vs. L.A. Raiders (OT)	41	26	436	4
Oct. 13, 1985	Phil Simms, N.Y. Giants vs. Cincinnati	62	40	513	1
Oct. 13, 1985	Dave Krieg, Seattle vs. Atlanta	51	33	405	4
Oct. 6, 1985	Phil Simms, N.Y. Giants vs. Dallas	36	18	432	3
Oct. 6, 1985	Joe Montana, San Francisco vs. Atlanta	57	37	429	5
Sept. 19, 1985	Tommy Kramer, Minnesota vs. Chicago	55	28	436	3
Sept. 15, 1985	Dan Fouts, San Diego vs. Seattle	43	29	440	4
Dec. 16, 1984	Neil Lomax, St. Louis vs. Washington	46	37	468	2
Dec. 9, 1984	Dan Marino, Miami vs. Indianapolis	41	29	404	4
Dec. 2, 1984	Dan Marino, Miami vs. L.A. Raiders	57	35	470	4
Nov. 25, 1984	Dave Krieg, Seattle vs. Denver	44	30	406	3
Nov. 4, 1984	Dan Marino, Miami vs. N.Y. Jets	42	23	422	2
Oct. 21, 1984	Dan Fouts, San Diego vs. L.A. Raiders	45	24	410	3
Sept. 30, 1984	Dan Marino, Miami vs. St. Louis	36	24	429	3
Sept. 2, 1984	Phil Simms, N.Y. Giants vs. Philadelphia	30	23	409	4
Dec. 11, 1983	Bill Kenney, Kansas City vs. San Diego	41	31	411	4
Nov. 20, 1983	Dave Krieg, Seattle vs. Denver	42	31	418	3
Oct. 9, 1983	Joe Ferguson, Buffalo vs. Miami (OT)	55	38	419	5
Oct. 2, 1983	Joe Theismann, Washington vs. L.A. Raiders	39	23	417	3
Sept. 25, 1983	Richard Todd, N.Y. Jets vs. L.A. Rams (OT)	50	37	446	2
Dec. 26, 1982	Vince Ferragamo, L.A. Rams vs. Chicago	46	30	509	3
Dec. 20, 1982	Dan Fouts, San Diego vs. Cincinnati	40	25	435	1
Dec. 20, 1982	Ken Anderson, Cincinnati vs. San Diego	56	40	416	2
Dec. 11, 1982	Dan Fouts, San Diego vs. San Francisco	48	33	444	5
Nov. 21, 1982	Joe Montana, San Francisco vs. St. Louis	39	26	408	3
Nov. 15, 1981	Steve Bartkowski, Atlanta vs. Pittsburgh	50	33	416	2
Oct. 25, 1981	Brian Sipe, Cleveland vs. Baltimore	41	30	444	4
Oct. 25, 1981	David Woodley, Miami vs. Dallas	37	21	408	3
Oct. 11, 1981	Tommy Kramer, Minnesota vs. San Diego	43	27	444	4
Dec. 14, 1980	Tommy Kramer, Minnesota vs. Cleveland	49	38	456	4
Nov. 16, 1980	Doug Williams, Tampa Bay vs. Minnesota	55	30	486	4
Oct. 19, 1980	Dan Fouts, San Diego vs. N.Y. Giants	41	26	444	3
Oct. 12, 1980	Lynn Dickey, Green Bay vs. Tampa Bay (OT)	51	35	418	1
Sept. 21, 1980	Richard Todd, N.Y. Jets vs. San Francisco	60	42	447	3
Oct. 3, 1976	James Harris, Los Angeles vs. Miami	29	17	436	2
Nov. 17, 1975	Ken Anderson, Cincinnati vs. Buffalo	46	30	447	2
Nov. 18, 1974	Charley Johnson, Denver vs. Kansas City	42	28	445	2
Dec. 11, 1972	Joe Namath, N.Y. Jets vs. Oakland	46	25	403	1
Sept. 24, 1972	Joe Namath, N.Y. Jets vs. Baltimore	28	15	496	6
Dec. 21, 1969	Don Horn, Green Bay vs. St. Louis	31	22	410	5
Sept. 28, 1969	Joe Kapp, Minnesota vs. Baltimore	43	28	449	7
Sept. 9, 1968	Pete Beathard, Houston vs. Kansas City	48	23	413	2
Nov. 26, 1967	Sonny Jurgensen, Washington vs. Cleveland	50	32	418	3
Oct. 1, 1967	Joe Namath, N.Y. Jets vs. Miami	39	23	415	3
Sept. 17, 1967	Johnny Unitas, Baltimore vs. Atlanta	32	22	401	2
Nov. 13, 1966	Don Meredith, Dallas vs. Washington	29	21	406	2
Nov. 28, 1965	Sonny Jurgensen, Washington vs. Dallas	43	26	411	3
Oct. 24, 1965	Fran Tarkenton, Minnesota vs. San Francisco	35	21	407	3
Nov. 1, 1964	Len Dawson, Kansas City vs. Denver	38	23	435	6
Oct. 25, 1964	Cotton Davidson, Oakland vs. Denver	36	23	427	5
Oct. 16, 1964	Babe Parilli, Boston vs. Oakland	47	25	422	4
Dec. 22, 1963	Tom Flores, Oakland vs. Houston	29	17	407	6
Nov. 17, 1963	Norm Snead, Washington vs. Pittsburgh	40	23	424	2
Nov. 10, 1963	Don Meredith, Dallas vs. San Francisco	48	30	460	3
Oct. 13, 1963	Charley Johnson, St. Louis vs. Pittsburgh	41	20	428	2
Dec. 16, 1962	Sonny Jurgensen, Philadelphia vs. St. Louis	34	15	419	5
Nov. 18, 1962	Bill Wade, Chicago vs. Dall. Cowboys	46	28	466	2
Oct. 28, 1962	Y.A. Tittle, N.Y. Giants vs. Washington	39	27	505	7
Sept. 15, 1962	Frank Tripucka, Denver vs. Buffalo	56	29	447	2
Dec. 17, 1961	Sonny Jurgensen, Philadelphia vs. Detroit	42	27	403	3

Nov. 19, 1961	George Blanda, Houston vs. N.Y. Titans	32	20	418	7
Oct. 29, 1961	George Blanda, Houston vs. Buffalo	32	18	464	4
Oct. 29, 1961	Sonny Jurgensen, Philadelphia vs. Washington	41	27	436	3
Oct. 13, 1961	Jacky Lee, Houston vs. Boston	41	27	457	2
Dec. 13, 1958	Bobby Layne, Pittsburgh vs. Chi. Cardinals	49	23	409	2
Nov. 8, 1953	Bobby Thomason, Philadelphia vs. N.Y. Giants	44	22	437	4
Oct. 4, 1952	Otto Graham, Cleveland vs. Pittsburgh	49	21	401	3
Sept. 28, 1951	Norm Van Brocklin, Los Angeles vs. N.Y. Yanks	41	27	554	5
Dec. 11, 1949	Johnny Lujack, Chi. Bears vs. Chi. Cardinals	39	24	468	6
Oct. 31, 1948	Sammy Baugh, Washington vs. Boston	24	17	446	4
Oct. 31, 1948	Jim Hardy, Los Angeles vs. Chi. Cardinals	53	28	406	3
Nov. 14, 1943	Sid Luckman, Chi. Bears vs. N.Y. Giants	32	21	433	7

Times 400 or More

102 times by 59 players . . . Marino 10; Fouts 6; Jurgensen, Montana 5; Kramer, Krieg 4; Namath, Simms 3; Anderson, Blanda, Cunningham, Esiason, Johnson, Kosar, Lomax, Meredith, O'Brien, Todd, Williams 2.

1,000 Yards Pass Receiving in a Season

Year	Player, Team	No.	Yards	Avg.	Long	TD
1989	Jerry Rice, San Francisco[4]	82	1,483	18.1	68	17
	Sterling Sharpe, Green Bay	90	1,423	15.8	79	12
	Mark Carrier, Tampa Bay	86	1,422	16.5	78	9
	Henry Ellard, L.A. Rams[2]	70	1,382	19.7	53	8
	Andre Reed, Buffalo	88	1,312	14.9	78	9
	Anthony Miller, San Diego	75	1,252	16.7	69	10
	Webster Slaughter, Cleveland	65	1,236	19.0	97	6
	Gary Clark, Washington[3]	79	1,229	15.6	80	9
	Tim McGee, Cincinnati	65	1,211	18.6	74	8
	Art Monk, Washington[4]	86	1,186	13.8	60	8
	Willie Anderson, L.A. Rams	44	1,146	26.0	78	5
	Ricky Sanders, Washington[2]	80	1,138	14.2	68	4
	Vance Johnson, Denver	76	1,095	14.4	69	7
	Richard Johnson, Detroit	70	1,091	15.6	75	8
	Eric Martin, New Orleans[2]	68	1,090	16.0	53	8
	John Taylor, San Francisco	60	1,077	18.0	95	10
	Mervyn Fernandez, L.A. Raiders	57	1,069	18.8	75	9
	Anthony Carter, Minnesota[2]	65	1,066	16.4	50	4
	Brian Blades, Seattle	77	1,063	13.8	60	5
	Mark Clayton, Miami[4]	64	1,011	15.8	78	9
1988	Henry Ellard, L.A. Rams	86	1,414	16.4	68	10
	Jerry Rice, San Francisco[3]	64	1,306	20.4	96	9
	Eddie Brown, Cincinnati	53	1,273	24.0	86	9
	Anthony Carter, Minnesota	72	1,225	17.0	67	6
	Ricky Sanders, Washington	73	1,148	15.7	55	12
	Drew Hill, Houston[3]	72	1,141	15.8	57	10
	Mark Clayton, Miami[3]	86	1,129	13.1	45	14
	Roy Green, Phoenix[3]	68	1,097	16.1	52	7
	Eric Martin, New Orleans	85	1,083	12.7	40	7
	Al Toon, N.Y. Jets[2]	93	1,067	11.5	42	5
	Bruce Hill, Tampa Bay	58	1,040	17.9	42	9
	Lionel Manuel, N.Y. Giants	65	1,029	15.8	46	4
1987	J.T. Smith, St. Louis[2]	91	1,117	12.3	38	8
	Jerry Rice, San Francisco[2]	65	1,078	16.6	57	22
	Gary Clark, Washington[2]	56	1,066	19.0	84	7
	Carlos Carson, Kansas City[3]	55	1,044	19.0	81	7
1986	Jerry Rice, San Francisco	86	1,570	18.3	66	15
	Stanley Morgan, New England[3]	84	1,491	17.8	44	10
	Mark Duper, Miami[3]	67	1,313	19.6	85	11
	Gary Clark, Washington	74	1,265	17.1	55	7
	Al Toon, N.Y. Jets	85	1,176	13.8	62	8
	Todd Christensen, L.A. Raiders[3]	95	1,153	12.1	35	8
	Mark Clayton, Miami[2]	60	1,150	19.2	68	10
	*Bill Brooks, Indianapolis	65	1,131	17.4	84	8
	Drew Hill, Houston[2]	65	1,112	17.1	81	5
	Steve Largent, Seattle[8]	70	1,070	15.3	38	9
	Art Monk, Washington[3]	73	1,068	14.6	69	4
	*Earnest Givins, Houston	61	1,062	17.4	60	3
	Cris Collinsworth, Cincinnati[4]	62	1,024	16.5	46	10
	Wesley Walker, N.Y. Jets[2]	49	1,016	20.7	83	12
	J.T. Smith, St. Louis	80	1,014	12.7	45	6
	Mark Bavaro, N.Y. Giants	66	1,001	15.2	41	4
1985	Steve Largent, Seattle[7]	79	1,287	16.3	43	6
	Mike Quick, Philadelphia[3]	73	1,247	17.1	99	11
	Art Monk, Washington[2]	91	1,226	13.5	53	2
	Wes Chandler, San Diego[4]	67	1,199	17.9	75	10
	Drew Hill, Houston	64	1,169	18.3	57	9
	James Lofton, Green Bay[5]	69	1,153	16.7	56	4
	Louis Lipps, Pittsburgh	59	1,134	19.2	51	12
	Cris Collinsworth, Cincinnati[3]	65	1,125	17.3	71	5
	Tony Hill, Dallas[3]	74	1,113	15.0	53	7
	Lionel James, San Diego	86	1,027	11.9	67	6
	Roger Craig, San Francisco	92	1,016	11.0	73	6
1984	Roy Green, St. Louis[2]	78	1,555	19.9	83	12
	John Stallworth, Pittsburgh[3]	80	1,395	17.4	51	11
	Mark Clayton, Miami	73	1,389	19.0	65	18
	Art Monk, Washington	106	1,372	12.9	72	7
	James Lofton, Green Bay[4]	62	1,361	22.0	79	7
	Mark Duper, Miami[2]	71	1,306	18.4	80	8
	Steve Watson, Denver[3]	69	1,170	17.0	73	7
	Steve Largent, Seattle[6]	74	1,164	15.7	65	12
	Tim Smith, Houston[2]	69	1,141	16.5	75	4
	Stacey Bailey, Atlanta	67	1,138	17.0	61	6
	Carlos Carson, Kansas City[2]	57	1,078	18.9	57	4
	Mike Quick, Philadelphia[2]	61	1,052	17.2	90	9
	Todd Christensen, L.A. Raiders[2]	80	1,007	12.6	38	7
	Kevin House, Tampa Bay[2]	76	1,005	13.2	55	5
	Ozzie Newsome, Cleveland[2]	89	1,001	11.2	52	5
1983	Mike Quick, Philadelphia	69	1,409	20.4	83	13
	Carlos Carson, Kansas City	80	1,351	16.9	50	7
	James Lofton, Green Bay[3]	58	1,300	22.4	74	8
	Todd Christensen, L.A. Raiders	92	1,247	13.6	45	12
	Roy Green, St. Louis	78	1,227	15.7	71	14
	Charlie Brown, Washington	78	1,225	15.7	75	8
	Tim Smith, Houston	83	1,176	14.2	47	6
	Kellen Winslow, San Diego[3]	88	1,172	13.3	46	8
	Earnest Gray, N.Y. Giants	78	1,139	14.6	62	5
	Steve Watson, Denver[2]	59	1,133	19.2	78	5
	Cris Collinsworth, Cincinnati[2]	66	1,130	17.1	63	5
	Steve Largent, Seattle[5]	72	1,074	14.9	46	11
	Mark Duper, Miami	51	1,003	19.7	85	10
1982	Wes Chandler, San Diego[3]	49	1,032	21.1	66	9
1981	Alfred Jenkins, Atlanta[2]	70	1,358	19.4	67	13
	James Lofton, Green Bay[2]	71	1,294	18.2	75	8
	Frank Lewis, Buffalo[2]	70	1,244	17.8	33	4
	Steve Watson, Denver	60	1,244	20.7	95	13
	Steve Largent, Seattle[4]	75	1,224	16.3	57	9
	Charlie Joiner, San Diego[4]	70	1,188	17.0	57	7
	Kevin House, Tampa Bay	56	1,176	21.0	84	9
	Wes Chandler, N.O.-San Diego[2]	69	1,142	16.6	51	6
	Dwight Clark, San Francisco	85	1,105	13.0	78	4
	John Stallworth, Pittsburgh[2]	63	1,098	17.4	55	5
	Kellen Winslow, San Diego[2]	88	1,075	12.2	67	10
	Pat Tilley, St. Louis	66	1,040	15.8	75	3
	Stanley Morgan, New England[2]	44	1,029	23.4	76	6
	Harold Carmichael, Philadelphia[3]	61	1,028	16.9	85	6
	Freddie Scott, Detroit	53	1,022	19.3	48	5
	*Cris Collinsworth, Cincinnati	67	1,009	15.1	74	8
	Joe Senser, Minnesota	79	1,004	12.7	53	8
	Ozzie Newsome, Cleveland	69	1,002	14.5	62	6
	Sammy White, Minnesota	66	1,001	15.2	53	3
1980	John Jefferson, San Diego[3]	82	1,340	16.3	58	13
	Kellen Winslow, San Diego	89	1,290	14.5	65	9
	James Lofton, Green Bay	71	1,226	17.3	47	4
	Charlie Joiner, San Diego[3]	71	1,132	15.9	51	4
	Ahmad Rashad, Minnesota[2]	69	1,095	15.9	76	5
	Steve Largent, Seattle[3]	66	1,064	16.1	67	6
	Tony Hill, Dallas[2]	60	1,055	17.6	58	8
	Alfred Jenkins, Atlanta	57	1,026	18.0	57	6
1979	Steve Largent, Seattle[2]	66	1,237	18.7	55	9
	John Stallworth, Pittsburgh	70	1,183	16.9	65	8
	Ahmad Rashad, Minnesota	80	1,156	14.5	52	9
	John Jefferson, San Diego[2]	61	1,090	17.9	65	10
	Frank Lewis, Buffalo	54	1,082	20.0	55	2
	Wes Chandler, New Orleans	65	1,069	16.4	85	6
	Tony Hill, Dallas	60	1,062	17.7	75	10
	Drew Pearson, Dallas[2]	55	1,026	18.7	56	8
	Wallace Francis, Atlanta	74	1,013	13.7	42	8
	Harold Jackson, New England[3]	45	1,013	22.5	59	7
	Charlie Joiner, San Diego[2]	72	1,008	14.0	39	4
	Stanley Morgan, New England	44	1,002	22.8	63	12
1978	Wesley Walker, N.Y. Jets	48	1,169	24.4	77	8
	Steve Largent, Seattle	71	1,168	16.5	57	8
	Harold Carmichael, Philadelphia[2]	55	1,072	19.5	56	8
	*John Jefferson, San Diego	56	1,001	17.9	46	13
1976	Roger Carr, Baltimore	43	1,112	25.9	79	11
	Cliff Branch, Oakland[2]	46	1,111	24.2	88	12
	Charlie Joiner, San Diego	50	1,056	21.1	81	7
1975	Ken Burrough, Houston	53	1,063	20.1	77	8
1974	Cliff Branch, Oakland	60	1,092	18.2	67	13
	Drew Pearson, Dallas	62	1,087	17.5	50	2
1973	Harold Carmichael, Philadelphia	67	1,116	16.7	73	9
1972	Harold Jackson, Philadelphia[2]	62	1,048	16.9	77	4
	John Gilliam, Minnesota	47	1,035	22.0	66	7
1971	Otis Taylor, Kansas City[2]	57	1,110	19.5	82	7
1970	Gene Washington, San Francisco	53	1,100	20.8	79	12
	Marlin Briscoe, Buffalo	57	1,036	18.2	48	8
	Dick Gordon, Chicago	71	1,026	14.5	69	13
	Gary Garrison, San Diego[2]	44	1,006	22.9	67	12
1969	Warren Wells, Oakland[2]	47	1,260	26.8	80	14
	Harold Jackson, Philadelphia	65	1,116	17.2	65	9
	Roy Jefferson, Pittsburgh[2]	67	1,079	16.1	63	9
	Dan Abramowicz, New Orleans	73	1,015	13.9	49	7
	Lance Alworth, San Diego[7]	64	1,003	15.7	76	4
1968	Lance Alworth, San Diego[6]	68	1,312	19.3	80	10
	Don Maynard, N.Y. Jets[5]	57	1,297	22.8	87	10
	George Sauer, N.Y. Jets[3]	66	1,141	17.3	43	3
	Warren Wells, Oakland	53	1,137	21.5	94	11
	Gary Garrison, San Diego	52	1,103	21.2	84	10
	Roy Jefferson, Pittsburgh	58	1,074	18.5	62	11
	Paul Warfield, Cleveland	50	1,067	21.3	65	12
	Homer Jones, N.Y. Giants[3]	45	1,057	23.5	84	7
	Fred Biletnikoff, Oakland	61	1,037	17.0	82	6
	Lance Rentzel, Dallas	54	1,009	18.7	65	6
1967	Don Maynard, N.Y. Jets[4]	71	1,434	20.2	75	10
	Ben Hawkins, Philadelphia	59	1,265	21.4	87	10
	Homer Jones, N.Y. Giants[2]	49	1,209	24.7	70	13
	Jackie Smith, St. Louis	56	1,205	21.5	76	9
	George Sauer, N.Y. Jets[2]	75	1,189	15.9	61	6
	Lance Alworth, San Diego[5]	52	1,010	19.4	71	9
1966	Lance Alworth, San Diego[4]	73	1,383	18.9	78	13
	Otis Taylor, Kansas City	58	1,297	22.4	89	8
	Pat Studstill, Detroit	67	1,266	18.9	99	5
	Bob Hayes, Dallas[2]	64	1,232	19.3	95	13
	Charlie Frazier, Houston	57	1,129	19.8	79	12
	Charley Taylor, Washington	72	1,119	15.5	86	12
	George Sauer, N.Y. Jets	63	1,081	17.2	77	5
	Homer Jones, N.Y. Giants	48	1,044	21.8	98	8
	Art Powell, Oakland[5]	53	1,026	19.4	46	11

1965	Lance Alworth, San Diego[3]	69	1,602	23.2	85	14
	Dave Parks, San Francisco	80	1,344	16.8	53	12
	Don Maynard, N.Y. Jets[3]	68	1,218	17.9	56	14
	Pete Retzlaff, Philadelphia	66	1,190	18.0	78	10
	Lionel Taylor, Denver[4]	85	1,131	13.3	63	6
	Tommy McDonald, Los Angeles[3]	67	1,036	15.5	51	9
	*Bob Hayes, Dallas	46	1,003	21.8	82	12
1964	Charley Hennigan, Houston[3]	101	1,546	15.3	53	8
	Art Powell, Oakland[4]	76	1,361	17.9	77	11
	Lance Alworth, San Diego[2]	61	1,235	20.2	82	13
	Johnny Morris, Chicago	93	1,200	12.9	63	10
	Elbert Dubenion, Buffalo	42	1,139	27.1	72	10
	Terry Barr, Detroit[2]	57	1,030	18.1	58	9
1963	Bobby Mitchell, Washington[2]	69	1,436	20.8	99	7
	Art Powell, Oakland[3]	73	1,304	17.9	85	16
	Buddy Dial, Pittsburgh[2]	60	1,295	21.6	83	9
	Lance Alworth, San Diego	61	1,205	19.8	85	11
	Del Shofner, N.Y. Giants[4]	64	1,181	18.5	70	9
	Lionel Taylor, Denver[3]	78	1,101	14.1	72	10
	Terry Barr, Detroit	66	1,086	16.5	75	13
	Charley Hennigan, Houston[2]	61	1,051	17.2	83	10
	Sonny Randle, St. Louis[2]	51	1,014	19.9	68	12
	Bake Turner, N.Y. Jets	71	1,009	14.2	53	6
1962	Bobby Mitchell, Washington	72	1,384	19.2	81	11
	Sonny Randle, St. Louis	63	1,158	18.4	86	7
	Tommy McDonald, Philadelphia[2]	58	1,146	19.8	60	10
	Del Shofner, N.Y. Giants[3]	53	1,133	21.4	69	12
	Art Powell, N.Y. Titans[2]	64	1,130	17.7	80	8
	Frank Clarke, Dall. Cowboys	47	1,043	22.2	66	14
	Don Maynard, N.Y. Titans[2]	56	1,041	18.6	86	8
1961	Charley Hennigan, Houston	82	1,746	21.3	80	12
	Lionel Taylor, Denver[2]	100	1,176	11.8	52	4
	Bill Groman, Houston[2]	50	1,175	23.5	80	17
	Tommy McDonald, Philadelphia	64	1,144	17.9	66	13
	Del Shofner, N.Y. Giants[2]	68	1,125	16.5	46	11
	Jim Phillips, Los Angeles	78	1,092	14.0	69	5
	*Mike Ditka, Chicago	56	1,076	19.2	76	12
	Dave Kocourek, San Diego	55	1,055	19.2	76	4
	Buddy Dial, Pittsburgh	53	1,047	19.8	88	12
	R.C. Owens, San Francisco	55	1,032	18.8	54	5
1960	*Bill Groman, Houston	72	1,473	20.5	92	12
	Raymond Berry, Baltimore	74	1,298	17.5	70	10
	Don Maynard, N.Y. Titans	72	1,265	17.6	65	6
	Lionel Taylor, Denver	92	1,235	13.4	80	12
	Art Powell, N.Y. Titans	69	1,167	16.9	76	14
1958	Del Shofner, Los Angeles	51	1,097	21.5	92	8
1956	Bill Howton, Green Bay[2]	55	1,188	21.6	66	12
	Harlon Hill, Chi. Bears[2]	47	1,128	24.0	79	11
1954	Bob Boyd, Los Angeles	53	1,212	22.9	80	6
	*Harlon Hill, Chi. Bears	45	1,124	25.0	76	12
1953	Pete Pihos, Philadelphia	63	1,049	16.7	59	10
1952	*Bill Howton, Green Bay	53	1,231	23.2	90	13
1951	Elroy (Crazylegs) Hirsch, Los Angeles	66	1,495	22.7	91	17
1950	Tom Fears, Los Angeles[2]	84	1,116	13.3	53	7
	Cloyce Box, Detroit	50	1,009	20.2	82	11
1949	Bob Mann, Detroit	66	1,014	15.4	64	4
	Tom Fears, Los Angeles	77	1,013	13.2	51	9
1945	Jim Benton, Cleveland	45	1,067	23.7	84	8
1942	Don Hutson, Green Bay	74	1,211	16.4	73	17

*First year in the league.

250 Yards Pass Receiving in a Game

Date	Player, Team, Opponent	No.	Yards	TD
Dec. 11, 1989	John Taylor, San Francisco vs. L.A. Rams	11	286	2
Nov. 26, 1989	Willie Anderson, L.A. Rams vs. New Orleans (OT)	15	336	1
Oct. 18, 1987	Steve Largent, Seattle vs. Detroit	15	261	3
Oct. 4, 1987	*Anthony Allen, Washington vs. St. Louis	7	255	3
Dec. 22, 1985	Stephone Paige, Kansas City vs. San Diego	8	309	2
Dec. 20, 1982	Wes Chandler, San Diego vs. Cincinnati	10	260	2
Sept. 23, 1979	*Jerry Butler, Buffalo vs. N.Y. Jets	10	255	4
Nov. 4, 1962	Sonny Randle, St. Louis vs. N.Y. Giants	16	256	1
Oct. 28, 1962	Del Shofner, N.Y. Giants vs. Washington	11	269	1
Oct. 13, 1961	Charley Hennigan, Houston vs. Boston	13	272	1
Oct. 21, 1956	Billy Howton, Green Bay vs. Los Angeles	7	257	2
Dec. 3, 1950	Cloyce Box, Detroit vs. Baltimore	12	302	4
Nov. 22, 1945	Jim Benton, Cleveland vs. Detroit	10	303	1

*First year in the league.

2,000 Combined Net Yards Gained in a Season

Year	Player, Team	Rushing Att.-Yds.	Pass Rec.	Punt Ret.	Kickoff Ret.	Fum. Runs	Total Yds.
1988	*Tim Brown, L.A. Raiders	14-50	43-725	49-444	41-1,098	7-0	154-2,317
	Roger Craig, San Fran.	310-1,502	76-534	0-0	2-32	2-0	390-2,068
	Eric Dickerson, Indianapolis	388-1,659	36-377	0-0	0-0	1-0	425-2,036
	Herschel Walker, Dallas	361-1,514	53-505	0-0	0-0	3-0	417-2,019
1986	Eric Dickerson, L.A. Rams	404-1,821	26-205	0-0	0-0	2-0	432-2,026
	Gary Anderson, San Diego	127-442	80-871	25-227	24-482	2-0	258-2,022
1985	Lionel James, San Diego	105-516	86-1,027	25-213	36-779	1-0	253-2,535
	Marcus Allen, L.A. Raiders	380-1,759	67-555	0-0	0-0	2-(-6)	449-2,308
	Roger Craig, San Fran.	214-1,050	92-1,016	0-0	0-0	0-0	306-2,066
	Walter Payton, Chicago	324-1,551	49-483	0-0	0-0	1-0	374-2,034
1984	Eric Dickerson, L.A. Rams	379-2,105	21-139	0-0	0-0	4-15	404-2,259
	James Wilder, Tampa Bay	407-1,544	85-685	0-0	0-0	4-0	496-2,229
	Walter Payton, Chicago	381-1,684	45-368	0-0	0-0	1-0	427-2,052
1983	*Eric Dickerson, L.A. Rams	390-1,808	51-404	0-0	0-0	1-0	442-2,212
	William Andrews, Atlanta	331-1,567	59-609	0-0	0-0	2-0	392-2,176
	Walter Payton, Chicago	314-1,421	53-607	0-0	0-0	2-0	369-2,028
1981	*James Brooks, San Diego	109-525	46-329	22-290	40-949	2-0	219-2,093
	William Andrews, Atlanta	289-1,301	81-735	0-0	0-0	0-0	370-2,036
1980	Bruce Harper, N.Y. Jets	45-126	50-634	28-242	49-1,070	3-0	175-2,072
1979	Wilbert Montgomery, Phil.	338-1,512	41-494	0-0	1-6	2-0	382-2,012
1978	Bruce Harper, N.Y. Jets	58-303	13-196	30-378	55-1,280	1-0	157-2,157
1977	Walter Payton, Chicago	339-1,852	27-269	0-0	2-95	5-0	373-2,216
	Terry Metcalf, St. Louis	149-739	34-403	14-108	32-772	1-0	230-2,022
1975	Terry Metcalf, St. Louis	165-816	43-378	23-285	35-960	2-23	268-2,462
	O.J. Simpson, Buffalo	329-1,817	28-426	0-0	0-0	1-0	358-2,243
1974	Mack Herron, New England	231-824	38-474	35-517	28-629	3-0	335-2,444
	Otis Armstrong, Denver	263-1,407	38-405	0-0	16-386	1-0	318-2,198
	Terry Metcalf, St. Louis	152-718	50-377	26-340	20-623	7-0	255-2,058
1973	O.J. Simpson, Buffalo	332-2,003	6-70	0-0	0-0	0-0	338-2,073
1966	Gale Sayers, Chicago	229-1,231	34-447	6-44	23-718	3-0	295-2,440
	Leroy Kelly, Cleveland	209-1,141	32-366	13-104	19-403	0-0	273-2,014
1965	*Gale Sayers, Chicago	166-867	29-507	16-238	21-660	4-0	236-2,272
1963	Timmy Brown, Philadelphia	192-841	36-487	16-152	33-945	2-3	279-2,428
	Jim Brown, Cleveland	291-1,863	24-268	0-0	0-0	0-0	315-2,131
1962	Timmy Brown, Philadelphia	137-545	52-849	6-81	30-831	4-0	229-2,306
	Dick Christy, N.Y. Titans	114-535	62-538	15-250	38-824	2-0	231-2,147
1961	Billy Cannon, Houston	200-948	43-586	9-70	18-439	2-0	272-2,043
1960	*Abner Haynes, Dall. Texans	156-875	55-576	14-215	19-434	4-0	248-2,100

*First year in the league.

300 Combined Net Yards Gained in a Game

Date	Player, Team, Opponent	No.	Yards	TD
Dec. 11, 1989	John Taylor, San Francisco vs. L.A. Rams	14	321	2
Nov. 26, 1989	Willie Anderson, L.A. Rams vs. New Orleans (OT)	15	336	1
Nov. 28, 1988	Tim Brown, L.A. Raiders vs. San Diego	12	306	1
Dec. 22, 1985	Stephone Paige, Kansas City vs. San Diego	8	309	2
Nov. 10, 1985	Lionel James, San Diego vs. L.A. Raiders (OT)	23	345	0
Sept. 22, 1985	Lionel James, San Diego vs. Cincinnati	20	316	2
Dec. 21, 1975	Walter Payton, Chicago vs. New Orleans	32	300	1
Nov. 23, 1975	Greg Pruitt, Cleveland vs. Cincinnati	28	304	2
Nov. 1, 1970	Eugene (Mercury) Morris, Miami vs. Baltimore	17	302	0
Oct. 4, 1970	O. J. Simpson, Buffalo vs. N.Y. Jets	26	303	2
Dec. 6, 1969	Jerry LeVias, Houston vs. N.Y. Jets	18	329	1
Nov. 2, 1969	Travis Williams, Green Bay vs. Pittsburgh	11	314	3
Dec. 18, 1966	Gale Sayers, Chicago vs. Minnesota	20	339	2
Dec. 12, 1965	Gale Sayers, Chicago vs. San Francisco	17	336	6
Nov. 17, 1963	Gary Ballman, Pittsburgh vs. Washington	12	320	2
Dec. 16, 1962	Timmy Brown, Philadelphia vs. St. Louis	19	341	2
Dec. 10, 1961	Billy Cannon, Houston vs. N.Y. Titans	32	373	5
Nov 19, 1961	Jim Brown, Cleveland vs. Philadelphia	38	313	4
Dec. 3, 1950	Cloyce Box, Detroit vs. Baltimore	13	302	4
Oct. 29, 1950	Wally Triplett, Detroit vs. Los Angeles	11	331	1
Nov. 22, 1945	Jim Benton, Cleveland vs. Detroit	10	303	1

Top 20 Scorers

Player	Years	TD	FG	PAT	TP
George Blanda	26	9	335	943	2,002
Jan Stenerud	19	0	373	580	1,699
Jim Turner	16	1	304	521	1,439
Mark Moseley	16	0	300	482	1,382
Jim Bakken	17	0	282	534	1,380
Fred Cox	15	0	282	519	1,365
Lou Groza	17	1	234	641	1,349
Pat Leahy	16	0	255	496	1,261
Chris Bahr	14	0	241	490	1,213
Gino Cappelletti	11	42	176	350	1,130
Ray Wersching	15	0	222	456	1,122
Don Cockroft	13	0	216	432	1,080
Garo Yepremian	14	0	210	444	1,074
Bruce Gossett	11	0	219	374	1,031
Nick Lowery	11	0	225	338	1,013
Sam Baker	15	2	179	428	977
Jim Breech	11	0	184	418	970
Rafael Septien	10	0	180	420	960
Lou Michaels	13	1	187	386	955
Eddie Murray	10	0	212	307	943

Cappelletti's total includes four two-point conversions.
Michaels's total includes one safety.

Top 20 Touchdown Scorers

Player	Years	Rush	Pass Rec.	Returns	Total TD
Jim Brown	9	106	20	0	126
Walter Payton	13	110	15	0	125
John Riggins	14	104	12	0	116
Lenny Moore	12	63	48	2	113
Don Hutson	11	3	99	3	105
Steve Largent	14	1	100	0	101
Franco Harris	13	91	9	0	100
Jim Taylor	10	83	10	0	93
Tony Dorsett	12	77	13	1	91
Bobby Mitchell	11	18	65	8	91
Leroy Kelly	10	74	13	3	90
Charley Taylor	13	11	79	0	90
Don Maynard	15	0	88	0	88
Lance Alworth	11	2	85	0	87
Eric Dickerson	7	82	4	0	86
Paul Warfield	13	1	85	0	86
Tommy McDonald	12	0	84	1	85
Pete Johnson	8	76	6	0	82
Art Powell	10	0	81	1	82
Marcus Allen	8	63	16	1	80

Top 20 Rushers

Player	Years	Att.	Yards	Avg.	Long	TD
Walter Payton	13	3,838	16,726	4.4	76	110
Tony Dorsett	12	2,936	12,739	4.3	99	77
Jim Brown	9	2,359	12,312	5.2	80	106
Franco Harris	13	2,949	12,120	4.1	75	91
John Riggins	14	2,916	11,352	3.9	66	104
O.J. Simpson	11	2,404	11,236	4.7	94	61
Eric Dickerson	7	2,450	11,226	4.6	85	82
Earl Campbell	8	2,187	9,407	4.3	81	74
Ottis Anderson	11	2,274	9,317	4.1	76	69

Player						
Jim Taylor	10	1,941	8,597	4.4	84	83
Joe Perry	14	1,737	8,378	4.8	78	53
Larry Csonka	11	1,891	8,081	4.3	54	64
Gerald Riggs	8	1,788	7,465	4.2	58	52
Mike Pruitt	11	1,844	7,378	4.0	77	51
Marcus Allen	8	1,781	7,275	4.1	61	63
Leroy Kelly	10	1,727	7,274	4.2	70	74
George Rogers	7	1,692	7,176	4.2	79	54
Freeman McNeil	9	1,605	7,146	4.5	69	30
John Henry Johnson	13	1,571	6,803	4.3	87	48
Wilbert Montgomery	9	1,540	6,789	4.4	90	45

Top 20 Combined Yards Gained

Player	Years	Tot.	Rush.	Rec.	Int. Ret.	Punt Ret.	Kickoff Ret.	Fumble Ret.
Walter Payton	13	21,803	16,726	4,538	0	0	539	0
Tony Dorsett	12	16,326	12,739	3,554	0	0	0	33
Jim Brown	9	15,459	12,312	2,499	0	0	648	0
Franco Harris	13	14,622	12,120	2,287	0	0	233	−18
O.J. Simpson	11	14,368	11,236	2,142	0	0	990	0
Bobby Mitchell	11	14,078	2,735	7,954	0	699	2,690	0
John Riggins	14	13,435	11,352	2,090	0	0	0	−7
Steve Largent	14	13,396	83	13,089	0	68	156	0
Greg Pruitt	12	13,262	5,672	3,069	0	2,007	2,514	0
Ollie Matson	14	12,884	5,173	3,285	51	595	3,746	34
Eric Dickerson	7	12,874	11,226	1,633	0	0	0	15
Tim Brown	10	12,684	3,862	3,399	0	639	4,781	3
Lenny Moore	12	12,451	5,174	6,039	0	56	1,180	2
James Brooks	9	12,436	6,343	3,005	0	565	2,523	0
Don Maynard	15	12,379	70	11,834	0	132	343	0
Charlie Joiner	18	12,367	22	12,146	0	0	194	5
Leroy Kelly	10	12,330	7,274	2,281	0	990	1,784	1
Ottis Anderson	11	12,206	9,317	2,882	0	0	0	7
Floyd Little	9	12,173	6,323	2,418	0	893	2,523	16
Abner Haynes	8	12,065	4,630	3,535	0	875	3,025	0

Top 20 Passers

Player	Years	Att.	Comp.	Pct. Comp.	Yards	TD	Pct. TD	Int.	Pct. Int.	Avg. Gain	Rating
Joe Montana	11	4,059	2,593	63.9	31,054	216	5.3	107	2.6	7.65	94.0
Dan Marino	7	3,650	2,174	59.6	27,853	220	6.0	125	3.4	7.63	89.3
Boomer Esiason	6	2,285	1,296	56.7	18,350	126	5.5	76	3.3	8.03	87.3
Dave Krieg	10	2,843	1,644	57.8	20,858	169	5.9	116	4.1	7.34	83.7
Roger Staubach	11	2,958	1,685	57.0	22,700	153	5.2	109	3.7	7.67	83.4
Bernie Kosar	5	1,940	1,134	58.5	13,888	75	3.9	47	2.4	7.16	83.4
Ken O'Brien	6	2,467	1,471	59.6	17,589	96	3.9	68	2.8	7.13	83.0
Jim Kelly	4	1,742	1,032	59.2	12,901	81	4.6	63	3.6	7.41	82.7
Neil Lomax	8	3,153	1,817	57.6	22,771	136	4.3	90	2.9	7.22	82.7
Sonny Jurgensen	18	4,262	2,433	57.1	32,224	255	6.0	189	4.4	7.56	82.6
Len Dawson	19	3,741	2,136	57.1	28,711	239	6.4	183	4.9	7.67	82.6
Ken Anderson	16	4,475	2,654	59.3	32,838	197	4.4	160	3.6	7.34	81.9
Danny White	13	2,950	1,761	59.7	21,959	155	5.3	132	4.5	7.44	81.7
Bart Starr	16	3,149	1,808	57.4	24,718	152	4.8	138	4.4	7.85	80.5
Fran Tarkenton	18	6,467	3,686	57.0	47,003	342	5.3	266	4.1	7.27	80.4
Tony Eason	7	1,536	898	58.5	10,987	61	4.0	50	3.3	7.15	80.3
Dan Fouts	15	5,604	3,297	58.8	43,040	254	4.5	242	4.3	7.68	80.2
Jim McMahon	8	1,831	1,050	57.3	13,335	77	4.2	66	3.6	7.28	79.2
Bert Jones	10	2,551	1,430	56.1	18,190	124	4.9	101	4.0	7.13	78.2
Johnny Unitas	18	5,186	2,830	54.6	40,239	290	5.6	253	4.9	7.76	78.2

1,500 or more attempts. The passing ratings are based on performance standards established for completion percentage, interception percentage, touchdown percentage, and average gain. Passers are allocated points according to how their marks compare with those standards.

Top 20 Pass Receivers

Player	Years	No.	Yards	Avg.	Long	TD
Steve Largent	14	819	13,089	16.0	74	100
Charlie Joiner	18	750	12,146	16.2	87	65
Art Monk	10	662	9,165	13.8	79	47
Charley Taylor	13	649	9,110	14.0	88	79
Ozzie Newsome	12	639	7,740	12.1	74	45
Don Maynard	15	633	11,834	18.7	87	88
Raymond Berry	13	631	9,275	14.7	70	68
James Lofton	12	607	11,251	18.5	80	57
Harold Carmichael	14	590	8,985	15.2	85	79
Fred Biletnikoff	14	589	8,974	15.2	82	76
Harold Jackson	16	579	10,372	17.9	79	76
Lionel Taylor	10	567	7,195	12.7	80	45
Wes Chandler	11	559	8,966	16.0	85	56
Lance Alworth	11	542	10,266	18.9	85	85
Kellen Winslow	9	541	6,741	12.5	67	45
John Stallworth	14	537	8,723	16.2	74	63
Stanley Morgan	13	534	10,352	19.4	76	67
J.T. Smith	12	526	6,749	12.8	77	33
Bobby Mitchell	11	521	7,954	15.3	99	65
Nat Moore	13	510	7,546	14.8	79	74

Top 20 Interceptors

Player	Years	No.	Yards	Avg.	Long	TD
Paul Krause	16	81	1,185	14.6	81	3
Emlen Tunnell	14	79	1,282	16.2	55	4
Dick (Night Train) Lane	14	68	1,207	17.8	80	5
Ken Riley	15	65	596	9.2	66	5
Dick LeBeau	13	62	762	12.3	70	3
Dave Brown	15	62	698	11.3	90	5
Emmitt Thomas	13	58	937	16.2	73	5
Bobby Boyd	9	57	994	17.4	74	4
Johnny Robinson	12	57	741	13.0	57	1
Mel Blount	14	57	736	12.9	52	2
Lem Barney	11	56	1,077	19.2	71	7
Pat Fischer	17	56	941	16.8	69	4
Willie Brown	16	54	472	8.7	45	2
Bobby Dillon	8	52	976	18.8	61	5

Player						
Jack Butler	9	52	826	15.9	52	4
Larry Wilson	13	52	800	15.4	96	5
Jim Patton	12	52	712	13.7	51	2
Mel Renfro	14	52	626	12.0	90	3
Bobby Bryant	13	51	749	14.7	56	3
Donnie Shell	14	51	490	9.6	67	2

Top 20 Punters

Player	Years	No.	Yards	Avg.	Long	Blk.
Sammy Baugh	16	338	15,245	45.1	85	9
Tommy Davis	11	511	22,833	44.7	82	2
Yale Lary	11	503	22,279	44.3	74	4
Rohn Stark	8	593	26,183	44.2	72	5
Horace Gillom	7	385	16,872	43.8	80	5
Jerry Norton	11	358	15,671	43.8	78	2
Don Chandler	12	660	28,678	43.5	90	4
Reggie Roby	7	394	17,105	43.4	77	2
Sean Landeta	5	301	13,025	43.3	71	1
Jerrel Wilson	16	1,072	46,139	43.0	72	12
Ralf Mojsiejenko	5	354	15,190	42.9	74	4
Norm Van Brocklin	12	523	22,413	42.9	72	3
Danny Villanueva	8	488	20,862	42.8	68	2
Bobby Joe Green	14	970	41,317	42.6	75	3
Sam Baker	15	703	29,938	42.6	72	2
Rich Camarillo	9	584	24,799	42.5	76	4
Jim Arnold	7	545	23,122	42.4	69	4
Ray Guy	14	1,049	44,493	42.4	74	3
Bob Waterfield	8	315	13,367	42.4	88	5
Curley Johnson	10	559	23,651	42.3	73	6

300 or more punts.

Top 20 Punt Returners

Player	Years	No.	Yards	Avg.	Long	TD
George McAfee	8	112	1,431	12.8	74	2
Jack Christiansen	8	85	1,084	12.8	89	8
Claude Gibson	5	110	1,381	12.6	85	3
Bill Dudley	9	124	1,515	12.2	96	3
Rick Upchurch	9	248	3,008	12.1	92	8
John Taylor	3	81	982	12.1	95	2
Billy Johnson	14	282	3,317	11.8	87	6
Vai Sikahema	4	157	1,846	11.8	76	3
Mack Herron	3	84	982	11.7	66	0
Billy Thompson	13	157	1,814	11.6	60	0
Henry Ellard	7	131	1,494	11.4	83	4
Louis Lipps	6	107	1,212	11.3	76	3
Rodger Bird	3	94	1,063	11.3	78	0
Bosh Pritchard	6	95	1,072	11.3	81	2
Bobby Joe Edmonds	4	105	1,178	11.2	75	1
Bob Hayes	11	104	1,158	11.1	90	3
Terry Metcalf	6	84	936	11.1	69	1
Jo Jo Townsell	5	110	1,206	11.0	91	2
Floyd Little	9	81	893	11.0	72	2
Les (Speedy) Duncan	11	202	2,201	10.9	95	4

75 or more returns.

Top 20 Kickoff Returners

Player	Years	No.	Yards	Avg.	Long	TD
Gale Sayers	7	91	2,781	30.6	103	6
Lynn Chandnois	7	92	2,720	29.6	93	3
Abe Woodson	9	193	5,538	28.7	105	5
Claude (Buddy) Young	6	90	2,514	27.9	104	2
Travis Williams	5	102	2,801	27.5	105	6
Joe Arenas	7	139	3,798	27.3	96	1
Clarence Davis	8	79	2,140	27.1	76	0
Lenny Lyles	12	81	2,161	26.7	103	3
Steve Van Buren	8	76	2,030	26.7	98	3
Bobby Jancik	6	158	4,185	26.5	61	0
Eugene (Mercury) Morris	8	111	2,947	26.5	105	3
Bobby Mitchell	11	102	2,690	26.4	98	5
Mel Renfro	14	85	2,246	26.4	100	2
Ollie Matson	14	143	3,746	26.2	105	6
Alvin Haymond	10	170	4,438	26.1	98	2
Noland Smith	3	82	2,137	26.1	106	1
Tim Brown	10	184	4,781	26.0	105	5
Al Nelson	9	101	2,625	26.0	78	0
Vic Washington	6	129	3,341	25.9	98	1
Dave Hampton	8	113	2,923	25.9	101	3

75 or more returns.

Annual Scoring Leaders

Year	Player, Team	TD	FG	PAT	TP
1989	Mike Cofer, San Francisco, NFC	0	29	49	136
	*David Treadwell, Denver, AFC	0	27	39	120
1988	Scott Norwood, Buffalo, AFC	0	32	33	129
	Mike Cofer, San Francisco, NFC	0	27	40	121
1987	Jerry Rice, San Francisco, NFC	23	0	0	138
	Jim Breech, Cincinnati, AFC	0	24	25	97
1986	Tony Franklin, New England, AFC	0	32	44	140
	Kevin Butler, Chicago, NFC	0	28	36	120
1985	*Kevin Butler, Chicago, NFC	0	31	51	144
	Gary Anderson, Pittsburgh, AFC	0	33	40	139
1984	Ray Wersching, San Francisco, NFC	0	25	56	131
	Gary Anderson, Pittsburgh, AFC	0	24	45	117
1983	Mark Moseley, Washington, NFC	0	33	62	161
	Gary Anderson, Pittsburgh, AFC	0	27	38	119
1982	*Marcus Allen, L.A. Raiders, AFC	14	0	0	84
	Wendell Tyler, L.A. Rams, NFC	13	0	0	78
1981	Ed Murray, Detroit, NFC	0	25	46	121
	Rafael Septien, Dallas, NFC	0	27	40	121
	Jim Breech, Cincinnati, AFC	0	22	49	115
	Nick Lowery, Kansas City, AFC	0	26	37	115
1980	John Smith, New England, AFC	0	26	51	129
	*Ed Murray, Detroit, NFC	0	27	35	116
1979	John Smith, New England, AFC	0	23	46	115
	Mark Moseley, Washington, NFC	0	25	39	114
1978	*Frank Corral, Los Angeles, NFC	0	29	31	118
	Pat Leahy, N.Y. Jets, AFC	0	22	41	107
1977	Errol Mann, Oakland, AFC	0	20	39	99
	Walter Payton, Chicago, NFC	16	0	0	96
1976	Toni Linhart, Baltimore, AFC	0	20	49	109
	Mark Moseley, Washington, NFC	0	22	31	97
1975	O.J. Simpson, Buffalo, AFC	23	0	0	138
	Chuck Foreman, Minnesota, NFC	22	0	0	132
1974	Chester Marcol, Green Bay, NFC	0	25	19	94
	Roy Gerela, Pittsburgh, AFC	0	20	33	93
1973	David Ray, Los Angeles, NFC	0	30	40	130
	Roy Gerela, Pittsburgh, AFC	0	29	36	123
1972	*Chester Marcol, Green Bay, NFC	0	33	29	128
	Bobby Howfield, N.Y. Jets, AFC	0	27	40	121
1971	Garo Yepremian, Miami, AFC	0	28	33	117
	Curt Knight, Washington, NFC	0	29	27	114
1970	Fred Cox, Minnesota, NFC	0	30	35	125
	Jan Stenerud, Kansas City, AFC	0	30	26	116
1969	Jim Turner, N.Y. Jets, AFL	0	32	33	129
	Fred Cox, Minnesota, NFL	0	26	43	121
1968	Jim Turner, N.Y. Jets, AFL	0	34	43	145
	Leroy Kelly, Cleveland, NFL	20	0	0	120
1967	Jim Bakken, St. Louis, NFL	0	27	36	117
	George Blanda, Oakland, AFL	0	20	56	116
1966	Gino Cappelletti, Boston, AFL	6	16	35	119
	Bruce Gossett, Los Angeles, NFL	0	28	29	113
1965	*Gale Sayers, Chicago, NFL	22	0	0	132
	Gino Cappelletti, Boston, AFL	9	17	27	132
1964	Gino Cappelletti, Boston, AFL	7	25	36	#155
	Lenny Moore, Baltimore, NFL	20	0	0	120
1963	Gino Cappelletti, Boston, AFL	2	22	35	113
	Don Chandler, N.Y. Giants, NFL	0	18	52	106
1962	Gene Mingo, Denver, AFL	4	27	32	137
	Jim Taylor, Green Bay, NFL	19	0	0	114
1961	Gino Cappelletti, Boston, AFL	8	17	48	147
	Paul Hornung, Green Bay, NFL	10	15	41	146
1960	Paul Hornung, Green Bay, NFL	15	15	41	176
	*Gene Mingo, Denver, AFL	6	18	33	123
1959	Paul Hornung, Green Bay	7	7	31	94
1958	Jim Brown, Cleveland	18	0	0	108
1957	Sam Baker, Washington	1	14	29	77
	Lou Groza, Cleveland	0	15	32	77
1956	Bobby Layne, Detroit	5	12	33	99
1955	Doak Walker, Detroit	7	9	27	96
1954	Bobby Walston, Philadelphia	11	4	36	114
1953	Gordy Soltau, San Francisco	6	10	48	114
1952	Gordy Soltau, San Francisco	7	6	34	94
1951	Elroy (Crazylegs) Hirsch, Los Angeles	17	0	0	102
1950	*Doak Walker, Detroit	11	8	38	128
1949	Pat Harder, Chi. Cardinals	8	3	45	102
	Gene Roberts, N.Y. Giants	17	0	0	102
1948	Pat Harder, Chi. Cardinals	6	7	53	110
1947	Pat Harder, Chi. Cardinals	7	7	39	102
1946	Ted Fritsch, Green Bay	10	9	13	100
1945	Steve Van Buren, Philadelphia	18	0	2	110
1944	Don Hutson, Green Bay	9	0	31	85
1943	Don Hutson, Green Bay	12	3	36	117
1942	Don Hutson, Green Bay	17	1	33	138
1941	Don Hutson, Green Bay	12	1	20	95
1940	Don Hutson, Green Bay	7	0	15	57
1939	Andy Farkas, Washington	11	0	2	68
1938	Clarke Hinkle, Green Bay	7	3	7	58
1937	Jack Manders, Chi. Bears	5	8	15	69
1936	Earl (Dutch) Clark, Detroit	7	4	19	73
1935	Earl (Dutch) Clark, Detroit	6	1	16	55
1934	Jack Manders, Chi. Bears	3	10	31	79
1933	Ken Strong, N.Y. Giants	6	5	13	64
	Glenn Presnell, Portsmouth	6	6	10	64
1932	Earl (Dutch) Clark, Portsmouth	6	3	10	55

*First year in the league.
#Cappelletti's total includes a two-point conversion.

Annual Leaders—Most Field Goals Made

Year	Player, Team	Att.	Made	Pct.
1989	Rich Karlis, Minnesota, NFC	39	31	79.5
	*David Treadwell, Denver, AFC	33	27	81.8
1988	Scott Norwood, Buffalo, AFC	37	32	86.5
	Mike Cofer, San Francisco, NFC	38	27	71.1
1987	Morten Andersen, New Orleans, NFC	36	28	77.8
	Dean Biasucci, Indianapolis, AFC	27	24	88.9
	Jim Breech, Cincinnati, AFC	30	24	80.0
1986	Tony Franklin, New England, AFC	41	32	78.0
	Kevin Butler, Chicago, NFC	41	28	68.3
1985	Gary Anderson, Pittsburgh, AFC	42	33	78.6
	Morten Andersen, New Orleans, NFC	35	31	88.6
	*Kevin Butler, Chicago, NFC	37	31	83.8
1984	*Paul McFadden, Philadelphia, NFC	37	30	81.1
	Gary Anderson, Pittsburgh, AFC	32	24	75.0
	Matt Bahr, Cleveland, AFC	32	24	75.0
1983	*Ali Haji-Sheikh, N.Y. Giants, NFC	42	35	83.3
	*Raul Allegre, Baltimore, AFC	35	30	85.7
1982	Mark Moseley, Washington, NFC	21	20	95.2
	Nick Lowery, Kansas City, AFC	24	19	79.2
1981	Rafael Septien, Dallas, NFC	35	27	77.1
	Nick Lowery, Kansas City, AFC	36	26	72.2
1980	*Ed Murray, Detroit, NFC	42	27	64.3
	John Smith, New England, AFC	34	26	76.5
	Fred Steinfort, Denver, AFC	34	26	76.5
1979	Mark Moseley, Washington, NFC	33	25	75.8
	John Smith, New England, AFC	33	23	69.7
1978	*Frank Corral, Los Angeles, NFC	43	29	67.4
	Pat Leahy, N.Y. Jets, AFC	30	22	73.3
1977	Mark Moseley, Washington, NFC	37	21	56.8
	Errol Mann, Oakland, AFC	28	20	71.4
1976	Mark Moseley, Washington, NFC	34	22	64.7
	Jan Stenerud, Kansas City, AFC	38	21	55.3
1975	Jan Stenerud, Kansas City, AFC	32	22	68.8
	Toni Fritsch, Dallas, NFC	35	22	62.9
1974	Chester Marcol, Green Bay, NFC	39	25	64.1
	Roy Gerela, Pittsburgh, AFC	29	20	69.0
1973	David Ray, Los Angeles, NFC	47	30	63.8
	Roy Gerela, Pittsburgh, AFC	43	29	67.4
1972	*Chester Marcol, Green Bay, NFC	48	33	68.8
	Roy Gerela, Pittsburgh, AFC	41	28	68.3
1971	Curt Knight, Washington, NFC	49	29	59.2
	Garo Yepremian, Miami, AFC	40	28	70.0
1970	Jan Stenerud, Kansas City, AFC	42	30	71.4
	Fred Cox, Minnesota, NFC	46	30	65.2
1969	Jim Turner, N.Y. Jets, AFL	47	32	68.1
	Fred Cox, Minnesota, NFL	37	26	70.3
1968	Jim Turner, N.Y. Jets, AFL	46	34	73.9
	Mac Percival, Chicago, NFL	36	25	69.4
1967	Jim Bakken, St. Louis, NFL	39	27	69.2
	Jan Stenerud, Kansas City, AFL	36	21	58.3
1966	Bruce Gossett, Los Angeles, NFL	49	28	57.1
	Mike Mercer, Oakland-Kansas City, AFL	30	21	70.0
1965	Pete Gogolak, Buffalo, AFL	46	28	60.9
	Fred Cox, Minnesota, NFL	35	23	65.7
1964	Jim Bakken, St. Louis, NFL	38	25	65.8
	Gino Cappelletti, Boston, AFL	39	25	64.1
1963	Jim Martin, Baltimore, NFL	39	24	61.5
	Gino Cappelletti, Boston, AFL	38	22	57.9
1962	Gene Mingo, Denver, AFL	39	27	69.2
	Lou Michaels, Pittsburgh, NFL	42	26	61.9
1961	Steve Myhra, Baltimore, NFL	39	21	53.8
	Gino Cappelletti, Boston, AFL	32	17	53.1
1960	Tommy Davis, San Francisco, NFL	32	19	59.4
	*Gene Mingo, Denver, AFL	28	18	64.3
1959	Pat Summerall, New York Giants	29	20	69.0
1958	Paige Cothren, Los Angeles	25	14	56.0
	*Tom Miner, Pittsburgh	28	14	50.0
1957	Lou Groza, Cleveland	22	15	68.2
1956	Sam Baker, Washington	25	17	68.0
1955	Fred Cone, Green Bay	24	16	66.7
1954	Lou Groza, Cleveland	24	16	66.7
1953	Lou Groza, Cleveland	26	23	88.5
1952	Lou Groza, Cleveland	33	19	57.6
1951	Bob Waterfield, Los Angeles	23	13	56.5
1950	*Lou Groza, Cleveland	19	13	68.4
1949	Cliff Patton, Philadelphia	18	9	50.0
	Bob Waterfield, Los Angeles	16	9	56.3
1948	Cliff Patton, Philadelphia	12	8	66.7
1947	Ward Cuff, Green Bay	16	7	43.8
	Pat Harder, Chi. Cardinals	10	7	70.0
	Bob Waterfield, Los Angeles	16	7	43.8
1946	Ted Fritsch, Green Bay	17	9	52.9
1945	Joe Aguirre, Washington	13	7	53.8
1944	Ken Strong, N.Y. Giants	12	6	50.0
1943	Ward Cuff, N.Y. Giants	9	3	33.3
	Don Hutson, Green Bay	5	3	60.0
1942	Bill Daddio, Chi. Cardinals	10	5	50.0
1941	Clarke Hinkle, Green Bay	14	6	42.9
1940	Clarke Hinkle, Green Bay	14	9	64.3
1939	Ward Cuff, N.Y. Giants	16	7	43.8
1938	Ward Cuff, N.Y. Giants	9	5	55.6
	Ralph Kercheval, Brooklyn	13	5	38.5
1937	Jack Manders, Chi. Bears		8	
1936	Jack Manders, Chi. Bears		7	

	Armand Niccolai, Pittsburgh	7
1935	Armand Niccolai, Pittsburgh	6
	Bill Smith, Chi. Cardinals	6
1934	Jack Manders, Chi. Bears	10
1933	*Jack Manders, Chi. Bears	6
	Glenn Presnell, Portsmouth	6
1932	Earl (Dutch) Clark, Portsmouth	3

First year in the league.

Annual Rushing Leaders

Year	Player, Team	Att.	Yards	Avg.	TD
1989	Christian Okoye, Kansas City, AFC	370	1,480	4.0	12
	*Barry Sanders, Detroit, NFC	280	1,470	5.3	14
1988	Eric Dickerson, Indianapolis, AFC	388	1,659	4.3	14
	Herschel Walker, Dallas, NFC	361	1,514	4.2	5
1987	Charles White, L.A. Rams, NFC	324	1,374	4.2	11
	Eric Dickerson, Indianapolis, AFC	223	1,011	4.5	5
1986	Eric Dickerson, L.A. Rams, NFC	404	1,821	4.5	11
	Curt Warner, Seattle, AFC	319	1,481	4.6	13
1985	Marcus Allen, L.A. Raiders, AFC	380	1,759	4.6	11
	Gerald Riggs, Atlanta, NFC	397	1,719	4.3	10
1984	Eric Dickerson, L.A. Rams, NFC	379	2,105	5.6	14
	Earnest Jackson, San Diego, AFC	296	1,179	4.0	8
1983	*Eric Dickerson, L.A. Rams, NFC	390	1,808	4.6	18
	*Curt Warner, Seattle, AFC	335	1,449	4.3	13
1982	Freeman McNeil, N.Y. Jets, AFC	151	786	5.2	6
	Tony Dorsett, Dallas, NFC	177	745	4.2	5
1981	*George Rogers, New Orleans, NFC	378	1,674	4.4	13
	Earl Campbell, Houston, AFC	361	1,376	3.8	10
1980	Earl Campbell, Houston, AFC	373	1,934	5.2	13
	Walter Payton, Chicago, NFC	317	1,460	4.6	6
1979	Earl Campbell, Houston, AFC	368	1,697	4.6	19
	Walter Payton, Chicago, NFC	369	1,610	4.4	14
1978	*Earl Campbell, Houston, AFC	302	1,450	4.8	13
	Walter Payton, Chicago, NFC	333	1,395	4.2	11
1977	Walter Payton, Chicago, NFC	339	1,852	5.5	14
	Mark van Eeghen, Oakland, AFC	324	1,273	3.9	7
1976	O.J. Simpson, Buffalo, AFC	290	1,503	5.2	8
	Walter Payton, Chicago, NFC	311	1,390	4.5	13
1975	O.J. Simpson, Buffalo, AFC	329	1,817	5.5	16
	Jim Otis, St. Louis, NFC	269	1,076	4.0	5
1974	Otis Armstrong, Denver, AFC	263	1,407	5.3	9
	Lawrence McCutcheon, Los Angeles, NFC	236	1,109	4.7	3
1973	O.J. Simpson, Buffalo, AFC	332	2,003	6.0	12
	John Brockington, Green Bay, NFC	265	1,144	4.3	3
1972	O.J. Simpson, Buffalo, AFC	292	1,251	4.3	6
	Larry Brown, Washington, NFC	285	1,216	4.3	8
1971	Floyd Little, Denver, AFC	284	1,133	4.0	6
	*John Brockington, Green Bay, NFC	216	1,105	5.1	4
1970	Larry Brown, Washington, NFC	237	1,125	4.7	5
	Floyd Little, Denver, AFC	209	901	4.3	3
1969	Gale Sayers, Chicago, NFL	236	1,032	4.4	8
	Dickie Post, San Diego, AFL	182	873	4.8	6
1968	Leroy Kelly, Cleveland, NFL	248	1,239	5.0	16
	*Paul Robinson, Cincinnati, AFL	238	1,023	4.3	8
1967	Jim Nance, Boston, AFL	269	1,216	4.5	7
	Leroy Kelly, Cleveland, NFL	235	1,205	5.1	11
1966	Jim Nance, Boston, AFL	299	1,458	4.9	11
	Gale Sayers, Chicago, NFL	229	1,231	5.4	8
1965	Jim Brown, Cleveland, NFL	289	1,544	5.3	17
	Paul Lowe, San Diego, AFL	222	1,121	5.0	7
1964	Jim Brown, Cleveland, NFL	280	1,446	5.2	7
	Cookie Gilchrist, Buffalo, AFL	230	981	4.3	6
1963	Jim Brown, Cleveland, NFL	291	1,863	6.4	12
	Clem Daniels, Oakland, AFL	215	1,099	5.1	3
1962	Jim Taylor, Green Bay, NFL	272	1,474	5.4	19
	*Cookie Gilchrist, Buffalo, AFL	214	1,096	5.1	13
1961	Jim Brown, Cleveland, NFL	305	1,408	4.6	8
	Billy Cannon, Houston, AFL	200	948	4.7	6
1960	Jim Brown, Cleveland, NFL	215	1,257	5.8	9
	*Abner Haynes, Dall. Texans, AFL	156	875	5.6	9
1959	Jim Brown, Cleveland	290	1,329	4.6	14
1958	Jim Brown, Cleveland	257	1,527	5.9	17
1957	*Jim Brown, Cleveland	202	942	4.7	9
1956	Rick Casares, Chi. Bears	234	1,126	4.8	12
1955	*Alan Ameche, Baltimore	213	961	4.5	9
1954	Joe Perry, San Francisco	173	1,049	6.1	8
1953	Joe Perry, San Francisco	192	1,018	5.3	10
1952	Dan Towler, Los Angeles	156	894	5.7	10
1951	Eddie Price, N.Y. Giants	271	971	3.6	7
1950	*Marion Motley, Cleveland	140	810	5.8	3
1949	Steve Van Buren, Philadelphia	263	1,146	4.4	11
1948	Steve Van Buren, Philadelphia	201	945	4.7	10
1947	Steve Van Buren, Philadelphia	217	1,008	4.6	13
1946	Bill Dudley, Pittsburgh	146	604	4.1	3
1945	Steve Van Buren, Philadelphia	143	832	5.8	15
1944	Bill Paschal, N.Y. Giants	196	737	3.8	9
1943	*Bill Paschal, N.Y. Giants	147	572	3.9	10
1942	*Bill Dudley, Pittsburgh	162	696	4.3	5
1941	Clarence (Pug) Manders, Brooklyn	111	486	4.4	5
1940	Byron (Whizzer) White, Detroit	146	514	3.5	5
1939	*Bill Osmanski, Chicago	121	699	5.8	7
1938	*Byron (Whizzer) White, Pittsburgh	152	567	3.7	4
1937	Cliff Battles, Washington	216	874	4.0	5
1936	*Alphonse (Tuffy) Leemans, N.Y. Giants	206	830	4.0	2
1935	Doug Russell, Chi. Cardinals	140	499	3.6	0
1934	*Beattie Feathers, Chi. Bears	101	1,004	9.9	8
1933	Jim Musick, Boston	173	809	4.7	5
1932	*Cliff Battles, Boston	148	576	3.9	3

First year in the league.

Annual Passing Leaders

Year	Player, Team	Att.	Comp.	Yards	TD	Int.
1989	Joe Montana, San Francisco, NFC	386	271	3,521	26	8
	Boomer Esiason, Cincinnati, AFC	455	258	3,525	28	11
1988	Boomer Esiason, Cincinnati, AFC	388	223	3,572	28	14
	Wade Wilson, Minnesota, NFC	332	204	2,746	15	9
1987	Joe Montana, San Francisco, NFC	398	266	3,054	31	13
	Bernie Kosar, Cleveland, AFC	389	241	3,033	22	9
1986	Tommy Kramer, Minnesota, NFC	372	208	3,000	24	10
	Dan Marino, Miami, AFC	623	378	4,746	44	23
1985	Ken O'Brien, N.Y. Jets, AFC	488	297	3,888	25	8
	Joe Montana, San Francisco, NFC	494	303	3,653	27	13
1984	Dan Marino, Miami, AFC	564	362	5,084	48	17
	Joe Montana, San Francisco, NFC	432	279	3,630	28	10
1983	Steve Bartkowski, Atlanta, NFC	432	274	3,167	22	5
	*Dan Marino, Miami, AFC	296	173	2,210	20	6
1982	Ken Anderson, Cincinnati, AFC	309	218	2,495	12	9
	Joe Theismann, Washington, NFC	252	161	2,033	13	9
1981	Ken Anderson, Cincinnati, AFC	479	300	3,754	29	10
	Joe Montana, San Francisco, NFC	488	311	3,565	19	12
1980	Brian Sipe, Cleveland, AFC	554	337	4,132	30	14
	Ron Jaworski, Philadelphia, NFC	451	257	3,529	27	12
1979	Roger Staubach, Dallas, NFC	461	267	3,586	27	11
	Dan Fouts, San Diego, AFC	530	332	4,082	24	24
1978	Roger Staubach, Dallas, NFC	413	231	3,190	25	16
	Terry Bradshaw, Pittsburgh, AFC	368	207	2,915	28	20
1977	Bob Griese, Miami, AFC	307	180	2,252	22	13
	Roger Staubach, Dallas, NFC	361	210	2,620	18	9
1976	Ken Stabler, Oakland, AFC	291	194	2,737	27	17
	James Harris, Los Angeles, NFC	158	91	1,460	8	6
1975	Ken Anderson, Cincinnati, AFC	377	228	3,169	21	11
	Fran Tarkenton, Minnesota, NFC	425	273	2,994	25	13
1974	Ken Anderson, Cincinnati, AFC	328	213	2,667	18	10
	Sonny Jurgensen, Washington, NFC	167	107	1,185	11	5
1973	Roger Staubach, Dallas, NFC	286	179	2,428	23	15
	Ken Stabler, Oakland, AFC	260	163	1,997	14	10
1972	Norm Snead, N.Y. Giants, NFC	325	196	2,307	17	12
	Earl Morrall, Miami, AFC	150	83	1,360	11	7
1971	Roger Staubach, Dallas, NFC	211	126	1,882	15	4
	Bob Griese, Miami, AFC	263	145	2,089	19	9
1970	John Brodie, San Francisco, NFC	378	223	2,941	24	10
	Daryle Lamonica, Oakland, AFC	356	179	2,516	22	15
1969	Sonny Jurgensen, Washington, NFL	442	274	3,102	22	15
	*Greg Cook, Cincinnati, AFL	197	106	1,854	15	11
1968	Len Dawson, Kansas City, AFL	224	131	2,109	17	9
	Earl Morrall, Baltimore, NFL	317	182	2,909	26	17
1967	Sonny Jurgensen, Washington, NFL	508	288	3,747	31	16
	Daryle Lamonica, Oakland, AFL	425	220	3,228	30	20
1966	Bart Starr, Green Bay, NFL	251	156	2,257	14	3
	Len Dawson, Kansas City, AFL	284	159	2,527	26	10
1965	Rudy Bukich, Chicago, NFL	312	176	2,641	20	9
	John Hadl, San Diego, AFL	348	174	2,798	20	21
1964	Len Dawson, Kansas City, AFL	354	199	2,879	30	18
	Bart Starr, Green Bay, NFL	272	163	2,144	15	4
1963	Y.A. Tittle, N.Y. Giants, NFL	367	221	3,145	36	14
	Tobin Rote, San Diego, AFL	286	170	2,510	20	17
1962	Len Dawson, Dall. Texans, AFL	310	189	2,759	29	17
	Bart Starr, Green Bay, NFL	285	178	2,438	12	9
1961	George Blanda, Houston, AFL	362	187	3,330	36	22
	Milt Plum, Cleveland, NFL	302	177	2,416	18	10
1960	Milt Plum, Cleveland, NFL	250	151	2,297	21	5
	Jack Kemp, L.A. Chargers, AFL	406	211	3,018	20	25
1959	Charlie Conerly, N.Y. Giants	194	113	1,706	14	4
1958	Eddie LeBaron, Washington	145	79	1,365	11	10
1957	Tommy O'Connell, Cleveland	110	63	1,229	9	8
1956	Ed Brown, Chi. Bears	168	96	1,667	11	12
1955	Otto Graham, Cleveland	185	98	1,721	15	8
1954	Norm Van Brocklin, Los Angeles	260	139	2,637	13	21
1953	Otto Graham, Cleveland	258	167	2,722	11	9
1952	Norm Van Brocklin, Los Angeles	205	113	1,736	14	17
1951	Bob Waterfield, Los Angeles	176	88	1,566	13	10
1950	Norm Van Brocklin, Los Angeles	233	127	2,061	18	14
1949	Sammy Baugh, Washington	255	145	1,903	18	14
1948	Tommy Thompson, Philadelphia	246	141	1,965	25	11
1947	Sammy Baugh, Washington	354	210	2,938	25	15
1946	Bob Waterfield, Los Angeles	251	127	1,747	18	17
1945	Sammy Baugh, Washington	182	128	1,669	11	4
	Sid Luckman, Chi. Bears	217	117	1,725	14	10
1944	Frank Filchock, Washington	147	84	1,139	13	9
1943	Sammy Baugh, Washington	239	133	1,754	23	19
1942	Cecil Isbell, Green Bay	268	146	2,021	24	14
1941	Cecil Isbell, Green Bay	206	117	1,479	15	11
1940	Sammy Baugh, Washington	177	111	1,367	12	10
1939	*Parker Hall, Cleveland	208	106	1,227	9	13
1938	Ed Danowski, N.Y. Giants	129	70	848	7	8
1937	*Sammy Baugh, Washington	171	81	1,127	8	14
1936	Arnie Herber, Green Bay	173	77	1,239	11	13
1935	Ed Danowski, N.Y. Giants	113	57	794	10	9
1934	Arnie Herber, Green Bay	115	42	799	8	12
1933	*Harry Newman, N.Y. Giants	136	53	973	11	17
1932	Arnie Herber, Green Bay	101	37	639	9	9

First year in the league.

Annual Pass Receiving Leaders

Year	Player, Team	No.	Yards	Avg.	TD
1989	Sterling Sharpe, Green Bay, NFC	90	1,423	15.8	12
	Andre Reed, Buffalo, AFC	88	1,312	14.9	9
1988	Al Toon, N.Y. Jets, AFC	93	1,067	11.5	5
	Henry Ellard, L.A. Rams, NFC	86	1,414	16.4	10
1987	J.T. Smith, St. Louis, NFC	91	1,117	12.3	8
	Al Toon, N.Y. Jets, AFC	68	976	14.4	5
1986	Todd Christensen, L.A. Raiders, AFC	95	1,153	12.1	8
	Jerry Rice, San Francisco, NFC	86	1,570	18.3	15

Year	Player, Team	No.	Yards	Avg	TD
1985	Roger Craig, San Francisco, NFC	92	1,016	11.0	6
	Lionel James, San Diego, AFC	86	1,027	11.9	6
1984	Art Monk, Washington, NFC	106	1,372	12.9	7
	Ozzie Newsome, Cleveland, AFC	89	1,001	11.2	5
1983	Todd Christensen, L.A. Raiders, AFC	92	1,247	13.6	12
	Roy Green, St. Louis, NFC	78	1,227	15.7	14
	Charlie Brown, Washington, NFC	78	1,225	15.7	8
	Earnest Gray, N.Y. Giants, NFC	78	1,139	14.6	5
1982	Dwight Clark, San Francisco, NFC	60	913	15.2	5
	Kellen Winslow, San Diego, AFC	54	721	13.4	6
1981	Kellen Winslow, San Diego, AFC	88	1,075	12.2	10
	Dwight Clark, San Francisco, NFC	85	1,105	13.0	4
1980	Kellen Winslow, San Diego, AFC	89	1,290	14.5	9
	*Earl Cooper, San Francisco, NFC	83	567	6.8	4
1979	Joe Washington, Baltimore, AFC	82	750	9.1	3
	Ahmad Rashad, Minnesota, NFC	80	1,156	14.5	9
1978	Rickey Young, Minnesota, NFC	88	704	8.0	5
	Steve Largent, Seattle, AFC	71	1,168	16.5	8
1977	Lydell Mitchell, Baltimore, AFC	71	620	8.7	4
	Ahmad Rashad, Minnesota, NFC	51	681	13.4	2
1976	MacArthur Lane, Kansas City, AFC	66	686	10.4	1
	Drew Pearson, Dallas, NFC	58	806	13.9	6
1975	Chuck Foreman, Minnesota, NFC	73	691	9.5	9
	Reggie Rucker, Cleveland, AFC	60	770	12.8	3
	Lydell Mitchell, Baltimore, AFC	60	544	9.1	4
1974	Lydell Mitchell, Baltimore, AFC	72	544	7.6	2
	Charles Young, Philadelphia, NFC	63	696	11.0	3
1973	Harold Carmichael, Philadelphia, NFC	67	1,116	16.7	9
	Fred Willis, Houston, AFC	57	371	6.5	1
1972	Harold Jackson, Philadelphia, NFC	62	1,048	16.9	4
	Fred Biletnikoff, Oakland, AFC	58	802	13.8	7
1971	Fred Biletnikoff, Oakland, AFC	61	929	15.2	9
	Bob Tucker, N.Y. Giants, NFC	59	791	13.4	4
1970	Dick Gordon, Chicago, NFC	71	1,026	14.5	13
	Marlin Briscoe, Buffalo, AFC	57	1,036	18.2	8
1969	Dan Abramowicz, New Orleans, NFL	73	1,015	13.9	7
	Lance Alworth, San Diego, AFL	64	1,003	15.7	4
1968	Clifton McNeil, San Francisco, NFL	71	994	14.0	7
	Lance Alworth, San Diego, AFL	68	1,312	19.3	10
1967	George Sauer, N.Y. Jets, AFL	75	1,189	15.9	6
	Charley Taylor, Washington, NFL	70	990	14.1	9
1966	Lance Alworth, San Diego, AFL	73	1,383	18.9	13
	Charley Taylor, Washington, NFL	72	1,119	15.5	12
1965	Lionel Taylor, Denver, AFL	85	1,131	13.3	6
	Dave Parks, San Francisco, NFL	80	1,344	16.8	12
1964	Charley Hennigan, Houston, AFL	101	1,546	15.3	8
	Johnny Morris, Chicago, NFL	93	1,200	12.9	10
1963	Lionel Taylor, Denver, AFL	78	1,101	14.1	10
	Bobby Joe Conrad, St. Louis, NFL	73	967	13.2	10
1962	Lionel Taylor, Denver, AFL	77	908	11.8	4
	Bobby Mitchell, Washington, NFL	72	1,384	19.2	11
1961	Lionel Taylor, Denver, AFL	100	1,176	11.8	4
	Jim (Red) Phillips, Los Angeles, NFL	78	1,092	14.0	5
1960	Lionel Taylor, Denver, AFL	92	1,235	13.4	12
	Raymond Berry, Baltimore, NFL	74	1,298	17.5	10
1959	Raymond Berry, Baltimore	66	959	14.5	14
1958	Raymond Berry, Baltimore	56	794	14.2	9
	Pete Retzlaff, Philadelphia	56	766	13.7	2
1957	Billy Wilson, San Francisco	52	757	14.6	6
1956	Billy Wilson, San Francisco	60	889	14.8	5
1955	Pete Pihos, Philadelphia	62	864	13.9	7
1954	Pete Pihos, Philadelphia	60	872	14.5	10
	Billy Wilson, San Francisco	60	830	13.8	5
1953	Pete Pihos, Philadelphia	63	1,049	16.7	10
1952	Mac Speedie, Cleveland	62	911	14.7	5
1951	Elroy (Crazylegs) Hirsch, Los Angeles	66	1,495	22.7	17
1950	Tom Fears, Los Angeles	84	1,116	13.3	7
1949	Tom Fears, Los Angeles	77	1,013	13.2	9
1948	*Tom Fears, Los Angeles	51	698	13.7	4
1947	Jim Keane, Chi. Bears	64	910	14.2	10
1946	Jim Benton, Los Angeles	63	981	15.6	6
1945	Don Hutson, Green Bay	47	834	17.7	9
1944	Don Hutson, Green Bay	58	866	14.9	9
1943	Don Hutson, Green Bay	47	776	16.5	11
1942	Don Hutson, Green Bay	74	1,211	16.4	17
1941	Don Hutson, Green Bay	58	738	12.7	10
1940	*Don Looney, Philadelphia	58	707	12.2	4
1939	Don Hutson, Green Bay	34	846	24.9	6
1938	Gaynell Tinsley, Chi. Cardinals	41	516	12.6	1
1937	Don Hutson, Green Bay	41	552	13.5	7
1936	Don Hutson, Green Bay	34	536	15.8	8
1935	*Tod Goodwin, N.Y. Giants	26	432	16.6	4
1934	Joe Carter, Philadelphia	16	238	14.9	4
	Morris (Red) Badgro, N.Y. Giants	16	206	12.9	1
1933	John (Shipwreck) Kelly, Brooklyn	22	246	11.2	3
1932	Ray Flaherty, N.Y. Giants	21	350	16.7	3

*First year in the league.

Annual Interception Leaders

Year	Player, Team	No.	Yards	TD
1989	Felix Wright, Cleveland, AFC	9	91	1
	Eric Allen, Philadelphia, NFC	8	38	0
1988	Scott Case, Atlanta, NFC	10	47	0
	Erik McMillan, N.Y. Jets, AFC	8	168	2
1987	Barry Wilburn, Washington, NFC	9	135	1
	Mike Prior, Indianapolis, AFC	6	57	0
	Mark Kelso, Buffalo, AFC	6	25	0
	Keith Bostic, Houston, AFC	6	–14	0
1986	Ronnie Lott, San Francisco, NFC	10	134	1
	Deron Cherry, Kansas City, AFC	9	150	0
1985	Everson Walls, Dallas, NFC	9	31	0
	Albert Lewis, Kansas City, AFC	8	59	0
	Eugene Daniel, Indianapolis, AFC	8	53	0

Year	Player, Team	No.	Yards	TD
1984	Ken Easley, Seattle, AFC	10	126	2
	*Tom Flynn, Green Bay, NFC	9	106	0
1983	Mark Murphy, Washington, NFC	9	127	0
	Ken Riley, Cincinnati, AFC	8	89	2
	Vann McElroy, L.A. Raiders, AFC	8	68	0
1982	Everson Walls, Dallas, NFC	7	61	0
	Ken Riley, Cincinnati, AFC	5	88	1
	Bobby Jackson, N.Y. Jets, AFC	5	84	1
	Dwayne Woodruff, Pittsburgh, AFC	5	53	0
	Donnie Shell, Pittsburgh, AFC	5	27	0
1981	*Everson Walls, Dallas, NFC	11	133	0
	John Harris, Seattle, AFC	10	155	2
1980	Lester Hayes, Oakland, AFC	13	273	1
	Nolan Cromwell, Los Angeles, NFC	8	140	1
1979	Mike Reinfeldt, Houston, AFC	12	205	0
	Lemar Parrish, Washington, NFC	9	65	0
1978	Thom Darden, Cleveland, AFC	10	200	0
	Ken Stone, St. Louis, NFC	9	139	0
	Willie Buchanon, Green Bay, NFC	9	93	1
1977	Lyle Blackwood, Baltimore, AFC	10	163	0
	Rolland Lawrence, Atlanta, NFC	7	138	0
1976	Monte Jackson, Los Angeles, NFC	10	173	3
	Ken Riley, Cincinnati, AFC	9	141	1
1975	Mel Blount, Pittsburgh, AFC	11	121	0
	Paul Krause, Minnesota, NFC	10	201	0
1974	Emmitt Thomas, Kansas City, AFC	12	214	2
	Ray Brown, Atlanta, NFC	8	164	1
1973	Dick Anderson, Miami, AFC	8	163	2
	Mike Wagner, Pittsburgh, AFC	8	134	0
	Bobby Bryant, Minnesota, NFC	7	105	1
1972	Bill Bradley, Philadelphia, NFC	9	73	0
	Mike Sensibaugh, Kansas City, AFC	8	65	0
1971	Bill Bradley, Philadelphia, NFC	11	248	0
	Ken Houston, Houston, AFC	9	220	4
1970	Johnny Robinson, Kansas City, AFC	10	155	0
	Dick LeBeau, Detroit, NFC	9	96	0
1969	Mel Renfro, Dallas, NFL	10	118	0
	Emmitt Thomas, Kansas City, AFL	9	146	1
1968	Dave Grayson, Oakland, AFL	10	195	1
	Willie Williams, N.Y. Giants, NFL	10	103	0
1967	Miller Farr, Houston, AFL	10	264	3
	*Lem Barney, Detroit, NFL	10	232	3
	Tom Janik, Buffalo, AFL	10	222	2
	Dave Whitsell, New Orleans, NFL	10	178	2
	Dick Westmoreland, Miami, AFL	10	127	1
1966	Larry Wilson, St. Louis, NFL	10	180	2
	Johnny Robinson, Kansas City, AFL	10	136	1
	Bobby Hunt, Kansas City, AFL	10	113	0
1965	W.K. Hicks, Houston, AFL	9	156	0
	Bobby Boyd, Baltimore, NFL	9	78	1
1964	Dainard Paulson, N.Y. Jets, AFL	12	157	1
	*Paul Krause, Washington, NFL	12	140	1
1963	Fred Glick, Houston, AFL	12	180	1
	Dick Lynch, N.Y. Giants, NFL	9	251	3
	Roosevelt Taylor, Chicago, NFL	9	172	1
1962	Lee Riley, N.Y. Titans, AFL	11	122	0
	Willie Wood, Green Bay, NFL	9	132	0
1961	Billy Atkins, Buffalo, AFL	10	158	0
	Dick Lynch, N.Y. Giants, NFL	9	60	0
1960	*Austin (Goose) Gonsoulin, Denver, AFL	11	98	0
	Dave Baker, San Francisco, NFL	10	96	0
	Jerry Norton, St. Louis, NFL	10	96	0
1959	Dean Derby, Pittsburgh	7	127	0
	Milt Davis, Baltimore	7	119	1
	Don Shinnick, Baltimore	7	70	0
1958	Jim Patton, N.Y. Giants	11	183	0
1957	*Milt Davis, Baltimore	10	219	2
	Jack Christiansen, Detroit	10	137	1
	Jack Butler, Pittsburgh	10	85	0
1956	Lindon Crow, Chi. Cardinals	11	170	0
1955	Will Sherman, Los Angeles	11	101	0
1954	Dick (Night Train) Lane, Chi. Cardinals	10	181	0
1953	Jack Christiansen, Detroit	12	238	1
1952	*Dick (Night Train) Lane, Los Angeles	14	298	2
1951	Otto Schnellbacher, N.Y. Giants	11	194	2
1950	*Orban (Spec) Sanders, N.Y. Yanks	13	199	0
1949	Bob Nussbaumer, Chi. Cardinals	12	157	0
1948	*Dan Sandifer, Washington	13	258	2
1947	Frank Reagan, N.Y. Giants	10	203	1
	Frank Seno, Boston	10	100	1
1946	Bill Dudley, Pittsburgh	10	242	1
1945	Roy Zimmerman, Philadelphia	7	90	0
1944	*Howard Livingston, N.Y. Giants	9	172	1
1943	Sammy Baugh, Washington	11	112	0
1942	Clyde (Bulldog) Turner, Chi. Bears	8	96	1
1941	Marshall Goldberg, Chi. Cardinals	7	54	0
	*Art Jones, Pittsburgh	7	35	0
1940	Clarence (Ace) Parker, Brooklyn	6	146	1
	Kent Ryan, Detroit	6	65	0
	Don Hutson, Green Bay	6	24	0

*First year in the league.

Annual Punting Leaders

Year	Player, Team	No.	Avg.	Long
1989	Rich Camarillo, Phoenix, NFC	76	43.4	58
	Greg Montgomery, Houston, AFC	56	43.3	63
1988	Harry Newsome, Pittsburgh, AFC	65	45.4	62
	Jim Arnold, Detroit, NFC	97	42.4	69
1987	Rick Donnelly, Atlanta, NFC	61	44.0	62
	Ralf Mojsiejenko, San Diego, AFC	67	42.9	57
1986	Rohn Stark, Indianapolis, AFC	76	45.2	63
	Sean Landeta, N.Y. Giants, NFC	79	44.8	61
1985	Rohn Stark, Indianapolis, AFC	78	45.9	68

	*Rick Donnelly, Atlanta, NFC	59	43.6	68
1984	Jim Arnold, Kansas City, AFC	98	44.9	63
	*Brian Hansen, New Orleans, NFC	69	43.8	66
1983	Rohn Stark, Baltimore, AFC	91	45.3	68
	*Frank Garcia, Tampa Bay, NFC	95	42.2	64
1982	Luke Prestridge, Denver, AFC	45	45.0	65
	Carl Birdsong, St. Louis, NFC	54	43.8	65
1981	Pat McInally, Cincinnati, AFC	72	45.4	62
	Tom Skladany, Detroit, NFC	64	43.5	74
1980	Dave Jennings, N.Y. Giants, NFC	94	44.8	63
	Luke Prestridge, Denver, AFC	70	43.9	57
1979	*Bob Grupp, Kansas City, AFC	89	43.6	74
	Dave Jennings, N.Y. Giants, NFC	104	42.7	72
1978	Pat McInally, Cincinnati, AFC	91	43.1	65
	*Tom Skladany, Detroit, NFC	86	42.5	63
1977	Ray Guy, Oakland, AFC	59	43.3	74
	Tom Blanchard, New Orleans, NFC	82	42.4	66
1976	Marv Bateman, Buffalo, AFC	86	42.8	78
	John James, Atlanta, NFC	101	42.1	67
1975	Ray Guy, Oakland, AFC	68	43.8	64
	Herman Weaver, Detroit, NFC	80	42.0	61
1974	Ray Guy, Oakland, AFC	74	42.2	66
	Tom Blanchard, New Orleans, NFC	88	42.1	71
1973	Jerrel Wilson, Kansas City, AFC	80	45.5	68
	*Tom Wittum, San Francisco, NFC	79	43.7	62
1972	Jerrel Wilson, Kansas City, AFC	66	44.8	69
	Dave Chapple, Los Angeles, NFC	53	44.2	70
1971	Dave Lewis, Cincinnati, AFC	72	44.8	56
	Tom McNeill, Philadelphia, NFC	73	42.0	64
1970	*Dave Lewis, Cincinnati, AFC	79	46.2	63
	*Julian Fagan, New Orleans, NFC	77	42.5	64
1969	David Lee, Baltimore, NFL	57	45.3	66
	Dennis Partee, San Diego, AFL	71	44.6	62
1968	Jerrel Wilson, Kansas City, AFL	63	45.1	70
	Billy Lothridge, Atlanta, NFL	75	44.3	70
1967	Bob Scarpitto, Denver, AFL	105	44.9	73
	Billy Lothridge, Atlanta, NFL	87	43.7	62
1966	Bob Scarpitto, Denver, AFL	76	45.8	70
	*David Lee, Baltimore, NFL	49	45.6	64
1965	Gary Collins, Cleveland, NFL	65	46.7	71
	Jerrel Wilson, Kansas City, AFL	69	45.4	64
1964	*Bobby Walden, Minnesota, NFL	72	46.4	73
	Jim Fraser, Denver, AFL	73	44.2	67
1963	Yale Lary, Detroit, NFL	35	48.9	73
	Jim Fraser, Denver, AFL	81	44.4	66
1962	Tommy Davis, San Francisco, NFL	48	45.6	82
	Jim Fraser, Denver, AFL	55	43.6	75
1961	Yale Lary, Detroit, NFL	52	48.4	71
	Billy Atkins, Buffalo, AFL	85	44.5	70
1960	Jerry Norton, St. Louis, NFL	39	45.6	62
	*Paul Maguire, L.A. Chargers, AFL	43	40.5	61
1959	Yale Lary, Detroit	45	47.1	67
1958	Sam Baker, Washington	48	45.4	64
1957	Don Chandler, N.Y. Giants	60	44.6	61
1956	Norm Van Brocklin, Los Angeles	48	43.1	72
1955	Norm Van Brocklin, Los Angeles	60	44.6	61
1954	Pat Brady, Pittsburgh	66	43.2	72
1953	Pat Brady, Pittsburgh	80	46.9	64
1952	Horace Gillom, Cleveland	61	45.7	73
1951	Horace Gillom, Cleveland	73	45.5	66
1950	*Fred (Curly) Morrison, Chi. Bears	57	43.3	65
1949	*Mike Boyda, N.Y. Bulldogs	56	44.2	61
1948	Joe Muha, Philadelphia	57	47.3	82
1947	Jack Jacobs, Green Bay	57	43.5	74
1946	Roy McKay, Green Bay	64	42.7	64
1945	Roy McKay, Green Bay	44	41.2	73
1944	Frank Sinkwich, Detroit	45	41.0	73
1943	Sammy Baugh, Washington	50	45.9	81
1942	Sammy Baugh, Washington	37	48.2	74
1941	Sammy Baugh, Washington	30	48.7	75
1940	Sammy Baugh, Washington	35	51.4	85
1939	*Parker Hall, Cleveland	58	40.8	80

**First year in the league.*

Annual Punt Return Leaders

Year	Player, Team	No.	Yards	Avg.	Long	TD
1989	Walter Stanley, Detroit, NFC	36	496	13.8	74	0
	Clarence Verdin, Indianapolis, AFC	23	296	12.9	49	1
1988	John Taylor, San Francisco, NFC	44	556	12.6	95	2
	JoJo Townsell, N.Y. Jets, AFC	35	409	11.7	59	1
1987	Mel Gray, New Orleans, NFC	24	352	14.7	80	0
	Bobby Joe Edmonds, Seattle, AFC	20	251	12.6	40	0
1986	*Bobby Joe Edmonds, Seattle, AFC	34	419	12.3	75	1
	*Vai Sikahema, St. Louis, NFC	43	522	12.1	71	2
1985	Irving Fryar, New England, AFC	37	520	14.1	85	2
	Henry Ellard, L.A. Rams, NFC	37	501	13.5	80	1
1984	Mike Martin, Cincinnati, AFC	24	376	15.7	55	0
	Henry Ellard, L.A. Rams, NFC	30	403	13.4	83	2
1983	*Henry Ellard, L.A. Rams, NFC	16	217	13.6	72	1
	Kirk Springs, N.Y. Jets, AFC	23	287	12.5	76	1
1982	Rick Upchurch, Denver, AFC	15	242	16.1	78	2
	Billy Johnson, Atlanta, NFC	24	273	11.4	71	0
1981	LeRoy Irvin, Los Angeles, NFC	46	615	13.4	84	3
	*James Brooks, San Diego, AFC	22	290	13.2	42	0
1980	J. T. Smith, Kansas City, AFC	40	581	14.5	75	2
	*Kenny Johnson, Atlanta, NFC	23	281	12.2	56	0
1979	John Sciarra, Philadelphia, NFC	16	182	11.4	38	0
	*Tony Nathan, Miami, AFC	28	306	10.9	86	1
1978	Rick Upchurch, Denver, AFC	36	493	13.7	75	1
	Jackie Wallace, Los Angeles, NFC	52	618	11.9	58	0
1977	Billy Johnson, Houston, AFC	35	539	15.4	87	2
	Larry Marshall, Philadelphia, NFC	46	489	10.6	48	0
1976	Rick Upchurch, Denver, AFC	39	536	13.7	92	4
	Eddie Brown, Washington, NFC	48	646	13.5	71	1
1975	Billy Johnson, Houston, AFC	40	612	15.3	83	3
	Terry Metcalf, St. Louis, NFC	23	285	12.4	69	1
1974	Lemar Parrish, Cincinnati, AFC	18	338	18.8	90	2
	Dick Jauron, Detroit, NFC	17	286	16.8	58	0
1973	Bruce Taylor, San Francisco, NFC	15	207	13.8	61	0
	Ron Smith, San Diego, AFC	27	352	13.0	84	2
1972	*Ken Ellis, Green Bay, NFC	14	215	15.4	80	1
	Chris Farasopoulos, N.Y. Jets, AFC	17	179	10.5	65	1
1971	Les (Speedy) Duncan, Washington, NFC	22	233	10.6	33	0
	Leroy Kelly, Cleveland, AFC	30	292	9.7	74	0
1970	Ed Podolak, Kansas City, AFC	23	311	13.5	60	0
	*Bruce Taylor, San Francisco, NFC	43	516	12.0	76	0
1969	Alvin Haymond, Los Angeles, NFL	33	435	13.2	52	0
	*Bill Thompson, Denver, AFL	25	288	11.5	40	0
1968	Bob Hayes, Dallas, NFL	15	312	20.8	90	2
	Noland Smith, Kansas City, AFL	18	270	15.0	80	1
1967	Floyd Little, Denver, AFL	16	270	16.9	72	1
	Ben Davis, Cleveland, NFL	18	229	12.7	52	1
1966	Les (Speedy) Duncan, San Diego, AFL	18	238	13.2	81	1
	Johnny Roland, St. Louis, NFL	20	221	11.1	86	1
1965	Leroy Kelly, Cleveland, NFL	17	265	15.6	67	2
	Les (Speedy) Duncan, San Diego, AFL	30	464	15.5	66	2
1964	Bobby Jancik, Houston, AFL	12	220	18.3	82	1
	Tommy Watkins, Detroit, NFL	16	238	14.9	68	2
1963	Dick James, Washington, NFL	16	214	13.4	39	0
	Claude (Hoot) Gibson, Oakland, AFL	26	307	11.8	85	2
1962	Dick Christy, N.Y. Titans, AFL	15	250	16.7	73	2
	Pat Studstill, Detroit, NFL	29	457	15.8	44	0
1961	Dick Christy, N.Y. Titans, AFL	18	383	21.3	70	2
	Willie Wood, Green Bay, NFL	14	225	16.1	72	2
1960	*Abner Haynes, Dall. Texans, AFL	14	215	15.4	46	0
	Abe Woodson, San Francisco, NFL	13	174	13.4	48	0
1959	Johnny Morris, Chi. Bears	14	171	12.2	78	1
1958	Jon Arnett, Los Angeles	18	223	12.4	58	0
1957	Bert Zagers, Washington	14	217	15.5	76	2
1956	Ken Konz, Cleveland	13	187	14.4	65	1
1955	Ollie Matson, Chi. Cardinals	13	245	18.8	78	2
1954	*Veryl Switzer, Green Bay	24	306	12.8	93	1
1953	Charley Trippi, Chi. Cardinals	21	239	11.4	38	0
1952	Jack Christiansen, Detroit	15	322	21.5	79	2
1951	Claude (Buddy) Young, N.Y. Yanks	12	231	19.3	79	1
1950	*Herb Rich, Baltimore	12	276	23.0	86	1
1949	Verda (Vitamin T) Smith, Los Angeles	27	427	15.8	85	1
1948	George McAfee, Chi. Bears	30	417	13.9	60	1
1947	*Walt Slater, Pittsburgh	28	435	15.5	33	0
1946	Bill Dudley, Pittsburgh	27	385	14.3	52	0
1945	*Dave Ryan, Detroit	15	220	14.7	56	0
1944	*Steve Van Buren, Philadelphia	15	230	15.3	55	1
1943	Andy Farkas, Washington	15	168	11.2	33	0
1942	Merlyn Condit, Brooklyn	21	210	10.0	23	0
1941	Byron (Whizzer) White, Detroit	19	262	13.8	64	0

**First year in the league.*

Annual Kickoff Return Leaders

Year	Player, Team	No.	Yards	Avg.	Long	TD
1989	Rod Woodson, Pittsburgh, AFC	36	982	27.3	84	1
	Mel Gray, Detroit, NFC	24	640	26.7	57	0
1988	Tim Brown, L.A. Raiders, AFC	41	1,098	26.8	97	1
	Donnie Elder, Tampa Bay, NFC	34	772	22.7	51	0
1987	Sylvester Stamps, Atlanta, NFC	24	660	27.5	97	1
	Paul Palmer, Kansas City, AFC	38	923	24.3	95	2
1986	Dennis Gentry, Chicago, NFC	20	576	28.8	91	1
	*Lupe Sanchez, Pittsburgh, AFC	25	591	23.6	64	0
1985	Ron Brown, L.A. Rams, NFC	28	918	32.8	98	3
	Glen Young, Cleveland, AFC	35	898	25.7	63	0
1984	*Bobby Humphery, N.Y. Jets, AFC	22	675	30.7	97	1
	Barry Redden, L.A. Rams, NFC	23	530	23.0	40	0
1983	Fulton Walker, Miami, AFC	36	962	26.7	78	0
	Darrin Nelson, Minnesota, NFC	18	445	24.7	50	0
1982	*Mike Mosley, Buffalo, AFC	18	487	27.1	66	0
	Alvin Hall, Detroit, NFC	16	426	26.6	96	1
1981	Mike Nelms, Washington, NFC	37	1,099	29.7	84	0
	Carl Roaches, Houston, AFC	28	769	27.5	96	1
1980	Horace Ivory, New England, AFC	36	992	27.6	98	1
	Rich Mauti, New Orleans, NFC	31	798	25.7	52	0
1979	Larry Brunson, Oakland, AFC	17	441	25.9	89	0
	*Jimmy Edwards, Minnesota, NFC	44	1,103	25.1	83	0
1978	Steve Odom, Green Bay, NFC	25	677	27.1	95	1
	*Keith Wright, Cleveland, AFC	30	789	26.3	86	0
1977	*Raymond Clayborn, New England, AFC	28	869	31.0	101	3
	*Wilbert Montgomery, Philadelphia, NFC	23	619	26.9	99	1
1976	*Duriel Harris, Miami, AFC	17	559	32.9	69	0
	Cullen Bryant, Los Angeles, NFC	16	459	28.7	90	1
1975	*Walter Payton, Chicago, NFC	14	444	31.7	70	0
	Harold Hart, Oakland, AFC	17	518	30.5	102	1
1974	Terry Metcalf, St. Louis, NFC	20	623	31.2	94	1
	Greg Pruitt, Cleveland, AFC	22	606	27.5	88	1
1973	Carl Garrett, Chicago, NFC	16	486	30.4	67	0
	*Wallace Francis, Buffalo, AFC	23	687	29.9	101	2
1972	Ron Smith, Chicago, NFC	30	924	30.8	94	1
	*Bruce Laird, Baltimore, AFC	29	843	29.1	73	0
1971	Travis Williams, Los Angeles, NFC	25	743	29.7	105	1
	Eugene (Mercury) Morris, Miami, AFC	15	423	28.2	94	1
1970	Jim Duncan, Baltimore, AFC	20	707	35.4	99	1
	Cecil Turner, Chicago, NFC	23	752	32.7	96	4
1969	Bobby Williams, Detroit, NFL	17	563	33.1	96	1
	*Bill Thompson, Denver, AFL	18	513	28.5	63	0
1968	Preston Pearson, Baltimore, NFL	15	527	35.1	102	2
	*George Atkinson, Oakland, AFL	32	802	25.1	60	0
1967	*Travis Williams, Green Bay, NFL	18	739	41.1	104	4
	*Zeke Moore, Houston, AFL	14	405	28.9	92	1
1966	Gale Sayers, Chicago, NFL	23	718	31.2	93	2

	*Goldie Sellers, Denver, AFL	19	541	28.5	100	2
1965	Tommy Watkins, Detroit, NFL	17	584	34.4	94	0
	Abner Haynes, Denver, AFL	34	901	26.5	60	0
1964	*Clarence Childs, N.Y. Giants, NFL	34	987	29.0	100	1
	Bo Roberson, Oakland, AFL	36	975	27.1	59	0
1963	Abe Woodson, San Francisco, NFL	29	935	32.2	103	3
	Bobby Jancik, Houston, AFL	45	1,317	29.3	53	0
1962	Abe Woodson, San Francisco, NFL	37	1,157	31.3	79	0
	*Bobby Jancik, Houston, AFL	24	826	30.3	61	0
1961	Dick Bass, Los Angeles, NFL	23	698	30.3	64	0
	*Dave Grayson, Dall. Texans, AFL	16	453	28.3	73	0
1960	*Tom Moore, Green Bay, NFL	12	397	33.1	84	0
	Ken Hall, Houston, AFL	19	594	31.3	104	1
1959	Abe Woodson, San Francisco	13	382	29.4	105	1
1958	Ollie Matson, Chi. Cardinals	14	497	35.5	101	2
1957	*Jon Arnett, Los Angeles	18	504	28.0	98	1
1956	*Tom Wilson, Los Angeles	15	477	31.8	103	1
1955	Al Carmichael, Green Bay	14	418	29.9	100	1
1954	Billy Reynolds, Cleveland	14	413	29.5	51	0
1953	Joe Arenas, San Francisco	16	551	34.4	82	0
1952	Lynn Chandnois, Pittsburgh	17	599	35.2	93	2
1951	Lynn Chandnois, Pittsburgh	12	390	32.5	55	0
1950	Verda (Vitamin T) Smith, Los Angeles	22	742	33.7	97	3
1949	*Don Doll, Detroit	21	536	25.5	56	0
1948	*Joe Scott, N.Y. Giants	20	569	28.5	99	1
1947	Eddie Saenz, Washington	29	797	27.5	94	2
1946	Abe Karnofsky, Boston	21	599	28.5	97	1
1945	Steve Van Buren, Philadelphia	13	373	28.7	98	1
1944	Bob Thurbon, Card.-Pitt	12	291	24.3	55	0
1943	Ken Heineman, Brooklyn	16	444	27.8	69	0
1942	Marshall Goldberg, Chi. Cardinals	15	393	26.2	95	1
1941	Marshall Goldberg, Chi. Cardinals	12	290	24.2	41	0

**First year in the league.*

Points Scored

Year	Team	Points
1989	San Francisco, NFC	442
	Buffalo, AFC	409
1988	Cincinnati, AFC	448
	L.A. Rams, NFC	407
1987	San Francisco, NFC	459
	Cleveland, AFC	390
1986	Miami, AFC	430
	Minnesota, NFC	398
1985	San Diego, AFC	467
	Chicago, NFC	456
1984	Miami, AFC	513
	San Francisco, NFC	475
1983	Washington, NFC	541
	L.A. Raiders, AFC	442
1982	San Diego, AFC	288
	Dallas, NFC	226
	Green Bay, NFC	226
1981	San Diego, AFC	478
	Atlanta, NFC	426
1980	Dallas, NFC	454
	New England, AFC	441
1979	Pittsburgh, AFC	416
	Dallas, NFC	371
1978	Dallas, NFC	384
	Miami, AFC	372
1977	Oakland, AFC	351
	Dallas, NFC	345
1976	Baltimore, AFC	417
	Los Angeles, NFC	351
1975	Buffalo, AFC	420
	Minnesota, NFC	377
1974	Oakland, AFC	355
	Washington, NFC	320
1973	Los Angeles, NFC	388
	Denver, AFC	354
1972	Miami, AFC	385
	San Francisco, NFC	353
1971	Dallas, NFC	406
	Oakland, AFC	344
1970	San Francisco, NFC	352
	Baltimore, AFC	321
1969	Minnesota, NFL	379
	Oakland, AFL	377
1968	Oakland, AFL	453
	Dallas, NFL	431
1967	Oakland, AFL	468
	Los Angeles, NFL	398
1966	Kansas City, AFL	448
	Dallas, NFL	445
1965	San Francisco, NFL	421
	San Diego, AFL	340
1964	Baltimore, NFL	428
	Buffalo, AFL	400
1963	N.Y. Giants, NFL	448
	San Diego, AFL	399
1962	Green Bay, NFL	415
	Dall. Texans, AFL	389
1961	Houston, AFL	513
	Green Bay, NFL	391
1960	N.Y. Titans, AFL	382
	Cleveland, NFL	362
1959	Baltimore	374
1958	Baltimore	381
1957	Los Angeles	307
1956	Chi. Bears	363
1955	Cleveland	349
1954	Detroit	337
1953	San Francisco	372
1952	Los Angeles	349
1951	Los Angeles	392
1950	Los Angeles	466
1949	Philadelphia	364
1948	Chi. Cardinals	395
1947	Chi. Bears	363
1946	Chi. Bears	289
1945	Philadelphia	272
1944	Philadelphia	267
1943	Chi. Bears	303
1942	Chi. Bears	376
1941	Chi. Bears	396
1940	Washington	245
1939	Chi. Bears	298
1938	Green Bay	223
1937	Green Bay	220
1936	Green Bay	248
1935	Chi. Bears	192
1934	Chi. Bears	286
1933	N.Y. Giants	244
1932	Green Bay	152

Total Yards Gained

Year	Team	Yards
1989	San Francisco, NFC	6,268
	Cincinnati, AFC	6,101
1988	Cincinnati, AFC	6,057
	San Francisco, NFC	5,900
1987	San Francisco, NFC	5,987
	Denver, AFC	5,624
1986	Cincinnati, AFC	6,490
	San Francisco, NFC	6,082
1985	San Diego, AFC	6,535
	San Francisco, NFC	5,920
1984	Miami, AFC	6,936
	San Francisco, NFC	6,366
1983	San Diego, AFC	6,197
	Green Bay, NFC	6,172
1982	San Diego, AFC	4,048
	San Francisco, NFC	3,242
1981	San Diego, AFC	6,744
	Detroit, NFC	5,933
1980	San Diego, AFC	6,410
	Los Angeles, NFC	6,006
1979	Pittsburgh, AFC	6,258
	Dallas, NFC	5,968
1978	New England, AFC	5,965
	Dallas, NFC	5,959
1977	Dallas, NFC	4,812
	Oakland, AFC	4,736
1976	Baltimore, AFC	5,236
	St. Louis, NFC	5,136
1975	Buffalo, AFC	5,467
	Dallas, NFC	5,025
1974	Dallas, NFC	4,983
	Oakland, AFC	4,718
1973	Los Angeles, NFC	4,906
	Oakland, AFC	4,773
1972	Miami, AFC	5,036
	N.Y. Giants, NFC	4,483
1971	Dallas, NFC	5,035
	San Diego, AFC	4,738
1970	Oakland, AFC	4,829
	San Francisco, NFC	4,503
1969	Dallas, NFL	5,122
	Oakland, AFL	5,036
1968	Oakland, AFL	5,696
	Dallas, NFL	5,117
1967	N.Y. Jets, AFL	5,152
	Baltimore, NFL	5,008
1966	Dallas, NFL	5,145
	Kansas City, AFL	5,114
1965	San Francisco, NFL	5,270
	San Diego, AFL	5,188
1964	Buffalo, AFL	5,206
	Baltimore, NFL	4,779
1963	San Diego, AFL	5,153
	N.Y. Giants, NFL	5,024
1962	N.Y. Giants, NFL	5,005
	Houston, AFL	4,971
1961	Houston, AFL	6,288
	Philadelphia, NFL	5,112
1960	Houston, AFL	4,936
	Baltimore, NFL	4,245
1959	Baltimore	4,458
1958	Baltimore	4,539
1957	Los Angeles	4,143
1956	Chi. Bears	4,537
1955	Chi. Bears	4,316
1954	Los Angeles	5,187
1953	Philadelphia	4,811
1952	Cleveland	4,352
1951	Los Angeles	5,506
1950	Los Angeles	5,420
1949	Chi. Bears	4,873
1948	Chi. Cardinals	4,705
1947	Chi. Bears	5,053
1946	Los Angeles	3,793
1945	Washington	3,549
1944	Chi. Bears	3,239
1943	Chi. Bears	4,045
1942	Chi. Bears	3,900
1941	Chi. Bears	4,265
1940	Green Bay	3,400
1939	Chi. Bears	3,988
1938	Green Bay	3,037
1937	Green Bay	3,201
1936	Detroit	3,703
1935	Chi. Bears	3,454
1934	Chi. Bears	3,900
1933	N.Y. Giants	2,973
1932	Chi. Bears	2,755

Yards Rushing

Year	Team	Yards
1989	Cincinnati, AFC	2,483
	Chicago, NFC	2,287
1988	Cincinnati, AFC	2,710
	San Francisco, NFC	2,523
1987	San Francisco, NFC	2,237
	L.A. Raiders, AFC	2,197
1986	Chicago, NFC	2,700
	Cincinnati, AFC	2,533
1985	Chicago, NFC	2,761
	Indianapolis, AFC	2,439
1984	Chicago, NFC	2,974
	N.Y. Jets, AFC	2,189
1983	Chicago, NFC	2,727
	Baltimore, AFC	2,695
1982	Buffalo, AFC	1,371
	Dallas, NFC	1,313
1981	Detroit, NFC	2,795
	Kansas City, AFC	2,633
1980	Los Angeles, NFC	2,799
	Houston, AFC	2,635
1979	N.Y. Jets, AFC	2,646
	St. Louis, NFC	2,582
1978	New England, AFC	3,165
	Dallas, NFC	2,783
1977	Chicago, NFC	2,811
	Oakland, AFC	2,627
1976	Pittsburgh, AFC	2,971
	Los Angeles, NFC	2,528
1975	Buffalo, AFC	2,974
	Dallas, NFC	2,432
1974	Dallas, NFC	2,454
	Pittsburgh, AFC	2,417
1973	Buffalo, AFC	3,088
	Los Angeles, NFC	2,925
1972	Miami, AFC	2,960
	Chicago, NFC	2,360
1971	Miami, AFC	2,429
	Detroit, NFC	2,376
1970	Dallas, NFC	2,300
	Miami, AFC	2,082
1969	Dallas, NFL	2,276
	Kansas City, AFL	2,220
1968	Chicago, NFL	2,377
	Kansas City, AFL	2,227
1967	Cleveland, NFL	2,139
	Houston, AFL	2,122
1966	Kansas City, AFL	2,274
	Cleveland, NFL	2,166
1965	Cleveland, NFL	2,331
	San Diego, AFL	2,085
1964	Green Bay, NFL	2,276
	Buffalo, AFL	2,040
1963	Cleveland, NFL	2,639
	San Diego, AFL	2,203
1962	Buffalo, AFL	2,480
	Green Bay, NFL	2,460
1961	Green Bay, NFL	2,350
	Dall. Texans, AFL	2,189
1960	St. Louis, NFL	2,356
	Oakland, AFL	2,056
1959	Cleveland	2,149
1958	Cleveland	2,526
1957	Los Angeles	2,142
1956	Chi. Bears	2,468
1955	Chi. Bears	2,388
1954	San Francisco	2,498
1953	San Francisco	2,230
1952	San Francisco	1,905
1951	Chi. Bears	2,408
1950	N.Y. Giants	2,336
1949	Philadelphia	2,607
1948	Chi. Cardinals	2,560
1947	Los Angeles	2,171
1946	Green Bay	1,765
1945	Cleveland	1,714
1944	Philadelphia	1,661
1943	Phil-Pitt	1,730
1942	Chi. Bears	1,881
1941	Chi. Bears	2,263
1940	Chi. Bears	1,818
1939	Chi. Bears	2,043
1938	Detroit	1,893
1937	Detroit	2,074
1936	Detroit	2,885
1935	Chi. Bears	2,096
1934	Chi. Bears	2,847
1933	Boston	2,260
1932	Chi. Bears	1,770

Yards Passing

Leadership in this category has been based on net yards since 1952.

Year	Team	Yards
1989	Washington, NFC	4,349
	Miami, AFC	4,216
1988	Miami, AFC	4,516
	Washington, NFC	4,136
1987	Miami, AFC	3,876
	San Francisco, NFC	3,750
1986	Miami, AFC	4,779
	San Francisco, NFC	4,096
1985	San Diego, AFC	4,870
	Dallas, NFC	3,861
1984	Miami, AFC	5,018
	St. Louis, NFC	4,257
1983	San Diego, AFC	4,661
	Green Bay, NFC	4,365
1982	San Diego, AFC	2,927
	San Francisco, NFC	2,502
1981	San Diego, AFC	4,739
	Minnesota, NFC	4,333
1980	San Diego, AFC	4,531
	Minnesota, NFC	3,688
1979	San Diego, AFC	3,915
	San Francisco, NFC	3,641
1978	San Diego, AFC	3,375
	Minnesota, NFC	3,243
1977	Buffalo, AFC	2,530
	St. Louis, NFC	2,499
1976	Baltimore, AFC	2,933
	Minnesota, NFC	2,855
1975	Cincinnati, AFC	3,241
	Washington, NFC	2,917
1974	Washington, NFC	2,978
	Cincinnati, AFC	2,804
1973	Philadelphia, NFC	2,998
	Denver, AFC	2,519
1972	N.Y. Jets, AFC	2,777
	San Francisco, NFC	2,735
1971	San Diego, AFC	3,134
	Dallas, NFC	2,786
1970	San Francisco, NFC	2,923
	Oakland, AFC	2,865
1969	Oakland, AFL	3,271
	San Francisco, NFL	3,158
1968	San Diego, AFL	3,623
	Dallas, NFL	3,026
1967	N.Y. Jets, AFL	3,845
	Washington, NFL	3,730
1966	N.Y. Jets, AFL	3,464
	Dallas, NFL	3,023
1965	San Francisco, NFL	3,487
	San Diego, AFL	3,103
1964	Houston, AFL	3,527
	Chicago, NFL	2,841
1963	Baltimore, NFL	3,296
	Houston, AFL	3,222
1962	Denver, AFL	3,404
	Philadelphia, NFL	3,385
1961	Houston, AFL	4,392
	Philadelphia, NFL	3,605
1960	Houston, AFL	3,203
	Baltimore, NFL	2,956
1959	Baltimore	2,753
1958	Pittsburgh	2,752
1957	Baltimore	2,388
1956	Los Angeles	2,419
1955	Philadelphia	2,472
1954	Chi. Bears	3,104

Year	Team	
1953	Philadelphia	3,089
1952	Cleveland	2,566
1951	Los Angeles	3,296
1950	Los Angeles	3,709
1949	Chi. Bears	3,055
1948	Washington	2,861
1947	Washington	3,336
1946	Los Angeles	2,080
1945	Chi. Bears	1,857
1944	Washington	2,021
1943	Chi. Bears	2,310
1942	Green Bay	2,407
1941	Chi. Bears	2,002
1940	Washington	1,887
1939	Chi. Bears	1,965
1938	Washington	1,536
1937	Green Bay	1,398
1936	Green Bay	1,629
1935	Green Bay	1,449
1934	Green Bay	1,165
1933	N.Y. Giants	1,348
1932	Chi. Bears	1,013

Fewest Points Allowed

Year	Team	Points
1989	Denver, AFC	226
	N.Y. Giants, NFC	252
1988	Chicago, NFC	215
	Buffalo, AFC	237
1987	Indianapolis, AFC	238
	San Francisco, NFC	253
1986	Chicago, NFC	187
	Seattle, AFC	293
1985	Chicago, NFC	198
	N.Y. Jets, AFC	264
1984	San Francisco, NFC	227
	Denver, AFC	241
1983	Miami, AFC	250
	Detroit, NFC	286
1982	Washington, NFC	128
	Miami, AFC	131
1981	Philadelphia, NFC	221
	Miami, AFC	275
1980	Philadelphia, NFC	222
	Houston, AFC	251
1979	Tampa Bay, NFC	237
	San Diego, AFC	246
1978	Pittsburgh, AFC	195
	Dallas, NFC	208
1977	Atlanta, NFC	129
	Denver, AFC	148
1976	Pittsburgh, AFC	138
	Minnesota, NFC	176
1975	Los Angeles, NFC	135
	Pittsburgh, AFC	162
1974	Los Angeles, NFC	181
	Pittsburgh, AFC	189
1973	Miami, AFC	150
	Minnesota, NFC	168
1972	Miami, AFC	171
	Washington, NFC	218
1971	Minnesota, NFC	139
	Baltimore, AFC	140
1970	Minnesota, NFC	143
	Miami, AFC	228
1969	Minnesota, NFL	133
	Kansas City, AFL	177
1968	Baltimore, NFL	144
	Kansas City, AFL	170
1967	Los Angeles, NFL	196
	Houston, AFL	199
1966	Green Bay, NFL	163
	Buffalo, AFL	255
1965	Green Bay, NFL	224
	Buffalo, AFL	226
1964	Baltimore, NFL	225
	Buffalo, AFL	242
1963	Chicago, NFL	144
	San Diego, AFL	255
1962	Green Bay, NFL	148
	Dall. Texans, AFL	233
1961	San Diego, AFL	219
	N.Y. Giants, NFL	220
1960	San Francisco, NFL	205
	Dall. Texans, AFL	253
1959	N.Y. Giants	170
1958	N.Y. Giants	183
1957	Cleveland	172
1956	Cleveland	177
1955	Cleveland	218
1954	Cleveland	162
1953	Cleveland	162
1952	Detroit	192
1951	Cleveland	152
1950	Philadelphia	141
1949	Philadelphia	134
1948	Chi. Bears	151
1947	Green Bay	210
1946	Pittsburgh	117
1945	Washington	121
1944	N.Y. Giants	75
1943	Washington	137
1942	Chi. Bears	84

Year	Team	
1941	N.Y. Giants	114
1940	Brooklyn	120
1939	N.Y. Giants	85
1938	N.Y. Giants	79
1937	Chi. Bears	100
1936	Chi. Bears	94
1935	Green Bay	96
	N.Y. Giants	96
1934	Detroit	59
1933	Brooklyn	54
1932	Chi. Bears	44

Fewest Total Yards Allowed

Year	Team	Yards
1989	Minnesota, NFC	4,184
	Kansas City, AFC	4,293
1988	Minnesota, NFC	4,091
	Buffalo, AFC	4,578
1987	San Francisco, NFC	4,095
	Cleveland, AFC	4,264
1986	Chicago, NFC	4,130
	L.A. Raiders, AFC	4,804
1985	Chicago, NFC	4,135
	L.A. Raiders, AFC	4,603
1984	Chicago, NFC	3,863
	Cleveland, AFC	4,641
1983	Cincinnati, AFC	4,327
	New Orleans, NFC	4,691
1982	Miami, AFC	2,312
	Tampa Bay, NFC	2,442
1981	Philadelphia, NFC	4,447
	N.Y. Jets, AFC	4,871
1980	Buffalo, AFC	4,101
	Philadelphia, NFC	4,443
1979	Tampa Bay, NFC	3,949
	Pittsburgh, AFC	4,270
1978	Los Angeles, NFC	3,893
	Pittsburgh, AFC	4,168
1977	Dallas, NFC	3,213
	New England, AFC	3,638
1976	Pittsburgh, AFC	3,323
	San Francisco, NFC	3,562
1975	Minnesota, NFC	3,153
	Oakland, AFC	3,629
1974	Pittsburgh, AFC	3,074
	Washington, NFC	3,285
1973	Los Angeles, NFC	2,951
	Oakland, AFC	3,160
1972	Miami, AFC	3,297
	Green Bay, NFC	3,474
1971	Baltimore, AFC	2,852
	Minnesota, NFC	3,406
1970	Minnesota, NFC	2,803
	N.Y. Jets, AFC	3,655
1969	Minnesota, NFL	2,720
	Kansas City, AFL	3,163
1968	Los Angeles, NFL	3,118
	N.Y. Jets, AFL	3,363
1967	Oakland, AFL	3,294
	Green Bay, NFL	3,300
1966	St. Louis, NFL	3,492
	Oakland, AFL	3,910
1965	San Diego, AFL	3,262
	Detroit, NFL	3,557
1964	Green Bay, NFL	3,179
	Buffalo, AFL	3,878
1963	Chicago, NFL	3,176
	Boston, AFL	3,834
1962	Detroit, NFL	3,217
	Dall. Texans, AFL	3,951
1961	San Diego, AFL	3,726
	Baltimore, NFL	3,782
1960	St. Louis, NFL	3,029
	Buffalo, AFL	3,866
1959	N.Y. Giants	2,843
1958	Chi. Bears	3,066
1957	Pittsburgh	2,791
1956	N.Y. Giants	3,081
1955	Cleveland	2,841
1954	Cleveland	2,658
1953	Philadelphia	2,998
1952	Cleveland	3,075
1951	N.Y. Giants	3,250
1950	Cleveland	3,154
1949	Philadelphia	2,831
1948	Chi. Bears	2,931
1947	Green Bay	3,396
1946	Washington	2,451
1945	Philadelphia	2,073
1944	Philadelphia	1,943
1943	Chi. Bears	2,262
1942	Chi. Bears	1,703
1941	N.Y. Giants	2,368
1940	N.Y. Giants	2,219
1939	Washington	2,116
1938	N.Y. Giants	2,029
1937	Washington	2,123
1936	Boston	2,181
1935	Boston	1,996
1934	Chi. Cardinals	1,539
1933	Brooklyn	1,789

Fewest Yards Rushing Allowed

Year	Team	Yards
1989	New Orleans, NFC	1,326
	Denver, AFC	1,580
1988	Chicago, NFC	1,326
	Houston, AFC	1,592
1987	Chicago, NFC	1,413
	Cleveland, AFC	1,433
1986	N.Y. Giants, NFC	1,284
	Denver, AFC	1,651
1985	Chicago, NFC	1,319
	N.Y. Jets, AFC	1,516
1984	Chicago, NFC	1,377
	Pittsburgh, AFC	1,617
1983	Washington, NFC	1,289
	Cincinnati, AFC	1,499
1982	Pittsburgh, AFC	762
	Detroit, NFC	854
1981	Detroit, NFC	1,623
	Kansas City, AFC	1,747
1980	Detroit, NFC	1,599
	Cincinnati, AFC	1,680
1979	Denver, AFC	1,693
	Tampa Bay, NFC	1,873
1978	Dallas, NFC	1,721
	Pittsburgh, AFC	1,774
1977	Denver, AFC	1,531
	Dallas, NFC	1,651
1976	Pittsburgh, AFC	1,457
	Los Angeles, NFC	1,564
1975	Minnesota, NFC	1,532
	Houston, AFC	1,680
1974	Los Angeles, NFC	1,302
	New England, AFC	1,587
1973	Los Angeles, NFC	1,270
	Oakland, AFC	1,470
1972	Dallas, NFC	1,515
	Miami, AFC	1,548
1971	Baltimore, AFC	1,113
	Dallas, NFC	1,144
1970	Detroit, NFC	1,152
	N.Y. Jets, AFC	1,283
1969	Dallas, NFL	1,050
	Kansas City, AFL	1,091
1968	Dallas, NFL	1,195
	N.Y. Jets, AFL	1,195
1967	Dallas, NFL	1,081
	Oakland, AFL	1,129
1966	Buffalo, AFL	1,051
	Dallas, NFL	1,176
1965	San Diego, AFL	1,094
	Los Angeles, NFL	1,409
1964	Buffalo, AFL	913
	Los Angeles, NFL	1,501
1963	Boston, AFL	1,107
	Chicago, NFL	1,442
1962	Detroit, NFL	1,231
	Dall. Texans, AFL	1,250
1961	Boston, AFL	1,041
	Pittsburgh, NFL	1,463
1960	St. Louis, NFL	1,212
	Dall. Texans, AFL	1,338
1959	N.Y. Giants	1,261
1958	Baltimore	1,291
1957	Baltimore	1,174
1956	N.Y. Giants	1,443
1955	Cleveland	1,189
1954	Cleveland	1,050
1953	Philadelphia	1,117
1952	Detroit	1,145
1951	N.Y. Giants	913
1950	Detroit	1,367
1949	Chi. Bears	1,196
1948	Philadelphia	1,209
1947	Philadelphia	1,329
1946	Chi. Bears	1,060
1945	Philadelphia	817
1944	Philadelphia	558
1943	Phil-Pitt	793
1942	Chi. Bears	519
1941	Washington	1,042
1940	N.Y. Giants	977
1939	Chi. Bears	812
1938	Detroit	1,081
1937	Chi. Bears	933
1936	Boston	1,148
1935	Boston	998
1934	Chi. Cardinals	954
1933	Brooklyn	964

Fewest Yards Passing Allowed

Leadership in this category has been based on net yards since 1952.

Year	Team	Yards
1989	Minnesota, NFC	2,501
	Kansas City, AFC	2,527
1988	Kansas City, AFC	2,434
	Minnesota, NFC	2,489
1987	San Francisco, NFC	2,484
	L.A. Raiders, AFC	2,727

Year	Team	
1986	St. Louis, NFC	2,637
	New England, AFC	2,978
1985	Washington, NFC	2,746
	Pittsburgh, AFC	2,783
1984	New Orleans, NFC	2,453
	Cleveland, AFC	2,696
1983	New Orleans, NFC	2,691
	Cincinnati, AFC	2,828
1982	Miami, AFC	1,027
	Tampa Bay, NFC	1,384
1981	Philadelphia, NFC	2,696
	Buffalo, AFC	2,870
1980	Washington, NFC	2,171
	Buffalo, AFC	2,282
1979	Tampa Bay, NFC	2,076
	Buffalo, AFC	2,530
1978	Buffalo, AFC	1,960
	Los Angeles, NFC	2,048
1977	Atlanta, NFC	1,384
	San Diego, AFC	1,725
1976	Minnesota, NFC	1,575
	Cincinnati, AFC	1,758
1975	Minnesota, NFC	1,621
	Cincinnati, AFC	1,729
1974	Pittsburgh, AFC	1,466
	Atlanta, NFC	1,572
1973	Miami, AFC	1,290
	Atlanta, NFC	1,430
1972	Minnesota, NFC	1,699
	Cleveland, AFC	1,736
1971	Atlanta, NFC	1,638
	Baltimore, AFC	1,739
1970	Minnesota, NFC	1,438
	Kansas City, AFC	2,010
1969	Minnesota, NFL	1,631
	Kansas City, AFL	2,072
1968	Houston, AFL	1,671
	Green Bay, NFL	1,796
1967	Green Bay, NFL	1,377
	Buffalo, AFL	1,825
1966	Green Bay, NFL	1,959
	Oakland, AFL	2,118
1965	Green Bay, NFL	1,981
	San Diego, AFL	2,168
1964	Green Bay, NFL	1,647
	San Diego, AFL	2,518
1963	Chicago, NFL	1,734
	Oakland, AFL	2,589
1962	Green Bay, NFL	1,746
	Oakland, AFL	2,306
1961	Baltimore, NFL	1,913
	San Diego, AFL	2,363
1960	Chicago, NFL	1,388
	Buffalo, AFL	2,124
1959	N.Y. Giants	1,582
1958	Chi. Bears	1,769
1957	Cleveland	1,300
1956	Cleveland	1,103
1955	Pittsburgh	1,295
1954	Cleveland	1,608
1953	Washington	1,751
1952	Washington	1,580
1951	Pittsburgh	1,687
1950	Cleveland	1,581
1949	Philadelphia	1,607
1948	Green Bay	1,626
1947	Green Bay	1,790
1946	Pittsburgh	939
1945	Washington	1,121
1944	Chi. Bears	1,052
1943	Chi. Bears	980
1942	Washington	1,093
1941	Pittsburgh	1,168
1940	Philadelphia	1,012
1939	Washington	1,116
1938	Chi. Bears	897
1937	Detroit	804
1936	Philadelphia	853
1935	Chi. Cardinals	793
1934	Philadelphia	545
1933	Portsmouth	558

Individual Records

Service
Most Games
- 5 Marv Fleming, Green Bay, 1967-68; Miami, 1972-74
  Larry Cole, Dallas, 1971-72, 1976, 1978-79
  Cliff Harris, Dallas, 1971-72, 1976, 1978-79
  D.D. Lewis, Dallas, 1971-72, 1976, 1978-79
  Preston Pearson, Baltimore, 1969; Pittsburgh, 1975; Dallas, 1976, 1978-79
  Charlie Waters, Dallas, 1971-72, 1976, 1978-79
  Rayfield Wright, Dallas, 1971-72, 1976, 1978-79
- 4 By many players

Most Games, Winning Team
- 4 By many players

Most Games, Coach
- 6 Don Shula, Baltimore, 1969; Miami, 1972-74, 1983, 1985
- 5 Tom Landry, Dallas, 1971-72, 1976, 1978-79
- 4 Bud Grant, Minnesota, 1970, 1974-75, 1977
  Chuck Noll, Pittsburgh, 1975-76, 1979-80

Most Games, Winning Team, Coach
- 4 Chuck Noll, Pittsburgh, 1975-76, 1979-80
- 3 Bill Walsh, San Francisco, 1982, 1985, 1989
- 2 Vince Lombardi, Green Bay, 1967-68
  Tom Landry, Dallas, 1972, 1978
  Don Shula, Miami, 1973-74
  Tom Flores, Oakland, 1981; L.A. Raiders, 1984
  Joe Gibbs, Washington, 1983, 1988

Most Games, Losing Team, Coach
- 4 Bud Grant, Minnesota, 1970, 1974-75, 1977
  Don Shula, Baltimore, 1969; Miami, 1972, 1983, 1985
- 3 Tom Landry, Dallas, 1971, 1976, 1979
  Dan Reeves, Denver, 1987-88, 1990

Scoring
Points

Most Points, Career
- 24 Franco Harris, Pittsburgh, 4 games (4-td)
  Roger Craig, San Francisco, 3 games (4-td)
  Jerry Rice, San Francisco, 2 games (4-td)
- 22 Ray Wersching, San Francisco, 2 games (7-pat, 5-fg)
- 20 Don Chandler, Green Bay, 2 games (8-pat, 4-fg)

Most Points, Game
- 18 Roger Craig, San Francisco vs. Miami, 1985 (3-td)
  Jerry Rice, San Francisco vs. Denver, 1990 (3-td)
- 15 Don Chandler, Green Bay vs. Oakland, 1968 (3-pat, 4-fg)
- 14 Ray Wersching, San Francisco vs. Cincinnati, 1982 (2-pat, 4-fg)
  Kevin Butler, Chicago vs. New England, 1986 (5-pat, 3-fg)

Touchdowns
Most Touchdowns, Career
- 4 Franco Harris, Pittsburgh, 4 games (4-r)
  Roger Craig, San Francisco, 3 games (2-r, 2-p)
  Jerry Rice, San Francisco, 2 games (4-p)
- 3 John Stallworth, Pittsburgh, 4 games (3-p)
  Lynn Swann, Pittsburgh, 4 games (3-p)
  Cliff Branch, Oakland-L.A. Raiders, 3 games (3-p)

Most Touchdowns, Game
- 3 Roger Craig, San Francisco vs. Miami, 1985 (1-r, 2-p)
  Jerry Rice, San Francisco vs. Denver, 1990 (3-p)
- 2 Max McGee, Green Bay vs. Kansas City, 1967 (2-p)
  Elijah Pitts, Green Bay vs. Kansas City, 1967 (2-r)
  Bill Miller, Oakland vs. Green Bay, 1968 (2-p)
  Larry Csonka, Miami vs. Minnesota, 1974 (2-r)
  Pete Banaszak, Oakland vs. Minnesota, 1977 (2-r)
  John Stallworth, Pittsburgh vs. Dallas, 1979 (2-p)
  Franco Harris, Pittsburgh vs. Los Angeles, 1980 (2-r)
  Cliff Branch, Oakland vs. Philadelphia, 1981 (2-p)
  Dan Ross, Cincinnati vs. San Francisco, 1982 (2-p)
  Marcus Allen, L.A. Raiders vs. Washington, 1984 (2-r)
  Jim McMahon, Chicago vs. New England, 1986 (2-r)
  Ricky Sanders, Washington vs. Denver, 1988 (2-p)
  Timmy Smith, Washington vs. Denver, 1988 (2-r)
  Tom Rathman, San Francisco vs. Denver, 1990 (2-r)

Points After Touchdown
Most Points After Touchdown, Career
- 9 Mike Cofer, San Francisco, 2 games (10 att)
- 8 Don Chandler, Green Bay, 2 games (8 att)
  Roy Gerela, Pittsburgh, 3 games (9 att)
  Chris Bahr, Oakland-L.A. Raiders, 2 games (8 att)
- 7 Ray Wersching, San Francisco, 2 games (7 att)

Most Points After Touchdown, Game
- 7 Mike Cofer, San Francisco vs. Denver, 1990 (8 att)
- 6 Ali Haji-Sheikh, Washington vs. Denver, 1988 (6 att)
- 5 Don Chandler, Green Bay vs. Kansas City, 1967 (5 att)
  Roy Gerela, Pittsburgh vs. Dallas, 1979 (5 att)
  Chris Bahr, L.A. Raiders vs. Washington, 1984 (5 att)
  Ray Wersching, San Francisco vs. Miami, 1985 (5 att)
  Kevin Butler, Chicago vs. New England, 1986 (5 att)

Field Goals
Field Goals Attempted, Career
- 7 Roy Gerela, Pittsburgh, 3 games
- 6 Jim Turner, N.Y. Jets-Denver, 2 games
  Rich Karlis, Denver, 2 games
- 5 Efren Herrera, Dallas, 1 game
  Ray Wersching, San Francisco, 2 games

Most Field Goals Attempted, Game
- 5 Jim Turner, N.Y. Jets vs. Baltimore, 1969
  Efren Herrera, Dallas vs. Denver, 1978
- 4 Don Chandler, Green Bay vs. Oakland, 1968
  Roy Gerela, Pittsburgh vs. Dallas, 1976
  Ray Wersching, San Francisco vs. Cincinnati, 1982
  Rich Karlis, Denver vs. N.Y. Giants, 1987
  Mike Cofer, San Francisco vs. Cincinnati, 1989

Most Field Goals, Career
- 5 Ray Wersching, San Francisco, 2 games (5 att)
- 4 Don Chandler, Green Bay, 2 games (4 att)
  Jim Turner, N.Y. Jets-Denver, 2 games (6 att)
  Uwe von Schamann, Miami, 2 games (4 att)
- 3 Mike Clark, Dallas, 2 games (3 att)
  Jan Stenerud, Kansas City, 1 game (3 att)
  Chris Bahr, Oakland-L.A. Raiders, 2 games (4 att)
  Mark Moseley, Washington, 2 games (4 att)
  Kevin Butler, Chicago, 1 game (3 att)
  Rich Karlis, Denver, 2 games (6 att)
  Jim Breech, Cincinnati, 2 games (3 att)

Most Field Goals, Game
- 4 Don Chandler, Green Bay vs. Oakland, 1968
  Ray Wersching, San Francisco vs. Cincinnati, 1982
- 3 Jim Turner, N.Y. Jets vs. Baltimore, 1969
  Jan Stenerud, Kansas City vs. Minnesota, 1970
  Uwe von Schamann, Miami vs. San Francisco, 1985
  Kevin Butler, Chicago vs. New England, 1986
  Jim Breech, Cincinnati vs. San Francisco, 1989

Longest Field Goal
- 48 Jan Stenerud, Kansas City vs. Minnesota, 1970
  Rich Karlis, Denver vs. N.Y. Giants, 1987
- 47 Jim Turner, Denver vs. Dallas, 1978
- 46 Chris Bahr, Oakland vs. Philadelphia, 1981

Safeties
Most Safeties, Game
- 1 Dwight White, Pittsburgh vs. Minnesota, 1975
  Reggie Harrison, Pittsburgh vs. Dallas, 1976
  Henry Waechter, Chicago vs. New England, 1986
  George Martin, N.Y. Giants vs. Denver, 1987

Rushing
Attempts

Most Attempts, Career
- 101 Franco Harris, Pittsburgh, 4 games
- 64 John Riggins, Washington, 2 games
- 57 Larry Csonka, Miami, 3 games

Most Attempts, Game
- 38 John Riggins, Washington vs. Miami, 1983
- 34 Franco Harris, Pittsburgh vs. Minnesota, 1975
- 33 Larry Csonka, Miami vs. Minnesota, 1974

Yards Gained

Most Yards Gained, Career
- 354 Franco Harris, Pittsburgh, 4 games
- 297 Larry Csonka, Miami, 3 games
- 230 John Riggins, Washington, 2 games

Most Yards Gained, Game
- 204 Timmy Smith, Washington vs. Denver, 1988
- 191 Marcus Allen, L.A. Raiders vs. Washington, 1984
- 166 John Riggins, Washington vs. Miami, 1983

Longest Run From Scrimmage
- 74 Marcus Allen, L.A. Raiders vs. Washington, 1984 (TD)
- 58 Tom Matte, Baltimore vs. N.Y. Jets, 1969
  Timmy Smith, Washington vs. Denver, 1988 (TD)
- 49 Larry Csonka, Miami vs. Washington, 1973

Average Gain

Highest Average Gain, Career (20 attempts)
- 9.6 Marcus Allen, L.A. Raiders, 1 game (20-191)
- 9.3 Timmy Smith, Washington, 1 game (22-204)
- 5.3 Walt Garrison, Dallas, 2 games (26-139)

Highest Average Gain, Game (10 attempts)
- 10.5 Tom Matte, Baltimore vs. N.Y. Jets, 1969 (11-116)
- 9.6 Marcus Allen, L.A. Raiders vs. Washington, 1984 (20-191)
- 9.3 Timmy Smith, Washington vs. Denver, 1988 (22-204)

Touchdowns

Most Touchdowns, Career
- 4 Franco Harris, Pittsburgh, 4 games
- 2 Elijah Pitts, Green Bay, 1 game
  Jim Kiick, Miami, 3 games
  Larry Csonka, Miami, 3 games
  Pete Banaszak, Oakland, 2 games
  Marcus Allen, L.A. Raiders, 1 game
  John Riggins, Washington, 2 games
  Jim McMahon, Chicago, 1 game
  Timmy Smith, Washington, 1 game
  Roger Craig, San Francisco, 3 games
  Tom Rathman, San Francisco, 2 games

Most Touchdowns, Game
- 2 Elijah Pitts, Green Bay vs. Kansas City, 1967
  Larry Csonka, Miami vs. Minnesota, 1974

Pete Banaszak, Oakland vs. Minnesota, 1977
Franco Harris, Pittsburgh vs. Los Angeles, 1980
Marcus Allen, L.A. Raiders vs. Washington, 1984
Jim McMahon, Chicago vs. New England, 1986
Timmy Smith, Washington vs. Denver, 1988
Tom Rathman, San Francisco vs. Denver, 1990

Passing
Attempts
Most Passes Attempted, Career
- 122 Joe Montana, San Francisco, 4 games
- 101 John Elway, Denver, 3 games
- 98 Roger Staubach, Dallas, 4 games

Most Passes Attempted, Game
- 50 Dan Marino, Miami vs. San Francisco, 1985
- 38 Ron Jaworski, Philadelphia vs. Oakland, 1981
    John Elway, Denver vs. Washington, 1988
- 37 John Elway, Denver vs. N.Y. Giants, 1987

Completions
Most Passes Completed, Career
- 83 Joe Montana, San Francisco, 4 games
- 61 Roger Staubach, Dallas, 4 games
- 49 Terry Bradshaw, Pittsburgh, 4 games

Most Passes Completed, Game
- 29 Dan Marino, Miami vs. San Francisco, 1985
- 25 Ken Anderson, Cincinnati vs. San Francisco, 1982
- 24 Joe Montana, San Francisco vs. Miami, 1985

Most Consecutive Completions, Game
- 13 Joe Montana, San Francisco vs. Denver, 1990
- 10 Phil Simms, N.Y. Giants vs. Denver, 1987
- 8 Len Dawson, Kansas City vs. Green Bay, 1967
    Joe Theismann, Washington vs. Miami, 1983

Completion Percentage
Highest Completion Percentage, Career (40 attempts)
- 68.0 Joe Montana, San Francisco, 4 games (122-83)
- 63.6 Len Dawson, Kansas City, 2 games (44-28)
- 63.4 Bob Griese, Miami, 3 games (41-26)

Highest Completion Percentage, Game (20 attempts)
- 88.0 Phil Simms, N.Y. Giants vs. Denver, 1987 (25-22)
- 75.9 Joe Montana, San Francisco vs. Denver, 1990 (29-22)
- 73.5 Ken Anderson, Cincinnati vs. San Francisco, 1982 (34-25)

Yards Gained
Most Yards Gained, Career
- 1,142 Joe Montana, San Francisco, 4 games
- 932 Terry Bradshaw, Pittsburgh, 4 games
- 734 Roger Staubach, Dallas, 4 games

Most Yards Gained, Game
- 357 Joe Montana, San Francisco vs. Cincinnati, 1989
- 340 Doug Williams, Washington vs. Denver, 1988
- 331 Joe Montana, San Francisco vs. Miami, 1985

Longest Pass Completion
- 80 Jim Plunkett (to King), Oakland vs. Philadelphia, 1981 (TD)
    Doug Williams (to Sanders), Washington vs. Denver, 1988 (TD)
- 76 David Woodley (to Cefalo), Miami vs. Washington, 1983 (TD)
- 75 Johnny Unitas (to Mackey), Baltimore vs. Dallas, 1971 (TD)
    Terry Bradshaw (to Stallworth), Pittsburgh vs. Dallas, 1979 (TD)

Average Gain
Highest Average Gain, Career (40 attempts)
- 11.10 Terry Bradshaw, Pittsburgh, 4 games (84-932)
- 9.62 Bart Starr, Green Bay, 2 games (47-452)
- 9.41 Jim Plunkett, Oakland-L.A. Raiders, 2 games (46-433)

Highest Average Gain, Game (20 attempts)
- 14.71 Terry Bradshaw, Pittsburgh vs. Los Angeles, 1980 (21-309)
- 12.80 Jim McMahon, Chicago vs. New England, 1986 (20-256)
- 12.43 Jim Plunkett, Oakland vs. Philadelphia, 1981 (21-261)

Touchdowns
Most Touchdown Passes, Career
- 11 Joe Montana, San Francisco, 4 games
- 9 Terry Bradshaw, Pittsburgh, 4 games
- 8 Roger Staubach, Dallas, 4 games

Most Touchdown Passes, Game
- 5 Joe Montana, San Francisco vs. Denver, 1990
- 4 Terry Bradshaw, Pittsburgh vs. Dallas, 1979
    Doug Williams, Washington vs. Denver, 1988
- 3 Roger Staubach, Dallas vs. Pittsburgh, 1979
    Jim Plunkett, Oakland vs. Philadelphia, 1981
    Joe Montana, San Francisco vs. Miami, 1985
    Phil Simms, N.Y. Giants vs. Denver, 1987

Had Intercepted
Lowest Percentage, Passes Had Intercepted, Career (40 attempts)
- 0.00 Jim Plunkett, Oakland-L.A. Raiders, 2 games (46-0)
    Joe Montana, San Francisco, 4 games (122-0)
- 2.13 Bart Starr, Green Bay, 2 games (47-1)
- 4.00 Dan Marino, Miami, 1 game (50-2)

Most Attempts, Without Interception, Game
- 36 Joe Montana, San Francisco vs. Cincinnati, 1989
- 35 Joe Montana, San Francisco vs. Miami, 1985
- 29 Joe Montana, San Francisco vs. Denver, 1990

Most Passes Had Intercepted, Career
- 7 Craig Morton, Dallas-Denver, 2 games
- 6 Fran Tarkenton, Minnesota, 3 games
    John Elway, Denver, 3 games
- 4 Earl Morrall, Baltimore-Miami, 4 games
    Roger Staubach, Dallas, 4 games
    Terry Bradshaw, Pittsburgh, 4 games
    Joe Theismann, Washington, 2 games

Most Passes Had Intercepted, Game
- 4 Craig Morton, Denver vs. Dallas, 1978
- 3 By eight players

Pass Receiving
Receptions
Most Receptions, Career
- 20 Roger Craig, San Francisco, 3 games
- 18 Jerry Rice, San Francisco, 2 games
- 16 Lynn Swann, Pittsburgh, 4 games

Most Receptions, Game
- 11 Dan Ross, Cincinnati vs. San Francisco, 1982
    Jerry Rice, San Francisco vs. Cincinnati, 1989
- 10 Tony Nathan, Miami vs. San Francisco, 1985
- 9 Ricky Sanders, Washington vs. Denver, 1988

Yards Gained
Most Yards Gained, Career
- 364 Lynn Swann, Pittsburgh, 4 games
- 363 Jerry Rice, San Francisco, 2 games
- 268 John Stallworth, Pittsburgh, 4 games

Most Yards Gained, Game
- 215 Jerry Rice, San Francisco vs. Cincinnati, 1989
- 193 Ricky Sanders, Washington vs. Denver, 1988
- 161 Lynn Swann, Pittsburgh vs. Dallas, 1976

Longest Reception
- 80 Kenny King (from Plunkett), Oakland vs. Philadelphia, 1981 (TD)
    Ricky Sanders (from Williams), Washington vs. Denver, 1988 (TD)
- 76 Jimmy Cefalo (from Woodley), Miami vs. Washington, 1983 (TD)
- 75 John Mackey (from Unitas), Baltimore vs. Dallas, 1971 (TD)
    John Stallworth (from Bradshaw), Pittsburgh vs. Dallas, 1979 (TD)

Average Gain
Highest Average Gain, Career (8 receptions)
- 24.4 John Stallworth, Pittsburgh, 4 games (11-268)
- 22.8 Lynn Swann, Pittsburgh, 4 games (16-364)
- 21.4 Ricky Sanders, Washington, 1 game (9-193)

Highest Average Gain, Game (3 receptions)
- 40.33 John Stallworth, Pittsburgh vs. Los Angeles, 1980 (3-121)
- 40.25 Lynn Swann, Pittsburgh vs. Dallas, 1979 (4-161)
- 38.33 John Stallworth, Pittsburgh vs. Dallas, 1979 (3-115)

Touchdowns
Most Touchdowns, Career
- 4 Jerry Rice, San Francisco, 2 games
- 3 John Stallworth, Pittsburgh, 4 games
    Lynn Swann, Pittsburgh, 4 games
    Cliff Branch, Oakland-L.A. Raiders, 3 games
- 2 Max McGee, Green Bay, 2 games
    Bill Miller, Oakland, 1 game
    Butch Johnson, Dallas, 2 games
    Dan Ross, Cincinnati, 1 game
    Roger Craig, San Francisco, 3 games
    Ricky Sanders, Washington, 1 game
    John Taylor, San Francisco, 2 games

Most Touchdowns, Game
- 3 Jerry Rice, San Francisco vs. Denver, 1990
- 2 Max McGee, Green Bay vs. Kansas City, 1967
    Bill Miller, Oakland vs. Green Bay, 1968
    John Stallworth, Pittsburgh vs. Dallas, 1979
    Cliff Branch, Oakland vs. Philadelphia, 1981
    Dan Ross, Cincinnati vs. San Francisco, 1982
    Roger Craig, San Francisco vs. Miami, 1985
    Ricky Sanders, Washington vs. Denver, 1988

Interceptions By
Most Interceptions By, Career
- 3 Chuck Howley, Dallas, 2 games
    Rod Martin, Oakland-L.A. Raiders, 2 games
- 2 Randy Beverly, N.Y. Jets, 1 game
    Jake Scott, Miami, 3 games
    Mike Wagner, Pittsburgh, 3 games
    Mel Blount, Pittsburgh, 4 games
    Eric Wright, San Francisco, 4 games
    Barry Wilburn, Washington, 1 game

Most Interceptions By, Game
- 3 Rod Martin, Oakland vs. Philadelphia, 1981
- 2 Randy Beverly, N.Y. Jets vs. Baltimore, 1969
    Chuck Howley, Dallas vs. Baltimore, 1971
    Jake Scott, Miami vs. Washington, 1973
    Barry Wilburn, Washington vs. Denver, 1988

Yards Gained
Most Yards Gained, Career
- 75 Willie Brown, Oakland, 2 games
- 63 Chuck Howley, Dallas, 2 games
    Jake Scott, Miami, 3 games
- 60 Herb Adderley, Green Bay-Dallas, 4 games

Most Yards Gained, Game
- 75 Willie Brown, Oakland vs. Minnesota, 1977
- 63 Jake Scott, Miami vs. Washington, 1973
- 60 Herb Adderley, Green Bay vs. Oakland, 1968

Longest Return
- 75 Willie Brown, Oakland vs. Minnesota, 1977 (TD)
- 60 Herb Adderley, Green Bay vs. Oakland, 1968 (TD)
- 55 Jake Scott, Miami vs. Washington, 1973

Touchdowns
Most Touchdowns, Game
- 1 Herb Adderley, Green Bay vs. Oakland, 1968
    Willie Brown, Oakland vs. Minnesota, 1977
    Jack Squirek, L.A. Raiders vs. Washington, 1984
    Reggie Phillips, Chicago vs. New England, 1986

Punting
Most Punts, Career
17   Mike Eischeid, Oakland-Minnesota, 3 games
15   Larry Seiple, Miami, 3 games
    Mike Horan, Denver, 3 games
14   Ron Widby, Dallas, 2 games
    Ray Guy, Oakland-L.A. Raiders, 3 games
Most Punts, Game
9   Ron Widby, Dallas vs. Baltimore, 1971
7   By eight players
Longest Punt
63   Lee Johnson, Cincinnati vs. San Francisco, 1989
62   Rich Camarillo, New England vs. Chicago, 1986
61   Jerrel Wilson, Kansas City vs. Green Bay, 1967

Average Yardage
Highest Average, Punting, Career (10 punts)
46.5   Jerrel Wilson, Kansas City, 2 games (11-511)
41.9   Ray Guy, Oakland-L.A. Raiders, 3 games (14-587)
41.3   Larry Seiple, Miami, 3 games (15-620)
Highest Average, Punting, Game (4 punts)
48.5   Jerrel Wilson, Kansas City vs. Minnesota, 1970 (4-194)
46.3   Jim Miller, San Francisco vs. Cincinnati, 1982 (4-185)
45.3   Jerrel Wilson, Kansas City vs. Green Bay, 1967 (7-317)

Punt Returns
Most Punt Returns, Career
6   Willie Wood, Green Bay, 2 games
    Jake Scott, Miami, 3 games
    Theo Bell, Pittsburgh, 2 games
    Mike Nelms, Washington, 1 game
    John Taylor, San Francisco, 2 games
5   Dana McLemore, San Francisco, 1 game
4   By seven players
Most Punt Returns, Game
6   Mike Nelms, Washington vs. Miami, 1983
5   Willie Wood, Green Bay vs. Oakland, 1968
    Dana McLemore, San Francisco vs. Miami, 1985
4   By six players
Most Fair Catches, Game
3   Ron Gardin, Baltimore vs. Dallas, 1971
    Golden Richards, Dallas vs. Pittsburgh, 1976
    Greg Pruitt, L.A. Raiders vs. Washington, 1984

Yards Gained
Most Yards Gained, Career
94   John Taylor, San Francisco, 2 games
52   Mike Nelms, Washington, 1 game
51   Dana McLemore, San Francisco, 1 game
Most Yards Gained, Game
56   John Taylor, San Francisco vs. Cincinnati, 1989
52   Mike Nelms, Washington vs. Miami, 1983
51   Dana McLemore, San Francisco vs. Miami, 1985
Longest Return
45   John Taylor, San Francisco vs. Cincinnati, 1989
34   Darrell Green, Washington vs. L.A. Raiders, 1984
31   Willie Wood, Green Bay vs. Oakland, 1968

Average Yardage
Highest Average, Career (4 returns)
15.7   John Taylor, San Francisco, 2 games (6-94)
10.8   Neal Colzie, Oakland, 1 game (4-43)
10.2   Dana McLemore, San Francisco, 1 game (5-51)
Highest Average, Game (3 returns)
18.7   John Taylor, San Francisco vs. Cincinnati, 1989 (3-56)
12.7   John Taylor, San Francisco vs. Denver, 1990 (3-38)
11.3   Lynn Swann, Pittsburgh vs. Minnesota, 1975 (3-34)

Touchdowns
Most Touchdowns, Game
None

Kickoff Returns
Most Kickoff Returns, Career
10   Ken Bell, Denver, 3 games
8   Larry Anderson, Pittsburgh, 2 games
    Fulton Walker, Miami, 2 games
7   Preston Pearson, Baltimore-Pittsburgh-Dallas, 5 games
    Stephen Starring, New England, 1 game
Most Kickoff Returns, Game
7   Stephen Starring, New England vs. Chicago, 1986
6   Darren Carrington, Denver vs. San Francisco, 1990
5   Larry Anderson, Pittsburgh vs. Los Angeles, 1980
    Billy Campfield, Philadelphia vs. Oakland, 1981
    David Verser, Cincinnati vs. San Francisco, 1982
    Alvin Garrett, Washington vs. L.A. Raiders, 1984
    Ken Bell, Denver vs. Washington, 1988

Yards Gained
Most Yards Gained, Career
283   Fulton Walker, Miami, 2 games
207   Larry Anderson, Pittsburgh, 2 games
177   Ken Bell, Denver, 3 games
Most Yards Gained, Game
190   Fulton Walker, Miami vs. Washington, 1983
162   Larry Anderson, Pittsburgh vs. Los Angeles, 1980
153   Stephen Starring, New England vs. Chicago, 1986
Longest Return
98   Fulton Walker, Miami vs. Washington, 1983 (TD)
93   Stanford Jennings, Cincinnati vs. San Francisco, 1989 (TD)
67   Rick Upchurch, Denver vs. Dallas, 1978

Average Yardage
Highest Average, Career (4 returns)
35.4   Fulton Walker, Miami, 2 games (8-283)
25.9   Larry Anderson, Pittsburgh, 2 games (8-207)
24.3   Darren Carrington, Denver, 1 game (6-146)
Highest Average, Game (3 returns)
47.5   Fulton Walker, Miami vs. Washington, 1983 (4-190)
32.4   Larry Anderson, Pittsburgh vs. Los Angeles, 1980 (5-162)
31.3   Rick Upchurch, Denver vs. Dallas, 1978 (3-94)

Touchdowns
Most Touchdowns, Game
1   Fulton Walker, Miami vs. Washington, 1983
    Stanford Jennings, Cincinnati vs. San Francisco, 1989

Fumbles
Most Fumbles, Career
5   Roger Staubach, Dallas, 4 games
3   Franco Harris, Pittsburgh, 4 games
    Terry Bradshaw, Pittsburgh, 4 games
    John Elway, Denver, 3 games
2   By six players
Most Fumbles, Game
3   Roger Staubach, Dallas vs. Pittsburgh, 1976
2   Franco Harris, Pittsburgh vs. Minnesota, 1975
    Butch Johnson, Dallas vs. Denver, 1978
    Terry Bradshaw, Pittsburgh vs. Dallas, 1979
    Joe Montana, San Francisco vs. Cincinnati, 1989
    John Elway, Denver vs. San Francisco, 1990

Recoveries
Most Fumbles Recovered, Career
2   Jake Scott, Miami, 3 games (1 own, 1 opp)
    Fran Tarkenton, Minnesota, 3 games (2 own)
    Franco Harris, Pittsburgh, 4 games (2 own)
    Roger Staubach, Dallas, 4 games (2 own)
    Bobby Walden, Pittsburgh, 2 games (2 own)
    John Fitzgerald, Dallas, 4 games (2 own)
    Randy Hughes, Dallas, 3 games (2 opp)
    Butch Johnson, Dallas, 2 games (2 own)
    Mike Singletary, Chicago, 1 game (2 opp)
    John Elway, Denver, 3 games (2 own)
Most Fumbles Recovered, Game
2   Jake Scott, Miami vs. Minnesota, 1974 (1 own, 1 opp)
    Roger Staubach, Dallas vs. Pittsburgh, 1976 (2 own)
    Randy Hughes, Dallas vs. Denver, 1978 (2 opp)
    Butch Johnson, Dallas vs. Denver, 1978 (2 own)
    Mike Singletary, Chicago vs. New England, 1986 (2 opp)

Yards Gained
Most Yards Gained, Game
49   Mike Bass, Washington vs. Miami, 1973 (opp)
37   Mike Hegman, Dallas vs. Pittsburgh, 1979 (opp)
21   Randy Hughes, Dallas vs. Denver, 1978 (opp)
Longest Return
49   Mike Bass, Washington vs. Miami, 1973 (TD)
37   Mike Hegman, Dallas vs. Pittsburgh, 1979 (TD)
19   Randy Hughes, Dallas vs. Denver, 1978

Touchdowns
Most Touchdowns, Game
1   Mike Bass, Washington vs. Miami, 1973 (opp 49 yds)
    Mike Hegman, Dallas vs. Pittsburgh, 1979 (opp 37 yds)

Combined Net Yards Gained
Attempts
Most Attempts, Career
108   Franco Harris, Pittsburgh, 4 games
73   Roger Craig, San Francisco, 3 games
66   John Riggins, Washington, 2 games
Most Attempts, Game
39   John Riggins, Washington vs. Miami, 1983
35   Franco Harris, Pittsburgh vs. Minnesota, 1975
34   Matt Snell, N.Y. Jets vs. Baltimore, 1969

Yards Gained
Most Yards Gained, Career
468   Franco Harris, Pittsburgh, 4 games
410   Roger Craig, San Francisco, 3 games
391   Lynn Swann, Pittsburgh, 4 games
Most Yards Gained, Game
239   Ricky Sanders, Washington vs. Denver, 1988
220   Jerry Rice, San Francisco vs. Cincinnati, 1989
213   Timmy Smith, Washington vs. Denver, 1988

Sacks
Sacks have been compiled since 1983.
Most Sacks, Game
2   Dwaine Board, San Francisco vs. Miami, 1985
    Dennis Owens, New England vs. Chicago, 1986
    Otis Wilson, Chicago vs. New England, 1986
    Leonard Marshall, N.Y. Giants vs. Denver, 1987
    Alvin Walton, Washington vs. Denver, 1988
    Charles Haley, San Francisco vs. Cincinnati, 1989
    Danny Stubbs, San Francisco, 1990

Team Records

Games, Victories, Defeats
Most Games
5   Dallas, 1971-72, 1976, 1978-79
    Miami, 1972-74, 1983, 1985

4 Minnesota, 1970, 1974-75, 1977
Pittsburgh, 1975-76, 1979-80
Oakland/L.A. Raiders, 1968, 1977, 1981, 1984
Washington, 1973, 1983-84, 1988
Denver, 1978, 1987-88, 1990
San Francisco, 1982, 1985, 1989-90

Most Consecutive Games
3 Miami, 1972-74
2 Green Bay, 1967-68
Dallas, 1971-72
Minnesota, 1974-75
Pittsburgh, 1975-76, 1979-80
Washington, 1983-84
Denver, 1987-88
San Francisco 1989-90

Most Games Won
4 Pittsburgh, 1975-76, 1979-80
San Francisco, 1982, 1985, 1989-90
3 Oakland/L.A. Raiders, 1977, 1981, 1984
2 Green Bay, 1967-68
Miami, 1973-74
Dallas, 1972, 1978
Washington, 1983, 1988

Most Consecutive Games Won
2 Green Bay, 1967-68
Miami, 1973-74
Pittsburgh, 1975-76, 1979-80
San Francisco, 1989-90

Most Games Lost
4 Minnesota, 1970, 1974-75, 1977
Denver, 1978, 1987-88, 1990
3 Dallas, 1971, 1976, 1979
Miami, 1972, 1983, 1985
2 Washington, 1973, 1984
Cincinnati, 1982, 1989

Most Consecutive Games Lost
2 Minnesota, 1974-75
Denver, 1987-88

Scoring
Most Points, Game
55 San Francisco vs. Denver, 1990
46 Chicago vs. New England, 1986
42 Washington vs. Denver, 1988
Fewest Points, Game
3 Miami vs. Dallas, 1972
6 Minnesota vs. Pittsburgh, 1975
7 By four teams
Most Points, Both Teams, Game
66 Pittsburgh (35) vs. Dallas (31), 1979
65 San Francisco (55) vs. Denver (10), 1990
59 N.Y. Giants (39) vs. Denver (20), 1987
Fewest Points, Both Teams, Game
21 Washington (7) vs. Miami (14), 1973
22 Minnesota (6) vs. Pittsburgh (16), 1975
23 Baltimore (7) vs. N.Y. Jets (16), 1969
Largest Margin of Victory, Game
45 San Francisco vs. Denver, 1990 (55-10)
36 Chicago vs. New England, 1986 (46-10)
32 Washington vs. Denver, 1988 (42-10)
Most Points, Each Half
1st: 35 Washington vs. Denver, 1988
2nd: 30 N.Y. Giants vs. Denver, 1987
Most Points, Each Quarter
1st: 14 Miami vs. Minnesota, 1974
Oakland vs. Philadelphia, 1981
2nd: 35 Washington vs. Denver, 1988
3rd: 21 Chicago vs. New England, 1986
4th: 14 Pittsburgh vs. Dallas, 1976; vs. Dallas, 1979; vs. Los Angeles, 1980
Dallas vs. Pittsburgh, 1979
Cincinnati vs. San Francisco, 1982
Washington vs. Miami, 1983
San Francisco vs. Cincinnati, 1989; vs. Denver, 1990
Most Points, Both Teams, Each Half
1st: 45 Washington (35) vs. Denver (10), 1988
2nd: 40 N.Y. Giants (30) vs. Denver (10), 1987
Fewest Points, Both Teams, Each Half
1st: 2 Minnesota (0) vs. Pittsburgh (2), 1975
2nd: 7 Miami (0) vs. Washington (7), 1973
Denver (0) vs. Washington (7), 1988
Most Points, Both Teams, Each Quarter
1st: 17 Miami (10) vs. San Francisco (7), 1985
Denver (10) vs. N.Y. Giants (7), 1987
2nd: 35 Washington (35) vs. Denver (0), 1988
3rd: 21 Chicago (21) vs. New England (0), 1986
San Francisco (14) vs. Denver (7), 1990
4th: 28 Dallas (14) vs. Pittsburgh (14), 1979

Touchdowns
Most Touchdowns, Game
8 San Francisco vs. Denver, 1990
6 Washington vs. Denver, 1988
5 Green Bay vs. Kansas City, 1967
Pittsburgh vs. Dallas, 1979
L.A. Raiders vs. Washington, 1984
San Francisco vs. Miami, 1985
Chicago vs. New England, 1986
N.Y. Giants vs. Denver, 1987
Fewest Touchdowns, Game
0 Miami vs. Dallas, 1972
1 By 16 teams
Most Touchdowns, Both Teams, Game
9 Pittsburgh (5) vs. Dallas (4), 1979

San Francisco (8) vs. Denver (1), 1990
7 N.Y. Giants (5) vs. Denver (2), 1987
Washington (6) vs. Denver (1), 1988
6 Green Bay (5) vs. Kansas City (1), 1967
Oakland (4) vs. Minnesota (2), 1977
Pittsburgh (4) vs. Los Angeles (2), 1980
L.A. Raiders (5) vs. Washington (1), 1984
San Francisco (5) vs. Miami (1), 1985
Chicago (5) vs. New England (1), 1986
Fewest Touchdowns, Both Teams, Game
2 Baltimore (1) vs. N.Y. Jets (1), 1969
3 In six games

Points After Touchdown
Most Points After Touchdown, Game
7 San Francisco vs. Denver, 1990
6 Washington vs. Denver, 1988
5 Green Bay vs. Kansas City, 1967
Pittsburgh vs. Dallas, 1979
L.A. Raiders vs. Washington, 1984
San Francisco vs. Miami, 1985
Chicago vs. New England, 1986
Most Points After Touchdown, Both Teams, Game
9 Pittsburgh (5) vs. Dallas (4), 1979
8 San Francisco (7) vs. Denver (1), 1990
7 Washington (6) vs. Denver (1), 1988
Fewest Points After Touchdown, Both Teams, Game
2 Baltimore (1) vs. N.Y. Jets (1), 1969
Baltimore (1) vs. Dallas (1), 1971
Minnesota (0) vs. Pittsburgh (2), 1975

Field Goals
Most Field Goals Attempted, Game
5 N.Y. Jets vs. Baltimore, 1969
Dallas vs. Denver, 1978
4 Green Bay vs. Oakland, 1968
Pittsburgh vs. Dallas, 1976
San Francisco vs. Cincinnati, 1982; 1989
Denver vs. N.Y. Giants, 1987
Most Field Goals Attempted, Both Teams, Game
7 N.Y. Jets (5) vs. Baltimore (2), 1969
San Francisco (4) vs. Cincinnati (3), 1989
6 Dallas (5) vs. Denver (1), 1978
5 Green Bay (4) vs. Oakland (1), 1968
Pittsburgh (4) vs. Dallas (1), 1976
Oakland (3) vs. Philadelphia (2), 1981
Denver (4) vs. N.Y. Giants (1), 1987
Fewest Field Goals Attempted, Both Teams, Game
1 Minnesota (0) vs. Miami (1), 1974
San Francisco (0) vs. Denver (1), 1990
2 Green Bay (0) vs. Kansas City (2), 1967
Miami (1) vs. Washington (1), 1973
Dallas (1) vs. Pittsburgh (1), 1979
Most Field Goals, Game
4 Green Bay vs. Oakland, 1968
San Francisco vs. Cincinnati, 1982
3 N.Y. Jets vs. Baltimore, 1969
Kansas City vs. Minnesota, 1970
Miami vs. San Francisco, 1985
Chicago vs. New England, 1986
Cincinnati vs. San Francisco, 1989
Most Field Goals, Both Teams, Game
5 Cincinnati (3) vs. San Francisco (2), 1989
4 Green Bay (4) vs. Oakland (0), 1968
San Francisco (4) vs. Cincinnati (0), 1982
Miami (3) vs. San Francisco (1), 1985
Chicago (3) vs. New England (1), 1986
3 In eight games
Fewest Field Goals, Both Teams, Game
0 Miami vs. Washington, 1973
Pittsburgh vs. Minnesota, 1975
1 Green Bay (0) vs. Kansas City (1), 1967
Minnesota (0) vs. Miami (1), 1974
Pittsburgh (0) vs. Dallas (1), 1979
Washington (0) vs. Denver (1), 1988
San Francisco (0) vs. Denver (1), 1990

Safeties
Most Safeties, Game
1 Pittsburgh vs. Minnesota, 1975; vs. Dallas, 1976
Chicago vs. New England, 1986
N.Y. Giants vs. Denver, 1987

First Downs
Most First Downs, Game
31 San Francisco vs. Miami, 1985
28 San Francisco vs. Denver, 1990
25 Washington vs. Denver, 1988
Fewest First Downs, Game
9 Minnesota vs. Pittsburgh, 1975
Miami vs. Washington, 1983
10 Dallas vs. Baltimore, 1971
Miami vs. Dallas, 1972
11 Denver vs. Dallas, 1978
Most First Downs, Both Teams, Game
50 San Francisco (31) vs. Miami (19), 1985
47 N.Y. Giants (24) vs. Denver (23), 1987
44 Cincinnati (24) vs. San Francisco (20), 1982
Fewest First Downs, Both Teams, Game
24 Dallas (10) vs. Baltimore (14), 1971
26 Minnesota (9) vs. Pittsburgh (17), 1975
27 Pittsburgh (13) vs. Dallas (14), 1976

Rushing

Most First Downs, Rushing, Game
- 16 San Francisco vs. Miami, 1985
- 15 Dallas vs. Miami, 1972
- 14 Washington vs. Miami, 1983
     San Francisco vs. Denver, 1990

Fewest First Downs, Rushing, Game
- 1 New England vs. Chicago, 1986
- 2 Minnesota vs. Kansas City, 1970; vs. Pittsburgh, 1975; vs. Oakland, 1977
     Pittsburgh vs. Dallas, 1979
     Miami vs. San Francisco, 1985
- 3 Miami vs. Dallas, 1972
     Philadelphia vs. Oakland, 1981

Most First Downs, Rushing, Both Teams, Game
- 21 Washington (14) vs. Miami (7), 1983
- 19 Washington (13) vs. Denver (6), 1988
     San Francisco (14) vs. Denver (5), 1990
- 18 Dallas (15) vs. Miami (3), 1972
     Miami (13) vs. Minnesota (5), 1974
     San Francisco (16) vs. Miami (2), 1985

Fewest First Downs, Rushing, Both Teams, Game
- 8 Baltimore (4) vs. Dallas (4), 1971
     Pittsburgh (2) vs. Dallas (6), 1979
- 9 Philadelphia (3) vs. Oakland (6), 1981
- 10 Minnesota (2) vs. Kansas City (8), 1970

Passing

Most First Downs, Passing, Game
- 17 Miami vs. San Francisco, 1985
- 16 Denver vs. N.Y. Giants, 1987
     San Francisco vs. Cincinnati, 1989
- 15 Minnesota vs. Oakland, 1977
     Pittsburgh vs. Dallas, 1979
     San Francisco vs. Miami, 1985

Fewest First Downs, Passing, Game
- 1 Denver vs. Dallas, 1978
- 2 Miami vs. Washington, 1983
- 4 Miami vs. Minnesota, 1974

Most First Downs, Passing, Both Teams, Game
- 32 Miami (17) vs. San Francisco (15), 1985
- 29 Denver (16) vs. N.Y. Giants (13), 1987
- 28 Pittsburgh (15) vs. Dallas (13), 1979

Fewest First Downs, Passing, Both Teams, Game
- 9 Denver (1) vs. Dallas (8), 1978
- 10 Minnesota (5) vs. Pittsburgh (5), 1975
- 11 Dallas (5) vs. Baltimore (6), 1971
     Miami (2) vs. Washington (9), 1983

Penalty

Most First Downs, Penalty, Game
- 4 Baltimore vs. Dallas, 1971
     Miami vs. Minnesota, 1974
     Cincinnati vs. San Francisco, 1982
- 3 Kansas City vs. Minnesota, 1970
     Minnesota vs. Oakland, 1977

Most First Downs, Penalty, Both Teams, Game
- 6 Cincinnati (4) vs. San Francisco (2), 1982
- 5 Baltimore (4) vs. Dallas (1), 1971
     Miami (4) vs. Minnesota (1), 1974
- 4 Kansas City (3) vs. Minnesota (1), 1970

Fewest First Downs, Penalty, Both Teams, Game
- 0 Dallas vs. Miami, 1972
     Miami vs. Washington, 1973
     Dallas vs. Pittsburgh, 1976
     Miami vs. San Francisco, 1985
- 1 Green Bay (0) vs. Kansas City (1), 1967
     Miami (0) vs. Washington (1), 1983
     Cincinnati (0) vs. San Francisco (1), 1989
     San Francisco (0) vs. Denver (1), 1990

Net Yards Gained Rushing and Passing

Most Yards Gained, Game
- 602 Washington vs. Denver, 1988
- 537 San Francisco vs. Miami, 1985
- 461 San Francisco vs. Denver, 1990

Fewest Yards Gained, Game
- 119 Minnesota vs. Pittsburgh, 1975
- 123 New England vs. Chicago, 1986
- 156 Denver vs. Dallas, 1978

Most Yards Gained, Both Teams, Game
- 929 Washington (602) vs. Denver (327), 1988
- 851 San Francisco (537) vs. Miami (314), 1985
- 782 Oakland (429) vs. Minnesota (353), 1977

Fewest Yards Gained, Both Teams, Game
- 452 Minnesota (119) vs. Pittsburgh (333), 1975
- 481 Washington (228) vs. Miami (253), 1973
     Denver (156) vs. Dallas (325), 1978
- 497 Minnesota (238) vs. Miami (259), 1974

Rushing
Attempts

Most Attempts, Game
- 57 Pittsburgh vs. Minnesota, 1975
- 53 Miami vs. Minnesota, 1974
- 52 Oakland vs. Minnesota, 1977
     Washington vs. Miami, 1983

Fewest Attempts, Game
- 9 Miami vs. San Francisco, 1985
- 11 New England vs. Chicago, 1986
- 17 Denver vs. Washington, 1988; vs. San Francisco, 1990

Most Attempts, Both Teams, Game
- 81 Washington (52) vs. Miami (29), 1983

- 78 Pittsburgh (57) vs. Minnesota (21), 1975
     Oakland (52) vs. Minnesota (26), 1977
- 77 Miami (53) vs. Minnesota (24), 1974
     Pittsburgh (46) vs. Dallas (31), 1976

Fewest Attempts, Both Teams, Game
- 49 Miami (9) vs. San Francisco (40), 1985
- 53 Kansas City (19) vs. Green Bay (34), 1967
- 55 San Francisco (27) vs. Cincinnati (28), 1989

Yards Gained

Most Yards Gained, Game
- 280 Washington vs. Denver, 1988
- 276 Washington vs. Miami, 1983
- 266 Oakland vs. Minnesota, 1977

Fewest Yards Gained, Game
- 7 New England vs. Chicago, 1986
- 17 Minnesota vs. Pittsburgh, 1975
- 25 Miami vs. San Francisco, 1985

Most Yards Gained, Both Teams, Game
- 377 Washington (280) vs. Denver (97), 1988
- 372 Washington (276) vs. Miami (96), 1983
- 337 Oakland (266) vs. Minnesota (71), 1977

Fewest Yards Gained, Both Teams, Game
- 171 Baltimore (69) vs. Dallas (102), 1971
- 174 New England (7) vs. Chicago (167), 1986
- 186 Philadelphia (69) vs. Oakland (117), 1981

Average Gain

Highest Average Gain, Game
- 7.00 L.A. Raiders vs. Washington, 1984 (33-231)
       Washington vs. Denver, 1988 (40-280)
- 6.22 Baltimore vs. N.Y. Jets, 1969 (23-143)
- 5.71 Denver vs. Washington, 1988 (17-97)

Lowest Average Gain, Game
- 0.64 New England vs. Chicago, 1986 (11-7)
- 0.81 Minnesota vs. Pittsburgh, 1975 (21-17)
- 2.23 Baltimore vs. Dallas, 1971 (31-69)

Touchdowns

Most Touchdowns, Game
- 4 Chicago vs. New England, 1986
- 3 Green Bay vs. Kansas City, 1967
     Miami vs. Minnesota, 1974
     San Francisco vs. Denver, 1990
- 2 Oakland vs. Minnesota, 1977
     Pittsburgh vs. Los Angeles, 1980
     L.A. Raiders vs. Washington, 1984
     San Francisco vs. Miami, 1985
     N.Y. Giants vs. Denver, 1987
     Washington vs. Denver, 1988

Fewest Touchdowns, Game
- 0 By 17 teams

Most Touchdowns, Both Teams, Game
- 4 Miami (3) vs. Minnesota (1), 1974
     Chicago (4) vs. New England (0), 1986
     San Francisco (3) vs. Denver (1), 1990
- 3 Green Bay (3) vs. Kansas City (0), 1967
     Pittsburgh (2) vs. Los Angeles (1), 1980
     L.A. Raiders (2) vs. Washington (1), 1984
     N.Y. Giants (2) vs. Denver (1), 1987

Fewest Touchdowns, Both Teams, Game
- 0 Pittsburgh vs. Dallas, 1976
     Oakland vs. Philadelphia, 1981
     Cincinnati vs. San Francisco, 1989
- 1 In seven games

Passing
Attempts

Most Passes Attempted, Game
- 50 Miami vs. San Francisco, 1985
- 44 Minnesota vs. Oakland, 1977
- 41 Baltimore vs. N.Y. Jets, 1969
     Denver vs. N.Y. Giants, 1987

Fewest Passes Attempted, Game
- 7 Miami vs. Minnesota, 1974
- 11 Miami vs. Washington, 1973
- 14 Pittsburgh vs. Minnesota, 1975

Most Passes Attempted, Both Teams, Game
- 85 Miami (50) vs. San Francisco (35), 1985
- 70 Baltimore (41) vs. N.Y. Jets (29), 1969
- 69 Denver (39) vs. Washington (30), 1988

Fewest Passes Attempted, Both Teams, Game
- 35 Miami (7) vs. Minnesota (28), 1974
- 39 Miami (11) vs. Washington (28), 1973
- 40 Pittsburgh (14) vs. Minnesota (26), 1975
     Miami (17) vs. Washington (23), 1983

Completions

Most Passes Completed, Game
- 29 Miami vs. San Francisco, 1985
- 26 Denver vs. N.Y. Giants, 1987
- 25 Cincinnati vs. San Francisco, 1982

Fewest Passes Completed, Game
- 4 Miami vs. Washington, 1983
- 6 Miami vs. Minnesota, 1974
- 8 Miami vs. Washington, 1973
     Denver vs. Dallas, 1978

Most Passes Completed, Both Teams, Game
- 53 Miami (29) vs. San Francisco (24), 1985
- 48 Denver (26) vs. N.Y. Giants (22), 1987
- 39 Cincinnati (25) vs. San Francisco (14), 1982

Fewest Passes Completed, Both Teams, Game
   19 Miami (4) vs. Washington (15), 1983
   20 Pittsburgh (9) vs. Minnesota (11), 1975
   22 Miami (8) vs. Washington (14), 1973

Completion Percentage
Highest Completion Percentage, Game (20 attempts)
  88.0 N.Y. Giants vs. Denver, 1987 (25-22)
  75.0 San Francisco vs. Denver, 1990 (32-24)
  73.5 Cincinnati vs. San Francisco, 1982 (34-25)
Lowest Completion Percentage, Game (20 attempts)
  32.0 Denver vs. Dallas, 1978 (25-8)
  37.9 Denver vs. San Francisco, 1990 (29-11)
  38.5 Denver vs. Washington, 1988 (39-15)

Yards Gained
Most Yards Gained, Game
  341 San Francisco vs. Cincinnati, 1989
  326 San Francisco vs. Miami, 1985
  322 Washington vs. Denver, 1988
Fewest Yards Gained, Game
   35 Denver vs. Dallas, 1978
   63 Miami vs. Minnesota, 1974
   69 Miami vs. Washington, 1973
Most Yards Gained, Both Teams, Game
  615 San Francisco (326) vs. Miami (289), 1985
  583 Denver (320) vs. N.Y. Giants (263), 1987
  552 Washington (322) vs. Denver (230), 1988
Fewest Yards Gained, Both Teams, Game
  156 Miami (69) vs. Washington (87), 1973
  186 Pittsburgh (84) vs. Minnesota (102), 1975
  205 Dallas (100) vs. Miami (105), 1972

Times Sacked
Most Times Sacked, Game
   7 Dallas vs. Pittsburgh, 1976
     New England vs. Chicago, 1986
   6 Kansas City vs. Green Bay, 1967
     Washington vs. L.A. Raiders, 1984
     Denver vs. San Francisco, 1990
   5 Dallas vs. Denver, 1978; vs. Pittsburgh, 1979
     Cincinnati vs. San Francisco, 1982; 1989
     Denver vs. Washington, 1988
Fewest Times Sacked, Game
   0 Baltimore vs. N.Y. Jets, 1969; vs. Dallas, 1971
     Minnesota vs. Pittsburgh, 1975
     Pittsburgh vs. Los Angeles, 1980
     Philadelphia vs. Oakland, 1981
   1 By nine teams
Most Times Sacked, Both Teams, Game
   10 New England (7) vs. Chicago (3), 1986
    9 Kansas City (6) vs. Green Bay (3), 1967
      Dallas (7) vs. Pittsburgh (2), 1976
      Dallas (5) vs. Denver (4), 1978
      Dallas (5) vs. Pittsburgh (4), 1979
      Cincinnati (5) vs. San Francisco (4), 1989
    8 Washington (6) vs. L.A. Raiders (2), 1984
Fewest Times Sacked, Both Teams, Game
   1 Philadelphia (0) vs. Oakland (1), 1981
   2 Baltimore (0) vs. N.Y. Jets (2), 1969
     Baltimore (0) vs. Dallas (2), 1971
     Minnesota (0) vs. Pittsburgh (2), 1975
   3 In three games

Touchdowns
Most Touchdowns, Game
   5 San Francisco vs. Denver, 1990
   4 Pittsburgh vs. Dallas, 1979
     Washington vs. Denver, 1988
   3 Dallas vs. Pittsburgh, 1979
     Oakland vs. Philadelphia, 1981
     San Francisco vs. Miami, 1985
     N.Y. Giants vs. Denver, 1987
Fewest Touchdowns, Game
   0 By 13 teams
Most Touchdowns, Both Teams, Game
   7 Pittsburgh (4) vs. Dallas (3), 1979
   5 Washington (4) vs. Denver (1), 1988
     San Francisco (5) vs. Denver (0), 1990
   4 Dallas (2) vs. Pittsburgh (2), 1976
     Oakland (3) vs. Philadelphia (1), 1981
     San Francisco (3) vs. Miami (1), 1985
     N.Y. Giants (3) vs. Denver (1), 1987
Fewest Touchdowns, Both Teams, Game
   0 N.Y. Jets vs. Baltimore, 1969
     Miami vs. Minnesota, 1974
   1 In five games

Interceptions By
Most Interceptions By, Game
   4 N.Y. Jets vs. Baltimore, 1969
     Dallas vs. Denver, 1978
   3 By nine teams
Most Interceptions By, Both Teams, Game
   6 Baltimore (3) vs. Dallas (3), 1971
   4 In six games
Fewest Interceptions By, Both Teams, Game
   1 Oakland (0) vs. Green Bay (1), 1968
     Miami (0) vs. Dallas (1), 1972
     Minnesota (0) vs. Miami (1), 1974
     N.Y. Giants (0) vs. Denver (1), 1987
     San Francisco (1) vs. Cincinnati (0), 1989

Yards Gained
Most Yards Gained, Game
   95 Miami vs. Washington, 1973
   91 Oakland vs. Minnesota, 1977
   89 Pittsburgh vs. Dallas, 1976
Most Yards Gained, Both Teams, Game
   95 Miami (95) vs. Washington (0), 1973
   91 Oakland (91) vs. Minnesota (0), 1977
   89 Pittsburgh (89) vs. Dallas (0), 1976

Touchdowns
Most Touchdowns, Game
   1 Green Bay vs. Oakland, 1968
     Oakland vs. Minnesota, 1977
     L.A. Raiders vs. Washington, 1984
     Chicago vs. New England, 1986

Punting
Most Punts, Game
   9 Dallas vs. Baltimore, 1971
   8 Washington vs. L.A. Raiders, 1984
   7 By seven teams
Fewest Punts, Game
   2 Pittsburgh vs. Los Angeles, 1980
     Denver vs. N.Y. Giants, 1987
   3 By nine teams
Most Punts, Both Teams, Game
   15 Washington (8) vs. L.A. Raiders (7), 1984
   13 Dallas (9) vs. Baltimore (4), 1971
      Pittsburgh (7) vs. Minnesota (6), 1975
   12 In three games
Fewest Punts, Both Teams, Game
   5 Denver (2) vs. N.Y. Giants (3), 1987
   6 Oakland (3) vs. Philadelphia (3), 1981
   7 In four games

Average Yardage
Highest Average, Game (4 punts)
  48.50 Kansas City vs. Minnesota, 1970 (4-194)
  46.25 San Francisco vs. Cincinnati, 1982 (4-185)
  45.29 Kansas City vs. Green Bay, 1967 (7-317)
Lowest Average, Game (4 punts)
  31.20 Washington vs. Miami, 1973 (5-156)
  32.38 Washington vs. L.A. Raiders, 1984 (8-259)
  32.40 Oakland vs. Minnesota, 1977 (5-162)

Punt Returns
Most Punt Returns, Game
   6 Washington vs. Miami, 1983
   5 By five teams
Fewest Punt Returns, Game
   0 Minnesota vs. Miami, 1974
   1 By 11 teams
Most Punt Returns, Both Teams, Game
   9 Pittsburgh (5) vs. Minnesota (4), 1975
   8 Green Bay (5) vs. Oakland (3), 1968
     Baltimore (5) vs. Dallas (3), 1971
     Washington (6) vs. Miami (2), 1983
   7 Green Bay (4) vs. Kansas City (3), 1967
     Oakland (4) vs. Minnesota (3), 1977
     San Francisco (5) vs. Miami (2), 1985
Fewest Punt Returns, Both Teams, Game
   2 Dallas (1) vs. Miami (1), 1972
     Denver (1) vs. N.Y. Giants (1), 1987
   3 Kansas City (1) vs. Minnesota (2), 1970
     Minnesota (0) vs. Miami (3), 1974
     Washington (1) vs. Denver (2), 1988
   4 L.A. Raiders (2) vs. Washington (2), 1984
     Chicago (2) vs. New England (2), 1986

Yards Gained
Most Yards Gained, Game
   56 San Francisco vs. Cincinnati, 1989
   52 Washington vs. Miami, 1983
   51 San Francisco vs. Miami, 1985
Fewest Yards Gained, Game
  −1 Dallas vs. Miami, 1972
   0 By five teams
Most Yards Gained, Both Teams, Game
   74 Washington (52) vs. Miami (22), 1983
   66 San Francisco (51) vs. Miami (15), 1985
   61 San Francisco (56) vs. Cincinnati (5), 1989
Fewest Yards Gained, Both Teams, Game
   13 Miami (4) vs. Washington (9), 1973
   18 Kansas City (0) vs. Minnesota (18), 1970
     Washington (0) vs. Denver (18), 1988
   20 Dallas (−1) vs. Miami (21), 1972
     Minnesota (0) vs. Miami (20), 1974

Average Return
Highest Average, Game (3 returns)
  18.7 San Francisco vs. Cincinnati, 1989 (3-56)
  12.7 San Francisco vs. Denver, 1990 (3-38)
  10.8 Oakland vs. Minnesota, 1977 (4-43)

Touchdowns
Most Touchdowns, Game
     None

Kickoff Returns

Most Kickoff Returns, Game
- 9 Denver vs. San Francisco, 1990
- 7 Oakland vs. Green Bay, 1968
  Minnesota vs. Oakland, 1977
  Cincinnati vs. San Francisco, 1982
  Washington vs. L.A. Raiders, 1984
  Miami vs. San Francisco, 1985
  New England vs. Chicago, 1986
- 6 By six teams

Fewest Kickoff Returns, Game
- 1 N.Y. Jets vs. Baltimore, 1969
  L.A. Raiders vs. Washington, 1984
- 2 By six teams

Most Kickoff Returns, Both Teams, Game
- 12 Denver (9) vs. San Francisco (3), 1990
- 11 Los Angeles (6) vs. Pittsburgh (5), 1980
  Miami (7) vs. San Francisco (4), 1985
  New England (7) vs. Chicago (4), 1986
- 10 Oakland (7) vs. Green Bay (3), 1968

Fewest Kickoff Returns, Both Teams, Game
- 5 N.Y. Jets (1) vs. Baltimore (4), 1969
  Miami (2) vs. Washington (3), 1973
- 6 In three games

Yards Gained

Most Yards Gained, Game
- 222 Miami vs. Washington, 1983
- 196 Denver vs. San Francisco, 1990
- 173 Denver vs. Dallas, 1978

Fewest Yards Gained, Game
- 17 L.A. Raiders vs. Washington, 1984
- 25 N.Y. Jets vs. Baltimore, 1969
- 32 Pittsburgh vs. Minnesota, 1975

Most Yards Gained, Both Teams, Game
- 279 Miami (222) vs. Washington (57), 1983
- 245 Denver (196) vs. San Francisco (49), 1990
- 231 Pittsburgh (162) vs. Los Angeles (79), 1980

Fewest Yards Gained, Both Teams, Game
- 78 Miami (33) vs. Washington (45), 1973
- 82 Pittsburgh (32) vs. Minnesota (50), 1975
- 92 San Francisco (40) vs. Cincinnati (52), 1982

Average Gain

Highest Average, Game (3 returns)
- 44.0 Cincinnati vs. San Francisco, 1989 (3-132)
- 37.0 Miami vs. Washington, 1983 (6-222)
- 32.4 Pittsburgh vs. Los Angeles, 1980 (5-162)

Touchdowns

Most Touchdowns, Game
- 1 Miami vs. Washington, 1983
  Cincinnati vs. San Francisco, 1989

Penalties

Most Penalties, Game
- 12 Dallas vs. Denver, 1978
- 10 Dallas vs. Baltimore, 1971
- 9 Dallas vs. Pittsburgh, 1979

Fewest Penalties, Game
- 0 Miami vs. Dallas, 1972
  Pittsburgh vs. Dallas, 1976
  Denver vs. San Francisco, 1990
- 1 Green Bay vs. Oakland, 1968
  Miami vs. Minnesota, 1974; vs. San Francisco, 1985
- 2 By four teams

Most Penalties, Both Teams, Game
- 20 Dallas (12) vs. Denver (8), 1978
- 16 Cincinnati (8) vs. San Francisco (8), 1982
- 14 Dallas (10) vs. Baltimore (4), 1971
  Dallas (9) vs. Pittsburgh (5), 1979

Fewest Penalties, Both Teams, Game
- 2 Pittsburgh (0) vs. Dallas (2), 1976
- 3 Miami (0) vs. Dallas (3), 1972
  Miami (1) vs. San Francisco (2), 1985
- 4 Denver (0) vs. San Francisco (4), 1990

Yards Penalized

Most Yards Penalized, Game
- 133 Dallas vs. Baltimore, 1971
- 122 Pittsburgh vs. Minnesota, 1975
- 94 Dallas vs. Denver, 1978

Fewest Yards Penalized, Game
- 0 Miami vs. Dallas, 1972
  Pittsburgh vs. Dallas, 1976
  Denver vs. San Francisco, 1990
- 4 Miami vs. Minnesota, 1974
- 10 Miami vs. San Francisco, 1985
  San Francisco vs. Miami, 1985

Most Yards Penalized, Both Teams, Game
- 164 Dallas (133) vs. Baltimore (31), 1971
- 154 Dallas (94) vs. Denver (60), 1978
- 140 Pittsburgh (122) vs. Minnesota (18), 1975

Fewest Yards Penalized, Both Teams, Game
- 15 Miami (0) vs. Dallas (15), 1972
- 20 Pittsburgh (0) vs. Dallas (20), 1976
  Miami (10) vs. San Francisco (10), 1985
- 38 Denver (0) vs. San Francisco (38), 1990

Fumbles

Most Fumbles, Game
- 6 Dallas vs. Denver, 1978

- 5 Baltimore vs. Dallas, 1971
- 4 By five teams

Fewest Fumbles, Game
- 0 By nine teams

Most Fumbles, Both Teams, Game
- 10 Dallas (6) vs. Denver (4), 1978
- 8 Dallas (4) vs. Pittsburgh (4), 1976
- 7 Pittsburgh (4) vs. Minnesota (3), 1975
  New England (4) vs. Chicago (3), 1986

Fewest Fumbles, Both Teams, Game
- 0 Los Angeles vs. Pittsburgh, 1980
- 1 Oakland (0) vs. Minnesota (1), 1977
  Oakland (0) vs. Philadelphia (1), 1981
  Denver (0) vs. Washington (1), 1988
- 2 In four games

Most Fumbles Lost, Game
- 4 Baltimore vs. Dallas, 1971
  Denver vs. Dallas, 1978
  New England vs. Chicago, 1986
- 2 In many games

Most Fumbles Lost, Both Teams, Game
- 6 Denver (4) vs. Dallas (2), 1978
  New England (4) vs. Chicago (2), 1986
- 5 Baltimore (4) vs. Dallas (1), 1971
- 4 Minnesota (2) vs. Pittsburgh (2), 1975
  Dallas (2) vs. Pittsburgh (2), 1979

Fewest Fumbles Lost, Both Teams, Game
- 0 Green Bay vs. Kansas City, 1967
  Dallas vs. Pittsburgh, 1976
  Los Angeles vs. Pittsburgh, 1980
  Denver vs. N.Y. Giants, 1987
  Denver vs. Washington, 1988
- 1 Washington (0) vs. Miami (1), 1973
  Miami (0) vs. Minnesota (1), 1974
  Oakland (0) vs. Minnesota (1), 1977
  Oakland (0) vs. Philadelphia (1), 1981
  Washington (0) vs. Miami (1), 1983
  Cincinnati (0) vs. San Francisco (1), 1989
- 2 In five games

Most Fumbles Recovered, Game
- 8 Dallas vs. Denver, 1978 (4 own, 4 opp)
- 5 Chicago vs. New England, 1986 (1 own, 4 opp)
- 4 Pittsburgh vs. Minnesota, 1975 (2 own, 2 opp)
  Dallas vs. Pittsburgh, 1976 (4 own)

Turnovers

(Number of times losing the ball on interceptions and fumbles.)

Most Turnovers, Game
- 8 Denver vs. Dallas, 1978
- 7 Baltimore vs. Dallas, 1971
- 6 New England vs. Chicago, 1986

Fewest Turnovers, Game
- 0 Green Bay vs. Oakland, 1968
  Miami vs. Minnesota, 1974
  Pittsburgh vs. Dallas, 1976
  Oakland vs. Minnesota, 1977; vs. Philadelphia, 1981
  N.Y. Giants vs. Denver, 1987
  San Francisco vs. Denver, 1990
- 1 By many teams

Most Turnovers, Both Teams, Game
- 11 Baltimore (7) vs. Dallas (4), 1971
- 10 Denver (8) vs. Dallas (2), 1978
- 8 New England (6) vs. Chicago (2), 1986

Fewest Turnovers, Both Teams, Game
- 1 N.Y. Giants (0) vs. Denver (1), 1987
- 2 Green Bay (1) vs. Kansas City (1), 1967
  Miami (0) vs. Minnesota (2), 1974
  Cincinnati (1) vs. San Francisco (1), 1989
- 3 Green Bay (0) vs. Oakland (3), 1968
  Pittsburgh (0) vs. Dallas (3), 1976
  Oakland (0) vs. Minnesota (3), 1977

Compiled by Elias Sports Bureau

Throughout this all-time postseason record section, the following abbreviations are used to indicate various levels of postseason games:

SB	Super Bowl (1966 to date)
AFC	AFC Championship Game (1970 to date) or AFL Championship Game (1960-69)
NFC	NFC Championship Game (1970 to date) or NFL Championship Game (1933-69)
AFC-D	AFC Divisional Playoff Game (1970 to date), AFC Second-Round Playoff Game (1982), AFL Inter-Divisional Playoff Game (1969), or special playoff game to break tie for AFL Division Championship (1963, 1968)
NFC-D	NFC Divisional Playoff Game (1970 to date), NFC Second-Round Playoff Game (1982), NFL Conference Championship Game (1967-69), or special playoff game to break tie for NFL Division or Conference Championship (1941, 1943, 1947, 1950, 1952, 1957, 1958, 1965)
AFC-FR	AFC First-Round Playoff Game (1978 to date)
NFC-FR	NFC First-Round Playoff Game (1978 to date)

Year references are to the season following which the postseason game occurred, even if the game was played in the next calendar year.

Postseason Game Composite Standings

	W	L	Pct.	Pts.	OP
Green Bay Packers	13	5	.722	416	259
San Francisco 49ers	15	8	.652	566	427
Pittsburgh Steelers	16	9	.640	582	494
Los Angeles Raiders*	19	12	.613	761	535
Detroit Lions	6	4	.600	221	208
Miami Dolphins	14	10	.583	535	468
Washington Redskins**	16	12	.571	569	523
Dallas Cowboys	20	16	.556	805	640
Kansas City Chiefs***	5	4	.556	159	182
Chicago Bears	12	11	.522	497	436
Denver Broncos	8	8	.500	323	426
Indianapolis Colts****	8	8	.500	285	300
New York Jets	5	5	.500	206	183
Philadelphia Eagles	7	7	.500	238	214
Houston Oilers	8	9	.471	258	387
Minnesota Vikings	13	15	.464	518	570
Seattle Seahawks	3	4	.429	128	139
Cincinnati Bengals	4	6	.400	195	223
New England Patriots†	4	6	.400	195	258
Los Angeles Rams††	13	20	.394	501	697
New York Giants	10	17	.370	443	504
Buffalo Bills	4	7	.364	195	236
Cleveland Browns	10	18	.357	567	650
San Diego Chargers†††	4	8	.333	230	279
Atlanta Falcons	1	3	.250	85	100
Tampa Bay Buccaneers	1	3	.250	41	94
Phoenix Cardinals††††	1	4	.200	81	134
New Orleans Saints	0	1	.000	10	44

*24 games played when franchise was in Oakland (won 15, lost 9, 587 points scored, 435 points allowed).

**One game played when franchise was in Boston (lost 21-6).

***One game played when franchise was Dallas Texans (won 20-17).

****15 games played when franchise was in Baltimore (won 8, lost 7, 264 points scored, 262 points allowed).

†Two games played when franchise was in Boston (won 26-8, lost 51-10).

††One game played when franchise was in Cleveland (won 15-14).

†††One game played when franchise was in Los Angeles (lost 24-16).

††††Two games played when franchise was in Chicago (won 28-21, lost 7-0), three games played when franchise was in St. Louis (lost 30-14, lost 35-23, lost 41-16).

Individual Records

Service
Most Games, Career
- 27 D. D. Lewis, Dallas (SB-5, NFC-9, NFC-D 12, NFC-FR 1)
- 26 Larry Cole, Dallas (SB-5, NFC-8, NFC-D-12, NFC-FR 1)
- 25 Charlie Waters, Dallas (SB-5, NFC-9, NFC-D 10, NFC-FR 1)

Scoring
Points
Most Points, Career
- 115 George Blanda, Chi. Bears-Houston-Oakland, 19 games (49-pat, 22-fg)
- 102 Franco Harris, Pittsburgh, 19 games (17-td)
- 95 Rafael Septien, L.A. Rams-Dallas, 15 games (41-pat, 18-fg)

Most Points, Game
- 19 Pat Harder, NFC-D: Detroit vs. Los Angeles, 1952 (2-td, 4-pat, 1-fg)
- Paul Hornung, NFC: Green Bay vs. N.Y. Giants, 1961 (1-td, 4-pat, 3-fg)
- 18 By 17 players

Touchdowns
Most Touchdowns, Career
- 17 Franco Harris, Pittsburgh, 19 games (16-r, 1-p)
- 12 John Riggins, Washington, 9 games (12-r)
- John Stallworth, Pittsburgh, 18 games (12-p)
- 11 Jerry Rice, San Francisco, 9 games (11-p)

Most Touchdowns, Game
- 3 Andy Farkas, NFC-D: Washington vs. N.Y. Giants, 1943 (3-r)
- Tom Fears, NFC-D: Los Angeles vs. Chi. Bears, 1950 (3-p)
- Otto Graham, NFC: Cleveland vs. Detroit, 1954 (3-r)
- Gary Collins, NFC: Cleveland vs. Baltimore, 1964 (3-p)
- Craig Baynham, NFC-D: Dallas vs. Cleveland, 1967 (2-r, 1-p)
- Fred Biletnikoff, AFC-D: Oakland vs. Kansas City, 1968 (3-p)
- Tom Matte, NFC: Baltimore vs. Cleveland, 1968 (3-r)
- Larry Schreiber, NFC-D: San Francisco vs. Dallas, 1972 (3-r)
- Larry Csonka, AFC: Miami vs. Oakland, 1973 (3-r)
- Franco Harris, AFC-D: Pittsburgh vs. Buffalo, 1974 (3-r)
- Preston Pearson, NFC: Dallas vs. Los Angeles, 1975 (3-p)
- Dave Casper, AFC-D: Oakland vs. Baltimore, 1977 (OT) (3-p)
- Alvin Garrett, NFC-FR: Washington vs. Detroit, 1982 (3-p)
- John Riggins, NFC-D: Washington vs. L.A. Rams, 1983 (3-r)
- Roger Craig, SB: San Francisco vs. Miami, 1984 (1-r, 2-p)
- Jerry Rice, NFC-D: San Francisco vs. Minnesota, 1988 (3-p)
- Jerry Rice, SB: San Francisco vs. Denver, 1989 (3-p)

Most Consecutive Games Scoring Touchdowns
- 8 John Stallworth, Pittsburgh, 1978-83
- 7 John Riggins, Washington, 1982-84
- Marcus Allen, L.A. Raiders, 1982-85 (current)
- 5 Duane Thomas, Dallas, 1970-71
- Franco Harris, Pittsburgh, 1974-75
- Franco Harris, Pittsburgh, 1977-79

Points After Touchdown
Most Points After Touchdown, Career
- 49 George Blanda, Chi. Bears-Houston-Oakland, 19 games (49 att)
- 41 Rafael Septien, L.A. Rams-Dallas, 15 games (41 att)
- 38 Fred Cox, Minnesota, 18 games (40 att)

Most Points After Touchdown, Game
- 8 Lou Groza, NFC: Cleveland vs. Detroit, 1954 (8 att)
- Jim Martin, NFC: Detroit vs. Cleveland, 1957 (8 att)
- George Blanda, AFC-D: Oakland vs. Houston, 1969 (8 att)
- 7 Danny Villanueva, NFC-D: Dallas vs. Cleveland, 1967 (7 att)
- Raul Allegre, NFC-D: N.Y. Giants vs. San Francisco, 1986
- Mike Cofer, SB: San Francisco vs. Denver, 1989 (8 att)
- 6 George Blair, AFC: San Diego vs. Boston, 1963 (6 att)
- Mark Moseley, NFC-D: Washington vs. L.A. Rams, 1983 (6 att)
- Uwe von Schamann, AFC: Miami vs. Pittsburgh, 1984 (6 att)
- Ali Haji-Sheikh, SB: Washington vs. Denver, 1987 (6 att)

Most Points After Touchdown, No Misses, Career
- 49 George Blanda, Chi. Bears-Houston-Oakland, 19 games
- 41 Rafael Septien, L.A. Rams-Dallas, 14 games
- 33 Chris Bahr, Oakland-L.A. Raiders, 11 games
- Matt Bahr, Pittsburgh-Cleveland, 10 games

Field Goals
Most Field Goals Attempted, Career
- 39 George Blanda, Chi. Bears-Houston-Oakland, 19 games
- 31 Mark Moseley, Washington-Cleveland, 11 games
- 27 Roy Gerela, Houston-Pittsburgh, 15 games

Most Field Goals Attempted, Game
- 6 George Blanda, AFC: Oakland vs. Houston, 1967
- David Ray, NFC-D: Los Angeles vs. Dallas, 1973
- Mark Moseley, AFC-D: Cleveland vs. N.Y. Jets, 1986 (OT)
- 5 Jerry Kramer, NFC: Green Bay vs. N.Y. Giants, 1962
- Gino Cappelletti, AFC-D: Boston vs. Buffalo, 1963
- Pete Gogolak, AFC: Buffalo vs. San Diego, 1965
- Jan Stenerud, AFC-D: Kansas City vs. N.Y. Jets, 1969
- George Blanda, AFC-D: Oakland vs. Pittsburgh, 1973
- Ed Murray, NFC-D: Detroit vs. San Francisco, 1983
- Mark Moseley, NFC: Washington vs. San Francisco, 1983
- Tony Franklin, AFC-FR: New England vs. N.Y. Jets, 1985
- Tony Zendejas, AFC-FR: Houston vs. Seattle, 1987 (OT)
- Chuck Nelson, NFC-D: Minnesota vs. San Francisco, 1987
- Luis Zendejas, NFC-D: Philadelphia vs. Chicago, 1988
- 4 By many players

Most Field Goals, Career
- 22 George Blanda, Chi. Bears-Houston-Oakland, 19 games
- 20 Toni Fritsch, Dallas-Houston, 14 games
- 18 Rafael Septien, L.A. Rams-Dallas, 15 games

Most Field Goals, Game
- 5 Chuck Nelson, NFC-D: Minnesota vs. San Francisco, 1987
- 4 Gino Cappelletti, AFC-D: Boston vs. Buffalo, 1963
- George Blanda, AFC: Oakland vs. Houston, 1967
- Don Chandler, SB: Green Bay vs. Oakland, 1967
- Curt Knight, NFC: Washington vs. Dallas, 1972
- George Blanda, AFC-D: Oakland vs. Pittsburgh, 1973
- Ray Wersching, SB: San Francisco vs. Cincinnati, 1981
- Tony Franklin, AFC-FR: New England vs. N.Y. Jets, 1985
- Jess Atkinson, NFC-FR: Washington vs. L.A. Rams, 1986
- Luis Zendejas, NFC-D: Philadelphia vs. Chicago, 1988
- Gary Anderson, AFC-FR: Pittsburgh vs. Houston, 1989 (OT)
- 3 By many players

Most Consecutive Field Goals
- 15 Rafael Septien, Dallas, 1978-82
- 9 Chuck Nelson, Minnesota, 1987
- 8 Tony Fritsch, Houston, 1978-79

Longest Field Goal
- 54 Ed Murray, NFC-D: Detroit vs. San Francisco, 1983
- 52 Lou Groza, NFC: Cleveland vs. Los Angeles, 1951
- Curt Knight, NFC-D: Washington vs. Minnesota, 1973
- Matt Bahr, AFC-FR: Cleveland vs. L.A. Raiders, 1982
- 51 Fuad Reveiz, AFC-D: Miami vs. Cleveland, 1985

Safeties
Most Safeties, Game
1 Bill Willis, NFC-D: Cleveland vs. N.Y. Giants, 1950
  Carl Eller, NFC-D: Minnesota vs. Los Angeles, 1969
  George Andrie, NFC-D: Dallas vs. Detroit, 1970
  Alan Page, NFC-D: Minnesota vs. Dallas, 1971
  Dwight White, SB: Pittsburgh vs. Minnesota, 1974
  Reggie Harrison, SB: Pittsburgh vs. Dallas, 1975
  Jim Jensen, NFC-D: Dallas vs. Los Angeles, 1976
  Ted Washington, AFC: Houston vs. Pittsburgh, 1978
  Randy White, NFC-D: Dallas vs. Los Angeles, 1979
  Henry Waechter, SB: Chicago vs. New England, 1985
  Rulon Jones, AFC-FR: Denver vs. New England, 1986
  George Martin, SB: N.Y. Giants vs. Denver, 1986
  D.D. Hoggard, AFC: Cleveland vs. Denver, 1987

Rushing
Attempts
Most Attempts, Career
400 Franco Harris, Pittsburgh, 19 games
302 Tony Dorsett, Dallas, 17 games
251 John Riggins, Washington, 9 games
Most Attempts, Game
38 Ricky Bell, NFC-D: Tampa Bay vs. Philadelphia, 1979
  John Riggins, SB: Washington vs. Miami, 1982
37 Lawrence McCutcheon, NFC-D: Los Angeles vs. St. Louis, 1975
  John Riggins, NFC-D: Washington vs. Minnesota, 1982
36 John Riggins, NFC: Washington vs. Dallas, 1982
  John Riggins, NFC: Washington vs. San Francisco, 1983

Yards Gained
Most Yards Gained, Career
1,556 Franco Harris, Pittsburgh, 19 games
1,383 Tony Dorsett, Dallas, 17 games
996 John Riggins, Washington, 9 games
Most Yards Gained, Game
248 Eric Dickerson, NFC-D: L.A. Rams vs. Dallas, 1985
206 Keith Lincoln, AFC: San Diego vs. Boston, 1963
204 Timmy Smith, SB: Washington vs. Denver, 1987
Most Games, 100 or More Yards Rushing, Career
6 John Riggins, Washington, 9 games
5 Franco Harris, Pittsburgh, 19 games
4 Larry Csonka, Miami, 12 games
  Chuck Foreman, Minnesota, 13 games
  Marcus Allen, L.A. Raiders, 7 games
Most Consecutive Games, 100 or More Yards Rushing
6 John Riggins, Washington, 1982-83
3 Larry Csonka, Miami, 1973-74
  Franco Harris, Pittsburgh, 1974-75
  Marcus Allen, L.A. Raiders, 1983
2 By many players
Longest Run From Scrimmage
80 Roger Craig, NFC-D: San Francisco vs. Minnesota, 1988 (TD)
74 Marcus Allen, SB: L.A. Raiders vs. Washington, 1983 (TD)
71 Hugh McElhenny, NFC-D: San Francisco vs. Detroit, 1957
  James Lofton, NFC-D: Green Bay vs. Dallas, 1982 (TD)

Average Gain
Highest Average Gain, Career (50 attempts)
6.71 Timmy Smith, Washington, 3 games (51-342)
6.67 Paul Lowe, L.A. Chargers-San Diego, 5 games (57-380)
6.46 Earnest Byner, Cleveland, 5 games (63-407)
Highest Average Gain, Game (10 attempts)
15.90 Elmer Angsman, NFC: Chi. Cardinals vs. Philadelphia, 1947 (10-159)
15.85 Keith Lincoln, AFC: San Diego vs. Boston, 1963 (13-206)
10.90 Bill Osmanski, NFC: Chi. Bears vs. Washington, 1940 (10-109)

Touchdowns
Most Touchdowns, Career
16 Franco Harris, Pittsburgh, 19 games
12 John Riggins, Washington, 9 games
9 Larry Csonka, Miami, 12 games
  Tony Dorsett, Dallas, 17 games
Most Touchdowns, Game
3 Andy Farkas, NFC-D: Washington vs. N.Y. Giants, 1943
  Otto Graham, NFC: Cleveland vs. Detroit, 1954
  Tom Matte, NFC: Baltimore vs. Cleveland, 1968
  Larry Schreiber, NFC-D: San Francisco vs. Dallas, 1972
  Larry Csonka, AFC: Miami vs. Oakland, 1973
  Franco Harris, AFC-D: Pittsburgh vs. Buffalo, 1974
  John Riggins, NFC-D: Washington vs. L.A. Rams, 1983
Most Consecutive Games Rushing for Touchdowns
7 John Riggins, Washington, 1982-84
5 Franco Harris, Pittsburgh, 1974-75
  Franco Harris, Pittsburgh, 1977-79
3 By many players

Passing
Pass Rating
Highest Pass Rating, Career (100 attempts)
104.8 Bart Starr, Green Bay, 10 games
97.5 Joe Montana, San Francisco, 17 games
93.3 Ken Anderson, Cincinnati, 6 games
Attempts
Most Passes Attempted, Career
536 Joe Montana, San Francisco, 17 games
456 Terry Bradshaw, Pittsburgh, 19 games
410 Roger Staubach, Dallas, 20 games
Most Passes Attempted, Game
64 Bernie Kosar, AFC-D: Cleveland vs. N.Y. Jets, 1986 (OT)
54 Randall Cunningham, NFC-D: Philadelphia vs. Chicago, 1988
  Jim Kelly, AFC-D: Buffalo vs. Cleveland, 1989

53 Dan Fouts, AFC-D: San Diego vs. Miami, 1981 (OT)
  Danny White, NFC-FR: Dallas vs. L.A. Rams, 1983

Completions
Most Passes Completed, Career
335 Joe Montana, San Francisco, 17 games
261 Terry Bradshaw, Pittsburgh, 19 games
223 Roger Staubach, Dallas, 20 games
Most Passes Completed, Game
33 Dan Fouts, AFC-D: San Diego vs. Miami, 1981 (OT)
  Bernie Kosar, AFC-D: Cleveland vs. N.Y. Jets, 1986 (OT)
32 Neil Lomax, NFC-FR: St. Louis vs. Green Bay, 1982
  Danny White, NFC-FR: Dallas vs. L.A. Rams, 1983
29 Don Strock, AFC-D: Miami vs. San Diego, 1981 (OT)
  Dan Marino, SB: Miami vs. San Francisco, 1984
  Warren Moon, AFC-FR: Houston vs. Pittsburgh, 1989 (OT)

Completion Percentage
Highest Completion Percentage, Career (100 attempts)
66.3 Ken Anderson, Cincinnati, 6 games (166-110)
62.5 Joe Montana, San Francisco, 17 games (536-335)
61.2 Dan Pastorini, Houston, 5 games (116-71)
Highest Completion Percentage, Game (15 completions)
88.0 Phil Simms, SB: N.Y. Giants vs. Denver, 1986 (25-22)
86.7 Joe Montana, NFC: San Francisco vs. L.A. Rams, 1989 (30-26)
84.2 David Woodley, AFC-FR: Miami vs. New England, 1982 (19-16)

Yards Gained
Most Yards Gained, Career
4,294 Joe Montana, San Francisco, 17 games
3,833 Terry Bradshaw, Pittsburgh, 19 games
2,791 Roger Staubach, Dallas, 20 games
Most Yards Gained, Game
489 Bernie Kosar, AFC-D: Cleveland vs. N.Y. Jets, 1986 (OT)
433 Dan Fouts, AFC-D: San Diego vs. Miami, 1981 (OT)
421 Dan Marino, AFC: Miami vs. Pittsburgh, 1984
Most Games, 300 or More Yards Passing, Career
5 Dan Fouts, San Diego, 7 games
  Joe Montana, San Francisco, 17 games
3 Terry Bradshaw, Pittsburgh, 19 games
  Danny White, Dallas, 17 games
  Dan Marino, Miami, 4 games
2 Daryle Lamonica, Buffalo-Oakland, 13 games
  Ken Anderson, Cincinnati, 6 games
  Bernie Kosar, Cleveland, 7 games
  John Elway, Denver, 11 games
Most Consecutive Games, 300 or More Yards Passing
4 Dan Fouts, San Diego, 1979-81
2 Daryle Lamonica, Oakland, 1968
  Ken Anderson, Cincinnati, 1981-82
  Terry Bradshaw, Pittsburgh, 1979-82
  Joe Montana, San Francisco, 1983-84
  Dan Marino, Miami, 1984
Longest Pass Completion
93 Daryle Lamonica (to Dubenion), AFC-D: Buffalo vs. Boston, 1963 (TD)
88 George Blanda (to Cannon), AFC: Houston vs. L.A. Chargers, 1960 (TD)
86 Don Meredith (to Hayes), NFC-D: Dallas vs. Cleveland, 1967 (TD)

Average Gain
Highest Average Gain, Career (100 attempts)
8.45 Joe Theismann, Washington, 10 games (211-1,782)
8.43 Jim Plunkett, Oakland-L.A. Raiders, 10 games (272-2,293)
8.41 Terry Bradshaw, Pittsburgh, 19 games (456-3,833)
Highest Average Gain, Game (20 attempts)
14.71 Terry Bradshaw, SB: Pittsburgh vs. Los Angeles, 1979 (21-309)
13.33 Bob Waterfield, NFC-D: Los Angeles vs. Chi. Bears, 1950 (21-280)
13.16 Dan Marino, AFC: Miami vs. Pittsburgh, 1984 (32-421)

Touchdowns
Most Touchdown Passes, Career
36 Joe Montana, San Francisco, 17 games
30 Terry Bradshaw, Pittsburgh, 19 games
24 Roger Staubach, Dallas, 20 games
Most Touchdown Passes, Game
6 Daryle Lamonica, AFC-D: Oakland vs. Houston, 1969
5 Sid Luckman, NFC: Chi. Bears vs. Washington, 1943
  Daryle Lamonica, AFC-D: Oakland vs. Kansas City, 1968
  Joe Montana, SB: San Francisco vs. Denver, 1989
4 Otto Graham, NFC: Cleveland vs. Los Angeles, 1950
  Tobin Rote, NFC: Detroit vs. Cleveland, 1957
  Bart Starr, NFC: Green Bay vs. Dallas, 1966
  Ken Stabler, AFC-D: Oakland vs. Miami, 1974
  Roger Staubach, NFC: Dallas vs. Los Angeles, 1975
  Terry Bradshaw, SB: Pittsburgh vs. Dallas, 1978
  Don Strock, AFC-D: Miami vs. San Diego, 1981 (OT)
  Lynn Dickey, NFC-FR: Green Bay vs. St. Louis, 1982
  Dan Marino, AFC: Miami vs. Pittsburgh, 1984
  Doug Williams, SB: Washington vs. Denver, 1987
  Jim Kelly, AFC-D: Buffalo vs. Cleveland, 1989
  Joe Montana, NFC-D: San Francisco vs. Minnesota, 1989
Most Consecutive Games, Touchdown Passes
10 Ken Stabler, Oakland, 1973-77
9 John Elway, Denver, 1984-89
8 Terry Bradshaw, Pittsburgh, 1977-82
  Joe Montana, San Francisco, 1981-84

Had Intercepted
Lowest Percentage, Passes Had Intercepted, Career (100 attempts)
1.41 Bart Starr, Green Bay, 10 games (213-3)
1.75 Phil Simms, N.Y. Giants, 8 games (228-4)
1.89 Jay Schroeder, Washington, 6 games (106-2)

Most Attempts Without Interception, Game
    48   Warren Moon, AFC-FR: Houston vs. Pittsburgh, 1989 (OT)
    47   Daryle Lamonica, AFC: Oakland vs. N.Y. Jets, 1968
    42   Dan Fouts, AFC-FR: San Diego vs. Pittsburgh, 1982

Most Passes Had Intercepted, Career
    26   Terry Bradshaw, Pittsburgh, 19 games
    19   Roger Staubach, Dallas, 20 games
    17   George Blanda, Chi. Bears-Houston-Oakland, 19 games
         Fran Tarkenton, Minnesota, 11 games

Most Passes Had Intercepted, Game
    6   Frank Filchock, NFC: N.Y. Giants vs. Chi. Bears, 1946
       Bobby Layne, NFC: Detroit vs. Cleveland, 1954
       Norm Van Brocklin, NFC: Los Angeles vs. Cleveland, 1955
    5   Frank Filchock, NFC: Washington vs. Chi. Bears, 1940
       George Blanda, AFC: Houston vs. San Diego, 1961
       George Blanda, AFC: Houston vs. Dall. Texans, 1962 (OT)
       Y.A. Tittle, NFC: N.Y. Giants vs. Chicago, 1963
       Mike Phipps, AFC-D: Cleveland vs. Miami, 1972
       Dan Pastorini, AFC: Houston vs. Pittsburgh, 1978
       Dan Fouts, AFC-D: San Diego vs. Houston, 1979
       Tommy Kramer, NFC-D: Minnesota vs. Philadelphia, 1980
       Dan Fouts, AFC-D: San Diego vs. Miami, 1982
       Richard Todd, AFC: N.Y. Jets vs. Miami, 1982
       Gary Danielson, NFC-D: Detroit vs. San Francisco, 1983
    4   By many players

Pass Receiving
Receptions
Most Receptions, Career
    73   Cliff Branch, Oakland-L.A. Raiders, 22 games
    70   Fred Biletnikoff, Oakland, 19 games
    67   Drew Pearson, Dallas, 22 games

Most Receptions, Game
    13   Kellen Winslow, AFC-D: San Diego vs. Miami, 1981 (OT)
       Thurman Thomas, AFC-D: Buffalo vs. Cleveland, 1989
    12   Raymond Berry, NFC: Baltimore vs. N.Y. Giants, 1958
    11   Dante Lavelli, NFC: Cleveland vs. Los Angeles, 1950
       Dan Ross, SB: Cincinnati vs. San Francisco, 1981
       Franco Harris, AFC-FR: Pittsburgh vs. San Diego, 1982
       Steve Watson, AFC-D: Denver vs. Pittsburgh, 1984
       John L. Williams, AFC-D: Seattle vs. Cincinnati, 1988
       Jerry Rice, SB: San Francisco vs. Cincinnati, 1988
       Ernest Givins, AFC-FR: Houston vs. Pittsburgh, 1989 (OT)

Most Consecutive Games, Pass Receptions
    22   Drew Pearson, Dallas, 1973-83
    18   Paul Warfield, Cleveland-Miami, 1964-74
       Cliff Branch, Oakland-L.A. Raiders, 1974-83
    17   John Stallworth, Pittsburgh, 1974-84

Yards Gained
Most Yards Gained, Career
  1,289   Cliff Branch, Oakland-L.A. Raiders, 22 games
  1,167   Fred Biletnikoff, Oakland, 19 games
  1,121   Paul Warfield, Cleveland-Miami, 18 games

Most Yards Gained, Game
   227   Anthony Carter, NFC-D: Minnesota vs. San Francisco, 1987
   215   Jerry Rice, SB: San Francisco vs. Cincinnati, 1988
   198   Tom Fears, NFC-D: Los Angeles vs. Chi. Bears, 1950

Most Games, 100 or More Yards Receiving, Career
    5   John Stallworth, Pittsburgh, 18 games
    4   Fred Biletnikoff, Oakland, 19 games
       Dwight Clark, San Francisco, 7 games
       Jerry Rice, San Francisco, 9 games
    3   Tom Fears, L.A. Rams, 6 games
       Cliff Branch, Oakland-L.A. Raiders, 22 games
       Tony Nathan, Miami, 10 games

Most Consecutive Games, 100 or More Yards Receiving, Career
    3   Tom Fears, Los Angeles, 1950-51
       Jerry Rice, San Francisco, 1988-89
    2   Lenny Moore, Baltimore, 1958-59
       Fred Biletnikoff, Oakland, 1968
       Paul Warfield, Miami, 1971
       Charlie Joiner, San Diego, 1981
       Dwight Clark, San Francisco, 1981
       Cris Collinsworth, Cincinnati, 1981-82
       John Stallworth, Pittsburgh, 1979-82
       Wesley Walker, N.Y. Jets, 1982
       Charlie Brown, Washington, 1983
       Steve Largent, Seattle, 1984-87

Longest Reception
    93   Elbert Dubenion (from Lamonica), AFC-D: Buffalo vs. Boston, 1963 (TD)
    88   Billy Cannon (from Blanda), AFC: Houston vs. L.A. Chargers, 1960 (TD)
    86   Bob Hayes (from Meredith), NFC: Dallas vs. Cleveland, 1967 (TD)

Average Gain
Highest Average Gain, Career (20 receptions)
  22.8   Harold Jackson, L.A. Rams-New England-Minnesota-Seattle, 14 games (24-548)
  21.1   Mark Jackson, Denver, 9 games (20-422)
  20.7   Charlie Brown, Washington, 8 games (31-643)

Highest Average Gain, Game (3 receptions)
  46.3   Harold Jackson, NFC: Los Angeles vs. Minnesota, 1974 (3-139)
  42.7   Billy Cannon, AFC: Houston vs. L.A. Chargers, 1960 (3-128)
  42.0   Lenny Moore, NFC: Baltimore vs. N.Y. Giants, 1959 (3-126)

Touchdowns
Most Touchdowns, Career
    12   John Stallworth, Pittsburgh, 18 games
    11   Jerry Rice, San Francisco, 9 games
    10   Fred Biletnikoff, Oakland, 19 games

Most Touchdowns, Game
    3   Tom Fears, NFC-D: Los Angeles vs. Chi. Bears, 1950
       Gary Collins, NFC: Cleveland vs. Baltimore, 1964

       Fred Biletnikoff, AFC-D: Oakland vs. Kansas City, 1968
       Preston Pearson, NFC: Dallas vs. Los Angeles, 1975
       Dave Casper, AFC-D: Oakland vs. Baltimore, 1977 (OT)
       Alvin Garrett, NFC-FR: Washington vs. Detroit, 1982
       Jerry Rice, NFC-D: San Francisco vs. Minnesota, 1988
       Jerry Rice, SB: San Francisco vs. Denver, 1989

Most Consecutive Games, Touchdown Passes Caught
    8   John Stallworth, Pittsburgh, 1978-83
    4   Lynn Swann, Pittsburgh, 1978-79
       Harold Carmichael, Philadelphia, 1978-80
       Fred Solomon, San Francisco, 1983-84
       Jerry Rice, San Francisco, 1988-89
       John Taylor, San Francisco, 1988-89 (current)
    3   By many players

Interceptions By
Most Interceptions, Career
    9   Charlie Waters, Dallas, 25 games
       Bill Simpson, Los Angeles-Buffalo, 11 games
    8   Lester Hayes, Oakland-L.A. Raiders, 13 games
       Ronnie Lott, San Francisco, 17 games
    7   Willie Brown, Oakland, 17 games
       Dennis Thurman, Dallas, 14 games

Most Interceptions, Game
    4   Vernon Perry, AFC-D: Houston vs. San Diego, 1979
    3   Joe Laws, NFC: Green Bay vs. N.Y. Giants, 1944
       Charlie Waters, NFC-D: Dallas vs. Chicago, 1977
       Rod Martin, SB: Oakland vs. Philadelphia, 1980
       Dennis Thurman, NFC-D: Dallas vs. Green Bay, 1982
       A.J. Duhe, AFC: Miami vs. N.Y. Jets, 1982
    2   By many players

Most Consecutive Games, Interceptions
    3   Warren Lahr, Cleveland, 1950-51
       Ken Gorgal, Cleveland, 1950-53
       Joe Schmidt, Detroit, 1954-57
       Emmitt Thomas, Kansas City, 1969
       Mel Renfro, Dallas, 1970
       Rick Volk, Baltimore, 1970-71
       Mike Wagner, Pittsburgh, 1975-76
       Randy Hughes, Dallas, 1977-78
       Vernon Perry, Houston, 1979-80
       Lester Hayes, Oakland, 1980
       Gerald Small, Miami, 1982
       Lester Hayes, L.A. Raiders, 1982-83
       Fred Marion, New England, 1985
       John Harris, Seattle-Minnesota, 1984-87
       Felix Wright, Cleveland, 1987-88

Yards Gained
Most Yards Gained, Career
   196   Willie Brown, Oakland, 17 games
   152   Ronnie Lott, San Francisco, 17 games
   151   Glen Edwards, Pittsburgh-San Diego, 17 games

Most Yards Gained, Game
    98   Darrol Ray, AFC-FR: N.Y. Jets vs. Cincinnati, 1982
    94   LeRoy Irvin, NFC-FR: L.A. Rams vs. Dallas, 1983
    88   Walt Sumner, NFC-D: Cleveland vs. Dallas, 1969

Longest Return
    98   Darrol Ray, AFC-FR: N.Y. Jets vs. Cincinnati, 1982 (TD)
    94   LeRoy Irvin, NFC-FR: L.A. Rams vs. Dallas, 1983
    88   Walt Sumner, NFC-D: Cleveland vs. Dallas, 1969 (TD)

Touchdowns
Most Touchdowns, Career
    3   Willie Brown, Oakland, 17 games
    2   Lester Hayes, Oakland-L.A. Raiders, 13 games
       Ronnie Lott, San Francisco, 17 games

Most Touchdowns, Game
    1   By 44 players

Punting
Most Punts, Career
   111   Ray Guy, Oakland-L.A. Raiders, 22 games
    84   Danny White, Dallas, 18 games
    73   Mike Eischeid, Oakland-Minnesota, 14 games

Most Punts, Game
    14   Dave Jennings, AFC-D: N.Y. Jets vs. Cleveland, 1986 (OT)
    12   David Lee, AFC-D: Baltimore vs. Oakland, 1977 (OT)
    11   Ken Strong, NFC: N.Y. Giants vs. Chi. Bears, 1933
       Jim Norton, AFC: Houston vs. Oakland, 1967
       Dale Hatcher, NFC: L.A. Rams vs. Chicago, 1985

Longest Punt
    76   Ed Danowski, NFC: N.Y. Giants vs. Detroit, 1935
    72   Charlie Conerly, NFC-D: N.Y. Giants vs. Cleveland, 1950
    71   Ray Guy, AFC: Oakland vs. San Diego, 1980

Average Yardage
Highest Average, Career (20 punts)
  44.5   Rich Camarillo, New England, 6 games (35-1,559)
  43.4   Jerrel Wilson, Kansas City-New England, 8 games (43-1,866)
  43.1   Don Chandler, N.Y. Giants-Green Bay, 14 games (53-2,282)

Highest Average, Game (4 punts)
  56.0   Ray Guy, AFC: Oakland vs. San Diego, 1980 (4-224)
  52.5   Sammy Baugh, NFC: Washington vs. Chi. Bears, 1942 (6-315)
  51.4   John Hadl, AFC: San Diego vs. Buffalo, 1965 (5-257)

Punt Returns
Most Punt Returns, Career
    25   Theo Bell, Pittsburgh-Tampa Bay, 10 games
    20   Gerald McNeil, Cleveland, 7 games
    19   Willie Wood, Green Bay, 10 games

Butch Johnson, Dallas-Denver, 18 games
Phil McConkey, N.Y. Giants, 5 games
Most Punt Returns, Game
  7 Ron Gardin, AFC-D: Baltimore vs. Cincinnati, 1970
      Carl Roaches, AFC-FR: Houston vs. Oakland, 1980
      Gerald McNeil, AFC-D: Cleveland vs. N.Y. Jets, 1986 (OT)
      Phil McConkey, NFC-D: N.Y. Giants vs. San Francisco, 1986
  6 George McAfee, NFC-D: Chi. Bears vs. Los Angeles, 1950
      Eddie Brown, NFC-D: Washington vs. Minnesota, 1976
      Theo Bell, AFC: Pittsburgh vs. Houston, 1978
      Eddie Brown, NFC: Los Angeles vs. Tampa Bay, 1979
      John Sciarra, NFC: Philadelphia vs. Dallas, 1980
      Kurt Sohn, AFC: N.Y. Jets vs. Miami, 1982
      Mike Nelms, SB: Washington vs. Miami, 1982
      Anthony Carter, NFC-FR: Minnesota vs. New Orleans, 1987
  5 By many players

Yards Gained
Most Yards Gained, Career
  237 Anthony Carter, Minnesota, 6 games
  221 Neal Colzie, Oakland-Miami-Tampa Bay, 10 games
  208 Butch Johnson, Dallas-Denver, 18 games
Most Yards Gained, Game
  143 Anthony Carter, NFC-FR: Minnesota vs. New Orleans, 1987
  141 Bob Hayes, NFC-D: Dallas vs. Cleveland, 1967
  102 Charley Trippi, NFC: Chi. Cardinals vs. Philadelphia, 1947
Longest Return
  84 Anthony Carter, NFC-FR: Minnesota vs. New Orleans, 1987 (TD)
  81 Hugh Gallarneau, NFC-D: Chi. Bears vs. Green Bay, 1941 (TD)
  79 Bosh Pritchard, NFC-D: Philadelphia vs. Pittsburgh, 1947 (TD)

Average Yardage
Highest Average, Career (10 returns)
  15.8 Anthony Carter, Minnesota, 6 games (15-237)
  12.6 Bob Hayes, Dallas, 15 games (12-151)
  12.4 Mike Fuller, San Diego-Cincinnati, 7 games (13-161)
Highest Average Gain, Game (3 returns)
  47.0 Bob Hayes, NFC-D: Dallas vs. Cleveland, 1967 (3-141)
  29.0 George (Butch) Byrd, AFC: Buffalo vs. San Diego, 1965 (3-87)
  25.3 Bosh Pritchard, NFC-D: Philadelphia vs. Pittsburgh, 1947 (4-101)

Touchdowns
Most Touchdowns
  1 Hugh Gallarneau, NFC-D: Chicago Bears vs. Green Bay, 1941
     Bosh Pritchard, NFC-D: Philadelphia vs. Pittsburgh, 1947
     Charley Trippi, NFC: Chicago Cardinals vs. Philadelphia, 1947
     Verda (Vitamin T) Smith, NFC-D: Los Angeles vs. Detroit, 1952
     George (Butch) Byrd, AFC: Buffalo vs. San Diego, 1965
     Golden Richards, NFC: Dallas vs. Minnesota, 1973
     Wes Chandler, AFC-D: San Diego vs. Miami, 1981 (OT)
     Shaun Gayle, NFC-D: Chicago vs. N.Y. Giants, 1985
     Anthony Carter, NFC-FR: Minnesota vs. New Orleans, 1987
     Darrell Green, NFC-D: Washington vs. Chicago, 1987

Kickoff Returns
Most Kickoff Returns, Career
  29 Fulton Walker, Miami-L.A. Raiders, 10 games
  21 Ken Bell, Denver, 9 games
  19 Preston Pearson, Baltimore-Pittsburgh-Dallas, 22 games
Most Kickoff Returns, Game
  7 Don Bingham, NFC: Chi. Bears vs. N.Y. Giants, 1956
     Reggie Brown, NFC-FR: Atlanta vs. Minnesota, 1982
     David Verser, AFC-FR: Cincinnati vs. N.Y. Jets, 1982
     Del Rodgers, NFC: Green Bay vs. Dallas, 1982
     Henry Ellard, NFC-D: L.A. Rams vs. Washington, 1983
     Stephen Starring, SB: New England vs. Chicago, 1985
  6 Wallace Francis, AFC-D: Buffalo vs. Pittsburgh, 1974
     Eddie Brown, NFC-D: Washington vs. Minnesota, 1976
     Eddie Payton, NFC-D: Minnesota vs. Philadelphia, 1980
     Alvin Hall, NFC-FR: Detroit vs. Washington, 1982
     Fulton Walker, AFC-D: Miami vs. Seattle, 1983
     Johnny Hector, AFC-FR: N.Y. Jets vs. New England, 1985
     Lorenzo Hampton, AFC: Miami vs. New England, 1985
     Albert Bentley, AFC-D: Indianapolis vs. Cleveland, 1987
     Eric Metcalf, AFC: Cleveland vs. Denver, 1989
     Darren Carrington, SB: Denver vs. San Francisco, 1989
  5 By many players

Yards Gained
Most Yards Gained, Career
  677 Fulton Walker, Miami-L.A. Raiders, 10 games
  481 Carl Garrett, Oakland, 5 games
  458 Cullen Bryant, L.A. Rams-Seattle, 19 games
Most Yards Gained, Game
  190 Fulton Walker, SB: Miami vs. Washington, 1982
  170 Les (Speedy) Duncan, NFC-D: Washington vs. San Francisco, 1971
  169 Carl Garrett, AFC-D: Oakland vs. Baltimore, 1977 (OT)
Longest Return
  98 Fulton Walker, SB: Miami vs. Washington, 1982 (TD)
  97 Vic Washington, NFC-D: San Francisco vs. Dallas, 1972 (TD)
  93 Stanford Jennings, SB: Cincinnati vs. San Francisco, 1988 (TD)

Average Yardage
Highest Average, Career (10 returns)
  30.1 Carl Garrett, Oakland, 5 games (16-481)
  27.9 George Atkinson, Oakland, 16 games (12-335)
  27.7 Eric Metcalf, Cleveland, 2 games (10-277)
Highest Average, Game (3 returns)
  56.7 Les (Speedy) Duncan, NFC-D: Washington vs. San Francisco, 1971 (3-170)
  51.3 Ed Podolak, AFC-D: Kansas City vs. Miami, 1971 (OT) (3-154)
  49.0 Les (Speedy) Duncan, AFC: San Diego vs. Buffalo, 1964 (3-147)

Touchdowns
Most Touchdowns
  1 Vic Washington, NFC-D: San Francisco vs. Dallas, 1972
     Nat Moore, AFC-D: Miami vs. Oakland, 1974
     Marshall Johnson, AFC-D: Baltimore vs. Oakland, 1977 (OT)
     Fulton Walker, SB: Miami vs. Washington, 1982
     Stanford Jennings, SB: Cincinnati vs. San Francisco, 1988
     Eric Metcalf, AFC-D: Cleveland vs. Buffalo, 1989

Fumbles
Most Fumbles, Career
  13 Tony Dorsett, Dallas, 17 games
  10 Franco Harris, Pittsburgh, 19 games
     Terry Bradshaw, Pittsburgh, 19 games
     Roger Staubach, Dallas, 20 games
  9 Chuck Foreman, Minnesota, 13 games
Most Fumbles, Game
  4 Brian Sipe, AFC-D: Cleveland vs. Oakland, 1980
  3 Y.A. Tittle, NFC-D: San Francisco vs. Detroit, 1957
     Bill Nelsen, AFC-D: Cleveland vs. Baltimore, 1972
     Chuck Foreman, NFC: Minnesota vs. Los Angeles, 1974
     Lawrence McCutcheon, NFC-D: Los Angeles vs. St. Louis, 1975
     Roger Staubach, SB: Dallas vs. Pittsburgh, 1975
     Terry Bradshaw, AFC: Pittsburgh vs. Houston, 1978
     Earl Campbell, AFC: Houston vs. Pittsburgh, 1978
     Franco Harris, AFC: Pittsburgh vs. Houston, 1978
     Chuck Muncie, AFC: San Diego vs. Cincinnati, 1981
     Andra Franklin, AFC-FR: Miami vs. New England, 1982
     Eric Dickerson, NFC-FR: L.A. Rams vs. Washington, 1986
  2 By many players

Recoveries
Most Own Fumbles Recovered, Career
  5 Roger Staubach, Dallas, 20 games
  4 Fran Tarkenton, Minnesota, 11 games
  3 Alex Webster, N.Y. Giants, 7 games
     Don Meredith, Dallas, 4 games
     Franco Harris, Pittsburgh, 19 games
     Gerry Mullins, Pittsburgh, 18 games
     Ron Jaworski, Los Angeles-Philadelphia, 10 games
     Lyle Blackwood, Cincinnati-Baltimore-Miami, 14 games
     Joe Montana, San Francisco, 17 games
     Warren Moon, Houston, 5 games
     Bernie Kosar, Cleveland, 7 games
Most Opponents' Fumbles Recovered, Career
  4 Cliff Harris, Dallas, 21 games
     Harvey Martin, Dallas, 22 games
     Ted Hendricks, Baltimore-Oakland-L.A. Raiders, 21 games
  3 Paul Krause, Minnesota, 19 games
     Jack Lambert, Pittsburgh, 18 games
     Fred Dryer, Los Angeles, 14 games
     Charlie Waters, Dallas, 25 games
     Jack Ham, Pittsburgh, 16 games
     Mike Hegman, Dallas, 16 games
     Tom Jackson, Denver, 10 games
     Mike Singletary, Chicago, 9 games
     Monte Coleman, Washington, 14 games
     Darryl Grant, Washington, 14 games
     Alvin Walton, Washington, 6 games
  2 By many players
Most Fumbles Recovered, Game, Own and Opponents'
  3 Jack Lambert, AFC: Pittsburgh vs. Oakland, 1975 (3 opp)
     Ron Jaworski, NFC-D: Philadelphia vs. N.Y. Giants, 1981 (3 own)
  2 By many players

Yards Gained
Longest Return
  93 Andy Russell, AFC-D: Pittsburgh vs. Baltimore, 1975 (opp, TD)
  60 Mike Curtis, NFC-D: Baltimore vs. Minnesota, 1968 (opp, TD)
     Hugh Green, NFC-FR: Tampa Bay vs. Dallas, 1982 (opp, TD)
  52 Wilber Marshall, NFC: Chicago vs. L.A. Rams, 1985 (opp, TD)

Touchdowns
Most Touchdowns
  1 By 22 players

Combined Net Yards Gained
Rushing, receiving, interception returns, punt returns, kickoff returns, and fumble returns.
Attempts
Most Attempts, Career
  454 Franco Harris, Pittsburgh, 19 games
  350 Tony Dorsett, Dallas, 17 games
  275 Chuck Foreman, Minnesota, 13 games
Most Attempts, Game
  40 Lawrence McCutcheon, NFC-D: Los Angeles vs. St. Louis, 1975
  39 John Riggins, SB: Washington vs. Miami, 1982
  38 Ricky Bell, NFC-D: Tampa Bay vs. Philadelphia, 1979
     Rob Carpenter, NFC-FR: N.Y. Giants vs. Philadelphia, 1981

Yards Gained
Most Yards Gained, Career
  2,060 Franco Harris, Pittsburgh, 19 games
  1,786 Tony Dorsett, Dallas, 17 games
  1,355 Roger Craig, San Francisco, 14 games
Most Yards Gained, Game
  350 Ed Podolak, AFC-D: Kansas City vs. Miami, 1971 (OT)
  329 Keith Lincoln, AFC: San Diego vs. Boston, 1963
  285 Bob Hayes, NFC-D: Dallas vs. Cleveland, 1967

Sacks

Sacks have been compiled since 1982

Most Sacks, Career

- 10.5   Richard Dent, Chicago, 7 games
- 8   Dexter Manley, Washington, 14 games
- 7.5   Mark Gastineau, N.Y. Jets, 6 games

Most Sacks, Game

- 3.5   Rich Milot, NFC-D: Washington vs. Chicago, 1984
  - Richard Dent, NFC-D: Chicago vs. N.Y. Giants, 1985
- 3   Richard Dent, NFC-D: Chicago vs. Washington, 1984
  - Garin Veris, AFC-FR: New England vs. N.Y. Jets, 1985
  - Gary Jeter, NFC-D: L.A. Rams vs. Dallas, 1985
  - Carl Hairston, AFC-D: Cleveland vs. N.Y. Jets, 1986 (OT)
  - Charles Mann, NFC-D: Washington vs. Chicago, 1987
  - Kevin Greene, NFC-FR: L.A. Rams vs. Minnesota, 1988
- 2.5   Lyle Alzado, AFC-D: L.A. Raiders vs. Pittsburgh, 1983
  - Jacob Green, AFC-FR: Seattle vs. L.A. Raiders, 1984
  - Larry Roberts, NFC-D: San Francisco vs. Minnesota, 1988

Team Records

Games, Victories, Defeats

Most Seasons Participating in Postseason Games

- 22   Cleveland/L.A. Rams, 1945, 1949-52, 1955, 1967, 1969, 1973-80, 1983-86, 1988-89
  - Cleveland, 1950-55, 1957-58, 1964-65, 1967-69, 1971-72, 1980, 1982, 1985-89
- 21   N.Y. Giants, 1933-35, 1938-39, 1941, 1943-44, 1946, 1950, 1956, 1958-59, 1961-63, 1981, 1984-86, 1989
- 18   Dallas, 1966-73, 1975-83, 1985
  - Chicago, 1933-34, 1937, 1940-43, 1946, 1950, 1956, 1963, 1977, 1979, 1984-88

Most Consecutive Seasons Participating in Postseason Games

- 9   Dallas, 1975-83
- 8   Dallas, 1966-73
  - Pittsburgh, 1972-79
  - Los Angeles, 1973-80
- 7   San Francisco, 1983-89

Most Games

- 36   Dallas, 1966-73, 1975-83, 1985
- 33   Cleveland/L.A. Rams, 1945, 1949-52, 1955, 1967, 1969, 1973-80, 1983-86, 1988-89
- 31   Oakland/L.A. Raiders, 1967-70, 1973-77, 1980, 1982-85

Most Games Won

- 20   Dallas, 1967, 1970-73, 1975, 1977-78, 1980-82
- 19   Oakland/L.A. Raiders, 1967-70, 1973-77, 1980, 1982-83
- 16   Washington, 1937, 1942-43, 1972, 1982-83, 1986-87
  - Pittsburgh, 1972, 1974-76, 1978-79, 1984, 1989

Most Consecutive Games Won

- 9   Green Bay, 1961-62, 1965-67
- 7   Pittsburgh, 1974-76
- 6   Miami, 1972-73
  - Pittsburgh, 1978-79
  - Washington, 1982-83
  - San Francisco, 1988-89

Most Games Lost

- 20   L.A. Rams, 1949-50, 1952, 1955, 1967, 1969, 1973-80, 1983-86, 1988-89
- 18   Cleveland, 1951-53, 1957-58, 1965, 1967-69, 1971-72, 1980, 1982, 1985-89
- 17   N.Y. Giants, 1933, 1935, 1939, 1941, 1943-44, 1946, 1950, 1958-59, 1961-63, 1981, 1984-85, 1989

Most Consecutive Games Lost

- 6   N.Y. Giants, 1939, 1941, 1943-44, 1946, 1950
  - Cleveland, 1969, 1971-72, 1980, 1982, 1985
- 5   N.Y. Giants, 1958-59, 1961-63
  - Los Angeles, 1952, 1955, 1967, 1969, 1973
  - Denver, 1977-79, 1983-84
  - Baltimore/Indianapolis, 1971, 1975-77, 1987 (current)
- 4   Washington, 1972-74, 1976
  - Miami, 1974, 1978-79, 1981
  - Chi. Cardinals/St. Louis, 1948, 1974-75, 1982 (current)
  - Boston/New England, 1963, 1976, 1978, 1982
  - Philadelphia, 1980-81, 1988, 1989 (current)

Scoring

Most Points, Game

- 73   NFC: Chi. Bears vs. Washington, 1940
- 59   NFC: Detroit vs. Cleveland, 1957
- 56   NFC: Cleveland vs. Detroit, 1954
  - AFC-D: Oakland vs. Houston, 1969

Most Points, Both Teams, Game

- 79   AFC-D: San Diego (41) vs. Miami (38), 1981 (OT)
- 73   NFC: Chi. Bears (73) vs. Washington (0), 1940
  - NFC: Detroit (59) vs. Cleveland (14), 1957
  - AFC: Miami (45) vs. Pittsburgh (28), 1984
- 71   AFC: Denver (38) vs. Cleveland (33), 1987

Fewest Points, Both Teams, Game

- 5   NFC-D: Detroit (0) vs. Dallas (5), 1970
- 7   NFC: Chi. Cardinals (0) vs. Philadelphia (7), 1948
- 9   NFC: Tampa Bay (0) vs. Los Angeles (9), 1979

Largest Margin of Victory, Game

- 73   NFC: Chi. Bears vs. Washington, 1940 (73-0)
- 49   AFC-D: Oakland vs. Houston, 1969 (56-7)
- 46   NFC: Cleveland vs. Detroit, 1954 (56-10)
  - NFC-D: N.Y. Giants vs. San Francisco, 1986 (49-3)

Most Points, Shutout Victory, Game

- 73   NFC: Chi. Bears vs. Washington, 1940
- 38   NFC-D: Dallas vs. Tampa Bay, 1981
- 37   NFC: Green Bay vs. N.Y. Giants, 1961

Most Points Overcome to Win Game

- 20   NFC-D: Detroit vs. San Francisco, 1957 (trailed 7-27, won 31-27)
- 18   NFC-D: Dallas vs. San Francisco, 1972 (trailed 3-21, won 30-28)
  - AFC-D: Miami vs. Cleveland, 1985 (trailed 3-21, won 24-21)
- 14   NFC-D: Philadelphia vs. Minnesota, 1980 (trailed 0-14, won 31-16)

-   NFC-D: Dallas vs. Atlanta, 1980 (trailed 10-24, won 30-27)
-   NFC-D: Washington vs. Chicago, 1987 (trailed 0-14, won 21-17)

Most Points, Each Half

- 1st: 38   NFC-D: Washington vs. L.A. Rams, 1983
  - 35   NFC: Cleveland vs. Detroit, 1954
    - AFC: Oakland vs. Houston, 1969
    - SB: Washington vs. Denver, 1987
  - 34   NFC: N.Y. Giants vs. Chi. Bears, 1956
- 2nd: 45   NFC: Chi. Bears vs. Washington, 1940
  - 30   SB: N.Y. Giants vs. Denver, 1986
    - AFC: Cleveland vs. Denver, 1987
  - 28   NFC: Chi. Bears vs. N.Y. Giants, 1941
    - NFC: Detroit vs. Cleveland, 1957
    - NFC-D: Dallas vs. Cleveland, 1967
    - NFC-D: Dallas vs. Tampa Bay, 1981
    - SB: San Francisco vs. Denver, 1989

Most Points, Each Quarter

- 1st: 28   AFC-D: Oakland vs. Houston, 1969
  - 24   AFC-D: San Diego vs. Miami, 1981 (OT)
  - 21   NFC: Chi. Bears vs. Washington, 1940
    - AFC: San Diego vs. Boston, 1963
    - AFC-D: Oakland vs. Kansas City, 1968
    - AFC: Oakland vs. San Diego, 1980
- 2nd: 35   SB: Washington vs. Denver, 1987
  - 26   AFC-D: Pittsburgh vs. Buffalo, 1974
  - 24   NFC-D: Chi. Bears vs. Green Bay, 1941
    - NFC: Green Bay vs. N.Y. Giants, 1961
- 3rd: 26   NFC: Chi. Bears vs. Washington, 1940
  - 21   NFC-D: Dallas vs. Cleveland, 1967
    - NFC-D: Dallas vs. Tampa Bay, 1981
    - AFC-D: L.A. Raiders vs. Pittsburgh, 1983
    - SB: Chicago vs. New England, 1985
    - NFC-D: N.Y. Giants vs. San Francisco, 1986
    - AFC: Cleveland vs. Denver, 1987
    - AFC: Cleveland vs. Denver, 1989
  - 17   NFC: Cleveland vs. Baltimore, 1964
    - NFC-D: Dallas vs. Chicago, 1977
    - SB: N.Y. Giants vs. Denver, 1986
- 4th: 27   NFC: N.Y. Giants vs. Chi. Bears, 1934
  - 24   NFC: Baltimore vs. N.Y. Giants, 1959
  - 21   AFC: Pittsburgh vs. Oakland, 1974
    - NFC: Dallas vs. Los Angeles, 1978
    - AFC-FR: N.Y. Jets vs. Cincinnati, 1982
    - NFC: San Francisco vs. Washington, 1983
- OT: 6   NFC: Baltimore vs. N.Y. Giants, 1958
  - AFC-D: Oakland vs. Baltimore, 1977
  - NFC-D: L.A. Rams vs. N.Y. Giants, 1989

Touchdowns

Most Touchdowns, Game

- 11   NFC: Chi. Bears vs. Washington, 1940
- 8   NFC: Cleveland vs. Detroit, 1954
  - NFC: Detroit vs. Cleveland, 1957
  - AFC-D: Oakland vs. Houston, 1969
  - SB: San Francisco vs. Denver, 1989
- 7   AFC: San Diego vs. Boston, 1963
  - NFC-D: Dallas vs. Cleveland, 1967
  - NFC-D: N.Y. Giants vs. San Francisco, 1986

Most Touchdowns, Both Teams, Game

- 11   NFC: Chi. Bears (11) vs. Washington (0), 1940
- 10   NFC: Detroit (8) vs. Cleveland (2), 1957
  - AFC-D: Miami (5) vs. San Diego (5), 1981 (OT)
  - AFC: Miami (6) vs. Pittsburgh (4), 1984
- 9   NFC: Chi. Bears (6) vs. Washington (3), 1943
  - NFC: Cleveland (8) vs. Detroit (1), 1954
  - NFC-D: Dallas (7) vs. Cleveland (2), 1967
  - AFC-D: Oakland (8) vs. Houston (1), 1969
  - AFC-D: Oakland (5) vs. Baltimore (4), 1977 (OT)
  - SB: Pittsburgh (5) vs. Dallas (4), 1978
  - AFC: Denver (5) vs. Cleveland (4), 1987
  - SB: San Francisco (8) vs. Denver (1), 1989

Fewest Touchdowns, Both Teams, Game

- 0   NFC-D: N.Y. Giants vs. Cleveland, 1950
  - NFC-D: Dallas vs. Detroit, 1970
  - NFC: Los Angeles vs. Tampa Bay, 1979
- 1   NFC: Chi. Cardinals (0) vs. Philadelphia (1), 1948
  - AFC: San Diego (0) vs. Houston (1), 1961
  - AFC-D: N.Y. Jets (0) vs. Kansas City (1), 1969
  - NFC-D: Green Bay (0) vs. Washington (1), 1972
- 2   In many games

Points After Touchdown

Most Points After Touchdown, Game

- 8   NFC: Cleveland vs. Detroit, 1954
  - NFC: Detroit vs. Cleveland, 1957
  - AFC-D: Oakland vs. Houston, 1969
- 7   NFC: Chi. Bears vs. Washington, 1940
  - NFC-D: Dallas vs. Cleveland, 1967
  - NFC-D: N.Y. Giants vs. San Francisco, 1986
  - SB: San Francisco vs. Denver, 1989
- 6   AFC: San Diego vs. Boston, 1963
  - NFC-D: Washington vs. L.A. Rams, 1983
  - AFC: Miami vs. Pittsburgh, 1984

Most Points After Touchdown, Both Teams, Game

- 10   NFC: Detroit (8) vs. Cleveland (2), 1957
  - AFC-D: Miami (5) vs. San Diego (5), 1981 (OT)
  - AFC: Miami (6) vs. Pittsburgh (4), 1984
- 9   NFC: Cleveland (8) vs. Detroit (1), 1954
  - NFC-D: Dallas (7) vs. Cleveland (2), 1967
  - AFC-D: Oakland (8) vs. Houston (1), 1969
  - AFC: Denver (5) vs. Cleveland (4), 1987
- 8   In many games

Fewest Points After Touchdown, Both Teams, Game
   0   NFC-D: N.Y. Giants vs. Cleveland, 1950
       NFC-D: Dallas vs. Detroit, 1970
       NFC: Los Angeles vs. Tampa Bay, 1979

Field Goals
Most Field Goals, Game
   5   NFC-D: Minnesota vs. San Francisco, 1987
   4   AFC-D: Boston vs. Buffalo, 1963
       AFC: Oakland vs. Houston, 1967
       SB: Green Bay vs. Oakland, 1967
       NFC: Washington vs. Dallas, 1972
       AFC-D: Oakland vs. Pittsburgh, 1973
       SB: San Francisco vs. Cincinnati, 1981
       AFC-FR: New England vs. N.Y. Jets, 1985
       NFC-FR: Washington vs. L.A. Rams, 1986
       NFC-D: Philadelphia vs. Chicago, 1988
       AFC-FR: Pittsburgh vs. Houston, 1989 (OT)
   3   By many teams
Most Field Goals, Both Teams, Game
   7   AFC-FR: Pittsburgh (4) vs. Houston (3), 1989 (OT)
   6   NFC-D: Minnesota (5) vs. San Francisco (1), 1987
       NFC-D: Philadelphia (4) vs. Chicago (2), 1988
   5   In many games
Most Field Goals Attempted, Game
   6   AFC: Oakland vs. Houston, 1967
       NFC-D: Los Angeles vs. Dallas, 1973
       AFC-D: Cleveland vs. N.Y. Jets, 1986 (OT)
   5   By many teams
Most Field Goals Attempted, Both Teams, Game
   9   NFC-D: Philadelphia (5) vs. Chicago (4), 1988
   8   NFC-D: Los Angeles (6) vs. Dallas (2), 1973
       NFC-D: Detroit (5) vs. San Francisco (3), 1983
       AFC-D: Cleveland (6) vs. N.Y. Jets (2), 1986 (OT)
       NFC-D: Minnesota (5) vs. San Francisco (3), 1987
       AFC-FR: Houston (4) vs. Pittsburgh (4), 1989 (OT)
   7   In many games

Safeties
Most Safeties, Game
   1   By 17 teams

First Downs
Most First Downs, Game
  34   AFC-D: San Diego vs. Miami, 1981 (OT)
  33   AFC-D: Cleveland vs. N.Y. Jets, 1986 (OT)
  31   SB: San Francisco vs. Miami, 1984
Fewest First Downs, Game
   6   NFC: N.Y. Giants vs. Green Bay, 1961
   7   NFC: Green Bay vs. Boston, 1936
       NFC-D: Pittsburgh vs. Philadelphia, 1947
       NFC: Chi. Cardinals vs. Philadelphia, 1948
       NFC: Los Angeles vs. Philadelphia, 1949
       NFC-D: Cleveland vs. N.Y. Giants, 1958
       AFC-D: Cincinnati vs. Baltimore, 1970
       NFC-D: Detroit vs. Dallas, 1970
   8   By many teams
Most First Downs, Both Teams, Game
  59   AFC-D: San Diego (34) vs. Miami (25), 1981 (OT)
  55   AFC-FR: San Diego (29) vs. Pittsburgh (26), 1982
  50   AFC: Oakland (28) vs. Baltimore (22), 1977 (OT)
       NFC-FR: St. Louis (28) vs. Green Bay (22), 1982
       AFC-FR: N.Y. Jets (27) vs. Cincinnati (23), 1982
       AFC: Miami (28) vs. Pittsburgh (22), 1984
       SB: San Francisco (31) vs. Miami (19), 1984
Fewest First Downs, Both Teams, Game
  15   NFC: Green Bay (7) vs. Boston (8), 1936
  19   NFC: N.Y. Giants (9) vs. Green Bay (10), 1939
       NFC: Washington (9) vs. Chi. Bears (10), 1942
  20   NFC-D: Cleveland (9) vs. N.Y. Giants (11), 1950

Rushing
Most First Downs, Rushing, Game
  19   NFC-FR: Dallas vs. Los Angeles, 1980
  18   AFC-D: Miami vs. Cincinnati, 1973
       AFC-D: Pittsburgh vs. Buffalo, 1974
  17   AFC-D: Cincinnati vs. Seattle, 1988
Fewest First Downs, Rushing, Game
   0   NFC: Los Angeles vs. Philadelphia, 1949
       AFC-D: Buffalo vs. Boston, 1963
       AFC: Oakland vs. Pittsburgh, 1974
       NFC-FR: New Orleans vs. Minnesota, 1987
       NFC: L.A. Rams vs. San Francisco, 1989
   1   NFC: N.Y. Giants vs. Green Bay, 1961
       AFC-D: Houston vs. Oakland, 1969
       NFC: Los Angeles vs. Dallas, 1975
       AFC-FR: Cleveland vs. L.A. Raiders, 1982
       NFC-D: N.Y. Giants vs. Chicago, 1985
       SB: New England vs. Chicago, 1985
       AFC-FR: Seattle vs. Houston, 1987 (OT)
       NFC-D: Philadelphia vs. Chicago, 1988
       AFC-D: Seattle vs. Cincinnati, 1988
   2   By many teams
Most First Downs, Rushing, Both Teams, Game
  25   NFC-FR: Dallas (19) vs. Los Angeles (6), 1980
  23   NFC: Cleveland (15) vs. Detroit (8), 1952
       AFC-D: Miami (18) vs. Cincinnati (5), 1973
       AFC-D: Pittsburgh (18) vs. Buffalo (5), 1974
  22   AFC: Miami (18) vs. Oakland (4), 1973
       AFC-D: Buffalo (11) vs. Cincinnati (11), 1981
       AFC-D: L.A. Raiders (13) vs. Pittsburgh (9), 1983

Fewest First Downs, Rushing, Both Teams, Game
   5   AFC-D: Buffalo (0) vs. Boston (5), 1963
   6   NFC: Green Bay (2) vs. Boston (4), 1936
       NFC-D: Baltimore (2) vs. Minnesota (4), 1968
       AFC-D: Houston (1) vs. Oakland (5), 1969
   7   NFC-D: Washington (2) vs. N.Y. Giants (5), 1943
       NFC: Baltimore (3) vs. N.Y. Giants (4), 1959
       NFC: Washington (3) vs. Dallas (4), 1972
       AFC-FR: N.Y. Jets (3) vs. Buffalo (4), 1981

Passing
Most First Downs, Passing, Game
  21   AFC-D: Miami vs. San Diego, 1981 (OT)
       AFC-D: San Diego vs. Miami, 1981 (OT)
       AFC-D: Cleveland vs. N.Y. Jets, 1986 (OT)
       NFC-D: Philadelphia vs. Chicago, 1988
  20   NFC-FR: Dallas vs. L.A. Rams, 1983
       AFC-D: Buffalo vs. Cleveland, 1989
  19   NFC-FR: St. Louis vs. Green Bay, 1982
       NFC-FR: Dallas vs. Tampa Bay, 1982
       AFC-FR: Pittsburgh vs. San Diego, 1982
       AFC-FR: San Diego vs. Pittsburgh, 1982
       NFC: Dallas vs. Washington, 1982
Fewest First Downs, Passing, Game
   0   NFC: Philadelphia vs. Chi. Cardinals, 1948
   1   NFC-D: N.Y. Giants vs. Washington, 1943
       NFC: Cleveland vs. Detroit, 1953
       SB: Denver vs. Dallas, 1977
   2   By many teams
Most First Downs, Passing, Both Teams, Game
  42   AFC-D: Miami (21) vs. San Diego (21), 1981 (OT)
  38   AFC-FR: Pittsburgh (19) vs. San Diego (19), 1982
  32   NFC-FR: St. Louis (19) vs. Green Bay (13), 1982
       AFC: Miami (18) vs. Pittsburgh (14), 1984
       SB: Miami (17) vs. San Francisco (15), 1984
Fewest First Downs, Passing, Both Teams, Game
   2   NFC: Philadelphia (0) vs. Chi. Cardinals (2), 1948
   4   NFC-D: Cleveland (2) vs. N.Y. Giants (2), 1950
   5   NFC: Detroit (2) vs. N.Y. Giants (3), 1935
       NFC: Green Bay (2) vs. N.Y. Giants (3), 1939

Penalty
Most First Downs, Penalty, Game
   7   AFC-D: New England vs. Oakland, 1976
   6   AFC-D: Cleveland vs. N.Y. Jets, 1986 (OT)
   5   AFC-FR: Cleveland vs. L.A. Raiders, 1982
Most First Downs, Penalty, Both Teams, Game
   9   AFC-D: New England (7) vs. Oakland (2), 1976
   8   NFC-FR: Atlanta (4) vs. Minnesota (4), 1982
   7   AFC-D: Baltimore (4) vs. Oakland (3), 1977 (OT)

Net Yards Gained Rushing and Passing
Most Yards Gained, Game
  610   AFC: San Diego vs. Boston, 1963
  602   SB: Washington vs. Denver, 1987
  569   AFC: Miami vs. Pittsburgh, 1984
Fewest Yards Gained, Game
   86   NFC-D: Cleveland vs. N.Y. Giants, 1958
   99   NFC: Chi. Cardinals vs. Philadelphia, 1948
  114   NFC-D: N.Y. Giants vs. Washington, 1943
Most Yards Gained, Both Teams, Game
 1,036   AFC-D: San Diego (564) vs. Miami (472), 1981 (OT)
 1,024   AFC: Miami (569) vs. Pittsburgh (455), 1984
  929   SB: Washington (602) vs. Denver (327), 1987
Fewest Yards Gained, Both Teams, Game
  331   NFC: Chi. Cardinals (99) vs. Philadelphia (232), 1948
  332   NFC-D: N.Y. Giants (150) vs. Cleveland (182), 1950
  336   NFC: Boston (116) vs. Green Bay (220), 1936

Rushing
Attempts
Most Attempts, Game
  65   NFC: Detroit vs. N.Y. Giants, 1935
  61   NFC: Philadelphia vs. Los Angeles, 1949
  59   AFC: New England vs. Miami, 1985
Fewest Attempts, Game
   9   SB: Miami vs. San Francisco, 1984
  10   NFC: L.A. Rams vs. San Francisco, 1989
  11   SB: New England vs. Chicago, 1985
       AFC-FR: Seattle vs. Houston, 1987 (OT)
Most Attempts, Both Teams, Game
 109   NFC: Detroit (65) vs. N.Y. Giants (44), 1935
  97   AFC-D: Baltimore (50) vs. Oakland (47), 1977 (OT)
  91   NFC: Philadelphia (57) vs. Chi. Cardinals (34), 1948
Fewest Attempts, Both Teams, Game
  45   AFC-FR: N.Y. Jets (22) vs. Buffalo (23), 1981
  46   AFC: Buffalo (13) vs. Kansas City (33), 1966
  48   AFC-D: Buffalo (12) vs. Boston (36), 1963
       AFC: Boston (16) vs. San Diego (32), 1963
       AFC-D: Buffalo (18) vs. Cleveland (30), 1989

Yards Gained
Most Yards Gained, Game
  382   NFC: Chi. Bears vs. Washington, 1940
  338   NFC-FR: Dallas vs. Los Angeles, 1980
  318   AFC: San Diego vs. Boston, 1963
Fewest Yards Gained, Game
   7   AFC-D: Buffalo vs. Boston, 1963
       SB: New England vs. Chicago, 1985
  17   SB: Minnesota vs. Pittsburgh, 1974
  18   AFC-D: Seattle vs. Cincinnati, 1988

Most Yards Gained, Both Teams, Game

- 430 NFC-FR: Dallas (338) vs. Los Angeles (92), 1980
- 426 NFC: Cleveland (227) vs. Detroit (199), 1952
- 404 NFC: Chi. Bears (382) vs. Washington (22), 1940

Fewest Yards Gained, Both Teams, Game

- 90 AFC-D: Buffalo (7) vs. Boston (83), 1963
- 106 NFC: Boston (39) vs. Green Bay (67), 1936
- 128 NFC-FR: Philadelphia (53) vs. Atlanta (75), 1978

Average Gain
Highest Average Gain, Game

- 9.94 AFC: San Diego vs. Boston, 1963 (32-318)
- 9.29 NFC-D: Green Bay vs. Dallas, 1982 (17-158)
- 7.35 NFC-FR: Dallas vs. Los Angeles, 1980 (46-338)

Lowest Average Gain, Game

- 0.58 AFC-D: Buffalo vs. Boston, 1963 (12-7)
- 0.64 SB: New England vs. Chicago, 1985 (11-7)
- 0.81 SB: Minnesota vs. Pittsburgh, 1974 (21-17)

Touchdowns
Most Touchdowns, Game

- 7 NFC: Chi. Bears vs. Washington, 1940
- 5 NFC: Cleveland vs. Detroit, 1954
- 4 NFC: Detroit vs. N.Y. Giants, 1935
  - AFC: San Diego vs. Boston, 1963
  - NFC-D: Dallas vs. Cleveland, 1967
  - NFC: Baltimore vs. Cleveland, 1968
  - NFC-FR: Dallas vs. Los Angeles, 1980
  - AFC-D: L.A. Raiders vs. Pittsburgh, 1983
  - SB: Chicago vs. New England, 1985

Most Touchdowns, Both Teams, Game

- 7 NFC: Chi. Bears (7) vs. Washington (0), 1940
- 6 NFC: Cleveland (5) vs. Detroit (1), 1954
- 5 NFC: Chi. Cardinals (3) vs. Philadelphia (2), 1947
  - AFC: San Diego (4) vs. Boston (1), 1963
  - AFC-D: Cincinnati (3) vs. Buffalo (2), 1981

Passing
Attempts
Most Attempts, Game

- 65 AFC-D: Cleveland vs. N.Y. Jets, 1986 (OT)
- 55 NFC-D: Philadelphia vs. Chicago, 1988
- 54 AFC-D: San Diego vs. Miami, 1981 (OT)
  - AFC-D: Buffalo vs. Cleveland, 1989
  - NFC-D: Minnesota vs. San Francisco, 1989

Fewest Attempts, Game

- 5 NFC: Detroit vs. N.Y. Giants, 1935
- 6 AFC: Miami vs. Oakland, 1973
- 7 SB: Miami vs. Minnesota, 1973

Most Attempts, Both Teams, Game

- 102 AFC-D: San Diego (54) vs. Miami (48), 1981 (OT)
- 96 AFC: N.Y. Jets (49) vs. Oakland (47), 1968
- 95 AFC-D: Cleveland (65) vs. N.Y. Jets (30), 1986 (OT)

Fewest Attempts, Both Teams, Game

- 18 NFC: Detroit (5) vs. N.Y. Giants (13), 1935
- 21 NFC: Chi. Bears (7) vs. N.Y. Giants (14), 1933
- 23 NFC: Chi. Cardinals (11) vs. Philadelphia (12), 1948

Completions
Most Completions, Game

- 34 AFC-D: Cleveland vs. N.Y. Jets, 1986 (OT)
- 33 AFC-D: San Diego vs. Miami, 1981 (OT)
- 32 NFC-FR: St. Louis vs. Green Bay, 1982
  - NFC-FR: Dallas vs. L.A. Rams, 1983

Fewest Completions, Game

- 2 NFC: Detroit vs. N.Y. Giants, 1935
  - NFC: Philadelphia vs. Chi. Cardinals, 1948
- 3 NFC: N.Y. Giants vs. Chi. Bears, 1941
  - NFC: Green Bay vs. N.Y. Giants, 1944
  - NFC: Chi. Cardinals vs. Philadelphia, 1947
  - NFC: Chi. Cardinals vs. Philadelphia, 1948
  - NFC-D: Cleveland vs. N.Y. Giants, 1950
  - NFC-D: N.Y. Giants vs. Cleveland, 1950
  - NFC: Cleveland vs. Detroit, 1953
  - AFC: Miami vs. Oakland, 1973
- 4 NFC-D: Dallas vs. Detroit, 1970
  - AFC: Miami vs. Baltimore, 1971
  - SB: Miami vs. Washington, 1982
  - AFC-FR: Seattle vs. L.A. Raiders, 1984

Most Completions, Both Teams, Game

- 64 AFC-D: San Diego (33) vs. Miami (31), 1981 (OT)
- 55 AFC-FR: Pittsburgh (28) vs. San Diego (27), 1982
- 53 SB: Miami (29) vs. San Francisco (24), 1984

Fewest Completions, Both Teams, Game

- 5 NFC: Philadelphia (2) vs. Chi. Cardinals (3), 1948
- 6 NFC: Detroit (2) vs. N.Y. Giants (4), 1935
  - NFC-D: Cleveland (3) vs. N.Y. Giants (3), 1950
- 11 NFC: Green Bay (3) vs. N.Y. Giants (8), 1944
  - NFC-D: Dallas (4) vs. Detroit (7), 1970

Completion Percentage
Highest Completion Percentage, Game (20 attempts)

- 88.0 SB: N.Y. Giants vs. Denver, 1986 (25-22)
- 87.1 NFC: San Francisco vs. L.A. Rams, 1989 (31-27)
- 80.0 NFC-D: Washington vs. L.A. Rams, 1983 (25-20)

Lowest Completion Percentage, Game (20 attempts)

- 18.5 NFC: Tampa Bay vs. Los Angeles, 1979 (27-5)
- 20.0 NFC-D: N.Y. Giants vs. Washington, 1943 (20-4)
- 25.8 NFC: Chi. Bears vs. Washington, 1937 (31-8)

Yards Gained
Most Yards Gained, Game

- 483 AFC-D: Cleveland vs. N.Y. Jets, 1986 (OT)
- 435 AFC: Miami vs. Pittsburgh, 1984
- 415 AFC-D: San Diego vs. Miami, 1981 (OT)

Fewest Yards Gained, Game

- 3 NFC: Chi. Cardinals vs. Philadelphia, 1948
- 7 NFC: Philadelphia vs. Chi. Cardinals, 1948
- 9 NFC: N.Y. Giants vs. Cleveland, 1950
  - NFC: Cleveland vs. Detroit, 1953

Most Yards Gained, Both Teams, Game

- 809 AFC-D: San Diego (415) vs. Miami (394), 1981 (OT)
- 747 AFC: Miami (435) vs. Pittsburgh (312), 1984
- 666 AFC-D: Cleveland (483) vs. N.Y. Jets (183), 1986 (OT)

Fewest Yards Gained, Both Teams, Game

- 10 NFC: Chi. Cardinals (3) vs. Philadelphia (7), 1948
- 38 NFC-D: N.Y. Giants (9) vs. Cleveland (29), 1950
- 102 NFC-D: Dallas (22) vs. Detroit (80), 1970

Times Sacked
Most Times Sacked, Game

- 9 AFC: Kansas City vs. Buffalo, 1966
  - NFC: Chicago vs. San Francisco, 1984
  - AFC-D: N.Y. Jets vs. Cleveland, 1986 (OT)
- 8 NFC: Green Bay vs. Dallas, 1967
  - NFC: Minnesota vs. Washington, 1987
- 7 NFC-D: Dallas vs. Los Angeles, 1973
  - SB: Dallas vs. Pittsburgh, 1975
  - AFC-FR: Houston vs. Oakland, 1980
  - NFC-D: Washington vs. Chicago, 1984
  - SB: New England vs. Chicago, 1985

Most Times Sacked, Both Teams, Game

- 13 AFC: Kansas City (9) vs. Buffalo (4), 1966
  - AFC-D: N.Y. Jets (9) vs. Cleveland (4), 1986 (OT)
- 12 NFC-D: Dallas (7) vs. Los Angeles (5), 1973
  - NFC-D: Washington (7) vs. Chicago (5), 1984
  - NFC: Chicago (9) vs. San Francisco (3), 1984
- 10 AFC-FR: Houston (7) vs. Oakland (3), 1980
  - NFC-D: N.Y. Giants (6) vs. San Francisco (4), 1984
  - SB: New England (7) vs. Chicago (3), 1985

Fewest Times Sacked, Both Teams, Game

- 0 AFC-D: Buffalo vs. Pittsburgh, 1974
  - AFC-FR: Pittsburgh vs. San Diego, 1982
- 1 In many games

Touchdowns
Most Touchdowns, Game

- 6 AFC-D: Oakland vs. Houston, 1969
- 5 NFC: Chi. Bears vs. Washington, 1943
  - NFC: Detroit vs. Cleveland, 1957
  - AFC-D: Oakland vs. Kansas City, 1968
  - SB: San Francisco vs. Denver, 1989
- 4 By many teams

Most Touchdowns, Both Teams, Game

- 7 NFC: Chi. Bears (5) vs. Washington (2), 1943
  - AFC-D: Oakland (6) vs. Houston (1), 1969
  - SB: Pittsburgh (4) vs. Dallas (3), 1978
  - AFC-D: Miami (4) vs. San Diego (3), 1981 (OT)
  - AFC: Miami (4) vs. Pittsburgh (3), 1984
  - AFC-D: Buffalo (4) vs. Cleveland (3), 1989
- 6 NFC-FR: Green Bay (4) vs. St. Louis (2), 1982
  - AFC: Cleveland (3) vs. Denver (3), 1987
- 5 In many games

Interceptions By
Most Interceptions By, Game

- 8 NFC: Chi. Bears vs. Washington, 1940
- 7 NFC: Cleveland vs. Los Angeles, 1955
- 6 NFC: Green Bay vs. N.Y. Giants, 1939
  - NFC: Chi. Bears vs. N.Y. Giants, 1946
  - NFC: Cleveland vs. Detroit, 1954
  - AFC: San Diego vs. Houston, 1961

Most Interceptions By, Both Teams, Game

- 10 NFC: Cleveland (7) vs. Los Angeles (3), 1955
  - AFC: San Diego (6) vs. Houston (4), 1961
- 9 NFC: Green Bay (6) vs. N.Y. Giants (3), 1939
- 8 NFC: Chi. Bears (8) vs. Washington (0), 1940
  - NFC: Chi. Bears (6) vs. N.Y. Giants (2), 1946
  - NFC: Cleveland (6) vs. Detroit (2), 1954
  - AFC-FR: Buffalo (4) vs. N.Y. Jets (4), 1981
  - AFC: Miami (5) vs. N.Y. Jets (3), 1982

Yards Gained
Most Yards Gained, Game

- 138 AFC-FR: N.Y. Jets vs. Cincinnati, 1982
- 136 AFC: Dall. Texans vs. Houston, 1962 (OT)
- 130 NFC-D: Los Angeles vs. St. Louis, 1975

Most Yards Gained, Both Teams, Game

- 156 NFC: Green Bay (123) vs. N.Y. Giants (33), 1939
- 149 NFC: Cleveland (103) vs. Los Angeles (46), 1955
- 141 AFC-FR: Buffalo (79) vs. N.Y. Jets (62), 1981

Touchdowns
Most Touchdowns, Game

- 3 NFC: Chi. Bears vs. Washington, 1940
- 2 NFC-D: Los Angeles vs. St. Louis, 1975
- 1 In many games

Punting
Most Punts, Game

- 14 AFC-D: N.Y. Jets vs. Cleveland, 1986 (OT)
- 13 NFC: N.Y. Giants vs. Chi. Bears, 1933

AFC-D: Baltimore vs. Oakland, 1977 (OT)
11 AFC: Houston vs. Oakland, 1967
AFC-D: Houston vs. Oakland, 1969
NFC: L.A. Rams vs. Chicago, 1985

Fewest Punts, Game
0 NFC-FR: St. Louis vs. Green Bay, 1982
AFC-FR: N.Y. Jets vs. Cincinnati, 1982
1 NFC-D: Cleveland vs. Dallas, 1969
AFC: Miami vs. Oakland, 1973
AFC-D: Oakland vs. Cincinnati, 1975
AFC-D: Pittsburgh vs. Baltimore, 1976
AFC: Pittsburgh vs. Houston, 1978
NFC-FR: Green Bay vs. St. Louis, 1982
AFC-FR: Miami vs. New England, 1982
AFC-FR: San Diego vs. Pittsburgh, 1982
AFC-D: Cleveland vs. Indianapolis, 1987
2 In many games

Most Punts, Both Teams, Game
23 NFC: N.Y. Giants (13) vs. Chi. Bears (10), 1933
22 AFC-D: N.Y. Jets (14) vs. Cleveland (8), 1986 (OT)
21 AFC-D: Baltimore (13) vs. Oakland (8), 1977 (OT)
NFC: L.A. Rams (11) vs. Chicago (10), 1985

Fewest Punts, Both Teams, Game
1 NFC-FR: St. Louis (0) vs. Green Bay (1), 1982
2 AFC-FR: N.Y. Jets (0) vs. Cincinnati (2), 1982
3 AFC: Miami (1) vs. Oakland (2), 1973
AFC-FR: San Diego (1) vs. Pittsburgh (2), 1982

Average Yardage
Highest Average, Punting, Game (4 punts)
56.0 AFC: Oakland vs. San Diego, 1980
52.5 NFC: Washington vs. Chi. Bears, 1942
51.3 AFC: Pittsburgh vs. Miami, 1972

Lowest Average, Punting, Game (4 punts)
24.9 NFC: Washington vs. Chi. Bears, 1937
25.3 AFC-FR: Pittsburgh vs. Houston, 1989
25.5 NFC: Green Bay vs. N.Y. Giants, 1962

Punt Returns
Most Punt Returns, Game
8 NFC: Green Bay vs. N.Y. Giants, 1944
7 By eight teams

Most Punt Returns, Both Teams, Game
13 AFC-FR: Houston (7) vs. Oakland (6), 1980
11 NFC: Green Bay (8) vs. N.Y. Giants (3), 1944
NFC-D: Green Bay (6) vs. Baltimore (5), 1965
10 In many games

Fewest Punt Returns, Both Teams, Game
0 NFC: Chi. Bears vs. N.Y. Giants, 1941
AFC: Boston vs. San Diego, 1963
NFC-FR: Green Bay vs. St. Louis, 1982
1 AFC: Miami (0) vs. Pittsburgh (1), 1972
AFC: Cincinnati (0) vs. San Diego (1), 1981
AFC-FR: Cincinnati (0) vs. N.Y. Jets (1), 1982
AFC-FR: San Diego (0) vs. Pittsburgh (1), 1982
NFC-D: Minnesota (0) vs. Washington (1), 1982
AFC: Seattle (0) vs. L.A. Raiders (1), 1983
AFC-D: Pittsburgh (0) vs. Denver (1), 1989
2 In many games

Yards Gained
Most Yards Gained, Game
155 NFC-D: Dallas vs. Cleveland, 1967
150 NFC: Chi. Cardinals vs. Philadelphia, 1947
143 NFC: Minnesota vs. New Orleans, 1987

Fewest Yards Gained, Game
−10 NFC: Green Bay vs. Cleveland, 1965
−9 NFC: Dallas vs. Green Bay, 1966
AFC-D: Kansas City vs. Oakland, 1968
−5 AFC-D: Miami vs. Oakland, 1970
NFC-D: San Francisco vs. Dallas, 1972
NFC: Dallas vs. Washington, 1972

Most Yards Gained, Both Teams, Game
166 NFC-D: Dallas (155) vs. Cleveland (11), 1967
160 NFC: Chi. Cardinals (150) vs. Philadelphia (10), 1947
146 NFC-D: Philadelphia (112) vs. Pittsburgh (34), 1947

Fewest Yards Gained, Both Teams, Game
−9 NFC: Dallas (−9) vs. Green Bay (0), 1966
−6 AFC-D: Miami (−5) vs. Oakland (−1), 1970
−3 NFC-D: San Francisco (−5) vs. Dallas (2), 1972

Touchdowns
Most Touchdowns, Game
1 By 10 teams

Kickoff Returns
Most Kickoff Returns, Game
10 NFC-D: L.A. Rams vs. Washington, 1983
9 NFC: Chi. Bears vs. N.Y. Giants, 1956
AFC: Boston vs. San Diego, 1963
AFC: Houston vs. Oakland, 1967
SB: Denver vs. San Francisco, 1989
8 By many teams

Most Kickoff Returns, Both Teams, Game
13 NFC-D: Green Bay (7) vs. Dallas (6), 1982
12 AFC: Boston (9) vs. San Diego (3), 1963
NFC: Dallas (6) vs. Green Bay (6), 1966
AFC-D: Baltimore (6) vs. Oakland (6), 1977 (OT)
AFC: Oakland (6) vs. San Diego (6), 1980
AFC-D: Miami (6) vs. San Diego (6), 1981 (OT)
NFC-D: N.Y. Giants (7) vs. San Francisco (5), 1981
AFC-FR: Cincinnati (8) vs. N.Y. Jets (4), 1982

NFC-D: L.A. Rams (10) vs. Washington (2), 1983
SB: Denver (9) vs. San Francisco (3), 1989
11 In many games

Fewest Kickoff Returns, Both Teams, Game
1 NFC: Green Bay (0) vs. Boston (1), 1936
2 NFC-D: Los Angeles (0) vs. Chi. Bears (2), 1950
AFC: Houston (0) vs. San Diego (2), 1961
AFC-D: Oakland (1) vs. Pittsburgh (1), 1972
AFC-D: N.Y. Jets (0) vs. L.A. Raiders (2), 1982
AFC: Miami (1) vs. N.Y. Jets (1), 1982
NFC: N.Y. Giants (0) vs. Washington (2), 1986
3 In many games

Yards Gained
Most Yards Gained, Game
225 NFC: Washington vs. Chi. Bears, 1940
222 SB: Miami vs. Washington, 1982
215 AFC: Houston vs. Oakland, 1967

Most Yards Gained, Both Teams, Game
379 AFC-D: Baltimore (193) vs. Oakland (186), 1977 (OT)
321 NFC-D: Dallas (173) vs. Green Bay (148), 1982
318 AFC-D: Miami (183) vs. Oakland (135), 1974

Fewest Yards Gained, Both Teams, Game
15 NFC: N.Y. Giants (0) vs. Washington (15), 1986
31 NFC-D: Los Angeles (0) vs. Chi. Bears (31), 1950
32 NFC: Green Bay (0) vs. Boston (32), 1936

Touchdowns
Most Touchdowns, Game
1 NFC-D: San Francisco vs. Dallas, 1972
AFC-D: Miami vs. Oakland, 1974
AFC-D: Baltimore vs. Oakland, 1977 (OT)
SB: Miami vs. Washington, 1982
SB: Cincinnati vs. San Francisco, 1988
AFC-D: Cleveland vs. Buffalo, 1989

Penalties
Most Penalties, Game
14 AFC-FR: Oakland vs. Houston, 1980
NFC-D: San Francisco vs. N.Y. Giants, 1981
13 AFC-FR: Houston vs. Cleveland, 1988
12 NFC-D: Chi. Bears vs. Green Bay, 1941
AFC-D: Pittsburgh vs. Baltimore, 1976
SB: Dallas vs. Denver, 1977
AFC-FR: N.Y. Jets vs. Cincinnati, 1982

Fewest Penalties, Game
0 NFC: Philadelphia vs. Green Bay, 1960
NFC-D: Detroit vs. Dallas, 1970
AFC-D: Miami vs. Oakland, 1970
SB: Miami vs. Dallas, 1971
NFC-D: Washington vs. Minnesota, 1973
SB: Pittsburgh vs. Dallas, 1975
NFC: San Francisco vs. Chicago, 1988
SB: Denver vs. San Francisco, 1989
1 By many teams

Most Penalties, Both Teams, Game
22 AFC-FR: Oakland (14) vs. Houston (8), 1980
NFC-D: San Francisco (14) vs. N.Y. Giants (8), 1981
AFC-FR: Houston (13) vs. Cleveland (9), 1988
21 AFC-D: Oakland (11) vs. New England (10), 1976
20 SB: Dallas (12) vs. Denver (8), 1977

Fewest Penalties, Both Teams, Game
2 NFC: Washington (1) vs. Chi. Bears (1), 1937
NFC-D: Washington (0) vs. Minnesota (2), 1973
SB: Pittsburgh (0) vs. Dallas (2), 1975
3 AFC: Miami (1) vs. Baltimore (2), 1971
NFC: San Francisco (1) vs. Dallas (2), 1971
SB: Miami (0) vs. Dallas (3), 1971
AFC-D: Pittsburgh (1) vs. Oakland (2), 1972
AFC-D: Miami (1) vs. Cincinnati (2), 1973
SB: Miami (0) vs. San Francisco (2), 1984
NFC: San Francisco (0) vs. Chicago (3), 1988
4 NFC-D: Cleveland (2) vs. Dallas (2), 1967
NFC-D: Minnesota (1) vs. San Francisco (3), 1970
AFC-D: Miami (0) vs. Oakland (4), 1970
NFC-D: Dallas (2) vs. Minnesota (2), 1971
SB: Denver (0) vs. San Francisco (4), 1989

Yards Penalized
Most Yards Penalized, Game
145 NFC-D: San Francisco vs. N.Y. Giants, 1981
133 SB: Dallas vs. Baltimore, 1970
128 SB: Chi. Bears vs. Green Bay, 1941

Fewest Yards Penalized, Game
0 By eight teams

Most Yards Penalized, Both Teams, Game
206 NFC-D: San Francisco (145) vs. N.Y. Giants (61), 1981
193 AFC-FR: Houston (118) vs. Cleveland (75), 1988
192 AFC-D: Denver (104) vs. Pittsburgh (88), 1978

Fewest Yards Penalized, Both Teams, Game
9 NFC-D: Washington (0) vs. Minnesota (9), 1973
15 SB: Miami (0) vs. Dallas (15), 1971
20 NFC: Washington (5) vs. Chi. Bears (15), 1937
AFC-D: Pittsburgh (5) vs. Oakland (15), 1972
SB: Pittsburgh (0) vs. Dallas (20), 1975
Miami (10) vs. San Francisco (10), 1984

Fumbles
Most Fumbles, Game
6 By 10 teams

Most Fumbles, Both Teams, Game
12 AFC: Houston (6) vs. Pittsburgh (6), 1978

10 NFC: Chi. Bears (5) vs. N.Y. Giants (5), 1934
SB: Dallas (6) vs. Denver (4), 1977
9 NFC-D: San Francisco (6) vs. Detroit (3), 1957
NFC-D: San Francisco (5) vs. Dallas (4), 1972
NFC: Dallas (5) vs. Philadelphia (4), 1980

Most Fumbles Lost, Game
4 NFC: N.Y. Giants vs. Baltimore, 1958 (OT)
AFC: Kansas City vs. Oakland, 1969
SB: Baltimore vs. Dallas, 1970
AFC: Pittsburgh vs. Oakland, 1975
SB: Denver vs. Dallas, 1977
AFC: Houston vs. Pittsburgh, 1978
AFC: Miami vs. New England, 1985
SB: New England vs. Chicago, 1985
NFC-FR: L.A. Rams vs. Washington, 1986
3 By many teams

Fewest Fumbles, Both Teams, Game
0 NFC: Green Bay vs. Cleveland, 1965
AFC: Buffalo vs. San Diego, 1965
AFC-D: Oakland vs. Miami, 1974
AFC-D: Houston vs. San Diego, 1979
NFC-D: Dallas vs. Los Angeles, 1979
SB: Los Angeles vs. Pittsburgh, 1979
AFC-D: Buffalo vs. Cincinnati, 1981
AFC-D: Cleveland vs. N.Y. Jets, 1986 (OT)
AFC-D: Denver vs. New England, 1986
SB: Denver vs. N.Y. Giants, 1986
1 In many games

Recoveries
Most Total Fumbles Recovered, Game
8 SB: Dallas vs. Denver, 1977 (4 own, 4 opp)
7 NFC: Chi. Bears vs. N.Y. Giants, 1934 (5 own, 2 opp)
NFC-D: San Francisco vs. Detroit, 1957 (4 own, 3 opp)
NFC-D: San Francisco vs. Dallas, 1972 (4 own, 3 opp)
AFC: Pittsburgh vs. Houston, 1978 (3 own, 4 opp)
6 AFC: Houston vs. San Diego, 1961 (4 own, 2 opp)
AFC-D: Cleveland vs. Baltimore, 1971 (4 own, 2 opp)
AFC-D: Cleveland vs. Oakland, 1980 (5 own, 1 opp)
NFC: Philadelphia vs. Dallas, 1980 (3 own, 3 opp)

Most Own Fumbles Recovered, Game
5 NFC: Chi. Bears vs. N.Y. Giants, 1934
AFC-D: Cleveland vs. Oakland, 1980
4 By many teams

Turnovers
(Numbers of times losing the ball on interceptions and fumbles.)
Most Turnovers, Game
9 NFC: Washington vs. Chi. Bears, 1940
NFC: Detroit vs. Cleveland, 1954
AFC: Houston vs. Pittsburgh, 1978
8 NFC: N.Y. Giants vs. Chi. Bears, 1946
NFC: Los Angeles vs. Cleveland, 1955
NFC: Cleveland vs. Detroit, 1957
SB: Denver vs. Dallas, 1977
NFC-D: Minnesota vs. Philadelphia, 1980
7 AFC: Houston vs. San Diego, 1961
SB: Baltimore vs. Dallas, 1970
AFC: Pittsburgh vs. Oakland, 1975
NFC-D: Chicago vs. Dallas, 1977
NFC; Los Angeles vs. Dallas, 1978
AFC-D: San Diego vs. Miami, 1982

Fewest Turnovers, Game
0 By many teams

Most Turnovers, Both Teams, Game
14 AFC: Houston (9) vs. Pittsburgh (5), 1978
13 NFC: Detroit (9) vs. Cleveland (4), 1954
AFC: Houston (7) vs. San Diego (6), 1961
12 AFC: Pittsburgh (7) vs. Oakland (5), 1975

Fewest Turnovers, Both Teams, Game
1 AFC-D: Baltimore (0) vs. Cincinnati (1), 1970
AFC-D: Pittsburgh (0) vs. Buffalo (1), 1974
AFC: Oakland (0) vs. Pittsburgh (1), 1976
NFC-D: Minnesota (0) vs. Washington (1), 1982
NFC-D: Chicago (0) vs. N.Y. Giants (1), 1985
SB: N.Y. Giants (0) vs. Denver (1), 1986
NFC: Washington (0) vs. Minnesota (1), 1987
2 In many games

Compiled by Elias Sports Bureau

Individual Records

Service
Most Games
- 9 *Ken Houston, Houston, 1971-73; Washington, 1974-79
  Joe Greene, Pittsburgh, 1971-77, 1979-80
  Jack Lambert, Pittsburgh, 1976-84
  Walter Payton, Chicago, 1977-81, 1984-87
  Harry Carson, N.Y. Giants, 1979-80, 1982-88
  Mike Webster, Pittsburgh, 1979-86, 1988
  Lawrence Taylor, N.Y. Giants, 1982-90
- 8 Tom Mack, Los Angeles, 1971-76, 1978-79
  *Franco Harris, Pittsburgh, 1973-76, 1978-81
  Lemar Parrish, Cincinnati, 1971-72, 1975-77; Washington, 1978, 1980-81
  Art Shell, Oakland, 1973-79, 1981
  Ted Hendricks, Baltimore, 1972-74; Green Bay, 1975; Oakland, 1981-82; L.A. Raiders, 1983-84
  *John Hannah, New England, 1977, 1979-83, 1985-86
  *Randy White, Dallas, 1978, 1980-86
  *Mike Haynes, New England, 1978-81, 1983; L.A. Raiders, 1985-87
  *Anthony Muñoz, Cincinnati, 1982-87, 1989-90
  Ronnie Lott, San Francisco, 1982-85, 1987-90
- 7 Ron Yary, Minnesota, 1972-78
  Elvin Bethea, Houston, 1972-76, 1979-80
  Roger Wehrli, St. Louis, 1971-72, 1975-78, 1980
  Jack Youngblood, Los Angeles, 1974-80
  Ray Guy, Oakland, 1974-79, 1981
  Robert Brazile, Houston, 1977-83
  Randy Gradishar, Denver, 1976, 1978-80, 1982-84
  James Lofton, Green Bay, 1979, 1981-86
  Mike Singletary, Chicago, 1984-90
  *Also selected, but did not play, in one additional game

Scoring
Points
Most Points, Career
- 30 Jan Stenerud, Kansas City, 1971-72, 1976; Green Bay, 1985 (6-pat, 8-fg)
- 26 Morten Andersen, New Orleans, 1986-89 (8-pat, 6-fg)
- 22 Eddie Murray, Detroit, 1981, 1990 (4-pat, 6 fg)

Most Points, Game
- 18 John Brockington, Green Bay, 1973 (3-td)
- 15 Garo Yepremian, Miami, 1974 (5-fg)
- 14 Jan Stenerud, Kansas City, 1972 (2-pat, 4-fg)

Touchdowns
Most Touchdowns, Career
- 3 John Brockington, Green Bay, 1972-74 (2-r, 1-p)
  Earl Campbell, Houston, 1979-82, 1984 (3-r)
  Chuck Muncie, New Orleans, 1980; San Diego, 1982-83 (3-r)
  William Andrews, Atlanta, 1981-84 (1-r, 2-p)
  Marcus Allen, L.A. Raiders, 1983, 1985-86, 1988 (2-r, 1-p)
- 2 By 11 players

Most Touchdowns, Game
- 3 John Brockington, Green Bay, 1973 (2-r, 1-p)
- 2 Mel Renfro, Dallas, 1971 (2-ret)
  Earl Campbell, Houston, 1980 (2-r)
  Chuck Muncie, New Orleans, 1980 (2-r)
  William Andrews, Atlanta, 1984 (2-p)
  Herschel Walker, Dallas, 1989 (2-r)

Points After Touchdown
Most Points After Touchdown, Career
- 8 Morten Andersen, New Orleans, 1986-89 (8 att)
- 6 Chester Marcol, Green Bay, 1973, 1975 (6 att)
  Mark Moseley, Washington, 1980, 1983 (7 att)
  Ali Haji-Sheikh, N.Y. Giants, 1984 (6 att)
  Jan Stenerud, Kansas City, 1971-72, 1976; Green Bay, 1985 (6 att)

Most Points After Touchdown, Game
- 6 Ali Haji-Sheikh, N.Y. Giants, 1984 (6 att)
- 4 Chester Marcol, Green Bay, 1973 (4 att)
  Mark Moseley, Washington, 1980 (5 att)
  Morten Andersen, New Orleans, 1986 (4 att), 1989 (4 att)

Field Goals
Most Field Goals Attempted, Career
- 15 Jan Stenerud, Kansas City, 1971-72, 1976; Green Bay, 1985
- 9 Eddie Murray, Detroit, 1981, 1990
- 8 Morten Andersen, New Orleans, 1986-89

Most Field Goals Attempted, Game
- 6 Jan Stenerud, Kansas City, 1972
  Ed Murray, Detroit, 1981
  Mark Moseley, Washington, 1983
- 5 Garo Yepremian, Miami, 1974
- 4 Jan Stenerud, Kansas City, 1976

Most Field Goals, Career
- 8 Jan Stenerud, Kansas City, 1971-72, 1976; Green Bay, 1985
- 6 Morten Andersen, New Orleans, 1986-89
  Eddie Murray, Detroit, 1981, 1990
- 5 Garo Yepremian, Miami, 1974, 1979

Most Field Goals, Game
- 5 Garo Yepremian, Miami, 1974 (5 att)
- 4 Jan Stenerud, Kansas City, 1972 (6 att)
  Ed Murray, Detroit, 1981 (6 att)
- 2 By many players

Longest Field Goal
- 51 Morten Andersen, New Orleans, 1989
- 48 Jan Stenerud, Kansas City, 1972
- 43 Gary Anderson, Pittsburgh, 1984

Safeties
Most Safeties, Game
- 1 Art Still, Kansas City, 1983
  Mark Gastineau, N.Y. Jets, 1985

Rushing
Attempts
Most Attempts, Career
- 81 Walter Payton, Chicago, 1977-81, 1984-87
- 68 O.J. Simpson, Buffalo, 1973-77
- 63 Eric Dickerson, L.A. Rams, 1984-85, 1987; Indianapolis, 1988-90

Most Attempts, Game
- 19 O.J. Simpson, Buffalo, 1974
- 17 Marv Hubbard, Oakland, 1974
- 16 O.J. Simpson, Buffalo, 1973
  Marcus Allen, L.A. Raiders, 1986

Yards Gained
Most Yards Gained, Career
- 368 Walter Payton, Chicago, 1977-81, 1984-87
- 356 O.J. Simpson, Buffalo, 1973-77
- 220 Earl Campbell, Houston, 1979-82, 1984

Most Yards Gained, Game
- 112 O. J. Simpson, Buffalo, 1973
- 104 Marv Hubbard, Oakland, 1974
- 85 Neal Anderson, Chicago, 1989

Longest Run From Scrimmage
- 41 Lawrence McCutcheon, Los Angeles, 1976
- 32 Randall Cunningham, Philadelphia, 1989
- 30 O.J. Simpson, Buffalo, 1975

Average Gain
Highest Average Gain, Career (20 attempts)
- 5.81 Marv Hubbard, Oakland, 1972-74 (36-209)
- 5.71 Wilbert Montgomery, Philadelphia, 1979-80 (21-120)
- 5.36 Larry Csonka, Miami, 1971-72, 1975 (22-118)

Highest Average Gain, Game (10 attempts)
- 7.00 O.J. Simpson, Buffalo, 1973 (16-112)
  Ottis Anderson, St. Louis, 1981 (10-70)
- 6.91 Walter Payton, Chicago, 1985 (11-76)
- 6.90 Earl Campbell, Houston, 1980 (10-69)

Touchdowns
Most Touchdowns, Career
- 3 Earl Campbell, Houston, 1979-82, 1984
  Chuck Muncie, New Orleans, 1980; San Diego, 1982-83
- 2 John Brockington, Green Bay, 1972-74
  O.J. Simpson, Buffalo, 1973-77
  Walter Payton, Chicago, 1977-81, 1984-87
  Marcus Allen, L.A. Raiders, 1983, 1985-86, 1988
  Herschel Walker, Dallas, 1988-89

Most Touchdowns, Game
- 2 John Brockington, Green Bay, 1973
  Earl Campbell, Houston, 1980
  Chuck Muncie, New Orleans, 1980
  Herschel Walker, Dallas, 1989

Passing
Attempts
Most Attempts, Career
- 120 Dan Fouts, San Diego, 1980-84, 1986
- 88 Bob Griese, Miami, 1971-72, 1974-75, 1977, 1979
- 57 Joe Montana, San Francisco, 1982, 1984-85, 1988

Most Attempts, Game
- 32 Bill Kenney, Kansas City, 1984
- 30 Dan Fouts, San Diego, 1983
- 28 Jim Hart, St. Louis, 1976

Completions
Most Completions, Career
- 63 Dan Fouts, San Diego, 1980-84, 1986
- 44 Bob Griese, Miami, 1971-72, 1974-75, 1977, 1979
- 33 Ken Anderson, Cincinnati, 1976-77, 1982-83

Most Completions, Game
- 21 Joe Theismann, Washington, 1984
- 17 Dan Fouts, San Diego, 1983
- 16 Dan Fouts, San Diego, 1986

Completion Percentage
Highest Completion Percentage, Career (40 attempts)
- 68.9 Joe Theismann, Washington, 1983-84 (45-31)
- 58.9 Ken Anderson, Cincinnati, 1976-77, 1982-83 (56-33)
- 52.5 Dan Fouts, San Diego, 1980-84, 1986 (120-63)

Highest Completion Percentage, Game (10 attempts)
- 90.0 Archie Manning, New Orleans, 1980 (10-9)
- 77.8 Joe Theismann, Washington, 1984 (27-21)
- 71.4 Joe Montana, San Francisco, 1985 (14-10)

Yards Gained
Most Yards Gained, Career
- 890 Dan Fouts, San Diego, 1980-84, 1986
- 554 Bob Griese, Miami, 1971-72, 1974-75, 1977, 1979
- 398 Ken Anderson, Cincinnati, 1976-77, 1982-83

Most Yards Gained, Game
- 274 Dan Fouts, San Diego, 1983
- 242 Joe Theismann, Washington, 1984
- 212 Phil Simms, N.Y. Giants, 1986

Longest Completion
- 64 Dan Pastorini, Houston (to Burrough, Houston), 1976 (TD)
- 57 James Harris, Los Angeles (to Gray, St. Louis), 1975
-     Ken Anderson, Cincinnati (to G. Pruitt, Cleveland), 1977
- 56 Dan Marino, Miami (to Allen, L.A. Raiders), 1985

Average Gain
Highest Average Gain, Career (40 attempts)
- 7.64 Joe Theismann, Washington, 1983-84 (45-344)
- 7.42 Dan Fouts, San Diego, 1980-84, 1986 (120-890)
- 7.11 Ken Anderson, Cincinnati, 1976-77, 1982-83 (56-398)

Highest Average Gain, Game (10 attempts)
- 11.40 Ken Anderson, Cincinnati, 1977 (10-114)
- 11.20 Archie Manning, New Orleans, 1980 (10-112)
- 11.09 Greg Landry, Detroit, 1972 (11-122)

Touchdowns
Most Touchdowns, Career
- 3 Joe Theismann, Washington, 1983-84
-   Joe Montana, San Francisco, 1982, 1984-85, 1988
-   Phil Simms, N.Y. Giants, 1986
- 2 James Harris, Los Angeles, 1975
-   Mike Boryla, Philadelphia, 1976
-   Ken Anderson, Cincinnati, 1976-77, 1982-83

Most Touchdowns, Game
- 3 Joe Theismann, Washington, 1984
-   Phil Simms, N.Y. Giants, 1986
- 2 James Harris, Los Angeles, 1975
-   Mike Boryla, Philadelphia, 1976
-   Ken Anderson, Cincinnati, 1977

Had Intercepted
Most Passes Had Intercepted, Career
- 8 Dan Fouts, San Diego, 1980-84, 1986
- 6 Jim Hart, St. Louis, 1975-78
- 5 Ken Stabler, Oakland, 1974-75, 1978

Most Passes Had Intercepted, Game
- 5 Jim Hart, St. Louis, 1977
- 4 Ken Stabler, Oakland, 1974
- 3 Dan Fouts, San Diego, 1986
-   Mark Rypien, Washington, 1990

Most Attempts, Without Interception, Game
- 27 Joe Theismann, Washington, 1984
-   Phil Simms, N.Y. Giants, 1986
- 26 John Brodie, San Francisco, 1971
-   Danny White, Dallas, 1983
- 21 Roman Gabriel, Philadelphia, 1974
-   Dan Marino, Miami, 1985

Percentage, Passes Had Intercepted
Lowest Percentage, Passes Had Intercepted, Career (40 attempts)
- 0.00 Joe Theismann, Washington, 1983-84 (45-0)
- 2.13 Dave Krieg, Seattle, 1985, 1989-90 (47-1)
- 3.41 Bob Griese, Miami, 1971-72, 1974-75, 1977, 1979 (88-3)

Pass Receiving
Receptions
Most Receptions, Career
- 18 Walter Payton, Chicago, 1977-81, 1984-87
- 17 Steve Largent, Seattle, 1979, 1982, 1985-88
- 14 John Stallworth, Pittsburgh, 1980, 1983, 1985
-   James Lofton, Green Bay, 1979, 1981-86
-   Marcus Allen, L.A. Raiders, 1983, 1985-86, 1988

Most Receptions, Game
- 8 Steve Largent, Seattle, 1986
- 7 John Stallworth, Pittsburgh, 1983
- 6 John Stallworth, Pittsburgh, 1980
-   Kellen Winslow, San Diego, 1982

Yards Gained
Most Yards Gained, Career
- 236 Steve Largent, Seattle, 1979, 1982, 1985-88
- 226 Wes Chandler, New Orleans, 1980; San Diego, 1983-84, 1986
- 206 James Lofton, Green Bay, 1979, 1981-86

Most Yards Gained, Game
- 114 Wes Chandler, San Diego, 1986
- 96 Ken Burrough, Houston, 1976
- 91 Alfred Jenkins, Atlanta, 1981

Longest Reception
- 64 Ken Burrough, Houston (from Pastorini, Houston), 1976 (TD)
- 57 Mel Gray, St. Louis (from Harris, Los Angeles), 1975
-   Greg Pruitt, Cleveland (from Anderson, Cincinnati), 1977
- 56 Marcus Allen, L.A. Raiders (from Marino, Miami), 1985

Touchdowns
Most Touchdowns, Career
- 2 Mel Gray, St. Louis, 1975-78
-   Cliff Branch, Oakland, 1975-78
-   Terry Metcalf, St. Louis, 1975-76, 1978
-   Tony Hill, Dallas, 1979-80, 1986
-   William Andrews, Atlanta, 1981-84
-   James Lofton, Green Bay, 1979, 1981-86
-   Jimmie Giles, Tampa Bay, 1981-83, 1986

Most Touchdowns, Game
- 2 William Andrews, Atlanta, 1984

Interceptions By
Most Interceptions By, Career
- 4 Everson Walls, Dallas, 1982-84, 1986
- 3 Ken Houston, Houston, 1971-73; Washington, 1974-79
-   Jack Lambert, Pittsburgh, 1976-84
-   Ted Hendricks, Baltimore, 1972-74; Green Bay, 1975; Oakland, 1981-82; L.A. Raiders, 1983-84
-   Mike Haynes, New England, 1978-81, 1983; L.A. Raiders, 1985-87
- 2 By seven players

Most Interceptions By, Game
- 2 Mel Blount, Pittsburgh, 1977
-   Everson Walls, Dallas, 1982, 1983
-   LeRoy Irvin, L.A. Rams, 1986
-   David Fulcher, Cincinnati, 1990

Yards Gained
Most Yards Gained, Career
- 77 Ted Hendricks, Baltimore, 1972-74; Green Bay, 1975; Oakland, 1981-82; L.A. Raiders, 1983-84
- 51 Jerry Gray, L.A. Rams, 1987-90
- 48 Joey Browner, Minnesota, 1986-90

Most Yards Gained, Game
- 65 Ted Hendricks, Baltimore, 1973
- 51 Jerry Gray, L.A. Rams, 1990
- 48 Joey Browner, Minnesota, 1986

Longest Gain
- 65 Ted Hendricks, Baltimore, 1973
- 51 Jerry Gray, L.A. Rams, 1990 (TD)
- 48 Joey Browner, Minnesota, 1986 (TD)

Touchdowns
Most Touchdowns, Game
- 1 Bobby Bell, Kansas City, 1973
-   Nolan Cromwell, L.A. Rams, 1984
-   Joey Browner, Minnesota, 1986
-   Jerry Gray, L.A. Rams, 1990
-   Mike Johnson, Cleveland, 1990

Punting
Most Punts, Career
- 33 Ray Guy, Oakland, 1974-79, 1981
- 19 Dave Jennings, N.Y. Giants, 1979-81, 1983
- 16 Jerrel Wilson, Kansas City, 1971-73
-   Tom Wittum, San Francisco, 1974-75

Most Punts, Game
- 10 Reggie Roby, Miami, 1985
- 9 Tom Wittum, San Francisco, 1974
-   Rohn Stark, Indianapolis, 1987
- 8 Jerrel Wilson, Kansas City, 1971
-   Tom Skladany, Detroit, 1982

Longest Punt
- 64 Tom Wittum, San Francisco, 1974
- 61 Reggie Roby, Miami, 1985
- 60 Ron Widby, Dallas, 1972

Average Yardage
Highest Average, Career (10 punts)
- 45.25 Jerrel Wilson, Kansas City, 1971-73 (16-724)
- 44.79 Reggie Roby, Miami, 1985, 1990 (14-627)
- 44.64 Ray Guy, Oakland, 1974-79, 1981 (33-1,473)

Highest Average, Game (4 punts)
- 49.57 Jim Arnold, Detroit, 1988 (7-347)
- 49.00 Ray Guy, Oakland, 1974 (4-196)
- 47.75 Bob Grupp, Kansas City, 1980 (4-191)

Punt Returns
Most Punt Returns, Career
- 13 Rick Upchurch, Denver, 1977, 1979-80, 1983
- 11 Vai Sikahema, St. Louis, 1987-88
- 10 Mike Nelms, Washington, 1981-83

Most Punt Returns, Game
- 7 Vai Sikahema, St. Louis, 1987
- 6 Henry Ellard, L.A. Rams, 1985
-   Gerald McNeil, Cleveland, 1988
- 5 Rick Upchurch, Denver, 1980
-   Mike Nelms, Washington, 1981
-   Carl Roaches, Houston, 1982

Most Fair Catches, Game
- 2 Jerry Logan, Baltimore, 1971
-   Dick Anderson, Miami, 1974
-   Henry Ellard, L.A. Rams, 1985

Yards Gained
Most Yards Gained, Career
- 183 Billy Johnson, Houston, 1976, 1978; Atlanta, 1984
- 138 Rick Upchurch, Denver, 1977, 1979-80, 1983
- 119 Mike Nelms, Washington, 1981-83

Most Yards Gained, Game
- 159 Billy Johnson, Houston, 1976
- 138 Mel Renfro, Dallas, 1971
- 117 Wally Henry, Philadelphia, 1980

Longest Punt Return
- 90 Billy Johnson, Houston, 1976 (TD)
- 86 Wally Henry, Philadelphia, 1980 (TD)
- 82 Mel Renfro, Dallas, 1971 (TD)

Touchdowns
Most Touchdowns, Game
- 2 Mel Renfro, Dallas, 1971
- 1 Billy Johnson, Houston, 1976
-   Wally Henry, Philadelphia, 1980

Kickoff Returns
Most Kickoff Returns, Career
10 Rick Upchurch, Denver, 1977, 1979-80, 1983
Greg Pruitt, Cleveland, 1974-75, 1977-78; L.A. Raiders, 1984
8 Mike Nelms, Washington, 1981-83
6 Terry Metcalf, St. Louis, 1975-76, 1978
Vai Sikahema, St. Louis, 1987-88
Most Kickoff Returns, Game
6 Greg Pruitt, L.A. Raiders, 1984
5 Les (Speedy) Duncan, Washington, 1972
Ron Smith, Chicago, 1973
Herb Mul-Key, Washington, 1974
4 By six players

Yards Gained
Most Yards Gained, Career
309 Greg Pruitt, Cleveland, 1974-75, 1977-78; L.A. Raiders, 1984
222 Rick Upchurch, Denver, 1977, 1979-80, 1983
175 Les (Speedy) Duncan, Washington, 1972
Most Yards Gained, Game
192 Greg Pruitt, L.A. Raiders, 1984
175 Les (Speedy) Duncan, Washington, 1972
152 Ron Smith, Chicago, 1973
Longest Kickoff Return
62 Greg Pruitt, L.A. Raiders, 1984
61 Eugene (Mercury) Morris, Miami, 1972
55 Ron Smith, Chicago, 1973

Touchdowns
Most Touchdowns, Game
None

Fumbles
Most Fumbles, Career
6 Dan Fouts, San Diego, 1980-84, 1986
4 Lawrence McCutcheon, Los Angeles, 1974-78
Franco Harris, Pittsburgh, 1973-76, 1978-81
Jay Schroeder, Washington, 1987
Vai Sikahema, St. Louis, 1987-88
3 O.J. Simpson, Buffalo, 1973-77
William Andrews, Atlanta, 1981-84
Joe Montana, San Francisco, 1982, 1984-85, 1988
Walter Payton, Chicago, 1977-81, 1984-87
Neil Lomax, St. Louis, 1985, 1988
Most Fumbles, Game
4 Jay Schroeder, Washington, 1987
3 Dan Fouts, San Diego, 1982
Vai Sikahema, St. Louis, 1987
2 By 11 players

Recoveries
Most Fumbles Recovered, Career
3 Harold Jackson, Philadelphia, 1973; Los Angeles, 1974, 1976, 1978 (3-own)
Dan Fouts, San Diego, 1980-84, 1986 (3-own)
Randy White, Dallas, 1978, 1980-86 (3-opp)
2 By many players
Most Fumbles Recovered, Game
2 Dick Anderson, Miami, 1974 (1-own, 1-opp)
Harold Jackson, Los Angeles, 1974 (2-own)
Dan Fouts, San Diego, 1982 (2-own)
Joey Browner, Minnesota, 1990 (2-opp)

Yardage
Longest Fumble Return
83 Art Still, Kansas City, 1985 (TD, opp)
51 Phil Villapiano, Oakland, 1974 (opp)
37 Sam Mills, New Orleans, 1988 (opp)

Touchdowns
Most Touchdowns, Game
1 Art Still, Kansas City, 1985
Keith Millard, Minnesota, 1990

Sacks
Sacks have been compiled since 1983.
Most Sacks, Career
7 Mark Gastineau, N.Y. Jets, 1983-86
Reggie White, Philadelphia, 1987-90
Howie Long, L.A. Raiders, 1984-88, 1990
Most Sacks, Game
4 Mark Gastineau, N.Y. Jets, 1985
Reggie White, Philadelphia, 1987
3 Richard Dent, Chicago, 1985
2 By many players

Team Records

Scoring
Most Points, Game
45 NFC, 1984
Fewest Points, Game
3 AFC, 1984, 1989
Most Points, Both Teams, Game
64 NFC (37) vs. AFC (27), 1980
Fewest Points, Both Teams, Game
16 NFC (6) vs. AFC (10), 1987

Touchdowns
Most Touchdowns, Game
6 NFC, 1984

Fewest Touchdowns, Game
0 AFC, 1971, 1974, 1984, 1989
NFC, 1987, 1988
Most Touchdowns, Both Teams, Game
8 AFC (4) vs. NFC (4), 1973
NFC (5) vs. AFC (3), 1980
Fewest Touchdowns, Both Teams, Game
1 AFC (0) vs. NFC (1), 1974
NFC (0) vs. AFC (1), 1987
NFC (0) vs. AFC (1), 1988

Points After Touchdown
Most Points After Touchdown, Game
6 NFC, 1984
Most Points After Touchdown, Both Teams, Game
7 NFC (4) vs. AFC (3), 1973
NFC (4) vs. AFC (3), 1980
NFC (4) vs. AFC (3), 1986

Field Goals
Most Field Goals Attempted, Game
6 AFC, 1972
NFC, 1981, 1983
Most Field Goals Attempted, Both Teams, Game
9 NFC (6) vs. AFC (3), 1983
Most Field Goals, Game
5 AFC, 1974
Most Field Goals, Both Teams, Game
7 AFC (5) vs. NFC (2), 1974

Net Yards Gained Rushing And Passing
Most Yards Gained, Game
466 AFC, 1983
Fewest Yards Gained, Game
146 AFC, 1971
Most Yards Gained, Both Teams, Game
811 AFC (466) vs. NFC (345), 1983
Fewest Yards Gained, Both Teams, Game
424 AFC (202) vs. NFC (222), 1987

Rushing
Attempts
Most Attempts, Game
50 AFC, 1974
Fewest Attempts, Game
15 AFC, 1989
Most Attempts, Both Teams, Game
80 AFC (50) vs. NFC (30), 1974
Fewest Attempts, Both Teams, Game
54 AFC (27) vs. NFC (27), 1983
AFC (18) vs. NFC (36), 1984

Yards Gained
Most Yards Gained, Game
224 NFC, 1976
Fewest Yards Gained, Game
64 NFC, 1974
Most Yards Gained, Both Teams, Game
425 NFC (224) vs. AFC (201), 1976
Fewest Yards Gained, Both Teams, Game
178 AFC (66) vs. NFC (112), 1971

Touchdowns
Most Touchdowns, Game
3 NFC, 1989
Most Touchdowns, Both Teams, Game
4 AFC (2) vs. NFC (2), 1973
AFC (2) vs. NFC (2), 1980

Passing
Attempts
Most Attempts, Game
50 AFC, 1983
Fewest Attempts, Game
17 NFC, 1972
Most Attempts, Both Teams, Game
94 AFC (50) vs. NFC (44), 1983
Fewest Attempts, Both Teams, Game
42 NFC (17) vs. AFC (25), 1972

Completions
Most Completions, Game
31 AFC, 1983
Fewest Completions, Game
7 NFC, 1972, 1982
Most Completions, Both Teams, Game
55 AFC (31) vs. NFC (24), 1983
Fewest Completions, Both Teams, Game
18 NFC (7) vs. AFC (11), 1972

Yards Gained
Most Yards Gained, Game
387 AFC, 1983
Fewest Yards Gained, Game
42 NFC, 1982
Most Yards Gained, Both Teams, Game
608 AFC (387) vs. NFC (221), 1983
Fewest Yards Gained, Both Teams, Game
215 NFC (89) vs. AFC (126), 1972

Times Sacked
Most Times Sacked, Game
9 NFC, 1985
Fewest Times Sacked, Game
0 NFC, 1971
Most Times Sacked, Both Teams, Game
17 NFC (9) vs. AFC (8), 1985
Fewest Times Sacked, Both Teams, Game
4 AFC (2) vs. NFC (2), 1978

Touchdowns
Most Touchdowns, Game
4 NFC, 1984
Most Touchdowns, Both Teams, Game
5 NFC (3) vs. AFC (2), 1986

Interceptions By
Most Interceptions By, Game
6 AFC, 1977
Most Interceptions By, Both Teams, Game
7 AFC (6) vs. NFC (1), 1977

Yards Gained
Most Yards Gained, Game
78 NFC, 1986
Most Yards Gained, Both Teams, Game
99 NFC (64) vs. AFC (35), 1975

Touchdowns
Most Touchdowns, Game
1 AFC, 1973, 1990
NFC, 1984, 1986, 1990

Punting
Most Punts, Game
10 AFC, 1985
Fewest Punts, Game
0 NFC, 1989
Most Punts, Both Teams, Game
16 AFC (10) vs. NFC (6), 1985
Fewest Punts, Both Teams, Game
5 NFC (0) vs. AFC (5), 1989

Average Yardage
Highest Average, Game
49.57 NFC, 1988 (7-347)

Punt Returns
Most Punt Returns, Game
7 NFC, 1985, 1987
Fewest Punt Returns, Game
0 AFC, 1984, 1989
Most Punt Returns, Both Teams, Game
11 NFC (7) vs. AFC (4), 1985
Fewest Punt Returns, Both Teams, Game
3 AFC (0) vs. NFC (3), 1984
AFC (0) vs. NFC (3), 1989

Yards Gained
Most Yards Gained, Game
177 AFC, 1976
Fewest Yards Gained, Game
0 AFC, 1984, 1989
Most Yards Gained, Both Teams, Game
263 AFC (177) vs. NFC (86), 1976
Fewest Yards Gained, Both Teams, Game
16 AFC (0) vs. NFC (16), 1984

Touchdowns
Most Touchdowns, Game
2 NFC, 1971

Kickoff Returns
Most Kickoff Returns, Game
7 AFC, 1984
Fewest Kickoff Returns, Game
1 NFC, 1971, 1984
AFC, 1988
Most Kickoff Returns, Both Teams, Game
10 AFC (5) vs. NFC (5), 1976
AFC (5) vs. NFC (5), 1986
Fewest Kickoff Returns, Both Teams, Game
5 NFC (2) vs. AFC (3), 1979
AFC (1) vs. NFC (4), 1988

Yards Gained
Most Yards Gained, Game
215 AFC, 1984
Fewest Yards Gained, Game
6 NFC, 1971
Most Yards Gained, Both Teams, Game
293 NFC (200) vs. AFC (93), 1972
Fewest Yards Gained, Both Teams, Game
99 NFC (48) vs. AFC (51), 1987

Touchdowns
Most Touchdowns, Game
None

Fumbles
Most Fumbles, Game
10 NFC, 1974
Most Fumbles, Both Teams, Game
15 NFC (10) vs. AFC (5), 1974

Recoveries
Most Fumbles Recovered, Game
10 NFC, 1974 (6 own, 4 opp)
Most Fumbles Lost, Game
4 AFC, 1974, 1988

Yards Gained
Most Yards Gained, Game
87 AFC, 1985

Touchdowns
Most Touchdowns, Game
1 AFC, 1985
NFC, 1990

Turnovers
(Number of times losing the ball on interceptions and fumbles.)
Most Turnovers, Game
8 AFC, 1974
Fewest Turnovers, Game
1 AFC, 1972, 1976, 1978, 1979, 1985, 1987
NFC, 1976, 1980, 1983
Most Turnovers, Both Teams, Game
12 AFC (8) vs. NFC (4), 1974
Fewest Turnovers, Both Teams, Game
2 AFC (1) vs. NFC (1), 1976

RULES

1990 NFL Roster of Officials

Art McNally, Director of Officiating
Jack Reader, Assistant Supervisor of Officials
Tony Veteri, Assistant Supervisor of Officials

No.	Name	Position	College	No.	Name	Position	College
25	Alderton, John	Line Judge	Portland State	108	Kemp, Stan	Side Judge	Michigan
115	Ancich, Hendi	Umpire	Harbor College	86	Kukar, Bernie	Field Judge	St. John's
81	Anderson, Dave	Head Linesman	Salem College	120	Lane, Gary	Side Judge	Missouri
34	Austin, Gerald	Side Judge	Western Carolina	18	Lewis, Bob	Field Judge	No College
22	Baetz, Paul	Back Judge	Heidelberg	49	Look, Dean	Side Judge	Michigan State
116	Baker, Bob	Line Judge	East Texas State	98	Lovett, Bill	Back Judge	Maryland
26	Baltz, Mark	Head Linesman	Ohio University	82	Mallette, Pat	Field Judge	Nebraska
55	Barnes, Tom	Head Linesman	Minnesota	9	Markbreit, Jerry	Referee	Illinois
14	Barth, Gene	Referee	St. Louis	38	Maurer, Bruce	Head Linesman	Ohio State
56	Baynes, Ron	Line Judge	Auburn	48	McCarter, Gordon	Referee	Western Reserve
17	Bergman, Jerry	Head Linesman	Duquesne	95	McElwee, Bob	Referee	Navy
83	Blum, Ron	Line Judge	Marin College	41	McKenzie, Dick	Line Judge	Ashland
110	Botchan, Ron	Umpire	Occidental	76	Merrifield, Ed	Field Judge	Missouri
101	Boylston, Bob	Umpire	Alabama	35	Miles, Leo	Head Linesman	Virginia State
94	Carey, Mike	Side Judge	Santa Clara	80	Millis, Tim	Back Judge	Millsaps
39	Carlsen, Don	Side Judge	Cal State-Chico	117	Montgomery, Ben	Umpire	Morehouse
63	Carollo, Bill	Side Judge	Wisconsin	36	Moore, Bob	Back Judge	Dayton
43	Cashion, Red	Referee	Texas A&M	20	Nemmers, Larry	Side Judge	Upper Iowa
24	Clymer, Roy	Back Judge	New Mexico State	51	Orem, Dale	Line Judge	Louisville
65	Coleman, Walt	Line Judge	Arkansas	77	Orr, Don	Field Judge	Vanderbilt
27	Conway, Al	Umpire	Army	10	Phares, Ron	Head Linesman	Virginia Tech
71	Coukart, Ed	Umpire	Northwestern	79	Pointer, Aaron	Head Linesman	Pacific Lutheran
61	Creed, Dick	Side Judge	Louisville	92	Poole, Jim	Back Judge	San Diego State
75	Daopoulos, Jim	Back Judge	Kentucky	5	Quirk, Jim	Line Judge	Delaware
78	Demmas, Art	Umpire	Vanderbilt	53	Reynolds, Bill	Line Judge	West Chester State
45	DeSouza, Ron	Line Judge	Morgan State	68	Richard, Louis	Back Judge	S.W. Louisiana
74	Dodez, Ray	Line Judge	Wooster	30	Riggs, Dennis	Umpire	Bellarmine
31	Dolack, Dick	Field Judge	Ferris State	121	Rivers, Sanford	Head Linesman	Youngstown State
6	Dooley, Tom	Referee	VMI	46	Robison, John	Field Judge	Utah
113	Dorkowski, Don	Field Judge	Cal State-Los Angeles	33	Roe, Howard	Referee	Wichita State
102	Douglas, Merrill	Side Judge	Utah	21	Schleyer, John	Head Linesman	Millersville
12	Dreith, Ben	Line Judge	Colorado State	122	Schmitz, Bill	Field Judge	Colorado State
57	Fiffick, Ed	Umpire	Marquette	70	Seeman, Jerry	Referee	Winona State
47	Fincken, Tom	Side Judge	Kansas State	109	Semon, Sid	Head Linesman	Southern California
111	Frantz, Earnie	Head Linesman	No College	118	Sifferman, Tom	Back Judge	Seattle
50	Gereb, Neil	Umpire	California	73	Skelton, Bobby	Field Judge	Alabama
72	Gierke, Terry	Head Linesman	Portland State	29	Slavin, Howard	Side Judge	Southern California
15	Glass, Bama	Line Judge	Colorado	119	Spitler, Ron	Side Judge	Panhandle State
23	Grier, Johnny	Referee	University of D.C.	91	Stanley, Bill	Field Judge	Redlands
40	Haggerty, Pat	Referee	Colorado State	103	Stuart, Rex	Umpire	Appalachian State
96	Hakes, Don	Field Judge	Bradley	52	Tompkins, Ben	Back Judge	Texas
104	Hamer, Dale	Referee	California, Pa., Univ.	4	Toole, Doug	Back Judge	Utah State
42	Hamilton, Dave	Umpire	Utah	32	Tunney, Jim	Referee	Occidental
44	Hampton, Donnie	Field Judge	Georgia	93	Vaughan, Jack	Field Judge	Mississippi State
105	Hantak, Dick	Referee	S.E. Missouri	100	Wagner, Bob	Umpire	Penn State
112	Haynes, Joe	Line Judge	Alcorn State	28	Wedge, Don	Side Judge	Ohio Wesleyan
85	Hochuli, Ed	Back Judge	Texas-El Paso	87	Weidner, Paul	Head Linesman	Cincinnati
54	Johnson, Jack	Line Judge	Pacific Lutheran	89	Wells, Gordon	Umpire	Occidental
114	Johnson, Tom	Head Linesman	Miami, Ohio	123	White, Tom	Referee	Temple
97	Jones, Nathan	Side Judge	Lewis & Clark	99	Williams, Banks	Back Judge	Houston
60	Jorgensen, Dick	Referee	Wisconsin	8	Williams, Dale	Head Linesman	Cal St.-Northridge
106	Jury, Al	Back Judge	San Bernardino Valley	84	Wortman, Bob	Field Judge	Findlay
107	Kearney, Jim	Back Judge	Pennsylvania	11	Wyant, Fred	Line Judge	West Virginia
67	Keck, John	Umpire	Cornell College				

1990 NFL Replay Officials

Bob Beeks—22 years as an NFL Line Judge. He officiated in five Super Bowls (XIV, XVI, XVIII, XXI, & XXIII). First year as Replay Official.

Mark Burns—Worked in League office for seven years with five years in Officiating Department. He has been a game observer since 1986. Fourth year as Replay Official.

Royal Cathcart—16 years as an NFL Line Judge and Side Judge. He is a former NFL player. Fourth year as Replay Official.

Bill Fette—25 years as a Field Judge in the PAC 10. Worked three Rose Bowls. Third year as Replay Official.

Jack Fette—23 years as an NFL Line Judge. He officiated in five Super Bowls (V, VIII, X, XII, & XXII). Third year as Replay Official.

Fritz Graf—24 years as an NFL Field Judge. He has been a game observer since 1984. He officiated in four Super Bowls (V, VIII, XV, & XVIII). Fifth year as Replay Official.

Dave Hawk—18 years as an NFL Side Judge. First year as Replay Official.

Chuck Heberling—22 years as an NFL Referee and Line Judge.

Fifth year as Replay Official.

Dave Kamanski—25 years as an NCAA Official. Referee in PAC 10 for 20 years. Worked three Rose Bowls, three East/West Games, and three Japan Bowls. Third year as Replay Official.

Tom Kelleher—28 years as an NFL Back Judge. He officiated in five Super Bowls (IV, VII, XI, XV, & XIX). Third year as Replay Official.

Grover Klemmer—19 years as an NFL Side Judge and Back Judge. Fourth year as Replay Official.

Cal Lepore—15 years as an NFL Head Linesman and Referee. He officiated in Super Bowl III. Fifth year as Replay Official.

Al Sabato—20 years as an NFL Head Linesman. He has been a game observer since 1982. He officiated in two Super Bowls (I & VI). Fifth year as Replay Official.

George Sladky—17 years as an NCAA Official. Nine years with the Big Ten and eight years with the Southwest Conference. He worked six bowl games. Fourth year as Replay Official.

Bill Swanson—21 years as an NFL Back Judge. He officiated in two Super Bowls (XI & XVI). Fifth year as Replay Official.

1990 Officials at a Glance

Referees

Gene Barth, No. 14, St. Louis, president, oil company, 20th year.

Red Cashion, No. 43, Texas A&M, chairman of the board, insurance company, 19th year.

Tom Dooley, No. 6, VMI, general contractor, 13th year.

Johnny Grier, No. 23, D.C. Teachers, planning engineer, 10th year.

Pat Haggerty, No. 40, Colorado State, retired teacher, 26th year.

Dale Hamer, No. 104, California (Pa.) University, vice-president, finance, 13th year.

Dick Hantak, No. 105, S.E. Missouri, educator, 13th year.

Dick Jorgensen, No. 60, Wisconsin, bank president, 23rd year.

Jerry Markbreit, No. 9, Illinois, trade and barter manager, 15th year.

Gordon McCarter, No. 48, Western Reserve, regional sales manager, 24th year.

Bob McElwee, No. 95, U.S. Naval Academy, owner, construction company, 15th year.

Howard Roe, No. 33, Wichita State, director of corporate insurance/administration, 7th year.

Jerry Seeman, No. 70, Winona State, district school administrator, 16th year.

Jim Tunney, No. 32, Occidental, president of motivation company and professional speaker, 31st year.

Tom White, No. 123, Temple, president, athletic sportswear, 2nd year.

Umpires

Hendi Ancich, No. 115, Harbor, longshoreman, 9th year.

Ron Botchan, No. 110, Occidental, college professor, former AFL player, 11th year.

Bob Boylston, No. 101, Alabama, stockbroker, 13th year.

Al Conway, No. 27, Army, director of operations, manufacturing, 22nd year.

Ed Coukart, No. 71, Northwestern, bank senior vice-president, 2nd year.

Art Demmas, No. 78, Vanderbilt, vice-president, institutional investments, 23rd year.

Ed Fiffick, No. 57, Marquette, podiatrist, 12th year.

Neil Gereb, No. 50, California, project manager, aircraft company, 10th year.

Dave Hamilton, No. 42, Utah, assistant executive director, 16th year.

John Keck, No. 67, Cornell, petroleum distributor, 19th year.

Ben Montgomery, No. 117, Morehouse, school administrator, 9th year.

Dennis Riggs, No. 30, Bellarmine, seminary vice-president, 3rd year.

Rex Stuart, No. 103, Appalachian State, insurance agent, 7th year.

Bob Wagner, No. 100, Penn State, executive director, 6th year.

Gordon Wells, No. 89, Occidental, chairman, college physical education department, 19th year.

Head Linesmen

Dave Anderson, No. 81, Salem, insurance executive, 7th year.

Mark Baltz, No. 26, Ohio, manufacturer's representative, 2nd year.

Tom Barnes, No. 55, Minnesota, manufacturer's representative, 5th year.

Jerry Bergman, No. 17, Duquesne, executive director, pension fund, 25th year.

Earnie Frantz, No. 111, vice-president and manager, land title company, 10th year.

Terry Gierke, No. 72, Portland State, real estate broker, 10th year.

Tom Johnson, No. 114, Miami, Ohio, teacher, 9th year.

Bruce Maurer, No. 38, Ohio State, administrator/associate director, recreational sports, 4th year.

Leo Miles, No. 35, Virginia State, retired, university athletic director, former NFL player, 22nd year.

Ron Phares, No. 10, Virginia Tech, president, general contracting firm, 6th year.

Aaron Pointer, No. 79, Pacific Lutheran, recreation supervisor, 4th year.

Sanford Rivers, No. 121, Youngstown State, university administrator, 2nd year.

John Schleyer, No. 21, Millersville, sales representative, 1st year.

Sid Semon, No. 109, Southern California, chairman, physical education department, 13th year.

Paul Weidner, No. 87, Cincinnati, marketing manager, 5th year.

Dale Williams, No. 8, Cal State-Northridge, business owner, 11th year.

Line Judges

John Alderton, No. 25, Portland State, vice-president, insurance, 2nd year.

Bob Baker, No. 116, East Texas State, teacher, counselor, 4th year.

Ron Baynes, No. 56, Auburn, high school administrator, coach, 4th year.

Ron Blum, No. 83, Marin College, P.G.A. golf professional, 6th year.

Walt Coleman, No. 65, Arkansas, president, dairy company, 2nd year.

Ron DeSouza, No. 45, Morgan State, vice-president, administration, 11th year.

Ray Dodez, No. 74, Wooster, communications consultant, 23rd year.

Ben Dreith, No. 12, Colorado State, retired high school teacher, 31st year.

Bama Glass, No. 15, Colorado, owner/manager, retail sales, 12th year.

Joe Haynes, No. 112, Alcorn State, deputy superintendent, public schools, 7th year.

Jack Johnson, No. 54, Pacific Lutheran, president, sports promotions, 15th year.

Dick McKenzie, No. 41, Ashland, financial services, 13th year.

Dale Orem, No. 51, Louisville, mayor, 11th year.

Jim Quirk, No. 5, Delaware, vice-president, government securities sales, 3rd year.

Bill Reynolds, No. 53, West Chester State, retired teacher, 16th year.

Fred Wyant, No. 11, West Virginia, life insurance company, investment management, former NFL player, 25th year.

Back Judges

Paul Baetz, No. 22, Heidelberg, financial consultant, 13th year.

Roy Clymer, No. 24, New Mexico State, district manager, gas company, 11th year.

Jim Daopoulos, No. 75, Kentucky, mortgage broker, 2nd year.

Jim Hochuli, No. 85, Texas-El Paso, attorney, 1st year.

Al Jury, No. 106, San Bernardino Valley, state traffic officer, 13th year.

Jim Kearney, No. 107, Pennsylvania, marketing manager, 13th year.

Bill Lovett, No. 98, Maryland, insurance sales, 1st year.

Tim Millis, No. 80, Millsaps, financial investigative consultant, 2nd year.

Bob Moore, No. 36, Dayton, attorney, 7th year.

Jim Poole, No. 92, San Diego State, college professor, 16th year.

Louis Richard, No. 68, S.W. Louisiana, sales manager, 5th year.

Tom Sifferman, No. 118, Seattle, manufacturer's representative, 5th year.

Ben Tompkins, No. 52, Texas, attorney, 20th year.

Doug Toole, No. 4, Utah State, physical therapist, orthopedic and sports medicine, 3rd year.

Banks Williams, No. 99, Houston, vice-president, general sales manager, 13th year.

Side Judges

Gerald Austin, No. 34, Western Carolina, associate superintendent, county schools, 9th year.

Mike Carey, No. 94, Santa Clara, owner/operator, ski accessory manufacturing, 1st year.

Don Carlsen, No. 39, Cal State-Chico, budget analyst, controller, 2nd year.

Bill Carollo, No. 63, Wisconsin, account executive, 2nd year.

Richard Creed, No. 61, Louisville, manager, real estate, 13th year.

Merrill Douglas, No. 102, Utah, deputy sheriff, former NFL player, 10th year.

Tom Fincken, No. 47, Emporia State, educator, 7th year.

Nate Jones, No. 97, Lewis and Clark, high school principal, 14th year.

Stan Kemp, No. 108, Michigan, vice-president, insurance executive, 5th year.

Gary Lane, No. 120, Missouri, divisional sales manager, former NFL player, 9th year.

Dean Look, No. 49, Michigan State, vice-president, instrument maker, former AFL player, 18th year.

Larry Nemmers, No. 20, Upper Iowa, high school principal, 6th year.

Howard Slavin, No. 29, Southern California, attorney, 4th year.

Ron Spitler, No. 119, Panhandle State, owner, service center, 9th year.

Don Wedge, No. 28, Ohio Wesleyan, sales executive, 19th year.

Field Judges

Dick Dolack, No. 31, Ferris State, pharmacist, 25th year.

Don Dorkowski, No. 113, Los Angeles State College, high school health director, 5th year.

Don Hakes, No. 96, Bradley, high school teacher, 14th year.

Donnie Hampton, No. 44, Georgia, president, mortgage company, 3rd year.

Bernie Kukar, No. 86, St. John's, owner/director, summer camp for boys, 7th year.

Bob Lewis, No. 18, retired U.S. government specialist, 15th year.

Pat Mallette, No. 82, Nebraska, real estate broker, 22nd year.

Ed Merrifield, No. 76, Missouri, sales representative, 16th year.

Don Orr, No. 77, Vanderbilt, mechanical contractor, 20th year.

John Robison, No. 46, Utah, high school counselor, 3rd year.

Bill Schmitz, No. 122, Colorado State, sales manager, 2nd year.

Bobby Skelton, No. 73, Alabama, industrial representative, 6th year.

Bill Stanley, No. 91, Redlands, college dean, athletic director, 17th year.

Jack Vaughan, No. 93, Mississippi State, financial services, 15th year.

Bob Wortman, No. 84, Findlay, retired supervisor, college basketball officials, 25th year.

Official Signals

1

TOUCHDOWN, FIELD GOAL, or SUCCESSFUL TRY
Both arms extended above head.

2

SAFETY
Palms together above head.

3

FIRST DOWN
Arm pointed toward defensive team's goal.

4

CROWD NOISE, DEAD BALL or NEUTRAL ZONE ESTABLISHED
One arm above head with an open hand.
With fist closed: **Fourth Down.**

5

BALL ILLEGALLY TOUCHED, KICKED, OR BATTED
Fingertips tap both shoulders.

6

TIME OUT
Hands crisscrossed above head.
Same signal followed by placing one hand on top of cap: **Referee's Time Out.**
Same signal followed by arm swung at side: **Touchback.**

7

NO TIME OUT or TIME IN WITH WHISTLE
Full arm circled to simulate moving clock.

8

DELAY OF GAME, ILLEGAL SUBSTITUTION, or EXCESS TIME OUT
Folded arms.

9

FALSE START, ILLEGAL SHIFT, ILLEGAL PROCEDURE, ILLEGAL FORMATION, or KICKOFF OR SAFETY KICK OUT OF BOUNDS

Forearms rotated over and over in front of body.

10

PERSONAL FOUL

One wrist striking the other above head.
Same signal followed by swinging leg:
Roughing Kicker.
Same signal followed by raised arm swinging forward:
Roughing Passer.
Same signal followed by hand striking back of calf: **Clipping**

11

HOLDING

Grasping one wrist, the fist clenched, in front of chest.

12

ILLEGAL USE OF HANDS, ARMS, OR BODY

Grasping one wrist, the hand open and facing forward, in front of chest.

13

PENALTY REFUSED, INCOMPLETE PASS, PLAY OVER, or MISSED GOAL

Hands shifted in horizontal plane.

14

PASS JUGGLED INBOUNDS AND CAUGHT OUT OF BOUNDS

Hands up and down in front of chest (following incomplete pass signal).

15

ILLEGAL FORWARD PASS

One hand waved behind back followed by loss of down signal (23).

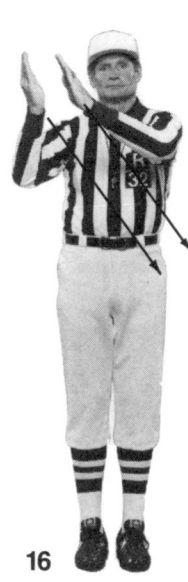

16

INTENTIONAL GROUNDING OF PASS

Parallel arms waved in a diagonal plane across body. Followed by loss of down signal (23).

17

INTERFERENCE WITH FORWARD PASS or FAIR CATCH
Hands open
and extended forward from
shoulders with hands vertical.

18

INVALID FAIR CATCH SIGNAL
One hand waved above head.

19

**INELIGIBLE RECEIVER
OR INELIGIBLE
MEMBER OF KICKING
TEAM DOWNFIELD**
Right hand touching top of cap.

20

ILLEGAL CONTACT
One open hand extended forward.

21

OFFSIDE or ENCROACHING
Hands on hips.

22

ILLEGAL MOTION AT SNAP
Horizontal arc with one hand.

23

LOSS OF DOWN
Both hands held behind head.

24

**CRAWLING, INTERLOCKING
INTERFERENCE, PUSHING, or
HELPING RUNNER**
Pushing movement of hands
to front with arms downward.

25

**TOUCHING A FORWARD
PASS OR SCRIMMAGE KICK**
Diagonal motion of
one hand across another.

26

**UNSPORTSMANLIKE
CONDUCT**
Arms outstretched, palms down.
(Same signal means continuous
action fouls are disregarded.)
Chop block.

27

**ILLEGAL CUT or
BLOCKING BELOW
THE WAIST**
Hand striking front of thigh
preceded by personal foul
signal (10).

28

ILLEGAL CRACKBACK
Strike of an open right hand
against the right mid thigh
preceded by personal foul
signal (10).

29

PLAYER DISQUALIFIED
Ejection signal.

30

TRIPPING
Repeated action of right foot
in back of left heel.

31

**UNCATCHABLE
FORWARD PASS**
Palm of right hand held
parallel to ground above head
and moved back and forth.

NFL Digest of Rules

This Digest of Rules of the National Football League has been prepared to aid players, fans, and members of the press, radio, and television media in their understanding of the game.

It is not meant to be a substitute for the official rule book. In any case of conflict between these explanations and the official rules, the rules always have precedence.

In order to make it easier to coordinate the information in this digest the topics discussed generally follow the order of the rule book.

Officials' Jurisdictions, Positions, and Duties

Referee—General oversight and control of game. Gives signals for all fouls and is final authority for rule interpretations. Takes a position in backfield 10 to 12 yards behind line of scrimmage, favors right side (if quarterback is right-handed passer). Determines legality of snap, observes deep back(s) for legal motion. On running play, observes quarterback during and after handoff, remains with him until action has cleared away, then proceeds downfield, checking on runner and contact behind him. When runner is downed, Referee determines forward progress from wing official and, if necessary, adjusts final position of ball.

On pass plays, drops back as quarterback begins to fade back, picks up legality of blocks by near linemen. Changes to complete concentration on quarterback as defenders approach. Primarily responsible to rule on possible roughing action on passer and if ball becomes loose, rules whether ball is free on a fumble or dead on an incomplete pass.

During kicking situations, Referee has primary responsibility to rule on kicker's actions and whether or not any subsequent contact by a defender is legal.

Umpire—Primary responsibility to rule on players' equipment, as well as their conduct and actions on scrimmage line. Lines up approximately four to five yards downfield, varying position from in front of weakside tackle to strongside guard. Looks for possible false start by offensive linemen. Observes legality of contact by both offensive linemen while blocking and by defensive players while they attempt to ward off blockers. Is prepared to call rule infractions if they occur on offense or defense. Moves forward to line of scrimmage when pass play develops in order to insure that interior linemen do not move illegally downfield. If offensive linemen indicate screen pass is to be attempted, Umpire shifts his attention toward screen side, picks up potential receiver in order to insure that he will legally be permitted to run his pattern and continues to rule on action of blockers. Umpire is to assist in ruling on incomplete or trapped passes when ball is thrown overhead or short.

Head Linesman—Primarily responsible for ruling on offside, encroachment, and actions pertaining to scrimmage line prior to or at snap. Keys on closest setback on his side of the field. On pass plays, Linesman is responsible to clear this receiver approximately seven yards downfield as he moves to a point five yards beyond the line. Linesman's secondary responsibility is to rule on any illegal action taken by defenders on any delay receiver moving downfield. Has full responsibility for ruling on sideline plays on his side, e.g., pass receiver or runner in or out of bounds. Together with Referee, Linesman is responsible for keeping track of number of downs and is in charge of mechanics of his chain crew in connection with its duties.

Linesman must be prepared to assist in determining forward progress by a runner on play directed toward middle or into his side zone. He, in turn, is to signal Referee or Umpire what forward point ball has reached. Linesman is also responsible to rule on legality of action involving any receiver who approaches his side zone. He is to call pass interference when the infraction occurs and is to rule on legality of blockers and defenders on plays involving ball carriers, whether it is entirely a running play, a combination pass and run, or a play involving a kick.

Line Judge—Straddles line of scrimmage on side of field opposite Linesman. Keeps time of game as a backup for clock operator. Along with Linesman is responsible for offside, encroachment, and actions pertaining to scrimmage line prior to or at snap. Line Judge keys on closest setback on his side of field. Line Judge is to observe his receiver until he moves at least seven yards downfield. He then moves toward backfield side, being especially alert to rule on any back in motion and on flight of ball when pass is made (he must rule whether forward or backward). Line Judge has primary responsibility to rule whether or not passer is behind or beyond line of scrimmage when pass is made. He also assists in observing actions by blockers and defenders who are on his side of field. After pass is thrown, Line Judge directs attention toward activities that occur in back of Umpire. During punting situations, Line Judge remains at line of scrimmage to be sure that only the end men move downfield until kick has been made. He also rules whether or not the kick crossed line and then observes action by members of the kicking team who are moving downfield to cover the kick.

Back Judge—Operates on same side of field as Line Judge, 17 yards deep. Keys on wide receiver on his side. Concentrates on path of end or back, observing legality of his potential block(s) or of actions taken against him. Is prepared to rule from deep position on holding or illegal use of hands by end or back or on defensive infractions committed by player guarding him. Has primary responsibility to make decisions involving sideline on his side of field, e.g., pass receiver or runner in or out of bounds.

Back Judge makes decisions involving catching, recovery, or illegal touching of a loose ball beyond line of scrimmage; rules on plays involving pass receiver, including legality of catch or pass interference; assists in covering actions of runner, including blocks by teammates and that of defenders; calls clipping on punt returns; and, together with Field Judge, rules whether or not field goal attempts are successful.

Side Judge—Operates on same side of field as Linesman, 17 yards deep. Keys on wide receiver on his side. Concentrates on path of end or back, observing legality of his potential block(s) or of actions taken against him. Is prepared to rule from deep position on holding or illegal use of hands by end or back or on defensive infractions committed by player guarding him. Has primary responsibility to make decisions involving sideline on his side of field, e.g., pass receiver or runner in or out of bounds.

Side Judge makes decisions involving catching, recovery, or illegal touching of a loose ball beyond line of scrimmage; rules on plays involving pass receiver, including legality of catch or pass interference; assists in covering actions of runner, including blocks by teammates and that of defenders; and calls clipping on punt returns.

Field Judge—Takes a position 25 yards downfield. In general, favors the tight end's side of field. Keys on tight end, concentrates on his path and observes legality of tight end's potential block(s) or of actions taken against him. Is prepared to rule from deep position on holding or illegal use of hands by end or back or on defensive infractions committed by player guarding him.

Field Judge times interval between plays on 45/25-second clock plus intermission between two periods of each half; makes decisions involving catching, recovery, or illegal touching of a loose ball beyond line of scrimmage; is responsible to rule on plays involving end line; calls pass interference, fair catch infractions, and clipping on kick returns; and, together with Back Judge, rules whether or not field goals and conversions are successful.

Definitions

1. **Chucking:** Warding off an opponent who is in front of a defender by contacting him with a quick extension of arm or arms, followed by the return of arm(s) to a flexed position, thereby breaking the original contact.
2. **Clipping:** Throwing the body across the back of an opponent's leg or hitting him from the back below the waist while moving up from behind unless the opponent is a runner or the action is in close line play.
3. **Close Line Play:** The area between the positions normally occupied by the offensive tackles, extending three yards on each side of the line of scrimmage.
4. **Crackback:** Eligible receivers who take or move to a position more than two yards outside the tackle may not block an opponent below the waist if they then move back inside to block.
5. **Dead Ball:** Ball not in play.
6. **Double Foul:** A foul by each team during the same down.
7. **Down:** The period of action that starts when the ball is put in play and ends when it is dead.
8. **Encroachment:** When a player enters the neutral zone and makes contact with an opponent before the ball is snapped.
9. **Fair Catch:** An unhindered catch of a kick by a member of the receiving team who must raise one arm a full length above his head while the kick is in flight.
10. **Foul:** Any violation of a playing rule.
11. **Free Kick:** A kickoff, kick after a safety, or kick after a fair catch. It may be a placekick, dropkick, or punt, except a punt may not be used on a kickoff.
12. **Fumble:** The loss of possession of the ball.
13. **Game Clock:** Scoreboard game clock.
14. **Impetus:** The action of a player that gives momentum to the ball.
15. **Live Ball:** A ball legally free kicked or snapped. It continues in play until the down ends.
16. **Loose Ball:** A live ball not in possession of any player.
17. **Muff:** The touching of a loose ball by a player in an unsuccessful attempt to obtain possession.
18. **Neutral Zone:** The space the length of a ball between the two scrimmage lines. The offensive team and defensive team must remain behind their end of the ball.
    Exception: The offensive player who snaps the ball.
19. **Offside:** A player is offside when any part of his body is beyond his scrimmage or free kick line when the ball is snapped.
20. **Own Goal:** The goal a team is guarding.
21. **Play Clock:** 45/25 second clock.
22. **Pocket Area:** Applies from a point two yards outside of either offensive tackle and includes the tight end if he drops off the line of scrimmage to pass protect. Pocket extends longitudinally behind the line back to offensive team's own end line.
23. **Possession:** When a player controls the ball throughout the act of clearly touching both feet, or any other part of his body other than his hand(s), to the ground inbounds.
24. **Punt:** A kick made when a player drops the ball and kicks it while it is in flight.
25. **Safety:** The situation in which the ball is dead on or behind a team's own goal if the impetus comes from a player on that team. Two points are scored for the opposing team.
26. **Shift:** The movement of two or more offensive players at the same time before the snap.
27. **Striking:** The act of swinging, clubbing, or propelling the arm or forearm in contacting an opponent.
28. **Sudden Death:** The continuation of a tied game into sudden death overtime in which the team scoring first (by safety, field goal, or touchdown) wins.
29. **Touchback:** When a ball is dead on or behind a team's own goal line, provided the impetus came from an opponent and provided it is not a touchdown or a missed field goal.
30. **Touchdown:** When any part of the ball, legally in possession of a player inbounds, is on, above, or over the opponent's goal line, provided it is not a touchback.
31. **Unsportsmanlike Conduct:** Any act contrary to the generally understood principles of sportsmanship.

Summary of Penalties

Automatic First Down

1. Awarded to offensive team on all <u>defensive fouls</u> with these exceptions:
   (a) Offside.
   (b) Encroachment.
   (c) Delay of game.
   (d) Illegal substitution.
   (e) Excessive time out(s).
   (f) Incidental grasp of facemask.
   (g) Prolonged, excessive or premeditated celebrations by individual players or groups of players.
   (h) Running into the kicker.

Loss of Down (No yardage)

1. Second forward pass <u>behind</u> the line.
2. Forward pass strikes <u>ground</u>, goal post, or crossbar.
3. Forward pass goes out of bounds.
4. Forward pass is first touched by eligible receiver who has gone out of bounds and returned.
5. Forward pass touches or is caught by an ineligible receiver on or behind line.
6. Forward pass thrown from behind line of scrimmage after ball once crossed the line.

Five Yards

1. Crawling.
2. Defensive holding or illegal use of hands (automatic first down).
3. Delay of game.
4. Encroachment.
5. Too many time outs.
6. False start.
7. Illegal formation.
8. Illegal shift.
9. Illegal motion.
10. Illegal substitution.
11. First onside kickoff out of bounds between goal lines and not touched.
12. Invalid fair catch signal.
13. More than 11 players on the field at snap for either team.
14. Less than seven men on offensive line at snap.
15. Offside.
16. Failure to pause one second after shift or huddle.
17. Running into kicker.
18. More than one man in motion at snap.
19. Grasping facemask of opponent.
20. Player out of bounds at snap.
21. Ineligible member(s) of kicking team going beyond line of scrimmage before ball is kicked.
22. Illegal return.
23. Failure to report change of eligibility.
24. Prolonged, excessive or premeditated celebrations by individual players or groups of players.
25. Loss of team time out(s) or five-yard penalty on the defense for excessive crowd noise.

10 Yards

1. Offensive pass interference.
2. Ineligible player downfield during passing down.
3. Holding, illegal use of hands, arms or body by offense.
4. Tripping by a member of either team.
5. Helping the runner.
6. Illegal batting or punching a loose ball.
7. Deliberately kicking a loose ball.

15 Yards

1. Chop block.
2. Clipping below the waist.
3. Fair catch interference.
4. Illegal crackback block by offense.
5. Piling on (automatic first down).
6. Roughing the kicker (automatic first down).
7. Roughing the passer (automatic first down).
8. Twisting, turning, or pulling an opponent by the facemask.
9. Unnecessary roughness.
10. Unsportsmanlike conduct.
11. Delay of game at start of either half.
12. Illegal blocking below the waist.
13. A tackler using his helmet to butt, spear, or ram an opponent.
14. Any player who uses the top of his helmet unnecessarily.
15. A punter, placekicker or holder who simulates being roughed by a defensive player.
16. A defender who takes a running start from beyond the line of scrimmage in an attempt to block a field goal or point after touchdown.

Five Yards and Loss of Down

1. Forward pass thrown from <u>beyond</u> line of scrimmage.

10 Yards and Loss of Down

1. Intentional grounding of forward pass (safety if passer is in own end zone). If foul occurs more than 10 yards behind line, play results in loss of down at spot of foul.

15 Yards and Loss of Coin Toss Option

1. Team's late arrival on the field prior to scheduled kickoff.

15 Yards (and disqualification if flagrant)

1. Striking opponent with fist.
2. Kicking or kneeing opponent.

3. Striking opponent on head or neck with forearm, elbow, or hands whether or not the initial contact is made below the neck area.
4. Roughing kicker.
5. Roughing passer.
6. Malicious unnecessary roughness.
7. Unsportsmanlike conduct.
8. Palpably unfair act. (Distance penalty determined by the Referee after consultation with other officials.)

15 Yards and Automatic Disqualification

1. Using a helmet that is not worn as a weapon.

Suspension From Game

1. Illegal equipment. (Player may return after one down when legally equipped.)

Touchdown

1. When Referee determines a palpably unfair act deprived a team of a touchdown. (Example: Player comes off bench and tackles runner apparently en route to touchdown.)

Field

1. Sidelines and end lines are <u>out of bounds</u>. The <u>goal line</u> is actually in the end zone. A player with the ball in his possession scores when the ball is on, above, or over the goal line.
2. The field is rimmed by a white border, a minimum six feet wide, along the sidelines. All of this is out of bounds.
3. The hashmarks (inbound lines) are 70 feet, 9 inches from each sideline.
4. Goal posts must be single-standard type, offset from the end line and painted bright gold. The goal posts must be 18 feet, 6 inches wide and the top face of the crossbar must be 10 feet above the ground. Vertical posts extend at least 30 feet above the crossbar. A ribbon 4 inches by 42 inches long is to be attached to the top of each post. The actual goal is the plane extending indefinitely above the crossbar and between the outer edges of the posts.
5. The field is 360 feet long and 160 feet wide. The end zones are 30 feet deep. The line used in try-for-point plays is two yards out from the goal line.
6. Chain crew members and ball boys must be uniformly identifiable.
7. All clubs must use standardized sideline markers. Pylons must be used for goal line and end line markings.
8. End zone markings and club identification at 50 yard line must be approved by the Commissioner to avoid any confusion as to delineation of goal lines, sidelines, and end lines.

Ball

1. The home club must have 24 balls available for testing by the Referee one hour before game time. In case of bad weather, a playable ball is to be substituted on request of the offensive team captain.

Coin Toss

1. The toss of coin will take place within three minutes of kickoff in center of field. The toss will be called by the visiting captain. The winner may choose one of two privileges and the loser gets the other:
   (a) Receive or kick
   (b) Goal his team will defend
2. Immediately prior to the start of the second half, the captains of both teams must inform the officials of their respective choices. The loser of the original coin toss gets first choice.

Timing

1. The stadium game clock is official. In case it stops or is operating incorrectly, the Line Judge takes over the official timing on the field.
2. Each period is 15 minutes. The intermission between the periods is two minutes. Halftime is 12 minutes, unless otherwise specified.
3. On charged team time outs, the Field Judge starts watch and blows whistle after 1 minute 50 seconds, unless television does not utilize the time for commercial. In this case the length of the time out is reduced to 40 seconds.
4. Referee may allow two minutes for injured player and three minutes for equipment repair.
5. Each team is allowed three time outs each half.
6. Time between plays will be 45 seconds from the end of a given play until the snap of the ball for the next play, or a 25-second interval after certain administrative stoppages and game delays.
7. Clock will start running when ball is snapped following all changes of team possession.
8. With the exception of the last two minutes of the first half and the last five minutes of the second half, the game clock will be restarted following a kickoff return, a player going out of bounds, or after all declined penalties on the Referee's ready signal.
9. Consecutive team time outs can be taken by opposing teams but the length of the second time out will be reduced to 40 seconds.
10. When, in the judgment of the Referee, the level of crowd noise prevents the offense from hearing its signals, he can institute a series of procedures which can result in a loss of team time outs or a five-yard penalty against the defensive team.

Sudden Death

1. The sudden death system of determining the winner shall prevail when score is tied at the end of the regulation playing time of all NFL games. The team scoring first during overtime play shall be the winner and the game automatically ends upon any score (by safety, field goal, or touchdown) or when a score is awarded by Referee for a palpably unfair act.
2. At the end of regulation time the Referee will immediately toss coin at center of field in accordance with rules pertaining to the usual pregame toss. The captain of the visiting team will call the toss.

3. Following a three-minute intermission after the end of the regulation game, play will be continued in 15-minute periods or until there is a score. There is a two-minute intermission between subsequent periods. The teams change goals at the start of each period. Each team has three time outs and general provisions for play in the last two minutes of a half shall prevail. Disqualified players are not allowed to return.

   Exception: In preseason and regular season games there shall be a maximum of 15 minutes of sudden death with two time outs instead of three. General provisions for play in the last two minutes of a half will be in force.

Timing in Final Two Minutes of Each Half

1. On kickoff, clock does not start until the ball has been legally touched by player of either team in the field of play. (In all other cases, clock starts with kickoff.)
2. A team cannot "buy" an excess time out for a penalty. However, a fourth time out is allowed without penalty for an injured player, who must be removed immediately. A fifth time out or more is allowed for an injury and a five-yard penalty is assessed if the clock was running. Additionally, if the clock was running and the score is tied or the team in possession is losing, the ball cannot be put in play for at least 10 seconds on the fourth or more time out. The half or game can end while those 10 seconds are run off on the clock.
3. If the defensive team is behind in the score and commits a foul when it has no time outs left in the final 30 seconds of either half, the offensive team can decline the penalty for the foul and have the time on the clock expire.
4. Fouls that occur in the last five minutes of the fourth quarter as well as the last two minutes of the first half will result in the clock starting on the snap.

Try-for-Point

1. After a touchdown, the scoring team is allowed a try-for-point during one scrimmage down. The ball may be spotted anywhere between the inbounds lines, two or more yards from the goal line. The successful conversion counts one point, whether by run, kick, or pass.
2. The defensive team never can score on a try-for-point. As soon as defense gets possession, or kick is blocked, ball is dead.
3. Any distance penalty for fouls committed by the defense that prevent the try from being attempted can be enforced on the succeeding kickoff. Any foul committed on a successful try will result in a distance penalty being assessed on the ensuing kickoff.
4. Only the fumbling player may advance a fumble during a try-for-point.

Players-Substitutions

1. Each team is permitted 11 men on the field at the snap.
2. Unlimited substitution is permitted. However, players may enter the field only when the ball is dead. Players who have been substituted for are not permitted to linger on the field. Such lingering will be interpreted as unsportsmanlike conduct.
3. Players leaving the game must be out of bounds on their own side, clearing the field between the end lines, before a snap or free kick. If player crosses end line leaving field, it is delay of game (five-yard penalty).
4. Substitutes who remain in the game must move onto the field as far as the inside of the field numerals before moving to a wide position.

Kickoff

1. The kickoff shall be from the kicking team's 35 yard line at the start of each half and after a field goal and try-for-point. A kickoff is one type of free kick.
2. Either a one-, two-, or three-inch tee may be used (no tee permitted for field goal or try-for-point plays). The ball is put in play by a placekick or dropkick.
3. If kickoff clears the opponent's goal posts it is not a field goal.
4. A kickoff is illegal unless it travels 10 yards OR is touched by the receiving team. Once the ball is touched by the receiving team it is a free ball. Receivers may recover and advance. Kicking team may recover but NOT advance UNLESS receiver had possession and lost the ball.
5. When a kickoff goes out of bounds between the goal lines without being touched by the receiving team, the ball belongs to the receivers 30 yards from the spot of the kick or at the out-of-bounds spot unless the ball went out-of-bounds the first time an onside kick was attempted. In this case the kicking team is to be penalized five yards and the ball must be kicked again.
6. When a kickoff goes out of bounds between the goal lines and is touched last by receiving team, it is receiver's ball at out-of-bounds spot.

Free Kick

1. In addition to a kickoff, the other free kicks are a kick after a safety and a kick after a fair catch. In both cases, a dropkick, placekick, or punt may be used (a punt may not be used on a kickoff).
2. On a free kick after a fair catch, captain of receiving team has the option to put ball in play by punt, dropkick, or placekick without a tee, or by snap. If the placekick or dropkick goes between the uprights a field goal is scored.
3. On a free kick after a safety, the team scored upon puts ball in play by a punt, dropkick, or placekick without tee. No score can be made on a free kick following a safety, even if a series of penalties places team in position. (A field goal can be scored only on a play from scrimmage or a free kick after a fair catch.)

Field Goal

1. All field goals attempted and missed from scrimmage line beyond the 20 yard line will result in the defensive team taking possession of the ball at the scrimmage line. On any field goal attempted and missed from scrimmage line inside the 20 yard line, ball will revert to defensive team at the 20 yard line.

Safety

1. The important factor in a safety is impetus. Two points are scored for the opposing team when the ball is dead on or behind a team's own goal line if the impetus came from a player on that team.

Examples of Safety:
(a) Blocked punt goes out of kicking team's end zone. Impetus was provided by punting team. The block only changes direction of ball, not impetus.
(b) Ball carrier retreats from field of play into his own end zone and is downed. Ball carrier provides impetus.
(c) Offensive team commits a foul and spot of enforcement is behind its own goal line.
(d) Player on receiving team muffs punt and, trying to get ball, forces or illegally kicks it into end zone where he or a teammate recovers. He has given new impetus to the ball.

Examples of Non-Safety:
(a) Player intercepts a pass with both feet inbounds in the field of play and his momentum carries him into his own end zone. Ball is put in play at spot of interception.
(b) Player intercepts a pass in his own end zone and is downed. Impetus came from passing team, not from defense. (Touchback)
(c) Player passes from behind his own goal line. Opponent bats down ball in end zone. (Incomplete pass)

Measuring

1. The forward point of the ball is used when measuring.

Position of Players at Snap

1. Offensive team must have at least seven players on line.
2. Offensive players, not on line, must be at least one yard back at snap. (**Exception:** player who takes snap.)
3. No interior lineman may move after taking or simulating a three-point stance.
4. No player of either team may invade neutral zone before snap.
5. No player of offensive team may charge or move, after assuming set position, in such manner as to lead defense to believe snap has started.
6. If a player changes his eligibility, the Referee must alert the defensive captain after player has reported to him.
7. All players of offensive team must be stationary at snap, except one back who may be in motion parallel to scrimmage line or backward (not forward).
8. After a shift or huddle all players on offensive team must come to an absolute stop for at least one second with no movement of hands, feet, head, or swaying of body.
9. Quarterbacks can be called for a false start penalty (five yards) if their actions are judged to be an obvious attempt to draw an opponent offside.

Use of Hands, Arms, and Body

1. No player on offense may assist a runner except by blocking for him. There shall be no interlocking interference.
2. A runner may ward off opponents with his hands and arms but no other player on offense may use hands or arms to obstruct an opponent by grasping with hands, pushing, or encircling any part of his body during a block. Hands (open or closed) can be thrust forward to initially contact an opponent on or outside the opponent's frame, but the blocker must work to bring his hands on or inside the frame.

   Note: Pass blocking: Hand(s) thrust forward that slip outside the body of the defender will be legal if blocker worked to bring them back inside. Hand(s) or arm(s) that encircle a defender—i.e., hook an opponent—are to be considered illegal and officials are to call a foul for holding. Blocker cannot use his hands or arms to push from behind, hang onto, or encircle an opponent in a manner that restricts his movement as the play develops.
3. Hands cannot be thrust forward above the frame to contact an opponent on the neck, face or head.

   Note: The frame is defined as the part of the opponent's body below the neck that is presented to the blocker.
4. A defensive player may not tackle or hold an opponent other than a runner. Otherwise, he may use his hands, arms, or body only:
   (a) To defend or protect himself against an obstructing opponent.

   Exception: An eligible receiver is considered to be an obstructing opponent ONLY to a point five yards beyond the line of scrimmage unless the player who receives the snap clearly demonstrates no further intention to pass the ball. Within this five-yard zone, a defensive player may make contact with an eligible receiver that may be maintained as long as it is continuous and unbroken. The defensive player cannot use his hands or arms to push from behind, hang onto, or encircle an eligible receiver in a manner that restricts movement as the play develops. Beyond this five-yard limitation, a defender may use his hands or arms ONLY to defend or protect himself against impending contact caused by a receiver. In such reaction, the defender may not contact a receiver who attempts to take a path to evade him.
   (b) To push or pull opponent out of the way on line of scrimmage.
   (c) In actual attempt to get at or tackle runner.
   (d) To push or pull opponent out of the way in a legal attempt to recover a loose ball.
   (e) During a legal block on an opponent who is not an eligible pass receiver.
   (f) When legally blocking an eligible pass receiver above the waist.

   Exception: Eligible receivers lined up within two yards of the tackle, whether on or immediately behind the line, may be blocked below the waist at or behind the line of scrimmage. NO eligible receiver may be blocked below the waist after he goes beyond the line.

Note: Once the quarterback hands off or pitches the ball to a back, or if the quarterback leaves the pocket area, the restrictions on the defensive team relative to the offensive receivers will end, provided the ball is not in the air.

5. A defensive player must not contact an opponent above the shoulders with the palm of his hand except to ward him off on the line. This exception is permitted only if it is not a repeated act against the same opponent during any one contact. In all other cases the palms may be used on head, neck, or face only to ward off or push an opponent in legal attempt to get at the ball.

6. Any offensive player who pretends to possess the ball or to whom a teammate pretends to give the ball may be tackled provided he is crossing his scrimmage line between the ends of a normal tight offensive line.

7. An offensive player who lines up more than two yards outside his own tackle or a player who, at the snap, is in a backfield position and subsequently takes a position more than two yards outside a tackle may not clip an opponent anywhere nor may he contact an opponent below the waist if the blocker is moving toward the ball and if contact is made within an area five yards on either side of the line.

8. A player of either team may block at any time provided it is not pass interference, fair catch interference, or unnecessary roughness.

9. A player may not bat or punch:
   (a) A loose ball (in field of play) toward his opponent's goal line or in any direction in either end zone.
   (b) A ball in player possession or attempt to get possession.
   Exception: A forward or backward pass may be batted, tipped, or deflected in any direction at any time by either the offense or the defense.
   Note: A pass in flight that is controlled or caught may only be thrown backward.

10. No player may deliberately kick any ball except as a punt, dropkick, or placekick.

Forward Pass

1. A forward pass may be touched or caught by any eligible receiver. All members of the defensive team are eligible. Eligible receivers on the offensive team are players on either end of line (other than center, guard, or tackle) or players at least one yard behind the line at the snap. A T-formation quarterback is not eligible to receive a forward pass during a play from scrimmage.
   Exception: T-formation quarterback becomes eligible if pass is previously touched by an eligible receiver.

2. An offensive team may make only one forward pass during each play from scrimmage (Loss of down).

3. The passer must be behind his line of scrimmage (Loss of down and five yards, enforced from the spot of pass).

4. Any eligible offensive player may catch a forward pass. If a pass is touched by one offensive player and touched or caught by a second eligible offensive player, pass completion is legal. Further, all offensive players become eligible once a pass is touched by an eligible receiver or any defensive player.

5. The rules concerning a forward pass and ineligible receivers:
   (a) If ball is touched accidentally by an ineligible receiver on or behind his line: loss of down.
   (b) If ineligible receiver is illegally downfield: loss of 10 yards.
   (c) If touched or caught (intentionally or accidentally) by ineligible receiver beyond the line: loss of 10 yards or loss of down.

6. The player who first controls and continues to maintain control of a pass will be awarded the ball even though his opponent later establishes joint control of the ball.

7. Any forward pass becomes incomplete and ball is dead if:
   (a) Pass hits the ground or goes out of bounds.
   (b) Hits the goal post or the crossbar of either team.
   (c) Is caught by offensive player after touching ineligible receiver.
   (d) An illegal pass is caught by the passer.

8. A forward pass is complete when a receiver clearly touches the ground with both feet inbounds while in possession of the ball. If a receiver would have landed inbounds with both feet but is carried or pushed out of bounds while maintaining possession of the ball, pass is complete at the out-of-bounds spot.

9. If an eligible receiver goes out of bounds accidentally or is forced out by a defender and returns to catch a pass, the play is regarded as a pass caught out of bounds. (Loss of down, no yardage.)

10. On a fourth down pass—when the offensive team is inside the opposition's 20 yard line—an incomplete pass results in a loss of down at the line of scrimmage.

11. If a personal foul is committed by the defense prior to the completion of a pass, the penalty is 15 yards from the spot where ball becomes dead.

12. If a personal foul is committed by the offense prior to the completion of a pass, the penalty is 15 yards from the previous line of scrimmage.

Intentional Grounding of Forward Pass

1. Intentional grounding of a forward pass is a foul: loss of down and 10 yards from previous spot if passer is in the field of play or loss of down at the spot of the foul if it occurs more than 10 yards behind the line or safety if passer is in his own end zone when ball is released.

2. It is considered intentional grounding of a forward pass when the ball strikes the ground after the passer throws, tosses, or lobs the ball to prevent a loss of yards by his team.

3. It is not intentional grounding when the defensive rushers have not put sufficient pressure on the passer to prevent him, for strategic purposes, from throwing the ball downfield in a natural and effective motion even though there is no apparent chance of completion.

Protection of Passer

1. By interpretation, a pass begins when the passer—with possession of ball—starts to bring his hand forward. If ball strikes ground after this action has begun, play is ruled an incomplete pass. If passer loses control of ball prior to his bringing his hand forward, play is ruled a fumble.

2. No defensive player may run into a passer of a legal forward pass after the ball has left his hand (15 yards). The Referee must determine whether opponent had a reasonable chance to stop his momentum during an attempt to block the pass or tackle the passer while he still had the ball.

3. No defensive player who has an unrestricted path to the quarterback may hit him flagrantly in the area of the knee(s) when approaching in any direction.

4. Officials are to blow the play dead as soon as the quarterback is clearly in the grasp and control of any tackler.

Pass Interference

1. There shall be no interference with a forward pass thrown from behind the line. The restriction for the passing team starts with the snap. The restriction on the defensive team starts when the ball leaves the passer's hand. Both restrictions end when the ball is touched by anyone.

2. The penalty for defensive pass interference is an automatic first down at the spot of the foul. If interference is in the end zone, it is first down for the offense on the defense's 1 yard line. If previous spot was inside the defense's 1 yard line, penalty is half the distance to the goal line.

3. The penalty for offensive pass interference is 10 yards from the previous spot.

4. It is pass interference by either team when any player movement beyond the offensive line significantly hinders the progress of an eligible player or such player's opportunity to catch the ball during a legal forward pass. When players are competing for position to make a play on the ball, any contact by hands, arms or body shall be considered incidental unless prohibited. Prohibited conduct shall be when a player physically restricts or impedes the opponent in such a manner that is visually evident and materially affects the opponent's opportunity to gain position or retain his position to catch the ball. If a player has gained position, he shall not be considered to have impeded or restricted his opponent in a prohibited manner if all of his actions are a bona fide effort to go to and catch the ball. Provided an eligible player is not interfered with in such a manner, the following exceptions to pass interference will prevail:
   (a) If neither player is looking for the ball and there is incidental contact in the act of moving to the ball that does not materially affect the route of an eligible player, there is no interference. If there is any question whether the incidental contact materially affects the route, the ruling shall be no interference.
   Note: Inadvertent tripping is not a foul in this situation.
   (b) Any eligible player looking for and intent on playing the ball who initiates contact, however severe, while attempting to move to the spot of completion or interception will not be called for interference.
   (c) Any eligible player who makes contact, however severe, with one or more eligible players while looking for and making a genuine attempt to catch or bat a reachable ball, will not be called for interference.
   (d) It must be remembered that defensive players have as much right to the ball as offensive eligible receivers.
   (e) Pass interference by the defense is not to be called when the forward pass is clearly uncatchable.
   (f) Note: There is no defensive pass interference behind the line.

Backward Pass

1. Any pass not forward is regarded as a backward pass or lateral. A pass parallel to the line is a backward pass. A runner may pass backward at any time. Any player on either team may catch the pass or recover the ball after it touches the ground.

2. A backward pass that strikes the ground can be recovered and advanced by offensive team.

3. A backward pass that strikes the ground can be recovered but cannot be advanced by the defensive team.

4. A backward pass caught in the air can be advanced by the defensive team.

Fumble

1. The distinction between a fumble and a muff should be kept in mind in considering rules about fumbles. A fumble is the loss of possession of the ball. A muff is the touching of a loose ball by a player in an unsuccessful attempt to obtain possession.

2. A fumble may be advanced by any player on either team regardless of whether recovered before or after ball hits the ground.

3. A fumble that goes forward and out of bounds will return to the fumbling team at the spot of the fumble unless the ball goes out of bounds in the opponent's end zone. In this case, the defensive team is to take possession at the spot of the fumble.

4. If an offensive player fumbles anywhere on the field during a fourth down play, or if a player fumbles on any down after the two-minute warning in a half, only the fumbling player is permitted to recover and/or advance the ball. If recovered by any other offensive player, the ball is dead at the spot of the fumble unless it is recovered behind the spot of the fumble. In that case, ball is dead at spot of recovery. Any defensive player may recover and/or advance any fumble.
   Exception: The fourth-down fumble rule does not apply if a player touches, but does not possess, a direct snap from center, i.e., a snap in flight as opposed to a hand-to-hand exchange.

Kicks From Scrimmage

1. Any punt or missed field goal that touches a goal post is dead.
2. During a kick from scrimmage, only the end men, as eligible receivers on the line of scrimmage at the time of the snap, are permitted to go beyond the line before the ball is kicked.
   Exception: An eligible receiver who, at the snap, is aligned or in motion behind the line and more than one yard outside the end man on his side of the line, clearly making him the outside receiver, REPLACES that end man as the player eligible to go downfield after the snap. All other members of the kicking team must remain at the line of scrimmage until the ball has been kicked.
3. Any punt that is blocked and does not cross the line of scrimmage can be recovered and advanced by either team. However, if offensive team recovers it must make the yardage necessary for its first down to retain possession if punt was on fourth down.
4. The kicking team may never advance its own kick even though legal recovery is made beyond the line of scrimmage. Possession only.
5. A member of the receiving team may not run into or rough a kicker who kicks from behind his line unless contact is:
   (a) Incidental to and after he had touched ball in flight.
   (b) Caused by kicker's own motions.
   (c) Occurs during a quick kick, or a kick made after a run, or after kicker recovers a loose ball. Ball is loose when kicker muffs snap or snap hits ground.
   (d) Defender is blocked into kicker.
   The penalty for running into the kicker is 5 yards. For roughing the kicker: 15 yards, an automatic first down and disqualification if flagrant.
6. If a member of the kicking team attempting to down the ball on or inside opponent's 5 yard line carries the ball into the end zone, it is a touchback.
7. Fouls during a punt are enforced from the previous spot (line of scrimmage). **Exception:** Illegal touching, illegal fair catch, invalid fair catch signal, and fouls by the receiving team during loose ball after ball is kicked.
8. While the ball is in the air or rolling on the ground following a punt or field goal attempt and receiving team commits a foul before gaining possession, receiving team will retain possession and will be penalized for its foul.
9. It will be illegal for a defensive player to jump or stand on any player, or be picked up by a teammate or to use a hand or hands on a teammate to gain additional height in an attempt to block a kick (Penalty 15 yards, unsportsmanlike conduct).
10. A punted ball remains a kicked ball until it is declared dead or in possession of either team.
11. Any member of the punting team may down the ball anywhere in the field of play. However, it is illegal touching (Official's time out and receiver's ball at spot of illegal touching). This foul does not offset any foul by receivers during the down.
12. Defensive team may advance all kicks from scrimmage (including unsuccessful field goal) whether or not ball crosses defensive team's goal line. Rules pertaining to kicks from scrimmage apply until defensive team gains possession.

Fair Catch

1. The member of the receiving team must raise one arm a full length above his head and wave it from side to side while kick is in flight. (Failure to give proper sign: receivers' ball five yards behind spot of signal.) **Note:** It is legal for the receiver to shield his eyes from the sun by raising one hand no higher than the helmet.
2. No opponent may interfere with the fair catcher, the ball, or his path to the ball. Penalty: 15 yards from spot of foul and fair catch is awarded.
3. A player who signals for a fair catch is not required to catch the ball. However, if a player signals for a fair catch, he may not block or initiate contact with any player on the kicking team until the ball touches a player. Penalty: snap 15 yards behind spot of foul.
4. If ball hits ground or is touched by member of kicking team in flight, fair catch signal is off and all rules for a kicked ball apply.
5. Any undue advance by a fair catch receiver is delay of game. No specific distance is specified for "undue advance" as ball is dead at spot of catch. If player comes to a reasonable stop, no penalty. For violation, five yards.
6. If time expires while ball is in play and a fair catch is awarded, receiving team may choose to extend the period with one free kick down. However, placekicker may not use tee.

Foul on Last Play of Half or Game

1. On a foul by defense on last play of half or game, the down is replayed if penalty is accepted.
2. On a foul by the offense on last play of half or game, the down is not replayed and the play in which the foul is committed is nullified.
   Exception: Fair catch interference, foul following change of possession, illegal touching. No score by offense counts.
3. On double foul on last play of half or game, down is replayed.

Spot of Enforcement of Foul

1. There are four basic spots at which a penalty for a foul is enforced:
   (a) Spot of foul: The spot where the foul is committed.
   (b) Previous spot: The spot where the ball was put in play.
   (c) Spot of snap, pass, fumble, return kick, or free kick: The spot where the act connected with the foul occurred.
   (d) Succeeding spot: The spot where the ball next would be put in play if no distance penalty were to be enforced.
      Exception: If foul occurs after a touchdown and before the whistle for a try-for-point, succeeding spot is spot of next kickoff.

2. All fouls committed by offensive team behind the line of scrimmage and in the field of play shall be penalized from the previous spot.
3. When spot of enforcement for fouls involving defensive holding or illegal use of hands by the defense is behind the line of scrimmage, any penalty yardage to be assessed on that play shall be measured from the line if the foul occurred beyond the line.

Double Foul

1. If there is a double foul during a down in which there is a change of possession, the team last gaining possession may keep the ball unless its foul was committed prior to the change of possession.
2. If double foul occurs after a change of possession, the defensive team retains the ball at the spot of its foul or dead ball spot.
3. If one of the fouls of a double foul involves disqualification, that player must be removed, but no penalty yardage is to be assessed.
4. If the kickers foul during a punt before possession changes and the receivers foul after possession changes, penalties will be offset and the down is replayed.

Penalty Enforced on Following Kickoff

1. When a team scores for touchdown, field goal, extra point, or safety and either team commits a personal foul, unsportsmanlike conduct, or obvious unfair act during the down, the penalty will be assessed on the following kickoff.

Procedures to Terminate or Temporarily Delay Completion of a Game

The National Football League holds to the position that all games should be played to their conclusion. However, if in the opinion of appropriate League authorities, it is impossible to begin or continue a game due to an emergency, or a game is deemed to be imminently threatened by any such emergency—e.g., severely inclement weather, lightning, flooding, power failure, interference by spectators, or other non-participants—then the following procedures will serve as guidelines for the Commissioner and/or his duly appointed representatives. The Commissioner will have the power to review the circumstances of each emergency and to adjust the following procedures in whatever manner he deems appropriate. If, in the Commissioner's opinion, it is reasonable to project that the resumption of an interrupted game would not change its ultimate result, he will be empowered to terminate the game.

1. The League employees vested with the authority to define emergencies under these procedures are the Commissioner, his representatives, and the game referee. In cases where neither the Commissioner nor his representatives are present, the referee shall have sole authority but he must make every effort to contact the Commissioner or representative for consultation. In all cases of significant delay, the League authorities will consult with the management of the participating clubs.
2. If, due to an emergency, a regular-season or postseason game is not started at its scheduled time and cannot be played at any later time that same day, the game, nevertheless, must be played on a subsequent date to be determined by the Commissioner.
3. If there is deemed to be a threat of an emergency (e.g., incoming tropical storm) that may occur during the playing of a game, the starting time of such game will not be moved to an earlier time unless there is clearly sufficient time to make an orderly change.
4. If an interrupted regular-season or postseason game cannot be completed on the same day, such game will be rescheduled by the Commissioner and resumed at that point.
5. In instances which require the Commissioner to reschedule a regular-season game, he will make every effort to set the game for no later than two days after its originally scheduled date, and if possible, at its original site. If unable to do so, he will schedule it at the nearest available facility. If it is impossible to schedule the game within two days after its original date, the Commissioner will attempt to schedule it on the Tuesday of the next calendar week in which the two involved clubs play other clubs no earlier than Sunday.
6. If an emergency interrupts a postseason game and such game cannot be resumed on that same date, the Commissioner will make every effort to arrange for its completion as soon as possible. If unable to schedule the game at the same site, he will select an appropriate alternate site. He will terminate the game short of completion only if in his judgment the continuation of the game would not be normally expected to alter the ultimate outcome.
7. In all instances where a game is resumed after interruption, the resumption will begin at the point at which the game was interrupted. The referee will call time out when it is necessary to declare an emergency interruption, and he will make a record of the team possessing the ball, position of the ball on the field, down, distance, time remaining in the period, and any other pertinent information required for an efficient and equitable resumption of play.

Note: In recent history, only two games, both preseason, have been terminated. In 1976, the Chicago College All-Star game was terminated due to thunderstorms with the Steelers leading the All-Stars 24-0, and the 1980 Pro Football Hall of Fame Game at Canton, Ohio, was called with 5:29 remaining due to severe thunder and lightning with the Chargers and Packers tied 0-0.

NOTES

NOTES

NOTES

NOTES

NOTES

NOTES

NOTES

NOTES

NOTES

NOTES

NOTES

NOTES